ISBN 978-0-266-59983-8
PIBN 10873586

FB &c Ltd, Dalton House, 60 Windsor Avenue, London, SW19 2RR.
Company number 08720141. Registered in England and Wales.

For support please visit www.forgottenbooks.com

Lade, (Sir) John (Bart.), s. John (Whithorne), of Isle of Jamaica, arm. UNIVERSITY COLL., matric. 3 May, 1738, aged 17; 2nd baronet, assumed the name of LADE in lieu of WHITHORNE, died 12 Feb., 1747, when the baronetcy expired.

Lade, (Sir) John (Bart.), s. John, of Westminster, baronet. CHRIST CHURCH, matric. 15 Nov., 1776, aged 17; 2nd baronet, died 10 Feb., 1838, when the baronetcy expired.

Ladyman, John, 1s. Joseph Harrison, of Norwich, gent. ST. JOHN'S COLL., matric. 12 Oct., 1878, aged 29.

Laffan, Rev. Robert Stuart de Courcy, 1s. Robert Michael, of London, arm. MERTON COLL., matric. 17 Oct., 1874, aged 21; B.A. 1878, M.A. 1884, senior classical master Derby Grammar School 1880-4, head-master King Edward School, etc., Stratford-on-Avon, 1885.

Laffer, Athanasius, s. John, of Alternan, Cornwall, gent. CHRIST CHURCH, matric. 13 Oct., 1798, aged 19; B.A. 1804, perp. curate St. Juliot, Cornwall, died in 1844. [5]

Lafont, Henry, M.A. TRINITY COLL., Dublin; incorp. 15 Sep., 1730. See *Cat. Grads.*

Lafont, John, of EMMANUEL COLL., Cambridge (B.A. 1820, M.A. 1823), adm. 'ad eundem' 1 July, 1835, rector of Hinxworth, Herts, and Sutton Bonnington, Notts, 1827, until his death 13 Oct., 1844.

Lafont, Ogle Russell, 1s. John, of Hinxworth, Herts, cler. ST. JOHN'S COLL., matric. 18 Feb., 1846, aged 18; B.A. 1849, M.A. 1852, rector of Hinxworth 1852-85.

Laidlaw, James, 1s. John, of Dominica, West Indies, arm. TRINITY COLL., matric. 26 June, 1827, aged 16.

Laidlay, Andrew, 1s. John, of Calcutta, East Indies, gent. QUEEN'S COLL., matric. 17 Oct., 1864, aged 19; B.A. 1868, B.C.L. & M.A. 1871, of Sea Cliff House, Haddingtonshire, and a commissioner of supply, bar.-at-law, Lincoln's Inn, 1872. See Foster's *Men at the Bar.* [10]

Laidler, Thomas, s. John, of Lowick, Northumberland, gent. ST. EDMUND HALL, matric. 2 July, 1773, aged 27.

Lainé, James Moullin, 2s. John Abraham, of St. Sampson's, Guernsey, gent. EXETER COLL., matric. 14 Oct., 1876, aged 18; scholar 1876-81, B.A. 1880, M.A. 1883. See *Coll. Reg.*, 168.

Laing, Allan Stewart, s. James, of Isle of Dominica, West Indies, arm. TRINITY COLL., matric. 26 Oct., 1805, aged 17; B.A. 1809, M.A. 1812, bar.-at-law, Middle Temple, 1812, a police magistrate at Hatton Garden, died 12 Feb., 1862.

Laing, Charles Miskin, o.s. Charles, of Rosherville, near London, arm. MAGDALEN COLL., matric. 15 Oct., 1881, aged 18; B.A. 1885, B.C.L. & M.A. 1888.

Laing, Rev. Francis, s. Alexander, of Edinburgh (city), gent. WORCESTER COLL., matric. 12 May, 1795, aged 22; B.A. from BALLIOL COLL. 1799, M.A. 1801, died at the Mythe, co. Gloucester, 24 Nov., 1861, aged 88. [15]

Laing, Francis Alexander. MERTON COLL., 1864. See WHITMORE.

Laing, Francis Henry. WADHAM COLL., 1838. See WHITMORE.

Laing, Francis Kelly, 2s. Samuel, of Sydenham, Kent, arm. CHRIST CHURCH, matric. 31 May, 1873, aged 18; a student of Lincoln's Inn 1873, died 1874.

Laing, John William, 2s. James, of Glasgow, arm. CHRIST CHURCH, matric. 7 June, 1865, aged 19; S.C.L. & B.A. from MAGDALEN HALL 1872, M.A. from CHRIST CHURCH 1872.

Laing, Joseph, 1s. George, of Tower Hill, London, arm. CORPUS CHRISTI COLL., matric. 16 Nov., 1822, aged 16. [20]

Laing, Joseph, 1s. George, of St. Katherine's, London, arm. UNIVERSITY COLL., matric. 17 Dec., 1823, aged 17; B.A. 1828.

Laing, Philip (Mathison Tovey), 2s. William, of Colchester, cler. NON-COLL., matric., 1881, aged 17; B.A. from ST. JOHN'S COLL. 1886.

Laing, Robert. WADHAM COLL., 1859, lecturer in law and modern history 1866-73. See CUTHBERT SHIELDS.

Laing, Thomas Josiah, o.s. Thomas, of St. Dunstan's-in-the-East, London, arm. MAGDALEN HALL, matric. 18 Nov., 1841, aged 30.

Lainson, John, 1s. John, of Bermondsey, arm. EXETER COLL., matric. 15 Oct., 1833, aged 17; a student of Lincoln's Inn 1839, father of the next named. [25]

Lainson, John Arthur, 1s. John, of Brighton, Sussex, arm. UNIVERSITY COLL., matric. 19 April, 1864, aged 19; B.A. 1868, M.A. 1870.

Laird, Egerton Knox, 5s. John, of Birkenhead, Cheshire, arm. NON-COLL., matric., 18 Feb., 1876, aged 28.

Laishley, George New, 1s. George, of Southampton, gent. ST. MARY HALL, matric. 19 Nov., 1840, aged 17.

Lake, (Sir) Atwell (Bart.), s. Bibye, of St. Helen's, London, Middlesex, baronet. JESUS COLL., matric. 29 April, 1731, aged 17; 2nd baronet, died 10 April, 1760 (? rector of St. Peter, West Lynn, Norfolk). See Foster's *Baronetage.*

Lake, Edward, 1s. Edward, of Hoo, near Rochester, Kent, gent. WADHAM COLL., matric. 22 Oct., 1856, aged 18; B.A. 1860, M.A. 1863. [30]

Lake, Gilbert, s. Gilbert, of Chippenham, Wilts, cler. QUEEN'S COLL., matric. 23 Oct., 1734, aged 16; B.A. 1738, M.A. 1741, vicar of Westport with Charlton, Wilts, 1749, and of Seagreen, Wilts, 1750.

Lake, Harry, 5s. John, of Hackney, Middlesex, arm. MAGDALEN HALL, matric. 19 June, 1851, aged 20.

Lake, Herbert John, 4s. Henry, of London, arm. NEW COLL., matric. 14 Oct., 1864, aged 19; B.A. 1868, M.A. 1871, bar.-at-law, Lincoln's Inn, 1870. See Foster's *Men at the Bar.*

Lake, John, s. James, of Truro, Cornwall, pleb. MAGDALEN HALL, matric. 28 March, 1757, aged 20; rector of Lanivet, Cornwall, 1770, until his death, buried there 4 June, 1805.

Lake, John James, s. John, of Lanivet, Cornwall, cler. EXETER COLL., matric. 30 May, 1797, aged 15; exhibitioner 1799, B.A. 1802, M.A. 1805, fellow 1805, until his death 31 Jan., 1809. See *Coll. Reg.*, 118.

Lake, Reginald John, 2s. George, of Islington, Middlesex, gent. NEW COLL., matric. 15 Oct., 1869, aged 19; B.A. 1872, bar.-at-law, Lincoln's Inn, 1874. See Foster's *Men at the Bar* & *Rugby School Reg.*, 472. [35]

Lake, Robert, s. Robert, of Charleton, Devon, gent. TRINITY COLL., matric. 1 April, 1732, aged 18.

Lake, Robert, s. Robert, of Scobel, Devon, arm. WADHAM COLL., matric. 19 May, 1779, aged 18.

Lake, Samuel, s. Robert, of St. Martin's, Salisbury, pleb. ORIEL COLL., matric. 10 Feb., 1738-9, aged 18.

Lake, William Charles, 1s. Charles, of London, arm. BALLIOL COLL., matric. 29 Nov., 1834, aged 17; scholar 1834-8, B.A. 1838, fellow 1838-59, M.A. 1841, tutor 1842-57, etc., proctor 1852-3, public examiner 1853, Whitehall preacher, rector of Huntspill, Somerset, 1858-69, preb. of Wells 1860-9, dean of Durham and D.D. 1869, and warden of Durham University 1869, etc. See *Rugby School Reg.*, 149.

Lake, William Hoblyn, s. John, of Lanivet, Cornwall, cler. WADHAM COLL., matric. 4 June, 1794, aged 14; B.A. 1798, M.A. 1803, fellow until 1812, when he was lost in the *Texel*, when chaplain of H.M.S. *St. George.* [40]

Lakes, Arthur, y.s. John, of Martock, Somerset, cler. QUEEN'S COLL., matric. 5 Feb., 1863, aged 19.

akin, John Marsh, y.s. John, of Birmingham, arm. WORCESTER COLL., matric. 26 Feb., 1835, aged 18; B.A. 1839, M.A. 1843, perp. curate Berrow, co. Worcester, 1849-51, rector of Gilmorton, 1851-81.

akin, Thomas Cooper, 1s. John, of Birmingham, arm. ORIEL COLL., matric. 21 March, 1833, aged 18.

ally, Meyrick, 2s. William Michael, of Drayton, co. Stafford, cler. WORCESTER COLL., matric. 19 Nov., 1829, aged 20.

ally, William Michael (LL.B. from ST. PETER'S COLL., Cambridge, 1803), 1s. Edmund, of Whitegate, Cheshire, cler. ST. JOHN'S COLL., incorp. 14 Nov., 1829, aged 54; D.C.L. 26 Nov., 1829, vicar of Little Missenden, Bucks, until 1809, rector of Drayton Bassett, 1799, until his death 15 June, 1857. See *Manchester School Reg.*, ii. 50.

Lamb, Alexander, s. Alexander, of Dartmouth, Devon, arm. EXETER COLL., matric. 5 June, 1817, aged 17; B.A. 1821. [5]

Lamb, Davies, fellow of ST. JOHN'S COLL., Cambridge (B.A. 1737, M.A. 1741); incorp. 14 June, 1748.

Lamb, Edmund George, s. Richard Westbrook, of Dublin, arm. MERTON COLL., matric. 17 Oct., 1882, aged 19; B.A. 1886.

Lamb, George, s. Edward, of Sandford, Westmoreland, pleb. QUEEN'S COLL., matric. 17 Dec., 1762, aged 20; B.A. 1766, M.A. 1777, rector of Hethe, Oxon, and of Eydon, Northants, 1777, until his death 10 Feb., 1801.

Lamb, George Augustus, s. Thomas Philips, of Rye, Sussex, arm. ORIEL COLL., matric. 8 July, 1799, aged 17; fellow MAGDALEN COLL. 1800-6, B.A. 1803, M.A. 1806, B.D. 1813, D.D. 1817, rector of Iden, Sussex, and of East Guildford with Playden 1807, until his death 31 Oct., 1864. See *Bloxam*, vii. 142.

Lamb, George Fleming, 3s. George Fleming, of Chunah, East Indies, cler. ORIEL COLL., matric. 21 Feb., 1861, aged 18; B.A. 1864, M.A. 1871, held various curacies 1865-73, rector of Broseley since 1873. [10]

Lamb, Rev. Henry William, 1s. George Warren, of Kettering, Northants, gent. CHRIST CHURCH, matric. 23 Jan., 1874, aged 18; B.A. 1878, M.A. 1883.

Lamb, Hubert, 3s. John, of Pocklington, Yorks, gent. NEW COLL., matric. 5 Feb., 1877, aged 20; B.Mus. 1881.

Lamb, James, s. John, of Hartley, Westmoreland, pleb. QUEEN'S COLL., matric. 31 March, 1773, aged 18; B.A. 1776, M.A. 1780, curate of Yoxall, Stafford, 1801, fellow, until he died at Kirkby Stephen, Oct., 1827.

Lamb, Sir James, Bart., s. George Burges, of Gibraltar, arm. UNIVERSITY COLL., matric. 7 Jan., 1770, aged 17 (as JAMES BLAND BURGES); created a baronet 31 Oct., 1795, assumed by royal licence the surname of LAMB in lieu of BLAND BURGES, etc., M.P. Helston 1787-96, etc., died 13 Oct., 1834. See Foster's *Baronetage*.

Lamb, John, s. Thomas, of Warcop, Westmoreland, gent. QUEEN'S COLL., matric. 17 April, 1776, aged 17; B.A. 1780, fellow, M.A. 1783, B. & D.D. 1797, curate and vicar of Banbury, Oxon, rector of Charwelton, Northants, 1805, and of Chipping Warden 1815, until his death 27 Dec., 1831. [15]

Lamb, John James Goodeve, o.s. John, of London, gent. QUEEN'S COLL., matric. 24 Oct., 1874, aged 19; scholar HERTFORD COLL. 1874-8, B.A. 1880, M.A. 1881, 2nd master Great Yarmouth Grammar School. See *St. Paul's School Reg.*

Lamb, John Thomas, 1s. John, of Pocklington, Yorks, gent. NEW COLL., matric. 5 Feb., 1877, aged 24.

Lamb, John White, s. Robert, of Hatfeild, co. York, pleb. LINCOLN COLL., matric. 10 April, 1731, aged 21.

Lamb, Joseph, 'manciple of Lincoln College;' privilegiatus 15 March, 1724-5.

Lamb, Matthew, s. Edward, of Sandford, Westmoreland, pleb. QUEEN'S COLL., matric. 24 Oct., 1751, aged 19; B.A. 1755, M.A. 1758, B. & D.D. 1773, principal Magdalen Hall 1786-88, chancellor of the diocese of Oxford, rector of Harvington, co. Worcester, and of Chipping Warden, Northants, preb. of Lichfield 1772, and of Worcester 1775, until his death 16 April, 1797. [20]

Lamb, Matthew, s. George, of Hethe, Oxon, cler. QUEEN'S COLL., matric. 6 July, 1793, aged 19; B.A. from LINCOLN COLL. 1797, M.A. 1800, rector of Eydon, Northants, 1801, until his death in 1825.

Lamb, Percy Stewart, 2s. Francis William, of Aldridge, co. Stafford, cler. WORCESTER COLL., matric. 18 Oct., 1883, aged 18.

Lamb, Richard, s. Michael, of Southwark, Surrey, arm. QUEEN'S COLL., matric. 30 Jan., 1810, aged 21.

Lamb, Robert, 8s. Thomas, of Cockerham, Lancashire, gent. ST. JOHN'S COLL., matric. 13 May, 1831, aged 19; B.A. 1835, M.A. 1841, perp. curate St. Mary's, Preston, 1844-49, rector of St. Paul's, Manchester, 1849-71, died 24 Dec., 1872.

Lamb, Thomas Davis, s. Thomas Phillips, of Rye, Sussex, arm. CHRIST CHURCH, matric. 11 Dec., 1793, aged 18; rector of Windlesham and Bagshot, Surrey, 1843-6, of West Hackney, 1846-68, vicar of All Saints, Bishopsgate Within 1868-72, etc. [25]

Lamb, Thomas Davis, 3s. George Augustus, of Marylebone, London, doctor. ST. JOHN'S COLL., matric. 11 Oct., 1834, aged 18.

Lamb, William, s. Edward, of Kidderminster, co. Worcester, pleb. PEMBROKE COLL., matric. 20 May, 1715, aged 18; B.A. 16 Jan., 1718-19.

Lamb, William, s. Edward, of Sandford, Westmoreland, pleb. QUEEN'S COLL., matric. 10 Oct., 1752, aged 16; brother of George 1762.

Lamb, William Pitt, 1s. George Augustus, of Iden, Sussex, doctor. CHRIST CHURCH, matric. 18 Jan., 1828, aged 18.

Lambard, Multon, s. Thomas, of Sevenoaks, Kent, arm. CHRIST CHURCH, matric. 1 June, 1774, aged 17; B.A. 1779, M.A. 1781, lieut.-colonel West Kent militia 1798, died 19 March, 1836. See *Alumni West.*, 399. [30]

Lambard, Thomas, s. Thomas, of Sevenoaks, Kent, arm. CHRIST CHURCH, matric. 5 June, 1724, aged 19; B.A. 1728, M.A. 1731, created D.C.L. 3 July, 1759, of Sevenoaks, Kent, bar.-at-law, Inner Temple, 1730, bencher 1761, died in 1769. See *Alumni West.*, 288.

Lambard, Thomas, s. Thomas, of Sevenoaks, Kent, arm. CHRIST CHURCH, matric. 5 June, 1776, aged 17; B.A. 1780, M.A. 1783, rector of Ashe and of Ridley, Kent, 1783, and also of Horsted, Sussex, died 19 April, 1811. See *Alumni West.*, 405.

Lambard, Thomas, s. Multon, of Sevenoaks, Kent, arm. CHRIST CHURCH, matric. 25 May, 1816, aged 18; student 1816-23, B.A. 1820, M.A. 1822, rector of Ridley 1821-40, and of Ashe, Kent, 1822-40. See *Alumni West.*, 480.

Lambard, William, s. Multou, of Sevenoaks, Kent, arm. CHRIST CHURCH, matric. 27 Oct., 1814, aged 17; of Beechmount, Sevenoaks, J.P., D.L., Kent, died 1 June, 1866.

Lambart, William Hugh, M.A. TRINITY COLL., Dublin, 1859 (B.A. 1850); adm. 'ad eundem' 10 Nov., 1859. [35]

Lambe, Henry, s. Henry, of Bucknell, co. Hereford, gent. CHRIST CHURCH, matric. 17 May, 1716, aged 19.

Lambe, John Percival George, s. John, of London, arm. BALLIOL COLL., matric. 17 May, 1815, aged 16; B.A. 1820.

Lambe, Lacon, s. William, of Dilling, co. Hereford, gent. BALLIOL COLL., matric. 6 June, 1717, aged 16; B.A. 1721, rector of Newton, co. Montgomery, 1733.

Lambe, Robert, s. Robert, of Addington, Northants, gent. LINCOLN COLL., matric. 14 April, 1743, aged 17; B.A. 25 Feb., 1746-7.

Lambe, Thomas Robert, o.s. Robert, of Oxton, Notts, gent. ST. MARY HALL, matric. 7 March, 1850, aged 19; S.C.L. 1853, incumbent of Coddington, Newark, died 21 Jan., 1861.

Lambe, William, s. John, of Durham (city), gent. EXETER COLL., matric. 18 March, 1724-5, aged 18, B.A. 1728; M.A. from MERTON COLL. 1732, died rector of Gateshead-on-Tyne 29 May, 1769.

Lambe, William, s. William, of Gateshead, co. Durham, cler. MERTON COLL., matric. 28 Nov., 1763, aged 17; B.A. 1767, M.A. 1770.

Lambert, Anthony Lewis, 'Mari Atlantico Natus,' 1s. Charles, arm. TRINITY COLL., matric. 24 Oct., 1821, aged 18; B.A. 1825, M.A. 1828, rector of Chilbolton, Hunts, 1848, until his death 21 March, 1869. See *Eton School Lists.*

Lambert, Aylmer Bourke, s. (Edmund), of Bath, Somerset, arm. ST. MARY HALL, matric. 26 Jan., 1779, aged 18; of Boyton House, Wilts, F.R.S., F.S.A., botanist, one of the original founders of the Linnean Society 1788, and its vice-president, bequeathed his collection and library to the British Museum, died at Kew Green 10 Jan., 1842. [5]

Lambert, Brooke, 3s. Francis John, of Chertsey, Surrey, arm. BRASENOSE COLL., matric. 8 June, 1854, aged 19: B.A. 1858, M.A. 1861, B.C.L. 1863, vicar of St. Mark, Whitechapel, 1865-71, of Tamworth 1872-8, and of Greenwich since 1880. See Foster's *Baronetage.*

Lambert, Burges, 4s. Robert, of Dorchester, Dorset, arm. BRASENOSE COLL., matric. 15 Jan., 1821, aged 18; B.A. from ST. JOHN'S COLL., Cambridge, 1825, M.A. 1829, vicar of Fritwell, Northants, 1833, until his death 28 May, 1843.

Lambert, Charles Lambert, 1s. Charles Joseph, of Coquimbo, Chili, arm. CHRIST CHURCH, matric. 15 Jan., 1869, aged 18; accidentally drowned at Hawaii, 20 Nov., 1874. See *Eton School Lists.*

Lambert, Daniel Henry, 1s. Benjamin, of Kensington, Middlesex, gent. KEBLE COLL., matric. 18 Oct., 1871, aged 19; B.A. 1874.

Lambert, Edmund, s. Edward, of Orcheston St. George, Wilts, cler. MAGDALEN COLL., matric. 4 Sep., 1724, aged 17; B.A. 1729. [10]

Lambert, Edmund, s. Edmund, of Boyton, Wilts, arm. MAGDALEN COLL., matric. 1 Feb., 1755, aged 19.

Lambert, Edward, s. Ed., of Orcheston St. George, Wilts, cler. PEMBROKE COLL., matric. 14 Dec., 1727, aged 16; demy MAGDALEN COLL. 1728-36, B.A. 1731, M.A. 1734, of Steeple Langford, Wilts, bar.-at-law, Middle Temple, 1738, deputy recorder of Salisbury. See *Bloxam*, vi. 218.

Lambert, Edward, s. Edmund, of Boyton, Wilts, arm. MAGDALEN COLL., matric. 29 July, 1755, aged 17.

Lambert, Edward, s. Edward, of Langford, Wilts, arm. MAGDALEN COLL., matric. 28 July, 1767, aged 18; demy 1767-70, rector of East Horsley, Surrey, and of Freshford, Somerset, died 17 March, 1818. See *Coll. Reg.*, vi. 349.

Lambert, Francis Henry, s. Robert, of Dorchester, Dorset, arm. NEW COLL., matric. 29 May, 1807, aged 19; died 15 Feb., 1810, 'late fellow.' [15]

Lambert, Francis John, s. Henry Anne, of —— Surrey, baronet. CHRIST CHURCH, matric. 6 May, 1818, aged 20; died 11 April, 1876, father of Brooke.

Lambert, Francis John, 1s. Edward Henry Gage, of Fordingbridge, Hants, gent. PEMBROKE COLL., matric. 27 Oct., 1885, aged 18. See Foster's *Baronetage.*

Lambert, Frederick Fox, 2s. Thomas, of Stockwell, Surrey, gent. CORPUS CHRISTI COLL., matric. 14 Oct., 1861, aged 18; B.A. 1865, M.A. 1868, vicar of Loversall, Yorks, 1868-72, chaplain to Marquis of Salisbury 1872, and rector of Clothall 1879.

Lambert, Greville Henry, 6s. Henry John, of London, baronet. MAGDALEN COLL., matric. 27 June, 1862, aged 19; B.A. 1866, M.A. 1870, rector of Emmington, Oxon, since 1872. See Foster's *Baronetage.*

Lambert, (Sir) Henry Edward Francis (Bart), 1s. Henry John, of Marylebone, London, bart. BALLIOL COLL., matric. 3 June, 1840, aged 17; B.A. 1843, M.A. 1847, 6th baronet, bar.-at-law, Inner Temple, 1847, died 15 June, 1872. See Foster's *Baronetage* & *Eton School Lists.* [20]

Lambert, (Sir) Henry Foley (Bart), 1s. Sir Henry Edward Francis, of London, bart. CHRIST CHURCH, matric. 31 May, 1879, aged 18; 7th baronet. See Foster's *Baronetage* & *Eton School Lists.*

Lambert, Hugh Biddulph, 1s. William Henry, of Ledbury, co. Hereford, cler. MERTON COLL., matric. 24 Oct., 1885, aged 17.

Lambert, James Hiley, 3s. James, of Durham (city), cler. ST. MARY HALL, matric. 3 Nov., 1868, aged 22; lay clerk New College 1866-71, clerk MAGDALEN COLL. 1875-6, B.A. & M.A. 1879, rector of Leigh, co. Worcester, 1886.

Lambert, John, s. Samuel, of Sherbourn, Dorset, gent. TRINITY COLL., matric. 2 April, 1726, aged 17.

Lambert, John, s. John, of Banbury, Oxon, gent. MERTON COLL., matric. 15 March, 1780, aged 18; B.A. from QUEEN'S COLL. 1783, M.A. 1786. [25]

Lambert, John Christopher, 1s. Alfred, of Richmond, Yorks, cler. NEW COLL., matric. 19 Oct., 1874, aged 33.

Lambert, Percival, 2s. William, of Leeds, gent. LINCOLN COLL., matric. 23 Oct., 1880, aged 20; B.A. 1883.

Lambert, Percival Beevor, 1s. Percival, of Hull, Yorks, gent. QUEEN'S COLL., matric. 17 Oct., 1864, aged 18; scholar 1865-70, B.A. 1868, bar.-at-law, Lincoln's Inn, 1873. See Foster's *Men at the Bar.*

Lambert, Richard. ST. EDMUND HALL, 1729. See LUMBERT.

Lambert, Richard Joseph Farran, 5s. Richard, of Horsfield, co. Gloucester, gent. ST. JOHN'S COLL., matric. 4 March, 1830, aged 19; B.A. 1834. [30]

Lambert, Richard William, 1s. Richard, of St. Stephen's, Bristol, gent. PEMBROKE COLL., matric. 18 Oct., 1819, aged 18; B.A. 1823, M.A. 1826, master of choristers of Bristol Cathedral 1824-40, vicar of Churchill, Somerset, 1833-40, and of Fivehead, Somerset, 1840.

Lambert, Robert Spears, 3s. Charles Joseph, of London, arm. CHRIST CHURCH, matric. 19 Feb., 1878, aged 18. See *Eton School Lists.*

Lambert, Thomas, s. Sam., of Sherbourn, Dorset, gent. TRINITY COLL., matric. 15 Oct., 1722, aged 16; bar.-at-law, Middle Temple, 1732.

Lambert, William, 1s. William, of East Indies, arm. EXETER COLL., matric. 7 Feb., 1833, aged 18; B.A. 1836, M.A. 1841, of Woodmansterne, Surrey, held various curacies 1837-49, vicar of Pennington, Hants, 1849.

Lambert, William, o.s. William Jonah, of Torquay, Devon, D.Med. ORIEL COLL., matric. 18 Oct., 1871, aged 18; commoner NEW INN HALL 1873, B.A. 1876, M.A. 1880, bar.-at-law, Lincoln's Inn, 1879. See Foster's *Men at the Bar* & *Rugby School Reg.*

Lambert, William George, 3s. Edmund, of Sloperton Cottage, Devizes, Wilts, arm. WADHAM COLL., matric. 9 Feb., 1822, aged 17; scholar CORPUS CHRISTI COLL. 1822-31, B.A. 1826, M.A. 1829, died in 1866. [35]

Lambert, William Henry, 4s. Henry John, of Aston Rowant, Oxon, bart. MERTON COLL., matric. 11 June, 1852, aged 18; postmaster 1852-6, B.A. 1857, M.A. 1859, rector of Stoke Edith, co. Hereford, 1858. See Foster's *Baronetage* & *Eton School Lists.*

Lambert, Willis Fleming Aston, 1s. George Patrick, of Milford, co. Pembroke, arm. WADHAM COLL., matric. 11 Oct., 1872, aged 18; B.A. 1876, M.A. 1879, vicar of Peterchurch, co. Hereford, 1887. See *Robinson*, 355.

Lambley, Richard Henry, y.s. William, of Morton, co. Lincoln, gent. NON-COLL., matric. 13 Oct., 1883, aged 25; B.A. from UNIVERSITY COLL. 1887.

Lamborn, Richard, s. 'Ovels,' of Oxford (city), arm. EXETER COLL., matric. 24 May, 1749, aged 19.

Lambourn, John, 'musician;' privilegiatus 9 Jan., 1750-1.

Lambton, Hon. Claud, 7s. John George, Earl of Durham. BALLIOL COLL., matric. 28 Jan., 1884, aged 19. See Foster's *Peerage.*

Lambton, Henry, s. Ralph, of Chester, co. Durham, arm. QUEEN'S COLL., matric. 16 July, 1715, aged 17; attorney to the bishop of Durham, M.P. Durham (city) in 4 parliaments, Jan. 1734, until his death, 26 June, 1761. See Foster's *Peerage,* E. DURHAM.

Lambton, Henry Ralph, 1s. William Henry, of Hebburn, co. Durham, arm. UNIVERSITY COLL., matric. 23 March, 1843, aged 18; of Winslow Hall, Bucks. See Foster's *Peerage,* E. DURHAM; & *Eton School Lists.* [5]

Lamert, George Frederick, 1s. George, of London, gent. WORCESTER COLL., matric. 14 Oct., 1865, aged 37; B.A. 1868, a student of the Inner Temple 1864, died 1870.

Lamert, Matthew, 3s. George, of Walthamstow, Essex, gent. ST. EDMUND HALL, matric. 18 April, 1861, aged 19; bible clerk 1861-5, B.A. 1865, M.A. 1871, Indian chaplain since 1869.

Laming, Henry, 3s. William Cotton, of Rotterdam, cler. QUEEN'S COLL. matric. 27 Oct., 1869, aged 19; B.A. 1873, M.A. 1877.

Lamont, Archibald, s. Archibald, of Kilfinan, co. Argyle, Scotland, arm. BALLIOL COLL., matric. 1 June, 1756, aged 13. [9]

Lamont, John Henry, 1s. James Archibald, of Edinburgh, arm. BRASENOSE COLL., matric. 7 March, 1872, aged 18; B.A. 1875, of Lamont, co. Argyle, J.P.

Lamotte, Digby Holden Rose Harwick, 1s. George Thomas Crespigny, of London, cler. TRINITY COLL., matric. 16 Oct., 1880, aged 18; B.A. 1885.

Lamotte, Francis Lagier, 3s. G. F., of Boulogne, France, gent. CHRIST CHURCH, matric. 21 Oct., 1840, aged 18; B.A. 1844, M.A. 1847.

Lamotte, George Thomas Crespigny, y.s. —— L., of Fulford, Yorks, arm. BALLIOL COLL., matric. 2 April, 1830, aged 18; B.A. 1834, M.A. 1838, rector of Denton, Kent, 1846-71, perp. curate Swingfield 1862-70, died 19 March, 1879.

Lamotte, James Henry, 2s. James, of Newcastle-upon-Tyne, Northumberland, gent. WADHAM COLL., matric. 27 March, 1824, aged 16.

Lamotte, John Lewis, 1s. James, of Taunton, Somerset, gent. WADHAM COLL., matric. 26 June, 1821, aged 18; B.A. 1826, M.A. 1829. [15]

Lamotte, Lewis, s. John, of Devonshire Street, London, gent. UNIVERSITY COLL., matric. 8 July, 1796, aged 17; B.A. 1800, bar.-at-law, Middle Temple, 1805, of the Jamaica bar, died in Spanish Town 23 Aug., 1814.

Lampen, Rev. Arthur George Nelson, 4s. (subs. 7s.) John, of Stoke, near Devonport, Devon, cler. ST. MARY HALL, matric. 9 April, 1867, aged 18; B.A. 1870, M.A. 1873.

Lampen, John, 1s. Richard, of Stoke Damerell, Devon, gent. EXETER COLL., matric. 17 April, 1822, aged 18; B.A. 1826, M.A. 1830, perp. curate St. John's, Devonport, 1831, rector of St. John's, Antony, Cornwall, 1863.

Lampen, Robert, s. Robert, of Plymouth, Devon, gent. EXETER COLL., matric. 11 May, 1808, aged 18; B.A. 1812, M.A. 1816, vicar of Probus, Cornwall, 1828, preb. of Exeter 1844, until his death 18 Aug., 1849.

Lampet, Lionel White, o.s. William Lionel, of Quatford, Salop, arm. ST. JOHN'S COLL., matric. 10 Dec., 1851, aged 18; B.A. 1855, a student of the Inner Temple 1855. [20]

Lampett, Lionell, s. Anton, of ——, co. Oxon, gent. EXETER COLL., matric. 6 Dec., 1728, aged 18; B.A. from ALL SOULS' COLL. 1732, M.A. 1736, vicar of Great Barford, Oxon, and rector of Pitsey, Berks, died at Steeple Aston 19 Jan., 1795.

Lamplugh, James Henry, 3s. Alfred, of Warrington, Lancashire, gent. LINCOLN COLL., matric. 15 Oct., 1878, aged 19.

Lamplugh, Richard, s. Robert, of Dovenby, Cumberland, gent. QUEEN'S COLL., matric. 3 March, 1725-6, aged 18; bar.-at-law, Gray's Inn, 1736, bencher 1749, treasurer 1758, dead before May, 1766.

Lamplugh, Thomas, s. Thomas, of York (city), cler. QUEEN'S COLL., matric. 4 Feb., 1745-6, aged 18; B.A. 1749, M.A. 1752, of Lamplugh Hall, Cumberland, rector of Copgrave, Yorks, 1754, and of Goldsborough, 1757, preb. of York 1758, until his death in 1783.

Lamplugh, William, s. Thomas, of Kensington, Middlesex, doctor. NEW COLL., matric. 15 July, 1719, aged 19; B.A. 1723, M.A. 1726, probably uncle of the last named. [25]

Lamprey, Thomas, s. Thomas, of Oxford (city), cler. ALL SOULS' COLL., matric. 15 April, 1752, aged 18; B.A. from NEW COLL. 1756, M.A. 1758, vicar of Stalisfield and of Halston, Kent (1760), until his death in 1800.

Lamprill, Edward Arthur, 1s. Frederick, of Brighton, Tasmania, arm. CORPUS CHRISTI COLL., matric. 20 Oct., 1886, aged 20.

L'Amy, John Alexander Ramsay Ramsay, 2s. John Ramsay, of Edinburgh, arm. CHRIST CHURCH, matric. 13 Oct., 1871, aged 19; B.A. 1875, M.A. 1878, minor canon of York.

Lancashire, Philip, 4s. Thomas, of Leigh, Lancashire, arm. BRASENOSE COLL., matric. 1 June, 1871, aged 18; B.A. 1875, M.A. 1878, vicar of St. Peter's, Oldham, 1883.

Lancaster, Daniel, s. Daniel, of Dean, Cumberland, gent. QUEEN'S COLL., matric. 12 April, 1783, aged 21; B.A. 1787, rector of Patney, Wilts, 1804, until his death 4 Dec., 1814. [30]

Lancaster, Ernest Le Crouler, 1s. William Lock, of London, arm. ST. JOHN'S COLL., matric. 13 Oct., 1879, aged 18; scholar 1879, B.A. 1883, B.Med. & M.A. 1887. See *Robinson,* 387.

Lancaster, Henry Hill, 5s. (subs. y.s.) Thomas, of Glasgow, Scotland, arm. BALLIOL COLL., matric. 17 May, 1849; B.A. 1853, M.A. 1872, died 24 Dec., 1875.

Lancaster, John, s. Robert, of Kirkby Ireleth, Lancashire, gent. QUEEN'S COLL., matric. 22 Feb., 1757, aged 20; B.A. 1760.

Lancaster, Peter, s. Peter, of Bowden, Cheshire, cler. BRASENOSE COLL., matric. 2 April, 1737, aged 18; B.A. 1741. See Ormerod's *Cheshire,* iii. 898. [34]

Lancaster, Richard Hume, s. Richard, of London, arm. MERTON COLL., matric. 23 March, 1790, aged 17; B.A. 1793, M.A. 1796, rector of Warneford, Hants, 1802, until his death 25 June, 1853.

Lancaster, Rev. Richard Thomas, s. Richard Hume, of St. Pancras, London, cler. EXETER COLL., matric. 4 July, 1815, aged 16; B.A. 1819, M.A. 1825, of Stanmer House, Cheltenham, died 24 Dec., 1882.

Lancaster, Rev. Robert Wharton, 1s. Joshua, of Ulverston, Lancashire, gent. NON-COLL., matric. 1 Nov., 1879, aged 22; B.A. from CHRIST CHURCH 1882.

Lancaster, Thomas, s. Samuel, of Barton, Westmoreland, pleb. QUEEN'S COLL., matric. 4 April, 1781, aged 21; B.A. 1784 (? chaplain to Lord Nelson), father of Thomas William.

Lancaster, Thomas Burne, 3s. Richard Hume, of Warneford, Hants, cler. MERTON COLL., matric. 30 Oct., 1822, aged 17; postmaster 1823-6, B.A. 1826, M.A. 1830, rector of Grittleton, Wilts, 1856, his until death 29 Jan., 1881.

Lancaster, Thomas Farrar, s. Thomas, of St. David's, Isle of Jamaica, arm. TRINITY COLL., matric. 10 Dec., 1806, aged 20. [40]

Lancaster, Thomas William, s. Thomas, of Fulham, Middlesex, cler. ORIEL COLL., matric. 26 Jan., 1804, aged 16, B.A. 1807; Michel scholar QUEEN'S COLL. 1808-9, fellow 1809-16, M.A. 1810, usher Magdalen College School 1840-9, vicar of Banbury 1815-49, Bampton lecturer 1831, select preacher 1832, rector of Over Worton, Oxon, 1849, until his death 12 Dec., 1859. See *Bloxam*, iii. 270.

Lance, Henry Porcher, 5s. John Edwin, of Buckland St. Mary, Somerset, cler. BRASENOSE COLL., matric. 1 July, 1852, aged 19; B.A. 1856.

Lancelot, John Bennett, 1s. Abraham, of Gresford, co. Denbigh, gent. JESUS COLL., matric. 18 Oct., 1883, aged 19; scholar 1883, B.A. 1887.

Lancy, Walter Graham de, 2s. William Jonathan Smith, of London, gent. NON-COLL., matric. 22 Jan., 1881, aged 37; B.A. 1885, M.A. 1887.

Lancy, Right Rev. William Heathcote de, D.D., created D.C.L. 23 June, 1852, bishop of Western New York 1839-65 (s. John Peter), B.A. YALE COLL., Newhaven, 1817, M.A. 1820, D.D. 1828, provost of University of Pennsylvania 1828-33, secretary of the House of Bishops of the American Church 1828-39, rector of St. Peter's, Philadelphia, 1836-9, died 6 April, 1865. **[5]**

Land, Henry, s. John, of Silverton, Devon, arm. BALLIOL COLL., matric. 8 May, 1744, aged 20, B.A. 20 Jan., 1747-8; M.A. from ORIEL COLL. 1751.

Land, Henry, s. Henry, of Woburn, Beds, cler. BALLIOL COLL., matric. 19 Oct., 1780, aged 18; B.A. 1784. (Rev. H. L. died at Colebrooke, Devon, Aug., 1807.)

Land, John, s. Schast., of Tiverton, Devon, gent. BALLIOL COLL., matric. 16 Feb., 1724-5, aged 17; B.A. 1728, M.A. 1731, proctor 1737 (? rector of Marsh Gibbon, Bucks, 1747, and vicar of Bampton, Oxon, 1751, until his death 14 June, 1757).

Land, John, s. Tristram, of Bread Street, London, cler. ST. JOHN'S COLL., matric. 10 July, 1760, aged 16; fellow 1760, B.A. 1764, M.A. 1768, lecturer and curate of St. Magnus the Martyr, London, rector of Hemyock, Devon, 1775, until his death 17 April, 1817. See *Robinson*, 110; & *Gent.'s Mag.*, i. 637.

Land, John, o.s. William, of Greenwich, Kent, arm. ST. EDMUND HALL, matric. 19 April, 1822, aged 18.

Land, Rev. Thomas, s. Henry, of Upton, Berks, cler. TRINITY COLL., matric. 16 April, 1782, aged 17 (? B.A. from SIDNEY SUSSEX COLL. 1788, died 12 Jan., 1835, aged 68). **[11]**

Landale, David Lewis, 3s. Thomas, of Paris, France, arm. BRASENOSE COLL., matric. 22 Nov., 1860, aged 17; B.A. 1864, bar.-at-law, Middle Temple, 1866.

Landale, Robert John, 1s. Robert, of Edinburgh, gent. EXETER COLL., matric. 11 Oct., 1872, aged 19; B.A. 1875, M.A. 1879.

Lander, John, 1s. John, of Gloucester, gent. PEMBROKE COLL., matric. 3 Dec., 1835, aged 18; B.A. 1839, M.A. 1865, rector of Donnington, co. Hereford, 1845.

Landon, George, born at St. Thomas's, Oxford, 3s. Whittington, dean of Exeter. WORCESTER COLL., matric. 4 July, 1823, aged 18; B.A. 1827, M.A. 1830, B.C.L. 1834, vicar of Branscombe, Devon, 1829-37, rector of Richards Castle (with Batchcott), Salop, 1837, until his death 6 Oct., 1873. **[15]**

Landon, George Charles Comyns, 1s. George, of Branscombe, Devon, cler. CHRIST CHURCH, matric. 23 May, 1850, aged 19.

Landon, Guy, 1s. Edward Henry, of Eastbourne, Sussex, cler. LINCOLN COLL., matric. 27 Oct., 1885, aged 19; scholar 1885.

Landon, Rev. Horace Richard, 1s. Whittington, of London, gent. WORCESTER COLL., matric. 29 Jan., 1878, aged 18; B.A. 1881, M.A. 1884.

Landon, James, born at St. Thomas's, Oxford, 2s. Whittington, dean of Exeter. WORCESTER COLL., matric. 18 May, 1822, aged 18; vicar of Bishops Tawton, Devon, 1827, died at Malden, Surrey, 13 Dec., 1878.

Landon, James, s. John, of Tedstone Delamere, cler. WORCESTER COLL., matric. 3 June, 1783, aged 18, B.A. 1787; fellow ORIEL COLL., M.A. 1789, B.D. 1799, proctor 1798, vicar of St. Mary the Virgin, Oxford, 1797, and of Aymestrey with Leinthall-Earls, co. Hereford, 1797, vicar of Aberford, Yorks, 1805, keeper of the University statutes 1806, died 2 March, 1850. **[20]**

Landon, James Timothy Bainbridge, o.s. James, of Aberford, Yorks, cler. WADHAM COLL., matric. 20 June, 1835, aged 18; scholar WORCESTER COLL. 1835-43, B.A. 1840, M.A. 1842; fellow MAGDALEN COLL. 1843-47, senior dean of arts 1845, public examiner 1849-50, chaplain Bromley College, Kent, vicar of Ledsham, Yorks, 1855, canon of York, 1877. See *Rugby School Reg.*, 174.

Landon, John, s. William, of Crednall, co. Hereford, pleb. BRASENOSE COLL., matric. 31 March, 1721, aged 20; B.A. from CHRIST CHURCH, 1725, rector of Nurstead with Ifield, Kent, 1754-61, died at Tedstone Court, co. Hereford, 3 June, 1777.

Landon, John, s. Thomas, of Credenhill, co. Hereford, pleb. BALLIOL COLL., matric. 29 Nov., 1740, aged 18; B.A. 1744, rector of Tedstone Delamere, co. Hereford, 1749-82, vicar of Donnington, co. Hereford, 1776, until his death in 1782, buried 2 Sep.

Landon, John Whittington Ready, born at Oxford (city), s. Whittington, dean of Exeter. WORCESTER COLL., matric. 7 May, 1818, aged 16, scholar 1818-26, B.A. 1822, M.A. 1824; fellow EXETER COLL. 1826, chaplain 1826-7, vicar of Braunton, Devon, 1823, and of Bishopstone, Wilts, 1826, until his death 14 Feb., 1880. See *Boase*, 126.

Landon, Thomas (Jones), s. Thomas, of Tedstone Delamere, co. Hereford, gent. WORCESTER COLL., matric. 3 July, 1805, aged 19; B.A. 1809, M.A. 1814, vicar of St. Brewards, Cornwall, 1815, until his death 1 Nov., 1850. **[25]**

Landon, Whittington, s, John, of Tedstone, co. Hereford, cler. WORCESTER COLL., matric. 13 Oct., 1775, aged 17; B.A. 1779, fellow 1782, M.A. 1782, B.D. 1790, D.D. 1795, provost 1796-1838, keeper of the archives 1796-1815, vice-chancellor 1802-6, select preacher 1808, rector of Croft with Yarpole, co. Hereford, 1796-1838, preb. of Norwich 1811-13, and of Salisbury 1821-38, dean of Exeter 1813-38, rector of Bishopstone, Wilts, 1822-6, vicar of Branscombe, Devon, 1827-30, incumbent of Elton, co. Hereford, died 29 Dec., 1838.

Landon, Whittington Henry, o.s. John, of Chelsea, Middlesex, gent. WORCESTER COLL., matric. 8 March, 1823, aged 18; B.A. 1827, M.A. 1830, vicar of Slebech, etc., co. Pembroke, 1851-77, died 23 Feb., 1883. See *Robinson*, 194.

Landor, Charles Savage, s. Walter, of Warwick (town), arm. WORCESTER COLL., matric. 10 March, 1795, aged 17; B.A. 1798, M.A. 1801, rector of Colton, co. Stafford, died July, 1849. See *Rugby School Reg.*, 59.

Landor, Charles Willson, o.s. Charles Savage, of Colton, co. Stafford, cler. WORCESTER COLL., matric. 5 March, 1831, aged 18; B.A. 1835, M.A. 1837, rector of Over Whitacre, vicar of Lindridge, co. Worcester, 1847-73, died 25 June, 1877. See *Rugby School Reg.*, 152.

Landor, John, s. Robert, of Rugeley, co. Stafford, arm. MAGDALEN HALL, matric. 8 Feb., 1755, aged 18; brother of Walter 1750. **[30]**

Landor, Robert Eyres, s. Walter, of St. Nicholas, Warwick (town), arm. WORCESTER COLL., matric. 21 June, 1797, aged 16; B.A. 1801, M.A. 1804, vicar of Hughenden, Bucks, chaplain-in-ordinary to the Prince Regent, rector of Birlingham, co. Worcester, 1829, until his death 26 Jan., 1869.

Landor, Walter, s. Robert, of Rugeley, co. Stafford, arm. WORCESTER COLL., matric. 29 Oct., 1750, aged 18, B.A. 1754, M.A. 1757; B.Med. from ST. ALBAN HALL, 1760, of Ipsley Court, co. Warwick, died Nov., 1805, father of Charles Savage, and of the last and next named.

Landor, Walter (Savage), s. Walter, of Warwick (town), arm. TRINITY COLL., matric. 13 Nov., 1792, aged 17; of Ipsley, co. Warwick, poet and miscellaneous writer, died at Florence, 17 Sep., 1864. See *Rugby School Reg.*, 54; & *Gent.'s Mag.*, ii. 791.

Landseer, Sir Edwin, R.A.; created D.C.L. 21 June, 1870 (son of John Landseer, engraver), A.R.A. 1825, R.A. 1830, declined the presidency 1866, knighted 3 July, 1850, died 1 Oct., 1873, buried in St. Paul's Cathedral.

Lane, Benjamin, s. — L., of St. Martin's, Worcester (city), gent. MERTON COLL., matric. 24 March, 1728-9, aged 16; B.A. 1733, M.A. 1735, rector of St. Andrew, Droitwich, 1744.

Lane, Cecil Thomas Edward Douglas, 3s. Richard Douglas Hay, of Brighton, arm. NON-COLL., matric. 8 June, 1878, aged 21. See *Eton School Lists.*

Lane, Charles, y.s. Rich., of St. Swithin's, Worcester (city), equitis. TRINITY COLL., matric. 28 Nov., 1723, aged 16; B.A. 1727, M.A. from MERTON COLL. 1732. [5]

Lane, Charles, s. Thomas, of St. Ann's, London, arm. QUEEN'S COLL., matric. 7 May, 1813, aged 20; B.A. 1815, M.A. 1817, perp. curate 1834-8, rector of Deal 1838-45, hon. canon Canterbury 1869, rector of Wrotham, Kent, 1845, until his death 23 March, 1879.

Lane, Charles Middleton Robert Douglas, 4s. Richard Douglas Hay, of Kemp Town, Sussex, arm. PEMBROKE COLL., matric. 3 May, 1883, aged 19.

Lane, Charles Pelham, 1s. Thomas, of Moseley, near Birmingham, gent. UNIVERSITY COLL., matric. 23 Jan., 1871, aged 19; B.A. 1874, M.A. 1877, of Moundsley Hall, co. Worcester, J.P. See *Rugby School Reg.*

Lane, Charlton, of JESUS COLL., Cambridge (B.A. 1820, M.A. 1823); adm. 'ad eundem' 8 June, 1842, perp. curate St. Mark's, Kennington, Surrey.

Lane, Charlton George, 1s. Charlton, of Kennington, Surrey, cler. CHRIST CHURCH, matric. 18 June, 1855, aged 19; B.A. 1860, M.A. 1867, rector of Little Gaddesden, Herts, 1870. [10]

Lane, Edmund, s. Thomas, of Newton Bushell, Devon, arm. ORIEL COLL., matric. 29 April, 1789, aged 18; B.A. 1793.

Lane, Edmund, 2s. John, of Stratford-upon-Avon, gent. MAGDALEN HALL, matric. 23 Oct., 1834, aged 18; B.A. 1839, M.A. 1850, B.C.L. 1850, rector of St. Mary, Manchester, 1844-56, incumbent of St. John, Selkirk, 1872.

Lane, Edward Henry, o.s. Charles, of Montreal, Canada, gent. MERTON COLL., matric. 27 Jan., 1832, aged 17; postmaster 1832-3.

Lane, Ernald, 5s. John Newton, of Kings Bromley, co. Stafford, arm. BALLIOL COLL., matric. 17 Oct., 1855, aged 18, B.A. 1860; fellow ALL SOULS' COLL. 1860-79, M.A., 1862, chaplain 1862-3, rector of Albury, Surrey, 1868-70, vicar of St. Michael, Handsworth, 1870-1, rector of Leigh, co. Stafford, 1870, archdeacon of Stoke and preb. of Lichfield 1888.

Lane, Francis Dalrymple, 4s. Henry, of Stratford-on-Avon, gent. ST. EDMUND HALL, matric. 18 Oct., 1879, aged 19. [15]

Lane, Frederick Coghlan, o.s. John, of St. Helier's, Isle of Jersey, arm. EXETER COLL., matric. 29 Jan., 1846, aged 17.

Lane, George, 3s. Joseph, of Stockport, Cheshire, arm. BRASENOSE COLL., matric. 11 Oct., 1827, aged 18.

Lane, Henry Alexander, 1s. Henry, of East Indies, arm. WORCESTER COLL., matric. 18 Oct., 1869, aged 19. See *Rugby School Reg.*

Lane, Henry Charles, 1s. Henry Thomas, of Westmeston, Sussex, arm. CHRIST CHURCH, matric. 16 Oct., 1850, aged 18; of Middleton, Sussex, J.P., late 2nd life guards. See *Eton School Lists.*

Lane, Henry Thomas, s. Thomas, of St. Mary-le-bone, London, arm. CHRIST CHURCH, matric. 31 Oct., 1811, aged 18; of Middleton House, Sussex, died 1834. See *Eton School Lists.* [20]

Lane, James Henry, s. James, of St. Mary Abbott, Middlesex, gent. WORCESTER COLL., matric. 9 June, 1817, aged 18; scholar 1817-22, B.A. 1821.

Lane, John, s. John, of Banbury, Oxon, pleb. WADHAM COLL., matric. 15 Feb., 1720-1, aged 18; B.A. 1724.

Lane, John, of KING'S COLL., Cambridge (B.A. 1725, fellow, M.A. 1729); incorp. 6 July, 1733.

Lane, John, s. William, of Hammersmith, Middlesex, arm. CHRIST CHURCH, matric. 9 Nov., 1778, aged 18; B.A. 1782, M.A. 1786 (? vicar of Sawbridgeworth, Herts, 1787, until his death 3 May, 1817).

Lane, John, o.s. John, of St. Pancras, Middlesex, gent. QUEEN'S COLL., matric. 12 Aug., 1830, aged 15; B.C.L. 1837, D.C.L. 1842, bar.-at-law, Inner Temple, 1843, died 25 Oct., 1850. [25]

Lane, John Bell, s. Robert, of Longford, Ireland, arm. BRASENOSE COLL., matric. 16 Dec., 1728, aged 18.

Lane, John George, 1s. John Croome, of Doncaster, Yorks, gent. ORIEL COLL., matric. 18 Oct., 1871, aged 19; B.A. 1874, M.A. 1878, rector of Over Whitacre, co. Warwick, 1883.

Lane, John Hamilton, s. John, of Fethard, co. Tipperary, arm. CHRIST CHURCH, matric. 9 Feb., 1775, aged 17.

Lane, (John) Henry Bagot Newton, 1s. John Newton, of Kings Bromley, co. Stafford, arm. CHRIST CHURCH, matric. 27 May, 1847, aged 18; student 1847-64, B.A. 1851, M.A. 1854, of Kings Bromley, J.P., lieut.-col. coldstream guards, died 22 March, 1886.

Lane, John Reynolds, 3s. Charles, of Henley-on-Thames, Oxon, arm. TRINITY COLL., matric. 30 Nov., 1854, aged 19; B.A. 1860, M.A. 1861, vicar of Roxby 1868-79, of Morhanger, Beds, 1879-83, and of Tatterford, Norfolk, since 1883. See *Eton School Lists.* [30]

Lane, John Samuel, 1s. John, of Cheltenham, arm. MERTON COLL., matric. 16 Oct., 1871, aged 17; scholar 1871-5, B.A. 1876.

Lane, Obadiah, of EMMANUEL COLL., Cambridge (B.A. 1756, M.A. 1759); incorp. 7 July, 1759.

Lane, Philip, s. John, of Sandford, Devon, gent. BALLIOL COLL., matric. 5 Dec., 1778, aged 18; B.A. 1782.

Lane, Raymond England, 3s. John, of Little Missenden, Bucks, arm. EXETER COLL., matric. 15 May, 1875, aged 18.

Lane, Richard, s. — L., of Thame, Oxon, arm. UNIVERSITY COLL., matric. 15 Dec., 1764, aged 17; B.A. 1768, M.A. 1771. [35]

Lane, Richard, 2s. Richard, of Coffleet, in Brixton, Devon, cler. QUEEN'S COLL., matric. 3 May, 1831, aged 19; B.A. 1836, vicar of Wembury, Devon, 1848-82, died 21 June, 1884. See *Eton School Lists.*

Lane, Richard Douglas Hay, 1s. Charles, of Fulham, Middlesex, cler. CHRIST CHURCH, matric. 19 Oct., 1842, aged 18; sometime captain 17th lancers.

Lane, Richard Ouseley Blake, 1s. Richard Ouseley Blake, of London, arm. TRINITY COLL., matric. Oct. 16, 1886, aged 18.

Lane, Robert, s. George, of St. Mary-le-Bow, London, arm. CHRIST CHURCH, matric. 19 Oct., 1750, aged 18.

Lane, Robert, s. John, of Sandford, Devon, gent. BALLIOL COLL., matric. 20 Nov., 1783, aged 18; B.A. 1788 (? 30 years master of Kingsbridge Grammar School, and Minister of Salcombe, Devon, died 27 May, 1840). [40]

Lane, Samuel, s. Thomas, of Totness, Devon, gent. EXETER COLL., matric. 26 Nov., 1776, aged 17; fellow 1780-94, B.A. 1780, M.A. 1783, rector of Hook, Dorset, 1791, until his death in 1827. See *Coll. Reg.*, 112.

Lane, Samuel, o.s. Samuel, of Totness, Devon, cler. EXETER COLL., matric. 2 Feb., 1821, aged 18; B.A. 1825, M.A. 1828, vicar of Holme, Devon, 1827-8, rector of Frome Vauchurch, Dorset, 1828, until his death 10 Dec., 1868.

Lane, Sidney Ernald Ralph, o.s. Sidney Leveson, of London, arm. BRASENOSE COLL., matric. 2 June, 1882, aged 18; B.A. 1886, bar.-at-law, Inner Temple, 1887.

Lane, Sidney Leveson, 2s. John Newton, of Bromley Manor, co. Stafford, arm. CHRIST CHURCH, matric. 31 May, 1849, aged 18; B.A. 1853, of Baldersby Park, Yorks, J.P., D.L., and of Manor House, Great Addington, Northants, bar.-at-law, Middle Temple, 1858. See Foster's *Men at the Bar.*

Lane, Theophilus, s. William, of Fanhope, co. Hereford, gent. BRASENOSE COLL., matric. 10 April, 1756, aged 15; B.A. 1759, M.A. 1763, rector of St. Michael's, Crooked Lane, London, died 7 June, 1816.

Lane, Theophilus, s. James, of Hereford (city), gent. BALLIOL COLL., matric. 30 April, 1792, aged 28; B.C.L. from MAGDALEN HALL 1801, D.C.L. 1814, preb. of Hereford 1801, died 19 July, 1814, father of Edward William Lane, translator and editor of the 'Arabian Nights.'

Lane, Thomas, s. Nicholas, of Gloucester (city), gent. EXETER COLL., matric. 10 Dec., 1744, aged 17; B.A. 16 March, 1749-50 (? vicar of Broadwater, co. Lincoln, 1755). [5]

Lane, Thomas, s. Thomas, of Bentley, co. Stafford, arm. PEMBROKE COLL., matric. 29 Nov., 1764, aged 18; B.A. 1768, M.A. 1772, rector of Handsworth, Staffordshire, 1776, until his death 12 Oct., 1802.

Lane, Thomas, s. Thomas, of Sevenoaks, Kent, gent. BRASENOSE COLL., matric. 29 Oct., 1771, aged 16.

Lane, Thomas Frederick, 1s. Thomas, of Worcester, gent. NEW COLL., matric. 5 Feb., 1877, aged 27.

Lane, Thomas Leveson, of ST. JOHN'S COLL., Cambridge (B.A. 1823, M.A. 1828); adm. 'ad eundem' 7 June, 1853 (2s. John, of Kings Bromley, co. Stafford), vicar of Wasperton, co. Warwick, 1834, and of Baswick, co. Stafford, 1836.

Lane, William, s. James, of St. John's, Hereford (city), gent. MERTON COLL., matric. 28 March, 1718, aged 18, B.A. 8 March, 1722-3; M.A. from ORIEL COLL. 1728, rector of Hampton Bishop and vicar of Stanhope, co. Hereford, preb. of Hereford 1730, treasurer 1732-44, preb. of Salisbury 1732, until his death 14 July, 1752. [10]

Lane, William Thomas, 2s. Odiarne Coates, of Clifton, near Bristol, gent. PEMBROKE COLL., matric. 22 Nov., 1855, aged 19.

Lanfear, (Rev.) Carl Sylvius Viereck, 1s. John Viereck, of Cassel, Germany, gent. WORCESTER COLL., matric. 4 June, 1881, aged 24; B.A. 1884.

Lane-Fox, George Sackville Frederick. CHRIST CHURCH, 1856. See FOX.

Lang, Alexander Denistoun, 1s. Gabriel Hamilton, of Richmond, Surrey, gent. MAGDALEN COLL., matric. 24 Jan., 1876, aged 18.

Lang, (Rev.) Algernon Herrmann, 1s. Herrmann, of London, gent. ST. JOHN'S COLL., matric. 26 June, 1871, aged 18; scholar 1871-6, B.A. 1876, M.A. 1878. See *Robinson*, 350. [15]

Lang, Andrew, 1s. John, of Selkirk (town), N.B., arm. BALLIOL COLL., matric. 28 Jan., 1865, aged 20, exhibitioner 1865-8; fellow MERTON COLL. 1868-76, B.A. 1869, M.A. 1875, the well-known writer.

Lang, Cosmo Gordon, 2s. John Marshall, of Fyvie, co. Aberdeen, gent. BALLIOL COLL., matric. 17 Oct., 1882, aged 17; scholar 1882-6, B.A. 1886, a student of Inner Temple, 1884.

Lang, Dashwood, 3s. Richard, of Broadclist, Devon, arm. ST. ALBAN HALL, matric. 7 Dec., 1825, aged 21; B.A. 1829, vicar of West Leigh, died 19 March, 1874.

Lang, Rev. Ernest, 3s. Alfred, of London, gent. NON-COLL., matric. 11 Oct., 1873, aged 20; B.A. 1877, M.A. 1886.

Lang, Ernest Augustus, 7s. Charles Henry, of St. Mary Abbots, Kensington, near London, D.Med. ST. JOHN'S COLL., matric. 5 March, 1845, aged 18; B.A. 1849, M.A. 1865, rector of St. Mary's, Manchester, 1857, until his death 5 March, 1872. [20]

Lang, Francis Charles, 2s. Oliver William, of Devonport, Devon, gent. QUEEN'S COLL., matric. 23 Oct., 1862, aged 19; B.A. 1867, M.A. 1869, chaplain royal navy since 1872.

Lang, James, s. Sam., of South Tawton, Devon, pleb. EXETER COLL., matric. 5 April, 1718, aged 20; B.A. 1721.

Lang, John Henry Graham, 4s. Hugh Morris, of Largs, co. Ayr, arm. BRASENOSE COLL., matric. 24 May, 1877, aged 18; B.A. 1880, M.A. 1886, bar.-at-law, Inner Temple, 1884. See Foster's *Men at the Bar.*

Lang, Nathaniel, s. Nath., of St. Mabyn, Cornwall, gent. EXETER COLL., matric. 22 March, 1731-2, aged 16; B.A. 1736.

Lang, Robert Lowman, 1s. Robert Lowman, of Fawley, Hants, gent. NON-COLL., matric. 20 Jan., 1883, aged 15, B.A. 1886; chorister CHRIST CHURCH 1878-83. [25]

Lang, Thomas William, 5s. John, of Selkirk, Scotland, arm. BALLIOL COLL., matric. 23 Jan., 1874 aged 19.

Lang, William Andrew, 1s. William, of Melbourne, gent. ORIEL COLL., matric. 1 June, 1882, aged 18; B.A. 1885, bar.-at-law, Inner Temple, 1887.

Lang, William Francis Dashwood, 1s. Dashwood, of Westleigh, Devon, cler. WADHAM COLL., matric. 27 Nov., 1861, aged 19; B.A. 1866, M.A. 1871, rector of Instow, Devon, 1869. See Foster's *Our Noble and Gentle Families.*

Langbridge, Frederick, 6s. Henry Charles, of Birmingham, arm. NON-COLL., matric. 17 Oct., 1874, aged 35; commoner ST. ALBAN HALL 1879, B.A. 1880, M.A. from MERTON COLL. 1883, rector of St. John's, Limerick, 1883, etc. See *Crockford.*

Langdon, Charles Baskerville, 3s. William Gregory, of Glasgow, gent. NON-COLL., matric. 15 Oct., 1870, aged 19. [30]

Langdon, Edward, 4s. Thomas, of Bampton, Devon, gent. EXETER COLL., matric. 24 June, 1859, aged 18; choral scholar NEW COLL. 1860-1, B.A. 1863, M.A. 1866.

Langdon, Rev. Frederick Edward Whitter, 3s. John Churchill, of Tatworth, Somerset, arm. CORPUS CHRISTI COLL., matric. 19 Oct., 1875, aged 19; B.A. 1879, M.A. 1883. See *Rugby School Reg.*

Langdon, Gilbert, s. Gilbert, of Woodbury, Devon, gent. WADHAM COLL., matric. 24 March, 1757, aged 18; B.A. from MERTON COLL. 1761, M.A. from MAGDALEN COLL., Cambridge, 1779, rector of Farley Hungerford, Somerset, with Winterbourne Haughton Dorset, 1782.

Langdon, Gilbert Henry, s. Gilbert, of Piddletown, Dorset, cler. EXETER COLL., matric. 26 May, 1797, aged 17; scholar 1797, rector of Weston Patrick 1813, and of Athelhampton, Dorset, 1818, and also of Rotherwick, Hants, died 28 Sep., 1840. See *Coll. Reg.*, 149.

Langdon, John, s. Tapper, of North Bovey, Devon, arm. TRINITY COLL., matric. 27 April, 1730, aged 18. [35]

Langdon, Richard, s. Charles, of Exeter (city), gent. EXETER COLL., matric. 13 July, 1761, aged 31; B.Mus. 18 July, 1761.

Langdon, Richard Northcote, 4s. John, of Chard, Somerset, gent. ST. ALBAN HALL, matric. 21 Oct., 1847, aged 20.

Langdon, Thomas William Spicer, 2s. John, of Chard, Somerset, arm. PEMBROKE COLL., matric. 18 May, 1839, aged 18; B.A. 1845, perp. curate Lopen, Somerset, 1859, until his death 24 June, 1871.

Langdon, William, s. Gilbert, of Longbredy, Dorset, cler. BALLIOL COLL., matric. 18 Nov., 1725, aged 18; B.A. 1729.

Langdon, William, s. William, of Mudford, Somerset, cler. ORIEL COLL., matric. 19 Nov., 1757, aged 17; B.A. 1761, M.A. 1783, B.D. 1783, chaplain to the king, rector of St. Paul's Cray, Kent, 1781, dispensation to hold Pylle with Montacute, Somerset, 1790.

Langdon, William Tobias, o.s. William, of St. Pancras, London, arm. WORCESTER COLL., matric. 6 Dec., 1832, aged 22; F.S.A., bar.-at-law, Middle Temple, 1842, died 26 Dec., 1863.

Langenberg, James Arthur Van, 2s. James, of Kandy, Ceylon, arm. MERTON COLL., matric. 28 Jan., 1886, aged 19; bar.-at-law, Inner Temple, 1888.

Langford, Augustus William Henry, o.s. William W., of Crowmarsh, Oxon, cler. BRASENOSE COLL., matric. 6 Feb., 1851, aged 18; B.A. 1855, held various curacies 1856-81, rector of Thorpe Falcon, Somerset, 1881.

Langford, Ayliffe, 1s. Thomas, of Islington, Middlesex, arm. QUEEN'S COLL., matric. 23 Feb., 1822, aged 18. See *Eton School Lists*. [5]

Langford, Edward, s. Edward, of Penzance, Cornwall, gent. BALLIOL COLL., matric. 20 Oct., 1796, aged 19; of Trungle, Cornwall, captain royal Cornwall militia, etc.

Langford, Edward, 3s. Edward, of Bath (city), arm. MERTON COLL., matric. 4 Dec., 1828, aged 20; postmaster 1828-31.

Langford, Edward Henry, s. Edward, of Windsor, Berks, cler. CHRIST CHURCH, matric. 3 Feb., 1817, aged 19.

Langford, Emanuel, s. Eman., of Chelsea, Middlesex, doctor. CHRIST CHURCH, matric. 15 July, 1721, aged 16; B.A. 1726, M.A. 1728.

Langford, Henry John, s. Harry, of Prestbury, Cheshire, arm. BRASENOSE COLL., matric. 14 Jan., 1788, aged 18; B.A. 1791. [10]

Langford, James, s. Jonas, of Antigua, gent. QUEEN'S COLL., matric. 7 July, 1739, aged 17.

Langford, James, 'cook;' privilegiatus 21 May, 1750.

Langford, John, s. David, of Ruthin, co. Denbigh, gent. JESUS COLL., matric. 10 July, 1733, aged 19; B.A. 1737.

Langford, John, 'chirurgus;' privilegiatus 28 July, 1775.

Langford, John Frere, 1s. John William, of Tannah, near Bombay, East Indies, arm. BALLIOL COLL., matric. 13 Oct., 1860, aged 19; B.A. 1864, M.A. 1868, chaplain Foundling Hospital, 1873-6, vicar of Bere Regis 1876-86, chaplain Holy Trinity, Nice, 1886. [15]

Langford, Joseph, s. Joseph, of Whitchurch, Salop, gent. CHRIST CHURCH, matric. 30 April, 1784, aged 16; B.A. 1788, rector 1st portion of Pontesbury, Salop, 1800.

Langford, Richard, s. Simon, of Holyhead, Anglesea, cler. JESUS COLL., matric. 10 March, 1737-8, aged 16; B.A. 13 Feb., 1741-2, M.A. 1744, B.D. 1752.

Langford, Robert, 'butler of Wadham College;' privilegiatus 11 April, 1747.

Langford, Samuel, s. Samuel, of ——, Devon, gent. EXETER COLL., matric. 10 July, 1732, aged 18.

Langford, Thomas, 7s. Stephen, of West Ham, Sussex, gent. WORCESTER COLL., matric. 19 Nov., 1851, aged 18; B.A. 1855, M.A. 1858, rector of Oxhill, co. Warwick, died 12 May, 1862. [20]

Langford, Thomas Frederick, 1s. Frederick, of Udimore, Sussex, arm. MERTON COLL., matric. 15 Oct., 1870, aged 18. See *Rugby School Reg.*

Langford, William, s. Emanuel, of Chelsea, Middlesex, doctor. CHRIST CHURCH, matric. 8 June, 1716, aged 20; B.A. 1720, M.A. 1723. See *Alumni West.*, 267.

Langford, William, 'cook of Jesus College;' privilegiatus 4 March, 1723-4.

Langford, William, 2s. Joseph, of St. Andrew's, Holborn, Middlesex, gent. MAGDALEN HALL, matric. 16 March, 1843, aged 21; bar.-at-law, Gray's Inn, 1854, sometime of EMMANUEL COLL., Cambridge, died 27 Dec., 1874.

Langford, William Thomas, 2s. John, of India, arm UNIVERSITY COLL., matric 20 Jan., 1866, aged 19, B.A. 1871, bar.-at-law, Lincoln's Inn, 1872. See Foster's *Men at the Bar*. [25]

Langham, Frederick Musgrave, 3s. James, of St. George's, Hanover Square, London, baronet. ST. ALBAN HALL, matric. 3 Nov., 1823, aged 16; died 9 March, 1832. See Foster's *Baronetage* & *Eton School Lists*.

Langham, Henry Burdett, 4s. James, of Marylebone, London, baronet. ST. ALBAN HALL, matric. 9 May, 1827, aged 18; died 30 Nov., 1876. See Foster's *Baronetage* & *Eton School Lists*.

Langham, (Sir) James (Bart.), s. William, of Rance, Northants, gent. LINCOLN COLL., matric. 26 Oct., 1753, aged 17; 7th baronet, M.P. Northamptonshire 1784-90, died 7 Feb., 1795, father of the next named.

Langham, (Sir) James (Bart.), s. James, of Marylebone, Middlesex, baronet. CHRIST CHURCH, matric. 27 Oct., 1794, aged 18; B.A. 1798, M.A. 1801, 10th baronet, bar.-at-law, Lincoln's Inn, 1802, M.P. St. Germans 1802-6, died 14 April, 1833. See Foster's *Baronetage* & *Eton School Lists*.

Langham, (Sir) James Hay (Bart.), 1s. James, of St. George's, Hanover Square, London, baronet. CHRIST CHURCH, matric. 20 Feb., 1821, aged 18; 11th baronet. See Foster's *Baronetage* & *Eton School Lists*. [30]

Langham, (Sir) John (Bart.), s. John, of Gayton, Northants, baronet. BALLIOL COLL., matric. 19 Aug., 1717, aged 19; 6th baronet, died s.p. Sep., 1766.

Langham, Purbeck, s. John, of Cottesbrook, Northants, baronet. UNIVERSITY COLL., matric. 22 May, 1745, aged 18; youngest brother of the last named.

Langham, Stephen, s. John, of Gayton, Northants, baronet. PEMBROKE COLL., matric. 23 March, 1726-7, aged 20; B.C.L. 1733, brother of the last named.

Langham, (Sir) William (Bart.), s. William, of Barrowden, Rutland, gent. LINCOLN COLL., matric. 26 Oct., 1753, aged 16; B.C.L. 1760, of Ramsbury Manor, Wilts, *j.u.*, took the name and arms of JONES, and was created a baronet 3 May, 1774, died 3 May, 1791, brother of James 1753.

Langhorne, Alexander Reginald, 2s. Alexander Grant Smith, of Broughton, Flints, gent. NON-COLL., matric. 4 Nov., 1884, aged 20. [35]

Langhorne, Charles Hartley, 2s. John, of Berwick-upon-Tweed, arm. EXETER COLL., matric. 25 May, 1837, aged 18; B.A. 1842, a student of Lincoln's Inn 1843, died in 1845.

Langhorne, Rev. Charles James, y.s. Thomas, of Musselburgh, near Edinburgh, cler. BALLIOL COLL., matric. 13 Dec., 1850, aged 20; B.A. 1856, M.A. 1857, exhibitioner 1859-60, died 19 Oct., 1874.

Langhorn, Thomas, s. Joseph, of London, gent. ST. EDMUND HALL, matric. 15 July, 1807, aged 15.

Langhorne, Thomas, 1s. Thomas, of Musselburgh, Edinburgh, cler. ST. JOHN'S COLL., matric. 6 March, 1844, aged 18; B.A. 1848, M.A. 1851, head-master Loretto School, near Edinburgh, 1848-61, vicar of Wroxton, Oxon, 1874-8, and of Elsfield 1878.

Langhorne, William Bailey, 1s. John Bailey, of Outwood, Yorks, arm. UNIVERSITY COLL., matric. 13 April, 1872, aged 19; B.A. 1876, a student of Lincoln's Inn 1876. [40]

L'Angle, John Maximilian de, s. Theo., of Tenterden, Kent, cler. CHRIST CHURCH, matric. 16 June, 1744, aged 17; B.A. 1748, M.A. 1752, rector of Danbury and Woodham Ferris, Essex, 1770, and vicar of Goodneston, Kent, died 30 May, 1783.

Langley, Adam, s. Adam, of Westminster (city), cler. TRINITY COLL., matric. 14 Oct., 1718, aged 15; B.A. 1722, brother of John 1723.

Langley, Rev. Archer John, s. John, of Ashford, Kent, arm. UNIVERSITY COLL., matric. 1 May, 1818, aged 18, B.A. 1822; fellow BALLIOL COLL. 1823-7, M.A. 1824, died 20 Feb., 1827.

Langley, Benjamin, s. Thomas, of Compton, Berks, cler. EXETER COLL., matric. 16 March, 1719-20, aged 15; B.A. 1725, fellow 1725-32, M.A. 24 March, 1728-9, rector of Compton, Berks, and of Mursley, Bucks, a benefactor to his college, died in 1777. See *Coll. Reg.*, 93.

Langley, James Robert, 3s. John Gace, of Buckden, Hunts, gent. NON-COLL., matric. 16 Oct., 1875, aged 18; B.A. 1879, M.A. 1883.

Langley, John, s. John, of Devorall Longbridge, Wilts, pleb. EXETER COLL., matric. 10 March, 1718-9, aged 18; B.A. 1722.

Langley, John, s. Adam, of Camberwell, Surrey, cler. TRINITY COLL., matric. 30 May, 1723; B.A. 1728, brother of Adam 1718. [5]

Langley, Rev. John, s. Samuel, of Checkley, co. Stafford, doctor. WORCESTER COLL., matric. 10 April, 1778, aged 15; B.A. 1782, M.A. 1784, fellow until his death 30 July, 1827.

Langley, John, s. John, of Bridgnorth, Salop, gent. CHRIST CHURCH, matric. 10 Oct., 1786, aged 18; B.A. 1790, M.A. 1793, chaplain Stafford County Gaol, died 5 Jan., 1835.

Langley, John, 2s. William, of Warminster, Wilts, gent. MAGDALEN HALL, matric. 14 Dec., 1818, aged 18; B.A. 1823, M.A. 1826 (? rector of St. Leonard's and St. Mary's, Wallingford, 1829-72, died 30 July, 1875).

Langley, John, o.s. John, of Stepney, Middlesex, gent. ORIEL COLL., matric. 24 Jan., 1874, aged 18; B.A. 1877, M.A. 1882, has held various curacies since 1878.

Langley, Samuel, s. Samuel, of Checkley, co. Stafford, cler. PEMBROKE COLL., matric. 18 May, 1738, aged 18; B.A. 26 Feb., 1741-2, M.A. 1758, B. & D.D. 1758, rector of Langton Peverel, Sussex, 1755, of Checkley, co. Stafford, and Steventon, Salop, 1759, until his death in 1791 (his widow died in Dec., 1812). [10]

Langley, Samuel, s. Samuel, of Checkley, co. Stafford, doctor. WORCESTER COLL., matric. 11 May, 1773, aged 17; B.A. 1777, M.A. 1780, rector of Checkley 1791, until his death 10 Feb., 1839.

Langley, Samuel, s. Samuel, of Isle of Sheppey, Kent, cler. WORCESTER COLL., matric. 9 May, 1807, aged 21.

Langley, Thomas, s. Samuel, of Checkley, co. Stafford, doctor. WORCESTER COLL., matric. 30 Oct., 1783, aged 16; B.A. 1787.

Langley, Thomas, s. Thomas, of Marlow, Bucks, gent. HERTFORD COLL., matric. 17 May, 1787, aged 18; B.A. 1791, M.A. 1794, rector of Whiston, Northants, 1800, until his death 28 July, 1801, author of the 'History and Antiquities of the Hundred of Desborough and Deanery of Wycombe, in Bucks, 1797.'

Langley, Thomas Bolland, 1s. John, of Meole Brace, Salop, cler. WORCESTER COLL., matric. 21 May, 1836, aged 19. [15]

Langley, Thomas William, 1s. Thomas, of Marylebone, London, gent. QUEEN'S COLL., matric. 5 June, 1824, aged 18.

Langley, William, s. James, of Birmingham, co. Warwick, gent. TRINITY COLL., matric. 17 March, 1739-40, aged 18, B.A. 1743; M.A. from MAGDALEN HALL, 1746 (? rector of Fenny Bentley, and 40 years headmaster Ashbourne Free Grammar School, died 6 Nov., 1795).

Langley, William Hawkes, s. John, of Newport, Salop, cler. CHRIST CHURCH, matric. 13 Oct., 1814, aged 18; B.A. 1819, M.A. 1821, curate of Wheatley, Oxon, 1823.

Langlois, Benjamin, s. Peter, of Leghorn, Italy, gent. CHRIST CHURCH, matric. 23 March, 1744-5, aged 18; created D.C.L. 8 July, 1773, M.P. St. Germans Dec., 1768-80.

Langman, Edward, s. John, of Totnes, Devon, gent. EXETER COLL., matric. 15 April, 1736, aged 20; B.A. from BALLIOL COLL. 1739. [20]

Langmead, George Winne, 2s. William, of St. Andrew's, Plymouth, arm. EXETER COLL., matric. 4 Feb., 1830, aged 17; B.A. 1834, M.A. 1847, army chaplain, died 18 April, 1873.

Langmead, Thomas Pitts (Taswell), o.s. Thomas of St. Giles-in-the-Fields, London, gent. ST. MARY HALL, matric. 23 Oct., 1862, aged 22; B.A. 1866, B.C.L. 1869, bar.-at-law, Lincoln's Inn, 1863, an associate of King's College, London, and of London University, died 8 Dec., 1882.

Langmead, William, 1s. William, of Plymouth, Devon, arm. BALLIOL COLL., matric. 14 Dec. 1826, aged 18. See *Eton School Lists.*

Langmore, Rev. Alfred Frederick, 2s. Erskine Graunt, of Rawul Pindee, India, arm. MERTON COLL., matric. 14 Oct., 1879, aged 19; B.A. 1883, M.A. 1886.

Langmore, Rev. Erskine William, 1s. Erskine Graunt, of Mowshera, East Indies, arm. KEBLE COLL., matric. 19 Jan. 1875, aged 19; B.A. 1878, M.A. 1885. [25]

Langran, James, 2s. Joseph, of London, gent. HERTFORD COLL., matric. 19 Oct., 1874, aged 38; B.Mus. 23 Oct., 1884.

Langridge, Arthur Bracy, 2s. Henry, of London, gent. CORPUS CHRISTI COLL., matric. 23 Oct., 1884, aged 18; scholar 1884.

Langsford, Sydney William, 2s. Richard Turner, of South Norwood, Surrey, gent. LINCOLN COLL., matric. 17 Oct., 1884, aged 19.

Langstaff, George William, o.s. William, of Andover, Hants, gent. MAGDALEN HALL, matric. 15 Dec., 1854, aged 28; B.A. 1859, M.A. 1861, vicar of Whatton, Notts, 1864-70, rector of Dalham, Suffolk, 1870, until his death 23 Sep., 1875.

Langston, Earle Augustus, 1s. Earle, of Manchester, arm. BRASENOSE COLL., matric. 16 Oct., 1861, aged 18; scholar 1861-4, B.A. 1865, M.A. 1870, held various curacies 1866-82, vicar of Hebburn-on-Tyne since 1882. [30]

Langston, Frederick Foyster, 4s. Stephen, of Horwood, Bucks, cler. ST. JOHN'S COLL., matric. 27 June, 1825, aged 19; B.A. 1829, M.A. 1835 (? died curate of Fenny Compton, Oxon, 7 Aug., 1838). See *Robinson*, 207.

Langston, James Haughton, s. John, of St. James's, Westminster, arm. CHRIST CHURCH, matric. 23 May, 1814, aged 17; created D.C.L. 23 June, 1819, of Sarsden House, Oxon, high sheriff 1819, M.P. Woodstock 1820-6, Oxford 1826-35, and 1841 until his death 19 Oct., 1863. See *Eton School Lists.*

Langston, Stephen, s. Stephen, of Greenwich, Kent, gent. CHRIST CHURCH, matric. 10 Dec., 1783, aged 17; B.A. 1787, M.A. 1790, rector of Hulcot and Little Horwood, Bucks, 1790, until his death 15 March, 1816. See *Robinson*, 137.

Langston, Stephen (Hurt), s. Stephen, of Little Horwood, Bucks, cler. WADHAM COLL., matric. 25 June, 1810, aged 17; scholar 1812-19, B.A. 1814, fellow 1819-25, M.A. 1820, rector of Aston Sandford, Bucks, 1828, perp. curate Southborough, Kent, 1847-72, died 15 March, 1878.

Langton, Arthur, 2s. Wenman Henry, of Leicester, cler. WADHAM COLL., matric. 17 June, 1819, aged 18; B.A. 1823, M.A. 1837, rector of Beeston Regis 1835 87, and of Matlaske and Plumstead 1837-71.

Langton, Bennet, s. Bennet, of Langton, co. Lincoln, arm. TRINITY COLL., matric. 7 July, 1757, aged 20; created M.A. 23 March, 1765, and D.C.L. 16 June, 1790, of Langton, captain Lincolnshire militia, Dr. Johnson's friend, died in 1801, father of George, 1790. [35]

Langton, Charles, 2s. George, of Lincoln (city), arm. TRINITY COLL., matric. 20 Oct., 1820, aged 19; B.A. 1824, M.A. 1827, a student of Lincoln's Inn 1823.

angton, Edward Grenville Gore, 3s. William Henry Powell Gore, of London, arm. CHRIST CHURCH, matric. 11 Oct., 1878, aged 19.

angton, Rev. Frederick William, 1s. Frederick Charles Rivers, of Rastrick, Yorks, gent. MERTON COLL., matric. 14 Oct., 1876, aged 19; B.A. 1880, M.A. 1883.

angton, George, s. Bennet, of Langton, co. Lincoln, arm. CHRIST CHURCH, matric. 1 March, 1790, aged 17; created M.A. from CORPUS CHRISTI COLL. 4 July, 1793, of Langton aforesaid.

angton, George Ferne, s. Bennet, of Langton, co. Lincoln, arm. TRINITY COLL., matric. 7 July, 1757, aged 18; died young.

angton, George Lewis, s. John, of Westminster, arm. MAGDALEN COLL., matric. 22 July, 1731, aged 15.

angton, George Thomas, s. William, of Buckingham, cler. ST. EDMUND HALL, matric. 5 April, 1797, aged 21; vicar of Kempston, Norfolk, 1809, and rector of Barton (St. Andrew's) 1837, until his death 18 Nov., 1841. **[6]**

angton, James, s. John, of St. Mary's, Warwick (town), pleb. ST. EDMUND HALL, matric. 20 May, 1724, aged 19; B.A. 22 March, 1727-8.

angton, Joseph, created D.C.L. 8 July, 1756; of Newton St. Loe, Somerset.

angton, Peregrine, s. Bennet, of St. Marylebone, Middlesex, arm. MERTON COLL., matric. 4 Dec., 1797, aged 17; B.A. 1801, of Gunby, co. Lincoln, assumed the name of MASSINGBERD, died at Exeter 23 Sep., 1856.

angton, Stephen St. Peter, o.s. Thomas, of Carmarthen, arm. MAGDALEN HALL, matric. 30 March, 1844, aged 29; B.A. 1849. **[10]**

angton, Wenman Henry, s. William, of Dublin (city), cler. WADHAM COLL., matric. 10 April, 1783, aged 19; B.A. 1787, M.A. 1793, B.D. 1800, D.D. 1810, rector of Warham St. Mary, with Waterden, Norfolk, 1789, chaplain-in-ordinary to Prince of Wales 1800, and sinecure rector of Longford, co. Derby, 1807, died 4 Nov., 1836.

Langton, Wenman Cavendish, s. Wenman Henry, of Langham, Norfolk, cler. WADHAM COLL., matric. 29 Nov., 1810, aged 17; scholar 1812-17, B.A. 1815.

Langton, William, s. George, of St. Ann's, Westminster, arm. QUEEN'S COLL., matric. 21 March, 1716-17, aged 18; B.A. from ALL SOULS' COLL. 1725, M.A. 1729, a student of the Middle Temple 1716.

Langton, William Gore, s. Edward Gore, of Kiddington, Oxon, arm. NEW COLL., matric. 19 Oct., 1776, aged 17; created M.A. 16 Dec., 1780, of Newton Park, Somerset, in right of his wife, whose surname and arms he assumed, M.P. Somerset 1795-1806, 1812-20, 1831-2, Tregony 1808-12, East Somerset 1832 until his death 14 March, 1847. See Foster's *Peerage*, E. ARRAN.

Langton, William Gore, s. William Gore, of Newton, Somerset, arm. CORPUS CHRISTI COLL., matric. 19 Oct., 1805, aged 18; of Combe Hay, died in his father's lifetime, half-brother of the next named. See Foster's *Peerage*, E. ARRAN. **[15]**

Langton, William Henry Gore, 3s. William Gore, of St. Marylebone, arm. MAGDALEN COLL., matric. 1 Nov., 1820, aged 18; of Clifton, Somerset, M.P. Bristol 1852-65, died 16 May, 1875.

Langton, William Henry Powell Gore, o.s. William, of Burdrop, Wilts, arm. CHRIST CHURCH, matric. 20 Oct., 1841, aged 17; B.A. 1848, M.A. 1849, of Newton Park and Hatch Beauchamp, Somerset, M.P. West Somerset 1851-9, 1863-8, died 11 Dec., 1873. See Foster's *Peerage*, D. BUCKINGHAM, & *Eton School Lists.*

Langton, William Stephen Gore, 1s. William Henry Powell Gore, of London, arm. CHRIST CHURCH, matric. 21 April, 1865, aged 17; B.A. 1871, of Newton Park, Somerset, M.P. Mid Somerset 1878, heir presumptive to the earldom of Temple of Stowe. See Foster's *Peerage*, D. BUCKINGHAM; & *Eton School Lists.*

Langton, Rev. Zachary, s. — L., pleb. MAGDALEN HALL, matric. 5 April, 1718; B.A. 1721, M.A. 1724, died at Oxford in 1786.

Langtry, Richard, s. Richard, of Gosport, Hants, pleb. PEMBROKE COLL., matric. 20 May, 1767, aged 16; B.A. 1771. **[20]**

Langwith, Oswald, s. James, of York (city), pleb. UNIVERSITY COLL., matric. 14 Oct., 1741, aged 19; B.A. 1745, B.C.L. 1767 (? died rector of Thornton, Yorks, 23 Feb., 1768).

Langworthy, Edward Martin, o.s. George, of Manchester, gent. NEW INN HALL, matric. 16 May, 1867, bar.-at-law, Inner Temple, 1873. See Foster's *Men at the Bar* & *Eton School Lists.*

Langworthy, George, s. Francis, of Charleton, Devon, cler. EXETER COLL., matric. 4 Feb., 1725-6, aged 19; B.A. 1729, rector of East Buckland, Devon, 1743.

Langworthy, John, o.s. John, of Crediton, Devon, arm. MAGDALEN HALL, matric. 9 Nov., 1839, aged 31; B.A. 1843, M.A. 1849, vicar of Backwell, Bristol, etc., 1843, until his death 24 Feb., 1882.

Langworthy, Rev. William Henry, o.s. — L., of Exeter (city), gent. WORCESTER COLL., matric. 30 May, 1849, aged 18; B.A. 1853. **[25]**

Lankester, Edward Forbes, 3s. Edwin, of London, D.Med. LINCOLN COLL., matric. 16 Oct., 1873, aged 18; scholar 1873, B.A. 1878, bar.-at-law, Middle Temple, 1878. See Foster's *Men at the Bar* & *St. Paul's School Reg.*, 347.

Lankester, Edwin Ray, 1s. Edwin, of London, arm. CHRIST CHURCH, matric. 14 April, 1866, aged 18, junior student 1866-7, B.A. 1868; Radcliffe travelling fellow 1870, fellow EXETER COLL. 1872, M.A. 1872, and lecturer on math. science (teacher in biology), scholar DOWNING COLL., Cambridge, 1864, professor of zoology and comparative anatomy in University College, London, 1874, F.R.S. 1875, professor of natural history, Edinburgh, in 1881, royal medallist (Royal Society) 1885, editor of 'Quarterly Journal of Microscopical Science' 1870. See *Boase*, 142, & *St. Paul's School Reg.*, 336.

Lanphier, William, s. William, of Gorth Meelis, co. Tipperary, gent. ST. MARY HALL, matric. 25 June, 1793, aged 22.

Lansdown, Joseph Ruscombe, 1s. Joseph Goodall, of St. James's, Bristol, gent. ST. EDMUND HALL, matric. 11 Dec., 1850, aged 18.

Lany, William, s. William, of St. Clement Danes, Westminster, gent. WADHAM COLL., matric. 6 June, 1728, aged 16 (? rector of Wramplingham, Norfolk, 1744). **[30]**

Lanyon, Charles, 2s. Charles, of Belfast, Antrim, Ireland, arm. (after knight). TRINITY COLL., matric. 6 Dec., 1858, aged 18; B.A. 1862, bar.-at-law, Inner Temple, 1865, died 27 Feb., 1877.

Lanyon, Lewis Mortimer, 4s. Charles, of Belfast, arm. (after a knight). PEMBROKE COLL., matric. 28 Oct., 1867, aged 21; brother of the last named. See Foster's *Baronetage.*

Laprimaudaye, Charles Henry, s. Peter, of London, gent. CHRIST CHURCH, matric. 1 March, 1782, aged 17; B.A. 1785, vicar of Leyton, Essex, 1800, until his death 25 March, 1848.

Laprimaudaye, Rev. Charles John, o.s. Stephen, of Calcutta, East Indies, gent. ST. JOHN'S COLL., matric. 23 April, 1825, aged 18; B.A. 1829, M.A. 1832, died at the Collegio Pio, Rome, 20 Jan., 1858.

Lapworth, James Edward, 3s. Alfred, of St. George's, Hanover Square, London, gent. PEMBROKE COLL., matric. 26 May, 1853, aged 19; B.A. 1857, M.A. 1860, bar.-at-law, Middle Temple, 1858, died 3 Jan., 1875.

Larcom, Arthur, 3s. Thomas Aitkin, of Dublin, 'equitis.' ORIEL COLL., matric. 1 March, 1866, aged 18; B.A. 1870, M.A. 1872, entered Foreign Office 1871, Oriental secretary at Teheran 1879, bar.-at-law, Inner Temple, 1875. See Foster's *Men at the Bar.* **[36]**

Larden, George Edge, s. George Harrison, of Chester (city), cler. BRASENOSE COLL., matric. 24 April, 1816, aged 17; B.A. 1820, M.A. 1822, rector of Doverdale, co. Worcester, 1831, vicar of Brotherton, Yorks, and of High Ercal, Salop, at his death 18 Oct., 1859.

Larden, Walter, 2s. George Edward, of Brotherton, Yorks, cler. MERTON COLL., matric. 25 Feb., 1875, aged 19; postmaster 1875-9, B.A. 1879, M.A. 1882, assistant-master of Cheltenham College 1880. See *Rugby School Reg.*

Lardner, William, s. Richard, of Witney, Oxon, pleb. NEW COLL., matric. 21 Oct., 1791, aged 20; B.A. 1795, M.A. 1798, clerk Magdalen College 1793-9, chaplain 1800-2, vicar of Seasalter and curate of Whitstable, Kent, minor canon of Canterbury, died 4 March, 1803. See *Bloxam*, ii. 114, 178.

Large, William John Agg, 1s. John, of Broughton Poges, Oxon, gent. ST. EDMUND HALL, matric. 18 Dec., 1848, aged 21.

Larken, Arthur Staunton, 3s. Edmund, of Tottenham, Middlesex, arm. ST. ALBAN HALL, matric. 17 May, 1834, aged 18; B.A. 1838, portcullis pursuivant of arms 1878-82, Richmond Herald 1882. [5]

Larken, Edmund Roberts, 1s. Edmund, of Tottenham, Middlesex, arm. TRINITY COLL., matric. 20 Oct., 1829, aged 19; B.A. 1833, M.A. 1836, rector of Burton-by-Lincoln 1843. See *Eton School Lists.*

Larkham, William, s. William, of Richmond, Surrey, gent. CORPUS CHRISTI COLL., matric. 1 Nov., 1735, aged 17; scholar 1735, B.A. 1739, M.A. and fellow 1742. See *Alumni West.*, 312.

Larkin, George, s. Josiah, of Bristol (city), gent. BALLIOL COLL., matric. 18 Oct., 1716, aged 15; B.A. 1720, M.A. 1723, B.Med. 1726, D.Med. 1737.

Larking, Lambert Blackwell, s. John, of East Malling, Kent, arm. BRASENOSE COLL., matric. 3 April, 1816, aged 19; B.A. 1820, M.A. 1823, vicar of Ryarsh 1830, and of Burham, Kent, 1837, until his death, 2 Aug., 1868. See *Eton School Lists.*

Larkins, Henry, s. John Pascal, of Greenwich, Kent, arm. UNIVERSITY COLL., matric. 25 Feb., 1813, aged 17; scholar 1814-21, B.A. 1817, M.A. 1819, bar.-at-law, Lincoln's Inn, 1819, died Dec., 1821.

Larkins, John Russell, 1s. Frederick, of Greenwich, Kent, gent. EXETER COLL., matric. 16 Oct., 1884, aged 18; scholar 1884-6, died at Auckland, N.Z., 31 May, 1886. [11]

Larkins, Walter Farquhar, 3s. John Pascal, of Calcutta, East Indies, arm. EXETER COLL., matric. 25 May, 1837, aged 17.

Larkworthy, Richard, s. Gregory, of Cannington, Somerset, cler. MERTON COLL., matric. 17 May, 1738, aged 19; B.A. 26 Feb., 1741-2.

Larnach, Donald Guise, 1s. William James Mudie, of Melbourne, gent. PEMBROKE COLL., matric. 1 May, 1879, aged 19; B.A. 1882, bar.-at-law, Inner Temple, 1887.

Laroche, Henry, s. John, of St. James's, Westminster, gent. MERTON COLL., matric. 10 Nov., 1752, aged 19; probably brother of Sir James Laroche, baronet, and died in 1802. [15]

Larpent, Frederic de Hochepied, 5s. John James, of Antwerp, Belgium, arm. ORIEL COLL., matric. 19 Oct., 1861, aged 18; of the Indian Civil Service. See Foster's *Baronetage.*

Larogue, Robert, s. Robert, of Thurleigh, Beds, cler. LINCOLN COLL., matric. 25 Oct., 1771, aged 18.

Lart, John, 1s. John, of Stratford, Essex, gent. NON-COLL., matric. 24 Oct., 1874, aged 19; a student of the Inner Temple, 1876. See *Robinson*, 364.

Lart, William Stanton, 2s. John, of Stratford, Essex, gent. NON-COLL., matric. 19 Oct., 1876, aged 19; B.A. from PEMBROKE COLL. 1880. See *Robinson*, 367.

Lascelles, Alfred George, 2s. Hon. George Edwin, of Harewood, Yorks. UNIVERSITY COLL., matric. 13 Oct., 1876, aged 19; B.A. 1881, bar.-at-law, Inner Temple, 1885. See Foster's *Peerage.* [20]

Lascelles, Arthur, 5s. (Henry), Earl of Harewood. CHRIST CHURCH, matric. 24 June, 1825, aged 18; B.A. 1828, of Norley Bank, Cheshire, died 19 July, 1880. See Foster's *Peerage.*

Lascelles, Brian Piers, 3s. Hon. Arthur, of Norley, Cheshire. MAGDALEN COLL., matric. 23 April, 1879, aged 19; B.A. 1882, M.A. 1885.

Lascelles, Hon. Daniel Henry, 2s. Henry Thynne, Earl of Harewood. CHRIST CHURCH, matric. 14 Oct., 1881, aged 19. See Foster's *Peerage* & *Eton School Lists.*

Lascelles, Edward, s. Henry, of Harewood, Yorks, arm. (after earl). CHRIST CHURCH, matric. 21 Oct., 1813, aged 17; Viscount Lascelles, died 17 Dec., 1839.

Lascelles, Edwin, s. Henry, Viscount L. (after earl). CHRIST CHURCH, matric. 22 May, 1818, aged 18; fellow ALL SOULS' COLL. 1822-65, B.C.L. 1826, D.C.L. 1831, bar.-at-law, Inner Temple, 1826, M.P. Ripon Feb., 1846-57, died 26 April, 1865. [25]

Lascelles, Edwin, 1s. John, of Whitehaven, Cumberland, arm. PEMBROKE COLL., matric. 20 Nov., 1856, aged 18; B.A. 1861, held various curacies 1861-78, rector of Newton St. Loe, since 1878.

Lascelles, Edwin Agar, 2s. Hon. William, of Wilton Crescent, London, arm. BALLIOL COLL., matric. 24 March, 1852, aged 18; B.A. 1856, bar.-at-law, Inner Temple, 1859, died 23 March, 1877.

Lascelles, Edwin John Moore, 1s. Edwin, of Brighton, cler. PEMBROKE COLL., matric. 24 Jan., 1882, aged 19.

Lascelles, Hon. George Edwin, 3s. Henry, Earl of Harewood. MERTON COLL., matric. 26 June, 1844, aged 17; B.A. 1848, of Sion Hill, Thirsk, bar.-at-law, Inner Temple, 1852, registrar West Riding of Yorkshire, captain Yorks yeomanry hussars 1859-69. See Foster's *Men at the Bar* & *Eton School Lists.*

Lascelles, Henry Thynne, 1s. Henry, Earl of Harewood. CHRIST CHURCH, matric. 12 May, 1842, aged 17; 4th earl, lieut.-colonel commanding Yorks (West Riding) yeomanry hussars 1859-70. See Foster's *Peerage* & *Eton School Lists.* [30]

Lascelles, Hon. James Walter, 4s. Henry, Earl of Harewood. EXETER COLL., matric. 3 May, 1849, aged 17; B.A. 1853, rector of Goldsborough, Yorks, since 1857. See Foster's *Peerage* & *Eton School Lists.*

Lascelles, John, 2s. John, of Whitehaven, Cumberland, arm. PEMBROKE COLL., matric. 13 Feb., 1867, aged 18; B.A. & M.A. 1873, brother of Edwin 1856.

Lascelles, Rev. Maurice George, 4s. Hon. George Edwin, of Harewood, Yorks. MERTON COLL., matric. 14 Oct., 1879, aged 19; B.A. 1883.

Lascelles, Robert, s. William, of Durham (city), gent. LINCOLN COLL., matric. 17 Nov., 1735, aged 16; B.A. 1739, vicar of Gilling and rector of Middleton-in-Teesdale, co. Durham, 1778, until his death 2 Nov., 1801.

Lascelles, Robert, s. Lascelles, of Helperby, Yorks, cler. MERTON COLL., matric. 29 Oct., 1796, aged 17. [35]

Lascelles, Rowley, s. Rowley, of Brighton, Sussex, arm. EXETER COLL., matric. 1 Feb., 1859, aged 20; B.A. 1862, vicar of Elson, Hants, 1865-73, rector of Woollavington, Sussex, since 1873.

Lascelles, Thomas, s. Francis, of Pontefract, Yorks, cler. UNIVERSITY COLL., matric. 3 May, 1735, aged 18; B.A. 10 Feb., 1738-9.

Laskey, Alexander, s. Joseph, of Morton Hamstead, Devon, pleb. EXETER COLL., matric. 2 April, 1726, aged 20; B.A. 1729.

Laskey, John, s. Edward, of Yealmpton, Devon, gent. EXETER COLL., matric. 10 July, 1738, aged 20; B.A. 1742.

Laskey, William, s. William, of Feock, Cornwall, gent. EXETER COLL., matric. 21 June, 1762, aged 18. [40]

Laski, Alexander de, 1s. Alexander, of Brighton, arm. MERTON COLL., matric. 24 Oct., 1885, aged 20.

assetter, Leslie Beauchamp, 2s. Frederick, of Sydney, Australia, arm. MAGDALEN COLL., matric. 16 Oct., 1884, aged 19; B.A. 1887.

atchmore, William, 'frumentarius et farinaus;' privilegiatus 10 Oct., 1817.

aterriere, Fenwick de Sales, 3s. Pierre, of London, D.Med. WORCESTER COLL., matric. 17 Feb., 1842, aged 18.

ates, Charles, s. John James, of Oxford (city), gent. MAGDALEN COLL., matric. 4 Nov., 1793, aged 22.

ates, James, 'musicae studiosus;' privilegiatus 18 Nov., 1763. [5]

Lates, John James, s. James, of St. Ebbs, Oxford, (city), pleb. ALL SOULS' COLL., matric. 14 Oct., 1786, aged 16; B.A. 1790, M.A. 1793, vicar of Winchcombe, co. Gloucester, 1793, rector of Sudeley 1817, and perp. curate Carlton Abbots 1820, until his death 3 Oct., 1831.

Latey, John, s. Richard, of South Molton, Devon, pleb. ST. EDMUND HALL, matric. 8 Dec., 1802, aged 22; B.A. 1806, M.A. 1809, a minor canon Bristol, and rector of Reed, Suffolk, 1813, and of Doynton, co. Gloucester, 1823, until his death 21 Oct., 1846.

Latham, Alexander Mere, 1s. George William, of Sandbach, Cheshire, arm. BRASENOSE COLL., matric. 10 June, 1881, aged 18; B.A. 1885.

Latham, Francis Law, y.s. John, of Sandbach, Cheshire, arm. BRASENOSE COLL., matric. 24 May, 1856, aged 18; scholar 1856-60, B.A. 1860, M.A. 1873, bar.-at-law, Inner Temple, 1864, advocate-general Bombay 1882. See Foster's *Men at the Bar*.

Latham, George William, 1s. John, of Marylebone, London, arm. BRASENOSE COLL., matric. 22 May, 1845, aged 18; B.A. 1849, M.A. 1852, bar.-at-law, Inner Temple, 1852, M.P. Cheshire (Crewe division) Dec., 1885 to June, 1886, died 4 Oct., 1886. See Foster's *Men at the Bar*. [10]

Latham, Henry, s. John, of St. Andrew's, Holborn, London, doctor. BRASENOSE COLL., matric. 8 April, 1812, aged 17; B.A. 1815, M.A. 1818, bar.-at-law, Lincoln's Inn, 1820, vicar of Selmeston with Alceston, Sussex, died 6 Sep., 1866. See *Manchester School Reg.*, i. 197.

Latham, Henry, 1s. Henry, of Harley Street, London, cler. BRASENOSE COLL., matric. 12 March, 1846, aged 17; B.A. 1849, M.A. 1863, bar.-at-law, Inner Temple, 1854, died 7 Jan., 1871.

Latham, John, s. James, of Frodsham, Cheshire, pleb. WADHAM COLL., matric. 29 March, 1737, aged 16; B.A. 10 Feb., 1740-1.

Latham, John, s. John, of Bunney, Notts, cler. ORIEL COLL., matric. 13 March, 1743-4, aged 18; B.A. 1747, perp. curate of Siddington, Cheshire, died 21 June, 1783, father of the next named. See *Manchester School Reg.*, i. 195.

Latham, John, s. John, of Gawsworth, Cheshire, cler. BRASENOSE COLL., matric. 2 June, 1778, aged 16; B.A. 1782, M.A. 1784, B.Med. 1786, D.Med. 1788, of Bradwall Hall, Cheshire, F.R.S., F.L.S., F.R.C.P. 1788, president 1813, physician to Middlesex Hospital 1780-93, to Magdalen Hospital 1789, and St. Bartholomew's 1793, physician extraordinary to the Prince of Wales 1795, and in 1821 when George IV., died 20 April, 1843. See Munk's *Roll*, ii. 393, & *Manchester School Reg.*, i. 195. [15]

Latham, John, s. Shenton, of Nantwich, Cheshire, gent. QUEEN'S COLL., matric. 14 Jan., 1791, aged 17.

Latham, John, s. John, of Oxford (city), doctor. BRASENOSE COLL., matric. 16 June, 1803, aged 16; fellow ALL SOULS' COLL. until 1821, B.C.L. 1810, D.C.L. 1815, of Bradwall Hall, died 30 Jan., 1853, father of John Henry. See *Manchester School Reg.*, i. 197; ii. 284.

Latham, John, y.s. Wilson, of Liverpool, gent. WADHAM COLL., matric. 16 Oct., 1883, aged 18; B.A. 1886.

Latham, John Alfred, o.s. William, of Northwich, Cheshire, arm. MERTON COLL., matric. 16 Oct., 1884, aged 19; B.A. 1887.

Latham, John Francis, s. Thomas, of Boxley, Kent, arm. ST. JOHN'S COLL., matric. 18 Nov., 1801, aged 19. [20]

Latham, John Henry, 1s. John, of London, arm. BRASENOSE COLL., matric. 18 Nov., 1840, aged 17; Craven scholar 1841, until his death 4 July, 1843. See *Rugby School Reg.*, 190.

Latham, John Larking, 2s. Samuel Metcalfe, of Dover, Kent, gent. WORCESTER COLL., matric. 10 Dec., 1846, aged 18; B.A. 1850, M.A. 1853, vicar of Lydden, Kent, since 1865.

Latham, John Mere, 1s. Francis Law, of London, arm. CORPUS CHRISTI COLL., matric. 26 Oct., 1885, aged 19; exhibitioner 1886.

Latham, John Patrick Alexander, 1s. David Macduff, of Greenock in Scotland, arm. BRASENOSE COLL., matric. 21 Oct., 1878, aged 20; B.A. 1882, M.A. 1887.

Latham, Lawrence, s. John, of Romsey, Hants, gent. PEMBROKE COLL., matric. 20 May, 1817, aged 18; B.A. 1821, perp. curate Ampney St. Mary, co. Gloucester, 1833-73, and rector of Quenington 1834-80. [25]

Latham, Lionel Henry, 6s. Charles, of Ingouville, near Havre, arm. MAGDALEN COLL., matric. 20 Oct., 1870, aged 21.

Latham, Mortimer Thomas, 3s. Thomas, of Billingboro', co. Lincoln, cler. BRASENOSE COLL., matric. 1 June, 1836, aged 19; B.A. 1840, vicar of Tattersall, co. Lincoln, since 1846.

Latham, Peter, s. John, of Prestbury, Cheshire, gent. BRASENOSE COLL., matric. 5 May, 1780, aged 19; B.A. 1783.

Latham, Peter Mayer (or Mere), s. John, of London, doctor. BRASENOSE COLL., matric. 18 June, 1806, aged 16; B.A. 1810, M.A. 1813, B.Med. 1814, D.Med. 1816, F.R.C.P. 1818, physician Middlesex Hospital 1815-24, and St. Bartholomew's Hospital 1824-41, physician extraordinary to Queen Victoria 1837, until his death 20 July, 1875. See *Manchester School Reg.*, i. 197; & Munk's *Roll.*, iii. 185.

Latham, Philip Arderne, 2s. Peter Mere, of St. George's, Hanover Square, London, arm. BRASENOSE COLL., matric. 21 Nov., 1861, aged 19; B.A. 1865, M.A. 1869. [30]

Latham, Raymond Mortimer, 1s. Mortimer Thomas, of Coningsby, co. Lincoln, —. EXETER COLL., matric. 15 May, 1875, aged 17; B.A. & M.A. 1882. See *Coll. Reg.*, 168.

Latham, Richard, 1s. Richard, of Sandbach, Cheshire, arm. BRASENOSE COLL., matric. 2 May, 1821, aged 17; scholar 1821-5, B.A. 1825, fellow 1825-36, M.A. 1827, senior bursar 1833, rector of Catworth-Magna, Hunts, 1835, until his death 10 Feb., 1873.

Latham, Robert, s. Nicholas, of Wigan, Lancashire, pleb. BRASENOSE COLL., matric. 22 May, 1770, aged 23; B.A. 1774, M.A. 1776, vicar of Dean, Cheshire, 1776.

Latham, Thomas, s. Charles, of Waltham, co. Leicester, gent. BRASENOSE COLL., matric. 3 May, 1788, aged 17; B.A. 1793, M.A. 1794, vicar of Billingborough, co. Lincoln, 1803, and of Sempringham 1826, until his death 11 May, 1846.

Lathbury, Daniel Connor, 1s. Thomas, of Wotton, near Northampton, cler. BRASENOSE COLL., matric. 21 June, 1850, aged 19; B.A. 1854, M.A. 1861, bar.-at-law, Lincoln's Inn, 1858. See Foster's *Men at the Bar*. [35]

Lathbury, Thomas, o.s. Henry, of Brackley, Northants, gent. ST. EDMUND HALL, matric. 7 April, 1821, aged 22; B.A. 1824, M.A. 1827, a theological writer, perp. curate St. Simon and St. Jude, Bristol, 1848, until his death 11 Feb., 1865.

Lathbury, Thomas Henry, 2s. Thomas, of Downend, near Bristol, cler. MAGDALEN HALL, matric. 12 June, 1852, aged 18; B.A. 1861.

Lathy, Maurice Frederick, 2s. Thomas, of Tillington, Sussex, gent. NON-COLL., matric. 16 Oct., 1886, aged 17.

Latimer, Digby, 3s. Edward, of All Saints, Oxford (city), gent. LINCOLN COLL., matric. 11 Oct., 1825, aged 17; B.A. 1831, M.A. 1833, bar.-at-law, Lincoln's Inn, 1835.

Latimer, Edward William Forty, 2s. Edward, of All Saints, Oxford, gent. LINCOLN COLL., matric. 1 Jan., 1822, aged 18; exhibitioner 1822-30, B.A. 1827, M.A. 1828, rector of Waddesdon, Bucks, 1829, until his death 14 March, 1881. See *Rugby School Reg.*, 125.

Latimer, George Burton Potts, 4s. Edward, of Holywell, Oxford (city), gent. PEMBROKE COLL., matric. 3 July, 1828, aged 19; B.A. 1833, M.A. 1852, perp. curate St. Paul's, Birmingham, 1848. See *Alumni West.*, 495.

Latimer, John Edward, 1s. — L., of All Saints, Oxford (city), gent. MERTON COLL., matric. 16 Dec., 1818, aged 17; postmaster 1819-22, B.A. 1824. [5]

Latimer, Rev. Roynon Charles Washington, 3s. Frederick, of Headington, Oxon, gent. ST. ALBAN HALL, matric. 4 Feb., 1881, aged 21.

Latimer, Rev. William, 7s. Edward, of Oxford (city), gent. LINCOLN COLL., matric. 4 March, 1830, aged 16; exhibitioner 1831-9, B.A. 1833, died 5 May, 1881.

Latter, Arthur Simon, 1s. Simon, of Stepney, London, gent. QUEEN'S COLL., matric. 4 June, 1846, aged 23; B.A. 1850, M.A. 1853, vicar of North Mimms, Herts, 1864-80, chaplain at Coblentz 1880-1, rector of Downham Market 1882.

Latter, Bertram Henry, 3s. Robinson, of Bromley, Kent, arm. CHRIST CHURCH, matric. 12 Oct., 1877, aged 19; exhibitioner 1877-81, B.A. 1881, M.A. 1884, bar.-at-law, Inner Temple, 1883. See Foster's *Men at the Bar.*

Latter, Edmund, of ST. JOHN'S COLL., Cambridge (B.A. 1727, M.A. 1731); incorp. 9 July, 1733. [10]

Latter, Hugh, 4s. Arthur Simon, of North Mimms, Herts, cler. CORPUS CHRISTI COLL., matric. 20 Oct., 1886, scholar 1886.

Latter, Oswald Hawkins, 2s. Arthur Symon, of Fulham, Middlesex, cler. KEBLE COLL., matric. 16 Oct., 1883, aged 19; B.A. 1887.

Lattimer, Robert Binney, 3s. William, of Carlisle, gent. QUEEN'S COLL., matric. 28 Oct., 1881, aged 18; exhibitioner 1881-2, scholar 1882-5, B.A. 1885.

Latton, Henry, s. William, of York Buildings, Middlesex, arm. WADHAM COLL., matric. 22 March, 1755, aged 17; B.A. 1758, M.A. 1762.

Latus, John, s. Ferdinand, of Cockermouth, Cumberland, arm. QUEEN'S COLL., matric. 8 March, 1720-1, aged 20. [15]

Laugharne, Hugh, s. David, of Ashton, Lancashire, pleb. CHRIST CHURCH, matric. 7 Feb., 1775, aged 16; chaplain Warwick Goal, vicar of Radford Semele 1789, and of Rowington 1812, until his death 2 July, 1843.

Laugharne, John, s. John, of Laugharne, co. Carmarthen, gent. JESUS COLL., matric. 1 June, 1715, aged 15; B.A. 16 Jan., 1718-9, M.A. 1721, B.D. 26 Feb., 1729-30 (? rector of Kilgerron, co. Pembroke, 1731).

Laugharne, John Philipps, s. Rowland P.-L., of St. Bride's, co. Pembroke, arm. JESUS COLL., matric. 20 Oct., 1770, aged 16; B.A. 1775, M.A. 1777, of Orlandon, co. Pembroke, father of Sir R. H. Laugharne-Philipps, 8th baronet. See Foster's *Baronetage.*

Laugharne, Thomas, s. John, of Llandawk, co. Carnarvon, gent. JESUS COLL., matric. 5 July, 1715, aged 17; B.A. 1719, M.A. 19 Jan., 1721-2.

Laugharne, Thomas Robert John, o.s. Thomas, c Walcot Bath, arm. JESUS COLL., matric. 18 Ma 1839, aged 18; B.A. 1843, M.A. 1845, of Laugharn Hall, co. Carmarthen, vicar of Burton-on-Wirra Cheshire, 1866-70, and of Rhayader, co. Radno since 1873. [20

Laugharne, Voil, s. Lewis, of St. Elwes, co. Pem broke, gent. ST. MARY HALL, matric. 17 Nov 1733, aged 19.

Laugharne, William, s. Francis, of White Churcl co. Pembroke, pleb. JESUS COLL., matric. 2 Marcl 1718-19, aged 19; B.C.L. 1725.

Laugharne, William, s. William, of Lanrythan, co Pembroke, gent. MAGDALEN HALL, matric. May, 1722, aged 19.

Laugharne, William, s. Arthur, of Lanunwas, cc Pembroke, cler. JESUS COLL., matric. 24 Marcl 1742-3, aged 18.

Laugharne, William Philipps. JESUS COLL., 181 See PHILIPPS. [25

Laughlin, Rev. Edward James, of TRINITY COLL. Dublin (B.A. 1851, M.A. 1857); adm. 'ad eundem 17 Dec., 1857, formerly in the army.

Laughlin, John William, scholar TRINITY COLL Dublin, 1837 (B.A. 1839, M.A. 1855); adm. 'a eundem' 8 March, 1860, rector of St. Peter, Saffro Hill, London, 1856-75, chaplain Victoria Par Hospital 1876, until his death 8 June, 1884, aged 8

Laughton, George, s. John, of Bridgewater, Some set, pleb. WADHAM COLL., matric. 3 April, 175 aged 18; B.A. 1757, M.A. 1771, B. & D.D. 177 J.P. co. Cambridge, vicar of Chippenham, co. Cam bridge, 1794, until his death in 1800.

Laughton, John, s. John, of Taunton, Somerset, plet EXETER COLL., matric. 2 July, 1743, aged 18; B.A 1747.

Laurence, Charles, o.s. Henry, of King-Somborne Hants, gent. NEW COLL., matric. 7 Nov., 187 aged 33. [30

Laurence, Charles, 2s. Henry, of Windsor, Berk arm. MAGDALEN HALL, matric. 13 Oct., 187 aged 22; (HERTFORD COLL.) B.Mus. 1875.

Laurence, Frederick John (Ross), 2s. Benjamin, ('Insula Zachynths,' arm. EXETER COLL., matri 17 May, 1838, aged 17; S.C.L. 1841, B.A. & M.A 1861, rector of Tiptree Heath 1866-82, and of Birch Essex, since 1882.

Laurence, French, s. Richard, of Bath (city), gen CORPUS CHRISTI COLL., matric. 5 March, 177 aged 16; Somerset scholar, B.A. 1777, M.A. 178 D.C.L. 1787, regius professor of civil law 1796-180 M.P. Peterborough Oct., 1796, until his death 2 Feb., 1809, brother of Richard 1778.

Laurence, Henry Hamilton, 5s. Percival, of Ea Claydon, Bucks, cler. NEW COLL., matric. 12 Oct 1883, aged 19; elected scholar of HERTFORD COLL 1882, scholar of NEW COLL. 1883, B.A. 1887.

Laurence, John, s. John, of Barnes, Surrey, arn ST. JOHN'S COLL., matric. 9 Feb., 1742-3, aged 17

Laurence, Richard, s. Jonathan, of Wrockwardin Salop, cler. PEMBROKE COLL., matric. 16 Ma 1727, aged 18; B.A. 21 Jan., 1730-1. [3

Laurence, Richard, s. Richard, of Bath, Somerse gent. CORPUS CHRISTI COLL., matric. 14 Jul 1778, aged 18, exhibitioner 1778, B.A. 1782, M.A 1785; B. & D.C.L. from UNIVERSITY COLL. 179 editor of the historical department of the 'Annu Register,' vicar of Coleshill, Wilts, 1787, and c Great Cheverell 179–, rector of Rolleston, Wilts, c Mersham, Kent, 1805, and of Stone, near Dartfor 181—, deputy professor of civil law 1796, Bampto lecturer 1804, regius professor of Hebrew, and canon of Christ Church 1814-22, archbishop of Cash 1822, until his death 28 Dec., 1838. See *Cotton*, i. 2

Laurence, Richard, o.s. Richard French, of Heading ton, Oxon, cler. NEW INN HALL, matric. 22 Oct 1878, aged 54.

Laurence, Richard French, s. John, of Eltham, Kent, gent. PEMBROKE COLL., matric. 4 Nov., 1814, aged 17; scholar 1814-21, B.A. 1818, M.A. 1821, fellow 1821-3, junior bursar 1822, Bodley's sub-librarian 1822, treasurer of Cashel, died 29 Sep., 1882. See *Robinson*, 188.

Laurence, Robert French, 5s. John, of Eltham, Kent, gent. CHRIST CHURCH, matric. 16 Dec., 1824, aged 17; student 1824-33, B.A. 1828, M.A. 1831, vicar of Chalgrove, Oxon, 1832. See *Robinson*, 200.

Laurence, Thomas French, 4s. John, of Eltham, Kent, gent. ST. JOHN'S COLL., matric. 28 June, 1824, aged 18; fellow 1824-34, B.A. 1828, M.A. 1832, dean of arts 1833, rector of East Farndon, Northants, 1834, until his death 27 Oct., 1837. See *Robinson*, 196.

Laurence, William Rogers, 1s. William Rogers, of Cheltenham, co. Gloucester, gent. QUEEN'S COLL., matric. 11 Dec., 1829, aged 18; B.A. from TRINITY COLL., Cambridge, 1835, perp. curate Whitchurch, Somerset, at his death 26 May, 1843.

Laurens, Gallais, 1s. John, of St. Heliers, Isle of Jersey, arm. JESUS COLL., matric. 31 March, 1854, aged 18; B.A. 1857. [5]

Laurent, Felix, s. Felix, of St. Giles, London, gent. WORCESTER COLL., matric. 20 March, 1812, aged 18; B.A. from ST. ALBAN HALL, 1817, M.A. 1820, master of Alford Grammar School 1822-47, vicar of Saleby, co. Lincoln, 1847, until his death 13 April, 1878.

Laurents, Hugh, s. Philip, of Isle of Jersey, pleb. PEMBROKE COLL., matric. 26 June, 1758, aged 19; chaplain to the Earl of Coventry, master of Kingston-upon-Thames Grammar School, rector of Grafton Flyford, co. Worcester, 1794, until his death 4 April, 1878.

Laurents, Philip, s. Philip, of St. Martin's, Isle of Jersey, pleb. PEMBROKE COLL., matric. 30 Oct., 1751, aged 20; B.A. 1755, master of Bury St. Edmund School 1776, until his death in Nov., 1787.

Laurie, Henry Montague, 4s. David Crawford, of London, D.Med. BALLIOL COLL., matric. 15 Oct., 1884, aged 18; B.A. 1887, Indian Civil Service 1884, bar.-at-law, Middle Temple, 1887.

Lavender, Charles Ernest, 2s. Thomas, of Canterbury, gent. ST. EDMUND HALL, matric. 5 Nov., 1885, aged 21. [10]

Lavers, William, s. William, of Totness, Devon, gent. HART HALL, matric. 30 March, 1720, aged 17; B.A. 6 March, 1723-4.

Laverty, Wallis Hay, 1s. John Nicholas, of St. Helens, Isle of Jersey, gent. QUEEN'S COLL., matric. 17 Oct., 1864, aged 17; scholar 1864-9, B.A. 1868, fellow 1869-73, M.A. 1871, public examiner and moderator in mathematics, rector of Headley, Hants, since 1872.

Lavicount, Stephen Wilkins, 1s. Joseph, of Honiton, arm. WORCESTER COLL., matric. 12 March, 1846, aged 19.

Lavie, Cecil Tudor, 1s. Tudor, of Vizianagram (*sic*), East Indies, arm. NEW COLL., matric. 10 Oct., 1884, aged 20.

Lavie, Germain, 1s. Germain, of St. John's, Hampstead, Middlesex, arm. CHRIST CHURCH, matric. 23 June, 1819, aged 19; B.A. 1823, M.A. 1831, auditor 1849-57, a student of Lincoln's Inn 1823, admitted a solicitor Easter term 1827, died 13 Jan., 1857. See *Eton School Lists*. [15]

Lavie, Germain, 3s. Tudor, of Westminster, arm. CHRIST CHURCH, matric. 8 June, 1854, aged 18; student 1854-61, B.A. 1858, M.A. 1861.

Lavie, Germain, 1s. Germain, of London, arm. CHRIST CHURCH, matric. 14 Oct., 1881, aged 19; B.A. 1886.

Lavie, John, s. Germain, of London, arm. HERTFORD COLL., matric. 27 Oct., 1775, aged 17; B.A. from EXETER COLL. 1781.

Lavie, Tudor, 2s. Tudor, of Madras, East Indies, arm. CHRIST CHURCH, matric. 23 May, 1850, aged 18; student 1850-4, father of Cecil Tudor. See *Alumni West*, 524.

Lavies, Joseph Samuel, o.s. John, of Westminster, Middlesex, gent. ST. MARY HALL, matric. 19 Jan., 1872, aged 47; D.Med., Edinburgh. [20]

Lavies, Robert Sherwood, 1os. Joseph Samuel, of London, D.Med. ST. MARY HALL, matric. 20 Oct., 1884, aged 18.

Lavine, Isaac, s. Isaac, of Isle of Barbados, arm. ST. MARY HALL, matric. 24 June, 1763, aged 22.

Lavington, Richard, s. Jo., of Newton, Bucks, cler. NEW COLL., matric. 20 Jan., 1717-8, aged 17, B.A. 1721; M.A. from CHRIST CHURCH 1724. (Memo.: Rev. Mr. L., of Exeter, died 11 Aug., 1759.)

Law, Alexander Patrick, 1s. Patrick Comerford, of North Repps, Norfolk, cler. CORPUS CHRISTI COLL., matric. 7 June, 1851, aged 19; commoner NEW INN HALL, 1856, B.A. & M.A. 1860. See *Rugby School Reg.*, 288.

Law, Archibald Fitzgerald, 4s. Michael, of Nizza, arm. ORIEL COLL., matric. 16 April, 1872, aged 19; B.A. & M.A. 1880, bar.-at-law, Inner Temple, 1879. See Foster's *Men at the Bar*. [25]

Law, Arthur, 4s. John, of Manchester, gent. WORCESTER COLL., matric. 8 June, 1850, aged 19.

Law, Benjamin, 1s. John, of Batley, Yorks, gent. QUEEN'S COLL., matric. 5 Feb., 1863, aged 18; B.A. 1867, M.A. 1869, bar.-at-law, Middle Temple, 1871. See Foster's *Men at the Bar*.

Law, David Edward, 4s. William John, of Marylebone, London, arm. BALLIOL COLL., matric. 3 June, 1857, aged 19, scholar 1857-62, B.A. 1863; fellow NEW COLL. 1864-73, M.A. 1865, died 9 April, 1873. See *Rugby School Reg.*

Law, Edmund, of ST. JOHN'S COLL., Cambridge (B.A. 1723, fellow CHRIST COLL., M.A. 1727, D.D. 1749); incorp. 8 July, 1732, archdeacon of Carlisle 1743, preb. of Lichfield 1763, and archdeacon of Stafford 1763, preb. of Lincoln 1764, and of Durham 1767, master of Peter House, Cambridge, 1756, chief librarian 1760, professor of theology 1764, bishop of Carlisle 1768, until his death 14 Aug., 1787. See Foster's *Peerage*, E. ELLENBOROUGH. [29]

Law, Edmund Christian, y.s. James Thomas, of Lichfield, co. Stafford, cler. BRASENOSE COLL., matric. 9 June 1846, aged 18; B.A. 1850, M.A. 1856, bar.-at-law, Inner Temple, 1856, some time principal surrogate, Lichfield. See Foster's *Men at the Bar*.

Law, Edward, s. Ewan, of St. George's, Westminster, arm. CHRIST CHURCH, matric. 27 May, 1808, aged 17; student 1808-16, B.A. 1812, M.A. 1815, B. & D.D. 1844, minister of Holy Trinity, Preston, chaplain to British Embassy, St. Petersburg, 1820, died 10 Nov., 1868. See Foster's *Peerage*, B. ELLENBOROUGH; & *Alumni West.*, 467.

Law, George Henry, of QUEEN'S COLL., Cambridge (B.A. 1781, fellow 1781-4, M.A. 1784, D.D. 1804); adm. 'ad eundem' 10 June, 1834, F.R.S., F.S.A., visitor of Wadham College, vicar of Torpenhow, Cumberland, 1787, rector of Kelsall, Herts, 1791, and of Willingham, co. Cambridge, 1802, preb. of Carlisle 1785, and of York 1812, vicar of Great Carleton, co. Lincoln, 1797, bishop of Chester 1812-24, and of Bath and Wells 1824, until his death 22 Sep., 1845, son of Edmund, bishop of Carlisle. See Foster's *Peerage*.

Law, George Still, o.s. George, of St. George the Martyr, London, arm. ORIEL COLL., matric. 25 Nov., 1830, aged 17; B.A. 1834, M.A. 1838, bar.-at-law, Lincoln's Inn, 1838. See Foster's *Men at the Bar*.

Law, Henry, 1s. Francis, of Bengal, arm. MAGDALEN HALL, matric. 21 May, 1835, aged 19. [34]

Law, James, s. John, of Banagher, co. Derry, Ireland, cler. PEMBROKE COLL., matric. 2 Feb., 1788, aged 16 (? if died at Bethelfield Manse, Kirkcaldy, 5 May, 1859, aged 83, in the 61st year of his ministry).

Law, John, s. William, of Langfield, Yorks, pleb. BRASENOSE COLL., matric. 11 April, 1747, aged 20.

Law, John, s. John, archdeacon of Rochester. ORIEL COLL., matric. 8 Feb., 1792, aged 18 (? lieutenant 77th foot, died in 1807).

Law, John, s. John, of Tawton, Devon, gent. EXETER COLL., matric. 15 Nov., 1817, aged 18; B.A. 1821, M.A. 1824, vicar of Bradworthy with Pancras Wyke, Devon, 1823, until his death 12 Jan., 1845.

Law, John Pilling, 1s. James, of Rochdale, co. Lancaster, arm. BRASENOSE COLL., matric. 19 Nov., 1863, aged 19; B.A. & M.A. 1875, a student of Inner Temple 1868.

Law, Markham John, 4s. William John, of Marylebone, London, arm. BALLIOL COLL., matric. 1 June, 1853, aged 19; B.A. 1858, bar.-at-law, Inner Temple, 1861, manager of the Consolidated Bank, Strand, London, died 7 March, 1880. See Foster's *Peerage* & *Rugby School Reg.*, 288.

Law, Robert, s. Walter, of Bucklebury, Berks, gent. BALLIOL COLL., matric. 19 June, 1806, aged 25.

Law, Robert Arbuthnot, 3s. Patrick Comerford, of North Repps, Norfolk, cler. ST. ALBAN HALL, matric. 1 Nov., 1881, aged 39; rector of Larling, Norfolk, 1869-70, and of Gunthorpe with Bale since 1870. [5]

Law, Rev. Robert Hartley, o.s. Thomas Charles, of Padiham, Lancashire, arm. BRASENOSE COLL., matric. 18 Oct., 1881, aged 19; scholar 1881-5, B.A. 1885.

Law, Samuel, s. Allen, of South Brent, Somerset, cler. ST. MARY HALL, matric. 30 May, 1734, aged 17; B.A. 1738.

Law, Samuel, s. Michael, of Dublin (city), doctor. UNIVERSITY COLL., matric. 10 May, 1777, aged 19; B.A. 1781.

Law, Stephen, s. William, of St. Mary's, Oxford (city), gent. QUEEN'S COLL., matric. 4 April, 1717, aged 18; B.A. 1720.

Law, Thomas, s. John, of Tawton, Devon, gent. EXETER COLL., matric. 15 Dec., 1796, aged 19; exhibitioner 1796, B.A. 1800, rector of Newton Tracey 1814, until his death 18 Feb., 1832. See *Coll. Reg.*, 149. [10]

Law, William, 3s. James, of Rochdale, Lancashire, arm. BRASENOSE COLL., matric. 9 June, 1870, aged 19; B.A. 1873, M.A. 1877, vicar of Holy Trinity, Hammersmith, since 1885.

Law, William Henry, o.s. Thomas S. —, of Barnstaple, Devon, gent. TRINITY COLL., matric. 27 Nov., 1850, aged 18. See *Eton School Lists.*

Law, William John, s. Ewan, of St. George's, Hanover Square, London, arm. CHRIST CHURCH, matric. 16 May, 1804, aged 17; student 1804-14, B.A. 1808, M.A. 1810, of Horsted, Sussex, bar.-at-law, Lincoln's Inn, 1813, a commissioner insolvent debtor's court 1824-53, chief commissioner 1853, until his death 5 Oct., 1869. See Foster's *Peerage*, B. ELLENBOROUGH; & *Alumni West.*, 461.

Law, Rev. William John, 1s. William, of Marston Trussell, Northants, cler. WORCESTER COLL., matric. 30 Oct., 1866, aged 19; a student of the Inner Temple 1869.

Law, William Smalley, 2s. William, of Northampton, gent. NON-COLL., matric. 17 Oct., 1885, aged 20. [15]

Lawes, James (Townsend), s. William, of Warminster, gent. ST. ALBAN HALL, matric. 1 Dec., 1797, aged 18; B.A. 1803, M.A. 1813, under-master Warminster School, master of Marlborough Grammar School 1808, perp. curate Easton, Wilts, vicar of Halberton, Devon, 1821, until his death 13 Oct., 1828.

Lawes, (Sir) John Bennet (Bart.), 1s. John Bennet, of Harlington, Herts, gent. BRASENOSE COLL., matric. 14 March, 1833, aged 18; of Rothamsted, Herts, J.P., created a baronet 19 May, 1882. See Foster's *Baronetage* & *Eton School Lists.*

Lawford, Edward Lancelot, o.s. Edward, of Leighton Buzzard, Beds, D.Med. EXETER COLL., matric. 3 June, 1876, aged 20.

Lawford, Henry Smith, 1s. Edward, of London, arm. CHRIST CHURCH, matric. 4 June, 1835, aged 19; B.A. 1839, M.A. 1841, solicitor to the secretary of State for India. See *Eton School Lists.*

Lawford, Herbert Browning, 4s. George, of Wandsworth, Surrey, arm. TRINITY COLL., matric. 29 Jan., 1883, aged 18; B.A. 1886. [20]

Lawford, Rev. John Grant, 2s. William (Robinson), of Leighton, Beds, gent. WADHAM COLL., matric. 1 July, 1828, aged 17; B.A. 1833, M.A. 1835, died at Brussels, 23 June, 1847.

Lawford, Lancelot Edward, 1s. Henry Smith, of London, arm. NEW COLL., matric. 14 Oct., 1871, aged 18; B.A. 1875, M.A. 1879, bar.-at-law, Inner Temple, 1877. See Foster's *Men at the Bar* & *Eton School Lists.*

Lawford, Robinson, s. William, of Gilsborough, Northants, gent. WADHAM COLL., matric. 13 July, 1764, aged 29.

Lawford, William, s. Samuel, of Cottesbrook, Northants, pleb. PEMBROKE COLL., matric. 18 Nov., 1730, aged 19; B.A. 1734.

Lawless, Hon. Cecil John, 2s. Valentine, Baron Cloncurry. CHRIST CHURCH, matric. 11 Dec., 1839, aged 19; M.P. Clonmel Sep., 1846, until his death 5 Nov., 1853. See Foster's *Peerage* & *Eton School Lists.* [25]

Lawless, Valentine Frederick, 1s. Edward, Baron Cloncurry. BALLIOL COLL., matric. 18 June, 1858, aged 17; B.A. from MAGDALEN HALL, 1861, 4th baronet. See Foster's *Peerage.*

Lawley, (Sir) Francis (Bart.), s. Robert, of Canwell, co. Warwick, baronet. CHRIST CHURCH, matric. 2c Oct., 1800, aged 18; fellow ALL SOULS' COLL. until 1815, B.C.L. 1808, D.C.L. 1813, 7th baronet, M.P. Warwickshire Nov., 1820-32, died s.p. 30 Jan., 1851. See Foster's *Peerage*, B. WENLOCK.

Lawley, Francis Charles, 4s. (Paul Beilby), Baron Wenlock. BALLIOL COLL., matric. 21 March, 1844, aged 18, B.A. 1848; fellow ALL SOULS' COLL. 1848-53, B.C.L. 1851, a student of the Inner Temple 1847, M.P. Beverley 1852 to July, 1854, special *Times*' correspondent during American war, and attached to the Confederate army 1862. See Foster's *Peerage* & *Rugby School Reg.*, 200.

Lawley-Thompson, Paul Beilby, s. Robert, of Canwell, co. Stafford, baronet. CHRIST CHURCH, matric. 11 Feb., 1803, aged 18, B.A. 1806; fellow ALL SOULS' COLL. 1806-17, B.C.L. 1810, D.C.L. 1815, 8th baronet, M.P. Wenlock 1826-32, Yorkshire (South Riding) 1833-37, assumed the final surname of THOMPSON by royal licence 1 June, 1839, created Baron Wenlock 13 May, 1839, died 9 May, 1852. See Foster's *Peerage* & *Rugby School Reg.*, 76.

Lawley, Stephen Willoughby, 3s. Paul Beilby, Baron Wenlock. BALLIOL COLL., matric. 27 May, 1841, aged 18; B.A. 1845, M.A. 1853, rector of Escrick Yorks, 1848-68, sub-dean of York 1852-62. See Foster's *Peerage* & *Rugby School Reg.*, 195. [30]

Lawley, William, o.s. William, of Wellington, Salop, arm. WORCESTER COLL., matric. 20 March, 1834, aged 20.

Lawrance, Henry, o.s. Eleazor, of Ipswich, arm. TRINITY COLL., matric. 16 Dec., 1828, aged 20.

Lawrance, Henry, 1s. Edward, of Isle of Barbados, arm. EXETER COLL., matric. 18 Oct., 1882, aged 19.

Lawrance, John, s. Edward, of Feok, Cornwall, arm. EXETER COLL., matric. 6 March, 1750-1, aged 16.

Lawrance, Thomas Dalton, 1s. John Compton, of Dunsby, co. Lincoln, arm. ORIEL COLL., matric. 27 Oct., 1883, aged 18; B.A. 1887. [35]

Lawrance, Robert, s. Robert, of Reading, Berks, gent. ST. EDMUND HALL, matric. 9 Dec., 1817, aged 28; B.A. 1821, M.A. 1824, rector of Bleadon, Somerset, 1850, until his death 16 Nov., 1871.

THE INNER QUADRANGLE, ST. JOHN'S.—*Reduced facsimile from Loggan.*

Lawrell, James, s. James, of Marylebone, Middlesex, arm. CHRIST CHURCH, matric. 5 Feb., 1800, aged 19; of Frimley, Surrey, died in 1842. See *Eton School Lists.*

Laurell, John, 5s. James, of Stoke, Surrey, arm. MERTON COLL., matric. 23 Oct., 1834, aged 18; B.A. 1838, M.A. 1841, a student of the Inner Temple 1835, died incumbent of St. Matthew's, City Road, London, E., 25 Oct., 1865.

Lawrence, Andrew, s. Thomas, of Devizes, Wilts, gent. HERTFORD COLL., matric. 20 March, 1777, aged 21; vicar of Longparish, Hants, at his death 31 July, 1821, brother of Sir Thomas, D.C.L.

Lawrence, Anthony Cocks, 3s. Walter Lawrence, of Brussels, Belgium, arm. MAGDALEN COLL., matric. 12 Dec., 1861, aged 18; B.A. 1865, rector of Whittington, co. Gloucester, 1868.

Lawrence, Arthur, s. Humphrey, of Launceston, Cornwall, gent. QUEEN'S COLL., matric. 10 Nov., 1773, aged 18; B.A. 1777. [5]

Lawrence, Arthur, 1s. Northmore Herle Pierce, of Launceston, Cornwall, gent. WADHAM COLL., matric. 18 June, 1851, aged 18; B.A. from ST. MARY HALL 1856, rector of St. Ewe, Cornwall, 1864-86, of Eversley, Hants, 1886.

Lawrence, Arthur Evelyn Barnes, 1s. Henry Frederick Barnes, of Bridlington, Yorks, cler. WORCESTER COLL., matric. 16 Oct., 1871, aged 19; exhibitioner 1873-76, B.A. 1876, M.A. 1878, vicar of St. Luke's, Liverpool 1883, assumed the additional surname of LAWRENCE in 1877.

Lawrence, Ashley Laurence Barnes, 3s. Henry Frederick Barnes, of Bridlington, Yorks, cler. ORIEL COLL., matric. 13 Oct., 1873, aged 19; B.A. 1877, M.A. 1880, vicar of Thornes, Yorks, 1881-6, and of Aberford, Yorks, 1886, assumed the additional surname of LAWRENCE in 1877.

Lawrence, Basil Keith Senior, 3s. Christopher, of Ash Priors, Somerset, cler. JESUS COLL., matric. 27 Oct., 1868, aged 18; scholar 1868-70.

Lawrence, Benjamin, s. John, of Builth, Brecon, gent. JESUS COLL., matric. 9 Nov., 1777, aged 18; B.A. 1782, rector of Darley Dale, co. Derby, 1808, until his death 18 Feb., 1838. [10]

Lawrence, Charles Arthur, 1s. Charles William, of Cirencester, co. Gloucester, arm. NEW COLL., matric. 13 Oct., 1876, aged 18; B.A. 1879, M.A. 1883.

Lawrence, Charles D'Aguilar, 2s. Charles, of Liverpool, cler. CHRIST CHURCH, matric. 18 Oct., 1867, aged 19; B.A. 1872, M.A. 1874, rector of Bermondsey, Surrey, 1871-9.

Lawrence, Charles Washington, 2s. Charles, of Liverpool, Lancashire, arm. BRASENOSE COLL., matric. 9 April, 1823, aged 18; B.A. 1827, M.A. 1830, incumbent of St. Luke's, Liverpool, at his death 20 Nov., 1861. See *Eton School Lists.*

Lawrence, Charles William, o.s. Charles, of Cirencester, arm. NEW COLL., matric. 30 June, 1840, aged 17; fellow 1840-50, B.A. 1844, M.A. 1848. See Foster's *Baronetage.*

Lawrence, Christian William, 2s. Walter, of Sandywell Park, near Cheltenham, arm. MAGDALEN COLL., matric. 7 June, 1855, aged 19; of Sandywell Park and Sevenhampton Manor, co. Gloucester, minister resident at Quito. [15]

Lawrence, Edward, 1s. Edward, of Liverpool, arm. BALLIOL COLL., matric. 20 Oct., 1874, aged 19; B.A. 1878, of the Indian Civil Service 1876, a student of the Inner Temple 1876. See *Rugby School Reg.*

Lawrence, Frederick Augustus, s. Richard James, of St. Marylebone, London, arm. QUEEN'S COLL., matric. 3 March, 1801, aged 20; B.A. 1804, M.A. 1807, captain 43rd regiment, died in Germany in 1841. See *Eton School Lists.*

Lawrence, George, s. George, of Brampton, co. Hereford, gent. ST. JOHN'S COLL., matric. 10 July, 1731, aged 17; B.A. 1735.

Lawrence, George, s. William, of Cirencester, co. Gloucester, pleb. ORIEL COLL., matric. 20 April, 1744, aged 17; B.A. 23 March, 1747-8.

Lawrence, George Alfred, 1s. Alfred Charnley, of Sandhurst, Kent, cler. BALLIOL COLL., matric. 29 Nov., 1845, aged 18; B.A. from NEW INN HALL 1850, novelist, author of 'Guy Livingstone,' etc., bar.-at-law, Inner Temple, 1852, died 29 Sep., 1876. See *Rugby School Reg.*, 228 [20]

Lawrence, George D'Aguilar, 1s. Arthur, of Larchfield, Surrey, knight. CHRIST CHURCH, matric. 11 Oct., 1878, aged 18; late lieutenant grenadier guards. See Foster's *Baronetage* & *Eton School Lists.*

Lawrence, George Guerard, o.s. George, of Château de Portail, near Tours, cler. ST. EDMUND HALL, matric. 25 June, 1841, aged 14; B.A. 1846, M.A. 1848, a student of Lincoln's Inn 1847, perp. curate Shirley, Hants, vicar of St. Paul's, Huddersfield, 1862, until his death 30 May, 1874.

Lawrence, George Patrick Charles, o.s. George Alfred, of Old Buckenham, Norfolk, arm. CORPUS CHRISTI COLL., matric. 8 Feb., 1878, aged 18; bar.-at-law, Lincoln's Inn, 1884. See Foster's *Men at the Bar* & *Eton School Lists.*

Lawrence, George Whitehorne, s. Benjamin, of Isle of Jamaica, arm. PEMBROKE COLL., matric. 14 March, 1761, aged 17.

Lawrence, Herbert Cecil Barnes, 2s. Henry Frederick Barnes, of Bridlington, Yorks, cler. TRINITY COLL., matric. 28 Jan., 1873, aged 20; scholar LINCOLN COLL. 1873-7, B.A. 1876, M.A. 1879, head-master Perse School, Cambridge, 1884, assumed the additional surname of LAWRENCE. [25]

Lawrence, Horace Hayes Montgomery, 3s. Richard Charles, of Lahore, East Indies, arm. NEW COLL., matric. 16 Oct., 1874, aged 19; B.A. 1878, a student of Lincoln's Inn 1876.

Lawrence, Hubert Carlton, 4s. Thomas Reginald, of Wolverhampton, gent. WORCESTER COLL., matric. 20 Oct., 1881, aged 19; scholar 1880-5, B.A. 1885.

Lawrence, Hugh Mullineux, 1s. Hugh Mullineux, of Manchester, gent. NON-COLL., matric. 26 Jan., 1885, aged 19.

Lawrence, Humphrey, 2s. Humphrey, of Lifton, Devon, arm. EXETER COLL., matric. 4 Feb., 1830, aged 18.

Lawrence, James, s. James, of Jamaica, arm. ST. MARY HALL, matric. 5 Dec., 1768, aged 17. [30]

Lawrence, James, 2s. James, of Liverpool, Lancashire, arm. BRASENOSE COLL., matric. 22 May, 1845, aged 17; B.A. 1849, M.A. 1852, perp. curate Ellel, Lancashire, 1856-64, died 4 April, 1885.

Lawrence, John, s. Thomas, of Pennsylvania, arm. UNIVERSITY COLL., matric. 17 Nov., 1741, aged 16; associate judge of the district of Pennsylvania. See *St. Paul's School Reg.*, 82.

Lawrence, John, s. John, of Sevenhampton, co. Gloucester, pleb. QUEEN'S COLL., matric. 18 June, 1751, aged 20; B.C.L. 1767.

Lawrence, John Hendrickson, 1s. Samuel, of Isle of Nevis, West Indies, arm. EXETER COLL., matric. 18 May, 1820, aged 18; B.A. 1824.

Lawrence, Sir John Laird Mair, Bart., created D.C.L. 6 July, 1859 (son of Lieut.-Col. Alex Lawrence), G.C.B. 1857, created a baronet 16 Aug., 1858, for services at Lahore in suppressing the Indian Mutiny; governor-general of India 1864-8, created Baron Lawrence 3 April, 1869, G.C.S.I. 1861, P.C. 1858, died 27 June, 1879, buried in Westminster Abbey. See Foster's *Peerage.* [35]

Lawrence, Rev. John Robert, 1s. John, of St. Ives, Hunts, gent. CHRIST CHURCH, matric. 14 Oct., 1870, aged 19; B.A. 1874, M.A. 1877, a student of the Inner Temple 1874. See *Rugby School Reg.*

Lawrence, Rev. John Thomas, 1s. Thomas, of Leeds, gent. MERTON COLL., matric. 1 May, 1878, aged 19; scholar 1878-82, B.A. 1882, M.A. 1886.

Lawrence, Lewis, 2s. Charles, of Llanelwedd, co. Radnor, arm. JESUS COLL., matric. 30 June, 1821, aged 18; B.A. 1825, curate of Brewood, co. Stafford, died 19 Dec., 1831.

Lawrence, Neville George Murray, 1s. John, of Hampstead, Middlesex, gent. QUEEN'S COLL., matric. 15 May, 1844, aged 18; B.A. 1849, M.A. 1851, vicar of Forebridge, co. Stafford, 1853-72, chaplain at Freiburg in Baden since 1880.

Lawrence, Philip, s. Philip, of Sutton, Wilts. pleb. MAGDALEN HALL, matric. 13 May, 1727, aged 18; B.A. from CHRIST CHURCH 17 March, 1730-1, M.A. 1734, vicar of Henley, and rector of Ash Bocking, Suffolk, 1740, until his death 24 Feb., 1793.

Lawrence, Philip, s. Philip, of Henley, Suffolk, cler. CHRIST CHURCH, matric. 26 April, 1758, aged 17; B.A. 1762, M.A. 1764.

Lawrence, Richard, s. Richard, of ——, Dorset, cler. EXETER COLL., matric. 22 Oct., 1730, aged 19; B.A. 1734. [5]

Lawrence, Richard Brissett, s. James, of Jamaica, West Indies, arm. BALLIOL COLL., matric. 2 Nov., 1813, aged 23.

Lawrence, Richard James, s. James, of Jamaica, West Indies, arm. ST. MARY HALL, matric. 29 Oct., 1762, aged 18; died 8 Nov., 1830. See biographical notice in *Gent.'s Mag.*, 472.

Lawrence, Robert, s. Walter, of Sevenhampton, co. Gloucester, gent. QUEEN'S COLL., matric. 7 June, 1743, aged 18; B.A. 1747.

Lawrence, Robert, s. Robert, of Shurdington, co. Gloucester, arm. ORIEL COLL., matric. 10 April, 1783, aged 17; B.A. 1787, M.A. 1790 (? B. & D.D. from WORCESTER COLL. 3 May, 1815, as R. L. TOWNSEND [see that name], rector of Alderton, co. Gloucester, 1795).

Lawrence, Robert, 4s. John, of Newport, co. Monmouth, gent. WORCESTER COLL., matric. 28 Jan., 1865, aged 19; B.A. 1869. [10]

Lawrence, Robert John Grewse, s. Benjamin, of Marylebone, Middlesex, cler. CHRIST CHURCH, matric. 9 Feb., 1815, aged 18.

Lawrence, Thomas, s. Thomas, of St. Margaret's, Westminster, gent. TRINITY COLL., matric. 20 March, 1726-7, aged 15; B.A. 1730, M.A. 1733, B.Med. 1736, D.Med. 1740, F.R.C.P. 1744, president 1767-74, died 6 June, 1783. See Munk's *Roll.*, ii. 150.

Lawrence, Thomas, s. John, of Builth, co. Brecon, pleb. JESUS COLL., matric. 3 April, 1770, aged 18.

Lawrence, Sir Thomas, created D.C.L. 14 June, 1820, then president of the Royal Academy (son of Thomas, a supervisor of excise), A.R.A. 1791, R.A. 1794, a principal painter in ordinary to the King 1792, knighted 20 April, 1815, born at Bristol 13 April, 1769, died unmarried 7 Jan., 1830, buried in St. Paul's Cathedral. See *Gent.'s Mag.*, 174.

Lawrence, Rev. Thomas, s. Thomas, of Demerara, West Indies, arm. EXETER COLL., matric. 2 July, 1816, aged 16; B.A. 1821, M.A. 1833, bar.-at-law, Lincoln's Inn, 1827, died 31 May, 1881. [15]

Lawrence, Thomas Edward, 4s. Henry, of Tenby, co. Pembroke, arm. JESUS COLL., matric. 31 May, 1860, aged 21; B.A. 1864, M.A. 1874, rector of Bridenbury, co. Hereford, 1872-4, vicar of Far Cotton, Northants, 1876-80, rector of Walgrave, Northants, 1880-2.

Lawrence, Thomas Northmore, 3s. Northmore Herle Pierce, of Launceston, Cornwall, arm. TRINITY COLL., matric. 16 June, 1862, aged 18; B.A. 1866, bar.-at-law, Lincoln's Inn, 1869, died 8 July, 1886. See Foster's *Men at the Bar*.

Lawrence, Walter, 4s. Edward Sampson, of London, gent. ST. JOHN'S COLL., matric. 13 Oct., 1877, aged 18; scholar 1877-84, B.A. 1881, bar.-at-law, Inner Temple, 1883. See *Robinson*, 369.

Lawrence, Walter Lawrence, s. William Morris, of Hempstead, co. Gloucester, arm. MAGDALEN COLL., matric. 4 July, 1817, aged 18; of Sandywell Park and Sevenhampton Manor, J.P., D.L., assumed the surname and arms of LAWRENCE in lieu of MORRIS by royal licence 25 Aug., 1815, a student of Lincoln's Inn, 1821, died 3 Dec., 1877.

Lawrence, Walter Roper, 6s. George, of Moreton-on-Lugg, co. Hereford, arm. BALLIOL COLL., matric. 17 Oct., 1877, aged 20; of the Indian Civil Service 1877, bar.-at-law, Inner Temple, 1883, assistant commissioner Punjab. See Foster's *Men at the Bar*. [20]

Lawrence, William Edwards, o.s. William, of Wotton-under-Edge, co. Gloucester, arm. BRASENOSE COLL., matric. 5 April, 1832, aged 18.

Lawrence, William Frederick, 1s. Charles Washington, of Liverpool, cler. CHRIST CHURCH, matric. 19 Jan., 1864, aged 19; B.A. 1867, M.A. 1872, of Cowesfield House, Wilts, J.P., bar.-at-law, Lincoln's Inn, 1871, M.P. Liverpool (Abercromby division) Nov., 1885. See Foster's *Men at the Bar* & *Eton School Lists.*

Lawrence, William Robert, 1s. William, of Chelsea, Middlesex, arm. WORCESTER COLL., matric. 8 Dec., 1842, aged 19.

Lawrence, Rev. Zante Webb, 1s. James Eli, of Wandsworth, Surrey, gent. EXETER COLL., matric. 22 Oct., 1880, aged 19; B.A. 1883.

Lawrenson, William Robert, o.s. William, of Dublin (city), arm. ORIEL COLL., matric. 12 Feb., 1819, aged 17; B.A. 1824. [25]

Lawrie, Andrew Douglas, 1s. Andrew, of London, gent. CHRIST CHURCH, matric. 16 Oct., 1874, aged 18; B.A. 1878, M.A. 1882, of Mount Mascal, Kent, bar.-at-law, Inner Temple, 1879. See Foster's *Men at the Bar* & *Eton School Lists.*

Lawrie, George James, s. Archibald, of Loudoun, co. Ayr, Scotland, cler. BALLIOL COLL., matric. 29 March, 1817, aged 20.

Lawry, Samuel Simon, s. John, of Lambeth, Surrey, cler. QUEEN'S COLL., matric. 24 Nov., 1772, aged 18; B.A. 1776, M.A. 1779, rector of Blunham, Beds, 1782, until his death in 1806.

Laws, Edward, 1s. John Milligen, of Lamphey Court, near Pembroke (town), arm. WADHAM COLL., matric. 28 May, 1856, aged 19; of Tenby, co. Pembroke, J.P.

Laws, Thomas Cox, s. John, of St. Ann's, London, Middlesex, gent. ST. JOHN'S COLL., matric. 10 Oct., 1715, aged 16; B.C.L. 1722. [30]

Lawson, Andrew, 2s. Marmaduke, of York (city), cler. MERTON COLL., matric. 1 Feb., 1819, aged 18; of Aldborough Manor, and Boroughbridge Hall, Yorks, J.P., D.L., M.P. Boroughbridge 1830 (unseated), Knaresborough 1835-7, and 1841-7, died 28 Feb. 1853. See Foster's *Yorkshire Collection.*

Lawson, Andrew Sherlock, 1s. Andrew, of Bramfield, Suffolk, arm. MERTON COLL., matric. 28 May, 1842, aged 17; postmaster 1842-4, of Aldborough Manor and Boroughbridge Hall, Yorks, J.P. D.L., died 22 May, 1872.

Lawson, Charles, s. Thomas, of East Kirkby, co. Lincoln, cler. CORPUS CHRISTI COLL., matric. 11 Feb., 1746-7, aged 18; scholar 1748-9, B.A. 21 March, 1750-1, M.A. 1753, 2nd master Manchester School July, 1749-64, high master 1764, until his death 19 April, 1807. See *Manchester School Reg.*, i. 121, etc.

Lawson, Charles, scholar ST. JOHN'S COLL., Cambridge, 1823 (B.A. 1824, M.A. 1827); adm. 'ad eundem' 2 July, 1829 (? archdeacon of Barbados).

Lawson, Charles Philip, 3s. Robert, of Tiverton, Devon, arm. BALLIOL COLL., matric. 14 March, 1850, aged 17; B.A. 1854, M.A. 1856, assistant-curate St. John's, Cheltenham, died 28 Dec., 1857.

Lawson, Francis, s. John, of Tavistock Street, London, arm. QUEEN'S COLL., matric. 18 Feb., 1752, aged 14; bar.-at-law, Inner Temple, 1758, father of the next named. [35]

Lawson, George, s. Francis, of London, arm. CHRIST CHURCH, matric. 26 May, 1785, aged 18; B.A. 1789, M.A. 1792 (? vicar of Heversham, Westmoreland, 1797). See *Alumni West.*, 419.

Lawson, George Mervyn, 2s. George, of London, gent. PEMBROKE COLL., matric. 29 Jan., 1885, aged 19.

Lawson, Harry Lawson Webster, 1s. Edward Levy, of London, gent. BALLIOL COLL., matric. 29 Jan., 1881, aged 18; B.A. 1884; a student of Inner Temple 1881, M.P. West St. Pancras since Nov., 1885. See *Eton School Lists.*

Lawson, Henry Graham, 4s. Charles, of Edinburgh, gent. WADHAM COLL., matric. 9 March, 1853, aged 17; B.A. 1856, M.A. 1859, bar.-at-law, Middle Temple, 1863. See Foster's *Men at the Bar.*

Lawson, James, s. John, of Canterbury (city), pleb. UNIVERSITY COLL., matric. 15 May, 1740, aged 18; B.A. from LINCOLN COLL. 26 Jan., 1743-4 (Memo.: Rev. J. Lawson, of Belvidere, Auchterarder, Scotland, died Aug., 1798, in his 75th year). [5]

Lawson, James, 3s. Marmaduke, of Aldborough, Yorks, cler. ST. ALBAN HALL, matric. 25 Nov., 1824, aged 18; B.A. 1828, M.A. 1831, vicar of Buckminster with Sewsterne, co. Leicester, 1834, until his death 19 March, 1872. See Foster's *Yorkshire Collection.*

Lawson, Rt. Hon. James Anthony, created D.C.L. 17 June, 1885 (son of James Lawson, of Waterford), scholar TRINITY COLL., Dublin, 1836, B.A. 1838, LL.B. 1841, LL.D. 1850, professor political economy 1840-5, bar.-at-law, King's Inns, Dublin, 1840, Q.C. 1857, sergeant-at-law 1860, legal adviser to Government in Ireland 1858-61, solicitor-general (I.) 1861-5, attorney-general (I.) 1865-6, a judge of Common Pleas (I.) 1868-87, M.P. Portarlington 1865-8, etc., P.C. England 1870, and Ireland 1865, died 10 Aug., 1887.

Lawson, John, s. Robert, of Newcastle-on-Tyne, Northumberland, arm. LINCOLN COLL., matric. 28 March, 1715, aged 17.

Lawson, John, s. John, of Barton, Beds, arm. LINCOLN COLL., matric. 13 Dec., 1735, aged 17.

Lawson, John, 4s. Marmaduke, of Boroughbridge, Yorks, cler. ST. ALBAN HALL, matric. 4 March, 1825, aged 17; B.A. 1829, M.A. 1833, vicar of Seaton Carew, co. Durham, since 1835. See Foster's *Yorkshire Collection.* [10]

Lawson, John Ancram, 2s. Joseph, of Clifton, co. Gloucester, gent. EXETER COLL., matric. 28 Jan., 1865, aged 18; B.A. 1868, M.A. 1873, rector of Copmanford, Hunts, 1881-5, vicar of Great Shelford, co. Cambridge, since 1885.

Lawson, John Grant, 2s. Andrew Sherlock, of Aldborough Manor, Yorks, arm. CHRIST CHURCH, matric. 15 Oct., 1875, aged 19; B.A. & M.A. 1882, bar.-at-law, Inner Temple, 1881. See Foster's *Men at the Bar.*

Lawson, Marmaduke Alexander, M.A. from TRINITY COLL., Cambridge, 2s. John, of Seaton Carew, co. Durham, cler. Incorp. from MAGDALEN COLL. 19 March, 1868, aged 28; Sherardian professor of botany 1868-83. See Foster's *Yorkshire Collection.*

Lawson, Richard, s. James, of Kirkham, Lancashire, pleb. BRASENOSE COLL., matric. 21 May, 1724, aged 18; B.A. 27 Feb., 1727-8.

Lawson, Richard, 6s. Andrew, of Wrangton, Suffolk, arm. MERTON COLL., matric. 1 Dec., 1853, aged 18; died May, 1863. See Foster's *Yorkshire Collection.* [15]

Lawson, Richard, 3s. Andrew, of Aldborough, Yorks, arm. CHRIST CHURCH, matric. 27 May, 1882, aged 18.

Lawson, Robert, 1s. Robert, of Richmond, Yorks, arm. CHRIST CHURCH, matric. 26 May, 1841, aged 19; student 1842-9, B.A. 1845, M.A. 1847, perp. curate Offenham, co. Worcester, 1848-64, rector of Upton-on-Severn 1864, hon. canon of Worcester 1874.

Lawson, Rev. Samuel, s. Henry, of Bolton, Lancashire, cler. BRASENOSE COLL., matric. 16 March, 1735-6, aged 17; B.A. 1739, M.A. 1742, died June, 1755. See *Manchester School Reg.*, i. 96.

Lawson, Walter Edward, 3s. William, of London, gent. NEW COLL., matric. 20 Oct., 1873, aged 26.

Lawson, West, s. William, of Boston, co. Lincoln, gent. BRASENOSE COLL., matric. 19 May, 1779, aged 18, exhibitioner 1779-82; demy MAGDALEN COLL. 1782-5, B.A. 1783, died 25 March, 1785. See *Manchester School Reg.*, i. 154; & *Bloxam*, vii. 65. [20]

Lawson, Wilfrid, 1s. Sir Wilfrid, of Netherhall, Cumberland, baronet. TRINITY COLL., matric. 15 Oct., 1881, aged 18; B.A. 1885, a student of Inner Temple 1883. See Foster's *Baronetage.*

Lawson, William, s. Wilfrid, of Isel, Cumberland, baronet. QUEEN'S COLL., matric. 26 Jan., 1714-5, aged 16; B.A. 1718, died unmarried.

Lawson, William, s. William, of Wigtoft, co. Lincoln, pleb. BRASENOSE COLL., matric. 15 May, 1777, aged 19; demy MAGDALEN COLL. 1779-82, B.A. 1781, fellow 1782-92, M.A. 1783 (? vicar of Marsham, Yorks, 1791), died in College 17 Jan., 1792. See *Manchester School Reg.*, i. 166; & *Bloxam*, vii. 55.

Lawson, William Crose, 1s. James Ashmer, of Armagh, Ireland, gent. EXETER COLL., matric. 7 June, 1870, aged 19.

Lawson, William John, 1s. William, of Longhirst, Bothall, Northumberland, arm. BRASENOSE COLL., matric. 9 June, 1841, aged 19; of Longhirst J.P., D.L., a student of Inner Temple 1843, died 6 Nov., 1859. [25]

Lawton, Hugh, s. Christopher, of Cork, Ireland, arm. ORIEL COLL., matric. 3 Feb., 1795, aged 16; of Lake Marsh, co. Cork, died 1859. See *Eton School Lists.*

Lawton, John, s. Robert, of Lawton, Cheshire, arm. BRASENOSE COLL., matric. 14 March, 1765, aged 18; of Lawton, died 25 March, 1804, father of the next named.

Lawton, John, s. John, of Hough, Cheshire, arm. BRASENOSE COLL., matric. 14 Dec., 1790, aged 19; B.A. 1794 (as LAWSON).

Lawton, John Thomas, 3s. Thomas, of Oldham, Lancashire, gent. NON-COLL., matric. 11 Oct., 1879, aged 22; B.A. from WADHAM COLL. 1882, M.A. 1886, vicar of Bedford, Leigh, Lancashire, 1886.

Lax, George Robert Gilling, 2s. Thomas Gilling, of Cheddar, Somerset, gent. WADHAM COLL., matric. 19 March, 1851, aged 18; B.A. 1856, M.A. 1878, assumed the additional surname of LAX by royal licence 20 May, 1868, rector of Fitzhead, Somerset, 1861. [30]

Lax, George Robert Gilling-, 1s. George Robert, of Old Werton, Hunts, cler. KEBLE COLL., matric. 14 Oct., 1879, aged 18; commoner CHARSLEY HALL 1879, B.A. 1885.

Laxton, Messing Thomas, 1s. Matthew, of Greetham, Rutland, arm. PEMBROKE COLL., matric. 30 May, 1850, aged 21; bar.-at-law, Lincoln's Inn, 1857. See Foster's *Men at the Bar.*

Laxton, Robert, s. Robert, of Leatherhead, Surrey, gent. PEMBROKE COLL., matric. 2 April, 1773, aged 18; fellow EXETER COLL. 1775-83, B.A. 1779, died in 1783. See *Boase*, 111.

Laxton, William, 1s, Matthew, of St. Augustines, Bristol, arm. EXETER COLL., matric. 15 May, 1828, aged 18; scholar TRINITY COLL. 1829-34, B.A. 1833, M.A. 1834; vicar of Atworth, Wilts, 1848-76, rector of Oddington, Oxon, 1876.

Laxton, William Holden Scott, 1s. William, of Holt, Wilts, cler. TRINITY COLL., matric. 14 Oct., 1872, aged 20; B.A. 1876, M.A. 1881, a master at Clifton College. [35]

Lay, George James Pattle, o.s. George, of Cawnpore, East Indies, arm. LINCOLN COLL., matric. 14 Feb., 1826, aged 18.

Lay, George William, o.s. James, of Southwark, Surrey, gent. ST. EDMUND HALL, matric. 2 July, 1873, aged 28.

Lay, William, 'cook of Brasenose College;' privilegiatus 21 May, 1778.

Layard, (Sir) Austen Henry, G.C.B., created D.C.L. 5 July, 1848 (son Henry Peter John Layard), attaché to H.M. embassy at Constantinople 1849-52, foreign under secretary 1852 and 1861-6, lord rector of Aberdeen 1855-6, commissioner of Works 1868-9, M.P. Aylesbury 1852-7, Southwark 1860-70, minister to Spain 1869-77, ambassador at Constantinople 1877-80, P.C. 1868, G.C.B. 1878. See Foster's *Baronetage*.

Layard, Daniel Peter, created D.C.L. 20 June, 1792, D.Med. Rheims 1742, F.R.S. London and Gottingen, licentiate of the College of Physicians 1752, died at Greenwich Feb., 1802, aged 82. See Munk's *Roll*, ii. 181.

Layard, Rev. Ernest Brownlow, 1s. Brownlow Edward, of Windsor, Berks, arm. KEBLE COLL., matric. 19 Oct., 1874, aged 17; B.A. 1878, M.A. 1886. See *Eton School Lists*. **[5]**

Laycock, James Akenhead, 1s. Joshua, of Harewood, Yorks, cler. WORCESTER COLL., matric. 15 Oct., 1864, aged 19; B.A. 1869, M.A. 1871.

Laycock, William, 2s. William, of Barnsley, Yorks, cler. ST. EDMUND HALL, matric. 19 Oct., 1865, aged 24; B.A. 1868, M.A. 1872, vicar of Hurdsfield, Cheshire, since 1877.

Laye, Arthur Henry Webb, o.s. Henry Thomas, of Scarborough, arm. BRASENOSE COLL., matric. 28 Nov., 1872, aged 18.

Laye, Henry Thomas, s. Francis, of Doncaster, Yorks, arm. CHRIST CHURCH, matric. 29 May, 1797, aged 19; vicar of Rampton, Notts, 1802, and of Pickering, Yorks, 1804, until his death in 1809. See *Alumni West.*, 449.

Layman, Edwin, 3s. Thomas, of St. George's, Southwark, gent. KEBLE COLL., matric. 13 Oct., 1873, aged 19; B.A. 1878, bar.-at-law, Middle Temple, 1878. **[10]**

Layng, Henry, s. Henry, of Wells, Somerset, doctor. BALLIOL COLL., matric. 30 May, 1715, aged 17; B.A. 6 Feb., 1718-19, M.A. 1722.

Layng, Henry, s. Henry, of Paul's Pury, Northants, cler. NEW COLL., matric. 19 Aug., 1749, aged 19; B.A. 1753, M.A. 1757.

Layng, William Wright, 1s. William, of Overstone, Northants, cler. ST. MARY HALL, matric. 6 Feb., 1866, aged 20; B.A. & M.A. 1873, vicar of Spilsby 1873-85, chaplain of Spilsby 1881-5, vicar of Hundleby 1883-5, rector of Rippingale, co. Lincoln, since 1885.

Layton, Charles Miller, o.s. Edward, of Chelsea, Middlesex, arm. ST. MARY HALL, matric. 6 May, 1842, aged 18; lieut. 35th regiment. See *Eton School Lists*.

Layton, Nicholas, s. Isaac, of Fenchurch Street, London, pleb. BALLIOL COLL., matric. 26 March, 1765, aged 18; B.A. 1768, M.A. 1772. **[15]**

Layton, Thomas Charles Litchfield, 1s. Charles, of Windsor, Berks, gent. PEMBROKE COLL., matric. 14 Nov., 1839, aged 16; scholar 1839-54, B.A. 1845, M.A. 1846, fellow 1854-6, rector of St. Aldate, Oxford, 1856-9, held various curacies 1859-77, vicar of Sempringham, co. Lincoln, since 1877.

Layton, William Edward, 2s. Edward, of Sidmouth, Devon, arm. EXETER COLL., matric. 1 Feb., 1862, aged 18; commoner ST. ALBAN HALL, 1865, B.A. & M.A. 1868, has held various curacies since 1869.

Lazarus, Adolf Max, 2s. Harry Moritz, of Manchester, gent. PEMBROKE COLL., matric. 23 Oct., 1879, aged 18; scholar 1879-84, B.A. 1883, B.C.L. & M.A. 1886, bar.-at-law, Inner Temple, 1886.

Lea, Abel Humphreys, 1s. Abel, of Kidderminster, co. Worcester, gent. WORCESTER COLL., matric. 18 June, 1846, aged 19; B.A. 1851, M.A. 1853, curate of Loxley, near Warwick, 1857-71, rector of Lighthorne, and vicar of Chesterton, co. Warwick, 1871, until his death 20 Oct., 1872.

Lea, Arthur Augustus, 1s. John, of Kidderminster, co. Worcester, gent. WADHAM COLL., matric. 13 April, 1842, aged 16; B.A. 1847, died 13 May, 1848, from the effects of a railway accident. **[20]**

Lea, Arthur Augustus, 3s. Frederick Simcox, of London, cler. CORPUS CHRISTI COLL., matric. 21 Oct., 1878, aged 18; scholar 1878-83, B.A. 1882, M.A. 1885, assistant-master at Haileybury College. See *Rugby School Reg.*

Lea, Benjamin, s. Thomas, of Kidderminster, co. Worcester, pleb. MERTON COLL., matric. 10 Oct., 1726, aged 18; B.A. 1730.

Lea, Edward Thomas, 2s. Thomas, of Falmouth, Isle of Jamaica, cler. ST. EDMUND HALL, matric. 22 Oct., 1883, aged 19; B.A. 1886.

Lea, Frederick Simcox, 1s. Thomas Simcox, of Hampstead, Middlesex, arm. WADHAM COLL., matric. 10 July, 1847, aged 23, B.A. 1851; fellow BRASENOSE COLL. 1853-6, M.A. 1854, of Astley Hall, co. Worcester, perpetual curate Holy Trinity, Stepney, 1855-72, vicar of Compton Dando, Somerset, 1872-3, rector of Tedstone Delamere since 1873, preb. of Hereford 1885.

Lea, George, 4s. John, of Kidderminster, co. Worcester, gent. WADHAM COLL., matric. 30 Jan., 1823, aged 18; B.A. 1826, M.A. 1829, perpetual curate of Christ Church, Birmingham, and preb. of Lichfield 1840-64, perpetual curate St. George, Edgbaston, 1864, until his death 10 May, 1883. **[25]**

Lea, James, s. Henry, of Westminster, pleb. CHRIST CHURCH, matric. 8 July, 1737, aged 17; B.A. 1741.

Lea, James, o.s. James, of Walsall, co. Stafford, gent. WORCESTER COLL., matric. 1 Dec., 1837, aged 18; B.A. 1842, M.A. 1845, bar.-at-law, Lincoln's Inn, 1845. See Foster's *Men at the Bar*.

Lea, James Herbert, 1s. Richard, of Tezpur, East Indies, arm. BALLIOL COLL., matric. 19 Oct., 1886, aged 19.

Lea, John, s. Samuel, of Newport, Salop, cler. CHRIST CHURCH, matric. 3 May, 1746, aged 19; B.A. 29 Jan., 1749-50, M.A. 1752.

Lea, John Joseph, 2s. Thomas, of Hagley, co. Worcester, gent. PEMBROKE COLL., matric. 29 Oct., 1840, aged 19; B.A. 1845, M.A. 1857. **[30]**

Lea, John Walter, 2s. John, of Blakebrook, Kidderminster, co. Worcester, arm. WADHAM COLL., matric. 22 Jan., 1845, aged 17; B.A. 1848.

Lea, Josiah Turner, 2s. William, of Stone, co. Worcester, arm. UNIVERSITY COLL., matric. 6 May, 1841, aged 18; B.A. 1845, vicar of Holy Trinity, Far Forest, co. Hereford, 1853. See *Rugby School Reg.*, 202.

Lea, Reginald Stephen, 2s. Thomas Simcox, of Astley, co. Worcester, arm. BRASENOSE COLL., matric. 8 June, 1865, aged 19; B.A. 1869, M.A. 1872. See *Rugby School Reg.*

Lea, Samuel, s. Samuel, of Stoke, co. Stafford, cler. MAGDALEN HALL, matric. 17 March, 1743-4, aged 18; B.A. from ST. EDMUND HALL, 1747, M.A. 1750.

Lea, Thomas, s. Thomas, of Henley-in-Arden, co. Warwick, arm. TRINITY COLL., matric. 5 Dec., 1811, aged 18; B.A. 1815, M.A. 1820, vicar of Bishops Itchington, co. Warwick, 1820, rector of Tadmarton, Oxon, 1824, until his death, 26 Oct., 1866. **[35]**

Lea, Rev. Thomas Simcox, 1s. Frederick Simcox, of Stepney, Middlesex, cler. BRASENOSE COLL., matric. 8 June, 1876, aged 19; scholar HERTFORD COLL. 1876-80, B.A. 1880, M.A. 1883.

Lea, William, 1s. William, of Stone, co. Warwick, arm. BRASENOSE COLL., matric. 6 June, 1838, aged 18; B.A. 1842, M.A. 1859, vicar of St. Peter's, Droitwich, 1849, hon. canon of Worcester 1858, archdeacon 1881. See *Rugby School Reg.*, 181.

Lea, William, 1s. Josiah Turner, of Ribbesford, co. Worcester, KEBLE COLL., matric. 18 Oct., 1881, aged 19; B.A. 1885.

Lea, William Arch, s. Benjamin, of Halesowen, Salop, cler. ALL SOULS' COLL., matric. 11 July, 1750, aged 17; B.A. 1754, chaplain R.N., curate of St. Kenelm's and Frankly Chapels, born 17 Jan., 1732, died at Halesowen, Salop, 19 Feb., 1802.

Lea, William Nowell, 1s. John Thomas Wildman, of Netherton, co. Worcester, gent. KEBLE COLL., matric. 18 Oct., 1881, aged 18.

Leach, Abraham, s. Abraham, of Pembroke (town), arm. HERTFORD COLL., matric. 26 June, 1783, aged 19; of Corston, co. Pembroke, J.P., died 20 March, 1843, father of Henry, 1813.

Leach, Rev. Alfred Wynter, 7s. Richard Howell, of Hampstead, Middlesex, arm. TRINITY COLL., matric. 18 Oct., 1875, aged 18; B.A. 1879.

Leach, Andrew John, 4s. Richard Howell, of London, gent. ST. JOHN'S COLL., matric. 17 April, 1871, aged 19; B.A. 1874, bar.-at-law, Lincoln's Inn, 1876. See Foster's *Men at the Bar.* [5]

Leach, Arthur Francis, 3s. Thomas, of Paddington, Middlesex, gent. NEW COLL., matric. 15 Oct., 1869, aged 18, scholar 1869-74, B.A. 1874; fellow ALL SOULS' COLL. 1874-82, M.A. 1877, bar.-at-law, Middle Temple, 1876. See Foster's *Men at the Bar.*

Leach, Francis Edwards, 2s. Henry, of Manerbere, co. Pembroke, arm. EXETER COLL., matric. 20 Oct., 1824, aged 18.

Leach, Francis George, s. Abraham, of Corston, co. Pembroke, gent. PEMBROKE COLL., matric. 12 May, 1815, aged 18; scholar 1817-20, B.A. 1819, fellow 1820-9, M.A. 1821 (as George Francis), rector of Stackpole and St. Petrox, co. Pembroke. See *Rugby School Reg.*, 104.

Leach, George, s. George, of Plymouth, Devon, arm. ORIEL COLL., matric. 23 Oct., 1802, aged 20; B.A. 1806.

Leach, George Pemberton, 1s. George Archibald, of Londonderry, Ireland, gent. ST. JOHN'S COLL., matric. 27 June, 1864, aged 19; scholar 1864-9, B.A. 1869, bar.-at-law, Lincoln's Inn, 1871, a commissioner under Government. See Foster's *Men at the Bar.* [10]

Leach, Henry, s. Abraham, of Pembroke (town), arm. ORIEL COLL., matric. 4 June, 1813, aged 19; of Corston, co. Pembroke, died 22 April, 1864.

Leach, John, s. Philip, of Monmouth (town), pleb. ALL SOUL'S COLL., matric. 18 Dec., 1732, aged 17; B.A. 1736 (? rector of Litchet Maltravers, Dorset, 1753, and Over Compton, Dorset, with Sutton Montague, Dorset, 1772).

Leach, (Sir) John; created D.C.L. 5 July, 1810, of St. Albans, Herts (son of Richard Leach, of Bedford, coppersmith), bar.-at-law, Middle Temple, 1790, bencher 1807, patent of precedency 1807, recorder of Seaford 1795, and M.P. July, 1806 until chancellor of the Duchy of Cornwall Feb., 1816, chief justice of Chester 1816, vice-chancellor and knighted 17 Jan., 1817, master of the rolls and privy councillor 1827, until his death 16 Sep., 1834.

Leach, John, o.s. John, of Pembroke (town), arm. UNIVERSITY COLL., matric. 25 April, 1844, aged 18.

Leach, Rev. John, 2s. George Charles, of Oxford (city), gent. MAGDALEN HALL, matric. 4 Feb., 1867, aged 23; servitor or exhibitioner CHRIST CHURCH 1867-70 B.A. 1870, M.A. 1878 [15]

Leach, John Frederick, 7s. Abraham, of Monckton, co. Pembroke, gent. BRASENOSE COLL., matric. 6 Feb., 1823, aged 18; B.A. 1827, M.A. 1831, bar.-at-law, Inner Temple, 1831.

Leach, John Henry, 5s. Thomas, of Barton-under-Needwood, co. Stafford, arm. BRASENOSE COLL., matric. 10 June. 1847, aged 17; B.A. 1851, fellow 1852-62, M.A. 1854, vicar of Gillingham, Kent, 1867-71, died 24 Dec., 1871.

Leach, Kenneth Henry, 1s. John Henry, of London, cler. NEW COLL., matric. 9 Dec., 1881, aged 18; B.A. 1885.

Leach, Octavius, 6s. Abraham, of Monckton, co. Pembroke, gent. PEMBROKE COLL., matric. 17 May, 1820, aged 17; scholar JESUS COLL. 1822-31, B.A. 1824, M.A. 1827, rector of Hubberstone, co. Pembroke, 1844, until his death 25 March, 1869.

Leach, Phil, s. Phil, of Castle Cary, Somerset, pleb. BALLIOL COLL., matric. 5 March, 1724-5, aged 14; B.A. 1728, M.A. 1733. [20]

Leach, Philip, s. Edward, of Monmouth, gent. ORIEL COLL., matric. 8 March, 1759, aged 19; B.A. 1762, rector of Larling and vicar of East Winch, Norfolk, 1765, until his death 24 May, 1817.

Leach, Robert, s. Robert, of Odcombe, Somerset, pleb. TRINITY COLL., matric. 30 March, 1751, aged 19; B.A. 1755.

Leach, Robert, s. George, of Mold, Flint, gent. JESUS COLL., matric. 22 Nov., 1779, aged 19.

Leach, Robert, s. Robert, of Compton, Somerset, cler. WADHAM COLL., matric. 28 Oct., 1780, aged 18. [24]

Leach, Rev. Robert, 3s. Robert, of Rochdale, Lancashire, arm. CORPUS CHRISTI COLL., matric. 4 Nov., 1869, aged 19; B.A. 1873, M.A. 1876.

Leach, Robert Burton, 2s. Walter Burton, of Sutton Montis, Somerset, cler. BRASENOSE COLL., matric. 6 Dec., 1855, aged 18, scholar 1855-9, B.A. 1859, M.A. 1862; a master St. Peter's College, Radley, 1862-4, rector of Sutton Montis 1864-71, and since 1875, and chaplain at Oporto 1871-8.

Leach, Thomas, 1s. Thomas, of St. Paul's, London, arm. MERTON COLL., matric. 9 June, 1831, aged 18; postmaster 1833-5, B.A. 1835, M.A. 1852, bar.-at-law, Middle Temple, 1840, died 23 March, 1881. See *Rugby School Reg.*, 146.

Leach, Thomas Cary, s. Philip, of Boconnoc, Cornwall, cler. EXETER COLL., matric. 26 April, 1771, aged 18; B.A. 1775, M.A. 1778, B.D. 1784, fellow 1776, until his death 1 June, 1785. See *Coll. Reg.*, 111.

Leach, Walter Burton, 1s. Robert, of Sutton Montis, Somerset, arm. WADHAM COLL., matric. 30 Oct., 1819, aged 18; B.A. 1823, M.A. 1827, vicar of Chilthorne Domer and rector of Sutton Montis and perp. curate Lovington, Somerset, 1825, until his death 24 Feb., 1860.

Leacock, William Thomas, s. John, of Isle of Barbados, West Indies, gent. QUEEN'S COLL., matric. 11 Oct., 1817, aged 19. [30]

Leacroft, John, s. Thomas, of Wirksworth, co. Derby, gent. UNIVERSITY COLL., matric. 28 Feb., 1723-4, aged 17; bar.-at-law, Lincoln's Inn, 1735, died 9 Sep., 1787.

Leadam, Isaac Saunders, 3s. Thomas Robinson, of London, arm. UNIVERSITY COLL., matric. 19 Oct., 1867, aged 18, scholar 1867-72, B.A. 1871; fellow BRASENOSE COLL. 1872-6, S.C.L. 1872, M.A. 1874, assistant classical tutor 1873-5, bar.-at-law, Lincoln's Inn, 1876, inspector of schools 1874-6, etc. See Foster's *Men at the Bar* & *Robinson*, 345.

Leader, Charles, s. John, of Great Dunmow, Essex, gent. NEW COLL., matric. 1 July, 1715, aged 18; B.A. 1719, M.A. 14 Jan., 1722-3 (? rector of Evenlode, co. Worcester, 1739).

Leader, John, s. John, of Drumtarrif, co, Cork, gent. ST. ALBAN HALL, matric. 2 May, 1817, aged 24.

Leader, John Temple, o.s. William, of Putney, Surrey, arm. CHRIST CHURCH, matric. 12 Feb., 1828, aged 17; M.P. Bridgewater 1835 to May, 1837, Westminster 1837-41. [35]

Leader, William, 1s. William, of Putney, Surrey, arm. CHRIST CHURCH, matric. 24 April, 1820, aged 18; B.A. 1824, a student of Lincoln's Inn, 1824, died at Oxford 28 Feb., 1826. See *Alumni West.*, 481.

Leader, William, 1s. Henry, of Inniskeel, co. Donegal, gent. PEMBROKE COLL., matric. 21 Feb., 1856, aged 19.

Leah, Thomas, of QUEEN'S COLL., Cambridge (B.A. 1831, M.A. 1838); adm. 'ad eundem,' 14 May, 1858, rector of St. Keyne, Cornwall, 1833.

Leah, William, 5s. John, of Everton, near Liverpool, gent. BRASENOSE COLL., matric. 24 Oct., 1865, aged 18; B.A. 1868.

Leahy, John White, 1s. John, of Dublin, arm. UNIVERSITY COLL., matric. 14 Oct., 1871, aged 19; B.A. 1876, of Southill, co. Kerry, J.P., high sheriff 1877, a student of the Inner Temple 1874. See *Eton School Lists.*

Leake, William, s. Joshua, of Wellington, Salop, gent. CHRIST CHURCH, matric. 13 Nov., 1769, aged 17; B.A. 1773, M.A. 1776.

Leake, Lieut.-Col. William Martin, created D.C.L. 26 June, 1816 (s. John Martin Leake, of Thorpe Hall, Essex), died 6 Jan., 1860. See *Gent.'s Mag.,* i. 303. [5]

Leakey, John Arundel, 1s. James, of St. David's, Exeter, gent. QUEEN'S COLL., matric. 28 Jan., 1841, aged 18; B.A. 1844, M.A. 1877, vicar of Topsham, Devon, 1857-80, rector of St. Gerrans 1880.

Leakey, Rev. John Arundell, 1s. John Arundell, of London, cler. NON-COLL., matric. 13 April, 1872, aged 19, B.A. 1876; M.A. from QUEEN'S COLL. 1877.

Leal, John, 3s. John, of Keith, Scotland, gent. NON-COLL., matric. 22 Oct., 1875, aged 32.

Lean, Arthur Stuckey, 2s. George Stuckey, of Bath, Somerset, arm. TRINITY COLL., matric. 16 Jan., 1875, aged 19; B.A. 1879, M.A. 1881, of Bath, banker. See *Rugby School Reg.*

Lean, George Stuckey, 1s. George Stuckey, of London, arm. TRINITY COLL., matric. 17 Oct., 1870, aged 19; B.A. 1874, M.A. 1877, bar.-at-law, Lincoln's Inn, 1877, died 26 Dec., 1884. See *Rugby School Reg.*

Lean, Hugh Vincent, 3s. James, of Calcutta, arm. NEW COLL., matric. 20 Jan., 1877, aged 19; B.A. 1880, M.A 1883. [11]

Leapingwell, William, of St. John's Street, Oxford, surgeon; privilegiatus 5 June, 1847.

Lear, Edward Denison, 1s. Francis, of Bishopstone, Wilts, cler. KEBLE COLL., matric. 19 Jan., 1875, aged 19; B.A. 1878, vicar of Blackmore, Hants, 1884.

Lear, Edward William, 3s. Francis, of Salisbury, Wilts, cler. NEW COLL., matric. 27 May, 1856, aged 21. See *Eton School Lists.*

Lear, Francis, s. Thomas, of Downton, Wilts, cler. ORIEL COLL., matric. 21 Oct., 1806, aged 17; demy MAGDALEN COLL. 1809-19, B.A. 1810, M.A. 1813, fellow 1819-22, B.D. 1821, rector of Chilmark, Wilts, 1824-42, and of Bishopstone 1842-50, preb. of Salisbury 1830, archdeacon 1836, dean 1846, until his death 23 March, 1850. [15]

Lear, Francis, born at Downton, Wilts, 1s. Francis, archdeacon of Salisbury. CHRIST CHURCH, matric. 12 May, 1842, aged 18; B.A. 1846, M.A. 1849, preb. of Salisbury 1856-64, chancellor 1861-4, precentor 1864-75, rector and vicar of Bishopstone 1850, canon residentiary of Sarum 1862, archdeacon 1875, etc.

Lear, Herbert Nelson, 2s. Francis, of Bishopstone, Wilts, cler. KEBLE COLL., matric. 19 Oct., 1880, aged 18; B.A. 1884.

Lear, Rev. Sidney Henry, born at Chilmark, Wilts, 2s. Francis, dean of Salisbury. CHRIST CHURCH, matric. 20 Oct., 1847, aged 18, B.A. 1851; fellow ALL SOULS' COLL. 1851-60, M.A. 1855, died 6 Feb., 1867.

Lear, Thomas, s. Thomas, of Angmering, Sussex, gent. NEW COLL., matric. 15 March, 1764, aged 19; B.A. 1767, M.A. 1771, a fellow of Winchester 1773, vicar of Downton, Wilts, and Peverell, Dorset, 1781-1824, died 27 March, 1828.

Leared, Arthur, D.Med. from TRINITY COLL., Dublin, 1860 (B.A. 1845, B.Med. 1847); adm. 'ad eundem' 7 Feb., 1861. [20]

Learmonth, Alexander, 1s. John, of Edinburgh, Scotland, arm. UNIVERSITY COLL., matric. 17 March, 1847, aged 17; of Dean, Midlothian, J.P., a student of the Inner Temple 1847, lieut.-col. 17th lancers, M.P. Colchester (Nov.) 1870-80, died 10 March, 1887. See *Eton School Lists.*

Leary, Philip Herbert, 6s. Cornelius, of Clapham, Surrey, arm. WADHAM COLL., matric. 24 Jan., 1873, aged 19; B.A. 1876, M.A. 1879, has held various curacies since 1876.

Leary, Thomas Humphrys Lindsay, 1s. Daniel, of Liverpool, Lancashire, gent. BRASENOSE COLL., matric. 6 Dec., 1845, aged 18, scholar 1845-8; B.A. from ST. MARY HALL 1853, M.A. 1859; D.C.L. from BRASENOSE COLL. 17 Dec., 1864, head-master Derby Grammar School 1859-65, vicar of St. Philip the Evangelist, Camberwell, 1883. See *Manchester School Reg.,* iii. 275.

Leasinby, John Bleay, s. — L., of Oxford (city), gent. ST. ALBAN HALL, matric. 14 Nov., 1789, aged 17, B.A. 1793; chorister MAGDALEN HALL 1780-9, M.A. 1799, chaplain 1802, until his death 10 June, 1818. See *Bloxam,* i. 200.

Leask, William Keith, 2s. James, of Aberdeen, arm. MERTON COLL., matric. 28 Jan., 1878, aged 20; scholar WORCESTER COLL. 1877-81. [25]

Leather, Percival Charles du Sautoy, 2s. Frederick John, of Cramond, near Edinburgh, arm. NEW COLL., matric. 23 Jan., 1886, aged 18.

Leatherbarrow, Jonathan, s. Jonathan, of Stockport, Cheshire, pleb. BRASENOSE COLL., matric. 17 March, 1717-8, aged 17; B.A. 1721, M.A. 1726.

Leatherdale, George Fenning, 2s. George, of Island of Mauritius, cler. QUEEN'S COLL., matric. 22 Oct., 1878, aged 18; exhibitioner 1878-83, B.A. 1882, M.A. 1885.

Leatherdale, Rev. Vincent John, 1s. George, of Mocha, Isle of Mauritius, cler. EXETER COLL., matric. 3 June, 1876, aged 19; B.A. 1879.

Leathes, Chaloner Stanley, s. Stanley, of Mundsley, Norfolk, gent. EXETER COLL., matric. 30 Jan., 1816, aged 19; B.A. 1819, M.A. 1824, rector of Ellesborough, Bucks, 1825, until his death 28 April, 1832. [30]

Leathes, John Beresford, 2s. Stanley, of London, D.D. NEW COLL., matric. 10 Oct., 1884, aged 19; scholar 1884.

Leathes, Stanley, s. Thomas, of Kirby Stephen, Westmoreland, cler. QUEEN'S COLL., matric. 7 Dec., 1731, aged 17; B.A. & M.A. 1740, rector of Plumstead, Norfolk, 1751.

Leathes, Stanley, of JESUS COLL., Cambridge (B.A. 1852, M.A. 1855, hon. fellow 1885); adm. 'ad eundem' 15 Nov., 1855, Boyle lecturer 1868-70, Hulsean lecturer (Camb.), 1873, Bampton lecturer (Oxon), 1874, Warburtonian lecturer, Lincoln's Inn, 1876-80, professor of Hebrew, King's College, London, 1863, member of Old Testament Revision Company 1870, preb. of St. Paul's 1876, rector of Cliffe-at-Hoo, Kent, 1880; for list of his works, see *Crockford.*

Leaver, Henry Cozens, 1s. William, of London, gent. PEMBROKE COLL., matric. 1 Dec., 1842, aged 18; B.A. 1847, M.A. 1849, vicar of Shepton Montague, Somerset, 1850-2, rector of Pen Selwood 1852, until his death 3 May, 1877.

Leaver, James John, 1s. John, of St. Luke's, London, gent. MAGDALEN HALL, matric. 16 Dec., 1851, aged 26. [35]

Leaver, Thomas, 'pharmacopola;' privilegiatus 26 Feb., 1714-5.

Leaver, Thomas Charles Hyde, o.s. Richard, of St. George's-in-the-East, London, gent. ST. JOHN'S COLL., matric. 25 June, 1832, aged 17; scholar 1832-41, B.A. 1836, M.A. 1840, rector of Rockhampton 1848-59, died 27 Jan., 1882. See *Robinson,* 230.

eaver, Rev. William Henry Acome, 1s. Henry Cozens, of Pen Selwood, Somerset, cler. ST. MARY HALL, matric. 19 Oct., 1874, aged 20.

eay, William, s. William, of Flyford Flavell, co. Worcester, cler. WORCESTER COLL., matric. 9 July, 1715, aged 17; B.A. 1719.

eay, William, 2s. William, of St. James's, Liverpool, gent. ST. EDMUND HALL, matric. 20 Feb., 1840, aged 32; B.A. 1843, M.A. 1846, vicar of Downside, Bath, since 1852.

eche, John Hurlestone, o.s. John Hurleston, of Carden Park, Cheshire, arm. BRASENOSE COLL., matric. 19 June, 1878, aged 19. See *Eton School Lists.*

eche, William, s. John, of 'Cawarden,' Cheshire, arm. BRASENOSE COLL., matric. 4 Dec., 1754, aged 19; of Carden Park, Cheshire, high sheriff 1774, died 8 May, 1812. **[5]**

echmere, Allen Whitmore, o.s. Thomas Allen, of Fownhope, co. Hereford, arm. PEMBROKE COLL., matric. 15 May, 1820, aged 18; B.A. 1824, perp. curate Brockhampton, co. Hereford, 1838, until his death 17 May, 1845.

echmere, (Sir) Anthony (Bart.), s. Edmund, of Hanley Castle, co. Worcester, arm. MERTON COLL., matric. 31 May, 1785, aged 18; of Rhyd Court, co. Worcester, created a baronet 10 Dec., 1818, receiver-general Worcestershire, and a banker, died 25 March, 1849. See Foster's *Baronetage.*

echmere, Anthony Berwick, 2s. Anthony, of Hanley, co. Worcester, baronet. CHRIST CHURCH, matric. 16 May, 1820, aged 17; B.A. 1824, M.A. 1826, hon. canon Worcester 1849, vicar of Eldersfield co. Worcester, 1826, of Welland, co. Worcester, 1828-76, and of Hanley Castle 1839, until his death 8 Oct., 1878. See Foster's *Baronetage.*

echmere, Edmund, s. Edmund, of Hanley Castle, co. Worcester, arm. QUEEN'S COLL., matric. 23 May, 1764, aged 16; B.A. 1768, M.A. 1770, of Staple Inn, bar.-at-law, Inner Temple, 1774, F.A.S., M.P. Worcester 1790-6, died 31 Oct., 1798, aged 51, half-brother of Anthony 1785.

echmere, (Sir) Edmund Anthony Harley (Bart.), o.s. Edmund Hungerford, of Malvern, co. Worcester, arm. (after a baronet). CHRIST CHURCH, matric. 15 May, 1845, aged 18; B.A. from ST. MARY HALL, 1849, M.A. 1852, 3rd baronet, M.P. Tewkesbury March, 1866-8, West Worcestershire July, 1876-85, Worcestershire (Bewdley division) since 1886. See Foster's *Baronetage.* **[10]**

echmere, (Sir) Edmund Hungerford (Bart.), s. Anthony, of Worcester (city), arm. CHRIST CHURCH, matric. 6 Feb., 1810, aged 17; B.A. 1813, M.A. 1816, 2nd baronet, died 2 April, 1856.

echmere, George Scudamore, 3s. Capel, of Lugwardine, co. Hereford, arm. MAGDALEN HALL, matric. 26 Oct., 1848, aged 21. See Foster's *Baronetage.*

echmere, John Scudamore, s. John Scudamore, of Fownhope, co. Hereford, gent. WORCESTER COLL., matric. 17 July, 1795, aged 20; of Fownhope, died 8 Jan., 1801.

echmere, Nicholas, s. Richard, of London, arm. WADHAM COLL., matric. 17 March, 1718-9, aged 18, B.A. 1723; M.A. from MERTON COLL. 1725, archdeacon of Winchester 1749, preb. 1750, until his death 15 Oct., 1770.

echmere, Richard, s. William, of Horton, Bucks, arm. QUEEN'S COLL., matric. 15 April, 1818, aged 18; B.A. 1822, M.A. 1845. **[15]**

echmere, Scudamore, s. Nicholas, of Fownhope, Hereford, arm. QUEEN'S COLL., matric. 2 May, 1729, aged 16.

echmere, Thomas, s. John Scudamore, of Fownhope, co. Hereford, arm. BALLIOL COLL., matric. 16 Dec., 1778, aged 19.

echmere, William Henry, 3s. Anthony, of St. Nicholas, Worcester (city), baronet. QUEEN'S COLL., matric. 4 June, 1845, aged 19; died s.p.

Lechmere, (Rev.) William (Oakley Milles) Lechmere, o.s. William, of London, gent. ST. MARY HALL, matric. 23 April, 1863, aged 17; B.A. 1867, M.A. 1877, bar.-at-law, Middle Temple, 1871, curate of St. John Baptist, Oxford, 1878-80. See Foster's *Men at the Bar.* **[19]**

Leckenby, Arthur Ernest, 1s. Richard, of Sible Heding-ham, Essex, gent. EXETER COLL., matric. 15 Oct., 1879, aged 19; scholar 1879-84, B.A. 1883, M.A. 1886.

Ledger, Rev. Charles George, 4s. John, of Upper Norwood, Surrey, gent. WADHAM COLL., matric. 17 Oct., 1878, aged 20; B.A. 1882.

Lediard, James, s. Thomas, of Bristol, Somerset, gent. BALLIOL COLL., matric. 9 June, 1777, aged 18; B.A. 1781, rector of Devizes, Wilts, 1789, until his death 18 April, 1833.

Ledlie, James Crawford, o.s. Alexander Homes, of Calcutta, gent. LINCOLN COLL., matric. 29 April, 1881, aged 21; scholar 1881-5, B.A. 1885, B.C.L. 1887, a student of the Middle Temple 1883.

Ledward, Edward Harris, 2s. Charles Ortt, of Claughton, Cheshire, arm. UNIVERSITY COLL., matric. 25 Jan., 1879, aged 19; B.A. 1883.

Ledward, Robert Harold, 3s. Charles Ortt, of Liverpool, gent. UNIVERSITY COLL., matric. 24 Jan., 1884, aged 18; B.A. 1887. **[25]**

Ledwich, Thomas, s. Edward, of St. Michael's (? St Michan's), Dublin, doctor. ST. JOHN'S COLL., matric. 31 Jan., 1769, aged 25.

Lee, Alfred Theophilus, scholar CHRIST'S COLL., Cambridge, 1850, B.A. 1853, M.A. 1856, and of TRINITY COLL., Dublin, 'ad eundem;' LL.B. & LL.D. 1866; adm. 'comitatis causa' 12 March, 1868, preacher to the Hon. Society, Gray's Inn, 1879, vicar of Elson, Hants, 1857, rector of Ahoghill, Ireland, 1858-72, died 19 July, 1883; for list of his works see *Crockford.*

Lee, Arthur Edmund Dennis Dillon, 16th Viscount Dillon. TRINITY COLL., 1829. See DILLON.

Lee, Arthur George, 3s. John Benjamin, of London, arm. UNIVERSITY COLL., matric. 28 Jan., 1868, aged 18; commoner ST. ALBAN HALL 1868, B.A. 1872, M.A. from UNIVERSITY COLL. 1877, vicar of Chippenham, co. Cambridge, 1878-86, rector of Langham, Suffolk, 1886.

Lee, Arthur Morier, 2s. George Philip, of Paddington, Middlesex, equitis. NEW COLL., matric. 18 Oct., 1867, aged 20; B.A. from BALLIOL COLL. 1872, M.A. 1875, bar.-at-law, Lincoln's Inn, 1877. See Foster's *Men at the Bar* & *Eton School Lists.* **[30]**

Lee, Cadwallader Blayney, 1s. William, of Church Town, Ireland, cler. CHRIST CHURCH, matric. 15 May, 1845, aged 19; B.A. 1849.

Lee, Edward, s. Edward, of Pinhoe, Devon, gent. ORIEL COLL., matric. 10 Dec., 1785, aged 17.

Lee, Edward, s. John, of Pusey, Wilts, gent. MERTON COLL., matric. 5 Nov., 1794, aged 19.

Lee, Edward Dyke, 2s. Nicholas, of London, cler. CHRIST CHURCH, matric. 23 May, 1861, aged 18; B.A. 1866, of Hartwell House, Bucks, J.P. See *Rugby School Reg.* **[34]**

Lee, Edward Henry, 4s. William, of Newington, Surrey, arm. NEW INN HALL, matric. 27 May, 1837, aged 19; B.A. 1841 (as Henry Edward) curate in charge Cliffe-at-Hoo, Kent, 1850-69, vicar of Boughton-under-Blean 1869-75, rector of Chiddingstone since 1875.

Lee, Frederick, s. Timothy Tripp, of Thame, Oxon, cler. PEMBROKE COLL., matric. 4 Nov., 1816, aged 17, scholar 1816-17; clerk MERTON COLL. 1817-21, B.A. 1821, chorister MAGDALEN COLL. 1806-16, chaplain 1822-6, M.A. 1823, rector of Easington, Oxon, 1833, minor canon of Windsor 1833, vicar of Stantonbury, Bucks, 1838, and rector of Stowe, Salop, 19 Oct., until his death 4 Nov., 1841. See *Bloxam,* i. 212.

Lee, Frederick George, 1s. Frederick, of Thame, Oxon, cler. ST. EDMUND HALL, matric. 23 Oct., 1851, aged 19; created D.D., of Washington, and Lee, Virginia, 1879, vicar of All Saints, Lambeth, since 1867, F.S.A. 1857; for list of his works see *Crockford.*

Lee, Frederick Hugh, 5s. John Benjamin, of London, arm. TRINITY COLL., matric. 19 Oct., 1874, aged 19; B.A. 1877.

Lee, Frederick Reginald Benedict Duncan, 1s. Frederick George, of Aberdeen, cler. ST. EDMUND HALL, matric. 24 April, 1884, aged 22; B.A. 1887.

Lee, (Sir) George, s. Thomas, of Hartwell, Bucks, baronet. CHRIST CHURCH, matric. 4 April, 1720, aged 19; B.C.L. 1724, D.C.L. 1729, M.P. Brackley Jan., 1733 to March, 1742, Devizes 1742-7, Liskeard 1747-54, and Launceston 1754-8, judge of the prerogative Court of Canterbury, and dean of the arches 1751-8, a lord of the Admiralty 1742, privy councillor 13 Feb., 1752, knighted 12 Dec., 1752, died 18 Dec., 1758.

Lee, (Sir) George (Bart.), s. William, of Westminster, baronet. ST. JOHN'S COLL., matric. 7 Dec., 1784, aged 17; B.A. 1788, M.A. 1791, 6th baronet, rector of Hartwell and vicar of Stowe, rector of Stratford until 1815, and of Beachampton 1815, until his death 27 Sep., 1827.

Lee, George, 1s. Lyon, of London, arm. WORCESTER COLL., matric. 29 Oct., 1840, aged 38. [5]

Lee, George Adolphus Irby, 1s. George Thomas, of Hythe, near Southampton, arm. ALL SOULS' COLL., matric. 7 June, 1855, aged 19; bible clerk, 1855-61, B.A. 1861.

Lee, George Henry, (2nd) Earl of Lichfield, created D.C.L. 19 Aug., 1732, custos brevium in the Court of Common Pleas, died 15 Feb., 1743.

Lee, George Henry, Viscount Quarendon, s. George Henry, Earl of Lichfield. ST. JOHN'S COLL., matric. 1 Jan., 1735-6, aged 17; created M.A. 14 Feb., 1737, and D.C.L. 25 Aug., 1743, D.C.L. by diploma 27 Sep., 1762, 3rd Earl of Lichfield, high steward of the University 1760, and chancellor 1762, M.P. Oxfordshire March, 1740, to Feb., 1743, lord of the bedchamber 1760, privy councillor 1762, vice-president of the Society of Arts, died 19 Sep., 1772.

Lee, George Holwell, 1s. George Robert, of Chelsea, Middlesex, gent. MAGDALEN HALL, matric. 22 May, 1847, aged 25; B.A. 1851, M.A. 1855, rector of East Clandon, Surrey, since 1881.

Lee, Rev. Godfrey Bolles, 7s. Robert Newton, of Coldrey, Hants, arm. NEW COLL., matric. 2 Jan., 1836, aged 18; fellow 1835-61, B.A. 1839, M.A. 1844, bursar 1860, warden of Winchester College 1861. See Foster's *Yorkshire Collection*, BOSVILE.

Lee, Harry, s. Eldred Lancelot, of Coton, Salop, arm. NEW COLL., matric. 3 Feb., 1741-2, aged 21; B.A. 1745, M.A. 1749, B. & D.D. 1764, warden of Winchester College 1763, rector of Rousham, Oxon, died 18 Nov., 1789. [11]

Lee, Harry, s. Harry, of Winchester (city), doctor. NEW COLL., matric. 1 Feb., 1782, aged 16; fellow 1782-9, B.A. 1785, M.A. 1789, fellow of Winchester 1789, vicar of Hound with Bursledon, Hants, 1812, and perp. curate Hamble 1815, and preb. of Hereford 1821, until his death 5 Feb., 1838.

Lee, Harry, s. Harry, of Winchester (city), cler. NEW COLL., matric. 31 Oct., 1811, aged 18; fellow 1812-27, B.A. 1815, M.A. 1819, B.D. 1827, dean of arts and bursar 1822, fellow of Winchester, vicar of North Bradley, Wilts, 1832, until his death 16 Sep., 1880.

Lee, Hector Edward, 6s. William, of London, gent. ST. JOHN'S COLL., matric. 17 Oct., 1885, aged 18; scholar 1885.

Lee, Henry, 1s. Henry, of London, gent. WORCESTER COLL., matric. 26 April, 1873, aged 18. [15]

Lee, Henry, 1s. George, of Upper Clapton, Middlesex, gent. TRINITY COLL., matric. 17 Jan., 1880, aged 18; B.A. 1882.

Lee, Henry Augustus Dillon, born in Brussels, s. Charles, Viscount Dillon. CHRIST CHURCH, matric. 21 Oct., 1795, aged 18; 13th Viscount Dillon, assumed the additional surname of LEE, created D.C.L. 7 June, 1815, M.P. Harwich 1799-1802, co. Mayo, in 4 parliaments, 1802-13, died 24 July, 1832. See Foster's *Peerage*.

Lee, Henry Austin, 2s. George, of Colombo, Isle of Ceylon, arm. PEMBROKE COLL., matric. 31 Jan. 1865, aged 17; scholar 1865-9, B.A. 1869.

Lee, Henry Philip, 1s. Henry, of Broseley, Salop, cler. KEBLE COLL., matric. 16 Oct., 1883, aged 18.

Lee, John, s. Nich., of Exeter (city), gent. EXETER COLL., matric. 21 Feb., 1727-8, aged 17; B.A. 1731, M.A. 1734. [20]

Lee, John, fellow of KING'S COLL., Cambridge (B.A. 1717, M.A. 1721); incorp. 9 July, 1733 (? rector of Kingston and Papworth Everard, co. Cambridge, 1755).

Lee, John, s. James, of Crediton, Devon, gent. BALLIOL COLL., matric. 5 July, 1756, aged 19; B.A. 1760.

Lee, John, 1s. John, of Whitchurch, Salop, gent. PEMBROKE COLL., matric. 30 May, 1850, aged 19; B.A. 1855, M.A. 1857, vicar of Tilstock, Salop, 1857.

Lee, John, 3s. William, of Roxburghe Manse, Scotland, D.D.. BALLIOL COLL., matric. 21 Oct., 1880, aged 20; exhibitioner 1880-5, B.A. 1885.

Lee, Rev. John Bond, 1s. Thomas, of Crediton, Devon, gent. EXETER COLL., matric. 29 June, 1858, aged 17; scholar 1858-63, B.A. 1862, M.A. 1865, headmaster Queen Elizabeth's Grammar School, Chipping Barnet, 1875. See *Coll. Reg.*, 158. [25]

Lee, John Edwards Vaughan, 2s. Vaughan Hanning Vaughan, of Llanharran, co. Glamorgan, arm. NEW COLL., matric. 15 Oct., 1881, aged 18.

Lee, John Simpson, 1s. John David, of Bangor Iscoed, co. Denbigh, gent. JESUS COLL., matric. 10 Nov., 1842, aged 18; B.A. 1846, M.A. 1849, curate of Moughtreg, co. Montgomery, died 19 March, 1867.

Lee, Joseph Henry Warburton, o.s. Joseph Henry, of Malpas, Cheshire, gent. CORPUS CHRISTI COLL., matric. 22 Oct., 1874, aged 19; scholar 1874-9, B.A. 1878, M.A. 1882, bar.-at-law, Lincoln's Inn, 1883. See Foster's *Men at the Bar*.

Lee, Lancelot Charles, s. Harry, of Winchester (city), doctor. NEW COLL., matric. 28 Jan., 1785, aged 16; fellow 1785-1826, B.A. 1788, M.A. 1793, a prisoner at Verdun until 1815, rector of Wootton, Oxon, 1825-36, died 28 Nov., 1841.

Lee, Lancelot John, 1s. John William Thomas, of Grouville, Isle of Jersey, cler. NEW COLL., matric. 9 July, 1852, aged 19; fellow 1852-74, B.A. 1856, M.A. 1859, bursar 1862, precentor 1865, senior bursar 1867, sub-warden 1869, perp. curate Sandford-on-Thames 1871-4, rector of Worthen, Salop, since 1874.

Lee, Matthew Henry, 4s. Joseph, of Redbrook, near Whitchurch, Salop, arm. BRASENOSE COLL., matric. 28 May, 1850, aged 18; scholar 1850-4, B.A. 1854, M.A. 1857, vicar of Hanmer, Flints, since 1867. [31]

Lee, Rev. Percy Thomas, 8s. John, of Brampton, arm. HERTFORD COLL., matric. 18 Oct., 1882, aged 18; B.A. 1885.

Lee, Philip Edward, 1s. George Philip, of London, equitis. BALLIOL COLL., matric. 16 Oct., 1865, aged 19; B.A. 1870, a student of Lincoln's Inn 1871. See *Eton School Lists*.

Lee, Philip Henry, 3s. — L., of Redbrook, co. Flint, arm. BRASENOSE COLL., matric. 10 Oct., 1823, aged 19; B.A. 1827, fellow 1827-37, M.A. 1830, senior bursar 1835, rector of Stoke Bruerne 1836, until his death 14 July, 1876.

Lee, Philip Henry, 3s. Joseph, of Redbrook, Malpas, co. Flint, gent. WORCESTER COLL., matric. 10 June, 1847, aged 18; B.A. 1851, M.A. 1854. [35]

Lee, Philip Henry, o.s. Philip Henry, of Huyton, Lancashire, cler. BRASENOSE COLL., matric. 23 Jan., 1858, aged 19; B.A. 1863, vicar of Pattishall, Northants, 1859-66, rector of Farnham, Hants, since 1866.

Lee, Richard Henry Beaumont, 3s. Thomas, of Leeds, Yorks, gent. LINCOLN COLL., matric. 4 May, 1820, aged 18; B.A. 1830, M.A. 1840, vicar of Aslackby, co. Lincoln, 1829-38, rector of Darley, co. Derby, 1838-47, and of Stepney, Middlesex, 1847, until his death 6 Aug., 1869.

ee, Richard Napoleon, 1s. Richard, of Brixton, Surrey, arm. ST. JOHN'S COLL., matric. 19 March, 1851, aged 18; bar.-at-law, Middle Temple, 1860.

ee, Robert Elton, 2s. Stanlake, of Broughton, Hants, cler. MAGDALEN COLL., matric. 12 Oct., 1872, aged 20; B.A. 1875, M.A. 1879, vicar of St. George, Tylehurst, Berks, 1881-2, rector of Padworth 1882-8, vicar of Stanford-in-the-Vale 1888.

ee, Robert Newton, s. Robert, of Louth, co. Lincoln, arm. QUEEN'S COLL., matric. 9 Dec., 1782, aged 17; of Coldrey, Hants, died 11 Feb., 1837. See Foster's *Yorkshire Collection*, BOSVILE.

ee, Robert Newton, s. Robert Newton, of Wickham, Hants, arm. BRASENOSE COLL., matric. 18 Oct., 1813, aged 18; of Taunton, brother of Godfrey Bolles.

ee, Sackville Usher Bolton, 1s. Edward, of Tranmore, co. Waterford, arm. ORIEL COLL., matric. 15 March, 1825, aged 18; B.A. 1828, M.A. 1832, rector of All Hallows on the Walls, Exeter, 1846-61, and of All Hallows in Goldsmith Street 1861-6, preb. of Exeter 1853, canon 1865, treasurer 1885, etc. [5]

Lee, Samuel, s. Henry, of Berwick, Wilts, arm. BALLIOL COLL., matric. 31 March, 1715, aged 18; demy MAGDALEN COLL. 1716-23, B.A. 1718, M.A. 1721, fellow 1723, until his death 12 Oct., 1724. See *Bloxam*, vi. 189.

Lee, Samuel, 2s. John, of Whitchurch, Salop, gent. PEMBROKE COLL., matric. 6 March, 1856, aged 18.

Lee, Sidney (formerly Solomon) Lazarus, 1s. Lazarus, of London, gent. BALLIOL COLL., matric. 19 Oct., 1878, aged 18; exhibitioner 1879-82, B.A. 1882, sub-editor 'Dictionary of National Biography.'

Lee, Stanlake, 3s. Henry Pineke, of White Waltham, Berks, gent. QUEEN'S COLL., matric. 18 Feb., 1836, aged 21; B.A. 1840, of Woolley Firs, Berks, rector of Broughton, Hants, since 1842.

Lee, Stanlake William Henry, 1s. Thomas Jones, of Banwell, Somerset, cler. WORCESTER COLL., matric. 28 Jan., 1874, aged 20. [10]

Lee, Thomas, s. Edward Henry, Earl of Lichfield. CORPUS CHRISTI COLL., matric. 16 Dec., 1721, aged 17; 10th son, died young.

Lee, Thomas, s. John, of Appleby, Westmoreland, pleb. QUEEN'S COLL., matric. 23 Feb., 1737-8, aged 22; B.A. 26 Feb., 1741-2, M.A. 1750.

Lee, Thomas, s. Lancelot, of Coton, Salop, gent. NEW COLL., matric. 11 Dec., 1745, aged 20.

Lee, Thomas, s. Joseph, of St. Nicholas, Warwick (town), gent. TRINITY COLL., matric. 12 March, 1778, aged 17; scholar 1778, B.A. 1781, fellow 1784, M.A. 1784, B.D. 1793, D.D. 1808, president 1808-24, and rector of Garsington, Oxon, 1808-24, vice-chancellor 1814-18, perp. curate St. Lawrence, Ipswich, 1790-1808, rector of Barton-on-the-Heath, co. Warwick, 1807-8, died 5 June, 1824.

Lee, Thomas, s. John, of West Cholderton, Wilts, arm. MERTON COLL., matric. 14 Dec., 1781, aged 26.

Lee, Thomas Booth, 1s. Thomas Wood, of Oakbank, near Whitchurch, Salop, gent. ST. JOHN'S COLL., matric. 24 March, 1859, aged 19. [16]

Lee, Thomas Faulkner, of QUEEN'S COLL., Cambridge (B.A. 1848, M.A. 1851, B.D. 1860, D.D. 1866); adm. 'ad eundem' 14 Jan., 1854, head-master Royal Grammar School, Lancaster, 1850, perp. curate Christ Church, Lancaster, 1857, until his death 12 Sep., 1875.

Lee, Thomas (Jones), 2s. John, of Maidenhead, Berks, arm. WORCESTER COLL., matric. 14 June, 1844, aged 18; scholar 1844-53, B.A. 1849, M.A. 1851, vicar of Christ Church, Luton, 1863, until his death 10 Feb., 1875.

Lee, Timothy, of TRINITY COLL., Cambridge (B.A. 1736, M.A. 1740, D.D. 1752); incorp. 30 July, 1741, vicar of Pontefract 1742, and rector of Felkirk, Yorks, 1743.

Lee, Timothy Tripp, s. Timothy, of Thame, Oxon, gent. PEMBROKE COLL., matric. 26 Nov., 1787, aged 17; fellow 1787, B.A. 1791, 26 years master of Free Grammar School, Thame, vicar of that parish 1795, until his death 29 Dec., 1840. [20]

Lee, William, s. William, of London, equitis (Lord Chief Justice). WADHAM COLL., matric. 19 Jan., 1742-3, aged 16; (? M.P. Appleby 1754 to Feb., 1756) died in 1778.

Lee, William, s. John, of Cholderton, Wilts, arm. NEW COLL., matric. 20 July, 1772, aged 18; B.A. 1776, M.A. 1781, B. & D.D. 1804, rector of Little Sandford, Essex, 1790.

Lee, William, s. William, of Isle of Dominique, West Indies, arm. CHRIST CHURCH, matric. 18 April, 1796, aged 17.

Lee, William, s. John Ellison, of Ottery St. Mary, Devon, arm. BRASENOSE COLL., matric. 10 Dec., 1817, aged 17; B.A. 1821, M.A. 1824, curate of Stanton-on-Arrow, co. Hereford, 1825-42, and vicar 1842, until his death 5 Jan., 1865.

Lee, William Blackstone, s. Henry of Winchester, Hants, cler. NEW COLL., matric. 25 Aug., 1812, aged 17; fellow 1812-36, B.A. 1816, M.A. 1820, dean of arts 1822, bursar 1823, sub-warden 1824, dean of divinity 1835, bar.-at-law, Middle Temple, 1820, rector of Wootton, Oxon, 1836, until his death 7 April, 1874. [25]

Lee, William Blackstone, o.s. William Blackstone, of Hastings, Sussex, cler. ORIEL COLL., matric. 21 April, 1860, aged 17; B.A. 1863, of Kingsgate House, Hants.

Lee, William Gurden, o.s. William, of Brackley, Northants, arm. LINCOLN COLL., matric. 10 May, 1845, aged 20; B.A. 1852, rector of Shelton, Northants, since 1866.

Lee, William Herbert, 5s. William, of London, arm. ST. JOHN'S COLL., matric. 13 Oct., 1883, aged 18; scholar 1883, B.A. 1887, of Indian Civil Service 1884.

Lee, William Lauriston Melville, 1s. Melville Lauriston, of Bridport, Dorset, cler. MAGDALEN COLL., matric. 16 Oct., 1884, aged 19.

Lee, William Randall, 1s. William Randall, of Brighton, arm. TRINITY COLL., matric. 22 Jan., 1872, aged 19; B.A. 1876, M.A. 1879. See *Eton School Lists*.

Leech, John, of ST. CATHERINE HALL, Cambridge (B.A. 1740, M.A. 1744); incorp. 8 April, 1747. [31]

Leech, John Langton, s. Savage, of Liverpool, Lancashire, gent. BRASENOSE COLL., matric. 3 May, 1780, aged 19, B.A. 1783; M.A. from PEMBROKE COLL., Cambridge, 1787, vicar of Askham 1795, and of Brigham, Cumberland, 1814, until his death in 1832.

Leech, Jos. s. Christopher, of Bootle, Cumberland, pleb. HART HALL, matric. 24 Jan., 1721-2, aged 15.

Leech, Joseph, s. John, of Darton, Yorks, cler. BRASENOSE COLL., matric. 22 May, 1729, aged 18; B.A. from LINCOLN COLL. 26 Feb., 1732-3.

Leech, Stephen, 2s. John, of Reddish, Lancashire, arm. MAGDALEN COLL., matric. 19 Oct., 1883, aged 19. [35]

Leech, William, s. William, of Whitehaven, Cumberland, pleb. QUEEN'S COLL., matric. 14 Feb., 1749-50, aged 18; B.A. 1753.

Leech, William, y.s. Daniel, of Drigg, Cumberland, gent. QUEEN'S COLL., matric. 18 Nov., 1825, aged 21; clerk 1825-9, B.A. 1829, M.A. 1833, vicar of Shernborne, Norfolk, 1833, perpetual curate Flitcham 1843, until his death Feb., 1871.

Leech, William Henry, s. John Langton, of Blackburne, Lancashire, cler. BRASENOSE COLL., matric. 28 May, 1813, aged 19.

Leeder, Forrest Bertram, 3s. John Mack, of Swansea, co. Glamorgan, gent. ST. MARY HALL, matric. 23 Oct., 1882, aged 17.

Leeds, Charles Edward, 1s. Edward Thurlow, of Eyebury, Northants, gent. EXETER COLL., matric. 16 Jan., 1864, aged 18; exhibitioner 1865-8, B.A. 1868, M.A. 1870, a solicitor 1873. See *Coll. Reg.*, 162. [40]

Leeds, Edward, 1s. Edward, of Manchester, arm. WADHAM COLL., matric. 2 May, 1855, aged 18; B.A. 1859, B.Med. & M.A. 1863.

Leeds, (Peregrine Hyde), Duke of. CHRIST CHURCH, 1731. See OSBORNE.

Leeds, Richard, s. Edward, of Hackney, Middlesex, arm. TRINITY COLL., matric. 15 Jan., 1794, aged 24; B.A. 1797.

Leeds, William Henry Arthur John, 2s. Henry, of Rangoon, arm. NEW COLL., matric. 18 Oct., 1883, aged 19; of the Indian Civil Service 1883.

Leeds, William Howard, 1s. George, of Swansea, co. Glamorgan, gent. NON-COLL., matric. 13 April, 1872, aged 18; B.A. 1876, held various curacies 1877-84, rector of St. George-super-Ely, Cardiff, 1886.

Leeke, John, s. Samuel, of Ashbourne, co. Derby, gent. MAGDALEN HALL, matric. 31 March, 1742, aged 20; B.A. 16 March, 1746-7.

Leeke, Ralph, 1s. Ralph, of Newport, Salop, arm. CHRIST CHURCH, matric. 16 Oct., 1868, aged 18; of Longford Hall, Salop, J.P. [5]

Leeke, Ralph Harvey, s. Ralph, of Longford, Salop, arm. CHRIST CHURCH, matric. 17 Oct., 1811, aged 18; B.A. 1816, M.A. 1820, of Ruckley Grange, Salop, rector of Longford 1825, died 4 April, 1849.

Leeke, Ralph Merrick, 1s. Thomas, of Canton, Salop, arm. CHRIST CHURCH, matric. 10 Nov., 1831, aged 18; of Longford Hall, Salop, J.P., D.L., high sheriff 1850, died 26 Nov., 1882.

Leeke, Richard, s. Samuel, of Lichborrow, Northants. gent. HART HALL, matric. 25 March, 1728, aged 16.

Leeke, Thomas, s. Ralph, of Shifnal, Salop, arm. CHRIST CHURCH, matric. 24 April, 1806, aged 17; B.A. 1810, of Longford Hall, Salop, J.P., bar.-at-law, Lincoln's Inn, 1813, high steward Newport 1829, died 25 Dec., 1836.

Leeke, William, s. Thomas, of Lincell, Salop, pleb. MAGDALEN HALL, matric. 21 March, 1715-6, aged 18; B.A. 1719. [10]

Leeman, William Luther, 4s. George, of York, gent. ST. EDMUND HALL, matric. 12 Feb., 1870, aged 21, F.R.G.S.; B.A. UNIVERSITY COLL., Durham, 1876, M.A. 1879, rector of Middleton St. George, 1874-6, vicar of Rosedale, Yorks, 1877-9, and of Seaforth, Lancashire, 1879-82, rector of Welton-le-Wold, co. Lincoln, 1882.

Leeming, Rev. Edward, o.s. Isaac, of Manchester, gent. BRASENOSE COLL., matric. 21 March, 1849, aged 19; scholar 1849-53, B.A. 1852, M.A. 1855.

Leeper, Alexander (scholar TRINITY COLL., Dublin, 1867), 2s. Alexander, of Dublin, cler. ST. JOHN'S COLL., matric. 12 Oct., 1872, aged 24; scholar 1873-5, principal Trinity College, Melbourne, Australia, 1877.

Lees, Rev. Alfred Harry Benden, o.s. Alfred, of Waldron, Sussex, gent. KEBLE COLL., matric. 18 Oct., 1871, aged 19; B.A. 1875, M.A. 1879, master of Minster Choir School, York, 1877.

Lees, Edward Brown, 1s. John, of Oldham, Lancashire, arm. EXETER COLL., matric. 2 May, 1862, aged 19; B.A. 1865, of Thurland Castle, Lancashire, of Kelbarrrow, Westmoreland, and of Clarksfield, near Oldham, Lancashire, J.P., etc. [15]

Lees, Elliott, o.s. Thomas Evans, of Oldham, Lancashire, arm. CHRIST CHURCH, matric. 31 May, 1879, aged 18; B.A. 1883, of Stone, Dorset, M.P. Oldham July, 1886. See *Eton School Lists*.

Lees, George John Dumville, 1s. John, of Gerwyn, near Wrexham, co. Flint, gent. WORCESTER COLL., matric. 27 Jan., 1868, aged 19; of Woodhill, Salop, J.P., etc.

Lees, James Arthur 1s. James, of Alkrington, Lancashire, arm. UNIVERSITY COLL., matric. 20 Jan., 1872, aged 19; B.A. 1876, of Alkrington Hall, Lancashire, J.P. bar.-at-law, Inner Temple, 1881. See Foster's *Men at the Bar* & *Eton School Lists*.

Lees, John Frederick, 1s. Edward, of Oldham, Lancashire, arm. BRASENOSE COLL., matric. 22 June, 1827, aged 18; B.A. 1831, of Werneth, Lancashire, M.P. Oldham (July), 1835-7, died 8 Sep., 1867. See *Manchester School Reg.*, ii. 150.

Lees, Joseph Crompton, 1s. Joseph, of Clarksfield, near Oldham, Lancashire, arm. EXETER COLL., matric. 2 May, 1862, aged 18. [20]

Lees, Richard, s. John, of Lillington, co. Warwick, gent. BALLIOL COLL., matric. 21 March, 1718-9, aged 16.

Lees, William Gilbert Hyde-, 2s. Charles, of Southport, Lancashire, gent. WADHAM COLL., matric. 19 Oct., 1885, aged 19.

Leese, John, s. John, of Blandford, Dorset, gent. PEMBROKE COLL., matric. 4 June, 1794, aged 19; B.A. 1798, M.A. 1801. See *St. Paul's School Reg.*, 183.

Leeson, Henry Beaumont, M.A. from CAIUS COLL., Cambridge, 1829 (B.A. 1826), 1s. of — L., arm. TRINITY COLL., incorp. 24 May, 1838, B.Med. 25 June, 1840, D.Med. 2 July, 1840.

Leeson, John Edmund, 2s. William, of Castle Donnington, co. Leicester, gent. NEW INN HALL, matric. 7 July, 1838, aged 27; perp. curate Old St. George's, Staleybridge, Lancashire, 1850, until his death 27 Aug., 1867. [25]

Leeson, Hon. William, s. Joseph, Earl of Milltown. ORIEL COLL., matric. 6 Sep., 1786, aged 16; died 7 Oct., 1819. See Foster's *Peerage*.

Leete, Henry Baird, 1s. Edward Stokes, of Newton-le-Willows, Lancashire, gent. WORCESTER COLL., matric. 18 Oct., 1883, aged 18; exhibitioner 1883, B.A. 1887.

Leetham, Arthur Richard, 1s. William, of Margate, Kent, gent. ST. MARY HALL, matric. 22 Oct., 1883, aged 19.

Leeves, Henry Daniel, s. William, of Wrington, Somerset, cler. CORPUS CHRISTI COLL., matric. 25 May, 1805, aged 15; scholar 1805-17, B.A. 1809, M.A. 1812, fellow 1817-20, B.D. 1820, chaplain at Athens, etc., died 8 May, 1845.

Leeves, Robert, s. Robert, of Stenning, Sussex, gent. PEMBROKE COLL., matric. 16 Oct., 1731, aged 18. [30]

Lefebvre, Philip Horton, 2s. Philip John, of St. Peter, Isle of Jersey, gent. QUEEN'S COLL., matric. 13 Dec., 1860, aged 18; B.A. 1865, a senior chaplain Bombay, 1879.

Lefeuvre, George, s. Peter, of Isle of Jersey, gent. EXETER COLL., matric. 19 Nov., 1789, aged 17; B.A. from PEMBROKE COLL. 1794, assistant chaplain British Embassy, Paris, where he died 20 Sep., 1848.

Lefeuvre, Philip Alfred, 1s. Philip, of St. Peter, Isle of Jersey, gent. WADHAM COLL., matric. 16 Oct., 1844, aged 18; B.A. 1849, M.A. 1841, vice-dean of Jersey, curate in charge of St. Heliers 1880.

Lefeuvre, Richard, s. Richard, of St. Mary's, Jersey pleb. JESUS COLL., matric. 7 March, 1734-5 aged 18; B.A. from PEMBROKE COLL. 5 March 1739-40, as FEUVRE. [34]

Lefevre, Charles Shaw, Viscount Eversley, speaker House of Commons (1839-57); created D.C.L. 16 June, 1858 (1s. Charles Shaw-Lefevre), M.P. Downton 1830-1, Hants 1831-2, North Hants 1832-57, bar.-at-law, Lincoln's Inn, 1819, bencher 1839 governor and captain-general Isle of Wight, created a viscount 11 April, 1857, A.D.C. to the Queen since 1860, etc., born 22 Feb., 1794. See Foster's *Peerage*

Lefevre, (Sir) John, George Shaw, K.C.B.; created D.C.L. 16 June, 1858, clerk of the Parliaments House of Lords, 1856-75, senior wrangler TRINITY COLL., Cambridge, and B.A. 1818, M.A. 1821 bar.-at-law, Inner Temple, 1825, bencher 1835 under-secretary Colonies 1833-4, poor-law commissioner 1834-41, F.R.S., etc., died 20 Aug., 1879 See Foster's *Peerage*, V. EVERSLEY, & *Eton School Lists*.

Lefroy, Anthony Cottrell, 2s. John Henry George, of Ashe, Hants, cler. CHRIST CHURCH, matric. 1[illegible] Dec., 1829, aged 17; B.A. 1834, M.A. 1839, perp. curate Cookham, Hants, 1841-68, vicar of Longdon, co. Gloucester, 1868, until his death 28 Sep. 1884.

froy, Augustus Henry Frazer, 2s. John Henry, of Toronto, Canada, arm. (after K.C.M.G.). NEW COLL., matric. 14 Oct., 1871, aged 19; B.A. 1875, M.A. 1880, bar.-at-law, Inner Temple, 1877. See Foster's *Men at the Bar* & *Rugby School Reg.*

froy, Benjamin, s. Isaac (Peter George), of Ashe, Hants, cler. MERTON COLL., matric. 14 Nov., 1809, aged 18; B.A. 1813, rector of Ashe 1823, until his death 27 Aug., 1829.

froy, Charles Edward, s. (John Henry) George, of Ashe, Hants, cler. CHRIST CHURCH, matric. 19 Feb., 1828, aged 17; B.A. 1832, M.A. 1836, of Ewshot House, Surrey, J.P., bar.-at-law, Lincoln's Inn, 1836, secretary to the Speaker and taxing officer of House of Commons, died 16 April, 1861.

froy, Charles Edward Cottrell, 2s. Henry Maxwell, of Fremantle, Australia, gent. KEBLE COLL., matric. 18 Oct., 1881, aged 18; B.A. 1886.

froy, Christopher Edward, s. Isaac (Peter George), of Ashe, Hants, cler. MAGDALEN HALL, matric. 6 June, 1810, aged 24; B.A. 1814, M.A. 1816, bar.-at-law, Middle Temple, 1819. **[5]**

efroy, Clement George, 2s. Charles Edward, of London, arm. CHRIST CHURCH, matric. 15 Jan., 1869, aged 18; bar.-at-law, Inner Temple, 1876. See Foster's *Men at the Bar*

efroy, Rev. Edward Cracroft, 1s. George Benjamin Austen, of London, gent. KEBLE COLL., matric. 19 Oct., 1874, aged 19; B.A. 1877, M.A. 1881.

efroy, George, s. Anthony, of Leghorn, Italy, arm. CHRIST CHURCH, matric. 4 April, 1764, aged 17, B.A. 1767; fellow ALL SOULS' COLL., M.A. 1771, rector of Ashe, Hants, with Compton, Surrey, 1783, until his death, 13 Jan., 1806.

efroy, George Benjamin Austen, o.s. Benjamin, of Alton, Hants, cler. ST. JOHN'S COLL., matric. 11 May, 1836, aged 17; of the Civil Service. See Foster's *Our Noble and Gentle Families.*

efroy, Henry Maxwell, 4s. (John Henry) George, of Ashe, Hants, cler. EXETER COLL., matric. 15 Dec., 1836, aged 18; B.A. 1840. **[10]**

efroy, John Henry George, s. Isaac Peter George, of Basingstoke, Hants, cler. CHRIST CHURCH, matric. 20 Oct., 1800, aged 18; B.A. 1804, of Ewshot, Hants, rector of Ashe, Hants, 1806, until his death 5 Sep., 1823.

efroy, William Chambers, 1s. Thomas Edward Preston, of London, arm. CHRIST CHURCH, matric. 30 May, 1868, aged 19; a junior student 1868-75, B.A. 1873, M.A. 1878, bar.-at-law, Lincoln's Inn, 1876. See Foster's *Men at the Bar.*

egard, Albert George, 3s. George, of Fangfoss, near Pocklington, Yorks, arm. BALLIOL COLL., matric. 17 Oct., 1864, aged 19; B.A. 1869, M.A. 1880, an inspector of schools. See Foster's *Baronetage.*

egard, (Sir) D'Arcy Widdrington (Bart.), 2s. Thomas Digby, of Ganton, Yorks, bart. ORIEL COLL., matric. 23 Jan., 1863, aged 19; 10th baronet, died 12 April, 1866.

egard, Digby Charles, 2s. Digby, of Etton, Yorks, arm. WADHAM COLL., matric. 28 Feb., 1833, aged 17; scholar UNIVERSITY COLL. 1837-41, B.A. 1837, M.A. 1839, rector of Lea, co. Linc., died 3 July, 1851.

egard, Digby Charles, o.s. Digby Charles, of Burton Agnes, co. York, cler. BRASENOSE COLL., matric. 17 March, 1870, aged 18; B.A. 1874. **[16]**

egard, Francis Digby, 1s. George, of York (city), arm. UNIVERSITY COLL., matric. 22 June, 1847, aged 18; scholar 1849-56, B.A. 1851, M.A. 1862, vicar of Whitwell, Yorks, 1858-73, rector of Stokesley 1873, until his death 20 Nov., 1883. See Foster's *Baronetage.*

egard, (Sir) Francis Digby (Bart.), 1s. Thomas Digby, of St. George's, Hanover Square, London, bart. ST. JOHN'S COLL., matric. 10 Dec., 1851, aged 18; 9th baronet, died 5 Jan., 1865.

egard, George, 1s. Digby, of Ganton, Yorks, arm. UNIVERSITY COLL., matric. 14 April, 1820, aged 17; scholar 1821-2, surveyor-general of the Duchy of Lancaster, died 31 Oct., 1882.

Legard, Henry Willoughby, 2s. Thomas, of Ganton, Yorks, bart. WORCESTER COLL., matric. 16 Oct., 1822, aged 17; of 9th lancers, died 21 Nov., 1845.

Legard, John Hawksworth, 2s. George, of Fangfoss, Yorks, arm. TRINITY COLL., matric. 19 May, 1856, aged 18; B.A. 1860. See Foster's *Baronetage.* **[21]**

Legard, Thomas Digby, 1s. Thomas, of Scarborough, Yorks, bart. MAGDALEN COLL., matric. 27 June, 1821, aged 18; B.A. 1824, 8th baronet, a student of Lincoln's Inn 1825, died 10 Dec., 1860.

Legard, William, s. Digby, of Ganton, Yorks, bart. MAGDALEN HALL, matric. 4 July, 1788, aged 23; B.A. 1792, vicar of Sherborne 1793, Ganton 1794, and of Lund 1817, until his death 19 Feb., 1826.

Legasicke, Henry, s. James, of Modbury, Devon, gent. PEMBROKE COLL., matric. 22 Oct., 1734, aged 17.

Legat, Alfred Henry, 1s. William, of Richmond, Yorks, gent. ORIEL COLL., matric. 19 Oct., 1870, aged 19; scholar 1870-5, B.A. 1875, M.A. 1877. **[25]**

Leggatt, Edward Owen Every, 1s. William Benjamin, of Chingleput, East Indies, arm. LINCOLN COLL., matric. 20 Oct., 1881, aged 17; scholar 1881-5, B.A. 1885, of the Indian Civil Service 1882. See *St. Paul's School Reg.*, 364.

Legg, William, 2s. George, of Gosport, Hants, gent. MAGDALEN HALL, matric. 14 Dec., 1855, aged 24; B.A. 1859, M.A. 1862, held various curacies 1859-72, rector of Hawkinge, Kent, since 1872.

Legge, Alfred Arthur Kaye, 2s. (Arthur Charles), of London, arm. CHRIST CHURCH, matric. 3 June, 1857, aged 17; B.A. 1862, M.A. 1868, bar.-at-law, of the Inner Temple, 1865-70, vicar of St. Andrew, Wigan, 1871-8. See *Foster's Peerage*, E. DARTMOUTH; & *Men at the Bar.*

Legge, Augustus, 5s. William Walter, Earl (of Dartmouth). CHRIST CHURCH, matric. 21 Oct., 1857, aged 17; B.A. 1861, M.A. 1864, vicar of St. Bartholomew, Sydenham, 1867-79, and of Lewisham, Kent, since 1879.

Legge, Hon. Augustus George, s. William, Earl of Dartmouth. CHRIST CHURCH, matric. 22 April, 1790, aged 17, B.A. 1794; M.A. from MERTON COLL. 1796, chaplain to George III. 1798, rector of Wonston 1797, and of Crawley, Hants, 18—, preb. of Lichfield 1801, archdeacon of Winchester 1814, preb. 1817, and chancellor 1820, rector of North Waltham 1820, until his death 21 Aug., 1828. **[30]**

Legge, Augustus George, 2s. Henry, of East Lavant, near Chichester, cler. CHRIST CHURCH, matric. 18 May, 1853, aged 18; B.A. 1857, M.A. 1870, of Mareland and Bramdean, Hants, vicar of North Elmham, Norfolk, since 1867.

Legge, Charles John, 2s. Thomas, of Liverpool, gent. ST. JOHN'S COLL., matric. 16 Jan., 1875, aged 18; B.A. 1879.

Legge, Hon. Edward, s. William, Earl of Dartmouth. CHRIST CHURCH, matric. 14 June, 1784, aged 17, B.A. 1788; fellow ALL SOULS' COLL. 1789, B.C.L. 1791, D.C.L. 1805, warden 1817-27, vicar of Lewisham, Kent, 1797-1827, preb. of Winchester 1795, and of Canterbury 1797, canon of Windsor 1802, and dean 1805, bishop of Oxford 1815, until his death 27 Jan., 1827. See Foster's *Peerage* & *Rugby School Reg.*, 51.

Legge, Hon. Edward Henry, 3s. William, Earl of Dartmouth. CHRIST CHURCH, matric. 12 June, 1851, aged 17; B.A. 1855, M.A. 1861, late lieut.-col. coldstream guards. See Foster's *Peerage* & *Eton School Lists.*

Legge, Rev. Eugene Ezekiel Pope, 2s. Ezekiel Pope, of Burton Bradstock, near Bridport, Dorset, arm. WADHAM COLL., matric. 18 June, 1862, aged 21; B.A. 1865, M.A. 1869, a student of Lincoln's Inn 1865, died 12 May, 1880. **[35]**

Legge, George (Viscount Lewisham), s. George, Earl of Dartmouth. MAGDALEN COLL., matric. 22 Jan., 1719-20, aged 15; M.P. Bedwin 1727, to Mar. 1729, died 29 Aug., 1732. See Foster's *Peerage.*

Legge, George, Viscount Lewisham, 1s. (William), Earl of Dartmouth. CHRIST CHURCH, matric. 22 Oct., 1771, aged 16; created M.A. 3 July, 1775, and D.C.L. 26 Oct., 1778, 3rd earl, M.P. Plymouth June, 1778-80, Staffordshire 1780-86 (elected also for Horsham and Malmesbury 1780), summoned to the House of Lords as Baron Dartmouth 15 June, 1801, P.C. 17 March, 1801, lord warden of the Stannaries, etc., 1783, president of the India Board 1801, lord steward of the Household 1802-4, lord chamberlain 1804, K.G. 27 May, 1805, died 10 Nov., 1810. See Foster's *Peerage*.

Legge, George Augustus, 1s. Hon. Augustus, of Wonston, Hants, cler. CHRIST CHURCH, matric. 25 April, 1820, aged 18; student 1820-5, B.A. 1824, vicar of Bray, Berks, 1825, until his death 16 June, 1826. See *Alumni West.*, 481.

Legge, Heneage, s. George, Earl of Dartmouth. MAGDALEN COLL., matric. 22 Jan., 1719-20, aged 14; bar.-at-law, Inner Temple, 1728, K.C. 1739, serjt.-at-law 1747, high steward of Lichfield 1734, baron of the Exchequer 1747, until his death 30 Aug., 1759.

Legge, Heneage, s. Heneage, of London, arm. ORIEL COLL., matric. 18 Oct., 1764, aged 17; died 1 Jan., 1827.

Legge, Heneage, s. William, Earl of Dartmouth. CHRIST CHURCH, matric. 23 Oct., 1777, aged 16; B.A. 1781, died 2 Sep., 1782. [5]

Legge, Hon. Heneage, s. George, Earl of Dartmouth. CHRIST CHURCH, matric. 24 Oct., 1805, aged 17; fellow ALL SOULS' COLL. 1812-28, B.C.L. 1812, D.C.L. 1818, bar.-at-law, Lincoln's Inn, 1815, M.P. Banbury Nov., 1819 to Feb., 1826, a commissioner of Customs died 12 Dec., 1844. See Foster's *Peerage* & *Eton School Lists.*

Legge, Henry, s. William, Earl of Dartmouth. CHRIST CHURCH, matric. 29 March, 1726, aged 17; created D.C.L. WADHAM COLL. 1 March, 1733-4, chancellor of the Exchequer 1754, and 1756-72, assumed the name of BILSON in lieu of LEGGE, M.P. East Looe Nov., 1740-1, Oxford 1741 to Dec., 1759, Hampshire Dec., 1759, until his death 23 Aug., 1764. See Foster's *Peerage.*

Legge, Hon. Henry, s. William, Earl of Dartmouth. CHRIST CHURCH, matric. 17 Oct., 1781, aged 16; B.A. 1785, M.A. 1788, a student until 1829, bar.-at-law, Middle Temple, 1790, bencher 1830, commissioner of the Navy, director of Greenwich Hospital, under secretary Irish affairs, died 18 April, 1844.

Legge, Henry, 3s. Augustus George, of Wonston, Hants, cler. CHRIST CHURCH, matric. 20 June, 1821, aged 17; B.A. 1824, of Mareland and Bramdean, Hants, rector of East Lavant, Sussex, 1828, until his death 8 Nov., 1879.

Legge, Hon. Henry 5s. George, Earl of Dartmouth. CHRIST CHURCH, matric. 22 Jan., 1822, aged 18, B.A. 1825; fellow ALL SOULS' COLL. 1825-42, B.C.L. 1835, D.C.L. 1840, vicar of Lewisham 1831-79, died 13 Feb., 1887. See Foster's *Peerage* & *Eton School Lists.* [10]

Legge, Henry Edward, 1s. Henry, of East Lavant, near Chichester, cler. CHRIST CHURCH, matric. 31 May, 1849, aged 18; B.A. 1853, M.A. 1856, a student of the Inner Temple 1853, died in Algiers 15 Dec., 1861. See *Eton School Lists.*

Legge, Henry James, 3s. James, of Silchester, Hants, gent. ST. ALBAN HALL, matric. 25 March, 1820, aged 20; B.A. 1823, M.A. 1835, vicar of Brimscombe, co. Gloucester, 1841, until his death 22 June, 1873.

Legge, James, 4s. Ebenezer, of Huntly, Aberdeen, arm. CORPUS CHRISTI COLL., matric. 9 June, 1876, aged 60; M.A. by decree 20 June, 1876, professor of Chinese language and literature 1876, father of the next named, and of Thomas M. 1882.

Legge, James Granville, 1s. James, of Hong Kong, arm (? cler). QUEEN'S COLL., matric. 15 May, 1880, aged 18; scholar 1880-5, B.A. 1884.

Legg, Joseph, s. Richard, of Market Lavington, Wil gent. QUEEN'S COLL., matric. 8 March, 177 aged 21; vicar of Maddington, Wilts, over 50 yea and 47 years rector of Holton, died at Maddingt 8 Feb., 1833. [1

Legge, Robert George, 2s. Hon. George Barringto of Leamington, cler. KEBLE COLL., matric. Oct., 1883, aged 19.

Legge, Thomas Morison, 2s. James, of Hong Kon Siam, D.D. NON-COLL., matric. 14 Oct., 18 aged 19; B.A. from TRINITY COLL. 1886.

Legge, Walter Douglas, 1s. Augustus George, North Elmham, Norfolk, cler. CHRIST CHURC matric. 31 May, 1884, aged 18.

Legg, William, Viscount Lewisham, s. George, E of Dartmouth. TRINITY COLL., matric. 14 Ja 1748-9, aged 17; created M.A. 21 March, 1750 and D.C.L. 28 April, 1756, 2nd earl, recorder Lichfield 1757, P.C. 1765, president Board of Tra 1765-6, Colonial secretary 1772-5, lord keel 1775-82, lord steward of the Household in 17 high steward University of Oxford 1786, died July, 1801. See Foster's *Peerage.*

Legge, William, s. William, of Westminster, ar (after Earl of Dartmouth). CHRIST CHURCH, matr 29 June, 1773, aged 16, B.A. 1776; M.A. from A SOULS' COLL. 1780, bar.-at-law, Middle Temp 1780, died 19 Oct., 1784. [2

Legge, William, Viscount Lewisham, s. George, E of Dartmouth. CHRIST CHURCH, matric. 3 M 1802, aged 17; B.A. 1805, created D.C.L. 13 Ju 1834, 4th Earl of Dartmouth, M.P. Milborne P Jan., to Nov., 1810, died 22 Nov., 1853. S Foster's *Peerage* & *Eton School Lists.*

Legge, William, 2s. Augustus, of Wonstone, Han cler. CHRIST CHURCH, matric. 2 June, 1821, ag 18; student 1821-7, B.A. 1825, of Mareland, Han rector of Ashtead, Surrey, 1826, until his death 6 No 1872. See Foster's *Peerage* & *Alumni West.*, 48

Legge, William Heneage (Viscount Lewisham), William Walter, Earl of Dartmouth. CHRIST CHUR matric. 19 May, 1869, aged 18; M.P. West Kent (M 1878-85, Lewisham since 1885, vice-chairman of Household 1885 and 1886. See *Eton School List*

Legge, William Walter (Viscount Lewisham), William, Earl of Dartmouth. CHRIST CHUR matric. 20 Oct., 1841, aged 18; B.A. 1844, M 1847, 5th Earl of Dartmouth, M.P. South Staffo shire Feb., 1849 to Nov., 1853. See Foster's *Peer* & *Eton School Lists.*

Legh, Ashburnham, s. Thomas, of Lalham, Lancash gent. BRASENOSE COLL., matric. 20 May, 17 aged 17, B.A. 1738; M.A. from ALL SOU COLL. 1742, of Golborne Park, Lancashire, d rector of Davenham, Cheshire, in 1775. [

Legh, Charles Henry Frederick Americus, o.s. Cha Richard Banastre, of Adlington, Cheshire, a CHRIST CHURCH, matric. 13 Oct., 1876, aged 18

Legh, Charles Richard Banastre, o.s. Thomas, Boulogne-sur-mer, arm. CHRIST CHURCH, mat 3 June, 1840, aged 19; of Adlington Hall Bonishall, Cheshire, J.P., D.L.

Legh, Cholmondeley (Leyburn), s. Ashburnham, Winwick, Lancashire, cler. BRASENOSE CO matric. 8 July, 1773, aged 17; B.A. from TRIN COLL. 1777, M.A. 1780, died at Lisbon 9 Feb., 1

Legh, Edmund Dawson, s. John, of Booth Cheshire, arm. BALLIOL COLL., matric. 13 Ma 1818, aged 17; B.A. 1821, M.A. 1830, perp. cu of St. Botolph's, Aldersgate, died 7 March, 1845

Legh, Fleetwood, s. Thomas, of London, gent. BRA NOSE COLL., matric. 25 May, 1721, aged 17 Bank, Lancashire, died 1725. [

Legh, George Cornwall, 1s. George John, of Rosth Cheshire, arm. CHRIST CHURCH, matric. 27 F 1823, aged 18; B.A. 1826, of High Legh, Chesl high sheriff 1838, M.P. North Cheshire 1841-7, June, 1848-68, Mid Cheshire 1868 to Feb., 1 died 16 June, 1877. See *Eton School Lists.*

gh, George John, created D.C.L. 6 July, 1810, of High Legh, Cheshire, high sheriff 1805 (son of Henry Cornwall Legh, of High Legh), died 17 March, 1832.

gh, Henry Cornwall, s. George, of Rosthern, Cheshire, arm. WADHAM COLL., matric. 17 April, 1751, aged 16; created M.A. 2 July, 1754, of High Legh, Cheshire, died high sheriff in 1791.

gh, Henry Cornwall, 2s. George John, of Rosthern, Cheshire, arm. BRASENOSE COLL., matric. 6 May, 1830, aged 18; B.A. 1834, M.A. 1836, incumbent of Welchhampton, Salop, 1840, until his death 24 Nov., 1847. See *Eton School Lists*.

gh, Henry Edmund, 3s. Edmund Dawson, of St. Botolph's, London, cler. BALLIOL COLL., matric. 13 May, 1859, aged 19; B.A. 1863, M.A. 1867, held various curacies 1864-75, vicar of Leigh, Surrey, 1874, etc.

egh, John Arthur, y.s. Robert, of Shrewsbury, arm. NEW INN HALL, matric. 3 May, 1884, aged 19. [5]

egh, John Pennington, 1s. Edmund Dawson, of St. Pancras, London, cler. WADHAM COLL., matric. 28 Jan., 1846, aged 18; B.A. 1849, M.A. 1870, of Norbury Booths, Cheshire, J.P.

egh, Peter, s. Thomas, of Prescot, Lancashire, gent. BRASENOSE COLL., matric. 2 July, 1725, aged 16; B.A. from ALL SOUL'S COLL. 1735, of Lyme, Cheshire, M.P. Newton, Lancashire, Dec., 1743-74, died 20 March, 1792.

egh, Peter, s. Richard, of Winstanley, Lancashire, gent. BRASENOSE COLL., matric. 12 May, 1730, aged 16.

egh, Richard, s. Henry, of Runcorn, Cheshire, arm. BRASENOSE COLL., matric. 6 Aug., 1720, aged 17; B.A. 29 Jan., 1724-5 (as LEIGH).

egh, Richard, s. Thomas, of Prestbury, Cheshire, gent. BRASENOSE COLL., matric. 15 May, 1721, aged 19.

Legh, Richard Cornwallis, 3s. George John, of Rostherne, Cheshire, arm. BRASENOSE COLL., matric. 13 May, 1837, aged 18; B.A. 1841. [11]

egh, Thomas, s. Thomas, of Lyme, Cheshire, arm. BRASENOSE COLL., matric. 15 June, 1810, aged 17; created D.C.L. 18 June, 1817, of Lyme Park, Cheshire, and of Haydock Lodge and Golborne Park, Lancashire, J.P.. M.P. Newton, Lancashire, April, 1814-32, died 8 May, 1857.

egh, Thomas (Peter), s. Ashburnham, of Davenham, Cheshire, cler. BRASENOSE COLL., matric. 8 Feb., 1773, aged 18; of Golborne, Lancashire, and of Lyme, Cheshire, colonel Lancashire fencible cavalry, M.P. Newton 1780, until his death 7 Aug., 1797.

egh, Thomas Wodehouse, 1s. William John, of Lyme Park, Cheshire, arm. CHRIST CHURCH, matric. 15 Oct., 1875, aged 18; B.A. 1880, of Lyme Park, Cheshire, J.P., of H.B.M. embassy, Paris, 1881-6, M.P. South-West Lancashire (Newton division) Aug., 1886. See *Eton School Lists*.

egh, William, s. Thomas Peter, of Winwick, Lancashire, arm. BRASENOSE COLL., matric. 9 Dec., 1816, aged 20. [15]

eicester, Frederick, 1s. Charles, of Middlewich, Cheshire, arm. WORCESTER COLL., matric. 3 May, 1821, aged 18; B.A. from QUEEN'S COLL. 1825, M.A. 1828, died 16 April, 1873. See Foster's *Peerage*, B. DE TABLEY.

eicester, George, Baron de Tabley, 1s. John Fleming, Baron de Tabley. CHRIST CHURCH, matric. 16 Oct., 1829, aged 17; 2nd baron, assumed the name of WARREN in lieu of LEICESTER by royal licence 8 Feb., 1832, a lord-in-waiting 1853-8, 1859-66, and treasurer of the Household 1868-72. See Foster's *Peerage* & *Eton School Lists*.

eicester, (Sir) Peter (Bart.), s. John Byrne, of Bruton, Cheshire, baronet. BRASENOSE COLL., matric. 30 May, 1750, aged 17; created M.A. 23 June, 1753, of Tabley Hall, Cheshire, 4th baronet, assumed the name of LEICESTER in lieu of BYRNE by Act of Parliament 1744, M.P. Preston March, 1767, to Nov., 1768, died 12 Feb., 1770. See Foster's *Peerage*, B. DE TABLEY.

Leigh, Arthur Egerton, 4s. Egerton, of High Legh, Cheshire, arm. BRASENOSE COLL., matric. 5 June, 1873, aged 19; B.A. 1877. See *Rugby School Reg.*

Leigh, Arthur Henry Austen, 4s. James Edward, of Speen, near Newbury, Berks, cler. BALLIOL COLL., matric. 30 May, 1855, aged 19; fellow ST. JOHN'S COLL. 1859-76, B.A. 1859, M.A. 1866, B.D. 1872, rector of Winterbourne, co. Gloucester, 1875. [20]

Leigh, Barnabas, s. Barnabas, of Shorewell, Isle of Wight, Hants, arm. CHRIST CHURCH, matric. 5 Nov., 1767, aged 19. See Berry's *Hants*, 122.

Leigh, Barnabas Eveleigh, s. John, of ——, Hants, arm. WADHAM COLL., matric. 11 Sep., 1723.

Leigh, Chandos, s. James Henry, of St. Marylebone, arm. CHRIST CHURCH, matric. 8 June, 1810, aged 18; of Adlestrop, Longborough, and Stoneleigh, co. Warwick, created Baron Leigh 11 May, 1839, died 27 Sep., 1850. See Foster's *Peerage*.

Leigh, Charles, s. George, of Isle of St. Christopher, arm. BRASENOSE COLL., matric. 7 May, 1760, aged 15.

Leigh, Charles Edward Austen, 2s. James Edward Austen, of Tring, Herts, cler. BALLIOL COLL., matric. 2 April, 1851, aged 18; clerk House of Commons. [25]

Leigh, Cholmeley Austen, 1s. James Edward Austen, of Tring, Herts, cler. BALLIOL COLL., matric. 17 March, 1847, aged 17; scholar TRINITY COLL. 1848-52, B.A. 1851, fellow 1852-64, M.A. 1856, bar.-at-law, Lincoln's Inn, 1856, on the council of King's College, London. See Foster's *Men at the Bar*.

Leigh, Edmund, 1s. William, of Llanelly, co. Carmarthen, cler. JESUS COLL., matric. 2 June, 1835, aged 18.

Leigh, Edward, s. Edward, Baron Leigh. BALLIOL COLL., matric. 9 Aug., 1726, aged 18; 3rd Lord Leigh, died March, 1737.

Leigh, Edward, s. John, of Brindle, Lancashire, pleb. WADHAM COLL., matric. 17 May, 1738, aged 18; B.A. 10 Feb., 1741-2. [29]

Leigh, Edward, Baron Leigh, s. (Thomas), Baron Leigh. ORIEL COLL., matric. 14 July, 1761, aged 18; created M.A. 13 Feb., 1764, and D.C.L. by diploma 29 April, 1767, then high steward of the University, 5th Lord Leigh, died 26 May, 1786.

Leigh, Edward, 2s. Edward, of Holywell, co. Flint, arm. JESUS COLL., matric. 24 March, 1857, aged 18.

Leigh, Edward Allesley Boughton Ward Boughton, 1s. John Ward Boughton, of Guilsborough, Northants, arm. CHRIST CHURCH, matric. 3 June, 1840, aged 18; of Brownsover Hall, co. Warwick, and of Guilsborough Hall, Northants, J.P., D.L., high sheriff 1874.

Leigh, Edward Chandos, 2s. Chandos, Baron Leigh. ORIEL COLL., matric. 7 Nov., 1851, aged 18; fellow ALL SOULS' COLL. 1855-71, B.A. 1855, M.A. 1858, bar.-at-law, Inner Temple, 1859, Q.C. 1881, bencher 1886, recorder of Stamford 1864-81, of Nottingham 1881, counsel to speaker of House of Commons, etc. See Foster's *Men at the Bar*.

Leigh, Edward Trafford, 1s. George Edward, of Stockport, Cheshire, cler. BRASENOSE COLL., matric. 17 May, 1820, aged 18; B.A. 1824, M.A. 1826, rector of Cheadle, Cheshire, 1829, until his death 7 Jan., 1847.

Leigh, Egerton, s. Peter, of Rosthern, Cheshire, cler. CHRIST CHURCH, matric. 18 July, 1721, aged 19; LL.B. from ST. JOHN'S COLL., Cambridge, 1728, LL.D. 1743, archdeacon of Salop (diocese of Hereford) 1741-60, preb. of Hereford 1742-60, until his death at Bath 5 Feb., 1760. [35]

Leigh, Egerton (B.A. from ST. JOHN'S COLL., Cambridge, 1756), s. Egerton, of Lymm, Cheshire, doctor. BRASENOSE COLL., incorp. 7 Feb. (or 3 March), 1758, aged 24; M.A. 8 July, 1758, preb. of Bangor 1758, 40 years rector of Lymm, preb. of Lichfield 1770, archdeacon of Salop (diocese of Lichfield) 1770, chancellor of Lichfield 1797, until his death 17 Sep., 1798.

Leigh, Francis, 1s. — L., of Cheadle, co. Stafford, arm. MAGDALEN HALL, matric. 11 Nov., 1836, aged 32; B.A. 1843.

Leigh, Francis Augustine, 1s. John, of Dublin, arm. CHRIST CHURCH, matric. 3 June, 1840, aged 17; of Rosegarland, co. Wexford, J.P., high sheriff 1867, sometime of 10th hussars. See *Eton School Lists.*

Leigh, Rev. Francis Joseph, of TRINITY COLL., Dublin (B.A. 1842, M.A. 1845), adm. 'ad eundem' 5 July, 1851.

Leigh, Francis William, 1s. William, of London, arm. NON-COLL., matric. 18 Oct., 1880, aged 20.

Leigh, George, 2s. George Edward, of Stockport, Cheshire, cler. BRASENOSE COLL., matric. 28 April, 1824, aged 17; B.A. 1828, M.A. 1830, brother of Edward Trafford. [5]

Leigh, George (Edward), s. John, of Oughtrington, Cheshire, arm. BRASENOSE COLL., matric. 12 March, 1790, aged 17; B.A. 1794, incumbent of St. Peter's, Stockport, died 5 May, 1808. See *Manchester School Reg.*, ii. 102.

Leigh, George Henry, s. Thomas, of Dunster, Somerset, gent. BALLIOL COLL., matric. 14 Dec., 1767, aged 18; B.A. 1771.

Leigh, Henry Devenish, 5s. Frederick, of Southampton, arm. NEW COLL., matric. 15 Oct., 1881, aged 17, scholar 1880-6, B.A. 1885; fellow CORPUS CHRISTI COLL. 1886, M.A. 1888, a student of Lincoln's Inn 1884.

Leigh, Henry Gerard, 1s. Henry Blundell, of Wigginton Lodge, near Tamworth, arm. CHRIST CHURCH, matric. 28 May, 1874, aged 17; lieutenant 1st life guards. See *Eton School Lists.*

Leigh, Rev. Howard Francis, 2s. Francis Joseph, of St. Paul's, Jersey, cler. MERTON COLL., matric. 14 Oct., 1879, aged 19; B.A. 1883, M.A. 1886. [10]

Leigh, James, s. William, of Adlestrop, co. Gloucester, arm. BALLIOL COLL., matric. 18 March, 1740-1, aged 16; of Adlestrop aforesaid, died 31 March, 1774, father of James Henry.

Leigh, James, s. Thomas, of Harden, Oxon, cler. ST. JOHN'S COLL., matric. 27 June, 1751, aged 15; assumed the surname of PERROTT, and died s.p.

Leigh, James Allett, s. Egerton, of Murston, Kent, cler. UNIVERSITY COLL., matric. 26 Feb., 1789, aged 18; B.A. 1792, M.A. 1795, of Leatherlake House, Runnymead, Surrey, vicar of Tollesbury, Essex, died 5 Feb., 1857.

Leigh, James Edward Austen, s. James Austen, of Dean, Hants, cler. EXETER COLL., matric. 10 Oct., 1816, aged 17; B.A. 1820, M.A. 1826, assumed the additional surname of LEIGH, perp. curate Knowl Hill 1841-52, vicar of Bray, Berks, 1852, until his death 8 Sep., 1874.

Leigh, James Gerard, 2s. Richard, of Halsell, near Liverpool, cler. CHRIST CHURCH, matric. 22 Oct., 1862, aged 18; B.A. 1867, M.A. 1871, vicar of Maghull, Lancashire, 1869-84, rector of Walton-on-the-Hill 1884. [15]

Leigh, James Henry, s. James, of Adlestrop, co. Gloucester, arm. CHRIST CHURCH, matric. 20 June, 1782, aged 17; of Adlestrop aforesaid, and of Stoneleigh, co. Warwick, M.P. Marlborough 1802-6, Bedwyn 1806 to March, 1818, Winchester March, 1818, to Feb., 1823, died 28 Oct., 1823, father of Chandos.

Leigh, James Mosley, 2s. James Heath, of Grappenhall, Cheshire, arm. BRASENOSE COLL., matric. 5 Feb., 1850, aged 17; a student of Lincoln's Inn 1854, died 14 Jan., 1858. See *Eton School Lists.*

Leigh, Rev. John, s. Robert, of St. Decuman's, Somerset, arm. ST. MARY HALL, matric. 9 April, 1813, aged 24; ecclesiastical commissary of Newfoundland, where he died in 1823, aged 34.

Leigh, John, s. Joseph, of Liverpool, Lancashire, arm. BRASENOSE COLL., matric. 9 May, 1815, aged 17; B.A. 1820, M.A. 1821, rector of Egginton, co. Derby, 1824, until his death 24 Oct., 1856. See *Eton School Lists.* [19]

Leigh, John Blundell, 2s. Henry Blundell, of Wiggin ton Lodge, near Tamworth, arm. CHRIST CHURCH matric. 24 May, 1877, aged 18. See *Eton School List*

Leigh, John Gerard, 1s. John Shaw, of Liverpoo Lancashire, arm. LINCOLN COLL., matric. 4 Marcl 1841, aged 19; of Luton Hoo Park, Beds, J.P a student of Lincoln's Inn 1843, died 24 Feb., 187 brother of Thomas 1844. See *Eton School Lists.*

Leigh, John Highfield, 4s. Henry, of Eccles, Lanca shire, arm. CORPUS CHRISTI COLL., matric. 2 Oct., 1878, aged 20; B.A. 1883, M.A. 188 bar.-at-law, Inner Temple, 1886.

Leigh, Rev. John Rowland, 1s. Daniel, of Llanivon co. Glamorgan, cler. ORIEL COLL., matric. 1 Nov 1881, aged 19; B.A. 1885.

Leigh, Rev. Neville Egerton, 3s. Egerton, of Hig Leigh, Cheshire, arm. BRASENOSE COLL., matri 1 June, 1871, aged 18; B.A. 1875, M.A. 1878. Se *Rugby School Reg.*

Leigh, Peter, s. Egerton, of Budworth, Cheshire, arn CORPUS CHRISTI COLL., matric. 10 May, 174 aged 16; B.C.L. 1749, rector of Lymm, Cheshir and of Middle, Salop, 1749, until he died in 175 See *Manchester School Reg.*, i. 154. [2

Leigh, Richard, s. Francis, of Sutton-at-Hone, Ken arm. CORPUS CHRISTI COLL., matric. 14 Marcl 1743-4, aged 16; B.C.L. 24 Jan., 1750-1, bar.-at-lav Middle Temple, 1753, serj.-at-law 1765, King's se jeant 1771, M.P. East Looe (Oct.) 1770-4, died 2 March, 1772.

Leigh, Richard, s. Richard, of London, arm. CHRIS CHURCH, matric. 13 April, 1778, aged 16.

Leigh, Richard, 3s. John, of Liverpool, Lancashir arm. BRASENOSE COLL., matric. 10 Oct., 182 aged 18; B.A. 1831, M.A. 1835, rector of Halsal Lancashire, 1843-63, of Walton-on-the-Hill, Lanca shire, 1868, until his death 9 April, 1884.

Leigh, (Sir) Robert Holt (Bart.), s. Holt, of Wiga Lancashire, arm. CHRIST CHURCH, matric. 25 Oct 1781, aged 18; B.A. 1837, M.A. 1838, of Hindle Hall, Lancashire, J.P., D.L., created a baronet 2 May, 1815, M.P. Wigan 1802-20, died s.p. 21 Jan 1843. See *Manchester School Reg.*, i. 217; & *Gent. Mag.*, vol. xix., N.S., 314.

Leigh, Roger, o.s. Thomas Yates, of Hindley, Lanca shire, arm. CHRIST CHURCH, matric. 16 Jun 1859, aged 19; of Hindley, Lancashire, J.P., an of Barham Court, Kent, J.P., M.P. Rochest 1880-5. [3

Leigh, Stanley, 1s. George, of Daresbury, Cheshir gent. WORCESTER COLL., matric. 9 April, 186 aged 20; B.A. 1868, B.C.L. & M.A. 1870, a studer of the Inner Temple 1869.

Leigh, Stratford, 4s. Thomas, of Wickham, Esse cler. ST. JOHN'S COLL., matric. 28 June, 184 aged 18; B.A. 1845, vicar of Hatfield Peverell, Esse 1850, until his death in 1875. See *Robinson*, 237.

Leigh, Thomas, s. Peter, of Rostherne, Cheshire, cle UNIVERSITY COLL., matric. 10 March, 1724- aged 18; B.A. 1728, M.A. 1731, rector (and patro of Murston, Kent, 1732, and rector of St. Ma garet's, Canterbury, died 19 April, 1774.

Leigh, Thomas, s. Edward, Baron Leigh. BALLIO COLL., matric. 8 Oct., 1731, aged 17; 4th Bar Leigh, died 30 Nov., 1749.

Leigh, Thomas, s. William, of Adlestrop, co. Glo cester, arm. BALLIOL COLL., matric. 23 Oct 1751, aged 17; demy MAGDALEN COLL. 1752-6 B.A. 1755, M.A. 1758, B.C.L. 1763, of Stoneleig Abbey, co. Warwick, vicar of Broadwell, co. Glo cester, 1762, rector of Adlestrop 1763, until his dea 26 June, 1813. See Foster's *Peerage*, B. LEIGH and *Bloxam*, vi. 292. [3

Leigh, Thomas, s. Thomas, of Heyford, Oxon, cle MAGDALEN COLL., matric. 13 March, 1753, ag 17; B.A. 1756 (? brother of James 1751).

Leigh, Thomas, 3s. John Shaw, of Walton, Lanca shire, arm. UNIVERSITY COLL., matric. 30 Ma 1844, aged 18; brother of John Gerard.

Leigh, Thomas Charles. CHRIST CHURCH, 1819. See TRACY.

Leigh, Thomas Gerard, 2s. John, of Liverpool, Lancashire, arm. BRASENOSE COLL., matric. 2 May, 1821, aged 17; B.A. 1825, M.A. 1827, rector of Walton-on-the-Hill, Lancashire, 1847, until his death 3 Nov., 1867. See *Eton School Lists.*

Leigh, Trafford, s. John, of Lymm, Cheshire, arm. BRASENOSE COLL., matric. 20 Jan., 1789, aged 18.

Leigh, Walter, 2s. Henry James, of Taunton, Somerset, gent. PEMBROKE COLL., matric. 20 May, 1845, aged 19; B.A. from ST. MARY HALL, 1862, held various curacies 1861-84, rector of Meshaw, Devon, 1884.

Leigh, William, s. William, pleb. BRASENOSE COLL., matric. 27 Aug., 1723, aged 15; B.A. 27 Feb., 1727-8.

Leigh, William, s. William, of London, arm. BALLIOL COLL., matric. 26 Oct., 1749, aged 17; rector of Little Ilford, Essex, born in parish of St. George's, Westminster, 1 April, 1732, died unmarried 2 April, 1764, brother of Thomas 1751. [5]

Leigh, William, s. John Burrige, of Rushall Hall, co. Stafford, arm. UNIVERSITY COLL., matric. 7 Dec., 1771, aged 19.

Leigh, William, s. Richard, of Atherston, co. Warwick, gent. HERTFORD COLL., matric. 20 Nov., 1795, aged 17, B.A. 1800; M.A. from WORCESTER COLL., 1820, curate and incumbent of Bilston, co. Stafford, 1813-35, rector of Pulham, Norfolk, 1835, until his death 12 April, 1858.

Leigh, William, o.s. William, of Liverpool, Lancashire, arm. BRASENOSE COLL., matric. 28 Oct., 1819, aged 16; of Woodchester Park, co. Gloucester. See *Eton School Lists.*

Leigh-Bennett, Ernest Edward. CORPUS CHRISTI COLL., 1868. See BENNETT. [10]

Leigh-Bennett, George Spencer. PEMBROKE COLL., 1864. See BENNETT.

Leighton, (Sir) Baldwin (Bart.), born at Sunderland, co. Durham, o.s. Baldwin, baronet. MAGDALEN COLL., matric. 15 March, 1823, aged 17; 7th baronet, M.P. South Shropshire 1859-65, died 26 Feb., 1871. See Foster's *Baronetage.*

Leighton, (Sir) Baldwin (Bart.), 1s. Baldwin, of Alderbury, near Shrewsbury, Salop, baronet. CHRIST CHURCH, matric. 8 June, 1854, aged 17; B.A. 1859, M.A. 1864, 8th baronet, a student of Lincoln's Inn 1858, M.P. South Shropshire Aug., 1877-85. See Foster's *Baronetage* & *Eton School Lists.*

Leighton, Baldwin Francis, 2s. Forester, of Shrewsbury, cler. CHRIST CHURCH, matric. 29 April, 1822, aged 18; B.A. 1827, curate, and perp. curate Ford, Salop, 1827-39, died 22 Dec., 1880.

Leighton, Edward, s. Baldwin, of Shrewsbury, arm. PEMBROKE COLL., matric. 14 April, 1764, aged 18; B.A. 1767, rector of Cardiston and of Pontesbury (2nd portion) 1769, died 11 May, 1804, brother of Forester next named. [15]

Leighton, Forester, s. Baldwin, of Shrewsbury, Salop, gent. PEMBROKE COLL., matric. 1 Nov., 1781, aged 18; B.A. 1785, rector of one of the portions of Pontesbury 1795, and vicar of Condover, Salop, died 12 May, 1807.

Leighton, Francis Henry, s. Francis, of Clewer, Berks, arm. UNIVERSITY COLL., matric. 3 Nov., 1770, aged 16; (? vicar of Didlington with rector of Colveston, Norfolk, 1787, and vicar of Eldon, Suffolk, 1791).

Leighton, Francis Knyvett, o.s. Francis Knyvett, of Ipswich, Suffolk, arm. TRINITY COLL., matric. 24 June, 1823, aged 16; demy MAGDALEN COLL. 1823-9, B.A. 1828; fellow ALL SOULS' COLL. 1829-43, M.A. 1831, D.D. 1858, of the Council of Keble College 1871-80, rector of Cardiston, Salop, 1828, vicar of St. Chad's, Shrewsbury, rector of Harpsden 1841-58, vice-chancellor Oxford 1866-70, canon of Westminster 1868, rector of Locking and warden of All Souls' College 1858, until his death 13 Oct., 1881. See *Rugby School Reg.*, 129; & *Bloxam*, vii. 290.

Leighton, Sir Frederick; president Royal Academy 1878, created D.C.L. 18 June, 1879, an associate 1864, royal academician 1868, hon. LL.D. Cambridge 1879, and Edinburgh 1879, hon. colonel artists' corps (volunteers) 20th Middlesex (son of Frederick Septimus Leighton, of London), created a baronet 11 Feb., 1886.

Leighton, Gerard, s. Edward, of Wattlesborough, Salop, baronet. NEW COLL., matric. 27 April, 1721, aged 18; a captain in the army. [20]

Leighton, Rev. John Francis, 1s. John, of Bath, cler. TRINITY COLL., matric. 20 Feb., 1879, aged 18; B.A. 1881.

Leighton, Robert, 1s. John Leighton Figgins, of Manchester, cler. BALLIOL COLL., matric. 21 Oct., 1867, aged 19; exhibitioner 1867-72, B.A. 1872, M.A. 1875, took the name of LEIGHTON in lieu of his patronymic in 1871, head-master Bristol Grammar School 1883.

Leighton, Stanley, 2s. (Baldwin), of Alderbury, Salop, baronet. BALLIOL COLL., matric. 21 March, 1855, aged 17; B.A. & M.A. 1864, of Sweeney Hall, Salop, J.P., D.L., bar.-at-law, Inner Temple, 1861, M.P. North Shropshire Feb., 1876-85, Shropshire (Oswestry division) since 1885. See Foster's *Men at the Bar.*

Leighton, Thomas, s. Robert, of Hartlepool, co. Durham, gent. LINCOLN COLL., matric. 24 March, 1736-7, aged 18; B.A. 1740, rector of St. Mary's, South Bailey, Durham, 1755. See *Gent.'s Mag.*, 1795, i. 357.

Leighton, Rev. Thomas Leighton, 3s. John Leighton, of Blackley, Lancashire, cler. UNIVERSITY COLL., matric. 8 June 1878, aged 20, exhibitioner 1877-9; commoner CHARSLEY HALL 1880, B.A. 1882; M.A. from UNIVERSITY COLL. 1885. [25]

Leinster, Augustus Frederick, Duke of. CHRIST CHURCH, 1810. See FITZGERALD.

Leir, Charles Edward, 2s. William Marriott, of Bruton, Somerset, cler. ORIEL COLL., matric. 18 Jan., 1861, aged 18; B.A. 1864, M.A. 1870, held various curacies 1865-76, rector of Charlton Musgrove, Somerset, 1876-86. See Foster's *Our Noble and Gentle Families.*

Leir, Charles Marriott, 2s. William, of Galhampton, Somerset, cler. TRINITY COLL., matric. 27 Oct., 1830, aged 18; B.A. 1834, rector of Charlton Musgrove 1845, until his death 12 Jan., 1864.

Leir, Frank William, 5s. Charles Marriott, of Charlton Musgrove, Somerset, cler. ST. JOHN'S COLL., matric. 20 Jan., 1877, aged 18.

Leir, John Macie, 2s. Thomas, of Weston, Somerset, arm. NEW INN HALL, matric. 14 March, 1837, aged 20; B.A. 1842, M.A. 1846, vicar (and patron) of Fingringhoe, Essex, 1846, until his death 24 June, 1849. [30]

Leir, Lewis Randolph Marriott, 4s. Charles Marriott, of Charlton Musgrove, Somerset, cler. MAGDALEN COLL., matric. 13 Oct., 1879, aged 19; B.A. 1883, M.A. 1886, rector of Charlton Musgrove 1886.

Leir, Paul, s. Thomas, of Charlton Musgrove, Somerset, cler. QUEEN'S COLL., matric. 4 June, 1788, aged 17; B.A. 1793, M.A. 1808, J.P. Somerset, rector (and patron) of Charlton Musgrove 1812, until his death 14 Feb., 1845.

Leir, Paul Methuen, s. Thomas, of Ditcheat, Somerset, cler. WADHAM COLL., matric. 25 June, 1772; brother of Thomas, 1756, and of William, 1757.

Leir, Thomas, s. Thomas, of Ditcheat, Somerset, cler. WADHAM COLL., matric. 18 March, 1719-20, aged 17; B.A. 1723, M.A. 1726, rector (and patron) of Ditcheat and Charlton Musgrove, Somerset, 1730, until his death in 1781.

Leir, Thomas, s. Thomas, of Ditcheat, Somerset, cler. ORIEL COLL., matric. 30 April, 1756, aged 18; B.A. from WADHAM COLL. 1760, rector (and patron) of Ditcheat and of Charlton Musgrove, Somerset, 1781, until his death in 1812. [35]

Leir, Thomas, s. Thomas, of Charlton Musgrove, Somerset, cler. QUEEN'S COLL., matric. 18 March, 1784, aged 18; B.A. 1787, of Jaggards House, Wilts, and of Weston, near Bath, J.P., died 7 May, 1836.

Leir, Thomas Macie, s. Thomas, of Lyme Regis, Dorset, arm. EXETER COLL., matric. 15 Dec., 1814, aged 19; of Jaggards House, Wilts, died 26 Nov., 1864.

Leir, William, s. Thomas, of Ditcheat, Somerset, cler. WADHAM COLL., matric. 21 Oct., 1757, aged 17; B.A. 1761, brother of Thomas, 1756, and of Paul M., 1772.

Leir, William, s. Thomas, of Charlton Musgrove, Somerset, cler. QUEEN'S COLL., matric. 13 June, 1787, aged 18; B.A. 1791, M.A. 1808, rector (and patron) of Ditcheat, Somerset, 1812, until his death 23 Dec., 1863.

Leir, William Marriott, 1s. William, of Ansford, Somerset, cler. WADHAM COLL., matric. 9 Dec., 1823, aged 18; B.A. 1828, M.A. 1835, rector of West Bagborough 1855-61, rector (and patron) of Ditcheat since 1861. See Foster's *Our Noble and Gentle Families.* [5]

Leith, John, s. William, of Tolquhoun Tarves, Aberdeen, Scotland, gent. BALLIOL COLL., matric. 26 June, 1729, aged 17; B.A. 9 March, 1733-4.

Leith, Lockhart, s. George, of Deal, Kent, arm. CHRIST CHURCH, matric. 9 Nov., 1778, aged 19; B.A. 1782.

Leith, William Forbes, 2s. James John, of Whitelough, co. Aberdeen, arm. WORCESTER COLL., matric. 9 Nov., 1854, aged 21; B.A. 1859, M.A. 1861, vicar of Wattisham, Suffolk, 1868.

Lely, John Mountney, 2s. John Lely Ostler, of Grantham, co. Lincoln, arm. MAGDALEN COLL., matric. 25 July, 1857, aged 17; demy 1857-63, B.A. 1862, M.A. 1864, assumed the surname of LELY in lieu of OSTLER May, 1862, bar.-at-law, Inner Temple, 1869. See Foster's *Men at the Bar* & *Coll. Reg.*, vii. 413.

Lely, Tracy, s. Peter, of Lincoln (city), gent. LINCOLN COLL., matric. 2 Dec., 1748, aged 18; demy MAGDALEN COLL. 1750-6, B.A. 1753, M.A. 1755, fellow 1756-62. See *Bloxam*, vi. 289. [10]

Leman, Charles Orgill, 3s. Naunton Thomas, of Brampton, Suffolk, cler. UNIVERSITY COLL., matric. 27 Oct., 1819, aged 18; died 25 Jan., 1845.

Leman, George Orgill, s. Naunton Thomas Orgill, of Beccles, Suffolk, cler. UNIVERSITY COLL., matric. 4 Nov., 1807, aged 18; scholar 1812-16, B.A. 1811, M.A. 1814, of Brampton Hall, Suffolk, incumbent of Stoven, 1823, his father assumed the additional surname of LEMAN in 1808, died 14 Dec., 1867.

Leman, James, s. James, of Clutton, Somerset, gent. MAGDALEN HALL, matric. 28 Oct., 1782, aged 16.

Leman, Robert Orgill, s. Naunton Orgill, of Brampton, Suffolk, cler. TRINITY COLL., matric. 2 Feb., 1818, aged 18; B.A. 1822, of Brampton Hall, Suffolk, died 24 Feb., 1869.

Leman, Thomas Orgill, 5s. Naunton Thomas, of Brampton, Suffolk, cler. WORCESTER COLL., matric. 10 May, 1822, aged 18; B.A. 1826, M.A. 1849, rector of Brampton, Suffolk, 1837, until his death 7 June, 1873. [15]

Lemarchand, Frederick Payne, 1s. Francis Wharton, of Ceylon, gent. QUEEN'S COLL., matric. 12 Nov., 1880, aged 18; B.A. 1886.

Lemon, Arthur Henry, 3s. William George, of Blackheath, Kent, arm. EXETER COLL., matric. 18 Oct., 1883, aged 19; scholar 1883, B.A. 1887.

Lemon, Charles, s. Samuel, of Germo, Cornwall, gent. EXETER COLL., matric. 10 April, 1771, aged 18; B.A. 1775.

Lemon, (Sir) Charles (Bart.), s. William, of Carclew, par. Milor, Cornwall, baronet. CHRIST CHURCH, matric. 21 Oct., 1803, aged 19; 2nd baronet, hon. M.A. Cambridge 1833, deputy warden of the Stannaries 1852, M.P. Penrhyn 1807-12, 1830-1, Cornwall 1831-2, West Cornwall 1832-57, died 12 Feb., 1868.

Lemon, James Frederick, 1s. James, of Rigarc House, near Helstone, Cornwall, arm. KEB COLL., matric. 18 Oct., 1875, aged 18; B.A. 18 M.A. 1882, vicar of Marazion, Cornwall, si 1883. [2

Lemon, Thomas William, o.s. Thomas, of Taunt Somerset, arm. MAGDALEN HALL, matric. 14 Ju 1865, aged 19; B.A. 1869, M.A. 1872, vicar Buckerell, Devon, 1878-84.

Lemon, William, s. William, of Penzance, Cornw arm. CORPUS CHRISTI COLL., matric. 17 No 1741, aged 16; of Carclew, Cornwall, father of next named.

Lemon, (Sir) William (Bart.), s. William, of Tru Cornwall, arm. CHRIST CHURCH, matric. 11 Ja 1765, aged 16; of Carclew, Cornwall, created baronet 3 May, 1774, M.P. Penrhyn Jan., 1770 Cornwall, in 11 parliaments, 1774, until his de 18 Dec., 1824.

Lemon, William, s. William, of London, baron CHRIST CHURCH, matric. 7 May, 1791, aged 1 died March, 1799.

Lempriere, Algernon Thomas, 2s. George Ourry, Southampton, Hants, arm. TRINITY COLL., matr 3 June, 1854, aged 18; B.A. 1858, M.A. 1861, ba at-law, Inner Temple, 1863. See Foster's *Men the Bar* & *Eton School Lists.* [2

Lempriere, Charles, s. John, of Grouville, Isle Jersey, cler. PEMBROKE COLL., matric. 29 Oc 1725, aged 17; B.A. 6 Feb., 1729-30.

Lempriere, Charles, s. Charles, Isle of Jersey, ar HERTFORD COLL., matric. 26 Oct., 1759, aged 1 commissary-general Jersey and Guernsey, brother William Charles.

Lempriere, Charles, 3s. John, of St. David's, Exet doctor. ST. JOHN'S COLL., matric. 26 June, 18 aged 18; scholar 1837, B.C.L. 1842, D.C.L. 18 dean of laws 1875, bar.-at-law, Inner Temple, 18 colonial secretary for the Bahamas. See Foste *Men at the Bar* & *Robinson*, 223.

Lempriere, Daniel Matthew, 5s. John, of St. Helie Isle of Jersey, gent. PEMBROKE COLL., matr 27 Oct., 1842, aged 18; B.A. 1847, M.A. 18 chaplain Jersey hospital and prison 1854-84, rector St. Clement's, Jersey, 1876.

Lempriere, Everard Philip, o.s. Henry, of Woolwi Kent, arm. ST. JOHN'S COLL., matric. 23 Ap 1870, aged 19; B.A. 1874. [3

Lempriere, George, s. James, of St. Helier's, Isle Jersey, gent. PEMBROKE COLL., matric. 4 Ap 1720, aged 19; B.A. 24 March, 1723-4, M.A. 172

Lempriere, George, s. James, of St. Helier's, Isle Jersey, arm. HERTFORD COLL., matric. 10 De 1760, aged 14.

Lempriere, John, s. Charles, of Isle of Jersey, ge PEMBROKE COLL., matric. 17 Jan., 1786, aged B.A. 1790, M.A. 1792, B.D. 1801, D.D. 1803, master Bolton Free Grammar School 1790, he master Abingdon Grammar School 1792, and Exeter Free Grammar School, vicar of Abingd 1800, rector of Meeth 1811, and of Newton Petrock, Devon, 1823, until his death 1 Feb., 18 author of 'Bibliotheca Classica,' etc.

Lempriere, Philip, s. Charles, of Isle of Jersey, ar CHRIST CHURCH, matric. 27 Jan., 1803, aged 18.

Lempriere, Reginald Raoul, 1s. William, of Ipswi Suffolk, cler. CHRIST CHURCH, matric. 3 Ju 1870, aged 18; commoner MAGDALEN HALL 18 B.A. from HERTFORD COLL. 1875, M.A. 1878, b at-law, Inner Temple, 1875, and advocate Ro Court of Jersey. See Foster's *Men at the Bar.*

Lempriere, William, 2s. Philip Raoul, of Isle Jersey, arm. CHRIST CHURCH, matric. 22 O 1835, aged 17, B.A. 1839, M.A. 1843; fell EXETER COLL. 1843-4, chaplain of Rozel Man Jersey, since 1869. See *Boase*, 135; & *Rugby Sch Reg.*, 172. [1

VIEW BY BEREBLOCK, 1566. [*Facsimile from Hearne.*]

Lempriere, William Charles, s. Charles, of Isle of Jersey, arm. HERTFORD COLL., matric. 29 April, 1773, aged 18; commissary-general of Jersey and Guernsey, advocate and jurat in Royal Courts, died 1 May, 1790.

Lendon, Abel, s. Philip, of Crediton, Devon, pleb. TRINITY COLL., matric. 22 May, 1729, aged 19; B.A. 26 Jan., 1732-3.

Lendon, Abel, s. William, of London, gent. CHRIST CHURCH, matric. 22 June, 1791, aged 19; B.A. 1795, M.A. 1798, perp. curate Totteridge, Herts, rector of Fryern Barnet, Herts, 1815, until his death 4 Aug., 1846. See *Alumni West.*, 433.

Lendon, Abel Seyer, 2s. Abel, of Finchley, Middlesex, cler. CHRIST CHURCH, matric. 14 Dec., 1827, aged 19; B.A. 1831, M.A. 1836, curate of Sutton and Upton, Northants. [4]

Lendon, Edwin Harding, 1s. Edwin, of Greenwich, Kent, arm. UNIVERSITY COLL., matric. 20 Jan., 1866, aged 17; B.A. 1870, B.Med. & M.A. 1876.

Lendon, William Seyer, 1s. Abel, of Finchley, cler. CHRIST CHURCH, matric. 12 Nov., 1824, aged 17; B.A. 1829, M.A. 1839, rector of Wymington 1839, and of Newton Bromswold, Northants, 1841, until his death 21 May, 1848.

Leney, Herbert, 4s. Frederick, of Malling, Kent, gent. ORIEL COLL., matric. 7 Feb., 1870, aged 19; B.A. 1874, M.A. 1882.

Lennard, Henry Arthur Hallam (Farnaby), 1s. John Farnaby, of Pickhurst, Kent, arm. (after baronet). CHRIST CHURCH, matric. 12 Oct., 1877, aged 18; commoner NEW INN HALL 1879, B.A. 1882. See Foster's *Baronetage* & *Eton School Lists.*

Lennard, Rev. Henry Barrett, s. Thomas, of St. George's, Hanover Square, London, baronet. MERTON COLL., matric. 17 Feb., 1816, aged 18; postmaster 1818-20, B.A. 1820, died 17 Aug., 1870. See Foster's *Baronetage.*

Lennard, Thomas Stirling George Barrett, 1s. 'John B.,' of George's, Hanover Square, London, arm. MERTON COLL., matric. 13 June, 1833, aged 17; B.A. 1837, of London, 'bill broker,' died 7 April, 1845. See *Alumni West.*, 509. [10]

Lennox, Charles Henry, Earl of March, 1s. Charles, Duke of Richmond. CHRIST CHURCH, matric. 20 Oct., 1836, aged 18; B.A. 1839, created D.C.L. 22 June, 1870, 5th Duke of Richmond and 1st Duke of Gordon, K.G. 1867, M.P. West Sussex 1841-60, president of the Council 1874-80, chancellor of the University of Aberdeen 1861. See Foster's *Peerage.*

Lennox, (Hon.) Charles Spencer Bateman Hanbury Kincaid, 2s. William Bateman Hanbury, of Kelmarsh, Northants, baronet (after baron). BRASENOSE COLL., matric. 5 July, 1845, aged 17, B.A. 1848; fellow of ALL SOULS' COLL. 1848-62, M.A. 1853, of Lennox Castle, Stirlingshire, D.L., assumed the additional surnames of KINCAID LENNOX by royal licence in 1862, M.P. Herefordshire 1852-7, Leominster 1858-65, sometime captain life guards, etc. See Foster's *Peerage*, B. BATEMAN; & *Eton School Lists.*

Lennox, Lord Henry George Charles Gordon, 3s. (Charles, 5th) Duke of Richmond. CHRIST CHURCH, matric. 21 Oct., 1840, aged 18; B.A. 1843, M.A. 1847, privy councillor, M.P. Chichester Feb., 1846-85, a lord of the Treasury 1852, 1858-9, secretary to the Admiralty 1866-8, president Board of Works 1874-6, died 29 Aug., 1886.

Lennox, Lord Walter Charles Gordon, 4s. Charles Henry, Duke of Richmond. CHRIST CHURCH, matric. 31 May, 1884, aged 18. See Foster's *Peerage.*

Lenny, Christian, of ST. JOHN'S COLL., Cambridge (B.D. 1842, D.D. 1847), adm. 'ad eundem' 4 July, 1848, and also 21 June, 1852, curate of St. James's, Stubbings, Berks, died 1 Jan., 1882. [15]

Lenthal, William, s. John, of Burford, Oxon, gent. BRASENOSE COLL., matric. 6 April, 1723, aged 17; of Burford, high sheriff Oxon, died in 1781.

Lenthal, William John, s. John, of Burford, Oxon, arm. JESUS COLL., matric. 30 May, 1783, aged 18; of Besselsleigh, Berks, high sheriff cos. Carnarvon and Merioneth, died March, 1855.

Lenthall, Maurice, 'pomarius et rerum conditarum venditor'; privilegiatus 24 Sep., 1801.

Leny, William Macalpine, 1s. James Macalpine, of Dumfries, Scotland, arm. CHRIST CHURCH, matric. 21 Oct., 1857, aged 17; of Dalswinton, co. Dumfries, J.P., sometime 15th hussars. See *Eton School Lists.*

Leon, George Alexander, 4s. George Isaac, of London, arm. UNIVERSITY COLL., matric. 16 Oct., 1875, aged 19; B.A. 1879, M.A. 1882, a student of Inner Temple 1877. [20]

Leonard, Arthur Allen, 3s. Francis Burford, of Penhow, co. Monmouth, cler. ORIEL COLL., matric. 25 Oct., 1869, aged 19; B.A. 1873, M.A. 1877, vicar of Fordington, Dorset, 1880-7. See *St. Paul's School Reg.*, 343.

Leonard, Francis Burford, o.s. Richard, of Brackley, Northants, cler. WADHAM COLL., matric. 21 May, 1823, aged 16; B.A. 1827, M.A 1831, curate of Mixbury, Oxon, 1831-46, head-master Aynhoe Grammar School 1831-47, rector of Kemeys Inferior, 1846, and perp. curate Llandevaud, co. Monmouth, 1853, until his death 13 May, 1886.

Leonard, Richard Weston, s. William, of Faringdon, Berks, pleb. QUEEN'S COLL., matric. 26 Feb., 1790, aged 15; B.A. 1796, M.A. 1823, rector of Newbottle and King's Sutton, Northants, 1810, until his death 4 Oct., 1861.

Leonard, Samuel Henry, 1s. John Hare, of Clifton, co. Gloucester, gent. LINCOLN COLL., matric. 16 Oct., 1873, aged 19; scholar 1873-7, B.A. 1877, B.C.L. & M.A. 1880, bar.-at-law, Lincoln's Inn, 1880. See Foster's *Men at the Bar.*

Leonard, William, s. William, of Abingdon, Berks, gent. ALL SOULS' COLL., matric. 26 April, 1775, aged 16; clerk MAGDALEN COLL. 1776-9, B.A. from EXETER COLL. 1779, 40 years curate of Hinton, Northants, incumbent of Hardwick 1799, and rector of Hethe, Oxon, at his death 2 Dec., 1840. See *Bloxam*, ii. 110. [25]

Leonard, William Slatter, 2s. Francis Burford, of Aynhoe, Northants, cler. ST. ALBAN HALL, matric. 20 Oct., 1864, aged 18, B.A. 1867; chaplain CHRIST CHURCH 1872-6, M.A. 1872, chaplain NEW COLL. 1873-5, vicar of Down Ampney since 1875.

Lepard, Arthur George Campbell, 1s. Samuel Campbell, of Canterbury, cler. WORCESTER COLL., matric. 19 Oct., 1882, aged 19; B.A. 1886.

Lepard, Samuel Campbell, 2s. Samuel, of Newington Butts, Surrey, gent. WORCESTER COLL., matric. 25 Oct., 1853, aged 21; B.A. 1857, M.A. 1860, chaplain H.M. prison, Canterbury, 1861-83, rector of St. Andrew, Canterbury, 1877-84, vicar of Tenterden since 1884.

Lernoult, Francis, s. Philip, of Canterbury, Kent, cler. WADHAM COLL., matric. 5 April, 1742, aged 16; B.A. 1745, M.A. 1749, proctor 1757.

Lerpiniere, Edward, s. Daniel, of Bishopsgate, London, gent. LINCOLN COLL., matric. 16 July, 1761, aged 18. [30]

Lesley, James, 1s. Henry James, of Sinnington, Yorks, arm. PEMBROKE COLL., matric. 29 Jan., 1866, aged 19; B.A. 1868, M.A. 1872, of Sinnington, Yorks, J.P.

Lesley, Robert, 2s. Henry James, of Sinnington, near Pickering, Yorks, gent. PEMBROKE COLL., matric. 26 Oct., 1868, aged 18; B.A. 1874.

Leslie, Andrew, s. John, Earl (of Rothes). CHRIST CHURCH, matric. 14 March, 1731-2, aged 19; B.A. 14 Jan., 1734-5, B.C.L. (by diploma) 18 March, 1739-40, equerry to the Princess Dowager of Wales, died 27 Aug., 1776.

Leslie, Cecil Edward St. Lawrance, 3s. Charles, of Kilmore, near Cavan, Ireland, cler. CHRIST CHURCH, matric. 12 Dec., 1861, aged 18; B.A. 1865. See Foster's *Baronetage.*

Leslie, (Sir) Charles (Bart.), s. Lucas, of Brighthelmstone, Sussex, baronet. CHRIST CHURCH, matric. 31 Jan., 1793, aged 19; 2nd baronet, commanded a troop of 7th dragoons, died 4 Feb., 1833.

Leslie, Charles, 1s. John, bishop of Elphin, in Ireland. CHRIST CHURCH, matric. 5 May, 1829, aged 18; B.A. 1833, M.A. 1836, bishop of Kilmore, Elphin, and Ardagh, 19 April, 1870, until his death 8 July following. See Foster's *Baronetage*.

Leslie, Charles Frederick Henry, 3s. Henry David, of London, arm. ORIEL COLL., matric. 19 Oct., 1880, aged 18.

Leslie, Charles (Powell), s. Charles Powell, of Dublin (city), arm. CHRIST CHURCH, matric. 30 April, 1784, aged 17; created M.A. 31 Jan., 1787, of Glaslough, co. Monaghan, high sheriff 1788, M.P. 1801-26, New Ross 1830-1, a colonel of militia, died 15 Nov., 1831. See Foster's *Baronetage*.

Leslie, Charles Powell, 1s. Charles Powell, of Donah, co. Monaghan, arm. CHRIST CHURCH, matric. 16 Oct., 1839, aged 18; of Glaslough, co. Monaghan, lord-lieut., and M.P. 1842, until his death 26 June, 1871. See Foster's *Baronetage*. [5]

Leslie, Charles Robert, MAGDALEN COLL., 1876. See FLETCHER.

Leslie, Edmund Douglas, 1s. James Edmund, of Edinburgh, Scotland, arm. ORIEL COLL., matric. 26 May, 1847, aged 18; of Leslie Hill, Ballymoney, and of Seaport Lodge, Bushmills, co. Antrim, etc.

Leslie, Edward, s. James, bishop of Limerick, Ireland. WADHAM COLL., matric. 29 June, 1765, aged 18; created M.A. 19 April, 1769, bar.-at-law, Middle Temple, 1777, brother of Richard 1765. See *Cotton*, vol. v., p. 60, & Foster's *Baronetage*.

Leslie, Edward, s. Charles Powell, of Glaslough, co. Monaghan, Ireland, arm. CHRIST CHURCH, matric. 13 March, 1812, aged 20; B.A. 1815, M.A. 1823, B.D. 1831, rector of Annahilt, co. Down, preb. and treasurer (diocese) Dromore 1817-47, died 2 Jan., 1865. See Foster's *Baronetage*.

Leslie, Rev. Edward Charles, 1s. Thomas, of Little Hothfield, Kent. arm. NON-COLL., matric. 29 April, 1881, aged 22; B.A. 1884. [10]

Leslie, Ferdinand Seymour, 1s. (John Charles) William, of Naples, Italy, cler. ORIEL COLL., matric. 17 May, 1864, aged 18; B.A. 1868, of 1st king's dragoon guards.

Leslie, Henry King, 4s. Charles, of Kilmore, Cavan, Ireland, cler. CHRIST CHURCH, matric. 5 Nov., 1863, aged 18. See Foster's *Baronetage*.

Leslie, James Edmund, s. James, of Belfast, co. Antrim, arm. CHRIST CHURCH, matric. 9 May, 1818, aged 18; B.A. 1821, of Leslie Hill and Seaport Lodge, co. Antrim, J.P., D.L., high sheriff 1854, a student of Lincoln's Inn 1820, died 17 Jan., 1881, father of Edmund Douglas.

Leslie, John, 2s. John, bishop of Dromore, Ireland, CHRIST CHURCH, matric. 23 May, 1833, aged 18; bar.-at-law, Middle Temple, 1841. See Foster's *Men at the Bar*.

Leslie, (Sir) John (Bart.), 2s. Charles Powell, of Dona, co. Monaghan, arm. CHRIST CHURCH, matric. 9 Dec., 1840, aged 17; B.A. 1844, M.A. 1865, of Glaslough House, co. Monaghan, J.P., D.L., high sheriff 1883, and of Pettigo, co. Donegal, J.P., sometime lieut. 1st life guards, M.P. co. Monaghan 1871-80, created a baronet 21 Feb., 1876. See Foster's *Baronetage*. [15]

Leslie, Rev. John Charles William, 4s. James, of Holywood, Belfast, co. Down, Ireland, arm. EXETER COLL., matric. 23 Feb., 1829, aged 20; B.A. 1832, died 29 Nov., 1877, father of Ferdinand.

Leslie, Richard, s. James, bishop of Limerick, WADHAM COLL., matric. 29 June, 1765, aged 16; brother of Edward 1765.

Leslie, Thomas, 3s. John, bishop of Dromore, Ireland. BALLIOL COLL., matric. 28 March, 1833, aged 18; B.A. 1841, M.A. 1847, bar.-at-law, Inner Temple, 1847, died 15 Feb., 1880. See Foster's *Baronetage*.

Leslie, William, 3s. Hugh Fraser, of Old Machar, co. Aberdeen, Scotland, arm. LINCOLN COLL., matric. 4 June, 1821, aged 17; B.A. 1825, M.A. 1829.

Lessey, Theophilus, s. William, of Stocklinch, Somerset, pleb. WADHAM COLL., matric. 9 April, 1720, aged 18; B.A. 1723. [20]

Lester, Rev. George Mackenzie Lester, 2s. Lester, of Swanage, Dorset, cler. UNIVERSITY COLL., matric. 16 Oct., 1880, aged 18; B.A. 1883.

Lester, Horace Frank, 2s. Frederick, of Bombay, arm. LINCOLN COLL., matric. 19 Oct., 1872, aged 19; exhibitioner UNIVERSITY COLL. 1873-7, B.A. 1876, bar.-at-law, Lincoln's Inn, 1879, and a journalist. See Foster's *Men at the Bar* & *Rugby School Reg.*

Lester, John Bingley Garland, 3s. Lester, of Swanage, Dorset, cler. UNIVERSITY COLL., matric. 11 Oct., 1884, aged 19.

Lester, John Moore, 1s. Frederick Parkinson, of Bombay, arm. UNIVERSITY COLL., matric. 23 Jan., 1871, aged 19; B.A. 1875, M.A. 1877, vicar of Stony Stratford, Bucks, 1880-4, incumbent of Holy Trinity, Ayr, 1884. See *Rugby School Reg.*

Lester, Rev. Joseph Dunn, 1s. John, of Aberystwith, co. Monmouth, gent. JESUS COLL., matric. 29 Jan., 1861, aged 19; scholar 1861-5, B.A. 1865, died 2 Dec., 1875. [25]

Lester, Lester Vallis, 1s. Lester, of Swanage, Dorset, cler. MAGDALEN COLL., matric. 13 Oct., 1879, aged 19, demy 1879-84, B.A. 1883, M.A. 1886; fellow St. John's College 1886, lecturer.

L'Estrange, (Rev.) Alfred Guy, (Kingan), o.s. Hilary Frederick, of Dublin (city), arm. EXETER COLL., matric. 12 June, 1851, aged 19; B.A. 1856, M.A. 1885. See *Eton School Lists*.

L'Estrange, Hamon Styleman, 1s. Henry L'Estrange Styleman, of Portman Square, London, arm. CHRIST CHURCH, matric. 27 May, 1858, aged 17; B.A. 1861, M.A. 1876, of Hunstanton Hall, Norfolk, J.P., D.L., high sheriff 1880.

L'Estrange, Henry George, 1s. George, of Dublin, arm. KEBLE COLL., matric. 14 Oct., 1872, aged 17; of Owendoon, co. Cavan. See *Eton School Lists*.

Le Strange, Henry Le Strange Styleman-, 1s. Henry, of Snettisham, Norfolk, arm. CHRIST CHURCH, matric. 25 Oct., 1832, aged 17; B.A. 1837, M.A. 1852, of Hunstanton, Norfolk, assumed the additional final surname of LE STRANGE in 1839, died 27 July, 1862. [30]

Letchworth, Arnold, 3s. Henry Finch, of St. Laurence Reading, Berks, arm. EXETER COLL., matric 14 June, 1859, aged 18; B.A. 1863, M.A. 1866 vicar of St. John Evangelist, Kingston-on-Thames since 1872.

Letchworth, Henry Howard, 2s. Henry Finch, of St. Laurence, Reading, arm. ORIEL COLL., matric 10 May, 1855, aged 18; B.A. 1859, M.A. 1861, held various curacies 1859-85, vicar of Holy Trinity Southampton, 1885-6, rector of Exton, Hants, since 1886.

Lethbridge, Ambrose Goddard, 2s. Thomas, of Bath (city), baronet. CHRIST CHURCH, matric. 24 May 1823, aged 18, B.A. 1827; fellow ALL SOULS COLL. 1827-52, M.A. 1831, proctor 1839, of East brook House, Somerset, J.P., D.L., bar.-at-law Middle Temple, 1832, recorder of Wells, died s.p 21 Nov., 1875. See Foster's *Baronetage*.

Lethbridge, Arthur, 1s. Thomas Arscot, of Woolwich Kent, gent. EXETER COLL., matric. 28 Jan., 1863 aged 18; B.A. 1867, M.A. 1872, vicar of Barrington, Somerset, 1878-85, rector of Shepton-Beauchamp since 1885.

Lethbridge, Charles, s. John, of Launceston, Cornwall, cler. ORIEL COLL., matric. 6 June, 1780, aged 17, B.A. 1785; M.A. from ST. JOHN'S COLL., Cambridge, 1792, rector of St. Thomas by Launceston 1791, of Salcombe, Devon, 1797, and of Stoke Climsland 1805, until his death 14 Dec., 1840.

Lethbridge, Charles, 1s. Thomas Prowse, of Brompton Ralph, Somerset, cler. BALLIOL COLL., matric. 21 June, 1854, aged 18. See Foster's *Baronetage.*

Lethbridge, Charles Henry, s. Charles, of St. Stephen's, juxta Launceston, Cornwall, cler. WADHAM COLL., matric. 9 June, 1810, aged 17; B.A. 1815 (? chaplain H.M.S. *Isis* 1823), perp. curate St. Stephen's by Launceston 1818, until his death 18 Jan., 1845.

Lethbridge, Christopher, s. Philip, of Santon Court, Devon, gent. BALLIOL COLL., matric. 26 May, 1748, aged 19; B.A. 1752. [5]

Lethbridge, Elford Copland, 5s. Robert, of Flushcombe, New South Wales, arm. MAGDALEN HALL, matric. 14 Feb., 1850, aged 20; B.A. 1855, M.A. 1858, curate of West Thurrock, Essex, 1858-63, vicar (with Purfleet) 1863-76, vicar of Charlestown (or St. George's, Pendleton), Lancashire, 1876-84, rector of Tolleshunt Knights, Essex, 1884.

Lethbridge, Francis Washington, born at Wood Green, Middlesex, 1s. Sir Roper, knight. EXETER COLL., matric. 28 Jan., 1886, aged 18.

Lethbridge, John, s. John, of Oakhampton, Devon, gent. BALLIOL COLL., matric. 5 April, 1742, aged 18, B.A. 1745; M.A. from PEMBROKE COLL., Cambridge, 1753, of Launceston, Cornwall, vicar of Dewstow, Cornwall, rector of Sutcombe, Devon, 1753, died at Exeter in 1796.

Lethbridge, John, s. John, of Pilton, Devon, arm. MAGDALEN COLL., matric. 18 Feb., 1764, aged 17; created M.A. 30 June, 1767.

Lethbridge, John Christopher Baron, 1s. John King, of Laneast, Cornwall, arm. ST. JOHN'S COLL., matric. 14 June, 1860, aged 20.

Lethbridge, John King, 2s. John King, of Tregeare, near Launceston, Cornwall, arm. WADHAM COLL., matric. 18 June, 1862, aged 18; B.A. 1867, M.A. 1869, vicar of Laneast, Cornwall, 1870-6, chaplain in the army since 1876. [10]

Lethbridge, Sir Roper (formerly Ebenezer), 1s. Ebenezer, of Plymouth, Devon, arm. EXETER COLL., matric. 1 Feb., 1859, aged 18; exhibitioner 1859-60, scholar 1860, B.A. 1863, M.A. 1866, bar.-at-law, Inner Temple, 1880, C.I.E. 1878, knighted by patent 14 Sep., 1885, sometime principal of Krishnagur College, Bengal, late government press commissioner India, and political agent India Office 1878, fellow Calcutta University, editor of *Calcutta Quarterly Review* 1871-8, M.P. North Kensington 1885. See Foster's *Men at the Bar* & *Coll. Reg.*, 158.

Lethbridge, (Sir) Thomas Buckler (Bart.), s. John, of Bishop's Lidiard, Somerset, arm. (after a baronet). ORIEL COLL., matric. 15 Nov., 1794, aged 16; 2nd baronet, M.P. Somerset 1806-12, 1820-30, died 17 Oct., 1849. See Foster's *Baronetage.*

Lethbridge, Thomas Prowse, 3s. Thomas Buckler, of Crawley, Hants, baronet. CHRIST CHURCH, matric. 14 June, 1828, aged 18; B.A. 1833, rector of Broad Nymet, Devon, 1837-45, of Bow (alias Nymet Tracy) 1839-45, and of Combe Florey, Somerset, 1845, until his death 27 June, 1851. See Foster's *Baronetage.*

Lethbridge, William, o.s. Charles Henry, of Hornby, Lancashire, gent. BRASENOSE COLL., matric. 19 Oct., 1882, aged 18; B.A. 1888.

Lethieullier, Charles, s. John, of London, arm. TRINITY COLL., matric. 15 Aug., 1728, aged 15; B.C.L. from ALL SOULS' COLL. 1735, D.C.L. 1740, bar.-at-law, Lincoln's Inn, 1739, died 10 Dec., 1759. See Berry's *Kent.* [15]

Lethieullier, Smart, s. John, of Little Ilford, Essex, arm. TRINITY COLL., matric. 19 Feb., 1719-20, aged 18; created M.A. 11 July, 1723, of Aldersbrook, Essex, died 27 Aug., 1760.

Letsome, Sampson, s. Sampson, of St. Martin's, Worcester (city), gent. MAGDALEN HALL, matric. 23 Feb., 1721-2, aged 18; B.A. 1725, M.A. 1728.

Lett, Charles, o.s. James, of Peckham, Surrey, arm. TRINITY COLL., matric. 8 April, 1829, aged 17.

Lett, Thomas, 'butler of Hertford College;' privilegiatus 26 Jan., 1762.

Letts, Ernest Frederick (B.A. from TRINITY COLL., Dublin, 1874), 4s. Thomas, of Sydenham, Kent, gent. ST. EDMUND HALL, incorp. 25 Jan., 1871, aged 20: chaplain of St. Edward's School, Oxford, 1875-8, and of New College 1877-8, minor canon and precentor of Manchester Cathedral 1878-85, rector of Newton Heath since 1885. [20]

Letts, Harold Arthur, 6s. Thomas, of Sydenham, Kent, gent. MERTON COLL., matric. 18 Oct., 1881, aged 20; postmaster 1881, until his death 27 Aug., 1884.

Leudesdorf, Charles, 1s. Henry, of Manchester, arm. WORCESTER COLL., matric. 2 Feb., 1870, aged 17, exhibitioner 1869-70, scholar 1870-3, B.A. 1873; fellow PEMBROKE COLL. 1873, M.A. 1876, mathematical lecturer 1874, junior bursar 1876, proctor 1887.

Leupolt, Albert Francis, 5s. Charles Benjamin, of Benares, East Indies, cler. BRASENOSE COLL., matric. 13 Oct., 1873, aged 19; scholar 1873, until his death in 1877.

Levander, Rev. Henry Charles, 1s. James, of Norwich (city), gent. PEMBROKE COLL., matric. 12 March, 1846, aged 19; B.A. 1850, M.A. 1863, a master at University College School, London, 1866-84, died 4 Dec., 1884. [25]

Lever, (Sir) Ashton, s. Darcy, of Alkrington, Lancashire, eq. aur. CORPUS CHRISTI COLL., matric. 1 April, 1748, aged 19; naturalist, scholar, and philanthropist knighted 1778, died 24 Jan., 1788. See *Manchester School Reg.*, i. 155.

Lever, (Sir) James Darcy, s. John, of Salford, Lancashire, arm. BRASENOSE COLL., matric. 6 Feb., 1721-2, aged 17; created D.C.L. 11 July, 1733, of Alkrington, Lancashire, high sheriff 1736, knighted 26 Jan., 1736-7, died 18 Aug., 1742, father of Sir Ashton last named.

Lever, Thomas, s. Samuel, of Wigan, Lancashire, cler. BRASENOSE COLL., matric. 26 Feb., 1732-3, aged 19; B.A. 1736.

Leveridge, Richard, 'Bampton carrier;' privilegiatus 18 Feb., 1752.

Leversage, John, s. John, of Horsley, co. Gloucester, gent. WORCESTER COLL., matric. 7 July, 1788, aged 17.

Leversage, William, s. Richard, of Nantwich, Cheshire, gent. BRASENOSE COLL., matric. 13 Dec., 1787, aged 17; B.A. 1791, M.A. 1794. [30]

Leversedge, Roger, s. Roger, of Frome Sellwood, Somerset, arm. BALLIOL COLL., matric. 8 June, 1722, aged 16.

Leverton, Edward Spry, 1s. Henry Spry, of Truro, Cornwall, gent. EXETER COLL., matric. 15 Oct., 1879, aged 20; scholar 1878-84, B.A. 1883, M.A. 1886.

Leverton, Rev. Henry Lewis, 2s. Henry Spry, of Truro, Cornwall, arm. ST. MARY HALL, matric. 28 Jan., 1880, aged 18, scholar 1880-1; commoner ORIEL COLL. 1881, B.A. 1884.

Levett, Edward, s. Richard, of Wycombe, Bucks, cler. CHRIST CHURCH, matric. 6 June, 1792, aged 17; student 1792-1812, B.A. 1796, M.A. 1799, rector of Ingestre, co. Stafford, until 1829, and of Deene, Northants, until 1834, died 18 Nov., 1845, brother of Richard 1790, and of Walter 1802. See *Alumni West.*, 435. [34]

Levett, Henry, s. Francis, of Aldermanbury, London, gent. EXETER COLL., matric. 26 Feb., 1718-9, aged 17; demy MAGDALEN COLL. 1720-6, B.A. 1722, M.A. 1725, died April, 1726. See *Bloxam*, vi. 197.

Levett, John, s. Theophilus, of Lichfield (city), gent. BRASENOSE COLL., matric. 23 Feb., 1738-9, aged 17; of Wychnor, co. Stafford, by purchase, 1765, bar.-at-law, Inner Temple, 1743, M.P. Lichfield 1761, until unseated Feb., 1762, died 22 Nov., 1799.

Levett, John, 1s. Theophilus, of Wichnor, co. Stafford, arm. TRINITY COLL., matric. 4 March, 1823, aged 18; created M.A. 7 June, 1826, of Wychnor Park and Packington Hall, died 19 Dec., 1853.

Levett, Nathaniel, o.s. Charles, of Staynton, co. Pembroke, gent. JESUS COLL., matric. 23 Oct., 1826, aged 18; B.A. 1830, M.A. 1834, curate of Hubberston, co. Pembroke, died 1837.

Levett, Norrison Dikes, 1s. Norrison, of North Ferriby, near Hull, gent. ST. EDMUND HALL, matric. 25 Oct., 1866, aged 20; B.A. 1874, M.A. 1875.

Levett, Richard, s. Theophilus, of Lichfield, co. Stafford, gent. CHRIST CHURCH, matric. 13 March, 1745-6, aged 19; B.A. from PEMBROKE COLL. 1749, M.A. 1752 (? rector of Little Berkhampstead 1753, rector of Wrotham, Kent, 1791), brother of John 23 Feb., 1738-9. [5]

Levett, Richard, s. Richard, of Blithfield, co. Stafford, doctor. CHRIST CHURCH, matric. 26 May, 1749, aged 18; B.A. 1753, M.A. 1756, vicar of West Wycombe, Bucks, 1765, until his death Jan., 1805. See *Alumni West.*, 349.

Levett, Richard, s. Richard, of Wycombe, Bucks, cler. CHRIST CHURCH, matric. 25 Oct., 1790, aged 17; fellow ALL SOULS' COLL., B.C.L. 1797, of Milford Hall, Stafford, curate to his father at Wycombe, died 25 Aug., 1843, father of the next named.

Levett, Richard Byrd, 1s. Richard, of Milford, co. Stafford, cler. CHRIST CHURCH, matric. 26 April, 1827, aged 16; of Milford Hall, co. Stafford, J.P., D.L., late lieut.-colonel commanding 3rd battalion Staffordshire rifles.

Levett, Theophilus, s. Thomas, of Whittington, co. Stafford, arm. CHRIST CHURCH, matric. 1 April, 1784, aged 18; of Wychnor Park, co. Stafford, high sheriff 1810, recorder of Lichfield, died 3 Dec., 1839.

Levett, Rev. Thomas, s. Thomas, of Whittington, co. Stafford, arm. CHRIST CHURCH, matric. 23 Oct., 1788, aged 18; B.A. 1792, of Packington Hall, co. Warwick, died 9 Oct., 1843. [10]

Levett, Thomas. TRINITY COLL., 1828. See PRINSEP.

Levett, Walter, s. Richard, of Stafford (town), cler. CHRIST CHURCH, matric. 29 May, 1802, aged 18; B.A. 1806, M.A. 1808, student until 1817, vicar of Carleton, Yorks, 1816-49, of Bray, Berks, 1823-5, and 1826, sub-dean of York 1827, died 27 Oct., 1860. See *Alumni West.*, 457.

Levien, Edward, 1s. John, of Marylebone, London, arm. BALLIOL COLL., matric. 25 Nov., 1837, aged 18; B.A. 1841, M.A. 1846.

Levien, Edward, 1s. Edward, of St. George the Martyr, London, arm. TRINITY COLL., matric. 2 May, 1839, aged 18; B.A. 1842, a student of Inner Temple 1840.

Levien, John, 2s. John, of Bath, gent. WADHAM COLL., matric. 1 March, 1838, aged 18; B.A. 1842, M.A. 1847, rector of Enmore, Somerset, 1860-75, and of Burnham Thorpe, Norfolk (and patron), since 1875, until his death 4 March, 1888. [15]

Levinge, Edward Vere, 2s. Harry Corbyn, of Cuttack, East Indies, gent. BALLIOL COLL., matric. 24 Oct., 1885, aged 18; of the Indian Civil Service 1885.

Levinge, (Sir) William Henry (Bart.), 1s. William James, of Dublin, arm. ORIEL COLL., matric. 19 Oct., 1867, aged 18; B.A. 1871, M.A. 1874, 9th baronet. See Foster's *Baronetage.*

Levinsohn, Henry Raphael, o.s. Lewis, of London, gent. MAGDALEN COLL., matric. 22 Oct., 1878, aged 18; B.A. 1882.

Levy, George, 2s. Abraham, of Sowerby, Westmoreland, gent. QUEEN'S COLL., matric. 7 June, 1834, aged 20; scholar 1834-8, B.A. 1838, M.A. 1847, incumbent Emmanuel Church, Bolton-le-Moors, Lancashire, 1841, until his death 27 Dec., 1853.

Levy, Henry Albert, 1s. Albert, of London, arm. HERTFORD COLL., matric. 28 Jan., 1879, aged 19. [20]

Levy, Thomas Bailey, 1s. Abraham, of Kirby Thore, Westmoreland, arm. EXETER COLL., matric. 18 Nov., 1830, aged 18; scholar QUEEN'S COLL. 1831-46, B.A. 1834, M.A. 1838, fellow 1846-72, chaplain 1843, bursar 1849-50, rector of South Weston, Oxon, 1855-56, and of Knights Enham, Hants, 1856, until his death 24 March, 1872.

Lewarne, Nathaniel Nicholas, 1s. Nicholas, of St. Columb, Cornwall, gent. NON-COLL., matric. 16 Oct., 1886, aged 28.

Lewes, David, s. James, of Doleheydd, co. Carmarthen, arm. PEMBROKE COLL., matric. 3 March, 1769, aged 18; a student of Lincoln's Inn 1770.

Lewes, John, s. Watkin, of Meline, co. Pembroke, cler. MERTON COLL., matric. 15 Dec., 1756, aged 18; B.A. 1760, M.A. 1764, D.C.L. 1768, rector of Ewell, Surrey, of St. George's, Southwark, 1768, and of Whippingham, Isle of Wight, 1777, until his death 9 Aug., 1802.

Lewes, Price, s. William, of Lengeler, co. Carmarthen, arm. BRASENOSE COLL., matric. 22 June, 1814, aged 18; of Gwastoed, co. Cardigan, bar.-at-law, Lincoln's Inn, 1826. See *Eton School Lists.* [25]

Lewes, Thomas, s. John, of Carmarthen (town), gent. TRINITY COLL., matric. 17 Nov., 1741, aged 18.

Lewes, Thomas, s. William, of Llysnewydd, co. Carmarthen, arm. BRASENOSE COLL., matric. 22 March, 1811, aged 17; B.A. 1815, M.A. 1817, rector of Paynton, Oxon, vicar of Great Barrington, Oxon, 1820, until his death 8 April, 1873. See *Eton School Lists.*

Lewes, Watkin, s. John, of Llantood, co. Pembroke, pleb. JESUS COLL., matric. 30 May, 1723, aged 19; B.A. 10 March, 1726-7 (? in holy orders and father of Watkin, bar.-at-law, Middle Temple, 1766).

Lewes, William, s. John, of Carmarthen, Wales, arm. TRINITY COLL., matric. 27 July, 1763, aged 16; created M.A. 23 June, 1767.

Lewin, Emilius, 7th & y.s. Thomas, of St. Giles's, London, arm. TRINITY COLL., matric. 27 June, 1829, aged 17; B.A. 1834. See *Eton School Lists.*

Lewin, Frederick Ellerker, 4s. Thomas Ellerker, of Clapham, Surrey, arm. CHRIST CHURCH, matric. 14 Oct., 1881, aged 19; junior student 1881, B.A. 1885. [31]

Lewin, Lionel Henry, 1s. Frederick Mortimer, of Combaconum, East Indies, arm. PEMBROKE COLL., matric. 25 Oct., 1871, aged 25; a student of Inner Temple 1872, died 20 Dec., 1874.

Lewin, Reginald Wynford Elphinstone, 2s. Gregory, of Marylebone, London, equitis. PEMBROKE COLL., matric. 10 Nov., 1853, aged 18; B.A. 1865.

Lewin, Spencer James, s. James, of Bushy, Herts, gent. WORCESTER COLL., matric. 26 Feb., 1784, aged 17; B.A. 1788, M.A. 1791, vicar (and patron) of Ifield, Sussex, 1790, rector of Rushden, Northants, 1807, and of Crawley, Sussex, 1817, until his death 25 April, 1842.

Lewin, Thomas, s. Thomas, of Madras, East Indies, arm. BRASENOSE COLL., matric. 11 July, 1804, aged 16; B.A. from CORPUS CHRISTI COLL. 1808, M.A. 1832, bar.-at-law, Inner Temple, 1811. [35]

Lewin, Thomas, 5s. Spencer James, of Ifield, Sussex, cler. WORCESTER COLL., matric. 29 Nov., 1823, aged 18; scholar TRINITY COLL. 1825-9, B.A. 1828, M.A. 1831, bar.-at-law, Lincoln's Inn 1833, author of legal and other works, died 5 Jan., 1877. See *Robinson*, 202.

Lewin, Wilfrid Hale, 2s. Edward Bernard Hale, of Wanstead, Essex, arm. UNIVERSITY COLL., matric. 21 May, 1875, aged 19; scholar 1875-8, B.A. 1878, bar.-at-law, Middle Temple, 1883. See Foster's *Men at the Bar.*

Lewington, Arthur Lord, 3s. John, of Maidenhead, Berks, arm. MAGDALEN HALL, matric. 23 March, 1868, aged 34, B.A. 1872; M.A. (HERTFORD COLL.) 1875, head-master St. Michael's Grammar School, Reading, 1865-8, fellow of St. Michael and St. Nicholas College, Lancing, and chaplain of Ardingly College 1872.

Lewis, Alfred Merlin, 1s. Titus, of Carmarthen (town), gent. JESUS COLL., matric. 31 Oct., 1861, aged 18; B.A. 1866, M.A. 1872, a student of the Inner Temple 1868, perp. curate Ryhill, Yorks, 1875-80, vicar of Huttons Ambo 1880-5, and of Ash, Somerset, 1885.

Lewis, Ambrose, s. Lewis, of Llangynhafal, co. Denbigh, cler. JESUS COLL., matric. 6 March, 1733-4, aged 17; B.A. 1737, M.A. 1740.

Lewis, Angelo John, 1s. John, of St. Pancras, Middlesex, arm. WADHAM COLL., matric. 24 Oct., 1855, aged 16; B.A. 1859, M.A. 1862, bar.-at-law, Lincoln's Inn, 1861. See Foster's *Men at the Bar.* [5]

Lewis, Arthur, s. John, of Brighthay, Dorset, gent. BALLIOL COLL., matric. 26 Feb., 1722-3, aged 16.

Lewis, Arthur, s. Richard, of Llanfaes, Isle of Anglesea, pleb. JESUS COLL., matric. 15 Dec., 1764, aged 19; B.A. 1768, M.A. 1771 (? rector of Fenford, Northants, 1774, until he died 12 Sep., 1786).

Lewis, Rev. Arthur, 5s. Henry, of Clifton, near Bristol, gent. QUEEN'S COLL., matric. 8 Feb., 1873, aged 18; clerk 1873-7, B.A. 1876, M.A. 1881, vice-president of St. John's Divinity School, Lahore, 1884.

Lewis, Arthur Bowen Wolseley, 1s. Thomas Wolseley, of Llanrwst, co. Denbigh, cler. TRINITY COLL., matric. 16 Oct., 1886, aged 20.

Lewis, Arthur Casson, 1s. Thomas, of Ruthin, co. Denbigh, arm. TRINITY COLL., matric. 14 Oct., 1872, aged 19; B.A. 1875, M.A. 1880. [10]

Lewis, Arthur Edward, 2s. John, of Wrexham, arm. CHRIST CHURCH, matric. 24 Jan., 1881, aged 19; B.A. 1884.

Lewis, Rev. Arthur Gardner, 3s. John Prothero, of Llandilo, co. Carmarthen, gent. JESUS COLL., matric. 30 Jan., 1873, aged 18; B.A. 1877, M.A. 1880.

Lewis, Arthur Griffith Poyer, 1s. Richard, of Denchworth, Berks, cler. (bishop of Llandaff). UNIVERSITY COLL., matric. 19 Oct., 1867, aged 19; B.A. 1871, M.A. 1884, bar.-at-law, Lincoln's Inn, 1873, official to archdeacon of St. David's 1874, registrar of diocese of Llandaff 1885. See Foster's *Men at the Bar* & *Eton School Lists.*

Lewis, Arthur James, born at Cananore, Bombay, East Indies, 2s. Robert, arm. TRINITY COLL., matric. 20 Nov., 1821, aged 20; B.A. 1825, bar.-at-law, Middle Temple, 1828, advocate-general Bombay 1857, and a member of Council, died 14 Nov., 1865.

Lewis, Arthur King, born in the Island of Ascension, 3s. James, gent. TRINITY COLL., matric. 16 Oct., 1886, aged 19; scholar 1886. [15]

Lewis, Barrington, s. Matthew, of Harley Street, Marylebone, Westminster, arm. CHRIST CHURCH, matric. 5 May, 1797, aged 19.

Lewis, Benjamin, s. John, of Kilrhedyn, co. Pembroke, gent. JESUS COLL., matric. 27 May, 1805, aged 19; B.A. 1809, M.A. 1812 (as LEWES), rector of Llanfihangel Penbedw 1815, rector of Kilrhedin, J.P. of cos. Carmarthen, Cardigan, and Pembroke, died 26 Jan., 1855, but see also *Gent.'s Mag.*, 1847, i. 670, for an apparently erroneous notice of death.

Lewis, Benjamin Williams, 3s. Roland, of Mothvey, co. Carmarthen, gent. JESUS COLL., matric. 26 April, 1860, aged 22.

Lewis, Charles, s. Francis, of Stanford, Notts, arm. MAGDALEN COLL., matric. 30 July, 1741, aged 17; demy 1741-5, B.A. 1745, fellow 1745-51, M.A. 20 Jan., 1747-8, died 12 March, 1762. See *Coll. Reg.*, vi. 252; & *Alumni West.*, 322.

Lewis, Charles, s. Thomas, of Martock, Somerset, pleb. QUEEN'S COLL., matric. 10 May, 1744, aged 18; B.A. 19 Feb., 1747-8. [20]

Lewis, Charles, s. Lewis, of Llangadoc, co. Carmarthen, pleb. JESUS COLL., matric. 5 July, 1753, aged 19.

Lewis, Charles, s. Marmaduke, of Linfield, Sussex, cler. CHRIST CHURCH, matric. 20 Jan., 1777, aged 15; student, B.A. 1781, died 6 Nov., 1782.

Lewis, Charles, s. James, of St. George-the-Martyr, London, gent. BRASENOSE COLL., matric. 1 July, 1803, aged 17.

Lewis, Charles Alexander, s. James, of Rockfield, co. Monaghan, Ireland, arm. ST. EDMUND HALL, matric. 11 Nov., 1816, aged 18.

Lewis, Charles Basset, 1s. Lewis, of Llangadoc, co. Carmarthen, arm. JESUS COLL., matric. 13 March, 1851, aged 19; of Gwinfe, co. Carmarthen, J.P.

Lewis, Charles Edward Llewellyn, 5s. David Phillips, of Guilsfield, co. Montgomery, cler. MERTON COLL., matric. 16 Oct., 1884, aged 19. [25]

Lewis, Charles Peter Herbert, 1s. Charles Tyrrel, of Exeter, arm. NON-COLL., matric. 19 April, 1879, aged 19.

Lewis, Charles Prytherch, 3s. Frederick, of Llanwrda, co. Carmarthen, gent. JESUS COLL., matric. 19 Oct., 1872, aged 19; B.A. 1876, M.A. 1879.

Lewis, Charles William Mansel, 1s. David, of London, arm. BALLIOL COLL., matric. 17 Oct., 1864, aged 18; B.A. 1869, of Stradey Castle, co. Carmarthen, J.P., D.L., high sheriff 1881. See *Eton School Lists.*

Lewis, Daniel Carter, s. Joseph, of Gloucester (city), gent. PEMBROKE COLL., matric. 26 March, 1781, aged 16; B.A. 1784, M.A. 1787, perp. curate Colnbrook, Bucks, 1788, minor canon Windsor 1794, vicar of Ruislip 1797, and of Newington, Kent, 1808, until his death 21 March, 1834. [30]

Lewis, Daniel Jones, 1s. William, of Llanerth, co. Cardigan, gent. JESUS COLL., matric. 30 Jan., 1873, aged 21; B.A. 1877, held various curacies 1878-86, vicar of Llanidan, etc., Anglesey, 1886.

Lewis, Rev. Daniel Rowland, 3s. Daniel, of Llandysilio, co. Cardigan, cler. BALLIOL COLL., matric. 24 Jan., 1876, aged 20; B.A. 1881.

Lewis, David, s. Thomas, of Gwnnws, co. Cardigan, cler. JESUS COLL., matric. 1 April, 1756, aged 20.

Lewis, David, s. Philip, of Llanvernoch, co. Pembroke, pleb. JESUS COLL., matric. 18 March, 1757, aged 21.

Lewis, David, B.A. from JESUS COLL. 3 Feb., 1761.

Lewis, David, s. Lewis, of Llanilid, co. Glamorgan, cler. JESUS COLL., matric. 27 March, 1760, aged 20. [35]

Lewis, David, s. Leyson, of Cayo, co. Carmarthen, gent. JESUS COLL., matric. 15 May, 1777, aged 19.

Lewis, David, s. David, of Abergwilly, co. Carmarthen, gent. JESUS COLL., matric. 7 June, 1782, aged 21. See *Gent.'s Mag.*, 1850, ii. 447.

Lewis, David, s. — L., of Dorston, co. Hereford, cler. CHRIST CHURCH, matric. 23 Oct., 1788, aged 19; B.A. 1792 (? rector of Monnington, co. Hereford, 1817).

Lewis, Rev. David, s. Lewis, of Llanerchaeron, co. Cardigan, gent. MAGDALEN HALL, matric. 21 Oct., 1807, aged 28; B.A. 1812, M.A. 1814, B. & D.D. 1826, died at Twickenham, Middlesex, 4 Jan., 1859, aged 80. [40]

Lewis, David, s. Thomas, of Llandilo, co. Carmarthen, arm. BRASENOSE COLL., matric. 10 Nov., 1814, aged 17; B.A. 1818, of Stradey, co. Carmarthen, M.P. 1835-7, bar.-at-law, Lincoln's Inn, 1823, died 16 Oct., 1872, father of Charles William Mansel.

Lewis, David, 1s. Evan, of Llanddeiniol, co. Cardigan, gent. JESUS COLL., matric. 6 March, 1834, aged 19; scholar 1834-9, B.A. 1837, fellow 1839-46, M.A. 1840, dean 1843, vice-principal 1845.

Lewis, David, 3s. Salmon, of Llanaber Barmouth, co. Merioneth, gent. JESUS COLL., matric. 16 Oct., 1845, aged 18; B.A. 1849, M.A. 1852, rector of Trefnant since 1855, preb. of St. Aidan 1884.

Lewis, David, 2s. William, of Cadoxton juxta Neath, co. Glamorgan, arm. JESUS COLL., matric. 22 March, 1854, aged 19; B.A. 1857, M.A. 1860, vicar of Briton Ferry 1863.

Lewis, David, 4s. Thomas, of Llanwinio, co. Carmarthen, gent. JESUS COLL., matric. 20 March, 1855, aged 20; B.A. 1859.

Lewis, Rev. David James, 3s. Thomas, of Clynfiew, co. Pembroke, arm. JESUS COLL., matric. 5 June, 1828, aged 17; scholar 1829-36, B.A. 1832, M.A. 1836, died in 1837.

Lewis, Edmund, s. Thomas, of Llancarfan, co. Glamorgan, gent. BALLIOL COLL., matric. 17 June, 1745, aged 17; B.A. 1749. [5]

Lewis, Edmund, s. Thomas, of Llanishen, co. Glamorgan, arm. JESUS COLL., matric. 22 March, 1745-6, aged 19.

Lewis, Edmund, 1s. William, of Abbotts Langley, Herts, cler. UNIVERSITY COLL., matric. 24 Nov., 1843, aged 18.

Lewis, Edmund Burke, s. James, of Littlehampton, Sussex, arm. CHRIST CHURCH, matric. 30 Nov., 1809, aged 17; B.A. 1813, M.A. 1816, rector of Toddington, Beds, 1816, until his death 1 Nov., 1846.

Lewis, Edward, of EMMANUEL COLL., Cambridge, M.A.; incorp. 22 June, 1738. Not found in *Cambridge List of Graduates.*

Lewis, Edward, s. Morgan, of St. Pierre, co. Monmouth, arm. UNIVERSITY COLL., matric. 29 April, 1778, aged 18; B.A. 1782, M.A. 1785, rector of Portskewett and St. Pierre, died 1 March, 1839, aged 79. [10]

Lewis, Edward Freke, o.s. Edward, of Portskewett, co. Monmouth, cler. UNIVERSITY COLL., matric. 2 Dec., 1819, aged 19; B.A. 1823, M.A. 1833, perp. curate Mounton 1839-79, rector of Portskewett 1839, until his death 2 July, 1880.

Lewis, Edward Lloyd, s. David, of Oswestry, Salop, cler. WADHAM COLL., matric. 8 July, 1814, aged 19.

Lewis, Edward Pilcher, 2s. Charles, of Exeter, arm. NON-COLL., matric. 15 April, 1882, aged 18; B.A. from EXETER COLL. 1887.

Lewis, Edward Samuel, 6s. John Wenham, of Westerham, Kent, arm. CHRIST CHURCH, matric. 17 Jan., 1829, aged 19; B.A. 1832, M.A. 1838. See *St. Paul's School Reg.*, 267.

Lewis, Ernest Arthur, 2s. Ernest A., of Mold, Flints, arm. EXETER COLL., matric. 12 Oct., 1878, aged 18; B.A. 1885. [15]

Lewis, Evan, s. Evan, of Darowen, co. Montgomery, pleb. JESUS COLL., matric. 12 May, 1785, aged 20.

Lewis, Evan, 2s. Evan, of Llanilar, co. Cardigan, gent. JESUS COLL., matric. 7 April, 1838, aged 19; B.A. 1841, M.A. 1863, vicar of Aberdare 1859-66, rector of Dolgelly 1866-84, chancellor of Bangor 1872-6, canon 1877-84, dean 1884.

Lewis, Forster, o.s. Charles Goring, of Malling, Sussex, arm. ST. JOHN'S COLL., matric. 19 March, 1851, aged 18; B.A. 1855, M.A. 1858, rector of Wotton-Fitzpaine, Dorset, 1864.

Lewis, Francis, s. Walter, of Abergavenny, co. Monmouth, gent. CHRIST CHURCH, matric. 5 July, 1734, aged 17; B.A. 1738, M.A. 10 March, 1740-1.

Lewis, Francis, s. Benjamin, of Llanelly, co. Brecon, gent. PEMBROKE COLL., matric. 15 April, 1736, aged 17. [20]

Lewis, Francis, s. Breynton, of Hereford (city), pleb. WADHAM COLL., matric. 8 June, 1736, aged 17; B.A. 15 Feb., 1739-40.

Lewis, Rev. Francis, s. Morgan, of St. Pierre, co. Monmouth, arm. ST. MARY HALL, matric. 14 Dec., 1779, aged 17; B.C.L. 1786, died 17 Sep., 1794.

Lewis, Francis, s. Charles, of Chepstow, co. Monmouth, arm. UNIVERSITY COLL., matric. 14 Dec., 1798, aged 16; B.A. 1803, M.A. 1805, B.D. 1826, vicar of Holme Lacy, co. Hereford, 1826, and rector of Llanvair Kilgiddin, co. Monmouth, 1831, until his death 20 Feb., 1872.

Lewis, Francis Samuel, 1s. Samuel, of Corsham, Wilts, gent. NON-COLL., matric. 15 Oct., 1881, aged 30; B.A. from QUEEN'S COLL. 1884, M.A. 1888, an assistant in Bodleian Library.

Lewis, Francis William, born at Bath, Somerset, s. John, dean (of Ossory). HERTFORD COLL., matric. 25 March, 1779, aged 19. [25]

Lewis, Frank Ball, 1s. Francis Theodore, of London, gent. QUEEN'S COLL., matric. 28 Oct., 1881, aged 18; B.A. 1884.

Lewis, Fuller Wenham, 1s. John Wenham, of Westerham, Kent, arm. CHRIST CHURCH, matric. 13 Oct., 1820, aged 19; B.A. 1827, M.A. 1830, a student of Lincoln's Inn 1824. See *Alumni West.*, 481.

Lewis, George, s. George, of St. Martin's-in-the-Fields, city of London, gent. CHRIST CHURCH, matric. 15 March, 1715-6, aged 16 (? entered as a student of the Inner Temple 15 Nov., 1714).

Lewis, George, s. George, of St. Martin's, Worcester (city), pleb. MAGDALEN HALL, matric. 28 Nov., 1722, aged 18.

Lewis, George, s. Thomas, of Salisbury, Wilts, gent. EXETER COLL., matric. 24 March, 1728-9, aged 21; B.A. 12 March, 1732-3. [30]

Lewis, George, s. George, of Westerham, Kent, cler. CHRIST CHURCH, matric. 22 June, 1731, aged 19; B.A. 1735, M.A. 1738, rector of Etchingham, Sussex, 1754, vicar of Westerham, Kent, until 1771. See *Alumni West.*, 302.

Lewis, Rev. George, 1s. Henry, of Carmarthen (town), arm. JESUS COLL., matric. 26 Jan., 1844, aged 18; B.A. 1847, died at Holyhead in 1850.

Lewis, George, 3s. Peter Jones, of Cwmyoy, co. Monmouth, cler. JESUS COLL., matric. 15 Oct., 1853, aged 18; clerk 1853, student of medicine 1857, B.A. 1860.

Lewis, Rev. George, 1s. George, of Monmouth, gent. BALLIOL COLL., matric. 18 Oct., 1881, aged 33; B.A. 1884.

Lewis, George Bridges, o.s. William, of Salisbury, arm. ORIEL COLL., matric. 10 March, 1842, aged 18; B.A. 1846, M.A. 1853, perp. curate Northaw, Herts, 1857-75, vicar of Kemsing, Kent, 1874. See *Eton School Lists.* [35]

Lewis, (Sir) George Cornewall (Bart.), 1s. Thomas Frankland, of St. George's, Hanover Square, London, arm. CHRIST CHURCH, matric. 10 Feb., 1824, aged 17; student 1828-39, B.A. 1829, M.A. 1831, created D.C.L. 24 June, 1857, 2nd baronet, bar.-at-law, Middle Temple, 1831, M.P. co. Hereford 1847-52, Radnor 1855-63, chief commissioner of poor laws 1839-47, etc., chancellor of Exchequer 1855-8, home secretary 1859, war secretary 1861-3, privy councillor, historian, philosopher, and critic, died 13 April, 1863. See Foster's *Baronetage* & *Eton School Lists.*

Lewis, George Harold, 2s. Walter Sunderland, of Ripon, Yorks, cler. CORPUS CHRISTI COLL., matric. 27 Oct., 1881, aged 19; B.A. 1886.

Lewis, George Tucker, 2s. Richard, of Honiton, Devon, cler. QUEEN'S COLL., matric. 8 April, 1835, aged 19; B.A. 1838, chaplain to the Devon County Asylum 1845-83.

Lewis, George William, 1s. David Baxter, of Rochester, Kent, gent. MAGDALEN HALL, matric. 2 June, 1829, aged 33; B.A. 1833, M.A. 1835, incumbent St. Peter's, Southwark, and vicar of Crich, co. Derby, died 7 Aug., 1858.

Lewis, Rev. Glynn Bodvill, s. Thomas, of Llanbeblig, co. Carnarvon, gent. JESUS COLL. matric. 23 Oct., 1806, aged 19; B.A. 1810, died at Mount Hazel, near Carnarvon, 7 March, 1832. [40]

ewis, Griffith, s. David, of Carmarthen (town), pleb. JESUS COLL., matric. 26 Jan., 1732-3, aged 19; B.A. 8 Feb., 1736-7.

ewis, Henry, s. Ellis, of Ruddland, co. Flint, cler. JESUS COLL., matric. 8 July, 1721, aged 18; B.A. 1725.

ewis, Henry, s. Henry, of Landaff, co. Glamorgan, pleb. JESUS COLL., matric. 22 March, 1745-6, aged 20; B.A. 1750, M.A. 1752, B.D. (by decree) 23 April, 1760.

ewis, Henry, s. Andrew, of Amberley, co. Monmouth, gent. WADHAM COLL., matric. 27 March, 1751, aged 17; B.A. 1754. See *Gent.'s Mag.*, 1795, i. 83.

ewis, Henry, s. Henry, of Cardiff, co. Glamorgan, gent. JESUS COLL., matric. 4 March, 1779, aged 17; B.A. from ST. ALBAN HALL, 1783, curate in charge of Ramsden Crays, and of Runwell, Essex, 1790-9, vicar of Broxted 1800, and of Mucking 1801, until his death 13 July, 1809. [5]

ewis, Henry, 1s. John, of Westfield, co. Pembroke, gent. PEMBROKE COLL., matric. 14 May, 1842, aged 19; B.A. 1846, M.A. 1848, vicar of Stowmarket 1861, until his death 31 July, 1876.

ewis, Henry, 1s. Thomas, of Blackburn, Lancashire, gent. CHRIST CHURCH, matric. 15 Oct., 1875, aged 18; student 1875-80, B.A. 1879, a student of the Middle Temple 1881.

ewis, Rev. Henry Ardern, 1s. Henry, of Broughton, near Manchester, gent. MAGDALEN HALL, matric. 6 March, 1866, aged 23, B.A. 1869; M.A. (HERTFORD COLL.) 1881.

ewis, Henry John, s. John, of St. George's, Hanover Square, London, gent. WORCESTER COLL., matric. 6 May, 1818, aged 18; B.A. 1821, M.A. 1827, vicar of St. Peter's, Worcester, 1831, chaplain of St. Oswald's Hospital, and a minor canon, died 15 Feb., 1835.

ewis, (Sir) Herbert Edmund Frankland (Bart.), 1s. Gilbert Frankland, of Monnington-upon-Wye, co. Hereford, baronet. CHRIST CHURCH, matric. 18 May, 1864, aged 18; 4th baronet, high sheriff, Radnor, 1886. See Foster's *Men at the Bar* & *Eton School Lists*. [10]

Lewis, Herbert Theodore, 5s. George, of Bristol, arm. CHRIST CHURCH, matric. 17 Feb., 1883, aged 19; student of music 1883, B.Mus. 1886.

Lewis, Hugh, s. John, of Dolbegey (? Dolgelly), co. Merioneth, pleb. JESUS COLL., matric. 8 July, 1720, aged 23; B.A. 1724.

Lewis, Hugh, s. Peter, of Llangower, co. Merioneth, pleb. JESUS COLL., matric. 15 Dec., 1758, aged 18; B.A. 1763.

Lewis, Hugh Mitchell, 3s. Robert Benjamin, of London, gent. UNIVERSITY COLL., matric. 18 Oct., 1886, aged 19; scholar 1886.

Lewis, Israel, s. Leyson, of Cayo, co. Carmarthen, cler. JESUS COLL., matric. 4 April, 1781, aged 20; B.A. from ST. ALBAN HALL, 1792, M.A. 1793, vicar of Long Ashton, Somerset, 1794, rector of Foxcote, near Bath, 1800, died 20 Feb., 1841. [15]

Lewis, James, s. James, of Llanfrynach, co. Pembroke, pleb. LINCOLN COLL., matric. 8 April, 1717, aged 18; B.A. 1720, M.A. 1723.

Lewis, James, s. Nathan, of Britford, Wilts, pleb. WADHAM COLL., matric. 22 March, 1747-8, aged 19; B.A. from CORPUS CHRISTI COLL. 1751 (? rector of St. Martin's, Salisbury, 1757).

Lewis, James, s. James, of Salisbury, Wilts, cler. CORPUS CHRISTI COLL., matric. 17 Dec., 1768, aged 15; demy MAGDALEN COLL. 1771-5, B.A. 1772, M.A. 1775, fellow 1779-88, B.D. 1782, bursar 1783, died 7 March, 1788. See *Bloxam*, vii. 38.

Lewis, James, 1s. James, of Isle of Jamaica, West Indies, arm. CHRIST CHURCH, matric. 30 May, 1828, aged 18; a student of the Middle Temple 1828, died in 1830. See *Eton School Lists*.

Lewis, James, 2s. Charles John, of St. James's, London, gent. WADHAM COLL., matric. 10 March, 1831, aged 15; clerk 1831-5, B.A. 1836. [20]

Lewis, James Edward, 1s. James, of Edgbaston, co. Warwick, gent. NON-COLL., matric. 21 Oct., 1871, aged 20; B.A. from MERTON COLL. 1875, a student of the Middle Temple 1875.

Lewis, Rev. James Harry, 5s. Titus, of Carmarthen, arm. TRINITY COLL., matric. 24 Jan., 1876, aged 20; B.A. 1880, M.A. 1882.

Lewis, James Sculthorpe, o.s. Evan, of Whittington, Salop, cler. CHRIST CHURCH, matric. 18 Oct., 1867, aged 19; a junior student 1867-72, B.A. 1871, M.A. 1874, exhibitioner 1876-7, vicar of Guilsfield, co. Monmouth, since 1881.

Lewis, Jenkin, s. Jenkin, of Talachddu, co. Brecon, pleb. JESUS COLL., matric. 1 June, 1739, aged 19; B.A. 1742.

Lewis, Jenkin, s. Lewis of Llanwinio, co. Carmarthen, pleb. HERTFORD COLL., matric. 25 Feb., 1746-7, aged 24; B.A. 1750. [25]

Lewis, John, s. Pierce, of Bangor, co. Carnarvon, cler. JESUS COLL., matric. 19 March, 1715-6, aged 17; B.A. 14 March, 1719-20.

Lewis, John, s. Maurice, of Amlwch, co. Anglesea, gent. JESUS COLL., matric. 15 May, 1716, aged 18; B.A. 1720.

Lewis, John, s. William, of St. John's, Hackney, Middlesex, gent. QUEEN'S COLL., matric. 14 May, 1719, aged 17; B.A. 1722, a student of the Middle Temple 11 Feb., 1720-1.

Lewis, John, s. Thomas, of St. Nicholas, co. Glamorgan, pleb. JESUS COLL., matric. 14 March, 1721-2, aged 17.

Lewis, John, s. David, of Llanddewi, co. Pembroke, pleb. JESUS COLL., matric. 24 March, 1728-9, aged 18; B.A. 1732. [30]

Lewis, John, s. John, of Tedbury, co. Gloucester, cler. ORIEL COLL., matric. 8 April, 1731, aged 18; B.A. 1735.

Lewis, John, s. John, of London, arm. CHRIST CHURCH, matric. 12 June, 1734, aged 17; B.A. 1738, M.A. 10 March, 1740-1, dean of Ossory, in Ireland, 1755, until his death 28 June, 1783, father of Francis William, and of Villiers William. See *Alumni West.*, 309.

Lewis, John, s. William, of Ross, co. Hereford, gent. BALLIOL COLL., matric. 10 Oct., 1739, aged 17.

Lewis, John, s. John, of Llanerchaeron, co. Cardigan, gent. QUEEN'S COLL., matric. 21 March, 1744-5, aged 18; a student of the Inner Temple 25 Jan., 1744-5. See *Gent.'s Mag.*, 1801, p. 1156. [34]

Lewis, John, s. John, of Queen Street, London, pleb. CHRIST CHURCH, matric. 14 April, 1755, aged 16.

Lewis, John, s. John, of Rhoscolyn, Isle of Anglesey, cler. ORIEL COLL., matric. 2 April, 1759, aged 18; B.A. 1762.

Lewis, John, s. John, of Llangattock, co. Monmouth, cler. CHRIST CHURCH, matric. 30 March, 1767, aged 19; B.A. 1771, M.A. 1775.

Lewis, John, s. John, of Landilo, co. Monmouth, arm. PEMBROKE COLL., matric. 8 Dec., 1770, aged 19; B.C.L. 1778.

Lewis, John, s. John, of Llanfair Clydogan, co. Cardigan, pleb. WADHAM COLL., matric. 27 May, 1773, aged 22.

Lewis, John, s. John, of Ceidio, co. Anglesey, cler. JESUS COLL., matric. 15 June, 1776, aged 19; B.A. 1781, M.A. 1792, rector of East Blatchington 1804, until his death 8 Dec., 1843. [40]

Lewis, John, s. Philip, of St. Melan's, co. Monmouth, arm. JESUS COLL., matric. 11 May, 1785, aged 17; B.A. 1790, rector of Ingatestone, with perp. curacy of Buttsbury, 1796, and rector of Rivenhall 1824, until his death 25 Feb., 1853.

Lewis, John, s. Richard, of Cowbridge, co. Glamorgan, pleb. JESUS COLL., matric. 31 Jan., 1788, aged 18; B.A. 1792, M.A. 1794, B.D. 1802, fellow until his death at Cowbridge 25 Feb., 1814.

Lewis, John, s. William, of Llanairon, co. Cardigan, arm. BRASENOSE COLL., matric. 12 Oct., 1810, aged 17.

Lewis, John, s. William, of Ross, co. Hereford, doctor. ST. MARY HALL, matric. 13 Feb., 1817, aged 24; a student of Gray's Inn 1820.

Lewis, John, 1s. Thomas, of Llanishen, co. Glamorgan, arm. JESUS COLL., matric. 12 March, 1827, aged 19.

Lewis, John Barnabas, s. Thomas Fry, of Curry-Mallet, Somerset, cler. QUEEN'S COLL., matric. 12 Dec., 1817, aged 18; B.A. from ST. ALBAN HALL, 1823.

Lewis, John (Daniel), s. James Bevan, of Monmouth, gent. ORIEL COLL., matric. 12 Nov., 1814, aged 18; B.A. 1819, M.A. 1821.

Lewis, John Evans, 2s. James, of Convil, co. Carmarthen, gent. JESUS COLL., matric. 6 Dec., 1823, aged 19. [5]

Lewis, John Felix Rogers, 1s. Thomas, of Aberayon, co. Cardigan, gent. CHRIST CHURCH, matric. 28 Jan., 1879, aged 20.

Lewis, John Glasgow, o.s. Jacob, of Isle of Barbados, West Indies, arm. PEMBROKE COLL., matric. 29 Jan., 1820, aged 19; B.A. 1823.

Lewis, John Henry, s. James, of Bloomsbury, London, arm. BRASENOSE COLL., matric. 29 Nov., 1806, aged 17; B.A. 1810, M.A. 1815, a student of the Middle Temple 1805.

Lewis, John Herbert, 1s. Enoch, of Whitford, Flints, gent. EXETER COLL., matric. 14 Oct., 1876, aged 17; B.A. 1879, M.A. 1884.

Lewis, Rev. John Herbert Wightman, 2s. John, of Shrewsbury, cler. WORCESTER COLL., matric. 19 Oct., 1882, aged 20; B.A. 1885. [10]

Lewis, John Howard, 2s. David, of Llandilo, co. Carmarthen, gent. NON-COLL., matric. 28 Jan., 1884, aged 19; B.A. 1887.

Lewis, Rev. John Jenkins, 1s. John Rees, of Cascob, co, Radnor, cler. KEBLE COLL., matric. 14 Oct., 1879, aged 19; B.A. 1882, M.A. 1886.

Lewis, Rev. John Price, 3s. Davis, of Birkenhead, cler. NON-COLL., matric. 13 Oct., 1877, aged 20; B.A. from NEW COLL. 1880.

Lewis, John Pryse, 1s. Lewis, of St. Asaph, co. Flint, cler. JESUS COLL., matric. 29 Oct., 1867, aged 19.

Lewis, John Timothy, 1s. John, of Caronuwchelawdd, co. Cardigan, gent. JESUS COLL., matric. 9 Feb., 1865, aged 19; B.A. 1868, M.A. 1871, rector of Llanfyrnach 1876. [15]

Lewis, John Wenham, s. George, of Westerham, Kent, arm. CHRIST CHURCH, matric. 27 Oct., 1794, aged 18.

Lewis, Rev. John William, o.s. John, of Wolverhampton, gent. KEBLE COLL., matric. 14 Oct., 1878, aged 23; B.A. 1882, M.A. 1887.

Lewis, Lewis, s. James, of Cilycwm, co. Carmarthen, pleb. JESUS COLL., matric. 24 March, 1715-6, aged 21.

Lewis, Lewis, s. Thomas, of St. James's, London, pleb. CHRIST CHURCH, matric. 5 July, 1753, aged 17; B.A. 1757.

Lewis, Lewis, s. Thomas, of Shrewsbury (town), cler. PEMBROKE COLL., matric. 11 Dec., 1780, aged 17; of Gwinfe, co. Carmarthen, J.P., D.L., rector of Clovelly, Devon, 1796, until he died in 1826. [20]

Lewis, Lewis. s. Rice, of Dolgelly, co. Merioneth, pleb. JESUS COLL., matric. 23 March 1782, aged 21.

Lewis, Lewis, 1s. Samuel, of Llanaber, co. Merioneth, gent. JESUS COLL., matric. 8 June, 1837, aged 18; B.A. 1841, fellow 1842-9, M.A. 1844, rector of Denbigh 1855, until his death 10 Oct., 1876.

Lewis, Lewis, 5s. Thomas, of Llanwinio, co. Carmarthen, arm. JESUS COLL., matric. 2 March, 1857, aged 20; B.A. 1860, M.A. 1864.

Lewis, Rev. Lewis, o.s. Frederick, of Pewsey, Wilts, gent. NON-COLL., matric. 25 Jan., 1873, aged 21; B.A. 1876, M.A. 1884.

Lewis, Lewis Elwyn, 1s. Lewis Woodward, of Mersham, Kent. cler. NON-COLL., matric. 20 Nov., 1880, aged 22. [25]

Lewis, Lewis Woodward, 3s. David, of Middlesex, doctor. LINCOLN COLL., matric. 15 March, 1849, aged 18; B.A. 1852, M.A. 1856, rector of Leysdown, with Isle of Sheppy, 1862-75, and of Meopham, Kent, since 1875. See *Robinson*, 283.

Lewis, Marmaduke, s. George, of Westerham, Kent, doctor. CHRIST CHURCH, matric. 14 June, 1748, aged 18; B.A. 1752, M.A. 1755, rector of East Garston, Berks, 1761, and of Lullingstone, Kent, 1772, until his death 21 July, 1806. See *Alumni West.*, 347.

Lewis, Matthew, s. William, of Isle, of Jamaica, arm. CHRIST CHURCH, matric. 13 June, 1765, aged 15; B.A. 1769, M.A. 1772, diplomatic secretary war department, father of Matthew G.

Lewis, Matthew Evan, 1s. Evan, of Llanfair, co. Montgomery, cler. JESUS COLL., matric. 4 May, 1824, aged 18; a student of the Inner Temple 1826.

Lewis, Matthew Gregory, s. Matthew, of Marybone, London, arm. CHRIST CHURCH, matric. 27 April, 1790, aged 15; B.A. 1794, M.A. 1797, a dramatic writer, and author of "The Monk," "Monk Lewis," etc., M.P. Hindon 1796-1802, died 16 May, 1818. [30]

Lewis, Maurice, s. William, of Amlwch, Isle of Anglesey, gent. JESUS COLL., matric. 13 Dec., 1725, aged 15; bar.-at-law, Middle Temple, 1733.

Lewis, Maurice, s. John, of Amlwch, co. Anglesea, cler. JESUS COLL., matric. 29 June, 1769, aged 19; B.A. 1773, M.A. 1776.

Lewis, Morgan, s. Morgan, of Llanwnda, co. Carnarvon, cler. JESUS COLL., matric. 27 Feb., 1716-7, aged 18; B.A. 1720.

Lewis, Morgan, s. David, of Carmarthen (town), gent. WORCESTER COLL., matric. 12 Feb., 1814, aged 17.

Lewis, Neil Elliott, 1s. Neil, of Hobart Town, Tasmania, gent. NON-COLL., matric. 27 April, 1878, aged 19; commoner BALLIOL COLL. 1878, B.A. 1882, B.C.L. & M.A. 1885, bar.-at-law, Inner Temple, 1883. See Foster's *Men at the Bar*. [35]

Lewis, Nicholas Hutchings, 1s. Charles, of Ash, Somerset, arm. QUEEN'S COLL., matric. 30 June, 1827, aged 17.

Lewis, Owen Evans, 2s. David, of Narberth, co. Pembroke, arm. CHRIST CHURCH, matric. 9 Dec., 1818, aged 19.

Lewis, Percival Cray, 1s. ——, of Lymington, Hants, arm. CHRIST CHURCH, matric. 20 Oct., 1847, aged 18.

Lewis, Philip, s. James, of Disart, co. Radnor, pleb. JESUS COLL., matric. 27 June, 1720, aged 17 (? rector of Llanbyster, co. Radnor, 1734).

Lewis, Philip, 1s. James, of Isle of Jamaica, arm. UNIVERSITY COLL., matric. 10 March, 1831, aged 18; B.A. 1835, M.A. 1836, perp. curate Bursledon, Hants, 1850-79, died 9 Aug., 1886. See *Eton School Lists*. [40]

Lewis, Pierce, s. Pierce, of Ruthin, co. Denbigh, pleb. JESUS COLL., matric. 27 Feb., 1716-7, aged 17.

Lewis, Rees, s. David, of Lanthoysant, co. Carnarvon, pleb. ALL SOULS' COLL., matric. 7 March, 1766, aged 18; B.A. 1770.

Lewis, Rice, s. John, of Llanfair Clydogan, co. Cardigan, pleb. WADHAM COLL., matric. 22 March, 1782, aged 22; B.A. from ORIEL COLL. 1785 (as Rees).

Lewis, Richard, s. Richard, of Llanfair, co. Montgomery, pleb. BALLIOL COLL., matric. 3 April, 1718, aged 19.

Lewis, Richard, s. Thomas, of St. Nicholas, co. Glamorgan, pleb. JESUS COLL., matric. 16 Dec., 1728, aged 19; B.A. 1732 (? M.A. from KING'S COLL., Cambridge, 1744, vicar of Bokerell, Devon, and rector of Tiddington, Somerset, 1765). [45]

Lewis, Richard, s. John, of Llandilo, co. Monmouth, arm. PEMBROKE COLL., matric. 7 March, 1768, aged 18; a student of Lincoln's Inn 1768.

Lewis, Richard, s. Richard, of Honiton, Devon, cler. BALLIOL COLL., matric. 12 Dec., 1792, aged 18; exhibitioner or clerk CORPUS CHRISTI COLL. 27 June, 1793, B.A. 1796, re-entered BALLIOL COLL. 26 Feb., 1811, M.A. 20 Jan., 1815, master of Honiton Grammar School, curate of Monkton, etc., died 26 March, 1843. See *Gent.'s Mag.*, 1843, i. 545.

Lewis, Richard, 1s. Richard, of Honiton, Devon, cler. MAGDALEN HALL, matric. 19 Jan., 1822, aged 18; B.A. 1825, M.A. 1829.

Lewis, Richard, 2s. John, of Henllan, arm. WORCESTER COLL., matric. 18 June, 1839, aged 18; scholar 1839-48, B.A. 1843, M.A. 1846, D.D. by diploma 1 March, 1883, bishop of Llandaff 1883, rector of Lampeter Velfry 1851-83, preb. of St. David's 1867-83, and archdeacon.

Lewis, Richard, 4s. David, of Colwinstone, co. Glamorgan, gent. JESUS COLL., matric. 11 March, 1856, aged 17 (subs. 'servius'); clerk 1856, scholar 1859-60, B.A. 1860, M.A. 1863.

Lewis, Rev. Richard David, 2s. David, of Aberystwith, co. Cardigan, gent. JESUS COLL., matric. 28 Jan., 1874, aged 20; B.A. 1878, M.A. 1880. **[5]**

Lewis, Robert, s. Ambrose, of Anglesey, cler. WADHAM COLL., matric. 31 March, 1726, aged 18; B.A. 1729, M.A. 1732, of Cemlyn in Anglesey, rector of Trefdaeth, and chancellor of the diocese of Bangor.

Lewis, Robert, s. Charles, of Disserth, co. Brecon, pleb. JESUS COLL., matric. 17 Feb., 1729-30, aged 18; B.A. 1733, M.A. 1746 (? vicar of Corwen, co. Merioneth, and 43 years vicar of Mold, died 23 June, 1792).

Lewis, Robert, s. Thomas, of St. Asaph (city), gent. JESUS COLL., matric. 8 July, 1737, aged 18; B.A. 1741.

Lewis, Robert George, y.s. John, of 'fossâ Shore' (Shoreditch), London, gent. WADHAM COLL., matric. 16 Nov., 1824, aged 17; B.A. 1828, M.A. 1831, perp. curate St. John, Blackheath, 1853-69, died 8 June, 1875.

Lewis, Robert Hely James Lynch-Blosse, o.s. James, of Llanblethian, co. Glamorgan, gent. MERTON COLL., matric. 30 Jan., 1865, aged 19; postmaster 1865, until his death 17 May, 1869, a student of the Inner Temple 1868. See *Eton School Lists.* **[10]**

Lewis, Roderick, s. Roderick, of Trefeglwys, co. Montgomery, cler. JESUS COLL., matric. 9 Dec., 1795, aged 19; B.A. 1799, his father died 3 Aug., 1802.

Lewis, Samuel, s. John, of Hilperton, Wilts, cler. ST. EDMUND HALL, matric. 26 May, 1757, aged 16.

Lewis, Thomas, s. Morgan, of Cilycwm, co. Carmarthen, gent. MAGDALEN HALL, matric. 22 Oct., 1718, aged 18.

Lewis, Thomas, s. Thomas, of Mothvey, co. Carmarthen, cler. JESUS COLL., matric. 16 March, 1718-9, aged 16; B.A. 1723.

Lewis, Thomas, s. Hugh, of Caerwys, co. Flint, cler. JESUS COLL., matric. 21 Feb., 1726-7, aged 21.

Lewis, Thomas, s. Gabriel, of Llanishen, co. Glamorgan, gent. BALLIOL COLL., matric. 27 Feb., 1737-8, aged 18. **[16]**

Lewis, Thomas, s. Herbert, of Harpton, Radnor, gent. UNIVERSITY COLL., matric. 24 March, 1737-8, aged 19 (? rector of New Radnor 1744).

Lewis, Thomas, s. Lewis, of Llangattock, co. Carmarthen, gent. JESUS COLL., matric. 9 April, 1747, aged 19; B.A. 1750, rector of Penboyr, co. Brecon, D.L. co. Carmarthen, father of Lewis 1780.

Lewis, Thomas, s. Thomas, of Talachddu, co. Brecon, cler. JESUS COLL., matric. 6 May, 1758, aged 21.

Lewis, Thomas, s. Thomas, of Pontypool, co. Monmouth, gent. ORIEL COLL., matric. 20 Feb., 1770, aged 17. B.A. 1774, M.A. 1776, bar.-at-law, Lincoln's Inn, 1781, and of Gray's Inn (ad eundem) 1797, died 1 Dec., 1813. **[20]**

Lewis, Thomas, s. Morgan, of St. Pierre, co. Monmouth, arm. ORIEL COLL., matric. 2 May, 1771, aged 20; of St. Pierre, died 17 June, 1796.

Lewis, Thomas, s. John, of Llanidloes, co. Montgomery, pleb. PEMBROKE COLL., matric. 6 April, 1781, aged 19; B.A. 1785.

Lewis, Thomas, s. Charles, of St. George's, Southwark, Surrey, cler. QUEEN'S COLL., matric. 31 May, 1781, aged 18; B.A. 1785.

Lewis, Thomas, s. Thomas, of St. Giles's, Middlesex, arm. MAGDALEN COLL., matric. 27 April, 1786, aged 18.

Lewis, Thomas, s. John, of Carmarthen (town), gent. WADHAM COLL., matric. 29 March, 1800, aged 18; B.A. 1804 (? rector of Merthyr, perp. curate Llanstephen and Llangunnoch, co. Carmarthen, 1815, until his death in 1842). **[25]**

Lewis, Thomas, s. Thomas, of London, arm. QUEEN'S COLL., matric. 17 May, 1806, aged 17; B.A. 1810, M.A. 1815, a student of Lincoln's Inn 1809.

Lewis, Thomas, o.s. John, of Llanbadarn-Fawr, Wales, gent. JESUS COLL., matric. 7 Dec., 1824, aged 20; B.A. 1829, rector of Manafon, co. Montgomery, 1851, until his death 12 Jan., 1872.

Lewis, Thomas, 1s. John, of Aberayon, cler. JESUS COLL., matric. 23 Oct., 1845, aged 16.

Lewis, Thomas (Curling), 2s. Samuel, of London, gent. ST. MARY HALL, matric. 31 Oct., 1868, aged 22; vicar of Harmondsworth, Middlesex, 1878-82, and of Sidcup, Kent, 1882-6.

Lewis, (Sir) Thomas Frankland (Bart.), s. John, of St. George's, Bloomsbury, Middlesex, arm. CHRIST CHURCH, matric. 24 April, 1798, aged 17; M.P. Beaumaris 1812-26, Ennis 1826-8, co. Radnor 1828-35, and Radnor (borough) 1847-55, on revenue commission 1821, 1822-5, joint secretary of the Treasury 1827, privy councillor 1828, vice-president Board of Trade 1828, treasurer of Navy 1830, commissioner of Poor Laws 1834-9, created a baronet 11 July, 1846, died 22 Jan., 1855. See Foster's *Baronetage & Eton School Lists.* **[30]**

Lewis, Thomas Freke, 2s. Francis, of Portskewett, co. Monmouth, cler. PEMBROKE COLL., matric. 22 Nov., 1849, aged 18; B.A. 1853, of Abbey Dore Court, co. Hereford, J.P., D.L.

Lewis, Rev. Thomas Winchester, s. Thomas, of St. Martin's, Ironmonger Lane, London, arm. ST. JOHN'S COLL., matric. 18 July, 1795, aged 17; B.A. 1799, M.A. 1802, died at Old Park, near Enfield, 13 June, 1813.

Lewis, Rev. Thomas Wolseley, 1s. Thomas, of Llanrwst, co. Denbigh, cler. JESUS COLL., matric. 23 June, 1854, aged 18; scholar 1855-9, B.A. 1859, M.A. 1861, a master Cheltenham College.

Lewis, Titus, 4s. Titus, of Carmarthen, gent. NON-COLL., matric. 18 April, 1874, aged 21; commoner PEMBROKE COLL. 1876, B.A. 1880, M.A. 1881.

Lewis, Tubal, s. Tubal, of Plymouth, Devon, gent. EXETER COLL., matric. 7 May, 1796, aged 19.

Lewis, Victor Arthur Nicolas, 1s. Arthur, of Plymouth, Devon, cler. MERTON COLL., matric. 29 May, 1873, aged 19. **[36]**

Lewis, Villiers William, born at Dartford, Kent, s. John, dean of Ossory. CHRIST CHURCH, matric. 16 May, 1772, aged 18; B.A. 1776. In the Dean's 'Entry Book' his name is set forth as VILLIERS WILLIAM LEWIS, though he matriculated under the Christian name of WILLIAM only.

Lewis, Walter, s. Walter, of Abergavenney, co. Monmouth, gent. CHRIST CHURCH, matric. 27 March, 1727, aged 15; B.A. 1730.

Lewis, Walter Reginald, 1s. Walter Sunderland, of Ripon, cler. NON-COLL., matric. 11 Oct., 1879, aged 18; B.A. 1885.

Lewis, William, s. William, of Stock Gaylard, Dorset, gent. EXETER COLL., matric. 3 March, 1720-1, aged 18; B.A. 1724. **[40]**

Lewis, William, s. William, of St. Andrew's, Holborn, gent. QUEEN'S COLL., matric. 4 July, 1722, aged 16; B.A. 1728.

Lewis, William, s. Charles, of Trethvin (*sic*), co. Monmouth, pleb. JESUS COLL., matric. 10 March, 1724-5, aged 15; B.A. 1728.

Lewis, William, s. William, of Richmond, Surrey, gent. CHRIST CHURCH, matric. 14 Oct., 1725, aged 17.

Lewis, William, s. John, of London, gent. CHRIST CHURCH, matric. 17 March, 1730-1, aged 17; B.A. 1734, M.A. 1737, B.Med. 1741, D.Med. 1745.

Lewis, William, s. Thomas, of Llandonna, Isle of Anglesey, pleb. JESUS COLL., matric. 15 Feb., 1733-4, aged 18; B.A. 1737, M.A. 1740.

Lewis, William, s. William, of Amlwch, co. Anglesea, pleb. JESUS COLL., matric. 17 March, 1737-8, aged 18; B.A. 16 Feb., 1741-2. [5]

Lewis, William, s. William, of Isle of Jamaica, arm. TRINITY COLL., matric. 8 June, 1765, aged 17 (William Lewis, fellow of the Linnæan Society, died 7 Feb., 1823). See *Gent.'s Mag.*, i. 185.

Lewis, William, s. William, of St. John's, Cardiff, co. Glamorgan, pleb. JESUS COLL., matric. 30 May, 1772, aged 17; B.A. 1777, M.A. 1779.

Lewis, William, s. John, of Rhôd-y-Geidio, co. Anglesey, cler. JESUS COLL., matric. 4 April, 1775, aged 19; B.A. 1779.

Lewis, William, s. John, of Llanerchaeron, co. Cardigan, arm. UNIVERSITY COLL., matric. 23 Oct., 1775, aged 19.

Lewis, William, s. Henry, of St. Peter's, Carmarthen (town), gent. JESUS COLL., matric. 13 Nov., 1777, aged 17. [10]

Lewis, Rev. William, s. Wyndham, of Coity, co. Glamorgan, gent. JESUS COLL., matric. 13 Dec., 1797, aged 16; B.A. 1802, died at Chenies, Bucks, 25 July, 1857, aged 78.

Lewis, William, s. William, of Hythe, Kent, arm. BRASENOSE COLL., matric. 25 Jan., 1815, aged 18; B.A. from ST. MARY HALL 1819, M.A. 1821 (? vicar of Abbots Langley, Herts, 1838, until his death 19 July, 1858).

Lewis, William Augustus, 1s. William, of Henllan, co. Denbigh, gent. JESUS COLL., matric. 23 Oct., 1885, aged 20.

Lewis, William Dickens, 2s. David, of Liverpool, gent. ST. ALBAN HALL, matric. 28 April, 1863, aged 24; B.A. 1867, M.A. 1874.

Lewis, William Frederick, 2s. James, of Spanish Town, Isle of Jamaica, arm. BALLIOL COLL., matric. 9 June, 1832, aged 17; B.A. from ST. MARY HALL 1836, bar.-at-law, Middle Temple, 1840, a judge in the Supreme Court of Jamaica, died in 1856. [15]

Lewis, William Hancock, 2s. Thomas, of Llanwinio, co. Carmarthen, gent. JESUS COLL., matric. 29 Oct., 1847, aged 19; scholar 1848-53, B.A. 1851, M.A. 1854.

Lewis, William Harry, 1s. Thomas Hodges, of Henwick, near Worcester, gent. NEW COLL., matric. 24 Jan., 1879, aged 19; B.A. 1882, died in 1882.

Lewis, William Henry, 1s. Thomas, of Manordeify, co. Pembroke, arm. TRINITY COLL., matric. 9 June, 1826, aged 17; of Clynfiew, co. Pembroke, J.P., D.L., high sheriff co. Carmarthen 1847, a student of the Middle Temple 1829.

Lewis, William Henry, 3s. Robert, of London, gent. LINCOLN COLL., matric. 13 Oct., 1866, aged 18; B.A. 1870, M.A. 1873, rector of West Allington, co. Lincoln, 1879-81, vicar of Hindon, Wilts, 1882-6, rector of Fonthill Gifford 1886.

Lewis, William Henry Denys Aston-, o.s. William, of Leadenham, co. Lincoln, D.Med. PEMBROKE COLL., matric. 23 Oct., 1872, aged 18; B.A. 1875, M.A. 1879, bar.-at-law, Lincoln's Inn, 1880. See Foster's *Men at the Bar*. [20]

Lewis, William James, 2s. John, of Llanwyddelan, co. Montgomery, cler. JESUS COLL., matric. 25 Oct., 1865, aged 18, scholar 1865-9, B.A. 1869; fellow ORIEL COLL. 1869, M.A. 1872, professor of mineralogy Cambridge University 1881.

Lewis, William John, s. John, of Llanerchymedd, Isle of Anglesey, cler. JESUS COLL., matric. 16 May, 1812, aged 18; B.A. 1815, M.A. 1818.

Lewis, Rev. William Lempriere, o.s. George, of Miltor Kent, arm. TRINITY COLL., matric. 20 June, 184[illegible] aged 18; scholar 1848-52, B.A. 1852, fellow 1852-[illegible] M.A. 1855, lecturer 1856, a student of the Inn[illegible] Temple 1851, died 18 Jan., 1872. See *Eton School List*

Lewis, Rev. William Lillington, s. William Lillingtor of Gloucester (city), gent. PEMBROKE COLL., matri[illegible] 18 Nov., 1760, aged 17; B.A. 1764, fellow, M.[illegible] 1767, died in 1772.

Lewis, Wyndham, s. Thomas, of Llanidan, co. Glan organ, arm. JESUS COLL., matric. 2 July, 175[illegible] aged 20; B.A. 1759, M.A. 1763 (? of Newhouse, c[illegible] Glamorgan, in holy orders, father of Wyndha[illegible] Lewis, M.P., born 1780, died 1838). [2[illegible]

Lewis, Wyndham, s. Thomas, of Llanishen, co. Gl[illegible] morgan, arm. JESUS COLL., matric. 14 May, 177[illegible] aged 21.

Lewis, Wyndham William, 1s. Henry, of Cardiff, c[illegible] Glamorgan, arm. WORCESTER COLL., matric. April, 1846, aged 18.

Lewman-Browne, Rev. John Burnard, 7s. Robe[illegible] Burnard, of Plymouth, gent. MAGDALEN HAL[illegible] matric. 21 Oct., 1841, aged 19; B.A. 1845, assistan[illegible] master Reading School 1871-9, in Felstead Scho[illegible] 1879-86, has assumed the additional surnames [illegible] LEWMAN-BROWNE.

Leworthy, George, s. George, of Charles, Devo[illegible] pleb. EXETER COLL., matric. 11 July, 1740, age[illegible] 18; B.A. 1746.

Lewthwaite, George, s. William, of Millom, Cumbe[illegible] land, arm. QUEEN'S COLL., matric. 11 April, 179[illegible] aged 18; B.A. 1795, M.A. 1797, B.D. 1805, rect[illegible] of Adel, Yorks, 1809, until his death 28 June, 1854.

Lewthwaite, George, 2s. George, of Adel, York[illegible] cler. UNIVERSITY COLL., matric. 14 April, 183[illegible] aged 19; B.A. 1842, M.A. 1843, curate of Ade[illegible] Yorks, 1842-60. See *Rugby School Reg.*, 176. [3[illegible]

Lewthwaite, Thomas, s. Thomas, of Kirk Andrew[illegible] Cumberland, cler. EXETER COLL., matric. 18 Feb. 1746-7, aged 28.

Lewton, Rev. Edward, s. Edward, of Bristol (city[illegible] pleb. WADHAM COLL., matric. 15 April, 178[illegible] aged 19; B.A. 1792, M.A. 1794, chaplain 1812-1[illegible] professor of classical and general literature, libraria[illegible] and registrar of the East India College, Haileybur[illegible] died 21 Feb., 1830.

Ley, Andrew, s. Hugh, of Redruth, Cornwall, cle[illegible] QUEEN'S COLL., matric. 22 May, 1735, aged 1[illegible] B.A. 26 Jan., 1738-9.

Ley, Augustine, 2s. William Henry, of Hereford (city cler. CHRIST CHURCH, matric. 13 April, 186[illegible] aged 19; a junior student 1861-6, B.A. 1865, M.[illegible] 1868, vicar of St. Weonard's, co. Hereford, 1878-8[illegible] curate of Sellack 1885. [3[illegible]

Ley, Carrington, s. John, of Tiverton, Devon, cle[illegible] BALLIOL COLL., matric. 8 July, 1806, aged 1[illegible] fellow 1806-18, B.A. 1810, M.A. 1814, vicar of Be[illegible] Regis, etc., Devon, 1818, until his death 24 Sep., 186[illegible]

Ley, Charles, s. Charles, of Wicomb, Essex, cle[illegible] MERTON COLL., matric. 7 July, 1733, aged 19.

Ley, George Frederick, 4s. Jacob, of Ashprington Devon, cler. CHRIST CHURCH, matric. 3 Jun[illegible] 1840, aged 18.

Ley, Gerald Lewis Henry, 2s. Henry, of London, ar[illegible] PEMBROKE COLL., matric. 3 Feb., 1874, aged 1[illegible] B.A. 1877, M.A. 1880, rector of Chagford, Devo[illegible] since 1886.

Ley, Henry, s. Henry, of St. Paul's, Devon, ar[illegible] CHRIST CHURCH, matric. 22 May, 1799, aged 1[illegible] B.A. 1803, M.A. 1806, rector of Kenn, Devon, 18[illegible] until his death 8 Jan., 1856. See *Alumni West.*, 45[illegible]

Ley, Jacob, 1s. Jacob, of Ashprington, Devon, cl[illegible] ST. ALBAN HALL, matric. 18 May, 1822, aged 1[illegible] student CHRIST CHURCH, 1822-59, B.A. 1826, M.[illegible] 1828, B.D. 1840, rhetoric reader 1833, censor 1836-[illegible] librarian 1840-5, catechist 1842, proctor 1839-[illegible] vicar of St. Mary Magdalene, Oxford, 1845-58, vic[illegible] of Staverton, Northants, 1858, until his death April, 1881. See *Alumni West.*, 490. [4[illegible]

ey, Jacob, s. Jacob, of Cockington, Devon, gent. BALLIOL COLL., matric. 23 March, 1787, aged 18; B.A. 1791, M.A. 1796, rector of Ashprington, Devon, 1795.

ey, Jacob, born at 'Algoniae,' in Canada, o.s. George, gent. CHRIST CHURCH, matric. 12 Jan., 1883, aged 19.

ey, John, 2s. Jacob, of Ashprington, Devon, cler. EXETER COLL., matric. 20 June, 1822, aged 17; B.A. 1826, M.A. 1829, fellow 1831-51, B.D. 1841, bursar 1839-41, rector of Waldron, Devon, 1851-80. See *Coll. Reg.*, 129.

ey, John Carrington, o.s. Carrington, of Bere Regis, Dorset, cler. CHRIST CHURCH, matric. 20 June, 1859, aged 18; B.A. 1864, bar.-at-law, Inner Temple, 1866, inspector of schools 1873. See Foster's *Men at the Bar.*

ey, John Henry, s. Henry, of Exeter, Devon, arm. CHRIST CHURCH, matric. 20 May, 1795, aged 17; student 1796, B.A. 1799, M.A. 1801, of Trehill, Devon, bar.-at-law, Middle Temple, 1803, bencher 1843, 2nd clerk assistant House of Commons 1801-14, clerk assistant (on the death of his uncle John) 1814-20, chief or deputy clerk 1820, until his death 21 Aug., 1850. See *Alumni West.*, 444. **[5]**

ey, John Henry, 1s. John Henry, of Dawlish, Devon, arm. CHRIST CHURCH, matric. 11 Dec., 1829, aged 17.

ey, John Henry (Francis), 1s. John Henry, of Kenn, Devon, arm. ST. JOHN'S COLL., matric. 16 Oct., 1866, aged 19; of Trehill, Devon, J.P., D.L., high sheriff 1873.

Ley, Rev. Richard, 3s. Thomas Hunt, of Maker, Devon, cler. BRASENOSE COLL., matric. 11 June, 1840, aged 18; scholar 1840-4, B.A. 1844, M.A. 1847, died 11 Dec., 1886.

ey, Spencer Edgcombe, 1s. Thomas Hunt, of Maker, Devon, cler. PEMBROKE COLL., matric. 9 Feb., 1832, aged 18; scholar 1832-5.

Ley, Thomas, s. Jerem., of Tavistock, Devon, gent. EXETER COLL., matric. 17 April, 1719, aged 17; B.A. from TRINITY COLL. 1723. **[10]**

Ley, Thomas, s. Richard, of Rain, Devon, gent. EXETER COLL., matric. 18 March, 1729-30, aged 18; B.A. from BALLIOL COLL. 1733, M.A. 1736 (? rector of Patrickston, Devon, 1736, and of Doddiscombeleigh and Ashton, Devon, 1754).

Ley, Thomas, s. William, of Ashburton, Devon, gent. EXETER COLL., matric. 3 April, 1762, aged 19.

Ley, Thomas, s. Thomas, of Doddiscombeleigh, Devon, cler. MERTON COLL., matric. 23 Feb., 1768, aged 18; B.A. 1772, 30 years curate of Shobrooke, rector of Bratton, Clovelly, 1807, and perp. curate of Linton and Contisbury, Devon, died 29 Feb., 1816.

Ley, Thomas (Hunt), s. John, of Exeter (city), gent. EXETER COLL., matric. 31 May, 1802, aged 16; B.A. 1812, M.A. 1813, of Maker, Devon.

Ley, William, s. Samuel, of Croydon, Surrey, cler. MAGDALEN HALL, matric. 6 May, 1741-2, aged 19; B.A. 1743. **[15]**

Ley, William, s. William, of Exeter (city), pleb. ST. EDMUND HALL, matric. 2 April, 1764, aged 24.

Ley, William Clement, 1s. William Henry, of St Augustine's, Bristol, cler. MAGDALEN COLL., matric. 4 March, 1858, aged 17; demy 1857-64, B.A. 1862, M.A. 1864, rector of Little Ashby, co. Leicester, 1874, vice-president Meteorological Society. See *Coll. Reg.*, vii. 413.

Ley, William Henry, 2s. Thomas Hunt, of Maker, Devon, cler. PEMBROKE COLL., matric. 3 Nov., 1831, aged 16; scholar 1831-2, and of TRINITY COLL. 1832-6, B.A. 1835, fellow 1836-9, M.A. 1838, dean 1838, vicar of Sellack, co. Hereford, 1841, until his death 23 March, 1887.

Leycester, Charles, s. Oswald, of Knutsford, Cheshire, cler. BRASENOSE COLL., matric. 20 April, 1814, aged 18; B.A. 1817.

Leycester, George (Hanmer), s. Ralph, of Sympson, Bucks, cler. CHRIST CHURCH, matric. 28 Jan., 1782, aged 18; B.A. from MERTON COLL. 1788, M.A. 1790, of Whiteplace, Berks, bar.-at-law, Lincoln's Inn, 1790, died 6 Oct., 1838. **[20]**

Leycester, Rev. Ralph, s. George, of London, gent. EXETER COLL., matric. 1 July, 1755, aged 18; B.A. 1759, of Whiteplace, Berks, died there 5 April, 1803, father of the last named.

Leycester, Ralph Oswald, 1s. Ralph Gerard, of Toft, near Knutsford, Cheshire, arm. CHRIST CHURCH, matric. 18 Jan., 1863, aged 18; of Toft Hall aforesaid.

Leyson, John, s. Morgan, of Longworth, Bucks, cler. JESUS COLL., matric. 9 May, 1749, aged 17; B.A. 1753.

Leyson, John, s. Thomas, of Bassaleg, co. Monmouth, cler. UNIVERSITY COLL., matric. 21 Jan., 1808, aged 18; B.A. from ST. ALBAN HALL 1813. See *Eton School Lists.*

Leyson, Thomas, s. John, of Cheslidon, Wilts, cler. JESUS COLL., matric. 11 Nov., 1774, aged 16; B.A. 1780, M.A. 1812, vicar of Bassaleg, co. Monmouth, 1782, and rector of Tredonnock and Pantleague 1812, until his death 8 Feb., 1838. **[25]**

Leyson, William, s. William, of Neath, co. Glamorgan, pleb. JESUS COLL., matric. 22 June, 1786, aged 18.

L'herondell, Francis, s. Francis, of Dublin, Ireland, cler. MAGDALEN COLL., matric. 22 Oct., 1746, aged 20 (? his father perp. curate Shields 1748; Dr. L. died at Chelsea, 1 Oct., 1752).

Lichfield, Alexander, s. Charles, of Oxford (city), pleb. WADHAM COLL., matric. 18 June, 1763, aged 17; B.A. 1767, fellow, M.A. 1773, proctor 1780, rector of Noke, Oxon, 1773, and of Wadhurst, Sussex, died 8 March, 1804.

Lichfield, Coventry, s. Leonard, of Peters-in-the East, Oxford (city), pleb. MAGDALEN HALL, matric. 26 May, 1726, aged 19; clerk 1728-31, B.A. 26 Jan., 1729-30, M.A. 1748, vicar of Stoke-cum-Woodcote, Oxon, 1752, 1st chaplain of Alnutt's Hospital, at Goring Heath, 1742, died 16 April, 1785. See *Bloxam*, ii. 89.

Lichfield, Coventry (Townshend Powys), s. Coventry, of South Stoke, Oxon, cler. MAGDALEN COLL., matric. 18 March, 1758, aged 17; chorister 1752-9, demy 1759-62, B.A. 1761, fellow 1762-83, M.A. 1764, B.D. 1774, D.D. 1778, senior dean of arts 1774, bursar 1775, vice-president 1779, dean of divinity 1780, rector of Boyton, Wilts, 1782, until his death, 1 May, 1810. See *Bloxam*, i. 164.

Lichfield, John, s. Coventry, of Goring, Oxon, cler. CORPUS CHRISTI COLL., matric. 18 May, 1763, aged 15; demy MAGDALEN COLL. 1768-80, B.A. 1769, M.A. 1772, fellow 1780-9, B.D. 1782, rector of Aston Tirrold-cum-Tubney 1787-1803, 2nd chaplain of Alnutt's Hospital 1785, died 3 Feb., 1803. See *Bloxam*, vi. 349. **[31]**

Lichfield, John, 'carpenter'; privilegiatus 1 Aug., 1780.

Lickorish, Richard, s. Joshua, of Brandon, par. Woolston, co. Warwick, gent. LINCOLN COLL., matric. 3 March, 1778, aged 18; B.A. 1782 (the wife of Rev. Dr. L., of Woolston, Coventry, died in 1810).

Lidbetter, Arthur Earle, 4s. Leonard, of Bramber, Sussex, gent. ORIEL COLL., matric. 7 Feb., 1870, aged 18; scholar 1869, until his death in 1871.

Liddell, (Hon. Sir) Adolphus Frederick Octavius (K.C.B.), 7s. Thomas Henry, Baron Ravensworth. CHRIST CHURCH, matric. 4 June, 1835, aged 17, B.A. 1839; fellow ALL SOULS' COLL. 1840-6, M.A. 1844, bar.-at-law, Inner Temple, 1844, Q.C. 1861, bencher 1861, K.C.B. 20 April, 1880, permanent under-secretary of State for Home department 1867, until his death 27 June, 1885. See Foster's *Men at the Bar* & *Eton School Lists.* **[35]**

Liddell, Adolphus George Charles, 1s. Hon. Adolphus, of Tadcaster, Yorks (K.C.B.). BALLIOL COLL., matric. 16 Oct., 1865, aged 19; B.A. 1870, M.A. 1873, bar.-at-law, Inner Temple, 1872, an examiner High Court of Justice 1884. See Foster's *Peerage*, E. RAVENSWORTH, & *Eton School Lists*.

Liddell, Charles John, 3s. Hon. Robert, of Barking, Essex, cler. CHRIST CHURCH, matric. 22 May, 1861, aged 17; B.A. 1866, a student of the Inner Temple 1868, of the British Museum library. See Foster's *Peerage*.

Liddell, Charles Lyon, o.s. Charles, of London, arm. CHRIST CHURCH, matric. 15 Oct., 1880, aged 19; B.A. 1885.

Liddell, Edward Thomas, 1s. Hon. (George) Augustus (Frederick), of Percy's Cross, near Walham, Middlesex, arm. CHRIST CHURCH, matric. 7 June, 1865, aged 20; B.A. 1869, M.A. 1883, rector of Wimpole, co. Cambridge, 1871-6, and of Jarrow-on-Tyne 1876-82, hon. canon of Durham 1881. See Foster's *Peerage*, E. RAVENSWORTH.

Liddell, Frederick Francis, 2s. (Henry) George, dean of Christ Church. CHRIST CHURCH, matric. 31 May, 1884, aged 18. [5]

Liddell, George William, o.s. George William Moore, of Sutton, Yorks, arm. MAGDALEN COLL., matric. 26 Jan., 1886, aged 18.

Liddell, Henry (George), s. Henry, of Lamesley, co. Durham, baronet. BRASENOSE COLL., matric. 16 Dec., 1805, aged 18; B.A. 1809, M.A. 1812, rector of Redmarshall, co. Durham, 1811-24, of Romaldkirk, Yorks, 1824-32, and of Easington, co. Durham, 1832, died 9 March, 1872. See Foster's *Peerage*, E. RAVENSWORTH.

Liddell, Henry George, 1s. Henry George, of bishop Auckland, co. Durham, cler. CHRIST CHURCH, matric. 9 May, 1829, aged 18; student 1830-46, B.A. 1833, M.A. 1835, B. & D.D. 1855, Greek reader 1840, censor 1845, dean 1855, vice-chancellor 1870-4, select preacher Oxford, 1842 and 1847, master of the schools 1843, public examiner 1844-5, Whitehall preacher 1845, Whyte's professor of moral philosophy 1845-6, senior proctor 1846, domestic chaplain to Prince Consort 1845, head-master Westminster School 1846-55, hon. LL.D., Edinburgh, 1884, joint author of Greek-English lexicon. See Foster's *Peerage*.

Liddell, Henry George, 1s. Hon. Henry Thomas Liddell, son of Baron Ravensworth. CHRIST CHURCH, matric. 15 May, 1839, aged 17; 2nd Earl Ravensworth, M.P. South Northumberland 1852-78, etc. See Foster's *Peerage* & *Eton School Lists*.

Liddell, Lionel Charles, 3s. Henry George, dean of Christ Church, Oxford. CHRIST CHURCH, matric. 15 Oct., 1886, aged 18. [10]

Liddell, Robert, 5s. Thomas Henry, baron Ravensworth. CHRIST CHURCH, matric. 13 Dec., 1826, aged 18; B.A. 1829; fellow ALL SOULS' COLL. 1831-6, M.A. 1834, vicar of Barking, Essex, 1836-51, and of St. Paul, Knightsbridge, 1851-81.

Liddell, Thomas, s. John, of Cirencester, co. Gloucester, pleb. EXETER COLL., matric. 24 March, 1742-3, aged 22.

Liddell, William Wren, 3s. Henry George, of Bolden, co. Durham, cler. CHRIST CHURCH, matric. 12 May, 1842, aged 18; B.A. 1846, M.A. 1849, vicar of South Cerney 1862-70, rector Cowley, co. Gloucester, since 1820. See Foster's *Peerage*, E. RAVENSWORTH.

Liddiard, Henry William, o.s. William, of Tenerwle, co. Glamorgan, cler. PEMBROKE COLL., matric. 23 Jan., 1822, aged 21.

Liddiard, John, s. John, of Ruckley, Wilts, gent. ST. MARY HALL, matric. 16 May, 1729, aged 18.

Liddiard, John, s. William, of Meysey Hampton, co. Gloucester, arm. BALLIOL COLL., matric. 11 April, 1753, aged 18; B.A. 1757, bar.-at-law, Middle Temple, 1759. [15]

Liddiard, William, s. William, of Marlborough, Wilt: arm. CORPUS CHRISTI COLL., matric. 18 Feb. 1757, aged 18; B.A. 1759, M.A. 1763.

Liddiard, William, s. William, of Ruckley, Wilts, cle UNIVERSITY COLL., matric. 27 Feb., 1792, aged 1 captain in the army; B.A. from TRINITY COLL Dublin, 1803, rector of Knockmark, co. Meath, die 11 Oct., 1841.

Liddiard, William Bedford, 1s. William, of Clapton Middlesex, gent. WORCESTER COLL., matric. 2 April, 1868, aged 18.

Liddon, Henry John, 1s. Henry, of St. Mary's Taunton, Somerset, arm. EXETER COLL., matric 2 June, 1852, B.A. & M.A. 1859, has held variou curacies since 1860. [20

Liddon, Henry Parry, 1s. Matthew, of Stoneham Hants, arm. CHRIST CHURCH, matric. 4 June 1846, aged 16; student 1846, B.A. 1850, M.A 1853, created D.C.L. 22 June, 1870, B. & D.D by decree 22 Nov., 1870, Dean Ireland's professo of exegesis of holy scripture 1870-82, canon of S Paul's 1870, chancellor of the cathedral 1886, vice principal of Cuddesdon Theological College 1854-9 preb. of Salisbury 1864-70, Oxford select preache 1863-5, 1870-2, 1877-9, 1884-5 (Cambridge 1884-5) Bampton lecturer 1866, on council of Keble Colleg 1871; for list of his works see *Crockford*.

Liddon, John, 3s. Matthew, of Colyton, Devon, arm CHRIST CHURCH, matric. 18 May, 1853, aged 18 B.A. 1857, M.A. 1860, bar.-at-law, Lincoln's Inn 1861. See Foster's *Men at the Bar*.

Liddon, William, s. William, of Rackenford, Devon arm. CORPUS CHRISTI COLL., matric. 30 Oct. 1775, aged 18 (? B.A. from EMMANUEL COLL. Cambridge, 1780, rector of Sandringham with Bab bingley 1797).

Lidgould, Charles, fellow of JESUS COLL., Cambridge B.A. 1716, M.A. 1720; incorp. 9 July, 1733.

Lidgould, John, of JESUS COLL., Cambridge, B.A 1716, M.A. 1721; incorp. 11 March, 1730-1. (Memo. — L., vicar of Harmesworth, Middlesex, died 27 Jan. 1760.) [25

Lidgould, John Michael, s. John, of Harmondsworth Middlesex, cler. LINCOLN COLL., matric. 9 Dec 1756, aged 21 (his father died 27 Jan., 1760).

Liebenrood, George Englebert, s. John Englebert of Reading, Berks, arm. ORIEL COLL., matric 26 Feb., 1818, aged 17. See *Eton School Lists*.

Liebenrood, John Englebert, Esq., created D.C.L. 6 July, 1810, of Prospect Hill, Berks, died at Leam ington 23 Sep., 1821.

Lieven, Count, created D.C.L. 15 June, 1814, D.C.L by diploma next day, ambassador extraordinary and minister plenipotentiary from the Emperor of Russ at the Court of St. James's 1812-34, governor to th Grand Duke Alexander, of Russia, 1834, created prince of the Russian empire, died 10th and buried Rome 12 Jan., 1839. See *Gent.'s Mag.*, 1857, i. 36

Lievre, Frederick William Stamp le, o.s. Frederick of St. Peter Port, Guernsey, gent. PEMBROK COLL., matric. 4 Feb., 1881, aged 18; scholar 1881- B.A. 1885, M.A. 1887. [30

Lievre, John Sturges, of ST. JOHN'S COLL., Cam bridge (B.A. 1815, M.A. 1819); adm. 'ad eundem Feb., 1860, rector of Little Ashby, co. Leicester, 183

Lifely, John, s. John, of Lechlade, co. Glouceste pleb. ST. JOHN'S COLL., matric. 1 June, 1739, ag 18; B.A. 8 March, 1742-3.

Light, Henry William Maure, 1s. Alexander Whale of Dundee, Scotland, arm. UNIVERSITY COLL matric. 22 March, 1828, aged 19; B.A. 1832, vic of Bramshaw, Hants, 1835-40, and of Wrought 1840, until his death 1 April, 1875.

Light, John, M.A. from TRINITY COLL., Dublin, 18 (B.A. 1845); adm. 'ad eundem' 21 June, 1860.

Lightbourn, Joseph Fraser, o.s. Francis, of Barbad East Indies, arm. JESUS COLL., matric. 16 Ma 1821, aged 18; B.A. 1825, rector of Pembroke a Devon, Bermuda, died 1 Feb., 1872. [3

Lightfoot, Francis Cuthbert, 1s. Nicholas Francis, of Cadbury, Devon, cler. ORIEL COLL., matric. 5 Nov., 1866, aged 19.

Lightfoot, Francis Lowry, 2s. John Prideaux, of Wootton, Northants, D.D. UNIVERSITY COLL., matric. 31 March, 1860, aged 18; B.A. 1863.

Lightfoot, George Herbert, 3s. John Prideaux, of Wootton, Northants, vice chancellor. UNIVERSITY COLL., matric. 16 Jan., 1863, aged 19; B.A. 1866, M.A. 1869, held various curacies 1869-81, vicar of Pickering, Yorks, 1881.

Lightfoot, Henry, 2s. Gabriel, of Moreton, Devon, gent. MAGDALEN HALL, matric. 10 Dec., 1833, aged 19.

Lightfoot, Henry Le Blanc, 4s. John Prideaux, of Wootton, Northants, D.D. UNIVERSITY COLL., matric. 23 Oct., 1868, aged 18; B.A. 1872. [5]

Lightfoot, Isaac, s. Isaac, of Wigton, Cumberland, gent. ST. ALBAN HALL, matric. 1 July, 1813, aged 28.

Lightfoot, John, s. Stephen, of Newent, co. Gloucester, gent. PEMBROKE COLL., matric. 26 March, 1753, aged 17; B.A. 1756, M.A. 1766, a botanist, F.R.S., F.L.S., rector of Shalden, Hants, 1765, and of Gotham and Sutton, Notts, and vicar of Sutton-upon-Lound with Scrooby, Notts, 1777, until his death 20 Feb., 1788.

Lightfoot, John, s. John, of Uxbridge, Middlesex, cler. MERTON COLL., matric. 10 Nov., 1802, aged 18; B.A. 1806, M.A. 1809, B.D. 1819, fellow until 1824, principal of postmasters and tutor 1822, vicar of Ponteland, Northumberland, 1823, until his death 23 Nov., 1863. See *Eton School Lists.*

Lightfoot, Rev. John Alfred, 1s. George, of Maryport, Cumberland, gent. NON-COLL., matric. 18 Oct., 1880, aged 19; B.A. from HERTFORD COLL. 1883, M.A. 1887. [9]

Lightfoot, John Nicholas, 6s. Gabriel, of Moreton Hampstead, Devon, gent. MAGDALEN HALL, matric. 7 Dec., 1843, aged 19; B.A. 1847, M.A. 1851, vicar of Cofton, Exeter, 1864, until his death in 1883.

Lightfoot, John Prideaux, 1s. Nicholas, of Crediton, Devon, cler. EXETER COLL., matric. 28 June, 1820, aged 17; B.A. 1824, fellow 1824-34, M.A. 1827, B. & D.D. 1854, tutor 1827-34, bursar 1828, dean 1830, proctor 1833, vice chancellor 1862-6, hon. canon of Peterborough 1853, rector of Wootton, Northants, 1834-54, rector of Exeter College 1854, and rector of Kidlington, Oxon, 1854, until his death 23 March, 1887. See *Coll. Reg.*, 125, 139.

Lightfoot, Joseph, s. John, of Abbey Holm, Cumberland, pleb. QUEEN'S COLL., matric. 17 June, 1784, aged 19; B.A. 1790, M.A. 1793, fellow until 1814, and tutor, vicar of Stanway, co. Gloucester, 1795-1814, and of Enham with Upton Gay, Hants, 1814, until his death 24 March, 1835.

Lightfoot, Joseph Barber, bishop of Durham (1879), created D.C.L. 18 June, 1879, scholar TRINITY COLL., Cambridge, B.A. 30th wrangler 1851, chancellor's medallist, fellow 1852-71, tutor 1853-62, M.A. 1854, D.D. 1864, D.D. Durham by diploma 1879, hon. D.D. Edinburgh 1884, LL.D. Glasgow 1879, and Dublin 1888, chaplain to Prince Consort 1861, Hulsean professor of divinity at Cambridge 1861-75, Margaret professor 1875-9, hon. chaplain in ordinary to the Queen 1862-79, Whitehall preacher 1866-7, canon residentiary St. Paul's 1861-79, select preacher at Oxford 1874-5, deputy clerk of the closet 1875-9; for list of his works see *Crockford.*

Lightfoot, Nicholas, s. Nicholas, of Morton Hampstead, Devon, gent. BALLIOL COLL., matric. 19 Oct., 1790, aged 18; B.A. 1794, perp. curate Churcheton, Devon, 1795, rector of Stockleigh Pomeroy 1831, until his death 7 April, 1847.

Lightfoot, Nicholas Francis, 2s. Nicholas, of Crediton, Devon, cler. EXETER COLL., matric. 3 Feb., 1829, aged 17; B.A. 1832, M.A. 1836, vicar of Cadbury, Devon, 1846-55, rector of Rislip 1855, until his death 19 Nov., 1881. [15]

Lightfoot, Reginald Prideaux, 1s. John Prideaux, of Wootton, Northants, doctor. BALLIOL COLL., matric. 30 May, 1855, aged 19; B.A. 1859, M.A. 1862, vicar of Preston Deanery, Northants, 1863-7, of Towcester 1867-71, hon. canon of Peterborough 1876-80, archdeacon of Oakham 1880, vicar of Wellingborough 1871.

Lightfoot, Thomas, 2s. Joseph, of Walworth, Surrey, arm. QUEEN'S COLL., matric. 25 Jan., 1827, aged 19.

Lightfoot, Thomas Streatfeild, 1s. Thomas, of St. James's, London, arm. EXETER COLL., matric. 8 June, 1825, aged 17; B.A. 1829, M.A. 1832, bar.-at-law, Middle Temple, 1833. See *Eton School Lists.*

Lightfoot, Thomas William, 2s. Thomas, of Valetta, Malta, arm. NON-COLL., matric. 4 Nov., 1884, aged 18.

Lightly, George Edwin, 4s. James, of Holyhead, Isle of Anglesey, gent. NON-COLL., matric. 13 Nov., 1874, aged 19. [20]

Lighton, Henry Chester, 2s. Thomas, of Chester (city), baronet. LINCOLN COLL., matric. 22 Feb., 1819, aged 20. See Foster's *Baronetage.*

Lilley, Edmund, 2s. Samuel Isaac, of Camberwell, Surrey, gent. WORCESTER COLL., matric. 9 Dec., 1825, aged 18; B.A. 1829, M.A. 1833, B.D. 1851, perp. curate of Smallhythe 1865-7, and vicar of Barrow Gurney, Somerset, 1869-81.

Lilley, Henry Thomas, 1s. John, of Dover, Kent, gent. BALLIOL COLL., matric. 17 Oct., 1877, aged 18; exhibitioner 1877-81, B.A. 1881, M.A. 1884.

Lilley, Samuel, 1s. Samuel, of Peckham, Surrey, gent. JESUS COLL., matric. 4 July, 1823, aged 16; B.A. 1827, scholar 1829-32, M.A. 1830.

Lillick, Samuel, s. Richard, of St. Augustine's, Cornwall, pleb. EXETER COLL., matric. 12 March, 1723-4, aged 18. [25]

Lillingston, Claude Augustus, 3s. Charles, of Ipswich, Suffolk, arm. WORCESTER COLL., matric. 1 March, 1855, aged 18; B.A. 1859.

Lillingston, George, 4s. Abraham (Spooner), of Lyme Regis, Dorset, arm. WORCESTER COLL., matric. 29 Jan., 1828, aged 20; B.A. 1832, M.A. 1836, incumbent of Southend, Middlesex, died 29 March, 1848.

Lillingston, George William. WORCESTER COLL., 1853. See JOHNSON.

Lillingston, Septimus Ernest Luke (Spooner), 7s. Edward, of Edgbaston, co. Warwick, cler. CHARSLEY HALL, matric. 13 Oct., 1881, aged 18; commoner HERTFORD COLL. 1884, B.A. 1886.

Lillington, Rev. Frederick, 2s. Richard, of Worcester (city), arm. BRASENOSE COLL., matric. 6 Dec., 1855, aged 18; scholar 1856-62, B.A. 1860, M.A. 1862. [30]

Lillington, George, s. Thomas, of Winfrith, Dorset, gent. WADHAM COLL., matric. 14 Oct., 1743, aged 16; B.C.L. 1750, rector of Leigh, Kent, 1758, master of Earl of Leicester's Hospital, Warwick, vicar of Hampden in Arden, died 2 March, 1794.

Lillington, Richard, s. George, of Leigh, Kent, cler. WORCESTER COLL., matric. 29 Nov., 1787, aged 21; B.A. 1791, vicar of Hampden in Arden 1792, until his death in 1826.

Lillington, Richard Dickson, s. Thomas, of Winfrith, Dorset, gent. HERTFORD COLL., matric. 3 March, 1740-1, aged 18; B.C.L. from WADHAM COLL. 1749, D.C.L. 1752, preb. of Salisbury 1773-86, chaplain to the King 1761, until his death in 1786.

Lilly, Charles James, 2s. Peter, of Kegworth, co. Leicester, cler. NON-COLL., matric. 8 Feb., 1877, aged 19.

Lilly, Edward, s. Robert, of Stourbridge, co. Worcester, gent. LINCOLN COLL., matric. 29 March, 1740, aged 18; B.A. 1743. [35]

Lilly, John, s. William, of Worcester (city), arm. BALLIOL COLL., matric. 14 March, 1787, aged 16; B.A. from ST. MARY HALL 1790, M.A. from MERTON COLL. 1795, B.C.L. 1801, rector of Stoke Lacy, co. Hereford, one of the six lecturers in the church of Bromyard 1801, preb. of Hereford 1813, and archdeacon 1823, until his death 30 Oct., 1825.

Limbrey, Charles, s. John, of Wootton, Hants, gent. QUEEN'S COLL., matric. 18 March, 1729-30, aged 18.

Limbrey, Henry, s. John, of Yateley, Hants, arm. WADHAM COLL., matric. 13 Feb., 1721-2, aged 18.

Limbrey, John, s. John, of Yateley, Hants, arm. WADHAM COLL., matric. 13 Feb., 1721-2, aged 17.

Limming, William, s. George, of St. Leonard's, London, gent. ST. ALBAN HALL, matric. 4 July, 1816, aged 27. [5]

Limpus, Henry Francis, 2s. Richard D., of Isleworth, Middlesex, gent. MAGDALEN HALL, matric. 6 Nov., 1856, aged 24; B.A. 1861, M.A. 1871, minor canon Llandaff 1867-8, Windsor 1868-74, vicar of Twickenham 1874.

Lind, Charles, s. Adam, of Edinburgh, Scotland, gent. MAGDALEN HALL, matric. 26 Feb., 1723-4, aged 17; B.A. from BALLIOL COLL. 1728, M.A. 1750, rector of Wivenhoe, and vicar of Ferring, Kent, 1750. See Foster's *Our Noble and Gentle Families*.

Lind, James (Player), s. John, of Haslar, Hants, doctor. WADHAM COLL., matric. 28 April, 1809, aged 18; B.A. 1813, M.A. & B.Med. 1816, D.Med. 1819, died 19 June, 1860. See Foster's *Our Noble and Gentle Families*, ii. 792.

Lind, John, s. Charles, of St. James's, Westminster, doctor. BALLIOL COLL., matric. 22 May, 1753, aged 15; B.A. 1757, M.A. 1761, bar.-at-law, Lincoln's Inn, 1776, F.R.S., a councillor to the King of Poland, died 12 Jan., 1781. See Foster's *Our Noble and Gentle Families*. [9]

Lindeman, Alfred Sanderson, 6s. Sidney Alfred, of London, gent. ST. MARY HALL, matric. 19 Oct., 1881, aged 17; exhibitioner 1881-5, B.A. 1886.

Linden, Dirk, Baron de, created D.C.L. 1 March, 1733-4, an attendant upon the Prince of Orange.

Linden, Edmund, Count von, 1s. Henry Count L., of Nurnberg, in Bavaria. CHARSLEY HALL, matric. 30 Oct., 1880, aged 18.

Lindesay, (Rev.) Frederick William, 1s. Frederick, of Loughry, co. Tyrone, arm. MERTON COLL., matric. 1 Feb., 1879, aged 21; commoner CHARSLEY HALL 1879, B.A. 1886.

Lindesay, Robert, s. John, of Derryloran, co. Tyrone, arm. CHRIST CHURCH, matric. 26 Feb., 1768, aged 20; of Loughry, co. Tyrone, assistant barrister for the county, M.P. Dundalk 1781-3, died 6 Jan., 1832.

Lindley, Charles Dalmar, 1s. Robert Charles, of Cromford, co. Derby, arm. MAGDALEN COLL., matric. 28 April, 1870, aged 21. [15]

Lindley, Finch, s. Francis, of Bowling, Yorks, arm. BRASENOSE COLL., matric. 1 July, 1720, aged 19; bar.-at-law, Inner Temple, 1727, died unmarried. See Foster's *Yorkshire Collection*, vol. ii., WOOD, of Hickleton.

Lindley, Herbert, o.s. John, of Derby, gent. NON-COLL., matric. 27 Jan., 1872, aged 17.

Lindley, Lennox Hannay, 3s. Sir Nathaniel, of London, knight. MAGDALEN COLL., matric. 21 Oct., 1886, aged 18.

Lindley, Walter Barry, 2s. Nathaniel, of London, arm. UNIVERSITY COLL., matric. 16 Oct., 1880, aged 18; B.A. 1883, M.A. 1887, bar.-at-law, Lincoln's Inn, 1887.

Lindley, Walter Delmar, 5s. Robert Charles, of Mansfield, Notts, gent. MAGDALEN COLL., matric. 19 Oct., 1883, aged 19; B.A. 1886. See *Eton School Lists*. [20]

Lindoe, Frederick Ekins, 1s. Robert Frederick, of Isle of Guernsey, gent. EXETER COLL., matric. 3 Nov., 1860, aged 18; B.A. 1864.

Lindon, Clement Hemery, 1s. Thomas Angell, Winford, Somerset, cler. MAGDALEN COL matric. 1 Feb., 1873, aged 19; demy 1872-7, B. 1877, B.C.L. 1881, bar.-at-law, Inner Temple, 18 See Foster's *Men at the Bar*.

Lindon, Thomas Angell, 2s. Joseph, of Plymou Devon, arm. ST. EDMUND HALL, matric. 2 De 1847, aged 25; B.A. 1851, M.A. 1854, vicar of Peter's, Halliwell, Lancashire, 1854-71, perp. cur St. Paul's, Jersey, 1871-80, vicar of Highclif Hants, 1880.

Lindop, Thomas Crump, 3s. William, of Newpo Salop, arm. CHRIST CHURCH, matric. 11 Oc 1861, aged 17; servitor 1861-4, B.A. 1864, M. 1868.

Lindop, William Crump, 2s. William, of Newpo Salop, gent. CHRIST CHURCH, matric. 20 Ap 1860, aged 17; servitor 1860-2. [2

Lindow, Henry Lindow, s. Henry (Rawlinson), Liverpool, Lancashire, arm. CHRIST CHURC matric. 18 April, 1795, aged 17; of Lower Slaugh House, co. Gloucester, assumed the surname LINDON in lieu of RAWLINSON in 1792, died in 18 See Foster's *Lancashire Collection*, RAWLINSON; *Rugby School Reg.*, 67.

Lindow, Henry William, 1s. Henry, of Cheltenha co. Gloucester, arm. ORIEL COLL., matric. March, 1842, aged 18; of Gawcomb, co. Glo cester, J.P., formerly an officer 17th lancers, died Feb., 1887. See Foster's *Yorkshire Collection*, RA LINSON; & *Rugby School Reg.*, 194.

Lindow, Jonas, 1s. John, of Egremont, Cumberlan gent. QUEEN'S COLL., matric. 30 Jan., 1866, ag 19: B.A. 1870, M.A. 1872, of Eben Hall a Ingwell, Cumberland, J.P., D.L., high she 1883.

Lindsay, Rev. Alexander Sutherland, 2s. Henry, Ide Hill, Kent, cler. KEBLE COLL., matric. Oct., 1879, aged 19; B.A. 1882.

Lindsay, Charles Dalrymple, s. James, Earl of B carres. BALLIOL COLL., matric. 1 Dec., 1779, ag 19; B.A. 1783, M.A. 1786, D.D. by diploma April, 1804, vicar of Sutterton, co. Linc., 1793, de of Christ Church, Dublin, bishop of Killaloe a Kilfenora 1803-4, bishop of Kildare 1804, until death 8 Aug., 1846. See Foster's *Peerage*, E. CRA FORD; & *Cotton*, ii. 235. [3

Lindsay, George Campbell, 2s. Thomas Sturn, Edinburgh, arm. WADHAM COLL., matric. 17 O 1882, aged 19.

Lindsay, Henry, born at Sutterton, Lincoln, s. H Charles, bishop of Kildare. UNIVERSITY COL matric. 19 Oct., 1818, aged 18; died 17 Feb., 18 See Foster's *Peerage*, E. CRAWFORD.

Lindsay, Rev. James, of TRINITY COLL., Cambri (B.A. 1854, M.A. 1857); adm. 'comitatis causa' June, 1863.

Lindsay, Robert Grant, 3s. Frederick Henry, Marylebone, London, arm. UNIVERSITY COL matric. 30 June, 1858, aged 18; B.A. 1862, a stud of the Inner Temple 1860.

Lindsay, Wallace Martin, y.s. Alexander, of Pitt weem, co. Fife, cler. BALLIOL COLL., matric. Oct., 1877, aged 19, exhibitioner 1877-82, B.A. 18 fellow JESUS COLL. 1882, M.A. 1885, assistant tu 1885. [

Lindsay, William, s. David, of St. James's, W minster, baronet. CHRIST CHURCH, matric. May, 1780, aged 18; of the Evelick family, in di matic service 1789-94, governor of the island Tobago 1794, until his death about June, 1796. *Alumni West.*, 412.

Lindsell, Arthur Knox, 2s. Robert Henry, of M chester, arm. TRINITY COLL., matric. 18 O 1869, aged 18; B.A. 1872, M.A. 1877.

Lindsell, Rev. Henry Bayly, 4s. Charles Samuel, Holme, Beds, arm. TRINITY COLL., matric. Oct., 1881, aged 18; B.A. 1885.

indsell, Henry Martin, 1s. Robert Henry, of Hertford (town), arm. BALLIOL COLL., matric. 16 Oct., 1865, aged 19; scholar TRINITY COLL. 1866-71, B.A. 1870, M.A. 1872, bar.-at-law, Inner Temple, 1872, inspector of schools 1875-6, junior examiner Education Department 1877. See Foster's *Men at the Bar*.

indsell, Robert Henry, 1s. Robert, of Biggleswade, Beds, arm. TRINITY COLL., matric. 18 March, 1837, aged 18; of Fairfield, Beds, J.P., D.L., high sheriff 1864, late lieut.-colonel 28th foot.

indsell, William Henry Barber, 3s. John, of London, arm. CORPUS CHRISTI COLL., matric. 16 Oct., 1866, aged 18; scholar 1866-71, B.A. 1871, journalist, bar.-at-law, Lincoln's Inn, 1875. See Foster's *Men at the Bar*.

indsey, William, s. John, of Antigua, West Indies, arm. CHRIST CHURCH, matric. 10 Oct., 1772, aged 19. [5]

ine, John, 'stationarius;' privilegiatus 18 Jan., 1803.

infield, Charles, s. John, of Horsham, Sussex, arm. QUEEN'S COLL., matric. 18 March, 1769, aged 16.

infield, Ralph Parkinson, o.s. Ralph, of Wakefield, Yorks, gent. QUEEN'S COLL., matric. 23 Oct., 1862, aged 19; B.A. 1866, M.A. 1869, vicar of Elton St. Stephen, Lancashire, 1882.

inford, Arthur Howard, 2s. William Thomas, of London, gent. MAGDALEN COLL., matric. 16 Oct., 1880, aged 19; B.A. 1886, a student of the Inner Temple 1884.

ing, John, s. Marmaduke, of Weston, Somerset, gent. MAGDALEN HALL, matric. 27 May, 1772, aged 16; B.A. 1776.

ingard, Edward Atherton, o.s. Edward Atherton, of Runcorn, Cheshire, gent. ST. EDMUND HALL, matric. 15 Oct., 1858, aged 18. [10]

ingard, Frank Chorlton, 2s. John Rowson, of Manchester, gent. EXETER COLL., matric. 22 Oct., 1880, aged 18; B.A. 1884, M.A. 1887.

Lingard, Rev. John, s. John, of Stockport, Cheshire, gent. BRASENOSE COLL., matric. 17 May, 1804, aged 18; B.A. 1808, M.A. 1810, B.D. 1820, died at Liverpool, 14 Jan., 1833. See *Manchester School Reg.*, ii. 228.

Lingard, John Rowson, o.s. John Rowson, of Stockport, Cheshire, arm. ORIEL COLL., matric. 29 Oct., 1857, aged 19.

Lingard, Joshua, 1s. Thomas, of Prestwich, Lancashire, gent. ST. MARY HALL, matric. 15 Dec., 1823, aged 25; B.A. 1827, M.A. 1831, incumbent of St. George's Church, Hulme, Lancashire, died 30 Nov., 1842. See *Manchester School Reg.*, ii. 106.

Lingard, Roger Rowson, BRASENOSE COLL., 1844. See GUTHRIE. [15]

Lingen, Charles James, 1s. Charles, of Hereford (city), arm. BALLIOL COLL., matric. 12 Oct., 1861, aged 17; died 8 June, 1864.

Lingen, Rev. Henry, s. Ralph, of Rock, co. Worcester, cler. WADHAM COLL., matric. 10 Oct., 1783, aged 18; B.A. 1787, fellow, M.A. 1793, died at Abberley, co. Worcester, 18 March, 1853, aged 87.

Lingen, Henry, s. Henry, of Abberley, co. Worcester, cler. WADHAM COLL., matric. 11 Dec., 1816, aged 17.

Lingen, Ralph, s. Henry, of Worcester (city), gent. WADHAM COLL., matric. 28 March, 1750, aged 18; B.A. 1753, M.A. 1756, rector of Castle Frome, co. Hereford, rector of Rock, co. Worcester, 1805, died in 1812, aged 80.

Lingen, Ralph Robert Wheeler, o.s. Thomas, of St. Martin's, Birmingham, gent. TRINITY COLL., matric. 22 May, 1837, aged 18, scholar 1837-41, B.A. 1841; fellow BALLIOL COLL. 1841-50, M.A. 1846, created D.C.L. 22 June, 1881, hon. fellow TRINITY COLL. 1886, bar.-at-law. Lincoln's Inn, 1847, secretary to committee of Council on Education 1849-70, permanent secretary to the Treasury 1870-85, K.C.B., 31 May, 1879, created Baron Lingen of Lingen, co. Hereford, 3 July, 1885. See Foster's *Men at the Bar* & *Rugby School Reg.*, xvi. [20]

Lingen, Robert. TRINITY COLL., 1744. See BURTON.

Lingen, Thomas, s. Thomas, of Radbrook, co. Gloucester, arm. TRINITY COLL., matric. 16 July, 1748, aged 18; brother of Robert last named, died unmarried.

Lingham, Charles, s. Charles, of St. Helen's, Worcester (city), gent. WORCESTER COLL., matric. 5 July, 1800, aged 17.

Linklater, Frederick Robert, 2s. J., of Brixton, Surrey, arm. CHRIST CHURCH, matric. 15 Oct., 1869, aged 18; a student of Lincoln's Inn 1859. See *Eton School Lists*.

Linklater, John Edmund, 1s. John, of Brixton, Surrey, arm. CHRIST CHURCH, matric. 12 June, 1867, aged 18; B.A. 1871, M.A. 1874, bar.-at-law, Inner Temple, 1872, registrar in Bankruptcy 1887. See Foster's *Men at the Bar* & *Eton School Lists*. [25]

Linley, Ozias Thurstan, s. Thomas, of Bath, Somerset, gent. CORPUS CHRISTI COLL., matric. 19 March, 1785, aged 18; B.A. 1789, a minor canon Norwich Cathedral 1790, vicar of Stoke Holy Cross, Norfolk, 1807, and of Trowse with Lakenham 1815, junior fellow and organist Dulwich College, died 6 March, 1831. See *Gent.'s Mag.*

Linsley, William Hessel, o.s. John Richard, of Sydney, gent. BALLIOL COLL., matric. 18 Oct., 1881, aged 20; B.A. 1886, bar.-at-law, Inner Temple, 1887.

Linton, Edward Francis, 4s. Henry, of Diddington, Hunts, cler. UNIVERSITY COLL., matric. 13 Oct., 1866, aged 18; B.A. 1871, M.A. 1873, rector of St. George's, Manchester, 1875-8, vicar of Sprowston, Norfolk, 1878.

Linton, Henry, s. John, of Freiston, co. Lincoln, cler. LINCOLN COLL., matric. 26 May, 1770, aged 17; demy MAGDALEN COLL. 1771-4, B.A. 1774, fellow 1774-1801, M.A. 1776, B.D. 1786, D.D. 1797, senior dean of arts 1786, bursar 1787, etc., vice-president 1795, dean of divinity 1797, rector of North Leverton, and vicar of Freiston, co. Leicester, 1782, rector of Dinton, Wilts, 1800, died 14 Feb., 1841. See *Bloxam*, vii. 37. [29]

Linton, Henry, 2s. John, of Freiston, co. Lincoln, arm. MAGDALEN COLL., matric. 26 July, 1821, aged 17; demy 1821-31, B.A. 1824, M.A. 1827, fellow 1831-5, senior dean of arts 1832, of Stirtloe, Hunts, curate of Diddington, Hunts, 1827-35, vicar 1835-56, rector of St. Peter-le-Bailey, Oxford, 1856-77, hon. canon CHRIST CHURCH 1871, died 14 April, 1887. See *Rugby School Reg.*, 125; & *Coll. Reg.*, vii.. 282.

Linton, Henry, 1s. Henry, of Diddington, Hunts, cler. WADHAM COLL., matric. 18 March, 1857, aged 18; B.A. 1860.

Linton, James, s. Thomas, of St. Nicholas, Worcester (city), pleb. MAGDALEN HALL, matric. 10 Dec., 1737, aged 17; B.A. 1741.

Linton, Rev. James, s. James, of Stamford, co. Lincoln, arm. BRASENOSE COLL., matric. 18 Oct., 1817, aged 18; demy MAGDALEN COLL. 1820-5, B.A. 1822, M.A. 1825, fellow 1825-33, dean of arts 1828, bursar 1829, of Hemingford House, Hunts, died 16 Oct., 1872. See *Rugby School Reg.* 122, & *Bloxam*, vii. 280.

Linton, Sydney, 3s. Henry, of Diddington, Hunts, cler. WADHAM COLL., matric. 12 Oct., 1860, aged 19; B.A. 1864, M.A. 1870, created D.D. 4 March, 1884, bishop of Riverina since 1884, vicar of Holy Trinity, Oxford, 1870-7, and of St. Philip, Heigham, 1877-84. See *Rugby School Reg.*

Linton, William Richardson, 4s. Henry, of Diddington, Hunts, cler. CORPUS CHRISTI COLL., matric. 21 Oct., 1869, aged 19; B.A. 1873, M.A. 1876, vicar of Shirley, co. Derby, 1886. [35]

Lintott, Joseph Cooper, 3s. George, of Fulham, Middlesex, gent. ST. ALBAN HALL, matric. 15 Oct., 1863, aged 20.

Linwood, Rev. William, o.s. William, of Birmingham, arm. CHRIST CHURCH, matric. 10 Dec., 1835, aged 18; student 1837-51, B.A. 1839, M.A. 1842, Hertford, Ireland, and Craven scholar 1836, and Boden Sanscrit scholar, public examiner 1850-1, died 7 Sep., 1878.

Linzee, Charles Arthur, y.s. Robert George, of Jermyns, near Romsey, Hants, arm. CHRIST CHURCH, matric. 15 Oct., 1880, aged 18.

Linzee, Edward Gordon, 1s. Robert George, of Jermyn, near Romsey, Hants, gent. NON-COLL., matric. 7 Dec., 1872, aged 19. See *Eton School Lists.*

Linzee, Edward Hood, 1s. Edward, of Penn, Bucks, cler. CHRIST CHURCH, matric. 4 June, 1835, aged 19; B.A. 1839, vicar of Bracknell, Berks, 1854-61. See *Rugby School Reg.*, 160.

Linzee, Robert George, 2s. Edward, of Penn, Bucks, cler. CHRIST CHURCH, matric. 15 May, 1839, aged 19; B.A. 1843, of Jermyns, Hants, J.P. See *Eton School Lists.* **[5]**

Linzey, Thomas, 'printer'; privilegiatus 21 July, 1747.

Lippincott, (Sir) Henry (Cann), s. Henry, of Stoke Bishop, co. Gloucester, bart. ORIEL COLL., matric. 29 Jan., 1794, aged 17; 2nd baronet, created M.A. 13 May, 1797, died s.p.l. 23 Aug., 1829.

Lippincott, Robert Cann, o.s. Henry C. L., of London, baronet (extinct). CHRIST CHURCH, matric. 19 May, 1836, aged 18; of Over Court, co. Gloucester. See *Eton School Lists.*

Lippitt, Alfred Joseph Warren, 1s. George Warren, of Vienna, arm. NEW COLL., matric. 13 Oct., 1876, aged 19; B.A. 1880, M.A. 1885, bar.-at-law, Inner Temple, 1884. See Foster's *Men at the Bar.*

Lipscomb, Arthur Morton, 6s. Christopher, bishop of Jamaica. BRASENOSE COLL., matric. 15 Oct., 1859, aged 18; B.A. 1868. **[10]**

Lipscomb, Charles Burton, 1s. Charles Henry, of Temple Ewell, Kent, cler. WORCESTER COLL., matric. 18 Jan., 1883, aged 19.

Lipscomb, Charles Henry, 2s. John Thomas, of St. Albans, Herts, gent. QUEEN'S COLL., matric. 14 May, 1840, aged 19; rector and vicar of Temple Ewell, Kent, 1862-71, rector of Norfolk, 1871.

Lipscomb, Christopher, s. William, of Pomfret, Yorks, cler. NEW COLL., matric. 12 July, 1800, aged 18; B.A. 1804, M.A. 1811, B. & D.D. 1824, dean of arts 1822, bursar 1823, fellow until 1825, vicar of Sutton Benger, Wilts, 1818, bishop of Jamaica 1824, until his death 4 April, 1843.

Lipscomb, Cyril, s. William, of Welbury, Yorks, cler. NEW COLL., matric. 26 Aug., 1812, aged 17; fellow 1812, until his death 25 Sep., 1815.

Lipscomb, Cyril William, 1s. Christopher, bishop of Jamaica. NEW COLL., matric. 29 June, 1848, aged 17; fellow 1848, B.C.L. & M.A. 1856, a student of Lincoln's Inn 1877. **[15]**

Lipscomb, Edwin Francis, 3s. William, of Winchelsea, Sussex, gent. ST. EDMUND HALL, matric. 16 Dec., 1867, aged 37; held various curacies 1870-83, rector of Aston-Botterell since 1883.

Lipscomb, Francis, s. William, of Welbury, Yorks, cler. CORPUS CHRISTI COLL., matric. 23 April, 1817, aged 19; exhibitioner 1817-18, and of UNIVERSITY COLL. 1818-24, B.A. 1821, M.A. 1824, rector of Welbury 1832, until his death 4 Aug., 1885.

Lipscomb, Francis, 1s. Francis, of Sevenoaks, Kent, cler. ST. JOHN'S COLL., matric. 24 May, 1844, aged 18. See *Rugby School Reg.*, 204.

Lipscomb, Frederick, 3s. John Thomas, of St. Albans, Herts, gent. QUEEN'S COLL., matric. 15 Feb., 1844 aged 19; B.A. 1847, M.A. 1850, held various curacies 1847-58, vicar of Frogmore since 1859.

Lipscomb, Frederick Bell, 1s. Frederick, of London, cler. ST. EDMUND HALL, matric. 19 Oct., 1872, aged 19; B.A. 1875, M.A. 1879, has held various curacies since 1878. **[20]**

Lipscomb, Henry Alchorne, 5s. John Thomas, of St. Albans, Herts, arm. EXETER COLL., matric. 25 May, 1858, aged 19; B.A. 1862, M.A. 1865, vicar of West Hyde, Herts, 1871-8, and of Sawbridgeworth since 1878.

Lipscomb, John Kempster, 1s. Kempster, of Portsea, Hants, arm. EXETER COLL., matric. 18 Nov., 1824, aged 18.

Lipscomb, John Streatfeild, 3s. Francis, of Hastings, Sussex, cler. PEMBROKE COLL., matric. 20 Feb., 1851, aged 18; B.A. 1855, M.A. 1858, died 1871.

Lipscomb, Maurice John, 2s. John Streatfeild, of Canterbury, arm. MAGDALEN COLL., matric. 23 Oct., 1885, aged 18.

Lipscomb, William, s. Thomas, of Winchester (city), gent. CORPUS CHRISTI COLL., matric. 6 July, 1770, aged 16; B.A. 1774, M.A. 1784, rector of Welbury, Yorks, 1789-1832, master of St. John's Hospital, Barnard Castle, died 25 May, 1842. **[25]**

Lipscomb, William Henry, 1s. William Henry, of Winchester, Hants, arm. UNIVERSITY COLL., matric. 14 Oct., 1865, aged 18; B.A. 1870, bar.-at-law, Lincoln's Inn, 1872. See Foster's *Men at the Bar.*

Lipscombe, Henry, 'cook of Corpus Christi College'; privilegiatus 18 April, 1738.

Liptrott, Bexworth, s. James, of Nuneaton, co. Warwick, gent. QUEEN'S COLL., matric. 30 Nov., 1726, aged 18; B.A. 1730, died 'minister' of Totteridge 18 July, 1784.

Liptrott, Rev. Boulton Brander, 2s. John, of Massoore, East Indies, arm. ST. JOHN'S COLL., matric. 13 Oct., 1877, aged 18; B.A. 1880, M.A. 1884.

Liptrott, James, s. John, of Broughton Astley, co. Leicester, cler. PEMBROKE COLL., matric. 2 June, 1753, aged 19; B.A. 1757, M.A. 1760, vicar of Thorpe (Egham), Surrey, 1774 (? rector of Offham, Kent, 1777), died 18 Oct., 1805. **[30]**

Liptrott, Rev. James, 1s. John, of Egham, Surrey, cler. WORCESTER COLL., matric. 17 Feb., 1827, aged 19; B.A. 1832, died 9 Sep., 1879. See *Rugby School Reg.*, 140.

Liptrott, John, s. Jacob (? James), of Nuneaton, co. Warwick, gent. BALLIOL COLL., matric. 21 March, 1718-9, aged 16; B.A. 1722, M.A. 1725, rector of Broughton Astley, co. Leicester, until his death in 1778. See Nichol's *Leicester*, iv. 61.

Liptrott, John, s. James, of Egham, Surrey, cler. WADHAM COLL., matric. 23 June, 1792, aged 18; B.A. from TRINITY COLL. 1796, M.A. 1805, rector of Broughton Astley, co. Leicester, 1812, until his death 16 Dec., 1848.

Lipyeatt, Jonathan, fellow of ST. JOHN'S COLL., Cambridge (B.A. 1741, M.A. 1745, 'in convoc.') incorp. 1 Oct., 1755, rector of Bovinger, Essex 1751, of Bubingworth and Meesden, Essex, 1756 and of Wath, Yorks, 1788, until his death 2 Jan., 1799.

Lipyeatt, Thomas, fellow of ST. JOHN'S COLL., Cambridge (B.A. 1731, M.A. 1735, B.D. 1743); incorp. 4 June, 1741, rector of Leyham and Girton, Suffolk 1756, and of Great Hallingbury, Essex, 1758, until his death 5 July, 1781. **[35]**

Lisle, Fermor, s. William, of Imley, Northants, gent. BALLIOL COLL., matric. 21 March, 1715-6, aged 18.

Lisle, Robert de, s. Robert Lisle, of Newcastle, Northumberland, arm. MAGDALEN COLL., matric. 1 Oct., 1811, aged 17. See Hodgson's *Northumberland*, 1., ii. 174; & *Eton School Lists.*

Lisle, Thomas, s. Edward, of Crux Eston, Hants, arm. MAGDALEN HALL, matric. 10 Sep., 1725, aged 16 demy 1726-32, B.A. 1729, M.A. 1732, fellow 1732-4[illegible] B.D. 1740, D.D. 1743, dean of arts 1740, bursar 1741, public orator 1746-9, rector of Wotton, Isle of Wight, 1737, and of Burghclere, Hants, died 2[illegible] March, 1767. See *Coll. Reg.*, vi. 210.

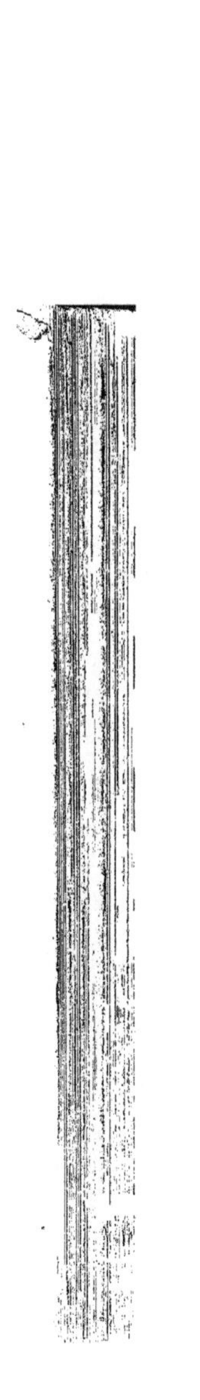

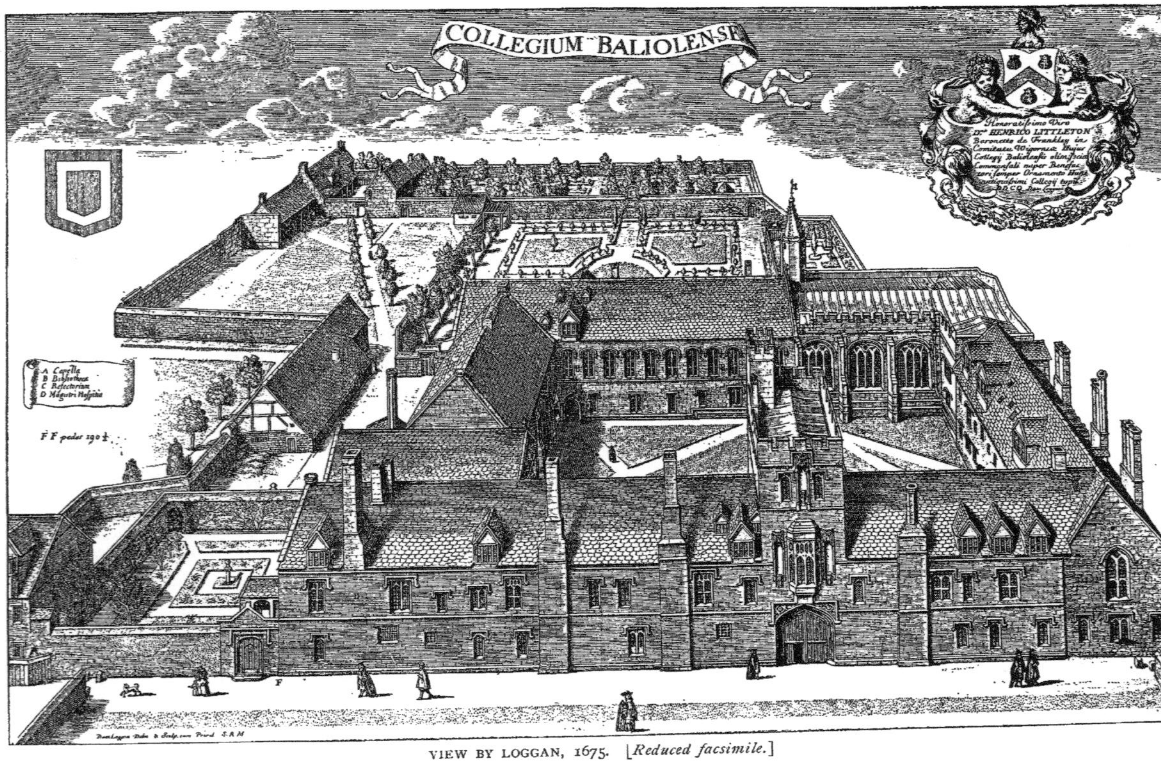

VIEW BY LOGGAN, 1675. [*Reduced facsimile.*]

Lissett, Richard, s. William, of Bampton, Oxon, gent. TRINITY COLL., matric. 13 March, 1716-7, aged 17; B.A. 1720, M.A. 1723.

Lister, Anthony, s. Anthony, of Giggleswick, Yorks, cler. WORCESTER COLL., matric. 26 Oct., 1762, aged 17.

Lister, Rev. Arthur Skidmore, 2s. James Stanley, of Bilston, co. Stafford, arm. KEBLE COLL., matric. 13 Oct., 1873, aged 18; scholar 1873-8, B.A. 1878, M.A. 1882.

Lister, Charles, 2s. Thomas, of Armitage, co. Stafford, arm. BALLIOL COLL., matric. 17 June, 1831, aged 19; of Anglesey, Hants, died 18 Aug., 1873. See Foster's *Peerage*, B. RIBBLESDALE.

Lister, Edward Longworth, o.s. Edward, of Whitegate, Cheshire, arm. BRASENOSE COLL., matric. 28 May, 1874, aged 18; B.A. 1879, M.A. 1881, of Cefn-Ila and Twyn Bell, co. Monmouth, J.P. **[5]**

Lister, Henry, 1s. Thomas, of London, gent. NEW COLL., matric. 19 Oct., 1874, aged 21; B.Mus. 1876.

Lister, James, 1s. James, of Seaforth, Lancashire, gent. UNIVERSITY COLL., matric. 13 Oct., 1883, aged 20.

Lister, James (Stovin), 1s. James, of Ousefleet, Yorks, arm. WORCESTER COLL., matric. 14 April, 1825, aged 18; B.A. 1829, M.A. 1833, vicar of Luddington, co. Lincoln, 1830, until his death 1 March, 1844.

Lister, John, 1s. John, of London, arm. BRASENOSE COLL., matric. 14 Oct., 1865, aged 18; B.A. 1868, M.A. 1872, of Shibden Hall, Yorks, bar.-at-law, Inner Temple, 1877. See Foster's *Men at the Bar*.

Lister, John James, 2s. John, of Overton, Flints, arm. MAGDALEN COLL., matric. 14 Oct., 1878, aged 19; B.A. 1882. **[10]**

Lister, John Joseph, s. Matthew Dymoke, of Manchester, Lancashire, gent. BRASENOSE COLL., matric. 15 May, 1789, aged 19; B.A. 1793, vicar of Burwell with Golceby, co. Lincoln, rector of Cranoe, co. Leicester, 1809-37, vicar of Farlethorpe, died 23 July, 1837. See *Manchester School Reg.*, ii. 72.

Lister, John Joseph, o.s. John Joseph, of Alford, co. Lincoln, cler. LINCOLN COLL., matric. 10 March, 1831, aged 17; B.A. 1835.

Lister, John Moore, 1s. John, of Doncaster, Yorks, arm. BRASENOSE COLL., matric. 24 June, 1859, aged 18; scholar 1859-62, B.A. 1862, M.A. 1866, of the Indian Civil Service 1861, rector of Barton-le-Street, Yorks, 1878-86, vicar of St. Andrew's, Newcastle-on-Tyne, 1886.

Lister, (Sir) Joseph (Bart.), created D.C.L. 9 June, 1880 (son of Joseph Jackson Lister, of Upton, Essex), F.R.S., professor clinical surgery King's College, London, surgeon extraordinary to the Queen, created a baronet 26 Dec., 1883.

Lister, Matthew Bancroft, s. Matthew Dymoke, of Broughton, Lancashire, arm. CHRIST CHURCH, matric. 16 Oct., 1784, aged 16; B.A. 1789, of Burwell Park, co. Lincoln, sheriff 1800, claimed the barony of Kyme, died 14 Oct., 1842. **[15]**

Lister, Matthew Dymoke, s. Matthew, of Lawford, parish of Newbold, co. Warwick, arm. QUEEN'S COLL., matric. 15 Dec., 1747, aged 17; created M.A. 27 Feb., 1752, of Burwell Park, co. Lincoln, died 9 Feb., 1772.

Lister, Nathaniel, s. Thomas, of Gisburne Park, Yorks, arm. LINCOLN COLL., matric. 14 Jan., 1743-4, aged 18; of Armitage Park, co. Stafford, M.P. Clitheroe, Lancashire, 1761-73, died 23 Sep., 1793. See Foster's *Peerage*, B. RIBBLESDALE.

Lister, Samuel Cunliffe, 1s. Samuel Cunliffe, of Ripon, Yorks, arm. ST. JOHN'S COLL., matric. 22 Oct., 1875, aged 19; B.A. 1878.

Lister, Stovin, elder son of Thomas Henry, of Luddington, co. Lincoln, cler. TRINITY COLL., matric. 11 Oct., 1879, aged 20; B.A. 1882. See *Eton School Lists*.

Lister, Thomas, s. Thomas, of Gisburne Park, Yorks, arm. BRASENOSE COLL., matric. 2 May, 1769, aged 17; created M.A. 26 June, 1772, and D.C.L. 8 July, 1773, M.P. Clitheroe 1773-90, created Baron Ribblesdale 26 Oct., 1797, died 22 Sep., 1826. See Foster's *Peerage*. **[20]**

Lister, Thomas, of EMMANUEL COLL., Cambridge (B.A. 1795, LL.B. 1798), s. Nathaniel, of Armitage, co. Stafford, arm. ST. MARY HALL, incorp. 25 June, 1801, aged 28; D.C.L. 17 June, 1802, of Armitage Park, died 24 Feb., 1828. See Foster's *Peerage*.

Lister, Hon. Thomas, s. Thomas, Baron Ribblesdale. CHRIST CHURCH, matric. 2 Nov., 1807, aged 17; 2nd baron, died 10 Dec., 1832.

Lister, Thomas, Baron Ribblesdale, 1s. Thomas, Baron Ribblesdale. CHRIST CHURCH, matric. 4 June, 1846, aged 18; 3rd baron, died 25 Aug., 1876. See Foster's *Peerage*.

Lister, Thomas Llewelyn, 1s. Thomas, of Cowbridge, co. Glamorgan, gent. JESUS COLL., matric. 19 April, 1858, aged 19; B.A. 1861, M.A. 1865, curate of St. Woolos 1862-75, vicar of St. Mark's, both in Newport, Monmouth, 1875.

Litchfield, Francis, s. Francis, of Northampton, arm. MERTON COLL., matric. 21 June, 1811, aged 19; postmaster 1812-5, B.A. 1815, M.A. 1818, rector of Elham, Kent, 1830, of Farthinghoe, and of Great Linford, Northants, 1836, until his death 9 Sep., 1876. See *Rugby School Reg.*, 90. **[25]**

Litchfield, George Arnold, 5s. William Edmund, of Kamptee, near Madras, East Indies, arm. EXETER COLL., matric. 9 Feb., 1860, aged 18; B.A. 1864.

Litchfield, Isaac Smith, 6s. Richard, of Torrington, Devon, arm. TRINITY COLL., matric. 11 June, 1819, aged 19; B.A. 1823, M.A. 1830, rector of Buckland Ripers, Dorset, 1841.

Lithgow, Andrew James, 1s. James, of Weymouth, Dorset, D.Med. EXETER COLL., matric. 13 Oct., 1877, aged 19; B.A. 1880.

Litler, Joseph Bellott, 1s. Robert, of Poynton, Cheshire, (cler.). BRASENOSE COLL., matric. 3 Feb., 1853, aged 18; scholar 1853, B.A. 1856, M.A. 1859, vicar of Brassington 1865-70, of Llantrissent, co. Monmouth, 1870-5, and of Hayton, Yorks, 1875.

Litler, Robert, s. Peter, of Northwich, Cheshire, pleb. BRASENOSE COLL., matric. 5 May, 1781, aged 20.

Litler, Robert, s. Robert, of Northwich, Cheshire, cler. BRASENOSE COLL., matric. 18 Oct., 1817, aged 16; scholar 1818-20, B.A. 1821, M.A. 1824, perp. curate Marple, Cheshire, and of Chadkirk, 1826, and of Poynton 1832, died 23 June, 1864. See *Manchester School Reg.*, iii. 104. **[31]**

Little, Andrew George, 2s. Thomas, of Marsh Gibbon, Bucks, cler. BALLIOL COLL., matric. 17 Oct., 1882, aged 19; B.A. 1887.

Little, Bryan Padgett Gregson, 1s. Samuel, of Stewart's Town, co. Tyrone, gent. ST. EDMUND HALL, matric. 16 Jan., 1833, aged 20.

Little, Charles Hardy (B.A. TRINITY COLL., Dublin, 1867), 9s. John, of Stewartstown, co. Tyrone, gent. Incorp. from ST. EDMUND HALL, 20 April, 1870, aged 24; M.A. 1874, perp. curate of St. John's, Peasedown, 1874-6.

Little, Edgar Hutchinson, 4s. Charles, of London, arm. BRASENOSE COLL., matric. 8 June, 1855, aged 17; scholar 1855-9, B.A. 1859, M.A. 1869, of the Indian Civil Service 1855, bar.-at-law, Middle Temple, 1871, died in 1874 or Feb., 1875. See Foster's *Men at the Bar*. **[35]**

Little, Ernest Knightley, 1s. George Arthur Knightley (formerly Howman), of Mitcham, Surrey, arm. MAGDALEN COLL., matric. 28 Jan., 1879, aged 18; B.A. 1882, of Newbold Pacey Hall, co. Warwick, J.P.

Little, Rev. Frederick Scratton, o.s. Augustus, of Marylebone, Middlesex, arm. TRINITY COLL., matric. 28 April, 1842, aged 17; B.A. 1846, M.A. 1848, died 5 April, 1865.

Little, George Arthur Knightley, 1s. George Ernest (formerly Howman), of Sonning, Berks, cler. BALLIOL COLL., matric. 27 May, 1841, aged 18; B.A. 1846, of Newbold Pacey Hall, co. Warwick, bar.-at-law, Inner Temple, 1849, changed his name to LITTLE, assistant manager Bank of England at Hull, died 26 Nov., 1879. See *Eton School Lists.*

Little, Rev. George Caruthers, 8s. John Caruthers, of Boston, co. Lincoln, arm. NON-COLL., matric. 29 Jan., 1878, aged 19; exhibitioner BALLIOL COLL. 1879-82, B.A. 1882, M.A. 1884.

Little, George Ernest, s. Arthur Howman, of Bristow, Surrey, cler. BALLIOL COLL., matric. 17 March, 1815, aged 17; B.A. 1818, M.A. 1821, of Newbold Pacey Hall, co. Warwick, assumed the name of LITTLE in lieu of his patronymic, master of St. Nicholas Hospital, Salisbury, 1824, vicar of Sonning, Berks, 1822-41, rector of Barnesley, co. Gloucester, 1841-74, hon. canon Bristol 1845-74, died 3 Aug., 1878.

Little, Henry Walmsley, 1s. Henry Walmsley, of London, gent. NEW COLL., matric. 18 Oct., 1875, aged 22; B.Mus. 1877, D.Mus. 1885.

Little, James Brooke, 2s. Robert Davis, of Chippenham, Wilts, arm. CHRIST CHURCH, matric. 15 Oct., 1869, aged 19; exhibitioner 1869-72, B.A. 1874, bar.-at-law, Inner Temple, 1876. See Foster's *Men at the Bar.* **[5]**

Little, John, 2s. William, of Westwood, Wilts, gent. MAGDALEN HALL., matric. 17 Nov., 1824, aged 24; B.A. 1832.

Little, John Brace, 1s. John, of Worcester (city), gent. BRASENOSE COLL., matric. 8 March, 1832, aged 20.

Little, John David George, o.s. Henry Alexander, of Blackrock, co. Dublin, arm. MERTON COLL., matric. 21 Oct., 1886, aged 18.

Little, Joseph, s. Joseph, of Bristol, Somerset, gent. PEMBROKE COLL., matric. 20 Oct., 1769, aged 17.

Little, Joseph Edward, 1s. Joseph Russell, of Tonbridge, Kent, cler. LINCOLN COLL., matric. 18 Oct., 1879, aged 18; B.A. 1883, M.A. 1886. **[10]**

Little, Robert William, 2s. William John, of St. Luke's, Finsbury, London, doctor. ORIEL COLL., matric. 5 Dec., 1857, aged 18; B.A. 1861, a student of Lincoln's Inn 1860. See *St. Paul's School Reg.*, 317.

Little, Sydney Hamilton, 10s. John, of Donaghendry, co. Tyrone, Ireland, gent. EXETER COLL., matric. 5 Feb., 1869, aged 19; exhibitioner 1869-71, B.A. 1872, M.A. 1878, vicar of Hordle, Hants, 1875-7. See *Coll. Reg.*, 164.

Little, Thomas Palling, 2s. John, of Standish, co. Gloucester, arm. TRINITY COLL., matric. 9 March, 1837, aged 19; B.A. 1841, M.A. 1843, vicar of Pauntley and Oxenhall, co. Gloucester, 1848-83, and of Edge since 1883.

Little, William, 1s. Robert, of Glasgow, gent. PEMBROKE COLL., matric. 2 Nov., 1838, aged 25.

Little, William, 1s. Francis, of Manchester, gent. CORPUS CHRISTI COLL., matric. 23 Oct., 1867, aged 19; scholar 1867-71, fellow 1871, B.A. 1872, M.A. 1874, lecturer and tutor 1870-83, librarian 1874, dean 1875, proctor 1879, vice president 1883, bar.-at-law, Lincoln's Inn, 1884. See Foster's *Men at the Bar.* **[15]**

Littledale, Charles Edward, 2s. Arthur, of Mymensing, East Indies, gent. QUEEN'S COLL., matric. 23 Oct., 1862, aged 19; B.A. 1868, M.A. 1869, vicar of St. Giles-in-the-Wood, Devon, 1870-8, and of Harpford since 1878.

Littledale, Charles Richard, 1s. Charles, of Marylebone, London, arm. CHRIST CHURCH, matric. 16 May, 1825, aged 18; student 1825-35, B.A. 1830, M.A. 1831, of Scarlets, Berks, J.P., bar.-at-law, Lincoln's Inn, 1833. See Foster's *Men at the Bar & Alumni West.*, 495.

Littledale, George Henry, o.s. George, of Liverpool, arm. BRASENOSE COLL., matric. 15 June, 1843, aged 18.

Littledale, Godfrey Armytage, 2s. Henry Anthony, of Bolton-by-Bolland, Yorks, arm. BRASENOSE COLL., matric. 5 June, 1873, aged 18; B.A. 1877, M.A. 1880, vicar of Chipping Norton, Oxon, 1886.

Littledale, Harold, 1s. Harold, of Liscard, near Wallasea, Cheshire, gent. CHRIST CHURCH, matric. 13 Oct., 1865, aged 19. **[20]**

Littledale, Henry Anthony, 1s. Anthony, of Liverpool, arm. BRASENOSE COLL., matric. 3 Nov., 1828, aged 18; B.A. 1840, M.A. 1842, of Bolton Hall, Lancashire, J.P., D.L., bar.-at-law, Inner Temple, 1842, died 6 July, 1859. See *Eton School Lists.*

Littledale, John, s. Henry, of Whitehaven, Cumberland, gent. QUEEN'S COLL., matric. 12 Oct., 1763, aged 16; B.A. 1769.

Littledale, Richard Frederick, scholar of TRINITY COLL., Dublin, 1852 (B.A. 1855, M.A. 1858, LL.B. & LL.D. 1862); adm. 'comitatis causa' 5 July, 1862, the controversialist and liturgical writer.

Littledale, William Dawson, 2s. Anthony, of Liverpool, arm. BRASENOSE COLL., matric. 26 May, 1831, aged 19; B.Mus. 1833.

Littledale, Willoughby Aston, 4s. Henry Anthony, of Bolton-by-Bolland, Yorks, arm. EXETER COLL., matric. 3 June, 1876, aged 18; B.A. 1879, M.A. 1884. **[25]**

Littlehales, Bendall, 1s. Bendall, of Plymouth, Devon, arm. ORIEL COLL., matric. 26 June, 1821, aged 17; B.A. 1825, J.P. Dorset, died 4 Oct., 1880. See Foster's *Baronetage*, BAKER.

Littlehales, Charles, s. John, of Winchester (city), doctor. NEW COLL., matric. 28 Feb., 1804, aged 20; fellow until 1815, B.C.L. 1810, B. & D.Med. 1820, physician Winchester Hospital, died 9 Feb., 1868, father of John Charles. See Munk's *Roll*, iii. 97.

Littlehales, John, s. John, of Bridgenorth, Salop, arm. PEMBROKE COLL., matric. 16 Oct., 1771, aged 17; B.A. 1775, M.A. 1778, B. & D.Med. 1782, F.R.C.P. 1787, physician Winchester Hospital, died 2 Jan., 1810 (monument in Winchester Cathedral), father of Richard 1805. See Munk's *Roll*, ii. 372.

Littlehales, Rev. John Charles, 1s. Charles, of St. Michael's, Winchester, D.Med. NEW COLL., matric. 10 Jan., 1839, aged 19; fellow 1838, until his death 6 Nov., 1843.

Littlehales, Joseph Gascoyne, s. Joseph Lawrence, of Clerkenwell, London, doctor. BRASENOSE COLL., matric. 25 June, 1793, aged 18; B.A. 1797, M.A. 1800, rector of Condecote, co. Gloucester, 1799, vicar of Little Bishop's Langham, Norfolk, 1814, rector of Shalstone, Bucks, 1821, and of Lillingstone Dayrell, 1848, until his death 2 June, 1854, father of Thomas 1819. See Foster's *Baronetage*, BAKER. **[30]**

Littlehales, Richard, s. John, of Winchester (city), doctor. NEW COLL., matric. 27 Feb., 1805, aged 18; B.A. 1809, fellow until 1813.

Littlehales, Thomas, 1s. Joseph Gascoyne, of Ambroseden, Oxon, cler. CHRIST CHURCH, matric. 21 May, 1819, aged 18; student 1819-45, B.A. 1823, M.A. 1826, vicar of Butler's Marston, co. Warwick, 1834-43, rector of Sheering 1834, until his death 19 April, 1849. See *Alumni West.*, 485.

Littlehales, Walter Gough, 4s. Charles, of St. Michael's, Winchester, Hants, gent. NEW COLL., matric. 12 Dec., 1854, aged 18; B.A. 1859, M.A. 1861, rector of Balvan, Essex, 1870.

Littlehales, William, 3s. Bendall Robert, of Swainswick, Somerset, arm. EXETER COLL., matric. 16 April, 1825, aged 18; B.A. 1829, M.A. 1846, vicar of Compton Bishop, Devon, 1848-79. See Foster's *Baronetage*, BAKER.

Littlejohn, David Harrower, 1s. David Stewart, of Broughty Ferry, near Dundee, gent. QUEEN'S COLL., matric. 27 Oct., 1869, aged 18; B.A. 1874, M.A. 1876.

Littleton, Cecil James, 5s. Edward Richard, Baron Hatherton. CHRIST CHURCH, matric. 16 Oct., 1868, aged 18; B.A. & M.A. 1874, vicar of Penkridge, co. Stafford, since 1880. See Foster's *Peerage* & *Eton School Lists.*

Littleton, Edward John, s. Moreton Walhouse, of Camberwell, Surrey, arm. BRASENOSE COLL., matric. 27 Jan., 1809, aged 17; created D.C.L. 18 June, 1817, a student of Lincoln's Inn 1810, M.P. co. Stafford 1812-35, P.C. England and Ireland, secretary for Ireland 1833-4, assumed the surname of LITTLETON in lieu of WALHOUSE by royal licence 23 July, 1812, created Baron Hatherton 11 May, 1835, died 4 May, 1863. See Foster's *Peerage* & *Rugby School Reg.*, 93.

Littleton, Edward Richard, 1s. Edward John, of Penkridge, co. Stafford, arm. (after baron). CHRIST CHURCH, matric. 14 May, 1834, aged 18; 2nd Baron Hatherton, M.P. Walsall 1847-52, South Stafford 1853-7. See Foster's *Peerage* & *Eton School Lists.*

Littleton, Hon. Henry Stuart, 3s. Edward Richard, Baron Hatherton. CHRIST CHURCH, matric. 19 Jan., 1864, aged 19. See Foster's *Peerage.* **[5]**

Littleton, Rev. Hugh, s. Thomas, of Trewin, Cornwall, gent. PEMBROKE COLL., matric. 27 Nov., 1789, aged 13; B.A. 1796, M.A. 1797, fellow until 1812, died in 1830.

Littleton, Richard Duppa, s. Littleton Duppa, of Wellington, Salop, pleb. JESUS COLL., matric. 10 Nov., 1752, aged 18; B.A. 1756, assumed the additional name of LITTLETON.

Littleton, Thomas, s. Richard, of Wellington, Salop, pleb. CHRIST CHURCH, matric. 28 April, 1722, aged 17; B.A. 18 Feb., 1725-6.

Littleton, Thomas, s. Hugh, of St. Germans, Cornwall, gent. EXETER COLL., matric. 3 April, 1734, aged 17; B.A. 1737.

Littleton, Hon. William Francis (C.M.G.), 4s. Edward Richard, Baron Hatherton. CHRIST CHURCH, matric. 27 April, 1866, aged 18; B.A. 1870, M.A. 1872, bar.-at-law, Inner Temple, 1872, C.M.G. 21 April, 1880. See Foster's *Men at the Bar* & *Eton School Lists.*

Littlewood, Alfred Samuel, 2s. Samuel, of Devizes, Wilts, cler. TRINITY COLL., matric. 23 March, 1848, aged 20; B.A. 1852, M.A. 1854, rector of Turnworth 1862, and of Winterbourne-Strickland 1885. **[11]**

Littlewood, Alfred Sidney, o.s. Alfred Samuel, of Turnsworth, Dorset, cler. UNIVERSITY COLL., matric. 18 Oct., 1886, aged 19; scholar 1886.

Littlewood, Rev. Benjamin Campbell, 2s. Benjamin, of Stourbridge, co. Worcester, arm. BRASENOSE COLL., matric. 23 May, 1872, aged 18; B.A. 1876, M.A. 1879.

Littlewood, Elijah Harrison, 4s. Samuel, of Edington, Wilts, cler. TRINITY COLL., matric. 12 Oct., 1861, aged 19; B.A. 1864, M.A. 1868, vicar of St. Augustine, Wisbech, 1876-83, and of All Saints, Newmarket, since 1883.

Littlewood, Henry Charles, 1s. Benjamin, of Alswinford, co. Worcester, arm. BRASENOSE COLL., matric. 20 May, 1869, aged 18; B.A. 1875, M.A. 1876, of the Hyde, co. Stafford, vicar of Goring, Berks, since 1885. See *Rugby School Reg.* **[15]**

Littlewood, James Lawrence, 2s. Samuel, of Edington, Wilts, cler. TRINITY COLL., matric. 22 May, 1858, aged 19; B.A. 1861, M.A. 1864, held various curacies 1863-78.

Littlewood, John, 3s. Samuel, of Edington, Wilts, cler. NON-COLL., matric. 25 Oct., 1869, aged 29; commoner EXETER COLL. 1870, B.A. 1872, M.A. 1876, held various curacies 1872-82, vicar of Ixworth, Suffolk, 1882.

Littlewood, Thomas Henry, 2s. William Edensor, of Hipperholme, Yorks, cler. CORPUS CHRISTI COLL., matric. 27 Oct., 1881, aged 19; exhibitioner 1881-2, scholar 1882-6, B.A. 1886.

Litton, Edward Arthur, 1s. Edward, of St. George's, Dublin, arm. BALLIOL COLL., matric. 6 April, 1832, aged 18, B.A. 1835; fellow ORIEL COLL. 1836-44, M.A. 1840, math. lecturer 1841, dean 1843, vice-principal St. Edmund Hall 1851-4, Bampton lecturer 1856, rector of St. Clement's, Oxon, 1858-60, and of Naunton, co. Gloucester, 1860, a student of Gray's Inn 1829, migrated to Lincoln's Inn 1839.

Litton, George John Letablere, o.s. John Letablere, of Dublin, arm. ORIEL COLL., matric. 14 Dec., 1885, aged 18. **[20]**

Liveing, Rev. Henry George Downing, 2s. Edward, of London, gent. ST. EDMUND HALL, matric. 5 Feb., 1879, aged 17; B.A. 1882.

Livera, Frederick John de, 2s. Frederick, of Colombo, Isle of Ceylon, arm. CHRIST CHURCH, matric. 7 June, 1865, aged 18; a student of Lincoln's Inn 1866.

Livera, Gerald Frederick de, 1s. Frederick, of Maturoe, Isle of Ceylon, arm. EXETER COLL., matric. 19 Oct., 1861, aged 17; B.A. from CHARSLEY HALL 1866, bar.-at-law, Lincoln's Inn, 1867. See Foster's *Men at the Bar.*

Livesay, John, s. William, of Halifax, Yorks, pleb. BRASENOSE COLL., matric. 3 April, 1718, aged 19; B.A. 1721.

Livesey, Ralph, s. William, of Blackburn, Lancashire, arm. ORIEL COLL., matric. 25 Feb., 1746-7, aged 18; of Livesey Hall, Lancashire, a governor of Blackburn Grammar School 1747, buried in Blackburn Church 9 Oct., 1766. **[25]**

Livesay, William, s. Charles, of Rushden, Northants, cler. BALLIOL COLL., matric. 22 Oct., 1716, aged 19; B.A. 12 March, 1718-19; M.A. from MAGDALEN HALL 1721.

Livesey, Harold, 2s. Thomas, of Knotty Ash, Lancashire, gent. NON-COLL., matric. 17 Oct., 1885, aged 19.

Livesey, John Cort, 1s. Thomas Alexander, of Worthen, Salop, cler. WORCESTER COLL., matric. 25 Jan., 1884, aged 19; B.A. 1887.

Livesey, Joseph, s. Thomas, of Manchester, Lancashire, arm. MAGDALEN COLL., matric. 28 June, 1794, aged 18.

Livesey, Robert, s. James, of Blackburn, Lancashire, arm. ST. ALBAN HALL, matric. 15 Nov., 1748, aged 17. **[30]**

Livesey, William Baldwin, 1s. William Harrison, of Stratford, gent. NON-COLL., matric. 18 Oct., 1880, aged 19.

Livett, John, s. Richard, of Potton, Beds, gent. BALLIOL COLL., matric. 28 Dec., 1747, aged 17; B.A. 1751, M.A. 1754.

Livingston, Henry Beekman, 1s. Henry Beekman, of New York, arm. CHRIST CHURCH, matric. 16 Oct., 1874, aged 20.

Livingston, Thomas Gott, 2s. James, of London, arm. MAGDALEN HALL, matric. 3 Feb., 1848, aged 18; B.A. 1852, M.A. 1854, minor canon Carlisle 1855-73, precentor 1855-8, vicar of Addingham, Cumberland, 1873.

Livingston, Warren, o.s. Robert Jay, of New York City, North America, gent. WORCESTER COLL., matric. 26 Oct., 1852, aged 18; B.A. 1856. **[35]**

Livingstone, Arthur Guinness, 5s. William, of Westport, co. Mayo, Ireland, gent. QUEEN'S COLL., matric. 26 Nov., 1861, aged 20; B.A. 1864, M.A. 1867, vicar of Forthampton, co. Gloucester, 1874-7, and of Mildenhall, Suffolk, 1877.

Livingstone, David, created D.C.L. 24 June, 1857, fellow of Royal Geographical Society (Victoria medal 1855), a licentiate of the Faculty of Physicians and Surgeons in Scotland 1838, African missionary and explorer 1840, until his death at Ulalu 1 May, 1873, buried in Westminster Abbey.

Livingstone, George Frederick James Fenton-, 4s. Thomas Livingstone, of Edinburgh, arm. MERTON COLL., matric. 18 Oct., 1880, aged 20.

Livingstone, Robert George, 4s. William, of Westport, co. Mayo, Ireland, gent. PEMBROKE COLL., matric. 15 May, 1856, aged 18; scholar ORIEL COLL. 1856-60, B.A. 1860, M.A. 1863, fellow PEMBROKE COLL. 1866, tutor 1864, junior dean 1866, sub-dean 1872, chaplain 1882, curate of St. Mary the Virgin 1863-7.

Livius, Henry George, 1s. Henry Samuel, of St. Augustine's, Bristol (city), cler. ST. EDMUND HALL, matric. 27 June, 1839, aged 17; exhibitioner 1839-43, B.A. 1844, M.A. 1848, rector of Keinton-Mandeville, Somerset, 1851, until his death 5 March, 1878.

Livius, Peter, created D.C.L. 24 March, 1775 (s. Peter Livius, of Lisbon, merchant), bar.-at-law, Middle Temple, 1775, as of Portsmouth, New Hampshire, New England, appointed a judge of Court of Common Pleas there by Judge Wentworth 1767, chief justice of Montreal 1775, created M.A. University of Cambridge, New England, died on his way to Brighton, 23 July, 1795.

Livius, Rev. Thomas Stiverd, 2s. Henry Samuel, of Clifton, co. Gloucester, cler. ORIEL COLL., matric. 3 June, 1846, aged 17; B.A. 1851, M.A. 1855. [5]

Livius, Rev. William Grinfield, 5s. Henry Samuel, of Clifton, near Bristol, co. Gloucester, cler. ST. EDMUND HALL, matric. 10 June, 1856, aged 19; B.A. 1860, M.A. 1867, died 21 Sep., 1877.

Llewellyn, Arthur James Cadwaladar, 1s. David, of Erchfont, near Devizes, Wilts, cler. QUEEN'S COLL., matric. 1 Dec., 1853, aged 20; B.A. 1857.

Lewellin, David Jones, 1s. Llewellyn, of Lampeter, co. Cardigan, D.C.L. JESUS COLL., matric. 19 June, 1852, aged 19.

Llewelin, Evan, s. Evan, of Swansea, co. Glamorgan, cler. JESUS COLL., matric. 28 March, 1724, aged 21.

Llewellin, Henry, s. Edward, of St. Fagan's, co. Glamorgan, gent. JESUS COLL., matric. 17 Dec., 1778, aged 17; B.A. 1782, M.A. 1785, B.D. 1793, rector of St. George's 1788, and of Michaelston-on-Ely with St. Bride's 1791, until his death 28 Dec., 1836. [10]

Llewellyn, Hopkin, 2s. Griffith, of Baglan, co. Glamorgan, gent. JESUS COLL., matric. 7 June, 1821, aged 20.

Llewelin, John, s. Evan, of Swansea, co. Glamorgan, cler. JESUS COLL., matric. 16 Nov., 1719, aged 17.

Llewelyn, John, s. John, of Cadoxton, co. Glamorgan, arm. ORIEL COLL., matric. 8 March, 1773, aged 17.

Llewellin, John, s. William, of Cardiff, co. Glamorgan, cler. JESUS COLL., matric. 26 Feb., 1798, aged 16; B.A. 1801, M.A. 1804.

Llewellin, John, 1s. John, of Rumney, co. Brecon, gent. JESUS COLL., matric. 10 May, 1826, aged 17; B.A. 1831, M.A. 1835, died curate of Wiveliscombe, Somerset, 28 Dec., 1869. [15]

Llewellin, John, 2s. William, of Haverfordwest, co. Pembroke, gent. BRASENOSE COLL., matric. 18 Oct., 1862, aged 18; B.A. 1867, vicar of Acaster-Selby, Yorks, 1871-3, chaplain royal navy 1873-9.

Llewellin, John Charles, 1s. John, of Llanedern, co. Glamorgan, cler. ST. JOHN'S COLL., matric. 16 Jan., 1875, aged 19; B.A. 1878, M.A. 1887.

Llewellyn, John Dillwyn, 1s. Lewis Weston Dillwyn, of Penllergare, co. Glamorgan, arm. ORIEL COLL., matric. 14 Dec., 1827, aged 17; of Penllergare, J.P., D.L., co. Glamorgan, high sheriff 1834, assumed the additional surname of LLEWELLYN, died 24 Aug., 1882.

Llewellyn, John Talbot Dillwyn, 1s. John Dillwyn, of Penllergare, near Swansea, co. Glamorgan, arm. CHRIST CHURCH, matric. 7 Dec., 1854, aged 18; B.A. 1858, M.A. 1861, of Penllergare and Ynisygerwn, co. Glamorgan, J.P., D.L., high sheriff 1887, a student of the Inner Temple 1859.

Llewellyn, John Harries, 1s. David, of Fonthill Bishop, Wilts, cler. QUEEN'S COLL., matric. 13 Nov., 1851, aged 19. [20]

Lewellin, Llewelyn, s. Richard, of Coyty, co. Glamorgan, gent. JESUS COLL., matric. 2 May, 1818, aged 19; scholar 1821-6, B.A. 1822, M.A. 1824, B.C.L. 1827, D.C.L. 1829, master of the schools 1825-6, principal of St. David's College, Lampeter, 1827-78, vicar of Lampeter, co. Cardigan, 1833, dean of St. David's 1840-78, died in Nov., 1878.

Llewelyn, Richard. MAGDALEN COLL., 1727. See LLUELLYN.

Llewellyn, Richard, s. Hopkin, of Margam, co. Glamorgan, gent. JESUS COLL., matric. 7 May, 1777, aged 17.

Llewellin, Richard, 1s. Richard, of Westbury, co. Gloucester, arm. UNIVERSITY COLL., matric. 1 July, 1819, aged 17; B.A. 1823, a student of Lincoln's Inn 1814.

Llewelyn, Thomas, s. John, of Neath, co. Glamorgan, pleb. JESUS COLL., matric. 1 April, 1717, aged 19. [25]

Llewellin, Thomas Johnes, 2s. William, of Abercorn, co. Monmouth, arm. UNIVERSITY COLL., matric. 26 Jan., 1881, aged 18; B.A. 1884.

Llewellin, William, s. John, of Peterstone-super-Eley, co. Glamorgan, gent. JESUS COLL., matric. 4 Nov., 1738, aged 19; B.A. 1742.

Llewellin, William, s. William, of Cardiff, co. Glamorgan, cler. JESUS COLL., matric. 26 March, 1773, aged 19; B.A. 1778.

Lewelyn, William, s. William, of Carmarthen (town), gent. ST. EDMUND HALL, matric. 22 May, 1781, aged 23.

Llewellyn, William, o.s. William, of Glennafon, co. Glamorgan, gent. MAGDALEN HALL, matric. 14 Jan., 1839, aged 18. [30]

Llewellyn, William, 1s. Llewellyn, of ——, co. Glamorgan, arm. EXETER COLL., matric. 14 Oct., 1861, aged 17.

Llewellin, William, 1s. William, of Mynyddsllesyn, co. Monmouth, arm. UNIVERSITY COLL., matric. 3 Nov., 1875, aged 19; B.A. 1879, bar.-at-law, Inner Temple, 1884. See Foster's *Men at the Bar.*

Llewellyn, William Mansel Dillwyn, 2s. John, of Penllergare, South Wales, arm. CHRIST CHURCH, matric. 4 June, 1857, aged 18. See *Eton School Lists.*

Lloyd, Alexander Ogilvie, 4s. George, of Thirsk, Yorks, arm. TRINITY COLL., matric. 3 Dec., 1851, aged 18; B.A. 1856, M.A. 1859, a student of Lincoln's Inn, 1857. See *Eton School Lists.* [34]

Lloyd, Alfred, 1s. Alfred, of Moseley, Birmingham, arm. WADHAM COLL., matric. 14 Oct., 1830, aged 18; scholar 1830-5, B.A. 1835, died 27 Dec., 1837. See Foster's *Our Noble and Gentle Families.*

Lloyd, Alfred Hart, 5s. George, of Cowesby, Yorks, arm. MERTON COLL., matric. 26 May, 1855, aged 17; scholar 1855-9, B.A. 1859. See Foster's *Lancashire Collection* & *Eton School Lists.*

Lloyd, Arthur, 'joyner'; privilegiatus 15 Oct., 1733.

Lloyd, Arthur Brooke, 3s. Bartholomew of Dublin, arm. BRASENOSE COLL., matric. 5 June, 1873, aged 17; B.A. 1877, B.C.L. 1880, bar.-at-law, Inner Temple, 1882. See Foster's *Men at the Bar.*

Lloyd, Arthur Gittins, 4s. John, of Newbridge, co. Denbigh, gent. QUEEN'S COLL., matric. 22 Oct., 1883, aged 18; B.A. 1886.

Lloyd, Arthur Percy, 3s. James Richard, of London, NON-COLL., matric. 9 May, 1873, aged 20. [40]

Lloyd, Arthur Philip, 1s. Henry James, of St. James's, Westminster, cler. CHRIST CHURCH, matric. 22 Oct., 1851, aged 18; of Leaton Knolls, Salop, J.P. See *Eton School Lists.*

Lloyd, Arthur Thomas, 2s. Henry William, of Cholsey, near Wallingford, Berks, cler. ST. EDMUND HALL, matric. 24 Jan., 1863, aged 18; B.A. 1865, M.A. 1870, vicar of Aylesbury 1876-82, vicar and hon. canon of St. Nicholas Cathedral, Newcastle-on-Tyne, 1882.

Lloyd, Baldwyn, s. Henry, of Llangollen, co. Denbigh, cler. WADHAM COLL., matric. 7 April, 1781, aged 17; B.A. 1787.

Lloyd, Bartholomew Clifford (B.A. TRINITY COLL., Dublin, 1828, M.A. 1832, LL.B. & LL.D. 1843), 2s. Bartholomew, of Dublin, D.D. incorp. from ST. JOHN'S COLL., 4 March, 1841, aged 30; M.A. 1865, of Losset, co. Cavan, bar.-at-law, King's Inns, Dublin, Q.C., died 28 April, 1872. See Foster's *Our Noble and Gentle Families.*

Lloyd, Benjamin, s. Howard, of Northop, Flint, arm. JESUS COLL., matric. 13 July, 1770, aged 18; B.A. 1774. **[5]**

Lloyd, Charles, s. David, of Llandevathew, co. Brecon, cler. JESUS COLL., matric. 21 Sep., 1742, aged 18; B.A. 1746, brother of Francis 1749.

Lloyd, Charles, s. Philip, of St. Martin's, Westminster, arm. CHRIST CHURCH, matric. 18 June, 1754, aged 19; student 1754, B.A. 1758, M.A. 1761, (? receiver-general and paymaster of the band of gentleman pensioners 1761), deputy teller of the exchequer 1767, until his death, 22 Jan., 1773. See *Alumni West.*, 362.

Lloyd, Charles, s. Thomas, of Bradenham, Bucks, cler. CHRIST CHURCH, matric. 4 Feb., 1803, aged 18; B.A. 1806, M.A. 1809, B.D. 1818, D.D. 1821, student 1804-22, censor 1820, a canon 1822-7, and regius professor of divinity 1822-9, preacher at Lincoln's Inn 1819, vicar of Bersted, Sussex, bishop of Oxford 1827, until his death 31 May, 1829, buried in the benchers' vault under the chapel of Lincoln's Inn. See *Eton School Lists.*

Lloyd, Charles, 3s. John, of Llandyssil, co. Cardigan, gent. JESUS COLL., matric. 25 May, 1825, aged 18; B.A. 1829, M.A. 1835.

Lloyd, Charles, o.s. Charles, of Kensington, Middlesex, arm. CHRIST CHURCH, matric. 10 Oct., 1827, aged 18; B.A. 1831, hon. canon 1868, rector of Hampden with Kimble 1840-59, and of Chalfont, St. Giles, Bucks, 1859, until his death 29 April, 1883.

Lloyd, Rev. Charles, o.s. Charles, bishop of Oxford. CHRIST CHURCH, matric. 21 April, 1841, aged 17; student 1841-62, B.A. 1845, M.A. 1847, tutor 1855, died 27 April, 1862. **[11]**

Lloyd, Charles, 1s. Charles, of Bettwys, co. Cardigan, cler. ORIEL COLL., matric. 13 April, 1869, aged 18; B.A. 1873, M.A. 1879, of Waunifor, co. Cardigan, J.P., high sheriff 1882.

Lloyd, Charles Corpe, 1s. William, of Barnet, Herts, arm. UNIVERSITY COLL., matric. 25 Jan., 1827, aged 18; bar.-at-law, Middle Temple, 1839. See Foster's *Men at the Bar.*

Lloyd, (Sir) Charles Cornwallis (Bart.), s. Charles, of Ludlow, Salop, baronet. CHRIST CHURCH, matric. 10 June, 1721, aged 15; 2nd baronet, a student of Lincoln's Inn 1720, died 25 Feb., 1729.

Lloyd, Charles Francis, 5s. John Ambrose, of Chester, gent. NEW COLL., matric. 5 Feb., 1877, aged 24; B.Mus. 17 Dec., 1878. **[15]**

Lloyd, Charles Harford, 6s. Edmund, of Thornbury, near Bristol, arm. MAGDALEN HALL, matric. 17 Oct., 1868, aged 19; scholar 1868, B.Mus. 1871, B.A. 1872, M.A. (HERTFORD COLL.) 1875, organist of Gloucester 1876-82, and of Christ Church 1882.

Lloyd, Clement Elphinstone, 1s. Morgan, of London, gent. ST. JOHN'S COLL., matric. 15 Oct., 1870, aged 19; B.A. 1874, bar.-at-law, Inner Temple, 1876. See Foster's *Men at the Bar.*

Lloyd, Clifford Bartholomew, 1s. Bartholomew Clifford, of St. Peter's, Dublin, gent. LINCOLN COLL., matric. 22 Oct., 1864, aged 19; B.A. 1871, of the Castle Killiney, co. Dublin, and of Losset, co. Cavan. See Foster's *Our Noble and Gentle Families.*

Lloyd, Clopton, s. Thomas, of Guildsfield, co. Montgomery, arm. TRINITY COLL., matric. 19 March, 1776, aged 16.

Lloyd, Daniel, s. William, of Laques, co. Carmarthen, arm. BALLIOL COLL., matric. 17 Dec., 1753, aged 17; of Laques aforesaid, high sheriff, co. Cardigan, 1760, bar.-at-law, Lincoln's Inn, 1759, died in 1792. **[20]**

Lloyd, Daniel, 2s. David, of Llandegai, co. Carnarvon, gent. JESUS COLL., matric. 27 Oct., 1868, aged 22; scholar 1869-73, B.A. 1872, M.A. 1886, vicar of Llandrygarn, Anglesey, since 1877.

Lloyd, Rev. Daniel Lewis, 2s. John, of Llanarth, co. Cardigan, gent. JESUS COLL., matric. 19 June, 1862, aged 18; scholar 1864-7, B.A. 1867, M.A. 1871, head-master of Dolgelly School 1867-72, of Friars School, Bangor, 1873-8, and of Christ's College, Brecon, 1878.

Lloyd, David, s. David, of Lledrod, co. Cardigan, gent. JESUS COLL., matric. 3 April, 1723, aged 16.

Lloyd, David, s. William, of Lureingfraid (*sic*), co. Montgomery, gent. JESUS COLL., matric. 8 April, 1728, aged 20; B.C.L. 18 March, 1734-5.

Lloyd, David, s. Edward, of Llanelian, co. Denbigh, pleb. JESUS COLL., matric. 11 Nov., 1731, aged 17; B.A. 5 March, 1735-6. **[25]**

Lloyd, David, s. David, of Llandyssil, co. Cardigan, gent. JESUS COLL., matric. 4 April, 1734, aged 16.

Lloyd, David, s. Richard, of Bettwys, co. Denbigh, pleb. JESUS COLL., matric. 12 May, 1735, aged 19.

Lloyd, David, B.A. from JESUS COLL. 20 Feb., 1738-9.

Lloyd, David, s. Edmund, of Maentwrog, co. Merioneth, pleb. JESUS COLL., matric. 30 May, 1754, aged 18; B.A. 1758.

Lloyd, David, s. Morgan, of Hay, co. Brecon, pleb. JESUS COLL., matric. 4 April, 1759, aged 19; B.A. 1763. **[30]**

Lloyd, David, s. David, of Llangwm, co. Denbigh, gent. CHRIST CHURCH, matric. 30 March, 1765, aged 19.

Lloyd, David, s. Llewellyn, of Cilcinnin, co. Cardigan, gent. JESUS COLL., matric. 11 June, 1765, aged 28 (B.A. 1778, M.A. 1780, D.C.L. 1783).

Lloyd, David, s. Rees, of Llangorse, co. Brecon, gent. PEMBROKE COLL., matric. 22 Oct., 1801, aged 25.

Lloyd, David, 4s. James, of Tynllyn, co. Cardigan, gent. KEBLE COLL., matric. 17 Oct., 1882, aged 21.

Lloyd, David Maurice, s. Maurice, of Llandervale, co. Merioneth, gent. HERTFORD COLL., matric. 15 May, 1793, aged 20; B.A. 1797, M.A. 1799, curate of Doddington, and after of Wichling and Kingsdowne, Kent, died 14 Oct., 1848. **[35]**

Lloyd, Rev. Edgar, 2s. Alfred, of Goldicote Alderminster, co. Warwick, arm. MERTON COLL., matric. June, 1834, aged 18; postmaster 1834-8, B.A. 1838, brother of Alfred 1830. See Foster's *Our Noble and Gentle Families.*

Lloyd, Edmund, s. Watkin, of Cardiff, co. Glamorgan, gent. JESUS COLL., matric. 6 Nov., 1724, aged 17.

Lloyd, Edward, s. Richard, of Oswestry, Salop, gent. JESUS COLL., matric. 27 May, 1717, aged 19, a student of Middle Temple 1717.

Lloyd, Edward, s. Edward, of John Baptist, Hereford (city), pleb. QUEEN'S COLL., matric. 29 April, 1725, aged 18.

Lloyd, Edward, s. John, of Llanwddyn, co. Montgomery, gent. JESUS COLL., matric. 22 March, 1726-7, aged 20; B.A. 1730.

Lloyd, Edward, s. John, of Llangollen, co. Denbigh, arm. JESUS COLL., matric. 18 Feb., 1752, aged 19.

Lloyd, Edward, s. John, of Llangurig, co. Montgomery, gent. JESUS COLL., matric. 4 June, 1767, aged 19; B.A. from BRASENOSE COLL. 1771, M.A. 1775.

Lloyd, Edward (Kenyon). CHRIST CHURCH, 1790. See WILLIAMS.

Lloyd-Edwards, Edward. ORIEL COLL. 1790. See EDWARDS. [5]

Lloyd, Edward, s. John, of Ruthin, co. Denbigh, arm. BRASENOSE COLL., matric. 10 May, 1796, aged 17; B.A. 1800, M.A. 1807 (? bar.-at-law, Gray's Inn, 1802). See *Alumni West.*, 436.

Lloyd, Edward, s. Edward, of Prescot, Lancashire, cler. BRASENOSE COLL., matric. 20 April, 1803, aged 17; B.A. 1807.

Lloyd, Rev. Edward, s. Thomas, of Bradenham, Bucks, cler. CHRIST CHURCH, matric. 12 May, 1810, aged 19; B.A. 1814, M.A. 1817, sometime of Peterley House, Bucks, died 10 Feb., 1850. See *Eton School Lists.*

Lloyd, Edward Honoratus, 2s. Horace, of Hawarden, Flints, arm. TRINITY COLL., matric. 31 May, 1879, aged 19; B.A. 1882, M.A. 1888, a student of Middle Temple 1878.

Lloyd, Edward Lewis, 8s. Ellis, of Ruthin, co. Denbigh, gent. JESUS COLL., matric. 16 Jan., 1869, aged 19; B.A. 1872, vicar of Carno, co. Montgomery, 1882-5, and of Dylife 1885. [10]

Lloyd, Edward Mostyn. CHRIST CHURCH, 1813. See MOSTYN.

Lloyd, Edward Owen Vaughan, 1s. Edward, of Llandyrnog, co. Denbigh, arm. NON-COLL., matric. 20 Jan., 1877, aged 19; commoner NEW INN HALL 1877, B.A. 1886, M.A. from BALLIOL COLL. 1887, of Rhagatt, co. Merioneth, and of Berth, co. Denbigh. See *Eton School Lists.*

Lloyd, Ernest Thomas, 3s. William Butter, of Monkmoor, near Salisbury, arm. CHRIST CHURCH, matric. 10 Oct., 1879, aged 19; exhibitioner 1879-82, B.A. 1884, of the Indian Civil Service 1879, a student of Middle Temple 1879.

Lloyd, Evan, s. John, of Llanycil, co. Merioneth, gent. JESUS COLL., matric. 22 March, 1750-1, aged 16; B.A. 1754, M.A. 1757 (? died vicar of Llanfair in 1775).

Lloyd, Evan, 1s. Thomas, of Troedyraur, co. Cardigan, gent. JESUS COLL., matric. 25 Oct., 1862, aged 20; B.A. 1868, M.A. 1871, held various curacies 1868-82, vicar of Bettws 1882. [15]

Lloyd, Francis, s. Rowland, of Machynleth, co. Montgomery, pleb. JESUS COLL., matric. 30 May, 1715, aged 17.

Lloyd, Francis, s. Francis, of Llandyrnog, co. Denbigh, cler. JESUS COLL., matric. 21 March, 1716-7, aged 17; B.A. 1720.

Lloyd, Francis, s. Richard, of Llansillian, Anglesey, gent. JESUS COLL., matric. 17 March, 1723-4, aged 16; B.A. 1727, M.A. 1730, B.Med. 1737.

Lloyd, Francis, s. John, of Llandowror, co. Carmarthen, pleb. TRINITY COLL., matric. 6 March, 1740-1, aged 22; B.A. 14 March, 1744-5, M.A. 1756.

Lloyd, Francis, s. David, of Llanvathen, co. Brecon, cler. JESUS COLL., matric. 11 May, 1749, aged 18; B.A. 1755, brother of Charles 1742. [20]

Lloyd, Francis, s. Edward, of Shrewsbury (town), arm. TRINITY COLL., matric. 10 April, 1764, aged 16; created M.A. 28 Feb., 1769 (? of Leaton Knolls, Salop, a student of Inner Temple 1766, M.P. Montgomeryshire 1795, until his death 19 Feb., 1799, father of Francis, 1800).

Lloyd, Francis, s. Daniel of Llanstephan, co. Carmarthen, arm. JESUS COLL., matric. 26 March, 1779, aged 17; B.A. 1782, M.A. 1785, brother of William, 1779.

Lloyd, Francis, s. Francis, of Burton, co. Stafford, arm. CHRIST CHURCH, matric. 5 Feb., 1800, aged 18; (? of Leaton Knolls, Salop, died 14 July, 1814). See *Eton School Lists.*

Lloyd, Francis, s. Eusebius, of Silchester, Hants, cler. CHRIST CHURCH, matric. 24 March, 1814, aged 18; student 1817-22, B.A. 1818, M.A. 1820.

Lloyd, Francis Llewellyn, scholar of ST. JOHN'S COLL., Cambridge 1837, fellow 1840-58, B.A. 1840, M.A. 1843, B.D. 1850; adm. 'ad eundem' 21 June, 1860, curate of Wilnecote, Tamworth. [25]

Lloyd, Francis Montague, 1s. Francis, of Bombay, arm. CHRIST CHURCH, matric. 16 Oct., 1872, aged 18; B.A. 1876, bar.-at-law, Inner Temple, 1878. See Foster's *Men at the Bar.*

Lloyd, Francis Sackville. CHRIST CHURCH, 1781. See WHEATE.

Lloyd, Frederick, s. John, of Caerwys, co. Flint, gent. QUEEN'S COLL., matric. 6 Dec., 1749, aged 18; B.A. 1753, M.A. 1756.

Lloyd, Frederick Assheton, 3s. William Iremonger, of Beaumaris, arm. PEMBROKE COLL., matric. 13 June, 1835, aged 19; scholar 1835-42, B.A. 1839, M.A. 1842, assumed the surname of LLOYD in 1872, vicar of Bullington 1857, until his death 14 Nov., 1887.

Lloyd, George, s. George, of Alkrington, Lancashire, arm. HERTFORD COLL., matric. 28 Feb., 1766, aged 17; of Manchester and York, bar.-at-law, Middle Temple, 1776, died 12 Oct., 1804. See Foster's *Lancashire Collection.* [30]

Lloyd, George, s. John, of Snitterfield, co. Warwick, arm. CHRIST CHURCH, matric. 3 July, 1787, aged 18; of Welcombe House, co. Warwick, high sheriff 1806, died 11 July, 1831. See Foster's *Lancashire Collection.*

Lloyd, George, 1s. Thomas, of Albrighton, Salop, cler. ST. MARY HALL, matric. 23 Feb., 1826, aged 21, B.A. 1829; M.A. from ST. JOHN'S COLL. 1833, B.Med. 1834.

Lloyd, George Frederick, 1s. John Charles, of Ludlow, Salop, gent. CHRIST CHURCH, matric. 16 Oct., 1885, aged 19; exhibitioner 1885.

Lloyd, George Kyrwan Carr, o.s. Robert James Carr, bishop of Chichester. CHRIST CHURCH, matric. 14 June, 1828, aged 17; of Lancing Manor, Sussex, J.P., D.L., high sheriff, assumed the additional surname of LLOYD in 1858, died 15 June, 1877.

Lloyd, Griffith, s. David, of Dolgelly, co. Merioneth, pleb. JESUS COLL., matric. 29 Feb., 1731-2, aged 20; B.A. 1735. [35]

Lloyd, Griffith, s. David, of St. Lawrence Jewry, London, gent. UNIVERSITY COLL., matric. 6 March, 1738-9, aged 16.

Lloyd, Gryffydd, s. Bell, of Llanfyllyn, co. Montgomery, arm. CHRIST CHURCH, matric. 22 Oct., 1793, aged 18, B.A. 1797; fellow ALL SOULS' COLL. 1801-9, M.A. 1801, rector of Chrisleton, Cheshire, 1809, until his death 25 Jan., 1843. See Foster's *Peerage*, B. MOSTYN.

Lloyd, Hedd, s. Howel, of St. Asaph's, co. Denbigh, gent. JESUS COLL., matric. 22 March, 1744-5, aged 17; B.A. 1748, M.A. 1751.

Lloyd, Henry, s. Ambrose, of Ruthin, co. Denbigh, pleb. JESUS COLL., matric. 29 March, 1740, aged 20.

Lloyd, Henry, s. Robert, of Llansilin, co. Denbigh, pleb. JESUS COLL., matric. 13 March, 1745-6, aged 18; B.A. 1749. [40]

Lloyd, Henry, s. Erasmus, of Worcester (city), gent. MERTON COLL., matric. 3 May, 1782, aged 18; B.A. 1786, M.A. 1788, rector of St. Clement's, Worcester, died 23 April, 1793, 'in the prime of life.'

Lloyd, Henry, 1s. William, of Lampeter, co. Cardigan, gent. JESUS COLL., matric. 18 April, 1863, aged 18.

Lloyd, Henry Frederick, 1s. Horace Charles, of Exeter, arm. ORIEL COLL., matric. 16 April, 1880, aged 18.

Lloyd, Henry (William), of MAGDALEN COLL., Cambridge (B.A. 1831, M.A. 1834), adm. 'ad eundem' 14 June, 1860, vicar of Cholsey-cum-Moulsford, Berks, 1837.

Lloyd, (Sir) Herbert (Bart.), s. Walter, of Lampeter, co. Cardigan, arm. JESUS COLL., matric. 15 March, 1737-8, aged 18; of Peterwell, co. Cardigan, baronet, so created 26 Jan., 1763, bar.-at-law, Inner Temple, 1742, M.P. Cardigan 1761-8, died 19 Aug., 1769.

Lloyd, Herbert, s. Percival, of Foy, co. Hereford, gent. TRINITY COLL., matric. 31 Oct., 1778, aged 17. **[5]**

Lloyd, Hoel, s. Hoel, of St. Asaph's, co. Flint, gent. JESUS COLL., matric. 31 March, 1742, aged 18.

Lloyd, Howard Meuric, o.s. Howard, of Dominica, East Indies, gent. EXETER COLL., matric. 24 Jan., 1873, aged 19; B.A. 1876, M.A. 1881, bar.-at-law, Inner Temple, 1878. See Foster's *Men at the Bar.*

Lloyd, Howel William, 3s. Edward, of Corwen, co. Merioneth, arm. BALLIOL COLL., matric. 10 April, 1835, aged 18; scholar JESUS COLL. 1838-42, B.A. 1839, M.A. 1841, in holy orders, but seceded to Rome. See *Rugby School Reg.*, 167.

Lloyd, Hugh, s. Hugh, of Mold, co. Flint, gent. CHRIST CHURCH, matric. 4 Dec., 1804, aged 19.

Lloyd, Hugh, 2s. David, of Llanbadarn Trefeglwys, co. Cardigan, gent. JESUS COLL., matric. 17 Jan., 1820, aged 22; B.A. 1823. **[10]**

Lloyd, Rev. Hugh Francis, 1s. Charles Albert, of Rand, co. Lincoln, cler. KEBLE COLL., matric. 28 Jan., 1879, aged 19; B.A. 1882, M.A. 1887.

Lloyd, Hugh Norris, 5s. William, of Maentwrog, co. Merioneth, cler. JESUS COLL., matric. 24 Oct., 1839, aged 19; scholar 1842-6, B.A. 1843, M.A. 1846.

Lloyd, Humphrey, s. John, of Dolgelly, co. Merioneth, pleb. CHRIST CHURCH, matric. 6 Nov., 1782, aged 18; B.A. 1786, vicar of Llanvawn, co. Merioneth, 1819, until his death 2 Nov., 1843.

Lloyd, Humphrey, D.D. TRINITY COLL., Dublin, created D.C.L. 20 June, 1855 (son of Bartholomew, D.D., provost Trinity College, Dublin), scholar TRINITY COLL., Dublin, 1819, B.A. 1820, fellow 1824-67, M.A. 1827, B. & D.D. 1840, provost 1867-81, president of the Royal Irish Academy 1846, and of the British Association 1857, F.R.S., died s.p. 17 Jan., 1881. See Foster's *Our Noble and Gentle Families.*

Lloyd, Humphrey Wilmot (B.A. TRINITY COLL., Dublin), 3s. Bartholomew Clifford, of Dublin, gent. QUEEN'S COLL., incorp. 23 June, 1870, aged 22.

Lloyd, Iorwerth Grey, 1s. Henry Robert, of Carew, co. Pembroke, cler. EXETER COLL., matric. 16 Jan., 1864, aged 19; B.A. 1867, M.A. 1872, held various curacies 1868-79, vicar of Hersham, Surrey, 1879-83, of Wiston, co. Pembroke, 1883, and of Clarbeston 1885. **[15]**

Lloyd, Rev. Jacob Youde William, 1s. Jacob William Hinde, of Ulverstone, Lancashire, arm. WADHAM COLL., matric. 14 May, 1835, aged 18; B.A. 1839, M.A. 1874, of Clochfaen, co. Montgomery, knight of the Saviour of Greece, assumed the name of LLOYD in lieu of HINDE, died at Ventnor, 14 Oct., 1887, aged 70.

Lloyd, James, s. James, of Lancing, Sussex, arm. UNIVERSITY COLL., matric. 5 Oct., 1737, aged 18; of Lancing, a student of Inner Temple 1737, died 16 March, 1798, father of James Martin.

Lloyd, James, s. Thomas, of Bronwydd, co. Cardigan, arm. BRASENOSE COLL., matric. 19 Oct., 1813, aged 18.

Lloyd, James David, s. John, of Pembroke (town), arm. JESUS COLL., matric. 21 June, 1806, aged 19; B.A. 1810, scholar 1812-14, M.A. 1813. **[20]**

Lloyd, (Sir) James Martin (Bart.), s. James, of Lancing, Sussex, arm. UNIVERSITY COLL., matric. 28 Jan., 1780, aged 17; of Lancing, baronet, so created 30 Sep., 1831, M.P. Steyning 1790-1, 1791-2, 1796-1806, 1806-18, Shoreham 1818-26, died 24 Oct., 1844.

Lloyd, James Martin Carr, 1s. George, of Brighton, Sussex, arm. MERTON COLL., matric. 10 April, 1869, aged 19; of Lancing Manor, Sussex, J.P. See *Eton School Lists.*

Lloyd, John, s. John, of Abergele, co. Denbigh, gent. JESUS COLL., matric. 4 April, 1715, aged 18 (? B.A. 17 Feb., 1718-19, M.A. 1722, B.D. 26 Feb., 1729-30).

Lloyd, John, s. Humphrey, of Llangeler, co. Montgomery, gent. JESUS COLL., matric. 29 Nov., 1715, aged 14 (? B.A. 1719).

Lloyd, John, s. William, of Newbery, Berks, cler. PEMBROKE COLL., matric. 6 March, 1717-8, aged 17; B.A. 26 Jan., 1721-2. **[25]**

Lloyd, John, s. Thomas, of Beaumaris, Isle of Anglesey, pleb. JESUS COLL., matric. 16 March, 1720-1, aged 18; B.A. 1724, M.A. 1727.

Lloyd, John, s. Morgan, of St. Martin's, Westminster, gent. JESUS COLL., matric. 1 March, 1721-2, aged 18.

Lloyd, John, s. John, of Mold, co. Flint, gent. JESUS COLL., matric. 9 May, 1722, aged 18.

Lloyd, John, B.A. from JESUS COLL. 14 Oct., 1725, M.A. 6 July, 1728.

Lloyd, John, s. Thomas, of Llanfair, co. Montgomery, pleb. JESUS COLL., matric. 20 March, 1724-5, aged 20. **[30]**

Lloyd, John, s. William, of Hartlebury, co. Worcester, cler. CHRIST CHURCH, matric. 3 Dec., 1725, aged 16; B.A. 1729, M.A. 1732.

Lloyd, John, s. Thomas, of Llanwgohllyn (*sic*), co. Merioneth, pleb. JESUS COLL., matric. 28 March, 1726, aged 19; B.A. from ST. EDMUND HALL 1730.

Lloyd, John, s. John, of St. Mildred's, Poultry, London, gent. ST. JOHN'S COLL., matric. 30 June, 1731, aged 17; B.A. 1735, M.A. 1738, B.D. 1745, D.D. 1756, proctor 1744, vicar of Stow Nine Churches 1754, and of Heyford, Northants, 1764, died 31 Dec., 1788. See *Robinson*, 55.

Lloyd, John, s. Edward, of Nantglyn, co. Denbigh, pleb. JESUS COLL., matric. 15 Dec., 1732, aged 19; B.A. 1736.

Lloyd, John, s. Walter, of Peterwell, co. Cardigan, arm. JESUS COLL., matric. 16 April, 1735, aged 17; bar.-at-law, Inner Temple, 1739 (? a commissioner of bankrupts), died 1790, brother of Herbert, 15 March, 1737-8. **[35]**

Lloyd, John, pleb. JESUS COLL., matric. 24 May, 1737.

Lloyd, John, s. Richard, of Knockin, Salop, pleb. JESUS COLL., matric. 27 March, 1738, aged 18.

Lloyd, John, s. Owen, of St. Asaph's, co. Denbigh, gent. JESUS COLL., matric. 17 Oct., 1738, aged 17.

Lloyd, John, B.A. from JESUS COLL. 6 Feb., 1740-1, M.A. 3 Nov., 1743.

Lloyd, John, B.A. from JESUS COLL., 17 July, 1742. **[40]**

Lloyd, John, s. Philip, of Laugharne, co. Carmarthen, pleb. JESUS COLL., matric. 29 March, 1740, aged 21.

Lloyd, John, B.A. from JESUS COLL., 7 March, 1743-4.

Lloyd, John, s. Thomas, of Llandryllio, co. Denbigh, cler. JESUS COLL., matric. 7 June, 1740, aged 17.

Lloyd, John, B.A. from ALL SOULS COLL., 10 May, 1744.

Lloyd, John, s. John, of Holywell, co. Flint, pleb. JESUS COLL., matric. 4 April, 1745, aged 19; B.A. 1748. **[45]**

Lloyd, John, s. George, of Hulme, Lancashire, arm. CORPUS CHRISTI COLL., matric. 26 June, 1752, aged 17; B.A. 1756, of Melbourne House, co. Warwick, F.R.S., died 8 June, 1777, father of George, 1787. See Foster's *Lancashire Collection & Manchester School Reg.*, i. 37.

Lloyd, John, s. Critchley, of Llandysilio, co. Denbigh, pleb. JESUS COLL., matric. 11 April, 1753, aged 19.

Lloyd, John, s. John, of Llanarmon-in-Yale, Flint, pleb. JESUS COLL., matric. 12 July, 1753, aged 20.

Lloyd, John, B.A. from JESUS COLL., 22 Feb., 1757.

Lloyd, John, s. Robert, of St. Michael's, Somerset, cler. JESUS COLL., matric. 31 Jan., 1754, aged 17.

Lloyd, John, s. Richard, of Holywell, Flint, cler. JESUS COLL., matric. 26 Feb., 1755, aged 17. **[5]**

Lloyd, John, B.A. from JESUS COLL., 14 Feb., 1759.

Lloyd, John, s. Evan, of Ruthin, co. Denbigh, pleb. JESUS COLL., matric. 12 March, 1756, aged 18; B.A. 1760.

Lloyd, John, s. William, of Llanstephan, co. Carmarthen, arm. JESUS COLL., matric. 15 Dec., 1758, aged 16; B.A. 1762, M.A. 1765, B.D. 1772, vicar of Holywell, Flints, died in 1803.

Lloyd, John, s. Charles, of Llandevalley, co. Brecknock, cler. JESUS COLL., matric. 4 June, 1767, aged 17; B.A. 1772.

Lloyd, John, s. Evan, of Cayo, co. Carmarthen, pleb. CHRIST CHURCH, matric. 11 July, 1767, aged 20; B.A. 1771 (? in holy orders, died in 1814). **[10]**

Lloyd, John, s. Rowland, of Dolgelly, co. Merioneth, gent. JESUS COLL., matric. 9 May, 1770, aged 21.

Lloyd, John, s. James, of Mabus, co. Cardigan, arm. UNIVERSITY COLL., matric. 21 May, 1771, aged 17.

Lloyd, John, s. John, of Wrexham, co. Denbigh, cler. QUEEN'S COLL., matric. 9 Nov., 1776, aged 17.

Lloyd, John, s. Morris, of Oswestry, Salop, arm. ST. ALBAN HALL, matric. 11 Dec., 1780, aged 22.

Lloyd, John, s. David, of Llanfair, co. Montgomery, pleb. JESUS COLL., matric. 20 May, 1790, aged 20; B.A. 1794, M.A. 1796 (? rector and vicar of Llandrillo, co. Merioneth, 1799, until his death in 1825).

Lloyd, John, created D.C.L. 5 July, 1793, then of Havodunos, co. Denbigh, F.R. & A.S.S. (son of Hoel, of Hafodunos, co. Denbigh, esq.), bar.-at-law, Middle Temple, 1781, bencher 1811, M.P. Flintshire, June 1797 to Oct. 1799, died in April 1815, aged 65. **[16]**

Lloyd, John, s. Humphrey, of Carnarvon (town), pleb. JESUS COLL., matric. 9 Dec., 1794, aged 19; B.A. 1798, M.A. 1801.

Lloyd, John, s. Frederick, of co. Limerick, arm. CHRIST CHURCH, matric. 20 Oct., 1804, aged 17.

Lloyd, John, 4s. Thomas, of Gwenther, co. Brecon, gent. JESUS COLL., matric. 30 May, 1829, aged 19; B.A. 1833.

Lloyd, John, 1s. Edward, of Rhagatt Corwen, co. Montgomery (*sic*), arm. CHRIST CHURCH, matric. 5 Feb., 1830, aged 18; of Rhagatt, co. Merioneth, J.P., D.L., high sheriff co. Denbigh 1863, a student of Lincoln's Inn 1834, died 22 May, 1865. **[20]**

Lloyd, John, 2s. Richard, of Midhurst, Sussex, cler. WORCESTER COLL., matric. 10 May, 1839, aged 19; bible clerk 1841-3, B.A. 1843, M.A. 1846, perp. curate Eridge, Kent, 1853-60, rector of Llanvapley, co. Monmouth, 1861.

Lloyd, John, 3s. John, of St. David's, co. Brecon, arm. ST. JOHN'S COLL., matric. 10 Dec., 1851, aged 18; of Huntington Court, co. Hereford, J.P. Brecon, bar.-at-law, Middle Temple, 1880. See Foster's *Men at the Bar.*

Lloyd, John Augustus, o.s. John Augustus, of Bath, Somerset, M.D. (subs. 'arm.'). ST. JOHN'S COLL., matric. 20 April, 1868, aged 19; B.A. 1872, M.A. 1874, vicar of Broadhinton, Wilts, 1877.

Lloyd, John Barclay, 1s. Frederick Giesler, of London, arm. MAGDALEN COLL., matric. 19 Oct., 1883, aged 19; exhibitioner 1884, B.A. 1887.

Lloyd, John Daniel, y.s. Nathaniel, of Uley, co. Gloucester, gent. QUEEN'S COLL., matric. 9 March, 1826, aged 19; B.A. 1829, curate of Blockley, co. Gloucester, rector of Clare portion of Tiverton 1837, until his death 2 March, 1855. **[25]**

Lloyd, John Edward, 2s. Charles, of Bettws, co. Cardigan, cler. ORIEL COLL., matric. 18 Oct., 1871, aged 18; B.A. 1874, M.A. 1879, vicar of Newbridge-on-Wye 1883.

Lloyd, John Edward, 1s. Edward, of Liverpool, arm. LINCOLN COLL., matric. 20 Oct., 1881, aged 20; exhibitioner 1884-5, B.A. 1886.

Lloyd, John George, 3s. George, of Kirby Fleetham, Yorks, arm. MERTON COLL., matric. 7 Dec., 1848, aged 19; B.A. 1854, died 13 Oct., 1856, brother of Alfred Hart. See Foster's *Lancashire Collection.*

Lloyd, John Hellings, 2s. John Daniel, of Tiverton, Devon, cler. BALLIOL COLL., matric. 4 Feb., 1859, aged 17; exhibitioner 1859-65, B.A. 1863, of Indian Civil Service 1862.

Lloyd, John Horatio, s. John, of Stockport, Cheshire, gent. QUEEN'S COLL., matric. 3 July, 1818, aged 19, B.A. 1822; fellow BRASENOSE COLL. 1823-6, M.A. 1824, bar.-at-law, Inner Temple, 1826, M.P. Stockport 1832-5, died 18 July, 1884. **[30]**

Lloyd, John Maurice Edward, 2s. John, of Montgomery (town), cler. TRINITY COLL., matric. 15 Oct., 1864, aged 20; B.A. 1869, M.A. 1872, bar.-at-law, Lincoln's Inn, 1872. See Foster's *Men at the Bar.*

Lloyd, John Philip, 1s. John William, of Deptford, arm. CHRIST CHURCH, matric. 24 June, 1825, aged 17.

Lloyd, John Rees, s. John, of Brecon, South Wales, arm. BALLIOL COLL., matric. 5 Nov., 1814, aged 17; bar.-at-law, Lincoln's Inn, 1824. See *Eton School Lists.*

Lloyd, John Vaughan, 2s. William, of Holyhead, Isle of Anglesey, cler. JESUS COLL., matric. 8 April, 1824, aged 19; scholar 1828-32, B.A. 1828, M.A. 1856.

Lloyd, Jonathan, s. Rice, of Llannording, co. Brecon, pleb. JESUS COLL., matric. 13 March, 1716-7, aged 22; B.A. 21 March, 1720-1. **[35]**

Lloyd, Joseph Skipp, 1s. Joseph, of Abinghall, co. Gloucester, arm. ST. JOHN'S COLL., matric. 12 March, 1829, aged 18; B.A. & M.A. 1864, of Abinghall House, co. Gloucester, bar.-at-law, Inner Temple, 1836, clerk of the cheque and adjutant of the royal body-guard 1852. See Foster's *Men at the Bar.*

Lloyd, Llewelyn, s. John, of Caerwys, co. Flint, cler. JESUS COLL., matric. 3 April, 1789, aged 18; B.A. 1793, rector of Nannerch, Flints, 1811, until his death 6 June, 1841.

Lloyd, Llewelyn Foster, 2s. Llewelyn, of Prestwich, Lancashire, arm. CHRIST CHURCH, matric. 24 Jan., 1881, aged 19.

Lloyd, Rev. Llewelyn Walter, 1s. Llewelyn, of Liverpool, arm. WADHAM COLL., matric. 19 Jan., 1872, aged 18; clerk 1871-6, B.A. 1876, M.A. 1878, 2nd master Ashby-de-la-Zouch Grammar School 1878-83, head-master since 1883.

Lloyd, Maurice, s. Maurice, of Llandderfel, co. Merioneth, pleb. JESUS COLL., matric. 18 March, 1722-3, aged 19; B.A. 28 Feb., 1726-7. **[40]**

Lloyd, Maurice, s. Maurice, of Oswestry, Salop, gent. HERTFORD COLL., matric. 8 May, 1784, aged 20; B.A. 1788, M.A. 1791, vicar of Lenham, Kent, 1791, until his death 16 May, 1810.

Lloyd, Nowes, s. John, of Epping, Essex, cler. ST. JOHN'S COLL., matric. 6 April, 1739, aged 19; B.A. 1742, M.A. 1747.

Lloyd, Oswald, 3s. Charles Albert, of Rand, co. Lincoln, cler. NON-COLL., matric. 18 Oct., 1883, aged 20; B.A. 1886.

Lloyd, Otho Holland, 1s. Horace, of London, arm. ORIEL COLL., matric. 17 Oct., 1876, aged 19; scholar 1876-80, B.A. 1883, a student of the Middle Temple 1878.

Lloyd, Owen, s. David, of Eglwysfach, co. Denbigh, cler. JESUS COLL., matric. 16 Dec., 1754, aged 18; B.C.L. 1764. **[45]**

Lloyd, Owen, s. Humphrey, of Dolgelly, co. Merioneth, pleb. TRINITY COLL., matric. 20 May, 1761, aged 19; vicar of Stapenhill, co. Derby, died at Dolgelly in 1813.

Lloyd, Owen, 2s. Robert, of Dublin, arm. ST. MARY HALL, matric. 5 Nov., 1873, aged 20.

Lloyd, Philip, s. Philip, of Greenwich, Kent, gent. CHRIST CHURCH, matric. 15 May, 1746, aged 17; B.A. 29 Jan., 1749-50, M.A. 1752, B. & D.D. 1763, vicar of Piddletown, Dorset, 1765, preb. of Westminster 1763-5, dean of Norwich 1765, until his death 31 May, 1790.

Lloyd, Pierce, s. Henry, of Ruthland, co. Flint, pleb. JESUS COLL., matric. 9 March, 1714-5, aged 19; B.A. 1718.

Lloyd, Pierce, s. Ed., of Llanelian, co. Denbigh, pleb. JESUS COLL., matric. 14 Oct., 1729, aged 18; B.A. 1733, M.A. 1736. [5]

Lloyd, Reginald Erasmus William, o.s. William, of Rushall, Wilts, cler. ST. ALBAN HALL, matric. 6 May, 1862, aged 22; B.A. 1865, M.A. 1869.

Lloyd, Rhys Jones, 3s. Thomas, of Kilne, co. Pembroke, arm. EXETER COLL., matric. 23 Jan., 1845, aged 18; B.A. 1849, rector of Troedyrawr 1852. See *Rugby School Reg.*, 211.

Lloyd, Rice, s. Thomas, of Langendeirne, co. Carmarthen, arm. JESUS COLL., matric. 22 May, 1729, aged 17.

Lloyd, Rice, s. William, of Llanfachreth, co. Merioneth, pleb. JESUS COLL., matric. 4 April, 1759, aged 20.

Lloyd, Richard, s. Richard, of Wimborne Minster, Dorset, cler. HART HALL, matric. 10 Oct., 1716, aged 17; B.A. 1720, M.A. 1723. [10]

Lloyd, Richard, s. Thomas, of Langadock, co. Carmarthen, arm. JESUS COLL., matric. 25 June, 1717, aged 16; B.A. from CHRIST CHURCH 1721.

Lloyd, Richard, s. Edward, of Myvod, co. Montgomery, arm. JESUS COLL., matric. 7 Nov., 1728, aged 17; a student of Lincoln's Inn 1729 (? died vicar of Llan Asaph, Flints 9 Jan., 1790, aged 80).

Lloyd, Richard, s. Thomas, of St. Peter's, Chester (city), gent. PEMBROKE COLL., matric. 4 July, 1733, aged 17.

Lloyd, Richard, s. John, of Whitford, co. Flint, pleb. JESUS COLL., matric. 4 April, 1734, aged 20.

Lloyd, Richard, s. Richard, of Waltham, co. Lincoln, gent. MERTON COLL., matric. 23 Nov., 1738, aged 17; B.A. 1742. [15]

Lloyd, Richard, s. Richard, of Llanfachreth, co. Merioneth, pleb. JESUS COLL., matric. 15 May, 1766, aged 22.

Lloyd, Richard, s. Thomas, of Abbotrenant, co. Cardigan, arm. CHRIST CHURCH, matric. 24 Nov., 1767, aged 18; B.A. 1771, M.A. 1781, rector of Rhosdie, and vicar of Llanbadarn, co. Cardigan, 1774.

Lloyd, Richard, 1s. Richard, of Llanrhystid, co. Cardigan, gent. JESUS COLL., matric. 28 Oct., 1830, aged 18; B.A. 1837.

Lloyd, Rev. Richard, 1s. Richard, of London, cler. MERTON COLL., matric. 27 Oct., 1836, aged 18; postmaster 1836-40, B.A. 1840, M.A. 1849. See *Eton School Lists*.

Lloyd, Richard Morgan, o.s. John, of Llanrhystid, co. Cardigan, cler. JESUS COLL., matric. 19 Jan., 1880, aged 19. [20]

Lloyd, Richard Myddelton, s. Richard, of Wrexham, co. Denbigh, gent. BALLIOL COLL., matric. 23 March, 1812, aged 18.

Lloyd, Robert, s. Thomas, of St. Asaph, co. Denbigh, gent. JESUS COLL., matric. 9 Feb., 1715-6, aged 18; B.A. 19 Feb., 1719-20, M.A. 1723.

Lloyd, Robert, s. John, of Llanguеslin, co. Carnarvon, gent. JESUS COLL., matric. 13 May, 1725, aged 17; B.A. 8 Feb., 1728-9, M.A. 1731.

Lloyd, Robert, s. David, of Henglwys, co. Anglesey, pleb. JESUS COLL., matric. 30 March, 1726, aged 18; B.A. 19 Feb., 1729-30.

Lloyd, Robert, s. Robert, of Festiniog, co. Merioneth, pleb. JESUS COLL., matric. 15 April, 1736, aged 12; B.A. 1739. [25]

Lloyd, Robert, s. Robert, of Cheam, Surrey, gent. JESUS COLL., matric. 12 Oct., 1737, aged 18.

Lloyd, Robert, s. William, of Ruthin, co. Denbigh, gent. JESUS COLL., matric. 20 May, 1809, aged 19.

Lloyd, Robert (B.A. TRINITY COLL., Dublin, 1828), 3s. Humphrey, of New Ross, co, Wexford, Ireland, arm. BRASENOSE COLL., incorp. 10 May, 1832, aged 43; M.A. 13 June, 1832, bar.-at-law, Lincoln's Inn, 1836. See Foster's *Our Noble and Gentle Families*, ii.

Lloyd, Roger, s. Meredith, of Corwen, co. Merioneth, gent. JESUS COLL., matric. 9 March, 1714-5, aged 19; B.A. 1718, M.A. 1721.

Lloyd, Rowley Young, 1s. (Edward), of Deal, Kent, arm. PEMBROKE COLL., matric. 9 March, 1837, aged 17; B.A. 1841, M.A. 1843, bar.-at-law, Inner Temple, 1845. [30]

Lloyd, Samuel, s. Thomas, of St. Chad's, Shrewsbury, pleb. JESUS COLL., matric. 29 Feb., 1731-2, aged 18; B.A. 16 March, 1735-6.

Lloyd, Samuel, s. Nathaniel, of Uley, co. Gloucester, gent. MAGDALEN COLL., matric. 26 Oct., 1815, aged 21; B.A. 1819, M.A. 1822, a student of Lincoln's Inn 1817, vicar of Horsley, co. Gloucester, 1825-49, died 16 March, 1863.

Lloyd, Rev. Simon, s. Simon, of Llanycil, co. Merioneth, gent. JESUS COLL., matric. 8 April, 1775, aged 18; B.A. 1779, died at Plasyndra, Bala, 6 Nov., 1836.

Lloyd, St. Vincent, 3s. John William, of Woolwich, Kent, arm. CHRIST CHURCH, matric. 4 June, 1828, aged 17.

Lloyd, Thomas, s. David, of Pennell, co. Merioneth, pleb. JESUS COLL., matric. 20 May, 1724, aged 19. [35]

Lloyd, Thomas, s. John, of Llandoget, co. Denbigh, pleb. JESUS COLL., matric. 2 March, 1724-5, aged 19; a student of the Middle Temple 1728.

Lloyd, Thomas, B.A. from JESUS COLL. 14 Feb., 1728-9.

Lloyd, Thomas, s. Thomas, of St. Peter's, Chester (city), gent. BRASENOSE COLL., matric. 12 April, 1736, aged 19; B.A. 1739.

Lloyd, Thomas, s. John, of Llanllawddog, co. Carmarthen, arm. CHRIST CHURCH, matric. 10 Oct., 1751, aged 18; B.A. 1755.

Lloyd, Thomas, s. Henry, of Llanrhaiadr, co. Denbigh, pleb. JESUS COLL., matric. 25 Oct., 1760, aged 20; B.A. 1765. [40]

Lloyd, Thomas, s. Thomas, of Llanvihangel, co. Cardigan, arm. ORIEL COLL., matric. 14 Jan., 1761, aged 16. (Memo.: Rev. T. L. vicar of Happisburgh 1781, and rector of Westwick 1787, died in 1814.)

Lloyd, Thomas, s. William, of Holywell, co. Flint, gent. CHRIST CHURCH, matric. 14 Dec., 1772, aged 18; a student of Lincoln's Inn 1772.

Lloyd, Thomas, s. David, of Llanvihangel Aberbythyck, co. Carmarthen, gent. JESUS COLL., matric. 26 March, 1774, aged 28.

Lloyd, Thomas, s. John, of Glynbrochan, co. Montgomery, gent. PEMBROKE COLL., matric. 19 May, 1778, aged 18; B.A. 1782.

Lloyd, Thomas, s. Roger, of Devynock, co. Brecon, cler. MAGDALEN HALL, matric. 23 March, 1779, aged 30; B.A. 1786, M.A. 1787. [45]

Lloyd, Thomas, s. Walter, of Llangoedmore, co. Cardigan, arm. UNIVERSITY COLL., matric. 3 July, 1779, aged 18; a student of Lincoln's Inn 1782.

Lloyd, Thomas, s. Evan, of Weobley, co. Hereford, gent. HERTFORD COLL., matric. 4 Nov., 1786, aged 18, B.A. 1790; M.A. from WORCESTER COLL. 1803 (? minor canon of Hereford, vicar of Norton 1797, of Marden 1799, rector of Stretton Sugwas 1800, died in 1809.)

Lloyd, Thomas, s. John, of Derwen, co. Denbigh, gent. JESUS COLL., matric. 21 May, 1803, aged 18; scholar, B.A. 1807, M.A. 1809, curate of Llanrwst, co. Denbigh, died 21 June, 1822.

Lloyd, Thomas, s. Thomas Griffith, of Guilsfield, co. Montgomery, arm. BRASENOSE COLL., matric. 17 May, 1810, aged 17; created M.A. 16 March, 1815.

Lloyd, Thomas, s. Thomas, of Cardigan (town), arm. MERTON COLL., matric. 6 Nov., 1812, aged 19.

Lloyd, Thomas, s. Bell, of Orgreave, co. Stafford, arm. CHRIST CHURCH, matric. 13 Dec., 1815, aged 19; B.A. 1819, M.A. 1824, bar.-at-law, Inner Temple, 1824, rector of Chrisleton, Cheshire. See Foster's *Peerage*, B. MOSTYN. [5]

Lloyd, Thomas, s. Thomas, of Beechmount, co. Limerick, arm. CHRIST CHURCH, matric. 1 May, 1818, aged 19. (Memo.: T. L., a King's Counsel, Ireland, M.P. co. Limerick 1826, until his death 17 Dec., 1829.)

Lloyd, Thomas, 1s. John, of Llandyssil, co. Cardigan, cler. JESUS COLL., matric. 22 Nov., 1821, aged 19; B.A. 1825, M.A. 1828 (? rector of Llanfairoellynn, co. Cardigan, 1831).

Lloyd, Thomas, 2s. William, of Ludlow, Salop, gent. CHRIST CHURCH, matric. 23 Oct., 1830, aged 19; B.A. 1834, M.A. 1837.

Lloyd, Thomas Conway, 1s. John, of Brecon, arm. CHRIST CHURCH, matric. 4 June, 1846, aged 17; of Dinas, co. Brecon, J.P., D.L., high sheriff 1878, etc.

Lloyd, (Sir) Thomas Davies (Bart.), 1s. Thomas, of Swansea, co. Glamorgan, arm. CHRIST CHURCH, matric. 5 Dec., 1838, aged 18; of Bronydd, co. Cardigan, M.P. 1865-8, baronet, so created 21 Jan., 1863, M.P. Cardigan district 1868-74, died 21 July, 1877. See Foster's *Baronetage*. [10]

Lloyd, Thomas Furley Forster, 5s. Arthur Forbes, of Instow, Devon, cler. ST. ALBAN HALL, matric. 20 Oct., 1863, aged 18; B.A. 1868.

Lloyd, Thomas Henry, 3s. Llewellyn, of Aigsburth, Lancashire, arm. BRASENOSE COLL., matric. 13 June, 1833, aged 18, B.A. 1837; fellow ALL SOULS' COLL. 1838-50, M.A. 1840, rector of Hamerton, Hunts, 1843, until his death 26 July, 1850.

Lloyd, Thomas John Edward, o.s. Thomas, of Lois Weeden, Northants, cler. MAGDALEN HALL, matric. 14 March, 1839, aged 21.

Lloyd, (Hon.) Thomas Pryce, 2s. Edward, of Bodfach, co. Montgomery, baronet (after Lord Mostyn). CHRIST CHURCH, matric. 22 Oct., 1818, aged 18; B.A. 1822, M.A. 1827, of Nannau, co. Merioneth, D.L., died 11 March, 1874. See Foster's *Peerage*.

Lloyd, Thomas Richard, 1s. John, of Caron, co. Cardigan, gent. QUEEN'S COLL., matric. 12 Dec., 1832, aged 18. [15]

Lloyd, Thomas Richard, 1s. John, of Denbigh (town), cler. JESUS COLL., matric. 24 Oct., 1839, aged 19; B.A. 1843, rector of Llanfynydd, co. Denbigh, 1843.

Lloyd, Trevor, 1s. Robert, of Ruthin, co. Denbigh, arm. MAGDALEN HALL, matric. 4 Nov., 1858, aged 24; B.A. & M.A. 1866.

Lloyd, William, s. Evan, of Trawsfynydd, co. Merioneth, pleb. JESUS COLL., matric. 19 March, 1715-6, aged 19; B.A. 1719.

Lloyd, William, s. Robert, of Bryncross, co. Carnarvon, pleb. JESUS COLL., matric. 29 Oct., 1719, aged 20; B.A. 1723.

Lloyd, William, s. Rosindale, of Wrexham, co. Denbigh, doctor. BRASENOSE COLL., matric. 28 March 1750, aged 18; B.A. 1753, M.A. 1756, of Aston Hall, Salop. [20]

Lloyd, William, s. John, of Llangower, co. Merioneth arm. JESUS COLL., matric. 26 Nov., 1759, aged 19

Lloyd, William, s. William, of London, gent. QUEEN'S COLL., matric. 15 Dec., 1764, aged 17.

Lloyd, William, s. William, of Bangor, co. Carnarvon cler. UNIVERSITY COLL., matric. 21 Feb., 1766 aged 17; B.A. 1769, M.A. 1773, B. & D.D 1802.

Lloyd, William, s. John, of Kingston, Hants, arm TRINITY COLL., matric. 2 April, 1773, aged 18.

Lloyd, William, s. William, of Beaconsfield, Bucks arm. WADHAM COLL., matric. 26 Oct., 1776 aged 16; B.C.L. 1784, keeper Ashmolean Museum 1796-1815. [25]

Lloyd, William, s. Daniel, of Llanstephan, co. Carmarthen, arm. JESUS COLL., matric. 26 March 1779, aged 18; B.A. 1782, M.A. 1785, high sheriff co. Cardigan 1807, died in 1840.

Lloyd, William, s. Evan, of Dolgelly, co. Merioneth gent. JESUS COLL., matric. 10 Dec., 1790, aged 19; B.A. 1794, M.A. 1797 (? of Blaenglynor, co. Merioneth, J.P., rector of Llanfaethlu, Anglesey 1828, until his death 3 June, 1844).

Lloyd, William, s. Robert, of Nevin, co. Carnarvon gent. JESUS COLL., matric. 7 Dec., 1797, aged 22 B.A. 1801.

Lloyd, William, s. Thomas, of Chetwynd, Salop, arm MERTON COLL., matric. 14 July, 1806, aged 18 rector of Drayton, Oxon, died 20 Oct., 1861. See *Eton School Lists*.

Lloyd, William, s. John, of London, arm. BRASENOSE COLL., matric. 1 April, 1818, aged 18; B.A 1822, M.A. 1825, rector of Lillingstone Lovell Bucks, 1826. [30]

Lloyd, William, o.s. William, of St. Mary's, Woolwich gent. JESUS COLL., matric. 20 May, 1825, aged 17 B.A. 1829, M.A. 1833.

Lloyd, William, 2s. John, of Lisyllt, co. Cardigan gent. NON-COLL., matric. 19 Jan., 1885, aged 23

Lloyd, Rev. William Forster, o.s. William, of Braderham, Bucks, cler. CHRIST CHURCH, matric. May, 1812, aged 17; student 1812-37, B.A. 181 M.A. 1818, Greek reader 1823, Drummond professor of political economy 1832-7, died 2 June, 1852. See *Alumni West.*, 475.

Lloyd, William Henry, o.s. Samuel, of Nailsworth co. Gloucester, cler. MAGDALEN COLL., matric. 20 Oct., 1852, aged 18; B.A. 1856, M.A. 185 vicar of Christ Church, Eastbourne, 1864-70, chaplain at Valparaiso 1870-83, vicar of Brimscombe co. Gloucester, 1866.

Lloyd, William Henry Cynric, 4s. Bell, of Woodstock Oxon, arm. JESUS COLL., matric. 16 Jan., 181 aged 17; scholar 1819-29, B.A. 1822, M.A. 182 rector of Norbury, and vicar of Nanton, co. Staff 1826, archdeacon of Durham 1869, until his death Jan., 1881. See Foster's *Peerage*, B. MOSTYN.

Lloyd, William Stowe, 2s. Thomas, of West Smethhurst, co. Stafford, gent. NON-COLL., matric. Oct., 1886, aged 20. [3

Lloyd, William Whitelocke, o.s. George Whitelock of Marly, near Dublin, arm. MAGDALEN COLL. matric. 17 Oct., 1874, aged 18. See *Eton School Lists*.

Lloyd-Edwardes, Thomas. QUEENS'S COLL., 186 See EDWARDES.

Lluellyn, Richard, s. Richard, of High Wickham Bucks, gent. MAGDALEN COLL., matric. 7 March 1726-7, aged 17; chorister 1720-8, clerk, 1729, demy 1729-32, B.A. 1730, fellow 1732-52, M.A. 1733, B.D. 3 Feb., 1741-2, junior dean of arts 1742, bursar 174 dean of divinity 1748, vice-president 1749, a student of Lincoln's Inn 1732, rector of Saunderton, Buck 1751, until his death 25 Dec., 1770. See *Bloxam*, 149; vi. 219.

lwyd, John, s. Lewis, of Llandeei Velfreiy, co. Pembroke, pleb. JESUS COLL., matric. 14 Oct., 1761, aged 24; rector of Swithland, co. Leicester, 1761, until his death 16 March, 1814.

lwyd, Thomas, s. Thomas, of Berllandowil, co. Carmarthen, gent. CHRIST CHURCH, matric. 13 May, 1735, aged 18; B.A. 1 March, 1738-9, M.A. 1745, died rector of Hornsey 4 May, 1775.

oaring, James 2s. William, of Winsham, Somerset, gent. NEW COLL., matric. 20 Oct., 1873, aged 37.

obb, Sydney Brooke, 3s. William, of Edmonton, Middlesex, arm. CHRIST CHURCH, matric. 15 Oct., 1856, aged 18; B.A. 1860, M.A. 1866, rector and vicar of Kennardington, Kent, 1873.

och, Rev. Charles Ramsey Fleming, 4s. William, of Berhampore, East Indies, arm. UNIVERSITY COLL., matric. 25 April, 1844, aged 19; B.A. 1848, died in 1868. See *Rugby School Reg.*, 230. [5]

och, Charles Stewart, 5s. George, of East Indies, arm. BALLIOL COLL., matric. 15 April, 1869, aged 19; B.A. 1875, a student of the Inner Temple 1873.

och, William Walker, 4s. George, of Bengal, East Indies, arm. BALLIOL COLL., matric. 9 April, 1864, aged 17; B.A. 1867, of the Indian Civil Service 1866.

ochée, Alfred Campbell, 3s. Alfred, of Canterbury, D.Med. KEBLE COLL., matric. 14 Oct., 1872, aged 18; B.A. 1876, M.A. 1879, chaplain at Aden 1879-80, garrison chaplain Bombay 1880.

ochée, Lewis Taswell, 1s. Alfred, of Canterbury, Kent, arm. EXETER COLL., matric. 19 Oct., 1867, aged 18; exhibitioner 1866-71, B.A. 1871, M.A. 1874, held various metropolitan curacies 1872-85, rector of Barnes, Surrey, 1885. See *Coll. Reg.*, 163.

ock, Campbell, of TRINITY COLL., Cambridge (B.A. 1861, M.A. 1864), adm. 'comitatis causa' 14 June, 1866. [10]

ock, Charles Snow, 5s. Thomas, of Pilton, Devon, arm. TRINITY COLL., matric. 12 March, 1840, aged 18; Blundell scholar BALLIOL COLL. 1840-6, B.A. 1844, M.A. 1851.

ock, Daniel, of TRINITY COLL., Cambridge (B.A. 1702, M.A. 1706); incorp. 10 July, 1722.

ock, George, s. William, of London, arm. CHRIST CHURCH, matric. 21 Oct., 1789, aged 18; B.A. 1794, M.A. 1796, rector of Lee, Kent, 1803, until his death 17 Nov., 1864.

ock, Rev. George Rideal, o.s. George, of Fareham, Hants, gent. WORCESTER COLL., matric. 27 Jan., 1881, aged 31; B.A. 1884, M.A. 1887.

ock, John, s. George, of Frome, Somerset, pleb. MAGDALEN COLL., matric. 15 July, 1727, aged 17; chorister 1722-8, clerk 1728-9. See *Coll. Reg.*, i. 150. [15]

ock, Matthew, s. Matt., of London, gent. QUEEN'S COLL., matric. 21 March, 1716-7, aged 18; a student of Lincoln's Inn 1716.

ock, Robert, 'servant to Mr. Stephens, of Magdalen College;' privilegiatus 15 Feb., 1725-6.

ock, Rev. Walter, 2s. Henry, of Dorchester, Dorset, arm. CORPUS CHRISTI COLL., matric. 16 Oct., 1865, aged 19, scholar 1865-9, B.A. 1869; fellow MAGDALEN COLL. 1869, M.A. 1872, junior dean of arts 1873, theological tutor 1873, bursar 1874, tutor of Keble College 1870, sub-warden 1881, dean and librarian 1874, on council 1885, divinity lecturer Worcester College 1882, proctor 1883.

ock, William Charles, s. John, of London, arm. QUEEN'S COLL., matric. 10 Dec., 1767, aged 19.

ocke, Alexander George, 3s. — L., of Teignmouth, Devon, arm. CHRIST CHURCH, matric. 15 Oct., 1880, aged 18. See *Eton School Lists.* [20]

ocke, Arthur Charles Edward, 1s. John Arthur, of Dawlish, Devon, arm. CHRIST CHURCH, matric. 18 April, 1879, aged 18. See *Eton School Lists.*

Locke, Charles John Georgius Courtenay, 1s. John, of Dawlish, Devon, arm. WORCESTER COLL., matric. 7 Feb., 1823, aged 19; rector of Newcastle, co. Limerick, died in Paris 16 Feb., 1848.

Locke, Richard, s. Richard, of Burnham, Somerset, gent. MAGDALEN HALL, matric. 29 Nov., 1788, aged 20 (? vicar of Long Bennington, co. Lincoln, and of Farndon-cum-Balderton, Notts, died 16 July, 1808).

Locke, Samuel, s. Thomas, of Taunton, Somerset, gent. WADHAM COLL., matric. 22 Oct., 1785, aged 17; B.A. 1789, M.A. 1796, B. & D.D. 1808, rector of Hilgay, Norfolk, 1816, chaplain to the Duke of Kent, died 20 Dec., 1849.

Locke, Samuel Charles, s. Samuel, of Guildford, Surrey, doctor. TRINITY COLL., matric. 28 Oct., 1811, aged 17; B.A. from ST. ALBAN HALL 1816. [25]

Locke, Thomas, s. Thomas, of Rochester, Kent, gent. CHRIST CHURCH, matric. 14 June, 1748, aged 18; B.A. 1752, M.A. 1755, usher Westminster School 1759. See *Alumni West.*, 347; & *Gent.'s Mag.*, 1801, ii. p. 1062.

Locke, Wadham, 1s. Wadham, of Rowde-Ford, Bromham, Wilts, arm. MERTON COLL., matric. 16 June, 1821, aged 17; postmaster 1822-5, B.A. 1825, of Cleve House, Wilts, J.P., high sheriff 1847, a student of the Inner Temple 1824, etc.

Locker, Arthur, 2s. Edward Hawke, of Greenwich, Kent, gent. PEMBROKE COLL., matric. 6 May, 1847, aged 18; B.A. 1851.

Locker, Samuel, 'butler of Queen's College;' privilegiatus 26 Jan., 1762.

Locker, William Algernon, y.s. Arthur, of London, arm. MERTON COLL., matric. 17 Oct., 1882, aged 18; B.A. 1886. [30]

Lockett, Charles, s. Thomas, of Rushton, co. Stafford, gent. WORCESTER COLL., matric. 20 Feb., 1789, aged 20; B.A. 1792, vicar of Sandbach, Cheshire, died in 1813.

Lockett, Henry, s. Timothy, of West Monkton, Somerset, gent. HART HALL, matric. 12 Dec., 1720, aged 15; B.A. 1724, M.A. 1727, rector of Chatworthy with Crocombe, Somerset, 1744.

Lockey, Charles, s. John, of Childrey, Berks, gent. CORPUS CHRISTI COLL., matric. 5 May, 1761, aged 17; B.A. from QUEEN'S COLL. 1765, M.A. 1767.

Lockey, Francis, s. Francis, of Reading, arm. TRINITY COLL., matric. 25 Nov., 1814, aged 17 (? perp. curate Blackford, parish of Wedmore, Somerset, 1825).

Lockey, Ralph, of PETER COLL., Cambridge (B.A. 1792, M.A. 1796), adm. 'ad eundem' 6 July, 1810, vicar of Much Dewchurch, co. Hereford, perp. curate Much Birch 1813, rector of Llanwarn 1818, until his death in 1833. [35]

Lockey, Richard, s. William, of Aldborough Hatch, Essex, gent. PEMBROKE COLL., matric. 8 June, 1736, aged 17; baptized at Barking 31 Jan., 1717-18.

Lockey, Rev. Richard, s. Richard, of Eastington, co. Gloucester, gent. PEMBROKE COLL., matric. 8 June, 1763, aged 17; B.A. 1768, died at Stinchcombe in 1826.

Lockey, Samuel Ralph, 1s. Ralph, of Llanwarne, co. Hereford, cler. PEMBROKE COLL., matric. 15 Nov., 1838, aged 18; B.A. 1843. See *Rugby School Reg.*, 181.

Lockhart, Alexander, s. William, of Edinburgh (city), arm. ST. MARY HALL, matric. 28 March, 1808, aged 20; B.A. 1811, M.A. 1814, rector of Stone 1822, and curate of Hartwell, Bucks, died at Ampthill in 1831.

Lockhart, Alexander Francis (Maxwell), 5s. Lawrence, of Inchinnan, co. Renfrew, cler. BALLIOL COLL., matric. 20 Oct., 1874, aged 20; scholar HERTFORD COLL. 1875-8, B.A. 1878, fellow 1878.

Lockhart, (Sir) Charles Macdonald (Bart.), s. (Sir Alexander Macdonald), baronet. BRASENOSE COLL., matric. 24 May, 1817; 2nd baronet, died 8 Dec., 1832. See Foster's *Baronetage.* [41]

Lockhart, Edgar Henry (born in Rome), 1s. James (of Sherfield House, Hants), arm. UNIVERSITY COLL., matric. 29 May, 1857, aged 18; B.A. 1861, M.A. 1865, Stowell fellow 1865-8, a student of Lincoln's Inn 1862, died 20 May, 1868.

Lockhart, George, s. George, of Edinburgh, Scotland, arm. ST. MARY HALL, matric. 27 Oct., 1742, aged 15 (? of the Carnwath family). See Foster's *Baronetage.*

Lockhart, James, s. James, of Westminster, arm. UNIVERSITY COLL., matric. 21 Feb., 1815, aged 20; B.A. 1819, M.A. 1823, of Sherfield English, Hants, bar.-at-law, Gray's Inn, 1824. See Foster's *Men at the Bar.*

Lockhart, James Augustus (born in Rome), 1s. James (of Sherfield House, Hants), arm. CORPUS CHRISTI COLL., matric. 2 Dec., 1852, aged 18; brother of Edgar Henry, 1857.

Lockhart, James Somerville, 4s. Laurence, of Inchinnan, co. Renfrew, cler. CORPUS CHRISTI COLL., matric. 19 Oct., 1870, aged 19, scholar 1870-5, classical lecturer and tutor 1875-9; fellow HERTFORD COLL. 1875, B.A. 1875, M.A. 1878, Latin lecturer, tutor, and Greek lecturer 1877, secretary to Civil Service Commission 1887. [5]

Lockhart, John Gibson, s. John, of Cambusnethan, co. Lanark, doctor. BALLIOL COLL., matric. 16 Oct., 1809, aged 16; B.C.L. 1817, created D.C.L. 13 June, 1834, editor of the 'Quarterly Review' 1825-53, bar.-at-law, Lincoln's Inn, 1831, auditor of the Duchy of Lancaster 1843, author of the 'Life of Scott,' died 25 Nov., 1854.

Lockhart, John Ingram. UNIVERSITY COLL., 1783. See WASTIE.

Lockhart, (Sir) Norman Macdonald (Bart.), 1s. Norman Macdonald, of Lanark, Scotland, baronet. CHRIST CHURCH, matric. 23 May, 1865, aged 20; 4th baronet, died 20 May, 1870. See Foster's *Baronetage* & *Eton School Lists.*

Lockhart, Philip, s. George, of Dryden Lothian, North Britain, arm. BALLIOL COLL., matric. 30 Aug., 1733, aged 17; B.A. 1737.

Lockhart, Samuel John Ingram, o.s. Samuel, of Kew, Middlesex, arm. LINCOLN COLL., matric. 6 Feb., 1823, aged 19; B.A. 1826, M.A. 1831, vicar of Hurstbourne Priors with St. Mary Bourne, Hants, 1843, until his death 26 Jan., 1887. [10]

Lockhart, William, o.s. Alexander, of Wallingham, Surrey, cler. EXETER COLL., matric. 17 May, 1838, aged 18; B.A. 1842.

Lockman, John, s. Christopher, of St. Martin's, London, gent. BALLIOL COLL., matric. 20 March, 1740-1, aged 19; B.A. 1744, M.A. 1748, B. & D.D. 1769, rector of Dunstable, Beds, 1753, of Drayton Beauchamp, Oxon, with West Iddersley, Bucks, 1786, master of St. Cross Hospital, Hants, canon of Windsor 1758, until his death 27 Dec., 1807.

Lockton, John, s. John, of West Illsley, Berks, cler. PEMBROKE COLL., matric. 7 Nov., 1751, aged 16; B.A. 1755, M.A. 1758.

Lockton, John, s. John, of Weyhill, Hants, cler. PEMBROKE COLL., matric. 3 Nov., 1784, aged 15; B.A. & fellow 1788, M.A. 1791, a student of the Inner Temple 1790, died 1796.

Lockton, John, 1s. Thomas, of Brampton Church, Northants, cler. MAGDALEN HALL, matric. 8 Dec., 1829, aged 18. [15]

Lockton, Philip, 3s. Thomas, of Brampton, Northants, cler. MAGDALEN HALL, matric. 28 May, 1841, aged 19; B.A. 1845, M.A. 1868, rector of Slapton 1875.

Lockton, Rev. Philip Sydney, 1s. Philip, of Windermere, Tasmania, cler. NON-COLL., matric. 14 Oct., 1876, aged 21; B.A. 1882. See *Robinson*, 358.

Lockton, Thomas, s. John, of Weyhill, Hants, cler. PEMBROKE COLL., matric. 3 Nov., 1784, aged 14; B.A. from CORPUS CHRISTI COLL. 1788, M.A. 1792, B.D. 1800, rector of Church Brampton, Northants, 1807, until his death 9 Feb., 1853.

Lockwood, Albert, 1s. Joseph Duke, of Workso[p], Notts, gent. MAGDALEN HALL, matric. 16 Jul[y], 1868, aged 37; commoner WORCESTER COLL. 187[ ], B.A. 1874, M.A. 1875, vicar of St. Anne's, Bue[l] Mills, Devon, 1874-82, died 1 May, 1884.

Lockwood, Rev. Edward, s. Richard, of Londo[n], Middlesex, arm. ST. JOHN'S COLL., matric. [ ] Feb., 1736-7, aged 17, B.A. 1740; M.A. from AL[L] SOULS' COLL. 1744, of Dews Hall, Essex, rector [of] Hanwell, Oxon, and of St. Peter's, Northampto[n] 1750, died 22 Jan., 1802. [20]

Lockwood, Edward. UNIVERSITY COLL., 1779. S[ee] PERCIVAL.

Lockwood, Edward (Isaac), of JESUS COLL., Can[m]bridge (B.A. 1820, M.A. 1823); adm. 'ad eundem' 1831, rector of Belstead, Suffolk, 1846.

Lockwood, George Palmer, of TRINITY COLL., Can[m]bridge (B.A. 1832, M.A. 1852); adm. 'ad eundem' 7 April, 1859, rector of South Hackney, Middlese[x] 1850.

Lockwood, John (Cutts), s. Edward, of London, cle[r]. CHRIST CHURCH, matric. 22 March, 1781, aged 18 B.A. 1784, M.A. 1787, vicar of Yoxford, 179[ ] 1816, rector of Topcroft, Norfolk, 1797-1816, vic[ar] of Croydon 1816, rector of Coulsdon 1820, until h[is] death in 1830, father of the next named.

Lockwood, John (William), s. John, of Yoxford, Su[f]folk, cler. CHRIST CHURCH, matric. 21 Dec., 181[ ] aged 16; student 1816-38, B.A. 1821 M.A. 182[ ] vicar of Chalgrove, Oxon, 1832, rector of Chelse[a] 1836, and of Kingham, Oxon, 1836, until his deat[h] 29 Nov., 1879. [25]

Lockwood, Richard, s. William, of Fifield, Essex, cle[r]. WADHAM COLL., matric. 15 June, 1780, aged 1[ ] B.A. 1784; M.A. from JESUS COLL., Cambridge, 180[ ] rector of Potter Heigham, and of Ashby, etc., No[r]folk, 1803, vicar of Lowestoft and Kessingland 180[ ] preb. of Peterborough 1824, died 1 Nov., 1830.

Lockwood, Samuel Davis, 4s. John William, of King[]ham, Hants, cler. ST. MARY HALL, matric. [ ] Feb., 1866, aged 24; B.A. 1869, rector of Woo[d]eaton, Oxon, 1871-80, and of Kingham since 1869.

Lockwood, Rev. William, s. Richard, of St. Michael['s], Pater Noster Row, London, arm. ORIEL COLL. matric. 21 Oct., 1743, aged 17; B.A. 1747, M.A. 1750, of Fifield, Essex, a student of the Inner Temp[le] 1743, father of Richard, 1780, and of William ne[xt] named.

Lockwood, William. ORIEL COLL., 1779. See MA[Y]DWELL.

Lockwood, William, 1s. St. George's-in-the-Eas[t], London, gent. MAGDALEN HALL, matric. 5 Jul[y], 1821, aged 41. [30]

Lockwood, William, 1s. William, of Easingwol[d], Yorks, arm. UNIVERSITY COLL., matric. 17 Dec., 1821, aged 17; scholar 1822-8, B.A. 1825, M.A. 1829, vicar of Kirkby Fleetham, Yorks, died [ ] May, 1854.

Lockyer, Edmund Leopold, 1s. Edmund, of S[t.] Andrew's, Plymouth, doctor. ST. MARY HAL[L], matric. 26 Oct., 1837, aged 21; B.A. from E[M]MANUEL COLL., Cambridge, 1847, M.A. 1850, Oxford ('ad eundem') 21 June, 1855, rector [of] Westcote, Barton, Oxon. See *Eton School Lists.*

Lockyer, Thomas, o.s. Thomas, of Plymouth, Devo[n], arm. MAGDALEN HALL, matric. 1 July, 1824, ag[ed] 19; of Wembury, Devon.

Locock, Sir Charles (Bart.), F.R.S., created D.C.L. [ ] Aug., 1868 (son of Henry Locock, of Northampto[n], M.D.), first physician accoucheur to the Quee[n], D.Med. Edinburgh 1821, F.R.C.P. 1836, created baronet 5 May, 1857 (having declined it in 184[ ]) and died 23 July, 1875. See Foster's *Baronetage* Munk's *Roll.*, iii. 270.

Locock, Charles Dealtry, 1s. Alfred Henry, [ ] Brighton, cler. UNIVERSITY COLL., matric. [ ] Oct., 1881, aged 19; B.A. 1886. See Foster['s] *Baronetage* [35]

ocock, David, s. Aaron, of Wellingborough, Northants. LINCOLN COLL., matric. 8 July, 1742, aged 17; of the baronet's family. See Foster's *Baronetage.*

ocock, Henry Thornton, 2s. Alfred Henry, of Brighton, cler. TRINITY COLL., matric. 15 Oct., 1883, aged 19; B.A. 1887.

oder, Charles, s. Seymour, of Hinton, Berks, cler. ORIEL COLL., matric. 26 March, 1743, aged 16; brother of John 1743.

oder, Francis, s. Charles, of Hinton, Berks, gent. EXETER COLL., matric. 5 March, 1715-6, aged 19; B.A. 20 Feb., 1719-20.

oder, Henry, 'apothecary;' privilegiatus 8 Feb., 1759. [5]

oder, John, s. Charles, of Hinton, Berks, gent. EXETER COLL., matric. 5 March, 1715-6, aged 20.

oder, John, s. Robert, of Dorchester, Dorset, gent. HART HALL, matric. 13 Feb., 1721-2, aged 17; B.A. 15 Feb., 1725-6.

oder, John, s. Seymour, of Hinton, Berks, cler. ORIEL COLL., matric. 26 March, 1743, aged 17; B.A. 1746, rector of Hinton 1750, until his death 18 May, 1805, brother of Charles 1743.

oder, Robert, s. Robert, of ——, co. Gloucester, gent. BALLIOL COLL., matric. 24 Jan., 1728-9, aged 18.

oder, William, 'tonsor;' privilegiatus 29 Oct., 1785. [10]

oder, William, 'stationarius,' 'tonsor;' privilegiatus 13 Dec., 1802.

oder, William; privilegiatus 26 Oct., 1813.

odge, Alfred, 3s. Oliver, of Penkhull, co. Stafford, gent. MAGDALEN COLL., matric. 1 Feb., 1873, aged 18, exhibitioner 1872-6, B.A. 1876; Fereday fellow ST. JOHN'S COLL. 1876, M.A. 1880.

odge, Aneurin Lloyd, 3s. Thomas, of Denbigh (town), gent. JESUS COLL., matric. 27 Feb., 1840, aged 18; B.A. 1844, M.A. 1864, rector of Wavertree 1859.

odge, Edmund, s. Edmund, of Newcastle, Northumberland, cler. LINCOLN COLL., matric. 25 Feb., 1725-6, aged 17; B.A. 1729. [15]

odge, Frederick, 2s. Lorenzo, of Queenborough, Tasmania, gent. NEW COLL., matric. 14 Oct., 1882, aged 19; B.A. 1885, a student of the Inner Temple 1884.

odge, John, s. John, of Deepdale, Yorks, gent. UNIVERSITY COLL., matric. 10 May, 1777, aged 20; B.A. 1782, rector of Coddington, co. Hereford, 1781-1801, vicar of Bosbury 1801, until his death in 1830.

odge, Rev. John, scholar TRINITY COLL., Cambridge, B.A. 1814, M.A. 1817; fellow MAGDALEN COLL., Cambridge, 1818-36, and proctor; adm. 'ad eundem' 1 July, 1829, University librarian (Cambridge) 1822-47, died at Keene Ground, Hawkshead, Lancashire, 27 Aug., 1850.

odge, John, s. Adam, of Liverpool, Lancashire, arm. BRASENOSE COLL., matric. 1 April, 1818, aged 17; B.A. 1821, M.A. 1828.

odge, John Alfred, 1s. James, of Abergavenny, co. Monmouth, gent. JESUS COLL., matric. 9 Feb., 1865, aged 21; B.A. 1867, vicar of Haverton Hill, co. Durham, 1875. [20]

odge, Oliver, 2s. Robert John, of Stepney, Middlesex, gent. ST. JOHN'S COLL., matric. 22 Oct., 1859, aged 19; scholar PEMBROKE COLL. 1860-5, B.A. 1863, bar.-at-law, Inner Temple, 1865. See Foster's *Men at the Bar* & *Robinson*, 306.

odge, Richard, s. John, of Enfield, Middlesex, arm. CHRIST CHURCH, matric. 17 Dec., 1759, aged 16.

odge, Richard, 4s. Oliver, of Penkhull, co. Stafford, arm. BALLIOL COLL., matric. 20 Oct., 1874, aged 19, exhibitioner 1874-5, scholar 1875-8; fellow BRASENOSE COLL. 1878, B.A. 1878, M.A. 1881, lecturer, junior bursar 1880, historical lecturer 1881-5, senior dean 1883, tutor 1884, librarian 1885.

Lodge, Samuel, 9s. Oliver, of Barking, Essex, cler. LINCOLN COLL., matric. 13 March, 1847, aged 18; B.A. 1851, M.A. 1853, rector of Scrivelsby, co. Lincoln, 1867, preb. of Lincoln 1879.

Loehnis, Herman William, 1s. Herman, of New York, arm. TRINITY COLL., matric. 14 Oct., 1876, aged 19; B.A. 1880, M.A. 1885, bar.-at-law, Inner Temple, 1882. See Foster's *Men at the Bar.* [25]

Lofft, Henry Capel, 1s. Robert Emlyn, of Troston, Suffolk, arm. EXETER COLL., matric. 28 Jan., 1847, aged 18; assumed the name of MOSELEY in lieu of his patronymic, died in 1866.

Loft, Charles Percival, 6s. John Henry, of Louth, co. Lincoln, arm. EXETER COLL., matric. 16 Dec., 1825, aged 18.

Loft, Henry, B.A. from SIDNEY SUSSEX COLL., Cambridge, 1732; fellow KING'S COLL., Cambridge, M.A. 1736, incorp. 7 July, 1738.

Loftie, John, s. William, of Sittingbourne, Kent, gent. CHRIST CHURCH, matric. 1 July, 1752, aged 17; B.A. 1756, vicar of St. Dunstan's, Canterbury, and curate of Wingham, Kent, died in 1800.

Loftus, Adam Robert Charles, 3s. John Henry, Marquis of Ely. BALLIOL COLL., matric. 16 May, 1834, aged 18; rector of Magheraculmoney, co. Fermanagh, died 25 Dec., 1866. See Foster's *Peerage.* [30]

Loftus, Arthur John, o.s. Arthur, of Rathangan, Ireland, gent. WORCESTER COLL., matric. 14 May, 1835, aged 18; of Rathangan, co. Kildare, keeper of the jewels in the Tower of London 1883, late gentleman usher to the Queen, late captain 18th hussars. See Foster's *Peerage,* M. ELY.

Loftus, Henry Yorke Astley, 5s. John Henry, Marquis of Ely. ORIEL COLL., matric. 21 May, 1840, aged 18; B.A. 1843, died 28 Feb., 1880. See Foster's *Peerage.*

Loftus, John, 2nd Marquis of Ely, K.P., created D.C.L. 3 July, 1810 (son of Charles, Marquis of Ely), M.P. co. Wexford 1790-1806, lord high-treasurer of Ireland and privy councillor, died 26 Sep., 1845.

Loftus, John Henry, Viscount, 1s. John, Marquis of Ely. CHRIST CHURCH, matric. 24 Oct., 1832, aged 18; 3rd marquis, M.P. Woodstock in 1845, died 15 July, 1857.

Loftus, John Henry (Wellington) Graham, 4th Marquis of Ely, 1s. John Henry, Marquis of Ely. MERTON COLL., matric. 10 April, 1869, aged 19. See Foster's *Peerage.* [35]

Loftus, William, 3s. John, of London, gent. ST. ALBAN HALL, matric. 20 Oct., 1865, aged 39; B.A. 1869, M.A. 1872, vicar of East Tytherley, Hants, 1876, until his death 28 Feb., 1888.

Logan, Alexander Cochrane, 1s. Alexander Cochrane, of Mandeville, Jamaica, arm. BALLIOL COLL., matric. 16 Oct., 1879, aged 18; of the Indian Civil Service 1879.

Logan, Joseph, 3s. James, of Liverpool, gent. PEMBROKE COLL., matric. 3 June, 1852, aged 18.

Logan, Logan, 1s. Joseph Dobinson, of St. Marylebone, London, gent. WADHAM COLL., matric. 10 Nov., 1836, aged 18; B.A. 1840, rector of Lookington, Yorks, 1853, assumed the name of LOGAN in lieu of DOBINSON.

Logan, Robert Henry, 1s. Robert, of Legerwood, co. Berwick, arm. BALLIOL COLL., matric. 28 Jan., 1878, aged 19; B.A. 1885, bar.-at-law, Middle Temple, 1884. See Foster's *Men at the Bar.* [40]

Loggin, Edward, s. William, of Beoley, co. Worcester, cler. TRINITY COLL., matric. 27 Oct., 1757, aged 19; B.C.L. from NEW COLL. 1766.

Loggin, Rev. George, s. George, of Rugby, co. Warwick, gent. HERTFORD COLL., matric. 16 Dec., 1801, aged 17, B.A. 1805; M.A. from TRINITY COLL. 1815, assistant master Rugby School 1809, until his death 12 July, 1824. See *Rugby School Reg.*, xiv., 71.

Loggin, John, s. John, of Swalecliffe, Oxon, cler. MERTON COLL., matric. 1 April, 1715, aged 18; B.A. 1718, M.A. 1721.

Loggin, John, s. John, of Sulgrave, Northants, cler. QUEEN'S COLL., matric. 4 June, 1747, aged 18.

Loggin, Thomas, s. John, of Long Marston, co. Gloucester, cler. TRINITY COLL., matric. 2 Dec., 1724, aged 16; B.A. 1728, M.A. 31 Jan., 1733-4.

Loggin, William, s. John, of Swalecliffe, Oxon, cler. TRINITY COLL., matric. 31 March, 1721, aged 17; B.A. 1724, probably brother of John 1715.

Loggin, William, s. William, of Beoley, Worcester, cler. MAGDALEN HALL, matric. 25 May, 1762, aged 17; B.A. 1766. [5]

Loggin, William, s. William, of Stratford-on-Avon, co. Warwick, cler. WORCESTER COLL., matric. 15 Dec., 1795, aged 18; B.A. from CORPUS CHRISTI COLL., Cambridge, 1809, rector (and patron) of Long Marston, co. Gloucester, 1808, and of Woolfardisworthy, Devon, 1830, until his death 28 April, 1831.

Loggon, Samuel, s. William, of ——, co. Hereford, pleb. BALLIOL COLL., matric. 23 Jan., 1729-30, aged 18; B.A. 1733, M.A. 1736.

Lohr, George Samuel Lewis, 1s. George Augustus, of Leicester, gent. (chorister MAGDALEN COLL. 1829-35). NEW COLL., matric. 19 Oct., 1874, aged 24.

Lomas, George, 3s. John, of Manchester, gent. ST. EDMUND HALL, matric. 22 Oct., 1869, aged 20; commoner MAGDALEN HALL 1870, S.C.L. & B.A. 1873, M.A. (HERTFORD COLL.) 1876, vicar of Musbury, Lancashire, since 1876.

Lomas, George, 2s. George, of Farnworth, Lancashire, gent. NEW COLL., matric. 18 Oct., 1875, aged 41; B.Mus. 26 Oct., 1876. [10]

Lomas, Henry, s. Thomas, of Gluton, co. Derby, pleb. WADHAM COLL., matric. 17 Oct., 1769, aged 21; B.A. 1773.

Lomas, Holland, 1s. George, of Farnworth, Lancashire, arm. BRASENOSE COLL., matric. 21 Jan., 1841, aged 19; B.A. from ST. MARY HALL, 1848, M.A. 1860, perp. curate St. Luke, Leeds, 1851-4, and of Walton Break, Lancashire, 1855-80, rector of Zeal Monachorum, Devon, 1885, until his death 7 July, 1886.

Lomas, John, 1s. William, of Strangways, near Manchester, gent. WORCESTER COLL., matric. 23 Feb., 1837, aged 33; B.A. 1840, M.A. 1843, perp. curate Walton Break, near Liverpool, 1846, until his death 6 Sep., 1854.

Lomas, Thomas, s. Edward, of Prestbury, Cheshire, gent. BRASENOSE COLL., matric. 3 April, 1780, aged 20; B.A. 1784, M.A. 1786, perp. curate Leeds, Kent, 1798, until his death 8-15 Nov., 1843. See *Manchester School Reg.*, ii., 13.

Lomax, Caleb, s. Caleb, of Childwickbury, Herts, arm. TRINITY COLL., matric. 16 Nov., 1745, aged 17; of Childwickbury, died 2 Dec., 1786. [15]

Lomax, Charles Henry, 1s. Thomas, of London, gent. CORPUS CHRISTI COLL., matric. 19 Oct., 1870, aged 19; exhibitioner 1871-4, B.A. 1873, M.A. 1879, bar.-at-law, Inner Temple, 1876. See Foster's *Men at the Bar* & *Rugby School Reg.*

Lomax, Edmund Shallett, s. Caleb, of St. Albans, Herts, arm. ST. JOHN'S COLL., matric. 9 Feb., 1771, aged 18; B.A. 1774, of Netley Place, Surrey.

Lomax, John, 4s. James, of Aldridge, co. Stafford, cler. MAGDALEN HALL, matric. 29 June, 1822, aged 31.

Lomax, Rev. John, s. Richard, of Bury, Lancashire, arm. QUEEN'S COLL., matric. 12 Feb., 1852, aged 18; a commoner MAGDALEN HALL 1855, B.A. 1859, M.A. (HERTFORD COLL.) 1876.

Lomax, John Acton, 1s. John, of Stibbard, Norfo cler. BRASENOSE COLL., matric. 22 Oct., 18 aged 19; scholar 1880-2. [2

Lombard, Rev. John, s. Edmund, of Kilshaich, Cork, cler. HERTFORD COLL., matric. 14 June, 17 aged 19; died 3 Jan., 1847. See *Gent.'s Ma* 1847, i., 445.

Lombard, John, M.A. TRINITY COLL., Dubl 1864, B.A. 1849, adm. 'comitatis causa' 16 Ju 1864 (son Rev. John Newman Lombard), rector Booterstown, co. Dublin, 1874, chaplain to the lo lieut. 1875. See Foster's *Our Noble and Gen Families*, ii.

Lomer, Edward Bridges, 2s. Edward, of Southampt Hants, gent. ORIEL COLL., matric. 2 Dec., 18 aged 19; B.A. 1852, M.A. 1854, bar.-at-law, In Temple, 1853, died 6 Aug., 1865. See *Rugby Sch Reg.*, 250.

London, John, 'tonsor'; privilegiatus 5 July, 1794.

London, William, 'tonsor'; privilegiatus 25 Fe 1825. [2

Long, Arthur Heathcote Montagu, 5s. William, London, arm. EXETER COLL., matric. 22 Ap 1865, aged 19; bar.-at-law, Inner Temple, 18 See Foster's *Men at the Bar.*

Long, Benjamin, o.s. Benjamin, of St. Mauri Winchester, gent. NEW COLL., matric. 3 Ju 1845, aged 43; B.Mus. 5 June, 1845.

Long, Charles, s. John, of Lopley, Hants, gent. PE BROKE COLL., matric. 1 Feb., 1717-8, aged 2 B.A. 21 Feb., 1721-2.

Long, Charles Beckford, s. Edward, of Chichest Sussex, arm. CHRIST CHURCH, matric. 10 Oc 1789, aged 18; B.A. 1794, student until 1812, di 1836.

Long, Rev. Charles Edward, 2s. William Charles, Beenham, Berks, arm. ST. JOHN'S COLL., matri 4 Dec., 1850, aged 19; B.A. 1855, M.A. 1858. [3

Long, Charles Newell, o.s. Charles Edward, Leamington, co. Warwick, cler. KEBLE COL matric. 19 Oct., 1886, aged 18.

Long, Claudius Horatius, 3s. Jeremiah, of St. Leonar Shoreditch, Middlesex, gent. EXETER COL matric. 22 Oct., 1859, aged 18; B.A. 1863, M. 1867.

Long, Donald Macdonald, o.s. Henry Nosworthy, Southsea, Hants, gent. ST. MARY HALL, matr 1 Dec., 1870, aged 21.

Long, Ernest Henry Kellett, 3s. Robert Kellett, Dunston, Norfolk, arm. CHRIST CHURCH, matr 13 Oct., 1865, aged 19; B.A. 1868, M.A. 18 rector of Tickencote, Rutland, 1880-4, and Newton Flotman, Norfolk, 1884, and vicar Dunston 1885. See Foster's *Our Noble and Gen. Families.*

Long, Fortescue Walter Kellett, 1s. Robert Kelle of Dunston, Norfolk, arm. CHRIST CHURC matric. 24 April, 1863, aged 19; B.A. 1867, M. 1871, of Dunston Hall aforesaid. See Foster's *O Noble and Gentle Families.* [3

Long, Rev. Francis, 2s. Michael, of Ashford, Ke gent. NON-COLL., matric. 22 Jan., 1881, aged 2 exhibitioner UNIVERSITY COLL. 1881-5, B.A. 18 M.A. 1887.

Long, Frank, 2s. William Edward, of New Wan worth, Surrey, arm. MAGDALEN COLL., matric. Oct., 1886, aged 22.

Long, Rev. Frederick Charles (Impey), 1s. Freder Charles, of Bala, co. Merioneth, cler. NON-COL matric. 22 Jan., 1876, aged 19; commoner NE COLL. 1876, B.A. 1879, M.A. 1882.

Long, Frederick Edward, scholar KING'S COLL., Ca bridge, 1835-8, fellow 1838-56, B.A. 1840, M. 1844; adm. 'ad eundem' 22 May, 1845, incumbe of Butterton, co. Stafford, 1856-75, rector of Wo ton, 1875.

Long, George, s. George, of Camberwell, Surrey, pl PEMBROKE COLL., matric. 30 May, 1770, aged 1 B.A. from NEW COLL. 1774. [4

ong, Henry, s. Henry, of St. Giles's, Oxon, pleb. MAGDALEN COLL., matric. 17 March, 1721-2, aged 18; chorister 1716-21, clerk 1722-5, B.A. 1725. See *Bloxam*, i. 143.

ong, Henry William, 2s. Walter, of Chalcot, near Westbury, Wilts, arm. TRINITY COLL., matric. 1 Dec., 1848, aged 19; B.A. 1852, M.A. 1858, rector of Hilperton, Wilts, 1854, until his death 30 Jan., 1876.

ong, James, s. James, of Wells (city), gent. LINCOLN COLL., matric. 29 March, 1721, aged 16; B.A. 1724.

ong, James, s. Lewis, of Wootton Bassett, Wilts, gent. QUEEN'S COLL., matric. 23 Sep., 1755, aged 16; B.A. 1760.

ong, (Sir) James (Tylney), s. Robert, of St. George's, Hanover Square, London, baronet. ORIEL COLL., matric. 2 Nov., 1756, aged 19; 7th baronet, M.P. Marlborough, (May) 1762-80, Devizes 1780-8, Wilts 1788-94, took the additional name of TYLNEY, died 28 Nov., 1794. **[5]**

ong, John, s. Richard, of Broad Clist, Devon, cler. BALLIOL COLL., matric. 24 March, 1715-6, aged 17.

ong, John, s. Richard, of Rood Ashton, Wilts, arm. MAGDALEN COLL., matric. 11 Oct., 1748, aged 17, B.A. 1752; fellow ALL SOULS' COLL. 1752, M.A. 1756, B.D. 1764, D.D. 1768, proctor 1763, rector of Freshford, Somerset, 1756-81, vicar of Whaddon, Wilts, 1770-81, rector of Chelsfield 1781, until his death 17 Oct., 1797. See *Bloxam*, vi. 275.

ong, John Bateman, s. Charles, of Lisbon, arm. CHRIST CHURCH, matric. 25 Nov., 1723, bar.-at-law, Inner Temple, 1730.

ong, John Neale Henry, 2s. William, of Bath, Somerset, arm. ST. MARY HALL, matric. 15 May, 1872, aged 22.

ong, John Speccott, s. Thomas, of Egloskerry, Cornwall, gent. EXETER COLL., matric. 27 July, 1736, aged 18. **[10]**

ong, Maurice St. Clair, 2s. Edwin, of London, gent. MERTON COLL., matric. 18 Oct., 1881, aged 19; B.A. 1885.

ong, Phipps, s. Samuel, of Shabbington, Bucks, cler. MAGDALEN COLL., matric. 27 Oct., 1789, aged 18, chorister 1784-90; B.A. from ALL SOULS' COLL. 1793, M.A. 1797, vicar of Shabbington 1799, until his death 8 Aug., 1846. See *Bloxam*, i., 201.

ong, Richard, s. Richard, of Lavington, Wilts, arm. MAGDALEN COLL., matric. 2 Dec., 1746, aged 18; created M.A. 1 April, 1754.

ong, Richard, s. William, of Kensington, Middlesex, pleb. UNIVERSITY COLL., matric. 14 May, 1748, aged 18.

ong, Richard, s. Beeston, of Bishopsgate Street, London, arm. ST. MARY HALL, matric. 27 March, 1778, aged 23; died unmarried. **[15]**

ong, Richard, s. Richard, of Rood Aston, Wilts, arm. BALLIOL COLL., matric. 23 May, 1814, aged 19; died in 1825.

ong, Richard Seymour, 1s. Richard England, of Liverpool, gent. NON-COLL., matric. 29 Jan., 1881, aged 18; exhibitioner BALLIOL COLL. 1882-5, B.A. 1884.

ong, (Sir) Robert (Bart.), s. James, of St. James's, Westminster, baronet. BALLIOL COLL., matric. 17 March, 1721-2, aged 16; 6th baronet, M.P. Wootton Bassett 1734-40, Wilts, 1741, until his death 10 Feb., 1767.

ong, Samuel, s. Charles, of Cheveley, Berks, doctor. CHRIST CHURCH, matric. 27 May, 1745, aged 18; B.A. 3 Feb., 1748-9, M.A. 1751.

ong, Thomas, M.A. TRINITY COLL., Dublin, 1860 (B.A. 1850); adm. 'ad eundem' 14 June, 1860, rector of St. Michan's, Dublin, 1873. **[20]**

ong, Walter, s. Walter, of Salisbury, Wilts, arm. QUEEN'S COLL., matric. 20 July, 1739, aged 16; bar.-at-law, Lincoln's Inn, 1747, and a bencher, 1772, F.S.A., 45 years judge of Sheriff's Court, London, died 20 March, 1807.

Long, Walter, s. John, of Preshaw, Hants, arm. ORIEL COLL., matric. 26 April, 1805, aged 16; B.A. 1809, M.A. 1812, of Preshaw and Muchelney, Hants, J.P., D.L., high sheriff 1824, a student of Lincoln's Inn 1809, died 5 Jan., 1871.

Long, Walter, s. Richard, of Bath, Somerset, arm. CHRIST CHURCH, matric. 17 Oct., 1811, aged 18; of Rood Ashton, Wilts, M.P. North Wilts in 7 parliaments 1835-65, died 31 Jan., 1867, father of the next named.

Long, Walter, 1s. Walter, of Marylebone, Middlesex, arm. CHRIST CHURCH, matric. 26 May, 1841, aged 17; died 17 April, 1847. See *Eton School Lists*.

Long, Walter Hume, 1s. Richard Penruddocke, of Bath, arm. CHRIST CHURCH, matric. 4 Nov., 1873, aged 19; of Rood Ashton and Wroxall, Wilts, J.P., D.L., M.P. North Wilts 1880-5, Wilts (Devizes division) 1885, etc., secretary to Local Government Board, 1886. **[25]**

Long, Walter Jervis, 1s. Walter, of Corhampton, Hants, arm. ORIEL COLL., matric. 17 May, 1834, aged 17; of Newton House and Woodlands, Somerset, J.P., etc.

Long, William, 2s. Walter, of Corhampton, Hants, arm. BALLIOL COLL., matric. 5 June, 1835, aged 17; B.A. 1839, M.A. 1844, of Wrington, Somerset, J.P., F.S.A.

Long, William Beeston, 1s. William, of Combe, Somerset, arm. CHRIST CHURCH, matric. 12 June, 1851, aged 18; B.A. 1856, of Hurts Hall, Suffolk, J.P., D.L., high sheriff 1879, a student of the Inner Temple 1856, etc.

Long, William Duncan, M.A. TRINITY COLL., Dublin, 1840 (B.A. 1837); adm. 'ad eundem' 14 June, 1860, rector of Bermondsey 1859-65, vicar of Godalming, Surrey, 1865, until his death 12 April, 1875. See *Crockford*.

Long, William Edward, elder son of William Edward, of Battersea, Surrey, arm. MAGDALEN COLL., matric. 16 Oct., 1880, aged 18, demy 1879-84, B.A. 1884; fellow QUEEN'S COLL. 1885, M.A. 1887. **[30]**

Long, William Nethersole, s. William, of Canterbury (city), arm. CHRIST CHURCH, matric. 12 Oct., 1789, aged 17.

Longbourne, Alfred, 5s. William Thomas, of Blackmoor, Essex, gent. LINCOLN COLL., matric. 7 Feb., 1870, aged 19. See *Eton School Lists*.

Longden, George, s. Robert, of Wormhill, co. Derby, gent. WADHAM COLL., matric. 29 April, 1771, aged 17; B.A. 1775.

Longden, Henry, s. Henry, of Fairfield, co. Derby, arm. BRASENOSE COLL., matric. 23 Oct., 1765, aged 18; B.A. from MERTON COLL. 1769, rector of Whitsbury, Wilts, 1777, and of Rockbourne, Hants, died 2 Feb., 1824.

Longden, Rev. Henry Isham, 1s. Charles Scudamore, of Lamport, Northants, arm. KEBLE COLL., matric. 14 Oct., 1878, aged 19; B.A. 1882, M.A. 1886. **[35]**

Longden, John, s. Robert, of Gloucester (city), pleb. ST. JOHN'S COLL., matric. 4 April, 1734, aged 15; B.A. 1737, M.A. 1740, rector of Winstone, and perp. curate of Barnwood and Flaxley, co. Gloucester, died 17 Oct., 1808.

Longdon, John, s. John, of Winston, co. Gloucester, cler. PEMBROKE COLL., matric. 25 March, 1773, aged 18.

Longe, Francis Davy, 2s. Robert, of Combs, Suffolk, cler. ORIEL COLL., matric. 17 May, 1850, aged 18; B.A. 1854, bar.-at-law, Inner Temple, 1858, Local Government Board inspector 1871. See Foster's *Men at the Bar*.

Longe, Henry Browne, of DOWNING COLL., Cambridge (B.A. 1825, M.A. 1828), adm. 'ad eundem' 24 Nov., 1859 (son of John, vicar of Coddenham, Suffolk), rector of Monewden, Suffolk, 1847.

Longe, Herbert Davy, 3s. John, of Sidmouth, Devon, cler. PEMBROKE COLL., matric. 26 Oct., 1881, aged 19.

Longfellow, Henry Wadsworth, created D.C.L. 27 July, 1869 (son of Stephen Longfellow, a member of Congress), American poet, professor of modern languages in Bowdoin College 1829-35, and in Harvard College 1836-54, LL.D. Cambridge, born at Portland, Maine, U.S.A., 27 Feb., 1807, died 24 March, 1882.

Longfield, Mountifort John Courtenay, o.s. Mountifort, of Castle Mary, co. Cork, arm. BRASENOSE COLL., matric. 14 Oct., 1876, aged 17; of Castle Mary, co. Cork. See *Eton School Lists.*

Longford, John, s. John, of Town Malling, Kent, gent. BRASENOSE COLL., matric. 1 Feb., 1774, aged 17.

Longford, Richard, s. John, of Malpas, Cheshire, cler. BRASENOSE COLL., matric. 14 Dec., 1744, aged 17. [5]

Longford, Thomas, s. William, of Stretton, co. Warwick, cler. QUEEN'S COLL., matric. 7 Dec., 1792, aged 18; B.A. 1796.

Longford, William, s. Thomas, of Sevenhampton, co. Gloucester, pleb. QUEEN'S COLL., matric. 3 July, 1754, aged 18; B.A. 1758, M.A. 1770.

Longford, William, s. William, of Stretton, co. Warwick, cler. PEMBROKE COLL., matric. 6 June, 1787, aged 16; B.A. 1792, M.A. 1794. (Memo.: William Hawes Longford, rector of Stretton-cum-Ditchford, co. Warwick, 1809.)

Longhurst, William Henry Roberts, 2s. Charles, of Bruntingthorpe, co. Leicester, cler. PEMBROKE COLL., matric. 10 June, 1858, aged 19; B.A. 1863, M.A. 1871, vicar of Holy Trinity, Worcester, 1871-9, and of Kempsey, co. Worcester, 1879.

Longland, Rev. Charles Boxall, 1s. Charles Pitman, of Rotherfield Greys, Oxon, cler. WORCESTER COLL., matric. 27 June, 1881, aged 19; B.A. 1885, M.A. 1888. [10]

Longlands, Rev. David, s. Thomas, of Greenwich, Kent, arm. CHRIST CHURCH, matric. 16 May, 1804, aged 18; B.A. 1808, M.A. 1810, student 1804, until his death in Oct., 1849. See *Alumni West.*, 461.

Longlands, Herbert (Penderel), 1s. William David, of Aston, near Stevenage, Herts, cler. BALLIOL COLL., matric. 6 April, 1848, aged 18; B.A. 1853, M.A. 1883.

Longlands, William David, s. Alexander, of Greenwich, Kent, gent. EXETER COLL., matric. 20 Feb., 1810, aged 18; Michel scholar QUEEN'S COLL. 1815-16, B.A. 1814, fellow BALLIOL COLL. 1816-22, M.A. 1816, a student of Lincoln's Inn 1811, rector of St. Gerrans, Devon, 1844, died 27 Dec., 1866.

Longley, Charles Thomas, s. John, of Rochester, Kent, arm. CHRIST CHURCH, matric. 9 May, 1812, aged 17; student 1812-28, B.A. 1815, M.A. 1818, B. & D.D. 1829, Greek reader 1822, tutor and censor 1825-8, proctor 1827, hon. student 1867-8, Whitehall preacher 1827, and rector of Tytherley, Hants, 1827, head-master Harrow, 1829-36, bishop of Ripon 1836-57, of Durham 1856-60, archbishop of York, 1860-2, archbishop of Canterbury 1862, until his death in Oct., 1868. See *Alumni West.*, 475.

Longley, Henry, 1s. Charles Thomas, bishop of Ripon. CHRIST CHURCH, matric. 2 June, 1852, aged 18; student 1853-61, B.A. 1856, M.A. 1859, B.C.L. 1863, bar.-at-law, Lincoln's Inn, 1860, 1st charity commissioner since 1885, etc. See Foster's *Men at the Bar* & *Rugby School Reg.*, 264. [15]

Longley, John, 3s. John, of Isle of Zante, arm. CHRIST CHURCH, matric. 18 Jan., 1856, aged 20; a merchant in India, died in Bombay in Dec., 1866. See *Rugby School Reg.*

Longley, John Augustine, o.s. Henry, of Lambeth, Surrey, arm. CHRIST CHURCH, matric. 30 May, 1885, aged 18.

Longman, Charles James, 2s. William, of London arm. UNIVERSITY COLL., matric. 15 Oct., 1870 aged 18; B.A. 1874, M.A. 1877.

Longman, Frederick William, 1s. William, of Paddingtou, Middlesex, arm. BALLIOL COLL., matric 17 Oct., 1864, aged 18.

Longman, Hubert Harry, 3s. William, of Chorlewood, Herts, gent. UNIVERSITY COLL., matric 16 Oct., 1875, aged 18. [20

Longman, John, s. James, of North Cadbury, Somerset, pleb. ST. MARY HALL, matric. 10 March 1729-30, aged 18; B.A. 27 Feb., 1734-5 (? of Cleyhiddon). See next entry.

Longman, John, s. John, of Cleyhiddon, Devon. cler TRINITY COLL., matric. 27 April, 1762, aged 19 B.A. 1766.

Longmire, George, s. James, of Windermere, Westmoreland, cler. QUEEN'S COLL., matric. 10 Oct. 1726, aged 20; B.A. 1731, M.A. 1735.

Longmire, James Fox, 3s. John Martyn, of Hargrave Northants, cler. WORCESTER COLL., matric. 1 June, 1829, aged 18; scholar 1830-3.

Longmire, John Martyn, 1s. John, of Wrestlingnorth Beds, cler. ST. EDMUND HALL, matric. 5 Feb. 1823, aged 17; B.A. 1828. [25

Longmire, Joseph Leopold, 2s. John Martyn, c Flangrave, Northants, cler. WORCESTER COLL. matric. 24 Nov., 1836, aged 18; exhibitioner LINCOLN COLL. 1838-45, B.A. 1840, M.A. 1844, recto of Sandiacre, co. Derby, 1849-79.

Longmore, Alexander, s. William, of Bath, Somerset arm. WADHAM COLL., matric. 22 Oct., 1776, age 22.

Longmore, Philip Alexander, scholar EMMANUE COLL., Cambridge, 1845, B.A. 1847, M.A. 1850 adm. 'comitatis causa' 2 June, 1865, incumbent c Hermitage, near Newbury, Berks, 1852.

Longmore, Samuel, s. Samuel, of St. Andrew's, Worcester (city), pleb. ST. MARY HALL, matric. 1 March, 1718-9, aged 18; B.A. 1722, died rector (All Saints, Worcester, in 1736.

Longridge, Rev. George, 5s. James Atkinson, (London, arm. BRASENOSE COLL., matric. 20 Ma 1875, aged 18; B.A. 1879. See *Eton School Lists.*

Longridge, James, 3s. James Atkinson, of Newcastle on-Tyne, Northumberland, arm. BRASENOSE COLL. matric. 4 June, 1868, aged 18; B.A. 1873, M.A 1876, curate of High Wycombe 1873-7, and of S John's, Hammersmith, 1877-85, vicar of St. Clement's City Road, London, 1885. [3

Longridge, Rev. William Hawks, 2s. James Atkinson, of Newcastle-on-Tyne, Northumberland, arm CORPUS CHRISTI COLL., matric. 20 Oct., 1868, age 19; exhibitioner 1871-3, B.A. 1873.

Longrigg, Rev. John Fallowfield, 1s. John, of Gre Strickland, Westmoreland, gent. QUEEN'S COLL matric. 22 Oct., 1878, aged 18; B.A. 1882, M.A 1886.

Longrigg, Joseph William, 2s. John, of Appleb Westmoreland, gent. QUEEN'S COLL., matric. May, 1867, aged 18; B.A. 1871, M.A. 1874, chapla R.N. since 1881.

Longrigg, William, 3s. John, of Maines, near Ki Oswald, Cumberland, gent. QUEEN'S COLL., matri 6 June, 1850, aged 18; taberbar 1850-4, B.A. 185 M.A. 1857. [3

Longsdon, John Wilson, 3s. Henry John, of Seacro Yorks, cler. ST. JOHN'S COLL., matric. 15 Oc 1881, aged 20, B.A. 1887. See *Robinson*, 382.

Longstaff, George Blundell, 2s. George Dixon, Wandsworth, Surrey, D.Med. NEW COLL., matri 16 Oct., 1868, aged 19; scholar 1868-73, B.A. 187 B.Med. & M.A. 1876. See *Rugby School Reg.*

Longstaff, Rev. Thomas, o.s. Thomas, of Londo gent. NON-COLL., matric. 11 Oct., 1873, aged 1 B.A. 1877, M.A. 1880.

Longueville, John Gibbons, 2s. Thomas, of Oswestry, Salop, arm. WADHAM COLL., matric. 25 March, 1829, aged 18; B.A. 1833, M.A. 1836, rector of Eccleston, Cheshire, 1854-80, died 14 July, 1882.

Longueville, Thomas, 1s. Thomas Longueville, of Mount, near Oswestry, Salop, arm. CHRIST CHURCH, matric. 27 Jan., 1865, aged 20.

Longvill, William, of ST. MARY HALL, created M.A. 17 July, 1777. See *Acts Book*.

Longworth, Edward Travers Dames, 1s. Francis Travers, of Dublin, arm. NEW COLL., matric. 16 Oct., 1880, aged 19; B.A. 1885, a student of the Middle Temple 1882.

Longworth, Francis, 1s. Francis, of Sparksbrook House, co. Warwick, arm. MERTON COLL., matric. 12 Dec., 1822, aged 19; died 1856. [5]

Longworth, Ralph, s. Edward, of Michaels, Lancashire, gent. QUEEN'S COLL., matric. 24 Jan., 1736-7, aged 17; B.A. 1740.

Longworth, Thomas James, 3s. Francis, of 'St. Phil.,' Birmingham, arm. JESUS COLL., matric. 9 Feb., 1826, aged 19; B.A. 1831, M.A. 1833, vicar of Bromfield, Salop, died 7 Nov., 1865.

Lonsdale, Arthur Pemberton (Heywood), y.s. Henry Gilbert, of Wakefield, Yorks, cler. BALLIOL COLL., matric. 14 March, 1853, aged 18; B.A. 1858, of Carntown, co. Louth, high sheriff 1877, of Drumgoon, co. Fermanagh, and of Shavington, Salop, J.P., D.L., bar.-at-law, Lincoln's Inn, 1862. See Foster's *Men at the Bar* & *Eton School Lists*.

Lonsdale, James Gylby, 1s. John, of Clapham, Surrey, cler. (after bishop of Lichfield). BALLIOL COLL., matric. 30 Nov., 1833, aged 17; scholar 1833-8, B.A. 1837, fellow 1838-64, M.A. 1840, tutor 1840, catechetical lecturer, moderator 1855-6, a student of Lincoln's Inn 1838, rector of Luffenham 1870-3, and of Huntspill, Somerset, 1873-8, professor of classical literature at King's College, London, 1865-70. See *Eton School Lists*.

Lonsdale, William, o.s. William Hilton, of Manchester, arm. ORIEL COLL., matric. 12 Dec., 1833, aged 18; B.A. 1837, bar.-at-law, Inner Temple, 1840. See Foster's *Men at the Bar* & *Rugby School Reg.*, 158. [10]

Lonsdall, John Grenehalgh, s. Miles, of Manchester, Lancashire, arm. QUEEN'S COLL., matric. 17 March, 1785, aged 18; B.A. 1789. See *Manchester School Reg.*, ii. 12.

Lonsdall, Miles, s. Miles, of Bury, Lancashire, gent. BRASENOSE COLL., matric. 26 Jan., 1754, aged 17; B.A. 1757, M.A. 1760, rector of Gawsworth, Cheshire, 1769, until his death 5 Dec., 1785.

Looker, Thomas, 'servant to Dr. Forster;' privilegiatus 19 May, 1778.

Loop, John, s. George, of Wareham, Dorset, gent. EXETER COLL., matric. 17 Dec., 1726, aged 19; B.A. from ST. EDMUND HALL 1731, vicar of Morden, Kent, 1737.

Loop, John, s. John, of Morton, Dorset, cler. WADHAM COLL., matric. 17 Oct., 1760, aged 19; B.A. 1764, vicar of Great Tudely with Capel, Kent, 1787. [15]

Lopes, Edmund Francis, 4s. Ralph, of Tamerton, Devon, baronet. ORIEL COLL., matric. 2 June, 1853, aged 19; died 28 Feb., 1867. See Foster's *Baronetage*.

Lopes, George Ludlow, 5s. Ralph, of Tamerton, Devon, baronet. EXETER COLL., matric. 12 Oct., 1855, aged 19; of Greenhill House, Wilts, J.P., D.L. See Foster's *Baronetage* & *Rugby School Reg.*

Lopes, (Right Hon. Sir) Henry Charles, 3s. Ralph, of Mainstow, Devon, baronet. BALLIOL COLL., matric. 12 Dec., 1845, aged 18; B.A. 1849, bar.-at-law, Inner Temple, 1852, Q.C. 1869, and bencher 1870, lord justice of appeal and privy councillor Dec., 1885, recorder of Exeter 1867-76, M.P. Launceston 1868-74, Frome 1874-6, a justice Common Pleas 1876-9, of Queen's Bench 1879-85. See Foster's *Men at the Bar*.

Lopes, Henry Ludlow, 1s. Sir Henry, of Maristow Devon, knight. BALLIOL COLL., matric. 22 Jan. 1885, aged 19.

Lopes, Henry Yarde Buller, 1s. Sir Massey, of Tamerton Folliott, Devon, baronet. BALLIOL COLL., matric. 31 May, 1879, aged 20; a student of the Inner Temple 1881. See Foster's *Baronetage* & *Eton School Lists*. [20]

Lopes, (Sir) Massey Lopes (Bart.), 1s. Ralph, of London, baronet. ORIEL COLL., matric. 14 June, 1838, aged 19; B.A. 1842, M.A. 1845, 3rd baronet, M.P. Westbury 1857-68, South Devon 1868-85, a civil lord of the admiralty 1874-80, privy councillor 1885. See Foster's *Baronetage*.

Lopes, (Sir) Ralph (Bart.), s. Abraham Franco, of London, arm. BRASENOSE COLL., matric. 21 April, 1807, aged 18; B.A. 1811, M.P. Westbury Dec., 1814, to May, 1819, 1831-47, South Devon 1849-54, deputy warden of the Stannaries, assumed the surname and arms of LOPES by royal licence 4 May, 1831 (having succeeded his uncle as 2nd baronet 26 March same year), died 26 Jan., 1854. See Foster's *Baronetage*.

Lopes, Ralph Kekewich, 1s. Ralph Ludlow, of London, arm. CHRIST CHURCH, matric. 13 Oct., 1871, aged 18; bar.-at-law, Inner Temple, 1877. See Foster's *Men at the Bar*.

Lopes, Ralph Ludlow, 2s. Ralph, of Tamerton, Devon, baronet. CHRIST CHURCH, matric. 3 June, 1840, aged 19; B.A. 1844, M.A. 1846, of Sandridge Park, Wilts, high sheriff 1869, bar.-at-law, Inner Temple, 1847, recorder of Devizes 1877. See Foster's *Men at the Bar*.

Loraine, Wilfrid Howard, 2s. Nevison, of Waterloo, Lancashire, cler. CHARSLEY HALL, matric. 10 May, 1883, aged 18. [25]

Lord, Arthur Owen, o.s. Hugh, of Masulipatam, East Indies, arm. TRINITY COLL., matric. 13 May, 1837, aged 18.

Lord, Cecil Gaisford, 1s. Arthur Owen, of London, arm. CHRIST CHURCH, matric. 23 May, 1872, aged 18.

Lord, Charles, s. Newdigate, of Shoreditch, London, gent. UNIVERSITY COLL., matric. 27 July, 1795, aged 17; B.A. 1800, vicar of Uffington with Barking and Woolstone, Berks, 1833, until his death 30 Dec., 1846.

Lord, Charles Henry, 1s. Thomas Wainwright, of Horden, Yorks, gent. NON-COLL., matric. 19 Oct., 1876, aged 27.

Lord, Rev. David William, 1s. David, of Lochlie, co. Forfar, gent. NON-COLL., matric. 14 Oct., 1882, aged 18; commoner HERTFORD COLL. 1882, B.A. 1886. [30]

Lord, Frederick Bayley, o.s. Samuel Curlew, of Tooting, Surrey, D.D. ST. JOHN'S COLL., matric. 11 Dec., 1861, aged 21.

Lord, Henry, s. William, of Northiam, Sussex, cler. ST. JOHN'S COLL., matric. 1 July, 1778, aged 17; scholar 1778, fellow 1781, B.A. 1782, M.A. 1792, B.D. 1792, D.D. 1801, 3rd master Merchant Taylor's School 1783-5, 2nd master 1785-96, rector of Barfreston, Kent, 1801, and of Northiam, Sussex, 1813, until his death 20 May, 1836. See *Robinson*, 136.

Lord, James, s. John, of Drayton Parslow, Bucks, cler. ST. MARY HALL, matric. 3 April, 1778, aged 19; B.A. 1781, rector (and patron) of Drayton Parslow 1817, until his death 13 Nov., 1835.

Lord, John, s. Lawrence, of Cotsford, Oxon, arm. HART HALL, matric. 1 April, 1732, aged 17; B.A. 1735, M.A. 1738 (? father of John next named and of William 1762).

Lord, John, s. John, of Marston Morton, Beds, cler. TRINITY COLL., matric. 20 Jan., 1756, aged 17; possibly chorister MAGDALEN COLL. 1750-6. See *Bloxam*, i. 164. [35]

Lord, Rev. John Frederick, 1s. John Pickup, of Cheltenham, arm. CHRIST CHURCH, matric. 24 Jan., 1879, aged 18; student of music 1879, B.A. & M.A. 1887. See *Eton School Lists*.

Lord, John Goodsir, 1s. Richard, of Crewe, Cheshire, D.Med. KEBLE COLL., matric. 22 Oct., 1885, aged 16.

Lord, John Pickup, 1s. John, of Wigan, Lancashire, arm. BRASENOSE COLL., matric. 10 June, 1840, aged 19; an officer 5th Lancashire militia, father of John Fredk.

Lord, Laurence, s. Laurence, of Cotsford, Oxon, arm. TRINITY COLL., matric. 13 March, 1721-2, aged 17, brother of John 1732, and of the next named.

Lord, Robert, s. Laurence, of Cotsford, Oxon, arm. EXETER COLL., matric. 9 Feb., 1726-7, aged 16; B.A. 21 Jan., 1730-1, sometime minister of a society of Protestant Dissenters at Knutsford, in Cheshire, died at Lenton, near Nottingham, 15 Dec., 1801. See *Gent.'s Mag.*, 1801, ii. 1157. [5]

Lord, Samuel Curlewis, s. Walter, of Tooting, Surrey, arm. WADHAM COLL., matric. 1 Dec., 1812, aged 19; B.A. 1816, M.A. 1820, B.D. 1827, D.D. 1830, vicar of West Barsham, Norfolk, 1818, rector of Farmborough, near Bath, 1853, until his death 21 March, 1867.

Lord, Septimus, 6s. Henry, of Northiam, Sussex, doctor. MAGDALEN HALL, matric. 30 Oct., 1834, aged 18.

Lord, William, s. John, of Drayton Parslow, Bucks, cler. BRASENOSE COLL., matric. 1 Dec., 1762, aged 19; demy MAGDALEN COLL. 1764-74, B.A. 1766, M.A. 1769, fellow 1774-1804, B.D. 1778, D.D. 1782, bursar, vice-president 1789, dean of divinity 1790, rector of Drayton Parslow, Bucks, and of Beaconsfield 1803, until his death 1 Nov., 1817. See *Bloxam*, vi. 341.

Lord, William Allwood, s. William, of Wingfield, co. Derby, gent. QUEEN'S COLL., matric. 17 Dec., 1796, aged 17; B.A. 1800.

Lorimer, Charles, 3s. James, of Toorak, near Melbourne, arm. EXETER COLL., matric. 19 Oct., 1882, aged 20; B.A. 1887, a student of the Inner Temple 1884. [10]

Lorimer, James, 2s. James, of Victoria, Australia, gent. NON-COLL., matric. 14 Oct., 1882, aged 22.

Loring, Arthur Mapletoft, 1s. Hector, of Isle of Malta, arm. BRASENOSE COLL., matric. 28 May, 1863, aged 20; B.A. 1866, M.A. 1870, vicar of Barnstaple (Holy Trinity) 1872, until his death 6 Sep., 1874.

Loring, Henry Lloyd, s. Joshua, of Englefield, Berks, gent. MAGDALEN COLL., matric. 27 July, 1802, aged 18; demy 1802-7, B.A. 1806, fellow 1807-16, M.A. 1809, D.D. (by decree) 17 June, 1818, archdeacon of Calcutta 1814, died 4 Sep., 1822. See *Coll. Reg.*, vii. 149.

Loring, Henry Nele, 1s. John Wentworth, of Fareham, Hants, arm. EXETER COLL., matric. 20 May, 1829, aged 17; B.A. 1833, M.A. 1837, held various curacies 1835-59, vicar of Boarhunt with Southwick, Hants, 1860-75.

Lort, Michael, fellow of TRINITY COLL., Cambridge, until 1780 (B.A. 1746, M.A. 1750, B.D. 1761, D.D. 1780); incorp. 7 July, 1759, regius professor of Greek 1759-71, preb. of St. Paul's 1780, F.R.S., F.S.A., died 5 Nov., 1790. See *Gent.'s Mag.* [15]

Lory, Frederick Aylmer Pendarves, 4s. William, of Meglor, near Falmouth, Cornwall, arm. EXETER COLL., matric. 16 April, 1858, aged 18; B.A. 1861, held various curacies 1863-75, vicar of Bagshot since 1875.

Lory, Jacob Withers Gordon, 1s. William, of St. Keverne, Cornwall, gent. EXETER COLL., matric. 9 May, 1844, aged 19.

Loscombe, Clifton Wintringham, s. Benjamin, of Bristol (city), arm. ORIEL COLL., matric. 18 Nov., 1803, aged 19.

Losh, William, s. William, of St. Mary's, Carlisle, Cumberland, pleb. QUEEN'S COLL., matric. 11 Oct., 1725, aged 16; B.A. 1730.

L'Oste, Charles, s. Charles, of Lowth, co. Lincoln, cler. HERTFORD COLL., matric. 17 Dec., 1740, aged 19; B.A. 1744, M.A. 1747. [20]

Loton, John, 1s. Nathan, of Uttoxeter, co. Stafford, gent. NON-COLL., matric. 16 Jan., 1875, aged 29; B.A. from ST. JOHN'S COLL. 1879.

Loton, John Lewis, s. John, of Lewisham, Kent, gent. HERTFORD COLL., matric. 10 July, 1742, aged 18.

Lott, Frederick Barnes, 1s. Frederick Edwin, of Leafield, Oxon, cler. CHRIST CHURCH, matric. 23 May, 1872, aged 18; a junior student 1872-9, B.A. 1876, M.A. 1880.

Lott, Frederick Edwin, 3s. Henry, of Tracey House, Devon, arm. BALLIOL COLL., matric. 30 March, 1833, aged 20; B.A. from ST. ALBAN HALL, 1841, M.A. 1844, a student of Inner Temple 1835, perp. curate Leafield and Ascott, Oxon, 1849, vicar of Bampton Lew, Oxon, 1857, until his death 12 Feb., 1869.

Lott, Harry Buckland, 1s. Harry, of Tracey Awlescomb, Devon, arm. BALLIOL COLL., matric. 1 Dec., 1825, aged 18; B.A. 1829, a student of Inner Temple 1829. [25]

Lott, John Browning, 1s. Charles, of Faversham, Kent, gent. NEW COLL., matric. 19 Oct., 1874, aged 21; B.Mus. 26 Oct., 1876.

Lott, Rev. Reginald Charles, 3s. Frederick Edwin, of Seafield, Oxon, cler. CORPUS CHRISTI COLL., matric. 17 Oct., 1876, aged 19; exhibitioner 1876-80, B.A. 1880, M.A. 1884.

Lott, William Buckland, 4s. Harry Baines, of Awlescombe, Devon, arm. BALLIOL COLL., matric. 16 May, 1839, aged 19; B.A. 1843, M.A. 1850, rector of Wymondham, co. Leicester, 1861-3, and of Barton Mills, Suffolk, since 1863.

Lough, Rev. Edward Inglis, 1s. John Francis Burnaby Lumley, of St. George's, Isle of Bermuda, cler. TRINITY COLL., matric. 16 Oct., 1880, aged 19; B.A. 1884, M.A. 1887.

Lough, John, s. John, of Milton, Kent, cler. QUEEN'S COLL., matric. 25 April, 1809, aged 18; B.A. 1813 (? garrison-chaplain Bermuda, died in 1839). [30]

Loughborough, Arthur, 1s. Thomas, of Lambeth, Surrey, arm. ST. JOHN'S COLL., matric. 1 July, 1861, aged 18; scholar 1861-4, B.A. 1864, bar.-at-law, Lincoln's Inn, 1867. See Foster's *Men at the Bar* & *Robinson*, 324.

Loughnan, Alfred Stack, 6s. Timothy, of Walcot, Bath, cler. PEMBROKE COLL., matric. 1 Feb., 1877, aged 19; scholar 1877-80, B.A. 1880.

Louis, Ferdinand, 'Linguæ Gallicæ Præceptor;' privilegiatus 29 July, 1765.

Lousada, Austin Percy, 1s. Percy, of Clifton, co. Gloucester, cler. ORIEL COLL., matric. 7 Feb., 1870, aged 19; B.A. 1873, bar.-at-law, Inner Temple, 1879. See Foster's *Men at the Bar*.

Lousada, Francis Baruh, 2s. Isaac Baruh, of Stamford, Middlesex, arm. EXETER COLL., matric. 11 April, 1832, aged 18. [35]

Lousada, Isaac Baruh, 1s. (Isaac) Baruh, of St George's, Bloomsbury, Middlesex, arm. QUEEN'S COLL., matric. 9 June, 1831, aged 22.

Lousada, Rev. Percy Martindale, o.s. David, of St. George's, Bloomsbury, Middlesex, arm. MERTON COLL., matric. 12 June, 1841, aged 18; a student of Inner Temple 1844, died 7 Sep., 1859, aged 36.

Lovat, John, s. Thomas, of Newcastle, co. Stafford pleb. BALLIOL COLL., matric. 26 March, 1743 aged 18; B.A. 1746.

Lovatt, Dale, s. Joseph, of Penkhull, co. Stafford gent. MAGDALEN HALL, matric. 4 Nov., 1738 aged 17; B.A. 1742.

Lovatt, Richard, s. Joseph, of Stoke, co. Stafford gent. MAGDALEN HALL, matric. 20 March, 1724-5 aged 17. [40]

Love, Benjamin, s. James, of London, gent. QUEEN'S COLL., matric. 16 Feb., 1776, aged 16; B.A. from SIDNEY SUSSEX COLL., Cambridge, 1783, rector of Hutesley, and vicar of Wemworth, Devon, died 22 Sep., 1797.

Love, Christopher James Christian Claude, s. James, of St. Martin's, Westminster, gent. MAGDALEN HALL, matric. 8 June, 1810, aged 17; B.A. 1816.

Love, John Garton William, 1s. George Alfred, of London, gent. WADHAM COLL., matric. 19 Oct., 1885, aged 27.

Love, Reginald Taverner, 2s. William, of Headcorn, Kent, arm. ORIEL COLL., matric. 14 Oct., 1864, aged 17; scholar 1864-9, B.A. 1868, M.A. 1872, vicar of Cowlinge, co. Cambridge, since 1883.

Love, Richard, 'servant to the Provost of Queen's College;' privilegiatus 26 Jan., 1762. [5]

Love, Samuel, s. Stephen, of Portishead, Somerset, gent. BALLIOL COLL., matric. 3 Dec., 1762, aged 18; B.A. 1766, M.A. 1769, a minor canon Bristol, vicar of Banwell, Somerset, at his death 17 Oct., 1773.

Love, Seymer, s. Joseph, of Londonderry, Ireland, arm. CHRIST CHURCH, matric. 6 Nov., 1765, aged 17; B.A. from ALL SOULS' COLL. 1770, M.A. 1774 (as Seymour).

Love, William Acworth, 3s. William, of Chertsey, Surrey, arm. ST. JOHN'S COLL., matric. 25 Jan., 1822, aged 18.

Loveband, Rev. Anthony William, 1s. — L., of Yarnscombe, Devon, gent. WORCESTER COLL., matric. 13 Feb., 1840, aged 18; B.A. 1843, M.A. 1846, of Pilton Abbey, Devon, died 25 Aug., 1878.

Loveday, Arthur, s. John, of Caversham, Oxon, arm. BRASENOSE COLL., matric. 15 July, 1784, aged 17; demy MAGDALEN COLL. 1784-99, B.A. 1788, M.A. 1791, B.D. 1799, fellow 1799-1827, D.D. 1815, vice-president 1802, dean of divinity 1807, rector of Chilton, Norfolk, 1800, and of Antingham (St. Mary) 1803, until he died 3 June, 1827. See *Bloxam*, vii. 91. [10]

Loveday, Arthur, 1s. Arthur, of St. Pancras, London, arm. BALLIOL COLL., matric. 5 March, 1845, aged 18; B.A. 1848, M.A. 1852, rector of Yattendon, Berks, 1873, until his death 26 Feb., 1885.

Loveday, George, y.s. Arthur, of London, arm. BRASENOSE COLL., matric. 4 Feb., 1847, aged 17; B.A. 1850, M.A. 1853, sometime of Doctors' Commons. See *Rugby School Reg.*, 245.

Loveday, John, s. Thomas, of Caversham, Oxon, arm. MAGDALEN COLL., 13 Feb., 1727-8, aged 17; B.A. 1731, M.A. 1734, of Caversham, father of the next named.

Loveday, John, s. John, of Caversham, Oxon, arm. MAGDALEN COLL., matric. 5 Feb., 1760, aged 17; B.C.L. 1766, D.C.L. 1771, died 4 March, 1809, father of the next named, and of Thomas 1806. See *Robinson*, 102.

Loveday, John, s. John, of Williamscote, Oxon, doctor. BRASENOSE COLL., matric. 18 May, 1802, aged 17; B.A. 1806, M.A. 1808 created D.C.L. 15 June, 1841, then of Williamscote, high sheriff Oxfordshire, died 19 Oct., 1864. [15]

Loveday, John Edward Taylor, 1s. Thomas, of East Ilsley, near Newbury, Berks, cler. EXETER COLL., matric. 11 June, 1862, aged 17; of Williamscote, Oxon, J.P., and of Arlescote, co. Warwick, J.P.

Loveday, Joseph, s. Joseph, of Taplow, Bucks, cler. HART HALL, matric. 29 March, 1732, aged 18; B.A. 1735.

Loveday, Thomas, s. John, of Williamscote, Oxon, doctor. MAGDALEN COLL., matric. 25 July, 1806, aged 17; demy 1806-17, B.A. 1810, M.A. 1813, fellow 1817-31, B.D. 1820, vice-president 1822, dean of divinity 1823, bursar 1824, select preacher 1819, 1823, rector of East Ilsley, Berks, 1831-66, died 22 Aug., 1873. See *Bloxam*, vii. 157.

Loveday, William, s. George, of Salisbury, Wilts, gent. MERTON COLL., matric. 29 March, 1757, aged 17.

Loveday, William Taylor, s. John, of Williamscote, Oxon, doctor. TRINITY COLL., matric. 14 Oct., 1805, aged 18; of Williamscote, Oxon, and Arlescote, co. Warwick, curate of Shotteswell, co. Warwick, died 2 April, 1875. [20]

Loveden, Edward (Loveden), s. Thomas, of Cirencester, co. Gloucester, gent. TRINITY COLL., matric. 10 April, 1767, aged 16; created D.C.L. 4 July, 1793, then of Buscot Park, Berks, F.R.S., F.S.A., M.P. Abingdon 1783-96, Shaftesbury 1802-12, died 4 Jan., 1822, father of the next named.

Loveden, Pryse, CHRIST CHURCH, 1792. See PRYSE.

Lovegrove, George Cuff, 2s. John, of St. Mary-de-Lode, Gloucester (city), arm. ST. JOHN'S COLL., matric. 25 March, 1857, aged 19.

Lovelace, John, s. James, of Exeter (city), pleb. EXETER COLL., matric. 25 March, 1737, aged 18; B.A. 1740 (? vicar of Great Waltham, Essex, died 20 March, 1797), father of the next named.

Lovelace, John, s. John, of Ailesbeare, Devon, cler. CHRIST CHURCH, matric. 27 May, 1762, aged 18. [25]

Loveland, John Douglas Errington, 1s. Richard Loveland, of London, arm. ST. JOHN'S COLL., matric. 13 Oct., 1883, aged 17.

Loveling, Benjamin, s. Benjamin, of Banbury, Oxon, cler. TRINITY COLL., matric. 13 July, 1728, aged 17.

Lovell, Charles Petre, 1s. Samuel, of London, gent. ST. JOHN'S COLL., matric. 15 Oct., 1881, aged 18; scholar 1881-5.

Lovell, Edmund, s. Edmund, of Pitney, Somerset, cler. EXETER COLL., matric. 9 April, 1717, aged 16; B.A. 1720, M.A. 1723.

Lovell, Edmund, s. Edmund, of Shepton Mallett, Somerset, cler. MERTON COLL., matric. 28 March, 1757, aged 17; B.A. 1760, M.A. 1763, D.C.L. 1768, preb. of Bath and Wells 1767, archdeacon of Bath 1786, until his death 18 July, 1798. [30]

Lovell, Edmund Charles, 2s. George, of Rookley, Hants, arm. MERTON COLL., matric. 26 March, 1824, aged 18; postmaster 1824-7.

Lovell, Edward Kerle, 1s. Edward, of Weymouth, Dorset, cler. UNIVERSITY COLL., matric. 11 Nov., 1841, aged 19; B.A. from ST. MARY HALL, 1846, curate of Oundle, Northants, died 1 Jan., 1851.

Lovell, Esdaile Lovell, 1s. Edwin, of Dinder, Somerset, arm. CORPUS CHRISTI COLL., matric. 29 Feb., 1856, aged 18; sometime a captain in the army.

Lovell, George, s. Edmund, of Wells (city), cler. EXETER COLL., matric. 9 April, 1767, aged 18; B.A. 1770, bar.-at-law, Middle Temple, 1775, (? died 1785).

Lovell, George Francis, o.s. Francis George, of London, arm. BALLIOL COLL., matric. 19 Oct., 1863, aged 19; B.A. 1867, M.A. 1870, B.D. 1876, lecturer Queen's 1882, and of Pembroke College 1885, vice-principal St. Edmund's Hall 1871, one of the four City lecturers at St. Martin Carfax, 1872.

Lovell, John, s. Robert, of Clewer, Berks, gent. JESUS COLL., matric. 7 Dec., 1715, aged 17; B.A. 1719. [35]

Lovell, Rev. John, s. John, of Bath, Somerset, arm. ORIEL COLL., matric. 14 March, 1778, aged 16; B.A. 1782, died 9 May, 1837, aged 76, brother of Peter H.

Lovell, Langford, s. Langford, of Isle of Antigua, America, arm. MAGDALEN COLL., matric. 14 Nov., 1793, aged 18.

Lovell, Peter Harvey, s. John, of Bath, Somerset, arm. ORIEL COLL., matric. 13 March, 1777, aged 17; of Cole Park, Wilts, died in 1841.

Lovell, Robert, s. Philip, of Christ Church, Isle of Barbados, arm. MERTON COLL., matric. 28 March, 1772, aged 18. [40]

Lovell, Samuel Walter, 3s. Samuel, of London, gent. LINCOLN COLL., matric. 3 Feb., 1886, aged 19; scholar 1885, died 7 April, 1887.

Lovell, Trefusis, s. Abraham, of Plymouth, Devon, gent. EXETER COLL., matric. 7 April, 1786, aged 19; B.A. 1790, chaplain to the Earl of Bristol, and rector of Aghadoe and of Duboe, co. Derry, preb. of Derry 1796-8, and archdeacon 1798-1813, rector of St. Luke's, Middlesex, 1813, until he died 10 Oct., 1844.

Lovell, Rev. William, s. Charles Henry, of London, gent. EXETER COLL., matric. 19 May, 1866, aged 17; scholar 1866-71, B.A. 1870, M.A. 1873. See *Coll. Reg.*, 162.

Lovell, William Faux, o.s. Isaac Samuel, of Thornby, Northants, gent. ST. JOHN'S COLL., matric. 14 Oct., 1871, aged 19; B.A. 1876, M.A. 1880, vicar of Houghton Regis, Beds, 1884.

Lovell, Rev. William Willes, 3s. Peter Harvey, of Malmsbury, arm. TRINITY COLL., matric. 27 June, 1834, aged 18; B.A. 1838, died 20 Feb., 1859. [5]

Lovely, Rev. Frederick Cecil, 2s. George, of Calcutta, cler. NON-COLL., matric. 3 June, 1876, aged 19; B.A. 1885.

Loveridge, Walter, 4s. Samuel, of Muchall, near Wolverhampton, gent. WORCESTER COLL., matric. 19 Oct., 1876, aged 18; B.A. 1879.

Lovesy, Conway Whithorne, 2s. Conway Whithorne, of Charlton Kings, co. Gloucester, gent. QUEEN'S COLL., matric. 17 Dec., 1834, aged 16; B.A. 1841, M.A. 1874, bar.-at-law, Middle Temple, 1845, police magistrate Trinidad 1871-3, puisne judge British Guiana 1873-8, died 5 Nov., 1885. See Foster's *Men at the Bar*.

Lovett, Harrington Verney, 2s. Robert, of Exeter, cler. BALLIOL COLL., matric. 17 Oct., 1882, aged 18; of the Indian Civil Service 1882.

Lovett, James, 'coachman to Dr. Blackstone;' privilegiatus 31 March, 1762. [10]

Lovett, Richard, s. Thomas, of Chirk, co. Denbigh, gent. MERTON COLL., matric. 12 Dec., 1799, aged 18.

Lovett, Thomas, 2s. John Henniker, of Whittington, Salop, arm. MAGDALEN COLL., matric. 19 Oct., 1883, aged 18; B.A. 1887.

Lovibond, Edward, s. Edward, of London, arm. MAGDALEN COLL., matric. 15 May, 1739, aged 16.

Low, Rev. Frederick William, 1s. William Henry, of London, gent. ST. JOHN'S COLL., matric. 12 Oct., 1878, aged 19; exhibitioner 1880-1, B.A. 1882, M.A. 1885. See *Robinson*, 379.

Low, George Peter, 1s. John, of St. Peter's, Dublin, arm. ORIEL COLL., matric. 12 April, 1861, aged 17; B.A. 1866, of Sunvale, co. Limerick, sometime captain 8th hussars. [15]

Low, Rev. Henry (scholar ST. JOHN'S COLL., Cambridge, 1853, 24th wrangler and B.A. 1834, M.A. 1837), 5s. John, of St. Aubin, Isle of Jersey, arm. EXETER COLL., incorp. 24 June, 1845, aged 36; fellow 1845-64, B.D. 1849, math. lecturer 1847-64, bursar 1853, dean 1863, died 18 Nov., 1864. See *Coll. Reg.*, 135.

Low, John, s. John, of Waly, Cheshire, pleb. BRASENOSE COLL., matric. 14 May, 1730, aged 20.

Low, Sidney James Mark, 1s. Maximilian, of Blackheath, Kent, gent. PEMBROKE COLL., matric. 12 Feb., 1876, aged 19, scholar 1875-6; exhibitioner BALLIOL COLL. 1876-7, scholar 1877-81, B.A. 1883 a student of the Inner Temple 1877.

Low, Simon, 1s. John, of Dublin, arm. ORIEL COLL., matric. 2 March, 1843, aged 18.

Low, Thomas, s. William, of Wigan, Lancashire, gent. BRASENOSE COLL., matric. 3 April, 1767, aged 20; B.A. 1770 (as LOWE). [20]

Low, Thomas, s. George, of London, gent. MAGDALEN HALL, matric. 6 Dec., 1788, aged 17; B.A. 1793.

Low, William Mackay, o.s. Andrew, of Newport, in America, arm. BRASENOSE COLL., matric. 22 Jan., 1880, aged 19.

Lowden, William, 2s. John, of St. Paul's, Covent Garden, gent. TRINITY COLL., matric. 8 July, 1843, aged 18.

Lowder, Charles Fuge, 1s. Charles, of Walcot Bath, arm. EXETER COLL., matric. 21 Feb., 1839, aged 18; B.A. 1843, M.A. 1845, vicar of St. Peter's (Old Gravel Lane), London, 1866, until his death 9 Sep., 1880.

Lowder, Samuel Molineux, s. Thomas, of Bristol (city), gent. ST. JOHN'S COLL., matric. 15 July, 1755, aged 15; B.A. 1759, M.A. 1763, B.D. 1768, vicar of Cardiff, co. Glamorgan, 1777. [25]

Lowder, William Henry, 2s. Charles, of Walcot, near Bath, gent. ST. EDMUND HALL, matric. 30 Oct., 1856, aged 25; B.A. 1860, M.A. 1863, held various curacies 1860-70, vicar of Alvanley, Cheshire, 1870-5, and of Hyde St. George 1875.

Lowdham, Caleb, of PEMBROKE HALL, Cambridge (B.A. 1724, M.A. 1728); incorp. 9 July, 1733, vicar of Diseworth.

Lowe, Alfred, 4s. George, of Burton-on-Trent, co. Stafford, gent. LINCOLN COLL., matric. 16 Oct., 1873, aged 19; scholar 1873-7, B.A. 1877, M.A. 1880, vicar of Rangemore, co. Stafford, since 1882.

Lowe, Cecil Henry, 2s. George William, of Great Dunmow, Essex, cler. CHRIST CHURCH, matric. 12 Oct., 1883, aged 20; B.A. 1887.

Lowe, Charles Bodington, 1s. Charles, of Erdington, co. Warwick, gent. WORCESTER COLL., matric. 14 Oct., 1865, aged 22; B.A. 1869, M.A. 1872, of Sheepy Hall, co. Leicester, J.P. [30]

Lowe, Charles Ernest, 2s. John Robert, of Ryhall, Rutland, gent. ST. EDMUND HALL, matric. 2 Feb., 1876, aged 17; B.A. 1880, M.A. 1882, rector of Kelling, Norfolk, 1884.

Lowe, (Sir) Drury Curzon (Drury) K.C.B., 2s. William Drury, of Aston, co. Derby, arm. CORPUS CHRISTI COLL., matric. 20 March, 1849, aged 19; major-general in the army, served in the Crimea and Indian Mutiny, commanded 17th lancers in Zulu War 1879, and cavalry brigade in South Africa 1881-2, and in Egypt 1882, K.C.B. 17 Nov., 1882.

Lowe, Edward Clarke, 7s. Samuel, of Everton, near Liverpool, gent. MAGDALEN HALL, matric. 15 Dec., 1842, aged 19; bible clerk LINCOLN COLL. 1844-6, B.A. 1846, M.A. 1849, B. & D.D. 1860, head-master St. John's College, Hurstpierpoint, 1850-73, provost of St. Chad's College, Denstone, 1873, canon of Ely 1873.

Lowe, Edward Jackson, 2s. George, of St. Mary de Lode, Gloucester (city), gent. ST. EDMUND HALL, matric. 7 Dec., 1848, aged 23; B.A. 1852, M.A. 1855, perp. curate New Buckenham, Norfolk, 1866-8, and of Bedford Chapel, Exeter, 1868, vicar of St. Margaret's, Tyler's Green, Bucks, 1868-73, rector of Great Gonerby, co. Lincoln, 1873-80, vicar of Stallingborough, 1880.

Lowe, Frederick Pyndar, 3s. Robert, of Bingham, Notts, cler. UNIVERSITY COLL., matric. 19 June, 1832, aged 19, B.A. 1836; fellow MAGDALEN COLL. 1836-42, M.A. 1839, rector of All Saints', Saltfleetby, 1842-67, died 12 Oct., 1782. See Foster's *Peerage*, V. SHERBROOKE. [35]

Lowe, George, 2s. Thomas Hill Peregrine Furye, of Corfton, Salop, cler. MERTON COLL., matric. 24 Nov., 1831, aged 18; postmaster 1831-5, B.A. 1836, vicar of Upper Ottery, Devon, 1841, until his death 2 Nov., 1885.

Lowe, Henry, o.s. Thomas, of Willingdon, Sussex, cler. CORPUS CHRISTI COLL., matric, 4 Feb., 1870, aged 18.

Lowe, Henry Parker, 2s. William, of Norwood, Surrey, gent. CHRIST CHURCH, matric. 16 Oct., 1885, aged 19; scholar 1883.

Lowe, Rev. Henry William, 5s. George, of Burton-on-Trent, arm. LINCOLN COLL., matric. 18 Oct., 1877, aged 18; B.A. 1880, M.A. 1884.

Lowe, Hubert Foster, 3s. William Bevington, of Ettington, co. Warwick, arm. BALLIOL COLL., matric. 16 Oct., 1879, aged 18; scholar 1879-83, B.A. 1883, M.A. 1886.

Lowe, Humphrey, s. Humphrey, of Bromsgrove, co. Worcester, arm. CHRIST CHURCH, matric. 17 Dec., 1728, aged 19.

Lowe, James Jackson, s. John, of Brotherton, Yorks, cler. BRASENOSE COLL., matric. 30 May, 1810, aged 17; scholar 1810-13, B.A. 1814, M.A. 1816, fellow 1817-25, tutor and dean 1822, rector of Fletton, Hunts, 1829, died 26 Oct., 1829.

Lowe, Jeremiah, s. Jeremiah, of Coventry, co. Warwick, arm. ORIEL COLL., matric. 27 Oct., 1788, aged 19; B.A. 1792, rector of Great Saxham, Suffolk, 1795, until his death 25 Aug., 1829. [5]

Lowe, John, s. Matthew, of Astbury, Cheshire, gent. BRASENOSE COLL., matric. 11 March, 1719-20, aged 16; B.A. 1723, M.A. 1726.

Lowe, John, s. Fran., of Ridgemont, Beds, arm. CORPUS CHRISTI COLL., matric. 15 July, 1732, aged 18.

Lowe, John, s. John, of Warrington, Lancashire, gent. BRASENOSE COLL., matric. 29 Feb., 1739-40, aged 18; B.A. 1743.

Lowe, John, s. John, of Ferrybridge, Yorks, gent. LINCOLN COLL., matric. 22 March, 1779, aged 21; B.A. 1782, M.A. 1785, rector of Tankersley, Yorks, 1803, preb. of York 1831-41, died 2 May, 1837.

Lowe, John, s. John, of Brotherton, Yorks, cler. LINCOLN COLL., matric. 27 June, 1809, aged 18; scholar 1812-14, B.A. 1813, M.A. 1839, perp. curate Swinton, Yorks, 1814-15, rector of Ardley, Oxon, 1815-73, died 18 March, 1874. [10]

Lowe, Joseph Peter, o.s. Joseph, of Salford, Lancashire, arm. MERTON COLL., matric. 21 Oct., 1886, aged 18; exhibitioner 1886.

Lowe, Julius Conran, o.s. Richard, of Marylebone, Middlesex, cler. QUEEN'S COLL., matric. 28 May, 1841, aged 18; B.A. 1845, M.A. 1854, sacristan Durham 1854-72, minor canon 1854, chaplain Durham County Prison 1873, until his death 4 Aug., 1887.

Lowe, Matthew, s. Uriah, of Knutsford, Cheshire, pleb. WADHAM COLL., matric. 1 April, 1732, aged 16; B.A. 5 March, 1735-6.

Lowe, Noel, 4s. Thomas Hill (Peregrine Furye), of Corfton, Salop, cler. QUEEN'S COLL., matric. 3 May, 1838, aged 20; B.A. 1842, vicar of Colyton Raleigh, Devon, 1844, until his death 3 April, 1857.

Lowe, Patrick Robert, 2s. Robert, of Perth, Scotland, arm. WORCESTER COLL., matric. 29 Jan., 1878, aged 18; B.A. 1881. [15]

Lowe, Paul, s. Paul, of Balsall, co. Warwick, cler. BRASENOSE COLL., matric. 18 July, 1719, aged 19; B.A. 1723.

Lowe, Ralph, M.A. ST. JOHN'S COLL., Cambridge; incorp. 13 Oct., 1733. (Memo.: Theophilus Lowe, fellow St. John's College, Cambridge, B.A. 1728, M.A. 1732.)

Lowe, Richard, s. Robert, of St. Alkmund, Derby (town), gent. QUEEN'S COLL., matric. 9 July, 1719, aged 20.

Lowe, Rev. Richard Thomas, of CHRIST'S COLL., Cambridge (B.A. 1825, M.A. 1831); adm. 'ad eundem' 28 June, 1843, chaplain at Madeira 1832-52, rector of Lea, co. Lincoln, 1852, until his death in 1875; for list of his works see *Crockford*.

Lowe, Robert, 2s. Robert, of Bingham, Notts, cler. UNIVERSITY COLL., matric. 16 June, 1829, aged 17, B.A. 1833; fellow MAGDALEN COLL. 1835-6, M.A. 1836, created D.C.L. 22 June, 1870, LL.D. Edinburgh 1867, bar.-at-law, Lincoln's Inn, 1842, M.P. Kidderminster 1852-9, Calne 1859-68, London University 1868-80, chancellor of the Exchequer 1868-73, Home secretary 1873-4, privy councillor, created Viscount Sherbrooke 25 May, 1880, G.C.B. 30 June, 1885. See Foster's *Peerage* & *Men at the Bar*. [20]

Lowe, Samuel, s. Samuel, of Southwell, Notts, arm. QUEEN'S COLL., matric. 14 May, 1736, aged 17; died in Aug., 1765, ancestor of Lord Sherbrooke.

Lowe, Thomas, s. Humphrey, of Bromsgrove, co. Worcester, arm. PEMBROKE COLL., matric. 6 April, 1734, aged 19; B.A. from NEW INN HALL 1737, M.A. 1740, rector of Chelsea.

Lowe, Thomas, o.s. John, of Rawmarsh, Yorks, cler. ORIEL COLL., matric. 10 June, 1835, aged 17; B.A. 1839, M.A. 1842, vice-principal Chichester Diocesan College and perp. curate of St. Bartholomew's, Chichester, 1843-50, vicar of Willingdon, Sussex, 1850, until his death 19 Dec., 1887.

Lowe, Rev. Thomas Hill, 1s. Noel, of Colyton, near Ottery St. Mary, Devon, cler. EXETER COLL., matric. 30 Nov., 1867, aged 19; B.A. from NEW INN HALL 1873, M.A. 1874.

Lowe, Thomas (Hill Peregrine Furye), s. Thomas, of Burford, co. Worcester, gent. TRINITY COLL., matric. 6 Nov., 1799, aged 17; B.A. 1805, M.A. 1818, a student of Lincoln's Inn 1804, vicar of Grimley with Hallow, co. Worcester, 1820, rector of Holgate (2nd portion), Salop, 1821, and of Holy Trinity, Exeter, 1837-40, vicar of Littleham with Exmouth 1840, precentor of Exeter 1832, canon residentiary 1832, and dean 1839, until his death 17 Jan., 1861. [25]

Lowe, William, s. Richard, of Chetwind, Salop, gent. CHRIST CHURCH, matric. 26 Feb., 1774, aged 20; B.A. 1780.

Lowe, William Drury, 1s. Robert Holden, of Spondon, co. Derby, arm. CHRIST CHURCH, matric. 15 March, 1822, aged 19; B.A. 1825, of Locko Park, co. Derby, high sheriff, 1854, assumed the name of LOWE in lieu of HOLDEN by royal licence 19 July, 1853 died 26 Feb., 1877.

Lowe, William John, o.s. William, of Edgbaston, co. Warwick, arm. MAGDALEN HALL, matric. 2 May, 1862, aged 23.

Lowell, James Russell, created D.C.L. 18 June, 1873, professor of modern literature at Harvard College, U.S., 1855, author of 'The Biglow Papers' and many other works, LL.D. Cambridge, 1874, born at Cambridge, Massachusetts, 22 Feb., 1819.

Lower, Henry, o.s. Henry Martyn, of St. John's, Newfoundland, cler. NEW COLL., matric. 15 Oct., 1881, aged 19; B.A. 1885. [30]

Lower, William Cornforth, s. John, of Ridley Hall, Northumberland, arm. UNIVERSITY COLL., matric. 23 June, 1806, aged 16.

Lowes, John, s. William, of 'Newcastle-upon-Tyne,' arm. UNIVERSITY COLL., matric. 17 Dec., 1764, aged 18; bar.-at-law, Lincoln's Inn, 1770, died in Dec., 1795.

Lowes, Thomas, s. William, of Haltwhistle, Northumberland, arm. UNIVERSITY COLL., matric. 25 Jan., 1771, aged 19.

Lowndes, Charles Arthur, 1s. Charles Clayton, of Windermere, Westmoreland, cler. BRASENOSE COLL., matric. 19 Oct., 1882, aged 18; exhibitioner 1882-6, B.A. 1886.

Lowndes, Charles Clayton, 1s. Matthew D., of Liverpool, Lancashire, arm. BRASENOSE COLL., matric. 25 Feb., 1843, aged 18, scholar 1843-6; B.A. from ST. MARY HALL 1850, M.A. 1853, vicar of Applewhaite, Cumberland, 1855, until his death 28 March, 1873. [35]

Lowndes, Edward, s. Matthew, of Buckfastleigh, Devon, cler. EXETER COLL., matric. 22 Feb., 1813, aged 20; B.A. from MAGDALEN HALL 1832, M.A. 1833, brother of Matthew 1804.

Lowndes, Ernest Campbell, 2s. Francis Dobson, of Wavertree, near Liverpool, arm. CORPUS CHRISTI COLL., matric. 20 Oct., 1879, aged 19; exhibitioner 1881-3, B.A. 1883, M.A. 1886, minor canon of Chester 1885.

Lowndes, George Rivers, 3s. Richard, of Poole Keynes, co. Gloucester, cler. NEW COLL., matric. 16 Oct., 1880, aged 18; scholar 1880-5.

Lowndes, Henry, s. William, of Edmonton, Middlesex, arm. CHRIST CHURCH, matric. 14 July, 1715, aged 16.

Lowndes, Henry Owen, s. William, of Marylebone, London, arm. BALLIOL COLL., matric. 4 June, 1813, aged 17; settled in America.

Lowndes, Rev. Jefferson, 1s. Jonathan William, of Oxford, gent. NON-COLL., matric. 9 April, 1875, aged 17; commoner HERTFORD COLL. 1877, B.A. 1880, M.A. 1883, head-master St. Kitts' Grammar School 1886.

Lowndes, Matthew, s. Matthew, of Buckfastleigh, Devon, cler. EXETER COLL., matric. 7 Nov., 1804, aged 17; bible clerk 1804, B.A. 1810, vicar of Buckfastleigh 1825. See *Coll. Reg.*, 149; & *Robinson*, 177.

Lowndes, Matthew, 1s. Matthew, of Buckfastleigh, Devon, cler. ST. ALBAN HALL, matric. 13 March, 1856, aged 21; B.A. 1859, vicar of Buckfastleigh, Devon, 1861. **[5]**

Lowndes, Milnes, s. Robert, of Chesterfield, co. Derby, arm. CHRIST CHURCH, matric. 13 July, 1782, aged 17; B.A. 1786, bar.-at-law, Middle Temple, 1794, brother of Thomas 1787, buried in the Temple Church 26 April, 1800.

Lowndes, Owen Charles Selby, o.s. Edward William Selby, of Winslow, Bucks, arm. LINCOLN COLL., matric. 29 Jan., 1864, aged 20; B.A. 1867, M.A. 1870, curate of Finedon, Northants, 1868-75, curate in charge of Blankney, co. Lincoln, 1876-8, vicar of Chapel Chorlton, co. Stafford, 1878.

Lowndes, Richard, s. Richard, of Sandbach, Cheshire, gent. BRASENOSE COLL., matric. 19 June, 1721, aged 18; of Bostock House and Hassall Hall.

Lowndes, Richard, s. Robert, of St. James's, London, arm. WORCESTER COLL., matric. 13 July, 1724, aged 17; created D.C.L. 8 July, 1756, of Winslow, Bucks, high sheriff 1742, M.P. 1741-74, died 6 Oct., 1775.

Lowndes, Richard, s. William, of Winslow, Bucks, arm. MERTON COLL., matric. 21 Oct., 1790, aged 19; B.A. 1794, M.A. 1799, fellow until 1814, rector of Gamlingay, Cambridge, and of Farley, Surrey, 1814, until his death 3 Feb., 1828. **[10]**

Lowndes, Richard, 1s. William Loftus, of Bloomsbury, London, arm. CHRIST CHURCH, matric. 3 June, 1840, aged 18; B.A. 1844, M.A. 1847, rector of Poole Keynes, Dorset, 1854-62, vicar of Sturminster-Newton since 1862, canon of Salisbury 1874.

Lowndes, Richard, 4s. Richard, of London, cler. KEBLE COLL., matric. 14 Oct., 1884, aged 18.

Lowndes, Robert, s. William, of Winslow, Bucks, arm. ST. MARY HALL, matric. 8 Nov., 1787, aged 17; B.C.L. 1794, rector of North Crawley and vicar of Astwood, Bucks, 1798, until his death 23 Sep., 1837.

Lowndes, Thomas, s. Robert, of Chesterfield, co. Derby, arm. PEMBROKE COLL., matric. 21 May, 1787, aged 21; B.A. 1791, brother of Milnes 1782.

Lowndes, Thomas, s. William Selby, of Winslow, Bucks, arm. MERTON COLL., matric. 24 March, 1794, aged 18; demy MAGDALEN COLL. 1795-1804, B.A. 1797, M.A. 1800, fellow 1804-24, B.D. 1807, bursar, vice-president 1813, dean of divinity 1814, vicar of East Worldham and perp. curate of West Tisted, Hants, 1823, until his death 19 April, 1860. See *Bloxam*, vii. 131. **[15]**

Lowndes, William. BALLIOL COLL., 1729. See STONE.

Lowndes, William (Selby), s. Richard, of St. Martin's, Westminster, arm. NEW COLL., matric. 16 Jan., 1754, aged 18; of Winslow and Whaddon, Bucks, assumed the additional name of SELBY, and died 3 May, 1813.

Lowndes, William. BRASENOSE COLL., 1769. See STONE.

Lowndes, William, s. Richard, of Liverpool, Lancashire, gent. BRASENOSE COLL., matric. 14 Jan., 1811, aged 19; B.A. 1814, M.A. 1817, bar.-at-law, Lincoln's Inn, 1818, Q.C. 1842, judge of small debts court 1847, died 31 March, 1850. See *Manchester School Reg.*, ii. 242.

Lowndes, William, 1s. William, of Whaddon, Bucks, arm. MAGDALEN COLL., matric. 22 March, 1827, aged 19; of Whaddon Hall and Winslow, Bucks, died 1 July, 1886. **[20]**

Lowndes, Rev. William, 1s. Richard, of Poole Keynes, co. Gloucester, cler. KEBLE COLL., matric. 14 Oct., 1878, aged 19; B.A. 1881, M.A. 1886, vice-principal Ely Theological College 1884.

Lowndes, William Charles, o.s. William Francis (Lowndes-Stone), of Remenham, Oxon, arm. CHRIST CHURCH, matric. 28 May, 1831, aged 18, died in the lifetime of his father 21 April, 1845. See *Eton School Lists.*

Lowndes, William Layton, o.s. Henry Dalston, of London, gent. ORIEL COLL., matric. 29 Oct., 1840, aged 18; B.A. 1844, M.A. 1848, of Broughton, Bucks, bar.-at-law, Lincoln's Inn, 1849. See Foster's *Men at the Bar.*

Lowndes, William (Selby), s. William (Selby), of Winslow, Bucks, arm. NEW COLL., matric. 18 June, 1785, aged 17; created M.A. 23 April, 1793, and also D.C.L. 5 July, 1810 (then of Seamore, Sussex), of Whaddon Hall, Bucks, M.P. 1810-20, took the additional name of SELBY (on his father's death, 1813), died 17 May, 1840.

Lowndes, Willoughby, 2s. Jonathan William, of Littlemore, Oxon, gent. NON-COLL., matric. 13 Oct., 1876, aged 17; died 1881, then of HERTFORD COLL. **[25]**

Lownds, John, s. James, of Paisley, Renfrew, Scotland, arm. QUEEN'S COLL., matric. 13 July, 1803, aged 19; B.A. 1808, M.A. 1810.

Lowrey, Francis, 2s. William, of Barmoor, Northumberland, gent. NEW COLL., matric. 16 Oct., 1874, aged 19; B.A. 1878, bar.-at-law, Inner Temple, 1880. See *Rugby School Reg.*

Lowry, Rev. Austin, 1s. Charles Henry, of Northleach, co. Gloucester, cler. ST. EDMUND HALL, matric. 23 Oct., 1875, aged 19; B.A. 1879, M.A. 1882.

Lowry, Charles, 2s. Charles Henry, of Northleach, co. Gloucester, cler. CORPUS CHRISTI COLL., matric. 23 Oct., 1877, aged 19; scholar 1877-82, B.A. 1881, M.A. 1885, assistant-master at Eton. See *Eton School Lists.*

Lowry, Charles Henry, 6s. Richard, of Stainwix, Cumberland, gent. QUEEN'S COLL., matric. 17 June, 1841, aged 18; scholar 1841-5, B.A. 1845, M.A. 1849, fellow 1849-55, head-master King's School, Carlisle, 1849-54, of Northleach Grammar School 1855-77, and of Carlisle Cathedral School 1877-81, vicar of Kirkby Ireleth since 1879. **[30]**

Lowry, Herbert, 3s. Charles Henry, of Northleach, co. Gloucester, cler. NON-COLL., matric. 11 Oct., 1879, aged 18; commoner HERTFORD COLL. 1877, B.A. 1883.

Lowry, Rev. James, s. James, of Desertcreight, co. Tyrone, Ireland, cler. CHRIST CHURCH, matric. 9 March, 1769, aged 15; B.A. 1773, of Rockdale, co. Tyrone, died 7 or 19 Jan., 1790. See Foster's *Peerage*, E. BELMORE.

Lowry, James, s. John, of Dungannon, co. Tyrone, Ireland, cler. TRINITY COLL., matric. 23 April, 1792, aged 19; B.A. 1794, rector of Clogherny, died 4 Nov., 1852. See *Eton School Lists.*

Lowry, John, s. Richard, of Kendal, Westmoreland, pleb. QUEEN'S COLL., matric. 21 Jan., 1723-4, aged 15; B.A. 1728, M.A. 1731, fellow 1736, proctor 1741, Whyte professor of moral philosophy 1742, rector of Charlton-on-Otmoor, Oxon, 1753, died 22 Feb., 1784. See *O. H. S.*, ix. p. 143.

Lowry, John, s. James, of Desertcreight, co. Tyrone, cler. CHRIST CHURCH, matric. 9 March, 1769, aged 16; B.A. 1774, rector of Clogherny, and of Donaghmore, Queen's County, died in 1822, father of James 1792. See Foster's *Peerage*, E. BELMORE.

Lowry, John Fetherston, 2s. Robert, of Pomeroy, co. Tyrone, arm. BRASENOSE COLL., matric. 16 June, 1836, aged 17; B.A. 1840, of Pomeroy aforesaid, a student of Lincoln's Inn 1840, bar.-at-law, King's Inns, Dublin, 1843, died 5 Feb., 1883. See Foster's *Peerage* & *Rugby School Reg.*, 181.

Lowry, Robert, s. James, of Desertcreight, co. Tyrone, cler. CHRIST CHURCH, matric. 3 March, 1770, aged 21; of Pomeroy House, co. Tyrone, died in 1802, father of the last named, and of Robert William.

Lowry, Robert Thomas Graves, 1s. Robert William, of Pomeroy, Ireland, arm. CHRIST CHURCH, matric. 16 Oct., 1874, aged 17. See Foster's *Peerage*, E. BELMORE; & *Eton School Lists.*

Lowry, Robert William, 1s. Robert William, of Desertcreight, co. Tyrone, arm. BRASENOSE COLL., matric. 24 March, 1836, aged 19; B.A. 1840; of Pomeroy House, co. Tyrone, J.P., D.L., high sheriff 1849, a student of Lincoln's Inn 1840, bar.-at-law, King's Inns, Dublin. See Foster's *Peerage*, E. BELMORE; & *Eton School Lists.* [5]

Lowth, Rev. Alfred Charles, 1s. Alfred James, of Branksea, Dorset, cler. KEBLE COLL., matric. 16 Oct., 1876, aged 19; B.A. 1880, M.A. 1883.

Lowth, Alfred James, 8s. Robert, of Chiswick, Middlesex, cler. EXETER COLL., matric. 21 Oct., 1836, aged 19; scholar 1838-41, B.A. 1841, M.A. 1844, perp. curate Branksea Island, Dorset, 1854-60, rector of Hamworthy, Dorset, 1860-2, and of St. Swithun, Winchester, 1865. See *Coll. Reg.*, 153; & *Eton School Lists.*

Lowth, Arthur, 7s. Robert Henry, of Hinton, Hants, cler. EXETER COLL., matric. 27 Jan., 1831, aged 17; B.A. 1834.

Lowth, Robert, s. William, of Hants, cler. ST. JOHN'S COLL., matric. 26 March, 1729, aged 18; fellow NEW COLL., B.A. 1733, M.A. 1737, D.D. (by diploma) 8 July, 1754, archdeacon of Winchester 1750, preb. of Durham 1755, professor of poetry 1741-51, bishop of St. David's 1766, of Oxford 1766-77, and of London 1777-87, declined the primacy, died 3 Nov., 1787. See *Gent.'s Mag.*

Lowth, Robert, s. Robert, bishop of London. CHRIST CHURCH, matric. 6 July, 1779, aged 17; B.A. 1783, M.A. 1786, preb. of St. Paul's 1789, and of Chichester 1792. [10]

Lowth, Thomas Henry, born at Chilbolton, Hants, s. Robert, bishop of Oxford. CHRIST CHURCH, matric. 14 Jan., 1772, aged 18; gold medallist for Latin verse, Winchester, 1770, fellow of NEW COLL., preb. of Chichester 1778.

Lowth, William, s. William, of Buriton, Hants, cler. HART HALL, matric. 13 May, 1724, aged 17; demy MAGDALEN COLL. 1724-32, B.A. 5 Feb., 1727-8, M.A. 1730, preb. of Winchester 1759, until his death 30 April, 1795, brother of Robert 1729. See *Bloxam*, vi. 205.

Lowth, William, 2s. Robert, of Hinton, Hants, cler. HART HALL, matric. 14 Oct., 1820, aged 18; B.A. from CHRIST CHURCH 1824, vicar of Leintwardine, co. Hereford, 1838, until his death 29 Oct., 1852.

Lowther, Arthur, s. Robert, of Cavendish (*sic*), Middlesex, arm. ST. EDMUND HALL, matric. 16 March, 1753, aged 23; an elder brother of James, 3rd Viscount Lonsdale.

Lowther, Beresford, 4s. Gorges, of St. Pancras, London, arm. EXETER COLL., matric. 31 May, 1827, aged 18; B.A. 1831, rector of Turnaston, co. Hereford, vicar of Vowchurch, co. Hereford, 1838-74. See Foster's *Peerage*, B. CROFTON. [15]

Lowther, Rev. Brabazon, 4s. (*sic*) Gorges, of Marybone, London, arm. MERTON COLL., matric. 13 May, 1829, aged 18; postmaster 1829-33, B.A. 1834, of Shrigley Hall, Cheshire, died 30 Dec., 1877. See Foster's *Peerage*, B. CROFTON.

Lowther, Chambre Brabazon Ponsonby, s. George, of Dublin, Ireland, arm. ORIEL COLL., matric. 14 Dec., 1793, aged 16; B.A. 1797, M.A. 1800, vicar of Cowarne Magna and Glasbury, and rector of Orcheston St. George, Wilts, 1813, until his death 11 May, 1830.

Lowther, Gorges Macdonald, 1s. Gorges P., of Longford, co. Derby, cler. QUEEN'S COLL., matric. 7 March, 1845, aged 20.

Lowther, Gorges Paulin, s. Gorges, of Clifton, co. Gloucester, arm. ST. MARY HALL, matric. 11 Feb., 1812, aged 19; B.A. 1815, M.A. 1823, curate of Shorwell, Isle of Wight, 1816-19, and of Longford, co. Derby, 1819-30, rector of Barton Blount, co. Derby, 1821, preb. of Salisbury 1841, rector of Orcheston St. George, Wilts, 1830, until his death 25 April, 1881, father of the last named.

Lowther, Henry Crofton, 2s. Brabazon, of Prestbury, Kent, cler. BALLIOL COLL., matric. 17 Oct., 1877, aged 19; B.A. 1881; M.A. 1887. See Foster's *Peerage*, B. CROFTON. [20]

Lowther, John, s. William, of Isel, Cumberland, pleb. QUEEN'S COLL., matric. 25 Oct., 1731, aged 17; B.A. 18 Jan., 1736-7 (? died rector of Otterden, Kent, 21 Oct., 1779).

Lowther, (Sir) William (Bart.), of TRINITY COLL., Cambridge (B.A. 1730, M.A. 1734); incorp. 9 July, 1734 (son of Christopher Lowther, of Little Preston, Yorks), rector of Swillington, and vicar of Welton, Yorks, 1742, preb. of York 1754, created a baronet 22 Aug., 1764, died 15 June, 1788. See Foster's *Baronetage.*

Lowther, William, o.s. Henry, of Distington, Cumberland, cler. MERTON COLL., matric. 28 Nov., 1833, aged 18.

Lowthian, Joseph, s. John, of Kirk Oswald, Cumberland, pleb. QUEEN'S COLL., matric. 30 May, 1778, aged 18; B.A. 1782, M.A. 1793, vicar of New Windsor 1800, rector of Thatcham, Berks, 1804, until his death 23 Feb., 1842.

Lowthian, Thomas, s. John, of Kirk Oswald, Cumberland, pleb. QUEEN'S COLL., matric. 22 Feb., 1742-3, aged 17; B.A. 17 March, 1747-8, taberdar 1748, M.A. 1751, fellow 1760, curate of Appledore, Kent, 1750, rector of South Weston and Hampton Poyle. See *O. H. S.*, ix., p. 1. [25]

Lowthian, Rev. William, 5s. John, of Brampton, Cumberland, cler. NON-COLL., matric. 10 April, 1869, aged 20; commoner QUEEN'S COLL. 1872, B.A. 1872, M.A. 1876.

Loxam or **Loxham,** William, s. William, of Longton, Lancashire, gent. BRASENOSE COLL., matric. 11 Oct., 1743, aged 18; B.A. 1747, M.A. 1750, rector of St. Matthew's, Bethnal Green, London, died at Longton aforesaid in 1809, aged 85.

Loxley, Arthur Smart, 1s. John, of Hackney, Middlesex, arm. EXETER COLL., matric. 30 Nov., 1864, aged 18; B.A. 1868, M.A. 1871, minor canon of Gloucester 1875-9, librarian 1876-9, vicar of Fairford, co. Gloucester, 1879, until his death 2 April, 1888.

Loxley, Rev. Francis Edwin, 2s. John Thomas, of Doncaster, Yorks, arm. QUEEN'S COLL., matric. 8 June, 1878, aged 19; exhibitioner 1878-83, B.A. 1882, M.A. 1885.

Loxley, Thomas, s. Thomas, of Chartingbrook, Yorks, pleb. ST. EDMUND HALL, matric. 3 June, 1742, aged 20; B.A. 13 March, 1745-6, died rector of Sprotborough, Yorks, 5 March, 1790. [30]

Loy, Henry Mills, 1s. James, of Darlaston, co. Stafford, cler. ST. JOHN'S COLL., matric. 31 Jan., 1878, aged 18; B.A. 1880.

Loyd, David, s. Thomas, of Langathen, co. Carmarthen, gent. TRINITY COLL., matric. 7 Dec., 1732, aged 18.

Loyd, Richard, s. Richard, of St. John's, Hereford (city), pleb. CHRIST CHURCH, matric. 4 March, 1717-8, aged 17.

Loyd, Samuel Jones, Lord Overstone, of TRINITY COLL., Cambridge, M.A.; created D.C.L. 8 June, 1854 (son of Lewis Loyd, of Overstone Park, Northants, and of London, banker), M.P. Hythe 1819-26, created Lord Overstone 5 March, 1860, died 16 Nov., 1883. See Foster's *Peerage* & *Eton School Lists*.

Luard, Bertram Selby, 2s. Robert Luard-Selby, of The Mote, Kent, arm. MAGDALEN COLL., matric. 25 Oct., 1871, aged 18; clerk 1871-3.

Luard, Frederick Peter, 3s. John, of Brighton, Sussex, arm. EXETER COLL., matric. 29 March, 1859, aged 23; lieut.-colonel Bengal staff corps. **[5]**

Luard, John Godfrey, o.s. John Godfrey, of Olveston, co. Gloucester, gent. EXETER COLL., matric. 20 Oct., 1881, aged 18; a student of the Inner Temple 1885.

Luard, Thomas Garnham, 2s. William Wright, of Witham, Essex, arm. WADHAM COLL., matric. 31 Oct., 1839, aged 18; B.A. 1843, M.A. 1851, hon. canon St. Albans 1882, vicar of Stansted-Mountfitchet, Herts, 1852, until his death 9 Jan., 1886.

Luard, Thomas Inglis, o.s. Thomas Garnham, of Henham, Essex, cler. WADHAM COLL., matric. 30 May, 1868, aged 19; B.A. 1873, M.A. 1877, perp. curate Perlethorpe, Notts, 1876-86.

Lubbock, Charles Western, 1s. Nevile, of North Cray, Kent, arm. BALLIOL COLL., matric. 1 Feb., 1882, aged 19. See Foster's *Baronetage* & *Eton School Lists*.

Lubbock, Sir John, 4th Bart., M.P., F.R.S.; created D.C.L. 9 June, 1875 (son of Sir John Lubbock, 3rd baronet), M.P. Maidstone 1870-80, London University since 1880, and vice-chancellor 1872-80, vice-president Royal Society. See Foster's *Baronetage* & *Eton School Lists*. **[10]**

Lubbock, John Birkbeck, 1s. John, of London, baronet. BALLIOL COLL., matric. 19 Oct., 1878, aged 20; B.A. & M.A. 1885, a student of Lincoln's Inn 1882. See *Eton School Lists*.

Lucas, Arthur, 1s. Arthur, of Darlington, co. Durham, arm. TRINITY COLL., matric. 15 Oct., 1881, aged 18; of the Indian Civil Service 1881.

Lucas, Arthur Henry Shakspeare, 3s. Samuel, of Stratford-on-Avon, co. Warwick, gent. BALLIOL COLL., matric. 17 Oct., 1870, aged 17; exhibitioner 1870-4, B.A. & M.A. 1877.

Lucas, Cecil James, 2s. Carr Ellison, of Hatfield, Herts, arm. EXETER COLL., matric. 25 Oct., 1821, aged 18; scholar 1821-4. See *Coll. Reg.* & *Eton School Lists*.

Lucas, Charles, s. William, of Daventry, Northants, gent. ORIEL COLL., matric. 15 July, 1786, aged 17. **[15]**

Lucas, Charles, s. Edward, of Castle Shane, co. Monaghan, Ireland, arm. HERTFORD COLL., matric. 29 Jan., 1788, aged 30; B.A. from EXETER COLL. 1791, M.A. 1793, of Castle Shane, bar.-at-law, King's Inns, Dublin, died in 1796, father of Edward 1806.

Lucas, Charles Belgrave, 1s. Charles, of Filby, near Norwich, cler. ST. JOHN'S COLL., matric. 21 Jan., 1871, aged 19; B.A. 1875.

Lucas, Rev. Charles Burrard, 2s. William Henry, of Lyndhurst, Hants, cler. BRASENOSE COLL., matric. 21 Oct., 1878, aged 18; scholar 1878-82, B.A. 1883.

Lucas, Charles Eden Lancaster, 2s. Samuel Lucas Lancaster, of Strontian, co. Argyle, arm. CHRIST CHURCH, matric. 10 Oct., 1873, aged 19; B.A. from CHARSLEY HALL 1879, a student of Lincoln's Inn 1877.

Lucas, Charles Halford, 4s. Richard, of Edith Weston, Rutland, cler. CHRIST CHURCH, matric. 8 June, 1854, aged 19; B.A. 1859, rector of Edith Weston 1860, until his death 17 March, 1885. **[20]**

Lucas, Charles Prestwood, 3s. Henry John, of Crickhowell, co. Brecon, D.Med. BALLIOL COLL., matric. 16 Oct., 1872, aged 19; exhibitioner 1872-7, B.A. 1884, bar.-at-law, Lincoln's Inn, 1885. See Foster's *Men at the Bar*.

Lucas, Edward, s. Charles, of Castle Shane, co. Monaghan, arm. CHRIST CHURCH, matric. 24 Oct., 1806, aged 18; of Castle Shane, high sheriff co. Monaghan, & M.P. 1834-41, under-secretary for Ireland 1841-6, and a privy councillor 1845, died 12 Nov., 1871.

Lucas, Edward Sampson. See EDWARD SAMPSON EARDLEY COUSINS EARDLEY, 10 April, 1839.

Lucas, Edward Scudamore, o.s. Fitzherbert Dacre, of Pau, France, arm. CHRIST CHURCH, matric. 13 Oct., 1871, aged 18; a commoner NEW INN HALL 1877, of Castle Shane, co. Monaghan.

Lucas, Henry, s. John, of Reynaldstone, co. Glamorgan, arm. JESUS COLL., matric. 30 April, 1760, aged 19. **[25]**

Lucas, Henry Jesse Andrews, 3s George William, of Redland, near Bristol, gent. WORCESTER COLL., matric. 19 Oct., 1886, aged 24.

Lucas, John, s. Charles, of St. Faith's, London, pleb. NEW INN HALL, matric. 20 June, 1715, aged 24; B.A. from EXETER COLL. 1719.

Lucas, John, fellow of JESUS COLL., Cambridge (B.A. 1705, M.A. 1709); incorp. 9 July, 1724.

Lucas, John, s. Henry, of Reynoldstone, co. Glamorgan, gent. JESUS COLL., matric. 1 July, 1726, aged 18; B.A. from BALLIOL COLL. 1735, a student of Middle Temple 1725.

Lucas, John, s. John, of Northampton (town), gent. LINCOLN COLL., matric. 14 July, 1738, aged 17, B.A. 1742; M.A. from ALL SOULS' COLL. 1746, licensed to practice medicine 20 July, 1748, B.Med. 1750. **[30]**

Lucas, John, s. Rich., of Llandilo Vawe, co. Carmarthen, pleb. JESUS COLL., matric. 16 Nov., 1738, aged 18; B.A. 1742, M.A. 1750.

Lucas, John, s. John, of Tingiwick, Bucks, gent. NEW COLL., matric. 19 Oct., 1759, aged 18; B.A. 1763, M.A. 1767.

Lucas, John, s. Benjamin, of Westminster, gent. QUEEN'S COLL., matric. 16 Dec., 1775, aged 18.

Lucas, John Ponsonby, 1s. Henry, of Reynoldstone, co. Glamorgan, arm. NEW INN HALL, matric. 10 June, 1848, aged 24; B.A. 1851, M.A. 1881, rector of Rhossili and vicar of Llangennith 1855.

Lucas, Noel, 1s. Rudd, of Long Ashton, Somerset arm. TRINITY COLL., matric. 18 Oct., 1869, aged 19; B.A. 1872, M.A. 1888, of Lulham Court, co. Hereford, held various curacies 1873-86. **[35]**

Lucas, Reginald Thomas Hall, 2s. William, of Rawreth, Essex, arm. LINCOLN COLL., matric. 21 May, 1861, aged 18, of the Indian Civil Service 1862, B.A. & LL.B. London University 1871, M.A. 1872, LL.D. 1875, head-master Moulton Grammar School 1873-80, of Bridgenorth School since 1880, rector of Tasley 1882. See *Robinson*, 327.

Lucas, Richard, s. Anthony, of London, gent. MERTON COLL., matric. 17 July, 1742, aged 17; demy MAGDALEN COLL. 1742-7, B.A. 1746, M.A. from EMMANUEL COLL., Cambridge, 1753, preb. of Lincoln 1767, and of Canterbury 1775, until his death Jan., 1789, aged 63. See also *Bloxam* vi., 262.

Lucas, Richard, s. William, of Cardigan (town), cler. WORCESTER COLL., matric. 16 Dec., 1788, aged 17; B.A. 1792, M.A. 1795, incumbent of Holwell, Beds, rector of Little Birch, co. Hereford, died 9 March, 1846.

Lucas, Richard Burroughs, o.s. Richard, of Hitchin, Herts, cler. WORCESTER COLL., matric. 17 June, 1841, aged 18; created M.A. from ST. MARY HALL, 14 Feb., 1850.

Lucas, Richard Gay, 5s. Gibson, of Yarmouth, Norfolk, cler. UNIVERSITY COLL., matric. 14 Nov., 1833, aged 18; B.A. 1837, M.A. 1867, rector of Mulbarton, Norfolk, 1842.

Lucas, Richard Hurd, s. Robert, of Ripple, co. Worcester, cler. BRASENOSE COLL., matric. 27 May, 1808, aged 18; B.A. 1812, M.A. 1814.

Lucas, Robert, s. Richard, of Durverton, Somerset, gent. BALLIOL COLL., matric. 11 Nov., 1731, aged 19.

Lucas, Robert, s. Robert, of Llangattock, co. Monmouth, arm. MERTON COLL., matric. 13 Dec., 1758, aged 17; B.A. 1762. **[5]**

Lucas, Samuel, 1s. Thomas, of Bristol, gent. QUEEN'S COLL., matric. 13 Oct., 1838, aged 20; B.A. 1842, M.A. 1846, bar.-at-law, Inner Temple, 1846, died 27 Nov., 1868.

Lucas, Samuel Francis, 4s. Joseph, of Upper Tooting, Surrey, gent. EXETER COLL., matric. 29 May, 1866, aged 18; B.A. 1870, M.A. 1873, a student of Inner Temple 1868, died in 1875.

Lucas, Thomas, s. Sim., of Coventry, co. Warwick, gent. ST. JOHN'S COLL., matric. 26 June, 1733, aged 16; B.A. 1737.

Lucas, Thomas Francis, o.s. Thomas, of Kinsale, arm. MAGDALEN HALL, matric. 20 June, 1834, aged 26.

Lucas, (Rev.) Vincent William, o.s. (subs. 'primus') William, of Oxford, gent. CHRIST CHURCH, matric. 18 Oct., 1869, aged 19; exhibitioner 1869-72, B.A. 1874, M.A. 1878. **[10]**

Lucas, William, s. Robert, of Langattock, co. Monmouth, gent. MERTON COLL., matric. 29 May, 1754, aged 19.

Lucas, Rev. William, s. Thomas, of Ashton, Lancashire, gent. LINCOLN COLL., matric. 30 Oct., 1767, aged 18; B.A. 1771, died 3 Feb., 1820, aged 70, late of Knightrider Street, London.

Lucas, William, s. William Reynolds, of Chelmsford, Essex, arm. EXETER COLL., matric. 18 March, 1780, aged 17; B.A. 1783, M.A. 1815, bar.-at-law, Lincoln's Inn, 1789, assumed the name of LUCAS in lieu of Reynolds. See *St. Paul's School Reg.*, 156.

Lucas, William Henry, 1s. Henry, of Newport Pagnell, Northants, arm. BRASENOSE COLL., matric. 21 Nov., 1839, aged 18; postmaster MERTON COLL., 1840-3, B.A. 1843; fellow BRASENOSE COLL. 1844-52, M.A. 1846, held various curacies 1848-66, vicar of Sopley, Hants, 1866.

Lucas, William Henry, 3s. Arthur, of Darlington, co. Durham, gent. NEW COLL., matric. 15 Oct., 1886, aged 19; of the Indian Civil Service 1886. **[15]**

Lucas, William Nelson, 1s. — L., of Yarmouth, Norfolk, cler. TRINITY COLL., matric. 8 March, 1838, aged 18; B.A. 1841, rector of Burgh St. Margaret's, Norfolk, died 21 Dec., 1861.

Lucas, Rev. William Orton, 1s. Orton, of London, arm. EXETER COLL., matric. 17 Oct., 1863, aged 19; B.A. 1867, M.A. 1870, died 23 Sep., 1874.

Lucas, William Robert, 2s. Charles, of Abury, Wilts, cler. LINCOLN COLL., matric. 27 Oct., 1831, aged 18.

Lucas, William Tindall, 1s. Francis, of Hatcham, Surrey, arm. PEMBROKE COLL., matric. 20 April, 1866, aged 18; B.A. 1869.

Luce, Edward, 3s. Francis Edward, of St. Laurence, Isle of Jersey, gent. NON-COLL., matric. 16 Oct., 1869, aged 18; scholar PEMBROKE COLL. 1870-4, B.A. 1874, M.A. 1876, perp. curate St. Gouray, Jersey, 1875-7, rector of St. John's, Jersey, 1877-80, and of St. Mary's, Jersey, since 1880. **[20]**

Luce, Francis, s. Thomas, of Whitleigh, Devon, gent. EXETER COLL., matric. 2 May, 1754, aged 17; B.A. 1758, vicar of Harpford and Fen Ottery, Devon, died in 1810.

Lucena, John Charles, s. John Charles, of London, arm. BRASENOSE COLL., matric. 10 Oct., 1817, aged 18; B.A. 1822, M.A. 1823, vicar of Anstey, co. Warwick, 1835, until his death 15 Feb., 1868.

Lucena, Lorenzo, created M.A. 5 June, 1877, hon. canon of Gibraltar 1842-60, Taylorian teacher of Spanish at Oxford 1858, died 24 Aug., 1881. See *Crockford.*

Lucena, Stephen Lancaster, 1s. Stephen Lancaster, of Enfield, Middlesex, arm. CHRIST CHURCH, matric. 30 May, 1885, aged 19.

Lucey, Rev. Algernon Charles, o.s. Ebenezer Curling, of Biddenden, Kent, cler. MAGDALEN COLL., matric. 16 Oct., 1880, aged 18; B.A. 1883, M.A. 1887.

Lucey, Ebenezer Curling, 5s. Charles, of Bermondsey, near Southwark, London, arm. LINCOLN COLL., matric. 21 June, 1854, aged 19; B.A. 1858, M.A. 1861, vicar of St. Margaret-at-Cliffe 1866-85, rector of Mersham, Kent, 1885. **[26]**

Luck, Charles Thomas, 1s. Charles, of Brooklyn, near New York, America, cler. EXETER COLL., matric. 13 May, 1856, aged 20; B.A. 1861, M.A. 1864, bar.-at-law, Lincoln's Inn, 1864, died 31 July, 1879. See *Eton School Lists.*

Luck, James, s. James, of Tunbridge, Kent, gent. ST. JOHN'S COLL., matric. 30 June, 1720, aged 18; B.A. 1724, M.A. 1728, B.D. 1733, D.D. 1738.

Luckie, Edgar George Fraser, 1s. David Fraser, of London, arm. BALLIOL COLL., matric. 18 Oct., 1881, aged 19; of the Indian Civil Service 1881.

Luckman, Arthur Weston, 1s. Samuel, of Mortlake, Surrey, gent. CHARSLEY HALL, matric. 2 Nov., 1886, aged 16. **[30]**

Luckman, Rev. William Arthur Grant, 1s. William Grant, of Bathwick, Somerset, cler. KEBLE COLL., matric. 19 Oct., 1876, aged 19; B.A. 1881, M.A. 1888.

Lucock, Joshua, s. Raisbeck, of Egremonte, Cumberland, arm. QUEEN'S COLL., matric. 19 Oct., 1790, aged 18.

Lucock, Raisbeck, s. Joshua, of Cockermouth, Cumberland, arm. QUEEN'S COLL., matric. 12 Oct., 1764, aged 16.

Lucy, Rev. Edward, s. William, of London, gent. BALLIOL COLL., matric. 29 March, 1745, aged 19; B.A. 1749, of Barley End, Bucks, died 14 Jan., 1778.

Lucy, George, s. Foulke, of Charlcote, co. Warwick, arm. BALLIOL COLL., matric. 17 March, 1732-3, aged 18; created D.C.L. 14 April, 1749, of Charlcote, died s.p. **[35]**

Lucy, George, s. John (formerly Hammond), of Charlcote, co. Warwick, cler. CHRIST CHURCH, matric. 22 Oct., 1807, aged 18; of Charlcote, high sheriff co. Warwck 1831, M.P. Fowey 1818-19 & 1820-30, died 7 July, 1845.

Lucy, Henry Spencer, 1s. George, of Compton Verney, near Stratford-upon-Avon, arm. CHRIST CHURCH, matric. 23 May, 1850, aged 19; of Charlcote Park, co. Warwick, D.L., high sheriff 1857.

Lucy, Reginald Aymer, 2s. George, of Charlcote, co. Warwick, arm. CHRIST CHURCH, matric. 8 June, 1854, aged 17.

Lucy, William Charles, 1s. William Charles, of Stratford-upon-Avon, co. Warwick, arm. TRINITY COLL., matric. 29 April, 1867, aged 19; B.A. 1871, M.A. 1873. See *Rugby School Reg.*

Luders, Alexander, s. Alexander, of St. George's, Bloomsbury, London, arm. BRASENOSE COLL., matric. 27 June, 1806, aged 17; B.A. 1810, M.A. 1815, rector of Woolstone, co. Gloucester, 1829, until his death 24 March, 1851. **[40]**

Ludford, Edward (Taylor), s. Thomas, of London, arm. CHRIST CHURCH, matric. 16 June, 1756, aged 18; B.A. from TRINITY COLL. 1760 (? rector of Berkswell, co. Warwick, 1762). See *Alumni West.*, 364.

Ludford, John (Newdigate), s. John (Bracebridge), of Ansley, co. Warwick, arm. UNIVERSITY COLL., matric. 11 Nov., 1774, aged 18; created M.A. 3 July, 1778, and D.C.L. 5 July, 1793, of Ansley Hall, co. Warwick, J.P., D.L., assumed the additional name of NEWDIGATE by royal licence, 5 July, 1808, bar.-at-law, Inner Temple, 1777, bencher 1811, died 16 May, 1825.

Ludgater, James, 2s. James, of Rotherhithe, Surrey, gent. LINCOLN COLL., matric. 3 June, 1835, aged 18.

Ludlam, Edward Thomas, 1s. Thomas, of Ellington, Hunts, cler. EXETER COLL., matric. 28 Jan., 1865, aged 19; scholar WORCESTER COLL. 1865-9, B.A. 1869.

Ludlam, William, s. Thomas, of London, arm. ORIEL COLL., matric. 15 Dec., 1791, aged 17; B.A. from TRINITY COLL., Cambridge, 1796, M.A. 1799.

Ludlow, Abraham, s. Abraham, of Bristol, co. Gloucester, arm. ORIEL COLL., matric. 14 July, 1796, aged 17; of Heywood House, Wilts, J.P., high sheriff 1810, died at Rouen 3 July, 1822. **[5]**

Ludlow, Arthur Rainey, 1s. Ebenezer, of St. Michael's, Bristol (city), arm. ORIEL COLL., matric. 30 May, 1827, aged 17; B.A. 1831, M.A. 1835, rector of Littleton-on-Severn 1855-69.

Ludlow, Ebenezer, s. Ebenezer, of Chipping Sodbury, co. Gloucester, gent. ORIEL COLL., matric. 28 June, 1791, aged 14; B.A. 1795, M.A. 1821, bar.-at-law, Gray's Inn, 1805, serjt.-at-law 1827, K.C. & Q.C., town clerk of Bristol, 1819, a commissioner of bankruptcy 1842, died 25 March, 1851.

Ludlow, Edmund, s. Thomas, of Warminster, Wilts, gent. TRINITY COLL., matric. 7 Nov., 1718, aged 18; B.A. 1722, died unmarried.

Ludlow, Edmund, s. Edmund, of Southampton (town), gent. QUEEN'S COLL., matric. 10 Dec., 1766, aged 21.

Ludlow, Edward, 2s. James, of Warminster, Wilts, arm. ST. EDMUND HALL, matric. 4 Nov., 1820, aged 19; B.A. 1824, M.A. 1827, held various curacies 1825-37, vicar of Winterbourne St. Martin's, Dorset, 1837. **[10]**

Ludlow, Henry Gaisford Gibbs, o.s. Abraham, of Westbury, Wilts, arm. CHRIST CHURCH, matric. 17 June, 1828, aged 18.

Ludlow, Henry John, o.s. John, of Hastings, Sussex, arm. EXETER COLL., matric. 27 April, 1881, aged 19.

Ludlow, John Thomas, 2s. Ebenezer, of St. Michael's, Bristol (city), arm. ORIEL COLL., matric. 25 Nov., 1830, aged 17; B.A. 1835, M.A. 1840, rector of Compton-Greenfield, co. Gloucester, 1846, until his death 10 Oct., 1873.

Ludlow, Thomas Binfield, 1s. Stephen of Cowley, Oxon, gent. CHRIST CHURCH, matric. 20 Oct., 1841, aged 19; servitor 1841-5, B.A. 1845, chaplain 1845-53, M.A. 1848, rector of Slapton, Bucks, 1853-74, vicar of St. Wendron, Cornwall, 1874-83, rector of Blyborough, co. Lincoln, 1883.

Ludlow-Bruges, William Heald, s. Benjamin Ludlow, of Melksham, Wilts, gent. QUEEN'S COLL., matric. 10 Nov., 1814, aged 17; B.A. 1818, M.A. 1822, of Seend, Wilts, J.P., D.L., assumed the additional surname of BRUGES by royal licence 1835, M.P. Bath 1837-41, Devizes (Feb.) 1844-8, bar.-at-law, Middle Temple, 1821, recorder of Devizes, died 23 June, 1855. **[15]**

Luffman, Samuel, 6s. John, of Milborne Port, Dorset, gent. NON-COLL., matric. 10 April, 1880, aged 25.

Luke, George Rankine, 2s. James, of West Church, Edinburgh, gent. BALLIOL COLL., matric. 8 Nov., 1855, aged 19, Snell exhibitioner, 1855, B.A. 1859; student CHRIST CHURCH 1859-62, tutor 1861, drowned at Oxford 3 March, 1862.

Luke, Rev. George Sercombe, s. Thomas, of Exeter (city), gent. QUEEN'S COLL., matric. 15 Dec., 1817, aged 23; B.A. 1822, died at Exeter 15 April, 1835.

Luke, William Henry Colbeck, o.s. William, of Calcutta, East Indies, arm. ORIEL COLL., matric. 14 Nov., 1849, aged 18; B.A. 1853, M.A. 1857, rector of Elmswell, Suffolk, 1863-78, vicar of St. Matthias, Earl's Court, London, 1878.

Luker, George Lewis, 'plumbarius et vitrarius;' privilegiatus 18 May, 1808. **[20]**

Lukin, George William, of CHRIST'S COLL., Cambridge, LL.B. 1797, s. Robert, of Braintree, Essex, gent. ST. ALBAN HALL, incorp. 20 June, 1798, aged 58; D.C.L. 23 June, 1798, rector of Felbrig and Aylmerton, Norfolk, preb. of Westminster 1797, dean of Wells 1799, until his death 27 Nov., 1812.

Lukin, James, 1s. James William, of Sydling, Dorset, arm. BRASENOSE COLL., matric. 26 March, 1846, aged 18; scholar 1846-51, B.A. 1849, rector of Hewelsfield, co. Gloucester, 1856-62, of Bradfield Combust, Suffolk, 1862-5, and of Pwllcrochan, co. Pembroke, 1865-9, vicar of Stetchworth, co. Cambridge, 1869-81, rector of Wickford, Essex, 1881.

Lukin, John, s. George William, of Saltash, Cornwall, doctor (after dean of Wells). ORIEL COLL., matric. 28 Feb., 1801, aged 18; B.A. 1804, M.A. 1807, preb. of Wells 1808, vicar of Combe St. Nicholas 1809, rector of Nursling, Hants, 1809, died 15 Dec., 1846. See *Eton School Lists.*

Lukin, Robert, s. George William, of Metton, Norfolk, cler. (after dean of Wells). EXETER COLL., matric. 13 July, 1791, aged 18, scholar 1791; demy MAGDALEN COLL. 1792-1802, B.A. 1795, M.A. 1799, fellow 1802-8, a first clerk in War Office 1831, secretary to the tennis club. See *Bloxam*, vii., 126; & *Boase*, 148.

Lukin, William Hugo, 2s. James William, of Sidling, Dorset, arm. BRASENOSE COLL., matric. 3 Feb., 1848, aged 18; scholar 1848-9. **[25]**

Lukis, William Collings, of TRINITY COLL., Cambridge (B.A. 1840, M.A. 1843); adm. 'ad eundem' 22 June, 1854, perp. curate East Grafton, Wilts 1846-50, vicar of Great Bedwyn, Wilts, 1850-5, rector of Collingbourne Ducis, Wilts, 1855-62, and of Wath, Yorks, 1862; for list of his works see *Crockford.*

Lukyn, Anthony, s. John, of Canterbury (city), arm. CHRIST CHURCH, matric. 13 July, 1744, aged 17; B.A. 1748; M.A. from KING'S COLL., Cambridge 1773, rector of St. Mildred and All Saints', Canterbury, vicar of Reculver and Hoath, Kent, died 1 Nov., 1778.

Lukyn, William, 'chirurgus;' privilegiatus 4 Dec. 1832.

Lumbert, Richard, s. Thomas, of Clapham, co. Gloucester, pleb. ST. EDMUND HALL, matric. 17 Oct. 1729, aged 18.

Lumby, John, s. Zeth, of St. Peter's, Paul's Wharf, London, pleb. QUEEN'S COLL., matric. 28 March 1724, aged 17; B.A. 20 March, 1727-8, M.A. 173[illegible] rector of Upway, Dorset, 1753, of Dipden, Hants preb. of Salisbury 1751, until his death 9 Jan., 175[illegible]

Lumley, Augustus William Savile. CORPUS CHRISTI COLL., 1847. See SAVILE. **[30]**

Lumley, Christopher, s. Hugh, of Penrith, Cumberland, arm. ORIEL COLL., matric. 17 Dec., 175[illegible] aged 18.

Lumley, Frederick Savile (2s.), born in St. George's Hanover Square, Westminster, arm. CORPUS CHRISTI COLL., matric. 27 Jan., 1842, aged 2[illegible] B.A. 1846, brother of Augustus, 1847, and of S[ir] John Savile Lumley.

Lumly, George, s. Thomas, of St. Nicholas, Newcastle, Northumberland, pleb. MERTON COLL., matric. 14 May, 1730, aged 17.

Lumley, George, s. Hugh, of — co. Cork, Ireland, arm. CHRIST CHURCH, matric. 15 July, 1755, aged 18.

Lumley, Henry, s. Hugh, of Cork, Ireland, arm. ORIEL COLL., matric. 17 Oct., 1751, aged 18. **[35]**

mley, Henry, s. Henry, of Whitechurch, Oxon, gent. MERTON COLL., matric. 15 Dec., 1786, aged 18; B.A. 1791, bar.-at-law, Lincoln's Inn, 1795.

mley, Joseph Robert, o.s. Joseph, of Wandsworth, Surrey, gent. ST. MARY HALL, matric. 29 Oct., 1840, aged 30.

mmis, Edward William, 1s. William, of Kingston-on-Hull, gent. WORCESTER COLL., matric. 22 Oct., 1885, aged 18; scholar 1884.

msdaine, Edwin Lumsdaine Sandys-, 1s. Edwin, of Upper Hardres, cler. ORIEL COLL., matric. 3 Feb., 1837, aged 18; B.A. 1841, M.A. 1843, bar.-at-law, Lincoln's Inn, 1846, died 30 April, 1853.

msdaine, Edwin Robert John Sandys-, 1s. Francis Gordon, of Canterbury, cler. CHRIST CHURCH, matric. 18 Jan., 1884, aged 19; B.A. 1887. [5]

msdaine, Edwin Sandys, s. Edwin Sandys, of Canterbury (city), arm. ST. JOHN'S COLL., matric. 20 May, 1803, aged 17; B.A. 1808, M.A. 1814, assumed the additional surname of LUMSDAINE, rector of Upper Hardres, Kent, 1815, until his death 3 July, 1871.

msdaine, Francis Gordon Sandys-, 3s. Edwin, of Upper Hardres, Kent, cler. CHRIST CHURCH, matric. 4 June, 1846, aged 18; student 1847-57, B.A. 1850, M.A. 1853, of Lumsdaine and Blanerne, co. Berwick, and Innergellie, co. Fife, curate of Upper Hardres, died 18 June, 1873. See *Rugby School Reg.*, 240.

msdaine, James Lumsdaine Sandys-, 2s. Edwin, of Hardres, Kent, cler. ORIEL COLL., matric. 12 Dec., 1839, aged 18; B.A. 1843, M.A. 1849, lieutenant 15th hussars, died 8 Dec., 1853.

msden, Hugh, s. Harry, of Aberdeen, Scotland, arm. WADHAM COLL., matric. 31 Oct., 1803, aged 20; of Pitcaple House, co. Aberdeen, J.P., D.L., etc., died 27 Jan., 1859.

msden, William Harry, 1s. William James, of Aberdeen, arm. MAGDALEN COLL., matric. 25 Oct., 1871, aged 19; B.A. 1875. [10]

ndie, Stow Compton, 2s. William Compton, of Spital House, Northumberland, cler. HERTFORD COLL., matric. 19 Oct., 1874, aged 19.

ndie, William Compton, 1s. William Compton, of Berwick-on-Tweed, cler. ORIEL COLL., matric. 18 Oct., 1871, aged 20.

ndy, Francis, s. Francis, of North Burton, Yorks, gent. UNIVERSITY COLL., matric. 22 March, 1768, B.A. 1771, M.A. 1774, 40 years rector of Lockington, Yorks, vicar of Lund, died 3 Oct., 1816, aged 67.

ndy, Francis, s. Francis, of Lockington, Yorks, cler. UNIVERSITY COLL., matric. 26 Oct., 1798, aged 18; B.A. 1802, M.A. 1805 rector (and patron) of Lockington, and perp. curate of Kilnwick-on-the-Wolds 1817, until his death 21 Nov., 1853.

ndy, Francis James, 1s. Francis, of Lund, Yorks, cler. UNIVERSITY COLL., matric. 16 May, 1833, aged 18. [15]

ney, Richard, 2s. William, of Launceston, Cornwall, gent. MAGDALEN HALL, matric. 14 Jan., 1822, aged 21; B.A. 1827, M.A. 1833.

ney, Thomas Hodson Radcliffe, 1s. Richard, of Bickleigh, Devon, cler. EXETER COLL., matric. 22 May, 1850, aged 18; B.A. 1855.

ngley, James, o.s. Peter, of Southampton, gent. NON-COLL., matric. 15 Oct., 1881, aged 18; B.A. from ST. JOHN'S COLL., 1886.

nn, Edward, of CORPUS CHRISTI COLL., Cambridge (B.A. 1728, M.A. 1732), s. William, archdeacon of Huntingdon; incorp. 11 July, 1747, rector of Elseworth, co. Cambridge, 1747, until his death 2 Nov., 1791. See Masters' *History of Benet Coll.*, p. 343.

nn, Matthew, s. Robert, of Norton, co. Worcester, pleb. MAGDALEN HALL, matric. 13 Dec., 1799, aged 19; B.A. 1807, M.A. 1810, minor canon Worcester Cathedral 1814, vicar of St. Peter's, Worcester, with Whittington Chapel 1815, vicar of Kempsey 1816, until his death 9 March, 1852. [20]

Luntley, Thomas, s. Thomas, of Hereford (city), gent. ST. JOHN'S COLL., matric. 22 June, 1759, aged 19; B.C.L. 1764, D.C.L. 1769, rector of Brampton Bryan, preb. of Hereford, until his death in 1800.

Lupton, Hugh, 5s. Francis, of Roundhay, near Leeds, gent. UNIVERSITY COLL., matric. 15 May, 1880, aged 19; B.A. 1884.

Lupton, James, 2s. James, of York (city), pleb. CHRIST CHURCH, matric. 7 July, 1819, aged 19; servitor 1819-23, B.A. 1823, chaplain 1823-7, M.A. 1825, chaplain NEW COLL. 1823-9, minor canon of St. Paul's and of Westminster Abbey 1829, vicar of Blackbourton, Oxon, 1827, and of St. Michael Queenhithe 1832, until his death 21 Dec., 1873.

Lupton, James Irvine, 1s. James, of Lambeth, Surrey, cler. ST. MARY HALL, matric. 17 Dec., 1849, aged 18, Nowell exhibitioner 1850-1.

Lupton, Sydney, 4s. Darnton, of Barwick-on-Elmet, Yorks, arm. CHRIST CHURCH, matric. 3 June, 1868, aged 18; a junior student 1870-5, B.A. 1871, M.A. 1875, sometime assistant-master at Harrow. See *Rugby School Reg.*, 121. [25]

Lupton, William Arthur, 1s. James Smithson, of Bramley, Yorks, gent. BALLIOL COLL., matric. 18 Oct., 1876, aged 18; B.A. 1879.

Luscombe, Arthur Morris, 2s. Richard James, of Moorlinch, Somerset, cler. ST. ALBAN HALL, matric. 14 Oct., 1879, aged 24; commoner MERTON COLL. 1880, B.A. 1882.

Luscombe, Edward Knighton, 2s. 'John L.,' of Plymouth, arm. CHRIST CHURCH, matric. 17 Dec., 1833, aged 17; student 1833-6, a minor canon Gloucester Cathedral 1845, died 3 Feb., 1867.

Luscombe, Edward Thornhill, s. Samuel, of Exeter (city), doctor. MAGDALEN HALL, matric. 9 May, 1804, aged 22.

Luscombe, John, s. John, of Charlington, Devon, arm. TRINITY COLL., matric. 29 April, 1729, aged 16. [30]

Luscombe, John Brooking, s. Edward, of Dittisham, Devon, gent. BALLIOL COLL., matric. 16 Dec., 1777, aged 18; B.A. 1781.

Luscombe, John Manning, s. Richard (Manning), of Kingsbridge, Devon, gent. PEMBROKE COLL., matric. 16 April, 1791, aged 18; of Combe Royal, Devon, assumed the surname of LUSCOMBE by royal licence, died 10 Jan., 1831.

Luscombe, Matthew Henry Thornhill, of CATHARINE HALL, Cambridge (B.A. 1798, M.A. 1805), s. Samuel, of Exeter, Devon, doctor. EXETER COLL., incorp. 29 Jan., 1810, aged 34; B.C.L. 1 Feb., 1810, D.C.L. 3 Feb., 1810, master of Haileybury College, 1806-19, bishop of the Episcopal Church of Scotland, 1824, and chaplain to the British Embassy at Paris, 1825 until his death at Lausanne, 24 Aug., 1846.

Luscombe, Richard James, s. Richard, of Totnes, Devon, gent. ST. MARY HALL, matric. 14 March, 1799, aged 18; of Moorlynch, Somerset, father of the next named.

Luscombe, Richard James, 1s. Richard James, of Moorlynch, Somerset, cler. WORCESTER COLL., matric. 13 May, 1829, aged 18; B.A. 1833, M.A. 1835, vicar of Moorlynch, Somerset, 1847, until his death 31 Oct., 1883. [35]

Luscombe, Samuel, 2s. Richard James, of Holne, Devon, cler. WORCESTER COLL., matric. 29 Oct., 1830, aged 18; B.A. 1834.

Lush, Percy John Frederick, y.s. Robert, of London, arm. CHRIST CHURCH, matric. 13 Oct., 1876, aged 18; a junior student 1876-83, B.A. 1880, M.A. 1884, B.Med. 1887.

Lush, Roland Gerald, y.s. Joseph, of Southsea, gent. NON-COLL., matric. 23 Oct., 1886, aged 18.

Lusher, Thomas, s. Thomas, of Alin, Berks, pleb. PEMBROKE COLL., matric. 26 Nov., 1715, aged 18; B.A. 1719 (as ROBERT LASHER).

Lushington, Charles, 3s. Henry, of St. George's, Bloomsbury, baronet. CHRIST CHURCH, matric. 14 Dec., 1822, aged 17; student 1822-35, B.A. 1826, M.A. 1830, vicar of Walton-on-Thames 1861-4. See Foster's *Baronetage*.

Lushington, Charles Manners, 6s. Stephen Rumbold, of St. James's, London, arm. ORIEL COLL., matric. 20 April, 1837, aged 17, B.A. 1841, M.A. 1843; fellow of ALL SOULS' COLL. 1843-6, of Norton Court, Kent, M.P. Canterbury 1854-7, died 27 Nov., 1864. See Foster's *Baronetage* & *Eton School Lists*.

Lushington, Edmund Law; created D.C.L. 21 June, 1876 (son of Edmund Henry), scholar TRINITY COLL., Cambridge, 1830-4, B.A. 1832, fellow 1834-42, M.A. 1835, hon. fellow 1885, senior classic, 1st chancellor's medallist, 1832, Greek professor Glasgow University 1858-75, lord rector 1884. See Foster's *Baronetage*.

Lushington, Franklin Guy, 5s. James Law, of Elstead, Surrey, arm. BALLIOL COLL., matric. 18 Oct., 1881, aged 19; B.A. 1885.

Lushington, Godfrey, 5s. Stephen, of St. Margaret's, Westminster, D.C.L. BALLIOL COLL., matric. 30 Nov., 1850, aged 18; fellow ALL SOULS' COLL. 1854-62, B.A. 1854, M.A. 1857, bar.-at-law, Inner Temple, 1858, permanent under-secretary Home Department 1885, etc. See Foster's *Men at the Bar* & *Rugby School Reg.*, 273. [5]

Lushington, Guy, 3s. Edward Harbord, of Calcutta, arm. UNIVERSITY COLL., matric. 16 Oct., 1885, aged 19; bar.-at-law, Middle Temple, 1887. See Foster's *Baronetage* & *Eton School Lists*.

Lushington, Henry, s. Stephen, of Sittingbourne, Kent, arm. WADHAM COLL., matric. 17 Dec., 1725, aged 16; B.A. 1729, M.A. 1732, B. & D.D. 1765, vicar of Eastbourne 1734, until his death 13 Jan., 1779. See Foster's *Baronetage*.

Lushington, Rev. Somerville Henry, 4s. Frederick Astell, of Lyndhurst, Hants, arm. EXETER COLL., matric. 15 Oct., 1875, aged 19.

Lushington, Stephen, s. Stephen, of Sittingbourne, Kent, arm. CHRIST CHURCH, matric. 13 June, 1726, aged 17; B.A. 1730, M.A. 1733, died s.p. See Foster's *Baronetage* & *Alumni West.*, 292.

Lushington, Stephen, s. Stephen, of Marylebone, Middlesex, baronet. CHRIST CHURCH, matric. 26 Oct., 1797, aged 15; fellow ALL SOULS' COLL. until 1821, B.A. 1802, M.A. 1806, B.C.L. 1807, D.C.L. 1808, bar.-at-law, Inner Temple, 1806, an advocate of Doctors' Commons 1808, judge of the Consistory Court 1828-38, and of the Court of Admiralty 1838-67, M.P. Yarmouth, Norfolk, 1866-8, Ilchester 1820-6 & 1831, Tregony 1826-30, Winchelsea 1831, and Tower Hamlets 1832-41, a privy councillor 1838, died 19 Jan., 1873. See Foster's *Baronetage* & *Eton School Lists*. [10]

Lushington, Stephen (George), s. Stephen Rumbold, of East Indies, arm. ORIEL COLL., matric. 10 Dec., 1816, aged 18; a commissioner of Customs, died unmarried 1 Feb., 1853. See Foster's *Baronetage* & *Eton School Lists*.

Lushington, Stephen Rumbold; created D.C.L. 12 June, 1839 (son of Rev. James Stephen Lushington), governor of Madras 1827-32, M.P. Rye 1807-12, Canterbury 1812-30 & 1835-7, chairman of committees House of Commons, joint secretary of the Treasury 1824-7, a privy councillor 1827, died 5 Aug., 1868. See Foster's *Baronetage* & *Rugby School Reg.*, 59.

Lushington, Sydney George, 2s. Edward Harbord, of Calcutta, arm. UNIVERSITY COLL., matric. 12 Oct., 1878, aged 19; B.A. 1884, B.C.L. & M.A. 1885, bar.-at-law, Inner Temple, 1884. See Foster's *Men at the Bar* & *Eton School Lists*.

Lushington, William Hurdis, 4s. Stephen Rumbold, of Binsted, Kent, arm. ORIEL COLL., matric. 17 March, 1826, aged 18; B.A. 1832, M.A. 1834, rector of Eastling, Kent, 1836, until his death 23 July, 1842. See Foster's *Baronetage* & *Eton School Lists*.

Lusignan, Constantine Adolphus, M.A. TRINI COLL., Dublin, 1865 (B.A. 1864); adm. 'comita causa' 8 July, 1865, curate-in-charge Wyresda Lancashire, 1856-63, perp. curate 1863-8, and vic 1868. [1

Lutener, J h , s. John, of Blackburn, Lancashi gent. BRASENOSE COLL., matric. 15 May, 17 aged 19; B.A. 1788, curate of Ludlow, and incu bent of Bradshaw, died in 1811. See *Manches School Reg.*, ii. 92.

Lutener, William Maurice Bonner, 1s. William, Harthill, Cheshire, cler. KEBLE COLL., matric. Oct., 1879, aged 19; B.A. 1884.

Lutley, Edward Chorley, 2s. Samuel Baker, of Exet Devon, gent. EXETER COLL., matric. 14 Oc 1865, aged 18; B.A. 1869, M.A. 1873, has h various curacies since 1861.

Lutley, Jenks, s. Philip, of Ludlow, Salop, ar MERTON COLL., matric. 21 Jan., 1726-7, aged 1 bar.-at-law, Lincoln's Inn, 1734, died about 1736.

Lutley, John Habington. CHRIST CHURCH, 18 See BARNEBY. [2

Lutt, Edward Kefford, of SIDNEY SUSSEX COL Cambridge (B.A. 1844, M.A. 1847); adm. ' eundem' 9 Dec., 1853, vicar of Harmston, co. L coln, 1862.

Luttrell, Alexander, s. Alexander, of Dunster, Som set, arm. CHRIST CHURCH, matric. 30 Oct., 17 aged 17.

Luttrell, Alexander Fownes, s. John, of Dunst Somerset, arm. EXETER COLL., matric. 6 M 1812, aged 18; rector of East Quantoxhead, Som set, 1817. See *Eton School Lists*.

Luttrell, Claude Mohun Fownes, 4s. George Fown of Kilve, Somerset, arm. MAGDALEN COLL., matr 21 Oct., 1886, aged 19.

Luttrell, Edward Fownes, 2s. Francis, of Kil Somerset, arm. CHRIST CHURCH, matric. 12 Ju 1851, aged 19; of Kilve Court, brother of Franc 1857, and of Reginald, 1858. See *Eton School Li*

Luttrell, Edward Fownes, 3s. George Fownes, Woodlands, Somerset, arm. NON-COLL., matr 1 Feb., 1879, aged 20. See *Eton School Lists*. [2

Luttrell, Francis Fownes, s. Henry, of Duns Somerset, arm. QUEEN'S COLL., matric. 29 Mar 1773, aged 17; created D.C.L. 5 July, 1793, Northway, Devon, bar.-at-law, Middle Tem 1782, a commissioner of customs, M.P. Mineh 1780-3, died 24 April, 1823, father of Henry Fow 1806.

Luttrell, Francis Fownes, s. John Fownes, of Duns Somerset, arm. CHRIST CHURCH, matric. 23 O 1810, aged 18; of Kilve Court and Wotton Ho Somerset, lieut.-colonel grenadier guards, died J 1862.

Luttrell, Francis Fownes, 4s. Francis Fownes, Kilve, Somerset, arm. ORIEL COLL., matric May, 1857, aged 19; brother of Edward 1851, Reginald 1858.

Luttrell, George Fownes, 1s. Francis Fownes, Kilve, Somerset, arm. CHRIST CHURCH, matri June, 1846, aged 19; B.A. 1850, of Dunster Ca Somerset, etc., J.P., D.L., high sheriff 1874, so time captain 11th Somerset rifle volunteers. *Eton School Lists*.

Luttrell, Henry, s. Simon, of Coton Hall, co. V wick, arm. CHRIST CHURCH, matric. 13 Jan., 1 aged 17.

Luttrell, Henry Acland Fownes, 1s. Alexander Fow of Quantoxhead, Somerset, cler. TRINITY Co matric. 10 May, 1845, aged 18; B.A. 1850, M 1852, of Badgworth Court, Somerset, J.P., D high sheriff 1881, lieut.-colonel 3rd Somerset volunteers. See *Eton School Lists*.

Luttrell, Henry Fownes, s. John Fownes, of North Devon, arm. QUEEN'S COLL., matric. 21 A 1741, aged 17; of Dunster Castle, Somerset, sumed the additional name and arms of LUTTR father of John F., 1770.

ttrell, Henry Fownes, s. Francis, of St. George's, London, arm. CHRIST CHURCH, matric. 17 May, 1806, aged 17; student 1806-13, B.A. 1810, a student of the Middle Temple 1809, secretary to the vice-chancellor of England, died 20 July, 1813. See *Alumni West.*, 464, & *Eton School Lists.*

ttrell, Henry Fownes, s. John, of Dunster Castle, Somerset, arm. BRASENOSE COLL., matric. 4 Feb., 1809, aged 18; B.A. 1812, of Dunster Castle, a student of the Middle Temple 1813, M.P. Minehead 1816-22, a commissioner of Board of Audit 1822-49, died 6 Oct., 1867.

ttrell, John Fownes, s. Henry, of Dunster, Somerset, arm. QUEEN'S COLL., matric. 3 Dec., 1770, aged 18; of Dunster Castle, M.P. Minehead 1784, until his death 16 Feb., 1816.

ttrell, John Fownes, s. John, of Dunster Castle, Somerset, arm. ORIEL COLL., matric. 8 Nov., 1805, aged 18; created M.A. 28 Nov., 1808, of Dunster Castle, J.P., D.L., M.P. Minehead 1812-32, died 11 Jan., 1857. See *Eton School Lists.*

ttrell, Reginald Fownes, 5s. Francis Fownes, of Kilve, Somerset, arm. ORIEL COLL., matric. 3 June, 1858, aged 19; brother of Edward, 1851, and of Francis, 1858. [5]

ttrell, Thomas (Fownes), s. John, of Dunster, Somerset, arm. EXETER COLL., matric. 26 May, 1814, aged 19; B.A. 1817, perp. curate Dunster 1821, vicar of Minehead 1822, and vicar of Carhampton, Somerset, 1834, until his death 17 Dec., 1871. See *Eton School Lists.*

twyche, Alfred James Peter, 1s. John, of St. Sepulchre's, London, gent. QUEEN'S COLL., matric. 28 Nov., 1828, aged 18; B.A. 1832, M.A. 1835, bar.-at-law, Middle Temple, 1840.

twyche, William, s. Thomas, of London, arm. BRASENOSE COLL., matric. 2 Sep., 1729, aged 17.

tyens, William Wynn, s. John, of St. Pancras, Middlesex, gent. PEMBROKE COLL., matric. 7 June, 1819, aged 17; B.A. 1823, M.A. 1826, chaplain E.I.C.S., died 29 June, 1862.

x, Richard, s. William, of Kenton, Devon, clerk. BALLIOL COLL., matric. 9 March, 1714-5, aged 18; B.A. 1718. [10]

xford, John Stewart Odiarne (Robertson), 1s. John, of Edinburgh, arm. CHRIST CHURCH, matric. 15 Oct., 1869, aged 18; B.A. 1873, of Higham, Sussex, bar.-at-law, Inner Temple, 1879, assumed the additional name of ROBERTSON. See Foster's *Men at the Bar* & *Eton School Lists.*

xmoore, Charles, s. John, of Broadwoodwidger, gent. EXETER COLL., matric. 7 Feb., 1718-9, aged 18; B.A. 1722.

xmoore, Charles, s. John, of Oakhampton, Devon, gent. BALLIOL COLL., matric. 28 Feb., 1743-4, aged 15; B.A. 1747.

xmoore, Charles Coryndon, o.s. Charles, of Eton, Bucks, cler. PEMBROKE COLL., matric. 10 June, 1858, aged 18; B.A. 1861, M.A. 1865, vicar of Fawley, Berks, 1866-84, and of Lapley, Stafford, since 1884. See *Eton School Lists.*

xmoore, Christopher, s. John, of Oakhampton, Devon, gent. PEMBROKE COLL., matric. 4 Dec., 1771, aged 18; B.A. 1776. [15]

xmoore, Edward, o.s. Thomas Coryndon, of Isle of St. Helena, arm. LINCOLN COLL., matric. 14 April, 1866, aged 18; scholar 1866-70, B.A. 1870, M.A. 1873, a schoolmaster at Ashford, near Staines. See *Eton School Lists.*

xmoore, Henry Elford, 2s. Henry, of Barnstaple, Devon, cler. PEMBROKE COLL., matric. 21 Jan., 1860, aged 18; scholar 1859-65, B.A. 1864, M.A. 1867.

uxmoore, John Stonhouse, 1s. John Reddaway, of Ashford, co. Derby, cler. EXETER COLL., matric. 18 Jan., 1883, aged 19.

Luxmoore, William, 5s. Coryndon, of Bridstow, Devon, cler. EXETER COLL., matric. 1 April, 1819, aged 19.

Luxton, Rev. Ernest William, 5s. Thomas, of Hatherleigh, Devon, gent. LINCOLN COLL., matric. 23 Oct., 1880, aged 21; B.A. 1883. [20]

Luxton, John, s. George, of Witheridge, Devon, gent. ST. MARY HALL, matric. 11 March, 1788, aged 19; B.A. 1791, 43 years perp. curate of Brushford, Devon, died in 1836.

Luxton, Laurence, s. Robert, of Brushford, Devon, gent. EXETER COLL., matric. 31 March, 1775, aged 18; B.A. 1778, preb. of Wells 1811-21, vicar of Holcombe Burnell, Devon, 1819.

Lyall, Charles James (C.I.E.), 1s. Charles, of St. James's, Paddington, Middlesex, arm. BALLIOL COLL., matric. 19 Oct., 1863, aged 18; B.A. 1867, M.A. 1879, of the Indian Civil Service 1865, a student of the Middle Temple 1865, secretary to Government of India in revenue and agricultural department, fellow of University of Calcutta, C.I.E., 1880.

Lyall, John Edwardes, 1s. George, of Bloomsbury, London, arm. BALLIOL COLL., matric. 31 March, 1829, aged 18; bar.-at-law, Inner Temple, 1837, advocate-general Bengal 1842, until his death 9 March, 1845. See *Eton School Lists.*

Lyall, Roger Campbell, 1s. John, of Sydney, Australia, arm. TRINITY COLL., matric. 27 Oct., 1869, aged 18; B.A. 1873, bar.-at-law, Inner Temple, 1877. See Foster's *Men at the Bar.* [25]

Lyall, William Hearle, y.s. George, of St. George's, Bloomsbury, London, arm. CHRIST CHURCH, matric. 15 May, 1845, aged 18; B.A. from ST. MARY HALL 1850, M.A. 1852, rector of St. Dionis Backchurch, London. See *Eton School Lists.*

Lybbe, Philip Lybbe Powys, 1s. Henry Philip Powys, of Broomfield, Middlesex, arm. BALLIOL COLL., matric. 18 March, 1836, aged 18; B.A. 1839, M.A. 1843, of Hardwick, Oxon, J.P., and of Broomfield, Middlesex, bar.-at-law, Inner Temple, 1843, M.P. Newport, Isle of Wight, 1859-65, assumed the additional surname of LYBBE by royal licence 18 Feb., 1863. See Foster's *Peerage*, LILFORD; & *Men at the Bar.*

Lycurgus, Alexander, created D.D. 19 Feb., 1870, archbishop of Syros and Tenos, vice-president of the Sacred Synod of Greece.

Lydal, Benjamin, s. Richard, of Kilncote, co. Leicester, pleb. WADHAM COLL., matric. 17 May, 1757, aged 21.

Lyddell, Charles, s. Dennis, of St. Olave's, London, arm. CHRIST CHURCH, matric. 15 Oct., 1716, aged 17; B.C.L. 1724, rector of Ardingley, Sussex, died 9 Jan., 1757, aged 59. [30]

Lyddon, William. CORPUS CHRISTI COLL., 1775. See LIDDON.

Lyde, Rev. James, s. John, of Berry Pomeroy, Devon, arm. EXETER COLL., matric. 29 March, 1760, aged 18; B.A. 1764, of Brent, near Modbury, Devon, died 1796.

Lyde, John Alan, s. John, of Berry Pomeroy, Devon, arm. TRINITY COLL., matric. 7 Nov., 1783, aged 24.

Lyde, Lionel William, 1s. William, of Wigton, Cumberland, cler. QUEEN'S COLL., matric. 23 Oct., 1882, aged 19; exhibitioner 1882-6, B.A. 1886.

Lyde, William, 'yeoman bedel-in-law;' privilegiatus 31 March, 1842. [35]

Lydiard. See LIDDIARD.

Lydiatt, Fran., s. Rich., of Warwick (town), cler. NEW COLL., matric. 5 July, 1728, aged 19; B.C.L. from MERTON COLL. 1738.

Lydiatt, Richard, s. Richard, of St. Mary's, Warwick (town), cler. NEW COLL., matric. 31 Oct., 1722, aged 16; B.A. 1726, M.A. 1730, proctor 1740 (? died vicar of Kimbolton, Hunts, 17 May, 1761).

Lydiatt, Thomas, s. Richard, of Warwick (town), cler. NEW COLL., matric. 14 Jan., 1729-30, aged 19; B.A. 1733, M.A. 1737.

Lye, Charles Henry Leigh, o.s. Benjamin Leigh, of Walcot, Bath, arm. WADHAM COLL., matric. 9 June, 1847, aged 17; B.A. 1851, M.A. 1854, chaplain Bombay 1857-79, and archdeacon 1864-79, rector of Badger, co. Hereford, 1880.

Lye, Edward Barton, s. George, of Warminster, Wilts, arm. EXETER COLL., matric. 17 Feb., 1813, aged 18; B.A. 1816, M.A. 1822, vicar of Raunds, Northants, 1820, until his death 6 Nov., 1854.

Lye, Fitzhardinge, 1s. John Gaunt, of Turnham Green, Middlesex, gent. QUEEN'S COLL., matric. 22 Oct., 1866, aged 18; a student of the Inner Temple 1867, died March, 1868. See *Eton School Lists.*

Lye (William), Mason, s. Richard, of Croome, co. Worcester, pleb. MAGDALEN HALL, matric. 20 March, 1734-5, aged 20; B.A. 1738. [5]

Lyell, (Sir) Charles (Bart.), s. Charles, of Kinnordy, co. Forfar, Scotland, arm. EXETER COLL., matric. 30 June, 1815, aged 17; B.A. 1819, M.A. 1821, created D.C.L. 20 June, 1855, bar.-at-law, Lincoln's Inn, 1822, professor of geology King's College, London, 1832, knighted 19 Sep., 1848, created a baronet 22 Aug., 1864, Copley medallist Royal Society 1858, president of Geographical Society 1836 & 1850, and of British Association 1864, died 22 Feb., 1875, buried in Westminster Abbey.

Lyford, Charles, y.s. Giles King, of Winchester (city), arm. ORIEL COLL., matric. 21 Feb., 1834, aged 18; B.A. from NEW INN HALL 1844, incumbent of St. Michael's, Shoreditch, died 28 July, 1867.

Lyford, Rev. John, s. John, of Basingstoke, Hants, gent. QUEEN'S COLL., matric. 1 Sep., 1786, aged 17; B.A. 1790, fellow, M.A. 1793, died at Basingstoke 12 June, 1799.

Lygon, Frederick, 2s. Hon. Henry Beauchamp, of St. George's, Hanover Square, London, arm. (after Earl Beauchamp). CHRIST CHURCH, matric. 15 Dec., 1848, aged 18, B.A. 1852; fellow ALL SOUL'S COLL. 1852-66, M.A. 1856, created D.C.L. 22 June, 1870, councillor of Keble College 1871-82; 6th Earl Beauchamp, M.P. Tewkesbury 1867-63, and West Worcestershire 1863-6, a lord of the Admiralty 1859, lord steward of the Household 1874-80, P.C., F.S.A., a student Inner Temple 1860. See Foster's *Peerage* & *Eton School Lists.*

Lygon, Henry Beauchamp, s. William, of Madresfield, co. Worcester, arm. (after Earl Beauchamp). CHRIST CHURCH, matric. 27 Jan., 1803, aged 18; 4th Earl Beauchamp, general in the army, colonel 10th hussars 1843, colonel 2nd regiment of life guards and gold-stick in waiting 1863, M.P. Worcestershire 1816-31, West Worcestershire 1832-53, died 8 Sep., 1863. See Foster's *Peerage* & *Alumni West.*, 457. [10]

Lygon, John (Reginald), s. William, of Madresfield, co. Worcester, arm. CHRIST CHURCH, matric. 29 May, 1802, aged 18; student 1802-12, B.A. 1806, M.A. 1808, took the name of PINDAR in lieu of LYGON by royal licence 22 Oct., 1813, succeeded as 3rd Earl Beauchamp 1823, died 22 Jan., 1853. See Foster's *Peerage* & *Alumni West.*, 457.

Lygon, William, s. Reginald (formerly Pyndar), of Madresfield, co. Worcester, arm. CHRIST CHURCH, matric. 2 May, 1764, aged 16; M.P. co. Worcester 1775, until created Baron Beauchamp 26 Feb., 1806, created Viscount Elmley and Earl Beauchamp 1 Dec., 1815, died 21 Oct., 1816. See Foster's *Peerage.*

Lygon, William Beauchamp, s. William, of Madresfield, co. Worcester, arm. (after Earl Beauchamp). CHRIST CHURCH, matric. 28 Jan., 1801, aged 18; B.A. 1804, M.A. 1808, 2nd Earl Beauchamp, M.P. co. Worcester 1806-16, died 12 May, 1823. See Foster's *Peerage* & *Alumni West.*, 457.

Lyman, Albert Benedict, 1s. Theodore Benedi of Hagerstown, Maryland, America, cler. WA HAM COLL., matric. 8 Dec., 1865, aged 19.

Lyme, Blackman, s. William, of Walton, Surrey, ge LINCOLN COLL., matric. 16 March, 1720-1, ag 18; bar.-at-law, Inner Temple, 17 June, 1727, di 27 Aug., 1752. [1

Lynam, Charles Cotteril, 1s. Charles, of Stoke-up Trent, gent. HERTFORD COLL., matric. 28 Ja 1879, aged 20; scholar 1878-83, B.A. 1883, M. 1886.

Lynam, Henry Byron, s. James, of Mansfield Wo house, Notts, cler. ST. MARY HALL, matric. April, 1791, aged 32; B.A. 1795.

Lynch, Dominick, s. Dominick, of Isle of Barbad arm. UNIVERSITY COLL., matric. 18 Nov., 17 aged 17.

Lynch, Edward Frederick Nicholas, 1s. Willi Nicholas, of London, arm. QUEEN'S COLL., matr 22 Oct., 1878, aged 18; B.A. 1883, bar.-at-la Middle Temple, 1883. See Foster's *Men at Bar.*

Lynch, Edward Melville, o.s. Thomas Toke, London, gent. LINCOLN COLL., matric. 18 O 1871, aged 19; scholar 1871-5, B.A. & M. 1879. [2

Lynch, John, s. John, of Lambeth, Surrey, dean Canterbury). CHRIST CHURCH, matric. 14 Ju 1753, aged 18; B.A. 1757, M.A. 1760, D.C. 1765, rector of All Hallows, Bread Street, 1761, a St. Dionis Backchurch, London, 1782, preb. Canterbury 1781, and archdeacon 1788, until death 1 May, 1803.

Lynch, John Finnis, 1s. Stephen, of —— near Bagd gent. BRASENOSE COLL., matric. 14 Oct., 18 aged 18; a student of Inner Temple, 1884.

Lynch, Mark Wilson, 1s. (John) Wilson, of Renmo co. Galway, arm. CHRIST CHURCH, matric. Jan., 1884, aged 17; B.A. 1887, of Duras, Galway, etc.

Lynch, Robert, s. George, of Ripple, Kent, doct CORPUS CHRISTI COLL., matric. 1 Dec., 1738, ag 16, B.A. 1742, fellow, M.A. 21 Feb., 1745-6, R cliffe travelling fellow UNIVERSITY COLL., B.M 1751, D.Med. 1756, died 2 Oct., 1783.

Linch, Thomas, M.A. from ST. JOHN'S COLL., Ca bridge; incorp. 5 June, 1724 (? JOHN LYN B.A. from ST. JOHN'S COLL. 1717, M.A. 17 D.D. 1728). [2

Lynch, William, s. William, of Newbury, Berks, pl MERTON COLL., matric. 31 Oct., 1732, aged B.A. 1736.

Lyne, Charles, s. Philip, of Trelevan, Cornw doctor. WADHAM COLL., matric. 3 May, 17 aged 19; B.A. 1800.

Lyne, Charles Felix Dixon, 1s. Charles Philip, of E Marden, Sussex, cler. PEMBROKE COLL., mat 16 March, 1837, aged 18; B.A. 1841.

Lyne, Charles Philip, s. Philip, of West Mard Sussex, gent. QUEEN'S COLL., matric. 3 D 1803, aged 17; B.A. 1808, M.A. 1826, vicar of E Marden, Sussex, 1817, and rector of West Thor 1833, until his death 1869.

Lyne, Charles Richard Nunez, 1s. Charles, of Li Petherick, Cornwall, cler. MAGDALEN HA matric. 9 Nov., 1853, aged 19; B.A. 1858, M 1860, curate in charge of St. John and St. Geo Exeter, 1868-70, rector 1870-5. [

Lyne, John, s. Rich., of Liskeard, Cornwall, p UNIVERSITY COLL., matric. 2 May, 1741, aged B.A. 14 Feb., 1744-5.

Lyne, John, s. John, of St. Ives, Cornwall, EXETER COLL., matric. 23 May, 1775, aged B.A. 1779; M.A. from CHRIST CHURCH 1 (his father, the rector of St. Ives, died 1791).

Lyne, Matthew, fellow of EMMANUEL COLL., C bridge (B.A. 1727, M.A. 1731, B.D. 1738); inc 9 July, 1733.

Lyon, John, s. Matthew, of Warrington, Lancashire, arm. QUEEN'S COLL., matric. 19 May, 1743, aged 18.

Lyon, John Daniel, o.s. — L., of Preston, Lancashire, gent. MAGDALEN HALL, matric. 13 May, 1831, aged 20.

Lyon, John Winder, s. Joseph, of St. George's, Bloomsbury Square, London, arm. TRINITY COLL., matric. 26 Oct., 1812, aged 18.

Lyon, Joseph, 1s. Edmund Brock, of Liverpool, arm. TRINITY COLL., matric. 6 Dec., 1853, aged 19; B.A. 1857, M.A. 1863, vicar of Maghull, Lancashire, 1865-9, and of Burton-in-Wirrall 1870-5.

Lyon, Hon. Kenneth Bowes, 6s. Claude, Earl Strathmore. CHRIST CHURCH, matric. 23 Jan., 1886, aged 18. [25]

Lyon, Percy Comyn, 4s. William, of St. Helier's, Jersey, arm. ORIEL COLL., matric. 18 Oct., 1881, aged 19; a student of the Inner Temple, 1881, and of the Indian Civil Service, 1881.

Lyon, Samuel Edmund, 3s. James Radcliffe, of Pulford, Cheshire, cler. WADHAM COLL., matric. 25 June, 1841, aged 19; B.A. 1845, perp. curate Farncombe, Surrey, 1849-59.

Lyon, Thomas Hayes, s. Joseph, of St. George's, Bloomsbury Square, London, arm. NEW COLL., matric. 20 June, 1808, aged 18; fellow 1808-37.

Lyon, Walter Sydney, 2s. Charles John, of Canterbury, gent. LINCOLN COLL., matric. 25 Oct., 1873, aged 18; scholar 1873-7, B.A. 1878, M.A. 1885.

Lyons, Admiral Sir Edmund, Bart., G.C.B. created D.C.L. 4 June, 1856 (son of John Lyons, of Antigua), minister plenipotentiary at Athens, knighted 25 Jan., 1835, vice-admiral of the White, created a baronet 29 July, 1840, and for his services in the Crimea was created Baron Lyons 23 June, 1856, G.C.M.G., G.C.H., died 23 Nov., 1858. See *Foster's Peerage* & *Gent.'s Mag.* [30]

Lyons, John Charles, s. Charles, of Mullingar, Ireland, arm. PEMBROKE COLL., matric. 21 May, 1810, aged 17; of Ledestown, co. Meath, J.P., D.L., high sheriff 1816, died in 1874.

Lyons, John Charles, 1s. John, of London, cler. QUEEN'S COLL., matric. 20 April, 1866, aged 19; held various curacies 1870-82.

Lyons, Joseph, s. Henry, of Isle of Antigua, gent. EXETER COLL., matric. 23 March, 1742-3, aged 17.

Lyons, Richard Bickerton Pemell, 1s. Edmund, of Lymington, Hants, arm. (after a baron). CHRIST CHURCH, matric. 4 June, 1835, aged 18; B.A. 1838, M.A. 1845, created D.C.L. 21 June, 1865, 2nd Baron Lyons, P.C., G.C.B. 1862, G.C.M.G. 1878, ambassador at Paris 1867-87, created Viscount Lyons 17 Nov., 1877, and was offered an earldom in 1887, but died 5 Dec., 1887, before the patent was executed. See Foster's *Peerage*.

Lyons, Samuel, s. John, of Tetworth, Hunts, arm. ST. EDMUND HALL, matric. 19 Oct., 1787, aged 19; B.A. 1791. [35]

Lyons, William, 1s. William, of Launceston, Van Dieman's Land, gent. ST. JOHN'S COLL., matric. 25 June, 1855, aged 18.

Lys, Francis John, 1s. Francis Daniel, of Bere Regis, Dorset, gent. WORCESTER COLL., matric. 19 Oct., 1882, aged 19; scholar 1882-6, B.A. 1886.

Lys, John Thomas, s. James, of Guildford, Surrey, arm. EXETER COLL., matric. 22 June, 1809, aged 17; fellow 1813-71, B.A. 1813, M.A. 1816, B.D. 1826, vicar of Merton, Oxon, 1826-33, and of Waterperry 1833, until he died 4 Oct., 1871. See *Coll. Reg.*, 121.

Lysaght, Edward, B.A. TRINITY COLL., Dublin, s. John, of Bunratty, co. Clare, Ireland, arm. ST. EDMUND HALL, incorp. 19 Oct., 1787, aged 25; M.A. 18 April, 1788, bar.-at-law, Middle Temple, 1788.

Lysaght, Frederick Percy, 3s. John, of Backwell, Somerset, gent. EXETER COLL., matric. 31 Jan., 1882, aged 18. [40]

Lysley, Warine Bayley Marshall, 2s. William John, of St. Pancras, London, arm. CHRIST CHURCH, matric. 12 June, 1851, aged 17; B.A. 1855, M.A. 1858, bar.-at-law, Inner Temple, 1859. See Foster's *Men at the Bar* & *Eton School Lists.*

Lysons, Daniel, s. Daniel, of Hempstead, co. Gloucester, arm. MAGDALEN COLL., matric. 2 March, 1744-5, aged 17; B.A. 1750, M.A. 1751, B.C.L. from ALL SOULS' COLL. 1755, licensed to practice medicine 5 July, 1756, D.C.L. 1759, commuted D.Med. 24 Oct., 1769.

Lysons, Daniel, s. Samuel, of Rodmarton, co. Gloucester cler. ST. MARY HALL, matric. 26 March, 1779, aged 16; B.A. 1782, M.A. 1785, of Hempstead Court, co. Gloucester, F.R.S., F.S.A., rector (and patron) of Rodmarton 1804, author of 'The Environs of London,' and 'Magna Britannia,' died 3 Jan., 1834.

Lysons, Daniel George, 3s. Samuel, of Hempstead Court, co. Gloucester, cler. EXETER COLL., matric. 26 May, 1863, aged 18; B.A. 1867, M.A. 1870, curate in charge of Rodmarton 1872-6, rector since 1877.

Lysons, John, s. Daniel, of Hempstead, co. Gloucester, gent. MAGDALEN HALL, matric. 15 May, 1724, aged 16; demy 1725-32, B.A. 1728, M.A. 1731, fellow 1732-60, D.C.L. 1750, senior dean of arts and bursar, vice-president 1751, died 12 Sep., 1760. See *Bloxam*, vi. 207. [5]

Lysons, Samuel, s. Daniel, of Hempstead, co. Gloucester, arm. ORIEL COLL., matric. 23 March, 1747-8, aged 17; B.A. 1751, M.A. 1755, of Hempstead Court, rector of Rodmarton and Cherrington, co. Gloucester, 1756, until his death 16 March, 1804.

Lysons, Samuel, 1s. Daniel, of Rodmarton, co. Gloucester, arm. EXETER COLL., matric. 24 Nov., 1826, aged 20; B.A. 1830, M.A. 1836, of Hempstead Court, co. Gloucester, F.S.A., rector of Rodmarton 1833-77, hon. canon Gloucester Cathedral 1867, died 27 March, 1877; for list of his works see *Crockford.*

Lyster, John, s. Henry, of Dublin (city), arm. UNIVERSITY COLL., matric. 30 May, 1775, aged 21; created M.A. 3 July, 1778 (? rector of Clonpriest, diocese of Cloyne, 1796, until his death in 1820).

Lyster, Richard, s. Richard, of Covent Garden, London, gent. JESUS COLL., matric. 25 Feb., 1764, aged 18; of Rowton Castle, Salop, died 23 May, 1807.

Lyster, Thomas, s. Thomas, of Westbury, Salop, cler. ORIEL COLL., matric. 3 March, 1737-8, aged 17; an uncle of the last named. [10]

Lyston, John, s. Maurice, of Alphington, Devon, arm. UNIVERSITY COLL., matric. 4 Feb., 1807, aged 19.

Lyte, Henry Churchill Maxwell, o.s. John Walker Maxwell, of London, arm. CHRIST CHURCH, matric. 23 May, 1866, aged 17; B.A. 1870, M.A. 1873, deputy-keeper public records 1886, a student of Lincoln's Inn 1869, F.S.A., author of 'History of Eton College,' 'History of the University of Oxford,' and 'Dunster and its Lords.' See *Eton School Lists.*

Lyte, Henry Francis, scholar TRINITY COLL., Dublin, 1813 (B.A. 1814, M.A. 1830); adm. 'ad eundem' 10 June 1834, perp. curate Lower Brixham, Devon, 1826, until his death at Nice 20 Nov., 1847, author of a metrical version of the Psalms, etc., and of the hymn 'Abide with me,' etc.

Lyte, Henry William Maxwell, 1s. Henry Francis, of St. Hilary Marazion, cler. CHRIST CHURCH, matric. 20 Oct., 1836, aged 18; died 3 June, 1856.

Lyte, John Walker Maxwell, 2s. Henry Francis, of Brixham, Devon, cler. NEW COLL., matric. 30 June, 1843, aged 18; died 28 July, 1848. [15]

Lyte, John Maxwell, 2s. Henry (William Maxwell), of St. Helier's, Isle of Jersey, arm. NON-COLL., matric. 10 April 1869, aged 18; commoner MAGDALEN COLL. 1869, B.A. 1873, M.A. 1875, chaplain to Bishop of Truro, died 28 Jan., 1887.

Lyttelton, Hon. Arthur Temple, M.A. Cantab, 5s George William, Lord Lyttleton. KEBLE COLL. incorp. 19 April, 1879, aged 27, tutor 1879-82, pre centor; B.A. from TRINITY COLL., Cambridge 1874, M.A. 1877, warden of Selwyn College, Cam bridge, 1881.

Lyttelton, Charles, s. Thomas, of Hagley, co. Wor cester, baronet. UNIVERSITY COLL., matric. 1 Oct., 1732, aged 18; B.C.L. & D.C.L. 1745, bar. at-law, Middle Temple, 1738, rector of Alvechurch co. Warwick, 1747, chaplain to the King, bishop o Carlisle 1762, until his death 21 Dec., 1768. Se Foster's *Peerage.*

Lyttelton, George, s. Thomas, of St. James's, West minster, baronet. CHRIST CHURCH, matric. 11 Feb. 1725-6, aged 17; 5th baronet, created Lord Lytteltor 19 Nov., 1737, M.P. Okehampton 1735-66, a lord o the Treasury 1744-54, cofferer to the Househol 1754-5, chancellor of the Exchequer 1755, P.C. 1754 died 25 Aug., 1773.

Lyttelton, George (Fulke), born in Jamaica, s. Williar Henry, Baron (Westcote and Lyttelton). BALLIO COLL., matric. 24 April, 1781, aged 17; 2nd Baro Westcote and Lyttelton, M.P. Bewdley 1790-6 Granard 1798-1800, died 12 Nov., 1828. [20

Lyttelton, George William, 4th Baron, K.C.M.G. created D.C.L. 22 June, 1870 (s. William Henry 3rd lord), B.A. & M.A. from TRINITY COLL. Cambridge, 1838, created LL.D. 1862, unde secretary of State for Colonies 1846, chief commi sioner of Endowed Schools, LL.D., F.R.S., P.C. died 18 April, 1876. See Foster's *Peerage.*

Lyttelton, Thomas, born at Hagley, Worcester, (George, Lord Lyttelton), Baron of Frankley CHRIST CHURCH, matric. 7 Nov., 1761, aged 17 2nd Baron Lyttelton, P.C. 1775, M.P. Bewdley 176 unseated Jan., 1769, died 27 Nov., 1779.

Lyttelton, William Henry, s. Thomas, of Londor baronet. ST. MARY HALL, matric. 22 June, 174 aged 17; created D.C.L. 23 Nov., 1781, 7th barone created Baron Westcote 29 July, 1776, and Baro Lyttelton 13 Aug., 1794, bar.-at-law, Middle Templ 1748, M.P. Bewdley 1748 to Feb., 1755, governor South Carolina 1755-60, of Jamaica 1760-6. envoy King of Portugal 1766-71, died 14 Sep., 1808. S Foster's *Peerage.*

Lyttelton, William Henry, s. William Henry, Barc Lyttelton. CHRIST CHURCH, matric. 24 Oct., 179 aged 16; B.A. 1802, M.A. 1805, student until 181 created D.C.L. 5 July, 1810, 3rd baron, M.P. Wo cestershire 1806-20, and lord-lieutenant, died 30 Apr 1837. See Foster's *Peerage.*

Lyttelton, William Henry Cornewall, 1s. Hon. Spence of Brighton, Sussex, arm. CHRIST CHURCH, matri 12 June, 1867, aged 18; died 22 May, 1881. [2

Lytton, Sir Edward George Earle Lytton Bulwe Bart., of TRINITY HALL, Cambridge (B.A. 182 M.A. 1835, LL.D. 1864), created D.C.L. 9 Jun 1853 (son of General William Earle Bulwer), t celebrated novelist, M.P. St. Ives 1831-2, Linc 1832-41, Herts 1852-66, created a baronet 18 Jul 1838, assumed the name of LYTTON by royal licen 10 Feb., 1844, secretary of State for the Coloni 1858-9, created Baron Lytton 14 July, 1866, lo rector of Glasgow University 1856-8, P.C. 18 G.C.M.G. 1869, died 18 Jan., 1873. See Foste *Baronetage.*

Lytton, John Robinson, s. William Robinson (af Lytton), of Knebworth, Herts, arm. JESUS COL matric. 2 May, 1741, aged 16; created D.C.L. Aug., 1746, of Knebworth, M.P. Bishop's Cas 1747-54, buried 12 April, 1762.

Lyus, Rev. Frederick Ormiston, 2s. George, of Sto market, Suffolk, gent. PEMBROKE COLL., mat 31 May, 1860, aged 19; B.A. 1863, M.A. 18 held various curacies 1870-81.

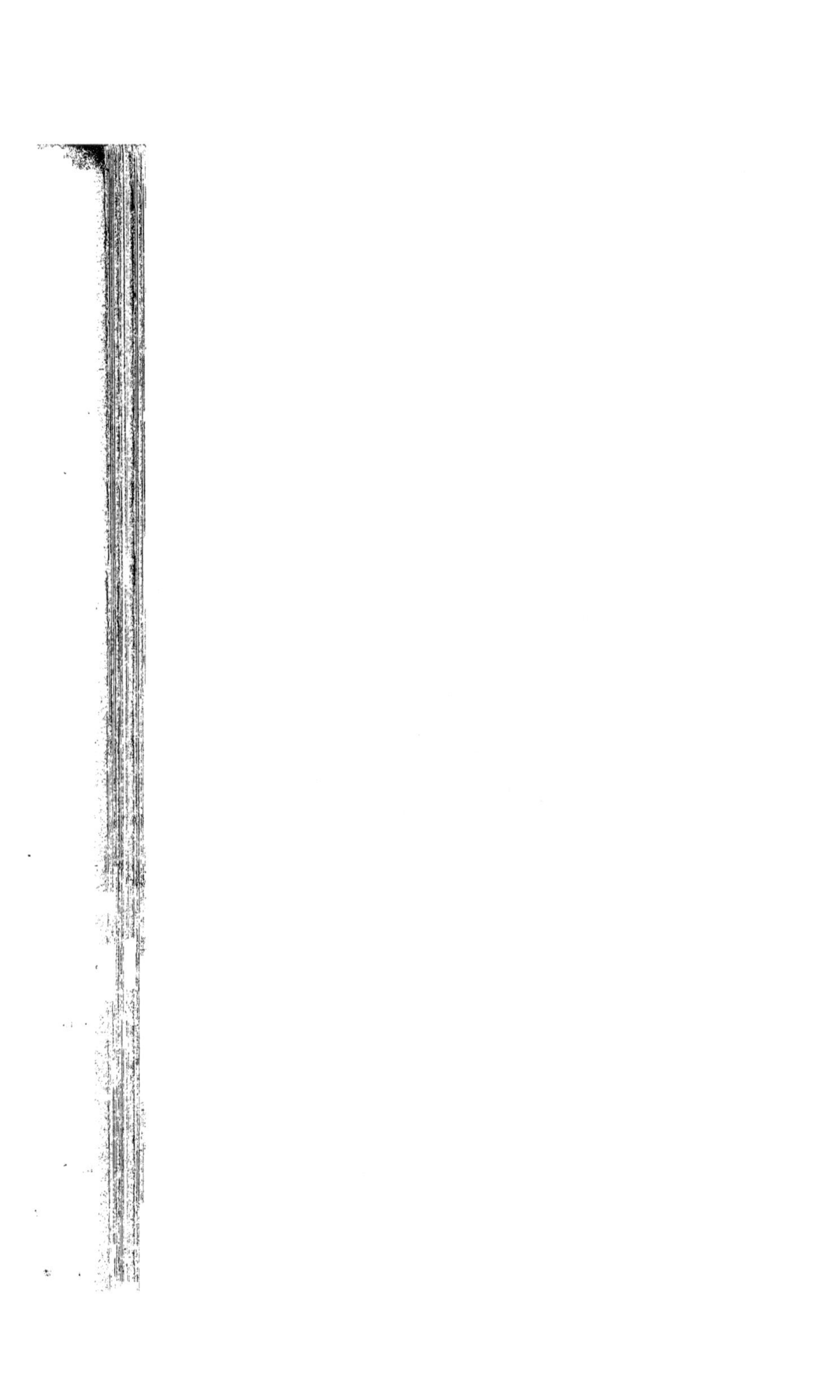

THE STAMFORD BRASENOSE.

Mabbott, Rev. Gilbert, s. Kymton, of Bath (city), Somerset, gent. CHRIST CHURCH, matric. 13 July, 1734, aged 18; B.A. from PEMBROKE COLL. 1738, M.A. 23 Jan., 1740-1, of Cassington, Oxon, father of the next named.

Mabbott, William, s. Gilbert, of Cassington, Oxon, cler. ST. JOHN'S COLL., matric. 18 July, 1766, aged 21.

Mabell, Rev. William, fellow of CHRIST COLL., Cambridge (B.A. 1723, M.A. 1727), incorp. 8 July, 1727, died Aug., 1735.

Maber, William Henry, 3s. John, of Swansea, co. Glamorgan, arm. BRASENOSE COLL., matric. 11 Nov., 1859, aged 19; scholar 1859-62, B.A. 1862, of the Indian Civil Service 1862.

Maberly, Alexander Cahill, 3s. Charles, of Owslebury, Hants, cler. QUEEN'S COLL., matric. 10 Oct., 1861, aged 17; clerk 1863-6, B.A. 1866, M.A. 1868, bar.-at-law, Lincoln's Inn, 1871. See Foster's *Men at the Bar*. [5]

Maberly, John, 2s. John, of Shirley, Surrey, arm. MAGDALEN COLL., matric. 14 Oct., 1826, aged 18; a student of Lincoln's Inn 1827. See *Eton School Lists*.

Maberly, Joseph James, 2s. Joseph, of St. Andrew's, Holborn, London, arm. BRASENOSE COLL., matric. 21 June, 1832, aged 16; B.A. 1836, M.A. 1845, of Hawkley Hurst, Hants, solicitor to Christ's Hospital. See *Eton School Lists*.

Maberly, Samuel Edward, 3s. Joseph, of St. Andrew's, London, arm. CHRIST CHURCH, matric. 20 Oct., 1836, aged 18; B.A. 1840, M.A. 1844, bar.-at-law, Lincoln's Inn, 1844, curate of Mells, Somerset, died 22 May, 1848. See *Eton School Lists*.

Maberly, Thomas Astley, 1s. Joseph, of St. George-the-Martyr, London, arm. CHRIST CHURCH, matric. 11 Oct., 1828, aged 17; B.A. 1832, M.A. 1836, of Mytten, Sussex, vicar of Cuckfield, Sussex, 1841, until his death 19 Nov., 1877. See *Eton School Lists*.

Maberly, Thomas Astley, 1s. Thomas Astley, of Cuckfield, Sussex, cler. CHRIST CHURCH, matric. 17 Oct., 1860, aged 18; B.A. 1865, M.A. 1871, of Mytten, Sussex, sometime captain rifle brigade. [10]

Maberly, William Leader, s. John, of London, arm. BRASENOSE COLL., matric. 6 April, 1815, aged 16; B.A. 1821, lieut.-colonel 76th regiment, secretary post-office, clerk to Ordnance, and a commissioner of Customs, M.P. Westbury 1819-20, Northampton 1820-30, Shaftesbury 1831-2, Chatham 1832-4, died 6 Feb., 1885. See *Eton School Lists*.

Mabson, Arthur, s. Arthur, of Long Island, America, gent. BALLIOL COLL., matric. 26 Feb., 1779, aged 16.

Maby, Charles Lockyer, s. Alexander, of Ilchester, Somerset, gent. BALLIOL COLL., matric. 20 Nov., 1755, aged 19; B.A. 1759 (as Charles).

Macalister, Alexander, o.s. John, of Edinburgh, arm. MERTON COLL., matric. 5 May, 1837, aged 18.

Macalister, John Henry, 1s. Alexander, of Edinburgh, gent. MERTON COLL., matric. 29 Jan., 1862, aged 18. [15]

McAll, Edward, 5s. Robert, of St. Ives, Cornwall, gent. ST. EDMUND HALL, matric. 11 Oct., 1826, aged 20; B.A. 1830, M.A. 1835, rector of Brighstone, Isle of Wight, 1840, until his death 29 Nov., 1866.

McAllister, Rev. William Marcus Coghlan, 1s. John, of Scotby, Cumberland, cler. QUEEN'S COLL., matric. 6 Nov., 1879, aged 18; B.A. 1883.

Macan, Rev. Henry Sneyd Robert, 2s. Turner, of Cheltenham, co. Gloucester, arm. UNIVERSITY COLL., matric. 15 May, 1850, aged 19; B.A. 1854, died 8 Feb., 1862. See *Eton School Lists*.

Macan, Reginald Walter, 3s. John, of Dublin, arm. CHRIST CHURCH, matric. 18 Oct., 1867, aged 19; scholar UNIVERSITY COLL. 1868-72, B.A. 1871, fellow and tutor 1884; student CHRIST CHURCH 1872-81, M.A. 1874, tutor 1875-82, lecturer ancient history, Brasenose College, 1882.

McAnally, David Lancaster, 1s. David, of Leamington, co. Warwick, cler. WORCESTER COLL., matric. 27 April, 1871, aged 18; B.A. 1875, M.A. 1878, chaplain in ordinary Hampton Court Palace 1886. See *Robinson*, 354. [20]

McArthur, James Fowler, 1s. James, of Glasgow, gent. BALLIOL COLL., matric. 17 Oct., 1882, aged 18; scholar 1881-6, B.A. 1886.

McArthur, Rev. John Donald Tilston, 1s. John, of Woolwich, Kent, gent. NON-COLL., matric. 9 April, 1875, aged 17; B.A. from QUEEN'S COLL. 1879.

Macartney, Coote, s. James, of Westminster, arm. UNIVERSITY COLL., matric. 5 May, 1743, aged 18; B.A. 11 Feb., 1746-7, died in Dublin 20 May following.

Macartney, Hugh, s. George, of Belfast, co. Antrim, Ireland, arm. MERTON COLL., matric. 4 June, 1729, aged 16; died in 1731.

Macartney, Mervyn Edmund, 4s. Maxwell, of London, D.Med. LINCOLN COLL., matric. 17 Feb., 1873, aged 19; B.A. 1877. [25]

Macartney, William Grey Ellison, 1s. John William, of Dublin, arm. EXETER COLL., matric. 30 May, 1871, aged 18; B.A. 1875, bar.-at-law, Inner Temple, 1878, M.P. South Antrim Dec., 1885. See Foster's *Men at the Bar* & *Eton School Lists*.

Macaulay, Colin Aulay, 1s. Colin Campbell, of Knighton, co. Leicester, arm. BALLIOL COLL., matric. 31 Jan., 1870, aged 18; died at Turin in May, 1873. See *Rugby School Reg.*

Macaulay, George Robert, o.s. James, of London, D.Med. QUEEN'S COLL., matric. 22 Oct., 1884, aged 19.

Macaulay, Henry William, 4s. Samuel Herrick, of Hodnet, Salop, cler. ORIEL COLL., matric. 17 Oct., 1876, aged 19. See *Eton School Lists.*

Macaulay, John, s. John, of St. Martin's, Middlesex, cler. PEMBROKE COLL., matric. 13 July, 1799, aged 44; B.A. from ST. ALBAN HALL 1801.

Macaulay, Kenneth, of JESUS COLL., Cambridge (B.A. 1835, M.A. 1839), adm. 'ad eundem' 20 June, 1844 (8s. Auley, vicar of Rothley, co. Leicester, deceased), bar.-at-law, Inner Temple, 1839, Q.C. and a bencher 1850, M.P. Cambridge 1852-3 and 1857-65, died 29 July, 1867.

Macaulay, John Jermy, 1s. John Simcoe, of Tarbet, near Limerick, arm. BRASENOSE COLL., matric. 27 Feb., 1845, aged 18; B.A. from NEW INN HALL 1849, M.A. 1851, bar.-at-law, Lincoln's Inn, 1852, died 9 Dec., 1859.

Macaulay, Thomas Babington, created D.C.L. 7 June, 1853 (son of Zachary Macaulay), scholar TRINITY COLL., Cambridge, 1820-4 (Craven scholar 1821), B.A. 1822, fellow 1824-52, M.A. 1825, historian and essayist, bar.-at-law, Lincoln's Inn, 1826, bencher 1850, M.P. Calne Feb., 1830-2, Leeds 1832 to Feb., 1834, Edinburgh June, 1839-46, and 1852 to Jan., 1856, a commissioner of bankrupts 1827, secretary to Board of Control 1832, 4th ordinary member of Council in India 1834, secretary of war 1839, paymaster to the forces 1846, lord rector of Glasgow University 1850, professor of ancient history, Royal Academy 1850, created Baron Macaulay, of Rothley, co. Leicester, 10 Sep., 1857, died 28 Dec., 1859, buried in Poets' Corner, Westminster Abbey. [5]

Macaulay, William, born at Upper Kingston, Canada, s. Robert, gent. QUEEN'S COLL., matric. 21 Jan., 1817, aged 22.

Macbean, Alexander, 2s. William Forbes, of St. Helena, arm. KEBLE COLL., matric. 14 Oct., 1879, aged 19; B.A. 1886.

Macbean, Frederick, 1s. William, of St. Peter Tavy, Devon, cler. MAGDALEN COLL., matric. 27 May, 1851, aged 20.

Macbean, William, s. William, of St. Ann's, Jamaica, West Indies, arm. CHRIST CHURCH, matric. 24 May, 1817, aged 19; B.A. & M.A. 1823, rector of St. Peter Tavy, Devon, 1825, until his death 13 July, 1855.

Macbride, John David, s. John David, of Plympton, Devon, arm. (admiral). EXETER COLL., matric. 28 March, 1795, aged 16; B.A. 1799, fellow 1800-5, M.A. 1802, B.C.L. & D.C.L. 1811, assessor of the Chancellor's Court 1812, lord almoner's professor of Arabic 1813, and principal MAGDALEN HALL 1813, until his death 24 Jan., 1868. [10]

MacCall, Archibald Noel Locke, 3s. George, of Guildford, Surrey, arm. MAGDALEN COLL., matric. 14 Oct., 1871, aged 18; a priest in the Oratory at Brompton. See *Eton School Lists.*

McCalmont, Frederick Haynes, 2s. Thomas, of Highfield, near Southampton, cler. ORIEL COLL., matric. 18 Oct., 1865, aged 19; B.A. 1869, B.C.L. & M.A. 1872, bar.-at-law, Inner Temple, 1872, died 3 Nov., 1880. See *Eton School Lists.*

McCalmont, Hugh, 1s. James, of Dublin, arm. CHRIST CHURCH, matric. 18 May, 1864, aged 19 (? major 7th hussars and brevet colonel). See *Eton School Lists.*

McCalmont, James, 4s. Hugh, of Belfast, Ireland, arm. MAGDALEN COLL., matric. 16 March, 1839, aged 19.

McCalmont, Rev. Thomas, B.A. TRINITY COLL., Dublin, 1829, 2s. Hugh, of Carnmoney, co. Antrim, Ireland, arm. WORCESTER COLL., incorp. 29 Oct., 1829, aged 20; died 16 March, 1872. [15]

McCance, John Stouppe Finlay, o.s. Finlay, of Belfast, arm. BRASENOSE COLL., matric. 22 April, 1884, aged 19; B.A. 1887, of Suffolk, co. Antrim.

McCandlish, Edward John, 1s. John McGregor, of Edinburgh, arm. MERTON COLL., matric. 21 Oct., 1886, aged 19.

McCann, Hugh O'Donoghue, 1s. Hugh O'Donoghue of Belfast, gent. QUEEN'S COLL., matric. 25 Oct. 1880, aged 19; scholar 1880-4, B.A. 1884, M.A. 1887

McCarogher, John Ommanney, o.s. Joseph, o Oving, Sussex, D.Med. MAGDALEN COLL., matric 27 July, 1843, aged 16; demy 1843-58, B.A. 1847 M.A. 1850, curate of Nuthurst, Sussex, 1851-9 rector 1859, preb. of Chichester 1867. See *Coll. Reg.*, vii. 374.

McCarthy, Charles, s. Charles, of Westminster, gent. EXETER COLL., matric. 24 Jan., 1788, aged 19 B.A. 1792. [20]

MacCartie, Charles Falkiner, 1s. Joseph, of Frankfort, Germany, cler. BRASENOSE COLL., matric. 1[9] Oct., 1867, aged 18; scholar 1867-8, of the Indian Civil Service 1868.

MacCartie, Joseph Fitzgerald, 2s. Joseph, of Manchester, cler. HERTFORD COLL., matric. 22 Nov., 1879, aged 18.

MacCartney, Samuel, 5s. Edward, of Dromore, gent. NON-COLL., matric. 10 May, 1879, aged 30.

MacCarty, Justin, s. Daniel, of Carrignavar, co. Cork, Ireland, arm. UNIVERSITY COLL., matric. 21 July, 1769, aged 16; died 1775.

McCaul, Alexander Israel, 3s. Alexander, of St. John's, Bethnal Green, London, D.D. ST. JOHN'S COLL., matric. 27 June, 1853, aged 18; B.A. 1858, M.A. 1860, curate of St. Magnus the Martyr, London, 1859-63, rector since 1863. See *Robinson*, 297. [25]

M'Caul, John, s. John, of Glasgow, Scotland, arm. BALLIOL COLL., matric. 4 May, 1805, aged 18; B.A. 1809, M.A. 1814 (as MACCAUL).

M'Caul, John Gordon, s. John, of Glasgow, Scotland, arm. BALLIOL COLL., matric. 4 May, 1805, aged 17; B.A. 1809, M.A. 1813 (as MAC CAUL).

McCaul, Samuel, 4s. Alexander, of St. Matthew's, Bethnal Green, Middlesex, doctor. ST. JOHN'S COLL., matric. 26 June, 1854, aged 18; B.A. 1860, B.C.L. 1863, M.A. 1864, bar.-at-law, Inner Temple, 1880. See Foster's *Men at the Bar* & *Robinson*, 302.

McCausland, Conolly Thomas, 1s. of Marcus, of Clifton, co. Gloucester, arm. CHRIST CHURCH, matric. 4 June, 1846, aged 18; of Drenagh, co. Londonderry, J.P., D.L., high sheriff 1866, sometime captain Derry militia, and in diplomatic service. See *Eton School Lists.*

McCausland, Frederic Hervey, s. Conolly, of Newton Limavaddy, co. Derry, Ireland, arm. TRINITY COLL., matric. 15 Dec., 1812, aged 18; B.A. 1816, died 1818.

M'Causland, Marcus, s. Conolly, of Ballykelly, Ireland, arm. CHRIST CHURCH, matric. 24 Oct., 1805 aged 18; of Fruit Hill, co. Derry, D.L., died 1[8] Jan., 1862. [31]

M'Causland, Robert Fannin, 1s. William Henry of Parsonstown, King's County, Ireland, cler WADHAM COLL., matric. 16 Oct., 1863, age[d] 19; B.A. 1868, vicar of Hawsker, Yorks, 1880.

McCheane, James Henry, 3s. William, of Liverpool gent. LINCOLN COLL., matric. 2 June, 1852, age[d] 18; scholar 1852-7, B.A. 1856, M.A. 1859, perp. curat[e] Holy Trinity, Leeds, 1862, until his death 1 Oct., 188[1]

McClellan, Rev. Edward James (Parsons), 5s. Jame[s] Creighton, of York (city), gent. QUEEN'S COLL. matric. 18 Oct., 1865, aged 19; B.A. 1869.

McClintock, Sir Francis Leopold; created D.C.L 20 June, 1860 (s. Henry, of Dundalk, co. Louth) the celebrated Arctic navigator, admiral R.N. 188[4] knighted 23 Feb., 1860, for services in search expe[dition] for Sir John Franklin, for which he als[o] received the Royal Geographical Society's go[ld] medal and the freedom of the city of London, nav[al] A.D.C. to the Queen 1868-71, F.R.S., created LL.D Cambridge 1860, and Dublin 1859. See Foster' *Peerage*, B. RATHDONNELL. [35]

McClymont, Colin Ritchie, 2s. Alexander, of Stran[raer], co. Wigton, gent. BALLIOL COLL., matri[c.] 20 Oct., 1868, aged 24; exhibitioner 1868-73, B.A. 1873, bar.-at-law, Inner Temple, 1873. See Foster *Men at the Bar.*

MacColl, Alexander, 1s. John, of Lochaber, Scotland, gent. NON-COLL., matric. 17 Feb., 1873, aged 45.

MacColl, Dugald Sutherland, o.s. Dugald, of Glasgow, cler. LINCOLN COLL., matric. 20 Oct., 1881, aged 22, scholar 1881-5, B.A. 1884; B.A. University of London 1879, M.A. 1881, fellow UNIVERSITY COLL., London.

McColl, John, 2s. John, of Kilmarley, co. Inverness, gent. NON-COLL., matric. 15 Oct., 1870, aged 44, B.A. 1874.

MacConechy, James, 1s. James, of Glasgow, Scotland, gent. BALLIOL COLL., matric. 18 May, 1854, aged 21; B.A. 1858, exhibitioner 1859-64, M.A. 1861, vicar of Christ Church, Watney Street, St. George's-in-the-East, London, 1868-71, and of All Saints', Paddington, 1871, in which year he died.

McConnell, Rev. Edward Alexander, 3s. James, of Wolverton, Bucks, arm. ST. JOHN'S COLL., matric. 13 Oct., 1877, aged 18; B.A. 1882, M.A. 1884. [5]

McConnell, Rev. Charles James, 2s. James Edward, of Wolverton, Bucks, arm. NON-COLL., matric. 26 Jan., 1878, aged 22; a commoner ST. MARY HALL 1879.

McConnell, Ronald Stafford, 4s. James Edward, of Wolverton, Bucks, arm. MERTON COLL., matric. 18 Oct., 1880, aged 20.

McCormack, Charles, s. Charles, of Rathkeal, near Limerick, Ireland, gent. ST. MARY HALL, matric. 18 July, 1783, aged 28; B.C.L. 1794.

McCormick, Samuel, s. Edward, of Edinburgh, Scotland, arm. BALLIOL COLL., matric. 8 July, 1805, aged 18.

McCorquodale, Harold, 4s. George, of Newton le Willows, Lancashire, arm. CHRIST CHURCH, matric. 18 Jan., 1884, aged 18. [10]

McCorquodale, Norman, 3s. George, of Newton le Willows, Lancashire, gent. PEMBROKE COLL., matric. 23 Oct., 1882, aged 18.

McCosky, Samuel Allen, D.D., bishop of Michigan, U.S.; created D.C.L. 23 June, 1852.

McCowan, Walter, o.s. Thomas James Craig, of Walton-on-Thames, Surrey, cler. KEBLE COLL., matric. 19 Oct., 1886, aged 20.

McCowen, Thomas James, 3s. James Thomas, of Cork, Ireland, arm. MAGDALEN HALL, matric. 10 April, 1862, aged 20.

McCrea, Henry Herbert, 3s. Henry Charles, of Halifax, Yorks, arm. BRASENOSE COLL., matric. 22 Nov., 1866, aged 19; B.A. 1870, M.A. 1878, vicar of Painswick, co. Gloucester, 1876-86. [15]

M'Creight, Daniel Chambers, D.Med. TRINITY COLL., Dublin, 1827 (B.A. 1820, B.Med. & M.A. 1823); incorp. MAGDALEN HALL 5 June, 1828.

McCririck, Thomas William, 1s. Thomas, of Bolton, Lancashire, gent. ST. ALBAN HALL, matric. 18 Oct., 1871, aged 27, perp. curate St. John Baptist, Stockton-on-Tees, 1871.

McCulloch, Bargeny, 1s. William, of Camber, co. Fife, cler. NEW COLL., matric. 18 Oct., 1883, aged 19; B.A. 1887.

Macculloch, Thomas, s. Archibald, of Westminster, MAGDALEN HALL, matric. 12 Dec., 1783, aged 20, vicar of Bradfield, Suffolk, 1794, rector of Wormley, Herts, 1798, until his death 11 May, 1832.

MacCunn, John, 3s. John, of Greenock, Scotland, gent. BALLIOL COLL., matric. 16 Oct., 1872, aged 26; Snell exhibitioner 1872-7, B.A. 1876, M.A. 1881; professor of philosophy at University College, Liverpool, 1881. [20]

McDermott, Cornelius William, 1s. Cornelius William, of Portsmouth, arm. CHRIST CHURCH, matric. 27 May, 1882, aged 19; B.A. 1886.

MacDermot, Edward Drane, B.Med. TRINITY COLL., Dublin (B.A. 1836, B.Med. 1845, M.A. & D.Med. 1848); adm. 'ad eundem' 10 July, 1847.

Macdona, Egerton Milne Cumming, o.s. John Cumming, of West Derby, Lancashire, arm. NEW COLL., matric. 15 Oct., 1886, aged 19.

Macdona, Henry Victor, M.A. TRINITY COLL., Dublin, 1863 (B.A. 1860); adm. 'comitatis causa' 1 Dec., 1865, vicar of St. Paul's, Kilburn, 1868-77, and of Cheadle Hulme, Cheshire, 1877.

Macdona, John Cumming, M.A. TRINITY COLL., Dublin, 1865 (B.A. 1858); adm. 'comitatis causa' 1 Dec., 1865, rector of Terrington St. Clement, Norfolk, 1873-5, and of Cheadle, Cheshire, 1874.

Macdona, Rev. Locke, 7s. George, of Dublin, gent. NON-COLL., matric. 20 Jan., 1872, aged 18; B.A. from QUEEN'S COLL. 1876. [25]

McDonald, Alexander, 1s. Alexander, of London, gent. CORPUS CHRISTI COLL., matric. 27 Oct., 1881, aged 19; exhibitioner 1882-5, B.A. 1886, M.A. 1888.

Macdonald, Alexander; created M.A. 24 April, 1883, Mr. Ruskin's master of drawing in the University Galleries 1866, father of the last named.

Macdonald, (Sir) Archibald (Bart.), s. Alexander, of Edinburgh, Scotland, baronet. CHRIST CHURCH, matric. 20 June, 1764, aged 17; B.A. 1768, M.A. 1772, bar.-at-law, Lincoln's Inn, 1770, K.C. 1778, bencher 1778, F.R.S. 1788, M.P. Hindon, Wilts, 1777-80, Newcastle-under-Lyme 1780-93, one of the judges of Wales 1780, solicitor-general 1784-8, serjt.-at-law 1793, attorney-general 1780-93, knighted 27 June, 1788, lord chief baron of the Exchequer 1793-1813, P.C. 1793, created a baronet 27 Nov., 1813, died 18 May, 1826, father of Sir James, 1801. See Foster's *Baronetage* & *Alumni West.*, 380.

Macdonald, Hon. Archibald, s. Alexander, of Edinburgh, Scotland, baron. ORIEL COLL., matric. 14 Dec., 1793, aged 16; B.A. 1796, M.A. 1815, died 5 Feb., 1861, father of the next named, and of James William 1828. See Foster's *Peerage*.

Macdonald, Archibald, 1s. Archibald, of Edinburgh, Scotland, arm. ORIEL COLL., matric. 8 June, 1821, aged 17; B.A. 1825, of Islay, died 3 May, 1873. See Foster's *Peerage* & *Eton School Lists.* [30]

Macdonald, Archibald Simon Lang, 3s. Simon, of Glasgow, arm. ST. MARY HALL, matric. 18 June, 1867, aged 27; exhibitioner MERTON COLL., 1868, B.A. 1873, fellow 1873-85, M.A. 1876, Millard lecturer in physics Trinity College 1873-6, died 13 Oct., 1885.

Macdonald, Charles John, 1s. Lachlan, of East Indies, gent. ST. JOHN'S COLL., matric. 16 Oct., 1886, aged 20.

Macdonald, Charles Reginald Yeatman, 1s. Charles Frederick Baxter, of London, gent. QUEEN'S COLL., matric. 21 Nov., 1873, aged 17.

Macdonald, David Macdonald Robertson, o.s. David Robertson, of Hastings, Sussex, arm. ST. JOHN'S COLL., matric. 16 Oct., 1875, aged 18; B.A. 1879, M.A. 1882, assumed the additional surname of MACDONALD, bar.-at-law, Inner Temple, 1881. See Foster's *Men at the Bar*. [35]

Macdonald, Rev. Frederick Charles, 4s. Thomas Moss, of Nottingham, cler. NON-COLL., matric. 18 Oct., 1880, aged 20; B.A. from ORIEL COLL. 1883, M.A. 1887. See *Robinson*, 380.

Macdonald, Frederick William, 1s. William, of Salisbury, Wilts, cler. QUEEN'S COLL., matric. 18 Oct., 1865, aged 17; B.A. (NON-COLL.) 1872; M.A. from QUEEN'S COLL. 1876, vicar of Stapleford 1877, and of Berwick St. James, 1880.

Macdonald, George, 3s. James, of Elgin, co. Moray, D.D. BALLIOL COLL., matric. 6 May, 1884, aged 22; B.A. 1887.

Macdonald, Godfrey (Bosvile), s. Alexander, of St. Cuthbert's, Edinburgh, baron. ORIEL COLL., matric. 17 Dec., 1792, aged 17; 3rd Baron Macdonald, a general in the army, died 13 Oct., 1832. See Foster's *Peerage*.

Macdonald, Grant William, 6s. William Pitt, of Trichinopoly, East Indies, arm. ST. MARY HALL, matric. 1 Nov., 1865, aged 19; B.A. 1872, vicar of St. Mark's, Holbeach, co. Lincoln, since 1879. [40]

Macdonald, Rev. Henry Francis, 1s. Thomas Moss, of Bromley, Kent, cler. MAGDALEN HALL, matric. 4 June, 1870, aged 19, scholar 1870, B.A. (HERTFORD COLL.) 1874, M.A. 1877, died 11 June, 1878.

Macdonald, Henry James, 1s. George Browne, of Manchester, gent. CORPUS CHRISTI COLL., matric. 11 March, 1854, aged 18; scholar 1854-8, of the Indian Civil Service 1858.

Macdonald, Jacob, 1s. Nicholas, of Wellow, Somerset, gent. ST. ALBAN HALL, matric. 1 Feb., 1820, aged 20; LL.B. from CAIUS COLL., Cambridge, 1829, vicar of Blewbury, etc., Berks, 1836, until his death 4 June, 1871, father of James William, 1842, and of Philip J. L., 1850.

Macdonald, (Sir) James (Bart.), s. Alexander, of Edinburgh, baronet. CHRIST CHURCH, matric. 9 May, 1759, aged 17; 8th baronet, died at Rome 26 July, 1766. See Foster's *Peerage*.

Macdonald, (Sir) James (Bart.), s. Archibald, of St. Martin's, London, equitis (after baronet). CHRIST CHURCH, matric. 15 May, 1801, aged 17; B.A. 1805, 2nd baronet, a student of Lincoln's Inn 1804, a clerk of the privy seal, M.P. Kirkwall burghs (June) 1805-6, Newcastle-under-Lyme 1806-12, Sutherlandshire 1812-16, Calne 1816-31, Hampshire 1831-2, a commissioner for Indian affairs 1827-8 & 1830-2, appointed lord high commissioner of the Ionian Islands 2 June, 1832, but died 29th of the same month. See Foster's *Scots M.P.'s* & *Alumni West.*, 455.

Macdonald, James, s. Thomas, of Edinburgh (city), arm. ST. MARY HALL, matric. 26 June, 1810, aged 26.

Macdonald, James Leonard, M.A. TRINITY COLL., Dublin, 1866 (B.A. 1860); adm. 'comitatis causa' 27 Feb., 1868. **[5]**

Macdonald, James William, 3s. Hon. Archibald, of Paddington, Middlesex, arm. CHRIST CHURCH, matric. 4 Dec., 1828, aged 17; B.A. 1832, bar.-at-law, Inner Temple, 1839. See Foster's *Peerage*.

Macdonald, Rev. James William, 1s. Jacob, of Garston, Wilts, cler. PEMBROKE COLL., matric. 10 Nov., 1842, aged 16; scholar 1842-52, B.A. 1847, M.A. 1849, brother of Philip J. L.

McDonald, John, 1s. John, of Glasgow, gent. ST. JOHN'S COLL., matric. 9 June, 1871, aged 20; B.A. 1876, M.A. 1878, bar.-at-law, Inner Temple, 1879. See Foster's *Men at the Bar*.

Macdonald, (Sir) John Alexander, created D.C.L. 21 June, 1865; LL.D. QUEEN'S UNIVERSITY, Canada, Canadian barrister 1836, Q.C., represented Kingston in Canadian Parliament 1844 (son of Hugh M., of Kingston, Canada), 'executive councillor in Canada,' attorney-general in Upper Canada 1854-62 & 1864-7, and for Canada 1867-73, prime minister 1867-73 & 1878, K.C.B. 1867, G.C.B. 21 Nov., 1884, and P.C. See Foster's *Baronetage*.

Macdonald, Kenneth Lachlan, 2s. Lachlan, of East Indies, gent. ST. JOHN'S COLL., matric. 16 Oct., 1886, aged 18. **[10]**

Macdonald, Norman Hilton, o.s. John, of St. George's, Bloomsbury, London, arm. ORIEL COLL., matric. 28 June, 1823, aged 16, B.A. 1827; fellow ALL SOULS' COLL. 1828-57, B.C.L. 1835, D.C.L. 1841, a student of Lincoln's Inn 1827.

Macdonald, Patrick Ogilvy, 2s. Patrick Arkley, of Montrose, co. Forfar, gent. LINCOLN COLL., matric. 17 Oct., 1884, aged 22; scholar 1884.

Macdonald, Philip James Lansdown, 2s. Jacob, of Garston, Wilts, cler. ST. JOHN'S COLL., matric. 8 May, 1850, aged 18, brother of James W. 1842.

Macdonald, Robert Estcourt, 2s. William, of Bishops Canning, Wilts, cler. NEW COLL., matric. 10 Oct., 1873, aged 19; B.A. from ST. ALBAN HALL 1882; M.A. from NEW COLL. 1887, a student of the Middle Temple 1874. **[15]**

Macdonald, Ronald, 2s. George, of London, LL.D. (the novelist). TRINITY COLL., matric. 14 Oct., 1882, aged 21; B.A. 1885.

Macdonald, Thomas Mosse, 2s. Thomas Mosse, of Nottingham, cler. BRASENOSE COLL., matric. 19 Oct., 1875, aged 19; scholar 1875-8, B.A. 1879.

McDonald, Rev. Walter Percy, 3s. James, of London, arm. ORIEL COLL., matric. 17 Oct., 1876, aged 19; B.A. 1879 M.A. 1886.

Macdonald, William, s. William, of St. Martin's, Perth, Scotland, arm. CHRIST CHURCH, matric. 11 May, 1798, aged 18.

Macdonald, William, s. John, of Carraden, Linlithgow, Scotland, arm. BALLIOL COLL., matric. 23 April, 1801, aged 17; B.A. 1805, M.A. 1807, vicar of Broad Hinton, Cricklade, Wilts, 1809, of Chitterne 1812, canon of Salisbury 1823, archdeacon of Wilts 1828, vicar of Bishops Canning, Wilts, 1815, until he died 24 June, 1862. **[20]**

Macdonald, William Henry, 1s. William, of Buckingham, gent. ST. EDMUND HALL, matric. 9 June, 1855, aged 19; B.A. from ST. MARY HALL 1860; M.A. from ST. EDMUND HALL 1862.

Macdonald, William Maurice, 2s. William, of Broad Hinton, Wilts, archdeacon (of Wilts). NEW COLL., matric. 2 July, 1833, aged 19; fellow 1833-9, rector of Calstone Willington, Wilts, 1841, until his death 17 April, 1880.

Macdonell, Alexander, 4s. James, of Inverness, arm. MERTON COLL., matric. 26 Oct., 1874, aged 22; postmaster 1874-9, B.A. 1878, Millard lecturer in physics Trinity College 1878-9.

Macdonell, Alexander (Ranaldson), s. Duncan, of Glengarry, Scotland, arm. UNIVERSITY COLL., matric. 12 Oct., 1790, aged 17; of Glengarry, died Jan., 1828.

McDonell, Angus, 3s. Æneas Ronald, of Lower Broughton, Lancashire, arm. UNIVERSITY COLL., matric. 17 Oct., 1885, aged 18. **[25]**

Macdonell, Arthur Anthony, 1s. Alexander Anthony, of Poonah, East Indies, arm. CORPUS CHRISTI COLL., matric. 17 Oct., 1876, aged 21; exhibitioner 1876-80, B.A. 1880, M.A. 1883, Taylorian teacher of German 1880, deputy professor of Sanskrit 1888.

Macdonell, William Robert, 1s. John, of Dufftown, co. Banff, gent. BALLIOL COLL., matric. 30 Jan., 1874, aged 21; scholar 1874-7.

MacDonell, John, s. Charles, of Ennis, co. Clare, Ireland, arm. MAGDALEN COLL., matric. 14 May, 1807, aged 18; of New Hall and Kilkee, co. Clare, high sheriff 1821, served in Spain in the Peninsular war, died 28 June, 1850. See *Eton School Lists*.

Macdonell, Lewis, s. Duncan, of Glengarry, Scotland, arm. UNIVERSITY COLL., matric. 12 Oct., 1790, aged 16; a captain in the army, died unmarried.

McDonnell, (Sir) Alexander, s. James, of Belfast, Ireland, doctor. CHRIST CHURCH, matric. 1 June, 1813, aged 18; student 1813-26, B.A. 1816, M.A. 1820, bar.-at-law, Lincoln's Inn, 1824, chief clerk charity commission, Ireland, privy councillor Ireland 1846, and a resident commissioner of education, died 21 Jan., 1875. See *Alumni West.*, 476.

Macdonnell, Randal William, Viscount Dunluce, o.s. Alexander, Earl of Antrim. CHRIST CHURCH, matric. 24 Oct., 1768, aged 18; created M.A. 1 June, 1769, 6th Earl of Antrim, K.B. 1779, created Marquis of Antrim 18 Aug., 1789, died 29 July, 1791. See Foster's *Peerage*. **[31]**

McDonnell, Hon. Schomberg Kerr, 5s. Mark Kerr, Earl of Antrim. UNIVERSITY COLL., matric. 13 Oct., 1879, aged 18. See Foster's *Peerage* & *Eton School Lists*.

Macdonnell, William Randall, Viscount Dunluce, 1s. Mark, Earl of Antrim. CHRIST CHURCH, matric. 19 May, 1869, aged 18; 6th Earl of Antrim of the last creation. See Foster's *Peerage*.

Macdonnogh, Felix, s. Felix, of Marylebone, Middlesex, arm. ORIEL COLL., matric. 3 July, 1784, aged 16; a student of Lincoln's Inn 1787.

Macdonough, Albert Irwin, scholar TRINITY COLL., Dublin, 1857 (B.A. 1858, LL.B. 1859, M.A. 1861, LL.D. 1863), adm. 'comitatis causa' 6 July, 1861. **[35]**

McDouall, Patrick George, 3s. William, of Ashby-de-la-Zouch, co. Leicester, cler. CHRIST CHURCH, matric. 26 May, 1841, aged 18; B.A. 1845, M.A. 1847, curate of Puttenham, Herts, 1846-9, of Uffington, co. Lincoln, 1849-56, vicar of Kirk Newton, Northumberland, 1856-77, rector of Cosgrove 1877. See Foster's *Peerage*, M. BUTE.

McDouall, William, s. John, of Glasgow, Scotland, arm. BALLIOL COLL., matric. 19 May, 1791, aged 16; B.A. 1795, M.A. 1798, vicar of Luton, Beds, 1827, and canon of Peterborough 1831, until his death 15 Dec., 1849, father of the last and next named.

McDouall, William Sutherland, 2s. William, of Ashby-de-la-Zouch, cler. CHRIST CHURCH, matric. 15 May, 1839, aged 18; B.A. 1843, M.A. 1845, rector of Ousden, Suffolk, 1854. See Foster's *Peerage*, M. BUTE.

McDougall, Rev. Archibald Blair, o.s. Robert Archibald, of Portsmouth, gent. LINCOLN COLL., matric. 18 Oct., 1879, aged 19; scholar 1879-83, B.A. 1883, M.A. 1886.

McDougall, Francis Thomas, o.s. William Adair, of Sydenham, Kent, gent. MAGDALEN HALL, matric. 28 Feb., 1839, aged 21; B.A. 1844, M.A. 1845, created D.C.L. 28 June, 1854, F.R.C.S., bishop of Labuan 1854-68, vicar of Godmanchester, Hunts, 1868-74, archdeacon of Huntingdon 1870-4, canon of Ely 1871-3, vicar of Milford, Hants, 1881-5, canon of Winchester 1873, archdeacon of the Isle of Wight 1874, rector of Mottistone with Shorewell, Isle of Wight, 1885, until his death 16 Nov., 1886. **[5]**

Macdougall, Henry, 7s. Alexander, of Abbots Langley, Herts, arm. BRASENOSE COLL., matric. 21 Jan., 1841, aged 21; B.A. 1845, M.A. 1847, chaplain to the forces 1847 (retired list 1861), rector of St. Michael, etc., Stamford, 1874.

Macdougall, James, 5s. Alexander, of Abbots Langley, Herts, arm. BRASENOSE COLL., matric. 2 July, 1830, aged 17; B.A. 1834, M.A. 1841, vicar of West and East Hanney, Berks, 1849.

McDougall, Samuel, 1s. William, of St. Giles, London, pleb. MERTON COLL., matric. 18 Feb., 1829, aged 24.

McDougall, Rev. Thomas Hugh, 2s. John, of Dundee, cler. ST. JOHN'S COLL., matric. 14 Oct., 1871, aged 20; B.A. 1876, M.A. 1878, a student of the Inner Temple 1874.

McDougall, Walter Kennedy, o.s. John, of Bath, gent. ORIEL COLL., matric. 14 Oct., 1878, aged 20; B.A. 1882, M.A. 1885. **[10]**

McDowall, Rev. Charles, o.s. Robert, of Sheffield, Yorks, arm. UNIVERSITY COLL., matric. 30 May, 1855, aged 18; scholar 1856-62, B.A. 1859, M.A. 1865, B. & D.D. 1882, head-master Cholmeley Grammar School, Highgate, since 1874, preb. of St. Paul's 1883.

McDowall, Robert Scott, 2s. Walter, of St. Bride's, London, gent. LINCOLN COLL., matric. 15 March, 1849, aged 18; B.A. 1852, M.A. 1861, held various curacies 1863-76, rector of North Poorton, Dorset, 1876-84, vicar of Yetminster 1884. See *St. Paul's School Reg.*, 303.

McDowall, William, 1s. Henry, of Johnstown, Renfrew, Scotland, arm. UNIVERSITY COLL., matric. 18 April, 1863, aged 19; probably died young.

McDowell, Rev. Frederick, 1s. Frederick, of Coventry, gent. NON-COLL., matric. 31 May, 1879, aged 37; B.A. from ST. ALBAN HALL 1882, M.A. from MERTON COLL. 1886.

Macduff, Alexander, 1s. Alexander, of Scone, Perth, arm. EXETER COLL., matric. 12 March, 1869, aged 19; of Bonhard, co. Perth, J.P. **[15]**

MacEvay, John, s. John, of Dublin (city), gent. MAGDALEN HALL, matric. 1 May, 1778, aged 24.

McEvoy, John Augustus Nisbit, s. John Augustus, of Warrington, Lancashire, cler. WORCESTER COLL., matric. 25 May, 1811, aged 30.

McEwen, Alexander Robertson, o.s. Alexander, of Edinburgh, D.D. BALLIOL COLL., matric. 17 Oct., 1870, aged 19; exhibitioner 1870-5, B.A. 1874, M.A. 1877.

Macfadyen, Dugald, 2s. John Allison, of Whalley Range, Lancashire, D.D. MERTON COLL., matric. 21 Oct., 1886, aged 18; exhibitioner 1886.

Macfadyen, William Allison, 1s. John Allison, of Manchester, D.D. BRASENOSE COLL., matric. 22 Oct., 1883, aged 18; scholar 1883, B.A. 1888. **[20]**

Macfarlane, Duncan Alwyn, 1s. James Duncan, of Staveley, co. Derby, cler. MAGDALEN COLL., matric. 22 April, 1876, aged 18; B.A. from ST. ALBAN HALL 1879.

Macfarlane, Rev. Edward Mactier, 3s. James, of Feltham, Middlesex, arm. LINCOLN COLL., matric. 22 Feb., 1838, aged 20; B.A. 1841, M.A. 1846, died 3 Nov., 1874.

Macfarlane, George Lewis, 4s. Robert, Lord Ormidale (of Session), of Edinburgh. ST. JOHN'S COLL., matric. 12 Oct., 1872, aged 18; B.A. 1876, a student of the Middle Temple 1873.

Macfarlane, James Duncan, 1s. James, of Feltham Hill, Middlesex, arm. ST. EDMUND HALL, matric. 23 Oct., 1834, aged 18; B.A. 1838, M.A. 1846, rector of Staveley, co. Derby, 1847, until his death 2 July, 1886.

Macfarlane, Robert, s. Andrew, of Inverness, Scotland, cler. BALLIOL COLL., matric. 27 Oct., 1807, aged 18; B.A. 1811, M.A. 1814. **[25]**

Macfarlane, William Alexander Comyn, o.s. William, of Edinburgh, D.Med. BALLIOL COLL., matric. 26 Jan., 1863, aged 20; scholar ST. JOHN'S COLL. 1864-8, B.A. 1866, M.A. 1869, vicar of Criftins, Salop, 1870-8, rector of Elmswell, Suffolk, 1878.

Macfarlane, William Charles, 2s. James, of Feltham, Middlesex, arm. MAGDALEN HALL, matric. 10 Feb., 1848, aged 30; B.A. 1852, M.A. 1855, vicar of Dorchester, Oxon, 1856, until his death 15 Nov., 1885.

Macfarren, (Sir) George Alexander; created D.Mus. 19 June, 1879 (s. George Macfarren, of London), professor of Music, and created D.Mus. Cambridge University 1875, M.A. from TRINITY COLL. 1878, knighted 22 May, 1883, principal of the Royal Academy of Music 1875, until his death 31 Oct., 1887.

MacGachen, John Drummond, 2s. John, of Cheltenham, co. Gloucester, arm. PEMBROKE COLL., matric. 17 Dec., 1844, aged 19; B.A. 1848, M.A. 1855, vicar of St. Bartholomew, Bethnal Green, London, 1860, until his death 10 April, 1886.

MacGachen, Nicholas Howard, 1s. John, of Edinburgh, arm. PEMBROKE COLL., matric. 14 Dec., 1844, aged 21; B.A. 1848, vicar of St. Mark, North End, Portsmouth, 1868-9, rector of St. George-the-Martyr, etc., Canterbury, 1869-81, vicar of Littleborne, Kent, since 1881. **[30]**

McGeachy, Forster Alleyne, o.s. Alexander, of Clifton, co. Gloucester, arm. BALLIOL COLL., matric. 22 March, 1828, aged 18; B.A. 1832, M.A. 1837, of Shenley Hill, Herts, J.P., D.L., high sheriff 1865, a student of Lincoln's Inn 1834, M.P. Honiton 1841-7, died 20 March, 1887.

McGhie, John Powlett, 4s. Robert, of Bishopshull, Somerset, arm. QUEEN'S COLL., matric. 17 April, 1823, aged 18; B.A. 1827, M.A. 1830, vicar of Portsmouth 1839, until his death 13 Jan., 1868.

McGilchrist, John, 1s. John, of Kilarron, co. Argyll, cler. BALLIOL COLL., matric. 19 Oct., 1886, aged 20; exhibitioner 1886.

McGilchrist, William, s. James, of Inchianan, Scotland, gent. BALLIOL COLL., matric. 17 Dec., 1728, aged 17; B.A. 1732, M.A. 1735.

McGildowny, John, o.s. Charles of Ballycastle, co. Antrim, arm. TRINITY COLL., matric. 14 March, 1839, aged 19; of Clare Park, co. Antrim, high sheriff 1843. **[35]**

McGill, George Henry, 2s. Robert, of Manchester, Lancashire, gent. BRASENOSE COLL., matric. 18 May, 1837, aged 19; scholar 1837-42, B.A. 1841, M.A. 1844, vicar of Stoke Ferry 1846-54, perp. curate Christ Church, St. George-in-the-East, 1854-67, rector of Bangor 1867. See *Manchester School Reg.*, iii. 220.

McGill, William Edward, 1s. William, of Camberwell, Surrey, arm. PEMBROKE COLL., matric. 6 May, 1859, aged 19; bible clerk, B.A. 1863, M.A. 1865.

M'Gowan, Edward, s. John, of Calcutta, East Indies, arm. UNIVERSITY COLL., matric. 14 Oct., 1811, aged 18.

McGrath, Henry Walter, o.s. Henry Walter, of Pendletou, near Manchester, cler. WADHAM COLL., matric. 18 Oct., 1862, aged 19; B.A. 1867, M.A. 1870, has held various curacies since 1868.

McGregor, Alexander, 3s. Walter Fergus, of Liverpool, arm. CORPUS CHRISTI COLL., matric. 18 Oct., 1871, aged 18; B.A. & M.A. 1880, a civil engineer. See *Rugby School Reg.* [5]

McGregor, Alexander John, 1s. Andrew, of Robertson, Cape of Good Hope, cler. ORIEL COLL., matric. 26 Jan., 1884, aged 19; exhibitioner 1885, B.A. 1887, a student of the Inner Temple 1884.

Macgregor, Peter, 2s. John, of Glasgow, gent. ST. EDMUND HALL, matric. 22 Oct., 1874, aged 17; B.A. 1879, M.A. 1881, B.C.L. 1883, bar.-at-law, Middle Temple, 1882 See Foster's *Men at the Bar.*

Macgregor, Peter Balderston, 1s. Alexander Balderston, of Helidon, Australia, gent. NON-COLL., matric. 2 June, 1884, aged 18; B.A. from BALLIOL COLL. 1888.

MacGregor, Robert Henry, 2s. Robert Brown, of Rochdale, Lancashire, arm. BRASENOSE COLL., matric. 17 June, 1839, aged 19.

MacGregor, William, 2s. Walter Fergus, of Liverpool, gent. EXETER COLL., matric. 30 Nov., 1867, aged 19; B.A. 1871, M.A. 1874, a student of the Inner Temple 1870, curate of St. Matthias, Liverpool, 1876-7, vicar 1877-8, vicar of Tamworth, etc., since 1878 (curate of Hopwas 1872-6). See *Rugby School Reg.* [10]

McGrigor, James Roderick Duff, 1s. Charles Roderick, of London, baronet. CHRIST CHURCH, matric. 20 May, 1875, aged 18. See Foster's *Baronetage* & *Eton School Lists.*

McGrotty, John, B.A. TRINITY COLL., Dublin, 1860, 4s. William, of Raphoe, Ireland, gent. Incorp. from MAGDALEN HALL 5 Nov., 1873, aged 44.

McGuiness, John Francis, 1s. John, of Aldershot, Hants, gent. NON-COLL., matric. 12 Oct., 1878, aged 15.

McGuire, William Walter, o.s. Samuel Edward, of Dublin, arm. BRASENOSE COLL., matric. 23 May, 1872, aged 19.

McGwire, William John, s. William, of Hillsborough, co. Down, Ireland, arm. CHRIST CHURCH, matric. 28 Jan., 1813, aged 17; of Carrigbawn, co. Down. See *Eton School Lists.* [15]

Macham, William, s. Joseph, of London, gent. ST. JOHN'S COLL., matric. 30 June, 1741, aged 18; B.C.L. 1749, D.C.L. 1754, an advocate in Doctors' Commons. See *Robinson*, 79.

Machell, James, 2s. James, of Ulverston, Cumberland, arm. BRASENOSE COLL., matric. 2 May, 1821, aged 18; B.A. 1827, M.A. 1829, incumbent of St. Mary's Egton, Lancashire, died at the Hall, Pennybridge, 15 May, 1864. See *Rugby School Reg.*, 125.

Machell, John Penny, 1s. James, of Colton, Lancashire, arm. CHRIST CHURCH, matric. 24 May, 1820, aged 18; of Pennybridge, Lancashire, died 19 Oct., 1884. See *Rugby School Reg.*, 125.

Machell, Richard, s. Lancelot, of Crackenthorpe, Westmoreland, gent. QUEEN'S COLL., matric. 17 Dec., 1731, aged 18; B.A. 1735, M.A. 1738, rector of Uldale 1752-70, of Asby and Brougham 1770, until his death 24 Feb., 1785.

Machell, Walter Leonard, o.s. Robert Scott, of Auckland, arm. EXETER COLL., matric. 23 Oct., 1885, aged 19. [20]

Machen, Edward, 1s. Edward, of Coleford, co. Gloucester, arm. EXETER COLL., matric. 3 March, 1836, aged 18; B.A. 1840, of Bicknor Court, and of Eastbach Court, co. Hereford, a student of the Inner Temple, 1840, rector of Micheldean, co. Gloucester, 1847-57, of Staunton 1857-74, and of Frome Bishop, co. Hereford, 1879-81. See *Rugby School Reg.*, 161.

Machen, John Edward Jones, 1s. Daniel Jones, of Cardiff, co. Glamorgan, cler. JESUS COLL., matric. 10 May, 1850, aged 18; B.A. 1854, M.A. 1857, took the additional name of MACHEN, curate of Alfreton, co. Derby, 1856-7, and of Llandegveth, co. Monmouth, 1864-74, rector of Llanthewy-Vach, co. Monmouth, 1858, until his death in 1887.

MacHutchin, Arthur, 1s. Mark Wicks, of Talke, co. Stafford, cler. CHARSLEY HALL, matric. 13 Oct., 1881, aged 18.

Macie, James Lewis, of London, arm. PEMBROKE COLL., matric. 7 May, 1782, aged 17; created M.A. 26 May, 1786. See SMITHSON.

Macie, John, s. David, of Weston, Somerset, arm. QUEEN'S COLL., matric. 27 Oct., 1736, aged 16; created D.C.L. 8 July, 1756, then of Weston, his widow died in 1800. [25]

McIlvaine, Charles Petit; created D.C.L. 9 June, 1853 (son of Joseph McIlvaine, of Burlington, New Jersey), minister Christ Church, Georgetown, D.C., 1820-5, chaplain to the (U.S.) Senate 1822-6, chaplain and professor of ethics U.S. Metropolitan Academy, minister at West Point 1825 to Dec., 1827, and of St. Anne's, Brooklyn, Jan., 1828-31, bishop of Ohio, 1831, until his death at Florence, 12 March, 1873.

MacInnes, Miles, 1s. John, of London, arm. BALLIOL COLL., matric. 22 March, 1849, aged 19; B.A. 1852, M.A. 1856, of Rickerby, Cumberland, J.P., D.L., M.P. Northumberland, Hexham division, Dec., 1885. See *Rugby School Reg.*, 245.

McIntire, Ninian Edward, 1s. Travis, of Barton Leonard, Yorks, cler. QUEEN'S COLL., matric. 25 Oct., 1880, aged 18; exhibitioner 1880-4, B.A. 1884, M.A. 1887.

McIntosh, Henry James, 2s. George, of Edinburgh, arm. CHRIST CHURCH, matric. 10 Oct., 1884, aged 19; of the Indian Civil Service 1884.

Macintosh, William Henry, 1s. William, of London, gent. WORCESTER COLL., matric. 19 Oct., 1875, aged 19; B.A. from QUEEN'S COLL. 1879, M.A. 1882. [30]

MacIver, William, o.s. William, of Liverpool, arm. BRASENOSE COLL., matric. 10 Oct., 1823, aged 17; B.A. 1827, M.A. 1830, a student of Lincoln's Inn, 1825, died rector of Lymm, Cheshire, 18 June, 1863.

Mack, Arthur Paston, 6s. John, of Paston Hall, Norfolk, gent. WORCESTER COLL., matric. 20 Oct., 1881, aged 18.

Mack, Rev. Edmund Ide, 1s. Martin Edmund, of Colombo, Ceylon, gent. LINCOLN COLL., matric. 22 Oct., 1874, aged 18; B.A. 1878, a student of the Middle Temple 1875, assistant-master St. Mark School, Windsor, 1886.

Mackail, John William, 1s. John, of Ascon Bute, cler. BALLIOL COLL., matric. 19 Oct., 1878, aged 19; exhibitioner 1877-82, hon. scholar 1878-82, B.A. 1881, fellow 1882, M.A. 1885.

Mackaness, John, s. John, of Beckley, Oxon, gent. BALLIOL COLL., matric. 3 Dec., 1783, aged 16; B.A. 1787, M.A. 1793, bar.-at-law, Middle Temple, 1794, recorder of Wallingford. [35]

Mackarness, Arthur John Coleridge, 3s. John Fielder, bishop of Oxford. TRINITY COLL., matric. 15 Oct., 1883, aged 18; B.A. 1886.

Mackarness, Charles Coleridge, 1s. John Fielder, of Tardebigge, co. Worcester, cler. EXETER COLL., matric. 17 May, 1869, aged 18; B.A. 1873, M.A. 1876, lecturer King's College, London, 1879-82, sometime chaplain, vicar of Aylesbury since 1882. See *Coll. Reg.*, 135, 164.

Mackarness, Frederick Michael Coleridge, 2s. John Fielder, bishop of Oxford. KEBLE COLL., matric. 19 Oct., 1874, aged 20; B.A. 1879, bar.-at-law, Middle Temple, 1879. See Foster's *Men at the Bar.*

Mackarness, George Richard, 2s. John, of Islington, Middlesex, arm. MERTON COLL., matric. 12 June, 1841, aged 18; postmaster 1841-5, B.A. 1845, M.A. 1848, created D.D. 10 March, 1874, vicar of Ilam, co. Stafford, 1854-74, bishop of Argyll and the Isles 1874, until his death 20 April, 1883.

Mackarness, John. See also MACKANESS, and MACKERNESS. [5]

Mackarness, John Fielder, 1s. John, of St. Mary, Islington, arm. MERTON COLL., matric. 22 Oct., 1840, aged 19, postmaster 1840-4, B.A. 1844; fellow EXETER COLL. 1844-6, M.A. 1847, D.D. by diploma 22 Dec., 1869, vicar of Tardebigge, co. Worcester, 1854-5, hon. canon of Worcester 1847-58, rector of Honiton 1855-69, preb. of Exeter 1858-69, bishop of Oxford 1870, and chancellor of the Most Noble Order of the Garter. See Foster's *Peerage, Boase* 135, & *Eton School Lists.*

Mackay, Æneas James George, o.s. Thomas George, of Edinburgh, arm. UNIVERSITY COLL., matric. 28 April, 1858, aged 18, B.A. 1862, M.A. 1865, hon. fellow King's College, London, 1883.

Mackay, Alexander Spencer Henry, o.s. Alexander, of Worthing, Sussex, arm. ST. JOHN'S COLL., matric. 17 Oct., 1865, aged 22; B.A. from NEW INN HALL 1875, bar.-at-law, Inner Temple, 1873. See Foster's *Men at the Bar.*

Mackay, Allan Douglas, y.s. Donald, of Southend, Kent, arm. WORCESTER COLL., matric. 16 Nov., 1848, aged 18; B.A. 1852, B.Med. 1856, a student of Lincoln's Inn 1851.

Mackay, Rev. Edward Bruce, 2s. Allan Douglas, of Stony Stratford Bucks, B.Med. WORCESTER COLL., matric. 23 April, 1879, aged 18; B.A. 1882, M.A. 1885. [10]

Mackay, Henry Falconer Barclay, 1s. Alexander Eugene, of Milford Haven, co. Pembroke, D.Med. MERTON COLL., matric. 19 Oct., 1883, aged 19; B.A. 1887.

Mackay, James Livingston, 1s. James, of New York, America, cler. WORCESTER COLL., matric. 18 Oct., 1862, aged 18.

Mackay, John, s. Daniel, of Monaghan, Ireland, gent. LINCOLN COLL., matric. 12 Oct., 1797, aged 16.

Mackay, John Archibald, 1s. John, of Rothsay, gent. CHRIST CHURCH, matric. 30 Oct., 1885, aged 24; exhibitioner 1885.

Mackay, John Macdonald, 4s. John, of Caithness, cler. BALLIOL COLL., matric. 28 Jan., 1878, aged 20; exhibitioner 1878-82, B.A. 1882. [15]

Mackay, Robert John, o.s. Robert Gordon, of Edinburgh, gent. UNIVERSITY COLL., matric. 15 Oct., 1881, aged 22; scholar 1881-3.

Mackay, Robert William, o.s. John, of St. James's, London, arm. BRASENOSE COLL., matric. 15 Jan., 1821, aged 17; B.A. 1824, M.A. 1828, bar.-at-law, Lincoln's Inn, 1828, died in Feb., 1882.

Mackay, Sween Macdonald, 2s. Donald, of Hadley, Middlesex, gent. WORCESTER COLL., matric. 18 May, 1843, aged 18; B.A. 1847, M.A. 1850, vicar of Skillington, co. Lincoln, 1850-9, and of Langton-by-Wragby, co. Lincoln, 1859.

Mackay, Thomas, 1s. Æneas John, of Edinburgh, arm. NEW COLL., matric. 16 Oct., 1868, aged 18; B.A. 1873, a student of the Inner Temple 1871.

McKee, John Reginald, o.s. John, of Belfast. EXETER COLL., matric. 28 Jan., 1886, aged 20.

Mackenzie, Alastair Oswald Morrison, 4s. Donald, of Edinburgh, arm. BRASENOSE COLL., matric. 21 Oct., 1878, aged 19; scholar 1878-82, B.A. 1884. [21]

Mackenzie, Rev. Alexander, s. John, of Bishopsgate, London, arm. CHRIST CHURCH, matric. 12 June, 1800, aged 18; B.A. 1804, M.A. 1807, died in college 21 July, 1809. See *Alumni West.*, 454.

Mackenzie, Alexander George, 1s. Alexander, of 'Avoch,' co. Ross, equitis. NEW COLL., matric. 2 June, 1838, aged 20; B.A. 1843, M.A. 1847, of Avoch House, bar.-at-law, Lincoln's Inn, 1844, born 14 Feb., 1818; his father, the celebrated explorer of North-West America, and the discoverer of the Mackenzie River, was knighted at St. James, 10 Feb., 1802, and died 12 March, 1820.

Mackenzie, Andrew Mitchell, 2s. Donald, of Edinburgh, arm. CORPUS CHRISTI COLL., matric. 16 Oct., 1866, aged 18, died at sea in 1885.

Mackenzie, Archibald, 2s. William, of Porto Bello, Scotland, arm. MAGDALEN HALL, matric. 26 Oct., 1848, aged 20; B.A. 1854, M.A. (HERTFORD COLL.) 1876. [25]

Mackenzie, Augustus Colin, 2s. Lewis, of Marylebone, Middlesex, arm. ST. JOHN'S COLL., matric. 12 May, 1841, aged 17; B.A. 1845, M.A. 1847, of Findon and Mountgerald, co. Ross, bar.-at-law, Inner Temple, 1847, died in Jan., 1865. See Foster's *Baronetage.*

Mackenzie, Charles, 2s. John, of Wellwyn, Herts, gent. PEMBROKE COLL., matric. 26 March, 1825, aged 18; scholar 1825-33, B.A. 1828, M.A. 1831, head-master St. Olave's Grammar School, Southwark, 1832-55, vicar of St. Helen's, Bishopsgate, 1836-46, rector of St. Benet Gracechurch, etc. 1846-66, principal of Westbourne College 1855-64, founder of the City of London College, preb. of St. Paul's 1852, rector of All Hallows, Lombard Street, etc., 1866, until his death 11 April, 1888. See Foster's *Baronetage & Robinson*, 198.

Mackenzie, Charles Frederick, scholar CAIUS COLL., Cambridge, 1846, 2nd Wrangler and B.A. 1848, fellow 1848-62, M.A. 1851; adm. 'ad eundem' 21 June, 1860 (son of Colin Mackenzie, of Portmore, N.B.), archdeacon of Natal 1854-9, bishop of the mission to the tribes dwelling in the neighbourhood of the Lake Nyassa and River Shiré (consecrated) 1 Jan., 1861, until his death in the island of St. Malo 31 Jan., 1862.

Mackenzie, Charles Kincaid, 1s. Alexander Kincaid, of Edinburgh, arm. UNIVERSITY COLL., matric. 16 Oct., 1875, aged 18; B.A. 1880, a student of Lincoln's Inn 1882.

Mackenzie, Donald, 1s. Donald, of Edinburgh, arm. CORPUS CHRISTI COLL., matric. 18 Oct., 1864, aged 20; B.A. 1867. [30]

Mackenzie, Edward Philip, 2s. Edward, of Nantes, Normandy, arm. ST. JOHN'S COLL., matric. 14 June, 1860, aged 18; of Downham Hall, Suffolk, J.P., high sheriff 1882, and of Auchenskeoch, Kirkcudbright, formerly 9th lancers, etc.

Mackenzie, Rev. Evan Charles, 5s. Henry, bishop suffragan of Nottingham. KEBLE COLL., matric. 28 Jan., 1879, aged 18; scholar 1879-82, B.A. 1883.

Mackenzie, Farquhar John Conrad, 5s. Donald, of Edinburgh, gent. KEBLE COLL., matric. 19 Oct., 1880, aged 19; scholar 1880-4, B.A. 1884.

Mackenzie, Francis Granville, 2s. Kenneth Smith, of London, (*soi-disant*) baronet. NEW COLL., matric. 10 Oct., 1884, aged 19.

Mackenzie, Frank, 2s. John Francis Campbell, of Ryde, Isle of Wight, arm. QUEEN'S COLL., matric. 5 Feb., 1879, aged 19. [35]

Mackenzie, Frederick Finch, 1s. Frederick William, of London, D.Med. WORCESTER COLL., matric. 20 Oct., 1868, aged 19.

Mackenzie, George William Russell, 1s. Alastair, of Nassau, New Providence, Bahamas, arm. MERTON COLL., matric. 25 Nov., 1858, aged 19; curate of Coton-in-the-Elms, co. Derby, 1866-8, vicar 1868-72, incumbent of Norwood Dickoya, Ceylon, 1872.

Mackenzie, Harold Montague, 3s. Alfred John, of Melbourne, arm. CHRIST CHURCH, matric. 31 May, 1879, aged 18.

McKenzie, Rev. Harry Ward, 3s. John Douglas, of St. Peter' St. Albans, Herts, gent. KEBLE COLL., matric. 18 Oct., 1870, aged 19; B.A. 1874, M.A. 1877, assistant-master and tutor Wellington College 1879-80, and since 1884, bursar 1884.

Mackenzie, Henry, 3s. John, of 'St. Steph.,' London, gent. PEMBROKE COLL., matric. 11 Oct., 1830, aged 22; B.A. 1835, M.A. 1838, created D.D. 17 Dec., 1869, master of Bancroft's Hospital 1837-40, perp. curate St. James's, Bermondsey, 1840-3, of Great Yarmouth, 1844-8, vicar of St.-Martin's-in-the-Fields 1848-55, rector of Tydd St. Mary 1855-66, preb. of Lincoln 1858-64, canon and sub-dean 1864, rector of South Collingham 1866-71, archdeacon of Nottingham 1866, suffragan bishop of Nottingham 1870-7, died 15 Oct., 1878. See Foster's *Baronetage; Robinson*, 200; & *Crockford*.

Mackenzie, Henry, 4s. William, of Bunkle, co. Berwick, arm. MAGDALEN HALL, matric. 31 May, 1849, aged 20; B.A. 1853, M.A. 1859, perp. curate St. Chad Malpas, Cheshire, 1859-68, rector of Overton, co. Denbigh, 1868, until his death 29 Sep., 1879. [5]

Mackenzie, Henry Gordon, 2s. Gordon Gates, of Montreal, arm. MAGDALEN COLL., matric. 24 Jan., 1876, aged 18: B.A. 1880, bar.-at-law, Inner Temple, 1880. See Foster's *Men at the Bar.*

Mackenzie, James, s. James, of Isle of Wight, Hants, arm. ORIEL COLL., matric. 12 Oct., 1790, aged 17.

Mackenzie, James Arundel, s. James, of Bishopstoke, Hants, arm. ORIEL COLL., matric. 28 Oct., 1818, aged 18. See *Eton School Lists.*

Mackenzie, John, s. John, of Brampton near Carlisle, Cumberland, arm. BALLIOL COLL., matric. 1 July, 1813, aged 18.

Mackenzie, John George Kenneth, 1s. John Henry, of London, arm. NEW COLL., matric. 14 Oct., 1882, aged 19; scholar 1882-6, B.A. 1886. [10]

Mackenzie, John Pendrill, born in Malta, 2s. John, gent. ST. MARY HALL, matric. 22 March, 1849, aged 24; B.A. 1852, M.A. 1859, of the Glack family, brother of Roderick.

Mackenzie, Keith William Stewart, 1s. James Alexander, of Urray, Scotland, arm. ST. JOHN'S COLL., matric. 17 Oct., 1835, aged 17; of Seaforth, co. Ross, J.P., D.L., died 18 June, 1881. See Foster's *Peerage*, E. GALLOWAY.

Mackenzie, Kenneth, 6s. Donald, of Edinburgh, arm. KEBLE COLL., matric. 16 Oct., 1883, aged 20; B.A. 1887.

Mackenzie, Kenneth Augustus Muir, 4s. John, of Delvin, Perth, baronet. BALLIOL COLL., matric. 17 Oct., 1864, aged 19; B.A. 1868, M.A. 1873, bar.-at-law, Lincoln's Inn, 1873, Q.C. 1886, a clerk of the Crown in Chancery 1885. See Foster's *Men at the Bar.*

Mackenzie, Kenneth John, 1s. Kenneth Smith, of Edinburgh, (*soi-disant*) baronet. NON-COLL., matric. 21 May, 1880, aged 18. [15]

Mackenzie, Lewis Mark, 1s. Lewis, of Marylebone, London, arm. EXETER COLL., matric. 30 May, 1839, aged 17; B.A. 1843, of Findon and Mountgerald, co. Ross, died 22 Jan., 1846. See Foster's *Baronetage.*

Mackenzie, Martin Edward, 1s. Hugh Munro, of Distington, Cumberland, gent. KEBLE COLL., matric. 17 Oct., 1882, aged 19; B.A. 1885.

Mackenzie, Montague Johnstone Muir, 5s. John Muir, of Dunkeld, Perth, baronet. BRASENOSE COLL., matric. 24 May, 1866, aged 18, scholar 1866-70, B.A. 1870; fellow HERTFORD COLL. 1874, bar.-at-law, Lincoln's Inn, 1873. See Foster's *Men at the Bar.*

Mackenzie, Robert Jamieson, 3s. Donald, of Edinburgh, arm. KEBLE COLL., matric. 16 Oct., 1876, aged 19; scholar 1876-80, B.A. 1880, M.A. 1885.

Mackenzie, Roderick Bain, born in Malta, 3s. John, arm. EXETER COLL., matric. 18 May, 1853, aged 18; B.A. 1858, M.A. 1860, vicar of St. Peter-at-Gowts, Lincoln, 1868-74, rector of Sudbrooke, co. Lincoln, 1874. [20]

McKenzie, William Bell, 2s. James, of Sheffield, Yorks, gent. MAGDALEN HALL, matric. 26 June, 1830, aged 24; B.A. 1834, M.A. 1837, incumbent of St. James's, Holloway, 1838, until his death 22 Nov., 1870.

Mackenzie, William Dalziel, 1s. Edward, of East Bank, Greenock, Scotland, arm. MAGDALEN COLL., matric. 12 June, 1858, aged 18; B.A. 1862, M.A. 1865, of Fawley Court, Oxon, J.P., high sheriff 1873, etc., bar.-at-law, Inner Temple, 1863, hon. major Queen's Own Oxfordshire hussars. See Foster's *Men at the Bar.*

Mackenzie, William Forbes, 1s. Colin, of Exmouth, Devon, arm. BRASENOSE COLL., matric. 19 Oct., 1824, aged 17; of Portmore, co. Peebles, M.P. 1837-52, and for Liverpool 1852-3, a lord of the Treasury, died 23 Sep., 1862.

Mackenzie, Rev. William Frederick, s. Frederick, of Exeter (city), gent. BALLIOL COLL., matric. 10 May, 1785, aged 19; B.A. from ST. ALBAN HALL 1791, died in 1808.

Mackenzie, William Roderick Dalziel, 1s. William Dalziel, of Harpesden, near Henley, arm. CHRIST CHURCH, matric. 22 April, 1884, aged 19. [25]

Mackerness, John, s. Matthew, of Stony Stratford, Bucks, pleb. BRASENOSE COLL., matric. 6 April, 1720, aged 19; B.A. 1723, M.A. 1726, rector of Heversham, Bucks, died 4 Sep., 1775.

Mackeson, Peyton Temple, 1s. George, of London, gent. UNIVERSITY COLL., matric. 11 Oct., 1872, aged 18; B.A. 1877, M.A. 1879.

Mackeson, William (Wyllys), 2s. John, of Jamaica, arm. QUEEN'S COLL., matric. 6 March, 1829, aged 16; B.A. 1836, bar.-at-law, Inner Temple, 1836, Q.C. and a bencher 1868. See Foster's *Men at the Bar.*

Mackesy, Thomas Lewis, 2s. Henry Vincent, of Waterford, arm. KEBLE COLL., matric. 18 Oct., 1881, aged 19; scholar 1881-5, B.A. 1885.

Mackett, Charles, s. Charles, of Southampton, Hants, arm. ORIEL COLL., matric. 7 March, 1806, aged 19. [30]

Mackett, William Henry, 1s. William Augustus, of Rochester, Kent, gent. NEW COLL., matric. 1[illegible] Oct., 1874, aged 30.

Mackey, Arthur Johnstone, 3s. John Alexander, of Heavitree, near Exeter, Devon, arm. CHRIST CHURCH, matric. 18 May, 1864, aged 18; a junior student 1864-71, B.A. 1869, bar.-at-law, Lincoln's Inn, 1871. See Foster's *Men at the Bar.*

Mackey, Bryan, s. William, of Kingston, Isle of Jamaica, gent. BRASENOSE COLL., matric. 11 Dec., 1788, aged 18; B.A. 1792, rector of Coates, co. Gloucester, 1799, until his death 25 Nov., 1847.

Mackey, Clement William, o.s. William Henry, of Stepney, Middlesex, gent. WORCESTER COLL., matric. 17 May, 1854, aged 19; B.A. 1858, M.A. 1861.

Mackey, John Alexander Dixie, 1s. John Brunt, of Croydon, Surrey, gent. CHRIST CHURCH, matric. 12 Oct., 1877, aged 19; B.A. 1885, bar.-at-law, Inner Temple, 1882. See Foster's *Men at the Bar & Robinson*, 379. [35]

Mackintosh, James Simon, 2s. Simon, of Aberdeen, Scotland, cler. ST. MARY HALL, matric. 25 Oct., 1864, aged 19; exhibitioner ORIEL COLL. 1865, B.A. 1867, M.A. 1882, of the Indian Civil Service 1865.

Mackintosh, Joseph, 1s. John, of Bangor, co. Carnarvon, gent. CHRIST CHURCH, matric. 13 Dec., 1837, aged 18; servitor 1837-41, B.A. 1841 (as MCINTOSH), perp. curate of Llanllugan 1851-60, rector of Llanerfyl, co. Montgomery, 1860, until his death 6 Feb., 1882. [20]

Mackintosh, Robert James, o.s. James, of Bombay, East Indies, eq. aur. NEW COLL., matric. 22 June, 1825, aged 18; fellow 1825-40, B.A. 1829, M.A. 1833, bar.-at-law, Lincoln's Inn, 1833.

Mackintosh, William Lachlan, 1s. Æneas, of Inverness, arm. ST. MARY HALL, matric. 23 Oct., 1882, aged 22; B.A. from PEMBROKE COLL. 1886.

Macklem, Sutherland, 2s. Thomas Clark, of Chippawa, Ontario, D.Med. NON-COLL., matric. 25 Oct., 1873, aged 20.

Macklin, Gerard Roseingrave Wilson, o.s. Roseingrave, of Derby (town), cler. TRINITY COLL., matric. 12 Oct., 1861, aged 18; B.A. 1865.

Macklin, John, s. William, of Monmouth (town), pleb. UNIVERSITY COLL., matric. 21 March, 1718-9, aged 20; B.A. 1722 (? vicar of Holy Trinity, Coventry, 1734). [25]

Mackmurdo, Arthur Heygate, 4s. Edward, of Edmonton, Middlesex, gent. NON-COLL., matric. 19 Oct., 1878, aged 26.

Mackness, George, 1s. Matthew George, of Wellingborough, Northants, gent. WADHAM COLL., matric. 29 June, 1852, aged 17; exhibitioner LINCOLN COLL. 1854-7, B.A. 1856, M.A. 1859, B. & D.D. 1871, held various curacies 1858-70, incumbent of St. Mary's, Broughty Ferry, N.B. 1870.

Mackness, George Owen Carr, 1s. George, of Hastings, D.D. CHRIST CHURCH, matric. 31 May, 1879, aged 18; a junior student 1879-84, B.A. 1883.

Mackonochie, Alexander Heriot, 3s. George, of Fareham, Hants, arm. WADHAM COLL., matric. 27 June, 1844, aged 18; B.A. 1848, M.A. 1851, curate of Westbury, Wilts, 1849-52, of Wantage 1852-8, and of St. George's-in-the-East 1858-62, perp. curate of St. Andrew's, Holborn, 1862-82, vicar of St. Peter's, London Docks, 1882-3, died 17 Dec., 1887.

Mackonochie, Rev. James Alison, 2s. James, of London, arm. CHRIST CHURCH, matric. 21 May, 1880, aged 19; B.A. 1884. [30]

Mackreth, Edmund Francis, 1s. George Edward, of London, arm. EXETER COLL., matric. 16 Jan., 1875, aged 19; B.A. 1878, M.A. 1881, minister of St. Mary's, Buxted, Sussex, 1885.

Mackreth, Samuel, s. William, of Candell, Westmoreland, pleb. QUEEN'S COLL., matric. 22 May, 1740, aged 17; B.A. 19 March, 1745-6, M.A. 1749.

Mackworth, (Sir) Digby (Bart.), s. Herbert, of Marylebone, London, baronet. MAGDALEN COLL., matric. 17 July, 1788, aged 22; created D.C.L. 18 June, 1799, 3rd baronet, and lieut.-colonel of the Oxford city loyal volunteers, 1798, 1803-4, died 2 May, 1838. See Foster's *Baronetage*.

Mackworth, Herbert, created D.C.L. 8 July, 1756, of Neath, co. Glamorgan (son of Sir Humphrey Mackworth, of Gnoll, co. Glamorgan, knight), M.P. Cardiff 1739, until his death 20 Aug., 1765, father of Herbert, 1753. See Foster's *Baronetage*.

Mackworth, (Sir) Herbert (Bart.), s. Herbert, of Neath, co. Glamorgan, arm. MAGDALEN COLL., matric. 15 Dec., 1753, aged 16; B.A. 1757, M.A. 1760, bar.-at-law, Lincoln's Inn, 1759, colonel of Glamorgan militia, M.P. Cardiff 1766-90, created a baronet 16 Sep., 1766, died 25 Oct., 1791. See Foster's *Baronetage*. [35]

Mackworth, Horace Eugene, 3s. (Digby), of Glen Uske, co. Monmouth, baronet. ST. EDMUND HALL, matric. 18 May, 1848, aged 19; B.A. 1852. See Foster's *Baronetage*.

Mackworth-Dolben, William Harcourt Isham, 4s. Digby, of Kingston, Berks, baronet. BALLIOL COLL., matric. 18 March, 1825, aged 18; B.A. 1829, assumed the additional name of DOLBEN by royal licence 20 July, 1835, died 2 Nov., 1872. See Foster's *Baronetage.*

MacLachlan, Alexander, s. 'Lachlan,' of St. Giles's, London, arm. TRINITY COLL., matric. 31 Jan., 1816, aged 17; exhibitioner 1817-19.

McLachlan, Angus, 4s. Thomas, of Darlington, co. Durham, arm. KEBLE COLL., matric. 19 Oct., 1886, aged 25.

Maclachlan, Archibald Campbell, 1s. Archibald Neil Campbell, of Newton Valence, Hants, cler. MAGDALEN COLL., matric. 16 Oct., 1884, aged 20.

Maclachlan, Archibald Neil Campbell, born at Boulogne-sur-Mer, 2s. Archibald, arm. EXETER COLL., matric. 8 Feb., 1838, aged 18; B.A. 1841, M.A. 1844, of Earls Island and Knocknakerna, co. Galway, vicar of Newton Valence, Hants, 1860.

MacLachlan, Ewan Hugh, 3s. Patrick, of Hackney, London, gent. PEMBROKE COLL., matric. 5 Dec., 1839, aged 20; scholar 1844-57, B.A. 1844, M.A. 1846, vicar of Monkton, Kent, 1871, until his death 7 Feb., 1884. [6]

McLachlan, Norman, 3s. Thomas, of Darlington, co. Durham, arm. KEBLE COLL., matric. 14 Oct., 1878, aged 20; B.A. 1882.

Maclagan, Charles Patrick Dalrymple, 1s. Robert, of Roorkee, East Indies, arm. EXETER COLL., matric. 15 May, 1875, aged 17; B.A. 1879, M.A. 1882, a student of the Inner Temple 1879.

Maclagan, Edward Douglas, 4s. Robert, of Murree, East Indies, arm. NEW COLL., matric. 12 Oct., 1883, aged 19; B.A. 1886, of the Indian Civil Service 1883.

Maclaine, William Osborne, born at Valenciennes, in France, baptized at Thornbury, co. Gloucester, o.s. Hector, arm. WADHAM COLL., matric. 23 Feb., 1837, aged 18; B.A. 1840, M.A. 1843, of Kyneton, co. Gloucester, J.P., D.L., bar.-at-law, Lincoln's Inn, 1884. See Foster's *Men at the Bar.* [10]

MacLaren, Archibald, 1s. James, of Alloa, co. Clackmannan, Scotland, arm. NEW INN HALL, matric. 17 Nov., 1864, aged 19.

MacLaren, Charles Edward, 2s. Henry, of Manchester, gent. EXETER COLL., matric. 11 Oct., 1872, aged 20; B.A. 1876, M.A. 1880, bar.-at-law, Lincoln's Inn, 1877. See Foster's *Men at the Bar.*

McLaren, Douglas, 4s. John Wingate, of London, arm. ORIEL COLL., matric. 23 Oct., 1885, aged 19.

McLaren, James, 1s. John, of Lybster, gent. NON-COLL., matric. 20 Jan., 1877, aged 26; B.A. 1881.

MacLaren, John Wallace Hozier, 3s. Archibald, of Summertown, near Oxford, gent. MAGDALEN COLL., matric. 16 Oct., 1880, aged 19; exhibitioner 1883-4, B.A. 1885, M.A. 1887. [15]

McLaughlin, Edward Crofton Leigh, 1s. Edward, of Southsea, Hants, arm. CHRIST CHURCH, matric. 8 June, 1878, aged 19; exhibitioner 1878, B.A. 1882, M.A. 1885, vicar of Whitwell, Yorks, 1886.

M'Laughlin, Hubert, M.A. TRINITY COLL., Dublin, 1831 (B.A. 1828); adm. 'ad eundem' 7 July, 1860 (son of Thomas, of Dublin), rector of Burford, Salop, 1838, preb. of Hereford 1857, sometime chaplain at Nice, died 15 Dec., 1882. See Foster's *Our Noble and Gentle Families.*

McLaughlin, Vivian Guy Ouseley, 4s. Edward, of Woolwich, Kent, arm. LINCOLN COLL., matric. 27 Oct., 1885, aged 20.

Maclaverty, Alexander, 2s. Alexander, of Glasgow, Scotland, doctor. CHRIST CHURCH, matric. 22 Oct., 1862, aged 18; B.A. 1865, M.A. 1869, vicar of Llangattock, etc., since 1875.

Maclay, Edwin Samuel, 3s. William, of Charlton, Kent, arm. NON-COLL., matric. 15 Jan., 1869, aged 19. [20]

Maclean, Alexander, 1s. Henry, of London, gent. CHRIST CHURCH, matric. 16 Oct., 1885, aged 18.

Maclean, Rev. Arthur James, 5s. John George, of London, gent. ST. JOHN'S COLL., matric. 13 Oct., 1879, aged 22; B.A. 1884, M.A. 1887. See *Eton School Lists.*

Maclean, Charles Hope, 6s. Alexander, of Stevenson, Haddington, Scotland, arm. BALLIOL COLL., matric. 24 May, 1822, aged 19; B.A. 1826, M.A. 1828, bar.-at-law, Middle Temple, 1829, one of the secretaries to the Statistical Society, died 14 Aug., 1839.

Maclean, Donald, s. Fitzroy Jeffreys Grafton, of Isle of Barbados, West Indies, arm. (after bart.). BALLIOL COLL., matric. 6 April, 1818, aged 18; Snell exhibitioner 1882, B.A. 1823, M.A. 1827, created D.C.L. 20 June, 1844, M.P. Oxford (city) 1835-47, bar.-at-law, Lincoln's Inn, 1827, died 21 March, 1874. See Foster's *Baronetage* & *Eton School Lists.*

McLean, Douglas Hamilton, 2s. John Donald, of Sydney, Australia, gent. NEW COLL., matric. 14 Oct., 1882, aged 19; B.A. 1887. See *Eton School Lists.* [25]

M'Lean, Frederick Benjamin, scholar of TRINITY COLL., Dublin, 1842 (B.A. 1844, M.A. 1847); adm. 'ad eundem' 14 Jan., 1858.

MacLean, George Gavin, 1s. George, of Lymington, Hants, arm. WADHAM COLL., matric. 8 Dec., 1854, aged 18; B.A. 1858, M.A. 1861, curate of Horsham, Sussex, 1862-72, vicar of Nutley, Sussex, 1872-82, and of Southrop, co. Gloucester, 1882.

McLean, Hector, 3s. John Donald, of Sydney, Australia, arm. NEW COLL., matric. 26 Jan., 1885, aged 20; died 20 Jan., 1888.

McLean, James Alfred, o.s. James, of London, arm. TRINITY COLL., matric. 11 April, 1826, aged 17.

Maclean, John, o.s. Hugh, of East Indies, gent. PEMBROKE COLL., matric. 11 Oct., 1861, aged 20.

MacLean, John Alexander, 4s. John Donald, of Sydney, Australia, arm. NEW COLL., matric. 16 Oct., 1885, aged 19. [31]

McLean, Norman, 1s. John Donald, of Hawthornden, Australia, arm. NEW COLL., matric. 24 Jan., 1881, aged 19; B.A. 1884. See *Eton School Lists.*

McLean, Thomas, s. John, of Isle of Jamaica, arm. CHRIST CHURCH, matric. 26 March, 1770, aged 17.

Macleane, Charles Donald, 1s. Arthur John, of St. Michael's, Cambridge (town), cler. EXETER COLL., matric. 19 Oct., 1861, aged 18; scholar 1861-5, B.Mus. 1862, B.A. & D.Mus. 1865, M.A. 1879, of the Indian Civil Service 1864. See *Coll. Reg.* 159.

Macleane, Douglas, 3s. Arthur John, of Bath, cler. PEMBROKE COLL., matric. 19 May, 1875, aged 18; scholar 1875-80, B.A. 1879, M.A. 1882, fellow 1882, divinity lecturer and chaplain 1882-4, rector of Codford St. Peter's, Somerset, 1884. [35]

Macleay, Oswell Sullivan, 3s. James Robert, of London, arm. BALLIOL COLL., matric. 25 Jan., 1871, aged 18; B.A. 1875, M.A. 1877, bar.-at-law, Inner Temple, 1878. See Foster's *Men at the Bar.*

Macleish, Hector Daniel, s. Hector, of St. Martin's, Westminster, gent. QUEEN'S COLL., matric. 3 Jan., 1801, aged 19; a student of Lincoln's Inn 1802.

Maclellan, George, s. Robert, of Bamaclellan, co. Galloway, gent. BALLIOL COLL., matric. 13 Aug., 1761, aged 14; B.A. 1765, M.A. 1771.

Maclellan, Robert, s. George, of Surfleet, co. Lincoln, cler. ST. ALBAN HALL, matric. 16 April, 179[illegible], aged 19.

Macleod, Alexander Normand, born at Madula, in the East Indies, s. Alexander, arm. CHRIST CHURCH, matric. 26 Jan., 1809, aged 18. [40]

Macleod, Donald Grant, of TRINITY COLL., Cambridge (LL.B. 1865, B.A. 1866, M.A. & LL.M. 1882); adm. 'comitatis causa' 8 June, 1865.

McLeod, Edward, 4s. — M., of Stirling, Scotland, arm. WORCESTER COLL., matric. 15 Oct., 183[illegible], aged 21; B.A. 1837, M.A. 1839.

acleod, Rev. Henry Crawford Crichton, 1s. Henry Dunning, of Boulogne-sur-Mer, arm. BALLIOL COLL., matric. 18 Oct., 1876, aged 19; exhibitioner 1876-81, B.A. 1881, M.A. 1884.

acleod, John George, 2s. Roderic, of London, D.Med. EXETER COLL., matric. 15 Feb., 1844, aged 17; B.A. 1847, M.A. 1851.

acleod, John Norman, born at Cawnpore, in the East Indies, s. Norman, arm. UNIVERSITY COLL., matric. 28 Nov., 1804, aged 16; M.P. Sudbury 1828-30, died 25 March, 1835, 'laird of the Isle of Skye.'

acleod, John William, born at Dingigal, in the East Indies, s. Alexander, arm. CHRIST CHURCH, matric. 17 Oct., 1811, aged 18; bar.-at-law, Lincoln's Inn, 1819, died 12 Aug., 1829.

acleod, Norman, s. John, of Dyke, co. Elgin, Scotland, arm. UNIVERSITY COLL., matric. 27 Nov., 1770, aged 16; 20th laird of Macleod, M.P. Inverness-shire 1790-6, died in Aug., 1801. See Foster's *Scots M.P.'s.* **[5]**

acleod, Norman, s. Roderick, of Aberdeen, Scotland, doctor. BALLIOL COLL., matric. 26 May, 1803, aged 16 (his father rector of St. Anne's, Soho, 1806, and chaplain of the Scottish Hospital, died 14 Dec., 1845, aged 91).

acleod, Norman Cranstoun, 3s. Robert Bruce Æneas, of Invergordon, co. Ross, arm. NEW COLL., matric. 16 Oct., 1885, aged 19.

acleod, William, s. John, of Gateshead, co. Durham, arm. UNIVERSITY COLL., matric. 16 Oct., 1802, aged 20; B.A. 1808, M.A. 1835, bar.-at-law, Inner Temple, 1812.

acleroy, Arthur Lloyd, 1s. Alexander Crawford, of Glasgow, arm. ST. MARY HALL, matric. 27 Jan., 1872, aged 18; scholar 1872-5, B.A. & M.A. 1879.

aclure, Edward Craig, 1s. John, of Manchester, arm. BRASENOSE COLL., matric. 28 Jan., 1852, aged 18; scholar 1852-6, B.A. 1856, M.A. 1858, vicar of Habergham Eaves 1863-77, and of Rochdale since 1877. **[10]**

aclure, Edward St. John, 1s. Edward Craig, of Burnley, Lancashire, cler. KEBLE COLL., matric. 16 Oct., 1883, aged 19; died 2 Sep., 1887.

cMahon, Rev. Bernard, o.s. Bernard, of Leamington Priors, co. Warwick, arm. MAGDALEN HALL, matric. 22 Jan., 1869, aged 23; died 3 Feb., 1887.

cMichael, William, s. William, of St. Mary's, Bridgnorth, Salop, gent. CHRIST CHURCH, matric. 23 Oct., 1800, aged 16; B.A. 1805, M.A. 1807, B.Med. 1808; Radcliffe travelling fellow UNIVERSITY COLL. 1811, D.Med. 1816, F.R.C.P. 1818, physician Middlesex Hospital 1822-31, physician extraordinary to the King 1829, in ordinary 1831, librarian to the King 1830, died 10 Jan., 1839. See Munk's *Roll*, iii. 182.

acmillan, Alexander, 2s. John, of Newton Stewart, Scotland, gent. BRASENOSE COLL., matric. 15 Oct., 1864, aged 19; scholar 1864-8, B.A. 1868, M.A. 1873, of the Indian Civil Service 1866, joint magistrate and deputy collector Allahabad, bar.-at-law, Inner Temple, 1883. See Foster's *Men at the Bar.*

acmillan, Alexander, created M.A. 25 March, 1881, late publisher to the University. **[15]**

cMillan, Charles Duncan Horatio, o.s. Charles, of Keynsham, near Bristol, gent. NON-COLL., matric. 13 Oct., 1884, aged 20.

cMillan, James, o.s. Robert, of Dumfries, gent. QUEEN'S COLL., matric. 10 Nov., 1885, aged 26; scholar 1885-6.

acmillan, Malcolm Kingsley, 1s. Alexander, of Cambridge, gent. BALLIOL COLL., matric. 20 Oct., 1875, aged 22; B.A. & M.A. 1884, a student of the Inner Temple 1884.

Macmillan, Michael, 4s. John, of Newton Stewart, co. Wigton, arm. BRASENOSE COLL., matric. 12 Oct., 1872, aged 19; scholar 1872-7, B.A. 1876. See *Rugby School Reg.*

Macmullen, Richard Gell, 2s. Stephen Henry, of Dobun, Kent, gent. CORPUS CHRISTI COLL., matric. 30 May, 1828, aged 13; scholar 1828-35, B.A. 1832, M.A. 1835, fellow 1835-46, B.D. 1845, Latin reader 1836, senior dean 1840, bursar 1844.

McMurdie, Joseph, s. John, of St. Bride's, London, gent. MAGDALEN HALL, matric. 21 Nov., 1814, aged 22; B.Mus. 24 Nov., 1814. **[21]**

Macnab, Arthur Alexander, 2s. Alexander, of Halifax, Canada, gent. UNIVERSITY COLL., matric. 17 Oct., 1885, aged 18.

McNair, Lindsay William, o.s. William, of Kensington, Middlesex, gent. PEMBROKE COLL., matric. 21 Oct., 1862, aged 27.

Macnamara, Charles Caroll, 1s. George Houseman, of Uxbridge, Middlesex, D.Med. ORIEL COLL., matric. 26 April, 1876, aged 18; B.A. 1879, bar.-at-law, Inner Temple, 1881, died 19 April, 1883.

Macnamara, Henry, 4s. Daniel, of Uxbridge, Middlesex, gent. LINCOLN COLL., matric. 22 April, 1847, aged 18; B.A. 1851, M.A. 1853, incumbent of St. Paul's, Dundee, 1875, until his death in 1885. **[25]**

Macnamara, Henry Danvers, 1s. Francis, of Calcutta, gent. MAGDALEN COLL., matric. 12 Oct., 1872, aged 18, clerk 1872-6; B.A. from ST. ALBAN HALL 1878, M.A. from MAGDALEN COLL. 1881, minor canon St. Paul's 1884.

Macnamara, Thomas Binstead, o.s. Thomas Pellew, of Cowes, Isle of Wight, gent. MAGDALEN HALL, matric. 30 March, 1843, aged 18; B.A. 1846, M.A. 1849, perp. curate Waterloo, Hants, 1852-62, rector of Kingston, Isle of Wight, 1883.

Macnaught, John, o.s. John, of Clarendon, Isle of Jamaica, D.Med. WADHAM COLL., matric. 18 Oct., 1843, aged 17; B.A. 1847, M.A. 1852, perp. curate St. Chrysostom, Everton, Lancashire, 1853-61, minister of Laura Chapel, Bath, 1867-71, of Holy Trinity, Conduit Street, 1871-5, vicar of St. Mary's, Northend, Fulham, 1881-6, rector of Covenham St. Bartholomew, co. Lincoln, 1886.

McNeile, Hector, 7s. Hugh, of Liverpool, D.D. CHRIST CHURCH, matric. 16 Oct., 1861, aged 18, a junior student 1860-5, B.A. 1865; fellow ST. JOHN'S COLL. 1865-71, M.A. 1869, math. lecturer 1865-6, a student of Lincoln's Inn 1865, vicar of Belvedere, Kent, 1881-6.

McNeill, Alexander, 4s. Alexander, of Edinburgh, arm. TRINITY COLL., matric. 15 Oct., 1881, aged 18; B.A. 1885. **[30]**

McNeill, Duncan, 1s. Malcolm, of London, arm. CORPUS CHRISTI COLL., matric. 19 Oct., 1883, aged 19; scholar 1883, B.A. 1887.

McNeill, Duncan Archibald, 2s. Archibald, of Edinburgh, arm. BALLIOL COLL., matric. 12 Oct., 1861, aged 20; exhibitioner 1861-6.

McNeill, Right Hon. Sir John, G.C.B., created D.C.L. 24 June, 1857 (son of John, of Colonsay, Scotland), P.C. 1857, D.Med. Bombay Medical Service 1834-6, envoy to Persia 1836-42, chairman Poor Law Board, Scotland, 1845-68, died 17 May, 1883.

MacNeill, John Gordon Swift, o.s. John Gordon Swift, of Dublin, cler. CHRIST CHURCH, matric. 19 Oct., 1868, aged 19; exhibitioner 1868-72, B.A. 1873, M.A. 1875, a student of the Inner Temple 1873, bar.-at-law, King's Inns, Dublin, 1876, M.P. South Donegal (Feb.) 1887.

McNeill, Ronald John, o.s. Edmund John, of Torquay, Devon, gent. CHRIST CHURCH, matric. 2 Feb., 1882, aged 20; B.A. 1886, of Craigdunn, co. Antrim, a student of Lincoln's Inn 1884. **[35]**

McNish, Alexander Copland, 2s. John, of Manchester, gent. BRASENOSE COLL., matric. 5 June, 1873, aged 18; B.A. 1877, M.A. 1880, bar.-at-law, Lincoln's Inn, 1879. See Foster's *Men at the Bar.*

McNish, Alexander William, s. Robert, of Isle of Antigua, gent. QUEEN'S COLL., matric. 16 Oct., 1817, aged 20; B.A. 1821.

Macock, Henry, s. Thomas, of Oxford (city), gent. LINCOLN COLL., matric. 10 May, 1758, aged 15; B.A. 1763, M.A. 1764, vicar of Harwell, Berks, and of Sellinge, Kent, where he died in 1816.

Macock, Rev. John, s. John, of Heyford-at-Bridge, Oxon, gent. MAGDALEN COLL., matric. 26 Aug., 1746, aged 13, B.A. 1750, M.A. 1753, B.D. from LINCOLN COLL. 1760, fellow until his death 19 Feb., 1773. See *Bloxam*, vi. 267.

Macock, Thomas, 'apothecary;' privilegiatus 12 April, 1742.

Maconochie, Alexander Francis, 1s. Alexander, of Mitcham, Surrey, gent. BALLIOL COLL., matric, 21 Oct., 1880, aged 17; of the Indian Civil Service 1880. [5]

Maconochie, John Allan. CHRIST CHURCH, 1867. See WELLWOOD.

Macphail, Edmund Whittingstall St. Maur, 1s. John Charles, of St. Maura, Ionian Islands, arm. JESUS COLL., matric. 2 June, 1853, aged 20; B.A. from LITTON HALL 1859, M.A. from JESUS COLL. 1863, rector of Plumpton, Northants, 1870-8, vicar of Balking, Berks, 1878-86, rector of Letcombe Bassett since 1886.

Macpherson, Alan, 2s. Allan, of Australia, arm. EXETER COLL., matric. 13 Oct., 1877, aged 20; B.A. 1881, M.A. 1886, bar.-at-law, Lincoln's Inn, 1881. See Foster's *Men at the Bar*.

Macpherson, Arthur Hoste, 2s. Arthur George, of Calcutta, arm. TRINITY COLL., matric. 17 Oct., 1885, aged 18.

Macpherson, Ewan Francis, 5s. Allan, of Bernera, Australia, arm. BRASENOSE COLL., matric. 22 Oct., 1883, aged 19; scholar 1883-6, exhibitioner 1886.

Macpherson, Rev. Hugh Alexander, 1s. William, of Calcutta, arm. ORIEL COLL., matric. 18 April, 1877, aged 19; B.A. 1881, M.A. 1884. [11]

McPherson, James John, 2s. Robert, of Clifford, co. Warwick, arm. QUEEN'S COLL., matric. 19 May, 1829, aged 17.

McPherson, John, 1s. Robert, of Inverness, Scotland, cler. TRINITY COLL., matric. 30 Nov., 1859, aged 18; scholar ST. JOHN'S COLL. 1860-3, B.A. 1863, bar.-at-law, Inner Temple, 1865, deputy conservator Forest Department India in 1882. See Foster's *Men at the Bar* & *Rugby School Reg.*

McPherson, Richard Robert James, 1s. Robert, of Chatham, Kent, arm. QUEEN'S COLL., matric. 31 Jan., 1826, aged 21; B.A. 1829, M.A. 1839, officiating minister of Midhurst, Sussex, where he died 23 June, 1841.

McPherson, Robert Arthur, 3s. John, of St. Andrew's, Scotland, gent. BALLIOL COLL., matric. 16 Oct., 1883, aged 19; of the Indian Civil Service 1883.

Macpherson, William Charteris, 2s. William, of London, arm. ORIEL COLL., matric. 18 Oct., 1881, aged 19; a student of the Middle Temple 1883. [16]

Macqueen, Archibald, 1s. John, of St. Bees, Cumberland. QUEEN'S COLL., matric. 25 Oct., 1886, aged 19; exhibitioner 1886.

McQueen, James Neville, 2s. John, of Kidderpore, near Calcutta, cler. UNIVERSITY COLL., matric. 29 May, 1857, aged 18; B.A. 1861.

McQueen, John Rainier, 1s. James, of Clifton, near Bristol, arm. BALLIOL COLL., matric. 18 June, 1858, aged 18; B.A. 1862, M.A. 1865, of Braxfield and Hardington, co. Lanark, and of Broughton, co. Peebles.

McQueen, Robert Rainier, 2s. James, of Brighton, Sussex, arm. EXETER COLL., matric. 29 May, 1860, aged 17; brother of the last named. [20]

McRae, Charles, 3s. Gilbert, of Limehouse, London, gent. EXETER COLL., matric. 3 June, 1876, aged 24; scholar 1875-80, B.A. 1879, M.A. 1883. See *Coll. Reg.*, 167.

Macrae, Charles Colin, 1s. Alexander, of Beng India, arm. UNIVERSITY COLL., matric. 11 Ju 1862, aged 18; scholar 1863-8, B.A. 1867, bar.-law, Lincoln's Inn, 1868. See Foster's *Men at Bar* & *Eton School Lists*.

Macrae, Isaac Vanden Heuvel, 5s. Colin, of N Haven, Connecticut, North America, arm. MA DALEN HALL, matric. 2 March, 1840, aged 20.

Macray, Charles Parish, 1s. John, of St. Panc Middlesex. MAGDALEN COLL., matric. 12 Ap 1841, aged 16; clerk 1841, until his death 21 Se 1844. See *Coll. Reg.*, ii. 120.

Macray, Walter Robert, 4s. William Dunn, of Du lingtou, Oxon, cler. NON-COLL., matric. 30 O 1882, aged 19; B.A. 1886. [2

Macray, William Edward, 1s. William Dunn, Oxford, cler. NON-COLL., matric. 3 March, 18 aged 19]; chorister MAGDALEN COLL. 1866- bible clerk ALL SOULS' COLL. 1877-80, B 1885.

Macray, William Dunn, 3s. John, of London, ge MAGDALEN COLL., matric. 17 Oct., 1844, aged clerk 1844-50, B.A. 1848; M.A. from NEW CO 1851, chaplain 1850-80, chaplain Christ Chu 1851-6, and Magdalen College 1856-70, curate St. Mary Magdalen, Oxford, 1850-67, special sistant in MS. department Bodleian library, F.S 1873, rector of Ducklington, Oxon, 1870; for of his numerous works see *Crockford*, & *Bloxa* ii. 121.

Macready, William Charles, 1s. William Charles, Elstree, Herts, arm. CHRIST CHURCH, matric. June, 1851, aged 18.

Macreight, Daniel Chambers, D.Med. TRINI COLL., Dublin, 1827, B.A. 1820, B.Med. & M. 1823, 4s. James, of Armagh, Ireland, gent. MA DALEN HALL, incorp. 4 June, 1828, aged 29.

Macreight, Edwin Chambers, 4s. Edwin Chamb of Queen Anne Street, London, doctor. PEMBRO COLL., matric. 11 June, 1857, aged 18. [

Macrorie, Basil Francis Newall, born at Accringt Lancashire, 1s. William Kennett, bishop of Mar burgh. BRASENOSE COLL., matric. 20 Oct., 18 aged 18.

Macrorie, William Kenneth, 1s. David, of Liverp arm. BRASENOSE COLL., matric. 2 Feb., 1 aged 17; B.A. 1852, M.A. 1855, created D.D. June, 1876, bishop of Maritzburgh 1869, D.C.L the University of the South, M.A. University of Cape 1876, perp. curate Wingates, Lancas 1860-1, rector of Wapping 1861-5, perp. cu Accrington 1865-9.

MacSparran, James, M.A., D.D. by diploma 5 A 1737, missionary in Rhode Island 1721.

McSwiney, John Henry Herbert, o.s. Daniel Brighton, Sussex, gent. PEMBROKE COLL., ma 19 Nov., 1846, aged 19; B.A. 1850, M.A. 1 rector of Barnoldby-le-Beck, co. Lincoln, 1886.

Mactaggart, James, o.s. James, of London, CHRIST CHURCH, matric. 23 Oct., 1834, 19.

McVicker, John William, 1s. Alexander, of Lon derry, gent. WORCESTER COLL., matric. 18 1883, aged 22; exhibitioner 1883-4.

Macy, Vincent Travers, 5s. Vincent Hardwic Oxhill, co. Warwick, cler. NON-COLL., matri Jan., 1886, aged 19.

Madan, Arthur Cornwallis, 3s. George, of Cam, Dursley, co. Gloucester, cler. CHRIST CHU matric. 16 Oct., 1869, aged 19; a junior st 1865-9, a senior student 1869, B.A. 1869, M.A. lecturer 1870, tutor 1871-80.

Madan, Falconer, 5s. George, of Cam, co. Glouc cler. BRASENOSE COLL., matric. 15 Oct., aged 19; scholar 1870-4, B.A. 1874, fellow 18 M.A. 1877, lecturer and librarian 1877, a sub-libr Bodleian Library 1880.

Maddock, Rev. Benjamin, of Corpus Christi Coll., Cambridge (B.A. 1842, M.A. 1847); adm. 'ad eundem' 10 May, 1850 (son of Benjamin, of Edgerton Lodge, Tadcaster), incumbent of Marple 1862, until his death 20 June, 1866.

Maddock, Edward North, 3s. Henry John, of Huddersfield, cler. Worcester Coll., matric. 3 Feb., 1840, aged 18; B.A. 1843, M.A. 1846.

Maddock, Rev. George Ashby, s. John, of Greenfields, Salop, arm. Brasenose Coll., matric. 6 Feb., 1807, aged 18; B.A. 1811, M.A. 1814, of Naseby, Northants, and Greenfields, Shrewsbury, died in 1836.

Maddock, Henry John, 1s. Henry John, of Enderby, co. Leicester, cler. Wadham Coll., matric. 21 Jan., 1829, aged 18; scholar Worcester Coll. 1830-5, B.A. 1833, fellow 1835-52, M.A. 1836, held various curacies 1852-63, rector of Bonchurch, Isle of Wight, 1869-83. **[20]**

Maddock, Henry William, 4s. Thomas, of Chester (city), cler. St. John's Coll., matric. 30 June, 1823, aged 18, B.A. 1827; fellow Brasenose Coll. 1827-36, M.A. 1830, vicar of Kington, co. Hereford, 1835-50, perp. curate All Saints, St. John's Wood, 1850, until his death 18 Feb., 1870. See *Robinson*, 202.

Maddock, Hinton, s. Thomas, of Chester (city), gent. Brasenose Coll., matric. 3 Feb., 1758, aged 18; B.A. 1761, died 6 April, 1775. See Ormerod's *Cheshire*, ii. 242, 681; & *Manchester School Reg.*, i. 65.

Maddock, Matthew, s. Robert, of Sandbach, Cheshire, gent. Brasenose Coll., matric. 1 March, 1737-8, aged 16; B.A. 26 Feb., 1741-2, M.A. 1744, proctor 1754, rector of Great Catworth, Hunts, and of Holywell with Needingworth at his death 22 Jan., 1788.

Maddock, Philip Harington, o.s. Philip Bainbrigge, of Trowbridge, Wilts, cler. Lincoln Coll., matric. 23 Oct., 1882, aged 19; scholar 1882-6, B.A. 1886.

Maddock. Richard, s. Richard, of Harberton, Devon, pleb. Hart Hall, matric. 25 May, 1721, aged 17.

Maddock, Rev. Robert North, 2s. Samuel, of Long Sutton, co. Lincoln, cler. Queen's Coll., matric. 26 Jan., 1832, aged 17; clerk 1832-5, B.A. 1836, M.A. 1839, principal of Mussoorie School on the Himalayas, where he died 7 March, 1867. **[26]**

Maddock, Samuel, 4s. Thomas, of Chester (city), cler. Brasenose Coll., matric. 1 Feb., 1819, aged 18; scholar 1819-22, B.A. 1822, M.A. 1825, rector of Abdon, Salop, at his death in 1828. See *Rugby School Reg.*, 123.

Maddock, Thomas, s. Samuel, of St. Mar., Chester (city), pleb. Brasenose Coll., matric. 10 April, 1731, aged 18; B.A. 24 March, 1734-5 (and ? M.A. from Queen's Coll., Cambridge, 1747), rector of Liverpool, 1772-83. See *Manchester School Reg.*, ii. 23.

Maddock, Thomas, s. Thomas, of Liverpool, Lancashire, cler. Brasenose Coll., matric. 14 Jan., 1780, aged 17; B.A. 1783, M.A. 1786, rector of Holy Trinity, Chester, 1786, preb. of Chester 1803, rector of Coddington, Cheshire, 1806-9, and of Northenden, Cheshire, 1809, until his death 12 Feb., 1825. See *Manchester School Reg.*, ii. 23.

Maddock, (Sir) Thomas Herbert, s. Thomas, of Chester (city), cler. Brasenose Coll., matric. 3 May, 1810, aged 17; entered H.E.I.C.S. 1817, resident at Lucknow 1831, special commissioner for Moorshedabad 1837, secretary to the Indian Government 1838-43, knighted by patent 25 April, 1844, deputy-governor of Bengal and president of the Council of India 1845-9, M.P. Rochester 1852-7, died 14 Jan., 1870. See *Manchester School Reg.*, iii. 20. **[30]**

Maddock, William, B.A. from Hart Hall 3 Feb., 1724-5. See *Acts Book*.

Maddock, Rev. William Herbert, 2s. Henry William, of Kington, co. Hereford, cler. St. John's Coll., matric. 28 June, 1858, aged 18; fellow 1858-64, B.A. 1862, M.A. 1865, has held various scholastic appointments since 1863. See *Robinson*, 312.

Maddocks, Robert, s. John, of Hanmer, co. Flint, pleb. PEMBROKE COLL., matric. 6 April, 1756, aged 18; B.A. 1760. (Memo.: Rev. Mr. Maddocks, of Queen's Square, died 26 Dec., 1766.)

Maddocks, Robert, s. — M., of Ruyton, Salop, gent. PEMBROKE COLL., matric. 10 Oct., 1792, aged 17; B.A. 1797, vicar of Leighton, Salop, 1816, and rector of Sidbury 1819, until his death 2 Aug., 1851.

Maddocks, Thomas, o.s. Thomas, of Woodlands, near Wem, Salop, arm. EXETER COLL., matric. 19 May, 1864, aged 18; B.A. 1867, of Woodlands aforesaid, J.P. Salop, formerly captain Salop rifle volunteers.

Maddox, Isaac, M.A. EDINBURGH UNIVERSITY (14 Feb., 1723); commoner QUEEN'S COLL. 15 June, 1724, incorp. and B.A. by decree of convocation 9 July, 1724, M.A. from QUEEN'S COLL., Cambridge, '*Com. Reg.*' 1728, D.D. 'per *Lit. Reg.*' 1731, preb. of Chichester 1725, dean of Wells 1734, bishop of St. Asaph 1736-43, bishop of Worcester 1743, until his death 27 Sep., 1759, father of the next named.

Maddox, Isaac Price, born at Hartlebury, co. Worcester, s. Isaac, bishop of Worcester. QUEEN'S COLL., matric. 6 May, 1757, aged 16. [5]

Maddox, John Mortimer, 1s. John Mortimer, of London, arm. PEMBROKE COLL., matric. 25 Oct., 1871, aged 19; B.A. & M.A. 1878, a student of the Middle Temple 1873, vicar of St. Mark, Bury, Lancashire, 1884.

Maddox, Stuart Lockwood, 2s. Ralph Henry, of Alleppey, East Indies, cler. WORCESTER COLL., matric. 22 Oct., 1885, aged 19; exhibitioner 1885, of the Indian Civil Service 1885.

Maddox, Walter Mynors, 1s. Thomas, of Welshpool, co. Montgomery, gent. JESUS COLL., matric. 28 Jan., 1874, aged 18; scholar 1876-9, B.A. 1877, M.A. 1880.

Maddox, William, s. William, of Bishops Hampton, co. Hereford, pleb. MERTON COLL., matric. 19 March, 1752, aged 18.

Maddy, Edwin, B.A. from PEMBROKE COLL., Cambridge, 1816, M.A. 1819, o.s. Philo., of Gloucester (city), arm. BRASENOSE COLL., incorp. 18 or 19 Feb., 1853, aged 39; B.C.L. 26 Feb., 1835, D.C.L. 5 March, 1835, bar.-at-law, Middle Temple, 1821, deputy chancellor diocese of Gloucester, died 13 Oct., 1867. [10]

Maddy, John, s. Joseph, of Dorston, co. Hereford, pleb. JESUS COLL., matric. 11 Oct., 1784, aged 18; B.A. 1788, M.A. 1791, B. & D.D. 1812, rector of Somerton, Suffolk, 1799, of Hartest with Boxted 1819, and of Stansted 1820, of Cambridge University 'ad eundem' 10 Dec., 1835, chaplain in ordinary to the King 1835, canon of Ely 1835, until his death 17 June, 1853.

Madeley, Walter, 1s. Frederick, of Handsworth, Stafford, gent. NEW COLL., matric. 10 Oct., 1884, aged 19; scholar 1884.

Madely, Clement, s. John Baily, of Uttoxeter, co. Stafford, gent. BRASENOSE COLL., matric. 16 Feb., 1792, aged 18; B.A. 1795, M.A. 1798, B. & D.D. 1828, vicar of Horncastle 1802, and of Stickford, co. Lincoln, 1829, until his death 21 March, 1845.

Madgett, Patrick, 'pharmacopola;' privilegiatus 23 Dec., 1826.

Madocks, John, s. John, of Talgarth, co. Brecon, pleb. JESUS COLL., matric. 12 July, 1775, aged 18; B.A. 1779, M.A. 1782. [15]

Madocks, John, s. John Edward, of North Cray, Kent, arm. CHRIST CHURCH, matric. 24 Oct., 1804, aged 18; of Vron Iw, and Glanywern, co. Denbigh, M.P., Denbigh (borough) 1832-3, died 20 Nov., 1837.

Madocks, John Edward, s. John, of Vron Iw, co. Denbigh, arm. MAGDALEN COLL., matric. 25 Aug., 1777, aged 17; created M.A. 15 Dec., 1781, of Vron Iw, father of John 1804.

Madocks, Joseph, s. John, of St. Andrew's, Holborn, London, arm. MAGDALEN COLL., matric. 17 March, 1781, aged 18; brother of John Edward, and of the next named.

Madocks, William Alexander, s. (John), of London, arm. CHRIST CHURCH, matric. 1 March, 1790, aged 16, B.A. 1793; fellow ALL SOULS' COLL. 1794-1818, M.A. 1799. See *Gent.'s Mag.*, 1809, ii. 685.

Maffei, (Francis) Scipio, Marquis of Verona, created D.C.L. 28 May, 1736, Italian writer and antiquary, F.R.S., died 11 Feb., 1755, aged 80. [20]

Magan, Rev. Charles Henry, 5s. Arthur, of St. Thomas, Dublin, arm. ST. JOHN'S COLL., matric. 7 June, 1821, aged 17; B.A. 1825, died 16 June, 1829.

Magee, Charles Smith, 1s. William Connor, bishop of Peterborough. EXETER COLL., matric. 15 Oct., 1879, aged 18; B.A. 1883, bar.-at-law, Middle Temple, 1886.

Magee, George, of TRINITY COLL., Cambridge, adm. 'comitatis causa' 19 April, 1866; B.A. TRINITY COLL., Dublin, 1827, rector of Acton Scott, co. Hereford, 1856.

Magee, William Connor, bishop of Peterborough (1868), created D.C.L. 21 June, 1870 (s. William, archbishop of Dublin), scholar TRINITY COLL., Dublin, 1838, B.A. 1842, M.A. & B.D. 1854, D.D. 1860, minister of the Octagon Chapel, Bath, 1851-6, perp. curate Quebec Chapel 1856-64, rector and vicar of Enniskillen, and precentor of Clogher 1860-4, dean of Cork 1864-8, and of the vice-regal chapel, Dublin 1866-9, select preacher Oxford 1880-2. See *Crockford*.

Magenis, Frederick Richard, 5s. Richard, of Cheltenham, arm. CHRIST CHURCH, matric. 14 May, 1834, aged 18. [25]

Magens, John Dorrien, o.s. Magens Dorrien, of St. Marylebone, arm. CHRIST CHURCH, matric. 1[illegible] April, 1821, aged 18.

Maggs, James, s. Thomas, of Bath, Somerset, gent. MERTON COLL., matric. 15 March, 1774, aged 24; vicar of Ewell, Surrey, 1802, until his death [illegible] Sep., 1824.

Magnay, Frederick William, 1s. Frederick Arthur, of Rickmansworth, Herts, arm. MERTON COLL., matric. 4 Nov., 1863, aged 20. See Foster's *Baronetage*.

Magnus, Harry, 2s. John, of Balham, Surrey, arm. MAGDALEN COLL., matric. 20 Oct., 1870, aged 19; demy 1869-71.

Magniac, Fry, s. Francis, of Clerkenwell, Middlesex, arm. TRINITY COLL., matric. 23 Oct., 180[illegible], aged 17. [30]

Magor, Edward Auriol, 2s. John Penburthy, of Redruth, Cornwall, arm. BRASENOSE COLL., matric. 3 Dec., 1868, aged 19; B.A. 1872, M.A. 1875, [illegible] Lamellen, Cornwall, J.P.

Magor, John Furnis, 1s. John Penburthy, of Redruth, Cornwall, arm. WADHAM COLL., matric. 2 Feb., 1848, aged 18; B.A. 1851.

Magor, Reuben Frederick, 2s. John Penburthy, [illegible] Redruth, Cornwall, arm. WADHAM COLL., matric. 31 Jan., 1849, aged 17; B.A. 1853.

Magor, Richard Martin, 2s. Martin, of Penzance, Cornwall, gent. WORCESTER COLL., matric. [illegible] Oct., 1883, aged 18.

Magrath, Charles Frederick, 4s. Nicholas, of St. Peter's, Isle of Guernsey, gent. PEMBROKE COLL., matric. 29 Jan., 1858, aged 17; scholar 1858-[illegible], B.A. 1861, of the Indian Civil Service 1861, di[ed] 13 Oct., 1881. [3[illegible]]

Magrath, John Richard, 3s. (Nicholas), of St. Peter Port, Isle of Guernsey, arm. ORIEL COLL., matr[ic.] 6 Dec., 1856, aged 17, scholar 1856-60, B.A. 186[illegible], fellow QUEEN'S COLL. 1860-78, M.A. 1863, B.[D. &] D.D. 1878, lecturer 1862-4, tutor 1864-77, and de[an] 1864-74, master of the schools 1864-5, chapl[ain] 1867-78, bursar 1874-8 (moderator 1866-7, sel[ect] preacher 1867-9, public examiner 1870-2, proc[tor] 1876-7), pro-provost 1877-8, provost since 18[illegible], curator of University chest 1885, etc., etc., vicar [of] Sparsholt, Berks, 1887.

aguire, James Rochefort, 2s. John Mulloch, of Boyle, Ireland, cler. MERTON COLL., matric. 17 Oct., 1874, aged 21, postmaster 1874-9, B.A. 1877; fellow ALL SOULS' COLL. 1879-86, M.A. 1881, bar.-at-law, Inner Temple, 1883. See Foster's *Men at the Bar.*

ahomed, Rev. James Dean Keriman, 2s. Frederick, of Brighton, gent. NON-COLL., matric. 11 Oct., 1873, aged 20; B.A. from KEBLE COLL. 1877, M.A. 1887.

ahon, Edward, 4s. William Vesey, of Rawmarsh, Yorks, baronet. EXETER COLL., matric. 4 June, 1881, aged 18; B.A. 1884.

ahon, George Augustus, o.s. James Nicholas, of St. Clement Danes, London, gent. MAGDALEN HALL, matric. 15 Nov., 1848, aged 20; B.A. 1852, M.A. 1856, vicar of Leigh-on-Mendip, Somerset, since 1860.

ahon, Rev. George Edward, 2s. George Augustus, of Leigh-on-Mendip, Somerset, cler. KEBLE COLL., matric. 19 Oct., 1880, aged 19; B.A. 1883, M.A. 1888. [5]

ahon, George William, o.s. William, of Swansea, Glamorgan, gent. PEMBROKE COLL., matric. 3 Dec., 1824, aged 16; scholar 1824-8, B.A. 1828, fellow 1828-37, M.A. 1831, garrison chaplain Fort St. George, Madras, died 3 Sep., 1865.

ahon, Rev. James Vesey, 3s. William Ross Vesey, of Rawmarsh, Yorks, baronet. EXETER COLL., matric. 23 Nov., 1878, aged 18; B.A. 1882, M.A. 1885, died 27 Jan., 1887. See Foster's *Baronetage.*

ahon, Ross, 1s. William Ross, of Rawmarsh, Yorks, cler. UNIVERSITY COLL., matric. 21 May, 1875, aged 19; died in 1875.

ahon, Thomas George Stacpoole, 1s. Charles, of Kingstown, near Dublin, arm. TRINITY COLL., matric. 12 Oct., 1867, aged 19; B.A. 1871, of Corbally, co. Clare, J.P., high sheriff 1880, bar.-at-law, Inner Temple, 1873. See Foster's *Men at the Bar.*

ahony, George Philip Gun, 1s. Peirce Kenifeck, of St. Peter's, Dublin, arm. ORIEL COLL., matric. 13 March, 1861, aged 18; B.A. 1866, of Kilmorna and Gunsborough, co. Kerry, J.P., D.L., high sheriff 1877, a student of the Inner Temple 1868. See *Rugby School Reg.* [10]

Mahony, John (Hickson), 2s. John Hickson, of Dingle, Kerry, arm. CHRIST CHURCH, matric. 4 June, 1835, aged 18; student 1835-49, B.A. 1839, M.A. 1842, of Tubrid, co. Kerry, J.P., assumed the name MAHONY in lieu of HICKSON. See *Alumni West.*, 511.

Mahony, Peirce Charles de Lacy, 3s. Peirce Kenifeck, of Dublin, arm. MAGDALEN COLL., matric. 29 Jan., 1870, aged 19; of Kilmorna, co. Kerry, J.P., assistant land commissioner 1881-4, M.P. North Meath July, 1886. See *Rugby School Reg.*

Mahony, Richard John, 1s. Denis, of Tralee, Kerry, cler. WORCESTER COLL., matric. 13 Nov., 1845, aged 17; B.A. 1849, of Dromore Castle, co. Kerry, J.P., D.L., high sheriff 1853.

Maidlow, John Mott, 2s. William, of Lambeth, Surrey, arm. QUEEN'S COLL., matric. 11 June, 1857, aged 18; taberdar 1857-62, B.A. 1861, fellow 1862-75, M.A. 1864, Eldon law scholar 1864-7, bar.-at-law, Lincoln's Inn, 1867. See Foster's *Men at the Bar.*

Maidman, James, s. John, of Henley, Oxon, gent. MERTON COLL., matric. 24 June, 1758, aged 16; rector of Little Greenford, Middlesex, 1789, and of Perrivale, Middlesex, and minister of Kingsland Chapel, died 19 Oct., 1809, his widow died 12 Sep., 1818. [15]

Maidment, Horace James, 2s. Thomas, of Henstridge, Somerset, gent. JESUS COLL., matric. 18 Oct., 1883, aged 18.

Main, Francis, 3s. Robert, of Greenwich, Kent, cler. PEMBROKE COLL., matric. 19 Oct., 1865, aged 22; B.A. 1868, M.A. 1872, bar.-at-law, Inner Temple, 1873, a master in Bristol Grammar School. See Foster's *Men at the Bar* & *Robinson*, 315.

Main, Francis Ingram, 1s. Robert, of Epsom, Surrey, gent. LINCOLN COLL., matric. 10 June, 1868, aged 17.

Main, James, 7s. William, of Burghead, near Elgin, pleb. NON-COLL., matric. 15 Oct., 1881, aged 26.

Main, Philip Thomas, scholar ST. JOHN'S COLL., Cambridge, 1859-63, 6th Wrangler and B.A. 1862, fellow 1863, M.A. 1865; adm. 'comitatis causa' 22 June, 1865. [20]

Main, Rev. Robert, 1s. Thomas, of Upnor, Kent, gent. PEMBROKE COLL., incorp. 12 Oct., 1860, aged 52; M.A. (by decree) 25 Oct., 1860; fellow of QUEEN'S COLL., Cambridge, 1836-8, 6th Wrangler and B.A. 1834, M.A. 1837, F.R.S. 1860, F.R.A.S., 1st assistant Royal Observatory, Greenwich, 1845-60, Radcliffe observer 1860, until his death 9 May, 1878, father of Francis 1865, and of Philip Thomas.

Maine, (Sir) Henry James Sumner (K.C.S.I.), 1s. James of Hockliffe, Beds, D. Med., fellow of CORPUS CHRISTI COLL. 1867-79, incorp. 26 Feb., 1870, aged 46; hon. fellow 1882, professor of jurisprudence 1869-79, created D.C.L. 21 June, 1865; B.A. from PEMBROKE COLL., Cambridge (senior classic, 1st chancellor's medallist), 1844; tutor TRINITY HALL 1844-7, M.A. 1847, LL.D. 1847, regius professor of civil law 1847, Rede lecturer 1875, bar.-at-law, Lincoln's Inn, 1850, and of the Middle Temple (*ad eundem*) 1862, bencher 1873, law member of the council of governor-general of India 1862-70, and a member of the council of Secretary of State for India 1871-88, K.C.S.I. 20 May, 1871; fellow London University and member of senate 1871-88; master of TRINITY HALL, Cambridge, 1877, until his death 5 Feb., 1888. See Foster's *Men at the Bar.*

Maingay, Frederick Thomas, 2s. William, of St. Petersburgh, gent. WADHAM COLL., matric. 8 March, 1854, aged 18.

Mainguy, James, 2s, Nicholas Maingy, of St. Peter's Port, Guernsey, arm. PEMBROKE COLL., matric. 31 Oct., 1822, aged 18; B.A. 1826, M.A. 1830, altered the spelling of his name, perp. curate of Shotwick, Cheshire, 1829, rector of St. Mary de Castro, Guernsey, 1843-60, and of St. Martin's, Guernsey, 1860-5, vicar of Hainton, co. Lincoln, 1865-79, and of South Willingham 1879, until his death 28 Jan., 1883, father of James and William Henry named below.

Mainguy, James, 1s. James, of Stanhope, co. Durham, cler. PEMBROKE COLL., matric. 3 June, 1852, aged 18. [25]

Mainguy, William Henry, 2s. James, of Stanhope, co. Durham, cler. CORPUS CHRISTI COLL., matric. 11 March, 1854, aged 17.

Maingy, Peter, s. John, of St. Peter's Port, Guernsey, gent. PEMBROKE COLL., matric. 13 June, 1809, aged 17; scholar 1812-17, B.A. 1814, M.A. 1815, curate of Bampton, Oxon, died in Guernsey 13 Dec., 1826.

Mainwaring, Rev. Algernon, 7s. Roland, of Whitmore, co. Stafford, arm. LINCOLN COLL., matric. 24 April, 1874, aged 21; B.A. 1879, M.A. 1881.

Mainwaring, Rev. Charles, s. Charles, of Bromborow, Cheshire, arm. BRASENOSE COLL., matric. 1 June, 1786, aged 17; B.A. 1790, M.A. 1792, of Oatley Park and Bromborough Hall, died 1 May, 1807, father of Townshend, 1825. See *Manchester School Reg.*, ii. 98-99.

Mainwaring, Charles, s. Thomas, of Lincoln (city), arm. CHRIST CHURCH, matric. 18 April, 1795, aged 17. [30]

Mainwaring, Charles Egerton Forbes Milman, 1s. Egerton Miles, of Isle of Mauritius, arm. MAGDALEN COLL., matric. 23 Oct., 1885, aged 18.

Mainwaring, Charles Henry, 3s. Roland, of Walcot, Bath, arm. ORIEL COLL., matric. 15 March, 1838, aged 18; B.A. 1843, rector of Whitmore, co. Stafford, 1848, until his death 3 April, 1878.

Mainwaring, Charles Kinaston, 1s. Charles, of Chester (city), cler. BRASENOSE COLL., matric. 2 May, 1821, aged 17; of Oatley Park and Bromborough Hall, Cheshire, high sheriff 1829, died 30 June, 1861.

Mainwaring, Charles Salnsbury, 1s. Townshend, of Marchwiel, co. Denbigh, arm. CHRIST CHURCH, matric. 27 May, 1863, aged 17; B.A. 1867, M.A. 1870, of Gaeltfaenan, co. Denbigh, J.P., a student of the Middle Temple 1866. See *Eton School Lists.*

Mainwaring, Edward, s. Thomas, of Nantwich, Cheshire, arm. BRASENOSE COLL., matric. 14 June, 1810, aged 16; B.A. 1814, perp. curate of Calverhall, Salop, 1843, until his death 6 July, 1869. See Foster's *Baronetage.*

Mainwaring, Edward Temple, 4s. John, of St. Aubin, Jersey, cler. WORCESTER COLL., matric. 26 April, 1873, aged 24.

Mainwaring, Frank Wodehouse Ramsay, 3s. John, of Swanswick, near Bath, cler. CHRIST CHURCH, matric. 15 Oct., 1875, aged 19; a junior student 1875-80, B.A. 1879.

Mainwaring, (Sir) Harry (Bart.), 1s. Henry, of Peover, Cheshire, baronet. CORPUS CHRISTI COLL., matric. 17 Jan., 1823, aged 18; 2nd baronet, died 23 Sep., 1875. See Foster's *Baronetage* & *Rugby School Reg.*, 128. [5]

Mainwaring, (Sir) Henry (Bart.), s. Henry, of Rosethorn, Cheshire. LINCOLN COLL., matric. 28 Feb., 1743-4, aged 17; created M.A. 23 May, 1747, 4th baronet, died unmarried 6 April, 1797.

Mainwaring, James, s. Charles, of Bromborough, Cheshire, arm. BRASENOSE COLL., matric. 28 March, 1775, aged 17; of Bromborough, died Feb., 1827, father of the next named.

Mainwaring, Rev. James, born at Besançon, 'Franche Comté,' s. James, arm. BRASENOSE COLL., matric. 15 Dec., 1806, aged 18; B.A. 1810, M.A. 1813.

Mainwaring, Percy Edward, 5s. Charles Henry, of Whitmore, co. Stafford, cler. PEMBROKE COLL., matric. 3 Feb., 1879, aged 20; B.A. 1882, rector of Whitmore since 1885.

Mainwaring, Randolph, 2s. Roland, of Whitmore, co. Stafford, arm. UNIVERSITY COLL., matric. 1 Dec., 1858, aged 19; B.A. 1862, of the Education Office, Christchurch, New Zealand. See *Rugby School Reg.* [10]

Mainwaring, Reginald Kynaston, 2s. Townshend, of Marchwiel, co. Denbigh, arm. CHRIST CHURCH, matric. 23 May, 1866, aged 18; B.A. 1871. See *Eton School Lists.*

Mainwaring, Richard, s. Rich., of London, pleb. ST. JOHN'S COLL., matric. 27 June, 1738, aged 17; until expelled 13 July, 1741. See *Robinson,* 169.

Mainwaring, Salusbury Kynaston, 1s. Charles Kynaston, of Oteley Park, near Ellesmere, Salop, arm. CHRIST CHURCH, matric. 17 April, 1863, aged 18; of Oteley Park, Salop, J.P., D.L., high sheriff 1870, and of Bromborough, Cheshire.

Mainwaring, Thomas, s. Thomas, of Lincoln (city), arm. BRASENOSE COLL., matric. 9 March, 1742-3, aged 18.

Mainwaring, Townshend, 2s. Charles Kynaston, of Oteley, Salop, arm. (? cler.). BRASENOSE COLL., matric. 3 Nov., 1825, aged 18; of Gaeltfaenan, co. Denbigh, high sheriff 1840, M.P. Denbigh 1841-68, died 25 Dec., 1883. See *Rugby School Reg.*, 140.

Maior, William, s. Thomas, of Market Harborough, co. Leicester, arm. MAGDALEN COLL., matric. 29 March, 1791, aged 17. See Nichol's *History of Leicestershire,* iv. 482. [16]

Mair, Rev. Henry Thomas, o.s. Henry, of Clifton, Somerset, cler. WADHAM COLL., matric. 28 Jan., 1846, aged 18; B.A. 1849, a student of Lincoln's Inn 1850, died 22 May, 1855.

Mair, John, 1s. John, of London, gent. WORCESTER COLL., matric. 27 Jan., 1868, aged 20.

Mairis, Henry Edwards Hale, 1s. Valentine Hale, of Aston, near Birmingham, arm. WADHAM COLL., matric. 30 Jan., 1839, aged 18.

Mairis, Robert, s. Robert, of Westminster, arm. ORIEL COLL., matric. 14 Oct., 1789, aged 17. [20]

Mairis, William, s. Robert, of St. Giles's, Middlese[x] gent. EXETER COLL., matric. 19 Jan., 1787, age[d] 19; B.A. 1791, M.A. 1808, B. & D.D. 1814, chap[lain] to the Duke of Kent, rector of St. Pete[r] Wallingford 1805, vicar of Bishops Lavington, Wilt[s] 1813, until his death, 1 May, 1828.

Maister, Rev. Arthur, 1s. John, of St. Pancra[s] London, arm. BALLIOL COLL., matric. 15 Ma[y] 1821, aged 18; B.A. 1826, M.A. 1829.

Maister, Henry, 1s. Arthur, of Winestead, York[s] arm. WADHAM COLL., matric. 17 May, 1832, age[d] 18; B.A. from NEW INN HALL 1839, M.A. 185[0] perp. curate of Thornaby, Yorks, 1845-50, curate [of] Routh, Yorks, 1850-7, vicar of Easington wit[h] Skeffling, etc., Yorks, 1858.

Maisterson, Henry, s. William, of Doncaster, York[s] gent. BRASENOSE COLL., matric. 2 April, 173[7] aged 18.

Maisterson, John, s. Rich., of Whitchurch, Salo[p] pleb. CHRIST CHURCH, matric. 23 Oct., 171[7] aged 19; B.A. 1721. [25

Maisterson, John, s. Thomas, of Nantwic[h] Cheshire, pleb. MAGDALEN HALL., matric. 1 April, 1739, aged 30. See Hall's *History of Nan[t]wich,* p. 420.

Maistre, Rev. Alexander Philip le, 3s. George Joh[n] of St. Brelads, Jersey, cler. LINCOLN COLL., matri[c] 23 Oct., 1880, aged 19; B.A. 1884, M.A. 1887.

Maistre, Francis William le, s. Francis, of St. Hillie[r] Isle of Jersey, Hants, gent. PEMBROKE COLL. matric. 22 June, 1730.

Maistre, James le, LL.D. TRINITY COLL., Dubli[n] 1856 (B.A. 1849, M.A. 1852, LL.B. & LL.D. 1856) adm. 'comitatis causa' 7 Nov., 1867.

Maistre, John Gustavus le, s. Stephen, of London, arm CHRIST CHURCH, matric. 5 July, 1786, aged 17 B.A. from QUEEN'S COLL. 1790, M.A. 1794, bar.-a[t] law, Lincoln's Inn, 1791. [30

Maistre, Philip le, 2s. Philip, of St. Bernard, Isle o[f] Jersey, gent. PEMBROKE COLL., matric. 31 May 1838, aged 19; scholar 1838-45, B.A. 1842, M.A. 184[5]

Maistre, Stephen Cæsar le, s. Cæsar, of London, arm CHRIST CHURCH, matric. 1 April, 1758, aged 20 bar.-at-law, Lincoln's Inn, 1760 (? died judge i[n] Bengal 1778).

Maistre, Rev. Sylvester John James Sullivan le, 2[s.] James, of Ingham, co. Lincoln, cler. KEBL[E] COLL., matric. 22 Jan., 1880, aged 20; B.A. 188[3] M.A. 1887.

Maistre, William de Villeneufre le, 4s. George Joh[n] of Jersey, cler. KEBLE COLL., matric. 16 Oct 1883, aged 20; B.A. 1887.

Maitland, Alexander Charles Richards, 2s. August[us] of Teignmouth, Devon, gent. CORPUS CHRIS[TI] COLL., matric. 28 April, 1865, aged 19; schol[ar] 1865-70, S.C.L. & B.A. 1870, M.A. 1872, bar.-at-la[w] Inner Temple, 1872. See Foster's *Baronetage* [&] *Men at the Bar.* [31

Maitland, Charles, s. Charles Maitland Barclay, Bath (city), arm. UNIVERSITY COLL., matric. [?] April, 1804, aged 18; rector of Little Langfor[d] Wilts, 1827, died Dec., 1844, father of Charles, 12[th] Earl of Lauderdale. See Foster's *Peerage.*

Maitland, Rev. Charles, 1s. Charles David, of Wo[ol]wich, Kent, cler. MAGDALEN HALL, matric. April. 1848, aged 33; B.A. 1852, author of 'T[he] Church in the Catacombs,' died 31 July, 1866. S[ee] Foster's *Our Noble and Gentle Families.*

Maitland, Edward Fuller-, 5s. Thomas, of W[ar]grave, Berks, arm. MAGDALEN COLL., matr[ic.] 14 Oct., 1878, aged 19; B.A. 1881.

Maitland, Elphinstone Vans Agnew, 2s. John, Madras, arm. MERTON COLL., matric. 26 Oc[t.] 1875, aged 19; postmaster 1875-7, a student of t[he] Inner Temple 1877.

Maitland, Frederick Henry, 4s. Augustus, of Exet[er] arm. CORPUS CHRISTI COLL., matric. 20 Oc[t.] 1868, aged 19; B.A. 1873. See Foster's *Baroneta[ge]* & *Rugby School Reg.* [4

Maitre, Alfred George le, 1s. Alfred William, of Twickenham, Middlesex, gent. ST. JOHN'S COLL., matric. 17 Oct., 1885, aged 19.

Majendie, Edward, born at Christleton, Cheshire, 6s. Henry William, bishop of Bangor. CHRIST CHURCH, matric. 16 Nov., 1821, aged 19; died at Milbrook, near Southampton, 15 July, 1825. See *Eton School Lists.*

Majendie, George John, born at Windsor, Berks, s. Henry (William), bishop of Bangor. CHRIST CHURCH, matric. 27 Oct., 1814, aged 19' student 1815-20, B.A. 1818; fellow MAGDALEN COLL. 1820-39, M.A. 1821, B.D. 1829, vicar of Stanton St. Bernard, Wilts. preb. of Sarum 1824, rector of Headington 1839, died 2 Nov., 1842. See *Eton School Lists.* **[20]**

Majendie, Henry Lewis, s. Lewis, of Hedingham Castle, Essex, arm. ORIEL COLL., matric. 29 April, 1814, aged 18; B.A. 1818, M.A. 1820, vicar of Great Dunmow, 1834, until his death 6 Jan., 1863.

Majendie, Henry William, 1s. George John, of Headington, Wilts, cler. EXETER COLL., matric. 22 Jan., 1858, aged 17; B.A. 1863, M.A. 1866, a student of the Middle Temple 1864, held various curacies 1866-75, vicar of Holy Trinity, Barnstaple, 1875-81, and of Tormohun, Devon, since 1884.

Majendie, Lewis Ashhurst, 1s. Henry Lewis, of Great Dunmow, Essex, cler. CHRIST CHURCH, matric. 19 May, 1853, aged 18; B.A. 1858, M.A. 1860, of Hedingham Castle, J.P., D.L., a student of Lincoln's Inn 1859, M.P. Canterbury 1874 to April, 1879, died 22 Oct., 1885.

Majendie, Rev. Severne Andrew Ashhurst, 3s. Henry Lewis, of Dunmow, Essex, cler. EXETER COLL., matric. 2 May, 1862, aged 19; B.A. 1867, M.A. 1868.

Majendie, Stuart, born at Windsor, Berks, 4s. Henry William, bishop of Bangor. CHRIST CHURCH, matric. 28 Jan., 1819, aged 19; B.A. 1822, vicar of Longdon, co. Stafford, rector of Barnwell, Northants, 1860, until his death 28 Sep., 1871. See *Eton School Lists.* **[25]**

Majendie, Stuart Routledge, 2s. Stuart, of Longdon, near Rugely, co. Stafford, cler. EXETER COLL., matric. 1 Dec., 1866, aged 18; B.A. 1870, minor canon of Gloucester 1878-83, sacrist 1878-81, librarian 1878-83, precentor 1882-3, vicar of Brookthorpe, co. Gloucester, since 1883.

Major, James, s. Alexander, of Londonderry (town), arm. QUEEN'S COLL., matric. 12 April, 1810, aged 18; a student of Lincoln's Inn 1815.

Major, John Henniker-, (2nd) Lord Henniker, created D.C.L. 26 June, 1816 (1s. John, 1st Lord Henniker), bar-at-law, Lincoln's Inn, 1777, assumed the surname and arms of MAJOR in 1792, M.P. Romney 1785-90, Steyning 1794-1802, Rutland 1805-12, Stamford 1812-18, died 5 Dec., 1821. See Foster's *Peerage.*

Major, Rev. John Richardson, 1s. John Richardson, of Thetford, Norfolk, cler. EXETER COLL., matric. 14 Nov., 1839, aged 18; B.A. 1845, M.A. 1846, master in King's College School, London, 1846-56, head-master Crypt School, Gloucester, 1863-7, master of Wye College, Kent, 1867, until his death 20 Feb., 1871.

Major, Rev. Thomas Noon Talfourd, o.s. William Wreford, of Putney, Surrey, arm. EXETER COLL., matric. 25 Jan., 1879, aged 19; B.A. 1884. **[30]**

Major, William, s. Jos., of St. Mary Aldermanbury, Middlesex, arm. BALLIOL COLL., matric. 21 Feb., 1716-7, aged 18; B.A. 1720.

Makepeace, John, s. William, of Swalcliffe, Oxon, pleb. CHRIST CHURCH, matric. 1 July, 1725, aged 18; B.A. 1729.

Makepeace, William, s. William, of St. Nicholas, town of Warwick, gent. MERTON COLL., matric. 29 March, 1715, aged 16, B.A. 6 Feb., 1718-9; M.A. from ORIEL COLL. 1722, bar.-at-law, Middle Temple, 1723, died 11 Nov., 1739.

Makgill, Arthur, 3s. George, of Kemback, co. Fife, Scotland, arm. UNIVERSITY COLL., matric. 22 May, 1861, aged 18; scholar 1861-6, B.A. 1865, M.A. 1879.

Makin, Thomas, fellow of CHRIST COLL., Cambridge (B.A. 1730, M.A. 1734); incorp. 13 July, 1741.

Makin, Thomas, s. Henry, of Prescott, Lancashire, gent. BRASENOSE COLL., matric. 17 March, 1755, aged 16; B.A. 1758.

Malaher, William Ernest, 1s. Lewis, of Reading, Berks, gent. ALL SOULS' COLL., matric. 22 April, 1865, aged 19; bible clerk 1865-9, B.A. 1869, M.A. 1872, curate of Royston, Herts, 1871-3, vicar 1874-7, rector of Weston Turville, Herts, since 1877. [4]

Malan, Rev. Alfred Henry, 4s. Solomon Cæsar, of Broadwindsor, Dorset, cler. ST. ALBAN HALL, matric. 31 Jan., 1870, aged 17; B.A. 1874, M.A. 1877.

Malan, Rev. Arthur Noel, 2s. Solomon Cæsar, of Broadwindsor, Dorset, cler. ORIEL COLL., matric. 18 Oct., 1865, aged 19; B.A. & M.A. 1872, head-master Eagle House School, Wimbledon, since 1874.

Malan, Edward Charles, 3s. Solomon Cæsar, of Bath, cler. WORCESTER COLL., matric. 17 Oct., 1868, aged 20; exhibitioner 1868-72, B.A. & M.A. 1876.

Malan, Solomon Cæsar, 1s. Cæsar, of Geneva, cler. ST. EDMUND HALL, matric. 6 July, 1833, aged 21, B.A. 1837; M.A. from BALLIOL COLL. 1843, created D.D. Edinburgh University 1880, vicar of Broadwindsor, Dorset, 1845-85, preb. of Salisbury 1870-5, secretary to Asiatic Society of Bengal 1839, etc.; for list of his works see *Crockford*.

Malbon, Samuel, 'pharmacopola;' privilegiatus 28 Sep., 1751. [9]

Malcolm, Archibald, of TRINITY COLL., Cambridge (B.A. 1828, M.A. 1832); adm. 'ad eundem' 7 March, 1845, curate of Wellesbourne, co. Warwick.

Malcolm, Gilbert, fellow TRINITY COLL., Cambridge, (B.A. 1796, M.A. 1799); adm. 'ad eundem' 26 June, 1816, incumbent of Todenham, co. Gloucester, 1812, until his death 16 April, 1855, a brother of Sir John.

Malcolm, James Aratoon, 4s. Aratoon, of Bashera, Persia, arm. BALLIOL COLL., matric. 10 Feb., 1886, aged 18.

Malcolm, Sir John, created D.C.L. 26 June, 1816 (son of George Malcolm, of Burnfoot, co. Dumfries), the celebrated Eastern diplomatist and historian, G.C.B., major-general E.I.C.S., minister plenipotentiary at the Court of Persia, knight of the Lion and the Sun (Persia) 22 Sep., 1812, knighted 15 Dec., 1812, G.C.B., nominated 26 Nov., 1819, installed 1821, major-general 1822, governor of Bombay 1827-31, M.P. Launceston 1831-2, died 30 May, 1833, statue in Westminster Abbey.

Malcolm, John, 3s. Neill, of St. George's, Hanover Square, London, arm. CHRIST CHURCH, matric. 6 Feb., 1824, aged 18; B.A. 1827, M.A. 1830, of Poltalloch, co. Argyll, J.P., D.L., and of Lamorbey, Kent, J.P., D.L., a student of Lincoln's Inn, 1829.

Malcolm, John Wingfield, 1s. John, of Hanover Square, London, arm. CHRIST CHURCH, matric. 16 Oct., 1850, aged 17; B.A. 1856, M.A. 1865, of Achnanama, Argyllshire, J.P., D.L., M.P. (July) 1886, and for Boston 1860-8, and 1874-8, etc. See *Eton School Lists*. [15]

Malcolm, Neill, s. Neill, of St. George's, Hanover Square, London, arm. CHRIST CHURCH, matric. 23 May, 1817, aged 19; B.A. 1824, M.A. 1826, of Poltollach, co. Argyle, J.P., a student of Lincoln's Inn 1818, M.P. Boston 1826-31, died 2 Oct., 1857.

Malcolm, Russell, y.s. George Russel, of Lambeth, Surrey, arm. UNIVERSITY COLL., matric. 8 Dec., 1825, aged 19; B.A. 1830. See *Eton School Lists.*

Malcolm, William Rolle, y.s. John, of Lamorbey, near Bexley, Kent, arm. BALLIOL COLL., matric. 28 May, 1858, aged 18, B.A. 1862; fellow ALL SOULS' COLL. 1864-75, M.A. 1865, bar.-at-law, Lincoln's Inn, 1865. See Foster's *Men at the Bar*.

Malcomson, Joseph, o.s. David, of Waterford, Ireland, arm. NEW INN HALL, matric. 23 Jan., 1882, aged 19. See *Eton School Lists.*

Malden, Bingham Sibthorpe, 2s. Charles Robert, of Ryde, Isle of Wight, arm. CORPUS CHRISTI COLL., matric. 23 March, 1849, aged 18; scholar 1849-50, held various curacies 1854-70, vicar of Sheldwich, Kent, 1870. [20]

Malden, Charles Scott, elder son Henry Charles, of Brighton, arm. TRINITY COLL., matric. 14 Oct., 1876, aged 18; B.A. 1880, M.A. 1883.

Malden, Percy, 2s. Bingham Sibthorpe, of Pattingham, co. Stafford, cler. CHARSLEY HALL, matric. 31 Oct., 1882, aged 19, B.A. from KEBLE COLL. 1887.

Male, Edward, scholar of CAIUS COLL., Cambridge, 1837, 21st Wrangler and B.A. 1840, M.A. 1843; adm. 'comitatis causa' 12 March, 1868, vicar of Rathmell, Yorks, 1854-6.

Male, Joseph, s. Joseph, of Birmingham, co. Warwick, gent. ST. EDMUND HALL, matric. 14 July, 1789, aged 25.

Male, Samuel, s. Joshua, of Halesowen, Salop, gent. WORCESTER COLL., matric. 1 July, 1737, aged 16; B.A. 1741, M.A. 1744. [25]

Maleborne, Godfrey. See MALLBONE.

Malet, Alexander, s. Baldwyn, of St. Audery, Somerset, arm. BALLIOL COLL., matric. 20 May, 1724, aged 19, B.A. 23 Jan., 1727-8; M.A. from KING'S COLL., Cambridge, 1735, rector of Combe Florey, Somerset, and Maiden Newton, 1732, preb. of Bath and Wells 1741, and of Gloucester 1761, died 21 Sep., 1775, father of Sir Charles Malet, Bart.

Malet, (Sir) Alexander (Bart.), 1s. Charles Warre, of Biddeston, Wilts, baronet. CHRIST CHURCH, matric. 19 Jan., 1819, aged 18; B.A. 1822, 2nd baronet, K.C.B. 1866, in diplomatic service 1824-66, died 28 Nov., 1886. See Foster's *Baronetage*.

Malet, Clement Drake Elton, 3s. William Wyndham, of Ardeley, near Buntingford, Herts, cler. PEMBROKE COLL., matric. 4 Feb., 1868, aged 22; B.A. 1871, rector of Lympston, Devon, 1879. See Foster's *Baronetage.*

Malet, (Sir) Edward Baldwin (G.C.B., G.C.M.G.), born in Holland, 2s. Alexander, baronet. CORPUS CHRISTI COLL., matric. 14 April, 1856, aged 18; minister plenipotentiary at Brussels 1883, and at Berlin 1884, G.C.B. 9 Feb., 1886, G.C.M.G. 26 June, 1885, privy councillor 1885, entered diplomatic service 1854. See Foster's *Baronetage* & *Eton School Lists.* [30]

Malet, William Wyndham, 3s. Charles Warre, of Newton Toney, Wilts, baronet. MAGDALEN HALL, matric. 15 Dec., 1834, aged 30; of Bombay Civil Service 1823-34, vicar of Ardeley, Beds, 1843, until his death 12 June, 1885. See Foster's *Baronetage.*

Malim, George, 1s. George Warcup, of Higham Ferrers, Northants, cler. LINCOLN COLL., matric. 23 April, 1825, aged 18; exhibitioner 1827-31, B.A. 1830, vicar of Higham Ferrers, Northants, 1837, until his death 7 April, 1868.

Malim, Henry, 4s. Wentworth, of St. Giles, Middlesex, gent. ST. JOHN'S COLL., matric. 22 Feb., 1839, aged 18; B.A. 1842, vicar of Great Wakering, Essex, since 1872. See *Robinson*, 232.

Malin, George (Pasley), s. Thomas, of Doncaster, Yorks, gent. BRASENOSE COLL., matric. 23 Oct., 1747, aged 18; B.A. 1751, rector of Harpole, and 40 years vicar of Higham Ferrers and Irtlingborough, Northants, died 14 Dec., 1802, aged 75.

Malin, Massey. BRASENOSE COLL., 1718. See MALYN. [35]

Maling, Henry Bromley, 1s. Thomas James, of Christchurch, New Zealand, gent. KEBLE COLL., matric. 16 Oct., 1883, aged 19; B.A. 1886.

Malkin, Benjamin Heath, from TRINITY COLL., Cambridge (B.A. 1792, M.A. 1802), s. Thomas, of St. Mary-le-Bow, London, arm. ST. MARY HALL, incorp. 2 or 3 March, 1810, aged 39; B.C.L. 6 March, 1810, D.C.L. 9 March, 1810, master of Bury St. Edmund's Grammar School 1809-28, F.S.A., died 26 May, 1842, father of Sir Benjamin, judge at Calcutta, who died there 21 Oct., 1837.

Mallabone, Robert, s. Robert, of Berkswell, co. Warwick, cler. TRINITY COLL., matric. 30 May, 1734, aged 17.

Mallaby, John Jackson, 3s. Joseph, of Birkenhead, co. Cheshire, arm. EXETER COLL., matric. 14 June, 1859, B.A. 1863, M.A. 1866, a student of the Inner Temple 1863, vicar of St. James's, Brighton, since 1873. See *Rugby School Reg.*

Mallack, John, s. John, of Pitminster, Somerset, gent. ST. JOHN'S COLL., matric. 18 Feb., 1735-6, aged 18; bar.-at-law, Inner Temple, 1743, J.P. Somerset, died in 1791.

Mallam, Benjamin, 5s. Thomas, of Oxford, gent. ST. JOHN'S COLL., matric. 29 June, 1846, aged 18; B.A. 1850, M.A. 1853, held various curacies 1853-62, rector of Poole-Keynes, co. Gloucester, 1862. See *Robinson*, 264.

Mallam, Charles George Cave, 4s. Thomas, of Oxon, arm. NON-COLL., matric. 12 Oct., 1878, aged 19; B.A. 1884, M.A. 1886. [5]

Mallam, Richard Freeborn, 3s. Richard, of Hook Norton, Oxon, gent. ST. ALBAN HALL, matric. 16 Oct., 1866, aged 18, B.A. 1876; M.A. from CHRIST CHURCH 1877, chaplain 1876-7, vicar of Stanway, co. Gloucester, 1884.

Mallam, Thomas William, 1s. Thomas, of St. Giles's, Oxford, gent. EXETER COLL., matric. 19 Jan., 1872, aged 19; B.A. & M.A. 1879.

Mallard, Charles Edward, o.s. Charles, of Liverpool, Lancashire, arm. TRINITY COLL., matric. 5 March, 1846, aged 19; B.A. 1850, M.A. 1853.

Mallbone, Godfrey, s. Godfrey, of Rhode Island, New England, arm. QUEEN'S COLL., matric. 22 June, 1742, aged 18; died at his seat in Pomfret, in the State of Connecticut, 12 Nov., 1785. See *Gent.'s Mag.*, 1786, i. 266.

Malleson, Cecil George, o.s. Alfred Brooks, of Melbourne, gent. PEMBROKE COLL., matric. 27 Oct., 1885, aged 19. [10]

Malleson, Edward, 3s. John, of St. James's, Westminster, gent. QUEEN'S COLL., matric. 26 May, 1849, aged 21; B.A. 1853, M.A. 1856, vicar of Wold Newton, Yorks, 1860-3, and of Baldersby, Yorks, 1863-80, rector of Great Bookham since 1880.

Malleson, Herbert Harry, 1s. Frederick Amadeé, of Birkenhead, cler. KEBLE COLL., matric. 14 Oct., 1884, aged 20.

Malleson, Mortimer Drewe, o.s. John Nesbitt, of Gilston, Herts, gent. CORPUS CHRISTI COLL., matric. 19 Oct., 1875, aged 19; scholar 1875-80, B.A. 1880, bar.-at-law, Lincoln's Inn, 1882. See Foster's *Men at the Bar*.

Malleson, Rodbard, o.s. Francis Rodbard, of Wimbledon, Surrey, gent. HERTFORD COLL., matric. 27 Oct., 1885, aged 18.

Mallet, Alfred Simonet, 1s. Robert Philip, of Grouville, Isle of Jersey, arm. PEMBROKE COLL., matric. 9 Dec., 1858, aged 20; B.A. 1862. [15]

Mallet, Bernard, 1s. Louis, of London, knight. BALLIOL COLL., matric. 19 Oct., 1878, aged 19. See Foster's *Baronetage*.

Mallet, Charles Edward, 1s. Charles, of London, gent. BALLIOL COLL., matric. 18 Oct., 1881, aged 18; B.A. 1885.

Mallet, David, s. James, of Perth, North Britain, gent. ST. MARY HALL, matric. 2 Nov., 1733, aged 28; B.A. 15 March, 1733-4, M.A. 1734.

Mallet, Rev. Henry Francis, 1s. John Louis, of St. Pancras, London, arm. BALLIOL COLL., matric. 16 May, 1839, aged 18; B.A. 1843, M.A. 1847.

Mallet, John, s. John, of Isle of Jersey, gent. EXETER COLL., matric. 9 Dec., 1788, aged 23; rector of Grouville, Jersey, 1808, until his death 6 Feb., 1851. [20]

Mallet, Louis Dupan, 3s. Louis, of London, a knight. BALLIOL COLL., matric. 16 Oct., 1883, aged 19, a brother of Bernard.

Mallet, Robert Philip, 3s. John, of St. John's, Isle of Jersey, cler. PEMBROKE COLL., matric. 12 Oct., 1825, aged 20; B.A. 1830, M.A. 1849.

Mallet, Thomas, s. Jonathan, of 'New York, North America, arm. ORIEL COLL., matric. 14 Dec., 1789, aged 18; B.A. 1793.

Mallet, William, s. William, of Meavey, Devon, gent. PEMBROKE COLL., matric. 7 July, 1721, aged 15.

Mallison, Henry, s. Isaac, of Hampstead, Middlesex, gent. TRINITY COLL., matric. 23 April, 1800, aged 17. [25]

Mallock, Charles Herbert, 1s. Charles Herbert, of Cockington, Devon, arm. EXETER COLL., matric. 14 June, 1859, aged 18; B.A. 1862, M.A. 1869, bar.-at-law, Inner Temple, 1865, died Feb., 1875.

Mallock, Henry Reginald Arnulph, 3s. William, of Cheriton Bishop, Devon, B.D. MAGDALEN HALL, matric. 16 April, 1872, aged 21.

Mallock, Rev. John Jervis, 3s. Charles, of Cockington, Devon, arm. EXETER COLL., matric. 15 Oct., 1875, aged 19; B.A. 1879, M.A. 1882.

Mallock, William Hurrell, 1s. William, of Cheriton Bishop, Devon, cler. BALLIOL COLL., matric. 25 April, 1870, aged 21.

Mallock, Roger, s. Roger, of Totness, Devon, cler. CHRIST CHURCH, matric. 5 Feb., 1814, aged 18; B.A. 1818, M.A. 1822, bar.-at-law, Gray's Inn, 1822.

Mallock, Rev. Roger, s. Samuel, of Colleton, Devon, cler. ORIEL COLL., matric. 22 Feb., 1791, aged 19; of Cockington, died in 1846. [31]

Mallock, Samuel, s. William, of Coombe Raleigh, Devon, pleb. BALLIOL COLL., matric. 20 Feb., 1745-6, aged 17; B.A. 1753, rector of Trusham, died in 1786.

Mallock, William, 7s, Roger, of Cockington, Devon, cler. BALLIOL COLL., matric. 14 Dec., 1827, aged 17; B.A. 1831, M.A. 1834, B.D. 1841, perp. curate Tormohun, Devon, 1833-44, rector of Cheriton Bishop 1844.

Mallory, George, s. George, of Mobberley, Cheshire, cler. CHRIST CHURCH, matric. 29 Nov., 1715, aged 19; rector of Mobberley, grandfather of John H., 1789.

Mallory, Rev. George, 1s. George, of Mobberley, Cheshire, cler. BRASENOSE COLL., matric. 17 June, 1851, aged 18; B.A. from ST. MARY HALL 1857, M.A. 1858, died 8 March, 1864 (his father, George, rector of Mobberley 1832, until his death 26 July, 1885, aged 79, said to have been of B.N.C.). See *Eton School Lists*. [35]

Mallory, Henry, s. Robert Harvey, of Wootton, co. Warwick, arm. BRASENOSE COLL., matric. 13 June, 1815, aged 17.

Mallory, John Holdsworth, s. Thomas, of Huyton, Lancashire, cler. BRASENOSE COLL., matric. 20 Jan., 1789, aged 17; B.A. 1792, M.A. 1795, rector (and patron) of Mobberley 1795, fellow of the Collegiate Church of Manchester 1814, until his death 25 May, 1832.

Malone, Anthony, s. Richard, of Dublin, Ireland, arm. CHRIST CHURCH, matric. 6 April, 1720, aged 18; a student of the Middle Temple 1720, bar.-at-law, King's Inns, May, 1726, created LL.D. TRINITY COLL., Dublin, 1737, M.P. co. Westmeath 1727-60 & 1769-76, Castlemartyr 1761-8, serjeant-at-law 1740-5, prime serjeant 1754, chancellor of the exchequer, Ireland, 1757-60, P.C., died 8 May, 1776.

Malone, Edmund, created D.C.L. 5 July, 1793, then of Senlis, co. Westmeath, Ireland, evidently the Shakespearian commentator (son of Edmund Malone, judge of Court of Common Pleas, Ireland), a student of the Inner Temple 1761; scholar TRINITY COLL., Dublin, 1760, B.A. 1762, created LL.D. 1801, bar.-at-law, King's Inns, 1767, died 25 May, 1812.

Malone, Henry, s. Richard, of Moystown, Ireland, arm. CHRIST CHURCH, matric. 11 Oct., 1759, aged 18; a student of the Inner Temple 1759, left a son, Richard.

Malone, Richard (B.A. TRINITY COLL., Dublin, 1759), s. Edmund, of London, arm. CHRIST CHURCH, incorp. 11 Oct. (14 Nov.), 1759, aged 21; a student of the Inner Temple 1757, M.P. Granard 1768-76, Banagher 1783, until created Lord Sunderlin 30 June, 1785, died s.p. 14 April, 1816.

Malone, Richard, scholar TRINITY COLL., Dublin, 1745 (B.A. 1747). Incorp. from CHRIST CHURCH 28 Feb., 1762 (probably elder son of Anthony Malone, Esq.), entered the Middle Temple 1753.

Malone, Rev. Richard, of TRINITY COLL., Cambridge; scholar QUEEN'S COLL. 1844, 1st senior optime & B.A. 1846, M.A. 1849; adm. 'ad eundem' 26 June, 1851 (son of Lieut. Edmond Malone, R.N.), vicar of St. Paul's, Cornwall, 1866-76, and of Potton, Beds, 1876.

Malpas, Rev. Henry, 1s. Joseph Henry, of Measham, co. Derby, cler. ST. EDMUND HALL, matric. 27 Oct., 1836, aged 19; B.A. 1840, M.A. 1849. [5]

Malpas, Joseph Henry, s. Henry, of Knightsbridge, Middlesex, gent. EXETER COLL., matric. 15 Dec., 1809, aged 21; B.A. 1813, M.A. 1816 (? vicar of Awre, co. Gloucester, 1826.

Malpas, Rev. William, 3s. Joseph Henry, of Measham, co. Derby, cler. PEMBROKE COLL., matric. 28 May, 1841, aged 17; scholar 1841-5, B.A. 1845, M.A. 1848.

Maltby, Edward Charles, 1s. Henry Joseph, of Eglingham, Northumberland, cler. UNIVERSITY COLL., matric. 11 June, 1862, aged 19; sometime lieutenant 9th regiment. See *Rugby School Reg.*

Maltby, Rev. Edward Secker, 4s. Brough, of Whatton, Notts, cler. KEBLE COLL., matric. 14 Oct., 1879, aged 19; B.A. 1885.

Maltby, James Chadwick, 2s. Brough, of Whatton, Notts, cler. KEBLE COLL., matric. 13 Oct., 1873, aged 20; B.A. 1876, M.A. 1882, rector of Apsley Guise, Beds, 1880. [10]

Malthus, Daniel, s. Sydenham, of St. Giles, London, arm. QUEEN'S COLL., matric. 18 May, 1747, aged 17. See Morant's *Essex*, ii. 543.

Malton, Rev. William Henry Castell, o.s. William Dawes, of Hastings, Sussex, arm. KEBLE COLL., matric. 23 Nov., 1877, aged 18; B.A. 1880.

Maltus, Rev. Farmer, s. William, of Scotton, co. Lincoln, pleb. LINCOLN COLL., matric. 1 Feb., 1723-4, aged 18; lecturer, of Bermondsey, Surrey, died 26 March, 1782.

Malyn, Massey, s. Robert, of St. Mary's, Nottingham (town), gent. BRASENOSE COLL., matric. 5 May, 1718, aged 30, B.C.L. 15 May, 1718; LL.D. from QUEEN'S COLL., Cambridge, 1723. [14]

Mammatt, Arthur Simmonds, 2s. Edward, of Ashby-de-la-Zouch, co. Leicester, arm. BALLIOL COLL., matric. 21 Oct., 1867, aged 19; B.A. 1872, M.A. 1875, vicar of Castle Donnington, co. Derby, 1880.

Manaton, Peirce, s. Peirce, of St. Clement's, London, gent. CHRIST CHURCH, matric. 7 April, 1720, aged 16; B.A. 1723, M.A. 1726, B.Med. 1729, D.Med. 15 Jan., 1732-3, died at Oxford, buried in the cathedral 8 March, 1742-3. See *Alumni West.*, 271.

Manaton, Robert, s. Robert, of St. Dunstan's, London, gent. CHRIST CHURCH, matric. 23 June, 1715, aged 20; B.A. 1719, M.A. 1722, proctor 1728. See *Alumni West.*, 266.

Manbey, Rev. George Henley, 2s. George, of St. Nicholas, Guildford, gent. KEBLE COLL., matric. 13 Oct., 1873, aged 18; B.A. 1877, M.A. 1880.

Manbey, William, 1s. William, of Stepney, Middlesex, gent. QUEEN'S COLL., matric. 21 Jan., 1825, aged 20; B.A. 1829, M.A. 1832.

Manby, Arthur Francis, 2s. Aaron, of Cockren, Yorks, cler. WADHAM COLL., matric. 16 Oct., 1880, aged 19; B.A. 1884. [20]

Manby, G. F. W., a commoner of TRINITY COLL., Cambridge; adm. 'ad eundem' 10 May, 1860.

Manby, John, s. Edward, of Agmondesham, Buck: arm. MERTON COLL., matric. 29 Oct., 1782, age 19; B.A. 1787, M.A. 1789, vicar of Lancaster 180(until his death 13 Feb., 1844.

Manby, John Ralph George, 1s. John, of Lancaste (town), cler. BRASENOSE COLL., matric. 27 Jun(1832, aged 18; B.A. 1836, M.A. 1840.

Manclarke, Richard Palgrave, 1s. Richard Beatniff(of Ashbourne, co. Derby, gent. WADHAM COLL matric. 28 Jan., 1846, aged 17; B.A. 1849, M.A. 185: perp. curate Kilnwick, Yorks, 1858-61, of Woodlanc Lancashire, 1861-7, vicar of St. James's, Barrow-ir Furness, 1867-78, rector of Anmer, Norfolk, 1878.

Mandell, John Heneage, o.s. John, of Owmby, cc Lincoln, cler. EXETER COLL., matric. 29 May 1855, aged 18; B.A. 1860, M.A. 1867, vicar (Haydon Bridge, Northumberland, 1879. [25

Mandell, William, 3s. Joseph, of Wigton, Cumbe land, gent. MAGDALEN HALL, matric. 6 July 1844, aged 29; B.A. 1850.

Mander, John, 'solicitor to the University;' priv: legiatus 30 April, 1745.

Mander, Thomas, s. Thomas, of Todenham, cc Gloucester, gent. ORIEL COLL., matric. 18 Feb. 1741-2, aged 16; B.A. 1745, M A. 1748 (? died recto of Woodbridge Hasketon, Suffolk, in 1762).

Manders, Edward Hacking, 3s. Thomas, of Hounslow Middlesex, arm. NON-COLL., matric. 30 Oct. 1875, aged 21; B.A. from CHRIST CHURCH 1878 M.A. 1882. [29

Manduell, Matthewman, 2s. John, of Wigton, Cum berland, gent. QUEEN'S COLL., matric. 18 April 1826, aged 19; B.A. 1830, vicar of Ashby Puerorum co. Lincoln, 1866, until his death 29 Nov., 1874.

Manduell, William Donald, y.s. John, of Aikton Cumberland, gent. QUEEN'S COLL., matric. 1: April, 1839, aged 18.

Manera, Arthur Christie Evelegh, 2s. Gourie, of New port, Isle of Wight, arm. NON-COLL., matric. 1(Nov., 1878, aged 18.

Manesty, Charles, s. James, of Crondall, Hants, cler ST. JOHN'S COLL., matric. 23 Oct., 1790, aged 16 B.A. 1794, M.A. 1798, rector of Purley, Berks, 180c until his death 11 Nov., 1844.

Manfield, William Hardy, 1s. William, of Dorchester Dorset, gent. PEMBROKE COLL., matric. 17 Oct. 1878, aged 18.

Mangey, Benjamin, s. Arthur, of Leeds, Yorks, gen UNIVERSITY COLL., matric. 10 Oct., 1716, age 16; B.A. from LINCOLN COLL. 1720, M.A. 172 (? died lecturer of St. Mildred's, city of Londor 20 Oct., 1730). [35

Mangey, John, s. Thomas, of Ealing, Middlese: doctor. ST. MARY HALL, matric. 22 July, 174: aged 17; B.A. 1749, M.A. 1752, vicar of Gre: Dunmow, Essex, 1754, and preb. of St. Paul's unt his death 1 Nov., 1782.

Mangey, Thomas, fellow of ST. JOHN'S COLL, Can bridge (B.A. 1707, M.A. 1711, LL.D. 1719); incor 4 May, 1720, D.D. 1725, re-incorporated 22 Jul: 1732.

Mangin, (Rev.) Alexander Reuben, 1s. Reuben Cai land, of Dublin (city), arm. (rear-admiral). S: ALBAN HALL, matric. 25 May, 1824, aged 18; B. 1828, M.A. 1833, died 27 Nov., 1848.

Mangin, Edward, s. Samuel Henry, of Dublin, Ir land, arm. BALLIOL COLL., matric. 9 June, 179 aged 19; B.A. 1793, M.A. 1795, preb. of St. Patrick' Dublin, 1800-3, of Dysart 1798-1800, and of Rath (bo in Killaloe) 1803, until his death 17 Oct., 1852, aged 8

Mangin, Edward Nangreave, 1s. Edward, of Ba (city), cler. WADHAM COLL., matric. 14 Ma 1835, aged 17; B.A. 1839, M.A. 1842, vicar Horsley, co. Gloucester, 1849-61, rector of Howic Northumberland, 1862-5, and vicar of Woodho 1865, until his death 23 July, 1879. [4(

Mangin, John Cailland Stuart, 3s. Reuben Caillan of St. Marylebone, London, arm. CHRIST CHURC matric. 12 Dec., 1829, aged 18.

Mangin, Rev. Joseph Wareing, 1s. Samuel Wareing, of London, cler. LINCOLN COLL., matric. 18 Oct., 1877, aged 19; B.A. 1881.

Mangin, Robert Rattray, 3s. Edward Nangreave, of Howick, Northumberland, cler. NEW COLL., matric. 4 Dec., 1882, aged 19; B.A. 1886.

Mangin, Samuel Wareing, 2s. Edward, of Bathwick, near Bath, cler. WADHAM COLL. matric. 24 Oct., 1838, aged 17; B.A. 1843, perp. curate of St. Matthias, Stoke Newington, 1854-8, of Headington Quarry, Oxon, 1858-63, vicar of St. Columba, Kingsland-Road, London, 1863-73, rector of St. Martin, Sarum, 1873-9, vicar of Bramshaw, Hants, 1881.

Mangin, William Nangreave, 2s. Edward Nangreave, of Horsley, co. Gloucester, cler. BRASENOSE COLL., matric. 3 Dec., 1874, aged 18.

Mangles, Albert, 5s. James, of Stoke, Somerset, arm. MERTON COLL., matric. 7 Feb., 1826, aged 16; postmaster 1828-9, B.A. 1829, M.A. 1832, a student of Lincoln's Inn 1829, vicar of Horsell, Surrey, 1840, until his death 2 Nov., 1875. [5]

Mangles, Arthur Onslow, 2s. Frederick, of Compton, near Guildford, Surrey, gent. MAGDALEN COLL., matric. 9 Dec., 1853, aged 19; B.A. 1858.

Mangles, George, s. Thomas, of Stoke Damerell, Devon, arm. QUEEN'S COLL., matric. 18 June, 1781, aged 18; B.A. 1785, M.A. 1794, vicar of Lewannick, Cornwall, 1797.

Mangles, Martin, 1s. Martin, of Brixton, Surrey, gent. WORCESTER COLL., matric. 24 April, 1845, aged 20.

Maningford, John Stuckey, o.s. — M., of Bristol (city), arm. MAGDALEN HALL, matric. 30 May, 1833, aged 26.

Manisty, James, 1s. James, of Edlingham, Northumberland, cler. LINCOLN COLL., matric. 13 Oct., 1824, aged 17; exhibitioner 1825-31, B.A. 1828, M.A. 1831, perp. curate Shildon, co. Durham, 1834-62, rector of Easington 1862, until his death 12 April, 1872. [10]

Manley, Augustus Frederick, 2s. Augustus East, of London, arm. MERTON COLL., matric. 22 Jan., 1872, aged 18; B.A. from ST. ALBAN HALL 1877. See *Eton School Lists.*

Manley, Francis Hardwicke, o.s. Henry John, of Jubbulpore, India, gent. EXETER COLL., matric. 15 Oct., 1870, aged 18; scholar 1870-5, B.A. 1874, M.A. 1877, vicar of Little Dunmow, Essex, 1885-8. See *Coll. Reg.*, 164.

Manley, Isaac George; created D.C.L. 5 July, 1810, admiral of the Red 1837 (son of John Manley, a bencher of the Middle Temple), sailed with Captain Cook on his first voyage round the world, died 14 Oct., 1837, father of John S. 1812.

Manley, John, s. John, of London, arm. EXETER COLL., matric. 6 March, 1733-4, aged 17; bencher of the Middle Temple, 1768, treasurer 1781, died 5 Sep., 1801, aged 85, father of Isaac George, D.C.L., and William 1773.

Manley, John, s. John, of St. George's, Bloomsbury, London, arm. UNIVERSITY COLL., matric. 17 June, 1809, aged 17; B.A. 1813, M.A. 1818, vicar of Godmersham and Westwell, Kent, rector of Merstham 1839, until his death 28 Dec., 1875. [15]

Manley, John, s. John, of Shobrooke, Devon, arm. WADHAM COLL., matric. 8 April, 1812, aged 18; scholar 1812-19, B.A. 1816, fellow 1819-23, M.A. 1821, rector of Upton Hellion, Devon, 1829, head-master Queen Elizabeth's Free Grammar School, Crediton, 1832, rector of Hittisleigh, Devon, 1857, until his death 13 March, 1865.

Manley, John Jackson, 1s. John, of Barking, Essex, D.Med. EXETER COLL., matric. 3 Feb., 1848, aged 18; B.A. 1852, M.A. 1855, vicar of Buckfastleigh, Devon, 1858-60, rector of Cottered 1861-70, etc., died 21 July, 1886. See *Eton School Lists.*

Manley, John Pearse, s. Edward, of Sidbury, Devon, arm. ST. JOHN'S COLL., matric. 25 Oct., 1790, aged 18; B.C.L. from ST. MARY HALL 1800, D.C.L. 1804, rector of Filton, co. Gloucester, 1816, until his death 25 Nov., 1823.

Manley, John Shawe, s. Isaac George, of Checkendon, Oxon, arm. CHRIST CHURCH, matric. 22 Oct., 1812, aged 18; of Manley Hall, co. Stafford, a student of Lincoln's Inn, 1814. See *Eton School Lists.*

Manley, Orlando, s. William, of Plymouth, Devon, cler. EXETER COLL., matric. 20 Nov., 1809, aged 19; B.A. 1814, perp. curate St. Peter's, Dartmouth, 1818. [20]

Manley, William, s. John, of Newton, Cheshire, gent. BRASENOSE COLL., matric. 21 Jan., 1773, aged 18; bar.-at-law, Middle Temple, 1779, serjt.-at-law, 1808.

Manley, William, s. Orlando, of Plymouth, Devon, gent. PEMBROKE COLL., matric. 1 July, 1780, aged 27; father of Orlando 1809.

Manlove, Joseph, s. Thomas, of Scraptoft, co. Derby, cler. MAGDALEN HALL, matric. 12 March, 1718-9, aged 17; B.A. 1722 (? died rector of Hertford, Herts, 6 July, 1753).

Manlove, Thomas, of EMMANUEL COLL., Cambridge (B.A. 1717, M.A. 1727); incorp. 1 June, 1738.

Manly, Thomas, s. Henry, of Halberton, Devon, gent. BALLIOL COLL., matric 23 Feb., 1729-30, aged 18; B.A. 1733. [25]

Mann, Archibald Henry, 3s. Gother Frederick, of Milford, co. Pembroke, arm. JESUS COLL., matric. 19 Oct., 1881, aged 18; B.A. 1887.

Mann, Arthur Henry, 3s. — M., of Norwich, gent. NEW COLL., matric. 2 Nov., 1872, aged 22; B.Mus. 1874, D.Mus. 1882.

Mann, Charles James, Viscount Brome, o.s. James, Earl Cornwallis. NEW COLL., matric. 10 April, 1832, aged 18; died 27 Dec., 1835.

Mann, James Hargrave, 1s. Joshua Hargrave Sams, of London, gent. LINCOLN COLL., matric. 18 Oct., 1879, aged 18; scholar 1879-83, B.A. 1883, M.A. 1886, a student of the Inner Temple 1884.

Mann, James Saumarez, o.s James Saumarez, of St. Peter's Port, Guernsey, gent. EXETER COLL., matric. 15 Oct., 1870, aged 19, scholar 1870-5, B.A. 1874, M.A. 1878; fellow TRINITY COLL. 1879. See *Coll. Reg.*, 164. [30]

Mann, William James, 2s. Samuel Laverack, of London, gent. QUEEN'S COLL., matric. 23 Oct., 1868, aged 18, B.A. 1871, M.A. 1875; associate in music TRINITY COLL., London, 1880, minor canon, Carlisle, 1875-8, precentor 1876-8, minor canon of Winchester 1878-82, and of Bristol since 1882, sacristan and precentor 1882. See *St. Paul's School Reg.*, 342.

Manners, Lord James, born at Belvoir, Rutland, s. (John), Duke of Rutland. UNIVERSITY COLL., matric. 1 Aug., 1739, aged 18; B.A. 1742, created D.C.L. 14 April, 1749. See Foster's *Peerage.*

Manners, John James Robert (7th Duke of Rutland); created D.C.L. 21 June, 1876 (son of John Henry, 5th Duke), G.C.B. 20 April, 1880, P.C. 1852; M.A. from TRINITY COLL., Cambridge, 1839, created LL.D. 1862, chancellor Duchy of Lancaster Aug., 1886, postmaster-general 1874-80 & 1885-6, chief commissioner of works 1852, 1858-9, & 1866-8, M.P. Newark 1841-7, Colchester 1850-7, North Leicestershire 1857-85, East Leicestershire 1885-8. See Foster's *Peerage* & *Eton School Lists.*

Manners, Moses, s. Edward, of All Souls, Newcastle-upon-Tyne, pleb. LINCOLN COLL., matric. 13 May, 1778, aged 18; B.A. 1782, M.A. 1785, usher of Newcastle Grammar School 1784, perp. curate St. Anne's, Newcastle-on-Tyne 1786, and rector of Charlton St. Peter, Norfolk, 1812, and of Thelverton, Norfolk, 1813, until his death 3 Feb., 1842.

Manners, Thomas, s. William, of Drayton, Middlesex, arm. (after lord). MERTON COLL., matric. 14 May, 1752, aged 20; B.C.L. 1760, rector of Ayleston, co. Leicester, 1755, and of Silk Willoughby, co. Lincoln, 1760, until his death in 1812, uncle of Sir William Manners, Bart. See Foster's *Peerage*, E. DYSART.

Manners, Walter, s. Edward, of Goadby Marwood, co. Leicester, arm. QUEEN'S COLL., matric. 30 March, 1811, aged 21; created M.A. 17 Nov., 1814.

Mannin, William, s. William, of Lambeth, Surrey, pleb. EXETER COLL., matric. 4 July, 1764, aged 19; B.A. 1768.

Manning, Charles, of GONVILLE and CAIUS COLL., Cambridge (B.A. 1735); incorp. 16 April, 1741.

Manning, Charles Downes, 1s. Charles John, of Marylebone, London, arm. BALLIOL COLL., matric. 1 Dec., 1847, aged 18; lieutenant 1st royal dragoons (? a nephew of Cardinal Manning). See *Eton School Lists*. [5]

Manning, Charles James, 2s. John Edge, of Sydney, New South Wales, arm. CORPUS CHRISTI COLL., matric. 17 April, 1861, aged 19; B.A. 1864, a student of Lincoln's Inn, 1862.

Manning, Charles James, o.s. James, of St. George's, Isle of Barbados, D.Med. QUEEN'S COLL., matric. 20 April, 1866, aged 19.

Manning, Frederick James, 2s. William, of St. Anne's, Soho, London, gent. LINCOLN COLL., matric. 20 March, 1839, aged 18; scholar 1839-43, B.A. 1842, M.A. 1845, B.C.L. & D.D. 1860, held various curacies 1845-66, vicar of St. John Baptist, Harlow, 1871-4, rector of St. Leonard's, Colchester, 1874-86, and of Fairstead since 1886.

Manning, George William, 4s. Isaac, of Easton Neston, Northants, gent. ST. ALBAN HALL, matric. 28 Jan., 1836, aged 26.

Manning, Henry, s. Thomas, of Harberton, Devon, pleb. HART HALL, matric. 1 March, 1721-2, aged 18; B.A. 17 March, 1725-6, father of the next named, and of Thomas 1749. [10]

Manning, Henry, s. Henry, of Upton Hellions, Devon, cler. WADHAM COLL., matric. 17 June, 1753, aged 18; B.A. from ALL SOULS' COLL. 1757, rector of Stokeinteignhead, 1758, and of Drewsteignton, Devon, 1808, until his death 13 March, 1810.

Manning, Henry Edward, 3s. William, of Totteridge, Herts, arm. BALLIOL COLL., matric. 2 April, 1827, aged 18, B.A. 1830; fellow MERTON COLL. 1832-7, M.A. 1833, rector of Lavington 1834-51, archdeacon of Chichester 1840-51, seceded to Rome, archbishop of Westminster and Metropolitan 1865, Cardinal 1875. See Foster's *Baronetage*, HUNTER.

Manning, John, s. Samuel, of Aldersgate, London, gent. ST. MARY HALL, matric. 5 July, 1773, aged 18; B.C.L. 1780, died at Frogmore Lodge, High Wycombe, 30 Sep., 1822, aged 68; Rev. John Manning, LL.B., an alderman of the corporation, mayor 1790. See *Gent.'s Mag.*

Manning, Thomas, s. Henry, of Silverton, Devon, cler. EXETER COLL., matric. 13 Dec., 1749, aged 18; B.A. from MERTON COLL. 1753.

Manning, William, s. Charles, of Cransley, Northants, cler. HART HALL, matric. 2 Dec., 1736, aged 19; B.A. 1740. See *Robinson*, 79. [15]

Manning, William Hubert, 2s. William Montagu, of Sydney, Australia, knight. EXETER COLL., matric. 19 Jan., 1872, aged 20; B.A. 1876, bar.-at-law, Lincoln's Inn, 1877. See Foster's *Men at the Bar*.

Manningham, John, s. Simon, of Eastbourne, Sussex, doctor. ST. JOHN'S COLL., matric. 5 March, 1743-4, aged 16; B.A. 1747.

Manoukian, Orshag Sarkis Senekerim, 3s. Senekerim, of Guedik, near Constantinople. BALLIOL COLL., matric. 17 Oct., 1882, aged 18; a commoner of NEW INN HALL in 1885.

Mansel, Bussy, born in St. Anne's, Westminster, s. Thomas, baron. CHRIST CHURCH, matric. 13 July, 1717, aged 16; 4th Baron Mansel, M.P. Cardiff 1727-34, Glamorganshire 1737-44, died 29 Nov., 1750.

Mansel, George Christopher, 1s. John, of London, gent. ST. JOHN'S COLL., matric. 16 Oct., 1875, aged 18; B.A. 1880, a student of the Middle Temple 1877. [20]

Mansel, Henry Longueville, 1s. Henry, of Cosgrove, Northants, cler. ST. JOHN'S COLL., matric. 1 July, 1839, aged 18; fellow 1839-55, and 1864-7, B.A. 1843, M.A. 1847, dean of arts 1847, tutor 1850, B.D. 1852, tutor 1850-64, hon. fellow 1868-71, regius professor of ecclesiastical history, and a canon of CHRIST CHURCH 1867-8, D.D. 1867, prælector of moral philosophy 1855-9, Bampton lecturer 1858, Waynflete professor of moral and metaphysical philosophy (Magdalen College) 1859-67, hon. canon of Peterborough, dean of St. Paul's 1868, until his death 29 July, 1871; for list of his works see *Crockford*, & *Robinson*, 243.

Mansel, James Temple, 1s. Mansel Dawkin, of Lathbury, Bucks, arm. CHRIST CHURCH, matric. 2 June, 1821, aged 18; student 1821-32, B.A. 1825, M.A. 1827, minister of the English Chapel at St. Servans, etc., died 1 Feb., 1880. See *Alumni West.*, 488.

Mansel, Lort, s. Thomas, of Pembroke, arm. TRINITY COLL., matric. 28 Feb., 1811, aged 19; B.A. 1815, vicar of Ministerworth, co. Gloucester, 1817, until his death in May, 1854.

Mansel, Raleigh Addenbroke, s. Raleigh, of Swansea, co. Glamorgan, arm. CHRIST CHURCH, matric. 1 June, 1813, aged 19; high sheriff co. Carmarthen 1844. See *Eton School Lists*.

Mansel, Rawleigh Dawkins, s. William, of Pennard, co. Glamorgan, arm. JESUS COLL., matric. 3 May, 1723, aged 18. [25]

Mansel, Thomas, Lord, s. Robert, of Westminster, arm. CHRIST CHURCH, matric. 5 June, 1736, aged 16; 2nd baron, died unmarried 28 or 29 Jan., 1743-4.

Mansel, William John, s. William, of St. Marylebone, baronet. UNIVERSITY COLL., matric. 20 Nov., 1809, aged 17; B.A. 1812, M.A. 1815, chaplain to George IV., rector of Hethe, Oxon, 1816, and of Ellesborough, Bucks, 1817, until his death 5 April, 1823.

Mansell, Rawleigh, s. Edward, of Pembrey, co. Carmarthen, baronet. JESUS COLL., matric. 8 July, 1715, aged 18; of the Trimsaran family.

Mansell, Rawleigh, s. Mansell (*sic*), of Swansey, co. Glamorgan, arm. JESUS COLL., matric. 17 Dec., 1762, aged 17 (? rector of Newick, Sussex, 1784).

Mansell, Waldemar, 3s. Alfred, of Copenhagen, Denmark, arm. UNIVERSITY COLL., matric. 7 May, 1856, aged 18; B.A. 1859, M.A. 1863. [30]

Mansfield, Arthur, 5s. Edward, of Bisley, co. Gloucester, cler. CHRIST CHURCH, matric. 4 June, 1846, aged 19; B.A. 1850, M.A. 1853, curate of Shirehampton, co. Gloucester, 1850-9, and vicar 1859-80, vicar of Elberton, co. Gloucester, 1880.

Mansfield, Edward, 2s. Edward, of Bisley, co. Gloucester, cler. EXETER COLL., matric. 17 May, 1838, aged 18; B.A. 1842, held various curacies 1843-76.

Mansfield, Edward Dillon, 1s. Joseph, of Bath, Somerset, cler. TRINITY COLL., matric. 15 Oct., 1864, aged 19; B.A. 1867, M.A. 1877.

Mansfield, John, s. William, of All Souls, Derby (town), pleb. BRASENOSE COLL., matric. 8 July, 1745, aged 21.

Mansfield, Joseph, 1s. Edward, of Bisley, co. Gloucester, cler. TRINITY COLL., matric. 21 Nov., 1833, aged 17; B.A. 1837, M.A. 1842, perp. curate New Swindon 1844-50, rector of Blandford St. Mary 1850-81. [35]

Mansfield, Robert Blachford, 2s. John, of Rowner, Hants, cler. UNIVERSITY COLL., matric. 1 Dec., 1842, aged 18; B.A. 1846, bar.-at-law, Inner Temple, 1849. See Foster's *Men at the Bar.*

Mansfield, Lieut.-General Sir William Rose, G.C.B., G.C.S.I., created D.C.L. 22 June, 1870 (5th son of James Mansefield, of Diggeswell House, Herts), served in the Sutlej and Punjab campaigns, chief of the staff during Indian Mutiny, commander-in-chief India 1865-70, colonel 38th regiment 1862-6, created Baron Sandhurst 28 March, 1871, died 23 June, 1876. See Foster's *Peerage.*

Manson, Alexander Thomas Grist, of TRINITY COLL., Cambridge, 1s. Alexander, of St. Mary's, Nottingham, D.Med. MAGDALEN COLL., incorp. 25 Oct., 1838, aged 22; B.C.L. 1840, D.C.L. 1849, vicar of Glossop, co. Derby, 1849, until his death 21 Dec., 1856.

Manson, Edward William Donoghue, o.s. Frederick Robert, of London, D.Med. BRASENOSE COLL., matric. 4 June, 1868, aged 18; scholar 1868-72, B.A. 1873, bar.-at-law, Middle Temple, 1878. See Foster's *Men at the Bar* & *St. Paul's School Reg.*, 341.

Manson, Rev. William Pitt, 1s. William Pitt, of Islington, Middlesex, arm. WADHAM COLL., matric. 25 Jan., 1862, aged 18; scholar 1861-6, B.A. 1866, M.A. 1869, died 15 April, 1873. [5]

Manston, Rev. Augustus Constantine, 1s. Augustus, of Liverpool, gent. NON-COLL., matric. 18 Oct., 1880, aged 19; B.A. from MERTON COLL. 1884.

Mant, Frederick Woods, born at Crawley, Hants, 2s. Richard, bishop of Down and Connor, in Ireland. NEW INN HALL, matric. 2 Nov., 1838, aged 29; B.A. 1844, vicar of Stanford, Norfolk, 1851-8, curate of Tottington 1851-8, vicar of Woodmancote 1858-70, and of Egham 1870-9.

Mant, Richard, s. Thomas, of Havant, Hants, gent. TRINITY COLL., matric. 11 Nov., 1761, aged 16, B.A. 1765, M.A. 1768; B. & D.D. from NEW COLL. 1793, rector of All Saints, Southampton, and of Fonthill-Bishop, Wilts, at his death 29 Jan., 1817.

Mant, Richard, s. Richard, of St. John's, Southampton, doctor. TRINITY COLL., matric. 16 Oct., 1793, aged 17, B.A. 1797; fellow ORIEL COLL. 1798, M.A. 1800, B. & D.D. 1815, lecturer 1812, vicar of Great Coggeshall, Essex, 1810, rector of St. Botolph's, Bishopsgate Street, 1815, and of East Horsley, Surrey, 1818, bishop of Killaloe 1820-3, vicar of Mountsea and rector of Killodiernan, diocese Killaloe, 1821, bishop of Down and Connor 1823, and of Dromore 1842, until his death 2 Nov., 1848; for list of his works see *Gent.'s Mag.*, 1849, i. 89; & *Cotton*, i., 473; iii., 213.

Mant, Walter Bishop, 1s. Richard, of Buritan, Hants, bishop of Down and Connor, in Ireland. ORIEL COLL., matric. 6 Feb., 1824, aged 16; B.A. 1827, M.A. 1830, died in 1869. [10]

Manton, Walter Henry, 2s. William, of Kenilworth, co. Warwick, gent. ST. ALBAN HALL, matric. 20 Oct., 1868, aged 19.

Manus, Rev. John, 1s. John, of Louth, co. Lincoln, cler. NON-COLL., matric. 26 Jan., 1877, aged 22.

Manwaring, Roger Manwaring, s. John Robert Parker, of Youghall, co. Cork, Ireland, arm. BRASENOSE COLL., matric. 8 April, 1812, aged 18; B.A. 1815, M.A. 1818.

Maples, Chauncy, 3s. Frederick, of Southgate, Middlesex, gent. UNIVERSITY COLL., matric. 23 Jan., 1871, aged 18; B.A. 1875, M.A. 1879, archdeacon of Nyassa, Central Africa, 1886.

Mapletoft, Francis, fellow of PEMBROKE COLL., Cambridge (11th Wrangler and B.A. 1752, M.A. 1755); incorp. 8 July, 1756, rector of Aynho, Northants, at his death 9 Dec., 1807, aged 78. [15]

Mapletoft, John, fellow of CLARE HALL, Cambridge (B.A. 1706, M.A. 1710); incorp. 11 July, 1719.

Mapletoft, John, fellow of PEMBROKE HALL, Cambridge (B.A. 1706, M.A. 1710); incorp. 12 July, 1718 (? vicar of Boltham, co. Lincoln, 1736).

Mapletoft, John, s. John, of Chester (city), cler. BRASENOSE COLL., matric. 7 March, 1746-7, aged 17; B.A. 1750.

Mapleton, David, s. David, of Reading, Berks, gent. ST. ALBAN HALL, matric. 19 July, 1783, aged 32.

Mapleton, David, 4s. James Henry, of Christ Church, Surrey, cler. ST. JOHN'S COLL., matric. 28 June, 1841, aged 18; B.A. 1845, M.A. 1863, vicar of Meanwood, Yorks, 1850-83, and hon. canon of Ripon, See *Robinson*, 238. [20]

Mapleton, Harvey Mallory, 5s. James Henry, of Christ Church, Surrey, cler. ST. JOHN'S COLL., matric. 5 March, 1845, aged 21; B.A. 1848, M.A. 1861, perp. curate Dunstall, co. Stafford, 1857-61, rector of Badgworth, Somerset, 1861.

Mapleton, Harvey William, 1s. Harvey Mallory, of Badgworth, Somerset, cler. ST. JOHN'S COLL., matric. 11 Oct., 1884, aged 19.

Mapleton, Henry Banbury, o.s. Henry, of London, D.Med. EXETER COLL., matric. 19 Oct., 1882, aged 19; B.A. 1886.

Mapleton, James, s. David, of Odiham, Hants, pleb. TRINITY COLL., matric. 10 Oct., 1732, aged 16; B.A. from QUEEN'S COLL. 1736, M.A. 1740.

Mapleton, James Henry, s. David, of Henley, Oxon, doctor. NEW COLL., matric. 8 Nov., 1797, aged 19; B.C.L. 1808, fellow until 1812, rector of Christ Church 1809, vicar of Whaddon, Bucks, 1810, and vicar of Mitcham, Surrey, died 10 Jan., 1859. [25]

Mapleton, James Henry, 1s. James Henry, of Christ Church, Surrey, cler. WORCESTER COLL., matric. 27 Feb., 1834, aged 19; B.A. 1838, rector of Aylton, co. Hereford, 1844, until his death 5 Jan., 1869.

Mapleton, James Henry Edward, o.s. James Henry, of Titley, co, Hereford, cler. BRASENOSE COLL., matric. 19 May, 1864, aged 19; a student of the Inner Temple 1868.

Mapleton, Reginald John, 3s. James Henry, of Christ Church, Surrey, cler. ST. JOHN'S COLL., matric. 27 June, 1836, aged 18; B.A. 1840, M.A. 1857, vicar of Great Glen, co. Leicester, 1851-5, incumbent of St. Columba, Kilmartin, North Britain, 1859, dean of Argyll and the Isles, and canon of Cumbræ 1886. See *Robinson*, 226.

Maypowdre, James, s. Richard, of St. Edmund's, Exeter, Devon, pleb. EXETER COLL., matric. 22 April, 1726, aged 18; B.A. from ST. MARY HALL 1730.

Mapowder, James, s. James, of Annington, Devon, cler. EXETER COLL., matric. 16 March, 1753, aged 18; B.A. 1756. [30]

Mapp, George, s. James, of Isle of Barbados, West Indies, arm. UNIVERSITY COLL., matric. 17 Nov., 1806, aged 18.

Mapp, James, s. James, of Isle of Barbados, West Indies, arm. CHRIST CHURCH, matric. 9 May, 1766, aged 16.

March, George Edward (C.M.G.), 3s. Thomas, of Brighton, Sussex, gent. ST. MARY HALL, matric. 24 April, 1850, aged 21; clerk in Foreign Office 1855, etc., secretary to Royal Commission on Extradition 1877, C.M.G. 1881.

March, John, s. Henry, of London, arm. ST. JOHN'S COLL., matric. 26 June, 1741, aged 17.

Marchant, Arthur William, 1s. Arthur, of Brixton, Surrey, gent. NEW COLL., matric. 5 Feb., 1877, aged 26; B.Mus. 1879. [35]

Marchant, Edward le, 2s. John, of St. Helen's, Isle of Wight, cler. EXETER COLL., matric. 27 May, 1847, aged 18.

Marchant, Francis Charles le, 2s. Denis, of London, arm. BALLIOL COLL., matric. 20 Oct., 1862, aged 18; B.A. 1867. See Foster's *Baronetage* & *Eton School Lists.*

Marchant, (Sir) Henry Denis le (Bart.), 1s. Denis, of Marylebone, London, baronet. CHRIST CHURCH, matric. 2 June, 1857, aged 18; B.A. 1862, M.A. 1863, 2nd baronet, bar.-at-law, Lincoln's Inn, 1865. See Foster's *Men at the Bar.*

Marchant, Henry Ernest, 6s. Thomas, of Brabourne, Kent, gent. NEW COLL., matric. 5 Feb., 1877, aged 39.

Marchant, James le, s. William, of ——, Hants, gent. PEMBROKE COLL., matric. 6 May, 1729, aged 15; B.A. from JESUS COLL. 19 Jan., 1732-3, M.A. 1735, B.D. 1744, proctor 1743.

Marchant, James le, s. John, of Southampton (town), arm. PEMBROKE COLL., matric. 26 March, 1789, aged 17.

Marchant, James Robert Vernam, 3s. Job, of Great Chishill, Essex, cler. WADHAM COLL., matric. 11 Oct., 1872, aged 19; scholar 1872-6, B.A. 1876, M.A. 1879, bar.-at-law, Gray's Inn, 1884. See Foster's *Men at the Bar.* **[5]**

Marchant, John, s. Thomas, of Hurstpierpoint, Sussex, gent. PEMBROKE COLL., matric. 23 Nov., 1726, aged 18. See *Sussex Archæological Collection,* xxv. 199.

Marchant, Rev. John le, s. Joshua, of Sidmouth, Devon, cler. EXETER COLL., matric. 31 March, 1810, aged 17; B.A. 1814, M.A. 1816, died at Ryde 21 July, 1864, aged 71.

Marchant, John le, s. Thomas, of St. Peter's Port, Isle of Guernsey, arm. PEMBROKE COLL., matric. 3 Oct., 1752, aged 17.

Marchant, John Gaspard le, 1s. (John) Gaspard, of Dublin, equitis. CHRIST CHURCH, matric. 16 June, 1859, aged 18. See Foster's *Baronetage.*

Marchant, Joshua le, s. Joshua, of St. Peter's Port, Guernsey, gent. PEMBROKE COLL., matric. 2 April, 1748, aged 16; B.A. 1751, M.A. 1754. **[10]**

Marchant, Joshua le, s. Joshua, of Isle of Guernsey, cler. PEMBROKE COLL., matric. 3 Dec., 1779, aged 16; fellow EXETER COLL. 1783-92, B.A. 1783, M.A. 1786. See *Boase,* 113.

Marchant, Joshua le, 1s. John, of Ryde, Isle of Wight, cler. TRINITY COLL., matric. 29 May, 1846, aged 18; B.A. from ST. MARY HALL 1851, held various curacies 1851-62, died 22 May, 1887.

Marchant, Richard, s. Jabez, of Tythrington, co. Gloucester, arm. EXETER COLL., matric. 27 Oct., 1789, aged 18.

Marchant, Thomas le, s. Elisha, of Castle, Isle of Guernsey, Hants, gent. PEMBROKE COLL., matric. 30 March, 1731, aged 15; fellow EXETER COLL. 1733-9, B.A. 4 March, 1736-7, M.A. 1737, died 3 Dec., 1739. See *Boase,* 98.

Marchant, Thomas le, s. Thomas, of St. Peter's Port, Guernsey, arm. LINCOLN COLL., matric. 4 May, 1748, aged 16. **[15]**

Marchant, Thomas, s. Thomas, of Edburton, Sussex, gent. BRASENOSE COLL., matric. 4 March, 1761, aged 18; B.A. 1764.

Marchant, William, s. William, of Hurstpierpoint, Sussex, pleb. TRINITY COLL., matric. 2 Nov., 1752, aged 17; B.A. 1756, died rector of Patcham, Sussex, 10 July, 1804.

Marchant, William Hirzell le, B.A. TRINITY COLL., Dublin, 2s. John, of Isle of Guernsey, arm. EXETER COLL., incorp. 22 May, 1839, aged 24; M.A. 10 Oct., 1839, B. & D.D. 1864, vicar of Haresfield, co. Gloucester. See Foster's *Baronetage.*

Marchmont, Arthur William, 2s. Henry, of Southgate, Middlesex, cler. PEMBROKE COLL., matric. 20 Oct., 1873, aged 20.

Marcon, Rev. Charles Abdy, 3s. Walter, of Edgefield, Norfolk, cler. CHARSLEY HALL, matric. 14 Jan., 1874, aged 20; B.A. 1878, M.A. 1882. **[20]**

Marcon, Walter, 4s. John, of Swaffham, Norfolk, arm. WORCESTER COLL., matric. 27 Oct., 1842, aged 18; B.A. 1846, rector of Edgefield Holt, Norfolk, 1848-76. See *Eton School Lists.*

Marcon, Walter Hubert, 1s. Walter, of Edgefield, Norfolk, cler. ST. ALBAN HALL, matric. 21 Oct., 1869, aged 18; B.A. 1873, M.A. 1878, rector of Edgefield since 1876.

Marcy, John, s. Richard, of Atterbury, Oxon, gent. MAGDALEN HALL, matric. 6 July, 1748, aged 19.

Mardenbrough, George Wright, s. Christopher, of St. Christopher's, West Indies, arm. ST. JOHN'S COLL., matric. 10 July, 1802, aged 21.

Marendaz, Francis, 2s. David Emanuel, of Margam, co. Glamorgan, gent. JESUS COLL., matric. 24 June, 1822, aged 19; scholar 1823-9, B.A. 1826, M.A. 1830, minister of St. Luke's, Berwick Street, St. James's, at his death 10 June, 1842. **[25]**

Marescoe, Peter, s. Peter, of Hayes, Middlesex, gent. QUEEN'S COLL., matric. 11 March, 1717-8, aged 17.

Marett. See also MARRETT, page 913.

Marett, Peter, s. Peter, of Grouville, Isle of Jersey, Hants, gent. PEMBROKE COLL., matric. 27 Feb., 1730-1, aged 19.

Marett, Robert Ranulph, o.s. Robert Pipon, of St. Brelade, Jersey, knight. BALLIOL COLL., matric. 22 Jan., 1885, aged 18; exhibitioner 1884, a student of the Inner Temple 1885.

Marfell, Cornelius, s. William, of Mitcheldean, co. Gloucester, pleb. ST. MARY HALL, matric. 22 Jan., 1778, aged 18, B.A. 1781; M.A. from CHRIST CHURCH 1786, chorister Magdalen College 1772-6. See *Bloxam,* i. 190. **[30]**

Margary, Samuel Lyde, s. Samuel, of King's Teignton, Devon, gent. MAGDALEN HALL, matric. 7 July, 1809, aged 28.

Margesson, Reginald Whitehall, 5s. William, of Ockley, Surrey, cler. MAGDALEN HALL, matric. 3 Dec., 1853, aged 25; B.A. from ST. MARY HALL 1857, rector of Virginstowe, Cornwall, 1879-81, and of Blendworth, Hants, 1881.

Margesson, William, s. William, of Broadwater, Sussex, arm. CHRIST CHURCH, matric. 1 May, 1811, aged 19; rector of Whatlington 1821, and of Mountfield, Sussex, 1836, until his death 20 May, 1871.

Margesson, William Anthony, 5s. Reginald Whitehall, of Mountfield, Sussex, cler. KEBLE COLL., matric. 19 Oct., 1886, aged 20.

Margetts, Francis Edward, 2s. Francis Thomas Clark, of Duxford, co. Cambridge, cler. NON-COLL., matric. 18 Oct., 1880, aged 20. **[35]**

Margetts, Walter William, 2s. William, of Sherborne, co. Gloucester, gent. NON-COLL., matric. 12 Oct., 1878, aged 21.

Margoliouth, David Samuel, o.s. Ezekiel, of Bethnal Green, London, gent. NEW COLL., matric. 13 Oct., 1877, aged 18 scholar 1877-81, B.A. 1880, fellow 1881, lecturer 1882, M.A. 1884, tutor 1884.

Mariett, John. BALLIOL COLL., 1720. See MARRIETT, page 914.

Mariett, Richard, s. Richard, of Alscot, co. Gloucester, arm. TRINITY COLL., matric. 8 Feb., 1736-7, aged 19.

Marindin, Henry Colvile, 1s. Samuel, of Worfield, near Chesterton, Salop, cler. BALLIOL COLL., matric. 14 March, 1853, aged 18; B.A. 1857, bar.-at-law, Lincoln's Inn, 1860, died 7 May, 1872. See Foster's *Baronetage,* WEDDERBURN; & *Eton School Lists.* **[40]**

Mariott, Edmund, s. John, of King's Langley, Herts, gent. CHRIST CHURCH, matric. 14 May, 1719, aged 18; B.A. 29 Jan., 1722-3, M.A. 1725.

Marjoribanks, Archibald John, 4s. Dudley Coutts, Lord Tweedmouth. ORIEL COLL., matric. 12 March, 1881, aged 19. See *Eton School Lists.*

Marjoribanks, Dudley Coutts, 2s. Edward, of Marylebone, London, arm. CHRIST CHURCH, matric. 17 Oct., 1838, aged 17; Baron Tweedmouth, of Edington, co. Berwick, so created 12 Oct., 1881, bar.-at-law, Middle Temple, 1848, M.P. Berwick 1853-68, 1874-81, created a baronet 25 July, 1866. See Foster's *Peerage* & *Men at the Bar.*

Markham, David, s. William, archbishop of York. CHRIST CHURCH, matric. 9 June, 1784, aged 17; served with the 7th and 76th regiments, major 20th regiment 1793, lieut.-colonel 1794, fell in action at St. Domingo 26 March, 1795. See Foster's *Yorkshire Collection* & *Alumni West.*, 418.

Markham, David Frederick, s. (William) of Aberford, Yorks, arm. CHRIST CHURCH, matric. 7 May, 1818, aged 18; B.A. 1822, M.A. 1255, vicar of Addingham, Cumberland, 1825, of Stillingfleet, Yorks, 1826-38, rector of Great Horkesley, Essex, 1838, canon of Windsor, 1827, until his death 31 March, 1853. See Foster's *Yorkshire Collection.*

Markham, David William Christian, 1s. David Frederick, of Stillingfleet, Yorks, cler. CHRIST CHURCH, matric. 20 Oct., 1847, aged 18; died at sea 17 May, 1850. **[20]**

Markham, Rev. Enoch, s. Enoch, of Limerick, Ireland, gent. CHRIST CHURCH, matric. 7 Feb., 1748-9, aged 24; B.A. 1752, M.A. 1756, master of Oakham Grammar School, died there 1769, uncle of the next named. See Foster's *Yorkshire Collection.*

Markham, George, s. Thomas, of London, arm. CHRIST CHURCH, matric. 1 July, 1771, aged 18; B.A. 1775, M.A. 1778, B. & D.D. 1791, vicar of Carlton in Craven, Yorks, 1780, rector of Tattenhall, Cheshire, died in 1816. See Foster's *Yorkshire Collection.*

Markham, George, s. William, archbishop of York. CHRIST CHURCH, matric. 24 May, 1780, aged 17; B.A. 1784, M.A. 1787, B. & D.D. 1803, preb. of Southwell 1787-1802, preb. of York and chancellor of York Cathedral 1787, rector of Beeford, Yorks, 1788-91, and of Stokesley 1791, commissary of Richmond 1790, canon residentiary of York and archdeacon of Cleveland 1797, dean of York 1802, until his death 29 Sep., 1822. See Foster's *Yorkshire Collection* & *Alumni West.*, 412.

Markham, Henry Robert, 1s. Henry, of Clifton, Notts, cler. CHRIST CHURCH, matric. 12 June, 1851, aged 18; of Clifton Hall, Notts, D.L., high sheriff 1875, assumed the name of CLIFTON in lieu of MARKHAM in Aug., 1869.

Markham, Henry Spencer, 2s. Robert, of York (city), doctor. CHRIST CHURCH, matric. 15 May, 1823, aged 18; B.A. 1828, M.A. 1830, rector of Clifton, Notts, 1830, vicar of Conisborough 1830, preb. of York 1830, canon residentiary of York 1833, died 2 Sep., 1844. **[25]**

Markham, John, s. John, of Bristol (city), Somerset, pleb. ORIEL COLL., matric. 21 March, 1725-6, aged 17; B.A. 6 Feb., 1729-30 (? died rector of Backwell, Somerset, at Cleve 29 March, 1786).

Markham, John, s. Alexander, of East Claydon, Bucks, cler. BRASENOSE COLL., matric. 16 Feb., 1771, aged 17; fellow and tutor WORCESTER COLL., B.A. 1774, M.A. 1777, perp. curate Northill, Beds, 1780, until his death 5 June, 1811.

Markham, John, 2s. William, of Aberford, Yorks, arm. ST. MARY HALL, matric. 20 March, 1820, aged 23; retired commander royal navy, died 26 Oct., 1870.

Markham, John, 1s. John, of St. Martin's-in-the-Fields, London, arm. CHRIST CHURCH, matric. 8 Dec., 1820, aged 19; B.A. 1825 (? died at Reigate 5 Feb., 1885).

Markham, Osborn, s. William, archbishop of York. CHRIST CHURCH, matric. 8 June, 1787, aged 18; B.A. 1791, M.A. 1794, bar.-at-law, Lincoln's Inn, 1794, chancellor of the diocese of York 1795, commissary of the prerogative court of York and a commissioner of bankrupts 1796, a commissioner of the navy 1803, M.P. Calne 1806-7, barrack-master-general 1807-22, died 22 Oct., 1827. See Foster's *Yorkshire Collection* & *Alumni West.*, 423. **[30]**

Markham, Robert, of ST. JOHN'S COLL., Cambridge B.A. 1748, M.A. 1752); incorp. from BRASENOSE COLL. 4 May, 1753, B. & D.D. 1768, a chaplain in ordinary to the King, rector of St. Mary, Whitechapel, 1768, until his death 24 Sep., 1786.

Markham, Robert, s. William, archbishop of York. CHRIST CHURCH, matric. 14 June, 1786, aged 18; student 1786, B.A. 1790, M.A. 1794, rector of Barton-in-Fabis, Notts, 1792-6, preb. of York 1792, archdeacon of the West Riding and chancellor of Richmond 1794, rector of Bolton Percy 1796, vicar of Bishopsthorpe 1797, preb. of Carlisle 1801, canon residentiary of York 1802, died 17 June, 1837. See Foster's *Yorkshire Collection* & *Alumni West.*, 421.

Markham, Robert, s. Robert, of Bishop Thorpe, Yorks, cler. CHRIST CHURCH, matric. 7 May, 1817, aged 18; captain 5th regiment, died at Fermoy in May, 1832.

Markham, Samuel, s. John, of London, gent. CHRIST CHURCH, matric. 30 May, 1741, aged 18; B.C.L. 1748, bar.-at-law, Inner Temple, 1748, a minor canon of Rochester, vicar of Leatherhead, Surrey, 1767, one of the evening preachers of St. Dunstan's-in-the-West, London, died 28 March, 1797. See Foster's *Yorkshire Collection* & *Alumni West.*, 324.

Markham, Thomas Hugh, 5s. Charles, of Northampton, arm. BRASENOSE COLL., matric. 21 March, 1844, aged 18; B.A. 1847, M.A. 1852, bar.-at-law, Inner Temple, 1851, died 19 Sep., 1868.

Markham, William, s. William, of Kingsale, Ireland, gent. CHRIST CHURCH, matric. 6 June, 1738, aged 18; B.A. 1742, M.A. 1745, B.C.L. & D.C.L. 1752, dean 1767-76, head-master Westminster School 1753-65, preb. of Durham 1759, chaplain to the king 1756, dean of Rochester 1765-71, vicar of Boxley, Kent, 1765-71, bishop of Chester 1771-6, archbishop of York 1776, until his death 3 Nov., 1807, buried in Westminster Abbey. See Foster's *Yorkshire Collection* & *Alumni West.*, 318. [5]

Markham, William, s. William, of Aberford, Yorks, arm. CHRIST CHURCH, matric. 9 May, 1815, aged 18; of Becca Hall, Yorks, D.L., colonel 2nd West Yorks militia, died 26 Jan., 1852. See Foster's *Yorkshire Collection* & *Alumni West.*, 474.

Markham, William Rice, 2s. John, of St. Martin's-in-the-Fields, London, arm. CHRIST CHURCH, matric. 8 Dec., 1820, aged 17; B.A. 1825, vicar of Morland, Cumberland, 1828, until his death 27 March, 1877.

Markheim, Henry William Gegg, 2s. Harrison Alfred Harrison, of Smyrna, Asia Minor, gent. UNIVERSITY COLL., matric. 17 Oct., 1863, aged 18, scholar 1864-9, B.A. 1869; fellow QUEEN'S COLL. 1871, M.A. 1871, a student of the Inner Temple 1873.

Markland, Daniel, s. John, of Astbury, Cheshire, gent. BRASENOSE COLL., matric. 31 March, 1718, aged 16; B.A. 1721.

Markland, Rev. John, s. Robert, of Manchester, Lancashire, arm. BRASENOSE COLL., matric. 26 April, 1797, aged 17; B.A. 1801, M.A. 1804, died 13 Dec., 1819. See *Eton School Lists.* [10]

Markland, James Heywood, F.R.S., F.A.S., created D.C.L. 21 June, 1849 (4s. Robert, of Withington, co. Lancaster), a student of the Inner Temple 1814, F.S.A., 1809, an original member of the Roxburghe Club 1812, F.R.S. 1816, died 28 Dec., 1864. See *Manchester School Reg.*, i. 66.

Markland, Rev. Ralph, s. John, of Wigan, Lancashire, gent. BRASENOSE COLL., matric. 26 Jan., 1732-3, aged 18; B.A. 1736, died unmarried.

Markoe, Peter, s. Abraham, of 'St. Croix, King's Quarter,' gent. PEMBROKE COLL., matric. 17 Feb., 1767, aged 16.

Marks, Alexander Christian, 3s. John, of Abridge, Essex, gent. NEW INN HALL, matric. 1 Dec., 1837, aged 21.

Marks, Hugh, 2s. John George, of Croydon, Surrey, gent. KEBLE COLL., matric. 16 Oct., 1883, aged 20; B.A. 1886. [15]

Marks, James Christopher, 1s. William, of Armagh, Ireland, gent. MAGDALEN HALL, matric. 24 June, 1863, aged 28; B.Mus. 25 June, 1863, D.Mus. 11 July, 1868.

Marks, John, s. John, of Dunyatt, Somerset, gent. BALLIOL COLL., matric. 10 April, 1742, aged 19; B.A. 1745.

Marks, Thomas Osborne, 3s. William, of Armagh, Ireland, gent. EXETER COLL., matric. 8 July, 1870, aged 25; B.Mus. from NEW COLL. 9 July, 1870.

Markwick, James, s. William, of Catsfield, Sussex, arm. ST. JOHN'S COLL., matric. 21 Sep., 1727, aged 16; bar.-at-law, Inner Temple, 1733.

Marle, Rev. William, 4s. Robert, of Birmingham, gent. NON-COLL., matric. 22 April, 1876, aged 28; B.A. from BALLIOL COLL. 1881. [20]

Marlen, Rev. Henry John, o.s. Henry, of St. Paul's, Canterbury, Kent, cler. WADHAM COLL., matric. 27 March, 1846, aged 20; clerk 1846-50, B.A. 1849, M.A. 1853, died Nov., 1881.

Marlen, Henry John Hopwood, 1s. Henry John, of Blackburn, Lancashire, cler. UNIVERSITY COLL., matric. 16 Oct., 1875, aged 19; B.A. 1880, M.A. 1882, a student of Inner Temple 1877. See *Rugby School Reg.*

Marler, Thomas, s. William, of Exeter (city), gent. BALLIOL COLL., matric. 1 April, 1789, aged 19; B.A. 1793, chaplain to British Factory at Oporto, died at Christ's Hospital, London, 30 Dec., 1807.

Marler, William, s. William, of Exeter (city), gent. BALLIOL COLL., matric. 11 April, 1783, aged 18; B.A. 1786, M.A. 1789.

Marling, Henry Hotspur, 1s. Nathaniel Samuel, of Stroud, co. Gloucester, arm. MAGDALEN HALL, matric. 22 March, 1849, aged 21; B.A. 1852, M.A. 1858, died at Stonehouse Court, co. Gloucester, 12 Nov., 1865. See Foster's *Baronetage.* [25]

Marlow, Michael, s. Michael, of St. Leonard's, London, gent. BRASENOSE COLL., matric. 9 April, 1728, aged 16, B.A. 1731; M.A. from CHRIST COLL., Cambridge, 1740, vicar of Nasing, Essex, 1752, chaplain of Aske's Hospital, Hoxton, rector of Lackford, Suffolk, 1761, and also of Freston St. Peter, until his death 30 Jan., 1795.

Marlow, Michael, s. Michael, of St. Leonard's, Middlesex, cler. ST. JOHN'S COLL., matric. 2 July, 1776, aged 17; scholar 1776, fellow 1779, B.A. 1780, M.A. 1784, B.D. 1789, D.D. 1795, president 1795-1828, vice-chancellor 1798-1802, select preacher 1805 & 1817, vicar of St. Giles's, Oxford, rector of Handborough, Oxon, 1795, preb. of Canterbury 1808, died 16 Feb., 1828. See *Robinson*, 128.

Marmion, Richard Walton, M.A. TRINITY COLL., Dublin, 1841, B.A. 1838; adm. 'comitatis causa,' 27 June, 1867.

Marnell, Richard, s. Richard, of St. Martin's, London, arm. CHRIST CHURCH, matric. 16 May, 1804, aged 17; B.A. 1808, M.A. 1811, a student until 1816, bar.-at-law, Inner Temple, 1814, an advocate before the Supreme Court of Bengal, counsel for paupers, Calcutta, died there 2 Aug., 1838. See *Alumni West.*, 461.

Marr, Rev. James Francis, 1s. James, of London, gent. ST. JOHN'S COLL., matric. 13 Oct., 1877, aged 19; scholar 1877-84, B.A. 1881, M.A. 1884. See *Robinson*, 365. [30]

Marr, Richard S., s. Patrick William, of Lewisham, Kent, arm. HERTFORD COLL., matric. 2 June, 1802, aged 15.

Marrable, Arthur George, 1s. George, of London, arm. UNIVERSITY COLL., matric. 14 Oct., 1882, aged 19; passed first at Sandhurst for the army in 1884.

Marras, Americo William, LINCOLN COLL. 1859. See BURRELL, p. 197.

Marrett, Clement Augustus, o.s. John, of St. Peter's, Guernsey, gent. PEMBROKE COLL., matric. 2 Oct., 1841, aged 18; scholar 1841-5, B.A. 1846.

Marrett, Edward Lawrence, 3s. Thomas, of Viznagrum (*sic.*), East Indies, arm. PEMBROKE COLL., matric. 13 Nov., 1845, aged 18; B.A. from ST. MARY HALL 1850, M.A. 1855, rector of Morborne, Hunts, 1854-8, vicar of Lesbury, Northumberland 1858-85, rector of Welbury, Yorks, 1885. [35]

Marriott, George Wharton, s. Robert, of Cotesbach, co. Leicester, doctor. CHRIST CHURCH, matric. 29 Oct., 1795, aged 17, B.A. 1799; fellow ALL SOULS' COLL., B.C.L. 1804, bar.-at-law, Middle Temple, 1810, a magistrate at Westminster Police Court and chairman of the Middlesex Sessions 1832, chancellor of the diocese of St. David's 1824, until his death 1 Feb., 1833, brother of John 1798. See *Rugby School Reg.*, 59.

Marriott, Harvey, s. William, of Dorking, Surrey, arm. WORCESTER COLL., matric. 17 Oct., 1798, aged 16; curate of Marston, co. Worcester, 1807, rector of Claverton, Bath, 1808, vicar of Loddiswell, Devon, 1847-62, vicar of Wellington, Somerset, 1862, until his death 18 Aug., 1865. See Foster's *Our Noble and Gentle Families.* **[20]**

Marriott, Henry Peter, 4s. James Powell Goulton-Constable (formerly Marriott), of Cotesbach, co. Leicester, cler. BRASENOSE COLL., matric. 13 Oct., 1873, aged 19; B.A. 1879, brother of George S., etc. See Foster's *Baronetage*, STRICKLAND.

Marriott, Hugh, s. Reginald, of Fulham, Middlesex, arm. QUEEN'S COLL. matric. 1 July, 1728, aged 17; bar.-at-law, Inner Temple, 1735, father of James 1761.

Marriott, James, s. Hugh, of St. Andrew's, Middlesex, arm. QUEEN'S COLL., matric. 14 Dec., 1761, aged 18; B.C.L. 1777, D.C.L. 1777, rector (and patron) of Horsmonden, Kent, 1785, until his death 31 July, 1809.

Marriott, James, 3s. (James Powell) Goulton-Constable (formerly Marriott), of Cotesbach, co. Leicester, cler. NON-COLL., matric. 21 Oct., 1871, aged 21; of Walcot, co. Lincoln, J.P., assumed the surnames of GOULTON-CONSTABLE in lieu of MARRIOTT in 1872. See Foster's *Baronetage*, STRICKLAND.

Marriott, James Powell. BALLIOL COLL., 1838. See CONSTABLE, p. 287, father of Charles 1867, George S. 1875, Henry P. 1873, James 1871, of John M., 1872, and of Robert 1865. **[25]**

Marriott, John, s. John, of Sunning, Berks, pleb. NEW INN HALL, matric. 9 Nov., 1722, aged 19 (? B.A. 1724, as William).

Marriott, John, s. Robert, of Cotesbach, co. Leicester, doctor. CHRIST CHURCH, matric. 10 Oct., 1798, aged 18; a student, B.A. 1802, M.A. 1806, a friend of Sir Walter Scott, curate of Broadclist, Devon, rector of Church Lawford with Newnham Chapelry, co. Warwick, 1807, until his death in 1825. See *Rugby School Reg.*, 65.

Marriott, John, 1s. John, of Church Lawford, co. Warwick, cler. ORIEL COLL., matric. 24 Nov., 1826, aged 17; B.A. 1830, M.A. 1833, vicar of Hythe, St. John's, 1863-78, died 13 Feb., 1881.

Marriott, John Arthur Ransome, 1s. Francis, of Bowdon, Cheshire, gent. NEW COLL., matric. 11 Oct., 1878, aged 19; B.A. 1882, M.A. 1885, lecturer in modern history Worcester College 1885, a student of the Inner Temple 1883.

Marriott, John Marmaduke, 4s. James Powell-Goulton Constable (formerly Marriott), of Cotesbach, co. Leicester, cler. BRASENOSE COLL., matric. 2 Nov., 1872, aged 19. **[30]**

Marriott, Randolph, s. John, of York (city), gent. UNIVERSITY COLL., matric. 31 Oct., 1796, aged 20; vicar of Ipplepen, Devon, 1814, until his death in 1843. See Foster's *Our Noble and Gentle Families.*

Marriott, Richard Walker, 2s. John, of Kibworth, co. Leicester, arm. EXETER COLL., matric. 22 Oct., 1847, aged 18; exhibitioner LINCOLN COLL. 1849-52, B.A. 1851, M.A. 1854, vicar of Aldborough, Yorks, 1863-86, rector of Shelton, Notts, 1886. See Foster's *Our Noble and Gentle Families*, vol. ii.

Marriott, Robert, s. Robert, of Braunston, Northants, gent. QUEEN'S COLL., matric. 5 July, 1760, aged 17; B.C.L. 1767, D.C.L. 1787, a student of Lincoln's Inn 1761, rector of Cotesbach, co. Leicester, 1767, and of Gilmorton 1787, until his death 18 July, 1808, father of John, 1798, and of Robert next named.

Marriott, Robert, s. Robert, of Cotesbach, co. Leicester, doctor. BRASENOSE COLL., matric. 14 Dec., 1792, aged 18; B.A. 1796, M.A. 1799, rector of Cotesbach 1808, until he died 5 Oct., 1841, father James P., 1831.

Marriott, Robert, 1s. James Powell (Goulton-Constable—formerly Marriott), of Cotesbach, near Lutterworth, co. Leicester, cler. CHRIST CHURCH, matric. 7 June, 1865, aged 18; died 14 May, 1868.

Marriott, Robert Thomas James, o.s. Robert, of St. Pancras, London, arm. MAGDALEN HALL, matric. 1 Nov., 1861, aged 18; scholar 1861, until his death in 1863.

Marriott, Samuel James, 1s. Matthew, of Welford, Northants, gent. NON-COLL., matric. 16 Oct., 1869, aged 25; B.A. 1874, M.A. 1876, vicar of Netherton, Dudley, 1878.

Marriott, Walter, s. William, of Pershore, co. Worcester, arm. WORCESTER COLL., matric. 28 Nov., 1815, aged 20; chaplain of the Bristol County Gaol, died 8 Oct., 1859. See Foster's *Our Noble and Gentle Families.* [5]

Marriott, Wharton Booth, 4s. (George W.), of St. George's, Bloomsbury, Middlesex, arm. TRINITY COLL., matric. 12 June, 1843, aged 19, scholar 1843-6; fellow EXETER COLL. 1846-51, B.C.L. 1851, M.A. 1856, B.D. 1870, select preacher 1868, assistant-master Eton College 1850-71, Grinfield lecturer on the Septuagint 1871, died 16 Dec., 1871; for list of works see *Crockford.* See also *Boase*, 136; & *Eton School Lists.*

Marriott, William, B.A. from NEW INN HALL, 29 Oct., 1724 (*Acts Book*). See John M., 1722.

Marriott, William, s. William, of Redland, co. Gloucester, arm. WORCESTER COLL., matric. 28 Nov., 1794, aged 20; died in India 18 Jan., 1805. See Foster's *Our Noble and Gentle Families*, vol. i.

Marriott, William, s. William, of Manchester, Lancashire, arm. BRASENOSE COLL., matric. 16 Oct., 1810, aged 18.

Marriott, William, 5s. John, of Glossop, co. Derby, arm. ST. ALBAN HALL, matric. 28 Nov., 1844, aged 21.

Marriott, William Edmund, 3s. Wharton Booth, of Eton, cler. PEMBROKE COLL., matric. 25 Jan., 1883, aged 19, scholar 1882-5; scholar HERTFORD COLL. 1881-2. [11]

Marriott, William Henry, 3s. John, of Kibworth, co. Leicester, cler. LINCOLN COLL., matric. 26 March, 1851, aged 18; exhibitioner 1851-6, B.A. 1855, M.A. 1857, vicar of Thrussington, co. Leicester, since 1867. See Foster's *Our Noble and Gentle Families*, vol. ii.; & *Rugby School Reg.*, 270.

Marriott, (Sir) William Henry Smith (Bart.), 1s. William Smith, of Horsmonden, Kent, cler. (after a baronet), BALLIOL COLL., matric. 12 Dec., 1854, aged 19; 5th baronet. See Foster's *Baronetage.*

Marriott, William Smith, 1s. John Bosworth Smith, of Sydling, Dorset, arm. CHRIST CHURCH, matric. 12 Oct., 1883, aged 18; B.A. 1887.

Marrow, Rev. William John (Williamson), 3s. William John, of Aigburth, Lancashire, arm. CHRIST CHURCH, matric. 20 May, 1875, aged 19; B.A. 1879, M.A. 1884. [15]

Marryat, Charles, 1s. Charles, of London, arm. QUEEN'S COLL., matric. 22 May, 1847, aged 19; B.A. 1851, M.A. (by decree) 16 March, 1854, incumbent of St. Paul's, Port Adelaide, 1853-68, vicar of Christ Church, North Adelaide, and archdeacon of Adelaide 1868. See *Eton School Lists.*

Marryat, Horatio, 5s. Joseph, of Wimbledon, Surrey, arm. CHRIST CHURCH, matric. 4 June, 1835, aged 17. See *Eton School Lists.*

Marryat, James, o.s. William, of Bishopsgate, London, gent. PEMBROKE COLL., matric. 13 April, 1831, aged 17; B.A. from NEW INN HALL 1838.

Marsden, Charles John, 1s. Anthony, of Gargrave, Yorks, cler. CHRIST CHURCH, matric. 15 May, 1834, aged 18; student 1836-43, B.A. 1838, M.A. 1840, vicar of Gargrave, Yorks, 1852. See *Eton School Lists.*

Marsden, Charles John Delabere, 1s. William Henry, of Darfield, Yorks, arm. LINCOLN COLL., matric. 5 May, 1828, aged 19; B.A. 1832, M.A. 1839, vicar of Bolton-upon-Dearne, Yorks, 1849-60, rector of Hooton-Roberts 1860, until his death 28 May, 1873. [20]

Marsden, Henry, s. Henry, of Melling, Lancashire, arm. QUEEN'S COLL., matric. 17 Feb., 1775, aged 17.

Marsden, John, s. William, of Barnsley, Yorks, arm. CHRIST CHURCH, matric. 26 May, 1749, aged 18 B.A. 1753, M.A. 1756, B. & D.D. 1777, precentor of St. Asaph's 1760, rector of Llandyssil 1761, preb. of Southwell 1762-96, vicar of Feliskirk, Yorks, 1765, rector of Bolton Percy 1774, vicar of Felkirk 1777-93, and preb. of York 1785, died 25 Feb., 1796. See *Alumni West.*, 349.

Marsden, Reginald Godfrey, 3s. John Howard, of Great Oakley, Essex, cler. MERTON COLL., matric. 24 April, 1865, aged 19; postmaster 1865-9, B.A. 1869, M.A. 1872, of Great Oakley, Essex, bar.-at-law, Inner Temple, 1872. See Foster's *Men at the Bar* & *Eton School Lists.*

Marsden, Stephen Weston, 3s. William Delabene, of Louth, co. Lincoln, cler. WORCESTER COLL., matric. 19 Oct., 1875, aged 19; B.A. 1880, M.A. 1884.

Marsden, Thomas, s. Thomas, of Wakefield, Yorks, gent. CHRIST CHURCH, matric. 30 May, 1777, aged 18; B.A. 1781, M.A. 1784, vicar of Skipton in Craven, and Kildwick, Yorks, Feb., 1790, died in 1805-6. See *Alumni West.*, 407. [25]

Marsden, William, created D.C.L. 28 June, 1786, born at Vervel, co. Wicklow (eldest son of John Marsden, D.D.), orientalist and antiquary, F.R.S. 1783, F.S.A. 1785, 2nd secretary to the admiralty about 1795, died 6 Oct., 1836.

Marsden, William, s. William, of Manchester, Lancashire, pleb. BRASENOSE COLL., matric. 24 March, 1790, aged 19; B.A. 1793, M.A. 1796, B.D. 1811, curate of St. George's, Wigan, 1817, vicar of Eccles 1837, until his death 15 Feb., 1861. See *Manchester School Reg.*, iii. 126.

Marsden, William, o.s. Richard, of Christ Church, Surrey, gent. WADHAM COLL., matric. 11 Oct., 1828, aged 18; B.A. 1833, M.A. 1835, rector of Everingham, Yorks, 1839, until his death 23 Dec., 1841.

Marsden, William Charles, 1s. Charles William, of Holywell, co. Flint, gent. JESUS COLL., matric. 27 Oct., 1877, aged 20.

Marsden, William Henry, s. John, of York (city), doctor. MERTON COLL., matric. 7 Nov., 1791, aged 14; B.A. 1795, a student of Lincoln's Inn 1796. [30]

Marsh, Arthur, 4s. Richard, of Leigh, near Manchester, gent. QUEEN'S COLL., matric. 29 Oct., 1867, aged 19; B.A. 1871, M.A. 1875, held various curacies since 1871.

Marsh, Bower, 2s. Bower, of Rochester, gent. EXETER COLL., matric. 23 Oct., 1885, aged 19; scholar 1885.

Marsh, Charles William, 3s. Matthew, of Winterslow, Wilts, cler. CHRIST CHURCH, matric. 23 May, 1833, aged 18.

Marsh, Edward Caldecott, 1s. Edward Newnham, of Belgaum, East Indies, arm. MERTON COLL., matric. 19 Oct., 1883, aged 18; B.A. 1887.

Marsh, Edward Garrard, s. John, of St. Thomas's, Salisbury, Wilts, arm. WADHAM COLL., matric. 19 July, 1800, aged 17, B.A. 1804; fellow ORIEL COLL. 1804-14, M.A. 1807, Bampton lecturer 1848, preb. of Southwell 1821, vicar of Sandon, Herts, 1828, and of Aylesford, Kent, 1841, until his death 20 Sep., 1862; for list of his works see *Crockford.*

Marsh, Edward Wulff, 3s. William, of Gwennap, Cornwall, cler. PEMBROKE COLL., matric. 3 June, 1852, aged 18. [36]

[M]arsh, George, s. George, of Ford, Northumberland, cler. LINCOLN COLL., matric. 8 Dec., 1750, aged 18; B.A. 1754, rector of Ford (on his father's death) 1760, until his (own) death 15 Oct., 1795.

[M]arsh, George Thomas, 2s. Matthew, of Winterslow, Wilts, cler. CHRIST CHURCH, matric. 17 Dec., 1830, aged 18; student 1830-7, B.A. 1834, M.A. 1838, vicar of Sutton Benger, Wilts, 1836, rector of Foxley 1840, until his death 24 Feb., 1862. See *Alumni West.*, 498.

[M]arsh, George Watkin, s. Watkin, of Newport, Salop, pleb. CHRIST CHURCH, matric. 20 Oct., 1790, aged 17; B.A. 1794, M.A. 1797.

[M]arsh, James Ernest, 3s. John, of St. Helen's, Lancashire, arm. BALLIOL COLL., matric. 16 Oct., 1879, aged 19; B.A. 1882.

[M]arsh, John, s. George, of Milton Abbas, Dorset, cler. ALL SOULS' COLL., matric. 30 March, 1720, aged 15; B.A. from BALLIOL COLL. 1723. Query, died vicar of St. Margaret-at-Cliffe, West Cliff (1733), and Buckland, near Dover, 1 Sep., 1773. [5]

[M]arsh, John, s. Thomas, of Llandinam, co. Montgomery, pleb. JESUS COLL., matric. 26 Oct., 1753, aged 20; B.A. 1757.

[M]arsh, John, s. William, of Crewkherne, Somerset, cler. BALLIOL COLL., matric. 1 June, 1756, aged 17; B.A. 1760.

[M]arsh, John, 1s. John, of Hursley, Hants, cler. NEW COLL., matric. 3 March, 1838, aged 18; fellow 1838-54, B.C.L. 1844, rector of Tingewick, Bucks, 1853, until his death 8 Feb., 1855.

[M]arsh, John Murdoch Wilmot, 1s. George, of Chelsea, Middlesex, cler. JESUS COLL., matric. 13 April, 1837, aged 17.

[M]arsh, John William, 2s. Edward Garrard, of Hampstead, Middlesex, cler. WADHAM COLL., matric. 19 Nov., 1840, aged 19; B.A. 1845, M.A. 1856, vicar of Bleasby 1848-74, rector of St. Michael, Winchester, 1874, until his death 14 Dec., 1882. [10]

[M]arsh, Martin William (James), o.s. Arthur, of London, arm. MERTON COLL., matric. 26 June, 1844, aged 18; died at Athens 10 Aug., 1846. See *Eton School Lists.*

[M]arsh, Matthew, s. Philemon, of York (city), cler. CHRIST CHURCH, matric. 28 Jan., 1788, aged 18; B.A. 1791, M.A. 1794, B.D. 1801, vicar of St. Mary Magdalen, Oxford, rector of Brinkworth, and of Winterslow 1804, chancellor of the diocese of Salisbury 1819, preb. of Salisbury 1823, sub-dean 1824, and canon 1825, until his death 30 July, 1840.

[M]arsh, Matthew Henry, 1s. Matthew of Winterslow, Wilts, cler. CHRIST CHURCH, matric. 16 May, 1828, aged 17; student 1828-41, B.A. 1833, M.A. 1835, bar.-at-law, Inner Temple, 1836, M.P. Salisbury 1857-68, died 26 Jan., 1881. See *Alumni West.*, 501.

[M]arsh, Rev. Richard, 6s. Thomas Edward, of Llanidloes, co. Montgomery, gent. WADHAM COLL., matric. 26 Oct., 1837, aged 18; B.A. 1841, died at Llanidloes 21 Aug., 1845.

[M]arsh, Richard Bayley, s. John, of Penn, co. Stafford, arm. ORIEL COLL., matric. 29 March, 1803, aged 18; created M.A. 18 June, 1806. [15]

[M]arsh, Thomas, 2s. Thomas, of Wigan, Lancashire, gent. ST. EDMUND HALL, matric. 15 Jan., 1844, aged 21; B.A. 1847.

[M]arsh, William, s. William, of Prescott, Lancashire, gent. BRASENOSE COLL., matric. 21 Feb., 1721-2, aged 18; B.A. 1726.

[M]arsh, Rev. William, s. Henry, of Crewkherne, Somerset, pleb. TRINITY COLL., matric. 24 May, 1726, aged 18; B.A. 1729, father of John 1756.

[M]arsh, William, s. John, of Lydford, Somerset, cler. WADHAM COLL., matric. 30 March, 1785, aged 17; B.A. 1789, M.A. 1794. (? died rector of Weston Bampfylde in 1824-5).

Marsh, William, s. Charles, of Reading, Berks, equitis. ST. EDMUND HALL, matric. 10 Oct., 1797, aged 22; B.A. 1801, M.A. 1807, B. & D.D. 1839, vicar of Basildon, Berks, 1802, rector of St. Peter's, Colchester, 1814, of St. Thomas's, Birmingham, 1829, and incumbent of St. Mary's, Leamington, 1843, hon. canon of Worcester 1848, died 24 Aug., 1864.

Marsh, William, 3s. James, of Exeter (city), gent. MAGDALEN HALL, matric. 27 Nov., 1819, aged 22; B.A. 1823, M.A. 1830, vicar of Ashburton, Devon, 1835, until his death 3 May, 1861. [21]

Marsh, William, o.s. John Hoskins, of Bath, arm. HERTFORD COLL., matric. 14 Oct., 1876, aged 19; scholar 1875-80, B.A. 1880, M.A. 1883.

Marsh, William, o.s. William Hobson, of Clayton, Yorks, gent. EXETER COLL., matric. 24 Jan., 1884, aged 21; scholar 1883, B.A. 1887.

Marsh, William Blencowe, 2s. William, of Gwennapp, Cornwall, cler. MAGDALEN HALL, matric. 10 May, 1848, aged 19.

Marsh, William Elliott, s. William, of Coventry (city), doctor. ST. JOHN'S COLL., matric. 30 June, 1817, aged 17; scholar & fellow 1817-71, B.C.L. 1826, D.C.L. 1831, bursar 1836, vice-president 1837, died in 1871. See *Rugby School Reg.*, 101. [25]

Marsh, William Nathaniel (Tilson). ORIEL COLL., 1833. See TILSON.

Marshall, Rev. Alfred, 5s. William Benjamin, of Neasdon, Middlesex, gent. ORIEL COLL., matric. 27 May, 1871, aged 18; B.A. 1874, M.A. 1878.

Marshall, Alfred, y.s. Henry, of Liverpool, gent. KEBLE COLL., matric. 18 Oct., 1881, aged 18; B.A. 1884.

Marshall, Alfred, scholar ST. JOHN'S COLL., Cambridge, 1862, fellow 1865-77 and 1885, 2nd Wrangler and B.A. 1865, M.A. 1868, 2s. William, of Sydenham, arm. BALLIOL COLL., incorp. 22 Oct., 1883, aged 41; fellow 1884-5, lecturer and tutor political economy 1883-4, professor political economy, Cambridge, 1884.

Marshall, Arthur, 2s. Robert, of London, arm. EXETER COLL., matric. 4 June, 1881, aged 18. [30]

Marshall, Arthur Young, 5s. John, of Hackney, London, arm. TRINITY COLL., matric. 27 March, 1847, aged 20; B.A. from ST. MARY HALL 1854.

Marshall, Bouchier, s. Thomas (Mervyn), of Bow, Devon, cler. EXETER COLL., matric. 30 May, 1805, aged 19; B.A. 1810, M.A. 1819, rector of Bow and Chawleigh, Devon, chaplain to the Duke of Kent, died in July 1827, father of the next named.

Marshall, Bouchier Mervyn, 1s. Bouchier, of Bow, Devon, cler. CHRIST CHURCH, matric. 21 Oct., 1840, aged 19; J.P. Devon, died 14 Jan., 1870.

Marshall, Carr Brackenbury, s. William, of Theddlethorpe, co. Lincoln, gent. LINCOLN COLL., matric. 12 April, 1810, aged 20; scholar 1810-14, B.A. 1813, rector of Brigsley, co. Lincoln, 1835, until his death 29 Sep., 1856. [34]

Marshall, Charles, s. Charles, of Barnstaple, Devon, gent. QUEEN'S COLL., matric. 1 June, 1768, aged 26.

Marshall, Charles, s. John, of Exeter (city), cler. EXETER COLL., matric. 23 Oct., 1788, aged 18; exhibitioner 1788, B.A. 1792, fellow 1793-7, M.A. 1795, rector of Lawhitton, Cornwall, 1798, until his death 24 July, 1826. See *Coll. Reg.*, 116, 147.

Marshall, Charles Alexander Leonard, 1s. Alexander, of Surbiton, Surrey, gent. ST. EDMUND HALL, matric. 1 Nov., 1877, aged 18; B.A. 1886.

Marshall, Charles Henry Tilson, 1s. William Knox, of Bridgnorth, Salop, cler. CHRIST CHURCH, matric. 21 Oct., 1858, aged 17.

Marshall, Charles Robert, s. Charles, of Theddlethorpe, co. Lincoln, arm. LINCOLN COLL., matric. 26 Nov., 1782, aged 18; B.A. 1786, M.A. 1789, B.D. 1799, rector of Cold Hanworth, co. Lincoln, 1802, and vicar of Exning, Suffolk, 1806, until his death 19 April, 1823.

Marshall, Douglas Hamilton, 5s. Hugh Graham, of Wells, Somerset, gent. WORCESTER COLL., matric. 19 Oct., 1886, aged 19; exhibitioner 1886. [40]

Marshall, Edward, s. William, of Ashprington, Devon, cler. EXETER COLL., matric. 18 March, 1748-9, aged 18; fellow 1751-8, B.A. 1754, M.A. 1755, vicar of Breage and Germoe, Cornwall, 1758, and of St. Eval 1782, until his death 3 May, 1803, brother of John 1747, of Richard 1741, and of William 1751. See *Coll. Reg.*, 104.

Marshall, Edward, s. Nicolas, of Enstone, Oxon, gent. PEMBROKE COLL., matric. 6 Nov., 1756, aged 17, B.A. 1760; fellow ORIEL COLL., M.A. 1763, vicar of Fordington, Dorset, died senior fellow 19 Sep., 1798.

Marshall, Edward. WORCESTER COLL., 1792. See HACKER, page 582.

Marshall, Edward, 3s. Charles, of Lawhitton, Cornwall, cler. EXETER COLL., matric. 16 April, 1823, aged 18.

Marshall, Edward, 1s. Edward (Marshall-Hacker, see page 582), of Ardley, Oxon, cler. ORIEL COLL., matric. 29 Jan., 1834, aged 18; scholar CORPUS CHRISTI COLL. 1834-6, fellow 1836-9, B.A. 1838, M.A. 1840, curate of St. Mary Magdalene, Oxford, 1846-60, vicar of Sandford St. Martin, Oxon, 1884, dropped the name of HACKER, brother of Jenner 1835; for list of his works see *Crockford*, and *Rugby School Reg.*, 155. [5]

Marshall, Edward Henry, 1s. Edward, of Oxford, cler. ORIEL COLL., matric. 28 April, 1870, aged 18; B.A. 1873, M.A. 1877, a student of the Inner Temple 1876.

Marshall, Rev. Edward Shearburn, 1s. Edward, of London, arm. BRASENOSE COLL., matric. 13 Oct., 1877, aged 19; scholar 1877-81, B.A. 1881, M.A. 1884.

Marshall, Ernest Theodore, 1s. Henry, of Dundalk, arm. CHARSLEY HALL, matric. 15 Oct., 1884, aged 18; B.A. from BRASENOSE COLL. 1887.

Marshall, Francis, s. Steph., of Enstone, Oxon, gent. UNIVERSITY COLL., matric. 17 Dec., 1730, aged 21; B.A. 1734.

Marshall, Francis Albert, 5s. William, of Grosvenor Street, London, arm. EXETER COLL., matric. 14 June, 1859, aged 18. [10]

Marshall, Francis Eden, 2s. Jenner, of Westcott Barton, Oxon, cler. ST. JOHN'S COLL., matric. 15 Oct., 1881, aged 18; B.A. 1884, M.A. 1888.

Marshall, Francis James, 4s. William, of St. Michael's, Oxford (city), pleb. NEW COLL., matric. 17 Dec., 1829, aged 17; chorister 1822-7, clerk 1829-34, B.A. 1834, M.A. 1837, chaplain 1834, until his death 26 Aug., 1843.

Marshall, Frederick Earnshaw, 1s. William, of Preston, Lancashire, arm. BRASENOSE COLL., matric. 22 May, 1839, aged 18; scholar 1839-40, B.A. 1843, M.A. 1848, of Penwortham Hall, Lancashire, J.P., bar.-at-law, Inner Temple, 1847, died in Aug., 1874. See *Rugby School Reg.*, 186.

Marshall, George, s. Nathaniel, of London, doctor. WORCESTER COLL., matric. 2 July, 1742, aged 18; B.A. 1746.

Marshall, George, s. Benjamin, of Naunton, co. Gloucester, cler. CHRIST CHURCH, matric. 19 May, 1743, aged 17; B.A. 1747. [15]

Marshall, George, s. George, of Bishops Waltham, Hants, gent. WADHAM COLL., matric. 5 Dec., 1772, aged 19. Query, vicar of Horsham, Sussex, 1784, until his death 7 Oct., 1819, aged 66.

Marshall, George, s. John, of Truro, Cornwall, gent. MAGDALEN HALL, matric. 4 April, 1788, aged 17.

Marshall, George (Clough), s. George, of Horsham, Sussex, cler. WADHAM COLL., matric. 2 Nov., 1803, aged 15; B.A. 1808, M.A. 1810, fellow until 1830, bar.-at-law, Inner Temple, 1811.

Marshall, George, 1s. James, of London, gent. CHRIST CHURCH, matric. 19 May, 1836, aged 18; student 1837-58, B.A. 1840, M.A. 1842, Greek reader 1846, censor 1849-57, several times moderator and public examiner, proctor 1850, vicar of Pyrton, Oxon, 1857-75, rector of Milton, Oxon, 1875.

Marshall, Gerald Keith Stirling, 3s. Stirling Frederick, of Farnham Royal, Bucks, cler. HERTFORD COLL., matric. 27 Oct., 1885, aged 19. [20]

Marshall, Henry Augustus, s. John, of Drogheda, co. Louth, Ireland, cler. CHRIST CHURCH, matric. 22 Oct., 1793, aged 16.

Marshall, Henry Bernard (Derham), 1s. — M., of Bawtry, Yorks, cler. WORCESTER COLL., matric. 6 June, 1856, aged 18; B.A. 1860, M.A. 1863, vicar of Hopton-Cangeford 1873-7, perp. curate Knowbury, Salop, 1877, vicar of Norton-Canon, 1877 (son of Rev. Henry Marshall, sometime of Bawtry, who died curate in charge of Spernal, co. Warwick, in 1845).

Marshall, Henry James, 5s. William, of Bath, Somerset, cler. CHRIST CHURCH, matric. 20 Oct., 1836, aged 18; exhibitioner CORPUS CHRISTI COLL. 1836-40, B.A. 1840, M.A. 1844, vicar of Bettws, co. Montgomery, 1854, until his death 25 Oct., 1881.

Marshall, Henry Johnson, o.s. Charles Henry, of Bath (city), arm. PEMBROKE COLL., matric. 14 June, 1834, aged 17; B.A. 1838.

Marshall, Jacob Kelk, 1s. John Hewson, of Great Grimsby, co. Lincoln, arm. PEMBROKE COLL., matric. 1 Feb., 1877, aged 17; B.A. 1879, M.A. 1883.

Marshall, James, 2s. James, of St. Sepulchre's, London, arm. CHRIST CHURCH, matric. 30 May, 1838, aged 18; B.A. 1842, M.A. 1846, assistant-master Westminster School, vicar of Pyrton, Oxon, 1875-80. [26]

Marshall, (Sir) James, 2s. James, of Edinburgh, Scotland, cler. EXETER COLL., matric. 3 Feb., 1848, aged 18; B.A. 1851, M.A. 1856, classical master in the school of the Oratory, Birmingham, 1865, bar.-at-law, Lincoln's Inn, 1868, chief justice Gold Coast Colony 1879-82, knighted at Windsor Castle 29 June, 1882, etc. See Foster's *Men at the Bar.*

Marshall, James McCall, o.s. James, of St. Philip's, Birmingham, gent. TRINITY COLL., matric. 8 June, 1857, aged 19, scholar 1857-62, B.A. 1862; fellow BRASENOSE COLL. 1863-6, M.A. 1864, classical lecturer 1863-4, master at Dulwich 1865-84, head-master Durham School 1884.

Marshall, Jenner, 2s. Edward Marshall (-Hacker), of Ardley, Oxon, cler. WORCESTER COLL., matric. 22 Oct., 1835, aged 18; B.A. 1839, M.A. 1843, of Westcott Barton Manor, Oxon, held various curacies 1841-58. See *Rugby School Reg.*, 175.

Marshall, John, s. William, of Bodmin, Cornwall, pleb. EXETER COLL., matric. 9 April, 1717, aged 19; B.A. from ST. MARY HALL 1720. [30]

Marshall, John, s. George, of Plaxtoll, Kent, gent. UNIVERSITY COLL., matric. 14 May, 1719, aged 17; B.A. 23 Jan., 1722-3, M.A. 1725.

Marshall, John, s. John, of Barnstaple, Devon, pleb. CORPUS CHRISTI COLL., matric. 2 April, 1726, aged 17; B.A. 1729, M.A. 26 Feb., 1732-3, rector of Heanton Punchardon 1744, father of Thomas M. 1771.

Marshall, John, s. William, of Ashprington, Devon, cler. EXETER COLL., matric. 2 June, 1747, aged 18; B.A. from PEMBROKE COLL. 1750, M.A. 1753, master of the Exeter Free Grammar School, and father of Charles 1788, brother of Edward 1749, of Richard 1741, and of William 1751.

Marshall, John, s. William, of Hurst, Sussex, gent. HERTFORD COLL., matric. 8 June, 1791, aged 17; B.A. 1795, M.A. 1798.

Marshall, John, s. Charles, of Lawhitton, Cornwall, cler. EXETER COLL., matric. 3 July, 1816, aged 17; B.A. 1820 (? rector of Evesham 1828, until his death 9 Dec., 1857). [35]

Marshall, John, 1s. Ralph, of Deersford, Kerry, Ireland, arm. MAGDALEN COLL., matric. 3 Feb., 1821, aged 17.

Marshall, John, 2s. Charles, of Broadway, co. Worcester, gent. WORCESTER COLL., matric. 6 April, 1821, aged 21; B.A. 1825, M.A. 1827.

Marshall, John, 1s. Thomas, of Huddersfield, Yorks, arm. ST. MARY HALL, matric. 6 Nov., 1824, aged 28; curate of Oldbury, near Bridgenorth, and curate of Sidbury, Salop, died at Manchester in 1835.

Marshall, Rev. Sampson, s. William, of Poundstock, Cornwall, cler. EXETER COLL., matric. 4 April, 1775, aged 17; died at Fremington, Devon, 29 Jan., 1833. [20]

Marshall, Samuel, 3s. William, of Upper Grosvenor Street, Grosvenor Square, London, arm. EXETER COLL., matric. 2 June, 1852, aged 18; B.A. 1857, a student of Lincoln's Inn, 1856, died 19 March, 1860. See *Rugby School Reg.*, 254.

Marshall, Stirling Frederick, 4s. William, of Widcombe, Somerset, cler. WADHAM COLL., matric. 5 March, 1835, aged 18; B.A. 1838, M.A. 1841, conduct of Eton College 1841-54, rector of Farnham Royal, Bucks, since 1854.

Marshall, Thomas, s. Thomas, of Notts, pleb. ST. MARY HALL, matric. 29 June, 1730, aged 20.

Marshall, Thomas, s. Thomas, of St. Margaret's, Westminster, pleb. CHRIST CHURCH, matric. 2 July, 1733, aged 17; B.A. 1737.

Marshall, Thomas, s. Thomas, of Padstow, Cornwall, gent. WADHAM COLL., matric. 26 March, 1765, aged 18; B.A. 1769. [25]

Marshall, Thomas, 1s. Thomas Horncastle, of Leeds, Yorks, arm. ST. JOHN'S COLL., matric. 1 July, 1850, aged 18; B.A. 1855, M.A. 1858, a student of Gray's Inn 1852, a solicitor at Leeds. See *Robinson*, 285.

Marshall, Thomas Ansell, o.s. Thomas, of Keswick, Cumberland, gent. TRINITY COLL., matric. 19 May, 1845, aged 18, scholar 1845-8; B.A. from NEW INN HALL 1850, M.A. 1868, a vice-master Cheltenham College 1851-9, principal Milford College, 1858-62, head-master Barnstaple Grammar School 1865-72, rector of St. Mary, Antigua, 1877-83.

Marshall, Thomas Harrison, 2s. Thomas Harrison, of Hull, Yorks, gent. MAGDALEN HALL, matric. 10 Oct., 1845, aged 24.

Marshall, Thomas Horatio, o.s. Thomas, of Hartford, Cheshire, arm. EXETER COLL., matric. 12 June, 1851, aged 18; B.A. 1856, M.A. 1865, of Hartford Beach, Cheshire, J.P., etc. See *Eton School Lists*.

Marshall, Thomas Mervin, . John, of Heanton Puncherdown, Devon, cler.s MAGDALEN HALL, matric. 20 March, 1771, aged 17; B.A. 1775 (as Thomas), rector of Bow, Devon, buried there 1795, father of Bouchier 1805. [30]

Marshall, Thomas Outram, 3s. Thomas, of Sukkar, East Indies, arm. NEW COLL., matric. 12 Oct., 1861, aged 18; scholar 1861-6, B.A. 1866, has held various curacies since 1866.

Marshall, Victor Alexander Ernest (B.A. from TRINITY COLL., Cambridge, 1864), 1s. James Garth, of Headingley, Yorks, arm. CHRIST CHURCH, incorp. 16 Oct., 1872, aged 30.

Marshall, Walter Gore, 2s. George, of London, arm. CHRIST CHURCH, matric. 27 May, 1863, aged 17; B.A. 1867, M.A. 1875, of Hambleton, Rutland, high sheriff 1884.

Marshall, Walter Langley, 2s. George, of Pyrton, Oxon, cler. CHRIST CHURCH, matric. 12 Oct., 1883, aged 18; B.A. 1887.

Marshall, Wilfrid George, 3s. James Earnshaw, of St. James's, near Taunton, Somerset, gent. EXETER COLL., matric. 13 Oct., 1871, aged 18; B.A. 1875, M.A. 1878, a student of the Inner Temple 1874. See *Eton School Lists*. [35]

Marshall, William, s. John, of St. Gennys, Cornwall, pleb. EXETER COLL., matric. 21 Feb., 1722-3, aged 19 (? B.A. 1726 as John).

Marshall, William, s. William, of St. Martin's-in-the-Fields, gent. QUEEN'S COLL., matric. 22 May, 1729, aged 17; a student of the Middle Temple 1730.

Marshall, William, s. Robert, of Kirkby Stephen, Westmoreland, gent. QUEEN'S COLL., matric. 8 May, 1736, aged 17; B.A. from NEW COLL. 3 Feb., 1740-1, M.A. 1744.

Marshall, William, s. Edward, of St. Gennys, Cornwall, pleb. EXETER COLL., matric. 9 April, 1747, aged 19.

Marshall, William, s. William, of Bunley, Devon, cler. EXETER COLL., matric. 27 March, 1751, aged 18; B.A. 1755, died 1808, father of William next-named, brother of Edward 1749, of John 1747, and of Richard 1741, and great grandfather of Edward S. 1877.

Marshall, William, s. William, of Totness, Devon, gent. CORPUS CHRISTI COLL., matric. 3 June, 1791, aged 16, B.A. 1795; fellow BALLIOL COLL. 1797-1816, M.A. 1797, proctor 1806, B.D. 1807, rector of Chickerell, Dorset, 1831, until his death 1 March, 1864.

Marshall, William, s. James, of Bath, Somerset, gent. CORPUS CHRISTI COLL., matric. 21 April, 1795, aged 16; B.A. 1799, M.A. 1803, died at Weston Zoyland, Somerset, 29 Dec., 1847, aged 69.

Marshall, William, 'musicæ supellectilis venditor;' privilegiatus 26 Aug., 1812.

Marshall, William, s. William, of Brompton, Yorks, arm. WORCESTER COLL., matric. 4 Dec., 1816, aged 17; created M.A. 29 Nov., 1822. [5]

Marshall, William, 2s. William, of St. Giles's, Oxford, gent. CHRIST CHURCH, matric. 9 Nov., 1826, aged 20; B.Mus. 7 Dec., 1826, D.Mus. 14 Jan., 1840, organist of St. John's College and of Christ Church 1825-46.

Marshall, William, 3s. William, of Penwortham, Lancashire, arm. UNIVERSITY COLL., matric. 14 March, 1849, aged 18; B.A. 1852, of Penwortham Hall, Lancashire, vicar of Ilton, Somerset, 1852, until his death 8 June, 1879. See *Rugby School Reg.*, 256.

Marshall, William, of CORPUS CHRISTI COLL., Cambridge (? B.A. 1838, M.A. 1843); adm. 'comitatis causa' 29 Nov., 1866.

Marshall, 'William C' (*i.e.*, Congreve), s. John, of Claverley, Salop, arm. BRASENOSE COLL., matric. 31 May, 1802, aged 18; B.A. 1806, M.A. 1809.

Marshall, William Julius, born in Mexico, 1s. William, gent. EXETER COLL., matric. 28 Jan., 1847, aged 18; B.A. 1850, M.A. 1860, bar.-at-law, Inner Temple, 1867, capt. West Suffolk militia, died in Aug., 1881. See *Eton School Lists.* [10]

Marshall, William Kennedy, 1s. Joseph, of Parsonstown, Ireland, cler. NON-COLL., matric. 23 Nov., 1876, aged 18; of Baronne Court, co. Tipperary, high sheriff King's County 1886.

Marshall, William Wilkinson, 1s. Charles, of Manchester, cler. HERTFORD COLL., matric. 24 Jan., 1876, aged 18; scholar 1875-80, B.A. 1879, B.C.L. & M.A. 1885, a student of the Inner Temple 1878.

Marsham, Charles, born in Westminster, s. Robert, Baron Romney. CHRIST CHURCH, matric. 28 Feb., 1763, aged 18; 3rd baron, M.P. Maidstone 1768-74, Kent 1774-90, created Viscount Marsham and Earl of Romney 22 June, 1801, died 1 March, 1811. See Foster's *Peerage*, ROMNEY.

Marsham, Charles, born in Westminster, s. Charles, Baron Romney. CHRIST CHURCH, matric. 15 Oct., 1795, aged 17; B.A. 1800, M.A. 1801, 2nd Earl of Romney, M.P. Hythe 1798-1802 & 1806-7, Downton 1803-6, died 29 March, 1845. See Foster's *Peerage* & *Eton School Lists.*

Marsham, Charles, s. Jacob, of Thurnham, Kent, doctor. CHRIST CHURCH, matric. 29 April, 1805, aged 17; B.A. 1809, M.A. 1811, rector of Ilsington, Devon, vicar of Stoke Lyne, and of Caversfield, Oxon, 1812, until his death 24 Aug., 1867. See Foster's *Peerage* & *Eton School Lists.* [15]

Marsham, Charles (Viscount), born at Wateringbury, Kent, 1s. Charles, Earl of Romney. CHRIST CHURCH, matric. 13 Oct., 1826, aged 18; B.A. 1829, 3rd earl, M.P. West Kent 1841-5, died 3 Sep., 1874. See Foster's *Peerage* & *Eton School Lists.*

Marsham, Charles (Viscount), born at Bexley, Kent, 1s. Charles, Earl of Romney. CHRIST CHURCH, matric. 20 Jan., 1860, aged 18; 4th earl. See Foster's *Peerage.*

Marsham, Charles Jacob Bullock, 1s. Robert Bullock, of Merton College, Oxford, arm. MERTON COLL., matric. 22 May, 1847, aged 18; B.A. 1851, M.A. 1855.

Marsham, Cloudesley Dewar Bullock, 3s. Rober Bullock, of St. John's, Oxford, doctor. MERTO COLL., matric. 20 Oct., 1853, aged 18; B.A. 185 M.A. 1860, rector of Edgcott 1861-8, vicar of Stok Lyne, Oxon, 1868. See Foster's *Peerage.*

Marsham, George, 1s. George (Frederick John), c Allington, Kent, cler. MERTON COLL., matric. 2 Oct., 1867, aged 18; of Hayle Place, Kent, and c Headfort, co. Antrim, D.L., high sheriff 1878. Se *Eton School Lists.* [20

Marsham, George Frederick John, 5s. Hon. Jacob, c Kirby Overblow, Yorks, doctor. CHRIST CHURCH matric. 17 May, 1824, aged 17; B.A. 1828, M.A 1831, rector of Allington 1831, and vicar of Halling bury, Kent, 1832-52, died rector of Edgcott, Buck 29 Jan., 1852. See Foster's *Peerage* & *Eton Scho Lists.*

Marsham, Jacob Joseph, 4s. Jacob, of Rocheste Kent, doctor. CHRIST CHURCH, matric. 13 March 1823, aged 19; B.A. 1826, M.A. 1830, vicar c Shorne, Kent, since 1837. See Foster's *Peerage* *Eton School Lists.*

Marsham, Jacob, born at Mote, Kent, s. Robert, Baro Romney. CHRIST CHURCH, matric. 25 Jan., 177 aged 17; fellow of KING'S COLL., Cambridge M.A. 1783, D.D. 1797, preb. of Bath and Well 1789, and of Rochester 1797, rector of Wilmington Kent, 1800, canon of Windsor 1805, until his deat 28 Jan., 1840. See Foster's *Peerage.*

Marsham, John, 2s. (Charles), Earl of Romney CHRIST CHURCH, matric. 14 Dec., 1860, aged 18 rector of Barton-Seagrave, Northants, 1868. Se Foster's *Peerage.*

Marsham, Robert, Baron Romney, s. Robert, Baro Romney. CHRIST CHURCH, matric. 10 July, 173 aged 18; created D.C.L. 11 July, 1733, 2nd baror president Society of Arts, F.R.S., died 19 Nov. 1793. [25

Marsham, Robert, born at Maidstone, 2s. Charle Earl of Romney. CHRIST CHURCH, matric. 4 Nov 1852, aged 17; B.A. 1855, M.A. 1859, attaché a Rio Janeiro 1855-9. See Foster's *Peerage* & *Eto School Lists.*

Marsham, Robert (Bullock), s. Jacob, of Thurnham Kent, doctor. CHRIST CHURCH, matric. 21 Oct 1803, aged 17, B.A. 1807; fellow MERTON COLL 1812-26, M.A. 1814, D.C.L. 1826, dean 1824, bar at-law, Lincoln's Inn, 1813, warden of Merton Co lege 1826, until his death 27 Dec., 1880, aged 9 See Foster's *Peerage*, E. ROMNEY; & *Eton Scho Lists.*

Marsham, Robert Henry Bullock, 2s. Robert Bulloc of Oxford (city), doctor. MERTON COLL., matri 25 Oct., 1851, aged 18; B.A. 1855, M.A. 185 bar.-at-law, Inner Temple, 1860, recorder of Mai stone 1868-79, police magistrate Greenwich ar Woolwich 1879. See Foster's *Men at the Bar.*

Marsland, George, 4s. Thomas, of Stockpo Cheshire, gent. BRASENOSE COLL., matric. Feb., 1830, aged 19; B.A. 1834, M.A. 1837, rect of Beckingham, Notts, 1837, until his death 15 No 1874.

Marson, Charles, o.s. Charles, of Southwark, Surre arm. CHRIST CHURCH, matric. 26 May, 1841, ag 19; B.A. 1845, M.A. 1847, held various curac 1845-61, vicar of Christ Church, Birmingham, a preb. of Lichfield 1864-71, vicar of Clevedon sin 1871. [3

Marson, Charles Latimer, 1s. Charles, of Wokin Surrey, cler. UNIVERSITY COLL., matric. 8 Ju 1878, aged 19; B.A. 1881, M.A. 1885, rector Orlestone, Kent, since 1886.

Marston, Francis, o.s. Francis, of Stokesay, Salo cler. WORCESTER COLL., matric. 3 Nov., 18 aged 18.

Martelli, Charles Henry Ansley, 2s. Horatio, Brighton, Sussex, arm. TRINITY COLL., matr 30 May, 1828, aged 16; B.A. 1833, M.A. 18 bar.-at-law, Inner Temple, 1836, died 30 May, 18

INTERIOR OF THE QUADRANGLE, QUEEN'S COLLEGE, demolished about 1720.—*From an engraving by Skelton after Green.*

Martelli, Francis, o.s. Thomas, of Marchwood, Hants, cler. KEBLE COLL., matric. 16 Oct., 1876, aged 19; scholar 1876-80, B.A. 1880, M.A. 1884.

Martelli, Horatio Francis Kingsford, 1s. Horatio, of St. Clement's, London, arm. BRASENOSE COLL., matric. 11 May, 1826, aged 18; of Marchwood Lodge, Southants, J.P., D.L., assumed the name of HOLLOWAY in lieu of MARTELLI; father of Charles B., see p. 680.

Martelli, Thomas Chessher, y.s. Horatio, of London, arm. BRASENOSE COLL., matric. 6 July, 1833, aged 20; B.A. 1841, M.A. 1844, (1st) incumbent of the district church of St. John, Marchwood, Southampton, 1843, until his death 7 Oct., 1859.

Marten, George Nisbet, 1s. Thomas Powney, of Ghazeepore, Bengal, East Indies, arm. PEMBROKE COLL., matric. 13 June, 1859, aged 18; B.A. 1862.

Marten, James, s. James, of Reigate, Surrey, gent. UNIVERSITY COLL., matric. 19 Feb., 1724-5, aged 16. **[5]**

Marten, John, s. Thomas, of London, gent. MERTON COLL., matric. 2 April, 1726, aged 14.

Marten, John Hawkins, s. Edmund, of Hammersmith, Middlesex, doctor. WORCESTER COLL., matric. 30 Oct., 1755, aged 18; B.A. 1759, M.A. 1762.

Marten, Richard, s. Richard, of Axbridge, Somerset, pleb. HART HALL, matric. 9 July, 1722, aged 16; B.A. 1726, M.A. 1728.

Marter, Richard, s. Richard, of Horsell, Surrey, arm. EXETER COLL., matric. 29 June, 1807, aged 19; rector of Bright Waltham, Berks, 1841, until his death 12 Dec., 1871.

Martin, Albert Bentinck, 3s. George, of Exeter, Devon, cler. QUEEN'S COLL., matric. 30 Oct., 1863, aged 19; a civil engineer, half-brother of George Edward and Henry Arthur. See *Rugby School Reg.* **[10]**

Martin, Alfred Trice, 6s. Samuel of London, gent. MAGDALEN HALL, matric. 8 June, 1872, aged 17; exhibitioner WORCESTER COLL. 1872-6, B.A. 1876, M.A. 1880.

Martin, Anthony Crosby, s. Robert, of Dangan, co. Galway, Ireland, arm. ST. MARY HALL, matric. 15 Dec., 1795, aged 24.

Martin, Arthur 2s. William, of Staverton, Devon, cler. UNIVERSITY COLL., matric. 12 March, 1850, aged 17; scholar CORPUS CHRISTI COLL. 1851-62, B.A. 1854, M.A. 1858, fellow 1862, vice-president 1873.

Martin, Arthur John Matthews, o.s. Arthur, of Evershot, Dorset, gent. WADHAM COLL., matric. 14 Oct., 1870, aged 19.

Martin, Charles, 5s. William, of Staverton, Devon, cler. NEW COLL., matric. 13 Oct., 1859, aged 18, scholar 1859-64, B.A. 1863; a senior student CHRIST CHURCH 1864-9, M.A. 1866, tutor 1865-9, select preacher 1869, assistant-master Harrow School 1869-70, warden of St. Peter's College, Radley, and vicar of Radley 1871-9, rector of Woodnorton 1879-83, and of Poulshot, Wilts, since 1883. **[15]**

Martin, Rev. Charles Herbert, s. Charles, of Chester (city), arm. EXETER COLL., matric. 4 June, 1813, aged 19; B.A. 1817, M.A. 1820, of Maisemore, co. Gloucester, died at Reading 22 Nov., 1865.

Martin, Charles Robert Hesketh, 1s. Henry, of Killegar, Ireland, cler. TRINITY COLL., matric. 14 Oct., 1882, aged 19; died 8 March, 1884.

Martin, Clifford Henry Williams, 3s. Edward, of Weston-super-Mare, arm. NON-COLL., matric. 19 Jan., 1884, aged 22.

Martin, Cornwallis Philip Wykeham-, 1s. Philip, of Leamington, co. Warwick, arm. MERTON COLL., matric. 18 Oct., 1873, aged 18; of Swadelands, Kent, J.P. See *Eton School Lists.*

Martin, David Basil, 2s. David, of London, gent. NON-COLL., matric. 13 Oct., 1877, aged 19; B.A. 1881, M.A. 1884. **[20]**

Martin, Denny, s. Denny, of Loose, Kent, arm. UNIVERSITY COLL., matric. 17 Dec., 1744, aged 19; B.A. 1748, M.A. 1751.

Martin, Douglas Eycott, 1s. William Eycott, of Rochester, cler. TRINITY COLL., matric. 17 Oct., 1885, aged 19.

Martin, Edward, s. John, of Kirkham, Lancashire, pleb. BRASENOSE COLL., matric. 10 July, 1718, aged 18; B.A. 1722.

Martin, Edward Brace, 3s. Thomas, of Reigate, Surrey, arm. EXETER COLL., matric. 29 May, 1855, aged 18; B.A. 1859, M.A. 1862, rector of West Grimstead, Wilts, since 1864.

Martin, Edward Kingdon, 1s. Edward William, of Laughton, co. Lincoln, cler. NON-COLL., matric. 14 Oct., 1876, aged 18. **[25]**

Martin, Edwin, s. Edwin, of Lombard Street, London, gent. CHRIST CHURCH, matric. 19 Oct., 1759, aged 18.

Martin, Fiennes Wykeham, 3s. Fiennes Wykeham, of Chacombe, Northants, arm. BALLIOL COLL., matric. 4 June, 1824, aged 20; died in June, 1828. See *Eton School Lists.*

Martin, Francis Pitney Brouncker, o.s. George, of Madras, East Indies, arm. WADHAM COLL., matric. 15 March, 1832, aged 17; B.A. 1842, M.A. 1843.

Martin, Francis William Wykeham, 4s. Fiennes, of Banbury, arm. BALLIOL COLL., matric. 16 Dec., 1828, aged 20; B.A. 1832, vicar of Chalcombe, Oxon, 1843, until his death 6 May, 1873. See *Eton School Lists.*

Martin, George, s. Joseph, of Leatherhead, Surrey, arm. CHRIST CHURCH, matric. 18 May, 1781, aged 16; B.A. 1785, M.A. 1788, vicar of Broad Windsor, Dorset, 1792, rector of Overbury and Cowley, co. Worcester, died at Ham Court 22 Aug., 1796. **[30]**

Martin, George, s. Allen, of Westminster, gent. QUEEN'S COLL., matric. 7 May, 1785, aged 26.

Martin, George, s. Joseph, of Bourton, co. Gloucester, cler. NEW COLL., matric. 5 Feb., 1810, aged 18; B.A. 1813, M.A. 1818, fellow until 1817, canon of Exeter 1816, chancellor of the diocese 1820, vicar of Harberton, Devon, 1820, died 27 Aug., 1860.

Martin, George, 'servant to St. John's College;' privilegiatus 17 Sep., 1832.

Martin, George, scholar ST. JOHN'S COLL., Cambridge, 1835, senior optime and B.A. 1837, M.A. 1840, B.D. 1847, D.D. 1852; adm. 'ad eundem' 10 July, 1852, hon. canon Truro 1880, principal Exeter Diocesan College 1839-51, rector of St. Pancras, Exeter, 1840-5, vicar of St. Breward, Cornwall, 1851, until his death in 1882.

Martin, George Clements, 1s. Thomas Clements, of Lambourne, Berks, gent. NEW COLL., matric. 8 June, 1868, aged 23; B.Mus. 12 June, 1868. **[35]**

Martin, George Edward, 1s. George, of Exeter, Devon, cler. CHRIST CHURCH, matric. 15 June, 1848, aged 18; postmaster MERTON COLL. 1848-52, B.A. 1853, of Ham Court, co. Worcester, J.P., D.L., high sheriff 1882, bar.-at-law, Lincoln's Inn, 1857, major Worcestershire yeomanry cavalry 1883. See Foster's *Men at the Bar* & *Eton School Lists.*

Martin, Gerard, s. Henry, of Bruton, Somerset, gent. PEMBROKE COLL., matric. 15 June, 1750, aged 18; bar.-at-law, Middle Temple, 1755.

Martin, Harold, 3s. Thomas, of Oughton, Lancashire, gent. LINCOLN COLL., matric. 17 Oct., 1884, aged 16.

Martin, (Sir) Henry (Bart.), o.s. Henry William, of St. Marylebone, Middlesex, baronet. ORIEL COLL., matric. 20 June, 1820, aged 18; 3rd baronet, died s.p. 4 Dec., 1863. See Foster's *Baronetage.*

Martin, Henry, 2s. Robert Marshall, of Southwark, Surrey, cler. ST. EDMUND HALL, matric. 22 Oct., 1868, aged 24; B.A. 1872, M.A. 1876, vice-principal Cheltenham College 1873-8, principal Winchester Training College 1878, chaplain 1881. See *Robinson*, 319. **[40]**

Martin, Henry Arthur, 2s. George, of Exeter (city), cler. CHRIST CHURCH, matric. 23 May, 1850, aged 18; B.A. from ST. MARY HALL 1855, M.A. 1857, vicar of Laxton (or Lexington), Notts, 1858. See *Eton School Lists.*

Martin, Henry Basil, 2s. Hezekia, of Folkestone, Kent, cler. BRASENOSE COLL., matric. 23 Oct., 1885, aged 19.

Martin, (Sir) Henry William (Bart.), s. — M., of Bishops Town, Ireland, arm. CORPUS CHRISTI COLL., matric. 18 Oct., 1786, aged 17; 2nd baronet, died 3 Feb., 1842. See Foster's *Baronetage.*

Martin, Henry Witte, 1s. James, of St. Botolph's, London, gent. MAGDALEN HALL, matric. 22 June, 1849, aged 31.

Martin, Hudson, s. Henry, of Bristol, Somerset, gent. JESUS COLL., matric. 26 March, 1728, aged 17; B.A. 1731, M.A. 1734.

Martin, Hugh Alexander, 2s. Peter, of Reigate, Surrey, D.Med. BRASENOSE COLL., matric. 21 Oct., 1878, aged 19. [5]

Martin, James, s. John, of London, cler. MERTON COLL., matric. 22 Dec., 1722, aged 14; B.A. from ST. MARY HALL 1728.

Martin, James, s. John, of Tardibeg, co. Worcester, gent. BRASENOSE COLL., matric. 18 Nov., 1732, aged 17; B.A. 1736.

Martin, James, s. James, of Sackmurthy, Cumberland, pleb. QUEEN'S COLL., matric. 17 Dec., 1776, aged 21; B.A. 1780, M.A. 1784.

Martin, John, s. Robert, of Pebworth, co. Gloucester, gent. PEMBROKE COLL., matric. 26 March, 1729, aged 19; B.A. 1732, M.A. 1735.

Martin, John, s. John, of Overbury, co. Worcester, arm. WORCESTER COLL., matric. 9 March, 1741-2, aged 17; created M.A. 22 Aug., 1746, of Hall Park and Overbury Hall, co. Worcester, M.P. Tewkesbury 1754-61, died 28 May, 1794. [10]

Martin, John, s. Robert, of Pebworth, co. Gloucester, arm. PEMBROKE COLL., matric. 16 March, 1748-9, aged 18; B.C.L. 1756.

Martin, John, 'chirurgus et pharmacopola;' privilegiatus 15 July, 1830.

Martin, John, 1s. William, of Coventry, co. Warwick, cler. HERTFORD COLL., matric. 18 Oct., 1883, aged 19; scholar 1881-6, B.A. 1886.

Martin, John Biddulph, 2s. Robert, of Eaton Square, London, arm. EXETER COLL., matric. 21 Jan., 1860, aged 18; B.A. 1862, M.A. 1867.

Martin, John Halliday, s. Samuel, of Marylebone, Middlesex, arm. PEMBROKE COLL., matric. 7 Nov., 1800, aged 18. [15]

Martin, John Pearson, 1s. John, of Maryport, Cumberland, gent. QUEEN'S COLL., matric. 22 Oct., 1884, aged 19.

Martin, John Sturges, 5s. Joseph, of Moreton-in-Marsh, co. Gloucester, cler. ORIEL COLL., matric. 7 Dec., 1821, aged 18; B.A. 1826, died 9 Aug., 1839, brother of Richard 1819.

Martin, Joseph, 4s. Edward, of Llangapelach, co. Glamorgan, arm. JESUS COLL., matric. 4 Dec., 1828, aged 20.

Martin, Joseph, 3s. John, of Croydon, Surrey, gent. WORCESTER COLL., matric. 26 April, 1873, aged 35; a student of the Inner Temple 1875.

Martin, Joseph John, s. Joseph, of Bourton-on-Hill, co. Gloucester, cler. CHRIST CHURCH, matric. 22 Oct., 1807, aged 17, B.A. 1811; fellow ALL SOULS' COLL. 1812-29, M.A. 1815, of Ham Court, co. Worcester, J.P., D.L., died 1873. [20]

Martin, Rev. Norman Jackson, 3s. George, of Liverpool, gent. CHRIST CHURCH, matric. 23 May, 1872; B.A. 1876, M.A. 1887, a student of the Inner Temple 1873, aged 18. See *Eton School Lists.*

Martin, Philip Wykeham, 1s. Charles Wykeham, of London, arm. BALLIOL COLL., matric. 23 March, 1847, aged 18; B.A. 1850, of Leed's Castle, Kent, Chacombe Priory, Northants, and Packwood Hall, co. Warwick, M.P. Rochester 1836, until his death 31 May, 1878, in the library of the House of Commons. See *Eton School Lists.*

Martin, Reginald Joseph, 3s. Robert Marshall, Bermondsey, Surrey, cler. ORIEL COLL., matri 13 Oct., 1873, aged 21; B.A. 1878, M.A. 188 rector of Greenstead, Essex, since 1883.

Martin, Richard, 5s. Joseph, of Exeter (city), cle ORIEL COLL., matric. 14 May, 1819, aged 16, B. 1823; fellow EXETER COLL. 1824-31, M.A. 182 bursar & tutor 1826, dean 1829, public examin 1830-1, vicar of Menheniot, Cornwall, 1831-83, ho canon Truro 1878, died 3 Feb., 1888. See *Boase,* 12

Martin, Richard, 2s. John, of St. Mary Woolnotl London, arm. NEW COLL., matric. 2 Feb., 182 aged 17; B.A. 1828, died in 1829. [2

Martin, Richard, 3s. William, of Staverton, Devo cler. CORPUS CHRISTI COLL., matric. 9 Marc 1854, aged 18; B.A. 1857, M.A. 1860, rector of Cha lacombe, Devon, 1861-80, rector of Swymbridge 188

Martin, Richard Biddulph, 1s. Robert, of Eatc Square, London, arm. EXETER COLL., matri 13 May, 1856, aged 18; B.A. 1859, M.A. 186 M.P. Tewkesbury 1880-5.

Martin, Robert, 4s. John, of St. Mary Woolnotl London, arm. EXETER COLL., matric. 22 Jan 1828, aged 19; of Overbury Court, co. Worceste high sheriff, 1877, father of the last named.

Martin, Robert, 3s. Thomas, of Deanes, Lancashir gent. ST. MARY HALL, matric. 25 Oct., 186 aged 19; B.A. 1867, M.A. 1871, B. & D.D. 188 vicar of Irlam, Lancashire, since 1872.

Martin, Robert Fanshawe. y.s. Thomas Byam, Plymouth, Devon, equitis. ORIEL COLL., matri 18 Feb., 1823, aged 17; lieut.-colonel in the arm died 13 July, 1846. See Foster's *Baronetage.* [3

Martin, Robert Marshall, 1s. Robert, of Cheshun Herts, gent. ST. EDMUND HALL, matric. 11 Dec 1837, aged 21; B.A. 1841, M.A. 1868, vicar Christ Church, Bermondsey, 1845-74, and of Thorp Surrey, since 1874.

Martin, Samuel, s. Adam, of Isle of Antigua, gen WADHAM COLL., matric. 11 April, 1717, aged 1 See Foster's *Baronetage.*

Martin, Samuel, s. Samuel, of Loughborough, c Leicester, cler. LINCOLN COLL., matric. 12 Marc 1718-9, aged 17; B.A. 1722, M.A. 1725.

Martin, Samuel, s. William, of East Indies, ar CHRIST CHURCH, matric. 2 Feb., 1798, aged (? See *Eton School Lists.*)

Martin, Septimus, 4s. Hezekiah, of Southtown, S folk, arm. JESUS COLL., matric. 27 Oct., 1864, ag 20; perp. curate St. Saviour's, Upper Sunbury, si 1881. [

Martin, Stephen Burfield, 1s. Robert Thomas, Hailsham, Sussex, gent. NON-COLL., matric. Jan., 1886, aged 19.

Martin, Thomas, s. Thomas, of New Sarum, Wi gent. BALLIOL COLL., matric. 16 Nov., 1733, a 18; B.A. 1737.

Martin, Thomas, 'butler to the dean of Christ Chur privilegiatus 19 May, 1778.

Martin, Thomas Alexander, 5s. John, of Berm arm. BALLIOL COLL., matric. 17 Oct., 1877, a 19; B.A. 1880, M.A. 1884, bar.-at-law, Ir Temple, 1882. See Foster's *Men at the Bar.*

Martin, Thomas Martin, 1s. James Thomas, of Leonard's, Shoreditch, arm. QUEEN'S Co matric. 8 Feb., 1844, aged 18. [

Martin, Walter Willasey, o.s. Walter Hattam, of Helier, Isle of Jersey, arm. BRASENOSE Co matric. 5 June, 1858, aged 18; B.A. 1861, M.A. 1 rector of Shepperton, Middlesex, since 1877.

Martin, William, s. William, of Warburton, Ches pleb. BRASENOSE COLL., matric. 26 June, 1 aged 22.

Martin, William, s. Adam, of Seaborough, Some gent. BALLIOL COLL., matric. 15 Feb., 1733-4, 19; B.A. 1737, bar.-at-law, Middle Temple, 174

Martin, William, s. William, of Dublin (city), do CHRIST CHURCH, matric. 26 May, 1785, aged See *Alumni West.*, 419.

Martyn, Claudius Robert, 1s. Thomas, of Evenley, Northants, cler. LINCOLN COLL., matric. 20 Nov., 1834, aged 18; exhibitioner 1836-42, B.A. 1838, M.A. 1841, rector of Ludgershall, Oxon, 1869, until his death in 1873. [20]

Martyn, Edward Joseph, 1s. John, of Masonbrook, co. Galway, arm. CHRIST CHURCH, matric. 24 May, 1877, aged 18.

Martyn, Francis Mountjoy, y.s. Charles Fuller, of Calcutta, East Indies, arm. TRINITY COLL., matric. 30 Oct., 1827, aged 18; colonel 2nd life guards.

Martyn, George Horace, 1s. John, of Ibberton, Dorset, cler. EXETER COLL., matric. 19 May, 1877, aged 19; B.A. 1880, M.A. 1887.

Martyn, John Lee, s. Nicholas, of St. George-the-Martyr, Middlesex, gent. TRINITY COLL., matric. 9 Nov., 1786, aged 19; B.A. 1792, M.A. 1793, B. & D.D. 1826, rector of St. George-the-Martyr, Queen Square, London, 1806, until his death 19 Aug., 1836.

Martyn, John Waddon, 3s. Thomas Waddon, of Lifton, Devon, cler. EXETER COLL., matric. 27 Jan., 1831, aged 18; B.A. 1835, M.A. 1836, of the office of Board of Trade, father of Thomas W. 1864. See *Eton School Lists.* [25]

Martyn, Northmore Herle Laurence, 2s. William Waddon, of Kingsteignton, Devon, cler. NON-COLL., matric. 13 Oct., 1876, aged 19; B.A. & M.A. from EXETER COLL. 1883.

Martyn, Orlando Bridgman, 1s. William, of Broughton, Middlesex, D.Med. MERTON COLL., matric. 17 Oct., 1874, aged 19; postmaster 1874-9, B.A. 1878, bar.-at-law, Inner Temple, 1880. See Foster's *Men at the Bar.*

Martyn, Richard Lomax, s. Nicholas, of St. George-the-Martyr, Westminster, arm. ORIEL COLL., matric. 14 Feb., 1789, aged 19; B.A. 1792, M.A. 1795, rector of Lurgashall, Essex, 1819, until his death 21 Sep., 1851.

Martyn, Robert, s. William, of North Tamerton, Cornwall, gent. EXETER COLL., matric. 2 April, 1747, aged 18; B.A. 14 March, 1750-1, vicar of Luffincott, father of Thomas Whaddon 1783, and of William 1783.

Martyn, Roger, s. John, of Tavistock, Devon, pleb. EXETER COLL., matric. 21 March, 1714-5, aged 17; B.A. from NEW INN HALL 1718, vicar of Awliscombe, Devon, 1723, until his death 6 July, 1763, father of Charles 1742, and of Thomas 1755. [30]

Martyn, Samuel Symons, o.s. Samuel Symons, of Isle of Man, arm. KEBLE COLL., matric. 26 Jan., 1886, aged 31.

Martyn, Thomas, s. Roger, of Awliscombe, Devon, cler. BALLIOL COLL., matric. 9 Dec., 1755, aged 18.

Martyn, Thomas, s. Claud, of Ludgershall, Bucks, cler. QUEEN'S COLL., matric. 5 June, 1810, aged 18.

Martyn, Thomas, 1s. John King, of Great Staughton, Hunts, cler. QUEEN'S COLL., matric. 10 Feb., 1820, aged 18; B.A. 1823, M.A. 1828.

Martyn, Thomas (Waddon), s. Robert, of Luffincott, Devon, cler. EXETER COLL., matric. 9 April, 1783, aged 17; B.A. 1787, curate of Lifton, Devon, 1798-1833, rector 1833, and of Luffincott 1794, until his death 31 Jan., 1837, father of John W. 1831, and of the next named. [35]

Martyn, Thomas Waddon, 2s. Thomas Waddon, of Lifton, Devon, cler. EXETER COLL., matric. 16 June, 1825, aged 17; B.A. 1829, died rector of Lifton and vicar of Thorverton, Devon, 6 March, 1846.

Martyn, Thomas Waddon, 1s. John Waddon, of Exeter, Devon, cler. MAGDALEN COLL., matric. 16 Jan., 1864, aged 19; demy 1863-8, rector of Hethe, Oxon, 1881-7, vicar of Aston Abbots 1887. See *Eton School Lists.*

Martyn, William, s. William, of Exeter (city), arm. BALLIOL COLL., matric. 13 Nov., 1742, aged 18; B.A. 1746.

Martyn, William, s. Robert, of Luffincott, Devon, cler. EXETER COLL., matric. 9 April, 1783, aged 19.

Martyn, William Edward, 2s. William, of London, D.Med. CHRIST CHURCH, matric. 15 Oct., 1875, aged 19; a junior student 1875-80, B.A. 1879.

Martyn, William Turnavine, 1s. William, of Saltash, Cornwall, gent. QUEEN'S COLL., matric. 23 Oct., 1882, aged 19; B.A. 1885.

Martyn, William Waddon, o.s. William Waddon, of St. Anstel, Cornwall, arm. TRINITY COLL., matric. 5 June, 1851, aged 18; B.A. 1855, of Tonacombe, Cornwall, and of Stoke Manor, Devon, rector of Lifton, Devon, since 1863. See *Eton School Lists.*

Marvin, Francis Sydney, 1s. Francis Bentham, of London, gent. ST. JOHN'S COLL., matric. 14 Oct., 1882, aged 19; scholar 1882, B.A. 1886.

Marvin, William Harry, o.s. John Higginson, of Shilton, co. Warwick, gent. ST. JOHN'S COLL., matric. 4 March, 1847, aged 18; B.A. 1850, M.A. 1854, rector of Higham Gobion, Beds, since 1857, and vicar of Hexton since 1868. [5]

Marvin, William Staresmore, s. William, of Clifton-upon-Dunsmore, co. Warwick, arm. UNIVERSITY COLL., matric. 19 Jan., 1813, aged 18; B.A. 1816, M.A. 1820, vicar of Shawbury, Salop, 1826, until his death 21 Nov., 1854. See *Rugby School Reg.*, 88.

Marwood, George, s. George Metcalfe, of Stanmer, Sussex, cler. CHRIST CHURCH, matric. 11 April, 1799, aged 17; B.A. 1803, of Little Busby Hall, Yorks, assumed the name of MARWOOD in lieu of METCALFE in 1809, vicar of Amport, Southants, died 9 Jan., 1842, father of the next named. See Foster's *Yorkshire Collection.*

Marwood, George, o.s. George of Amport,, Hants, cler. CHRIST CHURCH, matric. 19 June, 1827, aged 18; B.A. 1831, of Busby Hall, Yorks, J.P., D.L., died 7 April 1882.

Marwood, George Frederick, 1s. George, of Stokesley, Yorks, arm. EXETER COLL., matric. 14 Oct., 1876, aged 18; B.A. 1879, of Busby Hall, Yorks, J.P., bar.-at-law, Inner Temple, 1885. See Foster's *Yorkshire Collection.*

Marwood, James, s. Thomas, of Kilminton, Devon, gent. EXETER COLL., matric. 8 March, 1719-20, aged 18. [10]

Marwood, James Thomas Benedictus, 3s. James, of Chaffcomb, Somerset, arm. QUEEN'S COLL., matric. 22 Aug., 1764, aged 18; of Avishays, Somerset, died 20 Feb., 1811.

Marwood, Thomas, s. George Metcalfe, of Stanmer, Sussex, cler. ST. MARY HALL, matric. 6 Feb., 1804, aged 18; B.A. from MERTON COLL. 1808, Michel fellow QUEEN'S COLL. 1810-22, M.A. 1810, assumed the name of MARWOOD in lieu of METCALFE, rector of English Bicknor, co. Gloucester, 1822, until his death 25 Sep., 1832.

Marx, Francis Joseph Peter, o.s. George, of St. George's, Bloomsbury, London, arm. CHRIST CHURCH, matric. 4 June, 1835, aged 18; B.A. 1839, of Arlebury, Hants, J.P., died in 1876. See *Eton School Lists.*

Marychurch, Henry Weldy, 5s. Francis, of Bristol, gent. ST. EDMUND HALL, matric. 3 Feb., 1835, aged 24; B.A. 1838, M.A. 1855, perp. curate St. Paul's, Blackburn, 1850-70, vicar of Winksley, Yorks, 1870-5, and of Ingrow 1875-82.

Marychurch, William Thomas, 2s. Francis, of St. James's, Bristol, gent. ST. EDMUND HALL, matric. 2 June, 1826, aged 24; B.A. 1830, M.A. 1835, rector of Sudbourn with Orford, Suffolk, 1835, until his death 5 Aug., 1842. [15]

Mascall, Francis, s. Francis, of Eppleton, co. Durham, arm. UNIVERSITY COLL., matric. 9 Dec., 1780, aged 18; bar.-at-law, Lincoln's Inn, 1813, died 12 Nov., 1857.

Mascall, Robert, s. John, of Ashford, Kent, arm. ORIEL COLL., matric. 22 Nov., 1780, aged 18.

Mascall, Robert Curteis, s. Robert, of Ashford, Kent, arm. ORIEL COLL., matric. 26 April, 1811, aged 16; B.A. 1815, of Peasmarsh, Sussex, a student of Lincoln's Inn 1814, died at Nice 19 May, 1816.

Masham, Samuel, born in Kensington, Middlesex, s. Samuel, Baron M. CHRIST CHURCH, matric. 16 Dec., 1729, aged 17; 2nd Baron Masham, a lord of the bedchamber, remembrancer Court of Exchequer, F.R.S., died 14 June, 1776.

Mashborne, Philip, s. James, of Penshurst, Kent, cler. UNIVERSITY COLL., matric. 16 March, 1718-9, aged 14; B.A. 1722, M.A. 1725. [20]

Masheder, Rev. Richard, o.s. —— M., of Bury, Lancashire, cler. KEBLE COLL., matric. 15 Oct., 1877, aged 20; B.A. 1880, M.A. 1884.

Mashiter, Edward Holbech, s. Richard, of Solihull, co. Warwick, cler. MAGDALEN HALL, matric. 17 March, 1762, aged 18; B.A. 1765, M.A. 1768.

Mashiter, Richard, s. Roger, of Bolton, Lancashire, pleb. PEMBROKE COLL., matric. 23 Feb., 1737-8, aged 23; B.A. 6 March, 1741-2.

Maskell, William, o.s. William, of Shepton Mallet, Somerset, arm. UNIVERSITY COLL., matric. 9 June, 1832, aged 18; B.A. 1836, M.A. 1838.

Maskelyne, Edmund Mervin Booth Storey, 2s. Anthony Mervin Reeve, of Lydiard Tregoze, Wilts, arm. WADHAM COLL., matric. 2 Feb., 1848, aged 18; B.A. 1853, bar.-at-law, Lincoln's Inn, 1861. See Foster's *Men at the Bar.* [25]

Maskelyne, Anthony Mervin Reeve Storey, s. William Storey, of Hinton Martell, Dorset, cler. WADHAM COLL., matric. 10 Oct., 1806, aged 15; B.A. 1810, M.A. 1818, of Basset Down House, Wilts, in right of his wife he assumed the additional surname of MASKELYNE 1845, bar.-at-law, Inner Temple, 1816, died 15 May, 1879.

Maskelyne, Maurice, 1s. William, of Purton, Wilts, gent. PEMBROKE COLL., matric. 11 May, 1827, aged 20; brother of William 1827.

Maskelyne, Mervin Herbert Nevil Storey, 1s. Anthony Mervin Storey, of Lydiard Tregoze, Wilts, arm. WADHAM COLL., matric. 19 Nov., 1840, aged 17; B.A. 1845, M.A. 1849, hon. fellow 1873, a student of the Inner Temple 1846, lecturer in chemistry and physics Exeter College 1855-7, Waynflete professor of mineralogy 1856, sometime keeper of the mineral department British Museum, fellow of Institute of Chemistry; of Basset Down House, Wilts, etc., J.P., D.L., M.P. Cricklade 1880-5, North Wilts (Dec.) 1885, F.R.S., assumed the additional name of MASKELYNE.

Maskelyne, William, 2s. William, of Purton, Wilts, gent. PEMBROKE COLL., matric. 11 May, 1827, aged 19; B.A. 1831, M.A. 1834, rector (and patron) of Crudwell, Wilts, 1839, until his death 26 Nov., 1866.

Maskery, Rev. John 2s. Thomas, of Norbury, co. Derby, gent. WADHAM COLL., matric. 25 June, 1841, aged 17; B.A. 1846, M.A. 1855. [30]

Maskew, Arthur Fairclough, 2s. Thomas Ratsey, of Dorchester, Dorset, cler. NON-COLL., matric. 13 Oct., 1877, aged 23; B.A. 1881, vicar of St. Leonard's, Leicester, 1883-6, and of St. Paul's, Peterboro', 1886.

Maskew, Henry Edward, 4s. Thomas, of Milford, Hants, arm. MAGDALEN HALL, matric. 5 Dec., 1844, aged 19; chaplain of the forces at Zante 1854-76, incumbent of St. James's, Great Dollar, N.B., 1877.

Mason, Abraham, M.A. TRINITY COLL., Dublin, 1844 (B.A. 1840), 2s. Abraham, of Dublin, arm. BRASENOSE COLL., incorp. 6 July, 1844, aged 31; vicar of Broxted, Essex, 1846, until his death (? 1885).

Mason, Alexander Lyon Arthur, o.s. Chart Skinner, of Sherbourne, Dorset, cler. TRINITY COLL., matric. 18 Oct., 1869, aged 19; B.A. 1874, M.A. 1881, rector of Westley Waterless, co. Cambridge, since 1886.

Mason, Alfred Edward Woodley, 2s. William Woodley, of Camberwell, Surrey, gent. TRINITY COLL., matric. 11 Oct., 1884, aged 19. [35]

Mason, Arthur Brookland, 2s. Mashfield, of Sydney, Australia, gent. ST. JOHN'S COLL., matric. 1 July, 1861, aged 18; of Ceylon Civil Service 1866. See *Robinson*, 330.

Mason, Charles, fellow of TRINITY COLL., Cambridge (B.A. 1722, M.A. 1726); incorp. 27 Feb., 1730-1, B.D. 1736, D.D. 1749, Woodward professor of geology, Cambridge, 1734-62.

Mason, Charles, y.s. William, of Bilsby, co. Lincoln, cler. WORCESTER COLL., matric. 28 Oct., 1852, aged 19; B.A. 1856, curate of Bilsby, co. Lincoln, 1857-8, vicar 1858, of Farlsthorp since 1880.

Mason, Charles Arthur, 2s. Francis John Mills, of Waltair, East Indies, arm. BALLIOL COLL., matric. 17 Oct., 1877, aged 18; B.A. 1881, M.A. 1884, chaplain Madras railway 1886, brother of Francis W. R. 1871.

Mason, Edmund Robert, o.s. Henry William, of Deptford, Kent, gent. MAGDALEN HALL, matric. 19 Oct., 1867, aged 26; B.A. from QUEEN'S COLL. 1871, M.A. 1875, vicar of Christ Church, Birmingham, 1881, preb. of Lichfield 1881.

Mason, Francis, 1s. Henry Browne, of Seymour Street, St. George's, London, arm. MAGDALEN HALL, matric. 1 Feb., 1854, aged 20. [5]

Mason, Francis George Montagu, 1s. James Montagu, of Horrington, Somerset, cler. TRINITY COLL., matric. 22 May, 1874, aged 18; B.A. from NEW INN HALL 1879, M.A. 1881, bar.-at-law, Inner Temple, 1885. See Foster's *Men at the Bar.*

Mason, Francis Wheeler Randall, 1s. Francis John Mills, of Waltair, Madras, East Indies, arm. PEMBROKE COLL., matric. 27 April, 1871, aged 18; B.A. 1874, M.A. 1877, rector of Beesby, co. Lincoln, 1880, and of Steep, Hants, 1880, brother of Charles A. 1877.

Mason, Frederick La Tour, 3s. Richard, of Lincoln (city), arm. CORPUS CHRISTI COLL., matric. 15 Oct., 1859, aged 19; B.A. 1862, bar.-at-law, Lincoln's Inn, 1865. See Foster's *Men at the Bar* & *Rugby School Reg.*

Mason, George, s. John, of Porters, Herts, arm. CORPUS CHRISTI COLL., matric. 7 Feb., 1753, aged 17; bar.-at-law, Inner Temple, 1761.

Mason, George, B.A. from ST. JOHN'S COLL., Cambridge, 1760 (M.A. 1763), s. Miles, of Kirkby Stephen, Westmoreland, gent. NEW COLL., incorp. 10 Feb., 1780, aged 49, B. & D.D. 16 Feb., 1780, bishop of Man 1780, until his death 8 Dec., 1783. [10]

Mason, George, o.s. Thomas, of Bradford, Yorks, arm. BRASENOSE COLL., matric. 14 Jan., 1823, aged 18; B.A. 1827, M.A. 1829, of Copt Hewick Hall, Yorks, rector of Scruton, near Bedale, Yorks, 1834-57, died in Bohemia June, 1867. See *Manchester School Reg.*, iii. 133.

Mason, George, 4s. John, of Bengal, East Indies, arm. CHRIST CHURCH, matric. 24 Jan., 1823, aged 17.

Mason, George, 1s. Thomas, of Handley, Dorset, cler. ORIEL COLL., matric. 6 Nov., 1846, aged 17; B.A. from NEW INN HALL 1853, M.A. 1860, perp. curate of St. Stephen's, Devonport, 1858-62, archdeacon of Honolulu 1864-73, of Columbia 1880-4, dean of Victoria, Vancouver Island, 1878-80, vicar of Long Cross, Surrey, 1884. See *Crockford.*

Mason, George Miles, s. Miles, of London, gent. BRASENOSE COLL., matric. 21 Oct., 1807, aged 18; B.A. 1812, M.A. 1814, his father died 26 April, 1822, aged 70. See *Gent.'s Mag.*, 1822, i. 474.

Mason, Henry Allan, 2s. Nathaniel, of Islington, Middlesex, gent. MAGDALEN HALL, matric. 7 July, 1855, aged 26. [15]

Mason, Rev. Henry Bonner, 3s. Henry Brown, of Clifton, co. Gloucester, arm. CHRIST CHURCH, matric. 20 Oct., 1836, aged 19; B.A. from NEW INN HALL 1841, died 7 Feb., 1846. See *Rugby School Reg.*, 168.

Mason, Henry Cox, s. William, of London, gent. ST. EDMUND HALL, matric. 30 Nov., 1773, aged 18; B.A. 1777 (? M.A. from SIDNEY SUSSEX COLL., Cambridge, 1781), rector of St. Mary's, Bermondsey, chaplain to Lord Onslow, founder of the Deaf and Dumb School, died 3 Feb., 1804.

Mason, Henry Edward, 1s. Edward, of Tredegar, co. Monmouth, gent. JESUS COLL., matric. 5 Feb., 1863, aged 19; B.A. 1866, M.A 1869.

Mason, Henry Williams, 3s. William, of Carnarvon (town), D.Med. CHRIST CHURCH, matric. 31 May, 1844, aged 18; a student 1847-76, B.A. 1848, M.A. 1851, perp. curate Wigginton, Herts, 1858-75, vicar of Kirkham, Lancashire, 1875, hon. canon Manchester 1887, brother of John W. 1838, and of Rich. W. 1835.

Mason, Hugh, s. John, of Ruthin, co. Denbigh, pleb. JESUS COLL., matric. 14 July, 1763, aged 17; B.A. 1767.

Mason, Jacob, 3s. Abraham, of Dublin (city), arm. WORCESTER COLL., matric. 13 May, 1836, aged 18; brother of Thomas W. 1838. [21]

Mason, James Edward, 4s. Charles Adnam, of Tarrington, co. Hereford, gent. WORCESTER COLL., matric. 9 June, 1865, aged 19.

Mason, James Holman, s. Holman, of Oakhampton, Devon, gent. EXETER COLL., matric. 26 May, 1797, aged 17; B.A. 1801, M.A. 1804, vicar of Widdecombe-in-the-Moor, Devon, 1815, until his death 19 Jan., 1861.

Mason, James Wood, 1s. Joseph, of London, D.Med. QUEEN'S COLL. matric. 30 Jan., 1866, aged 20; a student of the Inner Temple 1867.

Mason, John, s. William, of Buckingham (town), gent. CHRIST CHURCH, matric. 14 Jan., 1716-7, aged 17; bar.-at-law, Middle Temple, 1727, bencher 1757, buried in the Temple Church, Friday, 11 Dec., 1761.

Mason, John, s. Thomas, of Westington, co. Hereford, gent. BALLIOL COLL., matric. 2 April, 1737, aged 18; B.A. 1740. [26]

Mason, John, s. John, of Syston, co. Lincoln, pleb. MAGDALEN HALL, matric. 12 Dec., 1738, aged 13.

Mason, John, 'tonsor;' privilegiatus 23 Sep., 1748.

Mason, John, s. John, of Denbigh (town), pleb. ORIEL COLL., matric. 21 Jan., 1788, aged 18; B.A. 1792, M.A. 1809. [29]

Mason, Rev. John, o.s. John Finch, of London, arm. CHRIST CHURCH, matric. 19 Oct., 1837, aged 18; B.A. from NEW INN HALL 1842, M.A. 1845, of Aldenham Lodge, Herts. See *Eton School Lists.*

Mason, John Mason, 2s. Thomas, of Kirkby Stephen, Westmoreland, gent. QUEEN'S COLL., matric. 6 June, 1839, aged 19; scholar ST. JOHN'S COLL., Cambridge, 1840, senior optime and B.A. 1844, rector of Whitfield, co. Durham, 1860, hon. canon of Durham.

Mason, John Williams, 2s. William, of Llanbeblig, co. Carnarvon, arm. JESUS COLL., matric. 3 May, 1838, aged 18; scholar 1840-4, B.A. 1842, rector of Furthoe 1843-80, and of Meldon, Northumberland, 1880, brother of Henry W. 1844, and of Richard W. 1835.

Mason, Joseph, 5s. Abraham, of St. Anne's, Dublin, gent. QUEEN'S COLL., matric. 13 Oct., 1836, aged 18; B.A. 1841, M.A. 1843, a chaplain to the forces in the Crimea, vicar of East Tytherley, Hants, 1851, until his death 5 Sep., 1876.

Mason, Richard, s. Charles, of High Ongar, Essex, arm. MAGDALEN COLL., matric. 28 April, 1733, aged 19.

Mason, Richard, o.s. Richard Shires, of Gargrave, Yorks, gent. QUEEN'S COLL., matric. 28 Oct., 1881, aged 20; B.A. 1885. [35]

Mason, Richard Williams, 1s. William, of Llanbeblig, co. Carnarvon, arm. JESUS COLL., matric. 26 Feb., 1835, aged 17; scholar 1835-44, B.A. 1839, M.A. 1841, perp. curate Penrhos-Llugwy, Anglesey, 1844-57, rector of Llanfair-Harlech 1859-70, and of Llantrisant 1870, until his death 2 June 1888, brother of H. W. 1844, and John W. 1838.

Mason, Robert, s. Thomas, of St. Swithin's, Lincoln (city), cler. QUEEN'S COLL., matric. 22 March, 1727-8, aged 19.

Mason, Robert, s. Robert, of Hurley, Berks, gent. ST. EDMUND HALL, matric. 12 Feb., 1807, aged 23; B.A. from QUEEN'S COLL. 1810, M.A. 1813, B.D. 1820, D.D. 1823, bequeathed his Egyptian papyri, etc., and £40,000 stock, to the Bodleian, and his Egyptian, Grecian, and Roman antiquities, together with £30,000 stock to Queen's College, died at Hurley 5 Jan., 1841.

Mason, Samuel, s. John, of Aswarby, co. Lincoln, cler. LINCOLN COLL., matric. 14 Dec., 1768, aged 18; B.A. 1772.

Mason, Simon, s. Charles, of Dinton, Bucks, gent. HART HALL, matric. 30 May, 1734, aged 19.

Mason, Sydney, 3s. Frederick, of Pietermaritzburg, gent. MERTON COLL., matric. 21 Oct., 1886, aged 19; postmaster 1886.

Mason, Thomas, 3s. Bryant, of Bengal, East Indies, arm. CHRIST CHURCH, matric. 1 Nov., 1820, aged 18; B.A. 1824, rector of Shapwick, Somerset.

Mason, Rev. Thomas Wall, M.A. TRINITY COLL. Dublin, 1831 (B.A. 1826), 1s. Abraham, of Dublin, gent. QUEEN'S COLL., incorp. 1 Feb., 1838, aged 34; died at Ropley, Hants, 9 Dec., 1860, brother of Jacob 1836. [5]

Mason, William, 'cook,' Oxford; 21 June, 1720.

Mason, William, 1s. Hamer, of Leintwardine, co. Hereford, gent. ST. JOHN'S COLL., matric. 30 May, 1829, aged 19.

Maspero, Gaston, hon. fellow QUEEN'S COLL. 1887, created D.C.L. 22 June, 1887, professor of Egyptology in the College de France, and a member of the Institut du France, and of the Academy of Inscriptions and Belles Lettres.

Massé, Edgar Francis Hubert Joseph, 1s. Joseph Francis Paul, of Sydenham, Kent, gent. WORCESTER COLL., matric. 21 Oct., 1880, aged 19; B.A. 1886.

Massé, Henri Jean Louis Joseph, 1s. Joseph Francis Paul, of Sydenham, Kent, gent. EXETER COLL., matric. 31 May, 1879, aged 18; migrated to WADHAM COLL. 1880, B.A. 1883. See *Robinson*, 370.

Massey, Augustus Shakespear Oliver, o.s. — M., of Mancetter, co. Warwick, arm. MAGDALEN COLL., matric. 21 Oct., 1847, aged 19. See *Eton School Lists*. [11]

Massey, Edwyn Reynolds, 3s. Thomas, of Hatcliffe, near Grimsby, co. Lincoln, cler. EXETER COLL., matric. 14 Oct., 1865, aged 18; exhibitioner 1866-70, B.A. 1870, M.A. 1872, vice-principal Lichfield College 1874-80, vicar of Merton, Oxon, 1880. See *Coll. Reg.*, 163.

Massey, Eyre, Baron Clarina, s. Nathaniel William, baron. CHRIST CHURCH, matric. 30 Jan., 1816, aged 17; B.A. 1819, 3rd baron, a representative peer 16 April, 1849, until his death 18 Nov., 1872. See Foster's *Peerage*.

Massey, Francis Elcocke, 1s. William, of Acton, Cheshire, arm. MAGDALEN COLL., matric. 29 Oct., 1841, aged 18; of Poole Hall, Cheshire, J.P., and of Carrickfergus co. Antrim, high sheriff 1875. See *Rugby School Reg.*, 199.

Massey, John Cooke, 2s. Thomas, of Hatcliffe, near Great Grimsby, co. Lincoln, cler. EXETER COLL., matric. 11 June, 1862, aged 20; B.A. 1865, M.A. 1869, rector of South Normanton, co. Derby, 1871, preb. of Southwell 1885. [15]

Massey, Leigh, s. James, of Oxmantown, near Dublin, Ireland, pleb. BRASENOSE COLL., matric. 30 May, 1718, aged 18; B.A. 31 Jan., 1721-2.

Massey, Peter, s. Thomas, of Chester (city), pleb. BRASENOSE COLL., matric. 11 May, 1758, aged 17; B.A. 1763. See *Manchester School Reg.*, i. 38.

Massey, Richard, 2s. Richard, of Manchester, gent. ST. ALBAN HALL, matric. 21 Oct., 1869, aged 37; B.A. 1874, M.A. 1877, vicar of Wereham, Norfolk, 1884.

Massey, William, s. William, of Chester (city), cler CHRIST CHURCH, matric. 29 Jan., 1791, aged 17; of Poole Hall, Cheshire, bar.-at-law, Lincoln's Inn, 1799, died in 1838, father of Francis E. 1841.

Massie, Edward, 9s. Richard, of St. Timothy's, Chester (city), cler. WADHAM COLL., matric. 14 Oct., 1825, aged 19; B.A. 1830, M.A. 1834, chaplain 1840-5, brother of the next named. [20]

Massie, Hugh Hamon, y.s. Richard, of Chester (city), cler. CORPUS CHRISTI COLL., matric. 17 Dec., 1835, aged 18; exhibitioner 1835-8.

Massie, John, scholar ST. JOHN'S COLL., Cambridge, 1864 (B.A. 1866, M.A. 1870), 1s. Robert, of Newton-le-Willows, Lancashire, arm. CORPUS CHRISTI COLL., incorp. 27 Nov. (or 9 Dec.), 1886, aged 43.

Massingberd, Algernon Langton, 1s. Peregrine, of Gunby, co. Lincoln, arm. CHRIST CHURCH, matric. 14 Nov., 1823, aged 19; of Gunby, died in 1844.

Massingberd, Charles Bolles, s. Thomas, of Millgreen, Essex, arm. ST. MARY HALL, matric. 15 Dec., 1792, aged 21; rector of Kettlethorpe, co. Lincoln, 1806, until his death 27 March, 1836. See Foster's *Baronetage*, MEUX.

Massingberd, Charles Burrell, s. William Burrell, of South Ormsby, co. Lincoln, arm. NEW COLL., matric. 29 Oct., 1767, aged 17; created M.A. 8 July, 1773 (as Charles), of Ormsby, co. Lincoln, and Braziers, Oxon, high sheriff, a student of Lincoln's Inn 1771, died in Nov., 1853. [25]

Massingberd, Charles John Henry Mundy, o.s. Charles Godfrey Mundy, of Ormsby, co. Lincoln, arm. CHRIST CHURCH, matric. 12 Dec., 1826, aged 18; of South Ormsby Hall, co. Lincoln, J.P., D.L., assumed the additional surname of MASSINGBERD by royal licence 8 May, 1863.

Massingberd, Francis, s. William, of Gunby, co. Lincoln, arm. UNIVERSITY COLL., matric. 4 Nov., 1774, aged 17; demy MAGDALEN COLL. 1775-81, B.A. 1778, M.A. 1781, fellow 1781-1824, rector of Braytoft and Gunby, co. Lincoln, at his death 25 June, 1824. See *Bloxam*, vii. 46.

Massingberd, Francis, s. Francis Burrell, of St. Bennet Fink, Middlesex, gent. HERTFORD COLL., matric. 11 July, 1780, aged 24, B.A. 1781; M.A. from ST. ALBAN HALL 1787, rector of Davenham, Essex, and of Washingborough, co. Lincoln, 1792, and preb. of Lincoln 1815, until his death 12 April, 1817.

Massingberd, Francis Charles, s. Francis, of Washingborough, co. Lincoln, cler. MAGDALEN COLL., matric. 25 July, 1818, aged 17; demy 1818-24, B.A. 1822, M.A. 1825, preb. of Lincoln 1847-62, chancellor 1862, rector of South Ormsby with Kettlesby, co. Lincoln, 1825, until his death 5 Dec., 1872. See *Bloxam*, vii. 272.

Massingberd, Henry Bolle, 4s. Charles Bolle, of Kettlethorpe, co. Lincoln, cler. LINCOLN COLL., matric. 21 Jan., 1829, aged 17; scholar 1829-30. See Foster's *Baronetage*, MEUX. [30]

Massingberd, Peregrine, s. Bennet Langton, of St. Marylebone, Middlesex, arm. MERTON COLL., matric. 4 Dec., 1797, aged 17; B.A. 1801, of Gunby, co. Lincoln, in right of his wife, whose name he assumed in lieu of his own, died at Exeter 23 Sep., 1856

Massingberd, Samuel, s. William, of Gunby, co Lincoln, arm. UNIVERSITY COLL., matric. 1(July, 1767, aged 18; B.A. from MAGDALEN COLL 1771, M.A. 1774, died unmarried, brother of Francis 1774.

Massingberd, William, s. Thomas Meux, of London gent. LINCOLN COLL., matric. 10 Oct., 1721 aged 18; of Gunby, co. Lincoln, assumed the nam of MASSINGBERD in lieu of MEUX in 1723, died i 1780, father of Francis, 1774. See Foster's *Baronet age*, MEUX; & *Robinson*, 38.

Massingberd, William Burrell, s. Burrell, of Sout Ormsby, co. Lincoln, arm. NEW COLL., matric. Dec., 1736, aged 17; of Ormsby, co. Lincoln, hig sheriff 1745, died 18 Aug., 1802.

Massingberd, William Burrell, s. (William Burrell of Ormsby, co. Lincoln, arm. UNIVERSITY COLL. matric. 28 Feb., 1775, aged 18; demy MAGDALE COLL. 1775-80, B.A. 1778, M.A. 1781, rector c South Ormsby with Kettlesby, co. Lincoln, 180(until his death 5 May, 1823. See *Bloxam*, vii. 50.

Massingberd, William Oswald, 2s. Francis Charle of London, cler. MAGDALEN COLL., matric. 2 April, 1867, aged 19; B.A. 1871, M.A. 1883, curat of South Ormsby, co. Lincoln, 1871-3, rector sinc 1873. See *Eton School Lists*. [3(

Massingham, Alfred Melancthon, 2s. John Deacon, of Derby, D.D. CHRIST CHURCH, matric. 22 Oct., 1872, aged 19; B.A. 1877, M.A. 1879.

Massingham, Edward Foley, 3s. John Deacon, of Derby, cler. ST. JOHN'S COLL., matric. 17 Oct., 1874, aged 19; died in 1875.

Massingham, Joseph John, 1s. Joseph, of Norwich, arm. BALLIOL COLL., matric. 15 Oct., 1873, aged 18; exhibitioner 1872-7; fellow MERTON COLL. 1877-8, B.A. 1878, a student of the Inner Temple 1875, died 7 Nov., 1878.

Massy, Edward Taylor, o.s. Hon. Edward, of Chester (city), arm. BRASENOSE COLL., matric. 18 May, 1826, aged 18; B.A. 1830, of Cottesmore, co. Pembroke, J.P., D.L., died 27 July, 1882. See Foster's *Peerage*, B. MASSY.

Massy, Hugh Ingoldsby, s. Hugh, of Ballabricken, Ireland, arm. MAGDALEN COLL., matric. 6 March, 1766, aged 16. See Foster's *Peerage*, B. CLARINA.

Massy, John, s. Hugh, of Duntrileague, co. Tipperary, Baron M. EXETER COLL., matric. 31 Oct., 1800, aged 17; of Barna, co. Limerick, died 6 July, 1869. See Foster's *Peerage*, B. MASSY. [5]

Master, Arthur Gilbert, 4s. Charles Gilbert, of London, arm. EXETER COLL., matric. 21 Oct., 1886, aged 19.

Master, Augustus Chester, 6s. William C., of Haywood, co. Stafford. UNIVERSITY COLL., matric. 1 Dec., 1842, aged 18; B.A. from NEW INN HALL 1847, perp. curate Perlethorpe, Notts, 1851-8, rector of Broadwas, co. Worcester, 1858-61, vicar of Preston, All Saints, 1861, until his death 10 Dec., 1887.

Master, Edward, s. Robert, of Vron, co. Flint, cler. BALLIOL COLL., matric. 15 May, 1790, aged 19; B.A. 1794, rector of Rufford, co. Lancashire, 1816, until his death in 1834.

Master, Frederick, s. Henry, of Lymington, Hants, arm. CHRIST CHURCH, matric. 3 June, 1802, aged 19; student 1802-17, B.A. 1806, M.A. 1808, vicar of Runcorn, Cheshire, 1816, until his death 2 May, 1845. [10]

Master, George Francis, 2s. William Chester, of Horton, Northants, arm. UNIVERSITY COLL., matric 15 June, 1835, aged 18; B.A. 1840, M.A. 1843, vicar of Baunton, co. Gloucester, 1843, rector of Stratton, 1844, until his death 6 May, 1875.

Master, George Streynsham, 1s. Robert Mosley, of Croston, cler. BRASENOSE COLL., matric. 9 June, 1841, aged 18; B.A. 1845, M.A. 1848, perp. curate of Welsh-Hampton, Salop, 1847-59, vicar of Twickenham 1859-65, rector of West Dean with East Grimstead, Wilts, 1865-86. See *Eton School Lists.*

Master, Gilbert Coventry, 2s. James S., of Chorley, Lancashire, cler. EXETER COLL., matric. 25 May, 1858, aged 19; B.A. 1862, M.A. 1865, held various curacies 1862-73, vicar of Rainford, Lancashire, 1873-9, rector of Chorley, Lancashire, 1879-80, vicar of Thurnham, Kent, since 1880. See *Rugby School Reg.*

Master, Gilbert Nathaniel Hoskins, 4s. Charles H., of Brighton, arm. CHRIST CHURCH, matric. 11 Oct., 1878, aged 18.

Master, James Henry, 1s. James, of Walcot, in city of Bath, arm. (admiral). BALLIOL COLL., matric. 9 June, 1821, aged 18. [15]

Master, James Streynsham, s. Streynsham, of Croston, Lancashire, cler. BALLIOL COLL., matric. 29 March, 1817, aged 18; scholar 1817-23, B.A. 1820, M.A. 1823, hon. canon of Manchester 1854, rector of Chorley, Lancashire, 1846, until his death 31 Dec., 1878. See *Manchester School Reg.*, iii. 101.

Master, John Whalley, s. Robert, of Croston, Lancashire, doctor. BRASENOSE COLL., matric. 24 Oct., 1786, aged 18; B.A. 1790, M.A. 1794, B.D. 1803, rector (and patron) of Chorley, Lancashire, 1798, until his death 13 Aug., 1846.

Master, Legh, s. Legh, of St. George's, Queen Square, London, arm. CORPUS CHRISTI COLL., matric. 16 Dec., 1737, aged 20; of New Hall, Lancashire, and of Codnor Castle, co. Derby, died in America in 1796.

Master, Legh Hoskins, s. Legh, of New Hall, parish of Winwick, Lancashire, arm. ST. ALBAN HALL, matric. 21 Nov., 1781, aged 27; of Codnor Castle, co. Derby, and of Barrow Green House, Surrey, rector of Lympsfield, Surrey, died 11 Jan., 1814.

Master, Oswald, 3s. Robert Moseley, of Burnley, Lancashire, cler. BRASENOSE COLL., matric. 12 March, 1846, aged 17; scholar 1847-50, B.A. 1849, M.A. 1852, held various curacies 1851-67, rector of Croston, Lancashire, 1867. [20]

Master, Robert, s. Legh, of New Hall, Lancashire, arm. BALLIOL COLL., matric. 17 March, 1745-6, aged 19, B.A. 1749; fellow ALL SOULS' COLL. 1749, M.A. 1753; B. & D.D. from ST. ALBAN HALL 1763, died rector of Croston 4 Aug., 1798. See *Manchester School Reg.*, ii. 30.

Master, Robert, s. William, of Friering, Essex, cler. NEW COLL., matric. 31 Jan., 1767, aged 19; B.A. 1770, M.A. 1774.

Master, Robert, s. Robert, of Croston, Lancashire, cler. BALLIOL COLL., matric. 24 June, 1785, aged 18; B.A. 1789, M.A. 1792, B.Med. 1792, physician to the British forces at St. Domingo, died 1797, brother of Streynsham, 1784. See *Manchester School Reg.*, ii. 30.

Master, Robert Moseley, s. Streynsham, of Croston, Lancashire, cler. BALLIOL COLL., matric. 2 Dec., 1811, aged 17; B.A. 1815, M.A. 1818, incumbent of Burnley, Lancashire, 1826-55, archdeacon of Manchester 1854, until his death 1 July, 1867. See *Eton School Lists.*

Master, Rev. Streynsham, s. Streynsham, knight (query created M.A. 2 July, 1751, as TRENCHARD MASTER, see below), uncle of Streynsham 1737. [25]

Master, Rev. Streynsham, s. Legh, of Ashton, Lancashire, arm. CORPUS CHRISTI COLL., matric. 12 Nov., 1737, aged 17; brother of Legh 1737, and of Robert 1746.

Master, Streynsham, s. Robert, of Croston, Lancashire, doctor. BALLIOL COLL., matric. 25 May, 1784, aged 17; B.A. 1788, M.A. 1791, rector of Croston, 1798, until his death 19 Jan., 1864, aged 98. See *Manchester School Reg.*, ii. 33.

Master, Streynsham Mosley, 1s. James Streynsham, of Chorley, Lancashire, cler. BALLIOL COLL., matric. 24 March, 1852, aged 17; B.A. 1856, M.A. 1860.

Master, Thomas, s. Thomas, of Cirencester, co. Gloucester, arm. BALLIOL COLL., matric. 12 May, 1735, aged 18; M.P. Cirencester 1747, until his death, buried at Cirencester 1 June, 1749.

Master, Thomas, created D.C.L. 22 May, 1736 (1s. of Thomas Master, M.P.), of the Abbey, Cirencester, father of Thomas 1735. [30]

Master, Thomas, s. Thomas, of Brislington, Somerset, arm. ORIEL COLL., matric. 22 May, 1761, aged 17; of the Abbey, co. Gloucester, etc., high sheriff 1771, M.P. 1784-96, inherited the Cann estates in 1782, and the Chester estates in Gloucestershire, etc., in 1799, died 12 May, 1823.

Master, Thomas, s. Thomas, of Chalfont, Bucks, arm. CHRIST CHURCH, matric. 26 Oct., 1786, aged 16; brigade-major 2nd dragoon guards, died 12 May, 1823.

Master, Thomas William Chester, 1s. William Chester, of St. George's, Hanover Square, London, arm. CHRIST CHURCH, matric. 17 Oct., 1833, aged 19; B.A. 1837, of Cirencester Abbey and Knole, co. Gloucester, J.P., high sheriff 1878, M.P. Cirencester 1837-44.

Master, Thomas William Chester, 1s. Thomas William Chester, of London, gent. CHRIST CHURCH, matric. 31 May, 1860, aged 19; M.P. Cirencester 1878-85.

Master, Rev. Trenchard, created M.A. 2 July, 1751. See *Cat. Grads.* [35]

Master, William, s. Richard, of Woodford, Essex, cler. NEW COLL., matric. 15 Dec., 1736, aged 21 (? of Friering, Essex, cler., father of Robert 1767).

Master, William, s. William, of Broughton, Hants, cler. NEW COLL., matric. 19 May, 1758, aged 18; B.C.L. 1766, rector of Paulers Pury, Northants, 1775, until his death in 1817.

Master, William, s. William, of Paulers Pury, Northants, cler. NEW COLL., matric. 19 Oct., 1815, aged 19; fellow 1815-34, B.C.L. 1821, dean of civil law 1828, rector of Bicester, Oxon, 1833, until his death 27 Feb., 1878. See *Rugby School Reg.*, 100.

Masterman, Henry, s. William, of Athelhampton, Dorset, gent. WADHAM COLL., matric. 14 March, 1795, aged 17; B.A. 1799, chaplain 1812-19, vicar of Milton Abbas and Alton Pancras, Dorset, 1823, until his death 7 Dec., 1841. See *Eton School Lists.*

Masterman, John, created D.C.L., 5 July, 1848, (son of William Masterman, of London, banker), of Leytonstone Hall, Essex, and of London, banker, M.P. 1841-57, a director of the East India Company, died 23 Jan., 1862, aged 82, father of Thomas 1842.

Masterman, John Story, 1s. Thomas, of Wallingford, Berks, cler. CORPUS CHRISTI COLL., matric. 20 Oct., 1868, aged 19, scholar 1868-73, B.A. 1873; fellow BRASENOSE COLL. 1873-7, M.A. 1875, assistant-master University College School, London, 1882. See *Rugby School Reg.* [5]

Masterman, Nevil, 2s. Thomas, of Garsington co., Oxford, cler. CORPUS CHRISTI COLL., matric. 19 Oct., 1870, aged 18; exhibitioner 1871-5, B.A. 1874, M.A. 1878. See *Rugby School Reg.*

Masterman, Rev. Thomas, 4s. John, of Walthamstow, Essex, arm. (after D.C.L.). WADHAM COLL., matric. 13 April, 1842, aged 17; B.A. 1846, M.A. 1849, died 22 Sep., 1856, father of John S. and of Nevil.

Masterman, William, s. William, of Friar Wadden, Dorset, gent. HART HALL, matric. 13 Feb., 1721-2, aged 17; B.A. 1725.

Masterman, William, 1s. Henry, of Clapton, Middlesex, arm. WADHAM COLL., matric. 14 Oct., 1864, aged 18; B.A. 1868, B.C.L. & M.A. 1871, D.C.L. 1881, bar.-at-law, Middle Temple, 1870. See Foster's *Men at the Bar.*

Masters, Allan Smith, 1s. William Cowburn, of St. Pancras, Middlesex, arm. EXETER COLL., matric. 17 May, 1838, aged 18; scholar 1840-4, B.A. 1842, M.A. 1844, of Camer, Kent, assumed the surnames of SMITH-MASTERS in lieu of his patronymic 1862, rector of Humber, co. Hereford, 1844-55, vicar of Tidenham, co. Gloucester, 1855-62, died 8 Oct., 1875. See *Coll. Reg.*, 153. [10]

Masters, George, s. George, of Whitchurch, Somerset, gent. WADHAM COLL., matric. 16 June, 1807, aged 18; B.A. from MAGDALEN HALL 1816, M.A. 1818, B. & D.D. 1827, died rector of Swingfield, Kent, 7 March, 1861.

Masters, George, 1s. George, of St. Giles's, London, D.D. WORCESTER COLL., matric. 15 Feb., 1838, aged 18; B.A. 1841, M.A. 1845.

Masters, John Ernest Cowburn Smith, 2s. Allan Cowburn Smith, of Tidenham, co. Gloucester, cler. KEBLE COLL., matric. 16 Oct., 1876, aged 20; B.A. 1880, M.A. 1883, vicar of St. George, Tylehurst, Berks, 1885.

Masters, John Smalman, o.s. William, of Greenwich, Kent, arm. JESUS COLL., matric. 1 Nov., 1820, aged 20; B.A. 1825, M.A. 1828, curate of Greenwich 1829-51, vicar of Christ Church, Shooter's Hill, 1865.

Masters, Robert, fellow of CORPUS CHRISTI COLL., Cambridge (B.A. 1734, M.A. 1738, B.D. 1746); incorp. 26 Jan., 1754. [15]

Masters, William, s. John, of Winchester, Hants, gent. MERTON COLL., matric 8 April, 1767, aged 18; B.A. from QUEEN'S COLL. 1776, M.A. 1781.

Masters, William Allan Smith, 1s. Allan, of Humber, co. Hereford, cler. BRASENOSE COLL., matric. 4 March, 1869, aged 18; B.A. 1873, M.A. 1875, of Camer, Kent, J.P., brother of John Ernest.

Masters, William Caldwall, 2s. John Smalman, of Greenwich, Kent, cler. MAGDALEN COLL., matric. 18 Oct., 1862, aged 18; B.A. 1865, M.A. 1869, vicar of Long Marston, Herts, 1871-85, rector of Stanton Fitzwarren, Wilts, since 1885.

Matcham, George, of ST. JOHN'S COLL., Cambridge (LL.B. 1814, LL.D. 1820); adm. 'ad eundem' 21 June, 1849 (son of George Matcham, by Catharine, sister of Horatio, Viscount Nelson), died 15 Jan., 1877. See Foster's *Peerage.*

Mather, Arthur, 5s. William, of West Derby, Lancashire, arm. LINCOLN COLL., matric. 1 Feb., 1873, aged 19; a student of the Inner Temple 1876. [20]

Mather, Charles, y.s. Robert, of Grantham, co. Lincoln, arm. EXETER COLL., matric. 29 May, 1855, aged 18.

Mather, Rev. Edward, 4s. James, of Radcliffe, near Manchester, arm. BRASENOSE COLL., matric. 25 May, 1853, aged 18; B.A. 1858, M.A. 1863.

Mather, Edward Lushington, 3s. John P., of Liverpool, Lancashire, arm. BRASENOSE COLL., matric. 6 June, 1844, aged 18; scholar 1846-50, B.A. 1848, M.A. 1851, vicar of Christ Church, Bootle, 1866-79, and of Over Tabley, Cheshire, 1881.

Mather, John, s. John, of Oxford (city), doctor. CORPUS CHRISTI COLL., matric. 4 Jan., 1733-4, aged 17; B.A. from NEW COLL. 1739, M.A. 14 Jan., 1742-3, rector of Biddenden, Kent, 1747.

Mather, Rev. John Cyril Vaughan, 1s. Frederick Vaughan, of Clifton, co. Gloucester, cler. KEBLE COLL., matric. 17 Oct., 1882, aged 20; B.A. 1885.

Mather, Robert, s. Robert, of St. Mary's, Shrewsbury, Salop, arm. BALLIOL COLL., matric. 27 Jan., 1717-8, aged 17; bar.-at-law, Middle Temple, 1726, and of the Inner Temple ('ad eundem') 1729, buried in the Temple Church, Thursday, 8 Jan., 1729-30. [26]

Mather, Roger, s. Thomas, of Chester (city), arm. BRASENOSE COLL., matric. 22 May, 1735, aged 16; B.A. 1738, M.A. 1741, B. & D.D. 1757, public orator 1749-60, rector of Whitechapel 1757, until his death in 1768.

Mather, Thomas, s. James, of St. Peter-le-Poor, London, gent. ST. MARY HALL, matric. 7 Nov., 1810, aged 39.

Mather, William, 1s. George, of Kensington, Middlesex, arm. ST. MARY HALL, matric. 25 Oct., 1864, aged 17.

Matheson, Rev. Charles, 3s. Charles, of Berbice, West Indies, arm. ST. JOHN'S COLL., matric. 1 July, 1850, aged 18; fellow 1850-6, B.A. 1854, M.A. 1857, head-master Clergy Orphan School, Canterbury, 1867. See *Robinson*, p. 273. [30]

Matheson, Heylyn Fraser, 1s. Charles, of Blackheath, Kent, cler. CHRIST CHURCH, matric. 13 Oct., 1876, aged 18; a junior student 1876-81, B.A. 1880, M.A. 1886.

Matheson, John, o.s. John, of Edinburgh, Scotland, gent. MAGDALEN HALL, matric. 6 Nov., 1826, aged 40.

Matheson, (Sir) Kenneth James (Bart.), 1s. Alexander, of London, arm. (after baronet). CHRIST CHURCH, matric. 28 May, 1874, aged 20; 2nd baronet. See Foster's *Baronetage.*

Matheson, Percy Ewing, 3s. James, of Nottingham, gent. BALLIOL COLL., matric. 17 Oct., 1877, aged 18, scholar 1876-81, B.A. 1881; fellow NEW COLL. 1881, M.A. 1884, lecturer 1883, tutor and sub-warden 1885, classical lecturer University College 1883-4.

Mathew, Bertie Bertie, 1s. Brownlow Bertie, of Clanfield, Hants, arm. CHRIST CHURCH, matric. 20 Nov., 1830, aged 18; lieut. 10th hussars, died at Rome 19 Nov., 1844. See Foster's *Our Noble and Gentle Families* & *Eton School Lists.* [35]

Mathews, Thomas, s. Thomas, of Llandaff, co. Glamorgan, arm. CHRIST CHURCH, matric. 3 Nov., 1758, aged 16; of Llandaff and Pencoed, co. Glamorgan, sheriff 1769, died 1782.

Mathews, Thomas Alexander, TRINITY COLL. 1832. See COOKE, page 290. [20]

Mathews, Thomas (William) s. Thomas, of Llandaff, arm. CHRIST CHURCH, matric. 6 April, 1728, aged 13; of Llandaff, a major in the army, M.P. co. Glamorgan, Dec., 1756-61.

Mathews, William, s. William, of Pitfield, co. Gloucester, gent. BRASENOSE COLL., matric. 4 June, 1747, aged 19; B.A. 1751. See *Manchester School Reg.*, i. 27.

Mathews, William, of Oxford (city), 'sartor;' privilegiatus 26 March, 1761; clerk Magdalen College 1759-91, yeoman bedel-in-law 1782, esquire bedel-in-divinity, died 25 Nov., 1791, father of William 1785. See *Coll. Reg.*, ii., 103.

Mathews, William s. William, of Cirencester, co. Gloucester, cler. MAGDALEN COLL., matric. 29 July, 1775, aged 14; demy 1775-92, B.A. 1779, M.A. 1782. See *Coll. Reg.*, vii, 50.

Mathews, Rev. William, s. William, of Oxford (city), gent. MAGDALEN COLL., matric. 17 Oct., 1785, aged 16; chorister 1778-85, clerk 1786-91, B.A. 1789, died 20 June, 1795. See *Coll. Reg.*, i. 199; ii. 113. [25]

Mathews, William, 'sculptor in aere;' privilegiatus 26 Feb., 1822.

Mathews, William, 2s. John, of St. Margaret's, Westminster, gent. MAGDALEN HALL., matric. 22 Oct., 1822, aged 20; B.A. from NEW COLL. 1826, chaplain 1825-31, curate of Romford, Essex, died 30 Dec., 1831.

Mathews, William Arnold, 1s. William, of Hatfield, Yorks, arm. CORPUS CHRISTI COLL., matric. 27 March, 1858, aged 18; B.A. 1861, M.A. 1864, vicar of Laughton, co. Lincoln, 1865-71, of Dacre, Cumberland, 1871-7, rector of Skelton, 1871-9, vicar of St. Mary, Carlisle, 1879-83, and of St. Lawrence, Appleby since 1883.

Mathias, Daniell, s. John, of Warrington, co. Lancaster, gent. BRASENOSE COLL., matric. 1 April, 1786, aged 18; scholar 1786-93, B.A. 1789, M.A. 1792, fellow 1793-1810, rector of St. Mary, Whitechapel 1807, until his death 24 July, 1837.

Mathias, Edward, 5s. William, of Eglwys Erw, co. Pembroke, gent. JESUS COLL., matric. 19 Oct., 1872, aged 19; scholar 1872-7, B.A. 1876, M.A. 1879. [30]

Mathias, George, of ST. JOHN'S COLL., Cambridge (B.A. 1838, M.A. 1842); 'ad eundem' 22 May, 1856, chaplain in ordinary to the Queen, chaplain Royal Hospital, Chelsea, 1846.

Mathias, Hugh Henry, 10s. Octavius, of Canterbury, New Zealand, cler. KEBLE COLL., matric. 14 Oct., 1884, aged 21; B.A. 1887.

Mathias, John, s. Lewis, of Llangwarren, co. Pembroke, arm. WADHAM COLL., matric. 26 Nov., 1795, aged 19.

Mathias, John Daniell, 1s. Daniell, of Whitechapel, London, cler. BRASENOSE COLL., matric. 1 July, 1830, aged 19; scholar 1830-7, B.A. 1834, curate of Great Mongeham, Essex, 1848-9, and of Norton, Somerset, died 19 June, 1866. See *Robinson*, 211.

Mathias, Lewis, 1s. Charles, of Wells, Somerset, arm. BRASENOSE COLL., matric. 29 March, 1832, aged 19; of Llanphey Court, and of Llangwarren, co. Pembroke, J.P., D.L., high sheriff 1856, died 1882. [35]

Mathias, Russell Frederick, 2s. Russell Matthias, of Tenby, co. Pembroke, gent. JESUS COLL., matric. 21 Oct., 1873, aged 19; scholar 1873-8, B.A. 1877, M.A. 1880; altered the spelling of his name.

Mathias, William, 2s. Charles, of Painswick, co. Gloucester, gent. BRASENOSE COLL., matric. 21 May, 1834, aged 18; B.A. 1839, M.A. 1841, incumbent of Burtle, Somerset, 1844, until his death 21 June, 1864.

Mathison, Gilbert Farquhar Graeme, 1s. Gilbert, of Middlesex, arm. ORIEL COLL., matric. 9 Dec., 1819, aged 16; of the Old Palace, Richmond, secretary of the Mint, and founder of Normal Schools, died at Therapia 1 Aug., 1854. See *Eton School Lists.*

Matolesi, Paul Biró, of Debreczin, Hungary. WADHAM COLL., privilegiatus 6 Dec., 1735.

Maton, Leonard James, 1s. Leonard Pitt, of Collingbourn Kingston, Wilts, arm. LINCOLN COLL., matric. 22 Oct., 1864, aged 19; B.A. 1867, a solicitor. See *Rugby School Reg.*

Maton, William George, s. George, of Salisbury (city), gent. QUEEN'S COLL., matric. 1 July, 1790, aged 16; B.A. 1794, M.A. 1797, B.Med. 1798, D.Med. 1801, F.R.C.P. 1802, physician to Westminster Hospital 1800-8, physician extraordinary to the Queen 1816, and to the Duchess of Kent and Princess Victoria 1820, died 30 March, 1835. See Munk's *Roll.*, iii. 6. **[5]**

Matson, Edward Fector, o.s. Edward, of St. James's, Dover, arm. ORIEL COLL., matric. 9 March, 1837, aged 17; bar.-at-law, Middle Temple, 1844.

Matson, Rev. Robert Bidwell, 1s. Robert, of Wilby, Northants, cler. NON-COLL., matric. 18 Oct., 1880, aged 29; B.A. from MERTON COLL. 1883.

Matthew, Charles, s. Philip, of Chudleigh, Devon, gent. BALLIOL COLL., matric. 16 Dec., 1786, aged 18; B.A. 1790, M.A. 1810, vicar (and patron) of All Saints' with St. Peter's, Maldon, 1809, rector of Layer Marney 1841, chaplain to the King of Hanover, died 13 June, 1844.

Matthew, Charles, 2s. John, of Kilve, Somerset, cler. BALLIOL COLL., matric. 17 April, 1823, aged 18.

Matthew, Henry, 3s. John, of Kilve, Somerset, cler. BALLIOL COLL., matric. 24 March, 1825, aged 18; rector of Eversholt, Beds, 1843, until his death 24 June, 1861. **[10]**

Matthew, John, s. Henry, of Barswell, co. Warwick, arm. PEMBROKE COLL., matric. 2 March, 1716-7, aged 16.

Matthew, John, s. Philip, of Chudleigh, Devon, gent. BALLIOL COLL., matric. 22 March, 1779, aged 17; B.A. 1782, M.A. 1785, rector of Kilve with Stringston, Somerset, 1797, until his death 10 March, 1837.

Matthew, John, s. John, of Kilve, Somerset, cler. BALLIOL COLL., matric. 16 June, 1817, aged 18; scholar 1818-23, B.A. 1821, M.A. 1830, rector of Chelvey, Somerset, 1831, until his death 28 Jan., 1886.

Matthew, Rowland George, 6s. David, of London, gent. ST. JOHN'S COLL., matric. 15 Oct., 1870, aged 18; scholar WADHAM COLL. 1870-5, B.A. 1875, M.A. 1877, vicar of St. Michael and All Angels, Wigan, 1881. See *Robinson*, 348.

Matthew, Thomas, s. John, of Burgh, Cumberland, pleb. QUEEN'S COLL., matric. 13 April, 1725, aged 15; B.A. 1730. **[15]**

Matthew, Walter Edmond, 3s. David, of Cambridge, arm. ST. JOHN'S COLL., matric. 15 June, 1866, aged 18; scholar 1869-73, B.A. 1870, M.A. 1873, archdeacon of Colombo, and incumbent of St. Paul's, Kandy, 1875. See *Crockford*, & *Robinson*, 338.

Matthews, Andrew, 2s. Andrew Hughes, of London, cler. LINCOLN COLL., matric. 7 March, 1833, aged 17; B.A. 1836, M.A. 1839, rector of Gumley, co. Leicester, since 1853.

Matthews, Andrew Hughes, s. James, of Oxford (city), gent. JESUS COLL., matric. 27 Nov., 1794, aged 12; B.A. 1798, M.A. 1801, B.D. 1809, fellow until 1812, rector of Stanton Harcourt, Oxon, 1810, vicar of Weston-on-the-Green, Oxon, 1822, and rector of Tilbrook, Beds, 1829, until his death 1 Sep., 1854.

Matthews, Andrew Marriott, 1s. Andrew Hughes, of Kelshall, Herts, cler. LINCOLN COLL., matric. 16 Oct., 1834, aged 21; brother of Henry Samuel R.

Matthews, Arthur, s. John, of Cheyhonger, co. Hereford, arm. BRASENOSE COLL., matric. 31 Oct., 1804, aged 16; B.A. 1808, M.A. 1811, B.D. 1818, fellow until 1840, librarian 1822, vice-principal 1817, vicar of Linton 1812, preb. of Hereford 1818, vicar of Wolhope with Fownhope and Fawley, co. Hereford, 1831, canon of Hereford 1831, until his death 23 Sep., 1840. **[20]**

Matthews, Arthur John, 1s. John, of London, arm. NEW COLL., matric. 13 Oct., 1877, aged 18; B.A. 1881, M.A. 1887, bar.-at-law, Inner Temple, 1884. See Foster's *Men at the Bar.*

Matthews, Charles Edward, 3s. Thomas, of Newark, Notts, gent. EXETER COLL., matric. 22 Oct., 1880, aged 19; B.A. 1883.

Matthews, Charles James, 3s. James R., of Lisbon, Portugal, arm. ORIEL COLL., matric. 30 March, 1844, aged 19; B.A. 1848.

Matthews, Frank Herbert, 2s. George Augustus, of London, gent. CORPUS CHRISTI COLL., matric. 21 Oct., 1880, aged 19; scholar 1880-5, B.A. 1884.

Matthews, Frank Paul, o.s. Michael, of Bedhampton, Hants, arm. WORCESTER COLL., matric. 14 Dec., 1852, aged 20. **[25]**

Matthews, George Fielding, 2s. Timothy Richard, of North Coates, co. Lincoln, cler. WORCESTER COLL., matric. 18 Oct., 1883, aged 21; B.A. 1887.

Matthews, Harold Francis, o.s. John Francis, of Stockwell, Surrey, gent. ST. EDMUND HALL, matric. 14 May, 1869, aged 19.

Matthews, Henry, s. Henry, of Shelderton, Salop, gent. BALLIOL COLL., matric. 19 March, 1760, aged 18; B.A. 1763.

Matthews, Henry, 1s. Henry, of Binfield, Berks, gent. QUEEN'S COLL., matric. 25 Jan., 1849, aged 20; B.A. 1852, M.A. 1855, held various curacies 1853-86, rector of Swineshead, co. Lincoln, since 1886. **[30]**

Matthews, Henry Samuel Ryder, 3s. Andrew Hughes, of London, cler. LINCOLN COLL., matric. 16 Oct., 1834, aged 17; bible clerk 1834-8, B.A. 1841, M.A. 1842, brother of Andrew M.

Matthews, Rev. Henry Usher, s. Joseph, of Sheffield, Yorks, gent. LINCOLN COLL., matric. 10 Oct., 1812, aged 20; scholar 1813-15, B.A. 1816 (formerly of TRINITY COLL., Cambridge), died 12 Jan., 1856.

Matthews, James, s. James, of St. Bride's, London, cler. BRASENOSE COLL., matric. 30 May, 1718, aged 20; B.A. 1721.

Matthews, James, s. James, of Barnett, co. Gloucester, pleb. JESUS COLL., matric. 17 Dec., 1757, aged 17; B.A. 1761, M.A. 1764.

Matthews, James, s. John, of Alton, Hants, gent. ST. EDMUND HALL, matric. 7 May, 1766, aged 30.

Matthews, James, s. James, of Oxford (city), gent. ST. JOHN'S COLL., matric. 1 July, 1794, aged 17; B.A. 1798, M.A. (by decree) 17 Dec., 1802, B.D. (by decree) 2 June, 1808, fellow and scholar until his death, assistant-chaplain 1822, bursar 1823, dean of divinity 1824, died in college 10 Dec., 1826. See *Robinson*, 157. **[36]**

Matthews, James, 1s. Thomas Pardo, of Ambrosden, Oxon, cler. WADHAM COLL., matric. 8 July, 1820, aged 17; B.A. 1826, M.A. 1828, vicar of Kirk Fenton, Yorks, 1830-69, and of Sherburn 1831, until his death in 1885, father of William P. P. 1857.

Matthews, John, s. William, of Linton, co. Hereford, arm. MERTON COLL., matric. 14 Feb., 1772, aged 16; B.A. 1778, M.A. 1779, B.Med. 1781, D.Med. 1782, F.R.C.P. 1783, physician to St. George's Hospital 1781-3, alderman and magistrate of Hereford, chairman Quarter Sessions, colonel 1st regiment Hereford militia, died 15 Jan., 1826. See Munk's *Roll*, ii. 332.

Matthews, John, 4s. John, of Market Drayton, Salop, pleb. CHRIST CHURCH, matric. 16 Oct., 1824, aged 20; servitor 1824-8, B.A. 1828, M.A. 1831, curate of Lacock, Wilts, died 3 Feb., 1853.

Matthews, John, o.s. John, of Broadclist, Devon, gent. EXETER COLL., matric. 11 Feb., 1841, aged 18; B.A. 1845, vicar of Knowstone, Devon, 1853, preb. of Exeter 1885.

Matthews, John Ebsworth, 2s. Charles Decimus, of Chipping Camden, co. Gloucester, gent. PEMBROKE COLL., matric. 25 March, 1857, aged 16; B.A. 1861, M.A. 1863, vicar of Swanwick, co. Derby, since 1877.

Matthews, Rev. John Henry Dudley, o.s. Charles, of Bradninch, Devon, arm. UNIVERSITY COLL., matric. 18 Oct., 1862, aged 18; B.A. 1866, M.A. 1869, tutor and assistant-master Wellington College 1869-84, head-master Leeds Grammar School 1884. See *Rugby School Reg.*

Matthews, John Holder, s. John, of Brompton, Middlesex, doctor. MERTON COLL., matric. 21 May, 1801, aged 18. [5]

Matthews, John Leonard, 3s. Thomas, of Bristol, gent. PEMBROKE COLL., matric. 28 Oct., 1867, aged 20; B.A. 1871, M.A. 1874, bar.-at-law, Inner Temple, 1872. See Foster's *Men at the Bar.*

Matthews, Joseph, s. Joseph, of Woodend, co. Gloucester, arm. UNIVERSITY COLL., matric. 15 Feb., 1772, aged 18.

Matthews, Richard, B.Med. JESUS COLL., Cambridge; adm. 'ad eundem' 28 June, 1860.

Matthews, Richard Miles, s. George, of Chipping Norton, Oxon, gent. LINCOLN COLL., matric. 17 May, 1805, aged 16; B.A. 1811, M.A. 1812.

Matthews, Rev. Richard Northon, 1s. Timothy Richard, of North Coates, co. Lincoln, cler. KEBLE COLL., matric. 18 Oct., 1881, aged 21; B.A. 1884.

Matthews, Stephen, 1s. John, of Cirencester, co. Gloucester, arm. BRASENOSE COLL., matric. 8 June, 1865, aged 18; B.A. 1868, M.A. 1872. [11]

Matthews, Thomas, s. Rice, of Langadock, co. Carmarthen, pleb. CHRIST CHURCH, matric. 7 May, 1761, aged 18; B.A. 1765, M.A. 1769.

Matthews, Thomas Killam. PEMBROKE COLL., 1878. See KILLAM. See page 793.

Matthews, Thomas Pardo, s. James, of Oxford (city), gent. JESUS COLL., matric. 2 July, 1792, aged 16; demy MAGDALEN COLL. 1793-1801, B.A. 1796, M.A. 1799, rector of Ambrosden, Oxon, died in 1821. See *Gent.'s Mag.*, 1821, i. 189; *Bloxam*, vii. 127; & *St. Paul's School Reg.*, 190.

Matthews, Tobias, s. Thomas, of Enderby, co. Leicester, cler. BRASENOSE COLL., matric. 11 Jan., 1722-3, aged 17; B.A. 1726. [15]

Matthews, William, s. James, of Repton, co. Derby, pleb. MAGDALEN HALL, matric. 28 March, 1751, aged 20.

Matthews, William, s. Joseph, of Cromhall, co. Gloucester, arm. TRINITY COLL., matric. 19 Oct., 1775, aged 18; B.A. 1779 (? vicar of Chaddesley Corbet, co. Worcester, 1798, until his death 1 June, 1805).

Matthews, William, 1s. David, of Llawrhydian, co. Glamorgan, gent. JESUS COLL., matric. 28 Jan., 1874, aged 27; clerk 1874, B.A. 1877, M.A. 1880, vicar choral St. David's Cathedral, master of the Cathedral School.

Matthews, William Edgar, 6s. Robert James, of Bath, Somerset, arm. PEMBROKE COLL., matric. 24 May, 1853, aged 20; B.A. 1857, a student of Lincoln's Inn 1857.

Matthews, William Edwin, 1s. William, of Sidney, Australia, gent. MAGDALEN HALL, matric. 16 Nov., 1848, aged 18. [20]

Matthews, William Hoskyns, s. John, of Kensington, Middlesex, doctor. MERTON COLL., matric. 31 March, 1798, aged 17; a student of Lincoln's Inn, 1800.

Matthews, William Prest Pardo, 1s. James, of Sherburn, Yorks, cler. QUEEN'S COLL., matric. 10 Dec., 1857, aged 19.

Matthews, Rev. William Stabb, 1s. John Redaway, of Torquay, Devon, gent. BRASENOSE COLL., matric. 8 June, 1860, aged 18; scholar 1860-3, B.A. 1864, head-master Leicester Grammar School 1871-8, and of Kirkham Grammar School 1878.

Matthewson, James, 'bibliopola;' privilegiatus 17 Nov., 1817.

Matthey, Percy St. Clair, 2s. George, of London, arm. EXETER COLL., matric. 18 Oct., 1882, aged 18; B.A. 1886. See *Eton School Lists.* [25]

Matthie, Hugh, s. Hugh, of Greenock, Scotland, gent. PEMBROKE COLL., matric. 19 April, 1825, aged 20; B.A. 1829, M.A. 1839, rector of Worthenbury, Flints, 1831, until his death 9 Dec., 1842.

Mattson, William, s. William, of Coningsby, co. Lincoln, pleb. LINCOLN COLL., matric. 13 June, 1759, aged 18; B.A. 1763.

Maturin, Charles Gabriel (Trewman), B.A. TRINITY COLL., Dublin, 1868, 1s. William, of Dublin, cler. ST. EDMUND HALL, incorp., 23 April, 1869, aged 23; rector of Amcotts, co. Lincoln, 1885.

Matuszewic, Adam, Count, created D.C.L. 10 June, 1834, minister plenipotentiary from the Emperor of Russia to the Court at St. James's. See *Gent.'s Mag.*, 1843, i. 425.

Maud, Arthur Roland, 4s. John Primatt, of Ancaster, co. Lincoln, cler. KEBLE COLL., matric. 19 Oct., 1886, aged 20. [30]

Maud, Charles Theobald, s. John, of St. Botolph's, London, arm. BALLIOL COLL., matric. 26 March, 1814, aged 17; B.A. 1818.

Maud, Edward, s. John, of Charwelton, Northants, pleb. LINCOLN COLL., matric. 26 Jan., 1730-1, aged 17; B.A. 1735, M.A. 1737.

Maud, Henry George, 5s. Henry Landon, of Assington, Suffolk, cler. UNIVERSITY COLL., matric. 18 Oct., 1886, aged 19; scholar 1886.

Maud, John Primatt, s. John, of Aldersgate, London, arm. MAGDALEN COLL., matric. 20 June, 1811, aged 18; B.A. from CAIUS COLL., Cambridge, 1815, M.A. 1819.

Maud, John Primatt, 1s. John, of Swainswick, Somerset, cler. CHRIST CHURCH, matric. 12 May, 1842, aged 18; student 1842-4, a commoner of NEW INN HALL 1844-5, LL.B. from TRINITY HALL, Cambridge, 1848, vicar of Ancaster, co. Lincoln, 1862, sometime lieutenant 5th Madras native infantry. See *Alumni West.*, 519. [35]

Maud, John Primatt, 1s. John Primatt, of Tranmere, Cheshire, cler. KEBLE COLL., matric. 14 Oct., 1879, aged 19; B.A. 1883, M.A. 1887.

Maude, Arthur, 3s. Thomas, of Lawford, near Colchester, Essex, cler. CHRIST CHURCH, matric. 23 May, 1861, aged 18; a junior student 1861-8, B.A. 1865, M.A. 1868, assistant-master St. Peter's College, Radley, 1867-76, rector of Burgh St. Andrew, Norfolk, 1886.

Maude, Charles Bulmer, 3s. Edmund, of Chapeltown, near Leeds, Yorks, gent. EXETER COLL., matric. 12 June, 1867, aged 19; B.A. 1871, M.A. 1874, vicar (and rector) of St. Cyprian, Kimberley, South Africa, 1875-80, perp. curate of Wilnecote, co. Stafford, 1881-6, vicar of Leek, co. Stafford, 1886.

Maude, Charles Edmund, 2s. Thomas William, of Canterbury, New Zealand, arm. MERTON COLL., matric. 16 Oct., 1884, aged 19; B.A. 1887.

Maude, Cornwallis, 3rd Viscount Hawarden, created D.C.L. 5 July, 1810 (s. Cornwallis, 1st Viscount Hawarden), an Irish representative peer 31 Oct., 1836, until his death 12 Oct., 1856. See Foster's *Peerage.* [40]

Maude, Eustace Addison, 1s. Robert, of Wallasey, Cheshire, arm. TRINITY COLL., matric. 17 April, 1882, aged 19.

Maude, Francis, s. Francis, of Wakefield, Yorks, gent. BRASENOSE COLL., matric. 10 Oct., 1816, aged 18; B.A. 1820, M.A. 1823, curate of Hoyland, Yorks, 1823, until his death 5 July, 1850.

Maude, Frederick, 1s. William, of Blackburne, Lancashire, arm. BRASENOSE COLL., matric. 14 Jan., 1824, aged 17; B.A. 1828, M.A. 1830, a student of the Inner Temple 1825.

Maude, Gerald Edward, 4s. Hon. Francis, of London, arm. CORPUS CHRISTI COLL., matric. 4 June, 1870, aged 18; B.A. 1874, bar.-at-law, Lincoln's Inn, 1876. See Foster's *Men at the Bar* & *Eton School Lists.*

Maude, James, s. Francis, of Wakefield, Yorks, arm. ORIEL COLL., matric. 21 Oct., 1742, aged 18; of Gildersome and Leathley, Yorks, died in 1778. See Foster's *Yorkshire Collection.*

Maude, John, s. Thomas James, of Osbaldwick, Yorks, arm. LINCOLN COLL., matric. 20 Oct., 1869, aged 20; postmaster MERTON COLL. 1869-74, B.A. 1874, M.A. 1887. See *Eton School Lists.*

Maude, John Barnabas, s. Joseph, of Kendal, Westmoreland, arm. QUEEN'S COLL., matric. 15 Jan., 1795, aged 14; B.A. 1798, M.A. 1802, fellow (senior) until 1851, bursar 1826, vicar of Monks Sherborne, Hants, 1829, domestic chaplain to Earl of Lonsdale, died 9 March, 1851. **[5]**

Maude, John Charles, born at Testwood, Hants, s. Cornwallis, Viscount Hawarden. CHRIST CHURCH, matric. 27 Jan., 1812, aged 18; B.A. 1815, M.A. 1818, rector of Enniskillen, died 21 June, 1860. See Foster's *Peerage.*

Maude, Rev. Joseph, s. Joseph, of Kendal, Westmoreland, arm. QUEEN'S COLL., matric. 2 March, 1792, aged 16; B.A. 1796, M.A. 1799, died 23 March, 1852.

Maude, Joseph, o.s. Joseph, of Reading, Berks, cler. QUEEN'S COLL., matric. 16 Oct., 1823, aged 18; Michel exhibitioner 1823-6, scholar 1826-30, B.A. 1827, M.A. 1830, fellow 1830-41, choral canon St. Asaph 1854, vicar of Chirk, co. Denbigh, 1852, until his death 11 Feb., 1874.

Maude, Rev. Joseph Hooper, 2s. Joseph, of Chirk, co. Denbigh, cler. CORPUS CHRISTI COLL., matric. 18 Oct., 1871, aged 19, scholar 1871-5; fellow HERTFORD COLL. 1875-84 and 1887, B.A. 1876, M.A. 1878, lecturer 1877, bursar 1878, dean 1881, tutor and lecturer 1884.

Maude, Ralph, 2s. Francis, of Wakefield, Yorks, arm. BRASENOSE COLL., matric. 2 June, 1819, aged 19; B.A. 1824, M.A. 1827, vicar of Mirfield, Yorks, 1827-70, died 15 Aug., 1880. **[10]**

Maude, Raymond William de Latham, 6s. Hon. Francis M., of London. MAGDALEN COLL., matric. 14 Oct., 1871, aged 19; B.A. 1875. See Foster's *Peerage*, V. HAWARDEN; & *Eton School Lists.*

Maude, Samuel, 1s. Joseph, of Newport, Isle of Wight, cler. WADHAM COLL., matric. 9 Dec., 1863, aged 18; B.A. 1868, M.A. 1871, held various curacies 1869-82, vicar of Needham Market since 1882.

Maude, Rev. Thomas, 2s. Thomas, of Newcastle, Northumberland, arm. UNIVERSITY COLL., matric. 20 Feb., 1819, aged 17; B.A. 1822, M.A. 1827, a student of the Inner Temple 1826, died at the rectory, Elvington, near York, 18 July, 1865; for list of his writings see *Gent.'s Mag.*, 1865, ii. 390; & Foster's *Yorkshire Collection.*

Maude, Thomas, 1s. Thomas William, of Christchurch, New Zealand, arm. HERTFORD COLL., matric. 18 May, 1883, aged 19; B.A. 1887, bar.-at-law, Inner Temple, 1888.

Maude, Thomas William, 1s. Thomas, of Elmstead, Essex, cler. BALLIOL COLL., matric. 14 March, 1850, aged 17; B.A. 1870, M.A. 1879, bar.-at-law, Lincoln's Inn, 1879. See Foster's *Men at the Bar.* **[15]**

Maude, Walter, 8s. Thomas James, of Rugby, gent. BALLIOL COLL., matric. 18 Oct., 1881, aged 19; of the Indian Civil Service 1881.

Maude, William Cassell, 1s. Arthur, of Rose Hill, near Rotherham, Yorks, gent. EXETER COLL., matric. 18 May, 1869, aged 18; B.A. 1873, B.C.L. & M.A. 1884, bar.-at-law, Lincoln's Inn, 1876. See Foster's *Men at the Bar.*

Maudson, Arthur Henry, 2s. Richard Thomas, of Leeds, gent. BRASENOSE COLL., matric. 20 Oct., 1886, aged 19; scholar 1886.

Maugham, Henry Macdonald, 3s. —M., gent. ORIEL COLL., matric. 7 Dec., 1848; B.A. 1852, M.A. 1855, held various curacies 1853-71, vicar of Whitstable, Kent, since 1871.

Maughan, Charles, s. John, of Bishop Wearmouth, co. Durham, arm. QUEEN'S COLL., matric. 15 March, 1790, aged 18. **[20]**

Maughan, Rev. Herbert, 2s. Nicolas, of Clapham, Surrey, arm. ST. JOHN'S COLL., matric. 1 Feb., 1870, aged 19; B.A. from NEW INN HALL 1876, M.A. 1878. See *Robinson*, 348.

Maughan, Veargitt William, o.s. Veargitt, of Clapton, Middlesex, gent. ST. JOHN'S COLL., matric. 11 Oct., 1884, aged 21; died at Oxford 29 May, 1888.

Maul, Charles, 1s. Charles, of Southampton, arm. WADHAM COLL., matric. 14 Oct., 1830, aged 18; scholar 1830-3.

Maule, George, s. William, of St. James's, Westminster, arm. CHRIST CHURCH, matric. 29 Oct., 1793, aged 17; B.A. 1797, M.A. 1800, bar.-at-law, Lincoln's Inn, 1801, joint solicitor to the Treasury, died in Nov., 1851.

Maule, George, 1s. George Frederick, of Godmanchester, Hunts, arm. UNIVERSITY COLL., matric. 14 Nov., 1833, aged 18; B.A. 1838, rector of Ampthill, Beds, 1846-75, and of Thoresway, co. Lincoln, since 1875. **[25]**

Maule, George Benjamin, 1s. George, of St. Margaret's, Westminster, arm. CHRIST CHURCH, matric. 2 Dec., 1828, aged 17; student 1832-47, B.A. 1833, M.A. 1835, bar.-at-law, Lincoln's Inn, 1838, died 14 Sep., 1850.

Maule, George Norman, o.s. John, of Bath, Somerset, arm. ST. JOHN'S COLL., matric. 4 Dec., 1845, aged 18; B.A. 1849, M.A. 1852, a barrister of Lincoln's Inn 1853. See Foster's *Men at the Bar* & *Eton School Lists.*

Maule, Henry Carteret, 1s. Thomas Carteret, of Cheam, Surrey, cler. ST. JOHN'S COLL., matric. 13 Oct., 1877, aged 19; B.A. 1880.

Maule, John, s. Stephen John, of Greenwich, Kent, gent. QUEEN'S COLL., matric. 17 Oct., 1788, aged 17; B.A. from MERTON COLL. 1792, M.A. 1800, incumbent of St. Mary-the-Virgin, Dover, 1817-42, died 17 Feb., 1866.

Maule, (Sir) John Blosset, 2s. George, of Kensington, Middlesex, arm. CHRIST CHURCH, matric. 4 June, 1835, aged 18; B.A. 1839, M.A. 1846, bar.-at-law, Inner Temple, 1847, Q.C. and a bencher 1866, treasurer 1882, recorder of Leeds 1861-80, director of public prosecutions 1880, knighted 7 Dec., 1882. See Foster's *Men at the Bar.* **[30]**

Maule, John Frederick, 2s. Richard Compton, of Rickinghall, Suffolk, cler. CHRIST CHURCH, matric. 12 June, 1867, aged 17; B.A. 1872, M.A. 1875, vicar of St. Paul's, Chichester, 1879-83, rector of Henley-on-Thames 1883. See *Eton School Lists.*

Maule, Montagu St. John, 3s. Henry St. John, of Bathwick, Bath, gent. PEMBROKE COLL., matric. 11 April, 1864, aged 17; B.A. 1868, a solicitor. See *Rugby School Reg.*

Maule, Nathaniel, 'carrier;' privilegiatus 5 Aug., 1737.

Maule, Thomas, s. William, of St. Nicholas, Worcester (city), pleb. CHRIST CHURCH, matric. 17 Jan., 1801, aged 19.

Maule, Thomas Carteret, 4s. William Henry, of Portsmouth, arm. ST. JOHN'S COLL., matric. 29 June, 1835, aged 17; scholar and fellow 1835-57, B.A. 1839, M.A. 1843, B.D. 1848, bursar 1854, vicar of St. Giles's, Oxford, rector of Cheam 1856, until he died 29 March, 1867. See *Robinson*, 223. **[35]**

Maund, Charles, s. Joseph, of Haverfordwest, co. Pembroke, pleb. JESUS COLL., matric. 31 March, 1792, aged 20; B.A. 1795.

Maund, John, o.s. John, of Pontypool, co. Monmouth, arm. BRASENOSE COLL., matric. 25 May, 1853, aged 18.

Maunder, Charles, scholar QUEEN'S COLL., Cambridge, 1836, B.A. 1839, M.A. 1842; adm. 'ad eundem' 9 May, 1844, perp. curate Holy Trinity, Bitton, 1845-54, and of Botleys, Surrey, 1854-5, vicar of Walton with Felixstow, Norfolk, 1857, until his death 22 July, 1882.

Maunder, Richard, s. Richard, of Exeter (city), cler. HART HALL, matric. 8 April, 1717, aged 18; B.A. 1720.

Maunder, Robert, s. Robert, of Tiverton, Devon, gent. EXETER COLL., matric. 4 June, 1794, aged 19; exhibitioner 1796, B.A. 1798, curate of North Molton 1798. See *Coll. Reg.*, 149.

Maunder, William, s. William, of Cruwys Morchard, Devon, gent. BALLIOL COLL., matric. 15 May, 1746, aged 17. [5]

Maundrell, Robert, s. Thomas, of Blackland, Wilts, gent. QUEEN'S COLL., matric. 15 Nov., 1782, aged 18.

Maunsell, Rev. Cecil Henry, o.s. George Edmond, of Thorpe Malsor, Northants, cler. ST. JOHN'S COLL., matric. 16 Oct., 1866, aged 19; B.A. 1870, M.A. 1873, of Thorpe Malsor, Northants.

Maunsell, George Edmond, 2s. Thomas Philip, of Rushton, Northants, arm. CHRIST CHURCH, matric. 11 Dec., 1834, aged 18; B.A. 1838, rector of Thorpe Malsor, Northants, 1841, until his death 29 Oct., 1875. See *Eton School Lists.*

Maunsell, George (Meares), s. Daniel, of Dublin, arm. ORIEL COLL., matric. 22 March, 1803, aged 17; B.A. 1807, of Ballywilliam, co. Limerick, J.P., high sheriff 1833, died in 1871.

Maunsell, Richard, s. William, of Limerick, Ireland, doctor. MERTON COLL., matric. 19 May, 1787, aged 21; B.A. 27 June, 1787, he probaby died young, his father archdeacon of Kildare and chancellor of Limerick. [10]

Maunsell, Richard Cecil, 2s. Frederick Webster, of Iwerne Courtney, Dorset, cler. WADHAM COLL., matric. 16 Oct., 1886, aged 19.

Maunsell, Thomas Cockayne, 3s. Thomas, of Kettering, arm. CHRIST CHURCH, matric. 20 Oct., 1836, aged 18; of Sparrows Herne Hall, Herts, J.P., sometime captain 12th royal lancers, and captain commanding royal Kettering yeomanry cavalry. See *Eton School Lists.*

Maunsell, William Thomas, 1s. Thomas Philip, of Rushton, Northants, arm. CHRIST CHURCH, matric. 21 May, 1831, aged 18; B.A. 1835, M.A. 1838, bar.-at-law, Middle Temple, 1837, recorder of Stamford 1859, died 13 March, 1862. See *Eton School Lists.*

Maurice, Charles Edmund, 2s. Frederick Denison, of Guy's Hospital, London, cler. CHRIST CHURCH, matric. 22 May, 1861, aged 17; B.A. 1865, bar.-at-law, Inner Temple, 1871. See Foster's *Men at the Bar.*

Maurice, David Theodore, s. Richard, of St. Martin's, London, gent. CHRIST CHURCH, matric. 14 Oct., 1743, aged 18; B.A. 1747. [15]

Maurice, Edward Arthur Bonnor-, 3s. Robert, of Bodynfoel Hall, near Llanfechain, co. Montgomery, arm. NEW COLL., matric. 24 Jan., 1868, aged 19; B.A. 1871, of Bodynfoel, co. Montgomery.

Maurice, Henry, s. Rowland, of Aberfraw, co. Anglesea, pleb. JESUS COLL., matric. 26 Feb., 1729-30, aged 17; B.A. 11 March, 1733-4.

Maurice, Rev. Horatio Charles, 1s. Thomas, of Harnhill, co. Gloucester, cler. EXETER COLL., matric. 12 Oct., 1860, aged 19; B.A. 1865, died Sep., 1870.

Maurice, John, s. Maurice, of Llanverothen, co. Carnarvon, pleb. JESUS COLL., matric. 16 May, 1774, aged 22.

Maurice, John Frederick Denison, o.s. Michael, of Lowestoft, Suffolk, gent. EXETER COLL., matric. 3 Dec., 1829, aged 24, B.A. 1831, M.A. 1835; scholar TRINITY COLL., Cambridge, 1825, migrated to TRINITY HALL 1826, subsequently incorporated of that university from TRINITY COLL. 1867, hon. M.A. 1867, professor of moral philosophy, Cambridge, 1866-72, chaplain and preacher to Honourable Society of Lincoln's Inn 1846-1860, professor of modern history and English literature King's College, London, 1840-6, and of ecclesiastical history 1846-53, founder and 1st principal of the Working Mens' College, London, 1854, perp. curate St. Peter's, Vere Street, London, 1860-6, vicar of St. Edward's, Cambridge, 1871, until his death 1 April, 1872; for list of his works see *Crockford.* [20]

Maurice, John Lloyd, 1s. Joseph, of Llanfwrog, co. Denbigh, gent. JESUS COLL., matric. 9 June, 1832, aged 20.

Maurice, John Meredith, 4s. Price, of Brighton, arm. BRASENOSE COLL., matric. 29 April, 1882, aged 17.

Maurice, John Pierce, s. Thelwall, of Marlborough, Wilts, gent. BRASENOSE COLL., matric. 4 May, 1815, aged 19; scholar 1816-19, B.A. 1819, M.A. 1821, rector of Michelmersh, Hants, 1840, until his death 17 July, 1874.

Maurice, Mortimer, 1s. Mortimer, of St. Paul's, Bristol, gent. ST. EDMUND HALL, matric. 19 March, 1842, aged 20; B.A. 1850.

Maurice, Peter, s. Peter, of Ruthin, co. Denbigh, cler. (after dean of Bangor). WADHAM COLL., matric. 1 July, 1737, aged 16; B.A. 1741, M.A. 1749, rector of Llanllechid and preb. of Penmynydd. See *Alumni West.*, 317. [25]

Maurice, Peter, s. Peter, of Glynne, co. Denbigh, pleb. JESUS COLL., matric. 27 May, 1738, aged 18; B.A. 1741.

Maurice, Peter, 2s. Hugh, of Greenwich, Kent, arm. JESUS COLL., matric. 19 Oct., 1822; B.A. 1826, chaplain NEW COLL. 1828-59, M.A. 1829, B.D. 1837, D.D. 1840, chaplain All Souls' College 1837-58, vicar of Yarnton, Oxon, 1858, until his death 30 March, 1878.

Maurice, Pryce, s. Pryce, of Llansilin, co. Denbigh, arm. QUEEN'S COLL., matric. 8 Feb., 1765, aged 18 (? died vicar of Towyn and rector of Clynnin, co. Merioneth, 19 April, 1803.

Maurice, Richard, s. Richard, of Llangedwin, co. Denbigh, cler. JESUS COLL., matric. 20 Nov., 1747, aged 18; B.A. 1751, M.A. 1754.

Maurice, Robert, s. Robert, of Denbigh (town), arm. JESUS COLL., matric. 13 May, 1742, aged 19.

Maurice, Robert, s. Richard, of Llangedwin, co. Denbigh, cler. JESUS COLL., matric. 12 March, 1749-50, aged 18; B.A. 1753, M.A. 1756, rector of Warmwell-cum-Poxwell and Bloxworth, Dorset, 1774, died at Blandford in 1817, aged 86. [31]

Maurice, Robert. ORIEL COLL. 1760. See MORRIS.

Maurice, Robert (Maurice) Bonnor, 2s. John Bonnor, of St. George-the-Martyr, London, arm. CHRIST CHURCH, matric. 21 May, 1823, aged 18; B.A. 1827, of Bodynfoel Hall, high sheriff co. Montgomery 1831, a student of the Inner Temple 1827, assumed the additional surname of MAURICE, died 1872.

Maurice, Thomas, s. Thomas, of Hertford (town), gent. ST. JOHN'S COLL., matric. 6 May, 1774, aged 19; B.A. from UNIVERSITY COLL. 1778, M.A. 1808, Oriental scholar and historian, chaplain 87th regiment about 1784, vicar of Wormleighton, co. Warwick, 1798-1824, and of Cudham, Kent, 1804-24, assistant-keeper of the MSS. British Museum, 1798, until his death 30 March, 1824.

Maurice, Thomas, 4s. Thelwall, of Marlborough, Wilts, arm. MERTON COLL., matric. 3 May, 1826, aged 19; B.A. 1830, M.A. 1833, J.P. cos. Gloucester and Wilts, rector of Harnhill, Wilts, and Driffield, co. Gloucester, 1840, until his death 26 June, 1881. [35]

Maurice, Thomas Calley, 1s. William Thelwall Blissett, of Swindon, Wilts, arm. UNIVERSITY COLL., matric. 27 Oct., 1840, aged 19.

Maurice, William James, 4s. Thomas, of Harnhill, near Cirencester, cler. KEBLE COLL., matric. 26 Jan., 1876, aged 18; B.A. 1879.

Mauzy, Lewis, s. Lewis, of Clonmell, co. Tipperary, Ireland, doctor. EXETER COLL., matric. 21 March, 1729-30, aged 20.

Mavor, John, s. William, of Woodstock, Oxon, doctor. WADHAM COLL., matric. 3 June, 1802, aged 16; fellow LINCOLN COLL. until 1826, B.A. 1806, M.A. 1808, B.D. 1816, sub-rector 1822, Greek lecturer 1823, claviger 1824, perp. curate Forest Hill, Oxon, 1823, and rector of Hadleigh, Essex, 1825, died in his cell on the debtor side of the Oxford County Gaol 19 June, 1853, his father, rector of Woodstock, was author of the well-known spelling-book, died 29 Dec., 1837.

Mavor, William Henry, 3s. William, of Woodstock, Oxon, doctor. TRINITY COLL., matric. 3 Dec., 1846, aged 18; B.A. from WORCESTER COLL. 1850. [5]

Mavrojani, Spyridion Alexander, o.s. Alexander, of London, arm. TRINITY COLL., matric. 17 Oct., 1885, aged 19.

Maw, George, s. John Henry, of Wakefield, Yorks, arm. LINCOLN COLL., matric. 24 Oct., 1812, aged 19; scholar 1813-15, B.A. 1819.

Mawdsley, Alfred Archibald, 1s. Peter Alfred, of Englefield, Flints, gent. LINCOLN COLL., matric. 19 Oct., 1883, aged 19; B.A. 1886.

Mawdesley, Arthur Leyland, o.s. John Leyland, of Liverpool, gent. ST. EDMUND HALL, matric. 29 Jan., 1886, aged 19.

Mawdesley, Robert, s. Robert, of Eccleston, Lancashire, gent. ORIEL COLL., matric. 10 July, 1724, aged 17. [10]

Mawdesley, Thomas, s. Robert, of Eccleston, Lancashire, gent. ORIEL COLL., matric. 10 July, 1724, aged 16; B.C.L. 1731.

Mawdesley, Thomas, s. John, of Liverpool, Lancashire, gent. BRASENOSE COLL., matric. 18 Feb., 1726-7, aged 17; B.A. 1730.

Mawdesley, Thomas, s. Thomas, of Leigh, Lancashire, cler. BRASENOSE COLL., matric. 30 March, 1776, aged 18; B.A. 1779, M.A. 1782, rector of St. Mary's, Chester, 1813, until his death 2 Sep., 1833.

Mawdesley, Thomas, s. Thomas, of Chester (city), cler. BRASENOSE COLL., matric. 16 Dec., 1805, aged 17; B.A. 1809, M.A. 1812, perp. curate of Chelford, Cheshire, 1816, until his death 21 Jan., 1839.

Mawdesley, William, s. Robert, of Eccleston, Lancashire, arm. BRASENOSE COLL., matric. 15 March, 1715-6, aged 20. [15]

Mawdsley, Richard, s. Edward, of Hutton, Lancashire, pleb. BRASENOSE COLL., matric. 10 Oct., 1741, aged 21.

Mawer, Thomas, s. George, of St. Botolph's, Aldersgate, London, arm. ST. JOHN'S COLL., matric. 25 May, 1722, aged 17; bar.-at-law, Inner Temple, 1730.

Mawry, William, s. William, of Exeter, Devon, pleb. EXETER COLL., matric. 11 March, 1715-6, aged 16.

Maxey, Lewis, s. John, of Wallingford, Berks, gent. CHRIST CHURCH, matric. 14 Jan., 1763, aged 16; B.A. 1766, clerk MAGDALEN COLL. 1767-8; M.A. from ST. CATHARINE COLL., Cambridge, 1772, minor canon Hereford Cathedral, rector of Byford, co. Hereford, 1782, vicar of Bridge Sollers, Preston, and Blakemere 1813, until he died 15 July, 1820. See *Bloxam*, ii. 104.

Maxey, William Seele, s. Joseph, of Islington, Middlesex, arm. QUEEN'S COLL., matric. 31 Oct., 1745, aged 22; B.A. 1749, rector of Northill, Beds, 1751, until his death 17 Sep., 1780. [20]

Maxse, James, s. John, of Brislington, Somerset, arm. UNIVERSITY COLL., matric. 5 Dec., 1809, aged 17.

Maxsted, Basil Eden, 2s. Edward Philip, of Hessle, Yorks, arm. PEMBROKE COLL., matric. 4 Feb., 1880, aged 17; B.A. 1882, M.A. 1886. See *Eton School Lists*.

Maxwell, Charles, 2s. Patrick, of Hatcham, Berks, cler. BALLIOL COLL., matric. 24 June, 1829, aged 18; B.A. 1833, rector of Wyddial, Herts, since 1836.

Maxwell, Edward, s. Robert, of Dumfries, Scotland, arm. UNIVERSITY COLL., matric. 14 Dec., 1771, aged 18.

Maxwell, Frederick David, 1s. James William, of St. Petersburgh, gent. CHRIST CHURCH, matric. 28 Nov., 1872, aged 21; B.A. 1876, M.A. 1880, bar.-at-law, Lincoln's Inn, 1879. See Foster's *Men at the Bar*. [25]

Maxwell, Frederick Mackenzie, 2s. Joseph, of Turks' Island, cler. BALLIOL COLL., matric. 17 Oct., 1882, aged 22; B.A. 1885.

Maxwell, George, 4s. Edward, of Rumbold's Wyke, Sussex, arm. ST. JOHN'S COLL., matric. 19 April, 1820, aged 18.

Maxwell, Rev. Gerald Speirs, 7s. Charles Francis, of London, arm. ORIEL COLL., matric. 15 Oct., 1877, aged 19; B.A. 1880, M.A. 1885.

Maxwell, Henry, B.A. TRINITY COLL., Dublin, 1745, s. John, of Dublin (city), arm. (after Baron Farnham). CHRIST CHURCH, incorp. 31 Oct., 1745, aged 21; dean of Kilmore 1761-5, bishop of Dromore 1765, and of Meath 1766, until his death 7 Oct., 1798. See Foster's *Peerage*, B. FARNHAM.

Maxwell, Henry, s. James, of St. George's, Westminster, arm. CHRIST CHURCH, matric. 23 May, 1765, aged 16; created M.A. 3 Nov., 1770. [30]

Maxwell, Henry George, 2s. Charles, of Wyddiall, Herts, cler. ST. JOHN'S COLL., matric. 31 Jan., 1865, aged 18; B.A. 1868, M.A. 1871, held various curacies 1870-82, assistant-chaplain her Majesty's Prison, Coldbathfields, 1882-6. See *Eton School Lists*.

Maxwell, (Sir) Herbert Eustace (Bart.), 1s. William, of Edinburgh, baronet. CHRIST CHURCH, matric. 12 Dec., 1863, aged 18; 7th baronet, M.P. Wigtownshire (April) 1880, a lord of the Treasury 1886. See Foster's *Baronetage*.

Maxwell, James Clerk, created D.C.L. 21 June, 1876 (only son of John C.-M., of Middleby, co. Dumfries), F.R.S., scholar TRINITY COLL., Cambridge, 1852-5, 2nd Wrangler and B.A. 1854, fellow 1855-8, M.A. 1857, hon. fellow 1872-9, professor natural philosophy Marischall College, Aberdeen, 1855, professor natural philosophy and astronomy King's College, London, 1859-71, and hon. fellow 1865-79, professor of experimental physics in Cambridge University 1871-9, president Cambridge Philosophical Society, and Rede lecturer 1878, died 5 Nov., 1879. See Foster's *Baronetage*, CLERK.

Maxwell, John, B.A. TRINITY COLL., Dublin, 1725; incorp. from ST. JOHN'S COLL. 22 or 23 Nov., 1726, created M.A. 7 July, 1727; M.A. TRINITY COLL., Dublin, 1728, B. & D.D. 1755, son of Robert F. Maxwell, of Falkland, co. Monaghan (? preb. of Connor 1721-59), archdeacon of Clogher 1762-83, died in 1784. See Cotton's *Fasti*, v. 218.

Maxwell, (Sir) John (Bart.), s. John, of Pollok, co. Renfrew, baronet. CHRIST CHURCH, matric. 26 Oct., 1809, aged 18; 8th baronet, M.P. Renfrewshire 1818-30, Lanarkshire 1832-7, died 6 June, 1865. See Foster's *Baronetage*, STIRLING-MAXWELL.

Maxwell, (Sir) John Robert Heron (Bart.), 1s. John Heron, of Bargally, Kircudbright, Scotland, baronet. EXETER COLL., matric. 13 May, 1856, aged 19; 7th baronet, sometime captain 15th hussars. See Foster's *Baronetage*. [35]

Maxwell, John William Perceval, 1s. Robert Perceval, of Dublin, arm. CHRIST CHURCH, matric. 21 Oct., 1858, aged 17; of Finnebrogue, co. Down, J.P., high sheriff 1873. See Foster's *Peerage*, E. EGMONT.

Maxwell, Joseph Renner, 1s. Thomas, of Sierra Leone, cler. MERTON COLL., matric. 14 Oct., 1876, aged 19; B.A. 1879, M.A. 1883, B.C.L. 1884, bar.-at-law, Lincoln's Inn, 1880. See Foster's *Men at the Bar*.

Maxwell, Louis Robert Meredith, o.s. Patrick, of Simla, East Indies, arm. CORPUS CHRISTI COLL., matric. 22 Oct., 1874, aged 18; passed first from Sandhurst 1876.

Maxwell, Patrick, s. Robert, of Minigoff, co. Galloway, arm. BALLIOL COLL., matric. 18 Jan., 1776, aged 18.

Maxwell, Patrick, s. Patrick, of Dundee, co. Angus, arm. BALLIOL COLL., matric. 16 Oct., 1786, aged 16; B.A. 1790, M.A. 1793, died at the rectory, Almer, Dorset, 13 Dec., 1830.

Maxwell, Patrick Hay, o.s. Thomas, of Maxweltown, co. Kirkcudbright, gent. WORCESTER COLL., matric. 29 May, 1857, aged 38; fellow commoner 1857, B.A. 1860. [5]

Maxwell, Robert Perceval, 1s. William Maxwell, of Ballinakill, Queen's County, cler. BRASENOSE COLL., matric. 25 May, 1831, aged 17; B.A. 1836, of Groomsport and Finnebrogue, co. Down, high sheriff 1841, and for co. Waterford 1864, a student of Lincoln's Inn 1834. See Foster's *Peerage*, E. EGMONT.

Maxwell, Thomas, s. Thomas, of Christ Church, Isle of Barbados, arm. CHRIST CHURCH, matric. 23 Aug., 1717, aged 14.

Maxwell, Wellwood (Herries), o.s. John Herries, of Munches, co. Kirkcudbright, arm. EXETER COLL., matric. 18 March, 1835, aged 17; of Munches, co. Kirkcudbright, J.P., D.L., M.P. 1868-74, a member of the Faculty of Advocates 1839.

Maxwell, William, s. William, of Carriden, co. Linlithgow, arm. CHRIST CHURCH, matric. 7 May, 1787, aged 19; created M.A. 16 June, 1791, possibly M.P. Linlithgow Burghs 1807-12. See Foster's *Scots M.P.'s*.

Maxwell, William George, s. George, of Cumberland, gent. MERTON COLL., matric. 10 Nov., 1789, aged 17; B.A. 1793, M.A. 1796, of Twyning House, near Tewkesbury, perp. curate of Great Washbourne, co. Gloucester, 1810, died 5 Nov., 1838. [10]

Maxwell, Hon. William George, born at Boulogne-sur-Mer, 9s. Henry, Baron Farnham, and cler. EXETER COLL, matric. 14 May, 1840, aged 19; died 12 April, 1876. See Foster's *Peerage*.

Maxwell, William Hall, 1s. John Hall, of Largs, co. Ayr, Scotland, arm. MERTON COLL., matric. 26 Jan., 1867, aged 19; of Dargavel, co. Renfrew, J.P., D.L.

Maxwell, William Jardine, 1s. Wellwood Herries, of Munches, co. Kirkcudbright, Scotland, arm. EXETER COLL., matric. 7 June, 1870, aged 18; B.A. 1873, M.A. 1879.

Maxwell, (Sir) William Stirling- (Bart.), created D.C.L. 21 June, 1876 (only son of Archibald Stirling, of Keir, co. Perth), 9th baronet, K.T., M.P. Perthshire 1852-65, 1874-80, lord rector of Edinburgh University 1872-4, chancellor Glasgow University 1875-8, a member of senate London University 1874-8, a trustee of the British Museum, assumed the additional surname of MAXWELL, died 15 Jan., 1878. See Foster's *Baronetage*.

May, Arthur, s. Joseph, of St. George's, Bloomsbury, London, arm. MERTON COLL., matric. 17 March, 1801, aged 21. [15]

May, Arthur Sigfrid, 2s. Frederick Schiller, of London, cler. ST. JOHN'S COLL., matric. 11 Oct., 1884, aged 18.

May, Arthur William, 1s. Samuel, of Worle, Somerset, gent. NON-COLL., matric. 13 Oct., 1883, aged 21.

May, Bowen Alexander, 3s. James Bowen, of Brighton, Sussex, gent. WORCESTER COLL., matric. 31 Jan., 1865, aged 18; B.A. & M.A. from CHARSLEY HALL 1871, bar.-at-law, Inner Temple, 1872. See Foster's *Men at the Bar*.

May, Edmund, 3s. Daniel, of Sunning, Oxon, gent. MERTON COLL., matric. 5 Dec., 1833, aged 17; B.A. 1837, M.A. 1840, vicar of Parwich, and perp. curate Alsop-le-Dale, co. Derby, 1867-9, rector of All Cannings, Wilts, 1869.

May, Rev. Edmund Bowen, o.s. James, of Ashbrittle, Somerset, cler. WORCESTER COLL., matric. 17 April, 1826, aged 18; B.A. 11 Feb., 1830, died in June same year. [20]

May, Edward, s. Edward, of Mayfield, Ireland, arm. ST. MARY HALL, matric. 21 March, 1800, aged 17.

May, Edward, 4s. George, of Herne, Kent, arm. CHRIST CHURCH, matric. 26 May, 1819, aged 18; B.A. 1824, bar.-at-law, Middle Temple, 1825.

May, Edward Henry Fox, 1s. Edward William, of West Allington, Dorset, cler. EXETER COLL., matric. 21 Oct., 1886, aged 19.

May, Edward John, o.s. Edward, of Marylebone, London, arm. WORCESTER COLL., matric. 24 Jan., 1839, aged 21; B.A. 1842, M.A. 1845, has held various curacies and scholastic appointments 1843-82. See *Crockford*. [24]

May, Edward Thomson, s. Samuel, of Fremington, Devon, cler. EXETER COLL., matric. 15 April, 1791, aged 18; B.A. 1795, curate of Braunton 1795, vicar of Fremington 1810, until his death in 1827.

May, Emanuel, s. Emanuel, of Fremington, Devon, gent. EXETER COLL., matric. 22 May, 1753, aged 17; fellow 1756-74, B.A. & M.A. 1760, B.D. 1771, vicar of Ilfracombe 1771, until his death, buried there 20 March, 1804, brother of James 1767. See *Coll. Reg.*, 105.

May, Frank Markland, 4s. Edmund, of Bath, cler. ST. EDMUND HALL, matric. 23 Oct., 1877, aged 18; Abbott scholar 1878, died in 1878.

May, Frederick Granville, 5s. Henry Thomas, of South Petherwyn, Cornwall, cler. NEW COLL., matric. 14 April, 1877, aged 19; B.A. 1881, rector of St. Mellion's, Cornwall, 1885.

May, George, s. George, of Maidstone, Kent, arm. ORIEL COLL., matric. 21 April, 1806, aged 16; B.A. 1810, M.A. 1814 (? died preb. of Lyddington, Wilts, 24 Dec., 1861. See *Gent.'s Mag.*).

May, George Charles, 1s. Henry William, of Uxbridge, Middlesex, arm. ST. JOHN'S COLL., matric. 16 Oct., 1886, aged 19. [30]

May, Henry, 1s. Thomas, of Deal, Kent, gent. MAGDALEN HALL, matric. 21 March, 1823, aged 20.

May, Henry, o.s. Joshua Bulkley, of Burslem, co. Stafford, arm. BRASENOSE COLL., matric. 17 Oct., 1874, aged 20; scholar 1874-9.

May, Henry Thomas, o.s. Thomas Charles, of Breamore, Hants, cler. NEW COLL., matric. 8 Oct., 1833, aged 18; fellow 1833-51, B.A. 1838, M.A. 1842, sub-warden 1848, dean of divinity 1849, proctor 1849, perp. curate Milton, Portsea, 1847-9, vicar of St. Petherwin, Cornwall, 1850.

May, Henry William, 1s. George, of Lydington, near Swindon, Wilts, cler. CHRIST CHURCH, matric. 17 Oct., 1860, aged 16; B.A. 1865, bar.-at-law, Lincoln's Inn, 1868.

May, Herbert Hine, 4s. William Hine, of Frome, Somerset, arm. WADHAM COLL., matric. 16 Oct., 1880, aged 19; scholar 1879-84, B.A. 1884, M.A. 1888.

May, James, s. Emanuel, of Tremington, Devon, gent. EXETER COLL., matric. 13 Nov., 1767, aged 18; B.A. 1771, rector of Cheldon 1779, and of Trevalga, Cornwall, 1793, until his death 11 Oct., 1831. [36]

May, James Bowen, s. James, of Cheldon, Devon, cler. BALLIOL COLL., matric. 1 May, 1795, aged 18; B.A. 1799, rector of St. Martin's, Exeter, 1825, until his death in 1827.

May, James (Six), s. George, of Maidstone, Kent, arm. CHRIST CHURCH, matric. 12 May, 1812, aged 17; B.A. 1815, M.A. 1820, vicar of Herne, Kent, 1831, until his death 17 May, 1866.

May, James Thomas, 1s. Thomas, of Penshurst, Kent, cler. UNIVERSITY COLL., matric. 20 Oct., 1848, aged 18; B.A. 1852, M.A. 1857, has held various curacies since 1853.

May, John, s. Charles Hughes, of Sittingbourne, Kent, arm. PEMBROKE COLL., matric. 2 June, 1791, aged 16.

May, John, o.s. John, of Richmond, Surrey, arm. EXETER COLL., matric. 2 Feb., 1822, aged 19; B.A. 1825, vicar of Ugborough, Devon, 1845, until his death 27 May, 1879. See *Eton School Lists.*

May, John Cecil, 2s. Thomas Henry, of Hampstead, Middlesex, gent. ST. EDMUND HALL, matric. 14 April, 1869, aged 27; B.A. & M.A. 1875, has held various curacies since 1877.

May, John Henry, 1s. Henry, of Maple Durham, Oxon, gent. PEMBROKE COLL., matric. 3 June, 1852, aged 18; B.A. 1857, M.A. 1859.

May, Joseph, born at Lisbon, Portugal, s. Joseph, arm. CHRIST CHURCH, matric. 10 Feb., 1786, aged 18; B.A. 1790, brother of Thomas Charles 1791. [5]

May, Joseph, s. Joseph, of St. James's, Westminster, arm. CHRIST CHURCH, matric. 22 May, 1818, aged 18.

May, Nathaniel, s. Thomas, of Brampton, Northants, cler. LINCOLN COLL., matric. 30 Oct., 1778, aged 17; B.A. 1783, M.A. 1785, rector of Digswell, Herts, 1795-1811, vicar (and patron) of Leigh, Kent, 1811, until his death 18 Jan., 1830. See *Robinson*, 135.

May, Philip James, 1s. Philip, of Hampton Wick, Middlesex, arm. NON-COLL., matric. 26 Jan., 1878, aged 19; a student of the Middle Temple 1878.

May, Robert Augustus, 5s. Edmund, of Parwich, co. Derby, cler. MERTON COLL., matric. 19 Oct. 1883, aged 18; B.A. 1887.

May, Samuel, s. Nath., of London, gent. ST. JOHN'S COLL., matric. 16 July, 1716, aged 17; B.A. 1720, M.A. 1723. [10]

May, Samuel, s. Samuel, of Fremington, Devon, pleb. EXETER COLL., matric. 31 March, 1718, aged 18; B.A. 1721.

May, Samuel, s. Eman., of Fremington, Devon, gent. EXETER COLL., matric. 16 Oct., 1750, aged 17; fellow 1750-5, B.A. 1755, died in 1782, father of Edward T. 1791. See *Coll. Reg.*, 105.

May, Samuel, 1s. Samuel, of Fremington, Devon, cler. LINCOLN COLL., matric. 16 April, 1823, aged 19.

May, Samuel (Thomson), s. Samuel, of Brynsworthy, Devon, cler. EXETER COLL., matric. 10 Oct., 1787, aged 18; B.A. 1791.

May, (Sir) Stephen (Edward, knight), s. James, of Clonegham, co. Waterford, Ireland, baronet. ST. MARY HALL, matric. 4 April, 1781, aged 18; M.P. Belfast 1814-16, then erroneously styled a baronet, collector of Customs, Belfast, April, 1816, and knighted 20 April 1816. [15]

May, Thomas, s. John, of Basing, Southampton, gent. LINCOLN COLL., matric. 2 Nov., 1731, aged 16; B.A. from CORPUS CHRISTI COLL. 1735, M.A. 10 Feb., 1738-9, B.D. 1746.

May, Thomas, s. Emanuel, of Fremington, Devon, gent. EXETER COLL., matric. 7 April, 1772, aged 18; B.A. 1776, rector (and patron) of Roborough, Devon, 1781, until his death 28 March, 1837.

May, Thomas Agnew, 1s. Henry Thomas, of South Petherwyn, Cornwall, cler. ST. MARY HALL, matric. 28 Jan., 1871, aged 19; scholar 1871-5, B.A. 1875, M.A. 1877.

May, Thomas Charles, born at Lisbon, Portugal, s. Joseph, arm. ORIEL COLL., matric. 13 July, 1791, aged 18; B.A. 1796, rector (and patron) of Breamore, Hants, 1797, until his death 26 March, 1837.

May, Sir Thomas Erskine, K.C.B., clerk of the House of Commons 1871-86, created D.C.L. 17 June, 1874, bar.-at-law, Middle Temple, 1838, bencher 1873, author of the 'Law, Privileges, Proceedings, and Usage of Parliament,' 'Constitutional History of England 1760-1870,' etc., knighted 6 July, 1866, created Baron Farnborough, of Farnborough, co. Southants, 11 May, 1887, died 17 May, 1887. See Foster's *Men at the Bar.* [20]

May, Rev. Thomas Henry, 2s. Thomas Henry, of Brompton, Middlesex, gent. WORCESTER COLL., matric. 26 Oct., 1868, aged 17; B.A. 1871, M.A. 1876.

May, Walter Barton, s. Walter, of Packham, Kent, arm. TRINITY COLL., matric. 10 Dec., 1801, aged 18; of Hadlow Castle, Kent, died 31 May, 1855, father of the next named.

May, Walter Horatio, o.s. Walter B., of Hadlow, Kent, arm. NEW INN HALL, matric. 27 Oct., 1842, aged 20.

May, William, s. William, of Plymouth, Devon, pleb. EXETER COLL., matric. 3 March, 1725-6, aged 18; B.A. from ST. MARY HALL 1729.

May, William, 1s. George, of Reading, Berks, gent. NEW COLL., matric. 4 June, 1881, aged 18; B.A. 1884. [25]

Maybery, Charles, s. John, of Brecon, pleb. BALLIOL COLL., matric. 4 Dec., 1782, aged 18.

Maybery, Charles, 2s. Thomas, of St. Mary's, Brecknock, arm. JESUS COLL., matric. 13 Nov., 1821, aged 17; scholar 1823-30, B.A. 1825, M.A. 1828, rector of Penderyn 1831, until his death 4 Jan., 1871.

Maybery, David Joseph, o.s. Joseph, of Llanelly, co. Carmarthen, gent. WORCESTER COLL., matric. 29 Jan., 1879, aged 19; B.A. 1884, M.A. 1886.

Maycock, Dottin, s. John, of Isle of Barbados, arm. ST. JOHN'S COLL., matric. 31 Oct., 1760, aged 17; bar.-at-law, Middle Temple, 1767.

Maycock, Herbert William, 3s. James, of Coventry, arm. MERTON COLL., matric. 19 Oct., 1883, aged 20; B.A. 1886. [30]

Mayd, William, s. William, of Tredington, co. Gloucester, gent. BALLIOL COLL., matric. 13 Dec., 1738, aged 19; B.A. 1742.

Mayd, William, s. William, of Moreton-in-Marsh, cler. WORCESTER COLL., matric. 10 July, 1765, aged 17.

Mayd, William, s. John Winslow, of Epsom, Surrey, gent. EXETER COLL., matric. 28 March, 1817, aged 19; B.A. 1822, M.A. 1823, vicar of Ewell, Surrey, 1826, and rector of Withersfield, Suffolk, 1827, until his death 22 Feb., 1879. See *Eton School Lists.*

Mayd, William, 2s. William, of Withersfield, Suffolk, cler. QUEEN'S COLL., matric. 18 May, 1848, aged 18; of Withersfield, Suffolk, bar.-at-law, Inner Temple, 1854, recorder of Bury St. Edmunds, Dec., 1877. See Foster's *Men at the Bar* & *Eton School Lists.*

Maydwell, Richard John Lockwood, 2s. William, of Kennington, Northants, cler. WADHAM COLL., matric. 17 June, 1823, aged 17; B.A. 1827, vicar of Southwick, Northants, 1832. [35]

Maydwell, Rev. William Lockwood, s. William Lockwood, of Fifield, Essex, cler. ORIEL COLL., matric. 31 Aug., 1779, aged 18; assumed the additional surname of MAYDWELL, died at Thrapstone, Northants, 12 June, 1836.

Mayer, Henry, s. Nathaniel, of Macclesfield, Cheshire, gent. BRASENOSE COLL., matric. 17 April, 1751, aged 17; B.A. 1755, M.A. 1758, proctor 1769.

Mayer, John. See MAYOR.

Mayer, John Henry, 1s. John, of Longton, co. Stafford, gent. WORCESTER COLL., matric. 17 March, 1852, aged 20; B.A. 1855, M.A. 1858, vicar of Wold Newton 1863-75, of Tandridge, Surrey, 1877-8.

Mayer, Peter, s. Nathaniel, of Macclesfield, Cheshire, gent. BRASENOSE COLL., matric. 7 March, 1745-6, aged 17; B.A. 27 Feb., 1749-50. [40]

Mayers, Edward Lascelles, s. Joseph, of Isle of Barbados, gent. QUEEN'S COLL., matric. 10 Oct., 1753, aged 18; bar.-at-law, Middle Temple, 1758.

Mayers, John, o.s. John Pollard, of Isle of Barbados, West Indies, arm. UNIVERSITY COLL., matric. 15 June, 1820, aged 19; B.A. 1825.

Mayers, Walter, s. Walter, of Gloucester (city), gent. PEMBROKE COLL., matric. 8 Dec., 1808, aged 18; scholar 1812-16, B.A. 1812, M.A. 1815, died curate of Over-Worton, Oxon, 22 Feb., 1828.

Mayhew, Anthony Lawson, 1s. Anthony, of Bury St. Edmunds, Suffolk, gent. WADHAM COLL., matric. 9 May, 1860, aged 18; B.A. 1863, M.A. 1868, chaplain and Hebrew lecturer 1880, vicar of Bearley, co. Warwick, 1872-3; for list of works see *Crockford.*

Mayhew, Rev. Cyril, o.s. William Augustus John, of Torino, arm. NON-COLL., matric. 21 Jan., 1882, aged 18.

Mayhew, Henry Courtney. TRINITY COLL., 1857. See COURTNEY.

Mayhew, Thomas, s. Thomas, of Colchester, Essex, gent. CHRIST CHURCH, matric. 8 Feb., 1728-9, aged 16. [5]

Mayhew, Thomas (Rabett), s. Thomas, of Saxmundham, Suffolk, gent. QUEEN'S COLL., matric. 4 Nov., 1835, aged 18; B.A. 1839, M.A. 1843, vicar of Darsham, Suffolk, and perp. curate of Dunwich 1851-66, rector of Warehorne, Kent, since 1866.

Maynard, Herbert John, 2s. Frederick Waite, of Wandsworth, Surrey, gent. ST. JOHN'S COLL., matric. 13 Oct., 1883, aged 18; scholar 1883, B.A. 1886, of the Indian Civil Service 1883.

Maynard, John, s. Walter, of Isle of Nevis, West Indies, arm. EXETER COLL., matric. 14 May, 1817, aged 18; B.A. 1822, M.A. 1824, rector of Sudborne, Suffolk, 1842, until his death 13 Sep., 1877.

Maynard, John Hothersall Pinder Adam Martin, 5s. Foster, of Charlton, Dorset, arm. PEMBROKE COLL., matric. 14 May, 1842, aged 19; B.A. 1847, M.A. 1850.

Maynard, John Seymour, 1s. John, of St. Stephen's, Bristol, cler. EXETER COLL., matric. 31 Jan., 1849, aged 19. [10]

Maynard, Robert, 5s. Thomas, of Pentonville, Middlesex, arm. WADHAM COLL., matric. 17 May, 1832, aged 17; B.A. 1836, M.A. 1838, vicar of Wormleighton, co. Warwick, 1841, until his death 2 April, 1869.

Maynard, Sydney Richard. See SYDNEY RICHARD MAYNARD-WALKER, 1858.

Maynard, Thomas, s. John, of Covent Garden, London, gent. BALLIOL COLL., matric. 24 March, 1742-3, aged 17; B.A. 1746.

Maynard, Thomas, s. John, of St. Michael's, Isle of Barbados, arm. EXETER COLL., matric. 27 Oct., 1770, aged 17; bar.-at-law, Middle Temple, 1775.

Maynard, Walter Edwin, 1s. Walter Fawkes, of Orford, Suffolk, cler. EXETER COLL., matric. 12 May, 1883, aged 17; B.A. 1886, died 2 Aug., 1887.

Maynard, Walter Fawkes, 2s. John, of St. Stephens, Bristol, cler. EXETER COLL., matric. 31 Jan., 1849, aged 17; B.A. 1853, M.A. 1856. [16]

Maynard, William, s. Samuel, of Isle of Barbados, arm. MAGDALEN COLL., matric. 19 Sep., 1721, aged 15.

Maynard, (Sir) William (Bart.), s. Henry, of Walthamstow, Essex, (baronet). QUEEN'S COLL., matric. 22 March, 1738-9, aged 17; 4th baronet, M.P. Essex 1759, until his death 18 Jan., 1772.

Mayne, Charles Cunninghame, 5s. Charles Otway, of Midsomer Norton, Somerset, cler. BRASENOSE COLL., matric. 7 June, 1866, aged 18; B.A. 1870.

Mayne, Charles Otway, 1s. Robert, of Limpsfield, Surrey, cler. CHRIST CHURCH, matric. 16 May, 1825, aged 17; student 1825-34, B.A. 1829, M.A. 1831, preb. of Wells 1840, vicar of Midsomer Norton, Somerset, 1833, until his death 28 April, 1867. See *Alumni West.*, 495. [20]

Mayne, Henry Blair, 2s. Robert, of Lympsfield, Surrey, cler. CHRIST CHURCH, matric. 21 May, 1831, aged 17; student 1831-46, B.A. 1835 M.A. 1838, bar.-at-law, Middle Temple, 1845, chief clerk private bills, House of Commons, since 1870. See Foster's *Men at the Bar* & *Alumni West.*, 506.

Mayne, John (Litchfield), s. John, of Oxford (city), gent. EXETER COLL., matric. 18 March, 1796, aged 20; B.A. from ST. ALBAN HALL 1802.

Mayne, Robert, s. Robert, of St. James's, Westminster, arm. CHRIST CHURCH, matric. 25 May, 1796, aged 18; B.A. 1800, M.A. 1803, rector of Lympsfield, Surrey, 1806, until his death 7 March, 1841, nephew of William, Lord Newhaven. See *Alumni West.*, 445.

Mayne, Robert Dawson, 2s. Richard, of London, equitis. BALLIOL COLL., matric. 14 Oct., 1861, aged 17; B.A. 1867, bar.-at-law, Lincoln's Inn, 1869, stipendiary justice, Port of Spain. See Foster's *Men at the Bar.*

Mayne, Samuel, s. Edward, of St. Aldate's, London (*sic.*), but query Oxford, gent. WADHAM COLL., matric. 6 July, 1715, aged 16. [25]

Mayne, William, s. Robert, of Dromore, co. Monaghan, arm. ST. JOHN'S COLL., matric. 8 July, 1805, aged 19.

Mayne, William Annesley, of TRINITY COLL., Dublin (B.A. 1842, LL.B. & LL.D. 1858); adm. 'ad eundem' 14 Jan., 1859.

Mayne, William G., M.A. TRINITY COLL., Dublin, 1832 (B.A. 1826); adm. 'comitatis causa' 21 June, 1867.

Mayo, Arthur, 5s. Herbert, of Oxford, arm. MAGDALEN HALL, matric. 2 May, 1862, aged 21; B.A. 1865, served in the Indian naval brigade during the Mutiny 1857, V.C. 25 Feb., 1862, assistant-curate St. Peter's, Plymouth, 1866, until he seceded to Rome in 1867.

Mayo, Augustus Frederick, 1s. Thomas, of Tunbridge Wells, D.Med. ORIEL COLL., matric. 14 June, 1838, aged 17; B.A. 1842, bar.-at-law, Inner Temple, 1846, died 20 April, 1869. [30]

Mayo, Benjamin, s. John, of Calne, Wilts, cler. QUEEN'S COLL., matric. 28 April, 1737, aged 17; B.A. 6 Feb., 1740-1, an apothecary at Calne, died 17 Nov., 1750.

Mayo, Charles, s. Charles, of St. Peter's, Hereford (city), gent. BRASENOSE COLL., matric. 3 March, 1728-9, aged 13; B.A. 1732, M.A. 1744, rector of Corringham, Essex, 1743-53, and of Castle Frome, co. Hereford, 1753, until his death 9 April, 1760.

Mayo, Charles, s. John, of Stoke, Wilts, cler. QUEEN'S COLL., matric. 29 April, 1767, aged 16; B.A. 1771, M.A. 1774, B.C.L. 1779, rector of Huish St. Nicholas 1775, and of Beechingstoke 1779, until his death 27 Nov., 1829.

Mayo, Charles, s. Herbert, of St. George's-in-the-East, Middlesex, doctor. ST. JOHN'S COLL., matric. 28 June, 1785, aged 18; B.A. 1789, M.A. 1793, B.D. 1798, Rawlinsonian professor of Anglo-Saxon 1795-1800, of Cheshunt, Herts, F.R.S., F.S.A., Whitehall preacher 1799-1800, morning lecturer of St. Michael's, Highgate, 1803-33, died 10 Dec., 1858. See *Robinson*, 141.

Mayo, Rev. Charles, s. Charles, of St. Botolph, Aldgate, gent. ST. JOHN'S COLL., matric. 25 June, 1810, aged 18; scholar 1810-13, fellow 1813-31, B.C.L. 1817, D.C.L. 1822, headmaster Bridgnorth Grammar School 1817, founder of 'the Pestalozzian' School, Cheam, died 23 Feb., 1846. See *Robinson*, 173.

Mayo, Charles, s. Charles, of St. Thomas, Winchester, Hants, gent. NEW COLL., matric. 3 July, 1856, aged 19; scholar and fellow 1856-77, B.A. 1859, Stud. Med. 1860, M.A. 1863, B.Med. 1865, D.Med. 1871, dean 1865, served in the American civil war, in the Franco-Prussian war, and in the Dutch campaign in Atchin, medical officer in the Fiji Islands, author of a 'History of Wimborne Minster,' died 15 July, 1877, at sea. See *History of the Mayo Family*, p. 60. [36]

Mayo, Charles Herbert, 2s. William, of Salisbury, Wilts, cler. LINCOLN COLL., matric. 13 April, 1864, aged 19; scholar 1864-8, B.A. 1868, M.A. 1871, vicar of Long Burton, Dorset, since 1872, author of the 'History of the Mayo and Elton Families'.' For lists of his works see *Crockford.*

Mayo, Charles Joseph, 1s. Charles Thomas, of Corsham, Wilts, arm. TRINITY COLL., matric. 11 Oct., 1884, aged 18.

Mayo, Charles Theodore, 1s. Charles, of Cheam, Surrey, D.C.L. BALLIOL COLL., matric. 2 April, 1851, aged 18; B.A. 1855, M.A. 1857, vicar of St. Andrew, Hillingdon, Middlesex, since 1865.

Mayo, Edmund Godfrey, 2s. Charles Thomas, of Corsham, Wilts, gent. TRINITY COLL., matric. 17 Oct., 1885, aged 18.

Mayo, Edward, 5s. Herbert, of Oxford, gent. ST. EDMUND HALL, matric. 27 Oct., 1864, aged 22; held various curacies 1870-84, vicar of Mogerhanger, Beds, since 1884.

Mayo, Rev. Francis Benjamin, 3s. Benjamin, of Melrose, Scotland, gent. WORCESTER COLL., matric. 18 Jan., 1883, aged 20; B.A. 1886. [5]

Mayo, Herbert, s. Charles, of Hereford (city), gent. BRASENOSE COLL., matric. 9 April, 1739, aged 18; fellow 1740-65, B.A. 1742, M.A. 1745, B.D. 1762, D.D. 1763, rector of Middleton Cheney, Northants, in 1764, and of St. George's-in-the-East 1764, vicar of Tollesbury, Essex, 1799, until his death, 5 Jan., 1802.

Mayo, Herbert Harman, 1s. Herbert, of London, gent. PEMBROKE COLL., matric. 26 May, 1847, aged 16; scholar 1847-52, B.A. 1851, vicar of Talland, Cornwall, 1874-6, etc.

Mayo, James, s. John, of Calne, Wilts, cler. QUEEN'S COLL., matric. 15 May, 1734, aged 18; B.A. 1738, curate of Avebury, Wilts, 1743, vicar 1746, with Winterbourne Monkton 1747, head-master Calne Grammar School 1758, rector of Ditteridge 1767, until his death 1 Sep., 1788.

Mayo, James, s. James, of Avebury, Wilts, cler. QUEEN'S COLL., matric. 23 March, 1774, aged 18; B.A. 1777, 2nd master Wimborne Minster Grammar School 1777-87, head-master 1787-1822, rector of Blackland, Wilts, 1779, and of Avebury-cum-Winterbourne Monkton 1789, until his death 1 Aug., 1822.

Mayo, James, s. James, of Wimbourne, Dorset, cler. QUEEN'S COLL., matric. 14 Jan., 1802, aged 17; B.A. from PEMBROKE COLL. 1805, M.A. 1810, 2nd master Wimborne Grammar School 1802, head-master 1822, vicar of Gussage All Saints 1817-33, vicar of St. Peter's, Shaftesbury, 1819-23, rector of Avebury-cum-Winterbourne Monkton 1823, until his death 18 Aug., 1851. [10]

Mayo, James, 2s. Charles, of Winchester, arm. Incorp. from WORCESTER COLL. 8 June, 1871, aged 30; B.A. from TRINITY COLL., Cambridge. 1862, M.A. 1865, B.D. 1868, sinecure rector of Buckland, Kent, 1874.

Mayo, John, s. William, of Child Okeford, Dorset, cler. QUEEN'S COLL., matric. 17 Nov., 1721, aged 17.

Mayo, John, s. John, of (Calne), Wilts, cler. QUEEN'S COLL., matric. 14 Oct., 1730, aged 17; B.C.L. 1737, rector of Beechingstoke 1737, vicar of Wilcot 1762, until his death 25 Jan., 1779.

Mayo, John, s. Thomas, of Hereford (city), gent. BRASENOSE COLL., matric. 1 June, 1778, aged 16, B.A. 1782; fellow ORIEL COLL., M.A. 1785, B.Med. 1787, D.Med. 1788, F.R.C.P. 1789, physician Foundling Hospital 1787-1809, and to the Middlesex Hospital 1788-1803, physician in ordinary to the Princess of Wales, buried at Speldhurst 8 Dec., 1818. See Munk's *Roll*, ii. 395.

Mayo, John Alderson, 2s. William Henry, of Ballyhooly, co. Cork, gent. MERTON COLL., matric. 12 Oct., 1878, aged 18; B.A. 1881. [15]

Mayo, Joseph, s. Joseph, of Westminster, arm. UNIVERSITY COLL., matric. 16 Jan., 1783, aged 18; B.A. 1786, M.A. 1789, rector of Ozleworth 1821, until his death 30 Dec., 1851.

Mayo, Joseph, s. Joseph, of Seend, Wilts, cler. BRASENOSE COLL., matric. 16 Jan., 1811, aged 17; scholar 1812-15, B.A. 1815, M.A. 1819, held various curacies in England, emigrated to the United States in 1839, rector of Liverpool, Ohio, for seven years, died 3 Sept., 1859.

Mayo, Matthias, s. William, of Brington, Northants, cler. HERTFORD COLL., matric. 10 May, 1743, aged 17; B.A. 27 Feb., 1746-7, M.A. 1749. (Memo.: Rev. Dr. Mayo, died at Clapham 28 Sep., 1786, aged 61.)

Mayo, Paggen William, s. Herbert, of St. George's, Middlesex, doctor. ST. JOHN'S COLL., matric. 30 June, 1784, aged 18; scholar 1784, fellow 1787, B.A. 1788, M.A. 1792, B.Med. 1792, D.Med. 1795, a physician to the forces 1793, physician Middlesex Hospital 1793-1801, F.R.C.P. 1796, died 6 July, 1836. See Munk's *Roll*, ii. 455; & *Robinson*, 139.

Mayo, Richard, s. Charles, of London, gent. ST. JOHN'S COLL., matric. 19 June, 1818, aged 18; B.A. 1822, M.A. 1826, perp. curate Plaxtol, Kent, 1841, died 30 April, 1864. See *Robinson*, 184. [20

Mayo, Robert, 3s. Thomas, of Tunbridge, Kent, D.Med. CHRIST CHURCH, matric. 12 June, 1851, aged 19; B.A. 1856, held various curacies 1857-69, brother of Augustus F. 1838. See *Robinson*, 282.

Mayo, Thomas, s. William, of Hope-under-Dinmore, co. Hereford, arm. TRINITY COLL., matric. 26 June, 1721, aged 16; bar.-at-law, Middle Temple, 1729, buried at Hope 13 July, 1730.

Mayo, Thomas, s. John, of London, doctor. ORIEL COLL., matric. 10 June, 1807, aged 17; B.A. 1811, fellow 1813-18, M.A. 1814, B.Med. 1815, D.Med. 1818, F.R.C.P. 1819, president 1857-62, F.R.S. 1835, physician in ordinary to the Duke of Sussex, died 13 Jan., 1871. See Munk's *Roll*, iii. 201.

Mayo, William, s. Charles, of Hereford (city), gent. BRASENOSE COLL., matric. 24 June, 1742, aged 16; scholar 1742, B.A. 1746, fellow, M.A. 1749 rector of Wootton Rivers, Wilts, 1768, until his death 15 May, 1800.

Mayo, William, 3s. Joseph, of Seend, Wilts, cler. MAGDALEN HALL, matric. 2 July, 1824, aged 22 B.A. 1828, M.A. 1831, rector of Folke, Dorset, and perp. curate North Wootton 1865, until his death 29 March, 1881. [25

Mayor, Andrew, s. John, of Manchester, Lancashire arm. WADHAM COLL., matric. 26 March, 1806 aged 23.

Mayor, Rev. Charles, of TRINITY COLL., Cambridge (B.A. 1837, M.A. 1840); adm. 'ad eundem' 3 Feb. 1842 (son of Joseph, rector of Collingburn, Notts) an assistant-master Rugby 1840, until his death 3 Aug., 1846.

Mayor, John, s. Thomas, of Dolgelly, co. Merioneth arm. WORCESTER COLL., matric. 4 March, 1774 aged 18; B.A. 1778, vicar of Shawbury, Salop 1781, until his death 22 May, 1826.

Mayou, Arthur Daniel, 4s. John Webster, of Fazeley near Tamworth, gent. NON-COLL., matric. 1 Nov. 1879, aged 18; B.A. 1883.

Mayou, Benjamin, 2s. John, of Appleby, co. Leicester gent. LINCOLN COLL., matric. 7 June, 1843, aged 18; held various curacies 1850-67, vicar of Baddesley Ensor, co. Warwick, 1867-76. [30

Mayow, Arthur Wynell-, 3s. Mayow, of Market Lavington, Wilts, cler. NON-COLL., matric. 1 April, 1872, aged 19; B.A. 1876, M.A. 1880, chaplain R.N. 1879-83, vicar of Frocester, co. Gloucester 1883.

Mayow, Mayow Wynell, 2s. Philip Wynell, of St. George's, Bloomsbury, arm. CHRIST CHURCH matric. 29 April, 1829, aged 18; student 1829-3 B.A. 1833, M.A. 1836, vicar of Market Lavington Wilts, 1836-60, perp. curate St. Mary, West Brompton, 1860-8, rector of South Heighton, Sussex 1868-71, of Southam 1871-8, and of Halstead, Kent 1878-81; for list of his works see *Crockford*.

[ayow, Philip Wynell, s. Philip Wynell, of Saltash, Cornwall, arm. WADHAM COLL., matric. 16 June, 1763, aged 17; B.A. 1767, M.A. 1770, curate of Plympton St. Mary, Devon, died 1800.

[ayow, Rev. Robert, s. John, of St. Stephen's, Cornwall, gent. EXETER COLL., matric. 12 July, 1797, aged 19; B.A. 1801, died at Ardwick, Lancashire, in 1816, aged 39.

[ayow, Robert Wynell, 2s. Robert, of Ardwick, Lancashire, cler. EXETER COLL., matric. 18 Feb., 1835, aged 18; B.A. from MAGDALEN COLL. 1839, M.A. 1841.

[ays, William Henry, 2s. James, of Bedford (town), gent. ST. ALBAN HALL, matric. 11 April, 1866, aged 21.

[aysey, Joseph, 'apothecary;' privilegiatus 19 April, 1750. See MEYSEY, p. 950. [5]

[aysmor, Humphrey, s. Humphrey, of Derwen, co. Denbigh, pleb. JESUS COLL., matric. 10 April, 1783, aged 19; B.A. 1787.

[ayson, Charles, s. Peter, of Frome, Somerset, cler. WADHAM COLL., matric. 5 April, 1769, aged 16; B.A. 1773, fellow, M.A. 1777, B.D. 1784, D.D. 1793, died rector of Lezant, Cornwall, 14 Jan., 1815.

[ason, Peter, s. Tho., of Brough, Cumberland, pleb. QUEEN'S COLL., matric. 13 March, 1739-40, aged 17; B.A. 1744, M.A. 1746 (as MAYSON).

[eacham, John, s. John, of Stratford-on-Avon, co. Warwick, gent. CHRIST CHURCH, matric. 8 April, 1783, aged 18.

[eackham, William Berkin, s. William Berkin, of St. Martin's, Westminster, arm. BALLIOL COLL., matric. 10 Oct., 1783, aged 17; B.C.L. 1790, D.C.L. 1798, took the additional name of MEACKHAM. [10]

[ead, Charles Clement, 2s. Clement John, of Gya, East Indies, arm. BALLIOL COLL., matric. 16 Oct., 1883, aged 18; of the Indian Civil Service 1883, died at Calcutta 31 May, 1888,

[ead, Charles Walter, 3s. Edward, of Scarborough-on-Hudson, America, cler. NON-COLL., matric. 21 Jan., 1882, aged 20; B.A. 1886.

[ead, Edward, s. Samuel, of Hornsey, Middlesex, gent. UNIVERSITY COLL., matric. 27 March, 1777, aged 19; bar.-at-law, Inner Temple, 1784.

[ead, Francis, s. Joseph, of Wellsborne, co. Warwick, arm. TRINITY COLL., matric. 2 April, 1778, aged 17, B.A. 1781; M.A. from MAGDALEN COLL. 1784, B.D. 1792, D.D. 1809, rector of Gayton-le-Marsh 1808, and of Candlesby, co. Lincoln, 1809, until his death in 1833. See *Rugby School Reg.*, 45.

[ead, George, 2s. Thomas Wynter, of Whipsnade, Beds, cler. ST. JOHN'S COLL., matric. 22 March, 1855, aged 19; B.A. 1859, M.A. 1864, held various curacies 1859-67, chaplain to the forces 1867. [15]

[ead, Richard, s. Richard, of London, doctor. CHRIST CHURCH, matric. 10 July, 1736, aged 18; created M.A. 28 June, 1739. (Rev. Mr. Mead, many years secretary to the late bishop of Lincoln and Salisbury, died 22 Sep., 1766.)

[ead, Richard Gawler, of ST. JOHN'S COLL., Cambridge (B.A. 1856, M.A. 1860); adm. 'comitatis causa' 6 June, 1861, rector of Balcombe, Sussex, 1868.

[ead, Thomas, s. Thomas, of Somerton, Somerset, pleb. LINCOLN COLL., matric. 12 May, 1750, aged 18.

[ead, Thomas Wynter, s. William, of Houghton Regis, Beds, cler. ST. JOHN'S COLL., matric. 28 June, 1802, aged 18; B.A. 1806, M.A. 1810, B.D. 1815, fellow until 1831, vicar of Studham, Beds, 1815, and of Great Staughton, Hunts, 1831, until his death 1 Nov., 1849. See *Robinson*, 163.

[ead, William, s. William, of Ilminster, Somerset, pleb. ST. MARY HALL, matric. 21 Oct., 1774, aged 18; B.A. 1780, M.A. 1781, minister of St. Marylebone Parochial Chapel, rector of Dunstable, Beds, 1800, until his death 29 Jan., 1822. [20]

Meade, Charles Hippisley, 3s. William, of Binegar, Somerset, cler. TRINITY COLL., matric. 11 Oct., 1884, aged 18; B.A. 1887.

Meade, De Courcy, 3s. Richard John, of Marston Bigot, Somerset, cler. EXETER COLL., matric. 13 May, 1842, aged 17; scholar 1842-8, B.A. 1846, M.A. 1849, rector of North and South Barrow, Somerset, 1870-8, rector of Tokenham, Wilts, 1878. See *Coll. Reg.*, 153.

Meade, Edward, s. John, Earl of Clanwilliam. WADHAM COLL., matric. 3 June, 1797, aged 16; killed in Egypt in 1801. See Foster's *Peerage.*

Meade, Edward, o.s. William, of North Cray, Kent, arm. WADHAM COLL., matric. 1 Nov., 1825, aged 18; B.A. 1829, M.A. 1832, perp. curate St. Peter's Malvern Wells, preb. of Salisbury, 1873, rector of Winkfield, Wilts, 1842, until his death 9 April 1887.

Meade, John Spencer, o.s. John, of Clifton, Bristol, equitis. BALLIOL COLL., matric. 27 May, 1830, aged 17 (his father, D.Med., deputy-inspector of hospitals, was knighted 5 Nov., 1816). [25]

Meade, Peirce, s. John, Earl of Clanwilliam. ST. JOHN'S COLL., matric. 27 Jan., 1797, aged 20; B.A. from WADHAM COLL. 1799, M.A. 1802, archdeacon of Dromore 1810-32, died 22 Nov., 1834. See Foster's *Peerage.*

Meade, Richard, s. James, of Kinsale, co. Cork, arm. HERTFORD COLL., matric. 7 March, 1767, aged 16; B.A. 1771.

Meade, Richard, Baron Gilford, s. John, Earl of Clanwilliam. CHRIST CHURCH, matric. 22 May, 1784, aged 18; 2nd Earl of Clanwilliam, died 3 Sep., 1805. See Foster's *Peerage.*

Meade, Richard, s. Edward, of Cripplegate, London, arm. WADHAM COLL., matric. 6 June, 1801, aged 18; exhibitioner 1802, B.A. 1805, perp. curate of Prince's Risborough, Bucks, and rector of Horsenden 1811, until his death 2 Aug., 1844. See *St. Paul's School Reg.*, 194.

Meade, Richard Charles, 3rd Earl of Clanwilliam, created D.C.L. 11 June, 1834 (son of Richard, 2nd earl), G.C.H., under-secretary of state for Foreign Affairs 1822, ambassador at Berlin 1823-8, died 7 Oct., 1879. See Foster's *Peerage.* [30]

Meade, Richard John, s. Thomas, of Cuddesdon, Oxon, arm. BALLIOL COLL., matric. 17 March, 1812, aged 18; B.A. 1815, M.A. 1822, rector of Marston Bigot 1821-34, perp. curate Christ Church, Frome Selwood, 1834-45, preb. of Wells 1863, canon 1865, precentor 1868, vicar of Castle Cary 1845, until his death 23 May, 1880. See *Eton School Lists.*

Meade, Robert, born in Isle of Madeira, 1s. Robert, arm. CHRIST CHURCH, matric. 8 Dec., 1827, aged 18; of 5th dragoon guards, died 22 Jan., 1851. See Foster's *Peerage* & *Eton School Lists.*

Meade, Robert, 2s. Robert, of North Curry, Somerset, gent. TRINITY COLL., matric. 28 June, 1859, aged 21; B.A. 1864, a student of the Inner Temple 1862.

Meade, Robert Henry, (C.B.) 2s. (Richard), Earl of Clanwilliam. EXETER COLL., matric. 7 Dec., 1854, aged 18; B.A. 1859, M.A. 1860, assistant under-secretary Colonial Office 1871, groom of the bedchamber to the Prince of Wales 1862-7, extra groom 1867. C.B. 21 March, 1885. See Foster's *Peerage.*

Meade, Sidney, 3s. Richard Charles Francis, Earl of Clanwilliam. EXETER COLL., matric. 21 Jan., 1861, aged 21; rector of Wylye, Wilts, 1869-82. [35]

Meade, Thomas Percy, 2s. Hon. Pierce, of Abergavenny, co. Monmouth, cler. BRASENOSE COLL., matric. 29 June, 1821, aged 18, B.A. 1825; fellow ALL SOULS' COLL. 1825-31, M.A. 1829, died 4 June, 1831. See Foster's *Peerage* & *Eton School Lists.*

Meade, William, 2s. Richard John, of Newton St. Philips, Somerset, cler. BALLIOL COLL., matric. 14 June, 1839, aged 18; B.A. 1843, M.A. 1847, rector of Binegar 1851.

Meades, William, s. Richard, of Wooton-under-Edge, co. Gloucester, gent. HART HALL, matric. 5 June, 1717, aged 17; B.A. 17 Feb., 1720-1.

Meadows, Douglas Spencer, 1s. William Spencer Harris, of Christ Church, Canterbury, cler. PEMBROKE COLL., matric. 19 June, 1851, aged 18; B.A. 1855, bar.-at-law, Lincoln's Inn, 1857, died in May, 1863.

Meadows, Rev. John Callander, o.s. John, of St. Helier, Isle of Jersey, gent. PEMBROKE COLL., matric. 24 Oct., 1827, aged 14; scholar 1827-38, B.A. 1835, M.A. 1836, died at Chelsea 14 July, 1847.

Meadows, William Spencer Harris, 1s. John Braham, of St. Anne's, Soho, London, gent. LINCOLN COLL., matric. 8 June, 1822, aged 20; B.A. 1826, M.A. 1829, took the name of MEADOWS in lieu of BRAHAM in 1851, vicar of Chigwell, Essex, 1855.

Meadows, William Walter, o.s. William, of Standish, Lancashire, gent. NON-COLL., matric. 18 Oct., 1875, aged 20. [5]

Meakin, James, s. George, of Sutton, Salop, pleb. CHRIST CHURCH, matric. 17 March, 1779, aged 19; B.A. 1782, M.A. 1785, preb. of Worcester, 1804, vicar of Wolverley, 1811, rector of St. John's, Bedwardine, 1814, vicar of Lindridge 1817, until his death 6 Oct., 1842.

Meakin, John Alexander Deverell, of ST. JOHN'S COLL., Cambridge (B.A. 1826, M.A. 1829); adm. 'ad eundem' 10 May, 1850, perp. curate Speenhamland, Berks, 1845.

Mealy, Pierce Owen, s. John, of St. George's, Middlesex, gent. JESUS COLL., matric. 1 March, 1776, aged 19; B.A. 1779, M.A. 1782, rector of Llanaltgo, co. Anglesey, buried in Bangor Cathedral 6 April, 1801.

Mealy, Rev. Richard Ridgeway Parry, o.s. Pierce Owen, of Bangor, co. Carnarvon, cler. ST. JOHN'S COLL., matric. 22 Jan., 1820, aged 18; B.A. 1823, M.A. 1827, died 22 Feb., 1870.

Meany, Edward Willcocks, 3s. Edward John, of Richmond, Virginia, gent. ST. MARY HALL, matric. 25 Oct., 1866, aged 22; B.A. 1870. [10]

Meard, David, s. John, of St. Anne's, Westminster, arm. UNIVERSITY COLL., matric. 10 Feb., 1734-5, aged 17; B.A. 1738, M.A. 1741.

Meare, John, s. Thomas, of Appleshaw, Hants, gent. ST. ALBAN HALL, matric. 17 Dec., 1787, aged 22.

Meares, Arthur, s. George, of Pwllcrochan, co. Pembroke, gent. JESUS COLL., matric. 15 Dec., 1732, aged 16.

Meares, George, o.s. George, of Aberystwith, co. Cardigan, arm. TRINITY COLL., matric. 17 April, 1833, aged 18.

Meares, Hawkewell, s. William, of Roscrowther, co. Pembroke, arm. PEMBROKE COLL., matric. 26 April, 1726, aged 18. [15]

Meares, Henry, 5s. John, of Frome, Somerset, gent. QUEEN'S COLL., matric. 15 Nov., 1832, aged 20.

Meares, Hugh, s. George, of Roscrowther, co. Pembroke, arm. ORIEL COLL., matric. 4 July, 1718, aged 15.

Meares, John, s. William Hawkwell, of Eastington, co. Pembroke, arm. MERTON COLL., matric. 25 May, 1772, aged 17; created M.A. 21 March, 1776.

Meares, John, 1s. Samuel Owen, of Haverfordwest, Pembroke, cler. BRASENOSE COLL., matric. 4 June, 1861, aged 18; B.A. 1868, vicar of St. Martin's, Haverfordwest, 1869-78, chaplain Northampton Prison 1878-80, rector of Haroldston West since 1880.

Meares, Noel Edgar, 1s. Thomas, of London, arm. EXETER COLL., matric. 16 Oct., 1884, aged 17. [20]

Mears, Edward, o.s. Edward, of Hartlepool, co. Durham, gent. QUEEN'S COLL., matric. 22 Oct., 1883, aged 18; scholar 1883, B.A. 1887.

Mears, Rev. Henry, s. Thomas, of Southampton, Hants, gent. MERTON COLL., matric. 23 Nov., 1799, aged 18; B.A. 1803, M.A. 1808, vicar of Hartley Wintney, Hants, 1819, 'late of Stowe Hill, Suffolk,' died 11 April, 1855.

Mears, Thomas, s. Thomas, of Southampton, Hants, gent. WADHAM COLL., matric. 10 May, 1785, aged 17; B.A. 1789, M.A. 1792, rector of St. John and of St. Lawrence, and vicar of St. Michael, Southampton, 1795, rector of All Saints', Southampton, 1817, until his death 24 April, 1835.

Mears, William, 2s. Thomas, of Southampton, Hants, cler. ST. ALBAN HALL, matric. 20 Nov., 1827, aged 18; B.A. from QUEEN'S COLL. 1832.

Mease, John, s. John, of Monmouth, pleb. JESUS COLL., matric. 28 May, 1731, aged 18; B.A. 1735, M.A. 1747, vicar of Elmeston Hardwicke, co. Gloucester, 1747. [25]

Meates, Thomas Arrowsmith, 1s. Thomas William, of Blythe Hill, near Lewisham, arm. UNIVERSITY COLL., matric. 20 Oct., 1876, aged 19; B.A. & M.A. 1886, bar.-at-law, Middle Temple, 1881. See Foster's *Men at the Bar*.

Mecklenburgh, Albert Ernest Gottlob, Duke of, Prince of Vandalia, etc., ambassador at the Court of Great Britain (*Cat. Grads.*); created D.C.L. 27 Sept., 1762 (son of Charles Louis Frederick, Duke of Mecklenburgh-Strelitz), born 27 Aug., 1742, died 27 Jan. 1814.

Mecklenburgh-Strelitz, Charles Frederick Augustus, Duke of, D.C.L. by diploma 16 June, 1814 (1st son of Charles Louis Frederick, Duke of Mecklenburgh-Strelitz), born 30 Nov., 1785, died 21 Sep., 1837.

Mecklenburg-Strelitz, Frederick William Charles George Ernest Adolphus Gustavus, reigning Grand Duke of, D.C.L. by diploma 6 June, 1853 (son of Grand Duke George Frederick Charles), born 17 Oct., 1819, married at Buckingham Palace 28 June, 1843, Princess Augusta, daughter of Adolphus Frederick, 1st Duke of Cambridge, and had issue. See Foster's *Peerage*. [30]

Medcalfe, George, s. Francis, of Lancaster (town), gent. UNIVERSITY COLL., matric. 26 March, 1717, aged 15; B.A. 1720.

Medd, Arthur Octavius, 8s. John, of Stockport, Cheshire, arm. UNIVERSITY COLL., matric. 30 May, 1860, aged 19; B.A. 1864, M.A. 1873, rector of Amble, Northumberland, 1869-82, vicar (and patron) of Bamburgh 1882-6, and rector of Rothbury 1886.

Medd, Charles Septimus, 7s. John, of Stockport, Cheshire, arm. UNIVERSITY COLL., matric. 21 March, 1857, aged 18; scholar 1857-62, B.A. 1861, fellow 1864-74, M.A. 1864, bar.-at-law, Inner Temple, 1869. See Foster's *Men at the Bar*.

Medd, John Charles, 1s. William Henry, of Heaton Norris, Kent, gent. UNIVERSITY COLL., matric. 13 Oct., 1877, aged 19; B.A. & M.A. 1884, a student of the Inner Temple 1878.

Medd, Peter Goldsmith, 1s. John, of Leyburn, Yorks, gent. ST. JOHN'S COLL., matric. 1 March, 1848, aged 18; scholar UNIVERSITY COLL. 1848-52, fellow 1852-77, B.A. 1852, M.A. 1854, tutor 1861-70, dean and librarian 1861, bursar 1856, on council of Keble College 1871, curate of St. John Baptist, Oxford, 1858-67, select preacher 1881, rector of Barnes 1870-6, hon. fellow King's College, London, 1861, hon. canon of St. Alban's 1877, rector of North Cerney, co. Gloucester, 1876. [35]

Medhurst, Charles. CORPUS CHRISTI COLL., 1812. See WHELER.

Medland, Samuel, s. William, of Launceston, Cornwall, gent. EXETER COLL., matric. 16 March, 1718-9, aged 19.

Medland, Thomas, 1s. Thomas, of St. Stephen's, Exeter, gent. BALLIOL COLL., matric. 6 Dec., 1820, aged 17; scholar CORPUS CHRISTI COLL. 1821-30, B.A. 1825, M.A. 1827, fellow 1830-41, B.D. 1836, junior dean 1836, vicar of Steyning, Sussex, 1840, until his death 8 Sep., 1882.

Medley, Dudley Julius, 2s. Julius George, of London, arm. KEBLE COLL., matric. 19 Oct., 1880, aged 19; B.A. 1883, M.A. 1887, modern history lecturer 1884.

Medley, John, s. John, of St. Martin's, co. Lincoln, gent. LINCOLN COLL., matric. 29 Oct., 1724, aged 18.

Medley, John, o.s. George, of Grosvenor Place, London, gent. WADHAM COLL., matric. 15 Nov., 1822, aged 17; B.A. 1826, M.A. 1830, D.D. by decree 15 March, 1845, perp. curate of St. John's, Truro, 1831-8, vicar of St. Thomas's, Exeter, 1838-45, preb. of Exeter 1842-5, bishop of Fredericton 1845, and metropolitan of Canada 1879.

Medley, John Bacon, born at Southleigh, Devon, 1s. John, bishop of Fredericton. EXETER COLL., matric. 23 Jan., 1850, aged 18; B.A. 1856, held various curacies 1855-75, rector of Orchardleigh-cum-Lullington, Somerset, 1875. [5]

Medley, Thomas, s. Thomas, of Friston, Sussex, arm. ST. JOHN'S COLL., matric. 15 Jan., 1732-3, aged 18; died in 1735.

Medlicott, Henry Edmonstone, 1s. Joseph, of Potterne, Wilts, cler. WADHAM COLL., matric. 21 May, 1858, aged 18; B.A. 1862, M.A. 1865, of Sandfield, Wilts, J.P., bar.-at-law, Middle Temple, 1866. See Foster's *Men at the Bar*.

Medlicott, John Pepper, s. Ossory, of Ireland, cler. HART HALL, matric. 29 Nov., 1726, aged 18 (his father vicar of Ticehurst, Kent, 1738).

Medlicott, Samuel, M.A. TRINITY COLL., Dublin, 1866 (B.A. 1853); adm. 'comitatis causa' 22 Feb., 1866, vicar of Leighland 1868-72, of Withiel-Florey, Somerset, 1872-7, rector of Bowness-on-Solway 1877.

Medlicott, Walter Edward, 2s. Joseph, of Potterne, near Devizes, Wilts, cler. CHRIST CHURCH, matric. 28 May, 1860, aged 18; B.A. 1864, M.A. 1867, vicar of Swanmore, Hants, 1871. [10]

Medlycott, Charles, s. Charles, of St. Martin's, Westminster, arm. MERTON COLL., matric. 11 Jan., 1717-8, aged 17.

Medlycott, Edward Bradford, 2s. William, of Milborn Port, near Sherborne, Somerset, baronet. MERTON COLL., matric. 19 March, 1851, aged 18; B.A. 1855, M.A. 1861, bar.-at-law, Lincoln's Inn, 1859. See Foster's *Men at the Bar*.

Medlycott, (Sir) William Coles (Bart.), o.s. William, of Milhorn Port, baronet. TRINITY COLL., matric. 25 March, 1825, aged 17; created D.C.L. 20 June, 1844, 2nd baronet, died 23 Dec., 1882. See Foster's *Baronetage*.

Medwin, Thomas, s. Thomas Charles, of Horsham, Sussex, arm. TRINITY COLL., matric. 2 Dec., 1805, aged 17.

Medwin, Thomas Rea, 1s. Thomas Peirce, of Greenford, Middlesex, gent. WORCESTER COLL., matric. 14 Oct., 1826, aged 15; bible clerk 1826-30, B.A. 1830, M.A. 1834, vicar of Bearley, co. Warwick, 1871-2, head-master Stratford-on-Avon, Grammar School 1843-68, vicar of Astwich with Arlesey, Beds, 1881, until his death 17 March, 1885. [15]

Mee, Edward Melford, 2s. John, of Riddings, co. Derby, cler. CORPUS CHRISTI COLL., matric. 19 Oct., 1872, aged 18, scholar 1872-7, B.A. 1876; fellow QUEEN'S COLL. 1879-86, M.A. 1879, tutor, junior bursar 1881-5, chaplain University College 1884-5, rector of Crawley, Hants, 1885.

Mee, Hugh, s. Richard, of Roston, Cheshire, gent. BRASENOSE COLL., matric. 21 Feb., 1716-7, aged 13; B.A. 1720, M.A. 1726.

Mee, John, 2s. John, of Nottingham, gent. Incorp. from QUEEN'S COLL. 24 Nov., 1879, aged 55; scholar CHRIST'S COLL., Cambridge, 1846, B.A. 1849, M.A. 1853, perp. curate Riddings, co. Derby, 1850-4, dean of Grahamstown 1861-4, vicar of St. Jude's, Southwark, 1864-71, rector and vicar of Westbourne, Hants, 1871, until his death 19 Sep., 1883.

Mee, Rev. John Henry, 1s. John, of Riddings, co. Derby, cler. QUEEN'S COLL., matric. 23 Jan., 1872, aged 19, scholar 1871-5, B.A. 1875; fellow MERTON COLL. 1875-9, M.A. 1878, B.Mus. 1882, succentor 1876-81, lecturer 1877-82, ancient history lecturer Worcester College 1882.

Meech, Charles Silvanus, s. Thomas, of Westbury, Wilts, arm. ST. EDMUND HALL, matric. 29 June, 1816, aged 21. [20]

Meech, Giles, s. Thomas, of Dorchester, Dorset, arm. CHRIST CHURCH, matric. 22 March, 1782, aged 18; B.A. 1785, M.A. 1801, rector of West Compton Abbas, Dorset, 1800, and vicar of Toller Porcorum 1800, until his death 1 Jan., 1849.

Meech, William John, 1s. Giles, of Charminster, Dorset, cler. NEW COLL., matric. 2 Sep., 1823, aged 21; fellow 1823-37, B.A. 1827, M.A. 1832, rector of Hammoon, Dorset, 1834, until his death 28 March, 1858.

Meek, Alexander Grant, 1s. Alexander, of Devizes, Wilts, arm. MAGDALEN COLL., matric. 1 Feb., 1862, aged 18; B.A. 1865.

Meek, John Demery, o.s. Daniel, of Worcester (city), gent. MAGDALEN HALL, matric. 17 June, 1852, aged 17.

Meeke, John, s. Samuel, of All Saints, Worcester (city), gent. BALLIOL COLL., matric. 17 March, 1717-18, aged 18; B.A. 13 March, 1721-2. [25]

Meeke, Rev. John, s. Auth., of St. Mary's, Strand, London, gent. PEMBROKE COLL., matric. 17 Dec., 1726, aged 17; B.A. 1730, M.A. 1733, died fellow 26 Sep., 1763.

Meeke, William Bewley, s. George, of Hull, Yorks, gent. MAGDALEN HALL, matric. 20 Feb., 1807, aged 21.

Meeres, Charles Edwin, 2s. Henry, of Aylesbury, Bucks, cler. ST. MARY HALL, matric. 6 Feb., 1866, aged 18; B.A. 1871, vicar of Pendeen, Cornwall, 1873-84, and of Perranzabulo since 1884.

Meeres, Eustace William Marriott, 1s. Horace, of Horsmonden, Kent, cler. NEW COLL., matric. 15 Oct., 1886, aged 19.

Meeres, Horace, 2s. Nathaniel, of Hampstead, Middlesex, cler. QUEEN'S COLL., matric. 10 Oct., 1856, aged 17; B.A. from EXETER COLL. 1860, M.A. 1863, vicar of Bradwell 1870. [30]

Meers, Ernest George, 1s. James Gray, of Ashford, Kent, gent. QUEEN'S COLL., matric. 17 Dec., 1877; B.Mus. 28 Nov., 1878.

Meerman, Gerard, created D.C.L. 3 July, 1759, envoy extraordinary at the Court of St. James's from Belgium, Dutch lawyer and bibliographer, author of 'Novus Thesaurus Juris Civilis,' died 15 Dec., 1771.

Meerfelt, Count, D.C.L. See MERVELDT, page 946.

Meeson, Edward, s. Roger, of Llanycefen, co. Flint, gent. HERTFORD COLL., matric. 6 April, 1797, aged 18; B.A. 1801.

Meetkerke, Adolphus, s. Adolphus, of Rushden, Herts, arm. NEW COLL., matric. 30 June, 1721, aged 17; died 8 Jan., 1784, buried at Rushden. [35]

Meetkerke, Adolphus, s. Adolphus, of Rushden, Herts, arm. NEW COLL., matric. 17 May, 1773, aged 19; of Julians, Herts, died 22 May, 1841.

Meetkerke, Charles, s. Adolphus, of Rushden, Herts, arm. TRINITY COLL., matric. 6 June, 1727, aged 16; B.C.L. 1734, died 10 Feb., 1774.

Megcough, Joshua, s. William, of Armagh, Ireland, gent. CHRIST CHURCH, matric. 3 Nov., 1767, aged 20.

Meggy, George William, 1s. George, of Chelmsford, Essex, gent. WADHAM COLL., matric. 24 March, 1857, aged 18; B.A. 1863, has held various curacies since 1866.

Meiklam, James, 1s. John, of Glasgow, Scotland, arm. CORPUS CHRISTI COLL., matric. 11 March, 1826, aged 18.

Meiklam, John Robert, 1s. Robert, of Rome, arm. CHRIST CHURCH, matric. 27 May, 1858, aged 18.

Meiklam, William, 3s. John, of Anderson, Glasgow, arm. CORPUS CHRISTI COLL., matric. 5 Feb., 1831, aged 18; B.A. 1835.

Meikleham, David Scott, 2s. William, of Glasgow, Scotland, cler. BALLIOL COLL., matric. 22 March, 1822, aged 18; B.A. 1826, M.A. 1829. [5]

Meiklejohn, Max John Christian, 1s. John Miller Dow, of Bowdon, Cheshire, arm. ORIEL COLL., matric. 23 Oct., 1884, aged 18; exhibitioner 1884.

Meinertzhagen, Daniel, 1s. Daniel, of St. Marylebone, London, arm. ORIEL COLL., matric. 21 Feb., 1861, aged 18; B.A. 1865.

Meire, John Evans, 1s. John, of Uckington, Salop, arm. ST. JOHN'S COLL., matric. 20 April, 1868, aged 19.

Melhuish, Rev. George Douglas, 1s. Walter William, of Clawton, Devon, arm. EXETER COLL., matric. 23 May, 1874, aged 18; B.A. 1877, M.A. 1881, a student of Lincoln's Inn 1879.

Melhuish, Rev. George Edward, 6s. John, of Walworth, near Newington, Surrey, arm. MERTON COLL., matric. 27 May, 1853, aged 17; postmaster 1854-7, B.A. 1858, M.A. 1860, died 9 April, 1874.

Melhuish, John Bremridge, s. Richard, of Sandford, Devon, gent. BALLIOL COLL., matric. 1 May, 1795, aged 18; B.A. 1799. [10]

Melhuish, John Edmund, 2s. John, of Croydon, Surrey, arm. CORPUS CHRISTI COLL., matric. 4 June, 1870, aged 18; scholar WADHAM COLL. 1870-5, B.A. 1875, M.A. 1879.

Melhuish, Richard, s. Thomas, of Witheridge, Devon, cler. EXETER COLL., matric. 15 March, 1771, aged 18.

Melhuish, Richard, s. Richard, of Sandford, Devon, gent. EXETER COLL., matric. 7 May, 1798, aged 18; B.A. 1802.

Melhuish, Thomas, s. Roger, of Northam, Devon, arm. EXETER COLL., matric. 21 March, 1737-8, aged 17; B.A. 1741, M.A. 1744, rector of Witheridge, Devon, 1745, until his death 14 March, 1793, father of the next named. [15]

Melhuish, Thomas, s. Thomas, of Cruwys Morchard, Devon, gent. EXETER COLL., matric. 23 May, 1765, aged 18; B.A. 1769, rector (and patron) of Ashwater, Devon, 1769-1811, rector of St. Ervan's, Cornwall, 1811, died in 1829.

Melhuish, Thomas, s. Thomas, of Ashwater, Devon, cler. EXETER COLL., matric. 7 May, 1796, aged 18; B.A. 1800, fellow 1800-9, M.A. 1803, perp. curate Clawton, Devon, 1811, rector (and patron) of Ashwater 1811, until his death 28 Oct., 1861. See *Coll. Reg.*, 118.

Melhuish, Thomas, s. John, of Exeter, Devon, gent. MAGDALEN HALL, matric. 12 Dec., 1815, aged 36.

Melhuish, Thomas Bremridge, 1s. Thomas, of Poughill, Devon, gent. EXETER COLL., matric. 4 Feb., 1830, aged 17; B.A. 1834, rector of Poughill, 1861, until his death 7 Oct., 1885.

Melhuish, Walter William, 2s. Thomas, of Ashwater, Devon, cler. MAGDALEN HALL, matric. 7 March, 1839, aged 18; B.A. 1842, of Court Barn, Devon, J.P. [20]

Melhuishe, William, s. Roger, of Northam, Devon, arm. EXETER COLL., matric. 9 June, 1735, aged 16; bar.-at-law, Middle Temple, 1742.

Melhuish, William, s. Thomas, of Poughill, Devon, gent. WADHAM COLL., matric. 30 May, 1772, aged 19; B.A. 1776, M.A. 1781.

Melhuish, William Shortrudge, s. Thomas, of Witheridge, Devon, cler. EXETER COLL., matric. 9 April, 1767, aged 17.

Melitus, Paul Gregory, 2s. Gregory Paul, of Calcutta, arm. BALLIOL COLL., matric. 19 Oct., 1878, aged 20; of the Indian Civil Service 1876.

Mellard, William, s. Thomas, of Cardiff, co. Glamorgan, gent. MAGDALEN HALL, matric. 22 Jan., 1817, aged 24; B.A. 1824, M.A. 1825, vicar of Caddington, Beds, 1829. [25]

Mellefont, Gilbert, s. David. of Dublin (city), arm. CHRIST CHURCH, matric. 20 June, 1775, aged 18; a student of the Middle Temple 1773, buried in the Temple Churchyard 13 July, 1780.

Mellen, Chase Hugo, 2s. William Proctor, of Cincinnati, America, arm. BRASENOSE COLL., matric. 21 Jan., 1884, aged 20; B.A. 1887.

Mellen, Clark Victor, 3s. William Proctor, of Cincinnati, America, arm. BRASENOSE COLL., matric. 22 April, 1884, aged 18.

Meller, Joseph, s. Joseph, of Wisbech, St. Peter's, Cambridge, pleb. ST. MARY HALL, matric. 8 May, 1733, aged 21; B.A. 1734 (query rector of Oddington, co. Gloucester, will proved C.P.C. 3 July, 1779).

Meller, Walter Clifford, 1s. Walter, of Paddington, Middlesex, gent. ST. JOHN'S COLL., matric. 16 Oct., 1869, aged 21; B.A. 1872, M.A. 1882. [30]

Melliar, Andrew Foster, 3s. Edward Foster, of Wells, Somerset, cler. WADHAM COLL., matric. 30 Jan., 1828, aged 17; B.A. 1832, M.A. 1834, of Wells, Somerset, assumed the additional name of MELLIAR by royal licence 13 Nov., 1840, died 10 May, 1841.

Melliar, Andrew Foster, 3s. Andrew Foster, of Wells, Somerset, arm. NEW COLL., matric. 13 Oct., 1860, aged 19; B.A. 1863, M.A. 1867, rector of Sproughton, Suffolk, since 1885.

Melliar, James, s. James, of Catcott, Somerset, gent. EXETER COLL., matric. 22 Nov., 1734, aged 16; bar.-at-law, Middle Temple, 1742.

Melliar, James, s. James, of Galhampton, Somerset, arm. WADHAM COLL., matric. 25 March, 1779, aged 24.

Melliar, William Foster, 1s. Andrew Foster, of Kingston, Somerset, arm. MERTON COLL., matric. 22 March, 1854, aged 17; B.A. 1858, of North Aston Hall, Oxon, J.P., high sheriff 1864. [35]

Mellish, Edward, s. Joseph, of Blyth, Notts, arm. CORPUS CHRISTI COLL., matric. 13 May, 1726, aged 18.

Mellish, (Sir) George, y.s. (Edward), of East Tuddenham, Norfolk, cler. (dean of Hereford). UNIVERSITY COLL., 8 May, 1833, aged 18; scholar 1833-9, B.A. 1837, M.A. 1839, hon. fellow 1872-7, created D.C.L. 17 June, 1874, bar.-at-law, Inner Temple, 1848, Q.C. and a bencher 1861, a lord justice of appeal in bankruptcy, died 15 June, 1877. See *Eton School Lists.*

Mellish, George Lilly, 2s. William, of Isle of Guernsey, arm. EXETER COLL., matric. 2 June, 1852, aged 17.

Mellish, Henry Edward, 1s. William Leigh, of Richmond, arm. BALLIOL COLL., matric. 20 Oct., 1875, aged 18; of Hodsock Priory, Notts, bar.-at-law, Inner Temple, 1882. See Foster's *Men at the Bar* & *Eton School Lists.*

Mellish, Peter Bertie, 2s. William John, of Orton, Notts, cler. CORPUS CHRISTI COLL., matric. 26 Oct., 1885, aged 18; exhibitioner 1885. [40]

Mellish, William, s. William, of Uxbridge, Middlesex, gent. QUEEN'S COLL., matric. 21 Feb., 1756, aged 17, B.A. 1759; M.A. from ST. EDMUND HALL 1762, bar.-at-law, Middle Temple, 1768.

Mello, Henry Jephson, 2s. William, of Blackheath, Kent, arm. CORPUS CHRISTI COLL., matric. 22 May, 1856, aged 18; B.A. 1859, a student of Lincoln's Inn 1860.

Mello, John Magens, 1s. John Arnold, of St. George's, London, gent. ST. JOHN'S COLL., matric. 26 June, 1854, aged 18; B.A. 1859, M.A. 1863, rector of Brampton St. Thomas, Chesterfield, 1863.

Mellor, Abijah, 5s. Charles, of Snenton, Notts, gent. JESUS COLL., matric. 10 May, 1826, aged 18; B.A. 1832.

Mellor, Cecil, 1s. Joseph, of Bolton, Lancashire, arm. ORIEL COLL., matric. 23 Oct., 1884, aged 19; B.A. 1887.

Mellor, George Henry, 4s. James, of Liverpool, gent. LINCOLN COLL., matric. 18 Oct., 1871, aged 18; scholar 1871-5, B.A. 1876, B.C.L. & M.A. 1878, bar.-at-law, Lincoln's Inn, 1877. See Foster's *Men at the Bar* & *Rugby School Reg.*

Mellor, Herbert Walton, 3s. George, of Ashton-under-Lyne, Lancashire, gent. QUEEN'S COLL., matric. 23 May, 1874, aged 19. [5]

Mellor, Stephen Wilkinson, 3s. Charles, of Snenton, Notts, gent. JESUS COLL., matric. 25 Oct., 1826, aged 22.

Mellor, William Henry, 4s. Jonathan, of Oldham, Lancashire, arm. ST. EDMUND HALL, matric. 30 April, 1846, aged 21; bar.-at-law, Inner Temple, 1861, died 13 May, 1872.

Melvill, Rev. Arthur Hardcastle, 2s. James Cosmo, of Hampstead, Middlesex, arm. ST. JOHN'S COLL., matric. 14 Oct., 1876, aged 23; B.A. 1880, M.A. 1885.

Melvill, Harry Edward, 1s. William Henry, of London, arm. UNIVERSITY COLL., matric. 11 Oct., 1884, aged 18.

Melvill, John Philip, s. John, of Calcutta, East Indies, arm. TRINITY COLL., matric. 28 Oct., 1815, aged 19. See *Eton School Lists.* [10]

Melville, Beresford Valentine, 2s. David, of Shelsley, co. Worcester, cler. BRASENOSE COLL., matric. 26 Jan., 1881, aged 23; B.A. 1885.

Melville, David, y.s. Robert, of Amsterdam, Holland, gent. PEMBROKE COLL., matric. 5 Dec., 1827, aged 19; scholar BRASENOSE COLL. 1832-5, B.A. 1836, M.A. 1839, tutor Durham University 1842-51, principal of Hatfield Hall 1846-51, created D.D. Durham 1882, rector of Shelsey-Beauchamp, co. Worcester, 1845-57, hon. canon of Worcester 1851-81, canon 1881, rector of Great Witley, co. Worcester, 1857.

Melville, David, 1s. David, of St. Pancras, London, arm. BRASENOSE COLL., matric. 28 June, 1832, aged 19.

Melville, George Fisher, o.s John, of Edinburgh, arm. BRASENOSE COLL., matric. 21 April, 1860, aged 18; B.A. 1863.

Melville, Robert, o.s. Michael Linning, of Sierra Leone, Africa, arm. MAGDALEN COLL., matric. 29 Oct., 1857, aged 16; B.A. 1861, M.A. 1864, of Hatfield Grove, Sussex, bar.-at-law, Lincoln's Inn, 1864. See Foster's *Men at the Bar.* [15]

Melville, (Hon.) Ronald Ruthven Leslie, 2s. Hon. John Thornton Leslie, of Roehampton, near Putney, Surrey, arm. CHRIST CHURCH, matric. 8 June, 1854, aged 18; B.A. 1858, M.A. 1865, heir presumptive to the Earl of Leven and Melville. See Foster's *Peerage* & *Eton School Lists.*

Menabrea, General Count, created D.C.L, 22 June, 1881, ambassador extraordinary from King of Italy.

Mence, Benjamin, s. Ben., of St. Helen's, Worcester (city), pleb. MAGDALEN HALL, matric. 5 March, 1739-40, aged 16; B.A. from MERTON COLL. 1746, M.A. from KING'S COLL., Cambridge, 1752, rector of All Hallows, London Wall, 1758. (Memo.: Rev. Joseph Mence, a celebrated singer, vicar of St. Pancras, who died at Worcester, 19 Dec., 1796, aged 74, was also rector of All Hallows aforesaid.)

Mence, Benjamin, s. John, of Barnsley, Yorks, cler. WORCESTER COLL., matric. 25 June, 1781, aged 16; B.A. 1785, M.A. 1788, perp. curate St. Mary's, Barnsley, Yorks, 1793, until his death 28 May, 1847.

Mence, John, s. George, of Worcester (city), pleb. ORIEL COLL., matric. 18 March, 1716-7, aged 19; B.A. 1720. [20]

Mence, John, s. John, of Barnsley, Yorks, cler. WORCESTER COLL., matric. 4 July, 1751, aged 17; B.A. 1755, perp. curate St. Mary, Barnsley, 1761, until his death, 8 March, 1806.

Mence, John, s. John, of Barnsley, Yorks, cler. WORCESTER COLL., matric. 25 June, 1781, aged 14; B.A. 1785, M.A. 1788, senior fellow at his death at Barnsley 1 Dec., 1816.

Mence, John William, 1s. William Cookes, of Barnsley, Yorks, gent. WORCESTER COLL., matric. 13 Nov., 1834, aged 18; B.A. 1839, M.A. 1844, incumbent of Prestwould, co. Leicester, 1842, until his death 9 Dec., 1854.

Mence, Richard, o.s. Samuel, of Highgate, Middlesex, cler. TRINITY COLL., matric. 26 June, 1835, aged 17; B.A. 1839, M.A. 1842, held various curacies 1840-64, vicar of Bockleton, co. Hereford, 1864.

Mence, Richard (Mugg), s. Richard, of St. Swithin's, Worcester (city), gent. CHRIST CHURCH, matric. 26 Oct., 1797, aged 17; B.A. 1802, M.A. 1804, bar.-at-law, Middle Temple, 1804. See *Rugby School Reg.*, 67. [25]

Mence, Samuel, s. Benjamin, of Worcester (city), gent. WORCESTER COLL., matric. 5 March, 1764, aged 21.

Mence, Samuel, s. Richard, of Worcester (city), gent. TRINITY COLL., matric. 26 Nov., 1798, aged 17; B.A. 1802, M.A. 1805, B.D. 1814, fellow until 1815, reader Highgate Chapel 1816, rector of Ulcombe, Kent, 1838, until his death 28 Nov., 1860. See *Rugby School Reg.*, 74.

Mence, William, s. Benjamin, of St. Helen's, Worcester (city), pleb. MERTON COLL., matric. 20 Oct., 1750, aged 18; B.A. 1754, M.A. 1757.

Mendez, Moses, created M.A. 19 June, 1750, of Mitcham, Surrey, and of Old Buckenham, Norfolk (o.s. of James Mendez, of Mitcham), buried 8 Feb., 1758, his widow and 3 sons were authorized to take the surname of HEAD in lieu of MENDEZ by royal licence 11 May, 1770, and his grandson, Francis Bond Head, was created a baronet 14 July, 1838. See Foster's *Baronetage.*

Mendham, John, s. John, of St. Olave's, Hart Street, London, arm. ST. EDMUND HALL, matric. 15 Oct., 1817, aged 17; B.A. 1821, M.A. 1825, rector of Clophill, Beds, 1844, until his death 23 April, 1869. [30]

Mendham, Rev. Joseph, s. Robert, of London, gent. ST. EDMUND HALL, matric. 27 Jan., 1789, aged 19; B.A. 1792, M.A. 1795, died at Sutton Coldfield, co. Warwick, 1 Nov., 1856.

Mendham, Rev. Robert Riland, s. Joseph, of Sutton Coldfield, co. Warwick, cler. WADHAM COLL., matric. 12 Nov., 1816, aged 18; B.A. 1820, M.A. 1824, died 15 June, 1857.

Mendl, Sigismund Ferdinand, 1s. Ferdinand, of London, gent. UNIVERSITY COLL., matric. 24 Jan., 1884, aged 17; B.A. 1887, a student of the Inner Temple 1884.

Mends, Joseph, s. Thomas, of Lyme Regis, Dorset, cler. ST. EDMUND HALL, matric. 29 March, 1803, aged 19; B.A. 1810, M.A. 1825, rector of Aller, Somerset 1809, until his death 19 Aug., 1828.

Mends, Thomas, s. John, of Haverfordwest, co. Pembroke, gent. ST. EDMUND HALL, matric. 8 Nov., 1791, aged 35; B.A. 1793, rector of Holbeton, Devon, 1784, until his death in 1829. [35]

Menet, John, o.s. John Francis, of Clapton, Middlesex, gent. EXETER COLL., matric. 6 May, 1841, aged 18; B.A. 1845, M.A. 1847, vicar of Hockerill, Beds, 1852.

Menteath, Francis Hastings Stuart, 5s. Charles, of Edinburgh, Scotland, arm. MAGDALEN HALL, matric. 28 June, 1828, aged 20; B.A. 1833, vicar of Thorpe Arch, Yorks, 1834, until his death 8 March, 1875. See Foster's *Baronetage* & *Rugby School Reg.*, 143.

Menteath, Rev. Granville Thorold Stuart, 1s. Granville Wheler, of Bolsover, co. Derby, cler. UNIVERSITY COLL., matric. 26 Nov., 1856, aged 18; B.A. 1861. See Foster's *Baronetage.*

Menteath, Granville Wheler, 7s. Charles, of Closeburn, Dumfries, Scotland, arm. MAGDALEN HALL, matric. 28 June, 1828, aged 17; B.A. 1832, M.A. 1835, vicar of Rauceby, co. Lincoln, 1843-54, rector of Hascomb 1854-60, perp. curate Grazeley 1861-8, rector of Morcot, Rutland, 1868-72, died 1 Sep., 1887.

Menteath, James (Stuart), s. William, of Burrowin, co. Perth, arm. BALLIOL COLL., matric. 9 April, 1736, aged 18; B.A. 1739, M.A. 1742, rector of Barrowby, co. Lincoln, died 15 July, 1802, grandfather of the next named.

Menteath, (Sir) James Stuart (Bart.), s. Charles, of Closeburn, co. Dumfries, arm., (after baronet). BRASENOSE COLL., matric. 11 June, 1812, aged 19; 2nd baronet, a Scottish advocate 1816, bar.-at-law, Middle Temple, 1834, died 27 Feb., 1870. See Foster's *Baronetage.*

Mentha, (Rev.) Frederick Henry (Fritz Harry in *Mat. Reg.*), o.s. Fritz, of Manchester, gent. HERTFORD COLL., matric. 14 Dec., 1874, aged 19; scholar 1874-9, B.A. 1879, M.A. 1881. [5]

Mentor, James, s. John, of Newbury, Berks, gent. MAGDALEN HALL, matric. 16 March, 1799, aged 25; B.A. 1802, M.A. 1808.

Menzies, Rev. Alfred, 4s. John, of Putney, Surrey, gent. WORCESTER COLL., matric. 29 Nov., 1828, aged 18; scholar TRINITY COLL. 1829-33, B.A. 1832, fellow 1833-6, lecturer in philosophy, died 24 Feb., 1836.

Menzies, Alfred Irvine, 2s. James Irvine, of Lambeth, Surrey, arm. MERTON COLL., matric. 17 Oct., 1882, aged 18; postmaster 1882, B.A. 1886. See *St. Paul's School Reg.*, 366.

Menzies, Rev. Alfred Sydney, 2s. William, of Winchester, cler. HERTFORD COLL., matric. 13 Oct., 1877, aged 19; scholar 1876-81, B.A. 1881.

Menzies, Fletcher Norton, 2s. Neil, of Edinburgh, baronet. UNIVERSITY COLL., matric. 23 June, 1837, aged 18; brother and heir of Sir Robert 1837. See Foster's *Baronetage.* [10]

Menzies, Francis Alleyn, 1s. William, of Winchester, cler. NON-COLL., matric. 13 Oct., 1876, aged 20; died commoner of NEW COLL., 31 May, 1879.

Menzies, Frederick, 5s. John, of Wavertree, Lancashire, gent. BRASENOSE COLL., matric. 5 Dec., 1833, aged 18; scholar 1835-7, fellow 1837-67, B.A. 1837, M.A. 1840, junior bursar, Hebrew lecturer, and Hulme lecturer in divinity 1850, vice-principal 1858, hon. canon of Christ Church 1883, rector of Great Shefford, Berks, 1866.

Menzies, George Champneys, 2s. Robert, of Harewood, Yorks, arm. ST. JOHN'S COLL., matric. 28 March, 1843, aged 19; brother of Robert William 1842.

Menzies, John, 2s. John, of Putney, Surrey, gent. CORPUS CHRISTI COLL., matric. 13 Oct., 1820, aged 16; scholar 1820-9, B.A. 1824, M.A. 1827, fellow 1829-38, B.D. 1836, rector of Wyke Regis with Weymouth 1837, until his death in 1847.

Menzies, John Graham, 3s. Graham, of Edinburgh, arm. BRASENOSE COLL., matric. 31 Jan., 1879, aged 18. [15]

Menzies, (Sir) Robert (Bart.), 1s. Neil, of Edinburgh, baronet. UNIVERSITY COLL., matric. 23 June, 1837; S.C.L. 1842, 7th baronet, sometime captain Perthshire rifles. See Foster's *Baronetage.*

Menzies, Robert, 1s. George, of Trentham, co. Stafford, gent. EXETER COLL., matric. 23 Oct., 1885, aged 19.

Menzies, Robert Stewart, 1s. Graham, of Edinburgh, arm. CHRIST CHURCH, matric. 20 May, 1875, aged 19; B.A. 1879, of Hallyburton House, N.B., J.P. cos. Perth and Forfar, bar.-at-law, Lincoln's Inn, 1887, M.P. East Perthshire Dec., 1885. See Foster's *Men at the Bar.*

ercer, William Thomas, 3s. George, of Edinburgh (city), arm. EXETER COLL., matric. 30 May, 1839, aged 17; B.A. 1843, M.A. 1851, a student of the Inner Temple 1842, colonial secretary and acting governor Hong Kong, died 23 May, 1879.

erchant, Rev. Charles, 1s. Charles Martin, of Bury, Lancashire, gent. WORCESTER COLL., matric. 29 Jan., 1879, aged 17; B.A. 1881, M.A. 1887.

erchant, Robert, s. Robert, of Fittleton, Wilts, cler. MAGDALEN HALL, matric. 31 March, 1757, aged 18; demy MAGDALEN COLL. 1757-67, B.A. 1760, M.A. 1763, fellow 1767-79, B.D. 1774, lecturer in moral philosophy 1772, bursar 1774, dean of divinity 1778, curate of East Tisted 1774, died 6 May, 1779, buried at Fittleton. See *Bloxam*, vi. 312.

erchant, William, s. William, of Bampton, Oxon, gent. MAGDALEN COLL., matric. 27 March, 1727, aged 17, chorister 1720 and 1725-7, expelled; then of EXETER COLL., whence he was also expelled; lastly a commoner of ST. EDMUND HALL, died 27 June, 1734. See *Bloxam*, i. 149.

ercier, Henry, scholar TRINITY COLL., Dublin, 1735 (B.A. 1736, M.A. 1739, fellow 1740, B.D. 1747, LL.D. 1750); incorp. 3 July, 1754, D.D. 1755, preb. of Christ Church, Dublin, 1761, until his death in 1769. [5]

ercier, Lewis Page, o.s. Francis, of St. Pancras, London, arm. TRINITY COLL., matric. 30 June, 1837, aged 17; scholar UNIVERSITY COLL. 1839-42, B.A. 1841, M.A. 1855, head-master Edgbaston School 1849-57, chaplain of the Foundling Hospital 1857-73, died 2 Nov., 1875.

eredith, Arthur Evan, 2s. David, of Elland, co. Derby, cler. CHRIST CHURCH, matric. 11 Oct., 1872, aged 20; migrated to TRINITY COLL., Cambridge, 1874, B.A. 1878, M.A. 1881.

eredith, Charles, 1s. Charles, of St. George's, Bloomsbury, London, arm. TRINITY COLL., matric. 30 May, 1857, aged 18; B.A. 1862, M.A. 1864.

Meredith, Rev. Charles John, o.s. John, of Oxford (city), pleb. MAGDALEN COLL., matric. 10 Oct., 1818, aged 18, chorister 1809-16, clerk 1818-23, B.A. 1822, chaplain 1823-6, M.A. 1825; fellow LINCOLN COLL. 1825-49, B.D. 1834, bursar 1830, sub-rector 1833, claviger 1837, rector of Waddington, co. Lincoln, 1848, until his death 18 July, 1851. See *Bloxam*, i. 213

Meredith, David, s. Thomas, of Cilycwm, co. Carmarthen, cler. CHRIST CHURCH, matric. 21 March, 1742-3, aged 18; B.A. 1747. [10]

Meredith, Edward, s. John, of Church Stretton, Salop, gent. CHRIST CHURCH, matric. 11 Oct., 1811, aged 17; servitor 1813-16, B.A. 1815, M.A. 1818, chaplain 1817-19, perp. curate Longdon-upon-Terne, 1845-65, rector of Ightfield, Salop, 1865, until his death 20 June, 1873.

Meredith, Eugene Samuel Isaac, 2s. Hireman, of Boston, America, gent. MERTON COLL., matric. 24 April, 1876, aged 21; B.A. 1882.

Meredith, George Edward, 1s. Edward, of Newport, Salop, cler. ST. JOHN'S COLL., matric. 24 Jan., 1863, aged 21; B.A. 1867, M.A. 1877.

Meredith, Henry, s. Henry, of Whitton, Radnor, cler. JESUS COLL., matric. 18 Oct., 1739, aged 19; B.A. 1743.

Meredith, Henry Hills, 2s. Charles, of London, arm. CHRIST CHURCH, matric. 8 Feb., 1872, aged 18; B.A. 1876, bar.-at-law, Inner Temple, 1879. See Foster's *Men at the Bar* & *Eton School Lists*. [15]

Meredith, James, s. James, of Colston, Wilts, cler. WADHAM COLL., matric. 14 Dec., 1724, aged 16; B.A. 1728, M.A. 1731, vicar of Stokeley, Somerset, 1732. (Memo.: Rev. J. M., of St. John's Street, died 2 May, 1777.)

Meredith, James, s. James, of Birmingham, co. Warwick, gent. ST. ALBAN HALL, matric. 31 May 1813, aged 15; created M.A. 17 June, 1841, brother of Samuel 1843.

Meredith, John, s. Henry, of Whitton, Radnor cler. JESUS COLL., matric. 20 March, 1755, aged 19.

Meredith, John, 3s. John, of Westbury, Salop, gent. CHRIST CHURCH, matric. 3 Dec., 1824, aged 20; B.A. 1828, M.A. 1831.

Meredith, Rev. John, 1s. Thomas Grubb, of Bishop Stortford, Herts, gent. NON-COLL., matric. 7 June, 1878, aged 36; B.A. 1884. [20]

Meredith, John Blunt, 2s. Edward, of Longdon, Salop, cler. ST. JOHN'S COLL., matric. 15 June, 1866, aged 19; B.A. 1870, vicar of Kinnerley, Salop, 1876.

Meredith, John (Lewis), 2s. William, of Eglwys-fach, co. Cardigan, gent. JESUS COLL., matric. 11 June, 1863, aged 20; clerk 1863-6, scholar 1866-8, B.A. 1868, M.A. 1877, vicar of Towyn 1873-80, rector of Gelligaer, co. Glamorgan, 1880.

Meredith, Joseph, 2s. Joseph, of Abergavenny, co. Monmouth, gent. JESUS COLL., matric. 4 May, 1865, aged 20; B.A. 1868, M.A. 1871, vicar of East Crompton, Lancashire, 1876, until his death 10 Nov., 1878.

Meredith, Myddelton, s. Thomas, of Wrexham, co. Denbigh, arm. JESUS COLL., matric. 3 April, 1723, aged 18; B.A. 22 March, 1726-7, uncle of Richard 1776.

Meredith, Richard, s. Thomas, of Pentrebychan, co. Denbigh, arm. ORIEL COLL., matric. 16 Nov., 1776, aged 18; died 1800, brother of Thomas 1778.

Meredith, Richard, 3s. Thomas, of Worcester (city), gent. ST. EDMUND HALL, matric. 16 Dec., 1819, aged 23; B.A. 1823, M.A. 1826, vicar of Hagbourne, Berks, 1825-68, rector of Westborough with Dry Doddington, co. Lincoln, 1868-85, died 3 Sep., 1886. [26]

Meredith, Robert Day, M.A. TRINITY COLL., Dublin, 1841 (B.A. 1838), 2s. William, of Dicksgrove, Kerry, gent. WORCESTER COLL., incorp. 25 June, 1841, aged 25; rector and vicar of Halstock, Dorset, 1843. See Foster's *Our Noble and Gentle Families*.

Meredith, Samuel, 4s. James, of Birmingham, co. Warwick, gent. ST. ALBAN HALL, matric. 26 May, 1843, aged 39; brother of James 1813.

Meredith, Samuel Readhead, 1s. David, of Meltham, Yorks, cler. BRASENOSE COLL., matric. 15 Oct., 1870, aged 20; B.A. 1874.

Meredith, Theophilus, s. Amos, of Prestbury, Cheshire, arm. CHRIST CHURCH, matric. 2 June, 1747, aged 16; B.A. from ST. EDMUND HALL 1761, M.A. 1762, vicar of Linton, co. Hereford, 1769, and rector of Ross 1771, until his death in 1775, brother of William 1742-3. [30]

Meredith, Thomas, s. Thomas, of Pentrebychan, co. Denbigh, arm. JESUS COLL., matric. 17 March, 1778, aged 17; B.A. 1782, M.A. 1784, B.Med. 1785, died in 1802.

Meredith, Thomas, 1s. James, of Hope, Flint, cler. EXETER COLL., matric. 9 April, 1864, aged 18; B.A. 1868, M.A. 1871, archdeacon of Singapore and surrogate 1882, and chaplain.

Meredith, Timothy, s. Thomas, of Chilcomb, co. Carmarthen, cler. CHRIST CHURCH, matric. 30 March, 1748, aged 21; B.A. 1752, M.A. 1755, vicar of Wootton Bassett, Wilts, 1753, and rector of Bawnden, co. Gloucester, 1772, until his death 15 April, 1793.

Meredith, (Sir) William (Bart.), s. Amos, of Chester (city), arm. CHRIST CHURCH, matric. 24 March, 1742-3, aged 18; created D.C.L. 14 April, 1749, then of Henbury, Cheshire, 3rd baronet, M.P. Wigan 1754-61, Liverpool 1761-80, a lord of the Admiralty 1764-5, died 2 Jan., 1790. See Ormerod's *Cheshire*, iii. 708.

Meredith, William George, o.s. George, of St. Marylebone, arm. BRASENOSE COLL., matric. 22 Jan., 1821, aged 17; B.A. 1824, M.A. 1829, a student of Lincoln's Inn 1823.

Meredith, Rev. William Henry Fitzgerald, 2s. Robert Fitzgerald, of Ottery St. Mary, Devon, cler. NON-COLL., matric. 16 Oct., 1875, aged 20; B.A. 1879.

Meredith, William Henry (Stewart) 1s. William, of London, arm. NON-COLL., matric. 13 Oct., 1877, aged 21; B.A. from MERTON COLL. 1883.

Meredith, William Macdonald, 7s. Richard, of Stapleton, co. Gloucester, cler. MAGDALEN HALL, matric. 20 April, 1868, aged 19; scholar 1869, B.A. 1871, M.A. (HERTFORD COLL.) 1886, vicar of Hagbourne. Berks, 1874-8, incumbent St. Paul's, Carrubber's Close, Edinburgh, 1877-8, senior chaplain of Edinburgh Cathedral 1879.

Meredyth, John, M.A. TRINITY COLL., Dublin, 1832 (B.A. 1826); adm. 'ad eundem' 7 June, 1853. [5]

Meredyth, (Sir) Richard Gorges (Bart.), s. Hamilton Gorges, of Clifford Street, London, arm. BRASENOSE COLL., matric. 11 July, 1752, aged 17; created M.A. 17 Feb., 1756, assumed the additional surname of MEREDYTH 1775, created a baronet of Ireland 28 Aug., 1787, died before 1809. See Foster's *Our Noble and Gentle Families.*

Meredyth, William Francis, M.A. TRINITY COLL., Dublin, 1854 (B.A. 1844); adm. 'ad eundem' 22 March, 1860, vicar of Crecora, co. Limerick, 1868, preb. of Limerick 1872-81, treasurer 1881-3.

Merefield, Samuel, s. William, of Woolmistone, Somerset, arm. EXETER COLL., matric. 28 March, 1735, aged 19; B.A. 1739.

Merest, James, s. James, of Westminster, arm. ORIEL COLL., matric. 30 May, 1775, aged 23; curate of Wortham, Suffolk for nearly 50 years, rector of Brandon Ferry and Wangford, Suffolk, 1796, vicar of Wroughton, Wilts, 1797, until his death 31 March, 1827.

Mereweather, John Davies, 2s. John, of St. James's, Bristol, gent. ST. EDMUND HALL, matric. 14 June, 1839, aged 22; B.A. 1843 (as John David M.), chaplain at Venice. [10]

Merewether, Charles George, 3s. Francis, of Great Yeldham, Essex, cler. WADHAM COLL., matric. 18 June, 1840, aged 17; B.A. 1845, bar.-at-law, Inner Temple, 1848, Q C. and a bencher 1877, recorder of Leicester 1868, M.P. Northampton 1874-80, died 24 June, 1884.

Merewether, Charles George, 2s. Francis Lewis, of Sydney, Australia, arm. CHRIST CHURCH, matric. 28 Jan., 1870, aged 20.

Merewether, Edward Christopher, 5s. Henry Alworth, of St. Andrew's, Holborn, London, arm. UNIVERSITY COLL., matric. 14 June, 1838, aged 18.

Merewether, Francis, s. John, of Chippenham, Wilts, doctor. ST. JOHN'S COLL., matric. 15 May, 1765, aged 27; B.C.L. 1776, rector of Foxcote and Combe Hay, Somerset, died 1 May, 1806.

Merewether, Francis, s. Henry, of Calne, Wilts, arm. CHRIST CHURCH, matric. 4 Feb., 1802, aged 18, B.A. 1805; M.A. from ST. JOHN'S COLL., Cambridge, 1809, re-admitted 'ad eundem' 7 June, 1853, rector of Coleorton 1816, and vicar of Whitwick, co. Leicester, 1818, until his death 21 July, 1864. See *Eton School Lists*, and for list of his writings see *Gent.'s Mag.*

Merewether, Francis Arthur Henry, 1s. Francis, of Australia, arm. NEW COLL., matric. 20 Oct., 1865, aged 17. [15]

Merewether, Francis Henry Shafton, o.s. Henry Robert, of Latchingdon, Essex, cler. KEBLE COLL., matric. 13 Oct., 1873, aged 20; NON-COLL. B.A. 1882.

Merewether, Henry Alworth, created D.C.L. 12 June, 1839 (1s. Henry, of Calne, Wilts, arm.), bar.-at-law, Inner Temple, 1809, serj.-at-law 1827, king's serjeant 1832, attorney-general to the Queen Dowager, recorder of Yarmouth and of Reading, town clerk of London 1842-59, died 22 July, 1864.

Merewether, Henry Alworth, 1s. Henry Alworth, of Combe Hay, Somerset, arm. WADHAM COLL., matric. 30 June, 1827, aged 15; migrated to TRINITY COLL., Cambridge, bar.-at-law, Inner Temple, 1837, Q.C. and a bencher 1853, recorder of Devizes 1842, until his death 29 Aug., 1877.

Merewether, Henry Robert, 2s. Francis, of Yeldham, Essex, cler. ST. ALBAN HALL, matric. 26 Oct., 1837, aged 21; B.A. 1840, held various curacies 1842-59, vicar of Tenterden 1859-83, and of East Peckham since 1883. See *Eton School Lists.* [20]

Merewether, John, s. John, of Marshfield, co. Gloucester, gent. QUEEN'S COLL., matric. 18 Oct., 1814, aged 18; B.A. 1818, M.A. 1822, B. & D.D. 1832, F.S.A. 1836, chaplain to the Duchess of Clarence 1824, and to the Queen 1830, rector of New Radnor 1828, dean of Hereford 1832, deputy-clerk of the closet 1833, vicar of Madeley 1836, until his death 4 April, 1850.

Merewether, John Francis, 1s. John, of Hampton, Middlesex (dean of Hereford). ORIEL COLL., matric. 27 May, 1842, aged 18.

Merewether, Walton Lockyer, 2s. Henry Alworth, of London, arm. CHRIST CHURCH, matric. 7 June, 1865, aged 18; B.A. 1870, bar.-at-law, Inner Temple, 1871. See Foster's *Men at the Bar* & *Eton School Lists.*

Merewether, Rev. William Henry Ernest, 2s. John, of Hampton, Middlesex, doctor (after dean of Hereford). ORIEL COLL., matric. 8 Nov., 1845, aged 17; B.A. 1849, died 13 June, 1855.

Merewether, Wyndham Arthur Scinde, 3s. Henry Alworth, of Bowden Hill, Wilts, arm. ORIEL COLL., matric. 18 Oct., 1871, aged 19; B.A. 1876, M.A. 1880, vicar of North Bradley, Wilts, 1885. [25]

Merivale, Charles (scholar ST. JOHN'S COLL., Cambridge, 1826, B.A. 1830, M.A. 1833, fellow 1833-48, B.D. 1840, D.D. 1870, hon. fellow 1874), created D.C.L. 13 June, 1866, chaplain to the House of Commons 1863-9, created LL.D. Edinburgh 1884, select preacher (Cambridge) 1838, Whitehall preacher 1840, rector of Lawford, Essex, 1848-70, Hulsean lecturer 1862, dean of Ely 1879 (brother of Herman named below); for list of his works see *Crockford.*

Merivale, George Montague, 2s. John Lewis, of Bushey, Middlesex, gent. NEW COLL., matric. 10 Oct., 1873, aged 18; B.A. 1878, a student of Lincoln's Inn 1878.

Merivale, Herman (C.B.), 1s. John Herman, of Dawlish, Devon, arm. ORIEL COLL., matric. 3 Nov., 1823, aged 17; scholar TRINITY COLL. 1825-8, B.A. 1827, fellow BALLIOL COLL. 1828-34, M.A. 1833, Drummond professor of political economy 1837-42, created D.C.L. 21 June 1870, bar.-at-law, Inner Temple, 1832, bencher 1865, recorder of Falmouth, Helston and Penzance 1841-8, under-secretary of state for the Colonies 1848-60, C.B. 1859, under-secretary of state for India 1860, until his death 8 Feb., 1874.

Merivale, Herman Charles, 1s. Herman, of London, arm. BALLIOL COLL., matric. 26 Jan., 1857, aged 17; B.A. 1861, bar.-at-law, Inner Temple, 1864. See Foster's *Men at the Bar.*

Merivale, Thomas. TRINITY COLL., 1721. See MERRIVALE. [30]

Merk, Frederick Holland, 4s. John Nepomuk, of Dhurmsala, East Indies, cler. BALLIOL COLL., matric. 17 Oct., 1882, aged 19; scholar 1882, exhibitioner 1886, B.A. 1887.

Merk, Walter Henry, 3s. John Nepomuk, of Dhurmsala, East Indies, cler. BALLIOL COLL., matric. 21 Oct., 1880, aged 19; scholar 1880-2, entered Indian Civil Service 1880, died in May or June, 1884.

Merrefield, George Nelmes, 2s. William, of Worcester (city), gent. MAGDALEN HALL, matric. 16 March, 1850, aged 24; B A. 1855, M.A. 1861, rector of St. James's, Manchester, rector of Gamston and vicar of Eaton, Notts, 1873-84.

Merrey, John, s. John, of Betton, Salop, gent. MAGDALEN HALL, matric. 28 March, 1729, aged 19; B.A. from WADHAM COLL. 1732, M.A. 1735 (as MURREY).

Merrick, George Purnell, 1s. William, of Clifton, near Bristol, gent. EXETER COLL., matric. 27 June, 1865, aged 23; B.Mus, 28 June, 1865, B.A. 1871, M.A. 1878, organist 1867-71, chaplain H.M. Prison, Westminster, 1878-83, and Milbank since 1883.

Merrick, James, s. John, of St. Lawrence, Reading, Berks, doctor. TRINITY COLL., matric. 14 April, 1736, aged 16; B.A. 1739, M.A. 1742, fellow 1744, author of a translation of the Psalms 1765, died in 1765. *O.H.S.*, ix. p. 24.

Merrick, John, s. John, of Reading, Berks, doctor. ST. JOHN'S COLL., matric. 8 July, 1721, aged 16; B.A. 1726, M.A. 21 March, 1729-30, B.Med. 1731, brother of the last named.

Merrick, John, s. John, of Haywood Lodge, co. Hereford, pleb. BRASENOSE COLL., matric. 19 June, 1783, aged 19; B.A. 1787. [5]

Merrick, John, 'tonsor;' privilegiatus 14 Nov., 1787.

Merrick, Marshall Montague, s. Sam., of London, gent. QUEEN'S COLL., matric. 5 May, 1738, aged 18; B.C.L. 1744, D.C.L. 1759, lecturer of St. Anne's, Westminster, and vicar of Reigate, Surrey, died 6 Sep., 1782.

Merrick, Rev. Robert, 4s. William, of Bradford, Wilts, gent. ST. MARY HALL, matric. 24 Oct., 1873, aged 26; B.A. 1876, M.A. 1880.

Merrick, Walter, s. Walter, of St. John Baptist, Hereford (city), pleb. NEW INN HALL, matric. 19 March, 1718-9, aged 20.

Merrick, William, s. John, of Reading, Berks, doctor. TRINITY COLL., matric. 29 June, 1732, aged 15; B.A. from ST. JOHN'S COLL. 1737, brother of James 1736, and of John 1721. [10]

Merriken, William Good, 1s. William Smith, of Hull, Yorks, gent. NEW COLL., matric. 24 Jan., 1881, aged 33; B.Mus. 1883.

Merriman, Edward Baverstock, 1s. Thomas Baverstock, of St. Mary's, Marlborough, Wilts, gent. EXETER COLL., matric. 21 Nov., 1857, aged 17; B.A. 1861, M.A. 1864.

Merriman, Edwin, s. John, of Newbury, Berks, gent. MAGDALEN COLL., matric. 26 July, 1798, aged 18; demy 1798-1803, B.A. 1802, M.A. 1805, fellow 1803-7, master of the Grammar School, Lewes, 1807, and rector of All Saints, Lewes, 1807, until his death 11 Feb., 1821. See *Coll. Reg.*, vii. 140.

Merriman, George, 2s. William Clark, of St. Peter's, Marlborough, Wilts, arm. EXETER COLL., matric. 13 May, 1856, aged 18; B.A. 1859, M.A. 1863, held various curacies 1861-76, vicar of Markham, Norfolk, since 1876.

Merriman, Harry Moubray, o.s. Henry Gordon, of Bridgnorth, D.D. BRASENOSE COLL., matric. 19 Oct., 1875, aged 18; B.A. 1879, M.A. 1883. [15]

Merriman, Henry Gordon, 7s. Thomas, of Marlborough, Wilts, arm. BRASENOSE COLL., matric. 18 May, 1842, aged 18; fellow NEW COLL. 1843-52, B.A. 1846, M.A. 1850, B. & D.D. 1861, tutor 1848-50, assistant-master Winchester College 1847-9, head-master Bridgnorth School 1850-9, of Royal Grammar School, Guildford, 1859-74, rector of Michelmarsh, Hants, 1874-84, and of East Woodhay 1884, died 10 Aug., 1887.

Merriman, Nathaniel James, 3s. Thomas, of Marlborough, Wilts, arm. BRASENOSE COLL., matric. 7 Feb., 1828, aged 18; B.A. 1831, M.A. 1834, created D.D. 14 June, 1877, archdeacon of Grahamstown 1847-68, dean 1868-71, bishop 1871, until his death 17 Aug., 1882.

Merriman, William Henry Robert, o.s. William H., of Hammersmith, Middlesex, arm. BRASENOSE COLL., matric. 9 June, 1842, aged 19; B.A. 1846, M.A. 1850, perp. curate Ditton Marsh, Wilts, 1851-8, and of Greinton, Somerset, 1859-61, died in 1886.

Merrin, William, 1s. William, of Heanor, co. Derby, gent. NON-COLL., matric. 29 Oct., 1874, aged 45.

Merriott, Rev. John Hepburne, 1s. Edwin, of Farnham, Surrey, gent. MERTON COLL., matric. 24 June, 1859, aged 18; postmaster 1859-64, B.A. 1864, M.A. 1874, assistant-master Eton College 1874. See *Robinson*, 308. [20]

Merrivale, Thomas, s. Thomas, of Dorking, Surrey, pleb. TRINITY COLL., matric. 26 Jan., 1720-1, aged 17.

Merry, Charles, s. Robert, of London, arm. BALLIOL COLL., matric. 29 Nov., 1776, aged 17.

Merry, George Ross, 5s. John, of Kilmarnock, Scotland, arm. LINCOLN COLL., matric. 20 Jan., 1866, aged 24; scholar 1866-70, B.A. 1870, M.A. 1882.

Merry, John, 1s. John, of Cofton, co. Worcester, arm. QUEEN'S COLL., matric. 2 Nov., 1838, aged 18; B.A. 1842, M.A. 1845, rector of Hawridge, Bucks, at his death 23 Sep., 1852.

Merry, Robert, 2s. John, of Newbiggin, Westmoreland, cler. EXETER COLL., matric. 10 June, 1833, aged 17; fellow JESUS COLL., B.A. 1839, M.A. 1841, vicar of Guilden Morden 1844, until his death 31 May, 1867. [25]

Merry, Robert Charles Thomas, 1s. Robert, of Guilden Morden, Cambridge, cler. QUEEN'S COLL., matric. 17 Oct., 1864, aged 18.

Merry, Theodore Arthur, 3s. Robert, of Guilden Morden, co. Cambridge, cler. BRASENOSE COLL., matric. 22 Jan., 1880, aged 19.

Merry, Rev. Walter Mansell, 1s. William Walter, of Oxford, cler. EXETER COLL., matric. 31 Jan., 1882, aged 18; B.A. 1885, M.A. 1888.

Merry, Rev. William, 2s. John, of St. Sidwell's, Exeter, cler. WORCESTER COLL., matric. 19 Oct., 1837, aged 17; B.A. 1842, M.A. 1848, died 17 May, 1859.

Merry, William Joseph Collings, 2s. William Walter, of Oxford, cler. MAGDALEN COLL., matric. 6 May, 1886, aged 18. [30]

Merry, William Walter, o.s. Walter, of Evesham, co. Worcester, arm. BALLIOL COLL., matric. 30 Nov., 1852, aged 17, scholar 1852-7, B.A. 1857; fellow LINCOLN COLL. 1859-84, M.A. 1859, B. & D.D. 1886, tutor and librarian 1860, tutor 1870-3, classical lecturer 1873-85, bursar 1884, rector 1885, public orator 1880, vicar of All Saints', Oxford, 1862-84, classical moderator 1863-4, 1869-71, 1874, 1877, 1882-3, select preacher 1878-9, Whitehall preacher 1883-4; for list of his works see *Crockford*.

Merryweather, Harry Hill, o.s. Henry, of Sheffield, D.Med. NON-COLL., matric. 27 May, 1882, aged 19; B.A. from WADHAM COLL. 1886, M.A. 1888.

Merryweather, John Henry Watson, y.s. John, of East Retford, Notts, arm. TRINITY COLL., matric. 12 Oct., 1867, aged 19; scholar 1867-72, B.A. 1872, M.A. 1877.

Mertens, Frederick Mounteney Dirs, 3s. Herman William, of Hackney, London, gent. QUEEN'S COLL., matric. 30 June, 1848, aged 18; B.A. 1852, M.A. 1856, assistant-master Lancing College 1852-8, head master St. Saviour's School at Shoreham 1858-70, and at Ardingly 1870, fellow of St. Nicholas' College 1858. See *Robinson*, 267.

Mertens, Lionel George, 3s. Herman Dirs, of Lucerne, Switzerland, —. UNIVERSITY COLL., matric. 17 Oct., 1885, aged 19. [35]

Mertens, Rowland Deane, 5s. Herman Dirs, of Lucerne, Switzerland, arm. ST. JOHN'S COLL., matric. 16 Oct., 1886, aged 19.

Merveldt, Maximilian, Count, D.C.L. by diploma 16 June, 1814, ambassador extraordinary and minister plenipotentiary from Vienna at the Court of St. James's.

Mervin, Edward, s. John, of Sturminster Newton, Dorset, gent. BALLIOL COLL., matric. 21 Feb., 1727-8, aged 17; B.A. 21 Jan., 1731-2.

Mervin, John, s. Richard, of Marwood, Devon, arm. EXETER COLL., matric. 12 March, 1732-3, aged 18; B.A. 1736, M.A. 1739.

Meryon, Charles Lewis, s. Lewis, of Rye, Sussex, arm. ST. JOHN'S COLL., matric. 29 March, 1803, aged 19; B.A. 1806, M.A. 1809, B.Med. & D.Med. 1817, F.R.C.P. 1821, died 11 Sep., 1877. See Munk's *Roll*, iii. 234; & *Robinson*, 166.

Mesham, Arthur, o.s. Arthur Bennet, of Wootton, near Canterbury Kent, cler. EXETER COLL., matric. 22 May, 1856, aged 18; B.A. 1862, of Pontypridd, Flintshire, J.P., D.L., high sheriff 1881, sometime captain 1st royal dragoons, and lieut.-colonel Denbigh yeomanry.

Mesham, Arthur Bennet, s. Robert, of Bromham, Beds, cler. CORPUS CHRISTI COLL., matric. 15 June, 1818, aged 16; scholar 1818-25, B.A. 1822, fellow 1825-34, M.A. 1825, B.D. 1833, dean 1832, rector of Wotton, Kent, 1834, until his death 4 May, 1870.

Mesham, Robert, s. Thomas, of Hawarden, Flint, gent. JESUS COLL., matric. 4 April, 1789, aged 18; B.A. 1792, M.A. 1795, vicar of Bromham-cum-Oakley, Beds, 1815, rector of Ripple, Kent, 1823, until his death in 1827. [5]

Mesman, Charles, s. Daniel, of Enfield, Middlesex, gent. HERTFORD COLL., matric. 26 June, 1789, aged 23; B.A. 1793, rector of Duntsbourne Abbots, co. Gloucester, 1794, until his death 20 Sep., 1842.

Messenger, George, s. James, of Ham, Surrey, gent. MAGDALEN HALL, matric. 5 July, 1805, aged 23; perp. curate Barton St. David's, Somerset, 1831, until his death 13 May, 1841.

Messenger, John Farnham, o.s. John Alexander, of Farnham, Surrey, gent. ST. JOHN'S COLL., matric. 25 June, 1855, aged 19; scholar LINCOLN COLL. 1856-9, B.A. 1859, M.A. 1862, curate of Farley, Wilts, 1863-74, vicar 1874-83, warden of Farley Hospital 1864-83, vicar of Newton-in-Mottram, Lancashire, 1883.

Messer, Allan Ernest, 4s. John, of Reading, gent. ST. JOHN'S COLL., matric. 13 Oct., 1883, aged 18; scholar 1883, B.A. 1887.

Messervy, Alfred, 3s. George, of St. Helier's, Isle of Jersey, gent. EXETER COLL., matric. 14 Oct., 1865, aged 20; scholar 1864-70, B.A. 1870, M.A. 1881, master of modern languages at Haileybury. See *Coll. Reg.*, 161. [10]

Messiter, Rev. George Malim, 1s. George, of Frome, Somerset, gent. WADHAM COLL., matric. 9 Feb., 1836, aged 18; scholar 1835-46, B.A. 1841, M.A. 1843, 2nd master Repton School 1852, until his death 19 May, 1874. See *Rugby School Reg.*, 173.

Messiter, George Terry Moulton, o.s. George, of Wincanton, Somerset, arm. EXETER COLL., matric. 3 June, 1857, aged 18; B.A. 1860, M.A. 1864, vicar of Payhembury, Devon, 1864.

Messiter, John, s. Moulton, of Wincanton, Somerset, arm. MERTON COLL., matric. 30 May, 1781, aged 17; B.A. 1785, rector of Bratton, Somerset, 1789, of Caundle Marsh, Dorset, 1790, chaplain royal artillery, rector of Romans Leigh, Devon, 1813, J.P. Kent, garrison chaplain, Woolwich, died 15 Nov., 1828.

Messiter, Richard, s. John, of Wincanton, Somerset, cler. WADHAM COLL., matric. 22 Oct., 1817, aged 17; exhibitioner CORPUS CHRISTI COLL. 1818-21, B.A. 1821, M.A. 1827, perp. curate Caundle Stourton, Dorset, 1830-64, rector of Caundle Purse 1829, and of Bratton, St. Maur's, Dorset, 1829, until his death 15 May, 1885.

Meston, James Scorgie, 1s. James, of Oldmachar, Aberdeen, gent. BALLIOL COLL., matric. 16 Oct., 1883, aged 18; of the Indian Civil Service 1883. [15]

Mesurier, Alfred John le, 1s. Abraham John, of St. Mary de Castro, Isle of Guernsey, arm. ORIEL COLL., matric. 10 Feb., 1853, aged 18.

Mesurier, George Frederick le, 2s. Frederick Henry, of East Woodhay, Hants, gent. EXETER COLL., matric. 14 May, 1851, aged 18; B.A. 1855, M.A. 1858, curate of Welford, Berks, 1857-65, and of Todmorton, co. Gloucester, 1865-70, rector of Didmarton, co. Gloucester, 1870.

Mesurier, Havilland le, 1s. Edward Algernon, of Genoa, Italy, arm. BALLIOL COLL., matric. 17 Oct., 1884, aged 18; of the Indian Civil Service 1884.

Mesurier, Henry le, s. William, of Isle of Guernsey, gent. PEMBROKE COLL., matric. 6 May, 1797, aged 16; B.A. from BRASENOSE COLL. 1800.

Mesurier, Rev. Henry le, 2s. Thomas, of Newton Longville, Bucks, cler. NEW COLL., matric. 11 Feb., 1824, aged 18; fellow 1824-32, B.A. 1828, M.A. 1831, dean of arts 1831, 2nd master Bedford Grammar School, died 24 May, 1874. [20]

Mesurier, John le, o.s. John, of Isle of Alderney, arm. CHRIST CHURCH, matric. 19 Oct., 1837, aged 19; B.A. 1841, M.A. 1844, vicar of Bembridge, Isle of Wight, 1851, hon. canon Winchester 1878.

Messurier, John Henry le, 1s. John Henry, of Guernsey, arm. JESUS COLL., matric. 19 Oct., 1881, aged 18; scholar 1881-5, B.A. 1886.

Mesurier, John Thomas Howe le, s. Paul, of Hackney, Middlesex, arm. BRASENOSE COLL., matric. 6 July, 1805, aged 19; B.A. 1809, M.A. 1812, chaplain to the forces in Malta 34 years, archdeacon of Malta, died 29 Sep., 1864.

Mesurier, Richard Arthur le, 7s. Thomas, of Haughton-le-Skerne, co. Durham, cler. CHRIST CHURCH, matric. 26 May, 1841, aged 18; scholar CORPUS CHRISTI COLL. 1841-8, B.A. 1845, M.A. 1848, fellow 1848-51, a student of the Inner Temple 1848, died 7 May, 1853.

Mesurier, Thomas le, s. ——, of Isle of Guernsey, arm. NEW COLL., matric. 27 June, 1774; B.A. 1778, fellow, M.A. 1782, B.D. 1813, Bampton lecturer 1807 (? if bar.-at-law, Middle Temple, 1781), rector of Newton Longueville, Bucks, and of Haughton-le-Skerne, co. Durham, 1812, until his death 14 July, 1822, aged 65. [25]

Metcalfe, (Sir) Charles Herbert Theophilus (Bart.), o.s. Theophilus John, of Simla, East Indies, baronet. UNIVERSITY COLL., matric. 28 May, 1874, aged 20; B.A. & M.A. 1881, 6th baronet. See Foster's *Baronetage*.

Metcalfe, Frederick, scholar ST. JOHN'S COLL., Cambridge, 1834 (B.A. 1838), 5s. Morehouse, of Gainsborough, co. Lincoln, gent. JESUS COLL., incorp. 31 Oct. (or 28 Nov.), 1844, aged 29; fellow LINCOLN COLL. 1844-85, M.A. 1845, B.D. 1855, bursar 1849, sub-rector 1851, Greek lecturer 1853, vicar of St. Michael's, Oxford, 1849, until his death 24 Aug., 1885.

Metcalfe, George. CHRIST CHURCH, 1799. See MARWOOD, page 923.

Metcalfe, George Morehouse, 1s. Henry Bentley, of Lincoln (city), cler. WORCESTER COLL., matric. 10 June, 1856, aged 18; B.A. 1860, M.A. 1863, curate in charge of Peterchurch, co. Hereford, 1852-74, vicar of Pipe, co. Hereford, 1874-85.

Metcalfe, Henry Bentley, 1s. John, of Brigg, co. Lincoln, arm. LINCOLN COLL., matric. 24 Jan., 1824, aged 19; scholar 1825-8, B.A. 1827. [30]

Metcalfe, Henry Geldart, 3s. James, of Clapham, Surrey, arm. TRINITY COLL., matric. 6 March, 1845, aged 20; B.A. 1848, M.A. 1851.

Metcalfe, John, s. John, of Richmond, Yorks, gent. UNIVERSITY COLL., matric. 11 April, 1764, aged 15; B A. 1768, M.A. 1770.

Metcalfe, John, s. John, of Thornthwaite, Yorks, gent. LINCOLN COLL., matric. 22 Nov., 1765, aged 18, B.A. 1769, M.A. 1772; fellow MAGDALEN COLL., B.D. 1780, D.D. 1783, Whitehall preacher 1792, rector of Clipston, Northants, 1791, died vicar of Fynden, Sussex, 21 Feb., 1807, aged 62.

Metcalfe, Rev. John, s. John, of Cannock, co. Stafford, cler. BRASENOSE COLL., matric. 31 May, 1802, aged 17; B.A. 1806, died in 1808.

Metcalfe, John, o.s. John, of Burton-upon-Trent, co. Stafford, cler. BRASENOSE COLL., matric. 10 Oct., 1826, aged 18; B.A. from MAGDALEN HALL 1831; M.A. from BRASENOSE COLL. 1870.

Metcalf, John Church, s. James, of Datchet, Bucks, cler. BRASENOSE COLL., matric. 15 Dec., 1720, aged 19.

Metcalfe, Maurice, 15s. Charles, of Wisbeach, co. Cambridge, arm. MAGDALEN HALL, matric. 23 May, 1868, aged 21.

Metcalfe, Rev. Reginald, 4s. John Bell, of Sydney, Australia, gent. ST. EDMUND HALL, matric. 23 Oct., 1873, aged 19; B.A. 1877, M.A. 1880.

Metcalfe, Thomas, s. Thomas, of Eisgart (Aysgarth), Yorks, pleb. CHRIST CHURCH, matric. 5 June, 1739, aged 19; B.A. 15 Feb., 1742-3. **[5]**

Metcalfe, Thomas, s. Jer., of Tunstall, Yorks, pleb. QUEEN'S COLL., matric. 10 June, 1740, aged 19; B.A. from UNIVERSITY COLL. 1744.

Metcalfe, Thomas. ST. MARY HALL, 1804. See MARWOOD.

Metcalfe, William, s. James, of St. Andrew's, Holborn, London, gent. TRINITY COLL., matric. 20 Jan., 1721-2, aged 17; B.A. 1725, M.A. 1728, B.Med. 1731.

Metcalfe, William, s. William, of Barton, co. Lincoln, pleb. LINCOLN COLL., matric. 23 Nov., 1726, aged 18; B.A. 1730.

Metford, Rev. George Augustus Seymour, 2s. J. Seymour, of Clifton, co. Gloucester, arm. ST. MARY HALL, matric. 20 Oct., 1879, aged 19; B.A. 1884, M.A. 1887. **[10]**

Methold, Henry, s. Francis, of Bath, Somerset, arm. TRINITY COLL., matric. 26 Feb., 1780, aged 18; of Beamish Park, co. Durham, captain commanding Durham fencible cavalry 1798, died May, 1799. See Foster's *Baronetage*, EDEN.

Methold, Thomas, s. Thomas, of London, arm. TRINITY COLL., matric. 6 April, 1781, aged 16; B.C.L. 1787, rector of Stonham Aspal, Suffolk, 1789, and of Wetheringsett-cum-Brockford 1791, preb. of Norwich 1804, until his death 17 June, 1836.

Methuen, Rev. Henry Hoare, 2s. Thomas Anthony, of All Cannings, Wilts, cler. EXETER COLL., matric. 16 Feb., 1837, aged 18; B.A. 1840, M.A. 1869, died 6 Oct., 1883. See Foster's *Peerage*.

Methuen, James, 1s. James, of Leith, near Edinburgh, gent. BRASENOSE COLL., matric. 2 June, 1882, aged 20; B.A. 1886.

Methuen, Rev. John Andrew, s. Paul, of Corsham, Wilts, arm. CHRIST CHURCH, matric. 16 Oct., 1813, aged 19; B.A. 1817, M.A. 1826, died 19 June, 1869. See Foster's *Peerage*. **[15]**

Methuen, Paul, s. Thomas, of Bradford, Wilts, arm. ORIEL COLL., matric. 4 April, 1741, aged 17; created M.A. 23 Aug., 1744, of Corsham, Wilts, M.P. Westbury 1747-8, Warwick 1762-74, Bedwyn 1774-81, died 22 Jan., 1795.

Methuen, Paul, s. Henry, of Bradford, Wilts, arm. CORPUS CHRISTI COLL., matric. 6 Oct., 1759, aged 19; created M.A. 8 July, 1763, bar.-at-law, Lincoln's Inn, 1762 (described as son-in-law of John Taylor, of Bristol), died 26 Oct., 1792.

Methuen, Paul, s. Paul, of Corsham, Wilts, arm. CHRIST CHURCH, matric. 26 Jan., 1797, aged 17; M.P. Wilts 1812-19, North Wilts 1833-7, created Baron Methuen 13 July, 1838, died 14 Sep., 1849. See Foster's *Peerage* & *Eton School Lists*.

Methuen, Paul Cobb, s. Paul, of Corsham, Wilts, arm. UNIVERSITY COLL., matric. 7 Nov., 1769, aged 17; of Luckman and Corsham, Wilts, M.P. Bedwin March, 1781-4, died Sep., 1816. See Foster's *Peerage*.

Methuen, Paul Mildmay, 1s. Paul, of St. George's, Hanover Square, London, arm. CHRIST CHURCH, matric. 25 Oct., 1832, aged 18; died 15 July, 1837. See *Eton School Lists*. **[20]**

Methuen, Thomas Anthony, s. Paul Cobb, of St. Marylebone, arm. ORIEL COLL., matric. 26 Oct., 1799, aged 18; B.A. 1803, M.A. 1806, a student of Lincoln's Inn 1801, rector of All Cannings, Wilts, 1809, and of Garsdon 1814, until his death 15 June, 1869. See Foster's *Peerage* & *Eton School Lists*.

Methven, David, 1s. David, of Kirkcaldy, co. Fife, gent. NON-COLL., matric. 2 Nov., 1878, aged 23.

Metivier, Charles, o.s. Charles, of Clifton, near Bristol, arm. PEMBROKE COLL., matric. 15 May, 1856, aged 18; B.A. 1859, M.A. 1863, held various curacies 1861-79.

Mettam, George, s. Thomas, of Nottingham (town), gent. MERTON COLL., matric. 6 July, 1786, aged 18; B.A. 1790, M.A. 1793, rector (& patron) of Barwell, co. Leicester, 1803, and vicar of Arnesby, co. Lincoln, 1820, until his death 18 June, 1853.

Metternich, H.H. Clement Wenceslaus Lotharius, Prince of; created D.C.L. 15 June, 1814, and diplomated the following day, Austrian minister at the Court of Dresden 1801, ambassador at Berlin 1803-4, and at Paris 1804-9, minister of state to the Emperor of Austria, created a prince of the Austrian Empire on the field of Leipsic 9 Sep., 1813, died 11 June, 1859. **[25]**

Meugens, Allan George Munro, 4s. Peter Joseph, of Penge, Surrey, gent. QUEEN'S COLL., matric. 22 Oct., 1866, aged 19; B.A. 1869, M.A. 1873, held various curacies 1870-8, vicar of Burton Joyce, Notts, 1878-83, rector of Carlton-in-the-Willows, Notts, 1883.

Meux, (Sir) Henry (Bart.), 1s. Henry, of North Cray, Kent, baronet. CHRIST CHURCH, matric. 4 June, 1835, aged 17; B.A. 1838, 2nd baronet, M.P. Herts 1847-59, died 1 Jan., 1883. See Foster's *Baronetage* & *Eton School Lists*.

Meux, Thomas, s. Thomas, of Littleton, Middlesex, arm. ST. JOHN'S COLL., matric. 9 April, 1728, aged 17; B.C.L. 27 March, 1735, of Fritwell, Oxon, died unmarried at Woodstock, brother of the next named. See *Robinson*, 46.

Meux, William. LINCOLN COLL. 1721. See MASSINGBERD.

Mew, James, o.s. George, of St. Andrew's, Holborn, London, gent. WADHAM COLL., matric. 23 March, 1855, aged 18; B.A. 1860, bar.-at-law, Inner Temple, 1864, and miscellaneous writer. See Foster's *Men at the Bar* & *Robinson*, 292. **[30]**

Mew, Samuel, s. Thomas, of Tewkesbury, co. Gloucester, pleb. MAGDALEN HALL, matric. 8 Dec., 1774, aged 19; B.A. 1779, vicar of Yardley, co. Warwick, 1788, until his death in 1805.

Meyer, William, s. William, of Baildon, Yorks, arm. UNIVERSITY COLL., matric. 15 April, 1791, aged 18.

Meyler, Hugh Harries, 2s. Eleazar, of Ambleston, co. Pembroke, gent. JESUS COLL., matric. 16 Oct., 1884, aged 19; scholar 1884-6.

Meyler, John, s. Thomas, of Marlbro', Wilts, cler. JESUS COLL., matric. 5 March, 1776, aged 15; B.A. from QUEEN'S COLL., 1779, M.A. 1782, vicar of Little Bedwin, Wilts, 1796, rector of Maulden, Beds, at his death 17 June, 1806.

Meyler, Richard, s. Jeremiah, of Isle of Jamaica, arm. CHRIST CHURCH, matric. 28 Oct., 1784, aged 18; created M.A. 8 Dec., 1787, a student of Lincoln's Inn, 1786, father of the next named. **[35]**

Meyler, Richard, s. Richard, of Melbrooke, arm. CHRIST CHURCH, matric. 26 Jan., 1809, aged 17; M.P. Winchester 1812, until his death while hunting at Melton, 3 March, 1818. See *Eton School Lists*.

Meyler, Thomas, s. William, of St. David's, co. Pembroke, pleb. JESUS COLL., matric. 23 March, 1737-8, aged 20; B.A. 1741, rector of St. Peter's, Marlborough and vicar of Preshute at his death 19 July, 1786.

Meyler, Thomas, s. John, of Marlborough, Wilts, cler. PEMBROKE COLL., matric. 20 May, 1817, aged 18; scholar 1817-20, B.A. 1820, M.A. 1824, master of Royal Free School, Marlborough, and vicar of Baydon, Wilts, 1834, until his death 28 Nov., 1852.

Meyler, Thomas, 5s. John, of St. Dogwell, co. Pembroke, gent. PEMBROKE COLL., matric. 14 June, 1844, aged 21.

Meyler, William, 1s. John, of St. Dogwell, co. Pembroke, gent. PEMBROKE COLL., matric. 24 March, 1831, aged 19; B.A. 1836, rector of Rudbaxton, co. Pembroke, 1844, until his death, 23 Feb., 1857.

Meynell, Godfrey, 2s. Godfrey, of Langley, co. Derby, arm. BRASENOSE COLL., matric. 17 Oct., 1838, aged 19; B.A. 1842, M.A. 1845, bar.-at-law, Middle Temple, 1845, brother of the next named.

Meynell, Henry, y.s. Godfrey, of Langley, co. Derby, arm. BRASENOSE COLL., matric. 9 June, 1846, aged 18; B.A. 1850, M.A. 1853, curate of Kidlington, Oxon, 1851-7, perp. curate Fauls, Salop, 1857-66, curate in charge of Denstone, co. Stafford, 1866-81, vicar 1881-5, vice-provost and fellow of College of St. John and St. Mary, Lichfield, hon. canon of Cumbrae 1874. **[5]**

Meynell-Ingram, Hugh Francis, 1s. Hugh Charles, of St. George's, Hanover Square, arm. CHRIST CHURCH, matric. 15 May, 1839, aged 18; of Temple Newsam, Yorks, and of Hoar Cross, co. Stafford (his father assumed the additional surname of INGRAM by royal licence 25 Oct., 1841), M.P. West Stafford 1868, until his death 26 May, 1871. See Foster's *Yorkshire Collection*.

Meynell, John, 1s. Godfrey, of Tapton, co. Derby, arm. BRASENOSE COLL., matric. 14 Jan., 1826, aged 18; B.A. 1829, died 19 May, 1851.

Meyrick, Arthur, s. Edward, of Ramsbury, Wilts, cler. TRINITY COLL. matric. 29 March, 1803, aged 16; B.A. 1806, M.A. 1809, vicar of Urchfont, Wilts, 1811-38, died 31 Dec., 1855, had six sons who matriculated.

Meyrick, Arthur, 2s. Arthur, of Ramsbury, Wilts, cler. CORPUS CHRISTI COLL., matric. 4 Nov., 1831, aged 17; scholar 1831-4, brother of Edward 1830, of Edwin 1832, and of Frederick 1843, etc.

Meyrick, Rev. Arthur, o.s. Edwin, of Chisledon, Wilts, cler. QUEEN'S COLL., matric. 13 Nov., 1868, aged 18; B.A. 1871, M.A. 1875, of the Grange, Crawley Downs, Sussex. **[10]**

Meyrick, David, s. David, of Langan, co. Glamorgan, gent. JESUS COLL., matric. 24 Jan., 1771, aged 19; B.A. 1775, J.P. co. Leicester, rector of Lutterworth at his death 22 July, 1801.

Meyricke, Edmond, s. Edm., of Bettws, co. Merioneth, gent. JESUS COLL., matric. 14 Oct., 1721, aged 18; B.A. 1725, M.A. 1728, B.D. 1736.

Meyrick, Edmund, s. Owen, of Westminster, arm. BRASENOSE COLL., matric 19 May, 1774, aged 18; brother of Owen P. 1769.

Meyrick, Edward, s. Hugh, of Dolgelly, co. Merioneth, pleb. JESUS COLL., matric. 14 May, 1730, aged 19; B.A. from CHRIST CHURCH 13 March, 1733-4, brother of John 1736.

Meyricke, Edward, s. Lewis, of Dolgelley, co. Merioneth, pleb. JESUS COLL., matric. 31 March, 1762, aged 18; B.A. 1766. **[15]**

Meyrick, Rev. Edward, 1s. Arthur, of Ramsbury, Wilts, cler. TRINITY COLL., matric. 3 April, 1830, aged 17; demy MAGDALEN COLL. 1831-6, B.A. 1833, M.A. 1836, fellow 1836-54, vice-president 1848, died 13 Dec., 1883. See *Bloxam*, vii., 326.

Meyrick, Edward Graves, s. Edward, of Hungerford, Wilts, cler. QUEEN'S COLL., matric. 27 March, 1795, aged 14; B.A. from ST. MARY HALL 1799, M.A. 1801, B. & D.D. from QUEEN'S COLL. 1814, vicar of Ramsbury, Wilts, 1811, rector of Winchfield, Hants, 1820, until his death 29 March, 1839. See also a notice of death, 31 Jan., 1830, in *Gent.'s Mag.*, p. 570.

Meyrick, Edwin, 3s. Arthur, of Ramsbury, Wilts, cler. QUEEN'S COLL., matric. 6 Dec., 1832, aged 17; B.A. 1836, M.A. 1839, vicar of Chisledon 1847-66, rector of Allington, Wilts, 1876-84.

Meyrick, Edwin James, o.s. James Coward, of Chelsea, Middlesex, arm. CHRIST CHURCH, matric. 3 June, 1840, aged 17.

Meyrick, Frederick, 3s. Edward, of Ramsbury, Wilts, D.D. TRINITY COLL., matric. 12 June, 1843, aged 16; scholar 1843-7, B.A. 1847, fellow 1847-60, M.A. 1850, proctor 1857, rhetoric lecturer and philosophy lecturer 1850, dean and assistant-tutor 1853, junior bursar 1852, tutor 1856-9, public examiner in lit. hum. 1856, Whitehall preacher 1856, select preacher 1855-6, 1865-6, 1875-6, an inspector of schools 1859-69, rector of Blickling, Norfolk, since 1868, brother of James 1835; for list of his works see *Crockford*.

Meyrick, (Sir) George Eliott Meyrick Tapps Gervis (Bart.), 1s. George William Gervis, of Dover, Kent, baronet. CHRIST CHURCH, matric. 4 June, 1846, aged 18; 3rd baronet, assumed the additional surname of MEYRICK by royal licence 16 March, 1876. See Foster's *Baronetage*. **[21]**

Meyrick, Henry Duffield, 1s. Arnold Garbett, of Tottenham, Middlesex, gent. NON-COLL., matric. 16 Oct., 1868, aged 19, B.A. 1881; chaplain MAGDALEN COLL. 1884, M.A. 1884, head-master St. Thomas's Collegiate School, Colombo, 1874-5, tutor and lecturer St. Thomas's College 1876-80, curate of Wytham 1880-1, rector since 1881.

Meyrick, James, 1s. Edward Graves, of Ramsbury, Wilts, cler. QUEEN'S COLL., matric. 13 Aug., 1835, aged 17; Michel exhibitioner 1835-8, scholar 1838-41, B.A. 1839, fellow 1841-8, M.A. 1842, vicar of Westbury, Wilts, 1847-50, died 15 Oct., 1854, brother of Frederick 1843.

Meyrick, John, s. Hugh, of Dolgelly, co. Merioneth, pleb. ST. MARY HALL, 1 June, 1736, aged 19; brother of Edward 1730.

Meyricke, John, s. Essex, of St. Mar., co. Pembroke, arm. NEW COLL., matric. 11 Feb., 1754. **[25]**

Meyrick, John (Francis), s. John, of Pembroke (town), arm. CHRIST CHURCH, matric. 20 Oct., 1788, aged 18; of Busby, co. Pembroke, died in college 11 Aug., 1790.

Meyrick, John Williams, 1s. — Williams, gent. NEW INN HALL, matric. 22 Nov., 1866; rector of Llandegfan with Beaumaris 1866, assumed the additional surname of MEYRICK.

Meyrick, Llewelyn, s. Samuel, of Christ Church, Surrey, doctor (after a knight). QUEEN'S COLL., matric. 16 Jan., 1818, aged 13; B.C.L. 1824, of Peterborough House, Middlesex, F.S.A., equerry to Duke of Sussex, died 14 Feb., 1837. See *Eton School Lists*.

Meyrick, Rev. Llewellyn, 6s. Arthur, of Ramsbury, Wilts, cler. MAGDALEN COLL., matric. 26 July, 1848, aged 17; demy 1848-54, B.A. 1852, fellow 1854-87, M.A. 1855, died 17 Nov., 1887. See *Bloxam*, vii. 382.

Meyrick, Maurice, 4s. Arthur, of Ramsbury, Wilts, cler. QUEEN'S COLL., matric. 14 June, 1838, aged 18; M.A. Lambeth 4 Aug., 1834, professor Latin Queen's College, Harley Street, London, minister of Barking Road School Church, Plaistow, 1867-9, vicar of Baydon, Wilts, 1871-3, of North Leigh, Oxon, 1883-5, and of Northmoor, Oxon, 1885. **[30]**

Meyrick, Owen John Augustus Fuller, 1s. Augustus Eliott Fuller, of St. Marylebone, London, arm. BRASENOSE COLL., matric. 18 Oct., 1822, aged 18; of Bodorgan, Anglesey, assumed the additional surname and arms of MEYRICK by royal licence 6 May, 1825, and died 12 Feb., 1876. See Foster's *Baronetage*, DRAKE and MEYRICK.

Meyrick, Owen Putland, s. Owen, of London, arm. BRASENOSE COLL., matric. 30 Nov., 1769, aged 17; created M.A. 30 March, 1773, of Bodorgan, co. Anglesey, and of Norden House, Surrey, died 24 March, 1825.

eyrick, Philip, s. Edward, of Trefry, co. Anglesey, gent. ORIEL COLL., matric. 7 April, 1736, aged 16.

eyrick, Richard, s. Owen, of Llangadwalader, co. Anglesea, arm. JESUS COLL., matric. 11 July, 1730, aged 17.

eyrick, (Sir) Samuel Rush (K.H.), s. John, of St. Margaret's, Westminster, arm. QUEEN'S COLL., matric. 27 June, 1800, aged 16; B.A. 1804, M.A. 1810, B.C.L. 1810, D.C.L. 1811, of Goodrich Court, co. Hereford, high sheriff 1834, F.S.A. 1810, an advocate of Doctors' Commons, created a knight of the Guelphic Order 22 Feb., 1832, the celebrated antiquary and writer on arms and armour, died 2 April, 1848.

eyrick, Thomas, s. Owen Lewis, of Holsworthy, Devon, cler. EXETER COLL., matric. 10 Nov., 1792, aged 18; B.A. 1796, rector of Covenham St. Mary, co. Lincoln, 1810, until his death 27 May, 1841. See *Manchester School Reg.*, ii. 161.

eyrick, Thomas, 4s. Arthur, of Ramsbury, Wilts, cler. CORPUS CHRISTI COLL., matric. 27 Feb., 1835, aged 17; scholar 1833-45, B.A. 1838, M.A. 1841. [5]

eyrick, William, s. Thomas, of Llanvechell, co. Anglesea, gent. JESUS COLL., matric. 14 May, 1774, aged 19.

eysey, Francis, s. John, of Bayton, co. Worcester, arm. WADHAM COLL., matric. 21 May, 1726, aged 18; of Shakenhurst, co. Worcester, bar.-at-law, Inner Temple, 1734, died in 1756.

eysey, John, s. John, of Bayton, co. Worcester, arm. WADHAM COLL., matric. 30 June, 1727, aged 18; B.A. 1731, of Shakenhurst, rector of Rock, co. Worcester, at his death 6 May, 1764.

eysey, Robert, s. Joseph, of Oxford (city), gent. MERTON COLL., matric. 24 May, 1773, aged 16. See JOSEPH MAYSEY, page 938.

eysey, Thomas, s. John, of Bayton, co. Worcester, arm. WADHAM COLL., matric. 28 March, 1729, aged 16; B.A. 1732, M.A. 1735, vicar of Mamble, co. Worcester, 1745, rector of Perton, co. Worcester, died in 1762. [10]

ichael, John, 2s. David, of Aberystwith, co. Cardigan, gent. NON-COLL., matric. 14 Jan., 1869, aged 23; B.A. from JESUS COLL. 1872, has held various curacies since 1872.

ichael, Walter Henry, 1s. Walter Amos, of London, gent. BALLIOL COLL., matric. 24 Oct., 1885, aged 19; of the Indian Civil Service 1885.

ichaelson, Thomas, s. Thomas, of Reading, Berks, arm. EXETER COLL., matric. 18 Nov., 1783, aged 18; B.A. 1787.

ichel, Christopher, s. David Robert, of Dewlish, Dorset, arm. ORIEL COLL., matric. 24 Feb., 1790, aged 18; in the army.

ichel, David Robert, s. John, of Kingston Russell, Dorset, arm. BRASENOSE COLL., matric. 27 June, 1753, aged 17; created M.A. 26 April, 1757, of Kingston Russell, M.P. Lyme Regis 1780-4, died in March, 1805. [15]

ichel, Henry Edward, born at Belfast, 3s. John, arm. NEW COLL., matric. 27 March, 1833, aged 18; B.A. 1837, grandson of the last named.

ichell, Arthur Tompson, 5s. Richard, of St. Giles's, Oxford, D.D. ORIEL COLL., matric. 7 Feb., 1871, aged 18; B.A. 1874, M.A. 1877, rector of Brampton, Norfolk, since 1885. See *Rugby School Reg.*

ichell, Charles Henry, 1s. Charles Henry Sampson, of Bruton, Somerset, arm. WORCESTER COLL., matric. 18 Jan., 1869, aged 23; NON-COLL. B.A. 1872.

ichell, Charles Nosworthy, s. Edward, of Bruton, Somerset, cler. ORIEL COLL., matric. 14 June, 1786, aged 16; B.A. 1791, M.A. 1797, rector of Witham Friary, Somerset, 1799, and of Llangattock-vibou-Avel, co. Monmouth, 1818, and of St. Maughans, near Monmouth, died s.p. 18 April, 1840.

Michell, Christopher, s. Christopher, of Ashwater, Devon, cler. EXETER COLL., matric. 21 March, 1737-8, aged 18; B.A. 1741, brother of Gilbert.

Michell, Edward, s. John, of Diptford, Devon, gent. EXETER COLL., matric. 7 March, 1755, aged 18; fellow 1758-63, B.A. 1762, master of Kingsbridge School, then of Bruton School, died rector of Witham Friary, Somerset, 1799. See *Coll. Reg.*, 106. [21]

Michell, Edward Blair, 1s. Richard, of St. Giles's, Oxford (city), cler. MAGDALEN COLL., matric. 19 Jan., 1861, aged 18, demy 1860-5, B.A. 1865, M.A. 1868; law lecturer HERTFORD COLL. 1874-7, bar.-at-law, Middle Temple, 1869, legal adviser to the King of Siam, Dec., 1885. See Foster's *Men at the Bar.*

Michell, Rev. Edward (Marshall), s. Edward, of Kingsbridge, Devon, cler. EXETER COLL., matric. 16 Dec., 1782, aged 18; B.A. 1786, of Bruton, Somerset, died in 1810. See *St. Paul's School Reg.*, 164.

Michell, Gilbert, s. Christopher, of Ashwater, Devon, cler. EXETER COLL., matric 17 March, 1739-40, aged 18; B.A. 1743.

Michell, Henry, s. Henry, of Richmond, Surrey, gent. CORPUS CHRISTI COLL., matric. 30 Nov., 1741, aged 15; B.A. 20 Feb., 1745-6. [25]

Michell, Henry Chicheley, 1s. Eardley Wilmot Lade, of Hurstmonceaux, Sussex, arm. QUEEN'S COLL., matric. 13 June, 1822, aged 18; B.A. from QUEEN'S COLL., Cambridge, 1828, M.A. 1832, perp. curate Baddesley, and curate of Lymington, Hants, died 12 Sept., 1851.

Michell, Herny Pye, 7s. James, of St. Neot, Cornwall, gent. MAGDALEN HALL, matric. 20 March, 1851, aged 29.

Michell, Henry William Robinson. TRINITY COLL., 1819. See JOHNSON, page 756.

Michell, Herbert William Cresswell, 4s. Richard, of Oxford, D.D. MAGDALEN HALL, matric. 8 June, 1868, aged 17, B.A. 1871, M.A. (HERTFORD COLL.) 1876.

Michell, Rev. James Charles, 1s. William, of Brighton cler. NEW COLL., matric. 13 Oct., 1876, aged 19; B.A. 1880. [30]

Michell, James Edward, 4s. Slyman, of Truro, Cornwall, arm. CORPUS CHRISTI COLL., matric. 19 Oct., 1882, aged 18; B.A. 1885.

Michell, John, s. John, of Huish, Somerset, gent. EXETER COLL., matric. 21 Feb., 1769, aged 18; B.C.L. 1797, D.C.L. 1814, preb. of Gloucester 1798, vicar of Fairford 1810, until his death 15 Sep., 1828.

Michell, John, s. John Taylor, of Isle of Wight, gent. MAGDALEN HALL, matric. 1 June, 1818, aged 19; B.A. 1823.

Michell, John, s. John, of St. Peter's Port, Isle of Guernsey, arm. PEMBROKE COLL., matric. 29 June, 1824, aged 17.

Michell, John, 2s. John, of Bruton, Somerset, gent. MAGDALEN HALL, matric. 30 May, 1828, aged 27. [35]

Michell, Octavius, s. Robert, of Taunton, Somerset, gent. EXETER COLL., matric. 21 June, 1803, aged 18; B.A. 1809, M.A. 1810.

Michell, Percy Turner, 2s. Samuel Vincent Pryce, of Helston, Cornwall, gent. QUEEN'S COLL., matric. 30 Oct., 1885, aged 18.

Michell, Richard, s. Simon, of St. Andrew's, London, arm. CHRIST CHURCH, matric. 27 April, 1720, aged 16.

Michell, Richard, s. John, of Totness, Devon, gent. WADHAM COLL., matric. 5 May, 1784, aged 18; B.A. 1788, M.A. 1793, B.D. 1804, D.D. 1811, fellow 1793-1812, proctor 1803, rector of Fryerning, and vicar of Eastwood, Essex, 1811, until his death 1 Jan., 1826. See *St. Paul's School Reg.*, 170.

Michell, Richard, 3s. Edward, of Bruton, Somerset, arm. WADHAM COLL., matric. 8 Dec., 1820, aged 15, B.A. 1824, M.A. 1827; fellow LINCOLN COLL. 1830-42, B.D. 1836, bursar 1832, tutor 1834-48, claviger 1835, public orator 1848-77, public examiner 1829-30, 1833-7, etc., prælector of logic 1839-49, Bampton lecturer 1849, rector of South Moreton, Berks, 1856, vice-principal MAGDALEN HALL 1848-68, D.D. 1868, principal 1868-74, 1st principal of HERTFORD COLL. 1874, until his death 29 March, 1877.

Michell, Richard Brooke, 2s. Richard, of Oxford, B.D. BALLIOL COLL., matric. 9 March, 1865, aged 19; B.A. & M.A. 1871, bar.-at-law, Lincoln's Inn, 1872, professor of law, Presidency College, Madras. See Foster's *Men at the Bar.*

Michell, Robert, s. William, of Maker, Cornwall, pleb. EXETER COLL., matric. 17 May, 1723, aged 17; B.A. 1726, fellow 1728, M.A. 1729, died 22 Dec., 1730. See *Coll. Reg.*, 93.

Michell, Robert Cary, s. Cary, of Virginia, America, gent. QUEEN'S COLL., matric. 7 June, 1788, aged 22; B.A. from ST. EDMUND HALL 1793, M.A. 1796, bar.-at-law, Lincoln's Inn, 1797.

Michell, Robert Frederick, s. Robert, of Chiltern, Wilts, arm. WADHAM COLL., matric. 12 May, 1795, aged 17.

Michell, Roland Lyons Nosworthy, 3s. Richard, of Oxford, B.D. CHRIST CHURCH, matric. 13 Oct., 1865, aged 18; a junior student 1865-70, B.A. 1870, H.M. commissioner in Cyprus 1879. **[5]**

Michell, Rowland Daniel, 5s. Edward, of Bruton, Somerset, gent. WADHAM COLL., matric. 1 July, 1833, aged 16; B.A. 1837, M.A. 1840, died 18 April, 1843, brother of Richard 1820.

Michell, Thomas, s. Ralph, of St. Mewer, Cornwall, cler. EXETER COLL., matric. 17 May, 1723, aged 18; B.A. 1727.

Michell, Thomas, s. Christopher, of Chittern, Wilts, gent. MERTON COLL., matric. 21 March, 1729-30, aged 18; B.C.L. 1736.

Michell, Thomas, s. Thomas, of Langfort, Somerset, gent. EXETER COLL., matric. 1 Dec., 1749, aged 18; B.A. 1753. **[10]**

Michell, Thomas, s. Thomas, of Michelmersh, Hants, cler. MERTON COLL., matric. 14 July, 1773, 17.

Michell, Thomas Hungerford, 1s. Thomas Penruddock, of Histon, co. Cambridge, cler. ORIEL COLL., matric. 30 May, 1846, aged 18; B.A. 1850, M.A. 1853, curate of Histon 1852-6, vicar 1856-65.

Michell, Thomas Penruddocke, s. Thomas, of Doler, Hants, arm. MERTON COLL., matric. 3 July, 1815, aged 18; postmaster 1816-19, B.A. 1819, M.A. 1823, of Stondus Hussey, Wilts, vicar of Histon, co. Cambridge, 1821-56, died 24 June, 1866. See *Eton School Lists.*

Michell, Walter Cecil, 2s. William Marwick, of London, arm. MERTON COLL., matric. 19 Oct., 1883, aged 19; B.A. 1887.

Michell, William, s. John, of Huish, Somerset, cler. EXETER COLL., matric. 15 June, 1801, aged 18; B.A. 1806, son of John 1769. **[15]**

Michell, William, 2s. James Charles, of Brighton, Sussex, arm. NEW COLL., matric. 25 May, 1848, aged 17; B.A. 1852, M.A. 1856, minister of All Saints', Guernsey, 1860-4, perp. curate Chantry, Somerset, 1864-72, preb. of Wells, and rector of Dinder, Somerset, since 1883; for list of his works see *Crockford.*

Michell, William Edwards, o.s. William, of Truro, Cornwall, arm. CHRIST CHURCH, matric. 18 Jan., 1861, aged 20; of Newquay, Cornwall, J.P., F.R.A.S., a special deputy warden of the Stannaries.

Michell, William Focord, s. Reynell, of Totness, Devon, arm. ORIEL COLL., matric. 16 Oct., 1783, aged 17: B.A. 1787, M.A. 1790, B. & D.D. 1810, chaplain to Lord Craven, rector of Throwleigh, Devon, dispensation to hold rectory of Lidford, Devon, 1793.

Michell, William Sloane, 1s. William Philip, of St. Tudy, Cornwall, cler. NON-COLL., matric. 9 Feb., 1878, aged 18.

Michell, William Walton, 1s. William Marwick, of London, arm. MERTON COLL., matric. 19 Oct., 1883, aged 20. **[20]**

Michelmore, Philip, 1s. Philip, of Painsford, Devon, arm. TRINITY COLL., matric. 17 Oct., 1885, aged 18.

Micholls, Edward Montefiore, 1s. Horace, of Manchester, gent. NEW COLL., matric. 14 Oct., 1871, aged 19; B.A. 1875, M.A. 1880, bar.-at-law, Inner Temple, 1877. See Foster's *Men at the Bar* & *Rugby School Reg.*

Micholls, Sydney Philip, 2s. Henry, of Manchester, gent. NEW COLL., matric. 16 Oct., 1868, aged 19; B.A. 1871, bar.-at-law, Inner Temple, 1875. See Foster's *Men at the Bar*, & *Rugby School Reg.*

Micklem, Henry, 2s. Nathaniel, of Henley, Oxon, arm. TRINITY COLL., matric. 11 July, 1846, aged 18.

Micklem, Leonard, 3s. Nathaniel, of Henley-on-Thames, Oxon, arm. MERTON COLL., matric. 14 Oct., 1865, aged 19; B.A. 1869, secretary to Bahia and San Francisco Railway. See *Eton School Lists.* **[25]**

Micklem, Nathaniel, s. Thomas, of Bisham, Berks, arm. WORCESTER COLL., matric. 4 April, 1810, aged 21.

Micklem, Nathaniel, 2s. Thomas, of Cookham, Berks, arm. NEW COLL., matric. 16 Oct., 1874, aged 20; B.A. 1877, B.C.L. & M.A. 1881, bar.-at-law, Lincoln's Inn, 1871. See Foster's *Men at the Bar.*

Middlemist, Francis John, 2s. John, of Uttoxeter, co. Stafford, gent. KEBLE COLL., matric. 18 Oct., 1870, aged 21; B.A. 1873, M.A. 1877, held various curacies since 1876.

Middlemist, Robert Walter, 3s. John, of Uttoxeter, co. Stafford, gent. NON-COLL., matric. 14 Oct., 1876, aged 21; B.A. 1884.

Middlemore, Samuel George Chetwynd, 2s. William, of Edgbaston, co. Warwick, arm. MERTON COLL., matric. 13 Oct., 1866, aged 17. **[30]**

Middleton, Alfred, 2s. Henry, of Wanborough, Wilts, cler. QUEEN'S COLL., matric. 16 Nov., 1849, aged 17; B.A. 1854, M.A. 1856, perp. curate Ponsonby 1857-60, head-master Kingsbridge Grammar School 1860-76, rector of Binton, co. Warwick, 1879.

Middleton, Arthur, 'tonsor;' privilegiatus 16 Nov., 1719.

Middleton, Bartholomew, s. Thomas, of Bampton, Oxon, cler. MAGDALEN COLL., matric. 15 Oct., 1779, aged 17; chorister 1774-9, clerk 1779-86, B.A. 1783, M.A. 1787, minor canon and sub-dean Chichester 1786, vicar of St. Peter the Great, Chichester, 1792, rector of Singleton, Surrey, and vicar of West Dean, Sussex, 1786, died 11 June, 1831. See *Bloxam*, i. 192.

Middleton, Conyers, of TRINITY COLL., Cambridge (B.A. 1702, M.A. 1706, D.D. 1717); incorp. 4 June, 1730, chief librarian 1721, Woodward professor of geology, Cambridge, 1731, died at Hildersham, co. Cambridge, 28 July, 1750, aged 66.

Middleton, David, s. Charles, of Carmarthen (town), gent. MAGDALEN HALL, matric. 9 July, 1778, aged 25; B.A. & M.A. 1794, rector of Crux Easton, Hants, 1823, until his death in 1827. **[35]**

Middleton, Erasmus, s. Erasmus, of Horncastle, co. Lincoln, pleb. ST. EDMUND HALL, matric. 4 June, 1767, aged 28; 'one of the six young men expelled the University,' a Methodist clergyman, rector of Turvey, Beds, 1804, until his death 25 April, 1805, editor of 'Biographia Evangelica.' See *Gent.'s Mag.*

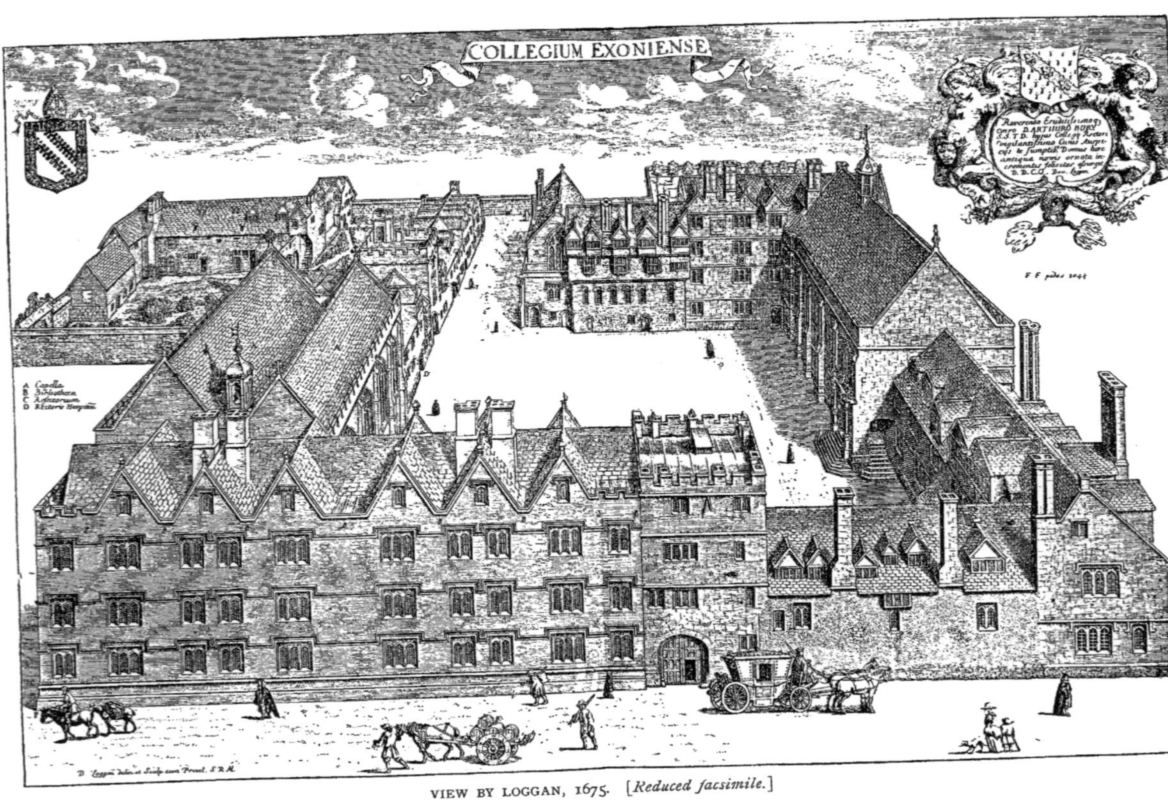

VIEW BY LOGGAN, 1675. [*Reduced facsimile.*]

Middleton, Frederick Graeme, 2s. John Charles, of Twyford, Hants, gent. PEMBROKE COLL., matric. 22 March, 1820, aged 17; demy MAGDALEN COLL. 1821-30, B.A. 1824, M.A. 1827, perp. curate of Bembridge, Isle of Wight, 1836, rector of Medsted, Hants, 1851, died 1 June, 1863. See *Bloxam*, vii. 283; & *Rugby School Reg.*, 127.

Middleton, Frederick Matthews, 1s. Frederick Graeme, of Hawkhurst, Kent, cler. UNIVERSITY COLL., matric. 15 May, 1850, aged 19; B.A. 1854, M.A. 1864, held various curacies 1855-68, vicar of Yorktown, Surrey, 1868, and chaplain of Farnborough Staff College 1880. See *Rugby School Reg.*, 283.

Middleton, Frederick Sholto, 1s. Sholto, of Tiverton, Devon, cler. BRASENOSE COLL., matric. 21 May, 1880.

Middleton, Frederick Thomas, 1s. Frederick Dobson, of Wallasey, Cheshire, arm. ORIEL COLL., matric. 1 June, 1882, aged 18.

Middleton, Hastings Burton, 1s. Hastings Nathaniel, of Brockham, Surrey, arm. MAGDALEN COLL., matric. 29 Oct., 1857, aged 18; demy 1857-62, B.A. 1863, M.A. 1868, of Bradford Peverell, Dorset, a student of the Middle Temple 1864, J.P. Dorset 1867, hon. secretary Salisbury Diocesan Synod 1880. See *Bloxam*, vii. 413. **[5]**

Middleton, Hastings Nathaniel, 1s. Hastings Nathaniel, of St. James's, Westminster, arm. MERTON COLL., matric. 4 April, 1827, aged 17; of Bradford Peverell, Dorset, J.P., D.L., high sheriff 1857, bar.-at-law, Inner Temple, 1834. See Foster's *Men at the Bar.*

Middleton, Henry, s. Bartholomew, of Chichester, Sussex, cler. ORIEL COLL., matric. 16 Jan., 1812, aged 17; demy MAGDALEN COLL. 1815-22, B.A. 1817, M.A. 1818, curate of Wanborough, Wilts, 1830-40. See *Bloxam*, vii. 260.

Middleton, Henry, 1s. Edward, of Southampton, Hants, D.Med. WADHAM COLL., matric. 29 March, 1832, aged 17; B.A. 1836.

Middleton, Henry Abdy, 1s. Henry, of Bishopstone, Wilts, cler. BRASENOSE COLL., matric. 24 June, 1843, aged 18; scholar 1844-8, B.A. 1847, M.A. 1856, chaplain H.M.S. *Crocodile* at his death at Malta 11 Dec., 1867.

Middleton, Henry Ochterlony, 1s. Henry Johnson, of Cawnpore, East Indies, arm. EXETER COLL., matric. 30 May, 1839, aged 19; B.A. from ST. MARY HALL 1844, M.A. 1846, perp. curate Denton, Yorks, 1862-6. **[10]**

Middleton, James William, o.s. James, of Agra, East Indies, gent. QUEEN'S COLL., matric. 30 May, 1868, aged 18; B.A. 1872, bar.-at-law, Lincoln's Inn, 1876. See Foster's *Men at the Bar* & *Eton School Lists.*

Middleton, Job, 'pistor;' privilegiatus 13 April, 1832.

Middleton, John, s. John, of Stoke, co. Stafford, gent. MAGDALEN HALL, matric. 10 Oct., 1732, aged 18; B.A. 1736, father of John 1766, and of Joshua H. 1763, and Thomas 1763.

Middleton, John, '2nd cook of Magdalen College;' privilegiatus 26 Jan., 1762.

Middleton, John, s. John, of Henley, co. Stafford, cler. WORCESTER COLL., matric. 10 April, 1766, aged 17; B.A. 1771, brother of Joshua H. 1763. **[15]**

Middleton, John Douglas, 1s. Stephen, of Lymington, Hants, cler. CORPUS CHRISTI COLL., matric. 14 Feb., 1851, aged 17; scholar 1851-6, B.A. 1855, M.A. 1858, perp. curate Selsley, co. Gloucester, 1862-4, vicar of Holy Trinity, West Cowes, 1867-84.

Middleton, John Henry, 1s. John, of York (city), arm. EXETER COLL., matric. 8 June, 1865, aged 18; Slade professor Fine Art, Cambridge, 1886, fellow KING'S COLL., Cambridge, 1888.

Middleton, John White, s. John, of Marylebone, Middlesex, gent. TRINITY COLL., matric. 20 June, 1794, aged 18; B.A. 1798, M.A. 1801 (as MIDDELTON).

Middleton, Joseph William Didcon, o.s. James, of Haigh Park, near Rothwell, Yorks, arm. LINCOLN COLL., matric. 22 May, 1861, aged 18.

Middleton, Joshua Heath, s. John, of Shelton, co. Stafford, cler. WORCESTER COLL., matric. 19 May, 1763, aged 16; brother of John, 1766. **[20]**

Middleton, Leonard, s. Thomas, of Hampstead, Middlesex, gent. TRINITY COLL., matric. 9 Nov., 1793, aged 18; B.A. 1797, M.A. 1801, rector of Great and Little Comberton 1819.

Middleton, Nathaniel, s. Nathaniel, of Stepney, Middlesex, arm. MERTON COLL., matric. 27 Oct., 1800, aged 19; probably father of Hastings N.

Middleton, Richard, s. Ric., of London, gent. QUEEN'S COLL., matric. 24 July, 1740, aged 18; B.A. 1744, M.A. 1747.

Middleton, Robert Marshall, 1s. George, of Highcross, Herts, arm. CORPUS CHRISTI COLL, matric. 25 Oct., 1876, aged 19; B.A. 1880, M.A. 1884, bar.-at-law, Inner Temple, 1883. See Foster's *Men at the Bar.*

Middleton, Samuel, s. Walter, of Hanchurch, co. Stafford, pleb. MAGDALEN HALL, matric. 10 Oct., 1723, aged 20; B.A. 1727. **[25]**

Middleton, Rev. Sholto, 3s. Henry, of Wanborough, Wilts, cler. BALLIOL COLL., matric. 29 June, 1853, aged 18; Blundell scholar 1853-9, B.A. 1857, M.A. 1860, head-master King's School, Bruton, 1864-9, etc.

Middleton, Rev. Stephen, s. John Douglas, of Frome, Somerset, gent. ST. ALBAN HALL, matric. 10 April, 1813, aged 27; B.D. from QUEEN'S COLL., Cambridge, 1826, died at Clifton 4 Oct., 1843.

Middleton, Thomas, s. Arthur, of All Saints, Oxford, pleb. QUEEN'S COLL., matric. 25 May, 1721, aged 16; B.A. 3 Feb., 1724-5.

Middleton, Thomas, s. Thomas, of 'Stendrape' (Staindrop), bishopric of Durham, gent. LINCOLN COLL., matric. 14 Oct., 1721, aged 18.

Middleton, Thomas, s. 'Mart.,' of Bradwell, co. Derby, pleb. UNIVERSITY COLL., matric. 23 May, 1750, aged 18; B.A. from LINCOLN COLL. 1754.

Middleton, Thomas, s. John, of London, doctor. TRINITY COLL., matric. 16 July, 1756, aged 17. **[31]**

Middleton, Thomas, s. John, of Shelton, co. Stafford, cler. WORCESTER COLL., matric. 19 May, 1763, aged 18 (? incumbent of Endon, near Leek, at his death in 1815).

Middleton, Thomas, 1s. Abraham, of Bethnal Green, London, gent. ST. EDMUND HALL, matric. 16 Oct., 1821, aged 18; B.A. 1825, M.A. 1828.

Middleton, Thomas Sholto, 2s. Bartholomew, of Chichester, Sussex, cler. BRASENOSE COLL., matric. 23 Jan., 1824, aged 18.

Middleton, William Frederick, 1s. John, of Glassart, co. Perth, arm. MAGDALEN COLL., matric. 14 Oct., 1871, aged 18; B.A. 1874. See *Eton School Lists.* **[35]**

Middleton, William Shortgrove, s. Tobias, of Clifton, co. Gloucester, arm. ST. MARY HALL, matric. 28 June, 1775, aged 22.

Midford, Gawen Aynsley, s. George, of Morpeth, Northumberland, arm. (surgeon). UNIVERSITY COLL., matric. 8 July, 1786, aged 19; a student of Lincoln's Inn 1786.

Midgley, Edward James, 2s. Jonathan, of Newcastle-upon-Tyne, arm. UNIVERSITY COLL., matric. 22 March, 1822, aged 18; B.A. 1827.

Midgley, William Holt, o.s. John, of Rochdale, Lancashire, arm. BRASENOSE COLL., matric. 22 May, 1845, aged 18. See *Eton School Lists*, 1910. **[39]**

Midwinter, Edward Adair, 2s. Nathaniel, of Winchester, Hants, cler. BRASENOSE COLL., matric. 14 Oct., 1865, aged 19; B.A. 1868, M.A. 1872, vicar of St. Paul's, Lisson Grove, London, 1880.

Midwinter, Henry Nathaniel, 3s. Nathaniel, of Winchester, Hants, cler. WORCESTER COLL., matric. 16 Oct., 1866, aged 18; exhibitioner 1866-70, B.A. 1872, M.A. 1873, chaplain (Bombay establishment) at Baroda 1878-83, Fort Belgaum since 1883.

Midwinter, John, 'pullarius' Oxford (city); privilegiatus 16 Oct., 1761, aged 25.

Midwinter, Nathaniel, 2s. William, of East Indies, arm. MAGDALEN HALL, matric. 24 May, 1838, aged 22; B.A. 1842, M.A. 1844, rector of St. Michael's, Winchester, 1844-74, vicar of Bleasby, Notts, 1874, until his death 7 Feb., 1888.

Midwinter, Stephen, s. William, of Essington, co. Gloucester, pleb. CHRIST CHURCH, matric. 2 Dec., 1726, aged 18.

Midwinter, William Colpoys, 1s. Nathaniel, of Fareham, Hants, cler. WADHAM COLL., matric. 18 June, 1862, aged 17; a student of the Inner Temple 1878. [5]

Miers, Henry Alexander, 3s. Francis Charles, of Rio Janeiro, Brazil, arm. TRINITY COLL., matric. 12 Oct., 1877, aged 19; scholar 1877-82, B.A. 1881, M.A. 1884, of the Natural History Department, South Kensington. See *Eton School Lists.*

Miers, John Nathaniel, s. Nathaniel, of Neath, co. Glamorgan, arm. MAGDALEN COLL., matric. 29 Nov., 1791, aged 18; of Ynyspenllwch, co. Glamorgan, etc., high sheriff 1808, died in 1814.

Miers, Reginald Hanbury, 1s. Richard Hanbury, of Little Dean, co. Gloucester, arm. BALLIOL COLL., matric. 17 Oct., 1882, aged 18.

Mieville, Louis, 2s John Louis, of London, gent. EXETER COLL., matric. 23 Oct., 1885, aged 18.

Miland, John, 'blacksmith and wheel-tire maker;' privilegiatus 7 March, 1747-8. [10]

Miland, John, 'blacksmith;' privilegiatus 21 Nov., 1758.

Milbank, Mark, s. Acclome, of Barningham, Yorks, gent. LINCOLN COLL., matric. 15 June, 1715, aged 16; died 26 April, 1758. See Foster's *Yorkshire Collection.*

Milbank, Mark, s. William, of Thorpe, near Bedale, Yorks, arm. ORIEL COLL., matric. 6 Nov., 1813, aged 18; of Thorpe Perrow and Barningham Park, Yorks, high sheriff 1832, M.P. Camelford, 1818-19, 1820-32, died 21 Oct., 1881. See Foster's *Baronetage.*

Milbanke, (Sir) Peniston (Bart.), born at Munich, Bavaria, 1s. John Ralph, baronet. CHRIST CHURCH, matric. 7 June, 1865, aged 18; 9th baronet. See Foster's *Baronetage.*

Milborne, Charles, s. George, of Red Lyon Square, Middlesex, arm. NEW COLL., matric. 29 Nov., 1754, aged 18. [15]

Milborne, George, s. Charles, of Hackney, Middlesex, arm. NEW COLL., matric. 22 June, 1716, aged 17; bar.-at-law, Middle Temple, 1724 (his father of Wonaston, co. Monmouth), father of the last named.

Milbourne, Samuel Lambert, s. Samuel, of Blandford, Dorset, gent. ORIEL COLL., matric. 16 May, 1743, aged 19; B.A. from MERTON COLL. 1747.

Mildert, William Van, s. Cornelius, of St. Mary Newington, Surrey, gent. QUEEN'S COLL., matric. 21 Feb., 1784, aged 18; B.A. 1787, M.A. 1790, B. & D.D. 1813, Boyle lecturer 1804, Bampton lecturer 1813, regius professor of divinity and canon of Christ Church 1813-20, rector of Bradden, Northants, 1795-6, of St. Mary-le-Bow, London, 1796, vicar of Farningham, Kent, 1807, preacher of Lincoln's Inn 1812, bishop of Llandaff 1819-26, and dean of St. Paul's 1820, bishop of Durham 1826, until his death 21 Feb., 1836, founder of the University of Durham. See *Robinson*, 146.

Mildmay, Aubrey Nevile St. John, 6s. Charles Arundell, of Long Marston, Yorks, cler. NEW COLL., matric. 10 Oct., 1884, aged 19; scholar 1883. See Foster's *Baronetage.*

Mildmay, Arundell Charles St. John, 3s. Paulet St. John, of Dogmersfield, Hants, arm. MERTON COLL., matric. 1 June, 1839, aged 18; B.A. 1843, fellow 1844-9, M.A. 1846, bursar & dean 1846, rector of Lapworth, co. Warwick, 1848-64, of Long Marston, Yorks, 1864-73, of Alvechurch, co. Worcester, 1873-9, and of Denton, Norfolk, 1879-83. See Foster's *Baronetage* & *Rugby School Reg.*, 184. [20]

Mildmay, Carew Anthony St. John, s. Henry, of Winchester, Hants, baronet. ORIEL COLL., matric. 3 June, 1818, aged 18; B.A. 1822, M.A. 1825, a student of the Inner Temple 1822, vicar of Burnham, Essex, 1827-58, rector of Chelmsford 1826, sinecure rector of Shorwell, Isle of Wight, archdeacon of Essex 1861, died 13 July, 1878. See Foster's *Baronetage* & *Eton School Lists.*

Mildmay, Charles William St. John, s. Henry Paulet St. John, of Dogmersfield, Hants, baronet. BRASENOSE COLL., matric. 2 May, 1812, aged 18; B.A. 1815; fellow MERTON COLL. 1816-30, M.A. 1821, perp. curate Holywell, Oxford, 1823, rector of Shorwell and Mottistone, Isle of Wight, at his death 16 Jan., 1830. See Foster's *Baronetage.*

Mildmay, Everard St. John, 4s. Paulet St. John, of London, arm. MERTON COLL., matric. 26 June, 1844, aged 18; B.A. 1848, a student of the Inner Temple 1849.

Mildmay, George St. John, 2s. Charles Arundell St. John, of Lapworth, co. Warwick, cler. CORPUS CHRISTI COLL., matric. 25 Jan., 1875, aged 18; B.A. 1879, bar.-at-law, Inner Temple, 1882. See Foster's *Men at the Bar.*

Mildmay, Henry Bingham, 2s. Humphrey, of St. James's, London, arm. CHRIST CHURCH, matric. 15 Oct., 1845, aged 17; of Shoreham Place, Kent, J.P., D.L., and of Flete, Devon, high sheriff, 1886. See Foster's *Baronetage* & *Eton School Lists.* [25]

Mildmay, (Sir) Henry (Carew) St. John (Bart.), s. Henry Paulet St. John, of Twyford, Hants, baronet. CHRIST CHURCH, matric. 28 Jan., 1805, aged 17; 4th baronet, M.P. Winchester 1807-18, died 17 Jan., 1848. See Foster's *Baronetage* & *Eton School Lists.*

Mildmay, Humphrey Francis, 1s. Humphrey, of St. George's, Hanover Square, arm. CHRIST CHURCH, matric. 31 May, 1844, aged 18; B.A. 1850, M.A. 1856, a student of the Inner Temple 1847, M.P. Herefordshire 1859-65, died 29 Nov., 1866.

Mildmay, Paulet Bertram St. John, 5s. Arundel Charles St. John, of Lapworth, co. Warwick, cler. KEBLE COLL., matric. 19 Oct., 1880, aged 18.

Mildmay, Walter St. John, s. Henry, of Winchester, Hants, baronet. BRASENOSE COLL., matric. 29 Nov., 1817, aged 19; rector of Mottestone and Shorwell 1824, of Abbotstone with Itchin Stoke 1829, and of Dogmersfield 1830 (all Hants), until his death 31 July, 1835. See Foster's *Baronetage.*

Miles, Rev. Albert Ray, 3s. William, of Southampton, gent. NON-COLL., matric. 14 Oct., 1876, aged 30; B.A. from QUEEN'S COLL. 1880, M.A. 1883.

Miles, Audley Charles, 2s. Charles William, of Malmesbury, Wilts, arm. BRASENOSE COLL., matric. 28 May, 1874, aged 18; B.A. 1879, M.A. 1883. [31]

Miles, Charles John, 3s. William, of Beesthorpe, Notts, arm. (after baronet). MERTON COLL., matric. 7 March, 1850, aged 18; captain 5th fusiliers, died 2 June, 1874. See Foster's *Baronetage* & *Eton School Lists.*

Miles, Charles Oswald, 5s. Robert Henry William, of Bingham, Notts, cler. TRINITY COLL., matric. 30 Jan., 1869, aged 18; B.A. 1873, M.A. 1875, warden of St. Cyprian College, Bloemfontein, 1877-82, canon and chancellor Bloemfontein, 1877-82, vicar of Shirehampton, co. Gloucester, 1884.

Miles, Edward, 2s. Lomas, of Willoughby, co. Leicester, cler. TRINITY COLL., matric. 29 Oct., 1867, aged 18; B.A. 1873, M.A. 1876, a solicitor.

Miles, Edward Pares, y.s. John, of Willoughby Waterless, co. Leicester, cler. WORCESTER COLL., matric. 3 Feb., 1837, aged 18; brother of Lomas 1828.

Miles, Edward Peach William, 7s. Philip John, of Bristol, Somerset, arm. CHRIST CHURCH, matric. 15 June, 1848, aged 18; of Shirehampton and Dauntesey, co. Gloucester. See Foster's *Baronetage* & *Eton School Lists.*

Miles, Frederick Montgomery McKay, 1s. Henry, of Loughor, co. Glamorgan, cler. JESUS COLL., matric. 23 April, 1877, aged 20; clerk 1877.

Miles, George, s. John, of St. Botolph, London, gent. WORCESTER COLL., matric. 17 Feb., 1818, aged 19. See *Eton School Lists.*

Miles, Henry, s. Lewis, of Llahilath, co. Monmouth, pleb. JESUS COLL., matric. 9 Dec., 1774, aged 20. [5]

Miles, Henry, s. John, of London, gent. ST. ALBAN HALL, matric. 15 March, 1817, aged 23, bar.-at-law, Lincoln's Inn, 1828 (? died 25 Jan., 1865).

Miles, Henry Cruger William, 9s. Philip John, of Abbott's Leigh, Somerset, arm. CHRIST CHURCH, matric. 16 Oct., 1850, aged 18. See Foster's *Baronetage* & *Eton School Lists.*

Miles, Henry Hugh, o.s. Henry, of Marylebone, London, arm. EXETER COLL., matric. 28 Jan., 1847, aged 18; B.A. 1851, M.A. 1853, of Downfield House, co. Hereford, rector of Clifton, Beds, 1858.

Miles, Henry Stewart, 3s. John, of Chessington, Surrey, gent. PEMBROKE COLL., matric. 5 May, 1870, aged 18; B.A. 1873, M.A. 1877, vicar of All Saints, Friern Barnet, 1882. See *Rugby School Reg.*

Miles, James Savile Henry, 1s. Robert, of Bingham, Notts, cler. EXETER COLL. matric. 17 Oct., 1863, aged 18. See Foster's *Baronetage.* [10]

Miles, John, s. Morgan, of St. Nicholas, co. Glamorgan, pleb. JESUS COLL., matric. 29 Oct., 1716, aged 17; B.A. from ST. EDMUND HALL 1720.

Miles, John, 'butler of St. John's College;' privilegiatus 16 March, 1721-2.

Miles, John, 1s. John, of Cowbridge, co. Glamorgan, gent. JESUS COLL., matric. 11 March, 1841, aged 19.

Miles, John William, 3s. Philip John, of Wraxall, Somerset, arm. CHRIST CHURCH, matric. 4 June, 1835, aged 17; B.A. 1839, M.A. 1865, of Underdown, co. Hereford, J.P., D.L., M.P. Bristol, April to June, 1868, died 5 Nov., 1878. See Foster's *Baronetage* & *Eton School Lists.*

Miles, Lomas, 3s. John, of Willoughby, co. Leicester, cler. QUEEN'S COLL., matric. 21 May, 1828, aged 17; B.A. 1832, M.A. 1835, rector of Willoughby-Waterless, co. Leicester, 1847-58, and of Coreley, Salop, 1858, until his death 22 March, 1875. [15]

Miles, Morgan, s. Morgan, of St. Nicholas, co. Glamorgan, pleb. JESUS COLL., matric. 27 March, 1727, aged 18; B.A. 1730.

Miles, Philip John, s. Philip, of Clifton, co. Gloucester, arm. CHRIST CHURCH, matric. 19 Oct., 1799, aged 18; this is *not* the father of Philip William, nor of William 1815.

Miles, Philip Napier, o.s. Philip William Skynner, of Westbury, co. Gloucester, arm. ORIEL COLL., matric. 26 April, 1884, aged 19; B.A. 1887.

Miles, Philip William Skynner, 2s. Philip John, of Clifton, co. Gloucester, arm. CHRIST CHURCH, matric. 15 May, 1834, aged 18; of King's Weston, co. Gloucester, M.P. Bristol, 1837-52, died 1 Oct., 1881. See Foster's *Baronetage* & *Eton School Lists.*

Miles, Richard, s. Thomas, of Wotton Bassett, Wilts, gent. BALLIOL COLL., matric. 14 May, 1766, aged 18; B.A. 1770, M.A. 1792, rector of Lydeard Tregoz, Wilts, 1780, until his death 4 Sep., 1839. [20]

Miles, Robert Fenton, 2s. Robert Henry, of Bingham, Notts, cler. TRINITY COLL., matric. 18 Oct., 1865, aged 19; B.A. 1868. See Foster's *Baronetage.*

Miles, Robert Henry William, 4s. Philip John, of Bristol (city), arm. CHRIST CHURCH, 20 Oct., 1836, aged 17; B.A. 1841, preb. of Lincoln 1864, rector of Bingham, Notts, 1845, until his death 25 Oct., 1883. See Foster's *Baronetage* & *Eton School Lists.*

Miles, Samuel Thomas, 1s. John, of Oadby, co. Leicester, cler. WORCESTER COLL., matric. 20 May, 1824, aged 18.

Miles, Vyvyan Charles, 3s. Charles William, of Burton Hill, Wilts, arm. CHRIST CHURCH, matric. 3 June, 1876, aged 19; B.A. 1880. See Foster's *Baronetage* & *Eton School Lists.*

Miles, William, s. Rich., of Hanslop, Bucks, pleb. UNIVERSITY COLL., matric. 19 Feb., 1724-5, aged 18; B.A. 1728, M.A. 1731. [25]

Miles, William, s. William, of Lanblethian, co. Glamorgan, cler. JESUS COLL., matric. 13 Dec., 1737, aged 18; B.A. 1741.

Miles, William, 'janitor of St. Mary Hall;' privilegiatus 26 Jan., 1762.

Miles, William, s. Stephen, of Kidderminster, co. Worcester, pleb. CHRIST CHURCH, matric. 25 May, 1773, aged 17; B.A. from CORPUS CHRISTI COLL. 1778. (W. M. sometime head-master Free Grammar School, Kidderminster, and officiating minister of Wribbenhall parish, died at Stourport in 1828.)

Miles, (Sir) William (Bart.), s. Philip John, of Bristol (city), arm. CHRIST CHURCH, matric. 18 Feb., 1815, aged 18; of Leigh Court, Somerset, baronet, so created 19 April, 1859, a student of Lincoln's Inn 1818, M.P. Chippenham 1818-20, Romney 1830-2, East Somerset 1834-65, died 17 June, 1878. See Foster's *Baronetage* & *Eton School Lists.*

Miles, William, s. — M., of Chenies, Bucks. ORIEL COLL., matric. 22 Oct., 1861, aged 25; bible clerk 1861-5, B.A. 1865. [30]

Miles, William Henry, 2s. William, of Beesthorpe, Notts, arm. BALLIOL COLL., matric. 28 June, 1848, aged 19; B.A. 1852, of Ham Green, Somerset, J.P. See Foster's *Baronetage* & *Eton School Lists.*

Milford, Archibald Locke, 4s. Frederick, of Exeter, gent. PEMBROKE COLL., matric. 2 May, 1882, aged 18.

Milford, Rev. Lionel Sumner, 1s. Robert Newman, of Farnham, Surrey, cler. PEMBROKE COLL., matric. 29 Oct., 1874, aged 19; scholar 1874-9, B.A. 1878, M.A. 1882, assistant-master Haileybury College 1879.

Milford, Reginald Stewart, 3s. Robert Newman, of Brightwell, Berks, cler. NEW COLL., matric. 10 Oct., 1884, aged 18; scholar 1884.

Milford, Robert Newman, 4s. John, of Exeter, arm. BALLIOL COLL., matric. 6 April, 1848, aged 19; B.A. 1851, M.A. 1854, rector of Brightwell, Berks, 1860-5, and of Bishop Knoyle, Wilts, 1865. See *Rugby School Reg.*, 261. [35]

Milford, Robert Theodore, 2s. Robert Newman, of Brightwell, Berks, cler. NEW COLL., matric. 16 Oct., 1880, aged 18; B.A. 1884, M.A. 1888.

Mill, James, of Arbroath, co. Forfar. TRINITY COLL., matric. 17 Oct., 1885, aged 23.

Mill, John, s. John, of Ashburton, Devon, pleb. WADHAM COLL., matric. 26 Feb., 1755, aged 19.

Mill, John, s. John, of Bentley, Hants, gent. ST. MARY HALL, matric. 7 Nov., 1744, aged 18.

Mill, John, s. John, of Hackney, Middlesex, arm. TRINITY COLL., matric. 21 Feb., 1811, aged 16; B.A. 1814, M.A. 1817, bar.-at-law, Middle Temple, 1819, assessor to the Court of Petty Sessions at Bombay. [40]

Mill, (Sir) John Barker (Bart.), 1s. John Barker, of Wareham, Dorset, arm. BRASENOSE COLL., matric. 17 Oct., 1822, aged 18; of Mottisfont Abbey, Hants, baronet, so created 16 March, 1836, having assumed the additional surname of MILL by royal licence 8 May, 1835, vicar of King Somborne, Hants, resigned 1836, took to training racehorses, died 20 Feb., 1860.

Mill, (Sir) John (Hoby, Bart.), s. Ri., of Woolbeding, Sussex, baronet. CHRIST CHURCH, matric. 16 June, 1738, aged 19; 7th baronet, assumed the additional name of HOBY, died in July, 1780, brother of Richard.

Mill, Nicholas, s. Nicholas, of Stoke Damerel, Devon, arm. EXETER COLL., matric. 26 Feb., 1790, aged 20; B.A. 1794, rector of Littleham, North Devon, 1799, until his death in 1828.

Mill, Richard, s. Ri., of Woolbeding, Sussex, baronet. NEW COLL., matric. 17 Feb., 1734-5, aged 18; created M.A. 12 July, 1738, 6th baronet, M.P. Hampshire 1765-8, died 17 March, 1770.

Mill, Thomas Harris Valetort, s. Nicholas, of Plymouth, Devon, gent. EXETER COLL., matric. 15 March, 1800, aged 18; B.A. 1804, minister of Northam, Devon, 1812, until his death 1 July, 1844. [5]

Mill, William, s. Hercules, of Montrose, Scotland, arm. TRINITY COLL., matric. 24 May, 1809, aged 18; B.A. 1813, M.A. 1817.

Mill, William Hodge, scholar and fellow of TRINITY COLL., Cambridge (6th Wrangler and B.A. 1813, M.A. 1816, D.D. 1829); adm. 'ad eundem' 10 May, 1839, principal of Bishops' College, Calcutta, 1820-38, Christian advocate (Hulse) 1839-44, rector of Brasted, Kent, 1843, regius professor of Hebrew and hon. canon of Ely 1848, until his death 25 Dec., 1853.

Millais, (Sir) John Everett (Bart.), R.A., created D.C.L. 9 June, 1880 (2s. John William Millais), created a baronet 16 July, 1885, born 8 June, 1829.

Millan, Samuel, s. Richard, of Friday Street, London, gent. TRINITY COLL., matric. 9 July, 1748, aged 18; B.A. 1752, M.A. 1755.

Millar, Rev. Charles John, 1s. Charles, of Sidmouth, Devon, D.Med. PEMBROKE COLL., matric. 27 Jan., 1875, aged 19; B.A. 1877, of Penrhos, co. Carnarvon. [10]

Millar, John, o.s. James, of Glasgow, Scotland, gent. BALLIOL COLL., matric. 28 May, 1819, aged 17.

Millar, John Hepburn, 1s. — Millar, Lord Craighill, of Edinburgh. BALLIOL COLL., matric. 17 Oct., 1882, aged 18; B.A. 1887.

Millard, Charles, s. Nathaniel, of Gloucester (city), gent. MAGDALEN COLL., matric. 16 Dec., 1766, aged 18; chorister 1761-7, clerk 1767-72, B.A. 1770, M.A. 1773, minor canon Norwich Cathedral 1771, and chancellor 1809, rector of Taverham 1793, vicar of Trowse with Lakenham, perp. curate Hemblington (all Norfolk), died 6 Nov., 1814. See *Bloxam*, i. 169.

Millard, Rev. Edward, 1s. Charles, of Norwich (city), cler. EXETER COLL., matric. 14 Jan., 1820, aged 17; B.A. 1824, died in London 13 Oct., 1844.

Millard, Frederick, o.s. Richard, of Craven Street, Strand, London, arm. QUEEN'S COLL., matric. 14 Feb., 1856, aged 18; Michel exhibitioner 1856-60, B.A. 1860, vicar of St. Catherine's, Tranmere, Cheshire, 1886, joint author Dr. Smith's 'English-Latin Dictionary.' [15]

Millard, Frederick Luke Holland, 1s. Frederick, of St. Kitts, West Indies, cler. ST. EDMUND HALL, matric. 26 Jan., 1884, aged 18; B.A. 1887.

Millard, Frederick Maule, 7s. William Salter, of Sprowston, near Norwich, gent. MAGDALEN COLL., matric. 27 July, 1853, aged 17; demy 1853-67, B.A. 1858, M.A. 1860, fellow 1867-70, head-master St. Michael's College, Tenbury, 1862-9, rector of Otham, Kent, 1869. See *Coll. Reg.*, vii. 401.

Millard, George Grantley, 5s. Samuel, of Llangarran, co. Hereford, gent. NON-COLL., matric. 15 Nov., 1873, aged 29.

Millard, James Elwin, 3s. William Salter, of St. George's, Norwich, gent. MAGDALEN HALL, matric. 18 Jan., 1842, aged 18; chorister MAGDALEN COLL. 1834-41, demy 1842-53, B.A. 1845, schoolmaster 1846-64, M.A. 1848, fellow 1853-65, B.D. 1855, D.D. 1859, junior dean of arts 1854, bursar 1855, dean of divinity 1861, vicar of Basingstoke 1864, hon. canon of Winchester, 1882. See *Bloxam*, i. 220; iii. 286; & vii. 352.

Millard, Jeffery Watson, 4s. William, of Sprowston, Norfolk, gent. WORCESTER COLL., matric. 15 March, 1849, aged 18; exhibitioner 1849-54, B.A. 1852, M.A. 1855, rector of Shimpling, Norfolk, since 1854. [20]

Millechamp, Elisha, s. Elisha, of Hereford (city), cler. CHRIST CHURCH, matric. 24 March, 1715-6, aged 18; B.A. from BALLIOL COLL. 1719.

Millechamp, Richard, s. Timothy, of Newnton, Wilts, cler. BALLIOL COLL., matric. 22 March, 1726-7, aged 13; B.A. 1731, M.A. 1735 (? his father died at Broadwater, Herts, 31 Jan., 1734).

Millechamp, Thomas, s. Timothy, of Newnton, Wilts, cler. BALLIOL COLL., matric. 22 March, 1726-7, aged 15; B.A. 1730.

Millechamp, Timothy. UNIVERSITY COLL., 1715. See MILLICHAMP.

Millechamp, Timothy, s. Tim., of Dursley, co. Gloucester, cler. BALLIOL COLL., matric. 10 May, 1722, aged 16; B.A. 1726, vicar of North Wootton, Norfolk, 1758. [25]

Miller, Alfred, 3s. Taverner John, of London, gent. EXETER COLL., matric. 15 Oct., 1864, aged 20; B.A. & M.A. 1872.

Miller, Alfred Welch, 3s. Thomas, of St. Vincent, Cape-de-Verd, gent. PEMBROKE COLL., matric. 6 Feb., 1878, aged 17; B.A. 1883.

Miller, Arthur, s. Arthur, of Mancetter, co. Warwick, gent. HERTFORD COLL., matric. 14 Oct., 1748, aged 17; B.A. 1752, M.A. 1755.

Miller, Arthur, s. Arthur, of Mancetter, co. Warwick, cler. ST. JOHN'S COLL., matric. 26 June, 1781, aged 17.

Miller, Augustus Jameson, 2s. Joseph Augustus, of Windsor, Berks, cler. EXETER COLL., matric. 14 Oct., 1871, aged 19; scholar 1870-5, B.A. 1875, M.A. 1878, vicar of Middleton, Yorks, 1880-7, rector of Wootton, Northants, 1887. See *Coll. Reg.*, 165.

Miller, Charles, s. Ernest, of Maidenhead, Berks, pleb. QUEEN'S COLL., matric. 16 Nov., 1716, aged 17; B.A. 1720, M.A. 1727. [31]

Miller, Charles, s. William, of Liverpool, Lancashire, gent. MERTON COLL., matric. 29 Jan., 1812, aged 18; postmaster 1812-15, B.A. 1815, M.A. 1818, rector of Thorpe, co. Derby. See *Eton School Lists*.

Miller, Charles, s. Charles Sanderson, of Harlow, Essex, cler. WORCESTER COLL., matric. 2 Feb., 1813, aged 16; demy MAGDALEN COLL. 1814-31, B.A. 1817, M.A. 1819, vicar of Harlow, Essex, 1831, until his death 10 May, 1885. See *Bloxam*, vii. 255; & *Rugby School Reg.*, 101.

Miller, Charles Davidson, 2s. Gerard Frederick, of Bromley, Kent, arm. LINCOLN COLL., matric. 8 June, 1878, aged 17.

Miller, Charles Hilliard, o.s. Charles, of Cheswardine, Salop, cler. WADHAM COLL., matric. 25 May, 1853, aged 18; B.A. 1857, M.A. 1860. [35]

Miller, Charles Sanderson, s. Sanderson, of Radway, co. Warwick, arm. ST. JOHN'S COLL., matric. 15 May, 1778, aged 16; B A. 1782, M.A. 1785, vicar of Harlow 1789, Lindsell 1790, and of Matching, Essex, 1825, until his death 21 April, 1837.

Miller, Rev. Charles Stewart, 2s. Dugald Stewart, of Richmond, Yorks, arm. BALLIOL COLL., matric. 19 Oct., 1878, aged 21; B.A. 1882, M.A. 1886.

Miller, Combe, s. John, of Lavant, Sussex, baronet. ORIEL COLL., matric. 9 Dec., 1763, aged 18; B.A. from NEW COLL. 1768, M.A. 1771, rector of Winfarthing and Snetterton, Norfolk, 1772, preb. of Chichester 1769, treasurer 1785, and dean 1790, until his death 18 Feb., 1814. See Foster's *Baronetage*.

Miller, Daniel, s. George, of Bath (city), gent. WADHAM COLL., matric. 8 Dec., 1812, aged 20; B.A. 1819.

Miller, Ebenezer, created M.A. 16 July, 1726, then of New England, D.D. by diploma 1 Dec., 1747, then a missionary.

Miller, Edward, s. Fiennes Saunderson, of Radway, arm. QUEEN'S COLL., matric. 19 Nov., 1801, aged 17; B.A. 1805, M.A. 1808, Michel fellow until 1819, vicar of Radway and Ratley, co. Warwick, died 28 July, 1857, aged 73. See *Rugby School Reg.*, 77.

Miller, Edward, 1s. Edward, of Radway, co. Warwick, cler. NEW COLL., matric. 1 Jan., 1844, aged 18; fellow 1843-57, B.A. 1847, M.A. 1851, tutor and dean of arts 1851, vicar of Butlers Marston, co. Warwick, 1868, rector of Bucknell, Oxon, 1879; for list of his works see *Crockford.*

Miller, Edward Alexander, 6s. Taverner John, of London, arm. EXETER COLL., matric. 21 May, 1872, aged 18; B.A. 1877, M.A. 1880, bar.-at-law, Lincoln's Inn, 1878. [5]

Miller, Edward Mansel, 1s. Edward, of Bognor, Sussex, cler. BRASENOSE COLL., matric. 2 Feb., 1849, aged 21, scholar 1849-51; demy MAGDALEN COLL. 1851-62, B.A. 1855, M.A. 1856, tutor 1851-6, fellow 1862, bursar 1872. See *Bloxam*, vii. 390.

Miller, Fiennes Sanderson, s. Sanderson, of Radway, co. Warwick, arm. BALLIOL COLL., matric. 17 March, 1778, aged 18; of Radway, died 1818.

Miller, Fiennes Sanderson (C.B.), 1s. Fiennes Sanderson, of Radway, co. Warwick, arm. WADHAM COLL., matric. 25 April, 1839, aged 18; of Radway, co. Gloucester, J.P., D.L., lieut.-colonel in the army, wounded at Waterloo when in command of the Inniskilling dragoons, died Sep., 1862.

Miller, Francis, 5s. Thomas, of St. Vincent, Cape de Verd, gent. PEMBROKE COLL., matric. 27 Oct., 1885, aged 18; brother of Alfred W. 1878.

Miller, Francis Richard, 6s. Charles Sanderson, of Harlow, Essex, cler. WORCESTER COLL., matric. 26 Feb., 1821, aged 16; B.A. 1824, M.A. 1827, vicar of Kineton, co. Warwick, 1834. See *Rugby School Reg.*, 125. [10]

Miller, Francis Wykeham, 1s. Francis Richard, of Kineton, co. Warwick, cler. BRASENOSE COLL., matric. 12 June, 1862, aged 17; B.A. 1865, M.A. 1869.

Miller, Rev. Frederick William, s. Sanders William, of Hasfield, co. Gloucester, cler. CORPUS CHRISTI COLL., matric. 17 April, 1807, aged 16; B.A. 1811, M.A. 1815, died 7 May, 1853.

Miller, George, 3s. Edward, of Radway, co. Warwick, cler. WORCESTER COLL., matric. 20 Nov., 1850, aged 18; vicar (and patron) of Radway since 1860.

Miller, George, 4s. Thomas, of Froyle, near Alton, Hants, baronet and cler. EXETER COLL., matric. 12 June, 1851, aged 17; scholar 1851-6, B.A. 1856, fellow 1857-65, M.A. 1858, lecturer 1858, bar.-at-law, Lincoln's Inn, 1863, examiner in the Education Office, London, 1865-84, assistant-secretary education department 1884. See Foster's *Baronetage* & *Coll. Reg.*, 140.

Miller, George Dempster, 1s. Robert, of St. Marylebone, London, gent. WADHAM COLL., matric. 17 May, 1832, aged 18; B.A. 1836, M.A. 1839, perp. curate Morley, Yorks, 1839-41, vicar of Skenfrett, co. Monmouth, 1841-6, and of Woodkirk, Yorks, 1846-72. [15]

Miller, George Russell, o.s. William Oliver, of Horley, Surrey, arm. BRASENOSE COLL., matric. 21 May, 1880, aged 20.

Miller, George Thomas, 2s. Patrick, of Exeter, D.Med. WORCESTER COLL., matric. 22 June, 1843, aged 18; B.A. 1848, curate of Broadclist, Devon, died 15 March, 1851.

Miller, Henry, 2s. Edward, of Radway, co. Warwick, cler. WORCESTER COLL., matric. 6 Feb., 1846, aged 17; demy MAGDALEN COLL. 1846-58, B.A. 1850, M.A. 1852, fellow 1858-60, vicar of Radway, co. Warwick, 1858-60, and of Ashbury, Berks, since 1860. See *Bloxam*, vii. 378.

Miller, Henry Walter, 2s. John Cale, of Chelsea, Middlesex, D.D. CORPUS CHRISTI COLL. matric. 21 Oct., 1862, aged 19; B.Mus. 1865 (B.A. from CHARSLEY HALL, 1867), M.A. 1875, held various curacies 1868-79, vicar of St. John the Divine, Richmond, 1879-85.

Miller, James, s. John, of Compton Valence, Dorset, cler. WADHAM COLL., matric. 11 July, 1726, aged 20. [20]

Miller, James, s. John, of Widnes, Lancashire, pleb. BRASENOSE COLL., matric. 13 Feb., 1738-9, aged 18; B.A. 1742.

Miller, James Boyd, 2s. James Boyd, of Exeter, arm. CHRIST CHURCH, matric. 10 Oct., 1879, aged 24; B.A. 1884.

Miller, James Gordon, o.s. James David, of Edinburgh, gent. NEW INN HALL, matric. 16 Oct., 1869, aged 26; of Hampden Hall, Devon.

Miller, James Webber, 2s. William, of St. Peter's, Chichester, cler. EXETER COLL., matric. 15 Nov., 1838, aged 19; B.A. 1842, M.A. 1861, rector of Birdham, Sussex, 1861, until his death 18 May, 1882.

Miller, John, s. John, of Buckingham (town), gent. ORIEL COLL., matric. 18 Dec., 1732, aged 15; B.A. 1736. [25]

Miller, John, s. Henry, of London, gent. WADHAM COLL., matric. 9 March, 1772, aged 18.

Miller, John, s. Peter, of Bockleton, co. Worcester, cler. WORCESTER COLL., matric. 21 June, 1804, aged 17; scholar 1806-10, B.A. 1808, fellow 1810-23, M.A. 1811, select preacher 1814, Bampton lecturer 1817, rector of Benefield, Northants, 1822-42, vicar of Bockleton 1855, until his death 18 Jan., 1858. See *St. Paul's School Reg.*, 223.

Miller, John, y.s. George, of London, gent. WADHAM COLL., matric. 16 Oct., 1886, aged 19.

Miller, John Cale, o.s. John, of Margate, Kent, gent. ST. JOHN'S COLL., matric. 27 March, 1832, aged 17; scholar LINCOLN COLL. 1834-6, B.A. 1835, M.A. 1838, B. & D.D. 1857, select preacher 1869, minister of Park Chapel, Chelsea, rector of St. Martin's, Birmingham, 1846-66, hon. canon Worcester 1852, canon 1871-3, treasurer 1871-3, vicar of Greenwich 1866, and canon of Rochester 1873, until his death 11 July, 1880.

Miller, (Sir) John Edward Augustus (Bart.), born in Paris, France, s. John, baronet. CHRIST CHURCH, matric. 15 Oct., 1789, aged 19; 2nd baronet, bar.-at-law, Lincoln's Inn, 1794, dead before June, 1826, father of John Riggs Miller, 1833. [30]

Miller, John Frederick, 4s. William, of London, arm. TRINITY COLL., matric. 25 Jan., 1871, aged 18; B.A. 1876, of London, solicitor. See *Rugby School Reg.*

Miller, John Harrison, o.s. Robert Marratt, of Dedham, Essex, D.D. WADHAM COLL., matric. 17 Oct., 1838, aged 17; scholar 1838-48, B.A. 1842, M.A. 1848, bar.-at-law, Inner Temple, 1851. See Foster's *Men at the Bar.*

Miller, John Riggs-, o.s. John, of Cork (city), baronet. TRINITY COLL., matric. 17 April, 1833, aged 17; B.A. 1837, M.A. 1841, of Goodneston, Kent, assumed the names of RIGGS-MILLER in lieu of MANVERS by royal licence 3 Aug., 1826. See *Eton School Lists.*

Miller, John Robert Charlesworth, 1s. John Robert, of Blackheath, Kent, gent. CORPUS CHRISTI COLL., matric. 10 Feb., 1855, aged 17; scholar 1855-65, B.A. 1859, M.A. 1861, fellow 1865-6, rector of Goddington, Oxon, 1866-78, vicar of Mottram in Longdendale, Lancashire, 1878.

Miller, Maxwell, 3s. Robert, of London, arm. WORCESTER COLL., matric. 15 Oct., 1850, aged 18, exhibitioner 1850; exhibitioner QUEEN'S COLL. 1851, member of Legislative Assembly, Hobart, Tasmania. See *St. Paul's School Reg.*, 306.

Miller, Richard Combe, 6s. Thomas Combe, of Froyle, Hants, baronet. EXETER COLL., matric. 8 Dec., 1860, aged 19, of Oakfield, Kent, J.P. See Foster's *Baronetage.*

Miller, Robert, s. Robert, of St. Anne's, London, gent. MAGDALEN COLL., matric. 13 Dec., 1769, aged 30; B.C.L. from ST. MARY HALL 1781, rector of Fimcote, co. Leicester, and vicar of St. Nicholas, Warwick, died 14 Nov., 1810.

Miller, Robert Burrington, 2s. George Dempster, of Woodchurch, Yorks, cler. WADHAM COLL., matric. 29 Jan., 1870, aged 16; B.A. 1873, M.A. 1876, perp. curate of All Saints', Sidmouth, 1883.

Miller, Robert Marratt, s. Robert, of Warwick (town), cler. WADHAM COLL., matric. 5 Nov., 1806, aged 20; B.A. 1810, M.A. 1813, B. & D.D. 1826, resident chaplain Lisbon 1811, vicar of Dedham, Essex, 1819, until his death 11 June, 1839. **[5]**

Miller, Robert Montgomerie, 2s. Boyd, of Mitcham, Surrey, arm. QUEEN'S COLL., matric. 17 Oct., 1844, aged 19.

Miller, Sanderson, s. Sanderson, of Radway, co. Warwick, gent. ST. MARY HALL, matric. 6 April, 1734, aged 17; of Radway, father of Fiennes 1778, and of Charles S. 1778.

Miller, Sanderson, s. Charles Sanderson, of Harlow, Essex, cler. NEW COLL., matric. 21 June, 1811, aged 20; fellow 1812, until his death 6 or 15 Dec., 1813.

Miller, Sanders William, s. William, of London, gent. PEMBROKE COLL., matric. 26 Nov., 1778, aged 18; B.A. 1782, M.A. 1810, rector of Hasfield, co. Gloucester, 1787, until his death in 1833.

Miller, Thomas, s. Thomas, of Over Whitakers, co. Warwick, gent. PEMBROKE COLL., matric. 11 May, 1716, aged 17. **[10]**

Miller, Thomas, 'janitor to Ratcliffe Library;' privilegiatus 24 Sep., 1759.

Miller, Thomas Frederick Dawson, 2s. Thomas Robson, of Gateshead, co. Durham, gent. TRINITY COLL., matric. 16 Oct., 1886, aged 18.

Miller, William, s. John, of Finedon, Northants, pleb. NEW COLL., matric. 11 April, 1798, aged 16, B.A. 1802, M.A. 1804; chorister Magdalen College 1789-98, clerk 1798-1807, minor canon, succentor and sub-treasurer Chichester Cathedral 1807, rector of East Wittering 1817, and of Birdham, Sussex, 1825, died 27 Feb., 1861. See *Bloxam*, i. 204.

Miller, William, s. Richard, of Boxwell, co. Gloucester, arm. TRINITY COLL., matric. 22 Nov., 1799, aged 18; possibly father of the next named.

Miller, William, 1s. William, of Chichester, cler. NEW COLL., matric. 25 Oct., 1832, aged 17; chorister 1825-32, clerk 1832-8, B.A. 1837, M.A. 1840. **[15]**

Miller, William, 1s. William, of Wigton, Cumberland, gent. HERTFORD COLL., matric. 18 Oct., 1883, aged 18; scholar 1882, B.A. 1887.

Miller, William Allen, F.R.S., created D.C.L. 17 June, 1868, professor of chemistry at King's College, London, B.Med. 1841, D.Med. 1842, fellow 1865-71, created LL.D., Cambridge, 1870, died 30 Sep., 1870.

Miller, William Duppa, 1s. William, of Tupsley, co. Hereford, arm. HERTFORD COLL., matric. 11 Nov., 1886, aged 18.

Miller, William Hallows, scholar ST. JOHN'S COLL., Cambridge, 1822-9, fellow 1829-44, and 1874-80, B.A. 1826, M.A. 1829, tutor 1830-44 (adm. 'ad eundem' 21 June, 1832), D.Med. 1841, mineralogy professor (Cambridge) 1832-80, created D.C.L. (Oxford) 21 June, 1876, F.R.S. 1838, died 20 May, 1880.

Miller, William Henry Archibald Christy-, o.s. Samuel, of London, gent. CHRIST CHURCH, matric. 14 Oct., 1870, aged 19; B.A. 1874, M.A. 1878, bar.-at-law, Inner Temple, 1877. See Foster's *Men at the Bar & Eton School Lists.* **[20]**

Miller, William Montague, 2s. Arthur Octavius, of Tottenham, Middlesex, gent. MAGDALEN HALL, matric. 29 Jan., 1873, aged 23; B.A. & M.A. (HERTFORD COLL.) 1882, vicar of Stony Stratford, Bucks, since 1885.

Miller, William Sanderson, 2s. Fiennes Sanderson, of Radway, co. Warwick, arm. NEW COLL., matric. 16 Oct., 1840, aged 18; fellow 1840-8, B.A. 1853, M.A. 1854, perp. curate Sibford Gower, Oxon, 1847-60, vicar of Morton-Murrell, co. Warwick, 1880-4.

Millerd, Thomas, s. Hugh, of ——, co. Cork, Ireland, gent. ST. JOHN'S COLL., matric. 29 June, 1731, aged 19.

Millerd, Thomas, s. James, of Rathcormac, co. Cork, Ireland, arm. CHRIST CHURCH, matric. 23 Jan., 1817, aged 18.

Milles, Isaac, s. Jeremiah, of Duloe, Cornwall, cler. BALLIOL COLL., matric. 17 March, 1732-3, aged 17; B.A. 22 Feb., 1736-7. **[25]**

Milles, Jeremiah, s. Jer., of Highclere, Hants, cler. CORPUS CHRISTI COLL., matric. 9 July, 1729, aged 15; B.A. 1733, M.A. 1735, B. & D.D. 1747, dean of Exeter 1762, F.A.S. 1741, and F.R.S., president of the Society of Antiquaries 1765, rector of Saltwood with Hythe, Kent, 1744, treasurer of Lismore Cathedral 1735, precentor of Waterford 1737-44, rector of St. Nicholas Acon, Lombard Street, with Merstham, Surrey, and sinecure rector of West Ferring, Sussex, precentor and preb. of Exeter 1747, died 13 Feb., 1784. See *Gent.'s Mag.*, p. 153.

Milles, Jeremiah, s. Jeremiah, of London, doctor. QUEEN'S COLL., matric. 7 Dec., 1768, aged 17, B.A. 1772; fellow MERTON COLL., M.A. 1775, of Pishiobury, Herts, bar.-at-law, Lincoln's Inn, 1776.

Milles, Richard, s. Jeremiah, of St. George's, Hanover Square, doctor. QUEEN'S COLL., matric. 3 Dec., 1770, aged 16; student CHRIST CHURCH, B.A. 1774, M.A. 1777, preb. of Exeter 1778, sinecure rector of West Ferring, Sussex, 1784, and vicar of Kenwyn in Cornwall, 1781.

Milles, Theodore, s. Jeremiah, of Duloe, Cornwall, cler. BALLIOL COLL., matric. 8 July, 1729, aged 18; B.A. 1733.

Milles, Thomas, s. Isaac, of Highclere, co. Southampton, cler. ORIEL COLL., matric. 4 Feb., 1733-4, aged 17; B.A. from BALLIOL COLL. 1737.

Milles, Thomas, s. Jeremiah, of St. Peter's, Exeter, doctor. QUEEN'S COLL., matric. 26 May, 1769, aged 16, B.A. 1773, M.A. 1776; fellow ALL SOULS' COLL. 1777-1830, B.C.L. 1779, D.C.L. 1790, bar.-at-law, Lincoln's Inn, 1777, K.C. and a bencher 1804, died 21 May, 1830. **[31]**

Milles, Thomas, o.s. Thomas, of Goudhurst, Kent, arm. TRINITY COLL., matric. 7 July, 1831, aged 17; B.A. 1835, vicar of St. Margaret's, Yalding, Kent, 1850-82.

Millett, Charles Frederick, 2s. Charles, of Hill Place, Hants, arm. CHRIST CHURCH, matric. 3 June, 1857, aged 18; B.A. 1860, M.A. 1878, bar.-at-law, Inner Temple, 1864-9.

Millett, Henry, 2s. Frederick, of Calcutta, arm. CHRIST CHURCH, matric. 26 May, 1858, aged 18; B.A. 1862, M.A. 1875, bar.-at-law, Lincoln's Inn, 1864, chief judge Calcutta Small Cause Court 1876, professor of law in Presidency College, Calcutta, 1870. See Foster's *Men at the Bar & Rugby School Reg.*

Millett, Humphrey, s. Humphrey, of St. Hilary, Cornwall, arm. EXETER COLL., matric. 11 March, 1762, aged 17. **[35]**

Millett, John Carnow, s. Richard Oke, of Phillack, Cornwall, gent. PEMBROKE COLL., matric. 2 April, 1789, aged 18; B.A. 1793 (as J. Curnow M.).

Mills, Barrington Stopford Thomas, o.s. Thomas, of Stutton, Suffolk, cler. CHRIST CHURCH, matric. 3 June, 1840, aged 18; B.A. 1844, M.A. 1847, of Stutton, rector of Lawshall, Suffolk, 1858. [20]

Mills, Barton Reginald Vaughan, 1s. Arthur, of London, arm. CHRIST CHURCH, matric. 13 Oct., 1876, aged 18; B.A. 1880, M.A. 1883, rector of Poughill 1887. See Foster's *Baronetage.*

Mills, Cecil, 2s. John, of Salisbury, Wilts, arm. CHRIST CHURCH, matric. 21 Oct., 1857, aged 17; B.A. from NEW INN HALL 1862, M.A. from CHRIST CHURCH 1864, rector of Barford, co. Warwick, since 1865. See Foster's *Baronetage.*

Mills, Rev. Charles Craigie, 1s. Charles Stewart, of Bahià, Brazil, arm. UNIVERSITY COLL., matric. 13 Oct., 1876, aged 18; B.A. 1879, M.A. 1883. See *Eton School Lists.*

Mills, Charles Henry, 1s. Charles, of Westminster, arm. CHRIST CHURCH, matric. 27 May, 1847, aged 17; B.A. 1851, M.A. 1854, Lord Hillingdon, so created 15 Feb., 1886, M.P. Northallerton 1865-6, West Kent 1868-85. See Foster's *Peerage* & *Eton School Lists.*

Mills, Daniel, B.A. from MERTON COLL. 22 Oct., 1740. See *Acts Book.* [25]

Mills, Daniel Yarnton, 1s. Daniel, of Miserden, co. Gloucester, arm. PEMBROKE COLL., matric. 19 Nov., 1835, aged 17.

Mills, David, 5s. William, of Vicksburgh, America, arm. MAGDALEN HALL, matric. 22 Jan., 1866, aged 18.

Mills, Edward, 1s. Edward, of London, gent. NEW COLL., matric. 5 Feb., 1877, aged 27; B.Mus. 1881.

Mills, Edward Francis James, 1s. Michael Edward, of Bhangulpore, East Indies, cler. ST. MARY HALL, matric. 22 Oct., 1883, aged 19.

Mills, Egremont John, 3s. Sir Charles Henry, of Ramsay, Kent, baronet (after Lord Hillingdon). CHRIST CHURCH, matric. 31 May, 1884, aged 17. [30]

Mills, Elliott, s. Daniel, of Stowell, co. Gloucester, pleb. PEMBROKE COLL., matric. 4 June, 1736, aged 19.

Mills, Ezekiel, s. Ezekiel, of Llanguntlo, co. Radnor, pleb. JESUS COLL., matric. 19 March, 1715-6, aged 17; B.A. 14 March, 1719-20.

Mills, Ezekiel, y.s. Ezekiel, of All Saints, Hereford (city), gent. ST. EDMUND HALL, matric. 1 Feb., 1838, aged 19.

Mills, Francis, s. John, of Barford, co. Warwick, cler. CHRIST CHURCH, matric. 9 Dec., 1777, aged 18; B.A. 1781, M.A. 1784, rector of Barford 1785-1841, died 23 April, 1851. See Foster's *Baronetage.*

Mills, Francis, s. William, of St. Marylebone, London, arm. CHRIST CHURCH, matric. 13 March, 1812, aged 18, B.A. 1815; fellow MERTON COLL. 1816-46, M.A. 1818, died in July, 1854. [35]

Mills, Francis, 1s. Henry, of Pillerton, co. Warwick, cler. CHRIST CHURCH, matric. 12 June, 1862, aged 18; B.A. 1866, M.A. 1869, of Manor House, Pillerton, bar.-at-law, Inner Temple, 1869. See Foster's *Men at the Bar.*

Mills, Frederick Charles, 4s. John Robert, of York (city), arm. UNIVERSITY COLL., matric. 19 Oct., 1867, aged 19; B.A. 1871, M.A. 1875, bar.-at-law, Lincoln's Inn, 1877. See Foster's *Men at the Bar.*

Mills, George Harry, 1s. Joseph, of Kingswinford, co. Stafford, gent. WORCESTER COLL., matric. 16 Oct., 1879, aged 17; B.A. 1883, M.A. 1886.

Mills, George Kaye, 2s. John, of Orton Waterville, Hunts, cler. QUEEN'S COLL., matric. 22 Oct., 1866, aged 19; clerk 1867-9, B.A. 1869, M.A. 1877.

Mills, Giles, s. William, of Bisley, co. Gloucester, pleb. PEMBROKE COLL., matric. 11 May, 1715, aged 16; B.A. 19 Feb., 1718-19, M.A. 1721 (? father or grandfather of Thomas 1765). [40]

Mills, Henry, 1s. Francis, of Barford, co. Warwick, cler. BALLIOL COLL., matric. 20 June, 1833, aged 18; B.A. 1837, M.A. 1840, of Manor House, Pillerton, co. Warwick, J.P., vicar of Pillerton Hersey 1841-64. See Foster's *Peerage* & *Rugby School Reg.*, 158.

Mills, Henry Maynard, 2s. Henry, of London, arm. LINCOLN COLL., matric. 13 Oct., 1866, aged 19; B.A. 1872, M.A. 1873, bar.-at-law, Inner Temple, 1875. See Foster's *Men at the Bar* & *St. Paul's School Reg.*, 338.

Mills, James, s. Samuel, of Tunbridge, Kent, gent. ST. JOHN'S COLL., matric. 2 July, 1776, aged 17; B.A. 1780, M.A. 1784.

Mills, James, o.s. Christopher John, of Gloucester (city), arm. CHRIST CHURCH, matric. 8 July, 1830, aged 19; of the Saxham Hall family.

Mills, James Bassnett, 3s. Samuel, of Portsmouth, Hants, gent. QUEEN'S COLL., matric. 25 March, 1825, aged 21; vicar of Hemswell, co. Lincoln, 1853, until his death 13 March, 1874. **[5]**

Mills, James Fuller Humfrys, o.s. John Pritchard, of St. Nicholas, Hereford (city), cler. ST. EDMUND HALL, matric. 26 May, 1849, aged 19; B.A. 1853, rector of Hockerton, Notts, 1850.

Mills, John, s. John, of Crewkherne, Somerset, pleb. WADHAM COLL., matric. 20 May, 1723, aged 18.

Mills, John, s. John, of St. Dunstan's-in-the-East, London, gent. BALLIOL COLL., matric. 3 June, 1728, aged 16; B.A. 21 Jan., 1731-2, M.A. 1735, rector of Barford and Oxhill, co. Warwick, 1760-85, died 21 March, 1791.

Mills, John, s. John, of Newcastle, Northumberland, gent. LINCOLN COLL., matric. 10 Oct., 1744, aged 18; B.A. 1748, M.A. 1753.

Mills, John, s. John, of Stockleigh, Devon, gent. BALLIOL COLL., matric. 11 April, 1753, aged 18; B.A. 1757. **[10]**

Mills, John, s. William, of Herts (*sic*), arm. CHRIST CHURCH, matric. 22 Oct., 1807, aged 18; of Bisterne, Hants, M.P. Rochester 1831-5, died 18 Feb., 1871, father of the next named. See Foster's *Baronetage.*

Mills, John, 1s. John, of London, arm. CHRIST CHURCH, matric. 15 Oct., 1856, aged 20; of Bisterne, Hants. See Foster's *Peerage* & *Eton School Lists.*

Mills, John, Frobisher, 2s. Charles Stewart, of Bahia, Brazil, arm. UNIVERSITY COLL., matric. 12 Oct., 1878, aged 19; B.A. 1882, bar.-at-law, Lincoln's Inn, 1886. See *Eton School Lists.*

Mills, John Pritchard, o.s. John, of St. John's, Hereford (city), gent. ST. EDMUND HALL, matric. 14 April, 1825, aged 23; B.A. 1829, rector of Hockerton, Notts, 1852, until his death 24 Dec., 1855, father of James F. H.

Mills, Joseph Langley, s. Moses, of Deddington, Oxon, gent. TRINITY COLL., matric. 11 Oct., 1805, aged 17; demy MAGDALEN COLL. 1806-12, B.A. 1809, M.A. 1812, fellow 1810-17, B.D. by decree 2 Nov., 1822, D.D. (by decree) 7 Nov., 1822, chaplain to the forces 1812, died at Quebec 13 Aug., 1832, father of Robert T. 1837. See *Bloxam*, vii. 159.

Mills, Lawrence Heyworth, D.D. of the University of New York, translator of a portion of the 'Zend Avesta,' and editor and translator of the 'Gathas of Zoroaster,' created M.A. 31 Jan., 1888. **[15]**

Mills, Markham, 6s. Henry Forster, of Bathwick, Somerset, cler. CHRIST CHURCH, matric. 10 Nov., 1831, aged 18; B.A. 1836, M.A. 1839.

Mills, Richard, s. Richard, of Tottenham High Cross, Middlesex, cler. HART HALL, matric. 5 Dec., 1735, aged 18.

Mills, Richard, 1s. Richard, of Eltham, Kent, arm. BRASENOSE COLL., matric. 6 June, 1844, aged 18; B.A. 1848, M.A. 1851, a student of Lincoln's Inn 1848.

Mills, Robert, s. Joseph, of Claverley Home, Salop, pleb. EXETER COLL., matric. 20 Feb., 1728-9, aged 18; B.A. 1732. **[20]**

Mills, Robert Twyford, born at Quebec, Lower Canada 1s. Joseph Langley, cler. MAGDALEN COLL., matric. 14 Nov., 1837, aged 18; clerk 1837-42, B.A. 1842, M.A. 1844, rector of Halse, Somerset, 1844, until his death 15 Sep., 1874. See *Bloxam*, ii. 120; & *Robinson*, 240.

Mills, Simon, s. William, of Leek, co. Stafford, arm. ORIEL COLL., matric. 1 April, 1745, aged 16; B.A. 1748, M.A. 1751, rector of Norbury, co. Derby, and vicar of Leek aforesaid at his death 18 June, 1785.

Mills, Thomas, s. John, of Llangunwls, co. Radnor, pleb. JESUS COLL., matric. 1 June, 1739, aged 18; B.A. 1743.

Mills, Thomas, s. Richard, of Brentford, Middlesex, cler. MERTON COLL., matric. 9 Dec., 1757, aged 17; B.A. 1761, vicar of Hillingdon, Middlesex, at his death 4 June, 1810 (his father, who was vicar of Hillingdon with Uxbridge more than 50 years, died 30 April, 1779).

Mills, Thomas, s. Giles, of Miserden, co. Gloucester, cler. PEMBROKE COLL., matric. 26 March, 1765, aged 18; B.A. 1768. **[25]**

Mills, Thomas, s. Joseph, of Cowbitt, Lincoln, cler. CHRIST CHURCH, matric. 17 Oct., 1792, aged 18; B.A. 1796, M.A. 1800, hon. canon Peterborough, rector of Northborough, Northants, 1833, until his death 21 July, 1856.

Mills, Thomas, s. Thomas, of Grove House, Surrey, arm. CHRIST CHURCH, matric. 23 Oct., 1810, aged 19; B.A. 1814, chaplain in ordinary to the King 1816, hon. canon of Norwich 1859, rector of Little Henery, Essex, 1821, and of Great Saxham 1821, with Stutton, etc., 1829, Suffolk, until his death 29 Sep., 1879. See *Eton School Lists.*

Mills, Thomas Richard, 1s. William, of Bath (city), arm. CHRIST CHURCH, matric. 19 May, 1836, aged 18.

Mills, Thomas Sturges, 2s. Moses, of Steeple Aston, Oxon, gent. MAGDALEN HALL, matric. 15 Dec., 1818, aged 27; J.P. D.L. cos. Lancashire, Cheshire and Yorks (West Riding), incumbent of Littleborough, Lancashire, at his death 1 Oct., 1864.

Mills, Thomas Wilgress, 2s. Richard, of Eltham, Kent, arm. BRASENOSE COLL., matric. 5 Feb., 1850, aged 18; B.A. 1853, M.A. 1856. **[30]**

Mills, Vandeleur, s. Samuel, of Tunbridge, Kent, pleb. ST. JOHN'S COLL., matric. 26 June, 1764, aged 15; B.C.L. 1771.

Mills, Walter Wilgress, o.s. Thomas Wilgress, of Eltham, Kent, arm. UNIVERSITY COLL., matric. 18 Oct., 1886, aged 19.

Mills, William, s. Hugh, of St. Clement's, London, gent. BRASENOSE COLL., matric. 10 Oct., 1716, aged 17.

Mills, William, s. Thomas, of Leek, co. Stafford, gent. HERTFORD COLL., matric. 9 May, 1763, aged 17.

Mills, William, s. John, of Miserden, co. Gloucester, gent. TRINITY COLL., matric. 22 Oct., 1785, aged 16; B.A. 1789, M.A. 1792, B.D. 1802, rector (and patron) of Miserden, co. Gloucester, 1797, and of Shellingford, Berks, 1810, until his death 15 March, 1848, father of William Y. 1822. **[35]**

Mills, William, s. Moses, of Deddington, Oxon, gent. LINCOLN COLL., matric. 23 Nov., 1809, aged 16; demy MAGDALEN COLL. 1810-20, B.A. 1813, M.A. 1816, fellow 1820-34, B.D. 1823, senior dean of arts 1822, bursar 1823, vice-president 1827, tutor 1829, dean of divinity 1830, Whyte's professor moral philosophy 1829, until his death 8 May, 1834. See *Bloxam*, vii. 246.

Mills, Rev. William, of QUEEN'S COLL., Cambridge (B.A. 1840, M.A. 1844), adm. 'ad eundem' 26 May, 1849, died 23 Dec., 1874.

Mills, William Woodward, 1s. Henry James, of St. Trinity, Port of Spain, Isle of Trinidad, gent. WADHAM COLL., matric. 18 April, 1850, aged 18; B.A. 1854, M.A. 1857, rector of Aylmerton, Norfolk, since 1872.

Mills, William Yarnton, 1s. William, of Miserden, co. Gloucester, cler. TRINITY COLL., matric. 29 June, 1822, aged 18; B.A. 1826, M.A. 1831, rector of Miserden 1848, until his death 22 May, 1870.

Millward, Edmund, s. Edmund, of Claydon, Bucks, cler. BRASENOSE COLL., matric. 11 Oct., 1782, aged 17; B.A. from MAGDALEN HALL 1783, rector of Farthinghoe, Northants, 1794, until his death 18 March, 1838.

Millward, Thomas Egerton, s. Edmund, of East Claydon, Bucks, cler. MAGDALEN HALL, matric. 25 March, 1789, aged 16; B.C.L. 1799.

Millwood, William, o.s. William, of Kensington, Middlesex, gent. PEMBROKE COLL., matric. 4 Feb., 1863, aged 18; B.A. 1867, M.A. 1869, bar.-at-law, Middle Temple, 1868. See Foster's *Men at the Bar*. [5]

Milman, Arthur, 2s. Henry Hart, of Reading, Berks, cler. CHRIST CHURCH, matric. 4 June, 1846, aged 17; student 1846-60, B.A. 1850, M.A. 1853, bar.-at-law, Inner Temple, 1853, commissary of the dean and chapter of St. Paul's 1869, registrar of the University of London since 1879. See Foster's *Men at the Bar* & *Alumni West.*, 522.

Milman, Francis, s. Francis, of Paignton, Devon, cler. EXETER COLL., matric. 3 April, 1718, aged 14; B.A. 1722, rector of East Ogwell, and vicar of Abbots Kerswell, Devon, died in 1773.

Milman, (Sir) Francis (Bart.), s. Francis, of East Ogwell, Devon, cler. EXETER COLL., matric. 5 July, 1760, aged 13; B.A. 1764, fellow 1765-80, M.A. 1767, B.Med. 1770, D.Med. 1776, B.D. 1778, one of Dr. Radcliffe's travelling physicians (or fellows) 1771-80, F.R.C.P. 1778, president 1811-13, physician Middlesex Hospital 1777-9, physician extraordinary to the Royal Household 1785, etc., and physician to George III. 1806, F.R.S., created a baronet 28 Nov., 1800, died 27 June, 1821. See Foster's *Baronetage; Coll. Reg.*, 107; & Munk's *Roll*, ii. 316.

Milman, Henry Clayton, 2s. George Alderson, of Shoeburyness, Suffolk, arm. KEBLE COLL., matric. 16 Oct., 1883, aged 19; B.A. 1887.

Milman, Henry Hart, s. Francis, of St. James's, Westminster, baronet. BRASENOSE COLL., matric. 25 May, 1810, aged 19; B.A. 1814, fellow 1814-9, M.A. 1816, B. & D.D. 1849, professor of poetry 1821-31, Bampton lecturer 1827, vicar of St. Mary's, Reading, 1817-35, rector of St. Margaret's, Westminster, and canon of Westminster 1835-49, dean of St. Paul's 1849, until his death 4 Sep., 1868, historian and poet. See *Eton School Lists*. [10]

Milman, Henry Salusbury, 2s. Francis Miles, of Bassaleg, co. Monmouth, arm. MERTON COLL., matric. 25 June, 1840, aged 18, postmaster 1840-4, B.A. 1844; fellow ALL SOULS' COLL. 1844-58, M.A. 1848, bar.-at-law, Inner Temple, 1848, a director of Society of Antiquaries 1880, assistant land commissioner 1882. See Foster's *Men at the Bar* & *Eton School Lists*.

Milman, Robert, 2s. William George, of Easton-in-Gordano, Somerset, baronet. EXETER COLL., matric. 9 May, 1833, aged 17; scholar 1834-8, B.A. 1838, M.A. 1867, created D.D. 30 Jan., 1867, bishop of Calcutta, 1867-76, vicar of Chaddleworth 1840-51, of Lamborne, Bucks, 1851-62, and of Great Marlow, Bucks, 1862-7, died 15 March, 1876. See Foster's *Baronetage* & *Coll. Reg.*, 152.

Millman, William, s. James, of Buckland Filleigh, Devon, pleb. EXETER COLL., matric. 18 Dec., 1738, aged 19; B.A. 1742.

Millman, William, s. William, of Beaford, Devon, cler. EXETER COLL., matric. 10 June, 1782, aged 19.

Milman, (Sir) William (Bart.), 1s. William, of Easton-in-Gordano, Somerset, baronet. BRASENOSE COLL., matric. 31 Jan., 1833, aged 19; B.A. 1837, 3rd baronet, bar.-at-law, Inner Temple, 1841, died 17 June, 1885. See Foster's *Baronetage*. [15]

Milman, (Sir) William George (Bart.), s. Francis, of St. George's, Westminster, doctor. EXETER COLL., matric. 22 May, 1798, aged 17; B.A. 1801, 2nd baronet, died 21 Aug., 1857. See Foster's *Baronetage* & *Eton School Lists*.

Milman, William Henry, 1s. Henry H., of Reading, Berks, cler. CHRIST CHURCH, matric. 9 June, 1843, aged 18; student 1843-58, B.A. 1847, M.A. 1850, rector of St. Augustine's with St. Faith under St. Paul's, London, 1857, minor canon of St. Paul's 1859. See *Alumni West.*, 526.

Milne, Rev. Ernest Arthur, y.s. Frank, of Monken Hadley, Herts, arm. KEBLE COLL., matric. 18 Oct., 1881, aged 19; B.A. 1886, M.A. 1888.

Milne, Francis Alexander, 1s. Francis, of Hadley, Middlesex, arm. KEBLE COLL., matric. 13 Oct., 1873, aged 19; B.A. 1877, M.A. 1880, bar.-at-law, Lincoln's Inn, 1880. See Foster's *Men at the Bar*.

Milne, Henry, 1s. William, of Manchester, arm. BRASENOSE COLL., matric. 6 March, 1834, aged 18; scholar 1835-7, B.A. 1838, M.A. 1840, rector (and patron) of Holme Hale, Norfolk, 1844. See *Manchester School Reg.*, iii. 223. [20]

Milne, Henry, 6s. Nathaniel, of Islington, Middlesex, arm. EXETER COLL., matric. 6 Dec., 1838, aged 19; B.A. from BRASENOSE COLL. 1842, M.A. 1845, vicar of Harlington, Beds, 1854-8, rector of Letchworth, Herts, 1859, until his death 20 April, 1885.

Milne, Henry Ernest, 4s. Nathaniel, of Radcliffe, Lancashire, cler. BRASENOSE COLL., matric. 4 March, 1879, aged 18; B.A. 1882, M.A. 1885, bar.-at-law, Inner Temple, 1884. See Foster's *Men at the Bar* & *Eton School Lists*.

Milne, John Bowker, 1s. Nathaniel, of Radcliffe, near Manchester, cler. BRASENOSE COLL., matric. 28 May, 1863, aged 19; B.A. 1867.

Milne, John Haworth, y.s. Oswald, of Preston, Lancashire, arm. BRASENOSE COLL., matric. 9 June, 1846, aged 18; B.A. 1850, M.A. 1854, vicar of Thatcham, Berks, 1855-62, rector of Itchingfield, Sussex, 1862-73, assistant-chaplain Dinan 1873-6, and at Avranches 1876.

Milne, Joseph Grafton, 2s. William, of Bowdon, Cheshire, gent. CORPUS CHRISTI COLL., matric. 20 Oct., 1886, aged 18; scholar 1886. [25]

Milne, Richard Henry, 1s. Henry, of Holme Hall, Norfolk, cler. BRASENOSE COLL., matric. 19 May, 1864, aged 19; B.A. 1868, held various curacies 1872-83, vicar of Goathland, Yorks, 1883.

Milne, Robert Duncan Gordon, 2s. George Gordon, of Cupar, co. Fife, cler. LINCOLN COLL., matric. 6 Nov., 1862, aged 18.

Milne, Robert Oswald, o.s. William Henry, of Prestwich, Lancashire, arm. BRASENOSE COLL., matric. 1 June, 1871, aged 18; B.A. 1876, of London, merchant. See *Rugby School Reg.*

Milne, Robert Matthew, 4s. Alexander George Matthew, of Charlton, Kent, gent. MAGDALEN HALL, matric. 25 Feb., 1836, aged 23; B.A. 1839.

Milne, Thomas (Milles), M.A. from CLARE HALL, Cambridge; incorp. 17 Dec., 1723, B.A. 1716, M.A. 1720. [30]

Milne, William, of ST. JOHN'S COLL., Cambridge (9th Wrangler and B.A. 1833, M.A. 1836); adm. 'ad eundem' 22 Oct., 1840.

Milne, William Charles Beaumont, 1s. William Charles, of Shanghai, China, arm. WADHAM COLL., matric. 26 April, 1867, aged 19.

Milne, William Herbert, 1s. William, of Bowdon, Cheshire, gent. BALLIOL COLL., matric. 21 April, 1882, aged 18; scholar 1881, until his death 16 Nov., 1884.

Milne, Rev. William Somerville, 4s. James, of Dundee, gent. NON-COLL., matric. 22 Nov., 1879, aged 29; B.A. 1884, M.A. 1886.

Milner, Alfred, o.s. Charles, of Giessen, Germany, D.Med. BALLIOL COLL., matric. 1 Feb., 1873, aged 18, scholar 1872-6, Jenkyns exhibitioner 1875-7; fellow NEW COLL. 1876, B.A. 1877, M.A. 1879, bar.-at-law, Inner Temple, 1881. See Foster's *Men at the Bar.*

Milner, Charles, 1s. Charles, of Farningham, Kent, arm. BRASENOSE COLL., matric. 22 Jan., 1820, aged 18; B.A. 1824, of Preston Hall, Kent. See *Eton School Lists.*

Milner, Rev. Charles James, 1s. James, of Stockton-on-Tees, co. Durham, cler. LINCOLN COLL., matric. 20 Oct., 1876, aged 19; B.A. & M.A. from NEW INN HALL 1883.

Milner, Dudley Francis, 4s. William, of Nun Appleton, Yorks, baronet. EXETER COLL., matric. 19 March, 1872, aged 18; died 1881. See *Rugby School Reg.* [5]

Milner, Edmund Taylor, 3s. Ralph, of Salford, Lancashire, gent. MERTON COLL., matric. 15 Oct., 1877, aged 18; scholar 1877-82, B.A. 1881, B.Med. & M.A. 1886.

Milner, Edward, 1s. Henry Beilby William, of Aldwark, Yorks, arm. CHRIST CHURCH, matric. 24 May, 1877, aged 19; See Foster's *Baronetage & Eton School Lists.*

Milner, (Sir) Frederick George (Bart.), 2s. William Mordaunt Edward, of Nun Appleton, near Tadcastle, Yorks, baronet. CHRIST CHURCH, matric. 30 May, 1868, aged 18; B.A. 1873, 7th baronet, M.P. Yorks 1883-4. See Foster's *Baronetage & Eton School Lists.*

Milner, Gamaliel, o.s. John Crosland, of Thurleston, Yorks, gent. CHRIST CHURCH, matric. 14 Oct., 1870, aged 18; B.A. 1873, M.A. 1880, held various curacies 1877-86, vicar of Hoyland Swaine, Yorks, 1886. See Foster's *Yorkshire Collection.*

Milner, George, s. William, of St. George's, Hanover Square, London, baronet. CHRIST CHURCH, matric. 17 Oct., 1811, aged 18; rector of Downham, and of Larling, Norfolk, died at Sandgate Dec., 1824. See Foster's *Baronetage & Eton School Lists.* [10]

Milner, George Ernest John, 1s. John, of Frating, Essex, cler. NON-COLL., matric. 14 Oct., 1882, aged 19; B.A. from HERTFORD COLL. 1885.

Milner, Henry, s. William, of Askham, Westmoreland, cler. ST. EDMUND HALL, matric. 6 June, 1744, aged 18; B.A. 1748, brother of William 1742.

Milner, Henry Beilby (William), 2s. William M., of Bolton Percy, Yorks, baronet. MERTON COLL., matric. 9 Feb., 1842, aged 18, B.A. 1845; fellow ALL SOULS' COLL. 1845-54, M.A. 1850, died 7 Ju , 1876. See Foster's *Baronetage & Eton School Lists.*

Milner, Henry Stephen, s. William, of London, baronet. CHRIST CHURCH, matric. 13 July, 1781, aged 17, B.A. 1785; B.C.L. from ALL SOULS' COLL. 1788, D.C.L. 1793, rector of Thribergh and Adwick-le-Street, Yorks, 1811, until his death 6 May, 1843. See Foster's *Baronetage.*

Milner, James Walker, 2s. Thomas, of Sheffield, Yorks, gent. LINCOLN COLL., matric. 18 March, 1842, aged 19; B.A. 1846, M.A. 1850, vicar of St. James's, Birkenhead, 1870. [15]

Milner, John, 1s. John, of Orton, Westmoreland, gent. QUEEN'S COLL., matric. 17 June, 1841, aged 19; scholar 1841-4, B.A. 1845, M.A. 1878, chaplain R.N. 1855, retired list 1873, F.R.G.S., vicar of Alston, Cumberland, 1873-5, chaplain in ordinary to H.R.H. Duke of Edinburgh 1875, rector of Middleton-in-Teesdale 1875.

Milner, Raper, s. George, of Hauxwell, Yorks, pleb. PEMBROKE COLL., matric. 8 April, 1813, aged 21; scholar 1813-16.

Milner, Richard John, 2s. Edward, of Liverpool, gent. EXETER COLL., matric. 2 June, 1868, aged 18; exhibitioner 1869-73, B.A. 1872, M.A. 1875, vicar of St. Michael's and All Angel's, Lower Sydenham, 1879-83, rector of Stock-Gaylard, Dorset, 1883. See *Coll. Reg.*, 164.

Milner, Robert Kennion, s. David, of Isle of Jamaica, arm. UNIVERSITY COLL., matric. 16 Jan., 1786, aged 17; B.A. 1790, M.A. 1794.

Milner, Thomas, 1s. James Walker, of Liverpool, cler. BALLIOL COLL., matric. 24 Oct., 1885, aged 20. [20]

Milner, Thomas Wheeler, s. David, of Kingston, Isle of Jamaica, gent. QUEEN'S COLL., matric. 22 Feb., 1780, aged 19.

Milner, Walter Hebden, 2s. Charles, of Clapham, Surrey, gent. ST. EDMUND HALL, matric. 19 Jan., 1861, aged 19; chaplain to the forces, Aldershot 1875-6, Malta 1876-83, Woolwich 1883.

Milner, Rev. Walter Metcalfe Holmes, 2s. John, of Greenock, cler. QUEEN'S COLL., matric. 22 Oct., 1878, aged 19; scholar 1878-82, B.A. 1882.

Milner, William, s. William, of Askham, Westmoreland, cler. QUEEN'S COLL., matric. 31 March, 1742, aged 17; B.A. 1745, M.A. 1753, vicar of Startforth, Yorks, nearly 50 years, and of Brigham, Cumberland, died 12 March, 1797.

Milner, (Sir) William Mordaunt (Bart.), s. William, of Appleton, Yorks, baronet. CHRIST CHURCH, matric. 19 Feb., 1798, aged 18; 4th baronet, died 25 March, 1855. See Foster's *Baronetage & Eton School Lists.* [25]

Milner, (Sir) William Mordaunt (Bart.), 1s. William Mordaunt Edward, of London, baronet. CHRIST CHURCH, matric. 23 May, 1866, aged 18; 6th baronet, died 14 April, 1880. See Foster's *Baronetage & Eton School Lists.*

Milner, (Sir) William Mordaunt Edward (Bart.), 1s. William, of Bolton Percy, Yorks, baronet. CHRIST CHURCH, matric. 30 May, 1838, aged 17; B.A. 1841, M.A. 1844, 5th baronet, M.P. York 1848-57, died 12 Feb., 1867. See Foster's *Baronetage & Eton School Lists.*

Milnes, Alfred, 2s. Benjamin, of Bolton, Lancashire, arm. LINCOLN COLL., matric. 18 Oct., 1871, aged 22; scholar 1871-5.

Milnes, Christopher, 2s. John, of Stixwold, co. Lincoln, arm. LINCOLN COLL., matric. 4 March, 1819, aged 18; B.A. 1822, M.A. 1825, B.D. 1833, rector of Scampton, co. Lincoln, 1828, and of Aisthorpe 1833, until his death 7 Feb., 1850.

Milnes, Edward, s. Thomas, of Henley, Oxon, cler. ALL SOULS' COLL., matric. 16 July, 1807, aged 19; B.A. 1811, vicar of Watlington, Oxon, 1814, until his death 11 July, 1841. [30]

Milnes, Edward, 1s. Edward, of Watlington, Oxon, cler. WORCESTER COLL., matric. 14 June, 1838, aged 18.

Milnes, Henry Walthall. TRINITY COLL., 1848. See WALTHALL.

Milnes, James, s. James, of Ingestre, co. Stafford, cler. HART HALL, matric. 10 May, 1723, aged 20; B.A. 14 Feb., 1726-7.

Milnes, John, s. John, of Wakefield, co. Worcester (*sic*), arm. WORCESTER COLL., matric. 6 July, 1818, aged 18; exhibitioner 1819-20.

Milnes, Nicholas Bourne, 2s. William, of Ashover, co. Derby, arm. TRINITY COLL., matric. 5 July, 1845, aged 19; B.A. 1849, M.A. 1853, rector of Collyweston, co. Lincoln, 1854. See *Rugby School Reg.*, 217. [35]

Milnes, Richard Monckton, created D.C.L. 20 June, 1855 (son of Robert Pemberton Milnes, of Fryston Hall, and Bawtry Hall, Yorks), M.A. from TRINITY COLL., Cambridge, 1831, and hon. fellow 1875-85, F.R.S., poet, M.P. Pontefract 1837-63, created Baron Houghton 20 May, 1863, died 11 Aug., 1885. See Foster's *Peerage.*

Minchin, Rev. Charles Humphrey, 1s. Henry, of Lyncombe, Somerset, cler. ST. MARY HALL, matric. 24 Oct., 1873, aged 18; B.A. 1876, M.A. 1880, aged 18.

Minchin, Edward Alfred, 2s. Charles Nicholl, of Weston-super-Mare, gent. KEBLE COLL., matric. 19 Oct., 1886, aged 20.

Minchin, Harry Christopher Montague, 3s. Henry Charles, of Wootton St. Mary, co. Gloucester, cler. WADHAM COLL., matric. 15 Oct., 1881, aged 19; scholar 1881-5, B.A. 1886.

Minchin, Harry Holdsworth, 4s. James Innes, of Farlington, Hants, arm. WADHAM COLL., matric. 19 March, 1851, aged 18; B.A. 1855, M.A. 1857, rector of Wormley, Herts, 1860-5, vicar of Woodford Halse, Northants, 1865-84, rector of Little Bromley, Essex, 1884. [25]

Minchin, Henry Charles, M.A. TRINITY COLL., Dublin, 1847 (B.A. 1833); adm. 'ad eundem' 30 June, 1854.

Minchin, John Champneys, 2s. Henry, of Botley, Hants, arm. NEW COLL., matric. 8 June, 1820, aged 19; fellow 1820-32, B.A. 1824, M.A. 1829, dean of arts 1829, rector of St. Mildred, London, etc., 1837, and of St. Olave, Jewry, 1872, until his death 22 Jan., 1880.

Minchin, Lawrence Harry Jackson, 1s. Harry Holdsworth, of Wormley, Herts, cler. CHRIST CHURCH, matric. 13 Oct., 1882, aged 19; exhibitioner 1882-3.

Minchinton, Edward Henry, s. Edward, of Mudford, Somerset, arm. WADHAM COLL., matric. 13 Nov., 1807, aged 20.

Mines, Francis, s. Thomas, of Hereford (city), pleb. JESUS COLL., matric. 17 Dec., 1762, aged 18; B.A. from CHRIST CHURCH 1766, M.A. 1769, vicar of Twining, co. Gloucester, and of Spilsbury, Oxon, at his death 4 June, 1792. [30]

Minet, Charles William, 1s. Isaac, of St. Marylebone, London, arm. UNIVERSITY COLL., matric. 4 April, 1821, aged 17; B.A. 1824.

Minet, William, o.s. James Lewis, of London, arm. UNIVERSITY COLL., matric. 15 Oct., 1870, aged 19; B.A. 1874, M.A. 1877, bar.-at-law, Inner Temple, 1876. See Foster's *Men at the Bar*.

Minett, Rev. Thomas Hopkins, o.s. William, of Wickwar, co. Gloucester, gent. KEBLE COLL., matric. 14 Oct., 1879, aged 19; B.A. 1882, M.A. 1886.

Minifie, Burnet, s. James, of Staplegrove, Somerset, cler. WADHAM COLL., matric. 16 Dec., 1755, aged 18.

Minifie, James, s. James, of Staplegrove, Somerset, gent. WADHAM COLL., matric. 15 March, 1724-5, aged 18; B.A. 1728, M.A. 1731. [35]

Minifie, James, s. James, of Staplegrove, Somerset, cler. WADHAM COLL., matric. 29 March, 1754, aged 18; B.A. 1757, rector of Goathurst, Norton Fitzwarren, and Staplegrove, at his death 24 July, 1789.

Minifee, John, s. Edward, of Bow, Devon, pleb. EXETER COLL., matric. 22 May, 1729, aged 19; B.A. 9 Feb., 1732-3.

Minoch, Justinian, s. Francis, of St. Olave's, Crutched Friars, London, gent. TRINITY COLL., matric. 13 June, 1801, aged 24.

Minor, Augustus Henry, 1s. John Bishton, of Astley, Salop, arm. BRASENOSE COLL., matric. 7 June, 1849, aged 18; B.A. 1853.

Minshull, Francis, s. William, of Aylesbury, Bucks, gent. JESUS COLL., matric. 15 May, 1787, aged 18; B.A. 1791, M.A. 1793, rector of Nunney, Somerset, 1797, until his death 28 June, 1817. [40]

Minshull, Thomas Freer, 4s. Thomas Evans, of Castle Bromwich, co. Warwick, cler. ST. EDMUND HALL, matric. 25 Oct., 1881, aged 20.

Minshull, Thomas Samuel, s. Thomas, of Salford, Lancashire, arm. BRASENOSE COLL., matric. 13 June, 1750, aged 17.

Minter, Stephen, s. William, of Barnham, Suffolk, gent. CHRIST CHURCH, matric. 25 May, 1745, aged 19; B.A. 174

Mintern, Henry, s. Henry, of Cheddington, Dorset, cler. WADHAM COLL., matric. 10 March, 1717-8, aged 18; B.A. 1721. See Hutchin's *Dorset*, iv., 422.

Minto, Walter, s. Robert, of Isle of Jamaica, arm. CHRIST CHURCH, matric. 22 Nov., 1798, aged 18.

Minto, William, 2s. James, of Alford, co. Aberdeen, arm. MERTON COLL., matric. 18 Oct., 1866, aged 21.

Minton, Charles Lee, 3s. Thomas, of Stoke, near Newcastle, co. Stafford, arm. QUEEN'S COLL., matric. 6 Dec., 1821, aged 21. [5]

Minton, Edward, s. Edward, of London, gent. WORCESTER COLL., matric. 29 March, 1757, aged 17; B.A. 1761.

Minton, Harry Herbert, 3s. Samuel, of Ryton, Salop, cler. NON-COLL., matric. 17 Oct., 1881, aged 20; B.A. from ST. JOHN'S COLL. 1886.

Minton, Samuel, 2s. Thomas, of Church Preen, Salop, gent. EXETER COLL., matric. 5 June, 1833, aged 19; B.A. 1837, M.A. 1841.

Minton, Samuel. WORCESTER COLL., 1837. See SENHOUSE.

Minton, Thomas Powel, 2s. Richard Roland, of Birkenhead, Cheshire, gent. NON-COLL., matric. 19 Oct., 1876, aged 18. [10]

Minty, Rev. Francis Arden, 2s. Richard George Pern, of Petersfield, Hants, gent. ST. EDMUND HALL, matric. 23 Oct., 1877, aged 19; B.A. 1880, M.A. 1884.

Minty, Henry Oliver, 1s. Oliver, of Cheltenham, gent. EXETER COLL., matric. 18 Oct., 1883, aged 20; exhibitioner 1882-6, B.A. 1887.

Mirehouse, Henry George, 1s. Henry John, of Easton-in-Gordano, Somerset, arm. MERTON COLL., matric. 18 Oct., 1880, aged 18; B.A. 1885.

Mirehouse, Richard Walter Byrd, 1s. Richard Byrd Levett, of Milford, near Berkswich, co. Stafford, arm. UNIVERSITY COLL., matric. 16 April, 1869, aged 19; of the Hall, Angle, co. Pembroke, assumed the additional surname of MIREHOUSE. See *Eton School Lists.*

Mirrielees, William, 3s. James, of Aberdeen, Scotland, arm. QUEEN'S COLL., matric. 27 March, 1847, aged 21; B.A. 1850, M.A. 1853, head-master Berwick-upon-Tweed Grammar School 1861-74, rector of Hawthorn, co. Durham, 1874-80, vicar of Whitworth, co. Durham, 1880, until his death 16 Nov., 1882. [15]

Missing, Rev. John, 2s. Richard William, of Bishops Sutton, Hants, gent. MAGDALEN HALL, matric. 26 Nov., 1822, aged 28; B.A. 1826, M.A. 1829, of Newdown, Bedford, died 20 Dec., 1840.

Mister, Samuel Wright, s. John, of Shipston-upon-Stour, co. Worcester, gent. ST. JOHN'S COLL., matric. 1 July, 1788, aged 18; B.A. 1792, fellow, M.A. 1796, B.D. 1801, of Batsford, co. Gloucester, rector of Little Rollwright, Oxon, 1797, until his death 7 May, 1836. See *Robinson*, 143.

Mitchel, John, s. John, of Knottingly, Yorks, pleb. UNIVERSITY COLL., matric. 5 March, 1752, aged 18, B.A. 1755; M.A. from EMMANUEL COLL., Cambridge, 1783, rector of Grendon, and vicar of Aldoty (or Austry), co. Warwick, sometime master of Atherstone School, died 26 Nov., 1790.

Mitchel, John, s. John, of Grendon, co. Warwick, cler. WORCESTER COLL., matric. 19 June, 1790, aged 18; B.A. 1794, M.A. 1797, rector of St. Nicholas, Cole Abbey, and St. Nicholas Olaves, London, 1817, until his death 4 April, 1846.

Mitchell, Albert George, 2s. Thomas, of Birmingham, gent. NEW COLL., matric. 19 Oct., 1874, aged 22; B.Mus. 1878. [20]

Mitchell, Alexander, 1s. Alexander, of Aberdeen, Scotland, arm. WADHAM COLL., matric. 19 June, 1848, aged 16; migrated to CHRIST CHURCH same year, a student of the Inner Temple 1850, M.P. Berwick-on-Tweed 1865-8, died 16 May, 1873. See *Eton School Lists.*

Mitchell, Andrew, 2s. Andrew, of New York, America, arm. TRINITY COLL., matric. 15 Oct., 1864, aged 20; B.A. 1868, M.A. 1872.

Mitchell, Andrew Alexander, o.s. Andrew, of Glasgow, gent. EXETER COLL., matric. 22 Jan., 1880, aged 20.

Mitchell, Rev. Arthur Fancourt, 2s. St. John, of Pentney, Norfolk, cler. LINCOLN COLL., matric. 18 Oct., 1879, aged 20; B.A. 1883.

Mitchell, Charles, 3s. John, of London, arm. WADHAM COLL., matric. 16 May, 1833, aged 18; B.A. 1837, M.A. 1839. [25]

Mitchell, David William, 1s. Alexander, of Gerard's Cross, Bucks, arm. CHRIST CHURCH, matric. 7 June, 1832, aged 18; B.A. 1836.

Mitchell, Edward, s. Edward Coupland, of Boston, co. Lincoln, gent. ST. JOHN'S COLL., matric. 29 June, 1846, aged 18; B.A. 1850, M.A. 1854, B.D. 1859, fellow 1846-78, dean of arts 1858, vice-president 1862, bursar 1863, vicar of Northmoor, Oxon, 1858-67, curate of Kemsing, Kent, 1872-4, took the name of MITCHELL in lieu of COUPLAND by royal licence 4 Jan., 1879. See *Robinson*, 261.

Mitchell, Ernest William John, o.s. James Johnstone, of Walcot, Bath, arm. KEBLE COLL., matric. 15 Oct., 1877, aged 18; B.A. 1880, M.A. 1884.

Mitchell, Frederick, 4s. John, of Kingsclere, Hants, cler. ORIEL COLL., matric. 22 Oct., 1840, aged 19; bible clerk 1840-3.

Mitchell, Henry, o.s. Samuel, of Chaddesley Corbett, co. Worcester, gent. LINCOLN COLL., matric. 1 June, 1837, aged 18; B.A. 1841, M.A. 1844, vicar of Bosham, Sussex, since 1845. See *St. Paul's School Reg.*, 279. [30]

Mitchell, Henry St. John, 1s. (Hon.) William Henry Fancourt, of Emberton, Australia, arm. EXETER COLL., matric. 10 Oct., 1873, aged 22; B.A. 1876.

Mitchell, Herbert Leonard, 3s. Francis Henry, of Marylebone, Westminster, London, arm. UNIVERSITY COLL., matric. 11 May, 1854, aged 18; B.A. 1879, M.A. 1883.

Mitchell, James, s. William, of Westminster arm. CHRIST CHURCH, matric. 2 June, 1751, aged 18.

Mitchell, James, s. James, of Richmond, Surrey, arm. CHRIST CHURCH, matric. 5 May, 1818, aged 18.

Mitchell, James, o.s. James, of Marylebone, London, arm. CHRIST CHURCH, matric. 12 Dec., 1826, aged 17; B.A. 1830, M.A. 1833, of Holbrook Hall, Suffolk, J.P., D.L., Herts, bar.-at-law, Lincoln's Inn, 1835. See Foster's *Men at the Bar.* [35]

Mitchell, James Dennistown, o.s. William Gillesbie, of Govan, co. Lanark, arm. NON-COLL., matric. 18 Oct., 1875, aged 22; B.A. from EXETER COLL. 1879, of Carwood, co. Lanark, a student of the Inner Temple 1879.

Mitchell, John, s. John, of Evesham, co. Worcester, cler. BALLIOL COLL., matric. 17 Dec., 1731, aged 18.

Mitchell, John, s. Josiah, of St. Sepulchre's, London, gent. ST. JOHN'S COLL., matric. 1 July, 1767, aged 17; B.A. 1771, M.A. 1776, B.D, 1781. See *Gent.'s Mag.*, 1793, i. 480; & *Robinson*, 118.

Mitchell, John, s. David, of Isle of Jamaica, arm. CHRIST CHURCH, matric. 5 Feb., 1800, aged 18; B.A. 1804, M.A. 1808, bar.-at-law, Lincoln's Inn, 1808, died in Nov., 1812. See *Alumni West.*, 447.

Mitchell, John, 1s. Thomas, of Skipton, Yorks, arm. UNIVERSITY COLL., matric. 23 Oct., 1868, aged 18; B.A. 1872, M.A. 1875, held various curacies 1872-83, perp. curate Minsterley, Salop, 1883. [40]

Mitchell, John Henry Turner. ORIEL COLL., 1856. See MOWBRAY.

itchell, Rev. John Thomas, o.s. Thomas, of Glasgow, arm. CORPUS CHRISTI COLL., matric. 19 Oct., 1882, aged 19; B.A. 1887.

itchell, Josiah, 8s. John, of Kingsclere, Hants, cler. ALL SOULS' COLL., matric. 8 Feb., 1853, aged 19; bible clerk 1853-7, B.A. 1856, M.A. 1859, vicar of Alberbury, Salop, 1866-86, rector of Barford, St. Martin, Wilts, 1886.

itchell, Lancelott, s. John, of Kingfair, Salop, gent. NEW COLL., matric. 28 Nov., 1723, aged 18; B.C.L. 1728 (as MICHELL).

itchell, Lancelot, o.s. Thomas Davis, of Herne Bay, Kent, arm. UNIVERSITY COLL., matric. 18 Oct., 1886, aged 18; exhibitioner 1886.

itchell, Moses, 4s. William, of Portsmouth, Hants, gent. MAGDALEN HALL, matric. 17 Feb., 1824, aged 17; B.A. 1829, M.A. 1830. **[5]**

itchell, Rev. Muirhead, 2s. John, of St. Pancras, London, arm. UNIVERSITY COLL., matric. 5 Feb., 1829, aged 19; B.A. 1832, M.A. 1835, H.M.'s inspector of schools, died 26 Feb., 1876.

itchell, Peter, s. Peter, of Merriott, Somerset, pleb. BALLIOL COLL., matric. 18 March, 1748-9, aged 20; B.A. 1753.

itchell, Peter, 'pharmacopola;' privilegiatus 8 Oct., 1772.

itchell, Peter Chalmers, 1s. Alexander, of Dunfermline, co. Fife, D.D. CHRIST CHURCH, matric. 10 Oct., 1884, aged 19; exhibitioner 1884.

itchell, Richard Arthur Henry, 1s. Richard, of Enderby, near Leicester, arm. BALLIOL COLL., matric. 12 Oct., 1861, aged 18; B.A. 1866, M.A. 1869, a master at Eton College. **[10]**

itchell, St. John, 6s. George Berkeley, of Leicester (town), cler. ST. EDMUND HALL, matric. 20 Nov., 1835, aged 19; B.A. 1839, vicar of Browne Edge, co. Stafford, 1847-51, vicar of Pentney, Norfolk, 1851-75, perp. curate West Bilney, Norfolk, 1852-75, chaplain St. Mark, Isle of Man, 1875-7, etc.

itchell, St. John Fancourt, 2s. Thomas Robinson, of Stranorlar, co. Donegal, D.Med. MERTON COLL., matric. 20 Jan., 1877, aged 36.

Mitchell, Theophilus 2s. Joseph Theophilus, of Lee, Kent, arm. MAGDALEN HALL, matric. 26 March, 1858, aged 18; B.A. & M.A. 1864, bar.-at-law, Inner Temple, 1876, died 16 Oct., 1881.

Mitchell, Thomas, s. John, of Kingsclere, Hants, cler. ORIEL COLL., matric. 17 Dec., 1835, aged 17; bible clerk 1835-40, B.A. 1840, held various curacies 1859-77, vicar of Great Tew, Oxon, since 1877.

Mitchell, Thomas Davis, 1s. Thomas, of Poole, Dorset, arm. MAGDALEN HALL, matric. 22 April, 1868, aged 32; bar.-at-law, Inner Temple, 1868, died 14 Feb., 1877. **[15]**

Mitchell, Sir Thomas Levingston; created D.C.L. 12 June, 1839 (son of John Mitchell), F.R.S., F.R.G.S., surveyor-general, joined the army in the Peninsula in 1809, was commissioned to survey the battlefields of the Peninsula, surveyor-general Eastern Australia 1827, knighted 17 April, 1839, colonel 1854, died 5 Oct., 1855.

Mitchell, William, s. William, of Honiton, Devon, gent. ST. MARY HALL, matric. 30 March, 1811, aged 30.

Mitchell, William, 1s. Ephraim Kershaw, of Mytholmroyd, near Halifax, Yorks, gent. ST. ALBAN HALL, matric. 22 Oct., 1867, aged 26; B.A. 1873, M.A. 1875, vicar of St. Luke, Bradford, 1881.

Mitchell, William, 2s. Thomas, of Skipton, co. York, gent. UNIVERSITY COLL., matric. 14 April, 1871, aged 18; NON-COLL. B.A. 1875, a student of Lincoln's Inn 1874. **[19]**

Mitchell, Rev. William Henry, 1s. William, of Arundel, Sussex, arm. TRINITY COLL., matric. 26 Jan., 1878, aged 19; B.A. 1881, M.A. 1884.

Mitchener, George Henry, 1s. — M., of Plymouth, Devon, arm. EXETER COLL., matric. 10 June, 1841, aged 18; B.A. 1845, assistant-curate Charles Church, Plymouth, at his death 13 Jan., 1847.

Mitchener, John, s. John, of St. Mary's, Warwick (town), gent. MAGDALEN HALL, matric. 13 June, 1716, aged 17; B.A. 1720.

Mitcheson, Richard Edmund, 1s. Richard Edmund, of Clapton, Middlesex, arm. ST. JOHN'S COLL., matric. 12 Oct., 1878, aged 18, scholar 1878-83, B.A. 1883; a senior student CHRIST CHURCH 1883, M.A. 1885, B.C.L. 1886, bar.-at-law of the Inner Temple, 1885. See *Robinson*, 380.

Mitchinson, John, o.s. John, of St. Mary-le-Bow, Durham (city), gent. PEMBROKE COLL., matric. 20 Feb., 1851, aged 17; scholar 1851-5, B.A. 1855, fellow 1855-81, M.A. 1857, D.C.L. 1864, hon. fellow 1884, select preacher 1872-3, D.D. by diploma Durham 1873, head-master King's School Canterbury, 1859-73, bishop of Barbados and the Windward Islands 1873-81, coadjutor to bishop of Antigua 1879-82, and to bishop of Peterborough 1881, Ramsden preacher at Cambridge 1883, hon. canon of Canterbury 1871, rector of Sibstone, co. Derby, 1881, archdeacon of Leicester 1886, etc. See *Crockford.*

Mitchison, Arthur Maw, 4s. William Anthony, of Sunbury, Middlesex, gent. PEMBROKE COLL., matric. 23 Oct., 1872, aged 17; B.A. 1876, bar.-at-law, Inner Temple, 1879. See Foster's *Men at the Bar* & *Eton School Lists.* **[25]**

Mitchison, Richard Stovin, 2s. William Anthony, of Sunbury, Middlesex, gent. PEMBROKE COLL., matric. 26 Oct., 1868, aged 18; B.A. 1873, M.A. 1875, rector of Barby, co. Warwick, since 1880. See *Eton School Lists.*

Mitford, Algernon Bertram (C.B.), 3s. Henry Reveley, of St. George's, Hanover Square, London, arm. CHRIST CHURCH, matric. 30 May, 1855, aged 18; of Batsford Park, co. Gloucester, J.P., D.L., entered Foreign Office 1858, secretary of Embassy at St. Petersburgh 1863-5, Pekin 1865-6, Japan 1866, secretary to Commissioners of Public Works, etc., 1874. See Foster's *Peerage*, E. REDESDALE; & *Eton School Lists.*

Mitford, Charles Lloyd, 2s. William Townley, of Pitshill, Sussex, cler. CHRIST CHURCH, matric. 31 May, 1879, aged 18; B.A. 1884.

Mitford, Gawen Aynsley. UNIVERSITY COLL., 1786. See MIDFORD.

Mitford, George Redesdale, 4s. Bertram, of Rocester, Northumberland, gent. ST. EDMUND HALL, matric. 12 Oct., 1861, aged 19. See Foster's *Peerage*, E. REDESDALE. **[30]**

Mitford, Henry Reveley, o.s. (Henry), of Marylebone, London, arm. MAGDALEN COLL., matric. 15 Oct., 1822, aged 18; of Exbury Park, Hants, an attaché at Florence 1825, died 21 Nov., 1883. See Foster's *Peerage* & *Eton School Lists.*

Mitford, John, s. William, of All Hallows, London, arm. QUEEN'S COLL., matric. 9 July, 1729, aged 17; of Newton House and Exbury, Hants, bar.-at-law, Lincoln's Inn, 1734, died 16 May, 1761. See Foster's *Peerage.*

Mitford, John, s. John, of Richmond, Surrey, arm. ORIEL COLL., matric. 6 March, 1801, aged 19; B.A. 1804, editor of the *Gent.'s Mag.* 1833-50, vicar of Benhall 1810, rector of Stratford St. Andrew 1824, and of Weston St. Peter 1815 (all Suffolk), until his death 27 April, 1859. See Foster's *Peerage.*

Mitford, John Reveley, 1s. John, of St. Pancras, London, arm. CHRIST CHURCH, matric. 1 June, 1826, aged 19; B.A. 1830, M.A. 1837, vicar of Manaccan, Cornwall, Jan., until his death 19 March, 1838. See Foster's *Peerage.*

Mitford, John (Thomas Freeman), o.s. John, of Portrush, co. Antrim, Baron Redesdale. NEW COLL., matric. 9 May, 1823, aged 17; B.A. 1825, M.A. 1828, created D.C.L. 7 June, 1853, 2nd baron, created Earl of Redesdale 3 Jan., 1877, chairman of committees of House of Lords, etc., 1851, until his death April, 1886. See Foster's *Peerage* & *Eton School Lists.* **[35]**

Mitford, William, s. William, of Exbury, Hants, arm. TRINITY COLL., matric. 22 March, 1731-2, aged 15; B.A. 1735, of Lovells Hill, and Maules, Berks, brother of John 1729.

Mitford, William, s. John, of St. Andrew's, London, arm. QUEEN'S COLL., matric. 16 July, 1761, aged 18; of Newtown, Hants, a student of the Middle Temple 1763, colonel Hampshire militia, M.P. Newport, Cornwall, 1785-90, Beeralston 1796-1802, and of Romney 1812-8, professor of ancient history at the Royal Academy, author of the 'History of Greece,' etc., died 10 Feb., 1827. See Foster's *Peerage*, E. REDESDALE.

Mitford, William, s. William, of Westminster, arm. CHRIST CHURCH, matric. 9 Aug., 1786, aged 19; died in 1790.

Mitford, William Townley, 1s. Charles, of London, arm. ORIEL COLL., matric. 12 Nov., 1835, aged 18; B.A. 1839, of Pitshill, Sussex, J.P., D.L., high sheriff 1847, M.P. Midhurst 1859-74. See *Foster's Peerage* & *Eton School Lists.*

Mitton, Henry, s. Robert, of Knaresborough, Yorks, cler. UNIVERSITY COLL., matric. 28 Oct., 1800, aged 18; B.A. 1804, M.A. 1807, rector of Harswell, Yorks, 1816, and of Newton Wold, co. Lincoln, 1833, until his death 30 Aug., 1854. [5]

Moberly, Charles Edward, 1s. William, of Islington, near London, arm. BALLIOL COLL., matric. 8 March, 1837, aged 16; scholar 1838-44, B.A. 1841, M.A. 1846, assistant-master Rugby School 1859-79, rector of Coln Rogers, co. Gloucester, 1879-83. See *Rugby School Reg.*

Moberly, Edward Hugh, 4s. George, of Winchester, D.D. CORPUS CHRISTI COLL., matric. 20 Oct., 1868, aged 18; B.A. 1872, M.A. 1875, priest vicar of Salisbury Cathedral 1875-7, vicar of Chute, Wilts, 1880-5.

Moberly, George, 7s. Edward, of Petersburg (city), Russia, arm. BALLIOL COLL., matric. 13 March, 1822, aged 18; B.A. 1825, fellow 1826-34, M.A. 1828, D.C.L. 1836, tutor and senior dean 1830, catechetical lecturer, public examiner 1830, 1833-5, select preacher 1833, 1858 and 1863, Bampton lecturer 1868, head-master Winchester College 1835-66, and fellow 1866-70, rector of Brightstone, Isle of Wight, 1866-9, canon of Chester 1868-9, preb. of Salisbury 1869, and bishop 1869, until his death 6 July, 1885; for list of his works see *Crockford.*

Moberly, George Herbert, 1s. George, of St. Swithin's, Winchester, Hants, doctor. CORPUS CHRISTI COLL., matric. 10 Feb., 1855, aged 18; scholar 1855-64, B.A. 1859, M.A. 1861, fellow 1864-70, lecturer in law and modern history, tutor, chaplain at Bonn 1869-71, rector of Duntesborne-Rous, co. Gloucester, 1871-80, principal Lichfield College, and preb. of Lichfield 1880-5, master of St. Nicholas Hospital, Salisbury, 1878, etc., rector of Monkton Farley 1887. See *Crockford.*

Moberly, Gerald Edward, 2s. Henry Edward, of Winchester, cler. NEW COLL., matric. 11 Dec., 1882, aged 18; B.A. 1885. [10]

Moberly, Henry Edward, 1s. Henry, of Madras, East Indies, arm. NEW COLL., matric. 6 March, 1841, aged 18; fellow 1841-60, B.A. 1845, M.A. 1849, tutor 1850, dean of divinity 1851, bursar 1853, sub-warden 1856, assistant-master Winchester College 1859-80, vicar of Heckfield, Hants, 1880-3, rector of St. Michael's, Winchester, 1883.

Moberly, John Cornelius, 4s. George, of Winchester, Hants, cler. NEW COLL., matric. 12 Oct., 1866, aged 18; B.A. 1869, M.A. 1873.

Moberly, Leonard Carr, 8s. William, of Lee, Kent, gent. ALL SOULS' COLL., matric. 12 April, 1864, aged 21; bible clerk 1864-8, B.A. 1868, died 27 Nov., 1874.

Moberly, Robert Campbell, 3s. George, of Winchester, Hants, D.C.L., cler. NEW COLL., matric. 16 Oct., 1863, aged 18; scholar 1863-7, B.A. 1867, a senior student CHRIST CHURCH 1867-80, M.A. 1870, lecturer 1868, tutor 1869-76, principal St. Stephen's House, Oxford, 1876-7, of Sarum College 1878-80, vicar of Great Budworth, Cheshire, 1880.

Moberly, Walter Allan, 6s. George, of Winchester, cler. CHRIST CHURCH, matric. 20 May, 1869, aged 18; B.A. 1874, M.A. 1879, private chaplain and secretary to the Bishop of Salisbury 1878-81, and to the Archbishop of Canterbury 1883, vicar of St. Philip's, Sydenham, 1881-3, vicar of the Church of the Ascension, Blackheath, 1884. [15]

Moberly, William Octavius, 1s. Charles Edward, of Shoreham, Sussex, cler. BALLIOL COLL., matric. 21 Oct., 1869, aged 18; B.A. 1873, M.A. 1877, assistant-master Clifton College. See *Rugby School Reg.*

Mocatta, Henry Elias, 1s. William Abraham, of St. Helen's, Lancashire, cler. PEMBROKE COLL., matric. 4 Feb., 1881, aged 19; B.A. 1885, M.A. 1887.

Mocatta, Maurice John, 2s. William Abraham, of Eccleston, Lancashire, cler. NEW COLL., matric. 12 Oct., 1883, aged 19; B.A. 1887.

Mocatta, William Abraham, M.A. TRINITY COLL., Dublin, 1856 (B.A. 1853); adm. 'ad eundem' 28 Feb., 1856, vicar of Bispham 1857-61, and of St. Thomas's, Eccleston, Lancashire, 1861, until his death 21 Dec., 1876.

Modd, John, s. George, of Marlborough, Wilts, gent. CORPUS CHRISTI COLL., matric. 17 Dec., 1762, aged 17, B.A. 1767, M.A. 1769; chorister Magdalen College 1755-63. See *Bloxam*, i. 166. [20]

Modlen, William, 3s. Robert, of Oxford, gent. NON-COLL., matric. 20 Jan., 1877, aged 18; exhibitioner WADHAM COLL. 1877, B.A. 1880.

Moe, Irenaeus, s. Cheesman, of Isle of Barbados, West Indies, arm. QUEEN'S COLL., matric. 10 Nov., 1802, aged 22; B.A. 1807. See *Robinson*, 98.

Moens, Seaburne May, 3s. James Benelotti, of Clapton, Middlesex, gent. MERTON COLL., matric. 11 June, 1852, aged 17; postmaster 1852-6, B.A. 1857, of the Indian Civil Service 1857, district and sessions judge at Allyghur, died 26 July, 1881. See *Robinson*, 307.

Moffat, Charles, s. William, of London, arm. BRASENOSE COLL., matric. 17 Jan., 1818, aged 16; B.A. 1822, M.A. 1824, held various curacies 1828-54.

Moffat, Charles William, 1s. Charles, of Brighton, Sussex, cler. EXETER COLL., matric. 3 Feb., 1848, aged 19; Michel exhibitioner QUEEN'S COLL. 1848-51, scholar 1851-5, B.A. 1851, M.A. 1854, fellow 1855, and chaplain until his death 3 June, 1856. See *Eton School Lists.* [25]

Moffat, Cornelius William, 4s. William, of Clapham, Surrey, arm. MERTON COLL., matric. 18 June, 1830, aged 18; postmaster 1830-4, B.A. 1835, M.A. 1837.

Moffat, Douglas, 1s. James Douglas, of Cawnpore, East Indies, arm. CHRIST CHURCH, matric. 16 Oct., 1861, aged 18; B.A. 1866, M.A. 1869, B.C.L. 1873, of Harperton and Edenhall, co. Roxburgh, bar.-at-law, Inner Temple, 1875. See Foster's *Men at the Bar.*

Moffatt, Harold Charles, o.s. George, of Basildon, Berks, arm. TRINITY COLL., matric. 23 Nov., 1878, aged 19; B.A. 1884, M.A. 1885, of Goodrich Court, co. Hereford, J.P., D.L. See *Eton School Lists.*

Moffatt, John Anderson Stanley Paget, 1s, Christopher William, of Kilmore, Ireland, cler. NON-COLL., matric. 4 Nov., 1884, aged 30; B.A. from EXETER COLL. 1888.

Moffat, William, 2s. Charles, of Sunbury, Middlesex, cler. WORCESTER COLL., matric. 19 May, 1864, aged 18; scholar 1864-9, B.A. 1869, held various curacies since 1870. [30]

Moger, George Ernest, 3s. Horace, of Widcombe, near Bath, arm. TRINITY COLL., matric. 15 Jan. 1883, aged 18; B.A. 1886.

Mogg, Arthur, 2s. Henry Hodges, of Chippenham, Wilts, cler. QUEEN'S COLL., matric. 10 Feb., 1832, aged 18; B.A. 1836, curate of Pauldon and Farringdon, Somerset, at his death in 1840.

Mogg, Charles Rees-, 4s. William, of Camely, near Bristol, arm. NON-COLL., matric. 2 May, 1877, aged 19.

Mogg, George, s. Jacob, of Farrington, Somerset, gent. ORIEL COLL., matric. 16 Feb., 1780, aged 19; bar.-at-law, Middle Temple, 1782.

Mogg, Henry Hodges, s. Jacob, of Farrington, Somerset, gent. ORIEL COLL., matric. 8 May, 1787, aged 17; B.A. 1791, M.A. 1794, vicar of High Littleton 1804, and of Chewton Mendip 1814, until his death 17 Jan., 1850. **[5]**

Mogg, Henry Hodges, 1s. Henry Hodges, of Chippenham, Wilts, cler. EXETER COLL., matric. 26 May, 1825, aged 18; B.A. 1829, M.A. 1833.

Mogg, Henry James Rees-, 2s. William, of Cholwell, Somerset, gent. EXETER COLL., matric. 15 Oct., 1870, aged 19; B.A. 1874, M.A. 1877, rector of Mixbury, Oxon, 1886.

Mogg, John George, 1s. George, of Bath (city), arm. ORIEL COLL., matric. 10 March, 1831, aged 17.

Mogg, John Rees, s. John Rees, of Wick, co. Glamorgan, gent. JESUS COLL., matric. 10 Oct., 1791, aged 19; B.A. 1795, preb. of Heytesbury, chaplain to the Duke of Cumberland, assumed the additional name of MOGG by royal licence in 1805, died at Cholwell House, Somerset, 20 Oct., 1835.

Mogg, Thomas, s. James, of Farrington, Somerset, gent. ORIEL COLL., matric. 22 March, 1779, aged 17; B.A. 1783, M.A. 1787, vicar of High Littleton at his death 10 Sep., 1803. **[10]**

Mogg, William (Clifton), 1s. Frederick George, of Pilmore, co. Durham, arm. EXETER COLL., matric. 19 Jan., 1866, aged 18; scholar 1865-70, B.A. 1870, M.A. 1872, vicar of Locking, Somerset, since 1880. See *Coll. Reg.*, 162.

Moggridge, Matthew Weston, 1s. Matthew, of Swansea, co. Glamorgan, arm. UNIVERSITY COLL., matric. 29 May, 1857, aged 18; B.A. 1863, a student of the Inner Temple 1861.

Mogridge, John, s. Philip, of Molland, Devon, gent. EXETER COLL., matric. 31 March, 1762, aged 17.

Mogridge, John, s. Anthony, of Himbleton, co. Worcester, cler. ST. ALBAN HALL, matric. 13 Dec., 1780, aged 33; B.A. & M.A. 1787, vicar of Pershore, co. Worcester, 1784, and of Avenbury, co. Hereford, 1783, until his death 2 March, 1796.

Mogridge, William Henry, s. John, of Pershore, co. Worcester, cler. JESUS COLL., matric. 15 Jan., 1816, aged 20; B.A. 1821, M.A. 1822, perp. curate Wick, co. Worcester, 1826, and minister of Balham Chapel, Surrey, 1828, until his death 15 Oct., 1847.

Mohun, Gilbert Maximilian, s. Gil. Max., of Fleet, Dorset, arm. HART HALL, matric. 15 Feb., 1725-6, aged 16. See Hutchins' *Dorset.* **[16]**

Mohun, William, s. Warwick, of St. Eva, Cornwall, arm. EXETER COLL., matric. 30 Oct., 1723, aged 17.

Moir, Robert William, o.s. George, of Edinburgh, arm. MAGDALEN COLL., matric. 12 June, 1863, aged 18. See *Eton School Lists.*

Moises, Hugh, s. Hugh, of Newcastle, Northumberland, cler. UNIVERSITY COLL., matric. 25 June, 1781, aged 18; B.A. 1785, M.A. 1789, fellow until 1813, rector of Whitchurch, Oxon, and vicar of East Farleigh, Kent, 1812, until his death 4 Nov., 1822; his father, the head-master of Newcastle Grammar School, died 5 July, 1806, aged 85.

Moises, William, s. Hugh, of Newcastle, Northumberland, cler. LINCOLN COLL., matric. 11 July, 1783, aged 18; B.A. 1787, M.A. from CHRIST COLL., Cambridge, 1802 (as WILLIAM BELL MOISES), of Dalton, Northumberland, vicar of Felton, Northumberland, and of Awthorne, Yorks. **[20]**

Moke, George Edward, o.s. George Lewis Augustus, of New York, arm. BRASENOSE COLL., matric. 16 Oct., 1879, aged 21; B.A. 1882, bar.-at-law, Inner Temple, 1885. See Foster's *Men at the Bar.*

Moland, Richard, s. Robert, of Dublin, arm. WADHAM COLL., matric. 28 June, 1759, aged 16; bar.-at-law, Middle Temple, 1767, died 22 May, 1797.

Molesworth, Arscott Ourry, 2s. Arscott Ourry, of Pencarrow, Cornwall, baronet. ORIEL COLL., matric. 28 April, 1831, aged 17; B.A. from NEW INN HALL 1835, a student of Lincoln's Inn 1836, died young.

Molesworth, Arthur Hilton, 4s. Rennell Francis Wynn, of Betteshanger, Kent, cler. PEMBROKE COLL., matric. 4 Feb., 1880, aged 19; B.A. from NEW INN HALL 1884, bar.-at-law, Inner Temple, 1885.

Molesworth, Hender. EXETER COLL., 1817. See ST. AUBYN. **[25]**

Molesworth, (Sir) John (Bart.), s. John, of London, baronet. BALLIOL COLL., matric. 14 March, 1748-9, aged 19; created M.A. 17 May, 1751, 5th baronet, M.P. Cornwall 1765, until his death 20 Oct., 1775. See Foster's *Baronetage.*

Molesworth, John, s. John, of Egloshayle, Cornwall, baronet. QUEEN'S COLL., matric. 17 Oct., 1781, aged 18; B.C.L. 1788, rector of St. Breock and of St. Ervan, Cornwall, at his death 18 Sep., 1811. See Foster's *Baronetage.*

Molesworth, John. ORIEL COLL., 1809. See ST. AUBYN.

Molesworth, John (Edward Nassau), s. John, of St. Clement's, Strand, London, arm. TRINITY COLL., matric. 3 Feb., 1808, aged 17; B.A. 1812, M.A. 1817, B. & D.D. 1838, vicar of Wirksworth, co. Derby, 1828, vicar of St. Martin's and St. Paul's, Canterbury, and one of the six preachers, vicar of Rochdale, Lancashire, 1839, until his death 21 April, 1877. See Foster's *Peerage.*

Molesworth, John Hilton, 2s. Rennell Francis Wynn, of Ramsgate, Kent, cler. KEBLE COLL., matric. 18 Oct., 1875, aged 19; B.A. 1878, M.A. 1882, vicar of St. Mark's, Peterborough, 1883. See Foster's *Peerage.* **[30]**

Molesworth, Rennell Francis Wynn, 5s. John Edward Nassau, of Millbrook, near Southampton, cler. BRASENOSE COLL., matric. 27 Feb., 1845, aged 18; scholar 1845-9, B.A. 1849, M.A. 1851, held various curacies 1850-67, vicar of Todmorden 1868-75, rector of Washington, co. Durham, since 1875. See Foster's *Peerage.*

Molesworth, St. George (Hamilton), s. Walter, of London, arm. WADHAM COLL., matric. 19 Aug., 1752, aged 21; B.A. 1757, M.A. 1760, a student of Lincoln's Inn 1748, vicar of Northfleet, Kent, 1763, until his death in Hamburgh 15 April, 1796. See Foster's *Peerage.*

Molesworth, William, s. John, of Pencarrow, Cornwall, baronet. BALLIOL COLL., matric. 28 March, 1751, aged 18; died 9 Feb., 1762.

Moleyns, (Rev.) Alured Bayfield de, 2s. William Bishop, of Westbury, co. Gloucester, cler. NON-COLL., matric. 16 Oct., 1869, aged 17; B.A. 1877, M.A. 1880. See Foster's *Peerage*, B. VENTRY.

Moleyns, Thomas Edward de, 1s. William Bishop, of Westbury-upon-Trym, co. Gloucester, cler. NON-COLL., matric. 16 Oct., 1868, aged 20, B.A. 1876; a scholar CAIUS COLL., Cambridge, 1866-8. See Foster's *Peerage*, B. VENTRY. **[35]**

Molineux, Arthur Ellison, 4s. George, of Lewes, Sussex, arm. CHRIST CHURCH, matric. 18 May, 1864, aged 18; B.A. 1869, M.A. 1871, vicar of Maiden Bradley, Wilts, 1877-83, and of Caversham, Oxon, 1883.

Molineux, Brian William, o.s. William, of Chester (city), cler. TRINITY COLL., matric. 22 Oct., 1832, aged 21; B.A. 1836.

Molineux, George, s. George, of Wolverhampton, co. Stafford, arm. CHRIST CHURCH, matric. 7 Feb., 1793, aged 19; B.A. 1796.

Molineux, John Davis, s. John, of 'Norward Monseratt,' gent. WADHAM COLL., matric. 11 Oct., 1725, aged 18.

Molineux, Thomas, 2s. George, of Lewes, Sussex, arm. TRINITY COLL., matric. 29 Nov., 1838, aged 18; rector of Waberthwaite, Cumberland, 1847-74.

Molins, John, s. John, of St. Martin's-le-Grand, London, gent. BRASENOSE COLL., matric. 10 July, 1718, aged 18.

Moll, Frederick, 1s. Henry, of London, gent. WORCESTER COLL., matric. 19 Oct., 1886, aged 20.

Moll, William Edmund, 1s. William, of Heigham, Norfolk, gent. WORCESTER COLL., matric. 19 Oct., 1875, aged 19; B.A. 1878, M.A. 1883, has held several curacies since 1879. [5]

Mollett, John William, 1s. John, of London, arm. BRASENOSE COLL., matric. 18 May, 1854, aged 19; B.A. 1865.

Molony, Charles Arthur, o.s. Edmund, of Calcutta, India, arm. LINCOLN COLL., matric. 30 Nov., 1844, aged 18; B.A. 1848, M.A. 1851, a student of Lincoln's Inn 1846, vicar of Hougham by Dover 1854-80, and of St. Laurence, Isle of Thanet, 1880. See *Eton School Lists.*

Molony, Rev. Francis Wheler, 2s. James, of Leamington, co. Warwick, arm. MERTON COLL., matric. 26 Nov., 1846, aged 17; B.A. from ST. MARY HALL 1853, M.A. 1856, died 1861. See *Eton School Lists.*

Molony, Rev. Henry William Eliott, 1s. Charles Walker, of Claremont, Cape of Good Hope, cler. NON-COLL., matric. 12 Oct., 1878, aged 20; bible clerk ALL SOULS' COLL. 1880-2, B.A. 1881, M.A. 1886.

Moltke, Count, created D.C.L. 11 Sep., 1768, of the Privy Council, and grand marshal of the Court to the King of Denmark; possibly Joachin Godske, Comte de Moltke, Danish minister of state, who died in 1818. [10]

Molyneux, Charles William, s. William Philip, Earl of Sefton. CHRIST CHURCH, matric. 12 June, 1816, aged 19; 3rd Earl of Sefton, M.P. South Lancashire, 1832-5, died 2 Aug., 1855. See Foster's *Peerage* & *Eton School Lists.*

Molyneux, Sir Francis, created D.C.L. 4 July, 1793, of Wellow, Notts, Bart. (son of Sir William Molyneux, baronet), knighted 18 Sep., 1765, gentleman usher of the black rod, died 9 June, 1812.

Molyneux, George More, s. James, of Loseley House, Surrey, arm. TRINITY COLL., matric. 7 July, 1815, aged 17; B.A. 1820, M.A. 1822, rector of Compton, Surrey, 1823, until his death 5 Nov., 1872.

Molyneux, Rev. Henry Walter More, 1s. George More, of Compton, Surrey, cler. CORPUS CHRISTI COLL., matric. 21 Oct., 1862, aged 19; B.A. 1866, M.A. 1869, died in 1871. See Foster's *Peerage* & *Eton School Lists.*

Molyneux, Howard William, 3s. John William Henry, of Hannington, Hants, cler. ST. MARY HALL, matric. 24 Oct., 1873, aged 22. [15]

Molyneux, James, s. James, of Loseley, Surrey, arm. CHRIST CHURCH, matric. 23 Jan., 1779, aged 19.

Molyneux, James More, s. More, of Loseley, near Guildford, Surrey, equitis. WADHAM COLL., matric. 27 Sep., 1742, aged 19; of Loseley, M.P. Haslemere 1754, until his death 24 June, 1759.

Molyneux, James More, 4s. James, of Loseley, Surrey, arm. TRINITY COLL., matric. 12 May, 1824, aged 19; of Loseley Park, Surrey, high sheriff, 1867, died 9 April, 1874.

Molyneux, Philip, 3s. Philip, of St. Giles's, Oxford, gent. NON-COLL., matric. 11 Oct., 1873, aged 17; B.A. from HERTFORD COLL. 1876, M.A. 1880, a student of the Inner Temple 1876.

Molyneux, Reginald Edward, 1s. Edward Molineux, of Manchester, gent. EXETER COLL., matric. 29 May, 1855, aged 18; B.A. 1859, M.A. 1862, held various curacies 1860-82, vicar of Christ Church, Virginia Water, 1883. [20]

Molyneux, Thomas More, s. — (More-Molyneux), of Guildford, Surrey, equitis. WADHAM COLL., matric. 8 April, 1742, aged 17; B.A. 1745, M.P. Haslemere 1759, until his death 3 Oct., 1776.

Molyneux, William, 5s. John, of Ludlow, Salop, arm. EXETER COLL., matric. 16 Nov., 1843, aged 19; and of CHRIST CHURCH 16 Oct., 1844, then 4th son, and aged 19, B.A. 1848, M.A. 1851, rector of Twineham, Sussex, 1859.

Molyneux, William More, 2s. James More, of Brightwell, Oxon, gent. PEMBROKE COLL., matric. 9 March, 1854, aged 18; B.A. 1857, M.A. 1865, of Loseley, Surrey, sometime a clerk in the House of Commons, a student of the Middle Temple. See *Rugby School Reg.*, 278.

Molyneux, William Philip, s. Charles William, Earl of Sefton. CHRIST CHURCH, matric. 25 April, 1789, aged 16; 2nd Earl of Sefton, M.P. Droitwich 1816-31, died 20 Nov., 1838. See Foster's *Peerage* & *Eton School Lists.*

Mompesson, William, of PETER COLL., Cambridge (B.A. 1719, M.A. 1723); incorp. 8 July, 1723. [25]

Monahan, Francis John, 2s. James Henry, of Dublin, arm. BALLIOL COLL., matric. 16 Oct., 1883, aged 18; of the Indian Civil Service 1883.

Monbrison, Etienne Conquéré de, 1s. George Conquéré, of Paris, arm. BALLIOL COLL., matric. 8 Nov., 1877, aged 17.

Moncaster, James, s. James, of Shields, co. Durham, gent. LINCOLN COLL., matric. 15 April, 1736, aged 18; B.A. 9 Feb., 1739-40, M.A. 1742.

Monck, Charles, s. John, of Walcot, Somerset, gent. NEW COLL., matric. 6 June, 1792, aged 19; B.A. 1796, fellow until 1832, bar.-at-law, Inner Temple, 1806, died about 1833, brother of George 1797, of Henry 1796, and of William Bligh 1788.

Monck, Rev. Edward Francis Berkeley, 2s. George Guthrie, of Guestling, Sussex, gent. PEMBROKE COLL., matric. 27 Oct., 1870, aged 19; B.A. 1873.

Monck, Rev. George, s. John, of Walcot, Somerset, gent. PEMBROKE COLL., matric. 3 July, 1797, aged 20; B.A. 1801, died 27 Feb., 1846. See Foster's *Peerage.* [31]

Monck, George (Gustavus), 1s. George, of Bath (city), gent. PEMBROKE COLL., matric. 30 Oct., 1834, aged 19; B.A. 1838, of Silver Hill, Sussex, J.P., died 22 July, 1885.

Monck, George Gustavus, 3s. John Bligh, of Reading, Berks, arm. BRASENOSE COLL., matric. 4 June, 1868, aged 18; B.A. 1872, M.A. 1875, vicar of Welsh Hampton, Salop, 1876-85.

Monck, Henry, s. John, of Bath, Somerset, arm. ORIEL COLL., matric. 12 Feb., 1796, aged 20; brother of Charles 1792, and of George 1797.

Monck, Henry Power Charles Stanley, 1s. Charles Stanley, Viscount Monck. CHRIST CHURCH, matric. 12 June, 1867, aged 18; B.A. 1871, sometime captain coldstream guards. See Foster's *Peerage* & *Eton School Lists.* [35]

Monck, Henry Stanley (2nd Viscount), born in Dublin, Ireland, s. Charles Stanley, Viscount Monk. CHRIST CHURCH, matric. 3 Feb., 1804, aged 18; created Earl of Rathdowne 12 Jan., 1822, died 20 Sep., 1848. See Foster's *Peerage* & *Eton School Lists.*

Monck, John, s. William, of Cecil Street, London, arm. CHRIST CHURCH, matric. 18 June, 1754, aged 19; B.C.L. 1761, bar.-at-law, Middle Temple, 1756, and of Lincoln's Inn (*ad eundem*) 1758, died at Bath 12 Nov., 1809. See Foster's *Peerage* & *Alumni West.*, 361.

Monck, John Bligh, 1s. John Berkeley, of Reading, Berks, arm. BRASENOSE COLL., matric. 27 June, 1829, aged 17; B.A. from NEW INN HALL 1833, of Coley Park, Berks, high sheriff 1845, a student of the Inner Temple 1834. See Foster's *Peerage* & *Eton School Lists.*

Monke, William, M.A. (by diploma) 9 Dec., 1755.

Monck, William Berkeley, 1s. John Bligh, of St. Mary's, Reading, Berks, arm. MAGDALEN COLL., matric. 20 Oct., 1860, aged 18; B.A. 1865, of Coley Park, Berks, bar.-at-law, Inner Temple, 1868. See Foster's *Men at the Bar.*

Monck, William Bligh, s. John, of Bath, Somerset, arm. ORIEL COLL., matric. 27 Oct., 1788, aged 20; died about 1813.

Monck, Rev. William Stanley, 2s. John Berkeley, of Reading, Berks, arm. UNIVERSITY COLL., matric. 11 Nov., 1841, aged 19; B.A. 1845, died at Leeds 11 July, 1847. See Foster's *Peerage* & *Eton School Lists.*

Monckton, Arthur, 2s. (Henry), of Stretton Hall, Penkridge, co. Stafford, arm. CHRIST CHURCH, matric. 18 May, 1864, aged 18; B.A. & M.A. 1871. See Foster's *Peerage*, V. GALWAY; & *Eton School Lists.*

Monckton, Edmund Gambier, born at Cuckney, Notts, 4s. William George Arundell, Viscount Galway. CHRIST CHURCH, matric. 19 Jan., 1829, aged 19; colonel West Yorks militia, died 7 Oct., 1872. [5]

Monckton, Edward, born at Fort St. George, East Indies, s. Edward, arm. CHRIST CHURCH, matric. 11 May, 1796, aged 18; B.A. 1800, M.A. 1803, of Somerford Hall, co. Stafford, bar.-at-law, Middle Temple, 1806, died 17 March, 1848.

Monckton, Francis, 1s. Henry, of Stretton, near Penkridge, co. Stafford, arm. CHRIST CHURCH, matric. 17 Oct., 1862, aged 18; of Somerford and Stretton, co. Stafford, J.P., D.L., M.P. West Staffordshire 1871-85. See Foster's *Peerage*, V. GALWAY.

Monckton, Frederick Smyth, born at Harworth, Notts, 5s. William George, Viscount Galway. CHRIST CHURCH, matric. 18 Oct., 1830, aged 19; B.A. 1833, incumbent of St. Peter's Church, Kingsland, died 31 May, 1861.

Monckton, George Edmund Milnes, 1s. Edward George Arundell Monckton Arundell, Viscount Galway. CHRIST CHURCH, matric. 27 May, 1863, aged 18; B.A. 1866, M.A. 1877, 7th viscount, M.P. North Notts 1872-85. See Foster's *Peerage* & *Eton School Lists.*

Monckton, George Edward Arundell, 1s. William George Arundell, Viscount Galway. CHRIST CHURCH, matric. 30 April, 1824, aged 19; B.A. 1827, 6th viscount, M.P. East Retford 1847, until his death 6 Feb., 1876. See Foster's *Peerage.* [10]

Monckton, Harewood Lascelles, o.s. Marshall, of Goole, Yorks, gent. NON-COLL., matric. 27 May, 1882, aged 17.

Monckton, Herbert Haden, 1s. Inglis George, of Coven, near Wolverhampton, cler. WADHAM COLL., matric. 16 Jan., 1880, aged 18; B.A. 1883.

Monckton, Hugh, s. Edward, of St. George's, London, arm. CHRIST CHURCH, matric. 8 June, 1810, aged 18; student 1812-17, B.A. 1814, M.A. 1816, rector of Seabon, Rutland, 1815, and vicar of Harringworth, Northants, 1815, until his death 31 Oct., 1842. See Foster's *Peerage*, V. GALWAY; & *Alumni West.*, 471.

Monckton, Inglis George, born at Futtyghur, Bengal, East Indies, 3s. William, gent. WADHAM COLL., matric. 24 Jan., 1850, aged 17; B.A. 1856, M.A. 1858, vicar of Coven, co. Stafford, 1857. See Foster's *Peerage*, E. GALWAY.

Monckton, John Lionel Alexander, 1s. John B., of London, knight. ORIEL COLL., matric. 19 Oct., 1880, aged 18; B.A. 1885, M.A. 1888, bar.-at-law, Lincoln's Inn, 1885. See Foster's *Men at the Bar.*

Monckton, Jonathan, of ST. JOHN'S COLL., Cambridge (B.A. 1733, M.A. 1737); incorp. 3 July, 1754. [15]

Monckton, Ralph Granville, 6s. Walter, of Brasted, Kent, gent. ST. EDMUND HALL, matric. 21 Oct., 1886, aged 18.

Moncrieff, Fitzroy Dundas, 3s. George, arm. BALLIOL COLL., matric. 18 April, 1872, aged 19.

Moncreiff, (Hon.) Frederick Charles, 4s. (James), of Edinburgh, arm. (after a baron). NEW COLL., matric. 12 Oct., 1866, aged 18; bar.-at-law, Middle Temple, 1874. See Foster's *Peerage.*

Moncreiff, George Robertson, 4s. James Wellwood, of Edinburgh, (*soi-disant*) baronet. BALLIOL COLL., matric. 29 Nov., 1834, aged 17; B.A. 1838, M.A. 1846, of Manor House, Hunts, rector of Tattenhall, Cheshire, 1842-55, H.M. inspector of schools 1850-73, a senior inspector 1873-84. See Foster's *Baronetage.*

Moncreiff, Henry, 1s. James, of Edinburgh (city), arm. NEW COLL., matric. 5 April, 1827, aged 17; B.A. 1831, D.D. Edinburgh, known as Sir Henry Wellwood Moncreiff, Bart., minister of St. Cuthbert's, Edinburgh, 1852, until his death 14 Nov., 1883. See Foster's *Baronetage.* [21]

Moncreiff, James, s. Henry, of Edinburgh, Scotland, (*soi-disant*) baronet. BALLIOL COLL., matric. 30 Nov., 1793, aged 17; B.C.L. 1800, a member of the Faculty of Advocates 26 Jan., 1799, a lord of Session and justiciary, Scotland, 1829, until his death 4 April, 1851, father of the last named.

Moncreiff, William (Wellwood), s. Henry, of Cavil, Fife, Scotland, (*soi-disant*) baronet. BALLIOL COLL., matric. 20 March, 1793, aged 17; B.A. 1797, M.A. 1799, B.C.L. & D.C.L. 1803, bar.-at-law, Middle Temple, 1800, king's advocate admiralty court, Island of Malta, died 5 Sep., 1813. See Foster's *Baronetage.*

Moncrieff, Patrick George, s. Patrick, of Auchtermuchty, co. Fife, Scotland, arm. EXETER COLL., matric. 6 Nov., 1807, aged 17.

Moncrieffe, David Stewart, s. William, of Bristol, doctor. QUEEN'S COLL., matric. 18 May, 1792, aged 19; B.A. 1796, M.A. 1798, rector of Loxton 1801, and of Weston-in-Gordano, Somerset, 1817, until his death 3 Aug., 1850. [25]

Money, Granville Erskine, 5s. James Drummond, of Honfleur, France, cler. TRINITY COLL., matric. 22 April, 1865, aged 19; B.A. 1868, M.A. 1874, rector of Byfleet, Surrey, 1884.

Money, John Kyrle Ernle, s. William, of Wellingborough, Northants, arm. ORIEL COLL., matric. 10 Nov., 1798, aged 17; B.A. 1803, M.A. 1832, commander H.E.I.C.S. (marine), died 6 Aug., 1825.

Money, Noel Ernest, 1s. Albert William, of Montreal, Canada, arm. CHRIST CHURCH, matric. 31 May, 1884, aged 17.

Money, Richard, s. Richard, of Westminster, arm. WORCESTER COLL., matric. 11 May, 1763, aged 18.

Money, Rowland Ernle Gambier, 2s. Rowland, of Alighur, near Agra, India, arm. MAGDALEN COLL., matric. 17 Oct., 1868, aged 18; demy 1868-71. [30]

Money, Walter McLachlan, 1s. Walter, of London, arm. NEW COLL., matric. 16 Oct., 1885, aged 19.

Money-Kyrle, William, s. William (Money), of Westow, Northumberland (*sic*), arm. ORIEL COLL., matric. 21 June, 1794, aged 17; B.A. 1798, M.A. 1824, of Homme House, co. Hereford, of Whetham, Wilts, and of Pitsford, Northants, rector of Yatesbury, Wilts, 1800-43, died 18 Jan., 1848.

Money, William. ORIEL COLL., 1826. See KYRLE.

Monins, John Henry, 1s. Richard Eaton, of Stradbrooke, Suffolk, cler. NEW INN HALL, matric. 22 Jan., 1872, aged 20; of Ringwould, Kent, J.P. See *Eton School Lists.*

Monk, Edwin George, 1s. George, of Frome, Somerset, gent. EXETER COLL., matric. 1 Dec., 1848, aged 28; B.Mus. 7 Dec., 1848, D.Mus. 15 March, 1856.

Monk, George, s. Richard, of Holland Lees, Lancashire, pleb. BRASENOSE COLL., matric. 3 April, 1773, aged 21; B.A. 1776, minister of St. Paul's Church, Liverpool, at his death in 1834. [35]

Monk, James Henry, scholar TRINITY COLL., Cambridge, 1801 (7th wrangler and B.A. 1804, fellow 1805-22, M.A. 1807, B.D. 1818, D.D. 1822); adm. 'ad eundem' 1831 (son of Charles Monk of 40th regiment), regius professor of Greek 1808-22, Whitehall preacher 1812, dean of Peterborough 1822-30, and rector of Fiskerton, co. Lincoln, 1822-30, canon of Westminster 1830, bishop of Gloucester 1830-6, of Gloucester and Bristol 1836, until his death 6 June, 1856.

Monk, John Boughey, fellow TRINITY COLL., Cambridge (12th wrangler and B.A. 1812, M.A. 1815); adm. 'ad eundem' 22 June, 1843, incumbent or chaplain of St. George's, Liverpool, 1829, until his death 20 Nov., 1861.

Monk, Mark James, 2s. Mark, of Hunmanby, Yorks, gent. NEW COLL., matric. 5 Feb., 1877, aged 18; B.Mus. 24 Oct., 1878, D.Mus. 24 March, 1888.

Monk, William, of ST. JOHN'S COLL., Cambridge (B.A. 1855, M.A. 1858); adm. 'ad eundem' 3 March, 1859, rector of Wymington, Beds, 1864, F.S.A. 1855, etc. See *Crockford.*

Monkhouse, Alfred William, 2s. Cyril John, of St. Martin's-in-the-Fields, London, arm. MAGDALEN HALL, matric. 21 March, 1850, aged 20; B.A. 1855, M.A. 1858, vicar of Barton, co. Cambridge, since 1871. See *St. Paul's School Reg.*, 296.

Monkhouse, Edward, s. William, of Newton, Cumberland, gent. ST. EDMUND HALL, matric. 11 April, 1794, aged 22; B.A. 1797, died at Brignall Rectory, Yorks, in 1834. **[5]**

Monkhouse, Isaac, s. Isaac, of Hugill, Cumberland, pleb. QUEEN'S COLL., matric. 20 Nov., 1772, aged 19; B.A. 1776, M.A. 1780, B.D. 1796, rector of Holwell, Somerset, 1797, until his death 29 Dec., 1834.

Monkhouse, John, s. Abraham, of Newbiggin, Cumberland, pleb. QUEEN'S COLL., matric. 3 July, 1779, aged 19; B.A. 1783, M.A. 1786, rector of Bramshot, Hants, 1809, until his death 15 Oct., 1828.

Monkhouse, John, o.s. John, of Lyzzick, near Keswick, Cumberland, cler. QUEEN'S COLL., matric. 17 June, 1852, aged 18; tabarder 1852-8, B.A. 1856, fellow 1858-62, M.A. 1859, rector of Church Oakley, Hants, 1862, until his death 6 May, 1879.

Monkhouse, Joseph Robert, 1s. Cyril (John), of Westminster, gent. QUEEN'S COLL., matric. 18 March, 1847, aged 18; B.A. from ST. ALBAN HALL 1851, bar.-at-law, Lincoln's Inn, 1854. See Foster's *Men at the Bar* & *St. Paul's School Reg.*, 294.

Monkhouse, Philip Edmund, 5s. Cyril John, of St. Martin's-in-the-Fields, London, gent. LINCOLN COLL., matric. 5 June, 1858, aged 19; clerk MERTON COLL. 1859-62, B.A. 1864, M.A. 1865, held various curacies and scholastic appointments 1865, until his death 28 May, 1883. See *St. Paul's School Reg.*, 314. **[10]**

Monkhouse, Richard. QUEEN'S COLL., 1774. See MUNKHOUSE.

Monkhouse, Robert, s. Robert, of Brathwaite, Cumberland, pleb. QUEEN'S COLL., matric. 17 Dec., 1785, aged 28; Rev. R. M. of Mottram in Lancashire, died 19 Aug., 1798.

Monkhouse, Thomas, s. William, of Longlands, Cumberland, pleb. QUEEN'S COLL., matric. 24 March, 1742-3, aged 17; B.A. 1748, M.A. 1751, B.D. 1768, D.D. 1780, fellow 1760, vicar of Sherborne Monachorum 1780, died 15 April, 1793. See *Gent.'s Mag.*, 1828, ii. 570; & *O.H.S.*, ix. p. 3.

Monkhouse, William, 3s. — M., of Stockdale Wath, Cumberland, cler. QUEEN'S COLL., matric. 22 June, 1824, aged 19; scholar 1826-39, B.A. 1828, M.A. 1832, fellow 1839-62, proctor 1842, B.D. 1853, bursar 1842, F.S.A. 1856, vicar of Goldington, Beds, 1836, until his death 14 June, 1862.

Monnington, Alfred, 5s. George, of Bitteswell, co. Leicester, cler. KEBLE COLL., matric. 14 Oct., 1872, aged 19; B.A. 1877, M.A. 1882. **[15]**

Monnington, George, 2s. Thomas, of Leinthall Starks, co. Hereford, pleb. WORCESTER COLL., matric. 2 July, 1821, aged 18; bible clerk 1822-5, B.A. 1825, M.A. 1856, vicar of Bitteswell, co. Leicester, 1844-81, died 14 June, 1886.

Monnington, George James, 1s. George, of Bitteswell, near Lutterworth, co. Leicester, cler. QUEEN'S COLL., matric. 30 Oct., 1863, aged 19; B.A. 1868, M.A. 1870, held various curacies since 1869. See *Rugby School Reg.*

Monnington, Thomas Pateshall, 2s. George, of Bitteswell, co. Leicester, cler. CORPUS CHRISTI COLL., matric. 16 Oct., 1866, aged 20; B.A. 1870, M.A. 1873, vicar of Downton, co. Hereford, 1873-6, rector of Letcombe Bassett, Berks, 1877-80, rector of Skelton, Carlisle, 1886.

Monnington, Walter, 3s. George, of Bitteswell, co. Leicester, cler. MAGDALEN HALL, matric. 5 Feb., 1869, aged 20; B.A. from WORCESTER COLL. 1873, bar.-at-law, Inner Temple, 1875. See Foster's *Men at the Bar.*

Monoux, (Sir) Humphrey (Bart.), s. Philip, of Wotton, Bedford, baronet. TRINITY COLL., matric. 19 Feb., 1719-20, aged 17; created M.A. 3 May, 1723, and also D.C.L. 11 July, 1733, 4th baronet, M.P. Tavistock 1723-34, Stockbridge 1734-41, died 3 Dec., 1757. **[20]**

Monpellier, Louis, 'linguæ Galliæ præceptor;' privilegiatus 28 Oct., 1761.

Monro, Alexander, 1s. Henry, of Portland, Australia, arm. ORIEL COLL., matric. 25 Oct., 1866, aged 19; scholar 1866-71, B.A. 1871, B.C.L. & M.A. 1879, bar.-at-law, 1874. See Foster's *Men at the Bar.*

Monro. Alexander Patrick Hale, 3s. Charles Hale, of York (city), arm. EXETER COLL., matric. 2 June, 1852, aged 18.

Monro, Charles, s. Charles, of London, arm. CHRIST CHURCH, matric. 24 Jan., 1805, aged 17; B.A. 1808, M.A. 1811, student until 1818, bar.-at-law, Inner Temple, 1815. See Foster's *Baronetage.*

Monro, Charles Hale, 1s. James, of Lymington, Hants, arm. EXETER COLL. matric. 3 June, 1824, aged 18; of Ingsdon, Devon, J.P., D.L., died 1867, father of Alexander P. H. **[25]**

Monro, Claude Frederick Hugh, 1s. Frederick Thomas, of London, arm. HERTFORD COLL., matric. 19 Oct., 1881, aged 18.

Monro, David, 2s. David, of Nelson, New Zealand, equitis. ORIEL COLL., matric. 28 March, 1867, aged 19.

Monro, David Binning, 1s. Alexander Binning, of Edinburgh, arm. BRASENOSE COLL., matric. 16 June, 1854, aged 17, scholar 1854; scholar BALLIOL COLL. 1854-9, B.A. 1858, fellow ORIEL COLL. 1859-82, M.A. 1862, sub-dean, junior treasurer, and classical lecturer 1862, tutor 1863-73, librarian 1871, history lecturer Lincoln College 1873-4, vice-provost of Oriel College 1874-82, provost 1882, a student of Lincoln's Inn 1859.

Monro, Edward, 1s. Edward Thomas, of St. George's, Bloomsbury, London, D.Med. ORIEL COLL., matric. 13 June, 1832, aged 17; B.A. 1836, M.A. 1839, select preacher 1862, perp. curate Harrow-Weald, Middlesex, 1842-60, vicar of St. John's, Leeds, 1860, until his death 13 Dec., 1866; for list of his writings see *Crockford.*

Monro, (Edward) Thomas, s. Thomas, of Bloomsbury, Westminster, doctor. ORIEL COLL., matric. 19 March, 1804, aged 14; B.A. 1809, M.A. 1810, B.Med. 1811, D.Med. 1814, F.R.C.P. 1816, treasurer 1845-54, died 25 Jan., 1856. See Foster's *Baronetage* & Munk's *Roll*, iii., 153. **[30]**

Monro, Frederick John, 2s. Robert, of Bridewell Hospital, London, cler. WADHAM COLL., matric. 8 May, 1861, aged 19; B.A. 1865, of London, solicitor. See Foster's *Baronetage* & *Rugby School Reg.*

Monro, Frederick Thomas, 8s. Edward Thomas, of Marylebone, London, D.Med. EXETER COLL., matric. 21 March, 1849, aged 17; B.A. 1852, a student of the Inner Temple 1853. See Foster's *Baronetage.*

Monro, Henry, 2s. Edward Thomas, of St. George's, Bloomsbury, London, doctor. ORIEL COLL., matric. 27 Nov., 1834, aged 17; B.A. 1839, B.Med. 1844, D.Med. 1863. See Foster's *Baronetage.*

Monro, Henry Theodore, 5s. Henry, of London, D.Med. MERTON COLL., matric. 22 Oct., 1877, aged 18; B.A. 1882. See Foster's *Baronetage.*

Monro, Hector Francis, 2s. Alexander, of Albury, Surrey, gent. ST. EDMUND'S HALL., matric. 21 June, 1855, aged 19. See Foster's *Baronetage.*

Monro, Horace, s. Thomas, of Selbourne, Hants, cler. UNIVERSITY COLL., matric. 27 June, 1816, aged 17; B.A. 1820, M.A. 1823, vicar of Kerry, co. Montgomery, 1830, until his death 31 Oct., 1836. See Foster's *Baronetage.*

Monro, Rev. Hugh, 7s. Edward Thomas, of London, D.Med. EXETER COLL., matric. 11 May, 1848, aged 18; B.A. 1852, died 14 March, 1881. See Foster's *Baronetage.*

Monro, John, s. James, of Greenwich, Kent, doctor. ST. JOHN'S COLL., matric. 26 June, 1733, aged 17, B.A. 1737, M.A. 1740; a Radcliffe travelling fellow UNIVERSITY COLL. 1741, B.Med. 1743, D.Med. by diploma 27 June, 1747, F.R.C.P. 1753, physician Bethlehem Hospital 1751, died 27 Dec., 1791. See Foster's *Baronetage,* MUNRO; Munk's *Roll,* ii. 183; & *Robinson,* 65. [5]

Monro, John, s. John, of St. Giles-in-the-Fields, Middlesex, doctor. ST. JOHN'S COLL., matric. 30 June, 1772, aged 17; B.A. 1776. See Foster's *Baronetage* & *Robinson,* 123.

Monro, Percy, 4s. Edward Thomas, of St. George's, Bloomsbury, London, D.Med. EXETER COLL., matric. 17 April, 1845, aged 19; B.A. 1849, M.A. 1859, vicar of Colden Common, Hants, 1851, until his death, 15 June, 1883. See Foster's *Baronetage.*

Monro, Robert, s. Thomas, of St. Martin's, London, doctor. MERTON COLL., matric. 9 June, 1815, aged 16; postmaster 1816-9, B.A. 1819, M.A. 1821, rector of Aston Sandford 1850, until his death, 1 Dec., 1857. See Foster's *Baronetage.*

Monro, Robert Douglas, 1s. Robert, of Bridewell, London, cler. WADHAM COLL., matric. 13 Dec., 1859, aged 19; B.A. 1862, M.A. 1866, vicar of the Slad, co. Gloucester, 1868-73, of Christ Church, Everton, Liverpool, 1875-8, and of St. Mark, Tollingtou Park, Middlesex, 1878-81. See Foster's *Baronetage* & *Rugby School Reg.*

Monro, Robert Webber, o.s. John Boscawen, of London, arm. BALLIOL COLL., matric. 3 June, 1857, aged 19; B.A. 1861, M.A. 1865, bar.-at-law, Lincoln's Inn, 1864, a clerk in the House of Lords since 1869. See Foster's *Men at the Bar.* [10]

Monro, Russell Henry, 1s. Henry, of London, arm. UNIVERSITY COLL., matric. 23 March, 1865, aged 18; B.A. 1869. See Foster's *Baronetage.*

Monro, Theodore Russell, 1s. Theodore, of London, arm. EXETER COLL., matric. 2 May, 1862, aged 19; B.A. 1866, M.A. 1868. See Foster's *Baronetage.*

Monro, Thomas, s. James, of Greenwich, Kent, doctor. CORPUS CHRISTI COLL., matric. 13 Feb., 1734-5, aged 18; B.A. 1738, M.A. 2 March, 1741-2, B.D. 1751, vicar of Burgate and rector of the two Worthams, Suffolk, at his death 23 Feb., 1781. See Foster's *Baronetage* & *Robinson,* p. 65.

Monro, Thomas, s. John, of St. Giles, London, doctor. ORIEL COLL., matric. 18 Feb., 1777, aged 17; B.A. 1780, M.A. 1783, B.Med. 1785, D.Med. 1787, F.R.C.P. 1791, physician Bethlehem Hospital 1792-1816, died 14 May, 1833. See Foster's *Baronetage* & Munk's *Roll,* ii., 414.

Monro, Thomas, s. Thomas, of Wargrave, Berks, cler. ST. MARY HALL, matric. 11 July, 1782, aged 17; demy MAGDALEN COLL. 1783-97, B.A. 1787, M.A. 1791, rector of Little Easton, Essex, 1800, until his death 25 Sep., 1815, father of Vere. See Foster's *Baronetage; Bloxam* vii. 81; & *Gent.'s Mag.,* ii. 378.

Monro, Tregonwell, 2s. Hector, of Bournemouth, Hants, arm. ST. JOHN'S COLL., matric. 17 Oct., 1885, aged 18. [15]

Monro, Rev. Vere, 2s. Thomas, of Thaxted, Essex, cler. UNIVERSITY COLL., matric. 8 March, 1819, aged 17; B.A. 1823, died at Malta 20 Oct., 1841.

Monro, William Agnew, 2s. Alexander, of Cheltenham, co. Gloucester, arm. ST. JOHN'S COLL., matric. 8 Dec., 1847, aged 17; died 8 April, 1864. See Foster's *Baronetage.*

Monsell, Rev. Charles Henry, B.A. TRINITY COLL., Dublin, 1837, y.s. Thomas Bewley, of St. Columbs, Londonderry, cler. Incorp. from WORCESTER COLL. 7 May, 1840, aged 24; M.A. 10 June, 1840, died at Naples 29 Jan., 1851. See Foster's *Peerage,* B. EMLY; & *Eton School Lists.*

Monsell, William, o.s. William, of Dublin, Ireland, arm. ORIEL COLL., matric. 10 March, 1831; Baron Emly, so created 12 Jan., 1874, M.P. co. Limerick, 1847-73, lord-lieut. 1873, postmaster-general 1869-73, etc., etc. See Foster's *Peerage* & *Eton School Lists.* [20]

Monson, (Sir) Edmund John (K.C.M.G., C.B.), 3s. William John, baron. BALLIOL COLL., matric. 24 March, 1852, aged 17, B.A. 1855; fellow ALL SOULS' COLL. 1858-82, M.A. 1859, minister to Uruguay 1879-84, envoy extraordinary and minister plenipotentiary to the Argentine Republic, etc., 1884-5, at Copenhagen 1885-8, and at Athens 1888, C.B. 3 Jan., 1878, K.C.M.G. 29 May 1886. See Foster's *Peerage* & *Eton School Lists.*

Monson, Evelyn John, 4s. William John, baron. MERTON COLL., matric. 24 March, 1859, aged 20; B.A. 1863, M.A. 1865, vicar of Croft, co. Lincoln, since 1865. See Foster's *Peerage.*

Monson, Frederick John (Baron), o.s. John George, baron. CHRIST CHURCH, matric. 31 March, 1827, aged 18; created D.C.L. 11 June, 1834, 5th baron, died 7 Oct., 1841.

Monson, Henry, fellow of TRINITY HALL, Cambridge, (LL.B. 1718, LL.D. 1726); incorp. 9 July, 1733, regius professor of civil law 1755 (brother of John, 1st Lord Monson), died 28 Feb., 1757. See Foster's *Peerage.*

Monson, Hon. John George, s. John, baron. CHRIST CHURCH, matric. 19 April, 1804, aged 18; 4th Lord Monson, died 14 Nov., 1809. [25]

Monson, William John, born at Negapatam, East Indies, s. William, arm. CHRIST CHURCH, matric. 27 Jan., 1814, aged 17; B.A. 1817, M.A. 1820, 6th Lord Monson, a student of Lincoln's Inn 1817, died 17 Dec., 1862.

Monson, William John, 1s. William John, baron. CHRIST CHURCH, matric. 28 Oct., 1846, aged 17; B.A. 1849, 7th Lord Monson, M.P. Reigate 1858-62, captain of the yeoman of the guard 1880-5. See Foster's *Peerage* & *Eton School Lists.*

Montagu, Charles Greville, s. Robert, Duke of Manchester. CHRIST CHURCH, matric. 12 Oct., 1759, aged 18; created D.C.L. 7 July, 1763, died in Jan., 1784.

Montagu, Rev. Edward, s. George, of Avisford, Sussex, arm. (after G.C.B. and admiral). BALLIOL COLL., matric. 10 Nov., 1814, aged 17; B.A. from ST. MARY HALL 1819, died 22 Dec., 1820. See Foster's *Peerage,* D. MANCHESTER.

Montagu, Edward (Wortley), s. Edward, of Elstree, Herts, arm. CHRIST CHURCH, matric. 1 June, 1768, aged 17; died at the Cape, made his will 25 Nov., 1777, proved 8 Dec., 1778. See *Alumni West.,* 387. [30]

Montagu, Ernest Edgar, 1s. Edgar, of London, arm. BRASENOSE COLL., matric. 4 June, 1868, aged 18; B.A. 1872, bar.-at-law, Inner Temple, 1874, died 11 Aug., 1875. See Foster's *Peerage,* D. MANCHESTER.

Montagu, Right Hon. Frederick, created D.C.L. 3 July, 1793, of Papplewick, Notts (son of Charles Montagu, of Lincoln's Inn), bar.-at-law, Lincoln's Inn, 1757, bencher 1782, privy councillor, M.P. Northampton (June) 1759-67, Higham Ferrers 1768-90, died 30 July, 1800, the last male descendant of George, son of Henry, 1st. Earl of Manchester.

Montagu, George, 2s. George, of Swaffham, Norfolk, cler. WORCESTER COLL., matric. 7 March, 1839, aged 18; B.A. 1843, rector of Thenford, Oxon, 1883. See Foster's *Peerage*, D. MANCHESTER.

Montagu, George Hervey, o.s. William, of Wheley, Essex, arm. BALLIOL COLL., matric. 18 March, 1823, aged 17; B.A. 1826.

Montagu, Gerrard, s. Edward, of Hampstead, Middlesex, arm. MAGDALEN COLL., matric. 17 March, 1775, aged 17; of Marlesford, Sussex, a student of Gray's Inn 1775, died 7 Oct., 1806. See Foster's *Peerage*, D. MANCHESTER.

Montagu, Henry James Montagu-Scott, Lord Montagu, created D.C.L. 11 June, 1834 (2s. Henry, 3rd Duke of Buccleuch, K.G., K.T.), Baron Montagu on the death of his grandfather, George, Duke of Montagu, in 1790, died 30 Oct., 1845.

Montagu, Rev. John, s. John, of Widley, Hants, arm. (admiral). UNIVERSITY COLL., matric. 30 June, 1767, aged 17, B.A. 1771; fellow ALL SOULS' COLL. 1771-1818, M.A. 1775, B.D. 1782, D.D. 1800, died in college 28 July, 1818. See Foster's *Peerage*, D. MANCHESTER. **[5]**

Montagu, John Edward, born at Hobart Town, Tasmania, 1s. John, arm. EXETER COLL., matric. 28 April, 1842, aged 17; registrar-general Cape of Good Hope, died 3 March, 1879. See Foster's *Peerage*, D. MANCHESTER.

Montagu, Hon. John Walter Edward Douglas-Scott-, 1s. Henry John, Baron Montagu. NEW COLL., matric. 27 Jan., 1886, aged 19. See Foster's *Peerage*.

Montagu, Robert, born at Lees, Essex, s. Charles, Duke of Manchester. CHRIST CHURCH, matric. 9 Feb., 1726-7, aged 16; 3rd Duke, M.P. Hunts 1734-9, died 10 May, 1762.

Montagu, Hon. Robert Henry Douglas Scott, 2s. Henry John, Baron Montagu. NEW COLL., matric. 15 Oct., 1886, aged 19. See Foster's *Peerage*.

Montagu, William Augustus, 2s. John, Earl of Sandwich, created D.C.L. 9 July, 1773, M.P. Huntingdon (Feb.) 1774, until his death 14 Jan., 1776. See Foster's *Peerage*. **[10]**

Montague, Charles Edward, 3s. Francis, of Ealing, Middlesex, gent. BALLIOL COLL., matric. 24 Oct., 1885, aged 18; exhibitioner 1884.

Montague, Francis Charles, 1s. Francis, of London, gent. BALLIOL COLL., matric. 18 Oct., 1876, aged 18, exhibitioner 1875-81, B.A. 1881; fellow ORIEL COLL. 1881, M.A. 1885, bar.-at-law, Lincoln's Inn, 1883. See Foster's *Men at the Bar*.

Montague, John, 3s. William, of Gloucester (city), gent. PEMBROKE COLL., matric. 30 Oct., 1834, aged 21; B.A. 1838, curate of Pyrton, Wilts, died at Gloucester 20 July, 1839.

Montague, John Monthermer, 2s. Charles, of Gloucester, gent. KEBLE COLL., matric. 18 Oct., 1871, aged 18; B.A. 1874, M.A. 1885.

Montague, William, s. Charles, of Surrey, arm. WADHAM COLL., matric. 22 April, 1814, aged 17.

Montalembert, (Charles Forbes de Tryon), Comte de, created D.C.L. 20 June, 1855, 'member of the French academy,' a distinguished politician, historian and theologian, died in Paris 13 March, 1870. **[16]**

Montblanc, Augustine Louis, created D.C.L. 26 June, 1816, sometime canon and vicar-general of the Metropolitan church of St. Saviour at Aix, in France.

Montefiore, Claude Joseph, 2s. Nathaniel, of London, arm. BALLIOL COLL., matric. 18 May, 1878, aged 19; B.A. 1882, M.A. 1885.

Montefiore, Rev. Durbin Brice, 3s. Thomas Law, of Charmouth, Dorset, cler. ST. ALBAN HALL, matric. 19 Oct., 1880, aged 19; B.A. from EXETER COLL. 1883.

Montefiore, Francis Abraham, s. Joseph Mayer, of Crawley, Sussex, arm. CHRIST CHURCH, matric. 10 Oct., 1879, aged 19. **[20]**

Montefiore, Leonard Abraham, 1s. Nathaniel, of London, arm. BALLIOL COLL., matric. 5 Feb., 1873, aged 19; B.A. 1878, a student of the Inner Temple 1875, died 6 Sep., 1879.

Montgomerie, Archibald William, Earl of Eglinton and Winton, created D.C.L. 7 June, 1853 (s. Archibald, Baron Montgomerie), 13th Earl of Eglinton, P.C. 1852, K.T. 1853, lord-lieutenant Ireland 1852-3, 1858-9, created Earl of Winton 23 June, 1859, died 4 Oct., 1861. See Foster's *Peerage*.

Montgomerie, Charles Waterton Edmonstone-, 2s. Hugh, of Sydenham, Kent, gent. CHRIST CHURCH, matric. 16 Oct., 1885, aged 19; of the Indian Civil Service 1885.

Montgomerie, Frederick Butler Molyneux, o.s. Frederick Molyneux, of Brighton, Sussex, arm. BALLIOL COLL., matric. 24 March, 1852, aged 19; B.A. 1855, M.A. 1859, bar.-at-law, Inner Temple, 1863. See Foster's *Men at the Bar* & *Eton School Lists*.

Montgomery, Archibald Vernon, 3s. Alexander, of Killoconnegan, co. Meath, arm. PEMBROKE COLL., matric. 26 Oct., 1877, aged 18; B.A. 1882. **[25]**

Montgomery, Archibald, s. Hugh, of Derry Gormathy, co. Fermanagh, Ireland, arm. EXETER COLL., matric. 4 Nov., 1800, aged 17.

Montgomery, Arthur Hope, 2s. Robert, of Longsight, Lancashire, gent. PEMBROKE COLL., matric. 27 Oct., 1885, aged 18; scholar 1885-6.

Montgomery, Arthur Samuel Law, 1s. Robert, of Cawnpore, East Indies, arm. EXETER COLL., matric. 19 May, 1864, aged 18.

Montgomery, Charles William, 2s. Archibald, of Whim, near Edinburgh, arm. ORIEL COLL., matric. 7 Dec., 1837, aged 19.

Montgomery, Edward, s. Francis, of Bodington, Northants, gent. HERTFORD COLL., matric. 17 Dec., 1746, aged 17; B.A. from LINCOLN COLL. 1750. **[30]**

Montgomery, Francis, s. Edward, of Duncot, Northants, cler. LINCOLN COLL., matric. 2 Nov., 1773, aged 18; B.A. 1777, M.A. 1780, rector of Harleston, Northants, 1809, vicar of Melbourne, co. Derby, at his death 26 Dec., 1830.

Montgomery, George Augustus, s. Augustus, of Islington, Middlesex, gent. ORIEL COLL., matric. 28 May, 1813, aged 18; B.A. 1817, M.A. 1821, rector of Bishopstoke, Wilts, 1821-42, preb. of Sarum, died in 1842.

Montgomery, (Sir) Graham Graham (Bart.), 1s. James, of Edinburgh, Scotland, baronet. CHRIST CHURCH, matric. 26 May, 1841, aged 17; B.A. 1845, M.A. 1864, 3rd baronet, M.P. Peeblesshire 1852-68, Peebles and Selkirk 1868-80, a lord of the Treasury 1866-8. and 1880, etc. See Foster's *Baronetage*.

Montgomery, Hugh, born at Florence, Italy, o.s. William, arm. CHRIST CHURCH, matric. 3 June, 1840, aged 18; of Grey Abbey, co. Down, J.P., D.L., high sheriff 1845. See *Eton School Lists*.

Montgomery, Hugh, 1s. John, of Belfast, Ireland, arm. CHRIST CHURCH, matric. 21 Oct., 1840, aged 18. **[35]**

Montgomery, Hugh de Fellenberg, 1s. Hugh Severin, of Leamington, co. Warwick, arm. CHRIST CHURCH, matric. 15 March, 1864, aged 19; B.A. 1868, M.A. 1883, of Blessingbourne, co. Tyrone, high sheriff co. Fermanagh 1871.

Montgomery, John Armstrong, s. John, of London, cler. WORCESTER COLL., matric. 29 May, 1805, aged 19; B.A. 1809 (as John), curate of Ledbury, co. Hereford, and chaplain to St. Katharine's Hospital at his death 16 March, 1842.

Montgomery, John Basil Hamilton, 2s. James, of Stobo, co. Peebles, baronet. CHRIST CHURCH, matric. 12 May, 1842, aged 17; of Newton, co. Lanark. See Foster's *Baronetage*.

Montgomery, Malcolm, 5s. James, of Brentford, Middlesex, arm. MAGDALEN HALL, matric. 15 May, 1844, aged 21.

Montgomery, Robert, o.s. Robert, of Bath, Somerset, gent. LINCOLN COLL., matric. 18 Feb., 1830, aged 22; B.A. 1833, M.A. 1838, 'the poet,' minister of Percy Chapel, St. Pancras, 1843, until his death 3 Dec., 1855.

Montgomery, William, 1s. William, of Christchurch, New Zealand, gent. BALLIOL COLL., matric. 24 Oct., 1885, aged 19.

Montgomery, William Percy, 1s. Robert, of Manchester, arm. MERTON COLL., matric. 16 Oct., 1884, aged 17; postmaster 1884, B.A. 1887.

Montmorency, Mervyn Standish de, 3s. John, of Dublin, arm. WADHAM COLL., matric. 9 Dec., 1863, aged 19; B.A. 1868, bar.-at-law, Inner Temple, 1870. See Foster's *Men at the Bar*, etc.

Montmorency, Reymond Hervey de, born at Jubbulpore, Bengal, India, o.s. Reymond Hervey, arm. PEMBROKE COLL., matric. 15 Oct., 1855, aged 20; major Bengal staff corps, deputy commissioner of Oudh, died 15 July, 1880. See Foster's *Peerage*, V. FRANKFORT; & *Eton School Lists*. [5]

Montolieu, Lewis, s. Lewis, of London, arm. CHRIST CHURCH, matric. 23 April, 1779, aged 17.

Monypenny, James Isaac, s. Thomas, of Idel, Sussex, gent. WADHAM COLL., matric. 10 June, 1816, aged 17; B.A. 1820, M.A. 1825, vicar of Hadlow 1841-73, died 14 Dec., 1881.

Monypenny, Robert Phillips Dearden, o.s. Robert, of Rolvenden, Kent, arm. TRINITY COLL., matric. 23 May, 1855, aged 19; B.A. 1859, of Maytham Hall, Kent, bar.-at-law, Lincoln's Inn, 1864. See Foster's *Men at the Bar*.

Mood, William Robert Lightfoot, 3s. John, of Edinburgh, gent. NON-COLL., matric. 11 Oct., 1879, aged 18.

Moody, Charles, s. Charles, of Bramshaw, Wilts, gent. MAGDALEN HALL, matric. 21 March, 1729-30, aged 18; B.A. from ORIEL COLL. 1733. [10]

Moody, Charles Aaron, s. Aaron, of Southampton, Hants, arm. ORIEL COLL., matric. 24 April, 1811, aged 18; of Kingsdon, Somerset, J.P., D.L., M.P. West Somerset 1847-63, died 17 Dec., 1867.

Moody, Clement, 6s. George, of Longtown, Cumberland, gent. MAGDALEN HALL, matric. 17 Dec., 1838, aged 27; B.A. 1844, M.A. 1845, vicar of St. Nicholas, Newcastle-upon-Tyne, 1853, until his death 23 Sep., 1871.

Moody, Henry Riddell, s. Robert Sadleir, of St. Mary-le-Bone, London, arm. ORIEL COLL., matric. 23 March, 1811, aged 18; B.A. 1815, M.A. 1817, of Aspley, Beds, hon. canon Canterbury 1866, rector of Chartham, Kent, 1822, until his death 16 March, 1873.

Moody, James Leith, 3s. Thomas, of Isle of Barbados, arm. ST. MARY HALL, matric. 15 Oct., 1835, aged 19; B.A. 1840, M.A. 1863, chaplain to the forces 1854, retired list 1876, rector of Virginstowe, Cornwall, 1876-9, vicar of St. John Baptist, Clay Hill, Enfield, 1879-85.

Moody, John Frederick Badger, 1s. John, of Derby, arm. EXETER COLL., matric. 18 Jan., 1883, aged 18. [15]

Moody, Nicholas James, y.s. Thomas Sloane, of All Saints, Southampton, gent. ORIEL COLL., matric. 7 March, 1839, aged 18; B.A. 1843, M.A. 1856, rector of St. Clement's, Oxford, died 5 July, 1858.

Moody, Peter, s. William, of Gosport, Hants, gent. MAGDALEN HALL, matric. 26 June, 1818, aged 20.

Moody, Richard, s. William, of Stratton, co. Gloucester, gent. TRINITY COLL., matric. 13 April, 1717, aged 16; B.A. 1720, M.A. 1723.

Moody, Robert Henry, 1s. Robert, of Winchester, gent. MAGDALEN HALL, matric. 17 Dec., 1835, aged 24.

Moody, Robert Sadleir, 1s. Henry Riddell, of Weald, Essex, cler. CHRIST CHURCH, matric. 3 June, 1840, aged 17; B.A. 1844, M.A. 1850, was in orders of the Church of England, seceded to Rome. See *Eton School Lists*. [20]

Moody, Lieut.-Colonel Thomas, created D.C.L. 13 June, 1834. See *Gent.'s Mag.*, 1838, i. 322.

Moody, William, s. Isaac, of Havant, Hants, gent. BALLIOL COLL., matric. 7 March, 1715-16, aged 17.

Moon, Arnold William, 2s. Robert, of London, arm. ORIEL COLL., matric. 14 Oct., 1878, aged 19.

Moon, Cecil Graham, 4s. Sir Edward Graham, of Fetcham, Surrey, baronet & cler. MAGDALEN COLL., matric. 21 Oct., 1886, aged 19.

Moon, (Sir) Edward Graham (Bart.), 1s. Francis Graham, of London, gent. MAGDALEN COLL., matric. 27 July, 1843, aged 18; demy 1843-51, B.A. 1847, M.A. 1850, held various curacies 1849-59, rector (and patron) of Fetcham, Surrey, since 1859. See Foster's *Baronetage*; *Bloxam*, vii. 374; & *Robinson*, 248. [25]

Moon, Edward Robert Pacy, 1s. Robert, of London, arm. NEW COLL., matric. 13 Oct., 1877, aged 19; scholar 1877-82, B.A. & M.A. 1884, bar.-at-law, Inner Temple, 1884. See Foster's *Men at the Bar*.

Moon, Francis Sidney Graham, 1s. Edward Graham, of Fetcham, Surrey, baronet. NON-COLL., matric. 20 Nov., 1874, aged 19.

Moon, Henry, s. Peter, of Lincoln (city), cler. EXETER COLL., matric. 15 May, 1793, aged 18; exhibitioner 1793, B.A. 1797, vicar of Chippenham, co. Cambridge, 1800, until his death in April, 1805. See *Coll. Reg.*, 148.

Moon, Robert Oswald, 3s. Robert, of London, arm. NEW COLL., matric. 10 Oct., 1884, aged 19.

Moor, Allen Page, of TRINITY COLL., Cambridge (B.A. 1846, M.A. 1849); adm. 'ad eundem' 13 June, 1850, sub-warden St. Augustine's College, Canterbury, 1849-66, vicar of St. Clement's, Truro, 1872, hon. canon of Truro 1883. [30]

Moor, Rev. Charles, 2s. John Frewen, of Ampfield, Hants, cler. KEBLE COLL., matric. 16 Oct., 1876, aged 19; B.A. 1880, M.A. 1883.

Moor, Charles Thomas, 3s. James Hoare Christopher, of Clifton-upon-Dunsmore, near Rugby, co. Warwick, cler. WORCESTER COLL., matric. 18 Oct., 1862, aged 19; B.A. 1866, M.A. 1870, vicar of Holy Trinity, the Sarn, Newtown, 1868-72, died 28 Feb., 1877.

Moor, Christopher, s. Christopher, of Arton, Cumberland, pleb. QUEEN'S COLL., matric. 24 Oct., 1751, aged 21; B.A. 1757, assistant-master Rugby School, vicar of Lilbourn, Northants, died at Rugby 11 March, 1803. See *Rugby School Reg.*, xiii.

Moor, Drayson, 1s. Thomas, of Stoke Newington, Middlesex, arm. MAGDALEN HALL, matric. 1 June, 1858, aged 22; B.A. 1863, M.A. 1865, held various curacies since 1864.

Moor, Edward Norman Peter, 4s. James Hoare, of Kingsbridge, Devon, cler. BALLIOL COLL., matric. 31 Jan., 1870, aged 19; scholar 1869-74, B.A. 1875, M.A. 1876, a master at Clifton College. [35]

Moor, Frederick, 2s. Henry Isaac, of Greenwich, Kent, arm. BRASENOSE COLL., matric. 16 Oct., 1833, aged 16.

Moor, Frederick, 1s. Frederick, of Hartfield, Sussex, arm. NEW COLL., matric. 14 Oct., 1864, aged 18; B.A. 1867, M.A. 1872, B.D. 1888, held various curacies 1869-77, rector of Whatlington, Sussex, since 1877.

Moor, Gerald Henry, 2s. Frederick, of Tunbridge Wells, Kent, arm. LINCOLN COLL., matric. 22 Oct., 1868, aged 18; B.A. 1872, M.A. 1875, held several curacies 1873-85, vicar of Lyminster, Sussex, 1885.

Moor, Gilbert Charles Francis John, 2s. James Hoare, of Exeter, cler. WORCESTER COLL., matric. 8 June, 1865, aged 18; scholar 1865-70, B.A. 1871, M.A. 1872, has held various curacies since 1871.

Moor, Rev. Henry Francis, 3s. Frederick, of East Grinstead, Sussex, arm. KEBLE COLL., matric. 18 Oct., 1875, aged 18; B.A. from CHARSLEY HALL 1883; M.A. from KEBLE COLL. 1884. [40]

Moor, Henry Peter, 2s. James Hoare Christopher, of Clifton-on-Dunsmore, near Rugby, cler. WADHAM COLL., matric. 9 Dec., 1863, aged 19; B.A. 1869.

Moor, Rev. James (Hoare), 1s. 'James H,' of Clifton, co. Warwick, cler. EXETER COLL., matric. 7 Feb., 1833, aged 16; demy MAGDALEN COLL. 1834-43, B.A. 1838, M.A. 1840, master of Kingsbridge School, died at Highwood, Uttoxeter, 21 (or 30) Oct., 1856. See *Bloxam*, vii. 335; & *Rugby School Reg.*, 146.

Moor, James Hoare Christopher, s. Christopher, of Rugby, co. Warwick, cler. MAGDALEN COLL., matric. 26 July, 1796, aged 16; demy 1796-1810, B.A. 1800, M.A. 1803, fellow 1810-15, B.D. 1811, assistant-master Rugby School 1800-31, fellow 1831, fifty years curate and vicar (1831) of Clifton-upon-Dunsmoor, near Rugby, and perp. curate St. George's, Donnington Wood, Salop, 1832, until his death 20 March, 1853. See *Rugby School Reg.*, xiii. 63; & *Bloxam*, vii. 133.

Moor, Rev. John Frewen, s. James Knight, of Sherborne, Dorset, cler. BRASENOSE COLL., matric. 19 Feb., 1817, aged 18; B.A. 1821, M.A. 1824, died 9 Dec., 1879. See *Rugby School Reg.*, 103.

Moor, John Frewen, o.s. John Frewen, of Bradfield, Berks, cler. ORIEL COLL., matric. 21 April, 1842, aged 18; B.A. 1846, M.A. 1848, vicar of Ampfield, Hants, since 1853.

Moor, Rev. Maurice Augustine, 6s. James Hoare, of Uttoxeter, co. Stafford, cler. NON-COLL., matric. 15 March, 1878, aged 21; B.A. 1886. [5]

Moor, Philip, 4s. John Frewen, of Ampfield, Hants, cler. KEBLE COLL., matric. 17 Oct., 1882, aged 19; B.A. 1886, died 20 June, 1887.

Moore, Adrian, s. Adr., of St. Clement Danes, London, gent. CORPUS CHRISTI COLL., matric. 15 Oct., 1716, aged 18.

Moore, Alexander Keys, 1s. Hugh, of Donegal, Ireland, cler. MERTON COLL., matric. 29 Oct., 1874, aged 22; postmaster 1874-9, B.A. 1879, a scholar Trinity College, Dublin, 1872, a student of the Inner Temple 1877.

Moore, Alfred, 5s. John, of Bishopwearmouth, co. Durham, arm. EXETER COLL., matric. 18 Oct., 1883, aged 19; B.A. 1887.

Moore, Alfred Percival, 3s. William Burton, of Evington, co. Leicester, cler. WADHAM COLL., matric. 19 Jan., 1877, aged 18; scholar 1876-81, B.A. 1881, B.C.L. 1885, classical lecturer or tutor 1881-2, a student of the Middle Temple 1881. [10]

Moore, Anthony, s. Thomas, of Grampound, Cornwall, gent. EXETER COLL., matric. 27 March, 1745, aged 18; B.A. 3 Feb., 1748-9, father of George 1779.

Moore, Arthur, 2s. Arthur, of Dublin, Ireland, arm. UNIVERSITY COLL., matric. 28 June, 1821, aged 17; B.A. 1825, M.A. 1832, brother of John Tydd 1810.

Moore, Arthur Collin, 1s. John Collingham, of Rome, gent. QUEEN'S COLL., matric. 30 Oct., 1885, aged 19.

Moore, Aubrey Lackington, 2s. Daniel, of Camberwell, Surrey, cler. EXETER COLL., matric. 12 June, 1867, aged 19, B.A. 1871; fellow ST. JOHN'S COLL. 1872-6, M.A. 1874, lecturer 1873, tutor 1874, assistant-tutor Magdalen College 1875-6 & 1880-1, tutor 1881, tutor Keble College 1880, and dean, rector of Frenchay, co. Gloucester, 1876-81, select preacher 1885-6, hon. canon of Christ Church 1887. See *St. Paul's School Reg.*, 340.

Moore, Rev. Cecil, 3s. Daniel, of Camberwell, Surrey, cler. EXETER COLL., matric. 14 Oct., 1870, aged 18; B.A. 1874, M.A. 1877, died 6 Aug., 1885. See *St. Paul's School Reg.*, 345. [15]

Moore, Charles, Baron Tullamore, M.A. TRINITY COLL., Dublin, 1730 (B.A. 1728); incorp. 15 Sep., 1730 (son of John, Baron Tullamore), governor of King's County, and muster-master-general of Ireland, created Earl of Charleville 16 Sep., 1758, died 17 Feb., 1764.

Moore, Charles, s. Richard, of Bruton, Somerset, pleb. CORPUS CHRISTI COLL., matric. 4 June, 1735, aged 19.

Moore, Charles, s. John, of St. Andrew's, Holborn, Middlesex, gent. ST. JOHN'S COLL., matric. 13 April, 1736, aged 17.

Moore, Charles, s. John, of St. John's, Westminster, arm. ST. JOHN'S COLL., matric. 11 Oct., 1740, aged 18; created D.C.L. 6 July, 1768, then of Appleby, co. Leicester, bar.-at-law, Middle Temple, 1742, died 18 May, 1775.

Moore, Charles, born at Durham, s. John, archbishop of Canterbury. CHRIST CHURCH, matric. 22 Dec., 1788, aged 17; B.A. 1792, M.A. 1795, M.P. Woodstock 1799-1802, of Heytesbury 1802-6 and 1807-12, died 14 Dec., 1826. [20]

Moore, Charles, s. John, of St. John's, Clerkenwell, Middlesex, cler. CORPUS CHRISTI COLL., matric. 19 Oct., 1790, aged 18; died in the East Indies March, 1802. See *Robinson*, 147.

Moore, Rev. Charles, 3s. George, of Creed, Cornwall, cler. EXETER COLL., matric. 25 June, 1825, aged 18; B.A. 1829, of Garlennick House, Grampound, Cornwall.

Moore, Charles Alfred, 4s. Thomas, of Sheffield, Yorks, gent. WORCESTER COLL., matric. 12 Oct., 1867, aged 18; B.A. 1871, B.C.L. & M.A. 1883, held various curacies 1873-82, chaplain H.B.M. legation, Copenhagen, 1883.

Moore, Rev. Charles Johnson, 2s. William Daniel, of Dublin, D.Med. MERTON COLL., matric. 17 Oct., 1874, aged 24; postmaster 1874-9, B.A. & M.A. 1881.

Moore, Charles Robert, 2s. Robert, of Hunton, Kent, cler. CHRIST CHURCH, matric. 5 June, 1828, aged 17; B.A. 1832, bar.-at-law, Inner Temple, 1835. See *Eton School Lists.* [25]

Moore, Charles Robert, 2s. Hon. (Edward) George, of Winkfield, Berks, cler. WORCESTER COLL., matric. 14 June, 1849, aged 17; died 2 Feb., 1853. See Foster's *Peerage*, E. MOUNTCASHELL; & *Eton School Lists.*

Moore, Charles Robert, 3s. John Walter, of Hordley, Salop, cler. CORPUS CHRISTI COLL., matric. 19 Oct., 1863, aged 19; scholar 1863-8, B.A. 1868, M.A. 1870, a master at Radley College. See *Eton School Lists.*

Moore, Charles Thomas John, 1s. Charles, of Moulton, co. Lincoln, cler. LINCOLN COLL., matric. 4 April, 1846, aged 18; of Frampton Hall, co. Lincoln, J.P., D.L., high sheriff 1856, hon. colonel and lieut.-colonel commanding 4th battalion Lincolnshire regiment.

Moore, Clement Harington, 3s. Robert, of St. Giles's, near Salisbury, cler. CHRIST CHURCH, matric. 14 Oct., 1864, aged 18; B.A. 1868, M.A. 1871.

Moore, Daniel, of ST. CATHERINE HALL, Cambridge (B.A. 1840, M.A. 1843); adm. 'ad eundem' 4 June, 1856, select preacher Cambridge 1844, 1851, and 1861, and Hulsean lecturer 1864, perp. curate Camden Church, Camberwell, 1844-66, vicar of Holy Trinity, Paddington, 1866, chaplain in ordinary 1870, preb. of St. Paul's 1880; for list of his works see *Crockford.* [30]

Moore, David, 4s. George, of Myton, near Warwick (town), arm. EXETER COLL., matric. 18 April, 1868, aged 18; B.A. 1871, M.A. 1876, perp. curate St. John Baptist, Alnmouth, Northumberland, 1877.

Moore, Denis Times, 1s. Francis, of Much Hadham, Herts, gent. EXETER COLL., matric. 21 Oct., 1854, aged 18; B.A. 1859, M.A. 1861, vicar of Woolton Hill, Hants, 1873-84. See *Eton School Lists.*

Moore, Edmund, s. Adam, of St. Clement Danes, London, arm. MERTON COLL., matric. 5 Nov., 1790, aged 25.

Moore, Edward, s. Edward, of St. Bartholomew-the-Less, London, gent. PEMBROKE COLL., matric. 5 July, 1721, aged 18; B.A. 1725.

Moore, Edward, s. Philip, of Romsey, Hants, pleb. WADHAM COLL., matric. 7 June, 1764, aged 17; B.A. 1768, M.A. 1772, vicar of Idmiston, and priest-vicar of Salisbury Cathedral at his death in 1812. [35]

oore, Edward, s. Glover, of Halsall, Lancashire, cler. BRASENOSE COLL., matric. 10 Oct., 1810, aged 18; B.A. 1814, M.A. 1817, rector of Gisleham, Suffolk, 1817-40, and of Whitchurch, Berks, 1840, until his death 11 Feb., 1880.

oore, Edward, 2s. George, of Wrotham, Kent, cler. CHRIST CHURCH, matric. 7 June, 1832, aged 18; B.A. 1836, M.A. 1840, rector of Frittenden, Kent, 1848-69, and of Davington, Kent, 1884-6. See *Eton School Lists.*

oore, Edward, 1s. Edward, of Norwood, Middlesex, cler. BRASENOSE COLL., matric. 7 July, 1837, aged 18; B.A. 1841, M.A. 1844, rector of Boughton Malherbe, Kent, 1843.

oore, Edward, 3s. John, of Cardiff, co. Glamorgan, gent. PEMBROKE COLL., matric. 26 May, 1853, aged 18, B.A. 1857; fellow QUEEN'S COLL. 1858-65, M.A. 1860, lecturer and tutor 1862, dean 1863, lecturer 1870-1, proctor 1871, principal of ST. EDMUND HALL 1864, B.D. 1867, D.D. 1878, and rector of Gatcombe, Isle of Wight, 1864.

oore, Edward Holmes, 4s. Edwin, of York (city), gent. QUEEN'S COLL., matric. 27 Oct., 1869, aged 19; exhibitioner 1869-74, B.A. 1874, M.A. 1878.

Moore, Edward James, s. — M. of Cradley, co. Stafford. CHRIST CHURCH, matric. 14 Oct., 1884, aged 19; B.A. 1887. [6]

Moore, Edward Loftus, s. Edward, Earl of Drogheda. CHRIST CHURCH, matric. 18 May, 1754, aged 17; B.A. 1756, chaplain to the Irish House of Commons, drowned with his father in crossing to Dublin, 28 Oct., 1758. See Foster's *Baronetage.*

Moore, Edward Marsham, 1s. Edward, of Frittenden, near Staplehurst, Kent, cler. CHRIST CHURCH, matric. 17 Oct., 1862, aged 18; B.A. 1867, M.A. 1870, curate of Ashbourne 1867-72, vicar 1872-6, rector of Benefield, Northants, 1876.

Moore, Edward William, 1s. Edward Wells, of Coleshill, near Farringdon, Berks, arm. WADHAM COLL., matric. 18 June, 1862, aged 18; exhibitioner 1866-7, B.A. 1866, M.A. 1869, minister of Brunswick Chapel, Marylebone, 1871-87, incumbent of Emanuel Church, Wimbledon, 1887.

Moore, Edward William, 1s. William Fernclough, of East Moulsey, Surrey, gent. NON-COLL., matric. 26 Oct., 1885, aged 19; scholar CHRIST CHURCH 1885. [10]

Moore, Ernest Alfred, 2s. Edwin, of Rochester, Kent, gent. UNIVERSITY COLL., matric. 13 Oct., 1879, aged 16; exhibitioner 1879-83, B.A. 1883, M.A. 1886.

Moore, Francis, s. William, of South Tawton, Devon, cler. EXETER COLL., matric. 13 March, 1773, aged 17; B.A. 1777, M.A. 1779, rector of Inwardleigh, Devon, at his death 25 Aug., 1795.

Moore, Francis, 2s. Francis, of Bridgnorth, Salop, gent. CHRIST CHURCH, matric. 13 Oct., 1827, aged 17; B.A. 1831, M.A. 1834, bar.-at-law, Inner Temple, 1836, died in May, 1841.

Moore, Francis Bell Grant, y.s. Henry Willoughby, of Barbados, cler. TRINITY COLL., matric. 2 Feb., 1882, aged 18; B.A. 1886.

Moore, Francis John, o.s. Francis, of North Church, Herts, arm. EXETER COLL., matric. 28 June, 1821, aged 17; B.A. 1826, M.A. 1829. [15]

Moore, George, s. Anthony, of Grampound, Cornwall, cler. EXETER COLL., matric. 22 Oct., 1779, aged 18; B.A. 1784, of Garlennick House, Cornwall, preb. of Lincoln 1790, vicar of Merther 1810, and rector of Ladock 1814, until his death 8 May, 1832, aged 70; father of George Anthony.

Moore, George, s. John, archbishop of Canterbury. CHRIST CHURCH, matric. 22 May, 1788, aged 17; B.A. 1792, M.A. 1795, registrar of the Faculty Office 1790, and a principal registrar of the prerogative court of Canterbury, preb. of Canterbury 1795, rector of Brasted, Kent, 1795, rector (and vicar) of Wrotham, Kent, 1800, until his death 9 Dec., 1845. See *Alumni West.*, 425.

Moore, George, o.s. George, of Snareston, co. Leicester, arm. CHRIST CHURCH, matric. 16 June, 1829, aged 17; of Appleby, co. Leicester, high sheriff co. Derby, 1837, died 26 Aug., 1871. See *Eton School Lists.*

Moore, George, 2s. George, of St. Nicholas, Warwick (town), arm. EXETER COLL., matric. 23 May, 1861, aged 18; exhibitioner 1861-5, B.A. 1865, M.A. 1869, held various curacies 1866-86, vicar of Great Wollaston, Salop, 1876-8, and of Denham, Suffolk, 1886. See *Coll. Reg.*, 160.

Moore, George, 5s. George, of Shadlow, co. Derby, gent. ST. ALBAN HALL, matric. 20 Oct., 1868, aged 25; B.A. from JESUS COLL. 1873, M.A. 1875, chaplain to forces at Oxford 1876, vicar of Cowley, 1875. [20]

Moore, George Anthony, s. George, of Grampound, Cornwall, cler. WADHAM COLL., matric. 14 Oct., 1814, aged 19; B.A. 1819, vicar of Talk-o'-the-Hill, co. Stafford, 1843, until his death 13 Sep., 1859.

Moore, George Augustus, o.s. George, of Burhampoota, East Indies, gent. QUEEN'S COLL., matric. 12 June, 1827, aged 18.

Moore, George Bridges, 1s. George, of Wrotham, Kent, cler. CHRIST CHURCH, matric. 15 June, 1827, aged 18; B.A. 1831, M.A. 1836, rector of Tunstall, Kent, 1837, until his death 13 Nov., 1885. See *Alumni West.*, 490.

Moore, George John, 1s. George, of Aston, co. Derby. arm. CHRIST CHURCH, matric. 18 Jan., 1861, aged 18; B.A. 1866, M.A. 1869, of Appleby Hall, co. Leicester, J.P., D.L.

Moore, George Pearce, 1s. George, of Dunington, arm. TRINITY COLL., matric. 20 June, 1827, aged 19.

Moore, George Ralph, 3s. Francis Wellington, of Duffield, co. Derby, cler. NON-COLL., matric. 22 Jan., 1881, aged 22. [26]

Moore, Glover, s. Nicholas, of Barton, Lancashire, pleb. BRASENOSE COLL., matric. 10 April, 1756, aged 18; B.A. 1760.

Moore, Rev. Halhed Sydney, 3s. Peter Halhed, of Lovington, Somerset, cler. KEBLE COLL., matric. 27 Jan., 1881, aged 19; exhibitioner 1882-4, B.A. 1884, M.A. 1888.

Moore, Harold Broadbent, 3s. William, of Stretford, Lancashire, gent. BRASENOSE COLL., matric. 20 Oct., 1886, aged 19; scholar 1886.

Moore, Harry Wilkinson, 3s. Arthur, of Drumcondra, Dublin, gent. TURRELL HALL, matric. 24 Jan., 1884, aged 33. [30]

Moore, Henry, s. Henry, of Kirkland (par.), Torpcuhow, Cumberland, gent. QUEEN'S COLL., matric. 11 Oct., 1805, aged 18; B.A. 1811.

Moore, Henry, 1s. Henry, of Bennet Street, London, gent. WORCESTER COLL., matric. 14 June, 1849, aged 18; scholar 1849-65. B.A. 1853, M.A. 1856, fellow 1865, has held various curacies since 1865.

Moore, Henry Dodwell, 2s. Philip Charles, of London, arm. PEMBROKE COLL., matric. 3 June, 1858, aged 19; B.A. 1862, M.A. 1865, vicar of Honington, co. Lincoln, 1867.

Moore, Henry Headley, 1s. Thomas, of Bilbrough, Yorks, gent. WORCESTER COLL., matric. 30 May, 1860, aged 21; B.A. 1864, M.A. 1869, vicar of St. John's, Darwen, Lancashire, 1869.

Moore, Henry (Kingsmill), 1s. Thomas, of Dublin, cler. BALLIOL COLL., matric. 15 Oct., 1873, aged 19; B.A. 1877, M.A. 1880, principal Church of Ireland Training College, Dublin, 1884. [35]

Moore, Henry Walter, 1s. John Walter, of Ellesmere, Salop, cler. MERTON COLL., matric. 9 July, 1859, aged 17, postmaster 1860-4; fellow EXETER COLL. 1864-6, B.A. 1864, M.A. 1866, classical lecturer 1864, died 4 Oct., 1866. See *Boase*, 142.

Moore, Herbert, 4s. Peter Halhed, of Pill, Somerset, cler. KEBLE COLL., matric. 17 Oct., 1882, aged 18; B.A. 1887.

Moore, Rev. Herbert Augustine, 3s. Daniel, of Camberwell, Surrey, cler. UNIVERSITY COLL., matric. 16 Oct., 1880, aged 20; B.A. 1884, M.A. 1887. See *St. Paul's School Reg.*, 359.

Moore, Rev. Herbert Daniel, 1s. George, of Banbury, Oxon, arm. BRASENOSE COLL., matric. 25 May, 1853, aged 17; scholar 1853-60, B.A. 1857, M.A. 1873, warden of Bishop's College, Pietermaritzburg, 1873.

Moore, Herbert Octavius, 8s. Edward, of Frittenden, Kent, cler. KEBLE COLL., matric. 13 Oct., 1873, aged 19; B.A. 1877, M.A. 1881, chaplain Bengal establishment 1885.

Moore, James, s. Arth., of Fetcham, Surrey, arm. WORCESTER COLL., matric. 10 Oct., 1717, aged 15; B.A. from ALL SOULS' COLL. 1722.

Moore, James, s. Acheson, of Dublin, Ireland, arm. BALLIOL COLL., matric. 16 June, 1743, aged 16; of Garvey House, co. Tyrone, died 1759. [5]

Moore, James, s. James, of All Souls, Hertford (town), cler. CORPUS CHRISTI COLL., matric. 28 Feb., 1804, aged 17.

Moore, James, of MAGDALEN COLL., Cambridge (LL.B. 1795), s. James, of Rotherfield, Surrey, arm. ST. JOHN'S COLL., incorp. 15 or 16 Dec., 1817, aged 49; D.C.L. 17 Dec., 1817.

Moore, James, 1s. Henry, of Douglas, Isle of Man, gent. WORCESTER COLL., matric. 1 March, 1855, aged 19; B.A. 1859, M.A. 1862, vicar of All Saints, Liverpool, 1870, until his death 5 Jan., 1879.

Moore, John, 'vinarius;' privilegiatus 7 Oct., 1723.

Moore, John, s. John, of Walls Wotton, co. Warwick, cler. BALLIOL COLL., matric. 28 March, 1732, aged 19. [10]

Moore, John, s. Thomas, of Stepney, Middlesex, pleb. ST. JOHN'S COLL., matric. 29 March, 1732, aged 18; B.A. 1735.

Moore, John, s. John, of Weobley, co. Hereford, pleb. PEMBROKE COLL., matric. 26 Oct., 1739, aged 17.

Moore, John, s. Thomas, of Gloucester (city), gent. PEMBROKE COLL., matric. 27 March, 1745, aged 15, B.A. 1748, M.A. 1751; a canon of CHRIST CHURCH 1763, B. & D.D. 1763, preb. of Durham 1761, rector of Ryton, co. Durham 1769, dean of Canterbury 1771-5, bishop of Bangor 1775-83, archbishop of Canterbury 1783, until his death 18 Jan., 1805.

Moore, John, s. Daniel, of Great Marlow, Bucks, arm. MERTON COLL., matric. 30 Oct., 1755, aged 18.

Moore, John, s. John, of St. Sepulchre's, London, cler. ST. JOHN'S COLL., matric. 28 June, 1759, aged 16; B.A. 1763, minor canon of St. Paul's, priest of the Chapel Royal, lecturer of St. Sepulchre's, and an examiner of Merchant Taylors' School, rector of St. Michael's Bassishaw, 1781, and Langdon Hills, Essex, 1798, until his death 16 June, 1821. See *Robinson*, 105. [15]

Moore, John, s. Richard, of St. Michael's, Gloucester (city), pleb. MAGDALEN COLL., matric. 17 Dec., 1774, aged 17, chorister 1770-5, clerk 1774-9, chaplain 1779-80; chaplain NEW COLL. 1776, B.A. 1778, M.A. 1781. See *Bloxam*, i. 177.

Moore, John, s. John, of Dublin, Ireland, doctor. CHRIST CHURCH, matric. 6 Dec., 1781, aged 18; of Tara House, co. Meath.

Moore, John, s. Francis, of Aspley, Beds, arm. EXETER COLL., matric. 2 Nov., 1785, aged 18.

Moore, John. EXETER COLL., 1802. See STEVENS.

Moore, John, s. John, archbishop of Canterbury. CHRIST CHURCH, matric. 20 Dec., 1803, aged 17; B.A. 1808. See *Eton School Lists.* [20]

Moore, John, s. John, of St. John's, Clerkenwell, London, cler. WORCESTER COLL., matric. 5 Feb., 1806, aged 18; scholar 1806-14, B.A. 1809, M.A. 1812, fellow 1814-8, proctor 1822 (? vicar of Alrewas, co. Stafford, 1832, until his death 11 June, 1851, aged 63).

Moore, John Henry, o.s. Henry John, of Clapham, Surrey, gent. EXETER COLL., matric. 25 Oct., 1882, aged 29.

Moore, John Tydd, s. Arthur, of Dublin (city), arm. UNIVERSITY COLL., matric. 1 Dec., 1810, aged 18; B.A. 1815, M.A. 1817, brother of Arthur 1821.

Moore, John Vaux, s. John Patrick, of Aspley, Beds, arm. EXETER COLL., matric. 5 April, 1816, aged 18; B.A. 1819, M.A. 1822, rector of Aspley Guise 1844, until his death 12 Jan., 1864.

Moore, John Walter, 3s. William, of St. George's, Hanover Square, London, arm. TRINITY COLL., matric. 25 May, 1831, aged 18; scholar EXETER COLL. 1833-7, B.A. 1835, M.A. 1838, rector of Hordley, Salop, since 1839. See *Boase*, 152. [25]

Moore, John Wilson, o.s. Ambrose, of St. Lawrence Jewry, London, arm. PEMBROKE COLL., matric. 10 Nov., 1853, aged 18; bar.-at-law, Inner Temple, 1871. See Foster's *Men at the Bar.*

Moore, Joseph, 1s. Joseph, of St. Charles-the-Martyr, Plymouth, arm. EXETER COLL., matric. 9 Feb., 1832, aged 18; scholar LINCOLN COLL. 1833-6, B.A. 1836, M.A. 1838, perp. curate of Littleworth 1838, and vicar of Buckland, Berks, 1842, until his death 26 April, 1876.

Moore, Joseph, 2s. John, of Moy, co. Tyrone, D.Med. MAGDALEN COLL., matric. 27 Oct., 1874, aged 19; exhibitioner 1874-9, B.A. 1878, M.A. 1882.

Moore, Joseph Christian, 1s. James, of Douglas, Isle of Man, gent. ST. EDMUND HALL, matric. 5 Nov., 1823, aged 21; B.A. 1827, M.A. 1844, perp. curate Measham, co. Derby, 1830-44, rector of Kirk-Andreas, Isle of Man, 1844, until his death 26 Feb., 1886.

Moore, Joseph Henry Hamilton, B.A. TRINITY COLL., Dublin, 1870 (2s. James Hamilton, of Dublin, gent.); incorp. from HERTFORD COLL. 18 April, 1876, aged 23; fellow 1875, M.A. 1877, philosophy lecturer, a student of the Middle Temple 1876. [30]

Moore, Lambert, s. Daniel, of Kingston, Isle of Jamaica, arm. UNIVERSITY COLL., matric. 2 June, 1808, aged 17.

Moore, Maurice Crosbie, s. Edward, of Waterford, Ireland, arm. CHRIST CHURCH, matric. 17 May, 1806, aged 17.

Moore, Melbourne Campbell, 1s. David, of Melbourne, Australia, arm. BRASENOSE COLL., matric. 19 Oct., 1875, aged 20.

Moore, Nathaniel, s. John, of St. Sepulchre's, London, cler. ST. JOHN'S COLL., matric. 5 July, 1762, aged 17; scholar 1762, B.C.L. 1770, D.C.L. 1773, rector of Winterbourne, co. Gloucester, 1795, until his death, 16 Nov., 1798. See *Robinson*, 111.

Moore, Oswald Allen, o.s. Robert Stephen, of Hulland, co. Derby, cler. MAGDALEN COLL., matric. 19 Oct., 1883, aged 19; B.A. 1887. [35]

Moore, Peter Halhed, 2s. Macartney, of Yateley, Berks, arm. BRASENOSE COLL., matric. 21 March, 1849, aged 18; scholar 1849-52, B.A. 1852, M.A. 1856, perp. curate Lovington 1858-63, and of Chadkirk, Cheshire, 1867.

Moore, Reginald Bowerman, 1s. William Walling, of Lyme Regis, Dorset, gent. NEW COLL., matric. 27 Jan., 1885, aged 34; B.Mus. 3 Dec., 1885.

Moore, Reginald William Bickerton, 1s. William Clark, of Ilfracombe, Devon, cler. HERTFORD COLL., matric. 18 Oct., 1883, aged 18; B.A. 1886.

Moore, Richard, s. Glover, of Halsall, Lancashire, cler. BRASENOSE COLL., matric. 10 Oct., 1810, aged 18; B.A. 1814, M.A. 1817, vicar of Lund, Lancashire, 1820, until his death in 1886.

Moore, Richmond, 1s. Peter Halhed, of Ham Green, Somerset, cler. KEBLE COLL., matric. 29 Jan., 1879, aged 20; scholar 1879-82, B.A. 1883, M.A. 1886. [40]

Moore, Robert, s. John, of St. Bride's, London, gent. LINCOLN COLL., matric. 10 April, 1778, aged 20; B.A. 1782.

Moore, Robert, s. John, Archbishop of Canterbury. CHRIST CHURCH, matric. 25 March, 1795, aged 17; B.A. 1799, M.A. 1802, registrar Prerogative Court of Canterbury, canon of Canterbury 1804-62, rector of Hunton, Kent, 1802, until his death 5 Sep., 1865. See *Eton School Lists.*

Moore, Robert, 3s. Robert, of Hunton, Kent, cler. CHRIST CHURCH, matric. 26 Nov., 1830, aged 18; B.A. 1834, died in 1857. See *Eton School Lists.*

Moore, Robert Eden, 1s. Robert, of Hunton, Kent, cler. CHRIST CHURCH, matric. 31 May, 1860, aged 18.

Moore, Robert Stephen, of ST. JOHN'S COLL., Cambridge (B.A. 1851, M.A. 1861); adm. 'comitatis causa' 6 June, 1861, has held various curacies 1852-73, vicar of Mickley, Yorks, 1874.

Moore, Stephen, 2s. Charles, of Moulton, co. Lincoln, cler. PEMBROKE COLL., matric. 5 Dec., 1862, aged 19. **[5]**

Moore, Stevenson Stewart, 1s. John James Stevenson, of Peel, Isle of Man, cler. KEBLE COLL., matric. 20 Jan., 1877, aged 18; B.A. 1880, bar.-at-law, Middle Temple, 1882. See Foster's *Men at the Bar.*

Moore, Thomas, s. John, of Norwich (city), arm. CHRIST CHURCH, matric. 23 June, 1726, aged 17.

Moore, Thomas, s. John, of St. Peter's, Hereford (city), cler. WADHAM COLL., matric. 27 April, 1730, aged 17; B.A. 7 March, 1733-4.

Moore, Thomas, fellow TRINITY COLL., Cambridge (B.A. 1712, M.A. 1716, D.D. 1733); incorp. 25 May, 1753.

Moore, Thomas, s. Thomas, of London, doctor. WORCESTER COLL. matric. 26 May, 1753, aged 15; B.A. 1757, M.A. 1759, rector of North Cray, Kent, 1765, and of Foot's Cray, 1768, until his death in 1823. **[10]**

Moore, Thomas. BALLIOL COLL., 1799. See STEVENS.

Moore, Thomas, 4s. John, of Warwick (town), arm. BRASENOSE COLL., matric. 24 May, 1866, aged 18; died Jan., 1869.

Moore, Thomas Barrington Geary, 3s. William, of Newport, Isle of Wight, doctor. PEMBROKE COLL., matric. 18 June, 1822, aged 18; B.A. 1827, M.A. 1832, vicar of Broxbourne, Herts, 1853-72, died 3 Feb., 1874. See *Eton School Lists.*

Moore, Thomas Coney Tunnard-, 1s. Charles Thomas John, of Frampton, co. Lincoln, arm. MAGDALEN COLL., matric. 18 Oct., 1873, aged 18; B.A. 1877, of Frampton Hall, co. Lincoln, J.P., bar.-at-law, Lincoln's Inn, 1879. See Foster's *Men at the Bar.*

Moore, Thomas James, s. Thomas, gent. MERTON COLL., matric. 16 Dec., 1808, aged 16; B.A. WADHAM COLL. 1814. **[15]**

Moore, Thomas Knackstone, 2s. George, of Barrington, Wilts, gent. MAGDALEN HALL, matric. 25 May, 1833, aged 20.

Moore, Thomas William, s. Thomas William, of New York, arm. WORCESTER COLL., matric. 9 Dec., 1788, aged 19.

Moore, Uriah Tonkin, EXETER COLL., 1807. See TONKIN.

Moore, Walter Gwyn, 4s. Edward Ackland, of Swindon, Wilts, gent. PEMBROKE COLL., matric. 23 Oct., 1875, aged 19.

Moore, William, s. William, of Wooton-under-Edge, co. Gloucester, arm. ST. JOHN'S COLL., matric. 15 June, 1737, aged 17. **[20]**

Moore, William, s. William, of London, gent. PEMBROKE COLL., matric. 26 March, 1781, aged 15; B.A. 1784, M.A. 1787, B.Med. 1788, D.Med. 1791, F.R.C.P. 1793, physician to the Duke of York and to the forces in the Flanders campaign, principal medical officer army depot Isle of Wight 1803, until his death at Ryde in 1832. See Munk's *Roll*, ii. 424-5.

Moore, William, s. Francis, of South Tawton, Devon, gent. WADHAM COLL., matric. 5 April, 1745, aged 17; B.A. 1748, M.A. 1751.

Moore, William, s. Blundell, of Byfleet, Surrey, arm. ST. MARY HALL, matric. 23 Oct., 1783, aged 18.

Moore, William, s. William, of Isle of Minorca, gent. WORCESTER COLL., matric. 28 Oct., 1786, aged 22.

Moore, William, s. Robert, of Tallow, co. Waterford, Ireland, cler. UNIVERSITY COLL., matric. 18 June, 1807, aged 18. See *Eton School Lists.* **[25]**

Moore, William, s. William, of Bisley, co. Gloucester, cler. PEMBROKE COLL., matric. 31 Oct., 1810, aged 14; scholar 1813-29, B.A. 1814, M.A. 1817, rector of Brimpsfield, co. Gloucester, 1829, until his death in June, 1879.

Moore, William, s. William, of Bow, London, gent. PEMBROKE COLL., matric. 3 Nov., 1812, aged 16; scholar 1812-17, B.A. 1816, M.A. 1819, curate of St. Edmund's, Salisbury, and of St. Thomas's Church, Ryde, where he died 27 Sep., 1851, aged 55.

Moore, William, 1s. Francis, of St. Mary Magdalen, Bridgnorth, gent. CHRIST CHURCH, matric. 14 Oct., 1825, aged 17; B.A. 1829, M.A. 1832.

Moore, William, 1s. William, of Cork, arm. CHRIST CHURCH, matric. 14 May, 1834, aged 18.

Moore, William, 2s. John Walter, of Hordley, near Ellesmere, Salop, cler. NEW COLL., matric. 12 Oct., 1861, aged 18, scholar 1861-6, B.A. 1866, M.A. 1870; fellow MAGDALEN COLL. 1872-9, junior dean of arts 1875, bursar 1877, lecturer of St. John's College 1875-7, rector of Appleton, Berks, 1878. **[30]**

Moore, William, 5s. Edward, of Boughton Malherbe, Kent, cler. ST. JOHN'S COLL., matric. 20 Jan., 1872, aged 20; B.A. 1875, a student of Lincoln's Inn 1879, rector of Kingston Deverill, Wilts, 1885.

Moore, William Clarke, o.s. Robert, of St. Giles's, Camberwell, Surrey, gent. ST. JOHN'S COLL., matric. 9 May, 1845, aged 18; B.A. 1849, M.A. 1851, vicar of St. Philip and St. James, Ilfracombe, 1857-73, and of Tulse Hill, Surrey, since 1873.

Moore, William Daniel, D.Med. TRINITY COLL., Dublin, 1860 (B.A. & B.Med. 1843); adm. 'comitatis causa' 26 June, 1862.

Moore, William Edward, 1s. William, of York, gent. QUEEN'S COLL., matric. 26 Oct., 1876, aged 18; exhibitioner 1876-80, B.A. 1880.

Moore, William (Huntridge), s. Samuel, of St. Stephen's, Exeter, gent. EXETER COLL., matric. 30 March, 1784, aged 17; exhibitioner 1784, B.A. 1790. **[35]**

Moore, William Robert, 1s. William, of Exeter, gent. WORCESTER COLL., matric. 26 April, 1873, aged 19.

Moore, William Withers, 1s. William Withers, of Doncaster, D.Med. ST. JOHN'S COLL., matric. 19 April, 1879, aged 23.

Moorhouse, Matthew Butterworth, 1s. Joshua, of Holmfirth, Yorks, arm. QUEEN'S COLL., matric. 18 March, 1858, aged 17; B.A. 1862, M.A. 1864, perp. curate Hepworth, Yorks, 1868-71, vicar of Bushbury, co. Stafford, 1872-80, and of St. Mary Bredin, Canterbury, 1880.

Moorsom, Arthur Addington, 2s. Robert, of Windsor, Berks, arm. CHRIST CHURCH, matric. 18 Jan., 1863, aged 18; B.A. 1869, M.A. 1879.

Moorsom, Joseph Robertson, 2s. Richard, of Whitby, Yorks, arm. UNIVERSITY COLL., matric. 18 Feb., 1839, aged 18; scholar 1839-48, B.A. 1843, M.A. 1846, rector of Southoe, Hunts, 1848. See *Rugby School Reg.*, 188. **[40]**

Moorsom, Launcelot Richard Purton, 2s. Robert Maude, of Sadberghe, co. Durham, cler. EXETER COLL., matric. 21 Oct., 1886, aged 20.

Moorsom, Richard, 1s. Richard, of Whitby, Yorks, arm. UNIVERSITY COLL., matric. 27 April, 1837, aged 18; B.A. 1841, vicar of Seaham, co. Durham, at his death 5 April, 1846. See *Rugby School Reg.*, 181.

Moorsom, Rev. Richard, o.s. Joseph Robertson, of Southoe, Hunts, cler. MERTON COLL., matric. 14 Oct., 1879, aged 19; B.A. 1884, M.A. 1888.

Mooyaart, Henry, 2s. James Nicholas, of Madura, Isle of Ceylon, arm. WORCESTER COLL., matric. 16 Oct., 1866, aged 38; B.A. 1872, M.A. 1874, sometime in Ceylon Civil Service, a student of the Inner Temple 1869, curate of St. Ebbe's, Oxford, 1874-7, vicar of Benhall, Suffolk, 1877-84, and rector of Uplowman, Devon, 1885.

Moran, Henry, 1s. Thomas, of St. Thomas's, Dublin, Ireland, pleb. JESUS COLL., matric. 9 June, 1823, aged 19.

Moran, John Henry, 3s. Francis Goldsberry, of Kilmore Moy, co. Sligo, Ireland, arm. MAGDALEN HALL, matric. 15 Feb., 1827, aged 18; B.A. 1830, vicar of St. Thomas's, liberty of the Rolls, 1866-86, etc. See *Crockford.*

Moran, Walter Isidore, 3s. Patrick Thomas, of Cheetham, Lancashire, arm. MERTON COLL., matric. 16 Oct., 1884, aged 19; postmaster 1884. [5]

Morant, Edward, s. John, of Isle of Jamaica, arm. ST. MARY HALL, matric. 7 March, 1746-7, aged 16; created D.C.L. 9 July, 1773, of Brockenhurst, Hants, M.P. Hindon 1761-8, Lymington 1774-80, Yarmouth, Isle of Wight, 1780-7, died 27 July, 1791.

Morant, George, s. John, of St. Marylebone, London, arm. CHRIST CHURCH, matric. 29 Jan., 1812, aged 20; of Farnborough Place, Hants, died 17 Dec., 1875.

Morant, Rev. James, of MAGDALEN COLL., Cambridge (B.A. 1834, M.A. 1837); adm. 'ad eundem' 14 June, 1849, of the H.E.I.C.S.

Morant, John, s. John, of Isle of Jamaica, arm. ST. JOHN'S COLL., matric. 11 April, 1741, aged 17; father of Edward.

Morant, John, s. Edward, of Brockenhurst, Hants, arm. UNIVERSITY COLL., matric. 2 April, 1773, aged 18; of Brockenhurst, died 2 March, 1794. [10]

Morant, John, s. John, of Westminster, arm. CHRIST CHURCH, matric. 24 Oct., 1804, aged 17; of Brockenhurst Park, Hants, high sheriff 1820, died 5 May, 1857. See *Eton School Lists.*

Morant, John, 1s. John, of Brockenhurst, Hants, arm. CHRIST CHURCH, matric. 9 June, 1843, aged 18; of Brockenhurst, high sheriff, Hants, 1869.

Morant, Robert Laurie, 1s. Robert, of London, arm. NEW COLL., matric. 15 Oct., 1881, aged 18; B.A. 1885.

Morant, William, s. John, of Jamaica, arm. ST. JOHN'S COLL., matric. 4 Nov., 1741, aged 16; brother of John 1741.

Morcom, William Genn, 2s. Joseph, of St. Austell, Cornwall, gent. EXETER COLL., matric. 26 May, 1858, aged 17; B.A. 1863, M.A. 1865, vicar of Little Grimsby 1866-71, rector of Georgham, Devon, 1871-80, and vicar of Braunton 1880. [15]

Mordacque, Louis Henry, 1s. Louis Alexander (Joseph), of Paris, France, gent. BRASENOSE COLL., matric. 18 May, 1842, aged 18; scholar 1842-6, B.A. 1846, M.A. 1849, perp. curate Haslingden, Lancashire, 1849, until his death 30 Jan., 1870. See *Manchester School Reg.*, iii. 264.

Mordaunt, Hon. Charles, born at York, s. John, Lord Mordaunt. BALLIOL COLL., matric. 13 Nov., 1727, aged 17; 4th Earl of Peterborough and 2nd Earl of Monmouth, died 1 Aug., 1779.

Mordaunt, Charles, s. Charles, of Walton, co. Warwick, baronet. CHRIST CHURCH, matric. 17 Dec., 1753, aged 16; B.A. 1757, M.A. 1760, rector of Little Massingham, Kent, 1761, until his death 22 Jan., 1820. See Foster's *Baronetage.*

Mordaunt, (Sir) Charles (Bart.), s. John, of Westminster, baronet. CHRIST CHURCH, matric. 1 Dec., 1788, aged 17; B.A. 1791, 8th baronet, M.P. Warwickshire 1804-20, died 30 May, 1823. See Foster's *Baronetage* & *Eton School Lists.*

Mordaunt, Charles, s. Charles, of Massingham, Norfolk, cler. CHRIST CHURCH, matric. 21 Dec., 1792, aged 18; B.A. 1796, M.A. 1800, rector of Badgeworth, Somerset, 1800, until his death 22 Jan., 1824, father of Charles, next named, and of John 1831. [20]

Mordaunt, Charles, 1s. Charles, of Ashton-water, Somerset, cler. BALLIOL COLL., matric. 6 April, 1832, aged 19; B.A. from NEW INN HALL 1836, rector of Badgworth, Somerset, 1838, until his death 11 Oct., 1861. See Foster's *Baronetage.*

Mordaunt, Charles, 1s. John, of London, baronet. CHRIST CHURCH, matric. 8 June, 1854, aged 18; 10th baronet, M.P. South Warwickshire 1859-68. See Foster's *Baronetage* & *Eton School Lists.*

Mordaunt, Charles Henry, s. Charles, Earl of Peterborough and Monmouth. CHRIST CHURCH, matric. 18 May, 1776, aged 18; 5th Earl of Peterborough, and 3rd Earl of Monmouth, died 16 June, 1814.

Mordaunt, Henry, s. Charles, of St. Anne's, Westminster, arm. CHRIST CHURCH, matric. 13 Nov., 1750, aged 18; B.A. 1755 (? brother of Charles 1753).

Mordaunt, John, s. John, of St. James's, London, baronet. NEW COLL., matric. 7 May, 1722, aged 17; B.C.L. 1729. [25]

Mordaunt, (Sir) John (Bart.), s. Charles, of Walton, co. Warwick, baronet. NEW COLL., matric. 26 Feb., 1752, aged 17; created M.A. 8 July, 1756, and D.C.L. 8 July, 1763, 7th baronet, a groom of the bedchamber, M.P. Warwickshire 1793-1802, died 18 Nov., 1806, father of the next named. See Foster's *Baronetage.*

Mordaunt, John, s. John, of London, baronet. CHRIST CHURCH, matric. 30 April, 1792, aged 17; B.A. 1796, M.A. 1798, rector of Wickin, Northants, at his death 27 Sep., 1806.

Mordaunt, (Sir) John (Bart.), 1s. Charles, of Farnborough, co. Warwick, baronet. CHRIST CHURCH, matric. 23 May, 1826, aged 17; B.A. 1829, M.A. 1832, 9th baronet, M.P. South Warwickshire 1835, until his death 27 Sep., 1845. See Foster's *Baronetage* & *Eton School Lists.*

Mordaunt, John, 2s. Charles, of Backwell (? Badgeworth), Somerset, cler. WADHAM COLL., matric. 27 Oct., 1831, aged 17; of 17th lancers, died 15 Nov., 1881, brother of Charles 1832.

Mordaunt, John Murray, 2s. John, of Walton, co. Warwick, baronet. CHRIST CHURCH, matric. 31 May, 1855, aged 17; of Staple Hill, co. Warwick, J.P., D.L. See Foster's *Baronetage.* [30]

Mordaunt, Osbert, 3s. John, of Walton House, co. Warwick, baronet. CHRIST CHURCH, matric. 17 Oct., 1860, aged 17; B.A. 1865, M.A. 1867, perp. curate Handsworth, Stafford, 1871-4, rector of Hampton Lucy, co. Warwick, 1874.

More, Henry, s. John, of Swinbroke, Oxon, pleb. ST. MARY HALL, matric. 17 Oct., 1719, aged 17.

More, Robert, s. Robert, of Shrewsbury (town), arm. PEMBROKE COLL., matric. 18 April, 1780, aged 22; of More, Linley, and Shelve, Salop, high sheriff, died 12 Jan., 1818, father of Thomas F. 1808.

More, Robert Bridgeman, s. Robert, of The More, Salop, arm. MAGDALEN COLL., matric. 6 Feb., 1807, aged 18; of Linley Hall, high sheriff Salop 1822, a student of Lincoln's Inn 1809, died in 1851.

More, Robert Jasper, o.s. Thomas Frederick, of Corley near Tenbury, co. Worcester, cler. BALLIOL COLL., matric. 27 June, 1855, aged 18; B.A. 1861, B.C.L. & M.A. 1862, of Linley Hall, Salop, and of the Hall, Cleobury North, J.P., D.L., high sheriff 1881, bar.-at-law, Lincoln's Inn, 1863, M.P. South Salop 1865-8, for Salop (Ludlow division) since Dec., 1885. See Foster's *Men at the Bar.* [35]

More, Thomas Frederick, s. Robert, of More, Salop, arm. EXETER COLL., matric. 31 Oct., 1808, aged 18; B.A. from PEMBROKE COLL., Cambridge, 1815, of Linley Hall, rector of Shelve, Salop, died 17 Dec., 1869.

Moreau, James Philip, s. James, of St. Martin's, Middlesex, gent. ST. EDMUND HALL, matric. 13 Dec., 1726, aged 18; B.A. from TRINITY COLL. 19 Feb., 1729-30.

Morehead, Robert, s. William, of Herbertshire, co. Stirling, Scotland, gent. BALLIOL COLL., matric. 4 Dec., 1795, aged 17; B.A. 1799, M.A. 1802, 2nd minister St. Paul's Episcopal Chapel, Edinburgh (D.D.), rector of Easington, Yorks, 1832-40, died 13 Dec., 1842.

Morehouse, Christopher, s. Stephen, of South Tawton, Devon, cler. WADHAM COLL., matric. 19 Feb., 1718-9, aged 18; B.A. 1722.

Carvalho-Moreira, Francisco Ignacio de, Brazilian minister at St. James's, created D.C.L. 2 July, 1862. [5]

Morel, Alphonso Charles de, 1s. Joseph Marie, of Marylebone, Middlesex, arm. UNIVERSITY COLL., matric. 16 March, 1843, aged 18.

Morel, Andrew Dominic, s. Nicholas, of St. James's, Westminster, arm. MERTON COLL., matric. 10 April, 1815, aged 18.

Moreland, Christopher Hudson, 2s. William Harrison, of Belfast, gent. LINCOLN COLL., matric. 22 Oct., 1886, aged 19; exhibitioner 1886.

Mores, Edward Rowe, s. Edward, of Tunstall, Kent, cler. QUEEN'S COLL., matric. 25 June, 1746, aged 16; B.A. 1750, M.A. 1753, one of the founders of the Society of Antiquaries, died 28 Nov., 1778. See *Robinson*, 96.

Moresby, Admiral Sir Fairfax, G.C.B., K.M.T., created D.C.L. 28 June, 1854 (son of Fairfax Moresby, of Stow House, Lichfield), entered the navy 1799, commander-in-chief in the Pacific 1850-5, G.C.B. 1855, admiral 1862, admiral of the Fleet 1870, commanded the *Menai*, *Pembroke* and *Canopus*, died 21 Jan., 1877, aged 90. [10]

Moresby, Henry, 6s. Fairfax, of Stow House, Lichfield, co. Stafford, arm. EXETER COLL., matric. 3 Nov., 1821, aged 16; B.A. 1826, M.A. 1828, bar.-at-law, Inner Temple, 1833.

Moresby, John, s. Fairfax, of Bath, Somerset, gent. ST. ALBAN HALL, matric. 11 Dec., 1816, aged 24.

Moreton, Hon. Augustus Henry (Macdonald), 2s. Thomas, baron (after Earl Ducie). MERTON COLL., matric. 4 Feb., 1823, aged 18; B.A. 1826, of Largie, co. Argyll, M.P. West Gloucesters. 1832-5, East Gloucesters. 1835-41, died 14 Feb., 1862.

Moreton, Hon. Berkeley Basil, born at Woodchester, co. Gloucester, 4s. Henry George, Earl Ducie. MAGDALEN COLL., matric. 9 Dec., 1853, aged 19; postmaster-general Queensland 1885. See Foster's *Peerage*.

Moreton, (Hon.) Percy, born at Woodchester, co. Gloucester, 3s. Thomas, Baron Ducie. CHRIST CHURCH, matric. 9 Nov., 1826, aged 18; captain 10th hussars, died 15 March, 1886. [15]

Moreton, Ralph, s. Ralph, of Woolstanton, co. Stafford, arm. WORCESTER COLL., matric. 26 Oct., 1770, aged 17; B.C.L. 1777.

Moreton, Robert, s. Nicol, of Suffolk, gent. BRASENOSE COLL., matric. 12 May, 1731, aged 17.

Moreton, Thomas, s. Charles, of Bolton, Lancashire, gent. BRASENOSE COLL., matric. 1 Feb., 1719-20, aged 18; B.A. from CORPUS CHRISTI COLL. 1723, M.A. 1726, B.D. 1734, D.D. 8 March, 1736-7.

Moreton, Thomas, s. Francis, Baron Ducie. EXETER COLL., matric. 24 March, 1792, aged 16; created M.A. 28 June, 1797, 5th baron, created Earl of Ducie, 28 Jan., 1837, died 22 July, 1840. See Foster's *Peerage & Eton School Lists*.

Moreton, Tudor Phillips, 1s. Julian, of Labuan, Isle of Borneo, cler. NON-COLL., matric. 23 Jan., 1886, aged 21. [20]

Morewood, Charles Rowland Palmer, 1s. Charles Rowland Palmer, of Southampton, Hants, arm. ST. JOHN'S COLL., matric. 18 Oct., 1862, aged 19; of Alfreton Hall, co. Derby, and of Ladbrooke, co. Warwick, high sheriff 1880. See Foster's *Peerage*, E. SELBORNE; & *Eton School Lists*.

Morewood, John, s. William, of Hartington, co. Derby, pleb. ST. EDMUND HALL, matric. 17 March, 1725-6, aged 20; B.A. 26 Feb., 1729-30.

Morewood, John, s. John, of Westbourn, Sussex, cler. QUEEN'S COLL., matric. 11 March, 1761, aged 17; B.A. 1764, M.A. 1767, rector of West Hallam, co. Derby, 1804, until his death in 1828.

Morewood, William Frederick Palmer, 2s. William Palmer, of Ladbrooke, co. Warwick, arm. CHRIST CHURCH, matric. 3 June, 1840, aged 18; B.A. 1844, bar.-at-law, Middle Temple, 1847, died 15 Aug., 1861. See Foster's *Peerage*, E. SELBORNE.

Morfill, William Richard, 1s. William, of Maidstone, Kent, gent. CORPUS CHRISTI COLL., matric. 28 May, 1853, aged 18; scholar ORIEL COLL. 1852-6, B.A. 1857, M.A. 1860, Ilchester lecturer in Sclavonic 1873. [25]

Morfitt, John, s. John, of Osgoldby, co. York, gent. QUEEN'S COLL., matric. 10 March, 1736-7, aged 23.

Morfitt, John, s. John, of Guiseley, co. York, cler. UNIVERSITY COLL., matric. 8 April, 1775, aged 17; bar.-at-law, Inner Temple, 1784.

Morgan, Alfred, 6s. George, of Biddlesdon, Bucks, arm. UNIVERSITY COLL., matric. 2 April, 1824, aged 19; B.A. 1826, M.A. 1832, bar.-at-law, Lincoln's Inn, 1835.

Morgan, Arthur John, 3s. Charles, Baron Tredegar. MERTON COLL., matric. 26 Oct., 1859, aged 19. See Foster's *Peerage*.

Morgan, Arthur Middlemore, 6s. Francis, of Catherington, Hants, arm. EXETER COLL., matric. 17 April, 1850, aged 18; B.A. 1854, M.A. 1857, held various curacies 1856-72, rector of Huish, North Devon, 1872-84, vicar of Mucking, Essex, 1884. [30]

Morgan, Benjamin, s. Benjamin, of Trelech, co. Carmarthen, cler. ST. ALBAN HALL, matric. 7 March, 1783, aged 27.

Morgan, Benjamin Ellis, o.s. Benjamin, of Aberdovey, co. Merioneth, cler. JESUS COLL., matric. 6 Feb., 1867, aged 20.

Morgan, Charles, s. Thomas, of Llanddewi-Felfry, co. Pembroke, cler. JESUS COLL., matric. 18 March, 1718-9, aged 18; B.A. 1722.

Morgan, Charles, s. Hugh, of Bettws, co. Radnor, gent. BRASENOSE COLL., matric. 10 April, 1742, aged 16; B.A. 11 March, 1745-6, M.A. 1748.

Morgan, (Sir) Charles (Bart.), 1s. King Gould, of St. Margaret's, Westminster, arm. CHRIST CHURCH, matric. 1 June, 1743, aged 17; B.A. 1747, M.A. 1750, created D.C.L. 8 July, 1773 (then) judge-advocate general 1771-1806, bar.-at-law, Middle Temple, 1750, chancellor of Salisbury 1772, M.P. Brecon, 1778-87, co. Brecon 1787-1808, knighted 5 May, 1779, created a baronet 15 Nov., 1792, and the next day assumed by royal licence the surname of MORGAN in lieu of GOULD, P.C. 1802, died 6 Dec., 1806, grandfather of Lord Tredegar. See Foster's *Peerage* & *Alumni West.*, 327. [35]

Morgan, Charles, s. Charles, of Llandovery, co. Carmarthen, gent. CHRIST CHURCH, matric. 30 June, 1750, aged 17; B.A. 1754, M.A. 1757.

Morgan, Sir Charles, 2nd Bart.; created D.C.L. 13 June, 1834 (s. Sir Charles Morgan, Bart.), lieut.-colonel in the army, M.P. Brecon, 1787-96, Monmouthshire 1796-1831, died 5 Feb., 1846. See Foster's *Peerage*, B. TREDEGAR.

Morgan, Charles, o.s. Charles, of Carmarthen (town), arm. EXETER COLL., matric. 18 March, 1835, aged 19; B.A. 1839, M.A. 1841, of Allt-y-Gog, co. Carmarthen, high sheriff 1857.

Morgan, Charles, 1s. James, of Bronllys, co. Brecon, cler. TRINITY COLL., matric. 6 Dec., 1855, aged 18; of Brooklands co. Monmouth, J.P., sometime captain 23rd royal Welsh fusiliers.

Morgan, Charles Augustus Samuel, 3s. Charles, of Brickendenbury, Hants, baronet. CHRIST CHURCH, matric. 27 June, 1821, aged 20; B.A. 1825, M.A. 1833, rector of Machen, co. Monmouth, 1831-73, chaplain in ordinary to the Queen 1829, chancellor of Llandaff 1851, died 5 Sep. 1875.

Morgan, Charles Edgar, 1s. William Henry, of Ystradyfodwg, co. Glamorgan, cler. KEBLE COLL., matric. 16 Oct., 1883, aged 23.

Morgan, Charles Henry, s. Walter, of Shepton Mallet, Somerset, gent. TRINITY COLL., matric. 2 March, 1802, aged 18; B.A. 1806, M.A. 1810, hon. canon Bristol 1853, vicar of Abbot's Leigh, 1852, until his death 1861.

Morgan, Charles James, 1s. Charles Henry, of Tiddenham, co. Gloucester, cler. LINCOLN COLL., matric. 16 June, 1836, aged 19; B.A. 1845, M.A. 1846, curate of Matherne, co. Monmouth, 1846-51, and of Reymerston, Norfolk, 1862-7. [5]

Morgan, Charles Leveson Gower, 2s. William, of Burton-on-Trent, co. Stafford, cler. WORCESTER COLL., matric. 17 Oct., 1868, aged 18; exhibitioner 1868-72, B.A. 1872.

Morgan, Charles Morgan Robinson, s. Charles, of St. Margaret's, Westminster, baronet. CHRIST CHURCH, matric. 8 May, 1811, aged 19; created D.C.L. 5 July, 1848, 3rd baronet, M.P. Brecon, 1812-18, 1830-2, 1835-47, created Baron Tredegar 16 April, 1859, lord-lieut. co. Monmouth 1866-75, died 16 April, 1875. See Foster's *Peerage*.

Morgan, Charles Octavius Swinnerton, 4s. Charles, of Ealing, Middlesex, baronet. CHRIST CHURCH, matric. 26 June, 1822, aged 18; B.A. 1825, M.A. 1832, of the Friars, Newport, co. Monmouth, M.P. 1841-74, F.R.S., F.S.A.

Morgan, Charles Tirrel, s. Charles, of Fairford, co. Gloucester, gent. EXETER COLL., matric. 17 Dec., 1759, aged 16; B.A. 1763, fellow 1764-5, M.A. 1767, proctor 1771, professor of moral philosophy 1772, bar.-at-law, Lincoln's Inn, 1769. See *Coll. Reg.*, 107.

Morgan, David, s. John, of Llanegwad, co. Carmarthen, pleb. JESUS COLL. matric. 17 March, 1717-8, aged 17. [10]

Morgan, David, s. David, of Llanycrwys, co. Carmarthen, pleb. JESUS COLL., matric. 18 March, 1748-9, aged 20.

Morgan, David, s. John, of Llandilo Fawr, co. Carmarthen, pleb. JESUS COLL., matric. 29 Feb., 1812, aged 19; B.A. 1815, M.A. 1818, died at Ham rectory 15 Jan., 1864, aged 71.

Morgan, David Howard, 1s. Thomas, of Paddington, Middlesex, arm. MAGDALEN COLL., matric. 13 Oct., 1821, aged 19; a student of Lincoln's Inn 1823.

Morgan, David (Parker), 4s. William, of Maesmynis, near Brecon, gent. JESUS COLL., matric. 8 May, 1862, aged 19; B.A. from MAGDALEN HALL 1866, vicar of Aberavon 1870-5, and of Aberdovey, North Wales, 1871-86, assistant-minister Church of Heavenly Rest, New York, 1881-5, and associate rector 1885.

Morgan, David Walter, s. William, of St. George's, Southwark, pleb. HERTFORD COLL., matric. 14 June, 1759, aged 25. [15]

Morgan, Edmond John, o.s. Charles Robert, of St. George's, Bloomsbury, London, gent. WADHAM COLL., matric. 30 Jan., 1839, aged 18; B.A. 1842, M.A. 1846, perp. curate St. Matthias, Malvern Link, 1849-52, rector of Great Fakenham 1856-86.

Morgan, Edmond Percy, 2s. William Bowyer, of Highgate, Middlesex, gent. ORIEL COLL., matric. 19 Oct., 1875, aged 17; B.A. 1881, M.A. 1882.

Morgan, Edward, s. Edward, of Aberdare, co. Glamorgan, gent. JESUS COLL., matric. 27 March, 1776, aged 17; B.A. 1779, M.A. 1782, B.D. 1790, proctor 1789, sinecure rector of Badgworth, co. Gloucester, 1796, and rector of Egloys Brewis, co. Glamorgan, at his death 30 July, 1832.

Morgan, Edward, s. William, of Brecon (town), cler. PEMBROKE COLL., matric. 27 March, 1778, aged 16; B.A. 1782.

Morgan, Edward, s. Nathaniel, of Bath, Somerset, cler. ORIEL COLL., matric. 12 July, 1794, aged 17; B.A. 1798, M.A. 1801, rector of Reresby, co. Leicester, at his death 1 Nov., 1812. [20]

Morgan, Edward, s. David, of Pyle, co. Glamorgan, gent. JESUS COLL., matric. 18 Oct., 1802, aged 18; B.A. 1806, M.A. 1811.

Morgan, Edward, s. William, of Aston Clinton, Bucks, doctor. EXETER COLL., matric. 2 April, 1816, aged 18; B.A. from ST. ALBAN HALL 1821, M.A. 1825.

Morgan, Edward Henry Elers, 1s. Edward, of Tunbridge Wells, arm. UNIVERSITY COLL., matric. 11 Oct., 1884, aged 19.

Morgan, Edward Strong, 2s. David Fortescue, of Bath, Somerset, cler. LINCOLN COLL., matric. 17 Oct., 1866, aged 20; scholar 1867-70, B.A. 1871.

Morgan, Evan Prichard, 1s. John, of Neath, co. Glamorgan, gent. JESUS COLL., matric. 19 Feb., 1823, aged 18; scholar 1827-31, B.A. 1827, M.A. 1833.

Morgan, Francis, s. James, of Oakfield, (par.) Mortimer, Berks, doctor. ORIEL COLL., matric. 19 May, 1794, aged 17; B.A. 1800, of Oakfield, brother of Henry Charles 1809. [25]

Morgan, Francis Augustine, 2s. Samuel Francis, of All Saints, Birmingham, cler. WADHAM COLL., matric. 11 March, 1856, aged 17; B.A. 1860, M.A. 1863, vicar of St. Paul's, Bath, 1869-85, and of Chepstow 1885.

Morgan, Francis Henry, 2s. Francis, of Chelsea, Middlesex, gent. WORCESTER COLL., matric. 3 March, 1842, aged 19; B.A. 1846, M.A. 1848, held various curacies 1846-61, rector of Guisborough, Yorks, 1862.

Morgan, Frederick, s. Francis, of Shepton Mallet, Somerset, arm. BALLIOL COLL., matric. 7 March, 1810, aged 18; B.C.L. from WORCESTER COLL. 1817.

Morgan, Frederick. ST. JOHN'S COLL., 1822. See PAYLER. [30]

Morgan, Frederick Francis, 1s. George Frederick, of Southall, Middlesex, cler. ST. MARY HALL, matric. 9 Feb., 1865, aged 17; B.A. 1869, M.A. 1871, held various curacies 1872-85, rector of Ludgarshall, Bucks, 1885.

Morgan, George, s. James, of Holbourn, London, arm. ORIEL COLL., matric. 29 April, 1757, aged 17; of Abercathy, co. Carmarthen, and of Billesden Park, Bucks, bar.-at-law, Lincoln's Inn, 1767, died 10 June, 1819, brother of James 1757.

Morgan, George, s. Francis, of Shepton Mallet, Somerset, arm. QUEEN'S COLL., matric. 25 Nov., 1802, aged 18; B.A. 1806, M.A. 1811.

Morgan, George, s. Thomas, of Lamphey, co. Pembroke, pleb. CHRIST CHURCH, matric. 15 Jan., 1807, aged 18; B.A. 1811, M.A. 1814, chaplain 1813-18, perp. curate Great Torrington, Devon, 1815, until his death 12 June, 1849.

Morgan, George, s. William, of Newent, co. Gloucester, cler. WADHAM COLL., matric. 27 Jan., 1812, aged 21 (? B.A. from ST. MARY HALL 1815, M.A. 1819); vicar of Stoke Great Milborough, Salop, 1819, until his death 16 Dec., 1866. See *Gent.'s Mag.*, 1867, i. 253. [35]

Morgan, George, s. George, of Sulhamstead, Berks, arm. ORIEL COLL., matric. 17 June, 1812, aged 18; a student of Lincoln's Inn 1817.

Morgan, George Cadogan, s. William, of Newcastle, co. Glamorgan, gent. JESUS COLL., matric. 10 Oct., 1771, aged 17, minister of a congregation at Norwich in 1776, and at Yarmouth 1785, etc., died 17 Nov., 1798. See *Gent.'s Mag.*, ii. 1144.

Morgan, George Frederick, 1s. George, of Great Torrington, cler. CHRIST CHURCH, matric. 19 Oct., 1837, aged 18; servitor 1837-41, B.A. 1841, M.A. 1844, rector of Teversall, Notts, 1877, until his death in 1887.

Morgan, George Osborne, born at Gottenburg, Sweden, 1s. Morgan, cler. BALLIOL COLL., matric. 30 Nov., 1843, aged 17; scholar WORCESTER COLL. 1847-50, B.A. 1848, fellow UNIVERSITY COLL. 1850-7, M.A. 1850, of Brymbo Hall, co. Denbigh, J.P., bar.-at-law, Lincoln's Inn, 1853, Q.C. and a bencher 1869, M.P. Denbighshire 1865-85, and East Denbighshire since 1885, privy councillor 1880, and judge advocate-general 1880-5, under-secretary for the Colonies Jan. to July, 1886. See Foster's *Men at the Bar*.

Morgan, Hanmer, 2s. Hugh Hanmer, of St. John's, Hereford (town), cler. CHRIST CHURCH, matric. 9 Dec., 1840, aged 19; B.A. from NEW INN HALL 1846, M.A. 1849, rector of St. Athan, co. Glamorgan. See *Eton School Lists*.

Morgan, Harington, 4s. Sir Walter, of Madras, knight. PEMBROKE COLL., matric. 27 Oct., 1883, aged 18; bar.-at-law, Middle Temple, 1887.

Morgan, Harris de Riemer, o.s. Edward, of Balycombe, Devon, arm. EXETER COLL., matric. 23 April, 1879, aged 19; B.A. 1884, M.A. 1886, a student of the Middle Temple 1883. **[5]**

Morgan, Hector Davies, s. Hector Davies, of St. George's, London, gent. TRINITY COLL., matric. 24 Feb., 1803, aged 18; B.A. 1806, M.A. 1815, Bampton lecturer 1819, curate of Castle Hedingham, Essex, 1809-46, canon of Brecon, died 23 Dec., 1850, father of John B. 1828.

Morgan, Henry, s. William, of Llanrhwydrus, Isle of Anglesey, gent. JESUS COLL., matric. 21 Feb., 1721-2, aged 17.

Morgan, Henry, s. William, of Newent, co. Gloucester, cler. WORCESTER COLL., matric. 12 Feb., 1814, aged 16.

Morgan, Henry Charles, s. James, of Southampton, Hants, arm. UNIVERSITY COLL., matric. 12 May, 1808, aged 18. **[9]**

Morgan, Henry Charles, s. James, of Mortimer, Berks, doctor. BRASENOSE COLL., matric. 12 Oct., 1809, aged 18; B.A. 1813, M.A. 1816, vicar of Goodrich, co. Hereford, 1830, until his death 29 July, 1875.

Morgan, Henry David, o.s. Morgan, of Llanrhian, co. Cardigan, gent. JESUS COLL., matric. 20 April, 1864, aged 18; B.A. 1868, rector of Tidmarsh, Berks, 1880.

Morgan, Henry Francis, o.s. Thomas Henry, of Tidenham House, co. Gloucester, arm. EXETER COLL., matric. 22 Jan., 1876, aged 18; B.A. from NEW INN HALL 1880.

Morgan, Henry George, 1s. Henry, of Camberwell, Surrey, cler. MERTON COLL., matric. 14 Oct., 1871, aged 19; postmaster 1872-7, B.A. 1876, M.A. 1878, vicar of Moreton Jeffries, co. Hereford, 1884, rector of Stoke Lacy 1886.

Morgan, Henry Thornhill, 1s. David Thomas, of Leytonstone, Essex, arm. TRINITY COLL., matric. 29 Jan. 1859, aged 18; B.A. 1864, M.A. 1865, curate of St. John's, Newbury, 1866, vicar 1871-84, vicar of Crowthorne, Berks, 1884.

Morgan, Hugh, s. Thomas, of Kingsland, co. Hereford, cler. BRASENOSE COLL., matric. 8 March, 1769, aged 16, B.A. 1772; M.A. from WORCESTER COLL. 1775, B. & D.D. 1803, vicar of Lugwardine, preb. of Hereford 1779, until his death 28 Aug., 1809.

Morgan, Hugh, 3s. Hugh, of Machynlleth, co. Montgomery, gent. JESUS COLL., matric. 3 June, 1843, aged 17; B.A. 1847, M.A. 1849, archdeacon and canon of St. Asaph 1877, vicar of Rhyl 1855, until his death 8 June, 1878. **[16]**

Morgan, Hugh (Hanmer), s. Hugh, of Ross, co. Hereford, cler. CHRIST CHURCH, matric. 8 May, 1800, aged 16; B.A. 1804, M.A. 1807, B.D. 1814, rector of Slapton, Bucks, 1805, preb. of Hereford 1808, inducted canon 1821, chancellor 1830, died 30 June, 1861. See *Eton School Lists*.

Morgan, Hugh Hanmer Rayer, 1s. Hanmer, of Hereford, cler. MERTON COLL., matric. 18 Jan., 1875, aged 18.

Morgan, Hugh Stratford. CHRIST CHURCH, 1837. See STRATFORD.

Morgan, Isaac, 1s. James, of Cork (city), arm. TRINITY COLL., matric. 7 April, 1835, aged 17; B.A. 1840, a student of the Inner Temple 1837.

Morgan, James, s. Thomas, of Ecclus Island, co. Glamorgan, pleb. JESUS COLL., matric. 18 March, 1718-9; B.A. 14 March, 1722-3. **[21]**

Morgan, James, s. James, of Holbourn, London, arm. ORIEL COLL., matric. 29 April, 1757, aged 16; B.A. 1761, M.A. 1764, B. & D.D. 1785, vicar of Llantrissant, co. Glamorgan, preb. of Gloucester 1803, until his death 2 June, 1816, father of Francis 1794, and of Henry Charles 1809.

Morgan, James, s. John, of Llanfihangel-y-Croyddin, co. Cardigan, pleb. JESUS COLL., matric. 12 May, 1796, aged 20.

Morgan, James, s. Ant., of Llanelly, co. Brecon, arm. UNIVERSITY COLL., matric. 27 March, 1732, aged 17.

Morgan, James, o.s. John, of Westbury, co. Gloucester, arm. TRINITY COLL., matric. 30 Nov., 1819, aged 17; B.A. 1823, M.A. 1826, vicar of Talgarth, co. Brecon, 1832, and of Llangorse 1836, died 6 May, 1871. **[25]**

Morgan, James Francis, 1s. Francis, of Hambledon, Hants, arm. WORCESTER COLL., matric. 25 April, 1839, aged 19; B.A. 1843, M.A. 1845, bar.-at-law, Lincoln's Inn, 1845, died 18 Dec., 1867.

Morgan, Rev. James Jones, 1s. William Wozencroft, of Penrock, co. Carmarthen, gent. JESUS COLL., matric. 26 Oct., 1874, aged 19; B.A. 1879, M.A. 1884.

Morgan, John, s. Edward, of Penderyn, co. Brecon, gent. JESUS COLL., matric. 14 Oct., 1717, aged 18; B.A. 1721, M.A. 1724, B.Med. 1727.

Morgan, (Sir) John (Bart.), s. Thomas, of St. Martin's-in-the-Fields, Middlesex, baronet. QUEEN'S COLL., matric. 20 June, 1726, aged 15; created M.A. 29 July, 1729, 4th baronet, of Kinnersley Court, M.P. Hereford 1734, and for Herefordshire 1755, until his death 20 April, 1767.

Morgan, John, s. Anthony, of Aberchydach, co. Brecon, gent. ORIEL COLL., matric. 4 June, 1733, aged 17; B.A. 1737, M.A. 1740. **[30]**

Morgan, John, s. Edward, of Brecknock (town), pleb. JESUS COLL., matric. 7 Dec., 1736, aged 18; B.A. from ORIEL COLL. 1741.

Morgan, John, s. Jenkin, of St. Bride's Major, co. Glamorgan, pleb. BALLIOL COLL., matric. 17 Dec., 1757, aged 19; B.A. 1761.

Morgan, John, s. Thomas, of Oxford (city), pleb. CHRIST CHURCH, matric. 14 July, 1775, aged 16; B.A. 1779, M.A. 1782, vicar of Tenbury, co. Warwick, 1845, until his death 21 Aug., 1848, aged 90.

Morgan, John, s. John, of Llanbadern, co. Cardigan, pleb. PEMBROKE COLL., matric. 28 March, 1776, aged 18; B.A. 1780.

Morgan, John, s. James, of Cowbridge, co. Glamorgan, gent. PEMBROKE COLL., matric. 20 Oct., 1783, aged 16; B.A. 1788. **[35]**

Morgan, John, s. Morgan, of Cayo, co. Carmarthen, cler. JESUS COLL., matric. 5 May, 1809, aged 22.

Morgan, John, 1s. Lewis, of Llansaintfraed, co. Cardigan, pleb. JESUS COLL., matric. 20 Oct., 1828, aged 20.

Morgan, John, 1s. Joel, of Llanbadarn Fawr, co. Cardigan, gent. JESUS COLL., matric. 18 May, 1839, aged 22; B.A. 1843, rector of Llandudno 1857, until his death in 1885. See *Eton School Lists*.

Morgan, John, 3s. John, of Convil-Cayo, co. Carmarthen, gent. JESUS COLL., matric. 28 May, 1841, aged 18; scholar 1841-8, B.A., 1845, M.A. 1847, vicar of Nantyglo 1857.

Morgan, John, 6s. Morgan, of Cil-y-cwm, co. Carmarthen, gent. JESUS COLL., matric. 2 Dec., 1852, aged 20; B.A. 1856, M.A. 1859, held various curacies 1857-82.

Morgan, John, 1s. Evan, of Llanddeiniol, co. Cardigan, cler. JESUS COLL., matric. 24 Oct., 1866, aged 20.

Morgan, John, of TRINITY COLL., Dublin (B.A. 1859, M.A. 1862, LL.B. & LL.D. 1864); adm. 'comitatis causa' 29 Nov., 1866, head of modern department Blackheath proprietary school 1856-74, vice-principal 1874-7, vicar of Humberston, co. Lincoln, 1877.

Morgan, Rev. John Anwyl Drury, 1s. John, of Llandudno, co. Carnarvon, cler. NON-COLL., matric. 2 Feb., 1878, aged 19; B.A. from MAGDALEN COLL. 1881, died 14 Jan., 1885. **[5]**

Morgan, John Blackstone, 1s. Hector Davies, of Islington, Middlesex, cler. TRINITY COLL., matric. 21 Feb., 1828, aged 19; B.A. 1831, curate of Garsington, Oxon, at his death 3 July, 1832.

Morgan, John Edward, born at Gottenburg, Sweden, 2s. Morgan, cler. UNIVERSITY COLL., matric. 3 Feb., 1848, aged 19; B.A. 1852, M.A. 1860, B.Med. 1861, D.Med. 1865, brother of George O. 1843.

Morgan, John Hammond, o.s. John, of Paddington, Middlesex, arm. TRINITY COLL., matric. 13 Oct., 1866, aged 19; B.A. 1871, M.A. 1873.

Morgan, John Holdsworth, 3s. John, of Greenwich, Kent, gent. ST. MARY HALL, matric. 14 Jan., 1868, aged 42.

Morgan, John Montague, s. John, of Daventry, Northants, gent. ST. EDMUND HALL, matric. 4 July, 1805, aged 26. **[10]**

Morgan, Rev. John Percy, 1s. John, of Pontnewnydd, co. Monmouth, cler. KEBLE COLL., matric. 18 Oct., 1881, aged 17; B.A. 1884.

Morgan, John Pugh, o.s. Evan Hugh, of Llanbadarnfawr, co. Cardigan, gent. JESUS COLL., matric. 20 April, 1864, aged 20; B.A. 1867, M.A. 1880, vicar of Dolfor, co. Montgomery, 1876.

Morgan, John Thomas, o.s. John, of Chapel Street, Belgrave Square, London, gent. JESUS COLL., matric. 19 Oct., 1860, aged 18; of Nantcaerio, co. Cardigan, J.P.

Morgan, John Woodrooffe, s. John, of Chelmsford, Essex, cler. UNIVERSITY COLL., matric. 14 Jan., 1811, aged 17; B.A. 1814, M.A. 1817, rector of St. Giles's, Colchester, 1818, until his death 13 June, 1857.

Morgan, Jonathan, s. John, of Llyswarney, co. Glamorgan, gent. JESUS COLL., matric. 8 March, 1761, aged 20; B.A. & M.A. 1773, B. & D.D. 1779, rector of Headley, Surrey, 1771, died at Cowbridge, co. Glamorgan, 15 May, 1823. **[15]**

Morgan, Jonas Couch, s. Jonas of Woodoris, Devon, arm. EXETER COLL., matric. 8 May, 1799, aged 19; B.A. from JESUS COLL. 1803.

Morgan, Joseph John, 1s. James Arthur, of Camden Town, near London, arm. UNIVERSITY COLL., matric. 21 Jan., 1864, aged 18.

Morgan, Lewis, s. William, of Lanedy, co. Carmarthen, gent. JESUS COLL., matric. 7 April, 1770, aged 21; B.A. 1774.

Morgan, Lewis, o s. Evan Thomas, of Gileston, co. Glamorgan, gent. JESUS COLL., matric. 10 May, 1845, aged 18; B.A. 1849, M.A. 1852, of the Grange, Llanblethian, co. Gloucester, and of Woolcombe House, Somerset, rector of St. Hilary, Cowbridge, since 1853, assumed the surname of MORGAN in lieu of THOMAS.

Morgan, Luke, s. Nat., of St. Peter's, Worcester (city), pleb. MERTON COLL., matric. 1 Feb., 1731-2, aged 17; B.A. 1736, M.A. 1738, rector of Whitburne, Herts, 1753, until his death in 1777. **[20]**

Morgan, Mordecai Jones, s. William, of Carleon, co. Montgomery, gent. JESUS COLL., matric. 7 April, 1772, aged 17; B.A. 1775.

Morgan, Morgan, s. Edward, of Cardiff, co. Glamorgan, gent. JESUS COLL., matric. 6 Feb., 1729-30, aged 16.

Morgan, Morgan, 1745. See MORGANS.

Morgan, Morgan, 1s. Morgan, of Porth Ystradvellte, co. Brecon, arm. TRINITY COLL., matric. 7 Feb., 1833, aged 17; B.A. 1837, M.A. 1845, vicar of Conway, co. Carnarvon, 1838, until his death 6 March, 1870.

Morgan, Morgan, 4s. Morgan, of Cil-y-cwm, co. Carmarthen, gent. JESUS COLL., matric. 11 Dec., 1855, aged 19; B.A. 1859, M.A. 1862, held various curacies 1859-70, incumbent of St. Peter's, Peterhead, N.B., 1880. **[25]**

Morgan, Rev. Moses, s. John, of Penzance, Cornwall, gent. PEMBROKE COLL., matric. 6 July, 1784, aged 22; of Bodmin Grammar School, died in 1810.

Morgan, Nathaniel, s. John, of Fotheringhay, Northants, cler. TRINITY COLL., matric. 16 Oct., 1759, aged 18; fellow KING'S COLL., Cambridge, B.A. 1764, M.A. 1767, rector of Glooston-on-Seir, and Corby, Northants, 1777, and of Dean, Northants, 1781, and master of Bath Grammar School at his death in 1811, father of Edward 1794.

Morgan, Nathaniel, 1s. Nathaniel, of Rearsby, co. Leicester, cler. BRASENOSE COLL., matric. 1 June, 1836, aged 19; B.A. 1840, M.A. 1843.

Morgan, Oatridge, s. Thomas, of Swindon, co. Gloucester, cler. PEMBROKE COLL., matric. 23 Oct., 1734, aged 17.

Morgan, Philip, s. Philip, of Llandeloy, co. Monmouth, gent. CHRIST CHURCH, matric. 4 March, 1729-30, aged 18; B.A. 1733, rector of Wasing, Berks, at his death 4 June, 1774. **[30]**

Morgan, Philip, s. Philip, of St. Bride's Minor, co. Glamorgan, pleb. JESUS COLL., matric. 23 March, 1771, aged 22.

Morgan, Philip Howell, 1s. John, of Devynock, co. Brecon, gent. JESUS COLL., matric. 30 June, 1834, aged 18; scholar 1835-42, B.A. 1839, M.A. 1841.

Morgan, Richard, s. Howell, of Llantrissent, co. Glamorgan, pleb. JESUS COLL., matric. 31 May, 1717, aged 19.

Morgan, Richard, s. Richard, of Drogheda, Ireland, arm. LINCOLN COLL., matric. 23 Nov., 1733, aged 19.

Morgan, Richard, s. David, of Llanfihangel Geneu-r-glyn, co. Cardigan, pleb. JESUS COLL., matric. 12 Nov., 1767, aged 22; B.A. & M.A. 1786. **[35]**

Morgan, Richard, s. Thomas, of Lamphey, co. Pembroke, pleb. CHRIST CHURCH, matric. 27 Feb., 1794, aged 19; B.A. 1797.

Morgan, Richard, 1s. Robert, of Henry's Mote, co. Pembroke, gent. JESUS COLL., matric. 10 May, 1826, aged 17; scholar 1831-5, B.A. 1830, M.A. 1832 (? vicar of Aberavon with Baglan, co. Gloucester, 1845, until his death 9 March, 1851).

Morgan, Richard Turnill, 2s. Major Butler, of St. Mary's, Lichfield, co. Stafford, arm. BRASENOSE COLL., matric. 13 Oct., 1860, aged 18; B.A. 1865, M.A. 1871, has held various curacies since 1865.

Morgan, Robert, s. Robert, of Llanaber, co. Merioneth, gent. JESUS COLL., matric. 4 June, 1778, aged 18; B.A. 1782.

Morgan, Robert, s. Robert, of Spanish Town, Isle of Jamaica, arm. MAGDALEN COLL., matric. 19 June, 1806, aged 18; B.A. 1810, a student of Lincoln's Inn 1809, rector of Sevington, Kent, 1840, until his death 19 April, 1867, aged 79. **[40]**

Morgan, Robert Bluett, 1s. Charles, of Carmarthen, South Wales, D.Med. UNIVERSITY COLL., matric. 11 Feb., 1830, aged 16; B.A. 1833.

Morgan, Samuel Christopher, 1s. Samuel Francis, of Winsor Lodge, near Birmingham, cler. WADHAM COLL., matric. 29 June, 1855, aged 18; B.A. 1859, M.A. 1862, B. & D.D. 1881, vicar of Aldershot 1864-9, of Christ Church, Greenwich, 1869-73, of Roxeth, Middlesex, 1873-6, of Swansea 1876-84, and of St. Mary's, Leamington, 1884.

Morgan, Samuel (Francis), s. Morgan, of Evesbatch, co. Hereford, cler. JESUS COLL., matric. 3 March, 1810, aged 18; scholar 1812-18, B.A. 1813, M.A. 1816, rector of All Saints, Birmingham, 1835-56, vicar of Chepstow 1856-71, and of Creech St. Michael 1871, until his death 3 May, 1872.

Morgan, Theophilus, 3s. Morgan, of Cwmyoy, co. Monmouth, cler. JESUS COLL., matric. 23 May, 1822, aged 18.

Morgan, Thomas, s. Thomas, of Pembray, co. Carnarvon, cler. JESUS COLL., matric. 23 Nov., 1726, aged 19; B.A. 1731, M.A. 1734, B.D. 1741, D.D. 1759, preb. of Salisbury 1770, until his death in 1782.

Morgan, Thomas, s. Lewis, of Cil-y-cwm, co. Carnarvon, cler. JESUS COLL., matric. 26 March, 1728, aged 17. [5]

Morgan, Thomas, s. William, of Tiverton, Devon, gent. EXETER COLL., matric. 18 March, 1729-30, aged 18; B.A. 1733.

Morgan, Thomas, s. Cann Wilkins, of St. George's, Somerset, arm. BALLIOL COLL., matric. 19 Feb., 1747-8, aged 18.

Morgan, Thomas, s. Richard, of Dursley, co. Gloucester, arm. MERTON COLL., matric. 2 July, 1761, aged 17, B.A. 1765; clerk MAGDALEN COLL. 1761-84. See *Bloxam*, ii. 103.

Morgan, Thomas, s. William, of Penderyn, co. Glamorgan, gent. PEMBROKE COLL., matric. 14 July, 1761, aged 17; B.A. 1765, bar.-at-law, Gray's Inn, 1774, bencher 1788, died 27 March, 1804, buried in Temple Churchyard 12 April.

Morgan, Thomas, s. John, of Llanbadarn, co. Cardigan, pleb. CHRIST CHURCH, matric. 22 Nov., 1763, aged 19; B.A. 1767. [10]

Morgan, Thomas, s. Philip, of Devynock, co. Brecon, gent. WADHAM COLL., matric. 14 Oct., 1786, aged 16; B.A. from JESUS COLL. 1790, M.A. 1793, B. & D.D. 1824, chaplain royal navy (four times in action) 1793-1801, perp. curate Talley 1801-52, rector of Llanvaches 1810-52, vicar of King's Langley, Herts, 1812-36, chaplain of Haslar Hospital 1815, of Plymouth Hospital 1816, and for Portsmouth Dockyard 1817, until his death 22 Nov., 1851.

Morgan, Thomas, s. William, of Brecknock (town), cler. JESUS COLL., matric. 13 March, 1787, aged 17; B.A. 1790, M.A. 1818.

Morgan, Thomas, s. William, of Bewdley, co. Worcester, cler. MAGDALEN HALL, matric. 15 Dec., 1788, aged 21; B.C.L. & D.C.L. 1808.

Morgan, Thomas, s. Richard, of London, gent. MAGDALEN HALL, matric. 8 March, 1794, aged 23; B.A. 1796, M.A. 1797.

Morgan, Thomas, 2s. Rees, of Mothvey, co. Carmarthen, gent. JESUS COLL., matric. 17 Dec., 1818, aged 19; B.A. 1822, M.A. 1830. [15]

Morgan, Thomas, 3s. William, of Eglwysilan, co. Glamorgan, gent. JESUS COLL., matric. 14 April, 1820, aged 19; B.A. 1824, M.A. 1827, curate of Llantillio-Pertholey, 1831-58, vicar 1858, until his death 5 Sep., 1872.

Morgan, Thomas, M.A. TRINITY COLL., Cambridge; adm. 'ad eundem' 1831.

Morgan, Thomas, o.s. George, of Letterston, co. Pembroke, gent. JESUS COLL., matric. 19 Oct., 1881, aged 19.

Morgan, Thomas Eyre, o.s. William Wright, of Whitchurch, Hants, gent. MAGDALEN HALL, matric. 15 Nov., 1855, aged 17.

Morgan, Thomas Holmes, 1s. Thomas Edward, of Swansea, co. Glamorgan, cler. CHARSLEY HALL, matric. 16 Oct., 1886, aged 19. [20]

Morgan, Thomas James, 2s. William, of Bristol, gent. NON-COLL., matric. 27 April, 1878, aged 49.

Morgan, Walter, s. William, of Llanarth, co. Monmouth, gent. MERTON COLL., matric. 17 Dec., 1776, aged 21; B.A. 1781.

Morgan, Walwyn, s. John, of Madeley, co. Hereford, gent. ST. JOHN'S COLL., matric. 28 March, 1724, aged 18; B.A. 27 Feb., 1727-8.

Morgan, Watkin, s. Philip, of Devynock, co. Brecon, arm. EXETER COLL., matric. 17 March, 1815, aged 21; brother of Thomas 1786. (Memo.: Rev. W. M., died at Brooke House, Monmouth, in 1835, aged 43.)

Morgan, William, s. Edward, of Penderyn, co. Brecon, gent. WADHAM COLL., matric. 31 March, 1715, aged 18. [25]

Morgan, William, s. John, of St. Peter's, Worcester (city), gent. MAGDALEN HALL, matric. 8 March, 1727-8, aged 17; B.A. 1731.

Morgan, William, s. Richard, of Dublin, Ireland, arm. CHRIST CHURCH, matric. 13 April, 1728, aged 16; B.A. 1731.

Morgan, William, s. William, of Merthyr, co. Glamorgan, cler. CHRIST CHURCH, matric. 30 Oct., 1734, aged 19; B.A. 1738.

Morgan, William, s. William, of Brecknock (town), gent. CHRIST CHURCH, matric. 29 March, 1739, aged 17; B.A. 1742, M.A. 1745.

Morgan, William, 1s. William, of Westminster, equitis. CHRIST CHURCH, matric. 9 June, 1743, aged 18; of Tredegar, co. Monmouth, M.P. 1747, until his death 16 July, 1763. [30]

Morgan, William, s. Edward, of Aberdare, co. Glamorgan, pleb. JESUS COLL., matric. 30 Oct., 1761, aged 20; B.A. 1765, M.A. 1768, B.D. 1775, D.D. 1787. (Memo.: W. M., died rector of Aston Clinton, Bucks, 21 Oct., 1798.)

Morgan, William, s. John, of Llanbadarn, co. Cardigan, pleb. CHRIST CHURCH, matric. 15 May, 1766, aged 19; B.A. 1770. (Memo.: W. M., vicar of Cwmtby, co. Monmouth, 1772, until his death in 1827.)

Morgan, William, s. William, of Llanedy, co. Carmarthen, gent. JESUS COLL., matric. 15 May, 1777, aged 19; B.A. 1781, M.A. 1784, B. & D.D. 1814. (Memo.: W. M., late chaplain Royal Naval Asylum, died at Greenwich 4 July, 1823.)

Morgan, William, s. Simon, of Llanddewi Felfry, co. Pembroke, cler. QUEEN'S COLL., matric. 8 May, 1793, aged 19; B.A. 1797, vicar of Llanddewi Felfry aforesaid, etc., 1809, and rector of Lampeter 1826, preb. of St. David's 1826, until his death in 1830.

Morgan, William, s. William, of Barnstaple, Devon, gent. EXETER COLL., matric. 21 March, 1795, aged 23; B.A. 1799, M.A. 1817. (Memo.: W.M., vicar of Tollesbury, Essex, 1826, until his death 17 Aug., 1842, aged 71.) [35]

Morgan, William, s. George, of Sulhamstead, Berks, arm. MAGDALEN COLL., matric. 25 July, 1812, aged 17; demy 1812-20, B.A. 1816, M.A. 1819, D.C.L. 1829, bar.-at-law, Lincoln's Inn, 1820, died in April, 1883. See *Coll. Reg.*, vii. 254; & *Rugby School Reg.*, 94.

Morgan, William, s. Jonathan, of Headley, Surrey, doctor. BALLIOL COLL., matric. 31 Jan., 1814, aged 15; demy MAGDALEN COLL. 1814-21, B.A. 1817, M.A. 1820, fellow 1821-54, bursar 1832-4-6-9 and 1843, vice-president 1834, died 12 Sep., 1881. See *Bloxam*, vii. 258.

Morgan, William, 1s. David, of Blaensenny, co. Brecon, gent. WADHAM COLL., matric. 25 March, 1829, aged 18; B.A. 1833.

Morgan, William, M.A. TRINITY COLL., Dublin, 1860; adm. 'ad eundem' 22 Nov., 1860.

Morgan, William, 6s. Thomas, of Gwnnws, co. Cardigan, gent. JESUS COLL., matric. 25 Jan., 1875, aged 20; B.A. 1878. [40]

Morgan, William Augustus, s. John, of South Pole, Devon, cler. WADHAM COLL., matric. 15 Dec., 1796, aged 20; perp. curate Tresmere, Devon, 1821, until his death 19 Aug., 1869.

Morgan, William Browning, 1s. William, of Bristol, gent. NON-COLL., matric. 13 Oct., 1876, aged 55.

Morgan, William Frederick Taylor, 1s. William Taylor, of London, D.Med. PEMBROKE COLL., matric. 27 Oct., 1884, aged 18; scholar 1884.

Morgan, William Lewis, 1s. William, of Merthyr Tydfil, co. Glamorgan, gent. NON-COLL., matric. 13 Nov., 1874, aged 23; B.A. from CHRIST CHURCH, 1878, M.A. from EXETER COLL. 1881 biology lecturer WADHAM COLL. 1879-85, natural science lecturer 1881-5 and 1885.

Morgan, William Taylor, 1s. John, of Llanbeblig, co. Carnarvon, arm. JESUS COLL., matric. 13 March, 1851, aged 19. **[5]**

Morgans, Morgan, s. Morgan, of Llanedarn, co. Monmouth, pleb. JESUS COLL., matric. 11 Dec., 1745, aged 18; B.A. 1749, M.A. 1752, B.D. 1759, vicar of Swanbourne, and rector of Addington, Bucks, 1779.

Moriarty, Arthur Stephen, 3s. Stephen Stack, of Dieppe, D.Med. BALLIOL COLL., matric. 19 Oct., 1878, aged 20; of the Indian Civil Service and a student of the Middle Temple 1878.

Moriarty, Gerald Patrick, y.s. Stephen Stack, of Dieppe, France, D.Med. BALLIOL COLL., matric. 18 Oct., 1881, aged 18; B.A. 1885.

Moriarty, Louis Martin, 2s. Stephen Stack, of Dieppe, France, D.Med. MAGDALEN COLL., matric. 17 Oct., 1874, aged 19; demy 1873-8, B.A. 1879, M.A. 1886.

Morice, Burton, s. William, of London, cler. HERTFORD COLL., matric. 12 Feb., 1784, aged 17; B.A. 1787, M.A. 1790, bar.-at-law, Lincoln's Inn, 1790, died 29 Aug., 1825. **[10]**

Morice, Charles, s. David, of Langley, Bucks, arm. MERTON COLL., matric. 3 March, 1761, aged 17; B.A. 1765, M.A. 1769, '32 years private chaplain to their Majesties at Windsor, and chaplain to the Duke of York,' died at Windsor 22 April, 1818.

Morice, Francis, s. William, of Westminster, arm. CHRIST CHURCH, matric. 10 June, 1740, aged 18; B.A. 1744, M.A. 1748, of Six-mile Bridge, co. Clare, said to have been a preb. of Limerick, and rector of Tradaree, died 2 Oct., 1778, brother of William 1750. See *Alumni West.*, 322.

Morice, Rev. Francis David, 1s. David Simpson, of London, arm. NEW COLL., matric. 12 Oct., 1866, aged 17, scholar 1866-70; fellow QUEEN'S COLL. 1871, B.A. 1871, M.A. 1873, lecturer 1871-4, succentor 1873-4, assistant-master Rugby School 1874.

Morice, George Thomas, 5s. David Robert, of Nigg, co. Kincardine arm. LINCOLN COLL., matric. 18 Oct., 1877, aged 19; B.A. 1881, bar.-at-law, Middle Temple, 1881. See Foster's *Men at the Bar.*

Morice, Henry, s. William, of St. Andrew's, Holborn, London, doctor. ST. JOHN'S COLL., matric. 20 Feb., 1795, aged 18; B.A. 1798, M.A. 1804, vicar of Ashwell, Herts, 1812, canon of Lincoln 1846, until his death 20 Dec., 1850, brother of William 1781. **[15]**

Morice, Harry Chalmers Gray, 4s. James, of Brixton, Surrey, gent. EXETER COLL., matric. 16 Oct., 1884, aged 18; scholar 1883.

Morice, Henry Edward, 2s. David Simpson, of London, gent. LINCOLN COLL., matric. 19 Oct., 1872, aged 19; scholar 1872-6, B.A. 1876.

Morice, James, 1s. James, of Moelumey, co. Cardigan, gent. JESUS COLL., matric. 27 Oct., 1842, aged 17; B.A. 1846.

Morice, Morice, s. James, of Llangowyddoh, co. Cardigan, pleb. CHRIST CHURCH, matric. 23 May, 1751, aged 21; B.A. 1755.

Morice, Richard Graves, s. Richard, of Dock, Devon, arm. ST. JOHN'S COLL., matric. 3 May, 1804, aged 18; rector of Knowle, Dorset, died 25 Nov., 1860. **[20]**

Morice, Rev. Thomas Richards, 3s. James, of Llanbadarnfawr, co. Cardigan, gent. JESUS COLL., matric. 6 May, 1847, aged 18; scholar 1849-52, B.A. 1851, fellow 1852, M.A. 1853, librarian 1854, catech. lecturer 1858.

Morice, (Sir) William (Bart.), s. Nicholas, of St. James's, Westminster, baronet. CORPUS CHRISTI COLL., matric. 24 Aug., 1724, aged 17; 3rd baronet, M.P. Newport, Cornwall, 1727, Launceston 1734, until his death 24 Jan., 1750.

Morice, William, s. William, of Westminster, gent. HERTFORD COLL., matric. 8 Dec., 1750, aged 17; B.A. 1754, M.A. 1757, rector of All Hallows, Bread Street, senior chaplain to the King, (D.D.), died 7 Jan., 1819, father of Henry 1795, and of William 1781, and brother of Francis 1740.

Morice, William, s. William, of London, cler. ST. JOHN'S COLL., matric. 3 July, 1781, aged 16; fellow 1781, B.A. 1785, M.A. 1789, B.D. 1794, rector of Tackley, Oxon, 1811, until his death 4 Feb., 1828. See *Robinson*, 137.

Morice, William Hallen, 4s. James, of Clarach, co. Cardigan, gent. JESUS COLL., matric. 26 June, 1851, aged 19; scholar 1852-8, B.A. 1855. **[25]**

Morier, Greville, o.s. James, of Boulogne-sur-Mer, arm. CHRIST CHURCH, matric. 3 June, 1840, aged 16; B.A. 1844.

Morier, (Sir) Robert Burnet David (G.C.B., G.C.M.G.), o.s. David Richard, of Paris, arm. BALLIOL COLL., matric. 5 March, 1845, aged 18; B.A. 1850, a student of Inner Temple 1847, entered diplomatic service 1853, envoy extraordinary and minister plenipotentiary to Portugal 1876-81, Spain 1881-4, ambassador to Russia 1884, P.C., G.C.M.G. 13 Feb., 1886, G.C.B. 30 Sep., 1887.

Morier, Victor Albert Louis, o.s. Robert Burnet David, of Darmstadt, arm. (after G.C.B.). BALLIOL COLL., matric. 11 May, 1886, aged 19.

Morison, Alexander James, 3s. Kenneth, of Hornsey, Middlesex, gent. NON-COLL., matric. 13 Oct., 1877, aged 16.

Morison, James Augustus Cotter, 4s. John, of St. Pancras, London, gent. LINCOLN COLL., matric. 23 March, 1850, aged 18; B.A. & M.A. 1859, 'positivist,' author of the 'Life and Times of St. Bernard,' etc., a student of Lincoln's Inn 1857, died 26 Feb., 1888. See *Times* obit. **[30]**

Morison, James Mitford, o.s. William, of Rothesay, Bute, N.B., arm. EXETER COLL., matric. 20 Nov., 1845, aged 19.

Morison, Rev. John Hall James, o.s. John Hall, of Glasgow, Scotland, gent. WORCESTER COLL., matric. 29 Oct., 1846, aged 20; B.A. 1850, M.A. 1853, sometime of Chingford, Essex, died at Malta 10 Nov., 1861.

Morison, William Thomson, 1s. Patrick, of Innerleithen, co. Peebles, arm. BALLIOL COLL., matric. 16 Oct., 1879, aged 19; of the Indian Civil Service 1879.

Morkill, John William, 1s. John, of Seacroft, Yorks, arm. ORIEL COLL., matric. 21 May, 1880, aged 19; B.A. 1884, M.A. 1887.

Morland, Benjamin, 2s. Benjamin, of Abingdon, Berks, arm. PEMBROKE COLL., matric. 10 Oct., 1822, aged 17; scholar 1822-7, of Sheepstead House, Berks, vicar of Shabbington, Bucks. **[35]**

Morland, Sir Francis Bernard, Bart., s. Scrope B.-M., of St. George's, Hanover Square, London, doctor. (after baronet). BRASENOSE COLL., matric. 14 July, 1806, aged 16; 5th baronet, died s.p. 22 June, 1876. See Foster's *Baronetage.*

Morland, Henry, 1s. Thomas, of Croydon, Surrey, arm. ST. JOHN'S COLL., matric. 15 June, 1869, aged 20; B.A. from MAGDALEN HALL 1873.

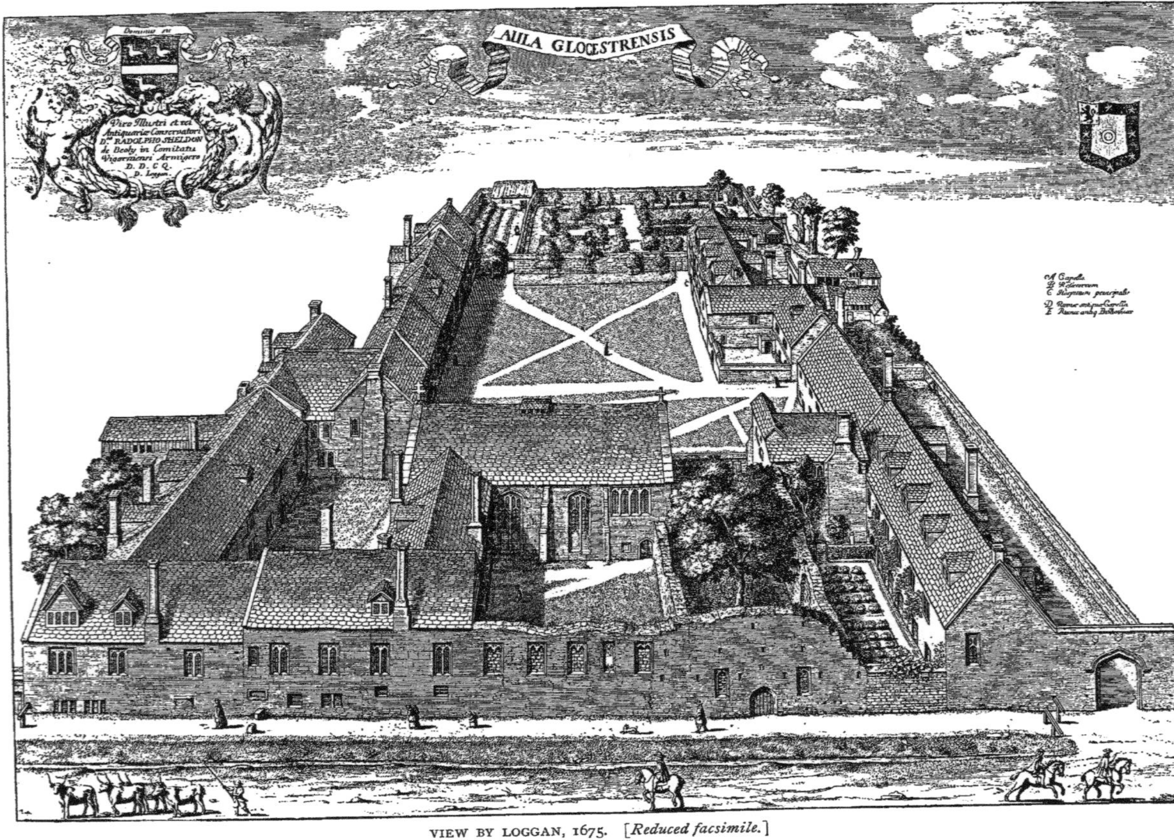

VIEW BY LOGGAN, 1675. [*Reduced facsimile.*]

Morland, James, 2s. Thomas, of Lancaster, gent. NEW COLL., matric. 19 Oct., 1877, aged 36.

Morland, John, 1s. Thomas, of Lancaster, gent. NEW COLL., matric. 19 Oct., 1874, aged 37.

Morland, Sir Scrope Bernard, Bart., s. Francis Bernard, of New Jersey, America, baronet. CHRIST CHURCH, matric. 13 April, 1775, aged 16; B.A. 1779, M.A. 1781, D.C.L. 1788, 4th baronet, M.P. Aylesbury 1789-1801, St. Mawes 1806-8, 1809-30, gentleman usher of the black rod Ireland 1787, under secretary State home department 1792, assumed the additional surname and arms of TYRRINGHAM by royal licence 8 May, 1789, and also by royal licence 15 Feb., 1811, the additional surname of MORLAND, died 18 April, 1830. See Foster's *Baronetage*, BERNARD.

Morland, William, s. John, of West Isley, Berks, pleb. TRINITY COLL., matric. 17 Dec., 1729, aged 20; B.A. from MERTON COLL. 17 Jan., 1733-4, M.A. 1736.

Morland, William Alexander, s. Thomas, of Lamberhurst, Kent, arm. CHRIST CHURCH, matric. 19 Oct., 1786, aged 19; B.A. 1790, of Lamberhurst, died 24 Dec., 1846. [5]

Morland, William Courtenay, o.s. Charles, of London, arm. CHRIST CHURCH, matric. 22 Oct., 1835, aged 17; B.A. 1839, M.A. 1842, of the Court Lodge, Lamberhurst, Sussex, high sheriff 1876, etc., bar.-at-law, Lincoln's Inn, 1843. See Foster's *Men at the Bar* & *Eton School Lists*.

Morley, Edward, M.A. from ST. JOHN'S COLL., Cambridge; incorp. 18 July, 1721.

Morley, Edward Dawson, s. George, of Newport Pagnell, Bucks, cler. ST. MARY HALL, matric. 19 Oct., 1861, aged 19; B.A. from MAGDALEN HALL 1867, M.A. 1871, held various curacies since 1869.

Morley, George, 1s. James, of St. Pancras, London, gent. WADHAM COLL., matric. 9 April, 1845, aged 18; B.A. 1849, M.A 1851, held various curacies 1850-72, vicar of Under River, Kent, 1878-80, lecturer at Causeway, Chiddingstone, 1874. See *Rugby School Reg.*, 223.

Morley, George Hart, 1s. George, of Newington, Surrey, arm. ST. JOHN'S COLL., matric. 2 Dec., 1830, aged 18; bar.-at-law, Inner Temple, 1839. [10]

Morley, James, o.s. James Alexander, of Manchester, Lancashire, arm. EXETER COLL., matric. 20 Oct., 1820, aged 18; a student of Lincoln's Inn, 1824.

Morley, John, s. Alexander, of Elworthy, Somerset, cler. ST. EDMUND HALL, matric. 21 March, 1740-1, aged 19; B.A. 1744, probably father of the next named.

Morley, John, s. John, of Elworthy, Somerset, cler. ORIEL COLL., matric. 20 Jan., 1780, aged 16; vicar of Aylesbury, Bucks, 1816, until his death 29 Sep., 1842.

Morley, John, 2s. Jonathan, of Blackburn, Lancashire, gent. LINCOLN COLL., matric. 5 Nov., 1856, aged 17; scholar 1856-60, B.A. 1859; M.A. 1874; bar.-at-law, Lincoln's Inn, 1875, hon. LL.D. Glasgow 1879, M.P. Newcastle-on-Tyne since Feb., 1883, chief secretary for Ireland Feb. to July, 1886, P.C. 1886, sometime editor of *Fortnightly Review* & *Pall Mall Gazette*. See Foster's *Men at the Bar*.

Morley, John Wilby, 2s. William, of Raithby, near Spilsby, co. Lincoln, cler. BRASENOSE COLL., matric. 16 June, 1857, aged 18. [15]

Morley, Josias, s. John, of Lancaster (town), arm. QUEEN'S COLL., matric. 3 March, 1734-5, aged 19; of Bethmesley (or Beamsley), and Giggleswick, Yorks, died in March, 1783. See Foster's *Yorkshire Collection*.

Morley, Sidney Frederick, 5s. George, of Hever, Kent, cler. UNIVERSITY COLL., matric. 17 Oct., 1885, aged 19; exhibitioner 1885.

Morley, Walter Francis, 2s. George, of Bexley Heath, Kent, cler. NON-COLL., matric. 13 Oct., 1876, aged 17; B.A. from WADHAM COLL. 1882, M.A. 1883.

Morley, William, 1s. William, of Leverton, co. Lincoln, cler. EXETER COLL., matric. 17 April, 1850, aged 18.

Morley, Rev. William Hammond, 4s. George, of Newport Pagnell, Bucks, cler. WORCESTER COLL., matric. 18 April, 1863, aged 19; B.A. 1867, M.A. 1871. [20]

Morphett, Eustace, 2s. George, of Adelaide, Australia, gent. ST. JOHN'S COLL., matric. 29 Jan., 1867, aged 19; B.A. 1870, M.A. 1875.

Morphett, John Cummins, 1s. John, of Adelaide, Australia, arm. PEMBROKE COLL., matric. 30 April, 1863, aged 18.

Morphew, Henry Leslie, 3s. William George, of Wrotham, Kent, gent. WORCESTER COLL., matric. 29 Jan., 1886, aged 19.

Morrall, Cyrus, 1s. Cyrus, of Liverpool, Lancashire, arm. BRASENOSE COLL., matric. 14 Jan., 1822, aged 18; B.A. 1825, M.A. 1828, of Plâs Yolyn, Salop, perp. curate St. Michael, Liverpool, 1833-56, vicar of North Leigh, Oxon, 1856-61, died 30 May, 1882.

Morrall, Cyrus, o.s. Cyrus, of Liverpool, cler. BRASENOSE COLL., matric. 5 June, 1873, aged 19; B.A. 1877, of Plâs Yolyn and Plâs Warren, Salop, J.P. [25]

Morrall, Rev. Henry, s. Charles, of Chester (city), arm. BRASENOSE COLL., matric. 26 Jan., 1808, aged 16; B.A. 1811, M.A. 1814 died at Rome, 3 Feb., 1868.

Morrall, Rev. John, s. Charles, of Chester (city), arm. BRASENOSE COLL., matric. 11 Dec., 1813, aged 18; B.A. 1817, fellow 1819-25, M.A. 1820, died 2 March, 1886.

Morrall, Luke, s. Richard, of Much Wenlock, Salop, pleb. CHRIST CHURCH, matric. 27 Oct., 1727, aged 16; B.A. 1731.

Morrell, Baker, 2s. Frederick Joseph, of St. Giles, Oxford (city), gent. ST. JOHN'S COLL., matric. 27 June, 1859, aged 18; B.A. 1863, M.A. 1866, chaplain E.I.C.S.

Morrell, Charles, o.s. Mark, of Winkfield, Berks, arm. TRINITY COLL., matric. 4 June, 1861, aged 18; of Burcote, Oxon, J.P., master of the South Oxfordshire hounds. See *Rugby School Reg.* [30]

Morrell, Charles Francis, 1s. Thomas Samuel, of London, gent. LINCOLN COLL., matric. 16 April, 1872, aged 19; B.A. 1875, bar.-at-law, Middle Temple, 1877. See Foster's *Men at the Bar*.

Morrell, Rev. Deacon, s. James, of St. Magdalen, Oxford (city), gent. CHRIST CHURCH, matric. 23 Oct., 1792, aged 17; B.A. 1796, M.A. 1799, student until 1813, of Moulsford, Berks, a student of Lincoln's Inn 1796, died 10 March, 1854.

Morrell, Edward, 3s. George Kidd, of Moulsford, Berks, cler. WADHAM COLL., matric. 16 Oct., 1866, aged 17; B.A. 1869, M.A. 1886. See *Eton School Lists*.

Morrell, Frederick Parker, 1s. Frederick Joseph, of St. Giles, Oxford (city), gent. ST. JOHN'S COLL., matric. 29 June, 1857, aged 18; B.A. 1861, M.A. 1864, steward 1883, and coroner, a solicitor in Oxford, his father steward of St. John's 1863-82. See *Rugby School Reg.*

Morrell, George Herbert, 1s. George Kidd, of Adderbury, Oxon, cler. EXETER COLL., matric. 26 May, 1863, aged 18; B.A. 1867, B.C.L. & M.A. 1870, of Headington Hill Hall, Oxon, J.P., D.L., high sheriff 1885, bar-at-law, Inner Temple, 1871, lieut.-colonel Oxford University rifle volunteers 1879. See Foster's *Men at the Bar* & *Rugby School Reg.* [35]

Morrell, George Kidd, 3s. Baker, of St. Mary Magdalen, Oxford (city), gent. ST. JOHN'S COLL., matric. 25 June, 1832, aged 18; scholar and fellow 1832-43, B.C.L. 1838, D.C.L. 1842, vicar of Moulsford, Berks, 1846-77, died 18 April, 1881. See *Robinson*, 222.

Morrell, Henry Cox, 1s. Henry, of St. George's, Bloomsbury, gent. CHRIST CHURCH, matric. 6 Feb., 1824, aged 16; chorister 1820-3, servitor 1824-9, B.A. 1829, M.A. 1831, chaplain 1831-7, vicar of Swilland, Suffolk, at his death 9 May, 1847.

Morrell, Herbert Hugh, 4s. Hopewell Baker, of Hay, co. Radnor, arm. ST. JOHN'S COLL., matric. 11 Oct., 1884, aged 18.

Morrell, Hopewell Baker, 2s. James Wright, of Forthampton, co. Gloucester, gent. WADHAM COLL., matric. 8 March, 1854, aged 17; of Moulsford Manor, Berks.

Morrell, James Wright, 1s. Baker, of Oxford (city), arm. TRINITY COLL., matric. 9 May, 1820, aged 17; died 9 May, 1873, father of the last named. [5]

Morrell, Nathaniel, s. Thomas, of Eton, Bucks, pleb. ST. JOHN'S COLL., matric. 17 Dec., 1723, aged 18.

Morrell, Robert Baker, 2s. George Kidd, of Adderbury, Oxon, cler. ORIEL COLL., matric. 6 June, 1865, aged 18; B.A. 1887.

Morrell, Robert Price, 2s. Baker, of Holywell, Oxford (city), arm. BALLIOL COLL., matric. 12 Dec., 1822, aged 16, B.A. 1826; fellow MAGDALEN COLL. 1827-33, M.A. 1829, dean of arts 1831, rector of Woodham Mortimer, Essex, 1835, until his death 8 June, 1872.

Morrell, Thomas, fellow KING'S COLL., Cambridge, B.A. 1726, M.A. 1733 (incorp. 6 July, 1733), D.D. 1743, re-incorporated 28 June, 1759, rector of Buckland, Herts, died at Scarborough in 1797.

Morrell, Thomas Baker, 5s. Baker, of Oxford (city), gent. BALLIOL COLL., matric. 30 Nov., 1832, aged 17; B.A. 1836, M.A. 1839, B. & D.D. 1863, bishop-coadjutor of Edinburgh 1863-9, died 5 Nov., 1877. [10]

Morrell, William John, 1s. William, of Tiverton, Devon, gent. BALLIOL COLL., matric. 24 Oct., 1885, aged 17; scholar 1884.

Morres, Arthur Philip, 3s. —— M., of Wokingham, Berks, arm. WADHAM COLL., matric. 19 Oct., 1853, aged 18; B.A. 1857, M.A. 1862, vicar of Britford, Wilts, 1868.

Morres, Elliot James, 2s. Elliot, of Reading, Berks, arm. TRINITY COLL., matric. 8 March, 1849, aged 18; B.A. 1852, a student of Lincoln's Inn 1853.

Morres, Harvey Redmond, s. Harvey, of Kilkenny, Ireland, Baron Mountmorres. CHRIST CHURCH, matric. 27 April, 1763, aged 17; B.A. 8 Feb., 1766, created M.A. 3 July, 1766, and also D.C.L. 8 July, 1773, 2nd Viscount Mountmorres, died 17 Aug., 1797. See Foster's *Peerage*.

Morres, Hugh Redmond, 5s. —— M., of Wokingham, Berks, cler. MAGDALEN COLL., matric. 14 Jan., 1858, aged 19; chorister 1849-55, clerk 1857-63, B.A. 1863, vicar of St. Sebastian, Wokingham, 1871, until his death 18 Sep., 1882. See *Coll. Reg.*, i. 224.

Morres, John, B.A. from BRASENOSE COLL., 1786. See MORRIS, page 987. [15]

Morres, Philip, o.s. John, of Nether Broughton, co. Leicester, cler. WORCESTER COLL., matric. 21 May, 1828, aged 18.

Morres, Robert, s. Thomas, of Hinckley, co. Leicester, doctor. BRASENOSE COLL., matric. 21 March, 1774, aged 16; B.A. 1777, M.A. 1780, vicar of Britford, Wilts, 1796, rector of Great Cheverell, Wilts, 1807, preb. of Salisbury 1805, until his death 18 Oct., 1841.

Morres, Robert Elliot, 1s. Elliot, of Nether Broughton, co. Leicester, arm. WADHAM COLL., matric. 22 Jan., 1845, aged 18; B.A. 1848, M.A. 1851, rector of Chedington 1863-4 & 1867-78, perp. curate Bicknoller, Somerset, 1864-7, rector of Langridge 1878, until his death in 1885.

Morres, Thomas, s. Thomas, of Burford, Salop, gent. JESUS COLL., matric. 21 March, 1732, aged 18, B.A. 1735, M.A. 1738; B.D. from HERTFORD COLL. 1751, D.D. 1751. [20]

Morres, Thomas, s. Robert, of Isleworth, Middlesex, cler. BRASENOSE COLL., matric. 23 Nov., 1813, aged 17; scholar 1813-17, B.A. 1817, M.A. 1820, rector of Wokingham 1820-72, master of Lucas Hospital, Wokingham, 1872, died 2 April, 1877.

Morrey, John, s. John, of Betton, Salop, gent. MAGDALEN HALL, matric. 28 March, 1729, aged 19.

Morrice, Andrew Ducarel, s. James, of Barford, co. Warwick, cler. CHRIST CHURCH, matric. 19 Oct., 1799, aged 17; B.A. 1803, M.A. 1806, a student until 1812, rector of Betteshanger, Kent, 1815, until his death 30 Sep., 1866. See *Rugby School Reg.*, 76.

Morrice, Frederick Francis James, o.s. Frederick Edward, of Newtown, Hants, arm. MERTON COLL., matric. 2 June, 1838, aged 18; of Betteshanger House, Kent.

Morrice, James, s. William, of Betteshanger, Kent, arm. CHRIST CHURCH, matric. 1 July, 1758, aged 18; B.A. 1762, M.A. 1767, rector of Betteshanger aforesaid, and 38 years vicar of Flower, Northants, died 9 Jan., 1815. [25]

Morrice, John George Selby, 1s. John, of Highbury, Middlesex, arm. EXETER COLL., matric. 2 June, 1868, aged 18; B.A. 1871.

Morrice, John Walter, 2s. John, of Wanstead, Essex, arm. JESUS COLL., matric. 18 May, 1839, aged 17; B.A. from EXETER COLL. 1843, M.A. 1845, bar.-at-law, Lincoln's Inn, 1846. See Foster's *Men at the Bar*.

Morrice, Richard, s. Morrice, of Llanrhyslyd, co. Cardigan, pleb. JESUS COLL., matric. 9 April, 1720, aged 21.

Morrice, Thomas, s. Barth., of Bishops Nympton, Devon, pleb. EXETER COLL., matric. 10 April, 1731, aged 21; B.A. 1734.

Morrice, William, 2s. William David, of Westbury, Wilts, cler. CORPUS CHRISTI COLL., matric. 18 Oct., 1871, aged 19; B.A. 1876, died in 1877. [30]

Morris, Adolphus Philipse, 5s. Henry Gage, of Worcester (city), arm. WORCESTER COLL., matric. 1 Dec., 1842, aged 18; B.A. 1846, M.A. 1851, chaplain Canterbury Association, New Zealand, 1851-2, missionary Upper Canada 1856-60, rector of St. Michael's, Brattleborough, Vermont, U. S., 1860-5, missionary at Michigan Lake, New York, 1866-9 vicar of Leeds, Kent, 1877, etc. See *Crockford*.

Morris, Albert John Thomas, 1s. James, of Southampton, Hants, gent. QUEEN'S COLL., matric. 14 June 1849, aged 19; B.A. 1854, incumbent of St. James's Muthill, co. Perth, 1858, and of Columba, Criefl N.B., 1861, until his death 7 June, 1882.

Morris, Alfred George, 4s. Thomas, of St. Wollos co. Monmouth, arm. JESUS COLL., matric. 1 March, 1851, aged 18; B.A. 1855, held variou curacies 1859-75, vicar of Roggiett, co. Monmouth 1878.

Morris, Alfred Tudor, 2s. James, of Oakwood, co Glamorgan, cler. JESUS COLL., matric. 18 Oct. 1882, aged 19; B.A. 1886.

Morris, Amherst Henry Gage, 1s. Francis Orpen, c Beechfield House, near Doncaster, Yorks, cler. ST MARY HALL, matric. 9 Feb., 1860, aged 23. [35

Morris, Arthur Gwilym, 2s. William, of Holywel Flints, gent. JESUS COLL., matric. 16 Jan., 186 aged 19.

Morris, Augustus William, 2s. George, of Madro Cornwall, cler. WORCESTER COLL., matric. 1 Jun 1837, aged 18; bible clerk, 1837-9.

Morris, Benjamin, s. William, of Waterford, Irelan arm. CHRIST CHURCH, matric. 26 Oct., 1809, age 18; B.A. 1814, brother of William 1804.

Morris, Charles, s. Edmund, of Loddington, co. Leicester, arm. MAGDALEN COLL., matric. 6 June, 1746, aged 18.

Morris, Charles, 2s. George, of Sarisbury, near Southampton, Hants, cler. CORPUS CHRISTI COLL., matric. 21 Oct., 1862, aged 18; B.A. 1867, vicar of Ston Easton, co. Gloucester, 1875-9, vicar of Street, Devon, 1882-8, vicar of Marston, Oxon, 1888, brother of George 1861.

Morris, Charles D'Urban, 6s. Henry Gage, of Charmouth, Dorset, arm. WORCESTER COLL., matric. 20 May, 1845, aged 18; scholar LINCOLN COLL. 1846-50, B.A. 1849; fellow ORIEL COLL. 1851-4, M.A. 1852, professor of Latin and Greek in John Hopkins University, Baltimore, 1876-85; died 7 Feb., 1886.

Morris, Charles Edward, 1s. Charles John, of Shrewsbury, arm. CHRIST CHURCH, matric. 14 Oct., 1881, aged 18; B.A. from NEW INN HALL 1885. See *Eton School Lists.*

Morris, Charles John, 1s. John, of St. Chads, Shrewsbury, arm. CHRIST CHURCH, matric. 31 May, 1849, aged 18; B.A. 1853, of Woodeaton, co. Stafford, etc., master of Shropshire foxhounds. See *Eton School Lists.* **[5]**

Morris, Charles Smyth, 1s. Thomas Charles, of Llanstephan, co. Carmarthen, gent. NEW COLL., matric. 18 Oct., 1867, aged 19; a student of Lincoln's Inn 1872. See *Rugby School Reg.*

Morris, David, 'carrier to ye Isle of Anglesea and Blew Morris' 18 Feb., 1718-9.

Morris, David, s. 'Morris David,' of Llanrwst, co. Denbigh, pleb. JESUS COLL., matric. 21 April, 1719, aged 18; B.A. 5 March, 1722-3, M.A. 1726.

Morris, David, s. Jonathan, of Llangynog, co. Merioneth, pleb. JESUS COLL., matric. 14 July, 1773, aged 27; B.A. from CHRIST CHURCH 1778.

Morris, David Melvill, 2s. Ebenezer, of Llanelly, co. Carmarthen, cler. JESUS COLL., matric. 18 April, 1863, aged 18; clerk 1863, B.A. 1866, M.A. 1876, vicar of Penally, co. Pembroke, 1873. **[10]**

Morris, Edward, s. Morris, of Llansilin, co. Denbigh, pleb. JESUS COLL., matric. 1 June, 1731, aged 20; B.A. 1736.

Morris, Edward, s. Thomas, of Newport, Salop, arm. ST. MARY HALL, matric. 21 May, 1818, aged 18.

Morris, Edward Ellis, 9s. John Carnac, of Madras, East Indies, arm. LINCOLN COLL., matric. 12 June, 1862, aged 18; B.A. 1866, M.A. 1869, assistant-master Haileybury, head-master Bedford County School, head-master Melbourne Grammar School, Australia, 1875, a professor in Melbourne University 1884. See *Rugby School Reg.*

Morris, Rev. Edward Henry, 1s. Thomas Edward, of Carleton, Yorks, cler. CHRIST CHURCH, matric. 4 June, 1881, aged 18; B.A. 1886.

Morris, Elias Walker, 1s. Richard, of Bampton, Oxon, pleb. NEW INN HALL, matric. 14 March, 1833, aged 23; B.A. 1837 (? assistant-minister of St. Paul's Church, Burslem), died at Newbury, Berks, 9 April, 1841. **[15]**

Morris, Francis Orpen, 1s. Henry Gage, of Cove of Cork, Ireland, arm. WORCESTER COLL., matric. 17 June, 1829, aged 19; B.A. 1834, ornithologist, vicar of Nafferton, Yorks, 1844-54, rector of Nun-Burnholme since 1854, for list of his works on ornithology, etc., see *Crockford.*

Morris, Frank Howe, o.s. Thomas, of Coventry, co. Warwick, gent. WORCESTER COLL., matric. 11 April, 1853, aged 19; B.A. 1859.

Morris, Frederick, s. Jeremiah, of Mere, Wilts, gent. QUEEN'S COLL., matric. 13 July, 1789, aged 22.

Morris, Frederick, 4s. Charles, of Wandsworth, Surrey, arm. BRASENOSE COLL., matric. 10 Oct., 1820, aged 18.

Morris, Frederick Philipse, 3s. Henry Gage, 'of Cove of Cork,' arm. WORCESTER COLL., matric. 13 June, 1833, aged 18; scholar LINCOLN COLL. 1836-8, B.A. 1838, M.A. 1841, bar.-at-law, Middle Temple, 1840. See Foster's *Baronetage.* **[20]**

Morris, Rev. Frederick William, 3s. William, of Holywell, Flints, gent. JESUS COLL., matric. 22 Jan., 1872, aged 19; scholar 1872-6, B.A. 1877, M.A. 1878, head-master Wotton-under-Edge School 1886.

Morris, Gabriel, s. Richard, of Llanfyllin, co. Montgomery, pleb. JESUS COLL., matric. 19 March, 1740-1, aged 17.

Morris, George, s. William, of Oxford (city), pleb. BALLIOL COLL., matric. 30 Nov., 1807, aged 15; scholar 1812-14, B.A. 1813, M.A. 1814.

Morris, George, o.s. Charles, of Southampton, Hants, arm. EXETER COLL., matric. 13 June, 1821, aged 16; scholar CORPUS CHRISTI COLL. 1822-30, B.A. 1825, M.A. 1828, vicar of King's Kerswell, Devon, 1859, until his death 9 July, 1880.

Morris, George, 1s. George, of Sarisbury, juxta Titchfield, Hants, cler. EXETER COLL., matric. 23 May, 1861, aged 19; B.A. 1865, brother of Charles 1862. **[25]**

Morris, George Eddison, 1s. George, of Penzance, cler. WORCESTER COLL., matric. 25 June, 1835, aged 18; B.A. 1839, M.A. 1856, sometime senior chaplain Madras presidency, rector of Middleton-Scriven, Bridgnorth, 1866.

Morris, Henry, o.s. Henry, of Ilminster, Somerset, gent. MAGDALEN HALL, matric. 11 May, 1836, aged 21.

Morris, Herbert, o.s. Huson, of Peckham, Surrey, gent. EXETER COLL., matric. 12 June, 1867, aged 15; B.A. 1870, M.A. 1876.

Morris, Herbert Forster, 2s. John, of Stretford, Lancashire, gent. WORCESTER COLL., matric. 19 Oct., 1886, aged 19.

Morris, Herbert Henry, 1s. Harvey, of Isle of Aseension, gent. QUEEN'S COLL., matric. 22 Oct., 1861, aged 17; scholar 1861-6, B.A. 1866, of the Indian Civil Service 1865, a student of the Middle Temple 1865. **[30]**

Morris, Hugh Chafin Grove, 1s. John Chafin, of Mere, Wilts, arm. CHRIST CHURCH, matric. 31 May, 1849, aged 19; servitor 1849-53, curate of Chard, died 24 Jan., 1854.

Morris, James, s. John, of Middleton, Lancashire, pleb. BRASENOSE COLL., matric. 18 Nov., 1736, aged 17; B.A. 1740, M.A. 1743 (? rector of Clayton cum Keymer, Sussex, at his death in 1793, 'formerly fellow of Brasenose').

Morris, James, s. John, of Leominster, co. Hereford, gent. BALLIOL COLL., matric. 15 Dec., 1803, aged 18; B.A. 1807.

Morris, James, M.A. TRINITY COLL., Dublin, 1840 (B.A. 1835), 2s. James, of Lucan, co. Dublin, gent. Incorp. from BRASENOSE COLL. 19 May, 1842, aged 37; B. & D.D. 1845, died 27 March, 1859.

Morris, James Taylor, 2s. William, of West Bromwich, near Birmingham, gent. MAGDALEN HALL, matric. 18 Dec., 1837, aged 28. **[35]**

Morris, John, s. John, of Newton St. Loe, Somerset, gent. NEW COLL., matric. 24 March, 1714-5, aged 17; B.A. 1718, M.A. 1721.

Morris, John, s. John, of Llandinam, co. Montgomery, pleb. JESUS COLL., matric. 21 March, 1718-9, aged 18.

Morris, John, s. Valent., of Isle of Antigua, arm. BALLIOL COLL., matric. 10 May, 1725, aged 18.

Morris, John, of ST. JOHN'S COLL., Cambridge (B.A. 1697, M.A. 1703); incorp. 9 July, 1733.

Morris, John, 'carrier;' privilegiatus 19 Feb., 1729-30.

Morris, John, s. Griffith, of Carmarthen (town), pleb. PEMBROKE COLL., matric. 31 May, 1750, aged 18. **[41]**

Morris, John, s. John, of Marshfield, co. Gloucester, cler. ST. EDMUND HALL, matric. 10 April, 1753, aged 18.

Morris, John, s. Michael, of Rochford, co. Hereford, gent. BRASENOSE COLL., matric. 10 April, 1782, aged 17; B.A. 1786, M.A. 1788 (as MORRES).

Morris, John, s. John, of Hagworthingham, co. Lincoln, pleb. LINCOLN COLL., matric. 28 Jan., 1796, aged 17; Michel fellow QUEEN'S COLL. B.A. 1799, M.A. 1802, B. & D.D. 1821, rector of Elstree, Herts, 1822, until his death 6 Nov., 1848, father of John Brande.

Morris, John, 3s. Thomas, of Glasbury, co. Brecon, gent. JESUS COLL., matric. 25 March, 1831, aged 18; B.A. 1834 (? died curate of St. David's at Brecon 14 Aug., 1846).

Morris, John, 3s. Lewis, of Carmarthen (town), gent. JESUS COLL., matric. 7 June, 1860, aged 21; B.A. 1864, M.A. 1868, rector of Girton, co. Cambridge, 1883-5, and of Narberth since 1885.

Morris, Rev. John, 1s. John, of Derwen, co. Denbigh, gent. JESUS COLL., matric. 30 Jan., 1877, aged 21; clerk 1877, B.A. 1882, M.A. 1886. [5]

Morris, John Baden, o.s. John Williams, of Bombay, East Indies, arm. UNIVERSITY COLL., matric. 15 March, 1821, aged 18; B.A. 1824.

Morris, John Bailey, o.s. Ebenezer, of Llanelly, co. Carmarthen, cler. JESUS COLL., matric. 8 April, 1835, aged 17.

Morris, John Brande, 1s. John, of Brentford, Middlesex, cler. (D.D.) BALLIOL COLL., matric. 17 Dec., 1830, aged 18, B.A. 1834; fellow EXETER COLL. 1837-46, M.A. 1837, Hebrew lecturer 1842, seceded to Rome, died in April, 1880. See *Boase*, 131.

Morris, John Edward, 2s. Henry, of Rugby, co. Warwick, arm. MAGDALEN COLL., matric. 14 Oct., 1878, aged 19; demy 1878-83, B.A. 1882, M.A. 1885.

Morris, Rev. John William, 1s. Joseph William, of Walcot, near Bath, arm. WORCESTER COLL., matric. 1 May, 1878, aged 19; B.A. 1881, M.A. 1885. [10]

Morris, Joseph, s. Joseph, of Claverley, co. Stafford, gent. WADHAM COLL., matric. 14 July, 1772, aged 19; B.A. 1777, rector of Tasley, Salop, nearly 60 years, died 19 July, 1837.

Morris, Joseph Ernest, 3s. Joseph, of Beddington, Surrey, gent. UNIVERSITY COLL., matric. 11 Oct., 1884, aged 18.

Morris, Joseph Lewis, o.s. Joseph, of Feltham, Kent, cler. WORCESTER COLL., matric. 18 May, 1843, aged 18; B.A. 1847, M.A. 1849, vicar of Fillongley, co. Warwick, 1856, until his death 2 May, 1884.

Morris, Lewis, 1s. Lewis, of St. Peter's, Carmarthen (town), arm. JESUS COLL., matric. 26 June, 1851, aged 18; scholar 1855, B.A. 1856, M.A. 1858, hon. fellow 1877, bar.-at-law, Lincoln's Inn, 1861, joint hon. secretary Aberystwith University since 1879. See Foster's *Men at the Bar.*

Morris, Marmaduke Charles Frederick, 3s. Francis Orpen, of Crambe, Yorks, cler. NEW COLL., matric. 16 Oct., 1863, aged 19; choral scholar 1863-8, B.A. 1867, B.C.L. 1870, M.A. 1872, head-master St. Michael's College, Tenbury, 1869-74, inspector of schools 1874-80, vicar of Newton-on-Ouse since 1879. [15]

Morris, Maurice O'Connor, 2s. Benjamin, of Seapoint, near Dublin, cler. WORCESTER COLL., matric. 24 June, 1844, aged 17; scholar 1844-9, bar.-at-law, Middle Temple, 1872. See Foster's *Men at the Bar.*

Morris, Mowbray Walter, 2s. Mowbray, of London, gent. MERTON COLL., matric. 14 Dec., 1865, aged 18; on the staff of the *Times'* newspaper. See *Eton School Lists.*

Morris, Owen, s. Henry, of Aberffraw, co. Anglesea, gent. JESUS COLL., matric. 18 Feb., 1777, aged 18.

Morris, Peter, s. John, of Oswestry, Salop, pleb. CHRIST CHURCH, matric. 28 March, 1745, aged 18; B.A. 1748.

Morris, Philip, s. William, of Clun, Salop, gent. ST. JOHN'S COLL., matric. 19 May, 1763, aged 18; J.P. co. Montgomery, rector of Sneade, died at the Hurst, Salop, 1 Sep., 1801. [20]

Morris, Philip, s. Philip, of Clun, Salop, cler. WORCESTER COLL., matric. 25 June, 1804, aged 18; created M.A. 12 May, 1807, bar.-at-law, Lincoln's Inn, 1812, died 16 Dec., 1872.

Morris, Richard, 2s. William George, of Stratford-upon-Avon, co. Warwick, gent. WADHAM COLL., matric. 12 March, 1819, aged 16; clerk 1820-3, B.A. 1823, M.A. 1831, vicar of Eatington, co. Warwick, 1833, until his death 16 April, 1859.

Morris, Rev. Richard, created M.A. 28 May, 1874, LL.D. Lambeth 1870, Winchester lecturer on English language and literature at King's College School, London, 1871.

Morris, Richard Edwards, 2s. Thomas, of Machynlleth, co. Montgomery, gent. NON-COLL., matric. 19 Oct., 1878, aged 26; B.A. from ST. JOHN'S COLL. 1882.

Morris, Robert, s. Thomas, of Ruthin, co. Denbigh, pleb. JESUS COLL., matric. 11 March, 1755, aged 19. [25]

Morris, Robert, s. David, of Maentwrog, co. Merioneth, cler. JESUS COLL., matric. 18 March, 1756, aged 19; B.A. 1760.

Morris, Robert, s. Robert, of Swansea, co. Glamorgan, arm. ORIEL COLL., matric. 22 May, 1760, aged 16; B.A. 1764, bar.-at-law, Lincoln's Inn, 1767, died in the East Indies 29 Nov., 1793. See Foster's *Baronetage.*

Morris, Robert, s. John, of Ruthin, co. Denbigh, pleb. CHRIST CHURCH, matric. 15 May, 1777, aged 18; B.A. 1781 (as MAURICE).

Morris, Robert, s. Thomas, of Clun, Salop, cler. JESUS COLL., matric. 30 Nov., 1785, aged 19; B.A. 1789.

Morris, Robert, s. Robert, of Llangwyvan, co. Denbigh, cler. JESUS COLL., matric. 6 Dec., 1804, aged 18; B.A. 1808, M.A. 1812. [30]

Morris, Robert, 1s. Robert, of St. George's, Bloomsbury, London, arm. CHRIST CHURCH, matric. 13 May, 1826, aged 18; B.A. 1830, M.A. 1833, perp. curate Holy Trinity, St. Giles's-in-the-Fields, 1838-50, rector of Fryern-Barnet, 1850-82.

Morris, Robert, 1s. Robert, of Llanilltyd, co. Merioneth, cler. JESUS COLL., matric. 16 June, 1836, aged 20.

Morris, Rev. Robert Leslie, 1s. Robert, of St. George's, Bloomsbury, London, cler. PEMBROKE COLL., matric. 8 May, 1857, aged 18; B.A. 1861, M.A. 1863, assistant-master Cholmeley School, Highgate, 1869.

Morris, Roger, s. James, of St. Mary's, Lambeth, Surrey, arm. ORIEL COLL., matric. 20 Feb., 1782, aged 17; lieut.-colonel Coldstream guards, fell at the battle of Alkmaar in Holland 19 Sep., 1799.

Morris, Rupert Hugh, 2s. William, of Holywell, co. Denbigh, gent. JESUS COLL., matric. 18 April, 1861, aged 18; scholar 1861-6, B.A. 1865, M.A. 1867, B. & D.D. 1884, principal of Training College for South Wales and Monmouth 1869-76, vicar of St. Mary, Park Street, Grosvenor Square, 1878-82, head-master Godolphin School, Hammersmith, 1876,-84, preb. of Manchester 1873, chaplain and librarian to the Duke of Westminster 1884. [35]

Morris, Samuel Sheppard Oakley, 3s. Ebenezer, of Llanelly, co. Carmarthen, cler. JESUS COLL., matric. 24 Oct., 1866, aged 19; scholar 1866-71, B.A. 1870, M.A. 1874, head-master of Dolgelly Grammar School 1872-8, chaplain R.N. since 1878.

Morris, Theodore Joseph, 1s. Joseph Ashby, of St. Nicholas Myton, co. Warwick, cler. LINCOLN COLL., matric. 5 Nov., 1856, aged 17; B.A. 1859, M.A. 1863, vicar of Nuthurst, co. Warwick, 1866-78 and of Hampton in Arden 1866.

Morris, Thomas, s. Thomas, of Antigua, gent. WADHAM COLL., matric. 11 Feb., 1716-7, aged 18.

Morris, Thomas, s. Thomas, of Ruthin, co. Denbigh, pleb. JESUS COLL., matric. 16 Feb., 1748-9, aged 18; B.A. 1753.

Morris, Thomas, s. John, of Llangyfelach, co. Glamorgan, arm. (after baronet). ORIEL COLL., matric. 26 May, 1800, aged 19; B.A. 1804, M.A. 1807, rector of St. James's, Dover, and vicar of Hingham, Kent, 1818, until his death 5 April, 1854. See Foster's *Baronetage* & *Eton School Lists*.

Morris, Thomas, s. John, of Wilmcot, co. Warwick, gent. MAGDALEN HALL, matric. 9 March, 1818, aged 24; B.A. 1825, M.A. 1827.

Morris, Thomas Dickin, o.s. Thomas Whitaker, of Heywood, Lancashire, cler. WADHAM COLL., matric. 14 June, 1867, aged 19; exhibitioner 1868-70, B.A. 1870, M.A. 1875, held various curacies 1871-81, vicar of Tottington, Lancashire, since 1881. [5]

Morris, Thomas Edward, 2s. John, of St. James's, London, D.D. CHRIST CHURCH, matric. 7 June, 1832, aged 18; student 1832-55, B.A. 1836, M.A. 1838, tutor 1838-45, rhetoric reader 1841, vicar of Carleton-in-Craven, Yorks, 1854, until his death 14 Dec., 1885. See *Alumni West.*, 507.

Morris, William, s. David, of Liverpool, Lancashire, gent. CHRIST CHURCH, matric. 12 July, 1716, aged 15.

Morris, William, s. William, of Pentrenant, co. Montgomery, gent. WORCESTER COLL., matric. 28 March, 1724, aged 17; bar.-at-law, Middle Temple, 1732, a judge of Court of Admiralty, and receiver-general of the casual revenue in the island of Barbados, died at Exeter 1795-6.

Morris, William, s. Cleaver, of Wells, Somerset, doctor. BALLIOL COLL., matric. 14 March, 1726-7, aged 17.

Morris, William, s. 'Morris Griffith,' of co. Montgomery, pleb. JESUS COLL., matric. 20 May, 1732, aged 19; B.A. 25 Feb., 1735-6. [10]

Morris, William, s. David, of Maentwrog, co. Merioneth, cler. JESUS COLL., matric. 17 May, 1759, aged 18; B.A. 1763.

Morris, William, s. Abraham, of Cork, Ireland, arm. WORCESTER COLL., matric. 10 Dec., 1799, aged 17; of the Dunkettle family.

Morris, William, s. William, of Waterford (town), Ireland, arm. CHRIST CHURCH, matric. 24 Oct., 1804, aged 17; a student of Lincoln's Inn 1807, a banker at Waterford, brother of Benjamin 1809. See *Eton School Lists*.

Morris, William, s. William, of St. Peter's, Oxford, pleb. ALL SOULS' COLL., matric. 31 Oct., 1805, aged 18; B.A. 1809, M.A. 1812, perp. curate of Wye, Kent, 1817, until his death 3 Sep., 1832.

Morris, William, s. Philip, of Clun, Salop, cler. UNIVERSITY COLL., matric. 12 June, 1806, aged 18; brother of Philip 1804. [15]

Morris, William, 1s. William, of St. John's, Walthamstow, Essex, gent. EXETER COLL., matric. 2 June, 1852, aged 18; B.A. 1856, M.A. 1875, hon. fellow 1882.

Morris, William, o.s. Daniel, of Pembrey, co. Carmarthen, gent. NON-COLL., matric. 16 Oct., 1875, aged 27.

Morris, Rev. William Alexander, 3s. Thomas, of Elmhirst, near Liverpool, gent. NEW COLL., matric. 15 Oct., 1875, aged 19; B.A. 1880.

Morris, William Chulmleigh, s. William, of Bridgetown, Isle of Barbados, West Indies, gent. QUEEN'S COLL., matric. 25 June, 1812, aged 18.

Morris, William John, 1s. Richard, of Northop, co. Flint, gent. JESUS COLL., matric. 1 Feb., 1878, aged 19; B.A. 1881, M.A. 1884. See *Robinson*, 370. [20]

Morris, William (O'Connor), 1s. Benjamin, of Kilkenny, cler. ORIEL COLL., matric. 15 June, 1843, aged 18; scholar 1844, B.A. 1853, of Gartnamona, King's County, J.P., a student of Lincoln's Inn 1852, bar.-at-law, King's Inns, 1854, County Court judge, etc., cos. Roscommon and Sligo.

Morris, William Robinson, 1s. William Bristow, of Kingston, Isle of Jamaica, arm. QUEEN'S COLL., matric. 6 Feb., 1862, aged 20; vicar of Low Wray, Westmoreland, 1869-77, of Lindale, Lancashire, 1877-9.

Morrish, William John, o.s. William, of Claines, co. Worcester, gent. MAGDALEN HALL, matric. 3 Nov., 1827, aged 19; B.A. & M.A. 1834, rector of Aylton, co. Hereford, 1869, until his death 28 Aug., 1880.

Morrison, Allan, y.s. James, of Marylebone, London, arm. BALLIOL COLL., matric. 13 April, 1861, aged 18; died in 1880.

Morrison, Archibald Charles Henry, s. Archibald, of Marylebone, London, arm. WADHAM COLL., matric. 17 Oct., 1811, aged 17; B.A. 1815, M.A. 1820, rector of Sezincote and vicar of Longborough, co. Gloucester, 1845, until his death 31 Oct., 1866.

Morrison, George, s. George, of ——, Berks, pleb. ST. JOHN'S COLL., matric. 20 Feb., 1728-9, aged 16; clerk MAGDALEN COLL. 1730-3, B.A. 1732, chaplain 1733-4; M.A. from CHRIST'S COLL., Cambridge, 1761 (? rector of Eastwood 1749, and of Great Sutton, Sussex, 1761, until his death 11 Dec., 1762). See *Bloxam*, ii. 91. [25]

Morrison, George, 5s. James, of Marylebone, London, arm. BALLIOL COLL., matric. 28 Jan., 1858, aged 18; died 4 April, 1884.

Morrison, Henry John, 2s. Alexander James William, of Monastereven, near Kildare, Ireland, cler. MAGDALEN HALL, matric. 4 Nov., 1864, aged 21.

Morrison, Rev. Hooper, s. Thomas, of Torrington, Devon, cler. UNIVERSITY COLL., matric. 30 May, 1754, aged 16; B.A. 1758, M.A. 1762, died at Bideford in 1798.

Morrison, John, s. Thomas, of Midhurst, Sussex, pleb. UNIVERSITY COLL., matric. 18 Nov., 1732, aged 19; B.A. 1736. [30]

Morrison, Thomas, s. Thomas, of Midhurst, Sussex, pleb. NEW COLL., matric. 22 May, 1723, aged 18; B.A. 26 Jan., 1726-7, M.A. 5 Feb., 1730-1.

Morrison, Thomas Hooper, s. Hooper, of Atherington, Devon, cler. NEW COLL., matric. 2 March, 1787, aged 18; B.A. 1790, M.A. 1794, J.P. Devon, vicar of Launcells, Cornwall, 1799, until his death 19 Dec., 1824.

Morrison, Walter, 4s. James, of Marylebone, London, arm. BALLIOL COLL., matric. 9 Dec., 1853, aged 17; B.A. 1857, M.A. 1862, of Malham Tarn, Yorks, high sheriff (W.R.) 1883, M.P. Plymouth 1861-74, and for Skipton division of Yorks (N.W.R.) July, 1886. See *Eton School Lists*.

Morrison, William, o.s. Archibald Charles Henry, of Stoneleigh, co. Warwick, cler. CHRIST CHURCH, matric. 30 March, 1852, aged 20; servitor 1852-5, B.A. 1856, M.A. 1858, chaplain 1856-68, vicar of Midsomer Norton, Somerset, 1867.

Morrison, Wilson Edward William, 2s. Robert William, of Dublin, cler. QUEEN'S COLL., matric. 22 Oct., 1870, aged 19; exhibitioner 1870-5, B.A. 1875. [35]

Morritt, Bacon, s. Bacon, of York (city), arm. TRINITY COLL., matric. 11 April, 1751, aged 18.

Morse, Edward, s. Jackman, of Awre, co. Gloucester, cler. MERTON COLL., matric. 7 Feb., 1737-8, aged 17; B.A. 21 March, 1742-3.

Morse, Edward, 3s. Herbert, of Emsworth, Hants, cler. ORIEL COLL., matric. 19 Oct., 1875, aged 18; B.A. 1878.

Morse, Edward Francis, o.s. John, of Stroud, co. Gloucester, gent. QUEEN'S COLL., matric. 5 May, 1831, aged 16; Michel exhibitioner 1831-3.

Morse, Francis, s. John, of Norwich (city), arm. CHRIST CHURCH, matric. 18 April, 1796, aged 18; of 6th Inniskilling dragoons, died 6 April, 1833.

Morse, Rev. Henry, s. George, of Lidbrooke, co. Gloucester, pleb. WORCESTER COLL., matric. 18 June, 1814, aged 18; B.A. 1819, M.A. 1822, died at Hereford in 1827.

Morse, Herbert, 1s. Herbert, of Emsworth, Hants, cler. LINCOLN COLL., matric. 23 April, 1873, aged 19; B.A. 1876, bar.-at-law, Lincoln's Inn, 1883. See Foster's *Men at the Bar*.

Morse, John, s. Jackman, of Awre, co. Gloucester, cler. PEMBROKE COLL., matric. 28 March, 1757, aged 18; B.A. 1761, rector of Blaisdon, co. Gloucester, 1778.

Morse, John, s. John, of St. Clement's, Norfolk, arm. CHRIST CHURCH, matric. 27 Oct., 1794, aged 18; of Sprowston Hall and Bagthorpe, Norfolk, high sheriff 1807, etc., died 28 Feb., 1844. [5]

Morse, John, s. Stephen, of Bloxam, co. Lincoln, cler. LINCOLN COLL., matric. 20 Nov., 1799, aged 18; B.A. 1804 (? died curate of Tewkesbury in 1812).

Morse, John, s. John, of Newent, co. Gloucester, gent. PEMBROKE COLL., matric. 7 Dec., 1810, aged 18; B.A. 1814, M.A. 1824, rector (and patron) of Huntley, co. Gloucester, 1817, and vicar of Oxenhall 1824, of Scone parsonage, Australia, died 11 April, 1852.

Morse, Leonard, y.s. Edward William, of Ealing, Middlesex, gent. LINCOLN COLL., matric. 27 March, 1838, aged 19; B.A. 1841, incumbent of St. Mary's, Montrose, at his death 10 Aug., 1848.

Morse, Robert, s. John, of Isle of Jamaica, arm. MAGDALEN COLL., matric. 28 July, 1769, aged 15; bar.-at-law, Lincoln's Inn, 1776-1801.

Morse, Stephen Herbert, 4s. Herbert, of Emsworth, Hants, cler. EXETER COLL., matric. 16 March, 1878, aged 19. [10]

Morse, Thomas, s. Robert, of Camden, co. Gloucester, cler. BALLIOL COLL., matric. 10 Nov., 1721, aged 18; B.A. 14 March, 1725-6, M.A. 1729.

Morse, Thomas, s. Leonard, of Northleach, co. Gloucester, pleb. WADHAM COLL., matric. 26 Oct., 1722, aged 18.

Morse, Thomas, s. Thomas, of Offchurch, co. Warwick, cler. ST. EDMUND HALL, matric. 3 July, 1754, aged 17; B.A. 1758.

Morse, Thomas, o.s. Thomas, of Cam, near Dursley, co. Gloucester, arm. QUEEN'S COLL., matric. 5 July, 1851, aged 17; of Ashmead House, co. Gloucester, J.P., sometime captain Gloucestershire militia. See *Eton School Lists*.

Morshead, Edmund Doidge Anderson, 3s. John Philip Anderson, of Lympstone, Devon, cler. NEW COLL., matric. 18 Oct., 1867, aged 18; scholar 1867-72, B.A. 1872, M.A. 1874, fellow 1874-9, master of Winchester School. [15]

Morshead, Edward, s. William, of Menhenniott, Cornwall, gent. EXETER COLL., matric. 8 July, 1742, aged 17; fellow 1744-60, B.A. 1747, M.A. 1749, vicar of Quethiock, Cornwall, 1759-1801, rector of Little Petherick, Cornwall, at his death 15 Nov., 1811. See *Coll. Reg.*, 102.

Morshead, Edward, s. William, of Menhenniott, Cornwall, arm. EXETER COLL., matric. 16 Dec., 1782, aged 18; fellow 1785-97, B.A. & M.A. 1789, rector of Hascombe, Surrey, 1791, of Calstock, Cornwall, 1796, of St. Dominick, in Cornwall, 1800-3, chaplain to the Prince of Wales and Duke of York 1823, died 17 Sep., 1852. See *Coll. Reg.*, 114.

Morshead, Francis Upton Anderson, 2s. John Philip, of Teignmouth, Devon, cler. UNIVERSITY COLL., matric. 13 Oct., 1866, aged 19; B.A. from ST. ALBAN HALL 1874, M.A. from UNIVERSITY COLL. 1874, brother of Edmund.

Morshead, Frederick, 2s. Henry John, of Kelly, Devon, cler. NEW COLL., matric. 21 Jan., 1853, aged 16; scholar 1853-66, B.A. 1857, M.A. 1859, tutor and dean 1863. See Foster's *Baronetage*.

Morshead, Henry, 1s. Henry, of Egg Buckland, Devon, arm. EXETER COLL., matric. 16 May, 1823, aged 17. [20]

Morshead, Henry John, 3s. Edward, of Calstock, Cornwall, cler. EXETER COLL., matric. 2 July, 1825, aged 18; B.A. 1829, M.A. 1832, rector of Kelly, Devon, and vicar of St. Cleather, Cornwall, 1837-80, died 25 Sep., 1881. See Foster's *Baronetage*.

Morshead, (Sir) John (Bart.), s. William, of Cartuther, Cornwall, arm. ORIEL COLL., matric. 15 May, 1766, aged 18; baronet, so created 22 Jan., 1784, M.P. Callington 1780-4, Bodmin 1784-1802, lord warden of the stannaries, and surveyor-general to the Prince of Wales, etc., died 10 April, 1813. See Foster's *Baronetage*.

Morshead, John, s. Philip, of Widey, Devon, arm. WORCESTER COLL., matric. 6 Nov., 1797, aged 18.

Morshead, John (Philip Anderson), 2s. Henry, of Isle of Madeira, arm. EXETER COLL., matric. 17 Feb., 1827, aged 17; B.A. 1831, M.A. 1845, vicar of Salcombe Regis, Devon, 1854, until his death 7 Sep., 1881.

Morshead, John Yonge Anderson, 1s. John Philip Anderson, of Newton St. Cyr, Devon, cler. UNIVERSITY COLL., matric. 24 April, 1865, aged 18; B.A. 1869, of Widey Court, Devon, J.P., bar.-at-law, Middle Temple, 1875. See Foster's *Men at the Bar*. [25]

Morshead, Pentyre Anderson, 3s. Pentyre, of Yealmpton, Devon, gent. ST. EDMUND HALL, matric. 23 Oct., 1875, aged 17; died 1879.

Morshead, Walter, 1s. Henry (John), of Kelly, Devon, cler. TRINITY COLL., matric. 23 May, 1853, aged 18; scholar BRASENOSE COLL. 1853-6, B.A. 1858, B.C.L. & M.A. 1860, of Treniffle, Cornwall, bar.-at-law, Lincoln's Inn, 1862, and of the Middle Temple (*ad eundem*) 1866, an examiner High Court of Justice 1884. See Foster's *Men at the Bar*.

Morshead, William, s. William, of Cartuther, Cornwall, arm. EXETER COLL., matric. 5 April, 1742, aged 19; high sheriff Cornwall 1753, buried 4 May, 1784, father of Sir John 1766.

Morson, Rev. James Collin Francis, 1s. James Henry, of London, arm. JESUS COLL., matric. 18 April, 1861, aged 18; scholar 1861-6, B.A. 1865, M.A. 1870, head-master Cowbridge Grammar School 1870, until his death 26 April, 1875.

Mort, Rev. Ernest, 5s. Thomas Sutcliffe, of St. Mark's, Sydney, N.S.W., arm. CHRIST CHURCH, matric. 16 Jan., 1880, aged 18; B.A. 1883. [30]

Mort, Henry Wallace, 1s. Henry, of Cussbrook, Queensland, gent. QUEEN'S COLL., matric. 22 Oct., 1866, aged 19; B.A. 1870, M.A. 1873, incumbent of All Saints', Woolhara, Sydney, N.S.W., 1876.

Mortan, Frederick, s. Edward, of Southampton, Hants, arm. ST. MARY HALL (MERTON COLL. in *Mat. Reg.*), matric. 6 Dec., 1817, aged 20.

Morth, Jeffery, s. John, of St. Stephen's, Cornwall, arm. EXETER COLL., matric. 4 July, 1718, aged 18; of Talland, Cornwall, left a daughter Margery.

Mortimer, Charles, s. Timothy, of York (city), gent. UNIVERSITY COLL., matric. 5 April, 1745, aged 19, B.A. 1748; fellow LINCOLN COLL., M.A. 1751, proctor 1755, B.D. 1759, D.D. 1781, rector 1781, until his death 26 Aug., 1784.

Mortimer, Charles, s. Timothy, of York (city), gent. BALLIOL COLL., matric. 21 March, 1793, aged 19.

Mortimer, Edward, s. Edward, of Trowbridge, Wilts, gent. EXETER COLL., matric. 7 March, 1736-7, aged 16. [36]

Mortimer, Edward Horlock, s. Edward, of Trowbridge, Wilts, arm. BRASENOSE COLL., matric. 17 April, 1804, aged 18.

Mortimer, George Ferris Whidborne, 1s. William, of Bishops Teignton, Devon, arm. BALLIOL COLL., matric. 18 March, 1823, aged 17; Michel exhibitioner QUEEN'S COLL. 1823-6, scholar 1826-30, B.A. 1826, M.A. 1829, B. & D.D. 1841, head-master City of London School, preb. of St. Paul's 1864, died 7 Sep., 1871.

Mortimer, George Frederick Lloyd, 3s. Mortimer Lloyd, of Walthamstow, Essex, cler. BALLIOL COLL., matric. 24 Oct., 1885, aged 19; in the army.

Mortimer, Henry Beaufoy, 8s. George Ferris Whidborne, of London, D.D. NEW COLL., matric. 14 Oct., 1870, aged 18; B.A. 1873, M.A. 1877.

Mortimer, Hugh Carstairs Jones-, 1s. Hugh Maurice, of St. Asaph, co. Denbigh, arm. MERTON COLL., matric. 21 Oct., 1886, aged 19.

Mortimer, Joseph, s. Joseph, of Trowbridge, Wilts, arm. ORIEL COLL., matric. 8 July, 1794, aged 18.

Mortimer, Rev. Percy, 1s. Francis William, of Swansea, co. Glamorgan, gent. JESUS COLL., matric. 18 Oct., 1882, aged 19; B.A. 1886. [5]

Mortimer, Thomas Gwynne, 1s. John Morgan, of Llanwnda, co. Pembroke, gent. JESUS COLL., matric. 15 March, 1849, aged 18; B.A. 1853, M.A. 1855, held various curacies 1854-65, rector of Castle Bigh, co. Pembroke, 1866.

Mortimer, William, 'cook of Queen's College;' privilegiatus 2 March, 1724-5.

Mortimer, William, o.s. William, of Lewisham, Kent, gent. WORCESTER COLL., matric. 9 Nov., 1854, aged 18; B.A. 1860, M.A. 1861.

Mortimer, William Basset, o.s. George, of Sidmouth, Devon, gent. PEMBROKE COLL., matric. 21 Feb., 1856, aged 19; B.A. 1862, M.A. 1865. [10]

Mortlock, Rev. Charles Frederick, 3s. Charles, of Leicester (town), cler. QUEEN'S COLL., matric. 30 May, 1868, aged 18; exhibitioner 1869-72, B.A. 1872, M.A. 1881.

Morton, Rev. D'Arcy Strangways, 2s. Edwin, of Malton, Yorks, arm. NON-COLL., matric. 23 Oct., 1880, aged 19; B.A. from WORCESTER COLL. 1884.

Morton, Edward James, 1s. Edward, of London, arm. WADHAM COLL., matric. 8 Dec., 1865, aged 19; B.A. 1868, M.A. 1872, of Heathfield, Wolverley, co. Worcester, J.P.

Morton, Francis Arthur, 3s. Charles, of Wakefield, Yorks, arm. UNIVERSITY COLL., matric. 11 Oct., 1884, aged 18; exhibitioner 1883.

Morton, James Cadell, o.s. Edwin Portlock, of Oxford, gent. NON-COLL., matric. 24 Oct., 1876, aged 19; B.A. 1881. [15]

Morton, James Elliot, 'Coll. Nov. Min.;' privilegiatus 13 May, 1829.

Morton, James Richmond, o.s. Hugh, of Newark-upon-Trent, Notts, arm. EXETER COLL., matric. 11 Feb., 1852, aged 17; B.A. 1856, M.A. 1858, held various curacies 1858-70, vicar of Huntington, Yorks, 1870.

Morton, John, s. John, of ——, Oxon, gent. TRINITY COLL., matric. 28 May, 1730, aged 15; created D.C.L. 14 April, 1749, then of Tackley, Oxon, bar.-at-law, Inner Temple, 1740, K.C. and a bencher 1758, chief justice Court of Sessions county palatine Chester 1762, attorney-general to the Queen, deputy high steward Oxford University, M.P. Abingdon 1747-70, Romney 1770-4, Wigan 1775, until his death 25 July, 1780.

Morton, John, s. Francis, of Eastnor, co. Hereford, gent. UNIVERSITY COLL., matric. 21 March, 1744-45, aged 18; B.A. 1748, M.A. 1752.

Morton, John, 2s. James, of London, gent. WORCESTER COLL., matric. 2 May, 1833, aged 18; B.A. 1837, M.A. 1844, vicar of Cleeve Prior 1857-72.

Morton, Rev. Matthew Calley, 1s. Henry, of Kirknewton, Northumberland, arm. EXETER COLL., matric. 20 April, 1837, aged 18; scholar 1838-42, B.A. 1841, M.A. 1844, warden of St. Columba College, Ireland, died 25 April, 1850. See *Coll. Reg.*, 153. [21]

Morton, Percy, 1s. William, of Hulme, Lancashire, gent. EXETER COLL., matric. 15 Oct., 1879, aged 19; scholar 1879-83, B.A. 1883, M.A. 1886.

Morton, Richard, s. John, of Tunbridge, Kent, gent. UNIVERSITY COLL., matric. 17 Nov., 1715, aged 15.

Morton, Richard, s. George, of Babworth, Notts, pleb. BALLIOL COLL., matric. 16 Dec., 1763, aged 18; B.A. from CHRIST CHURCH 1767; M.A. from WORCESTER COLL. 1770.

Morton, Samuel, s. Henry, of Oxendon, Northants, cler. LINCOLN COLL., matric. 11 April, 1753, aged 17; B.A. 1756. [25]

Morton Thomas, 1 Feb., 1719-20. See MORETON.

Morton, William, 1s. William, of Kent's Green, Powick, co. Worcester, arm. TRINITY COLL., matric. 8 July, 1853, aged 18; B.A. 1857, M.A. 1860, succentor St. Asaph 1872-86, cursal canon 1886.

Moscardi, Edward Henry, 1s. Lewis Donald, of Clifton, co. Gloucester, gent. WORCESTER COLL., matric. 16 Oct., 1871, aged 17; scholar 1871-5, B.A. 1874, M.A. 1886, of the Indian Civil Service 1874.

Moscardi, William, 3s. Lewis Donald, of Walcot, near Bath, gent. BALLIOL COLL., matric. 19 Oct., 1878, aged 18.

Mosditchian, Harootune Nisham, y.s. Nisham, of Cæsarea, in Asia Minor. BALLIOL COLL., matric. 18 Oct., 1881, aged 20; B.A. 1885. [30]

Moseley, Arthur, s. Joseph, of Earlswood, co. Warwick, gent. NON-COLL., matric. 31 Jan., 1871, aged 18.

Moseley, 'Edwin Sam,' 4s. Walter, of Buildwas, Salop, arm. BALLIOL COLL., matric. 3 June, 1857, aged 18; B.A. 1860, of the Indian Civil Service 1860, died in Dec., 1878.

Moseley, Henry, scholar ST. JOHN'S COLL., Cambridge, 1825, 7th wrangler & B.A. 1826, M.A. 1836; adm. 'ad eundem' 25 June, 1847, created D.C.L. 22 June, 1870, F.R.S., professor of natural philosophy and astronomy King's College, London, canon residentiary Bristol 1853-71, chaplain in ordinary to the Queen 1855, vicar of Olveston, co. Gloucester, 1854, until his death 20 Jan., 1872, father of Henry Nottidge 1864.

Moseley, Henry Capel, 1s. Robert Emlyn Lofft, of Troston, Suffolk, arm. EXETER COLL., matric. 28 Jan., 1847, aged 18; of Troston Hall and Glemham House, Suffolk, assumed the name and arms of MOSELEY, died in 1866.

Moseley, Henry John, 3s. Walter, of Buildwas, Salop, arm. NEW COLL., matric. 20 Oct., 1865, aged 18; B.A. from MAGDALEN COLL. 1871, bar.-at-law, Inner Temple, 1872, died in April, 1879. See *Rugby School Reg.* [35]

Moseley, Henry Nottidge, 1s. Henry, of Wandsworth, Surrey, cler. EXETER COLL., matric. 2 Feb., 1864, aged 19, B.A. 1868, M.A. 1872, fellow 1876-81; fellow MERTON COLL. 1882, Linacre professor of human and comparative anatomy 1881, Radcliffe travelling fellow 1869, member of the Government Eclipse Expedition to Ceylon 1871, etc., F.R.S. 1877. See *Boase*, 143.

Moseley, James, s. Acton, of Enfield, co. Stafford, arm. WADHAM COLL., matric. 2 April, 1737, aged 17; B.A. 1740, M.A. 1743, brother of Walter Acton 1733.

Moseley, James Fairclough, 2s. Joseph, of Manchester, gent. PEMBROKE COLL., matric. 23 Oct., 1882, aged 18; B.A. 1886.

Moseley, John, s. William, of Haresfield, co. Gloucester, cler. PEMBROKE COLL., matric. 26 March, 1729, aged 18; B.A. 1732, M.A. 1735.

Moseley, Reginald, 2s. Joseph, of Leamington, gent. ST. EDMUND HALL, matric. 2 May, 1876, aged 20; B.A. from WORCESTER COLL. 1887. [40]

Moseley, Thomas, s. William, of Almondbury, co. Gloucester, cler. MERTON COLL., matric. 9 March, 1744-5, aged 18; brother of William 1740-1.

Moseley, Thomas, 1s. Richard, of St. James's, Westminster, gent. ST. EDMUND HALL, matric. 23 March, 1821, aged 18; B.A. 1824, M.A. 1827, rector of St. Martin's, Birmingham, 1829-46, died 8 July, 1882.

Moseley, Tilson Humphrey, o.s. Thomas, of Birmingham, cler. WADHAM COLL., matric. 29 June, 1857, aged 18; B.A. 1860, M.A. 1864, bar.-at-law, Inner Temple, 1866. See Foster's *Men at the Bar.*

Moseley, Walter, o.s. Walter Matthew, of Astley, co. Worcester, arm. CHRIST CHURCH, matric. 13 Oct., 1820, aged 19; of Buildwas Park, Salop, high sheriff 1833, died 19 April, 1849. See *Eton School Lists.*

Moseley, Walter, 1s. Walter, of Buildwas, Salop, arm. TRINITY COLL., matric. 5 July, 1850, aged 18; of Bui'dwas aforesaid. See *Eton School Lists.*

Moseley, Walter Acton, s. Acton, of Enville, co. Stafford, arm. WADHAM COLL., matric. 5 July, 1733, aged 17; of The Mere, and of Glashampton, co. Worcester, died in 1793. [5]

Moseley, William, s. William, of Almondsbury, co. Gloucester, cler. PEMBROKE COLL., matric. 17 March, 1740-1, aged 17; B.A. 1744, brother of Thomas 1744-5.

Moseley, William, s. James, of St. Laurence, Ludlow, Salop, doctor. CHRIST CHURCH, matric. 31 Oct., 1804, aged 18.

Moseley, William Edward, s. Richard, of Chelmarsh, Salop, gent. MERTON COLL., matric. 10 Oct., 1734, aged 18.

Moseley, William Henry, s. Benjamin, of Witham, Essex, doctor. CHRIST CHURCH, matric. 20 Oct., 1794, aged 17; B.A. from ST. MARY HALL 1799, M.A. 1802, B.Med. 1802, D.Med. 1805.

Moseley, William Henry, 1s. William, of Leyton, near Stourbridge, co. Worcester, arm. BALLIOL COLL., matric. 24 March, 1852, aged 18; B.A. 1856, sometime captain 60th rifles. See *Rugby School Reg.*, 279. [10]

Mosenthal, Joseph, 6s. Adolphus, of London, gent. MERTON COLL., matric. 18 Oct., 1881, aged 18; B.A. 1884, bar.-at-law, Lincoln's Inn, 1886.

Moses, Samuel, 2s. Sylvester, of London, gent. TRINITY COLL., matric. 14 Oct., 1882, aged 18; scholar 1882-6, B.A. 1886, a student of the Inner Temple 1885.

Moses, Rev. William Stainton, 1s. William, of Dorrington, co. Lincoln, arm. EXETER COLL., matric. 25 May, 1858, aged 18; B.A. 1863, M.A. 1865.

Mosey, William, s. William, of Millingtown, Yorks, pleb. UNIVERSITY COLL., matric. 30 Oct., 1722, aged 22; B.A. 1726 (? died vicar of Lund, Yorks, 20 July, 1798).

Mosey, William, s. William, of Lund, Yorks, cler. UNIVERSITY COLL., matric. 24 April, 1758, aged 19; B.A. 1762, M.A. 1772. [15]

Mosley, Godfrey, 2s. Rowland, of Eggington, co. Derby, cler. CORPUS CHRISTI COLL., matric. 19 Oct., 1882, aged 19; B.A. 1886.

Mosley, Rev. Henry, 1s. Richard, of Rotherham, Yorks, cler. WORCESTER COLL., matric. 17 Oct., 1868, aged 19; B.A. 1872, M.A. 1877.

Mosley, John, s. Oswald, of Bolesworth, Cheshire, arm. BRASENOSE COLL., matric. 28 June, 1803, aged 17; died 31 Aug., 1804. See Foster's *Lancashire Collection.*

Mosley, Oswald, s. John, of Manchester, Lancashire, arm. BRASENOSE COLL., matric. 11 Nov., 1779, aged 18; of Bolesworth Castle, Cheshire, died 27 July, 1789, father of the next named and of the last named.

Mosley, (Sir) Oswald (Bart.), s. Oswald, of Moston, Cheshire, arm. BRASENOSE COLL., matric. 30 June, 1802, aged 17; created M.A. 18 June, 1806, and D.C.L. 5 July, 1810, 2nd baronet, M.P. Portarlington 1806-7, Winchelsea 1807-12, Midhurst 1817-8, North Staffordshire 1832-7, died 24 May, 1871. See Foster's *Baronetage* & *Manchester School Reg.*, i. 168.

Mosley, Oswald, 1s. Oswald, of Rolleston, co. Stafford, baronet. BRASENOSE COLL., matric. 18 June, 1822, aged 17; died 25 Sep., 1856. See Foster's *Baronetage* & *Eton School Lists.* [21]

Mosley, Paget Peploe, 1s. Paget Peploe, of Rolleston, co. Stafford, cler. EXETER COLL., matric. 28 May, 1854, aged 17. See Foster's *Baronetage.*

Mosley, Rowland, 4s. Ashton Nicholas, of Etwall, co. Derby, arm. EXETER COLL., matric. 31 Jan., 1849, aged 18; B.A. 1852, rector of Egginton, co. Derby, 1857. See Foster's *Baronetage.*

Mosley, Tonman, 2s. Tonman, of Anslow, co. Stafford, gent. (after a baronet). CORPUS CHRISTI COLL., matric. 20 Oct., 1868, aged 18; B.A. from ST. ALBAN HALL 1872, bar.-at-law, Inner Temple, 1874. See Foster's *Men at the Bar.*

Mosley, William Izod, s. William, of Cambden, co. Gloucester, arm. PEMBROKE COLL., matric. 7 May, 1766, aged 20. [25]

Moss, Charles, s. Charles, bishop of Bath and Wells. CHRIST CHURCH, matric. 8 Feb., 1780, aged 17; B.A. 1783, M.A. 1786, B. & D.D. 1797, chaplain House of Commons 1789, rector of Sherfield, Herts, and preb. of Salisbury 1786, of Westminster 1792, and of St. Paul's 1797, chancellor of Bath and Wells, bishop of Oxford 1807, until his death 16 Dec., 1811.

Moss, Charles, s. Charles, of Norwich (city), cler. WADHAM COLL., matric. 12 May, 1795, aged 18; B.A. 1799.

Moss, Edward Howard, o.s. Elkanah Howard, of Oldham, Lancashire, arm. WADHAM COLL., matric. 15 March, 1869, aged 19; of Ravenscroft Hall, Cheshire, J.P.

Moss, John, s. Joseph, of Crosby Garret, Westmoreland, pleb. QUEEN'S COLL., matric. 1 July, 1735, aged 21; B.C.L. 1746, D.C.L. 1747.

Moss, John Baron, s. John, of Wells, Somerset, arm. QUEEN'S COLL., matric. 5 July, 1771, aged 17.

Moss, John Edwards Edwards-, 1s. Thomas, of Roby, Lancashire, baronet. BALLIOL COLL., matric. 21 Oct., 1869, aged 18; B.A. 1873, M.A. 1875, a student of the Inner Temple 1871. See Foster's *Baronetage* & *Eton School Lists.* [31]

Moss, John Snow, 1s. Richard, of Brixton, Surrey, gent. CHRIST CHURCH, matric. 18 April, 1879, aged 19.

Moss, Joseph William, 1s. — M., of Dudley, co. Worcester, gent. MAGDALEN HALL, matric. 21 March, 1820, aged 17; B.A. 1825, M.A. 1827, B.Med. 1829.

Moss, Robert, s. Thomas, of Liverpool, Lancashire, gent. QUEEN'S COLL., matric. 13 March, 1740-1, aged 17; bar.-at-law, Inner Temple, 1752, recorder of Preston, died at Liverpool 25 Dec., 1791.

Moss, Samuel, s. William, of Middlewich, Chester, pleb. BRASENOSE COLL., matric. 21 March, 1718-9, aged 18; B.A. 1722, perp. curate of Horton, co. Stafford, for 50 years, vicar of Dilhorne, died 2 Feb., 1776. See *Manchester School Reg.*, i. 74. [35]

Moss, Samuel, 2s. Enoch, of Kilmarnock, Ayrshire, gent. ST. MARY HALL, matric. 19 Oct., 1874, aged 16; B.A. from WORCESTER COLL. 1878, B.C.L. & M.A. 1883, bar.-at-law, Lincoln's Inn, 1880. See Foster's *Men at the Bar.*

Moss, Thomas, s. John, of Manchester, Lancashire gent. BRASENOSE COLL., matric. 18 Nov., 1731 aged 19; B.A. 1735, M.A. 1738. See *Alumni West.*, 298.

Moss, Thomas, s. John, of Preston, Lancashire, pleb BRASENOSE COLL., matric. 15 July, 1738, aged 19.

Moss, Thomas, s. Robert, of Preston, Lancashire, arm UNIVERSITY COLL., matric. 1 June, 1782, aged 17 B.A. 1786, M.A. 1789, vicar of Walton-on-the Hill, Lancashire, 1812, until his death 22 Nov. 1842.

Moss, Tom Cottingham Edwards-, 2s. Thomas, of Roby, Lancashire, baronet. BRASENOSE COLL., matric. 28 May, 1874, aged 19; B.A. 1878, M.A. 1881, M.P. (Widnes division) South-West Lancashire (Dec.) 1885. See Foster's *Baronetage* & *Eton School Lists.*

Mosse, Benjamin, s. John, of Great Hampden, Bucks, cler. JESUS COLL., matric. 10 Oct., 1769, aged 12; B.A. from QUEEN'S COLL. 1773, M.A. 1776 (? died curate of East Stoke, Dorset, in 1809).

Mossman, Thomas Wimberley, 1s. Robert Hume, of Skipton, Yorks, gent. ST. EDMUND HALL, matric. 17 Dec., 1845, aged 19; B.A. 1849, created D.D. of the University of the South (U.S.A.) 1881, vicar of Randby, co. Lincoln, 1854-9, rector of East and West Torrington, co. Lincoln, 1859, until his death in 1885; for list of his writings see *Crockford.*

Mossop, John, s. Clement, of Rottington, Cumberland, gent. QUEEN'S COLL., matric. 21 Jan., 1792, aged 17; B.A. 1795, M.A. 1799, rector of Hothfield, Kent, 1802, until his death 3 Oct., 1849. See also *Gent.'s Mag.*, 1835, i. 103.

Mossop, John Henry, 1s. John, of Hothfield, Kent, cler. CHRIST CHURCH, matric. 7 June, 1865, aged 18. See *Eton School Lists.* [5]

Mostyn, Edward Mostyn Lloyd, s. Edward Pryce Mostyn, of Whitford, co. Flint, baronet (after baron). CHRIST CHURCH, matric. 28 Jan., 1813, aged 18; 2nd Baron Mostyn, assumed the additional surname and arms of MOSTYN by royal licence 9 May, 1831, M.P. Flints 1831-7, 1841-2, 1847-54, vice-admiral North Wales 1854, lord-lieutenant co. Merioneth 1840. See Foster's *Peerage.*

Mostyn, George Thornton, M.A. TRINITY COLL., Dublin, 1831 (B.A. 1828); adm. 'comitatis causa' 6 Feb., 1862.

Mostyn, Henry Porter, 1s. Robert I., of Caleot, co. Flint, gent. JESUS COLL., matric. 3 June, 1843, aged 19.

Mostyn, Hugh Wynne, born at Whitford, co. Flint, 5s. Edward, Baron M. CHRIST CHURCH, matric. 15 Oct., 1856, aged 18; B.A. 1860, M.A. 1863, rector of Buckworth, Hunts, 1863. See Foster's *Peerage.*

Mostyn, Humphrey, s. William, of Llanfechain, co. Montgomery, arm. JESUS COLL., matric. 4 March, 1736-7, aged 18; B.A. 1740, brother of William 1733. [10]

Mostyn, John, s. Roger, of Whitford, co. Flint, baronet. CHRIST CHURCH, matric. 25 June, 1728, aged 18; captain 2nd foot guards 1743, aide-de-camp to the King 1747, colonel King's Own royal fusiliers 1751, of 13th dragoons 1754, and of 5th dragoons 1758, a general in the army 1772, served in Flanders, M.P. Malton 1741-68, a governor of Chelsea Hospital 1768, died in Jan., 1779. See Foster's *Baronetage* & *Alumni West.*, 297.

Mostyn, John, s. John Ellis, of Holywell, co. Flint, gent. JESUS COLL., matric. 16 March, 1785, aged 18; B.A. from LINCOLN COLL. 1790, M.A. 1793.

Mostyn, John Meredith, s. John, of Llewesog Lodge (*sic?*), co. Denbigh, gent. MERTON COLL., matric. 12 May, 1792, aged 17; of Segrwyd, died 19 May, 1807.

Mostyn, Robert John, s. Samuel, of Bodfary, co. Flint, arm. JESUS COLL., matric. 7 Dec., 1812, aged 19.

Mostyn, (Sir) Roger (Bart.), s. Thomas, of London, baronet. CHRIST CHURCH, matric. 19 June, 1751, aged 16; 5th baronet, M.P. Flintshire 1758 until his death 26 July, 1796. [15]

Mostyn, Sydney Gwenffrwd, 2s. John, of Braintree, Essex, gent. EXETER COLL., matric. 16 Oct., 1884, aged 18; scholar 1884.

Mostyn, (Sir) Thomas (Bart.), s. Roger, of St. Martin's-in-the-Fields, Westminster, baronet. CHRIST CHURCH, matric. 13 Oct., 1720, aged 16; 4th baronet, M.P. Flintshire 1734-41, 1747 until his death 24 March, 1758.

Mostyn, Thomas, s. Thomas, of Whitford, co. Flint, baronet. CHRIST CHURCH, matric. 28 May, 1755, aged 18; B.A. 1759, M.A. 1762, rector of Christleton, Cheshire, 1775, and of Llanykil, co. Merioneth, 1775-82, vicar of Northenden, Cheshire, 1782, canon of St. Asaph 1773, preb. of Chester 1776, until his death 5 Dec., 1808. See Foster's *Baronetage* & *Alumni West.*, 362.

Mostyn, (Sir) Thomas (Bart.), s. Roger, of Christleton, Cheshire, baronet. CHRIST CHURCH, matric. 22 Oct., 1793, aged 17; 6th baronet, M.P. Flintshire 1796 (unseated, being under age), 1799, until his death 7 April, 1831.

Mostyn, Thomas Edward Mostyn Lloyd, 1s. Edward Mostyn Lloyd, of St. Asaph, co. Flint, arm. (after baron). CHRIST CHURCH, matric. 15 June, 1848, aged 18; B.A. 1851, M.P. Flintshire 1854, until his death 8 May, 1861. See Foster's *Peerage* & *Eton School Lists.* [20]

Mostyn, William, s. William, of Llanfechain, co. Montgomery, arm. JESUS COLL., matric. 8 May, 1733, aged 17; brother of Humphrey.

Mostyn, William, s. William, of Bryngwyn, co. Montgomery, arm. ORIEL COLL., matric. 18 April, 1761, aged 18.

Mothersill, Frank, 2s. Christopher, of Whalley Range, Lancashire, gent. PEMBROKE COLL., matric. 27 Oct., 1885, aged 20.

Motley, John Lothrop, created D.C.L. 20 June, 1860, American historian and diplomatist; B.A. HARVARD COLL., LL.D. 1860, advocate 1837, secretary of American legation at St. Petersburg 1841, United States minister at Vienna 1861-7, and at St. James's 1869-71, author of 'The Rise of the Dutch Republic,' died in England 29 May, 1877.

Motley, William, o.s. William Thomas, of Stroud, co. Gloucester, gent. MAGDALEN HALL, matric. 16 Dec., 1861, aged 39; B.A. 1867, M.A. 1869. [25]

Mott, John Stanley, 1s. John Thomas, of Blickling, Norfolk, arm. CHRIST CHURCH, matric. 4 June, 1857, aged 19; of Barningham Hall, Norfolk.

Mott, John Thomas, 1s. John, of Barningham, Norfolk, arm. CHRIST CHURCH, matric. 14 Dec., 1827, aged 18; B.A. 1831, of Barningham Hall, Norfolk, high sheriff, 1861, a student of the Inner Temple 1833, died 9 April, 1884.

Mott, John Thurston, s. Thomas Vertue, of Barningham Hall, Norfolk, arm. MAGDALEN COLL., matric. 19 March, 1803, aged 18; created M.A. 5 July, 1805, of Barningham Hall, high sheriff, Norfolk, 1800, died 12 Sep., 1847.

Mott, Stephen Light, s. John, of Lampleu, co. Stafford, cler. ST. MARY HALL, matric. 16 March, 1723-4, aged 17; B.A. from CHRIST CHURCH 1727, M.A. 1730.

Mott, William, 1s. John, of Lichfield (city), arm. CHRIST CHURCH, matric. 23 May, 1833, aged 18; B.A. 1837, of Wall, co. Stafford, J.P., D.L., a student of the Inner Temple 1836. See *Eton School Lists.* [30]

Mott, Rev. William Kynaston, 1s. William, of Wall, near Lichfield, co. Stafford, arm. CHRIST CHURCH, matric. 27 May, 1858, aged 18; B.A. 1864, M.A. 1865.

Motte. See also LAMOTTE.

Motte, William Gosford, s. William Gosford, of Oxford (city), pleb. BALLIOL COLL., matric. 15 Nov., 1802, aged 15; B.A. 1806.

Mottershead, John, s. Thomas, of Slaney, Cheshire, gent. BRASENOSE COLL., matric. 21 Feb., 1716-7, aged 16; B.A. 1720, M.A. 1723.

Mottershead, John, s. Matthew, of Buttley, Cheshire, pleb. BRASENOSE COLL., matric. 12 May, 1764, aged 19; B.A. 1768, M.A. 1770. [35]

Mottram, Charles John Macqueen, o.s. Charles, of Edinburgh, arm. MAGDALEN HALL, matric. 17 Nov., 1837, aged 23; B.A. 1841, M.A. 1855, vicar of St. John's, Kidderminster, 1852, until his death 26 March, 1872.

Mottram, Charles Piercy, 1s. Charles John McQueen, of Oxford, cler. MAGDALEN COLL., matric. 24 March, 1857, aged 18; B.A. 1861, M.A. 1872, rector of Doverdale since 1871.

Mottram, Joshua, 1s. Joshua, of London, cler. EXETER COLL., matric. 4 June, 1881, aged 30; B.A. 1885.

Moubray, John James, o.s. Robert, of Alloa, Scotland, gent. ST. JOHN'S COLL., matric. 16 Oct., 1875, aged 18; B.A. 1880, M.A. 1883, of Naemoor, co. Perth, etc.

Mould, Rev. George, 3s. John, of Appleby, co. Leicester, cler. PEMBROKE COLL., matric. 27 Jan., 1875, aged 20; B.A. 1878. **[5]**

Mould, James George, fellow CORPUS CHRISTI COLL., Cambridge, 1838-57 (B.A. 1838, M.A. 1841, tutor 1842-55, B.D. 1849); adm. 'ad eundem' 28 June, 1860, rector of Fulmodeston, Norfolk, 1868-86.

Mould, Thomas, s. Joseph, of Appleby, co. Leicester, pleb. ORIEL COLL., matric. 1 April, 1732, aged 18; B.A. from LINCOLN COLL. 1735, M.A. 1738.

Moulder, Thomas Jordan, 2s. Cornelius, of St. Lawrence, Kent, gent. NEW INN HALL, matric. 12 June, 1886, aged 38.

Moulding, Edward, s. John, of Walbrook, London, arm. WORCESTER COLL., matric. 14 March, 1736-7, aged 17; B.A. 6 Feb., 1740-1, M.A. 1743.

Moulding, John Bankes, s. Edward, of Worcester (city), cler. TRINITY COLL., matric. 30 May, 1774, aged 16; B.A. 1778, fellow and tutor, M.A. 1781, B.D. 1789, proctor 1788, died at the rectory of Rotherfield Gray's, Oxon, 1 April, 1814. **[10]**

Moule, Horatio, 6s. George, of Melksham, Wilts, gent. QUEEN'S COLL., matric. 23 Oct., 1824, aged 19; B.A. 1828, M.A. 1840, rector of Charmouth, Dorset, 1875-9, and of Road, Somerset, 1880, until his death 3 June, 1886.

Moule, Horatio Mosley, 4s. Henry, of Fordington, Dorset, cler. TRINITY COLL., matric. 16 June, 1851, aged 19, scholar 1851-4; migrated to QUEEN'S COLL., Cambridge, Hulsean prize 1858, died in 1873.

Moule, Philip, s. Francis, of Worcester (city), gent. HERTFORD COLL., matric. 1 Feb., 1764, aged 18.

Moullin, Charles William (Mansell), 2s. James Mansell, of Isle of Guernsey, D.Med. PEMBROKE COLL., matric. 26 Oct., 1868, aged 17; B.A. 1872, B.Med. & M.A. 1876, fellow 1877-86, D.Med. 1879.

Moullin, James Alfred, 1s. James Mansell, of Isle of Guernsey, D.Med. PEMBROKE COLL., matric. 26 Oct., 1868, aged 18; B.A. 1872, M.A. 1875, B.Med. 1877. **[15]**

Moullin, William Hilary (Baliol), 1s. William Baliol, of St. Peter's Port, Isle of Guernsey, arm. WADHAM COLL., matric. 18 April, 1863, aged 18; B.A. 1867, a barrister of Lincoln's Inn 1868. See Foster's *Men at the Bar.*

Moulsdale, Robert Owen, 1s. Robert Owen, of Llandrygan, co. Anglesey, gent. JESUS COLL., matric. 26 April, 1860, aged 17; scholar 1860-5, B.A. 1864, of Bryndyffryn, co. Denbigh, J.P., bar.-at-law, Middle Temple, 1869. See Foster's *Men at the Bar.*

Moulsdale, Thomas Gorst, 1s. Samuel, of Llanrwst, co. Denbigh, gent. JESUS COLL., matric. 23 Oct., 1806, aged 18; B.A. 1810, perp. curate Hope, Flints, 1830, died at Llanvairvie, co. Montgomery, 11 Dec., 1855.

Moulson, John, 1s. William Henry, of Sheffield, Yorks, gent. NEW COLL., matric. 16 Oct., 1874, aged 19; B.A. 1879, chaplain in India.

Moulton, John, 4s. Stephen, of New York, America, arm. PEMBROKE COLL., matric. 3 June, 1858, aged 19; B.A. 1862, M.A. 1865, of Kingston House, Bradford-on-Avon, bar.-at-law, Lincoln's Inn, 1864. See Foster's *Men at the Bar.* **[20]**

Moulton, Thomas William, 1s. Levi, of Kidgrove, co. Stafford, gent. NON-COLL., matric. 21 Jan., 1882, aged 21.

Moultrie, Austin, 4s. Gerard, of Barrow-Gurney, Somerset, cler. KEBLE COLL., matric. 22 Oct., 1885, aged 17.

Moultrie, Rev. Bernard, 1s. Gerard, of Houghton-le-Spring, co. Durham, cler. KEBLE COLL., matric. 28 Jan., 1879, aged 20; B.A. 1882.

Moultrie, Gerard, 1s. John, of Rugby, co. Warwick, cler. EXETER COLL., matric. 22 June, 1848, aged 18; B.A. 1852, M.A. 1856, chaplain Barrow-Gurney, Somerset, 1864-9, warden of St. James's College, Southleigh, 1873, until his death 25 April, 1885. See *Rugby School Reg.*, 233.

Moultrie, Rev. John, 2s. Gerard, of Bright Waltham, Berks, cler. NEW COLL., matric. 17 Jan., 1880, aged 19; B.A. 1883. **[25]**

Mounce, Samuel, s. John, of Tiverton, Devon, gent. BALLIOL COLL., matric. 30 May, 1718, aged 19.

Mounsey, John, s. John, of Cockermouth, Cumberland, pleb. QUEEN'S COLL., matric. 26 March, 1742, aged 17; B.A. 3 Feb., 1748-9, vicar of Tadcaster, Yorks, 1752, rector of Thoresby, co. Lincoln, 1775, and of Gawdley, co. Lincoln, 1782, of Market Rasen, co. Lincoln, died 29 May, 1806, aged 82.

Mount, Charles Bridges, 2s. Charles Milman, of Walcot, Bath, Somerset, cler. NEW COLL., matric. 1 Oct., 1845, aged 18; fellow 1845-66, B.A. 1849, M.A. 1854, bursar 1861, rector of Heyford Warren, Oxon, 1865-78.

Mount, Charles Milman, s. Thomas, of Cirencester, co. Gloucester, gent. TRINITY COLL., matric. 3 Nov., 1800, aged 16; fellow CORPUS CHRISTI COLL. until 1815, B.A. 1804, M.A. 1808, vicar of Hanington, Wilts, 1811, rector of Helmdon, Northants, 1814, rector of Great Tey, Essex, 1814, minister of Christ Church, Bath, 1821, preb. of Wells 1834, until his death 9 May, 1855.

Mount, Edward Shaw, 1s. Charles Milman, of Walcot, Somerset, cler. CORPUS CHRISTI COLL., matric. 16 Oct., 1834, aged 18, exhibitioner 1834-5; demy MAGDALEN COLL. 1835-77, B.A. 1838, M.A. 1841, bar.-at-law, Lincoln's Inn, 1846, died 19 April, 1879. See *Bloxam*, vii. 335. **[30]**

Mount, Francis John, 2s. (William), of Wasing, near Newbury, Berks, arm. ORIEL COLL., matric. 29 Jan., 1850, aged 18; B.A. 1854, M.A. 1856, vicar of West Firle, Sussex, 1871-7, and of Cuckfield 1877, preb. of Chichester 1875. See *Eton School Lists.*

Mount, William, s. William, of Tower Hill, London, arm. ORIEL COLL., matric. 13 Dec., 1805, aged 18; of Wasing Place, Berks, high sheriff 1826, M.P. Newport, Isle of Wight, 1831-2, died 10 April, 1869. See *Eton School Lists.*

Mount, William Arthur, 1s. William George, of Hartley Court, Berks, arm. NEW COLL., matric. 16 Oct., 1885, aged 19.

Mount, William George, 1s. William, of Wasing, Berks, arm. BALLIOL COLL., matric. 10 March, 1842, aged 17; B.A. 1845, M.A. 1848, of Wasing Place, Berks, J.P., D.L., high sheriff 1877, bar.-at-law, Inner Temple, 1849, M.P. Berkshire (South) since Dec., 1885. See Foster's *Men at the Bar & Eton School Lists.*

Mountain, Armine Wale, 1s. George Jehoshaphat bishop of Quebec, Canada. UNIVERSITY COLL., matric. 11 Nov., 1841, aged 18; B.A. 1845, M.A. 1854, incumbent of St. Michael's, Quebec, 1855, vicar of St. Mary, Wolverton End, 1872, until his death 31 Jan., 1885. **[35]**

Mountain, George Jehoshaphat, created D.C.L. 9 June, 1853, bishop of Quebec 1836-63 (2s. Jacob Mountain, 1st bishop of Quebec, 1793-1825), B.A. from TRINITY COLL., Cambridge, 1810, died 8 Jan., 1863.

Mountain, Jacob, 1s. 'Jacob Jehosaphat,' of Coteau Landing, Canada, cler. QUEEN'S COLL., matric. 28 Jan., 1869, aged 19; B.A. 1873, M.A. 1875, held various curacies 1873-85, rector of Hampton Poyle, Oxon, 1885.

Mountain, Jacob George, 2s. Jacob Henry Brooke, of Chalfont St. Giles, Bucks, cler. MERTON COLL., matric. 6 Nov., 1837, aged 19; postmaster 1837-41, B.A. 1841, M.A. 1847, principal of St. John's College, Newfoundland, where he died 10 Oct., 1856. See *Eton School Lists.*

Mountford, Thomas Newte, s. Thomas, of St. Pancras, London, arm. EXETER COLL., matric. 10 March, 1804, aged 19.

Mountfort, John, s. Samuel, of Kington, co. Hereford, pleb. JESUS COLL., matric. 21 Nov., 1796, aged 20; B.A. 1800, M.A. 1803. [5]

Mountfort, Simon Smyth, s. Simon, of Checkley, co. Stafford, arm. CHRIST CHURCH, matric. 11 April, 1799, aged 18; B.A. 1803.

Mountjoy, Rev. William, s. Robert, of Wotton-under-Edge, co. Gloucester, pleb. BRASENOSE COLL., matric. 2 April, 1748, aged 17; B.A. 1752. See *Manchester School Reg.*, i. 17.

Mountjoy, William John Jervis, o.s. William, of St. James's, Bristol, gent. ST. EDMUND HALL, matric. 6 July, 1844, aged 18.

Mountsteven, Hender, of PEMBROKE HALL, Cambridge (B.A. 1752), 4s. Hender M., of Bodmin, Cornwall, gent. Incorp. from EXETER COLL. 30 June (or 11 July), 1752, aged 22; fellow 1752-76, M.A. 18 April, 1755, B.D. 9 July, 1766, admitted to practice in medicine 11 July, 1792 (*Cat. Grads.*), rector of Little Petherick (St. Petrock Minor), Cornwall, 1782, died in 1812. See *Boase*, 105.

Mourant, Edward, o.s. Edward, of St. Clement, Isle of Jersey, gent. WADHAM COLL., matric. 9 March, 1853, aged 18; B.A. 1861, M.A. 1862, a student of Lincoln's Inn 1862. [10]

Mourant, Philip, s. Stephen, of Jersey, pleb. PEMBROKE COLL., matric. 17 Dec., 1717, aged 17; B.A. 1721.

Mousley, Francis, 3s. — M., of Derby (town), arm. NEW COLL., matric. 7 March, 1845, aged 18. See *Eton School Lists.*

Mousley, John, s. John, of Boswell, co. Warwick, gent. TRINITY COLL., matric. 26 Jan., 1793, aged 21, B.A. 1800, M.A. 1802; fellow BALLIOL COLL. 1802-16, B. & D.D. (by decree) 28 May, 1818, archdeacon of Madras at his death 31 Aug., 1819.

Mousley, William, s. Samuel, of Dordon, co. Warwick, pleb. CHRIST CHURCH, matric. 11 Dec., 1739, aged 16; B.A. 1743.

Mouton, Ludovic Charles Andre, o.s. Lewis, of Boulogue, France, arm. WADHAM COLL., matric. 27 Nov., 1868, aged 22; vicar of Hinton Admiral, Hants, 1876-7, rector of Woodchester, co. Gloucester, 1878-9, vicar of Brampford Speke, Devon, 1879-82, and of St. John the Evangelist, Sandown, Isle of Wight, 1882. [15]

Mowat, John Lancaster Gough, 3s. James, of St. Helier, Isle of Jersey, gent. EXETER COLL., matric. 14 Oct., 1865, aged 19, scholar 1865-70, B.A. 1869; fellow PEMBROKE COLL. 1871. M.A. 1872, lecturer, senior bursar and junior dean 1872, librarian 1885, proctor 1885, a student of Lincoln's Inn 1876. See *Boase*, 162.

Mowatt, Francis, o.s. Francis, of Australia, gent. ST. JOHN'S COLL., matric. 22 March, 1855, aged 17.

Mowatt, Frank Herbert, 1s. Frank, of London, arm. CORPUS CHRISTI COLL., matric. 20 Oct., 1886, aged 19.

Mowbray, Rev. Edmund George Lionel, 3s. John Robert, of Mortimer, Berks, arm. (after baronet) NEW COLL., matric. 11 Oct., 1878, aged 19; B.A. 1882, M.A. 1885. See Foster's *Baronetage* & *Eton School Lists.*

Mowbray, George, s. Teasdale, of Bishop Wearmouth, co. Durham, arm. QUEEN'S COLL., matric. 24 April, 1758, aged 18; of Ford, co. Durham, died 1 Aug., 1791. [20]

Mowbray, George, s. John (? George), of Bishop Wearmouth, co. Durham, arm. QUEEN'S COLL., matric. 19 April, 1788, aged 19; of Ford, born 29 Dec., 1769.

Mowbray, John Henry Turner Mitchell de, o.s. George Gardiner Mitchell, of London, arm. ORIEL COLL., matric. 7 Feb., 1856, aged 19; B.A. & M.A. from NEW INN HALL 1869, assumed the additional name of DE MOWBRAY in 1861, curate of Caistor, co. Lincoln, 1864-78, rector of Knossington, Rutland, 1878.

Mowbray, (Sir) John Robert (Bart.), o.s. Robert Stribling Cornish, of Exeter (city), arm. CHRIST CHURCH, matric. 23 May, 1833, aged 17, student 1835-47, B.A. 1837, M.A. 1839, created D.C.L. 30 Nov., 1869, hon. student 1876; hon. fellow HERTFORD COLL. 1875, created a baronet 3 May, 1880, and P.C. 1858, bar.-at-law, Inner Temple, 1841, assumed the surname of MOWBRAY in lieu of CORNISH by royal licence 26 July, 1847, M.P. Durham 1853-68, Oxford University since 1868; judge advocate general 1858-9 & 1866-8, Church Estates commissioner since 1871, member of Council of King's College, London, since 1877, etc. See Foster's *Barouetage* & *Men at the Bar.*

Mowbray, Reginald Ambrose, 2s. John Robert, of London, arm. (after a baronet). CHRIST CHURCH, matric. 20 Jan., 1871, aged 18; B.A. 1874, M.A. 1878.

Mowbray, Robert Gray Cornish, 1s. John Robert, of London, arm. (after baronet), BALLIOL COLL., matric. 19 Oct., 1868, aged 18, B.A. 1873; fellow ALL SOULS' COLL. 1873, M.A. 1875, bar.-at-law, Inner Temple, 1876, M.P. Prestwich or South-East division of Lancashire, July, 1886. See Foster's *Men at the Bar* & *Eton School Lists.* [25]

Mowbray, Teasdale, s. George, of Altondale, Northumberland, arm. QUEEN'S COLL., matric. 30 June, 1727, aged 20; father of George 1758. See Surtees' *Durham*, i. 242.

Mowbray, William, s. William, of London, arm. QUEEN'S COLL., matric. 5 June, 1739, aged 17.

Mower, John, s. John, of Leigh, co. Gloucester, cler. HART HALL, matric. 22 May, 1717, aged 16; B.A. from ALL SOULS' COLL. 24 March, 1720-1.

Moxon, Ernest Arthur, 4s. Francis Henry, of Sherburne, Yorks, gent. ST. EDMUND HALL, matric. 29 Jan., 1886, aged 19.

Moxon, William, 1s. George Dunhill, of Pontefract, Yorks, gent. NEW COLL., matric. 18 Oct., 1875, aged 32. [30]

Moy, Edward, s. Edward, of Trinity parish, Coventry, pleb. MAGDALEN HALL, matric. 23 June, 1726, aged 18; B.A. from PEMBROKE COLL. 1730.

Moyle, Rev. George, 1s. Richard, of Marazion, Cornwall, doctor. EXETER COLL., matric. 9 Feb., 1833, aged 17; scholar LINCOLN COLL. 1835-37, B.A. 1836, M.A. 1839, master of Chudleigh Grammar School 1850, until his death 22 Nov., 1861.

Moyle, John Baron, 2s. George, of Chudleigh, Devon, cler. NEW COLL., matric. 14 Oct., 1871, aged 18; scholar 1871-6, B.A. 1876, fellow 1876, M.A. 1878, B.C.L. 1879, tutor 1879, sub-warden 1880, junior bursar 1884, law lecturer Jesus College 1883, bar.-at-law, Lincoln's Inn, 1881. See Foster's *Men at the Bar.*

Moyle, Loftus Guillemand, born at sea between the Cape and Bombay, 4s. John Grenfell, arm. ST. EDMUND HALL, matric. 22 June, 1848, aged 18.

Moyle, Robert Edward, 5s. George, of Chudleigh, Devon, cler. CHRIST CHURCH, matric. 14 Oct., 1881, aged 19; a junior student 1881-2, scholar 1882-5, B.A. 1885, M.A. 1888.

Moyle, Vyvyan Henry, 9s. — M., of Penzance, Cornwall, gent. PEMBROKE COLL., matric. 3 March, 1853, aged 18; vicar of Ashampstead, Berks, 1885.

Moyle, Walter, 1s. George, of Chudleigh, Devon, cler. EXETER COLL., matric. 20 Jan., 1871, aged 19; exhibitioner WORCESTER COLL. 1871-5, B.A. 1876, M.A. 1878, rector of Ashcombe, Devon, 1885.

Moyle, Walter, s. Walter, of St. Germans, Cornwall, arm. EXETER COLL., matric. 25 June, 1728, aged 17; fellow 1730-1, died 16 Sep., 1732. See *Coll. Reg.*, 94.

Moyse, Henry Belward. QUEEN'S COLL. 1811. See BELWARD. [5]

Moysey, Abel, s. Abel, of Lime Street, London, pleb. ST. JOHN'S COLL., matric. 30 June, 1732, aged 16; B.A. 1736, M.A. 1739, B.Med. 1741, D.Med. 1745, a physician at Bath, purchased Charter House Hinton, died 11 Aug., 1780. See *Robinson*, 62.

Moysey, Abel, s. Abel, of Sherbourn, Dorset, doctor. CHRIST CHURCH, matric. 9 June, 1760, aged 16; B.A. 1764, M.A. 1767, of Charter House Hinton, Somerset, bar.-at-law, Lincoln's Inn, 1767, bencher 1802, a Welsh judge 1777, M.P. Bath 1774-90, deputy remembrancer of exchequer 1795, died July, 1831. See *Alumni West.*, 374.

Moysey, Abel, s. Abel, of St. Giles's, London, arm. CHRIST CHURCH, matric. 25 May, 1796, aged 18; B.A. 1800, M.A. 1803, of Charter House Hinton, Somerset, bar.-at-law, Lincoln's Inn, 1803, died 1839. See *Alumni West.*, 445.

Moysey, Charles Abel, s. Abel, of London, arm. CHRIST CHURCH, matric. 6 June, 1798, aged 18; B.A. 1802, M.A. 1805, B.D. 1818, D.D. 1818, Bampton lecturer 1818, of Charter House Hinton, Somerset, perp. curate, Southwick, Hants, and vicar of Hinton Parva, Wilts, 1808, rector of Martyr Worthy, Hants, 1810, and of Walcot, near Bath, 1817-39, archdeacon of Bath 1820-39, preb. of Wells 1826-39, died 17 Dec., 1859. See *Alumni West.*, 449.

Moysey, Frederick Luttrell, 2s. (Charles Abel), of Martyr Worthy, Hants, cler. CHRIST CHURCH, matric. 15 May, 1834, aged 18; student 1834-9, B.A. 1838, M.A. 1861, vicar of Combe St. Nicholas, Somerset, 1840-61, and of Sidmouth, Devon, 1861-5. See *Alumni West.*, 510. [10]

Moysey, Henry Gorges, 1s. Charles Abel, of Martyr Worthy, Hants, archdeacon, of Wells. ST. MARY HALL, matric. 21 May, 1836, aged 22; of Bathealton Court, high sheriff, Somerset, 1875.

Mozley, Alfred Dean, 5s. John, of Derby (town), gent. JESUS COLL., matric. 24 Oct., 1866, aged 18; scholar 1866-71, B.A. 1870, M.A. 1876, vicar of Kersey, Suffolk, 1878-9, rector of Wigginton, Oxon, 1879.

Mozley, Arthur, 6s. Henry, of St. Werburgh, Derby (town), arm. ORIEL COLL., matric. 9 March, 1837, aged 17; B.A. 1840, M.A. 1844, master Emanuel Hospital, Westminster, 1859-69, vicar of St. Peter, Great Windmill Street, Westminster, 1869-80, and of Saul, co. Gloucester, 1880-3.

Mozley, Rev. Francis Woodgate, 4s. John, of Derby (town), arm. NEW COLL., matric. 14 Oct., 1864, aged 18; scholar 1864-9, B.A. 1869, M.A. 1871, assistant-master Bedford Grammar School.

Mozley, James Bowling, 5s. Henry, of Gainsborough, co. Lincoln, arm. ORIEL COLL., matric. 1 July, 1830, aged 16, B.A. 1834, M.A. 1838; fellow MAGDALEN COLL. 1840-56, B.D. 1846, senior dean of arts 1842, bursar 1843, vice-president 1849, dean of divinity 1852, Bampton lecturer 1865, D.D. by decree 11 Nov., 1871, regius professor of divinity and canon of Christ Church 1871-8, canon of Worcester 1869-71, vicar of Old Shoreham, Sussex, 1856, until his death 4 Jan., 1878. [15]

Mozley, Thomas, 3s. Henry, of Gainsborough, co. Lincoln, arm. ORIEL COLL., matric. 17 Feb., 1825, aged 18; B.A. 1828, fellow 1829-37, M.A. 1831, junior treasurer 1835, perp. curate Moreton Pinckney, Northants, 1832-6, of Cholderton, Wilts, 1836-47, and of Plymtree, Devon, 1868-80, etc. See *Crockford.*

Muchall, Smith, s. William, of Breewood, co. Stafford, pleb. NEW INN HALL, matric. 9 May, 1716, aged 19; B.A. 20 Feb., 1719-20, vicar of Rowton, co. Stafford, 1732.

Muckalt, James, y.s. James, of Priest Hutton, Lancashire, gent. QUEEN'S COLL., matric. 6 March, 1828, aged 19; B.A. 1831.

Muckleston, Edward, o.s. Edward, of New Park, Salop, arm. WORCESTER COLL., matric. 28 Feb., 1839, aged 19; B.A. 1845, M.A. 1847, vicar of Ford, Salop, 1852-60, rector of Haseley, co. Warwick, 1865.

Muckleston, John s. John Fletcher, of Lichfield, doctor. CHRIST CHURCH, matric. 27 Jan., 1819, aged 18; B.A. 1822, perp. curate Wichnor 1832-72, died in July, 1877. See Foster's *Our Noble and Gentle Families*, ii. [20]

Muckleston, John Fletcher, s. John, of Shrewsbury, Salop, arm. CHRIST CHURCH, matric. 17 Oct., 1782, aged 18; B.A. 1786, M.A. 1789, B. & D.D. 1814, of Merrington, Salop, which he sold, perp. curate Weeford and Hints, co. Stafford, 1790, vicar of Wybunbury, Cheshire, 1802, preb. of Lichfield 1790, until his death 24 Oct., 1843.

Muckleston, Rowland, 2s. John Fletcher, 'of Close of Lichfield,' co. Stafford, D.D. WORCESTER COLL., matric. 18 Feb., 1830, aged 18; scholar 1831-7, B.A. 1833, M.A. 1836, fellow 1837-56, dean and tutor 1839-56, vice-proctor 1852, master of the schools 1838, public examiner 1847, etc., rector of Dinedor, co. Hereford, since 1855.

Muckleston, William Hawkins, s. Richard, of London, arm. BRASENOSE COLL., matric. 26 Jan., 1774, aged 18, B.A. 1777, M.A. 1780; B.Med. from PEMBROKE COLL. 1782, of London.

Muckleston, William Jeffryes, 2s. Samuel, of Kingston, Canada, arm. LINCOLN COLL., matric. 19 Oct., 1867, aged 18; B.A. 1870, M.A. 1874, curate of Ottawa, Canada, 1884.

Muddiman, Joseph George, 1s. Alexander Phillips, of Leighton Buzzard, Beds, gent. EXETER COLL., matric. 28 Jan., 1881, aged 19; B.A. 1885. [25]

Mudge, John, s. Thomas, of London, gent. PEMBROKE COLL., matric. 9 June, 1780, aged 17, B.A. 1784; M.A. from CHRIST'S COLL., Cambridge, 1792, vicar of Brampford Speke, Devon, 1790, and rector of Lustleigh 1791, until his death 3 May, 1847.

Mudge, Richard, s. Zachary, of Plymouth, Devon, cler. PEMBROKE COLL., matric. 24 March, 1734-5, aged 16; B.A. 1738, M.A. 1741 (? died rector of Bedworth 3 April, 1763).

Mudge, Zachary, o.s. Zachary, of Cockington, Devon, arm. (admiral). ORIEL COLL., matric. 5 March, 1831, aged 17; B.A. 1834, M.A. 1840, of Plympton, Devon, bar.-at-law, Lincoln's Inn, 1842, died 13 Dec., 1867.

Mudie, Arthur Oliver, 2s. Charles Edward, of London, gent. MAGDALEN COLL., matric. 17 Oct., 1874, aged 20; B.A. 1879, M.A. 1881.

Mugg, Rev. Henry, s. Henry, of Chudleigh, Devon, gent. ST. MARY HALL, matric. 5 Dec., 1781, aged 35; of Chudleigh, died 28 May, 1822, aged 76. [30]

Mugliston, Rev. John, 1s. James, of Repton, co. Derby, gent. WADHAM COLL., matric. 29 June, 1855, aged 17; scholar 1856-61, B.A. 1859, M.A. 1862, assistant-master of Cheltenham College since 1866.

Muir, John, Esq.; created D.C.L. 20 June, 1855, founder of the Sanskrit chair Edinburgh University (brother of Sir William Muir, K.C.S.I.), a judge in Upper India, retired 1855, died 7 March, 1882.

Muir, Kenneth, 2s. Andrew, of St. Petersburgh, arm. TRINITY COLL., matric. 17 Oct., 1885, aged 18.

Muir, Robert James, 1s. Robert, of Dumfries, Scotland, arm. MAGDALEN COLL., matric. 13 Oct., 1866, aged 19; demy 1866-71, B.A. 1872, M.A. 1873, inspector of schools, Scotland, 1879.

Muir, William, 1s. William, of Glasgow, gent. BALLIOL COLL., matric. 20 Oct., 1875, aged 25; exhibitioner 1875-80.

Muir, Sir William, K.C.S.I.; created D.C.L. 14 June, 1882 (son of William Muir, of Kilmarnock), lieut.-governor North-West Provinces Bengal 1868-74, member of Governor-General's Council 1874-6, and of Indian Council 1876, entered B.C.S. 1837, K.C.S.I. 8 Feb., 1867. See Foster's *Baronetage*.

Muirhead, James Patrick, o.s. Lockhart, of Hamilton, co. Lanark, doctor. BALLIOL COLL., matric. 6 April, 1832, aged 18; B.A. 1835, M.A. 1838, of Haseley Court, Oxon, J.P., a member of the Faculty of Advocates, Scotland, 1838. **[5]**

Muirhead, John Henry, 3s. John William, of Glasgow, arm. BALLIOL COLL., matric. 19 May, 1875, aged 20; exhibitioner 1875-80, B.A. 1879, M.A. 1887.

Muirhead, Lionel Boulton Campbell Lockhart, 1s. James Patrick, of Edinburgh, arm. BALLIOL COLL., matric. 18 Jan., 1864, aged 19; of Haseley Court, Oxon. See *Eton School Lists.*

Mulcahy, John Moore, s. Edmund, of Tipperary, Ireland, arm. EXETER COLL., matric. 18 April, 1810, aged 19.

Mules, Alfred Philip, o.s. Henry Charles, of Freston, Suffolk, arm. EXETER COLL., matric. 11 June, 1862, aged 18.

Mules, Charles Oliver, of TRINITY COLL., Cambridge (senior optime and B.A. 1860, M.A. 1863); adm. 'comitatis causa' 23 April, 1863 (s. John Hawks, cler.), archdeacon of Waimea, New Zealand, 1880, incumbent of Waimea 1868, etc. **[10]**

Mules, John (Hawkes), s. John, of Marwood, Devon, gent. EXETER COLL., matric. 1 Nov., 1773, aged 17, B.A. 1777; (Memo.: J. H. Mules, perp. curate Babington, and curate of Broadway, Somerset, 1811, master of Free Grammar School, Isle Abbots 1792-1822, vicar of Muchelney 1820, until his death in 1822), father of the next named.

Mules, John Hawkes, s. John, of Ilminster, Somerset, cler. ST. MARY HALL, matric. 23 May, 1798, aged 15, B.A. 1803; M.A. from ST. JOHN'S COLL., Cambridge, 1823, vicar of Ilminster 1822, until his death 5 Jan., 1858.

Mules, Philip, 1s. Philip, of Honiton, Devon, arm. BRASENOSE COLL., matric. 10 Oct., 1832, aged 19, B.A. 1836, fellow EXETER COLL. 1837-55, M.A. 1839, B.D. 1851, domestic chaplain to Duke of Rutland 1848. See *Boase*, 132; & *Eton School Lists.*

Mulgan, James Mason, 1s. William Edward, of Edenmore, co. Derry, cler. WORCESTER COLL., matric. 19 Oct., 1874, aged 19; scholar 1874-9, B.A. 1879, M.A. 1884, bar.-at-law, Inner Temple, 1882. See Foster's *Men at the Bar.*

Mulholland, Alfred John, 3s. John, of Ballywalter, Ireland, arm. BALLIOL COLL., matric. 20 Oct., 1875, aged 19; B.A. 1881. See *Eton School Lists.*

Mulholland, Andrew Walter, 1s. John, of Dublin, arm. BALLIOL COLL., matric. 18 Oct., 1871, aged 19; died in June, 1877. See *Eton School Lists.* **[15]**

Mulholland, Henry Lyle, 1s. John, of Craigavad, co. Down, arm. BALLIOL COLL., matric. 20 Oct., 1877, aged 23; B.A. 1881, of Ballywalter Park, co. Down, J.P., high sheriff 1883, M.P. North Derry division of Londonderry since Dec., 1885. See *Eton School Lists.*

Mullens, Charles, s. George, of The Close, Salisbury, doctor. NEW COLL., matric. 15 May, 1720, aged 19; B.C.L. 1729.

Mullens, John, s. William, of Old Jewry, London, gent. EXETER COLL., matric. 15 Dec., 1792, aged 19 B.A. 1800, M.A. 1802, minister of Balham Hill Chapel, died 19 June, 1834.

Mullens, Richard Carey, o.s. Richard, of East Pennard, Somerset, gent. NEW INN HALL, matric. 29 Oct., 1881, aged 19. **[20]**

Mullens, William, s. George, of Salisbury, Wilts, doctor. BALLIOL COLL., matric. 13 April, 1717, aged 17; B.A. from TRINITY COLL. 1720, M.A. 1723, B.Med. 1726.

Mullens, Robert George, 1s. Robert John, of Grahamstown, cler. KEBLE COLL., matric. 19 Oct., 1886, aged 19.

Müller, (Rev.) Carl (Frederick) o.s. Adolphus, of Hamyln, Hanover, arm. NON-COLL., matric. 27 April, 1878, aged 21; scholar ST. EDMUND HALL 1879, B.A. 1882, M.A. 1887, head-master Hereford County College, 1886.

Müller, Ernest Bruce Iwan-, o.s. Severe Félicité, of London, —. NON-COLL., matric. 29 May, 1873, aged 20; B.A. from NEW COLL. 1876, M.A. 1880.

Müller, Frederick Reynold, 3s. John Michael, of Molan, Germany, gent. EXETER COLL., matric. 2 Nov., 1872, aged 26; B.Mus. 1874. **[25]**

Müller, Friedrich Max, Ph.D. Leipzig, created M.A. from CHRIST CHURCH 4 Dec., 1851, M.A. 13 Dec., 1855, fellow ALL SOULS' COLL. 1858, Taylorian professor modern European languages 1854-68, Corpus professor of comparative philology 1868, Rede lecturer (Cambridge), 1868, Hibbert lecturer 1878.

Müller, William Grenfell Max, 1s. Friedrich Max, of Oxford, arm. UNIVERSITY COLL., matric. 17 Oct., 1885, aged 18.

Mullings, Joseph, 1s. Joseph Randolph, of Chichester, Wilts, gent. EXETER COLL., matric. 24 April, 1857, aged 20; died 30 June, 1860.

Mullins, Rev. George Henry, 1s. George, of Box, Wilts, cler. BRASENOSE COLL., matric. 8 June, 1855, aged 18; scholar 1855-8, B.A. 1859, M.A. 1862, assistant-master Uppingham School since 1864.

Mullins, Hugh Willoughby, 4s. John, of Brixton, Surrey, arm. MAGDALEN COLL., matric. 23 Oct., 1885, aged 18. **[30]**

Mullins, Rev. Joseph Denis, 1s. John, of Hulme, Lancashire, gent. PEMBROKE COLL., matric. 23 May, 1877, aged 18; scholar 1877-81, B.A. 1882, M.A. 1884.

Mullins, Robert Foster, scholar TRINITY COLL., Dublin, 1834 (B.A. 1836, LL.B. & LL.D. 1857); adm. 'comitatis causa' 22 June, 1865.

Mullins, Thomas, o.s. Thomas, of Goathurst, Somerset, gent. WORCESTER COLL., matric. 24 April, 1845, aged 17; B.A. 1849, M.A. 1851, bar.-at-law, Lincoln's Inn, 1858. See Foster's *Men at the Bar.*

Mulock, Thomas, s. Robert, of Dublin (city), arm. MAGDALEN HALL, matric. 20 June, 1817, aged 27.

Mulso, John, s. Thomas, of St. Ann's, Westminster, arm. ORIEL COLL., matric. 27 Nov., 1740, aged 19; B.A. 1744, M.A. 1747, preb. of Salisbury 1757, (? rector of Thornhill, Yorks, 1760), chaplain to the bishop of Winchester, preb. of Winchester 1770, rector of Meon Stoke and Bath Easton, Hants, 1776, until his death 21 Sep., 1791. **[35]**

Mulso, John, s. John, of Sunbury, Middlesex, cler. WORCESTER COLL., matric. 6 April, 1778, aged 18; B.A. 1781, M.A. 1784, of Thywell, Northants, vicar of South Stoneham, Hants, died 24 June, 1815.

Mulvany, Charles Mathew, of Dunville, Canada. MAGDALEN COLL., matric. 21 Oct., 1886, aged 19; demy 1886.

Mulvany, William Carpenter, 4s. Charles, of St. Helen's, Lancashire, gent. MAGDALEN COLL., matric. 17 Oct., 1868, aged 19; exhibitioner 1868-73, B.A. 1873, M.A. 1881, died in Feb., 1882.

Mumford, John, s. John, of Dartford, Kent, arm. MAGDALEN HALL, matric. 20 Oct., 1769, aged 17.

Mumford, Thomas Arthur, o.s. Thomas, of Stoke Damerell, Devon, arm. WADHAM COLL., matric. 14 Oct., 1820, aged 18.

Mumm, Arnold Louis, 2s. Jules, of London, gent. CORPUS CHRISTI COLL., matric. 20 Oct., 1879, aged 20; scholar 1879-84, B.A. 1883, M.A. 1886, a student of the Inner Temple 1883. See *Eton School Lists.*

Munby, John Pigott, 2s. Joseph, of York (city), gent. LINCOLN COLL., matric. 25 Feb., 1830, aged 18; scholar 1830-4, B.A. 1833, vicar of Hovingham, Yorks, 1842-76.

Munch, Oscar Charles de, Free Baron, 1s. Charles Freiherr de M., Free Baron, of Wurtemberg. BALLIOL COLL., matric. 11 March, 1885, aged 20.

Munday, John, s. Thomas, of Pangbourne, Berks, gent. ST. JOHN'S COLL., matric. 15 July, 1755, aged 16. [5]

Munday, Robert, s. Robert, of Knebworth, Herts, pleb. PEMBROKE COLL., matric. 26 June, 1761, aged 16; B.A. 1765.

Mundell, William Adams, 4s. Alexander, of Leatherhead, Surrey, gent. ST. JOHN'S COLL., matric. 23 June, 1832, aged 16; bar.-at-law, Middle Temple, 1847, bencher 1866.

Munden, John, s. John, of Bere Hacket, Dorset, gent. MERTON COLL., matric. 14 Dec., 1771, aged 18; B.A. 1775, M.A. 1778, D.C.L. 1788, rector of Bere Hacket and Corscombe at his death in 1821.

Munden, John Maber, s. George, of Chetnole, co. Gloucester, doctor. QUEEN'S COLL., matric. 12 Feb., 1801, aged 19; B.A. 1804, M.A. 1807 (as John), Michel fellow until 1816, rector of Bicknor English, co. Gloucester, 1815, vicar of Northover, Somerset, 1828, rector (and patron) of Corscombe, Dorset, 1821, until his death 17 Feb., 1842.

Munden, William, s. John, of Chetnole, Dorset, doctor. MERTON COLL., matric. 28 Feb., 1804, aged 17; B.A. 1808, M.A. 1811. [10]

Mundy, Alfred Edward Miller, 1s. Alfred Miller, of Shipley, co. Derby, arm. CHRIST CHURCH, matric. 20 May, 1869, aged 18; of Shipley Hall, co. Derby, J.P. See *Eton School Lists.*

Mundy, Charles Drayner Massingberd-, 1s. Charles Francis, of South Ormsby, co. Lincoln, arm. CHRIST CHURCH, matric. 18 Oct., 1886, aged 19.

Mundy, Charles Godfrey, s. Francis, of Newbury, co. Stafford, arm. CHRIST CHURCH, matric. 27 Oct., 1791, aged 17; B.A. 1795, M.A. 1799, of Burton Hall, co. Leicester, high sheriff, died 23 April, 1838.

Mundy, Charles John Henry. CHRIST CHURCH, 1826. See MASSINGBERD.

Mundy, Edward Miller, s. Edward, of Heanor, co. Derby, arm. CHRIST CHURCH, matric. 1 Feb., 1793, aged 18; of Shipley, co. Derby, died in 1834. See *Eton School Lists.* [15]

Mundy, Edward Miller, 1s. Edward Miller, of Heanor, co. Derby, arm. CHRIST CHURCH, matric. 8 July, 1819, aged 18; B.A. 1823, of Shipley, M.P. South Derbyshire 1841, until his death 29 Jan., 1849. See *Eton School Lists.*

Mundy, Fitzherbert Miller, 4s. Edward, of Walton-upon-Trent, co. Derby, arm. CHRIST CHURCH, matric. 23 May, 1833, aged 20; died in 1846. See *Eton School Lists.*

Mundy, Francis, s. Francis, of Market Bosworth, co. Leicester, arm. NEW COLL., matric. 26 Aug., 1738, aged 20; B.C.L. 1743, bar.-at-law, Inner Temple, 1743, recorder of Tamworth 1760.

Mundy, Francis, s. Francis, of Markeaton, co. Derby, arm. CHRIST CHURCH, matric. 10 Oct., 1788, aged 17; of Markeaton, M.P. Derbyshire 1822-31, died 6 May, 1837.

Mundy, Francis Noel, 1s. William, of Moreton, Dorset, arm. CHRIST CHURCH, matric. 12 June, 1851, aged 17; of Markeaton, co. Derby, D.L., high sheriff 1884, bar.-at-law, Lincoln's Inn, 1860. See Foster's *Men at the Bar.* [20]

Mundy, Francis (Noel Clarke), s. Wrightson, of Osbaston, co. Leicester, arm. NEW COLL., matric. 7 Nov., 1757, aged 18; created M.A. 21 May, 1761, of Markeaton, co. Derby, died 23 Oct., 1815.

Mundy, Frederick, s. Frederick Miller, of Shipley, co. Derby, arm. CHRIST CHURCH, matric. 9 March, 1797, aged 18, B.A. 1800; fellow ALL SOULS' COLL., M.A. 1805, rector of Windlestone, co. Durham, 1803, until his death 2 Jan., 1846. See *Eton School Lists.*

Mundy, Godfrey Basil, s. Edward Miller, of Shipley, co. Derby, arm. CHRIST CHURCH, matric. 27 Feb., 1794, aged 18; general in the army, died 14 March, 1848. See *Eton School Lists.*

Mundy, John Augustine (Massingberd), 2s. Charles John Henry, of Isle of Wight, arm. UNIVERSITY COLL., matric. 21 April, 1860, aged 19; B.A. 1863, died 29 April, 1864.

Mundy, Matthew, s. Matthew, of Budleigh Salterton, Devon, arm. EXETER COLL., matric. 26 May, 1814, aged 17; B.A. 1817, M.A. 1823, perp. curate Lynton 1832-61, vicar of Rockbeare, Devon, 1861, until his death 1 Sep., 1864. [25]

Mundy, Thomas, s. John, of Wickham, Berks, cler. TRINITY COLL., matric. 19 Jan., 1715-6, aged 17; B.A. 1720.

Mundy, Walter, 4s. Thomas Clement, of Upper Tooting, Surrey, gent. EXETER COLL., matric. 18 Oct., 1882, aged 18.

Mundy, William, fellow of PEMBROKE COLL., Cambridge (B.A. 1719, M.A. 1723); incorp. 27 Feb., 1730-1.

Mundy, William, o.s. Francis, of Mayfield, co. Stafford, arm. CHRIST CHURCH, matric. 16 Nov., 1820, aged 19; of Markeaton, high sheriff, Derbyshire, 1843, M.P. South Derbyshire 1849-57, 1859-65, died 10 April, 1877. See *Eton School Lists.*

Mundy, Wrightson, created D.C.L. 14 April, 1749, then of Osbaston, co. Leicester (s. Francis, of Osbaston), high sheriff, co. Derby, 1737, M.P. co. Leicester 1747-54, died 18 June, 1762. [30]

Munford, George, s. Benjamin, of Upton, Norfolk, gent. MAGDALEN HALL, matric. 14 Jan., 1818, aged 23; vicar of East Winch, Norfolk, 1849, until his death 17 May, 1871.

Munk, William Geoffrey, 1s. Edwin Isaac, of Exeter, gent. WORCESTER COLL., matric. 17 Oct., 1884, aged 19; B.A. 1887.

Munkhouse, Richard, s. Richard, of Winton, Westmoreland, gent. QUEEN'S COLL., matric. 9 Dec., 1774, aged 19; B.A. 1778, M.A. 1781, B. & D.D. 1795, vicar of Wakefield, Yorks, 1805, until his death in 1810.

Munn, George Shaw, 1s. George, of St. Saviour's, Southwark, arm. TRINITY COLL., matric. 29 Nov., 1838, aged 18; B.A. 1842, M.A. 1845, rector of Madresfield, co. Worcester, since 1856.

Munn, John (Read), 1s. Henry, of Beckley, Sussex, arm. WORCESTER COLL., matric. 25 Oct., 1824, aged 18; B.A. 1830, vicar of Ashburnham, Sussex, 1840, until his death 9 Dec., 1878. [35]

Munn, Rev. John Turner, 2s. Robert, of Newchurch, Lancashire, gent. UNIVERSITY COLL., matric. 14 Oct., 1882, aged 19; B.A. 1886.

Munn, Thomas, s. John, of Brookland, Kent, arm. ORIEL COLL., matric. 28 Nov., 1797, aged 19.

Munnings, Daniel, fellow of CAIUS COLL., Cambridge (B.A. 1720, M.A. 1724); incorp. 12 July, 1729.

Munns, Thomas Deason, 2s. Arnold Summers, of Sydenham, Kent, gent. NON-COLL., matric. 22 Jan., 1881, aged 18; migrated to EMMANUEL COLL., Cambridge, bar.-at-law, Middle Temple, 1887.

Munro, Alexander George, o.s. Alexander, of Dover, arm. BRASENOSE COLL., matric. 9 April, 1840, aged 19; B.A. 1844. [40]

Munro, Henry Acland, 2s. Alexander, of London, arm. NEW COLL., matric. 10 Oct., 1884, aged 18; B.A. 1888.

Munro, Henry Douglas, 2s. William, of Gloucester, arm. UNIVERSITY COLL., matric. 28 April, 1842, aged 17; B.A. from NEW INN HALL 1848.

Munro, Hugh, 1s. David, of Totteridge, Herts, gent. CHRIST CHURCH, matric. 14 Oct., 1881, aged 18; a junior student 1881, B.A. 1885.

Munro, Hugh Andrew Johnstone, s. Alexander, of 'Bedford S.', London, equitis. CHRIST CHURCH, matric. 23 May, 1814, aged 17; of Novar, co. Ross, N.B., a student of Lincoln's Inn 1816.

Munro, Hugh Andrew Johnstone, scholar TRINITY COLL., Cambridge, 1840-3 (B.A. 1842, fellow 1843-85, M.A. 1845, Litt.D. 1884), chancellor's medallist, Craven scholar 1841; adm. 'ad eundem' 8 March, 1860, Kennedy professor of Latin 1869-72, created D.C.L. 18 June, 1873, editor of 'Lucretius,' died 30 March, 1885. **[5]**

Munro, Hugh St. John Stuart, 1s. James St. John, of Monte Video, arm. TRINITY COLL., matric. 11 Oct., 1884, aged 18; B.A. 1887.

Munro, John Arthur Ruskin, 1s. Alexander, of London, gent. EXETER COLL., matric. 18 Oct., 1882, aged 18; scholar 1882-6, B.A. 1886.

Munro, Rev. Macdonald, 2s. Alexander, of Lynn, Norfolk, gent. NON-COLL., matric. 17 Oct., 1881, aged 31; B.A. from EXETER COLL. 1884, M.A. 1888.

Munro, (Sir) Thomas (Bart.), 1s. Thomas, baronet. CHRIST CHURCH, matric. 19 May, 1836, aged 16; 2nd baronet. See Foster's *Baronetage* & *Eton School Lists.*

Munroe, George Peabody, 4s. John, of Paris, arm. NEW INN HALL, matric. 16 Oct., 1883, aged 19.

Munsey, William, s. James, of All Saints, Hereford (city), gent. ALL SOULS' COLL., matric. 15 April, 1801, aged 18 (? B.A. from TRINITY HALL., Cambridge, 1809, vicar of Arundel, Sussex, 1811). **[11]**

Muntz, Charles Oscar, y.s. Philip Henry, of Smethwick, co. Stafford, arm. NEW COLL., matric. 14 Oct., 1871, aged 18; died 1872. See *Rugby School Reg.*

Muntz, Duncan Albert, 2s. Philip Albert, of Keresley, co. Warwick, arm. CORPUS CHRISTI COLL., matric. 20 Oct., 1886, aged 19.

Munyard, Joseph Daniel, 1s. Joseph, of Hampstead, Middlesex, arm. BRASENOSE COLL., matric. 14 Jan., 1830, aged 18. See *Eton School Lists.*

Murchison, Sir Roderick Impey, Bart., created D.C.L. 9 June, 1853 (son of Kenneth M., of Taradale, Ross-shire), the distinguished geologist, director-general of the Geological Survey of the United Kingdom 1855, established the Silurian and Devonian systems, served in the Peninsular war 1808-9, captain 6th dragoons, F.G.S. 1825, president Royal Society 1826, and four times president of the Geological Society, president of the Geographical Society 1862-71, knighted 11 Feb., 1846, president of the British Association 1846, created M.A. from TRINITY COLL., Cambridge, 1847, and LL.D. 1861, K.C.B. 1863, created a baronet 22 Jan., 1866, died 22 Oct., 1871.

Murchison, Roderick Leith, 1s. John Henry, of London, arm. TRINITY COLL., matric. 16 Oct., 1873, aged 20; B.A. 1879, held various curacies since 1877, minor canon of Bristol 1881. **[16]**

Murden, Jeffrey, M.A. from CHRIST COLL., Cambridge; incorp. 6 July, 1733.

Murdoch, Charles Edward Gambier, 1s. Charles Townsend, of London, arm. MAGDALEN COLL., 29 Jan., 1885, aged 19; B.A. 1887.

Murdoch, James, 1s. William, of Stonehaven, co. Kincardine, gent. WORCESTER COLL., matric. 16 Oct., 1879, aged 22; exhibitioner 1878-81, scholar 1879-81.

Mure, Alexander James, s. James, of St. Clement's, London, arm. CHRIST CHURCH, matric. 28 May, 1811, aged 17, B.A. 1814; fellow ALL SOULS' COLL. 1816-21, B.C.L. 1820, died 27 July, 1828. See *Alumni West.*, 472. **[20]**

Mure, James, s. William, of Beith, co. Ayr, arm. (a baron of exchequer, Scotland). CHRIST CHURCH, matric. 8 July, 1775, aged 15; B.A. 1779, bar.-at-law, Lincoln's Inn, 1784, and of Gray's Inn 'ad eundem' 1799, father of the last named, and of the next named, and of Philip W. 1819.

Mure, James, s. James, of St. Clement's, London, arm. CHRIST CHURCH, matric. 23 May, 1814, aged 17; student 1814-26, B.A. 1817, M.A. 1820, bar.-at-law, Inner Temple, 1824. See *Alumni West.*, 478.

Mure, James Edward Lockhart-, 1s. James Ochterlony, of Balmaghie, in Scotland, arm. BALLIOL COLL., matric. 16 Oct., 1883, aged 19; of Livingstone, co. Kirkcudbright.

Mure, Philip William, 3s. James, of St. Clement's, Westminster, arm. CHRIST CHURCH, matric. 21 May, 1819, aged 17; B.A. 1823, M.A. 1825, brother of James 1814. See *Alumni West.*, 486.

Mure, Reginald James, 1s. James, of Woodford, Essex, arm. CHRIST CHURCH, matric. 23 May, 1861, aged 18; a junior student 1861-8, B.A. 1866, M.A. 1873, bar.-at-law, Lincoln's Inn, 1869. See Foster's *Men at the Bar.* **[25]**

Mure, William, s. William, of Beith, co. Ayr, arm. (a baron of exchequer, Scotland). CHRIST CHURCH, matric. 8 July, 1775, aged 17; of Caldwell, co. Renfrew, vice-lieutenant, died 9 Feb., 1831, brother of James 1775.

Mure, Colonel William, created D.C.L. 9 June, 1853 (s. William, of Caldwell), of Caldwell, co. Renfrew, J.P., D.L., M.P. 1846-55, lord rector of Glasgow University 1847-8, 'the historian,' died 1 April, 1860. See Foster's *Scots M.P.'s.*

Murgatroyd, Thomas, fellow of TRINITY COLL., Cambridge (B.A. 1722, M.A. 1726); incorp. from CHRIST CHURCH 10 Oct., 1735, rector of Lofthouse and Kirkby, in Cleveland, at his death 23 May, 1780.

Muriell, Francis, s. Francis, of Maidstone, Kent, cler. MERTON COLL., matric. 17 May, 1738, aged 16.

Murison, William Alexander, 1s. John Barnett, of New Orleans, America, arm. TRINITY COLL., matric. 23 April, 1869, aged 19. **[30]**

Murley, Charles Hemsted, o.s. Stephen Hemsted, of Cheltenham, co. Gloucester, gent. WADHAM COLL., matric. 5 May, 1841, aged 18; B.A. 1845, M.A. 1849, chaplain 1855-67, died 28 Sep., 1873.

Murphy, Charles Henry, 2s. Thomas Edward, of Halifax, Nova Scotia, gent. QUEEN'S COLL., matric. 1 Nov., 1872, aged 17; B.A. 1875, M.A. 1879, minor canon of Gloucester 1883-5.

Murphy, Herbert, 1s. Joseph Patrick, of Preston, Lancashire, cler. BALLIOL COLL., matric. 21 Oct., 1880, aged 19; B.A. 1884.

Murphy, Patrick, scholar TRINITY COLL., Dublin, 1796, B.A. 1798, M.A. 1801, B. & D.Med. 1814, 2s. James, of Newtown Butler, co. Fermanagh, Ireland, gent. MAGDALEN HALL, incorp. 25 Jan., 1826, aged 57.

Murphy, Robert, LL.D. TRINITY COLL., Dublin; adm. 'comitatis causa' 28 March, 1863 (? James LL.B. & LL.D. 1842). **[35]**

Murray, Allan Robertson, o.s. Robert, of Greenock, Scotland, arm. MERTON COLL., matric. 16 Oct., 1866, aged 23; clerk 1866-8; exhibitioner BALLIOL COLL. 1867-72, B.A. 1870.

Murray, Alexander, 1s. William, of Greenlaw, co. Berwick, Scotland, arm. MAGDALEN HALL, matric. 29 Nov., 1825, aged 24; B.A. 1829, M.A. 1832, brother of George 1827.

Murray, Alexander Edward (Viscount Fincastle), 1s. George, Earl of Dunmore. CHRIST CHURCH, matric. 16 April, 1823, aged 18; 6th Earl of Dunmore, died 15 July, 1845. See Foster's *Peerage* & *Eton School Lists.*

Murray, Rev. Alexander William Oliphant, 1s. Patrick Oliphant, of Halebridge, Cornwall. NON-COLL., matric. 12 Oct., 1872, aged 18; B.A. from WORCESTER COLL. 1878, M.A. 1880.

Murray, Armstrong James, 1s. James, of Colesberg, near the Cape of Good Hope, gent. ORIEL COLL., matric. 20 Oct., 1860, aged 19; a student of the Middle Temple 1861.

Murray, Arthur Silver, 6s. Henry, of Douglas, Isle of Man, arm. EXETER COLL., matric. 12 Oct., 1878, aged 20; scholar 1878-83, B.A. 1882, M.A. 1886. See *Coll. Reg.*, 169.

Murray, Arthur Turnour, 1s. William Powell, of London, arm. UNIVERSITY COLL., matric. 26 Jan., 1878, aged 19; B.A. 1882, bar.-at-law, Lincoln's Inn, 1885. See Foster's *Men at the Bar*.

Murray, Barrington Boyle, 1s. George William, of Shrivenham, Berks, cler. KEBLE COLL., matric. 19 Oct., 1886, aged 18. [5]

Murray-Aynsley, Lord Charles, s. John, Duke of Athole. NEW COLL., matric. 30 June, 1789, aged 18; B.A. 1792, M.A. 1801, dean of Bocking, Essex, 1803, archdeacon of Sodor and Man 1803, assumed the additional surname of AYNSLEY 1793, died 5 May, 1808. See Foster's *Peerage*, D. ATHOLE.

Murray, Hon. Charles, s. David, Earl of Mansfield. CHRIST CHURCH, matric. 26 Oct., 1797, aged 16; major in the army, died 17 Sep., 1859. See Foster's *Peerage*.

Murray, Hon. (Sir) Charles Augustus (K.C.B.), 2s. George, Earl of Dunmore. ORIEL COLL., matric. 21 May, 1824, aged 17, B.A. 1827; fellow ALL SOULS' COLL. 1827-51, M.A. 1832, a student of Lincoln's Inn 1827, master of the Household 1839-45, extra groom-in-waiting 1845, envoy to Persia 1854, Saxony 1859, Denmark 1866, and to Portugal 1867-74, P.C. 1875, K.C.B. 23 June, 1866. See Foster's *Peerage*.

Murray, Hon. Charles John, 2s. (David) William, Earl of Mansfield. CHRIST CHURCH, matric. 30 March, 1827, aged 17; B.A. 1830, M.A. 1833, bar.-at-law, Lincoln's Inn, 1834, died 1 Aug., 1851. See Foster's *Peerage*.

Murray, Charles Robert Scott, o.s. Charles Scott, of Hambledon, Bucks, doctor. CHRIST CHURCH, matric. 11 May, 1837, aged 18; B.A. 1841, of Danesfield, Bucks, M.P. 1841-5, died 27 Aug., 1882. See *Eton School Lists*. [10]

Murray, Charles Scott, created D.C.L. 13 June, 1834, then of Danesfield Park (son of Charles Scott Murray), died 24 April, 1837, father of the last named.

Murray, David, s. David, Viscount Stormount. CHRIST CHURCH, matric. 28 May, 1744, aged 17; B.A. 1748, created D.C.L. 3 July, 1793, 2nd Earl of Mansfield, envoy extraordinary and plenipotentiary to the Court of Poland 1755, ambassador to Vienna 1763, and to Paris 1768, justice-general of Scotland 1778-95, secretary of State 1779, lord president of the Privy Council 1783 and 1794, a representative peer 1754-96, chancellor Marischal College, Aberdeen, 1793, died 1 Sep., 1796, buried in Westminster Abbey, his heart was carried to his seat at Kumlington, co. Dumfries. See Foster's *Peerage* & *Alumni West.*, 330.

Murray, David, s. Gideon, of Westminster, doctor. CHRIST CHURCH, matric. 15 Dec., 1764, aged 16; B.A. 1768, M.A. 1772, bar.-at-law, Lincoln's Inn, 1773, died 8 May, 1794. See Foster's *Peerage*, B. ELIBANK.

Murray, David Rodney, s. David, of St. Marylebone, arm. CHRIST CHURCH, matric. 8 June, 1810, aged 19; B.A. 1814, vicar of Beedon, Berks, 1828-74, rector of Cusop and of Brampton Bryan, co. Hereford, 1826, until his death 4 Nov., 1878. See Foster's *Peerage*, B. ELIBANK.

Murray, Douglas Stuart, 3s. George, of Southfleet, Kent, cler. EXETER COLL., matric. 25 Nov., 1871, aged 18; B.A. 1875, M.A. 1878, rector of Blithfield, co. Stafford, 1879. [15]

Murray, Douglas Wyndham Eustace Clare Grenville-, 2s. Eustace Clare, of London, arm. CHRIST CHURCH, matric. 23 May, 1866, aged 18; a junior student 1866-73, B.A. 1870, bar.-at-law, Lincoln's Inn, 1873. See Foster's *Men at the Bar*.

Murray, Eustace Clare, 2s. (Henry John), of London, gent. MAGDALEN HALL, matric. 1 March, 1848, aged 24; a student of the Inner Temple 1850, father of Douglas Wyndham, and of Reginald 1863.

Murray, Francis Henry, born at Kirk Michael, Isle of Man, 2s. George, bishop of Rochester. CHRIST CHURCH, matric. 19 Oct., 1837, aged 17; student 1839-47, B.A. 1841, M.A. 1845, rector of Chislehurst, Kent, 1846. See Foster's *Peerage*, D. ATHOLE.

Murray, Francis Peel, 2s. George William, of Handsworth, co. Stafford, cler. WADHAM COLL., matric. 20 Jan., 1871, aged 18; B.A. 1874.

Murray, Frederick Auriol, 1s. Frederick William, of Stone, Kent, cler. KEBLE COLL., matric. 14 Oct., 1884, aged 18; B.A. 1887. [20]

Murray, Frederick John George, 2s. Hon. Charles John, of Warren Wood, Herts, arm. MERTON COLL., matric. 2 June, 1858, aged 19; colonel 3rd dragoon guards. See Foster's *Peerage*, E. MANSFIELD.

Murray, Frederick William, born at Bromley, Kent, 5s. George, bishop of Rochester. CHRIST CHURCH, matric. 19 Oct., 1848, aged 17; B.A. 1852, M.A. 1855, rector of Leigh, Essex, 1856-9, of Stone, Kent, since 1859, hon. canon of Rochester since 1877. See Foster's *Peerage*, D. ATHOLE.

Murray, George, Viscount Fincastle, s. John, Earl of Dunmore. CHRIST CHURCH, matric. 9 Feb., 1778, aged 15; 5th earl, M.P. Liskeard 1800-2, died 11 Nov., 1836. See Foster's *Peerage*.

Murray, Lord George, s. John, Duke of Athole. NEW COLL., matric. 28 June, 1779, aged 18, B.A. 1782; D.D. by diploma 27 Nov., 1800, rector of Hurston, Kent, dean of Bocking, bishop of St. David's Dec., 1800, until his death 3 June, 1803. See Foster's *Peerage*.

Murray, Hon. George, s. David, Earl of Mansfield. CHRIST CHURCH, matric. 2 May, 1797, aged 17; lieut.-general in the army 1837, commanded the 2nd life guards in the Peninsula 1813 and 1814, auditor of the Exchequer in Scotland, died 30 Sep., 1848. See Foster's *Peerage*, E. MANSFIELD. [25]

Murray, George, born at Farnham, Surrey, s. George, bishop of St. David's. CHRIST CHURCH, matric. 22 Dec., 1801, aged 17; B.A. 1806, M.A. 1810, D.D. by diploma 13 March, 1814, bishop of Sodor and Man 1813-28, of Rochester 1828-60, died 16 Feb., 1860. See Foster's *Peerage*, D. ATHOLE.

Murray, General Sir George, G.C.B., G.C.H., created D.C.L. 14 June, 1820 (son of Sir William Murray, of Ochtertyre, Bart.), P.C. colonel 1st royals 1843, served in Flanders 1793, Holland 1799, and Egypt 1800, and in Spain and Portugal under Sir John Moore, nominated G.C.B. 11 Sep., 1813, installed 1821, M.P. Perthshire 1824-33, (May) 1834-5, F.R.S. 1824, secretary of state for Colonies 1828, master-general of the ordnance 1834-5, etc., colonel 42nd foot 1823-43, died 28 July, 1846. See Foster's *Scots M.P.'s*.

Murray, George, 4s. William, of Berwick-upon-Tweed, arm. MAGDALEN HALL, matric. 5 July, 1827, aged 20; B.A. 1831, M.A. 1834, brother of Alexander 1825.

Murray, George, o.s. James, of St. Pancras, London, gent. MAGDALEN HALL, matric. 22 March, 1850, aged 19; B.A. 1856.

Murray, George Edward, born in Kirk Michael, Isle of Man, 1s. George, doctor, and bishop of Rochester. CHRIST CHURCH, matric. 19 Oct., 1837, aged 19, B.A. 1841; fellow ALL SOULS' COLL. 1841-4, rector of South Fleet, Kent, 1843, until his death 28 Sep., 1854. See Foster's *Peerage*, D. ATHOLE. [30]

Murray, George Gilbert Aimé, 3s. Sir Terence Aubrey, of Sydney, Australia, knight. ST. JOHN'S COLL., matric. 11 Oct., 1884, aged 18; scholar 1884.

Murray, George Herbert, 1s. (George Edward), of Southfleet, near Gravesend, Kent, cler. CHRIST CHURCH, matric. 16 Oct., 1868, aged 19; B.A. 1873, of the Treasury. See Foster's *Peerage*, D. ATHOLE.

Murray, George Sholto Douglas, 2s. George William, of Kinlet, Salop, cler. WADHAM COLL., matric. 18 Oct., 1862, aged 18, scholar 1862-7, B.A. 1867; a senior student CHRIST CHURCH 1868-73, M.A. 1869, bar.-at-law, Lincoln's Inn, 1875, assistant charity commissioner 1880. See Foster's *Men at the Bar.*

Murray, George William, 5s. Charles, of St. Andrew's, London, arm. MERTON COLL., matric. 31 Oct., 1826, aged 20; B.A. 1830, M.A. 1833, rector of Handsworth, co. Stafford, 1848-61, hon. canon Worcester 1873, vicar of Bromsgrove 1861-82, died 26 July, 1887, father of the last named, and of William Frederick 1860. See *Robinson*, 200.

Murray, George William, o.s. George St. Vincent Nelson, of Cheltenham, co. Gloucester, arm. QUEEN'S COLL., matric. 15 June, 1846, aged 18, B.A. 1850; M.A. from JESUS COLL. 1853, rector of Welton-le-Wold, co. Lincoln, 1854-9, vicar of Shrivenham, Berks, 1859. See *Rugby School Reg.*, 244. **[5]**

Murray, Gideon, born at Ballencrix, Scotland, s. Alexander, Baron Elibank. BALLIOL COLL., matric. 24 Jan., 1728-9, aged 18; B.A. 1732, M.A. 1735, B. & D.D. 1761, preb. of Lincoln 1746, and of Durham 1761, died 21 June, 1776. See Foster's *Peerage.*

Murray, Henry Edward. CHRIST CHURCH, 1867. See ANDERDON.

Murray, Henry Stormont, 1s. Henry, of Richmond, Surrey, arm. CHRIST CHURCH, matric. 29 April, 1830, aged 18; B.A. 1834, M.A. 1836, bar.-at-law, Lincoln's Inn, 1838, died 12 Aug., 1863. See Foster's *Peerage*, E. MANSFIELD.

Murray, Herbert Harley (C.B.), born at Bromley, Kent, 4s. George, bishop of Rochester. CHRIST CHURCH, matric. 20 Oct., 1847, aged 17; a student 1848-59, B.A. 1851, M.A. 1856, a student of Lincoln's Inn 1851, treasury remembrancer Ireland, commissioner and deputy-chairman of H.M. Customs. See Foster's *Peerage*, D. ATHOLE.

Murray, James Augustus Henry, of BALLIOL COLL., created M.A. 10 Nov., 1885, president Philological Society 1878-80, 1882-4, editor of *New English Dictionary;* B.A. London 1873, LL.D. Edinburgh, D.C.L. Durham. **[10]**

Murray, James Fitzgerald, B.A. TRINITY COLL., Dublin, 1827, 2s. John, of Dublin, arm. Incorp. from NEW INN HALL 3 March, 1842, aged 31; incumbent of St. Andrew's, Wells Street, London, 1847, until his death 22 Feb., 1862.

Murray, James Henry, 1s. James, of St. Andrew's, Manchester, arm. CHRIST CHURCH, matric. 19 Oct., 1859, aged 18.

Murray, Jeffreys Wilkins, o.s. William, of Swansea, co. Glamorgan, arm. ORIEL COLL., matric. 28 June, 1838, aged 18; B.A. 1844, M.A. 1848, vicar of Mylor, Cornwall, 1868-74, rector of St. Enoder 1874 until his death 4 June, 1883.

Murray, John, s. Donald, of St. George's, Bloomsbury, Middlesex, arm. CHRIST CHURCH, matric. 20 May, 1784, aged 18; B.A. 1788, M.A. 1791.

Murray, John, 1s. John, of London, arm. MAGDALEN COLL., matric. 29 Jan., 1870, aged 18; B.A. 1872, M.A. 1876, publisher. See *Eton School Lists.* **[15]**

Murray, John Hale, o.s. John, of Widcombe, near Bath, gent. WORCESTER COLL., matric. 13 Oct., 1824, aged 18; B.A. 1832.

Murray, John Hubert Plunkett, 2s. Sir Terence Aubrey, of Sydney, in Australia, knight. MAGDALEN COLL., matric. 15 Oct., 1881, aged 19; demy 1881-5, B.A. 1886, bar.-at-law, Inner Temple, 1886.

Murray, John Rigby, 2s. Benjamin Rigby, of Ardwick, Lancashire, arm. NON-COLL., matric. 17 Jan., 1880, aged 22; B.A. from TRINITY COLL. 1883, M.A. 1886, bar.-at-law, Inner Temple, 1884. See Foster's *Men at the Bar* & *Eton School Lists.*

Murray, Patrick, 3s. Patrick, of Ochtertyre, co. Perth, baronet. EXETER COLL., matric. 20 Oct., 1830, aged 18; a member of the Scottish Faculty of Advocates 1836. See Foster's *Baronetage.*

Murray, Reginald Temple Strange Clare Grenville Nugent Grenville-, 1s. Eustace Clare, of London, arm. CHRIST CHURCH, matric. 16 Oct., 1863, aged 17. **[20]**

Murray, Robert Evelyn Hay, 1s. Robert Hay, of Kestern, Kent, arm. CHRIST CHURCH, matric. 29 Nov., 1870, aged 19; B.A. & M.A. 1878, a student of Gray's Inn 1881. See Foster's *Peerage* & *Eton School Lists.*

Murray, Robert Hay, born at Bath, 3s. George, bishop of Rochester. CHRIST CHURCH, matric. 16 Oct., 1844, aged 18; B.A. 1848, M.A. 1853, of Godinton Park, Kent, J.P., high sheriff Surrey 1869, bar.-at-law, Lincoln's Inn, 1853. See Foster's *Men at the Bar* & *Eton School Lists.*

Murray, Robert Hepburne, 2s. William, of Eccles, co. Berwick, Scotland, gent. ST. ALBAN HALL, matric. 20 May, 1827, aged 24; B.A. 1830, M.A. 1835, bar.-at-law, Lincoln's Inn, 1836, died 13 May, 1853.

Murray, Samuel, s. Samuel, of Dublin, Ireland, doctor. HERTFORD COLL., matric. 1 Nov., 1805, aged 21.

Murray, Sydney George Wolfe-, 3s. James, of Cringletie, co. Peebles, arm. EXETER COLL., matric. 23 May, 1874, aged 19. **[25]**

Murray, Thomas, s. Thomas, of West Chester, Cheshire, gent. QUEEN'S COLL., matric. 18 Nov., 1743, aged 17; B.A. 1747, M.A. 1750.

Murray, Thomas Douglas, 1s. Thomas B., of London, cler. EXETER COLL., matric. 29 May, 1860, aged 18; B.A. 1864, bar.-at-law, Lincoln's Inn, 1866. See Foster's *Men at the Bar, St. Paul's School Reg.*, 322; & *Rugby School Reg.*

Murray, William, s. David, Viscount Stormont. CHRIST CHURCH, matric. 18 June, 1723, aged 18; B.A. 1727, M.A. 1730, bar.-at-law, Lincoln's Inn, 1730, bencher 1743, serjt.-at-law 1756, M.P. Boroughbridge 1742-56, solicitor-general 1742-54, attorney-general 1754-6, lord chief justice of King's Bench 1756-88, and created Lord Mansfield 8 Nov., 1756, also created Earl of Mansfield 31 Oct., 1776, & 1 Aug., 1792, ex-officio chancellor of the exchequer 1757 and 1767, and thrice refused the seals of that office, died 20 March, 1793, buried in Westminster Abbey. See Foster's *Peerage* & *Alumni West.*, 281.

Murray, William, s. William, of ——, co. Stirling, N.B., arm. ST. MARY HALL, matric. 18 June, 1762, aged 17; probably of Touchadam and Polmaise, co. Stirling, died 1814, father of William 1793.

Murray, (Sir) William (Bart.), s. Robert, of Edinburgh, Scotland, baronet. CHRIST CHURCH, matric. 14 June, 1786, aged 17; B.A. 1790, M.A. 1793, 9th baronet, of Clermont, co. Fife, rector of Lavington, Wilts, 1795, and of Lofthouse, Yorks, 1802, until his death 14 May, 1842. See Foster's *Baronetage* & *Alumni West.*, 421. **[30]**

Murray, William, s. Alexander, of Edinburgh, arm. (after a judge). CHRIST CHURCH, matric. 22 June, 1791, aged 17; B.A. 1795, M.A. 1798, of Henderland, co. Peebles, bar.-at-law, Lincoln's Inn, 1800, also a Scottish advocate, a member of the board for poor relief, Scotland, 1851. See *Alumni West.*, 433.

Murray, William, s. William, of Edinburgh, Mid Lothian, Scotland, arm. CHRIST CHURCH, matric. 7 June, 1793, aged 19; probably of Touchadam and Polmaise, co. Stirling.

Murray, William, Viscount Stormont, 'Parisus natus,' s. David, Earl of Mansfield. CHRIST CHURCH, matric. 2 June, 1794, aged 17; 3rd Earl of Mansfield, K.T. 1835, died 18 Feb., 1840. See Foster's *Peerage & Alumni West*, 432.

Murray, William, s. William, of Dublin, Ireland, gent. PEMBROKE COLL., matric. 15 Dec., 1804, aged 18; B.A. 1809, died 19 April, 1810.

Murray, William, 2s. Charles, of Minstead, Hants, arm. CHRIST CHURCH, matric. 2 April, 1827, aged 18.

Murray, William, 1s. John, of Edinburgh, arm. MAGDALEN COLL., matric. 23 Oct., 1885, aged 19.

Murray, William Charles, 1s. Charles Frederick, of London, arm. ORIEL COLL., matric. 23 Oct., 1884, aged 18; B.A. 1887. [5]

Murray, William David (Viscount Stormont), 1s. William, Earl of Mansfield. CHRIST CHURCH, matric. 14 April, 1823, aged 17; 4th earl, M.P. Aldborough 1830-1, Woodstock 1831-2, Norwich 1832-7, Perthshire 1837-40, a lord of the Treasury 1834-5. See Foster's *Peerage & Eton School Lists.*

Murray, William Frederick, 1s. George William, of Kinlet, Salop, cler. BRASENOSE COLL., matric. 5 Nov., 1860, aged 18; B.A. 1864, of the Indian Civil Service 1863, died 2 July, 1865, brother of George S. D. 1862.

Murrey, William, s. William, of London, pleb. PEMBROKE COLL., matric. 10 May, 1722, aged 16; B.A. 18 Feb., 1726-7.

Murrin, John, 'porter of Christ Church;' privilegiatus 15 March, 1724-5.

Murrow, Henry, s. Walter, of 'Marid,' (*i.e.*, Carmarthen), pleb. JESUS COLL., matric. 11 April, 1717, aged 19. [10]

Murrow, Lloyd Edwards, 1s. James, of Liverpool, gent. ST. JOHN'S COLL., matric. 14 Oct., 1829, aged 22; bible clerk 1829-32.

Murthwaite, George, s. Richard, of Ravenstone Dale, Westmoreland, pleb. QUEEN'S COLL., matric. 17 Dec., 1750, aged 17; taberdar 1754, B.A. 1754, M.A. 1757, fellow 1765, B.D. 1775, rector of Charlton-on-Otmoor 1784, until his death 27 Oct., 1798. See *O.H.S.*, ix., p. 45.

Murton, Charles Duncan, 2s. Walter, of London, arm. UNIVERSITY COLL., matric. 11 Oct., 1884, aged 18.

Murton, Rev. George, 2s. Lewis, of Sharples, Lancashire, gent. PEMBROKE COLL., matric. 25 Oct., 1876, aged 20; B.A. 1879, M.A. 1883.

Muscroft, James Wilson, 4s. — M., of Pontefract, Yorks, gent. MAGDALEN HALL, matric. 22 Nov., 1855, aged 19. [15]

Muscut, James, s. John, of Mitcham, Surrey, gent. MERTON COLL., matric. 11 Dec., 1725, aged 16; B.A. from CORPUS CHRISTI COLL. 1729, M.A. 26 Feb., 1732-3, rector of Staughton, Beds, dead before 1796.

Musgrave, Chardin, s. Christopher, of Edenhall, Cumberland, baronet. ORIEL COLL., matric. 3 March, 1739-40, aged 16; B.A. 1743, M.A. 1746, B. & D.D. 1757, provost 1757, until his death 8 Jan., 1768. See Foster's *Baronetage.*

Musgrave, Charles Buxton, 1s. Charles, of Whitkirk, Yorks, archdeacon of Craven. CHRIST CHURCH, matric. 1 Dec., 1847, aged 19; a student 1848-64, B.A. 1851, M.A. 1854, bar.-at-law, Lincoln's Inn, 1855, died 12 Oct., 1881. See *Rugby School Reg.*, 234.

Musgrave, Christopher, s. Christopher, of Middlesex, baronet. CHRIST CHURCH, matric. 20 May, 1731, aged 17; B.A. from ORIEL COLL. 28 Jan., 1734-5, M.A. 1737; fellow ALL SOULS' COLL., B.D. 1745, D.D. 1749, rector of Barking, Essex, died in 1780.

Musgrave, Christopher, s. Philip, of Kempton Park, Middlesex, baronet. ORIEL COLL., matric. 16 Feb., 1778, aged 18; father of the next named and of William 1822. See Foster's *Baronetage.* [20]

Musgrave, Christopher, s. Christopher, of Strathfieldsaye, Berks, arm. MAGDALEN COLL., matric. 11 July, 1818, aged 18; brother of William 1829. See Foster's *Baronetage & Eton School Lists.*

Musgrave, (Sir) Christopher John (Bart.), s. John Chardin, of London, baronet. ORIEL COLL., matric. 24 May, 1816, aged 18; B.A. from ST. ALBAN HALL 1821, M.A. 1823, 9th baronet, rector of Crundall, Kent, 1826, died 11 May, 1834.

Musgrave, Edward, fellow PETER HOUSE, Cambridge (M.A. 1749); incorp. 9 July, 1751 (B.A. from PEMBROKE COLL., Cambridge, 1745).

Musgrave, George, s. George, of Chatham, Kent, arm. ORIEL COLL., matric. 11 May, 1758, aged 18; of Kepier, co. Durham, of Borden, Kent, of Shillington, and of Apsleybury, Beds, M.P. Carlisle 1768-74, died s.p.l. 27 March, 1814, brother of Joseph 1749.

Musgrave, (Sir) George (Bart.), 3s. John Chardin, of Sunbury, Middlesex, baronet. UNIVERSITY COLL. matric. 21 May, 1819, aged 19; 10th baronet, died 29 Dec., 1872. See Foster's *Baronetage.* [25]

Musgrave, George, 3s. John, of Whitehaven, Cumberland, arm. ST. JOHN'S COLL., matric. 11 Oct., 1873, aged 17; B.A. 1876, M.A. 1881.

Musgrave, George Musgrave, s. George, of St. Mary-le-Bone, Middlesex, arm. BRASENOSE COLL., matric. 17 Feb., 1816, aged 17; B.A. 1819, M.A. 1822, of Shillington Manor, Beds, and of Borden, Hall, Kent, rector of Bexwell, Norfolk, 1835-8, vicar of Borden 1838-54, died 26 Dec., 1883, father of Horace; for list of his works see *Crockford.*

Musgrave, Hans, s. Christopher, of St. James's, London, baronet. ORIEL COLL., matric. 26 Oct., 1734, aged 17; lieut.-colonel in the army.

Musgrave, Horace, 1s. George, of Martock, Somerset, cler. ORIEL COLL., matric. 22 June, 1848, aged 18; of the Cape mounted rifles, died 11 Oct., 1851.

Musgrave, James, s. James, of Kirby, Yorks, cler. ST. JOHN'S COLL., matric. 27 June, 1727, aged 17; B.C.L. 1734, D.C.L. 1738, rector of Chinnor, Oxon, 1750, until his death 7 Nov., 1780. See *Gent.'s Mag.*, 543. [30]

Musgrave, (Sir) James (Bart.), s. James, of Chinnor, Oxon, doctor. ST. JOHN'S COLL., matric. 30 June, 1769, aged 17; B.A. 1773, M.A. 1777, 8th baronet, died 27 April, 1814.

Musgrave, (Sir) James (Bart.), s. James, of Barnsley, co. Gloucester, arm. CHRIST CHURCH, matric. 21 Oct., 1803, aged 18; B.A. 1807, 9th baronet, died 6 Dec., 1858. See Foster's *Baronetage & Eton School Lists.*

Musgrave, (Sir) John Chardin (Bart.), s. Philip, of Sunbury, Middlesex, baronet. ORIEL COLL., matric. 27 Jan., 1775, aged 18; created M.A. 14 Nov., 1777, 7th baronet, died 24 July, 1806.

Musgrave, Joseph, s. George of Chatham, Kent, gent. ORIEL COLL., matric. 26 Oct., 1749, aged 18; of Kepier, co. Durham, died 7 June, 1807, brother of George 1758.

Musgrave, (Sir) Philip (Bart.), s. Christopher, of St. James's, London, baronet. ORIEL COLL., matric. 8 Jan., 1732-3, aged 20; 6th baronet, M.P. Westmoreland 1741-7, died 5 July, 1795. See Foster's *Baronetage.* [35]

Musgrave, (Sir) Philip (Christopher, Bart.), s. John Chardin, of Marylebone, London, baronet. CHRIST CHURCH, matric. 17 March, 1813, aged 18; 8th baronet, M.P. Petersfield June, 1820, to March, 1835, Carlisle April, 1825, until his death 26 June, 1827. See Foster's *Baronetage & Eton School Lists.*

Musgrave, (Sir) Richard (Bart.), s. Richard, of Croston, Yorks, baronet. QUEEN'S COLL., matric. 31 May, 1721, aged 18; created M.A. 18 June, 1723, then 4th baronet, died in 1739.

Musgrave, (Sir) Richard (Bart.), s. Ric., of Aspatria, Cumberland, baronet. ORIEL COLL., matric. 16 Feb., 1742-3, aged 18; 5th baronet, died in June, 1755.

Musgrave, (Sir) Richard (Bart.), s. Christopher, of Lismore, Ireland, arm. ORIEL COLL., matric. 14 May, 1764, aged 18; bar.-at-law, King's Inns, 1774, M.P. Lismore 1778-1800, author of 'History of the Irish Rebellion,' created a baronet 2 Dec., 1782, died 6 April, 1818. See Foster's *Baronetage*.

Musgrave, (Sir) Richard (Bart.), s. Christopher, of Mount Rivers, co. Waterford, arm. TRINITY COLL., matric. 7 June, 1809, aged 18; B.A. 1812, 3rd baronet, M.P. co. Waterford 1831-2 & 1835-7, died 7 July, 1859. See Foster's *Baronetage*.

Musgrave, Samuel, s. Richard, of Washfield, Devon, gent. QUEEN'S COLL., matric. 11 May, 1749, aged 16; B.A. from CORPUS CHRISTI COLL. 27 Feb., 1753-4, M.A. 5 March, 1756, Radcliffe travelling fellow UNIVERSITY COLL., B. & D.Med. 1775, physician Devon and Exeter Hospital 1766, F.R.C.P. 1777, died 4 July, 1780. See Munk's *Roll*, ii. 312; & *O.H.S.*, ix. 91.

Musgrave, Thomas, s. James, of Gransden, co. Cambridge, cler. ST. JOHN'S COLL., matric. 1 July, 1735, aged 18; B.A. 1739, M.A. 14 Jan., 1742-3, B.Med. 1745, brother of James 1720.

Musgrave, Thomas, s. George, of West Sandford, Devon, arm. NEW COLL., matric. 26 Nov., 1759, aged 18. **[5]**

Musgrave, Thomas, 4s. John Chardin, of St. Marylebone, Middlesex, baronet. UNIVERSITY COLL., matric. 21 May, 1819, aged 17; drowned near Iffley 12 June, 1822.

Musgrave, Wenman Aubrey Wykeham, 1s. Aubrey Wenman Wykeham, of Chinnor, Oxon, arm. CHRIST CHURCH, matric. 27 May, 1858, aged 18; of Barnsley Park, co. Gloucester, J.P., and of Thame Park, Oxon, J.P., D.L., high sheriff 1884, assumed the additional surname of MUSGRAVE by royal licence in 1879.

Musgrave, William, s. Philip, of Kingerby, co. Lincoln, gent. MERTON COLL., matric. 16 July, 1715, aged 17; B.A. 29 Feb., 1719-20, M.A. 24 Jan., 1721-2.

Musgrave, William, s. William, of Exeter (city), gent. (D.Med.). BALLIOL COLL., matric. 5 April, 1742, aged 18; B.A. 1745 (? M.A. from PETER HOUSE, Cambridge, 1757, LL.D. 1764), a student of the Middle Temple 1746.

Musgrave, William, s. James, of Chinnor, Oxon, doctor. ST. JOHN'S COLL., matric. 3 July, 1781, aged 14; B.C.L. 1788, fellow, D.C.L. 1796, lecturer St. Giles's, Oxford, 1796, rector of Chinnor, Oxon, 1804-9, and of Kington Bagpuize, at his death 4 Nov., 1809, brother of James 1769. See *Rugby School Reg.*, 49. **[10]**

Musgrave, William, 2s. Christopher, of Beach Hill, Berks, arm. CHRIST CHURCH, matric. 17 June, 1822, aged 17; a student of Lincoln's Inn 1829, brother of Christopher 1818. See Foster's *Baronetage* & *Eton School Lists*.

Musgrave, William Anthony Byam, 1s. Anthony, of Antigua, East Indies, knight. BALLIOL COLL., matric. 20 Oct., 1875, aged 19; B.A. 1879, B.C.L. & M.A. 1883, bar.-at-law, Inner Temple, 1881. See Foster's *Men at the Bar*.

Musgrave, (Sir) William Augustus (Bart.), s. James, of St. Mary-le-Bone, London, arm. (after a baronet). CHRIST CHURCH, matric. 17 May, 1809, aged 17; B.A. 1813, M.A. 1815, 10th baronet, rector of Emmingtou, 1827-72, and of Chinnor, Oxon, 1816, until his death 30 Sep., 1875. See *Alumni West.*, 470.

Musgrove, Patrick, 'cook of New College;' privilegiatus 26 June, 1730.

Musgrove, William, 'cook of St. Edmund Hall;' privilegiatus 3 May, 1723. **[15]**

Musgrove, William, 'cook of University College;' privilegiatus 27 Jan., 1762.

Musgrove, William, 'second cook of Christ Church College;' privilegiatus 21 May, 1778.

Mushet, Robert Smith, 1s. Robert, of Aldgate, London, arm. NEW COLL., matric. 13 Oct., 1877, aged 18; B.A. 1880, bar.-at-law, Lincoln's Inn, 1883 See Foster's *Men at the Bar*.

Musselwhite, Thomas Ralph, 1s. Thomas, of Devizes, Wilts, gent. MAGDALEN HALL, matric. 26 Nov., 1846, aged 31; B.A. & M.A. 1870, rector of St. Andrew Aston, Salop, vicar of West Mersey, Essex, 1863.

Mussendine, Carteret, s. John, of "Hilibarn,' (*i.e.* Hillsboro', Ireland), arm. WADHAM COLL., matric. 4 June, 1717, aged 18; of Great and Little Oakley, Essex, assumed the name of LEATHES in lieu of his patronymic in 1727, M.P. Sudbury 1727-34, and 1741-7, Harwich 1734-41, died 1787. **[20]**

Mussendine, Pudsey, s. William, of Holywell, Oxford (city), gent. MAGDALEN COLL., matric. 22 July, 1732, aged 14; chorister 1725-35. See *Coll. Reg.*, i. 156.

Musson, Bartholomew, s. Thomas, of Wigston, co. Leicester, gent. ST. MARY HALL, matric. 10 April, 1752, aged 19; died rector of Baginton, Coventry, 6 Aug., 1791.

Mustard, Daniel, 2s. David, of East Donyland, Essex, arm. ST. EDMUND HALL, matric. 5 July, 1821, aged 21.

Mustard, David, 1s. David, of Manningtree, Essex, gent. ST. MARY HALL, matric. 25 Oct., 1866, aged 20; B.A. 1869, M.A. 1879, held various curacies since 1869.

Musters, Charles, s. Mundy, of Colwick, Notts, arm. CHRIST CHURCH, matric. 3 May, 1734, aged 18; brother of Mundy 1730. **[25]**

Musters, John, s. Mundy, of Colwick, Notts, arm. NEW COLL., matric. 1 Nov., 1770, aged 17; of Colwick, high sheriff Notts 1777, died 25 Feb., 1827, father of the next named.

Musters, John, s. John, of Grosvenor Square, London, arm. CHRIST CHURCH, matric. 20 Oct., 1794, aged 17; of Colwick, Notts, master of the Pytchley hunt, died 8 Sept. 1849. See *Eton School Lists*.

Musters, John Chaworth, 1s. John George, of Wiverton, Notts, arm. CHRIST CHURCH, matric. 15 May, 1856, aged 18; of Annesley Park and Wiverton Hall, Notts, J.P., D.L., high sheriff 1864.

Musters, John Patrick Chaworth, 1s. T. Chaworth, of Oxton Hall, Notts, arm. CHRIST CHURCH, matric. 25 Jan., 1878, aged 18. See *Eton School Lists*.

Musters, Mundy, s. Mundy, of Colwick, Notts, arm. CHRIST CHURCH, matric. 22 June, 1730, aged 17; of Colwick, high sheriff Notts, 1753, died 15 Jan., 1770, father of John 1770. **[30]**

Musters, William Musters, 2s. John, of Annesley, Notts, arm. CORPUS CHRISTI COLL., matric. 13 Oct., 1828, aged 18; B.A. 1833, rector of St. John's, Colwick, 1834, and of West Bridgeford, Notts, 1834, until his death 16 Oct., 1870.

Musurus, Constantine, Pasha (1867), created D.C.L. 4 June, 1856 (son of Paul Musurus, a native of Retimo, in Crete), Turkish envoy extraordinary, etc., at Athens 1840-8, at Vienna 1848-51, and at St. James's 1851-85, with rank of ambassador, received rank of Muchir with title of Pasha 1867, etc.

Mutel, Francis, s. Charles, of Potterne, Wilts, cler. HART HALL, matric. 30 Oct., 1722, aged 17; B.A. from TRINITY COLL. 1725.

Mutlow, Thomas Anthony, s. Thomas, of Gloucester (city), gent. MAGDALEN COLL., matric. 19 Oct., 1793, aged 17; chorister 1788-93, clerk 1793-8, B.A. 1797, minor canon Canterbury Cathedral 1803-28, rector of St. Andrew's with St. Mary's Breadman, Canterbury, 1803, rector of St. Martin's, and vicar of St. Paul's, Canterbury, 1808, vicar of Preston, near Wingham, Kent, 1828. See *Bloxam*, i. 204.

Mutlow, William Wilton, s. William, of Gloucester (city), gent. PEMBROKE COLL., matric. 6 Dec., 1808, aged 18; scholar 1812-3, B.A. 1812, fellow 1813-7, M.A. 1815, a minor canon of Gloucester Cathedral 1815, vicar of Brockthorp, co. Gloucester, 1816, and rector of Rudford 1828. **[35]**

Mutter, George, s. George, of Westminster, arm. ST. EDMUND HALL, matric. 15 May, 1795, aged 18; B.A. 1799, M.A. 1802, rector of Chillenden, Kent, 1807.

Mutukisna, Henry Francis, 2s. Philip Rodrigo, of Taffna, Isle of Ceylon, arm. ORIEL COLL., matric. 27 Jan., 1865, aged 37; bar.-at-law, Lincoln's Inn, 1865.

Myddelton, Charles Panton, s. Thomas, of Prescot, Lancashire, gent. BRASENOSE COLL., matric. 6 April, 1785, aged 18; B.A. 1789, M.A. 1791, perp. curate Heaton Norris, Lancashire, 1809, until his death 10 Sep., 1843. See *Manchester School Reg.*, ii. 67.

Myddelton, Foulk, s. John, of Henllan, co. Denbigh, gent. JESUS COLL., matric. 17 Feb., 1729-30, aged 17; B.A. 1733, M.A. 1736.

Myddelton, John, s. William, of Denbigh (town), arm. ORIEL COLL., matric. 12 March, 1742-3, aged 18. [5]

Myddelton, John, 3s. William Price, of Worcester (city), cler. LINCOLN COLL., matric. 10 June, 1847, aged 19.

Myddelton, Philip Pryce, 1s. 'William P.,' of Loughborough, co. Leicester, cler. QUEEN'S COLL., matric. 6 July, 1833, aged 17; clerk 1833-6, B.A. 1839.

Myddelton, Richard, s. John, of Chirk Castle, co. Denbigh, arm. ST. JOHN'S COLL., matric. 19 March, 1743-4, aged 18; of Chirk Castle, M.P. Denbigh, 1747-88, died in March, 1795.

Myddelton, Richard, s. Richard, of Westminster, arm. CHRIST CHURCH, matric. 15 Oct., 1781, aged 17.

Myddelton, Robert, s. William, of Denbigh, arm. ORIEL COLL., matric. 24 May, 1748, aged 19; B.A. 1752. [10]

Myddelton, Thomas, s. John, of Henllan, co. Denbigh, gent. JESUS COLL., matric. 17 March, 1725-6, aged 17, B.A. 1729; M.A. from ORIEL COLL. 1732.

Myddelton, Thomas, s. George, of Wrexham, co. Denbigh, gent. ALL SOULS' COLL., matric. 13 July, 1734, aged 18, B.A. 1738; M.A. from ST. MARY HALL 1741.

Myddelton, William, s. John, of Henllan, co. Denbigh, gent. BRASENOSE COLL., matric. 16 July, 1715, aged 17.

Myddelton, William Price, s. Philip Price, of Hereford (city), doctor. QUEEN'S COLL., matric. 9 Dec., 1809, aged 22; B.A. 1813, M.A. 1818, assumed the additional name of MYDDELTON, chaplain Worcester County Gaol at his death in 1830.

Myers, Charles, 2s. Charles, of Aigburth, Lancashire, arm. BALLIOL COLL., matric. 20 Oct., 1875, aged 18; B.A. 1879, M.A. 1882, vicar of Lynn Regis, Dorset, 1888. See *Eton School Lists.* [15]

Myers, Charles John, scholar TRINITY COLL., Cambridge, 1822, 5th wrangler and B.A. 1823, fellow 1825-31, M.A. 1826; adm. 'ad eundem' 7 June, 1853, vicar of Flintham, Notts, 1829, rector of Ruskington, co. Lincoln, 1832.

Myers, Ernest James, 2s. Frederick, of Keswick, Cumberland, cler. BALLIOL COLL., matric. 26 Jan., 1863, aged 18, exhibitioner 1863-8, B.A. 1867; fellow WADHAM COLL. 1868-83, M.A. 1871, librarian 1870, bar.-at-law, Inner Temple, 1874. See Foster's *Men at the Bar.*

Myers, Frederick, fellow of CLARE HALL, Cambridge, 1833-9 (B.A. 1833, M.A. 1836); adm. 'ad eundem' 25 June, 1847, incumbent of St. John's Church, Keswick, 1839, until his death 20 July, 1851, father of Ernest J., last named, and of Frederick W. H., the poet and essayist.

Myers, George. See MYRES.

Myers, John, s. William, of Mitcham, Surrey, arm. PEMBROKE COLL., matric. 10 July, 1765, aged 18; B.A. 1769, M.A. 1772, rector of Walton-on-the-Hill, and vicar of Witley-cum-Thursley, Surrey, died at Ewell 28 Aug., 1815. [20]

Myers, Rev. John Duncan, 1s. John Powell, of Tenby, co. Pembroke, arm. ST. JOHN'S COLL., matric. 15 Nov., 1848, aged 19; B.A. 1853, died at Tenby 14 April, 1855.

Myers, Rev. John Morrison, 2s. William, of Isle of Jamaica, arm. EXETER COLL., matric. 14 June, 1834, aged 17; B.A. from NEW INN HALL 1843, head-master of Jamaica Free School, Walton St. Anne's, at his death 2 Feb., 1861.

Myers, Skinner, s. William, of St. Lawrence Jewry, London, arm. ORIEL COLL., matric. 9 April, 1746, aged 17.

Myers, Streynsham Derbyshire, s. William, of Mitcham, Surrey, arm. PEMBROKE COLL., matric. 24 March, 1768, aged 16; demy MAGDALEN COLL. 1770-7, B.A. 1771, M.A. 1774, vicar of Mitcham 1779, until his death 17 Sep., 1824. See *Bloxam*, vi. 352.

Myers, Thomas, o.s. Thomas, of St. George's, Hanover Square, London, arm. ORIEL COLL., matric. 12 March, 1822, aged 18; scholar TRINITY COLL., Cambridge, 1829, a senior optime and B.A. 1830, M.A. 1833, Hulsean prizeman 1829, Norrisian prizeman 1832-4, bar.-at-law, Lincoln's Inn, 1831, vicar of Sheriff Hutton, Yorks, 1848-57, rector of Holy Trinity, Goodramgate, etc., York, 1857-67, perp. curate Westgate, Stanhope, co. Durham, 1867-70. See *Eton School Lists.* [25]

Myers, Thomas Borron, 1s. William Joseph, of Liverpool, Lancashire, arm. CHRIST CHURCH, matric. 15 Oct., 1845, aged 19; of Porters, Herts, J.P., died 3 March, 1882. See *Eton School Lists.*

Myers, William, s. William, of London, gent. LINCOLN COLL., matric. 10 June, 1731, aged 18; B.A. 1735.

Myers, William, s. William, of Mitcham, Surrey, arm. PEMBROKE COLL., matric. 10 June, 1763, aged 19; brother of Streynsham.

Myers, William, 2s. William, of Penyghent, Yorks (*sic*), arm. HERTFORD COLL., matric. 29 April, 1878, aged 22.

Myers, William Henry, 1s. Charles, of Aigburth, Lancashire, arm. BALLIOL COLL., matric. 15 Oct., 1873, aged 18; B.A. 1877, M.A. 1880, of Swanmore House, Hants, J.P., bar.-at-law, Inner Temple, 1881. See Foster's *Men at the Bar* & *Eton School Lists.*

Myers, William Isaac, s. John, of Edenham, co. Lincoln, cler. LINCOLN COLL., matric. 18 April, 1792, aged 17; B.A. 1796, curate of Eltham, Kent, at his death in 1842. [31]

Myerscough, Samuel, 4s. John, of Salford, Lancashire, gent. MAGDALEN HALL, matric. 20 Oct., 1873, aged 19; B.Mus. (HERTFORD COLL.) 1881.

Myles, Alington, s. Alington, of Crumwar, co. Gloucester, cler. PEMBROKE COLL., matric. 24 March, 1715-6, aged 18; B.A. 1719.

Mylius, Frederick John, 1s. Frederick Henry, of Edgbaston, co. Warwick, cler. WORCESTER COLL., matric. 22 Nov., 1879, aged 19.

Mylne, George Francis, 1s. James, of Edinburgh, arm. BALLIOL COLL., matric. 13 May, 1859, aged 18; B.A. 1864. [35]

Mylne, James William, 1s. James, of Glasgow, Scotland, cler. BALLIOL COLL., matric. 25 March, 1820, aged 19; B.A. 1824, M.A. 1826, bar.-at-law, Lincoln's Inn, 1827, a Metropolitan commissioner of lunacy.

Mylne, John Eltham, 2s. James William, of Eltham, Kent, arm. CORPUS CHRISTI COLL., matric. 19 Oct., 1863, aged 19; B.A. 1867, B.C.L. & M.A. 1872, bar.-at-law, Lincoln's Inn, 1869, died in 1882.

Mylne, Louis George, 1s. Charles, of Paris, France, arm. CORPUS CHRISTI COLL., matric. 21 Oct., 1862, aged 19, B.A. 1866, M.A. 1870; tutor KEBLE COLL. 1871-6, created D.D. 7 March, 1876, bishop of Bombay 1876.

Mylne, Robert Scott, 1s. Robert William, of Westminster, gent. ORIEL COLL., matric. 13 Oct., 1873, aged 19; B.A. 1877, B.C.L. & M.A. 1880, chaplain and lecturer in divinity Pembroke College 1885. See *Eton School Lists.*

Mylne, William John Home, 2s. Robert William, of London, gent. ST. MARY HALL, matric. 25 Oct., 1875, aged 16; B.A. from QUEEN'S COLL. 1880, M.A. 1882. See *Eton School Lists.*

Mynors, Arthur Clinton Baskerville-, 2s. Robert, of Evancoyd, co. Radnor, arm. CHRIST CHURCH, matric. 20 May, 1875, aged 18.

Mynors, Aubrey Baskerville, 2s. Walter Baskerville, of Llanwarne, co. Hereford, cler. ORIEL COLL., matric. 26 Jan., 1884, aged 18; B.A. 1887.

Mynors, Edmund Baskerville, 2s. Peter, of Evencoyd, co. Radnor, arm. BALLIOL COLL., matric. 27 May, 1841, aged 18; B.A. from ST. MARY HALL 1845, M.A. 1848, rector of Ashley, Wilts. See *Eton School Lists.*

Mynors, Henry Walter Baskerville-, 1s. Walter Baskerville, of Llanwarne, co. Hereford, cler. BRASENOSE COLL., matric. 8 June, 1876, aged 18; B.A. 1879. [5]

Mynors, Peter Rickards, s. Peter, of Treago (parish), St. Welnard, co. Hereford, arm. MERTON COLL., matric. 22 March, 1808, aged 20; of Treago, co. Hereford, and Evancoyd, co. Radnor, high sheriff 1825, died 20 Jan., 1866.

Mynors, Robert, 1s. Robert Edward Eden, of Hartshorne, co. Derby, arm. UNIVERSITY COLL., matric. 7 May, 1835, aged 18; B.A. 1839, M.A. 1842, of Weatheroak, co. Worcester, J.P., D.L., bar.-at-law, Inner Temple, 1842. See Foster's *Men at the Bar* & *Rugby School Reg.*, 164.

Mynors, Robert Baskerville Rickards, 1s. Peter Rickards, of Bath, arm. CHRIST CHURCH, matric. 11 May, 1837, aged 17; B.A. 1841, of Treago, co. Hereford, J.P., D.L., and of Evancoyd, co. Radnor, high sheriff, 1856, a student of the Inner Temple 1841. See *Eton School Lists.*

Mynors, Robert Edward Eden, s. Robert, of Birmingham, co. Warwick, arm. UNIVERSITY COLL., matric. 19 June, 1806, aged 17; B.A. 1810, M.A. 1813, of Weatheroak, co. Worcester, a student of Lincoln's Inn 1806, died 15 Dec., 1842.

Mynors-Baskerville, Thomas Baskerville Mynors, s. Peter, of Treago, co. Hereford, arm. TRINITY COLL., matric. 22 Nov., 1808, aged 18; of Clyro Court, co. Radnor, assumed the additional surname and arms of BASKERVILLE by royal licence 1818, M.P. Herefordshire 1841-7, died 9 Sep., 1864. See *Eton School Lists.* [10]

Mynors, Thomas Baskerville, 4s. Peter Rickards, of Old Radnor, co. Radnor, arm. CHRIST CHURCH, matric. 19 May, 1853, aged 18; of Barland, co. Radnor.

Mynors, Thomas Hassall, 2s. Robert Edward Eden, of King's Norton, co. Worcester, arm. WADHAM COLL., matric. 11 May, 1838, aged 19; B.A. 1842, vicar of St. Patrick, Tamworth, co. Warwick.

Mynors, Walter Baskerville, 3s. Peter Rickards, of Evancoyd, co. Radnor, arm. ORIEL COLL., matric. 14 May, 1845, aged 18; B.A. 1850, rector of Llanwarne Ross, co. Hereford. See *Eton School Lists.*

Mynors, Willoughby Baskerville, 1s. Robert Baskerville, of Evancoyd, co. Radnor, arm. CHRIST CHURCH, matric. 31 May, 1873, aged 18.

Myott, Nathaniel, s. Thomas, of Greenwich, Kent, gent. MAGDALEN HALL, matric. 2 May, 1794, aged 26. [15]

Myres, George, s. John, of Bracelet, Lancashire, pleb. BRASENOSE COLL., matric. 6 April, 1745, aged 18; B.A. 1748.

Myres, William Miles, 1s. John James, of Preston, Lancashire, arm. BRASENOSE COLL., matric. 13 June, 1857, aged 18; B.A. 1861, M.A. 1864, perp. curate St. Paul's, Preston, 1867-79, vicar of Swanbourne, Bucks, 1879.

Myrtle, Frederick Septimus, 7s. William, of West Derby, Lancashire, gent. CORPUS CHRISTI COLL., matric. 27 Oct., 1881, aged 19.

Mytton, Rev. Benjamin, s. Thomas, of Shipton, Salop, arm. PEMBROKE COLL., matric. 24 Oct., 1787, aged 20; died at Shipton 6 Nov., 1793.

Mytton, Charles, s. Richard, of Halston, Salop, arm. WADHAM COLL., matric. 19 March, 1718-9, aged 16; B.A. from TRINITY COLL. 1724, M.A. 28 Jan., 1725-6, of Chester, father of the next named. [20]

Mytton, Charles, s. Charles, of Chester (city), arm. CHRIST CHURCH, matric. 27 March, 1760, aged 16; rector of Eccleston at his death 5 Sep., 1801, father of Charles next named.

Mytton, Charles. BRASENOSE COLL., 1788. See THORNYCROFT.

Mytton, Devereux, s. Devereux, of Guilsfield, co. Montgomery, gent. PEMBROKE COLL., matric. 23 Feb., 1770, aged 16; B.A. 1773, M.A. 1776, B.Med. 1781, D.Med. 1781, F.R.C.P. 1783, died 30 Sep., 1841. See Munk's *Roll.*, ii. 332.

Mytton, Devereux, s. John, of Liverpool, Lancashire, gent. BRASENOSE COLL., matric. 9 Nov., 1797, aged 18; B.A. 1801, M.A. 1804, rector of Llandyssil, co. Montgomery, 1807. See *Eton School Lists.*

Mytton, Henry, s. Thomas, of Cleobury, Salop, gent. BALLIOL COLL., matric. 19 Feb., 1719-20, aged 17; of Shipton, died in 1757. [25]

Mytton, James, s. Richard, of Guilsfield, co. Montgomery, arm. ST. JOHN'S COLL., matric. 14 April, 1739, aged 18.

Mytton, John, s. John, of Halston, Salop, arm. CHRIST CHURCH, matric. 27 May, 1785, aged 17; of Halston, died 8 Sep., 1798.

Mytton, John. BRASENOSE COLL., 1827. See THORNYCROFT.

Mytton, Richard, s. Richard, of Garth, co. Montgomery, arm. HERTFORD COLL., matric. 11 Oct., 1742, aged 19.

Mytton, Richard, s. Devereux, of Guilsfield, co. Montgomery, gent. PEMBROKE COLL., matric. 2 Nov., 1769, aged 18; B.A. 1773, bar.-at-law, Inner Temple, 1779, died 8 April, 1802. [30]

Mytton, Thomas, s. Henry, of Shipton, Salop, arm. BALLIOL COLL., matric. 18 May, 1754, aged 17; created M.A. 16 Dec., 1758, bar.-at-law, Middle Temple, 1761, died in July, 1787, father of Benjamin.

Mytton, Thomas, s. Thomas, of Shipton, Salop, gent. BALLIOL COLL., matric. 31 Jan., 1767, aged 24; of Cleobury North, Salop, bar.-at-law, Lincoln's Inn, 1769, died 2 Jan., 1830.

Nabb, Richard, s. John, of Halifax, Yorks, gent. BRASENOSE COLL., matric. 14 April, 1753, aged 18; exhibitioner 1753-5. See *Manchester School Reg.*, i. 37.

Nagel, David Henry, 1s. Henry, of Dundee, gent. TRINITY COLL., matric. 17 Oct., 1882, aged 19; scholar 1882, B.A. 1886.

Naghten, Arthur Robert, y.s. Thomas, of Titchfield, Hants, arm. WORCESTER COLL., matric. 18 Oct., 1848, aged 19; B.A. 1853, M.A. 1855, M.P. Winchester 1874-80, died 7 Aug., 1881. See *Eton School Lists.*

Naghten, Frederick, 3s. Thomas, of Tichfield, Hants, arm. ORIEL COLL., matric. 28 Nov., 1839, aged 17; scholar CORPUS CHRISTI COLL. 1839-45, B.A. 1843, died in 1845.

Nairn, Henry, s. William, of Berwick St. Leonard, Wilts, cler. TRINITY COLL., matric. 24 May, 1754, aged 18. [5]

Nairn, William Edward, 1s. William, of Widcombe, Bath, Somerset, arm. QUEEN'S COLL., matric. 21 Jan., 1830, aged 17; scholar LINCOLN COLL. 1830-4, B.A. 1833.

Naish, Richard, s. James, of Newark-upon-Trent, Notts, cler. WADHAM COLL., matric. 21 Oct., 1724, aged 17; B.A. 1728, M.A. 1731, rector of Batcombe-cum-Spargrove, Somerset, 1741.

Naish, Thomas, 1s. Thomas, of Shaftesbury, arm. LINCOLN COLL., matric. 16 Nov., 1837, aged 18; B.A. 1845, curate of Sible Hedingham, Essex, 1865, until his death 17 April, 1868.

Nall, Rev. George Herbert, 1s. George, of Yarmouth, gent. QUEEN'S COLL., matric. 15 May, 1880, aged 19; scholar 1880-5, B.A. 1884, classical master Westminster School 1886.

Nance, James, s. James, of St. Creed, Cornwall, gent. EXETER COLL., matric. 23 March, 1771, aged 26.

Nance, James Trengrove, 3s. James, of Eccleshall, co. Stafford, gent. NEW COLL., matric. 14 Oct., 1870, aged 18, scholar 1870-5, B.A. 1875; fellow ST. JOHN'S COLL. 1876-87, M.A. 1877, B.D. 1881, lecturer 1877, tutor 1878-86, dean of arts 1879, vice-president 1881, dean of divinity 1885, rector of Polstead, Essex, 1886. [10]

Nance, John, s. John, of Warlegan, Cornwall, arm. EXETER COLL., matric. 14 March, 1714-5, aged 18; B.A. 1718.

Nance, John, s. William, of Boxley, Kent, cler. WORCESTER COLL., matric. 20 June, 1794, aged 17; B.A. 1798, M.A. 1801, B. & D.D. 1813, rector of Old Romney 1810, and of Hope, All Saints, 1827, until his death 21 Feb., 1853.

Nance, William, s. James, of St. Creed, Cornwall, gent. EXETER COLL. matric. 17 May, 1768, aged 22; LL.B. from PETER COLL., Cambridge, 1779, vicar of Boxley, Kent, 1775, rector of Harbledown and Great Chart 1780, until his death in 1814.

Nanfan, James, s. George, of London, arm. WORCESTER COLL., matric. 15 April, 1736, aged 18; B.A. 1739. [15]

Nanjulian, Rev. Samuel, s. Samuel, of Uzella, Cornwall, gent. TRINITY COLL., matric. 14 Nov., 1778, aged 16; B.A. 1783, died at Plymouth Dock in Dec., 1786.

Nankivell, Edward, s. Thomas, of St. Agnes, Cornwall, gent. BALLIOL COLL., matric. 19 Feb., 1772, aged 17; B.A. 1776, died vicar of St. Stithian's in 1829, aged 75.

Nankivell, John Robert, 3s. John Thomas, of Truro, Cornwall, gent. EXETER COLL., matric. 17 April, 1845, aged 18; B.A. 1849, M.A. 1852, chaplain of Crediton, Devon, 1867, until his death 5 Nov., 1883.

Nankivell, Thomas, s. Benjamin, of St. Agnes, Cornwall, gent. PEMBROKE COLL., matric. 14 Nov., 1785, aged 19; B.A. 1790, vicar of St. Just 1814, until his death in 1825.

Nanney, Edward, s. John, of Dolgelly, co. Merioneth, pleb. JESUS COLL., matric. 31 Oct., 1720, aged 20. [20]

Nanney, Hugh, s. Lewis, of Dolgelly, co. Merioneth, gent. JESUS COLL., matric. 21 March, 1765, aged 17; B.A. 1769, M.A. 1772.

Nanney, Hugh John Ellis, 1s. Owen Jones Ellis, of Llanystwyndwy, co. Carnarvon, arm. ORIEL COLL., matric. 27 Jan., 1864, aged 18; a student of the Inner Temple 1866.

Nanney, Rev. Richard, s. Richard, of Clynog, co. Carnarvon, cler. JESUS COLL., matric. 26 May, 1757, aged 18; B.A. 1761, M.A. 1763, died in 1812.

Nanney, Robert, s. Lewis, of Dolgelly, co. Merioneth, arm. JESUS COLL., matric. 10 April, 1764, aged 18 (? died rector of Llanymowddy, and of Lwyn, co. Merioneth, 10 Dec., 1818).

Nanson, Arthur Cecil, 3s. John, of Carlisle, arm. NON-COLL., matric. 18 Oct., 1880, aged 19; B.A. from TRINITY COLL. 1884. [25]

Nanson, William, 1s. John, of Carlisle, Cumberland, arm. TRINITY COLL., matric. 17 Oct., 1868, aged 19; B.A. 1873.

Nanton, Edward William, 1s. John George, of Island of St. Vincent, arm. UNIVERSITY COLL., matric. 10 Dec., 1840, aged 18; a student of Lincoln's Inn 1841. See *Eton School Lists.*

Naper, James Lenox, 1s. James Lenox William, of Wellesbourne, co. Warwick, arm. CHRIST CHURCH, matric. 16 Oct., 1844, aged 18; of Loughcrew, co. Meath, high sheriff 1853. See Foster's *Peerage*, B. SHERBORNE; & *Eton School Lists.*

Naper, James Lenox William, s. William, of Cheltenham, co. Gloucester, arm. CHRIST CHURCH, matric. 26 April, 1809, aged 18; of Loughcrew, co. Meath, M.P. Weobley 1813-8, died 2 Sep., 1868. See Foster's *Peerage*, B. SHERBORNE; & *Eton School Lists.*

Naper, Robert, s. Robert, of Old Castle, co. Meath, Ireland, arm. CHRIST CHURCH, matric. 26 Jan., 1743-4, aged 19. See Foster's *Peerage*, B. SHERBORNE.

Naper, William, s. James Dutton (formerly NAPER or NAPIER), of Sherborne, co. Gloucester, arm. UNIVERSITY COLL., matric. 13 July, 1768, aged 19; of Loughcrew, co. Meath, brother of James, 1st Lord Sherborne, resumed the name of NAPER, died 28 Nov., 1791. See Foster's *Peerage*.

Napier, Arthur Sampson, 1s. George Webster, of Wilmslow, Cheshire, gent. EXETER COLL., matric. 23 May, 1874, aged 20, scholar 1874-8, B.A. 1878, M.A. 1881, fellow MERTON COLL. 1885, professor English language and literature 1885. See *Boase*, 167.

Napier, Bertram Harold, 1s. William Donald, of London, arm. CHRIST CHURCH, matric. 15 Oct., 1880, aged 19.

Napier, Charles Frederick, 2s. Hon. William, of London, arm. KEBLE COLL., matric. 19 Oct., 1880, aged 18; B.A. 1883, bar.-at-law, Middle Temple, 1885. [5]

Napier, Charles Walter Albyn, 2s. Gerard Martin Berkeley, of Penward, Somerset, arm. CHRIST CHURCH, matric. 19 May, 1836, aged 18; B.A. 1840, vicar of Evercreech, Somerset, 1843-50, rector of Wiston, Sussex, 1850.

Napier, Edward, s. Thomas, of Tintenhull, Somerset, gent. EXETER COLL., matric. 8 May, 1739, aged 18; B.A. 1742 (as NAPPER), father of Edward next named.

Napier, Edward, s. Edward, of Tintenhull, Somerset, cler. QUEEN'S COLL., matric. 11 July, 1764, aged 17 (? rector of Sutton Waldron, Dorset, 1782, until his death in 1816, aged 67). See Hutchins' *Dorset*, ii. 185, 779.

Napier, Edward (Berkeley), s. Andrew, of Westminster, arm. CHRIST CHURCH, matric. 11 Feb., 1778, aged 18; of Pylle House, Somerset, bar.-at-law, Middle Temple, 1783, died in 1798, father of Gerard Martin Napier 1809.

Napier, Edward Berkeley, 3s. Edward Berkeley, of Shepton Mallet, Somerset, arm. MERTON COLL., matric. 18 Oct., 1880, aged 18. [10]

Napier, Rev. George, 7s. Charles Walter Albyn, of Wiston, Sussex, cler. ST. MARY HALL, matric. 2 Feb., 1878, aged 18; B.A. 1881.

Napier, (Sir) Gerard (Bart.), s. Nathaniel, of Critchell, Dorset, baronet. BALLIOL COLL., matric. 11 May, 1719, aged 18; 5th baronet, died 25 Oct., 1759.

Napier, (Sir) Gerard (Bart.), s. Gerard, of Middle Marsh Hall, Dorset, baronet. TRINITY COLL., matric. 13 April, 1758, aged 18; 6th baronet, M.P. Bridport, 1761, until his death 25 Jan., 1765.

Napier, Gerard Martin Berkeley, s. Edward, of Pylle House, Somerset, arm. TRINITY COLL., matric. 16 Oct., 1809, aged 17; of Pennard House, Somerset, died 13 May, 1820, father of Charles 1836.

Napier, Hon. Henry Alfred, s. Francis, of Wilton Lodge, Roxburgh, Scotland, Baron Napier. CHRIST CHURCH, matric. 23 Jan., 1817, aged 19; B.A. 1820, M.A. 1822, rector of Swyncombe, Oxon, 1826, until his death 20 Nov., 1871. [15]

Napier, (Sir) John (Bart.), s. Archibald, of Luton Hoo, Beds. BALLIOL COLL., matric. 19 Jan., 1721-2, aged 16; 6th baronet, died in 1747.

Napier, Right Hon. Sir Joseph, Bart., created D.C.L. 7 June, 1853 (son of William Napier, of Belfast, merchant), B.A. TRINITY COLL., Dublin, 1825, M.A. 1828, LL.B. & LL.D. 1851, bar.-at-law, King's Inns, Easter, 1831, Q.C. 1844, attorney-general Ireland 1852, M.P. Dublin University 1848-58, lord chancellor of Ireland 1858-9, vice-chancellor of Dublin University 1867-82, P.C., created a baronet 9 April, 1867, died 9 Dec., 1882. See Foster's *Baronetage*.

Napier, Richard, s. George, of Celbridge, co. Kildare, Ireland, arm. ORIEL COLL., matric. 17 May, 1806, aged 18, B.A. 1810; fellow ALL SOULS' COLL. 1811-18, M.A. 1814, bar.-at-law, Lincoln's Inn, 1817, died in Jan., 1868.

Napier, Robert Cornelis, Lord Napier, of Magdala, created D.C.L. 26 June, 1878 (s. Major Charles Frederick Napier, R.A.), field-marshal in the army 1882, colonel commandant royal engineers 1874, commander-in-chief Bombay 1865-9, and in India 1870-5, commanded the Abyssinian Expedition 1867-8, governor of Gibraltar 1876-82, constable of the Tower 1886, created a peer 17 July, 1868, G.C.S.I. 16 Sep., 1867, G.C.B. 27 April, 1868. See Foster's *Peerage*.

Napier, Walter John, 2s. George Webster, of Wimslow, Cheshire, arm. CORPUS CHRISTI COLL., matric. 23 Oct., 1877, aged 20; B.A. 1880, B.C.L. & M.A. 1884, bar.-law, Lincoln's Inn, 1881. See Foster's *Men at the Bar* & *Rugby School Reg.* [20]

Napier, Wyndham, s. Nath., of Grange, Dorset, baronet. BRASENOSE COLL., matric. 12 Oct., 1723, aged 18; B.A. 1727, brother of Gerard 1719.

Napleton, John, s. John, of Pembridge, co. Hereford, cler. BRASENOSE COLL., matric. 22 March, 1755, aged 16; B.A. 1758, M.A. 1761, B. & D.D. 1789, rector of Would, Northants, 1777, canon of Hereford 1789, and chancellor of the diocese, master of the hospital at Ledbury, rector of Stoke Edith, and vicar of Lugwardine, co. Hereford, and prælector in divinity Hereford Cathedral 1810, died 9 Dec., 1817. See *Manchester School Reg.*, i. 153.

Napleton, John, o.s. John Charles, of Munderfield, co. Hereford, cler. WORCESTER COLL., matric. 16 Oct., 1872, aged 21; perp. curate Christ Church, Coventry, 1881-4, rector of Wymington 1885.

Napleton, John Charles, 9s. Timothy, of Powderham, Devon, cler. WORCESTER COLL., matric. 13 May, 1829, aged 18; bible clerk 1830-2, B.A. 1833, perp. curate Hatfield, co. Hereford, 1844-58, of Grendon Bishop 1849-58, of All Saints, Lambeth, 1858, until his death 13 April, 1867.

Napleton, Timothy, s. Marsh, of Tenbury, co. Worcester, gent. BRASENOSE COLL., matric. 4 April, 1772, aged 15, B.A. 1775; M.A. from TRINITY COLL., Cambridge, 1785, rector of Powderham, Devon, 1799, and of North Bovey 1802, until his death 16 Jan., 1816. See *Manchester School Reg.*, i. 153.

Napper, Campion, o.s. Campion, of Sutton-on-the-Forest, Yorks, cler. ST. ALBAN HALL, matric. 20 Oct., 1856, aged 21. [25]

Napper, Edward, 1s. Edward, of Ifold, Sussex, gent. PEMBROKE COLL., matric. 12 Feb., 1823, aged 18.

Nares, Edward, y.s. George, of London, equitis. CHRIST CHURCH, matric. 22 March, 1779, aged 16, B.A. 1783; fellow MERTON COLL. 1788-90, M.A. 1789, B. & D.D. 1814, Bampton lecturer 1805, regius professor modern history 1813-41, rector of Biddenden, Kent, 1798, until his death 20 Aug., 1841. See *Alumni West.*, 405.

Nares, Edward Robert, 1s. Edward, of Biddenden, Kent, doctor. MERTON COLL., matric. 2 Nov., 1821, aged 17; postmaster 1822-5, B.A. 1826, rector of Wittersham, and vicar of Brenzett, Kent, died 17 May, 1865.

Nares, Hon. Sir George, created D.C.L. 7 July, 1773 (son of George, of Albury, Oxon, gent.), educated at Magdalen College School; admitted to NEW COLL., bar.-at-law, Inner Temple, 1741, king's serjt.-at-law 1759, M.P. Oxford 1768 to Jan., 1771, and recorder, a judge of Court of Common Pleas, Jan., 1771 (knighted 27th), until his death 20 July, 1786, father of Edward 1779, and of George Strange 1776. [30]

Nares, George Strange, s. George, of London, equitis. CHRIST CHURCH, matric. 5 June, 1776, aged 17; captain 70th regiment of foot, died in the West Indies 1794. See *Alumni West.*, 405.

Nares, John Bever, s. John, of Llandwywydd, co. Cardigan, arm. MERTON COLL., matric. 8 June, 1803, aged 16.

Nares, Robert, s. James, of York (city), doctor. CHRIST CHURCH, matric. 30 May, 1771, aged 18; B.A. 1775, M.A. 1778, vicar of Easton Mauduit, Northants, 1782, vicar of Great Doddington 1784, usher Westminster School 1786-8, preacher at Lincoln's Inn 1788 to 1803, assistant librarian British Museum 1795, librarian MS. department until 1807, rector of Sharnford, co. Leicester, 1798-9, preb. of St. Paul's 1798, canon residentiary of Lichfield 1798, archdeacon of Stafford 1801, vicar of Dalby, co. Derby, vicar of St. Mary, Reading, 1805-18, rector of All Hallows, London Wall, 1818-29, F.S.A. 1795, F.R.S. 1804, vice-president Linnean Society 1823, died 23 March, 1829, author of 'A Glossary of Words,' etc. See *Alumni West.*, 395.

Nares, William Owen, 1s. Owen Alexander, of Haverfordwest, co. Pembroke, cler. JESUS COLL., matric. 21 Oct., 1878, aged 19; scholar 1878-80, B.A. 1882.

Narracott, John, s. Christopher, of Dittisham, Devon, arm. EXETER COLL., matric. 16 Oct., 1732, aged 18.

Nash, Alexander, o.s. Alexander, of Poonah, East Indies, arm. BRASENOSE COLL., matric. 19 May, 1864, aged 18; B.A. 1867, M.A. 1871, rector of Quedgley, co. Gloucester, since 1876.

Nash, Alfred Moses, 3s. Moses, of Twyford, Berks, gent. QUEEN'S COLL., matric. 22 Oct., 1870, aged 18; scholar 1870-4, B.A. 1873, M.A. 1877. **[5]**

Nash, Rev. Andrew John, 2s. George Augustus, of Edmonton, Middlesex, gent. ST. JOHN'S COLL., matric. 20 Oct., 1825, aged 18; died 24 April, 1888.

Nash, Arthur George, 2s. Frederick John, of Tulse Hill, London, gent. ST. EDMUND HALL, matric. 19 Oct., 1882, aged 20.

Nash, Augustus, 2s. Joseph Haynes, of Clifton, co. Gloucester, arm. TRINITY COLL., matric. 17 Oct., 1870, aged 18; B.A. 1874, bar.-at-law, Lincoln's Inn, 1876. See Foster's *Men at the Bar.*

Nash, Augustus John, s. Samuel, of Enstone, Oxon, cler. LINCOLN COLL., matric. 12 Nov., 1806, aged 18; exhibitioner until 1814.

Nash, Cecil William, 2s. George Lloyd, of Tolpuddle, Dorset, cler. KEBLE COLL., matric. 16 Oct., 1876, aged 19; B.A. 1881, M.A. 1883, incumbent of Christ Church, Kincardine O'Neil, Aberdeenshire, 1885.

Nash, Clifford Evans Fowler, 1s. David William, of Cheltenham, co. Gloucester, arm. PEMBROKE COLL., matric. 7 June, 1855, aged 18; B.A. 1859, M.A. 1862, bar.-at-law, Lincoln's Inn, 1862. See Foster's *Men at the Bar.* **[11]**

Nash, Edward Henry, 1s. Henry Fleetwood, of Slough, Bucks, arm. TRINITY COLL., matric. 14 Oct., 1872, aged 18; B.A. 1876, a solicitor in London. See *Rugby School Reg.*

Nash, Edward Henry, o.s. Henry Allden, of Banbury, cler. NON-COLL., matric. 16 Oct., 1886, aged 18.

Nash, Edward Jackson, 5s. George, of Weston, Notts, cler. LINCOLN COLL., matric. 23 Oct., 1880, aged 17; scholar 1880-4; B.A. 1885, M.A. 1887.

Nash, Edward Rowland, 4s. John, of Langley, Bucks, arm. LINCOLN COLL., matric. 19 Oct., 1872, aged 19. **[15]**

Nash, Francis, s. Francis, of Wallingford, Berks, gent. JESUS COLL., matric. 15 Oct., 1720, aged 15; B.A. 1724, M.A. 1728.

Nash, Rev. Francis Lochee, 3s. George, of Weston, Notts, cler. NEW COLL., matric. 10 Oct., 1873, aged 18; scholar 1873-8, B.A. 1877, M.A. 1880.

Nash, Rev. Francis Peel, 7s. Robert Seymour, of Old Sodbury, co Gloucester, cler. EXETER COLL., matric. 22 Oct., 1880, aged 19; B.A. 1884, M.A. 1887.

Nash, George, s. George, of Morkley, co. Worcester, gent. MAGDALEN HALL, matric. 9 July, 1725, aged 19. See Nash's *Worcestershire*, i. 327, & Supplement 25.

Nash, George, s. Richard, of Kempsey, co. Worcester, arm. CHRIST CHURCH, matric. 15 Feb., 1733-4, aged 15; B.A. 1737, M.A. 1740, died s.p. **[20]**

Nash, George, s. Salwey, of North Piddle, co. Worcester, cler. UNIVERSITY COLL., matric. 21 March, 1733-4, aged 18, B.A. 1737; M.A. from MAGDALEN COLL. 1741, brother of Salwey 1717.

Nash, George Lloyd, 4s. Thomas, of Lancing, Sussex, cler. CHRIST CHURCH, matric. 15 Oct., 1845, aged 18; student 1848-53, B.A. 1849, M.A. 1852, preb. of Salisbury 1869, vicar of Tolpuddle, Dorset, 1852. See *Eton School Lists.*

Nash, George Richard, s. Samuel, of Great Tew, Oxon, cler. LINCOLN COLL., matric. 13 April, 1810, aged 19.

Nash, Henry Allden, o.s. Charles, of London, gent. NON-COLL., matric. 29 April, 1881, aged 43, father of Edward Henry 1886.

Nash, Henry John, B.A. from WORCESTER COLL., 16 May, 1812 (*Acts Book*). **[25]**

Nash, Jacob, s. John, of Stanton Wick, Somerset, gent. PEMBROKE COLL., matric. 8 July, 1809, aged 32.

Nash, James s. Salwey, of Merthley, co. Worcester, cler. MAGDALEN HALL, matric. 1 March, 1721-2, aged 18; B.A. 1725.

Nash, James, s. Salwey, of Droitwich, co. Worcester, cler. WORCESTER COLL., matric. 30 June, 1752, aged 18; B.A. 1756 (? rector of St. Mary, Witton, and St. Andrew, Droitwich, 1775).

Nash, James (Ezekiel), 1s. James Ezekiel, of St. Augustine, Bristol, gent. TRINITY COLL., matric. 3 May, 1826, aged 18; B.A. 1830, M.A. 1833, vicar of St. Peter, Clifton Wood, 1855-72, and of Elberton, co. Gloucester, 1872-80, died 13 May, 1884.

Nash, Rev. James Okey, 2s. Thomas, of Pernambuco, arm. HERTFORD COLL., matric. 19 Oct., 1881, aged 18; scholar 1880-5, B.A. 1886. **[30]**

Nash, James Palmer, 1s. James, of Bristol, Somerset, cler. CHRIST CHURCH, matric. 22 May, 1861, aged 19; B.A. 1865, M.A. 1874, curate of Hedge-end, Hants, 1874-6, vicar 1876-86, rector of Bishopstoke, Hants, 1886.

Nash, John, s. John, of Tarrington, co. Hereford, cler. CHRIST CHURCH, matric. 21 March, 1718-9, aged 17; B.A. 1722, M.A. 1725.

Nash, Joseph William, s. John, of Tewksbury, co. Gloucester, gent. ST. MARY HALL, matric. 21 Nov., 1776, aged 31; B.A. 1780, M.A. 1783.

Nash, Nigel Fowler, 3s. David William, of Bedford Square, London, arm. PEMBROKE COLL., matric. 31 Jan., 1862, aged 19; B.A. 1865, M.A. 1868, held various curacies 1866-75, vicar of Aston Cantelow, co. Worcester, 1876-85, of Cotterstock, Northants, 1885-6, and of Geddington since 1886.

Nash, Okey, s. Joseph, of Chesham, Bucks, gent. MAGDALEN HALL, matric. 25 June, 1803, aged 24; B.A. 1812, M.A. 1814, vicar of Throwley, Kent, 1846, until his death 9 Feb., 1862. **[35]**

Nash, Richard, 1s. Gawen, of Walberton, Sussex, arm. BALLIOL COLL., matric. 18 May, 1738, aged 17; of Walberton, died in 1776.

Nash, Richard (Russell), s. Richard, of co. Worcester, arm. CHRIST CHURCH, matric. 4 June, 1730, aged 18; B.A. 1734, M.A. 1737, B. & D.D. 1751, preb. of Winchester 1742, until his death 18 Oct., 1757. See *Alumni West.*, 300.

Nash, Richard Skillicorne, s. Thomas, of Cheltenham, co. Gloucester, doctor. WORCESTER COLL., matric. 10 Oct., 1797, aged 18; B.A. 1801.

Nash, Salwey, s. Salwey, of North Piddle, co. Worcester, cler. MAGDALEN HALL, matric. 13 April, 1717, aged 17; B.A. 1721, father of James 1752, brother of George 1734, and James 1722.

Nash, Samuel, s. Samuel, of St. Mary-le-Bone, Middlesex, gent. ST. ALBAN HALL, matric. 24 March, 1790, aged 28. See *Gent.'s Mag.*, 1829, ii. 571.

Nash, Slade, s. Slade, of Bewdley, co. Worcester, arm. WORCESTER COLL., matric. 23 June, 1775, aged 17; B.A. 1779, M.A. 1791. **[41]**

Nash, Spencer Hampden, 6s. Charles, of Clifton, co. Gloucester, gent. BALLIOL COLL., matric. 18 Oct., 1881, aged 18; exhibitioner 1881, until his death in 1885.

Nash, (Sir) Stephen, s. Stephen, of Bristol, Somerset, arm. ORIEL COLL., matric. 2 March, 1780, aged 16; created M.A. 12 Nov., 1783, and D.C.L. 27 June, 1788, sheriff of Bristol, knighted 18 Aug., 1786, died about 1796.

Nash, Thomas, s. George, of Martley, co. Worcester, arm. UNIVERSITY COLL., matric. 27 March, 1735, aged 18; B.A. 1738.

Nash, Thomas, s. James, of New Town, co. Worcester, gent. WORCESTER COLL., matric. 6 July, 1761, aged 17; B.A. 1765, M.A. 1768, B.D. 1778, D.D. 1793, rector of Whitcombe, co. Gloucester, 1769, vicar of Ensham and Chelmarsh 1778, rector (and patron) of Salford 1800, until his death in 1826.

Nash, Thomas, 1s. William, of Stratford, Lancashire, arm. BALLIOL COLL., matric. 24 April, 1863, aged 18; exhibitioner 1863-8, B.A. 1867, M.A. 1870, bar.-at-law, Lincoln's Inn, 1872, died 28 Jan., 1885. [5]

Nash, Thomas Arthur, 3s. John, of Langley, Bucks, arm. LINCOLN COLL., matric. 19 Oct., 1867, aged 17; B.A. 1871, bar.-at-law, Lincoln's Inn, 1874. See Foster's *Men at the Bar.*

Nash, Thomas Augustus, 3s. William, of Newington Butts, Surrey, gent. WORCESTER COLL., matric. 25 Oct., 1853, aged 20; B.A. 1860, M.A. 1861, vicar of St. Philip's, Heigham, Norfolk, 1868-77, and of St. Paul's, Balls Pond, London, 1877-80, rector of Lowestoft 1880.

Nash, Rev. Thomas Gifford, o.s. Thomas Frederick, of Great Chesterford, Essex, gent. CHRIST CHURCH, matric. 12 Jan., 1883, aged 32; B.A. 1885.

Nash, Treadway (Russel), s. Richard, of Kemsey, co. Worcester, arm. WORCESTER COLL., matric. 14 July, 1740, aged 15; B.A. 1744, M.A. 20 Jan., 1746-7, B. & D.D. 1758, of Bevere, co. Worcester, F.S.A., rector of Leigh and of Strensham, co. Worcester, 1797, published 'Collections for a History of Worcestershire,' died 26 Jan., 1811.

Nash, William James, 3s. William, of Bowdon, Cheshire, arm. NEW COLL., matric. 20 Jan., 1877, aged 19; B.A. 1880. See *Rugby School Reg.* [10]

Nason, Charles, s. Charles, of Lymington, Hants, pleb. MAGDALEN HALL, matric. 22 Oct., 1718, aged 18; B.A. 1722.

Nason, Edward, s. Stephen, of Aston Cantlow, co. Warwick, cler. MAGDALEN HALL, matric. 27 Nov., 1776, aged 16; B.A. 1780, M.A. 1783.

Nason, John, s. John, of Headley, Surrey, cler. EXETER COLL., matric. 25 June, 1737, aged 17.

Nason, Stephen, s. Thomas, of Warwick (town), pleb. ST. MARY HALL, matric. 13 April, 1739, aged 20, B.A. 1742; M.A. from TRINITY COLL., Cambridge, 1749, vicar of Anstey, co. Warwick, 1750, vicar of Stratford-on-Avon with Bishopstone Castle (chapel), and rector of Clifford Chambers, co. Gloucester, 1776, his widow died early in 1799.

Nassau, Charles, Prince of, Count of Saarbruck and Saarwerde, etc., major-general of the Forces of the elector palatine of the Rhine, created D.C.L. 18 June, 1756 (son of William Henry, Prince of Nassau-Usingen), married 26 Dec., 1734, Christine Wilhelmine, daughter of Duke John William, of Saxe-Eisenach, and died 21 June, 1775, aged 63. [15]

Nassau, John Augustus, 2s. Frederick, of Windsor, Berks, arm. MAGDALEN COLL., matric. 24 June, 1819, aged 19. See *Eton School Lists.*

Naters, Edward Herbert, 2s. Charles John, of Horsforth, Oxon, cler. NON-COLL., matric. 13 Oct., 1884, aged 20.

Naters, Henry Trewhitt, 3s. Ralph, of Sandiford, near Newcastle-on-Tyne, gent. MAGDALEN HALL, matric. 22 June, 1843, aged 19.

Nation, Charles Codrington, y.s. William, of St. David's, Exeter, arm. ST. JOHN'S COLL., matric. 13 April, 1872, aged 18; B.A. 1875, M.A. 1880, vicar of All Saints, Pontefract, 1881-4, rector of Halesowen, co. Warwick, 1884.

Nation, Francis, s. Thomas, of Sanford Arundell, Somerset, gent. ORIEL COLL., matric. 24 Oct., 1724, aged 18. [20]

Nation, William Hamilton Codrington, 1s. William, of St. David's, Exeter, gent. ORIEL COLL., matric. 20 Oct., 1860, aged 17.

Natt, Anthony, s. Anthony, of Stepney, Middlesex, pleb. QUEEN'S COLL., matric. 5 May, 1733, aged 18; B.A. from WADHAM COLL. 3 Feb., 1736-7, fellow, M.A. 1739, rector of Standon, Herts, 1747, and of Netteswell, Essex, 1766, until his death 7 Nov., 1801. See *Robinson*, 63.

Natt, John, s. Nathan, of Netteswell, Essex, cler. ST. JOHN'S COLL., matric. 28 June, 1795, aged 16; B.A. 1799, M.A. 1803, B.D. 1808, scholar & fellow 1795-1831, librarian 1822, bursar 1824, vice-president 1826, lecturer of St. Giles's, Oxford, 1809, rector of St. Sepulchre's, London, 1829, until his death 12 Feb., 1843. See *Robinson*, 157.

Natteress, Joseph, s. Joseph, of Linton, Yorks, gent. QUEEN'S COLL., matric. 13 Sep., 1774, aged 18; B.A. 1778, M.A. 1785.

Naylor, Charles, 1s. Richard, of Gloucester (city), arm. ST. MARY HALL, matric. 14 Dec., 1822, aged 25. [25]

Naylor, Edmund, s. Richard, of Wigan, Lancashire, pleb. LINCOLN COLL., matric. 29 Oct., 1715, aged 19; B.A. 1719.

Naylor, Henry Paul Todd-, 3s. William Todd, of Hartford Grange, Cheshire, gent. UNIVERSITY COLL., matric. 16 Oct., 1880, aged 19; of the Indian Civil Service 1880.

Naylor, John, 1s. James, of Stanningley, Yorks, pleb. MAGDALEN HALL, matric. 3 Feb., 1863, aged 24; B.Mus. 5 Feb., 1863, D.Mus. 1872.

Naylor, North, s. Thomas, of Ashburton, co. Derby, cler. TRINITY COLL., matric. 15 Feb., 1772, aged 16.

Naylor, Oliver, s. Fermor, of Tawstock, Devon, cler. CORPUS CHRISTI COLL., matric. 18 June, 1722, aged 16, B.A. 1726; M.A. from KING'S COLL. Cambridge, 1746, vicar of Owthorne, Yorks, 1731, sinecure rector of Milton, co. Cambridge, 1747, rector of Morpeth, Northumberland 1746, until his death in 1775. [30]

Naylor, Robert, s. Christopher, of Turnham Green, Middlesex, cler. LINCOLN COLL., matric. 21 April, 1785, aged 17; of the Classical Academy, College Green, Bristol, died 21 Dec., 1822, his father head-master of King's College, Canterbury, died 4 April, 1816, aged 78.

Naylor, Samuel, o.s. Thomas, of St. Anne's, Westminster, gent. QUEEN'S COLL., matric. 1 July, 1831, aged 22; bar.-at-law, Middle Temple, 1845.

Naylor, Thomas Beagly, o.s. Thomas, of Weymouth, Dorset, gent. MAGDALEN HALL, matric. 29 May, 1827, aged 21; B.A. 1831, incumbent Episcopal Church, St. Andrew, Sydney (N.S.W.), died 22 Oct., 1849. See *Gent.'s Mag.*, 1850, i. 219.

Naylor, Rev. William Smethurst, 1s. William, of Longton, Lancashire, gent. WORCESTER COLL., matric. 19 Oct., 1882, aged 19; B.A. 1885.

Nazirsky, Dimitri Volkanoff, o.s. Dimitri Volkanoff, of Yemboly, in Bulgaria. NON-COLL., matric. 11 Oct., 1879, aged 25. [35]

Neal, Alfred Ernest, 3s. William, of London, arm. MAGDALEN COLL., matric. 24 Jan., 1874, aged 20.

Neal, Jeffery, 'common-room man Jesus College;' privilegiatus 19 May, 1778.

Neald, Charles, s. John, of Guildford, Surrey, gent. MERTON COLL., matric. 2 July, 1805, aged 18.

Neale, Charles, s. George, of Gloucester (city), pleb. EXETER COLL., matric. 13 Dec. 1735, aged 18; B.A. from CHRIST CHURCH 1739, rector of Harescombe with Pitchcombe, co. Gloucester 1741.

Neale, Charles, 3 & y.s. John, of Boddington, co. Gloucester, cler. QUEEN'S COLL., matric. 15 Oct., 1828, aged 24; B.A. 1832.

Neale, Edward, s. George Vansittart, of Calcutta, East Indies, arm. NEW COLL., matric. 20 May, 1788, aged 18; B.C.L. 1796, of Allesley Park, co. Warwick, assumed the surname of NEALE in lieu of his patronymic by royal licence 14 Nov., 1803, rector of Taplow 1803, until his death 21 Jan., 1850.

Neale, Edward Forster, o.s. Edward Pott, of Frittenden, Kent, cler. ST. JOHN'S COLL., matric. 30 June, 1845, aged 16; scholar and fellow 1845-55, B.C.L. 1851, bar.-at-law, Lincoln's Inn, 1853, died 4 March, 1855. See *Robinson*, 262.

Neale, Edward Henry, s. John, of Honiton, Devon, cler. ST. MARY HALL, matric. 14 Dec., 1812, aged 22.

Neale, Edward Vansittart, o.s. Edward, of Bath, Somerset, cler. ORIEL COLL., matric. 14 Dec., 1827, aged 17; B.A. 1831, M.A. 1836, of Allesley Park, co. Warwick, bar.-at-law, Lincoln's Inn, 1837. See Foster's *Men at the Bar*. [5]

Neale, Francis, s. John, of Staverton, co, Gloucester, cler. TRINITY COLL., matric. 4 July, 1816, aged 17; B.A. 1820, M.A. 1824, bar.-at-law, Lincoln's Inn, 1825.

Neale, Frederick, 3s. James, of Aylesbury, Bucks, gent. ST. ALBAN HALL, matric. 3 Dec., 1846, aged 40; B.A. 1850, M.A. 1853, vicar of Wootton, Beds, 1852, until his death 12 May, 1872.

Neale, John, s. Robert, of St. Martin's, Oxford (city), gent. BALLIOL COLL., matric. 14 May, 1719, aged 16; B.A. 1723, M.A. 1725.

Neale, John, s. John, of Tollerton, Notts, arm. MERTON COLL., matric. 9 March, 1748-9, aged 19.

Neale, John, s. James, of Henley, Oxon, cler. WORCESTER COLL,. matric. 15 Dec., 1775, aged 20; rector of Mary-le-Port, Bristol, 1792-1841, and vicar of Staverton with Boddington, co. Gloucester, 1794, until his death 26 Oct., 1841. [10]

Neale, John Alexander, 2s. Robert, of Chipping Sodbury, co. Gloucester, gent. QUEEN'S COLL., matric. 30 May, 1868, aged 19; exhibitioner 1869-71, B.A. 1873, B.C.L. & M.A. 1881, D.C.L. 1886, a student of Lincoln's Inn 1871.

Neale, John Blagdon, s. John, of Staverton, co. Gloucester, cler. PEMBROKE COLL., matric. 24 March, 1803, aged 16.

Neale, John Mason, of TRINITY COLL., Cambridge (B.A. 1840, M.A. 1845); adm. 'ad eundem' 24 June, 1846, (s. Cornelius, fellow St. John's College, Cambridge), founder of the Ecclesiological Society at Cambridge, incumbent of Crawley, Sussex, 1843, warden of Sackville College, East Grinstead, 1846, founded the East Grinstead Sisterhood, D.D. Hartford University 1861, composed the hymn 'Jerusalem the Golden,' died 6 Aug., 1866.

Neale, Pendock, s. John, of Tollerton, Notts, arm. MERTON COLL., matric. 16 Sep., 1743, aged 15.

Neale, Pendock, s. John, of Sibston, co. Leicester, cler. MAGDALEN COLL., matric. 26 Oct., 1775, aged 18; created D.C.L. 30 June, 1813, then of Tollerton, assumed the name of BARRY in lieu of NEALE, and became PENDOCK BARRY, of Rocleston Manor, Notts, J.P., high sheriff 1784, died 13 March, 1833. [15]

Neale, Pendock Barry, s. Pendock, of Tollerton, Notts, arm. MAGDALEN COLL., matric. 25 June, 1801, aged 18; created M.A. 26 June, 1805 (? became PENDOCK BARRY at the same time as his father). See *Eton School Lists*.

Neale, Philip Harris, 2s. Philip, of near Melbourne, gent. NON-COLL., matric. 24 April, 1877, aged 20.

Neale, Richard, s. Richard, of North Leach, co. Gloucester, pleb. QUEEN'S COLL., matric. 17 Feb., 1736-7, aged 14; B.A. 1741.

Neale, Robert, s. Robert, of Corsham, Wilts, arm. NEW COLL., matric. 4 April, 1755, aged 18; created M.A. 8 July, 1763.

Neale, Robert, s. James, of Henley, Oxon, cler. ST. EDMUND HALL, matric. 26 April, 1771, aged 19. [20]

Neale, Thomas, fellow of CLARE HALL, Cambridge (B.A. 1738, M.A. 1742); incorp. 8 July, 1756 (? died rector of Tollerton, Notts, and Sibston, co. Leicester, 29 March, 1782).

Neale, Thomas, 1s. Jonathan William, of Bromsgrove, co. Worcester, gent. WORCESTER COLL., matric. 19 Oct., 1886, aged 19; scholar 1885.

Neale, Thomas Tarver Mulliner, s. Thomas, of Ipswich, Suffolk, doctor. QUEEN'S COLL., matric. 6 May, 1784, aged 18; B.C.L. 1791.

Neale, Walter Erskine, 3s. Erskine, of Melton, Suffolk, cler. ST. JOHN'S COLL., matric. 29 June, 1857, aged 17; scholar 1857-60, B.A. 1861, of the Indian Civil Service 1861, magistrate and collector Muttra 1882, Bareilly 1883. See *Robinson*, 311.

Neale, William, s. William, of St. Albans, Herts, gent. BALLIOL COLL., matric. 3 April, 1723, aged 18; B.A. 1726, M.A. 1729. [25]

Neale, William, s. William, of Fenny Compton, co. Warwick, gent. MAGDALEN HALL, matric. 2 Dec., 1745, aged 18.

Neate, Arthur, scholar TRINITY COLL., Cambridge, 1825, senior optime 1826, B.A. 1827, 1s. Thomas, of Puddington, Beds, cler. Incorp. from TRINITY COLL. 5 (or 8) May, 1828, aged 25; M.A. 10 June, 1829, rector of Alvescot with Shilton, Oxon, 1829, until his death in 1870.

Neate, Arthur Edmond, o.s. Edmond, of Nantes, Brittany, arm. ST. MARY HALL, matric. 22 Oct., 1867, aged 27.

Neate, Charles, 2s. Thomas, of Adstock, Bucks, cler. LINCOLN COLL., matric. 2 June, 1824, aged 17, scholar 1826-8, B.A. 1828; fellow ORIEL COLL. 1828-79, M.A. 1830, senior treasurer 1845, lecturer in law and modern history 1856, Drummond professor political economy 1857-62, bar.-at-law, Lincoln's Inn, 1832, M.P. Oxford 1857 and 1863-8, died senior fellow 7 Feb., 1879, aged 72.

Neate, Rowland, 1s. Rowland, of London, arm. ORIEL COLL., matric. 31 Jan., 1868, aged 18. [30]

Neate, Thomas Arthur, 1s. Arthur, of Alvescot, Oxon, cler. ST. MARY HALL, matric. 1 Nov., 1865, aged 20; B.A. from ST. PETER'S COLL., Cambridge, 1873, bar.-at-law, Inner Temple, 1877. See Foster's *Men at the Bar*.

Neate, Walter, 3s. Arthur, of Alvescot, Berks, cler. NEW COLL., matric. 14 Oct., 1870, aged 18; B.A. 1874, M.A. 1887, rector of Alvescot 1878.

Neave, Francis Digby Spencer, 2s. William Augustus, of Neilgherry Hills, East Indies, arm. CHRIST CHURCH, matric. 31 May, 1860, aged 18; B.A. 1863. See Foster's *Baronetage*.

Neave, Henry Lyttelton, s. Thomas, of St. Andrew's, London, baronet. CHRIST CHURCH, matric. 24 Oct., 1816, aged 18; B.A. 1820, M.A. 1823, vicar of Epping, Essex, 1824, until his death 4 Aug., 1873. See *Eton School Lists*.

Neave, John Alexander, o.s. John, of London, gent. NON-COLL., matric. 10 April, 1880, aged 26. [35]

Neave, Richard, s. Richard, of Hackney, Middlesex, arm. CHRIST CHURCH, matric. 22 Oct., 1793, aged 19; bar.-at-law, Lincoln's Inn, 1800, deputy paymaster of the forces 1812, secretary and registrar Chelsea Hospital 1816, died 13 Jan., 1858. See Foster's *Baronetage*.

Neave, (Sir) Richard Digby (Bart.), s. Thomas, of St. Bartholomew's, London, arm. CHRIST CHURCH, matric. 28 Oct., 1812, aged 18; B.A. from ST. MARY HALL 1815, 3rd baronet, a student of Lincoln's Inn 1814, died 10 March, 1868.

Neave, Sheffield, s. Thomas, of London, baronet. CHRIST CHURCH, matric. 5 Dec., 1817, aged 18; B.A. 1821, a director of the Bank of England, governor 1857-8, died 24 Sep., 1868. See Foster's *Baronetage* & *Eton School Lists.*

Neave, Sheffield Henry Morier, 1s. Sheffield, of London, arm. BALLIOL COLL., matric. 16 Oct., 1872, aged 18; B.A. 1877, of Mill Green Park, Essex. See Foster's *Baronetage* & *Eton School Lists.*

Neave, Rev. William Alexander, 1s. William Augustus, of Salem, East Indies, arm. CHRIST CHURCH, matric. 31 May, 1860, aged 19; died 2 Oct., 1879.

Neaves, Charles, 1s. Charles, of Edinburgh, Scotland, arm. BALLIOL COLL., matric. 26 March, 1858, aged 18; B.A. from MAGDALEN HALL 1862.

Neblett, John, s. John, of Isle of Barbados, gent. EXETER COLL., matric. 16 Oct., 1759, aged 21. [5]

Neck, Aaron, s. Gregory Andrews, of St. Mary Church, Devon, gent. WADHAM COLL., matric. 23 March, 1787, aged 18; B.A. 1791, perp. curate Kings Kerswell, Devon, 1832, until his death 4 Oct., 1852.

Nedham, Charles, 5s. William, of Widcombe, near Bath, arm. EXETER COLL., matric. 15 June, 1843, aged 17; colonel in the army, etc. See Foster's *Peerage*, E. KILMOREY.

Nedham, Hampson, s. William, of Isle of Jamaica, arm. CHRIST CHURCH, matric. 4 Nov., 1724, aged 19; of Mount Olive, Jamaica, bar.-at-law, Inner Temple, 1730, died in Jamaica April, 1752, father of William D. 1748.

Nedham, Henry, s. Robert, of Spanish Town, Isle of Jamaica, arm. WORCESTER COLL., matric. 10 Oct., 1723, aged 15; died s.p. in Jamaica.

Nedham, John, s. William, of Hanover Square, London, arm. ORIEL COLL., matric. 2 Dec., 1793, aged 19, B.A. 1797; incorp. Cambridge University 1803, M.A. from ST. PETER'S COLL. 1803, rector of Oumby, co. Lincoln. [10]

Nedham, Robert, s. Robert, of Isle of Jamaica, arm. TRINITY COLL., matric. 30 May, 1723, aged 19; of Waresley Park, Hunts, of Howberry, Oxon, and of Morne Park, co. Down, M.P. Old Sarum 1734-41, died in 1762.

Nedham, William Dandy, s. Hampson, of London, arm. CHRIST CHURCH, matric. 25 June, 1748, aged 17; of Mount Olive, Jamaica, died in 1811.

Nedham, Rev. William Francis Longden, 1s. William Robert, of Dublin, arm. EXETER COLL., matric, 2 June, 1857, aged 18; B.A. 1861, died 7 June, 1864. See Foster's *Peerage*, E. KILMOREY.

Neech, Rev. Henry, 1s. George, of Windsor, Bucks, arm. MERTON COLL., matric. 11 May, 1819, aged 18; postmaster 1819-22, B.A. 1822, died 1 Feb., 1823. See *Eton School Lists.*

Need, Samuel William. TRINITY COLL., 1825. See WELFITT. [15]

Need, Thomas, 2s. John, of Mansfield, Notts, arm. UNIVERSITY COLL., matric. 5 May, 1826, aged 18; B.A. 1830.

Needham, Edward Leay, 1s. Edward Moon, of Birmingham, arm. BALLIOL COLL., matric. 25 Jan., 1871, aged 20; scholar 1870-5.

Needham, Francis Charles, Viscount Newry, 1s. Francis, Viscount Newry and Morne. CHRIST CHURCH, matric. 31 May, 1860, aged 17; B.A. 1864, M.A. 1867, 3rd Earl of Kilmorey, M.P. Newry 1871-4, a representative peer, Ireland, 1882. See Foster's *Peerage.*

Needham, George Arthur, 4s. Hon. Francis Henry. NON-COLL., matric. 25 May, 1872, aged 19; B.A. from KEBLE COLL. 1876.

Needham, Frederick, s. Thomas, of Cheapside, London, gent. PEMBROKE COLL., matric. 3 Dec., 1748, aged 18. [20]

Needham, (Hon.) Henry Colville, 2s. Francis Jack, Viscount Newry and Morne. CHRIST CHURCH, matric. 22 Oct., 1862, aged 18; B.A. 1865. See Foster's *Peerage*, B. KILMOREY; & *Eton School Lists.*

Needham, John, s. John, of Madresfield, co. Worcester, pleb. ST. MARY HALL, matric. 21 Oct., 1719, aged 19.

Needham, Peter, s. Peter, of Kings Somborne, Hants, cler. HART HALL, matric. 21 March, 1715-6, aged 17; B.A. from NEW COLL. 20 Feb., 1719-20.

Needham, Theophilus Henry Hastings, s. Thomas, of Lutterworth, co. Leicester, pleb. ALL SOULS' COLL., matric. 7 June, 1785, aged 17; B.A. 1789.

Neeld, Algernon William, 1s. John, of London, baronet. CHRIST CHURCH, matric. 18 May, 1864, aged 17; B.A. 1868, M.A. 1877. See Foster's *Baronetage.*

Neeld, Audley Dallas, 2s. John, of Avondale, Somerset, baronet. BRASENOSE COLL., matric. 13 June, 1867, aged 18; B.A. 1870, a student of the Inner Temple 1869, major 2nd life guards. [25]

Neell, John, s. John, of Sheviock, Cornwall, gent. EXETER COLL., matric. 13 March, 1728-9, aged 17.

Negus, John, s. John, of London, gent. ST. JOHN'S COLL., matric. 1 July, 1735, aged 16; B.A. 1739, M.A. 9 Feb., 1742-3, B.D. 1748, D.D. 1752, vicar of Great Staughton, Hunts, 1754, died 4 Sep., 1785. See *Robinson*, 64.

Neilder, John, s. John, of St. Stephen's (Saltash), Cornwall, cler. BALLIOL COLL., matric. 13 March, 1748-9, aged 18; B.A. 1753.

Neilson, Daniel Arthur, 2s. Daniel, of Liverpool, arm. ST. JOHN'S COLL., matric. 23 March, 1865, aged 19; B.A. 1870. [30]

Neilson, Horatio, 3s. John, of St. Augustine's, Bristol, arm. ST. EDMUND HALL, matric. 11 Oct., 1819, aged 18; B.A. 1823, rector of North Witham, co. Lincoln, 1846, until his death 23 Oct., 1860.

Neilson, John, s. John, of Bristol (city), gent. ST. EDMUND HALL, matric. 11 Oct., 1809, aged 22; B.A. 1813, M.A. 1816.

Neilson, John Backhouse, 4 & y.s. William, of Liverpool, arm. BALLIOL COLL., matric. 16 Dec., 1828, aged 18; B.A. from NEW INN HALL 1834.

Neilson, William, s. William, of Liverpool, Lancashire, arm. BRASENOSE COLL., matric. 10 Oct., 1817, aged 17; B.A. 1821. See *Eton School Lists.*

Neish, Edward William, 6s. William, of London, arm. UNIVERSITY COLL., matric. 13 Oct., 1883, aged 18. [35]

Neish, George Watson, 1s. William, of Dundee, co. Forfar, arm. CORPUS CHRISTI COLL., matric. 19 Jan., 1869, aged 19; B.A. 1871.

Nelmes, Richard, s. Thomas, of Bristol (city), gent. EXETER COLL., matric. 18 Feb., 1778, aged 18; B.A. 1782.

Nelson, Arthur, 2s. Edward Hamilton, of London, cler. ST. JOHN'S COLL., matric. 21 Oct., 1879, aged 19.

Nelson, Charles Meikle, o.s. Charles, of Dunbar, co. Haddington, D.Med. HERTFORD COLL., matric. 14 Oct., 1884, aged 19.

Nelson, Chris., s. Thomas, of Orton, Westmoreland, cler. QUEEN'S COLL., matric. 13 Oct., 1724, aged 17; brother of William 1726. [40]

Nelson, Edward Hamilton, of TRINITY COLL., Dublin (B.A. 1841, M.A. 1852); adm. 'ad eundem' 21 June, 1860, vicar of St. Stephen the Martyr, Marylebone, 1849, father of Ernest B. 1870.

Nelson, Edward John, 2s. Maurice Horace, of Sandford, Wilts, arm. HERTFORD COLL., matric. 22 Oct., 1886, aged 19.

Nelson, Ernest Beauchamp, 1s. Edward Hamilton, of Highgate, Middlesex, cler. CORPUS CHRISTI COLL., matric. 19 Oct., 1870, aged 19; B.A. 1875, M.A. 1877, bar.-at-law, Inner Temple, 1857. See Foster's *Men at the Bar.*

Nelson, George Henry, 1s. Richard, of Southowram, near Halifax, Yorks, gent. QUEEN'S COLL., matric. 18 April, 1864, aged 18; B.A. 1868, M.A. 1870.

Nelson, Rev. George Mawson, s. Richard, of Old Hutton, Westmoreland, gent. QUEEN'S COLL., matric. 3 July, 1812, aged 19, scholar 1815-19, B.A. 1816; fellow MAGDALEN COLL. 1819-33, M.A. 1819, B.D. 1826, junior dean of arts 1824, bursar 1825, died 20 Dec., 1859.

Nelson, Hector, 5s. John, of Rotherhithe, Surrey, gent. ST. JOHN'S COLL., matric. 30 June, 1834, aged 18; bible clerk 1834-8, B.A. 1838, M.A. 1842, preb. of Lincoln 1865, and principal of Lincoln Training College. See *Robinson*, 219.

Nelson, Horace Bertram, 5s. Thomas James, of Upper Clapton, Essex, gent. WORCESTER COLL., matric. 16 Oct., 1879, aged 18; B.A. 1883, B.C.L. & M.A. 1886, bar.-at-law, Gray's Inn, 1886.

Nelson, Horatio, Viscount, created D.C.L. 30 July, 1802, fell on board the *Victory* at the battle of Trafalgar 21 Oct., 1805. See Foster's *Peerage*. [5]

Nelson, James Henry, 3s. Thomas Wright, of London, arm. BRASENOSE COLL., matric. 23 May, 1861, aged 18. See *Eton School Lists*.

Nelson, James Park, 1s. Park, of Fulham, Middlesex, gent. EXETER COLL., matric. 25 Feb., 1853, aged 18; B.A. 1857, M.A. 1859, rector of Swilland, Suffolk, 1867, until his death 27 Dec., 1874.

Nelson, John, s. William, of St. James's, London, pleb. CHRIST CHURCH, matric. 10 Dec., 1761, aged 19.

Nelson, John, s. Richard, of Old Hutton, Westmoreland, gent. QUEEN'S COLL., matric. 10 July, 1794, aged 18; B.A. 1798, M.A. 1802, B. & D.D. 1848, fellow until 1816, a canon of Heytesbury, rector of Peterston-super-Ely, co. Gloucester, 1814, until his death 10 Dec., 1855.

Nelson, Rev. John, s. John William, of Portsmouth, Hants, gent. ST. JOHN'S COLL., matric. 19 June, 1818, aged 18; B.A. 1822, M.A. 1824. See *Gent.'s Mag.*, 1843, i. 327. [10]

Nelson, John, o.s. John, of Chester-le-Street, Durham, arm. ST. MARY HALL, matric. 2 July, 1840, aged 22.

Nelson, Richard Heydon, o.s. John, of Speen, Berks, cler. MAGDALEN COLL., matric. 25 July, 1835, aged 18; demy 1835, until his death 2 June, 1837. See *Coll. Reg.*, vii. 336.

Nelson, Thomas, s. Seth, of Ashcombe, Yorks, gent. UNIVERSITY COLL., matric. 16 Nov., 1726, aged 18; B.A. 1730, M.A. 1733.

Nelson, Hon. Thomas Horatio, 3s. Horatio, Earl Nelson, of Standlynch, Wilts. KEBLE COLL., matric. 16 Oct., 1876, aged 18. See Foster's *Peerage*.

Nelson, William, s. Thomas, of Orton, Westmoreland, cler. QUEEN'S COLL., matric. 25 Nov., 1726, aged 16; B.A. 1731, brother of Christopher 1724. [15]

Nelson, William, s. William, of St. Martin's, London, arm. CHRIST CHURCH, matric. 26 May, 1749, aged 18; B.A. 1753 (? rector of Strumpshaw-cum-Bradiston, Norfolk, 1764, until his death in 1812). See *Alumni West.*, 349.

Nelthorpe, (Sir) John (Bart.), s. (Henry), of Barton, co. Lincoln, baronet. TRINITY COLL., matric. 20 Feb., 1764, aged 18; created M.A. 10 March, 1768, 6th baronet, died 14 June, 1799.

Nelthorpe, Thomas, 'vintner;' privilegiatus 6 Oct., 1747.

Nepean, Charles Edward Burroughs, 8s. Evan, of London, cler. UNIVERSITY COLL., matric. 29 Jan., 1870, aged 18; B.A. from ST. ALBAN HALL 1873, M.A. from UNIVERSITY COLL. 1880, vicar of Lenham, Kent, 1876.

Nepean, Evan Alcock, 1s. Evan Colville, of Mitcham, Surrey, gent. UNIVERSITY COLL., matric. 11 Oct., 1884, aged 19; scholar 1884-6, in the University XI. 1887. [20]

Nepean, Evan Yorke, 2s. William, of Bombay, East Indies, arm. QUEEN'S COLL., matric. 26 April, 1844, aged 18; B.A. 1848, M.A. 1851, rector of Bucknall, co. Lincoln, 1859-68, vicar of Appleshaw, Hants, 1868. See Foster's *Baronetage*.

Neppred, Edward, s. William, of Pallington, Dorset, pleb. EXETER COLL., matric. 10 May, 1744, aged 19; B.A. 14 March, 1747-8.

Nesbitt, Albert John, 2s. Thomas, of Bideford, Devon, arm. BRASENOSE COLL., matric. 26 June, 1829, aged 18.

Nesbitt, Alfred Mortimer, 5s. Pearce Rogers, of Northampton, D.Med. CORPUS CHRISTI COLL., matric. 29 April, 1873, aged 18; scholar 1873-8, B.A. 1877, M.A. 1880, brother of Robert H.

Nesbitt, Cosby Thomas, 1s. John, of St. Giles's, London, arm. BRASENOSE COLL., matric. 16 Oct., 1833, aged 19; B.A. 1837, M.A. 1840, of Lismore House, co. Cavan, bar.-at-law, Inner Temple, 1843, died 1856. [25]

Nesbitt, John Downing, s. Alexander Downing, of King's County, Ireland, arm. WADHAM COLL., matric. 13 Nov., 1792, aged 21.

Nesbitt, Robert, 3s. Alexander, of Dulwich, Surrey, arm. UNIVERSITY COLL., matric. 24 May, 1877, aged 19; B.A. 1881.

Nesbitt, Robert Henry, 1s. Pearce Rogers, of Honiton, Devon, doctor. EXETER COLL., matric. 14 June, 1859, aged 19; scholar JESUS COLL. 1860-4, B.A. 1863, M.A. 1874, died May, 1881.

Nesfield, George Smart, 1s. Edward Dickinson, of Hutton Bushell, Yorks, arm. MERTON COLL., matric. 29 Jan., 1870, aged 23.

Nesfield, John Collinson, 2s. Charles William, of Stratton St. Margaret's, Wilts, cler. MERTON COLL., matric. 26 May, 1855, aged 18; postmaster 1855-9, B.A. 1860, M.A. 1862. [30]

Nesfield, Robert William Mills, y.s. William, of Brancepeth, co. Durham, cler. UNIVERSITY COLL., matric. 23 April, 1834, aged 18; B.A. 1838, M.A. 1840, of Castle Hill, co. Derby, J.P., D.L., bar.-at-law, Lincoln's Inn, 1841.

Ness, Edward, 1s. Richard Burdett, of Castle Godwin, co. Gloucester, arm. ST. MARY HALL, matric. 15 Dec., 1821, aged 17; B.A. 1826, M.A. 1832, rector of Elkstone 1846-77, died 26 Aug., 1884.

Ness, Francis Henry Derby, 2s. John Derby, of Morthoe, near Ilfracombe, Devon, cler. EXETER COLL., matric. 2 May, 1862, aged 18; B.A. 1868, M.A. 1870, held various curacies 1869-86.

Ness, John Derby, 2s. Richard, of Hanwell, Oxon, cler. LINCOLN COLL., matric. 13 Dec., 1821, aged 20; exhibitioner 1822-5, B.A. 1825, vicar of Morthoe, Devon, 1830.

Ness, Richard, s. Richard, of Broughton, Oxon, gent. MERTON COLL., matric. 19 March, 1785, aged 18; B.A. 1788, M.A. 1801, B. & D.D. 1823, rector of Abingdon, Northants, 1792, and of West Parley, Dorset, 1798, until his death 7 April, 1839. [35]

Ness, Richard Derby, s. Richard, of Hanwell, Oxon, cler. LINCOLN COLL., matric. 25 Nov., 1814, aged 17; exhibitioner 1815-23, B.A. 1819, M.A. 1822.

Nesselrode, Charles Robert, Count; D.C.L. by diploma 16 June, 1814, 'privy councillor and secretary of state to the Emperor of Russia,' Russian chancellor, died 23 March, 1862, aged 91.

Nethercote, Henry Osmond, y.s. John, of Moulton Grange, Northants, arm. BALLIOL COLL., matric. 8 June, 1837, aged 17; B.A. 1842, of Moulton Grange, high sheriff Northants 1872.

Netherlands, William Frederick George, King of the; D.C.L. by diploma 24 May, 1811, died 1 March, 1865.

Netherlands, H.R.H. Prince William Henry of the; D.C.L. by diploma 20 May, 1839 (3rd son of William II., King of the Netherlands), born 13 June, 1820. [40]

Nethersole, William Pierce, s. William, of Westminster, gent. HERTFORD COLL., matric. 20 March, 1773, aged 17; B.A. 1776, B.C.L. 1799, rector of Clophill, Beds, and vicar of Pulloxhill 1799, until his death 6 Dec., 1842.

Nettleship, Arthur, 4s. John, of Tickhill, Yorks, arm. TRINITY COLL., matric. 10 May, 1845, aged 18; scholar 1846-9, B.A. 1849, M.A. 1852, vicar of Minsterworth, co. Gloucester, 1854-77, rector of Barton-on-the-Heath 1877.

Nettleship, Henry, 1s. Henry John, of Kettering, Northants, gent. CORPUS CHRISTI COLL., matric. 3 April, 1857, aged 17, scholar 1857-61, B.A. 1861; fellow LINCOLN COLL. 1861-71, M.A. 1863, tutor and librarian 1862; lecturer in classics, Christ Church, 1873-8; fellow CORPUS CHRISTI COLL. 1873, tutor and librarian 1875, professor Latin literature since 1878.

Nettleship, Richard Lewis, 5s. Henry John, of Kettering, Northants, arm. BALLIOL COLL., matric. 16 Oct., 1869, aged 18; scholar 1864-9, fellow 1869, B.A. 1869, M.A. 1872, tutor 1871, dean 1872.

Nettleship, William, s. William, of Twickenham, Middlesex, gent. WORCESTER COLL., matric. 6 April, 1781, aged 18; B.A. 1784, M.A. 1787, rector of Ruckland with Farforth and Maidenwell, co. Lincoln, 1794, of Churchill, co. Worcester, 1811, and of Irby, co. Lincoln, 1814, until his death 18 Sep., 1841. [5]

Nettleship, William, 1s. William, of Stoke Pogis, Bucks, cler. MERTON COLL., matric. 11 Nov., 1823, aged 20; postmaster 1823-7, B.A. 1828, M.A. 1831. See *Eton School Lists.*

Neubauer, Dr. Adolph, of EXETER COLL.; M.A. by diploma 18 Feb., 1873, sub-librarian Bodleian library 1873, reader Rabbinical literature 1886.

Neucatre, James Sidney, 1776. See NEWCATER.

Neufville, 'Jacob,' s. 'Jacob,' of Isle of Jamaica, arm. TRINITY COLL., matric. 18 Nov., 1790, aged 17.

Neumann, Formby, 2s. John Stubbs, of Hockcliffe, near Leighton Buzzard, Beds, cler. WADHAM COLL., matric. 1 June, 1864, aged 19. [10]

Neve, Charles, s. Timothy, of Kensington, Middlesex, doctor. ST. JOHN'S COLL., matric. 3 July, 1779, aged 15; B.A. 1783, fellow, M.A. 1787, B.D. 1792, vicar of Cleve Prior, co. Worcester, vicar of Old Sodbury, co. Gloucester, 1795, and of Whitelady Aston, 1808, until his death 29 July, 1828. See *Robinson*, 133.

Neve, Charles, s. Titus, of Wolverhampton, co. Stafford, cler. PEMBROKE COLL., matric. 23 Oct., 1788, aged 21; B.A. 1793, vicar of Kilmersdon, Somerset, 1806, vicar of Brierley Hill, co. Stafford, 1809, until his death 2 June, 1833.

Neve, Rev. Charles, 1s. Richard, of Benenden, Kent, arm. EXETER COLL., matric. 19 May, 1877, aged 18; B.A. 1880, M.A. 1884, died 12 March, 1886.

Neve, Egerton Robert, s. Timothy, of Middleton Stoney, Oxon, doctor. MERTON COLL., matric. 15 Dec., 1783, aged 17; B.A. 1787, fellow, M.A. 1790, proctor 1799, one of H.M. preachers at Whitehall, rector of Middleton Stoney 1796, until his death 27 Sep., 1818.

Neve, Frederick Hervey, s. Timothy, of Oxford (city), doctor. MERTON COLL., matric. 10 Dec., 1793, aged 18; B.A. 1797, M.A. 1802, vicar of Llansantfraid-yr-Mechan, co. Montgomery, 1805, rector of Walwyn's Castle, co. Pembroke, 1815, and vicar of Southill, Beds, 1816, until his death 15 May, 1843. See *Robinson*, 155. [15]

Neve, Frederick Robert, 1s. Frederick, of Eton, Bucks, cler. ORIEL COLL., matric. 19 May, 1824, aged 17; B.A. 1828, M.A. 1833, seceded to Rome. See *Eton School Lists.*

Neve, Rev. Frederick William, 2s. George, of Benenden, Kent, gent. MERTON COLL., matric. 24 April, 1876, aged 20; B.A. 1879, M.A. 1883.

Neve, Timothy, s. Timothy, of Spalding, co. Lincoln, cler. (archdeacon of Huntingdon). CORPUS CHRISTI COLL., matric. 12 Nov., 1737, aged 13; scholar 1737-47, B.A. 1741, fellow 1747-62, M.A. 1744, B.D. 1753, D.D. 1758, chaplain of Merton College, Margaret professor of divinity 1783-98, rector of Letcomb Bassett 1762-4, and of Middleton Stoney 1762, and Geddington, Oxon, 1763, preb. of Worcester 1783, died 1 Jan., 1798. See Nichols' *Literary Anecdotes*, vol. vi., pp. 99-134; & *Gent.'s Mag.*, 1798, i-85.

Neve, Titus, s. Thomas, of Birch, co. Hereford, cler. BALLIOL COLL., matric. 16 May, 1738, aged 18; B.A. 1742, sacrist of the Collegiate Church at Wolverhampton, died about Jan., 1789. [19]

Nevell, William, 'pistor;' privilegiatus 22 Dec., 1826.

Neveu, Rev. Henry Godfray le, 1s. Thomas, of St. Helier's, Jersey, cler. WORCESTER COLL., matric. 23 May, 1877, aged 20; B.A. 1881, M.A. 1884.

Neveu, Thomas le, 1s. Thomas, of St. Clement's, Isle of Jersey, gent. ST. MARY HALL, matric. 19 Oct., 1849, aged 21; B.A. 1853, M.A. 1879, held various curacies 1852-63, rector of St. John, Jersey, 1863-75, and of St. Martin, Jersey, 1875.

Nevile, Charles, 2s. Christopher, of Scaftworth, Everton, Notts, arm. TRINITY COLL., matric. 10 June, 1835, aged 18; scholar 1836-41, B.A. 1839, M.A. 1842, curate of Thorney, Notts, 1839-44, and of Wickenby 1845-53, rector of Fledborough, Notts, 1853-77, vicar of Coates, co. Lincoln, 1869-75, preb. of Lincoln 1868, rector of Stow, co. Lincoln, 1877.

Nevile, Charles Swainston, 2s. Charles, of Fledborough, Notts, cler. KEBLE COLL., matric. 16 Oct., 1883, aged 19; B.A. 1886.

Nevile, Henry, 4s. Christopher, of Scaftworth, Notts, arm. TRINITY COLL., matric. 24 Nov., 1836, aged 18; B.A. 1840, rector of Wickenby, co. Lincoln, 1863, until his death 14 Feb., 1878. [25]

Nevill, Edmund Robert, 1s. Samuel Tarratt, bishop of Dunedin. LINCOLN COLL., matric. 17 Jan., aged 19; B.A. 1886.

Nevill, Edward, born at Sheffield Park, Fletching, Sussex, s. George, Baron Abergavenny. WADHAM COLL., matric. 5 Sep., 1721, aged 15; 13th baron, died 9 Oct., 1724.

Nevill, George, Baron Abergavenny, s. George, of St. Martin's-in-the-Fields. UNIVERSITY COLL., matric. 13 Sep., 1722, aged 20; 12th baron, died 5 Nov., 1723.

Nevill, George, Lord Abergavenny, born at Kidbrook, Sussex, s. William, Baron. CHRIST CHURCH, matric. 14 Feb., 1744-5, aged 17; 15th baron, created Viscount Nevill and Earl of Abergavenny 17 May, 1784, died 9 Sep., 1785. See Foster's *Peerage.*

Nevill, George, s. George Henry, of Croydon, Surrey, arm. CHRIST CHURCH, matric. 22 Oct., 1812, aged 20; rector of Chiltington, Sussex, 1819, until his death 20 Sep., 1825. See Foster's *Peerage*, B. ABERGAVENNY. [30]

Nevill, Rev. & Hon. George Henry, s. George, Baron Abergavenny. CHRIST CHURCH, matric. 10 Dec., 1778, aged 18; of Flower Place, Surrey, died 7 Aug., 1844.

Nevill, Henry, s. George, baron, after Earl of Abergavenny. CHRIST CHURCH, matric. 29 May, 1773, aged 18; created M.A. 8 March, 1776, 2nd earl, K.T., M.P. Seaford 1784, co. Monmouth 1784-5, recorder of Harwich, died 27 March, 1843.

Nevill, Henry Ralph, 4s. Richard Janion, of Lanelly, co. Carmarthen, arm. UNIVERSITY COLL. matric. 21 May, 1840, aged 18; B.A. 1844, M.A. 1850, perp. curate St. Mark, Lakenham, Norfolk, 1851-8, vicar of Great Yarmouth 1858-73, hon. canon Norwich 1860-73, vicar of St. Peter Mancroft, Norwich, 1881-4, canon of Norwich 1873, archdeacon 1874. See *Rugby School Reg.*, 186.

Nevill, Hugh, 1s. Charles William, of Llanelly, co. Carmarthen, arm. EXETER COLL., matric. 15 May, 1875, aged 20; B.A. 1878, M.A. 1882.

Nevill, James Yalden, 3s. Richard Janion, of Lanelly, co. Carmarthen, arm. ORIEL COLL., matric. 22 Feb., 1838, aged 18; B.A. 1842, M.A. 1848, curate of St. George's, Whitwick, co. Leicester, died 11 March, 1867.

Nevill, John, s. John, of Nottingham, Notts, arm. UNIVERSITY COLL. matric. 12 May, 1741, aged 16; B.A. 26 Feb., 1744-5.

Nevill, Hon. Ralph Pelham, 2s. William, Earl of Abergavenny. MERTON COLL., matric. 13 Dec., 1851, aged 19. See Foster's *Peerage* & *Eton School Lists.*

Nevill, Ralph William, 1s. Henry Ralph, of Yarmouth, cler. (after dean). KEBLE COLL., matric. 17 Oct., 1882, aged 19; B.A. 1886. [5]

Nevill, William, s. Edward, of Whitechapel, London (*sic*), arm. ORIEL COLL., matric. 30 April, 1716, aged 17; probably 14th Baron Abergavenny, who was captain of the yeomen of the guard 1737, master of the jewel office 1739, and died 21 Sep., 1744.

Nevill, William, s. William, Baron Abergavenny. CHRIST CHURCH, matric. 5 May, 1761, aged 19, B.A. 1764; M.A. from ALL SOULS' COLL. 1767, rector of Burghclere, Hants, and of Bishopstone, Wilts, died 22 July, 1810.

Nevill, William, s. Timmins, of Sutton Coldfield, co. Warwick, gent. ST. EDMUND HALL, matric. 28 March, 1801, aged 32. See *Gent.'s Mag.*, 1851, ii., 664.

Nevill, William, s. Henry, Earl of Abergavenny. CHRIST CHURCH, matric. 22 Oct., 1812, aged 20; M.A. from MAGDALEN COLL., Cambridge, 1816, 4th earl, rector of Birling, Kent, and vicar of Frant, Sussex, died 17 Aug., 1868.

Neville, Charles Fawcett. MAGDALEN HALL, 1834. See ROLFE. [10]

Neville, Frederick (formerly Frederick Howson Potter), 2s. William Potter, of Scarborough, Yorks, gent. QUEEN'S COLL., matric. 14 June, 1849, aged 19; B.A. 1853, M.A. 1856, perp. curate Holy Apostles, Charlton Kings, co. Gloucester, 1871-83, rector of Willersey, co. Worcester, 1883.

Neville, Hon. Richard, born at Buscombe, Berks, s. Richard Aldeworth, Baron Braybrooke. CHRIST CHURCH, matric. 17 Jan., 1801, aged 17; created D.C.L. 5 July, 1810, 3rd baron, M.P. Thirsk 1805-6, Saltash 1807, Buckingham 1807-12, Berks 1812-25, died 13 March, 1858. See Foster's *Peerage* & *Eton School Lists.*

Neville, Richard Aldworth Griffin-, s. Richard, of St. Margaret's, Westminster, arm. MERTON COLL., matric. 20 June, 1768, aged 17; created M.A. 4 July, 1771, and also D.C.L. 3 (or 5) July, 1810, 2nd Lord Braybrooke, M.P. Grampound 1774-80, Buckingham 1780-2, Reading 1782-97, assumed the additional surname of GRIFFIN by royal licence 27 July, 1797, died 28 Feb., 1825. See Foster's *Peerage.*

Neville, Strickland Charles Edward. WADHAM COLL. 1808. See ROLFE.

Neville, William, s. Robert, of Newton, Bucks, cler. CHRIST'S COLL., Cambridge, matric. 14 June, 1720, aged 19; B.A. 1723, fellow, M.A. 1727, incorp. 11 July, 1728. [15]

Neville, William, 1s. William Frederick, of Butleigh, near Glastonbury, Somerset, cler. MAGDALEN COLL., matric. 8 Feb., 1869, aged 18; clerk 1869-70, B.A. 1873, M.A. 1875, vicar of Watlington, Oxon, 1881-2, and of Butleigh since 1882.

Neville, William (Latimer), 1s. William, of St. Martin's, Birmingham, arm. QUEEN'S COLL., matric. 4 Nov., 1820, aged 18; B.A. 1826, M.A. 1828, curate Holy Trinity, Brompton, superintendent West Indian mission to Western Africa, where he died 7 July, 1861.

Neville, William Paine, o.s. William P., of Marylebone, Middlesex, arm. TRINITY COLL., matric. 7 March, 1844, aged 19; B.A. 1849, M.A. 1850.

Nevins, William Richard Feilding, 1s. William, of Frankfort-on-Maine, cler. ST. JOHN'S COLL., matric. 25 June, 1862, aged 20; B.A. 1869, died 24 Feb., 1878.

Nevinson, Basil George, 1s. George Henry, of Leicester, gent. EXETER COLL., matric. 19 Jan., 1872, aged 19; B.A. 1877, M.A. 1878, bar.-at-law, Lincoln's Inn, 1882. [20]

Nevinson, Rev. Charles, 2s. Edmund Henry, of Hampstead, Middlesex, arm. EXETER COLL., matric. 23 Jan., 1834, aged 17; scholar WADHAM COLL. 1834-41, B.A. 1838, M.A. 1840, fellow 1841-4, humanity lecturer 1842, warden of Browne's Hospital, Stamford, 1845, until his death 12 Aug., 1880.

Nevinson, Charles, 1s. Charles, of Stamford, co. Lincoln, cler. WADHAM COLL., matric. 12 Oct., 1866, aged 19.

Nevinson, Henry Woodd, 2s. George Henry, of Leicester, arm. CHRIST CHURCH, matric. 20 May, 1875, aged 18; a junior student 1875-80, B.A. 1879.

New, Edward Parris, s. James, of Bristol (city), gent. ST. JOHN'S COLL., matric. 26 June, 1818, aged 14; scholar and fellow 1818-32, B.A. 1822, M.A. 1825, B.D. 1831, dean of arts 1827, perp. curate Northmoor, Oxon, 1829, until his death 28 July, 1832.

New, Francis Thomas, y.s John, of Stapleton, co. Gloucester, arm. ST. JOHN'S COLL., matric. 3 Nov., 1824, aged 18; B.A. 1828, M.A. 1840. [25]

New, James, s. Samuel, of Nevis, in America, gent. ORIEL COLL., matric. 25 June, 1752, aged 17; B.A. 1756, vicar of St. Philip and St. Jacob, Bristol, 1772, and rector of Compton Greenfield, co. Gloucester, died 15 July, 1810.

New, John Cave, 1s. John, of Mangotsfield, co. Gloucester, arm. ST. JOHN'S COLL., matric. 4 March, 1847, aged 19; B.A. 1851, M.A. 1864, of Uffcuime, Devon, J.P., a student of the Inner Temple 1850, hon. lieut.-col. Devon artillery militia.

New, Nath., s. Thomas, of Oxford (city), gent. WADHAM COLL., matric. 13 March, 1716-7, aged 16.

New, Stafford. BALLIOL COLL., 1743. See NEWE, page 1015.

Newall, Edgar, 3s. Samuel, of Rugby, co. Warwick, cler. NEW COLL., matric. 10 Oct., 1873, aged 19; B.A. 1878, M.A. 1882. See *Rugby School Reg.*

Newbald, Clement Arthur, o.s. Samuel Wilberforce, of Pontefract, Yorks, cler. WADHAM COLL., matric. 16 Oct., 1886, aged 19. [31]

Newbald, Samuel Wilberforce, 3s. Charles, of H. Trinity, Hull, Yorks, gent. WADHAM COLL., matric. 23 Feb., 1837, aged 18; B.A. 1842, M.A. 1846, perp. curate Goole 1844-8, of Rawcliffe 1848-50, head-master King's School, Pontefract, 1850-68, vicar of Hooton Pagnell, Yorks, 1868, until his death in 1883.

Newbatt, Charles Henry, 1s. Edward, of Woolsthorpe, co. Lincoln, gent. CORPUS CHRISTI COLL., matric. 3 March, 1853, aged 18.

Newbattle, John William Robert, Baron. CHRIST CHURCH, 1813. See KERR.

Newbery, Francis, s. John, of Reading, Berks, gent. TRINITY COLL., matric. 1 April, 1762, aged 17; of Heathfield Park, Sussex, high sheriff, a commissioner of appeal for Surrey. See *Robinson*, 118.

Newbery, Henry James, s. Edward, of St. Bartholomew, London, arm. ST. EDMUND HALL, matric. 16 March, 1814, aged 22; rector of St. Gabriel, Fenchurch, with St. Margaret Pattens, London, 1834, until his death 21 July, 1886. [36]

Newbery, John, s. Henry, of Stoke, Surrey, pleb. MERTON COLL., matric. 20 Nov., 1721, aged 19; B.A. 1725.

Newbery, John, o.s. James, of St. Lawrence, Reading, gent. MAGDALEN COLL., matric. 5 May, 1837, aged 19; clerk 1837-8. See *Coll. Reg.*, ii. 120.

Newbery, John Fenton, 1s. John, of Haigh, Yorks, arm. CHRIST CHURCH, matric. 24 March, 1827, aged 19; B.A. 1831, died in Italy. See *Eton School Lists.*

Newbery, Sampson, s. Sampson, of Zeal, Devon, gent. EXETER COLL., matric. 26 May, 1750, aged 19; B.A. 1754, M.A. 1757, fellow 1758-86, B.D. 1768, vicar of Long Wittenham, Berks, 1778-85, rector of Bushey, Herts, 1785, until his death 7 March, 1794. See *Boase*, 106.

Newbery, Thomas, of QUEEN'S COLL., Cambridge (B.A. 1826, M.A. 1830); adm. 'ad eundem' 10 June, 1834 (s. William, of Manchester), perp. curate of Shipley with Heaton, Yorks, rector of Hinton St. George, 1846, and rector of Seavington St. Michael, Somerset, 1846, until his death 30 March, 1861. See *Manchester School Reg.*, iii. 296.

Newbigging, Robert, s. James, of Edinburgh (city), arm. ST. JOHN'S COLL., matric. 17 Oct., 1803, aged 20; B.A. 1813, M.A. 1814. [5]

Newbold, Arthur (George), 7s. Francis, of Macclesfield, arm. BRASENOSE COLL., matric. 13 June, 1833, aged 17; B.A. from MAGDALEN HALL 1839, vicar of Thornton, co. Lincoln, 1851, until his death 13 Jan., 1872.

Newbold, Clement Madely, 4s. Francis, of Prestbury, Cheshire, arm. BRASENOSE COLL., matric. 13 April, 1825, aged 16; B.A. 1829, fellow 1829, until his death in 1831.

Newbold, Francis George, 1s. Francis Stonehewer, of Macclesfield, D.D. BRASENOSE COLL. matric. 7 June, 1849, aged 18; B.A. 1853.

Newbold, Francis Stonehewer, s. Francis, of Macclesfield, Cheshire, arm. BRASENOSE COLL., matric. 24 April, 1816, aged 16; B.A. 1820, fellow 1821-7, M.A. 1822, B. & D.D. 1834, tutor & junior dean 1825, Greek lecturer 1826, rector of Stickney, co. Lincoln, 1828, died Jan., 1876.

Newbold, John Knifton, 1s. John, of King's Newton, co. Derby, gent. QUEEN'S COLL., matric. 11 June, 1828, aged 23; B.A. 1832. [10]

Newbolt, Francis George, 2s. Henry Francis, of Bilston, co. Stafford, cler. BALLIOL COLL., matric. 16 Oct., 1883, aged 20; B.A. 1887.

Newbolt, George Digby, 1s. William Robert, of London, cler. BRASENOSE COLL., matric. 30 June, 1848, aged 19; B.A. 1852, rector of Knotting with Souldrop, Beds, 1856.

Newbolt, Henry John, 1s. Henry Francis, of Bilston, co. Stafford, cler. CORPUS CHRISTI COLL., matric. 27 Oct., 1881, aged 19; scholar 1881-5, B.A. 1885, M.A. 1888, bar.-at-law, Lincoln's Inn, 1887.

Newbolt, (Sir) John (Henry), s. John Monk, of Winchester (city), cler. CHRIST CHURCH, matric. 13 March, 1787, aged 18, B.A. 1791; B.C.L. from ALL SOULS' COLL. 1794, of Portswood House, Hants, bar.-at-law, Lincoln's Inn, 1795, secretary of commission of peace 1794-1815, recorder of Bombay, chief justice of Madras, and knighted 17 April, 1810, died 22 Jan., 1823.

Newbolt, John Monk, s. Philip, of Winchester, Hants, gent. QUEEN'S COLL., matric. 14 Dec., 1754, aged 15; B.A. from MAGDALEN COLL. 1758, M.A. 1761. [15]

Newbolt, William Charles Edmund, 4s. William Robert, of Somerton, Somerset, cler. PEMBROKE COLL., matric. 29 May, 1863, aged 18; scholar 1863-8, B.A. 1867, M.A. 1870, vicar of Dymock, co. Gloucester, 1870-7, and of Malvern Link 1877.

Newbolt, William Henry, 1s. William, of Winchester, Hants, doctor. NEW COLL., matric. 14 March, 1825, aged 18; fellow 1825-44, B.A. 1829, M.A. 1833, rector of Pauler's Pury 1842, until his death 7 April, 1878.

Newbolt, William Hill, s. John, of Winchester, Hants, cler. ORIEL COLL., matric. 19 Oct., 1790, aged 19; B.A. 1794, M.A. 1799, B. & D.D. 1813, a minor canon of Winchester and rector of Morstead, Hants, 1804, until his death 25 Feb., 1833.

Newbolt, William Robert, 3s. John Henry, of Fulham, Middlesex, eq. aur. CHRIST CHURCH, matric. 15 March, 1820, aged 18; student 1821-8, B.A. 1824, M.A. 1826, vicar of Somerton, Somerset, 1833, until his death 4 April, 1857.

Newborough, John, s. Page, of Onibury, Salop, cler. BALLIOL COLL., matric. 28 March, 1740, aged 18; B.A. 1743, M.A. 1747, vicar of Thame, Oxon, 1761, until his death in 1795. [20]

Newborough, Thomas, Baron. CHRIST CHURCH 1820. See WYNN.

Newborough, William, s. John, of Oxford (city), cler. PEMBROKE COLL., matric. 24 Nov., 1764, aged 17; B.A. 1768, fellow, M.A. 1771, lecturer of Thame, Oxon, minister of Long Crendon, Bucks, died 15 Nov., 1787.

Newburgh, Broghil (or Brookhill), M.A. TRINITY COLL., Dublin, 1719 (B.A. 1716); incorp. from ST. EDMUND HALL 13 (or 16) May, 1728.

Newby, Henry, s. Charles, of Hooton Roberts, Yorks, gent. LINCOLN COLL., matric. 19 March, 1715-6, aged 16.

Newby, Henry, s. Isaac, of Applebuy (*sic*), co. Derby, cler. LINCOLN COLL., matric. 16 April, 1729, aged 19; B.A. 12 March, 1732-3. [25]

Newby, Henry, 1s. Joshua, of Wooton, co. Warwick, cler. WORCESTER COLL., matric. 11 Feb., 1841, aged 18; B.A. 1844, M.A. 1847, vicar of Mears Ashby, Northants, 1857, until his death 10 March, 1874. See *Rugby School Reg.*, 173.

Newby, Joshua, s. Henry, of Kildwick, Yorks, gent. BRASENOSE COLL., matric. 28 March, 1757, aged 18; B.A. 1760, fellow, M.A. 1763, rector of Great Rolwright, Oxon, died 12 Aug., 1811.

Newby, Joshua (Holmes), s. Joshua, of Great Rolwright, Oxon, cler. BRASENOSE COLL., matric. 23 April, 1806, aged 18; demy MAGDALEN COLL. 1808-17, B.A. 1810, M.A. 1813, rector of Haseley, co. Warwick, 1824, until his death 28 Jan., 1827. See *Bloxam*, vii. 177; & *Rugby School Reg.*, 86.

Newcater, James (Sidney), s. James, of Callessy, co. Fife, pleb. ST. EDMUND HALL, matric. 14 Nov., 1776, aged 26; B.A. 1780, M.A. 1783, rector of Wordwell, Suffolk, 1795, until his death 26 April, 1828.

Newcomb, Charles George, 1s. Joseph, of Battersea, Middlesex, arm. ORIEL COLL., matric. 19 Feb., 1835, aged 18; B.A. 1838, M.A. 1847, died vicar of Halberton, Devon, 20 June, 1862. [30]

Newcomb, Rev. Clement Ernest, 6s. William, of Kidderminster, gent. QUEEN'S COLL., matric. 22 Oct., 1884, aged 27; B.A. 1887.

Newcomb, Edward James, 1s. Edward James, of Kidderminster, co. Worcester, gent. MAGDALEN HALL, matric. 7 March, 1845, aged 20; B.A. 1849, M.A. 1852, curate of Leigh, near Worcester, died 4 Feb., 1865.

Newcomb, Frederick Baker, 5s. William, of Kidderminster, gent. QUEEN'S COLL., matric. 28 Oct., 1881, aged 25; B.A. 1884.

Newcomb, John, s. Thomas, of Stopham, Sussex, cler. NEW COLL., matric. 15 Dec., 1724, aged 16; B.A. 1728, M.A. 1731.

Newcomb, John Edward Waldron, o.s. John, of London, gent. ST. JOHN'S COLL., matric. 17 Oct., 1885, aged 19. [35]

Newcomb, John, fellow ST. JOHN'S COLL., Cambridge, B.A. 1704, M.A. 1708, B.D. 1715, D.D. 1725 (incorp. 9 July, 1733); master 1735-65, Lady Margaret professor of theology 1727-65.

Newcombe, James, s. Humphrey. of Exeter (city), pleb. CHRIST CHURCH, matric. 20 March, 1753, aged 19; B.A. from ORIEL COLL. 1758, chorister Exeter Cathedral 1743, dean's vicar, sub-treasurer and custos of Exeter Cathedral, and rector of Willand, Devon, 1810, curate of St. Sidwell's, died 4 Dec., 1816.

Newcombe, John, 1s. John, of Exeter, Devon, arm. EXETER COLL., matric. 4 May, 1738, aged 19.

Newcombe, John, s. Robert, of Exeter (city), arm. CORPUS CHRISTI COLL., matric. 9 Dec., 1778, aged 17; created M.A. (ORIEL COLL.) 14 June, 1782, bar.-at-law, Middle Temple, 1785.

Newcome, Edward William, 3s. Thomas, of Shenley, Herts, cler. BALLIOL COLL., matric. 3 June, 1840, aged 19; B.A. 1844, M.A. 1861, vicar of Leavesden, Herts, 1855.

Newcome, George William Frederick, s. Benjamin, dean of Rochester. ORIEL COLL., matric. 10 Feb., 1789, aged 16. [5]

Newcome, Henry Justinian, 1s. Thomas, of Shenley, Herts, cler. TRINITY COLL., matric. 14 Dec., 1833, aged 18; B.A. 1837, rector (and patron) of Shenley 1849, 'the ninth in direct continuous line of beneficed clerks from the Reformation to the present time.' See *Manchester School Reg.*, iii. 211; & *Eton School Lists.*

Newcome, Henry Neville, 1s. Edward William, of Leavesden, Herts, cler. CHARSLEY HALL, matric. 1 Nov., 1882, aged 18; B.A. from KEBLE COLL. 1886.

Newcome, John, s. Henry, of Hackney, Middlesex, gent. HERTFORD COLL., matric. 7 Feb., 1787, aged 18; B.A. 1791, M.A. 1795, died curate of Charleton, Hants, in 1797.

Newcome, Joseph, s. Joseph, of London, Middlesex, cler. MERTON COLL., matric. 15 Nov., 1744, aged 18; B.A. 1749, M.A. 1751, brother of William 1745.

Newcome, Noah Neale, of CORPUS CHRISTI COLL., Cambridge (B.A. 1742, M.A. 1746); incorp. 4 July, 1746. [10]

Newcome, William, s. Joseph, of Abingdon, Berks, cler. PEMBROKE COLL., matric. 31 Oct., 1745, aged 16, B.A. 1749; M.A. from HERTFORD COLL. 1753, B. & D.D. 1765, bishop of Dromore 1766-75, of Ossory 1775-9, of Waterford and Lismore 1779-95, archbishop of Armagh 1795, until his death 11 Jan., 1800. See *Cotton*, i. 133.

Newcome, William, born in Kilkenny, Ireland, s. (William), archbishop (of Armagh). CHRIST CHURCH, matric. 22 Jan., 1796, aged 17; B.A. 1799, M.A. 1802, of Hockwold Hall, Norfolk, rector of Belaugh with Scotton 1810, of Mundfort 1815, and of Langford with Ickburgh 1824 (all Norfolk), vicar of Sutton, Isle of Ely, 1838, until his death 22 May, 1846.

Newcome, William Charles, y.s. Richard, of Ruthin, co. Denbigh, archdeacon of Merioneth. TRINITY COLL., matric. 7 April, 1838, aged 19; B.A. 1843.

Newcomen, Charles Montgomerie, 2s. Arthur, of Kirkleatham, Yorks, arm. CHRIST CHURCH, matric. 18 May, 1864, aged 18.

Newcomen, John, s. George, of Chard, Somerset, pleb. PEMBROKE COLL., matric. 5 April, 1731, aged 18; B.A. 13 March, 1734-5 (? rector of Lanidon with Basildon, Essex, 1749, and vicar of Weybridge, Surrey, 1753). [15]

Newcomen, Thomas Gleadowe, s. William, of Dublin (city), baronet. CHRIST CHURCH, matric. 22 Oct., 1793, aged 16; B.A. from ST. MARY HALL 1796, 2nd baronet on the death of his father in 1807, and 2nd Viscount Newcomen on the death of his mother, M.P. Longford 1802-6, a student of Lincoln's Inn 1794, died unmarried 15 Jan., 1825. See *Eton School Lists.*

Newdegate, Charles Newdigate, 1s. Charles, of Harefield, Middlesex, arm. CHRIST CHURCH, matric. 15 May, 1834, aged 17; B.A. 1849, M.A. 1859, created D.C.L. 9 June, 1853, of Arbury, co. Warwick, P.C. 1886, M.P. North Warwickshire 1843-85, died 10 Aug., 1887. See *Eton School Lists.*

Newdegate, Jenkyn, s. George, of Hillingdon, Middlesex, arm. TRINITY COLL., matric. 18 March, 1739-40, aged 17.

Newdigate, Albert Lewis, 8s. Francis, of Blackheath, Kent, arm. CHRIST CHURCH, matric. 21 Oct., 1858, aged 18; B.A. 1861, M.A. 1868.

Newdigate, Alfred, 6s. Francis, of Astley, co. Warwick, arm. CHRIST CHURCH, matric. 20 Oct., 1847, aged 18; B.A. 1851, M.A. 1854, vicar of Kirk Hallam with Mapperley, co. Derby. See *Eton School Lists.* [20]

Newdigate, Charles John, 2s. Francis, of Astley, co. Warwick, arm. CHRIST CHURCH, matric. 20 Oct., 1841, aged 18; B.A. 1845, M.A. 1851, rector of West Hallam, co. Derby, 1848, until his death 21 July, 1876. See *Eton School Lists.*

Newdigate, (Sir) Edward (Bart.), s. Richard, of Arbury, co. Warwick (baronet). UNIVERSITY COLL., matric. 10 Oct., 1732, aged 17; 4th baronet, died 4 April, 1734. See *Alumni West.*, 307.

Newdigate, Francis, s. William Parker, of Salford, co. Warwick, arm. UNIVERSITY COLL., matric. 10 May, 1770, aged 18; of Kirk Hallam, co. Derby, assumed the surname and arms of NEWDIGATE in lieu of his patronymic, died in 1835.

Newdigate, Francis, s. Francis, of Keel, co. Stafford, arm. UNIVERSITY COLL., matric. 28 Nov., 1795, aged 21; of Kirk Hallam, died 21 May, 1862.

Newdigate, (Sir) Roger (Bart.), s. Richard, of Arbury, co. Warwick, arm. (baronet). UNIVERSITY COLL., matric. 9 April, 1736, aged 16; created M.A. 16 May, 1738, and D.C.L. 13 April, 1749, 5th baronet, M.P. Middlesex 1741-7, Oxford University 1750-80, died 23 Nov., 1806. See *Alumni West.*, 307. [25]

Newe, Stafford, s. Nathaniel, of Sandford, Oxon, gent. (see page 1013). BALLIOL COLL., matric. 14 Jan., 1742-3, aged 16; B.A. 1746, died rector of Hever, Kent, 30 Oct., 1796.

Newell, Ebenezer Josiah, 2s. Charles Wilkes, of Southwark, Surrey, gent. WORCESTER COLL., matric. 27 Jan., 1872, aged 18; exhibitioner 1871-6, B.A. 1876, M.A. 1878.

Newell, James Edward, s. Jeremiah, of Great Missenden, Bucks, cler. WORCESTER COLL., matric. 17 March, 1815, aged 19; B.A. 1819, M.A. 1821, perp. curate of Bromley, Kent, 1827, until his death 5 Jan., 1880.

Newell, John, s. William, of Adwell, Oxon, arm. MERTON COLL., matric. 16 Nov., 1720, aged 18; B.A. 1724, M.A. 1728.

Newell, Percy Joseph, o.s. Samuel Percy, of Wimborne, Dorset, arm. LINCOLN COLL., matric. 7 Dec., 1821, aged 19; B.A. from MAGDALEN HALL 1831. [30]

Newell, Samuel, s. Thomas, of Henley, Oxon, gent. UNIVERSITY COLL., matric. 11 May, 1765, aged 17; B.A. 1769, rector of Adwell, Oxon, and of Ickford, Bucks, 1775, until his death in 1802.

Newell, Thomas Blackman, s. Thomas, of Cheltenham, co. Gloucester, arm. CHRIST CHURCH, matric. 29 April, 1811, aged 17; B.A. 1815, M.A. 1817, perp. curate Cold Salperton, co. Gloucester, 1823, until his death 14 April, 1850.

Newell, William, s. William, of Adwell, Oxon, gent. CHRIST CHURCH, matric. 19 Feb., 1719-20, aged 18; B.A. 1723, M.A. 1726.

Newell, William Joseph, 2s. Percy Joseph, of Reading, Berks, cler. MAGDALEN HALL, matric. 17 Dec., 1852, aged 23.

Newenham, Rev. Arthur O'Brien, 3s. Baganell Burdett, of York, cler. QUEEN'S COLL., matric. 4 June, 1881, aged 19; B.A. 1884. [35]

LITTLE LION HALL, now demolished.—*From an engraving by Skelton*

Newenham, Edward Burdett, 1s. Bagenall Burdett, of West Farleigh, Kent, cler. QUEEN'S COLL., matric. 8 June, 1878, aged 19; B.A. 1881.

Newenham, William, s. Thomas, of Cork (city), Ireland, arm.. ST. JOHN'S COLL., matric. 14 July, 1722, aged 15; possibly great grandfather of the next named, and died in 1738.

Newenham, William Henry, s. William, of Walcot, in city of Bath, arm. CHRIST CHURCH, matric. 21 Oct,. 1803, aged 18; of Coolmore, co. Cork, died 4 Sep., 1842.

Newey, John, born at Itchin, Hants, s. John, dean of Chichester. MERTON COLL., matric. 27 Nov., 1728, aged 18; B.A. 1732, M.A. 1736.

Newhouse, Rev. Robert Perceval, 1s. Robert Brockman, of Coleshill, co. Warwick, gent. WORCESTER COLL., matric. 19 Feb., 1875, aged 19; exhibitioner 1874-5, scholar 1875-9, B.A. 1878, M.A. 1881. [5]

Newhouse, Thomas Postlethwaite, s. John, of Petworth, Sussex, gent. NEW COLL., matric. 16 April, 1783, aged 19; B.A. 1790, M.A. 1790.

Newill, Arthur Cotton, 2s. Henry, of Madras, arm. BALLIOL COLL., matric. 17 Oct., 1877, aged 19; Blundell scholar 1877-81.

Newington, Frank, 5s. Charles, of Ticehurst, Sussex, gent. ST. JOHN'S COLL., matric. 30 June, 1841, aged 20; B.A. 1845, perp. curate Wool 1860-73, vicar of Combe Keynes, Dorset, 1860-73, and of Osmington, Dorset, 1873, until his death 10 Oct., 1877.

Newington, John, s. Ben, of Southwark, Surrey, gent. QUEEN'S COLL., matric. 1 July, 1715, aged 17; B.A. 1719, M.A. 1722, B.Med. 1725, D.Med. 1728, fellow College of Physicians 1731, died 22 Jan., 1771. See Munk's *Roll*, ii. 117; & *Robinson*, 24.

Newington, Rev. Philip Playsted, 4s. Charles, of Ticehurst, Sussex, D.Med. WORCESTER COLL., matric. 1 Dec., 1837, aged 20; B.A. 1842, M.A. 1851, died 28 April, 1874. [10]

Newington, Samuel, 2s. Charles, of Ticehurst, Sussex, doctor. WORCESTER COLL., matric. 27 Feb., 1834, aged 19; B.A. from NEW INN HALL 1842, M.A. from WORCESTER COLL. 1868.

Newington, Thomas, s. William, of Offenham, co. Worcester, gent. BALLIOL COLL., matric. 8 April, 1731, aged 17.

Newington, William Broadley, 2s. Francis, of Broad Chalke, Wilts, cler. ST. JOHN'S COLL., matric. 24 Oct., 1874, aged 17.

Newland, Frederick William, 2s. Richard, of London, gent. MERTON COLL., matric. 14 Oct., 1876, aged 17; postmaster 1876-81, B.A. 1880, M.A. 1883.

Newland, Horace William, o.s. William, of Broadwater, Sussex, arm. TRINITY COLL., matric. 11 Oct., 1879, aged 19; B.A. 1882. [15]

Newland, Richard Bingham, s. James, of Havant, Hants, gent. QUEEN'S COLL., matric. 11 Feb., 1775, aged 17.

Newman, Alfred, 3s. William Jepson, of Badsworth, Yorks, cler. ORIEL COLL., matric. 13 April, 1866, aged 18; bible clerk 1866-9, B.A. 1869.

Newman, Augustus, 5s. Richard, of Stokenham, Devon, cler. ST. JOHN'S COLL., matric. 30 June, 1851, aged 19; B.A. 1855, M.A. 1858, B.Med. 1859.

Newman, Charles Durnford, 3s. Richard, of Dittisham, Devon, cler. WADHAM COLL., matric. 27 June, 1839, aged 18; B.A. 1843, M.A. 1854, head-master St. John's Academy, Newfoundland, 1845-55, etc., chaplain Dusseldorf 1869-70, vicar of St. Mary, Warwick, 1872, until his death 15 March, 1881.

Newman, Daniel, s. Francis, of Westbere, Kent, gent. UNIVERSITY COLL., matric. 24 March, 1757, aged 16; bar.-at-law, Lincoln's Inn, 1765, recorder of Maidstone, died at Westbere 1 Oct., 1781. [20]

Newman, Rev. David Herbert, 2s. William, of Gilston, Herts, cler. NON-COLL., matric. 20 Jan., 1877, aged 17; B.A. 1880.

Newman, Edwin, 1s. Edwin, of Yeovil, Somerset, arm. CHRIST CHURCH, matric. 11 Dec., 1846, aged 17; B.A. 1850, a student of Lincoln's Inn 1873.

Newman, Rev. Ernest Frederick, 3s. William Symons, of Coryton, Devon, cler. KEBLE COLL., matric. 15 Oct., 1877, aged 18; B.A. 1882, M.A. 1884.

Newman, Francis William, 3s. John, of London, arm. WORCESTER COLL., matric. 29 Nov., 1822, aged 17, B.A. 1826, hon. fellow 1883; fellow BALLIOL COLL. 1826-30, professor of Latin, University College, London, 1846-69, brother of Cardinal Newman.

Newman, Frederick, 4s. Richard, of Dartmouth, Devon, cler. QUEEN'S COLL., matric. 25 Nov., 1847, aged 20; B.A. 1851. [25]

Newman, Frederick Samuel, 3s. William Lewin, of St. Helen's, York (city), gent. QUEEN'S COLL., matric. 22 June, 1854, aged 19; B.A. 1858, M.A. 1861, held various curacies 1859-75, vicar of Marton in the Forest, Yorks, 1875.

Newman, George Henry, 2s. Edwin, of Yeovil, Somerset, gent. WADHAM COLL., matric. 31 Jan., 1849, aged 18; B.A. 1853, rector of West Lydford, Somerset, 1855, until his death 24 Feb., 1858.

Newman, Rev. George William, 2s. Henry, of Stroud, co. Gloucester, gent. PEMBROKE COLL., matric. 25 Oct., 1869, aged 19; scholar 1869-74, B.A. 1874, M.A. 1876.

Newman, Henry, s. Francis, of North Cadbury, Somerset, arm. WADHAM COLL., matric. 21 March, 1715-6, aged 18; B.A. 1719, M.A. 1722, brother of William 1718.

Newman, Henry, s. Charles, of Sherborne, Dorset, gent. ORIEL COLL., matric. 22 March, 1745-6, aged 19; B.A. 1749, rector of Shepton Beauchamp and Sparkford, Somerset, 1758, until his death 1 March, 1798. [30]

Newman, Henry, 3s. Edmund Lambert, of Cheltenham, co. Gloucester, arm. BALLIOL COLL., matric. 19 Oct., 1857, aged 19; B.A. 1861, M.A. 1864.

Newman, Henry Brown, s. Edwyn Sands, of Shepton Beauchamp, Somerset, cler. WADHAM COLL., matric. 6 Dec., 1815, aged 17; scholar 1816-25, B.A. 1819, M.A. 1825, fellow 1825-38, rector of Little Bromley, Essex, 1838, until his death 11 Jan., 1878.

Newman, James Steer, 3s. William, of Emsworth, Hants, cler. NON-COLL., matric. 10 April, 1880, aged 19.

Newman, John, s. Arthur, of Ringwood, Hants, gent. TRINITY COLL., matric. 3 Dec., 1776, aged 19; B.A. from NEW COLL. 1781.

Newman, John, s. John, of Barwick, Somerset, arm. TRINITY COLL., matric. 5 July, 1791, aged 18. [35]

Newman, John, 1s. John, of Aylesbury, Bucks, arm. TRINITY COLL., matric. 29 Nov., 1838, aged 18.

Newman, John, 2s. William, of Darfield, Yorks, gent. ORIEL COLL., matric. 30 June, 1848, aged 18; B.A. 1852, M.A. 1855, vicar of Worsborough, Yorks, since 1852.

Newman, John Henry, s. John, of Alton, Hants, arm. TRINITY COLL., matric. 14 Dec., 1816, aged 16, scholar 1819-22, B.A. 1820; fellow ORIEL COLL. 1822-45, M.A. 1823, B.D. 1836, tutor 1826-31, treasurer 1828, dean 1833, vice-principal St. Alban Hall 1825, hon. fellow Trinity College 1877, a student of Lincoln's Inn 1819, vicar of St. Mary-the-Virgin, Oxon, 1828-43, seceded to Rome 1845, head of the oratory of St. Philip Neri, at Birmingham, rector of the Catholic University, Dublin, 1854-8, cardinal 1879, brother of Francis William.

Newman, Morgan Henry, 2s. George, of Llandilo, co. Glamorgan, gent. JESUS COLL., matric. 31 Jan., 1870, aged 24; clerk 1870, B.A. 1874, M.A. 1877.

Newman, Philip, 6s. Richard, of Blackawton, Devon, cler. EXETER COLL., matric. 27 May, 1847, aged 17; B.A. 1852, M.A. 1854, bar.-at-law, Middle Temple, 1864. See Foster's *Men at the Bar*. [40]

Newman, Richard, of Kidlington, Oxon, 'carpenter;' 17 June, 1718.

Newman, Richard, s. William, of Dartmouth, Devon, arm. WADHAM COLL., matric. 16 Oct., 1805, aged 16; B.A. 1809, M.A. 1813, scholar until 1814, fellow 1814-5, rector of Coryton, Devon, 1830, until his death 13 Aug., 1853, father of Augustus 1851, of Charles Durnford 1839, of Frederick & Philip 1847, and of William S. 1835.

Newman, Thomas, s. Thomas, of St. Dunstan's-in-the-East, London, gent. WORCESTER COLL., matric. 10 May, 1722, aged 16.

Newman, Thomas, 'carpenter of the Theatre;' privilegiatus 7 July, 1724.

Newman, Thomas, 'groom of Merton College;' privilegiatus 27 Jan., 1762.

Newman, Thomas, s. William, of Whitchurch, Oxon, pleb. NEW COLL., matric. 16 Dec., 1774, aged 16; B.A. 1781, & chaplain, vicar choral Chichester Cathedral, vicar of Eastbourne and Durphorn, Sussex, at his death in April, 1809. [5]

Newman, Thomas Harding, 1s. Thomas, of Hornchurch, Essex, arm. WADHAM COLL., matric. 13 May, 1829, aged 17; demy MAGDALEN COLL. 1832-47, B.A. 1833, M.A. 1836, B.D. 1846, fellow 1846-73, D.D. 1847, dean of divinity 1849, bursar 1851, died 21 April, 1882. See *Bloxam*, vii. 330.

Newman, William, s. Francis, of North Cadbury, Somerset, arm. WADHAM COLL., matric. 11 July, 1718, aged 17; brother of Henry 1716.

Newman, William, s. William, of Frail, Hants, gent. WORCESTER COLL., matric. 31 Oct., 1722, aged 16.

Newman, Rev. William, o.s. John, of Worsborough, Yorks, cler. BRASENOSE COLL., matric. 8 June, 1876, aged 18; B.A. 1880, M.A. 1884.

Newman, William Abiah, M.A. TRINITY COLL., Dublin, 1842 (B.A. 1838), 1s. James, of St. Pancras, London, arm.; adm. 'ad eundem' 10 July, 1847, and incorp. from TRINITY COLL. 30 May, 1855, aged 44; B. & D.D. 7 June, 1855, dean of Capetown, died 7 Feb., 1864. [10]

Newman, William Alexander, 1s. William Abiah, of Wolverhampton, co. Stafford, cler. TRINITY COLL., matric. 30 June, 1859, aged 18; B.A. 1862, M.A. 1866, rector of Hatch Beauchamp, Somerset, 1869, until his death 21 July, 1885.

Newman, William Arthur, 1s. William Alexander, of Canterbury, cler. TRINITY COLL., matric. 11 Oct., 1884, aged 18.

Newman, William Frederick, 1s. William James, of Street, Devon, cler. ST. JOHN'S COLL., matric. 23 Jan., 1866, aged 20; B.A. 1870, M.A. 1875, vicar of Hockworthy, Somerset, 1880.

Newman, William James, o.s. William, of Dartmouth, Devon, arm. WADHAM COLL., matric. 20 June, 1838, aged 18; B.A. 1842, M.A. 1846, a student of the Inner Temple 1841, vicar of Hockworthy, Somerset, 1860, until his death 5 Jan., 1880.

Newman, Rev. William James Hermann, 1s. William, of Surbiton, Surrey, cler. NON-COLL., matric. 6 May, 1876, aged 20; B.A. 1879, M.A. 1886. [15]

Newman, William Jepson, 1s. William, of Darfield, Yorks, arm. ORIEL COLL., matric. 26 Feb., 1835, aged 18; B.A. 1838, M.A. 1841, died 15 Aug., 1859, father of Alfred 1866, and of William M. 1864.

Newman, William Lambert, 2s. Edward Lambert, of Cheltenham, co. Gloucester, gent. BALLIOL COLL., matric. 1 Dec., 1851, aged 17; scholar 1851-4, fellow 1854, B.A. 1857, M.A. 1858, historical lecturer and sub-dean 1863, reader of ancient history 1868-70, bar.-at-law, Lincoln's Inn, 1867. See Foster's *Men at the Bar*.

Newman, William Marmaduke, 1s. William Jepson, of Tankersley, near Barnsley, Yorks, cler. BALLIOL COLL., matric. 18 Jan., 1864, aged 18; B.A. 1868.

Newman, Wliliam Symons, 1s. Richard, of Dittisham, Devon, cler. WADHAM COLL., matric. 27 June, 1835, aged 17; B.A. 1840, M.A. 1842, rector of Coryton, Devon, 1853, until his death 27 April, 1880.

Newmarch, Charles Francis, o.s. Charles, of Cheltenham, co. Gloucester, gent. ST. ALBAN HALL, matric. 29 Jan., 1828, aged 17; B.A. 1833, M.A. 1834, rector of Leverton 1853, until his death 18 May, 1878. [20]

Newmarch, Francis Welles, 1s. Charles Francis, of Leverton, co. Lincoln, cler. BALLIOL COLL., matric. 1 Feb., 1873, aged 19; scholar CORPUS CHRISTI COLL. 1873-8, B.A. 1877.

Newmarch, Henry, 5s. John, of St. Trinity, Hull, Yorks, arm. ST. MARY HALL, matric. 16 May, 1823, aged 21; B.A. 1827, rector of Boultham, co. Lincoln, 1829-74, vicar of Hessle, Yorks, 1837, until his death 11 July, 1883.

Newmarch, Oliver Richardson (C.S.I.), 4s. Henry, of Cawnpore, East Indies, arm. MERTON COLL., matric. 27 May, 1853, aged 18; postmaster 1853-4, born 31 Oct., 1834, major-general, retired as colonel Bengal Staff Corps 1887, C.S.I. 1887, served with Agra brigade in 1857, assistant-secretary 1870-5, and accountant-general 1878 to military department, government of India.

Newnam, Thomas, s. Samuel, of Bristol (city), gent. CHRIST CHURCH, matric. 16 March, 1768, aged 20.

Newnham, Edward, s. James, of Chaddesley, co. Worcester, gent. UNIVERSITY COLL., matric. 13 March, 1740-1, aged 18. [25]

Newnham, Francis, s. Thomas, of Hatton Garden, Middlesex, gent. WADHAM COLL., matric. 18 June, 1798, aged 18; B.C.L. from WORCESTER COLL. 1805.

Newnham, Francis Brown, 3s. Thomas Garrett, of Llanllwchaiarn, co. Montgomery, gent. JESUS COLL., matric. 31 Jan., 1870, aged 20; B.A. & M.A. from NEW INN HALL 1883, a student of the Middle Temple 1878.

Newnham, Frederick John, y.s. George William, of Combe Down, Somerset, cler. MERTON COLL., matric. 14 Oct., 1879, aged 19; B.A. 1885, M.A. 1886.

Newnham, George William, o.s. William, of Bassingham, co. Lincoln, cler. CORPUS CHRISTI COLL., matric. 7 June, 1823, aged 16; scholar 1823-31, B.A. 1827, M.A. 1830, fellow 1831-3, perp. curate Coleford, Somerset, 1832-40, Shaw, Wilts, 1840-2, Monkton Combe, Somerset, 1845-63, and of Combe Down 1842-77.

Newnham, James, s. Thomas, of Broadwas, co. Worcester, arm. MERTON COLL., matric. 24 March, 1774, aged 19. [30]

Newnham, Lewis Edmund, 3s. George William, of Combe Down, Somerset, cler. MAGDALEN HALL, matric. 6 June, 1865, aged 19; B.A. 1869.

Newnham, Nathaniel John, 1s. Nathaniel, of Woodcote, near West Hampnett, Sussex, arm. WORCESTER COLL., matric. 11 Dec., 1852, aged 32; B.A. 1856.

Newnham, Philip Hankinson, 3s. William, of Farnham, Surrey, gent. WADHAM COLL., matric. 24 Jan., 1850, aged 17; B.A. 1854, M.A. 1857, rector of Frome-Vauchurch, Dorset, 1869-73, vicar of East Stonehouse, Devon, 1873-5, and of Maker, Cornwall, 1875-86, chaplain Devon and Exeter Hospital 1886.

Newnham, Thomas, s. Thomas, of Broadwas, co. Worcester, arm. NEW COLL., matric. 4 Feb., 1773, aged 19.

Newnham, William Heurtley, 1s. George W., of Coleford, near Bath, Somerset, cler. BALLIOL COLL., matric. 30 Nov., 1852, aged 18; B.A. 1856. M.A. 1869, bar.-at-law, Inner Temple, 1870, entered Indian Civil Service 1856, a judge at Poonah 1876-82. See Foster's *Men at the Bar* & *Eton School Lists*. [35]

Newnham, William (Moore), s. William, of Ash, Surrey, gent. CORPUS CHRISTI COLL., matric. 31 Oct., 1771. aged 16; B.A. 1775, fellow, M.A. 1779, B.D. 1787, rector of Bassingham, co. Lincoln, 1796, until his death 3 March, 1832.

Newport, Henry, of PEMBROKE COLL., Cambridge (B.A. 1845, M.A. 1849); adm. 'ad eundem' 21 June, 1860, head-master Exeter Grammar School 1852-76, rector of Wormshill, Kent, 1875-88, rector of Tarrant Hinton 1888.

Newport, Henry Allan Wakeman, 2s. Edward Ward Wakeman, of Salwarpe, near Droitwich, co. Worcester, cler. CHRIST CHURCH, matric. 16 June, 1859, aged 17; of Hanley Court, co. Worcester, assumed the additional name of NEWPORT in 1862. See Foster's *Baronetage*, WAKEMAN.

Newport, Henry Thomas, s. James, of Worcester (city), arm. TRINITY COLL., matric. 27 April, 1795, aged 18; B.A. 1799, M.A. 1802.

Newport, Rev. John, s. John, of Frome, Somerset, gent. ST. ALBAN HALL, matric. 4 April, 1805, aged 21; B.A. from WORCESTER COLL. 1808, died 22 Nov., 1868.

Newport, Right Hon. Sir John, created D.C.L. 3 July, 1810, then of New Park, co. Kilkenny, baronet so created 25 Aug., 1839 (son of Simon Newport, of Waterford), M.P. Waterford in 9 parliaments 1803-33, P.C. Ireland and chancellor of the exchequer 1806, comptroller of the exchequer, died 9 Feb., 1843. [5]

Newport, Robert, 3s. Robert, of Dunkittle, co. Kilkenny, gent. JESUS COLL., matric. 26 Oct., 1875, aged 19; scholar 1875-80, B.A. 1879, M.A. 1883.

Newport, Robert Edward, 5s. Henry, of St. David's, Exeter, cler. EXETER COLL., matric. 21 May, 1872, aged 17, exhibitioner 1873; migrated to ST. ALBAN HALL, Lent, 1875. See *Boase*, 166.

Newport, Simon, s. Simon, of Waterford (town), Ireland, gent. QUEEN'S COLL., matric. 19 Nov., 1773, aged 18; brother of Sir John Newport.

Newport, Simon George, s. William, of Waterford, Ireland, arm. BRASENOSE COLL., matric. 6 Nov., 1802, aged 17; lieut.-colonel 10th hussars. See *Eton School Lists*.

Newsam, Clement, s. Thomas, of Warwick (town), arm. MERTON COLL., matric. 15 Dec., 1756, aged 19. [10]

Newsam, Clement, s. Clement, of Dalkeith, Scotland, gent. WORCESTER COLL., matric. 24 June, 1793, aged 16; B.A. 1797, M.A. 1800, vicar of Portbury with Tickenham 1803, until his death 10 Feb., 1859.

Newsam, James, s. John, of Chadshunt, co. Warwick, arm. ST. MARY HALL, matric. 2 Nov., 1733, aged 18 (? M.P. St. Germans 1741-7, St. Mawes 1754-61, assumed the name of CRAGGS 175–).

Newsam, Peers, s. Thomas, of Warwick (town), arm. MERTON COLL., matric. 15 Dec., 1756, aged 17; B.A. 1760.

Newsam, Thomas Peers, s. Peers, of Dunchurch, co. Warwick, cler. MERTON COLL., matric. 28 Oct., 1783, aged 17; exhibitioner. See *Rugby School Reg.*, 46.

Newsham, Henry, s. John, of St. Peter's, Carmarthen, pleb. JESUS COLL., matric. 27 Feb., 1716-7, aged 16; B.A. 1720. [15]

Newsham, James, s. Edward, of London, Middlesex, gent. ST. MARY HALL, matric. 14 July, 1736, aged 19; B.A. 1740.

Newsholme, Joseph Wilkinson, 7s. John Wilkinson, of Settle, Yorks, arm. MERTON COLL., matric. 21 Oct., 1886, aged 19.

Newsom, John Alexander, 2s. John, of Curragh, co. Kildare, gent. CHRIST CHURCH, matric. 15 Oct., 1880, aged 19; exhibitioner 1880-4, B.A. 1884.

Newstead, William, s. Christopher, of York (city), gent. UNIVERSITY COLL., matric. 14 Oct., 1814, aged 19; scholar 1814-23, B.A. 1818.

Newte, John, s. Samuel, of Tiverton, Devon, cler. CORPUS CHRISTI COLL., matric. 19 Feb., 1772, aged 16; B.A. 1775, M.A. 1779, died rector of Tidcombe quarter, parish of Tiverton 2 Dec., 1792. [20]

Newte, Samuel, s. Samuel, of Titterton, co. Denbigh cler. ORIEL COLL., matric. 7 April, 1736, aged 18 B.A. 1739, M.A. 1742, rector of Bow, Devon 1742.

Newte, Samuel, s. Samuel, of St. Thomas, Devon, cler ORIEL COLL., matric. 22 April, 1763, aged 18; B.A. from NEW COLL. 1768, M.A. 1771, rector of Alphington 1768, until his death in 1772.

Newton, Arthur Edward, 2s. Francis Wheat, of Corfe, Somerset, arm. PEMBROKE COLL., matric. 26 Oct., 1881, aged 19; B.A. 1884. See *Eton School Lists*.

Newton, Augustus, 1s. John Frank, of Begbrooke, Oxon, arm. ST. MARY HALL, matric. 14 Feb., 1822, aged 20; bar.-at-law, Middle Temple, 1837.

Newton, Benjamin, of CLARE HALL, Cambridge (B.A. 1698, M.A. 1702); incorp. 6 July, 1722. (Rev. B. N. died at Gloucester, 4 April, 1735, father of John 1730.) [25]

Newton, Benjamin Wills, o.s. Benjamin Wills, of Devonport, Devon, gent. EXETER COLL., matric. 10 Dec., 1824, aged 16; fellow 1826-32, B.A. 1829, 'one of the early Plymouth Brethren.' See *Coll. Reg.*, 126.

Newton, Charles Farley, o.s. Charles, of Croydon, Surrey, gent. CHRIST CHURCH, matric. 13 Oct., 1882, aged 21.

Newton, Charles Stancliffe, 1s. Charles, of Sydney, Australia, arm. UNIVERSITY COLL., matric. 20 Jan., 1866, aged 19; a student of the Inner Temple 1870. See *Eton School Lists*.

Newton, (Sir) Charles Thomas (K.C.B.), 2s. Newton Dickinson Hand, of Clungunford, Salop, cler. CHRIST CHURCH, matric. 17 Oct., 1833, aged 17, student 1835-61, B.A. 1837, M.A. 1840; hon. fellow WORCESTER COLL. 1874, created D.C.L. 9 June, 1875, vice-consul at Mytilene, keeper of the department of Greek and Roman antiquities in the British Museum 1861, created LL.D. Cambridge 1879, and Ph.D. Strasburg 1879, C.B. 16 Nov., 1875, K.C.B. 21 June, 1887.

Newton, Charles William, 1s. James Banner, of Liverpool, arm. TRINITY COLL., matric. 17 Oct., 1885, aged 18. [30]

Newton, Francis Curzon, 2s. Charles Edmund, of Mickleover, co. Derby, arm. MERTON COLL., matric. 23 April, 1879, aged 17; B.A. 1883, a student of the Inner Temple 1882.

Newton, Francis James, 3s. Francis Rhodes, of St. Croix, East Indies, arm. UNIVERSITY COLL., matric. 13 Oct., 1876, aged 19; B.A. 1879, a student of the Inner Temple 1878, private secretary to the governor of the Cape of Good Hope. See *Rugby School Reg.*

Newton, Francis Murray, 1s. Francis Wheat, of Corfe, Somerset, gent. UNIVERSITY COLL., matric. 23 Jan., 1871, aged 18; B.A. & M.A. 1879, an inspector in school of practical mechanics at Eton. See *Eton School Lists*.

Newton, Francis Wheat, 2s. John, of Brentford, Middlesex, gent. PEMBROKE COLL., matric. 27 Jan., 1831, aged 17; B.A. 1835, of Barton Grange, Somerset, high sheriff 1861.

Newton, Frank Henry, 2s. William, of Ewerby Thorpe, co. Lincoln, arm. WADHAM COLL., matric. 12 Oct., 1866, aged 18. [35]

Newton, George, s. George, of London, gent. ORIEL COLL., matric. 4 March, 1747-8, aged 18; B.A. 1752, rector of Isfield, Sussex, 1755, until his death 18 Dec., 1791.

Newton, George, s. Samuel, of Mount Pleasant, Lancashire, arm. TRINITY COLL., matric. 22 Feb., 1817, aged 18; B.A. 1821. See *Eton School Lists*.

Newton, George Herbert, 4s. Francis, of Leeds, cler. NON-COLL., matric. 16 Oct., 1886, aged 19.

Newton, George William, s. Robert, of Heaton Norris, Lancashire, arm. BRASENOSE COLL., matric. 25 May, 1805, aged 16; B.A. 1809, M.A. 1814, brother of Robert 1800.

Newton, James, s. James, of Clerkenwell, Middlesex, gent. CHRIST CHURCH, matric. 13 Feb., 1732-3, aged 19; B.A. from CORPUS CHRISTI COLL. 1736.

Newton, James, s. James, of Withycombe, Somerset, pleb. ST. EDMUND HALL, matric. 11 Dec., 1762, aged 17; B.A. 1767.

Newton, James Antrobus, s. Robert, of Stockport, Cheshire, arm. BRASENOSE COLL., matric. 1 Feb., 1777, aged 17; of Cheadle Heath, Cheshire, died in 1823.

Newton, John, s. Benjamin, of co. Gloucester, cler. MAGDALEN COLL., matric. 25 Sep., 1730, aged 18, clerk 1730-1; M.A. from CHRIST'S COLL., Cambridge, 1738, vicar of Taynton, co. Gloucester. See *Bloxam*, ii. 92; & *Gent.'s Mag.*, 1790, ii. 1150.

Newton, John Frank, s. William, of St. Christopher's, West Indies, arm. CHRIST CHURCH, matric. 8 July, 1786, aged 19. [5]

Newton, John Horton, 1s. John, of Barnet, Middlesex, gent. EXETER COLL., matric. 19 April, 1882, aged 19; B.A. 1885.

Newton, Joseph, s. Joseph, of St. Nicholas, Leicester (town), pleb. LINCOLN COLL., matric. 17 March, 1721-2, aged 17; B.A. 1725, M.A. 1728, rector of Little Cheverell, Wilts, and vicar of Coleshill, Berks, 1759.

Newton, Newton, 1s. William Henry Davis, of Sandford, Oxon, gent. PEMBROKE COLL., matric. 29 May, 1860, aged 17; scholar 1860-5, B.A. 1863, M.A. 1869, assumed the surname of NEWTON in lieu of DAVIS, curate-in-charge of Princes Risborough 1876-80, died 1 Sep. (or March), 1881.

Newton, Newton Dickinson Hand, s. George Watson Hand, of St. Giles's, Cripplegate, London (archdeacon of Dorset, see page 599). ST. MARY HALL, matric. 2 June, 1802, aged 23; B.A. 1806, assumed the additional name of NEWTON, vicar (and patron) of Bredwardine 1829, and rector (and patron) of Brobury, co. Hereford, 1829, until his death 22 Nov., 1853, father of William 1831, and Charles Thomas 1833.

Newton, Peter, s. Peter, of St. Werburgh, Chester (city), cler. BRASENOSE COLL., matric. 24 March, 1715-6, aged 18; B.A. 20 Feb., 1719-20, M.A. 1722.

Newton, Philip, s. Philip, of Kilkenny (city), Ireland, arm. CHRIST CHURCH, matric. 2 June, 1813, aged 18. See *Eton School Lists.* [11]

Newton, Philip Arthur, o.s. Alfred Vincent, of Chiswick, Middlesex, arm. BRASENOSE COLL., matric. 19 June, 1878, aged 18.

Newton, Philip Jocelyn, 1s. Walter, of Dublin, arm. CHRIST CHURCH, matric. 20 Oct., 1836, aged 18; of Dunleckney Manor, co. Carlow, high sheriff 1846. See *Eton School Lists.*

Newton, Richard, 3s. Richard, of Ambleside, Westmoreland, gent. QUEEN'S COLL., matric. 29 Jan., 1834, aged 19; scholar 1834-6.

Newton, Robert, s. Robert, of Heaton Norris, Manchester, Lancashire, gent. BRASENOSE COLL., matric. 14 Jan., 1800, aged 16; B.A. 1803, fellow, M.A. 1806, died rector of St. Peter's Chapel, Stockport, 24 Feb., 1810. See *Rugby School Reg.*, 71. [15]

Newton, Thomas, fellow of TRINITY COLL., Cambridge (B.A. 1726, M.A. 1730); incorp. 13 Oct., 1733, D.D. 1745, preb. of Westminster 1757, bishop of Bristol 1761-82, dean of St. Paul's 1768, until his death 14 Feb., 1782.

Newton, Thomas, s. William, of Manchester, Lancashire, gent. BRASENOSE COLL., matric. 28 May, 1781, aged 18; B.A. from CHRIST'S COLL., Cambridge, 1785, M.A. 1788, rector of St. Cuthbert with St. Helen on the Walls, York, 1789, and vicar of Holy Trinity Church, Micklegate, 1789, perp. curate Coxwold, died in July, 1807. See *Manchester School Reg.*, i. 181.

Newton, Thomas, s. Lancelot, of Grasmere, Westmoreland, pleb. QUEEN'S COLL., matric. 9 July, 1724, aged 18.

Newton, Walter, s. Philip, of Bagnalstown, Carlow, Ireland, arm. CHRIST CHURCH, matric. 2 June, 1813, aged 20; of Dunleckney, co. Carlow, died 23 Aug., 1853. See *Eton School Lists.*

Newton, William, s. William, of Walton, co. Derby, cler. ST. JOHN'S COLL., matric. 22 March, 1730-1, aged 18. [20]

Newton, William, s. William, of Langdon, Devon, arm. ORIEL COLL., matric. 30 June, 1780, aged 17.

Newton, William, s. James, of Stowey, Somerset, cler. PEMBROKE COLL., matric. 27 March, 1801, aged 17; B.A. 1804. (Memo.: William N., M.P. Ipswich 1818-20, died at Elvedon Hall, Suffolk, 4 Nov., 1862, aged 80). See *Eton School Lists.*

Newton, William, 1s. Newton Dickinson, of Wrotham, Kent, cler. BALLIOL COLL., matric. 17 June, 1831, aged 18; B.A. 1836, rector of New Radnor.

Newton, William John, o.s. James, of Aberdeen, gent. CORPUS CHRISTI COLL., matric. 20 Oct., 1879, aged 18; B.A. 1883, a student of the Inner Temple 1881.

Newton, William Latham, 3s. John Fendall, of Whorlton, Yorks, arm. MAGDALEN COLL., matric. 16 Oct., 1880, aged 18. [25]

Newton, William Robert, 1s. William Leaper, of Derby, arm. BRASENOSE COLL., matric. 25 May, 1836, aged 19; of Birmington Hall, co. Derby, died 7 Nov., 1854.

Newtown-Butler, Brinsley, Baron of, born in St. Anne's, Dublin, s. Robert, Earl of Lanesborough. CHRIST CHURCH, matric. 27 Oct., 1801, aged 18; 4th Earl of Lanesborough, died 15 June, 1847. See Foster's *Peerage.*

Neycoe, Philip, of ST. JOHN'S COLL., Cambridge (? M.A.); incorp. 19 Oct., 1718.

Neyle, William, s. William, of Ipplepen, Devon, arm. EXETER COLL., matric. 8 April, 1742, aged 20; B.A. 1747, rector of West Ogwell, and chaplain of Naplais Royal, Nova Scotia, died at Great Ambrook 7 Sep., 1804.

Nias, Joseph Baldwin, 1s. Joseph, of Bath, Somerset, knight. EXETER COLL., matric. 16 Jan., 1875, aged 18; scholar 1876-9, B.A. 1879, B.Med. 1883. See *Coll. Reg.*, 168. [30]

Nibbs, George, s. James Langford, of Bettshanger, Kent, arm. ORIEL COLL., matric. 18 Oct., 1783, aged 18; B.A. 1787, vicar of Cutcombe with Luxborough, Somerset, 1791, until his death in 1832.

Nibbs, George Langford, o.s. George, of Cutcombe, Somerset, cler. PEMBROKE COLL., matric. 27 Oct., 1821, aged 20.

Nibbs, James Langford, s. James, of Isle of Antigua, gent. ST. JOHN'S COLL., matric. 9 Nov., 1758, aged 19.

Nibbs, James Langford, o.s. George Langford, of Stowey, Somerset, gent. WORCESTER COLL., matric. 9 June, 1852, aged 18.

Niblett, Arthur Edward, 1s. Edward Henry, of Haresfield, co. Gloucester, cler. EXETER COLL., matric. 13 Oct., 1871, aged 19; B.A. 1875, of Haresfield aforesaid, a student of the Inner Temple 1873.

Niblett, Edward Henry, 2s. Daniel John, of Haresfield, co. Gloucester, arm. EXETER COLL., matric. 29 April, 1830, aged 19; B.A. 1834, rector of Redmarley-d'Abitot, co. Gloucester, 1853, until his death 20 Oct., 1878. [36]

Niblett, Harry Edward, 5s. Charles, of Cheltenham, gent. TRINITY COLL., matric. 16 Oct., 1886, aged 20.

Niblett, Henry Morton, 2s. Edward Henry, of Redmarley, co. Worcester, cler. PEMBROKE COLL., matric. 20 Oct., 1873, aged 19; B.A. 1878, M.A. 1881, rector of Redmarley-d'Abitot, co. Gloucester, 1882.

Niblett, John (Daniel Thomas), 1s. John, of Haresfield, co. Gloucester, arm. EXETER COLL., matric. 1 March, 1827, aged 17; B.A. 1832, M.A. 1834, of Haresfield Court, co Worcester, died 1 Nov., 1833. See *Eton School Lists*.

Niblock, Joseph White, s. James, of Liverpool, Lancashire, gent. ST. EDMUND HALL, matric. 2 May, 1808, aged 21; B.A. 1812, M.A. 1824, B.D. 1825, D.D. 1825, curate of Hitchin, Herts, and master of the Free School 1820, undertook a private school in London, and called it the London High School, but without success, evening lecturer of St. Mary Somerset, Upper Thames Street, 1837, died in 1843.

Nicolls, Benjamin, s. William, of Isle of Barbados, arm. QUEEN'S COLL., matric. 11 Nov., 1748, aged 18.

Nicolls, Edward, s. Ed., of St. Michael's, Gloucester (city), pleb. PEMBROKE COLL., matric. 6 Nov., 1724, aged 20; B.A. 1728.

Nichol, John, o.s. John Pringle, of Montrose, Forfar, Scotland, doctor. BALLIOL COLL., matric. 24 April, 1855, aged 21; exhibitioner 1859-61, B.A. 1859, M.A. 1874, a student of Gray's Inn 1859, professor of English, Glasgow University, 1862. [5]

Nichol, John Pringle, 1s. John, of Glasgow, arm. BALLIOL COLL., matric. 22 Oct., 1883, aged 20; exhibitioner 1883, scholar 1883-6.

Nicholas, Charles, s. Robert, of Marylebone, London, arm. CHRIST CHURCH, matric. 1 June, 1813, aged 19; bar.-at-law, Middle Temple, 1818, died at Falmouth July, 1822.

Nicholas, Edmund Parry, 4s. George, of London, gent. EXETER COLL., matric. 17 Oct., 1863, aged 21; B.A. 1866, M.A. 1870, vicar of Worfield, Salop, 1872.

Nicholas, Edward, s. Edward, of South Stoneham, co. Southampton, arm. ST. MARY HALL, matric. 5 Dec., 1738, aged 18; brother of William 1734.

Nicholas, Edward Richmond, s. Edward, of Devizes, Wilts, gent. QUEEN'S COLL., matric. 14 June, 1748, aged 18; a physician, died in 1770, father of John 1781, and Robert 1774. [10]

Nicholas, Francis, s. George, of Ealing, Middlesex, doctor. WADHAM COLL., matric. 20 March, 1812, aged 16; B.A. 1815, M.A. 1818, D.C.L. 1839.

Nicholas, Rev. George, s. George, of Llantillio Crossenny, co. Monmouth, gent. WADHAM COLL., matric. 17 May, 1781, aged 17; scholar 1782, B.A. 1785, M.A. 1791, B. & D.C.L. 1793, died headmaster of Ealing School 20 Nov., 1829, father of the last named.

Nicholas, George Davenport, 1s. George, of Marylebone, London, gent. PEMBROKE COLL., matric. 22 Nov., 1855, aged 18; scholar 1855-60, B.A. 1859, M.A. 1862, perp. curate Clewer St. Stephen 1873. See *Robinson*, 294.

Nicholas, John, s. Edward, of Devizes, Wilts, doctor. QUEEN'S COLL., matric. 17 May, 1781, aged 17; B.C.L. 1788, D.C.L. 1800, rector of Fisherton Anger 1800, and Bremilham 1804, and vicar of Westport, Wilts, 1800, until his death 7 Oct., 1836.

Nicholas, Matthew, s. Matt., of Shalford, Surrey, cler. CORPUS CHRISTI COLL., matric. 30 May, 1723, aged 16; demy MAGDALEN COLL. 1726-31, B.A. 1727, M.A. 1730, fellow 1731-45, B.D. 1738, D.D. 18 Jan., 1742-3, senior dean of arts 1738, bursar 1739, dean of divinity 1744, presented to Willoughby 1740, rector of Swaby, co. Lincoln, 1743, vicar of Beeding, Sussex, 1744-87, rector of Penshurst, Kent, Dec., 1786, until his death 13 June, 1796, buried at Penshurst. See *Bloxam*, vi. 208. [15]

Nicholas, Robert, s. Math., of Shalford, Surrey, cler. MAGDALEN HALL, matric. 2 May, 1728, aged 16; B.A. 17 Feb., 1731-2.

Nicholas, Robert, s. Edward Richmond, of Devizes, Wilts, arm. QUEEN'S COLL., matric. 28 Nov., 1774, aged 16; F.S.A., bar.-at-law, Lincoln's Inn, 1782, M.P. Cricklade 1785 to March, 1790, chairman and commissioner board of excise 32 years, died 27 Dec., 1826, father of Charles 1813.

Nicholas, Tressilian George, 5s. George, of St. George's, Westminster, cler. and doctor. WADHAM COLL., matric. 25 April, 1839, aged 17; B.A. 1843, M.A. 1846, perp. curate West Molesey, Surrey, 1846-59, and since 1863, vicar of Lower Halstow, Kent, 1859-63.

Nicholas, William, s. Edward, of South Stoneham, co. Southampton, arm. NEW COLL., matric. 6 April, 1734, aged 16; brother of Edward 1738.

Nicholas, William Llewellyn, 10s. Thomas, of Fishguard, co. Pembroke, gent. JESUS COLL., matric. 27 Oct., 1868, aged 19; scholar 1869-73, B.A. 1873, M.A. 1879, rector of Flint since 1880. [20]

Nicholes, Philip, s. Jonathan, of Manchester, Lancashire, gent. BRASENOSE COLL., matric. 4 April, 1715, aged 16; B.A. 1718, M.A. 1722 (as NICHOLS).

Nicholes, William, s. John, of St. Mary's, Oxford (city), arm. MAGDALEN HALL, matric. 28 March, 1726, aged 15; B.A. from CORPUS CHRISTI COLL. 1729, M.A. 1732, B.D. 26 Feb., 1741-2.

Nicholetts, John, o.s. William, of Chipstable, Somerset, cler. PEMBROKE COLL., matric. 26 Oct., 1881, aged 19; B.A. 1886, M.A. 1888.

Nicholetts, William, 3s. John, of South Petherton, Somerset, gent. PEMBROKE COLL., matric. 30 May, 1849, aged 18; B.A. 1853, rector of Chipstable, Somerset, 1857.

Nicholl, (Sir) Charles Gounter, s. George Gounter, of Racton, Sussex, arm. NEW COLL., matric. 4 April, 1722, aged 17; knight of the Bath 1732, assumed the additional surname of NICHOLL, M.P. Peterborough 1721, until his death 24 Nov., 1733 (his only surviving daughter was Frances, Countess of Dartmouth.) [25]

Nicholl, Charles Iltid, 3s. Iltid, of Bloomsbury, London, arm. WORCESTER COLL., matric. 17 Dec., 1845, aged 24; B.A. 1849, perp. curate Hinton St. Mary, Dorset, 1863, until his death 26 Jan., 1869. See *Eton School Lists*.

Nicholl, Rev. Charles Southey, 5s. John Richard, of Streatham, Surrey, cler. KEBLE COLL., matric. 18 Oct., 1875, aged 19; B.A. 1879, M.A. 1882.

Nicholl, Conrad Ralm, 3s. John, of Islington, Middlesex, gent. EXETER COLL., matric. 18 May, 1853, aged 18; B.A. 1858, M.A. 1860. See *St. Paul's School Reg.*, 310.

Nicholl, David, o.s. Lewis Anthony, of St. Bride-super-Ely, co. Glamorgan, cler. JESUS COLL., matric. 22 June, 1859, aged 18; B.A. 1862, M.A. 1875, rector of St. George-super-Ely, co. Glamorgan, 1869-73, and of Edvyn-Loach, co. Hereford, 1873.

Nicholl, Edward Powell, 3s. John, of Merthyr Mawr, co. Glamorgan, D.C.L. BRASENOSE COLL., matric. 6 June, 1850, aged 18; B.A. 1855, M.A. 1857, vicar of Lacock, Wilts, 1864-71, and of Ascott-under-Wychwood, Oxon, 1883-5. See *Eton School Lists*. [30]

Nicholl, Frederick Hill, 2s. Frederick Iltid, of London, arm. MERTON COLL., matric. 23 Jan., 1871, aged 19.

Nicholl, George, s. Thomas, of Sutton, Middlesex, arm. BRASENOSE COLL., matric. 24 April, 1816, aged 18.

Nicholl, George Frederick, 1s. John, of Tipton, co. Stafford, gent. BALLIOL COLL., matric. 7 June, 1878, aged 45; M.A. by decree 5 Nov., 1878, hon. fellow 1888, Lord Almoner's professor and reader in Arabic 1878, lecturer in Oriental languages 1880, professor of Sanskrit and Persian, King's College, London, 1879.

Nicholl, Henry Frederick, 1s. Frederick, of London, arm. MERTON COLL., matric. 5 Feb., 1868, aged 18; B.A. 1872, M.A. 1874.

Nicholl, Henry Iltyd, 1s. Iltyd, of St. Bennet's, London, arm. ST. JOHN'S COLL., matric. 5 June, 1826, aged 17; B.A. 1830, M.A. 1833, D.C.L. 1841, an advocate Doctors' Commons, bar.-at-law, Inner Temple, 1833, died 24 Nov., 1845, father of the next named. See *Eton School Lists*. [35]

Nicholl, Iltyd, s. Whitlock, of Lantwit Major, co. Glamorgan, arm. JESUS COLL., matric. 7 May, 1761, aged 17; B.A. 1765, fellow, M.A. 1767, B.D. 1775, D.D. 1779, died rector of Tredington, co. Worcester, 9 Oct., 1787. See *St. Paul's School Reg.*, 111.

Nicholl, Iltyd, s. John, of Llanmaes, co. Glamorgan, gent. JESUS COLL., matric. 22 Aug., 1766, aged 15; B.A. 1770, M.A. 1773, died 23 Jan., 1786, grandfather of Henry Iltyd 1826.

Nicholl, Rev. Iltyd, 1s. Iltyd, of Usk, co. Monmouth, arm. EXETER COLL., matric. 20 Feb., 1833, aged 18; B.A. 1839, M.A. 1840, died 11 Feb., 1867.

Nicholl, Iltyd, 1s. Henry Iltyd, of Marylebone, London, doctor. CHRIST CHURCH, matric. 15 May, 1856, aged 19; B.A. 1860.

Nichol, John, s. Iltid, of Lantwit Major, co. Glamorgan, pleb. JESUS COLL., matric. 5 March, 1722-3, aged 19; B.A. 1726, M.A. 1769, of Lantwit Major, rector of West Ham, Sussex, 'Parson Nicholl' or 'Black Jack.' [5]

Nicholl, John, s. Whitlock, of Ham, co. Glamorgan, arm. JESUS COLL., matric. 24 Nov., 1764, aged 18; B.A. 1768, M.A. 1771, B.D. 1778, rector of Remenham, Berks (resigned 1798), died 16 July, 1830.

Nicholl, (Sir) John, s. John, of Llanmaes, co. Glamorgan, gent. ST. JOHN'S COLL., matric. 27 June, 1775, aged 16; B.C.L. 1780, D.C.L. 1785, of Merthyr Mawr, co. Glamorgan, F.R.S., P.C., M.P. Penrhyn 1802-6, Hastings 1806-7, Rye 1807-12, Bedwyn in 6 parliaments 1812-33, king's advocate-general 1798-1809, knighted 31 Oct., 1798, judge of Prerogative Court of Canterbury and dean of the arches 1809-34, judge High Court of Admiralty 1833-8, vicar-general to the Archbishop of Canterbury 1834, until his death 26 Aug., 1838.

Nicholl, John, s. John, of London, equitis. CHRIST CHURCH, matric. 12 June, 1815, aged 17; student 1816-22, B.C.L. 1823, D.C.L. 1825, of Merthyr Mawr, co. Glamorgan, bar.-at-law, Lincoln's Inn, 1824, M.P. Cardiff 1832-52, vicar-general to the Archbishop of Canterbury 1838-44, judge advocate-general 1841, and P.C. 1841, until his death 27 Jan., 1853, father of Edward P. 1850, and of Stephen H. F. 1854.

Nicholl, John Cole, 1s. John, of Merthyr Mawr, co. Glamorgan, D.C.L. CHRIST CHURCH, matric. 20 Oct., 1841, aged 18; of Merthyr Mawr, co. Glamorgan, high sheriff 1884. See *Eton School Lists*.

Nicholl, John Iltyd Dillwyn, 1s. John Cole, of Merthyr Mawr, co. Glamorgan, arm. CHRIST CHURCH, matric. 21 May, 1880, aged 19; B.A. 1884, a student of the Inner Temple 1881. See *Eton School Lists*. [10]

Nicholl, John Richard, 1s. Richard, of Pendhill, Surrey, arm. EXETER COLL., matric. 15 May, 1828, aged 18; B.A. 1832, M.A. 1835, rector of Streatham, Surrey, since 1843. See *Eton School Lists*.

Nicholl, John Whitlock. JESUS COLL. 1833. See CARNE, page 220.

Nicholl, Rev. Robert, s. Whitlock, of Llantwit Major, co. Glamorgan, arm. JESUS COLL., matric. 26 May, 1781, aged 18; B.A. 1785, M.A. 1787, of Dimlands, co. Glamorgan, assumed the surname of CARNE in lieu of NICHOLL by royal licence 16 Dec., 1842, died 10 Nov., 1848.

Nicholl, Samuel, s. Samuel, of London, gent. BALLIOL COLL., matric. 12 July, 1765, aged 20; B.A. 1769, M.A. 1772.

Nicholl, Stephen Henry Fox, 4s. John, of London, arm. ST. JOHN'S COLL., matric. 26 June, 1854, aged 18; B.A. 1861, M.A. 1862, rector of Llandough, co. Glamorgan, 1867, brother of Edward P.

Nicholl, Thomas, s. Thomas, of Clapham, Surrey, arm. EXETER COLL., matric. 26 April, 1815, aged 18. [15]

Nicholl, Thomas, of TRINITY HALL, Cambridge (B.A. 1828, M.A. 1832), 1s. Thomas, of Lambeth, Surrey, arm. Incorp. from WORCESTER COLL. 26 April, 1844, aged 47; B.D. 15 May, 1844, D.D. 25 May, 1844.

Nicholl, Thomas Beynon, 1s. William Thomas, of Abergwile, co. Carmarthen, cler. JESUS COLL., matric. 25 Oct., 1862, aged 19; B.A. 1866.

Nicholl, Whitlock, s. Iltyd, of Lantwit, co. Glamorgan, cler. JESUS COLL., matric. 28 April, 1737, aged 16; of the Ham, co. Glamorgan, high sheriff, 1746, died 21 Jan., 1788.

Nicholl, William Lewis, o.s. William, of Funchale, Isle of Madeira, D.Med. QUEEN'S COLL., matric. 25 Nov., 1841, aged 20. [20]

Nicholls, Benjamin, s. Peter, of St. Mary's, co. Pembroke, pleb. JESUS COLL., matric. 4 April, 1734, aged 17; B.A. 1737, M.A. 1740 (? vicar of Eccles, Lancashire, 1748).

Nicholls, Benjamin. QUEEN'S COLL., 1748. See NICCOLLS.

Nicholls, Benjamin Ernest, 1s. Henry, of Byfleet, Surrey, arm. MAGDALEN COLL., matric. 24 Jan., 1884, aged 19; B.A. 1886.

Nicholls, Charles Henry, 2s. Henry, of Kirdford, Sussex, arm. NEW COLL., matric. 18 Oct., 1886, aged 19.

Nicholls, Edward. PEMBROKE COLL., 1724. See NICCOLLS. [25]

Nicholls, Francis, s. John, of London (city), gent. EXETER COLL., matric. 14 March, 1714-5, aged 17; B.A. 1718, M.A. 1721, B.Med. 16 Feb., 1724-5, D.Med. 16 March, 1729-30, reader in anatomy, F.R.S. 1728, fellow College of Physicians 1732, physician to George II. 1753-60, died 7 Jan., 1778, father of John 1761. See Munk's *Roll*, ii. 123.

Nicholls, Francis, s. John, of London, arm. CHRIST CHURCH, matric. 3 Nov., 1790, aged 16; bar.-at-law, Lincoln's Inn, 1799, his father of Whitchurch, Oxon.

Nicholls, Francis Hamilton, 4s. Francis, of London, gent. WADHAM COLL., matric. 16 Oct., 1875, aged 20; B.A. 1879, M.A. 1882, vicar of St. Stephen, Islington, 1884.

Nicholls, Frank, 1s. Frank, of St. Gluvias, Cornwall, arm. EXETER COLL., matric. 27 July, 1831, aged 17.

Nicholls, George, s. Richard, of St. Clement's, London, arm. BRASENOSE COLL., matric. 8 April, 1731, aged 17. [30]

Nicholls, George, s. George, of Westminster, arm. BRASENOSE COLL., matric. 17 May, 1763, aged 18.

Nicholls, Henry, s. Henry, of Garrans, Cornwall, gent. EXETER COLL., matric. 13 Dec., 1791, aged 18, exhibitioner 1793, B.A. 1796; incorp. CAMBRIDGE UNIVERSITY 1808, M.A. from ST. PETER COLL. 1808, vicar of Peyhembury and Rockbear, Devon, 1831, until his death 5 Jan., 1860. See *Coll. Reg.*, 148.

Nicholls, Henry, o.s. Benjamin Elliott, of Walthamstow, Essex, cler. WADHAM COLL., matric. 2 May, 1855, aged 18; B.A. 1859, M.A. 1862.

Nicholls, Henry Cornelius, 1s. Henry, of Barnstaple, Devon, cler. EXETER COLL., matric. 23 Jan., 1850, aged 19. See *Rugby School Reg.*, 265.

Nicholls, Henry James, 2s. John George, of West Moulsey, Surrey, arm. QUEEN'S COLL., matric. 1 May, 1823, aged 17. See *Eton School Lists*. [35]

Nicholls, Jeremiah, s. Joseph, of Cary, Somerset, gent. BALLIOL COLL., matric. 22 March, 1747-8, aged 17; bar.-at-law, Lincoln's Inn, 1754.

Nicholls, John, s. John, of Worcester (city), gent. UNIVERSITY COLL., matric. 4 June, 1739, aged 17; B.C.L. 1748.

Nicholls, John, s. John, of Walgrove, Northants, pleb. LINCOLN COLL., matric. 13 March, 1739-40, aged 22.

Nicholls, John, s. Francis, of London, doctor. EXETER COLL., matric. 16 June, 1761, aged 16; B.A. 1765, of Goring, Oxon, bar.-at-law, Lincoln's Inn, 1767, M.P. Bletchingley 1783-7, Tregony 1798-1802, died 1832.

Nicholls, Robert Boucher, s. Isaac, of Barbados, gent. QUEEN'S COLL., matric. 2 Nov., 1762, aged 18; B.A. 1766, B.C.L. 1778 (as NICKOLLS).

Nicholls, Samuel, o.s. Samuel, of Bridgnorth, Salop, gent. PEMBROKE COLL., matric. 14 Nov., 1826, aged 16; B.A. 1830.

Nicholls, William, s. Richard, of Welton, Northants, pleb. LINCOLN COLL., matric. 23 Jan., 1718-19, aged 17; B.A. 1722.

Nicholls, William, s. Daniel, of Castlecomb, Wilts, pleb. BRASENOSE COLL., matric. 26 Feb., 1719-20, aged 17.

Nicholls, William, s. Peter, of Haverfordwest, co. Pembroke, pleb. JESUS COLL., matric. 26 Oct., 1736, aged 17; B.A. 1740. [5]

Nicholls, William Hunt Ward, 1s. Ward, of Calcutta, cler. WADHAM COLL., matric. 19 Oct., 1874, aged 18.

Nichols, Daniel, s. Richard, of Warrington, Lancashire, gent. BRASENOSE COLL., matric. 26 Oct., 1776, aged 18; B.A. 1780.

Nichols, Francis Morgan, 3s. John B., of Hampstead, Middlesex, gent. EXETER COLL., matric. 15 Feb., 1844, aged 17; scholar WADHAM COLL. 1844-9, B.A. 1847, fellow 1849-56, M.A. 1853, of Lawford Hall, Essex, J.P., bar.-at-law, Inner Temple, 1852. See Foster's *Men at the Bar.*

Nichols, George, s. John, of Cumner, Berks, pleb. MAGDALEN COLL., matric. 10 May, 1733, aged 16; chorister 1726, until expelled in 1734. See *Bloxam,* i. 156.

Nichols, John, s. John, of Coventry (city), pleb. ST. JOHN'S COLL., matric. 30 June, 1742, aged 18; B.A. 1746, fellow, M.A. 22 March, 1749-50, B.D. 1755, D.D. 1760, died vicar of St. Lawrence, Reading, 25 June, 1788. [10]

Nichols, John Bowyer Buchanan, 1s. Francis Morgan, of London, arm. BALLIOL COLL., matric. 16 Oct., 1879, aged 19; B.A. 1884.

Nichols, John Bruce, o.s. John Gough, of Wandsworth, Surrey, gent. ST. JOHN'S COLL., matric. 17 Oct., 1868, aged 19; B.A. 1872, M.A. 1876. See Walford's *County Families.*

Nichols, Philip. BRASENOSE COLL., 1715. See NICHOLES.

Nichols, Robert, B.A. from JESUS COLL., 13 Oct., 1726 (*Acts Book*).

Nichols, Rev. Sebastian Elijah, 4s. George, of Sheffield, co. York, pleb. MAGDALEN COLL., matric. 23 April, 1870, aged 21, clerk 1870-3, B.A. 1873; chaplain CHRIST CHURCH 1873-9, M.A. 1876, schoolmaster 1874-8. [15]

Nichols, Walter Buchanan, 2s. Francis Morgan, of London, arm. ORIEL COLL., matric. 15 Oct., 1879, aged 19.

Nichols, Walter Henry, 2s. George, of Sheffield, Yorks, gent. NEW COLL., matric. 7 Nov., 1871, aged 33.

Nichols, William. MAGDALEN HALL, 1726. See NICHOLES.

Nichols, William, s. Edward, of Linton, Devon, cler. QUEEN'S COLL., matric. 31 March, 1762, aged 18.

Nichols, Rev. William, s. William, of Chalmarsh, Salop, arm. CHRIST CHURCH, matric. 4 Dec., 1766, aged 16; B.A. 1770, M.A. 1775, died at Chalmarsh 4 Sep., 1801. [20]

Nichols, William Austin, 1s. John, of Bewdley, co. Worcester, arm. UNIVERSITY COLL., matric. 24 March, 1846, aged 18; bar.-at-law, Inner Temple, 1855.

Nichols, William Luke, 1s. Luke, of Gosport, Hants, arm. QUEEN'S COLL., matric. 28 Feb., 1821, aged 18; B.A. 1825, M.A. 1829, minister of Holy Trinity, Bath, 1839-46, vicar of Buckland Monachorum, Devon, 1846-51.

Nichols, William Powley, 1s. James, of London, gent. WORCESTER COLL., matric. 17 May, 1854, aged 19; B.A. 1859, M.A. 1861, rector of Little Cheverell, Wilts, 1868.

Nicholson, Arthur Carlton, 3s. William, of London, gent. CHRIST CHURCH, matric. 27 May, 1882, aged 17; B.A. 1885.

Nicholson, Arthur William, 1s. William Smith, of Gibraltar, arm. MAGDALEN COLL., matric. 1 June, 1870, aged 18; B.A. 1874, of Dukenfield, Cheshire, and of Arisaig, co. Inverness. [25]

Nicholson, Sir Charles, created D.C.L. 24 June, 1857, chancellor of the University of Sydney, New South Wales, 1854-60 (o.s. John Nicholson, of London), D.Med. Edinburgh, speaker of the Legislative Assembly, New South Wales, 1845-56, knighted by patent 1 March, 1852, created a baronet 8 April, 1859. See Foster's *Baronetage.*

Nicholson, Charles Archibald, 1s. Charles, of London, baronet. NEW COLL., matric. 15 Oct., 1886, aged 19.

Nicholson, Claude Humphry de Bohun, 1s. Horace, of Forest Hill, Essex, D.D. CHRIST CHURCH, matric. 15 Oct., 1886, aged 18.

Nicholson, Edward, s. Joseph, of Wigton, Cumberland, gent. QUEEN'S COLL., matric. 7 Nov., 1799, aged 16; B.A. 1803, M.A. 1807, rector of Pentridge, Devon, died 9 April, 1853.

Nicholson, Edward Elcock, 5s. John, of Penrith, Cumberland, arm. NON-COLL., matric. 29 Oct., 1877, aged 23; scholar WORCESTER COLL. 1877-80, B.A. 1881, died 2 Feb., 1886. [30]

Nicholson, Edward Henry, 1s. William Newzam, of Newark-on-Trent, Notts, arm. BALLIOL COLL., matric. 17 Oct., 1864, aged 19; B.A. 1869, M.A. 1873.

Nicholson, Edward Williams Byron, o.s. Edward, of St. Helier, Isle of Jersey, arm. TRINITY COLL., matric. 12 Oct., 1867, aged 18; scholar 1867-72, B.A. 1871, M.A. 1874, librarian of the London Institution 1873-82, Bodley's librarian 1882.

Nicholson, Frederick Augustus, 4s. Brinsley William Hewetson, of Islington, Middlesex, D.Med. LINCOLN COLL., matric. 20 Jan., 1866, aged 19.

Nicholson, Geoffry, s. Richard, of St. Bees, Cumberland, pleb. QUEEN'S COLL., matric. 10 Nov., 1720, aged 17; B.A. 26 Feb., 1724-5.

Nicholson, Henry Joseph Boone, s. John Payler, of Liston Green, London, cler. MAGDALEN HALL, matric. 22 May, 1817, aged 22; B.A. 1821, M.A. 1823, B.D. 1835, D.D. 1839, F.S.A., F.R.A.S., etc., rector of St. Albans 1835, hon. canon of Rochester 1862, until his death 27 July, 1866. [35]

Nicholson, Horatio Langrishe, scholar of TRINITY COLL., Dublin, 1851 (B.A. 1855, M.A. 1859); adm. 'ad eundem' 10 Nov., 1859, B. & D.D. 1880, vicar of St. Paul's, Southsea, since 1872.

Nicholson, Hugh Blomfield, 5s. William, of London, arm. NEW COLL., matric. 16 Oct., 1885, aged 18.

Nicholson, Rev. Hugh Smith, 6s. John, of Windermere, Westmoreland, arm. TRINITY COLL., matric. 16 Oct., 1880, aged 19; B.A. 1884, M.A. 1887.

Nicholson, James, s. James, of Warton, Lancashire pleb. QUEEN'S COLL., matric. 25 May, 1732, aged 16; B.A. 16 March, 1735-6 (Rev. J. P., of county palatine Durham, died 4 May, 1771).

Nicholson, James Nicholson, M.A. TRINITY COLL., Dublin, 1862 (B.A. 1860); adm. 'comitatis causa' 17 Dec., 1863, held various curacies 1871-86, chaplain City of London Cemetery 1886, took the name of NICHOLSON in lieu of CUSTIS. [40]

Nicholson, John, s. Henry, of Moresby, Cumberland, cler. ST. EDMUND HALL, matric. 2 June, 1813, aged 18.

Nicholson, John, 1s. Mark, of Isle of Barbados, West Indies, cler. QUEEN'S COLL., matric. 14 June, 1825, aged 16; B.A. 1830.

Nicholson, John, 3s. James. of Manchester, arm. BRASENOSE COLL., matric. 25 May, 1836, aged 19; scholar 1836-41, B.A. 1840. See *Manchester School Reg.,* iii. 243.

Nicholson, John Aldwell, scholar TRINITY COLL., Dublin, 1849 (B.A. 1852, M.A. 1858); adm. 'ad eundem' 7 July, 1859, consular chaplain at Gothenburg 1867-74, perp. curate Christ Church, Leamington, 1874-81, minister of St. Alban Martyr, Leamington, 1873.

Nicholson, John Harbottle, 1s. John, of Halliwell Dene, Northumberland, arm. CORPUS CHRISTI COLL., matric. 21 Oct., 1878, aged 19; B.A. 1882.

Nicholson, John (Payler), s. John, of London, arm. CHRIST CHURCH, matric. 17 June, 1778, aged 19; student 1778, B.A. 1782, M.A. 1786, master of St. Alban's free school 1796-1803, rector of St. Alban's 1796, until his death 9 May, 1817. See *Alumni West.*, 409.

Nicholson, John Ralph, 1s. William Middleton, of Liverpool, Lancashire, arm. CHRIST CHURCH, matric. 29 March, 1832, aged 20.

Nicholson, Rev. Mark, s. John, of Barton, Westmoreland, pleb. QUEEN'S COLL., matric. 11 Oct., 1790, aged 20; B.A. 1795, M.A. 1797, 25 years president of Codrington College, Barbados, died 16 June, 1838, father of John 1825. [5]

Nicholson, Nathaniel Alexander, 2s. John Armytage, of Dublin, arm. TRINITY COLL., matric. 26 Oct., 1843, aged 16; B.A. 1849, M.A. 1858, died 15 Feb., 1874.

Nicholson, Octavius, 8s. John, of Brigg, co. Lincoln, gent. ST. EDMUND HALL, matric. 14 Jan., 1851, aged 18.

Nicholson, Ralph, s. Francis, of Macclesfield, Cheshire, gent. BRASENOSE COLL., matric. 17 April, 1751, aged 17; B.A. 1755, fellow, M.A. 1757, rector of Dudcote, Berks, 1768, until his death 26 Dec., 1792, father of William 1794.

Nicholson, Ralph, s. Ralph, of Newington, Middlesex, arm. WORCESTER COLL., matric. 12 May, 1809, aged 22.

Nicholson, Rhodes, 2s. William Nicholson, of Heavitree, Devon, arm. LINCOLN COLL., matric. 15 March, 1849, aged 18. [10]

Nicholson, Richard, o.s. Richard, of Bahia, Brazil, gent. ORIEL COLL., matric. 30 May, 1846, aged 19; bible clerk 1846-50, B.A. 1850, M.A. 1852, perp. curate St. Mark, Easton, near Bristol, 1855-8, rector of Beechingstoke, Wilts, 1858, until his death 30 Sep., 1885.

Nicholson, Richard Thomas, 1s. Richard Thomas, of Maidstone, Kent, gent. UNIVERSITY COLL., matric. 14 Oct., 1882, aged 18; exhibitioner 1882-6, B.A. 1886.

Nicholson, Robert Laurence, 1s. Robert Laurence, of Cambridge, gent. ST. ALBAN HALL, matric. 13 Feb., 1868, aged 20.

Nicholson, Stansfield, 1s. Mark Anthony, of Accrington, Lancashire, cler. ST. EDMUND HALL, matric. 27 Oct., 1864, aged 18.

Nicholson, Thomas, s. Clement, of Whitehaven, Cumberland, pleb. QUEEN'S COLL., matric. 18 March, 1744-5, aged 17; taberdar 1748, B.A. 1750, M.A. 1754, fellow 1762, B.D. 1765, D.D. 1773, proctor 1764, vicar of Newbold Pacey 1781, died 25 Aug., 1803. See *O. H. S.*, ix., p. 14. [15]

Nicholson, Tom Marshall, 2s. William, of Leeds, gent. QUEEN'S COLL., matric. 10 Nov., 1885, aged 18.

Nicholson, William, s. Anton., of Crosby, Westmoreland, pleb. QUEEN'S COLL., matric. 12 July, 1734, aged 17, B.A. 1738, M.A. 1747.

Nicholson, William, s. Ralph, of Dudcote, Berks, cler. BRASENOSE COLL., matric. 23 May, 1794, aged 19; B.A. 1798.

Nicholson, William, s. John, of Thorpe, Westmoreland, gent. QUEEN'S COLL., matric. 18 Feb., 1802, aged 16; B.A. 1805, M.A. 1809, chaplain 1815-16, fellow 1816-29, rector of Bramshot, Hants, 1829, until his death in 1832.

Nicholson, William, 3s. Christopher Armytage, of Balrath, co. Meath, arm. TRINITY COLL., matric. 25 Oct., 1824, aged 19; B.A. 1829, M.A. 1831, rector of Welford with Wickham, Berks, 1836, until his death 15 Dec., 1878. [20]

Nicholson, William, 1s. William, of Sunderland, arm. BRASENOSE COLL., matric. 28 May, 1874, aged 18.

Nicholson, William Smith, 1s. William Henry, of Frindsbury, near the city of Rochester, arm. CHRIST CHURCH, matric. 2 June, 1852, aged 18; B.A. 1856, M.A. 1865. See Walford's *County Families.*

Nickalls, Guy, 3s. Tom, of Sutton, Kent, gent. MAGDALEN COLL., matric. 21 Oct., 1886, aged 19.

Nickalls, Hugh Patteson, 2s. Tom, of Bromley, Kent, gent. PEMBROKE COLL., matric. 27 Oct., 1884, aged 19.

Nickalls, Norman Tom, 1s. Tom, of Homesdale, Kent, arm. NEW COLL., matric. 12 Oct., 1883, aged 19. See *Eton School Lists.* [25]

Nickoll, Samuel Wilson, o.s. Samuel, of Elham, Kent, gent. QUEEN'S COLL., matric. 9 Nov., 1830, aged 17.

Nickolls, Robert Boucher. See NICHOLLS, p. 1022.

Nickson, William, s. Jonathan, of Malpas, Cheshire, gent. BRASENOSE COLL., matric. 10 Oct., 1805, aged 19; curate West Cowes, Isle of Wight, and of Farnham Royal, Bucks, died 26 Sep., 1841.

Nicol, Donald Ninian, o.s. John, of Liverpool, gent. QUEEN'S COLL., matric. 30 Oct., 1863, aged 20; B.A. 1867, M.A. 1872, of Ardmarnoch, co. Argyle, J.P., D.L., bar.-at-law, Middle Temple, 1870. See Foster's *Men at the Bar.*

Nicolas, Percy, 2s. Nicholas Harris, of St. George's, Bloomsbury, London, equitis. MAGDALEN HALL, matric. 16 March, 1854, aged 19. [30]

Nicolay, Baron, created D.C.L. 12 Jan., 1817, ambassador from the Emperor of Russia to the Court of Denmark, attending on the Grand Duke Nicholas.

Nicolay, George (Frederick Louisa), entered CHRIST CHURCH 24 Dec., 1781, B.A. 24 Nov., 1784, student, M.A. 26 April, 1787 (*Acts Book*), rector of St. Michael Royal and St. Martin Vintry, London, 1790, vicar of Little Marlow, Bucks, 1821, a brother of St. Katharine's Hospital, near the Tower of London, 1802, chaplain to the Duke of York, died at St. Katharine's, Regent's Park, 13 Dec., 1847, aged 83.

Nicolay, Nicholas, s. Frederick, of Westminster, arm. EXETER COLL., matric. 10 Nov., 1780, aged 15.

Nicoll, Alexander, s. John, of Monymusk, co. Aberdeen, gent. BALLIOL COLL., matric. 7 Dec., 1807, aged 14, B.A. 1811, M.A. 1814; canon CHRIST CHURCH and regius professor of Hebrew 1822-8, D.C.L. 1822, a sub-librarian Bodleian library, died 25 Sep., 1828. [34]

Nicoll, Charles, 1s. Samuel John, of Lyndhurst, Hants, arm. EXETER COLL., matric. 10 May, 1822, aged 17; B.A. 1827, vicar of Kings Sombourne, Hants, 1850, until his death 30 Sep., 1882.

Nicoll, Charles Alfred Samuel, o.s. Charles, of Stratford, Essex, cler. BRASENOSE COLL., matric. 31 May, 1860, aged 18; B.A. 1863, M.A. 1867, held various curacies 1865-74, rector of Bepton, Sussex, 1874-86.

Nicoll, John, s. John, of Westminster, doctor. CHRIST CHURCH, matric. 6 June, 1746, aged 18; B.A. 1750, M.A. 1753, rector of Meonstoke, Hants, preb. of Salisbury 1757, until his death 12 July, 1759. See *Alumni West.*, 337.

Nicoll, Richard, s. Thomas, of Preston Capes, Northants, cler. LINCOLN COLL., matric. 19 June, 1750, aged 17; B.A. 1755, fellow, M.A. 1757, B.D. 1764, D.D. 1775, rector of Drayton, Oxon, 1770, chancellor of Bath and Wells 1783, and preb. 1786, chaplain in ordinary to the King (resigned 1804), died 20 Jan., 1813.

Nicoll, (Thomas Vere) Richard, s. Richard, of Bodicot, Oxon, doctor. ORIEL COLL., matric. 7 May, 1788, aged 18; B.A. 1792, M.A. 1795, rector of Chevington, co. Warwick, 1796, until his death 22 Oct., 1841.

Nicolls, Edward Richard Jefferys, o.s. Richard, of Woolwich, Kent, arm. CHRIST CHURCH, matric. 18 April, 1873, aged 19; B.A. 1878, M.A. 1881, rector of Knipton, co. Lincoln, 1884. See *Rugby School Reg.*

Nicolls, Edward Trafford, s. Edward, of Liverpool, Lancashire, arm. CHRIST CHURCH, matric. 21 Oct., 1802, aged 19.

Nicolls, Ernest Hastings, 4s. Francis Hastings Gustavus, of Ashhorne, co. Warwick, arm. KEBLE COLL., matric. 14 Oct., 1879, aged 19; B.A. 1885.

Nicolls, Francis Hastings Gustavus, o.s. Jasper, of Calcutta, East Indies, equitis. ORIEL COLL., matric. 18 March, 1841, aged 19. **[5]**

Nicolls, Gustavus George, 1s. Jasper Hume, of Lennoxville, Canada, D.D. ST. MARY HALL, matric. 27 Oct., 1869, aged 17; bible clerk ORIEL COLL. 1870-3, B.A. 1873, M.A. 1881, incumbent of St. James's, Quebec.

Nicolls, Jasper Hume, 3s. Gustavus, of Isle of Guernsey, arm. ORIEL COLL., matric. 2 June, 1836, aged 17, B.A. 1840, M.A. 1843; Michel fellow QUEEN'S COLL. 1843-8, D.D. 1856, principal of Bishop's College, Lennoxville, Canada, died Aug., 1877.

Nicolls, Thomas, s. William, of Stafford (town), gent. ORIEL COLL., matric. 17 Dec., 1754, aged 19; B.C.L. from NEW COLL. 1763.

Nicolls, William, 2s. William, of Ware, Herts, gent. NON-COLL., matric. 10 April, 1869, aged 28; B.A. from HERTFORD COLL. 1874, M.A. 1876, has held various curacies since 1875.

Nicols, John, s. William, of Stockport, Cheshire, cler. MERTON COLL., matric. 18 July, 1719, aged 17; B.A. 1723, M.A. 1726, B. & D.D. 1759 (? rector of Dengey, Essex, 1761). **[10]**

Nicols, John Luke, s. John, of Montfield, Sussex, arm. ST. JOHN'S COLL., matric. 16 Nov., 1738, aged 17.

Nicolson, Arthur (C.M.G.) 2s. Frederick, of London, (*soi-disant*) baronet. BRASENOSE COLL., matric. 12 March, 1868, aged 18; secretary of legation at Teheran 1885, C.M.G. 6 Aug., 1886. See Foster's *Baronetage*, CHAOS.

Nicolson, Arthur Badenach, 1s. James Badenach, of Glenbervie, Scotland, arm. UNIVERSITY COLL., matric. 11 Oct., 1884, aged 19; B.A. 1887.

Nicolson, Clement, s. Clement, of 'Bondgate, city of London,' gent. QUEEN'S COLL., matric. 13 Nov., 1777, aged 18; B.A. 1781, M.A. 1784.

Nicolson, Edward Badenach, 2s. James, of Glenbervie, co. Kincardine, arm. BALLIOL COLL., matric. 19 Oct., 1886, aged 18. **[15]**

Nicolson, Jeremiah, s. Jere., of London, cler. ST. JOHN'S COLL., matric. 30 June, 1742, aged 18; B.A. 1746, M.A. 22 March, 1749-50, B.D. 1755, D.D. 1759, vicar of St. Lawrence, Reading, 1763, until his death 19 July, 1771. See *Robinson*, 82.

Nicolson, John Archibald Shaw-Stewart-, 2s. Michael Shaw-Stewart, of London (city), baronet. CHRIST CHURCH, matric. 27 May, 1847, aged 17; B.A. 1851, M.A. 1854, on council of Keble College 1871, and bursar 1876-80. See Foster's *Baronetage*.

Nicolson, Thomas, s. John, of Dalston, Cumberland, gent. QUEEN'S COLL. matric. 24 March, 1715-6, aged 16; B.C.L. 1723.

Nicolson, William, s. John, of Hoxded, Cumberland, gent. QUEEN'S COLL., matric. 17 Dec., 1722, aged 19; B.A. 13 June, 1723, M.A. 1726.

Nicolson, William, s. William, of St. Bees, Cumberland, pleb. QUEEN'S COLL., matric. 19 Sep., 1761, aged 18; B.A. 1766, M.A. 1769. **[20]**

Nightingale, Thomas, of ST. JOHN'S COLL., Cambridge (B.A. 1848, M.A. 1856); adm. 'ad eundem' 15 Nov., 1855, rector of St. Clement's, Hastings, 1855.

Nihill, Henry Daniel, 2s. Daniel, of Montgomery (town), cler. JESUS COLL., matric. 20 Nov., 1852, aged 18; scholar 1855-8, B.A. 1857, held various curacies 1857-67, vicar of St. Michael, Shoreditch, 1867 (curate 1865-7).

Nikitin, Basilius, of Russia; created M.A. ST. MARY HALL 2 May, 1770, also M.A. by diploma 2 June, 1775. See *Cat. Grads.*

Nind, Rev. Hubert George, 4s. Philip Henry, of Woodcote, Oxon, cler. UNIVERSITY COLL., matric. 17 May, 1864, aged 18; B.A. 1868, M.A. 1872, of Woodcote House, aforesaid. See *Eton School Lists.*

Nind, James, s. William, of ——, Middlesex, gent. TRINITY COLL., matric. 12 Nov., 1728, aged 17; B.A. 1732, rector of Englefield, Berks (? rector of Hackney 1753). **[25]**

Nind, Philip, s. Philip, of St. Martin's, London, gent. HERTFORD COLL., matric. 13 March, 1769, aged 18; B.A. 1772, vicar of Wargrave and Waltham St. Laurence, 1784, until his death in 1815, father of Philip Trant.

Nind, Philip Henry, 1s. Philip Trant, of Sunning, Berks, cler. CHRIST CHURCH, matric. 2 June, 1823, aged 17; student 1827-31, B.A. 1828, M.A. 1830, vicar of South Stoke, Oxon, 1844, until his death 13 Nov., 1886.

Nind, Philip Henry, 1s. Philip Henry, of Harehatch, near Maidenhead, Berks, cler. CHRIST CHURCH, matric. 23 May, 1850, aged 18; B.A. from NEW INN HALL 1857, M.A. 1858, gold commissioner British Columbia. See *Eton School Lists.*

Nind, Philip Trant, s. Philip, of Braughing, Herts, cler. MERTON COLL., matric. 27 Oct., 1795, aged 17; B.A. 1799 (as Philip), vicar of Wargrave 1816, until his death 30 Sep., 1826.

Ninis, Richard Duncan, 1s. George Wyatt, of Stockport, Cheshire, cler. KEBLE COLL., matric. 19 Oct., 1886, aged 19. **[30]**

Nisbet, John Marjoribanks, o.s. Josiah, of Madras, East Indies, arm. BALLIOL COLL., matric. 17 Dec., 1842, aged 18; B.A. 1846, M.A. 1851, rector of Deal 1856-61, vicar of Ramsgate 1861-7, rector of St. Giles'-in-the-Fields, London, and canon of Norwich, 1867.

Nisbet, Matthew Alexander, of JESUS COLL., Cambridge (B.A. 1860, M.A. 1863); adm. 'comitatis causa' 16 June, 1863, vicar of St. Luke, co. Gloucester, 1872-81, rector of Ringwould, Kent, 1881.

Nisbet, Walter, 2s. Harry, of Purneah, India, arm. MAGDALEN HALL, matric. 23 April, 1858, aged 22.

Nisbet, William, s. William, of Marlfield, Tiviotdale, arm. ST. MARY HALL, matric. 19 Nov., 1735, aged 15.

Niven, Robert, 1s. John, of Glasgow, gent. LINCOLN COLL., matric. 19 Oct., 1867, aged 21; scholar 1867-71, B.A. 1884, M.A. 1888, bar.-at-law, Lincoln's Inn, 1885. See Foster's *Men at the Bar*.

Nivernais, Louis Jules Barbou Mancini Mazarini, Duke de, Prince of the Holy Roman Empire, knight of the Order of the 'Sainct Esprit;' created D.C.L. 21 April, 1763, French ambassador at Rome, Berlin, and at the Court of St. James', where he negotiated the peace of 1763, imprisoned by the Republicans 1793, died 25 Feb., 1798, aged 82, author of several works. See *Biographie Universelle* & *Gent.'s Mag.*, 1798, i. 355. **[35]**

Nixon, Charles, s. Thomas, of Nuthall, Notts, cler. MERTON COLL., matric. 11 Oct., 1784, aged 18; B.A. 1788, vicar of Great Dalby, co. Leicester, 1791, rector of Nuthall 1797, preb. of Southwell 1825, until his death in 1837.

Nixon, Rev. Charles Farnsworth, y.s. John, of Nottingham, gent. LINCOLN COLL., matric. 2 June, 1841, aged 18; B.A. 1845, M.A. 1848, died 13 Dec., 1854.

Nixon, Charles Jones, 3s. William, of Woodlands, Walton Breck, near Liverpool, gent. WADHAM COLL., matric. 21 May, 1858, aged 18; B.A. 1862, M.A. 1865, bar.-at-law, Middle Temple, 1862. See Foster's *Men at the Bar.*

Nixon, Francis Russell, 2s. Robert, of North Cray, Kent, cler. ST. JOHN'S COLL., matric. 1 July, 1822, aged 18; scholar & fellow 1822-9, B.A. 1827, M.A. 1841, D.D. by decree 9 July, 1842, perp. curate Plaistow, Essex, and of Sandgate, Kent, chaplain at Naples, vicar of Ash-next-Sandwich, Kent, one of the six preachers of Canterbury, bishop of Tasmania 1842-63, rector of Bolton Percy, Yorks, 1864-5, died 7 April, 1879. See *Robinson*, 189.

Nixon, Frederick, 1s. James Lock, of Hackthorne, co. Lincoln, arm. BRASENOSE COLL., matric. 9 Dec., 1845, aged 20.

Nixon, Harry Vidal, 2s. Henry, of Norwood, Surrey, gent. BRASENOSE COLL., matric. 23 Oct., 1885, aged 20. **[5]**

Nixon, Rev. Howard, 3s. William, of London, gent. QUEEN'S COLL., matric. 6 Feb., 1878, aged 19; clerk 1877-82, B.A. 1882, M.A. 1884.

Nixon, James Lock, s. Thomas, of Berners Street, London, arm. CHRIST CHURCH, matric. 2 Feb., 1811, aged 17.

Nixon, John Evelyn, 2s. John, of Camden Villa, Cheltenham, arm. WADHAM COLL., matric. 13 Oct., 1866, aged 23, exhibitioner 1867-8; scholar Christ's College, Cambridge, 1863-6.

Nixon, Jonathan, s. Jonathan, of Ranow, Cheshire, pleb. BRASENOSE COLL., matric. 21 May, 1742, aged 24.

Nixon, Robert, s. Robert, of London, arm. CHRIST CHURCH, matric. 15 Nov., 1776, aged 17; B.A. 1780, M.A. 1783, B.D. 1790, died at Kenmure Castle, New Galloway, 5 Nov., 1837. **[10]**

Nixon, Robert, 1s. Thomas, of Oswald Kirk, Cumberland, gent. QUEEN'S COLL., matric. 22 June, 1854, aged 19.

Nixon, Thomas, s. Jeffery, of Nottingham, pleb. LINCOLN COLL., matric. 4 Nov., 1741, aged 18; B.A. 1745, rector of Old Dalby, co. Leicester, and rector of Nuthall and vicar of Hucknall, Notts, died 18 July, 1785.

Nixon, Thomas, 1s. John, of Nottingham, gent. LINCOLN COLL., matric. 1 Feb., 1823, aged 19; B.A. 1827, M.A. 1829, died vicar of Great Dalby, co. Leicester, 6 June, 1838.

Nixon, William, 1s. John, of Hackney, Middlesex, arm. WORCESTER COLL., matric. 9 June, 1848, aged 17; B.A. 1852, vicar of Sutton, Norfolk, 1855-72.

Noad, George Frederick, 1s. Humphrey Minchin, of Road and (*sic*) Woolverton, Somerset, gent. WORCESTER COLL., matric. 16 Dec., 1831, aged 19; exhibitioner 1831-8, B.C.L. 1838, D.C.L. 1846, held various scholastic appointments 1846-67, rector of Cold Norton, Essex, 1868, until his death 25 Nov., 1876.

Noble, George Harford, 1s. George James Luke, of St. Pancras, London, gent. QUEEN'S COLL., matric. 12 Dec., 1862, aged 21. **[15]**

Noble, Henry, s. Jos., of Cockermouth, Cumberland, pleb. QUEEN'S COLL., matric. 7 Nov., 1716, aged 18; father of next named.

Noble, Henry, s. Henry, of Croglin, Cumberland, cler. QUEEN'S COLL., matric. 4 Feb., 1745-6, aged 17; B.A. 1749, M.A. 1752.

Noble, Henry Lovell, s. Anthony, of Frolesworth, co. Leicester, cler. ALL SOULS' COLL., matric. 16 July, 1756, aged 18; B.A. 1760, died rector of Frolesworth 14 Feb., 1788.

Noble, John, s. Thomas, of Bampton, Westmoreland, pleb. QUEEN'S COLL., matric. 30 April, 1719, aged 17. **[20]**

Noble, John Henry Brunel, 3s. Andrew, of Newcastle-on-Tyne, arm. BALLIOL COLL., matric. 15 Oct., 1884, aged 19.

Noble, Joseph Horace, o.s. Joseph Alfred, of Fortis Green, Middlesex, arm. NEW COLL., matric. 16 Oct., 1874, aged 19; B.A. 1878, M.A. 1885.

Noble, Mark, 1s. Joseph William, of Leicester, doctor. MAGDALEN HALL, matric. 30 March, 1855, aged 21; B.A. 1858, M.A. 1860, a student of Lincoln's Inn 1859.

Noble, Robert, s. Mungo Henry Waller, of Ardbraccan, co. Meath, Ireland, cler. BRASENOSE COLL., matric. 11 June, 1814, aged 17; B.A. 1819, M.A. 1825, of Glass Drummond, co. Fermanagh, rector and vicar of Athboy, etc.

Noble, Thomas, s. Joseph, of Cockermouth, Cumberland, pleb. QUEEN'S COLL., matric. 9 Nov., 1722, aged 18; B.A. 1726, M.A. 1733, rector of Wolvey, co. Warwick, preb. of Lichfield, died 10 March, 1784. **[25]**

Noble, Walter Elliott Wheelock, 3s. Jeffrey Wheelock, of Plymouth, Devon, arm. WADHAM COLL., matric. 13 Oct., 1871, aged 19; B.A. 1875.

Noble, William, s. William, of Penrith, Cumberland, pleb. QUEEN'S COLL., matric. 7 Nov., 1716, aged 18; B.A. 1721 (? rector of Nettleworth, Essex, 1735).

Noble, William, s. Joseph, of Cockermouth, Cumberland, pleb. QUEEN'S COLL., matric. 4 March, 1723-4, aged 18.

Noble, William, 2s. John, of Abbey-town, near Carlisle, gent. ST. ALBAN HALL, matric. 24 March, 1874, aged 30; B.A. 1878, M.A. 1880, vicar of Newbottle, Oxon, 1873.

Noble, William James, born at Islington, Middlesex, 1s. John, of Little Over, co. Derby. KEBLE COLL., matric. 19 Oct., 1874, aged 19; scholar 1874-8, B.A. 1879, M.A. 1883, bar.-at-law, Inner Temple 1882. See Foster's *Men at the Bar.* **[30]**

Nocke, Richard, s. John, of Oldington, Salop, pleb. PEMBROKE COLL., matric. 8 May, 1733, aged 19; B.A. 3 March, 1737-8.

Nocton, Thomas, s. Thomas, of Washingborough, co. Lincoln, gent. LINCOLN COLL., matric. 10 May, 1758, aged 18; B.A. 1762, vicar of Bracebridge, co. Lincoln, 1769, until his death 24 March, 1809, aged 72.

Nodder, Joseph, s. John, of Chesterfield, co. Derby, arm. WADHAM COLL., matric. 13 June, 1806, aged 17; B.A. 1811, M.A. 1814, rector of Ashover, co. Derby, 1835, until his death 15 Jan., 1878.

Noel, Hon. Berkeley Octavius, s. Gerard, of Brighton, Sussex, baronet. MAGDALEN COLL., matric. 10 Feb., 1815, aged 20; died 28 March, 1841. See Foster's *Peerage*, E. GAINSBOROUGH.

Noel, Charles, 3s. John Perrott, of Bell Broughton, co. Worcester, arm. ST. JOHN'S COLL., matric. 29 June, 1821, aged 18; of Bell Broughton, high sheriff co. Worcester, 1853, died 3 Feb., 1877. **[35]**

Noel, Charles Francis Adderley, 1s. Berkeley Charles, of Warwick, arm. MERTON COLL., matric. 11 Oct., 1873, aged 19. See Foster's *Peerage*, E. GAINSBOROUGH; & *Eton School Lists.*

Noel, Rev. Clobery, s. Clobery, of Kirkby Mallory, co. Leicester, baronet. NEW COLL., matric. 23 April, 1735, aged 18; B.A. 15 Jan., 1738-9, M.A. 1742, died 27 Feb., 1763, brother of Edward, Viscount Wentworth.

Noel, Edward, s. Clobery, of Kirkby, co. Leicester, baronet. NEW COLL., matric. 23 July, 1733, aged 17; created M.A. 19 July, 1736, and also D.C.L. 23 Aug., 1744, 6th baronet in 1723, and Baron Wentworth, of Nettlested, in 1745, created Viscount Wentworth 5 May, 1762, died 31 Oct., 1774. See Foster's *Peerage.*

Noel, Rev. Edward Henry, 2s. Berkeley Charles Plantagenet, of Coleshill, near Birmingham, arm. CHRIST CHURCH, matric. 8 Feb., 1877, aged 17; B.A. 1880. See Foster's *Peerage* & *Eton School Lists.*

Noel, (Hon.) Francis James, s. Gerard Noel, of Marylebone, London, arm. TRINITY COLL., matric. 26 May, 1813, aged 19; B.A. 1817, M.A. 1820, vicar of Teston 1820, and rector of Nettlestead, Kent, 1820, until his death 30 July, 1854. See Foster's *Peerage*, E. GAINSBOROUGH.

Noel, James Gambier, 2s. Francis James, of Teston, Kent, cler. CHRIST CHURCH, matric. 11 Dec., 1845, aged 19; of the Admiralty.

Noel, John, s. Clobery, of Kirkby, co. Leicester, baronet. ORIEL COLL., matric. 28 March, 1735, aged 15, B.A. 1738; M.A. from BRASENOSE COLL. 1741, B.D. 1757, rector of Aston, co. Warwick, and of Steeple Aston, Oxon, 1762, until his death 3 Nov., 1790.

Noel, Montague Henry, 3s. Francis James, of Teston, near Maidstone, Kent, cler. CHRIST CHURCH, matric. 10 June, 1859, aged 18; B.A. 1863, M.A. 1866, vicar of St. Barnabas, Oxford, 1869. See Foster's *Peerage*, E. GAINSBOROUGH.

Noel, Rowney, s. Clobery, of Kirkby Mallory, co. Leicester, baronet. ST. JOHN'S COLL., matric. 1 Nov., 1743, aged 17; B.A. from ALL SOULS' COLL. 1747, M.A. 1751, B.D. 1759, rector of Kirkby Mallory and Elmsthorpe, co. Leicester, dean of Salisbury 1780, until his death 26 June, 1786. [5]

Noel, Thomas, s. Edward, Viscount Wentworth. BRASENOSE COLL., matric. 4 Nov., 1763, aged 17; created M.A. 29 April, 1766, and also D.C.L. 7 July, 1773, 2nd Viscount Wentworth, M.P. Leicester in 1774, died s.p. 17 April, 1815 (? father of Thomas 1792). See Foster's *Yorkshire Collection*.

Noel, Thomas, 1s. Thomas, of Kirkby Mallory, co. Leicester, cler. MERTON COLL., matric. 19 Feb., 1819, aged 19; B.A. 1824.

Noel, Thomas Noel, s. Thomas, of London, arm. (? viscount). CHRIST CHURCH, matric. 27 April, 1792, aged 18; B.A. 1796, M.A. 1801, rector of Kirkby Mallory, co. Leicester, 1801, until his death 22 Aug., 1853, father of Thomas last named.

Noel, Wyndham, 1s. David, of Llanwaton, co. Glamorgan, cler. NON-COLL., matric. 13 Oct., 1884, aged 19; B.A. from EXETER COLL. 1887.

Nogle, Henry, s. Daniel, of Challicombe, Devon, cler. EXETER COLL., matric. 2 Nov., 1756, aged 19; B.A. 1760. [10]

Nolan, Edward, 2s. Thomas, of Liverpool, Lancashire, cler. ST. JOHN'S COLL., matric. 27 June, 1864, aged 18; scholar 1867, until his death 4 Oct., 1870, a student of the Inner Temple 1869. See *Robinson*, 336.

Nolan, Frederick, of TRINITY COLL., Dublin, 1796, s. Edward, of St. Peter's, Dublin, arm. EXETER COLL., matric. 19 Nov., 1803, aged 22; B.C.L. & D.C.L. 1828, Boyle lecturer 1812-5, Bampton lecturer 1833, Warburton lecturer 1833-7, F.R.S., 1832, vicar of Prittlewell, Essex, 1822, until his death 16 Sep., 1864. For list of his writings see *Gent.'s Mag.*, 1864, ii. 788.

Nolan, Thomas, 1s. Thomas, of Liverpool, cler. ST. JOHN'S COLL., matric. 25 June, 1862, aged 18; scholar 1862-9, B.A. 1866, M.A. 1870, rector of Kingston-Bagpuze, Berks, 1877. See *Robinson*, 320.

Nolloth, Charles Frederick, 2s. Henry Ovenden, of Bexley, Kent, gent. ORIEL COLL., matric. 23 Oct., 1868, aged 18; B.A. 1872, M.A. 1875, vicar of Ashley Green, Bucks, 1875-80, rector of All Saints, Lewes, 1880.

Nolloth, Henry Edward, 1s. Henry Ovenden, of Bexley, Kent, gent. WORCESTER COLL., matric. 14 Oct., 1865, aged 19; B.A. 1868, M.A. 1872, B.D. 1880, perp. curate St. John Baptist, Plumstead, 1870-3, vicar of Christ Church, Chesham, 1873-80, and of Beverley Minster 1880. [15]

Noneley, Richard Marigold, 1s. Richard, of Market Drayton, Salop, gent. CHRIST CHURCH, matric. 11 Oct., 1819, aged 18.

Noott, Rev. Edgar Frank Cornwallin, 2s. Francis Harry, of Poole, Dorset, arm. MAGDALEN COLL., matric. 19 Jan., 1880, aged 20; B.A. 1883, M.A. 1886.

Norbury, John Frederick, 1s. Thomas, of Macclesfield, Cheshire, gent. TRINITY COLL., matric. 23 May, 1860, aged 18; B.A. 1863, M.A. 1866.

Norbury, Thomas, s. John, of Prestbury, Cheshire, gent. BRASENOSE COLL., matric. 4 April, 1720, aged 19.

Norbury, Thomas Coningsby Norbury, 1s. Thomas (formerly Jones), of Worcester (city), arm. CHRIST CHURCH, matric. 27 May, 1847, aged 18; of Sherridge, co. Worcester, sometime captain 6th dragoon guards, and colonel Worcestershire militia. See *Eton School Lists*. [20]

Norbury, Willoughby, 3s. Thomas, of Macclesfield, Cheshire, arm. BRASENOSE COLL., matric. 4 June, 1868, aged 19; B.A. 1871, M.A. 1875.

Norcliffe, Reginald (Miller), s. William, of London, arm. UNIVERSITY COLL., matric. 14 March, 1739-40, aged 18; died 22 Oct., 1740, M.I. Hatton, co. Warwick. See Foster's *Yorkshire Collection*.

Norcop, William Church, s. William, of Drayton, Salop, arm. CHRIST CHURCH, matric. 28 Jan., 1801, aged 17; of Betton Hall, Salop, acting high sheriff 1813, died 5 Sep., 1861.

Norcross, Thomas, s. William, of Boston, co. Lincoln, pleb. BRASENOSE COLL., matric. 8 Jan., 1714-5, aged 19; B.A. 1718.

Norcross, Thomas, s. John, of Hothfield, Kent, cler. TRINITY COLL., matric. 20 June, 1747, aged 17; B.A. 1751. [25]

Norgate, Gerald Le Grys, 1s. Charles, of East Dereham, Norfolk, gent. NON-COLL., matric. 13 Oct., 1884, aged 18; exhibitioner BRASENOSE COLL. 1886.

Norie, William Heather, o.s. John William, of Hackney, London, arm. CORPUS CHRISTI COLL., matric. 27 May, 1829, aged 17; bar.-at-law, Lincoln's Inn, 1837.

Norman, Rev. Alfred Ernest, 4s. Henry Burford, of Southsea, Hants, arm. MAGDALEN COLL., matric. 13 Oct., 1879, aged 18; B.A. 1883, M.A. 1887.

Norman, Rev. Alfred George, 4s. William, of Wanstead, Essex, cler. BRASENOSE COLL., matric. 29 Jan., 1878, aged 19; exhibitioner 1878-82, B.A. 1882, master high school Amritsar, Punjab.

Norman, Alfred Merle, 5s. John, of Exeter (city), arm. CHRIST CHURCH, matric. 15 Dec., 1848, aged 17; B.A. 1852, M.A. 1859, rector of Burmoor, co. Durham, 1866, hon. canon Durham 1885. [30]

Norman, Everard, 3s. George Blake, of Ilkeston, co. Derby, arm. LINCOLN COLL., matric. 18 Oct., 1870, aged 19, brother of George Allen 1861.

Norman, Rev. George, s. George, of Monk Silver, Somerset, gent. BALLIOL COLL., matric. 10 May, 1727, aged 19; B.A. 26 Jan., 1730-1, father of the next named.

Norman, George, s. George, of Monk Silver, Somerset, cler. ST. MARY HALL, matric. 14 March, 1750-1, aged 19; B.A. 1754.

Norman, George, of ST. PETER'S COLL., Cambridge (B.A. 1822, M.A. 1826); adm. 'comitatis causa' 6 June, 1861, perp. curate Marston 1836, and Whitgreave, co. Stafford, 1838, until his death about 1875.

Norman, George Allen, 1s. George Blake, of Ilkeston, co. Derby, arm. LINCOLN COLL., matric. 7 June, 1861, aged 18; B.A. 1866, B.Med. 1870, brother of Everard 1870. [35]

Norman, George Bethune, of TRINITY COLL., Cambridge (B.A. 1841, M.A. 1845); adm. 'ad eundem' 18 May, 1850 (son of James Ormond Norman, of Cuckfield, Sussex, and of London), minister of St. Mary Magdalen Chapel, and St. Margaret Chapel, Gloucester, 1846.

Norman, George Edward William, o.s. George, of St. Mary's, Stafford (town), cler. LINCOLN COLL., matric. 28 Feb., 1857, aged 18; scholar 1857-61, B.A. 1861, M.A. 1867, vicar of Marston, co. Stafford, 1875.

Norman, Henry, s. Henry, of Langford, Somerset, pleb. WADHAM COLL., matric. 21 March, 1729-30, aged 18; died rector of Bledon, Somerset, 13 Nov., 1780, father of Henry next named, and of William 1776.

Norman, Henry, s. Henry, of Langport, Somerset, cler. ALL SOULS' COLL., matric. 3 April, 1762, aged 19; B.A. 1765, rector of Morsted, near Winchester. See *Gent.'s Mag.*, 1788, ii. 935.

Norman, Henry, 3s. George, of Bromley, Kent, arm. CHRIST CHURCH, matric. 13 March, 1819, aged 17; B.A. 1822, a partner in the banking-house of Jones-Loyds. See *Eton School Lists.*

Norman, Rev. Henry Wilkins, 2s. John, of Congresbury, Somerset, arm. QUEEN'S COLL., matric. 26 March, 1840, aged 18; fellow NEW COLL. 1840-9, B.A. 1843, M.A. 1847, died 17 July, 1849. [5]

Norman, Herbert George Henry, 2s. Henry, of London, arm. CHRIST CHURCH, matric. 15 May, 1856, aged 18; B.A. 1859, bar.-at-law, Lincoln's Inn, 1863. See Foster's *Men at the Bar.*

Norman, James, s. James, of Cricklade, Wilts, gent. MERTON COLL., matric. 8 April, 1752, aged 16; B.A. 1756, M.A. 1759, B.D. 1776, proctor 1769, rector of Kibworth, co. Leicester, 1780, until his death 20 Dec., 1811.

Norman, James John Charles, 1s. Anthony, of Brailsford, Devon, cler. ST. EDMUND HALL, matric. 14 March, 1844, aged 22; clerk MAGDALEN COLL. 1846-8, S.C.L. 1852, B.A. 1853, M.A. 1856, rector of Warehorne, Kent, 1858-63, curate-in-charge of Berkeley 1863-9, vicar of Sevenhampton, Wilts, 1869-79, and of Highworth 1869. See *Bloxam*, ii. 122.

Norman, John, s. John, of H. Trinity, Isle of Jersey, pleb. PEMBROKE COLL., matric. 4 April, 1767, aged 22.

Norman, John Burton, o.s. Robert, of Kirk Andrews-on-Eden, Cumberland, gent. QUEEN'S COLL., matric. 10 June, 1847, aged 19; B.A. 1852, M.A. 1860, vicar of Grimsdale 1855-65, rector of Little Stanmore, Middlesex, 1865-7. [10]

Norman, John (Henry), s. John, of Hatton Garden, Middlesex, arm. TRINITY COLL., matric. 25 June, 1802, aged 17; B.C.L. 1811.

Norman, John Paxton, 1s. John, of Congresbury, Somerset, arm. EXETER COLL., matric. 16 Feb., 1837, aged 17; B.A. 1841, M.A. 1844, bar.-at-law, Inner Temple, 1852, a judge High Court of Bengal 1861, acting chief justice at Calcutta, at his death 21 Sep., 1871.

Norman, Richard Whitmore, o.s. Richard, of Bromley, Kent, arm. EXETER COLL., matric. 28 Jan., 1847, aged 17; B.A. 1851, M.A. 1853, warden St. Peter College, Radley, 1861-6, head-master St. Michael College, Tenbury, 1857-61, rector of St. James, Montreal, 1869-83, hon. canon Montreal, vice-chancellor of Bishop's College, Lennoxville, and D.C.L. 1878, rector of St. Matthias, Coté St. Antoine, 1883. See *Crockford.*

Norman, William, s. Henry, of Bledon, Somerset, cler. WADHAM COLL., matric. 23 May, 1776, aged 19; B.A. 1780, rector of Bledon on the death of his father in 1781, died 27 Sep., 1788.

Norman, William, o.s. John, of Hackney, Middlesex, arm. ST. EDMUND HALL, matric. 15 May, 1844, aged 19; B.A. 1848, M.A. 1850, perp. curate St. Jude's, Gray's Inn Road, 1853-7. [15]

Norman, William Eglesfield Bathurst, 3s. George Lewis, of Kingston, Canada, arm. EXETER COLL., matric. 16 April, 1880, aged 19; B.A. 1883, M.A. 1888, chaplain Bombay.

Norreys, (Sir) Charles Denham Orlando Jephson (Bart.), s. William Jephson, of Egham, Surrey, arm. BRASENOSE COLL., matric. 5 Feb., 1817, aged 17; B.A. 1827, M.A. 1828, of Mallow Castle, co. Cork, M.P. Mallow 1826-32, April, 1833-59, assumed the additional surname and arms of NORREYS by royal licence 18 July, 1838, and was created a baronet 6 Aug. in the same year. See Foster's *Baronetage.*

Norreys, Denham William Jephson, 1s. Denham Jephson, of Mallow, Ireland, baronet. EXETER COLL., matric. 30 May, 1839, aged 17; B.A. from NEW INN HALL 1844, died 6 May, 1888. See Foster's *Baronetage.*

Norreys, Robert Henry, o.s. Robert Josias Jackson, of Eccles, Lancashire, arm. TRINITY COLL., matric. 14 Feb., 1833, aged 20; of Davyhulme, Lancashire, J.P., D.L.

Norreys, Willoughby, Baron. MAGDALEN COLL., 1759. See BERTIE. [20]

Norris, Charles, s. Samuel, of London, gent. ALL SOULS' COLL., matric. 29 Nov., 1726, aged 19, B.A. 1730; B.C.L. from ST. EDMUND HALL 1733. (? died vicar of Brabourne, rector of Goodneston and minister of Nackington, Kent, 31 Jan., 1767).

Norris, Charles, s. John, of Marylebone, Middlesex, arm. CHRIST CHURCH, matric. 26 Oct., 1797, aged 18. See *Eton School Lists.*

Norris, Charles, s. Charles, of Norwich (city), gent. PEMBROKE COLL., matric. 14 Oct., 1818, aged 17; B.A. 1823.

Norris, Rev. Charles Leslie, 1s. Edward Samuel, of Highbury, Middlesex, arm. NEW COLL., matric. 16 Oct., 1880, aged 18; B.A. 1884, M.A. 1887, a student of the Inner Temple 1881.

Norris, Francis, 3s. William, of Netherhaven, Wilts, gent. QUEEN'S COLL., matric. 10 Nov., 1821, aged 20. [25]

Norris, George, s. William, of St. Andrew's, Middlesex, arm. TRINITY COLL., matric. 26 Oct., 1787, aged 20.

Norris, George Hugh, 2s. Henry, of Wroxton, near Banbury, Oxon, arm. EXETER COLL., matric. 11 June, 1862, aged 18; B.A. 1866, M.A. 1875, bar.-at-law, Inner Temple, 1870. See Foster's *Men at the Bar.*

Norris, George Poole, s. John, of Minehead Dulverton, Somerset, cler. EXETER COLL., matric. 9 Dec., 1811, aged 19.

Norris, George Withington, 3s. Robert, of Fairfield, near Liverpool, gent. EXETER COLL., matric. 16 Jan., 1875, aged 18; B.A. 1878, M.A. 1881, a student of Lincoln's Inn 1877.

Norris, Henry, s. William, of Sawbridgeworth, Herts, gent. MAGDALEN HALL, matric. 19 Jan., 1815, aged 22. [30]

Norris, Henry, o.s. Henry Handley, of Hackney, Middlesex, cler. BALLIOL COLL., matric. 22 March, 1828, aged 18; B.A. 1831, M.A. 1834, of Swalcliffe, Oxon. See Walford's *County Families.*

Norris, Henry Handley, of PETER HOUSE, Cambridge, B.A. 1797, M.A. 1806; adm. 'ad eundem' 23 Jan., 1817 (s. Henry Handley Norris, of Hackney), preb. of Llandaff 1819, and St. Paul's 1825, perp. curate (St. John's) South Hackney 1809-31 and rector 1831, until his death 4 Dec. 1850, father of Henry last named.

Norris, Hugh Littleton, 3s. John Pilkington, of London, B.D. TRINITY COLL., matric. 1 June, 1881, aged 18; B.A. 1885.

Norris, James, s. William, of Warblington, Hants, cler. TRINITY COLL., matric. 27 June, 1814, aged 17; scholar CORPUS CHRISTI COLL. 1815-22, B.A. 1818, M.A. 1822, fellow 1822-43, B.D. 1829, bursar 1830, D.D. 1843, president 1843, until his death 16 April, 1872.

Norris, James Hume, 1s. James, of Corpus Christi College, D.D. CORPUS CHRISTI COLL., matric. 19 Oct., 1863, aged 18. [35]

Norris, John, s. Robert, of St. Sepulchre's, London, gent. CHRIST CHURCH, matric. 23 Nov., 1738, aged 17; B.A. from MAGDALEN COLL. 1742, M.A. 1745, created D.C.L. 8 July, 1756.

Norris, John, s. Robert, of Exton, Somerset, cler. BALLIOL COLL., matric. 12 Nov., 1761, aged 18.

Norris, John, 'butler of Lincoln College;' privilegiatus 27 Jan., 1762.

Norris, John, s. John, of London, arm. MAGDALEN COLL., matric. 21 Jan., 1792, aged 18; B.A. 1795.

Norris, John, 'janitor bibliothecæ Bodleianæ;' privilegiatus 15 Oct., 1835. [5]

Norris, Rev. John Justice, 1s. John, of Newport, Salop, gent. CHRIST CHURCH, matric. 13 Oct., 1876, aged 19; exhibitioner 1876-80, B.A. 1881, M.A. 1883.

Norris, Richard, s. Richard, of Hampstead, Middlesex, arm. BRASENOSE COLL., matric. 10 Oct., 1805, aged 18.

Norris, Richard, 'serviens et virgefer;' privilegiatus 21 Nov., 1821.

Norris, Robert, s. William, of Brushford, Somerset, cler. BALLIOL COLL., matric. 8 Feb., 1730-1, aged 18; B.A. 1734, M.A. 1737.

Norris, Samuel, s. Edward, of Manchester, Lancashire, pleb. BRASENOSE COLL., matric. 21 Nov., 1729, aged 18; B.A. 1733. [10]

Norris, Samuel, s. Charles, of Brabourn, Kent, cler. CHRIST CHURCH, matric. 14 July, 1759, aged 19.

Norris, Thomas, of Mere, Wilts, 'organist;' privilegiatus 19 Oct., 1765.

Norris, Thomas, s. Samuel, of Bradford, Yorks, gent. MAGDALEN HALL, matric. 12 Dec., 1809, aged 25.

Norris, Thomas, o.s. William, of Hull, Yorks, arm. MAGDALEN HALL, matric. 10 Dec., 1825, aged 37.

Norris, William, s. John, of Nonsuch, Wilts, arm. MERTON COLL., matric. 12 March, 1735-6, aged 18. [15]

Norris, William, s. William, of Bromham, Wilts, arm. TRINITY COLL., matric. 23 Nov., 1772, aged 18.

Norris, William, s. James, of Portsmouth, Hants, gent. ST. MARY HALL, matric. 9 Dec. 1785, aged 23; B.A. 1790.

Norris, William, s. William, of Warblington, Hants, cler. TRINITY COLL., matric. 15 Dec., 1812, aged 17; exhibitioner 1814-16, B.A. 1816, M.A. 1819, curate of Warblington 1818-27, rector 1827-8, father of William Thomas 1848.

Norris, William Burrell, 3s. James, of Oxford, D.D. BRASENOSE COLL., matric. 9 June, 1870, aged 18; B.A. 1873, M.A. 1877, curate of Warblington, Hants, 1875-8, rector 1878.

Norris, William Foxley, 2s. — N., D.Med. TRINITY COLL., matric. 12 June, 1843; scholar 1843-8, B.A. 1848, M.A. 1850, vicar of Buckingham 1862-79, rector of Witney 1879. See *Rugby School Reg.*, 194. [20]

Norris, William Foxley, o.s. William Foxley, of Newbury, Berks, cler. TRINITY COLL., matric. 12 Oct., 1877, aged 18; B.A. 1881, M.A. 1884, vicar of Shirburn, Oxon, 1887.

Norris, Rev. William Smith, 1s. Richard, of Bury, Lancashire, arm. WORCESTER COLL., matric. 1 May, 1878, aged 19; B.A. 1884.

Norris, William Thomas, 1s. William, of Warblington, Hants, cler. CORPUS CHRISTI COLL., matric. 10 July, 1848, aged 18; exhibitioner 1848-52, B.A. 1852.

Norrish, Richard, s. Peter, of ——, Devon, gent. BALLIOL COLL., matric. 7 Feb., 1731-2, aged 18; B.A. 1735.

Norsworthy, George, 2s. William, of London, gent. MAGDALEN COLL., matric. 30 May, 1856, aged 18; B.A. 1861, M.A. 1863, bar.-at-law, Inner Temple, 1866. See Foster's *Men at the Bar.* [25]

Norsworthy, Henry, 3s. William, of Paddington, Middlesex, arm. MAGDALEN COLL., matric. 31 March, 1859, aged 19; B.A. & M.A. 1866, bar.-at-law, Inner Temple, 1866. See Foster's *Men at the Bar.*

North, Brownlow, y.s. (Francis), Earl of Guilford. TRINITY COLL., matric. (subs. 11 Jan.) 1760, aged 18, B.A. 1762; M.A. from ALL SOULS' COLL. 1766; canon of CHRIST CHURCH 1768-70, D.C.L. 1770, dean of Canterbury 1770, vicar of Lydd and Boxley, Kent, 1771, bishop of Lichfield 1771-4, of Salisbury 1774-81, prelate of the Order of the Garter, and bishop of Winchester 1781, until his death 12 July, 1820. See Foster's *Peerage*, E. GUILFORD.

North, Brownlow, o.s. Charles Augustus, of Chelsea, Middlesex, cler. MAGDALEN HALL, matric. 21 March, 1839, aged 29; B.A. 1842, of Dallas House, Morayshire, a well-known lay-preacher, died 9 Nov., 1875, father of Charles A. 1848. See Foster's *Peerage*, E. GUILFORD; & *Eton School Lists.*

North, Charles, s. Dan., of St. Olave's, London, pleb. ST. JOHN'S COLL., matric. 5 July, 1726, aged 18; B.A. 1730, M.A. 1735, died curate of St. Mary Magdalen, Bermondsey, 5 Dec., 1735. See *Robinson*, 46.

North, Charles (Augustus), s. Brownlow, bishop of Winchester. TRINITY COLL., matric. 26 Oct., 1803, aged 18; B.A. 1806, M.A. 1809, perp. curate of Gosport 1802, rector of Alverstoke and Havant 1809, preb. of Winchester 1812, until his death 13 Aug., 1825. See *Eton School Lists.* [30]

North, Charles Augustus, 1s. Brownlow, of Galway (town), Ireland, arm. EXETER COLL., matric. 3 Feb., 1848, aged 18; B.A. 1852, sometime captain Queen's own light infantry. See *Rugby School Reg.*, 239.

North, Dudley, Lord North, 1s. Francis, Earl of Guilford. CHRIST CHURCH, matric. 3 Dec., 1846, aged 17; died 28 Jan., 1860. See Foster's *Peerage* & *Eton School Lists.*

North, (Sir) Ford, 1s. John, of Liverpool, Lancashire, arm. UNIVERSITY COLL., matric. 30 June, 1848, aged 18; B.A. 1852, bar.-at-law, Inner Temple, 1856, Q.C. 1877, bencher 1881, justice Queen's Bench division 1881-3, Chancery division 1883, knighted 7 Dec., 1881. See Foster's *Men at the Bar.*

North, Francis, s. Francis, baron Guilford. TRINITY COLL., matric. 25 March, 1721, aged 16; 3rd baron Guilford 1729, 7th Lord North 1734, created Earl of Guilford 8 April, 1752, M.P. Banbury 1727 to Oct., 1729, died 4 Aug., 1790. See Foster's *Peerage.*

North, Francis, Earl of Guilford, s. Brownlow, bishop of Winchester. CHRIST CHURCH, matric. 16 Oct., 1790, aged 17; B.A. & M.A. from ST. MARY HALL 1797, 6th earl, rector of Alresford 1797-1850, and St. Mary, Southampton, 1797-1850, master of the hospital of St. Cross, Winchester, 1808, died 29 Jan., 1861. See Foster's *Peerage.* [35]

North, Francis Frederick. See FREDERICK 1796.

North, Frederick, s. Francis, baron (after Earl of Guilford). TRINITY COLL., matric. 12 Oct., 1749, aged 17; created M.A. 21 March, 1750, D.C.L. by diploma 10 Oct., 1772, 2nd Earl of Guilford, K.G., M.P. Banbury 1754-90, chancellor of the Exchequer 1769, first lord of the Treasury 1770, etc., chancellor of the University 1772, died 5 Aug., 1792. See Foster's *Peerage.*

North, Frederick, y.s. Frederick, Lord North, K.G. CHRIST CHURCH, matric. 18 Oct., 1782, aged 16; created D.C.L. 5 July, 1793, and D.C.L. by diploma 30 Oct., 1819, 5th Earl of Guilford, chancellor of the university of the Ionian Islands (Corfu) 1819, G.C.M.G. 26 Oct., 1819, chamberlain of the Exchequer 1779, M.P. Banbury 1792-4, F.R.S. 1794, secretary of state in Corsica 1795-7, governor of Ceylon 1798-1805, vice-admiral 1799-1805, created LL.D. Cambridge 1821, died 14 Oct., 1827. See Foster's *Peerage.*

North, Frederick (or Francis Frederick), s. Fountain, of Hampstead, Middlesex, arm. ORIEL COLL., matric. 22 Dec., 1796, aged 18; of Rougham, Norfolk, died 8 Oct., 1821. See Foster's *Peerage*, B. GUILFORD.

North, George Augustus, 1s. Frederick, Lord North, K.G. TRINITY COLL., matric. 1 Nov., 1774, aged 17; created M.A. 4 June, 1777, 3rd Earl of Guilford, M.P. Harwich 1778-84, Wootton Bassett 1784-90, Petersfield 1790, Banbury 1790-2, died 20 April, 1802.

North, James, 2s. Ford, of Liverpool, arm. BRASENOSE COLL., matric. 1 Nov., 1821, aged 19; B.A. 1825, M.A. 1828, perp. curate St. Catherine, Liverpool, 1833-73. See *Manchester School Reg.*, iii. 56.

North, James William, 1s. William, of Campfield, Lancashire, arm. NON-COLL., matric. 16 Oct., 1886, aged 22.

North, John, s. Samuel, of Crewkerne, Somerset, pleb. PEMBROKE COLL., matric. 30 May, 1734, aged 19; B.A. 17 March, 1737-8. [5]

North, John, s. John, of Bradenham, Bucks, cler. MERTON COLL., matric. 11 July, 1747, aged 19; B.A. 27 Feb., 1749-50, M.A. 1752 (? rector of Hawridge, Bucks, died in 1774).

North, Colonel John Sidney; created D.C.L. 12 June, 1839 (son of Lieut.-General Sir Charles William Doyle, K.C.B., G.C.H.), P.C. 1886, M.P. Oxon 1852-84, assumed the name of NORTH in lieu of DOYLE by royal licence 20 Aug., 1838, etc., father of William Henry John, Lord North. See below.

North, Nathaniel, s. Nathaniel, of Braunstone, Rutland, pleb. HART HALL, matric. 9 July, 1734, aged 16; B.A. 13 Feb., 1738-9.

North, Thomas, 1s. John, of Liverpool, Lancashire, arm. BRASENOSE COLL., matric. 17 June, 1830, aged 18; scholar 1830-4.

North, Walter Meyrick, 3s. William, of Lampeter, co. Cardigan, cler. BRASENOSE COLL., matric. 22 April, 1865, aged 19; B.A. 1870, bar.-at-law, Middle Temple, 1874. See Foster's *Men at the Bar*. [10]

North, William, 2s. George, of St. John's, Brecon, gent. JESUS COLL., matric. 13 June, 1825, aged 17; scholar 1830-5, B.A. 1829, M.A. 1832, professor of Latin in St. David's College, Lampeter, 1840-62, rector of Langoedmore 1845, archdeacon of Cardigan and preb. of St. David's 1860.

North, William Henry John, Lord, 1s. John Sidney, of Brighton, Sussex, arm. CHRIST CHURCH, matric. 8 June, 1854, aged 17; 11th Lord North. See Foster's *Peerage* & *Eton School Lists*.

Northcote, (Hon.) Amyas Stafford, 5s. Sir Stafford, baronet (after Earl of Iddesleigh). UNIVERSITY COLL., matric. 14 Oct., 1882, aged 17. See Foster's *Peerage*, E. IDDESLEIGH.

Northcote, Rev. Arthur Hugh, 1s. Hugh Stafford, of Nice, Italy, arm. ST. JOHN'S COLL., matric. 18 Feb., 1846, aged 19; B.A. 1850, died 2 Dec., 1860.

Northcote, (Hon.) Arthur Francis, 4s. Stafford Henry, of Upton Pyne, Devon, baronet (after earl). NEW COLL., matric. 14 Oct., 1871, aged 18; B.A. 1875, M.A. 1879, rector of Dodbrooke, Devon, 1884, and of Washfield since 1884. See *Rugby School Reg.* [15]

Northcote, Augustus Beauchamp, 1s. Augustus, of Camberwell, London, arm. QUEEN'S COLL., matric. 7 April, 1859, aged 27; B.A. 1862, M.A. 1865, lecturer in natural science Exeter College 1858-65, died 28 Dec., 1869.

Northcote, George Barons, s. Robert, of Buckerell, Devon, arm. CORPUS CHRISTI COLL., matric. 5 May, 1814, aged 17; of Somerset Court, Bridgwater, high sheriff 1855, died 2 April, 1875. See *Eton School Lists*.

Northcote, George Barons, 1s. George Barons, of Feniton, Devon, arm. EXETER COLL., matric. 25 May, 1837, aged 17; B.A. 1841, M.A. 1844, of Somerset Court, Somerset, and of Buckerell, Devon, rector (and patron) of Feniton since 1860.

Northcote, George Barons, 1s. George Barons, of Ilfracombe, Devon, cler. ST. MARY HALL, matric. 22 Oct., 1863, aged 18.

Northcote, George Russell, 8s. Henry Mowbray, of Monk Okehampton, Devon, cler. NEW COLL., matric. 14 Oct., 1882, aged 19; scholar 1882-6, B.A. 1886, fellow 1886. See Foster's *Peerage*, E. IDDESLEIGH. [20]

Northcote, (Sir) Henry (Bart.), s. Henry, of Tawstock, Devon, baronet. TRINITY COLL., matric. 23 April, 1729, aged 18; 5th baronet, M.P. Exeter 1735, until his death 28 May, 1743.

Northcote, Henry (Stafford), s. Stafford Henry, of Pyne House, Devon, baronet. CHRIST CHURCH, matric. 23 Oct., 1810, aged 18; B.A. 1813, M.P. Heytesbury 1826-30, died 22 Feb., 1850, father of Lord Iddesleigh.

Northcote, Henry Mowbray, 2s. Henry Stafford, of Streatham, Surrey, arm. NEW COLL., matric. 24 Jan., 1846, aged 19; B.A. 1849, rector of Monk Okehampton, Devon, died 6 Feb., 1878. See Foster's *Baronetage* & *Eton School Lists*.

Northcote, Hon. Sir Henry Stafford, Bart., C.B., 2s. Stafford Henry, of London, baronet (after earl). MERTON COLL., matric. 28 Jan., 1865, aged 18; B.A. 1869, M.A. 1873, baronet so created 23 Nov., 1887, entered Foreign Office 1868, financial secretary to War Office, June, 1885, to Jan., 1886, surveyor-general of the ordnance July, 1886, C.B. 20 April, 1880, M.P. Exeter since 1880. See Foster's *Baronetage* & *Eton School Lists*.

Northcote, Hugh, s. Henry, of Pynes, Devon, baronet. QUEEN'S COLL., matric. 4 April, 1759, aged 18; B.A. 1762, rector of Upton Pyne, died 25 July, 1787.

Northcote, James Spencer, 2s. George Barons, of Feulton, Devon, arm. CHRIST CHURCH, matric. 15 April, 1837, aged 15; scholar CORPUS CHRISTI COLL. 1837-42, B.A. 1841, M.A. 1844, Roman Catholic priest, late president Oscott College, near Birmingham. [26]

Northcote, Percy Williamson Barons, 2s. George Barons, of Lower, near Crieff, cler. NON-COLL., matric. 19 Oct., 1876, aged 19.

Northcote, Stafford Charles, s. Stafford, of Pynes, Devon, baronet. BALLIOL COLL., matric. 11 March, 1815, aged 18; B.A. 1819, M.A. 1821, rector of Upton Pyne, Devon, 1821, until his death 19 April, 1872. See Foster's *Baronetage*.

Northcote, Stafford Henry, 1s. Henry Stafford, of Marylebone, London, arm. BALLIOL COLL., matric. 3 March, 1836, aged 17; scholar 1836-42, B.A. 1839, M.A. 1842, created D.C.L. 17 June, 1863, 8th baronet, G.C.B. 20 April, 1880, bar.-at-law, Inner Temple, 1840, M.P. Dudley 1855-57, Stamford 1859-66, North Devon 1866-85, president Board of Trade 1866-7, secretary of state India 1867-8, chancellor of exchequer 1874-80, 1st lord of the Treasury 1885-6, lord rector of Edinburgh University 1883, created Earl of Iddesleigh 3 July, 1885, died 12 June, 1887. See Foster's *Men at the Bar* & *Eton School Lists*.

Northcote, Thomas, s. Joseph, of Newbury, Berks, gent. EXETER COLL., matric. 14 July, 1763, aged 36.

Northcote, Walter Stafford, 1s. Stafford, of London, baronet (after earl). BALLIOL COLL., matric. 19 Oct., 1863, aged 18; 2nd Earl of Iddesleigh, deputy chairman Inland Revenue Board 1886. See Foster's *Peerage*. [31]

Northey, Edward William, 1s. Edward Richard, of Epsom, Surrey, arm. CORPUS CHRISTI COLL., matric. 7 June, 1851, aged 19; B.A. 1855, M.A. 1858, of Woodcote House, Epsom, perp. curate Atlow, co. Derby, 1862-6, vicar of Christ Church, Long Lane, co. Derby, 1870-2, and of Chaddesden, co. Derby, 1872-9. See *Eton School Lists*.

Northey, William, created D.C.L. 2 July, 1754, then of Compton Basset, Wilts (son of William Northey, of the same), M.P. Calne 1747-60, Maidstone 1761-68, Bedwyn (Nov.) 1768-70, a groom of the bed-chamber to George III., a commissioner for trade, died 24 Dec., 1770.

Northmore, John, 2s. Thomas Welby, of Denton, co. Lincoln, cler. BRASENOSE COLL., matric. 9 Dec., 1845, aged 19; of Cleve House, Exeter, J.P. Devon, of Ceylon Civil Service 1846-54. See *Eton School Lists.*

Northmore, Thomas, s. John, of South Tawton, Devon, arm. EXETER COLL., matric. 25 May, 1754, aged 18; of Cleve House, Devon, died in Oct., 1777.

Northmore, Thomas Welby, 1s. Thomas Welby, of Dinapore, East Indies, cler. QUEEN'S COLL., matric. 13 May, 1841, aged 17; vicar of Kirk Hammerton, Yorks.

Norton, Alexander, 2s. Charles, of Rugby, arm. NON-COLL., matric. 12 Oct., 1878, aged 17. **[5]**

Norton, Cecil Grafton, 3s. David Evans, of Great Missenden, Bucks, cler. KEBLE COLL., matric. 22 Oct., 1885, aged 18.

Norton, David Evans, 3s. William, of St. Mark's, Kennington, Surrey, arm. ORIEL COLL., matric. 21 Feb., 1850, aged 18; B.A. 1854, M.A. 1856, head-master King's School, Bruton, 1872, vicar of Pitcombe 1880.

Norton, David Evans, 2s. David Evans, of Dover, cler. KEBLE COLL., matric. 18 Oct., 1881, aged 18; B.A. 1885, M.A. 1888.

Norton, Eardley, s. Eardley, of London, arm. UNIVERSITY COLL., matric. 24 Oct., 1801, aged 19; fellow 1801-9, B.A. 1805, M.A. 1808, vicar of Arncliffe, Yorks, 1809, perp. curate of Blythborough and Walberswick, Suffolk, 1816, until his death 26 Jan., 1835.

Norton, Edward, s. Edward, of Knaresborough, Yorks, gent. UNIVERSITY COLL., matric. 6 June, 1755, aged 19. See Foster's *Yorkshire Collection.*

Norton, (Hon.) Edward, 4s. Fletcher, of St. Giles's, London, eq. aur. (after baron). UNIVERSITY COLL., matric. 4 Nov., 1766, aged 16; B.A. 1770, M.A. 1773, bar.-at-law, Middle Temple, 1775, M.P. Haslemere 1780-4, Carlisle 1784, until his death in 1786. **[11]**

Norton, Sir Fletcher, Knight, created D.C.L. 20 Oct., 1762, solicitor-general 1761, knighted 25 Jan., 1762, bar.-at-law, Middle Temple, 1739, bencher 1754, attorney-general Dec., 1763, chief justice in Eyre 1763, recorder of Guildford, speaker of the House of Commons 1769-82, M.P. Appleby 1754-61, Wigan 1761-68, Guildford 1768-82 (son of Thomas Norton, of Grantley, Yorks), created Baron Grantley 9 April, 1782, died 1 Jan., 1789. See Foster's *Peerage.*

Norton, Fletcher, y.s. Fletcher, of Grantley, Yorks, equitis (after baron). UNIVERSITY COLL., matric. 22 Oct., 1762, aged 17; bar.-at-law, Middle Temple, 1769, bencher 1795, baron of exchequer Scotland 1775-1820, M.P. Appleby 1773-4, Carlisle 1774-5, died 19 June, 1820. See Foster's *Peerage.*

Norton, Frederick James, 5s. John David, of Little Stanmore, Middlesex, equitis. ORIEL COLL., matric. 3 June, 1846, aged 18; B.A. 1850, brother of John Bruce 1833.

Norton, George, s. John, of Shoreham, Sussex, gent. QUEEN'S COLL., matric. 16 Nov., 1809, aged 17; B.A. 1813, Michel scholar 1815-16, M.A. 1816, fellow 1816-20, bar.-at-law, Inner Temple, 1816, advocate-general Bombay 1823-54, died 13 July, 1876. **[15]**

Norton, (Hon. and Rev.) James, born at Edinburgh, Scotland, 4s. Fletcher, arm. (after baron). UNIVERSITY COLL., matric. 22 Nov., 1827, aged 18; B.A. 1831, M.A. 1835, of Annesley Park, Chertsey, etc., died 31 Oct., 1854. See Foster's *Peerage*, B. GRANTLEY.

Norton, James Lees, 7s. Henry, of Carmarthen, gent. NEW COLL., matric. 10 Oct., 1884, aged 19.

Norton, James Legge, 1s. John, of Williton, Somerset, gent. MERTON COLL., matric. 28 Jan., 1878, aged 18; postmaster 1878-82, B.A. 1882, M.A. 1885.

Norton, John, 2s. Silas, of Town Malling, Kent, gent. WADHAM COLL., matric. 19 March, 1851, aged 18; B.A. 1855, held various curacies 1856-76, vicar of Preston Wynne, co. Hereford, 1877.

Norton, John (Bruce), 1s. John David, of St. Pancras, London, gent. (after a knight). MERTON COLL., matric. 13 June, 1833, aged 17; postmaster 1833-7, B.A. 1838, bar.-at-law, Lincoln's Inn, 1841, advocate-general Madras, died 13 July, 1883. **[20]**

Norton, John Eardley, 1s. John Bruce, of Madras, arm. MERTON COLL., matric. 15 Oct., 1870, aged 18; B.A. 1874, bar.-at-law, Lincoln's Inn, 1876, coroner of Madras. See Foster's *Men at the Bar* & *Rugby School Reg.*

Norton, Thomas Brinsley, 2s. Hon. George Chapple, of Westminster, arm. UNIVERSITY COLL., matric. 5 July, 1850, aged 18; 4th Baron Grantley, died 24 Ju , 1877. See Foster's *Peerage* & *Eton School Lists.*

Norton, Thomas Herbert, 3s. Thomas, of Shelton, near Shrewsbury, gent. CHRIST CHURCH, matric. 14 Oct., 1871, aged 20; B.A. 1874, exhibitioner 1876-8.

Norton, Thomas Stringer, s. John, of Carlton, Yorks, gent. UNIVERSITY COLL., matric. 13 May, 1743, aged 19. See Foster's *Yorkshire Collection.*

Norton, Walter, s. William, of Tamworth, co. Warwick, gent. WADHAM COLL., matric. 15 May, 1777, aged 19; B.A. 1781. **[25]**

Norton, William, s. William, of Buckston, co. Derby, gent. BRASENOSE COLL., matric. 22 May, 1740, aged 17; B.A. 29 Feb., 1743-4.

Norton, William, s. Thomas, of Holsworthy, Devon, cler. PEMBROKE COLL., matric. 23 March, 1771, aged 18; B.A. 1775 (? died rector of Newton, in Cleveland, and curate of St. John, Beverley, 10 Dec., 1793).

Norton, William Francis, s. John, of Somerton, Somerset, gent. WADHAM COLL., matric. 5 March, 1801, aged 19.

Norway, Arthur, 1s. John, of St. Just, Roseland, Cornwall, arm. EXETER COLL., matric. 18 June, 1823, aged 17.

Norwood, Cornelius, s. Cornelius, of Winchester, co. Southampton, doctor. QUEEN'S COLL., matric. 6 March, 1733-4, aged 19; B.A. 1737, M.A. 1741.

Norwood, Curteis Henry, o.s. Curteis Young, of Willesborough, near Ashford, Kent, arm. BRASENOSE COLL., matric. 26 Nov., 1857, aged 18; B.A. 1862, M.A. 1864, held various curacies 1864-78, rector of Chaffcombe, Somerset, 1879. **[31]**

Norwood, Edward s. Edward, of Ashford, Kent, gent. CORPUS CHRISTI COLL., matric. 1 Feb., 1764, aged 18, B.A. 1767; M.A. from ORIEL COLL. 1770, rector (and patron) of Sevington 1777, and of Milstead 1822, until his death 2 July, 1831.

Norwood, George, s. Edward, of Ashford, Kent, cler. ORIEL COLL., matric. 25 May, 1797, aged 16; B.A. 1801, M.A. 1825, rector of Mersham, Kent, 1840, until his death, 24 May, 1876.

Norwood, Robert Pickman, 1s. George, of Oxford, gent. NON-COLL., matric. 21 Oct., 1871, aged 47; B.A. 1874, assistant Magdalen College School 1874-83, vicar of Fritwell, Oxon, 1883.

Norwood, Rev. Robert Pickman, 1s. Robert Pickman, of Oxford, cler. NON-COLL., matric. 10 May, 1879, aged 21. **[35]**

Norwood, Thomas, s. Thomas, of Leckhampton, co. Gloucester, cler. BALLIOL COLL., matric. 3 Dec., 1716, aged 18; B.A. 1720 (? he or his father died rector of Leckhampton 15 Aug., 1734).

Nosworthy, Matthias, s. John, of Moreton, Hampstead, Devon, arm. BALLIOL COLL., matric. 13 April, 1739, aged 20.

Nosworthy, Stephen, s. Stephen, of Manaton, Devon, pleb. ST. MARY HALL, matric. 10 Feb., 1792, aged 18; B.A. 1796, M.A. 1813, rector of Brushford, Somerset, 1811, until his death 8 Jan., 1835.

Notley, Rev. George, s. George, of Chillington, Somerset, gent. QUEEN'S COLL., matric. 10 April, 1742, aged 19; B.A. from MERTON COLL. 1745, father of the next named.

Notley, George, s. George, of Stoke Gomar, Somerset, cler. ST. MARY HALL, matric. 18 Nov., 1775, aged 21; died rector of Hatherleigh, Devon, 11 Aug., 1831.

Noton, Thomas, o.s. Thomas, of Kennington, Surrey, gent. ST. MARY HALL, matric. 19 Oct., 1874, aged 30.

Nott, Edward, s. John Neale Peydell, of Bath (city), arm. ORIEL COLL., matric. 14 May, 1793, aged 19, B.A. 1797, M.A. 1800, rector of Week, Hants, 1816, until his death 22 April, 1842. [5]

Nott, Fettiplace, s. Fettiplace, of Bicknall, co. Warwick, arm. BALLIOL COLL., matric. 9 April, 1720, aged 16; bar.-at-law, Middle Temple, 1726.

Nott, Fettiplace, s. Fettiplace, of Lichfield, co. Stafford, arm. PEMBROKE COLL., matric. 12 Sep., 1766, aged 17; B.A. 1770.

Nott, Rev. Frederick George, 4s. James George, of Rhyl, Flints, gent. JESUS COLL., matric. 28 Jan., 1874, aged 19; B.A. 1879, M.A. 1884.

Nott, Frederick Richard Harding, o.s. Richard, of Barnstaple, Devon, cler. EXETER COLL., matric. 18 Oct., 1883, aged 19.

Nott, George Frederick, s. Samuel, of St. James's, Westminster, cler. CHRIST CHURCH, matric. 30 Oct., 1784, aged 17, B.A. 1788; fellow ALL SOULS' COLL. until 1814, M.A. 1792, B.D. 1802, D.D. 1807, proctor 1801, Bampton lecturer 1802, F.S.A., perp. curate of Stoke Canon, Devon, 1807, vicar of Broadwindsor, Dorset, preb. of Winchester 1810, rector of Harrietsham and Woodchurch, Kent, 1812, until his death 25 Oct., 1841. [10]

Nott, Gilbert Harwood, 2s. William, of Bristol, gent. NON-COLL., matric. 17 Oct., 1885, aged 18.

Nott, John, s. Joseph, of Mynty, Wilts, gent. CHRIST CHURCH, matric. 11 May, 1716, of Braydon, Wilts, died 24 June, 1763, grandfather of Edward 1793.

Nott, John, s. John, of Monmouth, pleb. JESUS COLL., matric. 28 May, 1731, aged 17.

Nott, John, s. Francis, of South Molton, Devon, pleb. EXETER COLL., matric. 15 Oct., 1742, aged 16; B.A. 1747.

Nott, John Nott Pyke, 1s. John Pyke, of Barnstaple, Devon, cler. EXETER COLL., matric. 29 May, 1860, aged 19; scholar 1860-4, B.A. 1865, of Parracombe and Rowley, Devon, assumed the additional surname of NOTT. See *Coll. Reg.*, 159. [15]

Nott, Samuel, s. Edmund, of St. Michael in Bedwardine, co. Worcester, pleb. MERTON COLL., matric. 27 May, 1727, aged 17; B.A. from NEW COLL. 1731 (? died a minor canon of Worcester Cathedral 13 May, 1775).

Nott, Samuel, s. Samuel, of Worcester (city), cler. WORCESTER COLL., matric. 30 June, 1757, aged 17; B.A. 1761, M.A. 1764, preb. of Winchester 1770, rector of Houghton, Hants, 1776, vicar of Blandford, Dorset, chaplain to the King, died 27 May, 1793.

Nouaille, Julius, 2s. Peter, of Sevenoaks, Kent, gent. TRINITY COLL., matric. 24 May, 1823, aged 17; B.A. 1827, vicar of Ditchling, Sussex, 1845, until his death 2 Feb., 1855.

Nouaille, Peter, 1s. Peter, of Sevenoaks, Kent, gent. ST. JOHN'S COLL., matric. 14 Jan., 1820, aged 17; B.A. 1825.

Nourse, (Sir) Charles, 'chirurgus;' privilegiatus 4 May, 1739, knighted 15 Aug., 1786, died 19 April, 1789, aged 75. [20]

Nourse, Henry, s. John, of Wood Eaton, Oxon, arm. ORIEL COLL., matric. 6 Nov., 1765, aged 16; brother of John 1758.

Nourse, Henry Dalzell, 1s. John Henry Nurse, of Southampton, Hants, cler. TRINITY COLL., matric. 26 Nov., 1862, aged 18, B.A. 1866; M.A. from JESUS COLL. 1869; B.C.L. from TRINITY COLL. 1883, bar.-at-law, Lincoln's Inn, 1871, altered spelling of his name. See Foster's *Men at the Bar*.

Nourse, John, s. Francis, of London, arm. TRINITY COLL., matric. 1 July, 1729, aged 15.

Nourse, John, s. John, of Weston-sub-Penyard, Devon, arm. BALLIOL COLL., matric. 10 Oct., 1739, aged 17; fellow ALL SOULS' COLL., B.C.L. 1751, died in 1753. See Nichol's *Literary Anecdotes*, vol. i., p. 684.

Nourse, John, s. John, of Wood Eaton, Oxon, arm. TRINITY COLL., matric. 17 Jan., 1758, aged 17; brother of Henry 1765. [25]

Nourse, John, s. William, of Weston, co. Hereford, gent. BALLIOL COLL., matric. 5 May, 1772, aged 17; B.A. 1776, M.A. 1778, died in 1808.

Nourse, Timothy, s. William, of Weston, co. Hereford, arm. MERTON COLL., matric. 2 Feb., 1775, aged 17; died in America.

Nourse, William, s. William, of Liverpool (town), arm. ST. ALBAN HALL, matric. 13 July, 1798, aged 15; B.A. 1802, M.A. 1808, rector of Clapham, Sussex, 1821, until his death 4 April, 1871.

Nowell, Alexander Dawson, 1s. Josias Robinson, of Linton, Yorks, cler. BRASENOSE COLL., matric. 18 May, 1842, aged 19; B.A. 1846, M.A. 1849, of Netherside and Linton, Yorks, assumed the name of NOWELL in lieu of ROBINSON, rector of Linton in Craven (1st mediety), at his death 7 Jan., 1866.

Nowell, Cradock, s. Cradock, of Cardiff, co. Glamorgan, gent. ST. MARY HALL, matric. 16 March, 1780, aged 27 (? rector of Llanvigan, near Brecon, 1795, until his death in 1812). [30]

Nowell, Henry, s. Charles, of Giggleswick, Yorks, arm. ORIEL COLL., matric. 15 March, 1741-2, aged 18; B.A. 29 Jan., 1745-6.

Nowell, Henry Craddock, 2s. William, of Iffley, Oxon, arm. CORPUS CHRISTI COLL., matric. 23 Jan., 1826, aged 18; exhibitioner 1826-30, B.A. 1830, M.A. 1832. See *Eton School Lists*.

Nowell, Ralph Assheton, y.s. Josias Robinson, of Linton, Yorks, cler. BRASENOSE COLL., matric. 2 Feb., 1849, aged 18; lieut.-colonel Bengal Staff Corps (retired), assumed the name of NOWELL in lieu of ROBINSON. See Foster's *Lancashire Collection*.

Nowell, Roger, s. Roger, of Whalley, Lancashire, arm. BRASENOSE COLL., matric. 30 April, 1716, aged 18; of Read Hall, Lancashire, buried 11 Oct., 1734. See Foster's *Lancashire Collection*.

Nowell, Thomas, s. Cradock, of Cardiff, co. Glamorgan, pleb. ORIEL COLL., matric. 10 May, 1746, aged 16; B.A. 14 Feb., 1749-50, M.A. 1753, proctor 1761, B.D. 1764, D.D. from ST. MARY HALL 1764, principal 1764-1801, public orator 1760-76, regius professor of modern history 1771, until his death 23 Sep., 1801. [35]

Nowell, Thomas, s. Alexander, of Manchester, Lancashire, arm. BRASENOSE COLL., matric. 5 March, 1752, aged 16; B.A. 1755, lieutenant King's regiment of volunteers, died in 1765.

Nowell, Thomas Whitaker, 2s. Josias Robinson, of Linton, Yorks, cler. BRASENOSE COLL., matric. 18 May, 1842, aged 17; B.A. 1846, fellow 1848-62, M.A. 1849, of Netherside, Yorks, assumed the name of NOWELL in lieu of ROBINSON 1843, rector of Wapping 1853-60, of Poplar 1860.

Nowell, Walter Salmon, born at Ludyah, East Indies, 2s. Ralph Assheton, arm. BRASENOSE COLL., matric. 20 Oct., 1886, aged 19.

Nowell, William, s. Leonard, of Whalley, Lancashire, gent. BRASENOSE COLL., matric. 12 June, 1730, aged 16, B.A. 1734; M.A. from ORIEL COLL. 1738.

Nowell, William Atkinson, 3s. Josias Robinson, of Linton, Yorks, cler. BRASENOSE COLL., matric. 3 Feb., 1848, aged 18; B.A. 1851, M.A. 1854, assumed the name of NOWELL in lieu of ROBINSON 1843.

Nowers, George Philip, 4s. James Henry, of Etwall, co. Derby, cler. WADHAM COLL., matric. 1 Feb., 1870, aged 19; clerk 1872-4, B.A. 1875, M.A. 1876.

Nowers, Rev. James Edward Laurence, 1s. James Hey, of Dover, Kent, cler. QUEEN'S COLL., matric. 11 Oct., 1860, aged 18; scholar WADHAM COLL. 1861-6, Hody exhibitioner 1862-6, B.A. 1865.

Noyes, Eliot Warburton, 3s. Henry George, of Lee, Kent, arm. ORIEL COLL., matric. 15 Oct., 1879, aged 19. [5]

Noyes, Harry, 1s. Samuel Frederick, of London, arm. ST. JOHN'S COLL., matric. 12 Dec., 1865, aged 18; B.A. 1869.

Noyes, John Haighton, 2s. Henry Crine, of Hythe, near Southampton, arm. BALLIOL COLL., matric. 23 Oct., 1849, aged 17; Blundell scholar 1849-51.

Noyes, Robert, s. Philip, of Street, Wilts, pleb. MAGDALEN HALL, matric. 14 May, 1730, aged 19; B.A. from WADHAM COLL. 1734.

Noyes, Thomas Herbert, s. William, of Berkhampstead, Herts, gent. HERTFORD COLL., matric. 16 Feb., 1743-4, aged 16; bar.-at-law, Middle Temple, 1750.

Noyes, Thomas Herbert, s. Thomas Herbert, of Berkhampstead, Herts, arm. CHRIST CHURCH, matric. 16 Dec., 1775, aged 17; a student, B.A. 1779, M.A. 1782, vicar of Bath-Easton, Somerset, Dec., 1797, until his death 8 Aug., 1812. [10]

Noyes, Thomas Herbert, 1s. Thomas Herbert, of Bath-Easton, Somerset, cler. CHRIST CHURCH, matric. 21 May, 1819, aged 18; B.A. 1823, F.G.S., bar.-at-law, Lincoln's Inn, 1830. See Foster's *Men at the Bar*.

Noyes, Thomas Herbert, 1s. Thomas Herbert, of Gaddesden, Herts, arm. CHRIST CHURCH, matric. 11 Dec., 1845, aged 18; B.A. 1849, J.P. Sussex, a student of Lincoln's Inn 1853. See *Rugby School Reg.*, 241.

Nucella, Edward s. Timothy, of Cannon Street, London, gent. HERTFORD COLL., matric. 5 Dec., 1780, aged 21.

Nucella, Thomas, s. Timothy, of London, arm. MAGDALEN HALL, matric. 27 Nov., 1804, aged 32; B.A. from TRINITY HALL, Cambridge, 1809, M.A. 1812, rector of Glympton, Oxon, 1818, until his death 5 Feb., 1856.

Nugee, Andrew, 2s. Francis James, of St. James's, Westminster, gent. BRASENOSE COLL., matric. 16 Feb., 1832, aged 18; B.A. 1836, M.A. 1839, vicar of Wymering and rector of Widley, Hants, 1851, until his death 25 Dec., 1858. [15]

Nugee, Rev. Francis Edward, 1s. Andrew, of Wymering, Hants, cler. BALLIOL COLL., matric. 20 Oct., 1874, aged 19; B.A. 1879, M.A. 1882. See *Eton School Lists*.

Nugent, Alfred Frederick, 1s. John Venables, of Calcutta, arm. NON-COLL., matric. 13 Oct., 1877, aged 25.

Nugent, Claud, 4s. Edmund Charles, of London, arm. CHRIST CHURCH, matric. 16 April, 1886, aged 18.

Nugent, Edmund Lynch, 2s. Nicholas, of Isle of Antigua, arm. EXETER COLL., matric. 18 June, 1835, aged 16; B.A. 1839, bar.-at-law, Middle Temple, 1842, died 22 Oct., 1886.

Nugent, Edmund Frederick, 2s. Edmund Charles, of London, arm. CHRIST CHURCH, matric. 16 April, 1886, aged 20. [20]

Nugent, George, s. Thomas, of St. George's, Queen's Square, London, arm. MERTON COLL., matric. 10 March, 1768, aged 17; B.A. 1771, M.A. 1774, rector of Bygrave, Herts, 1791, until his death in 1830.

Nugent, Field-Marshal Sir George G.C.B., created D.C.L. 23 June, 1819; colonel 6th regiment, served in Holland and Flanders 1793, etc., lieut.-governor and commander-in-chief Jamaica 1801-6, created a baronet for military services 28 Nov., 1806, M.P. Charleville 1800-2, Buckingham 1790-1802, 1818-32, Aylesbury 1806-12, died 11 March, 1849. See Foster's *Baronetage*.

Nugent, (Sir) George Edmund (Bart.), born in the Isle of Jamaica, West Indies, 1s. George, baronet. CHRIST CHURCH, matric. 8 Dec., 1820, aged 18; B.A. 1823, 2nd baronet. See Foster's *Baronetage*.

Nugent, Hammond, 3s. John, of Dublin, D.Med. NEW COLL., matric. 14 Oct., 1871, aged 18; B.A. 1874.

Nugent, James Hartley, s. Edward, of Dublin, Ireland, arm. MAGDALEN HALL, matric. 28 Oct., 1812, aged 20. [25]

Nugent, John James, 1s. James, of Ramsgate, Kent, arm. NEW COLL., matric. 24 Jan., 1831, aged 18.

Nugent, Robert 3s. Christopher Richard, of Hartfield, Sussex, cler. CHRIST CHURCH, matric. 12 May, 1842, aged 19.

Nugent-Humble, John Nugent. CHRIST CHURCH, 1867. See HUMBLE. See page 713.

Nundy, George, 4s. Gopeenath, of Futtipore, East Indies, cler. NON-COLL., matric. 18 Feb., 1876, aged 19.

Nunn, John Joseph, 1s. John, of St. Peter's, Nottingham, arm. WADHAM COLL., matric. 8 March, 1854, aged 18; B.A. 1858, of 90th light infantry, died unmarried. [30]

Nunn, Thomas (Partridge), 1s. James H., of Great Yeldham, Essex, arm. ST. MARY HALL, matric. 30 March, 1843, aged 22; B.A. 1844, M.A. 1846, vicar of West Pennard since 1850.

Nunney, George, 'cæmentarius;' privilegiatus 20 May, 1817 (subs. 'plaisterer').

Nunney, William, 'tegularius et cæmentarius;' privilegiatus 18 May, 1808.

Nunns, William, s. Thomas, of Dalton, Lancashire, pleb. QUEEN'S COLL., matric. 17 Feb., 1720-1, aged 19; B.A. 1724.

Nurse, Bryan Taylor, s. Enoch, of Isle of Barbados, West Indies, gent. QUEEN'S COLL., matric. 17 June, 1818, aged 19; B.A. 1822. [35]

Nurse, Rev. James, s. John, of Isle of Barbados, West Indies, arm. WORCESTER COLL., matric. 20 May, 1817, aged 19; B.A. 1821, M.A. 1826, sometime of Lymington, died at Long Sutton vicarage, Somerset, 15 Aug., 1839.

Nurse, John, 1s. Joshua Bushel, of Barbados, West Indies, arm. MERTON COLL., matric. 15 June, 1827, aged 19; B.A. 1831, died curate of Bridgtown, Barbados, 5 Dec., 1839.

Nurse, Rev. John Henry, 1s. John Henry, of Isle of Barbados, gent. WORCESTER COLL., matric. 6 May, 1830, aged 18; B.A. 1834, M.A. 1844, died 11 Nov., 1861.

Nursey, Perry Fairfax, 3s. Perry, of Burlingham, Norfolk, cler. WADHAM COLL., matric. 26 Nov., 1862, aged 22; B.A. 1865, chaplain Holy Trinity, Rome, 1874-5, vicar of Norton, Radnors, 1878-86.

Nursey, Philip Lewis, 3s. Perry, of Burlingham, Norfolk, cler. WORCESTER COLL., matric. 12 Oct., 1861, aged 23. [40]

Nussey, Anthony Foxcroft, 3s. John, of St. James's, London, D.Med. EXETER COLL., matric. 22 Jan., 1858, aged 18; B.A. 1861.

Nussey, Edward Richard, 1s. John, of St. James's, Westminster, arm. ORIEL COLL., matric. 6 Nov., 1846, aged 18; B.A. 1851, held various curacies 1852-64, vicar of Longney, co. Gloucester, since 1865.

Nutcher, William, 3s. Thomas, of Hugglescote, co. Leicester, pleb. ST. MARY HALL, matric. 21 Feb., 1867, aged 31; clerk St. John's College 1861-5, master of the boys 1861-73.

Nuthall, William, s. John, of St. Paul's, Covent Garden, Middlesex, gent. BALLIOL COLL., matric. 27 April, 1720, aged 18.

Nutcombe, John Nutcombe Gould, 5s. John Gould, of Tratheage, Cornwall, arm. WADHAM COLL., matric. 5 June, 1823, aged 17; B.A. 1827, assumed the additional surname of NUTCOMBE, held various curacies, chaplain at Weisbaden and Frankfort-on-Maine, and chaplain R.N., rector of Stokeinteignhead 1847' until his death 19 Oct., 1878. See also *Gent.'s Mag.*, 1809, ii. 1237.

Nutt, Charles, s. George, of Speenhamland, Berks, arm. CORPUS CHRISTI COLL., matric. 9 May, 1816, aged 18, exhibitioner 1816-7; demy MAGDALEN COLL. 1817-22, B.A. 1820, M.A. 1824, vicar of East Harptree, Somerset, 1853, until his death 9 March, 1878. See *Bloxam*, vii. 271.

Nutt, Charles Henry, 1s. Charles, of Tiverton, Somerset, cler. MAGDALEN COLL., matric. 25 July, 1846, aged 17; demy 1846-61, B.A. 1851, M.A. 1853, rector and vicar of East Harptree 1864. See *Coll. Reg.*, vii. 379. **[5]**

Nutt, George, 3s. William Young, of Stoke, Surrey, cler. WORCESTER COLL., matric. 21 Nov., 1834, aged 18; B.A. 1838, vicar of Shaw and Whitley in Sarum.

Nutt, George, 1s. George, of Erle Stoke, near Melksham, Wilts, cler. NEW COLL., matric. 14 Oct., 1864, aged 18, scholar 1864-9, B.A. 1869; fellow EXETER COLL. 1869-77, M.A. 1871, classical lecturer 1869, a master at Cheltenham College and at Rugby 1874. See *Boase*, 142.

Nutt, George Arthur, o.s. Josiah, of London, gent. QUEEN'S COLL., matric. 25 Oct., 1880, aged 19; scholar 1880-4, B.A. 1885.

Nutt, Horace Young, 1s. Horace, of Stourbridge, co. Worcester, gent. ST. JOHN'S COLL., matric. 16 Oct., 1886, aged 22.

Nutt, John William, 3s. Charles, of Tiverton, Somerset, cler. CORPUS CHRISTI COLL., matric. 6 Feb., 1852, aged 17, scholar 1852-8, B.A. 1856, M.A. 1858; fellow ALL SOULS' COLL. 1858-75, chaplain 1873-9, inspector of schools 1860-7, Grinfield lecturer on the Septuagint 1874-6, sub-librarian Bodleian 1867-79, public examiner 1875, etc., rector of Harrietsham, Kent, 1879-88, and of Shelsfield 1888. See *Robinson*, 302. **[10]**

Nutt, Robert, 5s. William Young, of Burrow-in-Collem, co. Leicester, cler. WORCESTER COLL., matric. 8 July, 1843, aged 19; B.A. 1849, M.A. 1850, has held various curacies since 1854.

Nutt, Thomas, s. James, of Newport, Isle of Wight, pleb. BALLIOL COLL., matric. 8 Dec., 1806, aged 26; B.A. 1810, curate of Bodicote, Oxon, died 24 Jan., 1853.

Nutt, William, s. John, of Masefield, Sussex, gent. CHRIST CHURCH, matric. 10 June, 1721, aged 17. See *Sussex Archæological Journal*, vi. 238.

Nuttall, Rev. Ebenezer Appleby, y.s. James, of Barnoldswick, Yorks, gent. WORCESTER COLL., matric. 21 Oct., 1880, aged 19; B.A. 1883.

Nuttall, John, s. Robert, of Bury, Lancashire, arm. BALLIOL COLL., matric. 27 Feb., 1786, aged 16; died at Overleigh Hall, Cheshire, in Nov., 1813.

Nuttall, Thomas Kirkpatrick, o.s. Thomas, of Liverpool, gent. PEMBROKE COLL., matric. 26 Oct., 1881, aged 17; B.A. 1885. **[15]**

Nuttall, William, s. William, of Dean, Lancashire, pleb. BRASENOSE COLL., matric. 28 March, 1783, aged 20; B.A. & M.A. 1789, perp. curate Swinton, Lancashire, 1791, until his death in 1833.

Nutter, Ellis, s. Ellis, of Burnley, Lancashire, pleb. BRASENOSE COLL., matric. 31 March, 1726, aged 18.

Nutter, John, s. Richard, of Burnley, Lancashire, gent. ORIEL COLL., matric. 5 April, 1731, aged 17; B.A. 1735.

Nutting, Philip Henry, 4s. George Horace, of Bridgewater, Somerset, cler. EXETER COLL., matric. 13 Oct., 1871, aged 20. **[20]**

Oakden, Rev. Roger, 2s. Ralph, of Goudhurst, near Staplehurst, Kent, gent. PEMBROKE COLL., matric. 14 Oct., 1865, aged 19; B.A. 1870, M.A. 1872.

Oake, George, s. George, of Falmouth, Cornwall, arm. EXETER COLL., matric. 27 March, 1779, aged 17; B.A. 1782.

Oakeley, Arthur, 4s. Herbert, of Oakeley Lydham, Salop, cler. PEMBROKE COLL., matric. 28 Feb., 1834, aged 18; B.A. from NEW INN HALL 1840, M.A. 1841, rector of Lydham, Salop, 1842, until his death 2 Jan., 1870. See *Eton School Lists.*

Oakeley, Sir Charles, Bart., created D.C.L. 15 June, 1825 (s. William Oakeley, rector of Forton, Stafford, etc.), entered H.E.I.C.S. 1766, Governor of Madras 1790-4, created a baronet 5 June, 1790, died 7 Sep., 1826. See Foster's *Baronetage.*

Oakeley, (Sir) Charles (William Atholl, Bart.), 1s. Herbert, of Ealing, Middlesex, baronet. CHRIST CHURCH, matric. 4 June, 1846, aged 17; 4th baronet. See Foster's *Baronetage* & *Eton School Lists.* **[5]**

Oakeley, Edward de Clifford William, o.s. William Edward, of London, arm. CHRIST CHURCH, matric. 25 May, 1883, aged 18.

Oakeley, Frederick, 6s. Charles, of Holy Cross, Shrewsbury, baronet. CHRIST CHURCH, matric. 15 June, 1820, aged 17, B.A. 1824; fellow BALLIOL COLL. 1827-45, M.A. 1827, tutor 1831-7, senior dean 1834, catechetical and logic lecturer, bursar 1837, preb. of Lichfield 1832-45, incumbent of Margaret Chapel, Margaret Street, London, 1839-45, seceded to Rome, R.C. canon of Westminster 1852, died 29 Jan., 1880.

Oakeley, Rev. Herbert, s. Richard, of Croft, co. Hereford, arm. BALLIOL COLL., matric. 8 Dec., 1730, aged 17; B.A. 1734, M.A. 1737, died in 1788, father of the next named, and of John 1761.

Oakeley, Herbert, s. Herbert, of Firgrove, Salop, cler. BALLIOL COLL., matric. 10 April, 1767, aged 18; B.A. from NEW COLL. 1772, M.A. 1776, died rector of Hopton Castle and Lydham in 1812.

Oakeley, Herbert, s. John, of Lydham, Salop, arm. ORIEL COLL., matric. 27 Feb., 1797, aged 18; B.A. 1800, M.A. 1803, B.D. 1805, D.D. 1828, of Oakeley, Salop, rector (and patron) of Lydham 1812, preb. of Hereford 1817, until his death 5 Jan., 1830. **[10]**

Oakeley, (Sir) Herbert (Bart.), s. Charles, of Madras, East Indies, baronet. CHRIST CHURCH, matric. 25 April, 1807, aged 16; student 1807-23, B.A. 1811, M.A. 1813, 3rd baronet, preb. of St. Paul's 1816, of Lichfield 1816, and of Worcester 1817, dean and rector of Bocking 1834-45, archdeacon of Colchester 1841, vicar of Ealing, Middlesex, 1822-34, died 27 March, 1845.

Oakeley, (Sir) Herbert Stanley, 2s. Herbert, of Ealing, Middlesex, cler. and baronet. CHRIST CHURCH, matric. 17 Oct., 1849, aged 19; B.A. 1853, M.A. 1856, created D.Mus. 19 June, 1879, and D.Mus. Cambridge 1871, professor of music Edinburgh University, etc., 1865, knighted at Edinburgh 17 Aug., 1876. See Foster's *Baronetage* & *Rugby School Reg.*, 248.

Oakeley, James, 4s. Thomas, of Mitcheltroy, co. Monmouth, gent. JESUS COLL., matric. 6 April, 1848, aged 18; B.A. 1852, perp. curate of Llanishen, co. Monmouth, 1861-86.

Oakeley, Rev. James Bagnall Bagnall, 1s. William, of ——, co. Monmouth, cler. CORPUS CHRISTI COLL., matric. 21 Oct., 1873, aged 19; B.A. 1877.

Oakeley, John, s. Rowland, of South Kilworth, co. Leicester, cler. CORPUS CHRISTI COLL., matric. 21 March, 1715-6, aged 18; B.A. 1719. **[15]**

Oakeley, John, s. Herbert, of Lydbury, Salop, cler. BALLIOL COLL., matric. 3 Aug., 1761, aged 17; bar.-at-law, Inner Temple, 1771, brother of Herbert 1767.

Oakeley, John, 2s. Henry, of Croft, co. Hereford, arm. BRASENOSE COLL., matric. 28 May, 1874, aged 17; of Oakeley, Salop. See Foster's *Baronetage.*

Oakeley, Richard, s. Richard, of Hereford (city), arm. BALLIOL COLL., matric. 25 May, 1728, aged 18; of Oakeley, Salop, brother of Herbert 1730.

Oakeley, Robert, s. Jer., of St. Clement Danes, London, arm. CHRIST CHURCH, matric. 17 March, 1721-2, aged 17; B.A. 1725, M.A. 1728.

Oakeley, William, s. William, of Steventon, Salop, arm. BALLIOL COLL., matric. 4 March, 1736-7, aged 18; B.A. 6 March, 1740-1, M.A. 7 March, 1743-4, rector of Eaton-under-Heywood, and of Forton, co. Stafford, vicar of Holy Cross, Shrewsbury, 1782, until his death 3 Oct., 1863, father of Charles, D.C.L. See Foster's *Baronetage.* **[20]**

Oakeley, Rev. William (Bagnall), 3s. Thomas, of Mitcheltroy, co. Monmouth, gent. JESUS COLL., matric. 6 June, 1840, aged 18; scholar 1843-6, B.A. 1844, fellow 1846-54, M.A. 1847, father of James Bagnall B. 1873.

Oakeley, William Edward, o.s. William Edward, of Lichfield, co. Stafford, arm. CORPUS CHRISTI COLL., matric. 27 March, 1847, aged 18; of Plas, Tan-y-Bwlch, co. Merioneth, high sheriff 1874. See Foster's *Baronetage* & *Eton School Lists.*

Oakeley, William Gryffydd, s. William, of Shrewsbury, Salop, arm. CHRIST CHURCH, matric. 26 Jan., 1809, aged 18; B.A. 1812, of Tan-y-bwlch Hall, co. Merioneth, where he died 12 Oct., 1835.

Oakeley, Rev. William Pearce, 4s. Thomas William, of Mitcheltroy, co. Monmouth, gent. JESUS COLL., matric. 13 Oct., 1879, aged 19; B.A. 1883.

Oakes, Charles, 3s. Humphrey, of Bridgnorth, Salop, gent. ST. JOHN'S COLL., matric. 14 April, 1820, aged 18; B.A. 1824, M.A. 1827, rector of Kimberton, and vicar of Sutton Maddock, Salop, 1830, died 24 June, 1830. **[25]**

Oakes, Charles Henry, 4s. Henry, of Mitcham, Surrey, baronet. MERTON COLL., matric. 29 Nov., 1828, aged 18; B.A. 1832, M.A. 1835, bar.-at-law, Middle Temple, 1837, died 16 May, 1864. See Foster's *Baronetage.*

Oakes, James, 1s. Charles Henry, of Riddings, co. Derby, arm. TRINITY COLL., matric. 12 Oct., 1877, aged 19; B.A. 1880, M.A. 1885.

Oakeshott, Francis Benjamin, 5s. Jonathan, of Dalston, Middlesex, gent. JESUS COLL., matric. 18 Oct., 1882, aged 18; scholar 1882-6, B.A. 1886.

Oakeshott, Jonathan, 3s. Jonathan, of Dalston, Middlesex, arm. UNIVERSITY COLL., matric. 13 Oct., 1879, aged 19; scholar 1879-82, B.A. 1882, of the Indian Civil Service 1879, a student of the Middle Temple 1880.

Oakley, Charles Edward, o.s. Richard Cater, of Chatham, Kent, gent. PEMBROKE COLL., matric. 20 Feb., 1851, aged 19, scholar 1851 (exhibitioner WADHAM COLL. 1850); demy MAGDALEN COLL. 1853-5, B.A. 1855, B.C.L. & M.A. 1857, chaplain in the Crimea 1855, rector of Wickwar, co. Gloucester, 1856, and of St. Paul's, Covent Garden, 1863, until his death 15 Sep., 1865. See *Bloxam*, vii. 400; & *Rugby School Reg.*, 263. [5]

Oakley, Charles Selby, 4s. John, of Luton, near Chatham, Kent, arm. CORPUS CHRISTI COLL., matric. 19 Oct., 1863, aged 19; scholar 1863-8, B.A. 1868, M.A. 1871.

Oakley, Edward Banner, o.s. Richard, of Lambeth, Surrey, gent. ST. JOHN'S COLL., matric. 17 March, 1826, aged 19.

Oakley, Francis, s. Francis, of Dorchester, Dorset, gent. MAGDALEN HALL, matric. 7 Feb., 1818, aged 30; died vicar of Bradpole, Dorset, 6 Oct., 1843.

Oakley, John, 1s. John, of Frindsbury, Kent, gent. BRASENOSE COLL., matric. 11 June, 1852, aged 17; scholar 1852-9, B.A. 1857, M.A. 1859, B. & D.D. 1881, vicar of St. Saviour's, Hoxton, 1867-82, dean of Carlisle 1881-3, of Manchester 1883.

Oakley, Rev. Thomas, s. John, of Wigmore, co. Hereford, pleb. BRASENOSE COLL., matric. 26 April, 1787, aged 18; B.A. 1791, M.A. 1801, died 27 April, 1853. [10]

Oakman, Robert, s. William, of St. George's, Bloomsbury, London, gent. ST. ALBAN HALL, matric. 8 Dec., 1817, aged 26; B.A. 1822, curate of St. Peter's, Exeter, died at Martock vicarage 28 Aug., 1845, aged 55.

Oare, John, s. John, of Maidstone, Kent, gent. MAGDALEN COLL., matric. 17 Dec., 1736, aged 28; rector of Ditton, Kent, 1750.

Oates, Charles Cecil, 1s. John, of Scarborough, Yorks, cler. EXETER COLL., matric. 11 Oct., 1872, aged 18.

Oates, Francis, 1s. Edward, of Meanwoodside, near Leeds, Yorks, arm. CHRIST CHURCH, matric. 9 Feb., 1861, died near the Tati River, South Africa, 5 Feb., 1875. See Foster's *Yorkshire Collection.*

Oates, John, 2s. John, of Ripon (Risplith), Yorks, cler. LINCOLN COLL., matric. 30 March, 1843, aged 18; scholar 1844-7, B.A. 1846, M.A. 1850, held various curacies 1850-9, vice-principal Elizabeth College, Guernsey, 1860-8, principal 1868, chaplain All Saints, Guernsey, 1871. [15]

Oates, John William, 1s. Elkanah, of Leeds, Yorks, pleb. CHRIST CHURCH, matric. 31 May, 1855, aged 20; servitor 1855-9, B.A. 1859, M.A. 1862, held various curacies 1859-82, vicar of Ingrow, Yorks, 1882.

Oates, William Edward, 2s. Edward, of Leeds, Yorks, arm. CHRIST CHURCH, matric. 12 Dec., 1863, aged 21, brother of Francis 1861.

Oatley, George Edmund, s. Thomas, of Albrighton, Salop, gent. JESUS COLL., matric. 30 March, 1814, aged 18; B.A. 1817, M.A. 1820.

Obbard, Robert, 1s. Harry Smith, of Lucknow, East Indies, arm. BALLIOL COLL., matric. 20 April, 1871, aged 19; exhibitioner 1871-3, B.A. 1886, of the Indian Civil Service 1871.

O'Beirne, Hugh James, 2s. Hugh, of Dublin, arm. BALLIOL COLL., matric. 15 Oct., 1884, aged 18; of the Indian Civil Service 1884. [20]

Obins, Rev. Archibald Eyre, s. Michael, of Exmouth, Devon, arm. EXETER COLL., matric. 30 June, 1797, aged 21; B.A. 1799, M.A. 1811, died 6 Jan., 1867.

Obourn, Thomas, s. Thomas, of Salisbury (city), pleb. CORPUS CHRISTI COLL., matric. 1 June, 1736, aged 18; B.A. 29 Feb., 1739-40, M.A. 1743.

O'Brien, Algernon Æmilius MacMahon Stafford, 3s. Stafford, of Blatherwycke, Northants, arm. MAGDALEN HALL, matric. 29 Jan., 1846, aged 28. See Foster's *Peerage*, B. INCHIQUIN.

O'Brien, Donough (Acheson), s. Lucius, of ——, co. Clare, Ireland, baronet. PEMBROKE COLL., matric. 18 Oct., 1797, aged 16; a student of Lincoln's Inn 1803, died 22 Oct., 1847. See Foster's *Peerage*, B. INCHIQUIN.

O'Brien, (Sir) Edward (Bart.), s. Lucius, of London, BALLIOL COLL., matric. 12 Oct., 1721, aged 16; 2nd baronet, M.P. Peterborough 1727-8 (in English parliament), M.P. Clare (in Irish parliament) 1727, until his death 26 Nov., 1765. [25]

O'Brien, Edward, 1s. Henry, of Carrigallen, co. Leitrim, cler. NEW COLL., matric. 13 Oct., 1859, aged 19; scholar 1859-63, of the Indian Civil Service 1862, assistant commissioner Delhi. See Foster's *Peerage*, B. INCHIQUIN.

O'Brien, Francis Alexander, born at Ardmore, co. Wexford, 5s. James Thomas, bishop of Ossory, Ferns, and Leighlin. CHRIST CHURCH, matric. 19 May, 1869, aged 18; a junior student 1869-76, B.A. 1873, M.A. 1878, rector of Walton d' Eivile, co. Warwick, 1884.

O'Brien, George Edward, 3s. John, of Ashton-under-Lyne, Lancashire, cler. QUEEN'S COLL., matric. 22 Oct., 1866, aged 18; B.A. 1869, M.A. 1879, has held various curacies since 1872.

O'Brien, Horace Stafford, 1s. Henry, of Tixover Grange, near Stamford, Rutland, arm. CHRIST CHURCH, matric. 20 Jan., 1860, aged 17; of Cratloe Woods, co. Clare, etc. See Foster's *Peerage*, B. INCHIQUIN.

O'Brien, James, B.A. TRINITY COLL., Dublin, 1794, s. Edward, of Dromore, co. Clare, Ireland, arm. EXETER COLL., incorp. 27 June, 1800, aged 25. See Foster's *Peerage*, B. INCHIQUIN. [30]

O'Brien, James, 6s. Bryan, of Killorglin, co. Kerry, arm. MAGDALEN HALL, matric. 13 May, 1837, aged 23; brother of John 1843.

O'Brien, James, M.A., B. & D.D. TRINITY COLL., Dublin, 1859 (B.A. 1843); adm. 'ad eundem' 21 Feb., 1861, and incorp. from MAGDALEN HALL 17 Dec., 1863, founder and minister of St. Patrick's, Hove, Brighton, 1859, until his death 8 Jan., 1884.

O'Brien, John, B.A. TRINITY COLL., Dublin, 1843, 5s. Bryan, of Killorglin, Kerry, Ireland, gent. QUEEN'S COLL., incorp. 2 Nov., 1843, aged 29; M.A. 1846, vicar of Henfield, Sussex, 1851, until his death 14 Sep., 1872, brother of James 1837.

O'Brien, Peter Henry, 1s. Patrick, of Mooltan, East Indies, arm. BALLIOL COLL., matric. 21 Oct., 1880, aged 17; of the Indian Civil Service 1880.

O'Brien, Ranald Martin, 2s. Patrick, of Mooltan, East Indies, arm. BALLIOL COLL., matric. 19 Oct., 1886, aged 20. [35]

O'Brien, Timothy Carew, 1s. Timothy, of Dublin, arm. NEW INN HALL, matric. 3 May, 1884, aged 2[illegible]. See Foster's *Baronetage.*

O'Cahem, Daniel, 'master of arms,' 18 Aug. 1721.

O'Callaghan, Cornelius, s. Dennis, of Cork (city), Ireland, arm. BRASENOSE COLL., matric. 18 May, 1773, aged 15.

O'Callaghan, Cornelius, s. John, of Maryport, co. Clare, Ireland, arm. MAGDALEN COLL., matric. 4 Feb., 1806, aged 18; a student of Lincoln's Inn 1808.

O'Callaghan, Daniel, s. Donough, of Tulla, co. Clare, Ireland, arm. CHRIST CHURCH, matric. 2 March, 1769, aged 18, died 1772.

O'Callaghan, Donough, s. Cornelius, of Kelnoe, co. Clare, gent. ORIEL COLL., matric. 25 Nov., 1768, aged 19.

O'Callaghan, George Charles Martin, 1s. Cornelius, of St. Peter's, Dublin, arm. TRINITY COLL., matric. 18 May, 1839, aged 17; of Ballinalinch, co. Clare, high sheriff 1855.

O'Callaghan, George Ponsonby, 3s. Cornelius, Viscount Lismore. ORIEL COLL., matric. 6 March, 1834, aged 18; 2nd viscount, lord-lieut. Tipperary, high sheriff 1853. See Foster's *Peerage*. [5]

O'Callaghan, Patrick, B.A. TRINITY COLL., Dublin, 1822 (LL.B. & LL.D. 1864); adm. 'comitatis causa' 23 Feb., 1865.

Ockleshaw, Richard, s. Thomas, of Brentford, Middlesex, pleb. ST. MARY HALL, matric. 21 Feb., 1722-3, aged 14; B.A. 3 March, 1728-9, M.A. 1734.

O'Connell, John, 1s. Michael, of Newton, Queen's County, gent. NON-COLL., matric. 8 Feb., 1877, aged 30.

O'Connor, Alexander, 4s. Dennis Prittie, of Anderby, co. Lincoln, cler. ST. MARY HALL, matric. 22 Jan., 1869, aged 22; held various curacies 1870-80, rector of Nether Denton, Cumberland, 1880.

O'Connor, Arthur Patrick, 1s. Arthur, of London, gent. ST. MARY HALL, matric. 20 Oct., 1879, aged 19. [10]

O'Connor, Edward, 6s. Thomas, of Marchtown, co. Cambridge, gent. LINCOLN COLL., matric. 23 Oct., 1882, aged 18; scholar 1882-4, B.A. 1887.

O'Connor, George (M.A. QUEEN'S UNIVERSITY, Ireland), 3s. John, of Athenry, co. Galway, gent. PEMBROKE COLL., matric. 6 Nov., 1877, aged 23; scholar 1877, drowned in the Isis 7 June, 1878.

O'Connor, Harry King (B.A. TRINITY COLL., Dublin, 1872), 3s. Henry, of Kingstown, near Dublin, gent.; incorp. from QUEEN'S COLL. 6 March, 1872, aged 21; M.A. 1875, vicar of Locking, Somerset, 1876-80, chaplain India 1880.

O'Connor, John, s. Maurice, of Dublin, Ireland, arm. ST. MARY HALL, matric. 17 Dec., 1746, aged 18.

O'Connor, Rev. John Prittie, 3s. Dennis Prittie, of Anderby, co. Lincoln, cler. ST. MARY HALL, matric. 19 April, 1866, aged 19; B.A. 1869, M.A. 1874. [15]

Oddie, George Augustus, 2s. Henry Hoyle, of St. George's, Bloomsbury, London, arm. UNIVERSITY COLL., matric. 17 April, 1839, aged 18; B.A. 1843, rector of Aston, Herts, 1848, until his death 8 April, 1877. See *Eton School Lists*.

Oddie, John William, o.s. Thomas, of Blackburn, Lancashire, arm. WADHAM COLL., matric. 27 Nov., 1861, aged 22, B.A. 1865, classical lecturer 1866-7; fellow CORPUS CHRISTI COLL. 1867, M.A. 1868, tutor 1867-73, dean 1873, vice-president 1874.

Oddie, William, s. William, of Alford, co. Lincoln, cler. LINCOLN COLL., matric. 5 May, 1795, aged 18; demy MAGDALEN COLL. 1797-1801, B.A. 1799, M.A. 1801, fellow 1801-9, junior dean of arts 1804, prælector of moral philosophy 1805, bursar 1806, steward or clerk of accounts 1821-30, vicar of Iffley 1813-19, died 8 Nov., 1851. See *Bloxam*, vii. 138.

Oddy, John, s. John Lister, of Leeds, Yorks, gent. ST. MARY HALL, matric. 25 Oct., 1864, aged 22; bible clerk ALL SOULS' COLL. 1865-8.

Odell, Edward, 2s. John, of Marylebone, London, arm. CHRIST CHURCH, matric. 20 May, 1826, aged 18; B.A. 1830, M.A. 1834, of Carriglea, co. Waterford, died 1869. [20]

Odell, Francis John, 8s. Joseph, of Coventry, co. Warwick, gent. ST. JOHN'S COLL., matric. 20 Jan., 1877, aged 18; exhibitioner 1877-8, B.A. 1880, chaplain R.N. 1884.

Odell, John, s. John, of Waterford, Ireland, arm. CHRIST CHURCH, matric. 5 Feb., 1791, aged 16; of Carriglea, died 8 Feb., 1811, father of Edward and John.

Odell, John, 1s. John, of Lismore, co. Waterford, Ireland, arm. CHRIST CHURCH, matric. 23 June, 1821, aged 19; B.A. 1825, of Carriglea, high sheriff co. Waterford, died 17 May, 1847.

Odell, Richard, s. John, of Ardmore, Ireland, arm. NEW COLL., matric. 11 July, 1800, aged 18; B.A. 1804, M.A. 1808, fellow until 1825, curate of Barnham Overy & of Hockham, and chaplain to the Duke of Sussex, died 3 March, 1825.

Oder, John, s. Rich., of Pendina, co. Glamorgan, gent. ORIEL COLL., matric. 20 Oct., 1725, aged 19 (? died minister of Dummer, Hants, 19 Jan., 1731). [25]

Odling, William, o.s. George, of Southwark, Surrey, gent. Name entered *Mat. Reg.* 2 July, 1872, aged 42, from MAGDALEN COLL.; fellow of WORCESTER COLL. 1872 (vice-provost 1883), M.A. by decree 31 Oct., 1872, Waynflete professor of chemistry 1872; B.Med. LONDON UNIVERSITY 1851, examiner in forensic medicine 1862-7, in chemistry 1869-74.

O'Donnell, George Boodrie, 1s. George, of Mokunpoor, East Indies, gent. PEMBROKE COLL., matric. 27 Oct., 1870, aged 18; B.A. 1874.

O'Donoghue, Rev. Edward Geoffrey, o.s. Francis Talbot, of Sinnen, Cornwall, cler. EXETER COLL., matric. 16 Oct., 1874, aged 20; scholar 1873-8, B.A. 1878, head-master Kensington Grammar School 1886. See *Coll. Reg.*, 166.

O'Donnoghue, Hallifield (Cosgayne), s. Bartholomew, of Cork (city), Ireland, gent. ST. EDMUND HALL, matric. 16 April, 1806, aged 17, B.A. 1810; incorp. CAMBRIDGE UNIVERSITY 1813, M.A. from ST. JOHN'S COLL. 1813.

O'Donoghue, William Power, 1s. Daniel, of Cork (city), Ireland, arm. MAGDALEN HALL, matric. 28 June, 1864, aged 33; B.Mus. 30 June, 1864. [30]

O'Donohoe, James Patrick, 1s. Martin, of Shutford, Oxon, gent. UNIVERSITY COLL., matric. 16 Oct., 1880, aged 19; exhibitioner 1880-3, B.A. 1884.

O'Donovan, Morgan William, 1s. Henry Winthrop, of Cork, Ireland, arm. MAGDALEN COLL., matric. 29 Oct., 1881, aged 20; B.A. 1886.

O'Driscoll, William Justin, 2s. (Wm. Justin), of St. Peter's, Dublin, gent. ST. JOHN'S COLL., matric. 26 June, 1865, aged 18; B.A. 1870, B.C.L. 1872, of Belcourt, Bray, co. Dublin, bar.-at-law, Inner Temple, 6 June, 1871, died 18 Dec., 1882. See *Robinson*, 336.

O'Dwyer, Charles Philip Firmin, o.s. Charles Archer O'Rourke, of Chatham, Kent, gent. PEMBROKE COLL., matric. 27 Oct., 1885, aged 19; scholar 1885.

Oeschger, Henri, o.s. Lewis, of Paris, gent. NON-COLL., matric. 18 Oct., 1880, aged 22. [35]

Offer, Rev. John, s. Robert, of Devizes, Wilts, gent. ST. ALBAN HALL, matric. 9 Dec., 1815, aged 32; antiquary, died 23 Dec., 1822.

Offley, Charles, 2s. William, of Hastings, Sussex, arm. UNIVERSITY COLL., matric. 21 Nov., 1839, aged 18; B.A. 1843.

Offley, Henry Francis, s. Edward, of St. George, London, gent. ST. MARY HALL, matric. 17 Dec., 1795, aged 19.

Offley, William 1s. William, of Bennington, Herts, arm. UNIVERSITY COLL., matric. 30 April, 1828, aged 18; B.A. 1832.

Ogden, Alexander McRitchie, 3s. George Henry, of Bangor, gent. JESUS COLL., matric. 18 Oct., 1882, aged 18; B.A. 1886. [40]

Ogden, Richard Tynwald, of TRINITY COLL., Cambridge, LL.B. 1868; adm. 'comitatis causa' 12 March, 1868.

Ogden, Samuel, fellow of ST. JOHN COLL., Cambridge; B.A. 1737, M.A. 1741, B.D. 1748, D.D. 1753, incorp. 11 July, 1758, Woodward professor 1764-78, rector of Lawford, Essex, and of Stansfield, Suffolk, 1766, until his death 23 March, 1778.

Ogilvie, Charles Atmore, s. John, of Whitehaven, Cumberland, gent. BALLIOL COLL., matric. 27 Nov., 1811, aged 18; B.A. 1815, fellow 1816-34, M.A. 1818, tutor 1819-30, bursar, catechetical 1822, and senior dean, B. & D.D. 1842, regius professor of pastoral theology 1842, & canon of Christ Church 1849, and vicar of Ross, co. Hereford, 1839, until his death 17 Feb., 1873; for list of his writings see *Crockford.*

Ogilvie, George, of TRINITY HALL, Cambridge, LL.B. 1793, s. George, of St. George's, Westminster, arm. ST. MARY HALL, incorp. 9 (or 12) Feb., 1799, aged 30; D.C.L. 13 Feb., 1799.

Ogilvie, George, o.s. George Shadforth, of Calne, Wilts, arm. WADHAM COLL., matric. 22 Jan., 1845, aged 18; B.A. 1855, M.A. 1862, canon of St. George's Cathedral and rector of Rondebosch, Cape Colony, 1885. See *Crockford.*

Ogilvie, Glencairn Stuart, 5s. Alexander, of Haslemere, Surrey, arm. UNIVERSITY COLL., matric. 13 Oct., 1877, aged 19; B.A. 1881, bar.-at-law, Inner Temple, 1882. See Foster's *Men at the Bar & Rugby School Reg.* **[5]**

Ogilvie, James, Baron Deskfoord, o.s. James, Earl of Findlater and Seafield. CHRIST CHURCH, matric. 8 April, 1769, aged 18; 7th and last earl, died 5 Oct., 1811.

Ogilvie, James Christopher, s. James, of Westminster, gent. HERTFORD COLL., matric. 6 Dec., 1773, aged 17; B.A. 1777.

Ogilvie-Forbes, John Charles Matthias, 1s. George O.-F., of Aberdeen, arm. NON-COLL., matric. 21 Oct., 1871, aged 21; B.A. from KEBLE COLL. 1875, M.A. 1881, of Boyndlie, Aberdeenshire, sometime in holy orders.

Ogilvie, Robert Leveson James, 3s. John Hugh Donald, of Madras, East Indies, arm. ST. MARY HALL, matric. 28 Feb., 1864, aged 47.

Ogilvie, William Frederick, 1s. Edward David Stewart, of Sydney, Australia, arm. NON-COLL., matric. 23 May, 1885, aged 23. **[10]**

Ogilvy, Charles William Norman, 3s. John, of Baldovan Strathmartin, near Dundee, Scotland, baronet. CHRIST CHURCH, matric. 21 Oct., 1858, aged 19; B.A. 1864, M.A. 1865, rector of Barton-le-Street, Yorks, 1870-8, and of Hanbury, co. Worcester, 1878.

Ogilvy, David, 3s. Donald, of Logie Kirriemuir, co. Forfar, arm. WADHAM COLL., matric. 22 Jan., 1845, aged 18; B.A. 1852, a student of Lincoln's Inn 1854, died 20 July, 1857. See Foster's *Peerage,* E. AIRLIE.

Ogilvy, David Graham Drummond, 1s. David, Earl of Airlie. CHRIST CHURCH, matric. 9 Nov., 1843, aged 17; B.A. 1847, 7th earl, K.T., a representative peer 1851, lord high commissioner Church of Scotland 1872-5, died 25 Sep., 1881. See Foster's *Peerage.*

Ogilvy, Henry Thomas, 2s. John, of Baldovan House, near Dundee, baronet. BALLIOL COLL., matric. 17 Oct., 1855, aged 18; bar.-at-law, Lincoln's Inn, 1863. See Foster's *Men at the Bar.*

Ogilvy, (Sir) John (Bart.), 1s. William, of Edinburgh (city), baronet. CHRIST CHURCH, matric. 5 Nov., 1821, aged 18; 9th baronet, M.P. Dundee 1857-74. See Foster's *Baronetage.* **[15]**

Ogilvy, Reginald Howard Alexander, 1s. John, of Edinburgh (city), baronet. ORIEL COLL., matric. 5 Dec., 1850, aged 18; B.A. 1854, a student of Inner Temple 1860. See Foster's *Baronetage.*

Ogilvy, Walter, 2s. Hon. Donald, of Marylebone, London, arm. MAGDALEN HALL, matric. 15 June, 1839, aged 16; of Clova, co. Forfar, brother of David 1845.

Ogilwy, Alfred, 1s. Alfred Charles, of Windsor, gent. KEBLE COLL., matric. 14 Oct., 1879, aged 18; B.A. 1883, M.A. 1887.

Oglander, Henry, s. John, of Brading, Isle of Wight, baronet. NEW COLL., matric. 10 July, 1761, aged 18; B.A. 1765, M.A. 1769, B.D. 1776, fellow of Winchester College, rector of Widley, and vicar of Wymering and St. Helen's, died 16 March, 1814.

Oglander, (Sir) Henry (Bart.), 1s. William, of Marylebone, London, baronet. CHRIST CHURCH, matric. 29 May, 1829, aged 17; 7th baronet, died s.p. 1874. **[20]**

Oglander, (Sir) John (Bart.), s. William, of Brading, Hants, baronet. ST. JOHN'S COLL., matric. 10 Oct., 1721, aged 17; 4th baronet, died s.p. 11 May, 1767.

Oglander, John, s. John, of Nunwell, Isle of Wight, baronet. ST. JOHN'S COLL., matric. 29 Oct., 1756, aged 19; B.A. from NEW COLL. 1761, M.A. 1765, B.D. 1770, D.D. 1774, warden 1768, until his death 13 Jan., 1794.

Oglander, John, s. William, of Brading, Isle of Wight, baronet. TRINITY COLL., matric. 26 March, 1795, aged 17, B.A. 1798; fellow MERTON COLL. 1800-25, M.A. 1804, bursar 1822, sub-warden 1824, died 30 Oct., 1825, buried at Merton College.

Oglander, Peter, s. William, of London, baronet. ORIEL COLL., matric. 30 April, 1798, aged 18; B.A. 1802, died rector of East Stoke, Dorset, in 1807.

Oglander, (Sir) William (Bart)., s. John, of Nunwell, Isle of Wight, co. Southampton, baronet. NEW COLL., matric. 19 Sep., 1751, aged 18; B.A. 1754; B.C.L. ALL SOULS' COLL. 1760, 5th baronet, died 4 Jan., 1806. **[25]**

Oglander, (Sir) William (Bart.), s. William, of Parnham, Dorset, baronet. NEW COLL., matric. 3 March, 1787, aged 17; B.A. 1790, 6th baronet, M.P. Bodmin 1807-12, died 17 Jan., 1852.

Ogle, Ambrose Addington, 6s. James Ambrose, of Sutton, co. Derby, cler. KEBLE COLL., matric. 22 1885, aged 19.

Ogle, Arthur Joseph Savile, o.s. Richard, of Kynnersley, Salop, arm. ST. JOHN'S COLL., matric. 17 April, 1871, aged 20; B.A. 1875, vicar of Dunston, co. Stafford, 1882-6, and of Bishops Teignton, Devon, 1886.

Ogle, Bertram Savile, 1s. Arthur, of Durham (city), arm. CHRIST CHURCH, matric. 7 June, 1865, aged 18; B.A. 1870, of Hill House, Oxon, J.P., bar.-at-law, Lincoln's Inn, 1872. See Foster's *Men at the Bar & Eton School Lists.*

Ogle, Charles, s. John Savile, of Salisbury, Wilts, cler. CHRIST CHURCH, matric. 18 May, 1816, aged 16; died 13 Aug., 1820. See Foster's *Baronetage.* **[30]**

Ogle, Cyril, 3s. John William, of London, D.Med. TRINITY COLL., matric. 21 May, 1880, aged 19; B.A. 1884.

Ogle, Edward (Chaloner), s. John, of Knoyle, Wilts, cler. MERTON COLL., matric. 19 Oct., 1816, aged 18; B.A. 1820, M.A. 1823, of Kirkley Hall, Northumberland, vicar of Sutton Benger, Wilts, 1824, preb. of Salisbury 1828, died 7 Nov., 1869. See Foster's *Baronetage.*

Ogle, Rev. George, B.A. from PEMBROKE HALL, Cambridge, 1788 (M.A. 1791); adm. 'ad eundem' 19 June, 1817, of Purley Park, near Reading, died 25 June, 1828.

Ogle, Harman Chaloner, 1s. Nathaniel, of Orpington, Kent, arm. MAGDALEN COLL., matric. 1 Feb., 1862, aged 19; demy 1861-5, B.A. 1865, fellow 1865-87, usher 1866-7, M.A. 1868, tutor 1868-71, junior dean of arts 1868, bursar 1870, vice-president 1875, schoolmaster 1876-86, warden Queen's College, Birmingham, 1873-4, 2nd master Worcester Cathedral School 1874-6, rector of Tubney 1886, died 25 June, 1887.

Ogle, James, y.s. Chaloner, of Marter Worthy, Hants, equitis. MERTON COLL., matric. 8 Dec., 1794, aged 17; B.A. 1798, M.A. 1801, rector of Bishops Waltham 1802, and vicar of Crondall, Hants, 1811, until his death 19 May, 1833. See Foster's *Baronetage.*

Ogle, James Adey, s. Richard, of St. Giles's, London, arm. TRINITY COLL., matric. 13 April, 1810, aged 17; scholar 1812-19, B.A. 1813, M.A. 1816, B.Med. 1817, D.Med. 1820 (F.R.C.P. 1822), Aldrichian professor of the practice of medicine 1824-30, clinical professor 1830-57, regius professor of medicine 1851, until his death 25 Sep., 1857. See Munk's *Roll*, iii. 245; & *Eton School Lists.*

Ogle, James Ambrose, 1s. James Adey, of Oxford (city), D.Med. BRASENOSE COLL., matric. 18 May, 1842, aged 17; B.A. 1846, M.A. 1849, vicar of Sedgeford, Norfolk, 1858-74, rector of Southmere with Sedgeford 1874. See *Alumni West.*, 513.

Ogle, Rev. James Sayer, 1s. James, of Bishops Waltham, Hants, cler. NEW COLL., matric. 14 June, 1826, aged 17; fellow 1826-45, B.A. 1830, M.A. 1833, dean of arts 1833, bursar and tutor 1834, sub-warden 1835, died at Naples 30 April, 1845.

Ogle, John, s. John Savile, of Southampton, Hants, cler. CHRIST CHURCH, matric. 27 Oct., 1814, aged 18, B.A. 1818; fellow ALL SOULS' COLL. 1818-29, M.A. 1822, died 14 July, 1831. [5]

Ogle, John, 1s. John William, of London, D.Med. TRINITY COLL., matric. 28 Jan., 1874, aged 18; B.A. 1877, M.A. 1880, bar.-at-law, Inner Temple, 1879. See Foster's *Men at the Bar.*

Ogle, John Gilbert, 5s. James Ambrose, of Sedgeford, Norfolk, cler. KEBLE COLL., matric. 19 Oct., 1880, aged 18; B.A. 1884.

Ogle, John Savile, born at Ponteland, Cumberland, s. Newton, dean of Winchester. MERTON COLL., matric. 29 Oct., 1784, aged 17; B.A. 1788, M.A. 1791, preb. (or canon) Salisbury 1794, and of Durham 1820, until his death 1 April, 1838.

Ogle, John Savile, 1s. Edward Chaloner, of Sutton Benger, near Chippenham, Wilts, cler. CHRIST CHURCH, matric. 7 June, 1854, aged 18; of Kirkley Hall, Northumberland. See Foster's *Baronetage* & *Eton School Lists.*

Ogle, John William, o.s. Samuel, of Leeds, Yorks, arm. TRINITY COLL., matric. 7 March, 1844, aged 19; B.A. 1847, M.A. 1851, B.Med. 1851, D.Med. 1857. [10]

Ogle, Nathaniel, s. Nathaniel, of Newcastle-upon-Tyne, Northumberland, arm. BALLIOL COLL., matric. 25 Oct., 1731, aged 16; B.A. from ST. JOHN'S COLL., Cambridge, 1736, a student of the Middle Temple 1732, died in 1762.

Ogle, Nathaniel, born at Salisbury (city), s. Newton, dean of Winchester. MERTON COLL., matric. 17 Feb., 1783, aged 17; of Kirkley, Northumberland, died in May, 1813.

Ogle, Newton, s. Nathan., of Kirkley, Northumberland, arm. LINCOLN COLL., matric. 21 Oct., 1743, aged 17, B.A. 1747; M.A. from MERTON COLL. 1750, B. & D.D. 1761, preb. (or canon) of Sarum 1750, archdeacon of Surrey 1766, preb. of Durham 1768, dean of Winchester 1769, until his death 6 Jan., 1804.

Ogle, Octavius, 4s. James Adey, of Oxford (city), D.Med. WADHAM COLL., matric. 3 July, 1846, aged 17, scholar 1846-52, B.A. 1850; fellow LINCOLN COLL. 1852-9, M.A. 1853, tutor and claviger 1853, Greek lecturer 1855, librarian 1854, sub-rector 1855, moderator 1854, etc., public examiner 1879-80, master of the schools 1863, etc., chaplain Warneford Asylum, Oxford, 1864, a student of the Inner Temple 1881.

Ogle, Ponsonby Dugmore, 2s. William Reynolds, of Bishops Teignton, Devon, cler. NEW COLL., matric. 16 Oct., 1874, aged 18; scholar 1874-9, B.A. 1879. [15]

Ogle, Ralph, s. Ralph, of Heworth, Northumberland, arm. UNIVERSITY COLL., matric. 17 March, 1780, aged 18; B.A. 1784, died rector of Ingram, Northumberland, in 1790.

Ogle, Richard, s. John, of Winnington, co. Stafford, gent. MAGDALEN HALL, matric. 11 April, 1747, aged 17; B.A. from ST. EDMUND HALL 1750.

Ogle, Rev. Richard Jeston, 2s. James Adey, of Oxford (city), D.Med. TRINITY COLL., matric. 3 June, 1844, aged 19, scholar 1844-6; exhibitioner LINCOLN COLL. 1846-9, B.A. 1848, fellow 1849-51, M.A. 1851, died 16 July, 1851.

Ogle, Robert, s. Robert, of Alnwick, Northumberland, arm. BRASENOSE COLL., matric. 17 May, 1836, aged 18; scholar 1836-40, B.A. 1844, of Eglingham Hall, Northumberland, bar.-at-law, Inner Temple, 1846, died 15 March, 1879.

Ogle, Savile Craven Henry, 6s. John Savile, of Knoyle, Wilts, cler. CHRIST CHURCH, matric. 25 June, 1829, aged 18; B.A. 1833, bar.-at-law, Inner Temple, 1836, M.P. South Northumberland, 1841-52, died 11 March, 1854. See Foster's *Baronetage.* [20]

Ogle, Rev. Wilfrid (Rathmel), 2s. John William, of London, D.Med. TRINITY COLL., matric. 12 Oct., 1877, aged 18; B.A. 1881, M.A. 1884. See *Eton School Lists.*

Ogle, William, 3s. James Adey, of Oxford, doctor. CORPUS CHRISTI COLL., matric. 26 July, 1845, aged 17; scholar 1845-7, fellow 1847-64, B.A. 1849, M.A. 1852, B.Med. 1858, D.Med. 1861, junior bursar 1853, F.R.C.P. 1866. See *Rugby School Reg.*, 224.

Ogle, William Laurence, 3s. James Ambrose, of Sedgeford, Norfolk, cler. WORCESTER COLL., matric. 16 Oct., 1879, aged 18; scholar 1879-84, B.A. 1883, died 2 April, 1886.

Ogle, Rev. William Pomeroy, 3s. William Reynolds, of Bishops Teignton, Devon, cler. CHRIST CHURCH, matric. 11 Oct., 1878, aged 19; died 1 Aug., 1884.

Ogle, William Reynolds, 3s. John, of Preston, Salop, arm. TRINITY COLL., matric. 26 Nov., 1835, aged 19; B.A. 1839, M.A. 1842, vicar of Bishops Teignton, Devon, 1856, and of Luton, Devon, 1870, until his death 6 Jan., 1886. [25]

O'Gorman, Thomas Murray. MAGDALEN HALL, 1859. See GORMAN, page 542.

O'Grady, Frederick Standish, 5s. Paget Standish, Viscount Guillamore. ST. JOHN'S COLL., matric. 15 June, 1866, aged 19. See Foster's *Peerage.*

O'Grady, Thomas, s. William, of Dublin, Ireland, gent. ST. ALBAN HALL, matric. 27 June, 1787, aged 26.

O'Hanlon, Hugh Francis, 2s. Hugh Marmaduke, of Chester Place, London, arm. BRASENOSE COLL., matric. 11 Oct., 1861, aged 18; scholar 1861-4, B.A. 1865, a student of the Inner Temple 1867 died fellow of LINCOLN COLL. 8 Nov., 1867.

O'Hara, Charles, s. Kean, of Dublin (city), arm. BALLIOL COLL., matric. 7 Nov., 1720, aged 15; of Annaghmore, co. Sligo, high sheriff 1740, died 3 Feb., 1776. [30]

O'Hara, Charles, s. Charles, of Dublin, Ireland, arm. CHRIST CHURCH, matric. 26 Nov., 1763, aged 17; B.A. 1767, created M.A. 4 Dec., 1771, of Annaghmore, bar.-at-law, King's Inns, Dublin, 1770, a lord of the treasury in Ireland, M.P. Ballinakill 1761 to Nov., 1769, Armagh Nov., 1769-76, Dungannon 1776-83, Sligo 1783, until his death 19 Sep., 1822.

O'Hara, Henry, 1s. Henry, of Ballyahterton (*sic*), near Coleraine, arm. ST. JOHN'S COLL., matric. 6 June, 1840, aged 17.

O'Hara, William, s. Charles, of Ireland, arm. CHRIST CHURCH, matric. 12 Oct., 1764, aged 16; captain royal navy, died in 1790.

Ohren, Cecil, 1s. John, of Longton, co. Stafford, gent. UNIVERSITY COLL., matric. 17 Oct., 1885, aged 19.

Oke, William Samways, o.s. William Samuel, of Farnham, Surrey, doctor. WADHAM COLL., matric. 14 May, 1835, aged 19; B.A. 1839, vicar of Rowde, Wilts, 1871-4, rector of Road, Somerset, 1874, until his death 13 July, 1879.

Okeden, Edmund Robert Parry, 3s. William Parry, of Turnworth, Dorset, arm. EXETER COLL., matric. 6 Dec., 1870, aged 19; B.A. 1875, M.A. 1877, a student of the Inner Temple 1872. See *Eton School Lists.*

Okeden, Rev. Herbert George Parry, 4s. William Parry, of Turnworth, Dorset, arm. EXETER COLL., matric. 14 Oct., 1876, aged 19; B.A. 1879.

Okeden, William, s. William, of Red Lyon Square, London, arm. EXETER COLL., matric. 16 May, 1720, aged 17; died in 1753.

Okeden, William, s. Edmund, of Blandford, Dorset, gent. TRINITY COLL., matric. 10 March, 1753, aged 17; B.A. 1756, M.A. 1759, died in 1763. **[5]**

O'Keeffe, John Tottenham, s. John, of Cork (city), Ireland, gent. EXETER COLL., matric. 22 Nov., 1798, aged 23; B.A. 1801, probably a son of the celebrated dramatic author.

O'Kell, George, s. George, of Weaverham, Cheshire, gent. BRASENOSE COLL., matric. 24 Oct., 1783, aged 19; B.A. 1787, M.A. 1815, perp. curate Witton, Cheshire, 1818, until his death in 1833.

O'Kell, Robert, 1s. Thomas, of Warrington, Lancashire, gent. BRASENOSE COLL., matric. 7 June, 1860, aged 17; B.A. from NEW INN HALL 1868.

Okeover, Charles Gregory, s. Rowland Farmer, of Oldbury Hall, Atherstone, co. Warwick, arm. TRINITY COLL., matric. 29 Jan., 1811, aged 18; B.A. 1814, M.A. 1817, chaplain to the Duke of Sussex, perp. curate Merevale, co. Warwick, 1817, rector of Baxterley 1819, and vicar of Nether Whitacre 1819, until his death 1 Aug., 1826.

Okeover, Haughton Charles, o.s. Charles Gregory, of Atherstone, co. Warwick, cler. CHRIST CHURCH, matric. 19 Oct., 1843, aged 17; of Okeover, high sheriff co. Derby, 1862. See *Eton School Lists.* **[10]**

Okeover, Haughton Farmer, s. Rowland, of Weddington, co. Warwick, arm. CHRIST CHURCH, matric. 23 Oct., 1794, aged 18; created M.A. 28 June, 1797, of Okeover Hall, co. Stafford, high sheriff 1800. See *Eton School Lists.*

Okey, Thomas, 'servant to the warden of All Souls;' privilegiatus 16 May, 1778.

Olard, John, s. John, of St. James's, Westminster, Middlesex, pleb. UNIVERSITY COLL., matric. 21 Oct., 1717, aged 17; B.A. 1721.

Old, Thomas, s. Thomas, of Pancras-Wyke, Devon, pleb. EXETER COLL., matric. 15 Feb., 1721-2, aged 17; B.A. 1725.

Old, Thomas Trenham, s. William, of St. Mary-at-Hill, London, gent. MAGDALEN HALL, matric. 18 Feb., 1814, aged 27. **[15]**

Oldershaw, Henry, 3s. John, of Tarvin, Cheshire, doctor. BRASENOSE COLL., matric. 30 May, 1822, aged 18; B.A. 1826, M.A. 1829.

Oldershaw, John, s. John, of Market Bosworth, co. Leicester, gent. ST. MARY HALL, matric. 25 June, 1776, aged 16; B.C.L. 1783, D.C.L. 1819, vicar of Ranworth, Norfolk, 1795, and of Tarvin, Cheshire, 1796, until his death in 1824, father of Henry last named.

Oldershaw, Richard Loveland, o.s. John Percy, of St. Mary, Islington, Middlesex, gent. PEMBROKE COLL., matric. 1 March, 1860, aged 17.

Oldfield, Charles Bayley, 1s. George Biscoe, of East Woodhay, Hants, cler. NEW COLL., matric. 16 Oct., 1885, aged 18.

Oldfield, Christopher Campbell, 3s. Henry Swan, of India, arm. EXETER COLL., matric. 25 May, 1858, aged 19; brother of George B. **[20]**

Oldfield, Edmund, 2s. Thomas Brame, of Camberwell, Surrey, gent. WORCESTER COLL., matric. 11 May, 1837, aged 20; scholar 1837-40, B.A. 1839, fellow 1840-73, M.A. 1841, librarian 1852, commoner of TRINITY COLL., Cambridge, 1834, bar.-at-law, Inner Temple, 1842, died in Feb., 1885. See Foster's *Men at the Bar.*

Oldfield, Edmund Prescot, 1s. Henry Ambrose, of Calcutta, gent. KEBLE COLL., matric. 19 Oct., 1880, aged 18; B.A. 1883, M.A. 1888.

Oldfield, George Biscoe, 4s. Henry Swan, of Calcutta, East Indies, arm. EXETER COLL., matric. 22 Oct., 1859, aged 18; B.A. 1862, M.A. 1866, rector of Berwick-in-Tisbury with Sedgehill, Dorset, 1872.

Oldfield, George William, 1s. Joseph, of Dumdum, Calcutta, arm. WADHAM COLL., matric. 19 Jan., 1872, aged 18; B.A. 1875, M.A. 1878.

Oldfield, John Edward, o.s. Thomas, of Bettwys, near Abergele, co. Denbigh, gent. ORIEL COLL., matric. 13 April, 1869, aged 19; B.A. 1873. **[25]**

Oldfield, Josiah, 2s. David, of Ryton, Salop, gent. NON-COLL., matric. 15 April, 1882, aged 19; B.A. 1885.

Oldfield, Richard, s. Francis, of Isle of Jamaica, arm. QUEEN'S COLL., matric. 12 Sep., 1727, aged 16 (? M.P. Windsor 1738, unseated 1738).

Oldfield, William John, 1s. David, of Peyton, Salop, gent. CHRIST CHURCH, matric. 15 Oct., 1875, aged 18; exhibitioner 1876-9, B.A. 1879, M.A. 1882, rector of St. Mary Belize, British Honduras, 1881.

Oldham, Algernon Langston, 2s. James, of Brighton, Sussex, arm. TRINITY COLL., matric. 13 Oct., 1866, aged 19; B.A. 1869, M.A. 1873, rector of St. Leonard's, Bridgnorth, 1883, brother of George. See *Rugby School Reg.*

Oldham, Charles Edward Philip, 2s. Joseph, of Hatherleigh, Devon, arm. BRASENOSE COLL., matric. 13 Oct., 1860, aged 19; brother of D'Oyly, Egerton, and Ernest. **[30]**

Oldham, D'Oyly William, 3s. Joseph, of Hatherleigh, Devon, arm. EXETER COLL., matric. 12 March, 1864, aged 19; B.A. 1868, M.A. 1875, rector of Exbourne, Devon, 1877.

Oldham, Rev. Egerton Haslope, 7s. Joseph, of Oakfield, Devon, arm. LINCOLN COLL., matric. 27 April, 1876, aged 18; B.A. 1880, M.A. 1883.

Oldham, Ernest Joseph, 1s. Joseph, of Hatherleigh, Devon, arm. MAGDALEN COLL., matric. 28 May, 1857, aged 18; B.A. from MAGDALEN HALL 1862.

Oldham, Rev. George Townsend, 3s. James, of Brighton, Sussex, arm. ORIEL COLL., matric. 19 Oct., 1867, aged 18; B.A. 1870, M.A. 1874, brother of Algernon. See *Rugby School Reg.*

Oldham, Henry Yule, 5s. Thomas, of Dusseldorf, LL.D. JESUS COLL., matric. 18 Oct., 1882, aged 19; B.A. 1886. **[35]**

Oldham, James, 3s. Thomas, of Doverdale, co. Worcester, cler. TRINITY COLL., matric. 17 May, 1850, aged 19; scholar 1853, B.A. 1855, M.A. 1857, rector of Doverdale, co. Worcester, 1857-71, etc. See *Rugby School Reg.*, 255.

Oldham, Rev. John Basil, 2s. John, of Huddersfield, Yorks, cler. TRINITY COLL., matric. 18 Oct., 1862, aged 20; B.A. 1867, M.A. 1869, died 12 April, 1871.

Oldham, John Roberts, 1s. Adam, of Newington, Surrey, arm. ORIEL COLL., matric. 6 April, 1827, aged 19; B.A. 1830, M.A. 1833, vicar of Ottershaw, Surrey, 1865, until his death 16 June, 1882.

Oldham, Joseph, 1s. George Laing, of Tower Hill, London, arm. CORPUS CHRISTI COLL., matric. 16 Nov., 1822, aged 16; migrated to UNIVERSITY COLL. 17 Dec., 1823, B.A. 1828, of Strawbridge and Peters Marland Manor, Devon, assumed the name of OLDHAM in lieu of LAING in 1830, father of Charles, D'Oyly, Egerton, and Ernest.

Oldham, Joshua, 2s. Thomas, of Doverdale, co. Worcester, cler. BRASENOSE COLL., matric. 15 June, 1843, aged 18; B.A. 1847. See *Rugby School Reg.*, 211.

Oldham, Reginald Walter, 1s. Richard Samuel, of Glasgow, cler. KEBLE COLL., matric. 18 Oct., 1871, aged 19; B.A. 1875, M.A. 1880, rector of Trentishoe and Martinhoe, Devon, 1886.

Oldham, Richard Samuel, 3s. William, of St. George's, Southwark, Surrey, gent. WADHAM COLL., matric. 26 May, 1842, aged 19; B.A. 1846, M.A. 1849, incumbent of St. Mary, Glasgow, 1851-78, dean of Glasgow 1877-8, perp. curate Grosvenor Chapel 1878-81, rector of Little Chart, Kent, 1881.

Oldham, Thomas, s. James, of London, arm. ST. EDMUND HALL, matric. 3 July, 1800, aged 17; B.A. 1804, M.A. 1809 (? father of James and Joshua).

Oldisworth, John, s. William, of Fairford, co. Gloucester, gent. WADHAM COLL., matric. 13 July, 1779, aged 19; B.A. 1783. [5]

Oldnall, Edward, s. Edward, of St. Andrew's, Worcester (city), pleb. MERTON COLL., matric. 4 March, 1717-8, aged 19; B.A. 1721.

Oldnall, Samuel, s. John, of Claines, co. Worcester, gent. WORCESTER COLL., matric. 27 Nov., 1772, aged 18; B.A. 1776, M.A. 1779, rector of St. Nicholas, Worcester, and of North Piddle, co. Worcester, 1794, until his death 17 March, 1819, father of Sir William Oldnall Russell. See *post.*

Oldnall, William (Russell). CHRIST CHURCH, 1800. See RUSSELL.

Oldrey, Robert Blatchford, 1s. Robert, of London, gent. NON-COLL., matric. 14 Oct., 1876, aged 19.

Oldrid, John Henry, 1s. John, of Boston, co. Lincoln, gent. MAGDALEN HALL, matric. 18 Nov., 1830, aged 22; B.A. 1834, M.A. 1851, perp. curate Gawcott, Bucks, 1834-44, lecturer Boston 1844-63, vicar of Alford, etc., co. Lincoln, 1863-79. [10]

Oldrini, Thomas John, 1s. Gerard John, of Westminster, gent. QUEEN'S COLL., matric. 11 March, 1847, aged 21; B.A. 1850, M.A. 1853.

Oliphant, Rev. Charles James, 2s. George John, of London, gent. ST. MARY HALL, matric. 11 Nov., 1878, aged 24; B.A. 1882, M.A. 1885.

Oliphant, Cyril Francis, 1s. Francis Wilson, of London, arm. BALLIOL COLL., matric. 20 Oct., 1875, aged 18; B.A. 1883, a student of the Inner Temple 1878. See *Eton School Lists.*

Oliphant, David. QUEEN'S COLL. 1738. See OLYPHANT.

Oliphant, Francis Romano, 2s. Francis Wilson, of Rome, arm. BALLIOL COLL., matric. 28 Jan., 1879, aged 19; B.A. from NEW INN HALL 1883. See *Eton School Lists.* [15]

Oliphant, Frederick James, 7s. James, of Wimbledon, Surrey, arm. (cler. in *Mat. Reg.*). NEW COLL., matric. 25 Feb., 1863, aged 17; choral scholar 1863-6, B.A. 1866, M.A. 1871, vicar of Woking, Surrey, since 1878.

Oliphant, Laurence, s. Laurence, of Gask, co. Perth, arm. ORIEL COLL., matric. 28 May, 1818, aged 20; laird of Gask, died 31 Dec., 1824.

Oliphant, Laurence James, 1s. Laurence, of Condie House, near Forgandenny, co. Perth, arm. CHRIST CHURCH, matric. 18 May, 1864, aged 17; of Condie and Newton, co. Perth, lieut.-colonel grenadier guards.

Oliphant, Thomas Laurence Kington, 1s. Thomas Kington, of Clifton, near Bristol, arm. BALLIOL COLL., matric. 21 March, 1850, aged 18; B.A. 1854, M.A. 1858, of Gask, co. Perth, J.P., D.L., assumed the additional name of OLIPHANT in 1864, bar.-at-law, Inner Temple, 1858. See *Eton School Lists* & Foster's *Men at the Bar.*

Olivant, Thomas, s. Thomas, of Kirby Stephen, Westmoreland, gent. QUEEN'S COLL., matric. 2 April, 1757, aged 14. [20]

Olive, Carlton, 6s. John, of Hellingly, Sussex, cler. EXETER COLL., matric. 2 June, 1868, aged 19; B.A. 1871, M.A. 1878, held various curacies 1872-83.

Olive, Charles Daniel, 2s. Edward Crabbe, of Frome, Somerset, gent. CHRIST CHURCH, matric. 14 Oct., 1870, aged 19; a junior student 1870-4, B.A. 1875, M.A. 1877.

Olive, John, 1s. Edward, of Frome, Somerset, gent. WADHAM COLL., matric. 2 April, 1819, aged 18; B.A. 1822, M.A. 1825.

Olive, John, 2s. John, of Clifton, co. Gloucester, arm. WORCESTER COLL., matric. 5 Nov., 1822, aged 18; B.A. 1826, M.A. 1829, rector of Ayot St. Lawrence, Herts, 1830, until his death 3 Jan., 1874.

Olive, Rev. Leontine Wallace, 2s. Daniel, of Cheltenham, co. Gloucester, gent. WORCESTER COLL., matric. 16 Oct., 1872, aged 22; B.A. 1877, M.A. 1879. [25]

Olive, Lionel Albert, 1s. Lionel, of Clifton, co. Gloucester, arm. CHRIST CHURCH, matric. 12 June, 1867, aged 19; B.A. 1871. See *Eton School Lists.*

Olive, Richard, s. John, of Lacock, Wilts, pleb. ALL SOULS' COLL., matric. 30 June, 1721, aged 19, B.A. 1725; M.A. from NEW COLL. 1728 (? died vicar of Burnham, Somerset, 18 Feb., 1761).

Olive, Thomas, s. John, of Halsted, Essex, gent. MAGDALEN HALL, matric. 10 July, 1773, aged 25 (? vicar of Mucking, Essex, 1782, until his death 1 Feb., 1799).

Oliver, Alexander, 1s. Andrew, of Sydney, Australia, arm. EXETER COLL., matric. 1 June, 1855, aged 21; B.A. 1860, bar.-at-law, Inner Temple, 1862. See Foster's *Men at the Bar.*

Oliver, Arthur Pope, 3s. William Lomas, of Bollington, Cheshire, gent. EXETER COLL., matric. 18 Jan., 1883, aged 19. [30]

Oliver, Arthur Robert, o.s. Thomas, of St. George's, London, arm. WADHAM COLL., matric. 18 Oct., 1848, aged 18; B.A. & M.A. from ST. MARY HALL 1882.

Oliver, Rev. Arthur West, 6s. George Washington, of New Orleans, arm. QUEEN'S COLL., matric. 24 Jan., 1880, aged 21; B.A. 1883, M.A. 1886.

Oliver, Charles Goodrich, 1s. Charles, of Stepney, Middlesex, gent. ST. MARY HALL, matric. 7 March, 1871, aged 32.

Oliver, Frederick William, 1s. William Elliott, of St. George's, Hanover Square, London, arm. CHRIST CHURCH, matric. 18 May, 1853, aged 17; student 1853-61, B.A. 1857, M.A. 1860.

Oliver, George, s. George, of Ealing, Middlesex, gent. BRASENOSE COLL., matric. 4 March, 1800, aged 17. [35]

Oliver, George, 1s. Charles Wellington, of Uppingham, Rutland, arm. NON-COLL., matric. 11 Oct., 1873, aged 24; B.A. from NEW COLL. 1876, vicar of St. George, Darlaston, 1885.

Oliver, George Frederick, o.s. George, of Ashton-on-Mersey, arm. EXETER COLL., matric. 18 Jan., 1883, aged 21.

Oliver, Rev. Henry Francis, 1s. Harry, of London, gent. EXETER COLL., matric. 23 April, 1873, aged 19; B.A. 1877, M.A. 1880.

Oliver, Horace William, o.s. William, of Oxford, gent. QUEEN'S COLL., matric. 6 Feb., 1876, aged 18.

Oliver, James, s. James, of Abbotts Combe, Somerset, gent. HART HALL, matric. 15 March, 1722-3, aged 18. [40]

Oliver, John, s. John, of Audlem, Cheshire, cler. BRASENOSE COLL., matric. 30 May, 1715, aged 17; B.A. 26 Jan., 1718-9; M.A. 1722.

Oliver, John, s. Richard, of Pyworthy, Devon, gent. QUEEN'S COLL., matric. 10 Oct., 1770, aged 19; B.A. from EXETER COLL. 1775.

Oliver, John, s. Richard, of Pyworthy, Devon, gent. EXETER COLL., matric. 26 May, 1800, aged 19; B.A. 1804.

Oliver, Joseph, s. Joseph, of Bristol (city), gent. CHRIST CHURCH, matric. 20 April, 1761, aged 19; B.A. 1765, died at Bristol, 30 Sep., 1765.

Oliver, Peter, created D.C.L. 3 July, 1776, then chief justice in the province of Massachusett's Bay, America, died at Birmingham, 12 Oct., 1791, aged 78, his son Peter died at Shrewsbury 30 July, 1822, aged 81. See Ripley and Dana's *American Cyclopædia.*

Oliver, Peter, s. Peter, of Massachusett's Bay, New England, gent. QUEEN'S COLL., matric. 6 June, 1792, aged 17; a student of Middle Temple 1793 (? died in 1855). See Ripley and Dana's *American Cyclopædia.*

Oliver, Rev. Philip, s. Thomas, of Chester (city), arm. ORIEL COLL., matric. 25 April, 1780, aged 17; B.A. 1784, M.A. 1787, died in 1800. See *Gent.'s Mag.*, 1800, ii. 906.

Oliver-Gascoigne, Richard, s. Silver, of Castle Oliver, co. Limerick, Ireland, arm. MAGDALEN COLL., matric. 28 Oct., 1782, aged 19; created M.A. 26 Nov., 1789 (as RICHARD SILVER-OLIVER), of Parlington Hall, Yorks, high sheriff 1831, and of Castle Oliver, co. Limerick, assumed the additional surname of GASCOIGNE, died 14 April, 1843, father of Richard. See page 512. [5]

Oliver, Robert, s. Thomas, of 'Colleg. Civit Vigorn,' gent. WORCESTER COLL., matric. 15 June, 1727, aged 17, B.A. 1731; M.A. from MERTON COLL. 1734.

Oliver, Robert, s. Robert, of Dublin, Ireland, arm. CHRIST CHURCH, matric. 13 July, 1728, aged 18; of Castle Oliver, co. Limerick, M.P. Kilmallock, Oct., 1739, until his death 6 May, 1745.

Oliver, Rev. Robert, s. John (Ferneough), of Trafford, Cheshire, arm. MERTON COLL., matric. 2 Dec., 1815, aged 18; B.A. 1819, M.A. 1822, died 6 Jan., 1856, brother of Thomas L. 1815.

Oliver, Robert Bennett, of TRINITY COLL., Cambridge; B.A. 1859, M.A. 1862, adm. 'comitatis causa' 18 June, 1863, vicar of Whitwell, Isle of Wight, 1867.

Oliver, Robert Dudley Maunsell, o.s. John, of London, gent. CHRIST CHURCH, matric. 14 Oct., 1870, aged 17; B.A. 1875. [10]

Oliver, Robert Jewell, 1s. Robert, of Saltash, St. Stephen's Cornwall, gent. PEMBROKE COLL., matric. 9 May, 1833, aged 18; B.A. 1837, chaplain royal navy, died at Jerusalem 19 July, 1841.

Oliver, Roderic, 2s. Thomas, of Mile End, London, gent. QUEEN'S COLL., matric. 11 Oct., 1860, aged 19; B.A. 1864, M.A. 1878, a solicitor in London. See *St. Paul's School Reg.*, 320.

Oliver, Sydney James, 2s. James, of London, arm. MAGDALEN COLL., matric. 27 Oct., 1874, aged 19.

Oliver, Thomas, s. Thomas, of St. Marylebone, London, arm. MAGDALEN COLL., matric. 12 Oct., 1813, aged 18.

Oliver, Thomas Creswick, 1s. William Creswick Lomas, of Bollington, Cheshire, gent. NEW COLL., matric. 5 Feb., 1877, aged 18. [15]

Oliver, Thomas Long, s. John, of Trafford, Cheshire, arm. MERTON COLL., matric. 2 Dec., 1815, aged 19; a student of Lincoln's Inn 1817.

Oliver, Weston Ayles William, 1s. John, of Weymouth, Dorset, gent. NON-COLL., matric. 19 Oct., 1876, aged 17; B.A. from ST. MARY HALL 1880, M.A. 1883.

Oliver, William, of PEMBROKE COLL., Cambridge (B.Med. 1720, D.Med. 1725); incorp. 8 July, 1756.

Oliver, William, s. William, of Bath (city), doctor. CHRIST CHURCH, matric. 20 Jan., 1748-9, aged 18. [20]

Oliver, William Trevearnoe, s. William, of Exeter (city), doctor. BRASENOSE COLL., matric. 8 May, 1807, aged 18; B.A. 1811, brother of Robert 1815.

Oliverson, Cecil Henry, 1s. Richard, of London, arm. CHRIST CHURCH, matric. 15 Oct., 1886, aged 18.

Oliverson, Richard, 1s. Christopher, of Goosnargh, Lancashire, arm. EXETER COLL., matric. 6 June, 1851, aged 19; B.A. 1855, M.A. 1857, bar.-at-law, Middle Temple, 1858. See Foster's *Men at the Bar.*

Olivier, Dacres, 2s. (Henry Stephen), of Potterne, Wilts, arm. CHRIST CHURCH, matric. 31 May, 1849, aged 17; B.A. 1853, M.A. 1856, rector of Wilton, Wilts, 1867, canon and preb. of Salisbury, 1874. See *Rugby School Reg.*, 262.

Olivier, Dacres Edward, 1s. Dacres, of Great Yarmouth, cler. KEBLE COLL., matric. 14 Oct., 1878, aged 19; B.A. 1887.

Olivier, Daniel (Stephen), s. Daniel (Josias), of London, arm. ST. ALBAN HALL, matric. 30 April, 1777, aged 21; B.C.L. from CORPUS CHRISTI COLL. 1784, rector of Clifton, Beds, 1790, until his death 23 Dec., 1821. [25]

Olivier, Henry Arnold, 1s. Henry Stephen, of Devonport, Devon, arm. BALLIOL COLL., matric. 5 March, 1845, aged 19; B.A. 1849, M.A. 1854, rector of Crowhurst, Sussex, 1861-4, of Havant, Hants, 1870-4, and of Poulshot, Wilts, 1874-83, chaplain of Holy Trinity, Nice, 1885. See *Rugby School Reg.*, 211.

Olivier, Henry Eden, 3s. Dacres, of Wilton, Wilts, cler. NEW COLL., matric. 16 Jan., 1885, aged 18.

Olivier, Sydney Haldane, 2s. Henry Arnold, of Colchester, cler. CORPUS CHRISTI COLL., matric. 23 Oct., 1877, aged 18; exhibitioner 1878-81, B.A. 1883.

Ollivant, Joseph Earle, born at Lampeter, co. Cardigan, 3s. Alfred, bishop of Llandaff. BALLIOL COLL., matric. 22 Oct., 1858, aged 19; B.A. 1862, M.A. 1865, bar.-at-law, Inner Temple, 1873, chancellor diocese of Llandaff, master of Marlborough College. See Foster's *Men at the Bar* & *Rugby School Reg.*

Ollivant, Thomas. QUEEN'S COLL. 1757. See OLIVANT. [30]

Ollivant, William Spencer, born at Lampeter, co. Cardigan, 1s. Alfred, bishop of Llandaff. CHRIST CHURCH, matric. 3 March, 1853, aged 18; B.A. from CORPUS CHRISTI COLL. 1858, M.A. 1859, bar.-at-law, Lincoln's Inn, 1876, died 3 Oct., 1876. See *Rugby School Reg.*, 279.

Olliver, Eustace Herbert, 2s. George, of Kingston, Sussex, arm. EXETER COLL., matric. 13 April, 1872, aged 18.

Olliver, Thomas Stephen, 1s. William, of Goring, Sussex gent. WORCESTER COLL., matric. 27 Feb., 1856, aged 18.

Olphert, Rev. John, 1s. Thomas, of Limavady, co. Derry, cler. MERTON COLL., matric. 28 Jan., 1878, aged 19; B.A. & M.A. 1883.

Olyphant, David, s. David, of Isle of Jamaica, arm. QUEEN'S COLL., matric. 27 Feb., 1737-8, aged 16.

O'Malley, Owen, s. George, of Castlebar, co. Mayo, Ireland, gent. QUEEN'S COLL., matric. 16 May, 1793, aged 21; of Spencer Park, co. Mayo, high sheriff. [36]

Oman, Charles William Chadwick, o.s. Charles Philip Austin, of Mozufferporc, East Indies, gent. NEW COLL., matric. 11 Oct., 1878, aged 18, scholar 1878-82, B.A. 1882; fellow ALL SOULS' COLL. 1883, M.A. 1885.

Ombler, George Stuart, y.s. Edward, of Paul, Yorks, arm. UNIVERSITY COLL., matric. 3 June, 1833, aged 18; scholar 1834-42, B.A. 1846.

Ommanney, Edward Aislabie, 2s. Francis, of Mortlake, Surrey, equitis. EXETER COLL., matric. 9 March, 1824, aged 17; B.A. 1827, M.A. 1830, vicar of Chew Magna, Somerset, 1841-78, preb. of Wells 1848, until his death 21 Jan., 1884. See *Rugby School Reg.*, 133.

Ommanney, Erasmus Austin, o.s. Erasmus, of Southsea, Hants, arm. NON-COLL., matric. 31 May, 1879, aged 28; B.A. from MERTON COLL. 1882, M.A. 1886, retired commander R.N., curate of Clewer 1886. [40]

Ommanney, George Campbell, 2s. Octavius, of London, arm. WADHAM COLL., matric. 16 Oct., 1869, aged 18; exhibitioner 1870-1, B.A. 1872, M.A. 1876, vicar of St. Matthew, Sheffield, 1882. See *Robinson*, 345.

Ommanney, Walter Fabian, 3s. Edward, of Chew Magna, Somerset, cler. EXETER COLL., matric. 22 Oct., 1880, aged 19.

Omond, Thomas Stewart, 1s. Robert, of Edinburgh, D.Med. BALLIOL COLL., matric. 27 Jan., 1868, aged 21, exhibitioner 1868-72, B.A. 1872; fellow ST. JOHN'S COLL. 1872-8, M.A. 1874, librarian 1876, bursar 1877, bar.-at-law, Inner Temple, 1874. See Foster's *Men at the Bar*.

O'Neil, John Reynolds, 1s. John, of Chelsea, Middlesex, gent. CORPUS CHRISTI COLL., matric. 7 June, 1851, aged 18; exhibitioner 1852-5, B.A. 1855, M.A. 1858, a student of the Inner Temple 1859, died in July, 1876.

O'Neill, Arthur, 2s. William, of Ballynascreen, co. Derry, Ireland, cler. TRINITY COLL., matric. 26 Nov., 1862, aged 19. [5]

O'Neill, Charles Henry St. John, born at Shanes Castle, co. Dromore, Ireland, s. John, Viscount O'Neill. CHRIST CHURCH, matric. 23 Nov., 1795, aged 16; 2nd viscount, K.P., created Earl O'Neill Aug., 1800, one of the original 28 Irish representative peers 1801, died 25 March, 1841. See *Eton School Lists*.

O'Neill, Henry Arthur, o.s. John, of St. Peter's, Dublin, arm. QUEEN'S COLL., matric. 15 March, 1820, aged 17. See *Eton School Lists*.

O'Neill, John, s. Charles, of ——, co. Cork, Ireland, arm. CHRIST CHURCH, matric. 14 April, 1762, aged 22; created M.A. 15 June, 1762, of Shanes Castle, M.P. Randlestown, April, 1761-83, co. Antrim 1783-93, created Baron O'Neill 25 Oct., 1793, and Viscount O'Neill 3 Oct., 1795, died 17 June, 1798.

O'Neill, John Robert, o.s. Robert, of Talylyn, co. Brecon, arm. MAGDALEN HALL, matric. 5 Dec., 1844, aged 20.

O'Neill, (Hon.) Robert Torrens, 3s. William, of Mullavilly, co. Armagh, Ireland, cler. (after baron). BRASENOSE COLL., matric. 21 Jan., 1864, aged 19; B.A. & M.A. 1870, of Derrynoyd, co. Londonderry, high sheriff 1871, M.P. Mid Antrim, Dec., 1885. See Foster's *Peerage*. [10]

O'Neill, William Henry, 2s. William, of Lee, Kent, arm. JESUS COLL., matric. 20 Oct., 1886, aged 18; scholar 1886.

Ongley, Robert Henley, Baron, 1s. Robert Henley, Baron Ongley. CHRIST CHURCH, matric. 9 May, 1822, aged 19; 3rd baron, died s.p. 21 Jan., 1877. See Foster's *Peerage*.

Ongley, Samuel, s. Samuel, of St. Michael's, Cornhill, London, gent. ST. JOHN'S COLL., matric. 13 Dec., 1716, aged 19 (? M.P. Shoreham 1729-34, and Bedford 1734, until his death 15 June, 1747).

Onians, Anthony Seymore, s. John, of Stokesay, Salop, pleb. PEMBROKE COLL., matric. 23 Nov., 1720, aged 18.

Onions, John Henry, 1s. John Henry, of Market Drayton, Salop, gent. CHRIST CHURCH, matric. 14 Oct., 1871, aged 19; a junior student 1871-6, a senior student 1876, B.A. 1876, M.A. 1878, tutor 1878, and lecturer. [15]

Onley, George Deakin. ST. JOHN'S COLL., 1846. See PRATTENTON.

Onslow, Arthur, s. Richard, of St. Anne's, London, arm. EXETER COLL., matric. 19 Jan., 1764, aged 17, B.A. 1767; M.A. from ALL SOULS' COLL. 1771; canon of CHRIST CHURCH 1779-95, B.D. 1780, D.D. 1781, chaplain House of Commons 1774, rector of Gravesend 1782, archdeacon of Berks 1785, vicar of Kidderminster 1795, rector of Lindridge 1811, dean of Worcester 1795, until his death 15 Oct., 1817. See Foster's *Peerage*.

Onslow, Andrew George, 1s. Richard Foley, of Newent, co. Gloucester, arm. BRASENOSE COLL., matric. 7 June, 1849, aged 18; of Stardene, co. Gloucester, sometime captain 13th regiment. See Foster's *Peerage* & *Eton School Lists*.

Onslow, Arthur, s. George, of Ockham, Surrey, arm. MERTON COLL., matric. 17 May, 1791, aged 17; B.A. 1795, M.A. 1798, vicar of Chevering 1803, rector of Merrow, Surrey, 1812, and of Crayford, Kent, 1813, until his death 29 Nov., 1851. See Foster's *Peerage* & *Eton School Lists*.

Onslow, Arthur Andrew, 2s. Richard Francis, of Newent, co. Gloucester, archdeacon of Worcester. CHRIST CHURCH, matric. 23 Oct., 1834, aged 19; B.A. 1838, vicar of Claverdon, co. Warwick, 1842-50, of Newent, co. Gloucester, 1850, until his death 20 Dec., 1864. See Foster's *Peerage* & *Eton School Lists*. [20]

Onslow, Arthur Cyril (Phipps), born at Oxford, s. Arthur, dean of Worcester. CHRIST CHURCH, matric. 25 May, 1805, aged 16; student 1805-13, B.A. 1809, M.A. 1811, rector of St. Mary with St. Matthew, Newington, 1812, until his death 6 Feb., 1869. See *Alumni West.*, 462.

Onslow, Arthur George, s. Thomas, of Harley Street, Westminster, arm. (after earl). CHRIST CHURCH, matric. 4 Nov., 1795, aged 18; 3rd Earl of Onslow, died 24 Oct., 1870.

Onslow, Arthur George (Viscount Cranley), 1s. Arthur George, Earl of Onslow. CHRIST CHURCH, matric. 30 May, 1838, aged 17; B.A. 1841, M.A. 1844, died 2 Aug., 1856.

Onslow, Edward, s. George, of Westminster, arm. (after lord). CHRIST CHURCH, matric. 29 Oct., 1774, aged 16; M.P. Aldeburgh 1780-1, died unmarried.

Onslow, Francis Phipps, 2s. Phipps Vansittart, of Broadwas Hall, co. Worcester, arm. PEMBROKE COLL., matric. 15 June, 1854, aged 19; B.A. 1859, M.A. 1864, bar.-at-law, Lincoln's Inn, 1862. See Foster's *Men at the Bar* & *Rugby School Reg.*, 301. [25]

Onslow, Frederick Thomas, 4s. Thomas Cranley, of Alresford, Hants, arm. MAGDALEN HALL, matric. 20 June, 1839, aged 18; died 15 July, 1883.

Onslow, George, created D.C.L. 8 July, 1773, then of Ember Court, Surrey, P.C. 1767 (son of Arthur Onslow, speaker of the House of Commons 1727-61), 4th Baron Onslow, M.A. from PETER HOUSE, Cambridge, 1766, M.P. Rye, Sussex, 1754-60, Surrey 1761-76, a lord of the Treasury 1765-7, created Baron Cranley 20 May, 1776, and became 4th Baron Onslow 8 Oct. following, comptroller of the household 1777, treasurer 1779-80, lord of the bedchamber 1780, a colonel in the army, created Viscount Cranley and Earl of Onslow 19 June, 1801, died 17 May, 1814. See Foster's *Peerage*.

Onslow, (George) Augustus Cranley, 1s. Thomas Cranley, of St. George's, Hanover Square, London, arm. CHRIST CHURCH, matric. 28 April, 1831, aged 17; B.A. 1835, died 13 April, 1855.

Onslow, George Walton, s. George, of Ockham, Surrey, arm. CHRIST CHURCH, matric. 22 Dec., 1785, aged 16; B.A. 1792, M.A. 1795, vicar of Send 1792, of Shalford 1800, rector of Wisley, and vicar of Pyrford, Surrey, 1806, until his death 13 Feb., 1844. See Foster's *Peerage*.

Onslow, Henry Cope, 2s. Denzil, of Worthing, Sussex, arm. UNIVERSITY COLL., matric. 30 March, 1827, aged 18; demy MAGDALEN COLL. 1829-42, B.A. 1831, M.A. 1833, fellow 1842-3, died 25 April, 1870. See *Bloxam*, vii. 322. [30]

Onslow, Henry John (Hughes), 1s. Arthur, of Merrow, Surrey, cler. CORPUS CHRISTI COLL., matric. 12 June, 1830, aged 14; scholar 1830-7, B.A. 1834, of Alton Albany, Ayrshire, assumed the additional name of HUGHES 1840, died 31 July, 1870. See Foster's *Peerage* & *Eton School Lists*.

Onslow, Matthew Richard Septimus, 4s. Matthew Richard, of King's Langley, Wilts, baronet. NON-COLL., matric. 13 Oct., 1876, aged 19; B.A. from PEMBROKE COLL. 1880, M.A. 1883, chaplain royal navy. See Foster's *Baronetage.*

Onslow, Phipps, 1s. Phipps Vansittart, of Eltham, Kent, arm. EXETER COLL., matric. 6 May, 1841, aged 18; B.A. 1845, rector of Upper Sapey, co. Worcester, 1859. See Foster's *Peerage,* and for list of his works see *Crockford.*

Onslow, Richard Foley, 1s. (Richard Francis), of Kidderminster, Worcester, cler. CHRIST CHURCH, matric. 11 May, 1821, aged 18; B.A. 1825, of Stardene, co. Gloucester, died 12 March, 1879.

Onslow, Richard Francis, s. Arthur, of Reading, Berks, doctor. CHRIST CHURCH, matric. 20 Dec., 1793, aged 17; B.A. 1797, M.A. 1800, vicar of Kidderminster 1801, of Newent, co. Gloucester, 1804, rector of Stoke Edith 1834, archdeacon of Worcester 1815, preb. of Salisbury 1823, died 18 Oct., 1849. See Foster's *Peerage* & *Eton School Lists.*

Onslow, William Hillier, Earl of, o.s. Augustus Cranley, of Alresford, Hants, arm. EXETER COLL., matric. 15 April, 1871, aged 18; 4th earl, high steward of Guildford, a lord in waiting 1880, 1886. See Foster's *Peerage* & *Eton School Lists.* [5]

Openshaw, Rev. Thomas Williams, 3s. Laurence Rogers, of Bury, Lancashire, arm. BRASENOSE COLL., matric. 24 May, 1856, aged 18; scholar 1857-9, B.A. 1860, M.A. 1863.

Orange, Hugh William, o.s. William, of Broadmoor, Berks, D.Med. NEW COLL., matric. 16 Oct., 1885, aged 19; scholar 1884.

Orange, William Charles Henry Friso, Prince of; created D.C.L. 1 March, 1733-4 (posthumous son of John William, Prince of Nassau, who became also Prince of Orange, on the death of William III. of England), married 14 March, 1734, Anne, Princess Royal of England, daughter of George II., and died 22 Oct., 1751, grandfather of William, King of the Netherlands. See Foster's *Peerage,* xcix.

Orchard, Charles, s. Thomas, of Hartley, Devon, cler. BALLIOL COLL., matric. 21 May, 1726, aged 18.

Orchard, Charles, s. Charles, of Poughill, Cornwall, gent. MAGDALEN HALL, matric. 9 Nov., 1782, aged 22. [10]

Orchard, George (Randall), s. Abraham, of Bath, Somerset, gent. MAGDALEN HALL, matric. 14 Jan., 1815, aged 23; perp. curate North Bradley, Wilts, 1826, until his death 21 June, 1850.

Orchard, Henry Langhorne, 4s. George Briggs, of St. Ives, Cornwall, gent. PEMBROKE COLL., matric. 5 Feb., 1873, aged 30; B.A. 1876, M.A. 1879.

Orchard, Isaac, s. Isaac, of St. James's, Bath (city), gent. MAGDALEN HALL, matric. 24 May, 1817, aged 31.

Orchard, Paul, s. Paul, of Hartland, Devon, arm. EXETER COLL., matric. 25 June, 1757, aged 18; M.P. Callington 1784-1806, died 1 March, 1812.

Orchard, Robert George Hooper, o.s. George Randall, of North Bradley, Wilts, cler. MAGDALEN HALL, matric. 21 June, 1838, aged 16; B.A. 1844, M.A. 1858. [15]

Orchard, William, s. William, of Carhampton, Somerset, gent. BALLIOL COLL., matric. 29 Nov., 1743, aged 17.

Ord, Andrew John Blackett-, 2s. John Alexander, of Wolsingham, co. Durham, cler. QUEEN'S COLL., matric. 29 Oct., 1867, aged 18.

Ord, Charles Edward Blackett-, 4s. John Alexander, of London, cler. CORPUS CHRISTI COLL., matric. 17 Oct., 1876, aged 18; scholar 1876-81, B.A. 1880, M.A. 1886, vicar of Ovingham, co. Durham, 1886.

Ord, Craven, s. Craven, of St. Andrew's, Holborn, London, arm. UNIVERSITY COLL., matric. 2 March, 1803, aged 17; B.A. 1807, M.A. 1811, of Greensted Hall, Essex, preb. of Lincoln 1814, vicar of Gretton with Duddington, Northants, 1814-9, vicar of St. Mary-de-Wigtoft, Lincoln, 1809, until his death 14 Dec., 1836.

Ord, Edward Hamilton Blackett, 1s. John Alexander, of Heddon-on-the-Wall, Northumberland, cler. CHRIST CHURCH, matric. 23 May, 1861, aged 18. [20]

Ord, Henry Craven, s. John, of Fornham, Suffolk, doctor. TRINITY COLL., matric. 27 Jan., 1800, aged 21; B.A. 1802, rector of Wheathamstead, Herts, 1811-14, vicar of Stratfield Mortimer 1811, preb. of Lincoln 1814, until his death 1 Aug., 1840.

Ord, James, s. William, of Fenham, Northumberland, arm. CHRIST CHURCH, matric. 10 July, 1778, aged 19; B.A. 1782, M.A. 1785, of Langton Hall, co. Leicester, rector of Whitfield, co. Durham, 1784, until his death 29 Jan., 1843, father of the next named.

Ord, James Pickering, s. James, of Castle Eden, co. Durham, cler. UNIVERSITY COLL., matric. 4 Nov., 1807, aged 18; B.A. 1812, M.A. 1815, brother of Thomas Charles.

Ord, John, of CHRIST'S COLL., Cambridge (12th wrangler and B.A. 1772, M.A. 1786), s. Henry, of Middle Temple, London, arm. TRINITY COLL., incorp. 14 Jan., 1793, aged 42; B. & D.D. 17 Jan., 1793, chaplain in ordinary to Prince of Wales 1784, preb. of Lincoln 1796, and rector of Fornham St. Martin, Suffolk, 1796, and of Burgh and Ickborough, Norfolk, 1784, died 8 Sep., 1816, father of Henry Craven 1800.

Ord, John Alexander Blackett, 4s. Christopher Blackett, of Wylam, Northumberland, arm. CHRIST CHURCH, matric. 21 May, 1823, aged 20; B.A. 1827, vicar of Heddon-on-the-Wall, Northumberland, rector of Woolsingham, assumed the additional surname of ORD by royal licence 7 Dec., 1855, died 10 July, 1865, father of Andrew John, Charles Edward, and Edward Hamilton. [25]

Ord, John Thomas, o.s. John Norman, of Wheathamstead, Herts, cler. EXETER COLL., matric. 18 Feb., 1826, aged 18; B.A. 1830, of Fornham House, Suffolk, hon. colonel West Suffolk yeomanry cavalry.

Ord, Ralph, s. Ralph, of Durham (city), arm. CHRIST CHURCH, matric. 24 Jan., 1788, aged 17; B.A. 1791, M.A. 1794, student until 1813, rector of Semley, Wilts, 1812, until his death 15 Sep., 1855. See *Rugby School Reg.,* 57.

Ord, Richard, s. Ralph, of Sedgefield, co. Durham, arm. CHRIST CHURCH, matric. 4 Feb., 1802, aged 18.

Ord, Richard, 2s. Mark, of Hurworth, co. Durham, arm. BALLIOL COLL., matric. 19 Oct., 1868, aged 19; B.A. & M.A. 1876, of Sands Hall, co. Durham, J.P., bar.-at-law, Inner Temple, 1874. See Foster's *Men at the Bar.*

Ord, Thomas Charles, s. James, of St. Marylebone, London, cler. UNIVERSITY COLL., matric. 28 Jan., 1812, aged 17; B.A. 1815, M.A. 1819, rector of Galby and vicar of Norton, co. Leicester, 1826, until his death 6 Oct., 1844. See *Rugby School Reg.,* 92. [30]

Ord, William Wallis, 1s. William Miller, of Streatham, Surrey, D.Med. UNIVERSITY COLL., matric. 31 May, 1879, aged 19; B.A. 1883, B.Med. & M.A. 1887.

Orde, Charles William, o.s. Charles Ward, of Exeter (city), arm. UNIVERSITY COLL., matric. 6 March, 1828, aged 18; B.A. 1831, M.A 1836, of Nunnykirk, Northumberland, high sheriff, 1846, bar.-at-law, Lincoln's Inn, 1842, died 16 Sep., 1875.

Orde, James Henry, o.s. James, of Isle of Jersey, arm. ORIEL COLL., matric. 25 March, 1849; B.A. 1853, M.A. 1856, of Hopton House, Suffolk, a student of the Inner Temple, 1851, died 21 Feb., 1880. See Foster's *Peerage*, B. BOLTON.

Orde, John, s. John, of Weetwood, Northumberland, gent. LINCOLN COLL., matric. 23 Oct., 1788, aged 18; B.A. 1792, M.A. 1800, rector of Winslade, Yorks, 1811, of Wensley 1829, until his death 13 Jan., 1850. See Foster's *Peerage*, B. BOLTON.

Orde, (Sir) John Powlett (Bart.), o.s. John, of St. Marylebone, London, baronet. CHRIST CHURCH, matric. 10 April, 1821, aged 17; B.A. 1826, 2nd baronet, died 13 Dec., 1878. See Foster's *Baronetage* & *Eton School Lists.*

Orde, Leonard, s. John, of Weetwood, Northumberland, arm. UNIVERSITY COLL., matric. 9 May, 1787, aged 18; of Weetwood, lieut.-general in the army, died 2 Aug., 1850. See Foster's *Peerage*, B. BOLTON.

Orde, Thomas, s. John, of Norham, Northumberland, gent. LINCOLN COLL., matric. 17 Oct., 1721, aged 17; B.A. 1725. **[5]**

Orde, Thorley Launcelot Maximilian, 2s. Henry Powlett Shafto, of Chathill, Northumberland, arm. BALLIOL COLL., matric. 15 Oct., 1884, aged 19.

Orde, William, 1s. Charles William, of Edinburgh, arm. UNIVERSITY COLL., matric. 11 Oct., 1873, aged 19; B.A. 1878, of Nunnykirk, Northumberland. See *Eton School Lists.*

O'Reilly, Charles William, 3s. Edward, of Marylebone, Middlesex, arm. ST. MARY HALL, matric. 21 April, 1842, aged 22.

Orger, Edward Redman, 3s. William, of Sydenham, Kent, cler. PEMBROKE COLL., matric. 30 April, 1846, aged 19; B.A. 1849, M.A. 1852, vicar of Hougham-by-Dover 1880.

Orger, John Goldsmith, 2s. William, of Tooting, Surrey, cler. WADHAM COLL., matric. 27 Jan., 1841, aged 18; B.A. 1844, M.A. 1869, rector of Cranford, Northants, 1856-70, chaplain of Christ Church, Dinan, 1869. **[10]**

Orger, William, 2s. John, of Marylebone, London, gent. ST. EDMUND HALL, matric. 4 Dec., 1822, aged 33; B.A. 1826, M.A. 1829, died perp. curate Shirley, Hants, 2 May, 1859.

Orgill, George. UNIVERSITY COLL., 1807. See LEMAN, page 839.

Orgill, George Richard, s. William, of Isle of Jamaica, arm. UNIVERSITY COLL., matric. 31 Jan., 1798, aged 19.

Orgill, Thomas Tromp Tyrrell, 1s. Samuel Thomas, of Isle of Jamaica, gent. WORCESTER COLL., matric. 2 Nov., 1832, aged 21; B.A. 1836.

Orgill, Van Tromp Tyrrel, 1s. Thomas Tromp Tyrrel, of Port Anthony, Isle of Jamaica, cler. ST. ALBAN HALL, matric. 17 Oct., 1859, aged 19; B.A. 1862, M.A. 1872, rector of Cold Weston, Salop, 1870-5, & 1875-85, vicar of Ludford, etc., 1885. See *Crockford.* **[15]**

Orlebar, Arthur Bedford, 2s. Robert Charles, of Husborne-Crawley, Beds, arm. ST. JOHN'S COLL., matric. 3 Feb., 1829, aged 18; scholar LINCOLN COLL. 1830-3, B.A. 1832, M.A. 1842, professor of astronomy in Elphinstone College, Bombay, government inspector of schools, Melbourne, where he died 11 June, 1866. See *Manchester School Reg.*, iii. 216.

Orlebar, Augustus, 6s. Robert Charles, of Husborne-Crawley, Beds, arm. WADHAM COLL., matric. 3 May, 1843, aged 18; B.A. 1847, M.A. 1850, rector of Farndish, Beds, 1852-8, and vicar of Willington, Beds, 1858. See *Rugby School Reg.*, 203.

Orlebar, Augustus Scobell, 1s. Augustus, of Willington, Beds, cler. WORCESTER COLL., matric. 16 Oct., 1879, aged 19; scholar 1879-84, B.A. 1883, M.A. 1886, assistant-master Wellington College. See *Eton School Lists.*

Orlebar, Richard, 1s. Richard (Longuet), of Hinwick, Beds, arm. CHRIST CHURCH, matric. 11 Dec., 1851, aged 19; B.A. 1855, of Hinwick Hall, Beds, J.P. See *Rugby School Reg.*, 260.

Orloff, General Alexis Feodorovitch, Count, created D.C.L. 21 May, 1839, A.D.C. to the Emperor of Russia, died 20 May, 1861, aged 75. **[20]**

Orme, Rev. Edward Hartley, 1s. Edward, of St. George's, Hanover Square, London, arm. ST. MARY HALL, matric. 9 April, 1824, aged 19; B.A. 1829, M.A. 1831, died 20 April, 1839.

Orme, James Bond, 3s. George, of Merton, Surrey, arm. BRASENOSE COLL., matric. 18 March, 1858, aged 18; B.A. 1862, M.A. 1864, a student of the Inner Temple 1861, rector of East Angmering 1866.

Orme, Joseph, s. John, of Newport, Salop, gent. MAGDALEN HALL, matric. 11 Oct., 1725, aged 18; B.A. 1729.

Orme, William Henry, 1s. Thomas, of Ballina, Ireland, arm. ST. JOHN'S COLL., matric. 26 March, 1836, aged 20; B.A. 1840.

Orme, William Platt, 1s. John, of Leeds, Yorks, gent. LINCOLN COLL., matric. 29 Jan., 1881, aged 20.

Ormerod, Arthur Stanley, 7s. George, of Salcombe, Devon, arm. EXETER COLL., matric. 6 Feb., 1840, aged 18; B.A. 1843, M.A. 1846, vicar of Halvergate, Norfolk, 1853, until his death 22 Feb., 1884. See *Rugby School Reg.*, 192. **[25]**

Ormerod, Charles, 1s. Richard, of Kelvedon, Essex, cler. LINCOLN COLL., matric. 6 July, 1819, aged 23; possibly father of the next named.

Ormerod, Charles Holden Arthur, 1s. Charles, of London, arm. WADHAM COLL., matric. 18 Oct., 1848, aged 19; B.A. 1853, M.A. 1859.

Ormerod, George, s. George, of Manchester, Lancashire, gent. BRASENOSE COLL., matric. 21 April, 1803, aged 17; created M.A. 5 Feb., 1807, and also D.C.L. 17 Dec., 1818, of Sedbury Park, co. Gloucester, F.R.S., F.S.A., author of the 'History of Cheshire,' died 9 Oct., 1873.

Ormerod, George Thomas Bailey, 1s. Thomas Johnson, of Norwich (city), cler. BALLIOL COLL., matric. 9 April, 1864, aged 18; B.A. 1867, M.A. 1870, of Tildesley, Lancashire, bar.-at-law, Inner Temple, 1870, vicar of Oakridge, co. Gloucester, 1878-9. See Foster's *Men at the Bar.* **[30]**

Ormerod, George Wareing, 2s. George, of Leigh, Lancashire, arm. BRASENOSE COLL., matric. 31 Jan., 1829, aged 18; B.A. 1833, M.A. 1836, of Chagford, Devon, F.G.S.

Ormerod, Herbert Eliot, 2s. Charles, of Brighton, Sussex, arm. EXETER COLL., matric. 17 April, 1850, aged 18; postmaster MERTON COLL. 1850-4, B.A. from ST. MARY HALL 1854, M.A. 1857, bar.-at-law, Inner Temple, 1855. See Foster's *Men at the Bar.*

Ormerod, Rev. John Arderne, 3s. George, of Backford, Cheshire, arm. BRASENOSE COLL., matric. 8 Feb., 1832, aged 18; B.A. 1835, M.A. 1838, fellow 1838-64, senior bursar 1848, died 12 Dec., 1864. See *Rugby School Reg.*, 158.

Ormerod, Joseph Arderne, 2s. Thomas Johnson, of Starston, Norfolk, cler. CORPUS CHRISTI COLL., matric. 23 Oct., 1867, aged 19, scholar 1867-71, B.A. 1871; fellow JESUS COLL. 1871-5, B.Med. & M.A. 1875, D.Med. 1882. See *Rugby School Reg.*

Ormerod, Lawrence, s. Peter, of Ormerod, Lancashire, arm. BRASENOSE COLL., matric. 31 March, 1772, aged 18. **[35]**

Ormerod, Oliver, 1s. Richard, of Manchester, Lancashire, arm. BRASENOSE COLL., matric. 25 May, 1825, aged 18; B.A. 1829, M.A. 1832, a student of the Inner Temple 1825, perp. curate Birch, near Manchester, 1839-41, rector of Presteign 1841, until his death 14 Feb., 1880. See *St. Paul's School Reg.*, 258.

Ormerod, Thomas Holden, s. Richard, of Kensington, Middlesex, cler. NEW COLL., matric. 2 Dec., 1814, aged 17; fellow 1814, until his death 14 Sep., 1818.

Ormerod, Thomas Johnson, 1s. George, of Missenden, Bucks, arm. BRASENOSE COLL., matric. 18 May, 1826, aged 16; B.A. 1830, M.A. 1833, fellow 1831-8 (a student of the Inner Temple 1830), Hebrew lecturer 1832, junior bursar 1833, divinity lecturer 1836, select preacher 1845, archdeacon of Suffolk, 1846-68, rector of Redenhall, Norfolk, 1847, until his death 2 Dec., 1874. See *Manchester School Reg.*, i. 57.

Ormerod, William Piers; privilegiatus 19 Oct., 1846 (brother of the last named), F.R.C.S., London, surgeon Radcliffe Infirmary, Oxford, 1846-8, died 10 June, 1860, aged 42.

Ormond, Arthur William, y.s. James, of Melbourne, gent. BRASENOSE COLL., matric. 14 Oct., 1884, aged 20; B.A. 1887.

Ormond, Rev. David, gent. PEMBROKE COLL., matric. 27 June, 1787, died at Putney 29 June, 1802. [5]

Ormond, Ernest William, 2s. John, of Brighton, cler. NEW COLL., matric. 15 Oct., 1881, aged 18; B.A. 1886, bar.-at-law, Inner Temple, 1887.

Ormond, John, 3s. William, of Wantage, Berks, gent. PEMBROKE COLL., matric. 19 Nov., 1846, aged 17; scholar 1846-56, B.A. 1850, M.A. 1853, fellow 1856-7, vicar of Great Kimble and rector of Little Kimble, Bucks, 1857-72, consular chaplain Trieste 1881-3, rector of Horsenden 1886.

Ormiston, Thomas Lane, 2s. Thomas, of Malabar Hill, Bombay, arm. TRINITY COLL., matric. 16 Oct., 1886, aged 19; of the Indian Civil Service 1886.

Ormsby, Arthur, s. Arthur, of Westminster, arm. UNIVERSITY COLL., matric. 17 July, 1783, aged 17.

Ormsby, Henry Magee, o.s. John Blosset, of Powerscourt, near Wicklow, Ireland, cler. QUEEN'S COLL., matric. 11 Oct., 1860, aged 19; scholar 1860-5, B.A. 1865, M.A. 1870, assistant-master Rossall School. See *Rugby School Reg.* [10]

Ormsby, William Arthur, 2s. John, of Kirk Braddon, Isle of Man, arm. UNIVERSITY COLL., matric. 24 Feb., 1831, aged 18; B.A. 1834, M.A. 1837, curate of East Bradenham 1837-47, rector of Edgfield 1847-8, perp. curate St. James's, Norwich, 1848-53, rector of Smallburgh, Norfolk, 1853, and hon. canon Norwich 1871, until his death 15 Feb., 1881.

Ormsby, Rev. William Knox, o.s. William Arthur, of Norwich, cler. TRINITY COLL., matric. 28 Jan., 1873, aged 18; B.A. 1876, M.A. 1880.

Ornsbey, John, s. George, of Allenhead, Northumberland, cler. QUEEN'S COLL., matric. 19 March, 1727-8, aged 19; B.A. 17 Feb., 1731-2, (as ORMSBY).

Ornsby, Rev. George Radcliffe, 1s. George, of Whickham, co. Durham, cler. PEMBROKE COLL., matric. 25 Oct., 1869, aged 20; B.A. 1872, M.A. 1876, died 14 May, 1885.

Ornsby, John Arthur, 2s. George, of Whickham, co. Durham, cler. LINCOLN COLL., matric. 20 Oct., 1869, aged 19; B.A. 1873, M.A. 1876. [15]

Ornsby, Rev. Robert, 3s. George, of Lanchester, co. Durham, gent. LINCOLN COLL., matric. 8 Dec., 1836, aged 16, exhibitioner 1836-43, B.A. 1840; fellow TRINITY COLL. 1843-7, M.A. 1843, rhetorical lecturer 1844; fellow ROYAL UNIVERSITY, Ireland, 1882, seceded to Rome.

Oronhyatekha, Peter, 6s. 'Indiani,' of Grand River, or Ouse, Six Nations District, Canada. ST. EDMUND HALL, matric. 6 May, 1862, aged 21.

O'Rorke, Henry Thomas, M.A. TRINITY COLL., Dublin, 1859 (B.A. 1854); adm. 'ad eundem' 20 Oct., 1859, vicar of Sheriff-Hales, Salop, 1867-79, rector of Feltwell, Norfolk, 1879.

Orr, Alexander, 1s. James, of Belfast, arm. ORIEL COLL., matric. 25 Oct., 1832, aged 17; B.A. 1836, M.A. 1860, vicar of Lamby Connor, co. Antrim, 1847-60, and of Salehurst, Sussex, 1860-78, rector of Cheriton, Hants, 1878.

Orr, Andrew Aylmer, 1s. Robert Holmes, of Ballinasloe, Ireland, cler. CHRIST CHURCH, matric. 13 Oct., 1876, aged 18; B.A. 1879, B.Med. & M.A. 1885.

Orr, Charles Gathorne Edmund, 2s. Alexander, of Salehurst, Sussex, cler. ORIEL COLL., matric. 24 Nov., 1880, aged 18; B.A. 1883, M.A. 1887. [21]

Orr, Rev. Herbert Alexander, 2s. Alexander, of Lamby, co. Antrim, cler. UNIVERSITY COLL., matric. 23 April, 1870, aged 18; B.A. 1873, M.A. 1876, died 24 April, 1878.

Orr, James, 2s. James, of Holywood, co. Down, Ireland, arm. ORIEL COLL., matric. 18 Nov., 1841, aged 18; B.A. 1847. See *Rugby School Reg.*, 197.

Orr, James Stewart, 1s. Alexander, of Lamby, co. Antrim, Ireland, cler. TRINITY COLL., matric. 15 Oct., 1864, aged 17; B.A. 1867.

Orred, George, 1s. George, of Liverpool, arm. MERTON COLL., matric. 10 Dec., 1824, aged 17; of Tranmere, Cheshire, died in Oct., 1869. [25]

Orred, John, s. John, of Runcorn, Cheshire, arm. BRASENOSE COLL., matric. 8 May, 1795, aged 16; B.A. 1799, M.A. 1802, B.Med. 1803, died 23 June, 1805. See *Manchester School Reg.*, ii. 168.

Orred, John Randal, 3s. John, of Aigburth, Lancashire, D.Med. ST. JOHN'S COLL. matric. 31 May, 1879, aged 20; B.A. 1886, M.A. 1888, bar.-at-law, Inner Temple, 1887.

Orred, John Woodville, 1s. John, of Liverpool, arm. MERTON COLL., matric. 16 Jan., 1869, aged 18; a student of the Inner Temple 1872, died 23 Aug., 1877.

Orret, Henry, s. Henry, of Wigan, Lancashire, gent. BRASENOSE COLL., matric. 2 May, 1726, aged 17; B.A. 6 Feb., 1729-30, M.A. 1733.

Orrett, Thomas, s. John, of Warrington, Lancashire, pleb. BRASENOSE COLL., matric. 14 Oct., 1721, aged 19; B.A. 18 Feb., 1725-6, M.A. 1729. [30]

Orrett, William Green, s. William, of Warrington, Lancashire, arm. BRASENOSE COLL., matric. 2 Feb., 1802, aged 18; B.A. 1805, M.A. 1815, rector of Standish, Lancashire, 1825, until he died 12 June, 1841.

Orton, Francis, s. Francis, of Leicester (town), arm. ST. MARY HALL, matric. 3 Nov., 1817, aged 20; B.A. 1821, M.A. 1824, B.C.L. & D.C.L. 1833, incumbent of St. George's, Altrincham, and vicar of Hope, co. Derby, died 4 Feb., 1862.

Orton, George, s. George, of Slaugham, Sussex, cler. BRASENOSE COLL., matric. 2 Oct., 1722, aged 16.

Orton, John, s. George, of Preston, Sussex, cler. NEW COLL., matric. 18 Aug., 1721, aged 12.

Orton, Owen, 3s. John Swaffield, of Carisbrooke, Isle of Wight, arm. BALLIOL COLL., matric. 3 June, 1857, aged 18; scholar CORPUS CHRISTI COLL. 1858-62, B.A. 1861, M.A. 1864, rector of Normanton-on-Soar since 1868. [35]

Osbaldeston, George, s. George, of London, arm. BRASENOSE COLL., matric. 3 May, 1805, aged 18; the celebrated master of hounds, M.P. East Retford 1812-18, died 1 Aug., 1866. See *Eton School Lists*.

Osborn, Charles, s. Peter, of Highgate, Middlesex, gent. JESUS COLL., matric. 4 June, 1747, aged 20; B.A. 1748, M.A. 1749, an officer in 90th foot. See Foster's *Baronetage*.

Osborn, Edward, 1s. Edward Oliver, of Plymouth, Devon, arm. ORIEL COLL., matric. 14 May, 1824, aged 18; B.A. 1828, M.A. 1830.

Osborn, Edward Bolland, 1s. Edward Haydon, of London, arm. MAGDALEN COLL., matric. 6 Feb., 1885, aged 18; exhibitioner 1885.

Osborn, Edward Haydon, 1s. Edward, of Sutton Valence, Kent, cler. ST. JOHN'S COLL., matric. 18 Oct., 1852, aged 20, bible clerk 1852-5; demy MAGDALEN COLL. 1855-7, B.A. 1856, inspector of factories. See *Bloxam*, vii. 402. [40]

Osborn, Rev. Francis Wilfrid, 1s. Montagu Francis Finch, of Kibworth, co. Leicester, cler. KEBLE COLL., matric. 27 Jan., 1881, aged 18; exhibitioner 1881-5, B.A. 1884.

Osborn, (Sir) George Robert (Bart.), 1s. John, of Admiralty, St. Martin's, London, baronet. CHRIST CHURCH, matric. 10 Nov., 1831, aged 18; 6th baronet. See Foster's *Baronetage* & *Alumni West.*, 519.

Osborn, John, s. Danvers, of St. George's, Westminster, baronet. CHRIST CHURCH, matric. 20 May, 1760, aged 17; B.A. 1764, created D.C.L. 29 April, 1777, in diplomatic service, a minister at several foreign Courts.

Osborn, John, s. John, of London, arm. ORIEL COLL., matric. 1 Dec., 1763, aged 18; died young. See Foster's *Baronetage*.

Osborn, (Sir) John (Bart.), s. George, of Westminster, baronet. CHRIST CHURCH, matric. 22 April, 1790, aged 17; B.A. 1793, M.A. 1814, created D.C.L. 13 June, 1834, 5th baronet, M.P. Bedfordshire 1794-1817, 1818-20, Cockermouth 1807-8, Queenborough 1812-18, Wigton burghs 1821-4, a lord of the Admiralty 1811-29, a commissioner for auditing public accounts 1829, until his death 28 Aug., 1848. See Foster's *Baronetage* & *Alumni West.*, 519. [5]

Osborn, Montagu Francis Finch, 4s. John, of Marylebone, Middlesex, baronet. BALLIOL COLL., matric. 24 March, 1841, aged 16, B.A. 1845; fellow MERTON COLL. 1847-52, M.A. 1848, librarian 1848, dean 1850, rector of Kibworth-Beauchamp, co. Leicester, 1851-84, vicar of Embleton, Northumberland, 1884. See Foster's *Baronetage* & *Alumni West.*, 519.

Osborne, Lord Albert Edward Godolphin, s. George, Duke of Leeds. BALLIOL COLL., matric. 28 May, 1885, aged 19. See Foster's *Peerage*.

Osborne, Algernon Willoughby-, 2s. Willoughby, of Schole, East Indies, arm. HERTFORD COLL., matric. 20 Jan., 1883, aged 18; B.A. 1886.

Osborne, Charles, s. Charles, of Wolverhampton, co. Stafford, gent. ORIEL COLL., matric. 30 May, 1745, aged 17.

Osborne, Lord Conyers George Thomas William, 2s. George William Frederick, Duke of Leeds. CHRIST CHURCH, matric. 16 Oct., 1829, aged 17; killed accidentally in wrestling at Christ Church 19 Feb., 1831. [10]

Osborne, Edward, s. Jeremiah, of St. Radcliffe, Bristol (city), gent. PEMBROKE COLL., matric. 17 Dec., 1798, aged 19.

Osborne, Eric Willoughby, 3s. George Willoughby, of Hydrabad, East Indies, gent. WORCESTER COLL., matric. 24 Jan., 1863, aged 19.

Osborne, Francis Godolphin (Marquis of Carmarthen), o.s. Thomas, Duke of Leeds. CHRIST CHURCH, matric. 11 June, 1767; created M.A. 30 March, 1769, & D.C.L. 7 July, 1773, 5th duke, M.P. Eye 1774, Helston 1774-5, had summons to parliament as Baron Osborne 15 May, 1776, lord of the bedchamber 1776, home secretary 1783-9, died 31 Jan., 1799. See Foster's *Peerage*.

Osborne, Francis Godolphin, s. Francis, Duke of Leeds. CHRIST CHURCH, matric. 18 April, 1795, aged 17; created M.A. 28 June, 1797, M.P. Helston 1799-1802, Lewes 1802-6, Cambridge 1810-31, created Baron Godolphin 14 May, 1832, died 15 Feb., 1850. See Foster's *Peerage*, D. LEEDS.

Osborne, Francis Godolphin D'Arcy D'Arcy, Marquis of Carmarthen, s. George William Frederick, Duke of Leeds. CHRIST CHURCH, matric. 4 May, 1815, aged 16; 7th Duke of Leeds 1838, M.P. Helston 1826-30, summoned to parliament as Baron Osborne of Kiveton, Yorks, 2 July, 1838, assumed the additional name of D'ARCY 6 Aug., 1849, died 4 May, 1859. See Foster's *Peerage*. [15]

Osborne, George, s. Thomas, of St. Anne's, London, pleb. CORPUS CHRISTI COLL., matric. 27 March, 1723, aged 18; B.A. 1726.

Osborne, George, s. John, of Tamworth, co. Stafford, pleb. MERTON COLL., matric. 14 Dec., 1736, aged 19, B.A. 1740; M.A. from KING'S COLL., Cambridge, 1750.

Osborne, George, s. George, of Godmanstone, Dorset, cler. MERTON COLL., matric. 13 July, 1782, aged 17, B.A. 1786; M.A. from CLARE COLL., Cambridge, 1799, rector of Stainby-cum-Gunby, co. Lincoln, rector of Haselbeach, Northants, 1822, until his death 29 Oct., 1839.

Osborne, George Edward Caulfeilde, o.s. George Yarnold, of Fleetwood, Lancashire, cler. TRINITY COLL., matric. 17 Oct., 1885, aged 19.

Osborne, George Godolphin, born at Stapleford, co. Cambridge, 1s. Francis, arm. (after baron). CHRIST CHURCH, matric. 27 Nov., 1819; 2nd Baron Godolphin 1850, and 8th Duke of Leeds 1859, died 8 August, 1872. [20]

Osborne, Hamilton, y.s. Henry, of Dapto, New South Wales, arm. NEW INN HALL, matric. 12 June, 1868, aged 18.

Osborne, Henry, s. William, of Sculcoats, Yorks, arm. UNIVERSITY COLL., matric. 10 April, 1778, aged 19; B.A. 1782.

Osborne, Herbert Boyles, 1s. Edward, of Blendworth, Hants, cler. EXETER COLL., matric. 24 Jan., 1857, aged 19.

Osborne, Henry Bryan Godfrey Godfrey Faussett, 1s. Henry Godfrey Godfrey Faussett, of Littleton, co. Worcester, cler. CHRIST CHURCH, matric. 25 May, 1883, aged 18; B.A. 1887.

Osborne, Henry Godfrey Faussett, 2s. Godfrey Faussett, of Harefield, Middlesex, D.D. CHRIST CHURCH, matric. 20 Oct., 1841, aged 17; student 1842-55, B.A. 1845, M.A. 1848, of Hartlip Place, Kent, perp. curate South Littleton, etc., co. Worcester, 1854, until his death 18 Nov., 1878. [25]

Osborne, James, s. Samuel, of Barbados, arm. QUEEN'S COLL., matric. 15 July, 1738, aged 17; brother of Robert 1736.

Osborne, James, s. Robert Jonathan, of Isle of Barbados, arm. QUEEN'S COLL., matric. 31 Oct., 1745, aged 16; brother of Robert 1745.

Osborne, John, s. Samuel, of Husborn Tarrant, Hants, pleb. ST. MARY HALL, matric. 19 May, 1721, aged 18; B.A. 1724.

Osborne, John, s. Thomas, of Newtimber, Sussex, arm. UNIVERSITY COLL., matric. 25 May, 1732, aged 20; died rector of Newtimber 6 May, 1774.

Osborne, John, 2s. Jeremiah, of St. Michael's, Bristol (city), arm. TRINITY COLL., matric. 21 March, 1828, aged 17; B.A. 1831, M.A. 1834, bar.-at-law, Lincoln's Inn, 1835, Q.C. and a bencher 1863, died 23 Nov., 1872. [30]

Osborne, John Francis, 1s. John Francis, of Calcutta, East Indies, cler. WORCESTER COLL., matric. 15 Oct., 1864, aged 21; B.A. 1868, M.A. 1871, vicar of St. Peter, Highgate Hill, London, 1880.

Osborne, Leighton, s. Thomas, of Newtimber, Sussex, gent. UNIVERSITY COLL., matric. 11 July, 1728, aged 17; brother of John 1732.

Osborne, Peter Mann, s. Peter, of Exeter (city), gent. EXETER COLL., matric. 9 Nov., 1796, aged 18, B.A. 1800; incorp. CAMBRIDGE UNIVERSITY 1810, M.A. from SIDNEY SUSSEX COLL. 1810.

Osborne, Robert, s. Samuel, of Isle of Barbados, arm. QUEEN'S COLL., matric. 13 July, 1736, aged 17; brother of James 1738.

Osborne, Robert, s. Robert Jonathan, of Isle of Barbados, arm. QUEEN'S COLL., matric. 31 Oct., 1745, aged 18; brother of James 1745. [35]

Osborne, Lord Sidney Godolphin, s. Francis, Duke of Leeds. CHRIST CHURCH, matric. 21 Oct., 1808, aged 18; died 15 April, 1861. See Foster's *Peerage* & *Eton School Lists*.

Osborne, (Lord) Sidney Godolphin, born at Stapleford, co. Cambridge, 3s. Francis (after Lord Godolphin). BRASENOSE COLL., matric. 16 Dec., 1824, aged 16; B.A. 1830, rector of Stoke Poges, Bucks, 1832-41, and of Durweston and Bryanston 1841-75. See Foster's *Peerage*, D. LEEDS; & *Rugby School Reg.* 138.

Osborne, Sydney Rowlandson, 1s. Martin, of St. Ives, Hunts, arm. UNIVERSITY COLL., matric. 19 Oct., 1867, aged 18; B.A. 1872.

Osborne, Thomas (4th) Duke of Leeds, s. Peregrine, Duke of Leeds. CHRIST CHURCH, matric. 6 July, 1731, aged 17; created D.C.L. 9 April, 1733, F.R.S. 1739, K.G. 1749, P.C. 1753, cofferer of the household 1756-61, died 23 March, 1789. See Foster's *Peerage.*

Osborne, (Sir) Thomas (Bart.), s. William, of St. Peter's, Dublin, baronet. CHRIST CHURCH, matric. 18 April, 1769, aged 16; 8th baronet, M.P. Carysfort, 1776-97, died 3 June, 1821. See Foster's *Baronetage.*

Osborne, Thomas, s. Thomas, of London, gent. TRINITY COLL., matric. 16 Oct., 1792, aged 20. [5]

Osborne, William, s. Simon, of Penryn, Cornwall, gent. EXETER COLL., matric. 24 Jan., 1750-1, aged 18; B.A. 1755.

Osborne, Rev. William Alexander, o.s. William Alexander, of Macclesfield, Cheshire, cler. BRASENOSE COLL., matric. 13 May, 1862, aged 19; B.A. 1866.

Osgood, Lawrence, s. John, of Cheveley, Berks, gent. TRINITY COLL., matric. 13 Dec., 1737, aged 18.

Osgoode, William, s. William, of St. Martin's, London, gent. CHRIST CHURCH, matric. 12 July, 1768, aged 15; B.A. 1772, M.A. 1777, bar.-at-law, Lincoln's Inn, 1779, and of the Inner Temple (*ad eundem*) 1813, chief justice Upper Canada 1792, at Quebec 1795-1801, died 17 Jan., 1824.

Osler, Richard Smith, 3s. Timothy Smith, of Kingston, Surrey, arm. LINCOLN COLL., matric. 20 Oct., 1876, aged 19; scholar 1876-80, B.A. 1880, M.A. 1886. [10]

Osler, Rev. William Alban, 2s. Richard, of Falmouth, Cornwall, gent. MAGDALEN HALL, matric. 23 April, 1866, aged 25; commoner BENSON HALL 1867; (NON-COLL.) B.A. 1875, M.A. 1879, died 29 March, 1882.

Osma, Guillermo Joaquin de, 1s. John Ignatius, of Havannah, Island of Cuba, arm. PEMBROKE COLL., matric. 27 May, 1871, aged 18; B.A. 1874, M.A. 1879, attached to the Spanish Embassy in Paris.

Osman, Henry, s. Joseph, of Flamstead, Herts, gent. QUEEN'S COLL., matric. 11 July, 1754, aged 18; B.A. 1758.

Osman, Richard, 'plumbarius & vitrarius;' privilegiatus 31 May, 1813.

Osmaston, Francis Plumptre Beresford, 1s. John (formerly Wright), of Hulland, co. Derby, arm. UNIVERSITY COLL., matric. 20 Oct., 1876, aged 19; B.A. 1880, bar.-at-law, Inner Temple, 1885. [15]

Osmer, William, s. William, of Chiddingfold, Surrey, gent. CORPUS CHRISTI COLL., matric. 20 April, 1728, aged 12.

Osmond, Charles, s. Henry, of Tiverton, Devon, gent. TRINITY COLL., matric. 24 May, 1803, aged 16; J.P. Devon, rector of Ashton-sub-Edge, co. Gloucester, 1816, curate of Clare portion, Tiverton, died 17 Sep., 1830.

Osmond, Henry Fortescue, 1s. Charles, of Tiverton, Devon, cler. BALLIOL COLL., matric. 5 July, 1826, aged 17; scholar 1826-7.

Osmotherley, Salkeld, s. Cuthbert, of Langrigg, Cumberland, gent. ST. EDMUND HALL, matric. 4 May, 1725, aged 20.

Ostler, John Mountney. MAGDALEN COLL., 1857. See LELY, page 839. [20]

Ostler, William Grinfield, 1s. John Lely, of Grantham, co. Lincoln, arm. UNIVERSITY COLL., matric. 15 Nov., 1855, aged 17; B.A. 1860, of Framlingham Hall, Norfolk, and of Cawthorpe, co. Lincoln, has assumed the surname of LELY in lieu of OSTLER.

Ostrehan, Joseph Duncan, s. Joseph, of Isle of Barbados, West Indies, gent. WORCESTER COLL., matric. 22 May, 1818, aged 19; B.A. 1822, vicar of Creech St. Michael, Somerset, 1851, until his death 11 Sep., 1870.

Ostrehan, Joseph Duncan, 1s. Joseph Duncan, of Shepscore, co. Gloucester, cler. WORCESTER COLL., matric. 16 June, 1848, aged 18; B.A. from NEW INN HALL 1852, rector of Yarmouth, Isle of Wight, 1872-5, chaplain India, died 4 Feb., 1880.

Oswald, Alexander (Haldane), 1s. (Richard) Alexander, of St. Enoch, co. Lanark, arm. CHRIST CHURCH, matric. 17 March, 1831, aged 19; B.A. 1836, M.A. 1839, of Auchencruive, Ayrshire, M.P. 1843-52, assumed the additional name of HALDANE, died 6 Sep., 1868. See Foster's *Scots M.P.'s.*

Oswald, Henry Murray, 2s. John, of Dunnikier, co. Fife, Scotland (G.C.B., G.C.M.G.). CHRIST CHURCH, matric. 12 June, 1851, aged 18; B.A. 1855, M.A. 1860, vicar of St. Paul's, Alnwick, 1869-72, rector of Great Hallingbury 1873. [25]

Oswald, James Francis, 3s. William, of Stepney, Middlesex, gent. ST. EDMUND HALL, matric. 19 March, 1868, aged 28; bar.-at-law, Middle Temple, 1869. See Foster's *Men at the Bar.*

Oswald, James Townsend, s. James, of Kirkcaldy, Scotland, arm. ST. MARY HALL, matric. 17 Nov., 1766, aged 18; of Dunnikier, co. Fife, M.P. Kirkcaldy burghs 1768-74, Fifeshire 1776-9, secretary of Leeward Islands 1772, auditor of the Exchequer in Scotland 1779, died in 1813. See Foster's *Scots M.P.'s.*

Oswald, John, s. James, of Kirkcaldy, co. Fife, Scotland, gent. ST. MARY HALL, matric. 11 Nov., 1735, aged 19; B.C.L. 9 Feb., 1743-4, bishop of Clonfert 4 July, 1762, of Dromore 7 May, 1763, and of Raphoe 25 Aug., 1763, until his death 5 March, 1780. See *Cotton*, iii. 357.

Oswald, John, 1s. James Townsend, of Shirehampton, co. Gloucester, arm. BRASENOSE COLL., matric. 19 Oct., 1875, aged 19. See *Eton School Lists.*

Oswell, Rev. Edward Waring, 2s. William, of Wanstead, Essex, arm. CHRIST CHURCH, matric. 15 May, 1839, aged 18; B.A. 1843, M.A. 1845, died 8 Oct., 1853. [30]

Oswell, Frank, 2s. William Cotton, of Groombridge, Sussex, arm. CHRIST CHURCH, matric. 14 Oct., 1881, aged 18; B.A. 1885.

Oswell, George Devereux, 3s. Henry Lloyd, of Stoulton, co. Worcester, cler. KEBLE COLL., matric. 18 Oct., 1870, aged 19; B.A. 1873, M.A. 1887.

Oswell, Harrison, 3s. William Cotton, of Withyham, Sussex, arm. CHRIST CHURCH, matric. 30 May, 1885, aged 18.

Oswell, Henry Lloyd, 3s. Thomas, of Westbury, Salop, cler. CHRIST CHURCH, matric. 10 Nov., 1831, aged 18; B.A. 1835, M.A. 1838, perp. curate Stoulton, co. Worcester, 1843-51, vicar of Leighton, Salop, 1851-9, perp. curate Bobbington 1859-62, vicar of St. George's, Shrewsbury, 1866-72, rector of Llandinabo, co. Hereford, since 1872.

Oswell, William Henry, 1s. Henry Lloyd, of Stoulton, co. Worcester, cler. TRINITY COLL., matric. 24 Jan., 1863, aged 18; B.A. 1866, M.A. 1869, held various curacies 1867-75, vicar of South Kirkby, Yorks, 1875-85, rector of Saxby, co. Lincoln, 1885.

Otiwell, Thomas, M.A. from CLARE HALL, Cambridge; incorp. 9 July, 1733. [35]

Otley, Charles Bethell, s. Richard, of St. George's, Hanover Square, London, gent. WADHAM COLL., matric. 11 Oct., 1809, aged 17; B.A. 1813, M.A. 1822, rector of Welby, co. Lincoln, 1833, until his death 11 July, 1867.

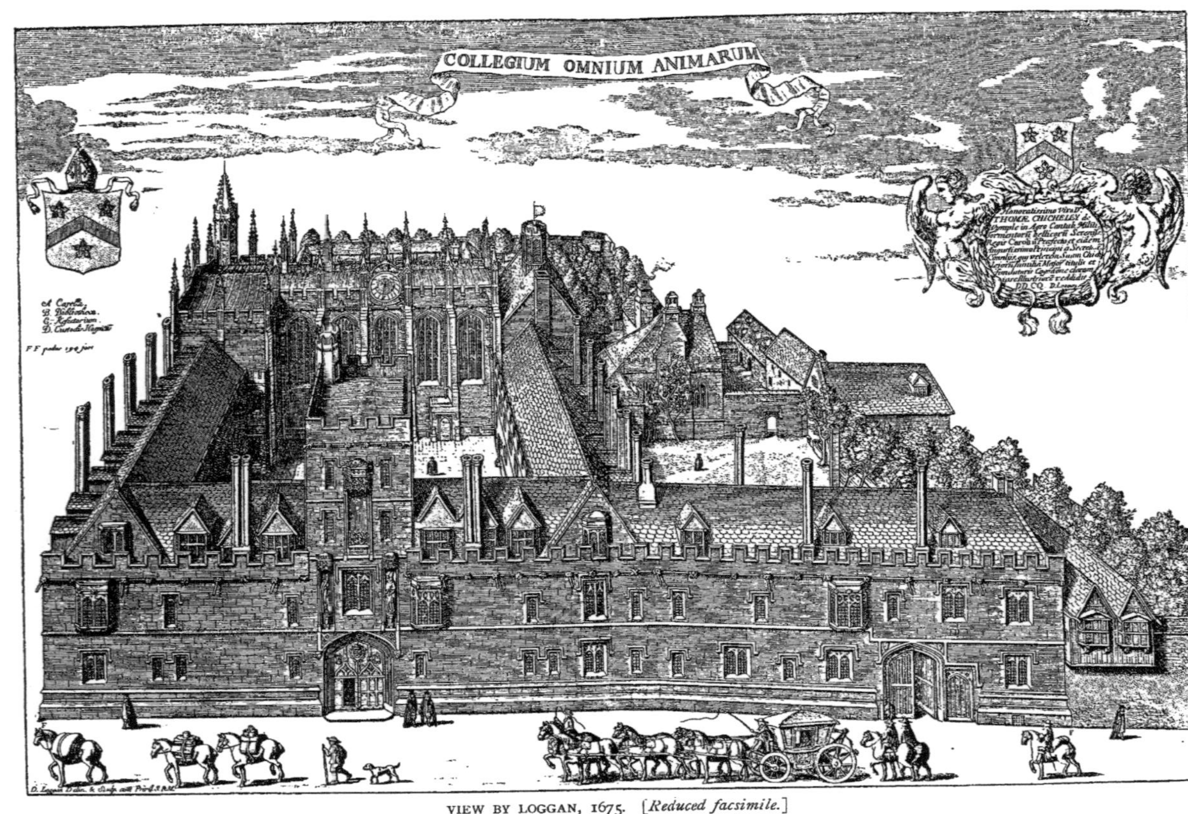

VIEW BY LOGGAN, 1675. [*Reduced facsimile.*]

O'Toole, Lorenzo Kirkpatrick. CHRIST CHURCH, 1827. See HALL.

Ottaway, Cuthbert John, o.s. James Cuthbert, of Dover, Kent, arm. BRASENOSE COLL., matric. 20 May, 1869, aged 18; scholar 1869-74, B.A. 1874, bar.-at-law, Inner Temple, 1876, died 2 April, 1878. See *Eton School Lists.*

Otté, Joachim, 1s. Walter, of Bideford, Devon, arm. WORCESTER COLL., matric. 4 June, 1850, aged 21.

Otter, Francis, 1s. Francis, of Gainsborough, co. Lincoln, gent. CORPUS CHRISTI COLL., matric. 1 March, 1850, aged 18; scholar 1850-61, B.A. 1854, M.A. 1856, fellow 1861-75, tutor, vice-president 1871, of Ranby Hall, co. Lincoln, J.P., bar.-at-law, Lincoln's Inn, 1867, M.P. Lincolnshire (Louth division) Dec., 1885, to June, 1886. See Foster's *Men at the Bar* & *Rugby School Reg.*, 257.

Otter, Henry Shirecliffe, 2s. Charles, of London, arm. CHRIST CHURCH, matric. 28 May, 1874, aged 18; a junior student 1874-9, B.A. 1878, of the Indian Civil Service 1876, and a student of Lincoln's Inn 1876, died 1879. [5]

Otter, John, 2s. Francis, of Gainsborough, co. Lincoln, gent. ST. MARY HALL, matric. 12 Dec., 1853, aged 19; B.A. 1858, M.A. 1861, vicar of Ranby, co. Lincoln, 1861-5, etc.

Otter, John Henry, elder son of Henry, of Tickhill, Yorks, arm. TRINITY COLL., matric. 13 Oct., 1866, aged 19; B.A. 1870.

Otter, Robert Henry (Arthur), 3s. Francis, of Gainsborough, co. Lincoln, gent. CORPUS CHRISTI COLL., matric. 5 Dec., 1854, aged 18; B.A. 1858, M.A. 1863. See *Rugby School Reg.*, 282.

Ottey, Rev. George Francis, s. Philip, of Kensington, Middlesex, gent. ORIEL COLL., matric. 11 Oct., 1811, aged 18; B.A. 1815, M.A. 1819, died Nov., 1861.

Ottey, Thomas, s. Beati, of Chester (city), gent. BRASENOSE COLL., matric. 1 Feb., 1736-7, aged 16; B.A. 1740, rector of Stoke, Suffolk, 1754; father of the next named. [10]

Ottey, Thomas Fairclough, s. Thomas, of Hadleigh, Suffolk, cler. MAGDALEN HALL, matric. 17 April, 1788, aged 32.

Ottley, Adam, s. Adam, of Pitchford, Salop, arm. BALLIOL COLL., matric. 11 May, 1736, aged 16, B.A. 18 Jan., 1739-40; M.A. from ALL SOULS' COLL. 1743, died rector of Pitchford 30 July, 1798.

Ottley, Adam, s. Thomas, of Stanley, Salop, arm. BRASENOSE COLL., matric. 25 June, 1762, aged 17; B.A. 1766.

Ottley, Brooke Taylor, s. (Richard), of Dunstan Park, Berks, arm. UNIVERSITY COLL., matric. 17 Dec., 1791, aged 17; of Delaford, co. Dublin, a commissioner of military accounts, and of public works, Ireland.

Ottley, Edward Bickersteth, 3s. Lawrence, of Richmond, Yorks, cler. NON-COLL., matric. 12 Oct., 1872, aged 19; B.A. from KEBLE COLL. 1876, M.A. 1879, principal of Theological College, Salisbury, 1880-3, minister of Quebec Chapel, London, 1883. See *Robinson*, 354. [15]

Ottley, Edward Byam, 2s. George Weatherill, of Isle of Antigua, arm. ST. EDMUND HALL, matric. 24 Jan., 1833, aged 21; died 9 Nov., 1835.

Ottley, Francis John, 1s. John Bridges, of Eling, Hants, cler. ORIEL COLL., matric. 8 Feb., 1844, aged 18; B.A. 1848, M.A. 1852, a mathematical master Eton College 1849, and assistant-master 1849-68, vicar of Seer Green 1868-70, and of Thorpe Acre, co. Leicester, 1879. See *Eton School Lists.*

Ottley, Henry Bickersteth, 2s. Lawrence, of Richmond, Yorks, cler. ST. JOHN'S COLL., matric. 28 June, 1869, aged 18; scholar 1869-76, B.A. 1874, M.A. 1876, vicar of Newton-on-Trent 1876-9, of St. Margaret Ilkley, Yorks, 1879-83, and of Horsham, Sussex, 1884. See *Robinson*, 355.

Ottley, Rev. Herbert Taylor, 8s. Lawrence, of Ripon, Yorks, cler. KEBLE COLL., matric. 14 Oct., 1878, aged 19; scholar 1878-82, B.A. 1882.

Ottley, John (Bridges) Hooker, s. Thomas Redman Hooker, of Rottingdean, Sussex, doctor (see p. 686). ORIEL COLL., matric. 17 June, 1815, aged 18; B.A. 1819, fellow 1822-5, M.A. 1823, assumed the additional surname of OTTLEY 2 Sep., 1820, vicar of Thorpe Acre, co. Leicester, 1845, until his death 12 March, 1879. See *Eton School Lists.* [20]

Ottley, Rev. Robert Lawrence, 3s. Lawrence, of Richmond, Yorks, cler. PEMBROKE COLL., matric. 29 Oct., 1874, aged 18, scholar 1874-8, B.A. 1878; a senior student CHRIST CHURCH 1878-86, M.A. 1881, tutor 1883-6; classical lecturer New College 1878-80, and at Keble College 1882-3, tutor 1881-2, vice-principal Cuddesdon College 1886.

Ottley, Thomas, s. Adam, of Pitchford, Salop, arm. BALLIOL COLL., matric. 16 Nov., 1733, aged 16; father of Adam 1762.

Ottley, Warner, 1s. Warner, of Walcot, in the city of Bath, arm., NEW COLL., matric. 30 Nov., 1826, aged 21.

Otway, Cooke, s. Henry, of Temple Derry, co. Tipperary, arm. CHRIST CHURCH, matric. 10 May, 1754, aged 21; of Castle Otway, co. Tipperary, died Dec., 1800. See Foster's *Baronetage.*

Otway, Rev. Cooke, M.A. TRINITY COLL., Dublin, 1827 (B.A. 1824); adm. 'ad eundem' 28 April, 1836 (son of Rev. Samuel Jocelyn Otway, of Leamington Priors, co. Warwick), died 9 March, 1882. See Foster's *Baronetage.* [25]

Otway, (Hon.) Robert, s. Henry, of Stanford, co. Leicester, arm. CHRIST CHURCH, matric. 9 Feb., 1815, aged 18; M.P. Leicester 1826-30, co. Tipperary 1832, until his death 29 Nov., 1844. See Foster's *Peerage*, B. BRAYE; & *Eton School Lists.*

Otway, Rev. Samuel Jocelyn, s. Cooke, of Anna, co. Tipperary, arm. MAGDALEN HALL, matric. 27 July, 1792, aged 23; B.A. 1796, died 26 Sep., 1855. See Foster's *Baronetage.*

Ougier, Peter, s. Peter, of Dartmouth, Devon, arm. ORIEL COLL., matric. 30 Oct., 1799, aged 18.

Ourry, Paul Treby. CHRIST CHURCH, 1775. See TREBY.

Ouseley, (Sir) Frederick Arthur Gore (Bart.), o.s. Gore, of St. George's, Hanover Square, baronet. CHRIST CHURCH, matric. 9 June, 1843, aged 17; B.A. 1846, M.A. 1849, B.Mus. 1850, D.Mus. 1854, hon. student 1867, professor of music 1855, precentor of Hereford 1855, warden of St. Michael College, and vicar of St. Michael and All Angels, near Tenbury, 1856, canon of Hereford 1886. See Foster's *Baronetage*, and for list of musical works see *Crockford.* [30]

Ouseley, Sir William, LL.D. TRINITY COLL., Dublin; created D.C.L. 23 June, 1819, the celebrated oriental scholar and traveller, knighted at Dublin Castle 11 Feb., 1800, died 1842. See Foster's *Baronetage.*

Ouseley, Sir William Gore, K.C.B.; created D.C.L. 20 June, 1855 (son of Sir William), minister at Rio Janeiro 1832, Buenos Ayres 1844, Monte Video 1846-7, etc., died 6 March, 1866.

Outhwaite, William Eugene, 2s. Thomas, of Auckland, New Zealand, arm. LINCOLN COLL., matric. 30 April, 1867, aged 20; S.C.L. & B.A. 1872, bar.-at-law, Inner Temple, 1873. See Foster's *Men at the Bar.*

Outram, Lieut.-General Sir James (Bart.); created D.C.L. 2 July, 1862 (son of Benjamin Outram, of Butterley Hall, co. Derby, civil engineer), a member of the Indian Council, G.C.B. 1857, and for services during the Indian Mutiny and the relief of Lucknow, created a baronet 10 Nov., 1858, died 11 March, 1863; buried in Westminster Abbey. See Foster's *Baronetage.*

Ouvaroff, Theodore, D.C.L. by diploma 16 June, 1814, general of Russian cavalry, died in 1824.

Ouvry, Arthur Garnault, 1s. Peter Thomas, of Wing, Bucks, cler. WADHAM COLL., matric. 24 Jan., 1879, aged 19; B.A. 1882, a student of Lincoln's Inn 1880, died 7 April, 1885.

Ouvry, Ernest Carrington, 2s. Peter Thomas, of Wing, Bucks, cler. WADHAM COLL., matric. 19 Oct., 1885, aged 19.

Overbury, Edward Noel, 2s. Nathaniel, of Lee, Kent, gent. NON-COLL., matric. 27 Jan., 1872, aged 28.

Overend, Frederick Laurence, 1s. Robert, of Manchester, gent. JESUS COLL., matric. 18 Oct., 1883, aged 19. [5]

Overend, Thomas George, 4s. James, of Tandraga, co. Armagh, gent. NON-COLL., matric. 16 Oct., 1868, aged 21; B.A. 1872, a student of Lincoln's Inn 1870.

Overend, Walker, 1s. Thomas, of Keighley, Yorks, gent. BALLIOL COLL., matric. 16 Oct., 1883, aged 24; scholar 1883, B.A. 1886.

Overend, Wilkinson, 2s. Thomas, of Keighley, Yorks, gent. KEBLE COLL., matric. 16 Oct., 1883, aged 19; scholar 1883, B.A. 1888.

Overman, George, s. William, of Lambeth, Surrey, arm. PEMBROKE COLL., matric. 10 April, 1728, aged 18; bar.-at-law, Lincoln's Inn, 1737.

Overton, Androwes, s. Androwes, of Queen-Camel, Somerset, gent. BALLIOL COLL., matric. 17 March, 1732-3, aged 18; B.A. 1737. [10]

Overton, Charles Frederick, 2s. Charles, of Clapham, Yorks, cler. WORCESTER COLL., matric. 21 March, 1857, aged 17; exhibitioner 1857-60, B.A. 1860, M.A. 1871, vicar of Warnham, Sussex, 1871-2.

Overton, Edmond Splugen, 3s. Charles, of Cottingham, Yorks, cler. PEMBROKE COLL., matric. 22 Feb., 1861, aged 17; scholar 1861-6, B.A. 1865.

Overton, Frederick Arnold, 1s. Samuel Charlesworth, of Hackness, Yorks, cler. NON-COLL., matric. 13 Oct., 1884, aged 22; exhibitioner EXETER COLL. 1884, B.A. 1887.

Overton, Isle Grant, 4s. Francis, of Louth, co. Lincoln, gent. CORPUS CHRISTI COLL., matric. 15 June, 1827, aged 17; scholar 1827-33, B.A. 1831, fellow 1833-44, M.A. 1834, B.D. 1841, junior dean 1838, rector of Rothwell, co. Lincoln, 1844, until his death in 1872.

Overton, John, 3s. Francis, of Waltham, co. Lincoln, gent. MAGDALEN HALL, matric. 17 Feb., 1831, aged 25; B.A. 1835, M.A. 1838, vicar of Rougham, Norfolk, 1846-82. [15]

Overton, John Henry, o.s. Francis, of Louth, co. Lincoln, gent. WADHAM COLL., matric. 24 Nov., 1853, aged 18; scholar LINCOLN COLL. 1854-8, B.A. 1858, M.A. 1860, vicar of Legbourne, co. Lincoln, 1860-83, canon of Lincoln Cathedral 1879, rector of Epworth 1883; for list of his works see *Crockford*. See *Rugby School Reg.*, 296.

Overton, Rev. Samuel Charlesworth, 1s. Charles, of Clapham, Yorks, cler. WORCESTER COLL., matric. 17 June, 1856, aged 19; bible clerk 1857-60, B.A. 1860, M.A. 1863.

Overy, Henry, 3s. Alfred, of Devizes, Wilts, gent. QUEEN'S COLL., matric. 27 Oct., 1869, aged 24; B.A. 1873, M.A. 1876, vicar of St. Veep, Cornwall, 1876.

Ovey, Richard, 1s. Richard, of London, arm. HERTFORD COLL., matric. 15 Oct., 1875, aged 19.

Owen, Arthur, s. Arthur, of Mounton, co. Pembroke, baronet. ORIEL COLL., matric. 4 July, 1718, aged 17; of the Orielton family, brother of John 1715.

Owen, Arthur Edwin Brisco, 1s. Brisco, of Remenham, Berks, cler. ORIEL COLL., matric. 22 Jan., 1877, aged 18; B.A. 1881, M.A. 1883, chaplain at Kadikeui, Constantinople, 1885. [21]

Owen, Rev. Arthur Frank Cowley, 3s. Edward, of East Dulwich, Surrey, arm. WADHAM COLL., matric. 26 Jan., 1881, aged 20; B.A. 1883, M.A. 1887.

Owen, Arthur Welsh, 2s. Arthur Smith, of Rockferry, Cheshire, gent. NON-COLL., matric. 12 Oct., 1872, aged 21; B.A. from CHRIST CHURCH 1876, M.A. 1879, rector of Wembworthy, Devon, 1878. See *Robinson*, 354.

Owen, Brisco, 5s. Owen, of Beaumaris, co. Anglesea, gent. JESUS COLL., matric. 14 Dec., 1824, aged 17; scholar 1826-32, B.A. 1829, M.A. 1831, fellow 1832-42, B.D. 1838, vice-principal and catechetical lecturer 1839, dean and Latin lecturer 1840, Greek lecturer 1841, rector of Remenham, Berks, 1841, until his death 25 Oct., 1864.

Owen, Bulkeley Hatchett Bulkeley, 1s. Thomas Bulkeley, of Tedsmore Hall, Salop, arm. CHRIST CHURCH, matric. 15 May, 1845, aged 19; of Tedsmore Hall, died 10 Aug., 1868. [25]

Owen, Charles, s. Charles, of Hereford (city), pleb. BRASENOSE COLL., matric. 11 May, 1719, aged 17; B.A. 21 Feb., 1722-3.

Owen, Charles, s. Morgan, of St. Andrew's, Holborn, London, arm. JESUS COLL., matric. 2 May, 1753, aged 18; bar.-at-law, Gray's Inn, 1756, bencher 1770, dead in 1784.

Owen, Charles Edward Jones, 1s. Evan Charles, of Dolgelly, co. Merioneth, cler. CHRIST CHURCH, matric. 13 Oct., 1876, aged 19. See *Eton School Lists*.

Owen, Charles Frederick, o.s. Eleazer, of Ystalyfera, co. Glamorgan, pleb. NON-COLL., matric. 21 Jan., 1882, aged 27.

Owen, Charles Gustavus, 2s. Henry Butts, of St. Olave, London, doctor. QUEEN'S COLL., matric. 26 June, 1819, aged 18; B.A. 1823, M.A. 1837, rector of Dodbrooke, vicar of Loddeswell, rector of Pinxton, co. Derby, 1864, until his death 18 Sep., 1879. See *Robinson*, 192. [30]

Owen, Charles Henry, 2s. Henry, of Clapham, Surrey, arm. ST. EDMUND HALL, matric. 30 June, 1843, aged 21; B.A. 1849, M.A. 1852, perp. curate Alderwasley, co. Derby, 1865.

Owen, Charles Mansfield, 7s. Herbert, of Stroud, co. Gloucester, arm. ST. ALBAN HALL, matric. 18 Oct., 1871, aged 18; B.A. 1874, M.A. 1878, vicar of Woolston, Hants, 1880-3, and of St. George's, Edgbaston, 1883.

Owen, Charles Mostyn, 4s. William, of West Felton, Salop, arm. TRINITY COLL., matric. 15 Feb., 1838, aged 19; B.A. 1842, M.A. 1858, chief constable Oxon, served in Caffre War 1845-7. See *Rugby School Reg.*, 186.

Owen, Corbett, s. Athelstane, of Rhiwsaeson, co. Montgomery, arm. CHRIST CHURCH, matric. 21 Nov., 1735, aged 19; brother of Richard 1740.

Owen, Daniel, s. Richard, of Llanidloes, co. Montgomery, gent. EXETER COLL., matric. 24 April, 1744, aged 20. [35]

Owen, David, s. Rowland, of Llanwnog, co. Montgomery, pleb. PEMBROKE COLL., matric. 15 Nov., 1749, aged 19.

Owen, David, s. Robert, of Llangathen, co. Carmarthen, pleb. JESUS COLL., matric. 1 Dec., 1789, aged 19; B.A. 1796. (Rev. David O., late of Broad Hinton, Wilts, died 3 Dec., 1849, aged 80.)

Owen, David Stanley, 1s. Daniel, of New Quay, co. Cardigan, gent. NON-COLL., matric. 13 Oct., 1877, aged 20; B.A. from QUEEN'S COLL. 1881, M.A. 1884, a student of the Inner Temple 1885.

Owen, Donald Millman, y.s. George Welsh, of Tiverton, Devon, arm. BALLIOL COLL., matric. 7 July, 1847, aged 17; scholar 1847-52, fellow 1852-66, B.A. 1852, M.A. 1857, B.D. 1877, librarian, catechetical lecturer and junior dean, 1863, rector of Marks Tey, Essex, 1868-78, of Ideford, Devon, 1878-86, and of Calverleigh since 1886.

Owen, Edmund John, 2s. Edmund Hemming, of Moore Hall, near Stoke St. Milborough, Salop, arm. BRASENOSE COLL., matric. 5 Feb., 1850, aged 18, scholar 1850-4; B.A. from ST. MARY HALL 1855, rector of Tretire, co. Ross, 1860. [40]

Owen, Edward, s. Edward, of Oxford (city), doctor. ST. JOHN'S COLL., matric. 6 June, 1744, aged 18; B.A. 1748, died rector of Southwick, Northants, in 1796.

Owen, Edward, s. David, of Llangurig, co. Montgomery, pleb. JESUS COLL., matric. 22 March, 1745-6, aged 17; B.A. 1749, M.A. 1752, master of the Free Grammar School, Warrington, and rector 1767, until his death in 1807. See *O.H.S.*, ix. 248.

Owen, Edward, s. Robert, of Dolgelly, co. Merioneth, pleb. JESUS COLL., matric. 8 March, 1758, aged 19.

Owen, Edward, s. John, of Llanaber, co. Merioneth, pleb. JESUS COLL., matric. 18 March, 1769, aged 19; B.A. 1772.

Owen, Edward, s. Lewis, of Gwalchmai, Isle of Anglesey, arm. JESUS COLL., matric. 4 June, 1778, aged 19; B.A. 1783. [5]

Owen, Edward, 1s. Edward, of 'Mancuo,' Jamaica, arm. (D.Med.). WORCESTER COLL., matric. 9 Nov., 1825, aged 17; B.A. 1830, M.A. 1833, curate of Gawsworth, Cheshire, died 31 July, 1848.

Owen, Edward, 2s. Hugh Davies, of Beaumaris, Isle of Anglesey, D.D. JESUS COLL., matric. 30 June, 1843, aged 17; scholar 1844-9, B.A. 1848, fellow 1849-63, M.A. 1850, B.D. 1858, librarian 1850, Latin lecturer 1852, chaplain to the Forces in the Crimea 1854-5, incumbent of Bodwrog and Llandrygan, died 6 May, 1864.

Owen, Edward Charles Everard, o.s. Edward Henry, of Forres, co. Moray, cler. BALLIOL COLL., matric. 16 Oct., 1879, aged 19, scholar 1879-84, exhibitioner 1882-4, B.A. 1883; fellow NEW COLL. 1884, M.A. 1886, classical lecturer 1884.

Owen, Edward Henry, s. William, of Felton, Salop, arm. CHRIST CHURCH, matric. 21 Oct., 1802, aged 18, B.A. 1806; fellow ALL SOULS' COLL. 1809-17, M.A. 1810, rector of Cound, Salop, 1816, until his death 28 Nov., 1838.

Owen, Edward John, o.s. Edward, of Wood Street, Cheapside, London, arm. QUEEN'S COLL., matric. 18 April, 1822, aged 17. [10]

Owen, Edward Robert, chirurgus, s. — O., doctor; privilegiatus 29 June, 1842, aged 33.

Owen, Edward Roberts, s. Robert, of Llanenddwyn, co. Merioneth, cler. CHRIST CHURCH, matric. 11 March, 1771, aged 17; B.A. 1774, M.A. 1783.

Owen, Rev. Edward Tudor, 2s. Richard, of Denbigh (town). JESUS COLL., matric. 24 March, 1857, aged 15; B.A. 1860, M.A. 1865.

Owen, Edwin James, 1s. Elias, of Llanllechid, co. Carmarthen, cler. NON-COLL., matric. 18 Oct., 1880, aged 21.

Owen, Ellis Anwyl, s. Richard, of Aberfraw, co. Anglesea, gent. JESUS COLL., matric. 27 March, 1809, aged 18; scholar 1812-17, B.A. 1812, M.A. 1815 (? rector of Llanystymdwy, co. Carnarvon, and chaplain to the Earl of Uxbridge 1841, died 22 May, 1846). [15]

Owen, Eugene, s. Owen, of Beaumaris, Isle of Anglesea, gent. JESUS COLL., matric. 28 May, 1813, aged 15.

Owen, Evan, s. Edward, of Llanglynin, co. Merioneth, pleb. JESUS COLL., matric. 15 Nov., 1716, aged 20.

Owen, Evan, s. Richard, of Cemmaes, co. Montgomery, pleb. BRASENOSE COLL., matric. 27 May, 1773, aged 19; B.A. 1777.

Owen, Francis, s. William, of Porkington, Salop, arm. PEMBROKE COLL., matric. 7 Dec., 1764, aged 18; created M.A. 4 Nov., 1768, died unmarried, brother of Robert 1751.

Owen, Francis, s. Thomas, of Llanfair, Isle of Anglesea, cler. CHRIST CHURCH, matric. 30 Nov., 1803, aged 17; B.A. 1807. (Memo.: Rev. — Owen, of Christ Church, died 1 July, 1808. See *Gent.'s Mag.*, 1808, ii. 660.) [20]

Owen, George Dorsett, 2s. George Dorsett, of Oswestry, Salop, gent. MAGDALEN HALL, matric. 27 March, 1851, aged 21.

Owen, George Titus, o.s. Titus, of London, gent. JESUS COLL., matric. 25 June, 1840, aged 18.

Owen, George Welsh, s. George, of Tiverton, Devon, arm. ORIEL COLL., matric. 23 Oct., 1801, aged 17.

Owen, George Welsh, 1s. George, of Tiverton, Devon, arm. TRINITY COLL., matric. 15 Oct., 1828, aged 18; B.A. from NEW INN HALL 1832, M.A. 1836 rector of Calverleigh, Devon, 1841-85.

Owen, Griffin (Griffith in *Mat. Reg.*), s. Griffith, of Dolgelly, co. Merioneth, pleb. JESUS COLL., matric. 19 March, 1771, aged 19; B.A. 1774, rector of Llanenddwyn, co. Merioneth, died in 1826. [25]

Owen, Griffith, s. Griffith, of Towyn, co. Merioneth, cler. JESUS COLL., matric. 29 March, 1803, aged 18; B.A. 1807, died rector of Dolbenmaen and Penmorfa, 18 Nov., 1853.

Owen, Goronwy (Gronovius), s. Owen, of Llanfair Mathafarn, pleb. JESUS COLL., matric. 3 June, 1742, aged 19; 'premier poet of Wales,' classical master at William and Mary College, Williamsburg, Va., 3 years minister of St. Andrew's, Brunswick County, Va., up to 1767, died 1769. See *Notes and Queries*, 7 April, 1888.

Owen, Henry, s. William, of Dolgelly, co. Merioneth, pleb. JESUS COLL., matric. 15 April, 1736, aged 19; B.A. 1739, M.A. 1743, B.Med. 1746, D.Med. 1753, rector of St. Olave, Hart Street, London, 1750-94, vicar of Edmonton, Middlesex, 1775, until his death 14 Oct., 1795; for list of his works see *Gent.'s Mag.*, 1795, ii. 884*b*.

Owen, Henry, s. William, of Holyhead, Isle of Anglesea, gent. ST. ALBAN HALL, matric. 14 Jan., 1815, aged 25.

Owen, Rev. Henry, of MAGDALEN COLL., Cambridge (B.A. 1827, M.A. 1830); adm. 'ad eundem' 5 June, 1845 (? rector of Heveningham, Suffolk, 1834). [30]

Owen, Henry, 4s. William, of Haverfordwest, co. Pembroke, arm. CORPUS CHRISTI COLL., matric. 17 May, 1862, aged 18; B.A. 1866, B.C.L. 1869.

Owen, Henry Butts, s. Henry, of Crutched Friars, London, doctor. ST. JOHN'S COLL., matric. 7 July, 1780, aged 16; fellow 1783, B.A. 1784, M.A. 1788, B.D. 1793, D.D. 1805, rector of St. Olave, Hart Street, 1794, and of Throcking, Herts, 1801, died 29 Nov., 1837. See *Robinson*, 135.

Owen, Henry Percy, 4s. Robert, of Sydney, Australia, gent. CHRIST CHURCH, matric. 8 May, 1880, aged 20; B.A. 1883, bar.-at-law, Inner Temple, 1885.

Owen, Herbert Dorset, 2s. John Maurice Dorset, of Hindringham, Norfolk, cler. WADHAM COLL., matric. 17 Oct., 1882, aged 19; scholar 1882, B.A. 1886.

Owen, Hugh, of ST. JOHN'S COLL., B.A. 22 June, 1721 (*Acts Book*). [35]

Owen, Hugh, s. Robert, of Holyhead, Isle of Anglesea, gent. ORIEL COLL., matric. 3 April, 1728, aged 17; bar.-at-law, Middle Temple, 1737.

Owen, Hugh (M.A. from JESUS COLL., Cambridge), s. John, of St. Ann's, Soho, Westminster, gent. JESUS COLL., incorp. 2 March, 1784, aged 35; B. & D.D. 15 March, 1790.

Owen, (Sir) Hugh (Bart.), s. Hugh, of Mounton, co. Pembroke, baronet. CHRIST CHURCH, matric. 28 Jan., 1801, aged 18; 6th baronet, M.P. Pembroke (town) 1809, until his death 8 Aug., 1809. See Foster's *Baronetage* & *Eton School Lists*.

Owen, Hugh Davies, s. Owen, of Beaumaris, Isle of Anglesea, gent. JESUS COLL., matric. 28 May, 1813, aged 16; scholar 1813-22, B.A. 1816, M.A. 1819, B. & D.D. 1834, rector of Trevdaeth, Bangor, 1849-80, died 4 Sep., 1881.

Owen, Hugh Davies, 3s. Hugh Davies, of Beaumaris, Isle of Anglesea, doctor. JESUS COLL., matric. 31 March, 1849, aged 18; B.A. 1852, M.A. 1855, of Glynafon, Anglesea, vicar of Penmynydd 1868, brother of Edward 1843.

Owen, (Sir) Hugh Owen (Bart.), 1s. John, of Lincoln's Inn, London, baronet. CHRIST CHURCH, matric. 19 June, 1822, aged 18; 2nd baronet, M.P. Pembroke 1826-38 & 1861-8. See Foster's *Baronetage.*

Owen, Hugh William, 1s. William, of Holyhead, gent. NON-COLL., matric. 14 Oct., 1876, aged 21.

Owen, Humphrey, s. Humphrey, of Myvod, co. Montgomery, gent. JESUS COLL. matric. 17 Nov., 1718, aged 16; B.A. 1722, fellow, M.A. 1725, B.D. 1733, D.D. 1763, principal 1763-8, Bodley's librarian 1747-68.

Owen, Humphrey, s. Owen, of Aberystwith, co. Cardigan, pleb. ST. JOHN'S COLL., matric. 10 April, 1742, aged 18; B.A. 13 March, 1745-6, M.A. 1762, built St. Michael's Church, Manchester, 26 years chaplain of the Collegiate Church, and also rector of St. Mary, Manchester, died 12 Nov., 1790. See *Manchester School Reg.*, i. 143. [5]

Owen, Humphrey, s. David, of Dolgelly, co. Merioneth, gent. MAGDALEN HALL, matric. 9 May, 1785, aged 22.

Owen, Humphrey Edward, 1s. Edward, of Dover, Kent, cler. MAGDALEN HALL, matric. 31 March, 1864, aged 24; B.Mus. 1866, B.A. & M.A. 1872, vicar of Leck, Lancashire, 1870-3, chaplain at Capri 1866-7, rector of South Moreton, Berks, 1877-78, chaplain at Toulon 1881-2, at Grasses 1882-3.

Owen, Rev. James Albert, 3s. William, of Haverfordwest, co. Pembroke, gent. CHRIST CHURCH, matric. 28 May, 1860, aged 18, a junior student 1860-5, B.A. 1864, M.A. 1867; fellow UNIVERSITY COLL. 1868-71, and lecturer, assistant-master of Cheltenham College 1870.

Owen, Rev. James Hughes, 1s. James Richard, of Rhyl, co. Flint, cler. JESUS COLL., matric. 6 April, 1859, aged 18, scholar 1859-64; B.A. from TRINITY COLL. 1862.

Owen, James Richard, 5s. Owen, of Beaumaris, Isle of Anglesey, gent. JESUS COLL., matric. 24 March, 1830, aged 18; scholar 1831-8, B.A. 1834, M.A. 1838, perp. curate Rhyl 1836-54, rector of Llanverres 1854-83, died 20 Oct., 1884. [10]

Owen, Jenkin, s. Jenkin, of Llanfwrog, co. Denbigh, pleb. JESUS COLL., matric. 16 April, 1729, aged 16; B.A. 19 Jan., 1732-3, M.A. 1737.

Owen, John, s. Arth., of Lansillin, co. Denbigh, baronet. ORIEL COLL., matric. 10 Nov., 1715, aged 17; lieut.-general in the army, died Jan., 1776.

Owen, John, s. 'Owen Roderick,' of Machynlleth, co, Montgomery, pleb. JESUS COLL., matric. 12 March, 1717-8, aged 19.

Owen, John, s. John, of St. Michael's, Coventry, gent. WADHAM COLL., matric. 11 Nov., 1719, aged 18.

Owen, John, s. John, of Bodedarn, Isle of Anglesey, arm. JESUS COLL., matric. 16 Nov., 1719, aged 17. [15]

Owen, John, s. Maurice, of Dolgelly, co. Merioneth, pleb. JESUS COLL., matric. 10 May, 1727, aged 21.

Owen, John, s. Owen, of Llanddyssyl, co. Cardigan, pleb. JESUS COLL., matric. 21 March, 1742-3, aged 20; B.A. 1747.

Owen, John, s. Thomas, of Beaumaris, Anglesea, cler. JESUS COLL., matric. 13 March, 1745-6, aged 17; B.A. 1749.

Owen, John, s. John, of Llandwrog, co. Carnarvon, cler. JESUS COLL., matric. 13 March, 1753, aged 17.

Owen, John, s. Lewis, of Barking, Essex. cler. ORIEL COLL., matric. 7 Feb., 1758, aged 16. [20]

Owen, John, s. Lewis, of Bodwink, co. Anglesea, arm. JESUS COLL., matric. 23 March, 1771, aged 18; B.A. 1775.

Owen, John, s. John, of Portsmouth, Hants, gent. WORCESTER COLL., matric. 6 Dec., 1771, aged 19; B.A. 1775.

Owen, John, s. John, of Llanynys, co. Denbigh, pleb. CHRIST CHURCH, matric. 30 March, 1787, aged 19; B.A. from ST. ALBAN HALL 1791 (Rev. J. O. died at Carmarthen 19 April, 1860, aged 92).

Owen, John, s. Thomas, of Llangurig, co. Montgomery, gent. HERTFORD COLL. matric. 21 Oct., 1793, aged 20, B.A. 1797; M.A. from CHRIST'S COLL., Cambridge, 1801.

Owen John, s. Watkin, of Llanrwst, co. Denbigh, pleb. CHRIST CHURCH, matric. 20 Oct., 1800, aged 18; B.A. 1804, M.A. 1807. [25]

Owen, John, s. Edward, of Conway, co. Carnarvon, cler. JESUS COLL., matric. 22 Oct., 1807. aged 18; B.A. 1811, M.A. 1814.

Owen, John, s. Owen, of Llanfairynghornwy, co. Anglesea, gent. JESUS COLL., matric. 4 April. 1811, aged 19; scholar 1812-16, B.A. 1816.

Owen, John, 2s. Hugh Owen, of Burton, co. Pembroke, arm. (after a baronet). MERTON COLL., matric. 18 June, 1846, aged 18; B.A. 1851, of Rose Bush, co. Pembroke. See Foster's *Baronetage* & *Rugby School Reg.*, 216.

Owen, John, 3s. Edward, of Llanfair, co. Montgomery, gent. JESUS COLL., matric. 11 Nov., 1847, aged 18; B.A. 1851, rector of Erryrys, Flints, 1862-86.

Owen, Rev. John, 1s. Griffith, of Llanengan, co. Carnarvon, gent. JESUS COLL., matric. 19 Oct., 1872, aged 18; scholar 1872-7, B.A. 1876, M.A. 1879, Welsh professor St. David's College, Lampeter, 1879-85, warden and head-master Llandovery College 1885. [30]

Owen, John, 2s. Evan, of Tall-y-llyn, co. Merioneth, gent. CHARSLEY HALL, matric. 20 Oct., 1880, aged 25.

Owen, John Arthur Edward, o.s. John, of North Brixton, Surrey, gent. WORCESTER COLL., matric. 18 Oct., 1861, aged 29; B.A. & M.A. 1871.

Owen, John Maurice Dorsett, 1s. George Dorsett, of Oswestry, Salop, arm. BRASENOSE COLL., matric. 18 June, 1846, aged 18; B.A 1850, M.A. 1853, vicar of Hindringham, Norfolk, 1860-77, and of Holy Trinity, Habergham Eaves, Lancashire, 1877.

Owen, John Ord, 3s. John, of Fulham, Middlesex, cler. MAGDALEN HALL, matric. 26 June, 1828, aged 21.

Owen, Rev. John Robert Blaney, 2s. — O., of St. Leonard's, Bucks, cler. QUEEN'S COLL., matric. 31 Jan., 1868, aged 19; B.A. 1870, M.A. 1877, head-master Hawkshead Grammar School, Westmorland, 1881-3, 2nd master Trent College 1872-81, head-master 1883. [35]

Owen, John Wellington, o.s. David, of Paddington, Middlesex, gent. JESUS COLL., matric. 29 Oct., 1867, aged 21; NON-COLL. B.A. 1878, incumbent of St. Paul's, Adelaide, South Australia, 1886. See *Crockford.*

Owen, Joseph. B.A. from JESUS COLL. 25 May, 1722. See *Cat. Grads.*

Owen, Joseph, s. John, of St. James's, Middlesex, arm. ST. ALBAN HALL, 23 March, 1784, aged 26; B.A. 1787.

Owen, Rev. Joseph Elias, 4s. Joseph, of Bettwys, co. Carnarvon, gent. JESUS COLL., matric. 10 April, 1869, aged 22; B.A. 1873.

Owen, Joshua William Theophilus, 3s. David, of Smethwick, near Birmingham, gent. NON-COLL., matric. 4 Feb., 1869, aged 19; S.C.L. & B.A. 1873, M.A. 1880, vicar of St. Paul, Forebridge, co. Stafford, 1876. [40]

Owen, Langer (Meade Loftus), 1s. William, of Sydney, Australia, arm. NEW COLL., matric. 4 June, 1881, aged 18; B.A. 1886, bar.-at-law, Lincoln's Inn, 1888.

Owen, Lewis, s. Lewis, of Llanfyhanlaby, co. Merioneth, pleb. JESUS COLL., matric. 30 May, 1723, aged 22.

Owen, Lewis, s. Robert, of Llanegryn, co. Merioneth, pleb. BALLIOL COLL., matric. 13 March, 1752, aged 19; B.A. 1756.

Owen, Lewis Edward, 1s. Lewis Welsh, of Colchester, Essex, cler. EXETER COLL., matric. 24 Jan., 1862, aged 18; B.A. 1866, vicar of Farndon, Cheshire, since 1878.

Owen, Lewis Welsh, 2s. George Welsh, of Tiverton, Devon, arm. BALLIOL COLL., matric. 21 Oct., 1830, aged 17; scholar 1830-6, B.A. 1834, M.A. 1838, fellow 1836-9, rector of Holy Trinity, Colchester, and vicar of Monks Tey, Essex, 1839-68, rector of Wadingham, co. Lincoln, 1868-70, preb. Lincoln 1869-76, rector of Wonston, Hants, 1870, until his death 4 Jan., 1884. [5]

Owen, Loftus Meade, 2s. Loftus, of Liverpool, cler. CORPUS CHRISTI COLL., matric. 19 Oct., 1883, aged 19; B.A. 1887.

Owen, Morris Williams Lloyd, 1s. Owen, of Havod, co. Pembroke, arm. ST. JOHN'S COLL., matric. 20 Jan., 1864, aged 19; of Cwmgloyne, co. Pembroke, high sheriff, 1870. See *Eton School Lists.*

Owen, Nicholas. s. Robert, of Llangevin, co. Anglesea, pleb. JESUS COLL., matric. 29 March, 1737, aged 17; B.A. 1740, M.A. 1743, rector of Llandyfrydog, father of the next named.

Owen, Nicholas, s. Nicholas, of Llandyfrydog, Isle of Anglesea, cler. JESUS COLL., matric. 30 June, 1769, aged 17; B.A. 1773, M.A. 1776 (? died rector of Bottwnog, co. Carnarvon, 17 June, 1811).

Owen, Octavius Edward, 8s. Herbert, of Boulogne-sur-Mer, arm. ST. MARY HALL, matric. 2 Nov., 1872, aged 18; B.A. from ORIEL COLL. 1879, M.A. 1883, a student of Inner Temple 1880, rector of Flempton, Suffolk, 1883. [10]

Owen, Octavius Freire, 5s. Henry Butts, of St. Pancras, London, doctor. CHRIST CHURCH, matric. 4 June, 1835, aged 19; B.A. 1839, M.A. 1843, perp. curate Stratton Audley 1842-6, vicar of St. Mary, Leicester, 1846-8, rector of Burstow, Surrey, 1848-55, vicar of Childs Wickham, co. Gloucester, 1855-8, chaplain Royal Arsenal, Woolwich, 1869, until his death 16 April, 1873; for list of his works see *Crockford.*

Owen, Owen, s. Owen, of Tolyatha, co. Merioneth, pleb. JESUS COLL., matric. 16 May, 1729, aged 18; B.A. 1 Feb., 1732-3.

Owen, Owen, s. Thomas, of Llanarmon, co. Denbigh, cler. JESUS COLL., matric. 10 Oct., 1765, aged 19.

Owen, Owen, s. Robert, of Dolgelly, co. Merioneth, pleb. JESUS COLL., matric. 3 April, 1770, aged 20; B.A. 1774, M.A. 1777, died rector of Llangyniew, co. Montgomery, 10 April, 1826, aged 76.

Owen, Owen, s. Morris, of Dolgelly, co. Merioneth, gent. JESUS COLL., matric. 17 Dec., 1779, aged 19; B.A. 1783. [15]

Owen, Owen, s. Owen, of Long House, parish of Llaurian, co. Pembroke, gent. ST. ALBAN HALL, matric. 16 March, 1785, aged 32; B.A. 1790.

Owen, Rev. Owen (s. Owen, of Glynavon, co. Anglesey), a commoner JESUS COLL. 1812, scholar 1816-22' B.A. 5 Dec., 1817, M.A. 27 Oct., 1819, fellow 1822-31, B.D. 1 Feb., 1827, Latin lecturer 1823, tutor 1830, assistant-master Rugby School 1819, lost in the *Rothsay Castle,* near Beaumaris, 17 Aug., 1831, brother of Hugh D. 1813, of Brisco 1824, and of James Richard 1830. See *Rugby School Reg.,* xiv.

Owen, Owen, 5s. Evans, of Llaniestyn, co. Carnarvon, gent. JESUS COLL., matric. 30 Jan., 1873, aged 22; scholar 1873-7, B.A. 1877, M.A. 1882.

Owen, Owen Anwyl, s. Richard, of Llanyngeneal, Isle of Anglesey, gent. JESUS COLL., matric. 16 Dec., 1816, aged 18; B.A. 1822, scholar 1822-5, curate of Llanrhyddiadd and Llanrhwydrus, Anglesey, died 20 March, 1857.

Owen, Philip Henry, 4s. Lewis Welsh, of Colchester, Essex, cler. ORIEL COLL., matric. 1 March, 1869, aged 19; B.A. 1872, vicar of Owlesbury, Hants, 1883. [20]

Owen, Reginald Solly, 3s. John, of Hooton, Cheshire, cler. CHRIST CHURCH, matric. 15 Oct., 1880, aged 18; a junior student 1880, B.A. 1884.

Owen, Richard, s. Athelstan, of Llanbrynmair, co. Montgomery, arm. HART HALL, matric. 13 Aug., 1740, aged 18; brother of Corbett 1735.

Owen, Richard, s. Rice, of Llanegryn, co. Merioneth, pleb. HERTFORD COLL., matric. 30 March, 1765, aged 19.

Owen, Richard, s. Thomas, of Llanganfalin, co. Cardigan, cler. WADHAM COLL., matric. 3 Nov., 1770, aged 20.

Owen, Richard, s. Nicholas, of Llandyfrydog, co. Anglesea, cler. JESUS COLL., matric. 14 May, 1774, aged 20; B.A. 1778. [25]

Owen, (Sir) Richard (K.C.B.); created D.C.L. 23 June, 1852 (son of Richard Owen, of Fulmer Place, Bucks), Hunterian professor of comparative anatomy and physiology, and conservator of the Museum of the Royal College of Surgeons, C.B. 3 June, 1873, late professor of physiology Royal Institution, superintendent natural history departments British Museum 1856-83, etc., K.C.B. 5 Jan., 1884.

Owen, Richard Evan, s. Evan, of Church Stoke, co. Montgomery, cler. BRASENOSE COLL., matric. 16 May, 1806, aged 17; B.A. 1810, M.A. 1813, perp. curate Hyssington, co. Montgomery, 1822, and rector of Snead 1849, until his death 1 March, 1870.

Owen, Richard Trevor, 1s. Richard, of Bodfary, co. Denbigh, arm. JESUS COLL., matric. 20 March, 1855, aged 18; scholar 1858-60, B.A. 1859, M.A. 1862, vicar of Llangedwyn 1869, editor of the 'Archæologia Cambrensis' 1879.

Owen, Robert, s. John, of Bodedern, co. Anglesea, arm. JESUS COLL., matric. 28 May, 1723, aged 16; B.A. 26 Jan., 1726-7, M.A. 1729.

Owen, Robert, s. Owen, of Dolgelly, co. Merioneth, pleb. JESUS COLL., matric. 16 May, 1727, aged 19. [30]

Owen, Robert, s. Hugh, of Dolgelly, co. Merioneth, pleb. JESUS COLL., matric. 2 June, 1747, aged 19; B.A. 1752.

Owen, Robert, s. William, of Porkington, Salop, arm. ORIEL COLL., matric. 24 Oct., 1751, aged 18; died unmarried, brother of Francis 1764.

Owen, Robert, 3s. David, of Dolgelly, co. Merioneth, gent. JESUS COLL., matric. 22 Nov., 1838, aged 18; scholar 1839-45, B.A. 1842, M.A. 1845, fellow 1845-64, B.D. 1852, Latin lecturer 1846, catechetical lecturer 1848, dean 1849, lecturer modern history 1858, public examiner in law, etc., 1859; for list of his works see *Crockford.*

Owen, Rev. Robert, 1s. Robert, of Edeyrn, near Pwlheli, gent. NON-COLL., matric. 17 Oct., 1874, aged 19; B.A. from NEW COLL. 1882.

Owen, Roger, s. Ellis, of Bridgnorth, Salop, gent. WADHAM COLL., matric. 31 March, 1784, aged 17; B.A. 1788, M.A. 1790. See *Gent.'s. Mag.,* 1850, i. 679. [35]

Owen, Rowland, s. Thomas, of Machynlleth, co. Montgomery, gent. BALLIOL COLL., matric. 1 Dec., 1727, aged 16.

Owen, Rowland, s. John, of Llanfawr, co. Merioneth, pleb. JESUS COLL., matric. 3 March, 1760, aged 17; B.A. 1764.

Owen, Sidney George, 1s. Sidney James, of ——, near Winchester, arm. BALLIOL COLL., matric. 17 Oct., 1877, aged 18; exhibitioner 1877-82, B.A. 1882, M.A. 1886.

Owen, Sidney James, 2s. Henry, of Worksop, Notts, gent. WORCESTER COLL., matric. 15 Dec., 1847, aged 19, B.A. 1853, M.A. 1856; tutor modern history Magdalen College 1866-80, lecturer Christ Church 1861-82, tutor 1871, Lees reader in law and history, modern history lecturer 1882-3, a senior student 1883, teacher of Indian law and history 1861, reader in Indian history 1878, bar.-at-law, Lincoln's Inn, 1871. See Foster's *Men at the Bar.*

Owen, Thomas, s. Henry, of Westcott, co. Gloucester, cler. LINCOLN COLL., matric. 7 April, 1715, aged 20.

Owen, Thomas, s. John, of Llanbedr, co. Anglesea, pleb. JESUS COLL., matric. 10 March, 1717-8, aged 19; B.A. 1721, M.A. 1725.

Owen, Thomas, s. Humphrey, of Llanfihangel, co. Cardigan, pleb. JESUS COLL., matric. 16 May, 1727, aged 19.

Owen, Thomas, s. Jenkin, of Llanfwrog, co. Denbigh, pleb. JESUS COLL., matric. 16 April, 1729, aged 17; B.A. 6 Feb., 1732-3, M.A. 1737. [5]

Owen, Thomas, s. Thomas, of Clyde, co. Pembroke, pleb. CHRIST CHURCH, matric. 8 July, 1730, aged 20; B.A. 1734.

Owen, Thomas, s. Thomas, of Beaumaris, co. Anglesea, cler. JESUS COLL., matric. 30 March, 1748, aged 17; B.A. 1751, M.A. 1754.

Owen, Thomas, s. Thomas, of Anglesea, pleb. JESUS COLL., matric. 20 March, 1767, aged 18, B.A. 1770; M.A. from QUEEN'S COLL. 1773, rector of Upton Scudamore 1779, until his death in 1812.

Owen, Thomas, s. Thomas, of Llanarmon, co. Denbigh, cler. PEMBROKE COLL., matric. 18 March, 1769, aged 20.

Owen, Thomas, s. Owen, of Fishguard, co. Pembroke, pleb. JESUS COLL., matric. 8 April, 1783, aged 19; B.A. from ST. ALBAN HALL 1787, M.A. 1791. See *Gent.'s Mag.*, 1833, ii. 88. [10]

Owen, Thomas, s. William, of Hodgeston, co. Pembroke, gent. CHRIST CHURCH, matric. 20 Jan., 1804, aged 18; B.A. 1808, M.A. 1810, chaplain 1812-3, rector of Hodgeston 1829, until his death 1 July, 1850; of the baronet's family.

Owen, Thomas. ORIEL COLL., 1842. See CHOLMONDELEY.

Owen, Thomas Cæsar, 5s. Thomas Ellis, of Llandyfrydog, Isle of Anglesey, cler. JESUS COLL., matric. 14 May, 1824, aged 19; B.A. 1828, perp. curate Gyffin 1836-52, rector of Llanbedrog 1852-80, died 28 Dec., 1883.

Owen, Thomas Ellis, s. William, of Conway, co. Carnarvon, arm. CHRIST CHURCH, matric. 26 May, 1785, aged 20; B.A. 1789, vicar of South Stoke, Oxon, 1792, rector of Llandyfrydog, Anglesey, 1794, until his death in 1814. See *Alumni West.*, 419.

Owen, Thomas Griffith, 2s. David, of Caerwys, co. Montgomery, gent. NON-COLL., matric. 28 Jan., 1884, aged 24; B.A. from EXETER COLL. 1888.

Owen, Thomas Mainwaring Bulkeley, 2s. Thomas Bulkeley, of Tedmore Hall, Salop, arm. CHRIST CHURCH, matric. 15 Oct., 1845, B.A. 1849, of Tedsmore Hall, Salop, vicar of Welsh Hampton 1863-70. See *Rugby School Reg.*, 217. [15]

Owen, Thomas William, 4s. James, of Llanidloes, co. Montgomery, gent. JESUS COLL., matric. 25 Oct., 1865, aged 22; scholar 1865-70, B.A. 1869, M.A. 1877, vicar of St. Nicholas, Leicester, 1875.

Owen, Walter Spottiswoode, 5s. Charles J., of Bath, Somerset, arm. MERTON COLL., matric. 26 April, 1871, aged 18.

Owen, William, s. Robert, of Holyhead, co. Anglesea, arm. JESUS COLL., matric. 17 Dec., 1715, aged 18.

Owen, William, s. John, of Bodedern, co. Anglesea, arm. JESUS COLL., matric. 1 April, 1717, aged 17. [20]

Owen, William, s. Owen, of Esger Lloyd, co. Montgomery, pleb. JESUS COLL., matric. 9 April, 1747, aged 24.

Owen, William, s. John, of Ceidio, co. Carnarvon, gent. BRASENOSE COLL., matric. 17 March, 1755, aged 17; B.A. 1758, M.A. 1761, perp. curate Ceidio, died 26 April, 1803. See *Manchester School Reg.*, i. 38.

Owen, William, s. Owen, of Berriew, co. Montgomery, gent. JESUS COLL., matric. 12 Oct., 1775, aged 17; fellow TRINITY COLL., Cambridge, 5th wrangler & B.A. 1782, M.A. 1785, bar.-at-law, Lincoln's Inn, 1787, K.C. and a bencher 1818, a commissioner of bankrupts, died at Glansevern, co. Montgomery, in 1837.

Owen, William, s. William, of St. James's, Westminster, arm. CHRIST CHURCH, matric. 5 May, 1818, aged 19; B.A. from ST. ALBAN HALL 1823. See *Gent.'s Mag.*, 1858, ii. 312.

Owen, William, 1s. William Daniel, of St. George's, Bloomsbury, London, gent. MAGDALEN HALL, matric. 7 Nov., 1849, aged 21; B.A. 1853, M.A. 1862, perp. curate of St. Stephen's, Tonbridge, 1856-62, vicar of Damerham, Wilts, 1862. [25]

Owen, William, 2s. John, of Holywell, co. Flint, gent. JESUS COLL., matric. 9 Feb., 1865, aged 20; B.A. 1869.

Owen, William Digby, 2s. George, of Oswestry, Salop, arm. TRINITY COLL., matric. 14 Oct., 1876, aged 19; B.A. 1880.

Owen, William Wynn, s. Edward, of Llanymonddy, co. Merioneth, cler. JESUS COLL., matric. 26 March, 1794, aged 19; B.A. 1798, M.A. 1800, rector of Llanymonddy, 1819, until his death in 1884.

Owen, Wyrriott, s. Charles, of Langum, co. Pembroke, arm. MAGDALEN HALL, matric. 23 May, 1722, aged 18; grandson of Sir Hugh, 2nd baronet.

Owens, Hugh Haydon, 2s. Zaccheus, of Ruthin, co. Denbigh, pleb. JESUS COLL., matric. 18 March, 1841, aged 18; B.A. 1845 (as OWEN). [30]

Owens, John, s. Thomas, of Ruthyn, co. Denbigh, pleb. JESUS COLL., matric. 17 Dec., 1717, aged 18.

Owens, John, s. 'Pierce Owen,' of Lanniglas, co. Montgomery, pleb. JESUS COLL., matric. 21 March, 1718-9, aged 21 (? B.A. 1722 as JOSEPH OWEN).

Owens, John, 1s. James, of Donnegor (? Donegal), co. Antrim, Ireland, gent. WORCESTER COLL., matric. 28 Oct., 1818, aged 17; B.A. 1822, M.A. 1826.

Owens, Owen, s. Maurice, of Dolgelly, co. Merioneth, pleb. JESUS COLL., matric. 13 Dec., 1721, aged 18.

Owens, Owen, s. Owen, of Berriew, co. Montgomery, cler. JESUS COLL., matric. 19 Feb., 1732-3, aged 19 (? B.A. 1736, or B.A. from QUEEN'S COLL. 1736, as OWEN). [35]

Owens, Owen, s. Owen, of Penmoyre, co. Carnarvon, pleb. JESUS COLL., matric. 19 Feb., 1732-3, aged 19 (? B.A. 1736, or B.A. from QUEEN'S COLL. 1736, as OWEN).

Owens, Owen, s. Rice, of Llanegrin, co. Merioneth, pleb. JESUS COLL., matric. 16 Dec., 1763.

Owens, Owen, s. Robert, of Llanystumdwy, co. Carnarvon, gent. ALL SOULS' COLL., matric. 14 June, 1781, aged 20; B.A. 1785. See *Gent.'s Mag.*, 1829, i. 378.

Owens, Robert, s. Watkin, of Llanrwyst, co. Carnarvon, pleb. JESUS COLL., matric. 3 March, 1714-5, aged 18; B.A. 3 March, 1718-9 (as OWEN).

Owens, Robert, s. Robert, of Llanfair, co. Denbigh, pleb. WADHAM COLL., matric. 5 June, 1783, aged 22. [40]

Owens, Walter, s. John, of Landibie, co. Carmarthen, pleb. CHRIST CHURCH, matric. 1 Dec., 1752, aged 17; B.A. 1756 (as OWEN).

Owens, William, s. Robert, of Bodfari, co. Flint, pleb. JESUS COLL., matric. 8 April, 1731, aged 19; B.A. 1734.

Owgan, Joseph Bullen, scholar TRINITY COLL., Dublin, 1839 (B.A. 1844, M.A. 1862, B. & D.D. 1864); adm. 'comitatis causa' 24 March, 1866.

Owsley, John, s. John, of Hallaton, co. Leicester, gent. QUEEN'S COLL., matric. 7 Dec., 1761, aged 19; B.A. from MERTON COLL. 1765, perp. curate Blaston, co. Leicester, 1768, until his death 26 July, 1835.

Owtram, Cuthbert Ellidge, 2s. Robert Hermon, of Surbiton, Surrey, gent. WORCESTER COLL., matric. 18 Oct., 1883, aged 19; B.A. 1887.

Oxenden, Ashton, 6s. Henry, of Barham, Kent, baronet. UNIVERSITY COLL., matric. 9 June, 1826, aged 17; B.A. 1831, M.A. 1859, D.D. by decree 10 July, 1869, rector of Pluckley, Kent, 1848-69, hon. canon Canterbury 1864, bishop of Montreal and metropolitan of Canada 1869-78, vicar of Hackington 1879-85. See Foster's *Baronetage*. [5]

Oxenden, Montagu, s. Henry, of Broom, Kent, baronet. EXETER COLL., matric. 28 Oct., 1817, aged 18; B.A. 1821, M.A. 1824, rector of Luddenham, Kent, 1827-78, and of Eastwell 1837, until his death 25 Jan., 1880, father of the next named. See Foster's *Baronetage* & *Eton School Lists*.

Oxenden, Percy Dixwell Nowell, 2s. Montagu, of Eastwell, Kent, cler. CHRIST CHURCH, matric. 15 Oct., 1856, aged 18. See Foster's *Baronetage*.

Oxenham, Edward Lavington, 2s. William, of Harrow, Middlesex, cler. MAGDALEN HALL, matric. 13 Oct., 1873, aged 30; bar.-at-law, Middle Temple, 1883. See Foster's *Men at the Bar*.

Oxenham, Rev. Frank Nutcombe, 2s. Nutcombe, of Moxbury, Devon, cler. EXETER COLL., matric. 15 Oct., 1858, aged 18; B.A. 1862, M.A. 1865.

Oxenham, George William, 3s. William, of Harrow, Middlesex, cler. EXETER COLL., matric. 16 Jan., 1869, aged 19. [10]

Oxenham, Henry Nutcombe, 1s. William, of Harrow, Middlesex, cler. BALLIOL COLL., matric. 30 Nov., 1846, aged 17; scholar 1846-54, B.A. 1850, M.A. 1854, seceded to Rome, died 23 March, 1888.

Oxenham, Nutcombe. See OXNAM.

Oxenham, Robert George, 1s. Nutcombe, of Modbury, Devon, cler. EXETER COLL., matric. 10 Oct., 1856, aged 18; B.A. 1860, M.A. 1867.

Oxenham, William, s. William, of South Tawton, Devon, arm. WADHAM COLL., matric. 19 Feb., 1718-9, aged 16; bar.-at-law, Inner Temple, 1726.

Oxenham, William, s. William, of Mamhead, Devon, arm. ORIEL COLL., matric. 19 Feb., 1749-50, aged 18. [15]

Oxford, Arnold Whitaker, 2s. Thomas, of Keynsham, Somerset, gent. CHRIST CHURCH, matric. 10 Oct., 1873, aged 19; a junior student 1873-8, B.A. 1876, M.A. 1880, vicar of St. Luke, Berwick Street, London, 1883.

Oxford & Mortimer, Edward, Earl of. CHRIST CHURCH, 1791. See HARLEY.

Oxlad, Francis, of Oxford, 'tonsor;' 29 June, 1719.

Oxlee, John, o.s. John, of Egton, Yorks, cler. ALL SOULS' COLL., matric. 12 Oct., 1826, aged 18; bible clerk 1826-9, his father died rector of Molesworth, Hunts, 30 Jan., 1854.

Oxlee, Richard Arthur Worsop, 2s. John, of Brington, Hunts, cler. WORCESTER COLL., matric. 24 Oct., 1861, aged 19; B.A. & M.A. 1868, perp. curate Scampton, Yorks, 1871-81, died 31 Aug., 1886. [20]

Oxley, Alfred James Rice, 6s. George, of Conisborough, Yorks, gent. NON-COLL., matric. 29 Oct., 1877, aged 21; B.A. from BALLIOL COLL. 1881, M.A. 1885.

Oxley, Charles Christopher, 1s. Charles, of Ripon, Yorks, arm. QUEEN'S COLL., matric. 19 March, 1829, aged 18.

Oxley, Thomas, 1s. Samuel, of Pontefract, Yorks, gent. QUEEN'S COLL., matric. 3 July, 1824, aged 18.

Oxley, Thomas, o.s. William, of King's Lynn, Norfolk, arm. ST. MARY HALL, matric. 2 April, 1830, aged 19.

Oxley, William Henry, 2s. Charles Christopher, of Redcar, Yorks, arm. ST. JOHN'S COLL., matric. 22 Oct., 1867, aged 18; B.A. 1870, M.A 1874, vicar of Grewelthorpe, Yorks, 1876-82, chaplain Sorrento 1883-5, of Palermo and Marsala 1885. [25]

Oxnam, George Nutcombe. s. William, of St. Paul's, Cornwall, cler. WADHAM COLL., matric. 11 Dec., 1816, aged 17, B.A. 1820; fellow EXETER COLL. 1820-30, M.A. 1823, bar.-at-law, Lincoln's Inn, 1825, died 15 Dec., 1873. See *Boase*, 124.

Oxnam, Nutcombe, 3s. William, of Exeter (city), Devon, cler. ORIEL COLL., matric. 19 March, 1828, aged 17; scholar TRINITY COLL. 1829-30; fellow EXETER COLL. 1832-4, B.A. 1834, M.A. 1839, preb. of Exeter 1850, vicar of Modbury, Devon, 1834, until his death 13 Sep., 1859. See *Coll. Reg.*, 130.

Oxnam, William, s. Richard, of Penzance, Cornwall, gent. ORIEL COLL., matric. 1 Dec., 1789, aged 19; B.A. 1794, M.A. 1798, preb. of Exeter, and rector of St. Petrock's, Exeter, 1803, until his death 23 Feb., 1844.

Oxnam, William, 2s. William, of Paul, Cornwall, cler. WADHAM COLL., matric. 1 April, 1819, aged 18; scholar 1819-26, B.A. 1823, M.A. 1826 (? vicar of Cornwood, Devon, 1824), 2nd master Harrow School 1841, until his death 13 Oct., 1863.

Ozanne, Herbert William, 2s. Richard James, of Tamworth, co. Derby, cler. EXETER COLL., matric. 16 Oct., 1868, aged 18; B.A. 1873. [30]

Ozanne, James Duncan, 3s. Joseph, of Launceston, Tasmania, gent. ST. EDMUND HALL, matric. 18 May, 1883, aged 19; B.A. 1886.

Ozanne, Martin, 2s. Peter, of Câtel, Isle of Guernsey, gent. PEMBROKE COLL., matric. 3 Nov., 1831, aged 17; scholar 1831-6.

Ozanne, Richard James, 1s. Richard Mansell, of Guernsey, gent. PEMBROKE COLL., matric. 10 June, 1841, aged 17; scholar 1841-5, B.A. 1846, M.A. 1848, vicar of Alfreton, co. Derby, 1852-4, perp. curate St. Matthew, Guernsey, 1854-8, rector of St. Andrew, Guernsey, 1858-70, and of St. Peter Port 1870, until his death 17 Dec., 1880.

Ozanne, Robert John Thorpe, 5s. John, of St. Peter Port, Guernsey, M.D. CORPUS CHRISTI COLL., matric. 1 Feb., 1881, aged 18; scholar 1881-5, B.A. 1884.

Ozaroffsky, Adam, Count, D.C.L. by diploma 15 June, 1814, lieut.-general in the Russian army. [35]

Pacey, Frederick William, 2s. Paul, of Oxford, gent. ST. MARY HALL, matric. 7 March, 1871, aged 24, B.Mus. 1873; chorister Christ Church 1857-61.

Pack, Arthur (Denis Henry Heber) Reynell, o.s. Arthur John Reynell, of Avisford, Sussex, arm. CHRIST CHURCH, matric. 31 May and 10 Oct., 1879, aged 18; of Netherton, Devon, late of Avisford aforesaid. See *Eton School Lists.*

Pack, John Christopher, 1s. Richard, of St. Bride's, London, arm. CHRIST CHURCH, matric. 7 Dec., 1825, aged 18; B.A. 1829.

Pack, Lewis, 2s. Richard, of Walthamstow, Essex, arm. BALLIOL COLL., matric. 11 May, 1837, aged 19; B.A. 1841.

Packe, Alfred Edmund, 3s. Edmund, of London, arm. CHRIST CHURCH, matric. 25 March, 1870, aged 18; B.A. 1873, B.C.L. & M.A. 1877, bar.-at-law, Lincoln's Inn, 1875. See Foster's *Men at the Bar* & *Eton School Lists.* [5]

Packe, Charles, 1s. Edmund, of Prestwold, co. Leicester, arm. CHRIST CHURCH, matric. 15 May, 1845, aged 18; B.A. 1849, of Stretton Hall, co. Leicester, J.P., bar.-at-law, Inner Temple, 1852. See Foster's *Men at the Bar* & *Eton School Lists.*

Packe, Charles James, s. Charles James, of Prestwold, co. Leicester, arm. EXETER COLL., matric. 29 March, 1776, aged 18; of Prestwold Hall, high sheriff, co. Leicester, 1822, lieut.-colonel Leicestershire militia, died 1 March, 1837.

Packe, Charles William, s. Charles James, of Carlby, co. Lincoln, arm. ORIEL COLL., matric. 20 Nov., 1810, aged 18; of Prestwold, co. Leicester, a student of Lincoln's Inn 1816, colonel Leicestershire yeomanry, M.P. South Leicester 1836, until his death 27 Oct., 1867. See *Eton School Lists.*

Packe, Christopher, s. Herbert, of Edinburgh (city), doctor. WORCESTER COLL., matric. 7 May, 1810, aged 18; B.A. 1814, M.A. 1825, minor canon of Windsor 1821, of St. Paul's 1817, preacher in ordinary to the Queen 1821, vicar of Ruislip 1834, until his death 4 June, 1878.

Packe, Henry Vere, 2s. Henry, of Harlestone, Northants, arm. BRASENOSE COLL., matric. 6 June, 1844, aged 18; B.A. 1848, rector of Shangton, co. Leicester, 1858. [10]

Packe, Horace, 4s. Henry Vere, of Shangton, co. Leicester, cler. WORCESTER COLL., matric. 22 Oct., 1885, aged 19.

Packe, William James, 2s. Edmund, of Paddington, Middlesex, arm. CHRIST CHURCH, matric. 22 Oct., 1851, aged 18; B.A. 1855, M.A. 1862, held various curacies 1858-73, vicar of Feering, Essex, since 1873, brother of Charles 1845. See *Eton School Lists.*

Packer, Arthur, 2s. Richard, of Barnstaple, Devon, gent. ST. EDMUND HALL, matric. 28 Jan., 1847, aged 27; B.A. 1852, M.A. 1858.

Packer, Edward, 2s. (Hon.) Charles, of Barbados, arm. EXETER COLL., matric. 26 Jan., 1878, aged 19.

Packer, Henry, s. Robert, of Shillingford, Berks, arm. TRINITY COLL., matric. 23 June, 1726, aged 18

Packer, Isaac George, 1s. George, of St. Nicholas, Nottingham (town), gent. WORCESTER COLL., matric. 27 June, 1854, aged 20; bible clerk 1856-7, B.A. 1859, M.A. 1884, vicar of Thurmaston, co. Leicester, 1866. [16]

Packer, Leonard Frederick, 6s. John Graham, of London, cler. MAGDALEN COLL., matric. 19 Oct., 1883, aged 18; B.A. 1887.

Packwood, Gery, s. Samuel, of co. Warwick, cler. ST. JOHN'S COLL., matric. 20 May, 1731, aged 16; bar.-at-law, Gray's Inn, 1734, bencher 1756.

Packwood, Josias, s. Jos., of Oldbury, co. Worcester, pleb. PEMBROKE COLL., matric. 18 Feb., 1726-7, aged 19.

Packwood, Rogers Porter, s. Charles Porter, of St. Mary, Warwick (town), arm. MERTON COLL., matric. 15 Oct., 1792, aged 17; B.A. 1796, M.A. 1799, fellow until 1812, vicar of St. Mary Church, Warwick, 1811, until his death 17 Aug., 1815. [20]

Packford, William, 2s. William, of Oxford, gent. ST. ALBAN HALL, matric. 20 May, 1878, aged 21.

Paddison, Richard, 1s. Howard, of Hampton, Middlesex, arm. BALLIOL COLL., matric. 17 Oct., 1882, aged 19; Blundell scholar 1882-6, B.A. 1887, a student of Lincoln's Inn 1882.

Paddon, Charles Edward, o.s. John Edward, of Fareham, Hants, gent. WADHAM COLL., matric. 18 March, 1857, aged 18; B.A. 1861.

Paddon, John, s. George, of Chawleigh, Devon, cler. EXETER COLL., matric. 21 Nov., 1774, aged 19; B.A. 1778, minister of St. Mary, Bungay, at his death 8 April, 1823 (his father rector of Chawleigh in 1743).

Paddon, Thomas Henry, 1s. Joseph, of Fareham, Hants, gent. TRINITY COLL., matric. 25 Oct., 1825, aged 18; B.A. 1829, M.A. 1853, vicar of High Wycombe 1844-69, incumbent of Emmanuel Church, Eastbourne, died 30 Oct., 1887. [25]

Paddon, William Francis Locke, 2s. Thomas Henry, of High Wycombe, Bucks, cler. WADHAM COLL., matric. 3 June, 1863, aged 18; B.A. 1866, incumbent of Kilmaine, co. Mayo, 1878.

Padley, Charles John Allen Newton, 2s. Alfred, of Alesford, Essex, cler. EXETER COLL., matric. 24 May, 1837, aged 17; B.A. 1841, M.A. 1857, rector of Enville, co. Stafford, 1874, until his death in 1887.

Padley, Henry Madeley, o.s. John Charles, of Retford, Notts, gent. NON-COLL., matric. 14 Oct., 1882, aged 20; B.A. 1886.

Padman, Jenner, s. Selby, of Hampstead, Middlesex, gent. CHRIST CHURCH, matric. 19 March, 1755, aged 17; B.A. 1758.

Padmore, Thomas, s. Charles, of Isle of Barbados, West Indies, arm. QUEEN'S COLL., matric. 30 Oct., 1800, aged 19. [30]

Padwick, Henry, o.s. Henry, of Horsham, Sussex, arm. BRASENOSE COLL., matric. 9 June, 1846, aged 17; B.A. 1850, M.A. 1853, of Manor House, Horsham, and of the Hermitage, East Grinstead, Sussex, J.P., D.L., bar.-at-law, Inner Temple, 1854. See Foster's *Men at the Bar.*

Page, Arnold Henry, 3s. William Bousfield, of Carlisle, gent. BALLIOL COLL., matric. 17 Oct., 1870, aged 19; B.A. 1875, M.A. 1877, bar.-at-law, Inner Temple, 1878, rector of Tendring, Essex, 1886. See Foster's *Men at the Bar.*

Page, Rev. Arthur Charles, 2s. Thomas, of East Dereham, Norfolk, arm. BRASENOSE COLL., matric. 17 Oct., 1874, aged 19; B.A. 1878, M.A. 1881, died 14 Feb., 1883.

Page, Cæsar, s. Richard, of Westminster (city), arm. CHRIST CHURCH, matric. 2 Feb., 1787, aged 19.

Page, Charles, s. John, of Northleach, co. Gloucester, gent. PEMBROKE COLL., matric. 27 March, 1733, aged 15; B.A. 3 Feb., 1736-7, M.A. 1741, of Northleach, co. Gloucester, died at Whitehall, near Bristol, 3 Feb., 1801, father of Charles 1777. [5]

Page, Charles, s. Robert, of Castle Eaton, Wilts, cler. QUEEN'S COLL., matric. 19 July, 1755, aged 16; B.A. 1761.

Page, Charles, s. Charles, of Bibury, co. Gloucester, cler. PEMBROKE COLL., matric. 9 May, 1777, aged 16; B.A. 1781.

Page, Charles, 1s. David, of Harrow, Middlesex, gent. ORIEL COLL., matric. 19 Oct., 1886, aged 18; scholar 1886.

Page, Cyril William, 1s. William, of St. Margaret's, Westminster, doctor. CHRIST CHURCH, matric. 9 May, 1823, aged 17; student 1823-73, B.A. 1827, M.A. 1829, perp. curate Christ Church, Westminster, 1843, until his death 11 April, 1873. See *Alumni West.*, 491.

Page, Rev. Edmund Skikelthorp, 1s. Edmund, of Gainsborough, co. Lincoln, gent. WORCESTER COLL., matric. 17 Oct., 1863, aged 19; B.A. 1866.

Page, Francis, s. Richard, of Ombersley, co. Worcester, arm. NEW COLL., matric. 29 April, 1743, aged 16; created M.A. 1 Aug., 1747, and also D.C.L. 14 April, 1749, then of Middle Aston, Oxon, M.P. Oxford University 1768-1801. [10]

Page, Frederick, s. Francis, of Newbury, Berks, arm. ORIEL COLL., matric. 14 July, 1786, aged 17; bar.-at-law, Inner Temple, 1792, bencher 1826, died 8 April, 1834.

Page, George, s. Thomas Hyde, of Betteshanger, Kent, equitis. WADHAM COLL., matric. 17 May, 1809, aged 18; created M.A. 26 June, 1811.

Page, Herbert Vivian, 3s. Alexander Shaw, of Lancashire, cler. WADHAM COLL., matric. 17 Oct., 1882, aged 19.

Page, Herbert William Cobbold, 2s. Luke Flood, of Woolpit, Suffolk, cler. CHRIST CHURCH, matric. 8 June, 1854, aged 18; B.A. from NEW INN HALL 1859. See *Eton School Lists.* [15]

Page, James, s. Richard, of Bath (city), pleb. MAGDALEN HALL, matric. 29 April, 1768, aged 18; curate of St. Peter and St. Paul, Bath, died at Liverpool in 1827, aged 78.

Page, John, s. Charles, of Bibury, co. Gloucester, cler. CORPUS CHRISTI COLL., matric. 21 Oct., 1774, aged 15; B.A. 1778, M.A. 1782.

Page, John, s. William Emanuel, of Frodsham, Cheshire, cler. BRASENOSE COLL., matric. 18 April, 1798, aged 17; B.A. 1802, M.A. 1804, B.D. 1815, D.D. 1825, fellow until 1823, vice principal 1816, vicar of Gillingham-cum-Lidsing, Kent, 1822, until his death 31 March, 1867. See *Manchester School Reg.*, ii. 202.

Page, John, 2s. Samuel, of Northaw, Herts, arm. EXETER COLL., matric. 3 May, 1849, aged 19; B.A. 1853, M.A. 1878. See *Eton School Lists.*

Page, John Charles, 1s. John, of Hockley, Essex, arm. BRASENOSE COLL., matric. 24 May, 1877, aged 18. [20]

Page, John Ernest, 2s. John William, of Bilston, co. Stafford, gent. WADHAM COLL., matric. 17 Oct., 1882, aged 20.

Page, Lawrence Bernard, 4s. William Bousfield, of Carlisle, gent. QUEEN'S COLL., matric. 20 Oct., 1873, aged 19; exhibitioner 1873-7, B.A. 1876, M.A. 1880.

Page, Philip, 'butler to Wadham College;' privilegiatus 19 May, 1778.

Page, Richard, s. Henry, of Wootton, Hants, pleb. WADHAM COLL., matric. 26 Oct., 1723, aged 19.

Page, Richard, s. Richard of Wembly, Middlesex, arm. UNIVERSITY COLL., matric. 15 Dec., 1767, aged 19. [25]

Page, Robert, s. Charles, of Northleach, co. Gloucester, pleb. PEMBROKE COLL., matric. 23 June, 1719, aged 17; B.A. 1723 (as Roger).

Page, Robert Henry Frederick, 1s. Robert Hyde, of Sidmouth, Devon, arm. WADHAM COLL., matric. 16 April, 1883, aged 28; a student of the Middle Temple 1883.

Page, Thomas, o.s. Thomas, of Ely, co. Cambridge, arm. TRINITY COLL., matric. 11 March, 1824, aged 17; J.P., D.L., co. Cambridge, a student of Lincoln's Inn 1825. See *Eton School Lists.*

Page, Thomas, 2s. Joseph, of St. Nicholas, Gloucester (city), gent. MAGDALEN HALL, matric. 18 May, 1825, aged 19; B.A. 1829, M.A. 1832, perp. curate St. Matthew's, Rugby, 1846, until his death 5 Nov., 1852.

Page, Thomas Douglas, 4s. Robert, of Charlton Mackerell, Somerset, gent. PEMBROKE COLL., matric. 1 March, 1855, aged 19; scholar 1855-61, B.A. 1859, M.A. 1861, fellow 1861-72, proctor 1872, bursar 1862, junior dean and historical lecturer 1863, lecturer in law and divinity 1869, etc., dean 1864, a student of Lincoln's Inn 1859, rector of Sibstone, co. Leicester, 1873, until his death 26 Sep., 1880. [30]

Page, Vernon, 5s. William, of Westminster (city), doctor. CHRIST CHURCH, matric. 13 May, 1836, aged 18; student 1836-59, B.A. 1840, M.A. 1842, perp. curate Maiden Bradley, Wilts, 1845-51, rector of St. Tudy, Cornwall, 1858, until his death 13 Oct., 1885. See *Alumni West.*, 512.

Page, Vernon Francis, o.s. Vernon, of St. Tudy, Cornwall, cler. ST. MARY HALL, matric. 21 Oct., 1878, aged 18; B.A. 1882, bar.-at-law, Middle Temple, 1885. See Foster's *Men at the Bar.*

Page, Walter Sylvester, y.s. John, of Brinton, Norfolk, gent. ST. ALBAN HALL, matric. 16 Oct., 1869, aged 21; incumbent of St. Andrew's, Exuma, Bahama Islands.

Page, William, s. William Emanuel, of Frodsham, Cheshire, cler. CHRIST CHURCH, matric. 3 June, 1795, aged 17; B.A. 1799, M.A. 1802, B.D. 1809, D.D. 1815, 2nd master Westminster 1802-14, headmaster 1814 to Aug., 1819, vicar of Willen, Bucks, 1806-19, vicar of Steventon and preb. of Westminster 1812-7, rector of Nunburnholme, Yorks, 1812-7, and of Quainton, Bucks, 1817, and sub-almoner 1817, until his death 20 Sep., 1819. See *Manchester School Reg.*, ii. 202; & *Alumni West.*, 443.

Page, William (Emanuel), s. John, of Oporto, Portugal, arm. CHRIST CHURCH, matric. 28 May, 1755, aged 18; B.A. 1759, M.A. 1762, chaplain to the factory at Oporto, rector of Frodsham, Cheshire, 1776, and preb. of Chester 1726, until his death 18 Jan., 1801. See *Alumni West.*, 362. [35]

Page, William Emanuel, 2s. William, of Westminster (city), doctor. CHRIST CHURCH, matric. 13 May, 1826, aged 18; student 1826-56, B.A. 1830, M.A. 1833, B.Med. 1834, D.Med. 1837, F.R.C.P. 1838, senior physician St. George's Hospital at his death 2 Jan., 1868. See *Alumni West.*, 497.

Page, William Robert, 1s. William Emanuel, of London, gent. QUEEN'S COLL., matric. 24 Oct., 1877, aged 18.

Paget, Hon. Sir Arthur (G.C.B.), s. Henry, Earl of Uxbridge. CHRIST CHURCH, matric. 8 June, 1787, aged 17; entered the diplomatic service in 1791, ambassador to the Sublime Port 1807, privy councillor, etc., M.P. Anglesey 1794-1807, etc., groom of the bedchamber, died 26 July, 1840. See Foster's *Peerage*, M. ANGLESEY; & *Alumni West.*, 423.

Paget, Arthur John Snow, 1s. John Moore, of Babington, Somerset, arm. TRINITY COLL., matric. 10 June, 1848, aged 17; died 16 April, 1863. See *Eton School Lists* & *Gent.'s Mag.*, 1863, i. 798.

Paget, Hon. Berkeley (Thomas), s. Henry, Earl of Uxbridge. CHRIST CHURCH, matric. 26 Oct., 1797, aged 17; a commissioner of Excise, M.P. Anglesey 1807-20, Milborne Port 1820-6, died 26 Oct., 1842. See Foster's *Peerage*, M. ANGLESEY.

Paget, Cecil George, 3s. Leopold Grimston, of Great Gaddesden, Herts, arm. CHRIST CHURCH, matric. 11 Oct., 1872, aged 19; a junior student 1872-6, B.A. 1877, M.A. 1879, vicar of Holt, Dorset, 1884.

Paget, Charles, s. William, of Barnet, Middlesex, cler. WADHAM COLL., matric. 3 Feb., 1815, aged 23. [5]

Paget, Edward Clarence, 3s. Edward James, of Swithland, co. Leicester, cler. KEBLE COLL., matric. 18 Oct., 1870, aged 19; B.A. 1874, M.A. 1877, principal Dorchester Missionary College 1878-84, assistant minister Davenport Cathedral, Iowa, U.S.A., 1886.

Paget, Edward Heneage, 4s. Edward, of Sandhurst, Berks, gent. (after G.C.B.). ST. JOHN'S COLL., matric. 10 Nov., 1847, aged 19; B.A. 1852, M.A. 1855, rector of Stuston, Suffolk, 1859-68, vicar of Hoxne, Suffolk, 1868-83, died 29 Sep., 1884. See Foster's *Peerage*, M. ANGLESEY; & *Eton School Lists*.

Paget, Edward James, 2s. Charles, of Rogate, Sussex, equitis. CHRIST CHURCH, matric. 5 Dec., 1828, aged 17; student 1828-42, B.A. 1832, M.A. 1835, rector of Swithland, co. Leicester, 1841-58, and of Steppingley, Beds, 1864, until his death 30 Aug., 1869. See Foster's *Peerage*.

Paget, Francis, 2s. James, of London (city), arm. (after baronet). CHRIST CHURCH, matric. 18 Oct., 1869, aged 18; a junior student 1869-73, B.A. 1873, M.A. 1876, a senior student 1873-83, tutor 1875-82, D.D. by decree 8 Dec., 1885, regius professor pastoral theology, and a canon 1885, Latin lecturer Hertford College 1874-5, Whitehall preacher 1881-3, vicar of Bromsgrove 1882-5.

Paget, Francis Edward, 1s. Edward, of St. George's, Hanover Square, London, equitis. CHRIST CHURCH, matric. 3 June, 1824, aged 18; student 1825-36, B.A. 1828, M.A. 1830, rector of Elford, co. Stafford, 1835, until his death 4 Aug., 1882. See Foster's *Peerage*, M. ANGLESEY; and for list of his works see *Crockford*. [10]

Paget, Sir George Edward (K.C.B.), created D.C.L. 22 June, 1870 (2s. Samuel Paget, of Great Yarmouth), president General Medical Council of the United Kingdom 1869-74; fellow CAIUS COLL., Cambridge, 1832-51 and 1881, 8th wrangler & B.A. 1831, D.Med. 1839, regius professor of physic, Cambridge, 1872, F.R.S. 1873, F.R.C.P. London, 1839, created D.Med. Dublin 1867, D.C.L. Durham 1870, and LL.D. Edinburgh 1871, knighted at Windsor Castle 9 March, 1886. See Foster's *Baronetage*.

Paget, Henry, s. Thomas, of Isleworth, Middlesex, baron. ST. JOHN'S COLL., matric. 25 Oct., 1738, aged 19; 2nd Earl of Uxbridge, died unmarried 17 Nov., 1769.

Paget, Henry Bayly, Lord Paget, created D.C.L. 7 July, 1773 (s. Sir Nicholas Bayly, Bart.), created Earl of Uxbridge 19 May, 1784, died 13 March 1812, father of Henry William, 1st Marquis of Anglesey.

Paget, Henry Luke, 3s. James, of London, baronet. CHRIST CHURCH, matric. 11 Oct., 1872, aged 18; B.A. 1876, M.A. 1880, vicar of St. Ives, Hunts, 1886, vicar of St. Pancras 1887. See Foster's *Baronetage*.

Paget, Henry William, s. Henry, Earl of Uxbridge. CHRIST CHURCH, matric. 14 Oct., 1784, aged 16; created M.A. 28 June, 1786, 2nd Earl of Uxbridge, K.G. 1818, G.C.B. 1815, G.C.H. 1816, etc., created Marquis of Anglesey 4 July, 1815, field-marshal 1846, wounded at Waterloo, M.P. Carnarvon 1790, Milbourne Port 1796-1804, 1806-10, lord-lieutenant of Ireland 1828-9, 1830-3, goldstick & colonel royal horse guards 1842, died 29 April, 1854. See Foster's *Peerage*. [15]

Paget, (Sir) James (Bart.), F.R.S., created D.C.L. 5 Aug., 1868 (3s. Samuel, of Great Yarmouth), surgeon extraordinary to the Queen 1858-67, sergeant-surgeon extraordinary 1867-77, and in ordinary 1877, surgeon to the Prince of Wales 1863, created a baronet 19 Aug., 1871, father of Francis 1869, Henry L. 1872, and of Stephen 1874. See Foster's *Baronetage*.

Paget, John, s. John, of Egham, Surrey, cler. PEMBROKE COLL., matric. 22 March, 1730-1, aged 16; B.A. 1734.

Paget, John, s. Thomas, of Basildon, Berks, cler. ORIEL COLL., matric. 22 March, 1745-6, aged 17; B.A. 1749, M.A. 1754, vicar of Doulton, Somerset, died 5 Oct., 1782.

Paget, John, s. John, of Hungerford, Berks, gent. QUEEN'S COLL., matric. 26 Feb., 1754, aged 18; B.A. 1757.

Paget, John, s. Richard, of Sherborne, Dorset, gent. ORIEL COLL., matric. 22 March, 1779, aged 17; of Newbery House and Cranmore Hall, Somerset, died 21 Aug., 1825. [20]

Paget, John Moore, s. John, of Kilmersdon, Somerset, arm. QUEEN'S COLL., matric. 12 April, 1810, aged 18; of Cranmore Hall, Somerset, high sheriff Rutland 1851, died 4 June, 1866.

Paget, Peter. PEMBROKE COLL., 1816. See PUGET.

Paget, Richard, s. Thomas, of Basildon, Berks, cler. ORIEL COLL., matric. 2 April, 1747, aged 16; B.A. from MAGDALEN COLL. 1751, M.A. 1753, of Newbery House and Cranmore Hall, Somerset, died 8 April, 1803.

Paget, Richard, s. Richard, of East Cranmore, Somerset, gent. MAGDALEN COLL., matric. 29 July, 1780, aged 14; demy 1780-94, B.A. 1784, M.A. 1787, curate of East Cranmore, died 9 Dec., 1794. See *Coll. Reg.*, vii. 58.

Paget, Robert, s. Thomas, of Mouseford, Berks, cler. QUEEN'S COLL., matric. 9 Dec., 1756, aged 17; demy MAGDALEN COLL. 1757-62, B.A. 1760, fellow 1762-93, M.A. 1763, B.C.L. 1773, D.C.L. 1777, vice-president 1778, etc., superior bedel in arts 1768, and also in law, died 10 Aug., 1793. See *Bloxam*, vi. 309. [25]

Paget, Stephen, 4s. James, of London, baronet. CHRIST CHURCH, matric. 16 Oct., 1874, aged 19; exhibitioner 1876-80, B.A. 1878, M.A. 1886, F.R.C.S. See Foster's *Baronetage*.

Paget, Thomas, s. John, of Pointington, Somerset, cler. QUEEN'S COLL., matric. 13 Nov., 1721, aged 15; fellow CORPUS CHRISTI COLL., B.A. 1725, M.A. 1728, B.D. 1738, proctor 1737, rector of St. Mewan, Cornwall, vicar of Clifton Maybank, Dorset, 1742, and of Bradford Abbas 1743, rector of Pointington 1745, and of Mells 1751, until his death 2 Jan., 1783.

Paget, Thomas Bradley, s. Thomas Bradley, of Tamworth, co. Warwick, gent. WADHAM COLL., matric. 2 May, 1800, aged 18; B.A. 1804, M.A. 1809, incumbent of Long Acre Episcopal Chapel, vicar of Evington, co. Leicester, 1842, until his death 20 March, 1846.

Pagett, Simon, s. Simon, of Glastonbury, par. of St. John's, Somerset, cler. BALLIOL COLL., matric. 10 Dec., 1737, aged 18; B.A. 1741, vicar of Ling 1787.

Pagett, William, s. John, of Chipping Norton, Oxon, gent. WADHAM COLL., matric. 19 June, 1745, aged 16; B.A. 1749, died rector of North Wingfield, co. Derby, 12 Dec., 1798. [30]

Paige, John, s. Nicholas, of East Allington, Devon, gent. ORIEL COLL., matric. 11 Dec., 1780, aged 19.

Paige-Browne, John Browne, 1s. John Browne, of Totnes, Devon, gent. EXETER COLL., matric. 10 June, 1833, aged 16; B.A. 1837, M.A. 1840, of Great Engleborne, Devon, assumed the additional name of BROWNE in 1870.

Paige, Robert, s. Thomas, of Thirsk, Yorks, gent. MERTON COLL., matric. 30 May, 1718, B.A. 1 Feb., 1721-2, M.A. from MAGDALEN COLL. 1724, B.D. 1733, D.D. 1736.

Paige, William Edward, 1s. William Michael, of Ilsington, Devon, cler. MERTON COLL., matric. 14 June, 1855, aged 19; clerk 1855-9, B.A. 1859, M.A. 1869, incumbent of St. Matthew Masterton, Wellington, New Zealand, 1880.

Pain, Andrew Reed, 4s. Richard, of Bletchley, Bucks, cler. PEMBROKE COLL., matric. 22 Nov., 1838, aged 19; B.A. 1843, rector of Bury, Hunts, 1848.

Pain, Rev. Frederick William Goodyer, 2s. Charles, of Kolapur, East Indies, gent. ST. ALBAN HALL, matric. 16 Oct., 1880, aged 22. **[5]**

Pain, John Lloyd, 2s. Thomas Lloyd, of Liverpool (town), cler. BRASENOSE COLL., matric. 6 Feb., 1851, aged 18; scholar 1851-5, B.A. 1854, M.A. 1857, held various curacies 1856-76, vicar of Holme, Westmoreland, 1876-7, and of Silverdale, Lancashire, 1877.

Pain, Montagu, 2s. George Henning, of Bridgewater, Somerset, gent. PEMBROKE COLL., matric. 20 Jan., 1864, aged 18; B.A. 1867, M.A. 1870, held various curacies 1869-86, rector of Penton Mewsey, Hants, 1886.

Pain, Philip, o.s. Philip, of Woodstock, Oxon, gent. LINCOLN COLL., matric. 28 May, 1841, aged 19; B.A. 1845, M.A. 1852.

Pain, Richard, s. John, of Banbury, Oxon, gent. PEMBROKE COLL., matric. 11 March, 1793, aged 18; B.A. 1796, B.C.L. 1820, rector of Little Wigborough, Essex, 1820, until his death 21 March, 1854. **[10]**

Pain, Richard Ernest, 1s. Edmund, of Stoke Hammond, Bucks cler. KEBLE COLL., matric. 19 Oct., 1874, aged 18; B.A. 1877, M.A. 1881.

Pain, Rev. Robert, 3s. John, of Banbury, Oxon, arm. QUEEN'S COLL., matric. 2 Dec., 1823, aged 17; B.A. 1828, died at Bloxham 3 May, 1836.

Pain, Thomas Holland, 1s. Thomas Lloyd, of Liverpool (town), cler. BRASENOSE COLL., matric. 7 June, 1849, aged 18; scholar 1850-3, B.A. 1853, M.A. 1856, curate of Stone, co. Worcester, 1859-71, vicar of Warton, Lancashire, 1871.

Pain, Thomas Lloyd, s. David, of Lugwardine, co. Hereford, arm. BRASENOSE COLL., matric. 23 Oct., 1817, aged 18; scholar 1817-21, B.A. 1821, M.A. 1824, perp. curate St. Thomas's, Liverpool, 1834, until his death 1876.

Paine, Ernest Charles, 2s. George William, of Forest Hill, Kent, gent. WADHAM COLL., matric. 19 Oct., 1885, aged 20. **[15]**

Paine, Gerald, 4s. Hammon, of Blackheath, Kent, gent. CHRIST CHURCH, matric. 25 May, 1883, aged 18.

Paine, Herbert Norman, 4s. John Marshall, of Addlestone, Surrey, arm. MAGDALEN COLL. matric. 26 Jan., 1886, aged 19.

Paine, John, s. John, of Wells, Somerset. ORIEL COLL., matric. 10 Oct., 1734, aged 17; B.A. 1738, M.A. 1741, sub-dean & preb. of Bath and Wells 1773, until his death in 1774.

Paine, John, s. John, of Patcham, Sussex, arm. ORIEL COLL., matric. 8 May, 1809, aged 19 (? perp. curate of St. John's, Dewsbury, 1827, until his death 4 March, 1858, aged 62).

Paine, Marshall Harcourt, 3s. John Marshall, of Addlestone, Surrey, arm. MERTON COLL., matric. 3 June, 1881, aged 18; B.A. 1884, a student of the Inner Temple 1884. **[20]**

Paine, William Henry, 1s. William Stephen, of London, arm. MAGDALEN COLL., matric. 21 Jan., 1882, aged 18; B.A. 1885.

Paine, William Worship, 3s. Thomas, of London, arm. NEW COLL., matric. 16 Oct., 1880, aged 18; B.A. 1884.

Painter, John, s. John, of St. Paul's, Shadwell, Middlesex, gent. ST. JOHN'S COLL., matric. 14 Dec., 1733, aged 17; B.A. 1737. See *Robinson*, 72.

Paitson, Leonard William, o.s. John, of Nether Wasdale, Cumberland, cler. LINCOLN COLL., matric. 20 Oct., 1881, aged 18.

Pakenham, Francis John, 7s. Thomas Michael, Earl of Longford. CHRIST CHURCH, matric. 17 Oct., 1849, aged 17; envoy extraordinary and minister plenipotentiary Buenos Ayres 1885. See Foster's *Peerage*. **[25]**

Pakenham, Rev. and Hon. Henry Robert, 5s. Thomas, Earl of Longford. BRASENOSE COLL., matric. 9 June, 1841, aged 18; B.A. 1845, M.A. 1853, died 7 April, 1856. See Foster's *Peerage*.

Pakenham, Thomas, s. Edward, of Westmeath, Ireland, arm. QUEEN'S COLL., matric. 11 July, 1729, aged 16; M.P. Longford borough 1745, until created Baron of Longford in Ireland 27 April, 1756, died 20 April, 1776. See Foster's *Peerage*.

Pakenham, Thomas, Lord Pakenham, 1s. William Lygon, Earl of Longford. CHRIST CHURCH, matric. 14 Oct., 1881, aged 16; B.A. 1885, 4th Earl of Longford 1887. See Foster's *Peerage*.

Pakenham, Thomas Cecil, 3s. Thomas Alexander, of Emsworth, Hants, arm. NEW COLL., matric. 12 Oct., 1883, aged 19; B.A. 1886. See Foster's *Peerage*.

Pakenham, William Lygon, 2s. Thomas, Earl of Longford. ORIEL COLL., matric. 4 May, 1836, aged 17; 3rd earl, G.C.B., general in the army 1881, under-secretary for war 1866-8, died 19 April 1887. See Foster's *Peerage*. **[30]**

Pakington, Herbert, s. Herbert, of Westwood, co. Worcester, baronet. TRINITY COLL., matric. 17 July, 1784, aged 18; brother of John 1778.

Pakington, Herbert Perrot Murray, 2s. John, of London (city), baronet (after baron). MERTON COLL., matric. 26 Jan., 1867, aged 18; B.A. 1870, M.A. 1875, bar.-at-law, Inner Temple, 1876. See Foster's *Men at the Bar*.

Pakington, (Sir) John (Bart.), s. Herbert, of Westwood, co. Worcester, baronet. WORCESTER COLL., matric. 8 July, 1778, aged 18; B.C.L. from ALL SOULS' COLL. 1786, 8th baronet, died 6 Jan., 1830.

Pakington, John Slaney, 1s. John Somerset, of Powick, co. Worcester, arm. (after baron). CHRIST CHURCH, matric. 16 Oct., 1844, aged 18 B.A. 1847, M.A. 1865, 2nd Baron Hampton, a student of Inner Temple 1846. See Foster's *Peerage* & *Eton School Lists*.

Pakington, John Somerset, s. William Russell, of Slaughter's Court, Powick, co. Worcester, arm. ORIEL COLL., matric. 13 Feb., 1818, aged 18; created D.C.L. 7 June, 1853, Baron Hampton, so created 6 March, 1874, created a baronet 13 July, 1846, G.C.B. 1859, M.P. Droitwich 1837-74, colonial secretary 1852, 1st lord of the Admiralty 1858-9, 1866-7, secretary of War 1867-8, etc., assumed the name of PAKINGTON in lieu of RUSSELL, died 9 April, 1880. See Foster's *Peerage* & *Eton School Lists*. **[35]**

Pakington, Thomas, s. John, of Westwood, co. Worcester, baronet. BALLIOL COLL., matric. 7 April, 1715, aged 19; died in Rome 1724.

Palairet, Rev. Charles, 2s. John, of Bath (city), arm. WADHAM COLL., matric. 26 June, 1821, aged 17; Michel exhibitioner QUEEN'S COLL. 1822-4, B.A. 1825, scholar 1824-7, fellow 1827-39, M.A. 1828.

Palairet, Henry Hamilton, 1s. Septimus Henry, of Bradford, Wilts, gent. EXETER COLL., matric. 26 May, 1863, aged 18; B.A. 1868, M.A. 1880, of Cattistock Lodge, Dorset, J.P. See *Eton School Lists.*

Palairet, Richard, 3s. John, of Walcot, Somerset, arm. WORCESTER COLL., matric. 6 Nov., 1824, aged 18; B.A. 1828, M.A. 1846, vicar of Norton St. Philip, Bath, 1837-66, preb. of Wells, 1855.

Palairet, Septimus Harry, s. John Walter, of Walcot, Bath (city), arm. WORCESTER COLL., matric. 14 Oct., 1825, aged 18; B.A. 1829.

Palatiano, Henry Leonidas Hartley de, o.s. Demetrius, of Athens, arm. EXETER COLL., matric. 2 June, 1857, aged 18; B.A. from CHARSLEY HALL 1865.

Paley, Algernon Herbert, 2s. Thomas, of Bowling, Yorks, arm. EXETER COLL., matric. 11 June, 1862, aged 18; B.A. 1867, bar.-at-law, Lincoln's Inn, 1872. See Foster's *Men at the Bar.* **[5]**

Paley, Edmund, s. William, archdeacon of Carlisle. QUEEN'S COLL., matric. 11 July, 1801, aged 18; B.A. 1805, M.A. 1808, vicar of Cawthorne, Yorks, 1809, rector of Gretford, co. Lincoln, 1837, until his death 1850.

Paley, James, s. William, archdeacon of Carlisle. QUEEN'S COLL., matric. 17 March, 1807, aged 22 (? B.A. from MAGDALEN COLL., Camb., 1813), vicar of Laycock, Wilts, 1814, until his death 9 Dec., 1863.

Paley, Thomas, 2s. John Green, of Bradford, Yorks, arm. UNIVERSITY COLL., matric. 5 Nov., 1821, aged 18; B.A. 1825, M.A. 1828, bar.-at-law, Lincoln's Inn, 1828.

Palgrave, Augustine Gifford, o.s. Reginald Francis Douce, of Reigate, Surrey, arm. MERTON COLL., matric. 21 April, 1885, aged 19.

Palgrave, Francis Milnes Temple, o.s. Francis Turner, of London, arm. TRINITY COLL., matric. 15 Oct., 1883, aged 19; B.A. 1887. **[10]**

Palgrave, Francis Turner, 1s. Francis, of Yarmouth, Norfolk, equitis. BALLIOL COLL., matric. 1 Dec., 1842, aged 18, scholar 1842-7; fellow EXETER COLL. 1847-62, B.A. 1851, M.A. 1856, professor of poetry 1885, vice-principal Kneller Hall, created LL.D. Edinburgh 23 April, 1878, assist.-sec. Education Department; for lists of works see *Boase*, 137.

Palgrave, William Gifford, 2s. Francis, of St. Margaret's, Westminster (city), equitis. TRINITY COLL., matric. 12 June, 1843, aged 17; scholar 1843-7, F.R.G.S., the celebrated traveller, consul-general Bulgaria 1879, Siam 1879, minister residentiary and consul-general in Uruguay 1884, author of several works.

Palin, Edward, o.s. Richard, of St. Luke's, Middlesex, gent. ST. JOHN'S COLL., matric. 26 June, 1843, aged 17; scholar & fellow 1843-66, B.A. 1848, M.A. 1851, B.D. 1856, lecturer 1859-64, dean of arts 1853, lecturer 1855, vice-president & tutor 1860, bursar 1862, public examiner 1861-2, perp. curate of Summertown, Oxford, 1856-60, vicar of Linton, co. Hereford, 1865. See *Robinson*, 268.

Palin, William, 7s. Richard, of Mortlake, Surrey, gent. ST. ALBAN HALL, matric. 17 Dec., 1829, aged 27; B.A. from TRINITY COLL., Cambridge, 1834, M.A. 1851, adm. 'comitatis causa' 21 June, 1861, rector of Stifford, Essex, 1834, until his death 16 Oct., 1882.

Paliologus, Nicholas Lower, 1s. Nicholas, of Calcutta, gent. PEMBROKE COLL., matric. 29 Oct., 1874, aged 18; B.A. from CHARSLEY HALL 1884, M.A. 1885, bar.-at-law, Inner Temple, 1880. See Foster's *Men at the Bar* & *Rugby School Reg.* **[15]**

Palk, Arthur George, 5s. Laurence, of Kenn, Devon, baronet. CHRIST CHURCH, matric. 20 April, 1826, aged 19; B.A. 1830, curate of Owston, Yorks, died 27 Nov., 1835. See Foster's *Peerage*, B. HALDON; & *Eton School Lists.*

Palk, Ashley, 1s. Robert John Malet, of Park Square, London, arm. UNIVERSITY COLL., matric. 1 Dec., 1852, aged 18; B.A. 1857, a student of the Inner Temple 1857, died 7 Oct., 1860. See Foster's *Peerage* & *Eton School Lists.*

Palk, Augustus, 3s. Laurence, of Kenn, Devon, baronet. EXETER COLL., matric. 30 June, 1843, aged 17; died 13 Sep., 1876.

Palk, (Hon.) Edward Arthur, 4s. Laurence, of London, baronet (after Lord Haldon). CHRIST CHURCH, matric. 11 Oct., 1872, aged 18; a student of the Inner Temple 1875. See Foster's *Peerage.*

Palk, Henry Laurence, 2s. Laurence Vaughan, of Dunchideock, Devon, baronet. ST. MARY HALL, matric. 14 May, 1840, aged 21; rector of Dunchideock with Shillingford 1846, and of Bridford, Devon, 1846, until his death 17 April, 1872. See Foster's *Peerage*, B. HALDON. **[20]**

Palk, Jonathan, s. Walter, of Ashburton, Devon, gent. EXETER COLL., matric. 9 May, 1780, aged 18; B.A. 1784.

Palk, (Sir) Laurence (Bart.), s. Robert, of Madras, East Indies, baronet. CHRIST CHURCH, matric. 29 March, 1784, aged 18; 2nd baronet, M.P. Ashburton 1787-96, Devonshire 1796-1812, died 20 June, 1813. See Foster's *Peerage*, B. HALDON.

Palk, Laurence Hesketh, 1s. Lawrence, of Kenn, Devon, baronet (after a baron). CHRIST CHURCH, matric. 14 Oct., 1864, aged 18; 2nd Baron Haldon. See Foster's *Peerage* & *Eton School Lists.*

Palk, (Sir) Laurence Vaughan (Bart.), s. Laurence, of St. George's, Hanover Square, Westminster, baronet. CHRIST CHURCH, matric. 29 Jan., 1812, aged 18; 3rd baronet, M.P. Ashburton 1818-31, died 16 May, 1860. See Foster's *Peerage* & *Eton School Lists.*

Palk, (Sir) Robert (Bart.), s. Walter, of Ashburton, Devon, pleb. WADHAM COLL., matric. 15 April, 1736, aged 18; B.A. 1739, governor of Madras 1763, M.P. Ashburton 1767-8 and 1774-87, Wareham 1768-72, created a baronet 19 June, 1782, died 29 April, 1798, ancestor of Lord Haldon. **[25]**

Palk, Robert, s. Robert, of Calcutta, East Indies, arm. ORIEL COLL., matric. 5 March, 1798, aged 17 (? a brother of Laurence 1784).

Pallavicino, Charles Alfred Alexander Manfrid Luserna d'Angrogno-, Marquis, 2s. Alexander Manfrid, Marquis, etc. CHRIST CHURCH, matric. 6 Nov., 1883, aged 18.

Pallett, Rev. Thomas Carter, 1s. Samuel Thomas, of Christ Church, London, gent. MAGDALEN HALL, matric. 15 April, 1856, aged 17; scholar LINCOLN COLL. 1857-60, B.A. 1860, M.A. 1862.

Palling, Edward, 2s. John, of Painswick, co. Gloucester, gent. QUEEN'S COLL., matric. 26 Oct., 1820, aged 18; B.A. 1824, M.A. 1827, perp. curate Tithby, etc., Notts, 1827-8, vicar of Cuckney, Notts, 1828, until his death in 1843.

Palliser, Joseph Marryat, 4s. Richard, of Dover, Kent, arm. PEMBROKE COLL., matric. 21 Oct., 1859, aged 16. **[30]**

Pallmer, Charles, s. John, of Isle of Jamaica, arm. ST. MARY HALL, matric. 30 March, 1763, aged 19.

Pallmer, Charles Nicholas, created D.C.L. 18 June, 1817, M.P. Ludgershall June, 1815, to June, 1817, Surrey 1826-30.

Palmer, Rev. Albert Reynolds, of JESUS COLL., Cambridge (LL.B. 1867, LL.M. 1870); adm. 'comitatis causa' 7 June, 1866.

Palmer, Alfred Zouch, 1s. William, of Marylebone, London, arm. MAGDALEN COLL., matric. 6 July, 1827, aged 18.

Palmer, Arthur, s. Charles, of Cranbury House, Middlesex, arm. UNIVERSITY COLL., matric. 16 Oct., 1759, aged 16. **[35]**

Palmer, Benjamin, s. Benjamin, of Solihull, co. Warwick, arm. ORIEL COLL., matric. 21 Feb., 1727-8, aged 16; B.A. from BALLIOL COLL. 1731, bar.-at-law, Middle Temple, 1733.

Palmer, Charles, s. Thomas, of ——, Salop, gent. UNIVERSITY COLL., matric. 3 July, 1731, aged 17; B.A. 1735, M.A. 1738, B.Med. 1741.

Palmer, Charles, s. John, of St. Michael's, Gloucester (city), cler. PEMBROKE COLL., matric. 9 April, 1777, aged 16; B.A. 1781, M.A. 1783, vicar of St. Mary-de-Lode, Gloucester, 1817-9, vicar of Churcham 1819, and perp. curate Quedgeley 1817, until his death in 1824.

Palmer, Charles, s. Charles, of Westminster (city), arm. WADHAM COLL., matric. 19 Nov., 1789, aged 18.

Palmer, Charles, s. John, of Bath, Somerset, arm. ORIEL COLL., matric. 16 Oct., 1793, aged 16; general in the army, M.P. Bath 1808-26, 1829, 1830-7, died 17 April, 1851. See *Eton School Lists*. His father died in 1818; see *Gent.'s Mag.*, 1818, i. 276.

Palmer, Charles, s. Charles, of Ladbroke, co. Warwick, arm. CHRIST CHURCH, matric. 28 Jan., 1801, aged 18; B.A. 1805, M.A. 1808, rector of Lighthorne and perp. curate Chesterton 1843, until his death 13 Feb., 1871. See Foster's *Peerage*, E. SELBORNE. [5]

Palmer, Charles Archdale, 2s. Charles Thomas, of Wanlip, co. Leicester, baronet. CHRIST CHURCH, matric. 17 Dec., 1831, aged 18; student 1831-8, B.A. 1835, M.A. 1838, rector of Wanlip 1837, until his death 27 March, 1860. See Foster's *Baronetage*.

Palmer, (Sir) Charles Harcourt (Bart.), s. Charles, of Dorney Court, Bucks. MAGDALEN COLL., matric. 14 Nov., 1777, aged 17; 6th baronet, died unmarried 1838 (father of Henry 1814, and John 1812). See Foster's *Baronetage*, CHAOS; & *Gent.'s Mag.*, 1833, i. 134.

Palmer, Charles Samuel, 5s. Henry, of Carlton Curlieu, co. Leicester, cler. EXETER COLL., matric. 22 June, 1848, aged 18; B.A. 1854, M.A. 1855, perp. curate Owston and rector of Withcote, co. Leicester, 1855-66, rector of Eardisley, co. Hereford, 1866. See Foster's *Baronetage*.

Palmer, (Sir) Charles Thomas (Bart.), s. Charles Grave Hudson, of London, arm. (after a baronet). CHRIST CHURCH, matric. 21 Oct., 1789, aged 18; B.A. 1794, 2nd baronet, a student of Lincoln's Inn 1793, assumed the surname and arms of PALMER only, by royal sign manual in 1813, died 30 April, 1827. See Foster's *Baronetage*.

Palmer, Charles Thomas, 1s. Charles Archdale, of Wanlip, co. Leicester, cler. EXETER COLL., matric. 23 May, 1861, aged 18; of Newland House, co. Gloucester. See Foster's *Baronetage*. [10]

Palmer, Edmund Charles, 3s. John, of Sydney, New South Wales, gent. WORCESTER COLL., matric. 20 March, 1857, aged 19; bar.-at-law, Inner Temple (as Charles Edmund), 1864, died 3 Feb., 1877.

Palmer, Edmund Richard Hopper Griffith, s. Charles, of Thurnscoe, Yorks, arm. QUEEN'S COLL., matric. 18 Nov., 1814, aged 19; B.A. 1818, M.A. 1869, rector of Greetham 1848-9, vicar of North Somercotes 1849-64, rector of South Somercotes 1864, until his death 24 Oct., 1886.

Palmer, Edward, s. Samuel, of Charlton, Dorset, cler. MERTON COLL., matric. 18 May, 1727, aged 18; B.A. 1732.

Palmer, Edward Davidson, 2s. Alfred William, of London, gent. NEW COLL., matric. 5 Feb., 1877, aged 30; B.Mus. 28 Nov., 1878.

Palmer, Edward, s. Edward, of Coleshill, co. Warwick, gent. ST. JOHN'S COLL., matric. 21 Oct., 1775, aged 18; B.A. 1779, perp. curate Moseley, co. Worcester, 40 years, and vicar of Stoke Courcy, Somerset, 1788, until his death 15 May, 1826 (father of William, perp. curate Lea Marston 1817, and vicar of Polesworth, co. Warwick, 1824, until his death 23 Jan., 1841). [15]

Palmer, Edwin, 4s. William Jocelyn, of Mixbury, Oxon, cler. BALLIOL COLL., matric. 25 Nov., 1841, aged 17; scholar 1841-5, B.A. 1845, fellow 1845-67, M.A. 1850, senior dean 1855, catechetical and philosophy lecturer, hon. fellow 1871; fellow Corpus Christi College 1870-8, vice-president 1877, hon. fellow 1878, Corpus professor of Latin literature 1870-8, archdeacon of Oxford, and a canon of CHRIST CHURCH 1877, D.D. (by decree) 7 May, 1878, select preacher 1865-6, 1873-4. See Foster's *Peerage*, E. SELBORNE.

Palmer, Felix, 3s. Philip, of St. Martin's, Westminster (city), gent. WADHAM COLL., matric. 19 Nov., 1840, aged 19; B.A. from BRASENOSE COLL. 1844, M.A. 1847, curate of Loughton, Essex, died 24 Jan., 1865.

Palmer, Felix Henry Price, 1s. Felix, of Loughton, Essex, cler. LINCOLN COLL., matric. 24 May, 1877, aged 19; B.A. 1882, M.A. 1885.

Palmer, Francis, s. William, of Kilmington, Somerset, cler. MAGDALEN HALL, matric. 12 Dec., 1799, aged 23 (? rector of Comb Pyne, Devon, 1805, or rector of Alcester, co. Warwick, 1807, until death 1 Dec., 1842).

Palmer, Francis, 3s. George, of Hadham, Herts, arm. CHRIST CHURCH, matric. 5 June, 1828, aged 17; B.A. 1832, bar.-at-law, Inner Temple, 1853. See Foster's *Men at the Bar*. [20]

Palmer, Francis, y.s. John Henry, of Rockingham, Northants, baronet. BRASENOSE COLL., matric. 12 March, 1846, aged 17; postmaster MERTON COLL. 1846-50, B.A. 1850, M.A. 1853, perp. curate St. George's Chapel, Albemarle Street, London, 1866. See Foster's *Baronetage* & *Eton School Lists*.

Palmer, Francis Beaufort, o.s. William, of London (city), cler. UNIVERSITY COLL., matric. 2 Dec., 1863, aged 18; bar.-at-law, Inner Temple, 1873. See Foster's *Men at the Bar*.

Palmer, Frederick William Henry, 2s. Jabez, of Dundee, Scotland, gent. NON-COLL., matric. 16 Oct., 1868, aged 18, B.A. 1871; M.A. from LINCOLN COLL. 1875, head-master Snettisham Grammar School 1875.

Palmer, (Sir) Geoffrey (Bart.), 1s. John Henry, of Skeffington, co. Leicester, baronet. CHRIST CHURCH, matric. 12 Dec., 1827, aged 18; B.A. 1830, 8th baronet, bar.-at-law, Inner Temple, 1838. See Foster's *Baronetage* & *Eton School Lists*.

Palmer, George, s. Edward, of Chadworth, co. Gloucester, pleb. ST. JOHN'S COLL., matric. 31 March, 1721, aged 19. [25]

Palmer, George Fortescue, 1s. Daniel, of Barnstaple, Devon, cler. WORCESTER COLL., matric. 8 Dec., 1819, aged 18.

Palmer, George Horsley, 3s. William Jocelyn, of Mixbury, Oxon, cler. EXETER COLL., matric. 16 Nov., 1843, aged 21; B.A. 1847, M.A. 1850, rector of Mixbury 1852-81. See Foster's *Peerage*, E. SELBORNE.

Palmer, George Hudson, 2s. George Joseph, of Wanlip, co. Leicester, baronet. BALLIOL COLL., matric. 31 Oct., 1859, aged 18; B.A. 1864, bar.-at-law, Lincoln's Inn, 1871. See Foster's *Men at the Bar*.

Palmer, (Sir) George Joseph (Bart.), 1s. Charles Thomas Hudson, of Wanlip, co. Leicester, baronet. CHRIST CHURCH, matric. 7 April, 1830, aged 18; 3rd baronet, died 22 Feb., 1866.

Palmer, Rev. George Thomas, 2s. George, of Christ Church, Surrey, arm. BRASENOSE COLL., matric. 31 May, 1820, aged 17; B.A. 1824, M.A. 1827, bar.-at-law, Lincoln's Inn, 1827, died 25 Dec., 1882.

Palmer, Gerard Walker, 3s. William James, of Langharne, co. Carmarthen, arm. KEBLE COLL., matric. 16 Oct., 1883, aged 18; B.A. 1886. [31]

Palmer, Greville Horsley, 1s. Edward Horsley, of London (city), arm. MAGDALEN COLL., matric. 23 Jan., 1864, aged 18; B.A. 1868. See Foster's *Peerage*, E. SELBORNE.

Palmer, Henry, s. Thomas, of St. Dionis, London, gent. ST. JOHN'S COLL., matric. 1 Feb., 1800, aged 19; B.A. 1804, M.A. 1806, died rector of Oare, Sussex, 7 Sep., 1815. See Foster's *Peerage*, E. SELBORNE.

Palmer, Henry, s. William, of Newington, Oxon, doctor. WORCESTER COLL., matric. 29 June, 1813, aged 16; B.A. 1820, perp. curate Broadway, co. Worcester, 1823, rector of Crichet Malherbe 1842, until his death 24 Feb., 1855.

Palmer, Henry, s. Charles, of Dorney, Bucks, baronet. CHRIST CHURCH, matric. 27 Jan., 1814, aged 16; B.A. 1817, M.A. 1820, vicar of Dorney 1832-56, died 20 Nov., 1865. See *Gent.'s Mag.*, 1866, i. 134.

Palmer, Henry, 3s. Richard, of Hurst, Berks, arm. CHRIST CHURCH, matric. 30 March, 1819, aged 19; B.A. 1822, M.A. 1826, rector of Little Laver, Essex, 1824, until his death 30 Oct., 1870.

Palmer, Henry, o.s. Henry, of St. Elizabeth, Isle of Jamaica, gent. MAGDALEN HALL, matric. 30 March 1830, aged 17. **[5]**

Palmer, Henry Edmund Michell, 4s. George Thomas, of Paramatta, Australia, arm. LINCOLN COLL., matric. 24 Nov., 1838, aged 17.

Palmer, Henry James, 4s. George Josiah, of Clapham, Surrey, gent. MAGDALEN COLL., matric. 16 Nov., 1854, aged 20; B.A. from MAGDALEN HALL 1861, M.A. 1867, incumbent of St. Mary's, Aberdeen, 1866-8, of St. Columba, Edinburgh, 1869-72, head-master Claremount School, Wallasey, 1872-84, vicar of Christ Church, Ashton-under-Lyne, 1884.

Palmer, Henry Marson, 1s. — P., of London, cler. LINCOLN COLL., matric. 11 June, 1859, aged 18; scholar 1859-63.

Palmer, Henry Norton, o.s. Henry Norton, of Old Buckenham, Norfolk, arm. WADHAM COLL., matric. 27 Nov., 1861, aged 18.

Palmer, Herbert, 1s. James Howard, of Bradfield, Berks, cler. MAGDALEN COLL., matric. 21 Oct., 1886, aged 19. **[10]**

Palmer, Hurly Pring, 2s. William, of Taunton, Somerset, arm. ST. MARY HALL, matric. 15 May, 1875, aged 18; B.A. from WADHAM COLL. 1879, M.A. 1885.

Palmer, Rev. James, s. William, of St. James's, Westminster (city), arm. ORIEL COLL., matric. 19 May, 1795, aged 23; B.A. 1799, M.A. 1801, killed by a fall from his horse 16 March, 1808.

Palmer, Rev. James Howard, 1s. John, of Claines, co. Worcester, cler. EXETER COLL., matric. 24 June, 1859, aged 17; B.A. 1862, M.A. 1866, assistant-master St. Andrew's College, Bradfield, 1862-9.

Palmer, James Nelson, o.s. James, of Headington, Oxon, cler. ST. JOHN'S COLL., matric. 4 May, 1821, aged 18; B.A. 1825, M.A. 1829, rector of Breamore, Hants, 1838, until his death 5 Nov., 1864.

Palmer, James Nelson, o.s. James, of Edmonton, Middlesex, cler. ST. JOHN'S COLL., matric. 6 March, 1850, aged 18; B.A. 1856, M.A. 1857, curate of Breamore, Hants, 1861-4, rector 1864-8. See *Eton School Lists.* **[15]**

Palmer, John, s. John, of Grafton Flyford, co. Worcester, gent. QUEEN'S COLL., matric. 5 July, 1723, aged 17; bar.-at-law, Middle Temple, 1730, died 22 Feb., 1734.

Palmer, John, s. John, of Gloucester (city), pleb. PEMBROKE COLL., matric. 5 Dec., 1734, aged 18; B.A. 1738, M.A. 1742.

Palmer, John, s. John, of Ilchester, Somerset, gent. WADHAM COLL., matric. 11 April, 1764, aged 17.

Palmer, John, s. John, of Bristol (city), gent. ST. ALBAN HALL, matric. 14 March, 1780, aged 30; B.C.L. from WADHAM COLL. 1795. **[19]**

Palmer, John, s. Charles Harcourt, of Dorney Court, Bucks, baronet. BRASENOSE COLL., matric. 6 Nov., 1812, aged 17; died in 1852, brother of Henry 1814. See *Herald and Genealogist*, vol. v., pp. 88 & 377-8.

Palmer, John, o.s. James, of Norton, co. Worcester, gent. WORCESTER COLL., matric. 17 Nov., 1826, aged 18; B.A. 1830, M.A. 1835, vicar of Bromyard, co. Hereford, 1855, until his death 15 Sep., 1867.

Palmer, John Cook, s. John, of Sutton Montacute, Somerset, cler. ST. MARY HALL, matric. 2 May, 1799, aged 18; B.C.L. & D.C.L. 1814.

Palmer, John Fox, s. William, of Alvechurch, co. Worcester, gent. WORCESTER COLL., matric. 30 June, 1792, aged 19; B.A. 1796, died chaplain of Moseley, co. Worcester, in 1826.

Palmer, (Sir) John Henry (Bart.), 1s. John, of Carlton, Northants, baronet. MAGDALEN COLL., matric. 11 July, 1795, aged 20; B.A. 1799, 7th baronet, died 26 Aug., 1865. See Foster's *Baronetage.*

Palmer, John Howard, 2s. John, of Lincoln, gent. EXETER COLL., matric. 18 Oct., 1882, aged 19; scholar 1882-6, B.A. 1886. **[25]**

Palmer, Jordan (Roquette Palmer), 3s. Arthur, of Bristol, Somerset, arm. LINCOLN COLL., matric. 10 June, 1847, aged 18; B.A. 1851, M.A. 1854, chaplain Royal Asylum of St. Anne 1861-75, F.S.A., F.R.G.S., died 30 April, 1885.

Palmer, Joseph, s. John, of Torrington, Devon, gent. EXETER COLL., matric. 19 March, 1766, aged 16; B.A. 1770, M.A. 1772, 'minister' of the Temple Church, London, chancellor of Ferns 1779-1801, precentor of Waterford 1801-29, dean of Cashel 1787, until his death at Bath 1 May, 1829.

Palmer, Joseph Blades, 3s. Benjamin, of Clapham, Surrey, gent. WORCESTER COLL., matric. 12 Oct., 1867, aged 18; B.A. 1871, held various curacies 1877-86, vicar of Easby, Yorks, 1886.

Palmer, Lewis Henry, 2s. John Henry, of Carlton, Northants, baronet. CHRIST CHURCH, matric. 20 Oct., 1836, aged 18; B.A. 1840, M.A. 1844, rector of East Carlton 1872-8. See Foster's *Baronetage.*

Palmer, Lyttelton, s. Samuel, of Brompton, co. Hereford, cler. CHRIST CHURCH, matric. 17 Dec., 1741, aged 18; B.A. 1745, M.A. 1748, rector of Corwen, co. Merioneth, 1748, until his death 29 Oct., 1749.

Palmer, Nicholas, s. Henry, of Plymouth, Devon, pleb. EXETER COLL., matric. 20 March, 1724-5, aged 18; B.A. 1729. **[31]**

Palmer, Peregrine, s. Nath., of Stoke Courcy, Somerset, BALLIOL COLL., matric. 3 July, 1719, aged 16, B.A. 1723; M.A. from ALL SOULS' COLL. 1727, created D.C.L. 12 April, 1749, then of Fairfield, Somerset, and M.P. for the University 1745, until his death 30 Nov., 1762.

Palmer, Ralph, s. Ralph, of Chelsea, Middlesex, arm. QUEEN'S COLL., matric. 14 May, 1730, aged 17.

Palmer, Ralph, s. William, of Devonshire Square, London, arm. CHRIST CHURCH, matric. 19 Nov., 1800, aged 17; B.A. 1804, bar.-at-law, Middle Temple, 1808, chief justice and commissary of the Vice-Admiralty Court, Madras, died in 1838. See Foster's *Peerage*, E. SELBORNE.

Palmer, Ralph Charlton, 3s. George, of Knightsbridge, London, arm. BALLIOL COLL., matric. 19 Oct., 1857, aged 18; B.A. 1862, bar.-at-law, Lincoln's Inn, 1864, clerk of the Crown in Chancery since 1880. See Foster's *Men at the Bar.* **[35]**

Palmer, Richard, s. Joshua, of Somersal-Herbert, co. Derby, pleb. QUEEN'S COLL., matric. 10 July, 1761, aged 21.

Palmer, Richard, s. Richard, of Hurst, Berks, arm. CHRIST CHURCH, matric. 1 June, 1813, aged 17; student 1813-25, B.A. 1816, M.A. 1819, a student of Lincoln's Inn 1819, rector of Blaby, co. Leicester, 1824-45, and of Purley, Berks, 1844, until his death 25 Oct., 1874. See *Alumni West.*, 476.

Palmer, Richard Frederick, 1s. Richard, of Newton Bushell, Devon, arm. EXETER COLL., matric. 22 Oct., 1859, aged 18; B.A. from NEW INN HALL 1865, M.A. 1866, rector of Clopton, Suffolk, 1868, until his death 8 May, 1879.

Palmer, Rev. Richard Thomas, 5s. John Henry, of Carlton, Northants, baronet. UNIVERSITY COLL., matric. 26 Nov., 1845, aged 18; B.A. 1849, M.A. 1852, died 19 Sep., 1861. See Foster's *Baronetage* & *Eton School Lists*.

Palmer, Rodber, 5s. George Thomas, of Paramatta, Australia, arm. ST. MARY HALL, matric. 22 June, 1843, aged 19.

Palmer, (Sir) Roger William Henry (Bart.), 1s. Roger, of Chester (city), baronet. CHRIST CHURCH, matric. 23 May, 1850, aged 18; 5th baronet, major-general in the army, commanded 2nd life guards, M.P. co. Mayo 1857-65. See Foster's *Baronetage* & *Eton School Lists*.

Palmer, Roundell, 2s. William Jocelyn, of Mixbury, Oxon, cler. CHRIST CHURCH, matric. 3 May, 1830, aged 17; scholar TRINITY COLL. 1830-4, B.A. 1834; fellow MAGDALEN COLL. 1834-48, M.A. 1836, hon. fellow 1862, created D.C.L. 2 July, 1862; hon. student Christ Church 1867, hon. LL.D. Cambridge, bar.-at-law, Lincoln's Inn, 1837, Q.C. and a bencher 1849, M.P. Plymouth 1847-52 & 1853-7, Richmond 1861-72, deputy steward Oxford University, and counsel to Oxford University 1861-3, solicitor-general 1861-3, knighted 5 Aug., 1861, attorney-general 1863-6, etc., lord high chancellor of Great Britain 1872-4 & 1880-5, created Baron Selborne 23 Oct., 1872, and Earl of Selborne and Viscount Wolmer 30 Dec., 1883. See Foster's *Men at the Bar*. [5]

Palmer, Rev. Rowland John, o.s. John Macquorie, of Petersham, Australia, arm. MAGDALEN HALL, matric. 20 Oct., 1868, aged 17; B.A. & M.A. from NEW INN HALL 1881.

Palmer, Samborne Stucley, o.s. Samborne, of Chumleigh, Devon, arm. EXETER COLL., matric. 12 Feb., 1821, aged 18; B.A. 1825.

Palmer, Samuel, s. Samuel, of Wyley, Wilts, cler. MERTON COLL., matric. 2 May, 1729, aged 18; B.A. 7 March, 1732-3, M.A. 25 Feb., 1735-6.

Palmer, Thomas, s. Thomas, of Isle of Barbados, arm. TRINITY COLL., matric. 24 Sep., 1720, aged 17.

Palmer, Thomas, s. Samuel, of Wickham, Hants, cler. NEW COLL., matric. 10 Dec., 1720, aged 18; B.C.L. 1728, D.C.L. 1732. [10]

Palmer, Thomas, s. John, of St. John's, Hereford (city), pleb. BRASENOSE COLL., matric. 28 March, 1724, aged 17; B.A. 1727.

Palmer, Rev. Thomas, s. Thomas, of London (city), gent. ST. JOHN'S COLL., matric. 6 July, 1790, aged 17; B.A. 1794, M.A. 1797, died at Dawlish 4 Jan., 1798.

Palmer, Thomas, 1s. Thomas, of Swindon, Wilts, gent. NEW COLL., matric. 5 Feb., 1877, aged 36; B.Mus. 1879.

Palmer, Walter Harvey, y.s. James, of Clifton, Somerset, gent. NEW COLL., matric. 19 Oct., 1874, aged 36.

Palmer, William, s. William, of Twining, co. Gloucester, gent. CHRIST CHURCH, matric. 21 March, 1729-30, aged 19; B.A. 1733. [15]

Palmer, William, s. William, of Combe Rawleigh, Devon, cler. EXETER COLL., matric. 3 April, 1750, aged 17; B.A. 1753, M.A. 1756.

Palmer, William, s. Charles, of Ladbroke, co. Warwick, arm. MAGDALEN COLL., matric. 8 May, 1754, aged 18; created M.A. 4 July, 1758, died unmarried.

Palmer, William, 'manciple of All Souls' College;' privilegiatus 26 Jan., 1762.

Palmer, William, o.s. Eliakim, of St. Peter's, London, gent. UNIVERSITY COLL. matric. 16 April, 1766, aged 17; created M.A. 9 July, 1773.

Palmer, William, s. William, of Chardstock, Dorset, cler. WORCESTER COLL., matric. 7 March, 1788, aged 17; B.A. from BALLIOL COLL. 1791, M.A. 1794, B. & D.D. 1812, vicar of Yarcombe, Devon, 1800, until his death 19 Nov., 1853. [20]

Palmer, William, s. William, of St. Botolph's, London, arm. ST. EDMUND HALL, matric. 13 Nov., 1795, aged 24; B.A. 1801 (? bar.-at-law, Lincoln's Inn, 1810; his father captain H.E.I.C.S.).

Palmer-Morewood, William, s. Charles, of Ladbroke, co. Warwick, arm. MAGDALEN COLL., matric. 6 Dec., 1797, aged 16, of Alfreton Hall, co. Derby, and of Ladbroke, co. Warwick, assumed the additional surname of MOREWOOD 1825, died 23 Feb., 1863.

Palmer, William, 2s. George, of St. Andrew's, Holborn, London, arm. ST. MARY HALL, matric. 16 Feb., 1822, aged 19; B.A. 1825, M.A. 1828, bar.-at-law, Inner Temple, 1830, professor civil law Gresham College, died 24 April, 1858. See Foster's *Peerage*, E. SELBORNE.

Palmer, William, 1s. William Jocelyn, of Mixbury, Oxon, cler. MAGDALEN COLL., matric. 27 July, 1826, aged 15; demy 1826-32, B.A. 1831, M.A. 1833, fellow 1832-55, bursar 1836, college tutor 1838-43, prælector of moral philosophy 1842, vice-president 1844, University examiner 1837-9, an Eastern traveller, tutor and censor, and member of the senate of Durham University 1833-6, joined the Church of Rome in 1855, died 5 April, 1879. See *Coll. Reg.*, vii. 297; & *Rugby School Reg.*, 147.

Palmer, William Henry, 4s. Edmund, of Brighton (town), gent. EXETER COLL., matric. 14 May, 1851, aged 17. [25]

Palmer, William James, 1s. James, of Lichfield, co. Stafford, arm. QUEEN'S COLL., matric. 7 May, 1841, aged 18.

Palmer, William (Jocelyn), s. William, of London (city), arm. BRASENOSE COLL., matric. 22 Feb., 1796, aged 18; B.A. 1799, M.A. 1802, B.D. 1811, rector of Mixbury, Oxon, 1802, and of Finmere 1814, until his death 28 Sep., 1853, father of Roundell, Earl Selborne. See Foster's *Peerage*.

Palmer, William (Patrick), B.A. TRINITY COLL., Dublin, 1824, o.s. William, of St. Mary's, Dublin (city), arm. MAGDALEN HALL, incorp. 20-23 Oct., 1828, aged 25; M.A. 28 Jan., 1829, vicar of Monkton-Wyld 1864-9, and of Whitchurch Canonicorum, Dorset, 1846, died in 1885 (styled himself a baronet).

Palmer, William Waldegrave, Viscount Wolmer, 1s. Roundell, Baron Selborne (after earl). UNIVERSITY COLL., matric. 12 Oct., 1878, aged 18; B.A. 1882, M.P. East (or Petersfield division) Hampshire since 1885.

Palmes, Arthur Lindsay, 2s. William Lindsay, of Hornsea, Yorks, cler. TRINITY COLL., matric. 14 Oct., 1872, aged 19; B.A. 1877, M.A. 1879, a student of Lincoln's Inn 1877, vicar of St. John Baptist, Penzance, 1881-3, and of Bodmin 1883. See Foster's *Yorkshire Collection* & *Rugby School Reg.* [30]

Palmes, George, 1s. William Lindsay, of Hornsea, Yorks, cler. LINCOLN COLL., matric. 18 Oct., 1870, aged 19; scholar 1870-4, B.A. 1875, M.A. 1878, of Naburn Hall, Yorks, a student of Lincoln's Inn 1875, vicar of Hill Farrance, Somerset, 1881-6, rector of Elston, Notts, 1887.

Palmour, John, 1s. John Dawkins, of Loveston, co. Pembroke, cler. JESUS COLL., matric. 4 March, 1852, aged 19; B.A. 1855, M.A. 1869, curate of St. Mary, Lancaster, 1858-73, vicar of Fulwood, Lancashire, 1873.

Panioty, Constantine Demetrius, 3s. Demetrius, of Calcutta, arm. EXETER COLL., matric. 15 May, 1880, aged 20; bar.-at-law, Lincoln's Inn, 1884. See Foster's *Men at the Bar*.

Panizzi, Sir Antonio, principal librarian of the British Museum 1856, created D.C.L. 6 July, 1859; D.C.L. Parma 1818, sentenced to death and his property confiscated (Oct., 1823) by the Italian Government for alleged association with the Carbonari, professor of Italian, University of London, 1828-31, extra assistant-librarian British Museum, keeper of printed books 1837-56, K.C.B. in 1869, died 8 April, 1879.

Pannell, John, s. John, of Bosham, Sussex, gent. ST. JOHN'S COLL., matric. 25 Oct., 1804, aged 19; B.A. from ST. MARY HALL 1809, M.A. 1811, rector of Ludgershall, Wilts, 1824, until his death 12 May, 1872.

Panter, Charles Edward, 2s. John Edward, of Fulham, Middlesex, arm. PEMBROKE COLL., matric. 31 May, 1873, aged 20; B.A. 1878, M.A. 1881, chaplain royal navy 1881.

Panter, Frederick Downes, 1s. John, of Fulham, Middlesex, arm. TRINITY COLL., matric. 15 May, 1827, aged 18; B.A. 1832, chaplain of Rushford, Norfolk, 1848, until his death 10 May, 1878.

Panter, Philip, s. William, of Camberwell, Surrey, gent. TRINITY COLL., matric. 7 Feb., 1804, aged 18; bible clerk ALL SOULS' COLL., B.A. from MAGDALEN HALL 1807, M.A. 1810, 16 years chaplain royal navy, died rector of Nettlecombe, Somerset, 2 Dec., 1832. See *Robinson*, 165. **[5]**

Pantin, Charles, 6s. James, of Middleton Square, London, gent. PEMBROKE COLL., matric. 19 Feb., 1852, aged 17; scholar 1851-3.

Pantin, James Henry, 2s. Thomas Pinder, of Camberwell, Surrey, cler. QUEEN'S COLL., matric. 21 March, 1844, aged 20; clerk 1844-5.

Pantin, John Wickliffe, 3s. Thomas, of Lutterworth, co. Leicester, cler. PEMBROKE COLL., matric. 13 Nov., 1845, aged 19; B.A. 1849, M.A. 1854, rector of Westcote, co. Gloucester, 1866. See *Robinson*, 257.

Pantin, Rev. Thomas, 1s. James Henry, of St. Sepulchre's, London, gent. PEMBROKE COLL., matric. 15 Nov., 1838, aged 18; scholar and exhibitioner 1838-44, B.A. 1843, M.A. 1845, master of the Grammar School, Abingdon, died 16 Sep., 1845.

Pantin, Thomas Pinder, s. Thomas, of St. Sepulchre's, London, arm. QUEEN'S COLL., matric. 24 June, 1817, aged 25; B.A. 1821, M.A. 1827, rector of Westcote, co. Gloucester, 1828, until his death 2 Sep., 1866. **[10]**

Pantin, William Edward Pinder, 1s. Charles, of London, gent. LINCOLN COLL., matric. 29 Jan., 1881, aged 18; scholar 1880-4, B.A. 1885.

Panting, George, s. John, of Brinkworth, Wilts, gent. PEMBROKE COLL., matric. 18 Jan., 1721-2, aged 18.

Panting, John, 4s. Thomas, of Shrewsbury, Salop, gent. MAGDALEN HALL, matric. 10 Oct., 1845, aged 35.

Panting, Matthew, s. Matthew, of St. Aldate's, Oxford (city), doctor. LINCOLN COLL., matric. 30 May, 1745, aged 15; demy MAGDALEN COLL. 1745-9, B.A. 1748; fellow ALL SOULS' COLL. 1749, M.A. 1752, B.D. 1763, rector of Brockhall, Northants, 1775. See *Bloxam*, vii. 266.

Panting, Richard, 5s. Thomas, of Shrewsbury (town), arm. CHRIST CHURCH, matric. 25 Oct., 1832, aged 18; B.A. 1836, M.A. 1839. **[15]**

Panting, Samuel, s. William, of Wootton-under-Edge, co. Gloucester, pleb. ORIEL COLL., matric. 17 Dec., 1755, aged 18; B.A. 1760.

Panting, Stephen, s. Samuel, of Wootton-under-Edge, co. Gloucester, pleb. BALLIOL COLL., matric. 30 March, 1751, aged 18; B.A. from TRINITY COLL. 1754, M.A. 1770.

Panting, Thomas, s. Matthew, of Oxford (city), doctor. LINCOLN COLL., matric. 27 Jan., 1749-50, aged 17; B.A. from MERTON COLL. 1753, M.A. 1765 (? died rector of St. Andrew's, Charlestown, South Carolina, in 1771).

Panting, William (Scott), s. John, of Wooton-under-Edge, co. Gloucester, pleb. ST. JOHN'S COLL., matric. 25 Oct., 1797, aged 18; B.A. 1801, 30 years curate of Beverstone and Kingscote, co. Gloucester, died 30 July, 1847.

Panton, David Brook, of CAIUS COLL., Cambridge (B.A. 1857, M.A. 1860); adm. 'ad eundem' 28 June, 1860. **[20]**

Panton, George Bryan, s. George, of Jamaica, West Indies, arm. UNIVERSITY COLL., matric. 11 Dec., 1813, aged 16; B.A. 1817, M.A. 1820, B.Med. 1821, inceptor candidate College of Physicians 1824. See Munk's *Roll*, iii. 285.

Panton, John Edward Wilson, s. George, of Isle of Jamaica, arm. UNIVERSITY COLL., matric. 7 Dec., 1816, aged 17; B.A. 1821, bar.-at-law, Middle Temple, 1826.

Panton, Richard, s. Richard Dunavan, of Isle of Jamaica, West Indies, arm. UNIVERSITY COLL., matric. 27 Jan., 1820, aged 17 (? B.A. from PETERHOUSE, Cambridge, 1825, died archdeacon of Surrey, Jamaica, 30 Aug., 1860, D.D.).

Pape, Daniel, s. Robert, of Newton Arlosh, Cumberland, gent. ST. MARY HALL, matric. 6 Nov., 1800, aged 43; vicar of Penn, co. Stafford, 1800, until his death 11 Dec., 1807.

Papendick, Rev. Frederick Henry, s. Christopher, of Windsor, Berks, arm. TRINITY COLL., matric. 8 Feb., 1803, aged 16; B.A. 1806, M.A. 1809, died at Morden, Surrey, 9 Feb., 1811. **[25]**

Papillon, Rev. Duncan, 5s. Alexander Frederick William, of Woolwich, Kent, arm. TRINITY COLL., matric. 19 Oct., 1874, aged 19; B.A. 1877, M.A. 1881.

Papillon, Godfrey Keppel, 3s. Philip Oxenden, of Colchester, arm. MERTON COLL., matric. 21 Oct., 1886, aged 19.

Papillon, John, 2s. Thomas, of Acrise, Kent, arm. UNIVERSITY COLL., matric. 16 March, 1825, aged 18; B.A. 1828, M.A. 1858, rector of Bonnington, Kent, 1831-41, and of Knowlton 1836-41, and of Lexden, Essex, 1841.

Papillon, Pelham Rawstorne, 1s. Philip Oxenden, of London, arm. UNIVERSITY COLL., matric. 13 Oct., 1883, aged 19; B.A. 1887.

Papillon, Philip, s. David, of Lee, Kent, arm. ORIEL COLL., matric. 5 June, 1777, aged 17; B.A. 1781, M.A. 1784, rector of Eythorne, Kent, 1784, and vicar of Tunbridge at his death 28 Jan., 1809. **[30]**

Papillon, Philip Oxenden, 1s. Thomas, of Barham, Kent, arm. UNIVERSITY COLL., matric. 14 Dec., 1844, aged 18; B.A. 1848, M.A. 1851, of Crowhurst Park, Sussex, J.P., and of Lexden Manor, Essex, J.P., D.L., M.P. Colchester 1859-65, a visitor of convict prisons since 1880, sometime major royal East Kent mounted rifles. See Foster's *Men at the Bar* & *Rugby School Reg.*, 226.

Papillon, Richard, 8s. Alexander Frederick William, of Reading, Berks, arm. EXETER COLL., matric. 18 Oct., 1882, aged 19; B.A. 1885.

Papillon, Thomas, 1s. Thomas, of Acrise, Kent, arm. CHRIST CHURCH, matric. 13 June, 1821, aged 18; of Crowhurst Park, Sussex, J.P., D.L., died 19 Aug., 1883, father of the next named.

Papillon, Rev. Thomas Henry, 2s. Thomas, of Denton, Kent, arm. UNIVERSITY COLL., matric. 29 April, 1854, aged 19; vicar of Stopsley 1872-5. See *Rugby School Reg.*, 289. **[34]**

Papillon, Thomas Leslie, o.s. John, of Lexden, Essex, cler. BALLIOL COLL., matric. 13 Oct., 1860, aged 19, scholar 1859-64, B.A. 1864; fellow MERTON COLL. 1865-9, M.A. 1867, tutor 1866, dean 1867; fellow NEW COLL. 1869-84, dean & tutor 1870-84, lecturer 1871, sub-warden 1874, junior bursar 1877-84, master of the schools 1877, etc., chaplain Balliol College 1881-3, moderator 1877-9 and 1885-7, Whitehall preacher 1877-9, vicar of Writtle, Essex, 1884.

Papillon, William, s. David, of Lee, Kent, arm. UNIVERSITY COLL., matric. 26 Oct., 1779, aged 18; B.A. 1783, M.A. 1786, vicar of Wymondham, Norfolk, 1788, until his death 26 Sep., 1836.

Papineau, Rossall William, 1s. William, of Bromley St. Leonard's, Middlesex, gent. ST. JOHN'S COLL., matric. 18 Oct., 1861, aged 19.

Paradise, John, F.R.S., created M.A. 14 April, 1769, and also D.C.L. 3 July, 1776 (*Acts Book*), a celebrated linguist, born at Salonichi, educated at Padua, died in London 12 Dec., 1795.

Paramore, David Robert, 1s. David Ramsey, of Muddy Plains, Launceston, Tasmania, gent. ST. JOHN'S COLL., matric. 28 June, 1858, aged 18; scholar & fellow 1858-69, B.A. 1864, M.A. 1866, rector of Codford St. Mary, Wilts, 1868, until his death 14 May, 1873. See *Robinson*, 301.

Paravicini, Francis de, 2s. Joseph, of Plumpton, Middlesex, arm. WORCESTER COLL., matric. 9 June, 1836, aged 20; B.A. 1840 (a baron), vicar of South Searle, Notts, 1846-57, rector of Avening, co. Gloucester, 1857. [5]

Paravicini, Francis de, 1s. Francis, of Wymondham, co. Leicester, cler. BALLIOL COLL., matric. 18 Oct., 1862, aged 19, scholar 1861-6; a senior student CHRIST CHURCH 1866-71, B.A. 1867, M.A. 1869; fellow BALLIOL COLL. 1878, classical lecturer 1872-8, and tutor since 1872, junior bursar 1875-9.

Parcq, John du, s. Amice, of Isle of Jersey, pleb. JESUS COLL., matric. 10 Oct., 1752, aged 17; B.A. from PEMBROKE COLL. 1756.

Pardew, John, 3s. Samuel, of Plymouth, Devon, gent. NEW COLL., matric. 19 Oct., 1874, aged 18.

Pardo, John, s. Paul, of Kidwelly, co. Carmarthen, gent. JESUS COLL., matric. 9 Dec., 1746, aged 17; B.A. 1750, M.A. 1753.

Pardoe, Geffrey, s. Geffrey, of Ombersley, co. Worcester, pleb. MAGDALEN HALL, matric. 15 Dec., 1738, aged 19. [10]

Pardoe, George, s. George, of Tenbury, co. Worcester, gent. BALLIOL COLL., matric. 4 Nov., 1773, aged 18; of Cleeton and Nash Court, Salop, died in 1798.

Pardoe, George, 2s. -- P., gent. ST. JOHN'S COLL., matric. 14 Dec., 1841; B.A. 1845, M.A. 1848, vicar of Alkham, Kent, 1864, until his death 1 Sep., 1881.

Pardoe, George (Dansey), s. George, of Nash (par. Burford), Salop, gent. BALLIOL COLL., matric. 15 Dec., 1804, aged 18; B.A. 1808, of Nash Court, rector of Hopton Castle, co. Hereford, 1812, until his death 28 May, 1856.

Pardoe, George Owen, 1s. Frederick, of Bishops Castle, Salop, arm. UNIVERSITY COLL., matric. 17 Oct., 1868, aged 19; B.A. 1872, vicar of Hyssington, co. Montgomery, 1874-85, and of Hinton Admiral 1885.

Pardoe, Thomas, s. Thomas, of Cleeton, Salop, gent. PEMBROKE COLL., matric. 14 Jan., 1724-5, aged 18; B.A. 1728. [15]

Pare, Edward Thomas, s. Edward, of Isle of Barbados, arm. ST. MARY HALL, matric. 30 March, 1763, aged 19.

Pare, Frederick Harry, s. John, of Exeter, Devon, arm. CHRIST CHURCH, matric. 16 Oct., 1817, aged 19; B.A. 1821, M.A. 1825, vicar of Cranborne, Dorset, 1830, died 15 May, 1877.

Pares, John Tylston, s. John, of Leicester (town), arm. UNIVERSITY COLL., matric. 4 Feb., 1817, aged 19; died Nov., 1831.

Parfect, John, s. Caleb, of Stroud, Kent, cler. ORIEL COLL., matric. 8 April, 1742, aged 17; B.A. 1745, M.A. 1748, B.D. 1764. See also PERFECT.

Parfitt, Peter Lewis, s. Edward, of Wells, Somerset, gent. BALLIOL COLL., matric. 12 Dec., 1795, aged 17; B.A. 1799, M.A. 1802, rector of Allerton, Somerset, 1814, and minor canon of Wells, until his death 17 Dec., 1857. [20]

Parfitt, Thomas, s. Edward, of Wells (city), gent. BALLIOL COLL., matric. 16 Dec., 1794, aged 18; B.A. 1798, M.A. 1801, B. & D.D. 1833, perp. curate Glastonbury with chapelry of Pennard 1812, until his death 13 Jan., 1865.

Pargeter, Rev. Robert, s. Robert, of Bloxham, Oxon, cler. MAGDALEN HALL, matric. 13 June, 1745, aged 18; B.A. from ST. EDMUND HALL 1750, rector of Stapleford, Herts, 1756, father of Robert and William.

Pargeter, Robert, s. Robert, of Buckingham (town), cler. BRASENOSE COLL., matric. 8 April, 1775, aged 16; demy MAGDALEN COLL. 1777-1803, B.A. 1778, M.A. 1781, died in London, 20 Feb., 1803. See *Bloxam*, vii. 54.

Pargeter, Rev. William, s. Robert, of Buckingham (town), cler. NEW COLL., matric. 15 Jan., 1777, aged 17; B.A. 1871, physician in the fleet at the battle of the Nile, died at Bloxham 17 April, 1810. See *Gent.'s Mag.*, i. 496.

Pargiter, Alfred Arthur, 7s. Robert, of Taunton, Somerset, cler. JESUS COLL., matric. 20 Oct., 1886, aged 19; scholar 1886. [25]

Pargiter, Frederick Eden, born at Jaffna, Ceylon, 1s. Robert, cler. EXETER COLL., matric. 25 April, 1870, aged 18; exhibitioner 1870-5, B.A. 1873, of the Indian Civil Service 1873, assistant collector and magistrate Bengal 1875. See *Coll. Reg.*, 165.

Pargiter, George Edgar Augustus, born at Jaffna, Ceylon, 4s. Robert, cler. MERTON COLL., matric. 24 Jan., 1876, aged 19; B.A. 1879, M.A. 1882, principal St. John's College, Agra, 1883.

Parham, Francis, 3s. William, of Sutton Veney, Wilts, gent. CHRIST CHURCH, matric. 19 Oct., 1853, aged 18; servitor 1853-7, B.A. 1857, M.A. 1860, curate of Broadwindsor 1869-83, vicar of Chardstock 1883.

Paris, John Ayrton, s. Thomas, of Cambridge; matric. from CAIUS COLL., Cambridge, 17 Dec., 1803, student 1804, B.Med. 1808, D.Med. 1813, F.R.S.; created D.C.L. 12 June, 1850, president of the College of Physicians 1844 until his death 24 Dec., 1856. See Munk's *Roll*, iii. 120.

Paris, John Hen., 2s. Archibald, of Enfield, Middlesex, arm. CHRIST CHURCH, matric. 26 May, 1819, aged 18. [30]

Paris, Joseph, s. Joseph, of Clapham, Surrey, gent. CHRIST CHURCH, matric. 30 March, 1736, aged 17.

Parish, Charles, s. Samuel, of Epsom, Surrey, pleb. ST. EDMUND HALL, matric. 16 Feb., 1815, aged 15; died at Epsom, 15 Dec., 1820.

Parish, Charles Samuel Pollock, 1s. Henry, of Dumdum, near Calcutta, cler., D.C.L. ST. EDMUND HALL, matric. 12 Dec., 1837, aged 15; B.A. 1841, chaplain at Moulmein 1852-76.

Parish, Henry, s. Samuel, of Epsom, Surrey, pleb. ST. EDMUND HALL, matric. 12 July, 1808, aged 17; B.A. 1813, M.A. 1815, D.C.L. 1820, chaplain H.E.I.C.S., died minister of Montpellier Chapel, Twickenham, 29 April, 1873.

Parish, Henry, 1s. Henry Headley, of Brasted, Kent, arm. CHRIST CHURCH, matric. 8 June, 1854, aged 19. See *Eton School Lists*. [35]

Parish, Samuel, s. William, of Warley Wiggan (par. Halesowen), co. Worcester, pleb. ST. EDMUND HALL, matric. 16 July, 1783, aged 23.

Parish, William, s. Samuel, of Epsom, Surrey, pleb. ST. EDMUND HALL, matric. 22 March, 1809, aged 20; B.A. 1819, chaplain H.E.I.C.S., died 25 Jan., 1863, at Ealing.

Parish, William Douglas, 5s. Woodbine, of Marylebone, London, equitis. TRINITY COLL., matric. 23 May, 1853, aged 19; vicar of Selmeston, Sussex, 1863, chancellor of Chichester Cathedral 1877; for list of his works see *Crockford.*

Park, Alexander Atherton, 2s. James Allan, of St. Giles's, Westminster, equitis. BALLIOL COLL., matric. 6 May, 1819, aged 16; B.A. 1822, M.A. 1825, bar.-at-law, Lincoln's Inn, 1827, (senior) master Court of Common Pleas 1826, until his death 21 Nov., 1871.

Park, Alexander Waldegrave, 2s. Alexander Atherton, of Bloomsbury, London, arm. TRINITY COLL., matric. 8 March, 1855, aged 18.

Park, Sir James Allan, knight; created D.C.L. 10 June, 1834 (s. James, of Edinburgh, surgeon), bar.-at-law, Lincoln's Inn, 1784, vice-chancellor Duchy of Lancaster 1791, recorder of Preston 1795, and of Durham 1802, K.C. 1799, attorney-general of Lancaster 1811, a judge of Common Pleas 1816 (knighted 14 May, 1816), until his death 8 Dec., 1838.

Park, James Allan, 1s. James Allan, of Barnes, Surrey, equitis. BALLIOL COLL., matric. 6 April, 1818, aged 17; B.A. 1821, M.A. 1825, hon. canon of Durham 1848, rector of Elwick Hall, co. Durham, 1828, until his death 8 Nov., 1871. **[5]**

Park, James Allan, 1s. James Allan, of Marlow, Bucks, cler. ORIEL COLL., matric. 26 May, 1847, aged 18; B.A. 1851, vicar of Methwold, Norfolk, 1853, until his death 4 Jan., 1875.

Park, James Allan, 2s. William W., of Ince, near Chester (city), cler. EXETER COLL., matric. 13 May, 1856, aged 17.

Park, Rev. Mungo Travers, 1s. Archibald, of Isle of Madeira, arm. LINCOLN COLL., matric. 1 Feb., 1861, aged 18; scholar 1861-5, B.A. 1865, M.A. 1870, head-master Louth Grammar School 1880-4, and of Oundle School 1884.

Park, Patrick Gray, 1s. John Steel, of Hackney, Middlesex, arm. EXETER COLL., matric. 11 May, 1848, aged 18.

Park, Rev. Philip Lees, o.s. Thomas, of Stoke Damerel, Devon, arm. TRINITY COLL., matric. 25 Jan., 1879, aged 18; B.A. 1882, M.A. 1885. **[10]**

Park, William Waldegrave, 3s. James Allan, of St. Giles's, London, eq. aur. BALLIOL COLL., matric. 6 April, 1824, aged 19; B.A. 1827, M.A. 1831, of Ince Hall, Cheshire, vicar of Kirk Whelpington, Northumberland, 1833, until his death 7 Dec., 1842.

Parke, Alfred Watlington, 3s. Charles Joseph, of Sturminster, Dorset, arm. ORIEL COLL., matric. 13 Oct., 1873, aged 18; NON-COLL. B.A. 1879, M.A. 1882, rector of Uplyme, Dorset 1883.

Parke, Charles Joseph, 1s. Charles, of Ham Common, Surrey, arm. ORIEL COLL., matric. 17 Dec., 1834, aged 18; B.A. 1842, M.A. 1846, of Henbury House, Dorset, J.P., high sheriff 1868, bar.-at-law, Inner Temple, 1847. See Foster's *Men at the Bar* & *Eton School Lists.*

Parke, Gilbert, s. Gilbert, of Westminster (city), arm. WADHAM COLL., matric. 10 April, 1783, aged 23; vicar of Wiggenhall, Norfolk, 1789, rector of Downham Market 1805, chaplain to the King, etc., died 24 Sep., 1824.

Parke, Roger Kennedy, 1s. George Thomas, of Ceylon, arm. ST. JOHN'S COLL., matric. 22 Oct., 1867, aged 19. **[15]**

Parke, William Alcock Whitbeck, 1s. William, of Piddletown, Dorset, arm. CHRIST CHURCH, matric. 16 Oct., 1885, aged 19.

Parker, Albert Edmund, Viscount Boringdon, o.s. Edmund, Earl Morley. BALLIOL COLL., matric. 19 Oct., 1861, aged 18; B.A. 1866, 3rd earl, a lord in waiting 1874, under secretary for war 1880-5. See Foster's *Peerage.*

Parker, Alfred, 1s. Timothy Methvett, of Malling, Kent, arm. EXETER COLL., matric. 25 Oct., 1838, aged 18.

Parker, Alfred John, 1s. George Ellis Ley, of Wednesbury, co. Stafford, gent. NON-COLL, matric. 23 Oct., 1886, aged 20.

Parker, Alfred Traill, 3s. Charles Stewart, of Aigburth, Lancashire, arm. UNIVERSITY COLL., matric. 7 May, 1856, aged 18; B.A. 1859, M.A. 1865. **[20]**

Parker, Algernon Robert, 3s. Thomas Augustus Wolstenholme, Earl of Macclesfield. CHRIST CHURCH, matric. 16 Oct., 1868, aged 18; B.A. & M.A. 1874, rector of Bix, Oxon, 1877. See Foster's *Peerage* & *Eton School Lists.*

Parker, Anthony, 1s. Standish Grady, of Dublin (city), cler. MAGDALEN COLL., matric. 18 April, 1863, aged 18; of Castle Lough, co. Tipperary, high sheriff 1876, brother of Robert G. 1864.

Parker, (Rev. and Hon.) Archibald, 8s. Thomas Augustus, Earl of Macclesfield. CHRIST CHURCH, matric. 25 Jan., 1878, aged 18; B.A. 1882, M.A. 1884. See Foster's *Peerage* & *Eton School Lists.*

Parker, Arthur Percy, 2s. Henry, of Newcastle-on-Tyne, arm. MAGDALEN COLL., matric. 21 Oct., 1886, aged 19.

Parker, Arthur William, o.s. Henry John Neil, of Shirley, Hants, arm. LINCOLN COLL., matric. 5 Feb., 1859, aged 17; scholar 1859-63, B.A. 1863, M.A. 1867, perp. curate Rowledge, Hants, 1871.

Parker, Banaster, s. Robert, of Burnley, Lancashire, arm. BRASENOSE COLL., matric. 15 March, 1715-6, aged 18; of Cuerden Hall, Lancashire, died in 1738. See Foster's *Lancashire Collection.* **[25]**

Parker, Banaster, s. Robert, of Cuerden, Lancashire, arm. BALLIOL COLL., matric. 24 Jan., 1777, aged 18; of Cuerden, died in 1788. See Foster's *Lancashire Collection.*

Parker, Cadowgan Francis, o.s. Pelley, of Edge, Cheshire, cler. EXETER COLL., matric. 16 Nov., 1843, aged 19.

Parker, Charles, s. Edward, of Hasfield, co. Gloucester, gent. PEMBROKE COLL., matric. 7 Nov., 1732, aged 18; B.A. 1736. See William 1752, and John 1774.

Parker, Charles, s. William, of Nottingham (town), arm. CHRIST CHURCH, matric. 11 June, 1773, aged 18; B.A. 1778, M.A. 1780, of Harefield Place, Middlesex, died 24 April, 1795. See *Alumni West.*, 397. **[30]**

Parker, Rev. Charles, s. Nathaniel, of London (city), arm. UNIVERSITY COLL., matric. 3 July, 1780, aged 19; B.A. 1784, M.A. 1787, died in June, 1805.

Parker, Charles, 3s. William, of Worton, Middlesex (*sic*), arm. QUEEN'S COLL., matric. 23 May, 1823, aged 18; B.A. 1827, M.A. 1830, chaplain E.I.C.S. 1830-7, died 3 June, 1882.

Parker, Charles, 4s. Henry, of Overton, Salop, D.Med. UNIVERSITY COLL., matric. 20 Nov., 1850, aged 18; B.A. 1854, M.A. 1857.

Parker, Rev. Charles Alexander Campbell, 2s. Joseph Timothy, of Kensington, Middlesex, cler. WADHAM COLL., matric. 22 Nov., 1867, aged 19; B.A. 1872, M.A. 1875, died 16 Oct., 1879.

Parker, Charles Arthur, 6s. Richard, of Claxby, co. Lincoln, cler. NON-COLL., matric. 4 June, 1881, aged 18. **[35]**

Parker, Charles Edward Neville, 1s. Edward, of Ashover, co. Derby, cler. MAGDALEN COLL., matric. 16 April, 1872, aged 19.

Parker, Charles Frederick, s. Thomas, of Churcham, co. Gloucester, cler. PEMBROKE COLL., matric. 3 Nov., 1802, aged 15; B.A. 1806, M.A. 1809, fellow until 1819, rector of Ringshall, Suffolk, 1819, until his death 30 April, 1870.

Parker, Charles (Hubert), 3s. William, of Tamworth, co. Stafford, arm. LINCOLN COLL., matric. 20 Oct., 1818, aged 18; B.A. 1822, M.A. 1825, rector of Great Comberton, co. Worcester, 1826, until his death in 1883.

Parker, Charles John, 1s. James, of Oxford, gent. NON-COLL., matric. 25 Jan., 1879, aged 18; B.A. 1882, M.A. 1885.

Parker, Charles John (Bullivant), 2s. William, of Swayfield, co. Lincoln, arm. EXETER COLL., matric. 29 Jan., 1846, aged 17; B.A. from NEW INN HALL 1850, of Beaconfield, co. Lincoln, J.P. See *Eton School Lists*.

Parker, Charles John Ernest, 1s. Charles John Bullivant, of Grantham, co. Lincoln, arm. MAGDALEN COLL., matric. 16 Oct., 1884, aged 20.

Parker, Charles Lewis, 2s. Joseph, of St. Michael's, Oxford (city), gent. WADHAM COLL., matric. 8 Dec., 1827, aged 17; B.A. 1831, M.A. 1835. [5]

Parker, Rev. Charles Lewis Edward, 1s. Charles Lewis, of London, arm. NEW COLL., matric. 16 Oct., 1880, aged 19; B.A. 1884, M.A. 1887.

Parker, Charles Pomeroy, 1s. Henry Melville, of Boston, U.S.A., arm. BALLIOL COLL., matric. 16 Oct., 1872, aged 20; B.A. 1876.

Parker, Charles Sandbach, 1s. Samuel Sandbach, of Aigburth, Lancashire, arm. UNIVERSITY COLL., matric. 13 Oct., 1883, aged 18; B.A. 1887.

Parker, Charles Stuart, 1s. Charles Stewart, of Aigburth, Lancashire, arm. BRASENOSE COLL., matric. 10 June, 1847, aged 18; scholar UNIVERSITY COLL. 1848-54, B.A. 1852, fellow 1854-69, M.A. 1855, tutor 1858-65, lecturer in modern history; of Fairlie, Ayrshire, M.P. Perthshire 1868-74, Perth 1878, etc. See Foster's *Scots M.P.'s* & *Eton School Lists*.

Parker, Charles William, 1s. Charles Hubert, of Great Comberton, co. Worcester, cler. WADHAM COLL., matric. 17 March, 1852, aged 19; B.A. 1856, M.A. 1859, rector of Bulphan, Essex, 1862-70, etc., vicar of Downton-on-the-Rock, co. Hereford, 1880, until his death 16 Dec., 1881. [10]

Parker, Christopher William, 1s. John Oxley, of Woodham, Essex, arm. ORIEL COLL., matric. 16 April, 1872, aged 19; B.A. 1875, M.A. 1879, of Woodham Mortimer.

Parker, Rev. Cuthbert Joseph, 1s. Joseph, of Stockport, Cheshire, gent. ORIEL COLL., matric. 19 Oct., 1875, aged 17; B.A. 1879, M.A. 1882.

Parker, Edmund, Viscount Boringdon, 1st & o.s. John, Earl Morley. CHRIST CHURCH, matric. 21 Jan., 1828, B.A. 1830, 2nd earl, died 28 Aug., 1864. See Foster's *Peerage*.

Parker, Edward, s. Thomas, of Gloucester (city), pleb. MAGDALEN COLL., matric. 17 March, 1780, aged 17; chorister 1775-80, clerk 1780-6, B.A. 1783, M.A. 1789, rector of St. Mary-le-bow, Durham (city), 1788, until his death 27 April, 1809. See *Coll. Reg.*, i. 194.

Parker, Edward, 1s. Joseph, of St. Michael's, Oxford (city), gent. ORIEL COLL., matric. 11 May, 1826, aged 17; B.A. 1830, M.A. 1832, vicar of Bicester, Oxon, 1836-43, rector of Oxenden Magna, 1843-85, hon. canon of Peterborough 1877, until his death in 1887. [15]

Parker, Edward Barnwell, 1s. Edward, of Bicester, Oxon, cler. PEMBROKE COLL., matric. 20 March, 1857, aged 18; scholar 1857-63, B.A. 1861, M.A. 1863, curate of Kirk Hallam, co. Derby, died 7 Nov., 1869. See *Rugby School Reg.*

Parker, Rev. Edward George, B.A. TRINITY COLL., Dublin, 1833 (M.A. 1844), o.s. Charles Lewis, of Bisham, Berks, arm. Incorp. from TRINITY COLL. 31 March, 1855, aged 46; chaplain to the forces, died 10 May, 1859, aged 50.

Parker, Edward Melville, 2s. Henry Melville, of Cambridge, Massachusetts, U.S.A., arm. KEBLE COLL., matric. 19 Oct., 1874, aged 19; B.A. 1878, M.A. 1882.

Parker, Edwin James, s. Thomas, of Churcham, co. Gloucester, cler. PEMBROKE COLL., matric. 3 Nov., 1810, aged 14; scholar until 1823, B.A. 1814, M.A. 1817, fellow 1823-54, B.D. 1837, bursar 1843, vicar of Waltham St. Lawrence, Berks, 1834, until his death 9 April, 1873.

Parker, Elliot Anderson, 1s. William, of London, arm. CHRIST CHURCH, matric. 15 Oct., 1869, aged 19; left 1872. [20]

Parker, Francis, s. Montagu, of Chudleigh, Devon, arm. ORIEL COLL., matric. 10 April, 1802, aged 19; of the Whiteway family, died 1822. See Foster's *Peerage*, E. MORLEY.

Parker, Francis, 4s. Thomas Augustus Wolstenholme, Earl of Macclesfield. CHRIST CHURCH, matric. 15 Oct., 1869, aged 18; S.C.L. & B.A. 1873, M.A. 1879, bar.-at-law, Inner Temple, 1875, M.P. South Oxfordshire July, 1886. See Foster's *Peerage* & *Men at the Bar*, & *Eton School Lists*.

Parker, Frederick Perrott, 1s. Charles Lewis, of Oxford (city), arm. ORIEL COLL., matric. 2 Dec., 1861, aged 18; B.A. 1866, M.A. 1868, rector of Colton, co. Stafford, 1874. See *Rugby School Reg.*

Parker, Frederick William, 2s. Charles, of Ringshall, Suffolk, cler. PEMBROKE COLL., matric. 14 May, 1842, aged 17; scholar 1842-5, B.A. 1846, M.A. 1849, vicar of Moughtrey 1863-70, rector of Aberbafesh, co. Montgomery, 1870-3, rector of Moutgomery 1873.

Parker, George, s. George, of Plympton St. Mary, Devon, arm. WADHAM COLL., matric. 15 May, 1718, aged 18; brother of John 1722. [25]

Parker, George, y.s. Thomas, of St. Giles's, London, equitis. EXETER COLL., matric. 15 Jan., 1753, aged 18; bar.-at-law, Inner Temple, 1759, of Almington, co. Stafford, died 19 Jan., 1819, father of Admiral Sir William Parker, Bart., G.C.B. See Foster's *Baronetage*.

Parker, George, (2nd) Earl of Macclesfield, created D.C.L. 3 July, 1759, M.P. Wallingford 1722-7, a teller of the exchequer 1719-64, president Royal Society 1752, until his death 17 March, 1764. See Foster's *Peerage*.

Parker, George, s. Thomas, Earl of Macclesfield. EXETER COLL., matric. 2 July, 1773, aged 18; created D.C.L. 28 June, 1797, 4th earl, M.P. Woodstock 1777-84, of Minehead 1790-5, lord of the bedchamber to the Prince of Wales 1780, comptroller of the household 1791-7, lord-lieutenant Oxon 1817, died 20 March, 1842. See Foster's *Peerage*.

Parker, George, 'Universitatis Clericus, Oxford;' privilegiatus 19 May, 1859, an assistant Bodleian library.

Parker, George, 2s. John Crabtree, of Halifax, Yorks, gent. ST. ALBAN HALL, matric. 2 May, 1865, aged 21; rector of Quainton 1885. [30]

Parker, George Augustus, 1s. Thomas Augustus Wolstenholme, Earl of Macclesfield. CHRIST CHURCH, matric. 25 Jan., 1862, aged 18; Viscount Parker. See Foster's *Peerage*.

Parker, George Bertie, o.s. George, of Oxford, gent. QUEEN'S COLL., matric. 26 Jan., 1885, aged 18.

Parker, George (Lane), s. George, Earl of Macclesfield. HERTFORD COLL., matric. 20 Jan., 1740-1, aged 17; B.A. 1743, M.A. 1750, lieut.-general in the army, M.P. Yarmouth, Isle of Wight, 1769-74, and Tregony 1774-80, died 6 Sep., 1791. See Foster's *Peerage*.

Parker, Gilbert, s. Samuel, of Oxford (city), gent. TRINITY COLL., matric. 7 June, 1739, aged 17; B.A. 1742, fellow, M.A. 1745, B.D. 1755, D.D. 1760, died rector of Oddington, Oxon, 1795.

Parker, Harry Clince, 1s. Robert Parker Little, of Madras, cler. KEBLE COLL., matric. 20 Jan., 1877, aged 19; B.A. 1882, M.A. 1883, assumed the name of PARKER in lieu of LITTLE by royal licence Dec., 1878, warden of Bishop Cotton Schools and College, incumbent of All Souls and chaplain of Fort Bangalore, Madras, 1884. [35]

Parker, (Sir) Henry (Bart.), s. Hyde, of Tredington, co. Worcester, cler. TRINITY COLL., matric. 22 June, 1731, aged 18; B.A. 1735, fellow, M.A. 1738, B.D., 1755, D.D. 1760, 4th baronet, rector of Rotherfield Greys 1767, and of Glympton, Oxon, 1776, until his death 10 July, 1782. See Foster's *Baronetage*.

Parker, Henry, s. Robert, of Salford, co. Warwick, cler. MERTON COLL., matric. 10 Oct., 1810, aged 22. See Robert 1721.

Parker, Henry, 2s. Samuel, of Low Elswick, near Newcastle-on-Tyne, arm. WORCESTER COLL., matric. 17 April, 1822, aged 19; B.A. 1826, M.A. 1836, rector of Ilderton, Northumberland, 1840, until his death 14 July, 1871.

Parker, Henry, 2s. Henry, of Overton, Flints, D.Med. UNIVERSITY COLL., matric. 20 March, 1846, aged 18, scholar 1846-51, B.A. 1850; fellow ORIEL COLL. 1851-85, M.A. 1852, a student of Lincoln's Inn 1851.

Parker, Henry, of Oxford (city), 'inspector of weights and measures;' privilegiatus 19 May, 1859. [5]

Parker, Henry, 3s. John, of Farnham, Surrey, cler. ST. MARY HALL, matric. 22 Oct., 1870, aged 18; B.A. 1876.

Parker, (Sir) Henry John (Bart.), s. Hugh, of St. Andrew's, Holborn. NEW COLL., matric. 7 July, 1721, aged 17; 3rd baronet, died in 1771. See Foster's *Baronetage*.

Parker, Henry John, s. Henry, of London (city), gent. ST. EDMUND HALL, matric. 25 June, 1790, aged 17; B.A. 1794 (as PARKES), M.A. 1797 (as PARKER), Gresham professor of divinity, rector of High Halden, Kent, 1837, died 19 Oct., 1867.

Parker, Henry Martyn, 3s. Edward, of Kirkdale, Lancashire, gent. LINCOLN COLL., matric. 18 Oct., 1870, aged 18; B.A. 1874, M.A. 1877.

Parker, Henry Royster, 1s. Henry, of Newcastle-on-Tyne, arm. BRASENOSE COLL., matric. 22 Jan., 1885, aged 19. [10]

Parker, Horace, s. John, of York (city), cler. LINCOLN COLL., matric. 8 May, 1799, aged 21; B.A. 1803, died an army chaplain on half-pay in 1833. See *Manchester School Reg.*, ii. 206.

Parker, Humphrey Timmins, 1s. William, of Walton, Surrey, arm. BALLIOL COLL., matric. 22 March, 1822, aged 17; B.A. 1827, M.A. 1831, vicar of Blandford, Dorset, 1836, until his death 25 Jan., 1853. See *Eton School Lists*, 103*a*.

Parker, James, s. John, of Bolton, Lancashire, gent. BRASENOSE COLL., matric. 21 March, 1718-9, aged 17; B.A. 1722, M.A. 1725, probably father of John 1747.

Parker, James, s. Richard, of Lisbon, Portugal, gent. BALLIOL COLL., matric. 26 March, 1740, aged 16; B.A. 1743.

Parker, James, o.s. John Henry, of Oxford, gent. TRINITY COLL. (name entered in *Mat. Reg.* 16 March, 1877, aged 43); created M.A. 6 March, 1877, of Oxford, publisher. [15]

Parker, James Benjamin, 2s. George Russell, of St. Pancras, London, gent. ST. MARY HALL, matric. 24 Nov., 1859, aged 18; B.A. 1863, M.A. 1867, held various curacies 1865-86.

Parker, James Edward, 3s. James, of Rothley, co. Leicester, arm. UNIVERSITY COLL., matric. 22 May, 1861, aged 18.

Parker, John, s. John, of Middlewich, Cheshire, gent. BRASENOSE COLL., matric. 15 May, 1716, aged 17.

Parker, John, s. John, of Bishopsgate, London, gent. BALLIOL COLL., matric. 13 April, 1717, aged 17; bar.-at-law, Inner Temple, 1752.

Parker, John, s. George, of Plympton St. Mary, Devon, arm. EXETER COLL., matric. 28 April, 1722, aged 18; of North Molton, Devon, died in 1768, father of John 1753, and brother of George 1718. [20]

Parker, John, s. Thomas, of St. Giles's, London, gent. MAGDALEN HALL, matric. 8 April, 1731, aged 18, B.A. 1734; chorister Magdalen College 1724-33. See *Bloxam*, i. 155.

Parker, John, s. John, of Woodthorpe, Yorks, gent. UNIVERSITY COLL., matric. 10 May, 1746, aged 18, B.A. 14 Feb., 1749-50; M.A. from BRASENOSE COLL. 1753 (*sic*), of Woodthorpe, a student of Lincoln's Inn, 23 Jan., 1746-7, died 6 Jan., 1794. See Foster's *Yorkshire Collection*.

Parker, John, s. John, of Bolton, Lancashire, arm. BRASENOSE COLL., matric. 11 Feb., 1746-7, aged 18; B.A. 1750 (? M.A. 1753).

Parker, John, s. John, of Saltram, Devon, arm. CHRIST CHURCH, matric. 23 Oct., 1753, aged 18; M.P. Bodmin 1761-2, Devonshire 1762, until created Lord Boringdon 18 May, 1784, died 27 April, 1788, father of John 1789.

Parker, John, 'apothecary;' privilegiatus 27 Sep., 1758.

Parker, John, s. William, of Bedford (town), gent. CORPUS CHRISTI COLL., matric. 6 May, 1769, aged 16; B.A. 1773, M.A. 1776, B.D. 1785, rector of St. John, Bedford, 1787, until his death at Kemble, Wilts, 1 June, 1828. [25]

Parker, John, s. John, of Hasfield, co. Gloucester, arm. MERTON COLL., matric. 25 March, 1774, aged 17. See Charles 1732, and William 1752.

Parker, John, s. John, of Newbold-npon-Avon, co. Warwick, cler. QUEEN'S COLL., matric. 14 May, 1774, aged 18; B.A. 1778, rector of Bilton, co. Warwick, and vicar of Newbold-upon-Avon 1787, until his death in 1817 (his father rector of Churchover with vicarage of Newbold 1743, until his death in 1787).

Parker, John, (2nd) Baron Boringdon, s. John, Baron Boringdon. CHRIST CHURCH, matric. 7 April, 1789; created D.C.L. 18 June, 1799, created Viscount Boringdon and Earl Morley 29 Nov., 1815, died 15 March, 1840. See Foster's *Peerage*.

Parker, John, s. George, of Lichfield, co. Stafford, arm. WORCESTER COLL., matric. 7 March, 1792, aged 16; B.A. 1795, M.A. 1798. [30]

Parker, John, s. John, of Liverpool, Lancashire, arm. TRINITY COLL., matric. 13 Nov., 1800, aged 18; created M.A. 15 June, 1803.

Parker, John, s. Thomas (Netherton), of Hatton Grange, Salop, gent. ORIEL COLL., matric. 31 Jan., 1816, aged 17; B.A. 1820, M.A. 1825, of Sweeney Hall, Salop, rector of Llanemarwic, co. Montgomery, 1827-44, vicar of Llan-y-Blodwell, Salop, 1844, until his death 13 Aug., 1860, brother of Thomas Browne 1817. See *Eton School Lists*.

Parker, John, s. Hugh, of Woodthorpe, Yorks, arm. BRASENOSE COLL., matric. 6 March, 1817, aged 17; B.A. 1820, M.A. 1823, of Darrington Hall, Yorks, bar.-at-law, Lincoln's Inn, 1824, M.P. Sheffield 1832-52, secretary to the Treasury and to the Admiralty, privy councillor, died 5 Sep., 1881. See Foster's *Yorkshire Collection*.

Parker, John Bartholomew, 1s. Lysimachus, of Louth, co. Lincoln, gent. QUEEN'S COLL., matric. 11 May, 1843, aged 19.

Parker, John Fleming, s. John, of Settle, Yorks, arm. BRASENOSE COLL., matric. 14 Jan., 1801, aged 18; B.A. 1804, M.A. 1807, preb. of Llandaff 1813, perp. curate Waddington, Yorks, 1818, rector of Bentham, Yorks, 1825, until his death 26 Nov., 1862. [35]

Parker, John Henry (C.B.) 'bibliopola,' privilegiatus, 4 Feb., 1832; created M.A. 27 June, 1867, keeper of the Ashmolean Museum 1870-84, C.B. 30 Oct., 1871, died 31 Jan., 1884, aged 77; father of James 1877.

Parker, John Oxley, o.s. Christopher Comyns, of Woodham Mortimer, Essex, arm. ORIEL COLL., 14 Dec., 1829, aged 17; B.A. 1833, of Woodham, Mortimer, high sheriff, Essex, 1883, died in 1887, father of Christopher W. 1872. See *Eton School Lists*.

Parker, John Paget, 1s. John, of St. Nicholas, Worcester (city), arm. ORIEL COLL., matric. 12 Nov., 1846, aged 18; B.A. 1852, M.A. 1855, of Woodside House, Worcester, vicar of Hindlip, co. Worcester, 1858-62, etc.

Parker, John Skipwith, 1s. John Thomas, of Newbold, co. Warwick, cler. CHRIST CHURCH, matric. 19 Oct., 1843, aged 18. See *Eton School Lists.*

Parker, John Thomas, s. John, of Newbold-on-Avon, co. Warwick, cler. CHRIST CHURCH, matric. 24 Oct., 1805, aged 18; B.A. 1809, M.A. 1812, rector of Bilton, and vicar of Newbold 1817, until his death 26 Oct., 1852. See *Rugby School Reg.*, 74.

Parker, John Webster, 2s. George, of Ulverstone, Lancashire, gent. BRASENOSE COLL., matric. 25 Feb., 1843, aged 18; scholar 1843-8, B.A. 1846, M.A. 1849, vicar of St. Alban, Rochdale, 1856, until his death 13 Aug., 1874.

Parker, Joseph, 'bibliopola;' privilegiatus 27 Jan., 1798.

Parker, Joseph Timothy, s. Timothy, of Hornby, Lancashire, gent. QUEEN'S COLL., matric. 5 June, 1818, aged 17; B.A. 1824, M.A. 1827, rector of Wyton, Hunts, until his death 28 May, 1862. [5]

Parker, Lewis James, 5s. James, of Newcastle-on-Tyne, gent. ST. ALBAN HALL, matric. 18 Oct., 1875, aged 26.

Parker, Marcus Aurelius, s. John, of York (city), cler. UNIVERSITY COLL., matric. 9 May, 1799, aged 20; migrated to ST. JOHN'S COLL., Cambridge, 1802, B.A. 1804, curate of Louth 1805-14, and of Warborough, Wilts, 1814, until his death 23 May, 1830. See *Manchester School Reg.*, ii. 206.

Parker, Montagu Edmund, s. John, of Saltram, Devon, arm. PEMBROKE COLL., matric. 28 Sep., 1757, aged 19; of Whiteway, Devon, died Jan., 1813, father of the next named.

Parker, Montagu Edmund, s. Montagu Edmund, of Chudleigh, Devon, arm. CHRIST CHURCH, matric. 22 April, 1796, aged 18; of Whiteway, Devon, died March, 1830, father of the next named.

Parker, Montagu Edmund Newcomb, 1s. Montagu Edmund, of Exeter (city), arm. ORIEL COLL., matric. 8 Dec., 1824, aged 17; B.A. 1830, M.A. 1832, of Whiteway, Devon, M.P. South Devon 1835-41, died 1 July, 1858. See Foster's *Peerage* & *Eton School Lists.* [10]

Parker, Pelley, s. Robert, of Hawton, Notts, cler. CHRIST CHURCH, matric. 22 Oct., 1807, aged 17; B.A. 1811, M.A. 1823, rector of West Hallam, co. Derby, 1828-49, of Hawton, Notts, 1849, until his death 18 Nov., 1865, father of Cadowgan 1843.

Parker, Peregrine, s. John, of York (city), cler. WORCESTER COLL., matric. 18 May, 1801, aged 18.

Parker, Reginald, 1s. Henry, of Hull, Yorks, arm. UNIVERSITY COLL., matric. 20 March, 1854, aged 18; scholar 1854-62, B.A. 1859, bar.-at-law, Lincoln's Inn, 1861. See Foster's *Men at the Bar* & *Rugby School Reg.*, 299.

Parker, Richard, s. Thomas, of Womborn, co. Stafford, gent. PEMBROKE COLL., matric. 18 March, 1716-7, aged 17; B.A. 1720, M.A. 1723.

Parker, Richard, s. Samuel, of St. Peter's, Oxford (city), gent. LINCOLN COLL., matric. 11 Oct., 1725, aged 13, scholar; a grandson of Samuel Parker, bishop of Oxford, and brother of Samuel 1730. See *Bloxam*, ii. 90. [15]

Parker, Richard, s. John, of Lechlade, co. Gloucester, gent. TRINITY COLL., matric. 9 Nov., 1756, aged 14; B.A. 1760, M.A. 1763.

Parker, Richard, 1s. John, of Oxford (city), gent. QUEEN'S COLL., matric. 30 June, 1854, aged 19; B.A. 1858, M.A. 1861, rector of Wykeham, Hants, 1863.

Parker, Richard, 3s. George Lloyd, of High Wycombe, Bucks, gent. WORCESTER COLL., matric. 9 Nov., 1854, aged 19.

Parker, Richard Thomas, 2s. John, of Leintwardine, Hereford, cler. ST. MARY HALL, matric. 16 Oct., 1866, aged 17; B.A. 1869, held various curacies 1871-80, rector of Mundford, Norfolk, 1881-4.

Parker, Richard William England, 1s. Richard, of Shidfield, Hants, cler. CHRIST CHURCH, matric. 13 Oct., 1882, aged 19; exhibitioner 1882-6, B.A. 1886. [20]

Parker, Robert, s. William, of Salford, co. Warwick, gent. BALLIOL COLL., matric. 31 May, 1721, aged 17; brother of William 1721. See also Henry, 1810.

Parker, Robert Gabbett, 2s. Standish Grady, of Limerick (city), Ireland, cler. WADHAM COLL., matric. 14 Oct., 1864, aged 18; B.A. 1869, M.A. 1873, of Ballyvalley, co. Clare, J.P., brother of Anthony 1863.

Parker, Robert John Crompton, o.s. Robert John, of York, gent. WADHAM COLL., matric. 11 Oct., 1884, aged 23; B.A. 1888.

Parker, Robert Townley, s. Thomas Townley, of Leyland, Lancashire, arm. CHRIST CHURCH, matric. 17 Oct., 1811, aged 18; of Cuerden Hall, Lancashire, high sheriff 1817, M.P. Preston 1837-41, 1852-7, constable of Lancaster Castle 1874, died 11 Aug., 1879. See Foster's *Lancashire Collection* & *Eton School Lists.*

Parker, Samuel, s. Samuel, of Holywell, Oxford (city), gent. MAGDALEN COLL., matric. 14 May, 1730, aged 26; clerk 1728-67, yeoman bedel of the University 1731. See *Coll. Reg.*, ii. 90. [25]

Parker, Samuel, s. William, of Atherston, co. Warwick, gent. ST. JOHN'S COLL., matric. 1 July, 1773, aged 17; B.A. 1777, M.A. 1781, B.D. 1786, rector of Winterbourne, co. Gloucester, and perp. curate Barford St. Michael's, Oxon, 1789, until his death 8 Sep., 1826.

Parker, Samuel Hay, o.s. Samuel Hay, of The Hague, Holland, arm. PEMBROKE COLL., matric. 2 May, 1823, aged 19; B.A. 1827, chaplain to the corporation of Stratford-on-Avon, and curate of Bishopton, died 24 Dec., 1845.

Parker, Samuel Perrott, s. Richard, of Lechlade, co. Gloucester, cler. TRINITY COLL., matric. 29 Jan., 1784, aged 16; B.A. from ORIEL COLL. 1787, fellow MERTON COLL. until 1810, M.A. 1790, proctor 1799, died vicar of Kingerby, co. Lincoln, 1810. See *Robinson*, 147.

Parker, Thomas, Viscount, s. (George), Earl of Macclesfield. HART HALL, matric. 10 May, 1740, aged 16; created M.A. 23 June, 1743, and D.C.L. 7 July, 1773, 3rd earl, M.P. Newcastle-under-Lyne 1747-54, Oxfordshire 1754-61, Rochester 1761-4, died 9 Feb., 1795. See Foster's *Peerage.*

Parker, Thomas, s. John, of Gloucester (city), pleb. PEMBROKE COLL., matric. 21 March, 1743, aged 17; B.A. 1747, M.A. 1755, rector of Taynton, co. Gloucester, and of Welsh Bicknor, co. Monmouth, at his death in 1800, father of Thomas 1771. [30]

Parker, Thomas, "bookbinder;" privilegiatus 9 July, 1745.

Parker, Thomas, 'janitor of Merton College;' privilegiatus 14 July, 1761.

Parker, Thomas, s. Thomas, of Gloucester (city), cler. PEMBROKE COLL., matric. 6 Nov., 1771, aged 18; B.A. 1775, M.A. 1778, vicar of Churcham with Bulling (Chapel), co. Gloucester, 1785, rector of Sunburie 1786.

Parker, Thomas, s. John, of Astle, Cheshire, cler. CHRIST CHURCH, matric. 5 May, 1784, aged 18; B.A. 1789, perp. curate Rainow 1796, and of Saltersford, Cheshire, 1815, until his death in 1835.

Parker, Thomas, s. Thomas, of St. Bartholomew, London, gent. QUEEN'S COLL., matric. 26 April, 1803, aged 18; B.A. 1807. See *St. Paul's School Reg.*, 211. [35]

Parker, Thomas (5th Earl of Macclesfield), created D.C.L. 11 June, 1834, died 31 March, 1850. See Foster's *Peerage.*

Parker, Thomas, 1s. Thomas, of Sunderland, co. Durham, gent. BRASENOSE COLL., matric. 23 Oct., 1885, aged 18.

Parker, Thomas Augustus Wolstenholme, 1s. Thomas, of Marylebone, London, arm. (after earl). CHRIST CHURCH, matric. 24 June, 1829, aged 18; 6th Earl of Macclesfield, M.P. Oxfordshire 1837-41. See Foster's *Peerage* & *Eton School Lists.*

Parker, Thomas Browne, s. Thomas Netherton, of Worcester (city), arm. ORIEL COLL., matric. 21 June, 1815, aged 18; a student of Lincoln's Inn 1817. See *Eton School Lists.*

Parker, Rev. Thomas Brownbill James, 2s. Joseph, of Stockport, Cheshire, gent. WORCESTER COLL., matric. 21 Oct., 1880, aged 20; B.A. 1883.

Parker, Thomas Comyns, 3s. Charles George, of Springfield, Essex, gent. WADHAM COLL., matric. 26 Jan., 1843, aged 20; B.A. 1847, bar.-at-law, Inner Temple, 1853, died 31 Aug., 1860.

Parker, Thomas Netherton, s. John, of Westminster, Middlesex, arm. ORIEL COLL., matric. 12 May, 1789, aged 17; B.A. 1793, M.A. 1795, father of Thomas Browne 1817, and of John 1816. **[5]**

Parker, Thomas (Townley), s. Robert, of Leyland, Lancashire, arm. BRASENOSE COLL., matric. 27 March, 1779, aged 18; of Cuerden, and of Astley, Lancashire, high sheriff, 1793, died during his shrievalty. See Foster's *Lancashire Collection.*

Parker, Thomas Townley, 1s. Robert Townley, of Leyland, Lancashire, arm. MAGDALEN COLL., matric. 29 Oct., 1841, aged 18; of Cuerden and of Astley, Lancashire. See Foster's *Lancashire Collection.*

Parker, Walter, o.s. William, of Shelton, co. Stafford, arm. WORCESTER COLL., matric. 13 Nov., 1845, aged 20.

Parker, William, s. William, of Salford, co. Warwick, gent. BALLIOL COLL., matric. 31 May, 1721, aged 16; bar.-at-law, Inner Temple, 1729, bencher 1761, brother of Robert 1721.

Parker, William, s. Thomas, of Enfield, Middlesex, gent. ST. JOHN'S COLL., matric. 29 Jan., 1724-5, aged 18; B.C.L. 1731. **[10]**

Parker, William, s. Moses, of St. Michael's, Coventry, co. Warwick, pleb. BALLIOL COLL., matric. 6 July, 1731, aged 17; B.A. 1735, M.A. 1738, B.D. 1751, D.D. 1754, rector of St. James's, Westminster, vicar of Catherine Cree, London, chaplain to the king, F.R.S., died 22 July, 1802.

Parker, William, s. William, of All Saints, Hereford (city), pleb. TRINITY COLL., matric. 3 Nov., 1731, aged 17, B.A. 1735, M.A. 19 Feb., 1740-1; chorister MAGDALEN COLL. 1728-31. See *Bloxam,* i. 158.

Parker, William, s. Thomas, of Kirkham, Lancashire, gent. BRASENOSE COLL., matric. 12 March, 1732-3, aged 19; B.A. 1736, M.A. 1739.

Parker, William, s. John, of Hasfield, co. Gloucester, gent. ORIEL COLL., matric. 12 May, 1752, aged 19. See Charles 1732, and John 1774.

Parker, William, s. William, of South Mimms, Middlesex, cler. PEMBROKE COLL., matric. 3 Nov., 1763, aged 18; B.A. 1767. **[15]**

Parker, William, 'bookbinder;' privilegiatus 21 May, 1778.

Parker, William, s. William, of Withley, co. Warwick, pleb. ST. ALBAN HALL, matric. 13 Jan., 1785, aged 29; B.A. 1790, M.A. 1791.

Parker, (Sir) William (Bart.), s. Harry, of Westminster (city), baronet. CHRIST CHURCH, matric. 29 April, 1789, aged 19; B.A. 1792, 7th baronet, died 21 April, 1830.

Parker, William, s. William, of Tamworth, co. Warwick, arm. TRINITY COLL., matric. 20 Jan., 1812, aged 18; B.A. 1815, M.A. 1818, rector of Little Comberton, co. Worcester, 1826, until his death 17 Dec., 1884.

Parker, William, 1s. William, of Swafield, co. Lincoln, arm. EXETER COLL., matric. 16 Nov., 1843, aged 19; B.A. 1847, of Hanthorpe House, co. Lincoln, hon. lieut.-colonel royal South Lincoln militia. See *Eton School Lists.* **[20]**

Parker, William George Gaskin, o.s. William George, of Bulkington, co. Warwick, cler. ORIEL COLL., matric. 14 June, 1860, aged 19.

Parker, William Hasell, 1s. William, of Yanwath, Westmoreland, gent. QUEEN'S COLL., matric. 24 Oct., 1874, aged 19; B.A. 1878, M.A. 1883, curate of All Saints, Cockermouth, 1881, vicar 1881.

Parker, William Henry, 4s. John, of Worcester (city), gent. WORCESTER COLL., matric. 12 May, 1852, aged 19.

Parker, William Herbert, 1s. James Smith, of Iffley, near Oxford, arm. NON-COLL., matric. 23 Oct., 1880, aged 21.

Parker, William (Hooper), s. John, of Kemble, Wilts, cler. NEW COLL., matric. 11 Nov., 1807, aged 17; fellow 1807-34, B.A. 1811, M.A. 1815, bar.-at-law, Middle Temple, 1821, hon. canon Norwich 1852, rector of Saham Tony, Norfolk, 1833, until his death 27 Aug., 1876. **[25]**

Parker, William John; privilegiatus 3 Feb., 1837.

Parker, William Ricketts, 3s. Thomas John, of Walcot, Bath (city), arm. ORIEL COLL., matric. 29 May, 1827, aged 17; B.A. 1831.

Parker, William Sackville, 6s. Edward, of Oxendon, Northants, cler. ST. JOHN'S COLL., matric. 14 June, 1870, aged 18; scholar 1872-6, B.A. 1875, M.A. 1878, rector of Anstey, co. Leicester, 1879-82, and Oxendon Magna 1882.

Parker, William Windsor, 1s. Windsor, of Mhow, Bengal, East Indies, arm. MERTON COLL., matric. 25 Oct., 1850, aged 19; B.A. 1855, M.A. 1857, bar.-at-law, Lincoln's Inn, 1861. See *Rugby School Reg.*, 268.

Parkes, Alfred Marshall, o.s. Alfred, of Chester, gent. ST. JOHN'S COLL., matric. 11 Oct., 1884, aged 18; B.A. 1887. **[30]**

Parkes, Francis (Barney), 3s. Richard, of Loppington, Salop, cler. CHRIST CHURCH, matric. 18 Oct., 1831, aged 19; servitor 1831-5, B.A. 1835, perp. curate Broughton, Salop, 1840-58, rector of Southwick, Sussex, 1858-73, vicar of Atcham, Salop, 1873, until his death 24 Sep., 1881.

Parkes, Harry Rutherford, 1s. Sir Harry, of London, knight. BRASENOSE COLL., matric. 17 March, 1881, aged 18; B.A. 1884.

Parkes, John, s. Abel, of Halesowen, Salop, gent. MAGDALEN HALL, matric. 14 March, 1780, aged 20; B.A. 1785, master of the Free Grammar School at Halesowen, and minister of Oldbury, died 29 Feb., 1796.

Parkes, John Augustine, 1s. David, of Sheffield, Yorks, gent. QUEEN'S COLL., matric. 18 April, 1864, aged 22.

Parkes, Richard, s. Pryn, of St. Martin's, co. Warwick, gent. ALL SOULS' COLL., matric. 30 Oct., 1778, aged 17; B.A. 1786, vicar of Hanmer, Flints, 1807-8, and of Loppington, Salop. **[35]**

Parkes, Robert, s. Robert, of Chilton Folliot, Wilts, pleb. PEMBROKE COLL., matric. 21 March, 1722-3, aged 18; B.A. 1726, M.A. 1731.

Parkhouse, William Heathman, 2s. Samuel Cawse, of Plymouth, Devon, gent. MAGDALEN HALL, matric. 6 May, 1859, aged 19; B.A. 1862, M.A. 1865, rector of All Hallows, Goldsmith Street, Exeter, 1867-74, vicar of Perranzabulo, Cornwall, 1874-84, rector of St. Paul, Exeter, 1884.

Parkhurst, Fleetwood, s. John, of Catesby, Northants, arm. QUEEN'S COLL., matric. 14 Nov., 1755, aged 18; B.A. 1759, of Ripple, co. Worcester, died 8 Sep., 1801.

Parkhurst, Fleetwood, s. Fleetwood, of St. Pancras, London, arm. TRINITY COLL., matric. 3 March, 1794, aged 20; B.A. 1797, M.A. 1801, vicar of Epsom 1804 (? died curate of Ripple, co. Worcester, 29 Oct., 1844).

Parkhurst, John, s. John, of Epsom, Surrey, cler. TRINITY COLL., matric. 25 March, 1775, aged 17; captain Northants militia, died in Dec., 1781. **[40]**

Parkhurst, Lewis Evan, 2s. Horace John, of Pontymoils, co. Monmouth, gent. JESUS COLL., matric. 18 Oct., 1882, aged 18; scholar 1882-6, B.A. 1886.

Parkhurst, Robert, s. Fleetwood, of St. James's, Westminster, arm. ORIEL COLL., matric. 27 Nov., 1807, aged 18; B.A. 1812, brother of Fleetwood 1794.

Parkhurst, William Horatio, 1s. Horatio John, of Ebbw Vale, co. Monmouth, gent. JESUS COLL., matric. 23 Oct., 1880, aged 19.

Parkin, Arthur Osborn, 2s. George Lewis, of London, arm. ST. JOHN'S COLL., matric. 15 Oct., 1881, aged 19; B.A. 1885. See *Eton School Lists.*

Parkin, Charles, s. Hugh, of Dacre, Cumberland, arm. BRASENOSE COLL., matric. 7 Feb., 1818, aged 18; B.A. 1821, M.A. 1824, brother of James 1815. [5]

Parkin, Rev. Charles Inglewood, 1s. Charles, of Lenham, near Maidstone, Kent, cler. BRASENOSE COLL. matric. 26 Nov., 1857, aged 19; B.A. 1861, M.A. 1865, died in 1886.

Parkin, George, 1s. James, of Ravenstonedale, Westmoreland, gent. BRASENOSE COLL., matric. 18 May, 1837, aged 18; scholar 1837-9. See *Manchester School Reg.*, iii. 235.

Parkin, George Robert, 5s. John, of Monston, New Brunswick, gent. NON-COLL., matric. 11 Oct., 1873, aged 27.

Parkin, James, s. Robert, of Exeter (city), gent. PEMBROKE COLL., matric. 24 Nov., 1755, aged 16; B.A. 1759, M.A. 1762 (? died rector of Oakford, Devon, in Sep., 1812), and father of the next named.

Parkin, James, s. James, of Oakford, Devon, cler. PEMBROKE COLL., matric. 3 Nov., 1806, aged 17; scholar 1806-13, B.A. 1810, M.A. 1813, rector of Oakford, aforesaid, 1813, until his death about 1870. [10]

Parkin, James, s. Hugh, of Shirsgill House, Dacre, Cumberland, arm. BRASENOSE COLL., matric. 2 Nov., 1815, aged 17; a student of Lincoln's Inn 1818, brother of Charles 1818.

Parkin, Lewis, 2s. George Patey, of Woolwich (town), gent. ST. JOHN'S COLL., matric. 29 June, 1840, aged 18; exhibitioner 1840, S.C.L. 1844, B.A. 1856, M.A. 1857, sometime a solicitor, rector of Ingatestone, Essex, 1860, until his death in 1887. See *Robinson*, 247.

Parkin, Miles, s. William, of Millom, Cumberland, pleb. QUEEN'S COLL., matric. 21 June, 1769, aged 19; B.A. 1773 (? died 1 Aug., 1788). See *Gent.'s Mag.*, ii. 753.

Parkin, Montagu Lewis, 1s. George Lewis, of London, gent. ST. JOHN'S COLL., matric. 14 Oct., 1876, aged 19; B.A. 1879, M.A. 1884, bar.-at-law, Lincoln's Inn, 1881. See Foster's *Men at the Bar.*

Parkin, William, s. John, of Mortomley, Yorks, gent. LINCOLN COLL., matric. 4 April, 1715, aged 18.

Parkins, Christopher, s. Thomas, of Chesham, Bucks, cler. UNIVERSITY COLL., matric. 24 March, 1784, aged 17; B.A. 1788, perp. curate Gresford, co. Denbigh, 1793, until his death 19 April, 1843. [16]

Parkins, Henry. TRINITY COLL., B.A. 1718. See PERKINS.

Parkins, John Bateman, s. John, of St. Martin-in-the-Fields, London, gent. MERTON COLL., matric. 7 April, 1720, aged 14.

Parkins, Thomas, s. Thomas, of Kingston-on-Hull, Yorks, pleb. LINCOLN COLL., matric. 3 June, 1742, aged 19.

Parkins, William Trevor, o.s. Christopher, of Gresford, co. Denbigh, cler. MERTON COLL., matric. 12 June, 1841, aged 19; postmaster 1841-2, S.C.L. 1850, B.A. & M.A. 1864, bar.-at-law, Inner Temple, 1851. See Foster's *Men at the Bar.* [20]

Parkins, William Trevor, 1s. William Trevor, of London, arm. BALLIOL COLL., matric. 21 Oct., 1869, aged 18; B.A. 1873, M.A. 1877, held various curacies 1875-83, vicar of Wychnor, co. Stafford, 1883.

Parkinson, Rev. Charles Luke, 3s. Luke, of Manchester, arm. BRASENOSE COLL., matric. 27 Feb., 1845, aged 18; scholar 1845-9, B.A. 1849, M.A. 1851, died 24 Dec., 1855.

Parkinson, Edward, s. Robert, of Ravendale, co. Lincoln, gent. BALLIOL COLL., matric. 27 March, 1779, aged 23; B.A. from HART HALL 1782, fellow LINCOLN COLL., M.A. 1787, B.D. 1797, Whitehall preacher 1785, rector of Great Leighs, Essex, 1803, until his death 18 Jan., 1819.

Parkinson, Israel, 3s. Richard, of Trawden, Lancashire, gent. QUEEN'S COLL., matric. 22 Oct., 1872, aged 22; B.A. 1875, M.A. 1879, vicar of St. George's, Ovenden, Halifax, 1877. [24]

Parkinson, James, s. James, of Birmingham, co. Warwick, cler. WADHAM COLL., matric. 6 June, 1717, aged 16; B.A. 20 Feb., 1720-1, M.A. 1724.

Parkinson, John, s. Robert, of Ravendale, co. Lincoln, gent. CORPUS CHRISTI COLL., matric. 24 Oct., 1770, aged 16, scholar 1770-2; demy MAGDALEN COLL. 1772-5, B.A. 1774, fellow 1775-98, M.A. 1777, B.D. 1786, D.D. 1797, junior dean of arts 1786, bursar 1787, rector of Brocklesby, co. Lincoln, 1785, and of Fittleton, Wilts, 1797, until his death at Ravendale 29 Aug., 1840. See *Bloxam*, vii. 38.

Parkinson, John, s. John, of Healing, co. Lincoln, cler. BALLIOL COLL., matric. 22 March, 1777, aged 18; B.A. 1780, M.A. 1787, vicar of Immingham, co. Lincoln, 1782, and rector of Healing 1793, until his death 11 Jan., 1837, father of William G. 1824.

Parkinson, John, 1s. William Grantham, of Stallingborough, co. Lincoln, arm. NEW COLL., matric. 12 Dec., 1851, aged 18; B.A. from ST. MARY HALL 1856, M.A. 1858.

Parkinson, John Posthumous, o.s. John Wilson, of Louth, co. Lincoln, doctor. LINCOLN COLL., matric. 15 June, 1827, aged 17; demy MAGDALEN COLL. 1827-34, B.A. 1831, M.A. 1834, fellow 1834-42, D.C.L. 1845, senior dean of arts 1840, proctor 1841-2, of Ravendale, co. Lincoln, J.P., assumed the name of PARKINSON in lieu of WILSON in 1840, perp. curate Marsh Chapel 1835-46, F.S.A., died 7 Dec., 1874. See *Bloxam*, vii. 320.

Parkinson, Rev. Richard, M.A. TRINITY COLL., Dublin, 1832, B.A. 1828 (s. Thomas, vicar of Stebannon, co. Louth); adm. 'ad eundem' 14 Jan., 1845, vicar of Northaw, Herts, died 3 Sep., 1868.

Parkinson, Robert Clarke, o.s. John, of Ravendale, co. Lincoln, cler. CHRIST CHURCH, matric. 21 March, 1828, aged 19. [31]

Parkinson, Robert John Hinman, 1s. John Posthumous Parkinson (formerly Wilson), of Ravendale, co. Lincoln, cler. MAGDALEN COLL., matric. 27 June, 1862, aged 18; B.A. 1866, B.C.L. & M.A. 1873, of Ravendale Hall, co. Lincoln, J.P., bar.-at-law, Inner Temple, 1873. See Foster's *Men at the Bar.*

Parkinson, Roger, s. James, of Blackburn, Lancashire, gent. CHRIST CHURCH, matric. 10 April, 1728, aged 17; B.A. 1731.

Parkinson, Thomas, s. Henry, of High Offley, co. Stafford, pleb. PEMBROKE COLL., matric. 15 April, 1736, aged 19; B.A. 5 March, 1739-40.

Parkinson, William, o.s. William Henry, of St. Leonard's, Shoreditch, London, gent. PEMBROKE COLL., matric. 8 Nov., 1822, aged 19. [35]

Parkinson, William, 1s. William, of London, arm. ORIEL COLL., matric. 15 Oct., 1877, aged 18; B.A. 1881, M.A. 1884.

Parkinson, William Grantham, o.s. John, of Healing, co. Lincoln, cler. LINCOLN COLL., matric. 31 March, 1824, aged 19; father of John 1851.

Parkyn, Frederick Silly, 1s. John, of Bodmin, Cornwall, gent. TRINITY COLL., matric. 2 July, 1828, aged 18.

Parkyn, William, s. Paul, of Elm, co. York, gent. HERTFORD COLL., matric. 3 June, 1742, aged 18.

Parkyns, (Sir) Thomas George Augustus (Bart.), born at Mondeville, near Caen in Normandy, 1s. Thomas Boultbee, arm. UNIVERSITY COLL., matric. 14 June, 1838, aged 17; 6th baronet. See Foster's *Baronetage.*

Parkyns, Thomas Mansfield Forbes, 1s. Thomas George Augustus, of Ruddington, Notts, baronet. BRASENOSE COLL., matric. 23 May, 1872, aged 19; bar.-at-law, Inner Temple, 1879. See Foster's *Men at the Bar* & *Eton School Lists.*

Parlby, Rev. John Hall, o.s. John, of South Stoneham, Hants, arm. UNIVERSITY COLL., matric. 5 Dec., 1823, aged 18; B.A. 1827, M.A. 1830, of Manadon, Devon, J.P., father of Walter C. H.

Parlby, Samuel, s. John, of Coningsby, co. Lincoln, gent. LINCOLN COLL., matric. 17 Dec., 1772, aged 17; B.A. 1776, rector of Market Weston 1799, died curate of Stoke-by-Nayland 18 March, 1803.

Parlby, Walter Coventry Hall, 3s. John Hall, of Plymouth, cler. ST. JOHN'S COLL., matric. 15 Oct., 1881, aged 19; B.A. 1885. [5]

Parminter, Henry, s. Henry, of Stoke Rivers, Devon, pleb. QUEEN'S COLL., matric. 4 April, 1750, aged 18, B.A. 1754.

Parmiter, Spurrier Clavell, 1s. John Spurrier, of Winchester, gent. BALLIOL COLL., matric. 24 Oct., 1885, aged 18; exhibitioner ORIEL COLL. 1886.

Parne, Thomas, fellow TRINITY COLL., Cambridge, 1717 (M.A. 1721, B.D. 1729, D.D. 1739); librarian 1734-41, incorp. 21 Oct., 1742.

Parnell, Rev. Arthur Henry, 2s. Richard, of London, cler. ST. MARY HALL, matric. 19 Oct., 1881, aged 20; B.A. from MERTON COLL. 1885. See *St. Paul's School Reg.*, 358.

Parnell, Francis, 1s. Charles Octavius, of St. George's, Hanover Square, London, arm. CHRIST CHURCH, matric. 15 May, 1856, aged 17; a junior student 1858-63, B.A. 1860, M.A. 1863, rector of Oxted, Surrey, 1869. [10]

Parnell, Paul, 3s. John, of St. George's, Hanover Square, London, gent. ST. JOHN'S COLL., matric. 1 July, 1839, aged 18; scholar & fellow 1839-49, B.C.L. 1848, bar.-at-law, Middle Temple, 1845, crown solicitor Perth, W. Australia, died 12 Nov., 1852. See *Robinson*, 236.

Parnell, Thomas Augustus, 4s. John, of St. George's, Hanover Square, gent. ST. JOHN'S COLL., matric. 29 June, 1840, aged 18; scholar 1840-5, B.A. 1844, held various curacies 1846-80, reader of Waddington Hospital, Clitheroe, 1886. See *Robinson*, 247.

Parnell, Thomas Parnell, 1s. John Griffin, of Clevedon, Somerset, arm. CHRIST CHURCH, matric. 5 June, 1875, aged 18; B.A. 1878, bar.-at-law, Inner Temple, 1883, assumed the name of PARNELL in lieu of GRIFFIN. See Foster's *Men at the Bar.*

Parnell, Victor Alexander Lionel Dawson, 6s. Henry, of London, arm. (Lord Congleton). CHRIST CHURCH, matric. 13 Oct., 1871, aged 19; B.A. 1877, bar.-at-law, Lincoln's Inn, 1877. See Foster's *Men at the Bar* & *Eton School Lists.*

Parnther, Robert, s. Robert, of London, arm. CHRIST CHURCH, matric. 26 Oct., 1791, aged 17; bar.-at-law, Inner Temple, 1798. See *Eton School Lists.* [15]

Parody, Augustus Lyon, 2s. Richard, of Gibraltar, gent. BALLIOL COLL., matric. 17 April, 1880, aged 20.

Parr, Arthur Dudley, 2s. Thomas Cart, of Cossington, co. Leicester, gent. BRASENOSE COLL., matric. 13 Oct., 1877, aged 18; bar.-at-law, Lincoln's Inn. See *Rugby School Reg.*

Parr, Bertie Chiverton, 3s. Thomas, of Grappenhall, Lancashire, arm. EXETER COLL., matric. 23 May, 1861, aged 19.

Parr, Cecil Francis, 5s. Thomas, of Grappenhall Heys, Lancashire, arm. EXETER COLL., matric. 25 Jan., 1868, aged 20; B.A. 1872, bar.-at-law, Inner Temple, 1874. See Foster's *Men at the Bar.*

Parr, Codrington, s. Bartholomew, of Exeter, gent. MAGDALEN COLL., matric. 1 Nov., 1817, aged 17; B.A. 1821, died in 1854, father of Henry D. 1848. See *Eton School Lists.* [20]

Parr, Edward, s. Thomas, of Rainhill, Lancashire, pleb. BRASENOSE COLL., matric. 9 April, 1739, aged 17; B.A. 1742.

Parr, Edward George Codrington, 1s. Samuel, of Dover, Kent, arm. BRASENOSE COLL., matric. 29 Jan., 1861, aged 19; B.A. 1865, M.A. 1874.

Parr, Henry, 4s. Thomas, of Condover, Salop, arm. MAGDALEN HALL, matric. 3 Feb., 1842, aged 26; vicar of St. Mary Magdalen, Taunton, 1849-58, curate-in-charge of Yoxford 1867-72, vicar 1872.

Parr, Henry Dimsdale, 2s. Codrington, of Dawlish, Devon, arm. EXETER COLL., matric. 3 Feb., 1848, aged 18. See *Eton School Lists.*

Parr, James, s. John, of Leigh, Lancashire, gent. BRASENOSE COLL., matric. 16 Jan., 1719-20, aged 18; B.A. 1723, M.A. 1726. [25]

Parr, John, 1s. John Edward, of Camberwell, Surrey, arm. EXETER COLL., matric. 14 May, 1851, aged 19; B.A. 1855, M.A. 1860, vicar of Parkstone, Dorset, 1858-72, of St. Mary, Marlborough, 1872. See *Eton School Lists.*

Parr, Rev. John, o.s. John David, of Plymouth, Devon, gent. EXETER COLL., matric. 30 May, 1871, aged 18; B.A. 1874, M.A. 1878.

Parr, John Edward, 3s. Thomas, of Poole, Dorset, gent. EXETER COLL., matric. 23 April, 1819, aged 19; bar.-at-law, Inner Temple, 1832, died 7 May, 1874. See *Eton School Lists.*

Parr, John Owen, s. John, of Bloomsbury, Westminster (*sic*), gent. BRASENOSE COLL., matric. 27 Feb., 1815, aged 16; scholar 1815-8, B.A. 1818, M.A. 1830, vicar of Durnford, Wilts, 1824, hon. canon of Manchester 1853, vicar of Preston, Lancashire, 1840, until his death 12 Feb., 1877.

Parr, John Owen, 1s. John, of Remenham, Berks, cler. EXETER COLL., matric. 23 Jan., 1845, aged 19; B.A. 1848, M.A. 1851, rector of Hinstock. [30]

Parr, John Walter, 2s. Robert, of Cheltenham, gent. MAGDALEN HALL, matric. 21 June, 1867, aged 19.

Parr, John Walter, 1s. John Robert, of Swinton, Lancashire, cler. NON-COLL., matric. 13 Oct., 1883, aged 19.

Parr, Percivall Chase, 4s. Thomas Chase, of Bromley, Kent, arm. NEW COLL., matric. 11 Oct., 1878, aged 18; scholar 1878-83, B.A. 1883, bar.-at-law, Inner Temple, 1885.

Parr, Robert, s. Robert, of Horstead, Norfolk, cler. TRINITY COLL., matric. 31 May, 1759, aged 18; demy MAGDALEN COLL. 1760-7, B.A. 1763, M.A. 1765, fellow 1767-76, vicar of Modbury, Devon, 1772, rector of St. Lawrence, Norwich, 1775-1802, and of Heigham 1781, until his death 3 July, 1812, his father died 13 Sep., 1759. See *Bloxam*, vi. 324.

Parr, Robert, 1s. Robert, of Tinwell, Rutland, arm. BALLIOL COLL., matric. 1 Feb., 1873, aged 20; B.A. 1878, bar.-at-law, Inner Temple, 1883. See Foster's *Men at the Bar.* [35]

Parr, Samuel, 2s. Bartholomew, of Exeter, Devon, doctor. EXETER COLL., matric. 5 May, 1821, aged 18; B.A. 1826, brother of Codrington 1817, his father died in 1813. See *Eton School Lists.*

Parr, Thomas Clements, 2s. George, of St. George's, Hanover Square, London, arm. CHRIST CHURCH, matric. 20 Jan., 1823, aged 19; B.A. 1828, M.A. 1831, bar.-at-law, Inner Temple, 1832. See Foster's *Men at the Bar* & *Eton School Lists.*

Parr, Thomas Henning, 1s. John, of Parkstone, Dorset, cler. WORCESTER COLL., matric. 18 Oct., 1883, aged 18; exhibitioner 1883.

Parr, Thomas Roworth, 1s. Thomas C., of Geneva, Switzerland, arm. ORIEL COLL., matric. 22 Feb., 1855, aged 18. See *Eton School Lists.*

Parr, Rev. Willoughby Chase, 3s. Thomas Chase, of Freelands, near Bromley, Kent, arm. MAGDALEN COLL., matric. 14 Oct., 1871, aged 18; B.A. 1875, M.A. 1881.

Parr, Wolstenholme, s. John, of Liverpool, Lancashire, gent. CORPUS CHRISTI COLL., matric. 17 Dec., 1778, aged 16; scholar 1778-89, B.A. 1782, M.A. 1786, fellow 1789-91, died in 1845. See *Manchester School Reg.*, i. 187.

Parratt, Charles, s. Henry, of London, cler. NEW COLL., matric. 25 Oct., 1732, aged 18; B.C.L. 1740 (? rector of Saham Tony, Norfolk, 1757).

Parratt, Walter, 2s. Thomas, of Huddersfield, Yorks, gent. MAGDALEN COLL., matric. 6 Nov., 1872, aged 31; B.Mus. 15 May, 1873, organist 1872-82, organist at Windsor 1882. **[5]**

Parris, Francis Sawyer, fellow SYDNEY SUSSEX COLL., Cambridge, B.A. 1723, M.A. 1728; (incorp. 8 July, 1732), B.D. 1735, D.D. 1747, master 1746-60, chief librarian 1756.

Parris, Paul Carrington, s. David, of Isle of Barbados, West Indies, arm. CHRIST CHURCH, matric. 21 Oct., 1808, aged 19.

Parrott, James Alfred, 4s. Thomas, of Sutton, near Macclesfield, arm. BRASENOSE COLL., matric. 15 Oct., 1870, aged 18; S.C.L. & B.A. 1873.

Parrott, Richard, 4s. John, of Clapham, Surrey, gent. WADHAM COLL., matric. 10 May, 1848, aged 17; B.A. 1852, M.A. 1858, vicar of Great Amwell, Herts, 1864.

Parry, Charles Clinton, 1s. Thomas Gambier, of Cheltenham, co. Gloucester, arm. CHRIST CHURCH, matric. 31 March, 1859, aged 18; died 7 July, 1883.

Parry, Charles David, s. Roger, of London, cler. CHRIST CHURCH, matric. 29 March, 1791, aged 19; B.A. 1794, M.A. 1815 (as David Charles). **[11]**

Parry, Charles Henry, s. Francis, of Mortimer, Berks, arm. QUEEN'S COLL., matric. 3 May, 1774, aged 17; B.C.L. from ST. EDMUND HALL 1782, vicar of Speen, Berks, 1780, until his death 11 Dec., 1788.

Parry, Charles Henry, 1s. Edward St. John, of Toronto, Canada, cler. EXETER COLL., matric. 11 Oct., 1872, aged 19; B.A. from ORIEL COLL. 1877, M.A. 1879.

Parry, Charles Hubert Hastings, 2s. Thomas Gambier, of Bournemouth, Dorset, arm. EXETER COLL., matric. 26 Jan., 1867, aged 18; B.Mus. 21 Feb., 1867, B.A. 1870, D.Mus. by decree 4 March, 1884, M.A. 1884, choragus of the University 1886. See *Eton School Lists.*

Parry, David, s. Thomas, of Lancolar, co. Denbigh, arm. BRASENOSE COLL., matric. 8 April, 1717, aged 19. **[15]**

Parry, David, s. William, of Cardigan (town), gent. ST. JOHN'S COLL., matric. 28 May, 1736, aged 16.

Parry, David, 3s. William, of Llanwnog, co Montgomery, gent. JESUS COLL., matric. 29 Oct., 1846, aged 18; B.A. 1850, rector of Darowen 1856-73, vicar of Llanwnog aforesaid 1873.

Parry, Edmond Wynne, 2s. Griffith, of Carnarvon, gent. NON-COLL., matric. 11 Oct., 1879, aged 24; a commoner of LINCOLN COLL.

Parry, Edward, s. Edward, of Nerquis, co. Flint, gent. JESUS COLL., matric. 7 April, 1772, aged 19.

Parry, Edward, s. Thomas, of Gwaenyscor, co. Flint, cler. JESUS COLL., matric. 1 Dec., 1779, aged 18; B.A. 1788 (? died rector of Caerwys, Flints, in 1816). **[20]**

Parry, Edward, 1s. Edward, of Sydney, Australia, equitis. BALLIOL COLL., matric. 22 March, 1849, aged 19; B.A. 1852, M.A. 1855, created D.D. 31 March, 1870, bishop suffragan of Dover 1870-83, rector of Acton, Middlesex, 1859-69, archdeacon and canon of Canterbury 1869, tutor Durham University 1853-6. See *Rugby School Reg.*, 247.

Parry, Edward, 1s. Thomas, of Chorlton-on-Medlock, gent. NON-COLL., matric. 21 Oct., 1871, aged 26; B.A. 1874, M.A. 1880.

Parry, Rev. Edward Archibald, 1s. Edward, bishop suffragan of Dover. ORIEL COLL., matric. 28 Jan., 1879, aged 18; B.A. 1883, M.A. 1885.

Parry, Edward Henry, 5s. Thomas Crook, of Birley, near Leominster, gent. BRASENOSE COLL., matric. 12 Oct., 1872, aged 19; scholar 1872-7, B.A. 1876, vicar of Dulas, co. Hereford, 1883.

Parry, Edward Hogarty, 2s. Edward St. John, of Toronto, Canada, cler. EXETER COLL., matric. 17 Oct., 1874, aged 19; exhibitioner 1874-8, B.A. 1878, M.A. 1882. See *Coll. Reg.*, 167. **[25]**

Parry, Edward Price, s. Edward, of Treyddynt (?), co. Flint, arm. JESUS COLL., matric. 13 May, 1815, aged 18; died fellow-commoner ST. JOHN'S COLL., Cambridge, 16 Jan., 1819, aged 22.

Parry, Rev. Edward St. John, 1s. Thomas, bishop of Antigua, West Indies. BALLIOL COLL., matric. 14 Dec., 1844, aged 19; B.A. 1848, M.A. 1851, a student of Lincoln's Inn 1849, sometime warden Queen's College, Birmingham, and principal Leamington College 1857-66. See *Rugby School Reg.*, 212.

Parry, Francis, s. Francis, of Llanaber, co. Merioneth, pleb. HERTFORD COLL., matric. 17 Dec., 1764, aged 21; B.A. 1768.

Parry, Francis, s. Edward, of Shrewsbury, Salop, gent. ST. JOHN'S COLL., matric. 12 Dec., 1787, aged 18.

Parry, Francis Charles. s. Charles Henry, of Speen, Berks, cler. UNIVERSITY COLL., matric. 27 Jan., 1798, aged 17; B.A. 1802, M.A. 1806, bar.-at-law, Middle Temple, 1806, a commissioner of bankrupts, deputy-registrar of the Bankruptcy Court, died 18 Dec., 1878. **[30]**

Parry, Frederick Sydney, 2s. Edward, bishop suffragan of Dover. BALLIOL COLL., matric. 21 Oct., 1880, aged 19; B.A. 1885.

Parry, George, 2s. Lewis, of Penywch, co. Cardigan, gent. QUEEN'S COLL., matric. 22 Oct., 1825, aged 21.

Parry, George Frederick, born at Tillicherry, East Indies, s. George, arm. WADHAM COLL., matric. 8 Feb., 1813, aged 18; B.A. from TRINITY COLL., Cambridge, 1817, M.A. 1822, bar.-at-law, Lincoln's Inn, 1821.

Parry, George Williams, 1s. George Williams, of Llidiade Llanilar, near Aberystwyth, arm. PEMBROKE COLL., matric. 23 May, 1872, aged 19.

Parry, Gregory, s. Gregory, of Llandevaylog, co. Brecon, cler. MERTON COLL., matric. 20 May, 1734, aged 17; B.A. 1737, M.A. 1740, rector of Vaynor, co. Brecon, 1749, preb. of Worcester 1772, until his death 1 Aug., 1785. **[35]**

Parry, Henry, s. Henry, of Machynlleth, co. Montgomery, pleb. JESUS COLL., matric. 2 June, 1720, aged 19; B.A. 28 Feb., 1723-4.

Parry, Henry, s. John, of Llanbachraeth, Isle of Anglesey, pleb. JESUS COLL., matric. 26 March, 1740, aged 20; B.A. 6 March, 1743-4.

Parry, Henry, s. Henry, of Llanuwchyllyn, co. Merioneth, pleb. JESUS COLL., matric. 1 June, 1786, aged 20; B.A. 1790, vicar of Llanasaph, co. Flint, 1798, and canon of St. Asaph 1833, until his death 17 Dec., 1854.

Parry, Henry, 1s. Henry, of Llanasa, near Holywell, co. Flint, cler. ALL SOULS' COLL., matric. 10 Dec., 1836, aged 17, bible clerk 1836-9; B.A. from NEW INN HALL 1842. **[39]**

Parry, Henry Hutton, 2s. (Thomas), bishop of Antigua. BALLIOL COLL., matric. 29 May, 1846, aged 19; B.A. 1851, M.A. 1859, tutor of Codrington College 1855-60, chaplain to the forces 1860-1, archdeacon of Barbados 1861-8, D.D. by diploma, Durham, 1876, bishop co-adjutor for Barbados 1868-76, bishop of Perth, Western Australia, 1876.

Parry, Hugh, s. John, of Llanundee, co. Carnarvon, pleb. JESUS COLL., matric. 17 Oct., 1730, aged 20.

Parry, Humphrey, s. Humphrey, of Llanfyllin, co. Montgomery, gent. JESUS COLL., matric. 10 Feb., 1738-9, aged 18.

Parry, James, s. Gregory, of Llandevalog, co. Brecon, cler. MERTON COLL., matric. 12 Feb., 1728-9, aged 18; B.A. 1732, bar.-at-law, Middle Temple, 1737 (? died 24 Sep., 1770).

Parry, James, 2s. Edward, of Bangor, co. Carnarvon, gent. JESUS COLL., matric. 25 March, 1831, aged 18; B.A. 1834.

Parry, James Patrick, 4s. William, of Eltham, Kent, arm. EXETER COLL., matric. 6 Dec., 1820, aged 17; B.A. 1825. [5]

Parry, John, s. John, of Llantrisant, Isle of Anglesey, pleb. JESUS COLL., matric. 26 March, 1731, aged 17; B.A. 1734.

Parry, John, s. Humphrey, of Pool, co. Montgomery, pleb. JESUS COLL., matric. 6 April, 1734, aged 18.

Parry, John, s. Joseph, of Abingdon, Berks, pleb. PEMBROKE COLL., matric. 15 July, 1740, aged 20.

Parry, John, s. Thomas, of Llanhoehannel, co. Pembroke, gent. WADHAM COLL., matric. 16 June, 1742, aged 18; B.A. 1746.

Parry, John, s. Thomas, of Newmarket, co. Flint, pleb. JESUS COLL., matric. 25 May, 1759, aged 18. [10]

Parry, John, s. James, of Aberporth, co. Cardigan, gent. CHRIST CHURCH, matric. 9 June, 1760, aged 16; B.A. 1764, M.A. 1767, died vicar of Skipton-in-Craven, Yorks, in 1777 or 1778. See *Alumni West.*, 374.

Parry, John, s. Thomas, of Batheaston, Somerset, gent. MAGDALEN HALL, matric. 7 Nov., 1765, aged 22; B.A. 1769. (Memo.: J. P., rector of Sturmer, Essex, 1789, until his death at Bath 14 July, 1799.)

Parry, John, s. Andrew, of Newington, Middlesex, gent. CHRIST CHURCH, matric. 3 July, 1770, aged 17; bar.-at-law, Lincoln's Inn, 1775 (? died 1810).

Parry, John, s. George, of Kellygare, co. Glamorgan, cler. ST. EDMUND HALL, matric. 27 June, 1780, aged 19; B.A. from ALL SOULS' COLL. 1784.

Parry, John, s. Simon, of Ruthin, co. Denbigh, pleb. WADHAM COLL., matric. 8 July, 1783, aged 19; B.A. 1792. [15]

Parry, John, s. Robert, of Liverpool, Lancashire, arm. BRASENOSE COLL., matric. 20 May, 1790, aged 20.

Parry, John, s. John, of Dulas, co. Hereford, pleb. JESUS COLL., matric. 20 May, 1791, aged 26. (Memo.: J. P., incumb. of Dulas and Ewyas Harold 1800, and of Clunbury, Salop, died in 1818.)

Parry, John, s. Edward, of Llanelidan, co. Denbigh, gent. JESUS COLL., matric. 24 May, 1798, aged 19; B.A. 1802. (Memo.: J. P., rector of Clocaenog, near Ruthin, 1834, until his death 31 Dec., 1845, aged 67.)

Parry, Rev. John, 1s. Henry, of Liverpool, Lancashire, gent. BRASENOSE COLL., matric. 14 Jan., 1822, aged 17; scholar 1822-5, B.A. 1825, fellow 1826-35, M.A. 1828, rector of Wapping 1833, until his death 13 Aug., 1852. See *Manchester School Reg.* iii. 130.

Parry, John Edward, 2s. John, of Blackwood, co. Monmouth, cler. NON-COLL., matric. 4 May, 1881, aged 22. [20]

Parry, John Jeffreys Bulkeley Jones-, 1s. John Parry, of Torpoint, Cornwall, arm. MAGDALEN COLL., matric. 16 Oct., 1882, aged 18.

Parry, John Morgan, 2s. John, of Wolverhampton, cler. WORCESTER COLL., matric. 22 Oct., 1885, aged 17.

Parry, John Parry Jones, s. Thomas Jones- (Parry in 1803), of St. James's, Westminster, arm. CHRIST CHURCH, matric. 13 May, 1807, aged 18; B.A. 1811, M.A. 1814, perp. curate Nevern, Carnarvon, 1820-5, rector of Edern 1821, and of Llangelynin, co. Merioneth, 1827, until his death 6 March, 1865. See *Alumni West.*, 466.

Parry, Joseph, s. Joseph, of Abingdon, Berks, pleb. PEMBROKE COLL., matric. 15 July, 1740, aged 19; B.A. 1744, M.A. 1747.

Parry, Joseph Henry, 1s. Joseph, of Allington, Wilts, gent. NEW COLL., matric. 13 Oct., 1877, aged 19; scholar 1877-82, B.A. 1881, a student of the Inner Temple 1882. [25]

Parry, Joshua, s. Thomas, of Holliwell, co. Flint, pleb. ST. MARY HALL, matric. 11 March, 1739-40, aged 21; B.A. from EXETER COLL. 1743.

Parry, Lewis James, 1s. John, of Amlwch, Isle of Anglesey, cler. JESUS COLL., matric. 21 Oct., 1873, aged 20; B.A. 1879.

Parry, Sir Love Parry Jones, K.C.H., s. Thomas Jones- (Parry in 1803), of Westminster, arm. CHRIST CHURCH, matric. 8 May, 1799, aged 17; B.A. 1803, M.A. 1811, of Madryn Park, co. Carnarvon (his father assumed the additional name of PARRY in 1803), lieut.-general in the army 1846, commanded a frontier brigade in Upper Canada, and had a horse shot under him at the battle of Lundy's Lane, K.C.H. 1835, M.P. Horsham 1806, Carnarvon 1835, high sheriff Anglesey 1840, entered Lincoln's Inn 1802, died 23 Jan., 1853. See *Alumni West.*, 452.

Parry, Morris Vivian, 1s. John, of Wolverhampton, cler. WADHAM COLL., matric. 17 Oct., 1882, aged 16; B.A. 1886.

Parry, Owen, s. Owen, of Ceidoe, co. Anglesea, gent. JESUS COLL., matric. 17 June, 1790, aged 18; B.A. 1794. [30]

Parry, 'Randolph,' s. 'Randolph,' of Osbeston (*sic*), Salop, pleb. JESUS COLL., matric. 17 March, 1725-6, aged 17; B.A. 1729, M.A. 1751, father of Robert 1756.

Parry, Rice, s. David, of Lanvihangel-y-Croydden, co. Cardigan, pleb. JESUS COLL., matric. 25 May, 1721, aged 18.

Parry, Richard, s. Hugh, of Westminster, gent. CHRIST CHURCH, matric. 10 June, 1740, aged 18; B.A. 1744, M.A. 1747, B.D. 1754, D.D. 1757, incumbent of Hawkhurst, Kent, 1748-51, preacher at Market Harborough 1754, rector of Wichampton, Dorset, 1757, died 9 April, 1780. See *Alumni West.*, 322.

Parry, Richard, s. Henry, of Llanelidan, co. Denbigh, gent. ST. MARY HALL, matric. 7 May, 1781, aged 36.

Parry, Richard Price, s. Francis, of Overton, co. Flint, arm. BRASENOSE COLL., matric. 20 June, 1753, aged 17. [35]

Parry, Robert, s. 'Randolphi,' of Osbaston (*sic*), Salop, cler. CHRIST CHURCH, matric. 11 Oct., 1756, aged 17.

Parry, Robert, s. Robert, of Llanvihangel, co. Merioneth, pleb. JESUS COLL., matric. 3 April, 1773, aged 24.

Parry, Robert, 3s. Griffith, of Carnarvon, arm. BRASENOSE COLL., matric. 22 Oct., 1878, aged 19; scholar 1878-82, B.A. 1882.

Parry, Robert Colt, s. Rowland, of Letton, co. Hereford, cler. BALLIOL COLL., matric. 1 June, 1742, aged 19.

Parry, Robert Lloyd Jones, 1s. Thomas Parry Jones, of Beaumaris, arm. JESUS COLL., matric. 20 Nov., 1834, aged 18; B.A. 1838, M.A. 1841, bar.-at-law, Lincoln's Inn, 1842. [40]

Parry, Rowland, of ST. JOHN'S COLL., Cambridge (M.A. 1710); incorp. 4 May, 1727.

Parry, Samuel Pryce, 2s. Thomas Pryce, of Oswestry, Salop, gent. QUEEN'S COLL., matric. 22 Oct., 1884, aged 18; B.A. 1888.

Parry, Sidney Llewellyn, o.s. Richard, of Brighton, arm. TRINITY COLL., matric. 18 Oct., 1875, aged 19.

Parry, Thomas, s. Edward, of Mold, co. Flint, pleb. JESUS COLL., matric. 1 April, 1732, aged 20; B.A. 19 Feb., 1739-40.

Parry, Thomas, s. Thomas, of Newmarket, co. Flint, pleb. JESUS COLL., matric. 13 Dec., 1749, aged 19.

Parry, Thomas, s. John, of Cloddock, co. Hereford, pleb. BRASENOSE COLL., matric. 7 Feb., 1757, aged 18; B.A. 1760.

Parry, Thomas, s. Richard, of St. David's, co. Pembroke, gent. ORIEL COLL., matric. 25 May, 1759, aged 15.

Parry, Thomas, s. Edward, of Castle Caerinion, co. Montgomery, pleb. JESUS COLL., matric. 13 June, 1768, aged 19; B.A. 1772. [5]

Parry, Thomas, s. Thomas, of Cwm, co. Flint, pleb. CHRIST CHURCH, matric. 26 Oct., 1787, aged 19.

Parry, Thomas, s. John, of Caerwys, co. Flint, gent. JESUS COLL., matric. 14 July, 1796, aged 18; B.A. 1800, M.A. 1803.

Parry, Rev. Thomas, s. Joseph, of Bangor, co. Carnarvon, pleb. JESUS COLL., matric. 9 May, 1799, aged 19; B.A. 1803, of Upper Bangor, died 28 June, 1855, aged 75.

Parry, Thomas, s. Llewellin, of Gernos, co. Cardigan, arm. WORCESTER COLL., matric. 6 Nov., 1802, aged 16.

Parry, Thomas, s. Edward, of Mold, co. Flint, cler. ORIEL COLL., matric. 27 April, 1812, aged 17, B.A. 1816; fellow BALLIOL COLL. 1818-25, M.A. 1819, tutor, senior dean, etc., 1823, D.D. (by decree) 9 July, 1842, archdeacon of Antigua 1824-40, and of Barbados 1837-42, bishop 1842, until his death 16 March, 1870. [10]

Parry, Thomas, 2s. John, of Aberystwith, co. Cardigan, arm. WADHAM COLL., matric. 31 May, 1824, aged 17; B.A. 1828, M.A. 1838, vicar of Walthamstow 1851.

Parry, Thomas Love Duncombe Jones, 1s. Love Parry, of Llanbedrog, co. Carnarvon, equitis. UNIVERSITY COLL., matric. 15 May, 1850, aged 18; of Madryn Castle, co. Carnarvon, high sheriff, 1854, M.P. 1868-74, M.P. Carnarvon burghs 1882-6. See *Rugby School Reg.*, 287.

Parry, Thomas Macdonald, o.s. Thomas Butler, of Killean and Kilchenzie, co. Argyle, arm. ST. MARY HALL, matric. 20 Oct., 1859, aged 20.

Parry, Thomas William, 1s. Thomas Edmund, of Carmarthen (town), gent. ST. MARY HALL, matric. 5 Dec., 1851, aged 23; B.A. 1856, rector of St. Nicholas, Hereford, 1859, until his death 27 July, 1871.

Parry, William, s. John, of Cluddock, co. Hereford, pleb. JESUS COLL., matric. 25 June, 1717, aged 18. [15]

Parry, William, s. William, of Easton, Wilts, gent. ORIEL COLL., matric. 14 Nov., 1724, aged 17.

Parry, William, s. Henry, of Llaneecil, co. Merioneth, cler. JESUS COLL., matric. 29 Feb., 1731-2, aged 19; B.A. 1735.

Parry, William, s. Griffith, of Dolgelly, co. Merioneth, pleb. JESUS COLL., matric. 29 Oct., 1750, aged 19; B.A. 1754.

Parry, William, s. James, of Oldcourt, co. Hereford, pleb. PEMBROKE COLL., matric. 27 Feb., 1756, aged 18.

Parry, William, s. John, of Llan-asaph, co. Flint, pleb. JESUS COLL., matric. 29 March, 1760, aged 22. [20]

Parry, William, 3s. Henry, of Rowton, Cheshire, gent. MAGDALEN HALL, matric. 13 June, 1850, aged 22; B.A. 1854, M.A. 1857, D.C.L. 1865, chaplain at Tirhoot, Bengal, 1860-2, vicar of Timsbury, Hants, 1863-9, resident at Mount Lebanon, and hon. chaplain in Syria 1869-74, rector of Johnston, co. Pembroke, 1876-80, rector of Fitz, Salop, 1880, member of the Royal Asiatic Society 1855.

Parry, William, s. Henry, of Monmouth (town), arm. ORIEL COLL., matric. 12 Dec., 1801, aged 17.

Parry, William Corbet Jones. WORCESTER COLL., 1843. See YALE.

Parry, Admiral Sir William Edward, created D.C.L. 1 July, 1829 (y.s. Caleb Hillier Parry, of Bath, D.Med.); the Arctic explorer, commanded the expedition of 1819, 1821-3, and 1827, knighted May, 1829, F.R.S., hydrographer to the admiralty 1823-6 and 1827-30, etc., captain-superintendent Greenwich Hospital, rear admiral 1852, died 8 July, 1855 (his father died 9 March, 1822, aged 66). See *Gent.'s Mag.*, 1855, ii. 206.

Parry, William Louis, 1s. William Harvey, of 'Tutonis,' France, arm. CORPUS CHRISTI COLL., matric. 18 Nov., 1844, aged 20; B.A. 1849. [25]

Parry, William (Warner), o.s. Robert Jones, of Birmingham, co. Warwick, gent. WORCESTER COLL., matric. 2 March, 1853, aged 20; B.A. 1858, M.A. 1859, chaplain royal navy 1866, retired list 1885.

Parslow, Daniel, s. John, of Woodstock, Oxon, gent. ST. ALBAN HALL, matric. 15 Jan., 1798, aged 31; B.A. 1804, curate of St. Giles'-in-the-Fields 1804, until his death 3 Feb., 1805.

Parson, Rev. Charles, s. John, of Chichester, Sussex, gent. NEW COLL., matric. 6 Dec., 1773, aged 15; B.A. 1778, M.A. 1780, died master of Midhurst Grammar School 11 Feb., 1795.

Parson, James Douglas, 4s. William Henry, of Pirbright, Surrey, cler. WORCESTER COLL., matric. 20 Oct., 1868, aged 19.

Parson, John, s. John, of Luxulian, Cornwall, gent. EXETER COLL., matric. 31 March, 1721, aged 19; B.A. 3 Feb., 1724-5 (as PARSONS). [30]

Parson, John, s. James Freakes, of Farnham, Surrey, gent. BRASENOSE COLL., matric. 15 July, 1802 aged 18; B.A. 1806 (as FREAKES), M.A. 1811 (as PARSON, which name he assumed), curate of Headley, rector of St. Peter, West Lynn, 1811, until his death 23 Nov., 1829.

Parson, John Campbell, 2s. William Henry, of Pirbright, Surrey, cler. TRINITY COLL., matric. 4 June, 1861, aged 18; B.A. 1865, M.A. 1868, vicar of Forestside, Hants, 1874.

Parson, Rev. Richard, 3s. James, of Guildford, Surrey, cler. MAGDALEN HALL, matric. 13 Dec., 1827, aged 19; B.A. 1832, M.A. 1834, died 5 Jan., 1880. See *Crockford.*

Parson, Thomas Hardwick, 8s. Joseph, of Greenwich, Kent, cler. MAGDALEN HALL, matric. 11 Nov., 1847, aged 20.

Parson, William Henry, 1s. James, of Chiddingfold, Surrey, cler. MAGDALEN HALL, matric. 14 Jan., 1823, aged 18; B.A. 1826, M.A. 1830, perp. curate Pirbright, Surrey, 1838-49, vicar of Lynchmere, Sussex, 1849, until his death 12 March, 1882. [35]

Parson, William Henry Onslow, 1s. William Henry, of Pirbright, Surrey, cler. WORCESTER COLL., matric. 29 June, 1859, aged 18; B.A. 1862, M.A. 1866, of Lynchmere, Sussex, held various curacies 1864-82, vicar of Lynchmere 1882.

Parsons, Andrew Evered, y.s. Henry, of Goathurst, Somerset, cler. WORCESTER COLL., matric. 21 June, 1844, aged 18; B.A. 1848, M.A. 1851, vicar of Haydon, Dorset, 1856, rector of Goathill, Somerset, 1864, until his death 12 Oct., 1876.

Parsons, Anthony, s. Duke, of St. Andrew's, Holborn, London, gent. CHRIST CHURCH, matric. 10 May, 1725, aged 19; B.A. 14 Feb., 1728-9, M.A. 1731, vicar of Marcham, Berks, 1739, and of Ardington 1751 until his death in 1778. See *Alumni West.*, 292.

Parsons, Charles, 3s. James, of Monmouth (town), pleb. JESUS COLL., matric. 30 June, 1848, aged 17; B.A. 1852, M.A. 1855, rector of Penarth, Cardiff, 1863.

Parsons, Charles, o.s. Charles, of Lewes, Sussex, gent. MAGDALEN COLL., matric. 14 Oct., 1871, aged 19; demy 1871-6, B.A. 1876, M.A. 1878, assistant-tutor 1876-8, bar.-at-law, Lincoln's Inn, 1881, died 25 May, 1888. See Foster's *Men at the Bar.*

Parsons, Rev. Charles James, 1s. Charles, of Cardiff, co. Glamorgan, cler. ST. JOHN'S COLL., matric. 22 Jan., 1876, aged 19; scholar KEBLE COLL. 1876-79, B.A. 1879, M.A. 1884.

Parsons, Rev. Charles Joseph, 3s. James, of Gloucester (city), cler. MAGDALEN HALL, matric. 14 Dec., 1822, aged 18; B.A. 1826, M.A. 1841.

Parsons, Daniel, 1s. John, of Clifton, co. Gloucester, cler. ORIEL COLL., matric. 20 May, 1828, aged 17; B.A. 1832, M.A. 1835, died 5 July, 1887.

Parsons, Edward, s. Richard, of Bristol (city), gent. ST. EDMUND HALL, matric. 11 Dec., 1788, aged 25; B.A. 1792. **[5]**

Parsons, Francis Crane, s. Henry, of Ham, Somerset, doctor. EXETER COLL., matric. 9 March, 1749-50, aged 18, B.A. 1753; M.A. from EMMANUEL COLL., Cambridge, 1785, vicar of Holbeton, Devon, 1777, rector of Rimpton and Limpsham, Somerset, 1785.

Parsons, Francis Crane, 1s. Henry, of Goathurst, Somerset, cler. WORCESTER COLL., matric. 6 May, 1826, aged 18; B.A. 1830, M.A. 1833, rector of Goathurst, Somerset, 1845, until his death 28 Sep., 1870.

Parsons, Frederick James, s. James, of Gloucester (city), cler. MAGDALEN COLL., matric. 26 July, 1815, aged 14; demy 1815-33, B.A. 1819, M.A. 1822, fellow 1833-42, B.D. 1834, math. lecturer 1827, bursar 1837, vice-president 1838, dean of divinity 1839, vicar of Selborne, Hants, 1842, until his death 31 Oct., 1875. See *Coll. Reg.*, vii. 264.

Parsons, Frederick William, 1s. Frederick James, of Houghton, Hunts, cler. MAGDALEN COLL., matric. 17 Oct., 1864, aged 18; demy 1863-8, B.A. 1869, M.A. 1876, rector of Tatsfield, Kent, 1884.

Parsons, George Lodowick, 5s. James, of Holywell, Oxford (city), cler. CHRIST CHURCH, matric. 21 Dec., 1827, aged 17; student 1827-49, B.A. 1832, M.A. 1834, vicar of Kirkham, Lancashire, 1848, until his death 27 May, 1852, father of James 1868. **[10]**

Parsons, Harold George, 1s. George, of Blackheath, Kent, gent. WADHAM COLL., matric. 16 Oct., 1886, aged 19; scholar 1885.

Parsons, Rev. Hector Laurence, 3s. Hon. Laurence, of Brighton, Sussex, arm. MAGDALEN COLL., matric. 16 Oct., 1862, aged 19; B.A. 1866. See Foster's *Peerage*, E. ROSSE.

Parsons, Henry, s. Henry, of Bridgewater, Somerset, gent. EXETER COLL., matric. 21 March, 1718-9, aged 18, B.A. 1722; M.A. from TRINITY COLL. 1729.

Parsons, Henry, s. Francis, of Bridgewater, Somerset, cler. EXETER COLL., matric. 10 Oct., 1781, aged 16, B.A. 1785; fellow ORIEL COLL. 1787, M.A. 1788, rector of Goathurst 1789-1845, vicar of Wembdon 1791, preb. of Wells 1791, died 9 Jan., 1845. See *Boase*, 146.

Parsons, Henry, s. Joseph, of Peterborough, Northants, cler. BALLIOL COLL., matric. 30 May, 1816, aged 18; scholar 1816-21, B.A. 1820, M.A. 1823, perp. curate Upton St. Leonards, co. Gloucester, 1833-46, rector of Sandhurst 1850, until his death 2 Jan., 1878. **[15]**

Parsons, Henry, 5s. Robert, of Aveton Giffard, Devon, gent. PEMBROKE COLL., matric. 3 March, 1831, aged 19.

Parsons, Henry, 2s. William, of Tamworth, gent. TRINITY COLL., matric. 6 March, 1856, aged 18; B.A. 1861, M.A. 1865, minor canon Llandaff 1870-9, rector of St. Mary Magdalen, Bridgnorth, 1879.

Parsons, Henry George Joseph, 1s. Henry James, of Arundel, Sussex, cler. MAGDALEN COLL., matric. 26 July, 1838, aged 17; demy 1838-44, B.A. 1842, fellow 1844-61, M.A. 1845, B.D. 1852, dean of divinity 1857, died in 1861. See *Coll. Reg.*, vii. 346.

Parsons, Henry James, s. Joseph, of Ashford, Kent, arm. CHRIST CHURCH, matric. 4 Dec., 1804, aged 17; demy MAGDALEN COLL. 1806-9, B.A. 1808, fellow 1809-20, M.A. 1811, B.D. 1818, rector of Saunderton, Bucks, 1819, and vicar of Arundel, 1828, until his death 3 Aug., 1844. See *Rugby School Reg.*, 78; & *Bloxam*, vii. 157.

Parsons, Henry James, 1s. John, of Bridgewater, Somerset, arm. LINCOLN COLL., matric. 27 March, 1863, aged 18; scholar 1863-5, of the Indian Civil Service 1865, assistant-judge at Ahmedabad, bar.-at-law, Lincoln's Inn, 1877. See Foster's *Men at the Bar* & *Eton School Lists.* **[20]**

Parsons, Herbert, 1s. John, of St. Mary-the-Virgin, Oxford (city), arm. BALLIOL COLL., matric. 29 Nov., 1838, aged 16; B.A. 1842, M.A. 1845.

Parsons, Herbert John, 1s. Herbert, of Elsfield, Oxon, arm. CHRIST CHURCH, matric. 19 Jan., 1877, aged 19. See *Eton School Lists.*

Parsons, Isaac, 'butler of Corpus Christi College;' privilegiatus 19 May, 1759.

Parsons, James, s. — P., of Cirencester, co. Gloucester, pleb. BALLIOL COLL., matric. 22 Oct., 1735, aged 16; B.A. 1739, M.A. 1750.

Parsons, James, s. George, of Sherborne, Dorset, gent. CHRIST CHURCH, matric. 18 June, 1754, aged 19; B.A. 1758, M.A. 1761, rector of Rulthorp, co. Gloucester, 1758, preb. of Exeter 1779, until his death before June, 1785. See *Alumni West.*, 361. **[25]**

Parsons, James, s. James, of Cirencester, co. Gloucester, cler. WADHAM COLL., matric. 16 Dec., 1777, aged 15, B.A. 1781, M.A. 1786; B.D. from ST. ALBAN HALL 1815, and vice-principal, perp. curate Newnham and Little Dean, co. Gloucester, 1800, until his death 6 April, 1847.

Parsons, James, o.s. George Lodowick, of Kirkham, Lancashire, cler. NEW COLL., matric. 16 Oct., 1868, aged 18; B.A. 1872, M.A. 1880, bar.-at-law, Inner Temple, 1876. See Foster's *Men at the Bar.*

Parsons, James Ramsay, o.s. John, of Bombay, gent. ST. JOHN'S COLL., matric. 12 Oct., 1872, aged 19; B.A. 1876, M.A. 1880, bar.-at-law, Inner Temple, 1879. See Foster's *Men at the Bar.*

Parsons, John, s. Henry, of Ledgborough, co. Worcester, gent. PEMBROKE COLL., matric. 13 April, 1725, aged 17; B.A. 1728, M.A. 1731.

Parsons, John, s. William, of St. Andrew's, Holborn, London, baronet. MERTON COLL., matric. 30 June, 1731, aged 15; B.A. 5 March, 1734-5, M.A. 1739, died young. **[30]**

Parsons, John, s. John, of York (city), arm. CHRIST CHURCH, matric. 19 June, 1759, aged 18; B.A. 1763, M.A. 1766, B.Med. 1769, D.Med. 1772, reader in anatomy 1769, clinical professor 1780-85, fellow College of Physicians 1775, died 9 April, 1785, buried in Christ Church Cathedral. See Munk's *Roll.*, ii. 303; & *Alumni West.*, 372.

Parsons, John, s. Joseph, of Upton Warren, co. Worcester, gent. WORCESTER COLL., matric. 22 June, 1762, aged 18; B.A. 1766, M.A. 1769.

Parsons, John, s. John, of Naunton, co. Gloucester, cler. QUEEN'S COLL., matric. 29 Oct., 1762, aged 18; B.A. 1766.

Parsons, John, s. John, of Lincoln (city), gent. BRASENOSE COLL., matric. 17 May, 1776, aged 17; B.A. 1780, fellow, M.A. 1782, B. & D.D. 1800, rector of Skegness, co. Lincoln, 1785, died rector of St. John's, Wapping, in 1833.

Parsons, John, s. Isaac, of Oxford (city), pleb. WADHAM COLL., matric. 30 June, 1777, aged 15, scholar 1780-5, B.A. 1782; fellow BALLIOL COLL. 1785, M.A. 1785, B. & D.D. 1799, master 1798-1819, vice-chancellor 1807-10, rector of All Saints' and St. Leonard's, Colchester, 1797-8, dean of Bristol 1810-13, bishop of Peterborough 1813, until his death 12 March, 1819.

Parsons, John, s. John, of Toddington, co. Gloucester, cler. ST. MARY HALL, matric. 10 Oct., 1788, aged 17 (? if the bar.-at-law, Middle Temple, 1797, who died in 1800).

Parsons, John, s. Francis, of Yeovil, Somerset, cler. WORCESTER COLL., matric. 23 May, 1798, aged 18; B.A. 1802, M.A. 1804, fellow until 1814, vicar of Oborne and Castleton, Dorset, 1811-54, curate of Sherborne 1803-11, vicar 1830, until his death 1 July, 1854.

Parsons, John, s. Daniel, of Isle of Barbados, West Indies, arm. UNIVERSITY COLL., matric. 24 June, 1800, aged 17, B.A. 1805; fellow ORIEL COLL. 1807-12, M.A. 1807, vicar of Marden, Wilts, 1816, until his death 31 July, 1844. See *Gent.'s Mag.*, ii. 1844; but see also *Gent.'s Mag.*, 1825, i. 378.

Parsons, John. BRASENOSE COLL., 1800. See HOPTON. [5]

Parsons, John, 2s. John, of Oxford (city), arm. TRINITY COLL., matric. 7 April, 1854, aged 19; B.A. 1858, M.A. 1860, of Oxford, banker. See *Rugby School Reg.*, 289.

Parsons, John, 4s. Joshua, of Peckington, Somerset, gent. CHRIST CHURCH, matric. 18 Oct., 1870, aged 18; exhibitioner 1870-2, B.A. 1874, M.A. 1881.

Parsons, John Clere, 2s. Laurence, Earl of Rosse in Ireland. MAGDALEN COLL., matric. 1 Feb., 1821, aged 18; B.A. 1822, a student of Lincoln's Inn 1822, died 10 Aug., 1828. See Foster's *Peerage*.

Parsons, John Tournay, 1s. Henry, of Upton St. Leonard, co. Gloucester, cler. BALLIOL COLL., matric. 21 March, 1844, aged 18; B.A. 1847, vicar of Much Dewchurch, co. Hereford, 1850, until his death 23 July, 1878. See *Eton School Lists*.

Parsons, Joseph, 'tonsor;' privilegiatus 28 Feb., 1754. [10]

Parsons, Joseph, s. Joseph, of Oxford (city), pleb. TRINITY COLL., matric. 17 March, 1779, aged 17; B.A. 1782, M.A. 1785, rector of Holwell, Beds, 1810, preb. of Peterborough 1815, rector of Glinton with Peykirk, Northants, 1816, until his death 1 Feb., 1829.

Parsons, Laurence, (4th) Earl of Rosse, created D.C.L. 22 June, 1870; chancellor Dublin University 1885, an Irish representative peer 1868. See Foster's *Peerage*.

Parsons, (Sir) Mark, (Bart.), s. William, of Westminster. CHRIST CHURCH, matric. 22 Dec., 1760, aged 19; created M.A. ORIEL COLL. 22 Nov., 1765, 4th baronet, died in 1812.

Parsons, Read, s. Ed., of Montserrat, America, gent. CHRIST CHURCH, matric. 20 May, 1731, aged 18.

Parsons, Robert, s. Philip, of Oakham, Rutland, cler. LINCOLN COLL., matric. 3 April, 1775, aged 17; B.A. 1778, M.A. 1782. (Rev. R. P. died at Sevenoaks 1 Aug., 1819. See *Gent.'s Mag.*, ii. 187). [15]

Parsons, Thomas, 'janitor of the theatre;' privilegiatus 23 Dec., 1746.

Parsons, Wallace Edward, 2s. John, of Oxon, gent. PEMBROKE COLL., matric. 3 Feb., 1874, aged 19.

Parsons, William, s. Richard, of Much Wenlock, Salop, pleb. CHRIST CHURCH, matric. 20 March, 1716-7, aged 18; B.A. 1720.

Parsons, William. TRINITY COLL., 1777. See HOPTON.

Parsons, William, s. Richard, of St. Anne's, Westminster, gent. MAGDALEN COLL., matric. 23 June, 1790, aged 42; B. & D.Mus. 26 June, 1790, then "master of H.M. band of musicians." [20]

Parsons, William, Baron Oxmantown, born at York, 1s. Laurence, Earl of Rosse, in Ireland. MAGDALEN COLL., matric. 1 Feb., 1821, aged 20; B.A. 1822, hon. fellow 1862-7, 3rd earl, M.P. King's County 1821-35, an Irish representative peer 1845, erected a monster telescope on his estate at Parsonstown about 1842, at a cost exceeding £20,000, F.R.S. 1824, president British Association 1843, and of Royal Society 1849-54, chancellor of the University of Dublin 1865, died 31 Oct., 1867. See Foster's *Peerage*.

Partington, Charles Edward, 3s. James Edge, of Manchester, Lancashire, gent. WORCESTER COLL., matric. 9 June, 1848, aged 22; B.A. 1852, M.A. 1854, vicar of Stoke Mandeville with Buckland 1858-72, rector of St. Ambrose, Manchester, 1884. See *Manchester School Reg.*, iii. 277.

Partington, Henry, 3s. Thomas, of Offham, Sussex, arm. CHRIST CHURCH, matric. 13 May, 1826, aged 18; student 1826-34, B.A. 1830, M.A. 1832, vicar of Wath-on-Dearne since 1833. See *Alumni West.*, 497.

Partington, Thomas, s. Thomas Walley, of Westminster, arm. CHRIST CHURCH, matric. 5 June, 1776, aged 16; B.A. 1780, M.A. 1783, of Offham, Sussex, bar.-at-law, Lincoln's Inn, 1784, chairman Lewes Quarter Sessions, died 5 April, 1842. See *Alumni West.*, 405.

Partington, Thomas, 1s. Thomas, of Hamsey, Sussex, arm. CHRIST CHURCH, matric. 18 May, 1822, aged 18; student 1822-30, B.A. 1826, M.A. 1828. See *Alumni West.*, 490. [25]

Partington, William Charles Mackenzie, 2s. William Henry, of Manchester, gent. QUEEN'S COLL., matric. 30 Oct., 1885, aged 20.

Partridge, Aubrey Arthur Hungerford, 1s. Arthur, of Handsworth, co. Stafford, arm. BALLIOL COLL., matric. 21 Oct., 1880, aged 20; B.A. 1884.

Partridge, Christopher, s. Christopher, of Hazlebury, Somerset, pleb. WADHAM COLL., matric. 6 April, 1734, aged 19; B.A. 1737, brother of Francis 1721.

Partridge, Christopher, s. John, of Witheridge, Devon, pleb. BALLIOL COLL., matric. 30 March, 1765, aged 18.

Partridge, Francis, s. Christopher, of Hazlebury, Somerset, pleb. WADHAM COLL., matric. 1 April, 1721, aged 19; B.A. 1724, brother of Christopher 1734.

Partridge, Henry, s. Henry, of Lincoln (city), pleb. PEMBROKE COLL., matric. 3 Dec., 1762, aged 18; B.A. from MAGDALEN COLL. 1766, M.A. 1769, brother of Samuel 1768. [31]

Partridge, Henry, s. Henry, of Lynn, Norfolk, arm. WADHAM COLL., matric. 10 Oct., 1764, aged 18; of Northwold and Lowbrooks, Norfolk, bar.-at-law, Middle Temple, 1770, K.C. and a bencher 1787, died 30 Dec., 1803, father of Henry Samuel and of John Anthony.

Partridge, Henry Champion, 1s. Henry Samuel, of Berwick, Norfolk, arm. BRASENOSE COLL., matric. 18 Oct., 1825, aged 18; B.A. 1829, M.A. 1833, bar.-at-law, Inner Temple, 1833, died 20 Oct., 1850.

Partridge, Henry Samuel, s. Henry, of St. Andrew's, London, arm. MAGDALEN COLL., matric. 22 June, 1801, aged 19; of Hockham Hall, Norfolk, J.P., D.L., died 1 Oct., 1858, father of the last named.

Partridge, James, s. Edm., of Burford, Oxon, gent. WORCESTER COLL., matric. 6 July, 1739, aged 17; B.A. 1743. [35]

Partridge, John, s. James, of Wormington, co. Gloucester, cler. MAGDALEN HALL, matric. 22 Oct., 1718, aged 18; B.A. 1722.

Partridge, John, s. William, of Goodrich, co. Hereford, arm. QUEEN'S COLL., matric. 30 April, 1812, aged 17.

Partridge, John Anthony, s. Henry, of Bedford Row, London, arm. BRASENOSE COLL., matric. 14 Jan., 1813, aged 18; B.A. 1817, M.A. 1820, rector of Cranwich and vicar of Freshwold, Norfolk, 1818, rector of Town Barningham 1819, of Wretham, Norfolk, 1831, and rector of Baconsthorpe and of Boldham, Norfolk, 1840, until his death 27 Feb., 1861, brother of Henry Samuel.

Partridge, Joseph Ashby, s. Joseph, of St. James's, Westminster, arm. CHRIST CHURCH, matric. 23 Oct., 1792, aged 18; B.A. from WORCESTER COLL. 1796, a student of Lincoln's Inn 1793.

Partridge, Lionel Stroud, 2s. Joseph Arthur, of Castle Bromwich, co. Warwick, arm. MAGDALEN COLL., matric. 16 Oct., 1884, aged 19; B.A. 1888.

Partridge, Richard William, 1s. William, of London, arm. WADHAM COLL., matric. 26 Nov., 1862, aged 18; bar.-at-law, Middle Temple, 1873. See Foster's *Men at the Bar.*

Partridge, Robert Wynyard, s. Robert, of Cawnpore, East Indies, arm. TRINITY COLL., matric. 26 March, 1817, aged 17.

Partridge, Samuel, s. Henry, of Lincoln (city), gent. CORPUS CHRISTI COLL., matric. 26 March, 1768, aged 17; demy MAGDALEN COLL. 1771-4, B.A. 1772, fellow 1774-82, M.A. 1775, fellow Society Antiquaries, rector of Leveston (south mediety), and vicar of Boston, co. Lincoln, 1785, and vicar of Wigtoff-cum-Quadring 1797, until his death in Aug., 1817, father of Thomas 1809. See *Bloxam*, vi. 353; & *Gent.'s Mag.*, 1817, ii. 186. **[5]**

Partridge, Samuel John, 1s. John William, of Stroud, co. Gloucester, gent. QUEEN'S COLL., matric. 9 June, 1836, aged 18; bar.-at-law, Gray's Inn, 1842, died 2 June, 1855.

Partridge, Thomas, s. Thomas, of North Perrott, Somerset, pleb. WADHAM COLL., matric. 19 March, 1729-30, aged 20; B.A. 1733.

Partridge, Thomas, s. Thos., of Isle of Jamaica, gent. ST. MARY HALL, matric. 13 Dec., 1759, aged 18.

Partridge, Thomas, s. Samuel, of Boston, co. Lincoln, cler. BRASENOSE COLL., matric. 15 Dec., 1809, aged 16; scholar 1812-6.

Partridge, Thomas Esbury, s. Thomas, of Hilsley, co. Gloucester, gent. MERTON COLL., matric. 10 Oct., 1785, aged 17; B.A. 1789, M.A. 1792, 'late of Hillsley,' rector of Uley, co. Gloucester, 1793, until his death 18 Jan., 1823. **[10]**

Partridge, William, s. Roger, of Lapford, Devon, gent. EXETER COLL., matric. 2 April, 1781, aged 18; B.A. 1785, rector of Romansleigh, Devon, 1797. See *Gent.'s Mag.*, 1828, ii. 378.

Partridge, William, 1s. John, of Monmouth (town), arm. CHRIST CHURCH, matric. 20 Oct., 1836, aged 18; B.A. 1840, M.A. 1860, of Wyelands, co. Gloncester, bar.-at-law, Middle Temple, 1843, stipendiary magistrate Wolverhampton 1860-3, police magistrate Westminster Police Court since 1863. See Foster's *Men at the Bar.*

Partridge, William Campbell, 1s. William, of King's Hill, near Wednesbury, co. Stafford, arm. MAGDALEN COLL., matric. 18 April, 1874, aged 18; demy 1873-5.

Partridge, William Edwards, 2s. Charles Anthony, of Blagdon, Somerset, arm. BRASENOSE COLL., matric. 26 April, 1827, aged 18; B.A. 1831, rector of Horsendon, Herts, 1844, until his death 18 May, 1886. See *Rugby School Reg.*, 144.

Partridge, William Robinson, o.s. William, of Edgbaston, co. Worcester, gent. PEMBROKE COLL., matric. 6 May, 1847, aged 19. **[15]**

Pasco, Thomas, 'alchymista;' privilegiatus 1 July, 1777.

Pascoe, James, s. Humphrey, of St. Ives, Cornwall, gent. EXETER COLL., matric. 17 March, 1740-1, aged 18; B.A. 1744, M.A. 1747.

Pascoe, James, 1s. James, of St. Keverne, Cornwall, cler. EXETER COLL., matric. 17 Feb., 1842, aged 18; B.A. 1845, M.A. 1849.

Pascoe, Richard, 2s. James, of St. Keverne, Cornwall, cler. EXETER COLL., matric. 7 June, 1854, aged 18.

Pascoe, Richard Corbett, 1s. Richard, of Stonehouse, Devon, arm. MAGDALEN HALL, matric. 25 Nov., 1847, aged 18, B.A. 1851; fellow EXETER COLL. 1853-68, M.A. 1854, lecturer 1855, vice-principal Lichfield Theological College 1855-61, principal Theological College 1861-7, rector of St. Stephen's, Exeter, 1862-3, died 9 June, 1868. See *Boase*, 139.

Pascoe, Thomas, s. Thomas, of Sithney, Cornwall, pleb. EXETER COLL., matric. 18 March, 1718-9, aged 18; B.A. 1722. **[21]**

Pascoe, Wellington Renton, y.s. Thomas, of Philipstown, Ireland, gent. LINCOLN COLL., matric. 19 Jan., 1885, aged 28.

Paske, George, s. George, of Alderley, co. Gloucester, arm. WADHAM COLL., matric. 28 March, 1726, aged 18; B.A. 1729, M.A. 1732, died vicar of Finchinfield June, 1753.

Pasley, General Sir Charles William, R.E., K.C.B., created D.C.L. 20 June, 1844, served at the siege of Copenhagen 1807, at the battle of Corunna 16 Jan., 1809, and in the Walcheren expedition 1809, C.B. 26 Sep., 1831, K.C.B. 21 Dec., 1846, inspector-general Board of Trade, colonel-commandant R.E., general 1860, died 19 April, 1861. See *Gent.'s Mag.*, i. 698.

Pasley, Hamilton Sabine, 4s. Thomas Sabine, of Windermere, Westmoreland, baronet. TRINITY COLL., matric. 5 June, 1855, aged 18; scholar 1855-60, B.A. 1859, sometime captain Cape mounted rifles. See Foster's *Baronetage.* **[25]**

Pasmore, John, s. John, of Helston, Cornwall, arm. EXETER COLL., matric. 19 March, 1766, aged 18; B.A. 1770, alderman of the borough of Helston, rector of St. Just 1793, until his death in 1803.

Pass, Robert, 1s. John, of Boston, co. Lincoln, gent. QUEEN'S COLL., matric. 22 June, 1854, aged 20.

Pass, William, o.s. John, of Stockport, Cheshire, arm. ST. MARY HALL, matric. 23 March, 1822, aged 18.

Passand, Henry, 'pharmacopola;' privilegiatus 25 April, 1789, father of the next named.

Passand, Henry John, o.s. Henry, of Oxford (city), gent. QUEEN'S COLL., matric. 15 March, 1820, aged 18; B.A. from ST. ALBAN HALL 1824, M.A. 1827, rector of Shipton-on-Cherwell, Oxon, 1831, until his death 16 Oct., 1867. See *Eton School Lists.* **[30]**

Passingham, Rev. Robert Townsend, s. Robert, of Richmond, Surrey, gent. WORCESTER COLL., matric. 14 Feb., 1818, aged 21; B.A. 1821, M.A. 1824, died at Tyfos, co. Merioneth, 8 April, 1847.

Passmore, Hugh Maire, s. John, of South Molton, Devon, gent. EXETER COLL., matric. 21 May, 1798, aged 18; B.A. 1802.

Passmore, William Philip, y.s. Francis Burdett, of North Molton, Devon, arm. NON-COLL., matric. 23 May, 1885, aged 33; B.A. from EXETER COLL. 1888.

Passow, John Claus de, s. — P., of Elsted, Kent, arm. TRINITY COLL., matric. 23 June, 1792, aged 19; B.A. 1796, M.A. 1799, rector of Hever, Kent, 1799, until his death 23 Feb., 1850.

Patch, Gayer, s. John, of Exeter (city), gent. WADHAM COLL., matric. 14 Dec., 1776, aged 21; B.A. 1780, M.A. 1783, rector of St. Leonard, Devon, 1780, until his death in 1825. See *St. Paul's School Reg.*, 140. **[35]**

Patch, James Terry, 1s. Thomas Lodge, of Singapore, East Indies, gent. EXETER COLL., matric. 25 May, 1858, aged 18; B.A. 1863, M.A. 1865, perp. curate of St. Stephen, Selly Hill, Birmingham, 1871-9.

Patch, John Barnes, 1s. Frederick Owen, of Tiverton, Devon, arm. MERTON COLL., matric. 19 June, 1852, aged 18; B.A. 1857.

Patch, Rev. Robert (Gayer), s. Robert, of Exeter, Devon, arm. WADHAM COLL., matric. 15 Oct., 1804, aged 16; B.A. 1809, M.A. 1813, scholar until 1813, fellow 1813-34, died in 1840.

Patch, Robert Burnett, s. John, of Exeter (city), gent. EXETER COLL., matric. 13 March, 1744-5, aged 18; fellow 1747-51, B.A. 22 March, 1750-1, schoolmaster at Crewkerne, Somerset. See *Coll. Reg.*, 103.

Patchell, Charles Watson, 1s. William Gibson, of Drove End, co. Lincoln, cler. LINCOLN COLL., matric. 21 Oct., 1878, aged 17; scholar 1878-82, B.A. 1882. **[40]**

Pater, Walter Horatio, 3s. Richard Glode, of London, arm. QUEEN'S COLL., matric. 11 June, 1858, aged 18, B.A. 1862; fellow BRASENOSE COLL. 1864, M.A. 1865, junior dean 1866, tutor 1867-83, dean 1871, lecturer 1873, writer on art, author of 'Marius the Epicurean,' etc.

Paterson, Archibald Robert, 6s. Robert, of Glasgow, arm. TRINITY COLL., matric. 12 Oct., 1878, aged 18; B.A. 1884.

Paterson, Arthur Bourne, 1s. Robert, of Coulter, co. Lanark, arm. HERTFORD COLL., matric. 18 Oct., 1880, aged 19, B.A. 1883.

Paterson, Rev. Francis, 3s. James, of Marylebone, London, arm. TRINITY COLL., matric. 16 March, 1849, aged 18; B.A. 1852, died at Funchal, Madeira, 28 March, 1854.

Paterson, George, 1s. George, of Edinburgh (city), arm. WADHAM COLL., matric. 11 May, 1836, aged 16; B.A. 1840, M.A. 1843, a member of the Scottish Faculty of Advocates 1842, J.P. co. Perth, died 25 Feb., 1867. [5]

Paterson, George Frederick, 1s. George, of Edinburgh, arm. MERTON COLL., matric. 20 Jan., 1877, aged 20; of Castle Huntly, co. Perth, D.L.

Paterson, George Mapletoft, 1s. John, of Putney, Surrey, arm. LINCOLN COLL., matric. 26 Nov., 1840, aged 19; B.A. 1844, M.A. 1847, rector of Brome, Norfolk, 1847, until his death 1 Aug., 1887.

Paterson, Gordon Walker, 4s. John, of St. Andrew's, N.B., gent. TRINITY COLL., matric. 14 Oct., 1882, aged 19; B.A. 1885.

Paterson, James, s. Thomas, of Greenwich, Kent, arm. CHRIST CHURCH, matric. 24 Oct., 1804, aged 17; B.A. 1809.

Paterson, James Alexander, 1s. Alexander, of Dalry, co. Kirkcudbright, cler. PEMBROKE COLL., matric. 20 Oct., 1873, aged 22; scholar 1873-7, B.A. 1876, M.A. 1880. [10]

Paterson, James Erskine, 1s. James, of Linlathen, co. Angus, arm. BALLIOL COLL., matric. 21 March, 1844, aged 18.

Paterson, Leslie Rimmer, 3s. Thomas Simpson, of Rock Ferry, Cheshire, gent. KEBLE COLL., matric. 22 Oct., 1885, aged 19.

Paterson, Noel Huntingdon, 2s. John, of Marylebone, London, gent. ST. JOHN'S COLL., matric. 29 June, 1863, aged 19; exhibitioner 1863, B.A. 1867, M.A. 1872, bar.-at-law, Middle Temple, 1869, killed on the Lyskamm, in Switzerland, 7 Sep., 1877. See *Robinson*, 321.

Paterson, Thomas Board, 2s. James, of Marylebone, Middlesex, arm. CHRIST CHURCH, matric. 20 Oct., 1841, aged 18.

Paterson, William Vautier, o.s. William B., of Kensington, gent. EXETER COLL., matric. 15 Oct., 1879, aged 18; B.A. 1882, M.A. 1886. [15]

Pateshall, John, s. Edmund, of Allensmore, co. Hereford, gent. PEMBROKE COLL., matric. 12 March, 1732-3, aged 18; B.A. 1736, died 1772.

Pateshall, Walter (Lechmere), s. Edmund, of Allensmore, co. Hereford, arm. ST. JOHN'S COLL., matric. 6 May, 1807, aged 19; B.A. 1811, M.A. 1814, perp. curate Grendon-Bishop, co. Hereford, 1815, until his death in 1820. See Foster's *Baronetage*, LECHMERE.

Patey, Charles Robert, 1s. George Edwin, of Plymouth, arm. EXETER COLL., matric. 28 Oct., 1872, aged 19; B.A. 1876, rector of Scremby, co. Lincoln, 1881.

Paton, Alexander, scholar of QUEEN'S COLL., Cambridge, 1833 (junior optime & B.A. 1835, M.A. 1839); adm. 'comitatis causa' 10 Oct., 1865, rector of Tuddenham St. Martin, Suffolk, 1846-75.

Paton, Alfred Vaughan, 1s. John Brown, of Sheffield Yorks, cler. TRINITY COLL., matric. 16 Oct., 1880, aged 18; scholar 1880-4, B.A. 1887, lecturer in the College of Science, University of Durham, a student of the Middle Temple 1883. [20]

Paton, Frederick Lechmere, 2s. George Blagrove (of Lincoln's Inn), arm. ORIEL COLL., matric. 19 Oct., 1870, aged 18; B.A. 1873, M.A. 1877, bar.-at-law, Lincoln's Inn, 1877. See Foster's *Men at the Bar.*

Paton, James, 2s. Henry, of London, arm. MAGDALEN HALL, matric. 25 Oct., 1871, aged 36; held various curacies, etc., 1866-80, vicar of Hemingborough, Yorks, 1880.

Paton, Rev. John Duguid, 3s. Alexander, of Tuddenham, Suffolk, cler. ST. EDMUND HALL, matric. 22 Jan., 1880, aged 23; B.A. 1881.

Paton, Walter Boldero, 3s. George, of London, gent. UNIVERSITY COLL., matric. 11 Oct., 1872, aged 19; B.A. 1876, M.A. 1879, bar.-at-law, Inner Temple, 1879. See Foster's *Men at the Bar.*

Paton, William Roger, 1s. John, of Grandholme, co. Aberdeen, arm. UNIVERSITY COLL., matric. 13 Oct., 1876, aged 19; of Grandholme aforesaid, a student of the Middle Temple 1878. See *Eton School Lists.* [25]

Patourel, Wallace Mackenzie le, 1s. Mesurier, of St. Peter Port, Guernsey, arm. BALLIOL COLL., matric. 19 Oct., 1886, aged 21.

Patriarche, John, s. Philip, of Hants, gent. PEMBROKE COLL., matric. 16 Oct., 1730, aged 17.

Patrick, Rev. John Arthur, 1s. William Smith, of Strensham, co. Worcester, arm. WADHAM COLL., matric. 16 Oct., 1874, aged 17; B.A. 1877, M.A. 1881.

Patrick, Robert, s. Robert, of Llanidlos, co. Montgomery, cler. JESUS COLL., matric. 22 March, 1730-1, aged 18.

Patridge, Sylvanus Roger, o.s. Roger, of Marylebone, London, arm. TRINITY COLL., matric. 13 May, 1837, aged 20. [30]

Patten, Alexander, 6s. James, of Edinburgh, arm. ORIEL COLL., matric. 31 Oct., 1882, aged 19.

Patten, James, 1s. John, of Edinburgh, arm. CHRIST CHURCH, matric. 24 Jan., 1868, aged 18; B.A. 1872, M.A. 1876, bar.-at-law, Inner Temple, 1873, a member of the Faculty of Advocates, Scotland, July, 1874. See Foster's *Men at the Bar.*

Patten-Bold, Peter, s. Thomas Patten, of Warrington, Lancashire, arm. CORPUS CHRISTI COLL., matric. 23 Oct., 1783, aged 19; created M.A. 4 July, 1793, and also D.C.L. 18 June, 1817 (see page 129), of Bank Hall, and of Bold Hall, Lancashire, assumed the additional surname and arms of BOLD, May, 1814, M.P. Newton, Lancashire, 1797-1806, Lancaster 1807-12, Malmesbury 1813-8, buried 17 Oct., 1819. See Foster's *Lancashire Collection.*

Patten, Thomas, s. Thomas, of Warrington, Lancashire, gent. BRASENOSE COLL., matric. 6 Feb., 1729-30, aged 16; B.A. from CORPUS CHRISTI COLL. 1733, M.A. 17 Feb., 1736-7, B.D. 1744, D.D. 1754, died rector of Childrey, Berks, 20 Feb., 1790, buried 28th. See Foster's *Lancashire Collection.*

Patten, Thomas, s. Thomas, of Warrington, Lancashire, arm. CORPUS CHRISTI COLL., matric. 14 Jan., 1748-9, aged 16; created M.A. 27 Feb., 1752, of Bank Hall, high sheriff, Lancashire, 1773, and of Cheshire 1775, lieut.-colonel royal Lancashire militia, died 19 March, 1806. See Foster's *Lancashire Collection.* [35]

Pattenden, Frederick William Waldebrand, 2s. George Edwin, of Boston, co. Lincoln, cler. NEW COLL., matric. 13 Oct., 1876, aged 19; scholar 1876-81, B.A. 1880, M.A. 1884, bar.-at-law, Inner Temple, 1884. See Foster's *Men at the Bar.*

Pattenden, George Edwin, of ST. PETER'S COLL., Cambridge (B.A. 1847, M.A. 1851), adm. 'ad eundem' 7 July, 1859, B.D. 1861, LL.D. 1871, head-master Boston School 1850, preb. of Lincoln 1883, vicar of Chertsey 1887.

Pattenson, Arthur Henry Tylden, 2s. William Hodges, of Biddenden, Kent, arm. BRASENOSE COLL., matric. 4 March, 1875, aged 18.

Pattenson, Charles, 1s. Charles, of East Indies, arm. MAGDALEN HALL, matric. 17 July, 1823, aged 17.

Pattenson, Christopher, s. John, of Penrithson, Cumberland, arm. QUEEN'S COLL., matric. 20 May, 1735, aged 17 (called PATTERSON in *Mat. Reg.*).

Pattenson, Robert Cane, 4s. John Edward, of Dacca, Bengal, gent. WADHAM COLL., matric. 18 June, 1835, aged 18; B.C.L. from ST. MARY HALL 1842, rector of Melmerby, Cumberland, 1844-81.

Pattenson, Thomas, s. Lancelot, of Melmerby, Cumberland, arm. ORIEL COLL., matric. 14 Dec., 1764, aged 17. [5]

Patterson, James Laird, 2s. William, of Marylebone, London, arm. TRINITY COLL., matric. 19 Nov., 1840, aged 18; B.A. 1846, M.A. 1847, curate of St. Thomas, Oxford, seceded to Rome 1850, president of St. Edmund's College, Ware, 1870-80, Roman Catholic bishop of Emmaus 1880 (Monsignor Patterson).

Patterson, James William, 1s. William, of Liskeard, Cornwall, gent. MAGDALEN HALL, matric. 22 April, 1869, aged 25.

Patterson, Rev. John Irwin, 2s. William, of Sandhurst, Berks, arm. NON-COLL., matric. 19 April, 1879, aged 19; B.A. from PEMBROKE COLL. 1882.

Patterson, Sutton, o.s. Robert, of Newcastle-on-Tyne, gent. NON-COLL., matric. 6 Feb., 1880, aged 31.

Patterson, William Harry, 1s. William, of London, arm. PEMBROKE COLL., matric. 6 Feb., 1878, aged 18; B.A. 1881. [10]

Patterson, William Talbot Nugent, 3s. Robert, of Lifford, co. Donegal (Ireland), arm. EXETER COLL., matric. 17 Oct., 1828, aged 18; a student of the Inner Temple 1835.

Patteson, Edward, s. William, of Birmingham, co. Warwick, gent. TRINITY COLL., matric. 1 Dec., 1750, aged 17; B.A. 1754, M.A. 1757.

Patteson, Rev. Edward, s. Edward, of Smethwick (par. Harborne), co. Stafford, cler. TRINITY COLL., matric. 31 March, 1781, aged 18; B.A. 1784, M.A. 1787, died at East Sheen 21 June, 1845.

Patteson, Edward, 2s. Edward, of Richmond, Surrey, cler. BALLIOL COLL., matric. 5 May, 1819, aged 17.

Patteson, James Henry, 2s. John, of Hindon, Wilts, arm. BALLIOL COLL., matric. 11 Dec., 1846, aged 18; B.A. 1850, M.A. 1853, bar.-at-law, Middle Temple, 1853, secretary of the Court of Probate 1858-63, sometime police magistrate Greenwich and Woolwich. See Foster's *Men at the Bar* & *Eton School Lists*. [15]

Patteson, John Coleridge, 1s. John, of St. Giles's, London, equitis. BALLIOL COLL., matric. 14 March, 1845, aged 17, B.A. 1848; fellow MERTON COLL. 1852-71, M.A. 1853, created D.D. 6 June, 1861, bishop of Melanesia 1861, until killed by natives at Mukapu 20 Sep., 1871. See *Eton School Lists*.

Patteson, Thomas, 3s. Henry, of Catton, Norfolk, cler. EXETER COLL., matric. 6 March, 1826, aged 18; B.A. 1830, M.A. 1832, vicar of Hambledon, Hants, 1841, until his death 4 June, 1874. See *Eton School Lists*.

Patteson, Thomas Charles, o.s. Thomas, of Putney, Wilts, cler. MERTON COLL., matric. 24 Nov., 1854, aged 18; postmaster 1854-8, B.A. 1858. See *Eton School Lists*.

Patteson, William, s. Edward, of Quath, Salop, cler. BALLIOL COLL., matric. 28 March, 1808, aged 20; B.A. 1811, M.A. 1817, rector of St. James's, Shaftesbury, 1833, until his death 17 March, 1859.

Pattinson, James Pearson, 1s. Thomas, of Congleton, Cheshire, gent. ORIEL COLL., matric. 14 Oct., 1878, aged 18; B.A. 1881, M.A. 1886. [20]

Pattinson, John, s. Thomas, of Holme Cultram, Cumberland, pleb. QUEEN'S COLL., matric. 19 Nov., 1773, aged 20; B.A. 1778, M.A. 1782, died curate of Northwood, Isle of Wight, in 1843.

Pattison, Mark, 1s. Mark James, of Hornby, Yorks, cler. ORIEL COLL., matric. 5 April, 1832, aged 18, B.A. 1836; fellow LINCOLN COLL. 1839-60, M.A. 1840, B.D. 1851, Greek lecturer 1841, tutor 1842-55, bursar 1843, sub-rector 1846, pro-vice-chancellor, delegate of the press and curator of the Bodleian library, rector of Lincoln College 1861, until his death 30 July, 1884, author of 'Life of Casaubon,' etc.

Pattison, Mark James, s. Mark, of Plymouth, Devon, arm. BRASENOSE COLL., matric. 21 Oct., 1805, aged 17; B.A. 1809, M.A. 1812, rector of Hawkeswell, Yorks, 1825, until his death 30 Dec., 1865.

Patton, Frederick Joseph, 1s. Joseph, of Bombay, arm. BALLIOL COLL., matric. 31 Jan., 1870, aged 19; B.A. 1875, bar.-at-law, Inner Temple, 1875. See Foster's *Men at the Bar* & *Eton School Lists*.

Patton, Rev. Thomas Lionel, 1s. Lionel, of Taunton, Somerset, gent. QUEEN'S COLL., matric. 28 Oct., 1881, aged 19; B.A. 1885. [25]

Pattrick, Arthur Henry Saint, 4s. Charles George Henry, of Worcester, gent. NON-COLL., matric. 9 April, 1875, aged 20; B.A. from QUEEN'S COLL. 1879, M.A. 1884, curate of Leysters, co. Hereford, 1880-2, 1885-6.

Pattrick, Beaufoy James Saint, 2s. Charles Thomas Saint, of Cradley, co. Hereford, cler. CHRIST CHURCH, matric. 26 May, 1841, aged 18; B.A. from ST. MARY HALL 1847, vicar of Weston Beggard, co. Hereford, 1853-80, rector of Chillesford, Suffolk, 1882.

Pattrick, Charles Thomas, s. George, of Blackheath, Kent, cler. ST. EDMUND HALL, matric. 10 Oct., 1808, aged 18; B.A. 1812, M.A. 1815.

Pattrick, Rev. John Brooke, 3s. John, of Dovercourt, Essex, arm. WADHAM COLL., matric. 9 Dec., 1864, aged 18; B.A. 1867, M.A. 1875.

Pattrick, Reginald Saint, 3s. Thomas Saint, of Sherborne, Dorset, cler. QUEEN'S COLL., matric. 22 June, 1854, aged 19; B.A. 1858, held various curacies 1862-74, vicar of Sellinge, Kent, 1874. [30]

Paty, George Perry Heywood, 1s. John, of Sydney, New South Wales, arm. LINCOLN COLL., matric. 26 March, 1851, aged 20; B.A. 1855, M.A. 1858.

Paul, Albert Saint, 1s. Charles, of Bristol, co. Gloucester, gent. ST. JOHN'S COLL., matric. 26 June, 1854, aged 18; B.A. 1858, M.A. 1862.

Paul, Alfred Wallis, 5s. Charles, of Redland, near Bristol, arm. WADHAM COLL., matric. 12 Oct., 1866, aged 19; scholar 1866-70, S.C.L. & B.A. 1870, of the Indian Civil Service 1868, a student of the Middle Temple 1868.

Paul, Charles Kegan, 1s. Charles, of Ilminster, Somerset, cler. EXETER COLL., matric. 29 Jan., 1846, aged 17; B.A. 1849, M.A. 1868, curate of Great Tew, Oxon, 1851-2, and of Bloxham 1852-3, conduct of Eton, and assistant-master 1854-62, vicar of Sturminster Marshall, Dorset, 1862-75, of London, publisher. See *Eton School Lists*. [34]

Paul, Dolben, 2s. Samuel Woodfield, of Finedon, Northants, cler. CHRIST CHURCH, matric. 23 May, 1850, aged 17; B.A. 1854, M.A. 1865, held various curacies 1857-67, rector of Bearwood, Berks, 1868.

Paul, Edward Clifford 3s. Theodore, of Llanbadawrfawr, co. Cardigan, gent. JESUS COLL., matric. 23 Oct., 1880, aged 17; B.A. 1884, M.A. 1877.

Paul, Rev. Frederick Campbell, 2s. William, of Waltham Cross, Herts, gent. MERTON COLL., matric. 18 Oct., 1880, aged 19; postmaster 1880-4, B.A. 1884, M.A. 1887.

Paul, Frederick William, 2s. William Henry, of Ash, Surrey, arm. WADHAM COLL., matric. 19 Jan., 1877, aged 18; scholar 1876-81, B.A. 1880, M.A. 1883, vicar of Emanuel Church, Nottingham, 1886.

THE VIRGIN'S CHAPEL OR LADY CHAPEL, CAT STREET, now a dwelling. [*From an Engraving by Skelton.*]

Paul, (Sir George) Onesiphorus (Bart.), s. Onesiphorus, of Woodchester, co. Gloucester, baronet. ST. JOHN'S COLL., matric. 8 Dec., 1763, aged 17; created M.A. 12 Dec., 1766, 2nd baronet, died 16 Dec., 1820.

Paul, George Woodfield, 1s. Samuel Woodfield, of Finedon, Northants, cler. WADHAM COLL., matric. 25 Oct., 1838, aged 18, B.A. 1842; fellow MAGDALEN COLL. 1842-8, M.A. 1845, vicar (and patron) of Finedon 1848.

Paul, Herbert Woodfield, 1s. George Woodfield, of Finedon, Northants, cler. CORPUS CHRISTI COLL., matric. 18 Oct., 1871, aged 18; scholar 1871-6, B.A. 1876, bar.-at-law, Lincoln's Inn, 1878. See Foster's *Men at the Bar* & *Eton School Lists.*

Paul, John, s. Dean, of Stroud, co. Gloucester, gent. CHRIST CHURCH, matric. 12 Oct., 1764, aged 19; of Salisbury, D.Med., died 15 June, 1815, father of Sir John Dean Paul, Bart. See Foster's *Baronetage.*

Paul, John, s. John, of Wallingford, Berks, arm. BALLIOL COLL., matric. 5 Nov., 1813, aged 18; B.A. 1817, died 14 Oct., 1817. **[5]**

Paul, John, 2s. John, of Chinnor, Oxon, gent. MAGDALEN HALL, matric. 18 March, 1837, aged 21; B.A. 1849, perp. curate Twigworth, co. Gloucester, minister of St. Peter Chapel, Pimlico, rector of St. Helen, Worcester, 1870-3, and of St. Alban, Worcester, 1870-81, died 26 May, 1883.

Paul, Sir John Dean, Bart., created D.C.L. 13 June, 1834 (son of John Paul, of Salisbury, D.Med.), created a baronet, 3 Sep., 1821, of London, banker, died 16 Jan., 1852. See Foster's *Baronetage* & *Eton School Lists.*

Paul, John Paul, s. (Josiah, formerly) Tippetts), of Tetbury, co. Gloucester, arm. QUEEN'S COLL., matric. 20 Nov., 1789, aged 17; created D.C.L. 22 June, 1814, then of High Grove, co. Gloucester, died 10 June, 1828, father of John 1813, and Walter M.

Paul, Joseph, s. Joseph, of East Chinnock, Somerset, gent. TRINITY COLL., matric. 10 May, 1725, aged 18; B.A. 22 Feb., 1728-9.

Paul, Joseph, s. Joseph, of Norton, Somerset, cler. NEW COLL., matric. 13 May, 1751, aged 17; B.A. 1755. **[10]**

Paul, Richard, s. William, of Gwennap, Cornwall, gent. EXETER COLL., matric. 2 April, 1781, aged 18; B.A. 1785, died rector of St. Mawgan 7 Dec., 1805. See *Coll. Reg.*, 147.

Paul, Robert Bateman, s. Richard, of St. Columb Major, Cornwall, cler. EXETER COLL., matric. 10 Oct., 1815, aged 17; B.A. 1820, M.A. 1822, fellow 1817-27, bursar and tutor 1825, public examiner Lit. Hum. 1826-7, vicar of Long Wittenham, Berks, 1826-9, of Llantwit Major 1829, vicar of St. John's, Kentish Town, 1846-50, archdeacon of Nelson, New Zealand, 1855-60, rector of St. Mary, Stamford, 1864-72, preb. of Lincoln 1867, confrater Browne's Hospital, Stamford, 1868, until his death 6 June, 1877. See *Coll. Reg.*, 122.

Paul, Robert Macleane, 3s. William, of Southleigh, Cornwall, arm. EXETER COLL., matric. 14 June, 1859, aged 18; B.A. 1862, M.A. 1866, a solicitor at Truro. See *Rugby School Reg.*

Paul, Samuel Paul, s. (Josiah, formerly Tippetts), of Tetbury, co. Gloucester, arm. NEW COLL., matric. 27 Nov., 1802, aged 21; vicar of Tetbury, co. Gloucester, 1825, until his death in 1828, brother of John Paul 1789.

Paul, Walter Matthews, s. John, of Highgrove, co. Gloucester, arm. BALLIOL COLL., matric. 30 Nov., 1814, aged 17; B.A. 1818, of Highgrove. **[15]**

Paul, William, s. William, of Gittisham, Devon, cler. QUEEN'S COLL., matric. 10 Oct., 1747, aged 17, B.A. 1751; M.A. from KING'S COLL., Cambridge, 1781, rector of Bratton Clovelly, Devon, rector of Lympston 1789.

Paulet, Charles Newton, 1s. — P., gent. MAGDALEN HALL, matric. 3 Feb., 1849, B.A. 1852, M.A. 1855, vicar of Kirk Hammerton, Yorks, 1855-74, curate-in-charge of Market Bosworth 1874-8.

Pauli, Charles Paine, 3s. (Paul) Emilius, of Marylebone, London, arm. PEMBROKE COLL., matric. 27 May, 1856, aged 18; B.A. 1861, bar.-at-law, Inner Temple, 1867. See Foster's *Men at the Bar.*

Pauli, Christian William Henry; privilegiatus 5 March, 1841, missionary of London Jews' Society 1841, died 4 May, 1877.

Pauli, Henry Samuel Benoni, 1s. Christian William Henry, of Westbourne, Sussex, cler. WORCESTER COLL., matric. 18 Oct., 1847, aged 18; B.A. 1851, curate of Escomb, Devon, died in Amsterdam 22 Dec., 1854. **[20]**

Pauli, Dr. Reinhold, professor of history at Gottingen, 1870-82; created D.C.L. 15 April, 1874, died at Bremen, 3 June, 1882, aged 55.

Paull, Henry Hugh Beams, 1s. Henry Andrew, of Doctors' Commons, London, gent. MAGDALEN HALL, matric. 10 May, 1845, aged 25.

Paull, Richard Beams, 3s. Henry Andrew, of St. James's, Clerkenwell, London, gent. MAGDALEN HALL, matric. 31 Oct., 1845, aged 19.

Paulson, Frederick George, 2s. George Robert, of Addington, Kent, cler. CHRIST CHURCH, matric. 18 Oct., 1869, aged 19; B.A. 1873.

Paulson, George Robert, s. Thomas Warre, of St. Marylebone, arm. BALLIOL COLL., matric. 24 April, 1816, aged 18; B.A. 1820, M.A. 1825, rector of Addington, Kent, 1834, until his death 14 Aug., 1869. See *Rugby School Reg.*, 90. **[25]**

Paulson, Richard Ellwyn, 4s. George Robert, of Addington, Kent, cler. HERTFORD COLL., matric. 1 Feb., 1881, aged 20.

Paulson, William Henry, 1s. George Robert, of Addington, Kent, cler. MAGDALEN COLL., matric. 26 Jan., 1867, aged 19; demy 1866-71, B.A. 1871.

Pauncefort-Duncombe, Philip Duncombe, s. George, of Bath (city), arm. CHRIST CHURCH, matric. 22 Oct., 1801, aged 17; of Great Brickhill Manor, Bucks, high sheriff 1824, and of Witham-on-the-Hill, co. Leicester, assumed the additional name of DUNCOMBE by royal licence 29 July, 1805, died 15 March, 1849. See Foster's *Baronetage.*

Pauncefote, Bernard, o.s. Bernard, of Cuddalore, East Indies, arm. BRASENOSE COLL., matric. 21 June, 1867, aged 18; B.A. 1870, a student of the Iuner Temple 1870, captain of University XI., died 24 Sep., 1882. See Foster's *Peerage*, B. CARRINGTON; & *Rugby School Reg.*

Pauncefote, Robert, s. Thomas Smith, of Nottingham, arm. WORCESTER COLL., matric. 14 Jan., 1804, aged 25; B.A. 1807, M.A. 1810, fellow until 1822, of Preston, co. Gloucester, bar.-at-law, Gray's Inn, 1808, died 22 Feb., 1843. See Foster's *Peerage*, B. CARRINGTON. **[30]**

Pavey, Alfred, 3s. James, of St. Ethelburga, London, gent. QUEEN'S COLL., matric. 24 Oct., 1850, aged 19; B.A. 1854, M.A. 1857, held various curacies 1854-67, vicar of Scarrington, Notts, 1867-73, and of Mansfield 1873, preb. of Southwell 1885.

Pavey, Alfred Katenbeck, 1s. Alfred, of Bingham, Notts, cler. HERTFORD COLL., matric. 18 Oct., 1883, aged 20; B.A. 1886.

Pavier, Thomas, 'tonsor;' privilegiatus 27 April, 1781.

Pawson, Louis, 2s. George Emmott, of Oxenhope, Yorks, gent. ST. EDMUND HALL, matric. 22 Oct., 1870, aged 20.

Pawson, William John, 1s. William, of Newcastle-on-Tyne, arm. CHRIST CHURCH, matric. 30 May, 1838, aged 20; of Shawdon, Northumberland, high sheriff 1861. **[35]**

Paxton, Francis Valentine, 5s. Henry, of Farleigh, Hants, arm. CHRIST CHURCH, matric. 8 June, 1854, aged 18; B.A. 1858, B.Med, 1864, M.A. 1865, brother of William A. 1837.

Paxton, Henry Arthur, 2s. George, of Bangalore, East Indies, arm. CHARSLEY HALL, matric. 22 Jan., 1884, aged 19.

Paxton, James Claudius, o.s. — P., of Buckby, Northants, gent. BRASENOSE COLL., matric. 28 June, 1837, aged 19; B.A. 1842, M.A. 1846, B.Med. 1847, Radcliffe travelling fellow University College 1847-8.

Paxton, William Archibald, 1s. Henry, of Barton, co. Warwick, arm. TRINITY COLL., matric. 23 Nov., 1837, aged 19; B.A. 1843, M.A. 1844, rector of Otterden, Kent, 1850.

Paxton, William Gill, s. Archibald, of St. Martin's, London, arm. MERTON COLL., matric. 9 July, 1805, aged 17; created M.A. 30 May, 1809, of Henbury House, Dorset, M.P. Plympton 1821-6, a student of Lincoln's Inn 1806, died in May, 1850.

Payler, Anthony (Charles), s. Thomas, of Ashford, Kent, arm. MERTON COLL., matric. 8 May, 1806, aged 17; B.A. 1810, M.A. 1818, vicar of Headcorn, Kent, 1822-36, rector of Chiddingstone St. Mary, Kent, 1836, until his death 28 Jan., 1852. [5]

Payler, Frederick Morgan, 5s. George Morgan, of Biddlesdon, Bucks, gent. ST. JOHN'S COLL., matric. 15 Nov., 1822, aged 19; B.A. 1827, M.A. 1832, assumed the additional name of PAYLER in 1854, held various curacies 1830-43, rector of Willey, co. Warwick, 1843. See *Rugby School Reg.*, 127.

Payler, Frederick Payler Morgan-, 1s. Frederick, of Turville, Bucks, cler. BRASENOSE COLL., matric. 7 March, 1861, aged 19; B.A. 1866, M.A. 1869, curate of Marton 1875-6. See *Rugby School Reg.*

Payler, Thomas Watkinson, s. Thomas (formerly Turner), of Kingston, Kent, arm. MERTON COLL., matric. 7 Nov., 1766, aged 18; of Heden.

Payler, William (Watkinson), s. Thomas, of Kingston, Kent, arm. MERTON COLL., matric. 16 Oct., 1793, aged 17; B.A. 1797, M.A. 1800, died rector of St. Mary Magdalen, Bermondsey, 19 June, 1814.

Payne, Abraham, s. Charles, of St. Christopher's, West Indies, gent. (after a baronet). ORIEL COLL., matric. 17 Dec., 1723, aged 17; brother of Sir Gillies, 2nd baronet. [10]

Payne, Alfred, 3s. Henry, of St. Mary's, Leicester (town), arm. TRINITY COLL., matric. 3 Dec., 1851, aged 19; B.A. 1856, M.A. 1859, rector of Enville, co. Stafford, 1869, until his death 25 June, 1874, brother of Arthur Frederick.

Payne, Alfred, 6s. Randolph, of Wandsworth, Surrey, gent. ST. EDMUND HALL, matric. 24 Nov., 1859, aged 18; held various curacies 1865-80, vicar of Baldersby, Yorks, 1880.

Payne, Alfred Dalrymple, of CAIUS COLL., Cambridge (B.A. 1856, M.A. 1860); adm. 'ad eundem' 13 Dec., 1860, held various curacies 1858-83.

Payne, Alfred Ernest, 2s. Frederick Alexander, of Kinnerley, Salop, gent. PEMBROKE COLL., matric. 22 April, 1869, aged 19; scholar 1869-73, B.A. & M.A. 1877, a student of the Inner Temple 1879.

Payne, Arthur Frederick, 2s. Henry, of St. Mary's, Leicester (town), arm. TRINITY COLL., matric. 3 Dec., 1851, aged 19; B.A. 1855, M.A. 1859, a student of Lincoln's Inn 1865, brother of Alfred 1851. [15]

Payne, Charles, s. Laurence, of Taunton, Somerset, cler. PEMBROKE COLL., matric. 17 March, 1743-4, aged 18.

Payne, Charles Gillies, s. Peter, of Stourton Castle, co. Stafford, arm. (*soi-disant* baronet). MERTON COLL., matric. 13 Dec., 1812, aged 18; postmaster 1812-15, B.A. 1815, M.A. 1818, bar.-at-law, Middle Temple, 1823, died 21 May, 1870, father of Salusbury G. 1884. See Foster's *Baronetage*, CHAOS.

Payne, Charles Henry, s. Simon, of Axbridge, Somerset, gent. PEMBROKE COLL., matric. 13 Dec., 1809, aged 18; bar.-at-law, Middle Temple, 1818, a commissioner of bankruptcy 1831, died 31 Aug., 1863.

Payne, Charles William Medows, s. Charles, of Stoke Clifton, co. Gloucester, arm. UNIVERSITY COLL., matric. 31 May, 1822, aged 18; B.A. 1826.

Payne, Charles Wynter, 2s. John, of Reigate, Surrey, gent. CHRIST CHURCH, matric. 11 Oct., 1878, aged 18; a junior student 1878-83, B.A. 1882, of the Indian Civil Service 1878, and a student of the Middle Temple 1879. See *Robinson*, 387. [20]

Payne, David Richards, o.s. John Edward, of Isle of Jamaica, arm. TRINITY COLL., matric. 5 March, 1835, aged 20.

Payne, Edward, s. William, of Crediton, Devon, pleb. EXETER COLL., matric. 12 March, 1732-3, aged 21; B.A. 1736.

Payne, Edward, s. Thomas, of Kinnerley, Salop, gent. CHRIST CHURCH, matric. 17 Oct., 1792, aged 18; B.A. 1796, M.A. 1799.

Payne, Edward, 1s. John, of St. Pancras, London, arm. NEW COLL., matric. 20 Feb., 1826, aged 16; fellow 1826-38, B.A. 1829, M.A. 1833, dean of arts 1833, bursar 1834, hon. canon Christ Church 1869-86, vicar of Swalcliffe, Oxon, 1837, until his death 30 June, 1886.

Payne, Edward John, 1s. Edward, of High Wycombe, Bucks, gent. MAGDALEN HALL, matric. 13 June, 1867, aged 22; B.A. from CHARSLEY HALL 1871; fellow UNIVERSITY COLL. 1872, M.A. 1874, bar.-at-law, Lincoln's Inn, 1874, recorder of Chipping Wycombe, Sep., 1883. See Foster's *Men at the Bar.* [25]

Payn, Francis, s. Francis, of Isle of Jersey, gent. PEMBROKE COLL., matric. 26 March, 1717, aged 17; B.A. 1721, M.A. 1723.

Payne, Rev. Frederick Edward Henry, 1s. Frederick Alexander, of Pentre Ucha, Salop, gent. ST. JOHN'S COLL., matric. 1 May, 1867, aged 18; B.A. 1871, M.A. 1876, died 18 May, 1885.

Payne, George, s. Capel, of St. Martin's-in-the-Fields, London, gent. MERTON COLL., matric. 3 Nov., 1746, aged 17; bar.-at-law, Inner Temple, 1753, and a bencher 1791, died 7 Dec., 1800.

Payne, George, 1s. George, of Northampton (town), arm. CHRIST CHURCH, matric. 12 April, 1823, aged 19; of Sulby Hall, Northants, high sheriff 1826, a well-known sportsman, died 2 Sep., 1878. See *Eton School Lists.*

Payne, George Augustus, 3s. Edward Henry, of Bridgnorth, Salop, cler. PEMBROKE COLL., matric. 20 Oct., 1829, aged 18; B.A. 1834, M.A. 1837, bar.-at-law, Lincoln's Inn, 1841, died 30 Nov., 1871.

Payne, Rev. George Speke, s. Samuel, of Weymouth, Dorset, cler. WADHAM COLL., matric. 6 April, 1797, aged 18; B.A. 1800, died 10 April, 1862. [31]

Payne, Harry Alfred, 4s. Alfred, of Groby, co. Leicester, cler. CHRIST CHURCH, matric. 10 Oct., 1879, aged 18. See *Eton School Lists.*

Payne, Henry, s. Edward, of Bushey, Herts, arm. ST. JOHN'S COLL., matric. 29 June, 1801, aged 18; B.C.L. 1807, D.C.L. 1812, scholar & fellow until 1828, vice-president 1822, dean of laws 1823, catechetical lecturer 1824, died 31 Aug., 1828. See *Robinson*, 162.

Payne, Henry (Thomas), s. Thomas, of Llangattock, co. Brecon, cler. WORCESTER COLL., matric. 21 Feb., 1777, aged 17; B.A. from BALLIOL COLL. 1780, M.A. 1784, vicar of Ystradvellty 1789, of Lanbedr and Patricio 1793, and of Devunnock 1799, canon of St. David 1810, archdeacon of Carmarthen 1827, until his death 22 April, 1832.

Payne, James, 2s. Edward Henry, of Wallingford, Berks, gent. QUEEN'S COLL., matric. 16 April, 1859, aged 18; B.A. 1863, B.C.L. 1868, D.C.L. 1873, vicar of Cogges, Oxon, 1872-84, etc. [35]

Payne, John Orlebar, of ST. PETER'S COLL., Cambridge (B.A. 1860, M.A. 1863); adm. 'comitatis causa' 25 June, 1863.

Payne, John Vaughan, 3s. William, of Colyton, Devon, arm. EXETER COLL., matric. 11 Nov., 1841, aged 18; B.A. from NEW INN HALL 1849, M.A. 1852, of Musbury, Devon, curate of Christ Church, Gloucester, 1863-8, vicar since 1868.

Payne, Joseph, s. Thomas, of Hereford (city), cler. CHRIST CHURCH, matric. 14 April, 1753, aged 32 (? of Buckland, died 31 March, 1786).

Payne, Joseph, s. Simeon, of Ealing, Middlesex, gent. QUEEN'S COLL., matric. 3 Nov., 1767, aged 24; B.C.L. 1774, bar.-at-law, Middle Temple, 1774.

Payne, Joseph, s. William, of St. Alphage, London, gent. ST. EDMUND HALL, matric. 6 May, 1818, aged 20; bar.-at-law, Lincoln's Inn, 1825, deputy assistant judge Middlesex Sessions, died 27 March, 1870.

Payne, Joseph Francis, 2s. Joseph, of St. Giles's, Camberwell, Surrey, gent. MAGDALEN COLL., matric. 25 Oct., 1858, aged 18; demy 1858-63, B.A. 1862, fellow 1863-83, B.Med. 1867, D.Med. 1880.

Payne, Peter George Stanhope, 3s. Salusbury Gillies, of Woburn Sands, Beds (*soi-disant* baronet). UNIVERSITY COLL., matric. 15 May, 1880, aged 18; B.A. 1884, bar.-at.law, Inner Temple, 1885. **[5]**

Payne, Rev. Peter Samuel Henry, 3s. Peter, of Handsworth, co. Warwick, arm. (*soi-disant* baronet). BALLIOL COLL., matric. 29 Nov., 1827, aged 17; scholar 1827-31, B.A. 1831, fellow 1831-41, M.A. 1835, bursar 1838, dean 1839, senior dean 1840, died 30 June, 1841, brother of Charles Gillies 1812.

Payne, Ralph, s. Abrah., of St. Christopher's, West Indies, gent. ORIEL COLL., matric. 17 Dec., 1722, aged 16; bar.-at-law, Middle Temple, 1730, father of Ralph, K.B., Lord Lavington, so created 1 Oct., 1795, and died 1 Aug., 1807. See Foster's *Baronetage*.

Payne, Ralph, s. Willet, of Isle of St. Christopher's, arm. ORIEL COLL., matric. 14 Feb., 1767, aged 17; B.A. 1770, M.A. 1773, probably a nephew of the last named.

Payne, Rev. Randolph, 2s. Randolph, of St. Paul's, Covent Garden, Westminster, gent. MAGDALEN HALL, matric. 30 March, 1843, aged 28; B.A. 1846, M.A. 1851.

Payne, Richard, s. Rich., of Barnesley, co. Gloucester, cler. PEMBROKE COLL., matric. 12 June, 1729, aged 17. **[10]**

Payne, Richard, 2s. John, of St. George's, Bloomsbury, London, arm. NEW COLL., matric. 20 Nov., 1829, aged 19; fellow 1829-41, B.C.L. 1837, vicar of Downton, Wilts, 1841-82, preb. of Salisbury 1861.

Payne, Robert Adair, 3s. William, of Clifton, Bristol, arm. ORIEL COLL., matric. 10 June, 1830, aged 18.

Payne, Salusbury Gillies, born in East Indies, o.s. Charles Gillies (*soi-disant* baronet). BRASENOSE COLL., matric. 22 June, 1848, aged 19; B.A. 1852, of Blunham House, Beds, J.P., barrister of the Middle Temple 1857. See Foster's *Baronetage*, CHAOS; & *Rugby School Reg.*, 261.

Payne, Samuel, s. George, of Whitchurch, Salop, gent. CHRIST CHURCH, matric. 19 Dec., 1722, aged 18; B.A. 1726, M.A. 1729.

Payne, Samuel, s. William, of Totnes, Devon, gent. BALLIOL COLL., matric. 19 May, 1743, aged 18; B.A. 20 Jan., 1746-7, rector of Hook, and Melbury-Bubb, Dorset, 1750. **[15]**

Payne, Samuel, s. Samuel, of Evershot, Dorset, cler. CORPUS CHRISTI COLL., matric. 4 May, 1757, aged 18; B.A. from TRINITY COLL. 1761 (? vicar of Winterbourne St. Martin, with rectory of Chickerell, Dorset, 1770), rector of Weymouth, and Portland with Wykeham Regis 1792, until his death 6 Dec., 1801, father of George Speke.

Payne, Samuel, s. William, of Tower of London, gent. ST. EDMUND HALL, matric. 31 Jan., 1810, aged 30; incumbent of Hunstanworth, co. Durham, died 2 Oct., 1864.

Payne-Gallwey, Stephen, s. Ralph, of Isle of St. Christopher's, arm. ORIEL COLL., matric. 14 Feb., 1767, aged 17; of Toft Hall, Norfolk, assumed the additional name of GALLWEY by act of parliament in 1762. See Foster's *Baronetage*.

Payne, Thomas, s. Thomas, of Hereford (city), cler. BRASENOSE COLL., matric. 26 March, 1736, aged 18; B.A. 1739, M.A. 1742, rector of Llangattock, canon residentiary of Wells 1766, until his death 31 Dec., 1797.

Payne, Thomas Charles Pigot, 1s. Samuel, of Nottingham (town), gent. UNIVERSITY COLL., matric. 5 Feb., 1858, aged 17. **[20]**

Payne, William, s. William, of Midhurst, Sussex, gent. MAGDALEN COLL., matric. 21 Feb., 1727-8, aged 18; clerk 1728-33, B.A. 1731, chaplain 1733, fellow 1733-53, M.A. 1734, B.D. 1744, D.D. 1745, junior dean of arts 1744, bursar 1745, vicar of Findon, Sussex, 1751, until his death in May, 1772. See *Coll. Reg.*, ii. 89.

Payne, William, s. William, of Crediton, Devon, gent. BALLIOL COLL., matric. 6 March, 1729-30, aged 19; B.A. 1733.

Payne, William, s. Samuel, of Evershott, Dorset, cler. CORPUS CHRISTI COLL., matric. 29 Feb., 1760, aged 17.

Payne, William, of TRINITY COLL., Cambridge, junior optime (B.A. 1851, M.A. 1854); adm. 'ad eundem' 20 May, 1857, vicar of St. John's, Reading, 1857.

Payne, William Arthur, 3s. Frederick, of Pentre Ucha, Salop, arm. PEMBROKE COLL., matric. 31 May, 1873, aged 17; scholar 1873-7, B.A. 1883. **[25]**

Paynter, John, s. James, of Boskenna, Cornwall, arm. ST. EDMUND HALL, matric. 20 June, 1808, aged 17; B.A. 1812, of Boskenna, died 2 Jan., 1847.

Paynter, John de Camborne, 3s. Francis of Penzance, Cornwall, arm. WADHAM COLL., matric. 5 June, 1861, aged 17.

Paynter, Thomas Beville, 4s. Francis, of Penzance, Cornwall, arm. WADHAM COLL., matric. 5 Dec., 1866, aged 19; B.A. 1870, rector of Christon, Somerset, 1879-84, of How Caple, co. Hereford, 1884.

Paynter, Rev. William Camborne, 2s. William, of London, arm. CHRIST CHURCH, matric. 19 Oct., 1848, aged 18; B.A. from ST. MARY HALL 1852, M.A. 1855, a student of Lincoln's Inn 1852. See *Eton School Lists*.

Paynton, George, 'surgeon;' privilegiatus 13 Oct., 1726.

Payton, Thomas Bartram, 8s. Thomas, of Cheltenham, gent. NON-COLL., matric. 18 April, 1874, aged 33. **[31]**

Peabody, George, created D.C.L. 26 June, 1867, merchant and philanthropist (son of Thomas Peabody, of Darwen, Mass.), died in London 14 Nov., 1869.

Peace, Albert Lister, o.s. Lister, of Huddersfield, Yorks, gent. NEW COLL., matric. 29 June, 1870, aged 26; (NON-COLL.) B.Mus. 30 June, 1870, D.Mus. 17 Dec., 1875, (as PEARCE).

Peace, Peter, s. Peter, of SS. Philip and James, Bristol (city), gent. WORCESTER COLL., matric. 10 Dec., 1829, aged 18; B.A. 1833, M.A. 1836, B.D. 1844, held various curacies 1835-70.

Peacey, Rev. William John, 3s. Arthur Thomas, of London, gent. NON-COLL., matric. 15 Oct., 1881, aged 21; B.A. from MERTON COLL. 1884, M.A. 1888.

Peach, Henry, s. Edward, of Whitchurch, Oxon, cler. ST. JOHN'S COLL., matric. 30 June, 1757, aged 16; B.A. 1761, M.A. 1765, B.D. 1770, vicar of Compton St. Nicholas, Berks, 1767, died rector of Cheam 10 March, 1813. See *Robinson*, 107. **[36]**

Peach, Henry, s. Henry, of Derby (town), gent. ST. JOHN'S COLL., matric. 14 July, 1772, aged 18; B.A. 1776.

Peach, Henry, s. Henry, of Twickenham, Middlesex, gent. PEMBROKE COLL., matric. 21 Nov., 1783, aged 18.

Peach, Henry (Peach) Keighly, 1s. (Henry Peach) Keighly, of Madras, East Indies, arm. TRINITY COLL., matric. 13 May, 1853, aged 19; of Idlicote, co. Warwick, assumed the name of PEACH in addition to KEIGHLY by royal licence 19 Oct., 1838. See *Eton School Lists*.

Peach, James Jarvis, s. John Cleaver, of Leeds, Yorks, cler. BRASENOSE COLL., matric. 16 May, 1793, aged 17; B.A. 1797, M.A. 1799, of Tockington, co. Gloucester, canon of Southwell 1820, rector of Holme Pierrepont, Notts, 1814, vicar of Appleton-le-Street, Yorks, and rector of Hawerby, co. Lincoln, took the name of PEACH instead of CLEAVER by royal licence 16 June, 1845, died 17 Feb., 1864.

Peach, John, s. Edward, of Whitchurch, Oxon, cler. ST. JOHN'S COLL., matric. 30 June, 1757, aged 18; B.C.L. 1764, bar.-at-law, Middle Temple, 1765, died 17 Sep., 1773. See *Robinson*, 107.

Peach, Paul, s. Paul, of St. Mary Magdalen, London, gent. ST. JOHN'S COLL., matric. 1 July, 1767, aged 18; left 1769. See *Robinson*, 120.

Peach, Samuel, s. Samuel, of Chalford, co. Gloucester, gent. HERTFORD COLL., matric. 17 Dec., 1762, aged 16; B.A. 1766, M.A. 1769, chaplain to the Duke of Cumberland, rector of Compton Beauchamp, Berks, died 7 March, 1803.

Peach, Samuel Cruger, s. Samuel (Peach Cruger, after Peach-Peach), of Old Tockington, co. Gloucester, arm. CHRIST CHURCH, matric. 21 Oct., 1813, aged 18; died 20 Dec., 1836. See *Eton School Lists*. **[5]**

Peach, Samuel Peach, s. Henry Cruger, of Bristol (city), arm. BALLIOL COLL., matric. 13 Nov., 1783, aged 16; of Tockington, co. Gloucester, took the name of PEACH in lieu of CRUGER by royal licence 9 May, 1788, died 25 Feb., 1845, father of the last named.

Peache, Alfred, 2s. James Courthope, of Lambeth, gent. WADHAM COLL., matric. 1 March, 1838, aged 19; B.A. 1841, M.A. 1844, curate of Mangotsfield with Downend, co. Gloucester, 1842-54, vicar 1859-74, and of Downend 1874-8, D.D., and chancellor of the Western division of Ontario 1885.

Peache, Gilbert Alan, 4s. Alfred, of Mangotsfield, co. Gloucester, cler. PEMBROKE COLL., matric. 28 Oct., 1886, aged 18.

Peachey, Charles, s. William, of Kirdford, Sussex, arm. QUEEN'S COLL., matric. 31 Jan., 1800, aged 17.

Peachey, (Sir) James (Bart.), s. John, of West Dean, Sussex, baronet. UNIVERSITY COLL. matric. 11 Dec., 1739, aged 17; 4th baronet in 1765, M.P. Seaford 1759-68, created Lord Selsey 13 Aug., 1794, died 1 Feb., 1808. **[10]**

Peachey, James Herbert, 1s. James Pearse, of London, arm. QUEEN'S COLL., matric. 25 Oct., 1886, aged 18; scholar 1886.

Peachey, (Sir) John (Bart.), s. John, of London, Middlesex, baronet. CHRIST CHURCH, matric. 17 Nov., 1737, aged 17; 3rd baronet, M.P. Midhurst 1744-61, died 30 June, 1765.

Peachey, John, s. Francis, of Chichester, Sussex, arm. NEW COLL., matric. 24 Oct., 1771, aged 19; of Rumboldswyke, Sussex, bar.-at-law, Middle Temple 1781, and a bencher 1821, died senior magistrate, Chichester, 28 May, 1831.

Peachy, Erlysman, s. John, of Alverstoke, Hants, gent. PEMBROKE COLL., matric. 23 Oct., 1723, aged 17; B.A. 1727, M.A. 1730, rector of Facombe-cum-Tangley, and vicar of Kingsclere, Hants, 1753.

Peachy, William, s. William, of Gosport, Hants, arm. TRINITY COLL., matric. 13 Nov., 1781, aged 18; B.C.L. 1790, D.C.L. 1813. **[15]**

Peacock, George, scholar TRINITY COLL., Cambridge, 1812-14, 2nd wrangler & B.A. 1813, fellow 1814-40, M.A. 1816, tutor 1823-39 (adm. 'ad eundem' 17 June, 1830), D.D. 1839, Lowndes professor of mathematics 1836, F.R.S., F.R.A.S., F.G.S., dean of Ely 1839, until his death 8 Nov., 1858.

Peacock, John, 2s. Wilkinson, of Thorpe Tilney, co. Lincoln, arm. LINCOLN COLL., matric. 8 March, 1838, aged 18; B.A. 1842, vicar of Wellingore, co. Lincoln, 1845-72, rector of Fulbeck 1872, until his death, 20 Feb., 1884.

Peacock, Mark Beauchamp, o.s. Mark Beauchamp, of Hornsey, Middlesex, gent. ST. JOHN'S COLL., matric. 6 Dec., 1854, aged 20; of Springfield Place, Essex, bar.-at-law, Lincoln's Inn, 1859. See Foster's *Men at the Bar* & *Eton School Lists*.

Peacock, Mark Beauchamp, 1s. Mark Beauchamp, of Brighton, arm. TRINITY COLL., matric. 17 Jan., 1880, aged 19; B.A. 1883, M.A. 1886, a student of Lincoln's Inn 1882.

Peacock, Matthew Henry, 1s. Matthew, of Leeds, Yorks, gent. EXETER COLL., matric. 14 Oct., 1876, aged 20; scholar 1876-81, B.A. 1880, M.A. 1883, head-master Wakefield School 1883. See *Coll. Reg.*, 168. **[20]**

Peacock, Walter Gilbert, 4s. Wilkinson Affleck, of Ulceby, co. Lincoln, cler. BALLIOL COLL., matric. 18 Oct., 1871, aged 18; B.A. 1875, rector of Ulceby, co. Lincoln, 1877.

Peacocke, George Montague Warren. NEW INN HALL, 1843. See SANDFORD.

Pead, Leonard Walter, 1s. Leonard, of London, arm. EXETER COLL., matric. 8 June, 1865, aged 19; B.A. 1869, M.A. 1874, a student of the Middle Temple 1874.

Pead, Prince, s. William, of St. Mary le Bone, London, gent. WADHAM COLL., matric. 6 April, 1734, aged 17; B.A. 1737, M.A. 1742, proctor 1749 (? died vicar of Aveley, Essex, 13 May, 1767).

Peake, Arthur Samuel, 2s. Samuel, of Leek, co. Stafford, gent. ST. JOHN'S COLL., matric. 13 Oct., 1883, aged 17; scholar 1883-5, B.A. 1887. **[25]**

Peake, Charles William, 1s. Charles Richard, of Tonbridge, Kent, arm. MAGDALEN COLL., matric. 19 Oct., 1883, aged 19; scholar (HERTFORD COLL.) 1884, B.A. 1887.

Peake, Edward, 2s. Richard, of Chepstow, co. Monmouth, arm. ORIEL COLL., matric. 20 Jan., 1880, aged 19; B.A. 1883, M.A. 1886.

Peake, George, s. George, of Leicester (town), gent. MERTON COLL., matric. 25 Oct., 1809, aged 18; postmaster 1810-13, B.A. 1813, M.A. 1822, vicar (and patron) of Aston, near Birmingham, 1823, until his death 8 Oct., 1830.

Peake, George, 1s. George, of Enderby, co. Leicester, cler. WORCESTER COLL., matric. 14 May, 1840, aged 18 (? vicar of Aston, Birmingham, 1872, until his death 9 July, 1876).

Peake, Rev. George Eden, 4s. Thomas, of St. Aldate's, Oxford (city), gent. MAGDALEN HALL, matric. 25 Nov., 1830, aged 18; B.A. 1835, M.A. 1837, died at Ruishton, Somerset, 10 June, 1848, aged 37. **[30]**

Peake, George Eden Frederick, 3s. George Eden, of Ruishton, Somerset, cler. ST. MARY HALL, matric. 23 Oct., 1865, aged 18; B.A. 1871, M.A. 1872, vicar of St. Margaret next Rochester 1878-84, and of St. John Eastover, Bridgwater, 1884.

Peake, Henry, 2s. Robert, of St. Augustine's, Bristol (city), gent. JESUS COLL., matric. 17 Dec., 1830, aged 22; B.A. 1834, head-master Grammar School 1834, and perp. curate Holy Trinity, Abergavenny, 1876, until his death 22 Feb., 1880.

Peake, Henry William, 2s. James Room, of Whitchurch, Salop, cler. CORPUS CHRISTI COLL., matric. 18 Oct., 1871, aged 21; B.A. 1875, M.A. 1881, a schoolmaster at Bournemouth. See *Rugby School Reg.*

Peake, Rev. James Room, 1s. Robert, of Bristol (city), gent. JESUS COLL., matric. 14 March, 1833, aged 25; scholar ST. JOHN'S COLL., Cambridge, 1825, scholar MAGDALEN HALL 1834, B.A. 1836, M.A. 1839, head-master Whitchurch Grammar School, Salop, 1839-82.

Peake, John, 2s. George, of Enderby, co. Leicester, cler. MAGDALEN HALL, matric. 28 April, 1842, aged 17; B.A. 1847. vicar of Ellesmere, Salop, 1864. See *Rugby School Reg.*, 176. **[35]**

Peake, Rev. Vincent William, 1s. John Horace, of Pershore, co. Worcester, gent. ST. EDMUND HALL, matric. 18 Oct., 1879, aged 19; B.A. 1883, M.A. 1887.

Peake, Walter Ancell, 1s. Frederick, of London, gent. EXETER COLL., matric. 30 May, 1871, aged 18.

Pearce, Alexander, 5s. Matthew, of Glasgow, arm. TRINITY COLL., matric. 18 Oct., 1865, aged 19; B.A. 1870.

Pearce, Baker, s. William, of London, gent. HERTFORD COLL., matric. 23 Feb., 1741-2, aged 18.

Pearce, Benjamin, s. Rich., of Wotton-under-Edge, co. Gloucester, pleb. ST. JOHN'S COLL., matric. 8 July, 1730, aged 18; B.A. 1734, M.A. 1737. [5]

Pearce, Charles, s. Charles, of St. John's, Hackney, Middlesex, gent. QUEEN'S COLL., matric. 13 Feb., 1778, aged 18.

Pearce, Francis, s. Francis, of Uffington, Berks, arm. HERTFORD COLL., matric. 13 Feb., 1773, aged 17.

Pearce, Francis Joseph, s. Thomas, of Idstone, Berks, arm. EXETER COLL., matric. 24 April, 1816, aged 20; B.A. 1820, father of Thomas 1838, and of the next named.

Pearce, Francis Joseph, 1s. Francis Joseph, of Hatford, Berks, cler. EXETER COLL., matric. 21 June, 1838, aged 19; brother of Thomas 1838.

Pearce, Henry, s. John, of Hereford (city), gent. CHRIST CHURCH, matric. 20 May, 1814, aged 19; servitor 1814-17, B.A. 1817, M.A. 1820, vicar of Yorkhill 1822, vicar choral Hereford Cathedral, etc., 1818, died 1 May, 1849. [10]

Pearce, James, B.Mus. 1860. See STEPHEN JAMES PEARCE.

Pearce, John, s. Wredenhall, of Downton, Salop, gent. ST. MARY HALL, matric. 12 June, 1751, aged 17; B.A. from BALLIOL COLL. 1755, M.A. 1758; brother of Wredenhall 1741.

Pearce, John, 2s. James, of Hill House, co. Monmouth, arm. QUEEN'S COLL., matric. 5 Dec., 1822, aged 18; B.A. 1829.

Pearce, John William Ernest, 1s. Henry Edwin, of Bristol, gent. MERTON COLL., matric. 18 Oct., 1881, aged 17; postmaster 1881-5, B.A. 1885, M.A. 1888.

Pearce, Joseph, s. Richard, of Stythians, Cornwall, gent. EXETER COLL., matric. 5 May, 1722, aged 18. [15]

Pearce, Joseph, s. Joseph, of Lymington, Hants, gent. QUEEN'S COLL., matric. 27 June, 1753, aged 19.

Pearce, Joseph, s. Richard, of St. Just, Cornwall, gent. EXETER COLL., matric. 16 Feb., 1761, aged 18; B.A. 1764.

Pearce, Maresco, 3s. Charles Thomas, of Camberwell, Surrey, arm. EXETER COLL., matric. 31 Jan., 1849, aged 17; B.A. 1852, M.A. 1864, a student of Lincoln's Inn 1853.

Pearce, Richard, s. Richard, of Westminster, arm. MAGDALEN HALL, matric. 9 May, 1787, aged 28.

Pearce, Robert, s. Thomas, of Hereford (city), pleb. CHRIST CHURCH, matric. 30 March, 1789, aged 18; B.A. from ST. ALBAN HALL 1792, M.A. 1795, vicar choral Hereford Cathedral 1792, custos of the College of Vicars 1840, and vicar of Marden 1797, of Holmer 1819, until his death 16 Feb., 1850. [20]

Pearce, Stephen Austen, 1s. Stephen, of Brompton, Kent, gent. NEW COLL., matric. 14 June, 1859, aged 22; B.Mus. 15 June, 1859, D.Mus. 9 July, 1864.

Pearce, (Stephen) James, 2s. — P., of Gillingham, Kent, gent. NEW COLL., matric. 6 June, 1860, aged 19; B.Mus. 14 June, 1860.

Pearce, Rev. Stephen Spencer, 1s. Stephen, of London, gent. LINCOLN COLL., matric. 18 Oct., 1879, aged 19; B.A. 1882, M.A. 1886.

Pearce, Thomas, s. Henry, of Wotton-under-Edge, co. Gloucester, pleb. ORIEL COLL., matric. 11 July, 1763, aged 17; B.A. 1767, M.A. 1771, B. & D.D. 1793, sub-dean of the Chapel Royal 1792, until his death at Lambeth 23 Feb., 1803.

Pearce, Thomas, s. Thomas, of Lambeth, Surrey, doctor. CORPUS CHRISTI COLL., matric. 24 March, 1801, aged 18, B.A. 1805; M.A. from EXETER COLL. 1807, vicar of Hartlip, Kent, 1810, and of Folkestone 1818, rector of Hawkinge 1818 (and of Mareston), until his death in 1854. See *Robinson*, 166.

Pearce, Thomas, s. Thomas, of Holsworthy, Devon, gent. EXETER COLL., matric. 31 May, 1802, aged 18; B.A. 1807 (? perp. curate Tywardreath, Cornwall, 1820). [25]

Pearce, Thomas, y.s. Francis Joseph, of Hatford, Berks, cler. LINCOLN COLL., matric. 23 June, 1838, aged 18; B.A. 1843, M.A. 1849, vicar of Morden, Dorset, 1853-83, rector of Charborough 1871, until his death 24 Sep., 1885.

Pearce, William, s. Thomas, of Westminster, arm. ST. MARY HALL, matric. 14 Jan., 1780, aged 17.

Pearce, William, s. William, of Boddington, co. Gloucester, gent. WORCESTER COLL., matric. 2 Dec., 1788, aged 17; B.A. 1792, M.A. 1795, vicar of Leigh, co. Gloucester, 1813, died at Staverton House, near Cheltenham, in 1825.

Pearce, Rev. William, 1s. James, of Chichester (city), gent. ST. EDMUND HALL, matric. 14 April, 1869, aged 23; B.A. 1870. [30]

Pearce, Wredenhall, s. Wredenhall, of Downton, Salop, arm. ORIEL COLL., matric. 21 April, 1741, aged 18; brother of John 1751.

Peard, Henry, s. Oliver, of Upway, Dorset, arm. PEMBROKE COLL., matric. 25 March, 1801, aged 17.

Peard, John, s. Thomas, of Budock, Cornwall, gent. EXETER COLL., matric. 3 June, 1763, aged 18; B.A. 1767, vicar of Manaccan, Cornwall, 1778.

Peard, John Whitehead, 2s. Shuldham, of Fowey, Cornwall, arm. EXETER COLL., matric. 4 March, 1829, aged 17; B.A. 1833, M.A. 1836, bar.-at-law, Inner Temple, 1837, colonel, known as 'Garibaldi's Englishman,' died 21 Nov., 1880. See *Annual Register*.

Peard, Oliver, s. Oliver, of Tiverton, Devon, gent. CORPUS CHRISTI COLL., matric. 17 May, 1779, aged 17. [35]

Peareth, John, s. John, of Aldworth, Berks, cler. WADHAM COLL., matric. 26 June, 1728, aged 16; B.A. 1732, M.A. 1734, bar.-at-law, Inner Temple, 1739.

Peareth, John Lennox, 3s. William, of Edyll, co. Forfar arm. BRASENOSE COLL., matric. 20 Oct., 1886, aged 19.

Peareth, William Jennens, s. William, of Washington, co. Durham, arm. CHRIST CHURCH, matric. 22 Oct., 1801, aged 17; died at Penzance 1804.

Pearkes, John, s. Benjamin, of Worcester (city), gent. WORCESTER COLL., matric. 9 April, 1755, aged 18; B.C.L. 1763, D.C.L. 1781, F.S.A., rector of St. Helen's, Worcester, and Breedon, co. Gloucester, 1781, until his death in 1787.

Pearman, Augustus John, 1s. John, of Maple Durham, Oxon, gent. PEMBROKE COLL., matric. 30 May, 1849, aged 17; B.A. 1853, M.A. 1856, vicar of Bethersden, Kent, 1857-66, and of Rainham, Kent, 1866-76, rector of Merstham, Surrey, 1876.

Pearman, Morgan Thomas, 2s. John, of Maple Durham, Oxon, gent. PEMBROKE COLL., matric. 3 March, 1853, aged 18; B.A. 1857, M.A. 1859, held various curacies 1858-71, vicar of Iwade, Kent, 1871. [41]

Pearman, Rev. William Allwright, 1s. Thomas Morgan, of Whitchurch, Oxon, gent. NON-COLL., matric. 17 Oct., 1879, aged 19; B.A. from PEMBROKE COLL. 1884, M.A. 1886.

Pears, Edmund Ward, 5s. James, of Pirbright, Surrey, cler. EXETER COLL., matric. 4 Feb., 1830, aged 16; demy MAGDALEN COLL. 1831-41, B.A. 1835, M.A. 1836, rector of St. Peter, Dorchester, 1864, until his death 1 July, 1878. See *Bloxam*, vii. 327.

Pears, Henry Temple, 1s. Steuart Adolphus, of Harrow, D.D. CORPUS CHRISTI COLL., matric. 23 Oct., 1867, aged 18; B.A. 1870, M.A. 1875.

Pears, Hugh Vaughan, 2s. Steuart Adolphus, of Repton, co. Derby, D.D. CORPUS CHRISTI COLL., matric. 25 Jan., 1875, aged 19; B.A. 1879, M.A. 1885.

Pears, James, s. James, of St. Mary Magdalen, Oxford (city), arm. NEW COLL., matric. 28 July, 1795, aged 17; B.C.L. from ST. MARY HALL 1810, classical master Marlow (Sandhurst), master of Bath Grammar School 1823, and rector of Charlecombe, Somerset, 1823, until his death 21 Jan., 1853.

Pears, Rev. James Robert, 1s. James, of Stanton St. John's, Oxon, cler. MAGDALEN COLL., matric. 27 July, 1820, aged 18; demy 1820-6, B.A. 1824, fellow 1826-34, M.A. 1827, dean of arts 1830, of Woodcote House, Windlesham, a student of the Inner Temple 1827, died 22 Aug., 1865. See *Coll. Reg.*, vii. 281.

Pears, Philip Walter, 2s. James Robert, of Bath, Somerset, cler. WADHAM COLL., matric. 9 Dec., 1863, aged 17; B.A. 1868.

Pears, Steuart Adolphus, 6s. James, of Pirbright, Surrey, cler. CORPUS CHRISTI COLL., matric. 15 June, 1832, aged 16; scholar 1832-9, B.A. 1836, M.A. 1839, fellow 1839-47, B.D. 1846, D.D. 1857, senior dean 1846, assistant-master Harrow School, head-master Repton School 1854-73, rector of Childrey 1874-5, died 15 Dec., 1875. See *Annual Register.*

Pearsall, John, s. Thomas, of Halesowen, Salop, gent. PEMBROKE COLL., matric. 15 April, 1736, aged 18; B.A. 1739, M.A. 1745 (? rector of Wareham 1761). [5]

Pearse, Arthur Henry, 2s. Thomas, of Westoning, Beds, cler. CORPUS CHRISTI COLL., matric. 23 March, 1849, aged 17; scholar 1849-58, B.A. 1852, M.A. 1855, missionary at Portneuf and Bourg-Louis, Canada, 1858-62, etc.

Pearse, Beauchamp Kerr Warren, 3s. Thomas, of Froyle, Hants, arm. UNIVERSITY COLL., matric. 30 May, 1855, aged 19; B.A. 1859, M.A. 1864, rector of Ascot Heath, Berks, 1864.

Pearse, Brice Hugh, 1s. Brice, of Woodford, Essex, arm. BRASENOSE COLL., matric. 19 May, 1845, aged 18; B.A. 1849, brother of Robert Wilson. See Foster's *Baronetage*, WILLIAMS-BULKELEY.

Pearse, George Wingate, o.s. George, of Harlington, Beds, arm. TRINITY COLL., matric. 12 June, 1841, aged 17; scholar CORPUS CHRISTI COLL. 1842-9, B.A. 1845, M.A. 1848, fellow 1849-51, rector of Walton, Fenny Stratford, 1851. [10]

Pearse, Henry Thornton, 1s. Henry, of Marylebone, London, arm. CHRIST CHURCH, matric. 14 May, 1856, aged 19; B.A. 1859, M.A. 1863, rector of Litchfield, Hants, 1865-72, rector of Larling, Norfolk, 1872.

Pearse, Herbert George, 2s. William, of Fairlight, Sussex, cler. BALLIOL COLL., matric. 21 Oct., 1867, aged 18; bar.-at-law, Lincoln's Inn, 1878, entered B.C.S. 1871, joint magistrate and deputy collector. See Foster's *Men at the Bar* & *Rugby School Reg.*

Pearse, John, s. John, of Morebath, Devon, gent. ORIEL COLL., matric. 11 Dec., 1745, aged 17; B.A. 1749. (Memo.: J. P., rector of East Thornton and vicar of Great Burstead, Essex, died 1 Dec., 1767.)

Pearse, John, s. John, of Chitway, Wilts, arm. QUEEN'S COLL., matric. 5 Nov., 1754, aged 19; demy MAGDALEN COLL. 1754-7, B.A. from EXETER COLL. 1758, M.A. 1761, rector of Nuffield, Oxon, 1760, until his death in 1826. See *Bloxam*, vi. 296.

Pearse, Nicholas, 2s. John, of Lincoln's Inn Fields, London, arm. BRASENOSE COLL., matric. 14 Jan., 1819, aged 18; B.A. 1823, M.A. 1826, bar.-at-law, Lincoln's Inn, 1826, died 21 April, 1830. [15]

Pearse, Rev. Reginald Vincent Beville, 1s. Vincent, of Barcheston, co. Warwick, cler. ST. EDMUND HALL, matric. 2 June, 1880, aged 18; B.A. from NEW INN HALL 1885.

Pearse, Richard, s. Hender, of Davidstowe, Cornwall, pleb. EXETER COLL., matric. 5 June, 1739, aged 20; B.A. 1742.

Pearse, Robert, s. Nic., of Madern, Cornwall, gent. MERTON COLL., matric. 12 March, 1739-40, aged 18.

Pearse, Robert Wilson, 2s. Brice, of London, arm. BRASENOSE COLL., matric. 12 March, 1846, aged 17; B.A. 1849, M.A. 1852, brother of Brice Hugh.

Pearse, Samuel Winter, s. Samuel, of Cadleigh, Devon, gent. EXETER COLL., matric. 22 May, 1800, aged 17; B.A. 1804. [20]

Pearse, Shortrudge, s. Thomas, of Tiverton, Devon, gent. EXETER COLL., matric. 26 March, 1779, aged 17; B.A. 1783, rector of Thelbridge 1793.

Pearse, Thomas, 1s. William, of Hanwell, Oxon, cler. WADHAM COLL., matric. 18 June, 1835, aged 19; demy MAGDALEN COLL. 1836-50, B.A. 1839, M.A. 1842, B.D. 1850, fellow 1850-5, vice-president 1852, dean of divinity 1853, rector of Fittleton, Wilts, 1855, until his death 25 Nov., 1885. See *Bloxam*, vii. 339; & *Rugby School Reg.*, 166.

Pearse, Thomas Deane, s. Thomas Deane, of Calcutta, Bengal, East Indies, arm. ORIEL COLL., matric. 9 June, 1795, aged 18.

Pearse, Vincent, 3s. William, of Hanwell, Oxon, cler. EXETER COLL., matric. 2 June, 1852, aged 18; exhibitioner LINCOLN COLL. 1854-8, B.A. 1857, M.A. 1859, rector of Hanwell, Oxon, 1861.

Pearse, William Bradley, 1s. James Langford, of Bangalore, Madras, arm. MERTON COLL., matric. 18 Jan., 1875, aged 19; of the Indian Civil Service 1874. [25]

Pearson, Albert Harford, 2s. Charles Buchanan, of Portland Place, London, cler. NEW COLL., matric. 29 March, 1859, aged 19; B.A. 1862, B.C.L. & M.A. 1865, bar.-at-law, Lincoln's Inn, 1867. See Foster's *Men at the Bar.*

Pearson, Alexander, 1s. Andrew Adam, of Edinburgh, arm. BALLIOL COLL., matric. 20 Oct., 1875, aged 19; B.A. 1879, of Luce, co. Dumfries, a member of the Scottish Faculty of Advocates 1882. See *Rugby School Reg.*

Pearson, Alexander, 1s. David A., of Edinburgh, arm. BRASENOSE COLL., matric. 7 June, 1884, aged 19.

Pearson, Alfred, 3s. Robert, of Brixton, Surrey, gent. NON-COLL., matric. 14 Jan., 1869, aged 20; B.A. from LINCOLN COLL. 1872, M.A. 1875, rector of St. Ebbe, Oxford, 1877-80, vicar of All Saints, Nottingham, 1880.

Pearson, Andrew, 2s. David Alexander, of Laurence Kirk, co. Kincardine, arm. BRASENOSE COLL., matric. 23 Oct., 1885, aged 19. [30]

Pearson, Arthur Cyril, 1s. Arthur, of Springfield, near Chelmsford, Essex, cler. BALLIOL COLL., matric. 16 Oct., 1856, aged 18; B.A. 1860, M.A. 1872, held various curacies 1862-77, rector of Drayton-Parslow, Bucks, 1877-86, and of Springfield, Essex, 1886.

Pearson, Arthur Hubert, 2s. Frederick Burnet, of Beenham, Berks, arm. UNIVERSITY COLL., matric. 28 May, 1874, aged 18; scholar 1874-8, B.A. 1878, bar.-at-law, Inner Temple, 1885, brother of Frederick J. N.

Pearson, Benjamin, s. Thomas, of Willersly, Westmoreland, pleb. QUEEN'S COLL., matric. 7 Nov., 1718, aged 18; B.A. 1724, M.A. 1728.

Pearson, Charles Buchanan, 1s. Hugh Nicholas, of Elmdon, co. Warwick, doctor. ORIEL COLL., matric. 23 March, 1825, aged 17; B.A. 1828, M.A. 1831, preb. of Salisbury 1832, rector of Knebworth, Herts, 1838-74, died 7 Jan., 1881. See *Eton School Lists.*

Pearson, Charles Henry, 4s. John Norman, of Islington, Middlesex, cler. ORIEL COLL., matric. 14 June, 1849, aged 18; scholar EXETER COLL. 1850-3, B.A. 1853, fellow ORIEL COLL. 1854-73, M.A. 1856, professor modern history King's College, London, 1855-65, lecturer on modern history Trinity College, Cambridge, 1869-71, professor of history University of Melbourne 1873. See *Rugby School Reg.*, 245; & *Boase*, 155. [35]

Pearson, Charles Hugh, elder son of Charles James, of Midhurst, Sussex, cler. TRINITY COLL., matric. 12 June, 1867, aged 18; scholar 1867-72, B.A. 1872, M.A. 1877.

Pearson, Charles John, 2s. Charles, of Edinburgh, arm. UNIVERSITY COLL., matric. 22 May, 1861, aged 17; scholar CORPUS CHRISTI COLL. 1862-6, B.A. 1865, M.A. 1868, bar.-at-law, Inner Temple, 1870, and a member of the Faculty of Advocates, Scotland, July, 1870. See Foster's *Men at the Bar.*

Pearson, Rev. Charles William, 1s. William, of Whitehaven, Cumberland, gent. NON-COLL., matric. 14 Oct., 1882, aged 34; B.A. 1886.

Pearson, Edward, s. Edward, of St. John's, Westminster, gent. CHRIST CHURCH, matric. 17 Dec., 1760, aged 16; B.A. 1764, M.A. 1767.

Pearson, Edward, 4s. Henry Robert, of Brompton, Middlesex, arm. WORCESTER COLL., matric. 16 Nov., 1848, aged 19; B.A. 1852, M.A. 1855, held various curacies 1852-82. [5]

Pearson, Ernest William, 1s. John, of Broughton, Lancashire, gent. LINCOLN COLL., matric. 18 Oct., 1879, aged 18; scholar 1879-83, B.A. 1886, bar-at-law Inner Temple, 1886.

Pearson, Francis Campbell, 1s. Francis Boyle, of Agra, India, arm. PEMBROKE COLL., matric. 23 Oct., 1872, aged 19; captain 4th hussars. See *Eton School Lists.*

Pearson, Frederick James Norman, 1s. Frederick Burnet, of Rome, arm. BALLIOL COLL., matric. 21 Oct., 1869, aged 18; B.A. 1874, bar.-at-law, Lincoln's Inn, 1877, an examiner High Court of Justice 1884. See Foster's *Men at the Bar.*

Pearson, Frederick Richard, 1s. James, of Formby, Lancashire, cler. KEBLE COLL., matric. 16 Oct., 1876, aged 19; B.A. & M.A. from MERTON COLL. 1884, vicar of Combe, Berks, 1856.

Pearson, Frederick Thorpe, 2s. Henry Robert, of Chelsea, Middlesex, gent. QUEEN'S COLL., matric. 29 Oct., 1840, aged 18; B.A. 1844, M.A. 1847, held various curacies 1852-64, vicar of Whitwick St. George, co. Warwick, 1865. [10]

Pearson, George, 2s. Hawtin, of St. Peter's-in-the-East, Oxford (city), gent. CHRIST CHURCH, matric. 4 June, 1846, aged 18; chorister 1836-40, servitor 1846-8; singing-man ST. JOHN'S COLL. 1844-6, B.A. from NEW INN HALL 1851, M.A. 1854.

Pearson, George Charles, 2s. William, of St. Pancras, London, arm. CHRIST CHURCH, matric. 7 June, 1832, aged 18; B.A. 1836, M.A. 1839, perp. curate Thanington, Kent, 1842-4, rector of St. Margaret, Canterbury, 1844-7, curate of St. Gregory the Great, Canterbury, 1852-61, one of the six preachers Canterbury Cathedral 1867-74, hon. canon Canterbury 1874.

Pearson, George Frederick, 2s. Richard, of London, gent. WORCESTER COLL., matric. 18 May, 1843, aged 18; B.A. 1847, M.A. 1858, perp. curate Pollington, Yorks, 1852-7, vicar-choral York 1857-62, priest-vicar Chichester Cathedral 1862-71, vicar of Felpham, Sussex, 1871-4, and of Funtington 1874.

Pearson, Henry, s. William, of York (city), doctor. CHRIST CHURCH, matric. 10 Oct., 1720, aged 16; B.A. 1724, M.A. 1727.

Pearson, Henry Daniel, 1s. Richard, of London, arm. WORCESTER COLL., matric. 14 May, 1840, aged 18; B.A. 1844, M.A. 1848, vicar of St. James's, Clapton, London, 1873, father of John H. [15]

Pearson, Henry Hollingworth, 1s. Henry, of Sheffield, co. York, cler. LINCOLN COLL., matric. 6 Feb., 1826, aged 18; B.A. 1829, M.A. 1833, vicar of Norton, Yorks, 1844.

Pearson, Herbert, 3s. George, of Pontefract, Yorks, arm. WADHAM COLL., matric. 12 Oct., 1877, aged 23.

Pearson, Hugh, 4s. Hugh (Nicholas), of Oxford (city), doctor (after dean of Salisbury). BALLIOL COLL., matric. 29 Nov., 1834, aged 17; B.A. 1839, M.A. 1841, canon of Windsor 1876, deputy clerk of the closet 1881, vicar of Sonning, Berks, 1841, until his death 13 April, 1882. See *Annual Register.*

Pearson, Hugh Nicholas, s. Hugh, of Lymington, Hants, arm. ST. JOHN'S COLL., matric. 16 July, 1796, aged 19; B.A. 1800, M.A. 1803, B. & D.D. 1821, proctor 1813, vicar of St. Helen's, Abingdon, with Radley and Drayton chapelries 1822, dean of Salisbury 1823, until his death 17 Nov., 1856.

Pearson, James Hugh, 1s. James Hackman, of Clerkenwell, Middlesex, arm. MAGDALEN HALL, matric. 30 June, 1859, aged 23; B.A. 1863, M.A. 1866, held various curacies 1864-85, vicar of Imber, Wilts, 1885. [20]

Pearson, John, s. Robert, of Crewkerne, Somerset, cler. WADHAM COLL., matric. 27 May, 1773, aged 18; bible clerk EXETER COLL. 1775, B.A. 1777. See *Boase,* 146.

Pearson, John, s. Thomas, of Tettenhall, co. Stafford, gent. CHRIST CHURCH, matric. 24 Oct., 1789, aged 17; bar.-at-law, Lincoln's Inn, 1802, advocate-general East India Company, Bengal, 1824-40, died 16 April, 1841. See *Gent.'s Mag.,* 1841, ii. 428.

Pearson, John, 2s. Thomas, of Bath (city), cler. EXETER COLL., matric. 26 June, 1822, aged 17; a commoner of MAGDALEN HALL 1827, B.A. 1830, M.A. 1838.

Pearson, John, 1s. William, of Tavistock Square, London, arm. BALLIOL COLL., matric. 4 June, 1824, aged 17; B.A. 1828, M.A. 1831, a student of Lincoln's Inn 1828. See *Eton School Lists.*

Pearson, Rev. John Armstrong, 2s. Thomas Aylmer, of Upton St. Leonards, co. Gloucester, gent. QUEEN'S COLL., matric. 22 Oct., 1866, aged 20; B.A. 1870, M.A. 1875. [25]

Pearson, John Henry, 1s. Henry Daniel, of Surbiton, Surrey, cler. CHRIST CHURCH, matric. 21 May, 1880, aged 22.

Pearson, John Noble, s. Michael Noble, of Outwell, Norfolk, cler. BRASENOSE COLL., matric. 16 May, 1805, aged 18.

Pearson, John Yardley, 4s. Joseph Hitchman, of West Bromwich, co. Stafford, gent. NEW COLL., matric. 11 Oct., 1878, aged 18; scholar 1878-83, B.A. 1883, M.A. 1888.

Pearson, Rev. Richard, s. Thomas, of Kirkby Stephen, Westmoreland, pleb. QUEEN'S COLL., matric. 23 Oct., 1761, aged 17; B.A. 1766, M.A. 1770, fellow until his death 20 March, 1791.

Pearson, Rev. Richard, s. Richard, of Birmingham, co. Warwick, doctor. ST. JOHN'S COLL., matric. 18 Jan., 1815, aged 20; B.A. 1818, M.A. 1821, died 11 Aug., 1853. [30]

Pearson, Robert, s. Henry, of Crewkerne, Somerset, pleb. PEMBROKE COLL., matric. 18 May, 1738, aged 20; B.A. 15 March, 1741-2, M.A. 1748.

Pearson, Robert, s. William, of Torpenhow, Cumberland, gent. QUEEN'S COLL., matric. 26 Oct., 1814, aged 18; scholar 1815-8, B.A. 1819, rector of Orton, Cumberland, 1845, until his death 20 Aug., 1857.

Pearson, Roland George, 2s. Edward, of Gainsborough, co. Lincoln, arm. HERTFORD COLL., matric. 22 Oct., 1886, aged 19.

Pearson, Thomas, s. Edward, of Wolverhampton, co. Stafford, gent. ST. EDMUND HALL, matric. 14 Feb., 1749-50, aged 17; B.A. from CHRIST CHURCH 1753, M.A. 1756.

Pearson, Thomas, s. John, of Kirkby Stephen, Westmoreland, pleb. QUEEN'S COLL., matric. 18 Dec., 1780, aged 20; B.A. 1784, fellow, M.A. 1788, B.D. 1797, vicar of Sparsholt, Berks, 1803, until his death 17 Feb., 1841, father of Thomas 1826. [35]

Pearson, Thomas, s. John, of Kendal, Westmoreland, gent. QUEEN'S COLL., matric. 15 June, 1816, aged 16; scholar 1816-29, B.A. 1820, M.A. 1823, fellow 1829-49, chaplain, librarian 1832, died at Kendal 10 Feb., 1849.

Pearson, Thomas, o.s. Thomas, of Sparsholt, near Berks, cler. QUEEN'S COLL., matric. 22 June, 1826, aged 17; Michel exhibitioner 1826-30, B.A. 1830, M.A. 1833, scholar 1830-3, fellow 1833-41.

Pearson, Thomas Horner, s. Robert, of Crewkerne, Somerset, cler. WADHAM COLL., matric. 27 April, 1768, aged 16; B.A. 1772, M.A. 1776, rector of Puddimore Milton, 1776, and vicar of Queen Camel, Somerset, 1785, until his death 13 May, 1832.

Pearson, Thomas Sherwin, 5s. Thomas Hook, of Barwell, co. Leicester, arm. CHRIST CHURCH, matric. 20 Jan., 1871, aged 19; B.A. 1876, a student of the Inner Temple 1873. See *Rugby School Reg.*

Pearson, William, s. William, of Kew, Surrey, arm. LINCOLN COLL., matric. 1 July, 1800, aged 16. [5]

Pearson, William, y.s. Henry, of Sheffield, Yorks, cler. QUEEN'S COLL., matric. 19 June, 1828, aged 17; scholar UNIVERSITY COLL. 1829-37, B.A. 1832, M.A. 1835, perp. curate North Rode, Cheshire, 1855-72.

Pearson, William, 3s. William, of Streatham, Surrey, arm. EXETER COLL., matric. 14 May, 1835, aged 19; B.A. 1839, M.A. 1842 (? vicar of Granborough, and died 1 April, 1867).

Pearson, William Henley. CHRIST CHURCH, 1831. See JERVIS, page 752.

Pearson, William Henry, 3s. Robert, of Rufford, Lancashire, cler. QUEEN'S COLL., matric. 17 Oct., 1848, aged 18; B.A. 1852, M.A. 1855.

Pearson, William Lawrence Wemyss, 2s. Francis Boyle, of Allahabad, arm. PEMBROKE COLL., matric. 29 Oct., 1874, aged 20; bar.-at-law, Inner Temple, 1881. See Foster's *Men at the Bar* & *Rugby School Reg.* [10]

Pearson, William Webster, 1s. William, of Bishop Auckland, co. Durham, gent. NEW COLL., matric. 5 Feb., 1877, aged 37.

Pearson, Wilson, s. Richard, of Redmayne, Cumberland, gent. QUEEN'S COLL., matric. 20 Oct., 1756, aged 19; bar.-at-law, Middle Temple 1765.

Peart, Francis, s. Francis, of St. John's, Worcester (city), pleb. MAGDALEN HALL, matric. 30 Oct., 1719, aged 19.

Pease, Frederick, 3s. Robert Copland, of Hull, Yorks, gent. MAGDALEN HALL, matric. 14 Dec., 1826, aged 19.

Pease, Henry Joseph Robinson, 1s. Joseph Walker, of Hesslewood, Yorks, arm. UNIVERSITY COLL., matric. 28 May, 1863, aged 19; of Hesslewood. See Foster's *Yorkshire Collection.* [15]

Pease, Howard, 1s. John William, of Saltwell, co. Durham, arm. BALLIOL COLL., matric. 17 Oct., 1882, aged 19; B.A. 1887. See Foster's *Baronetage.*

Pease, Peter Richard, s. William, of Steeple Morden, Cambridge, cler. MERTON COLL., matric. 19 Nov., 1768, aged 18.

Pease, William, s. Fran., of Clist St. George, Devon, cler. EXETER COLL., matric. 17 March, 1726-7, aged 16; B.A. 1730, fellow 1731-47, M.A. 1733, B.D. 1744, rector of Steeple Morden, co. Cambridge, 1746, vicar of Great Milton 1749. See *Coll. Reg.*, 94.

Peat, John, of ST. PETER'S COLL., Cambridge (B.A. 1833, M.A. 1836); adm. 'ad eundem' 21 Nov., 1839, held various curacies 1835-54, perp. curate Weald Chapel, Sevenoaks, 1854-60, rector of Hangleton, Sussex, 1860-4, vicar of East Grinstead 1863, until his death 11 May, 1871.

Peat, Thomas Heaviside, 1s. Thomas, of Manningtree, Essex, gent. ST. MARY HALL, matric. 27 Oct., 1869, aged 19; B.A. 1874, M.A. 1876, held various curacies 1875-86. [20]

Peat, William, s. Thomas, of 'Datsimcern' (? Dalesmain), Cumberland, pleb. QUEEN'S COLL., matric. 17 Dec., 1729.

Peatt, Joshua, s. John, of Holm Cultram, Cumberland, pleb. QUEEN'S COLL., matric. 15 June, 1744, aged 19.

Pech, James. NEW COLL., 1854. See PETCH.

Peche, Rev. George, s. Joseph, of Blandford, Dorset, gent. PEMBROKE COLL., matric. 21 June, 1808, aged 28; B.A. 1812, M.A. 1815, died at Dover 4 Aug., 1867.

Pechell, Augustus, s. Paul, of St. Clement's, London, arm. CHRIST CHURCH, matric. 17 June, 1772, aged 18; B.A. 1776, M.A. 1779, of Bartletts, Herts, bar.-at-law, Lincoln's Inn, 1779, commissioner of bankrupts, receiver-general of the Post-Office 1785, receiver-general of Customs 1790, died 19 Sep., 1820. See Foster's *Baronetage* & *Alumni West.*, 395.

Pechell, Augustus, s. Augustus, of London, arm. CHRIST CHURCH, matric. 17 May, 1809, aged 18; student 1809-20, B.A. 1813, M.A. 1815, bar.-at-law, Lincoln's Inn, 1817, chancellor of the diocese of St. David's (resigned 1843), died in 1863. See *Alumni West.*, 469. [25]

Pechell, Edward Rodney Cecil, 4s. Samuel George, of Berely House, East Meon, Hants, arm. WADHAM COLL., matric. 22 June, 1855, aged 17; hon. major in the army, died 11 Nov., 1880.

Pechell, (Sir) George Samuel (Bart.), 1s. Samuel George, of Chalfont St. Giles, Bucks, arm. TRINITY COLL., matric. 3 July, 1838, aged 19; 5th baronet, colonel Hants royal volunteers. See Foster's *Baronetage.*

Pechell, Horace Robert, s. Augustus, of Marylebone, arm. CHRIST CHURCH, matric. 8 June, 1810, aged 18, B.A. 1814; fellow ALL SOULS' COLL. 1814-27, M.A. 1817, perp. curate Nettleden 1819-22, rector of Bix 1822-70, chancellor and canon of Brecon, 1829, until his death 22 Feb., 1882. See Foster's *Baronetage.*

Pechell, (Sir) Thomas (Brooke, Bart.), s. Paul, of St. Clement's, London, arm. (after a baronet). CHRIST CHURCH, matric. 30 May, 1771, aged 18; B.A. 1775, M.A. 1779, 2nd baronet, a major-general in the army 1814, gentleman quarterly waiter to the Queen, gentleman usher, daily waiter 1795, assumed the additional surname of BROOKE by royal licence 22 Nov., 1800, M.P. Downton, died 17 June, 1826. See Foster's *Baronetage* & *Alumni West.*, 394. [30]

Peck, Awdry, 4s. Jasper, of Bath, Somerset, cler. WADHAM COLL., matric. 12 Oct., 1866, aged 19; B.A. 1870, M.A. 1885, M.R.C.S. 1875, L.R.C.P., London, 1875. See *St. Paul's School Reg.*, 337.

Peck, Edward, s. Robert, of Birmingham, co. Warwick, pleb. HART HALL, matric. 21 March, 1715-6, aged 18; B.A. 11 March, 1719-20.

Peck, Edward Ellis, 3s. William, of St. John Baptist, Bristol (city), gent. ST. EDMUND HALL, matric. 25 June, 1840, aged 22.

Peck, Henry Cecil, 2s. Jasper Kenrick, of Notton, Wilts, arm. UNIVERSITY COLL., matric. 11 Oct., 1884, aged 19; B.A. 1887.

Peck, Rev. Jasper, 2s. Kenrick, of Rushall, Wilts, cler. TRINITY COLL., matric. 1 June, 1822, aged 17; B.A. 1826, M.A. 1830, died 20 Nov., 1853. [35]

Peck, Kenrick, s. Kenrick, of London, arm. ORIEL COLL., matric. 4 May, 1790, aged 21; B.A. 1794, M.A. 1798, rector of Ightfield, Salop, 1820, died 16 Feb., 1837.

Peck, Philip, 3s. Jasper, of Bath, Somerset, cler. WADHAM COLL., matric. 14 Oct., 1864, aged 19; scholar 1864-9, B.A. 1869, a student of Lincoln's Inn 1868, minister in the Catholic Apostolic Church. See *St. Paul's School Reg.*, 331.

Peck, Philip Richardson, 'f.m.' Henry, of Rushall, Wilts, cler. TRINITY COLL., matric. 16 Nov., 1820, aged 18; of Cornish and Temple Coombe, Somerset, died in 1858.

Peck, Robert Holman, o.s. Robert William, of Fairfield, Manchester. NEW COLL., matric. 16 Oct., 1874, aged 19; scholar EXETER COLL. 1875-8, B.A. 1878, M.A. 1882, B.Med. 1884. See *Boase*, 167.

Peck, William Awdry, 1s. Jasper Kenrick, of London, arm. CHRIST CHURCH, matric. 15 Oct., 1880, aged 19; a junior student 1880, B.A. 1884, bar.-at-law, Lincoln's Inn, 1887.

Peckard, Henry, s. John, of Welbourne, co. Lincoln, cler. CORPUS CHRISTI COLL., matric. 15 Nov., 1744, aged 15.

Peckard, Peter, s. John, of Welbourne, co. Lincoln, cler. CORPUS CHRISTI COLL., matric. 20 July, 1734, aged 16, B.A. 1738, M.A. 2 March, 1741-2; fellow BRASENOSE COLL.; D.D. from MAGDALEN COLL., Cambridge (per *Lit. Reg.*), 1785, master 1781-97, vice-chancellor 1784, rector of Fletton, Hunts, and Tansor, Northants, 1777, rector of Abbotts Ripton, preb. of Southwell 1777, dean of Peterborough 1792, until his death 8 Dec., 1797.

Peckham, Harry, s. Henry, of Amberley, Sussex, cler. NEW COLL., matric. 8 Aug., 1759, aged 19; B.A. 1763, fellow, M.A. 1767, bar.-at-law, Middle Temple, 1768, K.C. and bencher 1782, recorder of Chichester, died 10 and buried in Temple Church 19 Jan., 1787.

Peckham, Harry John, o.s. Charles (formerly Smith), of Niton Hants, arm. BALLIOL COLL., matric. 19 Jan., 1861, aged 19; B.A. 1865, M.A. 1872, held various curacies 1870-82, vicar of Nutley, Sussex, 1882. **[5]**

Peckham, Henry, born at the Sub-Deanery, Chichester, Sussex, s. Hen., gent. TRINITY COLL., matric. 16 Dec., 1729, aged 17; B.A. 1733, rector of Tangmere, Sussex, died at Chichester in 1795, father of Harry 1759.

Peckham, Richard, s. Rich., of Compton, Sussex, arm. CHRIST CHURCH, matric. 14 March, 1731-2, aged 15.

Peckham, Richard, 1s. Thomas, of Allingbourne, Sussex, equitis. NEW COLL., matric. 10 April, 1734, aged 16; died 30 Aug., 1742.

Peckham, William, s. William, of Salehurst, Sussex, arm. MERTON COLL., matric. 3 Feb., 1735-6, aged 17.

Peckwell, Henry, s. Henry, of Chichester, Sussex, arm. ST. EDMUND HALL, matric. 17 May, 1770, aged 22. **[10]**

Peckwell, Robert Henry, s. Henry, of London, doctor. CHRIST CHURCH, matric. 23 Oct., 1792, aged 16; B.A. 1796, M.A. 1799, bar.-at-law, Lincoln's Inn, 1801, serjt.-at-law 1809, died in Jan., 1823.

Pedder, Arthur Lionel, o.s. William Henry, of Devon, arm. MAGDALEN COLL., matric. 21 Oct., 1886, aged 18; demy 1886.

Pedder, Edward, 2s. Edward, of Preston, Lancashire, gent. BRASENOSE COLL., matric. 6 June, 1838, aged 19; scholar 1838-41, B.A. 1842, M.A. 1845, hon. canon Manchester Cathedral 1870, vicar of St. John, Lancaster, 1862-80, died 21 March, 1881. See *Manchester School Reg.*, iii. 260.

Pedder, James, s. Richard, of Preston, Lancashire, gent. QUEEN'S COLL., matric. 29 Jan., 1749-50, aged 18; B.A. 1753, vicar (and patron) of Garstang, died in May, 1772. See *Manchester School Reg.*, ii. 42.

Pedder, Rev. John, of ST. JOHN'S COLL., Cambridge (B.A. 1826, M.A. 1829); adm. 'ad eundem' 14 June, 1849 (? died vicar of Garstang 16 July, 1859, aged 65, and grandson of James 1750). **[15]**

Pedder, John Leacock Kortright, 1s. Charles Lloyd, of St. Thomas, East Indies, arm. NON-COLL., matric. 16 Oct., 1875, aged 20.

Pedder, Rev. John Wilson, 1s. William, of Compton Dando, Somerset, cler. BRASENOSE COLL., matric. 9 June, 1870, aged 17; B.A. 1874, M.A. 1877.

Pedder, Thomas, 2s. Wilson, of Garstang, Lancashire, cler. NON-COLL., matric. 18 Oct., 1880, aged 19.

Pedder, William, s. George, of Carisbrook, Isle of Wight, gent. ST. EDMUND HALL, matric. 21 May, 1787, aged 26; B.A. 1792, vicar of Andover, Hants, 1793, until his death 18 March, 1823.

Pedder, William George (C.S.I.), 1s. William Newland, of Clevedon, Somerset, cler. WORCESTER COLL., matric. 21 Nov., 1849, aged 17; scholar EXETER COLL. 1850, B.A. 1854, Bombay Civil Service 1855-79, municipal commissioner for city of Bombay, secretary to Revenue Statistics and Commerce Department of Indian Office 1879, C.S.I. 29 May, 1886. See *Boase*, 156. **[20]**

Pedder, William Lewes, o.s. William, of Madras, East Indies, arm. EXETER COLL., matric. 27 June, 1856, aged 19.

Pedder, William Newland, s. William, of Andover, Hants, cler. WORCESTER COLL., matric. 16 Dec., 1814, aged 18; scholar 1817-19, B.A. 1818, M.A. 1821, fellow 1818-31, vicar of Clevedon, Somerset, 1830, until his death 15 June, 1871.

Pedder, Wilson, y.s. John, of Garstang, Lancashire, cler. BRASENOSE COLL., matric. 11 Feb., 1836, aged 17; B.A. 1840, M.A. 1842, vicar of Compton Dando 1847, perp. curate Horrington, vice-principal Wells Cathedral 1842-7, vicar of Garstang, Lancashire, 1859.

Peddie, James Dick, 2s. John Dick, of Edinburgh, arm. TRINITY COLL., matric. 14 Oct., 1876, aged 19; B.A. 1882.

Pedding, John, s. John, of St. Peter's, Marlborough, Wilts, pleb. MERTON COLL., matric. 7 April, 1715, aged 16. **[25]**

Peddle, John, s. Henry, of Yeovil, Somerset, gent. ST. MARY HALL, matric. 16 Oct., 1771, aged 19; B.C.L. 1778, vicar of Charlton Horethorne, Somerset, 1784, until his death in 1840.

Pedlar, George Henry Orchard. EXETER COLL., 1834. See SHIELD.

Pedley, James, s. James, of Manchester, Lancashire, gent. ST. EDMUND HALL, matric. 21 June, 1794, aged 48; B.A. & M.A. 1795, 40 years assistant-master Manchester School, curate of St. Thomas, Pendleton, 1776, until his death 29 June, 1825. See *Manchester School Reg.*, i. 78.

Pedley, James Thomas, s. James, of Manchester, Lancashire, cler. BRASENOSE COLL., matric. 17 May, 1804, aged 17; B.A. 1808, M.A. 1810, curate of Yaxley, and of Peakirk-cum-Glinton 1831-50, died 5 Dec., 1862. See *Manchester School Reg.*, ii. 198.

Pedley, Robert. BRASENOSE COLL., 1777. See DEVERELL. **[30]**

Peeke, Favell, s. John, of Isle of Jamaica, gent. MERTON COLL., matric. 14 Oct., 1721, aged 17.

Peel, Alfred Henry, 3s. Frederick, of Torquay, Devon, cler. ST. ALBAN HALL, matric. 28 Jan., 1882, aged 17.

Peel, Rev. Alfred Lennox, 3s. Lawrence, of London, arm. BALLIOL COLL., matric. 5 March, 1845, aged 17, B.A. 1849; fellow ALL SOULS' COLL. 1849-63, M.A. 1853, died 4 Nov., 1863. See Foster's *Baronetage* & *Eton School Lists.*

Peel, Archibald, 3s. Jonathan, of St. George's, Hanover Square, London, arm. TRINITY COLL., matric. 4 Dec., 1845, aged 17; B.A. 1850, M.A. 1852, of the Gerwyn, Wrexham. See Foster's *Baronetage* & *Eton School Lists.*

Peel, Arthur, 5s. Frederick, of Gainsborough, co. Lincoln, cler. ORIEL COLL., matric. 6 March, 1845, aged 18; B.A. 1848, M.A. 1852, bar.-at-law, Inner Temple, 1852, chief justice Island of Antigua, died 15 Oct., 1873. **[35]**

Peel, Arthur George Villiers, 2s. Arthur Wellesley, of London, arm. NEW COLL., matric. 15 Oct., 1886, aged 18.

Peel, Arthur Wellesley, 5s. Robert, of London, baronet. BALLIOL COLL., matric. 6 April, 1848, aged 18; B.A. 1852, M.A. 1865, created D.C.L. 22 June, 1887, of the Lodge, Sandy, Beds, a student of the Inner Temple 1853, M.P. Warwick 1865-85, Warwick & Leamington since 1885, patronage secretary to Treasury 1873-4, under-secretary Home Department, April to Dec., 1880, speaker of the House of Commons since Feb., 1884. See Foster's *Baronetage* & *Eton School Lists*

Peel, Charles Steers, 2s. William, of Liverpool, arm. WORCESTER COLL., matric. 24 Oct., 1839, aged 18; B.A. 1843, M.A. 1848, rector of Rousham, Oxon, 1859, until his death 10 Sep., 1873, brother of Francis William. See Foster's *Lancashire Collection.*

Peel, Edmund, 5s. Robert, of Accrington, Lancashire, gent. BRASENOSE COLL., matric. 28 Jan., 1836, aged 18; B.A. 1839, M.A. 1845, vicar of West Pennard, Somerset, 1849-50, of Wargrave-on-Thames 1850-5, and of Toot Baldon 1861-71, died 10 Nov., 1877. See Foster's *Baronetage.*

Peel, Edmund, 2s. John, of Swinton, Lancashire, arm. TRINITY COLL., matric. 1 Feb., 1862, aged 19; B.A. 1865, of Boxwell Court, co. Gloucester, died 9 June, 1885.

Peel, Edmund Yates, 3s. Giles Haworth, of Ince, Cheshire, cler. CHRIST CHURCH, matric. 16 Oct., 1844, aged 18; B.A. 1849, M.A. 1853, of Fern Hill, co. Carmarthen, died 29 Aug., 1861. See Foster's *Baronetage* & *Eton School Lists.*

Peel, Edward, 1s. Charles Wicksteed Ethelston, of Uplyme, Devon, cler. CHRIST CHURCH, matric. 15 May, 1845, aged 19; of Bryn-y-pys, Flints, etc., high sheriff 1870, and for co. Montgomery 1868, assumed the surname of PEEL in lieu of his patronymic by royal licence 29 March, 1831. See Foster's *Baronetage* & *Eton School Lists.* **[5]**

Peel, Edward Lennox, 1s. Charles, of Bowdon, Cheshire, arm. BALLIOL COLL., matric. 20 Oct., 1874, aged 18; B.A. 1879, M.A. 1882. See Foster's *Baronetage* & *Rugby School Reg.*

Peel, Francis William, 3s. William, of Caenby, co. Lincoln, arm. WORCESTER COLL., matric. 18 March, 1841, aged 18; B.A. 1845, M.A. 1847, vicar of Skelbrooke, Yorks, 1875-84, rector of Burghwallis since 1856. See *Rugby School Reg.*, 196.

Peel, Frederick, 4s. William Yates, of Bowne Hill, co. Stafford, arm. ORIEL COLL., matric. 3 March, 1853, aged 19; B.A. & M.A. 1859, of Barassie House, Malvern Link, vicar of Cowleigh, co. Worcester, 1866-75, and of Little Malvern since 1878.

Peel, Frederick, 3s. Edward, of Leeds, Yorks, gent. MAGDALEN HALL, matric. 7 March, 1871, aged 13; B.Mus. 6 July, 1872, vicar of Heslington, Yorks, 1880.

Peel, Gerald, 3s. John, of Swinton, Lancashire, arm. TRINITY COLL., matric. 24 Jan., 1866, aged 18; B.A. 1868, brother of Edmund 1862. **[10]**

Peel, Giles Haworth, s. Jonathan, of Accrington, Lancashire, arm. PEMBROKE COLL., matric. 26 March, 1801, aged 22; incumbent of Ince, Cheshire, died 23 Dec., 1854.

Peel, Herbert Richard, 2s. John, of Canterbury (city), doctor. CHRIST CHURCH, matric. 31 May, 1849, aged 18; B.A. 1853, M.A. 1856, rector of Handsworth, co. Stafford, 1860-73, died 2 June, 1885. See Foster's *Baronetage* & *Eton School Lists.*

Peel, John, s. Robert, of Bury, Lancashire, baronet. CHRIST CHURCH, matric. 18 Nov., 1817, aged 19; B.A. 1822, M.A. 1828, B. & D.D. 1845, vicar of Stone, co. Worcester, 1828, canon of Canterbury 1829-45, dean of Worcester 1845, until his death 20 Feb., 1875, father of the last named. See *Rugby School Reg.*, 112.

Peel, Lieut.-General Jonathan, 5s. Sir Robert Peel, Bart.; created D.C.L. 21 June, 1870, privy councillor, M.P. Norwich 1826-31, Huntingdon 1831-68, surveyor-general of ordnance 1841-6, secretary of state for war 1858-9, 1866-7, died 13 Feb., 1879. See Foster's *Baronetage.*

Peel, Lawrence, 6s. Robert, of Bury, Lancashire, baronet. CHRIST CHURCH, matric. 16 Oct., 1819, aged 18; M.P. Cockermouth, 1827-30. See Foster's *Baronetage.* **[15]**

Peel, Right Hon. Sir Lawrence; created D.C.L. 16 June, 1858, chief justice of Bengal 1842 (s. Joseph Peel, of Bowes Farm, Middlesex), bar.-at-law, Middle Temple, 1824, bencher 1856, M.P. Cockermouth 1827-50, privy councillor 1855, advocate-general Calcutta 1840, chief justice Bengal 1842, knighted 1842, governor and president Guy's Hospital, vice-president Legal Council, Bengal, 1854-5, a director East India Company 1857, president of the East India Association 1874, etc., died 22 July, 1884. See Foster's *Baronetage.*

Peel, (Sir) Robert (Bart.), s. Robert, of Bury, Lancashire, baronet. CHRIST CHURCH, matric. 21 Oct., 1805, aged 17; B.A. 1808, M.A. 1814, created D.C.L. 18 June, 1817, P.C. 1812, M.P. Cashel 1809-12, Chippenham 1812-7, Oxford University 1817-29, Westbury 1829-30, Tamworth 1830-50, Colonial under-secretary 1810, chief secretary Ireland 1812, Home secretary 1822 & 1828, first lord of the Treasury 1834-5 & 1841-6, died 2 July, 1850. See Foster's *Baronetage.*

Peel, Rev. Robert, s. Thomas, of Salkey (?), co. York, arm. ORIEL COLL., matric. 7 July, 1810, aged 18; scholar UNIVERSITY COLL. 1810-13, B.A. 1814, M.A. 1817, died 9 Sep., 1823.

Peel, (Sir) Robert (Bart., G.C.B.), 1s. Robert, baronet. CHRIST CHURCH, matric. 26 May, 1841, aged 19; 3rd baronet, G.C.B. 5 Jan., 1866, P.C. Great Britain and Ireland, chief secretary Ireland 1861-5, M.P. Tamworth 1850-80, Huntingdon 1884-5, Blackburn 1885-6, a lord of the Admiralty 1855-7. See Foster's *Baronetage.*

Peel, Robert, 1s. Robert, of London, baronet. TRINITY COLL., matric. 16 Oct., 1886, aged 17; migrated to BALLIOL COLL. 1887. **[20]**

Peel, Robert Augustus Lawrence, 1s. John, of Marylebone, cler. CHRIST CHURCH, matric. 9 June, 1843, aged 17; died 2 June, 1870, brother of Herbert Richard. See Foster's *Baronetage* & *Eton School Lists.*

Peel, Rev. Robert Kennedy, 1s. Jonathan, of London, arm. BALLIOL COLL., matric. 30 March, 1843, aged 17; B.A. 1847, bar.-at-law, Inner Temple 1850, died 17 April, 1863, brother of Archibald. See Foster's *Baronetage* & *Eton School Lists.*

Peel, St. Vincent, 1s. John, of Manchester, Lancashire, arm. MERTON COLL., matric. 24 June, 1862, aged 18; nephew of Edmund 1836.

Peel, Samuel, 1s. Frederick, of Godalming, Surrey, cler. NON-COLL., matric. 16 Oct., 1886, aged 22; chorister MAGDALEN COLL. 1874-80.

Peel, Sydney, 4s. John, of Crow Nest, near Sandbach, Cheshire, arm. TRINITY COLL., matric. 25 Jan., 1868, aged 18; B.A. 1871, M.A. 1874, bar.-at-law, Middle Temple, 1871, brother of Edmund 1862. See Foster's *Men at the Bar.* **[25]**

Peel, Rev. William, s. William, of Church Bank, Lancashire, arm. BRASENOSE COLL., matric. 24 April, 1816, aged 19; B.A. 1820, died in 1824. See Foster's *Lancashire Collection.*

Peel, William, o.s. Robert, of Church, Lancashire, gent. BRASENOSE COLL., matric. 28 March, 1822, aged 18; of Taliaris Park, co. Carmarthen, high sheriff 1843, died 16 March, 1883.

Peel, William, 1s. Giles Haworth, of Marcham, Berks, cler. WADHAM COLL., matric. 9 Nov., 1832, aged 18; of Swinton Park, Lancashire, died 10 Sep., 1864. See Foster's *Baronetage.*

Peel, William Augustus, 5s. Jonathan, of Brandon, Norfolk, arm. ST. JOHN'S COLL., matric. 28 June, 1852, aged 18; inspector Local Government Board, brother of Archibald and Robert Kennedy Peel.

Peel, William Frederick, 1s. Archibald, of London, arm. BALLIOL COLL., matric. 4 March, 1883, aged 21. **[30]**

Peel, William Robert Wellesley, 1s. Arthur Wellesley, of London, arm. BALLIOL COLL., matric. 24 Oct., 1885, aged 18.

Peers, Charles, of ST. JOHN'S COLL., Cambridge, M.A.; adm. 'ad eundem' 6 July, 1810 (B.A. 1799, M.A. 1804), created D.C.L. 14 June, 1820, then of Chislehampton, Oxon, high sheriff 1821 (s. Robert, of Chislehampton), F.S.A., bar.-at-law, Inner Temple, 1802, recorder of Henley-on-Thames, died 6 Feb., 1853.

Peers, Henry, s. Henry, of Isle of Barbados, arm. QUEEN'S COLL., matric. 16 Dec., 1729, aged 17; bar.-at-law, Inner Temple, 9 July, 1736, buried in Middle Temple vault, Temple Church, on Thursday, 12 Aug., 1736.

Peers, Henry, s. Richard, of Faringdon, Berks, cler. TRINITY COLL., matric. 2 July, 1734, aged 15; B.A. from BALLIOL COLL. 1738, M.A. 1742, vicar Upchurch, Kent, 1742 (? died at Egloshayle vicarage, Cornwall, 28 June, 1793).

Peers, Henry, s. Henry, of Linnee, in Southampton, Hants, arm. TRINITY COLL., matric. 1 Nov., 1810, aged 19.

Peers, Rev. Herbert James, 1s. Henry Robert, of Mossley Hill, Lancashire, gent. WORCESTER COLL., matric. 18 Oct., 1883, aged 18; B.A. 1887. **[5]**

Peers, John (Witherington), s. Charles, of Bromley, Middlesex, arm. MERTON COLL., matric. 9 Dec., 1763, aged 18; B.A. 1767, M.A. 1770, D.C.L. 1778, incumbent Chislehampton, Oxon, 1770, rector of Morden, Surrey, 1778, until his death 29 April, 1835, grandfather of John Witherington next named.

Peers, John Witherington, of CATHARINE COLL., Cambridge (B.A. 1833, M.A. 1836); 'ad eundem' 14 May, 1858, son of John Peers.

Peers, Richard, s. Richard, of St. Mich., Queenhythe, arm. QUEEN'S COLL., matric. 21 Jan., 1762, aged 18.

Peers, Robert, s. Charles, of Chislehampton, Oxon, arm. MAGDALEN HALL, matric. 10 Oct., 1763, aged 21, bar.-at-law, Inner Temple, 1766, and a bencher 1800, died at Chislehampton 4 Feb., 1818, father of Charles.

Peers, Samuel, s. William, of Christ Church, Kent, gent. HART HALL, matric. 28 May, 1723. B.A. from ST. MARY HALL 26 Jan., 1726-7. **[10]**

Peet, Arthur William, 4s. Joseph, of Mavelicara, India, cler. CHRIST CHURCH, matric. 18 Oct., 1867, aged 22.

Peet, Henry Herbert, 1s. John, of Shanklin, Isle of Wight, arm. NEW COLL., matric. 15 Oct., 1886, aged 19.

Peet, Rev. Thomas, 3s. Thomas, of Ormskirk, Lancashire, gent. NON-COLL., matric. 12 Oct., 1878, aged 34; B.A. 1881, M.A. 1885.

Peete, William Willox, s. William, of Dartford, Kent, arm. WADHAM COLL., matric. 20 Jan., 1815, aged 16; B.A. 1819, M.A. 1823.

Peeters, John, s. John, of Bromley, Kent, gent. ST. EDMUND HALL, matric. 18 March, 1812, aged 27. **[15]**

Pegge, (Sir) Christopher, s. Samuel, of Westminster, arm. CHRIST CHURCH, matric. 18 April, 1782, aged 17, B.A. 1786; fellow ORIEL COLL. 1788-90, M.A. 1789, B.Med. 1789; D.Med. from CHRIST CHURCH 1792, Lees reader in anatomy 1790, regius professor of medicine 1801-22, F.R.S. 1795, knighted 26 June, 1799, fellow College Physicians 1796, master of Ewelme Hospital, etc., died 3 Aug., 1822. See Munk's *Roll*, ii. 449.

Pegge, Samuel, fellow ST. JOHN'S COLL., Cambridge (B.A. 1725, M.A. 1729), created D.C.L. 8 July, 1791, preb. of Lichfield 1763, and of Lincoln 1772, rector of Whittington, co. Derby, died 14 Feb., 1796.

Peglar, John, s. John, of King's Norton, co. Worcester, gent. WORCESTER COLL., matric. 25 March, 1802, aged 18; B.A. 1805, M.A. 1808, perp. curate of Bishopston, co. Warwick, 1821, vicar of Alveston 1846, until his death 23 April, 1856. See *Eton School Lists.*

Pegler, John, s. Andrew, of Gloucester (city), pleb. PEMBROKE COLL., matric. 10 Oct., 1740, aged 19; B.A. 1744, M.A. 1748 (? died chaplain of Christ Church 1773, as PEGLAR).

Pegus, Frederick Edward, s. Peter, of Greenwich, Kent, gent. ST. JOHN'S COLL., matric. 25 June, 1817, aged 18; B.A. 1822, M.A. 1825, died curate of Little Missenden, Bucks, 27 March, 1848. See *Robinson*, 191. **[20]**

Peil, John Alexander, o.s. John, of Liverpool, gent. BALLIOL COLL., matric. 17 Oct., 1877, aged 18; exhibitioner 1877-81, B.A. 1881.

Peile, (Sir) James Braithwaite (K.C.S.I.), 2s. Thomas Williamson, of Liverpool, D.D. BRASENOSE COLL., matric. 17 June, 1851, aged 18; scholar ORIEL COLL. 1851-5, B.A. 1855, M.A. 1868, member of council of Governor of Bombay 1882, C.S.I. 29 July, 1879, K.C.S.I. in 1887.

Peile, James Hamilton Francis, 1s. James Braithwaite, of Gogha, East Indies, arm. (after K.C.S.I.). CORPUS CHRISTI COLL., matric. 19 Oct., 1882, aged 19; scholar 1882-6, B.A. 1886.

Peile, Walter Octavius, 7s. Thomas Williamson, of Repton, co. Derby, D.D. MAGDALEN COLL., matric. 19 Oct., 1863, aged 19; demy 1863-8, B.A. 1867, M.A. 1870, vicar of St. Paul's, South Hampstead, 1873-6, rector of Markshall, Essex, 1877-84, chaplain Bromley College 1884. See *Rugby School Reg.*

Peirce, Aaron, s. Aaron, of High Wickham, Bucks, pleb. WADHAM COLL., matric. 23 Nov., 1726, aged 19; B.A. 1735. **[25]**

Peirce, John, 'tonsor;' 24 April, 1719.

Peirce, John, 1s. John, of Lambourne, Berks, gent. ST. JOHN'S COLL., matric. 16 Oct., 1886, aged 18.

Peirse, Rev. Windham de la Poer Beresford-, 5s. Henry William de la Poer, of Bedale, Yorks, arm. KEBLE COLL., matric. 1 May, 1878, aged 19; B.A. 1881, M.A. 1884. See Foster's *Baronetage* & *Eton School Lists.*

Peirson, Peter, s. Edward, of St. Dunstan's West, London, Middlesex, gent. QUEEN'S COLL., matric. 24 March, 1728-9, aged 17; father of Peter, bencher of the Inner Temple 1800.

Peisley, Anthony, 'bookseller;' privilegiatus 17 Dec., 1724. **[30]**

Peisley, Bartholomew, s. Bartholomew, of Oxford (city), gent. TRINITY COLL., matric. 9 April, 1739, aged 16; B.A. 1742, M.A. 1745, B.D. 1755, D.D. 1760, died senior fellow 18 April, 1781.

Pelham, Augustus Thursby, 2s. Henry, of Penn, co. Stafford, cler. UNIVERSITY COLL., matric. 14 May, 1851, aged 18; B.A. 1855, M.A. 1858, perp. curate Clee St. Margaret 1860-4, rector of Cound, Salop, 1864.

Pelham, Charles Anderson, created D.C.L. 4 July, 1793, then of Brocklesby, co. Lincoln (son of Francis Anderson, of Manby, co. Lincoln); assumed the additional name of PELHAM, M.P. Beverley 1768-74, Lincolnshire 1774-94, recorder of Grimsby 1786, created Baron Yarborough 13 Aug., 1794, died 22 Sep., 1823. See Foster's *Peerage.*

Pelham, Henry Francis, 1s. John Thomas, bishop of Norwich. TRINITY COLL., matric. 22 April, 1865, aged 18, scholar 1865-9; fellow EXETER COLL. 1869-73 & 1882, B.A. 1869, M.A. 1872, classical lecturer 1869 & 1873-82, tutor 1882, proctor 1879, reader in ancient history 1887, etc. See Foster's *Peerage*, E. CHICHESTER; & *Boase*, 142.

Pelham, Henry Thursby, 2s. George Augustus Thursby, of Cound, Salop, cler. ORIEL COLL., matric. 27 April, 1818, aged 17; B.A. 1821, M.A. 1824, of Cound Hall, Salop, assumed the additional name of PELHAM in 1852, rector of Isham (inferior portion) 1825-39, and of Cound 1839-64, died 19 Dec., 1878. **[35]**

Pelham, Rev. Herbert, 4s. John Thomas, bishop of Norwich. MAGDALEN COLL., matric. 17 Oct., 1874, aged 19; B.A. 1878, died 30 May, 1881.

Pelham, John Thomas, 3s. Thomas, Earl of Chichester. CHRIST CHURCH, matric. 5 June, 1829, aged 17; B.A. 1832, M.A. 1857, D.D. by diploma 14 May, 1857, rector of Bergh Apton, Norfolk, 1837-52, perp. curate Christ Church, Hampstead, 1852-5, rector of St. Marylebone 1855-7, bishop of Norwich 1857. See Foster's *Peerage*, E. CHICHESTER.

Pelham, Sidney, 3s. John Thomas, bishop of Norwich. MAGDALEN COLL., matric. 17 Oct., 1863, aged 19; B.A. 1873, M.A. 1875, vicar of St. Peter Mancroft, Norwich, 1879-81. See Foster's *Peerage*, E. CHICHESTER.

Pelham, Walter Thursby, 1s. Henry, of Penn, co. Stafford, cler. ORIEL COLL., matric. 10 Feb., 1848, aged 17, B.A. 1852; M.A. from TRINITY COLL. 1857, died 15 Dec., 1874.

Pelicier, Paul Charles Jules, 3s. Henry Victor, of Yverdan, Switzerland, gent. NON-COLL., matric. 19 June, 1879, aged 19. [4]

Pell, (Sir) Albert, s. Robert, of St. George's, Middlesex, arm. ST. JOHN'S COLL., matric. 26 June, 1787, aged 18; B.C.L. 1793, D.C.L. 1798, scholar & fellow until 1813, bar.-at-law, Inner Temple, 1795, serjt.-at-law 1808, king's serjeant 1819, judge of the Court of Review (or Bankruptcy) 1831, knighted 7 Dec., 1831, died 6 Sep., 1832. See *Robinson*, 140.

Pell, Albert Julian, 1s. Beauchamp Henry St. John, of Ickenham, Middlesex, cler. MERTON COLL., matric. 17 Oct., 1882, aged 19; B.A. 1886.

Pell, Jens, o.s. Robert, of Tiverton, Devon, arm. EXETER COLL., matric. 2 July, 1829, aged 20; B.A. 1834, M.A. 1844.

Pell, Robert, s. Robert, of St. George's, Middlesex, arm. TRINITY COLL., matric. 13 July, 1787, aged 20; B.A. 1791, brother of Sir Albert. See *Robinson*, 139.

Pell, Robert, s. Robert, of Plymouth, Devon, arm. MERTON COLL., matric. 20 April, 1815, aged 18.

Pellatt, Henry, s. William, of Blechingley, Surrey, gent. PEMBROKE COLL., matric. 25 Nov., 1723, aged 19, B.A. 1727; M.A. from NEW COLL. 1730.

Pellatt, Thomas, 2s. Daniel Parker, of Banbury, Oxon, arm. TRINITY COLL., matric. 21 Jan., 1884, aged 19; B.A. 1887. [11]

Pellet, Stephen, s. John Baptist, of London, gent. HERTFORD COLL., matric. 8 July, 1769, aged 22, B.A. 1773; D.Med. Edinburgh 1779, a licentiate of the College of Physicians 1780, died 28 Nov., 1824. See Munk's *Roll*, ii. 324.

Pellew, Edward, Viscount Exmouth, created D.C.L. 18 Oct., 1816 (son of George Pellew); knighted 28 July, 1793, for the capture of the *Cleopatre*, created a baronet 18 March, 1796, for the capture of the French frigate *Virginie*, etc., created Baron Exmouth 1 June, 1814, and Viscount Exmouth 10 Dec., 1816, for bombarding Algiers, G.C.B., nominated 1816, installed 1821, M.P. Barnstaple 1802-4, vice-admiral of England 1832, died 23 Jan., 1833, brother of Samuel H. 1813. See Foster's *Peerage*.

Pellew, Edward, s. Edward, Viscount Exmouth. ORIEL COLL., matric. 4 March, 1818, aged 18; B.A. 1823, M.A. 1824, vicar of Christow, Devon, 1825, perp. curate Yarmouth, Norfolk, 1825, perp. curate St. James's, Bury St. Edmunds, 1845-65, died 29 Aug., 1869. See Foster's *Peerage* & *Eton School Lists*.

Pellew, Hon. Fleetwood John, 2s. Edward, Viscount Exmouth. ST. MARY HALL, matric. 18 May, 1849, aged 18; B.A. 1853, died 6 Nov., 1830. See Foster's *Peerage* & *Eton School Lists*. [15]

Pellew, George, s. Edward, of Flushing, Cornwall, baronet (after viscount). CORPUS CHRISTI COLL., matric. 20 March, 1812, aged 18; B.A. 1815, M.A. 1818, B.D. 1828, D.D. 1828, vicar of Nazing, Essex, 1819, and Sutton Galtries, Yorks, rector of St. George-the-Martyr, Canterbury, 1827, and of St. Dionis Backchurch, London, preb. of York and of Canterbury 1822-8, dean of Norwich 1828, and rector of Great Chart, Kent, 1852, until his death 13 Oct., 1866. See Foster's *Peerage* & *Eton School Lists*.

Pellew, George Israel, 2s. Hon. Edward, of Christow, Devon, cler. UNIVERSITY COLL., matric. 13 March, 1851, aged 19; B.A. 1854, chaplain at Avranche 1873-4, held various curacies 1855-82, curate of Peterston, co. Hereford, 1882-6, rector 1886. See Foster's *Peerage*.

Pellew, Henry Edward, of TRINITY COLL., Cambridge, B.A. 1850, M.A. 1853 (o.s. George, dean of Norwich); incorp. from UNIVERSITY COLL. 9 July, 1870, on council of Keble College 1871-3. See Foster's *Peerage*, V. EXMOUTH.

Pellew, Samuel Humphrey, s. (George), of Falmouth, Cornwall, arm. TRINITY COLL., matric. 2 July, 1813, aged 19; collector of customs, Falmouth, died 18 Feb., 1843, brother of Edward 1816.

Pelly, Francis, s. Henry Hinde, of Upton, Essex, arm. CHRIST CHURCH, matric. 2 Feb., 1799, aged 18; B.A. 1802, M.A. 1810, rector of Siston, co. Gloucester, 1815, until his death 3 July, 1844. See Foster's *Baronetage*. [20]

Pelly, Frederick William, 3s. Augustus Edward, of Liverpool, gent. LINCOLN COLL., matric. 24 April, 1874, aged 19, B.A. 1879; principal of St. John's College and chaplain to bishop of Qu'Appelle 1885-6, has held various curacies since 1879.

Pelly, Sir Harold, (4th) Bart., 1s. Sir George Henry, of Warnham Court, Sussex, baronet. CHRIST CHURCH, matric. 20 Jan., 1882, aged 18; B.A. 1886. See Foster's *Baronetage*.

Pelly, John, s. John, of Upton, Essex, arm. ST. MARY HALL, matric. 11 Feb., 1772, aged 17; B.C.L. 1778, rector of Weston-sub-Edge, died 17 Nov., 1809. See Foster's *Baronetage*.

Pelly, Theophilus, 1s. Francis, of Siston, Bristol, cler. CORPUS CHRISTI COLL., matric. 5 March, 1831, aged 17; scholar 1831-8, B.A. 1834, M.A. 1837, fellow 1838-54, B.D. 1845, senior dean 1843, bursar 1849, rector of Church Brampton, Northampton, at his death 4 Jan., 1856. See Foster's *Baronetage*.

Pember, Edward, s. John, of Worcester (city), gent. MAGDALEN HALL, matric. 17 March, 1743-4, aged 17; B.A. from WADHAM COLL. 1747. [25]

Pember, Edward Henry, 1s. John Edward Ross, of Stockwell, Surrey, arm. CHRIST CHURCH, matric. 23 May, 1850, aged 17; student 1854-61, B.A. 1854, M.A. 1857, of Vicars Hill House, Hants, J.P., bar.-at-law, Lincoln's Inn, 1858, Q.C. 1874, bencher 1876. See Foster's *Men at the Bar*.

Pember, Francis William, 1s. Edward Henry, of Hatfield, Herts, arm. BALLIOL COLL., matric. 21 Oct., 1880, aged 18, scholar 1880-4; fellow ALL SOULS' COLL. 1884, B.A. 1884, M.A. 1887, a student of Lincoln's Inn 1885.

Pember, Frederick, 3s. John Edward, of Brixton, Surrey, arm. CHRIST CHURCH, matric. 30 May, 1855, aged 17; B.A. 1859.

Pember, Howard Edward, 2s. Edward Henry, of Hatfield, Herts, arm. BALLIOL COLL., matric. 15 Oct., 1884, aged 19; exhibitioner 1884.

Pemberton, Bertram Roper Stote, 3s. Richard Lawrence, of Sunderland, co. Durham, arm. NEW COLL., matric. 25 Nov., 1886, aged 18. [30]

Pemberton, Charles Orlando Childe, 3s. William Lacon Childe, of Wrockwardine, Salop, arm. CHRIST CHURCH, matric. 17 March, 1831, aged 18; B.A. 1835, of Millichope Park, Salop, J.P., D.L., high sheriff 1859, entered the Inner Temple 1835, took the additional name of PEMBERTON, died 1 May, 1883.

Pemberton, Christopher Robert, 2s. Christopher, of St. George's, Westminster, doctor. CHRIST CHURCH, matric. 21 May, 1819, aged 18; student 1819-29, B.A. 1823, M.A. 1826, of Newton, co. Cambridge, high sheriff 1858, sometime a clerk in the Treasury, died 26 June, 1884. See *Alumni West.*, 485.

Pemberton, Edward, s. Thomas, of Warrington, Lancashire, gent. BRASENOSE COLL., matric. 22 May, 1810, aged 18; B.A. 1814, M.A. 1817. See James 1781.

Pemberton, Edward (John), 3s. Edward, of Mold, co. Flint, gent. JESUS COLL., matric. 11 Nov., 1847, aged 19; B.A. 1851, M.A. 1854, of Stour House, Sudbury, Suffolk, chaplain royal navy 1852-83, died in 1886. See *Rugby School Reg.*, 260.

Pemberton, Edward Leigh, 1s. Edward Leigh, of St. George's Bloomsbury, Middlesex, arm. ST. JOHN'S COLL., matric. 30 June, 1841, aged 18; B.A. 1845, of Torry Hill, Kent, J.P. M.P. East Kent, 1868-85, assistant under-secretary of State, home department, July, 1885. See Foster's *Men at the Bar*, & *Eton School Lists*.

Pemberton, Edward Robert, s. Thomas Butcher, of Northampton (town), arm. EXETER COLL., matric. 24 April, 1811, aged 18; B.A. from UNIVERSITY COLL. 1814, M.A. 1817, D.C.L. 1823, a student of the Inner Temple 1812, migrated to Lincoln's Inn 1813, vicar of St. Sepulchre's, Northampton, 1819-22, chaplain Chapel Royal, Brighton, 1822-30, rector of Milton, and perp. curate Hartwell, Northants, 1835-44, assumed the surname of PEMBERTON in lieu of BUTCHER 1842, vicar of Wandsworth 1844-50, rector of St. Mary Steps, Exeter, 1855-6, in charge of Sternfield, Suffolk, 1867-72, vicar of Shipley 1872-3, and of Somerby, co. Lincoln, 1873-4, rector of North Huish, Devon, 1874, until his death 11 Jan., 1879. See *Rugby School Reg.*, 87.

Pemberton Edward William Smythe, s. Edward, of Wroxeter, Salop, arm. CHRIST CHURCH, matric. 29 Jan., 1812, aged 18; of Condover, Salop, high sheriff 1819, assumed the surname of OWEN in lieu of his patronymic, died 9 April, 1863.

Pemberton, Francis Reginald, 6s. Stanley, of Little Hallingbury, Herts, cler. KEBLE COLL., matric. 17 Oct., 1882, aged 19; B.A. 1885. [5]

Pemberton, George, 2s. Edward, of Mold, co. Flint, arm. JESUS COLL., matric. 28 Nov., 1844, aged 18; scholar 1844-50, B.A. 1848, bar.-at-law, Lincoln's Inn, 1849. See Foster's *Men at the Bar*.

Pemberton, Rev. James, s. Edward, of Warrington, Lancashire, doctor. BRASENOSE COLL., matric. 13 Feb., 1781, aged 18; B.A. 1784, M.A. 1787, died at Warrington 14 Dec., 1798.

Pemberton, John, s. Richard, of Monk Wearmouth, co. Durham, gent. LINCOLN COLL., matric. 20 March, 1795, aged 16; B.A. 1799, M.A. 1801, of Sherburn Hall, co. Durham, bar.-at-law, Middle Temple, 1804, died 29 Jan., 1843.

Pemberton, John Stapylton Grey, 1s. Richard Laurence, of Bishopwearmouth, co. Durham, arm. NEW COLL., matric. 16 Oct., 1880, aged 19, B.A. 1884; fellow ALL SOULS' COLL. 1885, M.A. 1888, a student of the Middle Temple 1882. See *Eton School Lists*.

Pemberton, Joseph Hardwicke, 1s. Joseph, of Stepney, Middlesex, gent. WORCESTER COLL., matric. 6 March, 1872, aged 19. [10]

Pemberton, Ralph Hylton, 2s. Richard Laurence, of Sunderland, arm. NEW COLL., matric. 18 Oct., 1883, aged 19.

Pemberton, Randle Jackson, o.s. Edward Robert, of Tonbridge Wells, Kent, cler. WORCESTER COLL., matric. 2 July, 1846, aged 19.

Pemberton, Richard, s. Richard, of Crediton, Devon, gent. BALLIOL COLL., matric. 6 April, 1734, aged 18; B.A. 21 March, 1737-8.

Pemberton, Richard Laurence, o.s. Richard, of Bishop Wearmouth, co. Durham, arm. PEMBROKE COLL., matric. 19 June, 1851, aged 19; of Hawthorne Tower, co. Durham, high sheriff 1861, a student of Lincoln's Inn 1852. See *Eton School Lists*.

Pemberton, Robert, s. George, of St. Vedast als. Foster's, London, gent. ST. JOHN'S COLL., matric. 30 June, 1720, aged 17; B.A. 1724, M.A. 1728, B.D. 1733, D.D. 1742, 'preb. of Leckford 1743,' died in 1758. See *Robinson*, 35. [15]

Pemberton, Robert, s. John, of Hanmer, co. Flint, cler. PEMBROKE COLL., matric. 30 April, 1730, aged 17; B.A. 1734.

Pemberton, Robert s. Robert, of Isle of Nevis, arm QUEEN'S COLL., matric. 16 Dec., 1767, aged 18.

Pemberton, Robert, 1s. Robert Charles Boileau, of Calcutta, arm. UNIVERSITY COLL., matric. 18 Oct., 1886, aged 18.

Pemberton, Robert Norgrave, s. Robert, of Shrewsbury, Salop, arm. CHRIST CHURCH, matric. 26 Oct., 1809, aged 18; B.A. 1814, M.A. 1816, hon. canon of Hereford, rector of Church Stretton, Salop, 1818, until his death at Millichope Park 11 Oct., 1848.

Pemberton, Stanley, 6s. Christopher Robert, of St. George's, Hanover Square, London, D.Med. CHRIST CHURCH, matric. 2 June, 1830, aged 19; B.A. 1834, rector of Little Hallingbury, Essex, 1849, until his death 9 July, 1880. [20]

Pemberton, Stephen, s. John, of Bishop Wearmouth, co. Durham, gent. LINCOLN COLL., matric. 14 March, 1761, aged 17; B.A. from WORCESTER COLL. 1764, fellow ORIEL COLL., M.A., 1767, B.Med. 1770, of Bainbridge Holme, co. Durham, J.P., died 27 Nov., 1831.

Pemberton, Thomas, 'cler. Univ.;' privilegiatus 31 March, 1726.

Pemberton, Thomas, s. Robert, of Shrewsbury (town), gent. PEMBROKE COLL., matric. 8 March, 1779, aged 16; B.A. 1782, M.A. 1786, of Millichope Park, Salop, bar.-at-law, Lincoln's Inn, 1787, recorder of Wenlock, died in Feb., 1833.

Pemberton, Wilfrid Leigh, 2s. Edward Leigh, of London, arm. CHRIST CHURCH, matric. 11 Oct., 1872, aged 19; B.A. 1877, bar.-at-law, Lincoln's Inn, 1880. See Foster's *Men at the Bar*.

Pemberton, William, s. John, of Wrockwardine, Salop, arm. CHRIST CHURCH, matric. 4 Nov., 1748, aged 17; B.A. 1752, M.A. 1755 (? died rector of Rushbury, Salop, 20 Sep., 1813), uncle of the next named. [25]

Pemberton, William, s. Edward, of Wrockwardine, Salop, arm. TRINITY COLL., matric. 16 Nov., 1773, aged 18; cousin of Thomas 1779.

Pemberton, William, s. William, of Middleton, co. Durham, arm. UNIVERSITY COLL., matric. 11 Oct., 1790, aged 17; of Middleton St. George, died unmarried 11 March, 1801.

Pemberton, Rev. William Arthur, 4s. Arthur Gore, of Kensal Green, Middlesex, cler. NON-COLL., matric. 18 April, 1874, aged 20; B.A. 1885, M.A. 1887.

Pembroke, Charles John, o.s. Charles, of Chertsey, Surrey, doctor. QUEEN'S COLL., matric. 8 Feb., 1844, aged 18; B.A. from NEW INN HALL 1852.

Pembrey, Marcus Seymour, 2s. John Crips, of Oxford, gent. CHRIST CHURCH, matric. 16 Oct., 1885, aged 17. [30]

Pendarves, Edward William Wynne. TRINITY COLL., 1793. See STACKHOUSE, page 1339.

Pendarves, William Cole, 1s. John Wood, of Chelsea, Middlesex, arm. CHRIST CHURCH, matric. 14 Dec., 1859, aged 18; B.A. 1864, of Pendarves, Cornwall, J.P., D.L., high sheriff 1878, bar.-at-law, Lincoln's Inn 1868, deputy-warden of the Stannaries, assumed the surname of PENDARVES in lieu of WOOD 1861. See Foster's *Men at the Bar*.

Pendlebury, Rev. John Roger, o.s. James, of Bolton, Lancashire, arm. BRASENOSE COLL., matric. 6 June, 1879, aged 18; B.A. 1883, M.A. 1886. [33]

Pendlebury, William Henry, 1s. Thomas, of Bolton, Lancashire, merchant. CHRIST CHURCH, matric. 13 Oct., 1882, aged 20; scholar 1882, B.A. 1885.

Pendleton, John William, 1s. Joseph, of Bradford, Yorks, gent. ST. MARY HALL, matric. 21 Oct., 1871, aged 21; vicar of Oakworth, Yorks, 1878.

Pendrill, John, o.s. John, of St. Augustine's, Bristol (city), doctor. BALLIOL COLL., matric. 22 March, 1828, aged 18; B.A. from ST. JOHN'S COLL. 1835, British chaplain at Ghent. See *Eton School Lists*.

Penfold, Edward Bainbridge, 2s. James, of Thorley, Isle of Wight, cler. WORCESTER COLL., matric. 17 Oct., 1863, aged 20; B.A. 1867, M.A. 1870, held various curacies 1867-76, vicar of St. Michael, Camden Town, 1876.

Penfold, Edward Hollingworth, o.s. William, of Maidstone, Kent, arm. ST. JOHN'S COLL., matric. 28 March, 1843, aged 20; B.A. 1847.

Penfold, George Saxby, s. Hugh, of Epsom, Surrey, gent. MERTON COLL., matric. 13 June, 1788, aged 18; B.A. 1792, M.A. 1814, B. & D.D. 1825, rector of Pulham, Dorset, 1797, of Christ Church, Marylebone, 1825, of Trinity, Marylebone, 1828, and of Kingswinford, co. Stafford, 1832, until his death 13 Oct., 1846.

Penfold, John, s. Richard, of Steyning, Sussex, gent. ST. ALBAN HALL, matric. 6 Dec., 1788, aged 24; B.A. & M.A. 1798, vicar of Steyning 1792, and rector of Pycombe, Sussex, 1818, until his death in 1840.

Penfold, William, 3s. John, of Steyning, Sussex, cler. LINCOLN COLL., matric. 14 Dec., 1819, aged 19; B.A. 1823, M.A. 1826, perp. curate Wordesley, co. Stafford, 1831, rector of Ruardean, co. Gloucester, 1851, until his death 22 May, 1881. **[5]**

Penfold, William Thomas, 1s. Thomas Edward, of St. George-the-Martyr, London, gent. WADHAM COLL., matric. 17 March, 1852, aged 19; B.A. 1859, M.A. 1866, held various curacies 1861-78.

Penfound, William, s. James, of Exeter (city), pleb. ORIEL COLL., matric. 8 March, 1719-20, aged 19; B.A. 1723, M.A. 1740.

Pengelly, Henry, s. John Francis, of Peter Tavy, Devon, arm. TRINITY COLL., matric. 17 Nov., 1780, aged 21.

Penhall, William, 2s. John, of London, gent. EXETER COLL., matric. 7 June, 1854, aged 18.

Penleaze, John, 2s. John, of St. Marylebone, London, arm. MAGDALEN COLL., matric. 11 May, 1826, aged 17; B.A. 1831, rector of Black Torrington, Devon, 1834, until his death 24 June, 1879. **[10]**

Penleaze, John (Story), s. James David, of Christchurch, Hants, arm. MAGDALEN COLL., matric. 13 July, 1804, aged 18; bar.-at-law, Lincoln's Inn, 1812, M.P. Southampton 1831-2 & 1833-5, died 12 April, 1855, aged 69, father of John last named.

Penlington, Edmund Tom, 2s. Thomas, of London, arm. NEW COLL., matric. 16 Jan., 1885, aged 19.

Penlington, George, s. John, of Sandbach, Cheshire, gent. BRASENOSE COLL., matric. 9 March, 1741-2, aged 19.

Penlington, William, s. William, of Aston, Cheshire, gent. BRASENOSE COLL., matric. 23 Feb., 1737-8, aged 21.

Penn, Granville, s. Thomas, of Stoke Poges, Bucks, arm. MAGDALEN COLL., matric. 11 Nov., 1780, aged 18; of Stoke Park, F.S.A., died 28 Sep., 1844, father of the next named, of Thomas G., and of William; for list of his works see *Gent.'s Mag.*, 1844, ii. 545. **[15]**

Penn, Granville John, 1s. Granville, of Petersham, Surrey, arm. CHRIST CHURCH, matric. 19 May, 1820, aged 18; B.A. 1824, M.A. 1828, bar.-at-law, Lincoln's Inn, 1833.

Penn, James, s. John, of St. Bride's, London, pleb. BALLIOL COLL., matric. 4 July, 1745, aged 18; B.A. 1749.

Penn, Richard, s. Thomas, of Bucks, cler. TRINITY COLL., matric. 17 July, 1729, aged 17; B.A. 1733, M.A. 1736.

Penn, Thomas Gordon, 2s. Granville, of St. James's, Westminster, arm. CHRIST CHURCH, matric. 20 Jan., 1823, aged 19; B.A. 1827, M.A. 1833, perp. curate Edington and Shilton-super-Polden, Somerset, 1830, brother of Granville John and William.

Penn, William, 'Faber Lignarius;' privilegiatus 24 March, 1817. **[20]**

Penn, William, 3s. Granville, of St. George's, Hanover Square, London, arm. CHRIST CHURCH, matric. 5 June, 1829, aged 18; B.A. 1833, M.A. 1837, of Sennowe Hall, Norfolk, bar.-at-law, Lincoln's Inn, 1844. See Foster's *Men at the Bar.*

Penn, William Charles, 1s. William Stone, of Birmingham, gent. EXETER COLL., matric. 16 Oct., 1884, aged 21; B.A. 1888.

Pennant, Claud Douglas, 2s. Hon. Archibald Douglas, of London. NEW COLL., matric. 15 Oct., 1886, aged 18. See Foster's *Peerage*, B. PENRHYN.

Pennant, David, s. Thomas, of Chester (city), arm. CHRIST CHURCH, matric. 22 March, 1781, aged 17; B.A. 1784, of Bychton, Flints, high sheriff 1799, died 25 June, 1841, father of the next named.

Pennant, David, s. David, of Rose Hill, co. Flint, arm. CHRIST CHURCH, matric. 27 Jan., 1814, aged 18; died 15 Feb., 1835. **[25]**

Pennant, Edward, s. Roger, of Holywell, co. Flint, arm. JESUS COLL., matric. 17 May, 1717, aged 17; of Bagillt, Flints, died in 1741, father of the next named.

Pennant, Edward, s. Edward, of Holywell, co. Flint, arm. CHRIST CHURCH, matric. 3 May, 1746, aged 17; sold Bagillt Hall, high sheriff Flints 1753, died in 1778.

Pennant, George Sholto Gordon Douglas, 1s. Hon. (Edward Gordon) Douglas, of Linton Springs, Yorks, arm. (after baron). CHRIST CHURCH, matric. 8 June, 1854, aged 17; 2nd Lord Penrhyn, M.P. co. Carnarvon 1866-8 & 1874-80, etc. See Foster's *Peerage* & *Eton School Lists.*

Pennant, John, s. Peter, of Whitford, co. Flint, gent. JESUS COLL., matric. 11 March, 1719-20, aged 19; B.A. 1723, M.A. 1726, rector of Hadley and chaplain to the Princess Dowager of Wales, died rector of Compton Martin, Somerset, 28 Oct., 1770.

Pennant, Thomas, s. David, of Downing, co. Flint, arm. QUEEN'S COLL., matric. 7 March, 1743-4, aged 17; created D.C.L. 11 May, 1771, then of Downing aforesaid, zoologist and traveller, F.A.S. 1759-60, F.R.S. 1767, sheriff North Wales 1761, died 16 Dec., 1798, father of David 1781, and of the next named. See *Gent.'s Mag.*, 1798, p. 1144. **[30]**

Pennant, Thomas, s. Thomas, of Whitford, co. Flint, arm. CHRIST CHURCH, matric. 26 Oct., 1797, aged 17, B.A. 1801, M.A. 1804; fellow ALL SOULS' COLL. 1805-18, B.D. 1814, of Brynbella, Flints, rector of Weston Turville, Bucks, 1817, until his death 4 Dec., 1845.

Penneck, Henry, s. Charles, of Gwinear, Cornwall, gent. MERTON COLL., matric. 14 Dec., 1732, aged 18; B.A. 1737.

Penneck, Henry, of ST. PETER COLL., Cambridge (B.A. 1827, M.A. 1830); adm. 'ad eundem' 25 June, 1847, curate of Morvah, Cornwall, died 24 April, 1862. See obit. in *Gent.'s Mag.*, 1862, ii. 106.

Penneck, John, s. Charles, of Gwinear, Cornwall, gent. EXETER COLL., matric. 14 Dec., 1732, aged 18, B.A. 1736; M.A. from PEMBROKE COLL., Cambridge, 1746 (his son John, vicar of Gluvias 1772, died 11 March, 1789).

Penneck, Richard, of TRINITY COLL., Cambridge (B.A. 1749, M.A. 1753); incorp. 4 July, 1754, keeper of the reading-room British Museum, rector of Abinger, Surrey, 1764, and of St. John, Horsleydown, 1765, until his death 29 Jan., 1803. **[35]**

Pennefather, Charles Edward, 1s. Edward, of St. Peter's, Dublin, arm. CHRIST CHURCH, matric. 24 Jan., 1868, aged 18; captain on army reserve.

Pennefather, Edward, 1s. Edward, of St. Peter's, Dublin, arm. (C.J.Q.B., Ireland). BALLIOL COLL., matric. 2 April, 1827, aged 17; B.A. 1830, of Rathsallagh, co. Wicklow, J.P., D.L., a student of Lincoln's Inn 1831, bar.-at-law, King's Inns, Dublin, 1834, Q.C. 1858, and a bencher 1862, father of the last named.

Pennefather, Edward Graham, o.s. William, of Kiltennel, co. Wexford, cler. EXETER COLL., matric. 2 June, 1868, aged 18.

Pennefather, John, 2s. Richard, of Dublin (city), arm. (after baron of the Exchequer). BALLIOL COLL., matric. 25 May, 1833, aged 18; B.A. 1837, a student of the Inner Temple 1835, bar.-at-law, King's Inns, Q.C. and a bencher, died 8 April, 1855, father of Somerset Edward. See Foster's *Our Noble and Gentle Families.*

Pennefather, Joseph Lysaght, 4s. John, of Newport, co. Tipperary, (Ireland), cler. QUEEN'S COLL., matric. 18 Jan., 1819, aged 18; B.A. from ST. ALBAN HALL 1823, M.A. 1825, bar.-at-law, Lincoln's Inn, 1825.

Pennefather, Richard, 1s. Richard, of St. Peter's, Dublin, arm. BALLIOL COLL., matric. 24 June, 1824, aged 17; B.A. 1828, of Darling Hill, co. Tipperary, high sheriff, 1848, a student of Lincoln's Inn 1826, under secretary for Ireland, died in July, 1849. See *Eton School Lists.*

Pennefather, Somerset Edward, 2s. John, of St. Peter's, Dublin, arm. PEMBROKE COLL., matric. 25 Oct., 1871, aged 23; B.A. from TRINITY COLL., Dublin, 1876, M.A. 1876, vicar of Christ Church, Wakefield, 1874-5, of Kenilworth 1875-82, and of Jesmond, Newcastle-on-Tyne, 1882. **[5]**

Pennefather, William (Henry), 2s. Edward, of St. Peter's, Dublin, arm. BALLIOL COLL., matric. 22 March, 1828, aged 16; B.A. 1831, M.A. 1835, rector of Callan, co. Kilkenny, father of Edward G.

Pennell, Aubray Percival, 1s. Charles, of Minster, Kent, arm. CHRIST CHURCH, matric. 12 Oct., 1883, aged 18; scholar 1883-6, B.A. 1886, of the Indian Civil Service 1883, a student of the Middle Temple 1883.

Pennell, George Herbert, 1s. George Bryce, of Pentland Hill, near Melbourne, gent. LINCOLN COLL., matric. 18 Oct., 1879, aged 19; scholar 1879-83, B.A. 1884.

Pennell, Henry Lee, o.s. Henry L., arm. EXETER COLL., matric. 12 Oct., 1878, aged 18.

Pennell, Richard, s. Lovell, of Oporto, arm. MAGDALEN HALL, matric. 2 May, 1810, aged 33; B.A. 1814, M.A. 1819, chaplain to the British factory at Oporto 1813, died 21 Dec., 1857. **[10]**

Pennell, Richard Lewin, 1s, Richard Lewin, of Exeter, Devon, D.Med. CHRIST CHURCH, matric. 4 June, 1846, aged 18; B.A. 1850, M.A. 1853, missionary preacher Zanzibar, died there 27 June, 1872.

Pennell, Shelley Pilkington, s. Shelley, of Navenby, co. Lincoln, arm. BRASENOSE COLL., matric. 15 June, 1810, aged 16.

Penney, Johnston, 2s. David Johnston Eckford, of London, arm. TRINITY COLL., matric. 17 Oct., 1885, aged 19; of the Indian Civil Service 1885.

Penney, Rev. William Campbell, 1s. David Johnston Eckford, of Bombay, gent. HERTFORD COLL., matric. 19 Oct., 1881, aged 20; scholar 1880-5, B.A. 1886.

Penney, William Henry, o.s. Charles James, of London, arm. NON-COLL., matric. 17 Oct., 1874, aged 33; B.A. from ST. JOHN'S COLL. 1877, M.A. 1881, vicar of Northmoor, Oxon, 1879-80. **[15]**

Pennicott, William, s. William, of Westminster, gent. EXETER COLL., matric. 2 July, 1742, aged 16; B.A. 1746, M.A. 1749, rector of Long Ditton, Surrey, 1758, until his death 17 Feb., 1811.

Pennington, Arthur Delgarno, 1s. Arthur Robert, of Louth, co. Lincoln, cler. ST. MARY HALL, matric. 1 May, 1877, aged 20; B.A. 1885.

Pennington, Christopher, s. Christopher, of Bodmyn, Cornwall, gent. BALLIOL COLL., matric. 8 March, 1742-3, aged 19; B.A. 1746. See Maclean's *Trigg Minor*, i. 302.

Pennington, Frederick, o.s. Frederick, of Alderley Edge, arm. EXETER COLL., matric. 18 Jan., 1883, aged 19.

Pennington, George, s. William, of South Morton, Berks, cler. ST. ALBAN HALL, matric. 17 Dec., 1776, aged 18 (? vicar of Bassingbourn, co. Cambridge, 1801, until his death 21 Dec., 1832). **[20]**

Pennington, James, s. Thomas, of Deal, Kent, doctor. HERTFORD COLL., matric. 6 July, 1772, aged 14; B.A. 1776.

Pennington, John, s. John, of Truro, Cornwall, pleb. EXETER COLL., matric. 11 March, 1745-6, aged 19; B.A. 1749.

Pennington, Lowther Augustus John, Baron Muncaster, born at Cuckfield, Sussex, 1s. Lowther, Baron M. CHRIST CHURCH, matric. 17 Oct., 1821, aged 18; 3rd Baron Muncaster, and 7th baronet, died 30 April, 1838. See Foster's *Peerage & Eton School Lists.*

Pennington, Montagu, s. Thomas, of Mongeham, Kent, doctor. TRINITY COLL., matric. 23 Oct., 1777, aged 14; B.A. 1781, M.A. 1784, vicar of Northbourne and Shoulden, Kent, 1806, perp. curate St. George's Chapel, Deal, 1814, until his death 15 April, 1849.

Pennington, Thomas, s. Daniel, of Canterbury, pleb. EXETER COLL., matric. 16 July, 1747, aged 19; B.A. from CHRIST CHURCH 1751, M.A. 1754, B. & D.D. 1770, one of the six preachers Canterbury Cathedral, rector of Kingsdown, Kent, 1754, and of Tunstall 1766, until his death at Deal 26 Nov., 1802, father of James 1772. **[25]**

Pennington, William, s. Joseph. of Lowther, Westmoreland, arm. (after baronet). QUEEN'S COLL., matric. 19 Aug., 1726, aged 18; chief porter of the Tower 1727, died 8 April, 1734. See Foster's *Peerage*, B. MUNCASTER.

Pennington, William, s. William, of Yattenden, Berks, cler. MAGDALEN HALL, matric. 1 April, 1732, aged 17; chorister MAGDALEN COLL. 1727-33, clerk 1733-9, B.A. 1735, M.A. 1738, probably father of William 1764, and of George 1776. See *Bloxam*, i. 156.

Pennington, William, s. William, of Bodmyn, Cornwall, cler. BALLIOL COLL., matric. 22 March, 1744-5, aged 17; B.A. 1748, M.A. 1751.

Pennington, William, s. — P., of Wokingham, Berks, cler. TRINITY COLL., matric. 14 April, 1764, aged 14; demy MAGDALEN COLL. 1768-76, B.A. 1771, M.A. 1774. See *Bloxam*, vi. 350.

Penny, Rev. Benjamin, s. James, of Liverpool, Lancashire, gent. BRASENOSE COLL., matric. 23 May, 1798, aged 22; B.C.L. & D.C.L. 1834, died at Chester 28 Nov., 1857. **[30]**

Penny, Charles, 1s. Thomas, of Kennington, Somerset, gent. WADHAM COLL., matric. 3 Dec., 1824, aged 18.

Penny, Charles, 3s. Elias, of Sherborne, Dorset, gent. PEMBROKE COLL., matric. 2 Feb., 1827, aged 17; B.A. 1831, M.A. 1833, B. & D.D. 1850, head-master Crewkerne Grammar School 1838, and rector of Chaffcombe, Somerset, 1848, until his death 15 Dec., 1875.

Penny, Charles, 2s. Henry, of Yeovil, Somerset, gent. WORCESTER COLL., matric. 14 Oct., 1835, aged 19; B.A. 1840, M.A. 1842, rector of West Coker, Somerset, 1846-80, died in 1884.

Penny, Charles Joseph, 1s. Joseph, of Bath (city), gent. QUEEN'S COLL., matric. 19 March, 1833, aged 19; B.A. 1840, M.A. 1841.

Penny, Rev. Charles William, 2s. Charles, of West Ilsley, Berks, D.D. CORPUS CHRISTI COLL., matric. 22 May, 1856, aged 18; exhibitioner 1857-60, B.A. 1861, M.A. 1863, senior tutor and assistant-master Wellington College 1861. **[35]**

Penny, Edmund Henry, s. James, of Chelford, Cheshire, cler. BRASENOSE COLL., matric. 14 Dec., 1814, aged 17; scholar 1815-8, B.A. 1818, M.A. 1821, assistant-master and librarian of the Charterhouse, rector of Great Stambridge, Essex, 1839, until his death 28 May, 1879.

Penny, Edward, 2s. Thomas, of Liverpool, Lancashire, gent. ST. JOHN'S COLL., matric. 25 June, 1827, aged 18; B.A. 1831, M.A. 1835, rector of St. Andrew's, Canterbury, 1841, perp. curate Ash by Sandwich, 1842, rector of Great Mongeham, Kent, 1849, one of the six preachers Canterbury Cathedral 1843, and hon. canon 1866, died 24 Nov., 1869. See *Robinson*, 211.

Penny, Edward Lewton, 1s. Charles, of Sutton Courtney, Berks, doctor. PEMBROKE COLL., matric. 23 Nov., 1854, aged 18; B.A. 1859, M.A. 1861, D.D. 1882, held various curacies 1859-67, chaplain R.N. 1867.

Penny, Edward William, 2s. Edward, of Ash, Kent, cler. ST. JOHN'S COLL., matric. 25 June, 1862, aged 18; B.A. 1866, scholar 1867-70, M.A. 1870, vicar of Dersingham, Norfolk, 1875.

Penny, Fraser Hislop, 3s. Edward, of Ash, Kent, cler. ST. JOHN'S COLL., matric. 16 Jan., 1875, aged 30; B.A. 1878, M.A. 1881, curate of St. Giles's, Oxford, 1878.

Penny, Frederick Prescott, 3s. Robert, of Manchester, gent. ALL SOULS' COLL., matric. 16 Oct., 1876, aged 19; bible clerk 1876-80, B.A. 1881. **[5]**

Penny, Henry, s. Henry, of Somerton, Somerset, pleb. BALLIOL COLL., matric. 27 Nov., 1716, aged 18; B.A. from WADHAM COLL. 1720, upwards of 50 years vicar of Shipham and Christon, Somerset, died at Axbridge 12 July, 1791, in his 94th year.

Penny, Rev. Henry, s. Henry, of St. George's, Westminster, gent. ORIEL COLL., matric. 7 Feb., 1799, aged 18; B.A. 1803, M.A. 1807, died 30 April, 1850, father of the next named. See *Manchester School Reg.*, i. 118.

Penny, Henry Harwood, o.s. Henry, of Kitford, Surrey (*sic*), cler. ST. JOHN'S COLL., matric. 24 April, 1834, aged 24; bar.-at-law, Middle Temple, 1836.

Penny, James, s. Henry, of Knutsford, Cheshire, gent. BRASENOSE COLL., matric. 26 April, 1775, aged 18, B.A. 1779; M.A. from HERTFORD COLL. 1784, vicar of Preston, Lancashire, 1809, until his death 16 Oct., 1816. See *Manchester School Reg.*, i. 145.

Penny, John, 2s. Charles Joseph, of Bath (city), gent. ST. JOHN'S COLL., matric. 6 March, 1834, aged 19. **[10]**

Penny, Richard, s. Rich., of Cleobury, Salop, pleb. WADHAM COLL., matric. 4 March, 1723-4, aged 17; B.A. 1727, M.A. 1733.

Penny, Robert, s. Robert, of Castle Cary, Somerset, gent. ORIEL COLL., matric. 28 March, 1751, aged 19; B.A. 1755, fellow, M.A. 1757, B.D. 1774, D.D. 1774, rector of Wollaston with Cromhall, co. Gloucester, 1774, vicar of Badminton, rector of Cwmdu, co. Brecon, and of Troy with Cwm-carva, co. Monmouth, died at Badminton 31 July, 1809.

Penny, Robert George, o.s. John, of Great Grimsby, co. Lincoln, cler. ORIEL COLL., matric. 8 Dec., 1855, aged 18; scholar 1855-9, B.A. 1860, M.A. 1865, chaplain at Moscow 1866-79, curate in charge of Rotherfield, Sussex, 1879-86, rector of Warbleton 1886.

Penny, Thomas, 3s. Thomas, of St. Nicholas, Liverpool, gent. ST. JOHN'S COLL., matric. 27 June, 1831, aged 16; scholar 1831, drowned at Oxford 1832. See *Robinson*, 220.

Penny, William, s. James, of Ulverston, Lancashire, gent. QUEEN'S COLL., matric. 20 June, 1727, aged 18. **[15]**

Penny, William Goodenough, 1s. William, of Addingham, Yorks, cler. CHRIST CHURCH, matric. 23 May, 1833, aged 18; student 1833-42, B.A. 1837, M.A. 1839, curate of Ashenton and Dourton, Bucks, seceded to Rome in 1843. See *Alumni West.*, 508.

Penny, William Perkins, o.s. John, of Sherborne, Dorset, gent. PEMBROKE COLL., matric. 19 June, 1851, aged 18.

Pennyman, (Sir) James (Bart.), s. Ralph, of Beverley, Yorks, arm. CHRIST CHURCH, matric. 10 May, 1756, aged 19; 5th baronet, M.P. Scarborough 1770-4, Beverley 1774-96, died 27 March, 1808. See Foster's *Yorkshire Collection.*

Pennyman, John, s. Charles, of St. Clement Danes, Westminster, doctor. ORIEL COLL., matric. 21 Jan., 1723-4, aged 17.

Pennyman, John, s. James, of Little Ponton, co. Lincoln, gent. CHRIST CHURCH, matric. 3 April, 1773, aged 17; a student of Lincoln's Inn 1774, major Cinque Port light dragoons, buried at Ponton 25 Nov., 1795. **[20]**

Pennyman, (Sir) William Henry (Bart.), s. James, of Beverley, Yorks, baronet. MAGDALEN COLL., matric. 24 May, 1781, aged 17; 6th baronet, died 1852. See Foster's *Yorkshire Collection.*

Penrhyn, Arthur Leycester Leycester, 1s. Edward Hugh Leycester, of East Sheen, Surrey, arm. BALLIOL COLL., matric. 24 Oct., 1885, aged 19.

Penrhyn, Edward Hugh Leycester, 1s. Edward, of East Sheen, Surrey, arm. BALLIOL COLL., matric. 27 March, 1846, aged 18; B.A. 1849, M.A. 1852, of East Sheen, Surrey, J.P., D.L. See Foster's *Our Noble and Gentle Families* & *Eton School Lists.*

Penrhyn, Oswald Henry Leycester, 2s. Edward, of East Sheen, Surrey, arm. BALLIOL COLL., matric. 27 March, 1846, aged 17; B.A. 1849, M.A. 1852, perp. curate Bickerstaffe, Lancashire, 1858-69, vicar of Huyton 1869, hon. canon, Liverpool, 1880. See *Eton School Lists.*

Penrice, Harry, s. Humphrey, of Dodderhill, co. Worcester, cler. BALLIOL COLL., matric. 12 April, 1739, aged 17; B.A. 10 March, 1742-3, M.A. 1745.

Penrice, John, 1s. John, of Bromley, Essex, arm. BRASENOSE COLL., matric. 18 May, 1837, aged 18; B.A. 1841, of Bramerton, Norfolk, J.P., D.L. See *Eton School Lists.* **[26]**

Penrose, Charles, o.s. Charles Thomas, of Richmond, Surrey, cler. ORIEL COLL., matric. 22 Oct., 1872, aged 19; scholar 1872-6, B.A. 1877, M.A. 1880.

Penrose, John, s. Bernard, of Helston, Cornwall, gent. NEW COLL., matric. 26 Jan., 1716-7, aged 19; B.A. 1720 (? brother of Thomas 1734).

Penrose, John, s. Joseph, of Exeter (city), pleb. EXETER COLL., matric. 16 Oct., 1732, aged 19; B.A. 1736.

Penrose, John, s. John, of Penryn, Cornwall, cler. EXETER COLL., matric. 16 May, 1771, aged 17; exhibitioner 1770-4, fellow 1774-8, B.C.L. 1778, vicar of Cardynham 1777-82, of Perran-Uthnoe 1782, rector of Fledborough, Notts, 1783, and of Thorney 1803, until his death 14 Sep., 1829. See *Coll. Reg.*, 110, 145. **[30]**

Penrose, John s. John, of Cardynham, Cornwall, cler. EXETER COLL., matric. 3 July, 1795, aged 16; B.A. from CORPUS CHRISTI COLL. 1799, M.A. 1802, Bampton lecturer 1808, vicar of Bracebridge and Langton, co. Leicester, 1802, and perp. curate North Hykeham 1838, until his death 9 Aug., 1859.

Penrose, Rev. John, 1s. John, of Bracebridge, co. Lincoln, cler. BALLIOL COLL., matric. 6 July, 1832, aged 17, B.A. 1836; fellow LINCOLN COLL. 1837-43, M.A. 1839 of Craddock Cleve, Uffculme, Devon, assistant-master Rugby 1839-46, master of Exmouth School 1846, died in Norway 20 June, 1888. See *Rugby School Reg.*, xv.

Penrose, John, 1s. John, of Exmouth, Devon, cler. CHRIST CHURCH, matric. 15 Jan., 1869, aged 18; B.A. 1873, M.A. 1880, has held various curacies since 1874. See *Rugby School Reg.*

Penrose, Robert Uniacke (Fitzgerald), 2s. James, of Cork, Ireland, arm. EXETER COLL., matric. 15 Dec., 1819, aged 19; of Corkbeg and Lisquinlan, co. Cork, and of Water Castle, Queen's County.

Penrose, Rumney, s. Thomas, of Clifton, co. Gloucester, gent. MERTON COLL., matric. 17 Oct., 1717, aged 16; B.A. 1721, M.A. 1724.

Penrose, Rumney, s. Rumney, of Bristol (city), cler. WADHAM COLL., matric. 26 May, 1749, aged 16; B.C.L. from ST. JOHN'S COLL. 1756, and fellow, rector of St. Ewen's, Bristol 1762, until his death in 1786.

Penrose, Samuel, o.s. Samuel, of Cork, Ireland, arm. MAGDALEN HALL, matric. 24 April, 1850, aged 21; B.A. 1856, of Shandangan, co. Cork, has held various curacies since 1859.

Penrose, Thomas, s. Berdi. (? Bernard), of Helstone, Cornwall, pleb. CHRIST CHURCH, matric. 30 April, 1734, aged 18; B.A. 24 Jan., 1737-8, M.A. 1740, rector of Newbury, Berks, 1747, until his death in 1769, father of the last named.

Penrose, Thomas, s. Thomas, of Newbury, Berks, cler. WADHAM COLL., matric. 30 May, 1759, aged 16; B.A. from HERTFORD COLL. 1766, rector of Beckingham-cum-Standerwick, Somerset, died at Bristol 1779, father of the next named. [5]

Penrose, Thomas, s. Thomas, of Newbury, Berks, cler. NEW COLL., matric. 23 Feb., 1788, aged 18; B.C.L. 1803, D.C.L. 1818, fellow 1788-1815, of Shaw Place, Berks, chaplain at Florence, rector of Hampstead Marshall, Berks, vicar of Writtle-cum-Roxwell, Essex, 1814, until his death 8 Feb., 1851.

Penrose, Thomas (Trevenen), s. John, of Constantine, Cornwall, cler. CORPUS CHRISTI COLL., matric. 5 Feb., 1811, aged 17; exhibitioner 1811-14, B.A. 1815, fellow EXETER COLL. 1815-24, M.A. 1819, preb. of Lincoln 1834, vicar of Coleby 1828, and rector of Weston, Notts, 1834, until his death 5 July, 1862. See *Boase*, 122.

Penruddocke, Charles, s. Thomas, of Compton Chamberlain, Wilts, arm. ST. JOHN'S COLL., matric. 27 Oct., 1729, aged 20; of Compton Chamberlayne, high sheriff Wilts, 1741, died in 1769.

Penruddocke, Charles, 1s. Charles, of Bath, Somerset, gent. CHRIST CHURCH, matric. 20 Oct., 1847, aged 19; of Compton Park, Wilts, J.P., D.L., high sheriff 1861, F.G.H.S., bar.-at-law, Inner Temple, 1853. See Foster's *Men at the Bar*.

Penruddocke, Charles, s. Charles, of Compton Chamberlain, Wilts, arm. TRINITY COLL., matric. 23 Oct., 1761, aged 17; of Compton Chamberlayne, Wilts, 1770, until his death 30 Oct., 1788, father of John H. [10]

Penruddocke, Charles, s. Charles, of Compton, Wilts, arm. WADHAM COLL., matric. 18 March, 1796, aged 22; of Burcot, Somerset, died in Nov., 1799, grandfather of Charles 1847.

Penruddocke, John Hungerford, s. (Charles), of Compton Chamberlain, Wilts, arm. NEW COLL., matric. 9 Feb., 1789, aged 18; of Compton Chamberlayne, high sheriff Wilts, 1817, M.P. Wilton 1821-37, died 25 Dec., 1841.

Penruddocke, John Powys, 1s. John Hungerford, of Wilton, Wilts, cler. CHARSLEY HALL, matric. 18 April, 1882, aged 20.

Penruddocke, Thomas, 1s. Thomas, of Manningford, Wilts, arm. WADHAM COLL., matric. 10 April, 1821, aged 17; B.A. 1826, M.A. 1828, died vicar of Compton Chamberlayne, Wilts, 2 Sep., 1832.

Penruddocke, William Fielding, 4s. John Hungerford, of South Newton, Wilts, cler. KEBLE COLL., matric. 19 Oct., 1886, aged 20. [15]

Penry, James, s. Hugh, of Devynnock, Brecon, pleb. JESUS COLL., matric. 20 Oct., 1718, aged 18; B.A. 1722.

Penson, George Willis, o.s. George, of Bermondsey, Surrey, arm. ORIEL COLL., matric. 11 March, 1858, aged 18; B.A. 1862, bar.-at-law, Lincoln's Inn, 1866. See Foster's *Men at the Bar*.

Penson, John, s. John, of St. Thomas's, Oxford (city), pleb. CHRIST CHURCH, matric. 8 May, 1787, aged 17; B.A. 1791, M.A. 1795, died vicar of Brize-Norton, Oxon, 10 July, 1858.

Penson, John Pavitt, o.s. John, of Brize-Norton, Oxon, cler. WORCESTER COLL., matric. 18 Oct., 1827, aged 18; B.A. 1831, M.A. 1834, vicar of Clanfield, Oxon, 1836, until his death 3 June, 1864.

Penson, Peter, s. Robert, of Oxford (city), pleb. NEW COLL., matric. 6 Dec., 1804, aged 16; B.A. 1808, M.A. 1811, chaplain 1812-5, also of Christ Church 1812-16, clerk Magdalen College 1807-12, minor canon and precentor Durham Cathedral 1815, vicar of St. Oswald's, Durham, 1819, died in 1870. See *Bloxam*, ii. 117. [20]

Penton, Frederick Thomas, born at Boulogne, France, o.s. Henry, gent. CHRIST CHURCH, matric. 14 Oct., 1870, aged 18; of Sutton Park, Beds, M.P. Finsbury (central division), July, 1886, sometime captain 4th dragoon guards, hon. colonel 21st Middlesex rifle volunteers.

Penton, Henry, s. John, of St. Laurence, Winchester, arm. NEW COLL., matric. 31 Jan., 1721-2, aged 16; M.P. Tregony 1734-47, Winchester 1747-61, died 1 Sep., 1762.

Penton, Henry, s. John, of Bath (city), cler. ST. JOHN'S COLL., matric. 24 Nov., 1790, aged 20.

Penton, Thomas, 1s. Thomas, of Brinkworth, Wilts, cler. PEMBROKE COLL., matric. 1 Feb., 1820, aged 17; B.A. 1825. See *Gent.'s Mag.*, 1834, i. 662; & 1848, ii. 663. [25]

Pentreath, Arthur Godolphin, 1s. Frederick Richard, of Market Rasen, co. Lincoln, D.D. MAGDALEN COLL., matric. 16 Oct., 1884, aged 18; demy 1884.

Pentreath, Frederick Richard, 1s. Richard, of Madron, Cornwall, gent. EXETER COLL., matric. 18 May, 1853, aged 18; bible clerk WORCESTER COLL. 1854-6, scholar 1856-9, B.A. 1858, M.A. 1860, B.D. 1874, D.D. 1878, held various scholastic appointments 1857-84, rector of Dodbrooke, Devon, 1884-5.

Pentycross, Rev. Frederick John, 1s. Frederick, of Woodstock, Oxon, gent. NON-COLL., matric. 20 Jan., 1872, aged 22; B.A. 1876.

Penwarne, Thomas, s. William, of St. Veep, Cornwall, cler. PEMBROKE COLL., matric. 4 July, 1764, aged 18; B.A. 1768, perp. curate St. Germain's, Cornwall, 1772, until his death in 1822.

Penyston, Fairmedow, s. John, of Cornwell, Oxon, cler. BALLIOL COLL., matric. 8 Sep., 1737, aged 17; bar.-at-law, Middle Temple, 1744.

Penyston, Francis, s. Fairmedow, of Cornwell, Oxon, arm. BRASENOSE COLL., matric. 1 July, 1773, aged 16; created M.A. 2 July, 1776 (? bar.-at-law, Middle Temple, 1782). [30]

Penyston, Francis, s. Francis, of Cornwell, Oxon, arm. ORIEL COLL., matric. 10 March, 1812, aged 17; B.A. 1815, of Chipping Norton, Oxon, died about 1825. See *Eton School Lists*.

Pepall, Robert, 'butler to Merton College;' privilegiatus 19 May, 1759.

Pepin, Rev. John, 1s. John, of St. Helier's, Jersey, gent. JESUS COLL., matric. 27 Oct., 1877, aged 20; scholar 1877-82, B.A. 1881, M.A. 1884.

Peploe, John Birch, s. Daniel Webb, of Lamberhurst, Kent, arm. BRASENOSE COLL., matric. 10 Oct., 1818, aged 18; B.A. 1822, M.A. 1825, of Garnstone Castle, co. Hereford, assumed the surname of PEPLOE in lieu of his patronymic WEBB in 1866, preb. of Hereford 1844, vicar of King's Pyon, co. Hereford, 1825, and Weobley 1826, until his death 26 Jan., 1869.

Peploe, Samuel, s. Samuel, of Penrich, co. Stafford, cler. (after bishop of Chester). JESUS COLL., matric. 19 Feb., 1719-20, aged 18; B.C.L. from WADHAM COLL. 1726, D.C.L. 1763, preb. of Chester 1727-81, archdeacon of Richmond 1728, rector of Tattenhall, Cheshire, 1743, died chancellor of Chester 22 Oct., 1781. [35]

Peploe, Samuel, s. John, of Manchester, arm. CHRIST CHURCH, matric. 26 April, 1792, aged 17; of Garnstone Castle, co. Hereford. See *Eton School Lists*.

Pepper, Benjamin Huffum, s. John, of Winslade, Hants, cler. BRASENOSE COLL., matric. 16 Nov., 1738, aged 18; B.A. 1742.

Pepper, John, s. Michael, of Cork, Ireland, arm. ORIEL COLL., matric. 5 June, 1810, aged 19.

Pepper, Michael, s. Michael, of Stanstead, Herts, arm. ST. MARY HALL, matric. 21 Oct., 1780, aged 18.

Pepperell, William Royal, s. William, of Boston, New England, baronet. CHRIST CHURCH, matric. 18 Feb., 1794, aged 18; died 27 Sep., 1798.

Peppin, Arthur Hamilton, 1s. Stephen Francis Bedford, of Wells, Somerset, cler. WORCESTER COLL., matric. 19 March, 1884, aged 19; B.A. 1887. [5]

Peppin, Arthur Hamilton, 2s. John Hutton, of Edinburgh, arm. WORCESTER COLL., matric. 17 March, 1884, aged 30.

Peppin, Arthur Reginald Joseph, 3s. Arthur Bedford, of Lyme Regis, Dorset, arm. 'MR. LITTON'S HALL,' matric. 11 Oct., 1856, aged 19.

Peppin, Stephen Francis Bedford, 1s. Arthur Bedford, of Lyme Regis, Dorset, arm. ST. EDMUND HALL, matric. 12 April, 1851, aged 18; B.A. 1854, M.A. 1858, vicar of Horrington, Somerset, since 1865.

Peppin, Sydenham (Henry), s. Sydenham, of Exeter (city), gent. WADHAM COLL., matric. 19 March, 1807, aged 18; B.A. 1810, vicar of Branscombe, Devon, 1830, until his death 29 Sep., 1867. [9]

Pepys, Edmund, o.s. John, of Marylebone, arm. ORIEL COLL., matric. 28 Feb., 1823, aged 17; B.A. 1826, M.A. 1830, father of Henry and John Alfred.

Pepys, Henry, 3s. Edmund, of Marylebone, London, arm. ORIEL COLL., matric. 10 June, 1858, aged 18; bar.-at-law, Lincoln's Inn, 1862.

Pepys, John Alfred, 2s. Edmund, of Marylebone, London, arm. CHRIST CHURCH, matric. 15 May, 1856, aged 18; B.A. 1861, M.A. 1863, curate of Easingwold, Yorks. See *Eton School Lists*.

Pepys, (Sir) Lucas (Bart.), s. William, of London, arm. CHRIST CHURCH, matric. 3 July, 1760, aged 18; B.A. 1764, M.A. 1767, B.Med. 1770, D.Med. 1774, physician Middlesex Hospital 1769, fellow College of Physicians 1775, president 1804-10, physician extraordinary to the King 1777, and in ordinary 1792, created a baronet 22 Jan., 1784, physician-general to the army 1794, died 17 June, 1830. See Foster's *Peerage*, E. COTTENHAM; & Munk's *Roll*, ii. 304.

Pepys, (Sir) William Weller (Bart.), s. William, of London, arm. CHRIST CHURCH, matric. 28 Nov., 1758, aged 18; B.A. 1763, M.A. 1766, bar.-at-law, Lincoln's Inn, 1766, a master in Chancery 1775-1807, created a baronet 23 June, 1801, died 2 June, 1825, father of Charles, 1st Earl of Cottenham. See Foster's *Peerage* & *Eton School Lists*.

Perceval, Colonel Alexander, created D.C.L. 13 June, 1834 (2s. Philip, cler.), of Temple House, co. Sligo, M.P. 1831-41, serjt.-at-arms House of Lords, lieut.-colonel Sligo militia, died 9 Dec., 1858, aged 81, father of Philip 1832. See Foster's *Peerage*, E. EGMONT. [15]

Perceval, Arthur Philip, s. Charles George, Baron Arden. ORIEL COLL., matric. 19 March, 1817, aged 17, B.A. 1820; fellow ALL SOULS' COLL. 1821-5, B.C.L. 1824, chaplain to the King and to Queen Victoria 1826-50, rector of East Horsley, Surrey, 1824, until his death 11 June, 1853. See Foster's *Peerage*, E. EGMONT.

Perceval, Arthur (William) Bernard, 1s. Arthur Bernard, of Tresco, Scilly Isles, cler. NON-COLL., matric. 15 March, 1878, aged 18; B.A. from QUEEN'S COLL. 1883.

Perceval, Ascelin Spencer, 1s. Henry Spencer, of London, arm. EXETER COLL., matric. 16 Jan., 1875, aged 19; B.A. 1878, vicar of Mackworth, co. Derby, since 1886.

Perceval, Augustus George, 1s. Hon. Arthur Philip, of East Horsley, Surrey, cler. ORIEL COLL., matric. 4 June, 1847, aged 18; heir presumptive to Charles George, 7th Earl of Egmont.

Perceval, Charles George, s. Charles George, Baron Arden. CHRIST CHURCH, matric. 7 Dec., 1815, aged 18; rector of Calverton, Bucks, Jan., 1821, until his death 26 July, 1858, father of the next named. See Foster's *Peerage*. [20]

Perceval, Charles George, o.s. Charles George, of Calverton, Bucks, cler. UNIVERSITY COLL., matric. 28 May, 1863, aged 17; 7th Earl of Egmont, a student of the Inner Temple 1869, M.P. Midhurst 1874. See Foster's *Peerage*.

Perceval, Cyril Ambrose, 3s. Arthur Bernard, of Woolfardisworthy, Devon, cler. NON-COLL., matric. 13 Oct., 1883, aged 16; B.A. from QUEEN'S COLL. 1886.

Perceval, Dudley Montagu, 4s. Spencer, of Lincoln's Inn Fields, London, arm. CHRIST CHURCH, matric. 30 March, 1819, aged 18; B.A. 1822, a student of Lincoln's Inn, clerk of the Council at the Cape of Good Hope, deputy teller of the Exchequer 1828-34, died 2 Sep., 1856, brother of Henry and John Thomas.

Perceval, Henry, s. Spencer, of Hampstead, Middlesex, arm. BRASENOSE COLL., matric. 29 April, 1817, aged 17; B.A. 1820, M.A. 1823, rector of Charlton, Kent, and vicar of West Hoathley, Sussex, 1825-6, rector of Washington, co. Durham, 1826-37, and of Elmley-Lovett, co. Worcester, 1837-83, died 1 April 1885.

Perceval, John Thomas, 5s. Spencer, of St. Giles's, London, arm. MAGDALEN HALL, matric. 28 May, 1830, aged 27; brother of Henry and of Dudley. See Foster's *Peerage*, E. EGMONT. [25]

Perceval, Philip, 1s. Alexander, of Rathburn in Sligo, Ireland, arm. CORPUS CHRISTI COLL., matric. 30 May, 1832, aged 19; an officer in royal horse guards. See Foster's *Peerage*, E. EGMONT.

Perceval, Robert. BRASENOSE COLL., 1831. See MAXWELL.

Percival, Edward France, 2s. Stanley, of Liverpool, arm. BRASENOSE COLL., matric. 10 June, 1840, aged 18; scholar 1841-3, B.A. 1844, M.A. 1847, bar.-at-law, Inner Temple, 1847, died 12 Sep., 1849.

Percival, Edward Lockwood, s. Edward Lockwood, of Kingsthorpe, Northants, cler. UNIVERSITY COLL., matric. 12 Aug., 1779, aged 17, B.A. 1783; B.C.L. from ALL SOULS' COLL. 1786, assumed the additional surname of PERCIVAL, died at Dews Hall, 6 July, 1804, father of the next named.

Percival, Edward Lockwood, s. Edward, of Kingsthorpe, Northants, arm. CHRIST CHURCH, matric. 26 Oct., 1809, aged 18; B.A. 1813. [30]

Percival, Francis William, 6s. Samuel, of Northampton, arm. BRASENOSE COLL., matric. 19 March, 1863, aged 19; B.A. 1867, M.A. 1871, bar.-at-law, Inner Temple, 1878, F.S.A., etc. See Foster's *Men at the Bar*.

Percival, John, s. John, of Ardley, Oxon, cler. BRASENOSE COLL., matric. 19 Nov., 1734, aged 17.

Percival, John, s. John, of Mattersey, Notts, arm. WADHAM COLL., matric. 6 Dec., 1804, aged 16; B.A. 1808, M.A. 1814, scholar 1812-14, fellow 1814-32, senior bursar 1824.

Percival, John, 1s. William, of Brough, Westmoreland, gent. QUEEN'S COLL., matric. 22 June, 1854, aged 19; taberdar 1854-8, B.A. 1858, fellow 1858-63, M.A. 1861, select preacher 1882, head-master Clifton College 1862-78, preb. of Exeter 1871-82, president Trinity College 1878-87, canon of Bristol 1882-7, head-master of Rugby 1887. See *Rugby School Reg.*

Percival, John, 3s. John, of Buxton, co. Derby, gent. ST. EDMUND HALL, matric. 25 Nov., 1854, aged 25. [35]

Percival, John Guthrie, 2s. John, of Clifton, co. Gloucester, cler. MAGDALEN COLL., matric. 21 Oct., 1886, aged 20.

Percival, Lewis, 2s. Samuel, of St. Giles's, Northampton (town), arm. ORIEL COLL., matric. 14 Nov., 1850, aged 18; B.A. 1854.

Percival, Lovibond John Exley, 1s. Lovibond, of Cotham, Somerset, gent. BRASENOSE COLL., matric. 19 Oct., 1867, aged 18; scholar 1867-72, B.A. 1874.

Percival, Thomas Cozens, s. Thomas Basnet, of Manchester, Lancashire, cler. CHRIST CHURCH, matric. 8 May, 1815, aged 18; student 1815-26, B.A. 1819, M.A. 1821, rector of Horsheath, co. Cambridge, 1825, canon of Southwell 1829, rector of Barnborough, Yorks, 1848, until his death 19 July, 1863.

Percy, Algernon, Baron Prudhoe (1816), created D.C.L. 15 June, 1841, 4th Duke of Northumberland (on the death of his brother Hugh in 1847), K.G. 1853, admiral R.N. 1862, first lord of the admiralty in 1852, died 12 Feb., 1865.

Percy, Algernon George (6th Duke of Northumberland), created D.C.L. 21 June, 1870, M.P. Beeralston 1831-2, North Northumberland 1852-65, lord privy seal 1878-80. See Foster's *Peerage*. [5]

Percy, (Lord) Algernon Malcolm Arthur, 2s. Algernon George, Duke of Northumberland. CHRIST CHURCH, matric. 15 Jan., 1869, aged 17; B.A. 1871, M.A. 1878, M.P. Westminster 1882-5, and for St. George's, Hanover Square, 1885-7. See Foster's *Peerage* & *Eton School Lists*.

Percy, Algernon Payan, 2s. Henry, of Warkworth, Northumberland, cler. ST. JOHN'S COLL., matric. 15 June, 1866, aged 19. See Foster's *Peerage*, D. NORTHUMBERLAND.

Percy, Barnard Elliot, s. William, of Woolwich, Kent, cler. LINCOLN COLL., matric. 15 Jan., 1801, aged 16; B.A. 1805, bar.-at-law, Lincoln's Inn, 1807, perp. curate Felbridge, Surrey, and curate of Burstow, died 23 Nov., 1871. See *Alumni West.*, 451.

Percy, (Lord) Charles Greatheed-Bertie-, s. Algernon, Earl of Beverley. CHRIST CHURCH, matric. 15 May, 1812, aged 18; B.A. 1815, M.A. 1818, of Guy's Cliffe, co. Warwick, M.P. Newport, Cornwall, 1826-30, assumed the additional names of GREATHEED-BERTIE by royal licence 1 April, 1826, died 11 Oct., 1870. See Foster's *Peerage* & *Eton School Lists*.

Percy, Henry George (Earl Percy), 1s. Algernon, Earl Percy. CHRIST CHURCH, matric. 21 April, 1865, aged 18; M.P. North Northumberland 1868-85, treasurer of the household 1874-85, summoned to the House of Lords as Baron Lovaine 22 July, 1887. See Foster's *Peerage*. [10]

Percy, Hugh, of ST. JOHN'S COLL., Cambridge (M.A. 1805, D.D. 1825); adm. 'ad eundem' 10 June, 1834 (son of Algernon, Earl of Beverley), rector of Bishopsbourne, Kent, 1808, canon residentiary and preb. of Exeter 1810, chancellor of Salisbury Cathedral 1812, preb. of Canterbury 1816, and archdeacon 1822, bishop of Rochester 1827, of Carlisle 1827, until his death 5 Feb., 1856. See Foster's *Peerage* & *Eton School Lists*.

Percy, Thomas, bishop of Dromore 1782. See PIERCY.

Percy, Thomas, s. Anthony, of Southwark, Surrey, arm. ST. JOHN'S COLL., matric. 27 June, 1786, aged 17; B.C.L. 1792, fellow, D.C.L. 1797, vicar of Gray's Thurrock, Essex, 1793, edited the 4th edition of 'Percy's Reliques,' died 14 May, 1808. See *Robinson*, 140.

Percy, William, s. William, of Woolwich, Kent, cler. LINCOLN COLL., matric. 20 June, 1800, aged 17; lieutenant 1st Bombay native infantry 1803, died at Bombay 15 Nov., 1811. See *Alumni West.*, 454.

Percy, William Murray, o.s. William, of St. George's, Hanover Square, London, arm. EXETER COLL., matric. 23 April, 1822, aged 18; B.A. 1826. [15]

Pereira, Agostinho Henry, 1s. Henry Wall (formerly Tibbs), of Ormskirk, Lancashire, cler. ST. MARY HALL, matric. 22 Oct., 1870, aged 20.

Pereira, Henry Wall, scholar TRINITY COLL., Dublin, 1835 (B.A. 1839, M.A. 1842); adm. 'ad eundem' 14 June, 1860, assumed the surname of PEREIRA in lieu of TIBBS, vicar of Bobbington, Salop, 1862-71, F.S.A. Scotland, etc. See *Crockford*.

Pereira, Lynwode Charles, 2s. Henry Wall (formerly Tibbs), of Oxton, Notts, cler. ST. MARY HALL, matric. 15 Dec., 1870, aged 18.

Perfect, Caleb, s. Caleb, of Silton, Dorset, gent. TRINITY COLL., matric. 17 Dec., 1723, aged 17; B.A. 1727.

Perfect, Henry, s. William, of Dorchester (town), pleb. MAGDALEN COLL., matric. 4 Nov., 1736, aged 17; chorister 1729-38 (Rev. H. P., died at Kennington 19 May, 1801). See *Coll. Reg.*, i. 159.

Perfect, John, s. William, of Dorchester, Dorset, pleb. CHRIST CHURCH, matric. 31 Jan., 1733-4, aged 16; B.A. 1737 (? died rector of Sopworth, Wilts, 15 Oct., 1794). [21]

Perfect, John. ORIEL COLL., 1742. See PARFECT.

Perfect, Robert, s. William, of Wandsworth, Surrey, gent. QUEEN'S COLL., matric. 10 Dec., 1817, aged 18; B.A. 1823, M.A. 1825, M.P. Lewes 1847-52, died 29 July, 1875.

Perfect, Robert Frederick Strode, 3s. Robert, of Portland Place, Bath, arm. EXETER COLL., matric. 2 Feb., 1855, aged 19; B.A. 1859, M.A. 1862, vicar of St. Peter Malvern, Wells, 1871.

Perfect, Thomas. MAGDALEN COLL., 1822. See SOUTHBY. [25]

Perfect, William, s. William, of Leicester (town), pleb. MAGDALEN HALL, matric. 26 July, 1734, aged 22.

Perfect, William, 2s. Thomas William Chamberlain, of Hammersmith, Middlesex, gent. MAGDALEN HALL, matric. 19 Oct., 1822, aged 19; B.A. 1829, half brother of Thomas 1822.

Perfect, William Mosley, 2s. Mosley, of Settle, Yorks, arm. LINCOLN COLL., matric. 10 April, 1869, aged 19.

Periam, George, s. William, of Bemerton, Wilts, doctor. CHRIST CHURCH, matric. 15 May, 1735, aged 15; B.A. 1 March, 1738-9, M.A. 1741.

Periam, John, s. John, of Milverton, Somerset, gent. ST. JOHN'S COLL., matric. 6 March, 1718-9, aged 17 (? bar.-at-law, Middle Temple, 1723, M.P. Minehead 1742-7). [30]

Periam, John, s. James, of Wootton, Somerset, gent. EXETER COLL., matric. 19 April, 1732, aged 17.

Periam, John, s. John, of Butleigh Wootton, Somerset, pleb. EXETER COLL., matric. 8 May, 1739, aged 18.

Periam, Zac., s. John, of Milverton, Somerset, gent. ST. JOHN'S COLL., matric. 6 March, 1818-9, aged 16.

Pering, Benedict, s. Benedict, of Exeter (city), gent. ST. ALBAN HALL, matric. 31 Oct., 1774, aged 24; B.A. 1779, rector of St. Mary Arches and St. Olave, Exeter, 1778, until his death 29 Dec., 1814.

Pering, Benedict, s. Benedict, of St. Mary's, Exeter (city), cler. WADHAM COLL., matric. 15 May, 1801, aged 17; B.A. 1805, M.A. 1810, fellow 1812-17, rector of Fersfield, Norfolk, 1843, until his death 4 Nov., 1851. [35]

Pering, John, s. John, of Black Awton, Devon, gent. EXETER COLL., matric. 14 Feb., 1743-4, aged 17; B.A. 1750, M.A. 1751, fellow 1747, until his death in 1754. See *Coll. Reg.*, 103.

Pering, John, s. Richard, of Harberton, Devon, arm. CHRIST CHURCH, matric. 9 June, 1784, aged 19; B.A. 1788, M.A. 1791, vicar of Skipton and Kildwick, Yorks, 1806, until his death 30 April, 1843. See *Alumni West.*, 418.

Pering, Rev. John Symons, s. Benedict, of Alphington, Devon, cler. ORIEL COLL., matric. 25 Feb., 1814, aged 18; B.A. 1818, M.A. 1820, died in 1868.

Pering, Peter, 3s. Benedict, of St. Mary's, Exeter, Devon, cler. ORIEL COLL., matric. 26 Nov., 1818, aged 20; bible clerk 1818-22, B.A. 1822, M.A. 1826, vicar of Great Cornard, Suffolk, 1844-58.

Perkin, Frederick William, 3s. Richard Thornton, of Pimlico, Middlesex, arm. MAGDALEN HALL, matric. 11 Nov., 1847, aged 19.

Perkin, John, s. George, of Petrockstow, Devon, gent. EXETER COLL., matric. 5 April, 1742, aged 19.

Perkin, John Arthur, 3s. Robert, of Surbiton, Surrey, gent. EXETER COLL., matric. 20 Oct., 1881, aged 19; B.A. 1886; M.A. 1888.

Perkins, Algernon, 2s. Henry, of St. George's, Southwark, arm. ORIEL COLL., matric. 20 Oct., 1826, aged 17; B.A. 1831, M.A. 1833, a student of the Inner Temple 1831. [5]

Perkins, Benjamin Robert, 1s. Robert, of St. James's, Westminster, gent. LINCOLN COLL., matric. 16 Nov., 1820, aged 22, B.A. 1824; chaplain CHRIST CHURCH 1824-31, B.C.L. 1831, vicar of Wootton-under-Edge 1829-81, master of the Domus Scholarum Wootton 1838-82, died 7 Feb., 1886.

Perkins, Charles Mathew, 4s. Benjamin Robert, of Wootton-under-Edge, co. Gloucester, cler. LINCOLN COLL., matric. 12 June, 1855, aged 18; B.A. 1859, M.A. 1862, head-master Newland Grammar School 1868-73, and of St. Alban Grammar School 1873-80, rector of Sopworth, Wilts, 1880.

Perkins, Daniel, s. James, of Alerby, Cumberland, pleb. QUEEN'S COLL., matric. 24 Oct., 1727, aged 19; B.A. 1731, M.A. 1735, fellow 1744, B. & D.D. 1764 (vicar of Holyrood, Southampton, 1751), rector of Church Oakley and St. Cross, Southants, died at Southampton 14 Oct., 1772. See *O.H.S.*, ix. p. 30.

Perkins, Rev. Duncombe Steele, s. Shirley Farmer Steele, of Sutton Coldfield, co. Warwick, arm. TRINITY COLL., matric. 4 Nov., 1814, aged 19; B.A. 1820, of Orton Hall, co. Derby, died 3 Nov., 1882.

Perkins, Rev. Duncombe Steele, 1s. Duncombe Steele, of Cheltenham, co. Gloucester, cler. CHRIST CHURCH, matric. 2 June, 1857, aged 21; of Orton Hall, co. Leicester. See *Rugby School Reg.*, 103.

Perkins, Edmund, s. James, of Wington, Hants, arm. ST. MARY HALL, matric. 15 March, 1743-4, aged 18. [11]

Perkins, Frederick David, s. John David, of Heavitree, Devon, doctor. BRASENOSE COLL., matric. 25 May, 1810, aged 17; B.A. 1814, M.A. 1825, vicar of Stoke with Sowe, co. Warwick, 1817, rector of Swayfield, co. Lincoln, 1820, and Down Hatherley, co. Gloucester, 1827, chaplain to the King and Queen 1830, until his death 19 April, 1856. See *Eton School Lists.*

Perkins, Rev. George, 1s. John, of Sutton, Cheshire, gent. BRASENOSE COLL., matric. 18 May, 1842, aged 17; scholar 1842-5, B.A. 1846, M.A. 1849, held various scholastic appointments 1847-81, died 9 Dec., 1887. See *Manchester School Reg.*, iii. 267.

Perkins, George Joseph, 1s. Thomas, of Westbury, Wilts, gent. NON-COLL., matric. 8 June, 1878, aged 33.

Perkins, Henry, 1s. Henry, of West Square, London, arm. NEW COLL., matric. 17 May, 1823, aged 18.

Perkins, Hewlett Charles, o.s. Charles, of Chetnole, Dorset, arm. EXETER COLL., matric. 10 Oct., 1873, aged 19. [16]

Perkins, John, s. John, of St. Neots, Hunts, gent. WORCESTER COLL., matric. 4 June, 1772, aged 18; B.A. 1776, vicar of Arkesden, Essex, and Rampton Lisle, co. Cambridge, 1780.

Perkins, John, 1s. John, of Holywell, Oxford (city), gent. CHRIST CHURCH, matric. 20 June, 1820, aged 17, servitor 1820-4, B.A. 1824, M.A. 1827; chorister Magdalen College 1811-20, vicar of Lower Swell, co. Gloucester, 1833, lecturer at Carfax, Oxford, died 17 April, 1850. See *Bloxam*, i. 214.

Perkins, John David, s. John, of Staines, Middlesex, arm. MAGDALEN COLL., matric. 12 Oct., 1784, aged 20; B.A. from ST. MARY HALL 1789, M.A. 1792, B. & D.D. 1808, chaplain to the King 1816, rector of Laurence, Exeter, 1802, vicar of Dawlish 1807, rector of Mamhead, Devon, 1809, perp. curate East Teignmouth 1816, until his death 30 Sep., 1845.

Perkins, Oswald Thrale, 1s. Hugh, of Walton, Lancashire, gent. NEW COLL., matric. 13 Oct., 1877, aged 19; scholar 1877-82, B.A. 1881, M.A. 1884.

Perkins, Robert Cyril Layton, 2s. Charles Matthew, of Badminton, co. Gloucester, cler. JESUS COLL., matric. 23 Oct., 1885, aged 18; scholar 1885. [21]

Perkins, Samuel, s. Thomas, of Pelsdon, Dorset, gent. WADHAM COLL., matric. 17 March, 1714-5, aged 18; B.A. 1718, M.A. 1722.

Perkins, Samuel Wootton, s. James, of Leak Wootton, co. Warwick, gent. WADHAM COLL., matric. 19 June, 1811, aged 16; B.A. 1815, M.A. 1818, rector of Stockton, co. Warwick, 1822.

Perkins, Shirley Farmer Steele, s. Samuel Steele, of Orton-on-the-Hill, co. Leicester, gent. TRINITY COLL., matric. 27 Oct., 1784, aged 16; of Orton-on-the-Hill and Morebarne Grange, co. Leicester, bar.-at-law, Lincoln's Inn, 1792, a commissioner of Bankrupts for Birmingham 1794, died 18 Jan., 1852, father of Duncombe S. 1814.

Perkins, Vincent Robert, 1s. Benjamin Robert, of Cublington, Bucks, cler. WORCESTER COLL., matric. 9 June, 1848, aged 17. [25]

Perkins, William, s. William, of London, pleb. ST. JOHN'S COLL., matric. 4 July, 1734, aged 18; died in 1740. See *Robinson*, 65.

Perkins, William, s. Hutton, of Barnard's Castle, co. Durham, gent. LINCOLN COLL., matric. 14 March, 1763, aged 18; B.A. 1766, fellow, M.A. 1769, chaplain to the King, 45 years curate of Twyford, Bucks, vicar of Kingsbury, Somerset, died 18 May, 1820.

Perkins, William, s. William, of Twyford, Bucks, cler. LINCOLN COLL., matric. 14 April, 1812, aged 16; bible clerk 1812, B.A. 1818, M.A. 1820, curate of Goddington, Oxon, 1820-66, vicar of Twyford, Bucks, 1820, until his death 9 Feb., 1874. See *Robinson*, 190.

Perks, Bernard, 2s. Samuel Hollis, of Wolverhampton, arm. MAGDALEN COLL., matric. 23 Oct., 1885, aged 19.

Perks, Edwin Hollis, 1s. Samuel Hollis, of Newbridge, co. Stafford, arm. MAGDALEN COLL., matric. 16 Oct., 1882, aged 19; B.A. 1887. [30]

Perks, Ethelbert, s. Ethelbert, of Brockington, co. Gloucester, pleb. PEMBROKE COLL., matric. 19 April, 1735, aged 18; B.A. 1739, possibly brother of Walter 1749.

Perks, Francis, s. Thomas, of Ledbury, co. Hereford, pleb. BALLIOL COLL., matric. 13 Dec., 1738, aged 18.

Perks, Nathaniel, s. Robert, of Minchinhampton, co. Gloucester, gent. MERTON COLL., matric. 29 April, 1737, aged 17.

Perks, Walter, s. Ethel., of Cheltenham, co. Gloucester, pleb. QUEEN'S COLL., matric. 10 Oct., 1749, aged 20; possibly brother of Ethelbert 1735.

Pern, Andrew, s. John, of Napwell, Cambridge, cler. ORIEL COLL., matric. 5 May, 1766, aged 21 (? B.A. from PETER HOUSE, Cambridge, 1772, rector of Isham, Northants, 1781, and died rector of Abington, and Clay, Herts, 5 Dec., 1807). [35]

Perny, John (Anthony), s. Bernard, of Loughborough, Surrey, cler. MAGDALEN HALL, matric. 15 Oct., 1776, aged 18; B.A. 1780, M.A. 1812, B. & D.D. 1816, perp. curate Oxenden, co. Gloucester, 1811, rector of Hill Crome, co. Worcester, 1815, and of Pirton 1816, until his death 29 Sep., 1825.

Perowne, Edward Henry, fellow of CORPUS CHRISTI COLL., Cambridge, 1850-79, B.A. 1850, M.A. 1853 (adm. 'ad eundem' 27 June, 1857), tutor 1858-79, B.D. 1860, proctor 1871, D.D. 1873, master 1879, vice-chancellor 1879, etc., Lady Margaret professor 1877, preb. of St. Asaph 1877.

Perowne, John James Stewart, scholar CORPUS CHRISTI COLL., Cambridge, 1842, B.A. 1845, M.A. 1848, fellow 1849-64, hon. fellow 1886, B.D. 1856 (adm. 'ad eundem' 28 June, 1860), D.D. 1873; fellow Trinity College 1873-5, select preacher 1853, etc., vice-principal Lampeter College 1862-72, canon of Llandaff 1869-78, preb. of St. David's 1867-72, Hulsean professor of divinity 1875, hon. chaplain to the Queen 1875, dean of Peterborough 1878, hon. D.D. Edinburgh University.

Perrin, Louis, 1s. John, of Dublin, arm. MAGDALEN COLL., matric. 18 Oct., 1873, aged 19; B.A. 1877, bar.-at-law, Lincoln's Inn, 1880. See Foster's *Men at the Bar.*

Perrin, William Philp, s. — P., of London, arm. CHRIST CHURCH, matric. 7 Nov., 1761, aged 19; created M.A. 15 May, 1772 (as WILLIAM PERING).

Perrin, William Wilcox, 2s. Thomas, of Westbury, Somerset, arm. TRINITY COLL., matric. 29 April, 1867, aged 18; B.A. 1870, M.A. 1873, vicar of St. Luke's, Southampton, 1881.

Perrins, Charles William Dyson, o.s. James Dyson, of Worcester, gent. QUEEN'S COLL., matric. 23 Oct., 1882, aged 18. [5]

Perring, Albert Glenie, 1s. Jackson, of St. Peter, Colombo, Isle of Ceylon, gent. QUEEN'S COLL., matric. 9 July, 1853, aged 19; B.A. 1859, M.A. 1863, bar.-at-law, Lincoln's Inn, 1863. See Foster's *Men at the Bar.*

Perring, Charles, of PEMBROKE COLL., Cambridge (B.A. 1825, M.A. 1828); adm. 'ad eundem' 17 June, 1858, chaplain to the Clothworkers' Company 1827.

Perring, John Peter, s. John, of Mothecombe, Devon, arm. CORPUS CHRISTI COLL., matric. 7 April, 1813, aged 17; of Combe Flory, Somerset. See Foster's *Baronetage & Eton School Lists.*

Perring, John William Cowell, 1s. Philip, of Dartmouth, Devon, baronet & cler. BRASENOSE COLL., matric. 22 May, 1845, aged 18; died in India 13 July, 1852.

Perring, Peter, s. Philip, of Modbury, Devon, gent. EXETER COLL., matric. 19 Oct., 1792, aged 21; B.A. from ST. MARY HALL 1796, M.A. from EMMANUEL COLL., Cambridge, 1800, rector of North Huish, Devon, 1796, until his death 11 June, 1851. See Foster's *Baronetage.* [10]

Perring, (Sir) Philip (Bart.), s. John, baronet. BRASENOSE COLL., matric. 27 March, 1816, aged 19; B.A. 1820, M.A. 1822, 3rd baronet, domestic chaplain to the Duke of Cambridge, rector of North Huish, Devon, 1851, until his death 25 April, 1866. See Foster's *Baronetage & Eton School Lists.*

Perrott, Edward John, s. John, of Oxford (city), gent. HERTFORD COLL., matric. 10 Oct., 1741, aged 18; died 27 March, 1759.

Perrott, George St. John, 2s. Henry, of Stratford-on-Avon, gent. WORCESTER COLL., matric. 25 April, 1874, aged 17; B.A. 1878.

Perrott, George Wigley, s. George, of Pershore, co. Worcester, arm. WORCESTER COLL., matric. 28 Jan., 1803, aged 17; of Craycombe, co. Worcester, died 9 May, 1831, father of William Stafford and brother of John Wigley.

Perrott, Gregory, s. Greg., of Landegsed, co. Monmouth, cler. NEW INN HALL, matric. 17 Dec., 1725, aged 20; B.A. from JESUS COLL. 1729, rector of Gelligaer 1729, died 28 Dec., 1756, buried in Llandegveth church, father of William 1754. [15]

Perrott, Henry; created D.C.L. 11 July, 1733 (s. James Perrot), M.P. Oxford 1721, until his death in Paris 6 July, 1740. See *Perrott Notes,* p. 105.

Perrott, Humphrey, s. Thomas, of Bell Hall, co. Worcester, arm. BALLIOL COLL., matric. 20 March, 1727-8, aged 18; B.A. from UNIVERSITY COLL. 1731, fellow ORIEL COLL. until 1746, M.A. 1735, B.D. 1742, vicar of Dewley, buried at Bell Broughton 17 Dec., 1746.

Perrott, John, s. Thomas, of Broughton, co. Worcester, arm. BALLIOL COLL., matric. 6 April, 1723, aged 17; elder brother of the last named.

Perrot, John, s. William, of Bedwellty, co. Monmouth, pleb. EXETER COLL., matric. 22 Sep., 1737, aged 20; B.A. from CHRIST CHURCH 1741; one of these names was buried at Trevethin 12 May, 1743, leaving 4 children; another J.P., rector of Llanwern and Llanfihangel, vicar of Wiston, and perp. curate of Llandevand, died 23 Jan., 1803, aged 74.

Perrott, John, s. John, of Haverfordwest, co. Pembroke, pleb. CHRIST CHURCH, matric. 3 April, 1772, aged 19; B.A. 1776, M.A. 1778. [20]

Perrott, John (Stanford), s. Ben., of Bristol, Somerset, gent. ST. JOHN'S COLL., matric. 22 Oct., 1723, aged 19; died 21 May, 1768.

Perrott, Rev. John Wigley, s. George, of Fladbury, co. Worcester, arm. QUEEN'S COLL., matric. 16 June, 1814, aged 18; B.A. 1819, died in 1835, brother of George Wigley.

Perrott, Rev. Octavius George Dalhousie, born at sea, near India, 1s. Octavius, arm. ORIEL COLL., matric. 3 June, 1858, aged 18; B.A. 1862, M.A. 1870.

Perrott, Thomas, s, John, of St. Pancras, Middlesex, arm. UNIVERSITY COLL., matric. 2 July, 1788, aged 17; B.A. 1792, created D.C.L. 22 June, 1814, then of Kingston House, Bucks.

Perrott, Walter, 1s. David, of Llanspyddyd, co. Brecon, gent. JESUS COLL., matric. 20 March, 1855, aged 20. [25]

Perrott, William, s. Gregory, of Landegweth, co. Monmouth, cler. JESUS COLL., matric. 10 Oct., 1754, aged 18; B.A. 1758, died 19 March, 1779.

Perrott, William Stafford, 2s. George Wigley, of Fladbury, co. Worcester, arm. QUEEN'S COLL., matric. 27 June, 1833, aged 20.

Perry, Arthur John, 3s. John, of Breage, Cornwall, cler. ORIEL COLL., matric. 22 May, 1861, aged 18; B.A. 1864, M.A. 1871, held previous curacies 1866-74, vicar of St. Feock, Cornwall, 1874.

Perry, Charles, scholar TRINITY COLL., Cambridge, 1826-9 (senior wrangler, 1st Smith's prizeman 7th classic and B.A. 1828, fellow 1829-41, M.A. 1831, D.D. 1847); adm. 'ad eundem' 16 June, 1847, bishop of Melbourne 1847-76, perp. curate St. Paul, Camberwell, 1842-7, prelate of the most distinguished Order of St. Michael and St. George, preb. and canon of Llandaff 1878.

Perry, Charles Copland, s. Walter Copland, of London, gent. NON-COLL., matric. 28 Jan., 1871, aged 17; B.A. from NEW COLL. 1875, M.A. 1881.

Perry, Rev. Clement Raymond, o.s. Frederick, of Clifton, co. Gloucester, arm. CHRIST CHURCH, matric. 13 Oct., 1876, aged 19; B.A. 1881. [31]

Perry, Edward, 3s. Joseph, of Bilston, co. Stafford, arm. WORCESTER COLL., matric. 15 Oct., 1821, aged 19; B.A. 1826, a student of Lincoln's Inn 1825, vicar of Llangattock-vivon-Avel, etc., co. Monmouth 1844, until his death 19 July, 1875.

Perry, Rev. Edward John, 2s. Frederick, of Stratford, Essex, cler. NON-COLL., matric. 16 Jan., 1875, aged 19; scholar WORCESTER COLL. 1875-9, B.A. 1879, M.A. 1881, assistant-master Merchant Taylors' School 1882. See *Robinson,* 362.

Perry, Frederick, 1s. Isaac, of Lilleshall, Salop, gent. CHRIST CHURCH, matric. 14 Oct., 1881, aged 19; exhibitioner 1881-4.

Perry, Frederick Robert, 2s. William, of Paddington, Middlesex, arm. UNIVERSITY COLL., matric. 23 March, 1843, aged 18; B.A. 1846, M.A. 1849, incumbent of Cadmore End, Oxon, died 1 Dec., 1863.

Perry, Frederick Samuel, o.s. George Murray, of Neilpo, Australia, arm. EXETER COLL., matric. 22 Oct., 1880, aged 19. [36]

Perry, Frederick William George, 1s. Frederick, of Stratford, Essex, cler. WORCESTER COLL., matric. 16 Oct., 1872, aged 19; exhibitioner WADHAM COLL. 1873.

Perry, George Gresley, 1s. William, of Churchill, Somerset, arm. CORPUS CHRISTI COLL., matric. 3 March, 1837, aged 16, scholar 1837-42, B.A. 1840; fellow LINCOLN COLL. 1842-52, M.A. 1843, bursar 1847, tutor 1847-52, Greek lecturer 1848, preb. of Lincoln 1861, rector of Waddington 1852.

Perry, George Henry, 1s. George Gresley, of Waddington, co. Lincoln, cler. KEBLE COLL., matric. 13 Oct., 1873, aged 19; exhibitioner 1873-7, B.A. 1877, M.A. 1884, vicar of St. Matthew, City Road, 1884.

Perry, Rev. George Lockyer, s. George, of Westminster, gent. ST. JOHN'S COLL., matric. 29 Nov., 1790, aged 19; B.A. 1794, died at Aylesford vicarage, Kent, 9 April, 1843.

Perry, Herbert Louis, 3s. William Robert, of London, arm. HERTFORD COLL., matric. 14 Oct., 1884, aged 19; B.A. 1887.

Perry, Hugh, s. William, of Isle of Barbados, arm. BALLIOL COLL., matric. 20 Nov., 1759, aged 18.

Perry, John, s. Dan., of Pattingham, co. Stafford, pleb. PEMBROKE COLL., matric. 14 Nov., 1731, aged 18; B.A. 1736, vicar of Clent, co. Stafford, 1736, rector of Ashe and vicar of Farmingham, Kent, 1754. **[6]**

Perry, John, s. William, of Isle of Barbados, arm. BALLIOL COLL., matric. 24 Nov., 1757, aged 19; bar.-at-law, Middle Temple, 1765, one of his name was buried in the Temple Church 28 Sep., 1770, and another died a judge of the Court of Common Pleas, Jamaica, etc., 30 April, 1809.

Perry, John, 1s. William, of Churchill, Somerset, arm. BALLIOL COLL., matric. 11 Dec., 1821, aged 17; scholar 1823-9, B.A. 1826, M.A. 1832, vicar of Perranzabuloe, Cornwall, 1846, until his death, June, 1874, father of Walter C.

Perry, John Robert, 2s. William Parker, of Sibstone, co. Leicester, cler. EXETER COLL., matric. 24 Oct., 1849, aged 17; B.A. 1853, M.A. 1856.

Perry, Littleton, s. John, of Clent, co. Stafford, cler. MAGDALEN HALL, matric. 12 June, 1765, aged 19; B.A. 1769, vicar of Clent and Rowley Regis, 1781, until his death in 1816. **[10]**

Perry, Robert Charles, 2s. Robert Charles, of Peckham, Surrey, gent. ST. JOHN'S COLL., matric. 13 Oct., 1879, aged 18; scholar 1881-2, B.A. 1883, M.A. 1887. See *Robinson*, 376.

Perry, Septimus, s. William, of Chiswick, Middlesex, gent. MAGDALEN HALL, matric. 17 July, 1807, aged 16; B.A. 1811, M.A. 1814, died in 1871.

Perry, Thomas, s. George, of Wolverhampton, co. Stafford, pleb. BALLIOL COLL., matric. 15 March, 1720-1, aged 18; B.A. 1724.

Perry, Thomas, s. Ed., of Bilston, co. Stafford, gent. BALLIOL COLL., matric. 19 Nov., 1722, aged 17; B.A. 1726.

Perry, Thomas, s. William, of Isle of Barbados, arm. BALLIOL COLL., matric. 22 Oct., 1764, aged 18. **[15]**

Perry, Thomas Corbett, 2s. John, of Wolverhampton, co. Stafford, arm. LINCOLN COLL., matric. 8 May, 1828, aged 19; B.A. 1832.

Perry, Walter Churchill, 4s. John, of Perranzabuloe, Cornwall, cler. EXETER COLL., matric. 30 May, 1868, aged 19; scholar 1868-73, B.A. 1873, M.A. 1886, a master at Uppingham School. See *Coll. Reg.*, 163.

Perry, William, s. John, of Charles, Devon, gent. EXETER COLL., matric. 3 June, 1731, aged 18; B.A. 1734, M.A. 1737.

Perry, William, s. William, of Kingswinford, co. Stafford, gent. TRINITY COLL., matric. 5 July, 1773, aged 20.

Perry, William, s. William, of Chiswick, Middlesex, doctor. MAGDALEN HALL, matric. 6 April, 1802, aged 22; B.A. 1806, M.A. 1809. **[20]**

Perry, William Frederick Robert, 1s. William Parker, of Sibstone, co. Leicester, cler. EXETER COLL., matric. 3 May, 1849, aged 18.

Perry, William Parker, o.s. William, of St. Bride's, Fleet Street, London, gent. WADHAM COLL., matric. 17 June, 1823, aged 18; B.A. 1828, M.A. 1844, vicar of Chislehampton 1840, until his death 10 March, 1881.

Perry, William Payne, 1s. Robert Charles, of London, gent. ST. JOHN'S COLL., matric. 13 Oct., 1877, aged 19, scholar 1877-84, B.A. 1881, M.A. 1884. See *Robinson*, 371.

Perry, Right Rev. William Stevens, bishop of Iowa, United States, America, created D.D. 21 June, 1888.

Perryman, Richard, s. Richard, of Tregony, Cornwall, gent. EXETER COLL., matric. 6 June, 1774, aged 19; B.A. 1778. **[25]**

Perryn, Gerrard Alexander, 1s. Richard G., of Trafford, Cheshire, arm. BRASENOSE COLL., matric. 2 June, 1842, aged 18; scholar 1843-7, B.A. 1846, M.A. 1849, B. & D.D. 1871, of Trafford Hall, Cheshire, perp. curate Guilden-Sutton, Cheshire, 1851-68, died at Oxford 19 Jan., 1878. See *Rugby School Reg.*, 195.

Perryn, (Sir) Richard, s. Benjamin, of Flint (town), gent. QUEEN'S COLL., matric. 13 March, 1740-1, aged 17; bar.-at-law, Inner Temple, 1747, K.C. and a bencher 1771, vice-chamberlain of Chester, serjt.-at-law 1776, a baron of the Exchequer 1776-99, knighted 5 April, 1776, died 2 Jan., 1803.

Perryn, Richard, s. Richard, of St. Andrew's, London, arm. (after a knight). CHRIST CHURCH, matric. 17 June, 1772, aged 18; B.A. 1776, M.A. 1779, rector of Standish, Lancashire, 1779, until his death 31 Oct., 1825. See *Alumni West.*, 395.

Perryn, Richard George Henry, 1s. Richard Henry, of Yealand Conyers, Lancashire, arm. EXETER COLL., matric. 21 Jan., 1885, aged 20; B.A. 1888.

Perryn, Richard Gerrard, s. Richard, of Thornton, Cheshire, cler. CHRIST CHURCH, matric. 1 Feb., 1810, aged 18; B.A. 1814, M.A. 1816. **[30]**

Persehowse, Richard, s. William, of Reynolds Hall, co. Stafford, arm. MAGDALEN COLL., matric. 27 June, 1751, aged 18; created M.A. 2 July, 1754.

Persehowse, Thomas, s. Humphrey, of Ashbury, Berks, cler. LINCOLN COLL., matric. 20 May, 1724, aged 17, B.A. 1728; M.A. from TRINITY COLL., Cambridge, 1740, minor canon of Westminster. See *Alumni West.*, 289.

Pershouse, William Bradney, s. William, of Penn, co. Stafford, arm. ORIEL COLL., matric. 17 May, 1805, aged 18; of Pembroke Hall, co. Stafford.

Pertvee, Arthur, 8s. James, of Woodham Ferrers, Essex, gent. PEMBROKE COLL., matric. 17 June, 1856, aged 19; B.A. 1860, M.A. 1863, curate of Brancepeth, co. Durham, 1861-4, of St. Margaret, Leicester, 1865-72, vicar of Brightlingsea, Essex, 1872.

Pery, Hon. Edmund Sexten, s. Edmund, Earl of Limerick. CHRIST CHURCH, matric. 8 May, 1815, aged 18; of the Bury House, Cottingham, Northants, died 31 Dec., 1860. See Foster's *Peerage*.

Pery, John, s. John, of Hatton Garden, Middlesex, arm. CHRIST CHURCH, matric. 23 June, 1720, aged 17; B.A. 1724, M.A. 16 March, 1726-7, vicar of Ash, Kent, 1735, and of Farningham 1754, D.D. (probably a Lambeth degree), died 31 Oct., 1767, buried at Ash. See *Alumni West.*, 274 & 370*n.* **[36]**

Pery, John, s. John, of Ash, Kent, cler. CHRIST CHURCH, matric. 24 May, 1758, aged 18; B.A. 1762, M.A. 1765, rector of Ash, Kent, 1768, and of Houghton-cum-Wyton, and of Hemingford Abbots, Hunts, died at Wyton 27 March, 1811. See *Alumni West.*, 369.

Pery, Multon, s. John, of Ash, Kent, cler. CHRIST CHURCH, matric. 9 June, 1760, aged 17; B.A. 1764, died same year. See *Alumni West.*, 374.

Pescod, George, s. William, of Winchester, Hants, arm. NEW COLL., matric. 4 Sep., 1755, aged 19; bar.-at-law, Inner Temple, 1759.

Pescod, Robert (Peter in *Mat. Reg.*), arm. ST. MARY HALL, matric. 15 July, 1721; B.A. from MAGDALEN COLL. 1726, M.A. 1729.

Pescod, William, s. Robert, of St. Mary Calendar, Winchester (city), arm. NEW COLL., matric. 24 April, 1719, aged 18; B.A. 14 July, 1722-3, bar.-at-law, Inner Temple, 1725, recorder of Winchester, died 26 Feb., 1760.

Peshall, Samuel, s. John, of Guildford, Surrey, arm. PEMBROKE COLL., matric. 6 July, 1779, aged 17; B.A. & M.A. 1787, rector of Morton Baggot and Oldberrow, co. Worcester, 1800-20, died 4 Aug., 1835. [5]

Peshall, Samuel, o.s. Samuel D'Oyly, of Liseux, Normandy, cler. ST. MARY HALL, matric. 31 Oct., 1868, aged 19; B.A. 1871, M.A. 1875, curate of Oldberrow, co. Worcester, 1872-3, rector 1873. See *Rugby School Reg.*

Peshall, Samuel D'Oyly, s. Samuel, of Chiswick, Middlesex, cler. WORCESTER COLL., matric. 27 June, 1809, aged 17; B.A. 1813, M.A. 1815, rector of Morton Baggott, co. Warwick, 1820, and of Oldberrow, co. Worcester, 1835, until his death in 1859.

Pestell, William, s. Thomas, of Coleman Street, London, pleb. ST. JOHN'S COLL., matric. 6 July, 1723, aged 18; B.C.L. 1731, died at his fathers in London 28 May, 1732. See *Robinson*, 48.

Pester, John, s. Stephen, of North Perrott, Somerset, pleb. HART HALL, matric. 10 May, 1722, aged 18.

Pester, John, s. Robert, of Stocklinge, Somerset, cler. WADHAM COLL., matric. 27 Jan., 1749-50, aged 17; B.A. 1755. [10]

Pesterre, William Arthur, 1s. Thomas Arthur, of London, gent. MERTON COLL., matric. 12 Oct., 1861, aged 19; scholar 1861-6, B.A. 1866, M.A. 1871, died 10 March, 1886.

Petch, George, y.s. Robert, of Kirby Moorside, Yorks, gent. LINCOLN COLL., matric. 11 Nov., 1843, aged 17, scholar 1843-7, B.A. 1847; fellow TRINITY COLL. 1848-57, M.A. 1850, rhetorical reader 1849, tutor 1850, rector of Oddington, Oxon, 1857, until his death 1 Sep., 1875.

Petch, George Ellis, s. William, of Westminster (city), gent. ST. EDMUND HALL, matric. 9 Dec., 1795, aged 27; B.A. 1799.

Petch, James, o.s. James Butt, of Gravesend, Kent, gent. NEW COLL., matric. 7 June, 1854, aged 26; B.Mus. 3 June, 1854.

Peter, Edward, s. Samuel, of Plymouth, Devon, arm. TRINITY COLL., matric. 7 April, 1778, aged 18; B.C.L. 1784, rector of Great Wigborough, Essex, 1789, until his death 2 July, 1832. [15]

Peter, Rev. Hoblyn, s. Hoblin, of St. Merrin, Cornwall, gent. EXETER COLL., matric. 3 April, 1800, aged 19; B.A. 1804, of Porthcothan, died 22 Nov., 1846, aged 67.

Peter, John, s. Robert, of Mawnan, Cornwall, cler. BALLIOL COLL., matric. 2 March, 1799, aged 19; B.A. 1802, rector of Grade, Cornwall, 1817, until his death 12 Nov., 1852, father of Lewis M.

Peter, John Thomas Henry, 1s. William, of St. George's, Bloomsbury, London, arm. CHRIST CHURCH, matric. 4 June, 1829, aged 19, B.A. 1833; fellow MERTON COLL. 1836-56, M.A. 1836, bursar 1841, sub-warden 1844, proctor 1845, of Chiverton, Cornwall, high sheriff 1866, bar.-at-law, Inner Temple, 1840, died in 1883.

Peter, Lewis Morgan, 1s. John, of Redruth, Cornwall, cler. EXETER COLL., matric. 28 April, 1836, aged 19; B.A. 1840, M.A. 1843, vicar of Cornelly, Cornwall, 1868.

Peter, Robert, s. William, of Mawnan, Cornwall, cler. EXETER COLL., matric. 16 July, 1763, aged 19, B.A. 1767, vicar of Pellayne 1786, and rector of Sully, co. Glamorgan, 1802, until his death in 1822.

Peter, Robert Rous, s. Henry, of Harlyn, Cornwall, arm. EXETER COLL., matric. 6 July, 1809, aged 19, B.A. 1813, M.A. 1816; Michel fellow QUEEN'S COLL. 1816-28, a student of Lincoln's Inn 1815, died in 1858. [21]

Peter, William, s. Hen., of Endellion, Cornwall, gent. EXETER COLL., matric. 12 May, 1741, aged 19 (? of Harlyn, died in 1776).

Peter, William, s. William, of Mawnan, Cornwall, cler. BALLIOL COLL., matric. 16 March, 1752, aged 19; B.A. 1755, rector of Mawnan 1756, until his death 9 Oct., 1798.

Peter, William, s. Henry, of St. Merryn, Cornwall, arm. CHRIST CHURCH, matric. 27 Jan., 1803, aged 18; B.A. 1807, M.A. 1809, of Harlyn, Cornwall, bar.-at-law, Lincoln's Inn, 1813, M.P. Bodmin 1832-5, H.B.M. consul at Pennsylvania, died 6 Feb., 1853. See obit. *Gent.'s Mag.*, i. 441.

Peters, Arthur Edward George, 2s. Thomas, of Wellingtou, Somerset, cler. WORCESTER COLL., matric. 22 Oct., 1885, aged 19. [25]

Peters, Charles, s. Jonathan, of St. Clement's, Cornwall, gent. QUEEN'S COLL., matric. 30 May, 1786, aged 18; B.A. 1790, M.A. 1793, rector of 2nd portion of Pontesbury, Salop, 1803, until his death 7 April, 1824.

Peters, Charles Powell, 1s. Charles, of Pontisbury, Salop, cler. QUEEN'S COLL., matric. 26 March, 1828, aged 18; B.A. 1831, M.A. 1837, curate of Pitchford, Salop, 1844-65, rector 1865, until his death 9 Nov., 1879.

Peters, Edmund, s. William, of Doncaster, co. York, cler. CHRIST CHURCH, matric. 27 Oct., 1814, aged 18.

Peters, Edward, 'tonsor;' privilegiatus 15 June, 1759.

Peters, Frank Hesketh, 5s. Edward, of Chilgrove, near Chichester, arm. BALLIOL COLL., matric. 20 April, 1868, aged 18, scholar 1866-72, B.A. 1872; fellow UNIVERSITY COLL. 1874, M.A. 1875, librarian, & assistant-lecturer in modern history. See *Eton School Lists.* [30]

Peters, Jonathan, s. John, of Tregony, Cornwall, gent. EXETER COLL., matric. 31 Oct., 1738, aged 18; B.A. 1742, M.A. 1745, rector of St. Creed, Cornwall, 1750, father of Charles 1786.

Peters, Jonathan, s. John, of St. Austell, Cornwall, gent. QUEEN'S COLL., matric. 12 May, 1808, aged 19; B.A. 1813, M.A. 1818.

Peters, Rev. Michael Nowell, of ST. PETER'S COLL., Cambridge (B.A. 1822, M.A. 1844); adm. 'ad eundem' 1 July, 1851.

Peters, Richard, s. Ralph, of Liverpool, Lancashire, gent. WADHAM COLL., matric. 8 April, 1731, aged 20; D.D. by diploma 2 May, 1770, then rector of Christ Church and St. Peter, Philadelphia.

Peters, Thomas, 2s. Ralph, of Hinley, Lancashire, arm. ST. ALBAN HALL, matric. 25 May, 1831, aged 19; B.A. 1835, rector (and patron) of Eastington, co. Gloucester, 1837-83, brother of William Henry. See *Rugby School Reg.*, 154. [35]

Peters, William, s. Francis, of the Inner Temple, London, gent. QUEEN'S COLL., matric. 3 June, 1731, aged 16; a student of the Inner Temple 1728, (called PETER in *Mat. Reg.*)

Peters, William, s. Matthew, of Isle of Wight, gent. EXETER COLL., matric. 24 Nov., 1779, aged 37; B.C.L. 1788, chaplain to the Prince Regent, rector of Eaton, co. Leicester, 1783, of Knighton or Knipton, co. Leicester, and of Wolsthorp, co. Lincoln, 1788, and preb. of Lincoln 1795, until his death 20 March, 1814.

Peters, William Birdseye, s. Samuel, of 'Heborn, Connecticut,' North America, cler. TRINITY COLL., matric. 12 Oct., 1792, aged 18; a student of the Inner Temple 1792.

Peters, William Harold Stilwell, 2s. Joseph, of Rochester, arm. CHRIST CHURCH, matric. 30 May, 1885, aged 18.

Peters, William Henry, 3s. Ralph, of Hinley, Lancashire, arm. EXETER COLL., matric. 27 Feb., 1833, aged 19; of Harefield House, Devon, and of Park Postyn, Devon, high sheriff 1876.

Peterson, Arthur Frederick, 1s. William, of St. Kilda, Melbourne, gent. CORPUS CHRISTI COLL., matric. 4 Feb., 1879, aged 19; scholar 1879-83, B.A. 1883, M.A. 1886, bar.-at-law, Inner Temple, 1886.

Peterson, Edward, o.s. John, of Derby, gent. MAGDALEN HALL, matric. 13 Feb., 1868, aged 26.

Peterson, Peter, 1s. John, of Edinburgh, arm. LINCOLN COLL., matric. 10 April, 1869, aged 22; B.A. from BALLIOL COLL. 1872. [5]

Peterson, William, 5s. John, of Edinburgh, gent. CORPUS CHRISTI COLL., matric. 29 April, 1876, aged 19; scholar 1876-81, B.A. 1879, M.A. 1883, a student of the Inner Temple 1879, principal of University College, Dundee, 1882.

Pethon, William, s. Walter, of Tintagell, Cornwall, pleb. EXETER COLL., matric. 30 May, 1715, aged 18; B.A. 26 Feb., 1718-9.

Petit, Rev. John Lewis, scholar TRINITY COLL., Cambridge, 1822 (B.A. 1823, M.A. 1826); adm. 'ad eundem' 21 June, 1850.

Petit, Peter, s. Peter, of London, pleb. EXETER COLL., matric. 8 Nov., 1740, aged 20; clerk MAGDALEN COLL. 1743-7, B.A. 1744, M.A. 1747, vicar of Windham, Norfolk, 1755, commissary of Norfolk. See *Bloxam*, ii. 93.

Petley, Charles Robert Carter, 1s. Charles Carter, of Geanies, co. Ross, Scotland, arm. ST. JOHN'S COLL., matric. 6 May, 1826, aged 18; B.A. 1830, M.A. 1868, of Riverhead, Kent, J.P., father of the next named. [10]

Petley, Francis Woodgate, 2s. Charles, of Riverhead, near Sevenoaks, Kent, arm. MERTON COLL., matric. 18 April, 1868, aged 19; B.A. & M.A. 1875, died 21 April, 1877.

Petley, Rev. Henry, 3s. Charles Carter, of Chepstead, Keut, arm. WADHAM COLL., matric. 7 May, 1834, aged 18; B.A. 1838, M.A. 1843.

Petre, Oswald Henry Philip, 1s. Edward, of London, arm. CHRIST CHURCH, matric. 4 June, 1881, aged 19; exhibitioner 1884-5, B.A. 1886. See Foster's *Peerage*.

Petry, Henry James, 2s. William, of Quebec, Lower Canada, gent. QUEEN'S COLL., matric. 6 Dec., 1849, aged 21; B.A. 1853, incumbent of Danville, Quebec.

Pett, Phineas, s. John, of Maidstone, Kent, gent. CHRIST CHURCH, matric. 1 June, 1774, aged 18; B.A. 1778, M.A. 1781, censor 1783-91, proctor 1785, B.D. 1791, D.D. 1797, a canon 1815-30, treasurer 1828, principal of ST. MARY HALL 1801-15, Whitehall preacher 1788, vicar of Orton-on-the-Hill 1789, and of Cropredy, Oxon, 1789, rector of Wentnor, Salop, 1794, and of Chilbolton, Hants, 1795-1830, preb. of Salisbury 1801, rector of Newington, Oxon, 1802-30, refused the bishopric of Carlisle 1827, chancellor and archdeacon of Oxford 1797, until his death 4 Feb., 1830. See *Alumni West.*, 399. [15]

Pettat, Charles Richard, 2s. Thomas, of Gloucester (city), cler. UNIVERSITY COLL., matric. 3 March, 1831, aged 17; B.A. 1834, rector of Ashe, Hants, 1845, and of Deane, Hants, 1845, until his death 8 Jan., 1873. See *Rugby School Reg.*, 154.

Pettat, John, s. Thomas, of King Stanley, co. Gloucester, gent. BALLIOL COLL., matric. 10 May, 1756, aged 17; B.A. 1760, M.A. 1767, vicar of Stonehouse, co. Gloucester, 1771, rector of Quenington 1789, until his death 15 Jan., 1811.

Pettat, Thomas, s. John, of Stonehouse, co. Gloucester, cler. UNIVERSITY COLL., matric. 15 Dec., 1790, aged 18; B.A. 1794, M.A. 1797, rector of Hatherop, 1797, and of Beverstone, co. Gloucester, 1803, until his death 10 March, 1839.

Pettener, Thomas, s. John, of Worplesdon, Surrey, cler. CORPUS CHRISTI COLL., matric. 5 May, 1749, aged 15; B.A. 1753, M.A. 1756.

Petters, William Griffith, 1s. William, of Amlwch, Isle of Anglesey, gent. JESUS COLL., matric. 19 Nov., 1846, aged 20. [20]

Pettigrew, William Vesalius Davison, 2s. Augustus Frederick, of London, cler. KEBLE COLL., matric. 13 Oct., 1873, aged 19; died 29 Nov., 1874.

Pettingal, Charles Richard, 1s. Charles, of St. Margaret's, Westminster, cler. CHRIST CHURCH, matric. 14 Dec., 1826, aged 19.

Pettingal, Charles Thomas, s. John, of Leighton, Beds, arm. CHRIST CHURCH, matric. 12 June, 1800, aged 18; B.A. 1804, M.A. 1819, rector of Ore, Sussex, 1810, and of Little Braxted, Essex, 1819, until his death 28 Aug., 1858. See *Alumni West.*, 454.

Pettingal, Rev. George Hanbury, s. John, of Leighton Buzzard, Beds, gent. ST. MARY HALL, matric. 4 July, 1810, aged 23; B.A. 1815, died 18 Feb., 1838. See *Alumni West.*, 459.

Pettingal, John, s. Fran., of Newport, Monmouth, cler. JESUS COLL., matric. 15 March, 1724-5, aged 17, B.A. 1728; M.A. from CHRIST'S COLL., Cambridge, 1740, preacher Duke Street, Westminster, preb. of St. Paul's, 1757, until his death in 1781.

Pettingal, Thomas, s. John, of Westminster, doctor. CHRIST CHURCH, matric. 9 June, 1762, aged 17; B.A. 1766, M.A. 1769, tutor & censor 1774-9, B.D. 1778, proctor 1777, usher of Westminster School 1770-3, Whitehall preacher, rector of East Hampstead, Berks, 1782, until his death 8 April, 1826. See *Alumni West.*, 377. [25]

Pettipher, William, s. Henry, of Fenny Compton, co. Warwick, gent. BALLIOL COLL., matric. 16 Feb., 1714-5, aged 18; B.A. 1718.

Pettit, Charles William, o.s. William Fostey (or Fossey), of Leighton Buzzard, Beds, arm. KEBLE COLL., matric. 14 Oct., 1878, aged 17; drowned at king's weare in the Isis, near Oxford, 19 May, 1882.

Pettit, James, s. James, of Eltham, Kent, arm. QUEEN'S COLL., matric. 24 April, 1736, aged 17.

Pettman, Edward, s. William, of Ham, Kent, arm. TRINITY COLL., matric. 17 March, 1815, aged 19; B.A. 1818, M.A. 1838, chaplain Chatham Dockyard, died at Walmer 14 Sep., 1851. [30]

Pettman, Hatfield Edge, o.s. Thomas, of Llangfoist, co. Monmouth, arm. TRINITY COLL., matric. 19 May, 1836, aged 18; B.A. 1841, M.A. 1845.

Petty, James, s. James, of Grosvenor Street, Westminster, arm. CHRIST CHURCH, matric. 17 April, 1764, aged 17.

Petty, John, Earl of Shelburne, created D.C.L. 14 June, 1755 (2s. Thomas, Earl of Kerry), assumed the name of PETTY in lieu of FITZMAURICE, M.P. co. Kerry 1743-51, Chipping Wycombe, Bucks, 1754-60, P.C. Ireland, created Viscount FitzMaurice 7 Oct., 1751, and Earl of Shelburne 6 June, 1753, died 10 May, 1761, father of William, 1st Marquis of Lansdowne. See Foster's *Peerage*.

Petty, John Procter, B.A. TRINITY COLL., Dublin, 3s. Francis, of Otley, Yorks, gent. Incorp. from ST. EDMUND HALL 8 Feb., 1872, aged 25.

Petvin, John, s. William, of Little Baddow, Essex, cler. WADHAM COLL., matric. 28 June, 1759, aged 18, B.A. 1763; M.A. from EMMANUEL COLL., Cambridge, 1769, vicar of Burnham, Essex, 1767, and of Braintree 1778, until his death 28 Jan., 1796. [35]

Petvin, Joseph, s. John, of Haslebury, Somerset, gent. EXETER COLL., matric. 1 April, 1731, aged 18.

Petvin, William, s. John, of Haslebury, Somerset, pleb. WADHAM COLL., matric. 31 March, 1718 aged 18; B.A. 1721, M.A. 1725 (? died rector of Danbury and Woodham Ferrers, Essex, in 1770).

Peyton, Algernon Francis, 1s. Thomas, of Secunderabad, East Indies, baronet. MAGDALEN COLL. matric. 18 April, 1874, aged 18.

Peyton, (Sir) Henry (Bart.), s. Henry, of Emneth, co. Cambridge, baronet. CHRIST CHURCH, matric. 27 Jan., 1797, aged 17; created M.A. 2 May, 1800, 2nd baronet, M.P. Cambridgeshire 1802-6, died 24 Feb., 1854. See Foster's *Baronetage.*

Peyton, (Sir) Henry (Bart.), o.s. Henry, of St. George's, Hanover Square, London, baronet. CHRIST CHURCH, matric. 29 April, 1822, aged 17; 3rd baronet, M.P. Woodstock 1837-8, died 18 Feb., 1866.

Peyton, Thomas Griffith, 2s. Nicholson, of Colwall, co. Hereford, arm. ST. JOHN'S COLL., matric. 29 June, 1835, aged 18; B.A. from ST. MARY HALL 1843, M.A. from ST. JOHN'S COLL. 1844, of The Bartons, co. Hereford, J.P., D.L.

Peyton, Thomas Thornhill, 2s. Thomas, of Secunderabad, East Indies, baronet. MAGDALEN COLL., matric. 16 Oct., 1875, aged 18; B.A. 1879, M.A. 1888, rector of St. Mary March, co. Cambridge, 1882.

Phabayn, John Baron, 1s. John, of Charlton, Somerset, cler. LINCOLN COLL., matric. 17 Oct., 1866, aged 20. [5]

Phabayn, John Finden Smith, o.s. Thomas, of Alresford, Hants, gent. QUEEN'S COLL., matric. 12 May, 1828, aged 17; B.A. 1832, M.A. 1834, vicar of Charlton-Horethorn, Dorset, 1844, father of the last named.

Phaire, Robert, s. Robert, of Cork, Ireland, arm. WADHAM COLL., matric. 22 Oct., 1718, aged 17.

Pheasant, Rev. John Leslie Nevins, 1s. John, of Portglenone, Ireland, gent. NON-COLL., matric. 9 Feb., 1878, aged 22; B.A. 1881, M.A. 1886.

Pheasant, Rev. William, 2s. John, of Portglenone, co. Antrim, gent. NON-COLL., matric. 11 Oct., 1879, aged 21; B.A. 1883, M.A. 1887.

Phelips, Alfred Dering, 1s. Henry Plantagenet, of Guernsey, cler. KEBLE COLL., matric. 20 Jan., 1877, aged 19. [10]

Phelips, Charles, s. Edward, of Montacute, Somerset, arm. UNIVERSITY COLL., matric. 23 June, 1784, aged 18; B.A. 1788, M.A. 1821, rector of St. Margaret Pattens and St. Gabriel, Fenchurch, London, 1792, until his death 27 Oct., 1834.

Phelips, Charles James, 1s. Charles, of Marylebone, London, arm. CHRIST CHURCH, matric. 16 Oct., 1839, aged 18; B.A. 1843, of Briggins Park, Herts, a student of the Inner Temple 1843. See *Eton School Lists.*

Phelipps, Edward, s. Edward, of Westminster, arm. CHRIST CHURCH, matric. 23 April, 1741, aged 16; of Montacute, Somerset, M.P. 1774-80, died in 1797, father of Edward 1770.

Phelips, Edward, s. Edward, of Montacute, Somerset, arm. CHRIST CHURCH, matric. 15 June, 1770, aged 18; B.A. 1774, of Montacute, bar.-at-law, Middle Temple, 1778, M.P. Somersetshire 1784, until his death 5 Aug,, 1792. See *Alumni West.*, 391.

Phelipps, John, s. Edward, of Trent, Somerset, arm. CHRIST CHURCH, matric. 9 June, 1743, aged 17; B.A. 1747, M.A. 1750, vicar of Yeovil. [15]

Phelips, John, s. William, of Montacute, Somerset, cler. CHRIST CHURCH, matric. 21 Oct., 1802, aged 18; B.A. 1807, M.A. 1809, of Montacute, died 20 April, 1834.

Phelips, Richard Colston, 7s. William, of Montacute, Somerset, cler. TRINITY COLL., matric. 22 Feb., 1819, aged 18; B.A. 1822, M.A. 1825, vicar of Montacute 1826, rector of Cucklington 1833, until his death 15 March, 1862.

Phelips, Robert, s. William, of Cucklington, Somerset, cler. CHRIST CHURCH, matric. 8 June, 1810, aged 19; B.A. 1814, M.A. 1817, vicar of Yeovil 1815, rector of Lufton, Somerset, 1827, until his death 24 Feb., 1855.

Phelips, Rev. William, s. Edward, of Montacute, Somerset, arm. MERTON COLL., matric. 15 Dec., 1773, aged 18; B.C.L. 1780, father of Richard, Robert, and William.

Phelips, William, s. William, of Montacute, Somerset, cler. TRINITY COLL., matric. 8 June, 1807, aged 18; B.A. 1811, M.A. 1817, rector of Cucklington and Stoke Trister, Somerset, 1807, until his death 4 March, 1833. [20]

Phelp, John, s. John, of Benson, Oxon, gent. ST. JOHN'S COLL., matric. 12 Nov., 1734, aged 18.

Phelp, William Awbery, s. Philip, of St. Lawrence, Reading, Berks, gent. TRINITY COLL., matric. 14 Jan., 1784, aged 17; B.A. 1787, M.A. 1790, vicar of Stanwell, Essex, 1792, died 3 June, 1853.

Phelps, Rev. Abraham, s. Robert, of Porlock, Somerset, gent. EXETER COLL., matric. 5 June, 1739, aged 18; B.A. 1742, M.A. 1746, father of Charles.

Phelps, Arthur Whitmarsh, 2s. John, of Wilton, Wilts, cler. WORCESTER COLL., matric. 7 June, 1854, aged 19; bible clerk 1854-8, B.A. 1858, M.A. 1861, rector of Pertwood, Wilts, 1859-63, vicar of Compton Chamberlayne, Wilts, 1863-76, and of Amesbury 1876, brother of Philip A. and Robert.

Phelps, Charles, s. Abraham, of Bridgewater, Somerset, cler. EXETER COLL., matric. 11 May, 1769, aged 18. [25]

Phelps, Edward Robert, 1s. Edward Spencer, of Weston, Somerset, cler. CORPUS CHRISTI COLL., matric. 16 Oct., 1865, aged 18; B.A. 1868, M.A. 1872, chaplain at Madeira 1875-7, has held various curacies since 1870. See *Eton School Lists.*

Phelps, Edward Spencer, 2s. Thomas Spencer, of Maperton, Somerset, cler. WADHAM COLL., matric. 18 March, 1830, aged 18; B.A. 1835, chaplain R.N. 1836-71, chaplain at Bonn 1871-4.

Phelps, Ernest James, 2s. John Lecky, of Waterpark, co. Limerick, arm. MAGDALEN COLL., matric. 23 Oct., 1885, aged 18.

Phelps, Frederic Philip, 3s. William Whitmarsh, of Harrow-on-the-Hill, Middlesex, cler. WADHAM COLL., matric. 19 March, 1851, aged 18; B.A. 1855, M.A. 1863.

Phelps, Francis Robinson, 1s. Joseph Francis, of Newfoundland, cler. KEBLE COLL., matric. 18 Dec., 1882, aged 19; B.A. 1886. [30]

Phelps, Henry Cecil, 6s. John, of Little Langford, Wilts, cler. QUEEN'S COLL., matric. 3 Feb., 1865, aged 19; clerk 1866-9, B.A. 1868, M.A. 1871, vicar of St. James, Ashted, co. Warwick, 1873-85, rector of Upton 1885.

Phelps, Henry (Dampier), s. Thomas, of Sherborne, Dorset, cler. HERTFORD COLL., matric. 18 May, 1795, aged 18; B.A. 1799, M.A. 1801, rector of Snodland, Kent, 1804, until his death 30 July, 1865.

Phelps, Henry Dampier, 1s. Thomas Prankerd, of Thame, Oxon, cler. WADHAM COLL., matric. 23 June, 1829, aged 17; B.A. 1833, M.A. 1836, vicar of Birling, Kent, 1850, until his death 28 Oct., 1864.

Phelps, James, s. John Delafield, of Dursley, co. Gloucester, arm. ORIEL COLL., matric. 5 July, 1783, aged 16; B.A. 1787, M.A. 1790, rector of Brimpsfield and Cranham, and of Alderley, co. Gloucester, 1802, until his death 11 April, 1829.

Phelps, John, s. John, of Backwell, Somerset, cler. BALLIOL COLL., matric. 27 March, 1784, aged 18. [35]

Phelps, John, 2s. John, of 'Allington,' Wilts, gent. QUEEN'S COLL., matric. 15 June, 1820, aged 16; B.A. 1824, M.A. 1837, perp. curate Burcombe 1829-45, rector of Little Langford, Wilts, 1845-62, vicar of Hatherleigh, Devon, 1862, until his death 18 Feb., 1878.

Phelps, John, 2s. Robert, of Carew, co. Pembroke, gent. JESUS COLL., matric. 20 May, 1825, aged 18; scholar 1829-32, B.A. 1829, M.A. 1831, vicar of South Benfleet 1837-45, of Carew 1845-77, and of Rhydberth 1858-77, died 6 June, 1880.

Phelps, John, 1s. John, of Wilton, Wilts, cler. ALL SOULS' COLL., matric. 17 Dec., 1852, aged 19; bible clerk 1852-7, B.A. 1857, M.A. 1859, vicar of Houghton, Cumberland 1864.

Phelps, John Blagden, 3s. James, of Brimpsfield, co. Gloucester, cler. ORIEL COLL., matric. 30 May, 1833, aged 18; B.A. 1838.

Phelps, John Delafield, s. John Delafield, of Dursley, co. Gloucester, arm. ORIEL COLL., matric. 11 Dec., 1781, aged 17; B.A. 1785, bar.-at-law, Lincoln's Inn, 1789, an exchequer bill loan commissioner, died 1842.

Phelps, John Freeman, o.s. John, of Staynton, co. Pembroke, arm. JESUS COLL., matric. 14 Dec., 1825, aged 17.

Phelps, Rev. Lancelot Ridley, 3s. Thomas Prankerd, of Ridley, near Sevenoaks, Kent, cler. ORIEL COLL., matric. 22 Oct., 1872, aged 18; scholar 1872-7, B.A. 1877, fellow 1877, M.A. 1879, junior treasurer 1880, lecturer 1882, classical lecturer Pembroke College 1880-2, and St. Mary Hall 1880-5, vice-principal 1885, lecturer in political economy, Oriel College, 1882-5. [5]

Phelps, Philip Ashby, 5s. John, of Wilton, Wilts, cler. QUEEN'S COLL., matric. 1 Feb., 1859, aged 18; B.A. 1863, M.A. 1865, curate of Emanuel Church, Clifton, co. Gloucester, 1869-85, vicar of St. John's, Bristol, 1885, brother of Arthur W. and Robert.

Phelps, Richard, s. George, of Eye, co. Hereford, cler. TRINITY COLL., matric. 20 Oct., 1739, aged 19; B.A. from NEW COLL. 1744, M.A. 1748.

Phelps, Rev. Robert, 4s. John, of Wilton, Wilts, cler. ALL SOULS' COLL., matric. 4 April, 1857, aged 19; bible clerk 1857-61, B.A. 1861, M.A. 1863, died 10 June, 1878, brother of Arthur W. and Philip A.

Phelps, Thomas, s. George, of Ludchurch, co. Pembroke, pleb. PEMBROKE COLL., matric. 18 March, 1760, aged 19; B.A. 1764.

Phelps, Thomas, s. John, of Lougher, co. Glamorgan, pleb. ST. ALBAN HALL, matric. 28 May, 1789, aged 19; B.A. from JESUS COLL. 1793. [10]

Phelps, Thomas, s. John, of Berwick St. John, Wilts, arm. JESUS COLL., matric. 2 June, 1802, aged 19; B.A. 1806, M.A. 1809.

Phelps, Thomas, 1s. Thomas, of Alton, Dorset, gent. MAGDALEN HALL, matric. 3 Nov., 1857, aged 24; B.A. 1861, M.A. 1864, curate of Froxfield, Wilts, 1865-70, rector 1870-80.

Phelps, Thomas Prankerd, s. Thomas, of Shepton Mallet, Somerset, cler. HERTFORD COLL., matric. 4 May, 1799, aged 17; B.A. 1803, M.A. 1806, vicar of Tarrington, co. Hereford, 1832, until his death 28 April, 1854.

Phelps, Thomas Prankerd, 2s. Thomas Prankerd, of Thame, Oxon, cler. WORCESTER COLL., matric. 4 Nov., 1834, aged 20; B.A. 1838, rector of Ridley, Kent, 1840, hon. canon Rochester 1882-5.

Phelps, Thomas Spencer, s. William, of East Pennard, Somerset, gent. BALLIOL COLL., matric. 15 May, 1793, aged 18, B.A. 1797; M.A. from EMMANUEL COLL., Cambridge, 1836, rector of Maperton 1820, and of Weston Bampfyld, Somerset, 1836, until his death 6 Dec., 1856. [15]

Phelps, William, s. Samuel, of Bridgewater, Somerset, gent. TRINITY COLL., matric. 10 Dec., 1766, aged 18.

Phelps, William, s. John, of Flax Bourton, Somerset, cler. BALLIOL COLL., matric. 18 Nov., 1793, aged 17; B.A. from ST. ALBAN HALL 1797 (? F.S.A., vicar of Meare and Bicknoller, Somerset, 1824, and rector of Oxcombe, co. Lincoln, at his death 17 Aug., 1856).

Phelps, William Edward, 3s. John, of Wilton, Wilts, cler. MAGDALEN HALL, matric. 30 Oct., 1856, aged 20.

Phelps, William John, 2s. James, of Brimsfield, co. Gloucester, cler. ORIEL COLL., matric. 20 May, 1831, aged 17; B.A. 1835, M.A. 1838, of Chestal, Dursley, co. Gloucester, J.P., high sheriff 1860, bar.-at-law, Lincoln's Inn, 1839. See Foster's *Men at the Bar.*

Phelps, William (Whitmarsh), s. John, of Wilton, Wilts, gent. CORPUS CHRISTI COLL., matric. 20 Oct., 1815, aged 18; scholar 1815-22, B.A. 1819, M.A. 1822, fellow 1822-4, assistant-master Harrow, perp. curate Trinity, Reading, 1845-63, archdeacon and canon of Carlisle 1863, until his death 22 June, 1867. [20]

Phelps, William Whitmarsh, 1s. William Whitmarsh, of Chicklade, Wilts, cler. QUEEN'S COLL., matric. 4 June, 1845, aged 18; B.A. 1849, M.A. 1852, chaplain India.

Pheysey, Percy Alfred, 1s. Richard, of Sefton, Lancashire, gent. WADHAM COLL., matric. 16 Oct., 1886, aged 18.

Philbedge, Evan, s. John, of St. Mary's, Brecon (town), gent. WADHAM COLL., matric. 25 June, 1779, aged 16; B.A. 1783, M.A. 1787.

Philby, James Bridgen, 1s. Henry Adams, of Chigwell, Essex, arm. LINCOLN COLL., matric. 27 Jan., 1868, aged 19; S.C.L. & B.A. 1871, bar.-at-law, Lincoln's Inn, 1873, has held various curacies since 1879. See Foster's *Men at the Bar* & *Rugby School Reg.*

Philcox, Charles, 1s. James, of Preston, near Brighton, arm. HERTFORD COLL., matric. 22 Oct., 1886, aged 18. [25]

Philcox, Henry Edward, 2s. Henry Thomas Blair, of Brighton, Sussex, gent. EXETER COLL., matric. 12 June, 1867, aged 17; B.A. from MAGDALEN HALL 1874, M.A. (HERTFORD COLL.) 1877.

Philip, Alexander John Wilson, o.s. Wilson, of Worcester (city), arm. TRINITY COLL., matric. 13 April, 1836, aged 18; B.A. 1848.

Philipson, Hylton, 3s. Hilton, of Tynemouth, Northumberland, arm. NEW COLL., matric. 16 Oct., 1885, aged 19.

Philipson, Ralph Hilton, 1s. Hilton, of Tynemouth, Northumberland, arm. NEW COLL., matric. 15 Oct., 1881, aged 20; in the University XI. 1887. See *Eton School Lists.*

Phillimore, Arthur, 2s. George, of Willen, Bucks, cler. ORIEL COLL., matric. 25 Oct., 1866, aged 18; B.A. 1871, M.A. 1876, held various curacies 1873-83, rector of Castle Bromwich 1883-7, and of Enville 1887. See Foster's *Baronetage.* [30]

Phillimore, Egerton Grenville Bagot, o.s. John George, of London, arm. CHRIST CHURCH, matric. 28 May, 1874, aged 17; a junior student 1874-8, B.A. 1879, M.A. 1883, of Shiplake House, Oxon, a student of the Middle Temple 1877.

Phillimore, George, 1s. William, of St. Pancras, London, arm. CHRIST CHURCH, matric. 16 May, 1825, aged 17; student 1825-33, B.A. 1829, M.A. 1831, vicar of Willen 1832-51, and rector of Radnage, Bucks, 1851-86, father of Arthur. See *Alumni West.*, 495.

Phillimore, George Greville, 2s. Augustus, of Lostwithiel, Cornwall, arm. CHRIST CHURCH, matric. 15 Oct., 1886, aged 18; scholar 1886.

Phillimore, Greville, 4s. Joseph, of St. Martin's, Westminster, arm., D.C.L. CHRIST CHURCH, matric. 30 May, 1838, aged 17; student 1838-52, B.A. 1842, M.A. 1844, vicar of Down Ampney, co. Gloucester, 1851-67, and of Henley-on-Thames 1867, until his death 21 Jan., 1884. See Foster's *Baronetage.*

Phillimore, John Boucher, 1s. John, of The Ray, near Maidenhead, Berks, equitis. ST. MARY HALL, matric. 11 Dec., 1850, aged 19; B.A. 1855, M.A. 1856, died 5 May, 1865. [35]

Phillimore, John George, 1s. Joseph, of Gower Street, London, doctor. CHRIST CHURCH, matric. 28 May, 1824, aged 16; student 1824-9, B.A. 1828, M.A. 1831, of Shiplake House, Oxon, jurist and historian, bar.-at-law, Lincoln's Inn, 1832, Q.C. and bencher 1851, M.P. Leominster 1852-7, clerk in Board of Control 1827-32, died 27 April, 1865. See Foster's *Baronetage* & *Alumni West.*, 494.

Phillimore, Joseph, s. Robert, of Kensington, Middlesex, arm. CHRIST CHURCH, matric. 18 Feb., 1768, aged 17; a student of Lincoln's Inn 1764, vicar of Orton-on-the-Hill, co. Leicester, 1804, until his death 29 July, 1831. See Foster's *Baronetage* & *Alumni West.*, 439.

Phillimore, Joseph, s. Joseph, of Pancras, London, cler. CHRIST CHURCH, matric. 30 May, 1793, aged 17; B.A. 1797, B.C.L. 1800, D.C.L. 1804, regius professor civil law 1809-55, of Shiplake House, Oxon, an advocate Doctors' Commons 1804, king's advocate 1834, judge of the Cinque Ports 1809, chancellor of the diocese of Oxford, M.P. St. Mawes 1817-26, Yarmouth, Isle of Wight, 1826-30, a commissioner for Indian affairs 1822-8, created LL.D. Cambridge 1834, chancellor of the diocese of Oxford 1809, of Worcester 1834, and of Bristol 1842, commissary of St. Paul's 1834, judge of the Consistory Court at Gloucester 1846, F.R.S., died 24 Feb., 1855. See *Alumni West.*, 437.

Phillimore, Raymond Hawkeswood, 3s. William Phillimore, of Nottingham, arm. NON-COLL., matric. 3 June, 1876, aged 19.

Phillimore, Reginald Phillimore, 2s. William Phillimore, of Nottingham, arm. NON-COLL., matric. 3 June, 1876, aged 21; B.A. from QUEEN'S COLL. 1880. **[5]**

Phillimore, Richard, 6s. Joseph, of Shiplake, Oxon, D.C.L. (subs. doctor). CHRIST CHURCH, matric. 3 June, 1840, aged 16; student 1840, until drowned at Sandford Lasher 25 June, 1843, while attempting to rescue his friend William Gaisford (see p. 504). See *Alumni West.*, 516.

Phillimore, Robert, s. Joseph, of Pancras, Middlesex, cler. CHRIST CHURCH, matric. 29 May, 1802, aged 18; B.A. 1806, M.A. 1808, student 1802-15, usher of Westminster School 1805-7, a student of Lincoln's Inn 1808, perp. curate Hawkhurst 1812-4, vicar of Shipton-under-Wychwood 1814, and of Slapton, Bucks, 1815, until his death 25 Sep., 1852. See *Alumni West.*, 457.

Phillimore, (Sir) Robert Joseph (Bart.), 2s. Joseph, of St. Margaret's, Westminster, doctor. CHRIST CHURCH, matric. 16 May, 1828, aged 17; student 1828-39, B.A. 1832, B.C.L. 1835, D.C.L. 1838, bar.-at-law, Middle Temple, 1841, Q.C. 1858, bencher 1858, judge of Cinque Ports 1855-75, judge of High Court of Admiralty, and judge of Court of Arches 1867-75, judge advocate-general 1871-3, a justice High Court of Justice 1875-83, M.P. Tavistock 1853-7, knighted 17 Sep., 1862, P.C. 1867, created a baronet 21 Dec., 1881, died 4 Feb., 1885. See Foster's *Men at the Bar* & *Alumni West.*, 501.

Phillimore, (Sir) Walter George Francis (Bart.), 1s. Robert Joseph, of St. George's, Hanover Square, London, equitis. CHRIST CHURCH, matric. 27 May, 1863, aged 17, a junior student 1863-7, B.A. 1867; fellow ALL SOULS' COLL. 1867-71, B.C.L. 1870, D.C.L. 1875, 2nd baronet, bar.-at-law, Middle Temple, 1868, Q.C. 1883, chancellor of the diocese of Lincoln. See Foster's *Baronetage*.

Phillimore, William, s. Robert, of Kensington, Middlesex, arm. CHRIST CHURCH, matric. 21 Oct., 1767, aged 18; of Kendalls, Herts, entered Lincoln's Inn 1764, died 17 Oct., 1818. See Foster's *Baronetage* & *Alumni West.*, 439. **[10]**

Phillimore, William Phillimore Watts, 1s. William, of Nottingham, B.Med. QUEEN'S COLL., matric. 31 May, 1873, aged 19; B.A. 1876, B.C.L. & M.A. 1880.

Phillimore, William Robert, s. William, of St. George's, Middlesex, arm. ORIEL COLL., matric. 25 Jan., 1787, aged 18; of Kendalls, Herts, entered Lincoln's Inn 1786, died 2 May, 1829. See Foster's *Baronetage* & *Alumni West.*, 439.

Philips, Alexander, s. William, of Worcester (city), cler. MAGDALEN HALL, matric. 20 March, 1733-4, aged 18; clerk MAGDALEN COLL. 1736-8, B.A. 1737. See *Bloxam*, ii. 93.

Phillipps, Ambrose, s. William, of St. Andrew's, Holborn, Middlesex, arm. MAGDALEN COLL., matric. 18 July, 1724, aged 16 (? M.P. Leicestershire 1734, until his death 6 Nov., 1737).

Phillipps, Charles s. Thomas, of Llanarthy, co. Carmarthen, arm. JESUS COLL., matric. 4 July, 1720, aged 17. **[15]**

Phillips, Charles, s. Charles, of Walthamstow, Essex, gent. BRASENOSE COLL., matric. 14 March, 1744-5, aged 16; B.A. from ST. ALBAN HALL 20 Feb., 1748-9, vicar of Terling, Essex, died at Langford parsonage 18 Sep., 1801.

Phillips, Charles, s. Herbert, of St. Maughan's, co. Monmouth, gent. ORIEL COLL., matric. 29 April, 1788, aged 17; B.A. 1792, M.A. 1794 (? died vicar of Llangattock Vibonafel, and rector of Ragland, co. Monmouth, in 1818).

Philipps, Charles, s. John Lewis, of Llangynnor, co. Carmarthen, cler. JESUS COLL., matric. 22 April, 1801, aged 18; B.A. 1805, M.A. 1807, B.D. 1815, fellow until 1817, perp. curate Llanginning, co. Carmarthen, 1808, vicar of Pembroke 1809, and of St. Twinnell's, co. Pembroke, 1837, treasurer and canon of St. David's, died 18 Oct., 1853.

Phillipps, Charles, s. John, of Exton House, co. Hereford, cler. ORIEL COLL., matric. 24 Nov., 1815, aged 18.

Phillips, Charles, 3s. Henry, of Rugby, gent. EXETER COLL., matric. 16 Oct., 1875, aged 19; scholar 1875-80, B.A. 1879, M.A. 1885, a solicitor in Manchester. See *Boase*, 167; & *Rugby School Reg.*

Phillips, Charles Bannerman, 2s. Charles Palmer, of London, gent. NEW COLL., matric. 18 Oct., 1867, aged 18; scholar 1867-72, B.A. 1872, M.A. 1874. **[21]**

Phillips, Charles Edward, 2s. John, of Westbury, Salop, arm. CHRIST CHURCH, matric. 17 Oct., 1860, aged 19; B.A. 1864, died at Plumstead 6 April, 1867.

Phillips, Charles James, 1s. Charles John, of London, arm. BRASENOSE COLL., matric. 1 June, 1871, aged 18; B.A. 1874, M.A. 1879.

Phillips, Charles Maud, 2s. William Williams, of Pontypool, Monmouth, gent. QUEEN'S COLL., matric. 17 Oct., 1864, aged 18.

Phillips, Charles Palmer, 2s. William Edward, of Prince of Wales Island, arm. CHRIST CHURCH, matric. 15 May, 1839, aged 17; B.A. 1843, M.A. 1845, of Aldenham, Herts, bar.-at-law, Lincoln's Inn, 1846, a commissioner in lunacy since 1872. See Foster's *Men at the Bar* & *Eton School Lists*. **[25]**

Phillips, Charles Walter, 2s. Thomas, of Culham, Oxon, arm. EXETER COLL., matric. 21 April, 1874, aged 19.

Phillips, Daniel, s. Daniel, of Manchester, Lancashire, gent. BRASENOSE COLL., matric. 13 May, 1807, aged 18; B.A. 1811, M.A 1813. See *Manchester School Reg.*, ii. 208.

Philips, David, s. David, of Llandowroe, co. Carmarthen, pleb. NEW INN HALL, matric. 14 May, 1719, aged 18.

Phillips, Edward, s. Edward, of Llanvareth, co. Radnor, pleb. JESUS COLL., matric. 8 Nov., 1734, aged 18; B.A. 1738. **[29]**

Phillips, Edward, s. Edward, of Monmouth (town), gent. PEMBROKE COLL., matric. 27 March, 1745, aged 19; B.A. 1748, M.A. 1751, died vicar of West Tarring, and rector of Patching, Sussex, in 1803.

Philipps, Edward, s. Thomas, of Lampeter, co. Pembroke, gent. PEMBROKE COLL., matric. 14 Dec., 1754, aged 17; B.A. 1758.

Philipps, Edward, s. Edward, of London, gent. MAGDALEN HALL, matric. 14 Feb., 1786, aged 16; B.A. 1791, M.A. 1792 (as PHILLIPS).

Phillips, Edward, s. Elias, of Clifton, co. Gloucester, pleb. ST. EDMUND HALL, matric. 10 Oct., 1800, aged 23.

Philips, Edward, 2s. Robert, of Cheadle, co. Stafford, arm. ST. JOHN'S COLL., matric. 30 June, 1856, aged 23; B.A. & M.A. 1863, rector of Checkley with Hollington, Stafford, 1878.

Phillips, Edward Mowbray, 2s. Paul Winsloe, of Kingston, Canada, arm. ST. MARY HALL, matric. 1 Feb., 1873, aged 19. [5]

Philipps, (Sir) Erasmus (Bart.), s. John, of St. Martin's-in-the-Fields, Middlesex, baronet. PEMBROKE COLL., matric. 4 Aug., 1720, aged 20; of Picton Castle, 5th baronet, M.P. Haverfordwest 1726, until his death 15 Oct., 1743.

Philipps, Evan, 4s. John, of Trefaes, co. Cardigan, gent. JESUS COLL., matric. 28 Jan., 1874, aged 24.

Philipps, Faulkner Cecil Lloyd, 2s. John Philipps-Allen-Lloyd, of Dale, near Milford, Pembroke, arm. TRINITY COLL., matric. 30 May, 1857, aged 17; died in 1863.

Philips, Francis, 1s. Francis Aspinall, of Manchester, Lancashire, arm. CHRIST CHURCH, matric. 15 June, 1848, aged 18; B.A. 1852, M.A. 1857, of Lee Priory, Kent, and of Bank Hall, Lancashire, high sheriff 1871, bar.-at-law, Inner Temple, 1855, brother of George H. 1849. See Foster's *Men at the Bar* & *Eton School Lists.*

Phillips, Francis Angelo Theodore, 3s. George Robert, of London, arm. BALLIOL COLL., matric. 19 Oct., 1878, aged 21; of the Indian Civil Service 1878. [10]

Phillips, Francis Barclay Willmer, 1s. Barclay, of Hove, Sussex, gent. BALLIOL COLL., matric. 18 Oct., 1871, aged 18; exhibitioner 1871-5, B.A. 1875, B.Med. & M.A. 1885.

Phillips, Rev. Francis George Anderson, y.s. John, of Ludlow, Salop, cler. CHRIST CHURCH, matric. 31 May, 1879, aged 19; exhibitioner 1879-80, B.A. 1883, M.A. 1886.

Philips, Francis Maitland, 1s. Henry Lee, of Brighton, Sussex, arm. MERTON COLL., matric. 25 Jan., 1868, aged 19.

Phillips, Francis Roberts, 2s. William Joseph George, of Eling, co. Southampton, cler. TRINITY COLL., matric. 28 May, 1830, aged 18; B.A. 1834, vicar of Eling at his death 28 June, 1862.

Phillips, Frank Henry, 1s. William George, of Oxford, gent. NON-COLL., matric. 24 Oct., 1874, aged 19; B.A. & M.A. from MERTON COLL. 1884. [15]

Philips, Frederick, 1s. Frederick, of Erbistock, Overton, co. Flint, arm. CHRIST CHURCH, matric. 27 May, 1847, aged 18; B.A. 1852.

Philipps, Frederick Lewis Lloyd, 2s. (James Philipps) Lloyd, of Llanrhystid, co. Cardigan, arm. BRASENOSE COLL., matric. 6 June, 1844, aged 20; B.A. 1848, M.A. 1859, of Penty Park, co. Pembroke, J.P., etc.

Phillips, Frederick Parr, o.s. William, of St. Margaret's, Westminster, arm. CHRIST CHURCH, matric. 20 Oct., 1836, aged 17; B.A. 1840, M.A. 1844, rector (and patron) of Stoke d'Abernon, Surrey, 1862.

Phillips, George, s. Owen, of Spitle, co. Pembroke, gent. JESUS COLL., matric. 9 April, 1717, aged 17; B.A. 1720, M.A. 1723.

Phillips, George, s. George, of Haverfordwest, co. Pembroke, cler. HERTFORD COLL., matric. 27 Feb., 1752, aged 16; B.A. from JESUS COLL. 1755, M.A. 1758, B.Med. 1761, D.Med. 1765. [20]

Philips, George, s. Griffith, of Greenwich, Kent, arm. CHRIST CHURCH, matric. 26 Feb., 1754, aged 18.

Phillips, George, s. John, of St. Michael's, Barbados, gent. QUEEN'S COLL., matric. 28 Feb., 1772, aged 19.

Phillips, George, s. George, of St. Thomas's, Haverfordwest, co. Pembroke, doctor. JESUS COLL., matric. 5 June, 1794, aged 18; B.A. 1798 (?rector of New Moat, co. Pembroke, 1815, until his death in 1839).

Phillips, George, 3s. Francis, of Dunwich, Suffolk, gent. MAGDALEN HALL, matric. 19 June, 1824, aged 20.

Philips, George, 2s. John, of Minera, co. Denbigh, gent. QUEEN'S COLL., matric. 13 May, 1826, aged 18; B.A. 1830. [25]

Philipps, George, 3s. George, of Narberth, co. Pembroke, arm. JESUS COLL., matric. 31 Oct., 1844, aged 18; B.A. from NEW INN HALL 1850, M.A. 1851, held various curacies 1850-85.

Philips, George Henry, 2s. Francis Aspinall, of Ardwick, Lancashire, arm. CHRIST CHURCH, matric. 17 Oct., 1849, aged 18; B.A. 1853, M.A. 1857, of Abbey-cwm-Hir, co. Radnor, high sheriff 1860, brother of Francis 1848. See Foster's *Lancashire Collection* & *Eton School Lists.*

Phillips, George Newnham, 3s. William Joseph George, of Eling, co. Southampton, cler. MERTON COLL., matric. 9 June, 1832, aged 18; B.A. 1836, M.A. 1845, vicar of Eling, Hants, 1863, until his death 1 Sep., 1870.

Phillips, George Waller, 3s. George Allcroft, of Broughton, Lancashire, arm. BRASENOSE COLL., matric. 22 Jan., 1880, aged 18.

Philips, George Washington (Edward), s. Charles, of South Carolina, North America, gent. PEMBROKE COLL., matric. 22 Nov., 1811, aged 27; died vicar of Wendy, co. Cambridge, 24 Oct., 1865. [30]

Philips, Gilbert Henderson, 1s. John, of Childwall, Lancashire, arm. BRASENOSE COLL., matric. 9 June, 1841, aged 18; B.A. 1845, M.A. 1848, perp. curate Dringhouse, Yorks, 1848-67, vicar of Brodsworth, Yorks, 1867-83, canon of York 1878, rector of Bolton Percy, Yorks, 1883, until his death 3 Aug., 1885. See Foster's *Baronetage.*

Philipps, Griffith, 2s. — P., of Abergwilly, co. Carmarthen, arm. JESUS COLL., matric. 15 Dec., 1800, aged 18; B.A. 1806, M.A. 1807.

Philipps, Henry, s. Rich., of St. Clere, co. Carmarthen, pleb. JESUS COLL., matric. 30 March, 1726, aged 17; B.A. 1729.

Phillips, Henry, s. Thomas, of St. Peter's, Carmarthen (town), pleb. JESUS COLL., matric. 27 May, 1773, aged 19; B.A. 1777.

Philipps, Rev. Henry, s. William Hollingworth, of York (city), arm. QUEEN'S COLL., matric. 27 June, 1816, aged 19; B.A. 1821, M.A. 1835, brother of Sir James Evans Philipps, 11th baronet. See Foster's *Baronetage.* [35]

Phillips, Henry Charles Burnell, 2s. Edward James, of Monmouth, arm. NON-COLL., matric. 25 Jan., 1879, aged 19.

Phillips, Henry Frederick, 1s. William Spencer, of Cheltenham, co. Gloucester, cler. UNIVERSITY COLL., matric. 20 March, 1851, aged 18; B.A. 185[illegible], M.A. 1858, vicar of St. Peter, Rochester, 1860-8[illegible], hon. canon of Rochester 1878. See *Rugby School Reg.*, 278.

Phillips, Henry John, 1s. John, of Bishop's Castle, Salop, gent. WORCESTER COLL., matric. 17 Oct., 1863, aged 17; vicar of St. James's, Dudley 1873-[illegible] and of Kingsbury Episcopi since 1879.

Philipps, Henry March-, 1s. Charles Speucer, of London, arm. CHRIST CHURCH, matric. 24 Jan., 1873, aged 18.

Phillips, Herbert, s. Thomas, of Hilston, co. Monmouth, cler. WADHAM COLL., matric. 3 April, 1754, aged 18. [40]

Phillips, Herbert Edward, 2s. Charles John, of Mortlake, Surrey, arm. BRASENOSE COLL., matric. 1 Oct., 1879, aged 18; B.A. 1882, M.A. 1886.

Phillips, Rev. Howell Jones, 1s. Stephen, of St. Clement Danes, London, arm. WORCESTER COLL., matric. 23 May, 1828, aged 25; B.A. 1833, M.A. 1836, died at Carlton, Beds, 13 Sep., 1852.

Phillipps, Hugh March-, 2s. Charles Spencer, of Cove, Devon, arm. ST. ALBAN HALL, matric. 29 April, 1878, aged 18.

Phillips, Hugh Moreton, s. Revell, of Shifnal, co. Stafford, arm. CHRIST CHURCH, matric. 13 Oct., 1814, aged 18, servitor 1814-6; B.A. from WORCESTER COLL. 1818, M.A. 1822, perp. curate Dawley 1823-31, and of Stirchley, Salop, 1827, until his death 12 Oct., 1877.

Phillipps, James, s. James, of Holmer, co. Hereford, gent. TRINITY COLL., matric. 7 April, 1720, aged 17; B.A. from MAGDALEN HALL 16 March, 1723-4 (as PHILLIPS).

Phillips, James, s. William, of Llysyvrane, co. Pembroke, pleb. JESUS COLL., matric. 6 March, 1720-1, aged 20. [5]

Philips, James, s. John, of Lampeter, co. Pembroke, gent. JESUS COLL., matric. 26 June, 1723, aged 18 (? B.A. 1727, M.A. 17 Feb., 1729-30, B. & D.D. 1743 (as PHILIPPS), and of Colby, co. Pembroke, died in 1783, aged 80).

Philipps, James, s. James, of Carmarthen (town), arm. JESUS COLL., matric. 3 April, 1728, aged 18.

Philips, James, s. John, of Glascomb, co. Radnor, pleb. JESUS COLL., matric. 28 Nov., 1740, aged 19; B.A. 1744.

Phillips, James, 'musician;' privilegiatus 12 March, 1746-7.

Phillips, James, s. James, of London, arm. UNIVERSITY COLL., matric. 15 July, 1790, aged 17; B.A. 1794, M.A. 1797, lecturer of Wyrardisbury, Berks, died at Datchet 11 June, 1825. [10]

Phillipps, James, s. James, of Byngwyn, co. Hereford, arm. TRINITY COLL., matric. 6 March, 1817, aged 18.

Philipps, James, 1s. James, of Moylgrove, co. Pembroke, gent. JESUS COLL., matric. 4 May, 1829, aged 19; B.A. 1833.

Philipps, (Sir) James Erasmus (Bart.), o.s. James Evans, of Boyton, Wilts, cler. CHRIST CHURCH, matric. 19 Oct., 1842, aged 17; B.A. 1847, M.A. 1853, 12th baronet, vicar of Warminster, Wilts, 1859, preb. of Salisbury 1870. See Foster's *Baronetage.*

Philipps, (Sir) James Evans (Bart.), s. William Hollingworth, of Lyme Regis, Norfolk, arm. QUEEN'S COLL., matric. 8 July, 1813, aged 19; B.A. 1817, M.A. 1820, 11th baronet, vicar of Osmington, Dorset, 1832, until his death 13 Feb., 1873. See Foster's *Baronetage.*

Philipps, James Henry Alexander, of TRINITY COLL., Cambridge (B.A. 1838, M.A. 1841); adm. 'comitatis causa' 10 June, 1863 (son of Rev. Henry Gwyther, M.A., see page 580), of Picton Castle, co. Pembroke, assumed the surname of PHILIPPS in lieu of GWYTHER, vicar of Madeley, Salop, 1841-59, and of St. Mary, Haverfordwest, 1859, until his death 3 Dec., 1875. See Foster's *Baronetage.* [15]

Phillips, Jenkin, s. William, of Cardiff, co. Glamorgan, pleb. JESUS COLL., matric. 28 March, 1721, aged 18.

Philipps, Jeremiah, s. Thomas, of Lamboidy, co. Carnarvon, cler. LINCOLN COLL., matric. 26 Feb., 1718-9, aged 17.

Phillipps, John, s. Sam., of Poughill, Cornwall, gent. EXETER COLL., matric. 10 March, 1717-8, aged 18.

Philipps, (Sir) John (Bart.), s. John, of Slebech, co. Pembroke, baronet. PEMBROKE COLL., matric. 4 Aug., 1720, aged 19; created D.C.L. 12 April, 1749, 6th baronet, of Picton Castle, co. Pembroke, M.P. Carmarthen 1741-7, Petersfield 1754-61, Pembrokeshire 1761, until his death 23 June, 1764. See Foster's *Baronetage.*

Philipps, John, s. Edward, of Ford, co. Pembroke arm. JESUS COLL., matric. 30 Oct., 1722, aged 17.

Phillipps, John, s. Grismond, of Llandilo-faur, co Carmarthen, arm. CHRIST CHURCH, matric. 1 April, 1728, aged 17; his brother Griffith bar.-at-law Lincoln's Inn, 1741, of the family of Cwmgwilly, co. Carmarthen. [21]

Phillips, John, s. John, of Chedzoy, Somerset, pleb. UNIVERSITY COLL., matric. 19 March, 1729-30, aged 18; B.A. 1733.

Philipps, John, s. John, of Langenning, co. Carmarthen, gent. JESUS COLL., matric. 12 May, 1730, aged 18.

Philips, John, s. Robert, of Sommerton, Somerset, pleb. EXETER COLL., matric. 6 July, 1731, aged 19; B.A. 1735.

Phillips, John, s. Thomas, of St. David's, co. Pembroke, pleb. CHRIST CHURCH, matric. 7 Nov., 1732, aged 20; B.A. 1736, M.A. 1740 (as PHILIPPS). [25]

Philipps, John, s. Thomas, of Laugharne, co. Carmarthen, cler. JESUS COLL., matric. 13 Dec., 1733, aged 17; B.A. 1737, M.A. 1740, B. & D.D. 1765.

Phillipps, John, s. John, of Brecknock (town), gent. CHRIST CHURCH, matric. 10 March, 1742-3, aged 18.

Philipps, John, s. Owen, of Walwyn's Castle, co. Pembroke, cler. JESUS COLL., matric. 9 May, 1747, aged 17; B.A. 4 Feb., 1750-1, M.A. 1754 (? D.D. rector of Burton, co. Pembroke, died 13 Sep., 1830, father of Owen 1786). See Foster's *Baronetage,* SCOURFIELD.

Phillips, John, s. Gidney, of Bedford (town), gent. BALLIOL COLL., matric. 19 March, 1755, aged 18; B.A. from NEW COLL. 1758; M.A. from WORCESTER COLL. 1761.

Philipps, John, s. John, of Carmarthen (town), cler. CHRIST CHURCH, matric. 24 May, 1758, aged 18; B.A. 1762, M.A. 1765, preb. of St. David 1768, and of Brecknock 1787. See *Alumni West.*, 369. [30]

Phillipps, John, s. Thomas, of Eaton, co. Hereford, arm. BALLIOL COLL., matric. 4 June, 1764, aged 16; B.A. 1768, M.A. 1770.

Phillips, John, s. John, of St. Mary's, Haverfordwest, co. Pembroke, cler. JESUS COLL., matric. 19 March, 1771, aged 17; B.A. 1775, M.A. 1778.

Phillips, John, s. John, of Droitwich, co. Worcester, gent. QUEEN'S COLL., matric. 18 May, 1776, aged 17; B.A. from MERTON COLL. 1780, of Edstone, co. Warwick, high sheriff co. Worcester 1803, bar.-at-law, Inner Temple, 1792, died 30 Jan., 1836, brother of Richard 1785.

Phillipps, John, s. Joseph, of Mambury, Devon, gent. EXETER COLL., matric. 2 Dec., 1779, aged 27; fellow 1782-91, B.A. & M.A. 1786. See *Coll. Reg.*, 113.

Philipps, John, s. John, of London, gent. ST. MARY HALL, matric. 14 Oct., 1794, aged 18. [35]

Phillipps, John, s. John, of Hereford (city), cler. CHRIST CHURCH, matric. 27 Oct., 1814, aged 19.

Phillips, John, created D.C.L. 23 June, 1819, of Culham, Oxon, grandfather of John Shawe 1861.

Phillips, John, o.s. George, of Blockley, co. Worcester, gent. PEMBROKE COLL., matric. 26 March, 1829, aged 16; scholar 1829-37, B.A. 1833, M.A. 1836, curate of Brighouse, Yorks, died 21 Dec., 1851.

Phillips, John, 1s. John, of Marden, Wilts, gent. MAGDALEN COLL., matric. 25 Oct., 1853, aged 52; M.A. by decree 27 Oct., 1853, created D.C.L. 13 June, 1866, hon. fellow 1868-74, keeper of the Yorkshire Philosophical Society's Museum 1827, F.G.S. 1828, assistant-secretary British Association 1832, F.R.S. 1834, professor of geology King's College, London, and in Dublin University 1844, president Geological Society 1859-60, LL.D. Cambridge 1866, and Dublin 2 Sep. 1857, deputy-reader in geology at Oxford 1853-7, president British Association 1868, keeper of the Ashmolean Museum 1854-70, professor of geology and keeper of the University Museum 1857, until his death 24 April, 1874.

Phillips, Rev. John, 1s. John, of Aberayron, co. Cardigan, gent. NON-COLL., matric. 11 Oct., 1879, aged 20; B.A. from ST. JOHN'S COLL. 1882, M.A. 1887.

Phillips, John Bartholomew, s. John Bartholomew, of St. James's, Clerkenwell, London, pleb. ALL SOULS' COLL., matric. 22 Nov., 1832, aged 17; bible clerk 1832-6, B.A. 1836, M.A. 1839, rector of New-Church-in-Rossendale, Lancashire, 1850.

Phillips, John George, s. Griffith, of London, arm. BRASENOSE COLL., matric. 16 Dec., 1779, aged 18.

Philipps, John Henry. ORIEL COLL., 1825. See SCOURFIELD.

Philipps, John Lloyd, s. Levi, of Bombay, East Indies, arm. BRASENOSE COLL., matric. 8 April, 1818, aged 16; B.A. 1822, M.A. 1824. **[5]**

Phillips, John Shawe, 1s. John Shawe, of Culham, Oxon, arm. CHRIST CHURCH, matric. 23 May, 1861, aged 18; of Culham aforesaid.

Phillips, John Spencer, 1s. John Robert, of Writtle, Essex, arm. EXETER COLL., matric. 7 Feb., 1833, aged 18; B.A. 1837, of Riffham, Essex, bar.-at-law, Inner Temple, 1842. See Foster's *Men at the Bar.*

Philipps, John Wynford, 1s. James Erasmus, of Warminster, Wilts, cler. (after a baronet). KEBLE COLL., matric. 14 Oct., 1878, aged 18; B.A. 1882, M.A. 1885, bar.-at-law, Middle Temple, 1886, M.P. Mid Lanark, April, 1888. See Foster's *Baronetage.*

Phillips, Lewis Guy, 1s. Benjamin Guy, of London, arm. CHRIST CHURCH, matric. 23 May, 1850, aged 18; B.A. 1855, captain grenadier guards. See *Eton School Lists.*

Philips, Luke, s. James, of Llannynis, co. Brecon, gent. ST. EDMUND HALL, matric. 2 May, 1792, aged 40. **[10]**

Phillips, Martin Luther, o.s. David, of Llangynwid, near Bridgend, gent. NON-COLL., matric. 22 Jan., 1881, aged 25; B.A. from QUEEN'S COLL. 1884, M.A. 1887.

Philipps, Michael, s. John, of Newcastle, co. Carmarthen, gent. CHRIST CHURCH, matric. 11 July, 1754, aged 30.

Phillips, Moreton Hassall, 1s. Hugh Moreton, of Stirchley, Salop, cler. CHRIST CHURCH, matric. 19 Oct., 1843, aged 18.

Phillips, Nathaniel, s. Nathaniel, of Slebech, co. Pembroke, arm. CHRIST CHURCH, matric. 16 Oct., 1817, aged 19. See *Eton School Lists.*

Phillipps, Nicholas, s. William, of Rosemallen, Cornwall, arm. TRINITY COLL., matric. 5 Nov., 1777, aged 17. **[15]**

Phillips, Owen, s. Owen, of St. Peter's, Hereford (city), pleb. BALLIOL COLL., matric. 10 Oct., 1739, aged 18; B.A. 1743.

Philipps, Owen, s. John, of Burton, co. Pembroke, doctor. JESUS COLL., matric. 1 June, 1786, aged 14; B.A. 1790, M.A. 1792, of Williamston, co. Pembroke, bar.-at-law, Lincoln's Inn, 1779, died 11 Sep., 1830, father of Sir John Henry Scourfield, baronet.

Phillips, Rev. Percy Roberts, 2s. William George, of Northampton, gent. ST. ALBAN HALL, matric. 3 May, 1879, aged 20; B.A. from MERTON COLL. 1884, M.A. 1886.

Phillips, Philip, 'musician;' privilegiatus 3 Feb., 1741-2.

Philipps, Philip Lovell, o.s. John Randal, of Isle of Barbados, West Indies, arm. EXETER COLL., matric. 18 Feb., 1823, aged 17; B.A. 1826, M.A. 1829, B.Med. 1830, D.Med. 1833. **[20]**

Phillips, Philip Lovell, 1s. John Randall, of Isle of Barbados, gent. WORCESTER COLL., matric. 15 Oct., 1864, aged 19; B.A. 1869, M.A. 1880, bar.-at-law, Inner Temple, 1869, has held various curacies and livings in Barbados since 1877.

Phillips, Philip, s. William, of Lantrissant, co. Glamorgan, pleb. EXETER COLL., matric. 10 July, 1725, aged 18.

Phillipps, Richard, s. Richard, of Pemboyle, co. Carmarthen, gent. CHRIST CHURCH, matric. 31 March, 1720, aged 18.

Phillips, Richard, 'groome of Merton College;' privilegiatus 17 March, 1723-4.

Philips, Richard, s. William, of Swansea, co. Glamorgan, pleb. JESUS COLL., matric. 7 March, 1736-7, aged 16; B.A. 19 Feb., 1740-1, M.A. 1743 (as PHILIPPS). **[25]**

Philipps, Richard, s. John, of Picton Castle, co. Pembroke, baronet. PEMBROKE COLL., matric. 3 Feb., 1761, aged 18; Baron Milford, so created 22 July, 1766, M.P. Pembrokeshire 1765-70, and 1786-1812, Plympton 1774-9, Haverfordwest 1784-96, died 28 Nov., 1823.

Phillips, Richard, s. John, of Droitwich, co. Worcester, gent. TRINITY COLL., matric. 26 April, 1785, aged 20; B.A. 1789, M.A. 1792, brother of John 1776.

Phillips, Richard Ballard, s. Humphrey, of Barnstaple, Devon, gent. MAGDALEN HALL, matric 13 Dec., 1814, aged 20; B.A. 1822, M.A. 1823.

Phillips, Robert, s. Robert, of Kinlet, Salop, D.D. BALLIOL COLL., matric. 11 July, 1717, aged 18; B.A. 1721.

Phillips, Robert, 'cook of Wadham College;' 30 June, 1719. **[30]**

Phillips, Robert, s. Robert, of Holywell, Oxford (city), gent. WADHAM COLL., matric. 15 Dec., 1738, aged 16; B.A. 1742, M.A. 1746.

Phillipps, Robert Biddulph, s. Robert, of Hereford (city), arm. TRINITY COLL., matric. 12 June, 1816, aged 17; B.A. 1820, M.A. 1824, bar.-at-law, Middle Temple, 1825.

Philips, Roger, s. Rich., of Beaumaris, Isle of Anglesey, pleb. JESUS COLL., matric. 17 Dec., 1725, aged 18.

Phillips, St. John Knox Rickards-, 1s. Andrew Knox, of St. John's, Newfoundland, gent. WORCESTER COLL., matric. 18 Oct., 1883, aged 20.

Phillips, Samuel John, of PEMBROKE COLL., Cambridge (B.A. 1845, M.A. 1848); adm. 'comitatis causa,' 30 June, 1864, vicar of Tilney, Norfolk, 1878.

Phillips, Sidney, 1s. Sidney James, of London, arm. BRASENOSE COLL., matric. 16 June, 1859, aged 18; B.A. 1863, M.A. 1866, vicar of Castle Hedingham, Essex, 1868-75, and of Monmouth 1875-9, rector of Nuneham Courtney, Oxon, 1879. **[35]**

Phillips, Spencer William, 2s. William Spencer, of Gloucester (city), cler. UNIVERSITY COLL., matric. 9 June, 1852, aged 18; B.A. 1856, M.A. 1859, held various curacies 1857-69, vicar of St. Margaret-next-Rochester 1869-78, vicar of Wateringbury, Kent, 1878. See *Rugby School Reg.*, 286.

Philips, Stephen, s. Steph., of Eltham, Kent, cler. ST. MARY HALL, matric. 20 Nov., 1730, aged 20; B.A. from CHRIST CHURCH 19 June, 1734.

Phillips, Stephen, s. David, of Blanporth, co. Cardigan, pleb. CHRIST CHURCH, matric. 15 July, 1749, aged 22.

Philips, Stephen, 1s. Francis Holmes, of Islington, Middlesex, gent. ST. ALBAN HALL, matric. 3 May, 1864, aged 26; B.A. 1869; M.A. 1871, minor canon, etc., Peterborough, 1876-83, reader and chaplain Gray's Inn, 1884. **[40]**

Phillips, Sydney Archer, 1s. William, of New Hampton, Middlesex, gent. CORPUS CHRISTI COLL., matric. 23 Oct., 1884, aged 19; scholar 1884.

Phillips, Thomas, s. George, of Windsor, Berks, gent. CHRIST CHURCH, matric. 15 Oct., 1715, aged 17; B.A. 1719, M.A. 1722.

Phillipps, Thomas; B.A. from JESUS COLL. 18 June, 1720.

Phillipps, Thomas, s. James, of Huntingtown, co. Hereford, gent. TRINITY COLL., matric. 16 March, 1723-4, aged 17; bar.-at-law, Middle Temple, 1729.

Phillipps, Thomas, s. Thomas, of Bremenda, co. Carmarthen, arm. JESUS COLL., matric. 2 May, 1728, aged 17. **[45]**

Phillips, Thomas, s. William, of ——, co, Northampton, pleb. HART HALL, matric. 29 March, 1740.

Phillips, Thomas, s. Thomas, of Overbury, co. Worcester, cler. PEMBROKE COLL., matric. 18 March, 1748-9, aged 18; B.A. 1752.

Phillipps, Thomas, s. Thomas, of Eaton-Bishop, co. Hereford, arm. BALLIOL COLL., matric. 12 Feb., 1762, aged 16.

Phillips, Thomas, s. John, of Haverfordwest, co. Pembroke, cler. JESUS COLL., matric. 27 May, 1773, aged 17; B.A. from PEMBROKE COLL. 1777, M.A. 1779, proctor 1789.

Phillipps, Thomas, s. Nicholas, of Bodmin, Cornwall, gent. PEMBROKE COLL., matric. 20 May, 1809, aged 18. [5]

Phillipps, Thomas, s. Thomas, of Manchester, Lancashire, arm. UNIVERSITY COLL., matric. 19 Oct., 1811, aged 19; B.A. 1815, M.A. 1820.

Phillips, Thomas Falkner, 2s. George Allcroft, of Broughton, co. Lancashire, arm. BRASENOSE COLL., matric. 22 Jan., 1880, aged 19; B.A. 1884.

Phillipps, Thomas John, s. Thomas, of Tiverton, Devon, arm. BRASENOSE COLL., matric. 29 May, 1816, aged 18.

Phillips, Thomas Lloyd, 1s. Thomas, of Hay, co. Brecon, gent. MAGDALEN HALL, matric. 22 March, 1862, aged 30; B.A. from JESUS COLL. 1866, M.A. 1868.

Phillips, Thomas Shaw, 2s. Philip, of Stourbridge, co. Worcester, arm. MAGDALEN HALL, matric. 20 Jan., 1874, aged 38. [10]

Philips, Walter Alison, y.s. John, of Blackheath, Kent, arm. MERTON COLL. matric. 17 Oct., 1882, aged 17, exhibitioner 1882-6, B.A. 1886; Merchant Taylors' senior scholar ST. JOHN'S COLL. 1886.

Philips, Walter Hibbert, 1s. John, of Neath, co. Carmarthen, gent. JESUS COLL., matric. 25 Oct., 1869, aged 22; B.A. 1873, M.A. 1878.

Phillips, William, s. William, of Acton, co. Stafford, pleb. PEMBROKE COLL., matric. 23 May, 1722, aged 18; B.A. 1726.

Philips, William, s. William, of St. Michael's, Worcester (city), cler. MERTON COLL., matric. 1 July, 1724, aged 16.

Philipps, William, s. Rowland, of 'Man. Marid.,' Carmarthen, gent. JESUS COLL., matric. 8 Dec., 1729, aged 18. [15]

Philips, William, s. William, of Byton, co. Southampton, cler. JESUS COLL., matric. 9 April, 1739, aged 17.

Philips, William, s. John, of Camelford, Cornwall, gent. BALLIOL COLL., matric. 11 May, 1741, aged 18; B.A. 1744 (as PHILLIPPS).

Phillips, William, s. Benjamin, of Bristol (city), pleb. NEW COLL., matric. 22 Jan., 1768, aged 18; B.A. 1771, M.A. 1774, vicar of Great Bardfield, Essex, and of Cwmdu, co. Brecon, vicar of Appleby, Westmoreland, 1797, until his death 23 June, 1816, father of William Spencer 1810.

Philips, William, s. Nathaniel, of Manchester, Lancashire, gent. BRASENOSE COLL., matric. 6 April, 1785, aged 18. See Foster's *Lancashire Collection.*

Phillipps, William, s. Nicholas, of Roche, Cornwall, cler. QUEEN'S COLL., matric. 1 March, 1805, aged 17. [20]

Phillips, William, s. William, of Whitston, co. Monmouth, arm. TRINITY COLL., matric. 4 Oct., 1813, aged 17.

Phillips, William Alfred Maclure, 1s. Thomas William, of Woolston, Hants, gent. ST. JOHN'S COLL., matric. 14 Oct., 1876, aged 19; B.A. 1881.

Philipps, William Charles, 1s. Charles Allen, of Haverfordwest, co. Pembroke, arm. CHRIST CHURCH, matric. 25 June, 1830, aged 19.

Phillips, William Davies, y.s. Nathaniel, of Haverfordwest, gent. JESUS COLL., matric. 19 Jan., 1825, aged 19; B.A. 1829.

Phillipse, William George Thomas, s. William, of St. James's, Westminster, arm TRINITY COLL., matric. 6 Nov., 1797, aged 19; B.A. 1801 (as WILLIAM PHILLIPS). [25]

Phillips, William Hamilton, 2s. Edward, of Manchester, D.Med. (subs. arm.). CHRIST CHURCH, matric. 15 Jan., 1869, aged 18; S.C.L. & B.A. 1873, bar.-at-law, Inner Temple, 1877. See Foster's *Men at the Bar.*

Philipps, William Lewis, 1s. William Lewis, of Clyngwynne, co. Carmarthen, arm. CHRIST CHURCH, matric. 31 May, 1884, aged 17.

Phillips, William Lucas, s. Charles, of St. Luke's, Middlesex, gent. PEMBROKE COLL., matric. 21 Jan., 1757, aged 20.

Philips, William Morton, 1s. John William, of Checkley, co. Stafford, arm. MERTON COLL., matric. 2 June, 1870, aged 17; B.A. 1873. See *Eton School Lists.*

Phillips, William Page Thomas, o.s. Benjamin, of Marylebone, London, gent. EXETER COLL., matric. 11 Feb., 1852, aged 18; B A. 1855, M.A. 1858, of Melton Grange, Suffolk, J.P., D.L., bar.-at-law, Lincoln's Inn, 1857. See Foster's *Men at the Bar* & *Eton School Lists.* [30]

Phillips, William Parr, 1s. William Joseph George, of Ealing, Hants, cler. TRINITY COLL., matric. 1 June, 1826, aged 19; B.A. 1831.

Philipps, (Sir) William Philipps Laugharne, s. John P. L., of St. Bride's, Pembroke, arm. JESUS COLL., matric. 14 Dec., 1813, aged 19; 9th baronet, assumed the additional name of PHILIPPS, died 17 Feb., 1850.

Phillips, William Spencer, s. William, of Great Bardfield, Essex, cler. TRINITY COLL., matric. 27 Oct., 1810, aged 15; exhibitioner 1813-4, scholar 1814-22, B.A. 1815, M.A. 1817, B.D. 1827, fellow 1822-9, dean 1823, tutor 1824, philosophy lecturer 1828, vicar of New-Church with Ryde, Isle of Wight, and incumbent of St. John's Church, Cheltenham, died 13 May, 1863.

Philipps, William Thomas, s. William Hollingworth, of Brompton, Kent, arm. PEMBROKE COLL., matric. 18 Nov., 1806, aged 19; demy MAGDALEN COLL. 1808-20, B.A. 1811, M.A. 1813, fellow 1820-42, B.D. 1824, math. lecturer 1822, vice-president 1823, dean of divinity 1824, keeper of the Ashmolean Museum 1822-3, rector of Fittleton, Wilts, 1840, until his death 28 Sep., 1854. See Foster's *Baronetage* & *Bloxam*, vii. 178.

Phillips, Wilmot, 1s. Henry Stephen, of Newmarket, co. Cambridge, gent. WADHAM COLL., matric. 11 Oct., 1884, aged 20. [35]

Phillipson, William Wynne Burton, 1s. Richard B., of Pemarth, co. Merioneth, arm. JESUS COLL., matric. 23 Nov., 1843, aged 18; B.A. from NEW INN HALL 1849. M.A. 1873, chaplain at Wynberg, Cape of Good Hope, 1854-73, vicar of Bickerton, Cheshire, 1874-9, and of Burleydam 1882. See *Rugby School Reg.*, 202.

Phillott, Charles, s. Joseph, of Bath (city), gent. CHRIST CHURCH, matric. 8 May, 1792, aged 17; B.A. 1796, M.A. 1798, perp. curate Badley and Wickhamford, co. Worcester, 1808, vicar of Frome-Selwood, Somerset, 1813, until his death 26 Nov., 1851.

Phillott, Edward, 1s. James, of Stanton Prior, Somerset, cler. PEMBROKE COLL., matric. 28 April, 1825, aged 18; scholar 1825-33, B.A. 1829, M.A. 1836, rector of Brockley, co. Gloucester, 1868, until his death 5 Feb., 1874.

Phillott, Rev. Francis, 3s. James, of Stanton Prior, Somerset, cler. ST. JOHN'S COLL., matric. 23 March, 1841, aged 19; B.A. 1844, M.A. 1861, died 4 Sep., 1878. See *Crockford.*

Phillott, George Henry, o.s. Henry Wright, of Staunton-on-Wye, co. Hereford, cler. CHRIST CHURCH, matric. 13 Oct., 1871, aged 19; B.A. 1874.

Phillott, Henry Wright, 3s. Johnson, of Whitcombe, co. Gloucester, arm. CHRIST CHURCH, matric. 15 May, 1834, aged 17; student 1835-51, B.A. 1838, M.A. 1840, rector of Staunton-on-Wye 1850, preb. of Hereford 1864, chancellor of the choir 1886, and canon 1887; for list of his works see *Crockford.*

Phillott, Rev. Herbert, 4s. James, of Stanton Prior, Somerset, cler. CORPUS CHRISTI COLL., matric. 21 June, 1844, aged 20; exhibitioner 1844-8, B.A. 1848, died 22 Sep., 1854. See *Eton School Lists.*

Phillott, James, s. Joseph, of St. James's, Bath (city), gent. QUEEN'S COLL., matric. 20 Feb., 1766, aged 16; B.A. 1769, M.A. 1772, B. & D.D. 1786, rector and archdeacon of Bath 1798, rector of Stanton Prior, Somerset, preb. of Wells 1791, until his death 11 June, 1815.

Phillott, James, s. James, of Bath, Somerset, doctor. CORPUS CHRISTI COLL., matric. 29 Jan., 1795, aged 16; scholar 1792, B.A. 1798, M.A. 1802, rector of Stanton Prior, Somerset, 1815, until his death 30 Dec., 1865. [5]

Phillott, James Russell, s. John Hopkins, of Stanton Prior, Somerset, cler. WORCESTER COLL., matric. 9 Feb., 1821, aged 18; demy MAGDALEN COLL. 1821-9, B.A. 1824, M.A. 1827, fellow 1829-35. See *Bloxam*, vii. 283.

Phillott, John Stevens, s. James, of Bath, Somerset, cler. BALLIOL COLL., matric. 17 Dec., 1793, aged 17; B.A. 1797, M.A. 1800, vicar of Wookey 1801, and rector of Farmborough, Somerset, 1823, until his death 30 Aug., 1837.

Phillpot, William Edwin, o.s. Edwin, of Cheltenham, gent. NON-COLL., matric. 17 Oct., 1881, aged 18; B.A. from WORCESTER COLL. 1887.

Phillpotts, Rev. Barrington Henry Arthur, 1s. Octavius, of Plymouth, arm. ST. MARY HALL, matric. 22 Jan., 1883, aged 22; B.A. 1886.

Phillpotts, Edward Copleston, born in precincts of Durham Cathedral, 3s. Henry, bishop of Exeter. ORIEL COLL., matric. 1 Feb., 1832, aged 19; B.A. 1835, rector of Stokeinteignhead, Devon, 1838, and of Lezant, Cornwall, 1847, until his death 27 Jan., 1866. See *Alumni West.*, 500. [10]

Phillpotts, Henry, s. John, of Bridgewater, Somerset, gent. CORPUS CHRISTI COLL., matric. 7 Nov., 1791, aged 13; fellow MAGDALEN COLL. 1795-1804, B.A. 1795, M.A. 1798, B. & D.D. 1821, hon. fellow 1862-9, chaplain to bishop of Durham 1806, vicar of Kilmersdon, Somerset, 1804, of Bishop Middleham, 1805, and of Stanton-le-Street, co. Durham, 1806, rector of Gateshead 1808, preb. of Durham 1810-20, rector of Stanhope in Weardale 1820, dean of Chester 1828, visitor of Exeter College 1831, and bishop of Exeter 1831, until his death 18 Sep., 1869, father of John S.; for list of his works see *Crockford.*

Phillpotts, Henry John, born at Hallow, co. Worcester, 1s. William John, archdeacon of Cornwall. CHRIST CHURCH, matric. 23 May, 1850, aged 16; student 1852-62, B.A. 1855, M.A. 1858, vicar of Lamerton, Devon, 1860.

Phillpotts, Henry Robertson, 1s. Henry John, of Lamerton, Devon, cler. KEBLE COLL., matric. 19 Oct., 1886, aged 19.

Phillpotts, James Surtees, 3s. William John, of Hallow, co. Worcester, cler. NEW COLL., matric. 22 March, 1858, aged 18; fellow 1858-69, B.A. 1863, B.C.L. 1864, M.A. 1872, assistant-master Rugby 1862-74, head-master Bedford Grammar School 1874. See *Rugby School Reg.*

Phillpotts, John Hughes, 1s. Thomas, of St. Feock, Cornwall, cler. CHRIST CHURCH, matric. 27 May, 1863, aged 18; died in 1871. [15]

Phillpotts, John Scott, born at Durham, 6s. Henry, bishop of Exeter. EXETER COLL., matric. 8 March, 1838, aged 17.

Phillpotts, William Francis, 2s. William, of Hallow, co. Worcester, cler. NEW COLL., matric. 2 Nov., 1855, aged 18; fellow 1855-71, B.A. 1859, M.A. 1862, bar.-at-law, Middle Temple, 1864, and of Lincoln's Inn (ad eundem) 1866. See Foster's *Men at the Bar.*

Phillpotts, William John, 1s. Henry, of Bishop Middleham, co. Durham, doctor. ORIEL COLL., matric. 26 May, 1825, aged 18; B.A. 1830, M.A. 1832, vicar of Lezant, Cornwall, 1831, of Grimley, co. Worcester, 1832, of St. Gluvias, Cornwall, 1845, and archdeacon of Cornwall 1845, preb. of Exeter 1840, chancellor 1860, precentor 1870-2, died 10 July, 1888, father of Henry J., James S., and William F.

Philosofof, General, created D.C.L. 11 Sep., 1768, envoy extraordinary from Russia at the Court of Denmark.

Philp, William, s. Thomas, of Pyworthy, Devon, gent. EXETER COLL., matric. 4 June, 1747, aged 20. [20]

Philpin, Frederick Style, 1s. Moses, of Alcester, co. Warwick, gent. PEMBROKE COLL., matric. 16 Oct., 1866, aged 19.

Philpot, George Douglas, 2s. Benjamin, of Southwold, Suffolk, cler. PEMBROKE COLL., matric. 5 Dec., 1845, aged 18; died exhibitioner 8 Sep., 1846. See monumental inscription; *Rugby School Reg.*, 224.

Philpot, Hamley Stanley, o.s. William Benjamin, of Walesby, Cornwall (cler.). TRINITY COLL., matric. 18 Oct., 1875, aged 19; scholar 1875-80, B.A. 1879, M.A. 1882.

Philpot, John Gold, 1s. John, of London, arm. BRASENOSE COLL., matric. 25 Jan., 1868, aged 19; bar.-at-law, Middle Temple, 1877. See Foster's *Men at the Bar.*

Philpot, Joseph Charles, 2s. Charles, of Ripple, Kent, cler. WORCESTER COLL., matric. 14 Oct., 1820, aged 18; scholar 1821-6, B.A. 1824, M.A. 1827, fellow 1826-35. See *Robinson*, 192; & *St. Paul's School Reg.*, 252. [25]

Philpot, William, s. Thomas, of Esher, Surrey, gent. PEMBROKE COLL., matric. 28 April, 1785, aged 18; B.A. 1789, M.A. 1792.

Philpot, William Benjamin, 1s. Benjamin, of Southwold, Suffolk, cler. WORCESTER COLL., matric. 7 June, 1845, aged 22; scholar 1845-53, B.A. 1848, M.A. 1851, rector of Walesby, co. Lincoln, 1852-75, vicar of South Bersted, Sussex, 1875, father of Hamley. See *Rugby School Reg.*, 209.

Philpot, William Doveton, 1s. William, of Richmond, Surrey, cler. LINCOLN COLL., matric. 4 June, 1823, aged 18; B.A. 1828.

Philpott, Charles Barrington, 2s. Richard Stamper, of Horton, Surrey, cler. NON-COLL., matric. 25 Jan., 1879, aged 20; B.A. 1884.

Philpott, Rev. Francis Octavius, 6s. Henry Charles, of Severn-Stoke, co. Worcester, cler. ST. EDMUND HALL, matric. 12 June, 1867, aged 19; B.A. 1872, M.A. 1880. [30]

Philpott, Henry Charles, s. Thomas, of Worcester (city), cler. ST. JOHN'S COLL., matric. 5 Nov., 1812, aged 18; B.A. 1817, M.A. 1819, curate of Ripple, co. Worcester, 1818-25, and of Severn-Stoke 1826-55, rector of Earl's Croome 1855, until his death 21 Oct., 1873. See *Rugby School Reg.*, 93 and 108.

Philpott, Humphrey, s. Other, of Clent, co. Stafford, cler. ORIEL COLL., matric. 3 April, 1783, aged 17; B.A. 1786.

Philpott, John, s. Paul, of St. Peter's, co. Worcester, gent. BALLIOL COLL., matric. 24 March, 1723-4, aged 19.

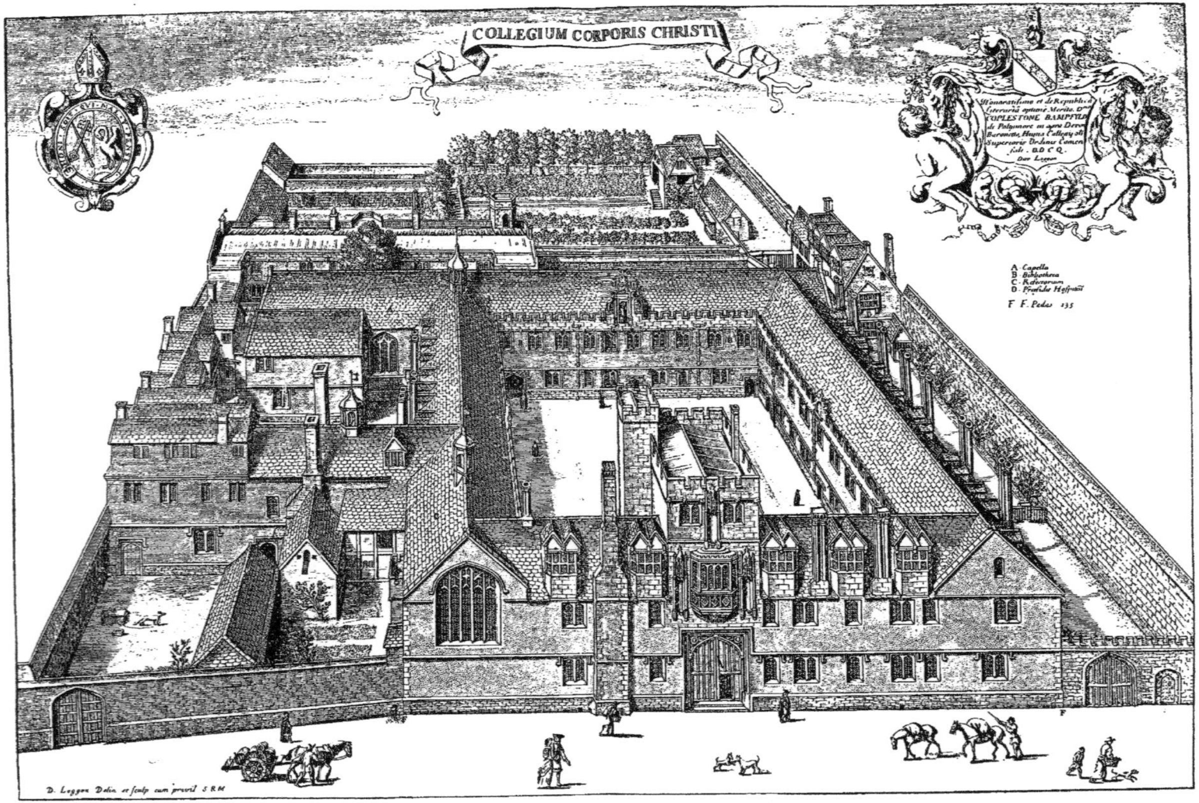

COLLEGIUM CORPORIS CHRISTI

A · Capella
B · Bibliotheca
C · Refectorium
D · Præsidis Hospitium

F F. Pedes 135

D. Loggan Delin. et sculp cum privil. S.R.M.

VIEW BY LOGGAN, 1675. [*Reduced facsimile.*]

Philpott, Rev. John Nigel, 3s. Richard Stamper, of Chewton Mendip, Somerset, cler. MAGDALEN COLL., matric. 16 Oct., 1877, aged 18; clerk 1877-81, B.A. 1882, M.A. 1887.

Philpott, Octavius, 8s. Henry Charles, of Severn-Stoke, co. Worcester, cler. BRASENOSE COLL., matric. 13 Oct., 1873, aged 18, scholar 1873-4; scholar JESUS COLL., Cambridge, 1874, senior optime & B.A. 1878.

Philpott, Other, s. Thomas, of Pedmore, co. Worcester, cler. CHRIST CHURCH, matric. 12 March, 1740-1, aged 17; B.A. 22 Feb., 1744-5, M.A. 1747, rector of Pedmore, died 18 Oct., 1792.

Philpott, Other, 3s. Thomas, of Pedmore, co. Worcester, cler. ST. JOHN'S COLL., matric. 11 June, 1823, aged 19; B.A. 1828, M.A. 1830.

Philpott, Thomas, s. Other, of Clent, co. Stafford, cler. ST. MARY HALL, matric. 9 March, 1779, aged 17; B.A. 1782, M.A. 1785, rector of Pedmore, co. Worcester, 1791, until his death 10 Sep., 1855. [5]

Philpott, Vaughan Williams, 1s. Thomas, of Haverfordwest, co. Pembroke, arm. CHRIST CHURCH, matric. 27 May, 1858, aged 18; B.A. 1862, M.A. 1869, rector of Avon Dassett, co. Warwick, 1878.

Philpott, William, 4s. Henry Charles, of Severn-Stoke, co. Worcester, cler. MAGDALEN COLL., matric. 6 March, 1863, aged 19; chorister 1855-60, clerk 1863-6, B.A. 1866.

Phinn, Charles Percival, 2s. Thomas, of Wilcot, Somerset, arm. BALLIOL COLL., matric. 30 Nov., 1846, aged 17; B.A. 1850, held various curacies and livings 1852-64, rector of Long Crichel, Dorset, 1864-85.

Phinn, Thomas, 1s. Thomas, of Exeter (city), arm. EXETER COLL., matric. 29 Oct., 1834, aged 20; scholar 1836-40, B.A. 1838, bar.-at-law, Inner Temple, 1840, Q.C. and a bencher 1854, recorder of Portsmouth 1848-52, and of Devonport 1852-5, M.P. Bath 1852-5, second secretary and counsel to the Admiralty, died 31 Oct., 1866. See *Coll. Reg.*, 152, & *Eton School Lists.*

Phipps, Rev. Barré, of ST. JOHN'S COLL., Cambridge (14th wrangler & B.A. 1797, M.A. 1800); adm. 'ad eundem' 24 April, 1845, rector of Nuthurst, Sussex, 1805, rector of Selsey 1817, canon of Chichester 1802, until his death 3 Jan., 1863. [10]

Phipps, Constantine, s. William, of London, arm. UNIVERSITY COLL., matric. 28 Nov., 1741, aged 19; M.P. Lincoln 1768-74, Huntingdon 1776-84, Newark 1784-90, created Baron Mulgrave in Ireland 3 Sep., 1767, died 13 Sep., 1775. See Foster's *Peerage*, M. NORMANBY.

Phipps, Rev. Constantine Osborne, 1s. Pownoll William, of Shepperton, Middlesex, cler. EXETER COLL., matric. 15 Oct., 1879, aged 18; B.A. 1884, M.A. 1886.

Phipps, Edmund, 3s. Henry, Earl of Mulgrave. TRINITY COLL., matric. 22 Nov., 1825, aged 16; B.A. 1828, M.A. 1831, entered Lincoln's Inn 1826, recorder of Scarborough and M.P. 1794-1818, and 1820-32, M.P. Queenborough 1818-20, died 27 Oct., 1857. See Foster's *Peerage*, M. NORMANBY.

Phipps, Edward James, 5s. Thomas, of Westbury, Wilts, arm. EXETER COLL., matric. 12 Dec., 1823, aged 17; B.A. 1828, rector of Devizes, Wilts, 1831-53, and of Stansfield, Suffolk, 1853, until his death 22 May, 1884.

Phipps, Frederick Hothersall, 4s. Charles Paul, of Liverpool, arm. CHRIST CHURCH, matric. 16 Oct., 1874, aged 18; B.A. 1879. See *Eton School Lists.* [15]

Phipps, James, s. George, of St. Mary Magdalen, Oxford (city), arm. PEMBROKE COLL., matric. 23 Oct., 1719, aged 17; B.A. 1723.

Phipps, James, s. Constantine, of Isle of Christopher, arm. ST. MARY HALL, matric. 16 Feb., 1761, aged 16; created M.A. 26 June, 1764, M.P. Peterborough 1780, until his death in Feb., 1786.

Phipps, John Capel Barré, y.s. Barré, of Abergavenny, co. Monmouth, arm. BRASENOSE COLL., matric. 2 June, 1882, aged 19.

Phipps, Pickering, o.s. Pickering, of Collingtree, Northants, gent. NEW COLL., matric. 16 Oct., 1880, aged 19; B.A. 1885.

Phipps, Pownoll William, 2s. Pownoll, of St. Margaret's, Westminster, gent. PEMBROKE COLL., matric. 15 June, 1854, aged 18; B.A. 1858, M.A. 1861, held various curacies 1859-71, vicar of Knapton-on-the-Hill, co. Warwick, 1871-3, rector of Upton Slough 1873-86, and of Chalfont St. Giles 1886. See *Rugby School Reg.*, 291. [20]

Phipps, Richard Leckonby Hothersall, o.s. John Lewis, of Doe Park, Walton, near Liverpool, arm. CHRIST CHURCH, matric. 17 Oct., 1862, aged 20; of Leighton House, Wilts, J.P., high sheriff, bar.-at-law, Inner Temple, 1868. See Foster's *Men at the Bar.*

Phipps, Thomas, s. William, of Duntsbourn Abbots, co. Gloucester, cler. HART HALL, matric. 21 Oct., 1717, aged 15.

Phipps, Thomas Hele, s. Thomas, of Westbury Leigh, Wilts, arm. HERTFORD COLL., matric. 19 March, 1766, aged 16; of Leighton House, died 10 Sep., 1790.

Phipps, Walter Tudway, 2s. Arthur Constantine, of Shepton Mallett, Somerset, arm. CHRIST CHURCH, matric. 14 Oct., 1864, aged 19; B.A. 1870, a student of Lincoln's Inn 1868.

Phipps, William (Wilton), 2s. Charles Paul, of Liverpool, gent. EXETER COLL., matric. 13 March, 1866, aged 19; B.A. 1869, M.A. 1873. See *Eton School Lists.* [25]

Phipson, Weatherley, 1s. Thomas Weatherley, of London, arm. BALLIOL COLL., matric. 17 Oct., 1864, aged 19; B.A. 1868, bar.-at-law, Inner Temple, 1879. See Foster's *Men at the Bar* & *Rugby School Reg.*, 457.

Phyn, John, s. James, of Albany, America, arm. CHRIST CHURCH, matric. 26 Oct., 1786, aged 15; B.A. 1791, M.A. 1795.

Piaget, 'Amy Petrus,' s. Peter, of Biggleswade, Beds, gent. CHRIST CHURCH, matric. 22 June, 1738, aged 18.

Picard, George. MERTON COLL., 1808. See CAMBRIDGE.

Picart, Samuel, s. Benjamin, of Christ Church, Spitalfields, London, gent. JESUS COLL., matric. 5 June, 1765, aged 17; left in 1766. See *St. Paul's School Reg.*, 110. [30]

Picart, Samuel, s. Samuel, of Carmarthen (town), cler. BRASENOSE COLL., matric. 22 May, 1792, aged 17; B.A. 1796, M.A. 1803, B.D. 1810, senior master Hereford School 1803, preb. of Hereford 1805, rector of Hartlebury 1817, until his death 28 Sep., 1835.

Piccop, John, s. George, of Manchester, gent. LINCOLN COLL., matric. 9 June, 1813, aged 25; scholar 1815-7, B.A. 1817, M.A. 1820, incumbent of St. Paul's, Manchester, 1822, perp. curate Farndon, Cheshire, 1844, until his death 10 Sep., 1854. See *Manchester School Reg.*, iii. 228.

Piccope, George John, 1s. John, of Manchester, cler. BRASENOSE COLL., matric. 6 June, 1838, aged 20; scholar 1838-42, B.A. 1842, M.A. 1845, curate of Brindle 1849-64, curate in charge of Yarwell, Northants, 1864, until his death 22 Feb., 1872. See *Manchester School Reg.*, iii. 241.

Pick, James, s. James, of Berkeley, co. Gloucester, gent. WORCESTER COLL., matric. 19 Nov., 1789, aged 19.

Pickard, Charles Edward, 4s. Henry William, of Hooton Roberts, Yorks, gent. ST. ALBAN HALL, matric. 20 Oct., 1864, aged 18; brother of Henry A.

Pickard, George, s. Jocelyn, of Bloxworth, Dorset, arm. MERTON COLL., matric. 7 July, 1774, aged 17; B.C.L. 1781, rector of Warmwell, Dorset, 1780, until his death 24 July, 1840, father of George 1808, and of John T. 1811. [35]

Pickard, Rev. Henry Adair, 1s. Henry William, of Forest Hill, near Mansfield, Notts, arm. CHRIST CHURCH, matric. 12 June, 1851, aged 19; student 1851-68, B.A. 1855, M.A. 1858, tutor 1858, Greek reader 1861, rhetoric reader 1863, of Sturminster Marshall, Dorset, inspector of schools 1864. See *Rugby School Reg.*, 254.

Pickard, William Jesse, 1s. William, of Great Yarmouth, Norfolk, gent. ST. MARY HALL, matric. 4 Feb., 1863, aged 27.

Pickard, John Trenchard. NEW COLL., 1811. See TRENCHARD.

Pickering, (Sir) Edward (Bart.), s. Gilbert, of Kensington, Middlesex, baronet. CHRIST CHURCH, matric. 25 May, 1732, aged 16; created M.A. 9 June, 1736, 4th baronet, died in July, 1749.

Pickering, Edward, 3s. Robert, of Liverpool, arm. BRASENOSE COLL., matric. 25 June, 1840, aged 18; scholar 1840-3, B.A. 1844, M.A. 1847, colonial chaplain Grahamstown, died 9 Jan., 1885. [5]

Pickering, Francis Percy Umfreville, 1s. James Henry, of Shipton, Yorks, cler. CHRIST CHURCH, matric. 8 June, 1870, aged 18. See *Eton School Lists.*

Pickering, Isaac Berwick, s. Isaac, of Lyndhurst, Hants, arm. BRASENOSE COLL., matric. 15 Dec., 1813, aged 19; B.A. 1817.

Pickering, James Bennett, 1s. Richard, of Kearsley, Lancashire, gent. ST. MARY HALL, matric. 23 Oct., 1882, aged 18.

Pickering, James Henry, 4s. Edward Rowland, of London, arm. CHRIST CHURCH, matric. 23 Oct., 1834, aged 18; B.A. 1838, vicar of Overton, Yorks, 1849-72, rector of West Chiltington, Sussex, 1872. See *Eton School Lists.*

Pickering, Rev. John, s. John, of Mackworth, co. Derby, cler. NEW COLL., matric. 30 March, 1757, aged 18; B.A. 1760, M.A. 1763, his widow died at Oxford 9 April, 1810. [10]

Pickering, John, s. Joseph, of 'St. Allaws,' London, gent. HERTFORD COLL., matric. 9 May, 1760, aged 18; bar.-at-law, Lincoln's Inn, 1766, brother of Joseph 1764.

Pickering, John Ferdinand Isaac, s. Isaac, of Kingston Lisle, Berks, arm. MAGDALEN COLL., matric. 27 March, 1801, aged 19.

Pickering, Joseph, s. Joseph, of London, gent. CHRIST CHURCH, matric. 26 Nov., 1764, aged 16; B.A. 1768, M.A. 1771, bar.-at-law, Lincoln's Inn, 1772. See *Gent.'s Mag.*, 1820, i. 566.

Pickering, Percival Spencer Umfreville, 1s. Percival André, of London, arm. BALLIOL COLL., matric. 22 Jan., 1877, aged 18; scholar 1876-80, B.A. 1880, M.A. 1883. See *Eton School Lists.*

Pickering, Percy Gilbert Umfreville, 2s. Edward Hayes, of Eton, Bucks, cler. MERTON COLL., matric. 30 Oct., 1860, aged 19; postmaster 1860-5, B.A. 1864, M.A. 1867, has held various curacies since 1867. [15]

Pickering, Richard, s. Thomas, of Acworth, Yorks, gent. LINCOLN COLL., matric. 29 Oct., 1784, aged 18; B.A. 1788, M.A. 1791, B.D. 1801, fellow until 1812, rector of Winterbourne Abbas with Steepleton 1811, rector (and patron) of Wilcot 1820, until his death 19 Aug., 1822.

Pickering, Samuel, s. John, of St. James's, Westminster, gent. QUEEN'S COLL., matric. 12 Dec., 1765, aged 17; B.A. 1769, M.A. 1772, died rector of Bishops Cleere, Somerset, in 1815.

Pickering, Thomas, s. Edmund, of St. Laurence, London, gent. ST. JOHN'S COLL., matric. 5 July, 1725, aged 16; senior fellow in 1748, B.A. 1729, M.A. 1733, B.D. 1738, D.D. 14 Jan., 1742-3, vicar of St. Sepulchre's, London, 1748, until his death 20 Jan., 1767. See *Robinson*, 39.

Pickering, Thomas Edward, 1s. Thomas, of Abbots Bromley, co. Stafford, arm. UNIVERSITY COLL., matric. 15 Oct., 1881, aged 20; scholar 1881-6, B.A. 1885.

Pickersgill, Richard Tennent, o.s. Frederick Richard, of London, arm. WADHAM COLL., matric. 11 Oct., 1879, aged 18; B.A. 1883, M.A. 1886. [20]

Pickford, Edward Matthew, s. Thomas, of Bowden, Cheshire, arm. BRASENOSE COLL., matric. 23 Jan., 1834, aged 19; B.A. 1838, M.A. 1844, rector of Tilston, Cheshire, 1850, until his death 18 Aug., 1869. See *Robinson*, 218.

Pickford, Rev. Francis Newland, 6s. John, of Newland, co. York, cler. NON-COLL., matric. 15 Oct., 1881, aged 18; B.A. from MERTON COLL. 1884.

Pickford, James John (B.A. TRINITY COLL., Dublin), 1s. James Hollins, of Brighton, Sussex, doctor. ST. MARY HALL, incorp. 14 May, 1858, aged 25; M.A. 1859, died curate of Great Gaddesden, Herts, 29 July, 1870.

Pickford, John, 1s. John, of Congleton, Cheshire, gent. QUEEN'S COLL., matric. 10 Feb., 1848, aged 17; B.A. 1851, M.A. 1854, held various curacies 1854-71, vicar of Newton-on-Rawcliffe, Yorks, 1871-82, rector of Newbourne, Suffolk, 1872. See *Manchester School Reg.*, iii. 106.

Pickford, John, 3s. William, of Manchester, arm. BRASENOSE COLL., matric. 17 Oct., 1863, aged 21; scholar 1863-6, B.A. 1867, M.A. 1870, head-master Alnwick Grammar School, incumbent of St. John, Baillieston, Glasgow, 1876-80, vicar of Tuddenham St. Martin, Suffolk, 1880. [25]

Pickford, Rev. Joseph, s. Joseph, of Royton, Lancashire, arm. CHRIST CHURCH, matric. 3 Feb., 1785, aged 18; B.A. 1789, M.A. 1791, died at Acomb, Yorks, 17 May, 1804. See Foster's *Baronetage*, RADCLIFFE; & *Manchester School Reg.*, i. 208.

Pickford, Joseph, s. Joseph, of Derby (town) gent. ORIEL COLL., matric. 18 May, 1790, aged 17; B.A. 1794, M.A. 1796.

Pickford, William, 2s. Thomas Edward, of Manchester, gent. EXETER COLL., matric. 2 June, 1868, aged 19; B.A. 1873, bar.-at-law, Inner Temple, 1874. See Foster's *Men at the Bar.*

Pickin, John Charles, s. William, of Whitesmore, Notts, gent. EXETER COLL., matric. 28 May, 1811, aged 17.

Pickin, Rev. Francis William, o.s. William John, of Perlethorpe, Notts, arm. MAGDALEN COLL., matric. 26 July, 1833, aged 17; demy 1833-43, B.A. 1837, M.A. 1840, fellow 1843, until his death 28 June, 1846. See *Coll. Reg.*, vii. 333; & *Rugby School Reg.*, 169. [30]

Pickmere, Edward Ralph, 1s. John Richard, of Warrington, Lancashire, arm. EXETER COLL., matric. 16 Oct., 1874, aged 19; B.A. 1879, M.A. 1881.

Pickthall, Henry, s. Robert, of Boothe, Cumberland, gent. QUEEN'S COLL., matric. 12 March, 1818, aged 25; B.A. 1821.

Pickwick, Rev. Charles, 2s. Aaron, of Bath, Somerset, gent. WORCESTER COLL., matric. 10 Oct., 1822, aged 19; B.A. 1826, died at Beckington rectory, Somerset, 12 Dec., 1834.

Pickwick, William, s. Eleazar, of Bath, Somerset (city), gent. ST. JOHN'S COLL., matric. 15 May, 1793, aged 16.

Picton, Edward, s. Thomas, of Rhydbaxton, co. Pembroke, arm. BRASENOSE COLL., matric. 4 June, 1778, aged 17; B.A. from NEW COLL. 1783, of Iscoed, near Carmarthen, vicar of Great St. Bride's super Ely with Wick, co. Glamorgan, 1798, until his death 2 Sep., 1835. [35]

Pidcock, Benjamin, s. John, of Ashborne, co. Derby, gent. WADHAM COLL., matric. 16 May, 1787, aged 18; B.A. 1791, M.A. 1793, perp. curate Elton 1812, and vicar of Youlgrave, co. Derby, 1812, until his death 28 Aug., 1835.

Pidcock, John Hyde, 1s. John Spencer, of Watford, Herts, doctor. WORCESTER COLL., matric. 12 May, 1837, aged 19.

idding, Benjamin, s. James, of St. James's, Bristol (city), cler. BALLIOL COLL., matric. 21 Feb., 1727-8, aged 17; B.A. 1731, M.A. 1739, rector (and patron) of Yatton Keynell, Wilts, at his death in 1764.

idding, James, s. James, of Bristol (city), gent. BALLIOL COLL., matric. 14 Jan., 1754, aged 18; B.A. 1757, rector (and patron) of Yatton Keynell, Wilts, 1764, until his death 12 Nov., 1821.

iddington, Benjamin, s. John, of Oxford (city), pleb. NEW COLL., matric. 7 April, 1769, aged 17; B.A. 1772, chaplain, minor canon Hereford Cathedral, died 15 June, 1774.

iddington, William, s. Thomas, of Cuddington, Bucks, gent. WADHAM COLL., matric. 10 March, 1717-8, aged 15; B.A. 1721, M.A. 1724 (? died lecturer of St. Bartholomew-the-Great, London, 18 Sep., 1734).

iddocke, Rev. John, s. John, of Ashby-de-la-Zouch, co. Leicester, gent. CHRIST CHURCH, matric. 24 Oct., 1781, aged 17; B.A. 1785, M.A. 1808, of Ashby-de-la-Zouch, where his wife died 14 July, 1798. **[5]**

idgeon, Winter Randell, o.s. Daniel, of London, arm. CHRIST CHURCH, matric. 11 Oct., 1878, aged 18; B.A. 1882, M.A. 1886.

idsley, Edward, s. Charles, of Bishopsteignton, Devon, gent. BALLIOL COLL., matric. 14 July, 1733, aged 19; B.A. 1737.

idsley, Edward, 3s. Simon, of Crediton, Devon, cler. WORCESTER COLL., matric. 18 Feb., 1830, aged 19; B.A. 1834.

idsley, Simon, s. William, of Colebrooke, Devon, gent. EXETER COLL., matric. 22 Oct., 1791, aged 18; B.A. 1795, M.A. 1815.

idsley, Sydenham, 2s. Simon, of Crediton, Devon, cler. WORCESTER COLL., matric. 27 Feb., 1826, aged 18; B.A. 1829, rector of Uplowman, Devon, 1832, until his death 25 Aug., 1857. **[10]**

Pidsley, William, 2s. Simon, of Crediton, Devon, cler. PEMBROKE COLL., matric. 29 Nov., 1821, aged 17; B.A. 1825.

Pidwell, Samuel, o.s. John Lawrence, of All Saints, London, arm. WORCESTER COLL., matric. 30 April, 1827, aged 19; B.A. 1835.

Pierantoni, Augusto, created D.C.L. 13 May, 1885, senator of the Kingdom of Italy, and professor of international law in the University of Rome.

Pierce, Rev. Charles, s. Thomas, of Bristol (city), arm. ORIEL COLL., matric. 26 March, 1787, aged 21; B.A. 1791, died at Redland, near Bristol, 17 Oct., 1809.

Pierce, Frederick, 2s. Frederick, of Madras, arm. QUEEN'S COLL., matric. 29 Jan., 1834, aged 20.

Pierce, Henry Glyn, 3s. Hugh, of Liverpool, gent. QUEEN'S COLL., matric. 29 Oct., 1867, aged 18; B.A. 1872. **[15]**

Pierce, James, s. Caleb, of Tiverton, Devon, gent. BALLIOL COLL., matric, 19 May, 1763, aged 18; B.A. 1767.

Pierce, John, s. David, of Llanynis, co. Denbigh, pleb. JESUS COLL., matric. 22 March, 1763, aged 19; B.A. from ALL SOULS' COLL. 1767.

Pierce, John, 1s. William, of St. James's, Westminster, gent. WORCESTER COLL., matric. 30 June, 1854, aged 18.

Pierce, Robert, s. William, of Cemets, co. Montgomery, pleb. CHRIST CHURCH, matric. 19 March, 1723-4, aged 18; B.A. 1727. **[20]**

Pierce, William, s. Pier., of Ceirchiog, Anglesea, pleb. JESUS COLL., matric. 1 April, 1717, aged 21; B.A. 1720.

Piercey, William, s. William, of Sowe, co. Warwick, gent. ST. EDMUND HALL, matric. 10 July, 1767, aged 22.

Piercy, Daniel, s. Jeremiah, of Ratcliff, co. Leicester, pleb. BALLIOL COLL., matric. 15 May, 1746, aged 16; B.A. 22 Feb., 1749-50, M.A. 1754.

Piercy, George Henry, s. Daniel, of Shrawley, co. Worcester, cler. WORCESTER COLL., matric. 4 July, 1786, aged 17; B.A. 1790, M.A. 1794, vicar of Cheddesley Corbet, co. Worcester, 1805, until his death 8 May, 1855.

Piercy, Rev. Peter, s. Thomas, of Harpsden, Oxon, arm. TRINITY COLL., matric. 24 March, 1809, aged 15; B.A. 1812, M.A. 1816, died at Henley-on-Thames 25 Jan., 1863. **[25]**

Piercy, Thomas, s. Arthur, of Bridgnorth, Salop, pleb. CHRIST CHURCH, matric. 7 July, 1746, aged 17, B.A. 1750, M.A. 1753; D.D. from EMMANUEL COLL., Cambridge, 1770, (as PERCY), re-admitted 'ad eundem' 4 July, 1793, vicar of Easton Mauduit, Northants, 1753-78, chaplain to George II. 1759, dean of Carlisle 1778-82, bishop of Dromore 1782, until his death 30 Sep., 1811, author of the 'Hermit of Warkworth,' and compiler of the 'Reliques of Ancient Poetry,' etc. See *Cotton*, iii. 285.

Pierpoint, Edward, s. Edward, of Prescott, Lancashire, pleb. BRASENOSE COLL., matric. 11 March, 1719-20, aged 19; B.A. 1723.

Pierpoint, Matthew Augustin, 1s. Matthew, of St. Nicholas, Worcester (city), gent. ST. JOHN'S COLL., matric. 11 Oct., 1843, aged 18; B.A. from NEW INN HALL 1850, held various curacies 1850-65, rector of Elsworthy, Somerset, 1867.

Pierpoint, Robert, 1s. Benjamin, of Warrington, Lancashire, arm. CHRIST CHURCH, matric. 6 Feb., 1865, aged 19; B.A. 1869, M.A. 1871, of St. Austin's, Warrington, bar.-at-law, Inner Temple, 1873. See Foster's *Men at the Bar* & *Eton School Lists.*

Pierrepont, Charles, created D.C.L. 4 July, 1793, of Thoresby, Notts (2s. Philip Medows), assumed the name of PIERREPONT in lieu of MEDOWS by royal sign manual 17 Sep., 1788, M.P. Notts 1778, until created Viscount Newark, etc., 23 July, 1796, and Earl Manvers 9 April, 1806, died 17 June, 1816. See Foster's *Peerage.* **[30]**

Pierrepont, Charles Evelyn, Viscount Newark, 1s. Charles, Earl Manvers. CHRIST CHURCH, matric. 21 Oct., 1823, aged 18; B.A. 1826, M.P. East Retford 1830-5, died 25 Aug., 1850.

Pierrepont, Edward Willoughby, o.s. Edward, of New York, arm. CHRIST CHURCH, matric. 24 Jan., 1879, aged 19; B.A. 1882.

Pierrepont, Hon. Edwards, created D.C.L. 26 June, 1878, late attorney-general United States, and subsequently envoy extraordinary and minister plenipotentiary to the Court of St. James.

Pierrepont, Evelyn (Henry Frederick), born at Richmond, Surrey, s. Charles, arm. (after Earl Manvers). ORIEL COLL., matric. 1 Feb., 1792, aged 17; created M.A. 5 July, 1793, died 22 Oct., 1801.

Pierrepont, Hon. Evelyn Henry, 2s. Sidney William Herbert, Earl Manvers. CHRIST CHURCH, matric. 20 May, 1875, aged 18. See Foster's *Baronetage.*

Pierrepont, Henry Bennet, o.s. William, of Godalming, Surrey, arm. NEW COLL., matric. 21 May, 1829, aged 18; B.A. 1833. **[35]**

Pierrepont, Henry Manvers, s. Charles, Viscount Newark. CHRIST CHURCH, matric. 26 Oct., 1797, aged 17; B.A. 1800, created D.C.L. 11 June, 1834, of Conholt Park, Hants, envoy to the Court of Denmark 1804-7, P.C. 1807, died 10 Nov., 1851. See Foster's *Peerage*, E. MANVERS.

Pierrepont, Philip Sidney, s. Charles, Earl Manvers. CHRIST CHURCH, matric. 3 May, 1803, aged 16; of Evenley Hall, Northants, high sheriff 1842, died 15 Feb., 1864.

Pierrepont, Sidney William Herbert, 2s. (Charles Herbert), Earl Manvers. CHRIST CHURCH, matric. 9 June, 1843, aged 18; B.A. 1846, 3rd Earl Manvers, M.P. South Notts 1852-60. See Foster's *Peerage* & *Eton School Lists.*

Piers, Octavius (B.A. TRINITY COLL., Dublin, 1809), s. William, of Dublin (city), baronet. MAGDALEN HALL, incorp. 3 (or 8) Feb., 1812, aged 23; vicar of Preston, near Weymouth, 1815, until his death 23 Feb., 1848. See Foster's *Baronetage*.

Pierson, Rev. Kirshaw Thomson, 4s. Mark, of Altrincham, Cheshire, arm. MAGDALEN HALL, matric. 29 April, 1870, aged 19, scholar 1870, B.A. 1874, M.A. (HERTFORD COLL.) 1883, has held various curacies since 1875.

Pierson, Thomas, s. Richard, of Sheffield, Yorks, pleb. BALLIOL COLL., matric. 5 May, 1730, aged 19 (? died vicar of Appleton-in-the-Street, Yorkshire, 6 Feb., 1764).

Pierson, William, 6s. George Bailey, of Holbeck, Yorks, gent. QUEEN'S COLL., matric. 22 Oct., 1872, aged 20; exhibitioner 1872-7, B.A. 1876, M.A. 1879.

Piggin, John Henry. TRINITY COLL., 1880. See FOWLER. [5]

Pigot, Arthur Cecil William, 3s. George, of Patshall, Stafford, baronet. NEW INN HALL, matric. 25 May, 1833, aged 19; died 9 May, 1865. See Foster's *Baronetage*.

Pigott, Arthur Gough, 1s. Gillery, baron and knight. EXETER COLL., matric. 12 June, 1867, aged 17; B.A. 1870, of Sherfield Hill, Hants, bar.-at-law, Middle Temple, 1873. See Foster's *Men at the Bar* & *Eton School Lists*.

Pigott, Arthur James, 3s. John Dryden, of Edgmond, Salop, cler. MERTON COLL., matric. 7 June, 1834, aged 17; postmaster 1834-8, B.A. 1838, vicar of Uffington, co. Lincoln, and Battlefield 1852-72, died 19 July, 1881.

Pigot, (Sir) Arthur (Leary), s. John, of Isle of Barbados, arm. TRINITY COLL., matric. 17 Oct., 1778, aged 26; bar.-at-law, Middle Temple, 1777, K.C. 1783, and a bencher 1799, attorney-general of Grenada, commissioner of public accounts 1780, solicitor-general to Prince of Wales 1784, attorney-general 1806-7, knighted 12 April, 1806, M.P. Steyning 1803-6, Arundel 1806-12, Horsham 1812-8, Arundel 1818, until his death 6 Sep., 1819.

Pigott, Benjamin, s. Robert, of Chetwynd, Salop, arm. EXETER COLL., matric. 26 June, 1733, aged 19; B.A. 1737, M.A. 1739, brother of John 1724. [10]

Pigott, Cecil Ernest, 2s. Gillery, of Brighton, knight. NON-COLL., matric. 7 March, 1874, aged 18; bar.-at-law, Middle Temple, 1885. See Foster's *Men at the Bar* & *Eton School Lists*.

Pigott, Cecil Hugh Smyth-, 1s. John Hugh, of Weston-super-Mare, arm. MAGDALEN COLL., matric. 28 Jan., 1879, aged 18.

Pigott, (Charles) Francis Corbet, 5s. John Dryden (Pigott, after Corbet), of Edgmond, Salop, cler. (see p. 296). CHRIST CHURCH, matric. 17 Oct., 1839, aged 19; B.A. 1843, M.A. 1865, rector of Llanwenarth, co Monmouth, 1861-5, rector of Edgmond, Salop, 1865, brother of George W.

Pigott, Dryden Walter, 1s. Robert, of Chetwynd, Salop, arm. CHRIST CHURCH, matric. 2 May, 1755, aged 17; brother of Edward 1764.

Piggott, Edmund James, 1s. John William Mose, of Guildford, Surrey, gent. LINCOLN COLL., matric. 19 Oct., 1875, aged 20; B.A. 1879, M.A. 1885, brother of Henry F. and John W. M. B. [15]

Pigott, Edward, s. Robert, of Chetwynd, Salop, arm. PEMBROKE COLL., matric. 10 April, 1764, aged 18; brother of Dryden W.

Pigot, Edward, 2s. James, of St. Helen's, Prescot, Lancashire, cler. BRASENOSE COLL., matric. 17 May, 1837, aged 18; scholar 1838-40, B.A. 1841, M.A. 1844, vicar of St. Thomas', Ashton-in-Makerfield, 1848-57, rector of Whittington, Lancashire, 1857.

Pigot, Rev. Edward Charles, 3s. Octavius Frederick, of Wigan, Lancashire, cler. QUEEN'S COLL., matric. 28 Oct., 1881, aged 21; B.A. 1884.

Pigott, Edward Frederick Smyth, 3s. John Hugh, of Brockley, Somerset, arm. BALLIOL COLL., matric. 17 Dec., 1842, aged 18; B.A. 1846, M.A. 1850, bar.-at-law, Lincoln's Inn, 1851, examiner of plays in the lord chamberlain's department since 1874, brother of George O. S. See Foster's *Men at the Bar* & *Eton School Lists*.

Pigot, Francis, s. George, of Isleworth, Middlesex, doctor. QUEEN'S COLL., matric. 17 Dec., 1736, aged 17; B.A. from NEW COLL. 1742, M.A. 1746, B.Med. 1749. [20]

Pigott-Stainsby-Conant, Francis 1s. Paynton, of Trunewell, Berks, arm. LINCOLN COLL., matric. 7 March, 1826, aged 17; M.P. Reading 1846-60, lieut.-governor Isle of Man, 1860, until his death 21 Jan., 1863 (his father assumed the additional names of Stainsby-Conant in 1836). See *Eton School Lists*.

Piggott, Fraser, 2s. Simon, of St. George's, Bloomsbury, London, arm. CHRIST CHURCH, matric. 2 June, 1852, aged 17; B.A. 1857, a student of Lincoln's Inn 1857.

Pigott, Frederick William, 8s. Paynton P. Stainsby Conant, of Sherfield, Hants, arm. ST. JOHN'S COLL., matric. 19 March, 1851, aged 19; of the Middle Temple.

Pigot, George, s. Charles, of St. David's, co. Pembroke, pleb. ST. JOHN'S COLL., matric. 8 July, 1729, aged 18; B.C.L. 1736, died fellow 2 Oct., 1737. See *Robinson*, 60.

Pigott, George, s. George, of Windlesham, Surrey, cler. ST. JOHN'S COLL., matric. 30 June, 1768, aged 17; B.A. 1772, M.A. 1776 (as PIGGOTT). See *Robinson*, 122. [25]

Pigott, George, o.s. George, of St. Luke's, London, arm. TRINITY COLL., matric. 16 March, 1826, aged 19; B.A. 1829.

Pigott, George Octavius Smyth, 4s. John Hugh, of Wroxall, Somerset, arm. EXETER COLL., matric. 22 May, 1845, aged 18; S.C.L. 1851, rector of Kingston Seymour, Somerset, 1854, brother of Edward F. S. See *Eton School Lists*.

Pigott, George William, 7s. John Dryden (Pigott, after Corbet), of Edgmond, Salop, cler. EXETER COLL., matric. 6 June, 1844, aged 19; B.A. 1848, rector of Upton Magna, Salop, 1854, preb. of Lichfield 1888, brother of Charles F. C.

Pigot, Harry Vernon, 3s. James Creswell, of Everton, Lancashire. NEW COLL., matric. 10 Oct., 1873, aged 19; scholar ORIEL COLL. 1874-9, B.A. 1877, M.A. 1885, a student of the Inner Temple 1875.

Pigott, Henry Frederick, 2s. John William Mose, of Guildford, gent. NON-COLL., matric. 1 May, 1886, aged 23; brother of Edmund J. and John W. M. B.

Pigot, Henry Orlando, 2s. George, of Patshall, co. Stafford, baronet. CHRIST CHURCH, matric. 11 May, 1826, aged 18; B.A. 1830, died Nov., 1840. See Foster's *Baronetage*. [31]

Pigot, Henry Septimus, 7s. Thomas, of St. Helen's, Lancashire, cler. BRASENOSE COLL., matric. 27 Feb., 1845, aged 18; B.A. 1848, M.A. 1851, vicar of Horwich, Lancashire, since 1853.

Pigot, Hugh, s. Charles, of Hodnet, Salop, gent. BRASENOSE COLL., matric. 10 Dec., 1716, aged 18; B.A. 1720, M.A. 1723. See Robert 1769.

Pigot, Hugh, 2s. Creswell, of Drayton, Salop, arm. BRASENOSE COLL., matric. 6 June, 1838, aged 18; B.A. 1842, M.A. 1845, vicar of Wisbech St. Mary 1863-9, rector of Stretham, co. Cambridge, 1869, until his death 22 Sep., 1884.

Pigot, Hugh Lindsay, 3s. John Tayleur, of Fremington, Devon, cler. KEBLE COLL., matric. 19 Oct., 1877, aged 19; B.A. 1880, M.A. 1886. [35]

Piggott, James, 1s. Simon Fraser, of St. George's, Bloomsbury, London, arm. UNIVERSITY COLL., matric. 5 March, 1845, aged 18; brother of Fraser 1852.

Pigot, James Creswell, 1s. James Creswell, of Liverpool, arm. LINCOLN COLL., matric. 20 Oct., 1869, aged 20; B.A. 1874, M.A. 1876, vicar of St. Thomas Eccleston, Lancashire, 1877, brother of Harry Vernon.

Pigott, James Noel, s. William, of Colton, co. Stafford, arm. WORCESTER COLL., matric. 18 Nov., 1801, aged 18; fellow until 1812, B.A. 1805, M.A. 1812, rector of Grendon Underwood, Bucks, 1808, until his death 9 April, 1855.

Pigott, John, s. Robert, of Chetwynd, Salop, arm. WADHAM COLL., matric. 24 March, 1723-4, aged 19; created M.A. 15 April, 1730, brother of Benjamin 1733.

Pigott, John, s. John, of Chaworth, Berks, gent. MAGDALEN HALL, matric. 12 March, 1750-1, aged 18; B.A. 1754, vicar of Gilling and Hornby, Yorks, 1770, and of Oswaldkirk 1774, until his death in Aug., 1812.

Pigott, John, s. John, of Brockley, Somerset, arm. CHRIST CHURCH, matric. 27 Feb., 1759, aged 17.

Pigott, John, s. John, of Limerick (Ireland), gent. CORPUS CHRISTI COLL., matric. 30 Oct., 1798, aged 16. **[5]**

Piggott, John David, 2s. Solomon, of Latchford, Cheshire, gent. MERTON COLL., matric. 24 June, 1833, aged 19; clerk and scholar 1833-7, B.A. 1837, rector of Cuxham 1853, brother of Samuel R.

Pigott, John Dryden, s. William, of Chetwynd, Salop, cler. CHRIST CHURCH, matric. 20 Nov., 1795, aged 18; B.A. 1800, M.A. 1802, rector of Habberley 1802, and of Edgmond, Salop (patron) 1811, until his death 17 April, 1845.

Pigott, John Dryden. CHRIST CHURCH, 1826. See CORBET, page 296.

Pigott, John Robert, s. William, of Chelmsford, Essex, arm. WORCESTER COLL., matric. 13 June, 1818, aged 18. **[10]**

Pigot, John Tayleur, 4s. Thomas, of Prescot, Lancashire, cler. BRASENOSE COLL., matric. 10 June, 1840, aged 19; scholar 1840-5, B.A. 1844, M.A. 1847, minor canon Rochester 1847-55, vicar of Fremington, North Devon, 1855, father of Hugh Lindsay.

Piggott, John William Mose Benjamin, 3s. John William, of Guildford, Surrey, gent. NON-COLL., matric. 13 Oct., 1884, aged 16; brother of Edmund J.

Pigott, Montague Horatio Mostyn Turtle, 1s. Robert Turtle, of London, arm. UNIVERSITY COLL., matric. 11 Oct., 1884, aged 19.

Pigot, Richard, s. George, of London, arm. ORIEL COLL., matric. 28 Jan., 1792, aged 18.

Pigott, Richard Paynton, 2s. Paynton, of Mortimer, Berks, arm. TRINITY COLL., matric. 2 April, 1829, aged 18; B.A. 1834, rector of Ellisfield, Hants, 1837, until his death 10 March, 1885. **[15]**

Pigott, Robert, s. Robert, of Chetwynd, Salop, arm. CHRIST CHURCH, matric. 21 Feb., 1717-8, aged 18; of Chetwynd Park, Salop, and of Chesterton Hall, Hunts, died in May, 1770, brother of John and Benjamin.

Pigot, Robert, s. Charles, of Peploe, Salop, arm. PEMBROKE COLL., matric. 11 July, 1769, aged 18. See Hugh, 1716.

Piggott, Robert Jackson, o.s. John Cornell, of Kendal, Westmoreland, gent. ST. MARY HALL, matric. 27 Oct., 1869, aged 19; B.A. 1876, vicar of Kentmere, Westmoreland, 1880.

Piggott, Samuel Rotton, 1s. Solomon, of St. Mary's, Nottingham (town), cler. ST. EDMUND HALL, matric. 21 Jan., 1830, aged 20; exhibitioner 1830-3, B.A. 1833, curate of Bredgar, Kent, 1838-49, vicar since 1849, brother of John David.

Pigott, Simon Fraser Cooke, s. Henry Cooke, of Bristol, arm. UNIVERSITY COLL., matric. 15 Feb., 1811, aged 17; B.A. 1814, M.A. 1817, bar.-at-law, Lincoln's Inn, 1817, took the additional surname of PIGOTT, vide *London Gazette* 17 Aug., 1824, died 24 June, 1865, father of James and Fraser. **[20]**

Piggott, Solomon, s. John, of Haddenham, Bucks, pleb. ST. EDMUND HALL, matric. 29 Jan., 1797, aged 17; B.A. 1800, M.A. 1803, rector of Dunstable, Beds, 1824, until his death 27 April, 1845, father of John D. and Samuel R.; for list of his works see *Gent.'s Mag.*, 1845, ii. 431.

Piggott, Theodore Caro, 2s. Henry James, of Padua, Italy, cler. CHRIST CHURCH, matric. 10 Oct., 1884, aged 16; scholar 1884, B.A. 1888, of the Indian Civil Service 1886.

Pigott, Thomas, s. Robert, of Shrewsbury, Salop, arm. BRASENOSE COLL., matric. 13 Oct., 1758, aged 18; brother of Dryden, Walter, and Edward, and of William 1759.

Pigot, Thomas, s. Thomas, of Hodnet, Salop, arm. CHRIST CHURCH, matric. 29 Oct., 1795, aged 17; B.A. 1799, M.A. 1802, died rector of Blymhill, co. Stafford, 25 Jan., 1840.

Pigott, Thomas Southwell, s. John, of Rosenarris, Queen's County (Ireland), arm. EXETER COLL., matric. 14 Sep., 1810, aged 18. **[25]**

Pigott, Wadham, s. John, of Brockley, Somerset, arm. ST. MARY HALL, matric. 9 June, 1768, aged 17; of Brockley Court, Somerset, rector of Quainton, Bucks, 1775, died in 1824, brother of John 1759.

Pigott, Wellesley Pole, 4s. George, of Kelavel, Ireland, baronet. BRASENOSE COLL., matric. 14 June, 1828, aged 18; B.A. from NEW INN HALL 1835, M.A. 1836, rector of Fuggleston St. Peter, with Bemerton, Wilts, 1836, and also of Fovant since 1836. See Foster's *Baronetage*.

Pigott, William, s. Robert, of Shrewsbury (town), arm. BRASENOSE COLL., matric. 25 May, 1759, aged 16; B.C.L. 1766, rector of Edgmond and Chetwynd, Salop, 1779, until his death 9 March, 1811.

Pigott, William, 4s. John, of Dover, Kent, arm. NEW COLL., matric. 26 March, 1831, aged 20; fellow 1831-51, B.C.L. 1839, bursar 1839, dean of civil law 1840, sub-warden 1844, vicar of Whaddon, Bucks, 1850, until his death 5 Oct., 1881.

Pigot, William Melville, o.s. Henry Becher, of Cromford, co. Derby, arm. BRASENOSE COLL., matric. 31 May, 1861, aged 19; B.A. 1865, M.A. 1868, vicar of Eaton, Norfolk, 1875. **[30]**

Pigou, Clarence, s. Frederick, of Putney, Surrey, arm. CHRIST CHURCH, matric. 2 Dec., 1815, aged 17, B.A. 1819; fellow MERTON COLL. 1821-58. See *Eton School Lists*, 61*a*.

Pigou, Frederick Hugo, 1s. Frederick Alexander Preston, of Dartford, Kent, gent. NON-COLL., matric. 13 May, 1884, aged 17.

Pigou, Henry Clarence, 3s. Henry Minchin, of Bancora, East Indies, arm. ORIEL COLL., matric. 20 Feb., 1840, aged 18; scholar UNIVERSITY COLL. 1841-7, B.A. 1844, M.A. 1848, rector of Wyke Regis, Dorset, 1855-83. See *Rugby School Reg.*, 182.

Pigou, Robert Richard, s. Frederick, of London, arm. CHRIST CHURCH, matric. 24 Oct., 1786, aged 18; fellow MERTON COLL. until 1823, B.A. 1790, M.A. 1795.

Pike, Arthur Leonard, 1s. John Bilton, of Clapham, Surrey, arm. NEW COLL., matric. 22 Nov., 1879, aged 18; B.A. 1883. **[35]**

Pike, Frederick Popham, 3s. John, of St. James's, Westminster, gent. PEMBROKE COLL., matric. 19 Oct., 1860, aged 19; B.A. 1865, M.A. 1867, bar.-at-law, Inner Temple, 1866, died 15 Sep., 1877.

Pike, Herbert Watson, 1s. Thelwell, of Weyhill, Hants, D.Med. NEW COLL., matric. 14 Oct., 1882, aged 19; B.A. 1885, of the Indian Civil Service 1882.

Pike, John, 1s. John, of Gray's Inn, London, gent. ST. ALBAN HALL, matric. 15 Oct., 1828, aged 27.

Pike, John William, 2s. John William, of Wareham, Dorset, arm. EXETER COLL., matric. 11 Oct., 1872, aged 19; a student of the Inner Temple 1885. See *Rugby School Reg.*

Pike, Rev. Josias John, s. Josiah, of Marylebone, Middlesex, gent. PEMBROKE COLL., matric. 2 July, 1788, aged 18; B.A. 1792, M.A. 1795, died 11 July, 1850. See *Robinson*, 147.

Pike, Luke Owen, o.s. Luke, of St. George's, Hanover Square, London, arm. BRASENOSE COLL., matric. 9 Dec., 1853, aged 18; scholar 1853-8, B.A. 1857, M.A. 1861, bar.-at-law, Lincoln's Inn, 1864. See Foster's *Men at the Bar.*

Pike, Marmaduke Christian, 3s. John William, of Wareham, Dorset, arm. BRASENOSE COLL., matric. 20 May, 1875, aged 20; B.A. 1878. See *Rugby School Reg.*

Pike, Thomas Mayer, 1s. John William, of Burslem, co. Stafford, arm. ST. JOHN'S COLL., matric. 12 Oct., 1872, aged 20; B.A. & M.A. 1882. See *Rugby School Reg.* [5]

Pike, Warburton Mayer, 4s. John William, of Wareham, Dorset, arm. BRASENOSE COLL., matric. 22 Oct., 1880, aged 19.

Pike, William Herbert, Ph.D., s. Warburton, of Clapham, arm. MERTON COLL., matric. 9 Dec., 1879, aged 28; created M.A. 11 Dec., 1879, professor of chemistry University College, Toronto, sometime one of the demonstrators of chemistry in the University laboratory.

Pilcher, Francis, 3s. Henry Incledon, of Tebarah, West Maitland, New South Wales, gent. ORIEL COLL., matric. 22 Oct., 1859, aged 19; B.A. 1862, M.A. 1868, rector of St. Clement's, Oxford, 1878.

Pilcher, George Loat, 1s. William, of London, gent. PEMBROKE COLL., matric. 23 Feb., 1848, aged 18; B.A. 1852, a student of Lincoln's Inn 1853. See *Eton School Lists.*

Pilcher, Giles Theodore, 2s. Jeremiah Giles, of Camberwell, Surrey, arm. CORPUS CHRISTI COLL., matric. 20 Oct., 1868, aged 19; scholar 1868-73, B.A. 1873, M.A. 1875, rector of Letcombe Bassett 1880-1. [10]

Pilcher, John Harry Warton, 1s. John Giles, of Egham, Surrey, arm. MAGDALEN COLL., matric. 16 Oct., 1884, aged 19; B.A. 1888.

Pilcher, Matthew, 3s. John Giles, of Stockwell, Surrey, gent. LINCOLN COLL., matric. 5 Nov., 1856, aged 18; bar.-at-law, Lincoln's Inn, 1860. See Foster's *Men at the Bar.*

Pile, Archibald Jones, 1s. Nathaniel Jones, of Isle of Barbados, arm. EXETER COLL., matric. 15 Oct., 1864, aged 18; B.A. 1867.

Pile, George Laurie, 1s. George Clarke, of the Island of Barbados, gent. EXETER COLL., matric. 3 June, 1876, aged 18; B.A. 1879.

Pilgrim, John, s. Joseph, of Red Lion Square, London, arm. TRINITY COLL., matric. 15 Nov., 1734, aged 17; bar.-at-law, Middle Temple, 1740 (? if took orders, and died at Windsor in 1778). [15]

Pilgrim, Thomas, fellow TRINITY COLL., Cambridge (B.A. 1703, M.A. 1707, B.D. 1716); incorp. 11 May, 1736, regius professor of Greek at Cambridge 1712-26.

Pilgrim, Robert Tegetmere, 2s. Charles, of Hampstead, Middlesex, arm. TRINITY COLL., matric. 20 May, 1822, aged 17; B.A. 1826, M.A. 1830, rector of Shaw, Berks, 1837, until his death 8 Nov., 1838.

Pilkington, Rev. Charles, s. Lyon, of Yorks, baronet. CHRIST CHURCH, matric. 16 June, 1730, aged 18; B.A. 1734, M.A. 1738, of St. Martin's-in-the-Fields, died in 1757. See Foster's *Yorkshire Collection.*

Pilkington, Charles, s. Richard, of Skendleby, co. Lincoln, gent. UNIVERSITY COLL., matric. 5 Dec., 1748, aged 16; demy MAGDALEN COLL. 1750-2, B.A. 1752, fellow 1752-74, M.A. 1755, B.D. 1762, D.D. 1768, junior dean of arts 1762, bursar 1763 & 1771, vice-president 1772, dean of divinity 1773, curate of Horspath 1771, vicar of Findon 1772, until his death 28 Jan., 1797. See *Bloxam*, vi. 288.

Pilkington, Charles, s. Charles, of Findon, Sussex, doctor. BRASENOSE COLL., matric. 26 May, 1794, aged 17; demy MAGDALEN COLL. 1794-8, B.A. 1798, M.A. 1801, preb. of Chichester 1803, and canon residentiary 1825, vicar of Chidham, Sussex, 1813, and of Eastergate, Chichester, 1825, until his death 21 Oct., 1828. See *Bloxam*, vii. 129. [20]

Pilkington, Charles, 1s. Charles, of St. Pancras, Chichester, cler. NEW COLL., matric. 5 July, 1820, aged 18; fellow 1820-35, B.C.L. 1827, M.A. 1861, rector of St. Laurence, Winchester, 1831, preb. of Chichester 1834, canon 1850, chancellor 1854, rector of Stockton, co. Warwick, 1835, until his death 10 Sep., 1870.

Pilkington, Charles Henry, 1s. Charles, of Stockton, co. Warwick, cler. NEW COLL., matric. 5 Oct., 1854, aged 16; fellow 1854-69, B.A. 1858, M.A. 1861, rector of Letton and Willersley, co. Hereford, 1868-71, vicar of Owslebury, Hants, 1871-5, and of the Tything, co. Worcester, 1875-82, rector of St. John's, Madder-market, Norwich, 1882.

Pilkington, Claude William Egerton Milborne Swinnerton, 3s. Lionel, of Chevet Park, Yorks, baronet. CHRIST CHURCH, matric. 13 Oct., 1882, aged 19; B.A. 1885. See Foster's *Baronetage* & *Eton School Lists.*

Pilkington, Frederick Wellington, 3s. William, of Denbigh (town), gent. JESUS COLL., matric. 18 June, 1829, aged 17.

Pilkington, Harrison, s. Lyon, of Wakefield, Yorks, baronet. CHRIST CHURCH, matric. 13 March, 1734-5, aged 18; of Chevet, Yorks, died 6 Dec., 1787. See Foster's *Yorkshire Collection.* [25]

Pilkington, Henry, s. William, of St. Margaret's, Westminster, arm. ORIEL COLL., matric. 12 June, 1805, aged 17; B.A. 1810, M.A. 1814, bar.-at-law, Gray's Inn, 1815, an assistant poor-law commissioner, died 26 Feb., 1859.

Pilkington, Herbert Walter Malony, 4s. William, of of Rathdowney, Ireland, arm. WORCESTER COLL., matric. 19 Oct., 1882, aged 20.

Pilkington, James, s. Edward, of Halsall, Lancashire, cler. BRASENOSE COLL., matric. 27 Oct., 1732, aged 17; B.A. 1736.

Pilkington, John, s. Edward, of Halsall, Lancashire, cler. ORIEL COLL., matric. 20 March, 1726-7, aged 18; B.A. 6 March, 1730-1. [29]

Pilkington, (Sir) Lionel (Bart.), s. Lyon, of Wakefield, Yorks, baronet. CHRIST CHURCH, matric. 14 May, 1725, aged 18; 5th baronet, M.P. Horsham 1748-68, died 7 Aug., 1778. See Foster's *Baronetage.*

Pilkington, Matthew, s. Thomas, of Bridgnorth, Salop, gent. PEMBROKE COLL., matric. 25 Nov., 1789, aged 18; B.A. 1793, M.A. 1797, incumbent of Alveley, Salop, 1804, until his death 15 Oct., 1847.

Pilkington, Richard, of QUEEN'S COLL., Cambridge (B.A. 1850, M.A. 1853); adm. 'ad eundem' 9 July, 1853.

Pilkington, (Sir) Thomas (Bart.), s. Michael, of Badsworth, Yorks, baronet. MERTON COLL., matric. 1 Aug., 1791, aged 17; created M.A. 5 July, 1793, 7th baronet, died 9 July, 1811.

Pilkington, (Sir) Thomas Edward (Bart.), 1s. (William), of Roystone, Yorks, baronet. UNIVERSITY COLL., matric. 16 Oct., 1847, aged 18; 9th baronet, died 8 Jan., 1854.

Pilkington, Thomas Edward Milborne Swinnerton, 1s. Lionel, of Chevet Park, Yorks, baronet. CHRIST CHURCH, matric. 13 Oct., 1876, aged 18; B.A. 1879, M.A. 1883. See Foster's *Baronetage* & *Eton School Lists.* [35]

Pilkington, Rev. William, 3s. Charles, of Chichester, Sussex, cler. TRINITY COLL., matric. 3 May, 1824, aged 17; demy MAGDALEN COLL. 1824-31, B.A. 1828, M.A. 1831, fellow 1831, until his death 2 June, 1832. See *Bloxam*, vii. 292.

Pilkington, William Lee, 1s. William, of Sutton Grange, Lancashire, gent. CHRIST CHURCH, matric. 3 Nov., 1875, aged 18.

illing, John Henry Rushworth, 1s. John Rushworth, of Oxford, cler. NON-COLL., matric. 15 May, 1869, aged 20, B.A. 1874; M.A. from ST. ALBAN HALL 1878, vicar of Wighton, Norfolk, 1883.

illing, John Rushworth, 1s. James, of Burmage, Lancashire, gent. MAGDALEN HALL, matric. 2 May, 1845, aged 18; B.A. 1849, M.A. (HERTFORD COLL.) 1874, vicar of Binham, Norfolk, 1863-4, of Longham 1864-9, rector of Barby, Northants, 1877-89, and of Walls-next-the-Sea 1880, until his death 19 Feb., 1886.

illing, Octavius Frank, 7s. John Rushworth, of Longham, Norfolk, cler. NON-COLL., matric. 17 Oct., 1885, aged 18.

illinger, John, of Park Street, Oxford; privilegiatus 4 March, 1848, yeoman-bedel of theology.

ilsworth, Thomas, s. Edward, of All Saints', Hereford (city), pleb. MAGDALEN HALL, matric. 15 May, 1727, aged 18. [5]

im, Henry Bedford, 1s. Bedford Clapperton Trevelyan, of London, arm. MERTON COLL., matric. 22 Oct., 1883, aged 20; B.A. 1886.

imblett, Charles Bradburn, 1s. James, of Burton-on-Trent, co. Stafford, cler. WADHAM COLL., matric. 19 Jan., 1884, aged 18; exhibitioner QUEEN'S COLL. 1884, B.A. 1887.

imlott, James, s. Richard, of Prestbury, Cheshire, gent. BRASENOSE COLL., matric. 15 Oct., 1792, aged 19.

inchback, Thomas, s. Joseph, of Bedworth, co. Warwick, gent. ST. EDMUND HALL, matric. 19 March, 1811, aged 30.

inchin, Hugh Tennent, y.s. John, of Southsea, Hants, gent. NON-COLL., matric. 23 Jan., 1886, aged 19. [10]

inchin, John Robert, 1s. John, of Landport, Hants, gent. NON-COLL., matric. 17 Oct., 1885, aged 20.

inching, Horace Henderson, 5s. Charles John, of Gravesend, Kent, gent. PEMBROKE COLL., matric. 23 Oct., 1875, aged 18; B.A. 1879, M.A. 1882.

Pinckard, Henry, s. Henry, of Hanley, Northants, gent. LINCOLN COLL., matric. 14 Dec., 1774, aged 17; B.A. 1778, M.A. 1781.

Pincke, Henry, s. Henry, of Damerham, Wilts, cler. TRINITY COLL., matric. 11 May, 1721, aged 16.

Pincke, Thomas, s. Alured, of Dodington, Kent, arm. HERTFORD COLL., matric. 9 May, 1781, aged 20; a student of Lincoln's Inn 1781. [15]

Pinckney, Charles Cotesworth, s. Charles, of Charlestown, South Carolina, arm. CHRIST CHURCH, matric. 19 Jan., 1764, aged 17; bar.-at-law, Middle Temple, 1769, brother of Thomas 1768.

Pinckney, Erlysman, o.s. Erlysman Charles, of St. James's, Salisbury, Wilts, arm. EXETER COLL., matric. 2 June, 1857, aged 18; B.A. 1861, M.A. 1864, of Wraxall Lodge, Bradford-on-Avon, bar.-at-law, Inner Temple, 1863. See Foster's *Men at the Bar.*

Pinckney, George, 1s. William, of Milford Hill, near Salisbury, arm. EXETER COLL., matric. 27 May, 1882, aged 18.

Pinckney, George Henry, 4s. John Hearne, of Laleham, Middlesex, cler. EXETER COLL., matric. 17 June, 1831, aged 19; B.A. 1835.

Pinckney, John Hearn, s. William, of Great Bedwin, Wilts, gent. CORPUS CHRISTI COLL., matric. 19 July, 1794, aged 16; B.A. 1798, M.A. 1802, B. & D.D. 1813, died at East Sheen, Surrey, 9 April, 1864. [20]

Pinckney, Miles, s. Charles, of Charlestown, America, arm. MAGDALEN COLL., matric. 7 July, 1787, aged 18.

Pinckney, Robert, 1s. Robert, of Amesbury, Wilts, arm. ST. JOHN'S COLL., matric. 5 April, 1848, aged 21; vicar of Cullompton 1857-61, rector of Chilfrome, Dorset, 1862-9, of Hittisleigh, Devon, 1869-70, vicar of Highcliffe, Hants, 1871-80, of Hinton Admiral, Hants, 1879, until his death in 1886.

Pinckney, Robert Arthur, 1s. John, of Salisbury, arm. EXETER COLL., matric. 19 Jan., 1877, aged 18; B.A. 1882. See *Eton School Lists.*

Pinckney, Thomas, s. Charles, of Charlestown, South Carolina, arm. CHRIST CHURCH, matric. 23 Nov., 1768, aged 18; bar.-at-law, Middle Temple, 1774, brother of Charles 1764.

Pinckney, William, 4s. Robert, of Amesbury, Wilts, arm. EXETER COLL., matric. 25 Feb., 1853, aged 18; B.A. 1857, M.A. 1859, of Milford Hill, Wilts, banker. See *Eton School Lists.* [25]

Pincott, Edward London, of CAIUS COLL., Cambridge (B.A. 1862, M.A. 1866); adm. 'comitatis causa' 18 May, 1866.

Pindar, John, s. Robert, of Owston, co. Lincoln, arm. LINCOLN COLL., matric. 15 Oct., 1722, aged 19; bar.-at-law, Inner Temple, 1729, brother of the next named.

Pindar, Robert, s. Robert, of Owston, co. Lincoln, gent. LINCOLN COLL., matric. 10 Nov., 1726, aged 19; B.A. 1730, M.A. 1733, probably father of Robert and Thomas next named.

Pindar, Robert, s. Robert, of Stockwith, co. Lincoln, cler. MERTON COLL., matric. 11 Dec., 1759, aged 19.

Pindar, Thomas, s. Robert, of Stockwith, Notts, cler. MERTON COLL., matric. 15 Dec., 1756, aged 19, B.A. 1760; M.A. from MAGDALEN COLL. 1763, D.C.L. 1772. [30]

Pinder, Edward, 2s. William Maynard, of Brighton, Sussex, arm. WADHAM COLL., matric. 15 June, 1843, aged 17; B.A. 1847, M.A. 1850, curate of Roydon, Norfolk, died 2 Oct., 1859.

Pinder, North, 3s. William Maynard, of Worcester, (city), arm. BALLIOL COLL., matric. 11 Dec., 1846, aged 17; scholar TRINITY COLL. 1847-51, B.A. 1850, fellow 1851-61, M.A. 1853, rhetoric lecturer, tutor, etc., 1856, dean 1859, etc., rector of Rotherfield Greys, Oxon, 1860. See *Rugby School Reg.*, 239.

Pinder, Reginald, s. Reginald, of Madresfield, co. Worcester, arm. MERTON COLL., matric. 12 March, 1732-3, aged 18.

Pine, (Sir) Benjamin (Chilley Campbell), 1s. Benjamin, of Maidstone, Kent, gent. ST. ALBAN HALL, matric. 4 July, 1828, aged 19; B.A. from TRINITY COLL., Cambridge, 1833, M.A. 1840, bar.-at-law, Gray's Inn, 1841, bencher 1880, lieut.-governor of Natal 1849-56, governor 1873-5, of Gold Coast Settlement 1856-9, and of Leeward Islands 1869-73, knighted at Windsor Castle 28 Nov., 1856, K.C.M.G. 29 Sep., 1871, etc. See Foster's *Men at the Bar.*

Pine, Edward, s. Ed., of East Down, Devon, arm. EXETER COLL., matric. 18 March, 1729-30, aged 18; B.A. 1735. [35]

Pine-Coffin, Rev. John, s. John Pine, of East Down, Devon, arm. EXETER COLL., matric. 29 March, 1754, aged 17; B.A. 1758, of East Down, Devon, and of Impington, co. Cambridge, assumed the additional surname of COFFIN by royal licence 1797, died at Bath, 29 April, 1824, father of Richard 1788.

Pine, Philip, s. Philip, of Totnes, Devon, cler. HERTFORD COLL., matric. 17 March, 1740-1, aged 18; B.A. 1744.

Pine-Coffin, Richard, s. John, of East Down, Devon, gent. BALLIOL COLL., matric. 5 Nov., 1788, aged 18; of East Down and Portledge, Devon, died 6 Oct., 1833.

Pinfold, Charles John, s. Charles, of Chicheley, Bucks, arm. BRASENOSE COLL., matric. 14 Jan., 1818, aged 17; B.A. from CHRIST'S COLL., Cambridge, 1825, died rector of Bramshall, co. Stafford, 21 Nov., 1856.

Pinfold, Joseph, 'cook of Worcester College;' privilegiatus 6 Oct., 1817. [40]

Ping, Andrew, 5s. John, of Rotherham, Yorks, arm. NON-COLL., matric. 23 May, 1885, aged 28; B.A. 1888.

Pinhey, Arthur Francis, 6s. Robert Hill, of Surat, East Indies, arm. (after knight). TRINITY COLL., matric. 14 Oct., 1882, aged 18; of the Indian Civil Service 1882, a student of the Inner Temple 1882.

Pinhey, Hugh Theodore, 3s. Robert Hill, of Satara, East Indies, arm. (after knight). KEBLE COLL., matric. 15 Oct., 1877, aged 18.

Pinhey, Robert William Spottiswoode, 1s. Robert Hill, of Poonah, East Indies, arm. (after knight). UNIVERSITY COLL., matric. 14 Oct., 1871, aged 18; B.A. 1875, bar.-at-law, Lincoln's Inn, 1877, advocate Bombay. See Foster's *Men at the Bar* & *Rugby School Reg.*

Pinhorn, Rev. Francis Reyner Brooksbank, 1s. George, of Brimfield, co. Hereford, cler. WADHAM COLL., matric. 11 Oct., 1878, aged 18; B.A. 1883, M.A. 1885.

Pinhorn, George, 2s. James, of Portsea, Hants, gent. ST. EDMUND HALL, matric. 17 May, 1827, aged 29; B.A. 1831, M.A. 1833, rector of Brimfield 1832, and vicar of Ashford-Bowler, co. Hereford, 1835, until his death 28 Jan., 1879. [5]

Pinkerton, John Saltwell, o.s. John, of Bloomsbury, London, gent. ST. JOHN'S COLL., matric. 29 June, 1829, aged 16; scholar and fellow 1829-56, B.A. 1834, M.A. 1837, B.D. 1843, dean of arts 1837, bursar 1842, vice-president 1845, chaplain 1857, proctor 1842-3, vicar of Leckford, Hants, 1855-70, rector 1870.

Pinkerton, Robert Hamilton, 3s. John, of Rutherglen, co. Lanark, arm. BALLIOL COLL., matric. 6 Feb., 1877, aged 21; exhibitioner 1877-9, B.A. 1881.

Pinkney, William, s. Philip, of Oxford (city), pleb. CHRIST CHURCH, matric. 5 March, 1732-3, aged 18; B.A. 1736, M.A. 1747.

Pinnell, Henry, s. John, of Fittleworth, Sussex, cler. CORPUS CHRISTI COLL., matric. 25 May, 1732, aged 15; B.A. 6 Feb., 1735-6, M.A. 1738, B.D. 27 Feb., 1747-8.

Pinnell, John, s. John, of Fittleworth, Sussex, gent. BALLIOL COLL., matric. 13 May, 1725, aged 15; demy MAGDALEN COLL. 1725-32, B.A. 1728, M.A. 1731, fellow 1732-48, B.D. 1739, rector of Burton and Coates, Sussex, preb. of Chichester 1744, rector of Ducklington 1747, until his death 22 Feb., 1798. See *Bloxam*, vi. 208. [10]

Pinnell, Peter, of TRINITY COLL., Cambridge (B.A. 1742, M.A. 1746); incorp. 14 July, 1752, vicar of Eltham, Kent, vicar of Shorne 1777 (? then D.D.), and preb. of Rochester 1775, until his death 16 Aug., 1783.

Pinney, John, s. John, of Isle of Nevis, West Indies, arm. TRINITY COLL., matric. 29 Nov., 1792, aged 19.

Pinney, William, 4s. William, of Exeter, gent. EXETER COLL., matric. 20 Oct., 1873, aged 28; B.Mus. 23 April, 1874.

Pinniger, Henry Herbert, o.s. Richard Broome, of Whichford, co. Warwick, cler. PEMBROKE COLL., matric. 21 Oct., 1859, aged 19; B.A. 1862, M.A. 1866.

Pinniger, Richard Broome, 4s. Broome, of Woodhill Park, near Marlborough, Wilts, arm. PEMBROKE COLL., matric. 8 Dec., 1821, aged 18; B.A. 1825, M.A. 1828, rector of Whichford, co. Warwick, 1839-85, died 3 June, 1887. [15]

Pinnock, James, s. James, of Isle of Jamaica, gent. PEMBROKE COLL., matric. 10 Oct., 1730, aged 18; died 20 June, 1736.

Pinnock, James, s. James, of London, gent. ORIEL COLL., matric. 9 May, 1755, aged 16; B.A. 1759, M.A. 1761, rector of Lasham, Hants, 1764-1822, rector of Husbands-Bosworth, co. Lincoln, 1822, vicar of Norton, Northants, morning preacher at the Foundling Hospital, died 5 June, 1828.

Pinnock, Tom, 2s. Thomas, of Newbury, Berks, gent. NON-COLL., matric. 11 Oct., 1879, aged 32.

Pinnock, William Henny, of CORPUS CHRISTI COLL., Cambridge (LL.B. 1850, LL.D. 1855); adm. 'ad eundem' 17 Dec., 1859, chaplain at Chantilly 1870-6, vicar of Pinner, Herts, 1880, until his death 2 Dec., 1885.

Pinwill, Edmund, 4s. William James, of Holbeton, Devon, cler. PEMBROKE COLL., matric. 12 Dec., 1860, aged 19; B.A. 1863, M.A. 1875, held various curacies 1864-80, vicar of Ermington, Devon, 1880. [20]

Pinwill, William James, of TRINITY COLL., Cambridge (B.A. 1824, M.A. 1828); adm. 'ad eundem' 22 April, 1857, vicar of Horley with Hornton, Oxon, 1853-78, died 10 Sep., 1885.

Pipe, James, s. Samuel, of Stafford (town), gent. PEMBROKE COLL., matric. 18 May, 1739, aged 17; B.A. 1742, M.A. 1745. See Shaw's *Staffordshire.*

Pipe, Samuel, s. Humphrey, of Birmingham, co. Warwick, cler. PEMBROKE COLL., matric. 26 March, 1736, aged 16; B.A. 1739, M.A. 1742.

Pipe, Samuel, s. Samuel, of Tamworth, co. Stafford, cler. PEMBROKE COLL., matric. 3 April, 1767, aged 16.

Pipon, James, s. James, of Brelade, Isle of Jersey, gent. WORCESTER COLL., matric. 28 Feb., 1785, aged 14. [25]

Pipon, James Clement Collier, 1s. James Kennard, of Plymouth, Devon, arm. LINCOLN COLL., matric. 4 May, 1860, aged 18; scholar 1860-4, B.A. 1864, M.A. 1870, a student of the Inner Temple 1866, hon. minor canon Chester 1878.

Pipon, Philip, s. Philip, of Isle of Jersey, gent. PEMBROKE COLL., matric. 20 March, 1717-8, aged 18; B.A. 1721, M.A. 1725, master of Bishop Stortford School 1733.

Pippin, Joseph, of SYDNEY SUSSEX COLL., Cambridge (B.A. 1713, M.A. 1717); incorp. 26 June, 1723.

Pirie, Francis Logie, 2s. Francis, of Fulham, Middlesex, arm. BALLIOL COLL., matric. 13 Oct., 1860, aged 19; B.A. 1863, M.A. 1872, a student of Lincoln's Inn 1863. See *Rugby School Reg.*

Pitcairn, Cecil Colvin, o.s. Walker, of Fetcham, Surrey, arm. MAGDALEN COLL., matric. 14 Oct., 1871, aged 19; B.A. 1876, M.A. 1878, died 1880.

Pitcairn, David, scholar JESUS COLL., Cambridge, 1855, 6th wrangler & B.A. 1858, 5s. John, of Twickenham, Middlesex, arm. MAGDALEN COLL., incorp. 28 July, 1859, aged 24; fellow 1859-71, M.A. 1861, junior dean 1864, bursar 1865, bar.-at-law, Lincoln's Inn, 1863. See Foster's *Men at the Bar.* [31]

Pitcairn, David Lee, 2s. David, of Torquay, Devon, D.D. MAGDALEN COLL., matric. 19 Oct., 1867, aged 19; demy 1867-72, B.A. 1871, M.A. 1875, vicar of Monkton Combe, Somerset, 1883.

Pitcairn, James, s. David, of Forfar, co. Fife (Scotland), arm. ST. MARY HALL, matric. 24 May, 1737, aged 22; possibly father of the next named.

Pitcairn, Robert, s. James, of West Kington, Wilts, cler. MERTON COLL., matric. 11 April, 1764, aged 18; B.A. from BALLIOL COLL. 1768, minister of Spring Gardens' Chapel, died 6 May, 1792.

Pitcairn, Robert, 1s. Robert, of Newton, near Buckingham, Tasmania, arm. ORIEL COLL., matric. 27 Jan., 1864, aged 21; bar.-at-law, Lincoln's Inn, 1867. See Foster's *Men at the Bar.* [35]

Pitcairne, William, D.Med. by diploma 10 April, 1749 (1s. David, minister of Dysart, co. Fife); D.Med. Rheims, private tutor to James, 6th Duke of Hamilton, when at Oxford, fellow College Physicians 1750, president 1775-85, treasurer 1784, died 25 Nov., 1791. See Munk's *Roll*, ii. 172.

Pitcher, Frederick Augustus, s. John, of Isle of St. Christopher, West Indies, arm. ORIEL COLL., matric. 29 Nov., 1814, aged 17.

tcher, Rev. John Earle, 4s. John Earle, of Marylebone, London, arm. ORIEL COLL., matric. 13 June, 1822, aged 18; B.A. 1826, M.A. 1829, died 16 Sep., 1836.

tchford, John, s. Richard, of Upton Magna, Salop, cler. CHRIST CHURCH, matric. 22 Oct., 1793, aged 19; B.A. 1797, M.A. 1800, vicar of Colwich, co. Stafford, 1807, until his death in 1828.

tman, Rev. Allan Acland, 4s. Samuel, of Bishop's Hull, Somerset, arm. MAGDALEN COLL., matric. 14 Oct., 1878, aged 19; B.A. 1881, M.A. 1885.

tman, Charles, 2s. William, of Andover, Hants, gent. QUEEN'S COLL., matric. 3 May, 1820, aged 18.

tman, Francis Edward, 2s. Henry Rogers, of Basford, Notts, cler. EXETER COLL., matric. 30 May, 1871, aged 19; B.A. 1874, chaplain royal navy 1882. [5]

tman, Frederick, 7s. James, of Dunchideock, Devon, arm. EXETER COLL., matric. 6 Feb., 1840, aged 18; B.A. 1843, M.A. 1846, died rector of Iddesleigh, Devon, 30 Sep., 1857.

tman, Harry Anderson, 5s. Frederick, of North Berwick, arm. NEW COLL., matric. 15 Dec., 1885, aged 19.

tman, James, s. Samuel, of Ide, Devon, arm. ORIEL COLL., matric. 20 March, 1797, aged 18; B.A. 1800, of Dunchideock, major East Devon militia, died 12 Feb., 1848.

tman, James Campbell, 4s. Frederick, of Edinburgh, arm. NEW COLL., matric. 8 Dec., 1883, aged 19; B.A. 1887.

tman, James Samuel, 1s. James, of Plymstock, Devon, arm. EXETER COLL., matric. 19 May, 1825, aged 18; of Dunchideock, high sheriff, Devon, 1856, died 27 March, 1868. See *Eton School Lists*. [10]

tman, James Walter, s. James, of Exeter (city), arm. BALLIOL COLL., matric. 27 Feb., 1759, aged 18. (Memo.: Rev. J. P., died at Alphington 10 June, 1791).

itman, John, s. John, of Alphington, Devon, cler. BALLIOL COLL., matric. 20 Feb., 1735-6, aged 17; B.A. 1739, M.A. 1742, rector of Alphington 1757, until his death 1 Feb., 1768.

itman, John, s. John, of Stow, co. Gloucester, pleb. MAGDALEN COLL., matric. 17 May, 1757, aged 18; chorister 1749-57, clerk 1757-62, B.A. 1761, chaplain 1764-9, M.A. 1765. See *Coll. Reg.*, i. 163.

itman, John, s. John, of Alphington, Devon, cler. BALLIOL COLL., matric. 21 Nov., 1768, aged 18, B.A. 1772; M.A. from ORIEL COLL. 1775.

itman, John, s. John, of Tiverton, Devon, cler. BALLIOL COLL., matric. 7 April, 1802, aged 18.

itman, Joseph, o.s. Joseph, of Stourbridge, co. Worcester, arm. TRINITY COLL., matric. 13 May, 1853, aged 19. [15]

itman, Maurice William, y.s. Henry Eyre, of Futteeghur, East Indies, arm. QUEEN'S COLL., matric. 2 May, 1844, aged 18; B.A. 1848, M.A. 1850, held various curacies 1849-66.

itman, Morgan, s. John, of Evershot, Dorset, pleb. TRINITY COLL., matric. 6 March, 1733-4, aged 19.

itman, Thomas, 2s. Thomas Dix, of St. Pancras, arm. WADHAM COLL., matric. 12 April, 1820, aged 18; B.A. 1826, M.A. 1827, vicar of Eastbourne since 1828, preb. of Chichester 1841, father of the next named.

itman, Thomas, 1s. Thomas, of Tooting, Surrey, cler. WADHAM COLL., matric. 27 Jan., 1847, aged 18; B.A. 1850, M.A. 1859, vicar of St. Jude's, Islington, 1855, until his death 9 Dec., 1863. See *Robinson*, 280. [20]

itman, William Daniel, 1s. William Parr, of Washfield, near Tiverton, Devon, cler. EXETER COLL., matric. 24 Jan., 1863, aged 18; scholar 1862-6, B.A. 1866, M.A. 1869, rector (and patron) of Aveton-Gifford, Devon, 1874. See *Coll. Reg.*, 160.

Pitman, William Edward, 1s. William, of Southsea Hants, arm. KEBLE COLL., matric. 12 Feb., 1883, aged 19.

Pitman, William Parr, 2s. James, of Dunchideock, Devon, arm. EXETER COLL., matric. 4 Feb., 1830, aged 18; B.A. 1834, M.A. 1838, rector of Aveton-Gifford, Devon, 1847, until his death 14 May, 1874.

Pitney, Matthew, s. Matth., of Lamyat, Somerset, cler. QUEEN'S COLL., matric. 24 March, 1728-9, aged 17.

Pitt, Charles, 4s. Joseph, of Cirencester, co. Gloucester, arm. CHRIST CHURCH, matric. 21 Nov., 1818, aged 18; B.A. 1822, M.A. 1825, rector of Ashton Keynes 1834-66, vicar of Malmesbury 1829, until his death 18 Oct., 1874, brother of Cornelius. [25]

Pitt, Charles Whitworth, o.s. London King, of Petersburg, Russia, doctor. BRASENOSE COLL., matric. 17 Jan., 1821, aged 18; B.A. 1824, M.A. 1829, rector of Stapleford Abbotts, Essex, 1841, until his death 23 Jan., 1867. See *Gent.'s Mag.*, i. 395.

Pitt, Christopher, s. Ch., of Blandford, Dorset, doctor. WADHAM COLL., matric. 3 April, 1718, aged 18; B.A. from NEW COLL. 1722, M.A. 1724, brother of Henry 1722. See Hutchin's *Dorset*.

Pitt, Cornelius, s. Joseph, of Cirencester, co. Gloucester, gent. ORIEL COLL., matric. 28 Oct., 1803, aged 16; B.C.L. 1810, bar.-at-law, Lincoln's Inn, 1813, rector of Hazleton, co. Gloucester, 1824, and of Rendcomb 1831, until his death 26 Feb., 1840, father of Joseph 1837, and brother of Charles.

Pitt, Edward Martin, o.s. Thomas Martin Ready, of Kensington, Surrey, cler. WADHAM COLL., matric. 3 Nov., 1858, aged 17; B.A. 1862, M.A. 1865, 'ad eundem' Cantab. 1867, assumed the name of PITT in lieu of READY, rector of Bagthorpe, Norfolk, 1875.

Pitt, Evans, . John, of Cricklade, Wilts, gent. CHRIST CHURCH, matric. 14 Dec., 1719, aged 16; B.A. 1723, M.A. 1726, B.Med. 1729, D.Med. 1733 (as Evan). [30]

Pitt, George, s. George, of Strathfieldsaye, Hants, arm. MAGDALEN COLL., matric. 26 Sep., 1737, aged 15; created M.A. 13 March, 1738-9, and also D.C.L. 21 Aug., 1745, of Strathfieldsaye, Hants, M.P. Shaftesbury 1747, Dorset 1747-74, envoy extraordinary Turin 1761, ambassador to Spain 1770, created Baron Rivers 20 May, 1776, lord of the bed-chamber, died 7 May, 1803. See Foster's *Peerage*.

Pitt, George, s. Thomas, of St. Marylebone, Middlesex, arm. CHRIST CHURCH, matric. 14 Oct., 1814, aged 18; died vicar of Audlem, Cheshire, 28 April, 1865.

Pitt, George Henry, s. Joseph, of Brentford, Middlesex, arm. UNIVERSITY COLL., matric. 22 Nov., 1811, aged 18. See *Eton School Lists*.

Pitt, George Lewis, 3s. Charles, of Malmesbury, Wilts, cler. PEMBROKE COLL., matric. 25 Oct., 1871, aged 18.

Pitt, Henry, s. Christop., of Blandford, Dorset, doctor. EXETER COLL., matric. 10 Oct., 1722, aged 16; fellow 1724, B.A. 1727, M.A. 1729, died 1733, brother of Christopher 1718. See *Coll. Reg.*, 93.

Pitt, James, s. George, of Strathfieldsaye, Hants, arm. MAGDALEN COLL., matric. 27 Nov., 1739, aged 17; died s.p., brother of George 1737, and of Thomas 1741. [35]

Pitt, James, s. James, of Gloucester (city), gent. EXETER COLL., matric. 30 May, 1741, aged 16; B.A. 1745, possibly father of the next named.

Pitt, James, s. James, of Maisemore, co. Gloucester, cler. WORCESTER COLL., matric. 12 July, 1776, aged 17, B.A. 1780; M.A. from ORIEL COLL. 1783, B.D. 1790, vicar of Modbury, Devon, 1792, died rector of Brimpsfield and Cranham, co. Gloucester, 6 March, 1806.

Pitt, John, s. George, of St. Martin's, London, arm. QUEEN'S COLL., matric. 6 July, 1722, aged 16; probably of Encombe, Dorset, M.P. Wareham 1734-47, 1748-51, 1761-8, Dorchester 1757-61, a commissioner of woods and plantations 1744, died 1787.

Pitt, John, s. James, of Felton, co. Hereford, pleb. WORCESTER COLL., matric. 16 Jan., 1788, aged 18; B.A. 1792, died perp. curate Amberley, co. Hereford, in Sep., 1812.

Pitt, Joseph, s. John, of Cirencester, co. Gloucester, arm. CHRIST CHURCH, matric. 27 Oct., 1814, aged 18; B.A. 1818, M.A. 1822, bar.-at-law, Lincoln's Inn, 1822. See *Eton School Lists.*

Pitt, Joseph, o.s. Cornelius, of Rendcombe, co. Gloucester, cler. ORIEL COLL., matric. 25 May, 1837, aged 18; B.A. 1841, M.A. 1844, rector of Rendcombe 1844.

Pitt, London King, s. Richard, of Tiverton, Devon, cler. ST. JOHN'S COLL., matric. 27 June, 1791, aged 18; B.A. 1795, fellow, M.A. 1801, B.C.L. 1807, D.C.L. 1807, rector of Hinton, co. Gloucester, 1805, and of Hanwell, Oxon, chaplain to the British factory, St. Petersburgh, where he died 6 May, 1813. See *Alumni West.*, 418; & *Robinson*, 152. [5]

Pitt, Nicholas, s. James, of Gloucester (city), arm. EXETER COLL., matric. 22 March, 1745-6, aged 17.

Pitt, Stephen, s. Stephen, of Kensington, Middlesex, arm. UNIVERSITY COLL., matric. 24 April, 1793, aged 17.

Pitt, Thomas, s. George, of Shroton, Dorset, arm. QUEEN'S COLL., matric. 8 April, 1741, aged 16; B.A. 14 Feb., 1744-5, died s.p., brother of George 1737, and James 1739.

Pitt, Thomas, s. Thomas, of Westminster, arm. MAGDALEN COLL., matric. 11 Oct., 1774, aged 19; bar.-at-law, Middle Temple, 1782.

Pitt, William, s. Robert, of Old Sarum, Wilts, arm. TRINITY COLL., matric. 14 Jan., 1726-7, aged 18; Earl of Chatham so created 4 Aug., 1766, M.P. Old Sarum 1735-47, Seaford 1747-54, Aldburgh 1754-56, Okehampton 1756-7, Bath 1757-66, paymaster-general 1746-55, privy councillor 1746, secretary of State 1756-61, lord keeper 1766-8, died 11 May, 1778. [10]

Pitt, William, s. Richard, of Stonehouse, co. Gloucester, gent. PEMBROKE COLL., matric. 8 March, 1757, aged 19; B.A. 1760.

Pitt, William Henry, s. Thomas, of Rosthern, Cheshire, arm. CHRIST CHURCH, matric. 26 April, 1809, aged 18. See *Eton School Lists.*

Pitt, William Morton, s. John, of London, arm. QUEEN'S COLL., matric. 14 March, 1772, aged 17; of Encombe, Dorset, M.P. 1790-1826, and for Poole 1780-90, died 28 Feb., 1836.

Pittar, Charles William Erskine, 2s. Charles Frederick, of Khidderpore, East Indies, gent. BALLIOL COLL., matric. 17 Oct., 1882, aged 18; of the Indian Civil Service 1882.

Pittaway, Stephen, 'Faber Ferrarius Universitatis;' privilegiatus 15 July, 1723. [15]

Pitter, John, 2s. Robert, of Hunton, Hants, gent. PEMBROKE COLL., matric. 1 March, 1855, aged 18.

Pitters, Robert, s. John, of Hunton, Hants, gent. NEW COLL., matric. 13 Aug., 1756, aged 17; B.C.L. 1763 (as PITTER).

Pittman, Joseph Matthew, 2s. Joseph, of Hawthorne, near Melbourne, arm. BALLIOL COLL., matric. 21 Oct., 1880, aged 16; scholar 1880-4, B.A. 1884.

Pitts, John, s. Thomas, of Friday Street, London, gent. PEMBROKE COLL., matric. 13 July, 1748, aged 17; B.A. 1752 (? rector of Great Brickhill, Bucks, 1761, until he died 6 July, 1793).

Pitts, Nicholas Alfred, 1s. Nicholas William Prettyjohn, of Churchstow, Devon, arm. MAGDALEN COLL., matric. 7 May, 1878, aged 20. [20]

Pix, George Banastre, 4s. Samuel, of Rolvenden, Kent, gent. LINCOLN COLL., matric. 20 March, 1843, aged 17; B.A. 1846, M.A. 1849, vice-principal York Training College, head-master Trinidad Grammar School 1853-6, perp. curate Acaster Selby, Yorks, 1859-68, rector of Caenby, and vicar of Saxby, co. Lincoln, 1868, until his death 6 Nov., 1874.

Pixell, John Pryn Parkes, s. John, of Birmingham, co. Warwick, gent. QUEEN'S COLL., matric. 13 March, 1743-4, aged 18.

Pixell, Thomas, s. John, of Birmingham, co. Warwick, pleb. MERTON COLL., matric. 24 May, 1734, aged 17; B.A. 1737, M.A. from TRINITY COLL., Cambridge, 1749, vicar of Icomb, and vicar of Grimley with Hallow, co. Worcester, 1768, until his death in 1792.

Pizey, Charles Edward, 1s. Charles Thomas, of Liverpool, cler. NON-COLL., matric. 4 Nov., 1876, aged 23.

Place, Conyers, of PEMBROKE COLL., Cambridge (B.A. 1723, M.A. 1727); incorp. 8 July, 1727. [25]

Place, Edward, s. Conyers, of Dorchester, Dorset, cler. ORIEL COLL., matric. 8 Feb., 1753, aged 18; B.A. 1757.

Place, Matthew, s. John, of Canford, Dorset, gent. WADHAM COLL., matric. 28 June, 1796, aged 18; B.A. 1800, rector of Hampreston, Dorset, 1806, until his death 15 March, 1834.

Place, Robert Harvey, 4s. John Conyers, of Marnhull, Dorset, cler. EXETER COLL., matric. 3 March, 1831, aged 18.

Plaisted, Henry, 3s. Edmund, of Caldicott, near Chepstow, co. Monmouth, gent. KEBLE COLL., matric. 18 Oct., 1871, aged 19; B.A. 1875, M.A. 1878.

Plaistowe, Richard, s. Henry, of Wendover, Bucks, gent. MERTON COLL., matric. 27 March, 1717, aged 18; B.A. from QUEEN'S COLL. 26 Feb., 1724-5. [30]

Plant, Arthur Blurton, y.s. Arthur, of Lichfield, co. Stafford, gent. NEW COLL., matric. 5 Feb., 1877, aged 22; B.Mus. 1882.

Plant, George Ralph, 5s. Samuel, of Weston-on-Trent, co. Stafford, cler. ST. EDMUND HALL, matric. 22 Oct., 1884, aged 19; B.A. 1887.

Plant, Henry Francis, 4s. Samuel, of Weston-upon-Trent, co. Derby, cler. ST. EDMUND HALL, matric. 14 June, 1883, aged 19.

Plant, Samuel, 2s. John, of Sandbach, Cheshire, gent. BRASENOSE COLL., matric. 11 June, 1840, aged 19; scholar 1840-5, B.A. 1844, M.A. 1847, vicar of Weston-on-Trent 1849, preb. of Lichfield 1878. See *Manchester School Reg.*, iii. 257-8.

Plantamour, Emile Duval, 3s. Duval, of Geneva, gent. NON-COLL., matric. 24 Jan., 1874, aged 18. [35]

Plarr, Victor Gustavus, o.s. Gustavus, of Strasburg. NON-COLL., matric. 14 Oct., 1882, aged 19; B.A. from WORCESTER COLL. 1886.

Plasket, Thomas, s. Thomas, of Kirkland Guards, Torpenhow, Cumberland, pleb. QUEEN'S COLL., matric. 11 March, 1783, aged 20; B.A. 1786, M.A. 1790, vicar of Shabbington, Bucks, 1798.

Plasted, Richard, s. Thomas, of St. Peter's-in-the-East, Oxford (city), pleb. QUEEN'S COLL., matric. 21 March, 1716-7, aged 17; B.A. 1720, M.A. 1723.

Platen, His Excellency Count de, created D.C.L. 20 June, 1860, then envoy extraordinary and minister plenipotentiary at St. James's from the King of Denmark.

Plater, Rev. Herbert, 2s. Charles Eaton, of Folkestone, Kent, cler. WORCESTER COLL., matric. 10 May, 1845, aged 18; postmaster MERTON COLL. 1845-9, B.A. 1849, M.A. 1851, head-master Newark Grammar School 1857. [40]

ater, Rev. William Edward, o.s. William, of Maidstone, gent. UNIVERSITY COLL., matric. 11 Oct., 1872, aged 18; B.A. 1876, M.A. 1879.

att, Alexander, 2s. Richard, of Brixton, Surrey, arm. WORCESTER COLL., matric. 8 March, 1838, aged 18.

att, Edward Bertrum Comyn, 1s. Thomas Duodecimus, of Melplash, Dorset, cler. MAGDALEN COLL., matric. 16 Oct., 1876, aged 18; chorister 1869-74, clerk 1876-7.

att, Hugh Edward Pigott, 2s. Thomas, of Hampstead, Middlesex, arm. TRINITY COLL., matric. 13 Oct., 1860, aged 17, scholar 1860-5, B.A. 1864; fellow LINCOLN COLL. 1868, M.A. 1868, assistant-tutor, proctor 1877, bar.-at-law, Lincoln's Inn, 1875. See Foster's *Men at the Bar*.

att, Noel, 7s. William, of Forest Lodge, Hants, gent. WORCESTER COLL., matric. 14 Oct., 1865, aged 21; B.A. 1869, chaplain Madras. **[5]**

att, Samuel, 2s. Thomas, of St. Andrew's, Holborn, London, arm. MAGDALEN HALL, matric. 2 April, 1821, aged 25; B.A. 1825, M.A. 1828, bar.-at-law, Inner Temple, 1825.

att, Sydney, 7s. John, of Oldham, Lancashire, arm. BALLIOL COLL., matric. 16 Oct., 1879, aged 18; of Bryn-y-neuadd, co. Carnarvon. See *Eton School Lists*.

att, William, 4s. Thomas, of St. George's, Bloomsbury, London, arm. BRASENOSE COLL., matric. 10 May, 1823, aged 19; B.A. 1827, M.A. 1830, bar.-at-law, Inner Temple, 1830. See Foster's *Men at the Bar*.

att, William, 7s. Samuel, of London, arm. MAGDALEN HALL, matric. 29 Jan., 1834, aged 26.

att, Winfrid Alured Comyn, 2s. Thomas Duodecimus, of London, cler. HERTFORD COLL., matric. 28 Jan., 1879, aged 19; bar.-at-law, Lincoln's Inn, 1885. See Foster's *Men at the Bar*. **[10]**

latten, Thomas Edward, 1s. Thomas Parlett, of Saffron Walden, Essex, cler. LINCOLN COLL., matric. 31 May, 1861, aged 19; B.A. 1865, M.A. 1868, vicar of St. George's, Old Brentford, 1874-7, and of Hindringham, Norfolk, 1877.

latts, John Thompson, 2s. Robert, of Calcutta, gent. BALLIOL COLL., matric. 1 Feb., 1881, aged 50; created M.A. 21 June, 1881, teacher of Persian 1880.

layer, Edward, s. Edward, of Bristol (city), gent. WORCESTER COLL., matric. 7 April, 1813, aged 18 (Memo.: Rev. E. P., died at Compton vicarage, near Salisbury, 15 July, 1851).

layfair, Arthur Grace, 3s. George William, of Salterton, Devon, arm. NON-COLL., matric. 28 Jan., 1884, aged 18.

layfair, Rev. Charles Stuart Macdonald, 2s. George William, of Edinburgh, arm. NON-COLL., matric. 4 Nov., 1880, aged 19; B.A. 1883. **[15]**

layne, Arthur Twisden, 2s. William, of Avening, co. Gloucester, arm. BRASENOSE COLL., matric. 22 Nov., 1860, aged 18; B.A. 1864, of Longfords, co. Gloucester, J.P.

lenderleath, William Charles, o.s. Charles, of Clifton, near Bristol, arm. WADHAM COLL., matric. 31 Jan., 1849, aged 17; B.A. 1852, M.A. 1855, rector of Cherhill, Wilts, 1860.

lessis, Peter du, s. Franc., of Shoreditch, London, cler. MERTON COLL., matric. 30 April, 1730, aged 16.

lestow, Charles Berners, s. John Davis, of Ipswich, Suffolk, cler. TRINITY COLL., matric. 9 May, 1815, aged 18.

lestow, John Davis, s. Thomas, of St. Mary, Aldermanbury, London, gent. ST. JOHN'S COLL., matric. 27 June, 1775, aged 16; B.A. 1779, M.A., 1783, B.D. 1788, rector (and patron) of Watlington, Norfolk, 1791, until his death 6 Feb., 1824. See *Robinson*, 129. **[20]**

Pleydell, Edmund Morton, s. Edmund Morton, of Milbourne St. Andrew, Dorset, arm. QUEEN'S COLL., matric. 5 April, 1742, aged 18.

Pleydell, Edmund Morton, s. Edmund, of Westminster, arm. UNIVERSITY COLL., matric. 2 Dec., 1773, aged 17.

Pleydell, Jonathan Morton, s. Edmund Morton, of Milbourne, St. Andrew's, Dorset, arm. QUEEN'S COLL., matric. 5 April, 1742, aged 17; created D.C.L. 8 July, 1756, then of Whatcombe, co. Gloucester, bar.-at-law, Lincoln's Inn, 1750, died in 1805, father of the next named.

Pleydell, Jonathan Morton, s. Jonathan Morton, of Bath (city), arm. UNIVERSITY COLL., matric. 7 Nov., 1783, aged 17; died s.p.

Pleydell, Thomas Morton, s. Edmund, of Lydiard Tregoze, Wilts, gent. QUEEN'S COLL., matric. 1 April, 1717, aged 15; died s.p. **[25]**

Plimley, Henry, s. Thomas, of Brewood, co. Stafford, arm. HERTFORD COLL., matric. 11 Dec., 1781, aged 17; B.A. 1789, M.A. 1791, vicar of St. Leonard, Shoreditch, 1801, vicar of Cuckfield, Sussex, 1817, and chancellor of the diocese of Chichester 1822, until his death 10 March, 1841.

Ploetz, Richard Adolf, 1s. Charles Julius, of Lubeck, Germany, arm. MAGDALEN COLL., matric. 17 Oct., 1868, aged 19; demy 1867-72, B.A. 1873, M.A. 1875.

Plomer, John, s. John, of Bristol, Somerset, gent. LINCOLN COLL., matric. 12 Dec., 1734, aged 17.

Plomer, Samuel, s. John, of Culworth, Northants, cler. LINCOLN COLL., matric. 21 Jan., 1740-1, aged 18; B.A. 1744, M.A. 1747 (his father vicar of Culworth, rector of Bilton, and master of Rugby School).

Plomer, William, s. William, of London, arm. BRASENOSE COLL., matric. 19 May, 1779, aged 17; B.A. 1783. **[30]**

Plow, Henry Anthony, 2s. Anthony, of St. George's-in-the-East, London, gent. MAGDALEN HALL, matric. 11 April, 1840, aged 30.

Plowden, Alfred Chichele, 1s. Trevor, of Murut, East Indies, arm. BRASENOSE COLL., matric. 12 June, 1862, aged 17; B.A. 1866, bar.-at-law, Middle Temple, 1870, recorder of Much Wenlock 1879-88, magistrate Great Marlborough Street Police Court 1888. See Foster's *Men at the Bar*.

Plowden, Charles Chichele, o.s. Charles Hood Chichele, of Marylebone, Westminster, arm. CHRIST CHURCH, matric. 16 Oct., 1844, aged 19; B.A. 1848, M.A. 1857.

Plowden, Francis, created D.C.L. 5 July, 1793, bar.-at-law, Middle Temple, 1796 (8s. William, of Plowden, Salop, esquire), author of a 'History of Ireland, 1172-1810,' died in Paris in 1829; for list of his works, see *Gent.'s Mag.*, 1829, i. 374.

Plowden, Thomas, s. James, of Bremer, Wilts, cler. MERTON COLL., matric. 3 Feb., 1766, aged 17.

Plowman, Henry, s. John, of Tolpuddle, Dorset, cler. ORIEL COLL., matric. 12 May, 1752, aged 17. **[35]**

Plowman, John, s. John, of Tolpuddle, Dorset, cler. WADHAM COLL., matric. 4 April, 1759, aged 17; B.A. 1763, M.A. 1765.

Plowman, John Warren, s. John, of Toller, Dorset, cler. ORIEL COLL., matric. 20 May, 1790, aged 18, Reynold's exhibitioner EXETER COLL. 1791; B.A. 1794, vicar of Toller Porcorum, Dorset, died at Milton Abbas, Dorset (then of Stogursey), 7 Nov., 1798. See *Boase*, 148.

Plows, William, 1s. William, of St. Dennis, York (city), gent. PEMBROKE COLL., matric. 6 May, 1847, aged 18; B.A. from ST. MARY HALL 1851, M.A. 1853, held various curacies, 1853-82, vicar of Haddenham 1882.

Plucknett, Charles, s. Charles, of Cheriton, Somerset, cler. ST. JOHN'S COLL., matric. 28 June, 1759, aged 18; B.A. 1763, M.A. 1767, B.D. 1772, rector of Bainton, Yorks. See *Robinson*, 108. **[40]**

Plucknett, Walter, 2s. George, of Finchley, Middlesex, arm. TRINITY COLL., matric. 19 Oct., 1874, aged 19. See *Eton School Lists.*

Plumb, Frederick, 2s. Josiah Burr, of Albany, N.Y., arm. CHRIST CHURCH, matric. 29 Nov., 1870, aged 19; B.A. 1875. See *Rugby School Reg.*

Plumb, Thomas Street, 1s. Josiah Burr, of Albany, near New York, gent. BALLIOL COLL., matric. 21 Oct., 1869, aged 19; B.A. 1874, bar.-at-law, Inner Temple, 1876. See Foster's *Men at the Bar* & *Rugby School Reg.*

Plumbe, Thomas, s. John, of Liverpool, Lancashire, gent. BRASENOSE COLL., matric. 16 Jan., 1719-20, aged 17; B.A. 1723, rector of Aughton, Lancashire.

Plumbe, William, s. William, of Liverpool, Lancashire, gent. BRASENOSE COLL., matric. 26 May, 1762, aged 18; B.A. 1767, rector of Aughton, died 1786. [5]

Plumer, Charles John, 'f.m.' Thomas, of Cannons, Middlesex, equitis. BALLIOL COLL., matric. 30 Nov., 1816, aged 16, B.A. 1820; fellow ORIEL COLL. 1821-30, M.A. 1823, rector of Elstree, Herts, 1849-68, vicar of Ilford, Sussex, 1868-82, died 22 March, 1887.

Plumer, Francis, s. Francis, of Westminster, arm. UNIVERSITY COLL., matric. 12 July, 1787, aged 17; B.A. 1791. (Memo.: Rev. F. P., of Twickenham, died 2 Nov., 1794.)

Plumer, Henry Richard Hugh, 3s. Thomas, of London, eq. aur. BALLIOL COLL., matric. 1 Dec., 1820, aged 17; scholar 1821-6, a student of Lincoln's Inn, 1825.

Plumer, Henry Thomas, 1s. Henry Richard Hugh, of Strickland Magna, near Morland, Westmoreland, arm. ORIEL COLL., matric. 16 Dec., 1853, aged 18.

Plumer, John Julius, 5s. Thomas, of Cannons, Middlesex, equitis. BALLIOL COLL., matric. 6 April, 1832, aged 18; B.A. 1836, M.A. 1839. [10]

Plumer, (Sir) Thomas, s. Thomas, of London, arm. UNIVERSITY COLL., matric. 10 June, 1771, aged 17; Vinerian scholar, B.A. 1775, fellow, M.A. 1778, B.C.L. 1783, of Cannons, Middlesex, bar.-at-law, Lincoln's Inn, 1778, K.C. and a bencher 1793, a commissioner of bankrupts 1781, a judge on North Wales circuit 1805, solicitor-general and knighted (15 April) 1807-12, M.P. Downton 1807-13, vice-chancellor 1813-18, Master of the Rolls 1818, until his death 24 March, 1824.

Plumer, Thomas Hall, 1s. Thomas, of Sugnall, co. Stafford, equitis. BALLIOL COLL., matric. 29 March, 1814, aged 18; B.A. 1816, M.A. 1819, bar.-at-law, Lincoln's Inn, 1819, clerk of the petty bag 1820, examiner in Court of Chancery 1821, a commissioner of bankrupts (? died 24 Dec., 1852). See *Eton School Lists.*

Plumer, Valentine, s. Richard, of Ludlow, Salop, pleb. CHRIST CHURCH, matric. 30 March, 1720, aged 17; B.A. 1723, vicar of Eye, co. Hereford, 1732.

Plummer, Alfred, 3s. Matthew, of Heworth, co. Durham, cler. EXETER COLL., matric. 14 June, 1859, aged 18, exhibitioner 1860-4, B.A. 1863; fellow TRINITY COLL. 1865-75, M.A. 1866, lecturer, tutor and dean 1867-74, librarian, 1866, master of the schools 1868-9, master of University College, Durham, 1874, junior proctor 1875, senior proctor 1877, created D.D. (Durham) 1882. See *Boase*, 159; and for list of his works see *Crockford.*

Plummer, Rev. Charles, 5s. Matthew, of St. Leonard's, Sussex, cler. CORPUS CHRISTI COLL., matric. 21 Oct., 1869, aged 18; scholar 1869-73, S.C.L. & B.A. 1873, fellow 1873, M.A. 1876, lecturer modern history 1875, chaplain 1875, dean and librarian 1882-6, divinity lecturer 1878, vice-president 1885. [15]

Plummer, Charles Scott, 1s. Charles Balfour Scott, of St. Andrew's, Edinburgh, arm. ORIEL COLL., matric. 18 May, 1839, aged 17; B.A. 1843, M.A. 1849, of Sunderland Hall, Selkirkshire, assumed the additional name of PLUMMER in 1839, died in Feb., 1880.

Plummer, Francis Bowes, 2s. Benjamin, of Whickham, co. Durham, arm. TRINITY COLL., matric. 17 Oct., 1870, aged 19; B.A. 1874, perp. curate St. John the Evangelist, Walton-on-the-Hill, 1883.

Plummer, George Thomas, s. William, of Truro, Cornwall, gent. EXETER COLL., matric. 25 March, 1795, aged 18; exhibitioner 1795, B.A. 1799, rector of North Hill, near Launceston, 1821, until his death in 1828. See *Coll. Reg.*, 148.

Plummer, John Taylor, 2s. John, of Carshalton, Surrey, arm. BRASENOSE COLL., matric. 18 May, 1842, aged 18; B.A. 1846, M.A. 1849, rector of Hartley Mauduit, Hants, 1847, until his death 12 May, 1869. See *Robinson*, 247.

Plummer, Joseph Walter Scott-, 2s. Charles, of London, arm. ORIEL COLL., matric. 31 May, 1879, aged 18; B.A. 1883. See *Eton School Lists.* [20]

Plummer, Rowland Taylor, 1s. John Taylor, of Hartley Mauduit, Hants, cler. PEMBROKE COLL., matric. 28 Oct., 1867, aged 19; B.A. 1871, M.A. 1874, rector of Hartley Mauduit 1875-9, vicar of St. Paul's, Bow Common, 1878.

Plummer, Seth Burge, 2s. William, of All Saints, Bristol (city), arm. UNIVERSITY COLL., matric. 20 March, 1823, aged 16; B.A. 1827, M.A. 1829.

Plumptre, Charles John, 1s. Charles Thomas, of Cleypole, co. Lincoln, cler. UNIVERSITY COLL., matric. 11 May, 1854, aged 18; B.A. 1858, M.A. 1865, of Fredville, Kent, high sheriff 1877, hon. colonel 1st volunteer battalion East Kent regiment, died in June, 1887. See *Times*, 20 June.

Plumptre, Charles Thomas, s. John, of Fredville, Kent, arm. UNIVERSITY COLL., matric. 29 April, 1817, aged 17; B.A. 1821, M.A. 1825, rector of Wickhambreux, Kent, 1842, until his death 3 Jan., 1862.

Plumptre, Edward Hayes, 3s. Edward Hallows, of Bloomsbury, London, arm. UNIVERSITY COLL., matric. 21 May, 1840, aged 18, scholar 1841-4, B.A. 1844; fellow BRASENOSE COLL. 1844-8, M.A. 1846, select preacher 1851-3, 1864-6, and 1872-3, Boyle lecturer 1866-7, Grinfield lecturer (on the septuagint) 1872-4, examiner in School of Theology 1872-4 (chaplain King's College, London, 1847-68, professor of pastoral theology 1853-63, professor of exegesis Holy Scripture 1863-81), assistant preacher Lincoln's Inn 1851-8, preb. of St. Paul's 1863-81, rector of Pluckley, Kent, 1869-73, vicar of Bickley, Kent, 1873-81, dean of Queen's College, Harley Street, 1855-75, principal 1875-77, dean of Wells 1881; for list of his works see *Crockford.* [25]

Plumptre, Francis Fitzherbert, 3s. John Bridges, of Goodneston, Kent, arm. ORIEL COLL., matric. 23 Oct., 1885, aged 21.

Plumptre, Frederick Charles, s. Charles, of Long Newton, co. Durham, cler. UNIVERSITY COLL., matric. 21 Oct., 1813, aged 17; B.A. 1817, fellow 1817-36, M.A. 1820, tutor 1820, dean and bursar 1821, B.D. 1836, D.D. 1837, vice-chancellor 1848-51, master 1836, until his death 21 Nov., 1870.

Plumptre, Henry Fitzwalter, 1s. John Bridges, of Goodneston, Kent, arm. UNIVERSITY COLL., matric. 16 Oct., 1880, aged 19; B.A. 1885.

Plumptre, Henry Scawen, born at Stone, co. Worcester, s. John, dean of Gloucester. MERTON COLL., matric. 1 Nov., 1809, aged 19; postmaster 1809-13, B.A. 1813, M.A. 1816, rector of Eastwood, Notts, 1819, vicar of Llanbethian with Cowbridge, etc., 1815, perp. curate Stonehouse, Devon, 1826, died 15 Sep., 1862. See *Eton School Lists.*

umptre, Henry Western, y.s. John, of Fredville, Kent, arm. UNIVERSITY COLL., matric. 9 May, 1821, aged 17; B.A. 1825, M.A. 1842, rector of Eastwood, Notts, 1827, and of Claypole, co. Lincoln, 1842, until his death 22 April, 1863.

umptre, Henry Western, 2s. Henry Western, of Eastwood, Notts, cler. UNIVERSITY COLL., matric. 20 March, 1854, aged 18; B.A. 1858, M.A. 1862, rector of Eastwood, Notts, 1863.

umptre, Henry Western, 1s. Charles John, of Nonington, Kent, arm. NEW COLL., matric. 15 Oct., 1886, aged 18; scholar HERTFORD COLL. 1886.

umptre, John Bridges, 1s. Henry Western, of Adisham, Kent, cler. UNIVERSITY COLL., matric. 27 April, 1852, aged 19; B.A. 1857, M.A. 1865, of Goodnestone, Kent.

lumptre, John Bridges, 2s. John Bridges, of Goodnestone, Kent, arm. ORIEL COLL., matric. 31 Oct., 1882, aged 19; B.A. 1887. [5]

lumptre, Robert Garland, 1s. Robert William, of Corfe Mullen, Dorset, cler. EXETER COLL., matric. 16 Oct., 1884, aged 19; scholar 1884.

lumptre, Robert William, 1s. Robert B., of Forthampton, co. Gloucester, cler. UNIVERSITY COLL., matric. 25 April, 1844, aged 18; B.A. 1848, M.A. 1850, held various curacies 1849-58, rector of Corfe Mullen, Dorset, 1858. See *Eton School Lists.*

lumptre, William Alfred, 4s. Edward Hall, of St. George-the-Martyr, Bloomsbury, London, arm. UNIVERSITY COLL., matric. 15 May, 1849, aged 18; B.A. 1853, M.A. 1858, S.P.G. missionary Madras 1858-62, vicar of Whatton, Notts, 1871-6, and of Bishop Norton, co. Lincoln, 1876, until his death 3 Sep., 1879.

lumridge, Henry, 1s. Henry, of Hursley, Hants, gent. ST. MARY HALL, matric. 7 March, 1871, aged 25; B.Mus. 15 June, 1871.

lunkett, Horace Curzon, 3s. Edward, Baron Dunsany. UNIVERSITY COLL., matric. 11 Oct., 1873, aged 18; B.A. 1878. See Foster's *Peerage* & *Eton School Lists.* [10]

'lunkett, Randall Edward, 1s. Edward, Baron Dunsany. CHRIST CHURCH, matric. 21 Oct., 1824, aged 19; B.A. 1833, 12th Baron Dunsany, M.P. Drogheda, 1835-7, died s.p. 7 April, 1852. See Foster's *Peerage* & *Eton School Lists.*

'lunkett, Randal Edward Sherborn, born at Sherborne, co. Gloucester, 1s. Edward, Baron Dunsany. CHRIST CHURCH, matric. 12 June, 1867, aged 18; B.A. 1872, M.P. West Gloucestershire 1874-80, died 25 Dec., 1883. See Foster's *Peerage* & *Eton School Lists.*

'lymley, Joseph. PEMBROKE COLL., 1776. See CORBETT, page 297.

'lymley, Panton. PEMBROKE COLL., 1800. See CORBETT, page 297.

'oate, Daniel, s. Richard, of Portsea, Hants, gent. MERTON COLL., matric. 13 Oct., 1756, aged 17; B.A. from CHRIST CHURCH 1760, M.A. 1763. [15]

'ochin, George, s. Thomas, of Loughborough, co. Leicester, cler. CHRIST CHURCH, matric. 24 Oct., 1806, aged 19; of Barkby Hall, co. Leicester, high sheriff 1828, died 29 Dec., 1831.

'ocklington, Rev. Duncan, 4s. Roger, of Walesby, Notts, cler. BRASENOSE COLL., matric. 7 June, 1860, aged 18; B.A. 1863, died 1 June, 1870.

'ocklington, Joseph. EXETER COLL., 1823. See SENHOUSE.

'ocklington, Roger, 1s. Roger, of Winthrope, Notts, arm. EXETER COLL., matric. 26 June, 1821, aged 18; B.A. 1825, M.A. 1829, vicar of Walesby, Notts, 1833, and rector of Skegnes, co. Lincoln, 1834, until his death 30 May, 1880. See *Eton School Lists.*

'ocock, Charles (Samuel), 4s. George, of St. George's, Hanover Square, London, baronet. CHRIST CHURCH, matric. 11 Feb., 1823, aged 17; B.A. 1826, M.A. 1830, rector of Rous Lench, co. Worcester, 1838, until his death in Jan., 1881. See Foster's *Baronetage.*

Pocock, Edward, 'tonsor;' privilegiatus 27 March 1734. [21]

Pocock, (Sir) George (Bart.), s. George, of Twickenham, Middlesex, Knight of the Bath. CHRIST CHURCH, matric. 10 Oct., 1783, aged 17; B.A. 1786, M.P. Bridgewater 1796-1806, 1807-20, created a baronet 18 Aug., 1821, died 14 July, 1840. See Foster's *Baronetage.*

Pocock, (Sir) George Edward (Bart.), s. George, of St. George-the-Martyr, London, arm. (after baronet). CHRIST CHURCH, matric. 29 Jan., 1812, aged 19; 2nd baronet, died 3 Sep., 1866. See Foster's *Baronetage* & *Eton School Lists.*

Pocock, Rev. Herbert Llewellyn, 2s. John Cowan, of Angle, co. Pembroke, cler. ST. EDMUND HALL, matric. 23 Oct., 1877, aged 18; B.A. 1882, M.A. 1886, a master at St. Columba's College, Rathfarnham.

Pocock, Isaac John Innes, 1s. Isaac, of Maidenhead, Berks, arm. BALLIOL COLL., matric. 11 May, 1837, aged 17; postmaster MERTON COLL. 1838-41, B.A. 1842, bar.-at-law, Inner Temple, 1847, died 28 May, 1886. See Foster's *Men at the Bar* & *Eton School Lists.* His father, artist and dramatist, died 23 Aug., 1835; see *Gent.'s Mag.*, 1835, ii. 657. [25]

Pocock, Rev. Nicholas, 1s. Nicholas, of Falmouth, Cornwall, arm. QUEEN'S COLL., matric. 3 Feb., 1831, aged 17; Michel exhibitioner 1831-4, scholar 1834-8, B.A. 1834, M.A. 1837, fellow 1838-48, math. lecturer 1847; for list of his works see *Crockford.*

Pococke, Ebenezer, 3s. George, of Bristol, gent. MAGDALEN HALL, matric. 5 July, 1838, aged 31.

Pococke, John, s. Hugh, of Chaddleworth, Berks, cler. CORPUS CHRISTI COLL., matric. 2 Nov., 1715, aged 17; B.A. 1720, M.A. 1722.

Pococke, John Blagrave, s. Samuel, of Inglefield, Berks, arm. ST. JOHN'S COLL., matric. 30 March 1792, aged 17.

Pococke, Richard, s. Richard, of St. John's, Southampton, cler. CORPUS CHRISTI COLL., matric. 13 July, 1720, aged 15; B.A. 1725, B.C.L. 1731, D.C.L. 1733, bishop of Ossory 1756, of Meath 1765, died 15 Sep., 1765. See *Cotton,* ii. 286; iii. 123. [30]

Pococke, Richard, s. Robert, of Calne, Wilts, pleb. BRASENOSE COLL., matric. 28 Jan., 1739-40, aged 18; B.A. 3 Feb., 1743-4.

Pode, Charles Coleridge, 3s. Thomas Julian, of Plympton St. Maurice (*sic*), Devon, gent. EXETER COLL., matric. 21 Jan., 1860, aged 18; scholar 1859-64, B.A. 1863, B.Med. 1868, M.A. 1872, Radcliffe travelling fellow 1867-9, died 25 May, 1873. See Foster's *Our Noble and Gentle Families* & *Coll. Reg.*, 158.

Pode, Edward, 4s. Thomas, of Plympton, Devon, arm. EXETER COLL., matric. 11 June, 1862, aged 19. See Foster's *Our Noble and Gentle Families.*

Pode, Ernest Duke Yonge, 1s. John Duke, of London, arm. KEBLE COLL., matric. 19 Oct., 1880, aged 18; B.A. 1884.

Pode, John (Duke), 1s. Thomas Julian, of Plympton St. Maurice (*sic*), Devon, arm. EXETER COLL., matric. 14 May, 1851, aged 18; fellow NEW COLL. 1853-61, B.A. 1855, M.A. 1858, of Slade, Devon, J.P., bar.-at-law, Inner Temple, 1858-76. See Foster's *Men at the Bar.* [35]

Podger, John, s. John, of Lavington, Somerset, pleb. BALLIOL COLL., matric. 30 May, 1745, aged 18, B.A. 7 Feb., 1748-9; M.A. from ST. MARY HALL 1771, B. & D.D. 1771.

Podmore, Claude, 3s. Thompson, of Elstree, Herts, cler. KEBLE COLL., matric. 19 Oct., 1886, aged 18.

Podmore, Frank, 3s. Thompson, of Elstree, Herts, cler. PEMBROKE COLL., matric. 29 Oct., 1874, aged 18; scholar 1874-8, B.A. 1877, M.A. 1883.

Podmore, George, s. John, of Edgmond, Salop, pleb. LINCOLN COLL., matric. 22 May, 1729, aged 18; B.A. from MAGDALEN HALL 7 March, 1732-3.

Podmore, George, 2s. Thompson, of Elstree, Herts, cler. KEBLE COLL., matric. 14 Oct., 1872, aged 19; B.A. 1877, M.A. 1880.

Podmore, Rev. Richard Hillman, of TRINITY COLL. Cambridge (B.A. 1844, M.A. 1847); adm. 'ad eundem' 6 June, 1850, vicar of Rockbeare, Devon, 1864.

Podmore, Thomas Edward, s. Richard, of Condover, Salop, cler. CHRIST CHURCH, matric. 6 Nov., 1772, aged 18; B.A. 1777.

Podmore, Thompson, 2s. Robert, of Hastings, Sussex, gent. ST. JOHN'S COLL., matric. 27 June, 1842, aged 18; scholar & fellow 1842-51, B.A. 1846, M.A. 1850, master Elstree Hill School, Herts, 1861-9, head-master Eastbourne College 1869-86, rector of Aston-le-Walls, Northants, 1886. See *Robinson*, 250. [5]

Pogose, Gregory Joakim, 1s. Joakim Gregory, of Dacca, Bengal, gent. QUEEN'S COLL., matric. 26 April, 1865, aged 19; bar.-at-law, Inner Temple, 1868. See Foster's *Men at the Bar.*

Pogose, Nicholas Joakim, 3s. Nicholas Joakim Gregory, of Dacca, Bengal, East Indies, arm. CHRIST CHURCH, matric. 19 May, 1869, aged 17. See *Eton School Lists.*

Pogson, Rev. Edward John, 3s. Thomas, of Kesgrave, Suffolk, arm. ST. JOHN'S COLL., matric. 30 June, 1834, aged 18; scholar & fellow 1834-46, B.C.L. 1840, D.C.L. (by decree) 14 June, 1844, died 24 March, 1846. See *Robinson*, 223.

Poingdestre, George, o.s. George, of St. Peter's, Isle of Jersey, arm. PEMBROKE COLL., matric. 28 Feb., 1839, aged 19; scholar 1839-45, B.A. 1844, M.A. 1853.

Poingdestre, Herbert Allen, o.s. John George, of Bahia, Brazil, arm. ST. ALBAN HALL, matric. 25 March, 1878, aged 19. [10]

Pointer, James, s. Henry, of London, gent. ST. JOHN'S COLL., matric 30 June, 1741, aged 16; rector of Southoe, Hunts, 1748, until his death 1 Nov., 1796.

Pole, Charles Chandos, o.s. Charles, of Liverpool, arm. WORCESTER COLL., matric. 9 June, 1842, aged 18; bar.-at-law, Middle Temple, 1849, died 20 Sep., 1881.

Pole, Charles Richard, s. Charles, of London, arm. ORIEL COLL., matric. 9 May, 1814, aged 17; B.A. 1818, M.A. 1821, of Wych Hill House, co. Gloucester, died 10 Aug., 1879. See Foster's *Baronetage* & *Eton School Lists.*

Pole, Edward, s. Reginald, of Stoke, Devon, arm. UNIVERSITY COLL., matric. 19 Oct., 1775, aged 17, B.A. 1779; fellow ALL SOULS' COLL., M.A. 1783, B.D. 1796, D.D. 1800, rector of Dibden, Hants, 1796, of Landreath, Cornwall, 1797, and of Barford St. Martin, Wilts, 1800, until his death 28 Dec., 1837, father of Edward 1824. See Foster's *Baronetage.*

Pole, Edward, born in Almeria, Spain, s. Edward Sacheverel, arm. TRINITY COLL., matric. 22 May, 1783, aged 22; B.C.L. from ST. ALBAN HALL 1795, rector of Egginton, co. Derby, 1795, until his death in 1824. [15]

Pole, Edward, 4s. Peter, of St. George's, Bloomsbury, London, baronet. BALLIOL COLL., matric. 13 June, 1822, aged 16; general in the army, colonel 12th lancers, died 3 Feb., 1879. See Foster's *Baronetage.*

Pole, Edward, 1s. Edward, of Barford, Wilts, doctor. EXETER COLL., matric. 24 Jan., 1824, aged 18; B.A. 1827, M.A. 1832, rector of Templeton, Devon, 1833-79, and of Rackenford since 1879. See Foster's *Baronetage.*

Pole, Edward Augustus, 1s. George Henry Law, of Plymouth, arm. NON-COLL., matric. 26 Jan., 1878, aged 17; B.A. 1888. See Foster's *Baronetage.*

Pole, Edward Sacheverell, s. Edward, of Radbourne, co. Derby, arm. CORPUS CHRISTI COLL., matric. 9 Dec., 1736, aged 18; B.A. 10 Feb., 1740-1, M.A. 1743, of Radbourne, colonel in the army, served at Fontenoy, Culloden, and through the Seven Years' War, at Minden, etc., died in 1780.

Pole, Edward Sacheverell Chandos, s. Sacheverell Chandos, of Radbourne, co. Derby, arm. ST. MARY HALL, matric. 14 Feb., 1817, aged 24; of Radbourne Hall, high sheriff, Derbyshire, 1827, died 19 Jan., 1863. [20]

Pole, Edward Sacheverell Chandos, 1s. E. S. Chandos, of Radbourne, co. Derby, arm. ORIEL COLL., matric. 9 May, 1844, aged 18; of Radbourne Hall, co. Derby, high sheriff, 1867, bar.-at-law, Middle Temple 1867, died in 1873. See *Eton School Lists.*

Pole, Evan William, y.s. William, of Westminster, D.Med. CHRIST CHURCH, matric. 11 Oct., 1878, aged 19; a junior student 1878-85, B.A. 1882, M.A. 1885.

Pole, George Henry Law, 1s. Reginald, of Hurcoth House, Baverstock, Wilts, cler. EXETER COLL., matric. 13 May, 1856, aged 18; postmaster MERTON COLL. 1856-7, captain R.E., died in 1876. See Foster's *Baronetage*, & *Our Noble and Gentle Families.*

Pole, German, s. German, of Conduit Street, London, arm. ST. MARY HALL, matric. 11 Feb., 1746-7, aged 18; died in 1763.

Pole-Gell, Henry Chandos, 2s. Edward Sacheverell Pole, of London, arm. ST. MARY HALL, matric. 6 May, 1847, aged 18; of Hopton Hall, co. Derby, high sheriff 1886, assumed the additional surname of GELL in 1863. See *Eton School Lists.* [25]

Pole, (Henry) Reginald Chandos, s. Sacheverell, of Radborne, co. Derby, arm. TRINITY COLL., matric. 30 June, 1815, aged 18; B.A. from ST. MARY HALL 1821, M.A. 1822, rector of Radborne 1824, and of Mugginton 1832, until his death 19 June, 1866.

Pole, Rev. Henry (Van Notten), s. John (or rather Charles), of Bishopsgate, London, baronet. CHRIST CHURCH, matric. 23 Oct., 1799, aged 17; B.A. 1803, M.A. 1806, of Waltham Place, Berks, died 24 May, 1865. See Foster's *Baronetage.*

Pole, Henry (Van Notten), 1s. Henry, of Wolverton, Hants, cler. CHRIST CHURCH, matric. 11 May, 1837, aged 17; of Waltham Place, Berks. See Foster's *Baronetage.*

Pole, John, s. Charles, of St. Breock, Cornwall, cler. BALLIOL COLL., matric. 18 May, 1738, aged 19. See Foster's *Baronetage.*

Pole, (Sir) John (Bart.), s. William, of Shute, Devon, baronet. NEW COLL., matric. 19 April, 1750, aged 17; 5th baronet, died 19 Feb., 1766. [30]

Pole, (Sir) John William (Bart.), s. John, of Salisbury (city), —. CORPUS CHRISTI COLL., matric. 8 June, 1776, aged 18; 6th baronet, M.P. West Looe 1796, died 30 Nov., 1799, called himself DE LA POLE.

Pole, Mundy, 4s. Charles, of St. Marylebone, London, arm. BALLIOL COLL., matric. 25 April, 1822, aged 17; B.A. 1826, major in the army, died in 1804.

Pole, Perriam, s. William, of Dublin (city), arm. CHRIST CHURCH, matric. 23 Nov., 1720, aged 18 (one of these names was M.P. Maryborough 1692-5, and died in Oct., 1704).

Pole, (Sir) Peter (Van Notten, Bart.), s. Peter, of St. Giles's, London, baronet. BRASENOSE COLL., matric. 30 May, 1818, aged 17; created M.A. 4 July, 1821, 3rd baronet, assumed the additional name of Van Notten 1853, died 20 May, 1887, aged 86. See Foster's *Baronetage.*

Pole-Carew, Reginald, s. Reginald Pole, of Stoke Damarel, Devon, arm. UNIVERSITY COLL., matric. 2 Feb., 1771, aged 17; of Antony, Cornwall, P.C., M.P. Penrhyn 1782-4, Reigate 1787-90, Lostwithiel 1790-6, 1812-16, Fowey 1796-9, 1802-12, under secretary Home department 1803-4, assumed the additional surname of CAREW, died 3 Jan., 1835. See Foster's *Baronetage*, POLE.

Pole, Reginald, 2s. Edward, of Barford, Wilts, doctor. EXETER COLL., matric. 30 Jan., 1819, aged 17; B.A. 1822, M.A. 1826, rector of Sheviocke 1825-39, and St. Mary Tavy, Devon, 1826-39, and of Yeovilton since 1839. See Foster's *Baronetage.*

Pole, Reginald Frederick, 3s. William Templer, of Marylebone, London, baronet. CHRIST CHURCH, matric. 11 May, 1837, aged 18; died 6 Oct., 1848.

Pole, Richard, 2s. Peter, of St. Giles's, Middlesex, baronet. BALLIOL COLL., matric. 22 June, 1819, aged 17; B.A. 1823, M.A. 1826, rector of Wolverton, 1844-79, and of Ewhurst 1847-79. See Foster's *Baronetage.*

Pole, Samuel, 3s. Peter, of St. Giles's, Middlesex, baronet. ST. MARY HALL, matric. 10 June, 1820, aged 17; major-general in the army, died 6 Feb., 1863. **[5]**

Pole, Watson Buller (Van Notten), 3s. Charles, of St. Marylebone, arm. BALLIOL COLL., matric. 8 May, 1821, aged 17; B.A. 1825, rector of Upper Swell, co. Gloucester, 1828-81, and of Condicote 1840-81. See Foster's *Baronetage* & *Rugby School Reg.*, 126.

Pole, William, s. Charles, of Wickhill, co. Gloucester, arm. BALLIOL COLL., matric. 30 May, 1816, aged 17; B.A. 1820, M.A. 1824, bar.-at-law, Middle Temple, 1823. See Foster's *Baronetage* & *Eton School Lists.*

Pole, William, 4s. Thomas, of Birmingham, co. Warwick, gent. ST. JOHN'S COLL., matric. 12 June, 1860, aged 46; B.Mus. 14 June, 1860, D.Mus. 17 Dec., 1867.

Pole, William Chandos, 3s. Edward Sacheverell Chandos, of Radbourne, co. Derby, arm. CHRIST CHURCH, matric. 20 Oct., 1852, aged 19; B.A. 1856, M.A. 1862, rector of Trusley, co. Derby, 1859-66, and of Radbourne since 1866. See *Eton School Lists.*

Pole, (Sir) William Edmund (Bart.), 2s. William, of Weymouth Street, London, baronet. CHRIST CHURCH, matric. 17 Oct., 1833, aged 17; student 1834-41, B.A. 1837, M.A. 1840, 9th baronet, bar.-at-law, Lincoln's Inn, 1841. See Foster's *Men at the Bar.* **[10]**

Pole, (Sir) William Templer (Bart.), s. John William Shute, of Shute, Devon, baronet. CHRIST CHURCH, matric. 24 April, 1801, aged 18; created M.A. 13 June, 1804, and also D.C.L. 5 July, 1810, 7th baronet, a student of Lincoln's Inn 1803, died 1 April, 1847. See Foster's *Baronetage* & *Eton School Lists.*

Polehampton, Arthur, 5s. Edward, of Greenford, Middlesex, cler. PEMBROKE COLL., matric. 7 March, 1850, aged 20.

Polehampton, Charles Arthur, 1s. Thomas Stedman, of Ross, co. Hereford, cler. ST. MARY HALL, matric. 23 April, 1884, aged 19; B.A. from MERTON COLL. 1887.

Polehampton, Edward Henry, 2s. Thomas Stedman, of Ellel, Lancashire, cler. QUEEN'S COLL., matric. 30 Oct., 1885, aged 19; scholar 1885.

Polehampton, Edward Thomas William, 1s. Edward, of Greenford, Middlesex, cler. PEMBROKE COLL., matric. 29 Oct., 1841, aged 18; scholar 1841-5, fellow 1845-60, B.A. 1847, M.A. 1848, perp. curate Great Bricett 1855-9, rector and vicar of Hartfield, Kent, 1859. See *Eton School Lists.* **[15]**

Polehampton, Henry Stedman, 2s. Edward, of Greenford, Middlesex, cler. PEMBROKE COLL., matric. 17 Nov., 1842, aged 18; scholar 1842-5, fellow 1845-56, B.A. 1846, M.A. 1849, curate of St. Chad's, Shrewsbury, chaplain to the residency at Lucknow, died in hospital there 1857-8. See *Eton School Lists.*

Polehampton, Herbert Edward, 3s. John, of Dover, cler. PEMBROKE COLL., matric. 23 Oct., 1883, aged 19.

Polehampton, John, 4s. Edward, of Greenford, Middlesex, cler. PEMBROKE COLL., matric. 7 Nov., 1844, aged 19; B.A. 1848, M.A. 1852, rector of Ightham, Kent, 1866.

Polehampton, Rev. John, 2s. John, of Leigh, near Tunbridge, cler. PEMBROKE COLL., matric. 26 April, 1880, aged 19; B.A. 1883, M.A. 1888.

Polehampton, Thomas Stedman, 4s. Edward, of Greenford, Middlesex, cler. PEMBROKE COLL., matric. 12 March, 1846, aged 18; scholar 1846-57, B.A. 1850, M.A. 1852, fellow 1857-63, held various curacies 1851-64, vicar of Ellel, Lancashire, 1864-9, and of St. Bartholomew the Less, London, etc., 1869-78, chaplain at Oporto 1878-85, etc. **[20]**

Poley, Arthur Pierre, 1s. Pierre, of London, gent. ST. JOHN'S COLL., matric. 16 Oct., 1875, aged 18; scholar 1875-82, B.A. 1880, bar.-at-law, Inner Temple, 1880. See Foster's *Men at the Bar* & *Robinson*, 365.

Poley, Thomas Weller, 2s. John Weller, of Boxted, Suffolk, arm. MERTON COLL., matric. 16 Oct., 1869, aged 18; B.A. 1874, M.A. 1883, bar.-at-law, Lincoln's Inn, 1878. See Foster's *Men at the Bar* & *Eton School Lists.*

Polhill, Charles, 1s. George, of Chipstead, Kent, arm. UNIVERSITY COLL., matric. 8 May, 1823, aged 17.

Polhill, Edward, s. Christopher, of Dinton, Wilts, gent. TRINITY COLL., matric. 10 Dec., 1754, aged 17; B.A. 1758, rector of Milstone 1762, of Brickmiston, Wilts, 1757, until his death 29 May, 1800.

Polhill, Frederick Campbell, 2s. George, of Chipstead, Kent, arm. UNIVERSITY COLL., matric. 20 June, 1827, aged 17; B.A. 1831, M.A. 1838, held various curacies 1834-50. **[25]**

Polhill, Henry Western Onslow, y.s. George, of Chipstead, Kent, arm. UNIVERSITY COLL., matric. 14 May, 1833, aged 17; scholar 1836-42, B.A. 1837, M.A. 1843.

Polhill, Robert, s. Edward, of Dinton, Wilts, cler. NEW COLL., matric. 23 Nov., 1720, aged 19; B.A. 1724, M.A. 1727, rector of Little Parndon, Essex, 1741.

Polhill, Robert, s. Richard, of Maidstone, Kent, gent. UNIVERSITY COLL., matric. 12 March, 1750-1, aged 17; B.A. 1754, M.A. 1757, rector of Goodhurst and Shadoxhurst, Kent, 1764.

Polhill, Rev. William, s. Richard, of Maidstone, Kent, gent. UNIVERSITY COLL., matric. 17 Dec., 1754, aged 18; B.A. 1758, died at Albury, near Guildford, 4 March, 1822.

Polhill, William, s. Robert, of Goudhurst, Kent, cler. UNIVERSITY COLL., matric. 27 Oct., 1785, aged 18; B.A. 1789. **[30]**

Pollard, Alfred William, 2s. Edward William, of London, arm. ST. JOHN'S COLL., matric. 13 Oct., 1877, aged 18; scholar 1877-82, B.A. 1881, M.A. 1885.

Pollard, Arthur Tempest, 2s. Tempest, of Rastrick, Yorks, gent. WADHAM COLL., matric. 24 Jan., 1873, aged 19; scholar 1872-7, B.A. 1876, M.A. 1879.

Pollard, Rev. Cecil Sherard, 3s. George Octavius, of London, arm. KEBLE COLL., matric. 14 Oct., 1878, aged 19; B.A. 1882, M.A. 1885, died in Aug., 1886.

Pollard, Edward, s. Edward, of St. Bartholomew's, London, pleb. ST. EDMUND HALL, matric. 16 Jan., 1823, aged 20; B.A. 1827, vicar of Ewerby, co. Lincoln, 1837-71, rector of Evedon 1837, until his death 5 Sep., 1874.

Pollard, George, s. William, of Bradford, Yorks, arm. UNIVERSITY COLL., matric. 20 April, 1814, aged 17.

Pollard, Henry Bargman, 1s. Henry Hinds, of Ryde, Isle of Wight, gent. CHRIST CHURCH, matric. 15 Oct., 1886, aged 17; scholar 1886.

Pollard, Henry Smith, 2s. Robert Blemell, of Chelsea, Middlesex, gent. LINCOLN COLL., matric. 1 April, 1830, aged 20; B.A. 1833, M.A. 1837, vicar of Edlington, co. Lincoln, 1852-7, died 4 Nov., 1884.

Pollard, John, s. John, of Baldon, Oxon, arm. MAGDALEN COLL., matric. 13 Nov., 1721, aged 14; demy 1721-6, B.A. 1725. See *Coll. Reg.*, vi., 201. [5]

Pollard, John, s. Thomas, of Isle of Barbados, doctor. QUEEN'S COLL., matric. 7 June, 1771, aged 18.

Pollard, John, s. William, of St. Swithin's, London, gent. BRASENOSE COLL., matric. 14 Nov., 1801, aged 18; B.A. 1805, M.A. 1808, rector of Bennington, Herts, 1813, until his death 23 Sep., 1851.

Pollard, Robert Crispe, 1s. Robert, of Chelsea, Middlesex. gent. EXETER COLL., matric. 20 May, 1825, aged 17; died young. See *Eton School Lists.*

Pollard, Seth, s. John, of Horsforth, Yorks, gent. UNIVERSITY COLL., matric. 13 Dec., 1749, aged 14; B.A. 1753, M.A. 1756.

Pollard, Thomas, o.s. Tobias, of St. Budeaux, Devon, arm. MAGDALEN HALL, matric. 22 June, 1865, aged 26. [10]

Pollard, William Joseph, 2s. Joseph, of Swansea, co. Glamorgan, gent. NON-COLL., matric. 14 Oct., 1882, aged 23.

Pollen, Arthur Joseph Hungerford, 6s. John Hungerford, of London, arm. TRINITY COLL., matric. 17 Jan., 1885, aged 18. See Foster's *Baronetage.*

Pollen, Benjamin, s. Edward, of Hodson, Herts, arm. QUEEN'S COLL., matric. 29 April, 1725, aged 18; of Little Bookham, Surrey, half-brother of Thomas 1717.

Pollen, George Pollen Boileau, s. John Peter Boileau, of Alcester, co. Warwick, arm. CHRIST CHURCH, matric. 15 April, 1818, aged 19; B.A. 1822, M.A. 1835, assumed the additional surname of POLLEN, rector of Little Bookham, Surrey, 1823, until his death 7 Nov., 1847. See Foster's *Baronetage,* BOILEAU.

Pollen, John, s. John, of Andover, Hants, gent. CORPUS CHRISTI COLL., matric. 17 Oct., 1719, aged 17; bar.-at-law, Lincoln Inn, 1726, bencher 1746, a Welsh judge, M.P. Andover 1734-54, died 24 July, 1775, father of the next named. [15]

Pollen, (Sir) John (Bart.), s. John, of Andover, Hants, arm. (after baronet). CORPUS CHRISTI COLL., matric. 16 May, 1759, aged 18; of Andover and Redenham, Hants, bar.-at-law, Lincoln's Inn, 1770, bencher 1802, created a baronet 15 May, 1795, died 7 Aug., 1814. See Foster's *Baronetage.*

Pollen, John Douglas Boileau, 1s. George P. B., of Little Bookham, Surrey, cler. CORPUS CHRISTI COLL., matric. 22 April, 1842, aged 17; scholar 1842-7, B.A. 1846, of Little Bookham, Surrey. See Foster's *Baronetage,* BOILEAU.

Pollen, John Hungerford, 2s. Richard, of St. James's, Westminster, arm. CHRIST CHURCH, matric. 30 May, 1838, aged 17, B.A. 1842; fellow MERTON COLL. 1842-52, M.A. 1844, proctor 1851, seceded to Rome. See Foster's *Baronetage* & *Eton School Lists.*

Pollen, (Sir) John Walter (Bart.), s. John, of Thruxton, Hants, baronet. CHRIST CHURCH, matric. 24 Nov., 1803, aged 19; 2nd baronet, M.P. Andover 1820-31 and 1835-41, died 2 May, 1863. See Foster's *Baronetage* & *Eton School Lists.*

Pollen, Richard, s. John, of Andover, Hants, arm. QUEEN'S COLL., matric. 12 April, 1764, aged 18; B.C.L. 1771, rector of Winchfield and vicar of Froyle, Hants, 1773, until his death 30 Dec., 1799 brother of John 1759. [20]

Pollen, Richard, s. John, of Thruxton, Hants, baronet. CHRIST CHURCH, matric. 9 March, 1804, aged 17, B.A. 1807; fellow MERTON COLL. 1812-15, M.A. 1814, of Rodbourne, Wilts, bar.-at-law, Lincoln's Inn, 1813, a six clerk in Chancery 1829, died 7 Feb., 1838. See Foster's *Baronetage* & *Eton School Lists.*

Pollen, (Sir) Richard Hungerford (Bart.), 1s. Richard, of Paddington, arm. CHRIST CHURCH, matric. 23 May, 1833, aged 17; B.A. 1837, 3rd baronet, a student of Lincoln's Inn 1837, died 8 April, 1881. See Foster's *Baronetage* & *Eton School Lists.*

Pollen, (Sir) Richard Hungerford (Bart.), 1s. Richard Hungerford, of London, baronet. CHRIST CHURCH, matric. 7 June, 1865, aged 18; 4th baronet. See Foster's *Baronetage* & *Eton School Lists.*

Pollen, Thomas, s. Edward, of Lincoln (city), gent. CORPUS CHRISTI COLL. matric. 29 May, 1717, aged 15; B.A. 17 Feb., 1720-1, M.A. 24 March, 1723-4, rector of Little Bookham, half-brother of Benjamin.

Polley, George, s. Thomas, of Nantwich, Cheshire, pleb. BRASENOSE COLL., matric. 14 July, 1721, aged 18; B.A. 1725, M.A. 1728. [25]

Pollexfen, John, s. John, of Halliton, Devon, arm. BALLIOL COLL., matric. 18 Nov., 1725, aged 16.

Pollington, Richard, 'musician;' privilegiatus 2 June, 1749.

Pollock, Arthur Williamson Alsager, o.s. William Paul, of Pau, arm. BRASENOSE COLL., matric. 23 May, 1872, aged 18.

Pollock, Frank, 4s. James Edward, of London, D.Med. TRINITY COLL., matric. 21 May, 1880, aged 22; B.A. & M.A. 1887.

Pollock, Frederick, fellow CORPUS CHRISTI COLL. 1882, professor of jurisprudence 1883, M.A. (by decree) 27 Feb., 1883; fellow TRINITY COLL., Cambridge, B.A. 1867, M.A. 1870 (1s. Sir William Frederick Pollock, baronet), bar.-at-law, Lincoln's Inn, 1871. See Foster's *Men at the Bar.* [30]

Pollock, Henry Alsager, o.s. Robert Carlisle, of North Rode, Cheshire, arm. BRASENOSE COLL., matric. 7 June, 1849, aged 17.

Pollock, James Francis Edward Blomart, 1s. John, of South Molton, Devon, arm. EXETER COLL., matric. 15 Feb., 1827, aged 18; B.A. 1832, died curate of Puddington, Devon, 23 Dec., 1834.

Pollock, James Samuel, M.A. TRINITY COLL., Dublin, 1861 (B.A. 1858); adm. 'comitatis causa' 21 June, 1866, curate in charge St. Alban-the-Martyr, Birmingham, 1865-71, incumbent 1871.

Pollock, James Wilson, 1s. James Edward, of Rome, doctor (subs. gent.). QUEEN'S COLL., matric. 29 Jan., 1867, aged 18.

Pollock, Thomas Benson, M.A. TRINITY COLL., Dublin, 1863 (B.A. 1859); adm. 'comitatis causa' 21 June, 1866, curate of St. Alban-the-Martyr, Birmingham. [35]

Pollock, Wilfred Douglas, 2s. Alfred Atkinson, of Hampstead, Middlesex, arm. CHRIST CHURCH, matric. 11 Oct., 1878, aged 18, exhibitioner 1878-80; B.A. from ST. ALBAN HALL 1882, M.A. from MERTON COLL. 1885.

Pollock, William James, B.A. TRINITY COLL., Dublin, 1853, 2s. John, of London, arm. WADHAM COLL., incorp. 3 June, 1864, aged 34; M.A. 9 June, 1864, rector of St. Saviour's, Bath, 1872-6, etc.

llok, Thomas, s. Thomas, of Grittleton, Wilts, doctor. TRINITY COLL., matric. 23 March, 1790, aged 17.

llok, William Pollok Morris, 1s. Robert Morris, of Glasgow, arm. TRINITY COLL., matric. 17 Jan., 1885, aged 17.

lson, Hugh, 1s. John Hugh Paysley, of Upton Helions, Devon, cler. EXETER COLL., matric. 9 Nov., 1825, aged 18; B.A. 1829.

lton, Thomas, s. Ed., of Exeter, Devon, gent. BALLIOL COLL., matric. 10 March, 1728-9, aged 18; B.A. 1732.

lwhele, Richard, s. Thomas, of Truro, Cornwall, arm. CHRIST CHURCH, matric. 3 March, 1778, aged 18; of Polwhele, Cornwall, the Cornish antiquary and historian, curate of Kenton 1782, vicar of Manaccan 1794, of Anthony 1809, and of Newlyn, a deputy warden of the Stannaries, author of the 'History of Cornwall,' and also of the 'History of Devonshire,' died March, 1838. [5]

olwhele, William, 6s. Richard, of Manaccan, Cornwall, cler. EXETER COLL., matric. 12 April, 1821, aged 18; exhibitioner 1821, B.A. 1825, vicar of St. Anthony in Meneage 1828-58. See *Coll. Reg.*, 151.

omeroy, Henry, s. Arthur, of Westminster, arm. CHRIST CHURCH, matric. 1 Feb., 1768, aged 18; a student of Lincoln's Inn 1771.

omeroy, John, s. John, of Bodmin, Cornwall, gent. EXETER COLL., matric. 23 March, 1771, aged 18; B.A. 1775.

omeroy, John James, s. John, of Urney, co. Derry, cler. (after viscount). CHRIST CHURCH, matric. 17 May, 1809, aged 18; 5th Viscount Harberton, lieutenant 20th light dragoons 1813, died 5 Oct., 1862. See Foster's *Peerage* & *Alumni West.*, 470.

omeroy, Joseph, s. John, of Foy, Cornwall, gent. EXETER COLL., matric. 8 March, 1744-5, aged 18. [10]

'omeroy, William Knox (B.A. TRINITY COLL., Dublin, 1835), 6s. John, Viscount Harberton. MAGDALEN HALL, incorp. 27 Feb., 1840, aged 26; bar.-at-law, Middle Temple, 1844, died 1 Nov., 1874. See Foster's *Peerage*.

'omeroy, William Knox, 2s. Hon. Arthur William, of Dromore, near Londonderry, Ireland, cler. BRASENOSE COLL., matric. 12 June, 1862, aged 19; B.A. 1865. See Foster's *Peerage*, V. HARBERTON; & *Rugby School Reg.*

'omery, John, s. Joseph, of St. Kew, Cornwall, cler. EXETER COLL., matric. 4 March, 1800, aged 18; B.A. 1804.

'omery, Joseph, s. John, of Leskard, Cornwall, gent. EXETER COLL., matric. 26 March, 1768, aged 18; B.A. 1771, M.A. 1774, vicar of St. Kew, Cornwall, 1777, until his death at Bodmin 7 Feb., 1837.

'omfret, George William Richard, Earl of. CHRIST CHURCH, 1843. See FERMOR, page 457. [15]

'omfrett, Josias, s. John, of Biddenden, Kent, cler. CORPUS CHRISTI COLL., matric. 9 Dec., 1715, aged 18; B.A. 1719, M.A. 1722.

'omphrey, John Lovell, s. George, of Bristol (city), gent. PEMBROKE COLL., matric. 25 Nov., 1756, aged 17; B.A. 1760.

'omphrey, Matthew, s. George, of Stoke Bishop, par. of Westbury, co. Gloucester, gent. QUEEN'S COLL., matric. 26 June, 1770, aged 16.

'onsford, James, s. Thomas, of Lockston, Somerset, cler. EXETER COLL., matric. 29 Oct., 1740, aged 17; B.A. 1744.

'onsford, William, s. William, of Puddicombe, Devon, arm. TRINITY COLL., matric. 3 April, 1816, aged 18; B.A. 1819, M.A. 1823, rector of Drewsteignton, Devon, 1846, until his death 1 Aug., 1869. [20]

Ponsonby, Frederick, Viscount Duncannon, 1s. William, Earl of Bessborough. CHRIST CHURCH, matric. 27 Oct., 1774, aged 16; created M.A. 22 April, 1777, and also D.C.L. 30 April, 1779, 3rd Earl of Bessborough, M.P. Knaresborough 1780-96, a lord of the Admiralty, died 3 Feb., 1844. See Foster's *Peerage*.

Ponsonby, Frederick John, 3s. Frederick, of Curzon Street, London, equitis. MERTON COLL., matric. 13 Dec., 1855, aged 18; B.A. 1861, M.A. 1862, rector of Brington, Northants, 1868-77, vicar of St. Mary Magdalen, Munster Square, London, 1877. See Foster's *Peerage*, E. BESSBOROUGH.

Ponsonby, George Glinn, 3s. William, of Isle of St. Vincent, arm. UNIVERSITY COLL., matric. 18 April, 1825, aged 19; B.A. 1829.

Ponsonby, John William, Viscount Duncannon, s. William, Earl of Bessborough. CHRIST CHURCH, matric. 14 Oct., 1799, aged 17; created M.A. 23 June, 1802, 4th Earl of Bessborough, M.P. 1805-6 and 1812, until created Baron Duncannon 19 July, 1834, chief commissioner of Woods and Forests, died 16 May, 1847. See Foster's *Peerage*.

Ponsonby, Maurice John George, 2s. Charles Frederick Ashley Cooper, Baron de Mauley. CHRIST CHURCH, matric. 19 May, 1865, aged 18; B.A 1869, M.A. 1873, vicar of Kirkstall, Yorks, 1875-8, of St. Paul's, Chichester, 1878-9, and of New Swindon 1879. See Foster's *Peerage* & *Eton School Lists*. [25]

Ponsonby-Barker, William, s. Chambrè Brabazon, of Dublin (city), arm. CHRIST CHURCH, matric 24 Feb., 1814, aged 19; of Kilcooly Abbey, co. Tipperary, high sheriff, 1844, his father assumed the additional name of BARKER, died 9 Jan., 1877. See Foster's *Peerage*, E. BESSBOROUGH.

Pont, Henry, s. Samuel, of Braughing, Herts, arm. CHRIST CHURCH, matric. 2 March, 1756, aged 18, B.A. 1759, M.A. 1762.

Pontifex, Reginald Dalton, 3s. William, of Pau, France, arm. MAGDALEN COLL., matric. 16 Oct., 1876, aged 19; B.A. 1880, B.C.L. & M.A. 1886, bar.-at-law, Lincoln's Inn, 1884. See Foster's *Men at the Bar*.

Ponton, Daniel, s. Dan., of Lambeth, Surrey, pleb. ORIEL COLL., matric. 11 March, 1725-6, aged 17; father of Thomas 1766.

Ponten, Jesse, s. John, of St. Clement's, London, pleb. PEMBROKE COLL., matric. 17 Jan., 1770, aged 18; B.A. 1774 (as PONTON). See *St. Paul's School Reg.*, 122. [30]

Ponton, Thomas, s. Daniel, of St. Mary's, Lambeth, Surrey, arm. ST. JOHN'S COLL., matric. 4 July, 1766, aged 17; B.A. 1770, M.A. 1774, bar.-at-law, Lincoln's Inn, 1772, died in Oct., 1821, father of Thomas next named. See *Robinson*, 118.

Ponton, Thomas, s. Thomas, of Battersea, Surrey, arm. BRASENOSE COLL., matric. 24 May, 1797, aged 16; created M.A. 28 March, 1800, bar.-at-law, Lincoln's Inn, 1804, one of the founders of the Roxburgh Club, died 13 April, 1853. See *Eton School Lists*.

Pooke, William Henry. WORCESTER COLL., 1828. See CHAMBERLAINE, page 235.

Poole, Alexander, s. Samuel, of Chelmsford, Essex, gent. ST. EDMUND HALL, matric. 17 June, 1818, aged 18; B.A. 1822.

Poole, Alexander, o.s. Samuel, of Gwersyllt, co. Denbigh, arm. TRINITY COLL., matric. 23 Nov., 1878, aged 19; B.A. 1882, M.A. 1885. [35]

Poole, Alfred, 2s. John Hall, of St. James's, Bristol, gent. ST. EDMUND HALL, matric. 30 March, 1844, aged 18; B.A. 1848, M.A. 1852, held various curacies 1848-58, vicar of Purbrook, Hants, 1861-86, rector of Laindon Hills, Essex, 1886.

Poole, Anthony, s. Auth., of Llambedar, co. Merioneth, pleb. JESUS COLL., matric. 19 March, 1727-8, aged 17; B.A. 1731.

Poole, Arthur James, 6s. Robert, of Ripon, Yorks, cler. EXETER COLL., matric. 2 June, 1857, aged 19.

Poole, Arthur Ruscombe, 1s. Gabriel Stone, of Bridgwater, Somerset, gent. TRINITY COLL., matric. 5 Nov., 1859, aged 19; B.A. 1863, M.A. 1866, bar.-at-law, Inner Temple, 1865. See Foster's *Men at the Bar* & *Rugby School Reg.*

Poole, Arthur William, 5s. Thomas Francis, of Shrewsbury, gent. WORCESTER COLL., matric. 18 Oct., 1869, aged 17; B.A. 1873, M.A. 1876, created D.D. 20 Oct., 1883, bishop in Japan 1883, until his death 14 July, 1885.

Poole, Charles, s. Thomas, of Bridgewater, Somerset, gent. BALLIOL COLL., matric. 15 Nov., 1792, aged 18; B.A. 1798.

Poole, Charles, s. Henry, of Whitchurch, alias Little Stanmore, Middlesex, cler. ST. JOHN'S COLL., matric. 5 July, 1796, aged 18. **[5]**

Poole, Charles, 6s. Thomas Francis, of Shrewsbury, gent. CHRIST CHURCH, matric. 10 Oct., 1873, aged 19; exhibitioner 1876-7, B.A. 1877.

Poole, Charles Henry, 4s. James, of Pitminster, Somerset, gent. ST. ALBAN HALL, matric. 7 Dec., 1872, aged 21.

Poole, Cudworth, s. Edward, of New Hall, Cheshire, pleb. MAGDALEN HALL, matric. 14 Nov., 1738, aged 19; B.A. 1739, died vicar of Eccles 11 Nov., 1768.

Poole, Cudworth Halsted, y.s. William Halsted, of Terrick Hall, Salop, arm. CHRIST CHURCH, matric. 23 May, 1866, aged 18; of Marbury Hall, Cheshire, high sheriff 1880. See *Eton School Lists.*

Poole, Domville, s. Domville, of Lymm, Cheshire, arm. BRASENOSE COLL., matric. 29 April, 1805, aged 17; brother of John 1808. **[10]**

Poole, Edward, 'clerk to Dr. Blackstone;' privilegiatus 31 March, 1762.

Poole, Francis, s. James, of St. Giles's, London, arm. BRASENOSE COLL., matric. 24 March, 1800, aged 18.

Poole, Frederick John, 2s. Robert, of Ripon, Yorks, cler. WORCESTER COLL., matric. 21 Nov., 1849, aged 19; B.A. 1853, M.A. 1860, vicar of Bishop Monckton, Yorks, 1865.

Poole, Rev. Frederick John, 4s. Thomas, of Letwell, co. Yorks, cler. LINCOLN COLL., matric. 18 Oct., 1871, aged 19; B.A. 1876, M.A. 1878.

Poole, Henry, s. Samuel, of Llanyhangell, co. Merioneth, pleb. JESUS COLL., matric. 27 March, 1760, aged 16; B.A. 1763, M.A. 1775, chaplain to the Prince of Wales, rector of Whitchurch, Edgware, Middlesex, 1776-1810, vicar of Herne Hill, Kent, died 5 Dec., 1810. **[15]**

Poole, Henry James, 2s. Thomas James, of Huntspill, Somerset, gent. QUEEN'S COLL., matric. 23 Oct., 1862, aged 19; B.A. 1866, M.A. 1870, held various curacies 1867-76, rector of Stowell, Dorset, 1876.

Poole, Henry John, 1s. John, of St. Clement's, Oxford (city), cler. PEMBROKE COLL., matric. 6 Dec., 1849, aged 19; B.A. 1853, M.A. 1856, incumbent of Wangaretta, Victoria, Australia, 1877, B.D.

Poole, Henry Lyte, s. Clement, of Ilchester, Somerset, arm. WADHAM COLL., matric. 26 March, 1806, aged 18.

Poole, Hugh, s. Anthony, of Caenst, co. Merioneth, cler. JESUS COLL., matric. 14 July, 1760, aged 18.

Poole, Hugh Ruscombe, 4s. Gabriel Stone, of Bridgewater, Somerset, gent. CHRIST CHURCH, matric. 28 Jan., 1867, aged 18; B.A. 1869, a solicitor. See *Rugby School Reg.* **[20]**

Poole, James, s. James, of Stretton, co. Hereford, cler. MERTON COLL., matric. 13 Dec., 1757, aged 17; B.A. from ALL SOULS' COLL. 1763, bar.-at-law, Inner Temple, 1764, bencher 1797, recorder of Hereford, died 22 Nov., 1801.

Poole, James, 1s. Edward, of Stretton Grandison, co. Hereford, arm. ORIEL COLL., matric. 3 July, 1829, aged 17; a student of Lincoln's Inn 1833.

Pool, John, s. William, of Hewthwaite, Cumberland, cler. QUEEN'S COLL., matric. 7 Dec., 1731, aged 16.

Poole, John s. John, of Over Stowey, Somerset, gent. BALLIOL COLL., matric. 6 March, 1788, aged 17, B.A. 1792; fellow ORIEL COLL. until 1812, M.A. 1794, rector of Enmore, Somerset, 1796, and of Swainswick 1811, until his death 16 May, 1857.

Poole, John, s. Domville, of Lymm, Cheshire, arm. BRASENOSE COLL., matric. 15 June, 1808, aged 17; B.A. 1813, M.A. 1814, brother of Domville 1808. **[25]**

Poole, John, 3s. Samuel, of Saffron Walden, Essex, gent. ST. EDMUND HALL., matric. 14 Oct., 1829, aged 21.

Poole, John, 3s. Joseph Ruscombe, of Bridgewater, arm. CHRIST CHURCH, matric. 3 June, 1840, aged 18; died 1842. See *Eton School Lists.*

Poole, John, 1s. Thomas Francis, of St. Mary's, Shrewsbury, gent. CHRIST CHURCH, matric. 17 Oct., 1862, aged 18; B.A. 1866.

Poole, John Henry, o.s. John, of Llantisilio, co. Montgomery, cler. JESUS COLL., matric. 27 Oct., 1866, aged 18; B.A. 1871, M.A. 1874, has held various curacies since 1872.

Poole, Josiah, s. David, of Chancery Lane, London, arm. QUEEN'S COLL, matric. 11 Feb., 1763, aged 17. **[30]**

Poole, Nath., s. John, of Nether Stowey, Somerset, pleb. BALLIOL COLL., matric. 2 March, 1723-4, aged 18; B.A. 1727.

Pool, Nathaniel, s. Nathaniel, of Gloucester (city), gent. MERTON COLL., matric. 30 March, 1737, aged 18; B.A. 17 March, 1740-1.

Poole, Reginald Lane, 2s. Edward Stanley, of London, arm. BALLIOL COLL., matric. 24 Oct., 1874, aged 17; B.A. 1878, M.A. 1881, modern history lecturer Jesus College 1886.

Poole, Richard, s. Auth., of Llambedar, co. Merioneth, pleb. JESUS COLL., matric. 19 March, 1727-8, aged 18.

Poole, Richard, 2s. Edward, of Stretton, co. Hereford, gent. BRASENOSE COLL., matric. 11 Feb., 1836, aged 19. See *Rugby School Reg.*, 151. **[35]**

Poole, Robert, 3s. Henry, of Churton, Somerset, cler. EXETER COLL., matric. 8 March, 1826, aged 18; B.A. 1829, died vicar of St. Decuman, Taunton, 4 May, 1884.

Poole, Robert, of CATHARINE HALL, Cambridge (B.A. 1823, M.A. 1826); adm. 'ad eundem' 10 Oct., 1845, minor canon and vicar of Ripon Cathedral 1824, perp. curate Bishop Monkton, Ripon, 1836.

Poole, Robert Blake, 1s. Thomas James, of Huntspill, Somerset, arm. BRASENOSE COLL., matric. 16 June, 1857, aged 17; B.A. 1860, M.A. 1864, held various curacies 1862-79, vicar of Ilton, Somerset, 1879.

Poole, Rev. Robert Burton, 1s. William Savage, of Leamington, co. Warwick, arm. UNIVERSITY COLL., matric. 14 June, 1859, aged 18; B.A. 1862, M.A. 1867, B.D. 1880, D.D. 1886, head-master Harpur Foundation Modern School, Bedford, 1877.

Poole, Robert Henry, 1s. Robert, of Ripon, Yorks, cler. WORCESTER COLL., matric. 6 Feb., 1845, aged 18; B.A. 1849, M.A. 1851, perp. curate St. Thomas, Leeds, 1854-6, and of Beeston, Leeds, 1856-8, rector of Rainton, co. Durham, 1859, until his death 7 March, 1875. **[40]**

Poole, Robert Henry John, 1s. Robert Henry, of Beeston, Yorks, cler. BRASENOSE COLL., matric. 13 Oct., 1877, aged 19; scholar 1877-80, B.A. 1881, M.A. 1884.

Poole, Samuel, 1s. Samuel, of St. Mary's, Isle of Jamaica, gent. PEMBROKE COLL., matric. 2 Nov., 1843, aged 18; B.A. 1848, M.A. 1850, incumbent of St. Thomas Motueka, Nelson, New Zealand, 1863. See *Crockford*.

Poole, Rev. Sealy, 3s. Thomas James, of Huntspill, Somerset, gent. EXETER COLL., matric. 7 Feb., 1870, aged 19; B.A. 1873, M.A. 1877, master of Evesham Grammar School 1879.

Poole, Stanley Edward Lane, 1s. Edward Stanley, of London, gent. CORPUS CHRISTI COLL., matric. 22 Oct., 1874, aged 19; exhibitioner 1875-6, B.A. 1878.

Pool, Thomas, s. John, of Jamaica, cler. ST. JOHN'S COLL., matric. 9 Oct., 1767, aged 18.

Poole, Thomas Eyre, 1s. Thomas, of Marylebone, London, arm. QUEEN'S COLL., matric. 28 March, 1827, aged 22; B.A. from MAGDALEN HALL 1833, M.A. 1836, a colonial chaplain, died at Freetown, Sierra Leone, 22 Jan., 1852. [5]

Poole, William, s. William, of Bristol (city), gent. ST. EDMUND HALL, matric. 3 Dec., 1804, aged 22.

Poole, William, 3s. Edward, of Stretton Grandison, co. Hereford, arm. ORIEL COLL., matric. 25 May, 1837, aged 17; B.A. 1841, M.A. 1845, perp. curate Little Dewchurch, co, Hereford, 1854, and also of Hentland 1854, preb. of Hereford 1857. See *Rugby School Reg.*, 164.

Poole, William Henry Wilkes, 1s. George Ayliffe, of Welford, Northants, cler. NON-COLL., matric. 23 April, 1870, aged 19; exhibitioner MAGDALEN COLL. 1870-5, B.A. 1874, M.A. 1877.

Poole, William James, 1s. William, of Carnarvon (town), gent. JESUS COLL., matric. 21 May, 1831, aged 18; scholar 1832-8, B.A. 1835, rector of Aberffraw, Bangor, 1850, until his death 25 Oct., 1872.

Poole, William Savage, 3s. Robert, of Kenilworth, co. Warwick, arm. MAGDALEN HALL, matric. 1 June, 1837, aged 20. [10]

Pooler, Henry, 3s. John, of Aderley, near Newport, Salop, gent. CHRIST CHURCH, matric. 16 Oct., 1855, aged 17; B.A. 1859, M.A. 1862.

Pooley, Henry, s. William, of Laddock, Cornwall, cler. ORIEL COLL., matric. 20 Feb., 1782, aged 18; B.A. 1786, M.A. 1791, vicar of Newlyn, Cornwall, 1821.

Pooley, Rev. Herbert, 4s. John Henry, of Scotter, co. Lincoln, cler. KEBLE COLL., matric. 18 Oct., 1875, aged 19; B.A. 1880, M.A. 1882.

Pooley, William, s. Henry, of London, gent. ORIEL COLL., matric. 25 March, 1757, aged 19; B.A. 1760, M.A. 1763, B.D. 1782.

Poore, Edward, s. Edward, of Andover, Hants, gent. MAGDALEN HALL, matric. 4 Dec., 1721, aged 17; bar.-at-law, Lincoln's Inn, 1729, bencher 1751, recorder of Salisbury, M.P. 1747-54, Downton 1756-61, died 19 May, 1780. [15]

Poore, Edward, s. Edward, of Bradford, Wilts, arm. ORIEL COLL., matric. 19 Oct., 1759, aged 16; created M.A. 8 July, 1763, of Wedhampton, Wilts, died 30 Dec., 1795, grandfather of Edward 1814.

Poore, Edward, s. George Webb, of Devizes, Wilts, gent. QUEEN'S COLL., matric. 14 Dec., 1761, aged 16; B.A. 1765, M.A. 1768, bar.-at-law, Lincoln's Inn, 1772.

Poore, (Sir) Edward (Bart.), s. Edward, of London, arm. MAGDALEN COLL., matric. 14 Oct., 1814, aged 18; 2nd baronet, died 13 Oct., 1838. See Foster's *Baronetage*.

Poore, Edward Dyke, s. William Dyke, of Tigheldean, Wilts, arm. ST. JOHN'S COLL., matric. 13 May, 1800, aged 18; a student of Lincoln's Inn 1803, father of Edward D. 1834, and of William D. 1833.

Poore, Edward Dyke, 1s. 'Edwd. D.,' of Tidworth, Wilts, arm. NEW COLL., matric. 17 June, 1834, aged 19; B.A. 1838. [20]

Poore, George Collins, s. George, of 'Egypt,' Isle of Wight, Hants, arm. ORIEL COLL., matric. 7 May, 1813, aged 17.

Poore, John, s. Robert, of Redbridge, Hants, gent. BRASENOSE COLL., matric. 16 Dec., 1793, aged 15; B.A. 1797, M.A. 1800, B. & D.D. 1826, curate of South Stoneham, Hants, rector of Murston, Kent, 1814-66, vicar of Rainham 1826, until his death 5 April, 1866.

Poore, Philip, 3s. Philip, of Andover, Hants, arm. QUEEN'S COLL., matric. 23 May, 1822, aged 18; B.A. 1828, rector of Fifield, Hants, 1830, until his death 28 July, 1837.

Poore, William Dyke, 2s. Edward, of Tidworth, Wilts, arm. EXETER COLL., matric. 5 June, 1833, aged 17; B.A. 1837, M.A. 1855, bar.-at-law, Lincoln's Inn, 1845. See Foster's *Men at the Bar*.

Pope, Arthur Frederick, o.s. Edward, of Marylebone, London, cler. CHRIST CHURCH, matric. 27 May, 1858, aged 18; a junior student 1859-64, B.A. 1863, M.A. 1865, vicar of Tring, Herts, 1872-81. [25]

Pope, Benjamin, s. Thomas, of All Saints, Worcester (city), pleb. CHRIST CHURCH, matric. 15 Jan., 1801, aged 18; B.A. 1804, chaplain 1806, M.A. 1807, minor canon of St. George's, Windsor, 1817-61, hon. canon 1861, vicar of Caversham, Oxon, 1809, vicar of Nether Stowey, Somerset, 1824, and of Ogbourne St. George, Wilts, 1826, until his death 22 Nov., 1871.

Pope, Charles Andrew, 3s. James, arm. WORCESTER COLL., matric. 19 Oct., 1875, aged 18; B.A. 1878, bar.-at-law, Inner Temple, 1879. See Foster's *Men at the Bar*.

Pope, Edward, s. Ebenezer, of Lincoln's Inn Fields, Westminster, arm. BRASENOSE COLL., matric. 8 April, 1812, aged 18; Michel exhibitioner QUEEN'S COLL. 1815-6, scholar 1816-20, B.A. 1816, M.A. 1819, fellow 1820-7, B. & D.D. 1836, died archdeacon of Jamaica, Feb., 1855. See *Alumni West.*, 469.

Pope, Edward Jesty, 2s. Francis, of Bradford Peverell, Dorset, gent. QUEEN'S COLL., matric. 23 Oct., 1868, aged 20; B.A. & M.A. 1876, rector of Bradford Peverell, Dorset, 1880.

Pope, Edwin, 6s. Horatio (or Horace), of Maidstone, Kent, gent. UNIVERSITY COLL., matric. 7 May, 1847, aged 18; B.A. 1851, M.A. 1853, vicar of Paddock Wood, Kent, 1859. [30]

Pope, Frederick Andrew, 4s. Septimus, of Christon, Somerset, cler. WADHAM COLL., matric. 23 Jan., 1874, aged 18.

Pope, Frederick Sherlock Willis, 2s. Frederick Sherlock, of Whitby, Yorks, cler. WORCESTER COLL., matric. 3 Dec., 1850, aged 19.

Pope, George Henry, 1s. George, of Stockwell, Surrey, arm. WADHAM COLL., matric. 11 June, 1858, aged 18; B.A. 1862, M.A. 1865, B.C.L. 1870, a student of Lincoln's Inn 1860, sometime a solicitor, secretary to Merchant Adventurers, Bristol, 1885. See *Rugby School Reg.*

Pope, George Uglow, created M.A. 2 Feb., 1886, teacher of Tamil and Telugu, 1886, D.D. Lambeth 1864, fellow of University of Madras 1859, etc. See *Crockford*.

Pope, Henry Edmunds, 1s. Simeon Lloyd, of Whittlesea, co. Cambridge, cler. ST. MARY HALL, matric. 30 March, 1864, aged 26; B.A. 1870, M.A. 1871.

Pope, Henry Montagu Randall, 1s. Peter Montagu, of West Malling, Kent, arm. ST. JOHN'S COLL., matric. 19 June, 1867, aged 18, scholar 1867-72, B.A. 1871; fellow LINCOLN COLL. 1872-4, M.A. 1874, bar.-at-law, Lincoln's Inn, 1873, died 18 Nov., 1880. See *Robinson*, 341. [36]

Pope, James, s. William, of Hillingdon, Middlesex, gent. ST. JOHN'S COLL., matric. 1 July, 1773, aged 16; B.A. 1777, fellow, M.A. 1781, B.D. 1786, died at Great Stoughton, Hunts, 1822, father of John 1825.

Pope, John, s. Abel, of Okeford, Dorset, pleb. PEMBROKE COLL., matric. 4 April, 1720, aged 18; B.A. 21 Feb., 1723-4.

Pope, John, 3s. James, of Great Stoughton, Hunts, cler. ST. JOHN'S COLL., matric. 24 Oct., 1825, aged 20; bible clerk 1825-9, B.A. 1829, M.A. 1835, minister of Barriefield Church, Kingston, Upper Canada, died 22 April, 1846.

Pope, John Billing, o.s. Charles, of Stoke Damerel, Devon, arm. BRASENOSE COLL., matric. 8 June, 1865, aged 18; B.A. 1868, bar.-at-law, Lincoln's Inn, 1872, died 8 Dec., 1881.

Pope, John O'Fallon, o.s. Charles (Alexander), of St. Louis, Missouri (U.S.A.), arm. CHRIST CHURCH, matric. 30 May, 1868, aged 17; B.A. 1871, M.A. 1876, a student of the Inner Temple 1870.

Pope, Montagu Mercer, 2s. Peter Montagu, of West Malling, Kent, D.Med. ST. JOHN'S COLL., matric. 14 Oct., 1871, aged 19; B.A. 1875, M.A. 1878, vicar of Milverton, co. Warwick, 1878.

Pope, Reginald Henry, y.s. John, of Exeter, arm. BRASENOSE COLL., matric. 19 Oct., 1882, aged 19; B.A. 1886. [5]

Pope, Richard William Massy, 2s. Richard Thomas Pembroke, of Bangor, co. Carnarvon, cler. WORCESTER COLL., matric. 27 April, 1867, aged 18; scholar 1869-72, S.C.L. & B.A. 1871, M.A. 1873, B.D. 1877, math. lecturer 1874-82, divinity lecturer 1875, master of the schools 1878-9, 1881-3, classical moderator 1880, proctor 1884, public examiner 1886 censor of Non-Collegiate students 1887.

Pope, Septimus, 7s. Andrew, of Bristol, gent. QUEEN'S COLL., matric. 15 Oct., 1829, aged 17; B.A. 1835, M.A. 1837, rector of Christon, Somerset, 1842, until his death 3 Nov., 1878.

Pope, Simeon Lloyd, o.s. Simeon, of All Hallows, London, arm. TRINITY COLL., matric. 14 March, 1820, aged 18; B.A. 1823, scholar 1823-4, M.A. 1829, vicar of Whittlesea St. Mary 1829, and curate of All Saints', Knightsbridge, died 14 Oct., 1855, father of Henry Edmund.

Pope, William, 2s. George, of Rochester, Kent, arm. UNIVERSITY COLL., matric. 30 June, 1859, aged 19; exhibitioner 1860-3, B.A. 1863, M.A. 1866, rector of Cossington, Somerset, 1866-76, and of St. Nicholas, Nottingham, 1876.

Pope, William, 1s. William, of Spencecoomb, Devon, gent. ST. JOHN'S COLL., matric. 16 Oct., 1869, aged 18; B.A. 1872. [10]

Pope, William Burt, 1s. William, of London, cler. NEW COLL., matric. 15 Oct., 1875, aged 20; B.A. 1879, M.A. 1882.

Pope, William Havens, 2s. William Havens, of Higham Ferrers, Northants, gent. WADHAM COLL., matric. 20 May, 1858, aged 18.

Pope, Rev. William Henry, 1s. William Henry, of Wolverhampton, D.Med. NON-COLL., matric. 15 Feb., 1879, aged 19; B.A. from JESUS COLL. 1884.

Pope, William Langley, o.s. William L., of Highweek, Devon, gent. PEMBROKE COLL., matric. 10 June, 1841, aged 17; B.A. 1845, M.A. 1852, B. & D.D. 1863.

Pope, William Law, s. William, of Hillingdon, Middlesex, arm. WORCESTER COLL., matric. 30 June, 1814, aged 17; scholar 1815-8, B.A. 1818, fellow 1818-79, M.A. 1820, vice-provost 1842, perp. curate chapel-of-ease, Tonbridge Wells, 1825, until his death 26 Feb., 1879. [15]

Pope, William Raymond, 1s. William John Pitfield, of Barnstone, Notts, cler. TURRELL HALL, matric. 15 Oct., 1886, aged 19.

Popham, Alexander, s. Alex., of Wellington, Somerset, gent. BALLIOL COLL., matric. 14 May, 1719, aged 16; demy MAGDALEN COLL. 1722-6, B.A. 1723, B.C.L. 1727, possibly father of Alexander 1746. See *Bloxam*, vi. 201.

Popham, Alexander, s. George, of Chilton, Wilts, cler. ST. JOHN'S COLL., matric. 18 June, 1735, aged 18; a cousin of Edward 1729.

Popham, Alexander, s. Alexander, of Monkton, Somerset, cler. BALLIOL COLL., matric. 11 Nov., 1746, aged 17; B.A. from ALL SOULS' COLL. 1751, M.A. 1755, bar.-at-law, Middle Temple, 1755, bencher 1785, a master High Court of Chancery 1786-1802, auditor of the duchy of Lancaster, M.P. Taunton 1765-80, and 1784-96, died 13 Oct., 1810, buried in the Temple Church.

Popham, Alexander, s. Thomas, of Bagborough, Somerset, arm. QUEEN'S COLL., matric. 19 Jan., 1761, aged 17; of Bagborough, died 6 Oct., 1792, father of Francis 1798. [20]

Popham, Alexander Hugh Leyborne, 4s. Edward William, of Chilton, Wilts, arm. UNIVERSITY COLL., matric. 2 May, 1840, aged 19; died 24 May, 1866.

Popham, Edward, s. Francis, of Littlecote, Wilts, arm. CHRIST CHURCH, matric. 28 March, 1729, aged 17; created D.C.L. 3 July, 1759, of Littlecote, M.P. Bedwyn 1734-41, and Wiltshire 1741, until his death in 1772, father of the next named.

Popham, Edward, s. Edward, of Littlecote, Wilts, arm. ST. MARY HALL, matric. 9 May, 1755, aged 16, B.A. 1759; fellow ORIEL COLL., M.A. 1762, B. & D.D. 1774, rector of Chilton Foliatt, Wilts, 1778, until his death 16 Sep., 1815.

Popham, Edward, 1s. William, of Tramore, co. Waterford (Ireland), cler. ST. ALBAN HALL, matric. 23 Oct., 1858, aged 18; B.A. 1861, M.A. 1868, a student of Lincoln's Inn 1860.

Popham, Edward William Leyborne, created D.C.L. 30 June, 1813, of Littlecote, Wilts, high sheriff 1839, lieut.-colonel Cambrian rangers and colonel in the army 1803, major-general 1810, lieut.-general 1814, and a general in the army 1837 (son of William Leyborne Leyborne, governor of Grenada, etc.), assumed the additional name of POPHAM, died 16 June, 1843.

Popham, Edward William Leyborne, 1s. Edward William Leyborne, of Houndstreet, Somerset, arm. ORIEL COLL., matric. 15 April, 1825, aged 17; of Littlecote and Hunstrete Park, Somerset, died 24 Jan., 1881. [25]

Popham, Edward William Leyborne, 1s. John Leyborne, of Chilton, Wilts, cler. QUEEN'S COLL., matric. 30 Oct., 1863, aged 18; scholar 1863-8, B.A. 1868, rector of Hemyock, Somerset, 1873.

Popham, Francis, s. Edward, of Littlecote, Wilts, arm. ST. MARY HALL, matric. 7 Jan., 1752, aged 18; of Littlecote and Hunstrete, died 1780, brother of Edward 1755.

Popham, Francis, s. Alexander, of Bagborough, Somerset, arm. BRASENOSE COLL., matric. 1 Nov., 1798, aged 18; created M.A. 18 July, 1801, of Bagborough, died 28 May, 1858.

Popham, Francis Leyborne, 2s. Edward William, of Chilton, Wilts, arm. UNIVERSITY COLL., matric. 15 March, 1827, aged 17, B.A. 1831; fellow ALL SOULS' COLL. 1831-43, M.A. 1834, bar.-at-law, Lincoln's Inn, 1837, died in 1880. [30]

Popham, Francis White, o.s. Richard Walton White, of Wotton, Isle of Wight, cler. UNIVERSITY COLL., matric. 30 Nov., 1848, aged 18; B.A. 1853, M.A. 1856, of Shanklin and Wotton, Isle of Wight, assumed the additional surname of POPHAM by royal licence 1853.

Popham, Francis William Leyborne, 1s. Francis Leyborne, of London, arm. BRASENOSE COLL., matric. 10 June, 1881, aged 19.

Popham, George, s. Francis, of Wellington, Somerset, gent. HART HALL, matric. 7 June, 1739, aged 18, B.A. (HERTFORD COLL.) 4 March, 1742-3; M.A. from BALLIOL COLL. 1748.

Popham, Hugh Francis Arthur Leyborne, 2s. Francis Leyborne, of London, arm. BRASENOSE COLL., matric. 19 Oct., 1882, aged 18; B.A. 1887.

Popham, John, s. John, of Winchester, Hants, arm. ST. JOHN'S COLL., matric. 18 March, 1726-7, aged 17; possibly ancestor of the next named. [35]

Popham, John, s. John, of Kitehill, Isle of Wight, arm. NEW COLL., matric. 22 Nov., 1810, aged 20; died 29 March, 1811.

Popham, John Leyborne, 3s. Edward William, of Ramsbury, Wilts, arm. WADHAM COLL., matric. 26 March, 1829, aged 18; B.A. 1832, M.A. 1838, preb. of Salisbury 1849, rector of Chilton Folliatt, Wilts, 1835, until his death 24 Sep., 1872.

Popham, Thomas, s. Alexander, of Wellington, Somerset, gent. EXETER COLL., matric. 17 March, 1717-8, aged 17; B.C.L. from NEW COLL. 1725.

Popham, Vyvyan Wallis, 1s. Christopher Wallis, of Sithney, Cornwall, arm. EXETER COLL., matric. 25 Feb., 1853, aged 19; B.A. 1856, M.A. 1871, curate of Ilminster 1857, of Fulke, Dorset, 1857-63, and of Illogan, Cornwall, 1863-79.

Popham, William, 1s. Edward, of Waterford, Ireland, arm. ORIEL COLL., matric. 9 Dec., 1830, aged 19; B.A. 1837, M.A. 1845, rector of Binstead, Isle of Wight, 1880-1, vicar of Christ Church, Bradford-on-Avon, 1848-72, father of Edward 1858.

Popkin, George Traherne, o.s. George Perry, of Llanwrst, co. Denbigh, gent. LINCOLN COLL., matric. 13 Oct., 1866, aged 19. **[5]**

Popkin, Robert, s. Thomas, of Swansea, co. Glamorgan, arm. BRASENOSE COLL., matric. 19 May, 1779, aged 18.

Popkin, Thomas, s. Robert, of Swansea, co. Glamorgan, arm. CHRIST CHURCH, matric. 1 March, 1736-7, aged 18; created D.C.L. 5 July, 1759, then of Kettlehill, co. Glamorgan, father of the last named.

Poppe, Philip Edward, o.s. Alexander, of London, gent. PEMBROKE COLL., matric. 1 March, 1860, aged 18.

Popplewell, William, 4s. William, of Leeds, Yorks, gent. JESUS COLL., matric. 25 Oct., 1865, aged 24; B.A. 1868, M.A. 1872, vicar of St. Thomas, Halliwell, Lancashire, 1876-8, vicar of All Souls, Bolton, 1878.

Porch, John, s. Rich., of Orpington, Kent, gent. MERTON COLL., matric. 4 April, 1723, aged 18 (called 'Perch' in *Mat. Reg.*). **[10]**

Porcher, Charles, s. Josiah Dupré, of St. Marylebone, London, arm. ORIEL COLL., matric. 13 April, 1818, aged 18; B.A. 1823, M.A. 1824, bar.-at-law, Lincoln's Inn, 1826, died in April, 1863.

Porcher, George Dupré, 1s. George, of Midgham, Berks, cler. BALLIOL COLL., matric. 10 March, 1842, aged 18; B.A. 1845, M.A. 1849, bar.-at-law, Inner Temple, 1849, died 10 March, 1876.

Porre, William de, 3s. Peter John, of Portsmouth, Hants, gent. MAGDALEN HALL, matric. 2 Dec., 1841, aged 19; B.A. 1845, died curate of Brownstone, Devon, 7 May, 1848.

Port, Bernard, s. John, of Ilam, co. Stafford, arm. BRASENOSE COLL., matric. 23 Jan., 1794, aged 17; B.A. 1797, M.A. 1800, vicar of Ilam 1804, until his death 30 Jan., 1854.

Port, George Richard, 1s. John of Wirksworth, co. Derby, arm. BRASENOSE COLL., matric. 21 April, 1819, aged 18; B.A. 1824, rector of Oxenton, co. Gloucester, 1838-55, and of Grafton-Flyford, co. Worcester, 1855-75, died in Dec., 1882. **[15]**

Port, John, s. John, of Ilam, co. Stafford, arm. BRASENOSE COLL., matric. 11 March, 1791, aged 17.

Portal, Andrew, s. William, of Clowne, co. Derby, cler. EXETER COLL., matric. 14 Jan., 1747-8, aged 22; B.A. 1761, M.A. 1765 (*sic*), vicar of St. Helen's, Abingdon, 1759 (? died 13 Sep., 1768), father of Thomas 1773.

Portal, Charles Septimus, s. William, of St. Marylebone, Middlesex, gent. MAGDALEN HALL, matric. 30 Nov., 1814, aged 34.

Portal, Edward Robert, 1s. William Thomas, of Northampton, gent. CHRIST CHURCH, matric. 31 May, 1873, aged 19; B.A. 1877, M.A. 1880, bar.-at-law, Inner Temple, 1880. See Foster's *Men at the Bar.*

Portal, George Raymond, 4s. John, of Whitchurch, Hants, arm. CHRIST CHURCH, matric. 15 May, 1845, aged 18; B.A. 1849, M.A. 1852, rector of Albury, Surrey, 1858-71, rector of Burghclere, Hants, 1871, hon. canon of Winchester 1882. See *Rugby School Reg.*, 222. **[20]**

Portal, Melville, 1s. John, of Laverstoke, Hants, arm. CHRIST CHURCH, matric. 30 May, 1838, aged 18; B.A. 1842, M.A. 1844, of Laverstoke House, Hants, high sheriff, 1863, bar.-at-law, Lincoln's Inn, 1845, M.P. North Hants 1849-57, etc. See Foster's *Men at the Bar.*

Portal, Melville Raymond, 1s. Melville, of Laverstoke, Hants, arm. BALLIOL COLL., matric. 19 May, 1875, aged 18.

Portal, Spencer John, 2s. Wynham Spencer, of Malshanger, Hants, arm. CHRIST CHURCH, matric. 13 Oct., 1882, aged 18.

Portal, Thomas, s. Andrew, of Abingdon, Berks, cler. HERTFORD COLL., matric. 13 Feb., 1773, aged 16.

Portal, William (Benjamin), s. William, of Westminster, gent. ST. JOHN'S COLL., matric. 28 June, 1785, aged 18; scholar & fellow 1785-1812, B.A. 1789, M.A. 1795, B.D. 1798, select preacher 1804, rector of Wasing, Berks, and vicar of Sandford, Oxon, died 27 June, 1812. See *Robinson*, 141. **[25]**

Portal, William Richard, 1s. Richard Brinsley, of Marylebone, London, gent. PEMBROKE COLL., matric. 20 Nov., 1856, aged 18; scholar 1856-62, B.A. 1860, M.A. 1863. See *Robinson*, 307.

Portal, William Wyndham, 1s. Wyndham Spencer, of Malshanger, Hants, arm. CHRIST CHURCH, matric. 15 Jan., 1869, aged 18; B.A. 1873, M.A. 1878, of Southington House, Hants, high sheriff, 1886. See *Eton School Lists.*

Portbury, Fisher, s. William, of Bampton, Devon, pleb. EXETER COLL., matric. 26 March, 1743, aged 18.

Portbury, George, s. Lewis, of St. Petrock, Exeter, gent. EXETER COLL., matric. 15 Oct., 1733, aged 17; B.A. 1737.

Porten, Stanier James, s. Stanier, of St. James's, Westminster, equitis. BRASENOSE COLL., matric. 29 June, 1798, aged 18; B.A. 1801, M.A. 1807, rector of Charlwood, Surrey, 1850, until his death 18 Nov., 1854. **[30]**

Porteous, David Scott, 1s. Alexander, of St. Cyres, co. Kincardine, arm. BRASENOSE COLL., matric. 1 June, 1871, aged 18.

Porter, Adrian Matthew, 6s. Henry, of St. Mary's Clyst, Devon, arm. MERTON COLL., matric. 13 Oct., 1860, aged 18.

Porter, Rev. Alfred, 4s. George Shepheard, of Bath, Somerset, cler. KEBLE COLL., matric. 18 Oct., 1875, aged 19; B.A. 1878, M.A. 1882, head-master diocesan Grammar School, King William's Town, Cape Colony, 1886.

Porter, Benjamin, s. Thomas Chinnall, of St. Giles's, London, arm. CHRIST CHURCH, matric. 3 Feb., 1814, aged 19; B.A. 1817. See *Eton School Lists.*

Porter, Charles, s. Thomas, of Manchester, Lancashire, gent. BRASENOSE COLL., matric. 13 April, 1799, aged 19; exhibitioner 1803, B.A. 1803, M.A. 1805, B.D. 1815, D.D. (by decree) 1 June, 1816, vice-principal St. Alban Hall, president King's College, Nova Scotia, 1806-36, rector of St. James's, Newport, N.S., 1816-36, died 25 Nov., 1864. See *Manchester School Reg.*, ii. 182. **[35]**

Porter, Rev. Charles Kirby, 2s. Charles, of Windsor, Nova Scotia, D.D. NEW INN HALL, matric. 18 Nov., 1841, aged 25; B.A. 1846, died 13 March, 1863.

Porter, George, s. George, of All Hallows the Great, London, pleb. QUEEN'S COLL., matric. 11 May, 1719, aged 19; B.A. 21 Feb., 1722-3.

Porter, George, born at Constantinople, s. James, equitis. CHRIST CHURCH, matric. 25 Nov., 1776, aged 17 (his father, minister at Brussels and ambassador, at Constantinople, knighted 21 Sep., 1763, died 9 Dec., 1776).

Porter, Rev. George, s. William, of St. Mary's, Carlisle, Cumberland, gent. QUEEN'S COLL., matric. 20 June, 1805, aged 15; B.A. 1809, M.A. 1812, fellow 1815-9, and on old foundation 1819-30, tutor 1819, junior bursar 1825, vicar of Baldon-Toot, vicar of Monks Sherborne, Hants, and perp. curate Pamber 1830, until his death 8 April, 1848.

Porter, George, 4s. Thomas, of Rockbeare, Devon, arm. EXETER COLL., matric. 14 Nov., 1844, aged 18; B.A. 1848, M.A. 1851, rector of Lympston, Devon, 1850-7, of Rackenford 1860-7, of Littleton, Middlesex, 1867-72, and of St. Leonard's, Exeter, 1872. See *Eton School Lists.*

Porter, Henry, s. Thomas, of Demerara, West Indies, arm. BRASENOSE COLL., matric. 24 April, 1811, aged 19; B.A. 1815, M.A. 1819, a student of Lincoln's Inn 1811.

Porter, Rev. Henry Blanc, 4s. Robert Tindal, of Masulipatam, East Indies, gent. EXETER COLL., matric. 15 Oct., 1870, aged 19; B.A. 1873, M.A. 1877. [5]

Porter, Rev. Henry Leech, 1s. John Leech, of Shipley, Yorks, cler. EXETER COLL., matric. 13 Oct., 1877, aged 19; scholar 1877-81, B.A. 1882. See *Coll. Reg.*, 168.

Porter, John, B.A. from HART HALL 11 Feb., 1725-6 (*Acts Book*).

Porter, John Robinson, 1s. Richard, of Islington, Middlesex, gent. MAGDALEN HALL, matric. 27 Aug., 1864, aged 25; vicar of Kniveton, co. Derby, 1870-1, and of Wartling, Kent, 1875.

Porter, Joseph, s. John, of St. Bees, Cumberland, gent. MAGDALEN HALL, matric. 16 Jan., 1795, aged 19; B.A. 1813, M.A. 1814, rector of St. John's, Bristol, 1826, until his death 2 Nov., 1833.

Porter, Lewis, 4s. Henry, of Dresden, Germany, gent. EXETER COLL., matric. 7 June, 1854, aged 17. [10]

Porter, Moses, s. Richard, of St. Andrew's Undershaft, London, gent. ST. JOHN'S COLL., matric. 10 July, 1753, aged 17; B.A. 1757, M.A. 1764, B.D. 1767, lecturer and curate Clapham, Surrey, died 5 Sep., 1791. See *Robinson*, 103.

Porter, Reginald, 3s. Henry, of Clyst St. Mary, Devon, gent. EXETER COLL., matric. 12 June, 1851, aged 18; B.A. 1855, M.A. 1858, rector of Kenn, Devon, 1858. See *Eton School Lists.*

Porter, Richard, s. Robert, of Lyng, Somerset, pleb. EXETER COLL., matric. 27 March, 1732, aged 19.

Porter, Richard, s. John, of Eskdale, Cumberland, gent. MAGDALEN HALL, matric. 23 April, 1812, aged 20; B.A. 1821.

Porter, Robert, s. William, of Wigan, Lancashire, gent. BRASENOSE COLL., matric. 23 May, 1792, aged 18; exhibitioner 1796, B.A. 1796, M.A. 1798, rector of Draycot-le-Moors, co. Stafford, 1806, until his death 25 March, 1838. See *Manchester School Reg.*, ii. 152. [15]

Porter, Robert Ibbetson, 8s. Robert Tindal, of Cheltenham, gent. PEMBROKE COLL., matric. 23 Oct., 1879, aged 18; scholar 1879-84, B.A. 1883, M.A. 1886.

Porter, Robert Waltham, 1s. Thomas, of Lower Norwood, Surrey, gent. BRASENOSE COLL., matric. 20 Oct., 1886, aged 18; scholar 1886.

Porter, Stafford, 3s. George, of Anstey, Herts, cler. ST. MARY HALL, matric. 23 Oct., 1876, aged 22.

Porter, Thomas, s. Thomas, of Lincoln (city), gent. LINCOLN COLL., matric. 29 March, 1737, aged 14; B.A. from PEMBROKE COLL. 10 Feb., 1740-1, M.A. 1743, perp. curate Northenden, Cheshire, 1752, until his death 25 May, 1802. See *Manchester School Reg.*, i. 117.

Porter, Thomas, 1s. Thomas, of Rockbeare, Devon, arm. ORIEL COLL., matric. 9 June, 1831, aged 17. See *Eton School Lists.* [20]

Porter, Thomas Chinnall, s. Benjamin, of London, arm. CHRIST CHURCH, matric. 12 Nov., 1777, aged 18; father of Benjamin 1814.

Porter, Rev. Thomas Cunningham, 1s. Christopher Waltham, of Bristol, gent. EXETER COLL., matric. 31 May, 1879, aged 19; scholar 1878-84, B.A. 1883, M.A. 1886, assistant-master Eton College 1885.

Porter, Walter, 4s. James, of Boston, co. Lincoln, gent. NEW COLL., matric. 5 Feb., 1877, aged 20.

Porter, Wilfrid King, 9s. Robert Tindal, of Cheltenham, arm. BALLIOL COLL., matric. 16 Oct., 1883, aged 18; B.A. 1888, entered the Indian Civil Service 1883, bar.-at-law, Gray's Inn, 1888.

Porter, Rev. William Warren, s. Moses, of Clapham, Surrey, cler. ST. JOHN'S COLL., matric. 1 July, 1794, aged 18; B.A. 1798, M.A. 1802, died 14 June, 1804. See *Robinson*, 155. [25]

Portington, Henry, s. John, of Bourne, co. Lincoln, gent. LINCOLN COLL., matric. 2 Nov., 1773, aged 17; B.A. 1779, fellow, M.A. 1780, rector of Winterbourne Abbas with Steepleton, Dorset, 1785, and of Wappenham, Northants, 1795, until his death 7 Dec., 1832.

Portis, John, s. James, of London, arm. UNIVERSITY COLL., matric. 15 Dec., 1786, aged 17; B.A. 1790, M.A. 1793, rector of Little Leigh, Essex, 1795, until his death 3 June, 1841.

Portlock, Benjamin, s. Benjamin, of London, arm. CHRIST CHURCH, matric. 23 Oct., 1733, aged 18.

Portman, Edward Berkeley, s. Edward Berkeley, of Bryanston, Dorset, arm. CHRIST CHURCH, matric. 20 Oct., 1817, aged 18; B.A. 1821, M.A. 1826, Viscount Portman, so created 28 March, 1873, (created Baron Portman 28 March, 1837), M.P. Dorset 1823-32, Marylebone 1833, lord warden of the Stannaries 1865, lord-lieut. Somerset 1860-4. See Foster's *Peerage* & *Eton School Lists.*

Portman, Edward William Berkeley, 1s. Hon. William Henry Berkeley, of London. CHRIST CHURCH, matric. 15 Jan., 1875, aged 18. See Foster's *Peerage* & *Eton School Lists.* [30]

Portman, Edwin Berkeley, 2s. Edward, Baron P. BALLIOL COLL., matric. 17 March, 1847, aged 16, S.C.L. & B.A. 1850; fellow ALL SOULS' COLL. 1850-7, B.C.L. 1854, bar.-at-law, Inner Temple, 1852, M.P. North Dorset, Dec., 1885. See Foster's *Men at the Bar* & *Rugby School Reg.*, 232.

Portman, Fitzharding Berkeley, 4s. Edward Berkeley, of Bryanston, Dorset, arm. CHRIST CHURCH, matric. 20 May, 1828, aged 17; fellow ALL SOULS' COLL. 1831-41, B.A. 1832, M.A. 1836, rector of Orchard Portman, etc., 1840-85, and of Staple Fitzpaine since 1840. See Foster's *Peerage* & *Eton School Lists.*

Portman, Henry Berkeley, 2s. Hon. William Henry, of London. NON-COLL., matric. 17 Oct., 1879, aged 19. See Foster's *Peerage* & *Eton School Lists.*

Portman, Henry Fitzhardinge Berkeley, 2s. Henry William Berkeley, of Child Okeford, Dorset, arm. MAGDALEN COLL., matric. 9 June, 1857, aged 18; B.A. 1863, rector of Pylle, Somerset, 1866-85, and of Orchard Portman, etc., 1885.

Portman, Henry William, s. Henry, of Bryanston, Dorset, arm. NEW COLL., matric. 4 July, 1755, aged 16; grandfather of Edward Berkeley, Viscount Portman, 1817. [35]

Portman, Walter Berkeley, 4s. Edward, Baron P. CHRIST CHURCH, matric. 30 May, 1855, aged 18; B.A. 1859, rector of Corton-Denham, Dorset, 1861. See Foster's *Peerage* & *Eton School Lists.*

Portman, (Hon.) William Henry Berkeley, 1s. (Edward Berkeley) Baron P. MERTON COLL., matric. 15 Oct., 1847, aged 18; M.P. Shaftesbury 1852-7, Dorsetshire 1857-85. See Foster's *Peerage & Eton School Lists.*

Portrey, David, s. David, of Lantwitt-Major, co. Glamorgan, pleb. JESUS COLL., matric. 10 Dec., 1744, aged 20.

Portney, John, s. Christopher, of Ystradgunlais, co. Brecon, gent. JESUS COLL., matric. 7 July, 1716, aged 18.

Post, Frederick Alfred, 2s. Wright Eli, of New York, America, arm. BRASENOSE COLL., matric. 3 Dec., 1868, aged 18.

Postance, Charles Groves, 5s. Henry, of Liverpool, cler. ST. MARY HALL, matric. 20 Oct., 1884, aged 19. [5]

Postance, Richard, 3s. Henry, of Tetbury, co. Gloucester, cler. ST. MARY HALL, matric. 22 Oct., 1870, aged 19; B.A. 1873, M.A. 1878, perp. curate St. Barnabas, Liverpool, 1879.

Postance, Rev. Walsham, 4s. Henry, of Birkenhead, Cheshire, cler. ST. MARY HALL, matric. 19 Oct., 1877, aged 22; B.A. 1881, M.A. 1884.

Postance, Rev. William Edmund, 2s. Richard, of London, cler. ST. MARY HALL, matric. 1 Feb., 1873, aged 19.

Poste, Edward, 3s. Beale, of Milstead, Kent, cler. ORIEL COLL., matric. 13 June, 1840, aged 17; B.A. 1844, fellow 1846, M.A. 1848, public examiner jurisprudence 1875-6, of Bydews Place, Kent, bar.-at-law, Lincoln's Inn, 1856, director Civil Service examinations. See Foster's *Men at the Bar.*

Postgate, John Lionel, 2s. John, of Birmingham, gent. QUEEN'S COLL., matric. 22 Oct., 1878, aged 19; Boden Sanskrit scholar, Eglesfield exhibitioner 1878-81, a student of Inner Temple 1880, drowned 1 June, 1881. [10]

Postlethwaite, George, 6s. John, of Furness, Lancashire, gent. NON-COLL., matric. 17 Oct., 1881, aged 21; B.A. 1886.

Postlethwayt, John, s. Mat., of Denton, Norfolk, cler. MERTON COLL., matric. 2 May, 1729, aged 18; B.A. 19 Feb., 1732-3, he or his father died rector of Denton 1750.

Postlethwaite, John, 1s. John, of Milnthorpe, Westmoreland, gent. QUEEN'S COLL., matric. 9 Feb., 1832, aged 20; B.A. 1836, M.A. 1858, rector of Tasley 1848-82.

Postlethwayt, Matthew, s. John, of Millum, Cumberland, pleb. QUEEN'S COLL., matric. 2 May, 1733, aged 17; B.A. 17 March, 1736-7.

Postlethwaite, Richard, 2s. Richard, of Roche, Cornwall, cler. ST. EDMUND HALL, matric. 23 Oct., 1822, aged 20; B.A. 1826. [15]

Postlethwaite, Thomas Marshall, 3s. Thomas, of Warton, Lancashire, cler. QUEEN'S COLL., matric. 19 March, 1829, aged 18; B.A. 1833, perp. curate Walney 1840-6, and of Witherslack 1846. See *Eton School Lists.*

Potemkin, James, D.C.L. by diploma 15 June, 1814; general in the Muscovite army.

Potenger, Richard, s. Thomas, of Isle of Guernsey, arm. UNIVERSITY COLL., matric. 16 Oct., 1810, aged 18; scholar PEMBROKE COLL. 1812-16, B.A. 1814, M.A. 1819, rector of St. Martin, Guernsey, 1832, until his death 5 Feb., 1860.

Potier, John, s. Stephen, of Lausanne, Switzerland, gent. ST. JOHN'S COLL., matric. 5 March, 1739-40, aged 24.

Potlrie, Charles, created D.C.L. 18 June, 1756; colonel of a regiment of foot in the Danish army, (late) governor of Prince of Nassau, etc., etc. [20]

Pots, John, s. John, of Barton, Cheshire, pleb. BRASENOSE COLL., matric. 15 April, 1736, aged 21.

Pott, Alfred, 2s. Charles, of Norwood, Surrey, arm. BALLIOL COLL., matric. 15 Dec., 1840, aged 18; demy MAGDALEN COLL. 1843-53, B.A. 1844, M.A. 1847, fellow 1853-5, B.D. 1854, hon. canon Christ Church 1858, vicar of Cuddesden and principal of Cuddesden College 1852-7, rector of East Hendred 1857-69, vicar of Abingdon 1869-75, archdeacon of Berks 1869, vicar of Sonning, Berks, 1882. See *Bloxam*, vii. 357; & *Eton School Lists.*

Pott, Arthur Sidney, 3s. Charles, of London, arm. BALLIOL COLL. matric. 6 April, 1848, aged 19; B.A. 1851, M.A. 1854, rector of Northill, Beds, 1858, until his death 12 March, 1866. See *Eton School Lists.*

Pott, Charles Percivall, 1s. Alfred, of East Hendred, Berks, B.D. KEBLE COLL., matric. 28 Jan., 1879, aged 18; died at Oxford 13 May, 1879. See *Eton School Lists.*

Pott, Edward, 2s. William, of Southwark, Surrey, gent. MERTON COLL., matric. 2 May, 1845, aged 18. See *Eton School Lists.* [25]

Pott, Francis, s. James, of St. Mary, Rotherhithe, London, pleb. ST. JOHN'S COLL., matric. 13 Feb., 1810, aged 17; B.A. 1813, M.A. 1818, vicar of Churchstowe with Kingsbridge, Devon, 1829, died in 1842.

Pott, Francis, 4s. William, of Southwark, Surrey, arm. BRASENOSE COLL., matric. 6 Feb., 1851, aged 18; B.A. 1854, M.A. 1857, held various curacies 1856-66, rector of Norhill, Beds, 1866.

Pott, John Arthur, 2s. Alfred, of London, cler. KEBLE COLL., matric. 14 Oct., 1884, aged 18.

Pott, John Lee, s. John, of Hereford (city), gent. NEW COLL., matric. 20 May, 1755, aged 19.

Pottell, William, s. William, of St. Mary, Blandford, Dorset, gent. NEW COLL., matric. 23 Oct., 1729, aged 18; B.A. 1734, M.A. 1738. [30]

Potter, Arthur Bayley, 3s. Thomas, of Manchester, arm. BALLIOL COLL., matric. 27 April, 1871, aged 18. See *Eton School Lists.*

Potter, Benjamin Conway, s. John Conway, of Soughton, co. Flint, cler. WORCESTER COLL., matric. 29 April, 1809, aged 18; B.A. 1813, M.A. 1815.

Potter, Charles, s. Christopher, of Holywell, Oxford (city), gent. CHRIST CHURCH, matric. 9 Dec., 1720, aged 19; B.A. 1724, M.A. 1727.

Potter, Charles Augustus, 2s. Edward, of Lisbon, Portugal, arm. MERTON COLL., matric. 24 June, 1862, aged 19; B.A. 1865, M.A. 1869, rector of Thimbleby, co. Lincoln, 1874.

Potter, Christopher, s. Christopher, of Holywell, Oxford (city), gent. QUEEN'S COLL., matric. 20 Jan., 1717-8, aged 17. [35]

Potter, Edward Arthur Smalley, 1s. Edward Smalley, of Ryde, Isle of Wight, arm. EXETER COLL., matric. 21 Oct., 1886, aged 18.

Potter, Emmanuel, s. John, of Ponsonby, Cumberland, pleb. QUEEN'S COLL., matric. 5 July, 1733, aged 18.

Potter, Fitzherbert, s. Fitzherbert, of Hanwell, doctor. LINCOLN COLL., matric. 17 Feb., 1756, aged 17; B.A. 1759.

Potter, Francis, s. Christ., of Toot Baldon, Oxon, gent. PEMBROKE COLL., matric. 17 Dec., 1729, aged 19; B.A. from NEW COLL. 1733, M.A. 1736, preb. of Bath and Wells 1749, archdeacon of Taunton 1748, and of Wells 1760, until his death 7 Oct., 1767.

Potter, Frederick Howson. QUEEN'S COLL., 1849. See NEVILLE, page 1013. [40]

Potter, Frederick William Cecil, 1s. Frederick, of Charlton Kings, co. Gloucester, cler. ST. JOHN'S COLL., matric. 14 April, 1877, aged 19; B.A. (NON-COLL.) 1884.

Potter, George, s. George, of Lowther, Westmoreland, pleb. QUEEN'S COLL., matric. 22 May, 1740, aged 18.

Potter, Rev. George Harries, 1s. Thomas, of Gosport, Hants, arm. QUEEN'S COLL., matric. 16 March, 1843, aged 18; clerk 1843-6, B.A. 1846, M.A. 1850, died at Malaga 3 Nov., 1854.

Potter, Rev. George Walpole, o.s. George Harries, of Gosport, Hants, cler. NEW COLL., matric. 20 Feb., 1872, aged 19; B.A. 1876, M.A. 1882.

Potter, The Right Rev. Horatio, created D.C.L. 7 July, 1860, bishop of New York, died 3 Jan., 1887, aged 84. See *Annual Register.*

Potter, John, born at Christ Church, s. John, bishop of Oxford. CHRIST CHURCH, matric. 5 Dec., 1727, aged 13; B.A. 1731, M.A. 1734, B.D. 1741, D.D. 1745, rector of Elme, Ely, 1738, vicar of Lydd, Kent, 1742 (? archdeacon of Oxford 1741, until his death 1767).

Potter, John Charles, 1s. John Gerald, of Manchester, arm. CHRIST CHURCH, matric. 31 May, 1873, aged 18; B.A. 1877, bar.-at-law, Inner Temple, 1880, J.P. Lancashire. See Foster's *Men at the Bar* & *Eton School Lists.* **[5]**

Potter, John Haslock, o.s. John, of Walsall, co. Stafford, gent. BRASENOSE COLL., matric. 11 April, 1866, aged 19; B.A. 1869, M.A. 1873, held various curacies 1870-82, vicar of Holy Trinity, Upper Tooting, 1882.

Potter, John Henry, 2s. Thomas, of Manchester, arm. MERTON COLL., matric. 21 May, 1869, aged 17; a student of the Inner Temple 1870. See *Eton School Lists.*

Potter, Rev. John Philips, s. John, of Manchester, arm. ORIEL COLL., matric. 5 June, 1809, aged 16; B.A. & M.A. 1815, died 8 Feb., 1861; for obituary notice of his son, see *Gent.'s Mag.*, 1847, ii. 100.

Potter, Peter, 1s. Peter, of Walsall, co. Stafford, arm. EXETER COLL., matric. 29 May, 1866, aged 24; B.A. 1872, perp. curate Minsterley, Salop, 1876-9, and of St. Thomas, Overmonnow, co. Monmouth, 1879.

Potter, Thomas, s. Thomas, of All Hallows', Steyning, London, gent. ST. JOHN'S COLL., matric. 2 April, 1726, aged 17; bar.-at-law, Inner Temple, 1736, died 9th, and buried in the Temple Church, Sunday, 12 April, 1741. **[10]**

Potter, Thomas, born at Cuddesden, Oxon, s. John, bishop of Oxford. CHRIST CHURCH, matric. 18 Nov., 1731, aged 13; B.A. 1735, M.A. 1738, bar.-at-law, Middle Temple, 1740, recorder of Bath, principal registrar province of Canterbury, joint vice-treasurer Ireland, M.P. St. German's 1747-54, Aylesbury 1754 to July, 1757, and Okehampton July, 1757, until his death 17 June, 1759.

Potter, Thomas Ashton, 1s. Thomas Bayley, of Eccles, near Manchester, arm. MERTON COLL., matric. 13 Oct., 1866, aged 19; B.A. 1871, M.A. 1874.

Potter, William, s. William, of Hartwell, Northumberland, gent. LINCOLN COLL., matric. 27 Feb., 1727-8, aged 17; B.A. 1731, M.A. 1734.

Potticary, George Brown Francis, 1s. Nathaniel, of St. Luke's, London, gent. MAGDALEN HALL, matric. 19 May, 1819, aged 23; B.A. 1824, M.A. 1825, rector of Girton, co. Cambridge, 1850-83.

Potticary, William, s. William, of Wily, Wilts, pleb. EXETER COLL., matric. 2 Nov., 1811, aged 17; chorister MAGDALEN COLL. 1802-11, a commoner of ST. EDMUND HALL 1815. See *Bloxam*, i. 208. **[15]**

Pottinger, Head, s. John, of Compton, Berks, gent. ST. JOHN'S COLL., matric. 17 Oct., 1776, aged 17; vicar of Compton, Berks, 1820, until his death 13 Jan., 1829. See Foster's *Baronetage.*

Pottinger, (Sir) Henry (Bart.), 2s. Henry, of East Indies, baronet. MERTON COLL., matric. 19 June, 1852, aged 18; B.A. 1856, 3rd baronet, bar.-at-law, Inner Temple, 1861. See Foster's *Men at the Bar* & *Eton School Lists.*

Pottinger, Henry Allison, 3s. William, of St. Mary Aldermary, London, pleb. WORCESTER COLL., matric. 21 April, 1842, aged 18; B.A. 1846, M.A. 1848, fellow 1883, modern history lecturer 1862-3, 1865-82, law lecturer since 1865, librarian 1884, lecturer and tutor in jurisprudence Corpus Christi College 1878-84, bar.-at-law, Lincoln's Inn, 1860. See Foster's *Men at the Bar.*

Potts, Andrew, o.s. George, of Brighton, gent. NON-COLL., matric. 16 Oct., 1875, aged 24; B.A. 1882.

Potts, Charles Henry, 1s. Charles William, of Chester (city), arm. BRASENOSE COLL., matric. 28 Nov., 1867, aged 19; B.A. from ST. ALBAN HALL 1873, M.A. 1874. **[20]**

Potts, Rev. Frederick Arthur, o.s. Frederick, of London, arm. MAGDALEN COLL., matric. 24 Jan., 1881, aged 18; B.A. 1884, M.A. 1887.

Potts, George William, o.s. Charles Hutton, of Sunderland, co. Durham, arm. MAGDALEN HALL, matric. 22 Oct., 1869, aged 18.

Potts, Henry John, 1s. Henry, of Chester (city), gent. EXETER COLL., matric. 14 Oct., 1865, aged 20; of Glanrafon, co. Denbigh, J.P., a student of the Inner Temple 1866.

Potts, John, s. Joseph, of Abbey, Cumberland, pleb. QUEEN'S COLL., matric. 10 Oct., 1781, aged 19.

Potts, Leonard Francis, 4s. Charles William, of Cheshire, arm. BALLIOL COLL., matric. 8 Feb., 1879, aged 19; B.A. 1883, M.A. 1885, a student of Lincoln's Inn 1881. See *Rugby School Reg.* **[25]**

Potts, Robert, of TRINITY COLL., Cambridge (B.A. 1832, M.A. 1835); adm. 'ad eundem' 6 June, 1850.

Potts, Robert Ullock, 1s. Robert Alfred, of London, gent. ORIEL COLL., matric. 23 Oct., 1884, aged 18.

Potts, Thomas Radford, 2s. Ralph Henry, of Bishopton, near Stratford-on-Avon, gent. NON-COLL., matric. 16 Jan., 1875, aged 20; B.A. from LINCOLN COLL. 1878, B.C.L. & M.A. 1882, bar.-at-law, Inner Temple, 1879. See Foster's *Men at the Bar.*

Pouchée, George John, o.s. Lewis John, of London, arm. TRINITY COLL., matric. 26 March, 1835, aged 18.

Poulden, Rev. James Bedford, 2s. James Bedford, of Fylton, co. Gloucester, cler. WORCESTER COLL., matric. 10 March, 1853, aged 18; B.A. 1856, M.A. 1860. **[30]**

Poulett, Anne, 4s. John, Earl Poulett. CHRIST CHURCH, matric. 19 May, 1729, aged 17; M.P. Bridgewater 1769, until his death 5 July, 1785.

Poulett, John, Viscount Hinton, born in London, s. John, Earl Poulett. BRASENOSE COLL., matric. 12 June, 1801, aged 17; 5th earl, died 20 June, 1864. See Doyle's *Baronage.*

Poulett, Vere, 3s. John, Earl Poulett. CHRIST CHURCH, matric. 19 May, 1729, aged 18; 3rd earl, died 14 April, 1788.

Poulett, Vere (Viscount Hinton), born at Hinton St. George, Somerset, 2s. (John), Earl Poulett. CHRIST CHURCH, matric. 26 May, 1841, aged 17; died 29 Aug., 1857.

Poulson, George, s. Clemen., of Chiping (*sic*), Yorks, gent. BRASENOSE COLL., matric. 10 Oct., 1722, aged 18. **[35]**

Poulson, George, 2s. John, of Petersfield, Hants, gent. ST. ALBAN HALL, matric. 11 Feb., 1823, aged 38.

Poulson, Thomas, s. John, of Stoke, co. Stafford, gent. MAGDALEN HALL, matric. 17 Feb., 1726-7, aged 17.

Poulter, Brownlow, o.s. Brownlow, of Buriton, Hants, cler. NEW COLL., matric. 10 May, 1844, aged 17; fellow 1844-51, B.A. 1848, M.A. 1851, bar.-at-law, Lincoln's Inn, 1856.

Poulter, Donald Francis Ogilvy, 1s. Brownlow, of Blackheath, Kent, gent. LINCOLN COLL., matric. 23 Oct., 1882, aged 20; exhibitioner 1884, B.A. 1887.

Poulter, Edmund Sayer, s. Edmund, of St. Marylebone, Middlesex, cler. TRINITY COLL., matric. 13 June, 1805, aged 17.

Poulter, John Sayer, s. Edmund Sayer, of Portman Square, London, cler. NEW COLL., matric. 13 Feb., 1810, aged 19; fellow until 1833, B.C.L. 1817 (as John), bar.-at-law, Middle Temple, 1819, M.P. Shaftesbury 1832-8.

Poulter, Thomas, s. William, of Bucks, pleb. BRASENOSE COLL., matric. 24 March, 1723-4, aged 17; B.A. 1727.

Poulton, Albert Henry Allen, 3s. Benjamin Wheeler, of Hammersmith, Middlesex, gent. WORCESTER COLL., matric. 17 June, 1859, aged 19; scholar 1859-65, B.A. 1863.

Poulton, Edward Bagnall, o.s. William Ford, of Reading, Berks, gent. JESUS COLL., matric. 21 Oct., 1873, aged 17; scholar 1873-8, B.A. 1876, M.A. 1880, lecturer in natural science since 1880, tutor Keble College 1882. [5]

Pound, Alfred John, 2s. William, of Norton, near Malton, Yorks, cler. EXETER COLL., matric. 29 May, 1866, aged 19; B.A. 1869, M.A. 1875, bar.-at-law, Lincoln's Inn, 1871, stipendiary magistrate British Guiana 1875-6. See Foster's *Men at the Bar* & *Eton School Lists*.

Pound, Rev. Robert William, 1s. William, of Norton, near Malton, Yorks, cler. BRASENOSE COLL., matric. 18 Oct., 1862, aged 19; scholar 1863-6, B.A. 1865, M.A. 1869.

Pound, Thomas, s. John, of Duloe, Cornwall, gent. BALLIOL COLL., matric. 17 Dec., 1737, aged 18.

Pouney, Henry, s. George, of East Indies, arm. CHRIST CHURCH, matric. 2 Dec., 1812, aged 19.

Pountney, Francis, 2s. Humphrey, of Wolverhampton, co. Stafford, cler. EXETER COLL., matric. 7 June, 1854, aged 18. [10]

Pountney, Humphrey, o.s. Humphrey, of St. Martin's, Birmingham, arm. QUEEN'S COLL., matric. 2 July, 1821, aged 18; B.A. 1825, M.A. 1828, vicar of St. John, Wolverhampton, 1831, until his death 31 Dec., 1857.

Poutiatine, Basil, 1s. 'Eupheme,' of St. Petersburg, Russia, arm. (subs. 'com.'). CHRIST CHURCH, matric. 16 Oct., 1863, aged 17; B.A. 1867, M.A. 1871.

Povah, Alfred, 2s. John, of Homerton, Middlesex, gent. WADHAM COLL., matric. 16 March, 1843, aged 19; clerk 1843-7, B.A. 1847, M.A. 1849, held various curacies 1847-60, rector of St. Olave, Hart Street, London, 1870.

Povah, Alfred, 1s. Alfred, of London, cler. BALLIOL COLL., matric. 21 Oct., 1867, aged 18; curate of St. Luke, West Holloway, London, 1871, until his death 5 Oct., 1873. See *St. Paul's School Reg.*, 337.

Povah, Francis, 4s. Richard, of St. James's, London, doctor. ST. JOHN'S COLL., matric. 27 June, 1825, aged 17; scholar & fellow 1825-34, B.C.L. 1832, a student of the Inner Temple 1831, died 29 July, 1834. See *Robinson*, 204. [15]

Povah, Francis Kohler, 2s. John Vidgen, of London, cler. CHRIST CHURCH, matric. 16 Oct., 1868, aged 19; B.A. 1873, M.A. 1876, rector of Necton, Norfolk, 1883.

Povah, John Richard, 1s. John Vidgen, of London, cler. UNIVERSITY COLL., matric. 13 Oct., 1866, aged 19; B.A. 1869, M.A. 1876.

Povah, Rev. Richard Worgan, s. Richard, of St. Leonard's, Shoreditch, London, cler. ST. JOHN'S COLL., matric. 1 July, 1813, aged 14; scholar & fellow 1813-83, B.A. 1817, M.A. 1820, minor canon St. Paul's, died 11 Jan., 1883. See *Robinson*, 183.

Powell, Alexander, s. Alexander, of Salisbury, Wilts, equitis. ORIEL COLL., matric. 22 Feb., 1779, aged 16.

Powell, Alexander, s. Francis, of Salisbury, Wilts, arm. EXETER COLL., matric. 26 May, 1800, aged 17; B.A. 1804, of Hurdcott House, Wilts, M.P. Downton, 1826-30, died 25 Dec., 1847, father of the next named. [20]

Powell, Alexander, 1s. Alexander, of Baverstock, Wilts, arm. EXETER COLL., matric. 15 May, 1827, aged 17; of Hurdcott House, died 31 Oct., 1882.

Powell, Arthur, s. William, of Westminster, arm. WADHAM COLL., matric. 11 May, 1784, aged 17.

Powell, Arthur Crofts, 1s. Arthur, of South Malling, Sussex (*sic*), arm. BRASENOSE COLL., matric. 4 June, 1863, aged 18; B.A. 1866, M.A. 1870. See Foster's *Our Noble and Gentle Families*.

Powell, Rev. Astell Drayner, 2s. William James, of Egremont, Cheshire, gent. NON-COLL., matric. 10 Feb., 1875, aged 23; B.A. from EXETER COLL. 1878, M.A. 1881.

Powell, Baden, s. Baden, of Hackney, Middlesex, arm. ORIEL COLL., matric. 25 April, 1814, aged 17; B.A. 1817, M.A. 1820, Savilian professor of geometry 1827-60, F.R.S. 1824, F.R.Astl.S., F.R.G.S., 1837, natural philosopher, etc., vicar of Plumstead 182-/7, died 11 June, 1860; for list of his works see *Crockford*. [25]

Powell, Charles, s. Henry, of Langattock, co. Carmarthen, cler. JESUS COLL., matric. 19 May, 1721, aged 19; B.A. 12 Oct., 1723-4.

Powell, Charles, s. William, of Abergavenny, co. Monmouth, cler. JESUS COLL., matric. 20 May, 1790, aged 18; B.A. 1794, M.A. 1796.

Powell, Charles, 2s. Baden, of Hackney, Middlesex, arm. TRINITY COLL., matric. 31 May, 1825, aged 17; B.A. 1829, M.A. 1833, bar.-at-law, Lincoln's Inn, 1832, J.P., D.L., co. Brecon, died 28 Oct., 1843.

Powell, Charles Marten, 1s. Thomas Wilde, of Blackheath, Kent, gent. CORPUS CHRISTI COLL., matric. 19 Oct., 1875, aged 20; scholar 1874-80, B.A. 1879.

Powell, Charles Watson, 1s. Charles, of London, arm. MERTON COLL., matric. 13 April, 1872, aged 19; B.A. & M.A. from ST. ALBAN HALL 1878, of Speldhurst, Kent, a student of the Inner Temple 1880.

Powell, Clement, 6s. Arthur, of Clapton, Middlesex, arm. ORIEL COLL., matric. 20 May, 1875, aged 19; B.A. 1879, M.A. 1882, rector of Newick, Sussex, 1885. [31]

Powell, Daniel Philip, s. Roger, of Gladestry, co. Radnor, cler. JESUS COLL., matric. 11 Oct., 1786, aged 21; B.A. 1790, rector of Sharnsfield, co. Hereford, 1799, until his death 27 Sep., 1851.

Powell, David, s. Llewellin, of Devynnock, co. Brecon, gent. JESUS COLL., matric. 15 Oct., 1762, aged 17; B.A. 1767.

Powel, David, 5s. Evan, of Abereyrnog, co. ——, gent. ST. MARY HALL, matric. 27 Jan., 1875, aged 19.

Powell, Rev. David Thomas, s. Thomas, of Westminster, arm. MAGDALEN HALL, matric. 21 March, 1798, aged 25; B.C.L. 1805, lieutenant 14th light dragoons, served in Flanders and Brabant in 1794, died 9 June, 1848. See *Gent.'s Mag.*, ii. 438. [35]

Powell, Edmund, s. Thomas, of Kenwin, Cornwall, gent. MAGDALEN HALL, matric. 27 March, 1759, aged 20; B.A. 1764.

Powell, Edmund, 2s. Philip, of Regent's Park, London, pleb. MAGDALEN COLL., matric. 23 Oct., 1845, aged 19, clerk 1845-6; scholar LINCOLN COLL. 1847-50, B.A. 1849, M.A. 1852, bar.-at-law, Inner Temple, 1852, died 31 Dec., 1864. See *Coll. Reg.*, ii. 122.

Powell, Rev. Edmund Nathaniel, 2s. Nathaniel, of Buckhurst Hill, Essex, arm. TRINITY COLL., matric. 12 Oct., 1878, aged 19; B.A. 1882, M.A. 1885.

Powell, Edward, s. Thomas, of Landow, co. Glamorgan, gent. JESUS COLL., matric. 31 March, 1721, aged 19.

Powel, Edward, s. Edward, of Storrington, Sussex, cler. ALL SOULS' COLL., matric. 17 July, 1730, aged 18. [40]

Powel, Edward, s. Edward, of Merthyr Dovan, co. Glamorgan, pleb. JESUS COLL., matric. 26 March, 1743, aged 19.

Powell, Edward, o.s. Thomas, of St. John's, Southwark, London, arm. MAGDALEN COLL., matric. 18 Oct., 1862, aged 18, demy 1862-5; scholar LINCOLN COLL. 1865-6, B.A. 1866.

Powell, Edward Henry, 2s. Walter Rice, of Maesgwynne, co. Carmarthen, arm. ST. JOHN'S COLL., matric. 6 March, 1844, aged 18; B.A. 1848, M.A. 1851, rector of Ludchurch, co. Pembroke, 1854-6, vicar of St. Anne's, Congresbury, Somerset, 1867.

Powell, Rev. Edward Parry, 1s. Edward Griffith, of Bangor, co. Carnarvon, arm. JESUS COLL., matric. 18 March, 1852, aged 18; died 15 June, 1882.

Powell, Evan, s. John, of Llangattock, co. Monmouth, cler. ST. ALBAN HALL, matric. 23 May, 1787, aged 19. [5]

Powell, Francis, s. Hugh, of Llowes, co. Radnor, pleb. HART HALL, matric. 10 Nov., 1718, aged 18.

Powell, Francis, s. Alexander, of St. Thomas, Salisbury, equitis. ORIEL COLL., matric. 27 March, 1776, aged 17; B.A. 1778, of Hurdcott House, Wilts, died in Jan., 1786, father of Alexander 1800.

Powell, Francis Sharp, scholar ST. JOHN'S COLL., Cambridge, 1846, senior optime & B.A. 1850, fellow 1851-4, M.A. 1853; adm. 'comitatis causa' 3 July, 1862 (s. Benjamin, cler.), of Horton Old Hall, Yorks, bar.-at-law, Inner Temple, 1853, M.P. Wigan 1857-9, Jan. to April, 1881, and 1885, Cambridge 1863-8, Yorks, West Riding (North division), 1872-4. See Foster's *Men at the Bar.*

Powell, Francis Smyth Baden-, 3s. Baden, of Oxford, cler. BALLIOL COLL., matric. 20 April, 1871, aged 20; B.A. 1876, M.A. 1878, bar.-at-law, Inner Temple, 1883. See Foster's *Men at the Bar* & *St. Paul's School Reg.*, 342.

Powell, Frank Joseph, 1s. John, of Chester, gent. NON-COLL., matric. 14 Oct., 1876, aged 18; B.A. 1879, M.A. 1883, vicar of Knotty Ash, Lancashire, 1885. [10]

Powell, Frederick, 1s. James, of St. Nicholas, Worcester (city), gent. CHRIST CHURCH, matric. 28 Jan., 1824, aged 18; servitor 1824-9, B.A. 1829.

Powell, Frederick Walter, 1s. Alfred, of Kempsey, co. Worcester, gent. LINCOLN COLL., matric. 19 Oct., 1883, aged 29; B.A. 1886.

Powell, Frederick York, 1s. Frederick, of London, arm. NON-COLL., matric. 27 Oct., 1868, aged 18; B.A. from CHRIST CHURCH 1872, M.A. 1876, a senior student 1884, lecturer in law 1874-84, bar.-at-law, Middle Temple, 1874. See Foster's *Men at the Bar* & *Rugby School Reg.*

Powell, Gabriel, s. Gabriel, of Swansea, co. Glamorgan, arm. ORIEL COLL., matric. 8 March, 1771, aged 17.

Powell, George, s. John, of Castleton, co. Hereford, gent. BRASENOSE COLL., matric. 24 May, 1781, aged 16, B.A. 1785; fellow BALLIOL COLL. 1786, until 1830, M.A. 1789, perp. curate Clifton, Oxon, 1797, vicar of Abbotsley and rector of Duloe, Cornwall, 1819, until his death 20 Feb., 1830. [15]

Powell, Rev. George Bather, 1s. Thomas, of Munslow, Salop, cler. WORCESTER COLL., matric. 17 Oct., 1868, aged 18; B.A. 1872.

Powell, George Ernest John, o.s. William Thomas Roland, of Cheltenham, co. Gloucester, arm. BRASENOSE COLL., matric. 23 May, 1861, aged 19.

Powell, George Francis Sydenham, 2s. Alexander, of Baverstoke, Wilts, arm. WADHAM COLL., matric. 1 March, 1838, aged 17; B.A. 1841, perp. curate Burcombe, Wilts, 1853-4, rector of Sutton Veney 1854.

Powell, George Gordon, 1s. George Thompson, of Croydon, gent. NON-COLL., matric. 20 Oct., 1884, aged 19.

Powell, (Sir) George Smyth Baden-, K.C.M.G., 3s. Baden, of Oxford, cler. BALLIOL COLL., matric. 18 Oct., 1871, aged 23; B.A. 1875, M.A. 1878, a student of the Inner Temple 1876, served in Bechuanaland 1885, M.P. Kirkdale division of Liverpool 1885, C.M.G. 24 May, 1884, K.C.M.G. 1888. See *St. Paul's School Reg.*, 338. [20]

Powell, Rev. Gervas, s. Reece, of Llanheron, co. Glamorgan, gent. HERTFORD COLL., matric. 3 Feb., 1741-2, aged 18; B.C.L. from UNIVERSITY COLL. 10 March, 1748-9, died in 1795.

Powell, Harry George, 2s. Joseph, of Buckhurst Hill, Essex, gent. NON-COLL., matric. 25 Jan., 1879, aged 18.

Powell, Harry James, 1s. Nathaniel, of Walthamstow, Essex, arm. TRINITY COLL., matric. 17 Oct., 1870, aged 17; B.A. 1873.

Powell, Henry, s. Hen., of Llangattock, co. Carnarvon, cler. JESUS COLL., matric. 5 April, 1731, aged 17.

Powell, Henry, s. Thomas, of Brecon (town), pleb. JESUS COLL., matric. 5 June, 1744, aged 18; B.A. 1748. [25]

Powell, Henry, 3s. Baden, of St. Helen's, London, arm. EXETER COLL., matric. 2 June, 1827, aged 18; B.A. 1831, B.Med. 1835, D.Med. 1839.

Powell, Henry Albert, 2s. George, of Holloway, Middlesex, gent. WADHAM COLL., matric. 20 March, 1868, aged 19; S.C.L. & B.A. 1873, M.A. 1874.

Powell, Henry Clark, 1s. Harry Townsend, of Stretton-on-Dunsmore, co. Warwick, cler. ORIEL COLL., matric. 14 May, 1857, aged 19; B.A. 1861, M.A. 1864, provost of Inverness Cathedral 1869-76, vicar of Stanton St. Bernard, Wilts, 1877-82, rector of Wylye, Somerset, 1882. See *Rugby School Reg.*

Powell, Henry Townsend, s. David, of Walthamstow, Essex, arm. ORIEL COLL., matric. 16 May, 1817, aged 17; B.A. 1821, M.A. 1824, vicar of Stretton-on-Dunsmore, co. Warwick, 1830, until his death 13 June, 1854.

Powell, Henry Townsend, 1s. Henry Clark, of All Saints, Dorset, cler. MAGDALEN COLL., matric. 23 Oct., 1885, aged 19; demy 1885. [30]

Powell, Herbert Andrews, 3s. Thomas Wilde, of Charlton, Kent, gent. CORPUS CHRISTI COLL., matric. 27 Oct., 1881, aged 18; B.A. 1885.

Powell, Hew David Steuart, s. Hew, of Blandford Forum, Dorset, arm. EXETER COLL., matric. 18 May, 1869, aged 18; B.A. & M.A. 1876.

Powell, Hew Steuart, y.s. Timothy, of Henbury, co. Gloucester, arm. TRINITY COLL., matric. 17 June, 1828, aged 17; B.A. 1832, M.A. 1835.

Powell, Howell, s. David, of Mothvey, co. Carmarthen, cler. JESUS COLL., matric. 15 Dec., 1758, aged 21; B.A. 1762 (? died vicar of Turville, Bucks 15 Dec., 1793).

Powell, Isaac Ormsby, M.A. TRINITY COLL., Dublin 1857 (B.A. 1844); adm. 'ad eundem' 7 April 1859, perp. curate St. Thomas's, Toxteth Park, Liverpool, 1853-63, vicar of Whaddon, co. Cambridge, 1863-81, and of Holybourne, Hants, 1881. [35]

Powell, James, s. James, of Devynnock, co. Brecon, pleb. JESUS COLL., matric. 2 Nov., 1725, aged 17; B.A. 1729, M.A. 1732.

Powell, James, s. Pierce, of Saintissa, Cornwall, cler. QUEEN'S COLL., matric. 22 March, 1763, aged 18.

Powell, James, s. James, of Church Lawford, co. Warwick, cler. JESUS COLL., matric. 10 Oct., 1765, aged 18.

Powell, James, B.A. from TRINITY COLL. 1769, M.A. 1772.

Powell, Rev. James, s. James, of Abingdon, Berks, gent. TRINITY COLL., matric. 13 Dec., 1788, aged 16; scholar, B.A. 1792, M.A. 1795, died 20 March, 1797. [40]

Powell, James, s. James, of London, arm. EXETER COLL., matric. 6 Dec., 1804, aged 26; created M.A. 22 Oct., 1807, a student of Lincoln's Inn 1807.

Powell, James, s. Samuel, of Maesmynis, Brecon, cler. JESUS COLL., matric. 27 May, 1805, aged 17; B.A. 1809, M.A. 1813.

Powell, James Baden, 1s. Henry, of Tunbridge Wells, Kent, doctor. EXETER COLL., matric. 23 May, 1861, aged 18; B.A. 1864, M.A. 1869, has held various curacies since 1867.

Powell, James Cotton, 1s. James, of St. Dunstan's-in-the-West, London, arm. TRINITY COLL., matric. 26 June, 1827, aged 18; B.A. 1831, M.A. 1834, a student of Lincoln's Inn 1834, died curate of St. James's, Clapton, Middlesex, 29 March, 1851.

Powell, James Howell Bevan, 5s. Walter Posthumus, of Madras, East Indies, cler. WORCESTER COLL., matric. 16 Oct., 1866, aged 20; chaplain S. W. India 1874-7, has held various curacies since 1870.

Powell, John, s. Joshua, of Herbrandston, co. Pembroke, cler. JESUS COLL., matric. 23 Feb., 1718-9, aged 17. [6]

Powell, John, s. Gab., of Swansea, co. Glamorgan, gent. JESUS COLL., matric. 12 Dec., 1721, aged 16.

Powell, John, B.C.L. from JESUS COLL. 10 June, 1726.

Powell, John, s. John, of Cantreff, co. Brecon, cler. JESUS COLL., matric. 13 March, 1739-40, aged 17.

Powell, John, s. Maurice, of Llanraider, co. Denbigh, pleb. JESUS COLL., matric. 29 March, 1740, aged 18. [10]

Powell, John, s. John, of Westminster, pleb. CHRIST CHURCH, matric. 22 May, 1740, aged 16; B.A. 1743.

Powell, John, s. John, of Little Sutton, Salop, gent. PEMBROKE COLL., matric. 11 March, 1745-6, aged 18; B.A. 1749.

Powell, John, s. Hugh, of Radnor (town), arm. MERTON COLL., matric. 15 March, 1758, aged 18; B.A. 1762.

Powell, John, s. John, of Lanmartin, co. Monmouth, cler. JESUS COLL., matric. 8 Dec., 1774, aged 22; B.A. 1778.

Powell, John, s. William, of Llyswen, co. Brecon, pleb. JESUS COLL., matric. 1 July, 1778, aged 23.

Powell, John, s. John, of Langattock, co. Monmouth, cler. WADHAM COLL., matric. 15 July, 1778, aged 17, B.A. 1783 (? M.A. from KING'S COLL., Cambridge, 1794, rector of Llansoy, co. Monmouth, 1796, until his death in 1836).[1] [16]

Powell, John, y.s. Henry, of Worcester, gent. ST. ALBAN HALL, matric. 10 Nov., 1875, aged 28.

Powell, John Folliott, s. Richard, of Abingdon, Berks, arm. ST. MARY HALL, matric. 6 Feb., 1795, aged 22; died 9 Nov., 1839. See Foster's *Lancashire Collection*.

Powell, John Harcourt, s. Harcourt, of St. James's, Middlesex, arm. UNIVERSITY COLL., matric. 29 April, 1777, aged 15; B.A. 1781 (? died vicar of Eccleshall, co. Stafford, and Dunchurch, co. Warwick, in 1822).

Powell, John Henry, s. John, of Westminster, gent. EXETER COLL., matric. 1 March, 1781, aged 24.

Powell, Rev. John Keal, 1s. Richard, of Saxby, co. Leicester, cler. NON-COLL., matric. 27 April, 1878, aged 18; B.A. 1884. [21]

Powell, (Sir) John Kynaston (Bart.), s. Roger Kynaston, of Shrewsbury, Salop, arm. PEMBROKE COLL., matric. 17 Oct., 1770, aged 17, B.A. 1774; B.C.L. from ALL SOULS' COLL. 1777, D.C.L. 1814, assumed the additional surname of POWELL 1797, created a baronet 8 Dec., 1818, M.P. Salop 1784, until his death 25 Oct., 1822.

Powell, John Robert, 1s. John Robert, of Monmouth, arm. JESUS COLL., matric. 15 March, 1849, aged 18; S.C.L. 1852, B.A. 1853, M.A 1857, curate of Monkton Farleigh, Somerset, 1853-63, vicar of St. Peter, Marland, Devon, 1863-75, rector of Buckland Filleigh 1875.

Powell, John Undershell, 1s. John, of Bonham, Wilts, cler. BALLIOL COLL., matric. 15 Oct., 1884, aged 19; scholar 1883.

Powell, John Welstead Sharp, 2s. Frederick, of Kingston-upon-Thames, Surrey, arm. ST. EDMUND HALL, matric. 11 Oct., 1826, aged 19; B.A. 1830, M.A. 1833, rector of Abinger, Surrey, 1850-77, died 25 Feb., 1881. [25]

Powell, Joseph, s. Ed., of Ross, co. Hereford, pleb. JESUS COLL., matric. 17 Dec., 1731, aged 20; B.A. 19 March, 1735-6.

Powell, Joseph, 'druggist;' privilegiatus 6 March, 1771.

Powell, Joseph, 1s. John, of Solihull, co. Warwick, gent. PEMBROKE COLL., matric. 23 April, 1823, aged 17.

Powell, Joshua, s. Rees, of Llantwyt Major, co. Glamorgan, pleb. JESUS COLL., matric. 14 April, 1739, aged 19.

Powell, Joshua, s. Joshua, of Llantwyt Major, co. Glamorgan, cler. CHRIST CHURCH, matric. 17 Dec., 1778, aged 20; B.A. 1782, M.A. 1785, vicar of Middlewich, Cheshire, 1787, until his death in Feb., 1797. See *Manchester School Reg.*; i. 205.

Powell, Legh Richmond, 3s. Henry Folliott, of Anglesea, Hants, arm. NON-COLL., matric. 10 April, 1880, aged 39. [31]

Powell, Lewis, s. William, of Devynnock, Brecon, pleb. MERTON COLL., matric. 7 March, 1743-4, aged 18; B.A. 1747, M.A. 1753. (Memo.: Rev. L. P., rector of St. Luke, Old Street, London, died at Donington, co. Lincoln, 14 Jan., 1792.)

Powell, Mansell, s. Matth., of Newcastle, Clun, Salop, gent. JESUS COLL., matric. 16 March, 1752, aged 19; B.A. 1755.

Powell, Martin, 'apothecary;' privilegiatus 11 Jan 1722-3.

Powell, Morgan, s. Howell, of Devynnock, co. Brecon, pleb. JESUS COLL., matric. 12 April, 1736, aged 20; B.A. 9 Feb., 1739-40. [35]

Powell, Morgan, s. Roderick, of Devynock, co. Brecon, pleb. JESUS COLL., matric. 30 March, 1748, aged 18.

Powell, Rev. Morgan Jones, 1s. Thomas, of Swansea, co. Glamorgan, gent. BALLIOL COLL., matric. 17 Oct., 1882, aged 19; B.A. 1886.

Powell, Peter (? Pierce), s. William, of Ruthin, co. Denbigh, pleb. JESUS COLL., matric. 3 March, 1714-5, aged 19; B.A. 12 March, 1718-9, M.A. 1721.

Powell, Pierce, s. Howell, of Pethklert, co. ——, pleb. JESUS COLL., matric. 27 March, 1727, aged 18.

Powell, Powys, s. Rog., of Moreton, co. Hereford, cler. MAGDALEN HALL, matric. 23 Feb., 1718-9, aged 19; B.A. 1722. [40]

Powell, Rees, s. Rees, of Lanharan, co. Glamorgan, gent. JESUS COLL., matric. 26 March, 1731, aged 16.

Powell, Rees, s. Rice (or Rees), of Llangamarch, co. Brecon, pleb. JESUS COLL., matric. 13 Oct., 1741, aged 19; B.A. 1745 (as Rice).

Powell, Richard, s. Jos., of Kinaston, parish of Hentland, co. Hereford, gent. HART HALL, matric. 5 June, 1717, aged 16; B.A. 13 March, 1720-1.

Powell, Richard, s. John, of Middlesex, pleb. CHRIST CHURCH, matric. 1 March, 1728-9, aged 22.

Powell, Richard, s. William, dean of St. Asaph, Flint, JESUS COLL., matric. 28 April 1752, aged 18. [45]

Powell, Richard, s. Thomas, of Bridgnorth, Salop, gent. CHRIST CHURCH, matric. 15 Nov., 1768, aged 18; B.A. 1772, M.A. 1775. See *Gent.'s Mag.*, 1825, i. 91.

Powell, Richard, s. Joseph, of Thame, Oxon, gent. PEMBROKE COLL., matric. 19 Jan., 1785, aged 17; B.A. from MERTON COLL. 1788, M.A. 1791, B.Med. 1792, D.Med. 1795, fellow College of Physicians 1796, physician to St. Bartholomew's Hospital 1801-24, died 18 Aug., 1834. See Munk's *Roll*, ii. 456.

Powell, Richard, s. Richard, of Munslow, Salop, cler. CHRIST CHURCH, matric. 16 Oct., 1797, aged 17; B.A. 1802, M.A. 1805, rector of Munslow 1806, until his death 8 Dec., 1845.

Powell, Robert (B.A. TRINITY COLL., Dublin, 1840), 3s. James White, of Sutton, near Macclesfield, arm. WORCESTER COLL., incorp. 26 March, 1840, aged 22; M.A. 1842, chaplain R.N. 1846, wounded before Sebastopol 1854, rector of Bellingham, Northumberland, 1860, until his death 20 Sep., 1886.

Powell, Roger, s. Roger, of Weobley, co. Hereford, cler. WORCESTER COLL., matric. 7 April, 1781, aged 17; B.A. 1784, M.A. 1787 (? died vicar of Lionshall, co. Hereford, 1816).

Powell, Samuel, s. Samuel, of Maesmynis, co. Brecon, cler. PEMBROKE COLL., matric. 19 March, 1807, aged 16; scholar 1812-13, B.A. 1812, M.A. 1815, rector of Stretford, co. Hereford, 1836, until his death in Dec., 1869.

Powel, Stewart McGregor, 1s. Thomas, of Llanblethian, co. Glamorgan, cler. JESUS COLL., matric. 23 June, 1854, aged 19. [5]

Powell, Thomas, s. John, of Llywl, co Brecon, pleb. JESUS COLL., matric. 1 June, 1715, aged 18.

Powell, Thomas, s. Thomas, of Carmarthen (town), gent. BALLIOL COLL., matric. 11 Dec., 1717, aged 17; B.A. 1721, M.A. 1724.

Powell, Thomas, s. William, of Cirencester, co. Gloucester, pleb. WADHAM COLL., matric. 14 Feb., 1718-9, aged 15; B.A. 1722, M.A. 1725.

Powell, Thomas, s. Thomas, of St. Andrew's, Holborn, London, arm. QUEEN'S COLL., matric. 26 April, 1737, aged 17.

Powell, Thomas, s. Thomas, of Ampney, co. Gloucester, cler. PEMBROKE COLL., matric. 27 March, 1745, aged 18; B.A. 1750. [10]

Powell, Thomas, s. John, of Llandetty, co. Brecon, pleb. JESUS COLL., matric. 31 March, 1747, aged 19.

Powell, Thomas, s. William, of Newtown, co. Montgomery, pleb. JESUS COLL., matric. 26 March, 1763, aged 21.

Powell, Thomas, born at Christleton, Cheshire, s. William, dean of St. Asaph. JESUS COLL., matric. 20 Oct., 1763, aged 18.

Powell, Thomas, B.C.L. from JESUS COLL. 13 July, 1770.

Powell, Thomas, s. William, of Nanteos, co. Cardigan, doctor. PEMBROKE COLL., matric. 7 Nov., 1763, aged 18; of Nanteos, died 1797, father of William Edward 1804. [15]

Powell, Thomas, s. Gabriel, of Swansea, co. Glamorgan, arm. BRASENOSE COLL., matric. 12 March, 1773, aged 18; B.A. 1776, M.A. 1780, perp. curate of Sedgeley, co. Stafford, 1793, until his death in 1828 (see *Gent.'s Mag.*, 1828, ii. 648), or died at Peterstone Court, co. Glamorgan, 2 Dec., 1832 (see *Gent.'s Mag.*, 1832, ii. 653).

Powell, Thomas, s. David, of Mothvay, co. Carmarthen, cler. JESUS COLL., matric. 9 Dec., 1774, aged 18; B.A. 1778.

Powel, Thomas, s. William, of Islington, Middlesex, pleb. CHRIST CHURCH, matric. 17 March, 1779, aged 18.

Powel, Thomas, s. David, of Nantmel, co. Radnor, pleb. JESUS COLL., matric. 16 May, 1782, aged 19; B.A. 1787.

Powell, Thomas, s. William, of Halesowen, Salop, gent. ST. MARY HALL, matric. 3 Dec., 1782, aged 18. [20]

Powell, Rev. Thomas, s. Thomas, of Sedgley, co. Stafford, cler. WORCESTER COLL., matric. 13 Dec., 1815, aged 18; scholar 1819-28, B.A. 1819, M.A. 1823, fellow 1828, until his death 17 Feb., 1865.

Powell, Thomas, s. Thomas, of Llanwetyd, co. Brecon, gent. JESUS COLL., matric. 27 Oct., 1868, aged 23; B.A. 1872, M.A. 1875.

Powell, Thomas Baden, s. James, of Hackney, Middlesex, arm. ORIEL COLL., matric. 17 April, 1804, aged 17; fellow 1808-12, B.A. 1808, M.A. 1810, hon. preb. Chichester 1849, rector of Newick, Sussex, 1818, until his death 25 April, 1868.

Powell, Thomas Baden, 1s. Thomas Baden, of St. Dunstan's, London, cler. EXETER COLL., matric. 20 May, 1829, aged 17; B.A. 1833, M.A. 1838.

Powell, Thomas Baden, 1s. William, of Newick, Sussex, cler. NEW COLL., matric. 15 Oct., 1884, aged 20. [25]

Powell, Thomas Crump, 1s. Richard, of Munslow, Salop, cler. BRASENOSE COLL., matric. 28 May 1834, aged 18; B.A. 1839, rector of Munslow, Salop since 1846. See *Rugby School Reg.*, 168.

Powell, Thomas Edmund, 2s. Thomas Wilde, of Blackheath, Kent, arm. ORIEL COLL., matric. 17 Oct., 1876, aged 19; scholar 1876-81, B.A. 1880.

Powell, Thomas Edward, 3s. David, of Hampstead, Middlesex, arm. ORIEL COLL., matric. 17 Feb., 1842, aged 18; B.A. 1845, M.A. 1848, vicar of Bisham, Berks, 1848.

Powell, Thomas Harcourt, s. John, of Titenham, co. Gloucester, arm. ORIEL COLL., matric. 8 March, 1771, aged 17; bar.-at-law, Lincoln's Inn, 1780, and of the Inner Temple 'ad eundem' 1809, bencher 1816, died at Peterstone Court, co. Brecon, May, 1822.

Powell, Thomas John, s. Thomas, of Cantreff, co. Brecon, cler. WORCESTER COLL., matric. 1 Nov., 1814, aged 19; B.A. from ST. ALBAN HALL 1818, M.A. 1824, rector of Cantreff and Llanhamlach, co. Brecon, died 7 April, 1864. [30]

Powell, Thomas Lewis, 2s. William, of Redcliff, Bristol, gent. ST. JOHN'S COLL., matric. 16 Feb., 1842, aged 20; S.C.L. from NEW INN HALL 1850, B.C.L. 1851.

Powell, Thomas (Prosser), o.s. Thomas, of Dorstone, co. Hereford, cler. ST. JOHN'S COLL., matric. 12 March, 1856, aged 18; B.A. 1860, assistant chaplain Buenos Ayres 1865-8, vicar of Peterchurch, co. Hereford, 1875.

Powell, Townsend, 2s. Harry Townsend, of Stretton-on-Dunsmore, co. Warwick, cler. EXETER COLL., matric. 19 Jan., 1866, aged 18; B.A. 1871, vicar of Quinton, co. Warwick, 1876.

Powell, Walter, s. John, of Llangattock, co. Monmouth, cler. JESUS COLL., matric. 24 May, 1792, aged 18; B.A. 1796, scholar 1816-23.

Powell, Walter, s. John, of Brecon, gent. JESUS COLL., matric. 6 Nov., 1813, aged 18; B.A. 1818, M.A. 1820. [35]

Powell, Walter Posthumus, o.s. Walter, of Bromsgrove, co. Worcester, cler. WORCESTER COLL., matric. 15 June, 1824, aged 18; scholar 1824-31, B.A. 1828, M.A. 1831, B.C.L. & D.C.L. 1836, chaplain Fort St. George (Madras), died 8 July, 1853.

Powell, Walter Rice, s. Walter Rice Howell, of Lanboidy, South Wales, arm. CHRIST CHURCH, matric. 28 Jan., 1813, aged 17.

Powell, Walter Rice Howell, 1s. Walter Rice Howell, of Haverfordwest, arm. CHRIST CHURCH, matric. 19 Oct., 1837, aged 18; of Maesg-wynne, co. Carmarthen, high sheriff 1849, M.P. 1880-5, M.P. North Carmarthenshire since 1885.

Powell, William, s. William, of Llangattock, co. Brecon, cler. CHRIST CHURCH, matric. 21 Oct., 1717, aged 17, B.A. 1721; M.A. from JESUS COLL. 1724.

Powell, William, s. Edward, of Storrington, Sussex, cler. LINCOLN COLL., matric. 14 May, 1736, aged 19; B.A. 29 Jan., 1739-40. [40]

Powell, William, s. Franklyn, of Lymington, Hants, cler. ORIEL COLL., matric. 25 March, 1738, aged 18.

Powell, William, s. Walter, of Abergavenny, co. Monmouth, pleb. CHRIST CHURCH, matric. 27 June, 1744, aged 18.

Powell, William, s. John, of Cantref, co. Brecon, cler. QUEEN'S COLL., matric. 18 March, 1744-5, aged 19.

Powell, William, created D.C.L. 8 July, 1763, then of Nanteos, Cardiganshire (3s. William), father of Thomas, 7 Nov., 1763.

Powell, William, s. William, of Abergavenny, co. Monmouth, cler. JESUS COLL., matric. 8 April, 1786, aged 16; B.A. 1789, M.A. 1792, B.D. 1800, a student of Lincoln's Inn 1795.

Powell, William, s. John, of Llandilo-Graban, co. Radnor, cler. JESUS COLL., matric. 26 May, 1803, aged 20; B.A. 1807.

Powell, William, 2s. Thomas Baden, of Farningham, Kent, cler. EXETER COLL., matric. 14 May, 1835, aged 17; B.A. 1839, M.A. 1841, bar.-at-law, Inner Temple, 1846, perp. curate Nutley 1851-4, rector of Newick, Sussex, 1868, until his death in 1885. [5]

Powell, William, 1s. John, of Abergavenny, gent. JESUS COLL., matric. 9 Nov., 1837, aged 15; B.A. 1844, MA. 1846, vicar of Mundon, Essex, until his death 27 Nov., 1865.

Powell, William Edward, s. Thomas, of Salop, arm. CHRIST CHURCH, matric. 20 Oct., 1804, aged 16; of Nanteos, co. Cardigan, lord-lieutenant, M.P 1816-54, died 10 April, 1854.

Powell, William George, 2s. William, of Newick, Sussex, cler. EXETER COLL., matric. 16 Oct., 1884, aged 19.

Powell, William Hawkins, 1s. Septimus, of Bristol, gent. MERTON COLL., matric. 21 Oct., 1886, aged 19.

Powell, William Wilfrid, o.s. Howell Worster, of Ripley, Yorks, cler. ST. JOHN'S COLL., matric. 15 June, 1866, aged 19. [10]

Powell, alias **Symonds,** William See SYMONDS, alias POWELL, 17 March, 1732-3.

Power, D'Arcy, 1s. Henry, of London, arm. NEW COLL., matric. 16 Oct., 1874, aged 18; exhibitioner EXETER COLL. 1876-8, B.A. 1878, M.A. 1881, B.Med. 1882, M.R.C.S. Eng. 1882. See *Robinson*, 374; & *Boase*, 168.

Power, Rev. Edward, 2s. John, of Atherstone, co. Warwick, gent. MAGDALEN HALL, matric. 15 Dec., 1821, aged 21; B.A. 1830, M.A. 1831, died master of Atherstone School 30 Dec., 1856.

Power, Guy Francis Thomas, 3s. Thomas Chandler, of Kaigalle, Isle of Ceylon, arm. ORIEL COLL., matric. 18 Oct., 1871, aged 18; scholar 1871-4, of the Indian Civil Service 1873.

Power, Henry Bolton, 3s. Manley, of Isle of Malta, eq. aur. ORIEL COLL., matric. 10 May, 1838, aged 17; B.A. 1842, M.A. 1846, vicar of Bramley, Surrey, 1847, until his death 15 March, 1882. [15]

Power, John, 1s. John, of Atherstone, co. Warwick, gent. ST. EDMUND HALL, matric. 16 Nov., 1843, aged 26; B.A. 1847, M.A. 1853, incumbent of St. Margaret's, Tyler's Green, Bucks, 1862-8, perp. curate Bedford Chapel, Exeter, 1868-71, rector of Dodbrooke, Devon, 1872-9, vicar of Altarnun, Cornwall, 1879, until his death 8 Feb., 1887.

Power, John Peckleton, of QUEEN'S COLL., Cambridge (B.A. 1843, M.A. 1846); adm. 'ad eundem' 21 June, 1855, rector of Acton Beauchamp, co. Worcester, 1867-70, vicar of Barkestone, Notts, 1873.

Power, Rev. Joseph, fellow CLARE COLL., Cambridge, 1823 & 1844-68, and librarian to that University 1845-68, 10th wrangler & B.A. 1821, M.A. 1824, fellow and tutor TRINITY HALL 1829-43, adm. 'ad eundem' 5 June, 1845.

Power, Manley, 2s. Henry Bolton, of Bramley, Yorks, cler. UNIVERSITY COLL., matric. 13 Oct., 1876, aged 19; B.A. 1881, incumbent of Christ Church, Milton, Brisbane, 1886.

Power, Philip Bennett, M.A. TRINITY COLL., Dublin, 1843 (B.A. 1846); adm. 'ad eundem' 3 June, 1854, perp. curate Christ Church, Worthing, 1855-65; for list of his writings, etc., see *Crockford*. [20]

Power, Philip Ernest de Poer, 1s. Philip Bennett, of Worthing, Sussex, cler. NEW COLL., matric. 16 Oct., 1880, aged 19; B.A. 1884.

Powers, George Wightman, 1s. George, of Barwell, co. Leicester, pleb. NEW COLL., matric. 12 Oct., 1883, aged 19; scholar 1883, B.A. 1887.

Powles, Allen Henry, 1s. Henry Charles, of Whitchurch, co. Hereford, cler. EXETER COLL., matric. 14 Oct., 1876, aged 19; scholar 1876-80, B.A. 1880, M.A. 1885. See *Coll. Reg.*, 168.

Powles, Ernest, 1s. Kenneth, of Liverpool, gent. WORCESTER COLL., matric. 19 Oct., 1886, aged 19.

Powles, Frederick James Endell, 3s. Henry Charles, of Rodmarton, co. Gloucester, cler. MERTON COLL., matric. 21 Oct., 1886, aged 19. [25]

Powles, George le Blanc, 3s. John Richard, of Warburton, Cheshire, arm. MAGDALEN COLL., matric. 17 Oct., 1864, aged 19; demy 1863-8, B.A. & M.A. 1874.

Powles, Henry Charles, 2s. James, of Monmouth (town), gent. ORIEL COLL., matric. 6 June, 1844, aged 18; B.A. 1848, M.A. 1851, rector of Ashelworth, co. Gloucester, 1877, until his death 11 Jan., 1881. See *Rugby School Reg.*, 207.

Powles, John Richard, 1s. John Diston, of Wandsworth, Surrey, arm. EXETER COLL., matric. 18 Nov., 1830, aged 17.

Powles, Louis Charles, 2s. Henry Charles, of Rodmarton, co. Gloucester, cler. CHRIST CHURCH, matric. 24 Jan., 1879, aged 18; B.A. 1882, M.A. 1885.

Powles, Louis Distou, 5s. John Diston, of St. Margaret's, Lothbury, London, arm. PEMBROKE COLL., matric. 16 Oct., 1861, aged 19; bar.-at-law Inner Temple, 1866, magistrate and judge in the Bahamas 1886-7. See Foster's *Men at the Bar*. [30]

Powles, Michael, s. Michael, of Ledbury, co. Hereford, gent. BRASENOSE COLL., matric. 7 April, 1772, aged 16; B.A. 1775, M.A. 1778.

Powles, Rev. Richard Cowley, 2s. John Diston, of London, arm. EXETER COLL., matric. 1 Feb., 1838, aged 18; exhibitioner 1839-42, fellow 1842-50, B.A. 1845, M.A. 1846, tutor 1846, held a school at Blackheath 1850-69, and then at Eversley, Hants. See *Coll. Reg.*, 134.

Powlett, Charles John, 1s. Percy William, of Rugby, co. Warwick, cler. WADHAM COLL., matric. 29 June, 1853, aged 18; scholar 1853-9, B.A. 1858, of the Indian Civil Service 1858.

Powlett, Harry George, born at Raby Castle, co. Durham, 3s. Harry Vane, Earl of Cleveland. ORIEL COLL., matric. 12 Feb., 1821, aged 17; B.A. 1829, created D.C.L. 21 June, 1876, 4th Duke of Cleveland, M.P. South Durham 1841-59, Hastings 1859-64, assumed the name of POWLETT in lieu of VANE, by royal licence 18 Nov., 1864, K.G. 10 April, 1865, created D.C.L. Durham University 27 June, 1882. See Foster's *Peerage*.

Powlett, Norton, s. Nort., of London, arm. EXETER COLL., matric. 17 Dec., 1722, aged 17; M.P. Winchester 1730-4, died 14 March, 1759, his father M.P. Petersfield in 6 parliaments 1705-34, died 18 June, 1741). [35]

Powlett, Percy William, 1s. Charles, of Dummer, Hants, cler. TRINITY COLL., matric. 3 Feb., 1820, aged 17, B.A. 1824; Michel fellow QUEEN'S COLL. 1828-34, M.A. 1828, assistant-master Rugby School 1825, rector of Frankton, co. Warwick, 1838, until his death 22 Sep., 1866. See *Rugby School Reg.*, xiv. & 105.

Powlett, Robert, s. William, of Aldgate, London, gent. MERTON COLL., matric. 2 June, 1743, aged 18; B.A. 1747.

Powley, Rev. Arthur Thomas, 2s. John, of Langwathby, Cumberland, gent. QUEEN'S COLL., matric. 28 Oct., 1881, aged 21; B.A. 1884.

Powley, Matthew, s. John, of Lowther, Westmoreland, pleb. QUEEN'S COLL., matric. 25 Sep., 1760, aged 19; B.A. 1764, M.A. 1768, vicar of Dewsburys and perp. curate Slackthwaite, Yorks, 1777, until his death 25 Dec., 1806.

Powley, Matthew, 7s. John, of Langwathby, Cumberland, gent. QUEEN'S COLL., matric. 5 July, 1845, aged 18; B.A. 1849, M.A. 1852, curate of Wallasey, Cheshire, 1850-9, chaplain at Malaga 1859-66, canon and chaplain Gibraltar 1866-9, vicar of Christ Church, Reading, 1869-81, rector of Purley, Berks, 1881.

Powley, Robert, 1s. John, of Langwathby, Cumberland, gent. QUEEN'S COLL., matric. 26 Oct., 1876, aged 19; B.A. 1880, M.A. 1883, chaplain 1882, assistant-master Oxford Military College, rector of Upton Scudamore 1888.

Pownall, Assheton, 3s. James, of Liverpool, arm. BRASENOSE COLL., matric. 9 June, 1841, aged 18; B.A. 1845, M.A. 1848, hon. canon Peterborough 1875-85, archdeacon of Leicester 1884, rector of South Kilworth 1847, until his death 24 Nov., 1886.

Pownall, Charles Colyear Beaty, of CLARE COLL., Cambridge (B.A. 1829, M.A. 1832); adm. 'comitatis causa' 6 June, 1861, assumed the additional surname of POWNALL.

Pownall, Francis, 2s. George, of London, arm. EXETER COLL., matric. 12 Oct., 1866, aged 18; B.A. 1870, M.A. 1873, bar.-at-law, Lincoln's Inn, 1873. See Foster's *Men at the Bar.* **[5]**

Pownall, William, s. William, of Liverpool, Lancashire, arm. UNIVERSITY COLL., matric. 25 May, 1784, aged 19.

Pownall, Rev. William Thomas Beaty-, 3s. Charles Colyear, of Milton Ernest, Beds, cler. MERTON COLL., matric. 28 Jan., 1865, aged 20; B.A. 1870, M.A. 1871.

Powne, Thomas, s. Ralph, of Llansalloss, Cornwall, cler. BALLIOL COLL., matric. 10 May, 1744, aged 19; B.A. 1748.

Powney, Rev. Henry, s. George, of East Indies, arm. CHRIST CHURCH, matric. 2 Dec., 1812, aged 19; B.A. from ST. ALBAN HALL 1816, M.A. 1819. See *Eton School Lists.*

Powney, Penyston, s. John, of Old Windsor, Berks, gent. QUEEN'S COLL., matric. 5 July, 1716, aged 17; created M.A. 15 March, 1720-1, and also D.C.L. 12 April, 1749, of Ives Place, Berks, M.P. 1739, until his death 8 March, 1757. **[10]**

Powney, Peniston, s. Peniston, of Ives Place, Berks, arm. QUEEN'S COLL., matric. 1 April, 1761, aged 17; created M.A. 23 March, 1765, and also D.C.L. 8 July, 1773, then of Ives Place, Berks (? M.P. Windsor 1780, until his death 17 Jan., 1794, as PENISTON PORTLOCK POWNEY).

Powney, Richard, s. John, of Old Windsor, Berks, gent. QUEEN'S COLL., matric. 19 March, 1718-9, aged 17; B.C.L. from ALL SOULS' COLL. 1726, D.C.L. 1731.

Powning, Frederick Edmonds, 2s. James, of Totnes, Devon, cler. ST. ALBAN HALL, matric. 28 Jan., 1882, aged 20.

Pownoll, Israel, s. Israel, of Deptford, Kent, arm. ST. MARY HALL, matric. 14 Dec., 1774, aged 24; B.A. 1778.

Powys, Atherton Legh, 4s. Thomas, Baron Lilford. CHRIST CHURCH, matric. 16 Oct., 1829, aged 20; M.A. from TRINITY COLL., Cambridge, 1834, rector of Titchmarsh, Northants, 1842-61. See Foster's *Peerage & Eton School Lists.* **[15]**

Powys, Rev. Charles Richard, 3s. Henry Philip, of Southgate, Middlesex, arm. EXETER COLL., matric. 30 April, 1846, aged 18, B.A. 1850; M.A. from ST. JOHN'S COLL. 1862, rector of Yelford, Berks, 1882. See Foster's *Peerage & Eton School Lists.*

Powys, Francis Arthur, 4s. Henry Philip, of Southgate, Middlesex, arm. ST. JOHN'S COLL., matric. 8 May, 1850, aged 19; scholar and fellow 1851-70, B.A. 1854, M.A. 1857, B.D. 1864, dean of arts 1859, bursar 1865, vice-president 1868, perp. curate Summertown, Oxford, 1860-4, vicar of St. Giles's, Oxford, 1864-9, rector of Winterslow, Wilts, 1869. See Foster's *Peerage* & *Eton School Lists.*

Powys, Henry, s. Thomas, of St. Cr., Salop, arm. ST. JOHN'S COLL., matric. 3 June, 1735, aged 17; probably brother of Thomas 1736.

Powys, Henry Leycester. BRASENOSE COLL., 1860. See KECK, page 781.

Powys, Henry Lyttleton, 2s. Horace, bishop of Sodor and Man. NON-COLL., matric. 16 Feb., 1878, aged 38. **[20]**

Powys, Henry Philip, s. Philip Lybbe, of Wargrave, Berks, arm. ST. JOHN'S COLL., matric. 17 Oct., 1808, aged 16; B.A. 1812, M.A. 1815, of Hardwick, Oxon, died 1 April, 1859. See Foster's *Peerage & Eton School Lists.*

Powys, Horace Annesley, 4s. Bransby William, of London, gent. ST. JOHN'S COLL., matric. 15 Oct., 1870, aged 19; scholar 1870-5, B.A. 1874, M.A. 1878, curate of Meanwood, Yorks, 1880-3, vicar 1883.

Powys, Hon. John, 2s. Thomas Lyttleton, Lord Powys. NON-COLL., matric. 21 Jan., 1882, aged 19; B.A. from BRASENOSE COLL. 1886.

Powys, Philip, y.s. Thomas, of St. Giles's, Middlesex, equitis. QUEEN'S COLL., matric. 15 July, 1721, aged 17; of Hardwick, Oxon, in right of his wife, father of Philip Lybbe, and of Thomas 1753.

Powys, Philip Barrington Lybbe, 1s. Philip, of Hardwick, Oxon, arm. ST. JOHN'S COLL., matric. 17 Oct., 1865, aged 17. See Foster's *Peerage & Eton School Lists.* **[25]**

Powys, Philip Lybbe, s. Philip, of Hardwick, Oxon, arm. ST. JOHN'S COLL., matric. 30 June, 1753, aged 18; B.C.L. 1761, of Hardwick, died 12 April, 1809.

Powys, Philip Lybbe. BALLIOL COLL. 1836. See LYBBE, page 884.

Powys, Richard, s. Rich., of St. Anne's, Westminster, arm. QUEEN'S COLL., matric. 20 Oct., 1725, aged 16.

Powys, Richard Thomas, s. Philip, of Hardwick, Oxon, arm. UNIVERSITY COLL., matric. 29 June, 1816, aged 18; B.A. 1820, M.A. 1823, vicar of Hullavington, Wilts, 1864, until his death 27 Jan., 1877. See Foster's *Peerage*, B. LILFORD; & *Eton School Lists.*

Powys, Thomas (s. Thomas), arm. UNIVERSITY COLL., matric. 27 July; 1736, of Lilford, Salop, born 24 Sep., 1719, died 2 April, 1767, father of Thomas, Lord Lilford. See Foster's *Peerage.* **[30]**

Powys, Thomas, s. John, of 'city of Salop,' arm. MAGDALEN COLL., matric. 26 April, 1750, aged 17; created M.A. 2 July, 1754.

Powys, Thomas, s. Philip, of Hardwick, Oxon, arm. ST. JOHN'S COLL., matric. 2 July, 1753, aged 16; B.A. 1757, M.A. 1760, B. & D.D. 1795, rector of Fawley, Bucks, and of Silchester, Hants, preb. of Hereford 1769, dean of Bristol 1779, canon of Windsor 1796-7, dean of Canterbury 1797, until his death 7 Oct., 1809. See Foster's *Peerage.*

Powys, Thomas, s. Philip Lybbe, of Hardwick, Oxon, arm. ST. JOHN'S COLL., matric. 30 June, 1784, aged 15; B.C.L. 1790, rector of High Roding, Essex, 1796, and of Fawley, Bucks, 1810, until his death 14 (or 17) Aug., 1817, father of the next named.

Powys, Thomas Arthur, 1s. Thomas, of Remenham, Berks, cler. ST. JOHN'S COLL., matric. 28 June, 1819, aged 17; scholar and fellow 1819-31, B.A. 1826, M.A. 1829, rector of Sawtry St. Andrew, Hunts, 1831, until his death 3 Sep., 1871.

Powys, Thomas Atherton, 1s. Thomas, Baron Lilford. CHRIST CHURCH, matric. 2 May, 1821, aged 19; B.A. 1824, 3rd baron, a lord-in-waiting, died 15 March, 1861. See Foster's *Peerage & Eton School Lists.* **[35]**

Powys, Thomas Lyttleton, 1s. Thomas, Baron Lilford. CHRIST CHURCH, matric. 12 June, 1851, aged 18; 4th Lord Lilford. See Foster's *Peerage.*

Powys, William Percy, 2s. Hon. Horatio, bishop of Sodor and Man. UNIVERSITY COLL., matric. 29 May, 1857, aged 19; B.A. 1861, M.A. 1864, curate of St. Mary, Reading, 1862-73, rector of Ashow, co. Warwick, 1873-7, and of Thorpe Achurch, Northants, 1877. See *Rugby School Reg.*

Poynder, Edmund Samuel, 2s. Thomas, of St. George's, Bloomsbury, arm. BRASENOSE COLL., matric. 9 June, 1837, aged 19.

Poynder, Frederick, 2s. John, of Clapham, Surrey, arm. WADHAM COLL., matric. 25 June, 1833, aged 17; B.A. 1838, M.A. 1840, chaplain 1847-9, assistant-master Charterhouse School 1838-9, second master 1858-72, chaplain Bridewell Hospital 1849-58.

Poynder, Frederick Cecil, o.s. Frederick, of London, cler. ST. JOHN'S COLL., matric. 16 Oct., 1880, aged 18; scholar 1880-4, B.A. 1884, M.A. 1887.

Poynder, (Sir) John Poynder Dickson, (Bart.), 1s. John Bourmaster Dickson, of Ryde, Isle of Wight (rear admiral). CHRIST CHURCH, matric. 30 May, 1885, aged 18; 6th baronet, assumed the additional name of POYNDER on attaining his majority. See Foster's *Baronetage.* **[5]**

Poynder, Thomas Henry Allen, 1s. Thomas, of St. George's, Bloomsbury, London, arm. BRASENOSE COLL., matric. 13 June, 1832, aged 18; B.A. 1836, M.A. 1839, bar.-at-law, Lincoln's Inn, 1839, died 26 Nov., 1873.

Poynder, William, s. Thomas, of Bishopsgate Street, London, arm. TRINITY COLL., matric. 3 Feb., 1808, aged 20; B.A. 1812, M.A. 1815, rector of Horne, Surrey, 1859, until his death 31 Jan., 1867.

Poynton, Arthur Blackburne, 4s. Francis John, of Kelston, Somerset, cler. BALLIOL COLL., matric. 24 Oct., 1885, aged 18; scholar 1884.

Poynton, Francis John, 2s. Thomas, of Chew Magna, Somerset, arm. EXETER COLL., matric. 29 May, 1846, aged 18; exhibitioner 1846, B.A. 1850, M.A. 1853, rector of Kelston, Somerset, 1858, etc. See *Crockford, & Coll. Reg.*, 155.

Poynton, Henry Hopwood, 3s. Francis John, of Kelston, Somerset, cler. NON-COLL., matric. 13 Oct., 1884, aged 18. **[10]**

Poyntz, Charles, s. Stephen, of St. James's, Westminster, arm. CHRIST CHURCH, matric. 13 Dec., 1752, aged 17; B.A. 1756, M.A. 1759, B. & D.D. 1769, rector of North Creak, Norfolk, 1760, and preb. of Llandaff and of Durham 1784, until his death 10 May, 1809.

Poyntz, James William, 2s. Stephen, of St. George's, London, arm. ST. MARY HALL, matric. 13 May, 1828, aged 21.

Poyntz, Nathaniel, s. Newdigate, of Tormarton, co. Gloucester, cler. ST. MARY HALL, matric. 23 Oct., 1801, aged 19; demy MAGDALEN COLL. 1802-6, B.A. 1805, of Alvescot House, Oxon, rector of Cranwich with vicarage of Methwold, Norfolk, 1813, died March, 1873. See Foster's *Our Noble and Gentle Families*, vol. i.; & *Bloxam*, vii. 149.

Poyntz, Nathaniel Castleton Stephen, 2s. Newdigate, of Tidenham, co. Gloucester, arm. PEMBROKE COLL., matric. 19 Oct., 1865, aged 19; B.A. 1868, M.A. 1887, held various curacies 1869-86, vicar of Dorchester, Oxon, 1886. See Foster's *Our Noble and Gentle Families*, vol. i.

Poyntz, Newdigate, s. Newdigate, of Hexton, Herts, arm. CHRIST CHURCH, matric. 15 June, 1770, aged 18; B.C.L. from ST. MARY HALL 17 April, 1771, rector of Tormarton, co. Gloucester, etc., 1777, until his death 19 Dec., 1825. **[15]**

Poyntz, Newdigate, 1s. Newdigate, of Tidenham, co. Gloucester, arm. PEMBROKE COLL., matric. 13 Dec., 1860, aged 18; B.A. 1864, M.A. 1867, vicar of Little Drayton, Salop, 1876-85, and rector of Stone, co. Stafford, 1885. See Foster's *Our Noble and Gentle Families*, vol. i.

Poyntz, William, s. Stephen, of St. Martin's, Westminster, arm. CHRIST CHURCH, matric. 17 Jan., 1752, aged 17; B.A. 1756, M.A. 1760, of Midgeham, Berks, died in 1809, father of William S. 1787.

Poyntz, William Dean, s. Dean, of St. James's, London, arm. UNIVERSITY COLL., matric. 4 June, 1767, aged 18; created M.A. 9 July, 1773 (as POINTZ).

Poyntz, William Stephen, s. William, of Westminster, arm. CHRIST CHURCH, matric. 29 June, 1787, aged 17; of Midgeham, Berks, and of Cowdray, Sussex, M.P. St. Albans 1800-7, Callington 1810-8, Chichester 1823-30, Ashburton 1831-2, Midhurst 1835-7, died 8 April, 1840.

Poyser, Arthur Horatio, 1s. Charles, of Ellesmere, Salop, arm. CHRIST CHURCH, matric. 16 Oct., 1868, aged 19; servitor 1868-79, exhibitioner 1876-9, B.A. 1872, M.A. 1875, bar.-at-law, Lincoln's Inn, 1873. See Foster's *Men at the Bar.* **[20]**

Praed, Charles Tyringham, 2s. James Backwell, of Tyringham, Bucks, arm. MERTON COLL., matric. 19 March, 1851, aged 18; of London, banker, M.P. St. Ives 1874-80. See Foster's *Baronetage*, MACKWORTH; & *Eton School Lists.*

Praed, Herbert, s. Humphrey, of Williamstrip, co. Gloucester, arm. ST. MARY HALL, matric. 31 Jan., 1769, aged 17; B.C.L. 1777, died rector of Ludgvan, Cornwall, in 1789, brother of William 1767.

Praed, Humphrey, s. William, of St. George's, Westminster, arm. BRASENOSE COLL., matric. 19 Feb., 1798, aged 15; of Southampton, died in 1837. See Foster's *Baronetage* & *Eton School Lists.*

Praed, James (Backwell), s. William, of St. George's, Westminster, arm. BRASENOSE COLL., matric. 19 Feb., 1798, aged 18; of Tyringham, Bucks, and Trevethoe, Cornwall, M.P. Bucks 1835-7, high sheriff 1807, died 13 Jan., 1837. See Foster's *Baronetage*, MACKWORTH.

Praed, Rev. John, s. William, of Tyringham, Bucks, arm. BRASENOSE COLL., matric. 21 Feb., 1814, aged 18; died 8 July, 1847. See Foster's *Baronetage* & *Eton School Lists.* **[25]**

Praed, John Mackworth, s. William, of Trevethoe, Cornwall, gent. UNIVERSITY COLL., matric. 9 April, 1733, aged 16; a student of the Middle Temple 1735.

Praed, William, s. Humphrey Mackworth, of Broughton, co. Stafford, arm. MAGDALEN COLL., matric. 2 March, 1767, aged 17; of Tyringham and Trevethoe, M.P. St. Ives 1774-5, 1780-1806, Banbury 1806-8, died 9 Oct., 1833.

Praed, William, s. William, of Tyringham, Bucks, arm. BRASENOSE COLL., matric. 19 Feb., 1798, aged 17; of Trevethoe, Cornwall, M.P. St. Ives 1838-46, died 8 July, 1846.

Praed, William Backwell. CHRIST CHURCH, 1848. See TYRINGHAM.

Prall, Richard Evans, 1s. Richard, of Rochester, arm. CHRIST CHURCH, matric. 27 May, 1882, aged 18; B.A. 1886, bar.-at-law, Lincoln's Inn, 1887. **[30]**

Prance, Charles Henry, 3s. Robert, of Hampstead, Middlesex, arm. CHRIST CHURCH, matric. 11 Dec., 1851, aged 19; B.A. 1856, M.A. 1858, bar.-at-law, Lincoln's Inn, 1862, died 8 July, 1878.

Prankerd, Archibald Arthur, y.s. John, of Langport, Somerset, gent. WORCESTER COLL., matric. 25 April, 1874, aged 23; B.A. 1879, B.C.L. & M.A. 1880, D.C.L. 1887, law lecturer Brasenose College 1883, University College 1883-6, and of Merton College 1884, bar.-at-law, Lincoln's Inn, 1877. See Foster's *Men at the Bar.*

Prankerd, Percy John, 1s. Peter Dowding, of Stepney, near Adelaide, Australia, arm. TRINITY COLL., matric. 12 Oct., 1878, aged 19; B.A. 1882, M.A. 1885, bar.-at-law, Inner Temple, 1884. See Foster's *Men at the Bar.*

Pratchet, James, s. Richard, of Allerton, Salop, pleb. QUEEN'S COLL., matric. 19 May, 1743, aged 18; vicar of Brinsep, co. Hereford, 1774, died rector of Holgate, Salop, 19 June, 1802.

Pratchet, James, s. James, of Adderley, Salop, cler. QUEEN'S COLL., matric. 19 May, 1774, aged 18.

Prater, Richard, s. Richard, of Frome, Somerset, gent. EXETER COLL., matric. 10 Oct., 1720, aged 17.

Prater, Thomas, 2s. Charles, of St. Martin's, London, arm. EXETER COLL., matric. 4 March, 1830, aged 17; B.A. 1833, M.A. 1836, rector of Hardwicke and Tusmore, Oxon, 1841-56, vicar of Leighton-under-the-Wrekin 1856-62.

Pratt, Charles Durham, o.s. Benjamin, of Belfast, gent. MAGDALEN HALL, matric. 23 Jan., 1874, aged 24. [5]

Pratt, Charles Ernest, o.s. Charles Tiplady, of Cawthorne, Yorks, cler. KEBLE COLL., matric. 19 Oct., 1886, aged 19.

Pratt, Charles Tiplady, 2s. John Slater, of Stokesley, Yorks, gent. QUEEN'S COLL., matric. 29 May, 1856, aged 17; B.A. 1860, M.A. 1863, curate in charge of Cawthorne, Yorks, 1866-74, vicar since 1874.

Pratt, Edward Haslope, 2s. George Isaac, of King's Norton, co. Worcester, gent. PEMBROKE COLL., matric. 26 May, 1853, aged 17; B.A. 1859.

Pratt, Frederick Thomas, scholar TRINITY COLL., Cambridge, scholar 1820, 1st senior optime & B.A. 1821, M.A. 1825, 3s. John, of Lambeth, gent. ST. JOHN'S COLL., incorp. 8 Dec., 1836, aged 37; B.C.L. 17 Dec., 1836, D.C.L. 6 April, 1837, an advocate of Doctors' Commons, died 13 April, 1868.

Pratt, Rev. George Edward Haslope, 1s. Edward Haslope, of Kidderminster, arm. ST. JOHN'S COLL., matric. 26 Oct., 1881, aged 19; B.A. 1885.

Pratt, George Henry, 1s. George Isaac, of King's Norton, co. Worcester, gent. WADHAM COLL., matric. 7 May, 1851, aged 18; B.A. 1855, M.A. 1858, vicar of St. Swithin, Lincoln, 1866. [11]

Pratt, Henry, s. John, of Tughill, co. Stafford, gent. UNIVERSITY COLL., matric. 24 Oct., 1747, aged 17; B.A. 1751, M.A. 1754, died vicar of Orpington and St. Mary Cray, Kent, 22 Oct., 1802, father of John 1790.

Pratt, Henry Edward, 2s. John, of Sedlescomb, Sussex, cler. UNIVERSITY COLL., matric. 11 Oct., 1833, aged 17; B.A. 1837, M.A. 1841, vicar of Wartling, Sussex, 1841, until his death 1 Sep., 1843.

Pratt, Henry Madan, o.s. Henry, of Peterborough, Northants, cler. PEMBROKE COLL., matric. 29 Oct., 1874, aged 19; B.A. 1879, M.A. 1881, rector of Great Witcombe, co. Gloucester, 1884-6, vicar of Sherborne with Windrush, Oxon, 1886.

Pratt, Jacob (Vivour), 3s. Robert, of Freetown, Sierra Leone, gent. CHRIST CHURCH, matric. 14 Oct., 1881, aged 24; B.A. 1887. [15]

Pratt, Rev. Jermyn, of TRINITY COLL., Cambridge (B.A. 1821, M.A. 1825); adm. 'ad eundem' 4 Dec., 1845 (3s. Edward Roger, of Ryston, Norfolk), of Ryston Hall, rector of Campsey Ashe, Suffolk, 1836-66, died 15 May, 1867.

Prat, John, s. George, of Chatham, Kent, cler. PEMBROKE COLL., matric. 11 July, 1746, aged 19; brother of Samuel 1745.

Pratt, John, s. Henry, of Orpington, Kent, cler. UNIVERSITY COLL., matric. 1 Dec., 1790, aged 17; B.A. 1794, M.A. 1797, rector of Sedlescomb, Sussex, 1803, until his death 6 Aug., 1861, father of John Joseph.

Pratt, John. o.s. John, of Lane Delph, co. Stafford, gent. PEMBROKE COLL., matric. 21 April, 1853, aged 18; B.A. from ST. MARY HALL 1858, M.A. 1859.

Pratt, John, 1s. John, of Oxford, arm. CORPUS CHRISTI COLL., matric. 6 Feb., 1878, aged 19; B.A. 1882; M.A. 1884. [20]

Pratt, Rev. John Joseph, 1s. John, of Sedlescomb, Sussex, cler. ST. JOHN'S COLL., matric. 29 June, 1829, aged 18; scholar & fellow 1829-62, B.A. 1834, M.A. 1838, died 11 March, 1880. See *Robinson*, 215.

Pratt, Josiah, s. Josiah, of Birmingham, co. Warwick, gent. ST. EDMUND HALL, matric. 22 June, 1789, aged 20; B.A. 1793, M.A. 1796, B.D. 1808, vicar of St. Stephen, Coleman Street, London, 1826, until his death 10 Oct., 1844.

Pratt, Julian, o.s. William, of Aldgate, London, arm. TRINITY COLL., matric. 28 May, 1841, aged 18; B.A. 1845, M.A. 1848, vicar of Challock 1870.

Pratt, Mervyn, 1s. Joseph, of St. George's, Dublin, arm. ST. MARY HALL, matric. 27 Oct., 1828, aged 21; of Cabra Castle, co. Cavan, high sheriff 1841, for co. Mayo 1843, and co. Meath 1875.

Pratt, Philip Edgar, 1s. Philip Proks, of Walsall, co. Stafford, gent. EXETER COLL., matric. 15 June, 1855, aged 18; scholar 1855-9, B.A. 1859, M.A. 1862, perp. curate of Minsterley, Salop, 1865-70, vicar of Diddlebury, Salop, 1870-80, and of Madley, co. Hereford, 1880. See *Coll. Reg.*, 157. [25]

Prat, Richard, s. John, of London, gent. QUEEN'S COLL., matric. 22 Nov., 1734, aged 18; B.A. 1738, rector of Glastonbury and vicar of Butcombe, Somerset, father of Richard 1787.

Prat, Richard, s. Richard, of Glastonbury, Somerset, cler. WADHAM COLL., matric. 10 April, 1783, aged 18; B.A. 1787, vicar of Littleham with Exmouth 1813, until his death 6 June, 1840.

Prat, Rev. Richard, o.s. Richard Periam, of Glastonbury, Somerset, gent. LINCOLN COLL., matric. 8 Feb., 1838, aged 18; postmaster MERTON COLL. 1839-43, B.A. 1842, died 14 Feb., 1878.

Pratt, Robert, s. John, of Covent Garden, London, arm. QUEEN'S COLL., matric. 14 Feb., 1744-5, aged 17; bar.-at-law, Inner Temple, 1751, M.P. Horsham 1763-74, a master in Chancery 1767, until his death 21 July, 1775.

Prat, Samuel, s. John, of St. Andrew's, Holborn, London, arm. QUEEN'S COLL., matric. 27 March, 1732, aged 18; bar.-at-law, Lincoln's Inn, 1738.

Prat, Samuel, s. George, of Boughton, Kent, cler. ORIEL COLL., matric. 10 Oct., 1745, aged 18; B.A. 27 Feb., 1749-50, brother of John 1746. [31]

Pratt, Thomas, s. Thomas, of St. James's, London, gent. CHRIST CHURCH, matric. 1 April, 1721, aged 18.

Pratt, Thomas Dowell, 1s. John Slater, of Stokesley, Yorks, gent. QUEEN'S COLL., matric. 22 June, 1854, aged 18; B.A. 1858.

Prat, Thomas Heaviside, 1s. Thomas, of Manningtree, Essex, gent. ST. MARY HALL, matric. 27 Oct., 1869, aged 19.

Pratt, William, s. David, of Blazeley, Northants, cler. WADHAM COLL., matric. 21 Jan., 1747-8, aged 16; B.A. 1753. [35]

Pratt, William, 3s. Owen Sturgis, of Northampton, gent. QUEEN'S COLL., matric. 24 Oct., 1874, aged 18; exhibitioner 1874-9, B.A. 1878, M.A. 1888.

Pratt, Rev. William Barrow, o.s. Charles O'Neill, of Macclesfield, Cheshire, cler. WADHAM COLL., matric. 13 Oct., 1865, aged 18.

Pratten, Caesar, s. Edward, of Bow, Middlesex, gent. TRINITY COLL., matric. 17 June, 1746, aged 18.

Prattenton, Edward, s. William, of Hartlebury, co. Worcester, pleb. UNIVERSITY COLL., matric. 3 March, 1714-5, aged 20; B.A. from ST. MARY HALL 1718.

Prattenton, Rev. George Deakin Onley, 1s. John Deakin Onley, of Bransford, co. Worcester, arm. ST. JOHN'S COLL., matric. 3 Dec., 1846, aged 19; B.A. 1850, M.A. 1865, assumed the additional surname of PRATTENTON. [40]

PART OF LITTLE GATE, now demolished. *From Skelton.*

Prattinton, James, s. James, of Bewdley, co. Worcester, gent. QUEEN'S COLL., matric. 9 Dec., 1783, aged 18; B.A. 1787.

Prattinton, Peter, s. William, of Bewdley, co. Worcester, gent. CHRIST CHURCH, matric. 6 May, 1789, aged 18; B.A. 1793, M.A. 1796, B. Med. 1797.

Pré, Arthur Michael Duncombe du, 2s. Michael Thomas, of Guiting, co. Gloucester, cler. (See page 397). LINCOLN COLL., matric. 22 Jan., 1880, aged 19; B.A. 1882.

Precavance, Thomas. MAGDALEN COLL., 1737. See PRICAVANCE. [5]

Preedy, Benjamin, s. William, of Evesham, co. Worcester, pleb. QUEEN'S COLL., matric. 3 Nov., 1739, aged 17; B.A. 1743, M.A. 1772, B. & D.D. 1772, rector of St. Alban's and of Dunton 1772, and also of Brington, Northants, 1777, until his death 26 March, 1796.

Preedy, Benjamin, s. William, of Evesham, co. Worcester, gent. MERTON COLL., matric. 16 June, 1790, aged 17; B.A. 1794, M.A. 1799, rector of Hinton-on-the-Green 1813, and Willersley, co. Gloucester, 1814, until his death 1 May, 1849.

Preedy, Charles, 2s. Charles Wooley, of Hunstanton, Norfolk, gent. NON-COLL., matric. 11 Oct., 1873, aged 18; B.A. from ST. EDMUND HALL 1876, M.A. 1884, has held various curacies since 1878.

Preedy, James, s. Benjamin, of Harding, Herts, cler. QUEEN'S COLL., matric. 14 May, 1771, aged 18; B.A. 1775, rector of Hasleton with Entworth, co. Gloucester, 1785.

Preedy, Rev. William, 2s. William Frederick, of Evesham, co. Worcester, arm. WADHAM COLL., matric. 9 Nov., 1832, aged 18; B.A. 1836, died 27 Oct., 1840. [10]

Preest, William Shuttleworth, s. William, of Birmingham, co. Warwick, gent. LINCOLN COLL., matric. 14 April, 1739, aged 18.

Prendergast, Lenox, 4s. Guy Lenox, of St. George's, Hanover Square, London, arm. CHRIST CHURCH, matric. 15 Dec., 1848, aged 18; late colonel royal Scots greys, served in the Crimea, severely wounded in the Balaclava charge. See Foster's *Our Noble and Gentle Families*, vol. i.; & *Eton School Lists.*

Prendergast, Michael, o.s. Michael, of Castlemaine, Australia, arm. PEMBROKE COLL., matric. 26 Oct., 1877, aged 20.

Prendergast, William Paul, 5s. Francis, of 'St. Morgan' (? St. Michan), Dublin (city), arm. TRINITY COLL., matric. 11 Nov., 1830, aged 17; B.A. 1834, bar.-at-law, Middle Temple, 1842. See Foster's *Men at the Bar.*

Prentice, George Hailey, 2s. Golden, of Prittlewell, Essex, arm. TRINITY COLL., matric. 28 April, 1841, aged 18; B.A. 1845, M.A. 1849, bar.-at-law, Inner Temple, 1849, died 28 March, 1878. [15]

Prentice, George Seward, 1s. Charles Brightly, of Cheltenham, co. Gloucester, gent. ST. MARY HALL, matric. 29 Oct., 1867, aged 20.

Prentice, Henry, 3s. Golding Nehemiah, of Rayleigh, Essex, arm. TRINITY COLL., matric. 11 March, 1847, aged 20; B.A. 1850, M.A. 1853, rector of Holford, Somerset, 1866.

Prescot, Charles Kenrick, s. Charles, of Stockport, Cheshire, cler. BRASENOSE COLL., matric. 11 April, 1804, aged 17; B.A. 1808, M.A. 1810, rector of Stockport 1820, until his death 4 May, 1875.

Prescot, Charless Warre, 2s. Kenrick, of Stockport, Cheshire, cler. BRASENOSE COLL., matric. 13 June, 1857, aged 19; B.A. 1861. M.A. 1876, a student of the Inner Temple 1885, a solicitor practising in High Court, Bombay. See *Rugby School Reg.*

Prescot, Edward, s. William, of Halifax, Yorks, arm. CHRIST CHURCH, matric. 17 June, 1778, aged 18; B.A. 1782, M.A. 1785, vicar of Long Preston, Yorks, 1789, until his death 16 Feb., 1809. See *Alumni West.*, 408; & *Manchester School Reg.*, i. 170. [20]

Prescot, Kelsall, s. Charles, of Stockport, Cheshire, cler. BRASENOSE COLL., matric. 16 April, 1806, aged 17; B.A. 1810, M.A. 1812, curate of Marple, died at Stockport 15 Dec., 1823.

Prescot, Kenrick, 1s. Charles Kenrick, of Stockport, Cheshire, cler. BRASENOSE COLL., matric. 22 June, 1848, aged 17, scholar 1848-52, B.A. 1852; fellow MERTON COLL. 1853-64, tutor 1854-61, M.A. 1855, tutor, lecturer in modern history and law 1854, dean 1855, vicar of Ponteland, Northumberland, 1864-78, and of Lapwith 1878.

Prescot, Oldfield Kelsall, o.s. William Henry, of Plemstall, Chester (city), cler. BRASENOSE COLL., matric. 4 Feb., 1847, aged 18; B.A. 1851, M.A. 1865, held various curacies 1853-67, vicar of Alderton, Wilts, 1867-75. See *Rugby School Reg.*, 247.

Prescot, Richard, s. Richard, of Dalton, Lancashire, gent. BRASENOSE COLL., matric. 2 April, 1747, aged 19; B.A. 1750, M.A. 1753.

Prescot, Rev. William Henry, s. Charles, of Stockport, Cheshire, cler. BRASENOSE COLL., matric. 16 April, 1817, aged 18; scholar 1818-21, B.A. 1821, M.A. 1823, of Bradshaw Hall, died 16 Nov., 1842. See *Manchester School Reg.*, iii. 38. [25]

Prescott, Benjamin Barton, 2s. George, of Liverpool, gent. PEMBROKE COLL., matric. 27 Oct., 1870, aged 19; B.A. 1874, M.A. 1877, vicar of Christ Church, Latchford, 1878.

Prescott, Charles John, 1s. James Jenkin, of Bridport, Dorset, gent. WORCESTER COLL., matric. 19 Oct., 1876, aged 19; exhibitioner 1874-80, B.A. 1880.

Prescott, Edgar Grote, 5s. Frederick Joseph, of St. Pancras, London, arm. EXETER COLL., matric. 2 June, 1857, aged 18; B.A. 1861. See Foster's *Baronetage.*

Prescott, Henry, 1s. Isaac Philip, of Portsmouth, Hants, cler. ORIEL COLL., matric. 18 Oct., 1862, aged 19. See Foster's *Our Noble and Gentle Families*, ii.

Prescott, Henry Frederick, 1s. Edgar Grote, of Sydenham, Kent, gent. QUEEN'S COLL., matric. 22 Oct., 1884, aged 18; B.A. 1887. [30]

Prescott, Isaac Philip, 1s. Henry, of Fareham, Hants, arm. ORIEL COLL., matric. 7 Nov., 1833, aged 17; B.A. 1837, M.A. 1840, held various curacies 1839-62, vicar of Priors Marston, co. Warwick, 1862-78, rector of Kelly, Devon, 1882, father of Henry, 1862.

Prescott, John, 1s. William Budd, of Walton, near Liverpool, gent. WADHAM COLL., matric. 19 Oct., 1853, aged 19; B.A. 1859, M.A. 1863, of Dalton Grange, Lancashire, a student of the Inner Temple, 1859.

Prescott, Rev. Peter, 2s. Thomas, of Bedford Leigh, Lancashire, gent. ST. MARY HALL, matric. 21 June, 1844, aged 22; exhibitioner 1848-9, B.A. 1852, M.A. 1853.

Prescott, William Hickling, of the United States; created D.C.L. 24 June, 1850 (son of William Prescott), author of the 'History of the Conquest of Mexico,' and also of the 'Conquest of Peru,' etc., died at Boston, U.S. 28 Jan., 1859.

Presland, Thomas, s. Thomas, of Walford, Salop, arm. BRASENOSE COLL., matric. 26 Nov., 1787, aged 17; of Walford, aforesaid, died vicar of Baschurch, Salop, 17 Sept., 1803. [35]

Pressey, Rev. William James, 2s. Arthur, of London, gent. WADHAM COLL., matric. 26 Jan., 1881, aged 22; B.A. 1884, M.A. 1887.

Prestidge, Thomas Kimbel, s. Thomas, of Culworth, Northants, pleb. BRASENOSE COLL., matric. 18 July, 1719, aged 16; B.A. 1723, M.A. 1726.

Preston, Aaron Necke, 2s. John, of St. Mary Church, near Torquay, gent. MAGDALEN HALL, matric. 21 May, 1840, aged 17.

Preston, Anthony, s. Ant., of Brougham, Westmoreland, cler. QUEEN'S COLL., matric. 12 Feb., 1742-3, aged 16; B.A. 1747.

Preston, Charles Moyes, 2s. William Mich. S., of Carlisle, Cumberland, cler. QUEEN'S COLL., matric. 14 June, 1844, aged 20; B.A. 1848, of Warcop Hall, vicar of Warcop, Cumberland, 1855.

Preston, Charles Sansome, 1s. Thomas Sansome, of London, gent. NEW COLL., matric. 10 Oct., 1884, aged 19; B.A. 1888.

Preston, Charles William Antony, 1s. Charles Moyes, of Warcop, Westmoreland, cler. CHRIST CHURCH, matric. 16 Oct., 1885, aged 20.

Preston, Franklin Roberts, 2s. James Franklin, of Llynyon, near Ruthin, co. Denbigh, gent. EXETER COLL., matric. 20 Jan., 1871, aged 19; B.A. 1874, M.A. 1877, vicar of Ellel Grange, Lancashire, 1884.

Preston, George, s. Isaac, of Beeston, Norfolk, arm. UNIVERSITY COLL., matric. 17 Dec., 1777, aged 17; B.A. 1783, M.A. 1784, of Stanfield Hall, Norfolk, rector of Beeston St. Lawrence, 1785, and of Tasburgh 1832, until his death 22 Oct., 1837. **[5]**

Preston, Rev. George Herbert, 3s. Thomas, of Swaffham Prior, co. Cambridge, cler. NON-COLL., matric. 27 April, 1878, aged 19; B.A. from CHARSLEY HALL 1884.

Preston, George Wooller 1s. Joseph, of Oxenhope, Yorks, arm. QUEEN'S COLL., matric. 24 Oct., 1877, aged 19; exhibitioner 1877-82, B.A. 1881.

Preston, Henry Jacob, 1s. Jacob Henry, of Beeston, Norfolk, baronet. UNIVERSITY COLL., matric. 14 Oct., 1871, aged 20; B.A. from ST. ALBAN HALL 1876. See Foster's *Baronetage* & *Eton School Lists.*

Preston, Isaac, s. Isaac, of Beeston, Norfolk, arm. UNIVERSITY COLL., matric. 2 July, 1772, aged 18; B.A. 1776, M.A. 1779, bar.-at-law, Lincoln's Inn, 1781, recorder of King's Lynn, died 1 May, 1796. See *Alumni West.*, 396.

Preston, Isaac. CHRIST CHURCH 1808. See JERMY, page 751. **[10]**

Preston, John, s. William, of Hampton Lucy, co. Warwick, cler. BALLIOL COLL., matric. 15 Oct., 1717, aged 18; B.A. from ALL SOULS' COLL. 1721, M.A. 1724.

Preston, John, s. George, of Edinburgh, baronet. BALLIOL COLL., matric. 26 Aug., 1735, aged 17; B.A. 1739, chaplain 26th regiment of foot, died 7 March, 1781. See Playfair's *Baronetage.*

Preston, John, s. John, of Staverton, Devon, gent. EXETER COLL., matric. 5 March, 1754, aged 22.

Preston, John, s. John, of Dublin, Ireland, arm. CORPUS CHRISTI COLL., matric. 23 June, 1783, aged 19.

Preston, John D'Arcy Jervis, s. D'Arcy, of Begbrook, Oxon, arm. MERTON COLL., matric. 10 June, 1813, aged 19; postmaster 1813-17, B.A. 1817, M.A. 1822, of Askham Bryan, Yorks, died 5 Aug., 1867. See Foster's *Our Noble and Gentle Families.* **[15]**

Preston, John D'Arcy (Warcop), 1s. John, of Askam Bryan, Yorks, cler. WORCESTER COLL., matric. 6 May, 1841, aged 17; B.A. 1845, M.A. 1849, chaplain to forces in Crimea 1853, etc., vicar of Sandgate, Kent, 1859-69, and of Stonegate, Sussex, 1869-71, rector of Freemantle, Hants, 1871. See Foster's *Our Noble and Gentle Families.*

Preston, John Wilby, o.s. Stephen, of Louth, co. Lincoln, cler. WADHAM COLL., matric. 14 June, 1854, aged 17; B.A. 1858, M.A. 1868, of Dalby Park, co. Lincoln.

Preston, John Wilby, 1s. John Wilby, of Dalby, co. Leicester, arm. MAGDALEN COLL., matric. 27 April, 1878, aged 18; B.A. 1881.

Preston, Martin Inett, 1s. Martin Inett, of Nottingham, gent. QUEEN'S COLL., matric. 23 May, 1874, aged 18; scholar 1874-8, B.A. 1878, M.A. 1881, a student of the Inner Temple 1875.

Preston, Nicholas, s. William, of St. Swithin's, Winchester (city), gent. NEW COLL., matric. 11 Feb., 1719-20, aged 19; B.A. 1723, fellow, M.A. 1727, died rector of Alton Barns, Wilts, 20 Dec., 1777, bequeathed £3,000 to New College. **[20]**

Preston, Richard, s. Thomas, of Long Preston, Yorks, pleb. CHRIST CHURCH, matric. 17 May, 1738, aged 19; B.A. 26 Jan., 1741-2, M.A. 1746.

Preston, Robert Arthur Berthon, 1s. Robert Berthon, of Geneva, gent. EXETER COLL., matric. 16 Jan., 1875, aged 19; B.A. 1878, M.A. 1881, bar.-at-law, Lincoln's Inn, 1881. See Foster's *Men at the Bar* & *Eton School Lists.*

Preston, Robert William Pigott Clarke Campbell-, 1s. William Colin, of Culross, co. Perth, cler. CHRIST CHURCH, matric. 31 May, 1884, aged 18.

Preston, Roland D'Arcy, 3s. John D'Arcy Warcop, of Sandgate, Kent, cler. EXETER COLL., matric. 21 Oct., 1886, aged 19; scholar 1886.

Preston, Samuel, s. William, of Oxford (city), pleb. MAGDALEN HALL, matric. 14 Oct., 1736, aged 17; B.A. 1740. **[25]**

Preston, Stephen, s. William, of Louth, co. Lincoln, gent. LINCOLN COLL., matric. 2 April, 1800, aged 18; fellow until 1833, B.A. 1803, M.A. 1806, B.D. 1815, curate of St. Michael's, Oxford, and of Little Grimsby and Conisholme, co. Lincoln, died 5 Dec., 1840, father of John Wilby 1854.

Preston, Thomas, 2s. Edmund, of Great Yarmouth, Norfolk, arm. EXETER COLL., matric. 3 Feb., 1836, aged 18; B.A. 1839, M.A. 1843, held various curacies 1840-56, vicar of Swaffham Prior since 1856.

Preston, Thomas Henry, 1s. Henry, of Moreby, Yorks, arm. CHRIST CHURCH, matric. 4 June, 1835, aged 18; of Moreby, sometime a captain 7th hussars, etc. See Foster's *Yorkshire Collection* & *Eton School Lists.*

Preston, William, s. William, of St. Martin's, Oxford, pleb. MERTON COLL., matric. 11 July, 1728, aged 15; B.A. 13 Feb., 1732-3, M.A. 1736.

Preston, William, s. William, of Hants, gent. ST. JOHN'S COLL., matric. 27 March, 1729, aged 18; demy MAGDALEN COLL. 1730-5, B.A. 1733, fellow 1734-48, M.A. 1736, B.D. 29 Jan., 1745-6, D.D. 1747, junior dean of arts 1745, bursar 1746, died 24 Oct., 1748. See *Bloxam*, vi. 227. **[30]**

Preston, William, s. William, of Brougham, Westmoreland, cler. QUEEN'S COLL., matric. 22 Feb., 1736-7, aged 16; B.A. 1741, M.A. by decree 24 Nov., 1744.

Preston, William, 4s. John D'Arcy Jervis, of Askham Bryan, Yorks, cler. ORIEL COLL., matric. 19 June, 1851, aged 18 (now William Warcup Peter Consett, of Brawith Hall, Yorks, assumed the name and arms of CONSETT in lieu of PRESTON. See Foster's *Our Noble and Gentle Families*, ii.

Preston, Rev. William Babington, 2s. James Blair, of Cuddalore, Madras, D.Med. KEBLE COLL., matric. 18 Oct., 1875, aged 19; B.A. 1879, M.A. 1887.

Preston, William Michael Stephenson, s. William Stephenson, of Warcop, Westmoreland, arm. QUEEN'S COLL., matric. 8 Dec., 1803, aged 18; B.A. 1807, M.A. 1811, fellow 1815-21, rector (and patron) of Warcop 1829, until his death 21 Sep., 1842, father of Charles Moyes 1844.

Preston, William Stephenson, 1s. William Michael, of Starford, Yorks, cler. ST. JOHN'S COLL., matric. 2 April, 1840, aged 18; B.A. 1845, of Warcop Hall, Cumberland, vicar of Warcop, 1851-5. **[35]**

Preston, William Thomas, 1s. Cooper, of Marsham, Yorks, arm. BRASENOSE COLL., matric. 10 May, 1832, aged 19; B.A. 1836, of Flasby Hall, Yorks, bar.-at-law, Inner Temple, 1840, died 17 Nov., 1877. See Foster's *Yorkshire Collection.*

Prestwich, Joseph, 1s. Joseph, of London, gent. CHRIST CHURCH, name entered in *Mat. Reg.*, 3 Nov., 1874, aged 62; M.A. (by decree) 11 Nov., 1874, professor of geology 1874-87, F.R.S., F.G.S., president Geological Society 1870-2, vice-president Royal Society 1870-1.

Prestwood, Thomas, s. Sebastian, of St. Sampson, Cornwall, arm. QUEEN'S COLL., matric. 23 March, 1726-7, aged 17.

Pretyman, Frederick, 2s. George Thomas, of Lincoln, cler. BALLIOL COLL., matric. 28 March, 1838, aged 18; demy MAGDALEN COLL. 1839-42, B.A. 1841, fellow 1842-58, M.A. 1844, B.D. 1852, junior dean of arts 1845, bursar 1847, dean of divinity 1854, rector of Great Carlton, co. Lincoln, 1850, preb. of Lincoln 1873. See *Bloxam*, vii. 347.

Pretyman, George, 1s. George Thomas, of Wheathamstead, Herts, cler. BALLIOL COLL., matric. 18 March, 1836, aged 18; B.A. from NEW INN HALL 1840, M.A. 1844, vicar of Great Carlton, co. Lincoln, 1844, until his death 6 April, 1850.

Pretyman, Henry George Middleton, 2s. John, of Sherington, Bucks, cler. ORIEL COLL., matric. 10 Dec., 1835, aged 18; B.A. 1839, M.A. 1843, a student of Lincoln's Inn 1839, rector of Lowick, Northants, 1856, until his death 11 May, 1870.

Pretyman, John Radclyffe, 1s. John, of Sherington, Bucks, cler. TRINITY COLL., matric. 17 May, 1834, aged 18; B.A. 1838, M.A. 1843.

Pretyman, Richard, of TRINITY COLL., Cambridge (B.A. 1814, M.A. 1817); adm. 'ad eundem' 24 April, 1834, canon residentiary and precentor of Lincoln 1817, rector of Walgrave, Northants, 1817, and of Middleton, Oxon, 1819. [5]

Prevost, Charles Thomas Keble, 1s. Charles, of Southsea, Hants, arm. KEBLE COLL., matric. 22 Oct., 1885, aged 19; B.A. 1888.

Prevost, (Sir) George (Bart.), o.s. George, of Isle of Dominica, West Indies, baronet. ORIEL COLL., matric. 23 Jan., 1821, aged 16; B.A. 1825, M.A. 1827, 2nd baronet, hon. canon of Gloucester 1859, archdeacon 1865-81, rector of Stinchcombe, co. Gloucester, 1834. See Foster's *Baronetage.*

Prevost, George Phipps, 1s. George, of Bisley, co. Gloucester, baronet. BALLIOL COLL., matric. 30 Nov., 1848, aged 18; B.A. from PEMBROKE COLL., 1852, colonel in the army, lieut.-colonel 23rd royal Welsh fusiliers, died 27 March, 1885. See Foster's *Baronetage.*

Priaulx, Peter, s. Peter, of Buckland, Surrey, doctor. CHRIST CHURCH, matric. 9 April, 1720, aged 16; demy MAGDALEN COLL. 1720-8, B.A. 1723, M.A. 1726, fellow 1728-43, B.D. 20 March, 1734-5, bursar 1737, dean of divinity 1741, rector of Candlesby 1738-42, and of East Bridgeford, Notts, 1742, until his death 18 March, 1783. See *Bloxam*, vi. 198.

Priaulx, Osmond, 1s. Osmond de Lancy, of Sydney, Australia, arm. CHRIST CHURCH, matric. 16 Jan., 1885, aged 18. [10]

Pricavance, Thomas, s. William, of Oxford (city), pleb. MAGDALEN COLL., matric. 2 April, 1737, aged 16; chorister 1731-41, B.A. 20 Jan., 1740-1, M.A. 1743. See *Bloxam*, i. 159.

Price, Andrew, s. Roger, of Leigh, Essex, cler. MAGDALEN COLL., matric. 24 Oct., 1771, aged 17; chorister 1767-72, B.A. 1775, M.A. 1778, usher of Magdalen College School 1772-88, chaplain Christ Church and of Bishop Warner's College at Bromley 1788-1800, rector of Brightwell Salome, co. Gloucester, 1782, and of Down Ampney 1788, until his death 7 June, 1851. See *Coll. Reg.*, i. 175; iii. 240.

Price, Arthur, s. Thomas, of Mydrim, co. Carmarthen, cler. JESUS COLL., matric. 16 March, 1718-9, aged 20.

Price, Arthur Henry, 2s. Thomas, of Kingsbury, co. Warwick, cler. WADHAM COLL., matric. 28 Oct., 1829, aged 18; B.A. 1833, M.A. 1838, vicar of Lugwardine, co. Hereford, 1862, until his death 12 May, 1884.

Price, Arthur Radcliffe, o.s. Henry Strong, of Glenelg, Australia, gent. PEMBROKE COLL., matric. 23 Oct., 1882, aged 19. [15]

Price, Aubrey, s. Dan., of Brecon (town), gent. NEW COLL., matric. 12 March, 1725-6, aged 21; B.A. 1729, M.A. 1733.

Price, Aubrey Charles, s. Aubrey, of Abbots-Stoke, Dorset, cler. NEW COLL., matric. 8 May, 1778, aged 18.

Price, Aubrey Charles, s. Aubrey Charles, of Broadwindsor, Dorset, cler. NEW COLL., matric. 10 Nov., 1806, aged 18; fellow 1806-27, B.A. 1810, M.A. 1815, proctor 1820, vicar of Chesterton, Oxon, 1826, until his death 29 Sep., 1848, father of George Frederick, and of the next named.

Price, Aubrey Charles, 1s. Aubrey, of Chesterton, Oxon, cler. NEW COLL., matric. 22 Dec., 1849, aged 20; fellow 1849-57, B.A. 1853, rector of Rusholme, co. Lancashire, 1856-60, vicar of St. James, Clapham, 1865-82, father of the next named, and of Langford.

Price, Aubrey Charles, 1s. Aubrey Charles, of Rusholm, Lancashire, cler. PEMBROKE COLL., matric. 25 Oct., 1876, aged 18; scholar 1876-81, B.A. 1880, M.A. 1883. [20]

Price, Bartholomew, s. Barthol., of London, arm. TRINITY COLL., matric. 31 Aug., 1763, aged 16; B.C.L. 1770.

Price, Bartholomew, 2s. William, of Coln St. Dennis, co. Gloucester, cler. PEMBROKE COLL., matric. 16 March, 1837, aged 18; scholar 1837-44, B.A. 1840, M.A. 1843, fellow 1844, junior dean 1844, tutor & math. lecturer 1845, bursar 1851, vicegerent 1864, public examiner 1847-8, 1853-5, moderator 1852, etc., proctor 1858, Sedleian professor of natural philosophy 1853, hon. fellow QUEEN'S COLL. 1868, F.R.S., F.R.Astr.S., visitor of Greenwich Observatory.

Price, Bonamy, 1s. Frederick, of St. Peter's Port, Isle of Guernsey, gent. WORCESTER COLL., matric. 14 June, 1825, aged 18; scholar 1828-35, B.A. 1829, M.A. 1832, hon. fellow 1883, Drummond professor of political economy 1868-88, assistant-master Rugby School 1830, hon. LL.D. Edinburgh, died 8 Jan., 1888. See *Rugby School Reg.*, xiv.

Price, Rev. Cadwgan Powell, 2s. Joshua, of Brynbeili, co. Brecon, gent. NON-COLL., matric. 22 Jan., 1876, aged 19; B.A. from LINCOLN COLL. 1879, M.A. 1883.

Price, (Sir) Charles (Bart.), s. Charles, of Jamaica, arm. TRINITY COLL., matric. 21 Oct., 1724, aged 16; created a baronet 16 Jan., 1768, speaker of the Assembly, Jamaica, died 26 July, 1772, brother of Thomas 1728. [25]

Price, Charles, s. Evan, of Llanelly, co. Carmarthen, pleb. JESUS COLL., matric. 12 March, 1735-6, aged 20; B.A. from MERTON COLL. 1739, M.A. 1742.

Price, Charles, s. Charles, of Blount's Court, Oxon, arm. BALLIOL COLL., matric. 3 Feb., 1743-4, aged 16.

Price, (Sir) Charles (Bart.), s. Charles, of Isle of Jamaica, arm. (after baronet). TRINITY COLL., matric. 14 May, 1752, aged 19; 2nd baronet, speaker of the Assembly, Jamaica, 1763, died 18 Oct., 1788. See Foster's *Baronetage.*

Price, Charles, of Blounts Court, Oxon, created D.C.L. 2 July, 1754, father of Charles 1744.

Price, Charles, s. Thomas, of Merriott, Somerset, cler. WADHAM COLL., matric. 30 Oct., 1793, aged 16; fellow until 1821, B.A. 1797, M.A. 1801, B.Med. 1802, D.Med. 1804, fellow College of Physicians 1805, physician Middlesex Hospital 1807-15, physician extraordinary to William IV. 1832, died 8 Sep., 1853. See Munk's *Roll.*, iii. 26. [30]

Price, Charles Cameron, 1s. Charles Parker, of Uxbridge, Middlesex, cler. PEMBROKE COLL., matric. 8 April, 1845, aged 16; B.A. 1849.

Price, Charles Godfrey, o.s. Peter, of Richmond, Surrey, cler. JESUS COLL., matric. 6 June, 1838, aged 17; scholar 1840-50, B.A. 1843, M.A. 1845, bar.-at-law, Inner Temple, 1854, died 11 June, 1882.

Price, Charles James Coverly, 2s. Henry, of St. Martin's, London, arm. BALLIOL COLL., matric. 16 Oct., 1856, aged 18, Blundell scholar 1856-64, B.A. 1861; fellow EXETER COLL. 1864, M.A. 1864, math. lecturer 1864-82, natural science lecturer 1865, junior bursar 1878. See *Boase*, 141.

Price, Charles Parker, o.s. Walter, of Beachley, co. Monmouth, gent. PEMBROKE COLL., matric. 16 Oct., 1820, aged 19; scholar 1821-7, B.A. 1824, M.A. 1827, vicar of Uxbridge, Middlesex, 1827, until his death 4 May, 1872.

Price, Chase, s. John, of Knighton, co. Radnor, arm. CHRIST CHURCH, matric. 24 May, 1749, aged 18; bar.-at-law, Inner Temple, 1757, M.P. Leominster 1759-67, Radnorshire 1768, until his death 28 June, 1777.

Price, Rev. Clement, 2s. Thomas, of Edgbaston, co. Warwick, cler. WORCESTER COLL., matric. 15 Oct., 1877, aged 19; exhibitioner 1877-81, B.A. 1881, M.A. 1884, sub-librarian.

Price, Corbet, s. John, of St. Mary's, Salop, arm. QUEEN'S COLL., matric. 22 May, 1723, aged 17; bar.-at-law, Inner Temple, 1730, buried in the Temple Church, Saturday, 31 Jan., 1735-6.

Price, Cormell, 1s. Samuel Cormell, of Stratford-upon-Avon, co. Warwick, gent. BRASENOSE COLL., matric. 5 July, 1854, aged 18; scholar 1854-8, B.A. 1859, M.A. 1865, B.C.L. 1867. [5]

Price, Cyril, 6s. Thomas, of Selby Oak, near Worcester, cler. WORCESTER COLL., matric. 22 Oct., 1885, aged 19.

Price, Daniel, s. Daniel, of Hereford (city), pleb. BRASENOSE COLL., matric. 20 Oct., 1756, aged 18; B.A. 1760, M.A. 1763, rector of Cradley, co. Hereford, etc., died 23 April, 1794.

Price, Rev. Daniel, s. Daniel, of Cradley, co. Hereford, cler. WORCESTER COLL., matric. 14 Feb., 1804, aged 16; B.A. 1807, M.A. 1810, died in 1817.

Price, David, s. Thomas, of Mydrim, co. Carmarthen, cler. JESUS COLL., matric. 11 May, 1719, aged 18; B.A. from UNIVERSITY COLL. 21 March, 1722-3, M.A. 1728.

Price, David, s. Rice, of Langamarch, co. Brecon, pleb. CHRIST CHURCH, matric. 2 June, 1719, aged 19; B.C.L. 1732. [10]

Price, David, s. Ric., of Mothvey, co. Carmarthen, gent. JESUS COLL., matric. 19 June, 1724, aged 18; B.A. 1728, M.A. 1738, B.D. 1739, vicar of Northleigh, and rector of Aston Clinton, Bucks, 1751, until his death 29 March, 1782.

Price, David, s. William, of Llangrannog, co. Cardigan, pleb. JESUS COLL., matric. 10 April, 1742, aged 19; B.A. 1745.

Price, David, s. Thomas, of Cylynin, co. Merioneth, pleb. JESUS COLL., matric. 26 March, 1743, aged 19; B.A. 1747.

Price, David, s. Thomas, of Abergele, co. Denbigh, cler. JESUS COLL., matric. 14 April, 1764, aged 18; B.A. 1768.

Price, David, 1s. David, of Cilcwm, co. Carmarthen, gent. JESUS COLL., matric. 23 April, 1841, aged 18; B.A. 1845, rector of Little Marcle, co. Hereford, 1865. [15]

Price, Edmund, 1s. Ralph Charles, of London, arm. UNIVERSITY COLL., matric. 11 May, 1854, aged 17; B.A. 1858, M.A. 1862, rector of Farnborough, Berks, 1862, until his death 15 Sep., 1872. See Foster's *Baronetage.*

Price, Edward, s. Edmund, of Clynnog, co. Carnarvon, cler. JESUS COLL., matric. 9 March, 1714-5, aged 18; B.A. from MAGDALEN HALL 6 March, 1718-9.

Price, Edward, s. Hugh, of St. Peter's Bailey, Oxford (city), cler. CHRIST CHURCH, matric. 1 June, 1719, aged 19. See *Alumni West.*, 272.

Price, Edward, s. Thomas, of Guilsfield, co. Montgomery, pleb. JESUS COLL., matric. 27 March, 1750, aged 18; B.A. 1753.

Price, Edward, s. Thomas, of Guilsfield, co. Montgomery, pleb. JESUS COLL., matric. 24 Nov., 1784, aged 19. [20]

Price, Edward, 1s. William, of Calcutta, East Indies, gent. MAGDALEN HALL, matric. 11 Feb., 1830, aged 17; B.A. 1834, M.A. 1836.

Price, Rev. Edward William, 1s. Edward, of Uttoxeter, co. Stafford, arm. ORIEL COLL., matric. 13 April, 1866, aged 18; B.A. 1869, died in 1871.

Price, Edwin Plumer, 2s. Thomas, of York (city), arm. LINCOLN COLL., matric. 13 Nov., 1834, aged 16; B.A. 1839, bar.-at-law, Inner Temple, 1841, Q.C. 1861, recorder of York 1866, a judge of County Courts 1874. See Foster's *Men at the Bar.*

Price, Eugene, s. Rowland, of Dolgelly, co. Merioneth, pleb. JESUS COLL., matric. 3 Nov., 1729, aged 19.

Price, Fowler Boyd, o.s. Fowler, of Huntington, co. Hereford, arm. ORIEL COLL., matric. 14 Nov., 1844, aged 18. [25]

Price, Francis, s. Francis, of Lanady, co. Carmarthen, arm. JESUS COLL., matric. 3 July, 1739, aged 18; B.A. 1743.

Price, Frederick Richard, 3s. John, of Llanrhaiadr, co. Denbigh, arm. QUEEN'S COLL., matric. 7 Oct., 1859, aged 19; B.A. 1866.

Price, George, s. Ralph, of Lyminge, Kent, cler. WADHAM COLL., matric. 12 Dec., 1798, aged 18; fellow until 1827, B.A. 1802, M.A. 1808, vicar of Eastwood, Essex, 1826-57, rector of Fryerning 1826, until his death 9 May, 1861.

Price, George, s. James, of High Wycombe, Bucks, cler. MAGDALEN HALL, matric. 30 May, 1818, aged 17; B.A. 1823, M.A. 1828, rector of Offord Cluny, Hunts, 1834, until his death 10 Feb., 1850.

Price, George, 2s. Barrington, of Langham Place, Middlesex, arm. TRINITY COLL., matric. 2 Nov., 1819, aged 18; B.A. from ST. ALBAN HALL 1824. [30]

Price, George Bowen Jordan, 1s. George, of Haverfordwest, co. Pembroke, arm. WADHAM COLL., matric. 21 Oct., 1825, aged 19.

Price, George Frederick, 2s. Aubrey Charles, of Chesterton, Oxon, cler. NEW COLL., matric. 7 Aug., 1851, aged 19; fellow 1851-73, B.A. 1855, M.A. 1859, B. & D.D. 1880, sub-warden 1864, rector of St. John-de-Madder-market, Norwich, 1863-72, and of Little Sampford, Essex, 1872-8, vicar and lecturer of Romford 1878-81, chaplain to Duke of Abercorn 1865-85, rector of Whitburn, co. Durham, 1881.

Price, George Herbert, 3s. Henry Stephens, of Somerstown, Middlesex, gent. BRASENOSE COLL., matric. 19 Oct., 1882, aged 19; exhibitioner 1882.

Price, George Winter, o.s. George, of Stepney, Middlesex, arm. EXETER COLL., matric. 13 June, 1850, aged 19; scholar MAGDALEN HALL 1851, died Nov., 1865.

Price, Griffith, s. Thomas, of Llangevelach, co. Glamorgan, arm. JESUS COLL., matric. 11 Nov., 1735, aged 16. [35]

Price, Henry, s. Henry, of Crutched Friars, London, pleb. CHRIST CHURCH, matric. 6 March, 1718-9, aged 16.

Price, Henry, s. Thomas, of Birmingham, co. Warwick, cler. CHRIST CHURCH, matric. 22 May, 1799, aged 17; demy MAGDALEN COLL. 1799-1815, B.A. 1804, M.A. 1806. See *Bloxam*, vii. 141.

Price, Rev. Henry Courtenay, 1s. Henry Stephen, of Chatham, Kent, gent. WORCESTER COLL., matric. 29 Oct., 1877, aged 18; B.A. 1882.

Price, Henry George, of TRINITY COLL., Dublin (B.A. 1842, LL.B. & LL.D. 1860); adm. 'ad eundem' 21 June, 1860.

Price, Henry Hugh, 1s. Hugh, of Bangor, co. Carnarvon, cler. WORCESTER COLL., matric. 13 Nov., 1845, aged 19; B.A. 1850, M.A. 1852, vicar of Ash, Salop, 1852-71. [40]

Price, Rev. Henry Malme, 3s. James, of Oxford, gent. BRASENOSE COLL., matric. 31 Jan., 1870, aged 18; B.A. 1874, M.A. 1876, died 29 March, 1878.

Price, Henry Samuel Benbow, 2s. Edward, of Uttoxeter, co. Stafford, arm. MERTON COLL., matric. 17 Oct., 1868, aged 18; postmaster 1868-73, B.A. 1873, bar.-at-law, Lincoln's Inn, 1876. See Foster's *Men at the Bar.*

Price, Henry Tilley, 2s. Hugh William, of Beaumaris, pleb. JESUS COLL., matric. 29 Oct., 1835, aged 15; servitor, B.A. 1840, M.A. 1846, sometime classical master Cheltenham College, rector of Elkstone, Cheltenham, 1877.

Price, Herbert, 3s. Thomas, of Birmingham, cler. QUEEN'S COLL., matric. 21 Oct., 1879, aged 19; scholar 1879-83, B.A. 1883.

Price, Herbert Chase Green-, 2s. Richard, of Knighton, Radnor, arm. (after baronet). BRASENOSE COLL., matric. 5 June, 1873, aged 18; B.A. 1878, M.A. 1881, curate in charge of Norton, Radnor, 1883-6, vicar 1886. See Foster's *Baronetage* & *Eton School Lists.*

Price, Herbert Coram, 1s. John, of Norwich, gent. ST. ALBAN HALL, matric. 21 April, 1874, aged 23. **[5]**

Price, Howel, s. Watkin, of Devynnock, co. Brecon, pleb. JESUS COLL., matric. 22 March, 1777, aged 18; B.A. 1780.

Price, Hugh, s. Rees, of Llanvachrath, co. Merioneth, pleb. JESUS COLL., matric. 26 March, 1731, aged 19; B.A. from BRASENOSE COLL. 1734.

Price, Hugh, s. John, of Llanynis, co. Brecon, gent. BALLIOL COLL., matric. 13 March, 1743-4, aged 16; B.A. 22 Feb., 1748-9.

Price, Hugh, s. Roger, of Llangamarch, co. Brecon, pleb. JESUS COLL., matric. 3 April, 1754, aged 17; B.A. 1757, M.A. 1766, of Castle Madoc, co. Brecon, rector of Rottendon and of Little Ilford, Essex, died 13 June, 1803, father of Hugh 1805.

Price, Hugh, s. Meshech, of Dolgelley, co. Merioneth, gent. JESUS COLL., matric. 6 Dec., 1804, aged 20; B.A. 1808, M.A. 1813, head-master Friars School, Bangor, junior vicar of Bangor 1838, until his death 31 Oct., 1850. **[10]**

Price, Hugh, s. Hugh, of Coln Rogers, co. Gloucester, cler. BRASENOSE COLL., matric. 20 June, 1805, aged 19; of Castle Madoc, co. Brecon, high sheriff, 1815, died 29 Aug., 1856.

Price, Hugh, o.s. Hugh, of Newton Toney, Wilts, cler. EXETER COLL., matric. 29 Jan., 1846, aged 18; B.A. from NEW COLL. 1851.

Price, Hugh, 4s. Thomas, of Edgbaston, co. Warwick, cler. WORCESTER COLL., matric. 19 Oct., 1882, aged 21; B.A. 1887.

Price, Hugh Bankes-, 1s. William, of Lampeter, co. Cardigan, gent. CHRIST CHURCH, matric. 10 Oct., 1884, aged 19, scholar 1884; brother of Llewellyn.

Price, Hugh Brocas, 3s. William Francis, of Monmouth, D.Med. MAGDALEN COLL., matric. 16 Oct., 1875, aged 20; demy 1874-6, brother of Llewellyn. **[15]**

Price, Rev. Hugh Pendrell, 1s. Thomas, of Cratfield, Suffolk, cler. ORIEL COLL., matric. 16 Oct., 1863, aged 19; B.A. 1867, M.A. 1870, assistant-master King's School, Sherborne, 1868.

Price, James, s. Ellis, of Holywell, co. Flint, cler. CHRIST CHURCH, matric. 2 April, 1734, aged 19; B.A. 1737, M.A. 1740.

Price, James, s. Thomas, of Llanfechan, co. Brecon, pleb. WADHAM COLL., matric. 15 March, 1743-4, aged 18; B.A. from CHRIST CHURCH 1747.

Price, James, s. James, of Bedwis, co. Monmouth, gent. ORIEL COLL., matric. 30 May, 1775, aged 18; rector of Cerrig-y-Druidion 1784, rector of Llanfechan, co. Montgomery, 1796, until his death 13 Nov., 1850, aged 94.

Price, James, s. James, of Chipping Wycombe, Bucks, cler. MERTON COLL., matric. 11 Dec., 1781, aged 18; B.A. 1785, M.A. 1788, vicar of High (or Chipping) Wycombe, Bucks, 1784, and rector of Great Munden, Herts, 1817, until his death 16 June, 1846. **[20]**

Price, James, s. John, of Amlwch, Isle of Anglesey, gent. JESUS COLL., matric. 2 May, 1818, aged 19.

Price, James, 6s. John, of Llandovery, co. Carmarthen, gent. MAGDALEN HALL, matric. 30 June, 1842, aged 23.

Price, James Higginbotham, s. James Higginbotham, of London, gent. MAGDALEN HALL, matric. 24 April, 1773, aged 15; created M.A. 21 Nov., 1777 (as J. H.), and also D.Med. 2 July, 1782 (as J. H. P.), then of Guildford, Surrey, F.R.S., assumed the additional name of PRICE. See *O.H.S.*, ix. 221.

Price, James Mansel, 1s. James, of Oxford (city), gent. ALL SOULS' COLL., matric. 3 Dec., 1845, aged 17; bible clerk 1845-9, B.A. 1849, M.A. 1852, vicar of Cuddington 1855.

Price, James Victor, 2s. Benjamin, of St. Martin's, Birmingham, gent. PEMBROKE COLL., matric. 5 Dec., 1851, aged 18; B.A. 1857, M.A. 1865. **[25]**

Price, John, s. John, of Rodstock, Somerset, cler. EXETER COLL., matric. 31 March, 1715, aged 18.

Price, John, s. John, of Ruthland, co. Flint, pleb. JESUS COLL., matric. 4 April, 1715, aged 17.

Price, John, s. Thomas, of Dremerchion, co. Flint, gent. JESUS COLL., matric. 27 Feb., 1716-7, aged 18.

Price, John, B.A. from JESUS COLL. 27 Oct., 1718.

Price, John, s. John, of St. Mary-de-Crypt, Gloucester (city), gent. PEMBROKE COLL., matric. 18 Nov., 1719, aged 18; B.A. from JESUS COLL. 1722. **[30]**

Price, John, s. Thomas, of Llangollen, co. Denbigh, gent. JESUS COLL., matric. 9 May, 1722, aged 16; B.A. 7 March, 1725-6, M.A. 1728, B.D. 1737, D.D. 1745.

Price, John, s. William, of Llanrhayadr, co. Denbigh, cler. JESUS COLL., matric. 1 June, 1731, aged 19.

Price, John, s. Ellis, of Skieviog, co. Flint, pleb. QUEEN'S COLL., matric. 9 April, 1736, aged 19; B.A. 1740.

Price, John, s. William, of Kidwelly, co. Carmarthen, pleb. JESUS COLL., matric. 8 June, 1736, aged 18; B.A. 20 March, 1739-40, M.A. 1743. **[34]**

Price, John, s. Robert, of Landegla, co. Denbigh, cler. JESUS COLL., matric. 26 March, 1754, aged 19; B.A. 1757, M.A. 1760, B.D. 1768, Bodley's librarian 1768-1813, vicar of Llangattock, co. Brecon, rector of Wollaston, and Alvington, co. Gloucester, died 11 Aug., 1813. See *Gent.'s Mag.*, 1813, ii. p. 400.

Price, John, s. John, of Penzance, Cornwall, arm. TRINITY COLL., matric. 18 Jan., 1757, aged 18.

Price, John, s. William, of Mothvey, co. Carmarthen, gent. JESUS COLL., matric. 30 Oct., 1770, aged 20.

Price, John, s. John, of Brecon (town), pleb. JESUS COLL., matric. 24 Jan., 1771.

Price, John, s. Samuel, of Coyty, co. Glamorgan, arm. JESUS COLL., matric. 22 Feb., 1771, aged 20.

Price, John, B.A. from JESUS COLL. 20 Feb., 1776.

Price, John, s. John, of Gwenddwr, co. Brecon, pleb. JESUS COLL., matric. 26 March, 1779, aged 19; B.A. from PEMBROKE COLL. 1783. See *Gent.'s Mag.*, 1829, i. 186. **[41]**

Price, John, s. David, of Llanelian, co. Denbigh, cler. JESUS COLL., matric. 8 April, 1783, aged 19; B.A. & M.A. 1801.

Price, John, y.s. Thomas, of Devynnock, co. Brecon, gent. JESUS COLL., matric. 29 Nov., 1820, aged 25; B.A. 1824, M.A. 1829.

Price, John, 3s. Rose, of Gulval, Cornwall, baronet. BRASENOSE COLL., matric. 21 May, 1827, aged 19; inspector-general penal department, murdered by convicts in Victoria 27 March, 1857. See Foster's *Baronetage.*

Price, John, 1s. John, of Clocasnog, co. Denbigh, gent. JESUS COLL., matric. 21 May, 1831, aged 19; scholar 1832-7, B.A. 1835, M.A. 1837. **[45]**

Price, John, 7s. Aubrey, of Wroughton, Wilts, cler. NEW COLL., matric. 5 Nov., 1834, aged 22; fellow 1834-45, B.A. 1839, brother of Rice 1826.

Pryce, John, 2s. Hugh, of Dolsalley, co. Monmouth, gent. JESUS COLL., matric. 11 Nov., 1847, aged 19; B.A. 1851, M.A. 1863, perp. curate Glanogwen 1856-64, vicar of Bangor 1864-80, rector of Trefedraeth 1880, canon of Bangor 1884, and archdeacon 1887, altered the spelling of his name.

Price, Rev. John, 3s. Thomas, of Llanganten, co. Brecon, gent. JESUS COLL., matric. 10 March, 1853, aged 18; B.A. 1857, M.A. 1865.

Price, John Alfred Parry, 2s. Howell, of Cyllybebill, co. Glamorgan, cler. QUEEN'S COLL., matric. 3 Nov., 1871, aged 18; B.A. 1875, B.Med. 1882, D.Med. 1885.

Price, John Arthur, o.s. John, of Shrewsbury, gent. BALLIOL COLL., matric. 18 Oct., 1881, aged 19; B.A. 1886. [5]

Price, John Charles, s. John, of Pall Mall, Westminster, arm. BRASENOSE COLL., matric. 26 Oct., 1764, aged 17.

Price, John Davis, s. Thomas, of Builth, co. Brecon, arm. JESUS COLL., matric. 12 Dec., 1806, aged 23.

Price, John Gilbert, 6s. Nicholas, of Rollston, co. Hereford, gent. JESUS COLL., matric. 14 June, 1826, aged 18.

Price, John Henry, 1s. David, of Bognor, Sussex, cler. ST. MARY HALL, matric. 24 Jan., 1877, aged 18; B.A. 1881, M.A. 1885, classical lecturer 1885.

Price, John Rice, s. Rice, of Llanfihangel-Bryn-Pabnan, co. Brecon, cler. WADHAM COLL., matric. 13 Oct., 1804, aged 19; B.A. 1808 (? died curate of Stonehouse, co. Gloucester, in 1826). See *Gent.'s Mag.*, 1849, i. 212. [10]

Price, Joseph, 2s. David, of All Saints, London, gent. MERTON COLL., matric. 14 March, 1828, aged 18.

Price, Langford Lovell Frederick Rice, 2s. Aubrey Charles, of London, cler. TRINITY COLL., matric. 15 Oct., 1881, aged 19, scholar 1881-5, B.A. 1885; fellow and treasurer ORIEL COLL. 1888, M.A. 1888.

Price, Lewis, s. John, of Conway, co. Carnarvon, cler. JESUS COLL., matric. 10 Feb., 1740-1, aged 18; B.A. 1744.

Price, Lewis Herbert, 4s. David, of Titley, co. Hereford, cler. NON-COLL., matric. 13 Jan., 1883, aged 19; B.A. from ST. MARY HALL 1886.

Price, Llewelyn Bankes, 2s. William, of Dolan, co. Cardigan, gent. JESUS COLL., matric. 20 Oct., 1886, aged 18; scholar 1886, brother of Hugh Bankes. [15]

Price, Lloyd John, 1s. John, of Llandissilio, co. Anglesea, gent. JESUS COLL., matric. 9 April, 1829, aged 19.

Price, Marmaduke Gwynne, 1s. Rees, of Brecon, cler. NON-COLL., matric. 17 Oct., 1881, aged 20; B.A. from WORCESTER COLL. 1885.

Price, Miles, s. Thomas, of Gloucester (city), gent. WADHAM COLL., matric. 15 Nov., 1774, aged 18.

Price, Morgan, s. Lewis, of Prignant, co. Cardigan, pleb. CHRIST CHURCH, matric. 10 Dec., 1768, aged 21; B.A. 1772, M.A. 1775 (? rector of Talachddu, co. Brecon, 1814, until his death in 1833).

Price, Owen Talbot, 1s. Charles John, of Surbiton, Surrey, gent. EXETER COLL., matric. 21 Oct., 1886, aged 18. [20]

Price, Peter, s. Robert, of Yspytty, co. Denbigh, gent. JESUS COLL., matric. 23 March, 1782, aged 19.

Price, Peter, s. Peter, of Yspytty, co. Denbigh, cler. JESUS COLL., matric. 17 Dec., 1813, aged 20; scholar 1817-22, B.A. 1817, M.A. 1820, rector of Erbistock, co. Denbigh, 1852, until his death 20 Aug., 1875.

Priceg Philip Richard, 1s. Philip, of Llantillio-Bertholey, co. Monmouth, gent. JESUS COLL., matric. 19 April, 1858, aged 18; B.A. 1862, M.A. 1864.

Price, Ralph, s. Bartholomew, of Wantage, Berks, gent. TRINITY COLL., matric. 7 Dec., 1733, aged 18; B.A. 1737.

Price, Ralph, s. Ralph, of Farnborough, Berks, cler. TRINITY COLL., matric. 11 May, 1763, aged 17; B.A. 1767, rector, vicar (and patron) of Lyminge, perp. curate of Paddlesworth and Stanford, Kent, died 7 July, 1811. See Foster's *Baronetage*. [25]

Price, Ralph, s. Ralph, of Lyminge, Kent, cler. TRINITY COLL., matric. 22 Jan., 1796, aged 17; B.A. 1800, M.A. 1803, rector, vicar (and patron) of Lyminge, died 9 July, 1863. See Foster's *Baronetage*.

Price, Randal Rose, 1s. George, of Dursany, co. Meath (Ireland), arm. TRINITY COLL., matric. 1 Dec., 1858, aged 18; of the Indian Civil Service 1860. See Foster's *Baronetage*.

Price, Rees Charles, 1s. Rees Charles, of Lympstone, Devon, gent. ST. EDMUND HALL, matric. 25 Oct., 1871, aged 19; B.A. 1876, M.A. 1878, has held various curacies since 1875.

Price, Rice, s. Rice, of Llanwair, co. Carmarthen, pleb. JESUS COLL., matric. 25 Feb., 1714-5, aged 18.

Price, Rice, s. Dan., of St. John's, Brecon (town), gent. NEW COLL., matric. 29 Dec., 1719, aged 18; founder's-kin fellow 1719-48, B.C.L. 1724, vacated his fellowship on being elected fellow of Winchester College in 1748, subsequently vicar of Andover, and then of Portsea. [30]

Price, Rice, s. John, of Llanavan, co. Brecknock, gent. PEMBROKE COLL., matric. 14 Feb., 1740-1, aged 24.

Price, Rev. Rice, 5s. Aubrey Charles, of Wroughton, Wilts, cler. NEW COLL., matric. 21 Jan., 1826, aged 19; fellow 1826-45, B.A. 1829, M.A. 1833, dean of arts 1834, bursar 1835, dean of divinity 1836, died 30 Nov., 1845, brother of John 1834.

Price, Richard, s. Thomas, of Llangollen, co. Denbigh, gent. JESUS COLL., matric. 24 March, 1715-6, aged 18; B.A. 1719, M.A. 1722.

Price, Richard, s. Henry, of Llangadwalladr, co. Anglesea, pleb. JESUS COLL., matric. 12 March, 1717-8, aged 20.

Price, Richard, s. John, of Mivord, co. Montgomery, gent. PEMBROKE COLL., matric. 15 March, 1724-5, aged 19; B.A. 1728. [35]

Price, Richard, s. John, of Richmond, Surrey, doctor. ST. JOHN'S COLL., matric. 24 March, 1724-5, aged 17; B.A. 12 Feb., 1728-9 (? M.P. Sudbury 1734-41).

Price, Richard, s. Richard, of Llandevilog, co. Carmarthen, pleb. JESUS COLL., matric. 18 May, 1727, aged 18; B.A. 1730.

Price, Richard, s. Richard, of Coychurch, co. Glamorgan, gent. JESUS COLL., matric. 6 Nov., 1734, aged 18; B.A. 1738, M.A. 1741.

Price, Richard, s. Henry, of Pembroke (town), pleb. JESUS COLL., matric. 21 March, 1738-9, aged 18.

Price, Richard, of BRASENOSE COLL., created M.A. 26 April, 1757 (*Acts Book*). See also PRYCE. [40]

Price, Richard, s. Richard, of Knighton, co. Radnor, arm. UNIVERSITY COLL., matric. 17 Nov., 1790, aged 17; B.A. 1794, lieut.-colonel Radnor militia, M.P. Radnor 1799-1847, died 10 April, 1861.

Price, Richard, s. Richard, of Ruthin, co. Denbigh, arm. MERTON COLL., matric. 9 Feb., 1799, aged 18.

Price, Richard, s. Thomas, of Llanfair-in-Builth, co. Brecon, arm. JESUS COLL., matric. 6 Dec., 1803, aged 17.

Price, Richard Edward, 2s. William, of Llangefni, Isle of Anglesey, cler. JESUS COLL., matric. 22 March, 1854, aged 20; B.A. 1858, M.A. 1860, rector of Llanymenech, Salop, 1876.

Price, Richard Henry, o.s. John, of Bristol, arm. CORPUS CHRISTI COLL., matric. 28 Jan., 1847, aged 17; exhibitioner 1847-52, died 2 May, 1851. [45]

rice, Richard John, 1s. Richard Watkin, of Llanfawr, co. Merioneth, arm. BRASENOSE COLL., matric. 14 Jan., 1822, aged 18; B.A. 1825.

rice, Richard John Lloyd, 1s. Richard, of Rhiwlas, co. Merioneth, arm. CHRIST CHURCH, matric. 16 Oct., 1861, aged 18; of Rhiwlas and Rhiwaedog, co. Merioneth, high sheriff 1868.

rice, Robert, s. John, of Yspytty, co. Denbigh, pleb. JESUS COLL., matric. 15 March, 1722-3, aged 18; B.A. 1726.

rice, Robert, s. Hugh, of Beaumaris, co. Anglesea, pleb. JESUS COLL., matric. 10 Feb., 1741-2, aged 18; B.A. from ST. MARY HALL 4 March, 1745-46.

rice, Robert, s. Thomas, of Denbigh (town), pleb. JESUS COLL., matric. 24 May, 1748, aged 18; B.A. from ALL SOULS' COLL. 1752. **[5]**

rice, Robert, s. Robert, of Yazor, co. Hereford, arm. CHRIST CHURCH, matric. 16 Dec., 1765, aged 17; B.C.L. from ALL SOULS' COLL. 1772, D.C.L. 1782, chaplain-in-ordinary to the King, canon of Salisbury 1785, and preb. of Durham 1795, died 7 April, 1823.

rice, (Sir) Robert (Bart.) s. Uvedale, of Yazor, co. Hereford, arm. (after baronet). CHRIST CHURCH, matric. 24 Oct., 1805, aged 19; 2nd baronet, M.P. Herefordshire 1818-41, and Hereford 1845, until his death 5 Nov., 1857, father of Uvedale T. S.

rice, Robert Albert, o.s. Robert, of Bristol, gent. NON-COLL., matric. 24 May, 1877, aged 19; a student of Inner Temple 1882.

rice, Robert Cholmeley, 5s. Barrington, of Langham Place, London, arm. CHRIST CHURCH, matric. 15 Dec., 1835, aged 18; student 1835-47, B.A. 1839, M.A. 1842, rector of Childe-Okeford, Dorset, 1868, until his death 17 Jan., 1873, brother of Thomas 1831.

rice, Roger, s. Ellis, of Skeiviog, co. Flint, cler. ST. MARY HALL, matric. 11 March, 1739-40, aged 17.

Price, (Sir) Rose (Bart.) s. John, of Penzance, Cornwall, arm. MAGDALEN COLL., matric. 5 Feb., 1787, aged 18; created a baronet 30 May, 1815, died 29 Sep., 1834. See Foster's *Baronetage*. **[11]**

Price, Rose Lambart, s. Rose, of Ampton, Suffolk, baronet. CHRIST CHURCH, matric. 16 Oct., 1817, aged 18; an officer royal marines, died 15 Jan., 1826. See Foster's *Baronetage, Eton School Lists, & Gent.'s Mag.*, 1826, i. 368.

Price, Salusbury, s. Thomas, of Westbury, Bucks, arm. TRINITY COLL., matric. 14 Dec., 1744, aged 19, B.A. 1748; M.A. from ALL SOULS' COLL. 1752, B.D. 1759, D.D. 1763, vicar of Little Marlow, Bucks, and rector of Buckland, Surrey, 1775.

Price, Rev. Salisbury James Murray, 2s. Campbell Knollys, of Haughend, near Dunkeld, Scotland, arm. PEMBROKE COLL., matric. 23 Oct., 1879, aged 21; B.A. 1884, M.A. 1886.

Price, Thelwall, s. Robert, of Ruthin, co. Denbigh, arm. QUEEN'S COLL., matric. 24 Nov., 1747, aged 17. **[15]**

Price, Theophilus, pleb. JESUS COLL., matric. 10 June, 1736.

Price, Thomas, s. David, of Yspytty, co. Carnarvon, pleb. JESUS COLL., matric. 18 March, 1722-3, aged 17; B.A. 1 March, 1726-7.

Price, Thomas, s. William, of Llanrhayader, co. Denbigh, cler. WADHAM COLL., matric. 31 March, 1726, aged 18.

Price, Thomas, s. Charles, of Kingston, Isle of Jamaica, gent. QUEEN'S COLL., matric. 8 April, 1728, aged 18; brother of Charles 1724. See Foster's *Baronetage*.

Price, Thomas, s. Thomas, of Landfoyet, co. Monmouth, arm. CHRIST CHURCH matric. 12 June, 1730, aged 17. **[20]**

Price, Thomas, s. Edward, of Milton, Northants, gent. LINCOLN COLL., matric. 24 March, 1742-3, aged 18; B.A. 1746.

Price, Rev. Thomas, s. David, of Bewdley, co. Worcester, cler. WADHAM COLL., matric. 8 April, 1747, aged 17; B.A. 1750, M.A. 1753, died a fellow 8 Sep., 1790.

Price, Thomas, s. William, of Hope Bagot, Salop, pleb. HERTFORD COLL., matric. 31 May, 1750, aged 18; B.A. from MAGDALEN COLL. 1754, M.A. 1756, usher Magdalen College School 1752-64, master of Lichfield Grammar School 1764-75, rector of Caldecote, co. Warwick, head-master Free Grammar School, Birmingham, 1775, until his death 12 Jan., 1797. See *Bloxam*, iii. 237.

Price, Thomas, s. Charles, of Porsett, co. Glamorgan, arm. JESUS COLL., matric. 15 March, 1769, aged 17; B.A. 1772, M.A. 1775, vicar of Merriott 1775, and rector of Fifehead and Swell 1782, until his death in 1832, father of William 1806.

Price, Thomas, s. Hugh, of Brecknock (town), cler. WORCESTER COLL., matric. 23 Oct., 1782, aged 18 (? vicar of St. Mellons with Llanedarn, co. Monmouth, 1808, until death, 28 Feb., 1846, aged 82). **[25]**

Price, Thomas, s. Richard, of Llansawell, co. Carmarthen, pleb. JESUS COLL., matric. 13 Dec., 1784, aged 18; B.A. 1788.

Price, Thomas, s. Thomas, of Lichfield, co. Stafford, cler. CHRIST CHURCH, matric. 3 May, 1792, aged 17; B.A. 1796, M.A. 1799, rector of Bredicot, co. Worcester, 1821, and of Enville 1824, until his death 4 Jan., 1837.

Price, Thomas, s. John, of Kewstocke, Somerset, cler. WADHAM COLL., matric. 22 Jan., 1802, aged 18.

Price, Thomas, s. David, of Aberystwith, co. Cardigan, cler. ST. EDMUND HALL, matric. 24 April, 1804, aged 27.

Price, Thomas, s. Walter, of Ystradgunlais, co. Brecon, gent. JESUS COLL., matric. 2 June, 1808, aged 20. See *Gent.'s Mag.*, 1847, i. 447. **[30]**

Price, Thomas, s. Rees, of St. Martin's, London, gent. ST. EDMUND HALL, matric. 14 Jan., 1812, aged 23; B.A. 1815, M.A. 1818 (? rector of Llanrothall, co. Hereford, 1826, until death 17 Sep., 1848).

Price, Thomas, s. Thomas, of Worcester (city), arm. TRINITY COLL., matric. 4 May, 1814, aged 19; B.A. 1818.

Price, Thomas, s. Watkin, of Cadoxton, co. Glamorgan, cler. JESUS COLL., matric. 14 March, 1818, aged 19; scholar 1818-21, B.A. 1821, fellow 1821-41, M.A. 1824, B.D. 1832, vice-principal 1833, Greek lecturer 1836, libarian 1837, junior bursar 1839.

Price, Thomas, 3s. Joseph, of Monmouth (town), arm. EXETER COLL., matric. 27 Jan., 1819, aged 17; B.A. 1823, M.A. 1827.

Price, Thomas, 3s. Barrington, of Sparsholt, Berks, arm. CHRIST CHURCH, matric. 1 July, 1831, aged 18; B.A. 1835, brother of Robert Cholmeley. **[35]**

Price, Thomas, 1s. Benjamin, of Edgbaston, co. Warwick, gent. MAGDALEN HALL, matric. 30 March, 1844, aged 18; B.A. 1847, M.A. 1851, assistant-master King Edward's School, Birmingham, 1847-62, vicar of St. Mary, Selly Oak, Birmingham, 1862.

Price, Thomas, 3s. David, of Trallong, co. Brecon, gent. JESUS COLL., matric. 14 March, 1850, aged 19; B.A. 1853, M.A. 1856, chaplain of Rûg Chapel, Merioneth, 1862-8, vicar of Prestatyn 1868.

Price, Thomas, 2s. Thomas, of Basendon, co. Gloucester, cler. ST. EDMUND HALL, matric. 30 April, 1870, aged 18.

Price, Rev. Thomas, 1s. Thomas, of Edgbaston, co. Warwick, cler. QUEEN'S COLL., matric. 23 Oct., 1875, aged 18; B.A. 1879, M.A. 1883.

Price, Thomas Charles, 1s. Thomas, of Bulmer, Yorks, arm. BRASENOSE COLL., matric. 29 Oct., 1835, aged 19; postmaster MERTON COLL. 1836-9, B.A. 1839, M.A. 1842, rector of Holtby, Yorks, 1845-51, vicar of St. Augustine the Less, Bristol, 1851, until his death 8 Nov., 1885.

Price, Thomas Phillips, o.s. William, of Llanarth, co. Monmouth, cler. UNIVERSITY COLL., matric. 16 Jan., 1863, aged 18; B.A. & M.A. 1869, of Triley Court, co. Monmouth, high sheriff 1882, bar.-at-law, Inner Temple, 1869, M.P. North Monmouthshire since Dec., 1885, captain royal Monmouthshire engineer militia 1879-83. See Foster's *Men at the Bar.*

Price, (Sir) Uvedale (Bart.), s. Robert, of Yazor, co. Hereford, arm. CHRIST CHURCH, matric. 13 Dec., 1763, aged 17; created a baronet 12 Feb., 1828, died 14 Sep., 1829, brother of Robert 1765, and father of Robert 1805.

Price, Uvedale Thomas (Shudd), o.s. Robert, of Salisbury (city), doctor. CHRIST CHURCH, matric. 15 Oct., 1823, aged 18; B.A. 1827, M.A. 1830, died unmarried. See *Eton School Lists.*

Price, Rev. Walter Lloyd, 4s. John Lloyd, of Llanllawddog, co. Carmarthen, arm. JESUS COLL., matric. 11 June, 1863, aged 18; scholar 1864-8, B.A. 1868, M.A. 1870. **[5]**

Price, Wilfred Thomas Rokeby, 2s. Hall Rokeby, of London, arm. NEW COLL., matric. 16 Jan., 1875, aged 19; B.A. 1879.

Price, William, s. Charles, of Michael Church, co. Hereford, pleb. BALLIOL COLL., matric. 3 Nov., 1726, aged 19; B.A. 1730.

Price, William, s. William, of St. George's, Bloomsbury, London, arm. JESUS COLL., matric. 25 Nov., 1735, aged 18.

Price, William, s. William, of Weobley, co. Hereford, cler. WADHAM COLL., matric. 10 Oct., 1739, aged 17; B.A. 1743, M.A. 1748.

Price, William, s. John, of Epsom, Surrey, cler. CHRIST CHURCH, matric. 17 Dec., 1751, aged 18; B.A. 1755, M.A. 1758. **[10]**

Price, William, s. David, of Minehead, Somerset, pleb. BALLIOL COLL., matric. 22 May, 1760, aged 18; B.A. 1764.

Price, William, s. Charles, of Bedwas, co. Monmouth, arm. JESUS COLL., matric. 17 March, 1779, aged 18; B.A. 1783, M.A. 1785.

Price, William, of TRINITY COLL., Cambridge (B.A. 1774, M.A. 1777), s. William, of Westminster, arm. HERTFORD COLL., incorp. 9 March, 1782, aged 29; D.C.L. 18 March, 1782, bar.-at-law, Lincoln's Inn, 1780.

Price, William, s. William Henry, of Wantage, Berks, gent. PEMBROKE COLL., matric. 4 Nov., 1799, aged 15; B.A. 1803, fellow, M.A. 1806, J.P. and tax commissioner co. Gloucester, chairman of the Board of Guardians, rector of Coln St. Dennis, co. Gloucester, 1809, and of Farnborough, Berks, 1815, until his death 13 April, 1860.

Price, William. QUEEN'S COLL., 1809. See MYDDELTON. **[15]**

Price, William, 2s. James, of Oxford (city), gent. CHRIST CHURCH, matric. 31 May, 1849, aged 18; chorister 1840-6, servitor 1849-53, B.A. 1853, M.A. 1856, chaplain 1853-74, schoolmaster 1858-74, vicar of Burton Abbots (or Black Bourton), Oxon, 1874.

Price, William, 3s. Aubrey Charles, of Chesterton, Oxon, cler. NEW COLL., matric. 8 June, 1854, aged 19; fellow 1854-8.

Price, William Arthur, 2s. Richard, Watkin, of Llanfaur, co. Merioneth, arm. BRASENOSE COLL., matric. 6 May, 1824, aged 18; B.A. 1828.

Price, William Arthur, 1s. Bartholomew, of Oxford, cler. NEW COLL., matric. 11 Oct., 1878, aged 18; scholar 1878-83, B.A. 1882, M.A. 1885.

Price, William Brinton, 1s. William Preston, of Margate, Kent, D.Med. CHRIST CHURCH, matric. 15 Oct., 1886, aged 18. **[20]**

Price, William George, 1s. William James, of Newport, Essex, gent. QUEEN'S COLL., matric. 4 Feb., 1884, aged 19; B.Mus. 1886.

Price, William Henry, 1s. William, of Coln St. Dennis, co. Gloucester, cler. PEMBROKE COLL., matric. 3 Nov., 1831, aged 18; scholar 1831-40, B.A. 1835, M.A. 1838, fellow 1840-59, bursar 1855, curate of Farnborough, Berks, 1836-61, Fawley, Berks, 1838-55, rector of Somerton, Oxon, 1861-74, and of Coln St. Dennis 1874.

Price, Rev. William Henry, scholar ST. JOHN'S COLL., Cambridge (B.A. 1880, M.A. 1883); incorp. from TRINITY COLL. 23 Feb., 1888.

Price, William Hughes Bankes-, 1s. John, of Marshfield, co. Glamorgan, cler. JESUS COLL., matric. 29 Jan., 1881, aged 19; B.A. 1884.

Price, William James, 2s. Thomas, of Crickhowell, co. Brecon, gent. JESUS COLL., matric. 14 June, 1860, aged 17; scholar 1861-5, B.A. 1866, M.A. 1868, held various curacies 1870-9, vicar of Lilleshall, Salop, 1879. **[25]**

Price, Rev. William Thomas, s. Thomas, of Merriott, Somerset, cler. WADHAM COLL., matric. 27 Oct., 1806, aged 16; B.A. 1811, M.A. 1813, of Hinton St. George, Somerset, died 30 Oct., 1838.

Prichard, Albert Herman, 4s. James Cowles, of Bristol, D.Med. MERTON COLL., matric. 8 June, 1849, aged 18; postmaster 1849-53, B.A. 1855, held various curacies 1867-78.

Prichard, Benjamin, s. Herbert, of Frieden (Friern Barnet), Herts, cler. ST. ALBAN HALL, matric. 5 March, 1736-7, aged 19.

Prichard, Rev. Benjamin, s. Benjamin, of Ewelme, Oxon, cler. BRASENOSE COLL., matric. 10 April, 1742, aged 21; demy MAGDALEN COLL. 1744-7, B.A. 1745, M.A. 1749, died 8 Nov., 1777, M.I. Ewelme. See *Bloxam*, vi. 264.

Prichard, Charles (Arthur), s. Charles, of London, arm. MERTON COLL., matric. 14 Oct., 1815, aged 18; postmaster 1815-8. **[30]**

Prichard, Charles Collwyn, 1s. Charles Edward, of Mitton, co. Worcester, gent. BRASENOSE COLL., matric. 15 Oct., 1864, aged 18; scholar 1864-8, B.A. 1869, M.A. 1871, vicar of Whalley, Lancashire, since 1881.

Prichard, Constantine Estlin, 3s. James, of Bristol, D.Med. BALLIOL COLL., matric. 25 Nov., 1837, aged 17; scholar 1837-42, B.A. 1841, fellow 1842-54, M.A. 1845, catechetical lecturer, vice-principal Wells College 1847, preb. of Wells 1852, rector of South Luffenham, co. Lincoln, 1854, until his death 6 Oct., 1869.

Prichard, David. s. John, of Llangadmore, co. Cardigan, pleb. JESUS COLL., matric. 8 May, 1730, aged 18.

Prichard, David, s. David, of Llangollen, co. Denbigh, pleb. JESUS COLL., matric. 14 Oct., 1748, aged 17; B.A. 1752, M.A. 1755 (as PRITCHARD).

Prichard, Evan, s. Evan, of Llantrissent, co. Glamorgan, pleb. JESUS COLL., matric. 7 Dec., 1801, aged 21 (? died rector of Colenna, co. Glamorgan, 1827). **[35]**

Prichard, Francis Augustine, 1s. Augustine, of Bristol, co. Gloucester, gent. PEMBROKE COLL., matric. 16 Oct., 1866, aged 19; scholar 1866-70, B.A. 1871, M.A. 1875.

Prichard, George, s. Basil, of Colwall, co. Hereford, gent. MERTON COLL., matric. 17 March, 1721-2, aged 17; bar.-at-law, Lincoln's Inn, 1727.

Prichard, George Herbert, 1s. Richard, of Newbold-on-Stour, co. Worcester, cler. MAGDALEN COLL., matric. 1 Feb., 1873, aged 19.

Prichard, Henry, s. Benjamin, of Ewelme, Oxon, cler. BRASENOSE COLL., matric. 10 Oct., 1767, aged 19; B.A. 1772, M.A. 1774, rector of Feltwell, Norfolk, 1778, until his death 19 April, 1823.

richard, Henry, 3s. William, of Llangwyllog, Isle of Anglesey, gent. JESUS COLL., matric. 25 Nov., 1818, aged 19.

richard, Hugh, 3s. Richard, of Llangaffo, Isle of Anglesey, cler. JESUS COLL., matric. 9 Dec., 1826, aged 19; B.A. 1830.

richard, James Cowles, s. Thomas, of Ross, co. Hereford, arm. ST. JOHN'S COLL., matric. 3 June, 1809, aged 23; D.Med. (by diploma) from TRINITY COLL. 3 July, 1835, president of the Ethnological Society of London, a commissioner of lunacy 1845, died 22 Dec., 1848. See *Gent.'s Mag.*, 1849, i. 208; & Duncomb's *Herts*, iii. 117, 118.

richard, Rev. James Cowles, 1s. James Cowles, of St. Augustine's, Bristol, doctor. TRINITY COLL., matric. 19 June, 1832, aged 18, scholar 1832-8, B.A. 1836; fellow ORIEL COLL. 1838-42, M.A. 1839, tutor 1839, junior treasurer 1840, vicar of Mitcham, Surrey, 1841-6, died 11 Sep., 1848.

richard, James Edward, 2s. Augustine, of Bristol, co. Gloucester, D.Med. (subs. arm.). WADHAM COLL., matric. 16 Oct., 1869, aged 20; B.A. 1873, B.Med. 1879. [5]

richard, John, s. Richard, of Lanarmon, co. Carnarvon, pleb. JESUS COLL., matric. 4 April, 1717, aged 18.

richard, John, s. Benjamin, of Ledbury, co. Hereford, cler. BRASENOSE COLL., matric. 22 May, 1717, aged 15; fellow 1719-38, B.A. 6 Feb., 1720-1, M.A. 1723, rector of Christ Church, Spitalfields, Middlesex, 1738, until his death 28 Sep., 1782.

richard, John, s. John, of Abernant, co. Carmarthen, cler. WADHAM COLL., matric. 21 May, 1776, aged 18.

richard, Rev. John, s. Richard, of Isle of Anglesey, cler. BRASENOSE COLL., matric. 20 Feb., 1815, aged 18; B.A. 1819, M.A. 1823, died 16 Nov., 1836.

richard, John James, s. Benjamin, of Hindley, Lancashire, cler. BRASENOSE COLL., matric. 22 May, 1760, aged 17. [10]

richard, Matthew Stewart, 3s. Charles Henry, of Brislington, Somerset, gent. NEW COLL., matric. 8 Dec., 1883, aged 18; B.A. 1887.

richard, Richard, B.A. from JESUS COLL. 1795, M.A. 1811, B.D. 1811 (*Cat. Grads.*), minor canon of Llandaff, rector of Llangan, co. Glamorgan, 1821, until his death 6 Oct., 1856.

richard, Richard, 2s. Richard, of Margam, co. Glamorgan, cler. JESUS COLL., matric. 22 Oct., 1827, aged 16; B.A. 1832, scholar 1832-5, M.A. 1834, fellow 1835-45, B.D. 1842, of Collenna, co. Glamorgan, rector of Newbold-on-Stour 1844, until his death 20 Sep., 1887.

richard, Bichard Bethell Allan, s. Richard, of Newbold-on-Stour, co. Worcester, cler. NEW COLL., matric. 13 Oct., 1876, aged 19; scholar 1876-9, a student of the Inner Temple 1880.

richard, Richard Posthumus, y.s. Evan, of Llantrissent, co. Glamorgan, cler. JESUS COLL., matric. 18 June, 1846, aged 18, (subs. serv.); B.A. 1850, M.A. 1855, vicar of Wilburton, co. Cambridge, 1861. [15]

richard, Robert, B.A. from JESUS COLL. 21 March, 1720-1.

richard, Robert, s. John, of Llangaffo, co. Anglesea, gent. JESUS COLL., matric. 26 March, 1784, aged 18; B.A. 1787, fellow, M.A. 1790, B.D. 1798, rector of Llanfihangel Glyn-y-Myvyr, co. Merioneth, 1800, and of Rotherfield Peppard, Oxon, 1808, until his death 30 March, 1848.

richard, Robert Anwyl, 1s. Robert, of Chester (city), gent. MAGDALEN HALL, matric. 13 Nov., 1834, aged 20; rector of Thelveton, Norfolk, 1864, until his death 21 Jan., 1886.

richard, Robert Robert (*sic*), 3s. David, of Beddgelert, co. Carnarvon, gent. JESUS COLL., matric. 9 Dec., 1825, aged 19.

Prichard, Roland, s. Roland, of Swansea, co. Glamorgan, arm. ORIEL COLL., matric. 7 Dec., 1789, aged 16. [20]

Prichard, Rev. Theodore Joseph, 4s. James Cowles, of Bristol, D.Med. ORIEL COLL., matric. 6 Dec., 1838, aged 17; demy MAGDALEN COLL. 1842-6, B.A. 1844, died 24 Feb., 1846. See *Bloxam*, vii. 349.

Prichard, Thomas, s. John, of Chirbury, Salop, gent. BALLIOL COLL., matric. 21 Feb., 1721-2, aged 18; B.A. 3 March, 1725-6.

Prichard, Thomas, s. Herbert, of Westminster (city), cler. BRASENOSE COLL., matric. 13 March, 1730-1, aged 16; B.A. 1734.

Prichard, Thomas, s. Benjamin, of Stepney, Middlesex, cler. ST. ALBAN HALL, matric. 9 Sep., 1739, aged 15; B.A. from TRINITY COLL. 1743, M.A. 1746.

Prichard, Timothy, s. Timothy, of Cleddock, co. Hereford, gent. QUEEN'S COLL., matric. 2 July, 1789, aged 30; B.A. 1798, M.A. 1799. [25]

Prichard, Walter, s. William, of Monmouth (town), gent. BALLIOL COLL., matric. 22 April, 1740, aged 16.

Prichard, Walter Henry, 1s. Constantine Estlin, of South Luffenham, Rutland, cler. QUEEN'S COLL., matric. 23 Oct., 1875, aged 18; exhibitioner 1875-9, B.A. 1880. See *Rugby School Reg.*

Prichard, William, s. William, of ——, co. Monmouth, gent. BALLIOL COLL., matric. 19 June, 1729, aged 16; B.A. 1733.

Prickard, Arthur Octavius, 4s. Thomas, of Llansantfraid Cwmdauddwr, co. Radnor, gent. NEW COLL., matric. 12 Oct., 1861, aged 18; scholar 1861-6, B.A. 1865, fellow 1866, M.A. 1868, lecturer, sub-warden & tutor 1873, dean 1874, etc., bar.-at-law, Lincoln's Inn, 1872. See Foster's *Men at the Bar.*

Prickard, Harry Seddon, 1s. William Edward, of Llandrindod, Radnor, cler. ORIEL COLL., matric. 23 Oct., 1884, aged 18. [30]

Prickard, Nathan Seddon, s. Thomas, of Westminster, arm. WADHAM COLL., matric. 24 March, 1787, aged 18; B.A. 1790.

Prickard, Thomas, o.s. Nathan Seddon, of Cwmdauddwr, co. Radnor, arm. ST. MARY HALL, matric. 17 Nov., 1820, aged 19; B.A. 1824, M.A. 1832.

Prickard, Thomas Charles, 2s. Thomas, of Cwmdauddwr, co. Radnor, arm. JESUS COLL., matric. 14 March, 1850, aged 18; B.A. 1854, of Dderw, co. Radnor, rector of New Radnor 1866-75.

Prickett, Giles, s. Giles, of Tiddington, Oxon, gent. NEW COLL., matric. 18 Dec., 1786, aged 14; B.A. 1790, M.A. 1794, rector of Ravenstone, co. Leicester, 1809, until his death 8 Feb., 1855.

Prickett, James, 'bibliopola;' privilegiatus 29 Dec., 1817. [35]

Prickett, Marmaduke Alan, 1s. Thomas William, of London, cler. NEW COLL., matric. 10 Oct., 1884, aged 20; scholar HERTFORD COLL. 1884.

Prickett, William Ward, s. Edward, of Warwick (town), gent. MAGDALEN HALL, matric. 5 Dec., 1807, aged 19.

Pridden, Frederick Swaby, 2s. William, of West Stow, Suffolk, cler. EXETER COLL., matric. 18 Oct., 1875, aged 21; B.A. 1878, M.A. 1882.

Pridden, John, s. John, of London, gent. QUEEN'S COLL., matric. 15 April, 1777, aged 19; exhibitioner 1778, B.A. 1781; M.A. from ST. JOHN'S COLL., Cambridge, 1789, F.S.A. 1785, rector of Caddington, Beds, 1797, vicar of Heybridge 1783-97, and of Wakering Parva, Essex, 1788-97, minor canon St. Paul's, 1782, of Westminster 1795, priest-in-ordinary Chapel Royal 1795, rector of St. George's, Botolph Lane, and of St. Botolph's, Bishopsgate, 1812, until his death 5 April, 1825. See *Gent.'s Mag.*, 1825, i. 467; & *St. Paul's School Reg.*, 130.

Pridden, William, 1s. William, of St. Saviour's, Southwark, Surrey, gent. PEMBROKE COLL., matric. 18 Feb., 1829, aged 21; B.A. 1832, M.A. 1835, rector of West Stow, Suffolk, 1846, until his death 3 Sep., 1872.

Pridden, William Henry, 1s. William, of West Stow, Suffolk, cler. MAGDALEN COLL., matric. 29 Jan., 1870, aged 18; demy 1868, until his death 1 July, 1873.

Prideaux, Charles Grevile, 1s. Neast Grevile, of St. Michael's, Bristol, arm. BALLIOL COLL., matric. 14 Dec., 1827, aged 17; B.A. 1831, M.A. 1834, bar.-at-law, Lincoln's Inn, 1836, and of the Middle Temple (ad eundem) 1847, Q.C. 1856, bencher Lincoln's Inn 1867, successively recorder of Helston 1868-76, of Exeter 1876-9, and of Bristol 1879. See Foster's *Men at the Bar*.

Prideaux, Hugh, s. James, of Camelford, Cornwall, gent. EXETER COLL., matric. 6 April, 1723, aged 17; B.A. 22 March, 1731-2.

Prideaux, Rev. Walter Thomas, o.s. Walter, of Totnes, Devon, arm. EXETER COLL., matric. 29 April, 1822, aged 17; died at Totnes in 1828. **[5]**

Prideaux, William Francis, 1s. Francis, of Marylebone, London, arm. CORPUS CHRISTI COLL., matric. 27 March, 1858, aged 17.

Prideaux, Rev. William Henry, 2s. Francis Greville, of Bristol, gent. LINCOLN COLL., matric. 30 March, 1848, aged 17; scholar 1848-52, B.A. 1852, M.A. 1855, head-master Queen Elizabeth's School, Worcester, and of Codrington Grammar School, Barbados 1870-8, died 4 June, 1880.

Pridham, Charles, 4s. Joseph, of St. Andrew's, Plymouth, arm. EXETER COLL., matric. 9 Feb., 1832, aged 19; B.A. 1836.

Pridham, Charles, 2s. John, of Farringdon, Berks, cler. LINCOLN COLL., matric. 22 Oct., 1840, aged 18; bible clerk 1842-4, B.A. 1844, bar.-at-law, Middle Temple, 1851. See Foster's *Men at the Bar*.

Pridham, John, s. Peter, of Brixham, Devon, gent. ST. EDMUND HALL, matric. 22 Oct., 1806, aged 25; B.A. 1811, M.A. 1814. **[10]**

Priest, Henry, 3s. William, of Bath, Somerset, gent. ST. ALBAN HALL, matric. 7 March, 1871, aged 33; B.Mus. 6 July, 1872.

Priest, John, s. John, of Cardiff, co. Glamorgan, gent. ORIEL COLL., matric. 26 March, 1763, aged 16; B.A. 1767.

Priest, Richard, s. Simon, of Bibury, co. Gloucester, cler. MAGDALEN COLL., matric. 20 May, 1737, aged 17, chorister 1733-41; B.A. from NEW COLL. 1741, M.A. 1744. See *Bloxam*, i. 159.

Priest, Richard, s. Richard, of Norwich (city), gent. HERTFORD COLL., matric. 30 March, 1750, aged 17; B.A. 1753, died rector of Reepham with Kerdiston, Norfolk, in 1799.

Priest, Simon, s. Simon, of Bibury, co. Gloucester, cler. MAGDALEN HALL, matric. 18 May, 1738, aged 20. **[15]**

Priest, Walter, s. Sim., of Bibury, co. Gloucester, cler. ST. JOHN'S COLL., matric. 28 Sep., 1733, aged 16, B.A. 9 Feb., 1739-40; M.A. from CHRIST CHURCH 13 March, 1740-1, vicar of Skipton, Yorks, 1748.

Priest, Rev. William John, 2s. William, of London, gent. ST. ALBAN HALL, matric. 17 Oct., 1865, aged 35; B.A. 1869, B.Mus. 1870, M.A. 1872, lecturer 1869-73, vice-principal 1873-82, master of the schools 1880-1, pass moderator 1881-2, lecturer in classics Merton College 1882.

Priestley, Albert Wesley, 2s. Midgley, of Thornton, Yorks, gent. QUEEN'S COLL., matric. 30 Oct., 1885, aged 20; exhibitioner 1885.

Priestley, Henry Samuel, 3s. John, of Hirdrefaig, Isle of Anglesea, arm. TRINITY COLL., matric. 22 May, 1858, aged 18; B.A. 1863, vicar of Talyllyn 1869.

Priestley, John, 2s. Samuel, of Leeds, Yorks, arm. TRINITY COLL., matric. 14 June, 1821, aged 18; B.A. 1825, M.A. 1829. **[20]**

Priestley, Joseph William, 1s. John, of Bradford, Yorks, arm. BRASENOSE COLL., matric. 24 June, 1830, aged 20.

Priestley, Richard Edwards, 2s. John, of Hirdrefaig, Isle of Anglesea, arm. TRINITY COLL., matric. 23 May, 1855, aged 18; B.A. 1859, vicar of Beddegelert 1863-79.

Priestley, Samuel Owen, 1s. Samuel, of Leeds, Yorks, arm. TRINITY COLL., matric. 18 Feb., 1820, aged 18; B.A. 1824.

Priestley, William, 3s. Henry, of Sheffield, Yorks, gent. LINCOLN COLL., matric. 22 Oct., 1868, aged 19; exhibitioner UNIVERSITY COLL. 1869-73, B.A. 1873, vicar of Oakenshaw, Bradford, Yorks, 1878.

Priestman, John Smith, o.s. Joseph, of Workington, Cumberland, gent. QUEEN'S COLL., matric. 14 Oct., 1823, aged 18; scholar 1824-7, B.A. 1827 (? died perp. curate Matfen, Northumberland, 18 June, 1861). **[25]**

Prime, Samuel Stansfield, s. Samuel, of London, arm. CHRIST CHURCH, matric. 26 Oct., 1791, aged 18; died in June, 1851. See *Eton School Lists*.

Primrose, Archibald Philip, Baron Dalmeny, 1s. 'Archibald Primrose,' of London, Baron Dalmeny. CHRIST CHURCH, matric. 20 Jan., 1866, aged 18; 5th Earl of Rosebery, lord privy seal 1885, chief commissioner of works 1885, secretary of State foreign affairs 1886, lord rector Aberdeen University 1878, of Edinburgh University 1880-3.

Primrose, Henry William (C.S.I.), 2s. Hon. Bouverie Francis, of Edinburgh, arm. BALLIOL COLL., matric. 16 Oct., 1865, aged 19; B.A. 1870, C.S.I. 1 Jan., 1885. See Foster's *Peerage*, E. ROSEBERY.

Prince, Arthur, 4s. John Franklin, of Manchester, gent. JESUS COLL., matric. 21 Jan., 1885, aged 20; B.A. 1888.

Prince, Charles, s. John, of North Leech, co. Gloucester, cler. MERTON COLL., matric. 28 March, 1735, aged 17; B.A. from PEMBROKE COLL. 1739.

Prince, Charles, s. Samuel, of Wallingford, Berks, cler. TRINITY COLL., matric. 11 March, 1757, aged 18; B.A. 1760. **[31]**

Prince, Daniel, 'bookseller;' privilegiatus 19 Sep., 1750.

Prince, Edward Becher, 4s. George Wilson, of Rendebosch, Cape of Good Hope, gent. MAGDALEN COLL., matric. 22 June, 1859, aged 18; B.A. 1862, M.A. 1866, curate, etc., in Capetown 1864-76, vicar of Cockington, Devon, 1879-82, and of Tormohun 1879-84.

Prince, George, s. George, of Wootton, Hants, cler. NEW COLL., matric. 2 July, 1743, aged 21; B.A. 1747, M.A. 14 Jan., 1750-1, died 15 Nov., 1763.

Prince, Harry Forth Wicksteed, o.s. Samuel, of Bonsall, co. Derby, arm. CHRIST CHURCH, matric. 20 Oct., 1882, aged 19. **[35]**

Prince, Henry Rhodes, o.s. Henry, of Taunton, Somerset, gent. NON-COLL., matric. 17 Oct., 1885, aged 21.

Prince, John, s. John, of St. Helen's, Berks, cler. MERTON COLL., matric. 29 March, 1729, aged 17.

Prince, John, s. John, of London, pleb. ORIEL COLL., matric. 10 April, 1772, aged 18; B.A. 1775, 40 years chaplain to the Magdalen Charity, Lambeth, vicar of Enford, Wilts, 1793, until his death 13 Nov., 1833, aged 80, father of Thomas 1805.

Prince, John, s. Vaugh., of Farringdon, Berks, gent. WORCESTER COLL., matric. 26 March, 1774, aged 16; B.C.L. from CORPUS CHRISTI COLL. 1782, D.C.L. 1801.

Prince, John Charles, s. John, of Winwick, Lancashire, cler. BRASENOSE COLL., matric. 15 Jan., 1810, aged 17; scholar 1812-13, B.A. 1813, M.A. 1821, perp. curate St. Thomas, Liverpool, 1825, until his death 24 Jan., 1851.

Prince, John Charles, 1s. John Charles, of Liverpool, cler. BRASENOSE COLL., matric. 18 May, 1842, aged 17; scholar CORPUS CHRISTI COLL. 1842-8, B.A. 1847, died in 1848.

Prince, Philip Cowling, o.s. Philip Alexander, of London, gent. MAGDALEN HALL, matric. 10 Oct., 1843, aged 24; B.A. 1851.

Prince, Robert, B.A. from MERTON COLL. 6 Feb., 1732-3 (*Acts Book*).

Prince, Samuel, o.s. Samuel, of Manchester, gent. ST. EDMUND HALL, matric. 25 June, 1840, aged 23. [5]

Prince, Thomas, s. John, of Aldermanbury, London, cler. WADHAM COLL., matric. 5 Nov., 1805, aged 17; B.A. 1809, scholar 1812-15, M.A. 1814, fellow 1815-30, B. & D.D. 1824, chaplain to the Prince Regent 1813, and to the British residents at the Hague 1825, died 22 Jan., 1830.

Prince, William, 'cook;' privilegiatus 17 March, 1723-4.

Prince, William, 'servant to Mr. Williamson, of Hertford College;' privilegiatus 21 May, 1778.

Pring, Rev. Daniel James, o.s. James Hurly, of Weston-super-Mare, D.Med. EXETER COLL., matric. 12 Oct., 1878; B.A. 1882, M.A. 1886.

Pring, Ellis Roberts, 4s. Joseph, of Penrallt, co. Bangor, doctor. MAGDALEN COLL., matric. 14 Dec., 1833, aged 18; chorister 1824-8, clerk 1833-7, B.A. 1838, perp. curate Talyllyn, co. Merioneth, 1843-68, rector of Penllech 1868. See *Coll. Reg.*, i. 217. [10]

Pring, Isaac, s. 'Jacob,' of Kensington, Middlesex, gent. NEW COLL., matric. 1 March, 1799, aged 21; brother of Joseph 1808.

Pring, Isaac Heathcote, 2s. Joseph, of Bangor, co. Carnarvon, gent. CHRIST CHURCH, matric. 19 March, 1823, aged 18; servitor 1823-8, B.A. 1828, died rector of Llanfrothen, co. Merioneth, 17 Dec., 1842, aged 38.

Pring, James Cubit, s. James, of Lewisham, Kent, gent. MAGDALEN HALL, matric. 27 June, 1797, aged 26.

Pring, Rev. John, s. William, of Sherborne, Dorset, gent. MAGDALEN HALL, matric. 28 Oct., 1794, aged 17; B.A. 1801, of Stanbrook House, Bristol, died 8 June, 1853.

Pring, Joseph, s. 'Jacob,' of Kensington, Middlesex, gent. MAGDALEN HALL, matric. 21 Jan., 1808, aged 32; B. & D.Mus. 27 Jan., 1808, brother of Isaac 1799. [15]

Pring, Joseph Charles, 1s. Joseph, of Bangor, co. Carnarvon, gent. JESUS COLL., matric. 23 March, 1820, aged 20, B.A. 1824; chaplain NEW COLL. 1825-73, M.A. 1826, vicar of Headington, Oxon, 1837, until his death 7 April, 1876.

Pring, William Mansfield, 2s. Charles Benjamin, of Great Cumberland Street, London, gent. QUEEN'S COLL., matric. 17 Oct., 1833, aged 18.

Pringle, John, s. Mark, of San Luce, Spain, arm. ST. MARY HALL, matric. 27 Jan., 1737-8, aged 18.

Pringle, John, s. Mark, of Edinburgh (city), arm. CHRIST CHURCH, matric. 16 Oct., 1813, aged 17; M.P. Linlithgow burghs 1819-20, died in 1831. See Foster's *Scots M.P.'s*.

Pringle, John Alexander Gordon, 1s. Mark, of Upper Nutwell, Devon, gent. EXETER COLL., matric. 12 June, 1851, aged 18. [20]

Pringuer, Henry Thomas, o.s. Samuel Freemoner, of Canterbury, gent. NEW COLL., matric. 5 Feb., 1877, aged 24; B.Mus. 25 Oct., 1877, D.Mus. 12 Nov., 1885.

Prinsep, Harry Stewart, 1s. Henry Auriol, of Lucknow, arm. ORIEL COLL., matric. 31 Oct., 1882, aged 19; B.A. 1887.

Prinsep, John, s. Reginald, of Tamworth, co. Stafford, gent. BALLIOL COLL., matric. 28 March, 1735, aged 18; B.A. 1738.

Prinsep, Thomas, 3s. Theophilus Levett, of Wychnor, co. Stafford, arm. TRINITY COLL., matric. 17 June, 1828, aged 17; he assumed the surname of PRINSEP in lieu of LEVETT. See *Eton School Lists*.

Prinsep, Thomas Levett, o.s. Thomas, of Bishops Teignton, Devon, arm. MERTON COLL., matric. 17 Oct., 1863, aged 18; of Croxhall Hall, co. Derby, J.P. [25]

Prioleau, Richard Trenholm, 3s. Charles Kuhn, of Liverpool, arm. CHRIST CHURCH, matric. 10 Oct., 1884, aged 19; B.A. 1887.

Prior, Rev. Charles Edward, 1s. Charles Edward, of Bedford (town), D.Med. (subs. gent.). QUEEN'S COLL., matric. 23 Oct., 1868, aged 18; scholar 1868-73, B.A. 1872, M.A. 1876, assistant-master in Merchant Taylors' School 1875.

Prior, Edward, fellow of TRINITY COLL., Cambridge (B.A. 1721, M.A. 1725); incorp. 9 July, 1733.

Prior, Frederick Henry, 2s. George Sayle, of Lisbon, Portugal, cler. MAGDALEN HALL, matric. 6 Feb., 1866, aged 18.

Prior, George, 1s. Benjamin, of Reading, Berks, gent. ST. EDMUND HALL, matric. 12 May, 1863, aged 32; B.Mus. 13 May, 1863, D.Mus. 7 July, 1876.

Prior, George Sayle, s. George, of Tewkesbury, co. Gloucester, gent. QUEEN'S COLL., matric. 4 Dec., 1817, aged 18; B.A. 1823, chaplain Lisbon 1840-61, rector of St. Breock, Cornwall, 1861-73, died 29 March, 1884. [31]

Prior, George Sayle, 1s. George Sayle, of Lisbon, Portugal, cler. MAGDALEN HALL, matric. 6 Feb., 1866, aged 20.

Prior, George Thurland, 1s. George Thomas, of Oxford, gent. MAGDALEN COLL., matric. 15 Oct., 1881, aged 18; demy 1881-6, B.A. 1885, M.A. 1888.

Prior, Henry Granger, o.s. James, of Tettenhall, co. Stafford, gent. HERTFORD COLL., matric. 25 April, 1877, aged 17.

Prior, Henry Lawrence, 2s. John Lawrence, of Teignmouth, Devon, cler. EXETER COLL., matric. 19 Jan., 1872, aged 18; B.A. 1875, bar.-at-law, Inner Temple, 1882. [35]

Prior, Henry Stansfield, 3s. Samuel Turner, of Blackheath, Kent, gent. ST. JOHN'S COLL., matric. 13 April, 1872, aged 23; B.A. & M.A. 1878, held various curacies 1878-86, priest in charge of St. Paul's, Kandy, Ceylon, 1886.

Prior, Herman Ludolph, 2s. John, of Clapham, Surrey, arm. TRINITY COLL., matric. 30 May, 1836, aged 17; scholar 1836-42, B.A. 1841, M.A. 1847, sometime commoner TRINITY HALL, Cambridge, bar.-at-law, Lincoln's Inn, 1850. See Foster's *Men at the Bar*.

Prior, John, s. Charles, of North Perrot, Somerset, pleb. MAGDALEN HALL, matric. 2 April, 1723, aged 17 (called BRIOR in *Mat. Reg.*).

Prior, John (Laurence), 1s. Andrew, of Walcot, Bath, arm. EXETER COLL., matric. 15 Nov., 1838, aged 17; B.A. 1842, M.A. 1846, vicar of Maldon, Essex, 1846-53, and of Lynby, Notts, 1853-75, rector of Horton, Bucks, 1875, until his death 30 Oct., 1879.

Prior, Rev. Jonathan Charles, o.s. Alfred Staff, of London, cler. ST. ALBAN HALL, matric. 16 Oct., 1872, aged 21. [40]

Prior, Richard Chandler Alexander, 1s. Richard Hayward Alexander, of Corsham, Wilts, gent. WADHAM COLL., matric. 13 April, 1826, aged 17; B.A. 1830, B.Med. 1835, D.Med. 1837, of Halse House, Somerset, assumed the additional name of PRIOR.

Prior, Thomas, s. John Murry, of Kilkenny (city), arm. QUEEN'S COLL., matric. 21 Aug., 1784, aged 22; B.A. 1785, brother of Andrew Murray Prior, of Rathdowney, Queen's County.

Prior, William, s. William, of Eton, Bucks, pleb. PEMBROKE COLL., matric. 29 March, 1740, aged 19; B.A. 1743.

Prise, James, s. Richard, of St. Peter's, Hereford (city), arm. BALLIOL COLL., matric. 9 March, 1721-2, aged 17; B.A. 1725, M.A. 1738, died vicar of Bridstow, co. Hereford, 14 Aug., 1779.

Pritchard, Rev. Albert Richard, 10s. William, of London, arm. LINCOLN COLL., matric. 7 June, 1860, aged 19; B.A. 1864, M.A. 1867, principal Wargrave Military College 1868.

Pritchard, Arthur, 3s. William Tarn, of Twickenham, Middlesex, gent. BALLIOL COLL., matric. 17 Oct., 1882, aged 19. [5]

Pritchard, Charles, scholar ST. JOHN'S COLL., Cambridge, 1829 (B.A. 1830, fellow 1832-5, hon. fellow 1886, M.A. 1833), 4s. William, of London, gent. Incorp. from NEW COLL. 7 March, 1870, aged 62; M.A. by decree 11 March, 1870, B. & D.D. 1880, fellow 1883, Savilian professor of astronomy 1870, formerly head-master of Clapham School, F.R.S. 1840, F.R.A.S., father of George.

Pritchard, Ebenezer, 5s. Thomas, of Broseley, Salop, gent. CHRIST CHURCH, matric. 31 Oct., 1834, aged 18; 'servitor' 1834-8, B.A. 1838.

Pritchard, Edward, s. Edward, of Machynlleth, co. Montgomery, gent. JESUS COLL., matric. 11 Dec., 1784, aged 19; B.A. 1788.

Pritchard, George Eric Campbell, o.s. Charles, of Freshwater, Isle of Wight, cler. HERTFORD COLL., matric. 31 Jan., 1884, aged 19; B.A. 1887.

Pritchard, Godfrey, 2s. Robert Albion, of Putney, Surrey, D.C.L. UNIVERSITY COLL., matric. 15 June, 1881, aged 19; B.A. from NEW INN HALL 1886.

Pritchard, Henry, 1s. Henry, of St. Olaves, Surrey, gent. MERTON COLL., matric. 27 May, 1837, aged 17, postmaster 1837-8; scholar CORPUS CHRISTI COLL. 1838-47, B.A. 1841, M.A. 1844, fellow 1847-57, B.D. 1853, senior dean 1851, math. lecturer 1852, proctor 1852, incumbent of Sheen, co. Stafford, died 14 April, 1857. [11]

Pritchard, Henry, 1s. Henry, of Isle of Anglesea, arm. ORIEL COLL., matric. 22 May, 1856, aged 17; B.A. 1860, M.A. 1863, bar.-at-law, Lincoln's Inn, 1865, died 13 Nov., 1867.

Pritchard, Lorenzo Alfred, 4s. Thomas, of Wednesbury, co. Stafford, gent. WADHAM COLL., matric. 11 Oct., 1884, aged 21; B.A. 1887.

Pritchard, Richard, s. John, of Llangaffo, co. Anglesea, gent. JESUS COLL., matric. 27 March, 1776, aged 19; B.A. 1780, of Dinam Hall, co. Anglesea, rector of Llanvair Pwllgwyngyll with Llandysilio 1785, and of Port Eynon, co. Glamorgan, 1803, until his death 3 March, 1850.

Pritchard, Richard, 2s. James, of Stratford-upon-Avon, co. Warwick, gent. MAGDALEN HALL, matric. 26 Nov., 1823, aged 18; B.A. 1828, curate of Whitchurch, co. Warwick, 1837-8, rector 1838, until his death 15 March, 1882. [15]

Pritchard, Rev. Richard Hughes, 1s. William, of Bangor, co. Carnarvon, gent. JESUS COLL., matric. 29 Oct., 1867, aged 17; scholar 1867-72, B.A. 1871, M.A. 1884.

Pritchard, Robert, s. Robert, of London, cler. NEW COLL., matric. 5 May, 1786, aged 17; fellow, B.A. 1790, died 25 Dec., 1795.

Pritchard, Robert Albion, 5s. William, of London, arm. LINCOLN COLL., matric. 3 Dec., 1846, aged 19; S.C.L. 1850, B.C.L. 1853, D.C.L. 1858, bar.-at-law, Inner Temple, 1855. See Foster's *Men at the Bar* & *St. Paul's School Reg.*, 290.

Pritchard, Robert Henry, 1s. Robert Albion, of London, arm. UNIVERSITY COLL., matric. 13 Oct., 1877, aged 19; B.A. 1882, bar.-at-law, Middle Temple, 1884. See Foster's *Men at the Bar.*

Pritchard, Rowland, y.s. William, of Ciltwllan, co. Carnarvon, pleb. NON-COLL., matric. 14 Oct., 1882, aged 19. [20]

Pritchard, Thomas John, o.s. Evan, of Walton, near Liverpool, arm. HERTFORD COLL., matric. 15 Oct., 1879, aged 21; B.A. from CHARSLEY HALL 1886.

Pritchard, Thomas Sirrell, 1s. Thomas, of Hereford (city), arm. BRASENOSE COLL., matric. 20 Jan., 1852, aged 17; B.A. 1855, M.A. 1858, bar.-at-law, Inner Temple, 1858, recorder of Wenlock, died 8 Aug., 1879.

Pritchard, Thomas William, 1s. William, of East Retford, Notts, D.Med. HERTFORD COLL., matric. 20 Jan., 1877, aged 17; B.A. 1880, M.A. 1883.

Pritchard, William, s. Thomas, of Richmond, Surrey, gent. WORCESTER COLL., matric. 25 June, 1799, aged 20.

Pritchett, George, s. Delabere, of Brimfield, co. Hereford, pleb. JESUS COLL., matric. 12 Oct., 1768, aged 17; B.A. 1772, vicar of Mathon, co. Worcester, 1794, until his death in 1835. [25]

Pritchett, John, s. Samuel, of Knightwick, co. Worcester, cler. WORCESTER COLL., matric. 25 June, 1778, aged 17; B.A. 1782, M.A. 1785.

Pritchett, John (Suckling), 1s. John Suckling, of King's Norton, co. Worcester, gent. BALLIOL COLL., matric. 26 April, 1873, aged 18; exhibitioner 1873-7, B.A. 1877, B.C.L. 1878, M.A. 1879, bar.-at-law, Inner Temple, 1881. See Foster's *Men at the Bar.*

Pritchett, Richard, s. Richard, of Narberth, co. Pembroke, pleb. JESUS COLL., matric. 27 March, 1727, aged 18; B.A. 27 Feb., 1730-1, rector of Richard's Castle, Salop, died 14 Oct., 1772.

Pritchett, Samuel, s. John, of Wichingford, co. Worcester, gent. LINCOLN COLL., matric. 10 Nov., 1726, aged 16; B.A. 1730, M.A. 1733.

Pritchett, Thomas Edward, o.s. Edward, of London, gent. NON-COLL., matric. 20 Jan., 1877, aged 23; B.A. from ST. ALBAN HALL 1880, curate Gingin, Perth, West Australia, 1884. [30]

Pritchitt, Rev. John Frederick Stephen, 2s. James John Joseph, of Southwark, arm. ST. MARY HALL, matric. 11 May, 1884, aged 22.

Pritt, Drinkall, s. James, of Hampstead, Middlesex, gent. ST. EDMUND HALL, matric. 2 Feb., 1815, aged 30.

Privett, Thomas, s. William, of Chilmark, Wilts, pleb. HART HALL, matric. 4 April, 1720, aged 16; B.A. 1723.

Probart, Francis, s. William, of Hanmer, co. Flint, pleb. PEMBROKE COLL., matric. 23 March, 1737-8, aged 20; B.A. 6 March, 1741-2.

Probert, Thomas, s. John, of Weobley, co. Hereford, pleb. HART HALL, matric. 21 Oct., 1724, aged 19. [35]

Probert, Thomas, s. John, of Weobley, co. Hereford, pleb. LINCOLN COLL., matric. 11 April, 1747, aged 17; B.A. 23 Feb., 1750-1.

Probert, William Geoffrey, 2s. William Richard, of Bedford, arm. LINCOLN COLL., matric. 27 Oct., 1885, aged 21.

Proberts, Charles, o.s. Charles, of Brecon (town), cler. JESUS COLL., matric. 22 May, 1847, aged 19.

Proby, John Joshua, Earl of Carysfort; created D.C.L. 3 July, 1810 (s. John, 1st Baron Carysfort), M.P. East Looe 1790, Stamford 1790-1801, ambassador at the Court of Berlin 1800, and of St. Petersburg 1801, created Earl of Carysfort 18 Aug., 1789, etc., died 7 April, 1828. See Foster's *Peerage.*

Proby, John Joshua, born at Powerscourt, Wicklow, 1s. Hon. Granville Leveson, arm. (after Earl of Carysfort). BALLIOL COLL., matric. 28 Nov., 1840 aged 17; B.A. 1844, Lord Proby, died 19 Nov., 1858. See Foster's *Peerage.* [40]

Probyn, Edmund, s. John, of Newland, co. Gloucester, arm. CHRIST CHURCH, matric. 11 June, 1752, aged 15; created M.A. 8 July, 1756 (as Edward), of Newland and Longhope, co. Gloucester, high sheriff, father of John 1777, and of William 1779.

Probyn, Edmund, s. John, of Abinghall, co. Gloucester, cler. UNIVERSITY COLL., matric. 29 Jan., 1806, aged 18; B.A. 1810, M.A. 1814, vicar of Longhope and rector of Abinghall, co. Gloucester, 1827, until his death 8 March, 1837.

Probyn, John, s. William (Hopkins), of Newland, co. Gloucester, gent. WADHAM COLL., matric. 10 Oct., 1727, aged 17; B.A. 1731, M.A. 1735, bar.-at-law, Lincoln's Inn, took the name of PROBYN in lieu of HOPKINS, M.P. Wootton Basset 1754-61, father of Edmund 1752.

Probyn, John, s. Edmund, of Newland, co. Gloucester, arm. CHRIST CHURCH, matric. 25 June, 1777, aged 16; of the Manor House, Longhope, co. Gloucester, dean and archdeacon of Llandaff 1796-1843, rector of Abinghall and vicar of Newland 1794-1837, vicar of Matherne with Caerwent, co. Monmouth, 1803, until his death 4 Oct., 1843, father of Edward 1806.

Probyn, William, s. Edmund, of Newland, co. Gloucester, arm. ST. MARY HALL, matric. 18 Feb., 1779, aged 16; B.A. 1783, M.A. 1785, vicar of Longhope, co. Gloucester, 1787, of St. Andrew's, Pershore, 1797, chancellor and canon residentiary of St. David's 1793, until his death in 1825. **[5]**

Procter, Charles Tickell, scholar and fellow KING'S COLL., Cambridge, 1850-68 (B.A. 1854, M.A. 1857); adm. 'ad eundem' 9 Dec., 1858, vicar of Richmond, Surrey, 1867, hon. canon of Rochester 1881.

Procter, James, s. Thomas, of Ilkley, Yorks, gent. UNIVERSITY COLL., matric. 2 May, 1792, aged 19.

Procter, James, s. James, of Pinner, Middlesex, gent. EXETER COLL., matric. 6 May, 1807, aged 18; B.A. 1811, rector of Garthorpe, co. Leicester, 1838, until his death 28 Oct., 1863.

Procter, John, 1s. John, of Lancaster (town), arm. BRASENOSE COLL., matric. 13 April, 1825, aged 18; B.A. 1829, died curate of Weston, Notts, 6 Dec., 1854.

Procter, John Mathias, 2s. Edward, of Macclesfield, Cheshire, arm. TRINITY COLL., matric. 12 June, 1854, aged 18, B.A. 1858; fellow JESUS COLL. 1859-65, M.A. 1861, vicar of Barkingside and Aldborough Hatch, Essex, 1864-78, rector of Laindon, Essex, 1878-83, hon. canon St. Alban's, 1882, rector of Thorley, Herts, 1883. **[10]**

Procter, Thomas, s. Henry, of Alton, co. Hereford, cler. BALLIOL COLL. matric. 31 March, 1753, aged 19; B.A. 1757.

Procter, Thomas, s. William, of Leeds, Yorks, gent. UNIVERSITY COLL., matric. 20 Oct., 1769, aged 18.

Procter, Thomas, s. Thomas, of Aberllunfi, co. Brecon, arm. JESUS COLL., matric. 9 May, 1818, aged 21, B.A. 1821; Michel fellow QUEEN'S COLL. 1824-6, M.A. 1824, chaplain to the forces at Calcutta, died in 1836.

Proctor, George, s. George, of Clewer, Berks, arm. ST. EDMUND HALL, matric. 20 May, 1813, aged 20, B.A. 1817; M.A. from WORCESTER COLL. 1820, B.D. 1828, D.D. 1829, rector of Monken-Hadley, Middlesex, 1846-60, chaplain to the Fishmonger's Almshouses, Maidenhead, 1860-80, died 7 Aug., 1881.

Proctor, George Henry, 1s. George, of Bridgnorth, Salop, cler. BALLIOL COLL., matric. 14 Dec., 1838, aged 18; B.A. 1842, M.A. 1845, assistant chaplain Crimea, died of fever at Scutari 10 March, 1855. **[15]**

Proctor, George Vizard, 1s. George, of Stroud, co. Gloucester, cler. WORCESTER COLL. matric. 12 Oct., 1867, aged 19; B.A. 1870, M.A. 1877, held various curacies 1871-7, vicar of Shippon, Berks, 1877-9.

Proctor, Gordon Percy, 1s. Francis Bartlett, of Cheltenham, cler. NON-COLL., matric. 17 Oct., 1885, aged 19.

Proctor, Henry, 3s. George, of Stroud, co. Gloucester, cler. UNIVERSITY COLL., matric. 15 Oct., 1870, aged 19; exhibitioner 1870-4, B.A. 1874, M.A. 1879, vicar of Coleford, co. Gloucester, since 1879.

Proctor, John Edward Ingleby, 1s. John M., of Aldborough Hatch, Essex, cler. NEW COLL., matric. 16 Jan., 1885, aged 19.

Proctor, Robert George Collier, o.s. Robert, of East Budleigh, Devon, arm. CORPUS CHRISTI COLL., matric. 20 Oct., 1886, aged 14; scholar 1886. **[20]**

Proctor, Thomas, s. Henry, of Clewer, Berks, arm. MERTON COLL., matric. 14 July, 1726, aged 18.

Proctor, Thomas, s. Samuel, of Newcastle-under-Lyne, Stafford, gent. BALLIOL COLL., matric. 26 March, 1728, aged 18; B.A. 1731.

Proctor, Thomas, s. Thomas, of Rownhill, Somerset, arm. QUEEN'S COLL., matric. 9 April, 1747, aged 18.

Proctor, Thomas, s. Thomas, of Taunton, Somerset, cler. ORIEL COLL., matric. 27 March, 1779, aged 18.

Proctor, William, s. Thomas, of Ammilton, Northumberland, arm. CHRIST CHURCH, matric. 8 July, 1718, aged 16; B.A. 1723, M.A. 1725. **[25]**

Proctor, Sir William Beauchamp, Bart., s. Thomas Beauchamp, of Tottenham, Middlesex, arm. MAGDALEN COLL., matric. 15 March, 1737-8, aged 15; created M.A. 17 Nov., 1742, assumed the additional surname and arms of PROCTOR by act of parliament 18 George II., M.P. Middlesex 1747-68, died 16 Sep., 1773. See Foster's *Baronetage*.

Proctor, William Henry, 5s. Edward, of Heversham, Westmoreland, gent. QUEEN'S COLL. matric. 23 Oct., 1882, aged 17; exhibitioner 1881-6.

Prodgers, Edwin, s. Edward, of St. Swithin's, Worcester (city), arm. TRINITY COLL., matric. 10 Oct., 1803, aged 17; B.A. 1807, M.A. 1810, B.D. 1827, rector of Ayott St. Peter, Herts, 1842, until his death 5 Dec., 1861, father of Edwin and Herbert.

Prodgers, Edwin, 1s. Edwin, of Brixton, Surrey, cler. CHRIST CHURCH, matric. 12 June, 1851, aged 17; B.A. 1855, M.A. 1859, of Ayot Bury, Herts. See *Eton School Lists*.

Prodgers, Herbert, y.s. Edwin, of Brixton, Surrey, cler. CHRIST CHURCH, matric. 8 June, 1854, aged 18; of Kington House, Wilts, J.P. See *Eton School Lists*. **[30]**

Propert, James, s. Thomas, of Trevaccoon, co. Pembroke, gent. CHRIST CHURCH, matric. 5 March, 1789, aged 20.

Propert, Thomas, s. Richard, of St. David's, co. Pembroke, gent. BRASENOSE COLL., matric. 2 Nov., 1769, aged 19; B.A. 1773, perp. curate Stony Stratford, Bucks, 1778, until his death 10 June, 1806.

Propert, William, s. David, of Llanryan, co. Pembroke, pleb. JESUS COLL., matric. 18 March, 1724-5, aged 19; B.C.L. 1732.

Propert, William (Gough), s. John, of St. David's, co. Pembroke, pleb. CHRIST CHURCH, matric. 7 Nov., 1785, aged 20; B.A. 1789.

Propert, William Peregrine, 1s. David, of Hubberstone, co. Pembroke, arm. JESUS COLL., matric. 2 Nov., 1849, aged 18; B.Mus. 21 June, 1850. **[35]**

Prosser, Francis Richard Wegg-, o.s. Francis Haggitt, of Nuneham, Oxon, D.D. BALLIOL COLL., matric. 10 March, 1842, aged 17; B.A. 1845, of Belmont, co. Hereford, high sheriff 1855, M.P. 1847-52, assumed the surnames of WEGG-PROSSER in lieu of HAGGITT in 1849. See *Eton School Lists*.

Prosser, Henry Paul, 1s. Thomas, of Monmouth, arm. WADHAM COLL., matric. 19 Jan., 1872, aged 18; B.A. 1875, M.A. 1878, vicar of All Saints, Hereford, 1886.

Prosser, James, s. Thomas, of Llanelweth, co. Radnor, pleb. JESUS COLL., matric. 14 March, 1761, aged 19. See *Gent.'s Mag.*, 1802, ii. 1171.

Prosser, James, of ST. CATHARINE COLL., Cambridge (B.A. 1832, M.A. 1835); adm. 'comitatis causa' 23 Feb., 1865, vicar of Thame, Oxon, 1841.

Prosser, John, s. Thomas, of Llangamarch, co. Brecon, pleb. JESUS COLL., matric. 2 April, 1736, aged 18; B.A. 1739.

Prosser, John, 2s. John, of Hereford (city), gent. MAGDALEN HALL, matric. 7 Nov., 1823, aged 19.

Prosser, John, 1s. William Samuel, of St. Peter's, Hereford (city), gent. ST. EDMUND HALL, matric. 10 Oct., 1838, aged 19; B.A. 1842. [5]

Prosser, Joseph Camplin, 3s. William, of Tewkesbury, co. Gloucester, cler. MAGDALEN HALL, matric. 21 Oct., 1829, aged 24; rector of Itton 1832, and vicar of Newchurch, co. Monmouth, 1829, until his death 1 Nov., 1870.

Prosser, Richard, s. John, of Monmouth (town), gent. WADHAM COLL., matric. 2 June, 1747, aged 17; B.A. 1 March, 1750-1.

Prosser, Richard, s. Humphrey, of Market Drayton, Salop, pleb. BALLIOL COLL., matric. 4 April, 1767, aged 19; B.A. 1770, fellow 1773, M.A. 1773, B.D. 1784, D.D. 1797, proctor 1783, of Belmont, near Hereford, rector of All Saints, Colchester, 1792-6, of Gateshead, co. Durham, 1796, preb. of Durham 1804, archdeacon of Durham and rector of Easington 1808, died 8 Oct., 1839.

Prosser, Robert, s. Thomas, of Dorston, co. Hereford, cler. BRASENOSE COLL., matric. 19 May, 1798, aged 17; B.A. from ALL SOULS' COLL. 1804.

Prosser, Samuel, s. Thomas, of Dorston, co. Hereford, cler. TRINITY COLL., matric. 2 Nov., 1739, aged 17; B.A. 1743. [10]

Prosser, Samuel, s. Thomas, of Dorston, co. Hereford, cler. WADHAM COLL., matric. 17 Dec., 1792, aged 19; rector of Southwick, Sussex, 1805, until his death in 1825.

Prosser, Samuel, s. Samuel, of Southwick, Sussex, cler. ST. JOHN'S COLL., matric. 13 June, 1818, aged 18; B.A. 1822, M.A. 1824, head-master Thame School, vicar of Holy Trinity, Margate, 1846 until his death 11 April, 1883. See *Robinson*, 187.

Prosser, Theophilus, s. Thomas, of Dorston, co. Hereford, cler. WADHAM COLL., matric. 18 July, 1767, aged 20.

Prosser, Theophilus, s. Theophilus, of Upton Bishop, co. Hereford, cler. BRASENOSE COLL., matric. 6 Dec., 1792, aged 18; B.A. 1797, M.A. 1799, died perp. curate of Upton Bishop, co. Hereford, in 1839.

Prosser, Thomas, s. Thomas, of Dorston, co. Hereford, cler. TRINITY COLL., matric. 22 May, 1723, aged 18; B.A. 1727. [15]

Prosser, Thomas, s. Thomas, of Peterchurch, co. Hereford, pleb. BALLIOL COLL., matric. 19 July, 1739, aged 19.

Prosser, Thomas, s. Thomas, of Dorston, co. Hereford, cler. JESUS COLL., matric. 31 May, 1759, aged 18.

Prosser, Thomas, s. Thomas, of Talgarth, co. Brecon, gent. WORCESTER COLL., matric. 4 Nov., 1774, aged 18; B.A. 1778, M.A. 1781, died vicar of Cwmdee, co. Brecon, 26 April, 1823.

Prosser, Thomas, s. Thomas, of Dorston, co. Hereford, cler. BRASENOSE COLL., matric. 16 Dec., 1789, aged 19; B.A. 1793, vicar of Dorston 1794, until his death 2 March, 1843.

Prosser, Walter Byron, o.s. Samuel, of Margate, Kent, cler. BRASENOSE COLL., matric. 13 June, 1867, aged 17; scholar 1867-71, B.A. 1871, bar.-at-law, Inner Temple, 1875. See Foster's *Men at the Bar.* [20]

Prosser, William, s. John, of Monmouth (town), gent. PEMBROKE COLL., matric. 27 June, 1789, aged 21. See *Gent.'s Mag.*, 1813, i. 395.

Prosser, William, 3s. John, of St. David's, co. Pembroke, gent. PEMBROKE COLL., matric. 28 Oct., 1829, aged 19 (? deacon 1845, preacher 1856, vicar of Ashby-Folville, co. Leicester, 1853, died 28 June, 1884, aged 85).

Prosser, William, 1s. William, of St. Mary's, Monmouth (town), cler. JESUS COLL., matric. 13 March, 1851, aged 18; S.C.L. from MAGDALEN HALL 1855, B.A. 1856, M.A. 1857, vicar of Ashby Folville, co. Leicester, 1866-8, and of Wrockwardine 1868-74, and of St. Luke, Bilston, 1880.

Prossor, Louis Anthony, 2s. Henry, of London, gent. NON-COLL., matric. 17 Oct., 1881, aged 18.

Prothero, David, s. William, of Llandilo. co. Carmarthen, gent. BRASENOSE COLL., matric. 12 June, 1792, aged 18; B.A. 1796, M.A. 1811, vicar of Llandilofawr, co. Carmarthen, 1809, and rector of Penboyre, etc., 1833, until his death 23 Nov., 1837. [25]

Prothero, Edward, s. Thomas, of Usk, co. Monmouth, gent. ORIEL COLL., matric. 18 Feb., 1818, aged 18.

Prothero, Edward Marsh, 2s. Thomas, of Whippingham, Isle of Wight, cler. MERTON COLL., matric. 23 Jan., 1860, aged 18; B.A. from ST. ALBAN HALL 1865, of Malpas Court, co. Monmouth, perp. curate Llanvihangel-Llantarnam 1872.

Prothero, Ernest Macdonald, 2s. Charles, of Llanvrechoa, co. Monmouth, arm. UNIVERSITY COLL., matric. 16 Oct., 1869, aged 18.

Prothero, Francis Thomas Egerton, 1s. Thomas, of The Close, Salisbury, cler. BALLIOL COLL., matric. 8 April, 1856, aged 18; B.A. 1860, of Malpas Court, co. Monmouth, J.P., bar.-at-law, Inner Temple, 1863. See Foster's *Men at the Bar.*

Prothero, George, 4s. Thomas, of St. Woolos, near Newport, co. Monmouth, arm. BRASENOSE COLL., matric. 8 Feb., 1838, aged 19; B.A. 1843, M.A. 1866, vicar of Clifton-on-Teme 1847-53, curate of Whippingham, Isle of Wight, 1853-7, rector 1857, chaplain in ordinary to the Queen 1866, canon of Westminster 1869. [30]

Prothero, Henry Allen, 3s. Thomas, of Whippingham, Isle of Wight, cler. BALLIOL COLL., matric. 21 Oct., 1867, aged 18; B.A. 1872.

Prothero, John Edwards, 1s. David, of Llandebie, co. Carmarthen, gent. JESUS COLL., matric. 5 Feb., 1863, aged 19; B.A. 1866, M.A. 1870, held various curacies 1868-81, rector of Orcheston St. George, Wilts, 1881.

Prothero, Michael Ernle Du Santoy, 4s. George, of Whippingham, Isle of Wight, cler. UNIVERSITY COLL., matric. 13 Oct., 1877, aged 20; B.A. 1880.

Prothero, Rowland Edmund, 3s. George, of Clifton, co. Worcester, cler. BALLIOL COLL., matric. 18 Oct., 1871, aged 20; fellow ALL SOULS' COLL. 1875, B.A. 1876, M.A. 1878, proctor 1883, bar.-at-law, Middle Temple, 1878. See Foster's *Men at the Bar.*

Prothero, Thomas, s. Thomas, of Llangattock, co. Carmarthen, cler. CHRIST CHURCH, matric. 3 Nov., 1737, aged 17; B.A. 6 March, 1741-2. [35]

Prothero, Thomas, s. Stephen, of Leighton, Salop, cler. CHRIST CHURCH, matric. 1 June, 1786, aged 19.

Prothero, Thomas, 1s. Thomas, of Newport, co. Monmouth, arm. BRASENOSE COLL., matric. 4 Feb., 1830, aged 18; B.A. 1833, M.A. 1837, of Malpas Court, co. Monmouth, chaplain to the Prince Consort 1848, chaplain-in-ordinary to the Queen 1853, until his death 11 June, 1870, father of Francis T. E., Henry Allen and Edward M.

Protheroe, Charles. MERTON COLL., 1738. See PRUTHEROE, page 1159.

Protheroe, Edward (Davis), s. Edward, of Bristol (city), arm. CHRIST CHURCH, matric. 3 Feb., 1817, aged 18; of Newnham, co. Gloucester, M.P. Evesham 1826-30, Bristol 1831-2, Halifax 1837-47, a commissioner of public records, took the additional surname of DAVIS in 1845, died 18 Aug., 1852.

Protheroe, William Ford, s. John, of Egremont, co. Carmarthen, gent. EXETER COLL., matric. 15 June, 1805, aged 16; rector of Stoke Talmage, Oxon, 1817.

Prout, John Arthur, 1s. John, of Rainham, Kent, cler. WADHAM COLL., matric. 10 March, 1842, aged 17; clerk 1842-5.

Prout, John William, 1s. William, of St. George's, Bloomsbury, London, doctor. WADHAM COLL., matric. 5 June, 1834, aged 17; B.A. 1839, M.A. 1841, bar.-at-law, Lincoln's Inn, 1841, died 2 June, 1881.

Prout, Thomas, s. Nicholas, of Denbury, Devon, gent. EXETER COLL., matric. 5 July, 1760, aged 15; B.A. 1765. [5]

Prout, Thomas Jones, 4s. William, of Edinburgh, D.Med. CHRIST CHURCH, matric. 12 May, 1842, aged 18; student 1842, B.A. 1846, M.A. 1848, tutor 1851, rhetoric reader 1852, censor 1857, librarian 1858, Wake librarian 1862, proctor 1859, vicar of Binsey 1857. See *Alumni West.*, 519.

Prout, William, s. John, of Cromwell, co. Gloucester, gent. CHRIST CHURCH, matric. 24 May, 1715, aged 16; B.A. 1719.

Prout, William Smart, 2s. John, of Rainham, Kent, cler. WORCESTER COLL., matric. 16 March, 1843, aged 17; bible clerk 1843-6, B.A. 1847.

Provand, Charles Maxwell, 1s. James, of Glasgow, Scotland, arm. MAGDALEN HALL, matric. 16 Nov., 1829, aged 31; B.A. 1833, M.A. 1836, and died perp. curate Coseley, co. Stafford, 9 April, 1843.

Provand, Henry John, 3s. James, of Cathcart, co. Renfrew, arm. BALLIOL COLL., matric. 22 May, 1828, aged 18. [10]

Prower, John, s. Robert, of Sturminster Newton, Dorset, gent. WADHAM COLL., matric. 20 Feb., 1766, aged 18; B.A. 1769, M.A. 1772, vicar of Purton, Wilts, 1771, until his death 29 Nov., 1826, father of John Mervin.

Prower, John Elton Mervin, o.s. John Mervin, cler. WADHAM COLL., matric. 25 March, 1829, aged 17; of Purton House, Wilts, high sheriff 1862, major royal Wilts militia, died 12 May, 1882.

Prower, John Mervin, s. John, of Purton, Wilts, cler. WADHAM COLL., matric. 5 Feb., 1802, aged 17; B.A. 1806, M.A. 1835, hon. canon of Bristol, vicar of Purton, Wilts, 1827, until his death 2 April, 1869, father of the last named.

Prower, Mervyn, 1s. John Elton Mervyn, of Purton, Wilts, arm. BRASENOSE COLL., matric. 24 May, 1866, aged 19; died in college, 28 Nov., 1867. See *Rugby School Reg.*

Prower, Nelson, 2s. James Elton Mervyn, of London, arm. BRASENOSE COLL., matric. 20 May, 1875, aged 18; B.A. 1878, M.A. 1882. See *Rugby School Reg.* [15]

Prowett, John, s. William, of Adderbury, Oxon, arm. NEW COLL., matric. 17 Dec., 1792, aged 18; B.A. 1796, fellow, M.A. 1801, rector of Edburton, Sussex, 1810, of Heigham, Norfolk, 1829, and of Catfield, Norfolk, 1833, sinecure rector of Great Tey, Essex, 1845, until his death 20 March, 1851.

Prowett, Rev. John Henry, 2s. John, of Edburton, Sussex, cler. TRINITY COLL., matric. 21 March, 1833, aged 19; scholar TRINITY HALL, Cambridge, 1836, LL.B. 1840, died in 1842.

Prowett, Richard, s. Ant., of Lilbourn, Northants, pleb. LINCOLN COLL., matric. 5 Feb., 1718-9, aged 18.

Prowse, George, s. John, of Old Cleeve, Somerset, gent. EXETER COLL., matric. 23 June, 1716, aged 17; B.A. 1720, M.A. 1723.

Prowse, George, s. George, of Yeovil, Somerset, arm. MAGDALEN COLL., matric. 1 Feb., 1755, aged 18. [20]

Prowse, George, s. Thomas, of Axbridge, Somerset, arm. MAGDALEN COLL., matric. 12 Nov., 1759, aged 19.

Prowse, George Bragge, s. George, of Yeovil, Somerset, arm. UNIVERSITY COLL., matric. 7 Nov., 1783, aged 17; created M.A. 17 Dec., 1787.

Prowse, James, s. John, of Kingston-juxta-Yeovil, Somerset, gent. TRINITY COLL., matric. 5 May, 1718, aged 17.

Prowse, John, s. Thomas, of St. George's, Bloomsbury, London, arm. CHRIST CHURCH, matric. 11 Feb., 1752, aged 18; created M.A. 21 Nov., 1754.

Prowse, John Arbuthnot, o.s. Richard, of Greenwich, Kent, arm. MAGDALEN HALL, matric. 24 March, 1820, aged 29. [25]

Prowse, Richard Orton, 1s. Richard Hopkins, of Woodbridge, Suffolk, cler. BALLIOL COLL., matric. 18 Oct., 1881, aged 19; B.A. 1885, M.A. 1888.

Prowse, Thomas, s. Rog., of St. Petrock, Exeter, gent. BALLIOL COLL., matric. 14 Jan., 1719-20, aged 17; B.A. 1723, M.A. 1726.

Prowse, Thomas, s. Thomas, of St. Andrew's, Holborn, Middlesex, arm. CHRIST CHURCH, matric. 21 Oct., 1724, aged 16.

Prowse, Rev. William, s. John, of Camerton, Somerset, cler. CHRIST CHURCH, matric. 30 May, 1778, aged 19; died at Taunton in 1807.

Prowse, William, s. James, of Stoke Damerel, Plymouth Dock, Devon, gent. ST. EDMUND HALL, matric. 14 May, 1812, aged 16; B.A. 1815, M.A. 1820, rector of Bickleigh and Sheepstone 1830. [30]

Prowse, William Charles Thomas, 2s. William, of Enham, Hants, arm. EXETER COLL., matric. 27 Nov., 1861, aged 18.

Pruen, George Griffiths, 2s. Septimus Conant, of Cleeve, Somerset, gent. CHRIST CHURCH, matric. 14 Oct., 1870, aged 19; a junior student 1870-5, B.A. 1874, M.A. 1877.

Pruen, Henry, 3s. Richard, of Cheltenham, co. Gloucester, gent. ORIEL COLL., matric. 11 Dec., 1821, aged 19; B.A. 1825, M.A. 1833, rector of Childs Wickham, co. Gloucester, 1828.

Pruen, Hudson Boyce, o.s. William Ashmead, of Fladbury, co. Worcester, cler. PEMBROKE COLL., matric. 29 Oct., 1841, aged 17; scholar 1841-5, B.A. 1846, M.A. 1850, curate-in-charge of Didbrook, co. Gloucester, 1851-73, of Twyning since 1873.

Pruen, John, s. Richard, of Cheltenham, co. Gloucester, gent. ST. JOHN'S COLL., matric. 12 Nov., 1816, aged 17; B.A. 1820, M.A. 1823, a student of Lincoln's Inn 1819. [35]

Pruen, John Ashmead, 3s. Alexander Conant, of Cheltenham, arm. BRASENOSE COLL., matric. 23 April, 1879, aged 19; B.A. 1883, M.A. 1887.

Pruen, Thomas, s. Richard, of Wotton, co. Gloucester, gent. PEMBROKE COLL., matric. 25 March, 1813, aged 16; scholar 1813-6.

Pruen, Thomas, 1s. Thomas, of Prestbury, co. Gloucester, cler. UNIVERSITY COLL., matric. 10 Feb., 1819, aged 19.

Pruen, William Ashmead, s. Thomas, of St. Mary-de-Crypt, Gloucester (city), gent. WORCESTER COLL., matric. 1 May, 1800, aged 17; B.A. 1805, M.A. 1808, B.D. 1819, perp. curate Fladbury, co. Worcester, 1809-38; vicar of Snitterfield, co. Warwick, 1838, until his death 4 June, 1840.

Prussia, Frederick William III., King of, D.C.L. by diploma 13 June, 1814, died 7 June, 1840. [40]

Prussia, Frederick William IV., King of, D.C.L. by diploma 15 June, 1814, died 2 Jan., 1861.

Prussia, William, King of, and German Emperor (2s. Frederick William III.), D.C.L. by diploma 15 June, 1814, died 9 March, 1888.

Prussia, Frederick III., King of, and German Emperor, D.C.L. by diploma 4 June, 1856 (then Prince Frederick William), succeeded his father 9 March, 1888, and died 15 June following.

Prussia, Prince Augustus of, cousin of Frederick William III., D.C.L. by diploma 15 June, 1814 (s. Prince Augustus Ferdinand, of Prussia), died 19 July, 1843.

Prussia, Prince Frederick of, nephew of Frederick William III., D.C.L. by diploma 15 June, 1814 (s. Prince Frederick Lewis Charles of Prussia), died 27 July, 1863.

Prussia, Prince William of, brother of Frederick William III., D.C.L. by diploma 15 June, 1814, died 28 Sep., 1851.

Prust, Joseph, s. William, of Hartland, Devon, pleb. MAGDALEN HALL, matric. 21 March, 1774, aged 19. [5]

Prust, Joseph Prust, s. Joseph Prust, of Woolfardisworthy, Devon, cler. EXETER COLL., matric. 30 April, 1799, aged 18; B.A. 1803, fellow 1805-23, M.A. 1806, B.D. 1817, proctor 1810, rector of West Worlington, Devon, 1805, of Virginstow 1811, and of Langtree 1822, until his death 13 May, 1839. See *Coll. Reg.*, 118.

Prust, Michael, s. William, of Hartland, Devon, gent. EXETER COLL., matric. 14 March, 1761, aged 19; B.A. 1764.

Prutheroe, Charles, s. Thomas, of Ystradveltey, pleb. MERTON COLL., matric. 10 March, 1737-8, aged 18; B.A. 1741.

Pryce, Alexander Thomas Albert, 1s. John, of Frant, Sussex, gent. QUEEN'S COLL., matric. 22 Nov., 1866, aged 25; of Withyham, Sussex.

Pryce, Alan Cameron Bruce, 1s. John Wyndham Bruce, of London, arm. EXETER COLL., matric. 2 Feb., 1855, aged 18; B.A. 1859, M.A. 1861, bar.-at-law, Lincoln's Inn, 30 April, 1862, assumed the additional surname of PRYCE in 1872, father of George Lewis Bruce, of Balliol College (see page 178). See Foster's *Peerage*, B. ABERDARE; & Foster's *Men at the Bar*. [10]

Pryce, Arthur Ivor, 2s. John, of Bangor, co. Carnarvon, cler. UNIVERSITY COLL., matric. 17 Oct., 1885, aged 18.

Pryce, Charles, s. William, of St. Dunstan's, London, gent. MERTON COLL., matric. 18 March, 1796, aged 18; B.A. 1800, M.A. 1802, vicar of Wellingborough 1810, and preb. of Hereford 1813, until his death 7 June, 1825. See *Eton School Lists*.

Pryce, Edmund, s. Richard, of Llansantfraid, co. Montgomery, gent. JESUS COLL., matric. 1 Dec., 1733, aged 17; B.A. 1738.

Pryce, Edward, s. Edmund, of Forden, co. Montgomery, arm. BALLIOL COLL., matric. 8 April, 1717, aged 18; of Gunley, co. Montgomery, high sheriff 1734, father of Edward 1742, and John 1752.

Pryce, Edward, s. John, of Whitton, co. Radnor, gent. JESUS COLL., matric. 5 Dec., 1722, aged 16. [15]

Pryce, Edward, s. Adam, of Lanvynling, co. Montgomery, arm. TRINITY COLL., matric. 24 May, 1726, aged 18; B.A. 18 March, 1729-30 (as PRICE).

Pryce, Edward, s. Edward, of Forden, co. Montgomery, arm. QUEEN'S COLL., matric. 1 June, 1742, aged 18; bar.-at-law, Middle Temple, 1748, brother of John 1759.

Pryce, Edward Stisted Mostyn, 1s. John Harryman, of Welshpool, co. Montgomery, arm. BALLIOL COLL., matric. 25 Jan., 1871, aged 19; B.A. 1874, M.A. 1877, of Gunley Hall, co. Montgomery, a student of the Inner Temple 1873.

Pryce, Francis, s. Samuel, of Llanvaughan, co. Brecon, pleb. CHRIST CHURCH, matric. 12 Feb., 1765, aged 18; B.A. 1768 (? died perp. curate Temple Guiting, co. Gloucester, in 1809, aged 64).

Pryce, John, s. William, of Penall, co. Merioneth, cler. JESUS COLL., matric. 2 June, 1720. [20]

Pryce, John, s. Thomas, of Welchpool, co. Montgomery, gent. JESUS COLL., matric. 6 Dec., 1722, aged 19.

Pryce, John, s. Richard, of Llansantfraid, co. Montgomery, gent. UNIVERSITY COLL., matric. 10 March, 1728-9, aged 19.

Pryce, John, s. Thomas, of Bettws, co. Montgomery, pleb. JESUS COLL., matric. 22 Oct., 1748, aged 19.

Pryce, Rev. John, s. Edward, of Gunley, co. Montgomery, gent. PEMBROKE COLL., matric. 22 Nov., 1752, aged 17; B.A. 1756, M.A. 1759, of Gunley, died in 1803, brother of Edward 1742, and father of Richard 1789.

Pryce, John, 2s. John, of Haddenham, Bucks, cler. CHRIST CHURCH, matric. 20 Oct., 1818, aged 18.

Pryce, John. JESUS COLL., 1847. See PRICE, page 1149. [26]

Pryce, John Devereux, 1s. John Devereux, of Shrawardine, Salop, arm. MAGDALEN HALL, matric. 14 Jan., 1840, aged 20.

Pryce, John Jones, 1s. John, of Brecon (town), arm. NON-COLL., matric. 14 Jan., 1869, aged 31.

Pryce, John Roland, 1s. John, of Bangor, cler. JESUS COLL., matric. 18 Oct., 1883, aged 18; B.A. 1887.

Pryce, Rev. Jonathan, s. Robert, of Prees, Salop, cler. JESUS COLL., matric. 20 May, 1809, aged 21; B.A. 1813, died at Whixall, Salop, 22 Aug., 1818.

Pryce, Joseph, s. Matthew, of Llansamblett, co. Glamorgan, gent. BALLIOL COLL., matric. 17 Dec., 1742, aged 18. [31]

Pryce, Richard, s. Morrice, of Berriew, co. Montgomery, pleb. CHRIST CHURCH, matric. 5 May, 1722, aged 18; B.A. 22 Feb., 1725-6 (as PRICE).

Pryce, Richard, s. Thomas, of Leintwardine, co. Hereford, cler. ALL SOULS' COLL., matric. 30 July, 1753, aged 19, B.A. 20 April, 1757; created M.A. from BRASENOSE COLL. 26 April, 1757.

Pryce, Richard, s. John, of Newport, Salop, cler. PEMBROKE COLL., matric. 17 Oct., 1789, aged 17; B.A. 1793, of Gunley, co. Montgomery, high sheriff, 1817, died 26 Oct., 1832.

Pryce, Rev. Richard Henry Mostyn, s. Richard, of Montgomery (town), gent. CORPUS CHRISTI COLL., matric. 13 Oct., 1817, aged 18; exhibitioner 1817-21, B.A. 1821, of Gunley, co. Montgomery, died 4 March, 1858. [35]

Pryce, Robert, s. Robert, of Llangedfan, co. Montgomery, gent. JESUS COLL., matric. 24 Nov., 1778, aged 19.

Pryce, Salusbury, s. Adam, of Llanfyllin, co. Montgomery, gent. JESUS COLL., matric, 17 March, 1732-3, aged 18; B.A. 1736, M.A. 1766, B. & D.D. 1766.

Pryce, Thomas, s. Thomas, of Burrington, co. Hereford, cler. TRINITY COLL., matric. 18 March, 1724-5, aged 18; B.A. 1728 (as PRICE).

Pryce, Thomas, s. Richard, of Burrington, co. Hereford, cler. WADHAM COLL., matric. 31 May, 1786, aged 18; B.A. 1790.

Pryce, Thomas William, s. Thomas, of Stockwell, Surrey, arm. UNIVERSITY COLL., matric. 5 Feb., 1814, aged 18. [40]

Pryce, William Henry, s. William, of Haddenham, Bucks, cler. ST. EDMUND HALL, matric. 18 March, 1817, aged 19; exhibitioner 1817-20, B.A. 1820.

Prynne, George Rundle, of CATHARINE COLL., Cambridge (B.A. 1840, M.A. 1861); adm. 'comitatis causa' 30 May, 1861, vicar of St. Peter, Plymouth, 1848.

Prynne, William Hunt, s. Dodington Hunt, of Charlton King's, co. Gloucester, arm. (see page 715). CORPUS CHRISTI COLL., matric. 12 Oct., 1791, aged 19; created M.A. 17 June, 1795, assumed the additional surname of PRYNNE.

Pryor, Arthur Vickris, 1s. Arthur, of Wandsworth, Surrey, arm. CHRIST CHURCH, matric. 18 May, 1864, aged 17; B.A. 1867, a partner in Truman and Hanbury's brewery. See *Eton School Lists*.

or, Edmund, 2s. Arthur, of Castle Rising, Norfolk, arm. CHRIST CHURCH, matric. 16 Oct., 1868, aged 18. See *Eton School Lists*.

or, Frederick Bell, 4s. John Izard, of Baldock, Herts, gent. NEW COLL., matric. 18 Jan., 1841, aged 18; fellow 1841-50, B.A. 1844, M.A. 1849, rector of Bennington, Herts, 1851, until his death 23 May, 1860.

or, Henry, s. Thomas, of Daventry, Northants, gent. LINCOLN COLL., matric. 5 Dec., 1716, aged 16; B.A. 1720.

or, Hubert Frederick, o.s. Frederick Bell, of Warneford, Hants, cler. ST. MARY HALL, matric. 15 April, 1871, aged 19.

or, John Eade, 1s. John, of Baldock, Herts, arm. MAGDALEN COLL., matric. 13 June, 1854, aged 18; B.A. 1858, M.A. 1861, rector of Bennington, Herts, 1860-81, died 5 July, 1884. See *Eton School Lists*. [5]

or, Michael, 6s. William, of St. Agnes, Cornwall, gent. NON-COLL., matric. 13 Oct., 1883, aged 20.

or, Morris, 2s. John Izard, of Baldock, Herts, gent. MAGDALEN HALL, matric. 13 Dec., 1823, aged 19.

or, Percival Arthur Leonard, 1s. John Eade, of Bennington, Herts, cler. MAGDALEN COLL., matric. 19 Oct., 1883, aged 18; B.A. 1887.

or, Reginald, 1s. Alfred, of Hatfield, Herts, arm. UNIVERSITY COLL., matric. 28 April, 1857, aged 18; scholar 1857-62, B.A. 1862 (as Alfred Reginald).

or, Richard Vickris, 1s. Vickris, of Baldock, Herts, arm. BALLIOL COLL., matric. 14 Dec., 1827, aged 18; B.A. 1831, M.A. 1834, rector of Spettisbury with Charlton, Dorset, 1841, until his death 24 Nov., 1851. [10]

yor, Roderick, 4s. Arthur, of Roehampton, Surrey, arm. BRASENOSE COLL., matric. 30 Jan., 1874, aged 18; B.A. 1877, M.A. 1883. See *Eton School Lists*.

yor, Thomas, 7s. Vickris, of Baldock, Herts, arm. CHRIST CHURCH, matric. 19 Oct., 1842, aged 17; B.A. 1847, of The Elms, Baldock. See *Eton School Lists*.

yse, Henry Louis Vanneck, o.s. Charles, of Hallgreen, co. Worcester, gent. ST. JOHN'S COLL., matric. 14 Oct., 1882, aged 18; B.A. 1886.

yse, John, s. John, of Kerry, co. Montgomery, gent. WADHAM COLL., matric. 3 March, 1741-2, aged 18; B.A. 25 Feb., 1745-6.

yse, John, s. Hugh, of Dolgelly, co. Merioneth, cler. JESUS COLL., matric. 12 March, 1766, aged 18. [15]

yse, John Pughe, s. Thomas, of Gogerddan, co. Cardigan, arm. ORIEL COLL., matric. 16 June, 1756, aged 17; created M.A. 21 May, 1760, died s.p.

yse, Lewis, s. Walter, of London, arm. ORIEL COLL., matric. 19 Aug., 1732, aged 15; of Gogerddan, died 12 March, 1798, father of the next named.

yse, Lewis, s. Lewis, of Woodstock, Oxon, arm. TRINITY COLL., matric. 21 Jan., 1768, aged 17; died 25 Sep., 1776.

yse, Lewis Thomas Loveden, 3s. Sir Pryse, of Llanbadarn-Fawr, co. Cardigan, baronet. EXETER COLL., matric. 18 Oct., 1883, aged 19. See Foster's *Baronetage*.

yse, Pryse, s. Edward Loveden Loveden, of Buscot, Berks, arm. (see page 874). CHRIST CHURCH, matric. 16 Feb., 1792, aged 18; of Gogerddan, co. Cardigan, high sheriff 1798, M.P. Carmarthen 1818-49, assumed the name of PRYSE in lieu of LOVEDEN, died 4 Jan., 1849. See Foster's *Baronetage*. [20]

yse, Thomas, s. John, of Cardigan, arm. ORIEL COLL., matric. 9 June, 1732, aged 15.

ytherch, Stephen, s. David, of Ruabon, Denbigh, pleb. JESUS COLL., matric. 14 April, 1739, aged 19; B.A. 1743, M.A. 1745, died vicar of Leighton and Wenlock, Salop, 12 Aug., 1786.

Puckle, Edwin, 4s. James William, of West Bromwich, co. Stafford, gent. MAGDALEN HALL, matric. 30 June, 1854, aged 22; B.A. 1858, rector of Alby, Norfolk, 1868.

Puckle, Frederick Craig, 2s. Richard, of Brighton, Sussex, arm. EXETER COLL., matric. 23 Oct., 1850, aged 18; B.A. 1854, M.A. 1861.

Puckle, Horace, 2s. James, of London, arm. NON-COLL., matric. 13 Oct., 1884, aged 19; B.A. from HERTFORD COLL. 1887. [25]

Puckle, John, o.s. John, of Pentonville, Islington, Middlesex, arm. BRASENOSE COLL., matric. 14 April, 1832, aged 19; scholar 1832-5, B.A. 1835, M.A. 1839, vicar of St. Mary-the-Virgin, Dover, 1842, hon. canon Canterbury 1869; for list of his works see *Crockford*.

Puckle, Thomas John, 1s. Thomas Broadhurst, of Pirbright, Surrey, gent. EXETER COLL., matric. 10 Oct., 1873, aged 19; B.A. 1877, M.A. 1880, vicar of Wrenthorpe, Yorks, 1883.

Puckridge, Jonathan Samuel, 1s. Jonathan, of London, gent. HERTFORD COLL., matric. 1 Dec., 1875, aged 18; B.A. 1878, M.A. 1883, held various curacies since 1880.

Puckridge, Richard, s. Thomas, of Rumsey, Hants, arm. ORIEL COLL., matric. 16 May, 1743, aged 18.

Puddicombe, Richard, s. Richard, of West Looe, Cornwall, gent. BALLIOL COLL., matric. 2 July, 1771, aged 17; vicar of Shebbeare and Sheepwash, Devon, 1779. [30]

Pudner, Humphrey, s. Humphrey, of Chartham, Kent, arm. UNIVERSITY COLL., matric. 12 Oct., 1734, aged 17. See Hasted's *Kent*, iv. 428.

Pudney, Henry, 2s. Thomas, of Halstead, Essex, gent. NON-COLL., matric. 25 Jan., 1879, aged 25.

Pudsey, Frederick William, 1s. William, of Eaglescliffe, co. Durham, cler. ST. ALBAN HALL, matric. 8 May, 1866, aged 26; curate of Aston, Yorks, 1867-70, vicar of Masborough, Yorks, 1870-84, and of Stainton in Cleveland 1884.

Puget, John Hey, 1s. John, of London, arm. NEW COLL., matric. 23 March, 1820, aged 17; B.A. from TRINITY COLL., Cambridge, 1825, M.A. 1828.

Puget, Peter, s. Peter, of Kensington, Middlesex, arm. PEMBROKE COLL., matric. 15 May, 1816, aged 17.

Pughe, Arthur Owen, 7s. Evan, of Llantrissant, Isle of Anglesey, cler. CHRIST CHURCH, matric. 12 Oct., 1883, aged 19; scholar 1883, B.A. 1888. [35]

Pughe, Charles Reay, 3s. Kenneth McKenzie, of 'Ins. of Cumbrae,' cler. WORCESTER COLL., matric. 16 Oct., 1871, aged 19; B.A. 1874, M.A. 1878, vicar of Ingleton, Yorks, 1879-83, rector of Castle Eaton, co. Gloucester, 1883, brother of Kenneth 1862.

Pugh, Cecil Rose, 2s. Charles, of Madeley, Salop, arm. MAGDALEN COLL., matric. 16 Oct., 1875, aged 19; B.A. 1878.

Pugh, David, s. Lewis, of Llanarth, co. Cardigan, pleb. MAGDALEN HALL, matric. 31 March, 1721, aged 18; B.A. from TRINITY COLL. 1725.

Pugh, David, s. Hugh, of Dolgelly, co. Merioneth, pleb. HERTFORD COLL., matric. 15 Dec., 1758, aged 19; B.A. 1762 (? died rector of Newport, co. Pembroke, in 1816). [40]

Pugh, David, s. Charles, of Sydenham, Kent, arm. TRINITY COLL., matric. 29 April, 1809, aged 19; recorder of Welshpool, and major Montgomeryshire yeomanry, M.P. Montgomery 1832-3, and 1847, until his death 20 April, 1861.

Pugh, David, 1s. David Heron, of Greenhill, co. Carmarthen, arm. BALLIOL COLL., matric. 6 April, 1824, aged 18; B.A. 1828, of Manoravon, co. Carmarthen, high sheriff 1874, M.P. 1857-68, and Dec., 1885, bar.-at-law, Inner Temple, 1837. See Foster's *Men at the Bar* & *Rugby School Reg.*, 123.

Pugh, David Richard, 1s. John, of Llantasarn, co. Cardigan, cler. JESUS COLL., matric. 20 Oct., 1886, aged 20.

Pughe, Edward, s. David, of Bryn Eglwys, co. Denbigh, gent. JESUS COLL., matric. 29 May, 1759, aged 18.

Pughe, Edward, 4s. Richard, of Llanegrin, co. Merioneth, cler. JESUS COLL., matric. 28 March, 1828, aged 19.

Pughe, Evan, s. Rice, of Caerwys, co. Flint, cler. JESUS COLL., matric. 20 May, 1779, aged 18 (? B.A. 1783, M.A. 1785).

Pugh, Evan, s. Lewis, of Llanegrin, co. Merioneth, pleb. JESUS COLL., matric. 24 June, 1779, aged 18 (? B.A. 1784 as PUGHE).

Pughe, Evan, 1s. Evan, of Llanfihangel Geneu-r-Glyn, cler. JESUS COLL., matric. 7 Dec., 1824, aged 18; B.A. 1828, vicar of Llanidloes 1837-50, senior vicar of Bangor, and vicar-choral of the cathedral 1850-63, rector of Llantrisant, etc., 1863, until his death 11 Aug., 1869. [5]

Pughe, Francis Heveningham, 3s. Evan, of Bangor, co. Carnarvon, cler. ALL SOULS' COLL., matric. 16 Oct., 1876, aged 18; bible clerk 1876-80, B.A. 1880, M.A. 1886, brother of Walter 1875.

Pugh, Frederick, 2s. Samuel, of Manchester, gent. NEW COLL., matric. 5 Feb., 1877, aged 19; B.Mus. 1885.

Pugh, George Augustus, 1s. Enoch, of Abergwili, co. Carmarthen, cler. JESUS COLL., matric. 16 Jan., 1869, aged 20; S.C.L. & B.A. 1872, M.A. 1876, curate of Wombourn, co. Stafford, 1837-82, vicar of Swindon, Stafford, 1882.

Pughe, George Richard Gould, 1s. Richard, of Golva, co. Montgomery, cler. TRINITY COLL., matric. 27 Nov., 1850, aged 19.

Pugh, Giles, 3s. Hugh, of Hinton Martel, Dorset, cler. MAGDALEN HALL, matric. 17 March, 1823, aged 19; B.A. 1827, chaplain to the British Embassy at Naples 1845-61, vicar of Shapwick 1864, until his death 28 Feb., 1875. [10]

Pugh, Henry Bruce, 3s. Giles, of South Newton, near Salisbury, cler. BALLIOL COLL., matric. 12 Oct., 1861, aged 19; B.A. 1865, M.A. 1868, rector of Dalham, co. Cambridge, 1876.

Pugh, Henry John, s. Henry, of Llanrwst, co. Denbigh, cler. BRASENOSE COLL., matric. 14 Nov., 1800, aged 19; B.A. 1804.

Pugh, Hugh, s. Lew., of Llanarth, co. Cardigan, pleb. JESUS COLL., matric. 1 April, 1717, aged 17.

Pugh, Hugh, s. Hugh, of Dolgelly, co. Merioneth, pleb. JESUS COLL., matric. 2 June, 1747, aged 18.

Pugh, Hugh, s. Howell, of Dolgelly, co. Merioneth, pleb. CHRIST CHURCH, matric. 22 Nov., 1754, aged 19; B.A. 1758, M.A. 1762 (Rev. H. P., of Brithdie, near Dolgelly, died in 1809). [15]

Pugh, Hugh, s. Morris, of Llanvihangel-y-Pennant, co. Merioneth, pleb. JESUS COLL., matric. 17 Dec., 1776, aged 19.

Pugh, Hugh, s. Hugh, of Llanvihangel-y-Traethan, co. Merioneth, pleb. JESUS COLL., matric. 10 Oct., 1782, aged 20; B.A. 1790, M.A. 1792 (? rector of Hinton Martel, Dorset, 1797, until his death 23 Sep., 1827, aged 72).

Pugh, Humphrey, s. Robert, of Lanvihangel-y-Traethan, co. Merioneth, pleb. JESUS COLL., matric. 19 March, 1766, aged 19; B.A. 1769.

Pugh, James Baldwyn, s. Thomas, of Rock, co. Worcester, cler. MERTON COLL., matric. 17 Dec., 1744, aged 19; B.A. 1748 (as James).

Pughe, John, s. Thomas, of Machynlleth, co. Montgomery, pleb. JESUS COLL., matric. 11 March, 1719-20, aged 20. [20]

Pugh, John, s. Thomas, of Hatherley, co. Gloucester, cler. BALLIOL COLL., matric. 8 March, 1720-1, aged 19.

Pugh, John, s. Thomas, of Lindridge, co. Worcester, cler. MAGDALEN HALL, matric. 21 March, 1740-1, aged 21.

Pughe, John, s. David, of Dolgelly, co. Merioneth pleb. JESUS COLL., matric. 27 March, 1750, aged 18; B.A. 1754.

Pugh, John, s. Hugh, of Dolgelly, co. Merioneth pleb. HERTFORD COLL., matric. 4 June, 1767 aged 23; B.A. 1771. See *Gent.'s Mag.*, 1799 i. 440.

Pughe, John, s. Hugh, of Llanvihangel, co. Merioneth gent. JESUS COLL., matric. 17 Dec., 1774, aged 18; B.A. 1778. [25]

Pughe, John, s. Rice, of Cerig-y-druidion, Denbigh cler. JESUS COLL., matric. 15 May, 1777, aged 19.

Pugh, John, s. Hugh Robert, of Llanfihangel, co. Merioneth, pleb. JESUS COLL., matric. 15 Dec. 1788, aged 23; B.A. 1792, M.A. 1796 (as PUGHE).

Pugh, John, s. Thomas, of London, gent. PEMBROKE COLL., matric. 24 May, 1791, aged 18; B.C.L. 1798.

Pughe, John, 3s. Richard, of Llanegryn, co. Merioneth, cler. JESUS COLL., matric. 4 Dec., 1819, aged 19; 'servitor,' B.A. 1823, M.A. 1828, perp. curate Llandecwyn and Llanvihangel-y-Traethan, co. Monmouth, died 2 July, 1861.

Pugh, John, s. Hugh, of Machynlleth, co. Montgomery, gent. MAGDALEN HALL, matric. 17 March, 1836, aged 27. [30]

Pugh, John Thomas, 3s. Richard, of Llanfihangel, co. Montgomery, cler. JESUS COLL., matric. 18 April, 1861, aged 19; B.A. 1865, M.A. 1884.

Pugh, John William, 2s. David, of Llandillo-Vawr, co. Carmarthen, arm. BALLIOL COLL., matric. 22 March, 1828, aged 18; B.A. 1832, M.A. 1834, vicar of Llandillo-Vawr, co. Glamorgan, 1838, until his death 14 July, 1852. See *Rugby School Reg.*, 141.

Pugh, Joshua, s. Thomas, of Cerig-y-druidion, co. Brecon, pleb. QUEEN'S COLL., matric. 18 March, 1718-9, aged 19.

Pughe, Kenneth Mackenzie, 1s. Kenneth Mackenzie, of Swanbourne, Bucks, cler. BRASENOSE COLL., matric. 19 June, 1862, aged 19; scholar 1862-7, B.A. 1865, M.A. 1869, curate of Irton, Cumberland, 1879-82, vicar 1882.

Pugh, Lewis, s. Maurice, of Llanvihangel-y-Pennant, co. Merioneth, pleb. JESUS COLL., matric. 16 May, 1774, aged 21. [35]

Pughe, Lewis, s. Hugh, of Llanvihangel, co. Merioneth, gent. JESUS COLL., matric. 16 May, 1782, aged 20.

Pughe, Lewis, s. Rice, of Llysfaen, co. Carnarvon, cler. JESUS COLL., matric. 10 April, 1783, aged 17.

Pughe, Lewis, s. Lewis, of Llanenddwyn, co. Merioneth, gent. JESUS COLL., matric. 9 May, 1799, aged 18.

Pugh, Lewis Pugh, 2s. John Evans, of Aberystwith, co. Cardigan, arm. CORPUS CHRISTI COLL., matric. 7 Dec., 1855, aged 18; B.A. 1859, M.A. 1862, of Abermaed, co. Cardigan, M.P. 1880-5, bar.-at-law, Lincoln's Inn, 1862, assumed the surname of PUGH in lieu of EVANS by royal licence 1868. See Foster's *Men at the Bar.*

Pugh, Lewis Pugh Evans, 1s. Lewis Pugh, of Calcutta, arm. CORPUS CHRISTI COLL., matric. 23 Oct., 1884, aged 19; a student of Lincoln's Inn 1884. [40]

Pugh, Maurice, s. Maur., of Bishop's Castle, Salop, gent. BALLIOL COLL., matric. 28 March, 1724 aged 18; B.A. 1727, M.A. 1731.

Pughe, Rev. Philip Alfred, 5s. Evan, of Bangor, cler. KEBLE COLL., matric. 14 Oct., 1879, aged 18; B.A. 1882, M.A. 1886, head-master Bewdley Grammar School.

Pugh, Rice, s. Rice, of Tallyllin, co. Merioneth, pleb. JESUS COLL., matric. 12 May, 1752, aged 21.

Pughe, Richard, s. Rich., of Darowen, co. Montgomery, pleb. JESUS COLL., matric. 14 Nov., 1726, aged 19; B.A. 1730, M.A. 1733.

ıgh, Richard, s. Hugh, of Dolgelly, co. Merioneth, pleb. JESUS COLL., matric. 10 Nov., 1752, aged 19.

ıghe, Richard, s. Richard, of Dolgelly, co. Merioneth, pleb. JESUS COLL., matric. 18 March, 1780, aged 17; B.A. 1785.

ıghe, Richard, s. Richard, of Llanegryn, co. Merioneth, cler. JESUS COLL., matric. 21 March, 1812, aged 19; B.A. 1815.

ıghe, Richard, o.s. William, of Mallwyd, co. Montgomery, cler. JESUS COLL., matric. 28 March, 1828, aged 19.

ıghe, Richard, 2s. William, of Darowen, co. Montgomery, gent. JESUS COLL., matric. 27 Nov., 1834, aged 22; B.A. 1838, M.A. 1841. **[5]**

ıgh, Robert, s. Hugh, of Beaumaris, gent. JESUS COLL., matric. 11 April, 1717, aged 21; B.A. from NEW INN HALL 11 July, 1719.

ıghe, Robert, s. John, of Dolgelly, co. Merioneth, pleb. JESUS COLL., matric. 7 May, 1761, aged 17.

ıgh, Robert, s. Hugh, of Dolgelly, co. Merioneth, pleb. EXETER COLL., matric. 26 March, 1768, aged 19; exhibitioner 1767, B.A. 1772, perp. curate Lee Brockhurst, Salop, vicar of Donnington, co. Lincoln, 1794, until his death 16 Feb., 1825. See *Coll. Reg.*, 145.

ıghe, Robert Parry, s. John, of Dolgelly, co. Merioneth, arm. JESUS COLL., matric. 14 May, 1807, aged 16.

ıghe, Rev. Walter Reginald Heveningham, 4s. Evan, of Bangor, cler. NON-COLL., matric. 16 Oct., 1875, aged 16; B.A. 1880, M.A. 1883, brother of Francis 1876. **[10]**

gh, Watkin, s. Lewis, of Llarth, co. Cardigan, pleb. JESUS COLL., matric. 12 May, 1730, aged 19; B.A. from CHRIST CHURCH 1733, M.A. 1737.

gh, William, s. John, of Knighton, co. Radnor, pleb. JESUS COLL., matric. 11 March, 1719-20, aged 18; B.A. 1723.

gh, William, s. William, of Llangentin, co. Brecon, pleb. JESUS COLL., matric. 4 Dec., 1740, aged 18; B.A. 26 Feb., 1744-5.

gh, William, s. David, of Bryngiwys, co. Denbigh, gent. JESUS COLL., matric. 15 May, 1755, aged 18.

gh, William, s. Hugh, of Dolgelly, co. Merioneth, pleb. JESUS COLL., matric. 3 April, 1770, aged 18; B.A. 1774, rector of Llanfair 1816, until his death 23 Dec., 1845, aged 95. **[15]**

gh, William, s. Richard, of Llanrwth, co. Denbigh, cler. CHRIST CHURCH, matric. 7 Nov., 1785, aged 19.

ghe, William, s. Richard, of Dolgelly, co. Merioneth, pleb. JESUS COLL., matric. 8 April, 1786, aged 20; B.A. 1790.

ghe, William, 4s. William, of Llanegrin, co. Merioneth, pleb. JESUS COLL., matric. 17 March, 1826, aged 19.

gh, William Owen, created D.C.L. 19 June, 1822, Welsh archæologist and lexicographer, died 4 June, 1835. See *Gent.'s Mag.*, ii. 216.

eston, Allen, s. Gerrard, of St. Dennis, London, gent. CHRIST CHURCH, matric. 16 Nov., 1719, aged 20. See *Alumni West.*, 272. **[20]**

eston, Edward, s. John, of Havod-y-wern, co. Denbigh, gent. JESUS COLL., matric. 26 Jan., 1714-5, aged 17; B.A. 1718, M.A. 1721, B.D. 1729.

eston, John, s. John, of Bangor, co. Denbigh, gent. JESUS COLL., matric. 15 Dec., 1732, aged 16; B.A. 1736.

eston, Philip, s. John, of Pickhill, co. Denbigh, arm. JESUS COLL., matric. 17 Dec., 1748, aged 17; B.A. 1752, M.A. 1755, B. & D.D. 1784, rector of Worthenbury, Flints, and vicar of Ruabon, co. Denbigh, 1784.

eston, Philip, s. Richard, of Chester (city), arm. BRASENOSE COLL., matric. 26 Nov., 1759, aged 18.

Puleston, Theophilus Henry Gresley, 4s. Richard, of Oswestry, Salop, baronet. BRASENOSE COLL., matric. 9 June, 1841, aged 19; B.A. 1845, rector of Worthenbury since 1848. See Foster's *Baronetage.*

Puleston, Watkin, s. John, of Bangor, co. Denbigh, gent. JESUS COLL., matric. 27 March, 1740, aged 16; B.A. 1743. **[25]**

Pulford, Alfred, 1s. Alfred, of London, gent. ST. JOHN'S COLL., matric. 24 Jan., 1874, aged 19.

Pulford, John, s. William, of Liverpool, Lancashire, pleb. BRASENOSE COLL., matric. 23 Oct., 1794, aged 16; B.A. 1799, M.A. 1811, B.D. 1816.

Pulford, Rev. William, s. William, of Liverpool, Lancashire, pleb. BRASENOSE COLL., matric. 25 June, 1791, aged 18; B.A. 1795, M.A. 1806, B. & D.D. 1816, died 26 July, 1849.

Pullan, Leighton, 2s. Charles, of Lewisham, Kent, gent. CHRIST CHURCH, matric. 10 Oct., 1884, aged 19; scholar 1884. **[30]**

Pullein, John, M.A. from CLARE COLL., Cambridge; adm. 'ad eundem' 10 June, 1859, B.A. 1836, M.A. 1840, vicar of Warmfield, Yorks, 1838-71, and of Weeton 1872-85, died 9 Jan., 1887.

Pullen, John, s. William, of Jamaica, arm. ST. JOHN'S COLL., matric. 5 Sep., 1777, aged 25.

Puller, (Sir) Christopher, s. Richard, of London, arm. CHRIST CHURCH, matric. 4 Feb., 1792, aged 18, B.A. 1795; fellow QUEEN'S COLL., bar.-at-law, Inner Temple, 1800, and of Lincoln's Inn 1812, K.C., and a bencher 1822, chief justice of Bengal 1823, until his death 31 May, 1824, father of Christopher 1825. See *Eton School Lists.*

Puller, Christopher Cholmeley, 3s. Christopher Giles, of Youngsbury, Herts, arm. BALLIOL COLL., matric. 28 June, 1858, aged 18; scholar 1858-63, B.A. 1863, M.A. 1864, a student of Lincoln's Inn 1872.

Puller, Christopher (William Giles), o.s. Christopher, of St. Giles'-in-the-Fields, London, equitis. CHRIST CHURCH, matric. 11 March, 1825, aged 17; student 1828-31, B.A. 1829, M.A. 1832, of Youngsbury, Herts, bar.-at-law, Lincoln's Inn, 1832, assumed the additional surname of GILES 1857, M.P. Herts, 1857, until his death 16 Feb., 1864, father of the last named. See *Eton School Lists.* **[35]**

Puller, George, s. Richard, of St. Peter-le-Poor, London, arm. MERTON COLL., matric. 27 Oct., 1810, aged 18; postmaster 1812-14, B.A. 1814.

Pulley, Harry, 2s. Charles Horton, of Homerton, Middlesex, gent. ST. MARY HALL, matric. 31 March, 1849, aged 24; B.A. 1852.

Pullin, Edward Tovey, s. John, of Bristol, Somerset, gent. ORIEL COLL., matric. 1 Nov., 1779, aged 18.

Pulling, Rev. Charles James, 3s. William, of Hereford (city), gent. MAGDALEN HALL, matric. 15 March, 1845, aged 27; B.A. 1848.

Pulling, Charles William Pulling, o.s. Charles James, of Cheetham Hall, Lancashire, cler. BRASENOSE COLL., matric. 15 Jan., 1883, aged 21. **[40]**

Pulling, Edward Herbert Langley, 3s. Frederick William, of Modbury, Devon, cler. NON-COLL., matric. 18 Oct., 1880, aged 21.

Pulling, Frederick Sanders, 1s. Frederick William, of Modbury, Devon, cler. EXETER COLL., matric. 19 Jan., 1872, aged 18; exhibitioner 1871-6, B.A. 1875, M.A. 1878, professor of history Yorkshire College, Leeds, in 1877, edited 'Life of Lord Salisbury.' See *Coll. Reg.*, 166.

Pulling, Henry George, 3s. William, of Eastnor, co. Hereford, cler. WORCESTER COLL., matric. 20 Oct., 1881, aged 19; scholar HERTFORD COLL. 1881-6, B.A. 1885.

Pulling, James, vice-chancellor of the University of Cambridge (1852-3), created D.C.L. 7 June, 1853; fellow CORPUS CHRISTI COLL. 1838-50, 11th wrangler & B.A. 1837, M.A. 1840, B.D. 1848, D.D. (per *Lit. Reg.*) 1855, master 1850-79, vicar of Belchamp St. Paul's 1863, until his death 26 Feb., 1879.

Pulling, Rev. John Lenten, o.s. John, of Deptford, Kent, gent. NON-COLL., matric. 25 Nov., 1868, aged 32; B.A. from CHRIST CHURCH 1874, B.C.L. 1876, M.A. 1878, died 23 Nov., 1887.

Pulling, William, 1s. William, of Hereford (city), arm. ORIEL COLL., matric. 9 June, 1832, aged 18, B.A. 1836; fellow BRASENOSE COLL. 1836-51, M.A. 1838, tutor, junior bursar, and Greek lecturer 1844, vicar of Tidenham, co. Gloucester, 1839-42, rector of Eastnor, co. Hereford, 1849, and of Pixley 1850, preb. of Hereford 1868.

Pullinger, Frank, 1s. William, of Oldham, Lancashire, gent. CORPUS CHRISTI COLL., matric. 23 Oct., 1884, aged 18; scholar 1884, B.A. 1888.

Pulman, Rev. Prockter Thomas, 1s. William Walker, of Wellington, Somerset, cler. PEMBROKE COLL., matric. 25 Oct., 1871, aged 20; B.A. 1876, B.C.L. & M.A. 1880, bar.-at-law, Middle Temple, 1879. See Foster's *Men at the Bar* & *Eton School Lists.*

Pulman, William Walker, 3s. James, of Westminster, arm. CHRIST CHURCH, matric. 12 May, 1842, aged 19; B.A. 1846, M.A. 1849, vicar of Wellington, Somerset, 1850, until his death 24 July, 1859. See *Eton School Lists.* [5]

Pulman, William Walker, 2s. William Walker, of Wellington, Somerset, cler. ST. JOHN'S COLL., matric. 12 Oct., 1872, aged 19; B.A. 1876, M.A. 1882, held various curacies 1876-85, rector of Westborough, co. Lincoln, 1885.

Pulsford, Charles, s. Luke, of Bradninch, Devon, doctor. MERTON COLL., matric. 9 July, 1799, aged 17; B.A. from JESUS COLL., Cambridge, 1807, canon residentiary of Wells 1826, vicar of Burnham, Somerset, 1827, until his death 15 March, 1841, aged 58 (as Charles Henry).

Pulsford, William, s. William, of Sanford, Devon, gent. EXETER COLL., matric. 19 March, 1718-9, aged 20; B.A. from ST. MARY HALL 3 Feb., 1723-4 (as PULESFORD).

Pulteney, John, s. Richard Fawcett, of Grendon, co. Warwick, doctor. CHRIST CHURCH, matric. 26 June, 1783, aged 16; of Chiswick, Middlesex, assumed the surname and arms of PULTENEY in lieu of FAWCETT by royal licence 9 Aug., 1813, died 24 June, 1849, father of the next named. See *Alumni West.*, 417.

Pulteney, John Apsley, 1s. John (formerly Fawcett), of Cumberland, arm. CHRIST CHURCH, matric. 18 April, 1823, aged 17; captain 12th lancers, died April, 1840. [10]

Pulteney, Richard Thomas Pulteney, 2s. John, of Ulverston, Lancashire, arm. TRINITY COLL., matric. 1 Dec., 1829, aged 18; B.A. 1833, rector of Ashley, Northants, 1853, until his death 22 June, 1874.

Pulton, Thomas, s. Thomas, of Gloucester (city), gent. PEMBROKE COLL., matric. 26 March, 1753, aged 17; B.A. 1756, M.A. 1759, rector of Hitcham, Bucks, 1784, and vicar of Chattisham, Suffolk, died in 1810.

Pulvertoft, Thomas, s. John, of Colnbrook, Bucks, gent. CHRIST CHURCH, matric. 22 March, 1781, aged 17.

Punchard, Elgood George, 2s. John Elgood, of Framlingham, Suffolk, gent. NEW INN HALL, matric. 28 Jan., 1868, aged 23; B.A. 1872, M.A. 1874, B.D. 1880, D.D. 1884, vicar of Linslade, Bucks, 1880-3, and of Christ Church, Luton, 1883.

Purbrick, Edward, 2s. James Clarke, of Birmingham, co. Warwick, gent. CHRIST CHURCH, matric. 15 Dec., 1848, aged 18; servitor 1848-50. [15]

Purbrick, Lewis, 5s. James, of St. Martin's, Oxford (city), gent. CHRIST CHURCH, matric. 20 Nov., 1820, aged 15; chorister 1819-20, servitor 1820-4, B.A. 1824, M.A. 1827, chaplain 1825-38, and of All Souls' College 1831-7, vicar of Chippenham, Wilts, 1837, until his death 26 Aug., 1860.

Purcel, Alexander, s. Emanuel, of Cowbridge, co. Glamorgan, pleb. JESUS COLL., matric. 15 March, 1724-5, aged 18; B.A. 1728, M.A. 1733, rector o Stoke Wade and Handford, Dorset, 1742.

Purcell, Agustus Henry D'Olier, o.s. William Henr D'Olier, of Sydenham Damarel, Devon, cler. KEBL COLL., matric. 14 Oct., 1884, aged 19.

Purcell, Rev. Edward, 2s. John, of Coventry, co. War wick, arm. LINCOLN COLL., matric. 14 April, 1866 aged 19; B.A. 1870, B.C.L. & M.A. 1872, lecture Queen's College 1880-1, public examiner 1879-80 1885-6.

Purcell, Francis (Talbot), 2s. James George, of Fox boro', Ireland, cler. MAGDALEN HALL, matric 11 March, 1868, aged 34; M.R.C.S. Edinburgh held various curacies 1864-83, rector of Edstaston Salop, since 1883. [20

Purcell, Gilbert Kenelm Treffry, 1s. Handfield Noel of Fowey, Cornwall, cler. EXETER COLL., matric 23 Oct., 1885, aged 18; B.A. 1888.

Purcell, Handfield Noel, 5s. Edward, of Dundalk co. Louth (Ireland), arm. EXETER COLL., matric 23 May, 1861, aged 18; B.A. 1864, M.A. 1869, vica of Fowey, Cornwall, 1867.

Purcell, Henry, s. George, of Hereford (city), pleb WADHAM COLL., matric. 13 Dec., 1759, aged 17 B.A. from CHRIST CHURCH 1763.

Purcell, John, s. John, of St. Giles's, London, doctor UNIVERSITY COLL., matric. 13 Oct., 1733, age 18.

Purcell, John, s. Henry, of Church Stoke, co. Mont gomery, pleb. QUEEN'S COLL., matric. 28 Feb. 1734-5, aged 19. [25

Purcell, John, s. John, of Stodasdon, Salop, cler CHRIST CHURCH, matric. 10 Oct., 1766, aged 17 B.A. 1770.

Purcell, Lionel Thomas, 3s. William, of Clifton, co Gloucester, cler. WORCESTER COLL., matric. 1 June, 1862, aged 19; B.A. 1865, M.A. 1872, hel various curacies 1868-80, rector of St. Paul, Exete 1880-4, vicar of St. Decuman's, Somerset, 1884.

Purcell, Matthew, s. John, of Kanturk, co. Cor (Ireland), arm. (after a knight). UNIVERSIT COLL., matric. 19 Oct., 1792, aged 19; B.A. 180 of Burton House, co. Cork, rector of Churchtow and Dungourney, died 1845.

Purcell-Llewellin, Richard Llewellin, 2s. Willia Purcell, of Clifton, co. Gloucester, cler. EXETE COLL., matric. 2 Feb., 1860, aged 18; B.A. 186 M.A. 1868, of Tregwynt, co. Pembroke, and c Eynant Hall, co. Montgomery, a student of Lir coln's Inn 1864, assumed the additional name c LLEWELLIN in 1871, brother of Lionel Thomas.

Purcell, Robert, s. Emanuel, of Coyty, co. Glamo gan, pleb. JESUS COLL., matric. 16 July, 172 aged 16; B.A. 1724. [30

Purcell, Robert, s. Robert, of Bristol (city), cle WADHAM COLL., matric. 24 Oct., 1751, aged 19.

Purcell, Thomas, s. John, of London, docto QUEEN'S COLL., matric. 5 May, 1738, aged 18.

Purchas, Rev. John, of CHRIST'S COLL., Cambridg (B.A. 1844, M.A. 1847); adm. 'ad eundem' 3 Jun 1854, minister of St. James' Chapel, Brighton, 186 until his death 18 Oct., 1872. See *Annual Registe*

Purdon, Hugh Arthur, 4s. William, of Glaston, Ru land, cler. MAGDALEN HALL, matric. 22 Apri 1861, aged 22; B.A. 1865.

Purdon, Robert Eyre Coote, s. Bartholomew, of Bat Somerset, arm. ST. MARY HALL, matric. 2 March, 1792, aged 26; of Ballyclough, co. Cor died s.p., his father took the additional surname c PURDON. See Foster's *Baronetage*, COOTE. [35

Purdon, Simon George, s. William, of Tinerana, cc Clare (Ireland), arm. TRINITY COLL., matric. Dec., 1815, aged 18; of Tinerana, high sheriff cc Clare 1829, died 7 Aug., 1862.

Purdon, Rev. William John, M.A. TRINITY COLL. Dublin, 1832 (B.A. 1814); adm. 'ad eundem' 2 Nov., 1852 (son of Simon Purdon).

rdue, George, 3s. James, of St. Peter's-in-the-East Oxford (city), pleb. MERTON COLL., matric. 30 March, 1843, aged 17; scholar 1843-5, vicar of East and West Challow, Berks, 1853.

rdue, George Henry, 1s. George, of Wantage, Berks, cler. KEBLE COLL., matric. 13 Oct., 1873, aged 19; B.A. 1877, M.A. 1880, vicar of Sbottermill, Surrey, 1884.

rdue, John, s. Stephen, of St. Sepulchre's, London, gent. TRINITY COLL., matric. 27 Feb., 1768, aged 17.

rdue, William ('virgifer Univ.'), s. William, of Holywell, Oxford (city); privilegiatus 24 Jan., 1820, aged 27.

rdy, Richard, s. Charles, of Greenwich, Kent, gent. QUEEN'S COLL., matric. 14 Jan., 1768, aged 15; B.A. 1771, M.A. 1781, B.D. 1782, D.D. 1800, vicar of Broad Hinton and of Cricklade, Wilts, and rector of Ashley 1791, until his death 15 Oct., 1808. See *Gent.'s Mag.*, 1812, ii. 587. [5]

refoy, Amyrald Dancer, 3s. Thomas, of Cloughjordan, Ireland, gent. ST. EDMUND HALL, matric. 3 May, 1873, aged 24.

refoy, George. CORPUS CHRISTI COLL., 1787. See JERVOISE, page 752.

refoy, Henry, s. Henry, of Shalstone, Bucks, arm. ORIEL COLL., matric. 13 Nov., 1719, aged 21; of Shalstone, high sheriff Bucks 1749, died 28 April, 1762.

refoy, Jervoise. WADHAM COLL., 1789. See JERVOISE, page 752.

rkis, John, s. John, of Titchfield, Hants, arm. MERTON COLL., matric. 14 Nov., 1783, aged 18; demy MAGDALEN COLL. 1785-93, B.A. 1787. See *Bloxam*, vii. 96. [10]

rlewent, Harry, s. Samuel, of Bath, Somerset, gent. ORIEL COLL., matric. 4 July, 1763, aged 16; fellow CORPUS CHRISTI COLL., B.A. 1767, M.A. 1771, B.D. 1779, died rector of Brampton St. Botolph, Northants, in July, 1807.

urlewent, Samuel, s. Robert, of Bath, Somerset, pleb. CORPUS CHRISTI COLL., matric. 10 Nov., 1722, aged 16; B.A. 1726.

urnel, William, s. Robert, of Wootton-under-Edge, co. Gloucester, gent. ORIEL COLL., matric. 22 Oct., 1718, aged 17.

urnell, Christopher, s. John, of Wickwar, co. Gloucester, gent. HART HALL, matric. 2 May, 1721, aged 15; brother of John next named, and of William Oldisworth 1738.

urnell, John, s. John, of Wickwar, co. Gloucester, gent. NEW COLL., matric. 24 March, 1726-7, aged 19; B.A. 1730, M.A. 1734, B.D. 1742, D.D. 1745, warden 1740-64, vice-chancellor 1747-50, brother of the last named, died 11 June, 1764. [15]

urnell, John Bransby, 1s. Purnell Bransby, of Stinchcombe, co. Gloucester, arm. CORPUS CHRISTI COLL., matric. 10 Oct., 1839, aged 19; of Stancombe Park, co. Gloucester, died 21 Aug., 1869. See Foster's *Baronetage*, COOPER.

urnell, Purnell Bransby, s. Robert Bransby Cooper, of Ferney Hill, co. Gloucester, arm. CHRIST CHURCH, matric. 23 Oct., 1810, aged 18; of Stancombe Park, assumed the surname of PURNELL in lieu of COOPER by royal licence 22 Feb., 1805, died 16 Nov., 1866, father of the last named. See Foster's *Baronetage*, COOPER; & *Eton School Lists*.

urnell, Robert Hughes (Wilkinson), 1s. Thomas, of Staverton, co. Gloucester, cler. EXETER COLL., matric. 12 June, 1867, aged 19; B.A. 1871, incumbent of Bunbury, Western Australia, 1879.

urnell, Thomas, o.s. Robert John, of Lyme, Dorset, arm. BRASENOSE COLL., matric. 18 March, 1834, aged 19; B.A. from NEW INN HALL 1838, vicar (and patron) of Staverton, co. Gloucester, 1841, father of the last named.

Purnell, Rev. William, s. John, of Dursley, co. Gloucester, gent. CHRIST CHURCH, matric. 27 June, 1720, aged 18; B.A. from ORIEL COLL. 1722, M.A. 1728, 2nd master Manchester Free Grammar School 1723-49, high master 1749, until his death in 1765. See *Manchester School Reg.*, i. 33. [20]

Purnell, William Oldisworth, s. John, of Wickwar, co. Gloucester, gent. NEW COLL., matric. 26 Aug., 1738, aged 19; B.A. 1742, M.A. 1746, brother of Christopher 1721, and of John 1727.

Purrier, Henry, 1s. Henry, of Kenilworth, co. Warwick, cler. WORCESTER COLL., matric. 16 Jan., 1822, aged 18; B.A. 1827, M.A. 1832, curate of Compton Beauchamp, Berks, died 7 Dec., 1857.

Purrier, Rev. Henry Thornton, 3s. John, of Frampton Cotterell, co. Gloucester, arm. MAGDALEN HALL, matric. 25 May, 1844, aged 20; B.A. 1848, M.A. 1852.

Purrier, John, y.s. Henry, of Cheshunt, Herts, cler. WORCESTER COLL., matric. 15 Jan., 1827, aged 19.

Pursell, John Reeves, 1s. John, of Stockbridge, Hants, D.Med. ST. JOHN'S COLL., matric. 15 Feb., 1851, aged 18, B.A. 1855; M.A. from MAGDALEN HALL 1862, rector of Eastwick, Essex, 1868. [25]

Purslove, Joseph, s. Matthew, of Lambcote Grange, Yorks, gent. UNIVERSITY COLL., matric. 14 Jan., 1743-4, aged 18; B.A. 1747.

Purt, Richardson, s. Mark, of Finborough, Suffolk, cler. TRINITY COLL., matric. 16 June, 1742, aged 19.

Purton, John, 3s. William, of Fanitree, Salop, arm. TRINITY COLL., matric. 29 June, 1824, aged 18; B.A. 1828, M.A. 1832, preb. of Hereford 1869, rector of Oldbury 1834, until his death 12 July, 1883.

Purton, William, 2s. William, of Chetton, Salop, arm. TRINITY COLL., matric. 26 June, 1822, aged 19; B.A. 1827, M.A. 1829, of the Woodhouse, near Cleobury Mortimer, Salop, died 18 Aug., 1876, father of the next named.

Purton, William, 1s. William, of Hampstead, Middlesex, arm. TRINITY COLL., matric. 5 June, 1851, aged 18; B.A. 1855, M.A. 1858, curate of St. Leonard's, Bridgnorth, 1856-63, curate in charge of Stottesdon, Salop, 1863-70, vicar of St. Ann's, Willenhall, 1870-80, and of St. Clement's, Bournemouth, 1880. [30]

Purves, John, 1s. William, of Edinburgh, gent. BALLIOL COLL., matric. 13 Oct., 1860, aged 20; exhibitioner 1860-5, B.A. 1864, fellow 1866, M.A. 1867, classical lecturer Wadham College 1864-6, and of Balliol College 1875, junior dean 1868, junior bursar 1872.

Purves, William Alexander, 3s. Richard, of Maryport, Cumberland, gent. QUEEN'S COLL., matric. 22 Oct., 1883, aged 18; scholar 1883, B.A. 1888.

Purvis, Robert Brownrigg Arthur, 1s. John Brett, of the Mauritius, arm. UNIVERSITY COLL., matric. 1 June, 1836, aged 18; captain 78th highlanders, died 12 Dec., 1856.

Purvis, Rev. Thomas Alexander, o.s. Thomas, of Guernsey, gent. NON-COLL., matric. 17 Oct., 1879, aged 27; B.A. from MERTON COLL. 1883, M.A. 1886.

Pusey, Edward Bouverie, 2s. Philip, of Pusey, Berks, arm. CHRIST CHURCH, matric. 28 Jan., 1819, aged 18, B.A. 1822; fellow ORIEL COLL. 1823-9, M.A. 1825; a canon of CHRIST CHURCH and regius professor of Hebrew 1828-82, B.D. 1832, D.D. 1836, on council of Keble College 1871-80, died 16 Sep., 1882; for list of his works see *Crockford*. See Foster's *Peerage*, E. RADNOR; & *Eton School Lists*. [35]

Pusey, Henry Bouverie, 1s. William Bouverie, of Middlesex, cler. CHRIST CHURCH, matric. 31 May, 1855, aged 18; B.A. 1860, M.A. 1862, lieutenant 76th foot, died at sea in 1869.

Pusey, Hon. Philip, s. Jacob, Viscount Folkestone. CHRIST CHURCH, matric. 23 Feb., 1765, aged 18; assumed the name of PUSEY in lieu of BOUVERIE by act of parliament 3 April, 1784, died 14 April, 1828, father of Edward B. 1819, of the next named, and of William 1828. See Foster's *Peerage*, E. RADNOR.

Pusey, Philip, s. Hon. Philip, of Pusey, Berks, arm. CHRIST CHURCH, matric. 22 Oct., 1817, aged 18; created D.C.L. 9 June, 1853, of Pusey aforesaid, M.P. Rye 1830, Chippenham 1830-1, Cashel 1831-2, Berkshire 1835-52, died 9 July, 1855, father of Sidney. See Foster's *Peerage* & *Eton School Lists*.

Pusey, Philip Edward, o.s. Edward Bouverie, of Christ Church, Oxford, D.D. CHRIST CHURCH, matric. 16 Oct., 1850, aged 20; B.A. 1854, M.A. 1857, died 15 Jan., 1880, aged 49.

Pusey, Sidney Edward Bouverie, 1s. Philip, of St. George's, Hanover Square, arm. CHRIST CHURCH, matric. 2 Feb., 1858, aged 18; B.A. 1861, M.A. 1872, of Pusey, Berks. See Foster's *Peerage*, E. RADNOR.

Pusey, William Bouverie, 3s. Philip, of St. George's, London, arm. ORIEL COLL., matric. 25 Jan., 1828, aged 17; B.A. 1831, M.A. 1834, rector of Langley, Kent, 1842, until his death 19 April, 1888. See Foster's *Peerage* & *Eton School Lists*. **[5]**

Putron, Godfrey Pierre de, 1s. Peter, of Tottenham, Middlesex, cler. PEMBROKE COLL., matric. 20 Oct., 1873, aged 19; B.A. 1877, M.A. 1880, curate of Telscombe with Piddinghoe, Essex, 1878-80, rector since 1880. See *Eton School Lists*.

Putron, Pierre de, 1s. Pierre, of St. Peter's, Isle of Guernsey, arm. PEMBROKE COLL., matric. 17 Feb., 1845, aged 19; B.A. 1848, M.A. 1851, held various curacies 1849-58, rector of Rodmell, Sussex, 1858.

Putt, Raymondo, s. William, of Gittisham, Devon, arm. (cler.). CHRIST CHURCH, matric. 17 Oct., 1792, aged 19; of Combe, Devon, captain South Devon militia.

Putt, Thomas, s. Raymundo, of Gittisham Devon, arm. QUEEN'S COLL., matric. 21 April, 1741, aged 18; bar.-at-law, Middle Temple, 1746, bencher 1783.

Putt, Thomas, s. Raymundo, of Plymouth, Devon, gent. CORPUS CHRISTI COLL., matric. 23 Oct., 1775, aged 17; B.A. 1779, M.A. 1783, B.D. 1792, rector of Farway, Devon, 1789, and of Trent, Somerset, 1802, until his death in 1832. **[10]**

Putt, Thomas, s. William, of Gittisham, Devon, cler. ORIEL COLL., matric. 28 Jan., 1794, aged 19; B.A. 1797, M.A. 1800, rector of Combe Rawleigh, 1817. See *Eton School Lists*.

Putt, Rev. William, s. Raymundo, of Gittisham, Devon, arm. BALLIOL COLL., matric. 9 July, 1744, aged 19; B.C.L. 1751, died at Combe, near Honiton, 20 Feb., 1797, father of Raymondo and of Thomas 1794.

Puxley, Edward Lavallin, 3s. John, of Clifton, arm. BRASENOSE COLL., matric. 11 June, 1852, aged 17; missionary in India 1859-66, B.D. Lambeth 1875, chaplain at Versailles 1875-6, rector of Great Catworth, Hunts, 1876, sometime lieutenant 4th dragoons. See *Eton School Lists*.

Puxley, Edward Lavallin, 2s. Henry Lavallin, of Beerham, co. Cork, arm. BRASENOSE COLL., matric. 22 Oct., 1880, aged 19; a student of the Inner Temple 1881. See *Eton School Lists*.

Puxley, Frank Lavallin Lavallin-, 1s. Edward, of Limerick, cler. BRASENOSE COLL., matric. 20 Oct., 1886, aged 18. **[15]**

Puxley, Henry Edmund Lavallin, 3s. Henry Lavallin, of Cork, arm. CORPUS CHRISTI COLL., matric. 20 Oct., 1886, aged 20.

Puxley, Henry Lavallin, 1s. John Lavallin, of Cork, Ireland, arm. BRASENOSE COLL., matric. 11 June, 1819, aged 19; B.A. 1823, a student of Lincoln's Inn 1823, died unmarried. See *Eton School Lists*.

Puxley, Henry Lavallin, 2s. John Lavallin, of Blackrock, near Cork, Ireland, arm. BRASENOSE COLL., matric. 17 June, 1851, aged 17; B.A. 1855, M.A. 1865, of Llangan, co. Carmarthen, high sheriff, 1864, and of Dunboy, co. Cork, high sheriff, 1865. See *Eton School Lists*.

Puxley, Herbert (Boyne) Lavallin, 4s. John, of Clifton, Somerset, arm. BRASENOSE COLL., matric. 30 Nov., 1854, aged 18; B.A. 1858, M.A. 1861, curate of Cockermouth 1859-65, vicar 1865-73, rector of Great Catworth, Hunts, 1873-5, vicar of Kimbolton, Hunts, 1875-9, rector of Catton with Stamford Bridge, Yorks, 1879.

Puxley, John, B.A. TRINITY COLL., Dublin, s. Henry, of Cork (city), Ireland, arm. TRINITY COLL., incorp. 10 June, 1795, aged 23; of Dunboy Castle, co. Cork, father of Henry 1819, and of the next named. **[20]**

Puxley, John Lavallin, 2s. John Lavallin, of Cork (city), Ireland, arm. BRASENOSE COLL., matric. 14 Jan., 1820, aged 18; B.A. 1824, of Dunboy Castle, co. Cork, a student of Lincoln's Inn 1824, died in 1837, father of John S., Henry, Edward, and Herbert. See *Eton School Lists*.

Puxley, John Lavallin, 1s. Henry Lavallin, of Limerick, arm. BRASENOSE COLL., matric. 21 May, 1880, aged 20. See *Eton School Lists*.

Puxley, John (Simon) Lavallin, 1s. John Lavallin, of Clifton, Somerset, arm. BRASENOSE COLL., matric. 22 June, 1848, aged 16; of Dunboy Castle, captain 6th dragoons, died in 1860. See *Eton School Lists*.

Puzey, Robert, s. John, of Wantage, Berks, pleb. HERTFORD COLL., matric. 24 Oct., 1776, aged 16.

Pybus, John, s. John, of Bencoolen, East Indies, arm. MAGDALEN COLL., matric. 21 Nov., 1771, aged 17. **[25]**

Pycroft, James, 2s. Thomas, of Pickwick, Wilts, arm. TRINITY COLL., matric. 25 May, 1831, aged 18; B.A. 1836, a student of Lincoln's Inn 1836, perp. curate St. Mary Magdalen, Barnstaple, 1845-56.

Pycroft, (Sir) Thomas (K.C.S.I.), 1s. Thomas, of Hampstead, Middlesex, arm. TRINITY COLL., matric. 13 May, 1826, aged 18; exhibitioner 1826-8, created M.A. 11 April, 1829, entered H.E.I.C.S. 1829, secretary of revenue, Madras, etc., 1843-62, member of council, Madras, 1862-7, K.C.S.I. 24 May, 1866.

Pyddoke, Henry Whateley, 1s. Edward, of Cheltenham, cler. NEW COLL., matric. 16 Oct., 1885, aged 19; scholar 1884, B.A. 1888.

Pye, Benjamin, s. Henry, of Westminster, arm. NEW COLL., matric. 10 May, 1744, aged 18; B.C.L. 1751, D.C.L. 1772, preb. of Salisbury 1760, rector of Whitburn, co. Durham, 1769, and vicar of Hart cum Hartingpost, co. Durham, 1770, archdeacon of Durham and rector of Easington 1791, until his death 26 March, 1808.

Pye, Charles, s. William, of Falmouth, Cornwall, gent. EXETER COLL., matric. 30 Oct., 1739, aged 19; B.A. 1743, rector of St. Mary, Truro, 1761, father of William 1774. **[30]**

Pye, George, s. George, of London, cler. MAGDALEN HALL, matric. 20 Feb., 1740-1, aged 19.

Pye, Henry, s. Hen., of Farringdon, Berks, arm. BALLIOL COLL., matric. 17 July, 1725, aged 15; created D.C.L. 6 July, 1759, of Farringdon, Berks, M.P. 1746, until his death 3 March, 1766, brother of Robert 1739.

Pye, Henry Anthony, s. Anthony, of St. Andrew's, Holborn, Middlesex, arm. MERTON COLL., matric. 16 Dec., 1782, aged 16; B.A. 1786, fellow, M.A. 1789, rector of Lapworth, co. Warwick, 1793, vicar of Cirencester 1805, preb. of Worcester 1818, rector of Harvington, co. Worcester, 1818, until his death 25 March, 1839.

Pye, Henry Anthony, s. Henry Anthony, of Lapworth, co. Warwick, cler. MERTON COLL. matric. 14 Dec., 1816, aged 16; demy MAGDALEN COLL. 1817-23, B.A. 1820, M.A. 1823, brother of William 1823. See *Bloxam*, vii. 271.

Pye, Henry James, s. Henry, of St. Anne's, Westminster, arm. MAGDALEN COLL., matric. 12 July, 1762, aged 17; created M.A. 3 July, 1766, and also D.C.L. 9 July, 1773, of Farringdon House, Berks, M.P. 1784-90, poet laureate 1790, magistrate Westminster Police Court 1792, died 11 May, 1813.

Pye, Henry John, of TRINITY COLL., Cambridge (B.A. 1848, M.A. 1852); adm. 'ad eundem' 14 Jan., 1853, of Clifton Hall, co. Stafford (1s. Henry John, of Clifton Hall), bar.-at-law, Inner Temple, 1876. See Foster's *Men at the Bar*.

Pye, James Thomas, 1s. James, of London, gent. NEW COLL., matric. 5 Feb., 1877, aged 26; B.Mus. 24 Oct., 1878.

Pye, Kellow John, 7s. Edmund, of Exeter, Devon, gent. MAGDALEN HALL, matric. 24 Jan., 1842, aged 29; B.Mus. 27 Jan., 1842. [5]

Pye, Richard, s. Ri., of Low, Oxon, gent. PEMBROKE COLL., matric. 12 Nov., 1740, aged 17; B.A. 1744, bar.-at-law, Lincoln's Inn, 1748.

Pye, Robert, s. Henry, of Faringdon, Berks, arm. NEW COLL., matric. 19 Dec., 1739, aged 20; B.C.L. 14 Jan., 1746-7, D.C.L. 1758, rector of Knotting Rise, Beds, 1743, rector of Odell, Beds, cum Tichmarsh, Northants, 1770, preb. of Rochester 1774, until his death 21 May, 1788, brother of Henry 1725.

Pye, William, s. Charles, of St. Austle, Cornwall, cler. EXETER COLL., matric. 11 Feb., 1774, aged 18; B.A. 1778, rector of Blisland 1780, died in 1834.

Pye, William, o.s. Henry Anthony, of Lapworth, co. Warwick, cler. CHRIST CHURCH, matric. 15 Oct., 1823, aged 18; student 1824-31, B.A. 1827, M.A. 1830, rector of Sapperton, co. Gloucester, 1833-83, brother of Henry Anthony 1816.

Pye, William Pye, 1s. William Antony Woolcock, of Cornwall, arm. TRINITY COLL., matric. 26 Nov., 1840, aged 17; B.A. 1844, M.A. 1850, assumed the name of PYE in lieu of WOOLCOCK, vicar of Countess Wear, Devon, 1858. [10]

Pyefinch, John, s. Henry, of Presteigne, co. Radnor, gent. PEMBROKE COLL., matric. 16 July, 1763, aged 17; B.A. 1767 (? died rector of 1st portion of Westbury, near Shrewsbury, in 1806).

Pyemont, John, 3s. Samuel, of Linwood, co. Lincoln, cler. LINCOLN COLL., matric. 4 Feb., 1825, aged 18; scholar 1825-9, B.A. 1830, M.A. 1838, undermaster Ipswich Grammar School, died curate of Eyke 15 Jan., 1842. See Foster's *Yorkshire Collection*.

Pyemont, Louis Oxley Pyemont, 3s. Samuel, of Whitwick, co. Leicester, cler. WORCESTER COLL., matric. 20 Oct., 1873, aged 19; scholar 1873-6, B.A. 1876.

Pyke, James Nott, 2s. John, of Barnstaple, Devon, cler. EXETER COLL., matric. 6 Feb., 1865, aged 19.

Pyke, John, s. Robert, of Clanville, Hants, gent. MERTON COLL., matric. 22 March, 1733-4, aged 19; B.A. 1738, M.A. 1740 (? died rector of Radstock, Somerset, 18 Feb., 1780). [15]

Pyke, John, s. Henry, of Pewsey, Wilts, gent. MERTON COLL., matric. 29 Oct., 1801, aged 17; B.A. 1805.

Pyke, John, s. John, of Barnstaple, Devon, gent. EXETER COLL., matric. 14 Jan., 1818, aged 19; B.A. 1821, M.A. 1825, rector of Parracombe, Somerset, 1826, until his death 25 Jan., 1868, father of the next named.

Pyke, John Nott. EXETER COLL., 1860. See NOTT, page 1031.

Pyke, Samuel, s. John, of Appledore, Devon, gent. EXETER COLL., matric. 14 Nov., 1810, aged 19.

Pyle, Edmund, fellow of CLARE COLL., Cambridge, D.D. 1740 (incorp, 11 July, 1746); of CORPUS CHRISTI COLL., Cambridge, B.A. 1723, M.A. 1727, archdeacon of York (West Riding) 1751, preb. of Winchester 1756, rector of Gedney, co Lincoln, 1743, died in 1776. [20]

Pyle, Samuel, s. Samuel, of Topsham, Devon, gent. EXETER COLL., matric. 18 June, 1802, aged 16; B.A. 1806, M.A. 1811.

Pym, Francis, 1s. Francis Leslie, of Radwell, Herts, arm. CHRIST CHURCH, matric. 24 Jan., 1868, aged 18; of The Hasells, Beds, and of Radwell, Herts. See *Eton School Lists*.

Pym, Frederick, 1s. Samuel, of Plympton St. Mary, Devon, arm. (after K.C.B.). WORCESTER COLL., matric. 31 May, 1822, aged 18; B.A. 1826, M.A. 1830, perp. curate Plymstock 1841-3, rector of Bickleigh, Devon, 1843, until his death 29 May, 1848.

Pym, Frederick William, 4s. Francis Leslie, of Brighton, arm. BRASENOSE COLL., matric. 13 Oct., 1877, aged 18.

Pym, Robert, 3s. Francis, of Sandy, Beds, gent. CHRIST CHURCH, matric. 26 May, 1819, aged 25; rector of Elmley, Yorks, 1830, until his death 17 Aug., 1862. [25]

Pyne, Anthony, s. John, of Charlton Mackerel, Somerset, arm. EXETER COLL., matric. 10 Nov., 1786, aged 18; scholar 1788-91, B.A. 1790, died rector of Pitney and Kingweston in 1819. See *Coll. Reg.*, 147.

Pyne, Arthur Thomas, 3s. William, of Pitney, near Langport, Somerset, cler. EXETER COLL., matric. 25 May, 1858, aged 17; B.A. 1862, M.A. 1865, bar.-at-law, Inner Temple, 1868. See Foster's *Men at the Bar*.

Pyne, Francis William, y.s. William, of London, cler. WORCESTER COLL., matric. 17 Dec., 1884, aged 18; B.A. 1888.

Pyne, George Masters, 1s. William Masters, of St. George's, Hanover Square, London, cler. WADHAM COLL., matric. 10 June, 1852, aged 19; B.A. 1858, M.A. 1859.

Pyne, Henry, 2s. John, of Canford, Dorset, arm. WADHAM COLL., matric. 24 Jan., 1879, aged 18; B.A. 1882. [30]

Pyne, John Ely, 1s. John, of Canford, Dorset, gent. ORIEL COLL., matric. 17 Oct., 1876, aged 19.

Pyne, Malachy, s. John, of St. Paul's, Exeter, gent. BALLIOL COLL., matric. 4 June, 1728, aged 18; B.A. 1732.

Pyne, Nathaniel, s. Abrah., of Ide, Devon, gent. EXETER COLL., matric. 21 March, 1734-5, aged 18; B.A. 1738.

Pyne, Thomas, s. Hugh, of Crowndle, Devon, gent. EXETER COLL., matric. 6 March, 1741-2, aged 16; B.A. 1745, fellow 1746-53, M.A. 1748, died in 1753. See *Coll. Reg.*, 103.

Pyne, William, s. Roger, of Heavitree, Devon, gent. BALLIOL COLL., matric. 27 March, 1742, aged 18; B.C.L. 1748. [35]

Pyne, William, 2s. Anthony, of East Charlton, Somerset, cler. PEMBROKE COLL., matric. 5 Dec., 1818, aged 18; B.A. 1822, M.A. 1825, rector of Pitney, near Langport 1825-52, rector of Sock Dennis, Somerset, 1852, until his death 28 July, 1881. See *Eton School Lists*.

Pyner, Francis, s. Francis, of St. Edmund the King and Martyr, London, gent. JESUS COLL., matric. 7 May, 1804, aged 16.

Pyott, Richard, s. John, of ——, co. Stafford, arm. UNIVERSITY COLL., matric. 7 May, 1730, aged 16; bar.-at-law, Lincoln's Inn, 1737.

Pyrke, Charles, s. Thomas, of Littledean, co. Gloucester, arm. BALLIOL COLL., matric. 23 April, 1737, aged 16; B.A. 23 Jan., 1740-1, brother of Thomas 1734.

Pyrke, Duncombe, 1s. Joseph, of Littledean, co. Gloucester, arm. ST. ALBAN HALL, matric. 26 Jan., 1832, aged 23; bar.-at-law, Lincoln's Inn, 1864. See Foster's *Men at the Bar*.

Pyrke, George, s. Joseph, of Littledean, co. Gloucester, arm. QUEEN'S COLL., matric. 19 Nov., 1801, aged 18; B.A. 1805, M.A. 1808, Michel fellow until 1816, rector of Whitchurch, co. Hereford, 1815, until his death 3 Dec., 1852.

Pyrke, Thomas, s. Thomas, of Littledean, co. Gloucester, arm. PEMBROKE COLL., matric. 22 Oct., 1734, aged 17; brother of Charles 1737.

Pyrke, Joseph, s. Joseph, of Grossmands, co. Monmouth, cler. WADHAM COLL., matric. 8 March, 1759, aged 18; verderer of the Forest of Dean, and deputy-constable of the Castle of St. Briavels, father of the next named.

Pyrke, Joseph, s. Joseph, of Littledean, co. Gloucester, arm. ORIEL COLL., matric. 18 May, 1792, aged 18; of Deane Hall, verderer of the Forest of Dean, died 9 Jan., 1851, father of Duncombe.

Pysing, William, s. William, of Canterbury, Kent, gent. CHRIST CHURCH, matric. 17 Dec., 1728, aged 17; B.A. 1732, M.A. 1735.

Q.

Quarington, John, s. Edward, of Gloucester (city), gent. PEMBROKE COLL., matric. 7 May, 1788, aged 17; B.A. 1792, M.A. 1808, B.D. 1808, vicar of Shopland, Essex, 1803, until his death 30 March, 1844.

Quarles, Thomas, s. Francis Thomas, of Foulsham, Norfolk, gent. EXETER COLL., matric. 22 June, 1816, aged 17; B.A. 1820, M.A. 1827, chaplain royal navy, author of the 'History and Antiquities of Foulsham,' died 18 July, 1845. [5]

Quarmby, George Jonathan, 1s. James, of Alford, co. Lincoln, cler. LINCOLN COLL., matric. 6 May, 1825, aged 19; scholar 1825-9, B.A. 1829, perp. curate St. George's, Portsea, 1854, until his death 2 Sep., 1869.

Quarmby, Rev. James Richard, 2s. James, of Alford, co. Lincoln, cler. LINCOLN COLL., matric. 4 Nov., 1830, aged 19; scholar 1831-5, B.A. 1834.

Quarme, George, s. Rob., of Padstow, Cornwall, gent. CHRIST CHURCH, matric. 9 June, 1735, aged 19; B.A. 1739, commissioner of Taxes 1762-3, of Excise 1766, until his death 10 May, 1775. See *Alumni West.*, 311.

Quarrell, Henry John, 2s. Richard, of Weston-super-Mare, cler. WORCESTER COLL., matric. 2 May, 1876, aged 19; B.A. 1881.

Quarrell, Thomas Read, 1s. Thomas Chance, of Bransford, co. Worcester, gent. EXETER COLL., matric. 22 Jan., 1880, aged 18; B.A. 1882, M.A. 1886. [10]

Quarrell, William Henry, 2s. Thomas Chance, of Leigh, co. Worcester, arm. EXETER COLL., matric. 15 May, 1880, aged 18; B.A. 1883, M.A. 1887, bar.-at-law, Lincoln's Inn, 1885. See Foster's *Men at the Bar*.

Quarrington, Frederick, s. William, of Reading, Berks, gent. PEMBROKE COLL., matric. 25 March, 1817, aged 17; scholar 1817-25, B.A. 1820, M.A. 1825, vicar of St. Peter, Walthamstow, 1851-85.

Quarterman, William, 1s. William, of Windsor, Berks, gent. MAGDALEN HALL, matric. 23 March, 1824, aged 24.

Quartley, Charles James, 2s. William James, of Shepton Mallet, Somerset, gent. ST. EDMUND HALL, matric. 23 Jan., 1834, aged 19; B.A. 1837, M.A. 1842, chaplain H.E.I.C.S., died 24 Feb., 1858.

Quartley, Henry, s. John, of Ashbrittle, Somerset, gent. ST. MARY HALL, matric. 26 March, 1734, aged 19; B.A. 1737, M.A. 1740, rector of Wichlive with Wicken, Northants, and Preston Bisset, Bucks, 1750, until his death 27 Dec., 1794. [15]

Quartley, Henry, s. William, of Huntsham, Devon, gent. MAGDALEN COLL., matric. 27 March, 1770, aged 16, chorister 1766-70, clerk 1770-8; Michel fellow QUEEN'S COLL. 1778, B.A. 1773, M.A. 1778, rector of Maids Moreton, Bucks, rector of Stapleford, Herts, 1790, vicar of Wolverton 1794, rector of Wicken, Northants, 1806, until his death 26 Jan., 1838. See *Bloxam*, i. 175; ii. 105.

Quartley, Henry Reade, s. Henry, of Wolverton, Bucks, cler. QUEEN'S COLL., matric. 29 March, 1803, aged 15; B.A. 1808, M.A. 1811, vicar of Stantonbury, Bucks, 1842-57, died 22 Oct., 1869.

Quartly, William, s. James, of Molland, Devon, gent. EXETER COLL., matric. 15 May, 1782, aged 19; B.A. 1786. [21]

Quayle, Daniel Fleming Wilson, 5s. Mark Hildersley, of Castletown, Isle of Man, arm. CHRIST CHURCH, matric. 12 June, 1867, aged 19; B.A. 1871, M.A. 1876, of Bridge House, Castletown, held various curacies 1872-86.

Quayle, William, 6s. Mark Hildersley, of Castletown, Isle of Man. BALLIOL COLL., matric. 18 Oct., 1871, aged 19; B.A. 1876, a student of the Inner Temple 1876.

Quekett, Arthur Edwin, 2s. John Thomas, of London, arm. BRASENOSE COLL., matric. 3 June, 1869, aged 18; B.A. 1873, M.A. 1876, a student of the Inner Temple 1876.

Quennell, William, 3s. Robert William, of Hornchurch, Essex, gent. WORCESTER COLL., matric. 15 June, 1857, aged 17; scholar 1857-63, B.A. 1861, M.A. 1864, 2nd master Brentwood Grammar School 1862-70, head-master 1870-9, vicar of Tring, Herts, 1881. [25]

Quentin, George Augustus Frederick, 1s. George Augustus Frederick, of Kirkee, East Indies, arm. ST. JOHN'S COLL., matric. 19 June, 1867, aged 19, B.A. 1872; M.A. from ST. ALBAN HALL 1882, a student of Lincoln's Inn 1872, rector of Shipdham, Norfolk, 1884.

Quesnel, Charles Michael, 2s. Michael, of Isle of Guernsey, gent. PEMBROKE COLL., matric. 7 Nov., 1844, aged 19; B.A. 1849, M.A. 1852, vicar of Preston-upon-Stour, co. Warwick, 1876.

Question, Thomas, s. Augustin, of Carhampton, Somerset, pleb. EXETER COLL., matric. 13 March, 1721-2, aged 18; B.A. 1725.

Quetville, John, s. Thomas, of Isle of Jersey, gent. PEMBROKE COLL., matric. 16 Feb., 1743-4, aged 16; B.A. 1748 (as John de Q.).

Quetteville, William de, 2s. Clement John, of Isle of Jersey, gent. PEMBROKE COLL., matric. 23 Feb., 1848, aged 18; fellow 1851-62, B.A. 1852, M.A. 1854, rector of Brinkworth, Wilts, 1861.

Quetteville, William Frederick Ludlow de, o.s. William, of Bath, cler. ORIEL COLL., matric. 27 Oct., 1883, aged 18; B.A. 1888.

Quibell, James Edward, 1s. John, of Newport, Salop, gent. CHRIST CHURCH, matric. 10 Oct., 1884, aged 16; exhibitioner 1884.

Quick, George Pring, 1s. George England, of Crewkerne, Somerset, pleb. ST. MARY HALL, matric. 25 Oct., 1866, aged 19; scholar 1867-71, S.C.L. & B.A. 1870, M.A. 1874, held various curacies 1871-85, chaplain in Chili 1876-8, in Brazil 1878-81, rector of St. Peter's, Cork, 1885-7, and of Douglas, co. Cork, 1887.

Quick, Humphrey, s. John, of Highbray, Devon, cler. BALLIOL COLL., matric. 12 May, 1721, aged 17; B.A. from ST. JOHN'S COLL. 16 March, 1724-5, M.A. from BALLIOL COLL. 1731. **[5]**

Quick, John, s. John, of Highbray, Devon, cler. CHRIST CHURCH, matric. 31 March, 1720, aged 18; B.A. 1723, M.A. 1726.

Quicke, Andrew, s. John, of Newton St. Cyres, Devon, gent. NEW COLL., matric. 23 Aug., 1805, aged 18; B.A. 1809, M.A. 1813, fellow until 1832, dean of arts 1825, bursar 1826, dean of divinity 1827, rector of Ashbrittle, Somerset, 1811-24, vicar of Newton St. Cyres 1824, fellow of Winchester College, rector of Biddeston, Wilts, 1832, until his death 14 Jan., 1864.

Quicke, Arthur Philip, 3s. Thomas Royle, of Twickenham, Surrey, arm. NON-COLL., matric. 13 Oct., 1877, aged 21; B.A. from HERTFORD COLL. 1880, M.A. 1884, bar.-at-law, Middle Temple, 1884. See Foster's *Men at the Bar.*

Quicke, Charles Penrose, 6s. John, of Walcot, near Bath, arm. TRINITY COLL., matric. 7 March, 1850, aged 18; B.A. 1854, rector of Ashbrittle, Somerset, 1859.

Quicke, Edward Cumming, s. John, of Newton St. Cyres, Devon, arm. NEW COLL., matric. 19 July, 1808, aged 18; B.C.L. 1816, fellow until 1848, dean of canon law 1822, and civil law 1839, bursar 1838, died 5 Jan., 1849. **[10]**

Quicke, Edward Henry, 4s. John, of Devizes, Wilts, arm. WADHAM COLL., matric. 21 May, 1840, aged 18; B.A. 1844, vicar of Newton St. Cyres, Devon, 1847, until his death 5 June, 1870.

Quicke, George Andrew, 3s. John, of Walcot, Bath, arm. NEW COLL., matric. 6 Aug., 1839, aged 20; fellow 1839-65, B.C.L. 1845, dean of civil law 1850, sub.-warden 1860, bursar 1861, dean of canon law 1859, dean 1863, rector of Ashbrittle, Somerset, 1855-90, and of Radclive, Bucks, 1864.

Quicke, John, s. John, of Newton St. Cyres, Devon, arm. MERTON COLL., matric. 11 Nov., 1800, aged 17; of Newton St. Cyres, high sheriff Devon 1833, captain king's dragoon guards, died 9 Sep., 1859. See *Eton School Lists.*

Quicke, John Mintern, 1s. Charles Penrose, of Ashbrittle, Somerset, cler. HERTFORD COLL., matric. 27 Oct., 1885, aged 20; scholar 1883.

Quilter, Frederick William, 4s. George, of Canwick, co. Lincoln, cler. LINCOLN COLL., matric. 26 June, 1851, aged 19; B.A. 1855, M.A. 1859, B. & D.D. 1872, incumbent of New Town, Tasmania, 1864-7, etc., chaplain at Geneva 1873-5, vicar of Shirebrook, Notts, 1876-8, rector of North Piddle, co. Worcester, 1878-85. **[15]**

Quin, Edward, s. Edward, of St. Pancras, Middlesex, gent. MAGDALEN HALL, matric. 26 Nov., 1812, aged 18; B.A. 1817, M.A. 1820, bar.-at-law, Lincoln's Inn, 1823, died 4 May, 1828.

Quin, Henry Bacon, 1s. Henry, of St. Mary's, Lambeth, Surrey, arm. MAGDALEN HALL, matric. 5 July, 1851, aged 18. See *Robinson*, 298.

Quin, Rev. John, s. Windham, of Adare, Ireland, arm. CHRIST CHURCH, matric. 11 May, 1780, aged 19; B.A. 1783, died 1789. See Foster's *Peerage,* E. DUNRAVEN.

Quin, Hon. Richard George, s. Valentine Richard, Baron Adare. ST. MARY HALL, matric. 30 May, 1811, aged 22; died 5 Oct., 1843.

Quin, (Valentine) Richard, s. Windham, of Adare, Ireland, arm. MAGDALEN COLL., matric. 31 May, 1769, aged 16; created a baronet 24 March, 1781, M.P. Kilmallock 1799-1800, created Baron Adare in 1800, Viscount Mount-Earl 1816, and Earl of Dunraven and Mount-Earl in 1822, died 24 Aug., 1824. **[20]**

Quin, Windham Henry (Wyndham), s. (Valentine) Richard, of Adare, co. Limerick, baronet (after earl). MAGDALEN COLL., matric. 28 May, 1799, aged 16; 2nd Earl of Dunraven, M.P. co. Limerick 1806-20, a representative peer Ireland 1839, assumed the additional surname and arms of WYNDHAM by royal licence 7 April, 1815, died 6 Aug, 1850. See *Eton School Lists.*

Quin, Windham Thomas Wyndham, Viscount Adare, 1s. Edwin Richard, Earl of Dunraven. CHRIST CHURCH, matric. 20 Oct., 1858 aged 17; 4th Earl of Dunraven, K.P. See Foster's *Peerage.*

Quincey, Henry de, s. Thomas Quincey, of Manchester, arm. BRASENOSE COLL., matric. 13 April, 1810, aged 17; brother of the next named.

Quincey, Thomas de, s. Thomas Quincey, of Green-Heys, near Manchester, Lancashire, arm. WORCESTER COLL., matric. 17 Dec., 1803, aged 18; the English opium-eater, assumed the prefix 'de,' died 8 Dec., 1859. See *Manchester School Reg.*, ii. 224-5.

Quine, Rev. John, 3s. William, of German, Isle of Man, gent. MERTON COLL., matric. 15 Oct., 1877, aged 20; postmaster 1877-81, B.A. 1882, M.A. 1887, head-master Douglas Grammar School 1883.

Quinlan, Andrew William Roche, o.s. Andrew William, of Bandon, co. Cork (Ireland), gent. MAGDALEN HALL, matric. 10 Oct., 1857, aged 21; B.A. 1861, M.A. 1864, chaplain India since 1868. **[26]**

Quinton, Edmund, s. Richard, of Wellingborough, Northants, gent. LINCOLN COLL., matric. 17 June, 1747, aged 19; B.A. 1751.

Quirk, George, 2s. James, of Douglas, Isle of Man, arm. WORCESTER COLL., matric. 17 Feb., 1842, aged 18; B.A. 1846, M.A. 1863, curate of Bringhurst, co. Leicester, 1847-60, vicar of Luton, Beds, 1860-2, rector of Martinsthorpe, Rutland, since 1849, and vicar of Over Kellet, Lancashire, since 1862.

Quirk, James Francis, 1s. James Richard, of Willoughby, co. Warwick, cler. QUEEN'S COLL., matric. 28 Jan., 1869, aged 18; B.A. & M.A. 1876, vicar of Grasby, co. Lincoln, 1879.

Quirke, James Richard, 1s. James, of Peel, Isle of Man, arm. ST. EDMUND HALL, matric. 10 Oct., 1837, aged 18; B.A. 1841, M.A. 1863, perp. curate Attleborough, co. Warwick, 1851-63, rector and vicar of Blandford Forum, Dorset, 1863, until his death, 11 Oct., 1876. **[30]**

Raban, Herbert, 2s. William, of Hatch Beauchamp, Somerset, arm. EXETER COLL., matric. 17 Nov., 1836, aged 16; B.A. & M.A. 1857.

Rabbits, Cicero, s. Hugh, of Maiden Bradley, Wilts, gent. WORCESTER COLL., matric. 29 March, 1817, aged 20; B.A. 1821.

Rabbitts, Edward Slade, 4s. Hugh, of Batcombe, Somerset, arm. TRINITY COLL., matric. 6 March, 1834, aged 19.

Rabett, Reginald, s. Reginald, of Bramfield Hall, Suffolk, arm. ST. EDMUND HALL, matric. 25 Jan., 1814, aged 19; of Bramfield Hall, vicar of Thornton, co. Leicester, 1831-57, and rector of Passenham, Northants, 1857, until his death 10 Sep., 1860.

Raby, Rev. Charles, s. Ephraim, of Grantham, co. Lincoln, arm. CORPUS CHRISTI COLL., matric. 12 July, 1797, aged 17; LL.B. from TRINITY HALL, Cambridge, 1804, died at Grantham 23 Nov., 1849.

Raby, Samuel, 1s. Joseph Cowell, of Tor Mohun, Devon, gent. WORCESTER COLL., matric. 15 Oct., 1864, aged 36. **[6]**

Race, Charles, 5s. John, of Biggleswade, Beds, arm. MAGDALEN HALL, matric. 30 May, 1846, aged 19.

Rackett, Thomas, s. Thomas, of Wandsworth, Surrey, arm. UNIVERSITY COLL., matric. 16 Nov., 1773, aged 17; B.A. 1777, M.A. 1780, rector of Spettisbury and Charlton, Dorset, at his death 29 Nov., 1840. See *Gent.'s Mag.*, 1841, i. 428.

Rackham, Hanworth Hart, 2s. Matthew, of Liverpool, gent. WORCESTER COLL., matric. 19 Oct., 1886, aged 26.

Rackham, Richard Belward, 3s. Matthew William, of Liverpool, gent. WORCESTER COLL., matric. 19 Oct., 1882, aged 18; exhibitioner 1882, B.A. 1886.

Ractcliff, George. MERTON COLL., 1802. See RATCLIFFE, page 1177. **[11]**

Radcliff, Joseph, o.s. Joseph, of Dublin, arm. TRINITY COLL., matric. 6 March, 1856, aged 17; B.A. 1860, M.A. 1862, bar.-at-law, Lincoln's Inn, 1864, died Sep., 1881. See *Eton School Lists.*

Radcliffe, Alan Fenwick, 1s. Frederick Adolphus, of Milston, Wilts, cler. CORPUS CHRISTI COLL., matric. 20 Oct., 1886, aged 18; scholar 1886.

Radcliffe, Alexander, s. Thomas, of Ormskirk, co. Lancashire, arm. ORIEL COLL., matric. 18 Oct., 1776, aged 17; B.A. from ALL SOULS' COLL. 1781, M.A. 1785, rector of Tichfield 1791, until his death 24 Dec., 1825.

Radcliffe, Alston William, 2s. George, of Salisbury (city), cler. BRASENOSE COLL., matric. 2 Dec., 1828, aged 18; B.A. 1832, M.A. 1837, rector of North Newnton, Wilts, 1843. **[15]**

Radcliffe, Arthur Caynton, 2s. John Alexander, of London, gent. CORPUS CHRISTI COLL., matric. 23 April, 1872, aged 18; exhibitioner 1872-6, B.A. 1875, M.A. 1880, vicar of Longfleet, Dorset, 1884-5, rector of Stoke Charity, Hants, 1885. See *Eton School Lists.*

Radcliffe, Copleston, s. Walter, of Tamerton, Devon, arm. EXETER COLL., matric. 4 July, 1763, aged 19; B.A. 1767, M.A. 1770, vicar of Tamerton 1774, rector of Stoke Climsland 1782, until his death 27 March, 1805. See *Gent.'s Mag.*, 1803, i. 600; & 1805, i. 384.

Radcliffe, Edmund Stringfellow, s. Edmund, of Manchester, Lancashire, arm. BRASENOSE COLL., matric. 30 April, 1794, aged 19; B.C.L. 1808, incumbent Walton-le-Dale, Lancashire, 1803, perp. curate Burnley 1817, until his death 20 Jan., 1826.

Radcliffe, Edward, 1s. Alfred, of Liverpool, Lancashire, gent. LINCOLN COLL., matric. 22 Oct., 1864, aged 18; B.A. from NEW INN HALL 1868.

Radcliffe, Francis Reynolds Yonge, 1s. John Alexander, of London, gent. CORPUS CHRISTI COLL., matric. 2 May, 1870, aged 18, exhibitioner 1871-4, B.A. 1874; fellow ALL SOULS' COLL. 1874-82, M.A. 1876, bar.-at-law, Inner Temple, 1876. See Foster's *Men at the Bar* & *Eton School Lists.* **[20]**

Radcliffe, Frank (Carew), 2s. Walter, of Warleigh, near Plymouth, arm. EXETER COLL., matric. 31 May, 1879, aged 18; B.A. 1883.

Radcliffe, George, s. John, of Acton, Cheshire, pleb. BRASENOSE COLL., matric. 20 Jan., 1789, aged 18; B.A. 1793, M.A. 1807, B. & D.D. 1818, vicar of Chute, Wilts, 1828, preb. of Sarum 1833, until his death 26 July, 1849 (name spelled RATCLIFF in *Mat. Reg.*), father of George next named, and of John Alexander 1857.

Radcliffe, Rev. George, s. George, of Southampton, Hants, cler. ST. MARY HALL, matric. 9 May, 1818, aged 15; B.A. 1822, M.A. 1824, died 20 May, 1862.

Radcliffe, Henry Delmé, 1s. Emelius Henry, of Hitchin Priory, Herts, arm. MAGDALEN COLL., matric. 25 April, 1822, aged 18; died 6 Nov., 1830. See *Eton School Lists.*

Radcliffe, Henry Eliot Delmé, 2s. Charles Delmé, of Holwell, Beds, cler. QUEEN'S COLL., matric. 19 June, 1851, aged 17; Michel exhibitioner 1851-5, scholar 1855-8, B.A. 1855, fellow 1858-63, M.A. 1858, rector of South Tidworth, Wilts, 1862. **[25]**

Radcliffe, Houstonne, s. John, of Liverpool, Lancashire, gent. BRASENOSE COLL., matric. 3 Feb., 1758, aged 19; B.A. 1761, fellow & tutor, M.A. 1764, B. & D.D. 1784, vicar of Gillingham and Bobbing, Kent, 1788, preb. of Ely 1787, preb. of Canterbury 1795, and archdeacon 1803, rector of Ightham, Kent, 1788, sub-dean Bath and Wells 1812, died 8 April, 1822. See *Manchester School Reg.*, i. 61.

Radcliffe, Houstonne John, 1s. John, of St. Anne's Limehouse, Middlesex, cler. BRASENOSE COLL., matric. 13 April, 1825, aged 17; died 1829.

Radcliffe, James, s. John, of St. Clement's, Worcester (city), pleb. CHRIST CHURCH, matric. 23 April, 1807, aged 18; B.A. 1811, M.A. 1813, chaplain New College 1814-5, a minor canon of Canterbury 1807, rector of St. Andrew and St. Mary Bredman, Canterbury, 1808, head-master Kirkham Grammar School and curate of Kirkham 1816, until his death 11 Feb., 1836, father of the next named.

Radcliffe, James, o.s. James, of Kirkham, Lancashire, cler. QUEEN'S COLL., matric. 14 March, 1850, aged 18.

Radcliffe, John, s. James, of Bolton, Lancashire, gent. BRASENOSE COLL., matric. 31 May, 1781, aged 16; B.A. 1785, M.A. 1787, fellow & tutor; Chetham's librarian, Manchester, 1787-92, rector of St. Anne's, Limehouse, Middlesex, 1807-50, vicar of Doddington, Kent, 1807, and of Teynham 1811, until his death 31 May, 1850, father of Houstonne John. See *Manchester School Reg.*, ii. 25.

Radcliffe, John, s. James, of Saddleworth, co. Yorks, pleb. MAGDALEN HALL, matric. 11 Nov., 1796, aged 23, clerk MAGDALEN COLL. 1799-1808; B.A. from CHRIST CHURCH 1800, M.A. from NEW COLL. 1803, chaplain Christ Church 1812-23, and precentor. See *Bloxam*, ii. 115.

Radcliffe, John, s. John, of Oldham, Lancashire, gent. WADHAM COLL., matric. 29 March, 1803, aged 23; B.A. from ST. MARY HALL 1807, M.A. 1809, vice-principal, vicar of Bramham, Yorks, 1823, vicar of Radley, Berks, chaplain Merton College 1835, until his death 22 Feb., 1852. [5]

Radcliffe, John Alexander, 5s. George, of Salisbury, D.D. MAGDALEN HALL, matric. 4 July, 1857, aged 34; brother of George 1818.

Radcliffe, John Randle, 5s. Edmund S., of Walton-le-Dale, Lancashire, cler. MAGDALEN HALL, matric. 2 May, 1844, aged 20; held various curacies 1852-77, vicar of Snitterfield, co. Warwick, 1877.

Radcliffe, Rev. John William, 1s. John, of St. Martin's, Westminster, arm. LINCOLN COLL., matric. 17 Dec., 1836, aged 19; B.A. 1840, M.A. 1845.

Radcliffe, Joseph Greaves, 1s. Robert Carr, of Blackburne, Lancashire, arm. ORIEL COLL., matric. 23 Oct., 1885, aged 18.

Radcliffe, Norman Cyril Wilmot, 4s. John Alexander, of London, arm. MAGDALEN COLL., matric. 16 Oct., 1882, aged 19; B.A. 1887. See Foster's *Lancashire Collection* & *Eton School Lists.* [10]

Radcliffe, Pollexfen Copleston Colemore, 1s. Copleston Lopez, of Plymouth, gent. NON-COLL., matric. 16 Oct., 1875, aged 20.

Radcliffe, Richard, s. Francis, of Crosthwaite, Cumberland, pleb. QUEEN'S COLL., matric. 18 Nov., 1743, aged 16; B.A. 1748, M.A. 1751, fellow 1762-93, bursar 1766, curate of Bucklebury, Berks, 1755, rector of Colsterworth, co. Lincoln, 1756-66, curate 1766-77, rector of Holwell, Dorset, 1777, until his death 18 Nov., 1793. *O.H.S.*, ix., p. v.

Radcliffe, Richard Duncan, 1s. Richard, of West Derby, Lancashire, arm. CHRIST CHURCH, matric. 16 Oct., 1863, aged 19; B.A. 1868, M.A. 1872, bar.-at.law, Middle Temple, 1872. See Foster's *Men at the Bar.*

Radcliffe, Walter, s. Walter, of St. Thomas's, Exeter, Devon, arm. EXETER COLL., matric. 10 April, 1753, aged 19; created M.A. 8 July, 1756, of Warleigh, Devon, died 9 April, 1803.

Radcliffe, Rev. Walter, s. Copleston, of Plymouth, Devon, cler. EXETER COLL., matric. 21 May, 1798, aged 19; of Warleigh, Devon, died 16 April, 1867, aged 88. [15]

Radcliffe, Walter (Copleston), s. Walter, of Plymouth, cler. EXETER COLL., matric. 7 May, 1834, aged 19; of Warleigh, Devon, died 12 Aug., 1876.

Radcliffe, William, s. Charles, of Barkisland, Yorks, pleb. UNIVERSITY COLL., matric. 9 April, 1720, aged 16; B.A. 4 March, 1723-4, M.A. 1726, of Whittle Place, Halifax, died 11 June, 1755. See Foster's *Yorkshire Collection.*

Radcliffe, William, s. William, of Huddersfield, Yorks, gent. UNIVERSITY COLL., matric. 9 July, 1729, aged 18; of Milnsbridge, Yorks, bar.-at-law, Middle Temple, 1735, died 26 Sep., 1795. See Foster's *Yorkshire Collection.*

Radcliffe, William, s. William, of London, gent. ORIEL COLL., matric. 26 March, 1783, aged 19; B.A. 1785.

Radcliffe, William, 1s. John, of Kingston, Jamaica, cler. BALLIOL COLL., matric. 20 Oct., 1875, aged 19; B.A. 1880, bar.-at-law, Inner Temple, 1882. See Foster's *Men at the Bar.* [20]

Radclyffe, Rev. Charles Edward, o.s. Charles Edward, of Eaton Church, co. Stafford, arm. BRASENOSE COLL., matric. 19 Nov., 1830, aged 29; B.A. 1834, M.A. 1837, of Little Park, Hants, died 15 April, 1862, father of the next named.

Radclyffe, Charles Edward, 1s. Charles E., of Oxford (city), cler. CHRIST CHURCH, matric. 19 May, 1853, aged 19. See *Eton School Lists.*

Radclyffe, Charles James, 1s. Charles James, of Hyde, near Blandford, Dorset, arm. CHRIST CHURCH, matric. 10 Dec., 1857, aged 18; of Foxdenton Hall, Lancashire, and of The Hyde, Dorset, high sheriff 1885. See Foster's *Lancashire Collection.*

Radclyffe, Robert, s. Alexander, of Foxdenton, Lancashire, arm. BRASENOSE COLL., matric. 27 June, 1724, aged 16; of Foxdenton, died 12 April, 1749, father of the next named.

Radclyffe, Robert, s. Robert, of Foxdenton, Lancashire, arm. BRASENOSE COLL., matric. 1 July, 1756, aged 19; of Foxdenton, died at Bath 18 Dec., 1783, father of the next named. See Foster's *Lancashire Collection.* [25]

Radclyffe, Robert, s. Robert, of Oldham, Lancashire, arm. QUEEN'S COLL., matric. 7 Feb., 1792, aged 18; of Foxdenton, high sheriff Dorset 1812, died 28 March, 1854, father of the next named, and of William Frederick.

Radclyffe, Robert, s. Robert, of Hillendon, Devon, arm. WORCESTER COLL., matric. 30 June, 1817, aged 18; B.A. 1821, died in 1838.

Radclyffe, William Frederick, 3s. Robert, of Hewish, Dorset, arm. QUEEN'S COLL., matric. 1 Dec., 1825, aged 19; B.A. 1829, M.A. 1837, rector of Tarrant Rushton and Tarrant Rawston, Dorset, 1852, until his death 8 June, 1880.

Radclyffe-Hall, Radclyffe. ST. JOHN'S COLL., 1869. See HALL, page 588.

Raddish, Thomas, s. William, of London, gent. UNIVERSITY COLL., matric. 19 March, 1782, aged 19; B.A. 1786, M.A. 1796. [30]

Radenhurst, John, s. Thomas, of Bunbury, Cheshire, cler. BRASENOSE COLL., matric. 28 March, 1751, aged 19; B.A. 1754.

Radenhurst, Thomas, s. Thomas, of Hanmer, co. Flint, pleb. CHRIST CHURCH, matric. 8 July, 1718, aged 17; B.A. 1722.

Radford, Alexander William (Norcopp), o.s. Alexander William N.-R., of Duffield, co. Derby, gent. PEMBROKE COLL., matric. 3 June, 1852, aged 18; of Betton Hall, co. Stafford, his father assumed the additional surname of NORCOPP by royal licence about 1862.

Radford, Arthur, o.s. John, of Smalley, co. Derby, arm. PEMBROKE COLL., matric. 28 Jan., 1869, aged 20; B.A. from ST. ALBAN HALL 1874, of Smalley aforesaid.

Radford, Arthur Smith, 3s. John, of Stanton, co. Derby, gent. QUEEN'S COLL., matric. 18 Oct., 1865, aged 19. [35

Radford, Arundel, s. William, of Lapford, Devon, cler. EXETER COLL., matric. 19 Feb., 1760, aged 17; fellow 1763-83, B.A. 1767, M.A. 1769, B.D. 1780, vicar of Gwennap, Cornwall, 1782, rector of Nymet Rowland, Devon, died 30 Oct., 1805. See *Coll. Reg.*, 107.

Radford, Arundel, s. John, of Lapford, Devon, cler. EXETER COLL., matric. 21 May, 1792, aged 19; B.A. 1796, curate of Nymet Rowland 1796, died at Wincanton 1824.

Radford, James, s. John, of Lapford, Devon, cler. EXETER COLL., matric. 17 May, 1790, aged 19; B.A. 1794.

Radford, John, s. William, of Nymet Rowland, Devon, cler. EXETER COLL., matric. 27 Feb., 1758, aged 17; B.A. 1762, fellow 1762, rector of Lapford 1763, father of William 1787, James 1790, Arundel 1792, and John 1792. See *Coll. Reg.*, 107.

Radford, John, s. John, of Lapford, Devon, cler. BALLIOL COLL., matric. 4 July, 1792, aged 17; B.A. 1796, vicar of Wincanton 1812, until his death 9 Jan., 1829. **[5]**

Radford, John, s. Thomas, of Attercliff, Yorks, cler. LINCOLN COLL., matric. 26 May, 1800, aged 18; fellow until 1834, B.A. 1804, M.A. 1807, B.D. 1815, D.D. 1834, tutor 1822, sub-rector 1823, rector 1834, and rector of Twyford, Bucks, 1834, until his death 21 Oct., 1851.

Radford, John Arundel, s. William, of Wivelescombe, Somerset, cler. QUEEN'S COLL., matric. 15 Dec., 1817, aged 18; B.A. from ST. ALBAN HALL 1823, rector of Nymet Rowland and Lapford, Devon, 1825.

Radford, Percival Charles, 2s. William Tucker Arundel, of Downe St. Mary, Devon, cler. UNIVERSITY COLL., matric. 15 June, 1881, aged 18; died 28 March, 1885.

Radford, William, s. John, of Witheridge, Devon, pleb. EXETER COLL., matric. 28 Feb., 1726-7, aged 19; B.A. 1730.

Radford, William, s. John, of Lapford, Devon, cler. EXETER COLL., matric. 21 May, 1787, aged 18; B.A. 1791, rector of Lapford 1799, and of Nymet Rowland 1806, until his death in 1824. **[10]**

Radford, William, s. Thomas, of Sheffield, Yorks, cler. TRINITY COLL., matric. 24 April, 1805, aged 18; B.A. 1809, M.A. 1811, scholar 1812-14, fellow 1814-15.

Radford, William Tucker Arundel, 1s. Benjamin Tucker, of Chumleigh, arm. EXETER COLL., matric. 17 Nov., 1836, aged 18; B.A. 1840, curate of Downe St. Mary, Devon, 1842-3, rector (and patron) since 1843.

Radford, William Tucker Arundel, 1s. William Tucker Arundel, of Downe St. Mary, Devon, cler. EXETER COLL., matric. 22 Jan., 1880, aged 18; B.A. 1885, M.A. 1886.

Radice, Evasio Hampden, 1s. Albert Hampden, of San Georgio, Naples, arm. UNIVERSITY COLL., matric. 11 Oct., 1884, aged 18; of the Indian Civil Service 1884.

Radley, Charles Ernest, 1s. Thomas, of Ashton-under-Lyne, cler. BRASENOSE COLL., matric. 16 Oct., 1879, aged 19; a student of Lincoln's Inn 1881. **[15]**

Radley, Edward Yelf, 2s. James, of Liverpool, gent. ST. JOHN'S COLL., matric. 17 Oct., 1885, aged 18.

Radley, James French, 1s. James, of Liverpool, gent. ST. JOHN'S COLL., matric. 11 Oct., 1884, aged 19.

Rae, Charles James, 2s. David Johnson, of Alexandria, Egypt, gent. WADHAM COLL., matric. 16 Oct., 1875, aged 17; B.A. 1881, a student of the Middle Temple 1878.

Rae, John Clayton, 1s. John, of Aberdeen, gent. JESUS COLL., matric. 23 Oct., 1885, aged 20; B.A. from ST. EDMUND HALL 1888.

Ragdale, John, s. Assael, of Atherston, co. Warwick, pleb. TRINITY COLL., matric. 31 Oct., 1729, aged 26 (? M.A. Cantab., per *Lit. Reg.*, 1764, and rector of Appleby, co. Leicester, and of Normanton, Notts, 1763). **[20]**

Ragg, Lonsdale, 5s. Thomas, of Wellington, Salop, cler. CHRIST CHURCH, matric. 16 Oct., 1885, aged 18; exhibitioner 1885.

Ragg, Philip Melancthon, 4s. Thomas, of Wellington, Salop, cler. CHRIST CHURCH, matric. 15 Oct., 1886, aged 18; exhibitioner 1886.

Raggett, Rev. Robert, o.s. Job Robert, of Maidstone, Kent, gent. NON-COLL., matric. 25 Jan., 1879, aged 21; B.A. 1884, M.A. 1886.

Raikes, Arthur Hamilton, 2s. Frederick Thornton, of Gravesend, Kent, cler. QUEEN'S COLL., matric. 26 Oct., 1876, aged 18; B.A. 1881, M.A. 1884.

Raikes, Charles (C.S.I.), 2s. John Matthew, of Cheshunt, Herts, arm. MAGDALEN HALL, matric. 10 March, 1838, aged 25; C.S.I. 24 May, 1866, judge of the Sudder Court, Agra, and commissioner at Lahore, died 16 Sept., 1885, father of the next named. See Foster's *Yorkshire Collection.* **[25]**

Raikes, Charles Hall, 1s. Charles, of Ghazepoor, India, arm. ORIEL COLL., matric. 12 Nov., 1857, aged 18; B.A. 1861, M.A. 1864, vicar of Chittoe, Wilts, 1867, until his death 14 Dec., 1885.

Raikes, Ernest Barkley, 2s. Francis, of Carleton Forehoe, Norfolk, cler. KEBLE COLL., matric. 17 Oct., 1882, aged 18; scholar 1881, B.A. 1887, bar.-at-law, Inner Temple, 1888.

Raikes, Francis, 3s. George, of Fulham, Middlesex, arm. EXETER COLL., matric. 11 Feb., 1841, aged 18; B.A. 1844, M.A. 1847, rector of Carleton-Forehoe, Norfolk, 1848-73, and of Barnham Broom 1873, until his death 19 Jan., 1879, brother of Walter 1843.

Raikes, Frederick, 3s. Job Matthew, of Cheshunt, Herts, arm. ORIEL COLL., matric. 29 Nov., 1832, aged 18; B.A. 1836. See Foster's *Yorkshire Collection.*

Raikes, Robert, 1s. Thomas, of Hull, Yorks, arm. EXETER COLL., matric. 9 Nov., 1837, aged 19; B.A. 1841, M.A. 1846, of Treberfydd, co. Brecon, high sheriff 1851. **[30]**

Raikes, Robert Napier, s. Robert, of Gloucester (city), gent. ORIEL COLL., matric. 27 March, 1802, aged 18; B.A. 1806, M.A. 1813, vicar of Gayton with Lynn 1811, rector of Hellesdon with Drayton, Norfolk, 1812, vicar of Long Hope 1837, and of Old Sodbury at his death 22 March, 1851.

Raikes, Robert Taunton, 1s. Robert, of Welton, Yorks, arm. MERTON COLL., matric. 14 June, 1862, aged 19; postmaster 1862-7, B.A. 1866, M.A. 1869, bar.-at-law, Inner Temple, 1869-79.

Raikes, Rev. Thomas Digby, o.s. Thomas, of Bellary, East Indies, arm. ORIEL COLL., matric. 23 Oct., 1868, aged 18; scholar 1868-73, B.A. 1873, M.A. 1875, assistant-master Radley College 1879. See Foster's *Yorkshire Collection.*

Raikes, Walter, 4s. George, of Fulham, Middlesex, arm. EXETER COLL., matric. 11 May, 1843, aged 19; of Canada. See Foster's *Yorkshire Collection.*

Raikes, William Alves, 3s. Charles, of Walthamstow, Essex, arm. ORIEL COLL., matric. 14 Oct., 1864, aged 19; B.A. 1868, bar.-at-law, Lincoln's Inn, 1870, brother of Charles H. See Foster's *Men at the Bar.* **[35]**

Railton, Ernest Henry, 1s. Harry, of Snittlegarth, Cumberland, arm. TRINITY COLL., matric. 11 Oct., 1879, aged 19; B.A. 1883, B.C.L. & M.A. 1887, of Snittlegarth aforesaid, bar.-at-law, Inner Temple, 1884. See Foster's *Men at the Bar* & *Rugby School Reg.*

Railton, Henry, o.s. Joseph, of Marylebone, London, arm. ST. JOHN'S COLL., matric. 3 Dec., 1856, aged 19.

ailton, Thomas, s. Jos., of St. Andrew's, Holborn, Middlesex, gent. QUEEN'S COLL., matric. 30 May, 1723, aged 16; B.A. 1728.

aincock, John Dawson, s. John, of St. Andrew's, London, gent. QUEEN'S COLL., matric. 17 Dec., 1779, aged 18.

aine, Alfred Octavius, 8s. William Surtees, of Gainford, co. Durham, arm. NEW COLL., matric. 10 Oct., 1873, aged 20; B.A. & M.A. 1887, a student of Lincoln's Inn 1877.

Raine, William, s. Joseph, of Balsford, co. Gloucester, gent. QUEEN'S COLL., matric. 20 May, 1791, aged 17; B.A. 1795, M.A. 1798, rector of Widford, co. Gloucester, 1812, and perp. curate of Swinbrook, Oxon, 1838, until his death 5 Jan., 1858.

Raine, William Surtees, o.s. William, of Halford Bridge, co. Warwick, cler. EXETER COLL., matric. 10 May, 1832, aged 18; B.A. 1836, of Gainford, co. Durham, and of Bradridge, Devon. See *Rugby School Reg.*, 150. [5]

Raines, Richard Edward Hodgson, 2s. Edward John, of York (city), cler. WORCESTER COLL., matric. 18 Jan., 1869, aged 22; S.C.L. & B.A. 1872, M.A. 1875, vicar of St. John, Carlton Hill, Brighton, 1879-86. See Foster's *Yorkshire Collection.*

Raines, William Easterby, 1s. Edward John, of York (city), cler. BRASENOSE COLL., matric. 27 June, 1857, aged 17; brother of the last named. See Foster's *Yorkshire Collection.*

Rainey, James Bryant, 1s. James Tuck, of Bath, gent. PEMBROKE COLL., matric. 28 Oct., 1867, aged 20; B.A. 1873, M.A. 1874, curate of Dulverton, Somerset, 1874-6, of Langford, Berks, 1876-84, vicar of Holwell, Oxon, 1884.

Rainier, George, 2s. David, of Islington, Middlesex, arm. BRASENOSE COLL., matric. 27 Jan., 1832, aged 18; B.A. 1835, vicar of Ninfield, Sussex, 1854, until his death 23 Oct., 1872.

Rainier, Peter, s. Daniel, of Sandwich, Kent, arm. ORIEL COLL., matric. 28 March, 1795, aged 17; B.A. 1798, M.A. 1801, B.Med. 1802, D.Med. 1805, fellow College of Physicians 1808, died 30 Oct., 1837. See Munk's *Roll*, iii. 64. [10]

Rainier, William Vashon, 4s. George, of Winkfield, Sussex, cler. NON-COLL., matric. 18 Oct., 1875, aged 18; B.A. from WADHAM COLL. 1879, M.A. 1882, chaplain R.N. 1882.

Rainy, George Haygarth, 1s. George, of St. Pancras, London, arm. UNIVERSITY COLL., matric. 18 April, 1863, aged 18.

Raisbeck, John s. Josiah, of Appleby, Westmoreland, pleb. QUEEN'S COLL., matric. 1 July, 1756, aged 30; probably father of the next named.

Raisbeck, John, s. John, of St. Laurence Wootton, Hants, cler. ST. EDMUND HALL, matric. 14 Dec., 1780, aged 19.

Rake, John, s. Samuel, of Penselwood, Somerset, gent. HART HALL, matric. 29 Nov., 1723, aged 17. [15]

Ralfe, William, s. James, of Durley, Wilts, gent. BRASENOSE COLL., matric. 3 April, 1762, aged 18; B.A. 1765, rector of Maulden, Beds, 1806, until his death 25 May, 1825, father of James, of Winchester.

Raleigh, Thomas, 1s. Samuel, of Edinburgh, arm. BALLIOL COLL., matric. 25 Jan., 1871, aged 20, exhibitioner 1870-5, B.A. 1875; fellow ALL SOULS' COLL. 1876, M.A. 1878, reader in English law 1886, bar.-at-law, Lincoln's Inn, 1877. See Foster's *Men at the Bar.*

Ralli, Alexander Pandia, 1s. Pandia Alexander, of Odessa, arm. TRINITY COLL., matric. 25 Jan., 1871, aged 18; S.C.L. & B.A. 1873, M.A. 1878.

Ralli, Antonio, 3s. Pandia, of Liverpool, arm. TRINITY COLL., matric. 31 May, 1879, aged 19; B.A. 1882, M.A. 1887.

Ralli, Constantine, 1s. Pandia, of London, arm. BRASENOSE COLL., matric. 5 June, 1873, aged 18. [20]

Ralli, Pandia, 2s. Pandia, of Liverpool, arm. TRINITY COLL., matric. 31 May, 1879, aged 20; B.A. 1882, M.A. 1887. See *Eton School Lists.*

Ralph, James, 3s. James, of St. Marylebone, London, arm. ST. EDMUND HALL, matric. 3 June, 1829, aged 30; B.A. 1833, M.A. 1842, rector of St. John's, Horsleydown, Surrey, 1845, until his death, 14 Nov., 1854.

Ralph, John Rowe Kelly, 1s. John, of Deal, Kent, arm. QUEEN'S COLL., matric. 10 April, 1845, aged 21; B.A. 1849, M.A. 1852, bar.-at-law, Lincoln's Inn, 1852, died 5 Dec., 1885. See Foster's *Men at the Bar.*

Ralph, Solomon (Kelly) Ferrier, 2s. John, of Deal, Kent, arm. BRASENOSE COLL., matric. 11 June, 1852, aged 21; B.A. 1856, M.A. 1859, rector of Kildalkey, co. Meath, 1875.

Ram, Abel John, s. Abel, of Westminster, arm. CORPUS CHRISTI COLL., matric. 19 June, 1795, aged 18; of Clonattin, co. Wexford, died 3 Nov., 1823, father of the next named. [25]

Ram, Abel John, o.s. Abel John, of St. George's, Hanover Square, London, arm. ORIEL COLL., matric. 29 March, 1822, aged 17; B.A. 1827, M.A. 1830, vicar of Towcester, perp. curate Beverley Minster 1840-4, vicar of West Ham 1845-68, hon. canon of Rochester 1867, rector of Rolleston, co. Stafford, 1868, until his death 18 Aug., 1883.

Ram, Abel John, 2s. Abel John, of Ilam, co. Stafford, cler. CORPUS CHRISTI COLL., matric. 14 Oct., 1861, aged 19; B.A. 1866, M.A. 1869, bar.-at-law, Inner Temple, 1872. See Foster's *Men at the Bar.*

Ram, George Stopford, 1s. Abel John, of Towcester, Northants, cler. WADHAM COLL., matric. 20 May, 1857, aged 18; B.A. 1861, M.A. 1864, of Clonattin, co. Wexford, perp. curate St. John's, Stratford, Essex, 1863-6, vicar of Brookfield St. Anne, Highgate Rise, 1868-81, vicar of St. Peter's, Bournemouth, 1881.

Ram, Stephen, s. Humphrey, of Westminster, arm. QUEEN'S COLL., matric. 2 Dec., 1760, aged 16; of Ramsfort, co. Wexford, bar.-at-law, Middle Temple, 1768, bencher 1797, M.P. Gorey 1764-89, died 8 March, 1821.

Ram, Stephen, 1s. Abel, of St. George's, Hanover Square, London, arm. CHRIST CHURCH, matric. 22 Oct., 1835, aged 17; of Ramsfort, co. Wexford, high sheriff 1840. See *Eton School Lists.* [30]

Ramadge, Francis Hopkins, B.Med. TRINITY COLL., Dublin (B.A. 1816, B.Med. & M.A. 1819), 1s. Thomas, of Dublin (city), gent. Incorp. from ST. ALBAN HALL 3-4 May, 1821, D.Med. 27 June, 1821, fellow College of Physicians 1822, died 8 June, 1867. See Munk's *Roll*, iii. p. 263.

Rammell, Thomas Easton, 1s. William Lake, of Sturry, Kent, arm. TRINITY COLL., matric. 16 Oct., 1886, aged 19; Ford student 1885.

Ramsay, Andrew Michael, created D.C.L. 10 April, 1730, knight of the Order of St. Lazarus, 'Chevalier Ramsay,' tutor of the children of the Chevalier de St. George, commonly called the Pretender, died 6 May, 1743.

Ramsay, Charles William Ramsay, o.s. William Ramsay, of Barnton Cramond, near Edinburgh, arm. CHRIST CHURCH, matric. 13 Dec., 1861, aged 17; of Barnton, N.B., died 30 Dec., 1865.

Ramsay, Frederick Allan, 3s. John Douglas, of Aldeborough, Suffolk, gent. ST. EDMUND HALL, matric. 5 Feb., 1879, aged 17. [35]

Ramsay, George Gilbert, 3s. George, of Fontainbleau, near Paris, France, arm. TRINITY COLL., matric. 8 June, 1857, aged 17; scholar 1857-62, B.A. 1862, M.A. 1864, professor of humanity Glasgow University. See *Rugby School Reg.*

Ramsay, George William, o.s. George Antrim, of Enfield, Middlesex, gent. WORCESTER COLL., matric. 17 Oct., 1863, aged 18.

Ramsay, Rev. Henry Havelock, 2s. Joseph, of London, gent. EXETER COLL., matric. 18 Oct., 1882, aged 18; B.A. 1885.

Ramsay, (Sir) James (Bart.), s. William, of Edinburgh, Scotland, baronet. CHRIST CHURCH, matric. 30 May, 1816, aged 18; 8th baronet, died 1 Jan., 1859. See Foster's *Baronetage*.

Ramsay, James Andrew Brown, 2s. George, Earl of Dalhousie. CHRIST CHURCH, matric. 24 Oct., 1829, aged 17; B.A. 1833, M.A. 1838, 10th earl, K.P., created Marquis of Dalhousie 25 Aug., 1849, M.P. Haddingtonshire 1837-8, governor-general of India 1847-56, assumed the additional surname of BROWN, died 19 Dec., 1860. See Foster's *Peerage*.

Ramsay, (Sir) James Henry (Bart.), 1s. George, of Versailles, France, arm. CHRIST CHURCH, matric. 26 June, 1851, aged 19; student 1854-61, B.A. 1855, M.A. 1858, 10th baronet, bar.-at-law, Lincoln's Inn, 1863. See Foster's *Men at the Bar* & *Rugby School Reg.*, 257.

Ramsay, John, of CORPUS CHRISTI COLL., Cambridge, M.A. 1714; incorp. from ST. JOHN'S COLL., Cambridge, 19 Oct., 1718. [5]

Ramsay, John, s. Gilbert, of Makerstown, co. Roxburgh, gent. BALLIOL COLL., matric. 8 Dec., 1747, aged 14; B.A. 1751, M.A. 1754.

Ramsay, John William, 1s. George, Earl of Dalhousie. BALLIOL COLL., matric. 20 Oct., 1875, aged 28; 13th earl, commander R.N., M.P. Liverpool, March to August, 1880, secretary for Scotland 1886, died 25 Nov., 1887. See Foster's *Peerage*.

Ramsay, Michael, s. David, of Lethindy, co. Stirling, gent. ST. MARY HALL, matric. 16 July, 1737, aged 30.

Ramsay, Rev. Norman Robert, o.s. William Fermor, of Leamington, arm. NEW COLL., matric. 15 Oct., 1881, aged 19; B.A. 1885.

Ramsay, William, born at Versailles, France, 2s. George, gent. (after baronet). CORPUS CHRISTI COLL., matric. 23 May, 1853, aged 18; of the Indian Civil Service 1855. See Foster's *Baronetage* & *Rugby School Reg.*, 257. [10]

Ramsay, William Ramsay, o.s. George, of Edinburgh, Scotland, arm. CHRIST CHURCH, matric. 1 Feb., 1828, aged 18; of Barnton, N.B., M.P. Stirlingshire 1831-2, Edinburghshire 1841-5, died 15 March, 1850, father of Charles William. See Foster's *Scots' M.P.'s*.

Ramsay, William Mitchell, 3s. Thomas, of Glasgow, gent. ST. JOHN'S COLL., matric. 12 Oct., 1872, aged 21, scholar 1872-7, B.A. 1879; fellow EXETER COLL. 1882-7, M.A. 1884, fellow LINCOLN COLL. 1885-6, and professor of archæology 1885-6, professor of Latin, Aberdeen University, 1886.

Ramsbotham, Cyril, 2s. Thomas, of Bury, Lancashire, cler. CHARSLEY HALL, matric. 17 Oct., 1877, aged 27.

Ramsbotham, Rev. Francis Shepley, 4s. John Hodgson, of Huddersfield, Yorks, D.Med. CORPUS CHRISTI COLL., matric. 19 Oct., 1870, aged 19; scholar 1870-5, B.A. 1875, M.A. 1877, assistant-master Charterhouse School 1875.

Ramsbotham, Herwald, 7s. James, of Wittingham, Sussex, gent. MAGDALEN COLL., matric. 14 Oct., 1878, aged 18; B.A. 1883, a student of the Inner Temple 1882. [15]

Ramsden, Arthur Charles, o.s. William, of Rushall, Wilts, cler. EXETER COLL., matric. 6 June, 1844, aged 18; of Stoneness, Kent. See Foster's *Baronetage*.

Ramsden, Charles, 1s. Walter Henry Fox, of Royton, Lancashire, gent. NON-COLL., matric. 13 Oct., 1884, aged 21; B.A. from WADHAM COLL. 1887.

Ramsden, Edward Plumptre, 2s. Robert John, of Ventnor, Isle of Wight, gent. WORCESTER COLL., matric. 12 Oct., 1867, aged 19. See Foster's *Baronetage*.

Ramsden, Frank, 1s. Frank, of Hexthorpe, Yorks, arm. CHRIST CHURCH, matric. 27 May, 1858, aged 18; B.A. 1862, M.A. 1884, of Hexthorpe aforesaid, bar.-at-law, Inner Temple, 1866. See Foster's *Men at the Bar*.

Ramsden, Frederick John, 2s. George, of Conisbro', Yorks, arm. CHRIST CHURCH, matric. 8 June, 1854, aged 17; B.A. 1859, M.A. 1861, rector of Uffington, co. Lincoln, 1861. See *Rugby School Reg.*, 289.

Ramsden, Frederick Plumptre, 1s. Frederick Selwyn, of Shirland, co. Derby, cler. ST. JOHN'S COLL., matric. 13 Jan., 1883, aged 19; B.A. 1886. [21]

Ramsden, Henry, 2s. Thomas Lagden, of Mitcham, Surrey, cler. BRASENOSE COLL., matric. 17 June, 1851, aged 18.

Ramsden, Rev. Henry Plumptre, 2s. Charles Henry, of Shirland, co. Derby, cler. WORCESTER COLL., matric. 17 Oct., 1868, aged 20; scholar 1868-73, B.A. 1873, diocesan inspector of schools 1881. See Foster's *Baronetage*.

Ramsden, John, s. John, of Southowram, Yorks, gent. UNIVERSITY COLL., matric. 14 March, 1761, aged 18.

Ramsden, (Sir) John (Bart.), s. John, of Byrom, Yorks, baronet. UNIVERSITY COLL., matric. 5 April, 1774, aged 18; 4th baronet, M.P. Grampound 1780-4, died 15 July, 1839. See Foster's *Baronetage*. [25]

Ramsden, John, s. John, of Doncaster, Yorks, cler. CHRIST CHURCH, matric. 29 Jan., 1812, aged 19; lieutenant Inniskilling dragoons, died 19 March, 1861. See Foster's *Baronetage*.

Ramsden, Thomas Lagden, o.s. Thomas, of Charterhouse, London, arm. ST. JOHN'S COLL., matric. 14 Nov., 1822, aged 17; B.A. 1826, M.A. 1829, vicar of Forest Gate, Essex, 1852, until his death 6 Jan., 1875, father of Henry.

Ramsden, William, s. George, of St. George's, Westminster, arm. CHRIST CHURCH, matric. 28 Jan., 1808, aged 18; B.A. 1812, M.A. 1828, rector of Linwood, co. Lincoln, 1828, (? and of Ashurst, Kent, 1834), until his death 4 Nov., 1860, aged 73. See Foster's *Baronetage*.

Ramsden, William Frescheville, 2s. Arthur Charles, of Ashurst, Kent, arm. CHRIST CHURCH, matric. 13 Oct., 1876, aged 19; B.A. 1880. See Foster's *Baronetage* & *Eton School Lists*.

Ramsey, Allan, 2s. William Billing, of Devonport, Devon, gent. PEMBROKE COLL., matric. 27 June, 1859, aged 18; B.A. 1863, M.A. 1866, chaplain in India since 1869. [30]

Ramsey, Edward, s. Edward, of Exeter (city), pleb. BALLIOL COLL., matric. 14 Dec., 1767, aged 23.

Ramsey, John, s. John, of Abbotts Langley, Herts, cler. ST. MARY HALL, matric. 13 Oct., 1741, aged 17; fellow EXETER COLL. 1744-82, B.A. 27 Jan., 1747-8, M.A. 1752, B.D. 1763, D.D. 1781, vicar of Abbotts Langley 1761, rector of Bushey, Herts, 1782, until his death 17 June, 1785. See *Coll. Reg.*, 102.

Ramsey, William, s. John, of Abbotts Langley, Herts, cler. EXETER COLL., matric. 15 Dec., 1744, aged 18; B.A. 10 March, 1748-9, brother of John last named.

Ramus, Henry, s. Charles, of Westminster, arm. EXETER COLL., matric. 16 Dec., 1800, aged 17.

Rand, Walter Charles, 1s. John, of Walton, Suffolk, gent. BALLIOL COLL., matric. 18 Oct., 1881, aged 18; of the Indian Civil Service 1881. [35]

Randall, Cyril Wilberforce, 4s. Richard William, of Lavington, Sussex, cler. MAGDALEN COLL., matric. 24 Jan., 1876, aged 19.

Randall, Edward, o.s. Frederick, of St. Benet's, Cambridge (town), gent. ORIEL COLL., matric. 8 Feb., 1849, aged 18; B.A. 1853, M.A. 1858, incumbent Canons Ashby, Northants, 1858-9, of St. Ninian, Castle Douglas, 1860-8, chaplain at Palæopyroo, Ægina, 1874-84, chaplain at Patras, Greece, 1884. See *Eton School Lists*.

Randall, Francis Henry, 5s. Richard William, of Graffham, Sussex, cler. KEBLE COLL., matric. 15 Oct., 1877, aged 19.

Randall, Henry Goldney, 2s. Richard, of St. Olave's, Old Jewry, London, gent. ST. JOHN'S COLL., matric. 25 June, 1827, aged 18; Michel scholar QUEEN'S COLL. 1831-4, B.A. 1831, fellow 1834-41, M.A. 1834, perp. curate St. Peter, Bishopworth, 1853-65, vicar of St. Mary, Redcliffe, Bristol, 1865-77, and of Bristol 1866-77, hon. canon 1868, archdeacon 1873, vicar of Christian Malford, Wilts, 1877, until his death 7 Aug., 1881. See *Robinson*, 201.

Randall, Henry Leslie, 1s. James Leslie, of Newbury, Berks, cler. CHRIST CHURCH, matric. 31 May, 1879, aged 18; B.A. 1884.

Randall, James, s. James, of Sparkeford, Hants, gent. TRINITY COLL., matric. 19 Oct., 1809, aged 19; scholar 1812-18, B.A. 1813, M.A. 1816, fellow 1818-21, assistant-master Rugby School 1813, bar.-at-law, Lincoln's Inn, 1818, rector of Binfield, Berks, 1831-59, archdeacon of Berks, 1855-69, canon of Bristol 1867-75, died 19 Nov., 1882. See *Rugby School Reg.*, xiv.

Randall, James Leslie, 2s. James, of Dorking, Surrey, cler. NEW COLL., matric. 6 May, 1848, aged 19; fellow 1848-56, B.A. 1852, M.A. 1855, hon. canon Christ Church 1878, rector of Newbury, Berks, 1857-78, of Sandhurst 1878-80, and of Mixbury, Oxon, 1881-5, archdeacon of Buckingham 1880.

Randall, James Lowndes, 3s. Richard William, of Lavington, Sussex, cler. ST. JOHN'S COLL., matric. 11 Oct., 1873, aged 18; B.A. from NEW INN HALL 1876, M.A. 1880. [5]

Randall, John, s. Thomas, of Surn, Dorset, gent. BALLIOL COLL., matric. 20 Oct., 1731, aged 17; B.A. 1735.

Randall, Onesiphorus, o.s. Onesiphorus, of London, gent. WORCESTER COLL., matric. 20 Oct., 1881, aged 19.

Randall, Richard, o.s. Henry Goldney, of Frant, Sussex, cler. EXETER COLL., matric. 19 May, 1864, aged 19; B.A. 1868, bar.-at-law, Lincoln's Inn, 1871. See Foster's *Men at the Bar.*

Randall, Richard William, 1s. James, of St. George's, Bloomsbury, cler. CHRIST CHURCH, matric. 12 May, 1842, aged 18; B.A. 1846, M.A. 1849, rector of Woollavington, Sussex, 1851-68, vicar of All Saints, Clifton, co. Gloucester, 1868.

Randall, Thomas, s. Thomas, of Eton, Bucks, pleb. CORPUS CHRISTI COLL., matric. 21 July, 1731, aged 20; B.A. 1735. [10]

Randall, Thomas Fitz, o.s. Thomas, of Walcot, near Bath, gent. TRINITY COLL., matric. 4 Dec., 1824, aged 18.

Randall, William, o.s. William, of Blackheath, Kent, arm. CORPUS CHRISTI COLL., matric. 13 June, 1833, aged 18; a student of the Inner Temple 1835.

Randall, William Richard, 3s. John, of Bridgend, co. Glamorgan, gent. JESUS COLL., matric. 29 Oct., 1867, aged 18; B.A. 1870.

Randall, William Sidney, 1s. William, of Colton, near Leeds, cler. WADHAM COLL., matric. 16 Oct., 1869, aged 19; B.A. from HERTFORD COLL. 1875, chaplain to the forces 1882.

Randell, James, 3s. George, of Bexley, Kent, arm. PEMBROKE COLL., matric. 13 Feb., 1867, aged 18; B.A. from ST. ALBAN HALL 1872, M.A. 1874, rector of Ifield, Kent, 1878, until his death 8 Nov., 1884. [15]

Randell, Joseph Knethell, s. Joseph, of St. Michael's, Dorset, gent. PEMBROKE COLL., matric. 17 May, 1804, aged 19; B.A. 1810, M.A. 1821.

Randell, Richard, s. Joseph, of Hanley, Dorset, gent. ST. ALBAN HALL, matric. 26 Nov., 1792, aged 22.

Randell, Rev. Thomas, 1s. George, of Stottesden, Salop, pleb. NON-COLL., matric. 6 Feb., 1880, aged 31; B.A. from ST. JOHN'S COLL. 1882, M.A. 1886, principal of Durham Training College 1885.

Randolph, Archibald Thomas, 1s. Edward John, of Dunnington, Yorks, cler. CHRIST CHURCH, matric. 18 Oct., 1867, aged 19.

Randolph, Benjamin, s. Caleb, of Ledbury, co. Hereford, gent. BRASENOSE COLL., matric. 23 March, 1726-7, aged 17. [20]

Randolph, Rev. Berkeley William, 4s. Cyril, of Riverhead, Kent, cler. BALLIOL COLL., matric. 22 Jan., 1877, aged 18; exhibitioner 1877-80, B.A. 1879, M.A. 1884.

Randolph, Bernard Montgomery, 7s. Thomas, of Much Hadham, Herts, cler. CHRIST CHURCH, matric. 2 June, 1852, aged 18; B.A. 1857.

Randolph, Brett, s. Brett, of Dursley, co. Gloucester, gent. ST. MARY HALL, matric. 18 March, 1777, aged 17.

Randolph, Cyril, 1s. George, of Eastry, Kent, cler. CHRIST CHURCH, matric. 9 June, 1843, aged 17; B.A. 1847, M.A. 1850, perp. curate Riverhead, Kent, 1850-63, rector of Staple, Kent, 1863-73, and of Chartham, Kent, 1873. See *Eton School Lists.*

Randolph, Edward John, 1s. Thomas, of St. James's, London, cler. CHRIST CHURCH, matric. 7 June, 1832, aged 18; student 1832-44, B.A. 1836, M.A. 1838, perp. curate Wigginton, Herts, 1839, and of Tring 1841-4, rector of Dunnington, Yorks, 1845, preb. of York 1848. See *Alumni West.*, 507. [25]

Randolph, Francis, s. Herbert, of Canterbury, Kent, arm. UNIVERSITY COLL., matric. 8 May, 1730, aged 16; fellow CORPUS CHRISTI COLL., B.A. 22 Feb., 1733-4, M.A. 17 Feb., 1736-7, B.D. 1744; D.D. from ST. ALBAN HALL 1763, principal 1759, rector of Shorwell, Isle of Wight, 1752, and perp. curate Warborough, Oxon, 1756, until his death 18 Feb., 1797, brother of George 1725, and of Thomas 1715.

Randolph, Francis Charles Hingeston, o.s. Francis Hingston, of St. Clement's, Truro, Cornwall, gent. EXETER COLL., matric. 12 Nov., 1851, aged 18; scholar 1850, B.A. 1855, M.A. 1858, P.C. Hampton-Gay, Oxon, 1858-60, rector of Ringmore, Devon, 1860, preb. of Exeter 1885, assumed the additional names of HINGESTON RANDOLPH in lieu of HINGSTON; for list of his works see *Crockford.* See *Coll. Reg.*, 155.

Randolph, Francis Piram Randolph Hingeston, 1s. Francis Charles Hingeston, of Ringmore, Devon, cler. KEBLE COLL., matric. 18 Oct., 1881, aged 20; B.A. 1884.

Randolph, George, s. Herbert, of Canterbury, Kent, arm. CORPUS CHRISTI COLL., matric. 2 Nov., 1725, aged 16, B.A. 1729; M.A. from ALL SOULS' COLL. 1733, B.Med. 1736, D.Med. 20 Feb., 1744-5, died at Bristol 22 April, 1764, aged 56.

Randolph, George, born at Oxford, s. John, bishop of London. CHRIST CHURCH, matric. 8 May, 1815, aged 18; student 1815-22, B.A. 1819, M.A. 1821, perp. curate Weald, Sevenoaks, 1821-2, vicar of Eastry, Kent, 1821-41, rector of Coulsdon, Surrey, 1841-63, died 10 June, 1880. See *Alumni West.*, 479. [30]

Randolph, Gower William, 5s. Edward, of Much Hadham, Herts. cler. CHRIST CHURCH, matric. 15 May, 1845, aged 18, student 1845-51, B.A. 1849; fellow ALL SOULS' COLL. 1851-63, B.C.L. 1852, D.C.L. 1857, a clerk in privy council office, died in Dec., 1863. See *Alumni West.*, 521.

Randolph, Henry Jones, s. William, of Bristol (city), gent. ST. EDMUND HALL, matric. 10 Oct., 1796, aged 18; B.A. 1800, M.A. 1804, rector of Newington Bagpath 1805, vicar of Hawkesbury, co. Gloucester, 1813, until his death 13 May, 1860, aged 82.

Randolph, Herbert, s. Herbert, of Deal, Kent, cler. CORPUS CHRISTI COLL., matric. 25 Oct., 1756, aged 17; B.C.L. from ST. ALBAN HALL 1763, preb. of Salisbury 1783, rector of Croxton, co. Lincoln, 1792, until his death 2 April, 1803 (his father died 6 Sep., 1755.

Randolph, Herbert, s. Thomas, of Petham, Kent, doctor. CORPUS CHRISTI COLL., matric. 26 March, 1762, aged 14, B.A. 1765; M.A. from MAGDALEN COLL. 1768, B.D. 1777, precentor of St. Paul's 1812, vicar of Canewdon, Essex, rector of Hanwell 1809, and perp. curate Wimbledon, Surrey, died 8 March, 1819.

Randolph, Herbert, s. Herbert, of Durnford, Wilts, cler. CORPUS CHRISTI COLL., matric. 22 May, 1787, aged 15; B.A. 1791, fellow, M.A. 1794, B.D. 1802, vicar of Chute, rector of Letcomb Bassett 1805, until his death at Rotterdam in 1828.

Randolph, Herbert, s. Herbert, of Wimbledon, Surrey, cler. CHRIST CHURCH, matric. 22 Dec., 1806, aged 17; student 1806-19, B.A. 1810, M.A. 1813, perp. curate Hawkhurst, Sussex, 1815-9, vicar of Marcham, Berks, 1819, until his death 13 March, 1875.

Randolph, Herbert, 1s. Herbert, of Letcombe, Berks, cler. BALLIOL COLL., matric. 17 March, 1826, aged 17; scholar 1826-32, B.A. 1830, M.A. 1842, incumbent of Holy Trinity, Melrose, 1849-55.

Randolph, James, s. Charles, of Langport, Somerset, arm. EXETER COLL., matric. 3 May, 1785, aged 18.

Randolph, John, s. Herbert, of Christ Church, Canterbury, arm. CORPUS CHRISTI COLL., matric. 29 Feb., 1719-20, aged 15; B.A. 1723. [6]

Randolph, John, s. Thomas, of Oxford (city), doctor. CHRIST CHURCH, matric. 17 June, 1767, aged 17; student, B.A. 1771, M.A. 1774, B.D. 1782, D.D. by diploma 30 Oct., 1783, professor of poetry 1776-83, proctor 1781, regius professor of Greek 1782-3, a canon of Christ Church and regius professor of divinity 1783-1807, preb. of Salisbury 1782, rector of Ewelme 1783, sinecure rector of Darowen 1797-1800, bishop of Oxford 1799-1806, Bangor 1806-9, and of London 1809-13, privy councillor 1809, F.R.S. 1811, died 28 July, 1813. See *Alumni West.*, 385.

Randolph, John, 1s. John Honywood, of Fulham, Middlesex, cler. BRASENOSE COLL., matric. 13 June, 1839, aged 18; B.A. 1843, M.A. 1847, chaplain Tattenhoe, etc., 1850-66, rector of Sanderstead, Surrey, 1866, until his death 11 July, 1881. See *Alumni West.*, 516.

Randolph, John Honywood, s. John, bishop of Bangor. CHRIST CHURCH, matric. 17 May, 1809, aged 18; student 1809-14, B.A. 1813, M.A. 1815, preacher to hon. Society of Gray's Inn 1815-7, rector of Burton Coggles, co. Lincoln, 1816, chaplain of the British Factory at St. Petersburg 1818, rector of Fobbing, Essex, 1822, and preb. of St. Paul's 1821, rector of Northolt, Middlesex, 1822-35, perp. curate St. Leonard's-on-Sea 1835, rector of Mistley-cum-Bradfield and Manningtree, Essex, 1839, and of Sanderstead, Surrey, 1845, died in June, 1868. See *Alumni West.*, 469.

Randolph, John James, 2s. Thomas, of Sheen, Surrey, cler. CHRIST CHURCH, matric. 15 May, 1834, aged 17, student 1834-40, B.A. 1838; fellow MERTON COLL. 1840, M.A. 1841, tutor and dean 1841, bursar 1842, sub-warden 1846, bar.-at-law, Lincoln's Inn, 1844. See Foster's *Men at the Bar* & *Alumni West.*, 510. [10]

Randolph, Joseph Randolph, 1s. Arthur Randolph, of Tor, Devon, arm. MAGDALEN COLL., matric. 21 Oct., 1886, aged 19.

Randolph, Leveson Cyril, 5s. Thomas, of Hadham, Herts, cler. CHRIST CHURCH, matric. 12 May, 1842, aged 17; student 1842-53, B.A. 1846, M.A. 1848, vicar of East Garston, Berks, 1853-70, and of St. Luke's, Lower Norwood, 1870, until his death 1 March, 1876. See *Alumni West.*, 519.

Randolph, Leveson John, 1s. Leveson Cyril, of Hemel Hempstead, Herts, cler. CHRIST CHURCH, matric. 25 Jan., 1878, aged 19; B.A. 1884, a student of the Inner Temple 1881. See *Eton School Lists.*

Randolph, Rodney Granville, 1s. George Granville, of Southsea, Hants, gent. CHRIST CHURCH, matric. 14 Oct., 1870, aged 18; B.A. 1874, M.A. 1877, curate of Leckhamstead, Bucks, 1880-2, rector 1882-3, vicar of South Kyme, co. Lincoln, 1884.

Randolph, Thomas, s. Herbert, of Canterbury (city), arm. CORPUS CHRISTI COLL., matric. 26 Nov., 1715, aged 14; B.A. 1719, M.A. 1 Feb., 1722-3, B.D. 1730, D.D. 1735, president 1748-83, vice-chancellor 1756-9, Margaret professor of divinity 1768-83, archdeacon of Oxford 1767, preb. of Worcester 1768, rector of Petham and Waltham, Kent, 1737, died 24 March, 1783. [15]

Randolph, Thomas, s. Thomas, of Islip, Oxon, doctor. CHRIST CHURCH, matric. 19 June, 1759, aged 18; B.A. 1763, M.A. 1766, rector of Saltwood-with-Hythe, Kent, 1769, vicar of Waltham and Petham 1783, until his death 18 July, 1808. See *Alumni West.*, 372.

Randolph, Thomas, s. John, bishop of Oxford. CHRIST CHURCH, matric. 17 May, 1806, aged 17; student 1806-13, B.A. 1810, M.A. 1812, preb. of St. Paul's 1812, chaplain in ordinary to the King 1825, rector of Much with Little Hadham, Essex, 1812, until his death 2 May, 1875. See *Alumni West.*, 464.

Randolph, William Cater, 1s. Henry Jones, of Hawkesbury, co. Gloucester, cler. TRINITY COLL., matric. 23 Nov., 1837, aged 19; B.A. 1842, M.A. 1844, of Yate House, co. Gloucester, sometime curate of Ermington, Devon.

Randolph, William, of ST. JOHN'S COLL., Cambridge (senior optime and B.A. 1840, M.A. 1843); adm. 'ad eundem' 20 June, 1844, incumbent of Aldershott, Dorset, 1854.

Randolph, Rev. William Frederick Herbert, 4s. Edward John, of Dunnington, Yorks, cler. CHRIST CHURCH, matric. 15 Oct., 1880, aged 17; scholar 1883-5, B.A. 1884, M.A. 1888. [20]

Rangeley, Rev. Isaac, o.s. Isaac, of Hayfield, co. Derby, gent. ST. MARY HALL, matric. 3 June, 1870, aged 22; B.A. from KEBLE COLL. 1874.

Ranger, Alfred Washington Guest, 1s. Josiah, of Brislington, Somerset, gent. WORCESTER COLL., matric. 16 Oct., 1872, aged 24; B.A. 1875, B.C.L. & M.A. 1879, D.C.L. 1884.

Ranken, Rev. Charles, s. Charles, of Belfast, Ireland, arm. CHRIST CHURCH, matric. 23 May, 1814, aged 17; student 1814-27, B.A. 1817, M.A. 1820, died 31 Oct., 1883. See *Alumni West.*, 478.

Ranken, Charles Edward, 1s. Charles, of Brislington, Somerset, cler. WADHAM COLL., matric. 15 Oct., 1845, aged 17; B.A. 1850, M.A. 1852, vicar of Sandford-on-Thames 1867-71, etc.

Ranken, Edward John, 2s. Charles, of Brislington, Somerset, cler. EXETER COLL., matric. 28 Jan., 1847, aged 17; B.A. from NEW INN HALL 1851.

Ranken, George Elliot, 1s. George Elliot, of Clifton, co. Gloucester, cler. UNIVERSITY COLL., matric. 21 Feb., 1845, aged 17; scholar 1845-51, B.A. 1849, M.A. 1883, a student of the Inner Temple 1849. See *Eton School Lists.* [26]

Ranken, John William, 1s. Charles, of St. George's, Bloomsbury, London, arm. CHRIST CHURCH, matric. 25 Oct., 1832, aged 17.

Ranken, Robert Burt, 1s. Thomas, of St. Mary's, Edinburgh, arm. BALLIOL COLL., matric. 29 Jan., 1859, aged 18; exhibitioner 1859-64, B.A. 1863, M.A. 1865.

Ranken, William Henry, 3s. Charles, of Brislington, Somerset, cler. CORPUS CHRISTI COLL., matric. 7 June, 1850, aged 17; scholar 1850-62, B.A. 1854, M.A. 1857, fellow 1862-9, junior bursar 1867, vicar of Sandford-on-Thames 1862-6, of Radley, Berks, 1865-7, of West Houghton, Lancashire, 1868-73, and of Marston Meysey, co. Gloucester, 1873-82, rector of Meysey Hampton, co. Gloucester, 1868-84, vicar of Christ Church, Surbiton, 1884.

Rankin, Daniel, 3s. Daniel, of Greenock, co. Renfrew, gent. BALLIOL COLL., matric. 17 Oct., 1882, aged 24; exhibitioner 1882, B.A. 1886. [30]

Rankine, Adam, o.s. John, of Liverpool, Lancashire, gent. BALLIOL COLL., matric. 16 Oct., 1866, aged 19; exhibitioner 1866-71, B.A. 1871.

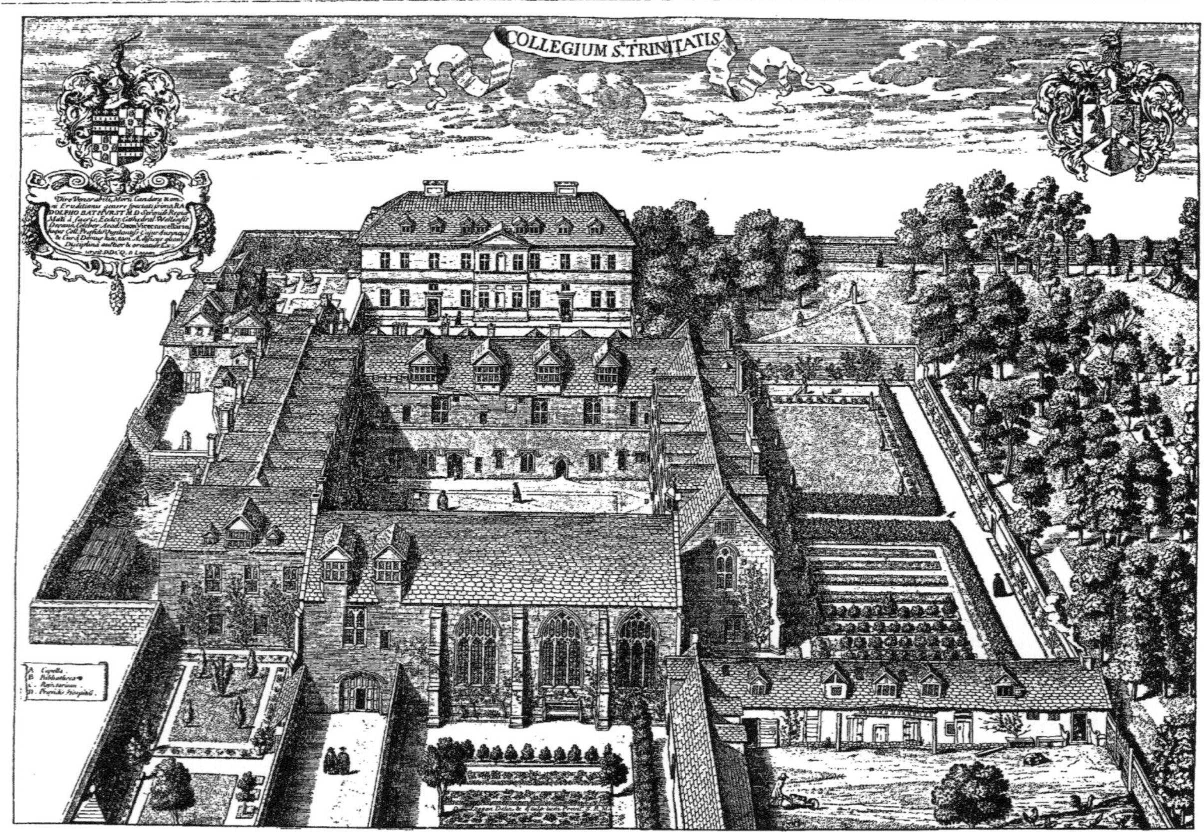

VIEW BY LOGGAN, 1675. [*Reduced facsimile.*]

Ranking, Devey Fearon, 6s. Robert, of Hastings, Sussex, arm. MAGDALEN HALL, matric. 21 Oct., 1867, aged 19; S.C.L. & B.A. 1873, M.A. 1874.

Ranking, John (Ebenezer), 7s. Robert, of Hastings, Sussex, gent. PEMBROKE COLL., matric. 26 Oct., 1868, aged 18; scholar MAGDALEN HALL 1869, B.A. 1872, B.Med. & M.A. (HERTFORD COLL.) 1876, D.Med. 1879.

Ranking, John Harvey, of CAIUS COLL., Cambridge (B.A. 1858, M.A. 1861); adm. 'comitatis causa' 11 July, 1863.

Rann, Charles Selwin, 'bibliopola;' privilegiatus 15 Oct., 1785.

Rann, Joseph, s. John, of West Bromwich, co. Stafford, cler. TRINITY COLL., matric. 28 Jan., 1729-30, aged 16; B.A. 1733. [5]

Rann, Joseph, s. John, of Birmingham, co. Warwick, gent. TRINITY COLL., matric. 10 Oct., 1751, aged 18; B.A. 1755, M.A. 1758, B.C.L. 1769, vicar of Holy Trinity, Coventry, 1773, until his death 21 Sep., 1811. See *Gent.'s Mag.*, 1811, ii. 394, & 1815, ii. 380.

Rann, Richard Edward, o.s. Thomas Burton, of Barnet, Middlesex, arm. QUEEN'S COLL., matric. 15 April, 1848, aged 19; B.A. 1851, M.A. 1856.

Ransom, Harry Alexander Vincent, o.s. Henry Spearman, of London, gent. ST. JOHN'S COLL., matric. 16 Oct., 1886, aged 18.

Ransom, Rev. Robert John, o.s. Robert, of Hastings, Sussex, gent. ST. MARY HALL, matric. 11 Nov., 1878, aged 21, B.A. 1883.

Ransome, Bernard Vincent Charles, 1s. Bernard Vincent Frederick, of Toowoomba, Australia, cler. WADHAM COLL., matric. 26 Jan., 1881, aged 18; B.A. 1884. [10]

Ransome, Cyril, 1s. Thomas, of Manchester, arm. MERTON COLL., matric. 16 Oct., 1869, aged 18; postmaster 1869-74, B.A. 1874, M.A. 1876.

Ransome, Walter Henry Alford, 2s. Vincent Frederick, of Chetnole, Dorset, cler. KEBLE COLL., matric. 17 Oct., 1882, aged 16; B.A. from CHARSLEY HALL 1886.

Raper, Charles Charnier, s. Henry, of Chelsea, Middlesex, arm. MERTON COLL., matric. 31 July, 1795, aged 18; B.A. 1799, in the War Office, died in 1845. See *Eton School Lists.*

Raper, Edward Bell, 1s. Joseph, of Ulverston, Lancashire, gent. PEMBROKE COLL., matric. 27 Oct., 1883, aged 19; scholar 1883-5, B.A. 1887.

Raper, Robert William, 1s. Timothy, of Llanwennerth, co. Monmouth, arm. BALLIOL COLL., matric. 13 April, 1861, aged 19; scholar TRINITY COLL. 1861-5, B.A. 1865, fellow QUEEN'S COLL. 1865-71, lecturer 1866, B.C.L. 1868, fellow TRINITY COLL. 1871, M.A. 1871, tutor 1869-82, lecturer 1865-9, dean 1875, bursar 1887. [15]

Rasbotham, Dorning, s. Dorning, of Dean, Lancashire, arm. BRASENOSE COLL., matric. 13 May, 1784, aged 17; B.A. 1788, M.A. 1790, chaplain Collegiate Church, Manchester, 1793, and fellow 1794, perp. curate St. Paul's, Manchester, 1795, rector of St. Mary's, Manchester, 1798, until his death 18 July, 1804. See *Manchester School Reg.*, i. 189.

Rasch, Arthur Warner, 1s. Arthur Augustus, of St. George's, Bloomsbury, London, arm. ST. JOHN'S COLL., matric. 18 Oct., 1861, aged 19.

Rashdall, Edward Montagu, 2s. John, of London, cler. NEW COLL., matric. 16 Oct., 1879, aged 19; B.A. 1883.

Rashdall, Hastings, 1s. John, of London, cler. NEW COLL., matric. 13 Oct., 1877, aged 19; scholar 1877-82, B.A. 1881, M.A. 1884; chaplain of University College and tutor in University of Durham 1884.

Rashdall, John of CORPUS CHRISTI COLL., Cambridge (B.A. 1833, M.A. 1836); adm. 'ad eundem' 7 June, 1843, vicar of Dawlish, Devon, 1864, until his death 5 Feb., 1867. [20]

Rashleigh, Rev. Arthur Stanhope, 1s. Stanhope, of Southgate, Middlesex, cler. UNIVERSITY COLL., matric. 13 Oct., 1879, aged 19; B.A. 1883.

Rashleigh, Charles Stackhouse, 1s. Jonathan Stackhouse, of Wickham, Hants, cler. MAGDALEN HALL, matric. 2 March, 1837, aged 23; died 22 April, 1867. See Foster's *Baronetage.*

Rashleigh, Charles Watson, s. John, of Penquite, par. St. Samson, Cornwall, arm. WADHAM COLL., matric. 2 Feb., 1803, aged 18. See Foster's *Baronetage.*

Rashleigh, Edward, 2s. Jonathan, of St. Andrew's, Holborn, London, arm. WADHAM COLL., matric. 13 May, 1829, aged 17; died s.p.

Rashleigh, Edward Stanhope, 2s. Stanhope, of Edmonton, Middlesex, cler. CORPUS CHRISTI COLL., matric. 23 Oct., 1884, aged 19; exhibitioner 1885. [25]

Rashleigh, Evelyn William, 2s. Jonathan, of London, gent. CHRIST CHURCH, matric. 15 Jan., 1869, aged 19; B.A. 1873, of Kilmarth, Cornwall, J.P.; bar.-at-law, Inner Temple, 1878. See Foster's *Men at the Bar.*

Rashleigh, George, s. Peter, of Boughton, Kent, cler. ORIEL COLL., matric. 13 Oct., 1801, aged 17; B.A. 1805, M.A. 1809, vicar of Horton Kirby, Kent, 1818, until his death 19 Feb., 1874. See Foster's *Baronetage.*

Rashleigh, George Burville, 1s. Henry Burville, of Horton Kirby, Kent, cler. EXETER COLL., matric. 12 June, 1867, aged 18; B.A. 1871, bar.-at-law, Lincoln's Inn, 1873, secretary to Master of the Rolls. See Foster's *Men at the Bar.*

Rashleigh, George Cumming, s. Jonathan, of Silverton, Devon, cler. NEW COLL., matric. 14 Nov., 1809, aged 18; fellow 1809-29, B.A. 1813, M.A. 1817, dean of arts 1826, proctor 1826, vicar of Andover 1829, perp. curate Hound 1850, and vicar of Hamble-le-Rice, Hants, 1850, until his death 1 April, 1874. See Foster's *Baronetage.*

Rashleigh, Henry Burvill, 1s. George, of Horton, Kent, cler. EXETER COLL., matric. 15 Nov., 1838, aged 18; B.A. 1842, curate of Horton Kirby, Kent, 1844-74, vicar (and patron) 1874. [30]

Rashleigh, Jonathan, s. Jonathan, of Wickham, co. Southampton, arm. MERTON COLL., matric. 9 Aug., 1758, aged 17, B.A. from UNIVERSITY COLL. 1763; M.A. from ALL SOULS' COLL. 1767, rector of Gedney, co. Lincoln, 1773, of Wickham, Hants, and of Silverton, Devon, 1784, until his death in Nov., 1806. See Foster's *Baronetage;* and also *Gent.'s Mag.*, 1788, ii. 661.

Rashleigh, Jonathan, 2s. William, of Ivy Church, Wilts, arm. BALLIOL COLL., matric. 22 March, 1839, aged 19; B.A. 1842, of Menabilly, Cornwall, high sheriff 1877, of Feniton, Devon, and of Lissadrone, co. Mayo. See Foster's *Baronetage.*

Rashleigh, Jonathan, 1s. Jonathan, of Menabilly, Cornwall, arm. CHRIST CHURCH, matric. 18 May, 1864, aged 18; B.A. 1869, a student of the Inner Temple 1868, died 8 Dec., 1872.

Rashleigh, Jonathan Stackhouse, s. Jonathan, of Wickham, Hants, cler. WADHAM COLL., matric. 3 July, 1801, aged 18; B.A. 1805, M.A. 1811, rector of Wickham, Hants, 1807, until his death 15 May, 1863.

Rashleigh, Peter, s. Jonathan, of Wykeham, Hants, arm. UNIVERSITY COLL., matric. 30 Oct., 1765, aged 20; fellow ALL SOULS' COLL., B.A. 1772, M.A. 1775, bar.-at-law, Middle Temple, 1772, rector of Worldham and New Romney, Kent, 1781, vicar of Barking, Essex, 1781, and rector of Southfleet 1788, until his death 8 Feb., 1836. See Foster's *Baronetage.* [35]

Rashleigh, Peter, s. Peter, of Boughton, Kent, cler. ORIEL COLL., matric. 25 Oct., 1804, aged 18.

Rashleigh, Philip, s. Jonathan, of Menabilly, Cornwall, arm. NEW COLL., matric. 15 July, 1749, aged 19; of Menabilly, father of the House of Commons, M.P. Fowey 1765-1802, died 26 June, 1811. See Foster's *Baronetage.*

Rashleigh, Stanhope, 4s. Jonathan Stackhouse, of Wickham, Hants, cler. MAGDALEN HALL, matric. 17 Dec., 1847, aged 18; B.A. 1852, vicar of St. Wenn, Cornwall, 1853-83.

Rashleigh, William, 1s. William Boys, of Farningham, Kent, gent. BRASENOSE COLL., matric. 23 Oct., 1885, aged 18; in the University XI. 1887. See Foster's *Baronetage*.

Rasoumoffsky, Adam, Count. D.C.L. by diploma 16 June, 1814; Russian privy councillor.

Ractcliff, George, s. Tristram, of Isle of Jamaica, West Indies, arm. MERTON COLL., matric. 12 Feb., 1802, aged 18. See *Eton School Lists*.

Ratcliffe, Gordon, 1s. Thomas, of Mylor, Cornwall, cler. KEBLE COLL., matric. 13 Oct., 1873, aged 19. [5]

Ratcliff, John, s. Robert, of Stonehouse, co. Gloucester, cler. PEMBROKE COLL., matric. 17 Nov., 1718, aged 18; B.A. 1722, M.A. 1725, B.D. 1737, D.D. 1739, master 1738, until his death 31 Oct., 1775.

Ratcliffe, Thomas, 7s. Thomas Wilkinson, of Ashbourne, co. Derby, arm. EXETER COLL., matric. 6 May 1841, aged 17.

Rathbone, Charles Bertie, s. John Rawbone (see next page), of St. Peter's, Oxford, cler. PEMBROKE COLL., matric. 4 Nov., 1800, aged 14; B.C.L. from ST. MARY HALL 1818, altered the spelling of his name (as RAWBONE), vicar of Coughton, co. Warwick, 1814, and of Buckland, Berks, 1825, until his death 3 May, 1828.

Rathbone, David, o.s. David, of Ashworth, Lancashire, cler. BRASENOSE COLL., matric. 25 May, 1853, aged 19; B.A. from ST. JOHN'S COLL. 1859, M.A. 1860, his father died 10 Feb., 1871.

Rathbone, Herbert Reynolds, 5s. Philip Henry, of Liverpool, arm. NEW COLL., matric. 15 Oct., 1881, aged 19; B.A. 1885. See Foster's *Lancashire Collection*. [10]

Rathbone, John Edward, 1s. Charles Bertie, of Buckland, Berks, cler. ORIEL COLL., matric. 13 June, 1833, aged 17.

Rathbone, John Egerton, s. John Rawbone (see next page), of St. Peter's, Oxford, cler. NEW COLL., matric. 28 July, 1795, aged 16; B.A. 1799, M.A. 1803, fellow until 1829, dean of arts 1823, bursar 1824, perp. curate Romford, Essex, 1828, until his death in 1838 (altered the spelling of his name).

Rathbone, Joseph, s. John, of Congleton, Cheshire, pleb. BRASENOSE COLL., matric. 13 Dec., 1749, aged 22.

Rathbone, Thomas, s. Richard, of Conway, co. Carnarvon, cler. JESUS COLL., matric. 26 March, 1779, aged 19; B.A. 1783 (? died vicar of Llandebrog, Anglesea, Dec., 1812).

Rathbone, Thomas, s. John Rawbone (see next page), of St. Peter's, Oxon, cler. LINCOLN COLL., matric. 12 Feb., 1798, aged 17; demy MAGDALEN COLL. 1801-7, B.A. 1802, M.A. 1805, fellow 1807-16, senior dean of arts 1810, bursar 1811, died 3 Feb., 1816, as RATHBONE (altered the spelling of his name). See *St. Paul's School Reg.*, 203; & *Bloxam*, vii. 143.

Rathbone, Thomas Ashton, 2s. William, of Liverpool, arm. UNIVERSITY COLL., matric. 27 Oct., 1874, aged 18; B.A. & M.A. 1882. [15]

Rathbone, William (Gail), 1s. William, of Wavertree, Lancashire, arm. UNIVERSITY COLL., matric. 17 Oct., 1868, aged 19; B.A. 1872. See Foster's *Lancashire Collection* & *Rugby School Reg.*

Rathborne, Rev. James, M.A. TRINITY COLL., Dublin, 1854 (B.A. 1849); adm. 'ad eundem' 13 Dec., 1860.

Rattey, Edwin, 2s. James, of Cambridge, gent. ST. MARY HALL, matric. 31 Oct., 1868, aged 21.

Rattigan, Henry Adolphus Boyden, 1s. William Henry, of Delhi, East Indies, arm. BALLIOL COLL., matric. 15 Oct., 1884, aged 20; B.A. 1888, a student of Lincoln's Inn 1885. [20]

Rattle, Henry, 3s. John, of Bath, Somerset, pleb. CHRIST CHURCH, matric. 19 May, 1853, aged 18; servitor 1853-7, B.A. 1857, M.A. 1860, assistant-curate St. Ebb's, Oxford, died in Feb., 1869.

Rattle, John Manley, 1s. John, of Bath, Somerset, pleb. CHRIST CHURCH, matric. 21 Oct., 1846, aged 19; servitor 1846-50, B.A. 1850, M.A. 1853.

Rattue, George, s. George, of Salisbury (city), pleb. WADHAM COLL., matric. 12 March, 1746-7, aged 20.

Raven, James, 1s. William, of Lexham, Norfolk, gent. NON-COLL., matric. 4 Nov., 1876, aged 38.

Ravenhill, Frederick Henry Harvey, 2s. Edward H., of Littlehampton, Sussex, cler. PEMBROKE COLL., matric. 25 Oct., 1856, aged 19; B.A. 1862. [25]

Ravenhill, Henry Everett, 3s. John, of Warminster, Wilts, arm. UNIVERSITY COLL., matric. 14 May, 1851, aged 19; B.A. 1855, M.A. 1858, vicar of Buckland Newton, Dorset, since 1860.

Ravenhill, Henry John, 1s. Henry, of Clapham, Surrey, arm. CHRIST CHURCH, matric. 28 Jan., 1870, aged 18; B.A. 1874.

Ravenhill, John, s. William, of Hereford (city), gent. BRASENOSE COLL., matric. 18 Feb., 1755, aged 17, B.A. 1758; fellow WORCESTER COLL., M.A. 1761, rector of Streynsham, co. Worcester, 1774.

Ravenhill, John, s. Timothy, of Cheshunt, Herts, arm. UNIVERSITY COLL., matric. 23 Nov., 1775, aged 22; B.A. 1779, M.A. 1813, B. & D.D. 1813, rector of Tooting, Surrey, 1805, until his death 14 Feb., 1833.

Ravenhill, Robert, s. Timothy, of Cheshunt, Herts, arm. UNIVERSITY COLL., matric. 1 July, 1778, aged 18; B.A. 1782, M.A. 1785. [30]

Ravenhill, Thomas Holmes, 3s. William Holmes, of Hereford (city), arm. WORCESTER COLL., matric. 6 Dec., 1838, aged 18; B.A. 1843, M.A. 1845, vicar of Arlingham, co. Gloucester, 1848.

Ravenhill, William Waldron, 5s. J , of Warminster, Wilts, arm. UNIVERSITY COLL., matric. 22 June, 1854, aged 18; S.C.L. 1858, B.A. & M.A. 1861, bar.-at-law, Inner Temple, 1862, recorder of Andover 1872. See Foster's *Men at the Bar*.

Ravenscroft, George, s. Edward, of Bombay, East Indies, arm. CHRIST CHURCH, matric. 29 Oct., 1795, aged 17.

Ravenscroft, John, s. Thomas, of Chester (city), gent. BRASENOSE COLL., matric. 14 April, 1739, aged 19; B.A. 1744, vicar of Hanmer, Flints, 1767, until his death in 1788.

Ravenscroft, John, 1s. John, of Birkenhead, Cheshire, gent. EXETER COLL., matric. 15 May, 1875, aged 18; B.A. 1879, M.A. 1882, a student of Lincoln's Inn 1876. See *Rugby School Reg.* [35]

Ravenscroft, Joseph, 2s. John, of Birkenhead, Cheshire, gent. EXETER COLL., matric. 14 Oct., 1876, aged 18.

Ravenscroft, Peter, s. George, of Wrexham, co. Denbigh, gent. JESUS COLL., matric. 31 May, 1775, aged 19; B.A. 1779, M.A. 1781, B.D. 1789, perp. curate Shocklach, Cheshire, 1780, until his death in 1832.

Ravenscroft, Thomas, s. Thomas, of Chester (city), arm. CHRIST CHURCH, matric. 3 July, 1728, aged 17. See Ormerod's *Cheshire*, iii. 207.

Ravenscroft, William, 'servant to Dr. Long, of All Souls' College;' privilegiatus 21 May, 1778.

Ravenscroft, William, s. William, of Oxford (city), pleb. PEMBROKE COLL., matric. 12 July, 1794, aged 17.

Ravenshaw, Edward, s. John, of Bracknell, Berks, arm. BRASENOSE COLL., matric. 11 Nov., 1800, aged 18; B.A. 1804, M.A. 1808, rector of West Kington, Wilts, 1816, until his death 13 Dec., 1854. See *Eton School Lists*. [41]

Ravenshaw, Thomas FitzArthur Torin, 7s. John Goldsborough, of London, arm. ORIEL COLL., matric. 3 June, 1847, aged 18; B.A. 1852, M.A. 1854, rector of Pewsey, Wilts, 1857-80, F.S.A., F.Z.S., F.R.B.S., died 26 Sep., 1882; for list of his works see *Crockford*.

awbone, John, s. John, of Drayton, Oxon, pleb. MAGDALEN HALL, matric. 2 May, 1740, aged 19; B.A. 7 March, 1748-9, M.A. 1765, vicar of Winslow and Granby, Bucks, 1765, until his death 17 Jan., 1775.

awbone, John, s. William, of Winslow, Bucks, pleb. MAGDALEN HALL, matric. 8 Dec., 1761, aged 18; chaplain MAGDALEN COLL. 1769-1821, B.A. 1765, M.A. 1768, vice-principal ST. MARY HALL, B.D. 1787, D.D. from MAGDALEN COLL. 1804, usher of the College School 1764-9, deputy-keeper of the archives, vicar of Cheddar, Somerset, vicar of Buckland, Berks, 1805, and rector of Hatford 1804, until his death 22 July, 1825, father of Charles B., John Egerton, and Thomas Rathbone. See *Bloxam*, ii. 176.

awbone, John, s. John, of Uxbridge, Middlesex, pleb. MAGDALEN HALL, matric. 10 Oct., 1791, aged 19; B.A. 1795, M.A. 1798.

awbone, John, 3s. George, of London, gent. MERTON COLL., matric. 12 Oct., 1878, aged 16.

awdon-Hastings, Francis, 1s. (John), Earl of Moira. UNIVERSITY COLL., matric. 23 Oct., 1771, aged 16; 2nd Earl of Moira in 1793, created Baron Rawdon 5 March, 1783, and Marquis of Hastings, etc., 13 Feb., 1817, K.G. 1812, G.C.B. & G.C.H. 1818, M.P. Randalstown 1780-3, assumed the additional surname and arms of HASTINGS 1790, general in the army 1803, privy councillor 1806, constable of the Tower 1806, governor-general Bengal and commissioner-in-chief India 1812-23, etc., died 28 Nov., 1826. [5]

awdon, Francis, s. John, of Glasslough, co. Monaghan, Ireland, arm. EXETER COLL., matric. 25 March, 1809, aged 30; B.A. 1812.

awdon-Hastings, George Augustus Francis, 1s. Francis, Marquis of Hastings. CHRIST CHURCH, matric. 9 Nov., 1826, aged 18; 2nd marquis, a lord of the bedchamber to William IV. 1830, and bearer of the golden spurs at the coronation in 1831, died 13 Jan., 1844.

Rawdon, George Wordsworth, 3s. Joshua, of Everton, near Liverpool, arm. BALLIOL COLL., matric. 3 June, 1857, aged 18; demy MAGDALEN COLL. 1858-63.

Rawdon, James Hamer, 1s. Joshua, of Liverpool, arm. BRASENOSE COLL., matric. 8 June, 1854, aged 18; B.A. 1858, M.A. 1861, held various curacies 1863-75, vicar of Crompton 1875-7, and of Preston, Lancashire, 1877.

Rawdon, William Frederick, 1s. William Frederick, of Naples, Italy, D.Med. WADHAM COLL., matric. 17 March, 1852, aged 19; B.A. 1856, M.A. 1859. See *Rugby School Reg.*, 282. [10]

Rawes, James, s. Gerard, of Kirby Lonsdale, Westmoreland, pleb. QUEEN'S COLL., matric. 29 Oct., 1735, aged 19; B.A. 1741, fellow, M.A. 1744, B.D. 1759, of Chedworth, co. Gloucester, died 6 June, 1785.

Rawes, Robert Booth, s. Richard, of Bromley, Kent, gent. ST. EDMUND HALL, matric. 3 July, 1801, aged 16; B.A. 1805, M.A. 1808.

Rawes, Rev. William, s. William, of Witton-le-Wear, co. Durham, cler. UNIVERSITY COLL., matric. 26 May, 1813, aged 17; B.A. 1817.

Rawkins, Silvester, s. Stephen, of Chardstock, Dorset, gent. BALLIOL COLL., matric. 6 June, 1753, aged 18; B.A. 1757.

Rawkins, Sylvester, s. Sylvester, of East Pennard, Somerset, cler. BALLIOL COLL., matric. 18 Oct., 1785, aged 17; B.A. 1789, M.A. 1792. [15]

Rawling, John, s. Cuthbert, of Stanton, Cumberland, pleb. QUEEN'S COLL., matric. 7 Nov., 1716, aged 17; B.A. 1722.

Rawling, John, s. John, of Kensington, Middlesex, arm. TRINITY COLL., matric. 13 March, 1793, aged 18.

Rawling, Robert, s. Luke, of Bolden, co. Durham, pleb. LINCOLN COLL., matric. 1 Dec., 1738, aged 18; B.A. 1742.

Rawlings, Rev. Charles, 4s. William, of Padstow, Cornwall, cler. EXETER COLL., matric. 24 Feb., 1823, aged 18.

Rawlings, James, s. John, of Witherington, co. Hereford, pleb. CHRIST CHURCH, matric. 19 Nov., 1724, aged 18; B.A. 1728. [20]

Rawlings, Philip, s. Mos., of Devizes, Wilts, pleb. QUEEN'S COLL., matric. 14 May, 1730, aged 16; B.A. 22 Feb., 1733-4.

Rawlings, William, s. William, of Padstow, Cornwall, gent. EXETER COLL., matric. 11 March, 1780, aged 18; scholar 1779, B.A. 1783, vicar of Padstow 1790, until his death 20 Dec., 1836, father of Charles, and William next named. See *Coll. Reg.*, 146.

Rawlings, William, s. William, of Padstow, Cornwall, cler. ST. EDMUND HALL, matric. 21 March, 1809, aged 18; B.A. 1813, rector of Lansallos, Cornwall.

Rawlings, William, 1s. Edward, of Stanton-super-Arrow, co. Hereford, gent. MAGDALEN HALL, matric. 5 June, 1824, aged 29; B.A. 1829, M.A. 1831.

Rawlins, Rev. Christopher, s. John, of Guildford, Surrey, arm. MERTON COLL., matric. 15 Dec., 1794, aged 17; B.A. 1798, M.A. 1826, died at Englefield Green 13 Dec., 1848, aged 72. [25]

Rawlins, Christopher, 1s. Christopher, of St. Pancras, London, cler. ORIEL COLL., matric. 2 May, 1827, aged 18; B.A. 1832, vicar of Thornton and Allerthorpe, Yorks, 1836, until his death 1 April, 1876.

Rawlins, Edmund, s. William, of Salford, co. Warwick, arm. WORCESTER COLL., matric. 14 June, 1771, aged 17; B.A. 1775, M.A. 1780, rector of Dorsington, 1816, until his death in 1830.

Rawlins, Edmund, s. William, of Pophills, co. Warwick, gent. WORCESTER COLL., matric. 1 Dec., 1802, aged 18.

Rawlins, Henry, s. Henry, of Wedmore, Somerset, gent. WADHAM COLL., matric. 11 May, 1769, aged 20; B.A. 1773, died rector of Staplegrove, Somerset in 1810.

Rawlins, Henry William, s. Henry, of Martock, Somerset, cler. BALLIOL COLL., matric. 17 Oct., 1801, aged 18; B.A. 1805, M.A. 1808, rector of Fiddington, 1821, and vicar of Kilton, Somerset, 1844, until his death 21 June, 1855. [30]

Rawlins, James, s. William, of St. Cross, Hants, cler. ST. JOHN'S COLL., matric. 16 July, 1808, aged 19; B.A. 1812, M.A. 1825.

Rawlins, James Murray Richard. BRASENOSE COLL., 1845. See WORKMAN.

Rawlins, John, s. John, of St. Aldate's, Oxford (city), pleb. HART HALL, matric. 20 May, 1724, aged 16; B.A. from CHRIST CHURCH 1727, M.A. 1730, rector of Haselton, co. Gloucester, and Ley, co. Worcester, 1752 (and also of Badley), until his death 3 Nov., 1784.

Rawlins, John, s. John, of Evesham, co. Worcester, cler. CHRIST CHURCH, matric. 5 Dec., 1764, aged 17, B.A. 1768; M.A. from MERTON COLL. 1772, B.D. 1782, vicar of Ponteland, Northumberland, 1788, until his death in 1811.

Rawlins, John, s. John, of Calcutta, East Indies, arm. MERTON COLL., matric. 10 May, 1810, aged 18; B.A. 1814, chaplain Bombay establishment, died at Cambay 24 Sep., 1817. See *Eton School Lists*.

Rawlins, John, 3s. Robert, of Whitchurch, Hants, arm. ST. JOHN'S COLL., matric. 1 March, 1848, aged 18; B.A. 1852, M.A. 1857. [35]

Rawlins, John Arthur, 3s. John, of Handsworth, co. Stafford, gent. EXETER COLL., matric. 29 May, 1860, aged 18; choral scholar NEW COLL. 1862-3, B.A. 1863, M.A. 1867, held various curacies 1865-80, vicar of St. Andrew's, Willesden, 1880.

Rawlins, John Fawsitt Herbert, s. John, of Bristol, co. Gloucester, gent. QUEEN'S COLL., matric. 24 Oct., 1789, aged 17; created M.A. 4 July, 1793, bar.-at-law, Inner Temple, 1798.

Rawlins, Michael, s. Michael, of Abingdon, Berks, pleb. PEMBROKE COLL., matric. 4 Nov., 1741, aged 19; B.A. 1745.

Rawlins, Richard, 'pharmacopola;' privilegiatus 12 June, 1772.

Rawlins, Richard, 3s. Samuel, of Cleobury Mortimer, Salop, gent. MAGDALEN HALL, matric. 26 Jan., 1822, aged 18; B.A. 1826, M.A. 1833, died curate of St. Anne's, Limehouse, 8 Sep., 1849.

Rawlins, Richard Randall, s. William, of St. Cross, Hants, cler. ST. JOHN'S COLL., matric. 29 Nov., 1804, aged 18; perp. curate Kneeton, Notts, 1836-67, died 24 Oct., 1874. **[5]**

Rawlins, Stedman, s. Stedman, of St. Christopher's, West Indies, arm. CHRIST CHURCH, matric. 22 Oct., 1801, aged 17.

Rawlins, Thomas, s. Richard, of Chatwall, Salop, gent. CHRIST CHURCH, matric. 12 Dec., 1794, aged 21.

Rawlins, Thomas Fraser Pye, 1s. Thomas Samuel Fraser, of Denchworth, Berks, cler. KEBLE COLL., matric. 14 Oct., 1884, aged 19; B.A. 1887.

Rawlins, Thomas Samuel Fraser, 2s. Richard, of Birmingham, co. Warwick, cler. LINCOLN COLL., matric. 14 Dec., 1847, aged 18; scholar WORCESTER COLL. 1848-53, B.A. 1852, fellow 1853-62, M.A. 1854, vicar of Denchworth, Berks, 1858-68, rector of Clifton-Campville, co. Stafford, 1868. See *St. Paul's School Reg.*, 301.

Rawlins, William, s. Thomas, of Stokegursey, Somerset, gent. HART HALL, matric. 14 April, 1739, aged 20. **[10]**

Rawlins, William, s. Anthony, of Fairford, co. Gloucester, gent. WADHAM COLL., matric. 31 May, 1775, aged 21; B.A. from ST. MARY HALL 1779, M.A. 1782, rector of Teversal, Notts, 1792, until his death 1 Jan., 1828.

Rawlinson, Abram Tyzack, s. Henry, of Liverpool, Lancashire, arm. CHRIST CHURCH, matric. 18 April, 1795, aged 17; died at Chadlington, Oxon, 1 Sep., 1849. See Foster's *Lancashire Collection* & *Rugby School Reg.*, 67.

Rawlinson, Edward Creswicke Scott, 2s. George, of Oxford, cler. KEBLE COLL., matric. 15 Oct., 1877, aged 18; drowned in river Cherwell 21 Jan., 1880.

Rawlinson, George, 3s. Abram, of Chadlington, Oxon, arm. TRINITY COLL., matric. 7 Nov., 1834, aged 21, B.A. 1838; fellow EXETER COLL. 1840-6, M.A. 1841, tutor 1841, sub-rector and divinity reader 1844, Bampton lecturer 1859, Camden professor of ancient history 1861, canon of Canterbury 1872, rector of All Hallows, Lombard Street, 1888, father of George Ernest 1867; for list of his works see *Crockford.* See also Foster's *Lancashire Collection & Boase*, 132.

Rawlinson, George, 5s. John, of St. George's, Bloomsbury, London, arm. ST. JOHN'S COLL., matric. 21 March, 1839, aged 18; B.A. 1842, M.A. 1846, perp. curate Bothamstall, Notts, 1848, until his death 26 Oct., 1850. **[15]**

Rawlinson, George Ernest, 1s. George, of Oxford, cler. BALLIOL COLL., matric. 4 May, 1867, aged 18; B.A. 1880.

Rawlinson, Major-General Sir Henry Creswicke, K.C.B., created D.C.L. 12 June, 1850 (son of Abram Tyzack Rawlinson, of Chadlington, Oxon), served in Indian army 1827-56, political agent at Candahar 1840-2, in Turkish Arabia 1843-55, consul at Bagdad 1844-51, consul-general 1851-6, envoy and minister plenipotentiary to Persia 1859-60, with rank of major-general, M.P. Reigate 1858, Frome 1865-9, president Royal Geographical Society 1871-5, a trustee British Museum 1878, member Indian Council 1858-9 and 1868, F.R.S., K.C.B. 4 Feb., 1856. See Foster's *Lancashire Collection.*

Rawlinson, Henry, 4s. John, of 'precincts of Winchester Cathedral,' arm. ST. JOHN'S COLL., matric. 27 March, 1832, aged 18; B.A. 1836, M.A. 1841, curate of Symondsbury, Dorset, 1839-63, rector 1863, until his death 10 June, 1881, father of the next named.

Rawlinson, Henry John, 1s. Henry, of Allington, Dorset, cler. ORIEL COLL., matric. 10 May, 1859, aged 18; B.A. 1863, M.A. 1866, vicar of Ivinghoe, Herts, since 1874.

Rawlinson, John Baldwin, 1s. Robert, of Whitehaven, Cumberland, arm. BRASENOSE COLL., matric. 23 Oct., 1885, aged 18; B.A. 1888. **[20]**

Rawlinson, Lionel Seymour, 3s. George, of Oxford, cler. NON-COLL., matric. 28 Jan., 1882, aged 17.

Rawlinson, William Chapman, 2s. Abraham, of Leyton, Essex, gent. MAGDALEN HALL, matric. 22 Oct., 1835, aged 18; B.A. 1839, M.A. 1843, rector of Chedburgh, Suffolk, 1853, until his death 25 Sep., 1864. See Foster's *Lancashire Collection.*

Rawnsley, Arthur Eden, 5s. Drummond, of Shiplake, Oxon, cler. HERTFORD COLL., matric. 19 April, 1879, aged 19.

Rawnsley, Edward, 1s. Thomas Hardwicke, of Halton, co. Lincoln, cler. BRASENOSE COLL., matric. 5 Feb., 1835, aged 18; B.A. 1838, M.A. 1842, of Raithby Hall, co. Lincoln, J.P., vicar of Hundleby, co Lincoln, 1849-60. See *Eton School Lists.*

Rawnsley, Edward Preston, o.s. Edward, of Raithby, co. Lincoln, cler. BRASENOSE COLL., matric. 9 June, 1870, aged 18; B.A. 1873, a student of the Inner Temple 1875. See *Eton School Lists.* **[25]**

Rawnsley, Hardwicke Drummond, 2s. Robert Drummond Burrell, of Shiplake, Oxon, cler. BALLIOL COLL., matric. 24 Oct., 1870, aged 19; B.A. 1875, M.A. 1883, vicar of Crosthwaite, Cumberland, 1883.

Rawnsley, Robert Drummond Burrell, 2s. Thomas Hardwick, of Spilsby, co. Lincoln, cler. BRASENOSE COLL., matric. 4 Feb., 1836, aged 18; demy MAGDALEN COLL. 1839-40, B.A. 1840, fellow 1840-2, M.A. 1843, preb. of Lincoln 1877, vicar of Shiplake, Oxon, 1849-61, rector of Halton Holgate, co. Lincoln, 1861, until his death 31 Aug., 1882. See *Bloxam*, vii. 346; & *Rugby School Reg.*, 165.

Rawnsley, Thomas Hardwicke, s. Thomas, of Bourn, co. Lincoln, gent. EXETER COLL., matric. 23 April, 1807, aged 17; scholar 1807, B.A. 1811, M.A. 1814, rector of Falkingham, co. Lincoln, 1814, and of Halton Holgate 1825, until his death 2 July, 1861, See *Coll. Reg.*, 150; & *Eton School Lists.*

Rawnsley, Walter Hugh, 4s. Robert Drummond Borrell, of Shiplake, Oxon, cler. MERTON COLL., matric. 14 Oct., 1876, aged 19; postmaster 1876-81, B.A. 1880. See *Eton School Lists.* **[29]**

Rawnsley, Willingham Franklin, 1s. Robert Drummond Burrell, of Little Hadham, Herts, cler. CHRIST CHURCH, matric. 18 Oct., 1864, aged 19; B.A. from CORPUS CHRISTI COLL. 1869, M.A. 1871.

Rawson, Edward Creswell, 6s. Samuel, of Parsloe, Essex, gent. BALLIOL COLL., matric. 19 Oct., 1878, aged 19; of the Indian Civil Service 1878.

Rawson, Henry Gilbert, 1s. Rawson, of Port Louis, Mauritius, arm. CHRIST CHURCH, matric. 8 June, 1870, aged 19; a junior student 1870, B.A. 1874, bar.-at-law, Inner Temple, 1877. See Foster's *Men at the Bar.*

Rawson, Jeremiah, s. Benjamin, of Bolton, Lancashire, arm. BALLIOL COLL., matric. 10 Oct., 1810, aged 19; a student of Lincoln's Inn 1815, of the Nidd Hall family. See Foster's *Yorkshire Collection.*

Rawson, Philip Heathcote, 2s. Philip, of Aigburth, Lancashire, arm. UNIVERSITY COLL., matric. 13 Oct., 1883, aged 19; B.A. 1886, a student of the Inner Temple 1884. See *Eton School Lists.*

Rawson, Richard Hamilton, 1s. Philip, of Aigburth, Lancashire, arm. BRASENOSE COLL., matric 10 June, 1881, aged 18. See *Eton School Lists*.

Rawson, William Henry, 1s. William, of Somerley, co. York. gent. EXETER COLL., matric. 30 Nov., 1867, aged 19; B.A. 1873, of Mill House, Yorks. See Foster's *Yorkshire Collection*.

Rawson, William Stepney, 3s. Rawson William, of Cape of Good Hope, arm. CHRIST CHURCH, matric. 31 May, 1873, aged 18; a junior student 1873-80, B.A. 1877, M.A. 1880.

Rawstorne, Atherton Gwillym, 1s. Robert Atherton, of Hutton Hall, Lancashire, cler. CORPUS CHRISTI COLL., matric. 18 Nov., 1873, aged 18; B.A. 1877, M.A. 1882, chaplain to the Bishop of Adelaide 1882. See *Eton School Lists* & Foster's *Lancashire Collection*.

Rawstorne, Henry Feilden, 2s. Robert Atherton, of Balderton Grange, Lancashire, cler. TRINITY COLL., matric. 12 Oct., 1878, aged 19; B.A. 1882, M.A. 1885, a student of the Inner Temple 1880. See Foster's *Lancashire Collection* & *Eton School Lists*. [5]

Rawstorne, Laurence, s. Laurence, of Preston, Lancashire, arm. BRASENOSE COLL., matric. 12 July, 1760, aged 17; of Newhall and Hutton, Lancashire, father of the next named. See Foster's *Lancashire Collection*.

Rawstorne, Laurence, s. Laurence, of Penwortham, Lancashire, arm. ORIEL COLL., matric. 17 May, 1794, aged 18; purchased Penwortham, high sheriff Lancashire 1814, etc., father of the next named.

Rawstorne, Lawrence, 1s. Laurence, of Penwortham, Lancashire, arm. CHRIST CHURCH, matric. 31 May, 1860, aged 17; B.A. 1864, M.A. 1883, of Penwortham aforesaid. See Foster's *Lancashire Collection*.

Rawstorne, Robert Atherton, s. Laurence, of Penwortham, Lancashire, arm. BRASENOSE COLL., matric. 11 Nov., 1796, aged 17; B.A. 1800, M.A. 1803, rector of Warrington, Lancashire, 1807-31, of South Thoresby, co. Lincoln, 1807-52, perp. curate Penwortham and Langton 1831, until his death 12 May, 1852. See Foster's *Lancashire Collection*.

Rawstorne, Robert Atherton, 1s. Robert A., of Warrington, Lancashire, cler. BRASENOSE COLL., matric. 18 May, 1842, aged 18; B.A. 1846, M.A. 1849, perp. curate Penwortham, Lancashire, 1852-8, vicar of Balderstone, Lancashire, 1859, archdeacon of Blackburne 1885. See Foster's *Lancashire Collection* & *Rugby School Reg.*, 199. [10]

Rawstorne, Robert Edward, 2s. William Edward, of Penwortham, Lancashire, cler. CHRIST CHURCH, matric. 13 Oct., 1882, aged 18; B.A. 1886.

Rawstorne, William, 1s. William Edward, of Penwortham, Lancashire, cler. BRASENOSE COLL., matric. 10 June, 1881, aged 18.

Rawstorne, William Edward, 1s. William, of Preston, Lancashire, arm. CHRIST CHURCH, matric. 30 May, 1838, aged 18; student 1841-6, B.A. 1842, M.A. 1844, rector of Galby, co. Leicester, 1845-50, vicar of Ormskirk 1850-3, vicar of Penwortham 1858, hon. canon of Manchester 1870. See Foster's *Lancashire Collection* & *Rugby School Reg.*, 173.

Rawstron, Rev. Reginald Heber, 5s. John, of Oakenham House, near Rochdale, arm. KEBLE COLL., matric. 14 Oct., 1879, aged 20; B.A. from CHARSLEY HALL 1884.

Ray, Benjamin, of ST. JOHN'S COLL., Cambridge (B.A. 1725, M.A. 1730); incorp. 9 July, 1733. [15]

Ray, Edmund Barker, 2s. Robert, of St. George's, London, arm. BRASENOSE COLL., matric. 14 Jan., 1823, aged 18; B.A. 1826, M.A. 1829.

Ray, John, s. John, of Winchester (city), gent. ORIEL COLL., matric. 21 July, 1753, aged 17; B.A. 1757, M.A. 1760, rector of West Dean, Wilts, 1761, until his death in 1778.

Ray, Rev. John, 1s. John, of Edmonton, Middlesex, gent. EXETER COLL., matric. 17 Oct., 1828, aged 18; B.A. 1833, died 26 Jan., 1844.

Ray, Washington, 4s. Charles, of London, gent. LINCOLN COLL., matric. 19 Oct., 1875, aged 18; scholar 1875-9, B.A. 1880, M.A. 1882.

Raye, William, s. George, of Quarrington, co. Lincoln, cler. HERTFORD COLL., matric. 2 May, 1754, aged 17; B.A. 1758. [20]

Ray, William (Carpenter), s. William, of Redland, Somerset, cler. PEMBROKE COLL., matric. 30 March, 1786, aged 18; B.C.L. 1795, vicar of Boreham, Essex, 1795, and of Pakenham, Suffolk, 1805, until his death 8 Jan., 1845.

Ray, William Carpenter Rishton, s. William, of Boreham, Essex, cler. WADHAM COLL., matric. 16 Dec., 1814, aged 18; rector of Eastwood, Essex, 1857, until his death 7 Nov., 1866.

Raybould, John Combet, s. Thomas, of Amblecoat, co. Stafford, gent. BALLIOL COLL., matric. 4 May, 1748, aged 17; B.A. 1752.

Raybould, William, s. John, of Clent, co. Stafford, gent. WORCESTER COLL., matric. 22 Oct., 1783, aged 18.

Rayer, Henry, 2s. William, of Tiverton, Devon, cler. TRINITY COLL., matric. 2 June, 1841, aged 18; B.A. 1847, M.A. 1848, died rector of St. Athan, co. Glamorgan, 22 Dec., 1853. [25]

Rayer, William, s. William, of St. Mary's, Middlesex, gent. TRINITY COLL., matric. 24 Nov., 1803, aged aged 18; B.A. 1807, M.A. 1810, rector of Tidcombe portion 1811, died in Dec., 1866. See Foster's *Baronetage*, CAREW.

Rayer, William, 3s. Richard, of Cuttsdean, co. Worcester, gent. PEMBROKE COLL., matric. 29 June, 1827, aged 18; B.A. from ST. MARY HALL 1831.

Rayer, William Carew, 1s. William, of Tiverton, Devon, cler. CHRIST CHURCH, matric. 15 May, 1839, aged 18; of Holcombe Rogus, Devon, sometime captain 1st Devon militia. See *Eton School Lists*.

Raymond, Gregory, s. George Syndercombe, of Symondsbury, Dorset, cler. BALLIOL COLL., matric. 26 Feb., 1799, aged 17; B.A. 1802, M.A. 1808, assumed the name of RAYMOND in lieu of SYNDERCOMBE, rector of Symondsbury 1806, until his death 2 Feb., 1863.

Raymond, John. s. John, of Limehouse, London, arm. EXETER COLL., matric. 30 March, 1762, aged 18. [30]

Raymond, John Storey, 1s. John Gatehouse, of Cann, Dorset, arm. EXETER COLL., matric. 10 Oct., 1873, aged 19; B.A. 1876, M.A. 1880, rector of Hemington, Somerset, 1882.

Raymond, John Tuckfield, 5s. George, of Lewisham, Kent, gent. ST. ALBAN HALL, matric. 16 Oct., 1866, aged 20; B.A. from ST. JOHN'S COLL., Cambridge, 1870, M.A. 1873, vicar of Upton Snodsbury, co. Worcester, 1879.

Raymond, Jonathan, y.s. Jemmett, of St. Peter's, Oxford (city), equitis. PEMBROKE COLL., matric. 17 Dec., 1723, aged 15.

Raymond, Thomas, s. William, of Thornbury, co. Gloucester, arm. ORIEL COLL., matric. 23 March, 1765, aged 18.

Raymond, Thomas Hampton, s. Thomas, of Hampton Court, Middlesex, arm. TRINITY COLL., matric. 16 Oct., 1812, aged 18. [35]

Raymond, William, s. John, of Rumsey, Hants, cler. WADHAM COLL., matric. 4 April, 1715, aged 19; B.A. 26 Feb., 1718-9.

Rayne, Thomas, s. Robert, of St. Lawrence Jewry, London, gent. CHRIST CHURCH, matric. 10 May, 1733, aged 17; B.A. 8 Feb., 1736-7, M.A. 10 March, 1740-1, vicar of Winwick, Northants, 1737, of Broadwindsor and Netherbury, Dorset, 1760 (preb. of St. Paul's, and chaplain to one of the regiments of guards), died at Oxford in 1789. See *Gent.'s Mag.*, 179.

Rayner, Alexander, s. William, of Barnstaple, Devon, cler. CHRIST CHURCH, matric. 17 May, 1716, aged 18, B.A. 29 Feb., 1719-20; M.A. from ORIEL COLL. 1722, B.Med. 1 Feb., 1726-7, D.Med. 1731.

Rayner, Edward, s. William, of Tiverton, Devon, cler. CHRIST CHURCH, matric. 16 March, 1724-5, aged 18, B.A. 1728; M.A. from ORIEL COLL. 1731, proctor 1738.

Rayner, Thomas, s. John, of Gate Burton, co. Lincoln, gent. LINCOLN COLL., matric. 6 May, 1757, aged 19.

Rayner, Thomas Dyson, 1s. Joseph, of Clifton, co. York, gent. EXETER COLL., matric. 16 Jan., 1875, aged 18; B.A. 1877.

Rayner, William, s. William, of Tiverton, Devon, cler. CHRIST CHURCH, matric. 27 May, 1715, aged 18; B.A. 10 March, 1718-9, M.A. 1722. **[5]**

Rayner, William John, s. Richard, of St. Martin's, Birmingham, gent. PEMBROKE COLL., matric. 23 Nov., 1814, aged 15; B.A. 1819.

Raynes, Rev. Herbert Alfred, 1s. Alfred Thomas, of Greenwich, Kent, cler. CHRIST CHURCH, matric. 14 Oct., 1881; exhibitioner 1881-5, B.A. 1885. See *St. Paul's School Reg.*, 364.

Raynolds, Edward and William. See REYNOLDS, page 1188.

Raynor, Edwin, 1s. William, of Nottingham, gent. NON-COLL., matric. 31 May, 1879, aged 31; held various curacies since 1874.

Raynor, John, o.s. John, of Plymouth, Devon, arm. TRINITY COLL., matric. 7 June, 1819, aged 18; B.A. 1823, M.A. 1826 (as RAYNER), died vicar of Tamerton Foliott, Devon, 5 Nov., 1829. **[10]**

Raynor, Rev. Philip Edwin, 4s. George, of Kelvedon, Hatch, Essex, cler. NEW COLL., matric. 15 Oct., 1875, aged 18; scholar 1875-80, B.A. 1879, M.A. 1882, warden of Christ's College, Hobart, Tasmania, 1886.

Raynsford, Francis, s. Francis, of Brixworth, Northants, arm. LINCOLN COLL., matric. 21 Oct., 1743, aged 18; B.A. 1747, M.A. 1750, died rector of Bugbrooke, Northants, 1785.

Raynsford, George (Nigel). CORPUS CHRISTI COLL., 1785. See EDWARDS, page 411.

Raynsford, John Nicolls, s. Francis, of Brixworth, Northants, arm. LINCOLN COLL., matric. 10 March, 1740-1, aged 17.

Raynsford, Justinian, s. Francis, of Brixworth, Northants, arm. LINCOLN COLL., matric. 13 Oct., 1742, aged 17. **[15]**

Raynsford, Nicolls, s. Justinian, of Brixworth, Northants, arm. MAGDALEN COLL., matric. 10 Feb., 1774, aged 18.

Raynsford, Richard, s. Richard, of Binfield, Berks, arm. UNIVERSITY COLL., matric. 10 Dec., 1761, aged 17.

Raynton, Francis, s. Nich., of Burr Street, London, arm. WADHAM COLL., matric. 23 March, 1726-7, aged 18.

Rayson, George, 1s. Joseph, of Renwick, Cumberland, gent. NON-COLL., matric. 17 Oct., 1874, aged 19; B.A. from QUEEN'S COLL. 1878.

Rayson, William, 2s. Robert, of Stockton-upon-Tees, Durham, gent. MAGDALEN HALL, matric. 14 Dec., 1852, aged 22; B.A. 1856, M.A. 1859, minor canon and sacristan of Worcester 1862-74, vicar of Lindridge, co. Hereford, since 1873. **[20]**

Rayson, Rev. William Robert, o.s. William, of Amesbury, Wilts, cler. KEBLE COLL., matric. 19 Oct., 1874, aged 19; B.A. 1878, M.A. 1883.

Rea, Carleton, 1s. Robert Tomkins, of Worcester, arm. MAGDALEN COLL., matric. 19 Jan., 1880, aged 18; B.A. 1883, B.C.L. & M.A. 1886, bar.-at-law, Inner Temple, 1884. See Foster's *Men at the Bar*.

Rea, James Thomas Roberts, o.s. Thomas, of Pembridge, co. Hereford, gent. ST. JOHN'S COLL., matric. 14 Oct., 1882, aged 18; B.A. 1886.

Rea, John Marcus Beaumont, 3s. George, of Middleton, near Alnwick, arm. BRASENOSE COLL., matric. 21 Oct., 1878, aged 18.

Read, Archibald, 3s. Robert Arthur, of Glastonbury, Somerset, gent. TRINITY COLL., matric. 16 Oct., 1886, aged 19. **[25]**

Read, Arthur, 1s. Robert, of Reigate, Surrey, gent. QUEEN'S COLL., matric. 19 April, 1869, aged 18; B.A. 1874. See *Robinson*, 347.

Read, Bagot, s. Bagot, of Llandinam, co. Montgomery, arm. BRASENOSE COLL., matric. 14 Jan., 1734-5, aged 18; father of the next named.

Read, Bagot, s. Bagot, of Chester (city), arm. BRASENOSE COLL., matric. 27 March, 1760, aged 18; of Llandinam Hall, co. Montgomery.

Read, Edmund Arthur Algernon, 2s. Edmund, of Blackheath, Kent, gent. NON-COLL., matric. 13 Oct., 1884, aged 20; B.A. 1887.

Read, Edward, s. Rich., of Cropredy, Oxon, gent. NEW INN HALL, matric. 6 Feb., 1724-5, aged 23. **[30]**

Read, Ernest Charles, 1s. Charles, of Honiton, Devon, arm. NEW COLL., matric. 16 Oct., 1880, aged 19; scholar 1880-5, B.A. 1884, died 13 July, 1886.

Read, Francis William, s. William, of Tenbury, co. Worcester, cler. BALLIOL COLL., matric. 14 Jan., 1740-1, aged 16; B.A. 1744, M.A. 1750.

Read, Frederick John, 2s. John, of Faversham, Kent, gent. NEW COLL., matric. 18 Oct., 1875, aged 17; B.Mus. 26 Oct., 1876.

Read, George, s. George, of ——, co. Lincoln, pleb. CHRIST CHURCH, matric. 1 June, 1716, aged 18; B.A. 1720, M.A. 1723.

Read, George Sydney, y.s. (subs. 4s.) David C., of Salisbury (city), gent. QUEEN'S COLL., matric. 10 June, 1841, aged 16; B.A. from ST. MARY HALL 1847, M.A. 1850, bar.-at-law, Lincoln's Inn, 1858. See Foster's *Men at the Bar*. **[35]**

Read, Herbert James, 2s. Charles, of Honiton, Devon, arm. BRASENOSE COLL., matric. 18 Oct., 1881, aged 18; scholar 1880-3, exhibitioner 1883, B.A. 1884, brother of Thomas 1879.

Read, James, s. Thomas, of Farmborough, Somerset, pleb. ST. MARY HALL, matric. 29 Oct., 1724, aged 18, B.A. 1728; M.A. from NEW COLL. 1731.

Read, John Offley Crewe, s. Offley Crewe, of Mucklestone, co. Stafford, cler. BRASENOSE COLL., matric. 28 Jan., 1808, aged 18; B.A. 1812, M.A. 1815; of Pen-y-bryn, co. Montgomery, and of Wern, Flints, assumed the additional surname of READ by royal licence 15 March, 1836, died 30 Nov., 1858. See Foster's *Peerage*, B. CREWE.

Read, Jones, s. Bagot, of Llandinam, co. Montgomery, gent. JESUS COLL., matric. 15 April, 1736, aged 17; B.A. 1739, fellow, M.A. 1742, B.D. 1749, D.D. 1755, died rector of Rotherfield Pepper, Oxon, 23 April, 1782.

Read, Joseph, s. Joseph, of Witney, Oxon, cler. MAGDALEN HALL, matric. 17 March 1721-2, aged 16; B.A. from BRASENOSE COLL. 1725. **[40]**

Read, Rev. Philip, 2s. Alexander, of Hyde, Cheshire, cler. LINCOLN COLL., matric. 22 Oct., 1868, aged 18; scholar 1868-72, B.A. 1872.

Read, Thomas, s. Thomas, of Shaftesbury, Dorset, pleb. ST. MARY HALL, matric. 12 March, 1717-8, aged 17; B.A. from ALL SOULS' COLL. 1721.

Read, Thomas, s. Thomas, of Evesham, co. Worcester, pleb. CHRIST CHURCH, matric. 7 Dec., 1734, aged 17; B.A. 1738.

Read, Thomas, s. Thomas, of Shaston, Dorset, cler. ALL SOULS' COLL., matric. 10 June, 1752, aged 16; B.A. from ORIEL COLL. 1756, M.A. 1759, B. & D.D. 1787, rector of Ufton and Patney, and vicar of Hale, Wilts, died 15 June, 1789.

Read, Thomas, s. Samuel, of Conway, co. Carnarvon, gent. JESUS COLL., matric. 16 May, 1812, aged 21; B.A. 1815, M A. 1818. **[45]**

ead, Rev. Thomas, (s. Charles) of Honiton, Devon, —. EXETER COLL., matric. 15 Oct., 1879, aged 18; scholar 1879-84, B.A. 1883, M.A. 1886, brother of Herbert I.

ead, Thomas Frederick Rudston, 3s. Thomas Cutler Rudston, of Sand Hutton, Yorks, cler. UNIVERSITY COLL., matric. 23 June, 1829, aged 18; scholar 1832-8, B.A. 1833, M.A. 1836, rector of Full Sutton, Yorks, 1836-45, of Winteringham, co. Lincoln, 1845-65, and of Withyham, Kent, 1865. See *Eton School Lists*.

ead, Rev. Trehane Symons, s. James, of Clutton, Somerset, doctor. EXETER COLL., matric. 2 May, 1801, aged 18; died in 1809.

ead, William, s. Henry, of Berhampoor, East Indies, gent. ST. EDMUND HALL, matric. 2 May, 1808, aged 18; B.A. 1812, M.A. 1814.

eade, Charles, 8s. John, of Ipsden, Oxon, arm. MAGDALEN COLL., matric. 26 July, 1831, aged 17; demy 1831-5, fellow 1835-84 B.A. 1835, Vinerian scholar 1835-42, Vinerian fellow 1842, M.A. 1838, D.C.L. 1847, junior dean of arts 1840, bursar 1843, vice-president 1850, bar.-at-law, Lincoln's Inn, 1843, novelist and writer, died 11 April, 1884. See Foster's *Baronetage* & *Coll. Reg.*, vii. 329. **[5]**

eade, Charles Darby, 2s. John, of Holbroke, Suffolk, arm. MAGDALEN HALL, matric. 12 March, 1840, aged 19; rector of Stow Bedon, Norfolk, 1850-60.

eade, Charles James, 3s, John Fielder, of Astbury, Cheshire, gent. ST. JOHN'S COLL., matric. 20 Jan., 1864, aged 19; B.A. 1867, M.A. 1870, vicar of Shotteswell, Oxon, 1872.

Reade, Chichester Arthur Wellesley, M.A. TRINITY COLL., Dublin, 1861 (B.A. 1858, LL.B. & LL.D. 1878); adm. 'comitatis causa' 7 Feb., 1867, chaplain Banstead Asylum 1877. See *Crockford*.

Reade, Compton, o.s. John Chandos, of London, baronet. TRINITY COLL., matric. 14 Feb., 1833, aged 18; died 31 July, 1851. See Foster's *Baronetage*.

Reade, Compton, 1s. Compton, of St. George's, Bloomsbury, London, gent. PEMBROKE COLL., matric. 25 Nov., 1852, aged 18; clerk MAGDALEN COLL. 1854-7, B.A. 1857, M.A. 1859, chaplain 1858-79, and of Christ Church 1861-7, vicar of Cassington, Oxon, 1867-9, rector of Elton, co. Durham, 1883-4, etc., lecturer Curzon Chapel, 1886. See *Bloxam*, ii. 122; and for list of his works see *Crockford*. **[10]**

Reade, Frederick William, 2s. Alfred, of Fredericton, New Brunswick, gent. ST. ALBAN HALL, matric. 28 Nov., 1866, aged 19; B.A. 1870, has held various curacies since 1872.

Reade, George, s. Richard, of Dublin (city), arm. ST. JOHN'S COLL., matric. 10 Jan., 1739-40, aged 21.

Reade, Gerald McCarthy Lewin, o.s. Charles William, of Brighton, Sussex, arm. EXETER COLL., matric. 30 May, 1871, aged 20; B.A. 1875, perp. curate Alphington, Devon, 1883. See *Eton School Lists*.

Reade, Rev. Henry St. John, 2s. William Barrington, of Streatley, Berks, arm. UNIVERSITY COLL., matric. 28 April, 1858, aged 18; scholar 1858-64, B.A. 1862, M.A. 1865, head-master Oundle Grammar School 1876, until his death 13 Feb., 1884.

Reade, Herbert Granville Revell, 2s. John Page, of London, arm. BALLIOL COLL., matric. 18 Oct., 1876, aged 19. See *Eton School Lists*. **[15]**

Reade, James Colquhoun Revell, 1s. John Page, of Harley Street, London, gent. CHRIST CHURCH, matric. 20 April, 1860, aged 20; B.A. 1864, of Crowe Hall, Suffolk, bar.-at-law, Middle Temple, 1869. See Foster's *Men at the Bar*.

Reade, (Sir) John (Bart.), s. John, of Shipton, Oxon, baronet. MAGDALEN COLL. matric. 18 Jan., 1780, aged 18; created M.A. 2 July, 1783, 5th baronet, died 7 Nov., 1789.

Reade, John, s. George, of Ipsden, Oxon, arm. ORIEL COLL., matric. 29 March, 1793, aged 17; of Ipsden, died 20 Oct., 1849. See Foster's *Baronetage*.

Reade, (Sir) John Chandos (Bart.), s. John, of Harley Street, London. CHRIST CHURCH, matric. 27 April, 1804, aged 19; 6th baronet, died 14 Jan., 1868.

Reade, John Page, 2s. George, of Madras, East Indies, arm. EXETER COLL., matric. 14 Nov., 1822, aged 17; B.A. 1828, of Crowe Hall, Suffolk, high sheriff 1865, died 28 Sep., 1880. **[20]**

Reade, Joseph, o.s. Joseph, of Shipton-under-Wychwood, Oxon, arm. BRASENOSE COLL., matric. 22 Oct., 1880, aged 17; B.A. 1884, M.A. 1888, a student of Lincoln's Inn 1884.

Reade, Richard, s. Richard, of Dublin, Ireland, arm. ST. JOHN'S COLL., matric. 22 May, 1739, aged 17.

Reade, Richard Bancroft, 2s. Richard, of Palgrave, Suffolk, cler. EXETER COLL., matric. 25 May, 1858, aged 19; died in Aug., 1864.

Reade, Thomas, s. Thomas, of Ipsden, Oxon, gent. HART HALL, matric. 17 July, 1725, aged 18.

Reade, William, o.s. George, of Alderholt Park, Dorset, arm. QUEEN'S COLL., matric. 24 May, 1822, aged 17; B.A. 1828, M.A. 1830, bar.-at-law, Lincoln's Inn, 1831, died 30 April, 1870. **[25]**

Reade, William Winwood, 1s. William Barington, of St. Finan, near Crief, Scotland, arm. MAGDALEN HALL, matric. 13 March, 1856, aged 17; died 24 April, 1875.

Reader, Edmund George, 3s. William, of Ewhurst, Hants, arm. QUEEN'S COLL., matric. 6 June, 1856, aged 18.

Reader, Harry Charles Lyon, 1s. William of Castlebar, co. Mayo, arm. MERTON COLL., matric. 4 March, 1871, aged 20; B.A. 1875, M.A. 1884, a priest of the Church of Rome. See *Rugby School Reg.*

Readhead, John, s. John, of Penrith, Cumberland, pleb. QUEEN'S COLL., matric. 6 March, 1731-2, aged 19; B.A. 1735.

Reading, James, s. William, of St. Alphage, London, cler. UNIVERSITY COLL., matric. 23 Nov., 1738, aged 16; B.A. 12 March, 1742-3, M.A. 1745, rector of Southwood, etc., and Reedham with Freethorpe, Norfolk, 1788, and of Stonesfield, Oxon, died in 1790. **[30]**

Reading, Philip, s. William, of St. Alphage, London, cler. UNIVERSITY COLL., matric. 27 March, 1738, aged 18. See *Gent.'s Mag.*, 1744, p. 676.

Reading, Thomas, s. William, of Hainton, co. Lincoln, cler. BRASENOSE COLL., matric. 31 Aug., 1723; B.A. 1727.

Ready, Arthur William, o.s. Thomas, of Wolverhampton, gent. WADHAM COLL., matric. 22 April, 1876, aged 20; scholar 1875-80, B.A. 1881.

Ready, Edward Martin. WADHAM COLL., 1858. See PITT, page 1120.

Ready, John, s. John, of Gloucester (city), gent. UNIVERSITY COLL., matric. 19 June, 1767, d 17. **[35]**

Ready, Robert, s. Alexander, of Filkins, Oxon, gent. NEW COLL., matric. 1 Dec., 1748, aged 18; B.A. 1752, M.A. 1756, rector of Buscot, and of Passmore and Cadmore, Bucks, 1761, until his death 1791.

Reay, Rev. Charles Lucas, o.s. William Lucas, of Liverpool, gent. QUEEN'S COLL., matric. 23 March, 1829, aged 17; B.A. 1834, died in New Zealand April, 1848.

Reay, Henry Joseph, s. Henry Ulrick, of Burn Hall, co. Durham, arm. MERTON COLL., matric. 25 Oct., 1811, aged 19.

Reay, Henry Ulric, s. Joseph, of Newcastle, Northumberland, arm. UNIVERSITY COLL., matric. 8 Oct., 1768, aged 18; B.A. 1772, M.A. 1775, bar.-at-law, Inner Temple, 1775.

Reay, Samuel, 1s. George, of Hexham, Northumberland, gent. NEW COLL., matric. 7 March, 1871, aged 46; B.Mus. 8 July, 1871. **[40]**

Reay, Stephen, s. John, of Montrose, Angus, Scotland, cler. ST. ALBAN HALL, matric. 26 May, 1814, aged 32; B.A. 1817, M.A. 1823, B.D. 1841, Bodley's sub-librarian 1828, Laudian professor of Arabic 1840, until his death 20 Jan., 1861.

Reay, Thomas Osmotherley, 5s. John, of All Hallows, London, gent. EXETER COLL., matric. 2 June, 1852, aged 18; B.A. 1857, M.A. 1862, vicar of Dovercourt, Essex, 1871-80, and of Prittlewell, Essex, 1880. See *Eton School Lists.*

Reay, William, s. Nic., of Denton, Cumberland, cler. QUEEN'S COLL., matric. 12 May, 1741, aged 19; B.A. 14 Feb., 1744-5, M.A. 1751.

Rebbeck, John, s. Benjamin, of Stockton, Wilts, gent. QUEEN'S COLL., matric. 21 Feb., 1809, aged 24.

Reddall, Enoch, 4s. Isaac, of Birmingham, gent. MAGDALEN HALL, matric. 14 Nov., 1850, aged 34. [5]

Reddall, Thomas, s. Luke, of Aldridge, co. Stafford, gent. ST. ALBAN HALL, matric. 23 June, 1815, aged 33.

Redfern, John Lemon, o.s. Tom, of Penrith, Cumberland, gent. QUEEN'S COLL., matric. 28 Oct., 1881, aged 19; B.A. 1884, M.A. 1888.

Redfern, Robert Scarr, 2s. Thomas, of Salford, near Manchester, gent. QUEEN'S COLL., matric. 4 July, 1840, aged 20; B.A. 1844, M.A. 1848, vicar of Acton, Cheshire, 1857, until his death 14 Feb., 1884.

Redfern, Thomas Robert, o.s. William Thomas, of Taunton, Somerset, cler. NEW COLL., matric. 12 Oct., 1866, aged 18; B.A. 1870, of the Indian Civil Service 1868, assistant-commissioner Oudh, bar.-at-law, Inner Temple, 1880. See Foster's *Men at the Bar.*

Redfern, William Thomas, 1s. Thomas, of Manchester, gent. MAGDALEN HALL, matric. 7 Nov., 1839, aged 21; B.A. 1845, M.A. 1846, vicar of St. James, Taunton, 1845, until his death 30 July, 1885. [10]

Redgrave, Jasper Alexander, 1s. Alexander, of Brompton, Middlesex, arm. CORPUS CHRISTI COLL., matric. 30 Jan., 1865, aged 19.

Redhead, Arthur Cecil Milne-, 2s. Richard, of Seedley, Lancashire, gent. BRASENOSE COLL., matric. 28 Jan., 1886, aged 20.

Redhead, Edward, 1s. Richard, of Bloomsbury, London, gent. MAGDALEN COLL., matric. 31 Oct., 1845, aged 32; B.Mus. 4 Dec., 1845.

Redhead, John Roberts, 1s. William, of Saffron Walden, Essex, gent. ST. EDMUND HALL, matric. 16 Dec., 1824, aged 20; B.A. 1828, vicar of Thurnby with Stoughton, co. Leicester, 1832, until his death 7 Jan., 1872.

Redhead, Theodore John, 1s. John Roberts, of Romaldkirk, co. York, cler. ST. EDMUND HALL, matric. 6 April, 1848, aged 17; exhibitioner 1848-51, B.A. 1851, M.A. 1856, perp. curate Emery-Down, Hants, 1864-8, vicar of Redlynch, Wilts, 1868-72, and of Thurnby, co. Leicester, since 1872. See *Robinson*, 289. [15]

Redifer, Alfred, 1s. William, of Stamford, co. Lincoln, gent. LINCOLN COLL., matric. 10 June, 1848, aged 18; B.A. from ST. MARY HALL 1852, M.A. 1855, held various curacies 1853-63, vicar of Finstock, Oxon, 1863.

Redington, Christopher Thomas Talbot, 1s. Thomas, of Dublin, equitis. CHRIST CHURCH, matric. 14 Oct., 1864, aged 17; B.A. 1869, of Kilcornan, co. Galway, high sheriff 1873, a senator of the Royal University of Ireland.

Redmayne, John Fitzgerald de Clare Studdert, 1s. John Marriner, of Kilrush, co. Clare, gent. MERTON COLL., matric. 1 Feb., 1879, aged 19; B.A. 1883, a student of the Inner Temple 1882.

Redmayne, Tunstal Fitzgerald, 3s. John Marriner, of Tynemouth, Northumberland, gent. NON-COLL., matric. 4 June, 1881, aged 18.

Redpath, Henry Adeney, 1s. Henry Syme, of Sydenham, Kent, gent. QUEEN'S COLL., matric. 29 Oct., 1867, aged 19; scholar 1867-72, B.A. 1871, M.A. 1874, organist, vicar of Wolvercote, Oxon, 1880-3, rector of Holwell, Dorset, 1883. See *Robinson*, 334. [20]

Redwood, Rev. Charles, s. Isaac, of Cowbridge, co. Glamorgan, pleb. JESUS COLL., matric. 10 March, 1736-7, aged 18.

Redwood, Jeremiah, s. Jeremiah, of London, arm. QUEEN'S COLL., matric. 5 July, 1764, aged 17.

Reece, Delahay, s. Richard, of Longtown, co. Hereford, cler. BRASENOSE COLL., matric. 10 Nov., 1752, aged 18; B.A. 1759.

Reece, George, s. William, of Colwall, co. Hereford, cler. MAGDALEN HALL, matric. 19 May, 1790, aged 22; B.A. 1797, M.A. 1798.

Reece, George Henry Walton, 4s. Richard Marsden, of London, arm. UNIVERSITY COLL., matric. 21 Jan., 1882, aged 20; B.A. 1885. [25]

Reece, Henry, 2s. Robert, of London, arm. BALLIOL COLL., matric. 16 Oct., 1879, aged 19; scholar UNIVERSITY COLL. 1880-3, a student of Lincoln's Inn 1880.

Reece, Joseph Frederick, 3s. Richard Marsden, of London, gent. CHRIST CHURCH, matric. 23 May, 1872, aged 18; a junior student 1872-6, B.A. 1877.

Reece, Richard, s. Richard, of Llangannon, co. Hereford, cler. JESUS COLL., matric. 13 May, 1727, aged 17; B.A. 1730.

Reece, Richard, s. William, of St. Peter's, co. Hereford, pleb. CHRIST CHURCH, matric. 18 June, 1766, aged 19; B.A. from QUEEN'S COLL. 1770.

Reece, Robert, o.s. Robert, of Isle of Barbados, West Indies, arm. EXETER COLL., matric. 5 March, 1825, aged 17; bar.-at-law, Inner Temple, 1850.

Reece, Robert, 1s. Robert, of Isle of Barbados, arm. BALLIOL COLL., matric. 28 Jan., 1857, aged 18; B.A. 1860, M.A. 1864, a student of the Inner Temple, 1850. [31]

Reed, Charles Francis, o.s. Charles, of Christ Church, Canterbury, New Zealand, gent. QUEEN'S COLL., matric. 7 March, 1874, aged 18; B.A. 1877.

Reed, Christopher, s. John, of Westminster, arm. EXETER COLL., matric. 9 May, 1815, aged 17; B.A. 1828, M.A. 1829, bar.-at-law, Middle Temple, 1824, his father of Chipchase Castle, Northumberland.

Reed, Edmond, s. Henry, of West Pennard, Somerset, cler. BALLIOL COLL., matric. 15 March, 1720-1, aged 15; B.A. 1724.

Reed, Rev. Francis, 2s. William, of Ottery St. Mary, Devon, gent. EXETER COLL., matric. 15 Oct., 1869, aged 18; B.A. 1873, M.A. 1876, vice-principal Fulland's School, Taunton, 1875-85, head-master Donington Grammar School 1885. [35]

Reed, Harold Martin, 2s. Martin, of Dover, Kent, gent. BALLIOL COLL., matric. 19 Oct., 1878, aged 18.

Reed, James, s. James, of Barnstaple, Devon, gent. MERTON COLL., matric. 20 Oct., 1787, aged 19; exhibitioner EXETER COLL. 1789, B.A. 1791, fellow 1792-1811, M.A. 1794, B.D. 1803, rector of Eversholt, Beds, 1810-43, vicar of Hampstead Norris, Berks, 1819-43, chaplain in ordinary to the Queen, died 10 Jan., 1843. See *Boase*, 116.

Reed, John, s. Robert, of Cripplegate, London, gent. LINCOLN COLL., matric. 30 Oct., 1778, aged 18; exhibitioner 1779. See *St. Paul's School Reg.*, 138.

Reed, Richard, s. John, of Buckland, Devon, pleb. QUEEN'S COLL., matric. 8 April, 1783, aged 19; bible clerk EXETER COLL. 1784, B.A. 1786. See *Boase*, 147.

Reed, Thomas, s. Richard, of Lugwardine, co. Hereford, gent. BALLIOL COLL., matric. 3 April, 1717, aged 16. [40]

eed, William, 1s. Hugh, of Isle of Jamaica, West Indies, gent. QUEEN'S COLL., matric. 13 Dec., 1827, aged 19; B.A. 1832, M.A. 1847, military chaplain Jamaica 1834-7, chaplain to bishop of Jamaica 1836-41, principal York and Ripon Training Schools 1841-8, of Training College, Carmarthen, 1848-65, canon and prebendary St. David's 1866, until his death 4 Jan., 1874.

eed, William, 1s. Benjamin Bradford, of Hamilton, co. Lanark, arm. WADHAM COLL., matric. 13 Oct., 1871, aged 18; B.A. 1874, M.A. 1878, vicar of Wandsworth 1885.

eed, William, o.s. John, of Montreal, in Canada, gent. NON-COLL., matric. 19 Oct., 1878, aged 19; organ scholar KEBLE COLL. 1879-82.

Reeks, Charles, s. John, of Yeovil, Somerset, pleb. CORPUS CHRISTI COLL., matric. 1 April, 1745, aged 15; B.A. 1748, M.A. 1752, B.D. 1759, died rector of Stratford St. Anthony in 1783.

Reeks, John, s. John, of Yeovil, Somerset, pleb. PEMBROKE COLL., matric. 5 April, 1731, aged 18; B.A. from CORPUS CHRISTI COLL. 1734, M.A. 7 Feb., 1737-8, B.D. 1745, D.D. 1756, rector of Stratford St. Anthony cum Hanny, Berks, 1769, until his death 29 June, 1770. [5]

Reeks, John, s. William, of Yeovil, Somerset, gent. ST. EDMUND HALL, matric. 16 Dec., 1779, aged 23.

Rees, Benjamin, 2s. Daniel, of Llanvihangel, Abercowen, co. Carmarthen, gent. JESUS COLL., matric. 28 May, 1830, aged 17; B.A. 1834, M.A 1837, died rector of St. Eglwscummin 8 Feb., 1847.

Rees, Charles Davies, 1s. William Price, of Llangevelach, co. Glamorgan, gent. JESUS COLL., matric. 5 July, 1833, aged 19; B.A. 1837.

Rees, Daniel, s. Ebenezer, of Llangeler, co. Carmarthen, pleb. JESUS COLL., matric. 12 June, 1815, aged 21; incumbent of Aberystruth, co. Monmouth, 1823, until his death 13 June, 1857.

Rees, David Rhys, 3s. William, of Llandengad, co. Carmarthen, arm. TRINITY COLL., matric. 14 April, 1869, aged 19. [10]

Rees, Delanoy, s. Thomas, of Llanon, co. Carmarthen, pleb. JESUS COLL., matric. 26 March, 1728, aged 19; B.A. 20 March, 1731-2.

Rees, Edward, s. Thomas, of St. Donats, co. Glamorgan, gent. JESUS COLL., matric. 30 March, 1750, aged 19.

Rees, Edward Wallace, 2s. Edward Watkins, of Cardigan, co. Glamorgan, arm. UNIVERSITY COLL., matric. 12 Oct., 1878, aged 19; scholar 1878-83, B.A. 1884.

Rees, Evan Joseph, 2s. David, of Cowbridge, co. Glamorgan, gent. JESUS COLL., matric. 29 Oct., 1867, aged 19; B.A. 1871, M.A. 1874.

Rees, George Edward, 2s. John, of Reynoldstone, co. Glamorgan, gent. JESUS COLL., matric. 19 Oct., 1872, aged 18; scholar 1872-7, B.A. 1876, M.A. 1879, rector of Bagendon, co. Gloucester, 1881. [15]

Rees, James, s. Henry, of Roch, co. Pembroke, pleb. CHRIST CHURCH, matric. 1 June, 1775, aged 18; B.A. 1779.

Rees, John (Thomas in *Mat. Reg.*), s. Griffith, of Llangundeirn, co. Carnarvon, pleb. HART HALL, matric. 17 June, 1719, aged 18; B.A. from ST. EDMUND HALL 1723 (as JOHN RICE).

Rees, John. JESUS COLL., 1791. See MOGG, page 966.

Rees, John Henry, o.s. Thomas Major, of Pontypool, co. Monmouth, cler. NON-COLL., matric. 16 Oct., 1886, aged 21.

Rees, Rev. John Hughes, 2s. David, of Llanbeblig, co. Carnarvon, gent. JESUS COLL., matric. 21 Oct., 1876, aged 19; scholar 1877-81, B.A. 1880, M.A. 1883. [20]

Rees, Rev. Leonard Herbert, 4s. David, of Cowbridge, co. Glamorgan, gent. JESUS COLL., matric. 20 Oct., 1873, aged 21; B.A. 1878, M.A. 1887.

Rees, Oakley, s. William, of Cappeldwey, co. Carmarthen, pleb. JESUS COLL., matric. 6 April, 1739, aged 18; B.A. 1742, M.A. 1745.

Rees, Rice, 1s. David, of Llandingat, co. Carmarthen, gent. JESUS COLL., matric. 15 May, 1822, aged 18; scholar 1825-8, B.A. 1826, fellow 1828-39, M.A. 1828, B.D. 1837, Welsh professor, tutor and librarian of St. David's College, Lampeter, died 20 May, 1839.

Rees, Samuel George, 2s. William, of North Walsham, Norfolk, cler. JESUS COLL., matric. 17 Dec., 1844, aged 18; scholar 1847-9, B.A. 1848, M.A. 1853, rector of Wasing, Berks, 1857-80, and of Abb Kettleby, co. Leicester, 1880.

Rees, Theophilus Aneurin, 5s. William, of Llandovery, co. Carmarthen, gent. JESUS COLL., matric. 27 Oct., 1877, aged 19; of Tonn, co. Carmarthen.

Rees, Thomas, s. Robert, of Carmarthen (town), pleb. PEMBROKE COLL., matric. 6 April, 1739, aged 18. [25]

Rees, Thomas, s. Thomas, of Tregaron, co. Cardigan, pleb. MAGDALEN COLL., matric. 21 March, 1750-1, aged 18; chorister 1744-52, clerk 1752-6, B.A. 1754, chaplain 1756-7, minor canon Winchester Cathedral 1757-69. See *Coll. Reg.*, i. 163.

Rees, Thomas Major, 2s. John, of Margam, co. Glamorgan, gent. JESUS COLL., matric. 6 April, 1859, aged 18; has held various curacies since 1864, father of John Henry 1886.

Rees, Thomas Williams, 5s. David, of Llanmydrisin, co. Carmarthen, gent. JESUS COLL., matric. 21 Oct., 1876, aged 22.

Rees, Walter Francis, 5s. David, of Cowbridge, co. Glamorgan, gent. LINCOLN COLL., matric. 16 Oct., 1873, aged 19; exhibitioner CHRIST CHURCH 1873-7, B.A. 1879, M.A. 1888. [30]

Rees, William, s. William, of Aberavon, co. Glamorgan, cler. JESUS COLL., matric. 28 April, 1809, aged 21; his father died 26 May, 1813.

Rees, William, s. James, of Haverfordwest, co. Pembroke, cler. PEMBROKE COLL., matric. 19 Oct., 1811, aged 18; B.A. 1816, M.A. 1821.

Rees, William Jenkins, s. Rees, of Llandingat, co. Carmarthen, gent. WADHAM COLL., matric. 12 April, 1791, aged 19; B.A. 1795, M.A. 1797, rector of Cascob, Radnor, 1807, and of Heyop 1813, preb. of Brecon 1820, F.S.A. 1840, died 18 Jan., 1855. See *Gent.'s Mag.*, 1855, i. 317.

Reeve, Alexander, 5s. Laurence, of Udimore, Sussex, gent. ST. EDMUND HALL, matric. 30 March, 1844, aged 25.

Reeve, Andrews, 1s. 'John A.,' of Locking, Somerset, gent. WADHAM COLL., matric. 14 May, 1835, aged 18; clerk 1835-8, B.A. 1839. [35]

Reeve, Rev. Edward Henry Lisle, 1s. Edward James, of Stanton, Essex, cler. ORIEL COLL., matric. 22 Jan., 1877, aged 18; B.A. 1880, M.A. 1883.

Reeve, (Sir) Henry (K.C.B.), created D.C.L. 21 June, 1870, registrar of the Privy Council 1837, editor of *Edinburgh Review* 1855, vice-president Society of Antiquaries, bar.-at-law, Middle Temple, 1839 (o.s. of Dr. Henry Reeve, of Norwich). See Foster's *Men at the Bar.*

Reeve, James Farr, 1s. James, of Lowestoft, Suffolk, gent. WADHAM COLL., matric. 23 Feb., 1837, aged 19; B.A. 1840, of Colne Park, Essex, rector of Thornham, Suffolk, 1850-72.

Reeve, John, 'chirurgus;' privilegiatus 14 Dec., 1829.

Reeve, (John), created D.C.L. 9 June, 1853 (son of William Reeve, of Leadenham, co. Lincoln), of Leadenham House, high sheriff co. Lincoln 1827, general in the army, colonel 61st regiment, died 3 Oct., 1864. [40]

Reeve, John Plumsted, s. Andrews, of Reading, Berks, arm. WADHAM COLL., matric. 12 June, 1792, aged 17; B.A. 1796, M.A. 1801.

Reeve, Joshua Robert, 1s. Charles, of Baldock, Herts, arm. BRASENOSE COLL., matric. 17 June, 1851, aged 17.

Reeve, Nevill Henry, 2s. Ellis, of Marylebone, London, arm. ORIEL COLL., matric. 11 March, 1858, aged 18; B.A. 1862, M.A. 1869, of The Hall, Ashby-de-la-Launde, co. Lincoln, sometime captain 45th regiment, served in Abyssinian campaign, at capture of Magdala 1868. See *Rugby School Reg.*

Reeve, Thomas, s. Thomas, of Withyham, Sussex, gent. TRINITY COLL., matric. 6 June, 1717, aged 18; B.A. 1720.

Reeve, Thomas, s. John, of Birmingham, co. Warwick, gent. ST. EDMUND HALL, matric. 30 June, 1742, aged 19; created M.A. 12 June, 1746 (as REEVES).

Reeves, Rev. Edgar Leo, 2s. Herbert William, of Richmond, Surrey, arm. UNIVERSITY COLL., matric. 31 May, 1879, aged 18; B.A. 1883, M.A. 1887.

Reeves, Frederick John Hawkes, 1s. Frederick, of Mangalore, East Indies, arm. MERTON COLL., matric. 11 Dec., 1829, aged 26; B.A. 1833, M.A. 1839, curate of Mortlake, Surrey, 1838-41, perp. curate 1841-52. [5]

Reeves, Herbert Kempson, 2s. Herbert Williams, of Richmond, Surrey, arm. ORIEL COLL., matric. 27 Oct., 1883, aged 17; B.A. 1886.

Reeves, John, s. John, of St. Martin's, London, pleb. MERTON COLL., matric. 31 Oct., 1771, aged 18, B.A. 1775; fellow QUEEN'S COLL. M.A. 1778, bar.-at-law, Middle Temple, 1779, bencher 1824, a commissioner of bankrupts 1780-91, F.S.A. 1789, F.R.S. 1790, chief justice Newfoundland 1791-2, superintendent of Aliens, law clerk to the Board of Trade, died 7 and buried in Temple Church 17 Aug., 1829. See *Gent.'s Mag.*, 1829, ii. 468.

Reeves, John, s. John, of Arborfield, Berks, arm. WADHAM COLL., matric. 23 March, 1798, aged 18.

Reeves, John Kingham, 1s. John Kingham, of West Hendred, Berks, arm. ORIEL COLL., matric. 15 Oct., 1879, aged 19; B.A. 1882.

Reeves, Thomas James, 2s. John Russell, of Brighton, Sussex, arm. EXETER COLL., matric. 22 April, 1865, aged 17; B.A. 1868. [10]

Reeves, Warwick William, 1s. John William, of Farley Chamberlayne, Hants, cler. WORCESTER COLL., matric. 2 Nov., 1872, aged 19.

Reeves, William Albert, 1s. William, of Oxford. NON-COLL., matric. 12 Oct., 1872, aged 16; chorister NEW COLL. 1865-71, B.A. (NON-COLL.) 1876, M.A. 1883.

Reibey, James Clack, o.s. James Haydock, of Moreton, Tasmania, cler. PEMBROKE COLL., matric. 28 Jan., 1869, aged 20. See *Eton School Lists.*

Reibey, James Haydock, 2s. Thomas, of Longford, Van Dieman's Land, arm. TRINITY COLL., matric. 30 May, 1840, aged 16; B.A. 1844, M.A. 1856, rector of Denbury, Devon, since 1859.

Reibey, Thomas, 1s. Thomas, of Longford, Van Dieman's Land, arm. TRINITY COLL., matric. 30 May, 1840, aged 18. [15]

Reich, John, 1s. Joel, of Lemberg, Austria, gent. ST. EDMUND HALL, matric. 17 Nov., 1819, aged 23.

Reichel, Charles Parsons, scholar TRINITY COLL., Dublin, 1841 (B.A. 1843, M.A. 1847, B.D. 1853, D.D. 1858); adm. 'comitatis causa' 18 June, 1863 (s. Charles Frederick), bishop of Meath 1885, professor of Latin, Queen's College, Belfast, 1850-64, vicar of Mullingar 1864-75, rector of Trim 1875-85, dean of Clonmacnois 1882-5, select preacher Cambridge 1876 & 1883, and Oxford 1880-2 & 1886. See *Crockford.*

Reichel, Henry Rudolf., 1s. Charles Parsons, of Belfast, cler. BALLIOL COLL., matric. 20 Oct., 1875, aged 19, scholar 1874-9; fellow ALL SOULS' COLL. 1880-7, B.A. 1881, M.A. 1882, modern history lecturer 1881-4, principal of North Wales University College, 1884.

Reichel, Oswald Joseph, 1s. Samuel Rudolph, of Ockbrook, co. Derby, arm. BRASENOSE COLL., matric. 24 June, 1859, aged 19; scholar QUEEN'S COLL. 1859-64, B.A. 1863, M.A. 1866, B.C.L. 1867, vice-principal Cuddesden College 1865-9, vicar of Sparsholt, Berks, 1869-86, F.R.S., F.R.H.S.; for list of his works see *Crockford.*

Reid, Adrian, s. John, of Isle of Jamaica, arm. ST. MARY HALL, matric. 23 March, 1767, aged 15.

Reid, Cecil Frederick, 2s. William, of Welwyn, Herts, arm. CHRIST CHURCH, matric. 23 May, 1861, aged 19. [21]

Reid, Charles Burton, of ST. JOHN'S COLL., Cambridge (B.A. 1835, M.A. 1838); adm. 'comitatis causa' 16 June, 1863, army chaplain.

Reid, David, 6s. Andrew, of Marylebone, London, arm. UNIVERSITY COLL., matric. 14 April, 1825, aged 17.

Reid, Dennis, s. George, of Isle of Jamaica, arm. CHRIST CHURCH, matric. 26 Jan., 1796, aged 17; B.A. 1799. See *Eton School Lists.*

Reid, George (Alexander), s. Andrew, of Barnet, Herts, arm. UNIVERSITY COLL., matric. 17 Dec., 1813, aged 19; B.A. 1817, M.A. 1822. [25]

Reid, George Benvenuto, 2s. William, of St. Kitts, West Indies, arm. EXETER COLL., matric. 24 Jan., 1884, aged 18; B.A. 1887.

Reid, George Boileau, 3s. Lestock Robert, of Bombay, East Indies, arm. CORPUS CHRISTI COLL., matric. 21 Oct., 1862, aged 19; B.A. 1867, of the Indian Civil Service 1865, a student of the Inner Temple 1863.

Reid, Hugh, 4s. Andrew, of Fitzroy Square, London, arm. UNIVERSITY COLL., matric. 29 Jan., 1882, aged 17.

Reid, James Hunter, 1s. James, of Westminster, D.Med. ST. JOHN'S COLL., matric. 28 June, 1847, aged 18; fellow 1847-71, B.A. 1851, M.A. 1855, B.C.L. 1857, D.C.L. 1861, lecturer in history 1855, in history and jurisprudence 1859-61, a student of Lincoln's Inn 1852, died 6 March, 1871. See *Robinson*, 277.

Reid, James Stafford, 4s. James, of Belfast, gent. LINCOLN COLL., matric. 23 Oct., 1882, aged 21; scholar 1882-3. [30]

Reid, Rev. John Edward, o.s. John, of Chingford, Essex, cler. WORCESTER COLL., matric. 27 April, 1871, aged 20; B.A. 1876, M.A. 1880.

Reid, John (Maitland), o.s. Edward Maitland, of London, gent. EXETER COLL., matric. 28 Jan., 1865, aged 19; scholar 1864-9, B.A. 1869, M.A. 1872, bar.-at-law, Lincoln's Inn, 1872, went on the Stock Exchange. See Foster's *Men at the Bar* & *Coll. Reg.*, 161.

Reid, John Lynch, o.s. John Lynch, of Isle of Jamaica, arm. QUEEN'S COLL., matric. 20 Nov., 1845, aged 19.

Reid, Robert, 2s. David, of Dunfermline, Fife, gent. WORCESTER COLL., matric. 14 Oct., 1865, aged 34; B.A. 1869, M.A. 1872, bar.-at-law, Inner Temple, 1872, M.P. Kirkcaldy burghs, 1874, until his death 30 March, 1875.

Reid, Robert Threshie, 2s. James John, of Isle of Corfu, equitis. MAGDALEN COLL., matric. 21 Oct., 1864, aged 18; scholar 1864-9, B.A. 1869, bar.-at-law, Inner Temple, 1871, Q.C. 1882, M.P. Hereford 1880-5, and Dumfries district, July, 1886. See Foster's *Men at the Bar.* [35]

Reid, William, s. David, of St. George's, London, arm. QUEEN'S COLL., matric. 24 Nov., 1747, aged 15; B.A. 1751, M.A. 1754.

Reid, William Cawley, o.s. Moses, of Coppenhall, Cheshire, cler. BRASENOSE COLL., matric. 3 Dec., 1874, aged 19; B.A. 1878, M.A. 1881, rector of Coppenhall, 1880.

Reid, William Pickering, s. William, of St. James's, Middlesex, cler. QUEEN'S COLL., matric. 2 March, 1782, aged 17.

illy, Anthony Miles William Adams, o.s. William Adams, of Mullingar, co. Westmeath (Ireland), arm. BRASENOSE COLL., matric. 15 March, 1855, aged 19; of Belmont, co. Westmeath, F.R.G.S., a student of the Inner Temple 1874. See *Rugby School Reg.*

eily, Edward, s. Richard, of Lismore, co. Waterford Ireland, arm. CHRIST CHURCH, matric. 15 Nov., 1777, aged 18 (? Keily).

einold, Arnold Wlliam, 1s. Arnold, of Hull, Yorks, arm. BRASENOSE COLL., matric. 17 Oct., 1863, aged 20, scholar 1863-6, B.A. 1866; fellow MERTON COLL. 1866-70, lecturer 1868; student CHRIST CHURCH 1869-73, M.A. 1870, Lee's reader in physics.

eiss, Charles Arthur, 1s. John, of Pendlebury, Lancashire, arm. BALLIOL COLL., matric. 31 Jan., 1870, aged 18.

eiss, Frederick Augustus, 2s. Leopold, of Highfield, near Manchester, Lancashire, arm. BALLIOL COLL., matric. 26 Jan., 1863, aged 19; B.A. 1867, M.A. 1869, rector of Rock, co. Worcester, 1870.

eith, Archibald William, 1s. Joseph, of Salisbury, gent. NEW COLL., matric. 18 Oct., 1867, aged 19; scholar 1867-72, B.A. 1871, M.A. 1874. **[5]**

elton, James, s. Henry, of Kirby Lonsdale, Westmoreland, pleb. QUEEN'S COLL., matric. 17 Dec., 1781, aged 18; vicar of Shirburn, Oxon, 1787, until his death in 1795. See *Gent.'s Mag.*, 1795, i. 357.

elton, John Rudge, s. James, of Watlington, Oxon, cler. QUEEN'S COLL., matric. 23 Jan., 1809, aged 19; B.A. 1812, M.A. 1816, perp. curate Marston Meysey, Wilts, 1817, until his death 27 Jan., 1856.

Remington, Daniel, s. Dan., of Gloucester (city), pleb. BRASENOSE COLL., matric. 18 March, 1731-32, aged 19; B.A. 1735, rector of St. John Baptist, Gloucester (city), 1741, until his death 19 July, 1768.

Remington, Reginald, 1s. Henry, of Ulverstone, Lancashire, gent. PEMBROKE COLL., matric. 19 June, 1851, aged 23; B.A. 1855, M.A. 1858, of the Crow Trees, Melling, Lancashire, held various curacies 1856-65, perp. curate Gilsland 1865-7, vicar (and patron) of Fritwell, Oxon, 1876-82. **[10]**

Remnant, James Farquharson, 4s. Frederick William, of London, arm. MAGDALEN COLL., matric. 16 Oct., 1880, aged 18; B.A. 1883, of Southwold, Suffolk, a student of Lincoln's Inn 1882.

Renaud, Daniel, s. Abraham, of 'Switzerland' (erased), gent. BRASENOSE COLL., matric. 29 Oct., 1716, aged 18; B.A. 1720, M.A. 1723, died rector of Whitchurch, co. Hereford, 1772.

Renaud, David, s. Daniel, of Whitchurch, co. Hereford, cler. BRASENOSE COLL., matric. 7 July, 1748, aged 18, B.A. 1752; M.A. from ST. JOHN'S COLL., Cambridge, 1769, vicar of Dewsall, co. Hereford, 1767, died rector of Havant, Hants, in 1807.

Renaud, George, 1s. George Daniel, of Havant, Hants, cler. CORPUS CHRISTI COLL., matric. 12 June, 1830, aged 15; scholar 1830-8, B.A. 1834, M.A. 1837, fellow 1838-9, perp. curate Clandown 1858-61, vicar of Silsoe, Beds, 1864-70, perp. curate Christ Church, Clevedon 1874-6, vicar of Flitton, Beds, 1876-83.

Renaud, George Daniel, s. David of Hannington, Hants, cler. ST. MARY HALL, matric. 28 Oct., 1793, aged 22; vicar of Dewsall Callon and perp. curate Aconbury 1808, vicar of Messingham, co. Lincoln, 1840, died 2 Dec., 1857. **[15]**

Renaud, William, 2s. George Daniel, of Havant, Hants, cler. EXETER COLL., matric. 8 June, 1836, aged 17; B.A. 1840, M.A. 1844, curate St. Thomas's, Salisbury, 1846-63, vicar 1863-74, rector of Havant 1874, preb. of Salisbury 1858.

Rendall, Charles Henry, 1s. Henry, of Great Rollright, Oxon, cler. HERTFORD COLL., matric. 24 Jan., 1876, aged 19; scholar 1875-80, B.A. 1879.

Rendall, Godfrey Arthur Harding, 6s. Henry, of Great Rollright, Oxon, cler. CORPUS CHRISTI COLL., matric. 20 Oct., 1886, aged 19; scholar 1886.

Rendall, Henry, 1s. Charles Henry, of Oxenwood, Berks, arm. TRINITY COLL., matric. 30 May, 1836, aged 18, scholar 1836-40, B.A. 1840; fellow BRASENOSE COLL. 1840-56, M.A. 1843, perp. curate Holy Trinity, Stepney 1847-55, rector of Great Rollright, Oxon, 1855.

Rendall, John, s. William, of Bridport, Dorset, gent. BALLIOL COLL., matric. 15 April, 1736, aged 19; B.A. 1739. **[20]**

Rendall, John, 2s. Charles Henry, of Shalbourne, Berks, arm. BALLIOL COLL., matric. 11 May, 1837, aged 18, B.A. 1841; fellow EXETER COLL. 1841-54, M.A. 1845, bar.-at-law, Inner Temple, 1845. See Foster's *Men at the Bar* & *Boase*, 133.

Rendall, Rev. Philip Pinckney, 2s. Thomas, of Wilsford, Wilts, arm. EXETER COLL., matric. 19 April, 1820, aged 18; B.A. 1824, M.A. 1827, of Salisbury, and of Winterbourne Dauntsey, died 2 Feb., 1832.

Rendall, Thomas Edward, 3s. Charles Henry, of Oxenwood, Berks, arm. TRINITY COLL., matric. 5 March, 1845, aged 24; B.A. 1850, M.A. 1852.

Rendel, James Meadows, 1s. Alexander Meadows, of London, arm. BALLIOL COLL., matric. 1 Feb., 1873, aged 18; exhibitioner 1872-81, B.A. 1878, bar.-at-law, Inner Temple, 1880, and of Lincoln's Inn, 'ad eundem,' 1881. See Foster's *Men at the Bar.*

Rendel, Stuart, 3s. James Meadows, of Plymouth, Devon, arm. ORIEL COLL., matric. 5 Nov., 1852, aged 18; B.A. 1857, M.A. 1859, of Plas Dinam, co. Montgomery, M.P. April, 1880, bar.-at-law, Inner Temple, 1861-77. See Foster's *Men at the Bar* & *Eton School Lists.* **[25]**

Rendell, Leigh Thomas, 1s. 'Thomas Leigh Tral,' of Tiverton, Devon, arm. BALLIOL COLL., matric. 12 Oct., 1861, aged 18; Blundell scholar 1861-6, B.A. 1866, M.A. 1872, vicar of Bishop's Tachbrook, co. Warwick, 1877-83, rector of Timsbury, Somerset, 1883.

Rendle, Charles Edmund Russel, 1s. Edmund Marchman Russel, of Plymouth, arm. NEW COLL., matric. 15 Oct., 1881, aged 19; B.A. 1886.

Rendle, Harry Richards, 3s. Edmund, of Plymouth, Devon, D.Med. BRASENOSE COLL., matric. 30 Nov., 1866, aged 19; B.A. 1870, M.A. 1873, curate of St. Barnabas, Oxford, 1871, until his death 30 March, 1874.

Rennell, George, s. Thomas, of Stockenham, Devon, cler. EXETER COLL., matric. 15 April, 1791, aged 18, B.A. 1795; M.A. from EMMANUEL COLL., Cambridge, 1804, rector of Greystead, Northumberland, 1818, until his death 31 Oct., 1841.

Rennell, Thomas, s. Thomas, of Drewsteinton, Devon, doctor. CHRIST CHURCH, matric. 24 May, 1737, aged 18; B.A. 1741, M.A. 1750, rector of Bernack and Woodford, Northants, 1770, and preb. of Winchester 1792, until his death 2 March, 1798, father of Thomas, dean of Winchester and master of the Temple. See *Gent.'s Mag.*, 1840, i. 654. **[30]**

Rennell, Thomas, s. Humphrey, of Bovey Tracey, Devon, gent. EXETER COLL., matric. 16 March, 1752, aged 19; B.A. 1756 (? vicar of Stokenham, Devon, and father of the next named).

Rennell, William, s. Thomas, of Stokenham, Devon, cler. ST. ALBAN HALL, matric. 30 March, 1792, aged 21; B.A. 1795, curate of Moreleigh, Devon, 1796, chaplain royal navy, died at Starcross, Devon, 1829.

Rennett, Hugh Percy, s. Godfrey, of St. Mary's, Lambeth, Surrey, gent. WORCESTER COLL., matric. 18 June, 1814, aged 22; B.A. 1819, M.A. 1821.

Rennie, John, 3s. Robert, of Borrow Stowness, co. Linlithgow, Scotland, D.D. MAGDALEN HALL, matric. 30 June, 1848, aged 31.

Rennie, John Henry Wyndham, 1s. William, of London, arm. NEW COLL., matric. 22 Nov., 1879, aged 18. See *Eton School Lists.* **[35]**

Rennison, Thomas, 1s. James, of Kirby Thore, Westmoreland, gent. QUEEN'S COLL., matric. 10 June, 1847, aged 19; scholar 1849-54, fellow 1854-75, B.A. 1851, chaplain, M.A. 1854, tutor 1858-66, bursar 1859-75, died 23 Jan., 1875.

Renouf, Elias George, o.s. Elias, of St. Martin's, Isle of Jersey, gent. PEMBROKE COLL., matric. 2 May, 1845, aged 21; B.A. 1849.

Renouf, Peter le Page, 1s. Joseph, of St. Peter's Port, Isle of Guernsey, gent. PEMBROKE COLL., matric. 12 March, 1840, aged 17; scholar 1840-2.

Renshaw, Samuel, s. John, of Liverpool, Lancashire, gent. BRASENOSE COLL., matric. 3 March, 1769, aged 16; B.A. 1772, M.A. 1775, rector of Liverpool 1794, until his death 19 Oct., 1829.

Rensselar, James Taylor Van, 2s. Maunsell, of New York, D.D. NEW COLL., matric. 27 Jan., 1886, aged 24. [5]

Renton, James Hall, 2s. James Hall, of Muswell Hill, Middlesex, gent. PEMBROKE COLL., matric. 4 Feb., 1881, aged 18; B.A. 1884, M.A. 1887.

Renton, James Henry, 2s. John Thornton, of London, arm. UNIVERSITY COLL., matric. 13 Oct., 1877, aged 18; B.A. 1881, M.A. 1884, bar.-at-law, Lincoln's Inn, 1884. See Foster's *Men at the Bar.*

Renton, John, s. John, of Edinburgh, Lothian, Scotland, arm. CHRIST CHURCH, matric. 2 April, 1726, aged 18.

Renwick, Thomas, 1s. Thomas, of Honiton, Devon, gent. (rear-admiral). CHRIST CHURCH, matric. 11 Dec., 1839, aged 20; servitor 1839-43, B.A. 1843, rector of Mottistone and vicar of Shorwell, Isle of Wight, 1854, until his death 12 Oct., 1874.

Repington, Gilbert, s. Gilbert, of Tamworth, co. Warwick, gent. CHRIST CHURCH, matric. 7 Dec., 1734, aged 21; B.A. 1740, M.A. 1742, brother of the next named. [10]

Repington, John, s. Gilbert, of Woodhouse, co. Warwick, gent. EXETER COLL., matric. 12 July, 1729, aged 18; died s.p.

Repton, Edward, s. Humfrey, of Sustead, Norfolk, arm. WADHAM COLL., matric. 29 May, 1800, aged 17; demy MAGDALEN COLL. 1801-8, B.A. 1804, M.A. 1806, perp. curate St. Philip's, Regent Street, London, 1820, canon of Westminster 1838, chaplain House of Commons, vicar of Shoreham, Kent, 1843, died 6 Aug., 1860. See *Bloxam*, vii. 143.

Repton, George Herbert, 2s. Edward, of Marylebone, London, cler. UNIVERSITY COLL., matric. 5 June, 1835, aged 21; B.A. 1839, a minor canon of Westminster and priest in ordinary to the Queen, died 8 April, 1862.

Repton, George William John, o.s. George Stanley, of St. George's, Hanover Square, London, arm. UNIVERSITY COLL., matric. 2 Feb., 1838, aged 19; M.P. St. Alban's 1841-52, Warwick 1852-68, 1874-85.

Repton, Guy George, o.s. George, of London, arm. BALLIOL COLL., matric. 21 Jan., 1880, aged 18; B.A. 1884. See *Eton School Lists.* [15]

Reserson, Thomas, s. Nicholas, of Isle of Guernsey, arm. PEMBROKE COLL., matric. 4 July, 1777, aged 22; B.A. 1781, M.A. 1785.

Restall, Henry, s. Henry, of All Saints, Oxford (city), gent. BALLIOL COLL., matric. 11 March, 1719-20, aged 16; B.A. 1723, M.A. 1726.

Reusch, John Antony, created D.C.L. 18 June, 1756, late 'institutor' of the Prince of Nassau.

Reuter, Herbert, 1s. Julian, of London, arm. BALLIOL COLL., matric. 18 Oct., 1871, aged 19.

Reveley, Henry, s. Willey, of Newby, Yorks, arm. UNIVERSITY COLL., matric. 25 May, 1736, aged 15; bar.-at-law, Gray's Inn, 1742, bencher 1756, died unmarried 1800. [20]

Reveley, Hugh, s. Henry, of Camberwell, Surrey, arm. CHRIST CHURCH, matric. 26 Oct., 1791, aged 19; B.C.L. 1799, of Bryn-y-gwin, co. Merioneth, high sheriff, 1811, secretary to Lord Redesdale, died 9 Nov., 1851, father of the next named.

Reveley, Hugh John, o.s. Hugh, of Dolgelley, co. Merioneth, arm. WADHAM COLL., matric. 26 Nov., 1829, aged 17; of Bryn-y-gwin, co. Merioneth, high sheriff 1852.

Revell, Charles John, 2s. George Richard, of Charlton, Kent, gent. NEW COLL., matric. 4 Feb., 188[illegible], aged 22; B.Mus. 1887.

Revell, Rev. Henry, s. Henry, of London, arm. TRINITY COLL., matric. 31 Oct., 1817, aged 18; a student of Lincoln's Inn 1818, died 5 Feb., 1832.

Rew, Charles, 4s. William Pell, of Finchley, Middlesex, gent. ST. JOHN'S COLL., matric. 28 June, 183[illegible], aged 16; scholar & fellow 1830-60, B.A. 1834, M.A. 1838, B.D. 1843, bursar 1846, vice-president 184[illegible], vicar of St. Giles', Oxford, 1846-53, and of Cranham, Essex, 1859, until his death 1 Jan., 1884. See *Robinson*, 216. [25]

Rew, William Andrew, 1s. William Pell, of Finchley, Middlesex, gent. ST. JOHN'S COLL., matric. 3[illegible] June, 1823, aged 18; scholar and fellow 1823-7[illegible], B.C.L. 1828, D.C.L. 1833, tutor 1828, vice-president, 1858, bar.-at-law, Inner Temple, 1844, died 23 Nov., 1870. See *Robinson*, 193.

Reynard, Charles, 4s. Horner, of Hutton Cranswick, Yorks, arm. WORCESTER COLL., matric. 25 Oct., 1836, aged 19.

Reynard, Edward Horner, 1s. Horner, of Ripon, Yorks, arm. LINCOLN COLL., matric. 12 Oct., 1827, aged 19; B.A. 1831, a student of Lincoln's Inn, 1829.

Reynardson, Rev. Edwin Thomas Birch, 2s. Henry Birch, of Hollywell, co. Lincoln, gent. CHRIST CHURCH, matric. 14 Oct., 1870, aged 18; B.A. 1876, M.A. 1879. See *Eton School Lists.*

Reynardson, Herbert Frederick Birch, 4s. Henry Birch, of Adwell, near Tetsworth, Oxon, arm. CHRIST CHURCH, matric. 24 April, 1875, aged 19; B.A. 1878, of the British Museum. See *Eton School Lists.* [30]

Reynardson, William John Birch, 1s. Henry Birch, of Bexley, Kent, arm. CHRIST CHURCH, matric. 17 April, 1868, aged 19; B.A. 1871, of Adwell House, Oxon, bar.-at-law, Inner Temple, 1875. See Foster's *Men at the Bar* & *Eton School Lists.*

Reynell, Carew, born at Bristol (city), s. Carew, bishop of Derry. NEW COLL., matric. 8 July, 1748, aged 18; B.A. 1752, M.A. 1756, vicar of St. Philip and St. James, Bristol, etc., 1759, perp. curate St. James 1772, and of Westbury-on-Trym, 1780, died 24 April, 1781, brother of William Henry. See *Gent.'s Mag.*, 1781, p. 242.

Reynell, Charles, s. Carew, of St. Philip's, Bristol, Somerset, cler. BALLIOL COLL., matric. 18 Dec., 1780, aged 18; B.C.L. from NEW COLL. 1793, fellow until 1812, vicar of Steeple Morden, co. Cambridge, 1811, until his death 27 Oct., 1829.

Reynell, Henry, s. Carew, of Covent Garden, London, gent. MERTON COLL., matric. 18 Dec., 1721, aged 17; B.A. from NEW COLL. 1726, M.A. 1729, B. & D.D. by decree 9 March, 1749.

Reynell, (Sir) Thomas (Bart.), s. Richard, of Laleham, Middlesex, baronet. BALLIOL COLL., matric. 21 Aug., 1716, aged 17; 3rd baronet, died 15 Sep., 1775. [35]

Reynell, William Henry, born at Bristol, co. Gloucester, s. Carew, bishop of Derry. NEW COLL., matric. 8 Aug., 1759, aged 18; B.A. 1763, M.A. 1767, bar.-at-law, Middle Temple, 1767, vicar of Hornchurch, Essex, and of St. Anthony Meneage, Cornwall, 1778, until his death 1809, brother of Carew 1748.

Reynolds, Arthur, 2s. Patrick, of Waterhead, Lancashire, cler. EXETER COLL., matric. 4 June, 1870, aged 19; scholar 1870-5, B.A. 1874, M.A. 1877, a master in Honiton Grammar School. See *Coll. Reg.*, 164.

Reynolds, Benjamin, s. Benj., of Hoggeston, Bucks, cler. TRINITY COLL., matric. 14 March, 1721-2, aged 17; B.A. 1725, M.A. 1736.

Reynolds, Benjamin, s. William, of Brocton, Salop, pleb. CHRIST CHURCH, matric. 31 Oct., 1760, aged 18; B.A. 1764.

Reynolds, Rev. Bernard, 2s. Joseph William, of Belper, co. Derby, cler. WADHAM COLL., matric. 15 Jan., 1869, aged 18; B.A. 1872, M.A. 1875, chief diocesan inspector of schools, London, 1886, preb. of St. Paul's 1887. See *Robinson*, 343.

Reynolds, Charles William, 1s. Charles, of St. Marylebone, London, arm. BRASENOSE COLL., matric. 19 May, 1831, aged 18; of Ramslade, Berks, sometime captain 16th lancers.

Reynolds, Edmund, s. Joseph, of London, arm. QUEEN'S COLL., matric. 20 Feb., 1773, aged 17.

Reynolds, Edward (Raynolds), s. William, of Abingdon, Berks, pleb. PEMBROKE COLL., matric. 7 Nov., 1732, aged 18; B.A. from ST. EDMUND HALL 7 Feb., 1737-8. [5]

Reynolds, Edward, 1s. Edward, of Wood Street, Cheapside, London, gent. WADHAM COLL., matric. 23 Feb., 1837, aged 19; B.A. 1840, vicar of Appledore, North Devon, 1842.

Reynolds, Edward, 2s. George William McArthur, of Hackney, Middlesex, arm. LINCOLN COLL., matric. 17 Nov., 1858, aged 16; B.A. 1862, bar.-at-law, Inner Temple, 1864, died at Lahore, India, 14 April, 1877.

Reynolds, Edward Swatman, 1s. Charles, of Great Fransham, Norfolk, cler. EXETER COLL., matric. 30 Jan., 1856, aged 16.

Reynolds, Rev. Evan Knatchbull Revell, 2s. Henry, of Croydon, Surrey, cler. WADHAM COLL., matric. 15 Oct., 1877, aged 19; B.A. 1881, M.A. 1885. See *Eton School Lists*.

Reynolds, Henry, 3s. Owen, of Conway, co. Carnarvon, cler. JESUS COLL., matric. 17 May, 1823 aged 17; scholar 1825-31, B.A. 1827, M.A. 1829, fellow 1831-49, B.D. 1841, librarian and tutor 1832, proctor 1835, vice-principal and lecturer 1836, Greek lecturer 1837, Latin lecturer 1841, senior bursar 1845, rector of Rotherfield Peppard, Oxon, 1848, until his death 25 Dec., 1869. [10]

Reynolds, Henry Revell, s. John, of Laxton, Notts, gent. LINCOLN COLL., matric. 17 March, 1763, aged 17; B.Med. from TRINITY COLL., Cambridge, 1768, D.Med. 1773, physician to Middlesex Hospital 1773-7, and to St. Thomas's Hospital, fellow College of Physicians 1774, physician extraordinary to George III. 1797, and physician in ordinary 1806, until his death 22 Oct., 1811. See Munk's *Roll*, ii. 299.

Reynolds, Henry Revell, of TRINITY COLL., Cambridge (B.A. 1850, M.A. 1853); adm. 'ad eundem' 28 May, 1856, curate of St. Andrew, Croydon, 1857-61, vicar 1861-3, vicar of Markham Clinton, Notts, 1863-72.

Reynolds, Henry Revell, 1s. Revell, of London, cler. NEW COLL., matric. 13 Oct., 1876, aged 19; B.A. 1880, M.A. 1884, a solicitor. See *Eton School Lists*.

Reynolds, Henry Walter, 1s. Joseph William, of Birmingham, cler. WADHAM COLL., matric. 13 Oct., 1865, aged 20; Hebrew exhibitioner 1865-71, B.A. 1870, M.A. 1872, vicar of St. Thomas, Agar Town, London, 1878. See *Robinson*, 336.

Reynolds, James, 'musicus'; privilegiatus 13 Sep., 1773. [15]

Reynolds, James Jones, 1s. James Jones, of Kentish Town, Middlesex, arm. ST. JOHN'S COLL., matric. 10 May, 1837, aged 18; B.A. 1841, held various curacies 1842-52, rector of Shaftesbury 1852-67, and of South Hykeham, co. Lincoln, 1867.

Reynolds, James William, 1s. William, of Lincoln, gent. NON-COLL., matric. 18 Oct., 1880, aged 31; B.A. from WORCESTER COLL. 1883.

Reynolds, John, fellow KING'S COLL., Cambridge, B.A. 1693, M.A. 1698; B.D. by diploma 7 Oct., 1718.

Reynolds, John, s. John of Bridgnorth, Salop, pleb. PEMBROKE COLL., matric. 12 July, 1733, aged 18; B.A. 1737.

Reynalds, John, s. John, of Morton Bagot, co. Warwick, cler. PEMBROKE COLL., matric. 20 March, 1734-5, aged 17; B.A. 1738, M.A. 1741.

Reynolds, Rev. John, s. Henry, of London, doctor. ORIEL COLL., matric. 8 May, 1799, aged 16; clerk in War Office 1803, died 15 Feb., 1862. See *Gent.'s Mag.*, 1862, i. 379; & *Alumni West.*, 446. [21]

Reynolds, John ('serviens.'), s. John. of Caerwys, Flint, pleb. WADHAM COLL., matric. 21 Nov., 1780, aged 19; B.A. from NEW COLL. 1784. See *Gent.'s Mag.*, 1803, p. 1189.

Reynolds, Rev. John Routh, 1s. Thomas John, of High Wycombe, Bucks, gent. WADHAM COLL., matric. 24 Oct., 1873, aged 20; B.A. NON-COLL. 1877, M.A. 1880.

Reynolds, Jonathan Robert, s. John, of London, arm. ST. JOHN'S COLL., matric. 12 Nov., 1779, aged 20.

Reynolds, Joseph, s. Thomas, of Marston Trussell, Northants, cler. MERTON COLL., matric. 29 March, 1734, aged 18; B.A. 1737. [25]

Reynolds, Joseph, s. William, of London, arm. ST. MARY HALL, matric. 26 May, 1769, aged 17.

Reynolds, Sir Joshua, Knt., created D.C.L. 9 July, 1773, president of the Royal Academy, F.R. & A.S., knighted 21 April, 1769 (s. Samuel, fellow of Balliol), died 23 Feb., 1792.

Reynolds, Llywarch Owain, 1s. Jonathan Owain, of Merthyr Tydvil, co. Glamorgan, gent. JESUS COLL., matric. 27 Oct., 1868, aged 26; B.A. 1875.

Reynolds, Owen, s. Samuel, of Llanwonog, co. Montgomery, pleb. JESUS COLL., matric. 26 Oct., 1753, aged 16; B.A. 1757.

Reynolds, Owen, s. Owen, of Oswestry, Salop, cler. JESUS COLL., matric. 1 June, 1786, aged 17, B.A. 1791; M.A. from JESUS COLL., Cambridge, 1819, rector of Aber, co. Carnarvon, and of Clocaenog, co. Denbigh, 1819, until his death in 1829. [30]

Reynolds, Richard, s. William, of Westbury, Salop, gent. BALLIOL COLL., matric. 1 April, 1731, aged 18.

Reynolds, Richard Williams, 1s. Daniel, of Liverpool, gent. BALLIOL COLL., matric. 19 Oct., 1886, aged 19; exhibitioner 1885.

Reynolds, Robert, s. Robert, of Cowley, co. Stafford, pleb. PEMBROKE COLL., matric. 14 Feb., 1740-1, aged 18; B.A. 1744, M.A. 1748.

Reynolds, Samuel Harvey, 1s. Samuel, of Stoke Newington, Middlesex, D.Med. EXETER COLL., matric. 17 April, 1850, aged 18, scholar 1850-4, B.A. 1854; fellow BRASENOSE COLL. 1855-72, M.A. 1857, tutor and Latin lecturer 1862, junior bursar 1866, a student of Lincoln's Inn 1858, vicar of East Ham, Essex, 1871. See *Coll. Reg.*, 155.

Reynolds, Seymour Baylie, o.s. James Jones, of Hartland, Devon, cler. ST. JOHN'S COLL., matric. 17 Oct., 1868, aged 18, B.A. 1872; chorister Magdalen College 1858-64, rector of Thorndon, Suffolk, 1878. See *Bloxam*, iii. 307. [35]

Reynolds, Sydney Montgomery, 4s. Thomas L., of Southwick, co. Stafford, gent. KEBLE COLL., matric. 17 Oct., 1882, aged 18; B.A. 1886.

Reynolds, Thomas, s. William, of Canterbury (city), pleb. UNIVERSITY COLL., matric. 19 Nov., 1740, aged 19; B.A. 1744.

Reynolds, Thomas, s. Joseph, of Marston Trussell, Northants, cler. LINCOLN COLL., matric. 18 Oct., 1769, aged 17; B.A. 1773, M.A. 1777, rector of Little Bowden, Northants 1776-1829, vicar of Dunton Bassett, co. Leicester 1776-1802, vicar of Lubbenham 1787, died 24 Dec., 1829, author of 'Iter Britanniarum.'

Reynolds, Walter, 1s. Thomas, of Lenton, Notts, gent. NON-COLL., matric. 22 Jan., 1876, aged 24; B.A. 1882.

Reynolds, William (Raynolds), s. William, of Abingdon, Berks, pleb. PEMBROKE COLL., matric. 27 Nov., 1717, aged 17; B.A. 23 Feb., 1721-2 (as REYNOLDS). [40]

Reynolds, William, s. John, of St. Laurence, Exeter, gent. EXETER COLL., matric. 24 July, 1721, aged 16; fellow 1723-41, B.A. 1728, M.A. 1732, one of the vicars of Bampton, Oxon, vicar of Veryan, Cornwall, 1741-3, master of Exeter School. See *Coll. Reg.*, 92.

Reynolds, William, 'butler of Merton College;' privilegiatus 10 May, 1733.

Reynolds, William. EXETER COLL., 1780. See LUCAS, page 880.

Reynolds, William Ferris, o.s. William Tellam, of Camborne, Cornwall, gent. MAGDALEN HALL, matric. 1 Nov., 1854, aged 20; B.A. 1858, M.A. 1863, chaplain King's College, Cambridge, 1866-73, vicar of East Moulsey, Surrey, 1873.

Reyroux, Rev. Frederick, 2s. Mark Anthony, of St. James's, Clerkenwell, London, gent. ST. EDMUND HALL, matric. 30 Nov., 1825, aged 24; B.A. 1829, M.A. 1835, B.D. 1845, died 5 Dec., 1881. [5]

Rhoades, Edward James, 1s. James Peter, of Clonmel, co. Tipperary, cler. PEMBROKE COLL., matric. 3 March, 1853, aged 19; B.A. 1858, M.A. 1859, vicar of Elmley Castle, co. Worcester, 1878. See *Rugby School Reg.*, 278.

Rhoades, Henry Tull, 3s. James Peter, of Clonmel, Ireland, cler. UNIVERSITY COLL., matric. 15 March, 1856, aged 18; scholar 1856-64, B.A. 1860, M.A. 1864, assistant-master Clifton College, head-master Lower School of Lawrence Sheriffe, Rugby, 1878. See *Rugby School Reg.*, 278.

Rhoades, James Peter, 3s. Thomas, of Chichester, Sussex, arm. WADHAM COLL., matric. 27 Jan., 1820, aged 17; scholar 1820-30, B.A. 1825, M.A. 1829, fellow 1830-2, rector of Clonmel, Ireland, died at Rugby 6 Nov., 1852.

Rhoades, Thomas, s. Tho., of Cirencester, co. Gloucester, pleb. TRINITY COLL., matric. 29 Feb., 1731-2, aged 16; B.A. 1735, M.A. 1738.

Rhoades, Willoughby Tho., 2s. James Peter, of Clonmel, Ireland, cler. PEMBROKE COLL., matric. 8 March, 1855, aged 19. [10]

Rhoades, Willoughby Westropp, o.s. Edward James, of Rugby, cler. PEMBROKE COLL., matric. 27 Oct., 1885, aged 19.

Rhodes, Alfred Henry, o.s. Alfred Dunston, of Birmingham, arm. CHRIST CHURCH, matric. 22 Oct., 1883, aged 19; exhibitioner 1883, B.A. 1887.

Rhodes, Ambrose, s. Ambr., of Modbury, Devon, arm. QUEEN'S COLL., matric. 23 Nov., 1722, aged 17; of Buckland House, Buckland Toussaint, brother of George 1723.

Rhodes, Ambrose Andrew, s. Ambrose, of Buckland, Devon, arm. EXETER COLL., matric. 24 May, 1748, aged 19; B.A. 1752, of Bellair, Devon, gentleman of the privy chamber 1786, died in 1800.

Rhodes, Rev. Ambrose William, s. George, of St. Erth, Cornwall, cler. WORCESTER COLL., matric. 9 Feb., 1799, aged 17; fellow until 1818, B.A. 1802, M.A. 1805, died in 1818. [15]

Rhodes, Cecil John, 4s. Francis William, of Bishop Stortford, Herts, cler. ORIEL COLL., matric. 13 Oct., 1873, aged 20; B.A. & M.A. 1881, a student of the Inner Temple 1876.

Rhodes, Charles Arthur, 1s. Charles Edward, of Dewsbury, Yorks, gent. EXETER COLL., matric. 16 Oct., 1884, aged 19.

Rhodes, Christopher, s. Christopher, of Middlesex, arm. CHRIST CHURCH, matric. 16 June, 1730, aged 17; B.A. 1734. See *Alumni West.*, 223.

Rhodes, Edward John, o.s. John, of Wetherby, Yorks, arm. UNIVERSITY COLL., matric. 18 May, 1864, aged 18.

Rhodes, Frank, 5s. Joseph, of Hawkes Bay, New Zealand, arm. ST. MARY HALL, matric. 9 May, 1881, aged 18; B.A. 1885, M.A. 1888, bar.-at-law, Inner Temple, 1887. [20]

Rhodes, (Sir) Frederick Edward, (Bart.), 1s. George Baker, of London, baronet. EXETER COLL., matric. 21 Oct., 1862, aged 19; B.A. 1866, assumed the surname of RHODES in lieu of BAKER by royal licence 29 Oct., 1878. See Foster's *Baronetage*.

Rhodes, Frederick John Madgwick, 3s. Arthur Charles, of Camberwell, Surrey, arm. BRASENOSE COLL., matric. 21 May, 1880, aged 17.

Rhodes, George, s. Ambr., of Modbury, Devon, arm. QUEEN'S COLL., matric. 21 Feb., 1722-3, aged 16; B.A. 5 Feb., 1727-8, died in 1772, father of the next named.

Rhodes, George, s. George, of Modbury, Devon, arm. EXETER COLL., matric. 14 March, 1761, aged 17; fellow 1764-9, B.A. & M.A. 1768, rector of South Pool, Devon, 1768, vicar of St. Erth and Uny Lelant, Cornwall, 1776-81, of Colyton, Devon, 1782, until his death 15 March, 1798. See *Coll. Reg.*, 107.

Rhodes, George Edward, 2s. Robert Heaton, of Canterbury, New Zealand, arm. BRASENOSE COLL., matric. 14 Oct., 1884, aged 18. [25]

Rhodes, George Hele, s. George, of Modbury, Devon, gent. ORIEL COLL., matric. 23 March, 1774, aged 17; died 1826.

Rhodes, Henry Brooke, 2s. John William, of Farnley Hall, Yorks, arm. TRINITY COLL., matric. 12 Dec., 1860, aged 18.

Rhodes, Rev. Henry Jackson, 4s. Thomas, of Market Rasen, co. Lincoln, gent. CORPUS CHRISTI COLL., matric. 5 March, 1841, aged 18; scholar 1841-6, B.A. 1844, M.A. 1847.

Rhodes, Hugh William, 1s. John, of Ripon, gent. WORCESTER COLL., matric. 22 Oct., 1885, aged 19; exhibitioner 1885.

Rhodes, Matthew John, of TRINITY COLL., Cambridge (B.A. 1839, M.A. 1843); adm. 'ad eundem' 18 May, 1843. [30]

Rhodes, Robert Heaton, 1s. George, of Levels, in Timain, New Zealand, gent. EXETER COLL., matric. 14 Oct., 1876, aged 19.

Rhodes, Robert Heaton, 1s. Robert Heaton, of New Zealand, arm. BRASENOSE COLL., matric. 22 Oct., 1880, aged 19; B.A. 1886, M.A. 1887, a student of the Inner Temple 1882.

Rhodes, William, s. George, of Birmingham, co. Warwick, gent. WORCESTER COLL., matric. 10 Dec., 1777, aged 17; B.A. 1781, M.A. 1784, vicar of Tadcaster, Yorks, 1811, until his death 31 Dec., 1829.

Rhodes, William, o.s. John, of Pudsey, near Leeds, gent. ORIEL COLL., matric. 29 Oct., 1867, aged 19; B.A. 1872, M.A. 1877, bar.-at-law, Lincoln's Inn, 1876, rector of Chale, Isle of Wight, 1883, until his death 15 Nov., 1884. See Foster's *Men at the Bar*.

Rhys, Charles Cureton, 2s. Charles Horton, of Brighton, Sussex, arm. BALLIOL COLL., matric. 25 April, 1870, aged 19; a student of the Middle Temple 1872. See Foster's *Our Noble and Gentle Families*. [35]

Rhys, Daniel Lewellin, o.s. Daniel, of Cardiff, co. Glamorgan, gent. BRASENOSE COLL., matric. 22 Oct., 1883, aged 19; scholar 1883, B.A. 1887.

Rhys, John, 1s. Hugh, of Llanbadarn-fawr, co. Cardigan, gent. JESUS COLL., matric. 25 Oct., 1865, aged 25; fellow MERTON COLL. 1869-73, B.A. 1870, M.A. 1873; hon. fellow JESUS COLL. 1877-81, fellow 1881, and bursar (Jesus College), professor of Celtic 1877.

Rhys, Rees Jenkin, 1s. Jenkin, of Aberdare, co. Glamorgan, arm. TRINITY COLL., matric. 18 Oct., 1875, aged 19; B.A. 1879, bar.-at-law, Inner Temple, 1881. See Foster's *Men at the Bar*.

Riach, Hugh Heugh, o.s. James Pringle, of Plymouth, Devon, arm. MAGDALEN COLL., matric. 19 April, 1869, aged 22; bar.-at-law, Lincoln's Inn, 1874. See Foster's *Men at the Bar*.

Riall, Samuel, s. William, of Clonmel, Ireland, gent. ST. MARY HALL, matric. 10 Oct., 1761, aged 20; B.C.L. 1768.

Ribblesdale, Thomas, Baron. CHRIST CHURCH, 1846. See LISTER, page 856.

Ricard, Francis, s. Francis, of Jersey, gent. PEMBROKE COLL., matric. 7 Dec., 1715, aged 17; B.A. 1719, another of the same name was appointed rector of St. John's, Jersey, 1790.

Ricard, John, 'lanista' (s. John); privilegiatus 18 Sep., 1776, aged 27.

Rice, Alwyne Compton Howard, 1s. Richard John Howard, of Sutton Courtney, Berks, cler. EXETER COLL., matric. 8 June, 1878, aged 19; exhibitioner 1878-81, B.A. 1882, M.A. 1885, chaplain royal navy 1886. See *Coll. Reg.*, 169. **[5]**

Rice, Arthur de Cardonnel, 1s. Francis William, of Fairford, co. Gloucester, cler. (after baron). CHRIST CHURCH, matric. 17 Oct., 1855, aged 19; B.A. 1861, M.A. 1865, 6th Baron Dinevor. See Foster's *Peerage*.

Rice, Bernard, s. Edward, of Alderminster, co. Worcester, cler. MAGDALEN HALL, matric. 10 Dec., 1766, aged 19; B.A. 1771, M.A. 1773.

Rice, Cecil Arthur Spring, 2s. Hon. Charles Spring, of London. BALLIOL COLL., matric. 28 Jan., 1878, aged 18; exhibitioner 1877-83. See Foster's *Peerage*, B. MONTEAGLE; & *Eton School Lists*.

Rice, Charles, s. Theo., of Talbenny, co. Pembroke, cler. JESUS COLL., matric. 8 May, 1744, aged 16.

Rice, Charles Allen Thorndyke, o.s. Henry, of Boston, U.S.A., arm. CHRIST CHURCH, matric. 28 Jan., 1870, aged 18; B.A. 1874, M.A. 1878. **[10]**

Rice, Charles Hobbes, 2s. David, of Stratford-upon-Avon, co. Warwick, gent. ST. JOHN'S COLL., matric. 30 June, 1851, aged 18; scholar & fellow 1851-68, B.A. 1855, M.A. 1859, B.D. 1864, tutor of St. Columba's College, co. Dublin, 1856-62, and vicar-choral of Armagh 1862-7, rector of Cheam, Surrey, 1867. See *Robinson*, 281.

Rice, Edward, s. Ed., of St. Aldate's, Oxford (city), pleb. JESUS COLL., matric. 4 June, 1728, aged 21; possibly father of Bernard.

Rice, Edward, s. George, of Hertford Street, St. George's, London, arm. CHRIST CHURCH, matric. 16 May, 1794, aged 17, B.A. 1798; M.A. from ALL SOULS' COLL. 1802, B. & D.D. 1820, precentor and preb. of York 1802, vicar of Sutton-in-the-Forest, York, 1804, rector of Great Barrington and of Great Rissington, co. Gloucester, 1810, preb. of Worcester 1815-25, rector of Oddington 1820, and dean of Gloucester 1825, until his death 15 Aug., 1862, brother of Lord Dinevor. See Foster's *Peerage*.

Rice, Edward Bennet, B.A. TRINITY COLL., Dublin, 1847, o.s. Edward M. G., of Newtown Stewart, co. Tyrone (Ireland), cler. PEMBROKE COLL., incorp. 7 Feb., 1850, aged 26; M.A. 1851, chaplain to Earl of Denbigh, died 26 Dec., 1851.

Rice, Edward Heming, 2s. Edward, of Christ Church, London, D.D. UNIVERSITY COLL., matric. 6 May, 1841, aged 18; died 1845. **[15]**

Rice, Edward Royd, s. Henry, of Dover, Kent, arm. ST. JOHN'S COLL., matric. 9 Dec., 1808, aged 18; B.A. from WORCESTER COLL., 1813, M.A. 1815, D.L. Kent, high sheriff 1830, M.P. Dover 1837-57, died 27 Nov., 1878, father of John M. 1842.

Rice, Evan, s. John, of Llanllawlhog, co. Carmarthen, pleb. JESUS COLL., matric. 27 March, 1732, aged 20; B.A. 1735.

Rice, Evan, s. Griffith, of Penbryn, co. Cardigan, pleb. PEMBROKE COLL., matric. 18 March, 1748-9, aged 19; B.A. 1753, M.A. 1755.

Rice, Francis William, 1s. Hon. Edward, of Barrington, co. Gloucester, doctor. CHRIST CHURCH, matric. 18 Oct., 1822, aged 18; B.A. 1826, M.A. 1847, 5th Baron Dinevor in 1869, vicar of Fairford, co. Gloucester, 1828, until his death 3 Aug., 1878. See *Alumni West.*, 484.

Rice, George, s. Edward, of London, arm. CHRIST CHURCH, matric. 26 Jan., 1741-2, aged 17; of Newton, co. Carmarthen, M.P. 1754-79, treasurer of his Majesty's chamber, died 3 Aug., 1779, father of Edward 1794, and of George next named. See Foster's *Peerage*, B. DINEVOR. **[20]**

Rice, George, s. George, of Westminster, arm. CHRIST CHURCH, matric. 1 Feb., 1783, aged 17; created M.A. 30 May, 1786, 3rd Baron Dinevor, M.P. Carmarthenshire 1790-3, died 9 April, 1852. See Foster's *Peerage*.

Rice, George Nelson, y.s. Pierce, of Cork (city), Ireland, gent. ST. EDMUND HALL, matric. 18 Jan., 1825, aged 19.

Rice, (Hon.) Henry, 3s. Edward, of Barrington, co. Gloucester, dean of Gloucester. CHRIST CHURCH, matric. 25 Oct., 1832, aged 19; B.A. 1836, vicar of Biddenham, Beds, 1850-6, rector of Great Rissington, co. Gloucester, 1856, brother of John Talbot and Francis William.

Rice, Hugh Goodenough, 3s. Richard, of Hampnett, co. Gloucester, cler. PEMBROKE COLL., matric. 27 Oct., 1884, aged 19; scholar 1884.

Rice, Jenkin, s. Jenkin, of Nevis, West Indies, gent. WADHAM COLL., matric. 19 Feb., 1718-9, aged 18.

Rice, John, B.A. from ST. EDMUND HALL 1723. See JOHN REES, page 1184. **[26]**

Rice, John, s. Richard, of Pembroke, cler. MERTON COLL., matric. 11 July, 1774, aged 19.

Rice, John, 3s. David, of Stratford-upon-Avon, co. Warwick, gent. PEMBROKE COLL., matric. 3 March, 1853, aged 18; B.A. 1857, M.A. 1860.

Rice, John Morland, 3s. Edward Royd, of Godmersham, Kent, arm. MERTON COLL., matric. 9 July, 1842, aged 19, postmaster 1842-6; demy MAGDALEN COLL. 1846-7, B.A. 1847, fellow 1847-64, MA. 1849, B.D. 1856, junior dean of arts 1853, bursar 1858, perp. curate Wye, Kent, 1854-8, rector of Boyton, Wilts, 1860-1, and of Bramber, Sussex, 1864. See *Bloxam*, vii. 378; & *Eton School Lists*.

Rice, (Hon.) John Talbot, 4s. Edward, of Worcester (city), doctor. EXETER COLL., matric. 26 Oct., 1837, aged 18; brother of Henry and of Francis William. See Foster's *Peerage*, B. DINEVOR. **[30]**

Rice, Morgan, s. Morgan, of Llandisilio, co. Carmarthen, pleb. JESUS COLL., matric. 24 March, 1742-3, aged 21; B.A. 12 March, 1746-7.

Rice, Morgan John, o.s. Horatio Morgan, of South Hill, Cornwall, cler. WADHAM COLL., matric. 28 Jan., 1867, aged 19; B.A. 1872, held various curacies 1879.

Rice, (Sir) Ralph, s. John, of Tooting, Surrey, arm. ORIEL COLL., matric. 29 June, 1798, aged 17; B.A. 1802, M.A. 1805, bar.-at-law, Inner Temple, 1805, recorder of Penang, senior puisne judge Supreme Court, Bombay, and knighted 29 May, 1817, died 3 July, 1850.

Rice, Richard, B.A. from JESUS COLL., 8 March, 1742-3 (rightly PRICE, see page 1149).

Rice, Richard, s. Richard, of Shireborn, co. Gloucester, cler. MERTON COLL., matric. 19 March, 1781, aged 19; B.C.L. 1795, rector (and patron) of Eaton Hastings, Berks, 1784, until his death 16 Dec., 1835. **[35]**

Rice, Richard, s. Richard, of Buscot, Berks, cler. MERTON COLL., matric. 19 June, 1810, aged 17; B.A. 1814, M.A. 1818, rector of Eaton Hastings, Berks, 1836, until his death 29 Sep., 1868.

Rice, Richard, 1s. Richard, of Hayton, Cumberland, cler. QUEEN'S COLL., matric. 17 June, 1841, aged 17; scholar 1841-5, B.A. 1846, M.A. 1851, 2nd master Northleach Grammar School 1849-68, vicar of Little Barrington, Oxon, 1866.

Rice, Richard John Howard, o.s. John Howard, of Marylebone, London, arm. EXETER COLL., matric. 20 May, 1846, aged 18; bible clerk 1846-9, B.A. 1850, M.A. 1852, vicar of Sutton Courtney, Berks, 1856.

Rice, Robert, 5s. David, of Stratford-on-Avon, co. Warwick, arm. ST. JOHN'S COLL., matric. 30 June, 1856, aged 18; servitor CHRIST CHURCH 1857-60, B.A. 1860, M.A. 1863, tutor St. Columba's College, co. Dublin, 1860-7, Winchester warden 1867, chaplain to lord-lieutenant of Ireland 1874.

Rice, Samuel, s. Evan, of Llanpedrog, co. Carnarvon, cler. ST. ALBAN HALL, matric. 5 June, 1783, aged 20; B.A. from CHRIST CHURCH 1787.

Rice, Theophilus, s. Richard, of Llanboidy, co. Carmarthen, pleb. MAGDALEN HALL, matric. 4 April, 1715, aged 19; B.A. 1720, M.A. 1722, one of these names was rector of Eccles St. Mary, Norfolk, 1773.

Rice, Vincent Edward, 6s. David, of Stratford-on-Avon, co. Warwick, arm. CHRIST CHURCH, matric. 22 Oct., 1862, aged 18; chorister MAGDALEN COLL. 1853-60. See *Bloxam*, i. 224.

Rice, Rev. and Hon. William Talbot, 3s. Francis William, Baron Dinevor. CHRIST CHURCH, matric. 21 May, 1880, aged 19; B.A. 1884, M.A. 1887. See Foster's *Peerage* & *Eton School Lists*. [5]

Rich, Charles, s. Lionel, of Dowdeswell, co. Gloucester, gent. BALLIOL COLL., matric. 22 Feb., 1722-3, aged 16; B.A. 1726, M.A. 1731 (? rector of Whittingtou and vicar of Coleshill, Berks, 1731).

Rich, (Sir) Charles Bostock (Bart.), s. John Bostock, of Windsor, Berks, doctor (see page 135). ST. JOHN'S COLL., matric. 30 June, 1768, aged 16; B.C.L. 1776, D.C.L. 1780, of Shirley House, Hants, assumed the surname and arms of RICH in lieu of BOSTOCK by royal licence 23 Dec., 1790, created a baronet 28 July, 1791, died 12 Sep., 1824. See Foster's *Baronetage* & *Robinson*, 123.

Rich, Charles David, 2s. John, of Ivinghoe, Bucks, cler. EXETER COLL., matric. 27 May, 1847, aged 19; lieut.-colonel 9th lancers, brother of John 1844. See Foster's *Baronetage*.

Rich, Daniel, s. Robert, of Sunning, Berks, baronet. ST. JOHN'S COLL., matric. 13 Feb., 1727-8, aged 17; a student of the Middle Temple 1734.

Rich, (Rev.) Edward John George Henry, 1s. Charles, of Shinfield, Berks, arm. NEW COLL., matric. 4 Dec., 1837, aged 21; fellow 1837-51, B.A. 1841, M.A. 1845, bursar 1845. [10]

Rich, Edward (Pickering), s. Ed., of London (city), gent. BALLIOL COLL., matric. 23 Jan., 1716-7, aged 17; B.A. 1722, M.A. 1724.

Rich, Edwin William Gordon, 1s. William Gordon, of Otago, New Zealand, arm. CHRIST CHURCH, matric. 15 Oct., 1875, aged 18.

Rich, George, s. John, of Darenth, Kent, gent. WORCESTER COLL., matric. 28 May, 1794, aged 19.

Rich, John, 1s. John, of Ivinghoe, Bucks, cler. CHRIST CHURCH, matric. 31 May, 1844, aged 18; student 1844-62, B.A. 1848, M.A. 1851, vicar of Chippenham 1861, rector of Kellaways 1884, hon. canon of Bristol 1882. See Foster's *Baronetage* & *Alumni West.*, 521.

Rich, Rev. Leonard James, 2s. Jabez Davidge, of Manchester, gent. KEBLE COLL., matric. 17 Oct., 1882, aged 19; B.A. 1885. [15]

Rich, Thomas, s. Thomas, of Over Stowey, Somerset, arm. QUEEN'S COLL., matric. 26 June, 1721, aged 16.

Rich, Thomas Lionel, 3s. Charles Lewis Henry Pye, of Shinfield, Berks, arm. WADHAM COLL., matric. 24 Oct., 1838, aged 18.

Rich, William, s. Sam., of Over Stowey, Somerset, pleb. TRINITY COLL., matric. 15 Oct., 1717, aged 19; B.A. 1721.

Rich, William Alexander, 4s. Obadiah, of Madrid, Spain, arm. MAGDALEN HALL, matric. 25 March, 1851, aged 24.

Rich, William Gordon, 3s. John, of Ivinghoe, Bucks, cler. CHRIST CHURCH, matric. 27 May, 1847, aged 18; student 1847-55, B.A. 1851. See Foster's *Baronetage* & *Alumni West.*, 523. [20]

Richards, Abraham, s. Thomas, Ystradmeurig, co. Cardigan, pleb. JESUS COLL., matric. 14 March, 1732-3, aged 22.

Richards, Alfred Bate, o.s. John, of Worcester (city), arm. EXETER COLL., matric. 19 Oct., 1837, aged 17; B.A. 1841, bar.-at-law, Lincoln's Inn, 1845, died 12 June, 1876.

Richards, Arthur Henry, 2s. John, of Greenwich, Kent, arm. ST. MARY HALL, matric. 27 Jan., 1864, aged 20.

Richards, Arthur James, 4s. Edward Few, of Farlington, Hants, cler. BRASENOSE COLL., matric. 12 June, 1862, aged 18; B.A. 1865, M.A. 1869, rector of Plumstead 1872-83.

Richards, Augustus Fulton, 4s. John, of Reading, cler. ORIEL COLL., matric. 15 Oct., 1879, aged 19; scholar 1879-84, of the Indian Civil Service 1879, died 3 Feb., 1885. [25]

Richards, Bisse, s. Ric., of St. Andrew's, Holborn, gent. MERTON COLL., matric. 10 May, 1732, aged 16; created M.A. 12 April, 1736, a student of Lincoln's Inn 1737, M.P. Hindon 1747, until his death 29 Dec., 1755.

Richards, Butler, s. Nicholas, of Calstock, Cornwall, cler. EXETER COLL., matric. 11 May, 1769, aged 18.

Richards, Charles, s. Escott, of Kentisbear, Devon, cler. BALLIOL COLL., matric. 20 March, 1739-40, aged 18; B.A. 1743.

Richards, Charles, s. Charles, of Bradninch, Devon, gent. CORPUS CHRISTI COLL., matric. 25 Nov., 1772, aged 18; B.A. 1781, M.A. 1783, fifty years master of Hyde Abbey School, near Winchester, vicar of St. Bartholomew's, Winchester, 1797, rector (and patron) of Chale, Isle of Wight, 1806, preb. of Winchester 1827, and vicar of Wanborough 1830, until his death 20 Jan., 1833, brother of George 1788, and of William P. 1792.

Richards, Charles, s. Charles, of Hyde, Hants, cler. CHRIST CHURCH, matric. 23 April, 1801, aged 18; demy MAGDALEN COLL. 1801-7, B.A. 1805, M.A. 1808, master of Hyde Abbey School, Winchester, vicar of South Stoneham, Hants, 1815, rector (and patron) of Chale, Isle of Wight, 1833, until his death in 1835. See *Bloxam*, vii. 146; & *Eton School Lists*.

Richards, Charles Henry, 2s. Henry, of Horfield, near Bristol, cler. BRASENOSE COLL., matric. 21 March, 1849, aged 18. [31]

Richards, Rev. Charles Henry, 4s. Henry Manning, of Sulham, Berks, cler. KEBLE COLL., matric. 18 Oct., 1875, aged 19; B.A. 1878, M.A. 1882, head-master All Saints' School, Clifton, 1885.

Richards, Rev. Charles Henry, 3s. John, of St. Thomas' Mount, Madras, cler. PEMBROKE COLL., matric. 26 Oct., 1877, aged 19; B.A. 1881, M.A. 1884.

Richards, Charles Reynell, 1s. William Henry, of Grays, Essex, cler. EXETER COLL., matric. 20 Oct., 1881, aged 18.

Richards, Rev. David, 1s. David, of Llanfair, co. Cardigan, gent. JESUS COLL., matric. 27 Oct., 1877, aged 19; scholar 1877-82, B.A. 1881, M.A. 1884. [35]

Richards, David, 2s. John, of Ponterwyd, co. Cardigan, arm. MERTON COLL., matric. 18 Oct., 1881, aged 19; postmaster 1881-5, B.A. 1885.

Richard, David, s. Rich., of Trawsfynydd, co. Merioneth, pleb. JESUS COLL., matric. 27 March, 1732, aged 20; B.A. 1735 (as RICHARDS).

Richard, David, s. John, of Towyn, co. Merioneth, pleb. JESUS COLL., matric. 16 May, 1774, aged 21.

Richards, Edward, s. David, of Lledrod, co. Cardigan, gent. JESUS COLL., matric. 15 May, 1789, aged 24. See *Gent.'s Mag.*, 1833, ii. 551.

Richards, Edward, s. Edward, of Gwytherin, co. Denbigh, cler. JESUS COLL., matric. 24 May, 1817, aged 19; scholar 1816-22, B.A. 1827. [40]

ichards, Edward, 4s. John, of Llangyniew, co. Montgomery, gent. JESUS COLL., matric. 25 Nov., 1858, aged 19; B.A. 1861, M.A. 1866.

ichards, Rev. Edward Bridges, 1s. Edward, of Epsom, Surrey, cler. JESUS COLL., matric. 28 Jan., 1823, aged 18; B.A. 1827, died at Epsom 1 Sep., 1832.

ichards, Edward Daubeny Griffith, 2s. Edward Griffith, of Weston-super-Mare, gent. CHARSLEY HALL, matric. 16 Oct., 1883, aged 19.

ichards, Edward Griffith, 1s. Henry, of Stapleton, co. Gloucester, cler. ORIEL COLL., matric. 30 June, 1843, aged 15; B.A. 1848, M.A. 1850.

ichards, Edward Saxon, 2s. Edward Tew, of Farlington, Hants, cler. TRINITY COLL., matric. 14 June, 1855, aged 18, exhibitioner 1854-6; demy MAGDALEN COLL. 1856, until his death 20 Jan., 1857. See *Bloxam*, vii. 406. **[5]**

ichards, Edward Tew, s. Griffith, of Farlington, Hants, cler. CORPUS CHRISTI COLL., matric. 30 Jan., 1816, aged 18; B.A. 1819, M.A. 1822, fellow 1822-4, rector (and patron) of Farlington, Hants, 1826, until his death 17 March, 1887. See *Eton School Lists.*

ichards, Edward Vaughan, 1s. William Parry, of London, arm. CHRIST CHURCH, matric. 3 June, 1840, aged 18; student 1840-54, B.A. 1844, M.A. 1846, bar.-at-law, Inner Temple, 1847, Q.C. and a bencher 1868, died in Sep., 1884. See *Alumni West.*, 516.

ichards, Edward Windsor, s. William, of 'Civit Landa' (Llandaff), arm. JESUS COLL., matric. 6 Dec., 1805, aged 17; B.A. 1810, M.A. 1812, rector of St. Andrew's, co. Glamorgan, 1828, until his death 15 Jan., 1848. See *Eton School Lists.*

ichards, Francis Arthur, 2s. Henry Manning, of Sulham, Berks, cler. NON-COLL., matric. 13 Oct., 1877, aged 19; B.A. from LINCOLN COLL. 1881, M.A. 1884, head-master Grammar School King William's Town, South Africa, 1884, until his death 7 Sep., 1886.

Richards, Franklin Thomas, 1s. Thomas, of Kensington, Middlesex, gent. QUEEN'S COLL., matric. 22 Oct., 1866, aged 19, scholar 1866-70, B.A. 1869; fellow TRINITY COLL. 1870-2, and again 1882, M.A. 1873, classical lecturer 1875-82, tutor 1881, proctor 1888. **[10]**

Richards, Frederick Jonathan, 2s. (William) Parry, of London, arm. MERTON COLL., matric. 1 Dec., 1842, aged 19; B.A. University College, Durham, 1849, M.A. 1853, vicar of Boxley, Kent, 1853, brother of Edward V. See *Eton School Lists.*

Richards, George, s. James, of ——, Dorset, gent. BALLIOL COLL., matric. 3 April, 1729, aged 16.

Richards, George, s. George, of Hadlow, Kent, cler. UNIVERSITY COLL., matric. 17 April, 1733, aged 19; B.A. 17 Feb., 1736-7.

Richards, George, s. George, of Longbredy, Dorset, arm. MERTON COLL., matric. 11 Oct., 1756, aged 17.

Richards, George, s. Michael, of Cardiff, co. Glamorgan, arm. JESUS COLL., matric. 7 July, 1759, aged 18; B.A. 1763. **[15]**

Richards, George, s. James, of Halesworth, Suffolk, cler. TRINITY COLL., matric. 10 March, 1785, aged 17, scholar 1786, B.A. 1788; fellow ORIEL COLL. 1790, M.A. 1791, B. & D.D. 1820, vicar of Bampton 1796, rector of Lillingstone Lovell, Oxon, 1795, rector of St. Martin's-in-the-Fields 1820, until his death, 30 March, 1837. See *Gent.'s Mag.*, i. 662.

Richards, George, s. Charles, of Bradninch, Devon, gent. CORPUS CHRISTI COLL., matric. 14 Jan., 1788, aged 18; B.A. 1791, M.A. 1800, brother of Charles 1772.

Richards, George, 4s. William, of Cheverill, Wilts, cler. ALL SOULS' COLL., matric. 2 Feb., 1826, aged 18; bible clerk 1826-9, B.A. 1829, M.A. 1840, chaplain 1836-47, rector of Thorneyburn, Northumberland, 1852-62, vicar of Chitterne, Wilts, 1862, until his death 24 Sep., 1874.

Richards, George, 1s. George, of St. George's, Hanover Square, gent. PEMBROKE COLL., matric. 27 April, 1837, aged 18; B.A. 1843, M.A. 1848, B. & D.D. 1858, senior tutor, chaplain, and Warneford professor of classics in Queen's College, Birmingham, 1846-55, rector of Marlingford, Norfolk, 1880.

Richards, George, 1s. George, of Warrington, Lancashire, cler. BRASENOSE COLL., matric. 12 Dec., 1854, aged 18. **[20]**

Richards, George Chatterton, 3s. John, of Churchover, near Rugby, gent. BALLIOL COLL., matric. 24 Oct., 1885, aged 18; scholar 1883.

Richards, George Cussans, s. George, of Isle of Jamaica, arm. TRINITY COLL., matric. 16 April, 1782, aged 17; bar.-at-law, Inner Temple, 1796, died 22 March, 1828, on the Bog Estate, Island of Jamaica.

Richards, Rev. George Harris, 1s. Edward Tew, of Droxford, Hants, cler. EXETER COLL., matric. 19 June, 1843, aged 18; B.A. 1848, M.A. 1850, died in Canada in 1863. See *Eton School Lists.*

Richards, George John, 1s. John William, of Manchester, cler. BRASENOSE COLL., matric. 24 May, 1856, aged 18; scholar 1856-60, B.A. 1860, of the Indian Civil Service 1859, died at Calcutta in Aug., 1862.

Richards, George John Knight, 2s. William Joseph, of Rednill, Cornwall, gent. ST. MARY HALL, matric. 31 Oct., 1868, aged 18; B.A. 1873. **[25]**

Richards, Griffith, s. Richard, of St. George's, London, arm. (after chief baron). QUEEN'S COLL., matric. 28 May, 1814, aged 17; B.A. 1818, M.A. 1820, bar.-at-law, Inner Temple, 1820, Q.C. and a bencher 1839, a commissioner of bankrupts, died 11 June, 1843. See *Alumni West.*, 478.

Richards, Harold Cotton, 3s. William Henry, of Grays, Essex, cler. QUEEN'S COLL., matric. 30 Oct., 1885, aged 18.

Richards, Henry, s. Robert, of Tawstock, Devon, gent. EXETER COLL., matric. 14 Oct., 1763, aged 16; B.A. 1767, fellow 1767-94, M.A. 1770, B.D. 1781, D.D. 1797, rector 1797-1807, Whitehall preacher 1787, vice-chancellor 1806-7, rector of Bushey, Herts, 1794, of St. Ebbe, Oxford, 1771, vicar of Longwittenham, Berks, 1789, died 19 Dec., 1807. See *Boase*, 108.

Richards, Henry, s. Charles, of Winchester, Hants, cler. MAGDALEN HALL, matric. 15 May, 1817, aged 22; B.A. 1824, M.A. 1829, vicar of Keevil, Wilts, 1830, until his death in 1839 (? father of Henry William 1843).

Richards, Henry, s. Griffith, of Farlington, Hants, cler. EXETER COLL., matric. 2 April, 1818, aged 19; B.A. 1822, M.A. 1824, B.D. 1834. **[30]**

Richards, Henry, 2s. John, of Llaneilar, co. Cardigan, gent. JESUS COLL., matric. 13 April, 1821, aged 21; B.A. 1824.

Richards, Henry Erle, 1s. Henry William Parry, of Isleworth, Middlesex, cler. NEW COLL., matric. 16 Oct., 1880, aged 18; B.A. 1885, bar.-at-law, Inner Temple, 1887. See *Eton School Lists.*

Richards, Henry Manning, o.s. John Barker, of St. George's, Hanover Square, arm. CHRIST CHURCH, matric. 7 Dec., 1836, aged 18; B.A. 1840, M.A. 1843, held various curacies 1841-71, rector of St. Laurence, Winchester, 1871. See *Eton School Lists.*

Richards, Henry Sillery Griffith, 1s. Edward Griffith, of Langford, Somerset, arm. ORIEL COLL., matric. 28 Jan., 1879, aged 20; a student of the Middle Temple, 1882.

Richards, Henry William, 2s. Henry, of Winchester, cler. MAGDALEN HALL, matric. 3 June, 1843, aged 19. **[35]**

Richards, Henry William Parry, 3s. William, of St. George-the-Martyr, London, arm. CHRIST CHURCH, matric. 15 May, 1845, aged 18; B.A. 1849, M.A. 1855, vicar of Isleworth, Middlesex, 1855, preb. of St. Paul's 1885. See *Eton School Lists.*

Richards, Herbert Paul, 2s. Thomas, of Kensington, Middlesex, arm. BALLIOL COLL., matric. 13 Oct., 1866, aged 17, scholar 1866-70, B.A. 1870; fellow WADHAM COLL. 1870, M.A. 1873, lecturer and librarian 1871, tutor 1873, proctor 1886.

Richards, Isaac, 4s. Isaac, of Tavistock, Devon, gent. EXETER COLL., matric. 16 Oct., 1878, aged 19; scholar 1878-82, B.A. 1882, M.A. 1885, incumbent of Remuera, Auckland, N.Z., 1885.

Richards, Ivor, o.s. William Steward, of Terwick, Hants, cler. ORIEL COLL., matric. 15 Oct., 1877, aged 19; B.A. 1881, M.A. 1884.

Richards, James, s. John, of St. Margaret's, Westminster, gent. CHRIST CHURCH, matric. 25 June, 1728, aged 18; B.A. 1732, M.A. 18 March, 1734-5. See *Alumni West.*, 297.

Richards, James Cotton, s. Charles, of St. Bartholomew, Winchester (city), cler. NEW COLL., matric. 25 Nov., 1809, aged 17; fellow 1809, until his death 14 Dec., 1814. **[5]**

Richards, John, s. William, of Grand Caroan, co. Glamorgan, pleb. JESUS COLL., matric. 3 April, 1723, aged 18; B.A. 1726.

Richards, John, s. James, of Lanblethian, co. Carmarthen, pleb. JESUS COLL., matric. 19 June, 1732, aged 24; B.C.L. 1747, D.C.L. 1758.

Richards, Rev. John, s. George, of Longbredy, Dorset, arm. BRASENOSE COLL., matric. 23 Jan., 1759, aged 17; B.C.L. 1765, died at Longbredy 14 Oct., 1803.

Richards, John, s. William, of Crowan, Cornwall, gent. EXETER COLL., matric. 25 May, 1772, aged 17.

Richards, John, s. Richard, of Llanegwad, co. Carmarthen, gent. JESUS COLL., matric. 11 July, 1774, aged 30. **[10]**

Richards, John, s. John, of St. Bride's, co. Glamorgan, pleb. JESUS COLL., matric. 9 Dec., 1774, aged 18.

Richards, John, entered ORIEL COLL. as bible clerk or servitor 1 March, 1776, B.A. 14 Jan., 1779, M.A. 17 May, 1783.

Richards, John, s. David, of Llanegwad, co. Carmarthen, cler. ST. EDMUND HALL, matric. 31 May, 1781, aged 21. See *Gent.'s Mag.*, 1843, ii. 551, 662.

Richards, John, o.s. John, of Cookham, Berks. arm. CHRIST CHURCH, matric. 15 Oct., 1886, aged 19.

Richards, John Alexander, s. John Alexander, of St. Mary Abchurch, London, pleb. MERTON COLL., matric. 16 May, 1764, aged 18. See *Robinson*, 115. **[15]**

Richards, John Alexander, 8s. Charles, of Llangollen, co. Denbigh, gent. JESUS COLL., matric. 21 Oct., 1878, aged 19; B.A. 1884.

Richards, John Cooper Allen, 1s. Edward England, of Martock, Somerset, arm. MERTON COLL., matric. 21 Oct., 1886, aged 18.

Richards, John Francis, 3s. Thomas, of London, arm. BALLIOL COLL., matric. 28 Jan., 1874, aged 20; exhibitioner 1874-8, B.A. 1877, M.A. 1880, head-master Huddersfield College 1882-7, and of Lancing College 1887.

Richards, John William, 2s. John, of Walcot in Bath, Somerset, cler. CORPUS CHRISTI COLL., matric. 13 Feb., 1827, aged 16; scholar 1825-34, B.A. 1831, M.A. 1834, fellow 1834-6, tutor, Greek reader 1835, high master Manchester Grammar School 1837-42, perp. curate East Harnham, Hants, 1855-9, etc., died 30 Oct., 1887.

Richards, Joseph, s. Philip, of Bristol (city), gent. EXETER COLL., matric. 22 Nov., 1784, aged 18; B.A. 1788, M.A. 1791, curate of Merton 1789, curate of Tamerton, and vicar of Wedmore, Somerset, 1825, until his death 27 Dec., 1826. **[20]**

Richards, Joseph Loscombe, s. Joseph, of Tamerton, Devon, cler. EXETER COLL., matric. 21 Oct., 1815, aged 17; fellow 1818-36, B.A. 1821, M.A. 1822, B.D. 1832, D.D. 1838, tutor 1822, sub-rector 1827, rector 1838-54, select preacher 1828, 1839, divinity reader 1834, rector of Bushey, Herts, 1835-8, chaplain to Prince Consort, died 27 Feb., 1854. See *Boase*, 122.

Richards, Lewis, 5s. Thomas, of Llanymwgddy, co. Merioneth, cler. JESUS COLL., matric. 18 May, 1820, aged 20; B.A. 1824.

Richards, Michael, s. Mich., of Cardiff, co. Glamorgan, gent. CHRIST CHURCH, matric. 14 Jan., 1723-4, aged 17.

Richards, Nicholas, s. William, of St. Just, Cornwall, gent. ST. MARY HALL, matric. 12 Dec., 1741, aged 32.

Richards, Philip Morgan, 1s. Edward, of Llandewy, co. Glamorgan, gent. JESUS COLL., matric. 30 March, 1827, aged 18; B.A. from NEW INN HALL 1835, died rector of Llanwyddelan, co. Montgomery, 25 Dec., 1861. **[25]**

Richards, Richard, s. Robert, of Beamister, Dorset, pleb. PEMBROKE COLL., matric. 15 April, 1736, aged 18; B.A. 1739.

Richards, (Sir) Richard, s. Thomas, of Dolgelly, co. Merioneth, pleb. JESUS COLL., matric. 19 March, 1771, aged 18; B.A. from WADHAM COLL. 1774, M.A. from QUEEN'S COLL. 1777, bar.-at-law, Inner Temple, 1780, K.C. and a bencher 1799, M.P. Helston 1796-9, serjt.-at-law 1814, Welsh judge or chief justice of Chester 1813, baron of exchequer 1814, knighted 11 May, 1814, chief baron 1817, until his death 11 Nov., 1823, buried in Temple Church 17th, father of Richard 1806, of William Parry 1806, and of Robert V. 1808.

Richards, Richard, s. Evan, of Llantrissent, co. Glamorgan, gent. JESUS COLL., matric. 10 Oct., 1791, aged 18.

Richards, Richard, s. Richard, of Dolgelly, co. Merioneth, arm. (after chief baron). CHRIST CHURCH, matric. 17 May, 1806, aged 18; B.A. 1810, M.A. 1812, of Caerynwch, co. Merioneth, M.P. 1836-52, bar.-at-law 1812, a commissioner of bankrupts 1814, accountant-general in Court of Exchequer 1820-41, master in Chancery 1841, died, 27 Nov., 1860, father of Richard M., and brother of Richard 1806, and of Robert V. 1808. See *Alumni West.*, 458.

Richards, Richard, 1s. Morgan, of Llechweddllwyfon, co. Cardigan, gent. JESUS COLL., matric. 21 Oct., 1873, aged 21; B.A. 1877. **[30]**

Richards, Richard Edward Lloyd, 1s. Richard Meredyth, of Caerymwch, co. Merioneth, arm. MAGDALEN COLL., matric. 24 Jan., 1884, aged 18; B.A. 1888.

Richards, Richard Meredyth, 1s. Richard, of St. Giles's, London, arm. MERTON COLL., matric. 2 Nov., 1838, aged 17; B.A. 1842, M.A. 1845, bar.-at-law, Inner Temple, 1846, died 4 Nov., 1873. See *Alumni West.*, 514.

Richards, Robert Bruce, 2s. George, of Isle of Barbados, West Indies, gent. EXETER COLL., matric. 17 June, 1831, aged 18.

Richards, Robert Maynard, o.s. James, of Liskeard, Cornwall, gent. MAGDALEN HALL, matric. 24 March, 1825, aged 18.

Richards, Robert Samuel, s. Thomas, of Kettering, Northants, gent. WORCESTER COLL., matric. 21 June, 1813, aged 18; B.A. 1817, M.A. 1820, bar.-at-law, Inner Temple, 1821. **[35]**

Richards, Robert Vaughan, s. Richard, of St. George's, Westminster, arm. CHRIST CHURCH, matric. 27 May, 1808, aged 17; student 1808-18, B.A. 1812, M.A. 1814, bar.-at-law, Inner Temple, 1819, Q.C. 1839, and a bencher 1839, died 2 July, 1846, brother of Richard 1806, and William Parry 1806. See *Alumni West.*, 467.

Richards, Samuel, 5s. Thomas, of Totnes Devon, gent. MAGDALEN COLL., matric. 22 Oct., 1835, aged 25; brother of Thomas 1824.

Richards, Simon, s. Edward, of Liddiard St. Lawrence, Somerset, pleb. ST. MARY HALL, matric. 8 May, 1735, aged 19; B.A. 1 March, 1738-9.

Richards, Simon, s. Samuel, of Creech, Somerset, gent. PEMBROKE COLL., matric. 19 March, 1779, aged 18.

Richards, Solomon Augustus, 1s. John Goddard, of Taney, co. Dublin, arm. TRINITY COLL., matric. 21 Oct., 1847, aged 19; B.A. 1850, of Ardamine, co. Wexford, and of Roebuck, co. Dublin, a student of Lincoln's Inn, 1849, died 13 Jan., 1874. See *Eton School Lists.*

Richards, Thomas, s. Thomas, of Cardigan (town), cler. TRINITY COLL., matric. 30 May, 1734, aged 17. See *Gent.'s Mag.*, 1798, i. 262. [5]

Richards, Thomas, s. Thomas, of Llangmawddwy, co. Merioneth, cler. JESUS COLL., matric. 15 Dec., 1812, aged 25.

Richards, Thomas, 1s. Thomas, of Totnes, Devon, gent. QUEEN'S COLL., matric. 17 June, 1824, aged 23; B.A. 1829, brother of Samuel 1835.

Richards, Rev. Thomas, 1s. David, of Merthyr Tydvil, co. Glamorgan, gent. JESUS COLL., matric. 23 Oct., 1880, aged 22; B.A. 1885.

Richards, Thomas Cynddelw, 1s. David, of Llansilin, co. Denbigh, cler. JESUS COLL., matric. 29 Oct., 1846, aged 20.

Richards, Thomas John, 2s. Alfred Smith, of Oak Village, near London, gent. BALLIOL COLL., matric. 16 Oct., 1879, aged 19, exhibitioner 1878-80; postmaster MERTON COLL. 1880-4, B.A. 1883.

Richards, Rev. Thomas Miller, 5s. Samuel, of St. Michael's, Bristol, gent. WADHAM COLL., matric. 30 Nov., 1829, aged 18; B.A. 1833, M.A. 1842, died 25 Sep., 1869. [11]

Richards, Thomas Watkin, s. Richard, of St. George-the-Martyr, London, arm. (after chief baron). QUEEN'S COLL., matric. 22 Aug., 1811, aged 17; B.A. 1815, Michel exhibitioner 1815-6, scholar 1816-18, M.A. 1818, fellow 1818-20, vicar of Seighford, co. Stafford, 1820, rector of Puttenham, Surrey, 1823, until his death, 30 Oct., 1859. See *Alumni West.*, 458.

Richards, Walter, s. John, of Tiverton, gent. BALLIOL COLL., matric. 30 March, 1751, aged 18; B.A. 1754, chaplain to garrison at Sheerness 1788.

Richards, Walter John Bruce, 1s. John, of Reading, Berks, arm. ST. MARY HALL, matric. 10 Feb., 1854, aged 18.

Richards, Wilfred Luke, o.s. John, of Tewkesbury, co. Gloucester, gent. EXETER COLL., matric. 17 Oct., 1865, aged 18; B.A. 1869. [15]

Richards, William, s. William, of Cardiff, co. Glamorgan, arm. ORIEL COLL., matric. 21 May, 1762, aged 17.

Richards, William, s. Richard, of Burton, Dorset, gent. TRINITY COLL., matric. 24 March, 1779, aged 18. See *Gent.'s Mag.*, 1823, ii. 645.

Richards, William, s. William, of Nether Stowey, Somerset, gent. ST. JOHN'S COLL., matric. 10 May, 1784, aged 17; B.A. 1789. See *St. Paul's School Reg.*, 162.

Richards, William, s. John, of Camborne, Cornwall, cler. EXETER COLL., matric. 14 March, 1810, aged 19.

Richards, William, s. Isaiah, of Llansamlet, co. Glamorgan, gent. ST. EDMUND HALL, matric. 11 Dec., 1810, aged 26. [20]

Richards, William, 3s. Thomas, of Totnes, Devon, gent. QUEEN'S COLL., matric. 23 June, 1827, aged 21; B.A. from NEW INN HALL 1844, M.A. 1845, vicar of Dawley Magna, Salop, 1849, until his death 5 April, 1870.

Richards, William, 1s. William, of St. Mary's, Reading, cler. QUEEN'S COLL., matric. 30 April, 1851, aged 19.

Richards, William Griffith, o.s. Frederick Jonathan, of Boxley, Kent, cler. MAGDALEN COLL., matric. 23 Nov., 1877, aged 18; B.A. 1881. See *Eton School Lists.*

Richards, William Henry, o.s. Henry, of Paris, France, arm. EXETER COLL., matric. 20 March, 1863, aged 19; of Croft House, Tenby, co. Pembroke, high sheriff 1878, mayor of Tenby 1881-6, a student of Lincoln's Inn 1863.

Richards, Rev. William Henry Holland, o.s. William Holland, of Chesterfield, co. Stafford, gent. PEMBROKE COLL., matric. 4 May, 1876, aged 20; B.A. 1880, M.A. 1883. [25]

Richards, William Lewis Jones, 1s. William, of Cardigan, cler. NON-COLL., matric. 17 Oct., 1881, aged 20; B.A. & M.A. from MERTON COLL. 1888, missionary at Alleppey, India, 1884.

Richards, William Nicholas (B.A. TRINITY COLL., Dublin, 1839), 2s. Goddard, of —— near Agra, East Indies, arm. WADHAM COLL., incorp. 2 May, 1839, aged 24; M.A. 1878.

Richards, William Page, s. Charles, of Silverton, Devon, gent. NEW COLL., matric. 21 Jan., 1792, aged 19; B.C.L. 1805, D.C.L. 1822, rector of Stoke Abbas, Dorset, and head-master Blundell's School, Tiverton, 1811, perp. curate East Teignmouth 1824, until his death 2 April, 1861, brother of George 1788.

Richards, William Parry, s. Richard, of Daventry, Northants, arm. QUEEN'S COLL., matric. 29 March, 1806, aged 16, B.A. 1809; fellow JESUS COLL. 1812-8, M.A. 1812, died 27 June, 1861, father of Edward V., Frederick J., and Henry William P., brother also of Richard 1806, and of Robert V. 1808.

Richards, William Steward, 3s. Edward, of Epsom, Surrey, cler. JESUS COLL., matric. 23 May, 1828, aged 19; B.A. 1832, scholar 1832-5, M.A. 1834, rector of Terwick, Hants, 1842, until his death 18 Oct., 1887. [30]

Richards, William Tanner, 6s. Samuel, of Bristol (city), gent. WADHAM COLL., matric. 27 Feb., 1834, aged 18.

Richards, William Upton, o.s. William, of Penryn, Cornwall, arm. EXETER COLL., matric. 29 April, 1829, aged 18; B.A. 1833, M.A. 1839, vicar of All Saints, Margaret Street, London, 1849, until his death 16 June, 1873.

Richardson, Albert Thomas, 1s. James Cope, of Darnford, co. Stafford, gent. HERTFORD COLL., matric. 19 Oct., 1881, aged 19; scholar 1880-5, B.A. 1885.

Richardson, Alfred Herman, 5s. Lawford, of Blackheath, Kent, gent. EXETER COLL., matric. 14 Oct., 1865, aged 19.

Richardson, Alfred Madeley, 1s. Alfred, of Southend, Essex, D.D. KEBLE COLL., matric. 26 Jan., 1886, aged 17; organ scholar 1885. [35]

Richardson, Arthur, 2s. Arthur Hill, of St. David's, co. Pembroke, cler. WORCESTER COLL., matric. 1 March, 1855, aged 18; B.A. 1859, vicar of St. Dogwell, Wolfs Island, co. Pembroke, 1866, and vicar of Ford 1876.

Richardson, Arthur, 2s. Frederick, of Bollington, Cheshire, cler. HERTFORD COLL., matric. 20 Jan., 1883, aged 18; B.A. 1886.

Richardson, Arthur James, 3s. John, of Clifton, co. Gloucester, cler. HERTFORD COLL., matric. 18 Oct., 1882, aged 19; scholar 1881-6, B.A. 1887.

Richardson, Arthur John, 2s. William Thomas, of Highgate, Middlesex, arm. MAGDALEN COLL., matric. 18 April, 1863, aged 18; demy 1862-7, B.A. 1868, M.A. 1871, perp. curate High Leigh, Cheshire, 1877-80, rector of East Blatchington, Sussex, 1880.

Richardson, Benjamin, s. John, of Churchill, Somerset, gent. CHRIST CHURCH, matric. 21 March, 1777, aged 18; B.A. 1781, rector of Hungerford Farley, Somerset, 1796, until his death 22 Jan., 1832.

Richardson, Charles Fletcher, 2s. John, of Cockermouth, Cumberland, gent. WORCESTER COLL., matric. 10 Feb., 1874, aged 33.

Richardson, Christopher, 1s. Christopher, of St. George's, Bloomsbury, London, arm. EXETER COLL., matric. 11 May, 1826, aged 18; B.A. 1830, of Field House, Whitby, Yorks, J.P., bar.-at-law, Lincoln's Inn, 1834. See Foster's *Men at the Bar.*

Richardson, Christopher Atley, s. John, of York (city), gent. MAGDALEN HALL, matric. 24 March, 1814, aged 26. See *Gent.'s Mag.*, 1841, i. 550.

Richardson, Edmund Augustine, o.s. Edmund, of Kendal, Westmoreland, cler. QUEEN'S COLL., matric. 22 June, 1854, aged 18; B.A. 1858, M.A. 1861, head-master Battersea Grammar School, 1878.

Richardson, Rev. Ford, s. Thomas, of Iron Acton, co. Gloucester, arm. UNIVERSITY COLL., matric. 4 Feb., 1813, aged 18; B.A. 1816, M.A. 1825, died at Iron Acton, 27 Nov., 1841. **[6]**

Richardson, Frederick Henry, 3s. Henry Kemp, of Leire, co. Leicester, cler. ST. JOHN'S COLL., matric. 8 June, 1860, aged 18; B.A. 1865, M.A. 1868, vicar of Belgrave, co. Leicester, 1872, until his death 6 Aug., 1887.

Richardson, George Billingsley, 3s. Ralph, of Nelson, New Zealand, D.Med. ST. JOHN'S COLL., matric. 13 April, 1872, aged 20; B.A. from NEW INN HALL 1876, bar.-at-law, Inner Temple, 1878. See Foster's *Men at the Bar.*

Richardson, George William, 2s. Joseph, of Leeds, Yorks, gent. NEW COLL., matric. 5 Feb., 1877, aged 26.

Richardson, Gerald, 2s. John, of Warwick, cler. ST. JOHN'S COLL., matric. 17 Oct., 1885, aged 19. **[10]**

Richardson, Godfrey Noel, 3s. Henry Mason, of Bolton-le-Moors, Lancashire, gent. NON-COLL., matric. 13 Oct., 1883, aged 17; B.A. 1887.

Richardson, Henry, s. Richard, of Brierley, Yorks, D.Med. (subs.). UNIVERSITY COLL., matric. 20 June, 1729, aged 18; B.A. 1733, M.A. 1736, died rector of Thornton in Craven, Yorks, 27 March, 1778, father of the next named. See Foster's *Yorkshire Collection.*

Richardson, Henry, s. Henry, of Thornton, Yorks, cler. UNIVERSITY COLL., matric. 9 April, 1777, aged 18; B.A. 1781, rector of Thornton in Craven 1783, took the name of CURRER in lieu of his patronymic, died 10 Nov., 1784.

Richardson, Henry, s. Samuel, of Pendoylyn, co. Glamorgan, arm. JESUS COLL., matric. 27 April, 1808, aged 16; B.A. 1812, scholar 1812-4. See *Gent.'s Mag.*, 1858, ii. 423.

Richardson, Henry, 1s. Thomas, of Balmescree, co. Londonderry, cler. EXETER COLL., matric. 10 June, 1828, aged 17. **[15]**

Richardson, Henry, 2s. George Gibson, of Beverley, Yorks, arm. CORPUS CHRISTI COLL., matric. 16 Oct., 1865, aged 19; B.A. 1868, M.A. 1872.

Richardson, Herbert Henley, 1s. Frederick Alexander, of St. Pancras, London, gent. ST. MARY HALL, matric. 28 Oct., 1854, aged 18; B.A. 1858, M.A. 1861, chaplain to the College of the Holy Spirit, Cambrae, 1863-72, hon. canon 1872-81, canon residentiary 1881, died 24 March, 1884.

Richardson, Rev. Henry Kemp, of TRINITY COLL., Cambridge (B.A. 1830, M.A. 1838); adm. 'ad eundem' 6 July, 1839, rector of Leire, co. Leicester, 1833, until his death 10 Aug., 1882, father of Frederick Henry.

Richardson, James, s. Richard Thomason, of Dean, Lancashire, pleb. BRASENOSE COLL., matric. 12 Oct., 1719; B.A 1723.

Richardson, James, s. John, of Kendal, Westmoreland, pleb. QUEEN'S COLL., matric. 8 July, 1732, aged 18; B.A. 1736. **[20]**

Richardson, James, s. William, of St. Bees, Cumberland, pleb. QUEEN'S COLL., matric. 12 July, 1779, aged 19; B.A. 1783, M.A 1786, probationary vicar of York Cathedral 1785, vicar-choral 1786, vicar of Holy Trinity, Goodramgate, with rector of St. Maurice, and rector of St. John, Delpyke, York, 1786-1804, also vicar of St. Martin, Coney Street, perp. curate St. John, Micklegate, York, 1804, vicar of Huntington, Yorks, 1804, perp. curate St. Paul, Heslington, Yorks, 1822, lecturer York Cathedral 1837, until his death 22 Dec., 1850.

Richardson, James Bernard, 1s. David, of Glasgow, arm. UNIVERSITY COLL., matric. 16 Jan., 1880, aged 18; lieut. 5th (royal Irish) lancers 1883, killed near Suakim 26 March, 1885.

Richardson, John, s. William, of Beighton, co. Derby, pleb. BALLIOL COLL., matric. 22 Feb., 1725-6, aged 19; B.A. 1729.

Richardson, John, s. Joseph, of Tideswell, co. Derby, gent. QUEEN'S COLL, matric. 21 Oct., 1757, aged 21; B.A. 1761, M.A. 1764. See *Gent.'s Mag.*, 1791, i. 489.

Richardson, John, s. George, of Edinburgh, Scotland, arm. WADHAM COLL., matric. 24 Nov., 1775, aged 34; M.A. (by diploma) 28 Feb., 1780, F.S.A., bar.-at-law, Middle Temple, 1781, author of a dictionary of Persian, Arabic, and English. **[25]**

Richardson, John, s. John, of St. George's, Middlesex, arm. ST. MARY HALL, matric. 8 Nov., 1787, aged 20.

Richardson, (Sir) John, s. Anthony, of London, arm. UNIVERSITY COLL., matric. 26 Jan., 1789, aged 17; B.A. 1792, M.A. 1795, bar.-at-law, Lincoln's Inn, 1803, serjt.-at-law 1818, a judge of common pleas Nov., 1818-24, knighted 3 June, 1819, died 19 March, 1841, father of Joseph John.

Richardson, John, s. Henry, of Patna, East Indies, arm. CHRIST CHURCH, matric. 23 Oct., 1794, aged 17; B.A. 1798.

Richardson, John, s. Thomas, of Warminghurst, Sussex, arm. TRINITY COLL., matric. 9 Feb., 1809, aged 18; died 20 July, 1825. See Foster's *Yorkshire Collection* & *Eton School Lists.*

Richardson, Rev. John 1s. William, of Grasmere, Westmoreland, gent. MAGDALEN HALL, matric. 11 Nov., 1825, aged 18; scholar QUEEN'S COLL. 1827-36, B.A. 1829, M.A. 1833. **[30]**

Richardson, John Hartley, 1s. John, of Mexborough, Yorks, cler. LINCOLN COLL., matric. 14 May, 1853, aged 20; B.A. 1857, M.A. 1860, curate of Godmanchester, died 10 Feb., 1863.

Richardson, Joseph, s. William, of London (city), gent. BALLIOL COLL., matric. 9 April, 1715, aged 18; B.A. from ALL SOULS' COLL. 1718, M.A. 1722.

Richardson, Rev. Joseph, s. Thomas, of Crosby Garratt, Westmoreland, gent. QUEEN'S COLL., matric. 12 Dec., 1785, aged 22; B.A. 1789, died in 1793, nephew of John. See *Gent.'s Mag.*, 1791, i. 489.

Richardson, Joseph, s. John, of Sebergham, Cumberland, pleb. ST. ALBAN HALL, matric. 6 Nov., 1798, aged 19; B.A. from QUEEN'S COLL. 1802, M.A. 1806, curate of Petworth, and master of Grammar School, Sheffield, Sussex, died in 1810.

Richardson, Joseph John, 1s. John, of St. Andrew's, Holborn, equitis. ORIEL COLL., matric. 18 Feb., 1824, aged 17; B.A. 1828, bar.-at-law, Lincoln's Inn, 1832, and of Inner Temple (ad eundem) 1837, died 23 March, 1842. **[35]**

Richardson, Michael, s. William, of Brampton, Westmoreland, pleb. QUEEN'S COLL., matric. 2 April, 1726, aged 18; B.A. 1730, M.A. 1734, B. & D.D. 1755.

Richardson, Murray Spenser, 1s. Murray, of Blackheath, Kent, arm. CHRIST CHURCH, matric. 18 May, 1864, aged 18; B.A. 1868, M.A. 1871, bar.-at-law, Inner Temple, 1871. See Foster's *Men at the Bar.*

Richardson, Oscar, 2s. Richard, of London, gent. WORCESTER COLL., matric. 21 Oct., 1880, aged 23.

Richardson, Piercy John, 3s. John, of Stratton, co. Gloucester, gent. NON-COLL., matric. 26 Jan., 1877, aged 35; B.A. from ST. JOHN'S COLL. 1880, M.A. 1884, held various curacies 1866-84, vicar of Seaton, Devon, 1884.

Richardson, Richard, s. Richard, of St. Lawrence Jewry, London, arm. NEW COLL., matric. 16 March, 1720-1, aged 18.

Richardson, Richard, s. Richard, of Bradford, Yorks, arm. BRASENOSE COLL., matric. 16 Aug., 1726, aged 17; of Bierley, Yorks, died 30 Jan., 1781. See Foster's *Yorkshire Collection.*

Richardson, Richard, s. Henry, of Thornton, Yorks, cler. UNIVERSITY COLL., matric. 21 April, 1773, aged 18; B.A. 1777, died at Lisbon 24 May, 1782. See Foster's *Yorkshire Collection.* [5]

Richardson, Richard, s. Richard, of Worcester (city), gent. BRASENOSE COLL., matric. 25 April, 1774, aged 21; B.A. 1778, M.A. 1782, B. & D.D. 1810, perp. curate Witton Gilbert, co. Durham, 1780, rector of Brancepeth, 1806, chancellor of St. Paul's 1792, and precentor of St. David's, died p., 1839.

Richardson, Richard, 1s. Richard, of Shotwick, Cheshire, arm. BRASENOSE COLL., matric. 10 June, 1830, aged 19; B.A. 1834, M.A. 1845, a student of the Inner Temple 1830, perp. curate Capenhurst, Cheshire, 1859-65, died 13 Aug., 1885.

Richardson, Richard Taswell, 1s. Richard, of Broughton, Hants, cler. UNIVERSITY COLL., matric. 20 Jan., 1872, aged 19; B.A. 1876, of Capenhurst, Cheshire, bar.-at-law, Inner Temple, 1879. See Foster's *Men at the Bar.*

Richardson, Robert, fellow EMMANUEL COLL., Cambridge, 14th wrangler and B.A. 1749, M.A. 1753 (incorp. 3 July, 1754), D.D. 1766.

Richardson, Robert, s. Samuel, of Dufton, Westmoreland, cler. QUEEN'S COLL., matric. 12 Oct., 1754, aged 18; B.A. 1758, M.A. 1762. [10]

Richardson, Samuel, s. Samuel, of Newent, co. Gloucester, arm. JESUS COLL., matric. 11 May, 1805, aged 16; B.A. 1809, M.A. 1811, bar.-at-law, Lincoln's Inn, 1812, died in Aug., 1813.

Richardson, Stephen, s. Stephen, of St. Giles's, Oxford (city), pleb. MAGDALEN HALL, matric. 16 July, 1720, aged 16; B.A. 1724.

Richardson, Thomas, s. Anthony, of Talbot, Maryland, America, arm. UNIVERSITY COLL., matric. 16 Oct., 1759, aged 18; B.A. 1763, M.A. 1766.

Richardson, Thomas, 1s. Peter D., of St. Dogwell's, co. Pembroke, cler. JESUS COLL., matric. 2 May, 1844, aged 18; scholar 1845-9, B.A. 1848, fellow 1849-52, M.A. 1851, curate of Fishguard, co. Pembroke, 1850-2, vicar 1852-4, minor canon of St. David's, and head-master Cathedral School 1854-67, vicar of Bayvill, co. Pembroke, 1867-77, of Aberdovey 1877, and of Rhyl 1878.

Richardson, Thomas Rumbold, 1s. Henry, of co. Derry (Ireland), arm. CHRIST CHURCH, matric. 4 June, 1857, aged 18; officer 1st life guards, died 7 (or 28) March, 1868. [15]

Richardson, Thomas Watkin, o.s. Thomas, of Ipswich, Suffolk, gent. ST. ALBAN HALL, matric. 7 July, 1820, aged 20.

Richardson, Thomas William, 2s. Thomas William, of 'Suaton in Cinences,' gent. NEW COLL., matric. 18 Oct., 1883, aged 18; of the Indian Civil Service 1884.

Richardson, William, s. William, of Beighton, co. Derby, pleb. BALLIOL COLL., matric. 2 March, 1724-5, aged 20; B.A. 1728.

Richardson, William, s. William, of Tuxford, Notts, cler. BALLIOL COLL., matric. 10 April, 1753, aged 19; B.A. 1757.

Richardson, William, s. Joseph, of Sheffield, Yorks, gent. QUEEN'S COLL., matric. 12 Dec., 1763, aged 19; B.A. 1767, M.A. 1773. See *Gent.'s Mag.*, 1823, i. 377. [20]

Richardson, William, s. William, of Rich Hill, Ireland, arm. CHRIST CHURCH, matric. 11 Oct., 1765, aged 16; created M.A. 1 June, 1769, and also D.C.L. 9 July, 1773, of Rich Hill, co. Armagh, M.P. 1807-20.

Richardson, William, s. William, of London, arm. TRINITY COLL., matric. 8 Feb., 1773, aged 18.

Richardson, William, s. John, of St. Bees, Cumberland, gent. LINCOLN COLL., matric. 16 Oct., 1800, aged 20; B.A. 1804. See *Gent.'s Mag.*, 1838, i. 214; & 1852, i. 423.

Richardson, William, s. Thomas, of Morland, Westmoreland, gent. QUEEN'S COLL., matric. 16 June, 1814, aged 17; scholar 1815-8. See *Gent.'s Mag.*, 1851, ii. 215.

Richardson, William, 1s. William, of Homerton, Middlesex, arm. EXETER COLL., matric. 16 June, 1823, aged 16; B.A. 1827, a student of Lincoln's Inn 1828. [25]

Richardson, William, 1s. William, of Ackworth, Yorks, cler. WADHAM COLL., matric. 13 June, 1827, aged 18, B.A. 1832; fellow MAGDALEN COLL. 1834-42, M.A. 1834, B.D. 1842, chaplain Sherburne Hospital, Durham, died 23 Nov., 1842.

Richardson, William, 2s. Peter Davies, of St. Dogwell's, co. Pembroke, cler. JESUS COLL., matric. 15 March, 1849, aged 19; scholar 1851-6, B.A. 1853, perp. curate St. Mary's, Llywdiarth, 1859-66, rector of Corwen 1866, hon. canon St. Asaph 1879.

Richardson, William Benson, 1s. William, of York (city), arm. UNIVERSITY COLL., matric. 5 March, 1845, aged 18; B.A. 1848, M.A. 1853, bar.-at-law, Inner Temple, 1883, Lord Mayor of York 1883. See Foster's *Men at the Bar.*

Richardson, William Cockin, 3s. John, of Wolverhampton, cler. ST. MARY HALL, matric. 24 Oct., 1885, aged 20.

Richardson, William Henry, 1s. William Henry, of Marylebone, London, equitis. ORIEL COLL., matric. 21 June, 1838, aged 18; B.A. 1844, M.A. 1845, of Chessel House, Hants, bar.-at-law, Inner Temple, 1846. See Foster's *Men at the Bar.* [30]

Richardson, William Henry, 1s. William Clarke, of Oxford (city), gent. ST. MARY HALL, matric. 25 Oct., 1864, aged 28; B.A. 1874, M.A. 1875, F.S.A. London 1881, sometime assistant-master in Christ Church Cathedral School, Oxford, and Queen Elizabeth's School, Ipswich.

Richardson, William King, 1s. Henry, of Boston, U.S.A., gent. BALLIOL COLL., matric. 1 Nov., 1880, aged 21; B.A. 1884.

Richardson, William Moore, 1s. Thomas, of Plymouth, Devon, cler. MERTON COLL., matric. 15 Oct., 1864, aged 19; postmaster 1864-9, B.A. 1869, M.A. 1879, vicar of Wolvercote, Oxon, 1883.

Richardson, William Ryder, 1s. William Ryder, of Manchester, gent. NON-COLL., matric. 22 Oct., 1881, aged 20.

Richardson, William Stevens, of TRINITY COLL., Cambridge (B.A. 1836, M.A. 1840); adm. 'ad eundem' 22 June, 1843, son of Sir John Richardson. See preceding page. [35]

Richardson, William Westbrook, s. Thomas, of Warminghurst, Sussex, arm. TRINITY COLL., matric. 22 Oct., 1808, aged 20; of Finden Place, Sussex, J.P., D.L. See Foster's *Yorkshire Collection.*

Richardson, Zaccheus, 'printer;' privilegiatus 20 Sep., 1756, brother of Stephen 1720.

Richey, James Bellett (C.S.I.), 1s. James, of Culmstock, Devon, cler. EXETER COLL., matric. 12 June, 1851, aged 17; scholar 1852-4, B.A. 1856, of the Indian Civil Service 1856, C.S.I. 25 May, 1878. See *Coll. Reg.*, 156.

Richings, Benjamin, s. Thomas, of Oxford (city), pleb. LINCOLN COLL., matric. 14 Dec., 1805, aged 17; B.A. 1811, M.A. 1812, vicar of Mancetter, co. Warwick, 1816, until his death 30 April, 1872.

Richings, Frederick Henry, 1s. Frederick Hartshill, of Atherstone, co. Warwick, cler. MAGDALEN HALL, matric. 14 June, 1865, aged 18; B.A. 1868, M.A. 1872, vicar of Upton Snodsbury 1870-5, rector of St. Clement, Worcester, 1875.

Richings, Herbert Athelstan, 2s. Frederick Hartshill, of Atherstone, co. Warwick, cler. ST. EDMUND HALL, matric. 2 Feb., 1867, aged 18; exhibitioner CHRIST CHURCH 1868-9, B.A. 1869, M.A. 1873, minor canon and librarian of Chester Cathedral 1873-4, minor canon Canterbury 1874, until his death 28 Jan., 1878.

Richman, Henry (John), s. — R., of Christchurch, Hants, gent. QUEEN'S COLL., matric. 16 Feb., 1775, aged 19; bible clerk CORPUS CHRISTI COLL. 1 Dec., 1775, B.C.L. 1802, master of the Free Grammar School, Dorchester, 1790-1813, rector of Holy Trinity, Dorchester, with Frome Whitfield, etc., 1813, until his death 28 Nov., 1824.

Richmond, George (R.A.), created D.C.L. 26 June, 1867, F.S.A., a celebrated portrait painter, father of William Blake and of Harry Inglis Richmond.

Richmond, Rev. George Edward, 1s. Henry James, of Bognor, Sussex, cler. UNIVERSITY COLL., matric. 12 Oct., 1878, aged 19; B.A. 1881, M.A. 1887. [5]

Richmond, Harry Inglis, 3s. George, of London, arm. BALLIOL COLL., matric. 27 Jan., 1868, aged 18; B.A. 1872, M.A. 1875, bar.-at-law, Lincoln's Inn, 1875, brother of William B. See Foster's *Men at the Bar*.

Richmond, Henry Charnley, 3s. John, of Liverpool, gent. WADHAM COLL., matric. 14 Oct., 1870, aged 19; scholar 1869-74.

Richmond, Henry Sylvester, 3s. Henry Sylvester, of Denton, near Canterbury, cler. ST. ALBAN HALL, matric. 18 April, 1864, aged 21; B.A. 1867.

Richmond, James, 1s. Richard, of Manchester, arm. MERTON COLL., matric. 25 Nov., 1871, aged 19; scholar 1871-6, B.A. 1875, M.A. 1880, B.Med. 1882.

Richmond, John, s. James, of Ayr (Scotland), cler. BALLIOL COLL., matric. 7 May, 1804, aged 19. [10]

Richmond, Joseph, s. Richard, of Crosby, Cumberland, pleb. QUEEN'S COLL., matric. 2 April, 1737, aged 17; B.A. 1742, M.A. 1745, fellow, B.D. 1759, D.D. 1762, rector of Newnham 1762, until his death 9 Jan., 1816, aged 98. See *O.H.S.*, ix. 22.

Richmond, Silvester, s. Silvester, of Liverpool, Lancashire, gent. BRASENOSE COLL., matric. 28 March, 1724, aged 17; B.A. 1727, died rector of Wallen, Lancashire, 1768.

Richmond, Thomas Henry, 1s. Thomas, of Kendal, Westmoreland, gent. NON-COLL., matric. 22 Nov., 1877, aged 25; B.A. from CHRIST CHURCH 1881, B.C.L. & M.A. 1884, bar.-at-law, Gray's Inn, 1885. See Foster's *Men at the Bar*.

Richmond, Thomas Knyvett, 1s. George, of Marylebone, London, gent. EXETER COLL., matric. 11 Feb., 1852, aged 18; B.A. 1858, M.A. 1859, rector of Hope Mansel, co. Hereford, 1868-74, vicar of Raughton Head 1874-8, of Crosthwaite, Cumberland, 1878-83, and of St. Mary, Carlisle, 1883, canon of Carlisle 1883, etc.

Richmond, Rev. Wilfrid John, 2s. John, of London, gent. NON-COLL., matric. 14 Jan., 1869, aged 20; B.A. from KEBLE COLL. 1873, M.A. 1875, tutor 1876-81, warden of Trinity College, Glenalmond, N.B., 1881-8. [15]

Richmond, William Alexander, 1s. Alexander Bailey, of St. Luke's, London, gent. LINCOLN COLL., matric. 10 May, 1853, aged 19; B.A. 1857, M.A. 1859, chaplain R.N. 1868-72.

Richmond, William Blake, of CHRIST CHURCH, M.A. (by decree) 18 Nov., 1879, Slade professor of fine art 1879-83, son of George Richmond, R.A., D.C.L., and brother of Harry Inglis.

Richter, Hans, created D.Mus. 25 April, 1885, the celebrated musical composer.

Rickaby, John, o.s. John, of Bridlington, Yorks, arm. BRASENOSE COLL., matric. 2 Feb., 1865, aged 19. See *Eton School Lists*.

Rickard, Rev. Herbert, 1s. John, of Derby, gent. JESUS COLL., matric. 18 Oct., 1882, aged 18; scholar 1882-6, B.A. 1886. [20]

Rickards, Arthur, 2s. Thomas Ascough, of Cosby, co. Leicester, cler. PEMBROKE COLL., matric. 22 June, 1857, aged 19; B.A. 1861, M.A. 1869.

Rickards, Arthur, 2s. Edward Henry, of St. Pancras, London, arm. CHRIST CHURCH, matric. 19 Jan., 1864, aged 19; of Manor House, West Drayton, sometime captain 6th dragoon guards. See *Eton School Lists*.

Rickards, Arthur George, o.s. George Kettilby, of London, arm. (after K.C.B.). BRASENOSE COLL., matric. 4 July, 1867, aged 19; B.A. 1872, bar.-at-law, Inner Temple, 1875. See Foster's *Men at the Bar* & *Eton School Lists*.

Rickards, Edwin, 4s. Thomas Ascough, of Cosby, co. Leicester, cler. ST. JOHN'S COLL., matric. 1 July, 1861, aged 19; B.A. 1864, B.Med. & M.A. 1872.

Rickards, Frederick Charles, 3s. Charles, of St. George's, Bloomsbury, arm. MERTON COLL., matric. 5 May, 1837, aged 19. [25]

Rickards, (Sir) George Kettilby (K.C.B.), 1s. George, of St. George's, Bloomsbury, London, arm. BALLIOL COLL., matric. 6 April, 1829, aged 17; scholar TRINITY COLL. 1829-35, B.A. 1833, M.A. 1836, Michel fellow QUEEN'S COLL. 1836-43, Drummond professor political economy 1852-7, of Fyfield House, Oxford, bar.-at-law, Inner Temple, 1837, bencher 1873, counsel to speaker of House of Commons, and referee on private bills 1851-82, member of Council King's College, London, 1871-3, K.C.B. 24 June, 1882. See Foster's *Men at the Bar* & *Eton School Lists*.

Rickards, Hely Hutchinson Keating, 3s. Richard Fowler, of Stroud, co. Gloucester, arm. MERTON COLL., matric. 27 Jan., 1831, aged 18, postmaster 1831-5; B.A. from NEW INN HALL 1835, of Llandough, co. Glamorgan, rector of Michaelstone-le-Pit 1839, and of Lechwith, etc., 1869, until his death 5 Dec., 1881.

Rickards, Rev. Marcus Samuel Cam, 4s. Robert Hillier, of Mount Radford, near Exeter, gent. WORCESTER COLL., matric. 27 April, 1872, aged 32; B.A. from MERTON COLL. 1875, M.A. 1878.

Rickards, Peter, s. Peter, of Old Radnor, co. Radnor, arm. BALLIOL COLL. matric. 20 May, 1735, aged 18; of Evenjob, co. Radnor, died in 1780, buried in Hereford Cathedral, grandfather of Peter Rickards Mynors, see page 1004.

Rickards, Richard Fowler, s. Robert, of Gloucester (city), cler. TRINITY COLL., matric. 4 April, 1786, aged 20. [30]

Rickards, Robert, s. Thomas, of Gladestry, co. Radnor, gent. CHRIST CHURCH, matric. 18 March, 1752, aged 18; died vicar of Llantrissent, co. Glamorgan, in 1810, aged 77.

Rickards, Robert Francis Bute, o.s. Robert, of Cape of Good Hope, arm. BALLIOL COLL., matric. 31 March, 1829, aged 17; B.A. 1832, M.A. 1840, vicar of Constantine, Cornwall, 1856, until his death 2 Nov., 1874.

Rickards, Robert Windsor, 1s. Robert, of Cheshire, arm. NEW COLL., matric. 23 Oct., 1885, aged 20.

Rickards, Samuel, s. Thomas, of Leicester (town), gent. ORIEL COLL., matric. 28 Jan., 1813, aged 17; B.A. 1817, fellow 1819-22, M.A. 1820, rector of Stowlangtoft, Suffolk, 1832, until his death 24 Aug., 1865.

Rickards, Thomas, 1s. Thomas Ascough of Cosby, co. Leicester, cler. WORCESTER COLL., matric. 17 June, 1851, aged 18; B.A. 1855, M.A. 1866, rector of Cressage, Salop, 1878. [35]

Rickards, Thomas Ascough, s. Thomas, of Leicester (town), arm. ORIEL COLL., matric. 5 May, 1810, aged 19; B.A. 1814, M.A. 1817, vicar of Cosby, co. Leicester, 1816-72, died 15 Jan., 1878, father of Arthur 1857, of Edwin, and of the last named.

Ricketts, Edward Jervis, s. William, of Westminster, arm. CHRIST CHURCH, matric. 19 Dec., 1783, aged 16; B.A. 1787, bar.-at-law, Lincoln's Inn, 1797, succeeded as 2nd Viscount St. Vincent 13 March, 1823, and assumed the surname of JERVIS in lieu of RICKETTS 7 May following, died 25 Sep., 1859. See Foster's *Peerage.*

Ricketts, Edward Woodville, 5s. George William, of Twyford, Hants, arm. ORIEL COLL., matric. 8 March, 1826, aged 17; sometime in the Treasury, brother of George R. G. See Foster's *Peerage.*

Ricketts, Frederick s. George Poyntz, of Marylebone, Middlesex, arm. CHRIST CHURCH, matric. 24 Oct., 1805, aged 16; student 1805-13, B.A. 1809, M.A. 1812, rector of St. James, Shaston, 1818, and of Eckington, co. Derby, 1819, until his death 23 March, 1843. See Foster's *Peerage.*

Ricketts, George Robert Goodin, s. George William, of Sutton, Hants, arm. CHRIST CHURCH, matric. 17 Oct., 1811, aged 19, brother of Edward W.

Ricketts, (Sir) George William, s. George (Crawford), of Isle of Jamaica, West Indies, arm. CHRIST CHURCH, matric. 26 Jan., 1809, aged 18; bar.-at-law, Middle Temple, 1818, a judge Supreme Court of Madras, and knighted 23 Mar., 1825, died 15 July, 1831. **[5]**

Ricketts, George William, 1s. George Henry Mildmay, of Allahabad, East Indies, arm. ORIEL COLL., matric. 27 Oct., 1883, aged 19; scholar 1883, B.A. 1888, in the University XI. 1887.

Ricketts, George Yeldham, WORCESTER COLL., 1828. See WILKINSON.

Ricketts, John, s. George, of Spanish Town, Isle of Jamaica, arm. UNIVERSITY COLL., matric. 8 May, 1810, aged 17.

Ricketts, John, 3s. John, of Talachddu, co. Brecon, gent. JESUS COLL., matric. 26 April, 1860, aged 19; B.A. 1864, M.A. 1867, held various curacies 1867-83, vicar of Llangunllo, Radnor, 1883.

Ricketts, Martin Henry, 1s. Martin, of Droitwich, co. Worcester, arm. EXETER COLL., matric. 15 June, 1843, aged 18; B.A. 1847, M.A. 1850, vicar of Hatfield, co. Hereford, 1862-74, and of Knighton 1878, preb. of Hereford 1886. **[10]**

Ricketts, Rev. Richard Ernest, 1s. Simpson Hicks, of Cheltenham, co. Gloucester, arm. TRINITY COLL., matric. 18 Oct., 1875, aged 19; B.A. 1879, M.A. 1882.

Ricketts, Sir Robert Tristram, Bart., K.C.B., created D.C.L. 18 June, 1828 (son of Robert Ricketts), created a baronet 15 Feb., 1828, rear-admiral 1830, vice-admiral of the Blue 1842, died 16 Aug., 1842. See Foster's *Baronetage.*

Ricketts, Rev. St. Vincent Fitzhardinge Lennox, 1s. St. Vincent William, of Taunton, Somerset, arm. ST. JOHN'S COLL., matric. 25 June, 1862, aged 19; B.A. 1865, M.A. 1869.

Ricketts, William, 4s. George William, of Laniston, near Sparsholt, Hants, arm. MERTON COLL., matric. 8 Dec., 1820, aged 17; postmaster 1820-4, B.A. 1824, fellow 1826-41 M.A. 1829, dean 1830, bursar 1831, sub-warden 1838, chaplain to the Duke of Cumberland 1829, rector of Kibworth, co. Leicester 1841, until his death 11 April, 1844.

Ricketts, William Henry, s. George, of Isle of Jamaica, arm. CHRIST CHURCH, matric. 11 April, 1761, aged 21; of Longwood, Hants, bar.-at-law, Gray's Inn, 1755, bencher 1769, died 5 Oct., 1799. See Foster's *Peerage*, V. ST. VINCENT. **[15]**

Rickman, John, s. Thomas, of Newburn, Northumberland, cler. MAGDALEN HALL, matric. 17 Nov., 1788, aged 17; B.A. from LINCOLN COLL., 1792, F.R.S. 1815, Speaker's secretary (Abbot) 1802-14, 2nd clerk assist. in the House of Commons 1814-20, clerk assist. 1820, until his death 11 Aug., 1840, compiler of the census returns of 1801, 1811, 1821 and 1831, and of returns of ancient parish registers, etc., died 11 Aug., 1840. See *Gent.'s Mag.*, 1841, i. 431.

Rickman, William Charles, o.s. John, of St. Margaret's, Westminster, arm. CHRIST CHURCH, matric. 21 Oct., 1829, aged 17; B.A. 1835.

Riddell, Campbell Drummond, s. Thomas, of Larbert, Stirling, arm. CHRIST CHURCH, matric. 28 Jan., 1813, aged 17; a member of the Scottish faculty of advocates 1819, member legislative council New South Wales, colonial treasurer, etc., died 27 Dec., 1858. See Foster's *Baronetage.*

Riddell, Charles Sydney Buchanan, 3s. John Charles Buchanan, of Harrietsham, Kent, cler. CHRIST CHURCH matric. 13 Oct., 1876, aged 18; B.A. 1880, M.A. 1883, university missionary to Central Africa 1884, died 11 June, 1886.

Riddell, Edward Francis, 1s. Francis, of London, arm. CORPUS CHRISTI COLL., matric. 19 Oct., 1883, aged 18; B.A. 1888. **[20]**

Riddell, George James, s. James, of Coxhoe, co. Durham, arm. MAGDALEN COLL., matric. 21 Feb., 1778, aged 19.

Riddell, George James, o.s. George James, of Tiverton, Devon, arm. TRINITY COLL., matric. 15 Oct., 1828, aged 18; B.A. from NEW INN HALL 1832.

Riddell, Henry Philip Archibald Buchanan (C.S.I.), 4s. John, of St. George's, Hanover Square, London, baronet. MERTON COLL., matric. 1 June, 1837; B.C.S. 1839-67, postmaster-general, N.W.P., India, C.S.I. 16 Sep., 1867. See Foster's *Baronetage* & *Eton School Lists.*

Riddell, James, s. Henry, of Little Govan, co. Renfrew, Scotland, arm. BALLIOL COLL., matric. 7 April, 1813, aged 18; B.A. 1816, M.A. 1819, rector of Easton, Hants, 1816-36, vicar of Hanbury, co. Stafford, 1836-63, died 13 May, 1878 father of the next named.

Riddell, James, 1s. James, of East Haddon, Northants, cler. BALLIOL COLL., matric. 28 Nov., 1840, aged 17; scholar 1840-5, B.A. 1845, fellow 1845-66, M.A. 1847, junior dean 1847, senior dean 1854, tutor 1857-66, math. and catech. lecturer, and philosoph. lecturer, proctor 1862, Whitehall preacher 1865, died 14 Sep., 1866. **[25]**

Riddell, (Sir) James Milles, (Bart.,) s. Thomas, of Larbert, co. Stirling. CHRIST CHURCH, matric. 19 April, 1804, aged 17; B.A. 1807, 2nd baronet, died 28 Sep., 1861. See Foster's *Baronetage.*

Riddell, John Charles Buchanan, 2s. John, of —— co. Roxburgh, baronet. CHRIST CHURCH, matric. 14 Feb., 1833, aged 18, B.A. 1837; fellow ALL SOULS' COLL. 1837-42, M.A. 1841, hon. canon Canterbury 1864, rector of Harrietsham, Kent, 1842, until his death 2 March, 1879. See Foster's *Baronetage* & *Eton School Lists.*

Riddell, John Walter Buchanan-, 1s. John Charles, of Harrietsham, Kent, cler. CHRIST CHURCH, matric. 12 June, 1867, aged 18; B.A. 1872, bar.-at-law, Inner Temple, 1874. See Foster's *Men at the Bar*, Foster's *Baronetage*, & *Eton School Lists.*

Riddell, Thomas, o.s. Thomas, of Lambeth, near London, gent. ST. EDMUND HALL, matric. 30 Jan., 1822, aged 19; B.A. 1825, M.A. 1828.

Riddell, (Sir) Walter Buchanan (Bart.), 1s. John, of Ramsgate, Kent, baronet. CHRIST CHURCH, matric. 14 June, 1828, aged 17; B.A. 1831, M.A. 1834, 10th baronet, bar.-at-law, Lincoln's Inn, 1834, recorder of Maidstone 1846-68, judge of county courts 1859-79. See Foster's *Men at the Bar*, Foster's *Baronetage*, & *Eton School Lists.* **[30]**

Riddell, William Adam, 1s. Adam, of London, gent. QUEEN'S COLL., matric. 12 Feb., 1869, aged 19; B.A. 1873.

Ridding, Arthur, 2s. Charles Henry, of Winchester College, cler. NEW COLL., matric. 9 Dec., 1845, aged 18; fellow 1845-76, B.A. 1850, M.A. 1854, dean and librarian 1863, died Aug., 1876.

Ridding, Charles Henry, s. John, of Winchester, Hants, arm. NEW COLL., matric. 31 March, 1815, aged 18; fellow 1815-24, B.C.L. 1823, 2nd master and fellow of Winchester College, rector of Rollstone, Wilts, 1824, and vicar of Andover, Hants, 1835, until his death 5 May, 1871.

Ridding, Charles Henry, 1s. Charles, of Winchester Hants, cler. TRINITY COLL., matric. 14 Nov. 1844, aged 18; demy MAGDALEN COLL. 1847-56 B.A. 1848, M.A. 1851, fellow 1856-66, junior dean of arts 1858, bursar 1861, vice-president 1863, rector of Slimbridge, co. Gloucester, 1865. See *Bloxam*, vii. 380.

Ridding, George, 3s. Charles Henry, of Winchester, Hants, cler. BALLIOL COLL., matric. 30 Nov., 1846, aged 18, B.A. 1851; fellow EXETER COLL. 1851-8, M.A. 1853, D.D. (by decree) 14 Jan., 1869, tutor 1852-64, catechist 1857, master of the schools 1855, proctor 1861, select preacher 1862-4, and master Winchester College 1863-7, head-master 1868-84, bishop of Southwell 1884. See *Boase*, 138.

Ridding, Thomas, s. Joseph, of St. James's, Westminster, gent. CHRIST CHURCH, matric. 16 March, 1726-7, aged 17; B.A. 1730, M.A. 1734, rector of Wonston, Hants, 1740, preb. of Winchester 1745, archdeacon of Surrey 1760, until his death 15 March, 1766.

Ridding, William, 4s. Charles Henry, of St. Mary's College, at Winchester, cler. NEW COLL., matric. 18 Dec., 1848, aged 18; fellow 1848-58, S.C.L. 1851, B.C.L. & M.A. 1856, vicar of Meriden, co. Warwick, 1860-73.

Ridding, William Caldecott, 2s. William, of Winchester, cler. EXETER COLL., matric. 18 Oct., 1883, aged 19; scholar 1883, B.A. 1887. **[5]**

Riddle, Arthur Esmond, 1s. Joseph Esmond, of Leckhampton, co. Gloucester, cler. WORCESTER COLL., matric. 18 April, 1872, aged 19; B.A. 1875, M.A. 1885, perp. curate Rydal, Westmoreland 1880-6, rector of Todmarton, Oxon, 1886.

Riddle, Arthur John, 2s. John, of Clevedon, Somerset, gent. JESUS COLL., matric. 17 April, 1866, aged 18; B.A. 1872, M.A. 1877, chaplain at Cronstadt 1885.

Riddle, John Brimble, 2s. Joseph B., of Bristol (city), gent. WADHAM COLL., matric. 10 Oct., 1833, aged 22; B.A. 1837, M.A. 1844, vicar of St. Thomas, Bristol, 1872.

Riddle, Joseph Esmond, 1s. Joseph, of St. Philip and St. James, Bristol (city), gent. ST. EDMUND HALL, matric. 18 Jan., 1825, aged 20; B.A. 1828, M.A. 1831, Bampton lecturer 1852, author of a 'Latin-English Dictionary,' incumbent of St. Philip and St. James, Leckhampton, co. Gloucester, 1840, until his death 27 Aug., 1859.

Rideout, George Meredyth, 2s. Henry Wood, of Avranches, France, gent. LINCOLN COLL., matric. 7 Nov., 1850, aged 19. **[10]**

Rideout, Gilbert Adolphus, 5s. Henry Wavel, of St. Peter's Port, Guernsey, arm. ST. JOHN'S COLL., matric. 30 May, 1860, aged 18; B.A. 1865, M.A. 1873, vicar of Fleet, Dorset, 1872-9, rector of Rusper, Sussex, 1885.

Rideout, John, s. Richard, of Framfield, Sussex, arm. UNIVERSITY COLL., matric. 1 Dec., 1744, aged 18; B.C.L. 1751, rector of Woodmancote, Sussex, 1755, died at Lewes in June, 1804.

Rideout, Peter (Richard), s. Philip, of Farnham, Dorset, cler. WADHAM COLL., matric. 10 Dec., 1795, aged 17; B.A. 1799, fellow, M.A. 1805, perp. curate of Motcombe 1808, until his death 15 Feb., 1850.

Rideout, Philip, s. Robert, of Fontmell Magna, Dorset, pleb. EXETER COLL., matric. 16 Nov., 1745, aged 17; B.A. 1749, M.A. 1752, rector of Farnham, Dorset, 1763.

Rideout, Philip, s. Philip, of Farnham, Dorset, cler. EXETER COLL., matric. 2 Nov., 1793, aged 18; B.A. 1797, rector of Farnham, Dorset, 1799, and vicar of Shapwick 1811, until his death 26 June, 1834.

Rider, Rev. Henry John, s. Edmund, of Longford, Essex, cler. ST. EDMUND HALL, matric. 21 Jan., 1789, aged 19; B.A. 1792, died 17 April, 1811. **[15]**

Rider, Ralph Carr, s. Ingram, of Leeds, Yorks, gent. MERTON COLL., matric. 3 Feb., 1786, aged 18; B.A. 1789, curate of Kentisbeare, Devon, and rector of Stoke, Kent, 1811, until his death 8 April, 1839.

Rider, Thomas, s. Ingram, of Leeds, Yorks, arm. UNIVERSITY COLL., matric. 19 May, 1783, aged 17; B.A. 1787, M.A. 1790, of Boughton Place, Kent, M.P. Kent 1831-2, West Kent 1832-3, died 6 Aug., 1847.

Rider, Thomas John, 1s. Thomas John, of Crickett, Salop, gent. BRASENOSE COLL., matric. 4 July, 1867, aged 19; B.A. 1871, M.A. 1874, perp. curate St. John's, Carrington, Notts, 1876-83, vicar of Baschurch, Salop, 1883.

Rider, William, s. John, of London, gent. ST. MARY HALL, matric. 22 June, 1739, aged 16; scholar JESUS COLL. 1744-9, B.A. 1745, chaplain to the Mercers' Company, lecturer of St. Vedast Foster, curate of St. Faith's, London, died 30 Nov., 1785. See *Gent.'s Mag.*, 1785, p. 1009; & *St. Paul's School Reg.*, 84.

Ridge, John, s. Thomas, of Northmore, Oxon, gent. PEMBROKE COLL., matric. 6 Dec., 1771, aged 19; B.C.L. 1780. **[20]**

Ridge, Richard, 'baker;' privilegiatus 25 Nov., 1760, probably father of Robert and Thomas.

Ridge, Robert, s. Richard, of Oxford (city), pleb. CHRIST CHURCH, matric. 27 March, 1779, aged 17.

Ridge, Thomas, s. Richard, of Oxford (city), pleb. BRASENOSE COLL., matric. 18 April, 1787, aged 16; B.A. 1791, M.A. 1793, rector of Knossington, co. Leicester, 1801, until his death in 1817.

Ridge, William Thomas, s. John, of Castle View, Queen's County, Ireland, cler. TRINITY COLL., matric. 12 April, 1804, aged 18. **[25]**

Ridger, Charles, 1s. George, of London, gent. NON-COLL., matric. 24 Jan., 1874, aged 27; B.A. from BALLIOL COLL. 1876, M.A. 1880, a student of Gray's Inn 1884.

Ridgeway, James, s. Tristram, of Wirksworth, co. Derby, gent. LINCOLN COLL., matric. 19 May, 1718, aged 16; B.A. 14 March, 1721-2.

Ridgeway, William Henry, 1s. Joseph, of High Roding, Essex, cler. MAGDALEN HALL, matric. 8 March, 1856, aged 19; scholar 1856, B.A. 1860, M.A. 1862, rector of Sternfield, Suffolk, 1865, until his death 30 Jan., 1880.

Ridgway, Francis Joseph, 1s. Isaac, of London, arm. BRASENOSE COLL., matric. 8 June, 1876, aged 18; B.A. 1880, bar.-at-law, Inner Temple, 1883. See Foster's *Men at the Bar*.

Ridgway, James, o.s. Tristram, of Huddersfield, Yorks, gent. LINCOLN COLL., matric. 1 July, 1847, aged 20; B.A. 1851, M.A. 1854, B.D. 1868, vice-principal North London College School 1855-62, principal Culham Training College 1862-73, hon. canon Christ Church, Oxon, 1870, F.S.A., died 19 July, 1881; for list of his works see *Crockford*. **[30]**

Ridgway, Rev. James Barnes, 1s. James William, of Kensington, Middlesex, arm. TRINITY COLL., matric. 31 Jan., 1870, aged 18; B.A. 1874, died 5 June, 1886.

Ridgway, John, s. Francis, of Leek, co. Stafford, pleb. UNIVERSITY COLL., matric. 24 June, 1715, aged 19.

Ridler, Samuel, s. Nath., of Chalford, co. Gloucester, arm. TRINITY COLL., matric. 24 March, 1720-1, aged 16; B.C.L. 1727. See *Gent.'s Mag.*, 1765, p. 199.

Ridley, Arthur William, 3s. Nicholas James, of Brighton, cler. CHRIST CHURCH, matric. 25 Nov., 1871, aged 19; B.A. 1876. See Foster's *Baronetage & Eton School Lists*.

Ridley, Charles John, s. Matthew White, of Heaton, Northumberland, baronet. UNIVERSITY COLL., 8 Nov., 1809, aged 17; B.A. 1813, fellow 1813-54, M.A. 1817, librarian, Rawlinsonian professor Anglo-Saxon 1822-7, rector of West Harling, Norfolk, 1826, until his death 8 Oct., 1854. See Foster's *Baronetage*.

Ridley, Charles William, 3s. Oliver Matthew, of West Harling, Norfolk, cler. UNIVERSITY COLL., matric. 16 Oct., 1875, aged 18; B.A. 1879, M.A. 1882, chaplain 1881-3, rector of St. Mary Wavertree, Liverpool, 1886. **[35]**

Ridley, Edward, 2s. Matthew White, of Blagdon, Northumberland, baronet. CORPUS CHRISTI COLL., matric. 21 Oct., 1862, aged 19, scholar 1862-6, B.A. 1866; fellow ALL SOULS' COLL. 1866-83, M.A. 1869, bar.-at-law, Middle Temple, 1868, M.P. South Northumberland 1878-80. See Foster's *Men at the Bar.*

Ridley, Francis Colborne, 5s. Oliver Matthew, of Worthing, Sussex, cler. NEW COLL., matric. 12 Oct., 1883, aged 18; B.A. 1887.

Ridley, George, 5s. Matthew White, of Marylebone, London, baronet. CHRIST CHURCH, matric. 11 May, 1837, aged 18; B.A. 1844, F.R.G.S., bar.-at-law, Middle Temple, 1843, M.P. Newcastle-on-Tyne 1856-60, copyhold enclosure and tithe commissioner 1860-80. See Fosters *Men at the Bar.*

Ridley, Gloster, s. Matthew, of Bencoolin, East Indies, gent. TRINITY COLL., matric. 14 Oct., 1721, aged 18; B.C.L. from NEW COLL. 1729, D.D. (by diploma) 25 Feb., 1767, rector of Romford, Essex, 1751, preb. of Salisbury 1766, died in 1774, father of James 1754. See *Gent.'s Mag.*, 1774, p. 542.

Ridley, Henry, s. Matthew, of Heaton, Northumberland, arm. UNIVERSITY COLL., matric. 22 Jan., 1770, aged 16; B.A. 1774, M.A. 1776, B. & D.D. 1802, preb. of Gloucester 1804, rector of Kirkby Underdale, Yorks, 1805, rector of St. Andrew cum St. Mary, Hertford, 1817, until his death 11 Oct., 1825, father of Henry John. [5]

Ridley, Henry (Colborne), s. Matthew, of St. Marylebone, Middlesex, baronet. CHRIST CHURCH, matric. 16 Oct., 1797, aged 17; B.A. 1801, M.A. 1804, rector of Hambledon, Bucks, 1804, until his death 26 Jan., 1832.

Ridley, Henry Colborne Maunoir, o.s. William Henry, of Hambledon, Bucks, cler. CHRIST CHURCH, matric. 24 Jan., 1873, aged 18.

Ridley, Henry John, s. Henry John, of Wallsend, Northumberland, doctor. CHRIST CHURCH, matric. 23 April, 1807, aged 17; B.A. 1811, M.A. 1813, preb. of Bristol 1816-32, rector of Newdigate, Surrey, 1814, Abinger 1821, and of Kirkby Underdale, Yorks, 1827, and preb. of Norwich 1832, until his death 11 Nov., 1834. See Foster's *Baronetage.*

Ridley, Henry Matthew, 2s. Nicholas James, of East Woodhay, Hants, cler. CHRIST CHURCH, matric. 19 May, 1869, aged 18; B.A. 1873, M.A. 1879, served in Egypt with 19th hussars, captain 7th hussars. See Foster's *Baronetage* & *Eton School Lists.*

Ridley, Henry Nicholas, 2s. Oliver Matthew, of West Harling, Kent, cler. EXETER COLL., matric. 23 May, 1874, aged 18; B.A. 1878, M.A. 1881. [10]

Ridley, Henry Richard, 3s. Matthew White, of Portland Place, London, baronet. UNIVERSITY COLL., matric. 15 May, 1833, aged 17; B.A. 1837, M.A. 1859, incumbent of Rock, Northumberland, 1849-51, vicar of Stranton, co. Durham, 1851-8, and of St. Cuthbert, Durham (city), 1858.

Ridley, Rev. Herbert, 2s. Henry, of Ipswich, gent. NON-COLL., matric. 17 April, 1880, aged 19; B.A. from NEW COLL. 1883, M.A. 1887.

Ridley, James, s. Glocester, of Poplar, Middlesex, cler. UNIVERSITY COLL., matric. 25 May, 1754, aged 18; B.A. from NEW COLL. 1760.

Ridley, James Francis, 5s. Nicholas James, of Newbury, Berks, cler. ST. JOHN'S COLL., matric. 14 Oct., 1876, aged 18. See Foster's *Baronetage* & *Eton School Lists.*

Ridley, Lancelot, 3s. Henry, of Ipswich, Suffolk, gent. LINCOLN COLL., matric. 25 Oct., 1873, aged 18; B.A. 1876, M.A. 1880, vicar of Chute, Hants, 1885. [15]

Ridley, Matthew, s. Richard, of Newcastle-on-Tyne, arm. ST. JOHN'S COLL., matric. 1 Dec., 1727, aged 16; created M.A. 1 July, 1730, bar.-at-law, Gray's Inn, 1732, bencher 1749, M.P. Newcastle-on-Tyne 1747-74, died 6 April, 1778. See Foster's *Baronetage.*

Ridley, (Sir) Matthew White (Bart.), s. Matthew, of Newcastle, Northumberland. CHRIST CHURCH, matric. 27 Feb., 1764, aged 18; 2nd baronet, M.P. Morpeth 1768-74, Newcastle-on-Tyne 1774-1812, died 9 April, 1813, brother of Matthew W. 1767. See Foster's *Baronetage.*

Ridley, (Sir) Matthew White (Bart.), s. Matthew, of Marylebone, Middlesex, baronet. CHRIST CHURCH, matric. 24 April, 1795, aged 17; B.A. 1798, 3rd baronet, M.P. Newcastle-on-Tyne 1812, until his death 14 July, 1836.

Ridley, (Sir) Matthew White (Bart.), 1s. Matthew White, of Newcastle, Northumberland, baronet. CHRIST CHURCH, matric. 20 June, 1825, aged 17; B.A. 1828, 4th baronet, M.P. North Northumberland 1859-68, died 25 Sep., 1877. See Foster's *Baronetage.*

Ridley, (Sir) Matthew White (Bart.), 1s. Matthew White, of London, baronet. BALLIOL COLL., matric. 12 Oct., 1861, aged 19, scholar 1860-5, B.A. 1865; fellow ALL SOULS' COLL. 1865-74, M.A. 1867, 5th baronet, a student of the Inner Temple 1864, M.P. North Northumberland 1868-85, Lancashire (Blackpool division) 1886, under-secretary Home department 1878-80, and for Foreign affairs 1885, financial secretary to the Treasury 1885-6. See Foster's *Baronetage.* [20]

Ridley, Nicholas, s. Matthew, of Heaton, Northumberland, arm. UNIVERSITY COLL., matric. 16 Oct., 1767, aged 18; bar.-at-law, Gray's Inn, 1773, bencher 1788, a master in Chancery 1802, until his death 1 Jan., 1805.

Ridley, Nicholas James, 2s. Henry Colborne, of Hambledon, Bucks, cler. CHRIST CHURCH, matric. 15 May, 1839, aged 18; B.A. 1843, M.A. 1845, of Hollington House, Hants, vicar of Woolton Hill, Hants, 1850-72, died 15 March, 1888. See Foster's *Baronetage.*

Ridley-Colborne, Nicholas William, s. Matthew, of St. Marylebone, Middlesex, baronet. CHRIST CHURCH, matric. 26 Oct., 1796, aged 17; B.A. 1800, of West Harling, Norfolk, a student of Gray's Inn 1795, assumed the additional surname and arms of COLBORNE by royal licence 21 June, 1803, represented seven constituencies in parliament 1805-37, created Baron Colborne 15 May, 1839, died 3 May, 1854.

Ridley, Oliver Matthew, 3s. Henry Colborne, of Hambledon, Bucks, cler. CHRIST CHURCH, matric. 12 May, 1842, aged 17; B.A. 1846, M.A. 1865, bar.-at-law, Inner Temple, 1850, rector of West Harling, Norfolk, 1855-60, vicar of Cobham, Kent, 1860-76, rector of Bishopstone, co. Hereford, 1876.

Ridley, Richard, s. Matthew, of Newcastle, baronet. UNIVERSITY COLL., matric. 14 Oct., 1799, aged 17; B.A. 1803, M.A. 1806, perp. curate Cramlington 1806, rector of Leathley, Yorks, 1826, until his death 21 Jan., 1845. [25]

Ridley, Stuart Oliver, 1s. Oliver Matthew, of London, cler. MAGDALEN COLL., matric. 20 Jan., 1872, aged 18; scholar EXETER COLL. 1873-7, B.A. 1875, M.A. 1881, a master in Friars School, Bangor, assistant British Museum 1878. See *Boase*, 166.

Ridley, Thomas, 1s. Thomas, of St. John Lee, Northumberland, gent. MAGDALEN HALL, matric. 3 Dec., 1829, aged 22; B.A. 1833, M.A. 1838, curate of East Bradenham 1833-5, Gosforth 1835-48, perp. curate St. Mary Sowerby, Yorks, 1848-67.

Ridley, Thomas Glynn, 2s. Thomas, of Cullercoats, Northumberland, arm. EXETER COLL., matric. 12 Oct., 1878, aged 20; B.A. 1883, B.C.L. & M.A. 1885, bar.-at-law, Lincoln's Inn, 1884. See Foster's *Men at the Bar.*

Ridley, Walter Colborne, 4s. Nicholas James, of Hollington House, Newbury, cler. BRASENOSE COLL., matric. 4 March, 1875, aged 19.

Ridley, William Charles, s. William, of Kimbolton, Hunts, gent. PEMBROKE COLL., matric. 25 April, 1809, aged 16; scholar 1812-3, died incumbent St. John's Episcopal Chapel, Glasgow, 12 May, 1855.

Ridley, William Henry, 1s. Henry Colborne, of Hambledon, Bucks, cler. CHRIST CHURCH, matric. 15 May, 1834, aged 18; student 1836-41, B.A. 1838, M.A. 1840, hon. canon 1871, rector of Hambledon, Bucks, 1840, until his death 17 Feb., 1882.

Ridlington, William, fellow TRINITY HALL, Cambridge, 1739 (M.A. 1743, LL.D. 1751); regius professor civil law 1757, incorp. 15 July, 1748.

Ridout, George, s. John, of London, gent. BALLIOL COLL., matric. 9 July, 1805, aged 17; B.C.L. 1812, lecturer of Newland, co. Gloucester, 1813, vicar 1832, until his death 26 Jan., 1871. See *St. Paul's School Reg.*, 215. [5]

Ridout, John, s. George, of Sherborne, Dorset, pleb. CORPUS CHRISTI COLL., matric. 9 March, 1748-9, aged 18; B.A. 1753.

Ridout, John Honyfield, s. John, of Blandford, Dorset, arm. MERTON COLL., matric. 22 Nov., 1785, aged 17.

Ridpath, Thomas Alan. Johnson, 1s. Thomas Alexander, of Hampstead, Middlesex, gent. KEBLE COLL., matric. 19 Oct., 1886, aged 18.

Ridsdale, Septimus Otter Barnes, 6s. George William Hughes, of Crowcombe, Somerset, cler. WADHAM COLL., matric. 11 June, 1858, aged 17; scholar 1858-63, B.A. 1861, Greek exhibitioner 1860-2, of the Indian Civil Service 1861, died 15 Nov., 1884.

Rigaud, Major-General Gibbes, created M.A. 14 Nov., 1874 (son of Stephen Peter Rigaud), served with 60th foot in Kaffir war 1851-3, and in China 1860, died 1 June, 1885. [10]

Rigaud, Rev. John, 4s. Stephen Peter, of Richmond, Surrey, arm. CORPUS CHRISTI COLL., matric. 14 May, 1840, aged 17; demy MAGDALEN COLL. 1840-9, B.A. 1844, M.A. 1846, B.D. 1854, fellow 1849-88, senior dean of arts 1850, bursar 1852, vice-president 1857, dean of divinity 1860, librarian 1874, commissary to Bishop of Antigua, died 27 July, 1888. See *Bloxam*, vii. 348.

Rigaud, Stephen Jordan, 1s. Stephen Peter, of Westminster, arm. EXETER COLL., matric. 23 Jan., 1834, aged 17; fellow 1838-41, B.A. 1841, M.A. 1842, B. & D.D. 1854, math. lecturer 1840, select preacher 1856, F.R.A.S., under-master Westminster School 1846-50, head-master Queen Elizabeth's School, Ipswich, 1850-7, Bishop of Antigua 1857, until his death 17 May, 1859. See *Coll. Reg.*, 132.

Rigaud, Stephen Peter, s. Stephen, of Richmond, Surrey, gent. EXETER COLL., matric. 15 April, 1791, aged 16; fellow 1794-1810, B.A. 1797, M.A. 1799, F.R.S., Savilian professor of geometry 1810-27, and of astronomy 1827-39, professor of experimental philosophy 1810-39, observer at Kew 1814, Radcliffe observer 1827, until his death 16 March, 1839. See *Coll. Reg.*, 117.

Rigby, Allan Danson, 4s. James Winstanley, of Liverpool, gent. WADHAM COLL., matric. 15 Oct., 1881, aged 19; scholar 1880-5, B.A. 1885.

Rigby, Arthur, '13s.' Edward, of Eccles, Lancashire, arm. BRASENOSE COLL., matric. 17 Oct., 1833, aged 18; B.A. 1837. [15]

Rigby, Christopher, s. Christopher, of Cosgrave, Northants, gent. ORIEL COLL., matric. 6 March, 1720-1, aged 18.

Rigby, Christopher, s. Christopher, of Monks Risborough, Bucks, gent. WADHAM COLL., matric. 14 April, 1790, aged 17; B.A. 1794, M.A. 1797, rector of Ringmore, and vicar of Ipplepen and Woodland, all in Devon, 1808.

Rigby, Edmund Winstanley, s. Edmund, of Brompton, Middlesex, arm. QUEEN'S COLL., matric. 20 May, 1795, aged 19.

Rigby, Edwin Budd, 1s. Tipping (Thomas), of St. Anne's, London, arm. LINCOLN COLL., matric. 20 Oct., 1827, aged 17; a student of the Inner Temple 1827. See *Eton School Lists*.

Rigby, Henry, M.A. ST. JOHN'S COLL., Cambridge; incorp. 6 July, 1733. [20]

Rigby, Henry, s. John, of Ickford, Bucks, cler. WADHAM COLL., matric. 28 May, 1759, aged 17; B.A. 1763, M.A. 1768, rector of Hadleigh, Essex, 1776, died at Salisbury 15 May, 1819, aged 77.

Rigby, Rev. Henry William, 1s. James, of Doncaster, gent. QUEEN'S COLL., matric. 4 June, 1881, aged 19; B.A. 1884, M.A. 1888.

Rigby, John, s. Thomas, of Wigan, Lancashire, pleb. CHRIST CHURCH, matric. 11 May, 1719, aged 18; B.A. 29 Jan., 1722-3, M.A. 1725.

Rigby, John, s. Christopher, of Cosgrave, Northants, gent. WADHAM COLL., matric. 15 Jan., 1727-8, aged 18; B.A. 1731, M.A. 1734, rector of North Meols, died at Harrock Hall, Lancashire, 29 Oct., 1793.

Rigby, Robert, s. Thomas, of Wigan, Lancashire, gent. ST. ALBAN HALL, matric. 13 July, 1795, aged 41; vicar of St. Mary's, Beverley, 1791, until his death 8 Jan., 1823, aged 69. [25]

Rigby, William, s. William, of Liverpool, Lancashire, arm. BRASENOSE COLL., matric. 14 Jan., 1817, aged 16; scholar 1817-20.

Rigden, Francis, 4s. Richard Henry, of Salisbury, gent. LINCOLN COLL., matric. 18 Oct., 1879, aged 19; B.A. 1882.

Rigden, Rev. Richard, 2s. Richard Henry, of Salisbury, gent. ST. JOHN'S COLL., matric. 16 Oct., 1875, aged 19.

Rigden, William, 1s. John Martin, of Lenham, Kent, gent. MAGDALEN HALL, matric. 29 Nov., 1827, aged 20; B.A. 1832, rector of Cann St. Rumbold, Dorset, 1857, until his death 26 May, 1870.

Rigg, Edward, 4s. Arthur, of Chester (city), cler. UNIVERSITY COLL., matric. 23 Oct., 1868, aged 18; scholar QUEEN'S COLL. 1868-73, B.A. 1872, M.A. 1877. [30]

Rigg, James Macmullen, 1s. James, of Brentford, Middlesex, cler. ST. JOHN'S COLL., matric. 17 Oct., 1874, aged 19; scholar 1874-9, B.A. 1878, bar.-at-law, Lincoln's Inn, 1881. See Foster's *Men at the Bar*.

Rigg, John, 1s. Wilson, of Manchester, Lancashire, cler. ST. EDMUND HALL, matric. 5 July, 1832, aged 21; B.A. from NEW INN HALL 1842, M.A. 1843, perp. curate New Mills, Glossop, co. Derby, 1848, until his death in Nov., 1860. See *Manchester School Reg.*, iii. 180.

Rigg, John, 1s. John, of Shrewsbury, cler. CHRIST CHURCH, matric. 13 Oct., 1882, aged 19; exhibitioner 1882, B.A. 1886.

Rigg, Robinson, 1s. Thomas, of Burgh-by-Sands, Cumberland, gent. QUEEN'S COLL., matric. 22 June, 1854, aged 18.

Rigg, William Harrison, 2s. Christopher Robert Pybus, of Scorton, Yorks, D.Med. ST. JOHN'S COLL., matric. 9 June, 1871, aged 21; B.A. 1876, M.A. 1881, took the name of RIGG in lieu of PYBUS, a student of the Inner Temple 1873, vicar of Anston, Yorks, 1883. [35]

Rigge, Herbert Miles, 1s. John Morton, of Shirehampton, co. Gloucester, gent. ST. EDMUND HALL, matric. 25 Oct., 1880, aged 24.

Riggs, Edward, s. Edward, of Binfield, Berks, arm. ST. JOHN'S COLL., matric. 23 Feb., 1736-7, aged 15.

Riggs, George, o.s. George, of Penrith, Cumberland, gent. QUEEN'S COLL., matric. 18 June, 1819, aged 20; scholar 1820-36, B.A. 1824, M.A. 1828, chaplain, math. lecturer, and tutor 1833-45, fellow 1836-46, bursar 1840, rector of Charlton-on-Otmoor, Oxon, 1846, until his death 4 Sep., 1855.

Righton, John Hayman, 3s. Edgar, of Trowbridge, Wilts, gent. NEW COLL., matric. 19 Oct., 1874, aged 33; B.Mus. 1883.

Riland, John, s. Richard, of Sutton Coldfield, co. Warwick, cler. QUEEN'S COLL., matric. 9 March, 1754, aged 17; B.A. 1757, M.A. 1760, rector of Sutton Coldfield 1790, until his death 13 March, 1822, father of John.

Riland, John, s. John, of Birmingham, co. Warwick, cler. ST. EDMUND HALL, matric. 8 Feb., 1797, aged 18; B.A. 1800, M.A. 1806.

Riland, Richard (Bisse), s. Richard, of Sutton Coldfield, co. Warwick, cler. QUEEN'S COLL., matric. 14 Feb., 1749-50, aged 16; B.A. 1753, M.A. 1756, rector of Sutton Coldfield 1758, until his death 17 Feb., 1790. See *O.H.S.*, ix. 268.

Riley, Rev. Edmund, 3s. Edward, of Hamstall Ridware, co. Stafford, gent. LINCOLN COLL., matric. 6 April, 1824, aged 19; B.A. 1827, M.A. 1831, died 10 May, 1862. [5]

Riley, Henry Thomas, scholar CHRIST'S COLL., Cambridge (B.A. from CLARE COLL. 1840, M.A. 1859), o.s. Henry, of Southwark, Surrey, gent. Incorp. from EXETER COLL. 16 June, 1870, aged 53; bar.-at-law, Inner Temple, 1847, editor of the 'Liber Albus,' etc., and of 'Memorials of London,' died 14 April, 1878.

Riley, John Athelstan Lawrie, o.s. John, of London, arm. PEMBROKE COLL., matric. 1 Feb., 1877, aged 18; B.A. 1881, M.A. 1883. See *Eton School Lists*.

Rimington, John Stewart, 5s. Michael, of Bow, Middlesex, arm. MAGDALEN HALL, matric. 1 Feb., 1858, aged 26; B.A. 1862.

Rimington, George Arthur, 1s. Michael, of Penrith, Cumberland, gent. QUEEN'S COLL., matric. 29 Jan., 1875, aged 18; B.A. 1878, bar.-at-law, Lincoln's Inn, 1885. See Foster's *Men at the Bar*.

Rimington, Michael Frederick, 2s. Michael, of Penrith, Cumberland, gent. KEBLE COLL., matric. 16 Oct., 1876, aged 18; B.A. 1879. [10]

Rimmer, Richard, o.s. Richard, of Liverpool, Lancashire, arm. EXETER COLL., matric. 17 April, 1845, aged 18; a student of the Inner Temple 1845.

Rimmer, Sydney Richard, o.s. John Whittle, of Seetapore, East Indies, arm. BRASENOSE COLL., matric. 23 Oct., 1885, aged 18.

Ring, Cornelius Percy, scholar TRINITY COLL., Dublin, 1836 (B.A. 1839, B.Med. 1840); adm. 'ad eundem' 18 May, 1843.

Ring, Nehemiah, s. Aaron, of St. Sepulchre's, London, pleb. MERTON COLL., matric. 14 March, 1747-8, aged 17; B.A. 1752.

Ring, Richard, s. William, of Shaftesbury, Dorset, arm. WORCESTER COLL., matric. 3 Feb., 1737-8, aged 18; B.A. 1741, M.A. 1744, vicar of Leckford, Hants, 1760, died vicar of Wherwell, Hants, in 1791. [15]

Ringer, Thomas, s. Thomas, of Forncett, Norfolk, gent. WORCESTER COLL., matric. 26 Jan., 1719-20, aged 17; B.A. 1723, M.A. 1726.

Ringrose, Charles Edward Leake, 1s. Christopher Leake, of Rotterdam, arm. CHRIST CHURCH, matric. 18 Oct., 1867, aged 18; B.A. 1871, bar.-at-law, Inner Temple, 1875, registrar of deeds Yorkshire, N.R., 1885. See Foster's *Men at the Bar* & *Rugby School Reg.*

Ringrose, Francis Davies, 4s. Robert Boyes, of Swanland, near Hull, arm. MERTON COLL., matric. 19 Oct., 1883, aged 20; B.A. 1887.

Ringrose, William Weaver, 2s. William, of Oxford, gent. NEW COLL., matric. 17 May, 1870, aged 31; B.Mus. 19 May, 1870.

Ringwood, John Ernest, 1s. Frederick Howe, of Dungannon, co. Tyrone, cler. WADHAM COLL., matric. 20 Jan., 1871, aged 19; scholar 1870-5, B.A. 1878, a student of the Middle Temple 1879. [20]

Riollay, Francis William, B.A. TRINITY COLL., Dublin, s. Christopher, of Guingamp, France, gent. HERTFORD COLL. incorp. 13 Jan., 1777, aged 29; M.A. 29 April, 1780, B.Med. 1782, D.Med. 1784 (not so named in *Cat. Grads.*, Dublin University), fellow College of Physicians 1785, died about 1797. See Munk's *Roll*, ii. 357.

Ripley, (Sir) Edward (Bart.), 1s. Henry, of Bradford, Yorks, arm. (after baronet). CHRIST CHURCH, matric. 19 Oct., 1859, aged 19; B.A. 1864, 2nd baronet, bar.-at-law, Inner Temple, 1870. See Foster's *Men at the Bar*.

Ripley, Frederick, 3s. Henry William, of Lightcliffe, Yorks, arm. (after baronet). CHRIST CHURCH, matric. 16 Oct., 1868, aged 21. See Foster's *Baronetage*.

Ripley, William Ernest, 1s. William Nottidge, of Earlham, Norfolk, arm. TRINITY COLL., matric. 12 Oct., 1878, aged 18; B.A. 1882.

Ripley, William Honeywood, 1s. Thomas Hyde, of Coggeshall, Essex, cler. UNIVERSITY COLL., matric. 13 Dec., 1832, aged 17; B.A. 1837, incumbent of Trinity Church, Toronto, 2nd master Canada College, etc., died 22 Oct., 1849. See *Rugby School Reg.*, 157. [25]

Ripley, Rev. William Joseph, o.s. William, of Liverpool, arm. WADHAM COLL., matric. 25 June, 1841, aged 17; B.A. 1845, M.A. 1848, died at Warrington 15 July, 1848. See *Rugby School Reg.*, 199.

Risdon, Anthony, s. Phil., of Budeaux, Devon, pleb. BALLIOL COLL., matric. 20 Nov., 1721, aged 18; B.A. from PEMBROKE COLL. 1725.

Risdon, George, 3s. John, of Peckham, Surrey, arm. UNIVERSITY COLL., matric. 27 March, 1821, aged 18.

Riseley, Thomas, 1s. George, of Clifton, co. Gloucester, gent. CHRIST CHURCH, matric. 20 Oct., 1873, aged 35; B.Mus. 1875.

Rishton, Henry, s. Geoffrey, of Kirkham, Lancashire, gent. QUEEN'S COLL., matric. 14 March, 1761, aged 17. [30]

Rishton, Martin Folkes, s. William, of Bristol (city), arm. ORIEL COLL., matric. 21 Nov., 1764, aged 17.

Rising, William Henry, s. John, of Marylebone, Middlesex, gent. TRINITY COLL., matric. 8 July, 1814, aged 18.

Risk, John Erskine, M.A. TRINITY COLL., Dublin, 1860 (B.A. 1847), adm. 'comitatis causa' 13 June, 1861; incorp. from MAGDALEN HALL, 9 June, 1864, aged 38 (1s. Andrew, of Dublin, arm.).

Risley, Herbert Hope, o.s. John Holford, of Akeley, Bucks, cler. NEW COLL., matric. 15 Oct., 1869, aged 18; scholar 1869-73, B.A. 1873, of the Indian Civil Service.

Risley, Holford Cotton, 1s. William Cotton, of Souldern, Oxon, cler. NEW COLL., matric. 14 March, 1850, aged 18; of Deddington, Oxon, high sheriff 1876. [35]

Risley, John, s. John, of St. Peter's, Beds, gent. NEW COLL., matric. 30 June, 1748, aged 19; B.A. 1752, fellow, M.A. 1757, 'father of the Wykehamists,' rector of Tingewick 1758, and of Thornton, Bucks, until his death 24 July, 1818.

Risley, John, s. John, of Barton, Bucks, cler. NEW COLL., matric. 17 Oct., 1787, aged 16; B.A. 1791, M.A. 1808, rector of Thornton, Bucks, and Aston, Northants, 1818, until his death 29 April, 1853, father of John H. 1832.

Risley, John Shuckburgh, 2s. Shuckburgh Norris, of Hildenborough, Kent, arm. MAGDALEN COLL., matric. 21 Oct., 1886, aged 18; exhibitioner 1886.

Risley, John Holford, y.s. (subs. 3 fil.), John, of Tingewicke, Bucks, cler. NEW COLL., matric. 25 Oct., 1832, aged 21; fellow 1832-50, B.C.L. 1840, M.A. 1865, rector of Akeley with Stockholt, Bucks, 1841-73, and of Nuffield 1873, until his death 16 Dec., 1883.

Risley, Robert Wells, 4s. William Cotton, of Deddington, Oxon, cler. EXETER COLL., matric. 2 Feb., 1855, aged 18; B.A. 1860, M.A. 1861, rector of Moulsoe, Bucks, 1883, until his death 23 Aug., 1884.

Risley, Shuckburgh Norris, o.s. Shuckburgh, of Muswell Hill, Middlesex, gent. PEMBROKE COLL., matric. 11 June, 1857, aged 19; bar.-at-law, Inner Temple, 1868. See Foster's *Men at the Bar.*

Risley, William Cotton, s. John, of Tingewick, Bucks, cler. NEW COLL., matric. 27 Nov., 1816, aged 18; fellow 1816-29, B.A. 1821, M.A. 1824, dean of arts 1824, bursar 1825, sub-warden 1826, vicar of Whaddon, Wilts, 1829, and of Deddington, Oxon, 1836-48, died 1 June, 1869.

Risley, William Cotton, 2s. William Cotton, of Souldern, Oxon, cler. EXETER COLL., matric. 11 Feb., 1852, aged 18; B.A. 1856, M.A. 1858, held various curacies 1858-76, vicar of Titley, co. Hereford, 1876-7, rector of Shelstone, Bucks, 1878.

Ritchie, Charles, 1s. Charles Thomson, of Woodford Bridge, Essex, arm. TRINITY COLL., matric. 11 Oct., 1884, aged 17; B.A. 1888 (his father president Local Government Board & P.C. 1886). [5]

Ritchie, Charles Edward, 3s. William, of Glasgow, gent. MAGDALEN COLL., matric. 19 Oct., 1883, aged 17; B.A. 1886.

Ritchie, Charles Foster, 1s. Robert, of Bickley, Kent, arm. NEW COLL., matric. 12 Oct., 1883, aged 18; B.A. 1888.

Ritchie, David, 2s. William, of Glasgow, gent. MAGDALEN COLL., matric. 19 Oct., 1883, aged 19; B.A. 1886.

Ritchie, David George, o.s. George, of Jedburgh, cler. BALLIOL COLL., matric. 26 May, 1874, aged 20, exhibitioner 1874-8, B.A. 1878; fellow JESUS COLL. 1878, M.A. 1881, Greek lecturer 1880, tutor 1881, librarian 1881-6, classical lecturer 1882, a student of the Inner Temple 1877.

Ritchie, Francis, 2s. Henry, of Islington, Middlesex, arm. LINCOLN COLL., matric. 23 May, 1866, aged 18; B.A. 1870, M.A. 1874, a student of the Inner Temple 1870. [10]

Ritchie, Harry Oliphant, 4s. William, of Dunnotter, co. Kincardine, arm. MERTON COLL., matric. 21 Oct., 1886, aged 19.

Ritchie, James, 4s. Henry, of London, gent. CORPUS CHRISTI COLL., matric. 19 Oct., 1875, aged 20; B.A. 1879, M.A. 1883.

Ritchie, James William, 1s. James Thompson, of Buckhurst Hill, Essex, arm. LINCOLN COLL., matric. 22 Oct., 1886, aged 18.

Ritchie, William, 5s. John, of Peterhead, Aberdeen, gent. ORIEL COLL., matric. 13 Oct., 1873, aged 19; scholar 1873-8, B.A. 1878, M.A. 1885.

Ritchie, William Hamilton, 1s. William, of Glasgow, arm. EXETER COLL., matric. 18 Jan., 1883, aged 21; B.A. 1885. [15]

Ritso, Frederick Henry James, s. George Frederick, of London, gent. CHRIST CHURCH, matric. 23 April, 1788, aged 16; B.A. 1792, M.A. 1795, bar.-at-law, Lincoln's Inn, 1814.

Ritson, John Holland, 3s. Caleb, of Bolton, Lancashire, gent. BALLIOL COLL., matric. 19 Oct., 1886, aged 18; scholar 1885.

Ritson, Joseph, 'Queen's College carrier;' privilegiatus 24 Oct., 1722.

Ritter, Frederick, 2s. Edward Frederick Christian, of Dieppe, arm. ST. JOHN'S COLL., matric. 12 Oct., 1878, aged 18, scholar 1878-9; B.A. from NEW INN HALL 1885, bar.-at-law, Inner Temple, 1885. See Foster's *Men at the Bar* & *Robinson*, 374.

Rive, His Excellency M. Auguste de la, created D.C.L. 2 July, 1860, minister plenipotentiary of the Helvetic Confederation at St. James's. [20]

Rivers, Arthur Richard, 2s. Richard, of Teignmouth, Devon, arm. ST. JOHN'S COLL., matric. 20 Jan., 1877, aged 19; B.A. 1881, M.A. 1884, minor canon and precentor of Sydney, New South Wales, 1884.

Rivers, Arthur Rivers Nunn-, o.s. John Parkinson Till, of Windsor, Berks, cler. WADHAM COLL., matric. 19 Jan., 1884, aged 19.

Rivers, Lieut.-General Augustus Henry Lane Fox Pitt-, F.R.S., created D.C.L. 30 June, 1886 (s. William Pitt Lane Fox), of Rusholme, Dorset, high sheriff 1884, served in the Crimea, president Anthropological Institute, assumed the additional names of PITT-RIVERS by royal licence 25 May, 1880. See Foster's *Peerage*, B. CONYERS.

Rivers, Charles Edmund, 2s. Josiah Charles, of Wynberg, Cape Town, arm. ORIEL COLL., matric. 18 Oct., 1881, aged 18; B.A. 1885.

Rivers, Elphinstone, 1s. Horace Elphinstone, of Greenwich, Kent, arm. NON-COLL., matric. 7 June, 1878, aged 18. [25]

Rivers, Francis, s. Francis, of Hammersmith, Middlesex, arm. WORCESTER COLL., matric. 2 Nov., 1808, aged 19.

Rivers, (Sir) James (Bart.), s. Peter, of Winchester (city), baronet. ST. MARY HALL, matric. 16 Nov., 1790, aged 18; B.A. 1794, 8th baronet, an officer of dragoons, died 27 Sep., 1805.

Rivers, (Sir) John (Bart.), s. Thomas, of Winchester (city), Hants. CHRIST CHURCH, matric. 4 Feb., 1736-7, aged 18; B.A. 1741, 5th baronet, died 1742.

Rivers-Gay, (Sir) Peter (Bart.), s. Thomas, of Winchester (city), doctor. CHRIST CHURCH, matric. 15 Oct., 1737, aged 16; B.A. from MAGDALEN COLL. 1741, M.A. 1744, 6th baronet, rector of Buttermere, Wilts, 1745-52, of Woolwich 1752, assumed the additional surname of GAY about 1760, preb. of Hereford 1760, and of Winchester 1766, and rector of Chelmsford 1774, until his death 20 July, 1790. See *Bloxam*, vi. 251.

Rivers, William, s. Peter, of Winchester (city), Bart. NEW COLL., matric. 24 May, 1793, aged 19; died 10 April, 1794. [30]

Rives, William Cabell, 1s. William Cabell, of Paris, arm. CORPUS CHRISTI COLL., matric. 19 Oct., 1870, aged 20; B.A. 1874, M.A. 1878.

Rivett, Lewis Culling Charles, s. Thomas, of Maresfield, Sussex, cler. UNIVERSITY COLL., matric. 30 March, 1816, aged 18.

Rivett-Carnac. See CARNAC, page 220.

Riviere, Briton, o.s. William, of London, arm. ST. MARY HALL, matric. 31 Jan., 1863, aged 22; B.A. 1866, M.A. 1873, the celebrated animal painter, royal academician 1881.

Rivington, Arthur William, 6s. Charles, of London, gent. CORPUS CHRISTI COLL., matric. 19 Oct., 1872, aged 18; exhibitioner 1872-6, B.A. 1876, M.A. 1879, a student of Lincoln's Inn 1875. [35]

Rivington, Rev. John Alfred, o.s. John, of Sydenham, Kent, arm. CHRIST CHURCH, matric. 7 June, 1865, aged 19; B.A. 1868, M.A. 1872. See *Rugby School Reg.*, 451.

Rivington, Luke, 4s. Francis, of St. James's, London, gent. MAGDALEN COLL., matric. 24 Jan., 1857, aged 18; demy 1856-62, B.A. 1861, M.A. 1863, held various curacies 1861-70, of St. John's Mission, Mazagon, Bombay. See *Bloxam*, vii. 406.

Rivington, Septimus, 7s. Francis, of Highgate, Middlesex, arm. TRINITY COLL., matric. 15 Oct., 1864, aged 18; B.A. 1868, M.A. 1871, a student of the Inner Temple, 1866.

Roach, Frederick Norman, 5s. Joseph Waterman, of Barbados, gent. ST. JOHN'S COLL., matric. 13 Oct., 1883, aged 19.

Roach, Reginald Black, 1s. Frederick, of Arreton, Isle of Wight, arm. QUEEN'S COLL., matric. 6 Feb., 1862, aged 19; B.A. & M.A. 1868, bar.-at-law, Middle Temple, 1867. See Foster's *Men at the Bar.*

Robartes, Thomas Charles Agar, o.s. Thomas James, of London, arm. (after a baron). CHRIST CHURCH, matric. 12 June, 1862, aged 18; B.A. 1867, M.A. 1869, 2nd Baron Robartes, bar.-at-law, Middle Temple, 1870, M.P. East Cornwall 1880-2. See Foster's *Men at the Bar.* [41]

Robartes, Thomas James Agar, 1s. Charles (Bagenal Agar), of St. George's, London, arm. CHRIST CHURCH, matric. 20 Oct., 1825, aged 17; B.A. 1830, M.P. Cornwall 1847-68, assumed the additional surname and arms of ROBARTES by royal licence 30 March, 1822, created Baron Robartes 13 Dec., 1869, died 9 March, 1882. See Foster's *Peerage.*

Robarts, Abraham George, 1s. Abraham Wildey, of Marylebone, London, arm. CHRIST CHURCH, matric. 1 March, 1828, aged 18; of London, banker, died Sep., 1860. See *Eton School Lists.*

Robarts, Abraham John, 1s. Abraham George, of Roehampton, Surrey, arm. CHRIST CHURCH, matric. 15 Oct., 1856, aged 17; B.A. 1859, of Lillingstone Dayrell, Bucks, high sheriff, 1869.

Robarts, Alfred, o.s. William, of Burnham, Bucks, arm. BRASENOSE COLL., matric. 26 Nov., 1840, aged 20; B.A. 1844, perp. curate Wootton Underwood, 1852, until his death 1 April, 1856.

Robarts, Charles Henry, 2s. Abraham George, of Sholebroke Lodge, Whittlebury, Northants, arm. CHRIST CHURCH, matric. 21 Oct., 1858, aged 18, B.A. 1862; fellow ALL SOULS' COLL. 1864, M.A. 1865, librarian 1870, sub-warden 1878, bar.-at-law, Lincoln's Inn, 1867, remembrancer city of London 1878-81. See Foster's *Men at the Bar.* [5]

Robarts, Charles Nathaniel, (of CHRIST'S COLL., Cambridge, B.A. 1858, M.A. 1861), 1s. Frederick, of London, arm. ST. JOHN'S COLL., incorp. 19 Dec., 1869, aged 35; chaplain Christ Church 1873, precentor 1879.

Robb, David Constable, s. Charles, of Blairgowrie, co. Perth, cler. NON-COLL., matric. 3 Nov., 1870, aged 19; exhibitioner WORCESTER COLL. 1872-3, scholar 1873-5, B.A. 1875.

Robb, William John, 1s. Hamilton, of Portadown, Ireland, gent. NON-COLL., matric. 13 Oct., 1877, aged 22.

Robberds, Walter John Forbes, 1s. Frederick Walter, of Burhampore, East Indies, cler. KEBLE COLL., matric. 17 Oct., 1882, aged 19; B.A. 1886.

Robbins, Albert James, 2s. George, of Bath, arm. QUEEN'S COLL., matric. 22 Oct., 1872, aged 18.

Robbins, Charles, 3s. William, of Hickling, Norfolk, cler. ST. EDMUND HALL, matric. 29 Jan., 1846, aged 18; exhibitioner 1846-8. [11]

Robbins, Frank, 4s. William, of Hickling, Norfolk, cler. CHRIST CHURCH, matric. 3 June, 1852, aged 19; 'servitor' 1852-6.

Robbins, George, 2s. Thomas, of Worcester (city), arm. MAGDALEN COLL., matric. 11 May, 1826, aged 18; B.A. 1831, M.A. 1834, sometime 17th lancers. See *Eton School Lists.*

Robbins, George, o.s. William, of West Bromwich, co. Stafford, gent. WORCESTER COLL., matric. 16 Feb., 1829, aged 17; chaplain, Tuscany, 1836-50, rector of Courteenhall, Northants, 1851, until his death 9 Feb., 1873.

Robbins, George William Francis, 3s. George, of Courteenhall, Northants, cler. BRASENOSE COLL., matric. 12 June, 1873, aged 19; B.A. 1878. [15]

Robbins, Rev. Henry, 2s. William, of Hickling, Norfolk, cler. WADHAM COLL., matric. 1 March, 1838, aged 18; clerk 1838-42, B.A. 1842, M.A. 1844, died 13 Oct., 1858.

Robbins, John, s. Walter, of Salisbury (city), cler. TRINITY COLL., matric. 7 Feb., 1718-9, aged 16; B.A. 1724 (as ROBINS).

Robbins, John, 1s. John, of St. George's, London, arm. CHRIST CHURCH, matric. 12 June, 1851, aged 19; B.A. 1856, M.A. 1859, B. & D.D. 1868, bar.-at-law, Inner Temple, 1858, chaplain at Wiesbaden 1860-2, vicar of St. Peter, Kensington, 1862-83, of Framfield, Sussex, 1883-6, and of Hemel Hempstead since 1886. See Foster's *Men at the Bar* & *Eton School Lists.*

Robbins, Leopold George Gordon, 1s. George, of Pisa, Italy, cler. TRINITY COLL., matric. 28 May, 1861, aged 19; scholar 1861-6, B.A. 1866, bar.-at-law, Lincoln's Inn, 1870. See Foster's *Men at the Bar.*

Robbins, Nathaniel, s. Nathaniel, of Golden, near Cashel, Ireland, gent. ST. MARY HALL, matric. 4 July, 1783, aged 25; B.A. 1784. [20]

Robbins, William, s. Walter, of Barnstaple, Devon, gent. EXETER COLL., matric. 1 March, 1779, aged 18; B.A. 1783.

Robbins, Rev. William, s. Benjamin, of St. George's, Hanover Square, London, gent. ST. EDMUND HALL, matric. 24 Feb., 1807, aged 20; B.A. 1810, M.A. 1813, died 24 Jan., 1856.

Robbins, William, 1s. William, of Hickling, Norfolk, cler. WORCESTER COLL., matric. 25 May, 1833, aged 19; B.A. 1837, M.A. 1845, vicar of Shropham, Norfolk 1850, until his death 4 March, 1886.

Robbs, Lewis, 5s. William Edward, of Stamford, co. Leicester, arm. BRASENOSE COLL., matric. 20 Oct., 1886, aged 18; exhibitioner 1886.

Robe, Francis William, s. William, of London, gent. MAGDALEN HALL, matric. 26 March, 1790, aged 18; B.A. from LINCOLN COLL. 1793, M.A. 1796.

Roberson, George Thomas, 1s. Thomas, of St. Michael's, Oxford (city), gent. LINCOLN COLL., matric. 19 April, 1820, aged 18; exhibitioner 1820-8, B.A. 1827, M.A. 1829. [25]

Roberson, John, s. Thomas, of Oxford (city), pleb. WADHAM COLL., matric. 8 May, 1770, aged 17; B.A. from CHRIST CHURCH 1774, M.A. 1779, chaplain MAGDALEN COLL. 1780-7. See *Bloxam,* ii. 177.

Roberson, John, s. John, of Oxford (city), cler. ST. JOHN'S COLL., matric. 25 June, 1804, aged 18; B.A. 1808, scholar and fellow 1809-24, M.A. 1812, B.D. 1817, under-master Merchant Taylors' School 1822 (3rd master in 1819), died curate of St. Michael's Bassishaw, 3 Jan., 1824. See *Robinson,* 167.

Roberson, Sidney Philip, 7s. Thomas, of St. Peter's-in-the-East, Oxford (city), gent. WORCESTER COLL., matric. 16 Dec., 1830, aged 19; B.A. 1836, perp. curate Rowton, Salop, 1850-76, died 7 March, 1879.

Roberson, William Henry Moncrieff, 2s. Thomas, of Oxford (city), gent. CHRIST CHURCH, matric. 15 Dec., 1819, aged 17, chorister 1812-8, servitor 1819-22; bible clerk LINCOLN COLL. 1821-5, B.A. 1825, M.A. 1826. [30]

Robert, Isaac Richard, 2s. Nicholas, of St. Marylebone, Middlesex, cler. MAGDALEN HALL, matric. 22 March, 1781, aged 21.

Roberton, James Matthew, 2s. James Matthew, of Limehouse, London, gent. MAGDALEN HALL, matric. 5 Nov., 1846, aged 21; B.A. 1851, M.A. 1853, vicar of St. Botolph's Without, Aldgate, London, 1860, until his death 1 Oct., 1885.

Roberts, Aaron, 1s. Aaron, of Denbigh (town), gent. JESUS COLL., matric. 2 June, 1853, aged 18; B.A. 1857, M.A. 1860.

Roberts, Albert James, 2s. Charles, of Westminster, gent. ST. JOHN'S COLL., matric. 27 May, 1846, aged 18; B.A. 1850, M.A. 1861, vicar of Tidebrook, Sussex, 1856.

Roberts, Alexander, 3s. John, of Clifton, near Bristol, arm. WADHAM COLL., matric. 22 April, 1870, aged 19; B.A. 1875, M.A. 1876, rector of Kimberley, Notts, 1878. [35]

Roberts, Alfred, s. Alfred William, of Southwark, Surrey, cler. TRINITY COLL., matric. 22 Oct., 1817, aged 18; B.A. 1822, M.A. 1824.

Roberts, Alfred Temple, 3s. Josiah, of Cheltenham, arm. MAGDALEN COLL., matric. 16 Oct., 1876, aged 18; demy 1875-80, B.A. 1880, M.A. 1883.

Roberts, Archibald Cameron, 1s. Thomas Archibald, of London, arm. JESUS COLL., matric. 18 Oct., 1883, aged 18; B.A. 1887. See *St. Paul's School Reg.,* 363.

Roberts, Arthur, 1s. William, of St. Giles's, London, arm. ORIEL COLL., matric. 16 March, 1819, aged 18; B.A. 1823, M.A. 1829, rector of Woodrising, Norfolk, 1831, until his death 3 Sep., 1886; for list of his works see *Crockford.*

Roberts, Arthur, 5s. John, of Wokingham, Berks, arm. WORCESTER COLL., matric. 14 March, 1833, aged 20; clerk MAGDALEN COLL. 1834-6, B.A. 1836, rector of Barkham, Berks, 1863, until his death 21 March, 1886, aged 72. See *Bloxam,* ii. 120.

Roberts, Arthur Carson, 1s. Thomas Howel Kyffin, of Frodsham, Cheshire, gent. BALLIOL COLL., matric. 17 Oct., 1882, aged 18; B.A. 1886, a student of the Inner Temple 1884.

Roberts, Arthur Llewelyn Wynne, 3s. H(ugh) Beaver, of Bangor, arm. MAGDALEN COLL., matric. 16 Oct., 1875, aged 20; B.A. 1878.

Roberts, Arthur Owen, 3s. Daniel, of Llangedwin, co. Denbigh, cler. JESUS COLL., matric. 24 Oct., 1866, aged 20. [5]

Roberts, Arthur Phillips, 1s. Arthur Troughton, of Mold, co. Flint, arm. BRASENOSE COLL., matric. 9 June, 1870, aged 18; B.A. 1873, bar.-at-law, Inner Temple, 1877. See Foster's *Men at the Bar* & *Eton School Lists.*

Roberts, Arthur William, 1s. Samuel, of Cheshunt, Herts, arm. LINCOLN COLL., matric. 25 Oct., 1869, aged 18; B.A. 1873, bar.-at-law, Inner Temple, 1874. See Foster's *Men at the Bar.*

Roberts, Barre Charles, s. Edward, of Westminster, arm. CHRIST CHURCH, matric. 24 Oct., 1805, aged 16; student, died 1 Jan., 1810. See *Gent.'s Mag.*, 1810, i. 179.

Roberts, Benjamin Chaffers, 2s. Robert, of Liverpool, gent. ST. JOHN'S COLL., matric. 1 May, 1867, aged 18.

Roberts, Browne Henry Eneas, 3s. Browne, of Marylebone, London, arm. ST. MARY HALL, matric. 1 May, 1849, aged 18; B.A. 1853. [10]

Roberts, Bryan, s. John, of Antony, Cornwall, arm. PEMBROKE COLL., matric. 21 Feb., 1771, aged 18; B.A. 1774, M.A. 1777, D.C.L. 1785.

Roberts, Cecil Wray Byng Wilkins, 2s. Claude Adolphus, of Richmond, Surrey, arm. WADHAM COLL., matric. 19 Jan., 1866, aged 20.

Roberts, Charles, s. Isaac, of Mortlake, Surrey, gent. MAGDALEN HALL, matric. 8 April, 1775, aged 18; B.A. 1779.

Roberts, Charles, s. William, of Monmouth (town), cler. MERTON COLL., matric. 7 April, 1791, aged 19.

Roberts, Charles Blissett, 1s. William Prouting, of Greenheys, near Manchester, gent. WADHAM COLL., matric. 26 Nov., 1870, aged 20; vicar of Otterford, Wilts, 1885. [15]

Roberts, Charles Edmund, 1s. Edmund Squire, of Chesterton, co. Cambridge, gent. NON-COLL., matric. 16 Oct., 1875, aged 18; B.A. from ST. JOHN'S COLL. 1879, M.A. 1884, chaplain Isle of Wight College 1886.

Roberts, Charles Edward Thornes, 3s. William, of Oswestry, Salop, arm. EXETER COLL., matric. 11 Oct., 1862, aged 19; exhibitioner 1865-6, B.A. 1866, M.A. 1883, classical master Ely Grammar School 1869-74, vicar of Brinsley, Notts, 1874-81. See *Coll. Reg.*, 162.

Roberts, Charles Henry, 1s. James, of Tidebrook, Sussex, cler. BALLIOL COLL., matric. 15 Oct., 1884, aged 19; scholar 1883.

Roberts, Charles Ingram, 3s. Thomas Turner, of Tenby, co. Pembroke, gent. WORCESTER COLL., matric. 10 June, 1852, aged 19; B.A. 1856, M.A. 1859, rector of St. Mary Hoo, Kent, 1875, until his death 17 Oct., 1886.

Roberts, Charles Philip, o.s. Philip, of Coleshill, co. Warwick, cler. TRINITY COLL., matric. 4 June, 1861, aged 18; B.A. 1864, M.A. 1868, vicar of Peel, Lancashire, 1871 [20]

Roberts, David, s. David, of Brentford, Middlesex, gent. ST. MARY HALL, matric. 13 July, 1781, aged 19.

Roberts, David, 1s. Robert, of Llanelidan, co. Denbigh, gent. JESUS COLL., matric. 7 Feb., 1833, aged 18; scholar 1834-9, B.A. 1837, M.A. 1840, rector of Llanelidan 1857, until his death in 1886.

Roberts, David, 9s. William, of Ceidiog, co. Carnarvon, cler. JESUS COLL., matric. 17 May, 1834, aged 18; B.A. 1838, M.A. 1839.

Roberts, David, 6s. David, of Aberystwith, gent. MAGDALEN HALL, matric. 3 Nov., 1836, aged 35; B.A. 1837, vicar of Bettws-Garmon, co. Carnarvon, 1868, until his death 1878.

Roberts, David Henry Bancroft, 1s. Henry, of Mold, Flints, cler. LINCOLN COLL., matric. 22 Oct., 1886, aged 19; scholar 1886. [25]

Roberts, Edmund, s. Henry, of Llandrisilio, co. Denbigh, gent. JESUS COLL., matric. 13 Feb., 1738-9, aged 19; B.A. 1742, M.A. 1745.

Roberts, Edmund, 2s. Alfred William, of St. Alban's, cler. MAGDALEN HALL, matric. 23 Jan., 1834, aged 21; B.A. 1840.

Roberts, Edward, s. Philip, of Crawley, Beds, arm. QUEEN'S COLL., matric. 6 April, 1753, aged 18; B.A. 1756.

Roberts, Edward, s. David, of Corwen, co. Merioneth, gent. JESUS COLL., matric. 16 Nov., 1769, aged 16; B.A. 1773, M.A. 1776. See *Gent.'s Mag.*, 1839, ii. 96.

Roberts, Edward, s. David, of Gwyddelwern, co. Merioneth, pleb. JESUS COLL., matric. 8 April, 1786, aged 20; B.A. 1790. [30]

Roberts, Edward, s. John, of Denbigh (town), gent. HERTFORD COLL., matric. 13 July, 1791, aged 19; B.A. 1795, M.A. 1798.

Roberts, Edward, s. David, of Tyddun Issa, co. Denbigh, pleb. BALLIOL COLL., matric. 24 Nov., 1800, aged 18; B.A. 1804. See *Gent.'s Mag.*, 1857, i. 495.

Roberts, Edward, s. James, of Bristol (city), doctor. LINCOLN COLL., matric. 1 June, 1808, aged 19.

Roberts, Edward, o.s. Edward, of Clerkenwell, London, gent. JESUS COLL., matric. 13 April, 1832, aged 20; B.A. 1835, M.A. 1838, vicar of Llangystenin, Isle of Anglesea, 1846.

Roberts, Edward, o.s. John, of Ruthin, co. Denbigh, gent. JESUS COLL., matric. 6 June, 1835, aged 20; B.A. from ST. MARY HALL 1841, M.A. 1863, vicar of Bunbury, Cheshire, 1864, until his death 5 Dec., 1887. [35]

Roberts, Edward, 1s. Daniel, of Southwark, Surrey, gent. EXETER COLL., matric. 30 April, 1846, aged 19.

Roberts, Edward (Dale), 1s. Edward, of Kingswood, co. Gloucester, cler. PEMBROKE COLL., matric. 30 May, 1868, aged 19; B.A. 1871, M.A. 1875, vicar of St. Paul's, Lozells, 1880.

Roberts, Edward Griffith, ('servitor'), o.s. Griffith, of Beaumaris, Isle of Anglesea, gent. JESUS COLL., matric. 15 March, 1832, aged 16.

Roberts, Edward Tufnell, 1s. H. T., of Milford, Hants, arm. ORIEL COLL., matric. 11 June, 1858, aged 18; scholar 1859-63, B.A. 1863, a student of Lincoln's Inn 1860.

Roberts, Edwin, 1s. Edwin, of Gloucester (city), gent. ST. MARY HALL, matric. 18 Nov., 1867, aged 23; exhibitioner MAGDALEN COLL. 1868-73, B.A. 1872, M.A. 1879, head-master Alford Grammar School 1877-80, and of Alton Grammar School 1880-3, rector of Candlesby, co. Lincoln, 1883. [40]

Roberts, Elliot Robert, 1s. Roger Eliot, of St. George's, Hanover Square, London, arm. CHRIST CHURCH, matric. 15 Jan., 1822, aged 16. See *Eton School Lists.*

Roberts, Ellis, s. John, of Ruthin, co. Denbigh, arm. JESUS COLL., matric. 27 May, 1814, aged 19; scholar 1815-22, B.A. 1818, M.A. 1821, vicar of Llanynys, co. Denbigh, 1824, until his death 12 Nov., 1844.

oberts, Ellis Gregory, 3s. Ellis, of St. David's, near Festiniog, cler. JESUS COLL., matric. 19 Jan., 1880, aged 20; scholar 1881-3, B.A. 1883.

oberts, Erasmus, s. John, of St. John's, Cornwall, gent. PEMBROKE COLL., matric. 18 Dec., 1809, aged 15.

oberts, Erasmus Coryton, 1s. John Coryton, of Trevael, Antony, Cornwall, arm. QUEEN'S COLL., matric. 5 July, 1851, aged 19; B.A. 1855, M.A. 1860, of Carbeale, Cornwall, J.P., D.L.

oberts, Ernest William, 2s. John Phillips, of Bampton, Oxon, cler. ST. MARY HALL, matric. 6 April, 1848, aged 18.

oberts, Evan, 1s. Robert, of Bangor, co. Carnarvon, gent. JESUS COLL., matric. 1 Dec., 1842, aged 20. **[5]**

oberts, Evan Killin, 1s. Robert, of Aberystwith, co. Cardigan, gent. JESUS COLL., matric. 27 Oct., 1877, aged 20.

oberts, Everett Ingram, o.s. Thomas, of Gloucester, cler. NON-COLL., matric. 16 Oct., 1875, aged 20.

oberts, Lieut.-General Sir Frederick Sleigh, Bart., G.C.B., G.C.I.E., created D.C.L. 8 Feb., 1881 (son of General Sir Abraham Roberts, G.C.B.), served throughout Indian Mutiny 1857-8, etc., and in Affghanistan 1879-80, V.C. 1858, C.I.E. 1 Jan., 1880, G.C.B. 21 Sep., 1880, created a baronet 11 June, 1881, G.C.I.E. 21 June, 1887, hon. LL.D. Dublin University. See Foster's *Baronetage* & *Eton School Lists.*

oberts, Rev. George, 3s. William, of Wokingham, Berks, gent. MAGDALEN HALL, matric. 31 May, 1827, aged 24; B.A. 1834, chorister MAGDALEN COLL. 1822-3, master of the Grammar School, Bampton, Oxon, died 9 Feb., 1847. See *Bloxam,* i. 217.

oberts, George, o.s. Charles, of Baldeston, Notts, gent. MAGDALEN HALL, matric. 28 Jan., 1836, aged 19; B.A. 1840, vicar of Norton Disney, co. Lincoln, 1852. **[10]**

oberts, George Blackmore Bayfield John, o.s. George, of London, cler. ORIEL COLL., matric. 17 Oct., 1866, aged 18; bible clerk 1866-72, B.A. 1872, vicar of Elmstone, co. Gloucester, 1879.

oberts, George Edmund, 1s, Owen, of Llanrwst, co. Denbigh, arm. MERTON COLL., matric. 16 Oct., 1884, aged 19.

oberts, George Farrar, 1s. Hugh, of Bangor, co. Carnarvon, gent. JESUS COLL., matric. 20 April, 1864, aged 19; B.A. 1867, M.A. 1870, vicar of Hollinfare, Lancashire, 1871.

oberts, George Quinlan, 1s. George Valentine, of Hobart Town, Tasmania, gent. NON-COLL., matric. 19 April, 1879, aged 19; of HERTFORD COLL. 1880.

oberts, Goodman, s. Thomas, of Ruthin, co. Denbigh, pleb. JESUS COLL., matric. 13 March, 1758, aged 18; B.A. from ORIEL COLL. 1762. **[15]**

oberts, Griffith, s. William, of Bettws, co. Carnarvon, pleb. JESUS COLL., matric. 17 Dec., 1762, aged 19; B.C.L. 1769, vicar of Aber, co. Carnarvon, 1773.

oberts, Griffith, B.A. TRINITY COLL., Dublin, 1822, 3s. — R., of Llanfihangel-Bachelleth, co. Carnarvon, cler. JESUS COLL., incorp. 30 May, 1822, aged 22; M.A. 1825.

oberts, Harry Bertie, 1s. Bertie, of Sandhurst, Berks, arm. BRASENOSE COLL., matric. 12 June, 1873, aged 18; B.A. 1876; rector of West Wickham, Kent, 1884. See *Eton School Lists.*

oberts, Henry, s. 'Patricius,' of Oakham, Kent, gent. MAGDALEN HALL, matric. 8 May, 1724, aged 15.

oberts, Henry, s. Henry, of Llantysilio, co. Denbigh, gent. JESUS COLL., matric. 26 Jan., 1729-30, aged 17. **[20]**

oberts, Henry, s. Henry, of Droitwich, co. Worcester, gent. WADHAM COLL., matric. 30 June, 1743, aged 17; B.A. 1747.

Roberts, Henry, s. James, of Warwick (town), cler. HERTFORD COLL., matric. 26 May, 1789, aged 19; B.A. 1793.

Roberts, Henry, s. William Haywood, of Eton, Bucks, doctor. TRINITY COLL., matric. 12 July, 1790, aged 18.

Roberts, Henry, 2s. John, of Kidderminster, co. Worcester, gent. ST. EDMUND HALL, matric. 14 April, 1825, aged 21; B.A. 1829, curate of Curry Rivell, Somerset, 1829-57, vicar 1857-64, vicar of Othery, Somerset, 1864, until his death 1 Oct., 1870.

Roberts, Henry, 2s. Robert, of Bala, co. Merioneth, pleb. CHRIST CHURCH, matric. 16 Oct., 1844, aged 19; servitor 1844-8, B.A. 1848, M.A. 1859, vicar of Dwygyvylchi, etc., 1867-71, and of Gwernafield, near Mold, 1871-9, rector of Llangerniew 1879, until his death 5 Aug., 1882. **[25]**

Roberts, Rev. Henry Charles Derham, 1s. Henry, of Naughton, Suffolk, cler. ST. EDMUND HALL, matric. 26 Jan., 1877, aged 20; B.A. & M.A. 1883.

Roberts, Rev. Henry Llewelyn, y.s. Thomas, of Uppingham, Rutland, cler. WORCESTER COLL., matric. 21 Nov., 1844, aged 21; B.A. 1848, died 13 March, 1851.

Roberts, Henry Mander, 5s. William, of Bampton, Oxon, gent. MAGDALEN COLL., matric. 10 Nov., 1827, aged 19; chorister 1816-25, clerk 1827-34, B.A. 1833, M.A. 1851, chaplain 1836-55, and of Merton College 1852-5, etc., rector of All Saints, Saltfleetby, co. Lincoln, 1855, until his death 17 Jan., 1867. See *Bloxam*, i. 216; ii. 119.

Roberts, Henry Seymour, of QUEEN'S COLL., Cambridge (LL.B. 1856, LL.D. 1861); adm. 'ad eundem' 1 July, 1858, head-master Thornbury Grammar School 1864-9, Wigton Grammar School 1869-70, and of Queen Elizabeth's Grammar School, Alford, 1870-6, etc., chaplain and secretary Dalston Refuge 1882.

Roberts, Henry Seymour Ward, 1s. Henry Seymour, of Bristol, LL.D. ST. ALBAN HALL, matric. 23 April, 1879, aged 22. **[30]**

Roberts, Henry Worsley, 1s. Henry T., of Lymington, Hants, arm. ORIEL COLL., matric. 7 Dec., 1843, aged 18.

Roberts, Herbert, 2s. John, of Yspytty, co. Denbigh, cler. JESUS COLL., matric. 23 March, 1858, aged 18; scholar 1860-2, B.A. 1862, held various curacies 1868-88, vicar of East Lulworth, Dorset, 1888.

Roberts, Rev. Horace, of MAGDALEN COLL., Cambridge (B.A. 1838, M.A. 1841); adm. 'ad eundem' 20 May, 1846.

Roberts, Hugh, 1s. Edward, of Llanaber, co. Merioneth, gent. JESUS COLL., matric. 4 May, 1829, aged 19.

Roberts, Hugh Edward, 4s. Robert Jones, of Denbigh, cler. JESUS COLL., matric. 21 Oct., 1873, aged 20. **[35]**

Roberts, Hugh Stewart, 1s. Hugh Beaver, of Bangor, co. Carnarvon. MAGDALEN COLL., matric. 15 Oct., 1870, aged 19; B.A. 1874. See *Eton School Lists.*

Roberts, Hugh Thomas, 1s. Hugh, of Chester, gent. CHRIST CHURCH, matric. 14 Oct., 1881, aged 19.

Roberts, James, s. James, of All Saints, Hereford (city), pleb. ST. JOHN'S COLL., matric. 7 Dec., 1715, aged 17.

Roberts, James, s. George, of Beckford, co. Gloucester, cler. ALL SOULS' COLL., matric. 14 June, 1749, aged 18, B.A. 1753; M.A. from MAGDALEN HALL 1762.

Roberts, James, s. Richard, of Kentchurch, co. Hereford, cler. WADHAM COLL., matric. 27 June, 1755, aged 15; B.A. 1759, M.A. 1762, rector of Kentchurch and preb. of Hereford 1797, until his death in 1816. **[40]**

Roberts, James, s. James, of Bissford, Northants, gent. LINCOLN COLL., matric. 5 Dec., 1780, aged 18; B.A. 1784, M.A. 1797, B. & D.D. 1804, rector of Abbey Dore and vicar of Much Marcle, chaplain to the Prince of Wales, died 3 April, 1809.

Roberts, James, s. James, of Warwick (town), cler. TRINITY COLL., matric. 12 Nov., 1783, aged 16; B.A. 1787, M.A. 1800, twenty years curate of Stoneleigh, co. Warwick, rector of Witherley, co. Leicester, 1805-33, died 6 Jan., 1842.

Roberts, James, s. Henry, of Clopton, co. Gloucester, gent. BRASENOSE COLL., matric. 7 June, 1791, aged 18; B.A. 1795. (Memo.: James Izod Roberts, rector of Saintbury, co. Gloucester, 1801, until his death in 1826.)

Roberts, James Clarke, 1s. James Foulkes, of Walthamstow, Essex, cler. MAGDALEN HALL, matric. 3 Feb., 1843, aged 20; B.A. 1848, M.A. 1853, vicar of Eastbury, Berks, 1868-9, and of West Wycombe 1869-72, rector of Ryton, Salop, 1872.

Roberts, James Corrall, s. James, of Stoneleigh, co. Warwick, cler. TRINITY COLL., matric. 21 Oct., 1813, aged 18; B.A. 1818, M.A. 1833, rector of Wolston, co. Warwick, 1819, and of Witherley, co. Leicester, 1846, until his death 6 Sep., 1871. **[5]**

Roberts, James Wrigley, s. Edward, of Liverpool, Lancashire, gent. BRASENOSE COLL., matric. 26 March, 1790, aged 21; B.A. 1793. (? See *Manchester School Reg.*, ii. 265.)

Roberts, Jeremiah, s. Jeremiah, of Worcester (city), pleb. MERTON COLL., matric. 22 May, 1760, aged 16; B.A. 1764, M.A. 1775, rector of Sedgeberrow, co. Worcester, 1787, until his death in 1825.

Roberts, John, s. John, of Denbigh (town), cler. JESUS COLL., matric. 18 March, 1722-3, aged 18.

Roberts, John, s. Griffith, of Llannawr, co. Merioneth, pleb. JESUS COLL., matric. 10 May, 1727, aged 21.

Roberts, John, s. Walter, of Ross, co. Hereford, gent. BALLIOL COLL., matric. 17 Oct., 1727, aged 18; B.A. 1731, M.A. 1734, B.Med. 1737. **[10]**

Roberts, John, s. Edward, of St. Werburgh, Chester (city), gent. CHRIST CHURCH, matric. 25 June, 1728, aged 16; B.A. 1732, M.A. 18 March, 1734-5.

Roberts, John, s. Robert, of Llanaber, co. Merioneth, pleb. ST. MARY HALL, matric. 29 March, 1735, aged 21; B.A. 1738.

Roberts, John, s. William, of Probus, Cornwall, pleb. EXETER COLL., matric. 11 March, 1745-6, aged 20; B.A. 1749.

Roberts, John, s. Henry, of St. David's, co. Pembroke, pleb. JESUS COLL., matric. 1 Nov., 1746, aged 16; B.A. from BRASENOSE COLL. 1750, M.A. 1753, rector of Llanbedrog in Lyne, co. Carnarvon, and vicar of Llanrhaiader, co. Denbigh, 1776, rector of Llantrissant, Anglesey, 1785, archdeacon of Merioneth 1785, until his death in 1802.

Roberts, John, s. Richard, of St. David's, co. Pembroke, cler. BRASENOSE COLL., matric. 7 March, 1747-8, aged 17; B.A. 1751. **[15]**

Roberts, John, s. Richard, of Wooton, par. St. Martin, co. Gloucester, gent. JESUS COLL., matric. 15 March, 1748-9, aged 17.

Roberts, John, s. Lewis, of St. Peter's, Dublin, Ireland, arm. CHRIST CHURCH, matric. 27 April, 1768, aged 21.

Roberts, John, s. Thomas, of St. Asaph, co. Flint, gent. JESUS COLL., matric. 7 March, 1772, aged 17.

Roberts, John, s. Robert, of Bottwnnog, co. Carnarvon, pleb. JESUS COLL., matric. 4 June, 1772, aged 17.

Roberts, John, s. John, of Llangantafal, co. Denbigh, gent. JESUS COLL., matric. 15 May, 1777, aged 19. **[20]**

Roberts, John, B.A. from JESUS COLL., 8 Feb., 1781, M.A. 10 Oct., 1783, B.D. 20 May, 1791.

Roberts, John, s. Robert, of Llanelidan, co. Denbigh, gent. JESUS COLL., matric. 15 May, 1777, aged 19.

Roberts, John, B.A. from JESUS COLL., 27 Feb., 1781.

Roberts, John, s. John, of Carnarvon (town), cler. JESUS COLL., matric. 24 May, 1788, aged 15; B.A. 1792, M.A. 1795.

Roberts, John, s. Peter, of St. Martin's, Salop, pleb. JESUS COLL., matric. 20 May, 1790, aged 20; B.A. 1794. **[25]**

Roberts, John, s. John, of Llanyfydd, co. Denbigh, gent. JESUS COLL., matric. 24 May, 1792, aged 17; B.A. 1796, M.A. 1799.

Roberts, John; privilegiatus 5 April, 1805.

Roberts, John, s. Bryan, of Drewsteignton, Devon, cler. PEMBROKE COLL., matric. 19 Oct., 1812, aged 15; scholar 1812-17.

Roberts, John, s. John, of St. Marylebone, London, arm. TRINITY COLL., matric. 9 Nov., 1813, aged 18. See *Gent.'s Mag.*, 1841, ii. 329.

Roberts, John, s. Owen, of Aberfraw, Isle of Anglesey, gent. JESUS COLL., matric. 3 Dec., 1817, aged 18 B.A. 1822, M.A. 1824. **[30]**

Roberts, John, 2s. Mark, of Tenby, co. Pembroke, gent. JESUS COLL., matric. 18 May, 1822, aged 18; B.A. 1827.

Roberts, John, 1s. John, of Amlwch, Isle of Anglesey arm. JESUS COLL., matric. 21 Oct., 1823, aged 18 B.A. 1829. See *Gent.'s Mag.*, 1845, ii. 432.

Roberts, John Arthur, o.s. Robert, of St. Asaph, co. Flint, gent. NON-COLL., matric. 13 Oct., 1883, aged 20; B.A. 1886.

Roberts, John Charles Aitken, 1s. John Philip, of Bampton, Oxon, cler. CHRIST CHURCH, matric. 20 Oct., 1847, aged 19; servitor 1847-8.

Roberts, John Farrar, 3s. Hugh, of Bangor, co. Carnarvon, gent. WORCESTER COLL., matric. 1 May, 1867, aged 19; B.A. 1871. **[35]**

Roberts, Rev. John Lindfield, 1s. John, of Hurstpierpoint, Sussex, arm. WORCESTER COLL., matric. 5 May, 1831, aged 18; B.A. from NEW INN HALL 1839, M.A. 1840, died 5 Feb., 1881. See *Crockford.*

Roberts, John Llewellyn, 2s. Job, of Buckingham, gent. QUEEN'S COLL., matric. 22 June, 1843, aged 18; Michel exhibitioner 1843-7, B.A. 1847, scholar 1847-50, M.A. 1850, fellow 1850-63, perp. curate St. John, Chatham, 1858-62, vicar of Spratton, Northants, 1862, hon. canon of Peterborough 1882.

Roberts, John Mortlock, o.s. William, of Sporle, Norfolk, cler. WORCESTER COLL., matric. 18 Oct., 1862, aged 19; B.A. 1865, M.A. 1882, held various curacies 1866-76, vicar of Long Compton, co. Warwick, 1876-82.

Roberts, John Phillips, s. William, of Oakingham, Berks, gent. NEW COLL., matric. 17 Oct., 1817, aged 18; clerk 1817-20, chaplain 1820-6, B.A. 1821, M.A. 1826, chaplain Christ Church 1824-8, rector of Eastergate, Sussex, 1849, until his death 12 Dec., 1882.

Roberts, John Rice, 2s. John, of Aberffraw, Isle o Anglesey, cler. JESUS COLL., matric. 11 March, 1856, aged 18; scholar 1858-60, B.A. 1860, M.A. 1862. **[40]**

Roberts, John Richard, y.s. Ellis, of Rhosymedre, co. Denbigh, cler. MERTON COLL., matric. 16 Oct., 1884, aged 19; postmaster 1884.

Roberts, John Richards, s. John, of Barnstaple, Devon gent. TRINITY COLL., matric. 8 Dec., 1794, aged 19; fellow until 1825, B.A. 1798, M.A. 1801, B.D. 1810, vice-president 1822, senior bursar 1823, F.S.A., rector of Hornblotton, Somerset, 1805, and of Rotherfield Greys, Oxon, 1824, until his death 20 June, 1843.

Roberts, John Varley, 4s. Joseph Varley, of Stanningley, near Leeds, gent. CHRIST CHURCH, matric. 7 March, 1871, aged 29; B.Mus. 8 July, 1871, D.Mus. 29 June, 1876, organist Magdalen College 1882.

BIBLIOTHECÆ BODLEIANÆ OXONIÆ *Prospectus interior ab Oriente*

A.A. *Introitus uterq; in Bibliothecam* B.B. *Sellæ foruliq; ex adverso positis in C.C. respondentes* D.

BIBLIOTHECÆ BODLEIANÆ OXONIÆ *Prospectus interior ab Occidente*

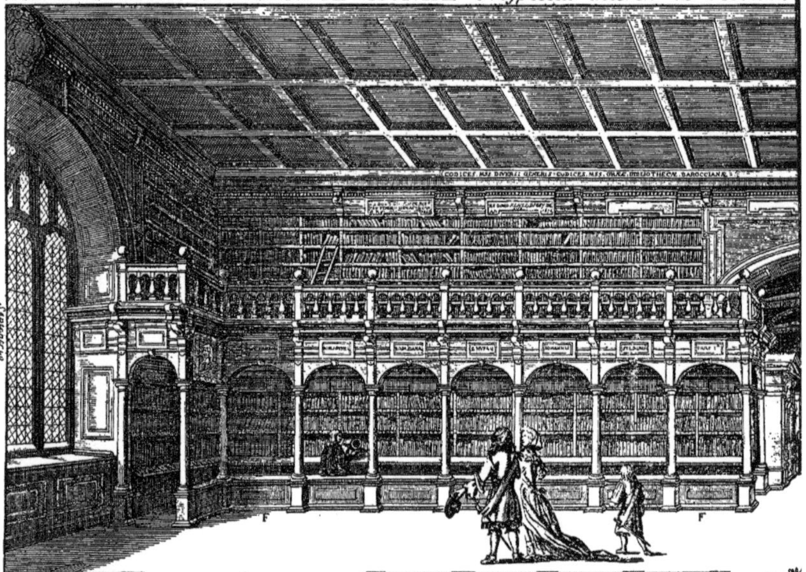

Viro admodum Reverendo vitæ integritate morum candore, spectatissimo; Scientiarum Academiæ ornamento; pro Dna Margareta Comitissa Richmondiæ Theologiæ Professori ANÆ Typum, Cui (dum IPSE præfuit) AUCTARIUM SELDENI Pelion sc. Ossæ gigan

Dav. Loggan delin. et

ide of ye Public or BODLEIAN LIBRARY in OXFORD from ye East

E. E. Sellæ foruliq; ex adverso positis in F F respondentes G. G. G. Fenestræ ad Occidentem

ide of ye Public or BODLEIAN LIBRARY in OXFORD from ye West

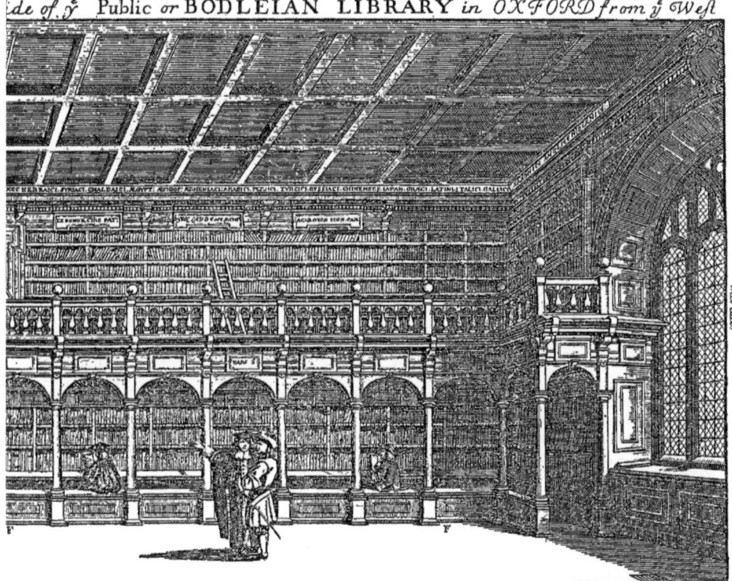

nnuum, Atlanti Dno THOMÆ BARLOVIO S.T. Dri Collegij Reginensis Præposito,
τιβρητω; et exteris hîc hospitantibus semper Patrono Hunc BIBLIOTHECÆ BODLEI
sed felici conjecit; optimo jure, debitâq; observantiâ D. D. C Q. Dav: Loggan

.SRM

oberts, John Williams, o.s. Robert, of Derwen, co. Denbigh, gent. JESUS COLL., matric. 21 May, 1831, aged 19; B.A. 1836, M.A. 1839.

oberts, John Williams, 1s. John, of Ruabon, co. Denbigh, gent. JESUS COLL., matric. 27 Feb., 1840, aged 17; scholar 1842-6, B.A. 1843.

oberts, Laurence Guilderdale, 3s. Augustus Morton, of Wadsley, Yorks, D.Med. NON-COLL., matric. 14 Oct., 1882, aged 19.

oberts, Lewis, 6s. William, of Bampton, Oxon, pleb. MERTON COLL., matric. 24 May, 1832, aged 19; clerk and scholar 1832-4 (chorister New College 1821-7).

oberts, Owen, 1s. Owen, of Clynnog, co. Carnarvon, gent. JESUS COLL., matric. 22 March, 1854, aged 18; scholar 1856-8, B.A. 1858, M.A. 1860, bar.-at-law, Inner Temple, 1865, on headquarters staff War Office 1859-66, clerk to the Clothworkers' Company. See Foster's *Men at the Bar*. **[5]**

oberts, Peter, s. John, of Eglwysfaih, co. Denbigh, pleb. JESUS COLL., matric. 19 Feb., 1729-30, aged 21.

oberts, Philip, s. Jeremiah, of Sutton Coldfield, co. Warwick, cler. MERTON COLL., matric. 22 May, 1793, aged 17; B.A. 1797 (? vicar of Claverdon, co. Warwick, 1813, until his death in 1817).

oberts, Richard, s. John, of Clannor, co. Carnarvon, pleb. JESUS COLL., matric. 5 June, 1716, aged 16.

oberts, Richard, s. Thomas, of St. David's, co. Pembroke, pleb. JESUS COLL., matric. 13 March, 1716-7, aged 20.

oberts, Richard, s. Walter, of Abergavenny, co. Monmouth, gent. JESUS COLL., matric. 17 Dec., 1717, aged 16; bar.-at-law, Middle Temple, 1725 (? died a bencher 27 Nov., 1772). See *Gent.'s Mag.* **[10]**

oberts, Richard, B.A. from JESUS COLL., 10 June, 1721, M.A. 18 April, 1724.

oberts, Richard, s. Ed., of Westbury, co. Gloucester, gent. PEMBROKE COLL., matric. 17 Dec., 1719, aged 17; B.A. 1723, M.A. 1726.

oberts, Richard, s. William, of Bristol (city), pleb. JESUS COLL., matric. 15 May, 1746, aged 17; servitor 1745-9, Pauline exhibitioner 1749-51, B.A. 22 Feb., 1749-50, M.A. 1759, B. & D.D. 1773, high-master St. Paul's School 1769-1814, died in 1823. See *St. Paul's School Reg.*, 82.

oberts, Richard, s. William Hancock, of Worcester (city), doctor. MERTON COLL., matric. 9 Nov., 1801, aged 17; B.A. 1805, M.A. 1815, minor canon Worcester Cathedral 1814, vicar of Stewkley, Bucks, 1830, until his death 21 Feb., 1859.

oberts, Richard Earnshaw, 1s. Joseph, of Almondsbury, Yorks, arm. ST. EDMUND HALL, matric. 4 July, 1828, aged 18; B.A. 1832, M.A. 1835, perp. curate St. George's, Barnsley, 1838-61, rector of Richmond, Yorks, since 1861. **[15]**

oberts, Richard Wightwick, 3s. John Coryton, of St. Anthony, Cornwall, gent. PEMBROKE COLL., matric. 26 June, 1854, aged 18; scholar 1854-62, B.A. 1859.

oberts, Robert, s. Robert, of Trewsfynydd, pleb. JESUS COLL., matric. 23 March, 1737-8, aged 18; B.A. 1741, M.A. 1744.

oberts, Robert, s. David, of Llanvair, co. Denbigh, pleb. JESUS COLL., matric. 22 March, 1744-5, aged 18; B.A. 1748, M.A. 1751, B.D. 1758.

oberts, Robert, s. Griffith, of Corwen, co. Merioneth, pleb. JESUS COLL., matric. 22 June, 1745, aged 18; B.A. 1749.

oberts, Robert, s. Ellis, of Llanfagrath, co. Merioneth, gent. JESUS COLL., matric. 21 Nov., 1765, aged 20. **[20]**

oberts, Robert, s. David, of Trawsfynydd, co. Merioneth, gent. JESUS COLL., matric. 15 May, 1766, aged 18; B.A. 1770.

oberts, Robert, s. Edward, of Ruthin, co. Denbigh, gent. JESUS COLL., matric. 28 March, 1787, aged 18; B.A. 1791. See *Gent.'s Mag.*, 1858, i. 111.

Roberts, Robert, s. Robert, of Llanynys, co. Denbigh, gent. JESUS COLL., matric. 20 March, 1793, aged 20; B.A. 1796, M.A. 1799.

Roberts, Robert, s. John, of Derwen, co. Denbigh, gent. HERTFORD COLL., matric. 3 Dec., 1796, aged 18; B.A. 1800.

Roberts, Robert, s. Robert, of Dolgelly, co. Merioneth, gent. JESUS COLL., matric. 13 March, 1799, aged 19. **[25]**

Roberts, Robert Jones, 1s. Robert Jones, of Llansannon, co. Denbigh, cler. ST. JOHN'S COLL., matric. 21 May, 1830, aged 18; B.A. from NEW INN HALL 1834, M.A. 1836, rector of Denbigh 1843-55, and of Ysceifiog, Flints, 1855, until his death 17 June, 1873.

Roberts, Robert Laurence, 2s. Roger Elliot, of St. George's, Hanover Square, London, arm. ORIEL COLL., matric. 27 June, 1829, aged 18; B.A. from ST. JOHN'S COLL. 1833, M.A. 1836.

Roberts, Robert Lloyd Anwyl, s. Robert, of Llanrhaiadr, co. Denbigh, cler. JESUS COLL., matric. 28 May, 1816, aged 18; B.A. 1820, M.A. 1825.

Roberts, Robert Prys, o.s. Francis, of Dolgelly, co. Merioneth, gent. JESUS COLL., matric. 4 May, 1829, aged 18.

Roberts, Roland Bennett Stokes, 2s. Edward Stokes, of St. Oswald's, Chester (city), arm. ORIEL COLL., matric. 7 April, 1859, aged 18; B.A. 1862. **[30]**

Roberts, Samuel, s. Richard, of Staverton, Northants, pleb. CHRIST CHURCH, matric. 27 Nov., 1728, aged 18; B.A. 1732.

Roberts, Samuel Wallis, s. Bryan, of Drewsteignton, Devon, doctor. PEMBROKE COLL., matric. 3 Nov., 1806, aged 14; fellow until 1839, B.A. 1813, M.A. 1814, B.D. 1834.

Roberts, Thomas, s. Ric., of city of St. David's, pleb. JESUS COLL., matric. 16 April, 1741, aged 18; B.A. 22 Feb., 1744-5.

Roberts, Thomas, s. John, of Soulbury, Bucks, pleb. TRINITY COLL., matric. 13 March, 1743-4, aged 19.

Roberts, Thomas, s. Philip, of Crawley, Beds, arm. QUEEN'S COLL., matric. 6 April, 1753, aged 16; B.A. 1756. **[35]**

Roberts, Thomas, s. Hugh, of St. George's, Middlesex, arm. BRASENOSE COLL., matric. 13 April, 1769, aged 18; B.A. 1773, M.A. 1776. See *Gent.'s Mag.*, 1816, i. 379; & 1824, ii. 570.

Roberts, Thomas, s. Morris, of Llanrhaiadr, co. Denbigh, pleb. CHRIST CHURCH, matric. 7 April, 1775, aged 18. See *Gent.'s Mag.*, 1829, ii. 377.

Roberts, Thomas, s. Thomas, of Denbigh (town), gent. JESUS COLL., matric. 16 May, 1782, aged 19; exhibitioner EXETER COLL. 1783, B.A. 1786, M.A. 1789. See *Boase*, 147.

Roberts, Thomas, s. John, of Bodean, co. Carnarvon, cler. HERTFORD COLL., matric. 12 April, 1783, aged 18; B.A. 1786, M.A. 1788.

Roberts, Thomas, 'vitrarius;' privilegiatus 2 Dec., 1788. **[40]**

Roberts, Thomas, s. Foulk, of Llandernog, co. Denbigh, pleb. HERTFORD COLL., matric. 26 May, 1800, aged 17; B.A. from JESUS COLL. 1804, vicar of Barholme with Stowe, and of Deeping St. James, co. Lincoln, 1815, and rector of St. Mary, Stamford 1828, until his death 13 April, 1847.

Roberts, Thomas, 1s. William (Prowting), of Bath (city), gent. WORCESTER COLL., matric. 17 June, 1851, aged 19; B.A. 1856, M.A. 1858, bar.-at-law, Inner Temple, 1858, rector of Belstone, Devon, 1869, until his death 28 Dec., 1876. See Foster's *Men at the Bar*.

Roberts, Thomas, 4s. John, of Llanbadarn-Faur, co. Cardigan, gent. JESUS COLL., matric. 21 Oct., 1873, aged 19; B.A. 1880, M.A. 1882, chaplain R.N. 1882.

Roberts, Thomas Arthur, 4s. Thomas, of Cheadle, Cheshire, arm. TRINITY COLL., matric. 16 Oct., 1873, aged 19; B.A. 1878, bar.-at-law, Inner Temple, 1881. See Foster's *Men at the Bar.*

Roberts, Thomas Aylesbury, s. Wilson Aylesbury, of Ribbesford, co. Worcester, arm. CHRIST CHURCH, matric. 28 Nov., 1793, aged 18; B.A. 1797, M.A. 1800, died vicar of Hagley, co. Worcester, in 1803, brother of Wilson A. 1778.

Roberts, Thomas Edward, o.s. Thomas, of Abererch, co. Carnarvon, cler. JESUS COLL., matric. 9 June, 1832, aged 18.

Roberts, Thomas Francis, 1s. Thomas, of Aberdovey, co. Merioneth, gent. NON-COLL., matric. 31 May, 1879, aged 18; scholar ST. JOHN'S COLL., 1879-84, B.A. 1883, M.A. 1888.

Roberts, Thomas Gough, o.s. Robert, of Llanrhaiadr, near Denbigh, gent. WADHAM COLL., matric. 20 Feb., 1840, aged 18. [5]

Roberts, Thomas Griffith, s. Thomas, of Ruthin, co. Denbigh, cler. BRASENOSE COLL., matric. 28 Jan., 1812, aged 18; B.A. 1815, M.A. 1818, fellow 1819-31, tutor 1820-5, a canon of St. Asaph 1830, rector of Llanrwst, co. Denbigh, 1831, until his death 28 Aug., 1852.

Roberts, (Sir) Thomas Howland (Bart.), 1s. Walter, of Cork, Ireland, Bart. BALLIOL COLL., matric. 24 April, 1823, aged 18; 3rd baronet, died 1 March, 1864. See Foster's *Baronetage* & *Eton School Lists.*

Roberts, Thomas Opie, 1s. John Ryland, of Lyncomb, Somerset, gent. WORCESTER COLL., matric. 14 Oct., 1865, aged 19; B.A. 1871, M.A. 1873, vicar of Haverhill, Suffolk, 1878.

Roberts, Thomas Turner, s. William, of Worcester (city), doctor. TRINITY COLL., matric. 3 May, 1794, aged 16; B.A. 1798.

Roberts, Thomas Walton, 2s. Thomas, of Britfield, co. Cork, baronet. TRINITY COLL., matric. 22 Nov., 1827, aged 18; of Glassenbury Castle, Kent, died 4 Oct., 1882. See Foster's *Baronetage.* [10]

Roberts, Walter, s. William, of Grosmount, co. Monmouth, gent. WADHAM COLL., matric. 11 May, 1749, aged 17; B.A. 1753.

Roberts, William, s. John, of Kidwelly, co. Carmarthen, pleb. JESUS COLL., matric. 13 March, 1716-7, aged 17; B.A. 1720.

Roberts, William, s. William, of Jacobstow, Devon, cler. EXETER COLL., matric. 16 March, 1729-30, aged 18; B.A. 1733, M.A. 1737.

Roberts, William, s. Thomas, of Rhoscolyn, co. Anglesea, gent. JESUS COLL., matric. 6 July, 1730, aged 16; B.A. 1734.

Roberts, William, s. Robert, of Chirk, co. Denbigh, cler. BRASENOSE COLL., matric. 18 May, 1737, aged 19; B.A. 27 Feb., 1740-1. [15]

Roberts, William, s. Robert, of Trawsfynydd, co. Merioneth, pleb. JESUS COLL., matric. 9 March, 1743-4, aged 19; B.A. 1747.

Roberts, William, 'Southam carrier;' privilegiatus 19 Dec., 1751, of Southam, Warwick.

Roberts, William, s. William, of Oswestry, Salop, cler. PEMBROKE COLL., matric. 23 Oct., 1766, aged 18; Rev. W. R. died at Oswestry 1816, aged 68.

Roberts, William, 'caementarius;' privilegiatus, 17 Jan., 1778.

Roberts, William s. John, of Carnarvon (town), gent. JESUS COLL., matric. 11 Nov., 1779, aged 18; B.A. 1783, M.A. 1787. [20]

Roberts, William, s. William, of Newington, Surrey, arm. CORPUS CHRISTI COLL., matric. 18 July, 1783, aged 16; B.A. 1787, M.A. 1791, bar.-at-law, Middle Temple, 1806, a commissioner of bankrupts, and charity commissioner, died in 1849.

Roberts, William, s. John, of Llanbedrog, co. Carnarvon, archdeacon of Merioneth. WORCESTER COLL., matric. 2 May, 1789, aged 18; B.A. 1793.

Roberts, William, of PEMBROKE COLL., Cambridge (B.A. 1788, M.A. 1791), s. William, of Monmouth, cler. MERTON COLL., incorp. 11 July, 1791, aged 24; B.Med. 7 July, 1792.

Roberts, William, s. Samuel, of Godalming, Surrey, gent. ST. EDMUND HALL, matric. 9 Dec., 1801, aged 22.

Roberts, William, s. John, of Eton, Bucks, doctor. WORCESTER COLL., matric. 27 May, 1811, aged 19.

Roberts, William, 1s. Richard, of Horton, Salop, gent. QUEEN'S COLL., matric. 26 Oct., 1837, aged 20. [25]

Roberts, William, o.s. David, of Tyn-y-Cornel, co. Merioneth, gent. JESUS COLL., matric. 26 Oct., 1875, aged 17; scholar 1875-9.

Roberts, William Anwyl, s. William, of Denbigh (town), arm. JESUS COLL., matric. 16 Dec., 1807, aged 23; B.A. 1811.

Roberts, William Anwyl, o.s. William A., of Llanrwst, co. Denbigh, cler. JESUS COLL., matric. 25 May, 1844, aged 18; B.A. 1848, held various curacies 1849-65, rector of Llanddyfnan, Anglesey, 1868.

Roberts, William Augustus, 1s. William, of Oxford, gent. NON-COLL., matric. 18 Oct., 1883, aged 19; B.A. 1886. [30]

Roberts, William David, 2s. John, of Amlwch, Isle of Anglesea, gent. JESUS COLL., matric. 17 June, 1830, aged 19; B.A. 1834, M.A. 1837.

Roberts, William David, 1s. David, of Caron, co. Cardigan, gent. JESUS COLL., matric. 21 Jan., 1885, aged 23.

Roberts, William Hancock, s. William, of Bushley, co. Warwick, gent. MAGDALEN HALL, matric. 14 July, 1769, aged 24; B.A. 1787, M.A. 1788, B. & D.D. 1788, rector of Broadwas, co. Worcester, 1783, until his death 10 Oct., 1814.

Roberts, William James Bethell Wynne, 2s. John, of Llangristiolus, Isle of Anglesea, cler. JESUS COLL., matric. 20 April, 1864, aged 19; B.A. 1868, M.A. 1870, vicar of Shelford, Notts, 1875-7.

Roberts, William Morris, 1s. Ellis, of Festiniog, co. Merioneth, cler. NON-COLL., matric. 22 Jan., 1876, aged 20; B.A. 1878, vicar of Bettws-y-Crwyn, co. Hereford, 1886. [35]

Roberts, William Robert, 3s. William, of Hubberston, co. Pembroke, gent. PEMBROKE COLL., matric. 16 Nov., 1848, aged 18; B.A. from ST. MARY HALL 1853, rector of Panteague 1855, until his death 1 June, 1856.

Roberts, William Robert, 1s. Thomas, of Milford Haven, co. Pembroke, arm. MERTON COLL., matric. 22 Oct., 1875, aged 19; of Hamilton House, Milford Haven, bar.-at-law, Inner Temple, 1887.

Roberts, William Walter, 1s. John Walter, of London, arm. MERTON COLL., matric. 15 March, 1849, aged 19.

Roberts, Wilson Aylesbury, s. Wilson Aylesbury, of Bewdley, co. Worcester, arm. CHRIST CHURCH, matric. 13 Feb., 1778, aged 17; M.P. Bewdley, 1818-32, died 28 Nov., 1853, brother of Thomas Aylesbury 1793.

Roberts, Wilson Aylesbury, 1s. Wilson Aylesbury, of Ledbury, co. Hereford, gent. QUEEN'S COLL., matric. 26 April, 1883, aged 37; B.A. 1886. [40]

Robertson, Abraham, s. Abraham, of Dunse, co. Berwick, pleb. CHRIST CHURCH, matric. 7 Dec., 1775, aged 22; B.A. 1779, M.A. 1782, B. & D.D. 1807, F.R.S. 1795, Savilian professor of geometry 1797-1810, of astronomy 1810, and Radcliffe observer 1810, until his death 4 Dec., 1826. See *Gent.'s Mag.*, 1827, i. 176.

Robertson, Alan Maxwell, 5s. Robert, of Torquay, Devon, arm. EXETER COLL., matric. 22 Oct., 1880, aged 19.

Robertson, Archibald, 1s. George Samuel, of Sywell, Northants, cler. TRINITY COLL., matric. 14 Oct., 1872, aged 19; scholar 1872-6, B.A. 1876, fellow 1876-86, M.A. 1879, lecturer 1876-83, and dean 1879-83, principal Hatfield Hall, Durham, 1883.

Robertson, Archibald, 2s. Archibald, of Plymouth, arm. ST. MARY HALL, matric. 15 March, 1872, aged 45; B.A. 1876, M.A. 1878, vicar of St. Saviour's, Brixton Hill, Surrey, 1875, until his death 3 Aug., 1879.

Robertson, Benjamin, 1s. Benjamin, of Dunphail, co. Moray, gent. BALLIOL COLL., matric. 16 Oct., 1883, aged 19; of the Indian Civil Service 1883.

Robertson, Casper Ludovic (Van Uytrecht), 3s. Charles, of Liverpool, gent. PEMBROKE COLL., matric. 26 Oct., 1877, aged 23.

Robertson, Charles, s. James, of Blair, co. Perth, arm. BALLIOL COLL., matric. 11 Jan., 1787, aged 17.

Robertson, Charles Alexander Lockhart, of CAIUS COLL., Cambridge (B.Med. 1856, D.Med. 1864); (adm. 'ad eundem' 4 April, 1857), Linacre demonstrator of anatomy 1860. [5]

Robertson, Charles Gray, o.s. Alexander Cunningham, of Simla, East Indies, arm. BALLIOL COLL., matric. 15 Oct., 1873, aged 18; lieutenant 8th foot in 1878, a student of the Inner Temple 1881.

Robertson, Divie, 3s. Divic, of St. Martin's, Middlesex, arm. CHRIST CHURCH, matric. 26 May, 1841, aged 18; B.A. 1845, M.A. 1849, held various curacies 1846-62, vicar of Henfield, Sussex, 1872; brother of Edward Lovett.

Robertson, Donald, s. Charles, of Perth, North Britain, pleb. CHRIST CHURCH, matric. 20 March, 1739-40, aged 19.

Robertson, Donald Ogilvy Morley, o.s. Duncan Stewart, of Edinburgh, arm. ST. MARY HALL, matric. 25 Oct., 1866, aged 19.

Robertson, Duncan Macpherson, 4s. William, of Victoria, Australia, gent. NEW INN HALL, matric. 23 April, 1883, aged 19. [10]

Robertson, Eben William, o.s. Francis, of Clapham, Surrey, arm. WORCESTER COLL., matric. 2 May, 1833, aged 17; B.A. 1837, bar.-at-law, Lincoln's Inn, 1845, died 3 June, 1874.

Robertson, Edgar William, 1s. Robert, of Edinburgh, gent. EXETER COLL., matric. 10 Oct., 1873, aged 20; of Auchenleeks, co. Perth, sometime captain Beds militia.

Robertson, Edmund, 1s. Edmund, of Kinnaird, co. Perth, gent. LINCOLN COLL., matric. 30 April, 1867, aged 21, scholar 1866-70, B.A. 1870; fellow CORPUS CHRISTI COLL. 1870, M.A. 1874, vice-president 1881, bar.-at-law, Lincoln's Inn, 1871, M.P. Dundee (Nov.) 1885. See Foster's *Men at the Bar*.

Robertson, Edward Hercules, 1s. Alexander, of Forfar, N.B., arm. NEW COLL., matric. 16 Oct., 1885, aged 18.

Robertson, Edward Lewis, 1s. Lewis Shuldham Barrington, of Lycombe, near Bath, gent. MAGDALEN COLL., matric. 15 Oct., 1870, aged 18; demy 1869-73.

Robertson, Edward Lovett, 2s. Divie, of St. Giles's, Bloomsbury, London, arm. EXETER COLL., matric. 27 Jan., 1831, aged 17; brother of Divle and father of Rowland. See *Eton School Lists*. [15]

Robertson, Frederick William, 1s. Frederick, of St. Anne's, Soho, London, arm. BRASENOSE COLL., matric. 4 May, 1837, aged 21; B.A. 1841, M.A. 1844, the well-known theologian, minister of Trinity Chapel, Brighton, 1847, until his death 14 Aug., 1853.

Robertson, George Arthur, 5s. Charles, of Walton, near Liverpool, gent. EXETER COLL., matric. 22 Jan., 1876, aged 18.

Robertson, George Chaplin, 4s. David Souter, of Edinburgh, arm. UNIVERSITY COLL., matric. 13 Oct., 1876, aged 19.

Robertson, George Manship, 3s. Frederick, of Painswick, co. Gloucester, arm. BRASENOSE COLL., matric. 16 Oct., 1879, aged 18; scholar 1879-84, B.A. 1883. [20]

Robertson, George Pringle, 3s. William, of Hobart Town, Tasmania, arm. TRINITY COLL., matric. 5 June, 1862, aged 18; B.A. 1866. See *Rugby School Reg.*

Robertson, George Samuel, o.s. Archibald, of Northampton (town), D.Med. EXETER COLL., matric. 12 Dec., 1843, aged 18; B.A. 1847, M.A. 1850, died 12 Nov., 1874. See *Rugby School Reg.*, 213.

Robertson, Gilbert Metcalfe, 1s. Thomas Campbell, of Calcutta, East Indies, arm. MERTON COLL., matric. 5 Dec., 1850, aged 18; sometime captain 1st royal engineers, had his horse shot under him at Balaclava. See *Eton School Lists.*

Robertson, Gordon, 2s. William Henry, of Chesterfield, co. Derby, doctor. UNIVERSITY COLL., matric. 15 Oct., 1859, aged 17; B.A. 1865, M.A. 1867, vicar of Earl-Sterndale, co. Derby, 1871.

Robertson-Barclay, James, s. James, of Dunfermline, co. Fife, arm. BALLIOL COLL., matric. 19 May, 1772, aged 19, B.A. 1776, M.A. 1778; Radcliffe travelling fellow UNIVERSITY COLL. 1780, B.Med. & D.Med. 1783, assumed the additional surname of BARCLAY, Oct., 1799, fellow College of Physicians 1787, physician to St. George's Hospital 1785-1800, F.R.S. 1790, physician extraordinary to Princess of Wales 1799, died in 1827. See Munk's *Roll*, ii. 371. [25]

Robertson, Rev. James, 3s. David, of East Hendred, Berks, gent. PEMBROKE COLL., matric. 20 Nov., 1827, aged 17; scholar 1827-35, B.A. 1831, M.A. 1834, died 22 April, 1875.

Robertson, James, 1s. Murdoch, of Edinburgh, gent. WORCESTER COLL., matric. 17 Oct., 1870, aged 19; B.A. 1876, a student of the Inner Temple 1872.

Robertson, James Alexander, o.s. James, of Calcutta, East Indies, arm. CHRIST CHURCH, matric. 24 May, 1823, aged 17.

Robertson, James Anderson, 4s. Robert, of Hobart Town, Tasmania, gent. ST. EDMUND HALL, matric. 22 Oct., 1874, aged 21; B.A. 1877, M.A. 1881.

Robertson, James Murray, 1s. James Murray, of Colombo, Ceylon, gent. NEW COLL., matric. 14 Oct., 1870, aged 19; of Ceylon, merchant. See *Rugby School Reg.* [30]

Robertson, Rev. James Richard Bagott, o.s. James, of Edinburgh, arm. WADHAM COLL., matric. 20 Jan., 1869, aged 20; B.A. & M.A. from HERTFORD COLL. 1875.

Robertson, James Scott, 2s. James Scott, of London, arm. QUEEN'S COLL., matric. 21 Oct., 1879, aged 18.

Robertson, John, 1s. James Alfred, of Melcombe Regis, Dorset, gent. QUEEN'S COLL., matric. 3 Nov., 1871, aged 19; B.A. 1875, M.A. 1878, vicar of Holy Trinity, Stroud Green, 1880-5, of St. Mary's, Kilburn, London, 1885.

Robertson, John Cunningham, o.s. Francis, of Isle of Jamaica, West Indies, arm. UNIVERSITY COLL., matric. 15 March, 1827, aged 17; B.A. 1831, M.A. 1835.

Robertson, John Elliot Pasley, 1s. Robert, of Greenwich, Kent, doctor. EXETER COLL., matric. 30 March, 1822, aged 17; B.C.L. & D.C.L. from MAGDALEN HALL 1835, advocate Doctors' Commons 1836, chancellor of the diocese of Rochester, and of St. Alban's, died 27 Feb., 1886. See Foster's *Men at the Bar*. [35]

Robertson, John Russell Thompson, 2s. James, of Edinburgh, arm. UNIVERSITY COLL., matric. 16 Oct., 1874, aged 18; B.A. 1878, M.A. 1882.

Robertson, Rev. Joseph, s. Joseph, of High Knipe, Westmoreland, pleb. QUEEN'S COLL., matric. 17 March, 1745-6, aged 19; B.A. 1749, died in London, 19 Jan., 1802, aged 75.

Robertson, Richard (Allin), 2s. James, of Southsea, Hants, cler. EXETER COLL., matric. 28 Jan., 1865, aged 18, scholar 1864-7; scholar PETER HOUSE, Cambridge, 1867, junior optime & B.A. 1871. See *Coll. Reg.*, 161.

Robertson, Rev. Robert, s. Robert, of Halesowen, Salop, pleb. MAGDALEN HALL, matric. 2 Dec. 1782, aged 19; B A. 1786, died head-master of the Free Grammar School, Halesowen in 1825.

Robertson, Robert, 1s. Robert, of London, arm. CHRIST CHURCH, matric. 23 Oct., 1834, aged 17; B.A. from NEW INN HALL 1841, a student of Lincoln's Inn 1838. See *Eton School Lists.*

Robertson, Robert Henry, 3s. Duncan, of Isle of Jamaica, arm. TRINITY COLL., matric. 6 June, 1860, aged 18.

Robertson, Rowland Edward, 1s. Edward Lovett, of Leghorn, Italy, gent. ST. JOHN'S COLL., matric. 20 Jan., 1864, aged 19.

Robertson, Thomas, s. Thomas, of Orton, Westmoreland, pleb. QUEEN'S COLL., matric. 4 April, 1759, aged 22; B.A. 1764, M.A. 1767.

Robertson, Thomas Herbert, o.s. Thomas Storm, of London, D.Med. (subs. arm.) MAGDALEN COLL., matric. 29 Jan., 1869, aged 19; B.A. 1872, bar.-at-law, Lincoln's Inn, 1873. See Foster's *Men at the Bar.* **[5]**

Robertson, Thomas Shute, o.s. James, of Edinburgh, gent. BALLIOL COLL., matric. 17 Oct., 1864, aged 19; B.A. 1869, bar.-at-law, Lincoln's Inn, 1871. See Foster's *Men at the Bar.*

Robertson, William, o.s. William, of Bath (city), doctor. EXETER COLL., matric. 26 June, 1820, aged 17; demy MAGDALEN COLL. 1824-36, B.A. 1825, M.A. 1828, fellow 1836-77, D.C.L. 1842, bursar 1844, bar.-at-law, Lincoln's Inn, 1828, died 17 June, 1877. See *Bloxam*, vii. 292.

Robertson, William, 2s. William, of Tasmania, gent. WADHAM COLL., matric. 28 Oct., 1857, aged 18; B.A. 1861, bar.-at-law, Middle Temple, 1863. See Foster's *Men at the Bar.*

Robertson, William Anstruther, 3s. William, of Edinburgh, arm. ORIEL COLL., matric. 10 June, 1858, aged 18.

Robertson, William Henry, 1s. William Henry, of Buxton, co. Derby, arm. CHRIST CHURCH, matric. 27 May, 1858, aged 18; B.A. 1863, M.A. 1866, minor canon Durham Cathedral 1866, sacrist 1872, sub-librarian 1874, until his death 2 Aug., 1885.

Robertson, William Ker, 2s. George Samuel, of Sywell, Northants, arm. MAGDALEN COLL., matric. 18 Oct., 1873, aged 18. **[11]**

Robertson, William St. Leonards, 1s. William, of Hobart Town, Tasmania, gent. WADHAM COLL., matric. 22 Oct., 1884, aged 20.

Robertson, William Theodore Melvill, 3s. Alexander, of Berwick-on-Tweed, gent. LINCOLN COLL., matric. 23 Oct., 1880, aged 18.

Robeson, Arthur Hemming, 1s. Hemming, of Forthampton, co. Gloucester, cler. UNIVERSITY COLL., matric. 15 Oct., 1881, aged 18; lieutenant 2nd batt. the King's (Shropshire light infantry) 1884.

Robeson, Hemming, o.s. William Henry, of Bromsgrove, co. Worcester, arm. BALLIOL COLL., matric. 30 Nov., 1850, aged 17; scholar 1850-7, B.A. 1855, M.A. 1858, curate of Bray, Berks, 1857-62, vicar of Forthampton, co. Gloucester, 1863-74, of Mildenhall, Suffolk, 1874-7, of Tewkesbury and Walton-Cardiff 1877, canon of Bristol 1884. **[15]**

Robeson, Herbert Edward, 3s. Hemming, of Forthampton, co. Gloucester, cler. ORIEL COLL., matric. 23 Oct., 1885, aged 19.

Robin, Arthur Hammond, o.s. James Hammond, of St. Saviour's, Jersey, arm. NEW COLL., matric. 14 Oct., 1870, aged 18; B.A. 1874, bar.-at-law, Inner Temple, 1876. See Foster's *Men at the Bar.*

Robin, Charles Janvrin, 1s. Charles William, of St. Helier's, Isle of Jersey, arm. UNIVERSITY COLL., matric. 19 Oct., 1867, aged 19; B.A. 1872, M.A. 1874, bar.-at-law, Inner Temple, 1875. See Foster's *Men at the Bar.*

Robin, John William, 4s. John Nicholas, of Naples, gent. PEMBROKE COLL., matric. 28 Oct., 1886, aged 18.

Robin, Leonard Philip, 2s. Philip Raulin, of Barnston, Cheshire, cler. HERTFORD COLL., matric. 4 June, 1881, aged 18. **[20]**

Robin, Percival Carteret, 1s. Philip Raulin, of Barnston, Cheshire, cler. ORIEL COLL., matric. 19 Oct., 1875, aged 19; B.A. 1879, M.A. 1882, vicar of Oxton, Cheshire, 1884.

Robin, Philip Raulin, 2s. John, of West Kirby, Cheshire, arm. BRASENOSE COLL., matric. 13 June, 1833, aged 18; B.A. 1837, M.A. 1840, rector of Woodchurch, Cheshire, 1861, hon. canon of Chester 1885.

Robins, Arthur, 2s. George Henry, of London, gent. MAGDALEN HALL, matric. 17 March, 1866, aged 32; M.A. Lambeth 1866, rector of Beaulieu, Hants, 1869-73, and of Nursling, Hants, 1873, rector of Holy Trinity, Windsor, 1873, hon. chaplain in ordinary to the Queen 1878-82, chaplain in ordinary 1882, chaplain to the Prince of Wales 1881, acting-chaplain to the forces 1873.

Robins, Arthur Geoffrey, 1s. Arthur, of Teddington, Surrey, cler. NON-COLL., matric. 11 Oct., 1879, aged 18; chorister MAGDALEN COLL. 1870-6.

Robins, Charles Matthew, 1s. Sanderson, of Cranbourn, Dorset, cler. ORIEL COLL., matric. 14 Nov., 1844, aged 17; B.A. 1848, M.A. 1851, curate of St. Clement Danes. See *Eton School Lists.* **[25]**

Robins, Daniel, s. John, of Wantage, Berks, gent. MAGDALEN HALL, matric. 31 May, 1775, aged 19; B.A. 1779.

Robins, George Augustus, 1s. George Henry, of Turnham Green, Chiswick, Middlesex, gent. PEMBROKE COLL., matric. 5 Dec., 1851, aged 19; B.A. 1855, M.A. 1861, rector of Bishopstone, co. Hereford, 1863-75, of Hedsor, Bucks, 1876-80, and of Eccleston, Cheshire, 1880.

Robins, John William, o.s. John, of St. Andrew's, London, arm. ST. JOHN'S COLL., matric. 21 Jan., 1842, aged 20; B.A. 1847, M.A. 1849, of the Elms, Watford.

Robins, Percy, y.s. George, of London, arm. BRASENOSE COLL., matric. 23 Nov., 1865, aged 19; B.A. 1869, a student of Lincoln's Inn 1869.

Robins, Sanderson, 2s. Matthew, of St. Mary's, Newington, Surrey, gent. EXETER COLL., matric. 28 Oct., 1818, aged 17; B.A. 1823, M.A. 1825, rector of Edmonsham, Dorset, 1826, and of St. James's, Dover, 1854-6, vicar of St. Peter's, Isle of Thanet, 1856, until his death 5 Dec., 1862. **[30]**

Robins, Stafford Denison, 2s. Arthur, of Caterham, Surrey, cler. ST. EDMUND HALL, matric. 17 May, 1880, aged 17.

Robins, Thomas, s. Thomas, of Bromham, Wilts, pleb. JESUS COLL., matric. 8 Dec., 1763, aged 12.

Robinson, Alexander Dawson. BRASENOSE COLL., 1842. See NOWELL, page 1031.

Robinson, Alfred, 5s. William Fothergill, of Liverpool, Lancashire, arm. UNIVERSITY COLL., matric. 30 May, 1860, aged 19, scholar 1860-5, B.A. 1864; fellow NEW COLL. 1865, M.A. 1867, precentor 1882, tutor 1865-75, and junior bursar 1868, sub-warden 1870, senior dean 1873, senior bursar 1875, lecturer 1875, a student of Lincoln's Inn 1865.

Robinson, Arthur, 5s. Augustus, of London, gent. EXETER COLL., matric. 13 Oct., 1871, aged 19.

Robinson, Arthur Dalgarno, of TRINITY HALL, Cambridge (B.A. 1856, M.A. 1860); adm. 'comitatis causa' 9 June, 1864, vicar of St. Clement's, Kensington, 1860. **[36]**

Robinson, Arthur Edward, 1s. John Ellill, of Charlton-upon-Otmoor, Oxon, cler. NEW COLL., matric. 3 Nov., 1853, aged 18; fellow 1853-78, B.A. 1857, M.A. 1860, rector of Stockton, co. Warwick, 1877-8, and of Wootton, Oxon, 1878, until his death 29 April, 1884, brother of Frederick 1864, and of George Croke.

Robinson, Augustine, o.s. Matthew, of Dulwich, Surrey, arm. BALLIOL COLL., matric. 16 Dec., 1834, aged 18; B.A. 1838, bar.-at-law, Lincoln's Inn, 1845, father of Julian. See Foster's *Men at the Bar.*

Robinson, Charles, 2s. Charles, of Grasmere, Westmoreland, arm. QUEEN'S COLL., matric. 29 Oct., 1846, aged 20; B.A. 1850, M.A. 1853, vicar of Bishop Burton, Yorks, 1853-72.

Robinson, Charles Ernest Russell, 1s. John, of Hollinwood, Lancashire, cler. NON-COLL., matric. 13 Oct., 1883, aged 18; B.A. 1888.

Robinson, Charles Edward Ricketts, of TRINITY COLL., Cambridge (B.A. 1852, M.A. 1855); adm. 'ad eundem' 10 Nov., 1859, hon. canon of Rochester 1866, incumbent of Holy Trinity, Milton-next-Gravesend, 1861-70, vicar of St. John, Torquay, 1870, until his death 4 Jan., 1881.

Robinson, Rev. Charles James, 1s. James Mould, of Beverley, Yorks, gent. QUEEN'S COLL., matric. 22 Nov., 1849, aged 18; B.A. 1854, M.A. 1856.

Robinson, Charles James, 1s. John, of Newton Heath, near Manchester, cler. CHRIST CHURCH, matric. 22 Oct., 1868, aged 19; exhibitioner 1868-72, B.A. 1872, M.A. 1875, perp. curate St. Matthias, Liverpool, 1878, an inspector of schools. See *Rugby School Reg.*, 274. [5]

Robinson, Charles Laurence Pemberton, 1s. Charles Richard, of York, arm. EXETER COLL., matric. 8 June, 1870, aged 18; B.A. 1873, a student of Lincoln's Inn 1872.

Robinson, Christopher, s. John, of Middlesex, Virginia, gent. ORIEL COLL., matric. 12 July, 1721, aged 18; B.A. 1724, M.A. 1729, fellow at his death 20 April, 1738. See Foster's *Baronetage.*

Robinson, Christopher, s. Christopher, of 'C. M. & in Virgin.' (*i.e.* Middlesex Co., Va.), gent. ORIEL COLL., matric. 21 May, 1724, aged 19; a student of the Middle Temple 1727, brother of Peter, and of William 1737.

Robinson, Christopher, s. Robert, of Monk Frystone, Yorks, gent. UNIVERSITY COLL., matric. 14 May, 1736, aged 17, B.A. 11 March, 1739-40; fellow MAGDALEN COLL. 1740, M.A. 1742, B.D. 1754, D.D. 1759, proctor 1753, rector of Albury, Oxon, and of Witham, Berks, 1760, until his death 24 Jan., 1802.

Robinson, (Sir) Christopher, s. Christopher, of Albury, Oxon, doctor. UNIVERSITY COLL., matric. 16 Dec., 1782, aged 16; demy MAGDALEN COLL. 1783-9, B.A. 1786, M.A. 1789, D.C.L. 1796, advocate, Mich. term 1793, King's advocate, and knighted 6 Feb., 1805, chancellor of the diocese of London, and judge of the Consistory Court, M.P. Callington 1818-20, a judge of the Admiralty Court 1828, and a member of the Privy Council 1828, died 21 April, 1833, father of Christopher Thomas, of John 1822, and of William 1819. See *Bloxam*, vii. 83. [10]

Robinson, Christopher, s. Christopher, of Penshaw, co. Durham, cler. LINCOLN COLL., matric. 12 March, 1812, aged 17; exhibitioner 1812-18, B.A. 1816, M.A. 1819, vicar of Kirk Newton, Northumberland, 1827, until his death 1 Feb., 1855.

Robinson, Christopher Thomas, 1s. Christopher, of London, equitis. BRASENOSE COLL., matric. 17 Jan., 1818, aged 17; B.A. 1822, M.A. 1825, died perp. curate Putney 7 March, 1861, brother of John 1822, and of William 1819.

Robinson, David, o.s. David, of Kensington, Middlesex, arm. QUEEN'S COLL., matric. 12 April, 1820, aged 17; B.A. 1824, M.A. 1826.

Robinson, Douglas, 1s. Douglas, of Edinburgh, arm. CHRIST CHURCH, matric. 31 May, 1873, aged 18; B.A. 1876.

Robinson, Edmund, s. Edmund, of Thorpe Green, Yorks, arm. BALLIOL COLL., matric. 21 March, 1817, aged 17; B.A. 1820, M.A. 1823, died curate of Great Ouseburne, Yorks, 26 March, 1846, father of Edmund 1851. [15]

Robinson, Edmund, s. Lancelot, of Manaton, Devon, gent. QUEEN'S COLL., matric. 18 Feb., 1752, aged 16.

Robinson, Edmund, o.s. Edmund, of Thorpe Green, Yorks, cler. ST. MARY HALL, matric. 27 March, 1851, aged 19.

Robinson, Edward Cecil, 2s. Charles Backhouse, of Liverpool, gent. EXETER COLL., matric. 8 Dec., 1868, aged 20; B.A. 1872, M.A. 1876, has held various curacies since 1873.

Robinson, Ellis Ashton, 4s. Francis, of Stonesfield, near Woodstock, Oxon, cler. BALLIOL COLL., matric. 9 April, 1864, aged 18; B.A. 1868, M.A. 1873.

Robinson, Ernest Keene, 2s. William Owen, of Erith, Kent, arm. LINCOLN COLL., matric. 23 Oct., 1882, aged 18; B.A. 1885. [20]

Robinson, Francis, s. Francis, of St. Dunstan's, London, gent. WADHAM COLL., matric. 5 Feb., 1730-1, aged 18.

Robinson, Francis, s. John, of Halton, Lancashire, pleb. WADHAM COLL., matric. 25 May, 1732, aged 16; subs. of QUEEN'S COLL., B.A. 5 March, 1735-6, M.A. 1738.

Robinson, Francis, 1s. Thomas, of St. Michael's, Oxford (city), arm. CORPUS CHRISTI COLL., matric. 16 Oct., 1819, aged 14; scholar 1819-26, B.A. 1823, M.A. 1826, fellow 1826-31, rector of Staughton Parva, Beds, 1831-81, and of Stonesfield, Oxon, 1834-82, died 17 Nov., 1886, father of Thomas Auriol and Walter Croke.

Robinson, Francis Douglas, 1s. William Kay, of Wymondham, co. Leicester, cler. JESUS COLL., matric. 23 Oct., 1885, aged 19.

Robinson, Francis Edward, 1s. Francis, of Begbroke, Oxon, cler. EXETER COLL., matric. 23 Jan., 1850, aged 17; B.A. 1853, M.A. 1857, vicar of Drayton, Oxon, 1878. [25]

Robinson, Francis Watson, 1s. Francis Kildale, of Whitby, Yorks, gent. WORCESTER COLL., matric. 15 Oct., 1864, aged 18; B.A. 1868, MA. 1871, vicar of St. Peter, Leicester, 1874.

Robinson, Francis Wrightson, 2s. Thomas, of Poonah, East Indies, cler. WORCESTER COLL., matric. 8 April, 1843, aged 18.

Robinson, Frank Edward, 1s. Edward Francis, of Dulwich, Surrey, gent. BALLIOL COLL., matric. 16 Oct., 1879, aged 19; of the Indian Civil Service 1879, a student of the Inner Temple 1880, killed by a tiger in India 27 April, 1886.

Robinson, Frederick, s. Thomas, of Kensington, Middlesex, gent. CHRIST CHURCH, matric. 25 Oct., 1787, aged 17.

Robinson, Frederick, 3s. John Ellill, of Chieveley, Berks, cler. WADHAM COLL., matric. 15 March, 1864, aged 18; B.A. 1867, M.A. 1871, has held various curacies, etc., since 1869, brother of Arthur Edward and of George Croke. [30]

Robinson, Frederick, 7s. John, of Rochdale, Lancashire, arm. EXETER COLL., matric. 28 May, 1885, aged 23.

Robinson, Frederick Godwin Johnson, 2s. Charles Richard, of York, arm. UNIVERSITY COLL., matric. 13 Oct., 1876, aged 20; B.A. 1880, M.A. 1884, rector of Castle Eden, co. Durham, 1885.

Robinson, Frederick John, Earl of Ripon, created D.C.L. 12 June, 1839 (2s. Thomas, Baron Grantham); M.P. Carlow 1806-7, Ripon 1807-27, chancellor of the Exchequer 1823, Colonial secretary and 1st lord of the Treasury 1827, created Viscount Goderich 28 April, 1827, lord privy seal and 1st lord of the Treasury 1833-4, created Earl of Ripon 10 April, 1833, president Board of Trade 1841, M.A. from ST. JOHN'S COLL., Cambridge, 1802, a student of Lincoln's Inn 1802, died 28 Jan., 1859. See Foster's *Peerage.*

Robinson, (Sir) Frederick Laud (Bart.), 4s. George Stamp, of Cranford, Northants, cler. and baronet. TRINITY COLL., matric. 5 June, 1862, aged 18; B.A. 1867, M.A. 1870, 9th baronet, rector (and patron) of Cranford St. Andrew, Northants, 1870. See Foster's *Baronetage* & *Rugby School Reg.*, 425.

Robinson, Frederick Sydney, 5s. John Charles, of London, gent. LINCOLN COLL., matric. 23 Oct., 1882, aged 20; scholar 1882-6, B.A. 1886. [35]

Robinson, Frederick William, o.s. Thomas Philip, Baron Grantham (after Earl de Grey). CHRIST CHURCH, matric. 14 Nov., 1827, aged 17; died 6 Feb., 1831. See Foster's *Yorkshire Collection.*

Robinson, George, 1s. Thomas, of Skibbereen, co. Cork, Ireland, arm. WADHAM COLL., matric. 13 May, 1829, aged 14; B.A. 1834, a student of Lincoln's Inn 1835.

Robinson, George, 1s. William Rose, of Edinburgh (city), arm. BALLIOL COLL., matric. 9 May, 1833, aged 20; Snell exhibitioner 1833, B.A. 1837, M.A. 1840.

Robinson, George, 2s. George, of Bedford, cler. NON-COLL., matric. 19 Jan., 1884, aged 22; B.A. from WADHAM COLL. 1888.

Robinson, George Croke, 2s. John (Ellill), of Chieveley, Berks, cler. CHRIST CHURCH, matric. 4 June, 1857, aged 18; student 1857-70, B.A. 1861, M.A. 1864, vicar of Benson, Oxon, 1867-79, etc. [5]

Robinson, George Edward, 1s. Edward, of Deythwet, co. Montgomery, arm. JESUS COLL., matric. 13 Oct., 1879, aged 18; B.A. 1883.

Robinson, George Frederick Samuel, Marquis of Ripon, K.G., created D.C.L 22 June, 1870, president of the Council 1869-73 (o.s. Frederick John, Earl of Ripon); M.P. Hull 1852-3, Huddersfield, 1853-7, Yorks (W.R.) 1857-9, gov.-general India 1880-4, etc., created Marquis of Ripon 23 June, 1871. See Foster's *Peerage.*

Robinson, George Gidley, 3s. Samuel Henry, of Howrah, East Indies, gent. EXETER COLL., matric. 31 May, 1873, aged 18; scholar 1873-8, B.A. 1877, M.A. 1880. See *Coll. Reg.*, 166.

Robinson, (Sir) George (Stamp), s. William, of Grafton, Northants, cler. NEW COLL., matric. 5 Dec., 1815, aged 18; fellow 1815-27, B.A. 1819, M.A. 1824, 7th baronet, rector of Cranford 1822-53, hon. canon of Peterborough 1853, until his death 9 Oct., 1873. See Foster's *Baronetage.*

Robinson, Rev. George Wharton, o.s. Jonathan, of Liverpool, gent. QUEEN'S COLL., matric. 27 Oct., 1869, aged 18; S.C.L. & B.A. 1873, M.A. 1875.

Robinson, Harry, 2s. William, of Melbourne, Australia, gent. KEBLE COLL., matric. 18 Oct., 1875, aged 18; B.A. 1878. [10]

Robinson, Harry Perry, 3s. Julius, of Chunar, East Indies, cler. CHRIST CHURCH, matric. 11 Oct., 1878, aged 18; a junior student 1878-82.

Robinson, Hedley Vicars, 1s. George, of Bedford, cler. NON-COLL., matric. 17 Jan., 1880, aged 21.

Robinson, Heneage, s. Heneage, of London, arm. ORIEL COLL., matric. 17 Oct., 1766, aged 18; B.A. 1770.

Robinson, Henry, s. Jocelyn, of Salisbury (city), gent. WADHAM COLL., matric. 22 Jan., 1756, aged 17. [15]

Robinson, Henry, 2s. William, of St. Leonard's, London, gent. ST. ALBAN HALL, matric. 25 Oct., 1838, aged 19; B.A. 1842, M.A. 1854, B. & D.D. 1871; a member of MERTON COLL. 1882, incorp. Durham University, M.A. 1868, D.D. 1872, a master in Christ's Hospital, London, 1849-57, rector of Kilkhampton, Cornwall, 1857-9, held several curacies in Northumberland and Durham 1859-72, died 4 Jan., 1887.

Robinson, Henry, 1s. Henry, of Huddersfield, Yorks, arm. WORCESTER COLL., matric. 18 Oct., 1869, aged 19.

Robinson, Henry, M.A. TRINITY COLL., Dublin, 1854 (B.A. 1851); adm. 'comitatis causa' 30 March, 1864, chaplain to the forces 1855-68, rector of St. Paul, St. Leonard's-on-Sea, 1868-78, vicar of Westfield, Sussex, 1881.

Robinson, Henry, 2s. Mark Antony, of York, gent. PEMBROKE COLL., matric. 3 Feb., 1872, aged 22; B.A. 1875, M.A. 1878, vicar of Grosmont, Yorks, since 1879.

Robinson, Henry, 2s. Charles, of Gravesend, Kent, gent. PEMBROKE COLL., matric. 28 Oct., 1886, aged 18. [20]

Robinson, Henry Charles Thorp, 1s. Samuel Henry, of Calcutta, East Indies, gent. EXETER COLL., matric. 30 Sep., 1865, aged 17; B.A. 1870, a student of Lincoln's Inn 1869.

Robinson, Henry Halliburton, 3s. William, of Halifax, N.S., arm. MAGDALEN COLL., matric. 16 Oct., 1875, aged 18; demy 1874-9, B.A. 1879.

Robinson, Henry Mowld, o.s. Henry, of Patras, Morea, Greece, gent. PEMBROKE COLL., matric. 11 June, 1857, aged 19; B.A. 1862, M.A. 1864, B. & D.D. 1877, head-master Bishop Cotton's School, Simla, 1885.

Robinson, Herbert Harold, 1s. Edmund Robert, of Clapham, Surrey, gent. EXETER COLL., matric. 12 June, 1851, aged 17; B.A. 1855, M.A. 1858, vicar of St. Andrew's, Burnley, 1867.

Robinson, Hubert Curwen, o.s. Albert Aretas, of Pully, near Lausanne, Switzerland, arm. BALLIOL COLL., matric. 16 Oct., 1879, aged 22; scholar 1875-84, B.A. 1884, died 8 Aug., 1888. [25]

Robinson, Hugh Malcolm, 1s. Hugh George, of York, cler. NEW COLL., matric. 15 Oct., 1875, aged 19; B.A. 1879, a student of the Middle Temple 1877.

Robinson, Rev. Jacob, 5s. James, of Ulverston, Lancashire, gent. ST. MARY HALL, matric. 19 Oct., 1874, aged 20; B.A. & M.A. from QUEEN'S COLL. 1882.

Robinson, James, s. James, of Littleton, co. Worcester, cler. UNIVERSITY COLL., matric. 17 Dec., 1715, aged 19; B.A. 1719.

Robinson, James, s. James, of St. Mary's, Lichfield (city), gent. ORIEL COLL., matric. 20 May, 1740, aged 17, B.A. 26 Jan., 1743-4; M.A. from WORCESTER COLL. 1746. See *Gent.'s Mag.*, 1792, ii. 767.

Robinson, James. TRINITY COLL., 1756. See HAYWARD, page 636. [30]

Robinson, James, o.s. Richard, of St. George's, Hanover Square, London, arm. PEMBROKE COLL., matric. 19 Nov., 1822, aged 18. See *Eton School Lists.*

Robinson, James, 2s. John, of (Temple) Sowerby, Westmoreland, cler. QUEEN'S COLL., matric. 10 June, 1847, aged 20.

Robinson, James Edward, 1s. John Park, of Grassendale, Lancashire, gent. NEW COLL., matric. 11 Dec., 1884, aged 19; B.A. 1887.

Robinson, Jeremiah, s. James, of Lichfield, gent. WORCESTER COLL., matric. 4 May, 1745, aged 18; B.A. 22 Feb., 1748-9, M.A. 1751.

Robinson, John, s. Thomas, of St. Nicholas, Newcastle, Northumberland, gent. MERTON COLL., matric. 24 April, 1729, aged 15; B.A. 19 Jan., 1732-3, M.A. 1739, B. & D.D. 1751, warden 1750, until his death 18 March, 1759. [35]

Robinson, John, s. John, of Cransley, Northants, arm. LINCOLN COLL., matric. 1 Feb., 1736-7, aged 17; a student of the Middle Temple 1737, he or his father created D.C.L. 14 April, 1749.

Robinson, John, s. John, of Stowe, co. Lincoln, cler. MAGDALEN HALL, matric. 15 Dec., 1746, aged 18; B.A. from ST. EDMUND HALL 1750.

Robinson, John, s. William, of St. Bride's, London, arm. MERTON COLL., matric. 16 Dec., 1761, aged 18.

Robinson, John, s. Samuel, of Liverpool, Lancashire, gent. BRASENOSE COLL., matric. 19 May, 1768, aged 25; B.A. 1772, M.A. 1774.

Robinson, (Sir) John (Bart.), s. William Freind, of Witney, Oxon, doctor. (See page 495.) CHRIST CHURCH, matric. 17 June, 1772, aged 18; B.A. 1776, M.A. 1779, preb. of Armagh, 1778, archdeacon 1786, precentor Christchurch, Dublin 1797-1823, assumed the name of ROBINSON (vide *London Gazette*, 30 Nov., 1793), created a baronet 14 Dec., 1819, died 16 April, 1832, father of William 1812. See Foster's *Baronetage* & *Alumni West.*, 395. [40]

Robinson, John, created D.C.L. 9 July, 1773 (1s. Charles, of Appleby, Westmoreland), of Appleby, M.P. Westmoreland 1764-74, and for Harwich 1774-1802, sec. to the Treasury 1770-82, surveyor of woods and forests, a student of Gray's Inn 1759, clerk of the peace for Westmoreland 1751-62, died 23 Dec., 1802.

Robinson, John, s. John, of Marylebone, Middlesex, gent. TRINITY COLL., matric. 11 July, 1783, aged 16; B.A. 1787, M.A. 1790. See *Gent.'s Mag.*, 1842, i. 559.

Robinson, John, s. John, of Southwold, Suffolk, gent. ST. MARY HALL, matric. 30 March, 1787, aged 27; B.A. 1791. See *Gent.'s Mag.*, 1825, i. 187.

Robinson, John, s. John, of Crosby Ravensworth, Westmoreland, pleb. QUEEN'S COLL., matric. 31 May, 1788, aged 18; B.A. 1792, M.A. 1796. [5]

Robinson, John, s. James, of Papplewick, Notts, arm. TRINITY COLL., matric. 20 Oct., 1812, aged 22; B.A. 1813, rector of Widmerpool, Notts, 1830, until his death 13 Nov., 1869. See *Eton School Lists.*

Robinson, John, s. John, of Ulverston, Lancashire, gent. BRASENOSE COLL., matric. 11 May, 1815, aged 17; migrated to LINCOLN COLL. 27 Nov., 1819, then aged 20; B.A. from ST. ALBAN HALL 1823.

Robinson, Rev. John, 3s. Christopher, of London, equitis. BRASENOSE COLL., matric. 17 April, 1822, aged 18; B.A. 1826, M.A. 1834, died in 1834, brother of Christopher T., and of William 1819.

Robinson, John, 2s. John, of West Ward, Cumberland, gent. QUEEN'S COLL., matric. 28 May, 1834, aged 18.

Robinson, John, 2s. William, of Settle, Yorks, arm. ORIEL COLL., matric. 8 April, 1843, aged 18; scholar 1843-7, B.A. 1846, M.A. 1853, chaplain Settle Union 1857-67, died in 1886.

Robinson, John, 1s. John, of Newbiggin, Westmoreland, cler. QUEEN'S COLL., matric. 22 June, 1843, aged 20; B.A. 1847, M.A. 1862, incumbent of St. James, Whitehaven, rector of Bowness 1855, until his death in 1877. [10]

Robinson, Rev. John, 1s. John James, of London, gent. MAGDALEN HALL, matric. 12 May, 1858, aged 28; B.A. 1862, M.A. 1864, died 22 Nov., 1864.

Robinson, John Alvaro, 2s. George, of Portalepe, Portugal, gent. NON-COLL., matric. 23 Oct., 1886, aged 25.

Robinson, (Sir) John Beverley (Bart.), created D.C.L. 20 June, 1855, chief justice of Upper Canada 1829-62, chancellor of Trinity College, Toronto, etc., died 30 Jan., 1863. See Foster's *Baronetage.*

Robinson, (Sir) John Blencowe (Bart.), 1s. George S., of Cranford, Northants, baronet. CHRIST CHURCH, matric. 15 June, 1848, aged 18; 8th baronet, died 10 Aug., 1877. See Foster's *Baronetage* & *Eton School Lists.*

Robinson, John Ellill, 2s. Thomas, of St. Michael's, Oxford (city), arm. CHRIST CHURCH, matric. 21 May, 1825, aged 17; B.A. 1829, M.A. 1832, a student of Lincoln's Inn 1829, vicar of Chieveley, etc., Berks, 1837-82, father of Arthur E., of Frederick 1864, and of George C. See *Alumni West.*, 496.

Robinson, John Gorges, 2s. William, of Lancaster, arm. CORPUS CHRISTI COLL., matric. 26 Oct., 1885, aged 19. [15]

Robinson, John Warburton, M.A. TRINITY COLL., Dublin, 1863 (B.A. 1859); adm. 'comitatis causa' 4 Feb., 1864, held various curacies 1864-76.

Robinson, Joshua, s. John, of Marylebone, Middlesex, gent. ST. MARY HALL, matric. 17 Dec., 1798, aged 28; B.C.L. 1806.

Robinson, Rev. Josias, s. Josias, of Clitheroe, Lancashire, arm. BRASENOSE COLL., matric. 24 April, 1811, aged 18; Hulme exhibitioner, B.A. 1814, M.A. 1817, fellow 1816-22, of Netherside and Linton, Yorks, rector of Alresford, Essex, 1841, until his death 20 May, 1843, his sons (Alexander Ralph and Thomas W.) assumed the name of NOWELL in lieu of ROBINSON. See page 1031.

Robinson, Julian, 4s. Augustine, of London, arm. BALLIOL COLL., matric. 21 Oct., 1867, aged 19; B.A. 1872, M.A. 1875, bar.-at-law, Inner Temple, 1874. See Foster's *Men at the Bar.* [20]

Robinson, Matthew, s. Laur., of Blyborough, co. Lincoln, cler. LINCOLN COLL., matric. 10 Oct., 1730, aged 17, B.A. 1734; M.A. from BRASENOSE COLL. 1737.

Robinson, Michael, s. Dav., of Fiskerton, co. Lincoln, gent. LINCOLN COLL., matric. 17 May, 1716; B.A. 16 Jan., 1719-20, M.A. 1722, B.D. 22 Feb., 1731-2.

Robinson, Nicholas, s. Nic., of London, D.Med. ST. MARY HALL, matric. 12 July, 1743, aged 15.

Robinson, Oswin, 5s. William, of St. Michael's, Coventry (town), gent. ST. JOHN'S COLL., matric. 6 March, 1844, aged 18; B.A. from NEW INN HALL 1849, M.A. 1854.

Robinson, Percy, 2s. Jonathan, of Lower Broughton, Lancashire, gent. CORPUS CHRISTI COLL., matric. 19 Oct., 1882, aged 19; exhibitioner 1882-6, B.A. 1886. [25]

Robinson, Peter, s. Christopher, of Virginia, gent. ORIEL COLL., matric. 2 April, 1737, aged 18; brother of Christopher 1724, and of William 1737.

Robinson, Proctor, s. Nicholas, of Thursby, Cumberland, cler. LINCOLN COLL., matric. 15 Dec., 1800, aged 20; B.A. 1804, M.A. 1808.

Robinson, Raphael, 3s. Eshell, of Cheetwood, Lancashire, gent. BRASENOSE COLL., matric. 23 Oct., 1885, aged 19; scholar 1885.

Robinson, Richard, s. William, of Martin, Surrey, arm. CHRIST CHURCH, matric. 13 June, 1726, aged 18; B.A. 1730, M.A. 1733, B. & D.D. 1748, 3rd baronet, preb. of York and rector of Etton, Yorks, 1738-52, rector of Hutton 1742, bishop of Killala 1752, of Ferns 1759, of Kildare 1761, archbishop of Armagh 1765, lord-almoner and vice-chancellor University Dublin, created Lord Rokeby 26 Nov., 1777, a lord justice of Ireland 1787, died 10 Oct., 1794. See *Cotton*, iii. p. 27; *Alumni West.*, 292.

Robinson, Richard, s. John, of East Stoke, Dorset, cler. BRASENOSE COLL., matric. 29 Feb., 1739-40, aged 18; B.A. 28 Feb., 1743-4. [30]

Robinson, Richard, s. Jonathan, of Egton, Yorks, cler. UNIVERSITY COLL., matric. 20 March, 1753, aged 18; B.A. 1756, died minister of Egton, etc., 20 April, 1806. See *Gent.'s Mag.*, 1806, i. 481.

Robinson, Richard, 1s. John James, of Gunthwaite Hall, Yorks, cler. WORCESTER COLL., matric. 26 June, 1862, aged 18, bible clerk 1862-3, scholar 1863-5; fellow QUEEN'S COLL. 1865-70, B.A. 1866, M.A. 1869, lecturer 1869, tutor & librarian, a student of the Inner Temple 1865, died 13 Nov., 1870.

Robinson, Richard Barton, 1s. Robert, of Preston, Lancashire, doctor. QUEEN'S COLL., matric. 10 Oct., 1822, aged 18; B.A. 1826, M.A. 1829, vicar of Lytham 1834-70, died 9 Aug., 1872.

Robinson, Robert, 4s. Thomas, of Stanwix, Cumberland, gent. QUEEN'S COLL., matric. 10 Dec., 1829, aged 20; B.A. 1835.

Robinson, Robert, 1s. John, of Appleby, Westmoreland, gent. QUEEN'S COLL., matric. 28 May, 1834, aged 20; scholar 1834-8, B.A. 1838, rector of St. Mary, Newmarket, 1851, until his death 20 Feb., 1856. See *Gent.'s Mag.*, 1856, i. 453. [35]

Robinson, Robert Alleyne, of JESUS COLL., Cambridge (B.A. 1862, M.A. 1865); adm. 'comitatis causa' 7 June, 1866, a student of the Middle Temple 1865, head steward of the Lonsdale estates.

Robinson, Robert Bertie Broughton, s. Christopher, of Albury, Oxon, doctor. CHRIST CHURCH, matric. 16 Dec., 1782, aged 18; B.A. 1786, M.A. 1789, rector of Waterstock, Oxon, and of Emmington, Bucks, 1790, until his death 24 Dec., 1826.

Robinson, (Sir) Septimus, s. William, of Martin Abbey, Surrey, arm. CHRIST CHURCH, matric. 14 May, 1730, aged 19; 'governor to the younger children of Frederick, Prince of Wales,' usher of the black rod 1760, knighted 10 April, 1761, died 5 Sept., 1765. See Foster's *Peerage*, B. ROKEBY; & *Alumni West.*, 300.

Robinson, Sydney Maddock, 1s. Walter Allen, of Kurrachee, East Ind'es, gent. NON-COLL., matric. 13 Oct., 1884, ag 18; B.A. from BRASENOSE COLL., 1888, bar.-at-law, Middle Temple, 1888.

Robinson, Thomas, s. Thomas, of Newcastle, Northumberland, gent. ORIEL COLL., matric. 17 May, 1716, aged 15; B.A. from LINCOLN COLL. 16 Jan., 1719-20, M.A. from MERTON COLL. 1722, B.D. 1731, D.D. 1733, proctor 1730, archdeacon of Northumberland 1758, until his death 6 Dec., 1761.

Robinson, (Sir) Thomas, (Bart.), s. William, of Rokeby, Yorks, arm. EXETER COLL., matric. 22 June, 1721, aged 18; of Rokeby aforesaid, a student of the Middle Temple 1722, created a baronet 10 March, 1730, M.P. Morpeth 1727, commissioner of excise 1735, governor of Barbados 1741-7, died 3 March, 1777, brother of Septimus. See Foster's *Peerage*, B. ROKEBY.

Robinson, Thomas, M.A. MAGDALEN COLL., Cambridge; incorp. 11 March, 1730-1.

Robinson, Thomas, s. John, of Stubbe Hall, Lancashire, pleb. QUEEN'S COLL., matric. 30 June, 1738, aged 20; B.A. 1742. [5]

Robinson, Thomas, s. Enoch, of Liverpool, Lancashire, gent. BRASENOSE COLL., matric. 2 May, 1741, aged 20.

Robinson, Thomas, s. Thomas, of All Saints, Oxford (city), gent. QUEEN'S COLL., matric. 14 Dec., 1762, aged 16; chaplain Merton College (until 1795), B.A. 1766, M.A. 1769, master Magdalen College School 1776-95, rector of Lillingstone Lovell, Oxon, 1784, until his death 4 Aug., 1795. See *Bloxam*, iii. 242.

Robinson, Thomas, s. Joseph, of Penruddock, par. Greystock, Cumberland, gent. QUEEN'S COLL., matric. 26 April, 1803, aged 18; B.A. 1807, M.A. 1810, fellow 1815-24, vicar of Milford-cum-Hordle, Hants, 1823, until his death 2 Aug., 1857.

Robinson, Thomas, scholar & fellow TRINITY COLL., Cambridge (13th wrangler & B.A. 1813, M.A. 1816); adm. 'ad eundem' 6 June, 1839, D.D. 1844, archdeacon of Madras, lecturer in Arabic 1837-55, master of the Temple 1845-69, and rector of Therfield, Herts, 1853-60, canon of Rochester 1854, until his death 13 May, 1873.

Robinson, Thomas, s. George, of Sedgebrook, co. Lincoln, arm. WADHAM COLL., matric. 3 June, 1863, aged 19; B.A. 1868, vicar of Heslington, Yorks, 1877-80, rector of Hinderclay, Suffolk, 1880-5, and of Brettenham, Norfolk, 1885. [10]

Robinson, Rev. Thomas Arthur, 1s. Thomas, of Merthyr, co. Glamorgan, gent. ST. ALBAN HALL, matric. 14 Oct., 1878, aged 22, B.A. 1881; M.A. from MERTON COLL. 1885.

Robinson, Thomas Auriol, 2s. Francis, of Stonesfield, Oxon, cler. CORPUS CHRISTI COLL., matric. 9 March, 1854, aged 18; brother of Walter Croke.

Robinson, Thomas Bond Bird, 1s. Thomas, of Milford, Hants, cler. CHRIST CHURCH, matric. 23 May, 1850, aged 19; B.A. 1854, M.A. 1874, vicar of Hinton Admiral, Hants, 1868-75, rector of Milton, Hants, 1875.

Robinson, Thomas Romney, created D.C.L. 26 June, 1867, F.R.S., M.R.I.A., scholar of TRINITY COLL., Dublin, 1808, B.A. 1810, fellow 1814, M.A. 1817, B.D. 1822, D.D. 1825, hon. LL.D. 1863, director of the observatory at Armagh, died 28 Feb., 1882, aged 89.

Robinson, Thomas William, 1s. William, of Oxford, merchant. NON-COLL., matric. 14 Oct., 1882, aged 21; B.A. 1885. [15]

Robinson, Thomas Wood, 2s. Thomas, of Llanymynach, co. Salop, gent. BALLIOL COLL., matric. 16 Oct., 1883, aged 18; scholar 1882, B.A. 1888.

Robinson, Rev. Walter, 3s. Thomas, of Swansea, co. Glamorgan, gent. EXETER COLL., matric. 22 Oct., 1880, aged 18; B.A. 1883.

Robinson, Walter Croke, 3s. Francis, of Stonesfield, Oxon, cler. NEW COLL., matric. 23 Jan., 1858, aged 18; fellow 1858, B.A. 1861, M.A. 1865, held various curacies 1863-73, brother of Thomas Auriol.

Robinson, William, s. James, of Lichfield, co. Stafford, gent. UNIVERSITY COLL., matric. 15 May, 1735, aged 17; B.A. 1 Feb., 1738-9, M.A. 1741, rector of Swinnerton and Stoke-upon-Trent, died 11 Sep., 1797; another of the same names and livings died in 1812.

Robinson, William, s. Christopher, of Virginia, gent. ORIEL COLL., matric. 2 April, 1737, aged 20; B.A. 1740, brother of Charles 1724, and of Peter 1737.

Robinson, William, s. John, of East Stoke, Dorset, cler. BRASENOSE COLL., matric. 17 March, 1737-8, aged 18. [21]

Robinson, William, s. William, of Withiel, Cornwall, cler. ORIEL COLL., matric. 21 Feb., 1764, aged 18; B.A. 1767.

Robinson, William, s. William, of St. Mary's, Kilkenny, Ireland, arm. UNIVERSITY COLL., matric. 17 Dec., 1776, aged 19; bar.-at-law, Inner Temple, 1784, died 4 Aug., 1805, buried in Temple Churchyard 8th.

Robinson, William, s. Roger, of Cambridge, pleb. ST. EDMUND HALL, matric. 19 Nov., 1792, aged 30; B.A. 1796.

Robinson, William, s. Carey, of Hanbury, co. Stafford, arm. BRASENOSE COLL., matric. 15 Dec., 1794, aged 17; B.C.L. 1801. [25]

Robinson, William, s. Charles Barnes, of Hill Ridware, co. Stafford, gent. WORCESTER COLL., matric. 6 July, 1805, aged 17; B.A. 1809, M.A. 1812, fellow 1812-36.

Robinson, William, s. William, of Barwick, Yorks, cler. MAGDALEN HALL, matric. 26 May, 1814, aged 21; B.A. 1818, M.A. 1822. See *Gent.'s Mag.*, 1855, i. 656.

Robinson, William, 2s. Christopher, of St. Paul's, London, equitis. BALLIOL COLL., matric. 25 Jan., 1819, aged 17; B.A. 1823, M.A. & D.C.L. 1829 (? died 11 July, 1870, aged 69), brother of Christopher Thomas and John 1822.

Robinson, William, 1s. William, of Settle, Yorks, arm. ORIEL COLL., matric. 25 Nov., 1841, aged 18, a student of the Middle Temple 1843.

Robinson, William Beauclerk, s. Daniel, of Gray's Inn, London, gent. MAGDALEN HALL, matric. 7 Dec., 1802, aged 20; B.A. 1806, M.A. 1811, rector of Litlington, Sussex, 1823-63, died 5 Oct., 1864.

Robinson, William Douglas. CHRIST CHURCH, 1870. See DOUGLAS, page 381. [31]

Robinson, William Frederick, o.s. John, of Bulwell, Notts, arm. TRINITY COLL., matric. 17 June, 1830, aged 18; B.A. 1835, of Markham Grange, Notts. See *Eton School Lists*.

Robinson, William, s. John (formerly Freind), of Dublin, Ireland, cler. CHRIST CHURCH, matric. 9 May, 1812, aged 18; student 1812-9, B.A. 1815, rector of Boveragh, co. Derry, died in Dec., 1834. See Foster's *Baronetage* & *Alumni West.*, 475.

Robinson, William George, 2s. William, of Kingswinford, co. Stafford, arm. ORIEL COLL., matric. 5 Feb., 1862, aged 18; B.A. 1866, M.A. 1872, bar.-at-law, Middle Temple, 1868. See Foster's *Men at the Bar*.

Robinson, William Grey, 1s. William, of Silksworth, co. Durham, arm. MAGDALEN COLL., matric. 16 June, 1865, aged 18; B.A. 1868, M.A. 1873, of Silksworth Hall, co. Durham. [35]

Robinson, William Hammond, o.s. William, of Manchester, cler. QUEEN'S COLL., matric. 25 Oct., 1886, aged 18; scholar 1886.

Robinson William Peart, 1s. William, of Burnley, Lancashire, arm. BALLIOL COLL., matric. 4 June, 1881, aged 19; B.A. 1886, of Reedley Bank, Lancashire.

Robinson, William Scott, 3s. George Abercrombie, of Marylebone, London, arm. EXETER COLL., matric. 21 March, 1823, aged 19; B.A. 1826, M.A. 1829, rector of Dyrham, co. Gloucester, 1828, and of Farleigh-Hungerford, Wilts, 1832, until his death 9 Jan., 1875. See Foster's *Baronetage*.

Robinson, William (Villiers), fellow TRINITY COLL., Cambridge (4th senior optime and B.A. 1789, M.A. 1792), 3s. George, baronet; adm. 'ad eundem' 6 July, 1810, rector of Grafton Underwood, and of Irchester-cum-Wollaston, Northants, 1794, until his death 14 Jan., 1829. See Foster's *Baronetage*.

Robley, Isaac, s. John, of Woodhouse, par. St. Mary, city of Carlisle, pleb. QUEEN'S COLL., matric. 8 June, 1727, aged 19; B.A. 1731; for one of these names see *Gent.'s Mag.*, 1849, ii. 662.

Robley, John Horatio, 1s. John, of St. George's, Bloomsbury, London, arm. EXETER COLL., matric. 16 May, 1823, aged 17.

Robotham, James, s. John, of St. Mellons, co. Monmouth, pleb. JESUS COLL., matric. 18 July, 1724, aged 20; B.A. 1728 (as Thomas).

Robson, Rev. Benjamin, 1s. George, of Notting Hill, Middlesex, arm. CHRIST CHURCH, matric. 27 Jan., 1865, aged 22; B.A. 1868. [5]

Robson, Edward Henry, 1s. John, of Ripon, Yorks, gent. WORCESTER COLL., matric. 24 April, 1845, aged 18; B.A. 1849, M.A. 1851, vicar of St. John's, Pendlebury, 1856.

Robson, George, s. James, of Westminster, gent. QUEEN'S COLL., matric. 25 Aug., 1791, aged 18; B.A. 1795, M.A. 1798, canon of St. Asaph 1803, vicar of Chirk 1804, rector of Erbistock 1805, until his death 7 Dec., 1851. See *Robinson*, 150.

Robson, George Young, 2s. Thomas, of Hornby, Yorks, arm. UNIVERSITY COLL., matric. 6 Dec., 1828, aged 18; scholar 1828-37, B.A. 1833, bar.-at-law, Inner Temple, 1838. See Foster's *Men at the Bar*.

Robson, James, s. James, of Durham (city), gent. LINCOLN COLL., matric. 14 Nov., 1747, aged 17; B.A. 1751, M.A. 1754.

Robson, James, s. James, of Sherborne, co. Durham, cler. LINCOLN COLL., matric. 16 Dec., 1794, aged 18; B.A. from UNIVERSITY COLL. 1800, M.A. 1801. [10]

Robson, John, s. John, of Sockbourne, co. Durham, gent. LINCOLN COLL., matric. 17 May, 1732, aged 17, B.A. 1735; M.A. from NEW INN HALL 1742.

Robson, John, s. John, of Durham (city), pleb. LINCOLN COLL., matric. 14 May, 1751, aged 18; B.A. 1755, M.A. 1758, vicar of Sockbourne, curate of St. Nicholas and St. Giles, Durham, died 28 April, 1802.

Robson, John Udny, 3s. Robert, of Newmarket, co. Cambridge, arm. MAGDALEN HALL, matric. 11 May, 1838, aged 26; B.A. 1842, M.A. 1845.

Robson, Robert, s. Robert, of Sebergham, Cumberland, pleb. QUEEN'S COLL., matric. 20 Oct., 1737, aged 16; B.A. 6 March, 1741-2.

Robson, Samuel, 1s. — R., of Wyham, co. Lincoln, gent. LINCOLN COLL., matric. 23 June, 1854, aged 17; B.A. 1858, M.A. 1869. [15]

Robson, Thomas (William), 1s. Thomas, of Holtby, Yorks, arm. UNIVERSITY COLL., matric. 3 Nov., 1825, aged 18; B.A. 1830, M.A. 1842, perp. curate Hudswell, Yorks, 1833-55, rector of Marske, Richmond, Yorks, 1855, until his death 29 Dec., 1878.

Robson, Thomas, 5s. Anthony Dent, of Kirkby Thore, Westmoreland, gent. MAGDALEN HALL, matric. 15 March, 1845, aged 24; B.A. 1851, vicar of Kirkleatham, Yorks, 1854-67, and of Marske-by-the-Sea since 1867.

Roch, George. s. George, of Freystrope, co. Pembroke, arm. JESUS COLL., matric. 30 March, 1762, aged 15.

Roch, James, s. Nicholas, of Manerbear, co. Pembroke, gent. JESUS COLL., matric. 1 June, 1786, aged 18; B.A. 1790.

Roch, John, s. Arthur, of Robeston, co. Pembroke, arm. JESUS COLL., matric. 11 Feb., 1758, aged 18; B.A. 1761, M.A. 1764, rector of Rudbaxton (or Robeston), and of Prendergast, co. Pembroke, 1777. [20]

Roch, Nicholas, s. Nicholas, of Paskeston, co. Pembroke, gent. CHRIST CHURCH, matric. 20 Nov., 1790, aged 18; B.A. 1794, M.A. 1797, B.D. 1811, D.D. 1811, rector of Talbenny 1805, and of Tenby, co. Pembroke, 1811, until his death 10 Sep., 1830.

Roch, Richard, B.A. from ST. EDMUND HALL, 1730. See ROCKE.

Roch, William, s. George, of Robeston, co. Pembroke, pleb. JESUS COLL., matric. 20 May, 1724, aged 17; B.A. 15 March, 1727-8, M.A. 1735, rector of Robeston 1735.

Roch, William, s. George, of St. Ishmael, co. Pembroke, arm. TRINITY COLL., matric. 30 June, 1814, aged 17; exhibitioner 1816-25, B.A. 1818, M.A. 1822, rector of Henry's Moat 1821, and of Herbranston 1827, and curate of Talbenny, co. Pembroke, died 31 Oct., 1858.

Roch, William Francis, 1s. George, of Haverfordwest, co. Pembroke, arm. CHRIST CHURCH, matric. 18 Oct., 1867, aged 18; of Butter Hill, co. Pembroke, high sheriff 1879. [25]

Roche, Francis William Alexander, 1s. John Webb, of Tregunter, arm. TRINITY COLL., matric. 18 April, 1872, aged 18; B.A. 1875, M.A. 1879, of Rochemount, co. Cork, of Tremadoc, co. Carnarvon, and of Tregunter, Brecon, high sheriff 1881.

Roche, Hallett Lyttleton, 3s. Henry Philip, of London, gent. NON-COLL., matric. 24 Oct., 1874, aged 19.

Roche, John Edward Fitzmaurice Hughes, 2s. John Webbe, of Tregunter, Brecon, arm. TRINITY COLL., matric. 24 Jan., 1876, aged 18; captain 3rd (Prince of Wales's) dragoon guards 1884.

Roche, William, 2s. Garrard, of St. George-the-Martyr, Westminster, arm. TRINITY COLL., matric. 11 Dec., 1826, aged 19; B.A. 1830, M.A. 1833, rector of Colney Heath, Herts, 1850, until his death 11 Aug., 1871.

Rocheid, Charles Henry Alexander Frederick Camille Everard James John, o.s. Charles Frederick, of Weimar, arm. TRINITY COLL., matric. 28 Jan., 1873, aged 19; B.A. 1876. See Foster's *Baronetage*, KINLOCH. [30]

Rochfort, Gustavus, born in Moose Island, America, 1s. Gustavus, arm. EXETER COLL., matric. 31 Oct., 1833, aged 18; captain 4th dragoon guards.

Rochfort, John Downes, 2s. (John Staunton), of Dublin, arm. CHRIST CHURCH, matric. 19 Oct., 1842, aged 19; of Lisnagree, co. Westmeath, bar.-at-law, Lincoln's Inn, 1850, died 24 May, 1885. See Foster's *Men at the Bar* & *Eton School Lists*.

Rocke, Alfred Beale, 9s. John, of Clungunford, Salop, cler. CHRIST CHURCH, matric. 12 June, 1851, aged 18; student 1854-61, B.A. 1855, M.A. 1858, a student of Lincoln's Inn 1858, died 13 June, 1887.

Rocke, James, s. John, of Catcott, Somerset, pleb. EXETER COLL., matric. 11 May, 1716, aged 18; B.A. from NEW INN HALL 1720.

Rock, Richard, s. John, of Catcott, Somerset, pleb. HART HALL, matric. 31 March, 1726, aged 17; B.A. from ST. EDMUND HALL 19 Feb., 1729 (as ROCH), vicar of Locking, Somerset, 1733 (as ROCHE), brother of the last named. [35]

Rocke, Richard, s. Thomas, of Bitterley, Salop, cler. WADHAM COLL., matric. 18 Feb., 1777, aged 18.

Rocke, Richard, s. Richard, of Moorshedabad, East Indies, arm. LINCOLN COLL., matric. 29 Jan., 1818, aged 19; B.A. 1821, rector of Lyndon, Rutland, 1828, until his death 27 July, 1830.

Rocke, Thomas, s. Francis, of Court-of-Hill, Salop, gent. WADHAM COLL., matric. 14 June, 1734, aged 17; B.A. 1738, M.A. 1744.

Rocke, Thomas, s. Thomas, of Bitterley, Salop, cler. CHRIST CHURCH, matric. 17 Nov., 1772, aged 18; B.A. 1776, vicar of Tenbury, co. Worcester, and rector of Silvington, Salop, 1777, until his death 5 April, 1827.

Rocket, Caleb, s. Caleb, of Honiton, Devon, gent. BALLIOL COLL., matric. 9 May, 1785, aged 19; B.A. from EXETER COLL. 1791, M.A. from JESUS COLL., Cambridge, 1803, preb. of Wells 1807, vicar of Weston Zoyland, Somerset, 1808, and of East Brent 1819, until his death 9 June, 1837.

Rockett, Hugh Joseph, o.s. Hugh, of Cheltenham, co. Gloucester, arm. WADHAM COLL., matric. 18 June, 1862, aged 20; held various curacies 1867-74.

Rodbard, Edward William Rodbard, o.s. Edward Whitley, of Merriott, Somerset, arm. ST. ALBAN HALL, matric 28 Nov., 1851, aged 20.

Rodbard, Henry, s. William, of Evercreech, Somerset, arm. UNIVERSITY COLL., matric. 27 May, 1773, aged 20.

Rodbard, William, s. William, of Norton, Somerset, arm. WADHAM COLL., matric. 10 May, 1768, aged 27. [5]

Rodd, Charles, 2s. Edward, of St. Just, Cornwall, cler. EXETER COLL., matric. 17 March, 1826, aged 18; B.A. 1829, rector of North Hill, Devon, 1832, until his death 16 Jan., 1885.

Rodd, Edward, s. Francis, of Trebartha Hall, par. Northill, Cornwall, arm. ORIEL COLL., matric. 18 Nov., 1785, aged 17, B.A. 1789; fellow EXETER COLL. 1791-1805, M.A. 1792, B.D. 1803, D.D. 1816, proctor 1802, rector of St. Just-in-Roseland, Cornwall, 1804, and of Dittisham, Devon, 1802, and vicar of Lamerton 1816, until his death 23 July, 1842. See *Boase*, 115.

Rodd, Francis, s. Francis, of Northill, Cornwall, arm. BALLIOL COLL., matric. 18 March, 1750-1, aged 18; of Trebartha Hall, Cornwall, colonel royal Cornwall militia, died 23 Jan., 1812, father of Francis H., next named.

Rodd, Francis Hearle, s. Francis, of Northill, Cornwall, arm. BRASENOSE COLL., matric. 13 July, 1784, aged 17; B.A. from ALL SOULS' COLL. 1788, M.A. 1792, of Trebartha, high sheriff 1818, died 22 April, 1836.

Rodd, Francis Rashleigh, 1s. Francis, of South Petherwin, Cornwall, arm. CHRIST CHURCH, matric. 27 May, 1858, aged 19; of Trebartha Hall Cornwall. [10]

Rodd, Henry Tremayne, 4s. Edward, of St. Just, Tregoney, Cornwall, 'D. Doctor.' EXETER COLL., matric. 4 Feb., 1830, aged 18; B.A. 1833, vicar of St. Gwinear, Cornwall, 1851.

Rodd, James Rennell, 1s. James Rennell, of London, arm. BALLIOL COLL., matric. 22 Jan., 1877, aged 18; B.A. 1881.

Rodd, John, s. John, of St. Peter's, Hereford (city), cler. TRINITY COLL., matric. 5 May, 1722, aged 15; B.A. 28 Jan., 1725-6, M.A. 1728, B.D. 1740, rector of Redmarley D'Abbitot, co. Worcester, 1731.

Rodd, John, s. Thomas, of Bridstow, co. Hereford, pleb. BALLIOL COLL., matric. 10 Oct., 1722, aged 18; B.A. 1726.

Roddon, Robert Lindsay, 2s. Robert Henry, of London, gent. KEBLE COLL., matric. 19 Oct., 1886, aged 20. [15]

Roden, Luke, s. Henry, of Offley, co. Stafford, gent. BALLIOL COLL., matric. 24 March, 1715-6, aged 18; B.A. 1720.

Rodenhurst, Thomas, B.A. from CHRIST CHURCH, 17 April, 1722 (rightly RADENHURST). See page 1170.

Roderick, David, s. Thomas, of Langathen, co. Carmarthen, pleb. QUEEN'S COLL., matric. 18 May, 1763, aged 18; B.A. 1767, M.A. 1769, a junior master Harrow School, vicar of Sherbourne and Windrush, co. Gloucester, perp. curate Cholesbury 1784, until his death 21 Aug., 1830.

Roderick, Rev. Evan Morgan, 2s. William, of Pantlluryfen, co. Carmarthen, gent. JESUS COLL., matric. 29 Jan., 1879, aged 19; scholar 1879-83, B.A. 1883, M.A. 1888. [19]

Roderick, Rev. Hugh Richard, o.s. Lewis, of Aberystwith, co. Cardigan, gent. JESUS COLL., matric. 19 Oct., 1872, aged 21; B.A. 1876, M.A. 1881.

Rodes, Rev. Cornelius Heathcote Reaston, M.A. ST. JOHN'S COLL., Cambridge, 1818 (B.A. 1814); adm. 'ad eundem' 25 May, 1826, of Barlborough, co. Derby, assumed the additional name of RODES.

Rodger, John Pickersgill, 2s. Robert, of London, arm. CHRIST CHURCH, matric. 8 June, 1870, aged 19; of Hadlow Castle, Twickenham, bar.-at-law, Inner Temple, 1877. See Foster's *Men at the Bar & Eton School Lists.*

Rodger, William Wallace, 1s. Robert, of London, gent. EXETER COLL., matric. 30 Nov., 1865, aged 18; of Hadlow Castle, Kent, bar.-at-law, Middle Temple, 1874. See Foster's *Men at the Bar & Eton School Lists.*

Rodgers, John, 5s. William, of Felling, near Gateshead, co. Durham, gent. MAGDALEN HALL, matric. 17 March, 1868, aged 45; perp. curate Worneth, Cheshire, 1849-55, minister of St. Barnabas, Holloway, 1855-63, vicar of St. Thomas's, Charterhouse, 1863, until his death 25 Oct., 1880.

Rodgers, John Edward, 1s. John, of London, cler. NON-COLL., matric. 18 Oct., 1880, aged 17. [25]

Rodgers, Rev. Robert Heywood, 2s. Herbert, of Gilmorton, co. Leicester, arm. BRASENOSE COLL., matric. 8 June, 1865, aged 18; scholar 1865-70, B.A. 1870, M.A. 1872, died 22 Sep., 1879. See *Crockford.*

Rodgerson, Rev. John Butler, s. William, of Spalding, co. Lincoln, gent. LINCOLN COLL., matric. 27 Nov., 1787, aged 17; fellow CORPUS CHRISTI COLL., B.A. 1791, M.A. 1795, died 5 Feb., 1807.

Rodick, Rev. John Tole, s. Archibald, of Wellingborough, Northants, gent. LINCOLN COLL., matric. 17 July, 1783, aged 18; died at Wellingborough 6 April, 1817.

Rodney, George (3rd baron), s. George, Baron R. CHRIST CHURCH, matric. 3 May, 1802, aged 18; created M.A. 7 Dec., 1803, and also D.C.L. 11 June, 1834, died 21 June, 1842. See Foster's *Peerage.*

Rodney, Harley, 1s. William Powell, of London, arm. CHRIST CHURCH, matric. 3 June, 1876, aged 17; B.A. 1879, M.A. 1883, of the public Record Office. See Foster's *Peerage & Eton School Lists.* [30]

Rodney, Henry, s. Henry, of St. Andrew's, London, gent. BALLIOL COLL., matric. 7 Dec., 1733, aged 17; died 1736.

Rodney, Spencer, s. George, Baron R. CHRIST CHURCH, matric. 20 Dec., 1803, aged 17; fellow ALL SOULS' COLL. 1807-44, B.A. 1807, M.A. 1811, 5th baron, rector of Elmley, Kent, 1805-18, died 15 May, 1846. See Foster's *Peerage.*

Rodocanachi, Emmanuel Michael, 2s. Michael Emmanuel, of London, arm. TRINITY COLL., matric. 19 Oct., 1874, aged 19; B.A. 1877, M.A. 1881, a student of the Middle Temple 1876.

Rodwell, Christopher, 1s. Christopher Brown, of Toller Porcorum, Dorset, cler. TRINITY COLL., matric. 1 Feb., 1868, aged 18; B.A. 1872, vicar of Shelford, Notts, 1880-2, and of Sproxton, co. Leicester, 1882-4, rector of Kimcote, co. Leicester, 1884.

Rodwell, George Edward Chippendale, 6s. Robert Mandeville, of High Laver, Essex, cler. KEBLE COLL., matric. 14 Oct., 1884, aged 19; B.A. 1887.

Rodwell, Robert Mandeville, 3s. William, of Ipswich, Suffolk, arm. EXETER COLL., matric. 14 May, 1840, aged 18; B.A. 1844, M.A. 1847, rector of Newcastle, co. Limerick, 1848-64, and of High Laver, Essex, 1864. [36]

Roe, Charles, 2s. John, of ——, co. York, arm. TRINITY COLL., matric. 13 June, 1828, aged 18; B.A. 1832, M.A. 1835, rector of Little Welnetham, Suffolk, 1849, until his death 5 April, 1878.

Roe, Charles Arthur, 4s. John Banister, of Blandford, Dorset, arm. EXETER COLL., matric. 14 June, 1859, aged 17; postmaster MERTON COLL. 1860-3, B.A. 1863, of the Indian Civil Service 1862.

Roe, (Sir) Frederick Adair (Bart.), s. William, of St. Marylebone, Middlesex, arm. CHRIST CHURCH, matric. 17 May, 1806, aged 17; student 1809-16, B.A. 1810, M.A. 1812, of Brundish, Suffolk, bar.-at-law, Lincoln's Inn, 1816, a king's counsel of Duchy of Lancaster, police magistrate Marlborough Street 1823, and at Bow Street 1832-9, knighted 5 Sep., 1832, and created a baronet 22 Feb., 1836, died 20 April, 1866. See *Alumni West.*, 464.

Roe, George Hamilton, D.Med. TRINITY COLL., Dublin (B.A., M.A., B. & D.Med. 1827), 1s. Peter, of New Ross, co. Wexford, arm. MAGDALEN HALL, incorp. 23 June (or 24 Jan.), 1828, aged 32; fellow Royal College Physicians 1835, physician to Westminster Hospital 1824-56, etc., died 13 Sep., 1873, father of William Gason. See Munk's *Roll*, iii. 275.

Roe, Henry Farwell, 1s. Henry Richard, of Totnes, Devon, arm. LINCOLN COLL., matric. 5 March, 1846, aged 19; B.A. 1850, M.A. 1852, a student of the Inner Temple 1850, rector of Lesnewth, Cornwall, 1854-71, and of Revelstoke, Devon, 1871.

Roe, Henry Richard, o.s. Henry, of Newton Ferrers, Devon, arm. EXETER COLL., matric. 8 Feb., 1820, aged 17; of Carswell House, near Holbeton, Devon.

Roe, James, s. James, of Macclesfield, Cheshire, cler. BRASENOSE COLL., matric. 10 May, 1777, aged 18; B.A. 1781, M.A. 1793, perp. curate Dorchester, Oxon, 1787, and rector of Newbury, Berks, 1796, until his death 9 July, 1838. See *Manchester School Reg.*, i. 168. **[5]**

Roe, James, s. James, of Pembroke (town), gent. TRINITY COLL., matric. 31 Oct., 1809, aged 18; B.A. 1815.

Roe, James, 2s. Thomas, of Kirkby-on-Bain, co. Lincoln, cler. WORCESTER COLL., matric. 23 June, 1836, aged 17; scholar 1836-44, B.A. 1841.

Roe, John, s. John, of Stourbridge, co. Worcester, pleb. MERTON COLL., matric. 21 Oct., 1724, aged 17; B.A. 1728.

Roe, John Colwell, 4s. Thomas, of Linton, Devon, cler. PEMBROKE COLL., matric. 19 March, 1825, aged 19.

Roe, Nicholas, s. Nicholas, of Totnes, Devon, cler. TRINITY COLL., matric. 1 April, 1732, aged 16; B.A. 1736, M.A. 1738, rector of Clystwick 1739, until his death in 1792. **[10]**

Roe, Peter, 1s. Robert, of Booterstown, co. Dublin, arm. NEW COLL., matric. 5 May, 1837, aged 17.

Roe, Reginald Heber, 7s. John Banister, of Blandford, Dorset, gent. BALLIOL COLL., matric. 21 Oct., 1869, aged 19; scholar 1869-74, B.A. 1875, M.A. 1876, head-master Brisbane School, Australia.

Roe, Robert, s. Charles, of Prestbury, Cheshire, gent. BRASENOSE COLL., matric. 18 May, 1774, aged 20.

Roe, Robert, s. William, of Warwick (town), gent. HERTFORD COLL., matric. 16 Dec., 1802, aged 23.

Roe, Thomas, s. Samuel, of Parwich, co. Derby, pleb. ST. EDMUND HALL, matric. 21 June, 1751, aged 20. **[15]**

Roe, Thomas, s. George, of Hayfield, co. Derby, cler. WADHAM COLL., matric. 2 Dec., 1790, aged 18; B.A. 1794, M.A. 1799, rector of Kirkby-on-Bain 1799, and of Sotby, co. Lincoln, 1797, until his death 17 July, 1827.

Roe, Thomas, s. Robert, of Exeter (city), gent. BALLIOL COLL., matric. 18 March, 1796, aged 18; B.A. 1799, rector of Brendon, Devon, 1831, and of Oare, Somerset, 1842, until his death 3 Jan., 1855.

Roe, Thomas, 2s. Thomas, of Lynmouth, Devon, cler. LINCOLN COLL., matric. 30 May, 1827, aged 19.

Roe, Thomas Turner, s. William Turner, of Whitchurch, Salop, arm. TRINITY COLL., matric. 15 Jan., 1806, aged 16; B.A. 1810, M.A. 1814, assumed the additional name of ROE in 1836, rector of Benington, co. Lincoln, 1820-34, of Swerford, co. Lincoln, 1834, until his death 14 July, 1836.

Roe, William, s. Thomas, of Castleton, co. Derby, cler. BRASENOSE COLL., matric. 2 June, 1720, aged 16; B.A. 21 Jan., 1723-4, M.A. 1727. **[20]**

Roe, William, s. Robert, of Bristol (city), arm. CHRIST CHURCH, matric. 30 June, 1768, aged 20.

Roe, William Dering Adair, 1s. William Thomas, of Marylebone, London, arm. CHRIST CHURCH, matric. 15 May, 1834, aged 18; ensign 15th foot, died in Canada in 1838. See *Alumni West.*, 440.

Roe, William Fletcher, B.A. TRINITY COLL., Dublin, y.s. Edward, of Strangford, co. Down, Ireland, cler. ST. MARY HALL, incorp. 23 June, 1853, aged 56; M.A. 17 Dec., 1853, of Pilton House, co. Down, rector of Hammoon 1863.

Roe, William Gason Hamilton John, 1s. George Hamilton, of Westminster, doctor. PEMBROKE COLL., matric. 29 May, 1846, aged 19; B.A. 1850, M.A. 1853, B.Med. 1855.

Roe, William Thomas, s. William, of Marylebone, Middlesex, arm. CHRIST CHURCH, matric. 18 June, 1794, aged 17; B.A. 1798, M.A. 1801, bar.-at-law, Lincoln's Inn, 1800, a commissioner of bankrupts 1804, and of customs 1819, until his death 25 April, 1834, father of William Dering and brother of Frederick Adair. See *Alumni West.*, 440. **[25]**

Roffey, John, o.s. John, of Ditchling, Sussex, gent. NON-COLL., matric. 17 Oct., 1881, aged 21; B.A. 1884.

Rogers, Aaron, 2s. John, of Walterstone, co. Hereford, cler. JESUS COLL., matric. 8 June, 1821, aged 19; B.A. 1825, M.A. 1828, chaplain royal navy 1832, perp. curate St. Paul's, Bristol, 1849-67, rector of St. Peter's, Bristol, 1867, until his death in 1872, father of John Henry 1861.

Rogers, Arthur George Liddon, 3s. James Edwin Thorold, of Oxford, arm. BALLIOL COLL., matric. 28 Jan., 1884, aged 19; B.A. 1887.

Rogers, Arthur Johnson, 1s. Robert Green, of Yarlington, Somerset, cler. ORIEL COLL., matric. 18 Oct., 1865, aged 19; B.A. 1869, M.A. 1873, rector (and patron) of Yarlington 1876.

Rogers, Rev. Augustus Mead Coxwell, y.s. William Coxwell, of Dowdeswell, co. Gloucester, cler. ST. JOHN'S COLL., matric. 13 Oct., 1877, aged 20; B.A. 1882, M.A. 1886. **[30]**

Rogers, Benjamin, s. James, of Kingston, co. Hereford, pleb. BRASENOSE COLL., matric. 1 March, 1715-6, aged 19; B.A. 1719.

Rogers, Benjamin, s. Robert, of Rainscombe, Wilts, cler. QUEEN'S COLL., matric. 20 Oct., 1738, aged 18; B.A. 1742, died vicar of Seagry, 23 Dec., 1802, father of James 1771.

Rogers, Benjamin Bickley, 3s. Francis, of Shepton Montague, Somerset, arm. WADHAM COLL., matric. 16 Oct., 1846, aged 17; scholar 1846-52, B.A. 1851, fellow 1852-61, M.A. 1854, bar.-at-law, Lincoln's Inn, 1856. See Foster's *Men at the Bar.*

Rogers, Bertram Mitford Heron, 2s. James (Edwin) Thorold, of Oxford, arm. NON-COLL., matric. 17 Jan., 1880, aged 19; B.A. from EXETER COLL. 1883.

Rogers, Charles, s. Charles, of Netherthorp, Yorks, gent. CHRIST CHURCH, matric. 22 March, 1750-1, aged 18. **[35]**

Rogers, Charles Coltman, 1s. John, of Aymestry, co. Hereford, cler. BRASENOSE COLL., matric. 20 March, 1873, aged 18; B.A. 1879, of Stanage Park, Radnor, M.P. 1884-5, high sheriff 1882, brother of John D. See *Eton School Lists.*

Rogers, Rev. Charles Fursdon, 2s. John Jope, of Camberwell, Surrey, arm. TRINITY COLL., matric. 12 Oct., 1867, aged 19; B.A. 1871, M.A. 1874, organizing secretary National Society 1877, brother of Francis B.

Rogers, Clement Francis, 5s. James Edwin Thorold, of Oxford, arm. JESUS COLL., matric. 23 Oct., 1885, aged 19.

Rogers, Edward, s. John, of Wentnor, Salop, gent. BALLIOL COLL., matric. 10 Oct., 1730, aged 18; B.A. 1734, M.A. 1739, rector of Mindtown, Salop, father of John 1760.

Rogers, Edward, 1s. Edward, of Ludlow, Salop, arm. WADHAM COLL., matric. 20 May, 1829, aged 17.

Rogers, Edward, 3s. Frederick Leman, of Marylebone, London, arm. (after baron). CHRIST CHURCH, matric. 11 May, 1837, aged 17; student 1839-76, B.A. 1841, M.A. 1843, rector of Odcombe, Somerset, 1875. See Foster's *Peerage*, B. BLACHFORD; & *Eton School Lists*.

Rogers, Edward FitzGerald, 1s. Edward Jordan, of Nassau, New Providence, Bahamas, cler. EXETER COLL., matric. 16 Jan., 1864, aged 19. [5]

Rogers, Edward Rogers, 1s. Charles, of Shipton, co. Gloucester, cler. MAGDALEN COLL., matric. 10 March, 1820, aged 18.

Rogers, Rev. Enys Henry, 1s. Henry, of Enys St. Gluvias, Cornwall, arm. KEBLE COLL., matric. 14 Oct., 1879, aged 18; B.A. 1883, M.A. 1887.

Rogers, Ernest, 3s. Henry, of Enys, Cornwall, arm. NEW COLL., matric. 10 Oct., 1884, aged 18; B.A. 1887, of the Indian Civil Service 1884.

Rogers, Francis, s. Robert, of Calne, Wilts, cler. QUEEN'S COLL., matric. 3 July, 1742, aged 18. See *Gent.'s Mag.*, 1800, i. 593.

Rogers, Francis Bassett, 8s. John Jope, of Porthleven, Cornwall, arm. MAGDALEN COLL., matric. 15 Oct., 1881, aged 19; B.A. 1885, brother of Charles Fursdon. [10]

Rogers, Francis James Newman, s. James, of Sherborne, Dorset, doctor. ORIEL COLL., matric. 5 May, 1808, aged 16; B.A. 1812, M.A. 1815, of Rainscombe, Wilts, bar.-at-law, Lincoln's Inn, 1816, and of the Inner Temple (ad eundem) 1820, Q.C. and a bencher 1837, recorder of Exeter 1835, deputy judge advocate 1842, died 19th, buried in Temple Church 25 July, 1851. See *Eton School Lists*.

Rogers, Francis Newman, 1s. Francis Newman, of St. James, Taunton, Somerset, arm. BALLIOL COLL., matric. 14 Dec., 1844, aged 18; B.A. 1848, bar.-at-law, Inner Temple, 1852, died 2 Sep., 1859. See *Eton School Lists*.

Rogers, Frederick, 1s. Frederick Leman, of Marylebone, London, arm. (after baronet). ORIEL COLL., matric. 2 July, 1828, aged 17; B.A. 1832, fellow 1833-45, M.A. 1835, B.C.L. 1838, senior treasurer 1838, Lord Blachford, so created 4 Nov., 1871, P.C., G.C.M.G. 1883, bar.-at-law, Lincoln's Inn, 1837, colonial land and emigration commissioner 1847-60, under-secretary Colonies 1860-71. cathedral commissioner 1880-4. See Foster's *Peerage, Men at the Bar*, & *Eton School Lists*.

Rogers, Frederick Evelyn, 7s. John Jope, of Penrose, near Helstone, Cornwall, arm. TRINITY COLL., matric. 17 Jan., 1880, aged 19; B.A. 1883, M.A. 1886, brother of Francis B. See *Eton School Lists*.

Rogers, George, s. John, of Leeke, co. Stafford, cler. CHRIST CHURCH, matric. 27 March, 1790, aged 19; B.A. 1793, M.A. 1796, and chaplain, vicar of Market Lavington, Wilts, 1805, until his death 29 May, 1836. [15]

Rogers, George Bourdieu, 1s. George, of Lavington, Wilts, cler. CHRIST CHURCH, matric. 7 June, 1828, aged 18; B.A. from PEMBROKE COLL. 1833, M.A. 1836.

Rogers, George Henvill, s. Richard, of Shroton, Dorset, cler. WADHAM COLL., matric. 13 Dec., 1787, aged 17; B.A. 1791, M.A. 1796, fellow until 1813, chaplain 1813-47, vicar of Southrop, co. Gloucester, 1812, until his death 25 July, 1847.

Rogers, Rev. Gerard Saltren, 1s. Saltren, of Gwennap, Cornwall, cler. CORPUS CHRISTI COLL., matric. 21 Oct., 1878, aged 19; B.A. 1882, M.A. 1885.

Rogers, Harry Spearing, 3s. William, of Maidstone, Kent, gent. NON-COLL., matric. 23 Oct., 1880, aged 20; B.A. & M.A. 1887.

Rogers, Henry, s. William, of Clodock, co. Hereford, pleb. BALLIOL COLL., matric. 23 June, 1732, aged 19; B.A. 1736. [20]

Rogers, Henry, s. Thomas, of Ystradveltte, co. Brecon, pleb. JESUS COLL., matric. 13 March, 1745-6, aged 20.

Rogers, Henry, s. Daniel, of Lincoln (city), arm. WADHAM COLL., matric. 28 Oct., 1817, aged 19; bar.-at-law, Lincoln's Inn, 1825.

Rogers, Henry, 7s. Milward, of Kinnerley, Salop, gent. JESUS COLL., matric. 4 Feb., 1826, aged 19; B.A. 1829.

Rogers, Henry, 3s. George, of Clifton, co. Gloucester, gent. UNIVERSITY COLL., matric. 21 Oct., 1830, aged 20; scholar 1830-3, B.A. 1834, M.A. 1837, vicar of All Saints, Bristol, 1841, until his death 7 Nov., 1849.

Rogers, Henry Chittenden, 1s. Henry, of Clifton, near Bristol, cler. CHRIST CHURCH, matric. 8 June, 1865, aged 18; servitor 1865-8, B.A. 1868, M.A. 1874, chaplain 1880-4, schoolmaster 1879-84, chorister Magdalen College 1856-62, rector of Wood Norton, Norfolk, 1884, etc. See *Bloxam*, i. 228. [25]

Rogers, Henry Hody, s. Richard Colmer, of Childe Okeford, Dorset, cler. WADHAM COLL., matric. 4 May, 1792, aged 17; B.C.L. 1799, rector of Pylle, Dorset, 1826, until his death 17 April, 1840, father of Philip H.

Rogers, Henry Middleton, 3s. John, of Sevenoaks, Kent, arm. BALLIOL COLL. matric. 13 May, 1859, aged 19; of the Indian Civil Service 1860.

Rogers, Herbert Goodenough, y.s. George, of Taunton, Somerset, gent. TRINITY COLL., matric. 26 Nov., 1862, aged 18; B.A. 1866, M.A. 1869, vicar of Cranbourne, Dorset, 1872-85.

Rogers, Hugh, s. John, of Penryn, Cornwall, gent. EXETER COLL., matric. 10 Oct., 1739, aged 19; of Treassowe, Cornwall, high sheriff 1770, died 1773, father of John 1768.

Rogers, Rev. Hugh St. Aubyn, 2s. Hugh, of Camborne, Cornwall, cler. EXETER COLL., matric. 17 May, 1838, aged 18; B.A. 1842. [30]

Rogers, Isaac, s. Thomas, of Bradford, Wilts, arm. ST. EDMUND HALL, matric. 21 Oct., 1803, aged 21.

Rogers, James, s. Benjamin, of Chippenham, Wilts, cler. BRASENOSE COLL., matric. 26 June, 1771, aged 16, B.A. 1775; M.A. from ORIEL COLL. 1780, D.D. 1800, rector of South Cadbury 1796, and Heddington, Wilts, 1800, until his death 11 Feb., 1831, father of Francis James N.

Rogers, James Beadon, 1s. 'Francis T.,' of Poole, Dorset, gent. MAGDALEN HALL, matric. 27 Oct., 1842, aged 19; B.A. 1847, M.A. 1874, vicar of Cornworthy, Devon, 1854-86.

Rogers, James Charles Warrington, 2s. 'John W.,' of Westminster, gent. EXETER COLL., matric. 8 Feb., 1844, aged 18; B.A. 1848, held various curacies 1849-77, rector of Great Blakenham, Suffolk, 1877, brother of John W.

Rogers, James Edwin Thorold, 9s. George Vining, of West Meon, Hants, gent. MAGDALEN HALL, matric. 9 March, 1843, aged 19; B.A. 1846, M.A. 1849, Drummond professor of political economy 1862-8 and 1888, lecturer on political economy since 1873, M.P. Southwark 1880-5, Bermondsey district 1885-6, examiner in political economy University of London, etc., etc., since 1888, sometime in holy orders, father of Arthur George, of Bertram, of Clement, and of Leonard J. [35]

Rogers, James John Warrington, 1s. J. Warrington, of Gillingham, Dorset, cler. ST. MARY HALL, matric. 29 April, 1873, aged 19: B.A. 1878, M.A. 1882, vicar of Aspull, co. Stafford, 1886, and of Bramfield, Suffolk, 1886.

Rogers, John, s. John, of Newent, co. Gloucester, gent. MERTON COLL., matric. 20 Nov., 1721, aged 18; (? rector of Dowdeswell, co. Gloucester).

Rogers, John, s. Matt., of Hewish, Somerset, pleb. LINCOLN COLL., matric. 13 March, 1721-2, aged 15.

Rogers, John, s. Sam., of Frome, Somerset, gent. CORPUS CHRISTI COLL., matric. 22 May, 1723, aged 17.

Rogers, (Sir) John (Bart.), 1s. John, of Cornwood, Devon, baronet. NEW COLL., matric. 13 Aug., 1724, aged 18; B.A. 1 March, 1726-7, 3rd baronet, unduly elected M.P. Plymouth 1739, high sheriff Devon 1755, colonel South Devon militia, died 20 Dec., 1773, brother of Robert 1723. See Foster's *Peerage*, B. BLACHFORD.

Rogers, John, s. Gilbert, of Landilo-Vaur, co. Carmarthen, pleb. JESUS COLL., matric. 2 April, 1726, aged 18; B.A. from CHRIST CHURCH 6 Feb., 1729-30, vicar of Carmarthen and Abergwilly 1752, until his death in Feb., 1796.

Rogers, John, s. John, of Bradford, Wilts, cler. ORIEL COLL., matric. 13 March, 1734-5, aged 18; B.A. 1738, M.A. 1741. [5]

Rogers, John, s. John, of Kilymancllyd, co. Carmarthen, pleb. JESUS COLL., matric. 10 May, 1746, aged 19; B.A. 22 March, 1749-50.

Rogers, John, s. John, of Abergavenny, co. Monmouth, pleb. JESUS COLL., matric. 30 March, 1751, aged 17.

Rogers, John, s. William, of Leekfrith, co. Stafford, pleb. BALLIOL COLL., matric. 21 March, 1752, aged 21; B.A. 1755.

Rogers, John, s. Edward, of Wentnor, Salop, cler. BALLIOL COLL., matric. 1 Dec., 1760, aged 16; B.A. 1764, M.A. 1768. See *Gent.'s Mag.*, 1792, i. 282 (see also Thomas Percival).

Rogers, John, s. Hugh, of Helston, Cornwall, arm. TRINITY COLL., matric. 11 June, 1768, aged 17; of Penrose and Treassowe, Cornwall, M.P. West Looe 1775-6, Penryn 1780-2, and Helston 1784-6, died 22 Feb., 1832, father of John 1797. [10]

Rogers, John, s. John, of Pilton, Devon, arm. ORIEL COLL., matric. 10 Feb., 1789, aged 17.

Rogers, John, s. John, of Plymouth, Devon, arm. TRINITY COLL., matric. 8 April, 1797, aged 18; B.A. 1801, M.A. 1810, of Penrose and Treassowe, Cornwall, canon of Exeter 1808, died 12 June, 1856, father of John Jope, of Saitren, and of William 1836. See *Eton School Lists*.

Rogers, John, s. William, of Hingston, co. Hereford, pleb. BALLIOL COLL., matric. 15 Dec., 1800, aged 20; B.A. 1804.

Rogers, John, o.s. John, of St. Swithin's, London, arm. BALLIOL COLL., matric. 17 March, 1826, aged 18; B.A. 1830 M.A. 1833, bar.-at-law, Inner Temple, 1836, died Aug., 1867.

Rogers, John, 3s. Thomas, of Liverpool, arm. BRASENOSE COLL., matric. 11 June, 1852, aged 18; scholar 1853-6, B.A. 1856, M.A. 1859, rector of Habberley, Salop, 1862-9, vicar of St. James, Accrington, 1869. See *Rugby School Reg.*, 291. [15]

Rogers, John Davenport, 3s. John, of Aymestry, co. Hereford, cler. BALLIOL COLL., matric. 20 Oct., 1875, aged 18, scholar 1874-9, B.A. 1879; fellow UNIVERSITY COLL. 1880-8, B.C.L. & M.A. 1882, of Stanage Park, co. Hereford, bar.-at-law, Inner Temple, 1883, brother of Charles C. See Foster's *Men at the Bar*.

Rogers, John Edwardes, o.s. John, of Llanewalle, co. Cardigan, doctor. WADHAM COLL., matric. 28 Jan., 1846, aged 19; B.A. 1849, of Abermeirig, co. Cardigan, high sheriff, 1872.

Rogers, John Henry, 1s. Aaron, of St. Paul's, Bristol, cler. WADHAM COLL., matric. 30 May, 1861, aged 17; B.A. 1865, M.A. 1868, perp. curate St. George's Chapel, Brighton, 1877-83, chaplain at Pau 1883.

Rogers, John Jope, 1s. John, of Mawnan, Cornwall, cler. TRINITY COLL., matric. 13 Nov., 1834, aged 18; B.A. 1838, M.A. 1841, bar.-at-law, Inner Temple, 1842. M.P. Helston 1859-65, died 2 April, 1880, father of Charles F., of Francis B., of Frederick Evelyn, and of Walter 1883.

Rogers, John Methuen, s. John, of Warminster, Wilts, cler. QUEEN'S COLL., matric. 4 April, 1767, aged 18; B.C.L. from NEW COLL. 1776, rector of Berkeley, Somerset, 1793, until his death 22 Aug., 1834. [20]

Rogers, John Pritt, 2s. Fletcher, of Grassendale, Lancashire, gent. ST. JOHN'S COLL., matric. 25 Jan., 1873, aged 18; B.A. 1877, M.A. 1879, has held various curacies since 1877.

Rogers, John Theodore, 1s. John, of South Church, near Bishop Auckland, co. Durham, cler. NON-COLL., matric. 11 Oct., 1879, aged 18; B.A. from CORPUS CHRISTI COLL. 1882, M.A. 1886.

Rogers, John Thornton, 1s. John, of Upper Tooting, Surrey, arm. BALLIOL COLL., matric. 8 Dec., 1852, aged 18; of River Hill, Kent, sometime captain 33rd regiment.

Rogers, John Warrington, 1s. John W., of St. Margaret's, Westminster, gent. MAGDALEN HALL, matric. 25 May, 1844, aged 22; created M.A. 18 Dec., 1854, bar.-at-law, Middle Temple, 1846, County Court judge, Melbourne, 1858, brother of James Charles W. See Foster's *Men at the Bar*.

Rogers, Leonard James, 2s. James Edwin Thorold, of Oxford, arm. BALLIOL COLL., matric. 21 Oct., 1880, aged 18; scholar 1879-84, B.Mus. & B.A. 1884, M.A. 1887, lecturer mathematics Wadham College 1885. [25]

Rogers, Lewis, s. Thomas, of Eglwsilan, co. Glamorgan, pleb. ST. EDMUND HALL, matric. 17 March, 1739-40, aged 19.

Rogers, Percy John Mackarness, 1s. Thomas Percival, of Batheaston, Somerset, cler. NON-COLL., matric. 22 Jan., 1876, aged 19; B.A. from BRASENOSE COLL. 1881.

Rogers, Philip Henville, o.s. Henry Hody, of Childe Okeford, Dorset, cler. WADHAM COLL., matric. 2 March, 1821, aged 19.

Rogers, Ralph Baron, 1s. William, of Mawnan, Cornwall, cler. EXETER COLL., matric. 22 Oct., 1880, aged 18; B.A. 1884, M.A. 1887. See *Eton School Lists*.

Rogers, Raymond Edward Lorance, s. John, of London, arm. ORIEL COLL., matric. 8 March, 1790, aged 17; B.A. 1793, died vicar of Bishop's Stortford, Herts, 2 Aug., 1816, aged 44. [30]

Rogers, Reginald Basset, 6s. Hugh, of Camborne, Cornwall, cler. ST. JOHN'S COLL., matric. 15 Nov., 1848, aged 18; B.A. 1852, held various curacies 1853-71, perp. curate of Cury with Gunwalloe, Cornwall, 1857-63, vicar of Sancreed 1879.

Rogers, Rev. Richard, s. Richard, of Dowdeswell, co. Gloucester, arm. PEMBROKE COLL., matric. 19 Oct., 1749, aged 16; B.C.L. 1756, brother of William 1749.

Rogers, Richard, s. William, of Gloucester (city), gent. ORIEL COLL., matric. 10 Oct., 1750, aged 17; B.C.L. 1757.

Rogers, Richard Colmer, s. Richard, of Sutton, Dorset, cler. MAGDALEN HALL, matric. 27 June, 1745, aged 16; B.A. from ST. EDMUND HALL 1749, M.A. 1752, B. & D.D. 1792, rector of Belchalwell and Stoke Wake, died 1812, aged 83.

Rogers, Richard Norris. MAGDALEN HALL, 1846. See GANDY, page 506. [35]

Rogers, Richard Rogers Coxwell, 2s. Charles Coxwell, of Shipton, co. Gloucester, cler. PEMBROKE COLL., matric. 21 Feb., 1822, aged 18; of Ablington Manor and Dowdeswell, co. Gloucester, J.P., D.L., high sheriff 1857, assumed the additional surname of ROGERS.

Rogers, Robert, s. John, of Cornwood, Devon, baronet. QUEEN'S COLL., matric. 22 Oct., 1723, aged 18; B.C.L. from WADHAM COLL. 1730, brother of John 1724.

Rogers, Robert, s. Robert, of Oxford (city), cler. PEMBROKE COLL., matric. 24 March, 1734-5, aged 15; demy MAGDALEN COLL. 1735-44, B.A. 1738, M.A. 1741, fellow 1744-61, B.D. 1750, junior dean of arts 1750, bursar 1751, vice-president 1760, rector of Swaby, co. Lincoln, Feb., 1761, until his death 20 April, 1761. See *Bloxam*, vi. 241.

Rogers, Robert Green, s. John, of Yarlington, Somerset, arm. ORIEL COLL., matric. 6 May, 1818, aged 17; B.A. 1822, M.A. 1825, rector of Yarlington, Devon, 1826, until his death in 1876.

Rogers, Roland, 4s. Joseph, of West Bromwich, co. Stafford, gent. NEW COLL., matric. 17 May, 1870, aged 22; B.Mus. 19 May, 1870, D.Mus. 17 June, 1875.

Rogers, Rowland, s. Gilbert, of Landilo, co. Carmarthen, pleb. JESUS COLL., matric. 21 March, 1740-1, aged 19; B.A. 1745.

Rogers, St. John, s. Richard, of Finchamstead, Berks, cler. TRINITY COLL., matric. 11 March, 1730-1, aged 16; B.A. 1734, M.A. 1737. [5]

Rogers, Saltren, 4s. John, of Mawnan, Cornwall, cler. EXETER COLL., matric. 6 May, 1841, aged 18; B.A. 1845, M.A. 1848, perp. curate Cury with Gunwalloe, Cornwall, 1849-56, vicar of Gwennap 1856, hon. canon Truro 1878, father of Gerard S.

Rogers, Samuel, s. William, of Gloucester (city), arm. CHRIST CHURCH, matric. 27 June, 1753, aged 19; student 1753-99, B.A. 1757, M.A. 1760, B.D. 1786, rector of St. Mary Magdalen, Oxford, 1763, and of Batsford, co. Gloucester, 1799, preb. of St. David's 1783, until his death 22 Dec., 1806. See *Alumni West.*, 360.

Rogers, Samuel, s. Samuel, of London, gent. WADHAM COLL., matric. 13 July, 1797, aged 17; B.A. & M.A. 1804, a student of Lincoln's Inn 1802, rector of Orton Longueville, Hunts, at his death 18 May, 1852.

Rogers, Thomas, s. Charles, of Bideford, Devon, gent. BALLIOL COLL., matric. 6 July, 1757, aged 17; B.A. from ALL SOULS' COLL. 1761.

Rogers, Thomas, 'Aula Magd. Principalis Auriga;' privilegiatus 20 May, 1778. [10]

Rogers, Thomas, 1s. Thomas, of Falmouth, Cornwall, gent. EXETER COLL., matric. 2 June, 1857, aged 18; choral scholar NEW COLL. 1859-63, B.A. 1862, M.A. 1864, minor canon Durham Cathedral 1864-84, precentor 1872-84, created D.Mus. (Durham) 1882, vicar of Roxwell, Essex, 1884.

Rogers, Thomas Alfred, 5s. Richard Cogan, of Stonehouse, Devon, arm. EXETER COLL., matric. 11 Oct., 1872, aged 19; scholar 1872-7, B.A. 1877. See *Coll. Reg.*, 166.

Rogers, Thomas Cooke, s. Edward, of St. Asaph, Flint, gent. BALLIOL COLL., matric. 25 Nov., 1793, aged 16; B.A. 1797, M.A. 1800, fellow until 1820, bursar 1813.

Rogers, Thomas Englesby, 1s. Francis, of Yarlington, Somerset, gent. CORPUS CHRISTI COLL., matric. 30 May, 1834, aged 17; scholar 1834-44, B.A. 1838, M.A. 1841, fellow 1844-6, of Yarlington House, Somerset, J.P., bar.-at-law, Lincoln's Inn, 1846, recorder of Wells 1872, chancellor of the diocese of Bath and Wells 1884. See Foster's *Men at the Bar.*

Rogers, Thomas Middleton, 1s. Thomas Eales, of Calcutta, East Indies, arm. ST. JOHN'S COLL., matric. 17 April, 1866, aged 18; B.A. 1869, of Ashburton, Devon, bar.-at-law, Lincoln's Inn, 1874. See Foster's *Men at the Bar.* [15]

Rogers, Thomas Oliver, s. Joseph, of Bristol (city), arm. WADHAM COLL., matric. 22 June, 1815, aged 18.

Rogers, Thomas Percival, 3s. John, of Wentnor, Salop, cler. CHRIST CHURCH, matric. 22 Oct., 1840, aged 19; student 1843-52, B.A. 1844, M.A. 1847, tutor 1850, vicar of Batheaston, Somerset, 1851, until his death 23 Feb., 1888.

Rogers, Walter, y.s. John Jope, of Penrose, Cornwall, arm. TRINITY COLL., matric. 15 Oct., 1883, aged 19; scholar 1883.

Rogers, Walter Francis, 5s. John, of Tooting, Surrey, arm. BALLIOL COLL., matric. 16 Oct., 1865, aged 19; B.A. 1870, M.A. 1872.

Rogers, Walter Lacy, 3s. Francis Newman, of Bloomsbury, London, arm. BALLIOL COLL., matric. 13 June, 1849, aged 18; B.A. 1853, M.A. 1864, bar.-at-law, Inner Temple, 1869, died 18 April, 1885. See Foster's *Men at the Bar* & *Eton School Lists.*

Rogers, William, s. William, of Burford, Oxon, pleb. ST. JOHN'S COLL., matric. 5 Dec., 1717, aged 15; B.A. 1721, M.A. 20 March, 1724-5. [21]

Rogers, William, s. John, of Gresford, co. Denbigh, pleb. JESUS COLL., matric. 23 Feb., 1726-7, aged 19; B.A. 1730.

Rogers, William, s. William, of Langhane, co. Carmarthen, pleb. JESUS COLL., matric. 15 March, 1737-8, aged 16; B.A. 1741.

Rogers, William* (subs.), s. Roger, of Westerton, co. Pembroke, pleb. PEMBROKE COLL., matric. 5 April, 1749, aged 16. (*Roger in *Mat. Reg.*)

Rogers, William, s. Richard, of Dowdeswell, co. Gloucester, arm. PEMBROKE COLL., matric. 1 June, 1749, aged 17; B.A. 1753, M.A. 1756, bar.-at-law, Lincoln's Inn, 1753, brother of Richard 1749. [25]

Rogers, William, 2s. John, of Mawnan, Cornwall, cler. EXETER COLL., matric. 28 April, 1836, aged 18; B.A. 1840, M.A. 1845, rector of Mawnan, Cornwall, 1842, father of Ralph B.

Rogers, William, 1s. William Lorance, of St. George's, Bloomsbury, London, arm. BALLIOL COLL., matric. 8 March, 1837, aged 17; B.A. 1842, M.A. 1844, perp. curate St. Thomas's, Charterhouse, 1844-63, chaplain in ordinary to the Queen 1857, preb. St. Paul's 1862, rector of St. Botolph's, Bishopsgate, 1863. See *Eton School Lists.*

Rogers, William Edwin, 3s. Thomas, of Salisbury, gent. ST. MARY HALL, matric. 7 Nov., 1871, aged 18.

Rogers, William Henry, of TRINITY COLL., Dublin (B.A. 1857, M.A. 1859); adm. 'comitatis causa' 5 Dec., 1861, rector of Heaton Norris, Lancashire, 1880.

Rogers, William Johnson, s. Benjamin, of Chippenham, Wilts, cler. BRASENOSE COLL., matric. 26 June, 1771, aged 17; brother of James 1771. [30]

Rogers, William Rogers Coxwell, 4s. Charles Coxwell, of Shipston Sollers, co. Gloucester, cler. EXETER COLL., matric. 30 April, 1829, aged 19; B.A. 1833, M.A. 1836, rector of Dowdeswell 1854, curate 1835-54, assumed the additional surname of ROGERS.

Rogerson, Alexander, 3s. William, of Gillesbie, near Lockerbie, co. Dumfries, arm. BRASENOSE COLL., matric. 24 Nov., 1864, aged 19; B.A. 1867, of St. Michael's, Lockerbie aforesaid.

Rogerson, Charles Joshua, 4s. Robert, of Shrewsbury, gent. NON-COLL., matric. 28 May, 1874, aged 19.

Rogerson, George, o.s. George, of Preston, Lancashire, gent. WORCESTER COLL., matric. 29 Jan., 1878, aged 19; B.A. 1882, M.A. 1884.

Rogerson, William, 2s. William, of Hewk, co. Dumfries, gent. QUEEN'S COLL., matric. 29 June, 1859, aged 17; of Gillesbie, co. Dumfries, lieut.-colonel 1st batt. Salop light infantry. [35]

Rohrweger, Frank, 2s. Julius Charles, of Camberwell, Surrey, arm. BRASENOSE COLL., matric. 24 May, 1877, aged 18; bar.-at-law, Inner Temple, 1885. See Foster's *Men at the Bar.*

Rokeby, Rev. Langham, s. Langham, of Spratton, Hants, cler. WORCESTER COLL., matric. 17 Oct., 1817, aged 33; created M.A. 23 June, 1819, of Arthingworth, Northants, died 16 Dec., 1826. See Foster's *Yorkshire Collection.*

Roles, William, s. James, of Maddington, Wilts, arm. ORIEL COLL., matric. 27 April, 1803, aged 16; B.A. 1808, M.A. 1812, vicar of Raunds, Northants, 1817, rector of Shorncot 1815, and of Upton Lovell 1820, until his death 6 Jan., 1834.

Rolfe, Arthur Fawcett Neville, 4s. Strickland C. E. N., of Painswick, co. Gloucester, cler. MAGDALEN HALL, matric. 3 June, 1843, aged 20; died 10 Dec., 1876.

Rolfe, Charles, 1s. Charles, of Lydd, Kent, gent. QUEEN'S COLL., matric. 28 Nov., 1820, aged 18; scholar LINCOLN COLL. 1821-5, B.A. 1824, rector of Shadoxhurst, Kent, 1838, until his death in 1877.

Rolfe, Charles Fawcett Neville, 1s. Strickland Charles Edward, of Marylebone, London, cler. MAGDALEN HALL, matric. 4 Dec., 1834, aged 19; B.A. 1840, of Heacham Hall, Norfolk, J.P., died in 1869.

Rolfe, Charles John, 3s. Robert Philemon, of Raynes, Essex, gent. ALL SOULS' COLL., matric. 11 Feb., 1870, aged 18; bible clerk 1870-4, B.A. 1874, has held various curacies since 1877. **[5]**

Rolfe, George Wilkinson, 1s. George Crabbe, of Hailey, Oxon, cler. CHRIST CHURCH, matric. 23 May, 1861, aged 17; servitor 1861-4, B.A. 1864, rector of Swanton Novers, Norfolk, 1884.

Rolfe, Henry Worsley, 6s. George Crabb, of Hailey, Oxon, cler. PEMBROKE COLL., matric. 3 Feb., 1879, aged 18; chorister MAGDALEN COLL. 1870-5.

Rolfe, Strickland Charles Edward Neville, s. Charles Neville, of Eltham, Kent, arm., (lieut.-general). WADHAM COLL., matric. 3 May, 1808, aged 18; B.A. 1812, M.A. 1816, vicar of Heacham, Norfolk, 1838-52, assumed the additional surname of ROLFE by royal licence 1 March, 1837, died 25 Dec., 1852.

Rolfe, Rev. Thomas Forster, 4s. George Crabb, of Hailey, Oxon, cler. NON-COLL., matric. 7 March, 1874, aged 18; bible clerk ALL SOULS' COLL. 1874-7, B.A. 1878, M.A. 1881, head-master Tamworth Grammar School 1884.

Rolland, Robert, 3s. Robert, of St. Vegean's, co. Forfar (Scotland), arm. ST. MARY HALL, matric. 4 Dec., 1824, aged 23; B.A. 1828, M.A. 1832. **[10]**

Rolland, Stewart Erskine, 1s. Peter, of St. Pancras, London, arm. CHRIST CHURCH, matric. 4 June, 1835, aged 18; served in 98th regiment, accompanied Dr. Layard to Nineveh. See *Eton School Lists.*

Rolle, Denys, s. John, of Stevenstone, Devon, arm. NEW COLL., matric. 19 Jan., 1741-2, aged 16; created M.A. 25 May, 1748, then of Hudscot, Devon, of Stevenstone 1750, M.P. Barnstaple 1761-74, died in June, 1797, father of John, Lord Rolle.

Rolle, Edward, s. Robert, of Meeth, Devon, gent. NEW COLL., matric. 10 July, 1723, aged 18; B.A. 1727, M.A. 1730, B.D. 1758, rector of St. John's, Wilts, and vicar of Moorlynch, Somerset, 1758, and preb. of Salisbury 1771, until his death 30 June, 1791.

Rolle, Henry, s. John, of St. Giles's, Devon, arm. NEW COLL., matric. 19 Oct., 1725, aged 16; created D.C.L. 30 April, 1731, M.P. Devonshire 1730-41, Barnstaple 1741-8, created Baron Rolle 8 Jan., 1747-8, died 17 Aug., 1750.

Rolle, John. NEW COLL., 1729. See JOHN ROLLE WALTER. **[15]**

Rolles, Edward, 2s. Robert, of St. Marylebone, London, arm. PEMBROKE COLL., matric. 21 Nov., 1826, aged 18; scholar 1826-31, B.A. 1831, M.A. 1833.

Rolles, Harry Robert Egerton, o.s. Robert John, of Cheltenham, co. Gloucester, cler. ST. MARY HALL, matric. 28 May, 1869, aged 17, exhibitioner 1869-70; B.A. from ORIEL COLL. 1873, M.A. 1877.

Rolles, Rev. Robert John, 1s. Robert, of Marylebone, arm. EXETER COLL., matric. 4 Feb., 1825, aged 18; migrated to NEW COLL. 1 April, 1826, aged 20; fellow 1826-45, B.A. 1830, M.A. 1833, bursar 1833, sub-warden 1836, died 11 Aug., 1875.

Rolleston, Frederick Christopher Lawrence, 3s. William Lancelot, of Scraptoft, co. Leicester, cler. ST. MARY HALL, matric. 24 Jan., 1884, aged 18.

Rolleston, George, s. Robert, of London, arm. MERTON COLL., matric. 2 July, 1810, aged 19; postmaster 1812-4, B.A. 1814, M.A. 1820, vicar of Maltby and of Stainton, Yorks, 1816, until his death 21 Feb., 1868. See *Eton School Lists.* **[20]**

Rolleston, George, o.s. Samuel, of Uttoxeter, co. Stafford, arm. NEW COLL., matric. 12 April, 1832, aged 19.

Rolleston, George, 2s. George, of Maltby, co. York, cler. PEMBROKE COLL., matric. 8 Dec., 1846, aged 17; scholar 1850-1, B.A. 1850, fellow 1851-62, M.A. 1853, B.Med. 1854, D.Med. 1857, hon. fellow 1862-81; fellow MERTON COLL. 1872-81, F.R.S. 1862, F.L.S., Lee's reader in anatomy, Linacre professor of human and comparative anatomy 1860, until his death 16 June, 1881.

Rolleston, John, s. Christopher, of London, arm. CHRIST CHURCH, matric. 24 Jan., 1805, aged 17; B.A. 1808, M.A. 1814, vicar of Burton Joyce, Notts, 1822, until his death 17 Nov., 1862.

Rolleston, Lancelot, s. Christopher, of London, arm. CHRIST CHURCH, matric. 24 Jan., 1805, aged 19; of Watnall Hall, Notts, M.P. 1837-49, colonel Notts militia, died 18 May, 1862.

Rolleston, Lancelot, 1s. Lancelot, of Watnall Hall, Notts, arm. CHRIST CHURCH, matric. 12 Oct., 1866, aged 19; of Watnall Hall aforesaid, high sheriff Notts 1877. **[25]**

Rolleston, Matthew, s. Samuel, of Southampton, Hants, arm. UNIVERSITY COLL., matric. 5 April, 1805, aged 17; B.A. 1808, M.A. 1811, bursar and tutor 1813 (select preacher 1815), fellow 1809, until his death 22 July, 1817.

Rolleston, Robert, 1s. George, of Stainton, co. Gloucester, cler. UNIVERSITY COLL., matric. 14 June, 1838, aged 18; B.A. 1842, perp. curate Seathwaite, Lancashire, 1855-7, and Holy Trinity, Warrington, 1860-3, rector of Sandford Rivers 1868.

Rolleston, Samuel, s. James, of St. Matthew's, London, gent. ORIEL COLL., matric. 9 May, 1722, aged 20, B.A. 1723; M.A. from MERTON COLL. 1725, (? rector of Stanton with Aston-upon-Trent 1744).

Rolleston, Samuel, s. Samuel, of Old Alresford, Hants, arm. MERTON COLL., matric. 31 Oct., 1793, aged 17.

Rollo, George, s. Robert, of Dundee (co. Angus), Scotland, gent. BALLIOL COLL., matric. 23 Feb., 1779, aged 21; B.A. 1782. **[30]**

Rollo, John Rogerson, Lord Rollo, of TRINITY COLL., Cambridge (M.A. 1856); adm. 'comitatis causa' 22 May, 1862, 10th baron, a Scottish representative peer 1861-5. See Foster's *Peerage.*

Rolls, Rev. Henry, B.A. from CHRIST'S COLL., Cambridge, 1816, 3s. Henry, of Southam, co. Warwick, gent. BALLIOL COLL., incorp. 9 Jan., 1819, aged 36; M.A. 15 Jan., 1819, rector of Barnwell St. Andrew 1818, and All Saints 1819, rector of Aldwinckle All Saints, Northants, 1820, until his death 24 July, 1838.

Rolls, John Allan, 1s. John, of The Hendre, near Monmouth, arm. CHRIST CHURCH, matric. 31 May, 1855, aged 18; of The Hendre aforesaid, M.P. co. Monmouth 1880-5, high sheriff 1875, sometime captain royal Gloucestershire hussars. See *Eton School Lists.*

Rolls, John Etherington Welch, 1s. John, of Bermondsey, Surrey, arm. CHRIST CHURCH, matric. 21 May, 1825, aged 18; of The Hendre, co. Monmouth, high sheriff 1842, died 27 May, 1870.

Rolph, John Mair, o.s. William, of Thornbury, arm. ORIEL COLL., matric. 21 June, 1838, aged 17.

Rolt, Cecil Henry, 3s. Henry George, of Limpsfield, Surrey, cler. NEW COLL., matric. 12 Oct., 1883, aged 18; B.A. 1887.

Rolt, Francis Wardlaw, 1s. Henry George, of Lympsfield, Surrey, cler. ORIEL COLL., matric. 30 Jan., 1882, aged 20.

Rolt, Rev. Henry George, 1s. John, of Athlone, Ireland, arm. (after a knight). BALLIOL COLL., matric. 12 Dec., 1845, aged 18; B.A. 1850, M.A. 1852. See Foster's *Our Noble and Gentle Families* & *Eton School Lists.*

Rolt, James, 2s. John, of London, knight. UNIVERSITY COLL., matric. 13 Oct., 1879, aged 19; B.A. 1883, a student of the Inner Temple 1882. See *Eton School Lists.* [5]

Rolt, John, s. Edward, of Saccomb, Herts, arm. MERTON COLL., matric. 27 May, 1736, aged 24; B.A. by decree 10 March, 1736-7, M.A. 17 June, 1737, rector of Bromham, Wilts, died 25 Oct., 1793. See Foster's *Our Noble and Gentle Families.*

Rolt, John, o.s. John, of Kennington, Surrey, arm. (M.P., Q.C.). UNIVERSITY COLL., matric. 25 Feb., 1853, aged 18; B.A. 1857, M.A. 1860, of Ozleworth Park, co. Gloucester, bar.-at-law, Inner Temple, 1859-74, died in 1876. See *Eton School Lists.*

Rolt, Samuel, s. Oliver, of Alderton, Northants, gent. WADHAM COLL., matric. 17 May, 1716, aged 18; B.A. 1719, M.A. 1722.

Romaine, William, s. William, of Hartlepool, Durham, pleb. HART HALL, matric. 10 April, 1731, aged 17; B.A. from CHRIST CHURCH 13 Feb., 1734, M.A. 1737, lecturer St. Botolph's, Bishopsgate, 1748, and of St. Dunstan's-in-the-West 1749-95, Gresham professor of astronomy, rector of St. Anne's, Blackfriars, 1764, until his death 25 July, 1795, author of 'The Life, Walk, and Triumph of Faith.'

Romaine, Rev. William, s. William, of Southwark, Surrey, cler. TRINITY COLL., matric. 15 April, 1774, aged 17; B.A. 1778, M.A. 1780, B. & D.D. 1791, died at Reading 11 March, 1826. [10]

Romanis, William, of EMMANUEL COLL., Cambridge (B.A. 1846, M.A. 1849); adm. 'ad eundem' 28 May, 1856, vicar of Great Wigston, co. Leicester, 1863.

Romer, Harry, 4s. Charles, of Brixton, Surrey, gent. CHRIST CHURCH, matric. 15 Oct., 1880, aged 17; B.A. 1884.

Romestin, Augustus Henry Eugene de, o.s. Augustus, of Paris, arm. ST. JOHN'S COLL., matric. 1 March, 1848, aged 17; B.A. 1852, M.A. 1854, perp. curate Woolland, Dorset, 1868-9, vicar of Freeland, Oxon, 1874-85, and of Stony Stratford 1885, warden of Great Maplestead House of Mercy 1885; for list of his works see *Crockford.*

Romestin, Rev. Eugene de, o.s. Augustus Henry Eugene, of Dresden, cler. NEW COLL., matric. 15 Oct., 1881, aged 19; B.A. 1885, M.A. 1885.

Romilly, Hugh Hastings, 3s. Frederick, of London, arm. CHRIST CHURCH, matric. 16 Oct., 1874, aged 18. See Foster's *Peerage.* [15]

Romley, John, s. William, of Burton, co. Lincoln, pleb. MAGDALEN HALL, matric. 13 Dec., 1735, aged 24.

Romman, William, s. Ric., of London, gent. ST. JOHN'S COLL., matric. 7 July, 1740, aged 17; B.C.L. 1747, rector of Upper Clatford, Hants, 1748, professor of geometry Gresham College, buried at All Hallows, Barking, 9 March, 1782. See *Robinson*, 81.

Romney, Francis Henry, 2s. James Watts, of Whitbourne, co. Hereford, gent. WORCESTER COLL. matric. 19 Oct., 1826, aged 22; B.A. 1830, M.A. 1833.

Romney, William. LINCOLN COLL., 1780. See RUMNEY, page 1234.

Rook, Clarence Henry, o.s. Henry John, of Faversham, Kent, gent. ORIEL COLL., matric. 18 Oct., 1881, aged 18; scholar 1881-6, B.A. 1886. [20]

Rooke, Daniel, M.A. from JESUS COLL., Cambridge; incorp. 7 July, 1759. (? Samuel Hooke, of JESUS COLL., Cambridge, B.A. 1703, M.A. 1707.)

Rooke, Edwin Frederick, 1s. Frederick John, of Rampisham, Dorset, cler. ORIEL COLL., matric. 23 Jan., 1863, aged 19.

Rooke, Rev. Francis Edward, 4s. Frederick John, of Rampisham, Dorset, cler. ORIEL COLL., matric. 21 May, 1880, aged 17; B.A. 1884.

Rooke, Frederick Darell, 5s. Frederick John, of Rampisham, Dorset, cler. NON-COLL., matric. 30 Oct., 1882, aged 19.

Rooke, Frederick John, 2s. Frederick William, of Corsham, Wilts, arm. ORIEL COLL, matric. 19 March, 1835, aged 17; B.A. 1838, M.A. 1841, rector of Rampisham, Dorset, 1845, preb. of Salisbury 1859. [25]

Rooke, George, s. Giles, of Lymington, Hants, equitis. MERTON COLL., matric. 21 April, 1814, aged 17; B.A. 1816, fellow 1821-31, M.A. 1822, dean 1823, principal of postmasters, and tutor 1824, hon. canon of Durham 1852, vicar of Embledon, Northumberland, 1830, until his death 17 Aug., 1874.

Rooke, (Sir) Giles, s. Giles, of London, arm. ST. JOHN'S COLL., matric. 26 Nov., 1759, aged 16, B.A. 1763; fellow MERTON COLL. 1766-85, M.A. 1766, bar.-at-law, Lincoln's Inn, 1766, serjt.-at-law 1781, King's serjeant 1793, a judge of Common Pleas 1793-1808, knighted 13 Nov., 1793, died 7 March, 1808.

Rooke, Giles, 1s. Giles, of Lymington, Hants, equitis. MERTON COLL., matric. 16 Dec., 1802, aged 16; B.A. 1805, a student of Lincoln's Inn 1805.

Rooke, James, s. James, of Brize Norton, Oxon, arm. ORIEL COLL., matric. 8 Feb., 1792, aged 16.

Rooke, Mortimer, 3s. Alexander Beaumont, of Corsham, Wilts, arm. ORIEL COLL., matric. 23 April, 1873, aged 19; B.A. 1877. [30]

Rooke, Robert, s. Thomas, of Whitehaven, Cumberland, pleb. QUEEN'S COLL., matric. 12 July, 1729, aged 20; B.A. 1733.

Rooke, Seton Paterson, 5s. Frederick William, of Greendown, Somerset, arm. ORIEL COLL., matric. 22 June, 1843, aged 18; B.A. 1847, M.A. 1850, brother of Frederick John.

Rooke, Thomas, s. Robert, of Southampton, cler. QUEEN'S COLL., matric. 19 Nov., 1773, aged 16; demy MAGDALEN COLL. 1774-96, B.A. 1777, M.A. 1780, assistant-master to Dr. Samuel Parr, at Colchester, 1777, and at Norwich 1778, died in Feb., 1796. See *Bloxam*, vii. 46.

Rooke, Thomas, M.A. & D.Med. TRINITY COLL., Dublin (B.A. 1848, M.A. 1851); adm. 'ad eundem' 7 July, 1860, vicar of Feckenham 1881.

Rooke, William Frederick, 5s. George, of Embleton, Yorks, cler. WORCESTER COLL., matric. 17 Oct., 1870, aged 19; exhibitioner 1870-5, B.A. 1874, M.A. 1877. [35]

Rooke, Willoughby John Edward, 2s. Henry Willoughby, of St. Mary's, Savoy, London, arm. BRASENOSE COLL., matric. 11 June, 1829, aged 19; B.A. 1833, M.A. 1836, vicar of Tunstall, Lancashire, 1847, domestic chaplain to H.R.H. the Duke of Cambridge, vicar of Little Wymondley, Herts, 1870-81.

Rookin, Henry, 1s. John, of Whitehaven, Cumberland, gent. QUEEN'S COLL., matric. 19 Oct., 1818, aged 16; scholar 1818-21, B.A. 1822, fellow 1822-36, M.A. 1826, vicar of Upton Grey, Hants, 1835, until his death 18 Jan., 1875. See *Rugby School Reg.*, 129.

Roope, Rev. Allen Colin, s. Charles, of Pulham, Norfolk, gent. QUEEN'S COLL., matric. 28 June, 1788, aged 21; died in July, 1802.

Roope, John, s. John, of Yarmouth, Norfolk, gent. ORIEL COLL., matric. 17 Dec., 1770, aged 20 (or 22); B.C.L. 1777. See *Gent.'s Mag.*, 1829, ii. 646.

Roope, Richard, 2s. 'Cabel' (or rather Robert), of Oporto, gent. WADHAM COLL., matric. 24 Oct., 1838, aged 18; B.A. 1842, M.A. 1845, bar.-at-law, Inner Temple, 1845, died 20 Jan., 1870.

Rooper, Archibald Henry, 1s. Henry Godolphin, of Langton, Kent, arm. BRASENOSE COLL., matric. 24 May, 1877, aged 18.

Rooper, Charles Frederick, 2s. Frederick James, of Abbots Ripton, Hunts, arm. ST. ALBAN HALL, matric. 20 Oct., 1881, aged 20.

Rooper, John George, 1s. Plumer Pott, of Chettle, Dorset, cler. EXETER COLL., matric. 27 May, 1871, aged 18; B.A. 1874, rector (and patron) of Abbots Ripton, Hunts, 1881. See *Rugby School Reg.*

Rooper, Plumer Pott, 2s. John Bonfoy, of London, arm. BRASENOSE COLL., matric. 9 June, 1846, aged 18; B.A. 1850, rector of Abbots Ripton, Hunts, 1853, until his death 18 May, 1881. See *Rugby School Reg.*, 215. [5]

Rooper, Thomas Godolphin, 2s. William Henry, of Abbots Ripton, Hunts, cler. BALLIOL COLL., matric. 13 Oct., 1866, aged 18; B.A. 1871, M.A. 1873, a student of Lincoln's Inn 1875, inspector of schools.

Rooper, William Henry, 1s. Thomas Richard, of Huntingdon, cler. UNIVERSITY COLL., matric. 22 June, 1825, aged 17; B.A. 1829, perp. curate St. Andrew's Chapel, Brighton, 1856-62.

Rooseboon, Frederick, Count, commissary of the Court of Admiralty, Amsterdam, in the suite of the Prince of Orange, created D.C.L. 1 March, 1733-4.

Rooth, John, 1s. John Wilcoxon, of London, arm. TRINITY COLL., matric. 15 Oct., 1883, aged 19; B.A. 1888.

Roots, George, 1s. George, of St. Pancras, juxta London, arm. BRASENOSE COLL., matric. 27 May, 1824, aged 17; B.A. 1828, bar.-at-law, Lincoln's Inn, 1832. See Foster's *Men at the Bar* & *Eton School Lists.* [10]

Roots, Thomas, s. Richard, of The Close of Sarum, cler. TRINITY COLL., matric. 7 Dec., 1727, aged 16. See *Gent.'s Mag.*, 1755, p. 284.

Roper, Alfred Francis, 5s. Thomas Henry, of Sulham, Berks, cler. NON-COLL., matric. 25 Oct., 1873, aged 20; B.A. from KEBLE COLL. 1877, M.A. 1880.

Roper, Charles, s. William, of Dublin (city), arm. BRASENOSE COLL., matric. 3 April, 1813, aged 17; B.A. 1816, of Rathfarnham Castle, etc., a student of Lincoln's Inn 1815, died 9 May, 1861. See Foster's *Peerage*, B. TEYNHAM.

Roper, Charles Blaney Trevor, 1s. Cadwallader Blaney Trevor, of Lewisham, Kent, arm. WORCESTER COLL., matric. 26 May, 1820, aged 20; of Plas Têg, Flints, high sheriff 1835, died 9 Feb., 1871.

Roper, Charles James Trevor-, 1s. Charles Blaney, of Hope, co. Southampton, arm. ST. JOHN'S COLL., matric. 5 March, 1845, aged 21; B.A. 1849, M.A. 1865, of Plas Têg, Flintshire, high sheriff 1878, a student of Lincoln's Inn 1845, sometime hon. colonel 6th battalion royal rifle corps. See Foster's *Peerage*, B. TEYNHAM. [15]

Roper, Charles Rodwell, s. Robert, of Wicken Hall, Bradwell, Suffolk, gent. ST. JOHN'S COLL., matric. 16 April, 1817, aged 14; bible clerk 1817-20, B.A. 1824, M.A. 1830, rector of St. Olave, Exeter, 1840-67, died 26 July, 1867.

Roper, Freeman, 1s. Freeman C. S., of London, gent. NEW COLL., matric. 15 Oct., 1881, aged 19; B.A. 1884.

Roper, Henry, s. Henry, Baron Teynham. ORIEL COLL., matric. 23 May, 1783, aged 19; created M.A. 16 Dec., 1785, 12th baron, died 10 June, 1800. See Foster's *Peerage.*

Roper, Henry Charles, 1s. Henry, of West Stoke, near Chichester, equitis. MERTON COLL., matric. 17 Oct., 1868, aged 18; B.A. 1872, bar.-at-law, Lincoln's Inn, 1874. See Foster's *Men at the Bar* & *Eton School Lists.*

Roper, John Anthony, 1s. Anthony, of Bengeworth, co. Worcester, gent. QUEEN'S COLL., matric. 21 June, 1827, aged 18. [20]

Roper, John Charles, 2s. John William, of Frant, Sussex, gent. KEBLE COLL., matric. 15 Oct., 1877, aged 18, B.A. 1881; chaplain BRASENOSE COLL. 1883-5, M.A. 1884, professor of theology, Toronto, 1886.

Roper, Philip, Baron Teynham, s. Henry, Baron Teynham. ST. JOHN'S COLL., matric. 8 July, 1723, aged 18; 9th lord, died unmarried 1 June, 1727. See Foster's *Peerage.*

Roper, Roper Stote Donnison Rowe, o.s. Thomas Rowe, of Hutton Henry, co. Durham, arm. UNIVERSITY COLL., matric. 10 May, 1832, aged 18; B.A. from ST. MARY HALL 1838.

Roper, Thomas Henry, 1s. Thomas, of Hampstead, gent. ST. JOHN'S COLL., matric. 8 Dec., 1836, aged 17; B.A. 1841, M.A. 1844, bar.-at-law, Lincoln's Inn, 1844, conduct of Eton College and curate of Eton 1855-63, rector of Puddlehinton, Dorset, 1863. See *Eton School Lists.*

Roper, Trevor Charles, s. Charles, of East Barnet, Middlesex, arm. CHRIST CHURCH, matric. 18 Nov., 1763, aged 18; 18th Lord Dacre, died 3 July, 1794. See Foster's *Peerage.* [25]

Roper, William, s. William, of King's Norton, co. Worcester, pleb. WORCESTER COLL., matric. 23 June, 1726, aged 17; B.A. 1730.

Roper, Rev. William, 2s. John, of Bridport, Dorset, gent. WORCESTER COLL., matric. 21 Oct., 1880, aged 18; B.A. 1884, M.A. 1887.

Roper, William John Duff, 3s. Thomas, of Hampstead, Middlesex, gent. LINCOLN COLL., matric. 14 June, 1849, aged 19.

Rorison, William Mitchell Macaulay, 1s. Gilbert, of Peterhead, Aberdeen, cler. ST. JOHN'S COLL., matric. 20 April, 1868, aged 21; scholar 1868-72, B.A. 1872.

Ros, Henry William Fitzgerald de, s. Henry, of St. Marylebone, London, arm. CHRIST CHURCH, matric. 21 Nov., 1812, aged 19; M.P. West Looe 1816-8, became 22nd Baron de Ros in 1831, died 29 March, 1839. See Foster's *Peerage* & *Eton School Lists.* [30]

Ros, William Lennox Lascelles Fitzgerald de, s. Hon. Henry, of Thames Ditton, Surrey, arm. CHRIST CHURCH, matric. 16 Dec., 1815, aged 18; student 1815-24, B.A. 1819, M.A. 1822, became 23rd Baron de Ros in 1839, colonel 4th hussars, lieut.-governor Tower of London, general in the army, died 5 Jan., 1874. See *Alumni West.*, 479.

Roscoe, Alfred, 3s. Robert, of Finchley, Middlesex, arm. WADHAM COLL., matric. 25 Jan., 1862, aged 20.

Roscoe, Edmund, 1s. Henry Enfield, of Manchester, arm. (after knight). MAGDALEN COLL., matric. 19 Oct., 1883, aged 19; died in Jan., 1885.

Roscoe, Sir Henry Enfield, F.R.S., created D.C.L. 22 June, 1887 (son of Henry Roscoe), B.A. University of London 1852, Ph.D. Heidelberg 1853, and hon. D.Med. 1886, created LL.D. Dublin 1878, Cambridge 1883, and Montreal 1884, president of Chemistry Society, London, 1850, and of Literary and Philosophical Society, Manchester, 1882, professor of chemistry at Owen's College (Victoria University), Manchester, 1858-86, F.R.S. 1863 (royal medal 1873), knighted 29 Nov., 1884, M.P. Manchester (South).

Roscoe, Henry William Kent, 2s. Edward Henry, of Chester (city), arm. CORPUS CHRISTI COLL., matric. 21 Oct., 1869, aged 19; scholar 1869-74, B.A. 1874, bar.-at-law, Lincoln's Inn, 1886. [35]

Rosdew, Joseph, s. Richard, of Yealmpton, Devon gent. EXETER COLL., matric. 31 May, 1786, aged 17; B.A. 1790, fellow 1792-1827, M.A. 1793, B.D. 1804, dean 1822, bursar 1824, vicar of South Newington 1808-18, rector of Bushey, Herts, 1827, until his death at Bushey 1 June, 1835. See *Coll. Reg.*, 115.

Rose, Bateman Lancaster, 5s. Philip, of London, gent. EXETER COLL., matric. 18 May, 1869, aged 17; B.A. from ST. ALBAN HALL 1874, M.A. 1879.

Rose, Charles, s. William Lucas, of Daventry, Northants, cler. LINCOLN COLL., matric. 29 Oct., 1807, aged 19; B.A. 1810, fellow 1812-36, M.A. 1812, B.D. 1819, tutor 1814-34, and Greek lecturer 1822, rector of Slapton, Northants, 1816, Whitehall preacher 1824, rector of Cublington, Bucks, 1834, until his death 12 Feb., 1845.

Rose, Daniel, 5s. James, of Cupar, Fife (Scotland), arm. BALLIOL COLL., matric. 18 Jan., 1864, aged 20; exhibitioner 1864-8.

Rose, Georges, 2s. James, of St. Clement Danes, Middlesex, gent. MAGDALEN HALL, matric. 28 May, 1841, aged 24; B.A. 1845, M.A. 1848, died 11 Nov., 1882. See Noble's *Biographical Anecdotes*, ix., p. 426. [5]

Rose, George Daniel Fullwood, 4s. David, of Wednesbury, co. Stafford, gent. PEMBROKE COLL., matric. 25 Oct., 1869, aged 19; B.A. 1872, M.A. 1876.

Rose, George Henry Boscawen, Earl of Falmouth. CHRIST CHURCH, 1829. See BOSCAWEN, page 135.

Rose, Henry Edward, 1s. Henry, of Croydon, Surrey, arm. KEBLE COLL., matric. 16 Oct., 1876, aged 19; scholar 1877-9.

Rose, Henry John, fellow ST. JOHN'S COLL., Cambridge, 1824-38 (14th wrangler & B.A. 1821, M.A. 1824, B.D. 1831); adm. 'ad eundem' 26 June, 1851, rector of Houghton Conquest, Beds, 1837-73, archdeacon of Bedford 1866, until his death 31 Jan., 1873.

Rose, Sir Hugh Henry, created D.C.L. 21 June, 1865, commanded Central India field force throughout the Indian Mutiny 1857-8, G.C.B., commander-in-chief in India 1860-5, colonel 92nd highlanders 1866-9, royal horse guards 1869-85, created Baron Strathnairn 31 July, 1866, field-marshal 1877, constable of the Tower 1880 (4s. Sir George Henry Rose, G.C.H., of Sandhills, Herts), died 16 Oct., 1885. See Foster's *Peerage*. [10]

Rose, Hugh James, fellow TRINITY COLL., Cambridge, 1817 (14th wrangler & B.A. 1817, chancellor's medallist, M.A. 1820, B.D. 1827); adm. 'ad eundem' 10 June, 1834, Hulsean Christian advocate 1829-33 (s. William, vicar of Glynde, Sussex), vicar of Horsham 1822-30, preb. of Chichester 1827-33, rector of Hadleigh, Suffolk, 1830-4, and of Fairsted, Essex, 1834-36, and perp. curate St. Thomas, Southwark, 1834, principal of King's College, London, 1836, until his death 22 Dec., 1838; for list of his works see *Gent.'s Mag.*, 1839, i. 319.

Rose, Hugh James, 1s. Henry John, of Houghton Conquest, Beds, cler. ORIEL COLL., matric. 20 Oct., 1860, aged 19; B.A. 1865, M.A. 1867, chaplain at Linares 1873-4, at Terez, Cadiz, etc., 1874, until his death 6 July, 1878.

Rose, James, 'Faber ferrarius;' privilegiatus 17 Nov., 1758 (subs. 'smith').

Rose, James, s. Hugh, of Mayo, co. Mayo (Ireland), arm. QUEEN'S COLL., matric. 6 Jan., 1796, aged 19.

Rose, James, o.s. James, of Bampton, Oxon, gent. EXETER COLL., matric. 31 May, 1873, aged 18; B.A. 1877, M.A. 1880. [15]

Rose, John, s. John, of Lambeth, Surrey, gent. ST. JOHN'S COLL., matric. 30 June, 1772, aged 17; B.A. 1776, M.A. 1785, B. & D.D. 1808, under-master Merchant Taylors' School 1779, rector of St. Martin's Outwich, 1795. See *Robinson*, 122.

Rose, John Henry, 'musicus;' privilegiatus 3 Nov., 1810.

Rose, John William, 2s. Henry, of Edinburgh, gent. BALLIOL COLL., matric. 21 Oct., 1880, aged 18; B.A. 1884, M.A. 1887.

Rose, Joseph, s. Joseph, of London, gent. TRINITY COLL., matric. 6 June, 1785, aged 20; B.A. 1789. See *Gent.'s Mag.*, 1830, ii. 378.

Rose, Joseph, s. Joseph, of Marylebone, Middlesex, cler. CHRIST CHURCH, matric. 22 Oct., 1801, aged 18; B.A. 1805, M.A. 1808. [20]

Rose, Richard Overend, 2s. William, of St. Pancras, London, arm. QUEEN'S COLL., matric. 3 Nov., 1871, aged 19; B.A. 1875, M.A. 1878, vicar of Staplefield, Sussex, 1884, and Markyate Street, Dunstable, 1885.

Rose, Samuel, s. John, of Northampton (town) gent. LINCOLN COLL., matric. 9 May, 1734, aged 17; B.A. 26 Jan., 1737-8.

Rose, Thomas, s. John, of Aberdeen, Scotland, cler. BALLIOL COLL., matric. 26 May, 1797, aged 15; B.A. 1801, M.A. 1803.

Rose, William, s. Joseph, of Doncaster, Yorks, arm. EXETER COLL., matric. 8 May, 1769, aged 18; B.A. 1773, M.A. 1778, rector of Carshalton, Surrey, and rector of Beckenham, Kent, 1776, until his death 2 April, 1829.

Rose, William, 'Faber ferrarius;' privilegiatus 11 Dec., 1787. [25]

Rose, William Francis, 2s. Henry John, of Houghton Conquest, Beds, cler. WORCESTER COLL., matric. 18 Oct., 1862, aged 20; B.A. 1867, M.A. 1871, vicar of Worle, Somerset, 1874.

Rose, William George, 1s. William, of Islington, Middlesex, arm. CHRIST CHURCH, matric. 26 Nov., 1830, aged 17.

Rose, William Somerset, 1s. John Capel, of Cransley, Northants, arm. BRASENOSE COLL., matric. 9 June, 1824, aged 18; of Cransley Hall, Northants, high sheriff 1867, died 1884.

Rosedale, Honyel Gough, 2s. William Lewis, of Willenhall, co. Stafford, cler. CHRIST CHURCH, matric. 4 June, 1881, aged 18; B.A. 1885, M.A. 1888.

Rosedale, William Elitto, 1s. William Lewis, of Willenhall, co. Stafford, cler. NON-COLL., matric. 20 Jan., 1877, aged 19; B.A. from NEW COLL. 1881, M.A. 1885, rector of Little Tintern, Monmouthshire, 1886. [30]

Rosenberg, Charles Bulkeley, s. Charles, of Bath, Somerset, gent. WADHAM COLL., matric. 21 Nov., 1811, aged 19.

Rosenstock, Rudolph, 2s. Julius, of Cassel, in Germany, gent. ST. EDMUND HALL, matric. 19 Oct., 1878, aged 18; B.A. 1882.

Rosenthal, Eugene Adolphus, 1s. Adolphus Lewis, of London, gent. EXETER COLL., matric. 23 Oct., 1885, aged 19.

Roskill, John Henry, 2s. Gustavus, of Manchester, gent. CORPUS CHRISTI COLL., matric. 20 Oct., 1879, aged 19; exhibitioner 1880-8, B.A. 1883, M.A. 1886, bar.-at-law, Inner Temple, 1883.

Roskilly, William, s. Thomas, of Llandreth, Cornwall, pleb. MAGDALEN HALL, matric. 7 July, 1783, aged 24; B.A. 1788, M.A. 1790, vicar of Kempsford, co. Gloucester, 1798, until his death in 1810. [35]

Ross, Alexander Adolphus, s. John, of Glenluce, co. Galloway (Scotland), arm. UNIVERSITY COLL., matric. 21 Sep., 1793, aged 17; B.A. 1797.

Ross, Alexander George Gordon, 2s. Alexander Henry, of London, arm. NEW COLL., matric. 16 Oct., 1885, aged 19.

Ross, Alexander Gordon, 1s. Henry James, of Esher, Surrey, gent. NON-COLL., matric. 3 Nov., 1883, aged 21.

Ross, Alexander Henry, 2s. Charles, of London, arm. CHRIST CHURCH, matric. 27 May, 1847, aged 17; B.A. 1851, M.A. 1865, bar.-at-law, Inner Temple, 1854, M.P. Maidstone 1880. See Foster's *Men at the Bar* & *Eton School Lists*.

Ross, Andrew, 1s. Philip, of Lower Wincraig, co. Ross, gent. WORCESTER COLL., matric. 22 April, 1885, aged 19. [40]

Ross, Benjamin Atkinson, 6s. Thomas Andrew, of Dundalk, co. Armagh, gent. NON-COLL., matric. 18 Oct., 1880, aged 19; B.A. from BALLIOL COLL. 1883, B.C.L. & M.A. 1887, bar.-at-law, Inner Temple. 1886.

Ross, Charles, s. Alexander, of Westminster, arm. CHRIST CHURCH, matric. 11 Feb., 1818, aged 18; B.A. 1822, M.A. 1824, created D.C.L. 13 June, 1834, M.P. Oxford 1822-6, St. Germains 1826-32, Northampton 1832-7, lord of the Admiralty 1830, of the Treasury 1832-5, a commissioner of audit 1849, until his death 21 March, 1860. See *Eton School Lists.*

Ross, Charles Douglas, 2s. Patrick, of Valetta, Isle of Malta, equitis. WADHAM COLL., matric. 1 July, 1843, aged 17; scholar 1843-8, B.A. 1847, M.A. 1853, fellow 1848-82, tutor 1853, dean 1855, died 16 Aug., 1882, aged 57.

Ross, Charles Sydenham, 2s. Archibald, of Lisbon, arm. MAGDALEN HALL, matric. 7 May, 1835, aged 17; B.A. 1839, M.A. 1841, held various curacies 1841-65, vicar of St. John, Glastonbury, 1865.

Ross, (Sir) Charles William Augustus (8th Bart.), born in Cheltenham, co. Gloucester, o.s. Charles, of Balnagowan, Scotland, baronet. CHRIST CHURCH, matric. 18 April, 1821, aged 19. See Foster's *Baronetage.*

Ross, David Melville, 1s. Charles Willert, of West Deeping, co. Lincoln, cler. NON-COLL., matric. 11 Oct., 1879, aged 18; scholar JESUS COLL. 1880-4, B.A. 1883, M.A. 1886. **[6]**

Ross, David Robert, s. Thomas, of Rosstrevor, co. Down (Ireland), cler. QUEEN'S COLL., matric. 26 Oct., 1814, aged 17; high sheriff co. Down 1837, M.P. Belfast 1842-7, governor of Tobago, 14 Feb., 1851, died 27 July, 1851.

Ross, George, 1s. George, of Cape of Good Hope, arm. LINCOLN COLL., matric. 13 Oct., 1820, aged 16; B.A. 1828, M.A. 1852, perp. curate Shepscomb, co. Gloucester, 1854-8, vicar of Tywardreath, Cornwall, 1863.

Ross, George Arthur Emilius, 9s. Edward Dalhousie, of Compigne, France, gent. PEMBROKE COLL., matric. 5 Dec., 1845, aged 17.

Ross, George Gould, o.s. George, of Wootton, Courtenay, Somerset, cler. ST. MARY HALL, matric. 23 March, 1850, aged 20; scholar 1851-5, S.C.L. 1855, B.C.L. 1856, M.A. 1860, D.C.L. 1875, chaplain at Dieppe 1869-75, acting principal Codrington College, Barbados, 1873, head-master St. Andrew Diocesan College, Grahamstown, 1875-81, and canon 1876-83, incumbent of St. Peter, Pietermaritzburg, 1882-3, etc. See *Crockford.* **[10]**

Ross, Rev. George Henry William Lockhart, 1s. John Lockhart, of Allanton, co. Lanark, cler. QUEEN'S COLL., matric. 31 May, 1873, aged 19; B.A. 1877. See Foster's *Baronetage* & *Robinson*, 359.

Ross, Henry Nickson, 3s. John, of Lowton, Lancashire, gent. CHRIST CHURCH, matric. 12 June, 1886, aged 19.

Ross, James Adolphus, 3s. Hew Dalrymple, of Hayton, Cumberland, equitis. EXETER COLL., matric. 23 Jan., 1845, aged 18; his father, who was 3rd son of Major John Ross, of Balkael, co. Galway, died a field-marshal and lieut.-governor of Chelsea Hospital, 10 Dec., 1868, aged 89.

Ross, Sir James Clark, captain R.N.; created D.C.L. 20 June, 1844, F.R.S., F.L.S., F.R.A.S, F.R.G.S. (3s. George, of Balsarroch, Galloway), entered the navy 1812, accompanied his uncle, Sir John Ross, in both his expeditions in search of a north-west passage, and also accompanied Parry in his three Arctic voyages 1819-25, discovered the position of the north magnetic pole 1829-33, commanded the *Erebus* in the Arctic expedition 1839-43, when he discovered Victoria land and the volcano 'Mount Erebus,' knighted 13 March, 1844, commanded an expedition in search of Sir John Franklin in 1848, Royal Geographical Society's gold medal 1841, died 3 April, 1862.

Rosse, John, of CORPUS CHRISTI COLL., Cambridge (M.A. 1720); incorp. from MERTON COLL. 13 Oct., 1722. **[15]**

Ross, John, fellow ST. JOHN'S COLL., Cambridge (B.A. 1740, M.A. 1740); incorp. 10 July, 1744, B.D. 1751, D.D. 1756, F.R.S., vicar of Frome, Somerset, 1760, preacher at the Rolls' Chapel, Bishop of Exeter 1778, until his death 14 Aug., 1792.

Ross, John Dawes, s. Richard, of Newton Harcourt, co. Leicester, pleb. ST. EDMUND HALL, matric. 19 Oct., 1757, aged 21; B.A. 1761, M.A. 1767.

Ross, John Lockhart, 1s. George, of Edinburgh, Scotland, arm. ORIEL COLL., matric. 27 June, 1829, aged 18; B.A. 1833, M.A. 1836, vicar of Fifield and Idbury, Oxon, 1840, and of Avebury, Wilts, 1852-63, rector of St. George-in-the-East 1863-73, and of St. Dunstan-in-the-East 1873; for list of his works see *Crockford.* See Foster's *Baronetage.*

Ross, John Pemberton, s. Andrew, of Isle of St. Vincent, West Indies, arm. BRASENOSE COLL., matric. 31 March, 1804, aged 18.

Ross, Reginald Robert Hamilton, 2s. John Lockhart, of Edinburgh, cler. ST. JOHN'S COLL., matric. 11 Oct., 1873, aged 18; scholar 1873-8, B.A. 1877, M.A. 1880. See Foster's *Baronetage* & *Robinson*, 359. **[20]**

'Ross of Bladensburg,' Robert Skeffington, 1s. Daniel, of Rosstrevor, co. Down, Ireland, arm. EXETER COLL., matric. 12 Oct., 1866, aged 19; B.A. & M.A. 1873, of Rosstrevor, co. Down, J.P., D.L., bar.-at-law, Lincoln's Inn, 1875, became a Jesuit priest 1884, sometime captain royal South Down militia. See Foster's *Men at the Bar.*

Rosser, Charles Adeane, 1s. Charles, of Gloucester (city), arm. ORIEL COLL., matric. 22 May, 1861, aged 18; B.A. 1864, M.A. 1868, chaplain to the forces 1871.

Rosseter, Robert Grafton, o.s. James Marmaduke, of Lambeth, arm. CHRIST CHURCH, matric. 3 June, 1840, aged 18; B.A. 1844, M.A. 1847, bar.-at-law, Lincoln's Inn, 1848, curate of Mayd Laver, Essex, died 19 July, 1861. See *Eton School Lists.*

Rossiter, Francis Seares, 1s. Charles, of London, gent. WADHAM COLL., matric. 19 Oct., 1885, aged 19; scholar 1884.

Rost, Reinhold, Ph. D.; created M.A. 22 June, 1886, librarian at the India Office. **[25]**

Rosthorn, Arthur de, 2s. Joseph, of Vienna, arm. NON-COLL., matric. 14 Oct., 1882, aged 20.

Roston, James, s. Thomas, of Draycot, Wilts, gent. QUEEN'S COLL., matric. 29 Oct., 1754, aged 18.

Rotch, William Dickason, o.s. Thomas Dickason, of London, arm. EXETER COLL., matric. 14 June, 1859, aged 18; B.A. 1862, bar.-at-law, Inner Temple, 1865. See Foster's *Men at the Bar.*

Roth, George Abraham, s. Richard, of ——, co. Kilkenny, Ireland, arm. CHRIST CHURCH, matric. 17 June, 1784, aged 17; a student of Lincoln's Inn 1784.

Roth, Walter Edmund, 5s. Matthew, of London, D.Med. MAGDALEN COLL., matric. 9 Dec., 1880, aged 19; demy 1880-5, B.A. 1885. **[30]**

Rotherham, Alan, 2s. John, of Coventry, gent. BALLIOL COLL., matric. 18 Oct., 1881, aged 19; B.A. 1886, bar.-at-law, Lincoln's Inn, 1888.

Rotherham, John, s. William, of Haydon Bridge, Northumberland, cler. QUEEN'S COLL., matric. 18 March, 1744-5, aged 19; B.A. 1748, M.A. by decree 11 Dec., 1753, Percy fellow University College 1760-7, rector of Houghton-le-Spring, and vicar of Seaham, co. Durham, 1769, until his death 24 July, 1789. See *O.H.S.*, ix. 27.

Rotherham, Thomas, s. William, of Haydon Bridge, Northumberland, cler. QUEEN'S COLL., matric. 24 May, 1737, aged 18; B.A. 6 Feb., 1740-1, M.A. 1744.

Rotherham, George Charles, o.s. Richard Kevett, of Coventry, co. Warwick, arm. ST. JOHN'S COLL., matric. 14 Dec., 1864, aged 19.

Rothschild, His Excellency Baron, created D.C.L. 24 June, 1857, envoy extraordinary and minister plenipotentiary of the King of Sweden at St. James's.

Rothwell, Francis Talbot, 1s. William Talbot, of Foxholes, Lancashire, gent. NON-COLL., matric. 15 Oct., 1870, aged 19.

Rothwell, James, s. Richard, of Bolton, Lancashire, cler. BRASENOSE COLL., matric. 31 March, 1787, aged 21; B.A. 1791, of Manor House, Much Hoole, died 6 Oct., 1824. See *Manchester School Reg.*, ii. 49.

Rothwell, Ralph, 2s. Ralph, of Preston, Lancashire, arm. BRASENOSE COLL., matric. 19 Nov., 1835, aged 19.

Rothwell, Richard, s. Richard, of Corley, co. Warwick, cler. HERTFORD COLL., matric. 14 Oct., 1748, aged 18; B.A. 1752. See *Gent.'s Mag.*, 1766, p. 247. [5]

Rothwell, Richard, s. Thomas, of Dublin, Ireland, arm. EXETER COLL., matric. 2 July, 1816, aged 17; B.A. 1820, of Rockfield, co. Meath, high sheriff 1839, died 13 Aug., 1853.

Rothwell, Richard Rainshaw, s. Richard, of Sharples, Lancashire, cler. BRASENOSE COLL., matric. 22 May, 1792, aged 20; B.A. 1799, M.A. 1800, rector of Sefton, 1801, until his death 5 April, 1863, his father died rector of Sefton 18 Sep., 1801. See *Manchester School Reg.*, ii. 130; & *Gent. s Mag.*, 1801, ii. 962.

Rothwell, Richard Rainshaw, o.s. Ralph, of Dunkirk, France, arm. BRASENOSE COLL., matric. 6 June, 1879, aged 18.

Rothwell, Richard Rainshaw, 1s. Ralph, of Preston, Lancashire, arm. BRASENOSE COLL., matric. 19 June, 1828, aged 19; B.A. 1833, M.A. 1835, of Sharples Hall, Lancashire, bar.-at-law, Inner Temple, 1847, Marquis and Count de Rothwell in the kingdom of Italy 1860. See Foster's *Men at the Bar* & *Manchester School Reg.*, ii. 130.

Rothwell, Thomas, 2s. Thomas, of Clonee, co. Dublin, arm. ORIEL COLL., matric. 1 March, 1832, aged 17; B.A. 1836, of Black Castle, co. Meath, and of Shantonagh, co. Monaghan, high sheriff 1841, assumed the surname and arms of FITZHERBERT in lieu of ROTHWELL by royal licence 19 Sep., 1863, died 29 April, 1879. [10]

Rothwell, Thomas, 1s. Richard, of Rockfield, co. Meath, Ireland, arm. MAGDALEN COLL., matric. 9 April, 1853, aged 18; B.A. 1857, of Rockfield House aforesaid, high sheriff co. Meath 1867.

Rotton, John, s. John, of Birmingham, co. Warwick, gent. ST. MARY HALL, matric. 27 Feb., 1784, aged 19.

Rotton, John Edward Whatton, o.s. John Stuart, of Cawnpore, East Indies, arm. ST. EDMUND HALL, matric. 15 Oct., 1840, aged 17.

Rotton, Walter, s. Robert, of Norton, co. Worcester, pleb. PEMBROKE COLL., matric. 13 March, 1721-2, aged 18; B.A. 1725.

Rotton, William, 3s. John, of Bath, gent. WADHAM COLL., matric. 27 June, 1844, aged 17; B.A. 1848, bar.-at-law, Inner Temple, 1853, died 9 June, 1865.

Rouch, Frederick, s. Thomas, of Bristol (city), gent. ST. JOHN'S COLL., matric. 24 May, 1817, aged 18; B.A. 1820, M.A. 1824, minor canon of Bristol 1825-7, and of Canterbury 1827-85, vicar of Lower Halston, Kent, 1840-59, and of Littlebourne, Kent, 1859-81, died 9 June, 1885. [15]

Rougemont, Edward, 3s. George, of Marylebone, London, arm. TRINITY COLL., matric. 29 Nov., 1849, aged 18; B.A. & M.A. 1856.

Roughead, Rev. William, of TRINITY COLL., Cambridge (B.A. 1856, M.A. 1859); adm. 'ad eundem' 9 Feb., 1860.

Roughsedge, Robert (Hankinson), s. Edward, of Liverpool, Lancashire, gent. BRASENOSE COLL., matric. 30 March, 1765, aged 18; B.A. 1769, M.A. 1771, incumbent of St. Peter's, Liverpool, 1796, until his death 10 Oct., 1829.

Round, Charles Gray, s. Charles, of Colchester, Essex, arm. BALLIOL COLL., matric. 22 Nov., 1814, aged 17; B.A. 1818, M.A. 1821, of Birch Hall, J.P., D.L., Essex, bar.-at-law, Lincoln's Inn, 1822, recorder of Colchester, M.P. North Essex, 1837-47, chairman Quarter Sessions, died 1 Dec., 1867. See Foster's *Our Noble and Gentle Families.* [20]

Round, Edmund, 3s. John, of St. James's, Westminster, arm. BALLIOL COLL., matric. 28 March, 1838, aged 17; B.A. 1841, M.A. 1844, of Wyvenhoe, Essex, bar.-at-law, Inner Temple, 1845, J.P. Essex, See Foster's *Men at the Bar.*

Round, Francis Richard, C.M.G., 2s. James Thomas, of Colchester, Essex, cler. BALLIOL COLL., matric. 17 Oct., 1864, aged 19; B.A. 1868, M.A. 1879, of the Colonial Office, C.M.G. 21 June, 1887.

Round, Frederick Peel, 2s. John, of Danbury Park, Essex, arm. BALLIOL COLL., matric. 18 March, 1836, aged 17; B.A. 1839, gentleman usher of the Green Rod, died 18 May, 1884.

Round, George, 1s. George, of St. Peter's, Colchester, arm. BALLIOL COLL., matric. 27 March, 1821, aged 18; of East Hill House, Colchester, and of East and West Mersea, Essex, high sheriff 1845, died 7 July, 1857.

Round, James, 1s. James Thomas, of Colchester, Essex, cler. CHRIST CHURCH, matric. 31 May, 1860, aged 18; B.A. 1864, M.A. 1872, of Birch, Essex, J.P., D.L., bar.-at-law, Inner Temple, 1868, M.P. East Essex 1868-85, and for Essex (Harwich division) since 1885, sometime major 4th battalion Essex regiment. See Foster's *Men at the Bar.* [25]

Round, James Thomas, 2s. Charles, of Birch Hall, Essex, arm. BALLIOL COLL., matric. 13 Dec., 1816, aged 18; scholar 1817-20, B.A. 1820, fellow 1820-35, M.A. 1823, B.D. 1830, proctor 1829, tutor 1824, senior dean 1825, bursar 1827, catechetical lecturer, preb. of St. Paul's 1843, rector of St. Reinwald's 1824-51, of St. Nicholas 1830-46, and of All Saints, Colchester, 1851, until his death 27 Aug., 1860.

Round, John, s. John, of St. Martin's, Colchester, Essex, arm. BALLIOL COLL., matric. 17 June, 1801, aged 18; B.A. 1805, M.A. 1808, created D.C.L. 16 June, 1814, of Danbury Park, Essex, J.P., D.L., high sheriff 1834, M.P. Ipswich 1812-8, Maldon 1837-47, high steward Colchester 1818, until his death 28 April, 1860. See Foster's *Our Noble and Gentle Families.*

Round, John, 1s. John, of St. George's, Hanover Square, London, arm. BALLIOL COLL., matric. 16 May, 1834, aged 18; B.A. 1838, M.A. 1841, of West Bergholt Hall, Essex, a student of the Inner Temple 1838, died 18 May, 1887.

Round, John Horace, o.s. John, of Brighton, Sussex, arm. BALLIOL COLL., matric. 20 Oct., 1874, aged 20; B.A. 1879, M.A. 1881, of West Bergholt Hall, Essex.

Round, Joseph Green, 3s. Charles, of St. James's, Colchester, arm. BALLIOL COLL., matric. 27 March, 1821, aged 17; B.A. 1825, M.A. 1827, rector of Woodham Mortimer, Essex, 1830, until his death 12 Sep., 1835. [30]

Round, Thomas Bennett, s. Charles, of Windsor, Berks, gent. ST. JOHN'S COLL., matric. 25 June, 1816, aged 18; B.A. 1821, M.A. 1822 (this name was originally spelt ROUNDS). See *Eton School Lists.*

Roundell, Charles Savile, 3s. Danson Richardson, of Clifton, co. York, arm. BALLIOL COLL., matric. 29 Nov., 1845, aged 18, B.A. 1850; fellow MERTON COLL. 1851-74, M.A. 1852, sub-warden 1860, of Oeborne, Fernhurst, Sussex, J.P., D.L., bar.-at-law, Lincoln's Inn, 1857, resumed his patronymic ROUNDELL in lieu of CURRER, M.P. Grantham 1880-5, private secretary to Earl Spencer when lord-lieut. Ireland 1868, a governor of Harrow School. See Foster's *Men at the Bar.*

Roundell, Danson, s. William, of Knaresborough, Yorks, gent. UNIVERSITY COLL., matric. 4 June, 1728, aged 18; B.A. 17 Feb., 1731-2, of Marton in Craven, J.P., D.L., died 30 May, 1770.

Roundell, Rev. Danson Richardson, s. William, of Marton, co. York, cler. CHRIST CHURCH, matric. 21 Oct., 1802, aged 18; B.A. 1806, M.A. 1809, assumed the surname and arms of CURRER 1806, resumed his patronymic by royal licence 21 Oct., 1851, died 10 March, 1873. See Foster's *Yorkshire Collection.*

Roundell, Henry, 1s. Henry Dawson, of Fringford, Oxon, cler. CHRIST CHURCH, matric. 9 June, 1843, aged 18; B.A. 1847, M.A. 1850, vicar of Buckingham, Oxon, 1854, until his death 26 Dec., 1864.

Roundell, Henry Dawson, s. William, of Marton, Yorks, cler. BRASENOSE COLL., matric. 12 April, 1804, aged 18, B.A. 1808; fellow MAGDALEN COLL. 1819, M.A. 1810, B.D. 1818, rector of Fringford, Oxon, 1815, until his death 17 Dec., 1852.

Roundell, Richard, s. Danson, of Marton, Yorks, gent. UNIVERSITY COLL., matric. 26 March, 1760, aged 18; B.A. 1763, a student of Lincoln's Inn 1765, died 11 Feb., 1772. [5]

Roundell, Richard Henry, s. William, of Marton, Yorks, cler. MAGDALEN COLL., matric. 6 April, 1796, aged 19; of Gledstone and Scriven, Yorks, high sheriff 1835, died 26 Aug., 1851.

Roundell, William, s. William, of Knaresborough, Yorks, gent. CHRIST CHURCH, matric. 28 March, 1726, aged 17; B.A. 1729, M.A. 1732, B.Med. & D.Med. 1740, of the city of York, died 31 May, 1762.

Roundell, Rev. William, s. Danson, of Marton, Yorks, gent. UNIVERSITY COLL., matric. 26 March, 1760, aged 17, B.A. 1763; fellow MAGDALEN COLL., M.A. 1766, of Gledstone House, Yorks.

Roundell, William, 1s. Danson Richardson, of Whitwell, co. York, cler. CHRIST CHURCH, matric. 4 June, 1835, aged 17; B.A. 1839, M.A. 1842, of Gledstone, Yorks, high sheriff (W.R.) 1881, bar.-at-law, Inner Temple, 1842, died 21 Sep., 1881. See Foster's *Yorkshire Collection.*

Roupell, George Charles Kynaston Pigott, 3s. Thomas Boone, of Madras, arm. CHRIST CHURCH, matric. 3 June, 1868, aged 18. [10]

Rouquet, James, s. Anthony, of London, pleb. ST. JOHN'S COLL., matric. 16 July, 1748, aged 18 (? died curate of St. Werburgh's 16 Nov., 1776).

Rouquet, James, s. James, of St. James's, Bristol, cler. MAGDALEN HALL, matric. 2 April, 1781, aged 19; B.A. from HERTFORD COLL. 1785, vicar of West Harptree, Somerset, 1789, until his death 22 March, 1837.

Rous, George, s. Thomas, of St. Michael Royal, London, arm. CHRIST CHURCH, matric. 16 Dec., 1760, aged 16; B.A. 1764, M.A. 1768, bar.-at-law, Inner Temple, 1768, bencher 1802, counsel to the East India Company, M.P. Shaftesbury 1776-80, died 11 June, 1802, buried in the Temple Church on the 18th.

Rous, Hugh Anthony, born at Henham, Suffolk, s. John, Baron R. BRASENOSE COLL., matric. 6 June, 1818, aged 17; B.A. 1821, M.A. 1824, vicar of Reyden, and perp. curate Southwold, Suffolk, 1826, until his death 29 Sep., 1828. See Foster's *Peerage*, E. STRADBROKE; & *Alumni West.*, 484.

Rous, John, s. Thomas, of Wotton-under-Edge, co. Gloucester, arm. CHRIST CHURCH, matric. 8 March, 1727-8, aged 18; of Piercefield, co. Monmouth, bar.-at-law, Lincoln's Inn, 1733. [15]

Rous, John, s. John, of Henham, Suffolk, baronet. MAGDALEN COLL., matric. 17 May, 1768, aged 17; created M.A. 8 Feb., 1771, 6th baronet, M.P. Suffolk 1780-96, created Baron Rous 14 July, 1796, and Earl of Stradbroke, etc., 18 July, 1821, died 17 Aug., 1827. See Foster's *Peerage.*

Rous, Richard, s. Thomas, of Topsham, Devon, gent. PEMBROKE COLL., matric. 9 Nov., 1770, aged 17; B.A. 1774, rector of Clystwick, Devon, 1792, vicar of Bickleigh with Shipton, Exeter, 1801, until his death in 1810, buried at Farringdon.

Rous, (Rev. & Hon.) Thomas Manners, born at Henham, Suffolk, 5s. John, Earl of Stradbroke. BALLIOL COLL., matric. 31 March, 1829, aged 18; B.A. 1832, died 31 May, 1841. See Foster's *Peerage.*

Rous, William John, o.s. Hon. William Rufus, of Worsted, Norfolk, arm. TRINITY COLL., matric. 5 July, 1851, aged 17; sometime lieut.-colonel Scots guards. See Foster's *Peerage*, E. STRADBROKE; & *Eton School Lists.*

Rousby, Edward Richard (Kendall), 1s. Edward, of Cottisford, Oxon, arm. MAGDALEN COLL., matric. 16 Oct., 1875, aged 18; B.A. from ST. ALBAN HALL 1880, a student of the Middle Temple 1876. [20]

Rousby, Henry, 2s. James Edward, of Souldern, Oxon, arm. LINCOLN COLL., matric. 28 Nov., 1839, aged 19.

Rouse, James, s. Ezekiel Athanasius, of Walton, Somerset, cler. PEMBROKE COLL., matric. 12 Dec., 1788, aged 17; B.A. 1793.

Rouse, John, s. John, of High Hampton, Devon, cler. PEMBROKE COLL., matric. 1 Aug., 1752, aged 14; rector of Tetcott, Devon, 1784-1811, and of St. Breock, Cornwall, 1811, until his death 7 March, 1818.

Rouse, Rev. John, 4s. Oliver, of 'Bay de Verde,' Newfoundland, cler. KEBLE COLL., matric. 16 Oct., 1883, aged 20; B.A. 1886.

Rouse, Oliver, s. Oliver, of Hatherleigh, Devon, gent. PEMBROKE COLL., matric. 15 Nov., 1794, aged 18; B.A. 1802. [25]

Rouse, Oliver, s. John, of Pyworthy, Devon, cler. PEMBROKE COLL., matric. 18 June, 1796, aged 15; rector of Tetcott, Devon, 1811, until his death 12 March, 1846.

Rouse, Robert Cecil, 4s. William, of Bradford, Yorks, gent. EXETER COLL., matric. 21 May, 1872, aged 18.

Rouse, Rolla Charles Meadows, scholar TRINITY COLL., Cambridge, 1855 (10th wrangler & B.A. 1856, M.A. 1859); adm. 'ad eundem' 21 June, 1860, rector and vicar of Southwold 1867-70, rector of Woodbridge 1870-87, rector of Rayleigh 1887.

Rouse, William, 'Bister carrier;' privilegiatus 6 Oct., 1741, probably father of the next named.

Rouse, William, s. William, of Bicester, Oxon, pleb. MAGDALEN COLL., matric. 4 April, 1754, aged 18; chorister 1745-55. See *Coll. Reg.*, i. 163. [30]

Rouse, Rev. William Gaskell, 1s. Benjamin, of Windsor, Berks, arm. CHRIST CHURCH, matric. 15 Oct., 1845, aged 19; B.A. 1849, M.A. 1852. See *Eton School Lists.*

Rouse, Rev. William George, 1s. William Felix, of Worcester, gent. MAGDALEN HALL, matric. 11 May, 1874, aged 17; scholar (HERTFORD COLL.) 1874-6.

Rousillon, Gabriel, s. Daniel, of South Stoneham, Hants, gent. MERTON COLL., matric. 9 July, 1716, aged 17; B.A. 1720, M.A. (6 June) 1729. (Memo.: G. R., D.D., died 7 July, 1729.) See *Historical Register.*

Routh, Anthony, s. John, of Sowerby, co. York, pleb. MERTON COLL., matric. 8 July, 1720, aged 19; B.A. 1726, M.A. 1737. See *Gent.'s Mag.*, 1759, p. 146.

Routh, Rev. Cuthbert, 1s. Oswald Forster, of Twickenham, Middlesex, gent. QUEEN'S COLL., matric. 22 Oct., 1861, aged 20; B.A. 1866, M.A. 1868.

Routh, John Martin, 1s. John William, of Tilehurst, Berks, cler. NEW COLL., matric. 20 Oct., 1865, aged 18; bar.-at-law, Inner Temple, 1872, Royal Humane Society's medallist 4 Aug., 1879. See Foster's *Men at the Bar.* [36]

Routh, John William, 2s. Samuel, of Andover, Hants, cler. QUEEN'S COLL., matric. 2 April, 1835, aged 17; demy MAGDALEN COLL. 1835-41, B.A. 1839, M.A. 1841, rector (and vicar) of Tylehurst, Berks, 1855. See *Bloxam*, vii. 336.

Routh, Martin Joseph, s. Peter, of Beccles, Suffolk, cler. QUEEN'S COLL., matric. 31 May, 1770, aged 14; demy MAGDALEN COLL. 1771-5, B.A. 1774, fellow 1775-91, M.A. 1776, proctor 1785, B.D. 1786, D.D. 1791, librarian 1781, junior dean of arts 1784, 1785, bursar 1786, president 1791-1854, rector of Tylehurst-cum-Theale 1810, born 18 Sep., 1755, died 22 Dec., 1854. See *Bloxam*, vii. 1.

Routh, Martin Joseph, 3s. Samuel Reginald, of Boyton, Wilts, cler. PEMBROKE COLL., matric. 26 Oct., 1837, aged 17; scholar 1837-46, B.A. 1842, M.A. 1845, fellow 1846-74, bar.-at-law, Inner Temple, 1847, died 6 Dec., 1874.

Routh, Reginald, 1s. Samuel, of Chertsey, Surrey, cler. QUEEN'S COLL., matric. 19 Nov., 1832, aged 19.

Routh, Robert Sheppard, 1s. Robert Alfred, of London, arm. CHRIST CHURCH, matric. 13 Oct., 1865, aged 18; B.A. 1870, M.A. 1873, held various curacies 1872-86, vicar of Longstock, Hants, 1886. See *Eton School Lists.* [5]

Routh, Samuel, s. Peter, of Beccles, Suffolk, cler. QUEEN'S COLL., matric. 12 Oct., 1782, aged 17; demy MAGDALEN COLL. 1785-91, B.A. 1786, fellow 1791-1811, M.A. 1789, B.D. 1799, dean of arts 1796-7, bursar 1798 & 1807, librarian 1796-1800, dean of divinity 1806, vicar of Wicklewood, Norfolk, 1802, and rector of Boyton, Wilts, 1810, until his death 1 Dec., 1822. See *Bloxam*, vii. 94.

Routledge, Allan, 'servant to Mr. Pitt of Christ Church;' privilegiatus 25 Nov., 1731.

Routledge, Alexander Leslie, 5s. William, of Aberdeen, gent. WADHAM COLL., matric. 13 Oct., 1871, aged 21; held various curacies 1874-83, vicar of Marshchapel, co. Lincoln, 1883.

Routledge, Arthur Allen, 'tonsor of St. Mary's, Oxford;' privilegiatus 5 July, 1760.

Routledge, Frederick, 4s. Robert Warne, of Hornsey, Middlesex, arm. BRASENOSE COLL., matric. 22 Jan., 1885, aged 18. [10]

Routledge, Herbert Hamilton, 1s. William, of Little Woolton, Lancashire, doctor (subs. cler.). ST. JOHN'S COLL., matric. 2 March, 1853, aged 17; B.A. 1857, M.A. 1879.

Routledge, John, s. William, of Glasgow, Scotland, cler. BALLIOL COLL., matric. 17 April, 1818, aged 19 (? vicar of Cransley, Northants, 1831).

Routledge, William Scoresby, 1s. William, of Melbourne, arm. CHRIST CHURCH, matric. 11 Oct., 1878, aged 19; B.A. 1882, M.A. 1887.

Row, Arthur Bryant, 4s. John Wall, of Crewkerne, Somerset, gent. BALLIOL COLL., matric. 19 Oct., 1878, aged 18; Blundell scholar 1878-80, B.A. 1881, M.A. 1885.

Row, Charles Adolphus, 3s. William, of St. John's, Cornwall, cler. PEMBROKE COLL., matric. 7 May, 1834, aged 17; scholar 1834-8, B.A. 1838, M.A. 1841, Bampton lecturer 1877, head-master Royal Free Grammar School, Mansfield, 1848-61, preb. of St. Paul's 1874; for list of his works see *Crockford.*

Row, John, s. John, of Plymouth, Devon, gent. MAGDALEN HALL, matric. 4 Nov., 1783, aged 28; chaplain St. Thomas's Hospital, Southwark, died 5 June, 1786. [15]

Row, John Kent, 1s. John, of Tiverton, Devon, arm. PEMBROKE COLL., matric. 13 Oct., 1823, aged 18; brother of Thomas K.

Row, Thomas, s. Thomas, of Penally, co. Pembroke, pleb. CHRIST CHURCH, matric. 21 Nov., 1786, aged 18; B.A. 1790, of Penally Court, died rector of Yerbeston and Loveston 18 June, 1810.

Row, Thomas Kent, 3s. John, of Tiverton, Devon, gent. ST. JOHN'S COLL., matric. 23 Feb., 1831, aged 18; brother of John K.

Row, William, s. William, of Plymouth, Devon, gent. EXETER COLL., matric. 10 April, 1794, aged 18; B.A. 1798, rector of St. John's, Cornwall, 1808, until his death 1 Dec., 1842. [20]

Rowan, William, s. George, of Bally McElligot, Kerry, Ireland, gent. ST. MARY HALL, matric. 27 Feb., 1787, aged 25; B.A. 17 Dec., 1787, M.A. 1790, bar.-at-law, King's Inns, father of archdeacon Rowan.

Rowbotham, John Frederick, o.s. Frederick, of Bradford, Yorks, cler. BALLIOL COLL., matric. 21 Oct., 1869, aged 19; exhibitioner 1868-74.

Rowbottom, Robert, s. Samuel, of Wigan, Lancashire, pleb. BRASENOSE COLL., matric. 20 March, 1728-9, aged 19; B.A. 26 Feb., 1732-3.

Rowcliffe, Henry, 4s. Charles, of Stogumber, Somerset, gent. ST. JOHN'S COLL., matric. 4 March, 1847, aged 18; B.A. 1851, M.A. 1854, bar.-at-law, Middle Temple, 1854, and of Lincoln's Inn (ad eundem), 1855, died 8 July, 1876.

Rowcliffe, Thomas, s. George, of Henstridge, Somerset, pleb. EXETER COLL., matric. 12 March, 1718-9, aged 17; B.A. 1723. See *Gent.'s Mag.*, 1737, p. 124. [25]

Rowcliffe, William Charles, 1s. William, of London, gent. ORIEL COLL., matric. 19 Oct., 1886, aged 19.

Rowden, Aldred William, 1s. George Croke, of Mortlake, Surrey, cler. BALLIOL COLL., matric. 19 Oct., 1868, aged 19; bar.-at-law, Lincoln's Inn, 1874. See Foster's *Men at the Bar* & *Rugby School Reg.*

Rowden, Edward, s. Francis, of Cuxham, Oxon, cler. NEW COLL., matric. 3 Dec., 1798, aged 18; B.A. 1802, M.A. 1806, fellow until 1812, vicar of Highworth, Wilts, 1804, until his death in March, 1869, father of Francis 1798, and of George C.

Rowden, Rev. Edward Wetherell, 1s. Edward, of Highworth, Wilts, cler. NEW COLL., matric. 27 Sep., 1833, aged 19; fellow 1833-51, B.A. 1838, M.A. 1842, D.C.L. 1856, bursar 1847, dean of arts 1848, sub-warden 1849, registrar 1853, until his death in 1870.

Rowden, Francis, s. Francis, of Palace Yard, Westminster, gent. MERTON COLL., matric. 26 March, 1743, aged 17; B.A. 1746, M.A. 1749, B.D. 1771, select preacher 1816, rector of Ibstone, Oxon, 1773, and of Cuxham 1774, preb. of Salisbury 1785, until his death 29 Dec., 1822. [30]

Rowden, Francis, s. Francis, of Cuxham, Oxon, cler. MERTON COLL., matric. 1 Aug., 1798, aged 16; B.A. 1802, M.A. 1805, proctor 1815, B.D. 1816, fellow until 1824, bursar 1822, rector of Cuxham and Ibstone, Oxon, 1823, until his death 18 Sep., 1852, brother of Edward 1798, and of George C.

Rowden, Francis, 1s. Francis, of Cuxham, Oxon, cler. WADHAM COLL., matric. 26 June, 1847, aged 18; B.A. 1851, bar.-at-law, Lincoln's Inn, 1854. See Foster's *Men at the Bar.*

Rowden, Francis Marmaduke, 2s. Edward, of Highworth, Wilts, cler. WADHAM COLL., matric. 16 May, 1833, aged 17; B.A. 1837, M.A. 1840, rector of Stanton-Fitzwarren, Wilts, 1851-84. See *Rugby School Reg.*, 159.

Rowden, Frederick, 6s. Francis, of Cuxham, Oxon, cler. NEW COLL., matric. 17 June, 1857, aged 18; fellow 1857, B.A. 1860, M.A. 1864, held various curacies 1864-78, rector of Birchanger 1878.

Rowden, George Croke, 3s. Edward, of Highworth, Wilts, cler. NEW COLL., matric. 20 Dec., 1836, aged 16; fellow 1836-47, B.C.L. 1842, D.C.L. 1848, precentor of Chichester died 17 April, 1863, father of Aldred William. [35]

Rowden, George Vere, 2s. Charles Wetherall, of Northaw, Middlesex, gent. PEMBROKE COLL., matric. 27 Oct., 1883, aged 19; B.A. 1887.

Rowden, Robert, 4s. Francis, of Cuxham, Oxon, cler. WADHAM COLL., matric. 22 Oct., 1851, aged 18; B.A. 1855, M.A. 1860, vicar of Winwick, Northants, 1863.

Rowe, Charles William, 2s. James John, of Littlehampton, Sussex, cler. WORCESTER COLL., matric. 7 June, 1845, aged 18; scholar LINCOLN COLL. 1847-50, B.A. 1849, incumbent of Bundawa, New South Wales, died 11 Dec., 1859.

Rowe, Edward, s. Edward, of Ipplepen, Devon, pleb. BALLIOL COLL., matric. 17 March, 1721-2, aged 19.

Rowe, George Duncan, 3s. Charles, of Valparaiso, Chili, arm. UNIVERSITY COLL., matric. 13 Oct., 1876, aged 18; B.A. 1881.

Rowe, Henry, s. Nathaniel, of London, arm. BRASENOSE COLL., matric. 27 Dec., 1768, aged 18. See *Gent.'s Mag.*, 1819, ii. 384.

Rowe, Henry Dickson, 1s. Henry Moore, of Maker, near Plymouth, arm. BRASENOSE COLL., matric. 17 June, 1851, aged 19; scholar 1851-6, B.A. 1855. [5]

Rowe, Hillary, s. Hillary, of Isle of Barbados, West Indies, arm. BALLIOL COLL., matric. 20 Oct., 1811, aged 18; B.A. 1815.

Rowe, Hutton, s. Anthony, of Newbottle, co. Durham, arm. ORIEL COLL., matric. 26 March, 1795, aged 18; brother of John 1797. See *Eton School Lists.*

Rowe, Rev. Hutton, 1s. Charles Hutton, of Tolesby Hall, Yorks, arm. MAGDALEN HALL, matric. 19 Feb., 1846, aged 19; B.A. 1850, M.A. 1853, died at Tolesby Hall 4 Nov., 1857.

Rowe, James, s. James, of Ideford, Devon, cler. BALLIOL COLL., matric. 13 March, 1740-1, aged 18; B.A. 1745.

Rowe, James, s. William, of Isle of Jamaica, gent. BALLIOL COLL., matric. 5 Nov., 1788, aged 18; brother of William 1790. [10]

Rowe, James John, 1s. James, of East Down, Devon, arm. MAGDALEN HALL, matric. 2 July, 1823, aged 27; B.A. 1827, M.A. 1830.

Rowe, John, s. John, of Silverton, Devon, gent. PEMBROKE COLL., matric. 15 June, 1774, aged 18; B.A. 1778, M.A. 1790, rector of Alvediscott, Devon, 1787, until his death 13 July, 1833.

Rowe, John, s. William, of Launceston, Cornwall, gent. EXETER COLL., matric. 7 May, 1796, aged 19; B.A. 1800, vicar of Stratton 1804, perp. curate Launceston 1808, until his death 8 March, 1837. See *Eton School Lists.*

Rowe, John, s. Anthony, of Newbottle, co. Durham, arm. ORIEL COLL., matric. 25 May, 1797, aged 18; B.A. 1801, brother of Hutton 1795.

Rowe, Richard Marrack, 3s. John, of Reginnys, Cornwall, gent. MAGDALEN HALL, matric. 29 April, 1847, aged 17, B.A. 1851; fellow EXETER COLL. 1852-61, M.A. 1854, theological tutor Queen's College, Birmingham, 1859-60, British chaplain Alexandria 1860, died 17 Dec., 1861. See *Boase*, 139.

Rowe, Samuel Nicholas Brooking, 1s. Samuel, of East Stonehouse, Devon, cler. WORCESTER COLL., matric. 6 March, 1850, aged 17; B.A. 1854. [16]

Rowe, Thomas, s. John, of Holne, Devon, cler. EXETER COLL., matric. 14 Feb., 1743-4, aged 18; B.A. 1747, died minister of Dean Prior, Devon, in 1805.

Rowe, William, s. James, of Isle of Jamaica, arm. ST. MARY HALL, matric. 6 July, 1765, aged 21; possibly father of James 1788, and of William next named.

Rowe, William, s. William, of Isle of Jamaica, arm. ORIEL COLL., matric. 30 April, 1790, aged 16; brother of James 1788.

Rowe, (Sir) William Carpenter, 1s. Coryndon, of Launceston, Cornwall, doctor. BALLIOL COLL., matric. 24 June, 1819, aged 18, scholar 1820-6, B.A. 1823; Michel fellow QUEEN'S COLL. 1827-38, M.A. 1827, bar.-at-law, Inner Temple, 1830, recorder of Plymouth 1838, Q.C. 1850, chief justice of Ceylon 1856, knighted 30 Jan., 1856, died 9 Nov., 1859, father of the next named. [20]

Rowe, William Henry Pendarves, 1s. William, of Kandy, Ceylon, equitis. BALLIOL COLL., matric. 18 Oct., 1876, aged 19; exhibitioner 1876, a student of Lincoln's Inn 1878, until his death 11 April, 1880.

Rowell, George, 'Automatarius;' privilegiatus 3 March, 1803.

Rowland, Charles, s. Nicholas, of Launcells, Cornwall, gent. ORIEL COLL., matric. 16 March, 1719-20, aged 17.

Rowland, Charles Browne, 4s. William, of Ramsbury, Wilts, arm. ST. JOHN'S COLL., matric. 28 June, 1852, aged 18; B.A. & M.A. 1859, held various curacies 1859-71, vicar of Pillerton Hersey, co. Warwick, 1871-5, and of Wolverley, co. Worcester, 1876.

Rowland, Charles Spenser, 1s. Charles Browne, of Martley, co. Worcester, cler. ST. JOHN'S COLL., matric. 14 Oct., 1882, aged 18; B.A. 1886. [25]

Rowland, Rev. Edward, 4s. Samuel, of Akenham Hall, Suffolk, gent. WORCESTER COLL., matric. 14 April, 1866, aged 19; B.A. 1869, M.A. 1872.

Rowland, Francis Oakley, 2s. John, of Upper Norwood, Surrey, gent. WORCESTER COLL., matric. 14 Oct., 1865, aged 18; B.A. 1871, M.A. 1872, perp. curate St. Benet and All Saints, Kentish Town, London, 1881.

Rowland, George, s. Thomas, of Aylesbury, Bucks, cler. QUEEN'S COLL., matric. 1 Dec., 1756, aged 17; created M.A. 20 June, 1760.

Rowland, George William, 3s. John Henry, of Norwood, Surrey, gent. WORCESTER COLL., matric. 12 Oct., 1867, aged 18.

Rowland, Henry Ratcliffe, 3s. Thomas, of Wrexham, co. Denbigh, arm. ST. JOHN'S COLL., matric. 25 Jan., 1879, aged 20; B.A. 1882. [30]

Rowland, John, s. John, of Llanddewi Brefi, co. Cardigan, cler. JESUS COLL., matric. 8 April, 1767, aged 22; a master of Shrewsbury Free Grammar School 55 years, rector of Llangeitho, co. Cardigan, died 1816, father of William G.

Rowland, Nathaniel, s. Daniel, of Llangeitho, co. Cardigan, cler. CHRIST CHURCH, matric. 16 July, 1767, aged 17; B.A. 1771, M.A. 1774.

Rowland, Richard, s. Richard, of Marham Church, Cornwall, pleb. EXETER COLL., matric. 21 Feb., 1716-7, aged 19; B.A. from NEW INN HALL 1721.

Rowland, Thomas Harding, s. George, of Ailesbury, Bucks, gent. PEMBROKE COLL., matric. 24 March, 1717-8, aged 16; B.A. 1721, M.A. 1724 (as Thomas).

Rowland, William, s. Henry, of Llanedwin, Isle of Anglesey, cler. JESUS COLL., matric. 28 June, 1785, aged 16; B.A. 1789, M.A. 1792, B.D. 1799, fellow until 1813. See *Gent.'s Mag.*, 1836, ii. 105, & 1842, i. 334. [35]

Rowland, William Gorsuch, s. John, of Shrewsbury, Salop, cler. CHRIST CHURCH, matric. 23 Oct., 1786, aged 16; B.A. 1790, M.A. 1793, preb. of Lichfield 1814, perp. curate St. Mary, Shrewsbury, 1828, until his death 28 Nov., 1851. See *Gent.'s Mag.*, 1852, i. 99.

Rowland, William John, 2s. Alexander William, of Sydenham, Kent, gent. WORCESTER COLL., matric. 9 April, 1864, aged 20; B.A. 1868, M.A. 1870, chaplain in Bengal 1873-83, vicar of Stoke-sub-Hamden 1884.

Rowlands, Ellis, s. Edward, of Dolgelly, co. Merioneth, pleb. JESUS COLL., matric. 15 May, 1766, aged 19; B.A. 1770.

Rowlands, Griffin, s. Antony, of Berch, co. Carnarvon, pleb. JESUS COLL., matric. 20 March, 1739-40, aged 19; B.A. 17 March, 1745-6 (as GRIFFITH ROWLAND).

Rowlands, Henry, s. John, of Llanllechyd, co. Carnarvon, gent. JESUS COLL., matric. 30 March, 1748, aged 17; B.A. 1751, M.A. 1754. [40]

Rowlands, Henry, s. Henry, of Isle of Anglesea, arm. UNIVERSITY COLL., matric. 24 March, 1784, aged 19, B.A. 1788; M.A. from CHRIST'S COLL., Cambridge, 1803, of Plasgwyn, Anglesea, vicar of Llanidan 1793, and rector of Newborough 1803, until his death 14 April, 1842.

Rowlands, Howel Pugh, s. John, of Dolgelly, co. Merioneth, gent. HERTFORD COLL., matric. 2 May, 1796, aged 18; B.A. 1800.

Rowlands, Hugh, s. Richard, of Bangor (city), gent. JESUS COLL., matric. 13 May, 1815, aged 19; B.A. 1819, M.A. 1821, rector of Llanrug, co. Carnarvon, 1836, until his death in 1843.

Rowlands, John Bowen, 2s. Thomas, of Haverfordwest, co. Pembroke, arm. TRINITY COLL., matric. 3 Dec., 1857, aged 18; B.A. from NEW INN HALL 1864, M.A. 1878, rector of Hubberston, co. Pembroke, 1869.

Rowlands, John Leche, o.s. John, of Ellesmere, Salop, gent. WADHAM COLL., matric. 17 May, 1832, aged 18. [5]

Rowlands, John Frederick, 1s. John, of Meole Brace, Salop, gent. NON-COLL., matric. 18 Oct., 1872, aged 20.

Rowlands, John Griffith, 1s. Daniel, of Llanidloes, co. Montgomery, arm. JESUS COLL., matric. 18 Oct., 1882, aged 19; B.A. 1886.

Rowlands, John Richard, 2s. William, of Worcester, gent. WADHAM COLL., matric. 23 March, 1859, aged 18.

Rowlands, Lewis, s. John, of Machynlleth, co. Montgomery, pleb. JESUS COLL., matric. 16 Dec., 1779, aged 20.

Rowlands, Owen, s. John, of Llanvair, co. Carnarvon, gent. JESUS COLL., matric. 16 May, 1782, aged 19; B.A. 1786, M.A. 1789. See *Gent.'s Mag.*, 1811, ii. 595. [10]

Rowlands, Parker, s. John, of Chester (city), arm. ST. JOHN'S COLL., matric. 12 July, 1744, aged 21.

Rowlands, Richard, s. Ric., of Talgarth, co. Merioneth, pleb. QUEEN'S COLL., matric. 2 April, 1723, aged 18.

Rowlands, Richard, s. John, of Kanunda, co. Carnarvon, pleb. JESUS COLL., matric. 26 Feb., 1729-30, aged 17.

Rowlands, Rev. Robert Evan, 1s. Owen Robert, of Bangor, gent. NON-COLL., matric. 13 Jan., 1883, aged 19; B.A. from QUEEN'S COLL. 1886.

Rowlands, Samuel, s. Owen, of Llanbedr, co. Merioneth, pleb. BRASENOSE COLL., matric. 31 May, 1781, aged 19; B.A. from ST. ALBAN HALL 1788. [15]

Rowlands, Thomas, s. John, of Bettws, co. Carnarvon, arm. JESUS COLL., matric. 15 May, 1716, aged 16.

Rowlands, William, 2s. Morris, of Llanfair, co. Merioneth, gent. JESUS COLL., matric. 22 Oct., 1870, aged 18; clerk 1870.

Rowlands, William Bowen, 1s. Thomas, of Haverfordwest, co. Pembroke, arm. JESUS COLL., matric. 22 March, 1854, aged 18; scholar 1855-8, B.A. 1859, M.A. 1865, of Glenmare, co. Pembroke, J.P., head-master of Grammar School, Haverfordwest, 1864, curate of Narberth, co. Pembroke, 1864, bar.-at-law, Gray's Inn, 1871, Q.C. and bencher 1882, M.P. Cardiganshire, July, 1886. See Foster's *Men at the Bar.*

Rowlands, William Edward, 2s. William, of Worcester (city), arm. WADHAM COLL., matric. 21 Nov., 1855, aged 18; B.A. 1859, M.A. 1873.

Rowlandson, Alfred, 8s. Michael, of Warminster, Wilts, D.D. QUEEN'S COLL., matric. 14 March, 1839, aged 18. [20]

Rowlandson, Arthur, 2s. Anthony, of Camberwell, Surrey, arm. BRASENOSE COLL., matric. 21 April, 1819, aged 17; B.A. 1823, M.A. 1825, bar.-at-law, Inner Temple, 1828.

Rowlandson, Edward, 1s. Michael, of Hungerford, Berks, doctor. QUEEN'S COLL., matric. 12 Nov., 1819, aged 16; Michel exhibitioner 1819-23, B.A. 1823, scholar 1823-6, fellow 1826-9, M.A. 1827, died curate of Kington St. Michael's, Wilts, 11 June, 1854.

Rowlandson, John, 5s. Michael, of Warminster, Wilts, doctor. QUEEN'S COLL., matric. 19 June, 1828, aged 17; B.A. 1832, M.A. 1840, died vicar of Kirkley Moorside, Yorks, 5 Aug., 1856.

Rowlandson, Michael, s. Edward, of Grassmere, Westmoreland, cler. ST. MARY HALL, matric. 24 Jan., 1800, aged 30, B.A. 1803, M.A. 1807; B. & D.D. QUEEN'S COLL. 1818, vicar of Warminster, Wilts, 1808, and rector of Monkton Farleigh 1819, until his death 8 July, 1824.

Rowlandson, Rev. Michael Edward, o.s. Edward, of Bradley, Wilts, cler. WADHAM COLL., matric. 3 May, 1854, aged 18; B.A. 1858, M.A. 1860. [25]

Rowlatt, Claudius Robert, 4s. William Henry, of St. Pancras, London, cler. MAGDALEN HALL, matric. 11 May, 1843, aged 18; B.A. 1848, M.A. 1850, ordained 1848, seceded to the Church of Rome 1858. See *St. Paul's School Reg.*, 286.

Rowlatt, James Clarke, o.s. James Clarke, of Hythe, Kent, pleb. MAGDALEN HALL, matric. 6 Feb., 1866, aged 23; B.A. from ORIEL COLL. 1869, M.A. 1878.

Rowlatt, John Clarke, of QUEEN'S COLL., Cambridge (B.A. 1841, M.A. 1844); adm. 'ad eundem' 16 June, 1847, curate of St. Mary-de-Lode, Gloucester.

Rowlatt, Thomas Mashiter, o.s. Charles Robert, of Cressing, Essex, cler. WORCESTER COLL., matric. 28 April, 1842, aged 19.

Rowley, Adam Clarke, 1s. James, of Stourport, co. Worcester, gent. WADHAM COLL., matric. 15 March, 1838, aged 18; B.A. 1842, M.A. 1846, vicar of St. Matthias Weir, Bristol, 1846-75, of Twigworth, co. Gloucester, 1875, and of Sutterton, co. Lincoln, 1875; for list of his works see *Crockford.* [30]

Rowley, Adam Clarke, 1s. Adam Clarke, of Bristol, cler. ST. MARY HALL, matric. 22 Oct., 1867, aged 19; B.A. 1882.

Rowley, Arthur, born in Dublin (s. Ormsby, Viscount, in *Mat. Reg.*). CHRIST CHURCH, matric. 6 Feb., 1768, aged 17; B.A. 1770, rather younger son of Right Hon. Hercules Langford-Rowley, M.P. co. Londonderry, by his wife Elizabeth Viscountess Langford, niece and heir of John Ormsby, Esq.; a student of Lincoln's Inn 1771, died young.

Rowley, Rev. Arthur, 3s. Adam Clarke, of Bristol, cler. NON-COLL., matric. 21 Oct., 1871, aged 20; B.A. 1878.

Rowley, George, s. George, of Richmond, Yorks, gent. UNIVERSITY COLL., matric. 1 Nov., 1799, aged 17; fellow 1807-21, B.A. 1803, M.A. 1806, B. & D.D. 1821, dean and tutor 1808-21, bursar 1815, vice-chancellor 1832-6, master 1821, and rector of Stanwick, Northants, 1823, until his death in Oct., 1836.

Rowley, Rev. Herbert Seddon, 3s. Thomas, of Riccarton, New Zealand, gent. QUEEN'S COLL., matric. 25 Oct., 1880, aged 19; B.A. 1883, M.A. 1887, chorister 1878-80. [35]

Rowley, Hercules Langford, s. Clotworthy, Baron Langford. CHRIST CHURCH, matric. 27 Jan., 1814, aged 18; 2nd baron, died 3 June, 1839. See Foster's *Peerage.*

Rowley, John, s. Joshua, of Kirkburton, Yorks, pleb. UNIVERSITY COLL., matric. 8 Nov., 1745, aged 24; B.A. 1749.

Rowley, John Arthur, 3s. Edwin, of Gawthorpe, Yorks, gent. PEMBROKE COLL., matric. 17 Oct., 1878, aged 18.

Rowley, Joseph, s. Benjamin, of Kirkburton, Yorks, pleb. QUEEN'S COLL., matric. 5 July, 1791, aged 18; B.A. 1795, M.A. 1804, chaplain Lancaster Castle, died 3 Jan., 1864.

Rowley, Richard, s. Thomas, of Broseley, Salop, pleb. QUEEN'S COLL., matric. 1 June, 1786, aged 19; B.A. 1790, M.A. 1795, died rector of Middleton Scriven in 1812, father of Thomas 1815.

Rowley, Richard, 2s. Thomas, of Bridgnorth, Salop, cler. CHRIST CHURCH, matric. 22 Oct., 1851, aged 18; student 1851-64, B.A. 1855, M.A. 1858, incumbent of Maiden Bradley, Wilts, died at Willey Rectory, Salop, 13 Aug., 1864.

Rowley, Thomas, s. Richard, of Middleton Scriven, Salop, cler. CHRIST CHURCH, matric. 19 Oct., 1815, aged 18; B.A. 1819, M.A. 1822, B. & D.D. 1839, head-master Bridgnorth School and vicar of Middleton Scriven, Salop, 1822-54, rector of Willey, co. Hereford, 1854, until his death in 1877.

Rowley, William, s. John, of Cawthorne, Yorks, gent. LINCOLN COLL., matric. 1 Nov., 1740, aged 18; B.A. from UNIVERSITY COLL. 1744, M.A. 1747 (? vicar of Aldborough and Friston, Suffolk, 1755).

Rowley, William, s. William, of St. Luke's, Middlesex, arm. ST. ALBAN HALL, matric. 28 Nov., 1780, aged 38; B.A. 1784, M.A. 1787, B.Med. 1788, 'a surgeon in the king's service 1760-5,' at the siege of Belleisle and the taking of Havannah, D.Med. St. Andrew's 1774, physician Marylebone Infirmary, died 17 March, 1806. See Munk's *Roll*, ii. 340. [5]

Rowley, William Walter, 1s. William, of Bilston, Staffords, gent. QUEEN'S COLL., matric. 13 Oct., 1831, aged 18; B.A. 1835, M.A. 1839, rector of Lympsham, Somerset, 1837-44, vicar of Emanuel Church, Weston-super-Mare, 1847-84, and of Woolavington, Somerset, 1884, preb. of Wells, 1875.

Rowney, Edward, s. Thomas, of St. Clement's, London, arm. CHRIST CHURCH, matric. 14 Jan., 1717-8, aged 16; B.A. 1721, M.A. 1724.

Rowning, John, fellow of MAGDALEN COLL., Cambridge (B.A. 1724, M.A. 1728); incorp. 1 April, 1731.

Roworth, William Selwyn, 1s. William, of Nottingham, arm. MAGDALEN HALL, matric. 19 Oct., 1860, aged 23; B.A, 1864.

Rowton, John, s. William, of Coventry, co. Warwick, pleb. ST. JOHN'S COLL., matric. 10 March, 1737-8, aged 17; B.A. 11 Feb., 1742-3. [10]

Roxburgh, Alexander Bruce, 2s. William, of North Leith, co, Edinburgh, D.Med. EXETER COLL., matric 12 Oct., 1878, aged 18; B.A. 1882.

Roxburgh, William Henry, 1s. William, of Portabello, co. Edinburgh, D.Med. BALLIOL COLL., matric. 28 Jan., 1878, aged 18; B.A. 1881.

Roy, Edmund, 4s. Robert, of St. George's, Hanover Square, London, arm. PEMBROKE COLL., matric. 11 May, 1821, aged 18; B.A. 1826, M.A. 1828, vicar of Westwood, co. Warwick, 1844, until his death 12 July, 1873.

Roy, John Wriothesley Russell, o.s. Thomas, of Woburn, Beds, cler. ALL SOULS' COLL., matric. 9 Dec., 1842, aged 17; bible clerk 1842-6, B.A. 1846.

Roy, Rev. Robert, s. (Robert), of Kensington, Middlesex, gent. MAGDALEN HALL, matric. 4 April, 1811, aged 19; died 1 Jan., 1863. [15]

Roy, Robert Evelyn, of CORPUS CHRISTI COLL., Cambridge (B.A. 1843, M.A. 1847); adm. 'ad eundem' 11 March, 1847, rector of Skirbeck, co. Lincoln, 1853.

Roy, William, s. Robert, of Kensington, Middlesex, gent. MAGDALEN HALL, matric. 14 May, 1811, aged 23; rector of Skirbeck 1834, until his death 2 Oct., 1852, styled D.D.

Royce, David, 3s. Matthew, of Pakham, gent. CHRIST CHURCH, matric. 20 Oct., 1836, aged 19; servitor 1836-40, B.A. 1840, chaplain 1844-51, M.A. 1845, perp. curate Cowley, Oxon, 1845-50, vicar of Nether or Lower Swell 1850.

Royds, Charles Leopold, 4s. John, of Marylebone, London, gent. WADHAM COLL., matric. 3 March, 1836, aged 19; B.A. 1839, vicar of Aldenham, Herts, 1850-84.

Royds, Edward, 1s. Edward, of Brereton, Cheshire, cler. BRASENOSE COLL., matric. 5 Feb., 1839, aged 18; B.A. 1842, M.A. 1845, rector of Brereton, Cheshire, 1845, brother of the next named. See *Rugby School Reg.*, 185. [20]

Royds, Francis Coulman, 4s. Edward, of Brereton, Cheshire, cler. BRASENOSE COLL., matric. 15 June, 1843, aged 17; B.A. 1847, M.A. 1850, rector of Coddington, Cheshire, 1855, vicar of Knowl Hill, Berks, 1873-9, rector of Haughton, co. Stafford, 1879. See *Rugby School Reg.*, 213.

Royds, Frederick Charles Alten, o.s. William, of Cowbridge, co. Glamorgan, arm. WORCESTER COLL., matric. 13 Nov., 1845, aged 18; died 10 Jan., 1863.

Royds, James, 1s. James, of Kermincham, Cheshire, arm. BRASENOSE COLL., matric. 4 March, 1840, aged 18; B.A. 1844, M.A. 1846, of Woodlands, Hartford, Cheshire, J.P., perp. curate Hartford 1846-63, died 14 May, 1886.

Royds, John, s. John, of Halifax, Yorks, arm. UNIVERSITY COLL., matric. 30 May, 1771, aged 21; created M.A. 7 July, 1774, bar.-at-law, Lincoln's Inn, 1771, died in Calcutta Sep., 1818.

Royds, Robert, s. Robert, of St. Stephen's, London, arm. CHRIST CHURCH, matric. 6 March, 1778, aged 18. [25]

Royle, Francis Edward Vernon, 1s. Thomas Vernon, of Chester, arm. ORIEL COLL., matric. 19 Oct., 1875, aged 17; B.A. 1879, a student of the Inner Temple 1878.

Royle, James, s. John, of Bala, co. Merioneth, cler. JESUS COLL., matric. 26 March, 1784, aged 18.

Royle, John, s. James Gwyder, of Llanrwst, co. Carnarvon, gent. ST. ALBAN HALL, matric. 1 Nov., 1810, aged 21; B.A. 1815. See *Gent.'s Mag.*, 1825, i. 91.

Royle, Thomas Richard Popplewell, 1s. Thomas Richard Popplewell, of Leeds, arm. MAGDALEN COLL., matric. 23 Oct., 1885, aged 21.

Royle, Rev. Vernon Peter Fanshawe Archer, 3s. Peter, of Sale, Cheshire, D.Med. BRASENOSE COLL., matric. 28 Jan., 1873, aged 18; B.A. 1878, M.A. 1884. [30]

Royle, William, s. James, of Daresbury, Cheshire, pleb. JESUS COLL., matric. 7 April, 1770, aged 21; B.A. 1775.

Royse, George, s. Nathaniel, of Winsham, Somerset, cler. MERTON COLL., matric. 12 April, 1783, aged 17.

Royse, Nathaniel Penn, s. William, of Winsham, Somerset, cler. MERTON COLL., matric. 8 July, 1727, aged 17; B.C.L. 1735.

Royse, Thomas, s. Nathan., of Winsham, Somerset, cler. TRINITY COLL., matric. 2 Feb., 1757, aged 17; B.A. 1760, M.A. 1763, B.D. 1773.

Royse, William, s. Nathaniel, of Winsham, Somerset, cler. WADHAM COLL., matric. 22 March, 1786, aged 25. [35]

Royse, William George, s. William, of Launceston, Cornwall, cler. WADHAM COLL., matric. 1 June, 1808, aged 18; B.A. 1812, M.A. 1814.

Rubie, Alfred Edward, 4s. John Parsons, of Portswood, Hants, gent. BALLIOL COLL., matric. 16 Jan., 1883, aged 19; exhibitioner BRASENOSE COLL. 1883, B.A. 1886.

Rubie, George, 2s. John Parsons, of Southampton, gent. NON-COLL., matric. 12 Oct., 1878, aged 18; B.A. from WORCESTER COLL. 1881, M.A. 1885, perp. curate, Winterslade, 1888.

Rubie, John Fonthill, 1s. John Parsons, of Fonthill Gifford, Wilts, gent. NEW COLL., matric. 20 Jan., 1877, aged 20; B.A. 1880, bar.-at-law, Inner Temple, 1883. See Foster's *Men at the Bar*.

Ruck, Laurence, 2s. Richard, of Newington, Kent, arm. MAGDALEN COLL., matric. 29 March, 1838, aged 18.

Ruck, William Ernest, 1s. William, of Croydon, Surrey, gent. ORIEL COLL., matric. 22 Oct., 1872, aged 18.

Rücker, Arthur William, 1s. Daniel Henry, of Clapham, Surrey, arm. BRASENOSE COLL., matric. 19 Oct., 1867, aged 18; scholar 1867-71, B.A. 1871, fellow 1871-6, M.A. 1874, prof. of mathematics at Yorkshire College, Leeds, 1875-86, F.R.S. 1884, prof. of physics at Royal School of Mines 1877.

Rücker, Frederick George, 2s. John Antony, of Blackheath, Kent, arm. BRASENOSE COLL., matric. 17 Oct., 1874, aged 18; scholar 1874-9, B.A. 1878, M.A. 1881, bar.-at-law, Middle Temple, 1879. See Foster's *Men at the Bar*.

Rücker, Reginald Wynn, 3s. Daniel Henry, of Clapham, Surrey, arm. BRASENOSE COLL., matric. 17 Oct., 1874, aged 19; scholar 1874-7, B.A. 1878, a student of the Inner Temple 1877. **[5]**

Rudall, Alfred, 2s. John Henry, of Kennington, Surrey, arm. WADHAM COLL., matric. 16 Jan., 1863, aged 22; Hebrew exhibitioner 1864-6, B.A. 1865, M.A. 1871, vicar of St. Paul, Penzance, 1866-8, incumbent of St. Mary's, Aberdeen, 1868-70, vicar of Carnmenellis, Cornwall, 1872-86, and of St. Agnes Scorrier 1886.

Rudall, Edward, 4s. John, of Crediton, Devon, cler. PEMBROKE COLL., matric. 10 Nov., 1819, aged 19; B.A. 1823, M.A. 1843.

Rudall, John, s. Thomas, of Plymouth, Devon, gent. EXETER COLL., matric. 15 March, 1771, aged 18; vicar of Crediton 1793-1832, died 7 Sep., 1835-7. See *Gent's Mag.*, 1835, ii. 554; & 1837, ii. 655.

Rudd, Abraham, s. Abraham, of London, cler. UNIVERSITY COLL., matric. 19 Oct., 1771, aged 18; B.A. 1775, M.A. 1778 (? died rector of Diddlebury, Salop, 11 Dec., 1794).

Rudd, Abraham Joseph, s. Sayer, of London, cler. ST. JOHN'S COLL., matric. 8 July, 1743, aged 18; B.A. 1747, M.A. 1750, curate of St. George's, Hanover Square, rector of Londesborough, Yorks, 1757, and of Burnby 1769. See *Robinson*, 84. **[10]**

Rudd, Charles Louis, 4s. William, of Cockermouth, Cumberland, gent. PEMBROKE COLL., matric. 4 June, 1861, aged 20; B.A. & M.A. 1868, vicar of Hempstead by Holt, Norfolk, 1873.

Rudd, Rev. Edward Miles, s. Edward, of Biggleswade, Beds, cler. ORIEL COLL., matric. 26 March, 1795, aged 18; B.A. 1799, M.A. 1801, fellow until his death 20 Dec., 1848. See *Eton School Lists*, 6a.

Rudd, George, 2s. William, of Staveley, Yorks, gent. NON-COLL., matric. 12 June, 1873, aged 31; B.A. & M.A. 1886, rector of Stand, Lancashire, 1876.

Rudd, George Edward, 1s. George, of York, cler. BRASENOSE COLL., matric. 14 Oct., 1884, aged 18; scholar 1884.

Rudd, Henry, 2s. Henry, of London, gent. CORPUS CHRISTI COLL., matric. 28 May, 1853, aged 20; B.A. 1857, M.A. 1860, B.C.L. & D.C.L. 1865, bar.-at-law, Inner Temple, 1866, died 15 Jan., 1880. **[15]**

Rudd, Henry Aytone Lindesay, 2s. Eric, of St. Helier's, Jersey, arm. JESUS COLL., matric. 20 Oct., 1886, aged 19; scholar 1886.

Rudd, John Bart, of ST. JOHN'S COLL., Cambridge (B.A. and senior optime 1835, M.A. 1838); adm. 'ad eundem' 28 Feb., 1856.

Rudd, Leonard Hampson, o.s. Thomas Anderson, of Bungay, Suffolk, gent. PEMBROKE COLL., matric. 30 March, 1833, aged 16; scholar 1833-41, B.A. 1837, M.A. 1840, perp. curate Ruscombe, Berks, 1844-64, died 26 March, 1888.

Rudd, Richard, s. Richard, of Kirkby Stephen, Westmoreland, gent. QUEEN'S COLL., matric. 10 Nov., 1792, aged 18.

Rudd, Richard, 5s. Philip, of Little Musgrave, Westmoreland, gent. QUEEN'S COLL., matric. 14 June, 1844, aged 19; B.A. 1848, M.A. 1851, vicar of Ebberston, Yorks, 1871, until his death 22 March, 1879. **[20]**

Ruddach, James Steuart Maynard, 1s. James Steuart, of Leamington, cler. ORIEL COLL., matric. 27 Oct., 1883, aged 19.

Ruddle, Thomas, s. Francis, of St. Andrew's, Hatton Garden, Middlesex, gent. ST. ALBAN HALL, matric. 12 Oct., 1790, aged 17.

Ruddock, Charles Lock, 2s. Thomas, of Norwich, gent. LINCOLN COLL., matric. 15 Oct., 1878, aged 19; B.A. 1884, M.A. 1885.

Ruddock, Edward Grevile, 2s. Noblett, of Bristol (city), cler. TRINITY COLL., matric. 8 Nov., 1823, aged 18; exhibitioner 1825-8, B.A. 1827, M.A. 1830, curate of Westbury cum Priddy, died at Wrington 2 Dec., 1856.

Ruddock, Mark Ernest, 1s. Henry John, of Sedgefield, co. Durham, gent. EXETER COLL., matric. 14 Oct., 1865, aged 19; B.A. 1869, M.A. 1872, vicar of Ardeley, Herts, 1885. **[25]**

Ruddock, Noblett, s. Noblett, of St. James's, Bristol, co. Gloucester, gent. TRINITY COLL., matric. 20 April, 1795, aged 17; B.A. 1799, M.A. 1802, vicar of Stockland, Bristol, and of Westbury cum Priddy 1814, until his death 27 April, 1851.

Ruddock, Rev. Noblett Henry Cranmer, 3s. John, of Bridgewater, Somerset, gent. NON-COLL., matric. 15 Oct., 1870, aged 19; B.A. & M.A. 1878, of Venne House, Somerset.

Ruddock, Noblett Surrage, o.s. Richard Beadon, of Bristol, gent. QUEEN'S COLL., matric. 22 Oct., 1866, aged 19; B.A. 1870, M.A. 1877.

Rudduck, Thomas, s. William, of Avisford, Somerset, gent. QUEEN'S COLL., matric. 6 April, 1723, aged 15; demy MAGDALEN COLL. 1724-8, B.A. 1726, died 5 June, 1728. See *Bloxam*, vi. 205.

Ruddock, Thomas David, 3s. Thomas, of Norwich, arm. ST. JOHN'S COLL., matric. 13 Oct., 1879, aged 18; B.A. 1882, B.C.L. & M.A. 1887. **[30]**

Rudgard, Rev. William Dore, 1s. William, of Lincoln, arm. CHRIST CHURCH, matric. 24 May, 1877, aged 19; B.A. & M.A. from NEW INN HALL 1884.

Rudge, Benjamin, s. Benjamin, of Thornhaugh, Northants, cler. UNIVERSITY COLL., matric. 31 Oct., 1744, aged 18; demy MAGDALEN COLL. 1746-50, B.A. 1748, M.A. 1751, rector of Wheatfield, Oxon, 1750, until his death 13 June, 1807. See *Bloxam*, vi. 267.

Rudge, Rev. Benjamin, s. Edward, of Salisbury (city), arm. ST. EDMUND HALL, matric. 12 Dec., 1791, aged 23; died 29 March, 1834.

Rudge, Edward, s. Edward, of St. Thomas's, Salisbury, Wilts, arm. QUEEN'S COLL., matric. 11 Oct., 1781, aged 18; of Abbey Manor House, Evesham, high sheriff Worcester 1829, F.R.S., died 3 Sep., 1846.

Rudge, Edward Laurence, o.s. Edward Drosier, of Fakenham, Norfolk, D.Med. EXETER COLL., matric. 16 Jan., 1875, aged 18; B.A. 1879, M.A. 1881. **[35]**

Rudge, Frederick, s. Thomas, of Haresfield, co. Gloucester, cler. PEMBROKE COLL., matric. 25 March, 1805, aged 17; vicar of Eardisland, co. Hereford, 1816.

Rudge, James (Horace), s. James, of Cromhill, co. Gloucester, gent. PEMBROKE COLL., matric. 24 March, 1801, aged 16, B.A. 1808; M.A. from CATHERINE HALL, Cambridge, 1813, F.R.S., lecturer of Limehouse 1815, and of St. Sepulchre's, London, 1821, styled D.D., chaplain to Prince Leopold 1820 (after King of the Belgians), Duke of York 1825, and to the Duke of Sussex 1831.

Rudge, John, s. Benjamin, of Thornhaugh, Northants, cler. NEW COLL., matric. 2 July, 1743, aged 19; B.A. 1747, M.A. 1750, bar.-at-law, Middle Temple, 1748, died 14 March, 1801.

Rudge, Rev. Selwyn Edward, 2s. Edward, of Norwood, Surrey, cler. NON-COLL., matric. 20 Jan., 1877, aged 20.

Rudge, Thomas, s. Thomas, of Gloucester (city), gent. MERTON COLL., matric. 7 April, 1770, aged 16, B.A. 1780; M.A. from WORCESTER COLL. 1783, B.D. 1784, rector of St. Michael's and St. Mary-de-Grace, Gloucester, 1784, vicar of Haresfield 1784, chancellor of the diocese of Hereford 1817, archdeacon of Gloucester 1814, until his death in 1825, author of 'The History of the County of Gloucester.'

Rudhall, John, 'bibliopola;' privilegiatus 30 Sep., 1726.

Ruding, Rogers, s. Rogers, of St. Martin's, Leicester (town), arm. MERTON COLL., matric. 21 June, 1768, aged 16; B.A. 1772, fellow, M.A. 1775, B.D. 1782, a numismatist, F.S.A., vicar of Malden, Surrey, 1793, until his death 16 Feb., 1820, author of 'Annals of the Coinage.'

Ruding, Skrymsher Rogers, s. Rogers, of St. Pancras, London, cler. MERTON COLL., matric. 21 April, 1814, aged 17; postmaster 1814-6.

Ruding, Walter, s. Walter, of Westcote, co. Leicester, arm. MERTON COLL., matric. 10 Oct., 1734, aged 17; B.A. 1738, M.A. 1741, B.Med. 1744, D.Med. 1748, died senior fellow 4 Jan., 1789. [5]

Ruding, Walter, s. Rogers, of Leicester (city), arm. MERTON COLL., matric. 24 Nov., 1764, aged 19. See Nichols' *Leicester*, iv. 568.

Rudyerd, Benjamin, s. John, of London, arm. TRINITY COLL., matric. 12 July, 1729, aged 15.

Rue, Warren de la, created D.C.L. 22 June, 1870 (son of Thomas de la Rue), vice-president of the Royal Society, born in Jan., 1815. See *Men of the Time.*

Ruell, David, s. James, of Llandewi Ystradenny, co. Radnor, gent. ST. EDMUND HALL, matric. 21 Oct., 1807, aged 24; B.A 1811, M.A. 1814, minister of St. James's Chapel, Pentonville, died 18 July, 1846.

Ruffer, Mark Armand, 3s. Alphonsé, of Lyons, arm. BRASENOSE COLL., matric. 29 Jan., 1878, aged 18; B.A. 1882, B.Med. & M.A. 1887. [10]

Rufford, Francis, s. Philip, of Worcester (city), gent. WADHAM COLL., matric. 21 Jan., 1772, aged 16; B.A. 1775, M.A. 1781, rector of Lower Sapey, co. Worcester, 1784, and of Kinwarton, co. Warwick, 1787, until his death 22 Jan., 1833.

Rufford, James, s. Francis, of Sapey, co. Worcester, gent. BALLIOL COLL., matric. 25 May, 1732, aged 16; B.A. 19 March, 1735-6.

Rufford, William, 1s. William Squire, of Pophills, co. Warwick, cler. MAGDALEN HALL, matric. 16 June, 1838, aged 18; B.A. 1843, rector of Lower Sapey, co. Worcester, 1846, until his death 13 April, 1868.

Rufford, William Squire, s. Francis, of Clifton, co. Worcester, cler. CHRIST CHURCH, matric. 27 April, 1804, aged 18; B.A. 1808, M.A. 1811, rector of Binton, co. Warwick, 1820, and of Lower Sapey, co. Worcester, 1831, until his death 17 April, 1836.

Rugeley, George, s. John, of Potton, Beds, gent. CORPUS CHRISTI COLL., matric. 28 May, 1758, aged 16; B.A. 1762, fellow, M.A. 1766, B.D. 1775, rector of Church Brampton, Northants, 1789, until his death in 1792. [15]

Rugg, John, s. John, of Bridgwater, Somerset, cler. BALLIOL COLL., matric. 24 March, 1723-4, aged 18; B.A. 1727, rector of Nettlecombe, and vicar of Bradford, Somerset, 1759.

Rugg, Rev. William Robert, 5s. George, of Debtling, Kent, gent. EXETER COLL., matric. 12 May, 1883, aged 27; B.A. from WORCESTER COLL. 1886.

Rugge, Rev. Charles, s. William, of Westminster, arm. EXETER COLL., matric. 15 Dec., 1762, aged 20; exhibitioner 1762, B.A. 1766, died in 1773. See *Coll. Reg.*, 145.

Rugge, William, s. William, of St. George's, Hanover Square, London, arm. BRASENOSE COLL., matric. 12 May, 1759, aged 18, B.A. 1763; M.A. from ALL SOULS' COLL. 1766, rector of Buckland, Surrey, 1776, until his death 2 Nov., 1786.

Rule, Ulric Zwingle, 3s. William Harris, of Gibraltar, Spain, gent. WORCESTER COLL., matric. 12 Oct., 1861, aged 21. [20]

Rumball, Charles, 3s. John Horner, of St. Albans, Herts, gent. MAGDALEN HALL, matric. 6 Dec., 1849, aged 20; B.A. 1859, M.A. (HERTFORD COLL.) 1875, vicar of Littlehampton 1864.

Rumbold, Charles Edmund, s. Thomas, of London, baronet. ORIEL COLL., matric. 7 March, 1806, aged 17; of Preston Candover, Hants, M.P. Great Yarmouth 1818-47, and 1848-57, died 31 May, 1857, See Foster's *Baronetage.*

Rumbold, George, s. George, of Crabble-juxta-Dover, Kent, baronet. BRASENOSE COLL., matric. 14 Jan., 1813, aged 18; died in the East Indies 1820.

Rumney, Edward, 1s. William, of Manchester, gent. HERTFORD COLL., matric. 6 June, 1882, aged 30.

Rumney, John, s. John, of Kirk Oswald, Cumberland, cler. QUEEN'S COLL., matric. 19 Oct., 1716, aged 19, B.A. 1720; M.A. from KING'S COLL., Cambridge, 1732 (? perp. curate Hexham, Northumberland, 1765, rector of Berwick 1768. [25]

Rumney, William, s. Joseph, of Berwick-upon-Tweed, cler. LINCOLN COLL., matric. 13 Dec., 1780, aged 18; B.A. 1784, M.A. 1787, rector (and patron) of Swindon, co. Gloucester, 1807, until his death in 1829 (as ROMNEY), evidently altered the spelling of his name.

Rumney, William, s. William, of Watermellock, Cumberland, pleb. QUEEN'S COLL., matric. 21 Nov., 1786, aged 20; B.A. 1790.

Rump, John, 4s. James, of Swanton Morley, Norfolk, arm. TRINITY COLL., matric. 15 March, 1832, aged 18; B.A. 1835, M.A. 1839, curate of Pakefield, Suffolk, 1837-56, rector 1856-9, rector of Bluntisham, Hunts, 1859.

Rumsey, Almaric, 2s. Lacy, of St. Luke's, Chelsea, Middlesex, arm. EXETER COLL., matric. 14 Nov., 1844, aged 18; B.A. from ST. MARY HALL 1849, bar.-at-law, Lincoln's Inn, 1857, assistant-solicitor H.M. Customs 1868-75, professor Indian jurisprudence King's College, London, 1879. See Foster's *Men at the Bar* & *Rugby School Reg.*, 226.

Rumsey, Henry Langston, 1s. Henry Wyldbore, of St. Mary-le-Crypt, Gloucester (city), gent. NEW COLL., matric. 3 June, 1857, aged 18; fellow 1857-74, B.A. 1861, M.A. 1864, rector of St. John, Madder-market, Norwich, 1872-82, vicar of Hoarcross, co. Stafford, 1882-5, vicar of Denstone 1885.

Rumsey, James, 4s. Henry, of Chesham, Bucks, gent. PEMBROKE COLL., matric. 14 May, 1842, aged 18; scholar 1842-5, B.A. 1846, M.A. 1849, tutor Hertford College 1874-83. [31]

Rumsey, John, s. John, of Trellick, co. Monmouth, arm. UNIVERSITY COLL., matric. 11 April, 1794, aged 15; B.A. 1800, M.A. 1802, of Trellick Court, perp. curate Chapel Hill, co. Monmouth, and vicar of Llangunneder, co. Carmarthen, died in 1821. (? See *Gent.'s Mag.*, 1828, ii. 91.)

Rumsey, Rev. John Thomas Medlycott, 2s. James, of Iffley, Oxon, cler. NON-COLL., matric. 10 Feb., 1874, aged 19; chorister Magdalen College 1864-7, B.A. from HERTFORD COLL. 1882, M.A. 1884.

Rumsey, Lacy Henry, 1s. Lacy, of Chelsea, near London, arm. BRASENOSE COLL., matric. 27 Feb., 1845, aged 20, scholar 1845-9; B.A. from NEW INN HALL 1850, M.A. 1853, sometime vice-principal Bishop's College, Jamaica, etc., and incumbent of Ipswich, Queensland, vicar of Llanstadwell, co. Pembroke, 1873.

Rumsey, Robert, s. John, of Cwmdau-ddwr, Brecon, pleb. JESUS COLL. matric. 24 March, 1728-9, aged 19; B.A. 26 Feb., 1732-3. [35]

Rumsey, Robert Frederick, 2s. Henry Wyldbore, of Gloucester (city), arm. BRASENOSE COLL., matric. 26 June, 1862, aged 19; scholar 1862-7, B.A. 1866, M.A. 1869, a student of the Inner Temple 1864, assistant-master Eton College 1873-7, vicar of Burnham, Berks, 1878.

Rundall, George William, 2s. John William, of Merkara, East Indies, arm. NEW COLL., matric. 14 Oct., 1871, aged 19; scholar 1871-6, B.A. 1876, M.A. 1879.

Rundell, Ernest William Matthew Carey, 1s. William Joseph, of Birkenhead, Cheshire, cler. MAGDALEN HALL, matric. 17 Oct., 1868, aged 19, S.C.L. & B.A. 1873, M.A. (HERTFORD COLL.) 1875, has held various curacies since 1872. See *St. Paul's School Reg.*, 341.

Rundle, Henry, s. Nicholas, of Sydenham, Devon, gent. EXETER COLL., matric. 10 Oct., 1733, aged 17; B.A. 1737, rector of Minster 1754, until his death in 1800.

Rundle, Samuel, 3s. Robert, of Devonport, Devon, arm. TRINITY COLL., matric. 11 May, 1831, aged 18; B.A. 1835, M.A. 1837, held various curacies 1835-75, rector of Stockleigh Pomeroy, Devon, 1875.

Rundle, Samuel, 1s. Samuel, of Plymouth, cler. ST. EDMUND HALL, matric. 30 April, 1870, aged 20; B.A. 1873, M.A. 1876.

Rundle, Thomas Sole, o.s. Thomas, of Devonport, Devon, gent. QUEEN'S COLL., matric. 4 Feb., 1870, aged 22; B.A. 1873, M.A. 1876, vicar of Cockington, Devon, 1882. [5]

Rusbridge, Edward, 'sutor;' privilegiatus 11 Dec., 1777.

Rusbridger, Rev. John, 1s. John, of Goodwood, Sussex, gent. WADHAM COLL., matric. 5 June, 1834, aged 17; B.A. 1839, M.A. 1841.

Ruscombe, Thomas, s. William, of Rannington, Somerset, gent. EXETER COLL., matric. 18 May, 1717, aged 17; B.A. 1721.

Rush, Henry John, s. Roger, of St. James's, Westminster, arm. WORCESTER COLL., matric. 24 June, 1808, aged 20; B.A. 1812, M.A. 1817, vicar of Hollington, Sussex, at his death 3 Nov., 1854.

Rush, Henry John, 1s. (Roger), of Crowhurst, Sussex, cler. WORCESTER COLL., matric. 21 March, 1839, aged 18; B.A. 1843, M.A. 1848, vicar of Rustington, Sussex, 1858-71. See *St. Paul's School Reg.*, 224.

Rush, John, s. Montague, of Heckfield, Hants, cler. ST. JOHN'S COLL., matric. 1 July, 1788, aged 18; B.C.L. 1795, rector of Hartwell, Bucks, 1803, vicar of Chelsea Old Church 1824, until his death 4 June, 1855. See *Robinson*, 147. [11]

Rush, Montague, y.s. John, of Streatley, Berks, equitis. ST. JOHN'S COLL., matric. 4 July, 1749, aged 17; B.A. 1753, M.A. 1757, B.D. 1762, rector of Elvetham, Hants, 1774.

Rush, Montague, s. Montague, of Heckfield, Hants, cler. ST. JOHN'S COLL., matric. 26 June, 1792, aged 18; B.A. 1796, M.A. 1800, vicar of Stone, Bucks, 1803-9. See *Robinson*. 153.

Rush, Samuel, s. Samuel, of Streatley, Berks, arm. ORIEL COLL., matric. 26 June, 1778, aged 19.

Rusher, William, 'apothecarius et parturientibus opem ferens;' privilegiatus 26 June, 1821. [15]

Rusher, William Eaton, 1s. William, of St. Peter's-in-the-East, Oxford (city), gent. MAGDALEN HALL, matric. 7 July, 1838, aged 18; B.A. 1842, M.A. 1852.

Rushforth, Collingwood McNeil, 2s. Daniel, of London, gent. ST. JOHN'S COLL., matric. 16 Oct., 1886, aged 17.

Rushforth, Gordon McNeil, 1s. Daniel, of London, gent. ST. JOHN'S COLL., matric. 15 Oct., 1881, aged 19; scholar 1881-5, B.A. 1885, M.A. 1888. See *Robinson*, 385.

Rushout, (Sir) Charles Rushout (Bart.), o.s. Charles Cockerell, of St. George's, London, baronet. CHRIST CHURCH, matric. 14 Jan., 1828, aged 18; 2nd baronet, assumed the surname of RUSHOUT in lieu of COCKERELL by royal licence 6 June, 1849. died 19 Sep., 1869. See Foster's *Baronetage*.

Rushout-Bowles, George, s. John, of St. James's, Westminster, baronet (after baron). CHRIST CHURCH, matric. 5 Feb., 1789, aged 18, B.A. 1792; M.A. from ALL SOULS' COLL. 1797, rector of Burford, Salop (3rd portion) 1799-1842, assumed the additional surname of BOWLES by royal licence 20 June, 1817, died 17 Oct., 1842, father of the next named. See Foster's *Peerage*, B. NORTHWICK, and *Gent.'s Mag.* 1842, ii. 655 [20]

Rushout, George, o.s. George, of Burford, Salop, arm. (*sic*). CHRIST CHURCH, matric. 16 Dec., 1829, aged 18; B.A. 1833, M.A. 1836, 3rd Lord Northwick, M.P. Evesham 1837-41, East Worcestershire 1847-59, died 18 Nov., 1887 See Foster's *Peerage*.

Rushout, John, s. John, of St. George's, Bloomsbury, baronet. CHRIST CHURCH, matric. 20 Oct., 1756, aged 18; 4th baronet in 1773, created Baron Northwick 26 Oct., 1797, M.P. Evesham 1761-96, died 20 Oct., 1800, father of George 1789.

Rushworth, Charles Powlett, s. Edward, of Isle of Wight, arm. ST. JOHN'S COLL., matric. 30 June, 1806, aged 15; fellow 1806-15, B.A. 1812, M.A. 1814, a commissioner of taxes 1818, until his death 15 Oct. 1854, father of Edward E.

Rushworth, Daniel, s. John, of Northampton (town), gent. NEW COLL., matric. 13 Feb., 1724-5, aged 18; B.C.L. 1731.

Rushworth, Edward, s. John, of Portsea, Hants. arm. TRINITY COLL., matric. 11 April, 1780, aged 24, of Faringford Hill, Isle of Wight, M.P. Yarmouth, Isle of Wight, Sep. 1780, until removed, April, 1781 (being in deacon orders), of Newport, Isle of Wight, 1784-90, and of Yarmouth June to Dec., 1790, and May, 1796, to March, 1797, mayor of Yarmouth, died 15 Oct., 1817, father of Charles P. [25]

Rushworth, Edward Everard, C.M.G., 1s. Charles Powlett, of Chelsea, arm. ST. JOHN'S COLL., matric. 30 June, 1834, aged 15; scholar & fellow 1834-55, B.C.L. 1840, D.C.L. 1844, died 10 Aug., 1877.

Rushworth, John, s. Thomas, of Holywell, city of Oxon, pleb. ST. JOHN'S COLL., matric. 2 July, 1716, aged 17; clerk MAGDALEN COLL., 1720, B.A. 1720, vicar of Fillongley, co. Warwick, 1732. See *Bloxam*, ii. 87.

Ruskin, John, 1s. John James, of London, arm. CHRIST CHURCH, matric. 20 Oct., 1836, aged 17, B.A. 1842, M.A. 1843, hon. student 1867; hon. fellow CORPUS CHRISTI COLL. 1871, Slade professor of fine art 1869-79 and 1883-5.

Russ, John, s. John, of Evercreech, Somerset, pleb. ORIEL COLL., matric. 13 May, 1740, aged 18; B.A. from CORPUS CHRISTI COLL. 1744, M.A. 1749.

Russell, Alexander Benn, 7s. Claude, of Binfield, Berks, arm. EXETER COLL., matric. 11 April, 1823, aged 19; LL.B. from EMMANUEL COLL., Cambridge, 1829, vicar of Westbury cum Priddy 1851-7, and rector of Laverton, Somerset, 1857, until his death 23 March, 1888 (his grandfather, John Russell, was born in Dec., 1672). See Foster's *Baronetage*.

Russell, Alexander Henry Monckton, 2s. Alexander Benn, of Wells, Somerset, cler. ST. MARY HALL, matric. 31 Jan., 1863, aged 19; B.A. 1869, M.A. 1872, chorister New College 1851-8, vicar of Westwood, co. Warwick, 1872-7, rector of Ashow, co. Warwick, 1877-84, and of Whitnash 1884. [31]

Russell, Alfred Francis, 1s. Francis, of London, arm. UNIVERSITY COLL., matric. 15 Oct., 1870, aged 19; B.A. 1874, M.A. 1877, rector of Chingford, Essex, 1878.

Russell, Arthur Eustace, 2s. Alfred Oliver, of Leytonstone, Essex, cler. BRASENOSE COLL., matric. 23 Oct., 1885, aged 19; exhibitioner 1885.

Russell, Arthur Goodacre, 2s. Arthur Tozer, of Caxton, co. Cambridge, cler. ST. MARY HALL, matric. 21 Oct., 1856, aged 18; bible clerk 1856-9, B.A. 1876, M.A. 1877, perp. curate St. Stephen, Cardiff, 1877.

Russell, Arthur Joseph, 1s. Charles, of London, arm. (after knight). NON-COLL., matric. 29 April, 1881, aged 20; B.A. from ORIEL COLL. 1886, bar.-at-law, Inner Temple, 1886. [35]

Russell, Benjamin, s. Jos., of Calne, Wilts, pleb. ST. EDMUND HALL, matric. 14 July, 1716, aged 17; B.A. from MERTON COLL. 1720.

Russell, Blois de Blois, o.s. John James, of West Bromwich, co. Stafford, arm. ST. JOHN'S COLL., matric. 12 March, 1856, aged 18.

ussell, Cecil Henry St. Leger, 1s. Richard, of Trinidad, West Indies, arm. TRINITY COLL., matric. 15 Oct., 1881, aged 19; scholar 1881-5, B.A. 1886.

ussell, Champion Branfill, 1s. Champion, of Stubbers, Essex, arm. UNIVERSITY COLL., matric. 18 Oct., 1879, aged 19; B.A. 1883.

ussell, Charles, s. William, of Wimbourne, Dorset, cler. NEW COLL., matric. 10 June, 1761, aged 19; B.A. 1765. See *Gent.'s Mag.*, 1833, i. 281.

ussell, Charles Martin, 1s. Garrett John, of Cork, cler. ST. ALBAN HALL, matric. 16 Oct., 1880, aged 41; vicar of Frampton-on-Severn, co. Gloucester, 1881.

ussell, Charles Watts, 2s. Jesse David Watts, of London, arm. CHRIST CHURCH, matric. 23 May, 1861, aged 17; B.A. 1871.

ussell, Charles William, s. Richard, of Ash, Hants, doctor. CHRIST CHURCH, matric. 30 May, 1764, aged 17, B.A. 1768; M.A. from ORIEL COLL. 1771, a student of Lincoln's Inn 1767. [5]

:ussell, Cyril, 3s. Charles, of London, arm. (after knight). UNIVERSITY COLL., matric. 24 Oct., 1883, aged 17; B.A. 1886.

:ussell, Dennis, s. Dennis, of Penryn, Cornwall, gent. WADHAM COLL., matric. 26 March, 1729, aged 17; B.A. 1733.

:ussell, Edward Cardale, 3s. David, of York, gent. KEBLE COLL., matric. 18 Oct., 1871, aged 25; has held various curacies since 1874.

:ussell, Rev. Edward Grant, 3s. Charles Dupré, of Bengal, East Indies, gent. ST. EDMUND HALL, matric. 1 Feb., 1849, aged 19; B.A. 1853, M.A. 1861, died 20 May, 1883. See Foster's *Baronetage*.

:ussell, Edward James, 1s. Edward James Richard, of Dorking, Surrey, gent. ST. MARY HALL, matric. 22 Oct., 1867, aged 23; B.A. 1870, M.A. 1875, vicar of St. James's, Heywood, Lancashire, 1876-83, of Todmorden 1883. [10]

tussell, Edward Oldnall, 1s. William Oldnall, of St. Pancras, London, arm. (after knight). ST. JOHN'S COLL., matric. 10 Nov., 1847, aged 18.

tussell, Edward Watts, y.s. (subs. 5s.) Jesse Watts, of Ham, near Ashbourne, co. Stafford, arm. CHRIST CHURCH, matric. 20 Oct., 1863, aged 18; a junior student 1863-8, B.A. 1867, bar.-at-law, Lincoln's Inn, 1870. See Foster's *Men at the Bar*.

tussell, Francis, s. William, of St. George's, Hanover Square, arm. CHRIST CHURCH, matric. 23 Oct., 1810, aged 17; lieut.-colonel in the army, M.P. Tavistock 1831, until his death 24 Nov., 1832. See Foster's *Peerage*, D. BEDFORD.

tussell, Francis Albert Rollo, 3s. John, Earl Russell. CHRIST CHURCH, matric. 3 June, 1868, aged 18; B.A. 1873, M.A. 1878. See Foster's *Peerage*.

tussell, Francis (Shirley), 2s. James, of Aden, co. Aberdeen (Scotland), arm. BALLIOL COLL., matric. 21 Jan., 1860, aged 19; B.A. 1862, lieut.-colonel 1st royal dragoons. [15]

:ussell, Francis Xavier Joseph, 4s. Charles, of London, knight. ORIEL COLL., matric. 19 Oct., 1886, aged 19; brother of Arthur Joseph 1881, and of Cyril 1883.

:ussell, Frederick, o.s. Thomas, of Colchester, Essex, arm. QUEEN'S COLL., matric. 13 Nov., 1820, aged 17; B.A. from ST. MARY HALL 1828, M.A. 1828. See *Eton School Lists*.

:ussell, Hon. Frederick Gustavus Hamilton, 2s. William Viscount Boyne. CHRIST CHURCH, matric. 18 Oct., 1886, aged 19. See Foster's *Peerage*.

:ussell, Rev. George born in Isle of Minorca, s. Christopher, arm. ST. MARY HALL, matric. 28 May, 1746, aged 18; B.A. 1750, died 1767.

:ussell, (Sir) George (Bart.), s. John, of Knightsbridge, Middlesex, baronet. CHRIST CHURCH, matric. 24 Oct., 1798, aged 17; 10th baronet, of Chequers, Bucks, a student of Lincoln's Inn 1802, died 25 April, 1804. See *Eton School Lists*. [20]

Russell, (Sir) George (Bart.), 3s. Henry, of Swallowfield, Berks, baronet. EXETER COLL., matric. 4 June, 1846, aged 17; B.A. 1850, M.A. 1853, 4th baronet, bar.-at-law, Lincoln's Inn, 1853, recorder of Wokingham 1862, a judge of County Courts 1866-84, M.P. East Berks, Dec., 1885. See Foster's *Baronetage, Men at the Bar*, & *Eton School Lists*.

Russell, George William Erskine, 2s. (Lord) Charles James Fox, of London. UNIVERSITY COLL., matric. 11 Oct., 1872, aged 19; exhibitioner 1872-7, B.A. 1876, M.A. 1880, a student of the Inner Temple 1875, M.P. Aylesbury 1880-5. See Foster's *Peerage*.

Russell, George William Francis Sackville, 1s. Hastings, of London, arm. (after Duke of Bedford). BALLIOL COLL., matric. 22 Oct., 1870, aged 18; B.A. 1874, M.A. 1877, Marquis of Tavistock, a student of the Inner Temple 1871, M.P. Beds 1875-85. See Foster's *Peerage*.

Russell, Giles Banger, 1s. Thomas, of Beaminster, Dorset, arm. TRINITY COLL., matric. 5 July, 1850, aged 18. See John Cox, 1802; and also *Eton School Lists*.

Russell, Henry Vane, 3s. Harry, of Lewisham, Kent, arm. CORPUS CHRISTI COLL., matric. 7 June, 1828, aged 19; B.A. 1832, M.A. 1835, vicar of Stottesden, Salop, at his death 21 May, 1846. [25]

Russell, Henry Lloyd, 1s. Henry, of Albany, New York, America, gent. ST. MARY HALL, matric. 25 Feb., 1858, aged 20; vicar of Church of Annunciation, Chislehurst, 1870.

Russell, Henry Stuart, 1s. Samuel Henry, of St. George's, Hanover Square, London, arm. CHRIST CHURCH, matric. 30 May, 1838, aged 19.

Russell, Herbert, 2s. Francis, of London, arm. KEBLE COLL., matric. 27 Jan., 1872, aged 19; B.A. 1875, bar.-at-law, Inner Temple, 1881. See Foster's *Men at the Bar*.

Russell, Herbert David, 2s. David, of York (city), arm. WADHAM COLL., matric. 26 Nov., 1862, aged 18; B.A. 1866.

Russell, Lord Herbrand Arthur, 2s. Hastings, Duke of Bedford. BALLIOL COLL., matric. 24 Jan., 1877, aged 18. See Foster's *Peerage*. [30]

Russell, James, 4s. William, of Faringdon, Devon, gent. MAGDALEN HALL, matric. 29 June, 1858, aged 29; B.Mus. 1 July, 1858, D.Mus. 22 June, 1865.

Russell, James Cholmeley, 1s. James, of St. George's, Bloomsbury, London, arm. MAGDALEN COLL., matric. 22 March, 1860, aged 18; B.A. 1864, bar.-at-law, Lincoln's Inn, 1867. See Foster's *Men at the Bar*.

Russell, James Robert Neville Graves, 4s. Lechmere, of Ashford Hall, Salop, arm. CHRIST CHURCH, matric. 12 Oct., 1866, aged 19. See *Eton School Lists*.

Russell, (Jesse) David Watts, 1s. Jesse Watts, of St. Marylebone, London, arm. CHRIST CHURCH, matric. 21 Oct., 1830, aged 18; B.A. 1835, of Biggin Grange, Northants, M.P. North Stafford 1841-7, died 7 March, 1879, father of Charles Watts 1861. See *Eton School Lists*.

Russell, Jesse (Watts), s. Jesse, of Whitechapel, London, arm. WORCESTER COLL., matric. 13 Nov., 1804, aged 18; B.A. 1808, M.A. 1811, created D.C.L. 23 June, 1819, of Ilam Hall, co. Stafford, assumed the additional surname of WATTS by royal licence 28 March, 1817, M.P. Gatton 1820-6, died 26 March, 1875. [35]

Russell, John, s. John, of Blandford, Dorset, pleb. ORIEL COLL., matric. 25 May, 1723, aged 18.

Russell, John, s. Henry, of Northleach, co. Gloucester, pleb. MAGDALEN HALL, matric. 24 March, 1726-7, aged 19.

Russell, John, s. Thomas, of London, pleb. BRASENOSE COLL., matric. 26 June, 1741, aged 27.

Russell, John, s. John, of Soulderne, Oxon, cler. CORPUS CHRISTI COLL., matric. 14 Nov., 1755, aged 16; scholar 10 Nov., 1755, B.A. 1759, M.A. 1763, B.D. 1772, proctor 1771, rector of Helmdon, Northants, 1783, and of Ilmington, co. Warwick, 1783, until his death 26 April, 1802 (his father died 17 March, 1772), father of John 1803.

Russell, (Sir) John (Bart.), s. Charles, of St. James's, Westminster. CHRIST CHURCH, matric. 24 May, 1758, aged 17; B.A. 1762, M.A. 1765, 8th baronet, bar.-at-law, Lincoln's Inn, 1766, died 8 August, 1783. See Foster's *Baronetage* & *Alumni West.*, 369.

Russell, (Sir) John (Bart.), s. John, of Knightsbridge, Middlesex, baronet. CHRIST CHURCH, matric. 29 Oct., 1795, aged 18; 9th baronet, died 11 June, 1802.

Russell, John, s. Henshaw, of Walthamstow, Essex, gent. MAGDALEN HALL, matric. 8 April, 1802, aged 22; B.A. 1806, vicar of Sutton Courtney, Berks, died 26 Aug., 1828.

Russell, John, s. John, of Helmdon, Northants, cler. CHRIST CHURCH, matric. 3 May, 1803, aged 16; B.A. 1806, M.A. 1809, B.D. 1817, D.D. 1820, head-master Charterhouse School 1811-32, canon of Canterbury 1827-32, rector of St. Botolph's, Bishopsgate Without, 1832, until his death 3 June, 1863, father of John 1833. [5]

Russell, John s. John, of Sheepfields, Cumberland, gent. QUEEN'S COLL., matric. 31 May, 1809, aged 19; B.A. 1813, fellow 1815-23, M.A. 1816.

Russell, John, s. John, of Dartmouth, Devon, cler. EXETER COLL., matric. 9 Nov., 1814, aged 18; B.A. 1818, rector of Swymbridge, Devon, 1832-80, and of Black Torrington 1880, until his death 28 April, 1883, known as Jack Russell, 'the Sporting Parson.'

Russell, John, 1s. John, of Charterhouse, London, doctor. CHRIST CHURCH, matric. 23 May, 1833, aged 19.

Russell, John, 1s. John, of Nottingham, arm. BALLIOL COLL., matric. 19 Oct., 1868, aged 18; B.A. 1873, M.A. 1875.

Russell, John Cecil, 1s. Alexander James, of Edinburgh, gent. NEW COLL., matric. 9 Dec., 1858, aged 19. [10]

Russell, John Cox, s. John Banger, of Beaminster, Dorset, gent. BALLIOL COLL., matric. 12 Nov., 1802, aged 18; B.A. from HERTFORD COLL. 1806, rector of North Poorton, Dorset, died 20 Aug., 1819.

Russell, John Fenn, 2s. William, of Shepperton, Middlesex, cler. WADHAM COLL., matric. 28 Jan., 1846, aged 18; B.A. 1849.

Russell, John Francis Stanley, Earl, 1s. John, Viscount Amberley. BALLIOL COLL., matric. 16 Oct., 1883, aged 18. See Foster's *Peerage*.

Russell, John Francis Vickers, 1s. John, of Neath, co. Glamorgan, gent. JESUS COLL., matric. 20 Oct., 1886, aged 19; scholar 1886.

Russell, John Montague, 3s. James, of London, arm. MAGDALEN COLL., matric. 24 Jan., 1868, aged 18; B.A. 1870. [15]

Russell, John Somerset, ORIEL COLL., 1818. See PAKINGTON, page 1058.

Russell, John Wellesley, 4s. Edward, of Kidderminster, co. Worcester, cler. BALLIOL COLL., matric. 21 Oct., 1869, aged 17, exhibitioner 1869-71, scholar 1870-3; fellow MERTON COLL. 1873, B.A. 1873, M.A. 1876, lecturer in mathematics 1881, and tutor Balliol College 1872.

Russell, Joseph Burnett, 4s. James, of Edinburgh, D.Med. MAGDALEN HALL, matric. 20 Oct., 1868, aged 24; B.A. 1872, M.A. (HERTFORD COLL.) 1875, curate of St. John, Folkestone, 1880-3, vicar 1883-5.

Russell, Louis Pitman, 3s. John Alexander, of London, arm. TRINITY COLL., matric. 17 Oct., 1868, aged 17; S.C.L. & B.A. 1872, bar.-at-law, Middle Temple, 1875, an advocate before the High Court of Judicature, Bombay. See Foster's *Men at the Bar* & *Rugby School Reg.*

Russell, Matthew, s. William, of Sunderland, co. Durham, arm. UNIVERSITY COLL., matric. 28 March, 1781, aged 16; of Brancepeth Castle, co. Durham, M.P. Saltash 1802 to Feb., 1807, and 1812, until his death 8 May, 1822. [20]

Russell, Michael, s. Dennis, of Bideford, Devon, gent. EXETER COLL., matric. 10 Oct., 1718, aged 17.

Russell, Michael, s. Michael, of Bideford, Devon, pleb. EXETER COLL., matric. 23 March, 1737-8, aged 19; B.A. from CHRIST CHURCH 13 Feb., 1741-2, M.A. 1745.

Russell, Michael, 1s. — R., gent. ST. JOHN'S COLL., admitted 28 Oct., 1841, aged 60; D.C.L. (by decree) 29 Oct., 1841, M.A. Glasgow University 1806, LL.D 1820, dean of Edinburgh 1831-7, bishop of Glasgow and Galloway 1837, until his death 2 April, 1848.

Russell, Michael Watts Watts, 2s. Jesse Watts, of Ilam, co. Stafford, arm. CHRIST CHURCH, matric. 12 Dec., 1833, aged 18; B.A. 1838, M.A. 1841, rector of Benefield, Northants, seceded to Rome, died 16 March, 1875. See *Eton School Lists*.

Russell, Ratcliffe, s. William, of Preston, Lancashire, pleb. BRASENOSE COLL., matric. 8 March, 1727-8, aged 17. [25]

Russell, Richard, s. William, of Basingstoke, Hants, gent. CHRIST CHURCH, matric. 8 June, 1716, aged 20; B.C.L. 1723, D.C.L. 1743, rector of Ashe and vicar of Overton, Hants, father of Charles William 1764. See *Alumni West.*, 268.

Russell, Richard, s. Ric., of St. John the Baptist, Hereford (city), cler. NEW COLL., matric. 11 Sep., 1728, aged 17.

Russell, Richard, s. Richard, of South Malling, Sussex, arm. CHRIST CHURCH, matric. 17 Dec., 1750, aged 17; B.A. 1754, M.A. 1757, brother of William 1743.

Russell, Robert, 3s. John, of Leek, co. Stafford, arm. ORIEL COLL., matric. 22 Oct., 1859, aged 18; B.A. 1863, M.A. 1866, vicar of St. Barnabas, Rotherhithe, 1873.

Russell, Robert, 1s. Robert, of Ockham, Surrey, arm. CHRIST CHURCH, matric. 16 Oct., 1868, aged 20; a student of the Inner Temple 1870. [30]

Russell, Robert, o.s. Robert, of Durban, Natal, arm. MERTON COLL., matric. 28 Jan., 1886, aged 18.

Russell, Robert Bruce, 2s. James, of Walmer, Kent, arm. MAGDALEN COLL., matric. 9 Feb., 1863, aged 18; B.A. 1867, bar.-at-law, Inner Temple, 1871. See Foster's *Men at the Bar*.

Russell, (Sir) Robert Frankland (Bart.), s. Thomas Frankland, of York (city), baronet. CHRIST CHURCH, matric. 31 Oct., 1803, aged 19; 7th baronet, M.P. Thirsk in 7 parliaments April, 1815, until March, 1834, assumed the additional surname of RUSSELL, and died 11 March, 1849. See Foster's *Baronetage*.

Russell, (Sir) Robert Greenhill (Bart.), s. John Greenhill, of Missenden, Bucks, doctor. CHRIST CHURCH, matric. 24 May, 1780, student until 1836, B.A. 1784, M.A. 1787, bar.-at-law, Lincoln's Inn, 1790, assumed the additional surname of RUSSELL in 1815, created a baronet 15 Sep., 1831, M.P. Thirsk in 8 parliaments 1806-33, died 12 Dec., 1836. See *Alumni West.*, 412.

Russell, Sambrooke (Nicholas), s. John, of Basingstoke, Hants, gent. QUEEN'S COLL., matric. 17 Dec., 1750, aged 17; B.A. 1754, M.A. 1757, rector of Bruntingthorpe, died 29 Dec., 1795. [35]

Russell, Samuel (or ? John), M.A. from ST. JOHN'S COLL., Cambridge; incorp. 2 Nov., 1725.

Russell, Samuel Henry, 1s. Thomas, of St. Anne's, Blackfriars, London, gent. ST. JOHN'S COLL., matric. 25 June, 1832, aged 18; scholar & fellow 1832-57, B.A. 1836, M.A. 1840, B.D. 1845, 2nd master Merchant Taylors' School, London, 1836-57, vicar of Charlbury, Oxon, 1857, until his death 10 Sep., 1873. See *Robinson*, 216.

Russell, Rev. Spencer Cecil, 3s. Cecil, of Tyrrell's Pass, near Westmeath, Ireland, cler. CORPUS CHRISTI COLL., matric. 16 Oct., 1866, aged 19; scholar 1866-70, B.A. 1870, fellow 1870, until his death 17 Aug., 1873.

Russell, Terence, B.A. TRINITY COLL., Dublin, 1713 (M.A. 1715); incorp. 24 March, 1717-8.

Russell, Theodosius Stuart, 1s. Edmund, of Pontefract, Yorks, cler. EXETER COLL., matric. 10 Oct., 1856, aged 20; chief constable Yorkshire (West Riding), sometime captain 1st West York militia, etc. See Foster's *Our Noble and Gentle Families*, vol. ii.

Russell, Thomas, s. John, of West Wickham, Bucks, pleb. BALLIOL COLL., matric. 6 Feb., 1729-30, aged 17; B.A. 1733, M.A. 1736, B. & D.D. 1765, vicar of Lugwardine and Brampton Bryan, co. Hereford, master of Ledbury Hospital, canon residentiary and preb. of Hereford 1752, until his death 17 Jan., 1785. [5]

Russell, Thomas, s. William, of Worcester (city), gent. CHRIST CHURCH, matric. 17 Dec., 1764, aged 15; B.A. 1768, M.A. 1772.

Russell, Rev. Thomas, s. John, of Beaminster, Dorset, gent. NEW COLL., matric. 29 Dec., 1780, aged 19; B.A. 1784, died a fellow 31 July, 1788.

Russell, Thomas, s. John, of Guildford, Surrey, pleb. MERTON COLL., matric. 27 Oct., 1783, aged 35; B.C.L. 1790, rector of West Clandon, Surrey, 1788, until his death 18 July, 1822, author of a 'History of Guildford.'

Russell, Thomas, 3s. Thomas, of London, gent. ST. JOHN'S COLL., matric. 26 June, 1848, aged 18; B.A. 1852, M.A. 1855, held various curacies 1853-61, master Banbury Grammar School 1861-5, and of Brackley Grammar School 1865-70. See *Robinson*, 268.

Russell, Thomas, 1s. Thomas, of Beaminster, Dorset, arm. TRINITY COLL., matric. 1 June, 1853, aged 18. [10]

Russell, Thomas Artemidorus, 3s. Thomas Artemidorus, of Cheshunt, Herts, gent. ST. JOHN'S COLL., matric. 12 March, 1829, aged 18; died in 1863.

Russell, Timothy, s. James (Jocobi in *Mat. Reg.*), of Downton, Wilts, gent. BALLIOL COLL., matric. 12 Nov., 1743, aged 18.

Russell, Western Francis, 2s. Sydenham Francis, of Willesborough, Kent, cler. CHRIST CHURCH, matric. 15 Oct., 1880, aged 18; a junior student 1880-5; B.A. 1884.

Russell, William, s. William, of Wimborne Minster, Dorset, pleb. HART HALL, matric. 10 Oct., 1716, aged 17; B.A. 1720, M.A. 1723.

Russell, William, s. Peter, of Shadwell, Middlesex, gent. QUEEN'S COLL., matric. 10 Oct., 1719, aged 15; B.A. 1723. [15]

Russell, William, s. Richard, of Malling, Sussex, arm. CHRIST CHURCH, matric. 17 Dec., 1743, aged 17; B.A. 23 March, 1747-8, M.A. 1750, bar.-at-law, Lincoln's Inn, 1751, brother of Richard 1750.

Russell, Lord William, s. Francis, of Bloomsbury, Middlesex, arm. (after Marquis of Tavistock). CHRIST CHURCH, matric. 2 Nov., 1784, aged 17; created M.A. 30 March, 1787, and also D.C.L. 3 July, 1793, M.P. Surrey 1789-1807, Tavistock 1807-19, and 1826-31, born (posthumous) 20 Aug., 1767, murdered by his valet 6 May, 1840, father of Francis 1810.

Russell, William, s. Thomas, of Lyleshayes, Salop, arm. PEMBROKE COLL., matric. 3 Nov., 1762, aged 24.

Russell, William, s. John, of Helmden, Northants, cler. MAGDALEN COLL., matric. 26 July, 1804, aged 16; demy 1804-15, B.A. 1808, M.A. 1811, fellow 1815-31, B.D. 1819, proctor 1818, dean of divinity 1822, bursar 1823, vice-president 1822, died 26 Nov., 1831. See *Bloxam*, vii. 156.

Russell, William, s. Hugh, of St. Andrew's, London, gent. MAGDALEN HALL, matric. 25 Jan., 1808, aged 30. [20]

Russell, William, 1s. Francis, Marquis of Tavistock (after duke). CHRIST CHURCH, matric. 10 May, 1827, aged 17; 8th Duke of Bedford, died 26 May, 1872. See Foster's *Peerage*, & *Eton School Lists*.

Russell, William, 3s. John, of London, doctor. CHRIST CHURCH, matric. 19 May, 1836, aged 18; B.A. from NEW INN HALL 1840, M.A. 1843, rector of Aber-Edw with Llanfarith 1846.

Russell, William, 2s. Edward James Richard, of Dorking, Surrey, gent. CHRIST CHURCH, matric. 7 July, 1865, aged 19; B.Mus. 8 July, 1865.

Russell, William, y.s. William, of London, gent. EXETER COLL., matric. 20 Oct., 1881, aged 19; exhibitioner 1881-5, B.A. 1885, M.A. 1888.

Russell, William, 5s. Archibald, of Cambuslang, co. Lanark, arm. CORPUS CHRISTI COLL., matric. 20 Oct., 1886, aged 18. [25]

Russell, William Allan, 1s. James, of Westminster, gent. QUEEN'S COLL., matric. 29 Oct., 1847, aged 19; Lusby scholar MAGDALEN HALL 1849, B.A. 1852, M.A. 1855, bishop of missions in North China 1872, until his death 5 Oct., 1879.

Russell, William Ernest, 5s. David, of Clifton, Yorks, arm. CORPUS CHRISTI COLL., matric. 18 Oct., 1871, aged 19; B.A. 1875, M.A. 1878, a master at Haileybury College.

Russell, William Henry, 1s. Henry Emanuel, of New Britain, America, gent. ORIEL COLL., matric. 13 Oct., 1873, aged 19; B.A. 1876.

Russell, William Herbert, s. William, of Powick, co. Worcester, arm. CHRIST CHURCH, matric. 20 Feb., 1813, aged 19. See Foster's *Peerage*, B. Hampton; & *Eton School Lists*.

Russell, (Sir) William Oldnall, s. (Samuel) Oldnall, of Worcester (city), cler. CHRIST CHURCH, matric. 22 Dec., 1801, aged 16; a student until 1812, B.A. 1804, M.A. 1807, bar.-at-law, Lincoln's Inn, 1809, serjt.-at-law 1827, altered his names RUSSELL OLDNALL to OLDNALL RUSSELL, chief justice Bengal, knighted 22 Feb., 1832, died 22 Jan., 1833, father of Edward O. 1847. [30]

Russell, William Robert, o.s. Joseph, of St. Albans, Herts, gent. QUEEN'S COLL., matric. 22 Oct., 1878, aged 18.

Russell, William Tyrrell, s. John, of Southill, Cornwall, cler. LINCOLN COLL., matric. 9 May, 1818, aged 19; B.A. 1822.

Russia, Alexander I., Emperor of; D.C.L. by diploma 15 June, 1814, died 1 Dec., 1825.

Russia, Alexander II., Emperor of (then Grand Duke and Hereditary Prince); D.C.L. by diploma 20 May 1839, died 13 March, 1881.

Russia, Michael, Grand Duke of, 3rd brother of Alexander I.; D.C.L. by diploma 16 Oct., 1818, died 9 Sep., 1849. [35]

Russia, Nicholas, Grand Duke of, 2nd brother of Alexander I.; D.C.L. by diploma 11 Jan., 1817, died 2 March, 1855.

Russwurm, Alexander, 1s. Alexander, of Kilkenny, Ireland, arm. CHRIST CHURCH, matric. 15 June, 1848, aged 19; servitor 1848-52, B.A. 1852, head-master Portsmouth Grammar School 1855-74, vicar of Marcham, Berks, 1875.

Rust, Clement Ernest, 3s. George, of London, cler. ST. JOHN'S COLL., matric. 16 Oct., 1875, aged 19; B.A. 1879, died in 1881. See *St. Paul's School Reg.*, 353.

Rust, Rev. Edward Aldridge, o.s. James, of Chelmsford, Essex, arm. WADHAM COLL., matric. 20 Jan., 1871, aged 23.

Rust, George, s. James, of Huntingdon (town), arm. BRASENOSE COLL., matric. 8 April, 1812, aged 16; B.A. 1815, M.A. 1818, of Cromwell House, Hunts, died in 1876. See *Rugby School Reg.*, 96.

Rust, Rev. George, 1s. Richard, of Bishop's Stortford, Herts, pleb. PEMBROKE COLL., matric. 9 June, 1836, aged 17; scholar 1836-40, B.A. 1841, M.A. 1844, classical master King's College School 1849, and master of the Lower School 1868, until his death 6 March, 1874.

Rust, George John, 1s. George, of Huntingdon (town), arm. UNIVERSITY COLL., matric. 15 May, 1849, aged 18; B.A. 1853, of Alconbury House, Hunts, J.P., D.L., bar.-at-law, Lincoln's Inn, 1858. See *Eton School Lists.*

Rust, James, s. James, of Gransden, Hunts, arm. UNIVERSITY COLL., matric. 20 March, 1816, aged 17; scholar 1818-23, B.A. 1819, M.A. 1822, fellow 1823-31, bar.-at-law, Lincoln's Inn, 1825, M.P. Huntingdonshire 1852-9, chairman Hunts Quarter Sessions, died 24 July, 1875. See *Rugby School Reg.*, 96. [5]

Ruston, James, of JESUS COLL., Cambridge (B.A. 1851, M.A. 1856); adm. 'ad eundem' 5 July, 1856, vicar of Hordle, Hants, 1861-75.

Rutherford, Arthur, 5s. William, of Crosby, Lancashire, gent. WORCESTER COLL., matric. 19 Oct., 1882, aged 16; scholar BRASENOSE COLL. 1883-5, exhibitioner 1885, B.A. 1886.

Rutherford, Rev. William Gunion, 2s. Robert, of Glasgow, cler. BALLIOL COLL., matric. 26 April, 1873, aged 19; exhibitioner 1873-7, B.A. 1877, M.A. 1880, fellow and prælector UNIVERSITY COLL. 1883, LL.D. St. Andrew's 1885, head-master Westminster School 1883.

Ruthven, Walter Hore, s. William Hore, of Shelmaker, co. Wexford, Ireland, arm. CHRIST CHURCH, matric. 11 May, 1802, aged 17; of Harperstown, co. Wexford, J.P., high sheriff 1828, assumed the additional surname of RUTHVEN. See Foster's *Peerage*, 1883, B. RUTHVEN. [9]

Rutson, Albert Osliff, 3s. William, of Newby Wiske, Yorks, arm. UNIVERSITY COLL., matric. 20 March, 1855, aged 18, scholar 1855-60, B.A. 1859; fellow MAGDALEN COLL. 1860-70, M.A. 1861, junior dean of arts 1865, bar.-at-law, Lincoln's Inn, 1864. See Foster's *Men at the Bar* & *Rugby School Reg.*, 378.

Rutter, Evan, 2s. John Snoulton, of Chartham, Kent, gent. MAGDALEN HALL, matric. 13 Nov., 1851, aged 18; B.A. 1856, M.A. 1858, held various curacies 1858-71, vicar of Spittal St. John, Berwick-on-Tweed 1871. See *St. Paul's School Reg.*, 308.

Rutter, Rev. John Hagley, o.s. John, of Ilminster, Somerset, gent. EXETER COLL., matric. 10 Oct., 1873, aged 17; B.A. 1876, M.A. 1880.

Rutter, Thomas, s. Ellis, of St. Asaph, co. Flint, pleb. JESUS COLL., matric. 7 March, 1721-2, aged 18; B.A. 1725.

Rutter, William, s. William, of Salwarp, co. Worcester, pleb. BALLIOL COLL., matric. 23 Feb., 1726-7, aged 19; B.A. 1730.

Rutton, Isaac, s. Matthias, of Ashford, Kent, gent. UNIVERSITY COLL., matric. 5 March, 1728-9, aged 17; B.A. 1732, M.A. 1735, B.Med. 1741, died 1792, father of the next named. [15]

Rutton, Matthias, s. Isaac, of Ashford, Kent, gent. ST. ALBAN HALL, matric. 24 Nov., 1775, aged 27; rector of Sheldwick 1781, and of Cowling, Kent, 1783, died rector of Badlesmere in 1818.

Rutton, William Isaac, s. Isaac, of Isle of Sheppey, Kent, arm. CHRIST CHURCH, matric. 8 June, 1787, aged 18. See Berry's *Kent*, 184; & *Alumni West.*, 423.

Ruxton, John Fitzherbert, s. William, of Dublin, Ireland, arm. CHRIST CHURCH, matric. 13 April, 1807, aged 17; of Ardee House, co. Louth, high sheriff 1823, died in 1826, father of the next named.

Ruxton, William, 1s. John Fitzherbert, of Ardee, co. Louth, arm. ORIEL COLL., matric. 3 Dec., 1840, aged 17; of Ardee aforesaid, high sheriff co. Louth, 1848.

Ryall, Charles, s. Christopher, of Sherbourn, Dorset, gent. HART HALL, matric. 3 July, 1716, aged 18; B.A. 1720. [20]

Ryall, Narcissus, s. Richard, of South Cambray, Somerset, gent. ST. MARY HALL, matric. 19 March, 1778, aged 19; rector of Lydford, Somerset, 1784, until his death in 1829.

Ryan, Alfred Thomas, 3s. Vincent William, bishop of Mauritius. WADHAM COLL., matric. 7 June, 1871, B.A. 1875, vicar of Corton, Suffolk, 1884-5.

Ryan, Frederick, s. Stanart, of Dublin (city), arm. MERTON COLL., matric. 28 Oct., 1773, aged 16.

Ryan, Richard, s. John, of Isle of Demerara, West Indies, arm. QUEEN'S COLL., matric. 4 Nov., 1814, aged 18.

Ryan, Vincent John, 1s. Vincent William, of Edge Hill, near Liverpool, bishop of Mauritius. WADHAM COLL., matric. 8 June, 1867, aged 17; B.A. 1871, M.A. 1874, perp. curate Wibsey, Yorks, 1873-75, vicar of Christ Church, Bradford, 1875. [25]

Ryan, Vincent William, 2s. John, of Cork (city), Ireland, gent. MAGDALEN HALL, matric. 7 Dec., 1837, aged 20; B.A. 1841, M.A. 1848 D.D. 1853, curate of Edgehill, Liverpool, and vice-principal of Liverpool College 1847-50, principal of Highbury Training College 1850-3, bishop of Mauritius 1853-68, archdeacon of Suffolk 1868-9, rector of St. Nicholas, Guildford, and commissary of bishop of Winchester 1869-70, vicar of Bradford 1870-80, archdeacon of Craven 1875-80, vicar of St. Peter, Bournemouth, 1880-1, rector of Middleham, Yorks, 1881-3, commissary and assistant-bishop to bishop of Ripon 1870, rector of Stanhope, co. Durham, 1883, until his death 11 Jan., 1888.

Ryan, William Gladstone, o.s. Charles Lister, of London, arm. TRINITY COLL., matric. 15 Oct., 1883, aged 18.

Rycroft, Ellis, s. Richard, of Isle of Barbados, gent. QUEEN'S COLL., matric. 15 Dec., 1718, aged 17.

Ryde, Rev. John Gabriel, 1s. William, of St. Swithin's, London, gent. ST. JOHN'S COLL., matric. 16 Feb., 1842, aged 18; B.A. 1846, M.A. 1848, died 7 Dec., 1868.

Ryde, Rev. Lewis Forbes, 3s. John Gabriel, of Melrose, Scotland, cler. NON-COLL., matric. 18 Oct., 1880, aged 21; B.A. from ST. JOHN'S COLL. 1883, M.A. 1887. [30]

Ryde, Walter Cranley, 3s. Edward, of London, arm. CHRIST CHURCH, matric. 20 May, 1875, aged 18; a junior student 1875-82, B.A. 1879, M.A. 1888, bar.-at-law, Inner Temple, 1882. See Foster's *Men at the Bar.*

Ryder, Dudley, Earl of Harrowby, created D.C.L. 16 June, 1814 (2nd baron), lord president of the Council 1812-27, M.A. from ST. JOHN'S COLL., Cambridge, 1787, created LL.D. 1833, M.P. Tiverton 1784-1803, created Viscount Sandon and Earl of Harrowby 19 July, 1809, died 26 Dec., 1847. See Foster's *Peerage.*

Ryder, Dudley, Viscount Sandon, s. Dudley, Earl of Harrowby. CHRIST CHURCH, matric. 19 Oct., 1816, aged 18; B.A. 1820, M.A. 1832, created D.C.L. 5 July, 1848, 2nd Earl of Harrowby, K.G. 1859, M.P. Tiverton 1819-31, Liverpool 1831-47, chancellor Duchy of Lancaster 1855, lord privy seal 1855-7, died 19 Nov., 1882. See Foster's *Peerage.*

Ryder, Dudley Francis Stuart, Viscount Sandon, 1s. Dudley, Earl of Harrowby. CHRIST CHURCH, matric. 31 May, 1849, aged 18; B.A. 1853, M.A. 1878, 3rd earl, M.P. Lichfield 1856-9, Liverpool 1868-82, president Board of Trade 1878-80, etc. See Foster's *Peerage.*

Ryder, Edward Lisle, o.s. Alfred Philipps, of Lichfield, arm. ORIEL COLL., matric. 23 Oct., 1872, aged 19; B.A. 1876, a student of Lincoln's Inn 1874.

Ryder, Rev. George Dudley, born at Lutterworth, co. Leicester, 3s. Henry, bishop of Lichfield and Coventry. ORIEL COLL., matric. 6 March, 1828, aged 17; B.A. 1833, M.A. 1834, died 19 June, 1880.

Ryder, Granville Richard, 2s. Hon. Granville Dudley, of Hemel Hempstead, Herts, arm. CHRIST CHURCH, matric. 12 June, 1851, aged 17; S.C.L. 1858, B.A. & M.A. 1860, bar.-at-law, Inner Temple, 1859, M.P. Salisbury 1874-80. See Foster's *Men at the Bar.*

Ryder, Henry Dudley, born at Garendon Park, co. Leicester, 1s. Henry, bishop of Gloucester. ORIEL COLL., matric. 22 Jan., 1821, aged 17; B.A. 1825, M.A. 1828, vicar of Tarvin, Cheshire, and of High Offley, co. Stafford, canon of Lichfield 1833, until his death 19 Jan., 1877.

Ryder, Henry Dudley, 2s. Henry Dudley, of Tarvin, Cheshire, cler. WADHAM COLL., matric. 18 Oct., 1851, aged 17; scholar 1851-7, B.A. 1857, died 14 June, 1880. [5]

Ryder, Henry Dudley, 2s. Dudley, Earl of Harrowby. CHRIST CHURCH, matric. 8 June, 1854, aged 18. See Foster's *Peerage.*

Ryder, Henry Stewart, 3s. Hon. Granville, of Bovingden, Herts, arm. MERTON COLL., matric. 1 Dec., 1853, aged 18; lieutenant rifle brigade, fell before Sebastopol, 8 Sep., 1855.

Ryder, James Octavius, 2s. William Dudley, of St. Philip's, Birmingham, co. Warwick, gent. PEMBROKE COLL., matric. 23 Oct., 1845, aged 18, B.A. 1849; fellow ALL SOULS' COLL. 1850-67, M.A. 1853, rector of Elmley, Kent, 1852-66, rector of Welwyn, Herts, 1866, until his death 24 April, 1870.

Ryder, Richard Calthorpe Whitmore, born at St. Andrew's, Wells, 8s. Henry, bishop of Lichfield and Coventry. ORIEL COLL., matric. 13 June, 1840, aged 17; scholar WADHAM COLL. 1841-9, B.A. 1844, fellow 1849, M.A. 1850, bar.-at-law, Inner Temple, 1848. See Foster's *Men at the Bar.*

Ryder, Samuel, s. Sam., of St. Margaret's, Westminster, arm. LINCOLN COLL., matric. 1 Dec., 1742, aged 19. [10]

Ryder, Spencer Charles Dudley, 1s. Spencer Charles Dudley, of Dinapore, East Indies. KEBLE COLL., matric. 18 Oct., 1871, aged 19.

Ryder, Thomas Dudley, 5s. Henry, of Lutterworth, bishop of Lichfield and Coventry. ORIEL COLL., matric. 21 March, 1833, aged 17, B.A. 1837, M.A. 1840, bar.-at-law, Gray's Inn, 1856, registrar of the diocese of Manchester, died 23 Jan., 1886. See Foster's *Peerage*, E. HARROWBY; & *Rugby School Reg.*, 163.

Ryder, Thomas Richard, s. Thomas, of Hendon, Middlesex, arm. EXETER COLL., matric. 1 May, 1812, aged 17; B.A. from PEMBROKE COLL. 1817, M.A. 1821, vicar of Ecclesfield, Yorks, 1825, until his death 24 July, 1839.

Ryder, William Charles, 1s. William Bromwich, of Manchester, arm. CHRIST CHURCH, matric. 18 Jan., 1884, aged 19.

Ryder, William Dudley, born at Wells, Somerset, 4s. Henry, bishop of Lichfield and Coventry. EXETER COLL., matric. 27 Jan., 1831, aged 17; B.A. 1835, M.A. 1839, bar.-at-law, Lincoln's Inn, 1840, arbitrator in the Mixed Court, New York. See Foster's *Peerage*, E. HARROWBY. [15]

Rye, George, s. William Beauchamp, of Dallington, Northants, doctor. CHRIST CHURCH, matric. 6 July, 1770, aged 17.

Rye, George, s. John, of Ryecourt, co. Cork, Ireland, arm. MAGDALEN COLL., matric. 3 June, 1780, aged 17; died s.p.

Rye, George Augustus, s. John, of Hopton, Suffolk, arm. EXETER COLL., matric. 26 June, 1815, aged 18.

Rye, John Tonson, s. Richard Tonson, of co. Cork, Ireland, arm. BRASENOSE COLL., matric. 21 Oct., 1814, aged 17; of Ryecourt, co. Cork.

Rye, Joseph Jekyll, s. William Beauchamp, of Northampton (town), doctor. PEMBROKE COLL., matric. 5 May, 1778, aged 18; B.A. 1782, M.A. 1792. [20]

Rye, Peter Hugh Jekyll Lewis, o.s. Peter, of Great Grimsby, co. Lincoln, arm. LINCOLN COLL., matric. 23 Jan., 1827, aged 19.

Rye, Rev. Robert Drury, s. William Beauchamp, of Northampton, doctor. CHRIST CHURCH, matric. 23 May, 1776, aged 19; demy MAGDALEN COLL. 1776-80, B.A. 1780, M.A. 1782, died at Colworth, Northants, in 1796. See *Bloxam*, vii. 54.

Rye, William Beauchamp, s. George, of Islip, Oxon, archdeacon of Oxford. CHRIST CHURCH, matric. 13 Dec., 1739, aged 15; B.A. 1743, M.A. 1747, B.Med. 1751, D.Med. 1759, father of George, Joseph J. and Robert D.

Ryland, Archer, s. Richard, of St. Olave's, London, gent. ST. JOHN'S COLL., matric. 25 June, 1810, aged 18; scholar & fellow 1810-20, B.C.L. 1817, bar.-at-law, Gray's Inn, 1818, bencher 1841, died 20 Feb., 1857. See *Robinson*, 172.

Ryle, Arthur Johnston, 3s. John Charles, of London, cler. (after bishop). NEW COLL., matric. 13 Oct., 1877, aged 20; B.A. 1881, M.A. 1885. See Foster's *Peerage* & *Eton School Lists.* [25]

Ryle, Frederick William, 2s. John, of Prestbury, Cheshire, arm. CHRIST CHURCH, matric. 17 Oct., 1838, aged 18, B.A. 1842; fellow BRASENOSE COLL. 1843-6, M.A. 1845, incumbent of Elson, at his death 1 May, 1846. See *Eton School Lists.*

Ryle, John Charles, 1s. John, of Macclesfield, arm. CHRIST CHURCH, matric. 15 May, 1834, aged 18; B.A. 1838, M.A. 1871, D.D. by diploma 4 May, 1880, bishop of Liverpool 1880, rector of St. Thomas's, Winchester 1843-4, and of Helmingham, Suffolk, 1844-61, vicar of Stradbroke, Suffolk, 1861-80, hon. canon of Norwich 1872-80, select preacher Cambridge 1873-4, at Oxford 1874-6, and 1879-80, father of Arthur J., and of the next named. See *Eton School Lists*, and for list of his works see *Crockford.*

Ryle, Reginald John, 1s. John Charles, of London, cler. (after bishop). TRINITY COLL., matric. 28 Jan., 1874, aged 19; B.A. 1877, B.Med. & M.A. 1884.

Ryley, Edward, o.s. Samuel, of Preston, Lancashire, arm. TRINITY COLL., matric. 29 Nov., 1849, aged 20; B.A. 1853, M.A. 1856, rector of Sarratt, Herts, 1859.

Ryley, Geoffrey Charles Edward, 1s. Edward, of Sarratt, Herts, cler. TRINITY COLL., matric. 16 Oct., 1886, aged 19. [30]

Rymer, John, s. Richard, of Yarm, Yorks, gent. ST. EDMUND HALL, matric. 13 March, 1788, aged 26; B.A. 1791, M.A. 1808, vicar of Ruskington, co. Lincoln, and of Littleham, Devon, 1803.

Rymer, Thomas, of QUEEN'S COLL., Cambridge (B.A. 1729, M.A. 1733); incorp. 9 July, 1733.

Ryves, Arthur Edward, o.s. Thomas James, of Allahabad, East Indies, arm. TRINITY COLL., matric. 11 Oct., 1884, aged 19; B.A. 1888.

Ryves, George Thomas, 3s. William Harding, of London, arm. BRASENOSE COLL., matric. 3 Feb., 1853, aged 19; B.A. 1857, M.A. 1860, vicar of Buildwas, Salop, 1871-4, and of Upper Tean, co. Stafford, 1874.

Ryves, Francis, s. Dudley, of Dublin, Ireland, arm. BRASENOSE COLL., matric. 1 April, 1773, aged 16.

Ryves, Henry Pleydell, s. Thomas, of Ranston, Dorset, arm. MERTON COLL., matric. 20 June, 1776, aged 16; rector of Chesleborne, Dorset, preb. of Chichester at his death in 1817. [35]

Ryves, James Alfred, 5s. William Harding, of Brighton, Sussex, arm. ST. JOHN'S COLL., matric. 25 March, 1857, aged 20.

Ryves, John William Dudley, s. Dudley, of Windsor, Berks, arm. EXETER COLL., matric. 19 Nov., 1777, aged 19; B.A. 1781, M.A. 1796 (as Dudley).

Ryves, William John Francis, 1s. William Harding, of Brighton, Sussex, gent. PEMBROKE COLL., matric. 25 Nov., 1847, aged 19.

SAPIENTIÆ
ET
FELICITA-
TIS.

Lightning Source UK Ltd.
Milton Keynes UK
UKHW011831281118
333023UK00011B/980/P